2009

Our Sunday Visitor's

CATHOLIC ALMANAC

Matthew Bunson, D.Min.
General Editor

Our Sunday Visitor Publishing Division
Our Sunday Visitor, Inc.
Huntington, Indiana 46750

OUR SUNDAY VISITOR'S CATHOLIC ALMANAC
2009 EDITION

STAFF

Greg Erlandson
Editor-in-Chief

Dr. Matthew E. Bunson
General Editor

Murray W. Hubley
Production Editor

Cathy Dee
Web Editor

Contributors to the 2009 Edition
Dr. John Borelli,
Barbara Fraze,
Dr. Eugene Fisher,
Brother Jeffrey Gros, F.S.C.,
Rev. Ronald Roberson, C.S.P.
Rev. C. Eugene Morris,
Russell Shaw,
Rev. Francis Tiso

Jane Cavolina, Editorial Consultant
Carrie Bannister, Assistant

ACKNOWLEDGMENTS: Catholic News Service, for coverage of news and documentary texts; *The Documents of Vatican II*, ed. W. M. Abbott (Herder and Herder, America Press: New York 1966), for quotations of Council documents; *Annuario Pontificio* (2008); *Statistical Yearbook of the Church* (2008); *L Osservatore Romano* (English editions); *The Official Catholic Directory* Excerpts of statistical data and other material, reprinted with permission of *The Official Catholic Directory*, ' 2008 by Reed Reference Publishing, a division of Reed Publishing (USA) Inc. Trademark used under license from Reed Publishing (Nederland) B.V.; *The Papal Encyclicals*, 5 vols., ed. C. Carlen (Pierian Press, Ann Arbor, MI); *Newsletter of the U.S. Bishops Committee on the Liturgy*; Kathleen Bullock, Associate for Operations, The United States Catholic Mission Assoc. (3029 Fourth St. N.E., Washington, DC 20017), for U.S. overseas-mission compilations and statistics; *Catholic Press Directory* (2008); *Annuaire Directiore*, Canadian Conference of Catholic Bishops, for latest available Canadian Catholic statistics; Rev. Thomas J. Reese, S.J., for names of dioceses for which U.S. bishops were ordained; other sources as credited in particular entries. Special thanks are owed to Rev. Mr. William Kokesch, Dir.-Communications Service, Canadian Conference of Catholic Bishops; Msgr. Michael Servinsky; and Rev. Jorge Francisco V zquez Moreno, adjunct secretary of the *Conferencia del Episcopado Mexicano*.

2009 Catholic Almanac

Published annually by Our Sunday Visitor Publishing Division, Our Sunday Visitor, Inc., 200 Noll Plaza, Huntington, IN 46750
ISBN: 978-1-59276-441-9
ID: T678
Library of Congress Catalog Card No. 73-641001
International Standard Serial Number (ISSN) 0069-1208

Editorial Note: Comments, corrections, and suggestions should be addressed to the editorial offices of the *Catholic Almanac*: 6105 Chapel Pines Run, Fort Wayne, IN 46804; (260) 444-4398; E-mail: almanac@osv.com.

Visit us online at www.CatholicAlmanac.com, and at the Our Sunday Visitor web site at www.OSV.com.

CONTENTS

PART ONE: NEWS AND EVENTS
Year in Review:
September 2007-August 2008 5
Deaths 53
News in Depth:
Pope Benedict XVI: 2007-2008
Pope Benedict XVI in America 55
Papal Encyclical: *Spe Salvi* 59
New Cardinals 60
Pope Benedict XVI and Islam 61
Papal Trips 2007-2008 55
Austria, Austria, Sept. 7-9 62
United States of America, Apr. 15-21 66
Sydney, Australia, WYD, July 12-21. 67
Papal Documents and Announcements:
The Year of St. Paul 73
CDF: The Ordination of Women 73
CDF: On the Validity of Baptism 73
CDF: Note on Evangelization 74
Holy See Finances 75
Special Reports — International News:
Fernando Lugo and Paraguay 76
Christians in Iraq 77
Special Reports — National News:
Sexual Abuse Scandal 78
Catholics and the Election 79
Life Issues:
Hydration and the Vegetative State 80
Stem-Cell Research 82
United States Conference of Catholic Bishops:
Meetings of U.S. Bishops 2007-08 84

PART TWO: THE TEACHINGS OF THE CATHOLIC CHURCH
Doctrine of the Catholic Church:
Catechism of the Catholic Church 87
Lumen Gentium 89
Pope, Teaching Authority, Collegiality 92
Revelation 93
The Bible 96
Apostles and Evangelists 105
Apostolic Fathers, Fathers, Doctors 106
Creeds 109
Christian Morality 110
Moral Teachings of Pope John Paul II 112
Catholic Social Doctrine 114
Social Doctrine Under Pope John Paul II 115
Social Encyclicals of Pope John Paul II 116
Socio-Economic Statements by Bishops 117
Blessed Virgin Mary 119
Redemptoris Mater 121
Apparitions of the Blessed Virgin Mary 123
The Code of Canon Law 125
Glossary 128
The Church Calendar 161
2009 Calendar 165
Holy Days and Other Observances 171
Liturgical Life of the Church 175
Mass, Eucharistic Sacrifice, Banquet 178
Liturgical Developments 182
The Sacraments of the Church 189
Matrimony 197
Communion of Saints 204
Saints — Patrons and Intercessors 211

Beatifications, 2007-08 215

PART THREE: THE CHURCH UNIVERSAL
Dates, Events in Catholic History 218
Ecumenical Councils 228
The Papacy and the Holy See:
Pope Benedict XVI 231
Pope John Paul II 232
Popes of the Catholic Church 236
Popes of the Twentieth Century 241
Papal Encyclicals — 1740 to Present 246
Canonizations by Leo XIII and Successors 251
Beatifications by Pope John Paul II 253
Beatifications by Benedict XVI 255
Roman Curia 255
Vatican City State 261
Diplomatic Activities of the Holy See 263
U.S.-Holy See Relations 270
Pontifical Academies 271
Hierarchy of the Catholic Church 273
Synod of Bishops 275
College of Cardinals 276
Cardinals' Biographies and Statistics 277
Electing the Pope: the Conclave 297
The Universal Church:
The Church Throughout the World 298
Catholic World Statistics 335
Episcopal Conferences 336
International Catholic Organizations 340
Eastern Catholic Churches:
Jurisdictions and Faithful 344
Eastern Catholic Churches in U.S. 348
Byzantine Divine Liturgy 349
Code of Canons of the Eastern Churches 351
The Catholic Church in the U.S.:
Chronology of U.S. Catholic History 352
U.S. Catholic History 358
Missionaries to the Americas 363
Franciscan Missions 365
Church-State Relations in the U.S. 366
Catholics in the U.S. Government 371
United States Hierarchy:
Jurisdictions, Hierarchy, Statistics 373
Ecclesiastical Provinces 373
Archdioceses, Dioceses,
Archbishops, Bishops 374
Chancery Offices 384
Cathedrals in the United States 388
Basilicas in the United States 389
Shrines and Places of Interest, U.S. 390
Biographies of American Bishops 394
United States Conference
of Catholic Bishops 420
Hispanic, African-American,
and Native-American Catholics:
Hispanic Catholics in the U.S. 424
African-American Catholics in the U.S. 427
Native-American Catholics 429
Missionary Activity of the Church 429
U.S. Catholic Mission Association 430
Statistics of the Church in the U.S.:
U.S. Statistics and Summary 432
Percentage of Catholics
in the Total U.S. Population 433

Catholic Population, U.S. 435
Receptions into the Church, U.S....................439
The Catholic Church in Canada **441**
Ecclesiastical Jurisdictions of Canada 442
Canadian Conference of Catholic Bishops.....446
Canadian Shrines......................................446
Statistical Summary 447
The Catholic Church in Mexico........................449
Ecclesiastical Jurisdictions of Mexico 451
Mexican Conference of Catholic Bishops 455
Statistical Summary 456

PART FOUR: THE LIFE OF THE CHURCH IN THE WORLD
Consecrated Life:
Institutes of Consecrated Life.........................458
Religious Institutes of Men in the U.S. 458
Membership, Religious Institutes of Men 467
Religious Institutes of Women 468
Membership, Religious Institutes of Women ..487
Organizations of Religious 489
Secular Institutes...490
Third Orders 493
Apostolates and Ministries:
Laity in the Church 494
Special Apostolates and Groups 495
Catholic Youth Organizations 497
Campus Ministry...497
Associations, Movements, Societies 498
Catholic Social Services.....................................508
Facilities for Retired and Aged Persons 511
Facilities for Disabled Children, Adults 520
Retreats, Spiritual Renewal Programs.............525
Education:
Legal Status of Catholic Education 532
Education Vouchers......................................532
Ex Corde Ecclesiae 533
Catholic School Statistics Summary................534
Catholic Schools and Students in U.S. 535
Catholic Universities, Colleges in U.S. 539
Diocesan, Interdiocesan Seminaries...............544
Pontifical Universities....................................546
World and U.S. Seminary Statistics 547
Ecclesiastical Faculties 548
Pontifical Universities, Institutes in Rome 550

Catholic Communications:
Catholic Press Statistics 551
Newspapers, Magazines, Newsletters 551
Books 565
Canadian Catholic Publications 566
International Catholic Periodicals....................567
Catholic News Agencies................................567
Radio, Television, Theatre...............................568
Film (includes "best lists") 569
Roman Catholic Internet Sites........................570
Developments in Communications 571
Message of the Holy Father
    for World Communications Day................571
Pontifical Honors and Awards... 573
Awards 575
Ecumenism, Interreligious Dialogue:
Ecumenism..578
Directory on Ecumenism...............................580
Ecumenical Agencies....................................580
International Bilateral Commissions 583
U.S. Ecumenical Dialogues 584
Common Declarations 584
Ecumenical Statements 589
Separated Eastern Churches:
The Orthodox Churches................................590
Jurisdictions 591
Eastern Ecumenism......................................591
Relations With the Orthodox Church..............592
Recent Developments 593
Oriental Orthodox Churches 595
Reformation Churches:
Leaders and Doctrines of the Reformation 596
Protestant Churches in the U.S......................598
Anglican-Catholic Dialogue..........................601
Lutheran-Catholic Dialogue..........................603
Interreligious Dialogue:
Judaism..606
Catholic-Jewish Relations 607
We Remember: A Reflection on the Shoah....608
Papal Statements..608
Millennium Events 609
International Liaison Committee.....................610
Islam...613
Message for the End of Ramadan 614
Hinduism and Buddhism 615
Index **617**

Year In Review
September 2007 to
August 2008

SEPTEMBER 2007

VATICAN

Pope and Youth On Sept. 2, Pope Benedict XVI addressed half a million young people, advising them to become daring Christians. The Holy Father spoke at the closing Mass today in Loreto, where the Holy Father arrived Saturday for an encounter with youth from Italy and around the world. Many of the young pilgrims had spent the night under the stars or in large tents. There were 150 bishops and 2,000 priests who concelebrated the Eucharist with the Pope. "The message is this: Do not follow the way of pride but the way of humility. Go against the current: Do not listen to the interesting and seductive voices that today from many parts propose as models lives of arrogance and violence, of despotism and success at all costs, of appearances and having, of harm to being," he announced. "Do not be afraid, dear friends, to prefer the 'alternative' ways indicated by true love: a sober way of life attentive to others; affectionate relationships that are sincere and pure; an honest commitment in study and work; deep interest in the common good." The Holy Father also urged the young people to re-forge an alliance between man and the earth. "To the new generations the future of the planet is entrusted, in which there are evident signs of a development that has not always known how to safeguard the delicate equilibriums of nature. Before it is too late, it is necessary to make courageous decisions that reflect knowing how to recreate a strong alliance between man and the earth. A decisive 'yes' to the protection of creation is necessary and a firm commitment to reverse those tendencies that run the risk of bringing about situations of unstoppable degradation."

Priest-Survivor On Sept. 2, Fr. Giancarlo Bossi, the Italian missionary who was kidnapped for 39 days in the Philippines, was in Loreto with Benedict XVI to express his gratitude for having survived his ordeal. The Pope spoke of Fr. Bossi during his address, saying: "In [Fr. Bossi] I would like to greet and thank all those who spend their existence for Christ on the frontiers of evangelization," he said. Fr. Bossi then thanked the Holy Father for his deliverance from captivity. Fr. Bossi was taken hostage June 10 and held for more than five weeks. He plans to return to the Philippines to continue his missionary service.

Suicide at Vatican It was reported on Sept. 3 that there was an apparent suicide of a member of the Vatican police force. Jesuit Father Federico Lombardi, director of the Vatican press office, released a statement today, expressing the Pope's grief at the event. Alessandro Benedetti, aged 26 and a member of the Corps of the Gendarmerie of Vatican City State, was found in a bathroom of the Gendarmerie's barracks in a very grave condition with a gunshot wound. The young man was taken immediately to Santo Spirito Hospital where he died at around 9 a.m. Initial evidence would seem to suggest that the young man committed suicide.

Mother Teresa On Sept. 5, Pope Benedict XVI celebrated the 10th anniversary of the death of Blessed Teresa of Calcutta by urging the faithful to care for the poor as she did in her lifetime. At the end of the general audience in St. Peter's Square, the Holy Father greeted a group of Missionaries of Charity, the group founded by Mother Teresa. He counseled these religious "to always faithfully serve God in the poor and needy. Continue following her example and be instruments of divine mercy in every setting."

Syrian Official On Sept. 5, Pope Benedict XVI received Farouk al-Charaa, the vice president of Syria, in an audience. They reportedly discussed the plight of Christians in that Middle Eastern country. The vice president of the Syrian Arab Republic delivered a personal message from Bashar al-Assad, president of Syria. Farouk al-Charaa later met with Abp. Dominique Mamberti, Vatican secretary for relations with states.

Papal Concert On Sept. 5, Pope Benedict XVI attended a musical concert in the inner courtyard of the apostolic palace at Castel Gandolfo. The event was organized by the Bamberg Symphony Orchestra as part of the celebrations marking the 100th anniversary of the archdiocese of that German city. The Holy Father commented that music "has the power to lead us back ... to the Creator of all harmony, creating a resonance within us which is like being in tune with the beauty and truth of God, with the reality which no human knowledge or philosophy can ever express."

Ecumenical Assembly On Sept. 5, Pope Benedict XVI expressed his hopes that the 3rd European Ecumenical Assembly will "create meeting spaces for unity" while respecting legitimate diversity. The Holy Father sent this message to the meeting under way through Sunday in Sibiu, Romania. The papal message continued: "In an atmosphere of mutual trust, and with the awareness that our shared roots are much deeper than our divisions, it will be possible to overcome a false sense of self-sufficiency and ... spiritually to experience the shared foundation of our faith"

Israeli President On Sept. 6, Pope Benedict XVI received Israeli President Shimon Peres in an audience at Castel Gandolfo, where they discussed hopes for an end to the 60 years of conflict in the Holy Land. The president also met with Cardinal Tarcisio Bertone, secretary of state, Abp. Dominique Mamberti, secretary for relations with states, and Oded Ben-Hur, Israeli ambassador to the Holy See. The Holy Father and Peres also were reported as having discussed Israeli-Holy See relations. Hope was also expressed "for a rapid conclusion to the important negotiations currently under way, and for the creation of constant dialogue between the Israeli authorities and the local Christian communities with a view to the full participation of those communities in constructing the common good." President Peres also renewed the invitation to the Holy Father to visit the Holy Land.

Asian Bishops On Sept. 6, at Castel Gandolfo, Pope Benedict XVI received in audience bishops from Laos and Cambodia, in Italy for their five-yearly visit. "You carry out your ministry at the service of the Church," the Holy Father told the prelates, "in often difficult conditions and in a great variety of situations. Be sure that you have my fraternal support and the support of the universal Church in your service to the people of God." He also stated that one of the most important elements of the bishops' ministry is the announcement of the Christian faith. He concluded with an appeal to the bishops to care for the underprivileged, calling this "a specific sign of the authenticity" of faith.

Pope in Austria On Sept. 7, Pope Benedict XVI arrived in Vienna as a pilgrim, and was welcomed at the Vienna International Airport. Austrian President Heinz Fischer, Chancellor Alfred Gusenbauer and Cardinal Christoph Schönborn, Abp. of Vienna, were among the civil and religious leaders on hand to welcome the Pope. The Holy Father went immediately to the Marian shrine of Mariazell and to Vienna's Am Hof Platz today, site of the Mariensaeule — a bronze Marian column dating from 1667 — where he presided over a liturgical prayer service from the balcony of the Church of the Nine Angelic Choirs. Pope Benedict XVI also visited the Holocaust memorial in Vienna's Judenplatz, where he was received by Austrian chief rabbi, Paul Chaim Eisenberg, and the president of the Jewish community in Austria, Ariel Muzikant. Addressing the government and diplomatic officials in the reception hall of Vienna's Hofburg Palace, the Holy Father announced: "Europe cannot and must not deny her Christian roots. These represent a dynamic component of our civilization as we move forward into the third millennium." On Saturday during the open-air Mass he presided over at the Marian shrine of Mariazell in Austria, which commemorated the 850th anniversary of the founding of the pilgrimage site. In his homily, the Holy Father told the tens of thousands who participated in the Mass near the shrine's basilica that Jesus alone "is the bridge that truly brings God and man together ... the one universal mediator of salvation, valid for everyone and, ultimately, needed by everyone." On Sunday, Sept. 9, Pope Benedict XVI celebrated at St. Stephen's Cathedral in Vienna, on the last day of his three-day apostolic trip to Austria. About 40,000 people followed the Mass on large screens placed in St. Stephen's Square, since not all of the participants were able to be accommodated inside. After the Mass, the Holy Father recited the Angelus in St. Stephen's Square. As he was leaving, the pilgrims waved yellow handkerchiefs and banners from countries such as Germany, Israel, Austria and even Iran, chanting the Pope's name in Italian, "Be-ne-de-tto! Be-ne-de-tto!" The Holy Father ended his visit to Austria, expressing his hopes that the country will offer a contribution to Europe by salvaging the wealth found in its Christian roots at the Vienna-Schwechat airport Sunday with a farewell ceremony. Austrian President Heinz Fischer and the president of the Austrian bishops' conference, Cardinal Schönborn, were in attendance.

Slovakian Ambassador On Sept. 14, Pope Benedict XVI received in audience the new ambassador of Slovakia to the Holy See, Jozef Dravecky, who presented his letters of credence to the Pope. Next year Slovakia will mark 15 years of diplomatic relations with the Holy See, but the Holy Father noted at the meeting that the "bonds uniting the Bishop of Rome to the people of your country stretch back to the time of Saints Cyril and Methodius." The Holy Father also commented that diplomatic cooperation "has been especially fruitful in recent years, as evidenced by your government's ratification of two of the four items contained in the Basic Agreement signed in 2000."

10th Inter-Christian Symposium On Sept. 17, Pope Benedict XVI sent a message to the 10th Inter-Christian Symposium between Catholics and Orthodox being held on the Island of Tinos in Greece. Cardinal Walter Kasper, president of the Pontifical Council for Promoting Christian Unity, received the papal message. The symposium, with the theme "St. John Chrysostom: Bridge Between East and West," is held every two years, and alternately hosted by the Catholic and Orthodox Churches. In his message, the Holy Father reflected on the figure of St. John Chrysostom; the 1,600th anniversary of the saint's death was Friday, and invoked the aid of the Holy Spirit and the intercession of Mary, under her title of "*Theotokos.*"

Aid to the Church in Need Pope Benedict XVI, on Sept. 18 greeted the leaders of the charity organization Aid to the Church in Need, saying their work is "an eloquent testimony to the love of God." The organization's directors attended the papal Angelus as part of an international conference last Thursday through Sunday to mark the organization's 60th anniversary. The Holy Father expressed "the prayers and gratitude of the Successor of Peter," and he encouraged Aid to the Church in Need to continue its work of investing resources in the formation of vocations and committed laypeople. The Holy Father concluded by giving his apostolic blessing to all the staff and benefactors of the Germany-based charity organization.

Newly Beatified On Sept. 18, Pope Benedict XVI praised three recently proclaimed blessed and invited the Church to follow the "luminous testimony" of the new beati. He particularly mentioned the beatification in Poland of Fr. Stanislaus Papczynski. Cardinal Secretary of State Tarcisio Bertone celebrated the Mass of the beatification, and the Holy Father sent his greeting to the faithful gathered there, saying Fr. Papczynski was "a priest who was exemplary in preaching, in the formation of the laity, a father of the poor and an apostle of intercessory prayer for the dead." The Holy Father also mentioned that Cardinal José Saraiva Martins, prefect of the Congregation for Saints' Causes, was in Bordeaux in the Pope's name to proclaim as blessed Sister Marie-Céline of the Presentation of the Blessed Virgin Mary, a French nun from the Second Order of St. Francis. The Holy Father honored as well Fr. Basile Antoine-Marie Moreau, who was beatified Saturday in Le Mans by Cardinal Saraiva Martins. The founder of the Congregation of the Holy Cross, Fr. Moreau was 73 when he died in 1873.

Benin Bishops On Sept. 20, Pope Benedict XVI received the bishops of Benin at Castel Gandolfo, encouraging them to continue to be courageous defenders of the values of life and family. The prelates were in Rome on their five-yearly visit. The Holy Father noted how, over recent years, the bishops from the west African nation had "shown great evangelical courage in guiding the people of God through numerous difficulties," The Holy Father then recalled how the bishops had publicly defended, "courageously and in various circumstances, the values of the family and of respect for life" against "ideologies that propose models or attitudes opposed to an authentic concept of human life."

International Gypsy Meeting On Sept. 23, participants of the first international meeting of Gypsy priests, deacons and religious, gathered today to pray the Angelus at Castel Gandolfo, Pope Benedict XVI, greeting them, announced: "May the theme of your conference: 'With Christ at the Service of Gypsy People,' become a greater reality in each of your lives. I pray for this and I entrust you all to the protection of the Virgin Mary." The meeting, organized by the Pontifical Council for Migrants and Travelers, took place in the Vatican and is the result of the 2006 document "Guidelines for the Pastoral Care of Gypsies," which provides ideas and norms for ministry. The participants also conducted a pilgrimage to the Shrine of Our Lady of Divine Love in Rome, where they prayed the rosary in honor of Blessed Ceferino Giménez Malla, a Spanish martyr and the first beatified Gypsy.

Ukraine Bishops On Sept. 24, Pope Benedict XVI received in audience at Castel Gandolfo the bishops of the Latin rite of Ukraine, in Italy for their five-yearly visit and accompanied by Greek-Catholic bishops from that country. The Holy Father recommended an intensified collaboration between the Latin-rite bishops and the Greek-Catholic bishops in Ukraine "for the good of the entire Christian people." He also suggested to the Latin and Greek-Catholic bishops that they meet at least once a year, reaching "agreement between yourselves in order to make pastoral activity ever more harmonious and effective. I am convinced that fraternal cooperation between pastors will be an encouragement and a stimulus for all the faithful to grow in unity and apostolic enthusiasm, and that it will also favor fruitful ecumenical dialogue."

Vatican Stamp and Coin Museum It was reported on Sept. 25 that a new museum featuring all the stamps and coins minted in Vatican City State since 1929 is open to the public. The Philatelic and Numismatic Museum of Vatican City State, located within the Vatican Museums, and offers sections of sketches, printing plates, plaster models, bronze casts and other materials illustrating the various phases in the production of stamps and coins. Visitors can also see a presentation on the history of the postal service of the Papal State during the period from 1852 to 1870.

Castel Gandolfo Farewell On Sept. 28, Pope Benedict XVI met with Bp. Marcello Semeraro of Albano, the diocese in which Castel Gandolfo is located, as well as local religious communities, the civil authorities and the personnel in charge of security during his stay in the summer residence south of Rome. The Holy Father was saying farewell, as he planned to return to Rome. "I would like to be able to pause and speak to each of you," he said, "to thank you personally for the willingness and generosity with which you have contributed to the smooth functioning of the Pope's activities here in Castel Gandolfo." He added: "It is often the case, that such contributions remain unseen and compel you to work tiring hours, remaining away from your homes for long periods. Thus, your families are also involved in the sacrifices you have to face. For this reason, I would like to assure you once again of my most heartfelt appreciation, which I also extend to your relatives."

GENERAL AUDIENCES
St. Gregory of Nyssa (2), Sept. 5.
Apostolic Journey to Austria, Sept. 12.
St. John Chrysostom (1), Sept. 19.
St. John Chrysostom (2), Sept. 26.

INTERNATIONAL
Scottish Commemoration On Sept. 2, Abp. Mario Conti

of Glasgow attended a pilgrimage commemorating the 1982 papal visit and encouraged Scots to stay loyal to their Catholic faith, even as society makes it more difficult. Abp. Conti also quoted Pope John Paul II's words to the young people of Scotland: "Do not let the sight of the world in turmoil shake your confidence in Jesus. Not even the threat of nuclear war. Remember his words: 'Be brave: I have conquered the world.' Let no temptation discourage you. Let no failure hold you down. There is nothing that you cannot master with the help of the One who gives you strength." Abp. Conti then referred to a pastoral letter prepared by the prelates to mark the occasion of the papal visit, announcing: "Today, at a distance of 25 years, we need to reflect on those words. In so many areas of life 'the most fundamental principles of our Christian life' are not only questioned, but ridiculed and threatened with sanction." He also offered an invitation to Scottish Catholics: "To join us confidently in preaching the Gospel to the nonbelievers and the unchurched of our land."

Alexy II It was reported on Sept. 4 that Orthodox Patriarch Alexy II has recognized the Vatican's representative in Russia for his efforts in establishing good relations between the two Churches. Alexy II of Moscow and All Russia has awarded Abp. Antonio Mennini the Order of the Holy Prince Daniel of Moscow, third degree, "in recognition of his efforts for establishing good relations between the Russian Orthodox and the Roman Catholic Churches and on the occasion of his 60th birthday." Abp. Mennini has served as the Vatican's representative in Russia since November 2002.

Excommunicated It was reported on Sept. 12 that certain members of the Community of the Lady of All Nations, a movement commonly known as the Army of Mary, have incurred excommunication. The Congregation for the Doctrine of the Faith issued a declaration of excommunication that applies to certain members of the group. The Canadian bishops' conference stated: "Following earlier consultations with the bishops of Canada and also with the Congregation for Institutes of Consecrated Life and Societies of Apostolic Life, the Congregation for the Doctrine of the Faith has issued a declaration of excommunication that applies to various members of the Army of Mary. Despite repeated warnings by the bishops of Canada, including Cardinal Marc Ouellet, Abp. of Quebec City, members of the Army of Mary earlier this year participated in ordinations forbidden by and not recognized by the Catholic Church. The actions obliged the congregation to issue the declaration, it states, because of 'the very grave situation' and given there was no 'hope of another solution.'" The Vatican declaration states the excommunications are "*latae sententiae*," incurred automatically.

Cause Opened It was announced on Sept. 17 that Cardinal François-Xavier Nguyên Van Thuân's cause for beatification has been opened five years after the Vietnamese prelate died at age 74. Cardinal Renato Martino, who succeeded Cardinal Nguyên Van Thuân as president of the Pontifical Council for Justice and Peace, made the announcement at a Mass that he celebrated on Sunday, exactly five years after the prelate died. During his homily, Cardinal Martino recalled his predecessor as an example "of unshakeable faith, of steadfast hope and of limitless charity." Cardinal Van Thuân suffered at the hands of the Vietnamese Communists during 13 years of imprisonment. Cardinal Martino said his predecessor nourished Christian faith with the Eucharist. Speaking about the Eucharist just before he died, Cardinal Van Thuân said: "Jesus gives us everything we need in the Eucharist: love, the art of loving, loving always, loving with a smile, loving right away and loving our enemies, loving by forgiving, forgetting having forgiven." Also in attendance at the memorial Mass were Cardinals Angelo Sodano and Roger Etchegaray, president of the College of Cardinals and retired president of the Pontifical Council for Justice and Peace, respectively.

Belarus Deportations On Sept. 21, Belarusian Deputy Prime Minister Aleksandr Kosinets said that all foreign Catholic priests would be banned from the country over the next few years. Of the approximately 350 Catholic priests in the country, the majority are foreign and almost all of those are Polish. Belarus has been targeting foreign Catholics since last year, deporting all those without papers. Now the ban is extended to all foreign Catholic priests. Kosinets stated that "foreign priests cannot conduct religious activities in Belarus because they do not understand the mentality and traditions of the Belarusian people."

City Mission Gathering It was reported on Sept. 22 that Cardinal Peter Erdö had welcomed hundreds of European Catholics to his archdiocese for the Fifth International Congress for New Evangelization, which coincided with Budapest's City Mission. The City Mission program is an evangelization effort directed at large European cities; A discussion was held by Cardinal Erdö and the prelates of the previous four host cities: Abp. (now Cardinal) André Vingt-Trois of Paris; and Cardinals Christoph Schönborn of Vienna, Austria; Godfried Danneels of Mechelen-Brussels, Belgium; and Jose da Cruz Policarpo, patriarch of Lisbon, Portugal concerning the outreach programs and evangelization efforts for urban residents.

Marian Apparitions Dismissed On Sept. 24, the Holy See was reported as dismissing the claims of a woman in England who says Mary has visited her outside her home for more than 20 years. Declaring that such claims are "highly questionable," the Vatican also has refused to approve the statutes of the community she founded. Patricia De Menezes stated that the apparition has been appearing to her at her home in Surbiton, England since 1984. She stated also that she received a divine message that the Church must proclaim aborted babies to be martyrs. De Menezes founded the Community of Divine Innocence, which has about 3,000 members in 43 countries, many coming from the pro-life movement. Abp. Angelo Amato, secretary of the Vatican's Congregation for the Doctrine of the Faith, announced the decision in a letter to Abp. Kevin McDonald of Southwark, the archdiocese in which De Menezes lives.

Priest Killed in Sri Lanka On Sept. 26, Fr. Nicholas Pillai Pakiaranjith, 40, was killed in a blast from a claymore mine. He was driving food and supplies to displaced people near Kilinochchi, an area under Tamil control. Fr. Pakiaranjith coordinated the work of Jesuit Refugee Service in Sri Lanka's Mannar district, where control is divided between government forces and the Liberation Tigers of Tamil Elam. One of the priest's assistants also was injured in the blast. Bp. Rayappu Joseph of Mannar praised Fr. Pakiaranjith's deep commitment to the poor and marginalized. "It is a heinous crime to attack and kill such peace-loving and unarmed heroes of our society," he stated.

NATIONAL

World's Poor On Sept. 5 Catholic leaders urged the U.S. Senate to support funding for urgent humanitarian and development activities for the world's poorest countries, but not for abortion services. Bp. Thomas Wenski of Orlando, chairman of the U.S. bishops' conference international policy committee, and Ken Hackett, president of Catholic Relief Services sent a letter to the Senators who were considering the state/foreign operations appropriations bill for 2008. Of particular concern, the letter explained, was the provision of adequate funding for the Millennium Challenge Account/ Corporation (MCA), which helps vulnerable countries to make key reforms.

Cardinal Keeler Honored On Sept. 6, nearly 2,000 people gathered at the Baltimore Convention Center Sept. 6 to honor Cardinal William H. Keeler as he steps down after heading the Baltimore Archdiocese for 18 years. Cardinal Keeler plans to spend time to ecumenical and interfaith endeavors in his retirement. In October, the cardinal said he plans to go to Ravenna, Italy, as part of the International Catholic-Orthodox Commission. He also will continue serving as moderator for Jewish-Catholic affairs for the U.S. bishops.

Respect Life Sunday On Sept. 6, it was reported that U.S. dioceses were preparing for Respect Life Sunday, to be celebrated on Oct. 7, Cardinal Justin Rigali chairman of the Committee for Pro-Life Activities at the U.S. bishops' conference, announced: "We will not see the day when all human life is respected and defended unless we address a deeper problem. As Pope Benedict XVI has said: 'If truth does not exist for man, then neither can he ultimately distinguish between good and evil. And then the great and wonderful discoveries of science become double-edged: They can open up significant possibilities for good, for the benefit of mankind, but also, as we see only too clearly, they can pose a terrible threat, involving the destruction of man and the world. We need truth.'" The theme of this year's Respect Life Sunday is "The Infant in My Womb Leaped for Joy."

Nuns Excommunicated On Sept. 17, it was reported that six women religious of the Monastery of Our Lady of Charity and Refuge in Hot Springs, Arkansas were excommunicated by the Catholic Church for their involvement in a schismatic association, the Community of the Lady of All Nations, also known as the Army of Mary. The Army of Mary is no longer considered a Catholic organization because of its false teachings and was so declared by the Vatican's Congregation for the Doctrine of the Faith. The nuns have been followers of the Army of Mary for decades.

40 Days for Life A nationwide campaign to end abortion was announced on Sept. 26 as planned in some 80 cities in 33 states are launching the largest simultaneous pro-life mobilization in American history. The 40-day time frame was chosen from examples in biblical history. Bp. Samuel Aquila of Fargo, North Dakota, is encouraging all in his diocese to participate in the 40 Days of Life. The bishop asked especially for prayer vigils to be held at the state's only abortion clinic, located in Fargo. The 40 Days for Life concludes on Nov. 4.

Lasting Monument On Sept. 26, Abp. Edwin F. O'Brien dedicated the new headquarters of the U.S. Archdiocese for the Military Services in the northeast section of Washington, DC. The archbishop expressed his hopes that the building would serve as "a lasting monument" to the service and sacrifices of American military personnel and the chaplains who minister to them. Abp. O'Brien, who was installed Oct. 1 as archbishop of Baltimore had served as the head of the archdiocese that coordinates the spiritual care of nearly 1.5 million Catholics around the world, including active-duty and reserve military personnel and National Guard members, their families, U.S. government workers overseas and residents of Veterans Affairs hospitals.

OCTOBER 2007

VATICAN

Galaxy Conference On Oct. 1, the Vatican Observatory called together some of the world's top astronomers for a major conference that offered considerations of the creation and evolution of disk galaxies. Such a conference was designed to better understand the nature of the universe. More than 200 men and women from 26 countries, all noted astronomers, attended the Rome gathering. The observatory director, Argentine Jesuit Fr. Jose Funes, said they were able to attract top scientists and scholars for the meeting because "the Vatican Observatory is a prestigious institute, and the Holy See is well recognized in this field of astronomy."

Vatican Calendar It was reported on Oct. 3 that the first official wall calendar featuring images of Pope Benedict XVI had been released by the Vatican photo service. Photos of the papal 2007 Alpine vacation were included in the calendar which was available in bookshops and newsstands near the Vatican and online. The 2008 calendar depicted the Holy Father posing in front of an Alpine lake, a pine forest, a small Marian shrine, and with local residents.

Theological Commission On Oct. 5, Pope Benedict XVI addressed members of the International Theological Commission who had been working on a document on the foundations of natural moral law and, specifically, on how those principles form the basis of a "universal ethic" that can be recognized and shared by all peoples of all religions. The growing assumption that there are no ethical absolutes, the Holy Father warned, threatens the fundamental rights of human beings and imposes "enormous and serious consequences on the civil and social order," The members of the International Theological Commission agreed that the commission's report was to serve as an important part of a project being promoted by the Congregation for the Doctrine of the Faith to encourage universities, associations and individual scholars.

Jesus of Nazareth It was reported on Oct. 5 that 2 million copies of Pope Benedict XVI's book, *Jesus of Nazareth*, have been sold worldwide. The work depicts biblical accounts and details the moral implications of his teachings. The book has been number one on the Catholic Best-Sellers List for the past three months, according to the Catholic Book Publishers Association. *Jesus of Nazareth* also ranked among the top 10 hardcover nonfiction books on the New York Times Best Sellers' list after its English release and stayed on the list for several weeks.

South Korean Ambassador On Oct. 11, Pope Benedict XVI received the letters of credence of Francis Ji-Young Kim, the new South Korean ambassador to the Holy See. The Holy Father praised the efforts made by South Korea to establish reconciliation on the Korean peninsula. He also warned that South Korea's success in scientific research and development cannot come at the cost of manipulating human life. South Korea is known as a leader in stem cell research. The South Korean Ministry of Health and Welfare announced last month that it would allow scientists to conduct research on cloning human embryos to create embryonic stem cells.

Spanish Martyrs It was announced on Oct. 12 that Pope Benedict XVI has approved the beatification rites of 490 more people, the majority of them martyrs from the religious persecution in 1930s Spain. Individuals were scheduled to be beatified in their native countries, and on Oct. 28, in St. Peter's Square, 498 martyrs of the religious persecution in Spain

(1936-1939) were scheduled by the Holy See to be beatified. This group of martyrs for the faith is the largest ever group of people to be beatification at the same time. Two rites of beatification were also scheduled for November and another for December with the Holy Father's approval. The complete list and remarkable stories of the martyrs can be found at: www.conferenciaepiscopal.es/ santos/martires/alfabetico.html.

Apostolic Palace Doors On Oct. 12, Pope Benedict XVI officially inaugurated the restored bronze door of the Apostolic Palace in the Vatican. Over 24 feet tall and 13 feet wide, the doors were fashioned out of and bronze taken from ancient Roman temples and were put in place by Bernini, the famed architect of the colonnade surrounding St. Peter's Square. The portals have a steel core and weigh 12,130 pounds. Abp. John P. Foley, pro-grand master of the Knights of the Holy Sepulcher, and members of the Catholic chivalric order greeted the Holy Father at the ceremony. The knights, along with an Italian bank, funded the restoration. Vatican officials, Swiss Guards, the restorers and benefactors who paid for the two-year project participated in the ritual held at the northwest end of the colonnade. "Now," the Holy Father announced, the bronze door "has returned to its place and function, under the beautiful mosaic of the Madonna and Child with Sts. Peter and Paul. Precisely because it marks the point of access to the house of the person called by the Lord to guide, as father and pastor, the entire People of God, this door assumes a symbolic and spiritual significance. Those who come to meet Peter's Successor pass through here. Pilgrims and visitors to the various offices of the apostolic palace cross this threshold."

Sacred Music On Oct. 15, Pope Benedict XVI visited the newly refurbished Pontifical Institute of Sacred Music, where he was welcomed by Cardinal Zenon Grocholewski, prefect of the Congregation for Catholic Education and chancellor of the Pontifical Institute of Sacred Music, and the institute's president, Monsignor Valentin Miserachs Grau. The Holy Father noted the pre-eminence of sacred music over other art forms, explaining "that, as sacred song united to the words, it forms a necessary or integral part of the solemn liturgy. Precisely for this reason, the ecclesial authorities must undertake to guide ... the development of such an important form of music, not by 'freezing' its heritage but by seeking to combine the legacy of the past with the worthwhile novelties of the present, so as to achieve a synthesis worthy of the exalted mission [sacred music] has in the service of God." The Holy Father encouraged the professors and students in their "demanding yet passionate" task, asking them to be "conscious that it has a value of great relevance for the very life of the Church."

New Cardinals On Oct. 17, Pope Benedict XVI announced the names of 23 new cardinals for the Church, including the head of a Texas archdiocese. The consistory, the second of the Pope's pontificate, was scheduled for Nov. 24, the eve of the solemnity of Christ the King. "The new cardinals," the Holy Father explained, "come from various parts of the world. And the universality of the Church, with the multiplicity of her ministries, is clearly reflected in them. Alongside deserving prelates who work for the Holy See are pastors who dedicate their energies to direct contact with the faithful." Two of the new cardinals were U.S. prelates: Abp. John Patrick Foley, pro-grand master of the Equestrian Order of the Knights of the Holy Sepulcher of Jerusalem and Abp. Daniel DiNardo of Galveston-Houston, Texas. Ireland was represented in this group, and there were six new cardinals from Italy, three from Spain and two from Argentina. The rest were chosen from Mexico, Iraq, Germany, Poland, France, Senegal, India, Brazil and Kenya. After the consistory, the College of Cardinals had 202 members, of whom 121 were electors. The Holy Father entrusted the future cardinals "to the protection of Mary Most Holy asking her to help each of them in their new tasks, that they may know how to bear courageous witness in all circumstances to their love for Christ and for the Church." [See also **News in Depth** on p. 60.]

Chilean Leader On Oct. 18, Pope Benedict XVI received in audience the president of Chile, Michelle Bachelet and other civil leaders from Chile. Following her 40-minute audience with the Holy Father, President Bachelet met with his secretary of state, Cardinal Tarcisio Bertone, and Abp. Dominique Mamberti, secretary for relations with states. "The cordial discussions provided an opportunity for an exchange of information and ideas on the sociopolitical situation of the country and its role in Latin America," the Vatican reported. President Bachelet gave the Holy Father a sculpture and a book, representing Chilean culture. He gave her a papal medallion.

Mennonites At Vatican On Oct. 19, Pope Benedict XVI received at the Vatican delegates from the Mennonite World Congress. The Holy Father told the delegates: "In the ecumenical spirit of recent times, we have begun to have contacts with each other after centuries of isolation. Since it is Christ himself who calls us to seek Christian unity, it is entirely right and fitting that Mennonites and Catholics have entered into dialogue in order to understand the reasons for the conflict that arose between us in the 16th century. To understand is to take the first step towards healing. Mennonites are well known for their strong Christian witness to peace in the name of the Gospel, and here, despite centuries of division, the dialogue report 'Called Together to be Peacemakers' has shown that we hold many convictions in common." The Holy Father concluded, "It is my hope that your visit will be another step toward mutual understanding and reconciliation."

Congolese Bishops Pope Benedict XVI on Oct. 19 received in audience eight prelates from the Congolese Catholic bishops' conference, who were completing their five-yearly visit, the required *ad limina*. About half of Congo's 65 million inhabitants are Catholic. The Holy Father addressed a variety of topics relevant to the situation in Congo, giving special attention to the issue of Christian families in Congo, and the formation of priests. He urged the prelates to concern themselves "with the initial and permanent Christian formation of the faithful, ensuring they understand the Christian mystery, and base themselves on the reading of Scripture and sacramental life." And he asked them to help priests to lead "an ever more dignified and holy existence, rooted in a profound spiritual life and an emotional maturity lived in celibacy."

Tanzanian President Pope Benedict XVI, on Oct. 10, received in an audience Tanzanian President Jakaya Mrisho Kikwete and other civil leaders from that nation. The Holy Father and the president discussed the need for peaceful coexistence between Christians and Muslims during the African leader's visit. Secretary of state, Cardinal Tarcisio Bertone, and Abp. Dominique Mamberti, secretary for relations with state were also present. The president was in Italy also to attend the 21st International Encounter of Peoples and Religions, organized by the Catholic lay Sant'Egidio Community and the Archdiocese of Naples. Of the nearly 40 million inhabitants of Tanzania, some 35% are Muslim and 30% Christian. A large percentage of the population follows the beliefs of traditional religions.

Benedict XVI in Naples On Oct. 21, Pope Benedict XVI visited Naples and spoke to a group of interreligious leaders, urging them to promote peace and the "spirit of Assisi." Addressing the leaders in the archdiocesan seminary of Capodimonte on the first day of the 21st International Encounter of Peoples and Religion, the Holy Father announced: "Faced with a world lacerated by conflicts, where at times violence is justified in the name of God, it is important to re-emphasize that religion can never be a vehicle of hate; never, in the name of God, can we justify evil and violence." "On the contrary," he added, "because they speak of peace to the human heart, religions can offer precious resources for building a peaceful humanity." The Holy Father celebrated Mass in Naples' historic Piazza del Plebiscito. He stopped to embrace Orthodox Ecumenical Patriarch Bartholomew of Constantinople, Anglican Abp. Rowan Williams of Canterbury and other leaders of Christian churches. After the Mass, they were joined by representatives of the Jewish, Islamic, Buddhist, Hindu and other religions for a meeting and lunch. Patriarch Bartholomew, Abp. Williams and Ezzedine Ibrahim, a Muslim scholar from the United Arab Emirates, were among the nine guests at the Holy Father's table. Ibrahim was one of 138 Muslim leaders and scholars who signed an Oct. 11 letter to the pope and other Christian leaders proposing a dialogue based on the shared beliefs that there is only one God, that God loves the people he created and that he calls believers to love others.

Iraqi Priests Freed On Oct. 21, it was reported that Pope Benedict XVI received with joy the news that the two priests kidnapped in Iraq over a week ago, had been set free. The two priests, Fr. Mazen Ishoa, 35, and Fr. Pius Afas, 60, were kidnapped on their way to celebrate Mass on Oct. 13 at Our Lady of Fatima Parish Church in the al-Faisaliya neighborhood. They were released on a street in Mosul. It has not been confirmed whether a ransom was paid for the two priests. The kidnappers, who did not make any claims about political allegiance, had asked for a $1 million ransom, and had set a payment deadline for Saturday.

Bosnian Pact On Oct. 25, a ceremony of ratification was held in the Vatican as the Basic Agreement and the Additional Protocol between the Holy See and Bosnia and Herzegovina entered into effect. Cardinal Tarcisio Bertone, the Pope's secretary of state, and President Zeljko Komsic, each accompanied by their respective delegations, exchanged the instruments of ratification of the agreement and its additional protocol, signed last April 19 and Sept. 29, respectively. Pope Benedict XVI also received in audience the Bosnian leader, who officially invited the Pontiff to visit his country. With the agreement, elements of the life and activity of the Catholic community in Bosnia and Herzegovina will be clarified, such as "the recognition of the juridical status of the Catholic Church and its institutions in civil society, its independence in worship and in apostolate, and of its specific contribution in the cultural, educational, pastoral, military, aid and charity fields, and in the press," Cardinal Bertone said.

Knights Templar On Oct. 25, it was reported that Vatican officials and laypeople presented *Processus Contra Templarios* ("Trial Against the Templars"), a compendium of reprints of the original acts of the hearings against the Knights Templar, the group novelist Dan Brown linked to the Holy Grail in *The Da Vinci Code*. The volume is the third in the *Exemplaria Praetiosa* series of the Vatican Secret Archives, issued in collaboration with the Scrinium publishing house. The 799 available copies of the volume have been sold to collectors, scholars and libraries from all over the world, reported the Vatican press office. The 800th copy will be given to Benedict XVI. The military order of the Poor Knights of Christ and of the Temple of Solomon was founded in Jerusalem in 1118 to protect Christians in the Holy Land. The order was suppressed in 1312 and its vast holdings and wealth seized by various crowns across Christendom.

Leader of Iceland On Oct. 26, Pope Benedict XVI received in audience Geir Haarde, the Prime Minister of Iceland. The leader then met with the Holy Father's secretary of state, Cardinal Tarcisio Bertone, and Abp. Dominique Mamberti, secretary for relations with states. The audience with Benedict XVI was a first for Haarde, a Protestant, who showed enthusiasm when presenting the Holy Father a cross and a Bible translated to Icelandic. The Holy Father gave the prime minister pontifical metals and rosaries. Only about 2% of Iceland's 300,000 citizens are Catholic.

Paraguayan President On Oct. 29, Pope Benedict XVI received in audience Óscar Nicanor Duarte Frutos, the president of Paraguay. The two discussed the role of Church and state in political life, and afterward, the South American leader met with the Pontiff's secretary of state, Cardinal Tarcisio Bertone, and Abp. Dominique Mamberti, secretary for relations with states. "The cordial meetings served to consider questions concerning the current situation of Paraguay, with particular attention being given to the specific roles of Church and state in political life and in the human, moral, educational and socioeconomic development of the nation," the Vatican press office reported.

General Audiences

St. Cyril of Alexandria, Oct. 3.
St. Hilary of Poitiers, Oct. 10.
St. Eusebius of Vercelli, Oct. 17.
St. Ambrose of Milan, Oct. 24.
St. Maximus of Turin, Oct. 31.

INTERNATIONAL

Amnesty International On Oct. 3, the Australian Catholic Bishops' Conference announced that it has severed all ties between Amnesty International and the Catholic Church in Australia. Amnesty International has come under fire around the world because of its support of abortions. "It is with much regret that we are now in a position of having to advise that member-

ship of Amnesty International is no longer compatible with Catholic teaching and belief on this important point," Abp. Philip Wilson of Adelaide, president of the bishops' conference, stated. "After due consideration we now also urge Catholics and all people who believe in the dignity of the human person from natural conception until natural death to seek other avenues of defending human rights," the archbishop said.

Polish Convent It was reported on Oct. 10 that a police unit evicted several dozen former nuns from the Sisters of the Family of Bethany convent in Kazimierz. The former nuns had refused a series of court orders to leave and had been expelled from their order earlier this year. The eviction was handled peacefully. Former Franciscan Fr. Roman Komaryczko, however, was arrested for showing aggressive behavior during the police activities. The women residents of the convent, including five from Russia and Belarus, who were scheduled to be deported, were relocated.

Muslim Scholars On Oct. 12, it was announced that Muslim scholars had written to Benedict XVI and the heads of Christian churches to propose that the two faiths cooperate in creating peace and understanding in the world. This communication was sent a year after 38 Muslim scholars sent an open letter to the Pope in the wake of his address given at the University of Regensburg in September. The 138 signatories of this year's letter offer an open invitation to Christians to unite with Muslims over what is most essential to their respective faiths — the commandment of love. The document calls for tolerance, understanding and moderation, and is signed by Muslim leaders, politicians and academics. [See also **News in Depth** on p. 61.]

John Paul II It was reported on Oct. 16 that a photograph of a bonfire that was taken in southern Poland depicts a silhouette resembling that of Pope John Paul II. Polish cameraman Gregorz Lukasic took the photo an Apr. 2 at Beskid Zywiecki, at a memorial service commemorating the second anniversary of the Pontiff's death. He took many pictures of the event, but only in the photograph taken at the exact time of the Holy Father's death a silhouette appears resembling that of the Pope. The image was published by Vatican Service News, and the image was picked up by the international press.

Catholic Military Chaplains The 2nd International Conference for the formation of Catholic military chaplains was reported on Oct. 16 as having taken place in Rome. Cardinal Renato Martino, president of the Pontifical Council for Justice and Peace, presided at the event. Having the theme of "Human Dignity and Humanitarian Rights: The Role of Religions," the conference was co-sponsored by the Pontifical Councils for Justice and Peace, Interreligious Dialogue and Promoting Christian Unity, along with the Congregation for Clergy. Military chaplains, other members of the armed forces, academics and civil society representatives from more than 30 countries, gathered for the meetings. The chaplains and other guests paid special attention to current issues in the area of humanitarian rights, such as the struggle against terrorism, the status of nuclear weapons, and new ways of waging war, including the military use of biotechnology.

Traditional Anglicans It was reported on Oct. 24 that three Church of Ireland parishes have joined traditional Anglicans from 12 other countries in requesting that the Catholic Church receive them into full communion. The decision to petition for the move "seeking full, corporate, sacramental union" was made during an early Oct. plenary meeting of the Traditional Anglican Communion, the umbrella organization for traditional Anglicans At the Vatican, officials would not comment on the letter, although they confirmed the doctrinal congregation had received it. If the appeal of these Anglicans is approved by the Vatican, some 400,000 traditional Anglicans worldwide would be admitted into the Catholic Church. Entire parish communities are asking to be received into the Catholic Church in an appeal for corporate communion, which means that every member of the parish becomes Catholic and the parish effectively becomes part of the Catholic Church.

NATIONAL

Human Life Witnesses It was reported on Oct. 1 that Cardinal Justin Rigali of Philadelphia, chairman of the U.S. bishops' Committee on Pro-Life Activities, called on Catholics and "all people of good will to witness to the truth about the incomparable dignity and right to life of every human being." He offered this challenge in the statement for Respect Life Sunday, celebrated in Catholic parishes in the United States on Oct. 7. Cardinal Rigali also noted that education is necessary to alert the faithful to life issues, including embryonic stem-cell research, partial-birth abortion and euthanasia. In 1972 the U.S. bishops launched the Respect Life program and designated the first Sunday in Oct. as Respect Life Sunday.

Orange Diocese On Oct. 2, Bp. Tod D. Brown of Orange was reported as agreeing to settle four sexual abuse cases involving lay employees of the church and female high-school students for nearly $7 million. This settlement was in addition to a $100 million settlement in 2005 involving 90 claimants alleging sexual abuse by clergy of the diocese. "The settlement of these civil cases represents the moral obligation of the church for such behavior by adults in positions of responsibility," Bp. Brown said in a statement. "By settling these cases I sincerely hope that it will enable the women who brought these actions to begin the process of healing and reconciliation."

St. Mother Theodore On Oct. 3, the Sisters of Providence and hundreds of Catholics gathered at St. Mary-of-the-Woods to celebrate the feast day of St. Mother Theodore Guerin. St. Mary-of-the-Woods is the site of the National Shrine of Our Lady of Providence and the National Shrine of St. Mother Theodore Guerin. A Mass was celebrated at the Church of the Immaculate Conception at the motherhouse in honor of the occasion. The celebrant of the Mass, Fr. Daniel Hopcus, the congregation's chaplain, offered gratitude to God for the life of St. Mother Theodore and noted her faithful love, compassion and dedication to those in need.

Sainthood Cause Opened On Oct. 5, Oklahoma Catholics gathered in Okarche's Holy Trinity Church to witness the formal start of the sainthood cause for Fr. Stanley Francis Rother, a priest of the Oklahoma City Archdiocese. The faithful celebrated the Eucharist and prayed for the canonization of the Fr. Rother, who was brutally murdered in 1981 in the Guatemalan village where he ministered to the poor. "This is the very first time in history that a canonization process has been initiated here in Oklahoma," said Abp. Eusebius J. Beltran of Oklahoma City. "It is my hope and my prayer that almighty God will bring to a happy conclusion this good work which he has begun in us." Abp.

Beltran commissioned a canonization committee and named an assistant coordinator.

Liturgical Music Statement It was reported on Oct. 6 that the U.S. Conference of Catholic Bishops is considering an updated version of a 35-year-old statement on liturgical music when they convene in Baltimore for their annual fall general meeting. Originally named "Music in Catholic Worship," the document will offer a directory of liturgical songs for use in U.S. parishes. The planned directory is an outgrowth of the 2001 Vatican instruction *Liturgiam Authenticam* ("The Authentic Liturgy"), which called on each bishops' conference to compile a "directory or repertory of texts intended for liturgical singing."

Thank Your Priest On Oct. 25 it was reported that a nationwide campaign in the United States to "celebrate the priesthood" had been set for the last Sunday of October. The U.S. Council of Serra International, a lay group dedicated to promoting vocations, was coordinating the event, which was organized at a parish level by lay people who wanted "to express appreciation for the devoted priests who serve them so faithfully." Suggestions for liturgies and celebrations, as well as posters and guides were made available. "Affirming and supporting our priests are some of the most important things that we can do as Serrans," says Gary Davis, president of the U.S. Council of Serra International. "Our priests give of themselves every day in so many different ways. It is an honor to recognize them in a manner in which entire parishes may join together in an outpouring of appreciation."

$9.5 Million to U.S. Poor The Catholic Campaign for Human Development reported on Oct. 26 that donations from the annual national collection taken up in parishes before Thanksgiving totaled some $9.5 million this year. The funds were slated to aid more than 300 poverty-fighting organizations, and the Catholic Campaign for Human Development distributed the money to 314 projects in 46 states, the District of Columbia and Puerto Rico in 2007. These local organizations address the specific concerns of their poor and low-income members and work for economic justice, fair housing, health care access, living wages, and immigrant and worker rights. When the donations are taken up each year, 25% of the funds remain in each diocese for local Catholic Campaign programs.

Miller Apology On Oct. 26, the Miller Brewing Company issued a formal apology for "the offense caused by the use of Miller brand logos on a poster promoting the Folsom Street Fair in San Francisco with an irreverent take on Leonardo da Vinci's "The Last Supper." The Milwaukee based company issued the apology after it had completed "an exhaustive audit of its marketing procedures for approving local marketing and sales sponsorships" and will tighten "compliance procedures" to ensure such an incident will not happen again. The Catholic League for Religious and Civil Rights and other Christian groups had expressed outrage over the poster, which had what critics described as a sadomasochistic theme. The Catholic League had called for a boycott of Miller products and countered with a statement that the apology was inadequate because it did not address "the anti-Catholic nature of the event itself."

NOVEMBER 2007

VATICAN

Called to Holiness On All Saints' Day, Nov. 1, Pope Benedict XVI greeted the pilgrims gathered in St. Peter's Square for the Angelus, announcing that sainthood is only for the "chosen few." He added that becoming a saint "is the task of every Christian, and what's more, we could even say it's the task of everyone!" The Holy Father said that that the Christian is already holy, "because baptism unites him to Jesus and the paschal mystery, but at the same time he has to become holy, conforming himself to Jesus ever more intimately." The Holy Father made a private visit today to the Vatican Grottoes to pray for the repose of the souls of the Pontiffs entombed there, and for all the faithful departed.

Translation of Liturgy On Nov. 2, the chairman of the International Commission on English in the Liturgy, Bp. Arthur Roche of Leeds, was reported as announcing that the draft phase of the process to translate the 2002 *Roman Missal* from Latin to English has been completed. The last installment, the appendices, of the draft version of the English translation was sent to the episcopal member conferences. The bishops were expected to submit changes to be incorporated into a final proposed version. Bp. Roche estimated that the process would be completed by the end of 2008. The 11-member conferences of the international commission include Australia, Canada, England & Wales, India, Ireland, New Zealand, Pakistan, the Philippines, Scotland, South Africa and the United States. This effort has long been awaited by the faithful.

Damien of Molokai It was reported on Nov. 2 that the medical commission of the Vatican Congregation for the Causes of Saints had ruled that the healing of a Hawaiian woman of lung cancer more than 10 years ago was "unexplainable according to available medical knowledge." The woman prayed to Blessed Damien de Veuster and made pilgrimages to Kalaupapa, where he labored among the Lepers and suffered from the disease after years of dedicated service. According to Sacred Hearts Father Bruno Benati, the postulator of Blessed Damien's cause, the five-physician commission's Oct. 18 ruling was unanimous, and this decision moves the Cause for Canonization forward. Kalaupapa remains a shrine to Blessed Damien's sacrifices. It is likely that Bl. Damien will be canonized in 2009.

Turkey-Kurd Conflict On Nov. 4, Pope Benedict XVI expressed his concern for the Kurdish people residing in northern Iraq. The Holy Father stated his appeal for peace in the region after praying the Angelus with more than 50,000 people who had gathered in St. Peter's Square. "I cannot forget that in that region numerous people, fleeing from the uncertainty and terrorism that have made life in Iraq difficult in these years, have found refuge." He also commented on the fact that among these Kurds there are many Christians. The current crisis is linked to the presence of Kurdish rebels of the Kurdistan Workers' Party (PKK) in northern Iraq.

New Families On Nov. 4, it was reported that Pope Benedict XVI met with some 400 participants in the International New Families Meeting, which marked the 40th anniversary of the organization's foundation. The New Families movement, sponsored by the Catholic lay Focolare movement, is a network of 800,000 families living in 182 countries and promoting family values and virtues. Calling the family a "sacred and sanctifying place," the Holy Father praised the commitment to the "silent and profound evangelization" that New Families promotes, and the organization's four guiding principles, which are spirituality, education, sociability, and solidarity.

Saudi King On Nov. 6, Pope Benedict XVI received in audience King Abdallah bin Abdulaziz Al Saud of Saudi Arabia, marking the first time in history that such a visit from a Saudi ruler took place. The two discussed the need for collaboration among Christians, Muslims and Jews in the various regions of the world, especially in supporting the value of the family. The Saudi Arabian leader then went on to meet with the Pope's secretary of state, Cardinal Tarcisio Bertone, and Abp. Dominique Mamberti, secretary for relations with states. As king, the Saudi Arabian ruler also is the guardian of Islam's sacred mosque in Mecca, where the founder of Islam, Mohammed, was born, and of Medina, where Mohammed's tomb is located. Saudi Arabia and the Holy See do not maintain diplomatic relations, as there is no ambassador from that nation in attendance at the Vatican. There is an apostolic delegate to the Arabian Peninsula, a post held by the Nuncio in Kuwait and Lebanon and who resides in Lebanon.

Romanian Prime Minister On Nov. 7. Pope Benedict XVI received in audience In Romanian Prime Minister Calin Popescu Tariceanu, who thanked the Holy Father for encouraging tolerance in migration. The prime minister also expressed the hope that such a positive attitude should continue. Tariceanu's comments came amid rising tension in Italy over the immigration issue involving Romanians, especially Gypsies. Italy passed a decree allowing the deportation of European Union citizens considered to be dangerous. Some 20 Romanians were later deported, mostly Gypsies, on that basis.

Mozambique President Pope Benedict XVI, on Nov. 8, received in audience Armando Guebuza, the Mozambique president. They discussed the work of the Church in that country and noted that Catholics are committed to a greater presence in the university sector and in the public health sectors.. The president of the southeast African nation then went on to meet with the Holy Father's secretary of state, Cardinal Tarcisio Bertone, and Abp. Dominique Mamberti, secretary for relations with states. About 23% of Mozambique's almost 21 million people are Catholic.

Indonesian Ambassador On Nov. 12, Pope Benedict XVI received the papers of Indonesia's new ambassador to the Holy See, Suprapto Martosetomo. The Holy Father announced that he deeply appreciated Indonesia's position of condemning terrorist violence, under whatever pretext it occurs, and he noted Indonesia's role in promoting interreligious cooperation. "As Indonesia now sits as a non-permanent member of the United Nations Security Council," the Holy Father continued, "I take the present occasion to express my confidence that the principles which inspire your own national policies of pacification, dialogue and tolerance will enable Indonesia to make a fruitful contribution to the solution of global conflicts and the promotion of a peace based on international solidarity and concern for the integral development of individuals and peoples."

Portuguese Bishops It was announced on Nov. 13 that Pope Benedict XVI received in audience the Portuguese bishops, in Rome for their required five-year visit, the *ad limina*.

The Holy Father told the bishops that the Church "should not, above all, speak of itself, but of God. With this, I don't mean to say that we don't have to discuss the best organization of the Church and the distribution of responsibilities: There are always imbalances that need corrections." He also discussed "the authentic mission of the Church." He then counseled: "Given the growing wave of Christians that are not practicing in your dioceses, perhaps it is worthwhile to verify the efficiency of the current processes of initiation, to better help Christians to mature with the educative activities of our communities, and to take on in their lives an authentically Eucharistic stamp that makes them capable of giving reason for their hope in an adequate way for our times."

Relics of St. Thérèse On Nov. 14, Pope Benedict XVI greeted the faithful from the French Diocese of Bayeux and Lisieux, and Bp. Pierre Auguste Pican, who are in Rome on pilgrimage, with the relics of St. Thérèse of the Child Jesus and the Holy Face. The Holy Father then recalled how "120 years ago, Thérèse of Lisieux came to Rome to ask permission of Pope Leo XIII to enter the Carmelite order, despite her youth. Eighty years ago, Pope Pius XI proclaimed her patron saint of missions, and in 1997, Pope John Paul II declared her a doctor of the Church." "In this audience," he continued, "I will have the joy of praying before her relics, as will many faithful over the course of this week in various churches in Rome."

Primacy of Rome On Nov. 15, it was announced that the Catholic-Orthodox theological commission's recognized the primacy of the Bishop of Rome. And that was an "important first step," says the director of the Vatican press office, Fr. Federico Lombardi. The concluding document of the Oct. 8-14 plenary assembly of the Joint International Commission for Theological Dialogue Between the Catholic Church and the Orthodox Church, held in Ravenna, Italy, was titled "Ecclesiological and Canonical Consequences of the Sacramental Nature of the Church: Ecclesia Communion, Conciliarity and Authority." The document also stipulated the need to study and understand the functions of the Bishop of Rome, how his primacy is to be exercised, and the scriptural and theological foundations of it. The meeting was held in Ravenna under the presidency of Cardinal Walter Kasper, president of the Pontifical Council for Promoting Christian Unity, and Metropolitan Ioannis of Pergamo.

Missionary Superiors Pope Benedict XVI received in audience on Nov. 16 some 100 superiors-general from missionary societies of apostolic life. These superiors were in Rome to participate in a meeting organized by the Congregation for the Evangelization of Peoples. "Your assembly," the Holy Father told the group, "bears eloquent witness to the continuing vitality of the missionary impulse in the Church and the spirit of communion uniting your members [...] to the Successor of Peter and his universal apostolic ministry." He expressed his gratitude to all the missionaries who, "today as in the past [...] continue to leave their families and homes, often at great sacrifice, for the sole purpose of proclaiming the good news of Christ and serving him in their brothers and sisters. Many of them, also in our time, have heroically confirmed their preaching by the shedding of their blood, and contributed to establishing the Church in distant lands."

Euthanasia On Nov. 18, Pope Benedict XVI warned against the temptation to euthanize the elderly sick, which he called a symptom of the culture of death. He addressed this modern manifestation while receiving in audience participants in the 22nd international conference promoted by the Pontifical Council for Health Care Ministry. The theme of the meeting, which was held last week in the Vatican, was on "The Pastoral Care of Elderly Sick People." The Holy Father added that euthanasia "appears as one of the more alarming symptoms of the culture of death that is advancing above all in the society of well-being."

New Encyclical It was announced on Nov. 23 that Pope Benedict XVI's second encyclical, *Spe Salvi*, would be signed and released to the public Nov. 30, the feast of St. Andrew the Apostle. The Vatican also stated that the encyclical would also be released that in eight languages, including English. As the Church prepares for the Year of St. Paul, the title, *Spe Salvi*, refers to Paul's Letter to the Romans, 8:24: "For in hope we were saved." The Holy Father's second encyclical continues with a reflection on the theological virtues: faith, hope and love. His 2005 encyclical, *Deus Caritas Est*, considered love. (See **News in Depth**.)

New Cardinals On Nov. 24, Pope Benedict XVI created 23 new cardinals from 14 countries. The group included U.S. Cardinal John P. Foley, grand master of the Knights of the Holy Sepulcher, and Cardinal Daniel N. DiNardo of Galveston-Houston. The ceremony opened with a greeting, followed by the Pope's reading of the formula of creation while solemnly proclaiming the names of the new cardinals. The Liturgy of the Word, the Pontiff's homily, and the profession of faith followed. Each cardinal then took an oath, knelt before the Holy Father and received the cardinal's biretta, before being assigned a title or deaconry. Pope Benedict XVI also assigned the cardinals a Roman church as a sign of their participation with the Bishop of Rome in the pastoral care of the city. The cardinals' rings were bestowed at a concelebrated Mass on the next day. The cardinals' rings represent the dignity, pastoral care and the most solid communion with the See of Peter. As a result of this ceremony, the College of Cardinals had 201 members, of whom 120 were electors, that is, under the age of 80. (See **News in Depth** for other details.)

Muslims Letter On Nov. 29, Pope Benedict XVI responded to an open letter sent to him by 138 Muslim scholars. The Holy Father affirmed in his reply the importance of dialogue and mutual respect and acceptance and his willingness to receive Prince Ghazi and a delegation of the signatories of the letter. The papal response further affirmed the readiness of the Pontifical Council for Interreligious Dialogue, in collaboration with other specialized pontifical institutes, to organize a working meeting. The Muslims' letter, sent Oct. 13, was written on the occasion of the end of the month of Ramadan, and titled "A Common Word Between Us and You." The Holy Father's responding letter, signed by his secretary of state, Cardinal Tarcisio Bertone, was addressed to Prince Ghazi bin Muhammad bin Talal, president of the Aal al-Bayt Institute for Islamic Thought, one of the signatories of the original letter.

Slovenian Prime Minister On Nov. 29, Pope Benedict XVI received in audience the Slovenian prime minister, Janez Jansa, who invited the Holy

Father to visit his country in 2009 and expressed his nation's gratitude for the Holy See's concern ever since Slovenia gained independence. The prime minister later met with the Holy Father's secretary of state, Cardinal Tarcisio Bertone. Cardinal Bertone expressed in a communiqué issued after the meeting his hope that the Slovenian presidency would help bring peace and stability to the region of southeastern Europe. Slovenia gained independence in 1991. About 58% of its 2 million inhabitants are Catholic.

Vatican and NGOs It was reported on Nov. 30 that Vatican officials would meet with Catholic nongovernmental organizations for the first time. Some 85 civil society associations will take part in the encounter, organized by the Pope's Secretariat of State. According to a Vatican statement, the participating organizations all "have as a point of reference the evangelical teaching and social doctrine of the Church." Nongovernmental organizations, known as NGOs, are legally constituted entities directed by private citizens with no participation or representation of any government and work as advocates of social causes such as human rights, poverty and religious freedom. Cardinal Tarcisio Bertone, the Pope's secretary of state, Abp. Dominique Mamberti, secretary for relations with states, and Abp. Celestino Migliore, permanent observer to the United Nations, have been scheduled to address the meeting. Delegates will be received in a papal audience.

GENERAL AUDIENCES

St. Jerome (1), Nov. 7.
St. Jerome (2), Nov. 14.
Aphraates, "the Sage," Nov. 21.
St. Ephrem, Nov. 28.

INTERNATIONAL

Death Penalty Petition On Nov. 4, a group called the World Coalition Against the Death Penalty delivered to the United Nations a petition signed by 5 million people from 154 countries calling for an end to capital punishment. The delegation visiting the UN was also led by the Community of Sant'Egidio. The human rights committee of the General Assembly was presented with a draft resolution on this occasion signed by the countries of Angola, Albania, Brazil, Croatia, Gabon, Mexico, the Philippines, Portugal (representing the European Union), and New Zealand, and. more than 70 nations signing on as co-sponsors.

"Jesus of Nazareth" On Nov. 5, it was reported that Franco Zeffirelli, the noted director, credited Pope Paul VI with making the television miniseries "Jesus of Nazareth" a success. Pope Paul VI had personally thanked Zeffirelli for the masterpiece of filming. Zeffirelli spoke of the miniseries in a lecture marking the new academic year at the Pontifical Lateran University of Rome. The renowned director recalled some of what went on behind the scenes during the filming of the more than six hours of "Jesus of Nazareth," which is just one of the some two dozen productions that Zeffirelli directed. Zeffirelli was also director of the famed biography of St. Francis of Assisi, *Brother Sun, Sister Moon* (1972).

Venezuelan Persecution On Nov. 5, Abp. Ramon Perez Morales, retired archbishop of Los Teques, stat-ed that President Hugo Chavez's government is persecuting Catholic Church leaders in an effort to quiet their criticism of his policies. The archbishop said that there is a "systematic campaign of persecution by government-controlled media to quiet the church." Abp. Morales insisted, however, that it was impossible for the church to keep quiet while Venezuela is being declared a socialist, Marxist, Leninist state. Chavez has labeled his Catholic critics as "ignorant," "perverse" and "liars."

Romanian Benedictines On Nov. 6, it was reported that a Benedictine monastery, Mater Unitatis, was dedicated last month for cloistered women religious in the town of Piatra Neant. The project of establishing the Roman Catholic convent began in 1994 by Bp. Petru Gherghel of Iasi, Romania, and was greatly aided by the Vatican and an Italian Benediction convent. The monastery is set among three Orthodox monasteries, which is an unusual situation in that nation.. Officially the monastery is called Monastic Center 'Mother of Unity,' to which the Romanian government gave juridical status in 2002, but the Benedictine roots are recognized by the local populace.

Argentine Beatification On Nov. 12, Cardinal Tarcisio Bertone, the Vatican secretary of state, beatified Ceferino Namuncurá in a small Argentine village. Blessed Ceferino is the first of the Mapuche indigenous peoples to be so honored. Blessed Ceferino (1886-1905) was a student of the Salesian Society in Argentina, and a Mapuche. The Mapuche are the indigenous inhabitants of southern and central Chile and southern Argentina. On the same day, in St. Peter's Square, Pope Benedict XVI greeted the pilgrims from Argentina and the Salesians present at the audience. He announced: "We give thanks to the Lord for the extraordinary testimony of this young 19-year-old student, who, inspired by his devotion for the Eucharist and love for Christ, wanted to be a Salesian and a priest to show his fellow Mapuche the path to heaven. With his life, he lightens our path to sanctity, inviting us to love our brothers with the love with which God loves us." Cardinal Bertone celebrated the beatification ceremony in the place where Blessed Ceferino was born, announcing that Aug. 26, Ceferino's birthday, will be his liturgical feast day.

Persecution of Christians On Nov. 21, it was reported that the European Parliament joined its voice to that of many Church leaders who are condemning the persecution of Christians in several nations. The Parliament in a resolution asked governments to protect the rights of all citizens and combat acts of discrimination and intolerance. The Parliament further promised that aid to countries will hinge on the condition of respect for religious freedom. Mario Mauro, vice president of the European Parliament and primary promoter of the resolution, said in a public statement, "The persecution of Christians in the world is one of the fiercest contemporary challenges to the dignity of the person." The parliamentary resolution cited concrete cases of intimidation, abductions and assassinations in Iraq, attacks on Christian churches, the assassination of a Protestant bishop, a bombing at a school directed by missionaries in Pakistan, the assassination of a professor at a Christian library in Gaza, and the assassination of two Coptic men in Egypt. Mauro affirmed that "religious liberty is the litmus test to reveal if there is respect for all other freedoms and human rights."

Schoenstatt Apostolate It was reported on Nov. 27 that the Schoenstatt Apostolate has undertaken programs to provide a variety of ministries in Paraguay and other nations for Catholics who have experienced broken marriages. The organization received papal encouragement from Pope Benedict XVI and has been served by a couple from Paraguay, Sonia, and Eduardo Morales, of the Catholic Schoenstatt movement. The Morales had already taken the first steps in a ministry for divorced and remarried couples in 2005, at a meeting of the Latin American bishops' council. Two years ago, *Pastoral de Esperanza* ("Ministry of Hope") was added to the pastoral initiatives of the movement's family ministry, along with courses for dating and engaged couples and other ministries. The ministry works by offering a yearlong cycle of formative talks and monthly get-togethers, in which leaders seek to strengthen the couples in their Christian faith and support them in their roles as parents. Spiritual retreats also form part of the process, during which the movement seeks to teach the couples that the Church loves them, is not distant from them, and suffers for their situation.

NATIONAL

U.S. Bishops Lobby It was reported on Nov. 2 that the conference of U.S. bishops had run an ad campaign in Capital Hill publications urging Congress to support the Mexico City Policy, which ensures that government money does not fund abortions abroad. The House Committee on Foreign Affairs convened a hearing Wednesday on the Mexico City Policy, the same day the bishops' conference placed full-page ads in *Roll Call*, *The Hill*, *CQ Today*, and *Congress Daily AM*. The Knights of Columbus funded the ad that featured the image of a woman from the developing world holding her child, paired with a quotation from Grace Olivarez, dissenting member of John D. Rockefeller III's federal advisory commission on population: "The poor cry out for justice and equality and we respond with legalized abortion."

Envoy to Holy See It was announced on Nov. 5 that Mary Ann Glendon, who has served in key Vatican posts for years, would soon represent her native country to the Holy See. U.S. President George W. Bush announced his intention to nominate Glendon, Harvard law professor and president of the Pontifical Academy for Social Sciences, as ambassador of the United States to the Holy See. The nomination, with confirmation by the Senate, made Glendon successor toFrancis Rooney, who held the post since 2005. Well-known and much admired in the legal profession and among her peers at Harvard, Glendon began her work with the Vatican in 1994 when Pope John Paul II appointed her to lead the Holy See delegation to the U.N. 4th World Conference on Women in Beijing. She was also appointed to the newly formed Pontifical Academy of Social Sciences. She was named the academy's first female president in 2004, the second woman to be appointed to lead a Vatican council.

Abortion Group On Nov. 6 it was reported that the Catholic bishops of Colorado decried the secrecy that surrounded the new acquisition of new Planned Parenthood facilities in their state, and said the public deserves to know the truth about the organization. Abp. Charles Chaput of Denver, Bp. Michael Sheridan of Colorado Springs and Bp. Arthur Tafoya of Pueblo issued a joint statement on the recent ground breaking of the new Planned Parenthood of the Rocky Mountains' headquarters and clinic in northeast Denver. Planned Parenthood acquired the property for the new clinic, under the guise of a different name and planned to complete the entire project in secrecy.

Military Archdiocese On Nov. 11, Veterans Day, the U.S. military archdiocese paid tribute to "every man and woman who faithfully served in the noble causes of securing peace and freedom in the military service of our great nation." Auxiliary Bp. Richard B. Higgins, archdiocesan administrator and vicar for veterans affairs of the U.S. Archdiocese for the Military Services, announced, "To our courageous and honorable veterans, we thank you. The archdiocese ... stands ready to serve your spiritual and pastoral needs wherever you find yourself in the journey of life."

USCCB Affairs On Nov. 11, the U. S. Conference of Catholic Bishops, attending their meeting in Baltimore, approved a $147.7 million budget for 2008 and a 16 percent reduction in the diocesan assessment to fund the USCCB. The bishops accepted as well recommendations of the USCCB Committee on Priorities and Plans for the interim plans of conference offices and committees and continued vital ministries. The U.S. bishops, two days later, elected Cardinal Francis E. George of Chicago as their president and Bp. Gerald F. Kicanas of Tucson, Ariz., as their vice president.

Knights' Donation It was reported on Nov. 11 that the Knights of Columbus would donate 2,000 wheelchairs to veterans. In ceremonies held in Washington, Chicago, Los Angeles and Bonham, Texas, the Knights of Columbus distributed 2,000 wheelchairs to military veterans recovering from battle wounds.. "As our nation pauses to honor these men and women on Veterans Day, we are honored to be able to reach out to help veterans in need," Supreme Knight Carl A. Anderson announced. The Knights of Columbus partnered with the Wheelchair Foundation to distribute the wheelchairs.

Oratorio Premiere On Nov. 27.it was announced that the world premiere of Russian Orthodox Bp. Hilarion Alfeyev's newest musical work was scheduled for December 17 at the Basilica of the National Shrine of the Immaculate Conception. It was performed by the Russian Defense Ministry Symphony Orchestra together with the Choir of the Tretyakov Gallery and the Youth Choir of the Musical College by the Moscow Conservatory. The Washington Boys Choir joined the Russian musicians at the finale of the "Oratorio." "At the heart of this composition lies the Gospel narrative of the birth and early days of Jesus Christ's life on earth," Bp. Alfeyev of Vienna and Austria explained. Hilarion Alfeyev, 41, studied violin, piano and composition before entering monastic life at age 20. He was consecrated bishop at age 35. He is the representative of the Moscow Patriarchate to the European Union in Brussels and a member of the Mixed Commission for the Dialogue Between the Roman Catholic Church and the Orthodox Church.

DECEMBER 2007

VATICAN

Spe Salvi On Dec. 2, Pope Benedict XVI summarized the central message of his second papal encyclical, *Spe Salvi*, before reciting the midday Angelus with the thousands of pilgrims gathered in St. Peter's Square. He also spoke on the meaning of Advent, declaring that the season of Advent "is the propitious time to reawaken in our hearts the expectation of him 'who is, who was and who is coming.'" The Pontiff regarded the First Sunday of Advent as "a most appropriate day to offer to the whole Church and all men of good will my second encyclical, which I wanted to dedicate to the theme of Christian hope." [See **News in Depth** on p. 59.]

Asian Martyrs On Dec. 3, Pope Benedict XVI received in audience the Korean bishops and prelate for Mongolia The Holy Father spoke of the endurance of the Asian martyrs' testimony, which speaks eloquently of the fundamental concept of *"communio"* that unifies and vivifies ecclesial life. The Korean episcopal conference, and the prefect apostolic for Ulaanbaatar, Mongolia, were in Rome for their five-yearly visit. "The Church in your countries has made remarkable progress since the arrival of missionaries in the region over 400 years ago, and their return to Mongolia just 15 years ago," the Holy Father stated. "This growth is due in no small part to the outstanding witness of the Korean martyrs and others throughout Asia who remained steadfastly faithful to Christ and his Church,"

AIDS Victims The Apostleship of Prayer announced on Dec. 4 that Pope Benedict XVI would pray during Dec. for the victims of AIDS, especially children and women. "That human society may be solicitous in the care of all those stricken with AIDS, especially children and women, and that the Church may make them feel the Lord's love." The Holy Father also chooses an apostolic intention for each month. In December he would pray, "That the incarnation of the Son of God, which the Church celebrates solemnly at Christmas, may help the peoples of the Asiatic continent to recognize God's envoy, the only Savior of the world, in Jesus."

Financial Pact On Dec. 4 it was announced that the Holy See and Albania signed an agreement concerning, in part, the fiscal status of Catholic Church organizations in the country. The agreement was signed in the office of the Albanian minister of finance in Tirana by Abp. Giovanni Bulaitis, apostolic nuncio in Tirana, and by Ridvan Bode, Albania's finance minister. The accord between the two countries concluded in 2002. The current agreement creates a juridical framework for the fiscal treatment of ecclesiastical institutions recognized as nonprofit juridical entities.

Lourdes Jubilee It was announced on Dec. 5 that Pope Benedict XVI would grant the faithful a plenary indulgence for the occasion of the 150th anniversary of the apparition of the Blessed Virgin Mary at Lourdes. The Holy See published a decree of the Apostolic Penitentiary stating that a plenary indulgence is granted to faithful who take part in the jubilee year, which was scheduled to last through Dec. 8, 2008. The Immaculate Conception was defined a dogma on Dec. 8, 1854.

World Peace Day On Dec. 5 it was reported that Pope Benedict XVI had chosen the family to be the theme for the World Day of Peace 2008. The message for the peace day was titled "The Human Family: Community of Peace." The World Day of Peace was scheduled to be observed Jan. 1.

Eastern Christianity On Dec. 6, Pope Benedict XVI received a delegation from the Pontifical Oriental Institute, which was marking its 90th Anniversary. The Holy Father declared that the wisdom of Eastern Christianity is a heritage that the Church values as he met with 280 members of the institute, which was founded by Pope Benedict XV in 1917. The Holy Father explained how his predecessor favored the Eastern Churches, which came to "enjoy a regime more in keeping with their traditions, under the gaze of the Roman Pontiffs who have never ceased to show their concern with concrete gestures of support."

Catholic-Baptist Dialogue On Dec. 6, Pope Benedict XVI addressed the members of the joint international commission, sponsored by the Baptist World Alliance and the Pontifical Council for Promoting Christian Unity, meeting in Rome. The Holy Father advised the members that dialogue between Baptists and Catholics can move forward only when points of disagreement are confronted in a spirit of openness, respect and fidelity to the truth of Christ. The theme of the meeting was "The Word of God in the Life of the Church: Scripture, Tradition and *Koinonia*." The dialogue continues through 2010.

Polish Leader Pope Benedict XVI on Dec. 7 received in audience the new prime minister of Poland, Donald Tusk, who succeeded Jaroslaw Kaczynski. The cordial discussion included the present situation in Poland, where the moral and religious values are being challenged by modern trends; also discussed was the European and international roles of Poland. Prime Minister Tusk met afterward with Cardinal Tarcisio Bertone, the Pope's secretary of state, and Abp. Dominique Mamberti, Vatican secretary for relations with states.

Metropolitan Kirill On Dec. 7, Pope Benedict XVI received in audience Metropolitan Kirill of Smolensk and Kaliningrad, the president of the Department of External Affairs of the Moscow Patriarchate. The Holy Father reportedly discussed with Metropolitan Kirill topics concerning Orthodox-Catholic relations, as well as the need to cooperate on an international level to promote commonly-held Christian values. He also extended greetings to Patriarch Alexy II of Moscow and All Russia. Metropolitan Kirill marked the feast of St. Catherine of Alexandria with a visit to the Orthodox parish in Rome that bears her name. He later attended a concert by the Choir of the Monastery of St. Daniel of Moscow in the Basilica of St. Mary of the Angels and Martyrs. In his greeting to those present, reported by Vatican Radio, the Orthodox metropolitan said that "Catholics and Orthodox feel that they belong to the same family, since they share the same Christian values.

Albanian President On Dec. 7, Pope Benedict XVI received in audience President Bamir Topi of Albania The president visited the Holy Father to express gratitude for the Catholic contributions offered to the

Albanian people. The leader also met with the Pope's secretary of state, Cardinal Tarcisio Bertone, and the secretary for the relations with states, Abp. Dominique Mamberti.

Immaculate Conception On the Solemnity of the Immaculate Conception, it was reported on Dec. 9, Pope Benedict XVI reflected on today's youth, who are "growing up in an environment saturated by messages that propose false models of happiness." Addressing thousands of pilgrims gathered in St. Peter's Square the Holy Father announced that "young men and women run the risk of losing hope because they often seem orphans of true love, the love that fills life with meaning and joy." He added: "How sad it is when the young lose wonder, the enchantment of the best sentiments, the value of respect for the body, manifestation of the person and his inscrutable mystery!"

Michelangelo Sketch On Dec. 10, the Vatican announced the discovery of a design for the cupola of the Basilica of St. Peter's presumed to have been drawn by Michelangelo. The design was to be presented to Cardinal Angelo Comastri, president of the Fabbrica di San Pietro, the office in charge of construction matters and maintenance related to St. Peter's. The design was also scheduled to be officially presented to the information organizations and made public in the Press Office of the Holy See. The sketch was dated 1563, the year before Michelangelo's death, and experts who analyzed it believe that it deals with instructions the artist sent to the carvers who were cutting the stone blocks of the basilica.

Bible Online On Dec. 10, it was reported that the Vatican Congregation for the Clergy launched a Web site that allows researchers to access Bible verses with exegeses from doctors of the Church or cross reference liturgical texts with commentaries from Church Fathers. The Website at www.bibliaclerus.org offers six categories in nine languages. It also gives the option of downloading the site's content. The nine translations of the Bible, including Hebrew and Greek, can be read side-by-side, as can the Eastern and Latin Codes of Canon Law.

Ecumenical Taizé Meeting It was reported on Dec. 11 that Pope Benedict XVI sent a message to the young people gathering in Geneva for an ecumenical encounter organized by the Taizé Community. The message was sent in his name by his secretary of state, Cardinal Tarcisio Bertone, to the 40,000 youth in Switzerland. The program includes moments of prayer, silence, song, and testimonies from the ecumenical community of Taizé. The message stated: "Dear young people gathered in Geneva by the Taizé Community for a new stage of the pilgrimage of trust on earth launched by Brother Roger, the Pope assures you of his spiritual closeness and asks the Lord that these days may be for you a time of grace and a powerful experience of Church."

New Ambassadors On Dec. 13, Pope Benedict XVI welcomed seven new ambassadors to the Holy See, coming from Thailand, Seychelles, Namibia, Gambia, Suriname, Singapore, and Kuwait. At a formal audience, the Holy Father told the diplomats that their task was particularly important in today's world, "to show that, in all the situations of international life, dialogue must overcome violence, and the desire for peace and brotherhood should prevail over confrontation and individualism, which only causes tensions and resentment, impeding progress in the reconciliation of societies." He also turned his attention to youth, calling them "a country's greatest wealth." He concluded by offering his encouragement to "all people who participate in this beautiful mission of educating youth to continue tirelessly in their task, convinced that an adequate formation of youth prepares a promising tomorrow."

Venezuelan Cardinal On Dec. 13, Pope Benedict XVI sent a message to Cardinal Jorge Urosa Savino, after the Caracas archbishop was attacked by a group of Hugo Chávez supporters called "The Hot Corner." The cardinal was attacked verbally and physically Friday by the Venezuelan president's supporters in the capital's central Bolivar Plaza, as local police stood by. The message stated: "As a sign of consolation and esteem, I cordially send you my apostolic blessing, which extends to all the pastors and faithful of that beloved nation." Cardinal Urosa received several verbal attacks from Chávez during the campaign for the referendum on the socialist constitutional reform, which was defeated in the ballot boxes.

Christmas at St. Peter's It was announced on Dec. 13 that the 85-foot Christmas tree in St. Peter's Square, decorated with more than 2,000 ornaments, will be officially lit Friday. Cardinal Giovanni Lajolo, president of the Governorate of Vatican City State, was designated to preside at the official lighting ceremony. The 140-year-old, 3-ton fir is to stand beside the Nativity scene in the square, which was still under construction. Civil and religious authorities from the region of Bolzano in northern Italy, which donated this year's tree, will attend. The Nativity scene, which was scheduled to be unveiled on Christmas Eve, contained 17 life-size statues. Of these, nine are the original figures donated by St. Vincent Pallotti for the Nativity scene in the Roman Church of Sant'Andrea della Valle in 1842. The other eight figures added over the years. As in 2006, the Italian province of Trento has provided more sculpted wooden figures and animals, as well as household utensils for the depiction of daily life. It was also announced that Paul VI Hall would also be adorned with a tree and a Nativity scene designed by Mexican artists.

New Church Dedicated On Dec. 16, Pope Benedict XVI blessed the new church of Santa Maria del Rosario ai Martiri Portuensi in Magliana, located in the western part of the Diocese of Rome. Referring to the fact that it was Gaudete Sunday, the Holy Father said: "In truth, all of Advent is an invitation to rejoice because 'the Lord is coming,' because he is coming to save us." He added: ... "Today, there is another reason for us to rejoice. ... It is the dedication of the new parish church which is built on the same site where my beloved predecessor, the Servant of God John Paul II, celebrated Holy Mass on the occasion of his pastoral visit on Nov. 8, 1998."

Japanese Bishops On Dec. 17, Pope Benedict XVI received in audience bishops from Japan, in Rome for their five-yearly visit. "Indeed the world is hungry for the message of hope that the Gospel brings," the Holy Father told the prelates. "Even in countries as highly developed as yours, many are discovering that economic success and advanced technology are not sufficient in themselves to bring fulfillment to the human heart. Anyone who does not know God is ultimately without hope, without the great hope that sustains the whole of life." He added: "You have made the voice of the Church heard on the enduring importance of this witness, all the greater in a world where armed conflicts bring so much suffering to the innocent," he said. "I encourage you to continue to speak on matters of public concern in the life of your nation, and to ensure that your statements are promoted and widely disseminated, so that they may be properly heard at all levels within society."

Causes of Saints In an address to the postulators of the Vatican Congregation for Saints' Causes, Pope Benedict XVI, on Dec. 17, announced that those who work in the causes of saints need to be at the exclusive service of truth. The Holy Father received these postulators in an audience. "Through beatifications and canonizations," Benedict XVI added, the Church "gives thanks to God for the gift of those of his children who have responded generously to divine grace, honoring them and invoking them as intercessors." And the Church "presents these shining examples for the imitation of all the faithful, called through baptism to sanctity, which is the aim and goal of every state of life."

Papal Christmas Schedule On Dec. 17, the Office for the Liturgical Celebrations of the Supreme Pontiff published the calendar of events at which the Pope would preside during the Christmas season. The Holy Father was scheduled to celebrate Midnight Mass on Monday, Dec. 24, in St. Peter's Basilica. The next day, at noon from the central balcony of St. Peter's, he was scheduled to deliver his Christmas message to the world and will impart his blessing *urbi et orbi* (to the city of Rome and the world). On New Year's Eve, at 6 p.m. in St. Peter's Basilica, he was to preside at first vespers of the solemnity of Mary Mother of God. This was to be followed by the exposition of the Blessed Sacrament, the singing of the traditional "*Te Deum*" hymn of thanksgiving for the conclusion of the civil year, and the Eucharistic blessing.

French President On Dec. 20, Pope Benedict XVI welcomed French President Nicolas Sarkozy to the Vatican for talks focused on Europe, the Middle East, Africa and the role of religions in society. President Nicolas Sarkozy visited the Holy Father in his private library for 30 minutes, his first visit to the Pontiff as president of France. Afterward, Sarkozy went on to meet with the Pope's secretary of state, Cardinal Tarcisio Bertone, and Abp. Dominique Mamberti, secretary for relations with states. At the end of the conversation, best wishes were exchanged for the forthcoming feasts of Christmas and the New Year. Before leaving the Vatican, Sarkozy visited the tomb of Pope John Paul II.

Midnight Mass Homily On Dec. 24, Pope Benedict XVI preached a homily at the Christmas Midnight Mass in St. Peter's Basilica, The Holy Father spoke of St. Gregory of Nyssa's interpretation of the stable in which Christ was born, announcing: "Thus, according to Gregory's vision, the stable in the Christmas message represents the ill-treated world. What Christ rebuilds is no ordinary palace. He came to restore beauty and dignity to creation, to the universe: This is what began at Christmas and makes the angels rejoice. The earth is restored to good order by virtue of

the fact that it is opened up to God, it obtains its true light anew, and in the harmony between human will and divine will, in the unification of height and depth, it regains its beauty and dignity. Thus Christmas is a feast of restored creation."

Muslim Scholars It was reported on Dec. 24 that an international group of Muslim scholars has accepted an invitation from Pope Benedict XVI. The Muslim scholars also sent a Christmas greeting to "our Christian neighbors all over the world." Jordan's Prince Ghazi bin Muhammad bin Talal, architect of the Muslim scholars' project, said the group planned to send representatives to the Vatican in February or March.

Christmas Prayer On Dec. 25, Pope Benedict XVI offered a prayer from the central balcony of St. Peter's Basilica during his traditional Christmas address. Before giving his blessing *urbi et orbi* (to the city of Rome and the world) he offered a Christmas greeting in 63 languages, including, this year, Guarani, the language of an indigenous South American people. The Holy Father expressed his wish that the light of Christ, "which comes to enlighten every human being," would "shine forth and bring consolation to those who live in the darkness of poverty, injustice and war; to those who are still denied their legitimate aspirations for a more secure existence, for health, education, stable employment, for fuller participation in civil and political responsibilities, free from oppression and protected from conditions that offend against human dignity."

GENERAL AUDIENCES
St. Chromatius of Aquileia, Dec. 5.
St. Paulinus, Bishop of Nola, Dec. 12.
Christ's Birth, Dec. 19.

INTERNATIONAL
Basilica of St. Teresa It was reported on Dec. 3 that the Diocese of Salamanca hopes to finish the Basilica of St. Teresa of Avila, where the incorrupt body of the mystical doctor is reserved, before the 400th anniversary of her beatification. The basilica, located in Alba de Tormes, in the western province of Salamanca, was begun in 1898 by Bp. Tomás de Cámara y Castro of Salamanca. Teresa de Cepeda y Ahumada, born in Avila in 1515, died in Alba de Tormes in 1582. .The estimated cost of the total project is 4.3 million (\$6.32 million). The Diocese of Salamanca currently counts on little more than 1 million (\$1.47 million), and is in need of raising more than 3 million (\$4.41 million) to complete the project.

Climate Change Meeting On Dec. 4, a Vatican delegation attended the 13th session of the U.N.-led climate change conference on the Indonesian island of Bali. The Holy See is usually represented at such meetings with a delegation led by the apostolic nuncio and made up of experts from the area. More than 180 countries were meeting in Bali to draft a climate change framework that will succeed the Kyoto Protocol, the treaty on reducing greenhouse gas emissions that expires in 2012.

Red Cross Conference Abp. Silvano Tomasi, permanent observer of the Holy See to the Office of the United Nations and Specialized Institutions in Geneva, was reported on Dec. 6 as attending the 30th International Conference of the Red Cross and the Red Crescent Movement. The conference, entitled

"Together for Humanity," took place in Geneva. Addressing the international aid agency, Abp. Tomasi said: "Beyond the tragedies and shortcomings of man-made conflicts, tensions and natural disasters, defacing the dignity of every person, a realistic and long-range solution to enhance humanitarian protection rests on the realization that the human family is really one."

Jubilee Year in Lourdes On Dec. 11, Cardinal Ivan Dias, prefect of the Vatican Congregation for Evangelization of People, opened the jubilee celebrations in France on Saturday, feast of the Immaculate Conception, the title with which Mary introduced herself when she appeared to Bernadette Soubirous in 1858. Cardinal Dias said that the struggle between the forces of good and evil "began at the beginning of human history, and will continue until the end." He added that today "this battle is even bloodier than in Bernadette's time." The world finds itself terribly deceived in the spiral of relativism that desires to create a society without God, a relativism that erodes the permanent and unchange-able values of the Gospel; and of religious indifference that remains unconcerned before the higher good of things relat-ing to God and the Church."

Priest Stabbed On Dec. 16 it was reported that an Italian priest, Capuchin Fr. Adriano Franchini, the superior of the Custody of Turkey, was stabbed at the end of Mass in the Bayrakli parish church, in Izmir. He was the latest victim of violence against Christians in Turkey. Three people were arrested as suspects. Another Italian priest was killed in Trabzon in February 2006. In January, a Christian journalist was killed in Istanbul, and in April, three Christians were killed at a Bible publishing house in Malatya.

Cuban Beatification On Dec. 10, it was reported that Abp. Juan García Rodríguez of Camaguey announced this month that the beatification of José Olallo Valdés is expected for November 2008. The cause for his beatification has been under way for about two decades. Father Olallo Valdés was a reli-gious nurse of the Order of Hospitallers who lived in the 19th century in a convent-hospital. The first Cuban to be raised to the altar was Augustinian Brother José López Piteira, a native of San Jose de Jatibonico, who was beatified in Rome on Oct. 28, together with 497 other martyrs, the majority of whom were Spanish.

Tony Blair Conversion On Dec. 21, former British Prime Minister Tony Blair became a Catholic during a private ceremony in London. Blair. He was received into full communion with the Catholic Church by Cardinal Cormac Murphy-O'Connor of Westminster at Archbishop's House, the cardinal's private resi-dence. The cardinal said. "My prayers are with him, his wife and family at this joyful moment in their jour-ney of faith together." Blair served as British prime minister from May 1997 until June 2007.

NATIONAL

Pope's Visit It was reported on Dec. 4 that The Catholic University of America has launched a website dedicated to Benedict XVI's visit to the school in April. The Pope has been scheduled to visit the univer-sity Thursday, April 17, as part of his apostolic visit to the United States. "Even though we're five months away from welcoming the Holy Father to Catholic University, excitement about his upcoming visit is run-ning very high," said university president Father David O'Connell. "In recognition of this excitement and to satisfy the desire for as much information and transparency as possible, we have created this special Catholic University of America website."

Bishops Fault Book On Dec. 10, it was reported that the U.S. bishops are drawing attention to "pervading ambiguities and equivocations that could easily con-fuse or mislead the faithful" in a book by a chairman at Georgetown University's theology department. Father Peter Phan. The work, titled "Being Religious Interreligiously: Asian Perspectives on Interfaith Dialogue," was discussed by the bishops' Committee on Doctrine, which was requested to review the book by the Vatican Congregation for the Doctrine of the Faith asked the U.S. conference to review the book. "The way the book addresses some theological issues," the bishops wrote, "raises serious concerns." Though the author was asked to respond to the issues in his book, the bishops said he "did not provide the needed clarifications." They added that "since the ambiguities in the book concern matters that are cen-tral to the faith, the Committee on Doctrine decided to issue a statement that would both identify problematic aspects of the book and provide a positive restatement of Catholic teaching on the relevant points."

Guadalupe Center On Dec. 12, some 2,000 Hispanic Catholics attended St. Edward Church's new Our Lady of Guadalupe Center in Nashville for a Mass. The center is the new home of the parish's Hispanic ministry. Celebrated on the feast of Our Lady of Guadalupe, who is the patroness of the Americas and the Diocese of Nashville, the Mass was preceded by a procession.

Cardinal George On Dec. 12, Cardinal Francis George, the newly elected president of the U.S. bish-ops' conference announced that the World Day of Peace message of Pope Benedict XVI was urgent for the world. Cardinal George noted particularly two of the papal message: nuclear disarmament and protec-tion of the environment. "Pope Benedict XVI's call for nations to show 'greater determination' for 'a pro-gressive and mutually agreed dismantling of existing nuclear weapons' is urgent and should be of the high-est priority for citizens of the world," the Cardinal said, adding: "The Pope's concern for the environment is also paramount."

U.S. Envoy to Holy See On Dec. 21, the U.S. Senate confirmed President George Bush's nomination of Mary Ann Glendon as the U.S. ambassador to the Holy See. Ambassador Glendon will succeed Francis Rooney, who has represented the United States before the Holy See since 2005. A date for her succession has not been set. Glendon is the president of the Pontifical Academy of Social Sciences and a law professor at Harvard University. In 1994, Pope John Paul II appointed her to lead the Holy See delegation to the U.N. 4th World Conference on Women in Beijing.

Ground Zero On Dec. 24, the 2007 Christmas Eve Midnight Mass at ground zero was the last official Mass on the former site of the World Trade Center. Franciscan Fr. Brian Jordan from St. Francis of Assisi Church in Manhattan had celebrated Christmas Midnight Mass every year at the site since 2001. The priest was an unofficial chaplain at ground zero after the towers collapsed. Port Authority officials had informed him that future construction work would pre-vent celebrations of the Mass there.

JANUARY 2008

VATICAN

Agent of Peace On World Day of Peace, Jan. 1, Pope Benedict XVI stated: "We have begun a new year, and I wish that it will be for all peaceful and prosperous." The day also commemorated the solemnity of Mary, the Mother of God: "In Bethlehem, in the fullness of time, Jesus was born of Mary: The Son of God was made man for our salvation, and the Virgin truly became Mother of God. This immense gift that Mary received was not reserved only for her, but for us all." The Holy Father also recognized the efforts of various ecclesial organizations, and in particular the marches organized by the Community of Sant' Egidio, to promote the World Day of Peace.

Family March On Jan. 1, Pope Benedict XVI greeted more than 2 million participants in a pro-family march in Madrid, Spain, urging them to be witnesses "of the beauty of human love." The Holy Father gave this greeting before praying the Angelus with the thousands gathered in St. Peter's Square. His words could be heard via video link by those congregated in the Plaza de Colon in Madrid to promote the Christian family. The event in Madrid was organized by the archdiocese with the support of ecclesial movements as well as pro-life and pro-family organizations. The Holy Father said, "I invite all Christian families to experience the loving presence of the Lord in their lives. I encourage them, inspired by love of Christ for all mankind, to give witness before the world of the beauty of human love, marriage and family."

Papal Intention It was announced on Jan. 1 that Pope Benedict XVI's monthly prayer intention was focused on unity. The Apostleship of Prayer announced the general intention chosen by the pope: "That the Church may strengthen her commitment to full visible unity in order to manifest in an ever growing degree her nature as community of love, in which is reflected the communion of the Father, the Son and the Holy Spirit." The Holy Father also prayed that "the Church in Africa, which is preparing to celebrate her Second Special Assembly of the Synod of Bishops, may continue to be the sign and instrument of reconciliation and justice in a continent which is still marked by war, exploitation and poverty."

World Stability Speaking to the Vatican diplomatic corps on Jan. 7, Pope Benedict XVI described the security and stability of the world as fragile. The Holy See maintains diplomatic relations with 176 nations. The Holy Father also gave special mention to places affected by "appalling natural disasters," announcing: "I am thinking of the hurricanes and floods which have devastated certain regions of Mexico and Central America, as well as countries in Africa and Asia, especially Bangladesh, and parts of Oceania; mention must also be made of the great fires." He spoke as well of the conflict in the Middle East and noted that hope is almost vanquished in the conflict in the Darfur region of Sudan. "The Catholic Church is not indifferent to the cries of pain that rise up from these regions," he said. "She makes her own the pleas for help made by refugees and displaced persons, and she pledges herself to foster reconciliation, justice and peace."

Epiphany On the feast of the Epiphany, Jan. 7, Pope Benedict XVI announced that the Church completes its mission when it reflects the light of Christ to nations enveloped in a "dense fog." He stated this during his homily at a Mass on the solemnity of the Epiphany of the Lord, held in St. Peter's Basilica. He also said that the feast is when the Church celebrates "Christ, light of the world, and his 'manifestation' to all people," and called for austerity in order to avoid wasting wealth when so many people suffer in extreme poverty.

St. Lawrence Jubilee On Jan. 8, Pope Benedict XVI launched the jubilee year of St. Lawrence, which marks the 1,750th anniversary of the martyrdom of the saint. Card. Camillo Ruini presided over the opening Mass of the jubilee year, held in the Basilica of St. Lawrence Outside the Walls. St. Lawrence was one of seven deacons of Rome condemned by Emperor Valerian I in 258 to die on a grill. He lived in Rome and served by administering the goods of the Church and caring for the poor. St. Lawrence is also the patron of the city of Huesca, Spain, where people venerate the memory of his parents, Sts. Orencia and Paciencia.

English Missal On Jan. 10, Card. Francis Arinze, prefect of the Congregation for Divine Worship and the Sacraments, was reported as sharing satisfaction with translation experts and other concerned Vatican officials over the new English translation of the Roman Missal, which nears completion. The Congregation for Divine Worship and the Sacraments explained the progress of the Vox Clara Committee in a press release. Vox Clara was formed in 2001 to serve as a panel of bishops who provide advice to the Holy See concerning English-language liturgical books. The committee's 15th meeting ended last month, and focused extensively on the Green Book draft translations of several Masses from the International Commission on English in the Liturgy (ICEL). ICEL sends its proposed translation to bishops and experts for study and comment (Green Book). After the comments are incorporated, the texts are proposed for canonical vote by the episcopal conferences (Gray Book). The text, once approved by the bishops' conference, is sent to Rome for approval (White Book). The press release also stated: "Considerable time was also devoted to a careful review of the ICEL Gray Book for the Proper of Seasons in the light of those recommendations provided to the mixed commission by the congregation following Vox Clara's review of the ICEL Green Book for this segment last year. This review was conducted in preparation for the submission of White Book translations following the canonical approval of these texts by the English-language episcopal conferences in the coming months and the subsequent and concluding review by the congregation in preparation for the granting of the 'recognitio.'" Vox Clara also studied the "confirmation of the Order of Mass, including the fine-tuning of several points of translation in the Eucharistic prayers." Card. Arinze expressed the congregation's thanks for the contribution the committee members and advisers have given to the English-language edition of the Roman Missal. The Vox Clara committee will meet again in September.

Pope Baptizes Babies On Jan. 13, Pope Benedict XVI baptized 13 babies, giving them the sacrament that he said opened heaven for them. Eight baby girls and five baby boys were brought to the Sistine Chapel, where the Holy Father expressed his joy at imparting the first sacrament of Christian life to the newborns, "one of the most expressive moments of our faith." In his homily for the feast of the Baptism of the Lord, the Holy Father reflected on the "mystery of life": of the "human life represented here by the newborns and the divine life that God gives to the baptized." The children's parents, employees of Vatican City, were accompanied by the babies' godparents and a small group of relatives.

Benin President Pope Benedict XVI, on Jan. 13, received in audience the president of the West African country of Benin, Thomas Yayi Boni. President Boni was accompanied by his wife and an entourage and had a 15-minute private conversation with the Holy Father in French. The audience reportedly focused on Benin's difficult socioeconomic situation, deepened by last October's floods.

Holy Land Bishops On Jan. 14, Pope Benedict XVI received in audience prelates from the Conference of Latin Bishops in the Arab Regions. Abp. Michel Sabbah, patriarch of Jerusalem, was among them. The bishops, from countries such as Israel, Iraq, and Saudi Arabia, visited the pope during their five-yearly visit to Rome. They discussed with him the phenomenon of the emigration of Christians from the Holy Land, the problems of justice and peace, and the formation of priests and laypeople. The prelates closed their tour with a meeting with the Middle East bishops.

Pope Cancels University Visit It was announced on Jan. 15 that Pope Benedict XVI canceled his visit to Rome's Sapienza University amid protests from 67 professors and students regarding the Church's role in science. The visit was planned for Thursday, but a group of professors and students signed a letter protesting the visit by a pope whom they claimed is "hostile to science," and occupied the rector's office in protest. Giorgio Israel, a Jewish mathematician and professor at the university, noted in *L'Osservatore Romano* that a 1990 speech by then Card. Ratzinger actually defended Galileo.

Christian Unity On Jan. 16, Pope Benedict XVI invited the Church to pray without ceasing for Christian unity, so that all believers may profess Christ as their savior. He made his appeal at the end of today's general audience in preparation for the Week of Prayer for Christian Unity, which began Friday. The Pontiff recalled that the theme for the week is the invitation of St. Paul to the Thessalonians: "Pray without Ceasing."

"Royal Door" On Jan. 18, Pope Benedict XVI announced that prayer is the "royal door" of ecumenism. The Holy Father said this on the first day of the Week of Prayer for Christian Unity to members of a Catholic-Lutheran pilgrimage from Finland. The pope addressed the delegation, which was in Rome for an annual visit on the occasion of the feast of St. Henrik, patron of Finland. The group, sponsored by the Evangelical Lutheran Church of Finland, and led by Lutheran Abp. Kari Makinen of Turku and Catholic Bp. Józef Wróbel of Helsinki, coincided with the beginning of the Week of Prayer for Christian Unity.

Roman Affection On Jan. 20, some 200,000 people gathered at the Vatican to support Pope Benedict XVI days after protests led him to cancel a visit to a Roman university. The Holy Father's visit to La Sapienza University for the inauguration of the academic year had been planned, but a group of professors signed a letter objecting to the visit by the Holy Father, whom they labeled as "hostile to science." At the behest of Card. Camillo Ruini, the pope's vicar for Rome, throngs of professors, students, families, and politicians gathered in St. Peter's Square today for the weekly Angelus to show their affection for the Holy Father in what the Italian media tagged "Pope Day." Those gathered in St. Peter's Square held up banners with slogans such as "Holy Father We Love You" and "The Truth Sets Us Free," while tens of thousands more watched video links of the event outside the Milan cathedral and in Verona.

World Day of Sick It was reported on Jan. 20 that Pope Benedict XVI announced that pain is the door by which the faithful can enter into the mystery of redemption, and reach peace and happiness with Christ. He stated this as part of his message for the 16th World Day of the Sick, to be celebrated on the diocesan level on Feb. 11. Catholics throughout the world celebrate this day in honor of those who suffer and endure physical disabilities and illnesses. The caregivers of such patients are also remembered in prayers. St. Agnes's Feast On the feast of St. Agnes, Jan. 21, Pope Benedict XVI blessed two live lambs whose wool will be used to weave pallia. The animals were blessed in the Apostolic Palace. The pallia woven from the lambs' wool were to be bestowed on new metropolitan archbishops on June 29, the solemnity of Sts. Peter and Paul. The pallium is a white band embroidered with six black crosses and worn over the shoulders. It has two hanging pieces, front and back. Worn by the Holy Father and by metropolitan archbishops, the pallium symbolizes authority and expresses the special bond between the bishops and the Roman Pontiff.

Togo Leader On Jan. 21, it was reported that Pope Benedict XVI received in audience Faure Essozimna Gnassingbe, the president of Togo. They discussed the situation of the thousands of refugees in that West African country. The president is the son of Etienne Gnassingbe Eyadema, who was also president of the small African country. After being received by the Holy Father, the president met with the pope's secretary of state, Card. Tarcisio Bertone, and Abp. Dominique Mamberti, secretary for relations with states. Togo has a population of 5.7 million. About half of Togolese belong to traditional African religions; another 29% are Christian and 20% are Muslim.

Media Overstepping On Jan. 24, Pope Benedict XVI commented that rather than reporting on reality, mass media sometimes create reality, thus wielding tremendous power over all dimensions of human life. The Holy Father affirmed this in a message released for World Communications Day, to be celebrated May 4. "In view of their meteoric technological evolution, the media have acquired extraordinary potential, while raising new and hitherto unimaginable questions and problems," the Holy Father stressed in the message. He also noted disturbing trends in the use of mass media: "Unfortunately, though, they risk being transformed into systems aimed at subjecting humanity to agendas dictated by the dominant interests of the day." The Holy Father explained: "This is what happens when communication is used for ideological purposes or for the aggressive advertising of consumer products. While claiming to represent reality, it can tend to legitimize or impose distorted models of personal, family or social life." He added: "When communication loses its ethical underpinning and eludes society's control, it ends up no longer taking into account the centrality and inviolable dignity of the human person. As a result it risks exercising a negative influence on people's consciences and choices and definitively conditioning their freedom and their very lives."

Slovenian Bishops On Jan. 24, Pope Benedict XVI received in audience bishops from the Slovenian Episcopal conference who had just completed their five-yearly visit to the Vatican. In his address to them, the Holy Father considered the changes the country has seen over the past years, including its entry into the European Union. Recalling the pastoral letter written by Slovenian bishops in 2004, the pope noted that it remains valid because, "if Europe wishes to remain—and ever more to become—a land of peace, maintaining the dignity of the human person as one of its fundamental values, it cannot relinquish the principle spiritual and ethical component of its foundation: Christianity." The Holy Father then went on to consider the "main challenge" facing the Church in Slovenia: "Western-style secularism, which is different and perhaps more underhanded than Marxist secularism." Referring to the National Eucharistic Congress, which will be held in Slovenia in 2009, the Holy Father stated that the Eucharist and the Word of God "constitute the true treasure of the Church. Faithful to the teaching of Christ, each community must use earthly goods simply, in the service of the Gospel."

Ecumenical Cause On Jan. 25, Pope Benedict XVI received in audience members of the Joint Working Group between the World Council of Churches and the Catholic Church. The group was in Rome to begin a new phase of work. "The Joint Working Group, which began in 1965, has worked assiduously to strengthen the 'dialogue of life,' which my predecessor, Pope John Paul II, called the 'dialogue of charity,'" the Holy Father announced, citing *"Ut Unum Sint."* "This cooperation has given vivid expression to the communion already existing between Christians and has advanced the cause of ecumenical dialogue and understanding." The Holy Father and Reverend Doctor Samuel Kobia, the secretary-general of the World Council of Churches, along with high-level representatives of both the Catholic Church and the council, marked together the 100th anniversary of the Week of Prayer for Christian Unity. "The centenary of the Week of Prayer for Christian Unity offers us an opportunity to thank almighty God for the fruits of the ecumenical movement, in which we can discern the presence of the Holy Spirit fostering the growth of all Christ's followers in unity of faith, hope and love," the pope said. "To pray for unity is itself 'an effective means of obtaining the grace of unity' since it is a participation in the prayer of Jesus himself. When Christians pray together, 'the goal of unity seems closer,' for the presence of Christ in our midst fosters a profound harmony of mind and heart: We are able to look at each other in a new way, and to strengthen our resolve to overcome whatever keeps us apart." He concluded, "Dear friends, I pray that the new Joint Working Group will be able to build on the commendable work already done, and thus open the way to ever greater cooperation, so that the Lord's prayer 'that they all may be one' will be ever more fully realized in our time."

World Day of Leprosy On Jan. 27, Pope Benedict XVI asked Christians to be missionaries of the Good News not only in word but also in "active charity." After praying the Angelus today from the window of his study, the pope greeted those suffering from leprosy, "assuring [them] of a special prayer," which he extended to "those who, in various ways, assist them." He also invited "political and health officials to commit themselves still further to those who suffer from" Hanson's disease, urging: "May all our contemporaries stand beside their brothers and sisters in humanity. Each one of you is called by Christ and must be a missionary of the Good News in word and in active charity."

GENERAL AUDIENCES
Mary, Mother of God, Jan. 2.
St. Augustine of Hippo (1), Jan. 9.
St. Augustine of Hippo (2), Jan. 16.
Week of Prayer for Christian Unity, Jan. 23.
St. Augustine of Hippo (3), Jan. 30.

INTERNATIONAL
Christmas Holiday It was reported on Jan. 1 that the Christian feast of Christmas was among nine religious and ethnic feasts the Nepalese government has added to the country's list of public holidays. The designation resulted from pressure from minority ethnic and religious groups. The Nepalese Home Affairs Ministry announced that Christmas and Eid al-Fitr, the Muslim feast that follows the fasting month of Ramadan, were among the new public holidays. Good Friday and Easter public holidays were also designated as holidays.

2007 Violent Deaths It was reported on Jan. 5 that twenty-one people involved in Catholic ministry suffered violent deaths in 2007. The Vatican Congregation for the Evangelization of Peoples released the list of names of the dead, including priests and deacons. One seminarian, one brother, and one woman religious are also included. 2007's statistics show three fewer deaths than in 2006 and four less than two years ago, and include 15 priests. Sister Anne Thole of the Franciscan Sisters of the Holy Family perished when a hospital for AIDS patients caught fire in South Africa. She died heroically trying to save the patients.

Venezuelan Priest Slain On Jan. 6 it was reported that Fr. Pedro Orellana Hidalgo, a diocesan priest was murdered Sunday in what investigators believe was a case of robbery turned homicide. He was strangled. Several objects were stolen from the priest's residence, including a television and money. Fr. Orellana was born in Caracas and carried out his pastoral work for years in the Archdiocese of Cumana. His most recent ministry was in the Immaculate Heart of Mary Parish in Caracas.

Hong Kong Cardinal On Jan. 13, Card. Joseph Zen Ze-kiun of Hong Kong and some 200 lay Christians and clergy attended a prayer rally before joining thousands protesting the central government's decision not to allow direct elections for Hong Kong officials in 2012. Card. Zen announced that he was very angry the Chinese government in Beijing ignored the aspirations of Hong Kong residents in this manner. "We hope for respect and dialogue. We will hold on to our stance [for universal suffrage in 2012] right to the end and believe in the power of prayer," he added.

Iraqi Christian Exodus It was reported on Jan. 15 that the Catholic exodus from Iraq might resume in the wake of recent attacks against Christian holy places. This alarm was sounded by the charity organization Aid to the Church in Need, based on reports it collected from Christians in Iraq after a series of attacks in early January. "The attacks had the goal of terrorizing Christians so they leave the region, and to make those Iraqi Christians who have emigrated and are hoping to return cancel their plans," an organization statement said. Aid to the Church in Need considers that "given the small extent of the material damage caused by the bombs, it is not very likely that the attackers aimed to cause injuries or greater damage." Abp. Louis Sako of Kirkuk said he thinks the bombings are a political message, directed at terrorizing the Christian community of the area, which had suffered relatively few acts of violence or intimidation.

Priest Murdered It was reported on Jan. 16 that an Oblate of Mary Immaculate Fr. Reynaldo Roda was shot and killed in the southern region of Mindanao in what appeared to be an attempted kidnapping. The 54-year-old priest spent the last 10 years as a missionary in the area where he was slain. He was the parish priest of Our Lady of the Most Holy Rosary Church in Tabawan, in the Apostolic Vicariate of Jolo. Fr. Roda was praying in a chapel in the village of Likud Tabawan when about 10 men attacked him. He resisted until one of the men took out a handgun and shot the priest in the head. A teacher who was with Fr. Roda was captured by the gunmen. The southern island of Mindanao is a region known for the presence of Islamic fundamentalists. The largest group is the Moro Islamic Liberation Front. The movement of Abu Sayyaf ("Sword Bearers") is associated with al-Qaida and is also active in the area.

Kenyan Priest Slain On Jan. 27, it was announced that a Catholic priest of the western Kenyan Diocese of Nakuru was murdered as vicious interethnic violence claimed more lives in the Rift Valley town. Fr. Michael Kamau Ithondeka, 41, was killed Saturday morning at an illegal roadblock set up by armed youth. He was vice rector at St. Mathias Mulumba Senior Seminary in Tindinyo. Fr. Ithondeka was born in Kiambu, near Nairobi, in 1966, and was ordained a priest of Nakuru Diocese in 1993.Israeli President On Jan. 29, the president of Israel, Shimon Peres, visited Nazareth on Monday, welcomed by the Franciscan caretakers of the Holy Land. The Israeli president was also received by Nazareth's mayors and other civil and religious leaders. After the official welcome, Peres visited Nazareth's basilica and was given an explanation of the sanctuary. He then gave an address.

NATIONAL

Merging Congregations It was reported on Jan. 3 that the merger of seven congregations of Dominican women religious has been approved by the Vatican. The official date for the foundation of the new congregation, which has not yet been named, is Easter 2009. The congregations uniting are: the Dominican Sisters, St. Mary of the Springs in Columbus, OH; the Sisters of St. Dominic of the Immaculate Heart of Mary in Akron, OH; the Congregation of St. Rose of Lima in Oxford, MI; the Dominican Sisters, Congregation of St. Mary, and the Eucharistic Missionaries of St. Dominic, both in New Orleans; the Dominican Sisters of Great Bend, KS; and the Congregation of St. Catharine of Siena in St. Catharine, KY.

Pilgrim Bush It was reported on Jan. 11 that U.S. President George Bush made time for a stop at traditional Christian pilgrimage sites today during his peace-seeking tour in the Middle East. Franciscan Fr. Pierbattista Pizzaballa, Custodian of the Holy Land,

accompanied the president during his stop in Capernaum. President Bush also visited the Church of the Nativity in Bethlehem and the Mount of the Beatitudes, and was described as interested in the archaeology of the house of St. Peter at Capernaum. He read several passages of Scripture related to the site.

Peru Churches It was reported on Jan. 16 that the Church in the United States has planned to assist Cubans construct a cathedral and Peruvians to rebuild their churches after last year's earthquake. Funds for such projects will be provided by the 2008 Collection for the Church in Latin America, scheduled to be taken up in most U.S. parishes Jan. 26-27. The theme this year is "Forming Disciples and Missionaries of Jesus Christ." The annual collection has been conducted for more than 45 years. In 2007, some $7.7 million dollars was distributed to Latin American dioceses, parishes, seminaries, and other programs. That was almost $2 million more than in 2006.

Black Catholics It was reported on Jan. 22 that the National Black Catholic Apostolate for Life invited U.S. Catholics to participate in its annual "Black Catholic Rosary Across America for Life." Last year more than 20,000 people participated in the program. The rosary was planned to coincide with the Jan. 22 March for Life in Washington and other related events, including a Jan. 21 vigil Mass at the Basilica of the National Shrine of the Immaculate Conception.

Post-Communist Lands It was reported on Jan. 26 that the Collection for the Church in Central and Eastern Europe will be taken up in most U.S. parishes on Feb. 6, Ash Wednesday, or the First Sunday of Lent, Feb. 10. "Love Is the Only Light," a theme taken from Pope Benedict XVI's first encyclical, is the theme for the 2008 collection. The collection was established shortly after the fall of Communism and has provided more than $100 million to Catholics in post-Communist Russia and Central and Eastern Europe. These funds have supported more than 3,500 Church projects in more than 25 countries. "As a result of this severe [Communist] repression, the bishops of the region today face the formidable tasks of restoring church structures and, more importantly, of rebuilding the spiritual centers of their communities," said Card. Justin Rigali, chairman of the Subcommittee on Aid to the Church in Central and Eastern Europe. "Now more than ever, the ecclesial needs of Catholics in Central and Eastern Europe must be tenderly cared for."

Sainthood Cause On Jan. 27, Card. Edward M. Egan of New York presided over a Mass that marked the opening of the cause for canonization of Fr. Isaac Thomas Hecker, the founder of the Paulist Fathers. Card. Egan noted: "He was a person who suffered, who made his way through life bearing crosses and who taught that sanctity can be captured in many different ways." The ceremony also marked the 150th anniversary of the Church of St. Paul the Apostle, the parish that Fr. Hecker established on Columbus Avenue in New York. More than 1,000 people attended the bilingual Mass, and Card. Egan blessed the tomb of Fr. Hecker in the church. Fr. Hecker served the American Church during a turbulent and difficult period.

FEBRUARY 2008

VATICAN

Ukrainian Bishops On Feb. 1, Pope Benedict XVI welcomed bishops of the Greek-Catholic Church of Ukraine, expressing his joy that their Churches have "rediscovered freedom." The bishops visited the Vatican for their five-yearly visit, the first they have been able to make in 70 years. "Now that your Churches have rediscovered their complete freedom," the Holy Father announced, "you are here to represent your communities, reborn and vibrant in the faith, which have never ceased to feel their full communion with Peter's Successor. You are welcome, dear brothers, in this house in which intense and incessant prayers have always been said for the beloved Greek-Catholic Church of Ukraine."

Mentally Handicapped It was announced on Feb. 1 that Pope Benedict XVI's general prayer intention for Feb. would focus on the well-being of the mentally handicapped. The Apostleship of Prayer issued the general intention chosen by the pope: "That the mentally handicapped may not be marginalized, but respected and lovingly helped to live in a way worthy of their physical and social condition." The Holy Father also planned to pray, "That the institutes of consecrated life, which are so flourishing in mission countries, may rediscover the missionary dimension and, faithful to the radical choice of evangelical counsels, be generous in bearing witness to and announcing Christ to the ends of the earth."

Tridentine Rite Prayer On Feb. 5, it was reported that Pope Benedict XVI reformulated a prayer for the Jews in the Good Friday liturgy according to the 1962 Roman Missal. The changes to the prayer were publicized in a message from the Vatican Secretariat of State. The non-official English translation of the Latin prayer is: "Let us also pray for the Jews, that God our Lord should illuminate their hearts, so that they will recognize Jesus Christ, the Savior of all men. Let us pray. Let us genuflect. Rise. All-powerful and eternal God, you who wish that all men be saved and come to the recognition of truth, graciously grant that when the fullness of peoples enters your Church all of Israel will be saved. Through Christ Our Lord, Amen."

Slovenian Leader On Feb. 5, Pope Benedict XVI received in audience the president of Slovenia, Danilo Turk. The two spoke of the nation's current presidency of the European Union and the Balkans. President Turk later met with the Holy Father's secretary of state, Card. Tarcisio Bertone, and the secretary for relations with states, Abp. Dominique Mamberti. The visit provided an opportunity for the two to examine a number of matters concerning the current international scene, in particular the situation in the Balkans, also in the light of the Slovenian presidency of the European Union.

Ash Wednesday Mass On Feb. 6, Pope Benedict XVI celebrated an Ash Wednesday Mass at Rome's Basilica of Santa Sabina. Dressed in the purple vestments of the Lenten season, the Holy Father presided over the liturgy that began with a procession from the nearby Church of St. Anselm on the Aventine Hill. He then placed ashes on the prelates, clergy, a long line of cardinals, bishops, priests, and lay faithful. The Holy Father's homily focused on the value of prayer,

silence, and sacrifice during Lent, comments that he used on several occasions for the seasonal observances.

Money to Bolivia It was announced on Feb. 7 that through the Pontifical Council Cor Unum, Pope Benedict XVI showed his solidarity with flood-drenched Bolivia, giving some $50,000 to the relief effort. Cor Unum is the agency that coordinates and promotes the world's Catholic institutions of assistance and volunteering. Bolivia, along with Argentina and Ecuador, was hit by torrential rains, and deaths have been reported. The Holy Father invited the Church "to reflect about the value and the practice of almsgiving. Gospel almsgiving is not simple philanthropy: Rather it is a concrete expression of charity, the theological virtue which demands interior conversion to love of God and of our brothers."

Lenten Time On Feb. 7, Pope Benedict XVI received the parish priests of the Diocese of Rome, and described the holy season of Lent, saying: "It seems to me that the time of Lent should be a time of fasting from words and images, because we need a little silence, a little space, without being constantly bombarded with images. We need to create spaces of silence [...] to open our hearts to the true image, to the true word." The Pontiff also underlined the importance of the clergy giving witness that "we can truly know God. That we can be his friends, and walk with him."

Costa Rican Bishops On Feb. 6, Pope Benedict XVI received in audience the bishops of Costa Rica, led by the president of the episcopal conference, Bp. José Francisco Ulloa Rojas of Cartago. The bishops were in Rome for their five-yearly visit. "The people of Costa Rica," said the Holy Father, "must constantly revitalize their [...] profound Christian roots, their vigorous religiosity, and their deep Marian devotion; may these bring the fruits of a life worthy of the disciples of Jesus."

Sister Lucia's Beatification On Feb. 13, Pope Benedict XVI announced that he would dispense with the five-year waiting period established by Canon Law to open the cause of beatification of Sister Lucia, one of the three Fatima visionaries. The news was announced today in the cathedral of Coimbra, Portugal, on the third anniversary of the Carmelite's death. Lucia de Jesus dos Santos was 10 years old when, on May 13, 1917, she saw for the first time a lady she later identified as the Blessed Virgin Mary, in the Cova de Iria. She saw the vision with her cousins Francisco and Jacinta Marto, who were beatified by John Paul II in Fatima, in 2000. The mortal remains of the Carmelite were moved in 2006 to the Shrine of Fatima. The body of the nun, who died at age 97, is buried next to Jacinta. Francisco is buried in the same basilica.

The Transfiguration On Feb. 17, Pope Benedict XVI at the midday Angelus in St. Peter's Square presented the story of the Transfiguration, announcing: "The transfiguration is an event of prayer. Praying, Jesus is immersed in God, he is united intimately to him, he adheres with his human will to the Father's will of love, and in this way light invades him and the truth of his being appears visibly: He is God, light from light. Even his robes become white and luminous." The Holy Father added that this image recalls the sacrament of baptism and "the white robes worn by the neophytes. Those who are reborn in baptism are clothed in light, anticipating heavenly existence, which the Book of Revelation represents with the symbol of white robes."

Sanctorum Mater On Feb. 18, Card. José Saraiva Martins, the prefect of the Congregation for Saints' Causes, presented the instruction *Sanctorum Mater*, regarding diocesan or eparchial enquiries in the causes of saints. The cardinal explained that the aim of the document "is to contribute to ensuring that current norms for the diocesan inquiry of a cause of beatification and canonization are applied with ever greater care." The instruction is divided into six sections.

Vocation Crisis On Feb. 19, Pope Benedict XVI addressed the executive committee of the International Union of Superiors General, who were meeting in the Vatican. In his address, the Holy Father said: "We are all aware how, in modern globalized society, it is becoming ever more difficult to announce and bear witness to the Gospel. The process of secularization that is advancing in contemporary culture does not, unfortunately, spare even religious communities."

Vocation Day Message In his message for the 45th World Day of Prayer for Vocations, dated Dec. 3 and released on Feb. 22, Pope Benedict XVI announced that the number of baptized persons increases every year due to the work of priests wholly consecrated to the salvation of their brothers and sisters. The World Day of Prayer was scheduled to be celebrated on Apr. 13 and is dedicated this year to "Vocations at the Service of the Church on Mission." "The Church prays every day to the Holy Spirit for the gift of vocations. Gathered around the Virgin Mary, Queen of the Apostles, as in the beginning, the ecclesial community learns from her how to implore the Lord for a flowering of new apostles, alive with the faith and love that are necessary for the mission," the Holy Father said.

St. Peter's Patio On Feb. 22, Pope Benedict XVI dedicated the north patio of St. Peter's Basilica to St. Gregory the Illuminator, the national saint and patron of Armenia. The brief ceremony was attended by Abp. Nerses Bedros XIX, patriarch of Cilicia of the Armenian Catholics, and a group of prelates of the Armenian Catholic Church. The Holy Father said: "St. Gregory was called the illuminator precisely because in him the Lord's face is reflected in an extraordinary way." The Holy Father asked that the "Armenian people, through the intercession of this illustrious and distinguished son, continue their journey along the paths of faith, letting themselves be guided, as they have for centuries, by Christ and by his Gospel, which has indelibly marked their culture."

Peter's Pence Pope Benedict XVI received on Feb. 22 the members of the Circle of St. Peter, who presented to him the Peter's Pence donations collected every year in the parishes and institutes of Rome's diocese. Addressing the members of the society he emphasized that their service "has always distinguished you for your unconditional faithfulness to the Church and its universal pastor, the Roman Pontiff." The Holy Father also expressed gratitude for the presentation of the Peter's Pence, which "represents concrete assistance offered to the pope so that he might respond to the many petitions that come from around the world, espe-

cially from the poorest countries."

Death's Moments On Feb. 25, Pope Benedict XVI announced that it was the duty of Christians to accompany those who are dying, and no believer should die alone. The Holy Father said this while receiving in audience participants in the international congress of the Pontifical Academy for Life titled "Close by the Incurable Sick Person and the Dying: Scientific and Ethical Aspects." "Death concludes the experience of earthly life, but through death there opens for each of us, beyond time, the full and definitive life. For the community of believers, this encounter between the dying person and the source of life and love represents a gift that has a universal value, that enriches the communion of the faithful." He once again recalled "the firm and constant ethical condemnation of all forms of direct euthanasia, in keeping with the centuries-long teaching of the Church."

El Salvador Bishops On Feb. 26, Pope Benedict XVI received in audience the prelates from the episcopal conference of El Salvador, who have recently completed their five-yearly visit. The Holy Father highlighted how most Salvadoran people "are characterized by their living faith and deep religious sentiment. The Gospel, taken there by the first missionaries and fervently preached by pastors full of love for God such as Abp. Oscar Arnulfo Romero, has become deeply rooted in that beautiful land, bringing abundant fruits of Christian life and sanctity." An estimated 83% of El Salvador's almost 7 million people are Catholic.

Feminist "Baptism" On Feb. 29, the Congregation for the Doctrine of the Faith clarified that two formulae for baptism that remove the masculine names for God are invalid and undermine faith in the Trinity. The congregation's statement, made public today, responded to two questions concerning the validity of baptism conferred without referring to God the Father and Son. Pope Benedict XVI, during a recent audience with Card. William Levada, prefect of the Congregation for the Doctrine of the Faith, approved these responses, which were adopted at the ordinary session of the congregation. The pope ordered their publication.

New Statistics On Feb. 29, Pope Benedict XVI received from his secretary of state the 2008 edition of the *Annuario Pontificio*. Card. Tarcisio Bertone was accompanied by Abp. Fernando Filoni, *sostituto* for General Affairs, and the officials responsible for compiling and printing the volume. The yearbook provides new statistics, such as the fact that in 2007, eight new episcopal sees were created, as well as one apostolic prefecture, two metropolitan sees, and one apostolic vicariate; 169 new bishops were also appointed. From year-end 2005 to year-end 2006, the latest date for which numbers are available, the number of Catholics in the world increased from 1.115 billion to 1.131 billion, a growth of 1.4%. Over the same period, the number of bishops grew from 4,841 to 4,898, an increase of 1.2%. The number of religious and diocesan priests moved from 406,411 in 2005 to 407,262 in 2006 (a growth of 0.21%). The number of priests has grown steadily from 2000 to 2006.

General Audiences
Lenten Season, Feb. 6.
St. Augustine of Hippo (4), Feb. 20.
St. Augustine of Hippo (5), Feb. 27.

INTERNATIONAL
Vietnam Nunciature On Feb. 1, it was reported that the Vietnamese authorities had decided to return the

former apostolic nunciature in Hanoi to the Catholic Church. Catholics were occupying the property in protest demonstrations against the refusal of the government to restore the building to the Church. The civil authorities decided to let the church have the building "to show good will and respect toward the pope." The announcement of the breakthrough came a day after the Vatican secretary of state, Card. Tarcisio Bertone, sent a letter to Abp. Joseph Ngo Quang Kiet of Hanoi.

Dignity of Women On Feb. 1, Bp. Agustinus Agus of Sintang, Indonesia, attended a meeting in Malaysia to reflect on how to promote the dignity of women. The meeting is focused on "Challenges to Women and the Family in the 21st Century," and is sponsored by the Office of Laity and Family of the Federation of Asian Bishops' Conferences. Participants came from Thailand, Vietnam, Indonesia, Malaysia, Sri Lanka, Mongolia, and the Philippines. Bp. Agus gave the inaugural address. He encouraged ministry focusing on the dignity of women at both the diocesan and parish levels. The bishop's address was followed by a series of presentations from nongovernmental organizations on the situations of women in their respective Asian countries.

Incorrupt Heart Stolen It was reported on Feb. 1 that the incorrupt heart of Servant of God Bp. Mamerto Esquiú has been stolen from the site in Catamarca, Argentina, where it was kept. A spokesman of the Franciscan Province of the Assumption in Argentina reported this second theft of the heart. Bp. Esquiú was the prelate of Cordoba, Argentina, and died in 1883. His body was laid to rest in that city's cathedral, but his heart was found to be incorrupt, and was kept at the Franciscan monastery in Catamarca. The bishop was declared a Servant of God in 2005 and the cause for his beatification is progressing.

Lourdes Apparitions On Feb. 12 it was reported that Orthodox and Russians gathered in Minsk with Catholics of Belarus to celebrate the 150th anniversary of Mary's apparitions in Lourdes and to consider Our Lady's role in their personal and national history. Abp. Tadeusz Kondrusiewicz of Minsk led the celebration, titled "Into the Future with the Immaculata." The symposium also featured the testimonies of the faithful about the role of the Virgin in their lives.

Praying in Algeria On Feb. 13, Catholic priest Fr. Pierre Wallez was sentenced by the tribunal of Oran, a city in northwestern Algeria, to a year in prison for having "directed a religious ceremony in a place which has not been recognized by the government." Fr. Wallez is the first victim of legislation approved in Mar. 2006 regarding the exercise of the practices of non-Muslim worship in this Muslim North African country. A young Muslim doctor was condemned to two years without parole for using medicines paid for by Caritas.

Apostolic Nunciature Bombed It was announced on Feb. 18 that a bomb was set off outside the offices of the apostolic nunciature in Caracas,Venezuela. In response, the Venezuelan bishops urged their government to protect the pope's "house in Venezuela." The bombing caused only minor damages, but the façade of the structure was also vandalized with political graffiti. A statement from the Venezuelan bishops' conference expressed the prelates concern, both for this attack and the "eruption of political violence in vari-

ous regions of the country." The bishops called for calm, prudence, and respect for constitutional rights and liberties.

John Paul II Memorial It was reported on Feb. 19 that the Vatican secretary of state, Card. Tarcisio Bertone, would visit the island of Cuba and unveil a memorial to Pope John Paul II in Santa Clara, where he would celebrate Mass. The seven-day visit by Card. Bertone commemorates the 10th anniversary of Pope John Paul II's apostolic journey to Cuba. He was scheduled to meet with Cuban bishops, visit seminarians, and then preside over Mass in the plaza of Havana's cathedral. Thousands of Cuban Catholics were expected for the Mass. The cardinal and the group accompanying him also went to Santiago de Cuba, where he prayed the rosary with youth and celebrated Mass in the Diocese of Guantánamo-Baracoa. Card. Bertone addressed the University of Havana, and had dinner with representatives of the Cuban government.

Holy Land Pilgrims The Franciscan Custos of the Holy Land, Fr. Pierbattista Pizzaballa, announced on Feb. 24 that pilgrims are returning to the Holy Land. He stated this at a conference Wednesday on the situation of the Middle East organized by the Community of Sant'Egidio. Card. Leonardo Sandri, prefect of the Congregation for Eastern Churches, also participated in the conference, which was titled "Christians in the Middle East: Between Future, Tradition and Islam." Card. Sandri said that pilgrimages to the Holy Land are one of the three ways to help the area and the minority group of Christians that live there, just 1% of the population, a total of 170,000.

Pakistani Extremists On Feb. 2, Abp. Lawrence Saldanha of Lahore, the president of Pakistan's episcopal conference, called on the government to protect Christians in the wake of increased violence and pressure to convert to Islam. The archbishops cited the growing "hatred and intolerance" of militant groups whom, he said, were contravening Pakistan's constitution by trying to force Christians to turn to Islam. He also noted the case of a young Catholic father of four who was kidnapped and threatened with death but escaped his captors. His kidnappers were part of Jamaat-ul-Dawah, which has been classified as a terrorist organization by the United Kingdom, Pakistan, and other countries. Stressing how religious freedom is enshrined in Pakistan's constitution, Abp. Saldanha called on the government to crack down on extremism. He also described the plight of Christian girls who are abducted and forced to marry Muslim boys and change their religion. Some 500 Christians have received anonymous letters warning of violent retribution if a mass conversion to Islam did not follow within 10 days.

Cardinal's Office Invaded It was reported on Feb. 28 that Card. Jorge Urosa, archbishop of Caracas, appealed for peace in the wake of escalating political violence, this time after supporters of President Hugo Chávez took temporary possession of the archiepiscopal palace. A group of "students and other revolutionaries" took possession of the archbishop's offices, forcing those working in the building to leave. The group read a declaration ratifying "that our fight is for the power of the sovereign people and for socialism as the only possible alternative for the development of the country." The Card. announced: "This escalation of violence should cease, and that is the work of the government."

NATIONAL

Archbishop Sheen On Feb. 3, a ceremony was held in the Peoria Cathedral to mark the closing of the diocesan phase of the sainthood cause of Abp. Fulton J. Sheen. A Mass of thanksgiving marking the end of five years of preliminary research into Abp. Sheen's life and virtues was celebrated. A prolific writer and gifted orator, Abp. Sheen became known nationwide as the host of pioneering radio and television programs, including "The Catholic Hour" and "Life Is Worth Living." Abp. Sheen received an Emmy Award as television's "Most Outstanding Personality" in 1952.

Catholic Identity It was reported on Feb. 3 that Abp. Raymond L. Burke of St. Louis announced that those who represent Catholic institutions have an obligation to "show respect for the teachings of the church." He also cautioned against taking public positions contrary to those teachings. The archbishop was speaking of a local priest who attended a political rally and identified himself as "pro-choice, personally" and "very much an advocate for stem-cell research," although he did not specifically mention embryonic stem-cell research. He also identified himself as a Catholic.

Bishops' Survey A nationwide survey on U.S. Catholic attitudes and practices regarding marriage, commissioned in Apr. 2007 by the U.S. bishop's Committee on Marriage and Family Life, was presented on Feb. 11. The survey was carried out by the Center for Applied Research in the Apostolate at Georgetown University via the Internet polling firm Knowledge Networks. Abp. Joseph E. Kurtz of Louisville, KY, chairman of of the bishops' newly renamed Committee on Laity, Marriage, Family Life and Youth, stated: "This is the first time that such a varied and comprehensive body of data about Catholic patterns in marriage has been collected and analyzed." According to the survey, 70% of currently married Catholics in the United States were either married in the Church or had their marriage blessed. A slight majority of Catholics (55%) say their views about marriage have been at least "somewhat" informed by Church teaching. Abp. Kurtz also noted that the survey showed preparation the Church offers to engaged couples is helping marriages, but that Catholic couples do not consistently turn to the Church for help with struggles during marriage. "We must find ways to offer couples a more integrated, continuous, and varied ministry that will help them to grow in happiness and holiness through the entire lifecycle of a marriage," he said.

New Religious Foundation The Daughters of Mary, Mother of Israel's Hope, a new community of sisters in the Archdiocese of St. Louis with the permission of Abp. Raymond L. Burke was announced on Feb. 13. The community is being founded by Rosalind Moss, an author, an Eternal Word Television Network TV host, and one of the network's radio hosts. "The purpose of this religious community is to flood the world with holy habits as signs to God," she explained.

Alaska Diocese On Feb. 13, the Diocese of Fairbanks announced that it would file for bankruptcy. Bp. Donald J. Kettler of Fairbanks made the announcement. More than 140 people have filed about 150 claims against the diocese. The most recent abuse asserted in a claim took place in the 1980s, although some cases go back to the 1950s. Filing for bankruptcy is "the best way to bring all parties together and to provide for fair and equitable treatment of all who have been harmed," the bishop said. "I am legally and morally bound to both fulfill our mission and to pursue healing for those injured."

Aparecida The 35th meeting of the Bishops of the Church in America was reported on Feb. 15 as being conducted in Huntington, NY. It was the eighth such meeting since Pope John Paul II issued his apostolic exhortation *"Ecclesia in America."* The annual meetings gather bishops from the entire American continent, including representatives from the Canadian episcopal conference and the Latin American Episcopal Council, which represents 22 bishops' conferences from Mexico to Chile. The theme of this year's meeting was the final document resulting from the 5th General Conference of the Bishops of Latin America and the Caribbean, held last May near the shrine of Our Lady of Aparecida, and inaugurated by Pope Benedict XVI. That conference declared a "continental mission" to bring people back to the faith, or deeper into it.

Chair of Peter On Feb. 22, the Cardinal Newman Society invited Catholics to take advantage of the feast of the Chair of St. Peter to pray for Catholic education's fidelity to the teaching authority of the pope. The Cardinal Newman Society labors to strengthen and renew Catholic identity at Catholic colleges and universities. The organization said the appeal is leading up to Pope Benedict XVI's Apr. 17 visit to the Catholic University of America in Washington, DC, where the Holy Father will address Catholic college presidents and diocesan education officials. Patrick Reilly, the president of the society, said, "This feast day allows us a special opportunity to pray for Pope Benedict and consider his important role as shepherd to the Church, with vital implications for Catholic education."

Katharine Drexel Shrine On Feb. 28, the U.S. episcopal conference designated the shrine of St. Katherine Drexel as a national shrine, making it the 27th with that title in the United States. "It was with great pleasure that I received the news that the Shrine of St. Katharine Drexel has been elevated in status to a National Shrine," said Card. Justin Rigali, abp. of Philadelphia. "This designation is especially gratifying because Mother Katharine's love of the Holy Eucharist and care for God's poor and oppressed was formed in the archdiocese of Philadelphia. I pray that the honor bestowed upon the shrine will open opportunities for others to hear God's word and reflect upon St. Katharine's message of love and service to all." St. Katharine Drexel was born in Philadelphia in 1858. Her life was devoted to the Eucharist and to serving the poor and socially oppressed among Native and African Americans. Pope John Paul II beatified her in 1988, and almost 12 years later, aided by the 1994 healing of a deaf girl accepted as attributable to miraculous intercession, she was canonized in 2000.

MARCH 2008

VATICAN

Salesians Encouraged On Mar. 1, Pope Benedict XVI sent a message to the rector major of the Salesians, Fr. Pascual Chávez Villanueva and to the participants in the 26th general chapter of the congregation, which was held in Rome. The Holy Father stated that the theme chosen for this general chapter— *"Da mihi animas, cetera tolle"* ("Give me souls, take away all else")—expresses "that same program of spiritual and apostolic life that Don Bosco made his own." He added, "It is vitally important for the Salesians to draw continual inspiration from Don Bosco, to know him, study him, love him, imitate him, invoke him and make their own that apostolic passion which flows from the heart of Christ." The Holy Father also thanked the congregation "for the research and educational activities of the Pontifical Salesian University."

Prelate's Release On Mar. 2, Pope Benedict XVI appealed again for the release of the Chaldean archbishop of Mosul, Iraq, who was kidnapped. After leading the midday Angelus in St. Peter's Square today, the Holy Father repeated his appeal for the release of Abp. Paulos Faraj Rahho. He was taken captive as he was leaving Mosul's Church of the Holy Spirit after participating in the Way of the Cross. Three men who accompanied him, including his driver, were killed.

Satellite Unity On Mar. 3, Pope Benedict XVI prayed the rosary with university students from 10 European and American cities and then entrusted them the duty of being builders of peace and unity. The Holy Father thus participated in the 6th European Day for Universities, held in Paul VI Hall and linked via satellite to Naples, Italy; Bucharest, Romania; Toledo, Spain; Avignon, France; Minsk, Belarus; Washington DC; Mexico City; Havana, Cuba; Aparecida, Brazil; and Loja, Ecuador. The Council of European Episcopal Conferences and the vicariate of Rome's office for pastoral care in universities promoted the satellite union, with the theme "Europe and the Americas Together to Build a Civilization of Love." Some 40,000 university students participated.

Catholic-Muslim Forum It was reported on Mar. 4 that the representatives of the Holy See and the 138 Muslim scholars who wrote to Pope Benedict XVI last October proposing a new dialogue have established the Catholic-Muslim Forum. The forum conducted a planning session and will sponsor a seminar in Rome. Pope Benedict announced that he will meet with the seminar participants in November. Accepting the central topic suggested by the 138 in their letter to the pope and other Christian leaders, the seminar planners have said the theme will be "Love of God, Love of Neighbor." The Nov. 4 session will focus on the theological and spiritual foundations of Christian and Muslim teachings about the obligation to love God and one's neighbor.

Patriarch of Constantinople On Mar. 6, Pope Benedict XVI received in audience the Orthodox Patriarch Bartholomew I of Constantinople, who is in Rome to mark the 90th anniversary of the Pontifical Oriental Institute, where he himself received a doctorate. They also prayed together in Latin in the Urban VIII Chapel of the Apostolic Palace. The Holy Father

first met Bartholomew I when the pope traveled to Turkey in 2006, on the occasion of the feast of St. Andrew. They met again last October during the Holy Father's trip to Naples for the 21st International Encounter of Peoples and Religions.

Bishops of Guatemala On Mar. 6, Pope Benedict XVI received the bishops of Guatemala in audience at the conclusion of their five-yearly visit to Rome. The pope invited the prelates "to continue with renewed energy the Church's evangelizing mission in the context of modern cultural movements and globalization." The Holy Father noted the impact on evangelization of the 2nd American Missionary Congress held in Guatemala in 2003, and the 5th General Conference of the Episcopate of Latin America and the Caribbean that took place in Brazil last year.

Luxembourg Prime Minister On Mar. 7, Pope Benedict XVI received in audience Prime Minister Jean-Claude Juncker of Luxembourg, which is set to become the third country in Europe to legalize euthanasia. Juncker's Christian Social Party, aided by the Church in the country, attempted to block the legislation, but the bill passed 30–26 in a vote in Parliament last month. The bill still needs to pass a second reading for it to become law. The measure is expected to pass and could come into force before summer. During the audience, the cordial discussions included the subject of euthanasia and international affairs. The Luxembourg leader met afterward with Abp. Dominique Mamberti, secretary for relations with states.

Historical Sciences On Mar. 7, Pope Benedict XVI met with members of the Pontifical Committee for Historical Sciences, and he commented that these scholars work "in a field that is of great interest for the life of the Church." The Holy Father noted how during the pontificate of Leo XIII, "historiography was guided by the spirit of the times and hostile to the Church." Hence, that Pope "opened the archives of the Holy See to researchers [...] in the conviction that the study and description of the true history of the Church could not but be favorable to her." Today, he said, "it is no longer just a question of tackling a historiography hostile to Christianity and to the Church. Today it is historiography itself that is going through a serious crisis, having to fight for its very existence in a society ruled by positivism and materialism. These two ideologies have led to a boundless enthusiasm for progress, which [...] influences the view of life of large sectors of society. The past thus appears as a dark backdrop against which the present and future glitter with misleading promise."

Church Values On Mar. 10, Pope Benedict XVI received in audience members of the Pontifical Council for Culture at the conclusion of its plenary session on "The Church and The Challenge of Secularization." "Today more than ever," the Holy Father told the participants, "reciprocal openness between cultures is an important field for dialogue between men and women committed to seeking authentic humanism, over and above the differences that separate them." Secularization, he said, "invades all aspects of daily life and causes the development of a mentality in which God is effectively absent, entirely or in part, from human life and conscience." This "is not just an external threat to believers," added the pontiff, "but has for some time been evident in the bosom of the Church herself." The Holy Father urged the Pontifical Council for Culture to remain committed to "fruitful dialogue between science and faith," respecting the ambition and methodology of each of them, in order "to serve man and humanity, favoring the integral development and growth of each and of all."

Death of Iraqi Prelate Pope Benedict XVI, on Mar. 13, sent a telegram of condolence to the leader of the Church in Iraq, expressing his condolences at the death of the archbishop of Mosul, Abp. Paulos Faraj Rahho, who was kidnapped on Feb. 29. In the telegram to Card. Emmanuel III Delly, patriarch of Babylon of the Chaldeans, the pope expressed his closeness "to the Chaldean Church and to the entire Christian community," reaffirming his "condemnation for an act of inhuman violence which offends the dignity of human beings and seriously damages the cause of the fraternal coexistence of the beloved Iraqi people."

Bolivian Ambassador On Mar. 14, Pope Benedict XVI received the letters of credence of the nation's new ambassador to the Holy See, Carlos Federico de la Riva Guerra. At the beginning of his Spanish-language address, the Holy Father recalled how "Bolivia's deep Christian roots have sustained its people, accompanied the vicissitudes of its history and promoted a sense of respect and reconciliation, so necessary in the difficult moments the nation has had to face." The Holy Father also noted that Bolivia "is experiencing a process of profound change that is producing difficult and at times worrying situations. [...] We cannot remain indifferent when social tension is increasing and a climate unfavorable to understanding is spreading." Bolivia's population of some 9 million is about 95% Catholic.

Palm Sunday On Mar. 16, Pope Benedict XVI celebrated the Palm Sunday Mass in St. Peter's Square. The Holy Father centered his homily on the Gospel passage of the cleansing of the temple, when Christ drives out of the house of his Father those who had made it a "den of thieves." "From the story of the 12-year-old Jesus, we know that he loved the temple as the house of his Father, as his paternal house," the pontiff said. "Now he comes again to this temple, but his journey goes beyond it: The ultimate goal of his ascent is the cross." The Holy Father stated that Christ's zeal for the temple should lead Christians of today to reflect: "Is our faith pure and open enough that, beginning from it, the 'pagans'—the persons today who are seeking and have their questions—can also intuit the light of the one God, can associate themselves with our prayer in the atriums of faith and by their seeking perhaps become worshippers? Does the awareness that greed is idolatry also reach our heart and our life practices? Do we not perhaps also allow idols to enter even into the world of our faith? Are we disposed to let the Lord purify us again and again, allowing him to chase out of us and the Church what is contrary to him?" The Holy Father concluded by affirming that to recognize this loving God, "we must abandon the pride that blinds us, that wants to drive us far away from God, as if God were our competitor. To meet God it is necessary to become capable of seeing with the heart," he announced. "We must learn to see with a young heart that is not hindered by prejudices and blinded by interests."

Greek Ambassador On Mar. 17, Pope Benedict XVI received the letters of credence of Miltiadis Hiskakis, the new ambassador of Greece to the Holy See. In his English-language address to the diplomat, the Holy Father first considered the path of Christian unity, and progress in relations between Catholics and Orthodox. He also recalled the "valiant efforts" made by the recently deceased Christodoulos, abp. of Athens and all Greece, "to mend the breach between Christians in the East and West." After reiterating his "eagerness to work together as we travel the road towards Christian unity," the Holy Father recalled that "honesty and trust will be required from all parties if the important questions raised by this dialogue are to continue to be addressed effectively." The Holy Father then thanked the ambassador "for the assurance of your government's resolve to address administrative issues concerning the Catholic Church in your nation. Among these, the question of its juridical status is of particular significance."

Agreement With Andorra On Mar. 17, the Holy See signed an agreement with Andorra, further consolidating its collaboration with the tiny European nation. The agreement is made up of a preamble and 16 articles divided into six parts that cover the juridical status of the Catholic Church in Andorra, canonical marriage, the teaching of religions in schools, the economic system of the Catholic Church in Andorra, and the local bishopric. The document was signed by Benedict XVI's secretary of state, Card. Tarcisio Bertone, and for Andorra by Albert Pintat, head of government. The agreement will come into force following the exchange of instruments of ratification.

Dialogue in Tibet On Mar. 19, Pope Benedict XVI is asking for dialogue and tolerance to overcome the crisis in Tibet. "I follow with deep unrest the news that in these days is coming from Tibet. My fatherly heart feels sadness and sorrow at the suffering of so many people," the pope said at the end of the general audience in Paul VI Hall. "The mystery of the passion and death of Jesus, that we live again in this Holy Week, helps us to be particularly sensitive to their situation," the Holy Father affirmed. "With violence, problems are not solved, only aggravated."

Holy Thursday On Mar. 20, Pope Benedict XVI celebrated the Mass of the Lord's Supper in the Basilica of St. John Lateran. In his homily, the Holy Father reflected on the need for interior purification as a condition to living in communion with God and with each other. "This is what Holy Thursday exhorts," he said. "Do not let rancor toward others become poison for the soul. It exhorts us to continually purify our memory, forgiving each other from the heart, washing one another's feet, so as to be able to go all together toward the banquet of God. Day after day we are covered by numerous forms of filth, of empty words, prejudices, reduced and altered wisdom; a multiplicity of falsities filter in continuously to our most intimate being. All this obscures and contaminates our soul, it threatens us with being incompetence with regard to the truth or the good." The Holy Father said Christ synthesized charity and purification with the gesture of washing the feet of his disciples. During the liturgy, the Holy Father washed the feet of a dozen priests, and during the presentation of the gifts, the pontiff was presented a monetary offering that will be sent to the orphanage *"La Edad De Oro"* ("The Golden Age") in Havana.

Priesthood Is Service On Mar. 20, Pope Benedict XVI celebrated the Holy Thursday Chrism Mass with 1,600 bishops and priests at St. Peter's Basilica. The bishops and priests renewed the promises they made on the day of their ordination. "To be present before the Lord should always be, in its depths, to take charge of mankind before the Lord who, for his part, takes charge of all of us before the Father," the Holy Father declared. He also said that this service is manifested in a concrete way in the Eucharistic celebration. There, he said, what the priest does "is serve, to complete a service to God and a service to man." The Holy Father concluded with an allusion to the washing of the feet, with which Christ, "the true High Priest of the world" wants "to be the servant of all. […] With the gesture of love to the end, he washes our soiled feet; with the humility of his service, he purifies us of the illness of our pride."

Way of the Cross On Mar. 21, Pope Benedict XVI conducted the Way of the Cross in the Roman Colosseum. Tens of thousands of the faithful were present for the ceremony and the meditations, which were written this year by Card. Joseph Zen, bishop of Hong Kong. "Is it possible to remain indifferent before the death of the Lord, of the Son of God?" the Holy Father asked. "For us, for our salvation he became man, so as to be able to suffer and die. Let us pause to contemplate his cross. The cross, fount of life and school of justice and peace, is the universal patrimony of pardon and mercy. It is permanent proof of a self-emptying and infinite love that brought God to become man, vulnerable like us, unto dying crucified."

Easter Message On Mar. 23, Pope Benedict XVI celebrated Easter in St. Peter's Basilica before thousands of the faithful, a ceremony broadcast on some 102 television stations in 67 countries around the world. After celebrating the Easter Mass, and before imparting the blessing *"urbi et orbi"* (to the city of Rome and the world), the Holy Father read a message in which he highlighted the need for peace in Darfur, the Holy Land, Iraq, Lebanon, and Tibet. "The death and resurrection of the Word of God incarnate is an event of invincible love, it is the victory of that Love which has delivered us from the slavery of sin and death," the Holy Father Pontiff said from the balcony of St. Peter's Basilica to the crowds gathered in the square below on a rainy Easter morning. He added, "It has changed the course of history, giving to human life an indestructible and renewed meaning and value. Through the death and resurrection of Christ, we too rise to new life today, and uniting our voice with his, we proclaim that we wish to remain forever with God, our infinitely good and merciful Father."

John Paul II It was reported on Mar. 31 that the report documenting the heroic virtues of Pope John Paul II is nearly completed. Such a report on the former pope's virtue is a necessary and definitive step in the beatification process, Monsignor Slawomir Oder announced. "In recent days, I have turned in a nearly definitive draft of the *'positio,'* the report that collects all of the documents ordered in a systematic and organized way about his pontificate," the monsignor stated. Card. José Saraiva Martíns, prefect of the Congregation for Saints' Causes, announced earlier, "I can guarantee that as soon as we receive the *'positio,'* we will study it immediately without losing a moment, since obviously this dicastery desires that John Paul II arrives as soon as possible to the altars and can be called 'blessed,' and thus respond to the shouts in St. Peter's Square, *'santo subito'* (sainthood now)." Theologians will study the document and if it is approved Pope Benedict XVI could then grant a decree in recognition of John Paul II's heroic virtue. This would permit proclaiming John Paul II as venerable.

General Audience

St. Leo the Great, Mar. 5.
Boethius and Cassiodorus, Mar. 12.
The Easter Triduum, Mar. 19.
Octave of Easter, Mar. 26.

INTERNATIONAL

"House of Prayer" On Mar. 3, the archbishop of Tuam clarified that the "House of Prayer," founded by a woman who claims to have been visited by the Virgin Mary, does not have Church approval. Abp. Michael Neary released a public statement last clarifying the Church's stance on the Achill Island prayer house, founded by Christina Gallagher. A diocesan commission was established to "investigate certain claims regarding and emanating from this work." Gallagher claims to receive regular messages from Our Lady and to have the stigmata. "I respect the faith and devotion of many people who have been impressed by this work in the past, some of whom have expressed their sadness at my stance," the archbishop acknowledged but, he concluded, "The House of Prayer has no Church approval and the work does not enjoy the confidence of the diocesan authorities."

St. Padre Pio It was reported on Mar. 5 that the body of St. Padre Pio of Pietreclina has been exhumed and would be ready for public veneration beginning in Apr. The Vatican delegate who oversees the shrine of the saint, Abp. Domenico Umberto D'Ambrosio of Manfredonia-Vieste-San Giovanni Rotondo announced earlier that the Vatican Congregation for Saints' Causes authorized the exhumation of the Capuchin friar's body to verify the condition of his mortal remains, and to ensure its future preservation. Abp. D'Ambrosio himself presided over the three-hour liturgy that ended after midnight. A large crowd spontaneously gathered to attend the liturgy. The body of the Capuchin friar will be conserved and put in a part-glass coffin in the crypt of the old Church of St. Mary of Grace in San Giovanni Rotondo, where his remains had been kept for 40 years.

Azerbaijan Catholic Church On Mar. 9, Card. Tarcisio Bertone, the Vatican Secretary of State, presided over the dedication of the Church of the Immaculate Conception in Baku, Azerbaijan, the first Catholic Church in that country. The church was built on land donated to Pope John Paul II by President Heydar Aliyev, father of the nation's current head of state, on the eve of the pontiff's visit to the country in 2002.

Turkish Cave Church It was announced on Mar. 12 that the Cave Church of St. Peter, considered the first

Christian church in Antioch, has been closed due to structural concerns. Turkish authorities closed the church Mar. 1 for fear that the structure could cave in. Also known as St. Peter's Grotto, the church is a natural cave on the western face of Mount Stauris, which towers over Antioch. It is widely believed that St. Peter himself dug the cave as a place for the first community of Christians in Antioch to gather.

Opus Dei Anniversary On Mar. 13, Opus Dei celebrated the 25th anniversary of its status as a personal prelature. Personal prelatures favor the Church's evangelizing organizations. The jurisdiction of a prelate is assigned to a certain group of faithful from one or more dioceses, rather than to a geographical area. Various cardinals were present at the anniversary meeting. The current prelate of Opus Dei, Bp. Javier Echevarría, explained that the juridical state of the personal prelature is best suited to the pastoral phenomenon that the founder, St. Josemaría Escrivá, envisioned in 1928, when Opus Dei was founded.

Qatar Catholic Church On Mar. 16, Pope Benedict XVI's special envoy, Card. Ivan Dias, the prefect of the Congregation for the Evangelization of Peoples, welcomed the nation's first Catholic church, Our Lady of the Rosary, built in the seaside capital city of Doha. Thousands of the faithful joined with the cardinal in the inaugural celebration Friday. Card. Dias came as the pope's special envoy, bearing a chalice sent by the pontiff. Qatar, a peninsular nation in the Persian Gulf, bordering Saudi Arabia, has a population of less than 1 million, with a strong majority of Muslims. The Catholic population is multiethnic, including many of the foreign workers in the booming business of natural gas and oil production. Mass will be celebrated at the Church of Our Lady of the Rosary in 14 languages.

NATIONAL

Catholic University Rosary On Mar. 1, students at The Catholic University of America in Washington prayed the rosary with Pope Benedict XVI via satellite from the Vatican. The event celebrated the sixth Day of Prayer for European and American University Students. Students from Havana; Mexico City; Toledo, Spain; Aparecida, Brazil; Loja, Ecuador; Naples, Italy; Avignon, France; Bucharest, Romania; and Minsk, Belarus, joined the Washington students in the prayers. Abp. Donald W. Wuerl presided at the prayer service, joined by Abp. Pietro Sambi, apostolic nuncio to the United States.

Chicago Cathedral On Mar. 7, the Archdiocese of Chicago announced that Holy Name Cathedral will remain closed until early May for needed repairs. The cathedral's ceiling and roof structure needed renovations. The cathedral has been closed in Feb., after the structural damage was determined after a piece of decorative wood fell from the ceiling. Parish Masses and other services have been celebrated in the parish center.

Thousands Converting On Mar. 11, it was reported that tens of thousands of Americans planned to join the Catholic Church this Holy Saturday through the Rite of Christian Initiation of Adults. Many such converts participated in the Rite of Election with their bishops at the beginning of Lent and are scheduled to be bap-

tized, confirmed, and receive Communion for the first time this Saturday. More, who already have been baptized, will embrace full membership in the Catholic Church. The numbers vary across dioceses. The Diocese of Orange, CA, had 650 converts, the Archdiocese of Detroit had 589 catechumens receiving full initiation, the Archdiocese of Cincinnati had 437 catechumens and 541 candidates for a total of 978 people; and another 65 candidates were brought into the Church at other times during the year. Most of those coming into the Church through the RCIA program were adults, but in some instances children were part of both groups, usually as members of a family that enters the Church together. The 2007 Official Catholic Directory listed almost 64,500 adults baptized in the Catholic Church and nearly 93,000 who came into full communion. It is estimated that more than a million infant baptisms will take place in the U.S. during 2008.

Knights Founder It was announced on Mar. 16 that the founder of the Knights of Columbus, Fr. Michael McGivney, was declared venerable by Pope Benedict XVI, furthering his process toward possibly becoming the first American-born priest to be canonized. The Holy Father approved a decree recognizing the heroic virtue of Fr. Michael McGivney. "All of us who are members of the Knights of Columbus are profoundly grateful for this recognition of the holiness of our founder," said Supreme Knight Carl Anderson. "The strength of the Knights of Columbus today is a testament to his timeless vision, his holiness and his ideals." Fr. McGivney founded the Knights of Columbus with the help of several men of St. Mary's Parish in New Haven in 1882. He was born in Connecticut in 1852 to parents who were natives of Ireland and immigrants to the United States. The Knights of Columbus is the world's largest Catholic fraternal organization with more than 1.7 million members in the United States, Canada, Mexico and Central America, the Caribbean islands, the Philippines, Guam, and, most recently, Poland.

Airport Welcome It was reported on Mar. 18 that President George Bush would greet Pope Benedict XVI when the he arrived for a six-day visit to the United States. The Holy Father was scheduled to arrive on Apr. 15 at Andrews Air Force Base on an Alitalia flight dubbed "Shepherd One." Accompanying him on the plane will be several Vatican officials and members of the Vatican press corps. The welcoming ceremony was to include Abp. Pietro Sambi, Vatican nuncio to the United States; Card. Francis George of Chicago, president of the U.S. episcopal conference; Abp. Donald Wuerl of Washington, DC; and Abp. Timothy Broglio of the U.S. Archdiocese for the Military Services. The Holy Father was scheduled to visit President Bush at the White House on the next morning. Several hundred guests were invited for this occasion.

Papal Visit Blog On Mar. 24, it was reported that a new Papal Visit Blog was opened and included preparations for the Apr. 15–20 papal visit, views from the pew during the visit, and post-visit reflections on the event. The blog was orchestrated by the U.S. episcopal conference's Department for Communications. The site also had information for both the general public and the media covering the event about venues, background information, and teaching resources.

APRIL 2008

VATICAN

Papal Intention It was reported on Apr. 1 that Pope Benedict XVI's general prayer intention for April is for Christians, that they never tire of announcing the news of Christ's resurrection. The Apostleship of Prayer announced the general intention chosen by the pope: "That Christians, even in the difficult and complex situations of present-day society, may not tire of proclaiming with their lives that Christ's resurrection is the source of peace and of hope." The Holy Father also chooses a general intention for each month. In April he will pray: "That the future priests of the young Churches may be constantly more formed culturally and spiritually to evangelize their nations and the whole world."

John Paul II Video On Apr. 1 it was announced that the H2Onews.org has launched a series of videos that highlight the main events surrounding the death and funeral of the pontiff. On the eve of the anniversary, the Catholic multimedia organization released the first video that includes the tolling of the bell that announced the death of the Holy Father, and the announcement made by Joaquín Navarro Valls, then director of the Vatican press office. The minute-and-a-half video also showed clips of the millions of people who came to bid their final farewell to John Paul II. The series of videos showed clips from John Paul II's funeral, the conclave, and the election of Card. Joseph Ratzinger as pope.

Mercy Congress On Apr. 2, Pope Benedict XVI inaugurated the 1st World Apostolic Congress. The Holy Father addressed the participants of the Mercy Congress during his homily at a Mass celebrated for John Paul II in St. Peter's Square. The first session of the Mercy Congress was held in the Basilica of St. John Lateran and included contributions from Card. Christoph Schönborn, abp. of Vienna and promoter of the congress, and Card. Camillo Ruini, the pope's vicar for Rome. Card. Stanislaw Dziwisz, abp. of Krakow and longtime secretary of John Paul II, also spoke.

Grandparents' Roles It was announced on Apr. 2 that the plenary assembly of the Pontifical Council for the Family would be dedicated this year to the theme of grandparents. The assembly on "Grandparents: Their Testimony and Presence in the Family" was held in the Vatican. Organizers of the conference highlighted the role of grandparents in keeping families together, as well as supporting and caring for grandkids; and in mediating the relationship of the couple, and the relationship between parents and children. Card. Alfonso López Trujillo, president of the Pontifical Council for the Family, will begin the assembly, followed by Abp. Fernando Filoni of the Vatican secretariat of state, who spoke on the role of the elderly in the Church and society. Couples from Australia, Congo, Chile, and the Philippines gave a round-table discussion.

Message of Hope On Apr. 8, Pope Benedict XVI announced in a video message to the American people that he was going to the United States to bring the message that Jesus Christ is the hope for all mankind. "Before setting off, I would like to offer you a heartfelt greeting and an invitation to prayer," the Holy Father said. "As you know, I shall only be able to visit two cities: Washington and New York. The intention behind my visit, though, is to reach out spiritually to all Catholics in the United States. At the same time, I earnestly hope that my presence among you will be seen as a fraternal gesture toward every ecclesial community, and a sign of friendship for members of other religious traditions and all men and women of good will." He added: "I am especially grateful to all who have been praying for the success of the visit, since prayer is the most important element of all. Dear friends, I say this because I am convinced that without the power of prayer, without that intimate union with the Lord, our human endeavors would achieve very little. Indeed this is what our faith teaches us. It is God who saves us, he saves the world, and all of history. He is the shepherd of his people. I am coming, sent by Jesus Christ, to bring you his word of life."

Papal Foundation On Apr. 4, Pope Benedict XVI personally thanked members of the Papal Foundation for a check for more than $7.5 million, provided to assist him in carrying out his ministry to the universal Church. The Holy Father received in audience today members of the foundation, which organizes annual fundraisers to support the Holy Father's charitable endeavors, and offers grants, projects, and scholarships to developing countries. "Dear friends, I am pleased to have this occasion to express my gratitude for the generous support the Papal Foundation offers through aid projects and scholarships which assist me in carrying out my apostolic ministry to the universal Church," the Holy Father announced. "I ask for your prayers, and I assure you of my own." The Papal Foundation was established in 1990 and has given more than $41 million in grants for the building of churches, seminaries, schools, hospitals and other projects for the care of the poor around the world.

Syro-Orthodox Priest On Apr. 6, Pope Benedict XVI said he was "profoundly saddened" by the death of Syro-Orthodox Fr. Youssef Adel Abudi, who was murdered in his home in Baghdad. Fr. Adel was killed by a group of armed men at the entrance to his house in Karrada, an area in central Baghdad. The pope sent a message of condolence to Mar Saverius Jamil Hawa, the Syro-Orthodox bishop of Baghdad, to offer to Fr. Adel's wife and family his "deepest sympathy." The note was signed by the pope's secretary of state, Card. Tarcisio Bertone.

Caribbean Bishops On Apr. 7, Pope Benedict XVI received in audience bishops from the Antilles Episcopal Conference, of the Caribbean area, who had just completed their five-yearly visit. The Antilles refers to the islands forming the greater part of the West Indies in the Caribbean Sea. The Antilles are divided into two major groups: the "Greater Antilles" to the north including the larger islands of Cuba, Jamaica, Haiti and the Dominican Republic, and Puerto Rico; and the smaller "Lesser Antilles" on the southeast. The Holy Father spoke of the fact that "your shores have been battered by negative aspects of the entertainment industry, exploitative tourism and the scourge of the arms and drugs trade; influences which not only undermine family life and unsettle the foundations of traditional cultural values, but tend to negatively affect local politics." He then encouraged

the prelates: "Be audacious witnesses to the light of
Christ, which gives families direction and purpose,
and be bold preachers of the power of the Gospel,
which must permeate their way of thinking, standards
of judgment, and norms of behavior." He also urged
them to support local seminaries and religious vocations.

Venezuelan Bishops On Apr. 8, it was reported that Pope
Benedict XVI received in audience the directors of the
Venezuelan episcopal conference. The bishops presented to
the Holy Father their greetings and they informed him about
the unity of the bishops, priests. and religious, and of the
Church in general. They also discussed the general situation
in the country, and the Holy Father reiterated his closeness to
the Church, the bishops, and the Venezuelan people. The
Church in Venezuela has recently suffered verbal and physical attacks. In Feb., supporters of President Hugo Chávez
took temporary possession of the archiepiscopal palace.
Some days earlier, a bomb was set off outside the offices of
the apostolic nunciature in Caracas.

29 Ordained in Rome On Apr. 27, Pope Benedict
XVI sent forth 29 newly ordained priests to spread the
"joy of Christ" in a world that is "often sad and negative." The Holy Father presided at an ordination
Mass today in St. Peter's Basilica in which, as Bishop
of Rome, he bestowed the sacrament of holy orders on
candidates from his own diocese. All of the men studied for the priesthood in Rome, although seven of the
new priests are from outside of Italy. The non-Italian
priests are from Iraq, Colombia, Chile, Paraguay,
France, Haiti, and India. In his homily Benedict XVI
explained that today a new mission was beginning for
them. Being missionaries of the Gospel, he said, they
must "proclaim and witness to joy."

Missionary Character Pope Benedict XVI, on Apr. 13, the
World Day of Prayer for Vocations, led the praying of the
midday Regina Caeli with thousands gathered in St. Peter's
Square. The Holy Father told the faithful that St. Paul, for
whom "vocation and mission are inseparable," is a model for
all Christians, particularly "those men and women who dedicate themselves totally to announcing Christ to those who
still have not known him: a vocation which continues to
maintain all of its validity." The Holy Father then prayed that
there would be "an increasing number of those who decide to
radically live the Gospel through the vows of chastity, poverty and obedience—men and women who have a primary role
in evangelization." He said, "Some of them dedicate themselves to contemplation and prayer, others to a multifaceted
educational and charitable work. All of them, nevertheless,
are united in the same objective: to give witness to the primacy of God over all and to spread his Kingdom in every sphere
of society." He also affirmed that those called to Christian
marriage should also give their lives a missionary flavor.

Sanctification of Priests On Apr. 14, in honor of the World
Day of Prayer for the Sanctification of Priests, the Vatican
Congregation for Clergy reminded priests that their number
one priority must be prayer. The congregation affirmed this in
a message directed to all the priests of the world on the occasion of the feast, which will be held May 30, the feast of the
Sacred Heart of Jesus. Signed by Card. Claudio Hummes and
Abp. Mauro Piacenza, respectively prefect and secretary of
the congregation, the message encouraged contemplating the
"perfect and fascinating humanity of Christ, live and acting
now."

Pope Greeting Russians On Apr. 16, Russia marked Pope
Benedict XVI's 81st birthday by offering a televised life of

the Holy Father, including a televised greeting from him to
the Russian people. A state television channel was scheduled
to broadcast a documentary sponsored by the Germany-based
organization Aid to the Church in Need. The documentary
concludes with a message from the Holy Father to Russian
Orthodox Patriarch Alexy II, Orthodox Christians, and to all
Russians. He said, "Russia is truly great, in a variety of different waysin her sheer geographical scale, in her long history, in her magnificent spirituality, in her multiplicity of artistic expression. During the past century the horizon of your
noble land, like that of other regions on the European continent, was obscured by shadows of suffering and violence,
shadows that were however opposed and overcome by the
splendid light of so many martyrs—Orthodox, Catholics and
other believers, who perished under the oppression of ferocious persecutions." The film was produced in St. Petersburg
by the interdenominational Christian media agency
Blagovest Media, under the direction of Nikolaj Goryachkin
in collaboration with the Germany-based Catholic Radio and
Television Network.

Musical Concert On Apr. 24, a concert marking the third
anniversary of Pope Benedict XVI was offered. The concert
was a gift from the president of Italy, Giorgio Napolitano.
The Holy Father attended the concert, held in Paul VI Hall,
accompanied by the president. The pope's older brother,
Monsignor Georg Ratzinger, was also there. Milan's
Giuseppe Verdi orchestra and symphonic choir, directed by
Oleg Caetani and Erina Gambarini, respectively, interpreted
musical compositions from Luciano Berio, Luigi Boccherini,
Brahms, and Beethoven. Before the concert, the pope and the
president had a meeting in the study of Paul VI Hall.

Former USSR Bishops On Apr. 24, Pope Benedict
XVI received in audience prelates from the region,
which includes all of Armenia and the majority of
Georgia and Azerbaijan, all part of the former Soviet
Union countries of the southern Caucasus region. The
bishops are in Rome for their five-yearly visit. "Since
the fall of the Soviet Union," the Holy Father said,
"your peoples have seen significant social changes
along the road to progress. Yet difficult situations per-
sist: many are the poor, the unemployed, and the
refugees whom war has forced from their homes." He
described the Catholic community in the region as "a
small flock" in which "Catholics of Armenian, Latin
and Chaldean rites coexist with Orthodox, Armenian-
Apostolic, Jews and Muslims. In such a multi-reli-
gious context, it is important for Catholics to continue
and to intensify their collaboration with other
Churches and with the followers of other religions, as
already happens in many places."

Eastern Easter Greetings On Apr. 27, Pope Benedict XVI
sent greetings to the Eastern Churches that are celebrating
Easter. The Holy Father announced before praying the
Regina Caeli with several thousand people gathered in St.
Peter's Square: "Today many Eastern Churches, following
the Julian Calendar, celebrate the great solemnity of Easter. I
would like to express my fraternal spiritual nearness to these
brothers and sisters of ours. I cordially greet them, praying
that the God who is one and three will confirm them in the
faith, fill them with the splendorous light that emanates from
the resurrection of the Lord and to comfort them in the difficult situations that they often find themselves living and witnessing to the Gospel." He added, "I invite all to join with
me in invoking the Mother of God, that the road of dialogue
and collaboration that was started upon sometime ago will
soon lead to a more complete communion among all the dis-

ciples of Christ, that they may be a luminous sign of hope for all humanity."

Faith-Reason Dialogue On Apr. 30, Pope Benedict XVI received representatives of Catholicism and Islam considering faith and reason in their respective creeds. The Holy Father expressed satisfaction with the theme chosen by the Pontifical Council for Interreligious Dialogue and the Tehran-based Center for Interreligious Dialogue of the Islamic Culture and Relations Organization, "Faith and Reason in Christianity and Islam." The participants, with the help of six papers presented by three scholars from each side, examined the faith-reason topic, which was developed through three subthemes from the point of view of Catholics and Shiite Muslims.

Vatican Clarifications On Apr. 30, the bishops' conference of England and Wales reported that the Vatican had clarified the celebration of holy days of obligation when celebrating the extraordinary form of the Roman rite according to the 1962 Missal. The episcopal conference submitted a query to the Pontifical Commission Ecclesia Dei, which confirmed that in the Roman rite, whichever form of the liturgy is being celebrated, the holy days of obligation are to be held in common. Where the obligation has been removed and the holy day transferred to the Sunday, this is to be followed in both ordinary and extraordinary celebrations of Mass, the pontifical commission clarified. Catholics are obliged to go to Mass on holy days of obligation. Some holy days of obligation vary according to the decisions made by local episcopal conferences.

General Audience

St. Benedict, Apr. 9.
Apostolic Journey to the United States of America, Apr. 30.

INTERNATIONAL

Sister Lucia's Cause On Apr. 2, Spanish Fr. Ildefonso Moriones was named the postulator of the cause of beatification of Sister Lucia, one of the three Fatima visionaries. In Feb., on the third anniversary of Sister Lucia's death, Benedict XVI dispensed the five-year waiting period established by Canon Law to open her cause of beatification. A vice postulator is still to be named. The dispensation of the five-year waiting period has only been given in two other cases: Pope John Paul II and Blessed Teresa of Calcutta.

Westminster Lecture On Apr. 3, former British Prime Minister Tony Blair addressed 1,600 people gathered in London's Westminster Cathedral about the power of religious faith. Blair, a former Anglican who was received into the Catholic Church before Christmas, said he wanted to promote the "idea of faith itself as something dynamic, modern and full of present relevance." His remarks came in a lecture on the subject of "Faith and Globalization," the first in a series of six speeches hosted by the Archdiocese of Westminster on "Faith and Life in Britain."

Lebanese Bishops On Apr. 4, Card. Nasrallah Sfeir, head of the Maronite Catholic bishops, issued a statement Wednesday calling for justice and peace. The Lebanese bishops noted that the Arab Summit held in Damascus, which was not attended by their country and slighted by other members of the Arab League, "insisted upon a commitment toward the Arab initiative for the treatment of the Lebanese crisis." The

bishops lamented that the working class is struggling under the high cost of living and threatens to strike. They also decried a lack of justice from the state, noting problems with the government ignoring court rulings against it in a few cases, as well as a failure to bring justice to conflicts over land and water. "The critical circumstance Lebanon is going through requires from all Lebanese cooperation and joined efforts to overcome the ordeal and face it with a strong will," the bishops affirmed. "The Lebanese must ask God to enable them to get through this ordeal by finding the right solution." Pope Benedict XVI prayed for Lebanon during his Feb. 17 Angelus address. Maronite Catholics make up the largest percentage of Lebanon's Christian population, which is itself about 39% of the entire population of the nation.

L'Osservatore Romano Display It was reported on Apr. 7 that the Milan exhibition of L'Osservatore Romano provided glimpses of the principal events of Italy and the Church in the last 147 years. The Catholic University of the Sacred Heart sponsored this "rereading of history from the point of view of the Holy See and 11 pontificates—from Leo XIII to Benedict XVI—that cannot but provoke surprises and clear up errors." Similar displays were presented in Rome, in 2006, and in Messina the following year. Among the documents in the exhibition "From Rome to the World: 147 Years of History Seen Through the Pages of the Pope's Newspaper" is Pope Pius XI's encyclical about the economic crisis of the 1930s and the alarming statements about the consequences of the first persecutions of the Jews in Nazi Germany.

French Converts On Apr. 7, as many as 150 to 200 Muslims convert to Catholicism each year in France, many of them the children of mixed marriages. Bp. Michel Dubost of Evry has worked with the program of dialogue with Islam that has resulted in a dozen Muslims being baptized every year in his diocese. The situation of Catholic converts from Muslim is often dire. The majority reportedly face misunderstandings from those around them, and others reproach them for having "disowned their culture." Some have hidden their conversion even from members of their family. Despite their growing numbers, converts from Islam to Christianity, including all confessions, do not exceed the number converting to Islam. In Aug. of 2006, the French daily La Croix reported that some 3,600 people in France convert to Islam every year.

English Missionary Slain On Apr. 11, it was reported that Brother Brian Thorp, an English missionary, was killed in Kenya, the victim of unknown assailants in the Lamu parish in the Archdiocese of Mombasa. Investigations were under way, but Brother Thorp was apparently the victim of an armed robbery. He was a Mill Hill Missionary who had served also in the Congo and Uganda. In 1999, he returned to Kenya, and was appointed to Lamu Island where he renovated the parish buildings.

Church in Kazakhstan It was announced on Apr. 17 that the episcopal conference of the Church in the former Soviet republic of Kazakhstan was formally accepted into the Federation of Asian Bishops' Conferences. The conference was officially accepted as a new member of the FABC. The Church in Kazakhstan consists of the Archdiocese of Astana, two dioceses—Karaganda and Almaty—and the Apostolic Administration in Atyrau. Of the 15 million inhabitants of Kazakhstan, some 60% are Shiite Muslims, while some 40% are Christians, mainly Orthodox. There are approximately 250,000 Roman Catholics in the country. The presence of the Church in Kazakhstan goes back to the second century. The Kazakhstan bishops' site reports that the first Christians there were among the Roman soldiers who had been taken prisoner after a battle they lost against the Persians. A bishop's see existed in the land in the fourth century, and at the end of the fourth and the beginning of the fifth centuries, there was a Melkite monastery. The Archdiocese of Astana and the Diocese of Almaty were established in 2003.

Jubilee in Lourdes It was announced on Apr. 24 that journalists and all those involved in the field of social communications would join in a special jubilee celebration in Lourdes as part of the itinerary marking the 150th anniversary of the apparitions of Our Lady. The May 29–30 jubilee was organized by the communications council of the French episcopal conference, various French Catholic press organizations, and "Secours Catholic" of the aid organization Caritas. The bishop of Lourdes was designated to inaugurate the event.

Damascus Focus On Apr. 24, Patriarch Gregorios III Laham of Antioch of the Melkite Greek Catholic Church, announced that with the help of the Franciscan custodians of the Holy Land, and in some cases, civil leaders, he planned to oversee the activities focused on St. Paul. The jubilee year marking the second millennium of Paul's birth was scheduled is from June 28, 2008, to June 29, 2009. Patriarch Gregorios III also explained that the preparations are under way in Damascus, which is the seat of the Melkite Greek Church. "We have spoken about it with the president of the republic, Bashar al-Assad, and with the minister of information, Mohsen Bilal," Patriarch Gregorios III said. "Both are interested in the framework of the celebrations in Damascus, capital of Arab culture in 2008, and because the faith of St. Paul is also a cultural theme of this city. This wide-ranging program, to be carried out in cooperation with the Franciscan Friars Minor of the Custody of the Holy Land—who are the caretakers of the Church of St. Ananias in Damascus—has begun this year, so as to later continue, to enable us to discover our faith of today in the teaching of St. Paul."

NATIONAL

Texas Co-Cathedral On Apr. 2, the new Co-Cathedral of the Sacred Heart in Houston was dedicated. Card. Daniel N. DiNardo of Galveston-Houston was the main celebrant for the three-hour Mass of the celebration. The dedication provided a cathedral for the 1.3 million Catholics in the Archdiocese of Galveston-Houston. Many American and visiting bishops took part in the ceremonies.

Bush Interview On Apr. 10, President George W. Bush was interviewed by Raymond Arroyo, lead anchor for EWTN Global Catholic Network, on the eve of Pope Benedict XVI's arrival in the country. The interview was aired just days ahead of the Papal visit. President Bush discussed U.S. relations with the Holy See, the papal visit, and Iraq. The interview was televised from EWTN's studio at the John Paul II Cultural Center in Washington, DC, aired on "The World Over."

Pope's Visit Pope Benedict XVI arrived on Apr. 15 to begin his pastoral visit of the United States. Landing at Andrews Air Force Base, the Holy Father was welcomed to the United States today in an unprecedented reception by President George Bush., accompanied by his wife and daughter Jenna. Pope Benedict XVI flew to the United States aboard an Alitalia Boeing 777, called Shepherd One. The Holy Father resided at the apostolic nuncio, and celebrated his 81st birthday with a morning reception at the White House and a private meeting with the president. Pope Benedict XVI emerged from the apostolic nuncio's residence in the U.S. capital this morning to be greeted by children's voices wishing him a happy birthday in his native German language. Thousands of people gathered to welcome Pope Benedict XVI to America during his drive through the streets of Washington, DC, in the Popemobile. He then met with Catholic groups and addressed some 350 bishops in the crypt of the Basilica of the National Shrine of the Immaculate Conception. The Apr. 17 Mass in Nationals Park reflected the diversity of Catholic heritages in the Archdiocese of Washington, and was attended by 45,000 people. The prayer of the faithful was recited in six languages—English, Spanish, Korean, Vietnamese, Tagalog, and Igbo. The Holy Father then met with Jewish leaders and with Catholic educators. On Apr. 18, he addressed the U.N. General Assembly in the morning, shortly after having arrived in New York for the second leg of his two-city U.S. tour. The U.N. Secretary-General Ban Ki-moon welcomed the Holy Father, with staff members. On Apr. 19, Pope Benedict XVI celebrated Mass in St. Patrick's Cathedral with bishops, priests, religious, and seminarians. On Apr. 20, the Holy Father began the final day of his U.S. visit by blessing the site of the Sept. 11, 2001, terrorist attacks on the World Trade Center, and meeting with survivors and relatives of the victims. At Yankee Stadium that afternoon, a site transformed into an open-air church, he urged more than 57,000 Catholics to "move forward with firm resolve" in continuing the legacy of faith set in motion by the country's first Catholics. "Follow faithfully in the footsteps of those who have gone before you!" he told those present. Some 4,000 people, including Vice President and Mrs. Cheney, were at John F. Kennedy International Airport when the Holy Father departed from the United States that evening.

Communion Reception On Apr. 29, Card. Edward Egan, the Archbishop of New York, announced that Rudolph Giuliani, the city's former pro-abortion mayor, should not have received the Eucharist at the Mass held in Yankee Stadium during Pope Benedict XVI's trip to the United States. "Throughout my years as archbishop of New York," Card. Egan stated, "I have repeated this teaching in sermons, articles, addresses and interviews without hesitation or compromise of any kind. Thus it was that I had an understanding with Mr. Giuliani when I became archbishop of New York and he was serving as mayor of New York, that he was not to receive the Eucharist because of his well-known support of abortion. I deeply regret that Mr. Giuliani received the Eucharist during the papal visit here in New York, and I will be seeking a meeting with him to insist that he abide by our understanding."

MAY 2008

VATICAN

Cuban Bishops On May 2, Pope Benedict XVI received in audience the bishops of Cuba during their five-yearly visit to the Vatican. "At this historic moment, the Church in Cuba is called to offer all Cuban society the only true hope: Our Lord Jesus," the Holy Father announced. "This means that the nourishing of ecclesial life must be given a central role in your aspirations and your pastoral projects." He then expressed the hope that the forthcoming beatification of Fr. José Olallo Valdés "may give fresh impulse to your service to the Church and the people of Cuba, always being a leavening for reconciliation, justice and peace."

Media Council On May 2, Pope Benedict XVI sent a message to the Pontifical Council for Social Communications for World Communications Day. The Holy Father's message notes that there are many people who now see a need for infoethics, similar to bioethics, in the field of medicine and scientific investigation. According to Abp. Celli, president of the council, the Holy Father's words "put us on the alert even more because social communications are profoundly linked to man, and therefore, they invite us to zealously defend the human person in every respect and in everything that man is and is called to be. They are certainly words that encourage us. If the media is a challenge, it is before all else a challenge for human intelligence," he said. "And the Church is not afraid of intelligence or of reason."

Ascension of Christ On May 4, Pope Benedict XVI prayed the Regina Caeli with thousands of the faithful gathered in St. Peter's Square, and he announced: "Today the solemnity of the Ascension of Christ into heaven is celebrated in Italy and in various other countries. After the Ascension the first disciples remain together in the cenacle around the Mother of Jesus in fervent expectation of the gift of the Holy Spirit promised by Jesus. On this first Sunday of May, the month of Mary, we too relive this experience, more intensely feeling Mary's spiritual presence."

Charismatic Renewal On May 4, Pope Benedict XVI sent a message through Secretary of State Card. Tarcisio Bertone encouraging and praising the work of the Charismatic Renewal in its commitment to promote communion. The message was sent to the members of the Catholic Charismatic Renewal *(Rinnovamento nello Spirito)*, gathered near Rimini, Italy, for their 31st meeting. The annual celebration focused on the theme "Regenerated by the Word of God" (1 Pt 1:23).

Social Sciences On May 4, Pope Benedict XVI addressed participants in the plenary session of the Pontifical Academy of Social Sciences. Their meeting was focused on "Pursuing the Common Good: How Solidarity and Subsidiarity Can Work Together." "How can solidarity and subsidiarity work together in the pursuit of the common good in a way that not only respects human dignity, but allows it to flourish?" the Holy Father asked. "This is the heart of the matter which concerns you. And though certain elements can help to understand these concepts," he said, "the solidarity that binds the human family, and the subsidiary levels reinforcing it from within, must however always

be placed within the horizon of the mysterious life of the Triune God, in whom we perceive an ineffable love shared by equal, though nonetheless distinct, Persons."

Swiss Guard On May 5, Pope Benedict XVI spoke to 33 new recruits of the Swiss Guard and praised their commitment to serving God by serving Christ's Vicar. The Swiss Guards were accompanied by their families and other members of the corps. The following day, May 6, is the traditional swearing-in day for new recruits of the Pontifical Swiss Guard because on that day in 1527, some 150 members of the Swiss Guard lost their lives during the sack of Rome, protecting Pope Clement VII and the Church from the onslaught of Emperor Charles V's troops. "The love for the Catholic Church remains the same, to which you bear witness, rather than with words, with your bodies, which—thanks to the characteristic uniforms—are easily recognizable at the entrance to the Vatican and to pontifical audiences," the Holy Father stated. "Your historic uniforms speak [...] of your commitment to serve God by serving the 'servant of his servants.'"

Archbishop of Canterbury On May 5, Pope Benedict XVI received in audience Rowan Williams, the archbishop of Canterbury, who acknowledged that the Anglican Communion is going through an "unprecedentedly difficult time." The Anglican leader was in Rome for the 7th Building Bridges seminar with Christian and Muslim scholars. The Anglican Communion is facing a fracture because parts of the group, notably the Episcopal Church in the United States, have approved the ordination of women and homosexuals as bishops.

Papal Rosary On May 5, Pope Benedict XVI led the praying of the rosary Saturday at the Basilica of St. Mary Major. "In the experience of my generation, May evenings evoke pleasant memories of evening appointments to pay homage to the Virgin Mary," the Holy Father said. "Today we together confirm that the holy rosary is not some pious practice relegated to the past, a prayer of distant times to be thought of nostalgically. Indeed, the rosary is experiencing what is almost a new springtime." He added: "The rosary, when it is prayed in an authentic manner—not mechanically and superficially, but profoundly—brings peace and reconciliation. It contains the healing power of the Most Holy Name of Jesus, invoked with faith and love at the heart of each Hail Mary."

Condolences to Myanmar On May 6, Pope Benedict XVI expressed his sympathy for the victims of Cyclone Nargis that pounded Myanmar (Burma). In a telegram sent by the pope's secretary of state, Card. Tarcisio Bertone, to Abp. Paul Zinghtung Grawng of Mandalay, president of the bishops' conference of Myanmar, the Holy Father expressed his sorrow and promised prayers. The telegram said: "Deeply saddened by news of the tragic aftermath of the recent cyclone, the Holy Father expresses his heartfelt sympathy. With prayers for the victims and their families, he invokes God's peace upon the dead and divine strength and comfort upon the homeless and all who are suffering." The death toll rises by the minute in Myanmar, with state radio announcing today that more than 22,000 are confirmed dead and some 41,000 are missing.

Chinese Mozart Concert On May 7, the

Philharmonic Orchestra of China and the Choir of the Shanghai Opera House performed Mozart's Requiem at the Vatican, in honor of Pope Benedict XVI. The Holy Father expressed his gratitude, commenting: "Another high-quality musical performance sees us gathered once again in the Paul VI audience hall. For me and for all of us here, it takes on a particular value and meaning, [I]t puts us in touch, as it were, with the living reality of the world of China. I thank the choir and orchestra for this generous tribute and I congratulate the organizers and the artists for their skillful, refined and elegant performance of a musical work that forms part of the artistic heritage of all humanity... Finally, as I thank you once again for this most welcome tribute, I send my greetings, through you, to all the people of China as they prepare for the Olympic Games, an event of great importance for the entire human family." And he ended, saying in Chinese, "I thank you all and I offer you my best wishes."

Melkite Patriarch On May 8, Pope Benedict XVI received some 300 members of the Melkite Greek Catholic Patriarchate, headed by Patriarch Gregorios III Laham. The group is on pilgrimage in Rome. The Holy Father praised "the vitality of the Melkite Church, despite the difficulties of the [Mideast] region's social and political situation." The Holy Father also invited the patriarch to carry out "an intense pastoral outreach" to awaken in the faithful "a new impetus to know ever more closely the person of Christ, thanks to a renewed reading of Paul's writings. This focus will also guarantee a thriving future for the Melkite Church."

Latin American Bishops On May 9, Pope Benedict XVI received in audience Abp. Raymundo Damasceno Assis of Aparecida, Brazil, and Aux. Bp. Víctor Sánchez Espinosa of Mexico City, the president and secretary-general of the Latin American bishops' council, respectively. They are in Rome for the celebration of the 50th anniversary of the Pontifical Commission for Latin America and to present to the Holy Father with the results of the 3rd American Missionary Congress in Quito, Ecuador, and subsequent missions. The prelates also gave him the guiding document for the continental mission, and the commemorative video of the 5th General Conference of the Bishops of Latin America and the Caribbean.

Latin Edition The Vatican's official Web site launched an edition in the Church's official language—Latin on May 9. Visitors to the site can now select "*Santa Sedes—Latine*" from the home page. A menu appears offering texts of the popes, the Bible, the Catechism of the Catholic Church, the Code of Canon Law, the texts of the Second Vatican Council, and documents from the Roman Curia. *Summi Pontifices*, the pages covering the papacy, contain information about the last five popes and include encyclicals, speeches, sermons, and messages.

Pentecost On May 11, Pope Benedict XVI celebrated on the feast of Pentecost in St. Peter's Square, announcing: "In the event of Pentecost it is made clear that multiple languages and different cultures belong to the Church; they can understand and make each other fruitful. St. Luke clearly wants to convey a fundamental idea, namely, in the act itself of her birth the Church is already 'catholic,' universal. She speaks all languages from the very beginning, because the Gospel that is entrusted to her is destined for all peoples, according to the will and the mandate of the risen Christ. The Church that is born at Pentecost is not above all a particular community—the Church of Jerusalem—but the universal Church, that speaks the language of all peoples." The Holy Father continued, "From her, other communities in every corner of the world will be born, particular Churches that are all and always actualizations of the one and only Church of Christ. The Catholic Church is therefore not a federation of churches, but a single reality: The universal Church has ontological priority. A community that is not catholic in this sense would not even be a Church."

Hungarian Bishops On May 12, Pope Benedict XVI received bishops from the Hungarian bishops' conference, at the end of their five-yearly visit to Rome. "The people entrusted to your care now stand before us spiritually, with their joys, their plans, their suffering, their problems and their hopes," the Holy Father said. "The long period of communist rule left a deep mark on the Hungarian people, and even today its consequences are evident, particularly in the difficulty many find in trusting others, a typical trait of people who have long lived in an atmosphere of suspicion." He also affirmed that the unity characterizing the Hungarian prelates "in following the teachings of the Church, is for me a cause of serenity and comfort."

Prayer for Church in China On May 16 it was announced that Pope Benedict XVI had composed a prayer to Our Lady of Sheshan to mark the Day of Prayer for the Church in China this month. In his pastoral letter to Catholics in China last May, which the Holy Father had designated as May 24. The day is the feast of Our Lady, Help of Christians, who is venerated at the Marian Shrine of Sheshan, located 21 miles from Shanghai. "Look upon the People of God," the pope wrote in the prayer, "and, with a mother's care, guide them along the paths of truth and love, so that they may always be a leaven of harmonious coexistence among all citizens."

Corpus Christi On May 22, Pope Benedict XVI celebrated the feast of Corpus Christi in the Basilica of St. John Lateran. After the Mass, he led a Eucharistic procession through the streets of Rome to the Basilica of St. Mary Major. The congregation included Missionaries of Charity, boy scouts, cardinals, Knights of the Holy Sepulcher, pilgrims from around the world, and even some homeless people curious about the celebration. Meditating on the Eucharistic mystery, the Holy Father cited the phrase from St. Paul: "There is neither Jew nor Greek, there is neither slave nor free person, there is not male and female; for you are all one in Christ Jesus." He added. "The Eucharist can never be a private event, reserved to people chosen on the basis of affinity or friendship. The Eucharist is a public worship that has nothing of esotericism or exclusivity. We have not decided with whom we want to gather; we have come and found ourselves together with each other, gathered by faith and called to become one body, sharing the only Bread that is Christ. We are united beyond our differences of nationality, profession, social class, political ideas: We open ourselves to each other to become one in him."

Mausoleum Restored It was reported on May 27 that one of the most important monuments of the

Roman necropolis located under the Vatican Basilica is restored and ready for viewing. Card. Angelo Comastri, archpriest of the Basilica of St. Peter's, presented the results of the recently-completed restoration of the Valerii Mausoleum. The crypt dates from the second century and is famous for its stucco decorations. It is located in the middle of the route through the old necropolis that leads to the tomb of St. Peter.

Women's Ordination Invalid The Vatican's doctrinal congregation decisively decreed that the ordination of women is invalid on May 30. The general decree "On the Delict of Attempted Sacred Ordination of a Woman" was to "come into force immediately." The Congregation for the Doctrine of the Faith states that it is acting to protect "the nature and validity of the sacrament of holy orders" and affirms that "he who shall have attempted to confer holy orders on a woman, as well as the woman who may have attempted to receive Holy Orders, incurs in a *latae sententiae* excommunication," that is, an automatic excommunication. The decree is signed by the dicastery's prefect, Card. William Levada, and the secretary of the Vatican congregation, Abp. Angelo Amato. The decree also affirms that the ordination of a woman to the priesthood is invalid or null, and that "only baptized men can by ordained validly." In regard to the automatic excommunication, the excommunicated person is barred "from taking part in any way as minister in the celebration of the sacrifice of the Eucharist or in any other ceremony of public worship," from "celebrating sacraments or sacramentals and from receiving the sacraments," as well as from "exercising functions in offices or ministries or ecclesiastical endeavors no matter what they are" or from "acts of governance."

General Audience

Pentecost, May 7.
Pseudo-Dionysius the Areopagite, May 14.
St. Romanus the Melodist, May 21.
St. Gregory the Great (1), May 28.

INTERNATIONAL

Marian Apparitions Approved On May 4, it was reported that Bp. Jean-Michel di Falco of the Diocese of Gap officially recognized the apparitions of the Virgin Mary to Benoite Rencurel at the sanctuary of Laus in the area of Hautes-Alpes, France. The pronouncement was made during a Mass in the Basilica of Notre Dame in Laus. Among those present were the apostolic nuncio to France, Bp. Fortunato Baldelli, and 30 cardinals and bishops from around the world. Rencurel, a poor shepherdess, was born in 1647. The Virgin Mary started appearing to her in 1664 and continued visiting her throughout the rest of her life. Rencurel died in 1718. The holy site now draws 120,000 pilgrims annually. Numerous physical healings have also been associated with the site, especially when oil from a lamp is applied on the wounds according to the directives the Virgin Mary gave to Rencural.

Holy Land Website It was announced on May 5 that a website was launched by the Assembly of Catholic Ordinaries of the Holy Land. Providing information in five languages—English, Italian, French, Arabic, and Hebrew—the website plans to become an authentic news agency for the Catholic Church in the Holy Land. Abp. Michel Sabbah of Jerusalem said: "The new website is important to reflect the variety found in the Holy Land. A land that belongs to its inhabitants, but also the land where every Christian is born. To have up-to-date information on the Holy Land is important for every Christian."

Australians "Reconnect" On May 8, the Australian episcopal conference announced that it planned to bring fallen-away Catholics back to the Church with a pastoral plan to reach out to Catholics who no longer practice their faith. A pastoral letter was to be read to parishes, urging them to become places of welcome. A six-week program titled "Reconnect" was also part of the strategy. A national advertising campaign inviting Catholics to reconnect with the Church community was designated as well.

St. Thérèse's Parents On May 8, the bodies of Louis and Zélie Martin were exhumed and moved into the crypt of the basilica dedicated to their daughter, as part of the process for the beatification of the parents of St. Thérèse of Lisieux. Louis (1823–1894) and Zelie (1831–1877) Martin were proclaimed venerable by Pope John Paul II in Mar. 1994.

Cause Opened It was reported on May 19 that the Catholic Church in Poland had started the cause for the canonization of a peasant couple, Jozef and Wiktoria Ulm, shot by the Nazis for hiding Jews in their farmhouse during the Holocaust. The couple's six small children died with their parents. "This was a poor family, but a resourceful and hardworking one," said Abp. Jozef Michalik of Przemysl, president of the Polish bishops' conference. "They knew sheltering Jews carried a death sentence and that several neighbors had already been executed for it. Despite this, they offered themselves—not even the children were afraid."

Priests Are Targets On May 27 it was announced that Zimbabwean priests were in hiding as a result of being made targets of the Mugabe enforcers. The assailants were part of an intimidation campaign leading up to the June 27 runoff election between President Robert Mugabe, 84, and opposition leader Morgan Tsvangirai. The Catholic Church joined with other denominations earlier this month to speak out about the situation and to protest the country's organized violence against those who did not vote for Mugabe.

NATIONAL

Prohibiting Hybrids On May 2, Card. Justin Rigali, chairman of the Bishops' Committee on Pro-Life Activities, welcomed bills introduced in the U.S. House and Senate that would prohibit the creation of animal-human hybrids. He also commended the congressmen who introduced the identical bills in both the House and the Senate. "Their legislation offers an opportunity to rein in an egregious and disturbing misuse of technology to undermine human dignity," the cardinal said. "While this subject may seem like science fiction to many, the threat is all too real." He noted as well: "The alleged promise of embryonic stem cells has already been used in attempts to justify destroying human embryos, and even to justify creating them solely for destructive research. Now, the same utilitarian argument is being used to justify an especially troubling form of genetic manipulation, to create partly human creatures as mere objects for research or commercial use."

Communion Decisions On May 5, the archbishop of

Washington, Donald Wuerl, announced that the decision of whether or not to give Communion to pro-abortion politicians rests on the shoulders of local bishops. The issue was brought to national attention when several pro-abortion politicians received Communion during Benedict XVI's visit to the United States. Card. Edward Egan, abp. of New York, released a statement stating that former New York mayor Rudolph Giuliani should not have received the Eucharist during the pope's visit. Abp. Wuerl added the Church's position on abortion, citing one of his previous articles: "Abortion and support for abortion are wrong. No informed Catholic can claim that either action is free of moral implications."

Cause Opened On May 11, the cause for beatification for a 20th-century Massachusetts-born priest, Fr. Theodore Foley (1913-1974), officially opened in Rome. For 10 years, Fr. Foley was the superior general of the Congregation of the Passion, also known as the Passionists. Daniel Foley was born in 1913 in Springfield to a family of Irish immigrants. He attended the schools of the Passionist Fathers, where he heard the call to the priesthood. He entered the Passionists congregation in 1932 and in the following year made his first profession, taking the name Theodore. He was ordained a priest in 1940 and became the general consultor and assistant to the superior-general of the Passionists. He was himself elected superior-general in 1964, a post he held until his death on Oct. 9, 1974.

Governor Restricted On May 12, Abp. Joseph Naumann of Kansas City, KS, asked local pro-abortion politicians to refrain from receiving the Eucharist, and repeated a request to Governor Kathleen Sebelius not to receive Communion. Abp. Naumann said: "What makes the governor's actions and advocacy for legalized abortion, throughout her public career, even more painful for me is that she is Catholic. Sadly, Governor Sebelius is not unique in being a Catholic politician supporting legalized abortion. Since becoming archbishop, I have met with Governor Sebelius several times over many months to discuss with her the grave spiritual and moral consequences of her public actions by which she has cooperated in the procurement of abortions performed in Kansas. My concern has been, as a pastor, both for the spiritual well-being of the governor but also for those who have been misled—scandalized—by her very public support for legalized abortion."

Church in Detroit It was reported on May 20 that the Archdiocese of Detroit celebrated its 175th anniversary, with celebrations including services in Blessed Sacrament Cathedral. Card. Adam Maida, the abps. of Detroit, reflected on the foundation and development of the local Church in Detroit during his homily at the ceremonies. "Every anniversary affords us an opportunity to pause and remember, to consider with joy and gratitude, the blessings we have received," he said. "With the serenity of time, we can put into perspective the events, people, and experiences that have made us who we are today. Even now, 175 years later, many of the things that have happened, and the way they have happened, have no obvious human logic or clear explanation; ultimately, our personal and communal history is always something of a mystery." The cardinal noted: "Missionaries brought

us the faith and we must be missionaries to the next generation and the generations to come as our children and grandchildren call forth from us ever-new responses of faith, hope and love."

Lebanese Cardinal On May 22, the Maronite patriarch of Antioch, Card. Nasrallah Pierre Sfeir, met with U.S. President George Bush on Wednesday, seeking his help to keep Lebanon peaceful and independent. The two met in the Oval Office to discuss the unique and important role of the Maronite Christian community in Lebanon and their common vision of an independent, sovereign and peaceful Lebanon. Card. Sfeir was on a multi-continent trip that he began May 4. His first stops included Qatar and South Africa, and during the U.S. leg of the trip, he stopped in New York, Philadelphia, and Houston. A week ago, he addressed the U.N. Security Council, where he spoke of the various issues facing Lebanon. He also met privately with Secretary-General Ban Ki-moon.

Cardinal's E-mail On May 28, it was reported that Card. Sean O'Malley, the abp. of Boston, was involved in the "Weekly E-mail from Cardinal Sean & the Pilot." The service was said to include messages from the cardinal, notes from his blog, press releases from the archdiocese, and links to current stories from the archdiocesan paper. The cardinal explained: "This weekly e-mail initiative will increase communication and connection among Catholics across the archdiocese. As we celebrate our bicentennial year, we have been reminded how Catholics have innovated to ensure that the saving message of Jesus Christ reaches as many people as possible. We want to continue that spirit of innovation and evangelization by utilizing the many new communication tools made possible by the recent advances in technology. I encourage every Catholic of the archdiocese with an e-mail account to sign up."

Excommunication of Group On May 29, it was announced that the Congregation for the Doctrine of the Faith confirmed an earlier declaration from Abp. Raymond Burke of St. Louis that the board of directors of the St. Stanislaus Kostka Corporation and the priest they hired are excommunicated. The corporation is associated with what used to be St. Stanislaus Kostka parish. Abp. Burke recently noted that in 2005, he "was obliged to declare the excommunication of the members of the board of directors of St. Stanislaus Kostka Corporation because of their persistence in schism." The members of the board had committed the most grievous delict of schism by hiring a suspended priest, that is, a priest not in good standing in the Church, for the purpose of attempting to celebrate the sacraments and sacramentals at St. Stanislaus Kostka Church, all outside of the communion of the Catholic Church." The priest involved, Fr. Marek Bozek of the Diocese of Springfield-Cape Girardeau, had left his priestly assignment against the expressed will of his bishop and was suspended from all acts of the power of Holy Orders and of governance. The board appealed for a review, but the Congregation for the Doctrine of the Faith took two actions, the abp. explained: "First, it has rejected the recourse presented by the Board of Directors of St. Stanislaus Kostka Corporation, including Reverend Bozek. In other words, it has found the recourse to be without foundation. Secondly, the Congregation has confirmed my decrees of Dec. 15, 2005, by which I declared that the members of the Board of Directors had incurred the canonical penalty of excommunication because of persistence in schism."

JUNE 2008

VATICAN

China and Myanmar On June 1, Pope Benedict XVI called for world solidarity with China and Myanmar as they deal with the effects of natural disasters. The Holy Father appealed on behalf of the victims of Cyclone Nargis and the Chinese earthquake during the midday Angelus in St. Peter's Square. "Once again I would like to invoke the Virgin's maternal intercession for the people of China and Myanmar, stricken by natural disasters, and for those who are dealing with the many situations of suffering, of sickness and material and spiritual misery that mark the journey of humanity," the pontiff said. The Chinese authorities have again updated the number of victims of the earthquake that struck May 12. The death toll is now above 69,000 and the number of missing persons is more than 18,000.

Decree for Pauline Year It was announced on June 1 that the Holy See would allow the Mass for the feast of the Conversion of St. Paul to be said on a Sunday in 2009, during the Pauline jubilee year. The Congregation for Divine Worship and the Sacraments published the decree authorizing the Mass to be said Jan. 25, 2009, which falls on the Third Sunday in Ordinary Time. Some feasts that coincide with a Sunday are moved to a weekday since the normal Sunday liturgy usually takes precedence. Pope Benedict XVI declared the jubilee year marking the 2,000th anniversary of Paul's birth. It was scheduled to be held from June 28, 2008, to June 29, 2009.

Southeast Asian Bishops On June 6, Pope Benedict XVI received in audience the bishops of Malaysia, Singapore, and Brunei, in Rome for their five-yearly visit. Quoting the apostolic letter *"Ecclesia in Asia,"* the Holy Father announced: "The Church's faith in Jesus is a gift received and a gift to be shared; it is the greatest gift which the Church can offer to Asia." He also encouraged the Southeast Asian bishops to continue their "commitment to interreligious dialogue."

Italian Premier Pope Benedict XVI, on June 6, received in audience today Silvio Berlusconi, the premier of Italy, who was accompanied by Gianni Letta and Paolo Bonaiuti, undersecretaries of state to the presidency of the Council of Ministers. Berlusconi and Letta met privately with the Holy Father. "They discussed the questions concerning the situation in Italy and the Catholic Church's contribution to the life of the nation, as well as the situation in the Middle East and the social development of the European continent." Upon greeting Letta, the pope said, "I greet an old friend—young, but old." Turning to Bonaiuti, the Holy Father said, "I meet him in person. I always see him on television."

Interreligious Dialogue On June 8, Pope Benedict XVI received in audience participants in the plenary meeting of the Pontifical Council for Interreligious Dialogue. Card. Jean-Louis Tauran, president of the Vatican dicastery, greeted the pope and explained to him the issues that were discussed during the dicastery's meeting, which focused on the theme "Dialogue in Truth and Charity: Pastoral Orientations." The Holy Father commented: "Religious collaboration offers the opportunity of expressing the highest ideals of every religious tradition. Helping the sick, giving suc-

cor to victims of natural disasters and violence, care of the elderly and the poor: These are some of the sectors in which persons of different religions can work together."

Pontifical Ecclesiastical Academy Students from the Pontifical Ecclesiastical Academy, the institution that trains candidates for the Holy See diplomatic service, were received in audience by Pope Benedict XVI on June 9. The students were accompanied by Abp. Beniamino Stella, president of the academy. The group was made up of some 25 priests from 15 nations. "Apart from the necessary juridical, theological and diplomatic training," the Holy Father told them, "what is most important is that your lives and activities should reflect a faithful love for Christ and for the Church that brings forth in you a friendly pastoral concern for everyone." He added: "Whatever work you undertake in the Church, ensure that you always remain his true friends, faithful friends who have met him and have learned to love him above all else. Communion with him, the divine master of our souls, will ensure you serenity and peace even in the most complex and difficult moments."

University Professors On June 9, Pope Benedict XVI addressed participants in the 6th European Symposium of University Professors. The Holy Father said that, in the face of the present crisis of modernity, it is urgent to re-launch a "fruitful dialogue" between philosophy and theology. Card. Camillo Ruini, the pope's vicar for Rome, and professors from 26 European countries, were received by the Holy Father in the Vatican's Clementine Hall, at the conclusion of their June 5–8 symposium on the topic "To Extend the Horizons of Rationality: Perspectives for Philosophy."

Islamic Group On June 11, Pope Benedict XVI received in audience the participants of the Islamic-Catholic committee established by the Pontifical Council for Interreligious Dialogue and the Saudi Arabia-based International Islamic Forum for Dialogue. Card. Jean-Louis Tauran and Abp. Pier Luigi Celata, president and secretary, respectively, of that Vatican dicastery participated. The committee met on the theme "Christians and Muslims: Witnesses of the God of Justice, Peace and Compassion in a World That Suffers Violence."

Bangladesh Bishops The bishops of Bangladesh were received in audience by Pope Benedict XVI on June 12. The bishops of Bangladesh were in Rome for their five-yearly visit. The Holy Father told them: "Bishops are called to be patient, mild and gentle in the spirit of the beatitudes. In this way they lead others to see all human realities in the light of the Kingdom of Heaven. Many of your people suffer from poverty, isolation or discrimination, and they look to you for spiritual guidance that will lead them to recognize in faith, and to experience in anticipation, that they are truly blessed by God." The Holy Father also noted: "Like the first Christians, you live as a small community among a large non-Christian population. Your presence is a sign that the preaching of the Gospel, which began in Jerusalem and Judea, continues to spread to the ends of the earth in accordance with the universal destination the Lord willed for it." Bangladesh's population of some 153 million is majority Muslim, with a large Hindu population. All other religions combined make up less than 1% of the population.

President Bush On June 13, Pope Benedict XVI received U.S. President George Bush. The president visited the pope in the Vatican today as part of his tour of Europe. In response to the president's unprecedented welcome of the Holy Father to the United States last April, this meeting included a "unique protocol." The Holy Father welcomed the president, accompanied by his wife, Laura, and the ambassador to the Holy See, Mary Ann Glendon, in the entrance of St. John's Tower in the Vatican Gardens. After the welcome, the two leaders had a private meeting in the upper level study of the tower. "Such an honor, such an honor," President Bush announced later. The Holy Father and President Bush strolled about the Vatican Gardens after the meeting, until they reached the nearby grotto of Our Lady of Lourdes. There the choir of the Sistine Chapel performed two motets for them.

Beatifications Planned The Vatican announced on June 13 that the beatification cause for some 250 Spaniards who died in Valencia or other parts of Spain during the 1934–1939 religious persecution has been approved. This has been noted as the most numerous group of Valencian martyrs to be recognized by the Church. Abp. Agustín García-Gasco of Valencia opened the cause in June of 2004, and it includes 183 priests, six men religious, four women religious, and 57 lay faithful.

Pope Pius XII On June 1, the Vatican announced that a conference and exhibition on the pontificate of Pope Pius XII and his service before his election to the See of Peter would commemorate the 50th anniversary of the Servant of God's death and would be held in Nov. Pius XII served as Supreme Pontiff from 1939–1958. Bp. Salvatore Fisichella, rector of the Pontifical Lateran University, spoke of the pontiff's "great stature, especially in spiritual terms, but also intellectually and diplomatically." Pope Pius XII led the Church during various significant historical situations and issued 43 encyclicals "that marked his pontificate, and the many discourses in which he examined the most controversial questions of his time." The conference was scheduled to be held at two universities where the future pope studied, the Gregorian and Lateran Universities. The exhibition was also scheduled to be on display in the Charlemagne Wing off St. Peter's Square from Oct. 21 to Jan. 6.

Pakistan Bishops On June 19, Pope Benedict XVI received in audience the bishops of Pakistan, in Rome for their five yearly visit. He told them that their presence in the Vatican "not only provides me with an opportunity to rejoice with you over the fruits of your labors, but to listen to your account of the hardships which you and your flock must endure for the sake of the Lord's name." Hindus and Christians combined make up only 3% of the population in Pakistan, which is majority Sunni Muslim. The Holy Father told the Pakistani bishops: "Your priests, united by a special bond to Christ the Good Shepherd, are heralds of Christian hope as they proclaim that Jesus lives among his people to ease their anguish and strengthen them in their weakness."

Congo President Pres. Joseph Kabila of Congo was received in audience by Pope Benedict XVI on June 19. The two discussed the need for human rights and the necessity of a security pact in the Great Lakes Region. The discussions also focused on the political and social situation in the country. Concerning the future of the country, the two discussed as well particular emphasis was given to the importance of the education and formation of the young, for whom the Church is always ready to make her specific contribution. One-half of Congo's 66 million inhabitants are Catholic; some 20% of the population is Protestant.

Radio's Mission On June 20, Pope Benedict XVI received in audience participants in a symposium titled "The Identity and Mission of Catholic Radio Today." The symposium was organized by the Pontifical Council for Social Communications. In his address, the Holy Father said, "Today, even though you make use of modern communication technologies, the words you broadcast are also humble, and sometimes it may seem to you that they are completely lost amid the competition of other noisy and more powerful mass media. But do not be disheartened! The words you transmit reach countless people, some of whom are alone and for whom your word comes as a consoling gift, some of whom are curious and are intrigued by what they hear, some of whom never attend church because they belong to different religions or to no religion at all, and others still who have never heard the name of Jesus Christ, yet through your service first come to hear the words of salvation." The congress has gathered representatives from 50 countries and some 63 Catholic radio stations at the Pontifical Urbanian University.

Eucharistic Message Pope Benedict XVI, on June 23, spoke in a video message for youth attending the 49th International Eucharistic Congress. The congress ended Sunday in Quebec City. Speaking in French and English, the Holy Father announced: "Do not forget that the Sunday Eucharist is a loving encounter with the Lord that we cannot do without. When you recognize him 'at the breaking of bread,' like the disciples at Emmaus, you will become his companions. He will help you to grow and to give the best of yourselves. Remember that in the bread of the Eucharist, Christ is really, totally and substantially present. It is therefore in the mystery of the Eucharist, at Mass and during silent adoration before the Blessed Sacrament of the altar, that you will meet him in a privileged way."

Catholic Biblical Federation On June 24, Pope Benedict XVI greeted members of the Catholic Biblical Federation plenary assembly in Tanzania. His words were sent to Bp. Vincenzo Paglia of Terni-Narni-Amelia, Italy, president of the Catholic Biblical Federation. The federation has a plenary assembly every six years. This year's assembly is under way in Dar-es-Salaam, capital of Tanzania, with the topic: "The Word of God: Source of Reconciliation, Justice and Peace." The Holy Father stated: "The fact that your meeting is being held in Dar-es-Salaam is an important gesture of solidarity with the Church in Africa, more so in view of next year's special Synod for Africa. The message you bring to Dar-es-Salaam is clearly a message of love of the Bible and love of Africa."

Orthodox Patriarch It was announced on June 24 that the ecumenical patriarch of Constantinople, Bartholomew I, planned to attend the inauguration of the Pauline Jubilee Year and Mass celebrated by Benedict XVI. Supreme Pontiff, Bartholomew I planned to participate in Saturday's celebration of vespers at the Basilica of St. Paul's Outside the Walls. With this event, Benedict XVI will officially inaugurate the Pauline year. Representatives of other Christian communities are also scheduled to attend. On Sunday, the feast of Sts. Peter and Paul, Bartholomew I will participate in the Mass celebrated by the pope in St. Peter's. The patriarch and the Holy

Father will pronounce the homily; together they will recite the profession of faith and impart the blessing. The pope will concelebrate Mass with the new metropolitan archbishops, upon whom he will impose the pallium during the course of the ceremony.

Malayalam L'Osservatore Pope Benedict XVI expressed his appreciation on June 25 for the first Malayalam-language version of the L'Osservatore Romano. The message of the Holy Father announced: "The publication is a highly significant event in the life of the Church in India, since it will keep the over six million Catholics in Kerala State fully informed about the ministry of the pope and the work of the Holy See and strengthen the bonds of faith and ecclesial communion linking the Catholic community to the See of Peter. I willingly take this occasion to offer my prayerful good wishes for this important undertaking, together with my heartfelt thanks to the directors of the Carmel International Publishing House and to all those who in any way have contributed to its realization." Some six million Catholics speak Malayalam in Kerala.

Honduran Bishops On June 25 Pope Benedict XVI received in audience the Honduran bishops, in Rome for their five-yearly visit. The Holy Father highlighted the bishops' role in this service of charity, and added: "I know well how the poverty, which affects so many of your fellow-countrymen, afflicts you." He also assured the bishops that he shares their concern at the "increase in violence, emigration, destruction of the environment, corruption, and lack of education, among other grave problems." Some 70% of Honduras' 7 million inhabitants are below the poverty line.

Gabonese Ambassador On June 26, Pope Benedict XVI received in audience the new Gabonese representative at the Holy See, Firmin Mboutsou. "Through your mediation, Lord Ambassador, I invite all authorities and men of good will, in particular on the beloved African continent, to be ever more committed to a peaceful, fraternal and solidaristic world," the Holy Father announced. Gabon is on the western coast of Africa and bordered by Congo, and is one of Africa's richest nations and its population of close to 1.5 million is between 55% and 75% Christian.

Chinese Bishops Pope Benedict XVI, on June 27, received the bishops of the Chinese dioceses of Hong Kong and Macao at the conclusion of their five-yearly visit. Hong Kong and Macao are the two special administrative regions of China, and are allowed govern themselves with a high degree of sovereignty. "I hope and pray to the Lord that the day will soon come when your brother bps. from mainland China come to Rome on pilgrimage to the tombs of the Apostles Peter and Paul, as a sign of communion with the Successor of Peter and the Universal Church," the Holy Father said. "I willingly avail myself of the occasion to send to the Catholic community of China and to all the people of that vast country the assurance of my prayers and my affection."

Pauline Year On June 30, Pope Benedict XVI announced that the Pauline Year would involve the entire Church before praying the Angelus with thousands gathered in St. Peter's Square. The Pauline Year was inaugurated at a ceremony at the Basilica of St. Paul Outside the Walls by the Holy Father. He said the "horizon of the Pauline Year cannot but be universal because St. Paul was, par excellence, the apostle of those who, in regard to the Jews, were 'distant,' and who, 'thanks to the blood of Christ,' were drawn 'near.' For this reason, today too, in a world that has become 'small,' but where many have not yet met the Lord Jesus, the Jubilee of St. Paul invites all Christians to be missionaries of the Gospel," the pope affirmed. "This missionary dimension must always be accompanied by that of unity, represented by St. Peter, the 'rock' on which Jesus Christ built his Church."

General Audience
St. Gregory the Great (2), June 4.
St. Columban, June 11.
St. Isidore of Seville, June 18.
St. Maximus the Confessor, June 25.

INTERNATIONAL
Religious Mobilize It was reported on June 4 that the International Union of Generals Superior sponsored an international congress in Rome, organized by the religious superiors and the World Organization of Migrations. Religious from 20 countries and 31 congregations participated in the weeklong event, which aimed to educate women religious in the fight against trafficking, reinforce existing national and regional networks, and create the foundations for an international network. Studies presented during the first day of the congress indicated that between 600,000 and 820,000 are victims of transnational trafficking per year. To date over 4,000 religious have participated.

Scottish Cardinal On June 6, Card. Keith O'Brien spoke at a Mass in the Crypt of the House of Commons, where he reminded members of Parliament and the House of Lords that society is currently living a "time of confusion over the most basic questions about our society and the values we hold dear." The abp. of St. Andrews and Edinburgh added that the country needed its legislators to follow their conscience, even at the expense of political difficulty. Parliament voted May 19 in favor of the "Human Fertilization and Embryology Bill," which allows for the creation of human-animal hybrids, made by introducing human DNA into animal ova.

Neocatechumenate Approved It was reported on June 12 that the Catholic lay Neocatechumenal Way received the Church's final approval of its statutes. Card. Stanislaw Rylko, president of the Pontifical Council for the Laity, issued the document of approval. The group began in Spain in 1964, the mid 1960s. It is parish-based and forms small communities of renewal within parishes.

Dialogue With Islam On June 13, it was announced that "Catholics and Muslims in Today's France" has been issued by the French bishops. The French prelates also released "How Christians and Muslims Speak of God" at the end of May, which aims to respond to questions that come from the faithful regarding the Christian and Muslim understanding of God. The note was signed by Abp. Pierre-Marie Carré, president of the conference's doctrinal commission.

Islamic-Catholic Panel It was announced on June 16 that the Islamic-Catholic Liaison Committee in Rome issued five conclusions from the 14th meeting of the committee, which was held in the Vatican. The Catholic delegation was headed by Card. Jean-Louis Tauran, president of the Pontifical Council for Interreligious Dialogue, while the Islamic delegation was headed by Professor Hamid bin Ahmad Al-Rifaie, president of the International Islamic Forum for Dialogue, of Jeddah, Saudi Arabia. The meeting had the theme "Christians and Muslims as Witnesses of the God of Justice, of Peace and of Compassion in a World Suffering From Violence."

International Eucharistic Congress On June 16, Card. Josef Tomko opened the 49th International Eucharistic Congress. As the Holy Father's special envoy for the event, the cardinal presided at the opening mass of the weeklong congress in Quebec. Pope Benedict XVI was scheduled to address the participants live via satellite. Some 11,000 pilgrims, 50 cardinals and more than 100 bishops gathered for the inaugural Mass of the congress.

Vietnam Relations It was announced on June 16 that a Vatican delegation led by the undersecretary for relations with states left Vietnam after gaining agreement on a timetable for enhancing bilateral relations. Msgr. Pietro Parolin and the Holy See delegation were in Vietnam for their annual visit. They met with Vietnam's Deputy Prime Minister and Foreign Minister Pham Gia Khiem and with Vietnamese government officials headed by Committee for Religious Affairs Chairman Nguyen The Doanh. Vietnam is about 7% Catholic. The Church does not have diplomatic relations with the communist nation, though in Jan. 2007, Vietnamese Prime Minister Nguyen Tan Dung made a historic visit to Benedict XVI.

Diocesan Ban on Filming It was reported on June 17 that the Rome diocesan officials have denied Hollywood producers permission to film the prequel to *The Da Vinci Code* inside its churches in Rome. Producers of the film, *Angels and Demons*, were turned down because the movie is a work of "fantasy that damages common religious sentiment." Producers of the new movie, currently being filmed in Rome and due for release next spring, had asked for permission to film scenes inside the churches of Santa Maria del Popolo and Santa Maria della Vittoria about a year ago.

Holy See Display On June 19, it was reported that the Vatican pavilion at the international exposition on "Water and Sustainable Development" being held in Zaragoza, Spain, was attracting thousands of visitors. The Holy See's booth offers a reflection on the divine and human dimensions of water. El Greco's *The Baptism of Christ* captured the visitors' attention. Also of great interest was the tapestry of *Creation,* on loan from the Vatican Museums and placed in the main room of the pavilion, as well as the bronze and silver baptismal font given to Pope John Paul II in 1996 and used by pontiffs on special occasions, such as the celebration of baptisms at the Easter Vigil.

NATIONAL

Father Damien's Canonization It was announced on June 3 that the Vatican has recognized a miracle attributed to the intercession of Blessed Belgian Blessed Damien de Veuster, known as the Apostle of Lepers in Molokai, Hawaii. Fr. Bruno Benati, general postulator of Fr. Damien's cause, announced earlier this month that the Congregation for Saints' Causes ruled that a Hawaiian woman's cure from cancer was a miracle linked to her prayers to Fr. Damien (1840-1889). This moves the blessed one step closer to being declared a saint. Born Jozef De Veuster, he entered the novitiate of the Congregation of the Sacred Hearts of Jesus and Mary in Leuven, Belgium. Damien was sent as a missionary to Honolulu in 1864, and shortly afterward was ordained a priest. He labored in Hawaii before asking for permission to be assigned to Kalaupapa, a leprosy settlement on the island of Molokai. He arrived on May 10, 1873. There he estab-

lished the Parish of St. Philomena and attended to the lepers medical needs, built homes and beds and even coffins, and dug graves. Fr. Damien was 49 when he died of leprosy on Apr. 15, 1889. He was declared blessed in 1995.

Papal Visit Aftermath On June 11, the Vatican nuncio for the United States, Abp. Pietro Sambi, announced that American Catholics have changed their image of Benedict XVI and the Catholic Church after the pope's April visit to the nation. He added that the American people "discovered" the Holy Father during his visit, which they viewed in an overwhelmingly positive way. "The Pope has been 'discovered' as an attentive expert on what happens in the heart of the man of today, as a bearer of substantial and life-giving answers, offered with clarity, with humility, almost with timidity," the nuncio commented. And in response to this, he also affirmed that "the affection, attention, respect and love of a whole population has exploded." He added: "Even the press, which normally makes no secret of its sharpness with the Catholic Church, has written of and transmitted the visit of the pope with interest, respect and liking." The secular press "defined the visit as 'an event that exceeded every expectation.' And, given the power and resonance of the U.S. mass media, a success here implies a success in the whole world."

Paulist Anniversary On June 19, the Paulist Fathers' 150th anniversary convocation opened at the Catholic University in Washington, DC. Paulist Fr. Lawrence Boadt addressed the gathering and discussed the evangelization efforts used today. The Missionary Society of St. Paul the Apostle was founded in 1858 by Fr. Isaac Thomas Hecker, a New York City native, and began its missionary apostolate to America.

U.S. Religiosity On June 25 Abp. Donald Wuerl, chairman of the Bishops' Committee on Evangelization and Catechesis, and abp. of the Archdiocese of Washington, DC, responded to the results of the Pew Forum on Religion and Public Life survey just released. The survey was based on answers from more than 35,000 American adults and reveals that a vast majority of Americans, nearly 92%, believe in God or a universal spirit. "History testifies that religious faith is very important to Americans," Abp. Wuerl noted. "At every juncture of our past, Americans have called upon God for guidance, protection and direction. There is a clear identification with religion in America which, for Catholics, reflects the dedicated efforts of priests, catechists and teachers in our history." The Pew study also states that 74% of Americans believe in heaven and only 59% in hell.

Cause to Open On June 26, it was announced that the canonization cause for Fr. Emil Kapaun, a military chaplain who was captured when he stayed behind with wounded soldiers, was scheduled to be opened. He was taken prisoner in 1950 during the Korean War and spent seven months ministering in prison. After a blood clot in his leg immobilized him, he was moved to a hospital where he was denied medical treatment. He died in 1951. The cause was opened by Bp. Michael Jackels of Wichita, who will preside over the diocesan phase of the canonization process. Emil Kapaun was born in 1916. He was ordained a priest of the Diocese of Wichita in 1940 and entered the U.S. Army Chaplain Corps in 1944. In 1946, he returned to diocesan work, but only for two years, as he reentered the military chaplaincy in 1948. In 1950, Fr. Kapaun was sent to Korea, where he would die a prisoner.

JULY 2008

VATICAN

Peace Day Message On July 1, the World Day of Peace message of Pope Benedict XVI was announced. "Combating Poverty: Building Peace" is the theme chosen by the Pope for this World Day of Peace, celebrated on the first day of each year. The statement noted how the Pope — in a June 2 message addressed to the U.N. Food and Agriculture Organization – denounced the scandal of world poverty in the following terms: "Poverty and malnutrition are not a simple fatality, provoked by adverse environmental situations or by disastrous natural calamities. [...] Purely technical and economic considerations must not prevail over the duties of justice toward people suffering from hunger."

Castel Gandolfo On July 1, it was announced that Pope Benedict XVI would go to the papal summer residence at Castel Gandolfo. During the summer period, all private and special audiences were scheduled to be suspended. On the first and last Sundays of July (the 6th and 27th) the Pope planned to pray the Angelus from the courtyard there. For the other two Sundays, he would be in Australia for World Youth Day. General audiences were scheduled to be resumed again regularly on Wednesday, Aug. 13.

Fourth Crusade It was announced on July 1 that a study of the 4th Crusade of the 1204 has been published by the Vatican. The Vatican Publishing House (*Libreria Editrice Vaticana*) released a volume collecting the addresses in various languages from a conference held in 2004 on the 4th Crusade. That year was the 800th anniversary of the crusade that went awry. The 13th-century event is considered to have cemented the Great Schism with the Orthodox that had occurred in 1054. The 2004 conference was organized by the Pontifical Committee of Historical Sciences, in collaboration with the Institute of Byzantine History of the University of Athens and the Institute of Byzantine and Neo-Greek Studies of the University of Vienna.

Colombian Conference On July 2, it was reported that Pope Benedict XVI had sent a message addressed to the Colombian bishops' conference for the 100th anniversary of that institution. The bishops were gathered in plenary assembly through Saturday. In his message, the Holy Father highlighted how the episcopal conference, established in 1908, and assured them of his "prayers and spiritual closeness in the efforts you are making to ensure the Gospel rings out in all parts of Colombian territory, through initiatives in the fields of pastoral care in education and in universities, and in the concern you show for the imprisoned, the sick, the elderly, indigenous peoples, workers, the displaced, the young and families." More than 3 million people in Colombia have been forced to flee their homes during decades of fighting between guerrilla groups, paramilitaries and the army.

Solomon Islands Leader On July 3, Pope Benedict XVI received in audience the governor general of the nation, Nathaniel Rahumaea Waena. The meeting took place at Castel Gandolfo, where Waena also met with Abp. Dominique Mamberti, secretary for relations with states. The Holy Father and the Solomon Island leader discussed the current political and social situation of the country, and on the significant contribution of the Catholic Church in the region.

Miracles Noted On July 3, Pope Benedict XVI authorized the promulgation of decrees attributing miracles to five causes, including that of Blessed, Father Damien de Veuster, Belgian professed priest of the Congregation of the Sacred Hearts of Jesus and Mary (1840-1889) and Louis and Marie-Celie Martin, parents of St. Thérèse of Lisieux. The Holy Father received in private audience today Cardinal José Saraiva Martins, prefect of the Congregation for Saints' Cause and authorized the promulgation of the decrees.

Women Bishops On July 8, the Pontifical Council for Promoting Christian Unity responded to the vote of the Church of England to pave the way for the episcopal ordination of women. The council announced that the decision is an obstacle to union with the Catholic Church. The general synod of the Church of England affirmed "that the wish of [the synod's] majority is for women to be admitted to the episcopate…We have regretfully learned the news of the Church of England vote that paves the way for the introduction of legislation that will lead to the ordaining of women to the episcopacy." In reply to these events, the Pontifical Council for Promoting Christian Unity stated: "The Catholic position on the issue has been clearly expressed by Popes Paul VI and John Paul II. Such a decision signifies a break with the apostolic tradition maintained by all of the Churches since the first millennium and is, therefore, a further obstacle to reconciliation between the Catholic Church and the Church of England."

Top Donors It was announced on July 9 that the dioceses in Germany, the United States and Italy contributed the most in 2007 to cover the Holy See's expenses. The Council of Cardinals for the Study of Organizational and Economic Questions of the Apostolic See reported this today after meeting last Thursday and Friday in the Vatican. Dioceses contributed a total of $29,552,843 (some 18.7 million) to the Holy See in 2007. These three countries contributed large percentages of this total. Germany contributed the most at 31.57%, followed by the United States at 28.31%. Italy contributed 18.9%. Austria, Canada and Spain contributed more than 3% each, and Korea contributed 2.31% (See also **News in Depth**.)

Peter's Pence On July 10, it was reported that the annual collection for the Pope's charitable activities brought in nearly $80 million (over 50 million) in 2007, down some $20 million from the previous year. The Council of Cardinals for the Study of Organizational and Economic Questions of the Apostolic See reported the result after meeting last Thursday and Friday in the Vatican. The Peter's Pence collection is made up of the totality of donations destined to assist the Pope in his charitable apostolic mission. The Holy Father has allocated the Peter's Pence collection to charitable works for peoples in several countries of the world hit by natural disasters, to the support of numerous initiatives of ecclesial communities of the Third World, and to help the poorest local Churches. [See also **News in Depth**.]

King of Bahrain Pope Benedict XVI received in audience at Castel Gandolfo King Hamad Bin Isa Al-Khalifa of Bahrain. King Hamad also met with Abp. Dominique Mamberti, secretary for relations with states. The Holy Father and Vatican authorities used the occasion to thank the king for the welcome he has shown to many Christian immigrants. The king also invited the Holy Father to visit his country. Bahrain is the smallest of the Gulf countries. It has a population of more than 700,000 inhabitants, 35% of whom are immigrants. Even though the official religion is Islam, there are minority populations of Jews and Christians that enjoy religious liberties. Bahrain has maintained diplomatic relations with the Vatican since 2000.

Papal Visit in Australia On July 13, Pope Benedict XVI arrived at Richmond Royal Australian Air Force Base, located northwest of Sydney. He was greeted by Prime Minister Kevin Rudd and Cardinal George Pell, the archbishop of Sydney. Pope Benedict XVI rested for three days at the Opus Dei-run Kenthurst Study Center, located northwest of Sydney and then at the Sydney cathedral house. The first papal public event was a welcome ceremony at Sydney's Government House, after which the Holy Father visited the Blessed Mary MacKillop Memorial Chapel. In the afternoon the Holy Father boarded the ship "Sydney 2000" and traveled by sea to Barangaroo East Darling Harbor. The sight of the flotilla of 13 vessels, dubbed the papal "boat-a-cade" set off the chants — *"Ben-e-det-to"* and *"Viva il Papa"* — from approximately 500,000 youth and locals lining the shores. Pope Benedict XVI was welcomed by aboriginal representatives, and delivered his first address to the youth pilgrims. An ecumenical meeting in the crypt of St. Mary's Cathedral followed, where he met with some 40 representatives of other religions. On Saturday he celebrated Mass with Australian bishops, seminarians and men and women religious novices, and consecrated the new altar, and in the afternoon the Holy Father presided at the World Youth Day Vigil. The weeklong event culminated with an open-air Mass on July 20 at Randwick Racecourse. Some 500,000 people attended. The Holy Father also received a visit from the Taronga Zoo Mobile in Sydney with animals such as a koala bear, a carpet python, a red-necked wallaby, shingle back lizards, a parrot, a possum, a baby crocodile, an echidna, and a kangaroo. He was also greeted by the Australian Federation of Islamic Councils. A concert was also held with 10,000 World Youth Day pilgrims from Asia at Olympic Park for the Fifth Asian Youth Gathering. The event organized by the Federation of Asian Bishops' Conferences included music, testimonies and prayers in English, Mandarin and Cantonese. At the end of the 23rd World Youth Day, Benedict XVI told the young people that he would see them again in Madrid in 2011.

His last farewell was made before boarding the plane that would take him back to Rome. The Holy Father thanked the government officials present at his departure ceremony, including Prime Minister Kevin Rudd and Governor-General, Major-General Michael Jeffery.

Saudi-Organized Conference On July 24 it was reported that Pope Benedict XVI sent a message to the World Conference on Dialogue, held in Madrid, Spain, and sponsored by the Mecca-based Muslim World League. Cardinal Jean-Louis Tauran, president of the Pontifical Council for Interreligious Dialogue, who delivered the meeting's closing address, transmitted the papal message to participants. King Juan Carlos of Spain and spiritual representatives of virtually all religions attended the conference, held from July 16-18 and convoked by King Abdullah of Saudi Arabia.

Iraqi Leader On July 25, Pope Benedict XVI received Prime Minister Nouri Kamel Al-Maliki at Castel Gandolfo. The two conversed and used this opportunity to examine a number of fundamental aspects of the situation in Iraq, including the many Iraqi refugees both inside and outside the country. The prime minister invited the Holy Father to visit Iraq. Maliki paid a visit to the tomb of Pope John Paul II in the Vatican Grottoes and met also with the Pope's secretary of state, Card. Tarcisio Bertone, and Abp. Dominique Mamberti, secretary for relations with states.

Mountain Retreat On July 28 Pope Benedict XVI arrived in Bressanone, a city of 20,000 inhabitants in the province of Bolzano, in the mountainous region of Trentino-Alto Adige in northern Italy. The Holy Father was scheduled to Pope spend his summer holidays there until Aug. 11. Bp. Wilhelm Emil Egger of Bolzano-Bressanone welcomed him at Bolzano's airport along with local authorities. The Holy Father then proceeded to Bressanone's seminary, where he had often vacationed prior to his election to the papacy. He was greeted by the sound of bells of the cathedral, and children singing in German, the language of the majority of the people of the area.

Anglican Request On July 30, Cardinal William Levada, prefect of the Congregation for the Doctrine of the Faith, announced that the Holy See was following with "serious attention" the request from the Traditional Anglican Communion for "full, corporate, sacramental union" with Rome. The letter was written before the beginning of the Lambeth Conference, the once-a-decade gathering of Anglican leaders. The Lambeth Conference was facing unprecedented controversy, and some bishops boycotted it altogether. The conflict within the Communion has arisen over debate about the possibility of ordaining homosexual bishops and blessing homosexual marriages. A synod decision this summer to pave the way for the episcopal ordination of women further alienated some Anglican leaders, many of whom were in disagreement with the Communion's decision to ordain women as priests. The Traditional Anglican Communion stated that its aim was "to recall Anglicanism to its heritage, to heal divisions caused by departures from the faith, and to build a vibrant church for the future based on powerful local leadership." By some counts, it has about 400,000 faithful. If the request for "corporate union" is deemed possible, it would imply the entrance of entire parish communities into communion with Rome.

General Audience
The Great Apostle St. Paul, July 2.

INTERNATIONAL
Cause Opened On July 1, it was reported that the cause for Friar Albert Beretta, brother of St. Gianna Beretta, opened in Italy last month. Friar Albert was an Italian missionary in Brazil for 33 years. Albert Beretta was born in Milan in 1916. He was already a doctor and surgeon when he was ordained a priest in the Capuchin Order in 1948. He left for Brazil a year later. He was described as "a witness of the beatitudes. [...] He was a witness of God's presence in every person, from the beginning to the end."

Nepal Priest Slain It was reported on July 1 that Fr. John Prakash, 62, a Salesian priest from India was killed Monday in Nepal when armed men broke into his residence and detonated an explosive device. Fr. Prakash directed a school in Sirsiya in the Morang district of the South Asian country. The assassination is linked to a Hindu extremist group. Bp. Anthony Sharma, the apostolic vicar of Nepal, that since the nation's classification as a lay state in 2006, some Hindu extremists "have felt deprived of their privileges." Nepal was previously the world's only Hindu nation. The population of some 29.5 million is 80% Hindu. The group suspected in the slaying of Father Prakash was also implicated in the bombing of a prayer meeting of a Muslim community.

Canadian Abortionist On July 3, the Canadian bishops conference decried the appointing of an abortionist to the Order of Canada. The bishops said they were "dismayed" by the appointment of Dr. Henry Morgentaler to the group, which aims to "recognize outstanding achievement and service in various fields of human endeavor." The Order of Canada's motto is *desiderantes meliorem patriam,* "they desire a better country." The Canadian bishops declared that "Far from improving our country, Morgentaler's actions continue to create controversy and division in our nation."

"Reformed Catholic Church" On July 4, the Catholic bishops of Venezuela stated that the Reformed Catholic Church in Venezuela was not recognized in any way by the Catholic Church and the faithful were urged not to associate themselves with it. The group presented itself in Venezuela two weeks ago. It was started by former Lutherans, Anglicans and Catholics, including two priests who Cardinal Jorge Urosa Savino described as "in bad canonical situations." The members profess support for President Hugo Chávez. The Anglican Communion in the country also issued a communiqué stating that they do not recognize the group.

Miraculous Medal The Association of the Miraculous Medal, on July 8, celebrated the centennial anniversary of pontifical approval 100 years ago. Vincentian Father Gregory Gay, superior-general of the association, announced that the centenary would run through Nov. 20, 2009, with its third international meeting. The association, established after the apparitions of the Virgin Mary to St. Catherine Labouré, was recognized formally on July 8, 1909. The miraculous medal was manifested by the Blessed Virgin to St. Catherine in Paris in 1830. The medal shows Our Lady standing on a globe with her arms outstretched and with the rays of light streaming from her fingers. Framing the figure is the inscription: "O Mary, conceived without sin, pray for us who have recourse to thee." The back of the medal has 12 stars encircling a large "M" from which arises a cross. Below are two hearts with flames arising from them. One heart is encircled in thorns and the other is pierced by a sword. It noted that the principal apostolate has been prayer to promote a greater devotion to the Virgin Mary.

"Magnanimous Gestures" On July 9, it was reported that an Anglican bishops was seeking "magnanimous gestures" from Benedict XVI to facilitate the entrance of Anglicans into the Catholic Church. In a letter to be published in this week's edition of Britain's *Catholic Herald* newspaper, Anglican Bp. Andrew Burnham of Ebbsfleet said "traditional Anglo-Catholics" now face the decision of staying in the Church of England in "what, for a while, will be a protected colony – where the sacramental ministry of women bishops and priests is neither acknowledged nor received – or to leave." In a vote Monday, the general synod of the Church of England decided to allow the ordination of women bishops. Though a "code of practice" was discussed for those who do not in conscience accept the ordination of women bishops, it was not clearly defined. Bp. Burnham acknowledged that the decision is not easy. "You don't become a Catholic, for instance, because of what is wrong with another denomination or faith," he said. "You become a Catholic because you accept that the Catholic Church is what she says she is and the Catholic faith is what it says it is. In short, some Anglo-Catholics will stay and others will go." The bishop mentioned the

similar decision already faced in 1992, when the Church of England decided to ordain women priests. "What we must humbly ask for now is for magnanimous gestures from our Catholic friends, especially from the Holy Father, who well understands our longing for unity, and from the hierarchy of England and Wales," Bp. Burnham said. "Most of all we ask for ways that allow us to bring our folk with us."

Mary MacKillop Coin On July 9 it was announced that Australia is honoring Blessed Mary MacKillop, who will likely be the country's first saint, by featuring her on a collector's coin. The $1 uncirculated coin is the first of the Royal Australian Mint's series which commemorates unique Australians who have made an extraordinary contribution to the nation. The Royal Australian Mint coin designer Vladimir Gottwald depicted MacKillop as "guiding future generations." Pope John Paul II beatified Sister Mary MacKillop in 1995.

St. Pius X Society It was reported on July 14 that a group of monks close to the traditionalist Society of St. Pius X asked for and received canonical good standing and communion with the Holy See. The vicar-general of the Transalpine Redemptorists, Father Michael Mary, reported this month on the group's blog that "our community now truly rejoices in undisputed and peaceful possession of communion with the Holy See because our priests are now in canonical good standing." He had asked the Holy See, in the presence of the members of the Pontifical Commission Ecclesia Dei, for the priestly suspensions to be lifted. The Transalpine Redemptorists are based on Papa Stronsay, an island in Orkney, north of Scotland. Father Michael Mary went on to say: "We are very grateful to our Holy Father Pope Benedict XVI for issuing, last July, the *'Motu Proprio Summorum Pontificum'* which called us to come into undisputed and peaceful communion with him."

Lambeth Conference Cardinal Walter Kasper was reported on July 18 as having joined with some 650 Anglican leaders at the Lambeth conference. Cardinal Kasper, the president of the Pontifical Council for Christian Unity, was invited by the Anglican Communion's spiritual leader, Abp. Rowan Williams. The Lambeth conference is held once every 10 years. The communion is threatened by schism. One of the main issues causing conflict is the Episcopalian resolve to ordain openly homosexual bishops. The Episcopal church is the portion of the Anglican Communion in the United States.

Iraqi Christians It was reported on July 29 that the Christian communities of southern Iraq have begun a campaign for the restoration of churches that have been damaged due to negligence and the war. Father Imad Aziz Al Banna, of the Archdiocese of Basra of the Chaldeans, announced that the local Christian community requested that the government finance the project. The community is working in cooperation with the office in charge of non-Muslim groups, and other government ministries. The recent reopening of the church of Um Al Azhan in Al-Amarah demonstrates the effectiveness of this campaign. The church, built in 1880, was restored. A Mass and baptism were held there, celebrated by Father Al Banna at the end of June. Although less numerous than that of Baghdad and northern Iraq, the Christian community of the nation's south has ancient roots which, according to

Syro-Orthodox Father Sam'an Khaz'al, date back to the 4th century.

NATIONAL

Lay Leaders On July 1, it was reported that the Lay Center in Rome welcomed the faithful of American dioceses to a conference focused on "Collaborators in the Lord's Vineyard: Called to Communion, Called to Mission." The delegates addressed the specific tasks of the laity in the Church. The U.S. bishops' Secretariat for the Laity, Marriage, Family Life and Youth collaborated in sponsoring the conference. Cardinal John Patrick Foley opened the conference with a Eucharistic celebration. Ecclesial ministries, leadership programs, and catechetical or pastoral work depend upon the dedication of lay ministers who work in collaboration with priests, deacons and bishops; and have the formation and education to carry out their roles. The conference concerned all of those aspects of lay leadership.

Millions Southward The U.S. bishops' conference, on July 2, reported that approval had been given for an additional set of grants for the Church in Latin America. The total for the first half of 2008 is thus set at \$4 million. The Church in the United States supports Latin American faithful with grants each year, with the majority of the funds coming from a Sunday collection, taken up in most parishes in January. The financial support provides aid for seminary and religious formation, religious education, catechesis and youth ministries, evangelization, lay formation and ministry, diaconate training, and research.

US Youths It was reported on July 3 that some 15,000 young men and women from the United States and 50 of their bishops were headed to Australia for World Youth Day. This has been listed as the largest delegation representing any country outside of Australia. Cardinal Francis George, archbishop of Chicago and president of the episcopal conference, is one of the prelates set to attend. Some of the young people were going to the celebration with their families. World Youth Day was the 23rd celebration since Pope John Paul II started the events in 1985. For the first time at a World Youth Day, the U.S. episcopal conference will sponsor a Mass for all U.S. groups in Sydney. Cardinal George will preside and deliver the homily on Saturday, July 19, at an outdoor location in the center of Sydney.

Liturgy Translation The translation of the Proper of Seasons for use in the United States was reported on July 8 as being stalled, after it failed to garner the approval of two-thirds of the nation's Latin rite bishops. The bishops voted on the translation of that section of the *Missale Romanum* in their June general assembly. There were not enough bishops there to fulfill the voting requirements for approval or rejection of the translation. Successive voting by mail did not bring enough votes for the approval. This text, the "Gray Book," is the second stage in the draft translation of the Proper or Seasons prepared by the International Commission for English in the Liturgy. The commission submitted it to the bishops of English-speaking countries for approval. Some of the 11 conferences that belong to the liturgical commission have already approved it. The U.S. prelates will not send this Gray Book back to the International Commission for English in the Liturgy, intending instead to handle the process with the episcopal conference's Committee on Divine Worship.

Missal Translation The U.S. episcopal conference reported on July 28 that it had received the *recognitio* from the Holy See for the Order of the Mass, the main section of the missal. The Vatican Congregation for Divine Worship and the Sacraments approved the first section of the new English translation of the Roman Missal. This is the first of 12 sections of the translation of the third edition of the Roman Missal. The translations of each section of the Roman Missal are being prepared by the International Commission for English in the Liturgy. The commission submits the drafts to the 11 episcopal conferences of English-speaking countries. Once the bishops have given their approval, it falls to the Vatican to give final approval. The Vatican congregation, in its letter granting approval for the Order of the Mass, pointed out that while the texts are binding, the approval "does not intend that these texts are to be put into use immediately."

Excommunication Lifted It was reported on July 28 that three leaders of a former St. Louis parish who incurred excommunication for hiring a suspended priest have been reconciled with the Church. According to a statement last week from the Archdiocese of St. Louis, Bernice Krauze, Stanley Rozanski, and Robert Zabielski, members of the Board of Directors of St. Stanislaus Parish Corporation, met in June with Abp. Raymond Burke to be reconciled fully with the Church. "They are once again in full communion with the Catholic Church and are no longer under any censure," the archdiocese reported. The St. Stanislaus Parish Corporation is associated with what used to be St. Stanislaus Kostka parish. The board of directors incurred excommunication in December 2005, a penalty that was later confirmed by the Vatican. The priest involved, Father Marek Bozek of the Diocese of Springfield-Cape Girardeau, had left his priestly assignment against the expressed will of his bishop, Bp. John Leibrecht, in order to be hired by the St. Stanislaus Kostka Corporation. The three board members who gained back their communion with the Church have joined other parishioners of the former St. Stanislaus Kostka parish in filing a lawsuit against the St. Stanislaus Parish Corporation, the archdiocese reported.

Desecration of Host The Confraternity of Catholic Clergy was reported on July 29 as proposing Friday as a national day of prayer and fasting in the wake of the desecration of the Eucharist by a Minnesota professor. Paul Myers, a professor of biology at the University of Minnesota at Morris, says he desecrated the Eucharist by piercing it with a rusty nail, then he threw it into the trash. The self-professed atheist wrote about the incident on his blog and posted a photo of the desecrated host. The statement of the Confraternity of Catholic Clergy said it found the actions of Myers "reprehensible, inexcusable, and unconstitutional. His flagrant display of irreverence by profaning a consecrated Host from a Catholic Church goes beyond the limit of academic freedom and free speech." The congregation asked the faithful to make a holy hour before the Eucharist on Aug. 1, the feast of St. Alphonsus Ligouri, and to fast in "reparation for the sacrilegious desecration of the Holy Eucharist."

AUGUST 2008

VATICAN

Grand Mufti On Aug. 1, Vatican Radio reported that the grand mufti of Syria, Ahmad Bader Hassoun, had invited Pope Benedict XVI to Damascus to celebrate the Year of St. Paul. The invitation was made during a session with Italian reporters visiting Damascus as part o their own celebration of the special Pauline Year. The Mufti said also that he hoped to meet with the Holy Father in Rome.

Papal Olympic Greeting On Aug. 3, Pope Benedict XVI extended his best wishes to all of the participants in the upcoming Summer Olympic Games in Beijing, China. The Holy Father declared: "I am happy to send the host country, the organizers and participants — especially the athletes — my cordial greeting with the hope that each one can give the best of his, or herself, in the genuine Olympic spirit."

Papal Q and A On Aug. 6, Pope Benedict XVI had a closed-door meeting with over 400 priests and religious in the northern Italian city of Bressanone and answered questions from the participants. The session was held in the city where the Holy Father was vacationing. While not open to reporters, it was subsequently reported that the pope answered various questions on pastoral care.

China and the Gospel On Aug. 6, Pope Benedict XVI visited the church of Oies, the birthplace of the missionary St. Josef Freinademetz and spoke on the importance of the Gospel for the future of China. The Holy Father said, "It is important that this great country should open itself to the Gospel. St. Josef Freinademetz shows us that faith is not an alienation for any culture or any people, because all cultures are waiting for Christ, and are not destroyed by the Lord, but rather come to their maturity."

Benedict and Georgia On Aug. 10, Pope Benedict XVI made a heartfelt appeal for the immediate cessation to military operations in the republic of Georgia and its province of South Ossetia after Russian forces launched a violent operation against the one-time Soviet republic. The pope said, "It is my earnest hope that the military action may cease immediately, and that, partly in the name of a shared Christian heritage, further violent conflict and retaliation may be avoided, which could degenerate into a much more widespread conflict."

Those who Pray On Aug. 13, Pope Benedict XVI reflected on the witness of the martyrs, in particular Sts. Edith Stein and Maximilian Kolbe. Speaking at his vacation spot in the northern Italian city of Bressanone, the Holy Father stressed that "those who pray never lose hope, not even in difficult situations, even situations that are desperate in human terms. This is what the Church's history teaches us." He added, Edith Stein and Maximilian Kolbe "both concluded their earthly existence with martyrdom in Auschwitz. In human terms, their lives could seem like a defeat, but they are instead proof of the victory of love."

Benedict on the Assumption On Aug. 15, Pope Benedict XVI meditated on the Assumption and the "maternal solicitude" of the Blessed Virgin Mary. The Holy Father spoke in the courtyard of the pontifical retreat in Castel Gandolfo, the traditional summer residence of the popes. The Holy Father said, "Assumed into heaven, Mary points out to us the ultimate destination of our earthly pilgrimage. She reminds us that our entire being - spirit, soul, and body - is destined for the fullness of life; that those who live and die in the love of God and of neighbor will be transfigured in the image of the glorious body of the risen Christ; that the Lord humbles the proud and raises up the lowly (cf. Lk 1:51-52)." The pope also focused on his upcoming trip to Lourdes in September, to celebrate the 150th anniversary of the Marian apparitions there.

Georgia Crisis On Aug. 18, Pope Benedict XVI used his Angelus delivered at the papal summer residence at Castel Gandolfo to call for humanitarian relief Georgia that has been severely troubled since the invasion of Georgia by Russia on Aug. 7 over the status of the disputed regions of South Ossetia and Abkhazia. The Holy Father declared, "I appeal for a prompt opening of humanitarian corridors between the region of South Ossetia and the rest of Georgia, so that the dead who are still abandoned can receive a worthy burial and the wounded may be adequately attended, and that those who long to be reunited with their loved ones may be permitted to do so."

Road Rage It was reported on Aug. 18 that Pope Benedict XVI had encouraged Christians to be mindful of their behavior while driving their cars. Speaking before praying the midday Angelus to the crowd at the papal summer residence at Castel Gandolfo, the Holy Father declared, "Human life is too precious and it is too unworthy of man to meet death or become an invalid due to causes that could mostly be avoided." He added, "There is certainly a need for a greater sense of responsibility, above all by drivers, as accidents are often caused by excessive speed and imprudent conduct. Christians must above all make a personal examination of conscience on their own conduct as drivers."

Overcoming Racism On Aug. 18, Pope Benedict XVI took time before praying the midday Angelus with crowds at the papal summer residence at Castel Gandolfo to speak about overcoming racism and added this will be crucial for the progress of the 21st century. He said, "How important it is, especially in our time, that every Christian community be ever more conscious of this, in order to help civil society to overcome every possible temptation to racism, intolerance and exclusion, and to organize itself with options that are respectful of the dignity of every human being." The Holy Father added, "One of humanity's great victories is precisely the overcoming of racism. Unfortunately, however, there are new worrying manifestations of the latter, often linked to social and economic problems, which, however, can never justify contempt and racial discrimination."

General Audiences

Greeting to Pilgrims, Aug. 13.

INTERNATIONAL

Lambeth Conference From July 16-Aug. 4, the Lambeth Conference brought together representatives of the worldwide Anglican Communion in London and dealt with controversial and divisive issues such as the ordination of women priests and bishops, same-sex unions, the ordination of openly gay men and women, and unity in the Anglican community. During the conference, Card. Walter Kasper, president of the Pontifical Council for Promoting Christian Unity, gave an assessment of these issues from the Roman Catholic perspective. On Aug. 7, Msgr. Donald Bolen, an official of the pontifical council, expressed his confidence that dialogue with the Anglican Communion would continue even in the aftermath of the recent conference.

Indian Stampede On Aug. 3, a stampede took place at

Naina Devi Temple in Bilaspur, India, in which more than 230 people were injured. There were 146 Hindus who were killed, including 42 children and 50 women. The tragedy was marked by India's Catholic bishops who offered prayers and statements of concern for the victims. The prayers were not for Catholics but an expression of outreach to the Hindu majority in the country.

Indonesia Protests On Aug. 4, more than 3,500 Christians marched in Jayapura, the capital of Indonesian Papua, to protest the recent introduction of *Sharia*, Islamic law, as the main law of the region. The protests included the participation of Catholic leaders in the region who are also aware of the growing threat of the imposition of Sharia across the whole of Indonesia. The demonstration also expressed concern that special legislative autonomy was granted to the region seven years ago that permitted the recent actions.

Cardinal Newman It was reported on Aug. 11 that the British government's Ministry of Justice granted permission for the exhumation of Card. John Henry Newman's body. The famed convert and Cardinal is a candidate for canonization, and the permission was requested to exhume his remains from the small grave just outside Birmingham, England, and transfer them to a marble sarcophagus in a Birmingham church. According to British law, it is illegal to move bodies from cemetery graves to church tombs, but a special exemption was made by the British authorities.

Animal Rights On Aug. 14, it was reported that an Italian animal rights organization had organized a petition to urge Pope Benedict XVI to stop wearing ermine on his hats and robes. The organization, the Italian Association for Defense of Animals and the Environment, gathered the petition of more than 2,900 signatures in recognition of the Holy Father's famous love and concern for animals, especially cats. The Holy Father has worn the traditional fur-trimmed cap, called a *camauro*, and fur-trimmed capes in the winter and early spring months. The petition specifically asks the pope to act "with respect for life in all its forms and to remember that animals also are creatures of God."

Priest Murdered It was reported on Aug. 18 that Fr. Thomas Pandipally, a 37-year old Carmelite of Mary Immaculate priest, had been found on Aug. 17 near Yellareddy, a town 200 miles northwest of the state capital, Hyderabad, in India, according to the UCA News, an Asian Church news agency. The priest's mutilated body was discovered on a deserted road. He had celebrated Mass in the mission station of Burgiga, some miles from Yellareddy and had apparently been stabbed to death. Abp. Marampudi Joji of Hyderabad declared of the murder, "Father Thomas is a martyr: He sacrificed his life for the poor and marginalized. But he did not die in vain, because his body and his blood enrich the Church in India, particularly the Church in Andhra Pradesh — the southeastern state where he died."

NATIONAL

Housing Bill On Aug. 1, Bp. William F. Murphy of Rockville Centre, N.Y., chairman of the Bishops' Committee on Domestic Justice and Human Development of the USCCB, issued a statement praising the recent passage of the Housing and Economic Recovery Act of 2008 that was signed on July 30 by Pres. George W. Bush and that included provision for the creation of a national Housing Trust Fund. The USCCB worked for the last decade to bring about a national Housing Trust Fund, and the new bill includes $300 million for the fund. Bp. Murphy declared, "The Bishops' conference has worked for years to enact a national

Housing Trust Fund because affordable housing is vitally important to the stability and sustainability of families and communities throughout the country. This new institution and resources are welcome signs that the Administration and Congress can work together across party lines to make the housing needs of low-income families a common national priority."

School Choice On Aug. 4, Circuit Court Judge John C. Cooper ruled that a decision by the Florida Taxation and Budget Reform Commission to permit two proposed amendments to the state constitution on the Nov. 4 ballot were legal and did not exceed its authority. The first amendment, Ballot Initiative 7, would repeal a provision of the state constitution prohibiting public spending on religious institutions; the second amendment, Ballot Initiative 9, would revise a section of the constitution to allow public funding for scholarships to include religious and other private schools. The decision was greeted warmly by Catholic leaders in Florida. D. Michael McCarron, executive director of the Florida Catholic Conference, praised the ruling, "We are pleased with the ruling because it is a pivotal step toward safeguarding health, education and social service programs in which Floridians benefit through the participation of faith-based providers. All Floridians, particularly the vulnerable and in need, deserve the opportunity to benefit from programs with a secular purpose provided by religious organizations."

Pilgrims Killed On Aug. 8, 17 parishioners from a Houston, Texas area Vietnamese Catholic parish were killed when the pilgrimage bus taking them to Marian Days in Carthage, Mo., crashed while on a highway overpass near Dallas. The pilgrims belonged Our Lady of Lavang and Vietnamese Martyrs churches in Houston. Twelve pilgrims died at the scene of the accident while five others died after reaching local hospitals.

Yahweh Rule It was reported on Aug. 8 that Bp. Arthur J. Serratelli of Paterson, NJ, chairman of the Bishops' Committee on Divine Worship of the USCCB, had sent a letter to his fellow bishops regarding new Vatican directives on the use of "the name of God" (Yahweh) in the sacred liturgy. The letter noted that the Vatican directive would not entail changes to official liturgical texts or to the ongoing effort of the bishops on the translation of the Missal. Rather, the directives would have "some impact on the use of particular pieces of liturgical music in our country as well as in the composition of variable texts such as the general intercessions for the celebration of the Mass and the other sacraments." The communiqué from the Congregation for Divine Worship and the Discipline of the Sacraments had been dated to June 29 and referred to the Tetragrammaton — YHWH, the Hebrew notation for the name of God. It made clear the philological reasons for the decision as well as the need to be faithful to the Church's tradition that "from the beginning, that the sacred Tetragrammaton was never pronounced in the Christian context nor translated into any of the languages into which the Bible was translated."

Chicago Settlement On Aug. 12, the Archdiocese of Chicago announced that it had agreed to pay 16 victims of clergy sex abuse more than $12.6 million in a settlement. The archdiocese also agreed to release files related to the cases and other information. Speaking of the settlement, Card. George, archbishop of Chicago, stated, "I apologize again today to the survivors and their families and to the whole Catholic community. We must continue to do everything in our power to ensure the safety of the children in our care."

DEATHS — AUGUST 2007 TO AUGUST 2008

Abbott, Father Walter, S.J., 84, Mar. 5, 2008, Jesuit priest, biblical scholar, and expert in ecumenism and interreligious dialogue; born in Somerville, MA, he entered the Jesuit order in 1941, was ord. a priest in 1956, and took his final vows in 1959; he worked for many years in the Vatican, including as director of the North American section of Vatican Radio and at the Vatican Office for Common Bible Work; edited one of the most popular English-language translations of the documents of Vatican II and was also a founding general secretary and treasurer of the World Catholic Federation of the Biblical Apostolate and was features editor of *America* magazine.

Arzube, Bishop Juan A., 89, Dec. 25, 2007, auxiliary bishop of Los Angeles from 1971 to 1993; born in Guayaquil, Ecuador, he studied at Rensselaer Polytechnic Institute in Troy, NY, and St. John's Seminary in Camarillo, CA; ord. a priest on May 5, 1954; consecrated titular bp. of Civitate and auxiliary bishop of Los Angeles on Mar. 25, 1971; he was one of the first Hispanic bishop in the United States; ret., Sept 7, 1993; he received numerous awards and honors, including the John Anson Ford Human Relations Award and the Campaign for Human Development's Empowerment Award.

Bertie, Fra Andrew, 78, Feb. 7, 2008, Grand Master of the Knights of Malta; in full, Andrew Willoughby Ninian Bertie, he was born in London and was educated at Oxford and London before serving in the Scots Guards; a member of the British aristocracy, he was a descendant through his mother of Britain's royal Stuart family; he worked as a financial journalist and a language teacher and joined the Knights of Malta in 1956; took his vows in 1981; elected for life as grand master on Apr. 8, 1988 by the Council of State, he was the 78th grand master of the 900-year-old charitable order; as grand master, he oversaw extensive development and modernization of the order's global humanitarian programs and increased its membership and diplomatic missions to assist charitable work; he was the first Englishman to be elected grand master.

Boyle, Bishop Paul M., C.P., 81, Jan. 10, 2008, apostolic vicar of Mandeville, Jamaica, from 1991 to 1997 and bishop from 1997 until his retirement in 2004; born in Detroit, MI, he studied at the Passionist houses of study and the Lateran Univ. in Rome; professed in the Cong. of the Passion on July 9, 1946; ord. a priest on May 30, 1953; he served as pres. of the Conference of Major Superiors of Men from 1969 to1974; superior general of the Passionists, from 1976 to1988; ord. titular bp. of Canapium and first vicar apostolic of Mandeville, Jamaica, July 9, 1991; ret. Jul. 6, 2004.

Buckley Jr., William F., 82, Feb. 27, 2008, one of the most influential figures in the modern American Conservative movement, a writer and intellectual; born in New York, he served in the U.S. Army from 1944 to 1946 and then studied at Yale University; he published his first book in 1951, *God and Man at Yale: The Superstitions of Academic Freedom*, critiquing the university bias against religion and capitalism; he went on to author over 50 books, including both fiction and non-fiction; he founded the famed conservative magazine *National Review* in 1955 and served as its editor until 1990; in 1997, he wrote on his own Catholic faith in *Nearer, My God: An Autobiography of Faith*; he also hosted the PBS program *Firing Line* for three decades.

Burghardt, Father Walter, S.J., 93, Feb. 16, 2008, a leading American theologian and editor of the journal *Theological Studies*; born in New York City, he entered the Society of Jesus and was ordained a priest in 1941; he taught at Woodstock College for two decades; editor of *Theological Studies* for four decades, he was also co-editor of *The Woodstock Papers*, Catholic consultant to the American Heritage Dictionaries, co-founder of the journal *The Living Pulpit*, founder of *Preaching the Just Word* to improve homiletics, president of the Catholic Theological Society of America, the Mariological Society of America and the North American Academy of Ecumenists; consultor to the Vatican's Pontifical Council for Promoting Christian Unity.

Buswell, Bishop Charles A., 94, June 14, 2008; bishop of Pueblo from 1959 to 1979; born in Homestead, OK, he studied St. Louis Preparatory Seminary, Kenrick Seminary, and the American College at the Univ. of Louvain in Belgium; ord. a priest for Oklahoma City on July 9, 1939; cons. bp. of Pueblo on Sept. 30, 1959, he resigned, Sept. 18, 1979; as bishop, he attended all four sessions of the Second Vatican Council; he was also an outspoken peace and civil rights activist; after his retirement he was arrested during an antinuclear protest.

Castillo Lara, Cardinal Rosalio, S.D.B., 85, Oct. 16, 2007, Venezuelan Cardinal and a long-time Vatican official; born in San Casimiro, Venezuela; ord. a priest on Sept. 4, 1949 for the Salesians, he completed his studies in canon law at the Salesian University in Turin, Italy, and taught canon law there and at the Pontifical Salesian University in Rome; provincial superior of the Salesians in Venezuela, he was elected in 1967 to the general council of Salesians as regional superior for Latin America; cosecrated titular bp. of Precausa on May 24, 1973, he was coadj. bp. of Trujillo from 1973 to1976; called to Rome in 1975, he was made an archbishop on May 26, 1982 and became the first president of the Pontifical Commission for the Authentic Interpretation of the Code of Canon Law when it was instituted in 1984, made a cardinal deacon in 1985 (titular church, Our Lady of Coromoto in St. John of God); transf. to the order of cardinal priests, Jan. 29, 1996; served as pres. of the Administration of Patrimony of the Holy See from 1989 to 1995 and pres. of the Pontifical Commission for the State of Vatican City State from 1990 to 1997; after he retired and returned to Venezuela, he was a fearless critic of leftist President Hugo Chavez.

Champlin, Msgr. Joseph, 77, Jan. 17, 2008, noted priest, author, and liturgist; born in Hammondsport, NY, he studied at Phillips Academy in Andover, MA, Yale Univ., the Univ. of Notre Dame, and St. Bernard's School of Theology; ord. a priest on Feb. 2, 1956; he served as assoc. dir. of the liturgy secretariat for the then National Conference of Catholic Bishops from 1968 to 1971; rector of the Syracuse cathedral from 1995-2005; he was the author of more than 50 books with more than 20 million copies.

Christodoulos, Archbishop, 69, Jan. 28, 2008, Archbishop of Athens and All Greece and primate of the Autocephalous Orthodox Church of Greece from 1998 until his death and a leading figure in modern Catholic-Orthodox dialogue; born Christos Paraskevaidis in Xanthi, Thrace, in Northern Greece, he attended high school at the Roman Catholic Marist Leonteion Lyceum of Athens; after studies at the University of Athens, he was ordained a priest in 1965; elected bishop of Demetrias in Volos, Thessaly, in 1974; he was elected archbishop of Athens in 1998; he was a leader in Catholic-Orthodox ecumenical efforts and helped organize the visit of Pope John Paul II to Athens in 2001 and visited Pope Benedict XVI in Rome in 2006.

Corripio Ahumada, Cardinal Ernesto, 89, Apr. 10, 2008, Mexican Cardinal and archbishop of Mexico City and primate of Mexico from 1977 to 1994; born in Tampico, Mexico, he was ordained a priest on Oct. 25, 1942, in Rome, where he remained until almost the end of World War II; he earned a doctorate in philosophy from the Pontifical Gregorian University, and licentiates in theology, canon law, and church history; back in Mexico, he taught and held various positions in local seminary of Tampico; consecrated the titular bp. of Zapara and aux. bp. of Tampico, Mar. 19, 1953; bp. of Tampico from 1956 to 1967, he also served as abp. of Antequera from 1967 to 1976; abp. of Puebla de los Angeles from 1976 to 1977; transf. to the metropolitan see of México, July 19, 1977; made a cardinal priest on June 30, 1979 (titular church, Mary Immaculate al Tiburtino) resigned on Sept. 29, 1994; he played a key role in the renewing of diplomatic relations between the Holy See and México.

Deiss, Father Lucien, C.S.Sp., 86, Oct. 9, 2007, Holy Ghost priest, Scripture scholar, and noted liturgical music composer; a native of France, he entered the Congregation of the Holy Spirit and became a specialist in biblical exegesis and at one time occupied the chair of Sacred Scripture and Dogmatic Theology at the Grand Scholasticat des Peres du Saint-Esprit in Paris; he was best known for his work in liturgical music and the liturgical reforms of the Second Vatican Council, including the Lectionary during Vatican II; he was a member of the Concilium on Liturgy and served as liturgical editor of the magazine *Assemblee Novelle*; he composed a number of hymns that were in vogue immediately after the Council.

De Paoli, Archbishop Ambrose, 73, Oct. 10, 2007, longtime Vatican diplomat and Vatican nuncio to Australia; born in Jeannette, PA, he grew up in Miami; ordained a priest on Dec. 18, 1960, in Rome; after studies at the North American College and Lateran Univ. in Rome, he entered the papal diplomatic service and held posts in Canada, Turkey, Africa and Venezuela; ord. titular abp. of Lares, Nov. 20, 1983, in Miami and served as apostolic pro-nuncio to Sri Lanka from 1983 to 1988; apostolic delegate in southern Africa and pro-nuncio to Lesotho, 1988; first apostolic nuncio to South Africa, 1994; apostolic nuncio to Australia, 2004.

Dery, Cardinal Peter Poreku, 89, Mar. 6, 2008, Cardinal from Ghana, archbishop of Tamale from 1977 to 1994; born in Ko, Ghana, he was baptized in 1932 and ordained a priest on Feb. 11, 1951; named bp. of Wa on Mar. 16, 1960, he introduced liturgical inculturation to the diocese; appointed apostolic admin. of Tamale in 1972, he became bp. of Tamale on Nov. 18, 1974 and the first abp. of Tamale, May 30, 1977; ret. as abp. June 30, 1994; named a cardinal priest on Mar. 24, 2006 (titular church, Diaconia di Sant'Elena fuori Porta Prenestina).

Ehringer, Abbot Claude, 98, Sept. 17, 2007, Benedictine Abbot and founder of Prince of Peace Abbey in Oceanside, Calif.; born, Charles Perrette Ehringer in Jeffersonville, IN, he entered St. Meinrad Preparatory School at St. Meinrad, IN, in 1922 and the Benedictines in 1929; he professed his Solemn Vows in 1933 and was ordained a priest on May 22, 1934; with other Benedictines, he helped start the Oceanside community in 1958; elected prior in 1965, he was elected the first abbot in 1983 and retired in 1994.

Frey, Bishop Gerard L., 93, Aug. 16, 2007, bishop of Savannah from 1967 to 1972 and bishop of Lafayette, LA, from 1972 to 1989; born in New Orleans, LA, he studied at Notre Dame Seminary in New Orleans and was ord. a priest for New Orleans on Apr. 2, 1938; cons. bp. of Savannah, Aug. 8, 1967, he was transf. to Lafayette on Nov. 7, 1972 and installed on Jan. 7, 1973; he retired on May 15, 1989; he took part in the Second Vatican Council and appointed the first

woman chancellor in the U.S.

Gallagher, Father Joseph V., 85, Nov. 16, 2007, president of the Paulist Fathers from 1986 to 1994; born in New York City, he studied at the University of Notre Dame and served in the Navy during World War II; after the war, he earned a law degree from Fordham University; he joined the Paulists in 1956 and was ordained in 1961; vice president of the Paulist Fathers from 1978 to 1986, when he was elected president; as head of the Paulists, he oversaw a national capital campaign.

Gagnon, P.S.S., Cardinal Edouard, 89, Aug. 25, 2007, member of the Sulpicians, president of the Pontifical Council for the Family from 1985 to 1990, and a Cardinal from 1985; born on Jan. 15, 1918, in Port Daniel, Quebec, Canada; he was ordained a priest for the Sulpicians on Aug. 15, 1940; cons. bp. of St. Paul in Alberta, Mar. 25, 1969, he was rector of Canadian College in Rome from 1972 to1977; vice president-secretary of Vatican Committee for the Family from 1973 to 1980, he was appointed titular abp. of Giustiniana Prima on July 7, 1983 and pro-president of Pontifical Council for the Family in 1983; named a cardinal deacon on May 25, 1985 (with the deaconry of St. Elena fuori Porta Prenestina); he was transf. to the order of cardinal priests on Jan. 29, 1996 with the titular church of St. Marcellus; he also served as president of Pontifical Committee for International Eucharistic Congresses, 1991 to 2000.

Gantin, Cardinal Bernardin, 86, Cardinal from Benin, prefect of the Congregation for Bishops, from 1984 to 1998, and dean of the College of Cardinals from 1993 to 2002; born in Toffo, Bénin, he studied at the Pontifical Urbanian Athaenaeum and at the Pontifical Lateran Athenaeum and was ordained a priest on Jan. 14, 1951; named titular bp. of Tipasa di Mauritania and auxiliary of Dahomey, Dec. 11, 1956; cons. Feb. 3, 1957, named abp. of Cotonou, Jan. 5, 1960 and was the first African metropolitan archbishop; adjunct sec. of the Cong. for Evangelization of Peoples, Mar. 5, 1971; secr. for the congregation, Feb. 26, 1973; vice-president of the Pontifical Commission *Iustitia et Pax*, Dec. 19, 1975; pro-president, Dec. 16, 1976; made a cardinal deacon on June 27, 1977; pres. of the Pontifical Commission *Iustitia et Pax*, June 29, 1977; resigned on Apr. 8, 1984; pres. of the Pontifical Council *Cor Unum*, 1978-1984; took part in the conclaves of 1978; prefect of the Cong. for Bishops and president of the Pontifical Commission for Latin America, 1984 to 1998; transf. to the cardinal priests on June 25, 1984 and cardinal bishops of the suburbicarian see of Palestrina, Sept. 29, 1986; dean of the College of Cardinals and bishop of the title of the suburbicarian see of Ostia, retaining the title of the suburbicarian see of Palestrina, June 5, 1993; res. the deanship of the College of Cardinals and the title of the suburbicarian see of Ostia, and became dean emeritus, Nov. 30, 2002; he was the first African to be both the head of a Vatican dicastery and dean of the College of Cardinals.

Garey, Gerard S., 90, Feb. 29, 2008, president of the Raskob Foundation for Catholic Activities; after studies at The Catholic University of America in Washington, he served as a captain in the U.S. Army during World War II; he then worked for E.I. du Pont de Nemours & Co. and in 1966 was appointed executive vice president of the Raskob Foundation; he was elected president in 1985 and oversaw an expansion of programs.

Goulet, Robert, 73, Oct. 30, 2007, famed singer and entertainer; born in Lawrence, MA, to a French Canadian family, he grew up in Canada and attended the Royal Conservatory of Music in Toronto on a scholarship; his first big break was in 1960 when he played the role of Lancelot in the Lerner and

Loewe stage production of "Camelot"; he went on to a long career in theater, radio, television, and film and earned Grammy and Tony awards; in 2006 he received a star on Canada's Walk of Fame and also received a star on the Hollywood Walk of Fame.

Hamao, Cardinal Stephen Fumio, 77, Nov. 8, 2007, Japanese Cardinal and president of the Pontifical Council for Migrants and Travelers from 1998 to 2006; born in Tokyo, Japan, he converted to Catholicism in 1946 and entered the seminary in 1949; after studies in Rome at the Pontifical Urbanian University and Pontifical Gregorian University, he was ord. a priest on Dec. 21, 1957; cons. titular bp. of Oreto and auxiliary bp. of Tokyo on April 29, 1970; named bp. of Yokohama in 1979, he was appointed head of the Pontifical Council for Pastoral Care of Migrants and Itinerants in 1998 and made a cardinal deacon on Oct. 21, 2003 (deaconry, St. John Bosco in Via Tuscolana); he resigned in 2006.

Hart, Bishop Daniel A., 80, Jan. 14, 2008, bishop of Norwich from 1995 to 2003; born in Lawrence, MA, he studied for the priesthood at St. John's Seminary, Brighton, MA, and was ord. a priest on Feb. 2, 1953; he held degrees in theology, business administration, education, and pastoral counseling; app. aux. bp. of Boston on Aug. 30, 1976, he was cons. on Oct. 18, 1976; app. bishop of Norwich on Sept. 12, 1995, he was installed on Nov. 1, 1995; ret. Mar. 11, 2003.

Hyde, Henry J., 83, Nov. 29, 2007, Republican Congressman from Illinois who served from 1976 to 2006 and was a leading advocate for the Pro-Life cause; born in Chicago, IL, he studied at Georgetown University in Washington and the Loyola University Law School in Chicago; after service in the U.S. Navy during World War II, he worked as a lawyer; elected to the Illinois House of Representatives in 1967, he became majority leader in 1971; elected to the U.S. House in Nov. 1974, he was re-elected 15 times; in Congress, he worked tirelessly to end federal funding of abortions; he also served as chairman of the House International Relations Committee and the House Judiciary Committee; as chairman in 1998, he introduced legislation to investigate the case for the impeachment of Pres. Bill Clinton and led the impeachment hearings; in 2006 he was named a Knight of St. Gregory by Pope Benedict XVI; in 2007, he was awarded the Presidential Medal of Freedom.

Karcher, Carl Nicholas, 90, Jan. 11, 2008, Catholic entrepreneur and founder of the Carl's Jr. restaurants; born near Upper Sandusky, OH, he moved to California in 1939; that same year, he married Margaret (Heinz) Karcher (they were married for 66 years); he started his first business in 1941 and opened the first Carl's Drive-In Barbeque in 1944; the first two Carl's Jr. restaurants opened in 1956; currently, there are 3,036 franchised or company-operated restaurants in the Carl's Jr. and Hardee's chains; he served on many boards for charitable organizations and received numerous awards; he opened Mercy House in 1998 for the homeless.

Kozlowiecki, Cardinal Adam, S.J., 96, Sept. 28, 2007, Polish Cardinal who spent six years in Nazi concentration camps; born in Huta Komorowska, Poland; entered the Jesuits on July 30, 1929 and took his final vows on Aug. 15, 1945; ord. a priest on June 24, 1937, he was arrested by the Gestapo in Nov. 1939 and was sent to the Auschwitz concentration camp in 1940 and then Dachau from Dec. 1940 to April 29, 1945, when he was freed by the U.S. army; after teaching at the Jesuit School, Pullach, he volunteered as a missionary to the Jesuit mission in North Rhodesia, now Zambia; named tit. Bp. of Diospoli inferiori and apostolic vicar of Lusaka, Zambia, on June 4, 1955, he was cons. on Sept. 11, 1955; promoted to the metropolitan see of Lusaka,

Apr. 25, 1959, he resigned in 1969 so that an African prelate could be named archbishop; transf. to the titular see of Potenza Picena, May 29, 1969; from 1969 to 1989, he was director of the Pontifical Missionary Society of Zambia; made a companion of the Order of Freedom of the Republic of Zambia in 1987 and received the *Legion d'honneur* from France in 2006; made a cardinal priest on Feb. 21, 1998 (titular church, St. Andrew on the Quirinal).

Lopez Trujillo, Cardinal Alfonso, 72, Apr.19, 2008, Colombian Cardinal and president of the Pontifical Council for the Family from 1990; born in Villahermosa, Colombia, he was ord. a priest on Nov. 13, 1960, in Rome; after studies at the Pontifical University of St. Thomas Aquinas where he earned a doctorate in philosophy, he returned to Colombia and taught philosophy; named an aux. bp. of Bogota on Feb. 25, 1971 and consecrated a bishop on Mar. 25, 1971; elected CELAM general secretary in 1972; named coadj. abp. of Medellin on May 22, 1978, he acceded to the see on June 2, 1979; pres. of CELAM from 1979 to 1983, he helped organize the 1979 Puebla Conference in which Pope John Paul II participated; named cardinal in Feb. 2, 1983 (titular church, St. Prisca); promoted to cardinal bishop, Nov. 17, 2001 (with the suburbicarian see of Frascati); named President of the Pontifical Council for the Family in 1990; he was a leading defender of the family around the world.

Lorscheider, Cardinal Aloisio, O.F.M., 83, Dec. 23, 2007, Brazilian cardinal and Franciscan and a prominent spokesperson for the poor in South America; he entered the Franciscans in 1933, made his solemn vows in 1945, and was ord. a priest on Aug. 22, 1948; after studies in Rome, he taught theology at the Antonianum, Rome, and was director of Franciscan international house of studies; ord. bp. of Santo Angelo, Brazil on May 20, 1962; abp. of Fortaleza in 1973; he was also president of CELAM from 1975 to 1979; named a cardinal on May 24, 1976 with the titular church of S. Pietro (in Montorio); named abp. of Aparecida in 1995; he resigned on Jan. 28, 2004; he was an advocate for the poor and defended Father Leonardo Boff's writings.

Lubich, Chiara, 88, Mar. 14, 2008, beloved founder of the Focolare movement, one of the most important ecclesial movements in the modern Church; born in Trent, Italy, she adopted the name Chiara in honor of St. Clare of Assisi; in 1943, she consecrated herself to God and began forming what became a new movement that took its name from the Italian word for a hearth, *focolare*; diocesan approval was granted in 1947 and Vatican approval was given in 1962; Lubich spent the rest of her life guiding the movement; she received a host of awards and honorary doctorates, including the 1977 Templeton Prize and the 1998 Prize for Human Rights by the Council of Europe; the movement currently has more than 140,000 members and 2 million adherents and friends in 182 countries.

Maciel Degollado, Father Marcial, 87, Jan. 30, 2008, founder of the Legionaries of Christ; born in Cotija de la Paz in the Mexican state of Michoacán, he founded the Legion of Christ on Jan. 3, 1941, with the support of the Bishop of Cuernavaca, and was ord. a priest Nov.26, 1944; he founded the Regnum Christi Movement (the movement for laypeople) in 1959; the Legion of Christ and Regnum Christi grew swiftly over the next decades and ultimately opened universities and many other charitable institutes; the Pontifical Athenaeum *Regina Apostolorum* in Rome is highly respected for its programs in theology, philosophy, and canon law; he retired in Jan. 2006 after being the subject of an investigation by Vatican authorities regarding sexual impropriety; no trial was conducted because of Fr. Maciel's poor health and advanced age; currently, the Legion has 600 priests and 2,500 seminarians worldwide.

Montrose, Bishop Donald W., 84, May 7, 2008, bishop of Stockton from 1985 to 1999; born in Denver, CO, he studied at St. John's Seminary, Camarillo, CA, and was ordained a priest for Los Angeles on May 7, 1949; ord. titular bp. of Forum Novum and aux. bp. of Los Angeles on May 12, 1983, he was named bp. of Stockton on Dec. 17, 1985 and installed on Feb. 20, 1986; he retired on Jan. 19, 1999; as bishop, he presided over the growth of the diocese in the 1980's and was noted for his pastoral care for Latinos in the diocese.

Moraczewski, Father Albert S., O.P., 87, May 1, 2008, first president of the National Catholic Bioethics Center and one of the pioneers in bioethics; born in Chicago, IL, he was ord. a priest in 1954; he earned a doctorate in pharmacology from the University of Chicago in 1958 with many other honorary degrees, including the great honor of master of sacred theology in 1989; he taught psychopharmacology, theology and ethics at the University of Chicago, the Houston State Psychiatric Institute and Baylor College of Medicine in Houston; he founded the Pope John XXIII Medical-Moral Research Center, now the National Catholic Bioethics Center in Philadelphia, in 1972; in 2004 the Catholic Health Association presented him with a lifetime achievement award.

Niedergeses, Bishop James D., 90, Nov. 16, 2007, bishop of Nashville from 1975 to 1992; born in Lawrenceburg, TN, he studied at St. Bernard College in St. Bernard, AL, St. Ambrose College in Davenport, IA, Mt. St. Mary Seminary of the West and Athenaeum in Cincinnati, OH, and was ord. a priest on May 20, 1944; cons. bp. of Nashville on May 20, 1975; he retired on Oct. 13, 1992; as bishop, he launched the Catholic Foundation of Tennessee to assist the Church in rural parts of Tennessee.

Renner, Gerald, 75, Oct. 24, 2007, religion reporter and editor; born in Philadelphia, he studied at Georgetown University and worked as a journalist for the U.S. Navy during the Korean War; he subsequently worked for *The Reading Eagle* in Pennsylvania, *United Press* in Washington, associate director of public information for the then National Conference of Catholic Bishops and U.S. Catholic Conference, editor and director of Religion News Service from 1980 to 1984, and religion reporter for *The Hartford Courant* from 1985 until his retirement in 2000; won the Templeton Prize given by the Religion Newswriters Association; in 1997, he broke the story about allegations against the founder of the Legion of Christ, Fr. Maciel Degollado.

Russert, Tim, 58, June 13, 2008, renowned American journalist best known as the moderator for 16 years of NBC's *Meet the Press* and NBC News' Washington bureau chief; born in Buffalo, NY, he earned a B.A. in 1972 from John Carroll University and a law degree with honors from the Cleveland-Marshall College of Law in 1976; he worked as a special counsel to Sen. Daniel Patrick Moynihan of New York from 1978-83 and was a counselor to Gov. Mario Cuomo of New York from 1983-84; he joined NBC in 1984 and became moderator of *Meet the Press* in 1991; he received 48 honorary doctorates and numerous awards for excellence in journalism.

Snow, Tony (Robert Anthony), 53, July 12, 2008, popular television news anchor and radio host, syndicated columnist, musician, and White House Press Secretary under Pres. George W. Bush; born in Berea, KY, and raised in Cincinnati, OH, he earned a B.A. in philosophy from Davidson College in 1977 and began his journalism career in 1979 as an edito-

rial writer for *The Greensboro Record* in NC; he also worked at *The Daily Press* in Newport News (1982-84), *The Detroit News* (1984-87), *The Washington Times* (1987-91), and *USA Today* as a Counterpoint Columnist (1994-2000); from 1993 to 2000, he was a syndicated columnist; from 1996 to 2003, he served as the first host of Fox News Sunday for the Fox News Channel and was a frequent guest host for Rush Limbaugh's radio show; his own radio program, *The Tony Snow Show*, was nationally syndicated; in 1991, became deputy assistant to the president for communications and director of speechwriting for Pres. George H.W. Bush; he was also White House Press Secretary from May 2006 to Sept. 2007.

Stickler, Cardinal Alfons, S.D.B., 97, Dec. 12, 2007, Austrian Cardinal and Librarian and Archivist of the Holy Roman Church from 1985 to 1988; born in Neunkirchen, Austria; entered the Salesians of Don Bosco in 1927 and was ord. a priest on Mar. 27, 1937; he earned a doctorate in *utroque iure*, both canon and civil law, in July 1940, taught canon law at the Salesian University in Turin (later Rome), and served as rector from 1958 to 1966; named prefect of the Apostolic Vatican Library, Mar. 25, 1971; named titular abp. of Bolsena and pro-librarian of Holy Roman Church, Sept. 8, 1983; pro-archivist of Holy Roman Church, July 9, 1984; made a cardinal deacon on May 25, 1985 (deaconry of S. Giorgio in Velabro), May 25, 1985; librarian and archivist of the Holy Roman Church, May 27, 1985; resigned, July 1, 1988; transf. to the order of cardinal priests, Jan. 29, 1996.

Suárez Rivera, Cardinal Adolfo, 81, Mar. 22, 2008, Mexican Cardinal and archbishop of Monterrey from 1983 to 2002; born in San Cristobal, Mexico, he was ordained a priest on Mar. 8, 1952; after seminary studies in Rome at the Pontifical Latin American College and the Pontifical Gregorian University, he served in pastoral positions until his consecration as bp. of Tepic on Aug. 15, 1971; transf. to the diocese of Tlalnepantla on May 8, 1980, he was named abp. of Monterrey on Nov. 8, 1983; appointed a cardinal priest on Nov. 26, 1994 (titular church, Our Lady of Guadalupe on Monte Mario); as archbishop, he was elected president of the Mexican bishops' conference in 1988 and 1991, helped negotiate the 1992 constitutional reforms extending legal recognition to the Catholic Church in Mexico for the first time in more than 70 years, and worked to end the bloodshed in Chiapas, Mexico during the unrest caused by the Zapatista National Liberation Front.

Wyman, Jane, 90, Sept. 10, 2007, Oscar-winning actress and one-time wife of future president Ronald Reagan; born Sarah Jane Fulks in St. Joseph, MO, she started her long career as a radio singer and in 1936 began appearing in films; she earned fame for her performance in *The Lost Weekend* (1945) and earned an Oscar nomination for *The Yearling* (1946); she then won an Oscar for her portrayal of a deaf-mute rape victim in Johnny Belinda (1948) and was nominated again twice for *The Blue Veil* (1951) and *Magnificent Obsession* (1954); she later worked in television; from 1940 to 1948, she was married to Ronald Reagan; an adult convert, she supported Hollywood's Covenant House and Our Lady of Angels Monastery; the Arthritis Foundation named its Jane Wyman Humanitarian Award in her honor.

Zahn, Gordon, 89, Dec. 9, 2007, co-founder of Pax Christi USA; born in Milwaukee, he was drafted in 1944 and then declared himself a conscientious objector during World War II and did public service instead; after the war, he earned a doctoral degree from The Catholic University of America; he helped establish Pax Christi USA in 1972; he received numerous awards and honors.

News In Depth

POPE BENEDICT XVI

2007-2008

Pope Benedict XVI in America

Pope Benedict XVI visited Washington, DC, and New York from Apr. 15-21, on the eighth foreign apostolic journey of his pontificate. The visit marked the occasion of the 200th anniversary of the declaration of Baltimore as the first metropolitan see of the United States and the creation of the suffragan sees Bardstown (KY), Boston, New York, and Philadelphia. The pontiff also visited the United Nations. The official announcement was made regarding the papal visit during the U.S. Bishops' meeting in Baltimore in November 2007.

The papal visit was the first for the pontiff to the U.S. since his election in April 2005; prior to his election, then Cardinal Joseph Ratzinger had visited the United States several times and expressed great fondness for the country. His earliest encounter with Americans took place immediately after the Second World War when the young Ratzinger was held in a prisoner-of-war camp for six weeks by American soldiers.

Pope Benedict was received with genuine enthusiasm and great affection both in Washington, DC, and in New York, and his presence and teachings were considered timely and important for Catholics in the United States. Despite being elected three years ago and entering the papacy as one of the best known Cardinals of the late 20th century, the pontiff was unfamiliar to Americans (and American Catholics in particular) who had heard only of his work as head of the Congregation for the Doctrine of the Faith or as a "conservative" theologian.

The trip allowed the Holy Father to make direct contact with Americans and American Catholics and to give expression to the theme, "Christ Our Hope." The theme was reiterated throughout the homilies and speeches of the pope.

The Sex Abuse Scandal

In the lead up to the visit, American media speculated intensely on whether and how the pontiff would deal with the issue of the sex-abuse scandal that created such a severe crisis for the Church in the United States from 2002. The media were thus taken entirely by surprise when Pope Benedict addressed the issue directly on the flight from Italy to Washington, DC. He declared:

"I am ashamed and we will do everything possible to ensure that this does not happen in future. I think we have to act on three levels: the first is at the level of justice and the political level. I will not speak at this moment about homo-

sexuality: this is another thing. We will absolutely exclude paedophiles from the sacred ministry; it is absolutely incompatible, and whoever is really guilty of being a paedophile cannot be a priest. So at this first level we can do justice and help the victims, because they are deeply affected; these are the two sides of justice: one, that paedophiles cannot be priests and the other, to help in any possible way the victims. Then there is a pastoral level. The victims will need healing and help and assistance and reconciliation: this is a big pastoral engagement and I know that the bishops and the priests and all Catholic people in the United States will do whatever possible to help, to assist, to heal. We have made a visitation of the seminaries and we will do all that is possible in the education of seminarians for a deep spiritual, human and intellectual formation for the students. Only sound persons can be admitted to the priesthood and only persons with a deep personal life in Christ and who have a deep sacramental life."

As events transpired, the Holy Father addressed the crisis several more times during his American tour, including an unannounced meeting with four sex abuse victims from the archdiocese of Boston at the apostolic nunciature in Washington, DC.

During the celebration of vespers and a meeting with the Bishops of the United States of America at the National Shrine of the Immaculate Conception in Washington on Apr. 16, the pope again noted that the scandal was "sometimes very badly handled," quoting an earlier observation by Cardinal Francis George of Chicago. In his homily during the celebration of Holy Mass at the Washington Nationals Stadium on Apr. 17, Pope Benedict said:

"...I acknowledge the pain which the Church in America has experienced as a result of the sexual abuse of minors. No words of mine could describe the pain and harm inflicted by such abuse. It is important that those who have suffered be given loving pastoral attention. Nor can I adequately describe the damage that has occurred within the community of the Church. Great efforts have already been made to deal honestly and fairly with this tragic situation, and to ensure that children — whom our Lord loves so deeply (cf. Mk 10:14), and who are our greatest treasure — can grow up in a safe environment. These efforts to protect children must continue."

Impact of the Trip

The consensus both among the media and the general public was that the papal visit had been an immense opportunity for Americans and American Catholics to get to know the pontiff better. This was accomplished during the five days of the trip, and the Holy Father's brief stay in America was hailed immediately as the source of hope and renewal for a Church in the United States in need of both.

In an interview granted to *L'Osservatore Romano* by Abp. Pietro Sambi, the papal nuncio to the United States, stress was placed upon the hope that the Holy Father brought to the United States. The nuncio noted that American Catholics were able to discover Pope Benedict and came away with an overwhelmingly positive view. The nuncio said, "Benedict XVI was little and badly known in the United States. Those who expected an 'inflexible policeman of the Holy Office' have been conquered by the pastor, the father, the persuasive teacher…The Pope has been 'discovered' as an attentive expert on what happens in the heart of the man of today, as a bearer of substantial and life-giving answers, offered with clarity, with humility, almost with timidity."

Abp. Sambi added that crucial to the deep connection forged between the pope and the American people were the papal reflections on hope. The nuncio noted, "Speaking of hope, the Pope has touched on a theme that is profoundly rooted in the history and the culture of this people, and he has struck a particularly sensitive chord for these times…The success of the Pope can be explained by Benedict XVI's capacity to understand the motivations of the American people and to contribute, with humility, the answers they need."

The long-term impact of the papal visit was seen by the nuncio in clear terms of courage. He reported that after the visit, "the Catholic Church has been renewed in courage. We are getting reports from parishes that many of the faithful who had for some time abandoned their religious practices, have returned to confession and Sunday Mass."

Program
(Complete texts of papal addresses, remarks and homilies can be found at www.vatican.va.)

Washington, DC

Welcoming ceremony on the South Lawn of the White House in Washington (April 16, 2008)
Pope Benedict was given a formal welcome at the White House by Pres. George W. Bush, joined by First Lady Laura Bush, and most of the Congressional leadership. In attendance were also 12,000 representatives of the Church in the United States. The Holy Father said in part:

"In the next few days, I look forward to meeting not only with America's Catholic community, but with other Christian communities and representatives of the many religious traditions present in this country. Historically, not only Catholics, but all believers have found here the freedom to worship God in accordance with the dictates of their conscience, while at the same time being accepted as part of a commonwealth in which each individual and group can make its voice heard. As the nation faces the increasingly complex political and ethical issues of our time, I am confident that the American people will find in their religious beliefs a precious source of insight and an inspiration to pursue reasoned, responsible and respectful dialogue in the effort to build a more humane and free society.

"Freedom is not only a gift, but also a summons to personal responsibility. Americans know this from experience – almost every town in this country has its monuments honoring those who sacrificed their lives in defense of freedom, both at home and abroad. The preservation of freedom calls for the cultivation of virtue, self-discipline, sacrifice for the common good and a sense of responsibility towards the less fortunate. It also demands the courage to engage in civic life and to bring one's deepest beliefs and values to reasoned public debate. In a word, freedom is ever new. It is a challenge held out to each generation, and it must constantly be won over for the cause of good (cf. *Spe Salvi*, 24)."

A Joint declaration between the Holy See and the Office of the President of the United States of America was released at the end of the private meeting between the Holy Father Benedict XVI and U.S. President George W. Bush (April 16, 2008).

Meeting with the Bishops of the United States of America at the National Shrine of the Immaculate Conception in Washington (April 16, 2008)
Pope Benedict XVI celebrated vespers and had a meeting with the Bishops of the United States of America at the National Shrine of the Immaculate Conception in Washington. During the session with the U.S. Bishops, Among the remarks of the pontiff were the words:

"As my predecessor, Pope John Paul II taught, 'The person principally responsible in the Diocese for the pastoral care of the family is the Bishop ... he must devote to it personal interest, care, time, personnel and resources, but above all personal support for the families and for all those who ... assist him in the pastoral care of the family' (*Familiaris Consortio*, 73). It is your task to proclaim boldly the arguments from faith and reason in favor of the institution of marriage, understood as a lifelong commitment between a man and a woman, open to the transmission of life. This message should resonate with people today, because it is essentially an unconditional and unreserved 'yes' to life, a 'yes' to love, and a 'yes' to the aspirations at the heart of our common humanity, as we strive to fulfill our deep yearning for intimacy with others and with the Lord. Among the countersigns to the Gospel of life found in America and elsewhere is one that causes deep shame: the sexual abuse of minors. Many of you have spoken to me of the enormous pain that your communities have suffered when clerics have betrayed their priestly obligations and duties by such gravely immoral behavior. As you strive to eliminate this evil wherever it occurs, you may be assured of the prayerful support of God's people throughout the world. Rightly, you attach priority to showing compassion and care to the victims. It is your God-given responsibility as pastors to bind up the wounds caused by every breach of trust, to foster healing, to promote reconciliation and to reach out with loving concern to those so seriously wronged."

As part of the session, Pope Benedict gave responses to questions posed by the American Bishops. The questions covered a variety of pastoral concerns including ways to bring inactive Catholics back to the Church.

Celebration of Holy Mass at the Washington Nationals Stadium (April 17, 2008)
Pope Benedict celebrated Mass at Nationals Stadium in front of an estimated crowd of over 50,000. He declared in

part of his homily:

"The world needs this witness! Who can deny that the present moment is a crossroads, not only for the Church in America but also for society as a whole? It is a time of great promise, as we see the human family in many ways drawing closer together and becoming ever more interdependent. Yet at the same time we see clear signs of a disturbing breakdown in the very foundations of society: signs of alienation, anger and polarization on the part of many of our contemporaries; increased violence; a weakening of the moral sense; a coarsening of social relations; and a growing forgetfulness of Christ and God. The Church, too, sees signs of immense promise in her many strong parishes and vital movements, in the enthusiasm for the faith shown by so many young people, in the number of those who each year embrace the Catholic faith, and in a greater interest in prayer and catechesis. At the same time she senses, often painfully, the presence of division and polarization in her midst, as well as the troubling realization that many of the baptized, rather than acting as a spiritual leaven in the world, are inclined to embrace attitudes contrary to the truth of the Gospel…

"'In hope we were saved!' (*Rom* 8:24). As the Church in the United States gives thanks for the blessings of the past two hundred years, I invite you, your families, and every parish and religious community, to trust in the power of grace to create a future of promise for God's people in this country. I ask you, in the Lord Jesus, to set aside all division and to work with joy to prepare a way for him, in fidelity to his word and in constant conversion to his will. Above all, I urge you to continue to be a leaven of evangelical hope in American society, striving to bring the light and truth of the Gospel to the task of building an ever more just and free world for generations yet to come."

Meeting with the representatives of other religions at the "Rotunda" Hall of the Pope John Paul II Cultural Center of Washington (April 17, 2008)

After his session with Catholic educators, the Holy Father had a meeting with representatives of other religions. During the encounter, the pontiff received several gifts from young people of different faiths.

Meeting with representatives of the Jewish community in Washington D.C. (April 17, 2008)

Following his meeting with representatives of other religions, Pope Benedict met with representatives of the Jewish community in Washington, D.C. He also delivered a message to the Jewish community on the occasion of the feast of Pesah.

New York

On April 18, the Holy Father flew from Washington, D.C. to New York City to begin the second part of his visit. Included in the New York journey was a significant address to the United Nations General Assembly.

Address of the Holy Father to the General Assembly of the United Nations Organization in New York (April 18, 2008)

The third pontiff (after Popes Paul VI and John Paul II) to address the United Nations General Assembly, Pope Benedict XVI centered his remarks on the sixtieth anniversary of the Universal Declaration of Human Rights. He declared:

"Through the United Nations, States have established universal objectives which, even if they do not coincide with the total common good of the human family, undoubtedly represent a fundamental part of that good. The founding principles of the Organization – the desire for peace, the quest for justice, respect for the dignity of the person, humanitarian cooperation and assistance – express the just aspirations of the human spirit, and constitute the ideals which should underpin international relations. As my predecessors Paul VI and John Paul II have observed from this very podium, all this is something that the Catholic Church and the Holy See follow attentively and with interest, seeing in your activity an example of how issues and conflicts concerning the world community can be subject to common regulation. The United Nations embodies the aspiration for a 'greater degree of international ordering' (John Paul II, *Sollicitudo Rei Socialis*, 43), inspired and governed by the principle of subsidiarity, and therefore capable of responding to the demands of the human family through binding international rules and through structures capable of harmonizing the day-to-day unfolding of the lives of peoples. This is all the more necessary at a time when we experience the obvious paradox of a multilateral consensus that continues to be in crisis because it is still subordinated to the decisions of a few, whereas the world's problems call for interventions in the form of collective action by the international community. Indeed, questions of security, development goals, reduction of local and global inequalities, protection of the environment, of resources and of the climate, require all international leaders to act jointly and to show a readiness to work in good faith, respecting the law, and promoting solidarity with the weakest regions of the planet. I am thinking especially of those countries in Africa and other parts of the world which remain on the margins of authentic integral development, and are therefore at risk of experiencing only the negative effects of globalization. In the context of international relations, it is necessary to recognize the higher role played by rules and structures that are intrinsically ordered to promote the common good, and therefore to safeguard human freedom.

"These regulations do not limit freedom. On the contrary, they promote it when they prohibit behaviour and actions which work against the common good, curb its effective exercise and hence compromise the dignity of every human person. In the name of freedom, there has to be a correlation between rights and duties, by which every person is called to assume responsibility for his or her choices, made as a consequence of entering into relations with others. Here our thoughts turn also to the way the results of scientific research and technological advances have sometimes been applied."

Greetings to the staff and the personnel of the United Nations in New York (April 18, 2008)

Following his address to the General Assembly, the pope spoke to the staff and personnel of the United Nations.

Meeting with representatives of the Jewish community at Park East Synagogue in New York and Ecumenical Prayer Service at St Joseph's Parish in New York (April 18, 2008)

Later in the day on the 18th, Pope Benedict met with Jewish representatives at the venerable Park East Synagogue in New York City and conducted an ecumenical prayer service at St. Joseph's parish. At both events, the Holy Father received a very warm reception and reaffirmed his commitment to interreligious dialogue and ecumenical outreach.

Homily during the celebration of a Votive Mass for the Universal Church with priests, men and women religious in St. Patrick's Cathedral, New York (April 19, 2008)

On April 19, the pontiff celebrated Mass in St. Patrick's Cathedral, making him the first pope to say Mass in that famed and beloved cathedral (Pope John Paul II had conducted prayer services there). The Mass provided him with an opportunity for an encounter with men and women religious. The pope was given a thunderous welcome.

Meetings with young people having disabilities at St. Joseph Seminary in Yonkers, New York and with young people and seminarians at St. Joseph Seminary in Yonkers, New York (April 19, 2008)

After the Mass at St. Patrick's Cathedral, the pontiff was taken to St. Joseph Seminary in Yonkers where he had an emotional meting with young people with disabilities and also with young people and seminarians.

Prayer during the visit to Ground Zero in New York (April 20, 2008)

The next day, on Apr. 20, the pope paid a visit to Ground Zero in lower Manhattan, the site of the terrorist attacks on September 11, 2001. The Holy Father recited a prayer on the occasion:

O God of love, compassion, and healing, look on us, people of many different faiths and traditions, who gather today at this site, the scene of incredible violence and pain.

We ask you in your goodness to give eternal light and peace to all who died here—the heroic first-responders: our fire fighters, police officers, emergency service workers, and Port Authority personnel, along with all the innocent men and women who were victims of this tragedy simply because their work or service brought them here on September 11, 2001.

We ask you, in your compassion to bring healing to those who, because of their presence here that day, suffer from injuries and illness.

Heal, too, the pain of still-grieving families and all who lost loved ones in this tragedy. Give them strength to continue their lives with courage and hope.

We are mindful as well of those who suffered death, injury, and loss on the same day at the Pentagon and in Shanksville, Pennsylvania.

Our hearts are one with theirs as our prayer embraces their pain and suffering.

God of peace, bring your peace to our violent world:

peace in the hearts of all men and women and peace among the nations of the earth.

Turn to your way of love those whose hearts and minds are consumed with hatred.

God of understanding, overwhelmed by the magnitude of this tragedy, we seek your light and guidance as we confront such terrible events. Grant that those whose lives were spared may live so that the lives lost here may not have been lost in vain. Comfort and console us, strengthen us in hope, and give us the wisdom and courage to work tirelessly for a world where true peace and love reign among nations and in the hearts of all.

Homily during the celebration of Holy Mass at New York's Yankee Stadium (April 20, 2008)

On the afternoon of Apr. 20, the Holy Father's visit climaxed with Mass at Yankee Stadium. The Holy Father's homily touched on the legacy of faith of American Catholics and the immense challenges faced by the Church in the United States today. He said in part:

"Our celebration today is also a sign of the impressive growth which God has given to the Church in your country in the past two hundred years. From a small flock like that described in the first reading, the Church in America has been built up in fidelity to the twin commandment of love of God and love of neighbor. In this land of freedom and opportunity, the Church has united a widely diverse flock in the profession of the faith and, through her many educational, charitable and social works, has also contributed significantly to the growth of American society as a whole…

Today we recall the bicentennial of a watershed in the history of the Church in the United States: its first great chapter of growth. In these two hundred years, the face of the Catholic community in your country has changed greatly. We think of the successive waves of immigrants whose traditions have so enriched the Church in America. We think of the strong faith which built up the network of churches, educational, healthcare and social institutions which have long been the hallmark of the Church in this land. We think also of those countless fathers and mothers who passed on the faith to their children, the steady ministry of the many priests who devoted their lives to the care of souls, and the incalculable contribution made by so many men and women religious, who not only taught generations of children how to read and write, but also inspired in them a lifelong desire to know God, to love him and to serve him. How many 'spiritual sacrifices pleasing to God' have been offered up in these two centuries! In this land of religious liberty, Catholics found freedom not only to practice their faith, but also to participate fully in civic life, bringing their deepest moral convictions to the public square and cooperating with their neighbors in shaping a vibrant, democratic society. Today's celebration is more than an occasion of gratitude for graces received. It is also a summons to move forward with firm resolve to use wisely the blessings of freedom, in order to build a future of hope for coming generations.

PAPAL ENCYCLICAL: SPE SALVI

On Nov. 30, 2007, Pope Benedict XVI issued his second encyclical, Spe Salvi, *that focuses on the theological virtue of hope. The title was taken from St. Paul's letter to the Romans, specifically, Roman 8:24, "Spe salvi facti sumus" ("in hope we are saved").*

His first encyclical, *Deus Caritas Est* ("God Is Love") in 2005, examined the theological virtue of love. The Holy Father's third encyclical is expected to center on Catholic social teachings, although the pontiff will also likely reflect in the future on the theological virtue of faith. The encyclical is divided into eight chapters with an introduction and is approximately 19,000 words long.

In his introduction, Pope Benedict approaches his task with the clarity that has been a hallmark of his papal writings:

"According to the Christian faith, 'redemption' — salvation — is not simply a given. Redemption is offered to us in the sense that we have been given hope, trustworthy hope, by virtue of which we can face our present: the present, even if it is arduous, can be lived and accepted if it leads towards a goal, if we can be sure of this goal, and if this goal is great enough to justify the effort of the journey. Now the question immediately arises: what sort of hope could ever justify the statement that, on the basis of that hope and simply because it exists, we are redeemed? And what sort of certainty is involved here?" (No. 1).

He begins answering this question in the first chapter by discussing the relationship between faith and hope. He traces the development of faith in the Old Testament and then centers especially on Paul's letter to the Ephesians and notes, "To come to know God—the true God—means to receive hope" (No. 3). This stands in contrast to the despair known by those who do not know God, a contrast made all the more real by Benedict's example of St. Josephine Bakhita, a one-time slave who came to Christ.

In the next chapter, "The concept of faith-based hope in the New Testament and the early Church," Benedict asks can our encounter with the God who in Christ has shown us his face and opened his heart be for us too not just "informative" but "performative"—that is to say, can it change our lives, so that we know we are redeemed through the hope that it expresses?" (No. 4). The reflection that follows seamlessly weaves together the writings of St. Paul with the Church Fathers to demonstrate that Jesus "tells us who man truly is and what a man must do in order to be truly human. He shows us the way, and this way is the truth. He himself is both the way and the truth, and therefore he is also the life which all of us are seeking. He also shows us the way beyond death; only someone able to do this is a true teacher of life" (no. 6). To show this, Benedict uses as the example of early Christian sarcophagi that depict Jesus as philosopher and shepherd, especially the image of the philosopher in the ancient world as one who teaches the art of living authentically.

In the chapter "Eternal life — what is it?" Benedict asks, "is the Christian faith also for us today a life-changing and life-sustaining hope?" (No. 10). He shows that death is a part of existence and that "we want life itself, true life, untouched even by death; yet at the same time we do not know the thing toward which we feel driven" (No. 12). What drives us, Benedict teaches, is the longing for "eternal life." This is not some endless prolongation of human life but "a plunging ever anew into the vastness of being, in which we are simply overwhelmed with joy" (No. 12).

Moving on to the chapter "Is Christian hope individualistic?," the pontiff develops the idea of this vastness of being and relies on such renowned theologians as Henri de Lubac, Augustine of Hippo, Bernard of Clairvaux, and Benedict of Nursia to present the social reality of salvation.

From here, the pope proceeds to "The transformation of Christian faith-hope in the modern age," and the question of how we arrived "at this interpretation of the 'salvation of the soul' as a flight from responsibility for the whole, and how did we come to conceive the Christian project as a selfish search for salvation which rejects the idea of serving others?" (no. 16). In answering this, Benedict observes the impact of Francis Bacon, Immanuel Kant, Friedrich Engels, and Karl Marx in shaping the notion that salvation is possible in this world meaning that salvation for the next world is no longer needed. This critique of modernity and false progress is summed up by the pope, that: "Given the developments of the modern age, the quotation from St. Paul with which I began (Eph 2:12) proves to be thoroughly realistic and plainly true. There is no doubt, therefore, that a 'Kingdom of God' accomplished without God—a kingdom therefore of man alone—inevitably ends up as the 'perverse end' of all things as described by Kant: we have seen it, and we see it over and over again" (No. 23).

In the next chapter "The true shape of Christian hope" Benedict returns to the question, "what may we hope? And what may we not hope?" He reiterates, "It is not science that redeems man: man is redeemed by love. This applies even in terms of this present world... Our relationship with God is established through communion with Jesus—we cannot achieve it alone or from our own resources alone" (nos. 26, 28). This is a reminder of the dangers of modern philosophy, of communism, and also of liberation theology.

In "Settings for learning and practicing hope," he discusses how we can learn from hope and cites three ways: Prayer as a school for hope; Action and suffering as settings for learning hope; and Judgment as a setting for learning and practicing hope. In demonstrating these facets, Benedict makes references to the revered Vietnamese Cardinal Nguyen Van Thuan who suffered for so long alone in prison, the philosophers Max Horkheimer and Theodor W. Adorno, the Russian writer Fyodor Dostoevsky, and Plato. In a memorable passage, the Holy Father notes the power of suffering:

"We can try to limit suffering, to fight against it, but we cannot eliminate it. It is when we attempt to avoid suffering by withdrawing from anything that might involve hurt, when we try to spare ourselves the effort and pain of pursuing truth, love, and goodness, that we drift into a life of emptiness, in which there may be almost no pain, but the dark sensation of meaninglessness and abandonment is all the greater. It is not by sidestepping or fleeing from suffering that we are healed, but rather by our capacity for accepting it, maturing through it and finding meaning through union with Christ, who suffered with infinite love" (no. 37).

In his closing chapter, "Mary, Star of Hope," Pope Benedict honors the Blessed Mother:

"Life is like a voyage on the sea of history, often dark and stormy, a voyage in which we watch for the stars that indicate the route. The true stars of our life are the people who have lived good lives. They are lights of hope. Certainly, Jesus Christ is the true light, the sun that has risen above all the shadows of history. But to reach him we also need lights close by—people who shine with his light and so guide us along our way. Who more than Mary could be a star of hope for us? With her "yes" she opened the door of our world to God himself; she became the living Ark of the Covenant, in whom God took flesh, became one of us, and pitched his tent among us (cf. Jn 1:14)" (No. 49).

THE SACRED COLLEGE OF CARDINALS

Pope Benedict XVI continued to shape the future direction of the Church and made another significant mark upon the eventual election of his successor when he announced the creation of 23 new cardinals on Oct. 17, 2007.

The new members of the College of Cardinals, including two Americans — Abps. Daniel N. DiNardo, of Galveston-Houston, and Abp. John P. Foley, Grand Master of the Knights of the Holy Sepulcher — were from 14 countries and included seven officials based in Rome, 11 heads of archdioceses around the globe, and five clerics over the age of 80 who were honored for their long service to the Church but who are not eligible to participate in any future conclave.

In naming the 23 cardinals, Pope Benedict exceeded by one the maximum limit of 120 cardinal electors set by Pope Paul VI in 1973. Pope John Paul II set aside the limit on several occasions during his pontificate.

The appointment of Abp. DiNardo of Galveston-Houston is especially significant as it marks the first time that a cardinal has been named for the Texas see that was raised to the rank of an archdiocese by Pope John Paul II only three years ago. The archdiocese is the 10th largest in the U.S., and the designation reflects the rapid growth in recent decades of the Catholic population in the South and Southwest and the increasing diversity of the Church in Texas.

Abp. Foley, now the Grand Master of the Knights of the Holy Sepulchre of Jerusalem, is best known for serving as the popular president of the Pontifical Council for Social Communications from 1984 until June of this year. His voice is familiar to millions around the world as he customarily provided the narration for the televised Midnight Mass at Christmas from the Vatican.

Among the other notable new cardinals are:

Abp. Leonardo Sandri, prefect of the Congregation for Eastern Churches, from Argentina, a former nuncio (papal ambassador) to Mexico and undersecretary of state for general affairs in the Vatican. It was Sandri who delivered the official announcement in St. Peter's Square in 2005 that John Paul II had passed away.

Abp. Seán Brady of Armagh, Ireland, has become one of his country's most articulate voices for peace in Northern Ireland and the dangers of growing secularism in the Isle. His recent meeting with the controversial anti-Catholic Protestant leader Ian Paisley was hailed a major breakthrough in Northern Ireland's troubled religious history.

Abp. Angelo Bagnasco of Genoa, Italy, is considered a rising star in European Catholicism, especially with his appointment as head of the influential Italian Bishops' Conference. In April 2007, following a condemnation of same-sex unions, he was the target of death threats from gay-rights activists and was given police protection.

Abp. Odilo Scherer of São Paulo, Brazil, the first non-Franciscan archbishop in São Paulo in 37 years, recently was in charge of the important meeting of the Council of Latin American Bishops' Conferences (CELAM) in Brazil that was attended by Pope Benedict. He has spoken extensively on the crises facing the Church in Latin America, including the rise of secularism, the inroads of the Pentecostal Movement, and the perpetuation of poverty and social injustice.

Abp. Théodore-Adrien Sarr of Dakar, Senegal, is revered for his defense of human rights and promotion of peace in western Africa. He and his fellow bishops received threats of violence in 2004 for their work, in a country that is 95% Muslim and barely 5% Catholic.

Abp. Emmanuel III Delly, the Patriarch of Babylon for the Chaldeans and head of the Chaldean Catholic Church with his base in Baghdad, became patriarch at the end of 2003 and has served throughout the difficult post-Saddam era in Iraq. Wounded accidentally by shattered glass in the fighting, he has labored to hold together the Christian population in the country while forging good relations with the new government and negotiating for the release of kidnapped hostages.

All of the cardinals were installed officially at a special consistory on Nov. 24, 2007. At that time, there were 202 total cardinals with 121 of them eligible to participate in any conclave. As of Aug. 15, 2008, there were 194 cardinals from 68 countries or areas. There were 116 electors from 60 countries: 58 are from Europe, 20 from North America, 16 from South America, 9 from Africa, 11 from Asia and two from Oceania.

Of the current cardinal electors, thirty were named by Benedict XVI and 86 by John Paul II.

The United States has the second largest number of voting cardinals, at 13, behind only Italy which has 21.

The New Cardinals

Abp. Leonardo Sandri, 63, from Argentina, prefect of the Congregation for Eastern Churches.

Abp. John P. Foley, 71, from the United States, Grand Master of the Knights of the Holy Sepulchre of Jerusalem and president emeritus of the Pontifical Council for Social Communications.

Abp. Giovanni Lajolo, 72, from Italy, former Vatican foreign minister presently in charge of the administration of the Vatican City State.

Abp. Paul-Josef Cordes, 73, from Germany, president of the Pontifical Council Cor Unum that coordinates Catholic aid around the world.

Abp. Stanislaw Rylko, 59, from Poland, president of the Pontifical Council for the Laity.

Abp. Angelo Comastri, 64, from Italy, archpriest of St. Peter's Basilica and president of the Fabric of Peter.

Abp. Raffaele Farina S.D.B., 74, from Italy, a Salesian and the archivist of the Holy Roman Church and head of the Vatican Library.

Abp. Agustin Garcia-Gasco y Vicente, 76, archbishop of Valencia, Spain.

Abp. Seán Brady, 68, archbishop of Armagh, Ireland.

Abp. Lluís Martínez Sistach, 70, archbishop of Barcelona,

Spain.
Abp. André Vingt-Trois, 64, archbishop of Paris, France.
Abp. Angelo Bagnasco, 64, archbishop of Genoa, Italy.
Abp. Théodore-Adrien Sarr, 70, archbishop of Dakar, Senegal.
Abp. Oswald Gracias, 62, archbishop of Bombay, India.
Abp. Francisco Lopez Ortega, 58, archbishop of Monterrey, Mexico.
Abp. Daniel Nicholas DiNardo, 58, archbishop of Galveston-Houston.
Abp. Odilo Scherer, 58, archbishop of São Paulo, Brazil.

Abp. John Njue, 63, archbishop of Nairobi, Kenya.
There were also five new cardinals over the age of 80 and so ineligible to vote in a conclave: Abp. Emmanuel III Delly, 80, Patriarch of Babylon of the Chaldeans. Abp. Giovanni Coppa, 81, from Italy, former apostolic nuncio to Czechoslovakia, the Czech Republic, and Slovakia. Abp. Estanislao Esteban Karlic, 81, Abp. emeritus of Paraná, Argentina. Fr. Urbano Navarrete Cortés, S.J., 87, from Italy, a Jesuit and rector emeritus of the Gregorian University in Rome. Fr. Umberto Betti, OFM, 85, from Spain, a Franciscan and rector emeritus of the Lateran University in Rome.

POPE BENEDICT XVI AND ISLAM

Dialogue between the Church and many religious and political leaders of Islam. In 2006, much was made of the so-called Regensburg Controversy when the Holy Father's speech on faith and reason sparked protests, riots, and violence by Muslims when he included a disparaging quote about Muhammad from a 14th century Byzantine Emperor. However, in the months that followed, Pope Benedict won over many of his critics through his trip to Turkey and his appeals for authentic dialogue with Islam that includes the principle of reciprocity (that Christians in Muslim countries should enjoy the same rights as those given Muslims in Western nations) and the promotion of human dignity, peace, and religious tolerance.

In November 2007, the pontiff welcomed King Abdullah of Saudi Arabia to the Vatican, marking the first time that a Saudi king had officially spoken with the Pope. On the agenda of their discussions were religious freedom, inter-religious and inter-cultural dialogue, and the need to solve the Israeli-Palestinian conflict. Pope Benedict used the occasion to raise the situation of Christian workers who live in Saudi Arabia and noted to the Saudis "the positive and industrious presence of Christians" in the kingdom.

The royal visit was only one of several surprises in late 2007. On October 11, 2007, one year after the release of an open letter to the Pope from 38 prominent Muslim clerics from around the world accepting his "apology" over the Regensburg remarks, an even more impressive group of 138 Muslim scholars, clerics and intellectuals sent another open letter, titled *A Common Word Between Us and You*, to Pope Benedict and other Christian leaders.

The letter was unprecedented in several respects. First, it was signed by prominent Muslim leaders, politicians and academics, from the leading branches of Islam and the school of Islamic jurisprudence, such as the Sunni, Shiite, Salafi and the Sufi, representing more than 40 countries, including Iran, Iraq, Saudi Arabia, Syria, Egypt and Pakistan. The letter thus represented a key consensus opinion of Islamic theologians.

The stress upon consensus becomes important in light of the letter's contents. The Muslim leaders argue that the twin commands of love of God and love of neighbor provide common ground between the two traditions. "Whilst Islam and Christianity are obviously different religions – and whilst there is no minimizing some of their formal differences – it is clear that the two greatest commandments are ... a link between the Quran, the Torah and the New Testament." There is, consequently, no necessary antagonism between the two faiths. They go on to quote the Quran by writing, "As Muslims, we say to Christians that we are not against them

and that Islam is not against them – so long as they do not wage war against Muslims on account of their religion, oppress them and drive them out of their homes."

Equally, the Muslim leaders maintain that the numbers of Christians and Muslims make cooperation essential. "Christianity and Islam," they argue, "are the largest and second largest religions in the world and in history…The relationship between these two religious communities [is] the most important factor in contributing to meaningful peace around the world."

Cardinal Angelo Scola, patriarch of Venice and a leader in Catholic-Muslim dialogue through his journal *Oasis*, noted the significance of the letter in an interview with the Italian media. "The document," he observed, "in the perspective of that double love, of God and one's neighbor, underscores a vein of the Muslim tradition which has been partially placed in the shade due to the growth of fundamentalism." The cardinal noted as well that the text affirms that man has "mind or the intelligence, which is made for comprehending the truth; the will which is made for freedom of choice, and sentiment which is made for loving the good and the beautiful." But it also condemns terrorists, declaring "to those who nevertheless relish conflict and destruction for their own sake or reckon that ultimately they stand to gain through them, we say [...] to sincerely make every effort to make peace and come together in harmony."

The Vatican's response was delivered initially in late November by Cardinal Secretary of State Tarcisio Bertone. The reply expressed the pope's gratitude "for the positive spirit which inspired the text and for the call for a common commitment to promoting peace in the world." It then invited a representative group of the signatories to gather at the Vatican.

The diplomatic reply was not surprising. What was highly unusual, however, was the speed with which plans have advanced. While circumspect in his optimism and realistic in his awareness of the difficulties that attend progress in dialogue, Cardinal Jean-Louis Tauran, the top Vatican official in charge of relations with Islam, said in early January that he expected to meet with Muslim representatives in February or March to lay the groundwork for the meeting.

Only time will tell what lasting progress can be made, but the change in atmosphere from the post-Regensburg violence and hostility points to the success of Pope Benedict in sparking a global conversation that has been engaged within Islam as well. Such debates and dynamic self-examination within Islamic circles could be a key start to effecting genuine change in Islam, achieving the slow marginalization of radicals and Islamists, and giving voice at long last to moderate Muslims who have been fearful of speaking out. Such a change in the culture of the Islamic world might bring with it prospects for peace on a global level as well as hopes for a better and more secure life for the average non-Muslim. The prospects in the short term seem limited, but the benefit of dialogue were stressed by Pope Benedict when he declared in

November of last year, "Dialogue, respect for the convictions of others, and collaboration in the service of peace are the surest means of securing social concord. These are among the noblest goals which can bring together men and women of good will, and, in a particular way, all those who worship the one God who is the Creator and beneficent Lord of the whole human family."

PAPAL TRIPS 2007-2008

Vienna, Austria, Sept. 7-9.

Pope Benedict XVI visited Vienna, Austria from Sept. 7 to 9, on the seventh foreign apostolic journey of his pontificate. The visit marked the occasion of the 850th anniversary of the foundation of the Shrine of Mariazell.

Program

Welcome ceremony at the international airport of Vienna/Schwechat (Sept. 7, 2007)

Prayer before the Mariensäule at Am Hof Square in Vienna (Sept. 7, 2007)

Meeting with the public authorities and the Diplomatic Corps at Hofburg Palace in Vienna (Sept. 7, 2007)

Holy Mass on the occasion of the 850th anniversary of the foundation of the Shrine of Mariazell (Sept. 8, 2007)

Celebration of Marian Vespers with Priests, Religious, Deacons and Seminarians at the Basilica of Mariazell (Sept. 8, 2007)

Holy Mass in St. Stephen's Cathedral in Vienna (Sept. 9, 2007)

Recitation of the Angelus Domini (Sept. 9, 2007)

Visit to Heiligenkreuz Abbey (Sept. 9, 2007)

Meeting with representatives of volonteer organizations at the Wiener Konzerthaus (Sept. 9, 2007)

Farewell ceremony at the international airport of Vienna/Schwechat (Sept. 9, 2007)

Excerpts from Addresses and Homilies

Welcome ceremony at the international airport of Vienna/Schwechat (September 7, 2007)

With great joy I am now setting foot, for the first time since the beginning of my Pontificate, in the land of Austria, a country which I know well, not least from its geographical closeness to my birthplace. I thank you, Mr President, for the cordial words with which you have welcomed me in the name of the whole Austrian people. You know how close I feel to your native land and to many of the people and places in your country. This cultural space in the heart of Europe transcends borders and brings together ideas and energies from various parts of the continent. The culture of this country is deeply imbued with the message of Jesus Christ and the activity which the Church has carried out in his name. All this, and much more, gives me a vivid sense, dear Austrian friends, of being "at home" here in your midst.

The reason for my coming to Austria is the 850th anniversary of the shrine of Mariazell. This Marian sanctuary in some way represents the maternal heart of Austria, and has always had a particular importance also for Hungarians and the Slavic peoples. It symbolizes an openness which not only transcends physical and national frontiers, but, in the person of Mary,

reminds us of an essential dimension of human beings: their capacity for openness to God and his word of truth.

In this way, I would like, during these three days here in Austria, to go as a pilgrim to Mariazell. In recent years, I have been pleased to notice among many people an increased interest in the idea of pilgrimage. Journeying as pilgrims, young people in particular have found a new way to reflect and meditate; they come to know one another and together they encounter creation and the history of faith which, often and perhaps unexpectedly, they experience as a source of strength for the present. I intend my pilgrimage to Mariazell to be a journey made in the company of all the pilgrims of our time. In this spirit I will soon lead the people in prayer in the centre of Vienna, prayer which, like a spiritual pilgrimage, will accompany these days throughout your country.

Mariazell does not only represent 850 years of history, but shows us on the basis of that history – as reflected in the statue of the Blessed Mother pointing to Christ her Son – the way to the future. In view of this, today I would like, along with Austria's political authorities and the representatives of international organizations, to take another look at our present and our future.

Tomorrow, the Feast of the Nativity of Mary, the patronal feast of Mariazell, will bring me to that holy place.

Prayer before the Mariensäule at Am Hof Square in Vienna (September 7, 2007)

As the first stop of my pilgrimage to Mariazell I have chosen the Mariensäule, to reflect briefly with all of you on the significance of the Mother of God for Austria past and present, and her significance for each one of us. I offer a cordial greeting to all those gathered here to pray beneath the Mariensäule. I thank you, dear Eminence, for the warm words of welcome at the beginning of our celebration. I greet the Mayor of the capital and the other Authorities present. I particularly greet the young people and the representatives of the foreign-language Catholic communities in the Archdiocese of Vienna, who will gather after this Liturgy of the Word in the church and will remain until tomorrow in adoration before the Blessed Sacrament. I have heard that you have been here for three hours already. I can only express my admiration and say Vergelt's Gott! With this adoration you will very concretely accomplish what all of us wish to do in these days: with Mary, to look to Christ...

Meeting with the public authorities and the Diplomatic Corps at Hofburg Palace in Vienna (September 7, 2007)

It is my great joy and honour to meet you today, Mr President, together with the members of the Federal Government and representatives of the political and civic life of the Republic of Austria. Our meeting here in the Hofburg reflects the good relations, marked by reciprocal trust, which exist between your country and the Holy See, relations to which you, Mr President, have just alluded. For this I am most pleased.

Relations between Austria and the Holy See are part of that vast network of diplomatic relations in which Vienna serves as an important crossroads, inasmuch as a number of international Organizations have their headquarters in this city. I am pleased by the presence of many diplomatic representatives, whom I greet with respect. I thank you, distinguished Ambassadors, for your dedicated service, not only to the countries which you represent and to their interests, but also to the common cause of peace and understanding between peoples.

This is my first visit as Bishop of Rome and Supreme Pastor of the universal Catholic Church to this country, which I know well from many earlier visits. It is – may I say – truly a joy for me to be here. I have many friends here and, as a Bavarian neighbour, Austria's way of life and traditions are familiar to me. My great predecessor of blessed memory, Pope John Paul II, visited Austria three times. Each time he was received most cordially by the people of this country, his words were listened to attentively, and his apostolic journeys left their mark...

We are gathered in an historical setting, which for centuries was the seat of an Empire uniting vast areas of Central and Eastern Europe. This time and place thus offer us a good opportunity to take a far-ranging look at today's Europe. After the horrors of war and traumatic experiences of totalitarianism and dictatorship, Europe is moving towards a unity capable of ensuring a lasting order of peace and just development. The painful division which split the continent for decades has come to an end politically, yet the goal of unity remains in great part still to be achieved in the minds and hearts of individuals. If, after the fall of the Iron Curtain in 1989, certain excessive hopes were disappointed, and on some points justified criticisms can be raised about certain European institutions, the process of unification remains a most significant achievement which has brought a period of unwonted peace to this continent, formerly consumed by constant conflicts and fatal fratricidal wars. For the countries of Central and Eastern Europe in particular, participating in this process is a further incentive to the consolidation of freedom, the constitutional state and democracy within their borders. Here I would like to recall the contribution made by my predecessor, Pope John Paul II, to that historic process. Austria too, as a bridge-country situated at the crossroads of West and East, has contributed much to this unification and has also – we must not forget – greatly benefited from it…

Nowadays we hear much of the "European model of life". The term refers to a social order which combines a sound economy with social justice, political pluralism with tolerance, generosity and openness, but also means the preservation of the values which have made this continent what it is. This model, under the pressure of modern economic forces, faces a great challenge. The oft-cited process of globalization cannot be halted, yet it is an urgent task and a great responsibility of politics to regulate and limit globalization, so that it will not occur at the expense of the poorer nations and of the poor in wealthier nations, and prove detrimental to future generations.

Certainly – as we know – Europe has also experienced and suffered from terribly misguided courses of action. These have included: ideological restrictions imposed on philosophy, science and also faith, the abuse of religion and reason for imperialistic purposes, the degradation of man resulting from theoretical and practical materialism, and finally the degeneration of tolerance into an indifference with no reference to permanent values. But Europe has also been marked by the capacity for self-criticism, which gives it a distinctive place within the vast panorama of the world's cultures.

It was in Europe that the notion of human rights was first formulated. The fundamental human right, the presupposition of every other right, is the right to life itself. This is true of life from the moment of conception until its natural end. Abortion, consequently, cannot be a human right – it is the very opposite. It is "a deep wound in society", as the late Cardinal Franz König never tired of repeating…

Another great concern of mine is the debate on what has been termed "actively assisted death". It is to be feared that at some point the gravely ill or elderly will be subjected to tacit or even explicit pressure to request death or to administer it to themselves. The proper response to end-of-life suffering is loving care and accompaniment on the journey towards death – especially with the help of palliative care – and not "actively assisted death". But if humane accompaniment on the journey towards death is to prevail, structural reforms would be needed in every area of the social and healthcare system, as well as organized structures of palliative care. Concrete steps would also have to be taken: in the psychological and pastoral accompaniment of the seriously ill and dying, their family members, and physicians and healthcare personnel. In this field the hospice movement has done wonders. The totality of these tasks, however, cannot be delegated to it alone. Many other people need to be prepared or encouraged in their willingness to spare neither time nor expense in loving care for the gravely ill and dying.

Finally, another part of the European heritage is a tradition of thought which considers as essential a substantial correspondence between faith, truth and reason. Here the issue is clearly whether or not reason stands at the beginning and foundation of all things. The issue is whether reality originates by chance and necessity, and thus whether reason is merely a chance by-product of the irrational and, in an ocean of irrationality, it too, in the end, is meaningless, or whether instead the underlying conviction of Christian faith remains true: *In principio erat Verbum* – in the beginning was the Word; at the origin of everything is the creative reason of God who decided to make himself known to us human beings.

Holy Mass on the occasion of the 850th anniversary of the foundation of the Shrine of Mariazell (September 8, 2007)

With our great pilgrimage to Mariazell, we are celebrating the patronal feast of this Shrine, the feast of Our Lady's Birthday. For 850 years pilgrims have been travelling here from different peoples and nations; they come to pray for the intentions of their hearts and their homelands, bringing their deepest hopes and concerns. In this way Mariazell has become a place of peace and reconciled unity, not only for Austria, but far beyond her borders. Here we experience the consoling kindness of the Madonna. Here we meet Jesus Christ, in whom God is with us, as today's Gospel reminds us – Jesus, of whom we have just heard in the reading from the prophet Micah: "He himself will be peace" (5:4). Today we join in the great centuries-old pilgrimage. We rest awhile with the Mother of the Lord, and we pray to her: Show us Jesus. Show to us pilgrims the one who is both the way and the destination: the truth and the life.

Making a pilgrimage means setting out in a particular direction, travelling towards a destination. This gives a beauty of its own even to the journey and to the effort involved. Among the pilgrims of Jesus's genealogy there were many who forgot the goal and wanted to make themselves the goal. Again and again, though, the Lord called forth people whose longing for the goal drove them forward, people who directed their whole lives towards it. The awakening of the Christian faith, the dawning of the Church of Jesus Christ was made possible, because there were people in Israel whose hearts were searching – people who did not rest content with custom, but who looked further ahead, in search of something greater: Zechariah, Elizabeth, Simeon, Anna, Mary and Joseph, the Twelve and many others. Because their hearts were expectant, they were able to recognize in Jesus the one whom God had sent, and thus they could become the beginning of his worldwide family. The Church of the Gentiles was made possible, because both in the Mediterranean area and in those parts of Asia to which the messengers of Jesus travelled, there were expectant people who were not satisfied by what everyone around them was doing and thinking, but who were seeking the star which could show them the way towards Truth itself, towards the living God.

We too need an open and restless heart like theirs. This is what pilgrimage is all about. Today as in the past, it is not enough to be more or less like everyone else and to think like everyone else. Our lives have a deeper purpose. We need God, the God who has shown us his face and opened his heart to us: Jesus Christ. Saint John rightly says of him that only he is God and rests close to the Father's heart (cf. *Jn* 1:18); thus only he, from deep within God himself, could reveal God to us – reveal to us who we are, from where we come and where we are going. Certainly, there are many great figures in history who have had beautiful and moving experiences of God. Yet these are still human experiences, and therefore finite. Only HE is God and therefore only HE is the bridge that truly brings God and man together. So if we Christians call him the one universal Mediator of salvation, valid for everyone and, ultimately, needed by everyone, this does not mean that we despise other religions, nor are we arrogantly absolutizing our own ideas; on the contrary, it means that we are gripped by him who has touched our hearts and lavished gifts upon us, so that we, in turn, can offer gifts to others. In fact, our faith is decisively

opposed to the attitude of resignation that considers man incapable of truth – as if this were more than he could cope with. This attitude of resignation with regard to truth, I am convinced, lies at the heart of the crisis of the West, the crisis of Europe. If truth does not exist for man, then neither can he ultimately distinguish between good and evil. And then the great and wonderful discoveries of science become double-edged: they can open up significant possibilities for good, for the benefit of mankind, but also, as we see only too clearly, they can pose a terrible threat, involving the destruction of man and the world. We need truth. Yet admittedly, in the light of our history we are fearful that faith in the truth might entail intolerance. If we are gripped by this fear, which is historically well grounded, then it is time to look towards Jesus as we see him in the shrine at Mariazell. We see him here in two images: as the child in his Mother's arms, and above the high altar of the Basilica as the Crucified. These two images in the Basilica tell us this: truth prevails not through external force, but it is humble and it yields itself to man only via the inner force of its veracity. Truth proves itself in love. It is never our property, never our product, just as love can never be produced, but only received and handed on as a gift. We need this inner force of truth. As Christians we trust this force of truth. We are its witnesses. We must hand it on as a gift in the same way as we have received it, as it has given itself to us.

Celebration of Marian Vespers with Priests, Religious, Deacons and Seminarians at the Basilica of Mariazell (September 8, 2007)

We have come together in the venerable Basilica of our *Magna Mater Austriae* in Mariazell. For many generations people have come to pray here to obtain the help of the Mother of God. We too are doing the same today. We want to join Mary in praising God's immense goodness and in expressing our gratitude to the Lord for all the blessings we have received, especially the great gift of the faith. We also wish to commend to Mary our heartfelt concerns: to beg her protection for the Church, to invoke her intercession for the gift of worthy vocations for Dioceses and religious communities, to implore her assistance for families and her merciful prayers for all those longing for freedom from sin and for the grace of conversion, and, finally, to entrust to Mary's maternal care our sick and our elderly. May the great Mother of Austria and of Europe bring all of us to a profound renewal of faith and life!

At the heart of the mission of Jesus Christ and of every Christian is the proclamation of the Kingdom of God. Proclaiming the Kingdom in the name of Christ means for the Church, for priests, men and women religious, and for all the baptized, a commitment to be present in the world as his witnesses. The Kingdom of God is really God himself, who makes himself present in our midst and reigns through us. The Kingdom of God is built up when God lives in us and we bring God into the world. You do so when you testify to a "meaning" rooted in God's creative love and opposed to every kind of meaninglessness and despair. You stand alongside all those who are earnestly striving to discover this meaning, alongside all those who want to make something positive of their lives. By your prayer and intercession, you are the advocates of all who seek God, who are journeying towards God. You bear witness to a hope which, against every form of hopelessness, silent or spoken, points to the fidelity and the loving concern of God. Hence you are on the side of those who are crushed by misfortune and cannot break free of their burdens. You bear witness to that Love which gives itself for humanity and thus conquered death. You are on the side of all who have never known love, and who are no longer able to believe in life. And so you stand against all forms of injustice, hidden or apparent, and against a growing contempt for man. In this way, dear brothers and sisters, your whole life needs to be, like that of John the Baptist, a great, living witness to Jesus Christ, the Son of God incarnate. Jesus called John "a burning and shining lamp" (*Jn* 5:35). You too must be such lamps! Let your light shine in our society, in political and economic life, in culture and research. Even if it is only a flicker amid so many deceptive lights, it nonetheless draws its power and splendour from the great Morning Star, the Risen Christ, whose light shines brilliantly – wants to shine brilliantly through us – and will never fade.

Holy Mass in St. Stephen's Cathedral in Vienna (September 9, 2007)

"*Sine dominico non possumus!*" Without the gift of the Lord, without the Lord's day, we cannot live: That was the answer given in the year 304 by Christians from Abitene in present-day Tunisia, when they were caught celebrating the forbidden Sunday Eucharist and brought before the judge. They were asked why they were celebrating the Christian Sunday Eucharist, even though they knew it was a capital offence. "*Sine dominico non possumus*": in the word *dominicum/dominico* two meanings are inextricably intertwined, and we must once more learn to recognize their unity. First of all there is the gift of the Lord – this gift is the Lord himself: the Risen one, whom the Christians simply need to have close and accessible to them, if they are to be themselves. Yet this accessibility is not merely something spiritual, inward and subjective: the encounter with the Lord is inscribed in time on a specific day. And so it is inscribed in our everyday, corporal and communal existence, in temporality. It gives a focus, an inner order to our time and thus to the whole of our lives. For these Christians, the Sunday Eucharist was not a commandment, but an inner necessity. Without him who sustains our lives, life itself is empty. To do without or to betray this focus would deprive life of its very foundation, would take away its inner dignity and beauty.

Does this attitude of the Christians of that time apply also to us who are Christians today? Yes, it does, we too need a relationship that sustains us, that gives direction and content to our lives. We too need access to the Risen one, who sustains us through and beyond death. We need this encounter which brings us together, which gives us space for freedom, which lets us see beyond the bustle of everyday life to God's creative love, from which we come and towards which we are travelling.

Of course, if we listen to today's Gospel, if we listen to what the Lord is saying to us, it frightens us: "Whoever of you does not renounce all that he has and all links with his family cannot be my disciple." We would like to object: What are you saying, Lord? Isn't the family just what the world needs? Doesn't it need the love of father and mother, the love between parents and children, between husband and wife? Don't we need love for life, the joy of life? And don't we also need people who invest in the good things of this world and build up the earth we have received, so that everyone can share in its gifts? Isn't the development of the earth and its goods another charge laid upon us? If we listen to the Lord more closely, and above all if we listen to him in the context of everything he is saying to us, then we understand that Jesus does not demand the same from everyone. Each person has a specific task, to each is assigned a particular way of discipleship. In today's Gospel, Jesus is speaking directly of the specific vocation of the Twelve, a vocation not shared by the many who accompanied Jesus on his journey to Jerusalem. The Twelve must first of all overcome the scandal of the Cross, and then they must be prepared truly to leave everything behind; they must be prepared to assume the seemingly absurd task of travelling to the ends of the earth and, with their minimal education, proclaiming the Gospel of Jesus Christ to a world filled with claims to erudition and with real or apparent education – and naturally also to the poor and the simple. They must themselves be prepared to suffer martyrdom in the course of their journey into the vast world, and thus to bear witness to the Gospel of the Crucified and Risen Lord. If Jesus's words on this journey to Jerusalem, on which a great crowd accompanies him, are addressed in the first instance to the Twelve, his call naturally extends beyond the historical moment into all subsequent centuries. He calls people of all times to count exclusively on him, to leave everything else behind, so as to be totally available for him, and hence totally available for others: to create oases of selfless love in a world where so often only power and wealth seem to count for anything. Let us thank the Lord for giving us men and women in every century who have left all else behind for his sake, and have thus become radiant signs of his love. We need only think of people like Benedict and Scholastica, Francis and Clare of Assisi, Elizabeth of Hungary and Hedwig of Silesia, Ignatius of Loyola, Teresa of Avila, and in our own day, Mother Teresa and Padre Pio. With their whole lives, these people have become a living interpretation of Jesus's teaching, which through their lives becomes close and intelligible to us. Let us ask the Lord to grant to people in our own day the courage to leave everything behind and so to be available to everyone.

Yet if we now turn once more to the Gospel, we realize that the Lord is not speaking merely of a few individuals and their specific task; the essence of what he says applies to everyone. The heart of the matter he expresses elsewhere in these words: "For whoever would save his life will lose it; and whoever loses his life for my sake, he will save it. For what does it profit a man if he gains the whole world and loses or forfeits himself?" (*Lk* 9:24f.). Whoever wants to save his life just for himself will lose it. Only by giving ourselves do we receive our life. In other words: only the one who loves discovers life. And love always demands going out of oneself, it always demands leaving oneself. Anyone who looks just to himself, who wants the other only for himself, will lose both himself and the other. Without this profound losing of oneself, there is no life. The restless craving for life, so widespread among people today, leads to the barrenness of a lost life. "Whoever loses his life for my sake ... ", says the Lord: a radical letting-go of our self is only possible if in the process we end up, not by falling into the void, but into the hands of Love eternal. Only the love of God, who loses himself for us and gives himself to us, makes it possible for us also to become free, to let go, and so truly to find life. This is the heart of what the Lord wants to say to us in the seemingly hard words of this Sunday's Gospel. With his teaching he gives us the certainty that we can build on his love, the love of the incarnate God. Recognition of this is the wisdom of which today's reading speaks to us. Once again, we find that all the world's learning profits us nothing unless we learn to live, unless we discover what truly matters in life…

In this Sunday's Opening Prayer we call to mind firstly that through his Son God has redeemed us and made us his beloved children. Then we ask him to look down with loving-kindness upon all who believe in Christ and to give us true freedom and eternal life. We ask God to look down with loving-kindness. We ourselves need this look of loving-kindness not only on Sunday but beyond, reaching into our everyday lives. As we ask, we know that this loving gaze has already been granted to us. What is more, we know that God has adopted us as his children, he has truly welcomed us into communion with himself. To be someone's child means, as the early Church knew, to be a free person, not a slave but a member of the family. And it means being an heir. If we belong to God, who is the power above all powers, then we are fearless and free. And then we are heirs. The inheritance he has bequeathed to us is himself, his love. Yes, Lord, may this inheritance enter deep within our souls so that we come to know the joy of being redeemed. Amen.

Visit to Heiligenkreuz Abbey (September 9, 2007)

On my pilgrimage to the *Magna Mater Austriae*, I am pleased to visit this Abbey of Heiligenkreuz, which is not only an important stop on the *Via Sacra* leading to Mariazell, but the oldest continuously active Cistercian monastery in the world. I wished to come to this place so rich in history in order to draw attention to the fundamental directive of Saint Benedict, according to whose *Rule* Cistercians also live. Quite simply, Benedict insisted that "nothing be put before the divine Office".[1]

For this reason, in a monastery of Benedictine spirit, the praise of God, which the monks sing as a solemn choral prayer, always has priority. Monks are certainly – thank God! – not the only people who pray; others also pray: children, the young and the old, men and women, the married and the single – all Christians pray, or at least, they should!

In the life of monks, however, prayer takes on a particular importance: it is the heart of their calling. Their vocation is to be men of prayer. In the patristic period the monastic life was likened to the life of the angels. It was considered the essential mark of the angels that they are worshippers. Their very life is worship. This should hold true also for monks. Monks pray first and foremost not for any specific intention, but simply because God is worthy of being praised. "*Confitemini Domino, quoniam bonus!* – Praise the Lord, for he is good, for his mercy is eternal!": so we are urged by a

number of Psalms (e.g. *Ps* 106:1). Such prayer for its own sake, intended as pure divine service, is rightly called *officium*. It is "service" par excellence, the "sacred service" of monks. It is offered to the triune God who, above all else, is worthy "to receive glory, honour and power" (*Rev* 4:11), because he wondrously created the world and even more wondrously renewed it.

Meeting with representatives of volonteer organizations at the Wiener Konzerthaus (September 9, 2007)

I have looked forward with particular joy to this meeting, which takes place near the end of my visit to Austria. And naturally there is the further joy of having heard not only a marvellous piece by Mozart, but also, unexpectedly, the "Vienna Choir Boys". Heartfelt thanks! It is good to meet people who are trying to give a face to the Gospel message in our communities; to see people, young and old, who concretely express in Church and society the love which we, as Christians, must be overwhelmed: the love of God which enables us to see others as our neighbours, our brothers and sisters! I am filled with gratitude and admiration when I think of the generous volunteer work done in this country by so many people of all ages. To all of you, and to those who hold honorary and unremunerated positions in Austria, I would like today to express my special appreciation. I thank you, Mr. President, you, Archbishop Kothgasser, and, above all, you, the young people representing volunteer workers in Austria, for your beautiful and profound words of greeting.

Farewell ceremony at the international airport of Vienna/Schwechat (September 9, 2007)

Once again I was able to experience Mariazell as a particularly grace-filled place, a place which in these days welcomed all of us and gave us inner strength for the road ahead. The throngs of people who joined in our celebration in the Basilica, in Mariazell itself and throughout Austria should inspire us, with Mary, to look to Christ and, as persons whom God looks upon with love, and to face with confidence the path to the future. It was nice that the wind and the bad weather could not stop us, but, in the end, added even more to our joy.

At the very beginning of my pilgrimage, our common prayer in the Square "Am Hof" brought us together in a way which transcended national borders and directly showed us Austria's open hospitality, which is one of this country's finest qualities. CA

United States of America, April 15-21, 2008

Pope Benedict XVI visited Washington, DC, and New York from Apr. 15-21, on the eighth foreign apostolic journey of his pontificate. The visit marked the occasion of the 200th anniversary of the declaration of Baltimore as the first metropolitan see of the United States and the creation of the suffragan sees Bardstown (KY), Boston, New York, and Philadelphia. The pontiff also visited the United Nations. (See above for full coverage.) CA

Sydney, Australia, World Youth Day, July 12-21, 2008

Pope Benedict XVI visited Sydney, Australia from July 12-21 on the occasion of the 23rd World Youth Day. The apostolic journey marked the ninth of his pontificate.

The trip was marked by the Holy Father's memorable meetings with young people form all over the world, including a harbor sail in Sydney and a Mass at Randwick Racecourse in Sydney on July 20 that drew a crowd estimated at 500,000. The event at Randwick was the largest gathering in the history of Australia.

The papal visit marked as well as an opportunity for the Catholic Church in Australia to embark on genuine renewal after years of blows to morale as a result of the secularization of Australian society and a severe sex abuse scandal. Much like the Holy Father's visit to the United States, Benedict's time in Australia was a much needed time for healing and revitalization for the Catholic community.

In his homilies, the pope stressed to young people the urgency of allowing the Holy Spirit to direct their lives in the faith: "We need to understand the person of the Holy Spirit and his vivifying presence in our lives. This is not easy to comprehend. Indeed the variety of images found in scripture referring to the Spirit — wind, fire, breath — indicate our struggle to articulate an understanding of him. Yet we do know that it is the Holy Spirit who, though silent and unseen, gives direction and definition to our witness to Jesus Christ."

The pontiff also took the opportunity to address directly the sex abuse scandal that has troubled the Catholic Church in Australia for the last years. In his Mass at St. Mary's Cathedral in Sydney with the Bishops of Australia, Pope Benedict took the opportunity to speak to the scandal. He declared: "Here I would like to pause to acknowledge the shame which we have all felt as a result of the sexual abuse of minors by some clergy and religious in this country. Indeed, I am deeply sorry for the pain and suffering the victims have endured, and I assure them that, as their pastor, I too share in their suffering. These misdeeds, which constitute so grave a betrayal of trust, deserve unequivocal condemnation. They have caused great pain and have damaged the Church's witness."

Program

Welcoming ceremony at the Government House of Sydney (July 17, 2008)

Welcoming celebration by the young people at Barangaroo East Darling Harbor of Sydney (July 17, 2008)

Ecumenical Meeting in the Crypt of St. Mary's Cathedral in Sydney (July 18, 2008)

Meeting with representatives of other religions in the Chapter Hall of St. Mary's Cathedral in Sydney (July 18, 2008)

Prayer at the beginning of the Way of the Cross in the square in front of St. Mary's Cathedral in Sydney (July 18, 2008)

Meeting with a group of handicapped young people at the Convalescent Unit of the University of Notre Dame in the Church of the Sacred Heart in Sydney (July 18, 2008)

Holy Mass with the Australian Bishops, seminarians and novices (with the Consecration of the new altar) at St. Mary's Cathedral in Sydney (July 19, 2008)

Vigil with the young people at Randwick Racecourse in Sydney (July 19, 2008)

Holy Mass for the 23rd World Youth Day at Randwick Racecourse in Sydney (July 20, 2008)

Recitation of the *Angelus Domini* at Randwick Racecourse in Sydney (July 20, 2008)

Meeting with benefactors and organizers of the 23rd World Youth Day at the Reception Hall of the Cathedral House and in the Chapter Hall of St. Mary's Cathedral in Sydney (July 20, 2008)

Greeting to volunteer workers for the 23rd World Youth Day in the Domain of Sydney (July 21, 2008)

Farewell ceremony at the International Airport of Sydney (July 21, 2008)

Excerpts from Addresses and Homilies

(Complete texts of papal addresses, remarks and homilies can be found at www.vatican.va.)

Welcoming ceremony at the Government House of Sydney (July 17, 2008)

Some might ask what motivates thousands of young people to undertake what is for many a long and demanding journey in order to participate in an event of this kind. Ever since the first World Youth Day in 1986, it has been evident that vast numbers of young people appreciate the opportunity to come together to deepen their faith in Christ and to share with one another a joyful experience of communion in his Church. They long to hear the word of God, and to learn more about their Christian faith. They are eager to take part in an event which brings into focus the high ideals that inspire them, and they return home filled with hope and renewed in their resolve to contribute to the building of a better world. For me it is a joy to be with them, to pray with them and to celebrate the Eucharist with them. World Youth Day fills me with confidence for the future of the Church and the future of our world. …Dear Australian friends, once again I thank you for your generous welcome and I look forward to spending these days with you and with the young people of the world. May God bless all who are present, all the pilgrims and all who live in this land. And may he always bless and protect the Commonwealth of Australia.

Welcoming celebration by the young people at Barangaroo East Darling Harbor of Sydney (July 17, 2008)

What a delight it is to greet you here at Barangaroo, on the shores of the magnificent Sydney harbor, with its famous bridge and Opera House. Many of you are local, from the outback or the dynamic multicultural communities of Australian cities. Others of you have come from the scattered islands of Oceania, and others still from Asia, the Middle East, Africa and the Americas. Some of you, indeed, have come from as far as I have, Europe! Wherever we are born, we are here at last in Sydney. And together we stand in our world as God's family, disciples of Christ, empowered by his Spirit to be witnesses of his love and truth for everyone!

I wish firstly to thank the Aboriginal Elders who welcomed me prior to my boarding the boat at Rose Bay. I am deeply moved to stand on your land, knowing the suffering and injustices it has borne, but aware too of the healing and hope that are now at work, rightly bringing pride to all Australian citizens. To the young indigenous - Aboriginal and Torres Strait Islanders - and the Tokelauans, I express my thanks for your stirring welcome. Through you, I send heartfelt greetings to your peoples…

This evening I wish therefore to recall briefly something of our understanding of Baptism before tomorrow considering the Holy Spirit. On the day of your Baptism, God drew you into his holiness (cf. 2 Pet 1:4). You were adopted as a son or daughter of the Father. You were incorporated into Christ.

You were made a dwelling place of his Spirit (cf. 1 Cor 6:19). Indeed, towards the conclusion of your Baptism, the priest turned to your parents and those gathered and, calling you by your name, said: "you have become a new creation" (*Rite of Baptism*, 99).

Dear friends, in your homes, schools and universities, in your places of work and recreation, remember that you are a new creation! As Christians you stand in this world knowing that God has a human face - Jesus Christ - the "way" who satisfies all human yearning, and the "life" to which we are called to bear witness, walking always in his light (cf. ibid., 100).

Ecumenical Meeting in the Crypt of St. Mary's Cathedral in Sydney (July 18, 2008)

This year we celebrate the two thousandth anniversary of the birth of St. Paul, a tireless worker for unity in the early Church. In the scripture passage we have just heard, Paul reminds us of the tremendous grace we have received in becoming members of Christ's body through baptism. This sacrament, the entryway to the Church and the "bond of unity" for everyone reborn through it (cf. *Unitatis Redintegratio*, 22), is accordingly the point of departure for the entire ecumenical movement. Yet it is not the final destination. The road of ecumenism ultimately points towards a common celebration of the Eucharist (cf. *Ut Unum Sint*, 23-24; 45), which Christ entrusted to his Apostles as the sacrament of the Church's unity *par excellence*. Although there are still obstacles to be overcome, we can be sure that a common Eucharist one day would only strengthen our resolve to love and serve one another in imitation of our Lord: for Jesus' commandment to "do this in memory of me" (Lk 22:19) is intrinsically ordered to his admonition to "wash one another's feet" (Jn 13:14). For this reason, a candid dialogue concerning the place of the Eucharist — stimulated by a renewed and attentive study of scripture, patristic writings, and documents from across the two millennia of Christian history (cf. *Ut Unum Sint*, 69-70) — will undoubtedly help to advance the ecumenical movement and unify our witness to the world...

Dear friends, your presence fills me with the ardent hope that as we pursue together the path to full unity, we will have the courage to give common witness to Christ. Paul speaks of the importance of the prophets in the early Church; we too have received a prophetic calling through our baptism. I am confident that the Spirit will open our eyes to see the gifts of others, our hearts to receive his power, and our minds to perceive the light of Christ's truth. I express heartfelt thanks to all of you for the time, scholarship and talent which you have invested for the sake of the "one body and one spirit" (Eph 4:4; cf. 1 Cor 12:13) which the Lord willed for his people and for which he gave his very life. All glory and power be to him for ever and ever. Amen!

Meeting with representatives of other religions in the Chapter Hall of St. Mary's Cathedral in Sydney (July 18, 2008)

A harmonious relationship between religion and public life is all the more important at a time when some people have come to consider religion as a cause of division rather than a force for unity. In a world threatened by sinister and indiscriminate forms of violence, the unified voice of religious people urges nations and communities to resolve conflicts through peaceful means and with full regard for human dignity. One of the many ways religion stands at the service of mankind is by offering a vision of the human person that highlights our innate aspiration to live generously, forging bonds of friendship with our neighbors. At their core, human relations cannot be defined in terms of power, domination and self-interest. Rather, they reflect and perfect man's natural inclination to live in communion and accord with others.

The religious sense planted within the human heart opens men and women to God and leads them to discover that personal fulfillment does not consist in the selfish gratification of ephemeral desires. Rather, it leads us to meet the needs of others and to search for concrete ways to contribute to the common good. Religions have a special role in this regard, for they teach people that authentic service requires sacrifice and self-discipline, which in turn must be cultivated through self-denial, temperance and a moderate use of the world's goods. In this way, men and women are led to regard the environment as a marvel to be pondered and respected rather than a commodity for mere consumption. It is incumbent upon religious people to demonstrate that it is possible to find joy in living simply and modestly, generously sharing one's surplus with those suffering from want.

Friends, these values, I am sure you will agree, are particularly important to the adequate formation of young people, who are so often tempted to view life itself as a commodity. They also have an aptitude for self-mastery: indeed, in sports, the creative arts, and in academic studies, they readily welcome it as a challenge. Is it not true that when presented with high ideals, many young people are attracted to asceticism and the practice of moral virtue through self-respect and a concern for others? They delight in contemplating the gift of creation and are intrigued by the mystery of the transcendent. In this regard, both faith schools and State schools could do even more to nurture the spiritual dimension of every young person. In Australia, as elsewhere, religion has been a motivating factor in the foundation of many educational institutions, and rightly it continues to occupy a place in school curricula today. The theme of education frequently emerges from the deliberations of the Interfaith Cooperation for Peace and Harmony, and I warmly encourage those participating in this initiative to continue the conversation about the values that integrate the intellectual, human and religious dimensions of a sound education.

The world's religions draw constant attention to the wonder of human existence. Who can help but marvel at the power of the mind to grasp the secrets of nature through scientific discovery? Who is not stirred by the possibility of forming a vision for the future? Who is not impressed by the power of the human spirit to set goals and to develop ways of achieving them? Men and women are endowed with the ability not only to imagine how things might be better, but to invest their energies to make them better. We are conscious of our unique relationship to the natural realm. If, then, we believe that we are not subject to the laws of the material universe in the same way as the rest of creation, should we not make goodness, compassion, freedom, solidarity, and respect for every individual an essential part of our vision for a more humane future?

Yet religion, by reminding us of human finitude and weakness, also enjoins us not to place our ultimate hope in this passing world. Man is "like a breath, his days are like a passing shadow" (Ps 144:4). All of us have experienced the disappointment of falling short of the good we wish to accomplish and the difficulty of making the right choice in complex situations.

The Church shares these observations with other religions. Motivated by charity, she approaches dialogue believing that the true source of freedom is found in the person of Jesus of

Nazareth. Christians believe it is he who fully discloses the human potential for virtue and goodness, and he who liberates us from sin and darkness. The universality of human experience, which transcends all geographical boundaries and cultural limitations, makes it possible for followers of religions to engage in dialogue so as to grapple with the mystery of life's joys and sufferings. In this regard, the Church eagerly seeks opportunities to listen to the spiritual experience of other religions. We could say that all religions aim to penetrate the profound meaning of human existence by linking it to an origin or principle outside itself. Religions offer an attempt to understand the cosmos as coming from and returning to this origin or principle. Christians believe that God has revealed this origin and principle in Jesus, whom the Bible refers to as the "Alpha and Omega" (cf. Rv 1:8; 22:1).

My dear friends, I have come to Australia as an ambassador of peace. For this reason, I feel blessed to meet you who likewise share this yearning and the desire to help the world attain it. Our quest for peace goes hand in hand with our search for meaning, for it is in discovering the truth that we find the sure road to peace (cf. *Message for World Day of Peace*, 2006). Our effort to bring about reconciliation between peoples springs from, and is directed to, that truth which gives purpose to life. Religion offers peace, but more importantly, it arouses within the human spirit a thirst for truth and a hunger for virtue. May we encourage everyone — especially the young — to marvel at the beauty of life, to seek its ultimate meaning, and to strive to realize its sublime potential!

With these sentiments of respect and encouragement, I commend you to the providence of Almighty God, and I assure you of my prayers for you and your loved ones, the members of your communities, and all the citizens of Australia.

Meeting with a group of handicapped young people at the Convalescent Unit of the University of Notre Dame in the Church of the Sacred Heart in Sydney (July 18, 2008)

The text is available at: www.vatican.va/holy_father/benedict_xvi/speeches/2008/july/documents/hf_ben-xvi_spe_20080718_darlinghurst_en.html.

Holy Mass with the Australian Bishops, seminarians and novices (with the Consecration of the new altar) at St. Mary's Cathedral in Sydney (July 19, 2008)

In this noble cathedral I rejoice to greet my brother Bishops and priests, and the deacons, religious and laity of the Archdiocese of Sydney. In a very special way, my greeting goes to the seminarians and young religious who are present among us. Like the young Israelites in today's first reading, they are a sign of hope and renewal for God's people; and, like those young Israelites, they will have the task of building up the Lord's house in the coming generation. As we admire this magnificent edifice, how can we not think of all those ranks of priests, religious and faithful laity who, each in his or her own way, contributed to the building up of the Church in Australia? Our thoughts turn in particular to those settler families to whom Father Jeremiah O'Flynn entrusted the Blessed Sacrament at his departure, a "small flock" which cherished and preserved that precious treasure, passing it on to the succeeding generations who raised this great tabernacle to the glory of God. Let us rejoice in their fidelity and perseverance, and dedicate ourselves to carrying on their labors

for the spread of the Gospel, the conversion of hearts and the growth of the Church in holiness, unity and charity!

We are about to celebrate the dedication of the new altar of this venerable cathedral. As its sculpted frontal powerfully reminds us, every altar is a symbol of Jesus Christ, present in the midst of his Church as priest, altar and victim (cf. *Preface of Easter* V). Crucified, buried and raised from the dead, given life in the Spirit and seated at the right hand of the Father, Christ has become our great high priest, eternally making intercession for us. In the Church's liturgy, and above all in the sacrifice of the Mass consummated on the altars of the world, he invites us, the members of his mystical Body, to share in his self-oblation. He calls us, as the priestly people of the new and eternal covenant, to offer, in union with him, our own daily sacrifices for the salvation of the world.

In today's liturgy the Church reminds us that, like this altar, we too have been consecrated, set "apart" for the service of God and the building up of his Kingdom. All too often, however, we find ourselves immersed in a world that would set God "aside." In the name of human freedom and autonomy, God's name is passed over in silence, religion is reduced to private devotion, and faith is shunned in the public square. At times this mentality, so completely at odds with the core of the Gospel, can even cloud our own understanding of the Church and her mission. We too can be tempted to make the life of faith a matter of mere sentiment, thus blunting its power to inspire a consistent vision of the world and a rigorous dialogue with the many other visions competing for the minds and hearts of our contemporaries.

Yet history, including the history of our own time, shows that the question of God will never be silenced, and that indifference to the religious dimension of human existence ultimately diminishes and betrays man himself. Is that not the message which is proclaimed by the magnificent architecture of this cathedral? Is that not the mystery of faith which will be proclaimed from this altar at every celebration of the Eucharist? Faith teaches us that in Jesus Christ, the incarnate Word, we come to understand the grandeur of our own humanity, the mystery of our life on this earth, and the sublime destiny which awaits us in heaven (cf. *Gaudium et Spes*, 24). Faith teaches us that we are God's creatures, made in his image and likeness, endowed with an inviolable dignity, and called to eternal life. Wherever man is diminished, the world around us is also diminished; it loses its ultimate meaning and strays from its goal. What emerges is a culture, not of life, but of death. How could this be considered "progress"? It is a backward step, a form of regression which ultimately dries up the very sources of life for individuals and all of society.

We know that in the end — as Saint Ignatius of Loyola saw so clearly — the only real "standard" against which all human reality can be measured is the Cross and its message of an unmerited love which triumphs over evil, sin and death, creating new life and unfading joy. The Cross reveals that we find ourselves only by giving our lives away, receiving God's love as an unmerited gift and working to draw all men and women into the beauty of that love and the light of the truth which alone brings salvation to the world.

It is in this truth — this mystery of faith — that we have been "consecrated" (cf. Jn 17:17-19), and it is in this truth that we are called to grow, with the help of God's grace, in daily fidelity to his word, within the life-giving communion of the Church. Yet how difficult is this path of consecration! It demands continual "conversion," a sacrificial death to self which is the condition for belonging fully to God, a change of mind and heart which brings true freedom and a new breadth of vision. Today's liturgy offers an eloquent symbol of that progressive spiritual transformation to which each of us is called. From the sprinkling of water, the proclamation of God's word and the invocation of all the saints, to the prayer of consecration, the anointing and washing of the altar, it's being clothed in white and apparelled in light — all these rites invite us to re-live our own consecration in Baptism. They invite us to reject sin and its false allure, and to drink ever more deeply from the life-giving springs of God's grace.

Dear friends, may this celebration, in the presence of the Successor of Peter, be a moment of rededication and renewal for the whole Church in Australia! Here I would like to pause to acknowledge the shame which we have all felt as a result of the sexual abuse of minors by some clergy and religious in this country. Indeed, I am deeply sorry for the pain and suffering the victims have endured, and I assure them that, as their pastor, I too share in their suffering. These misdeeds, which constitute so grave a betrayal of trust, deserve unequivocal condemnation. They have caused great pain and have damaged the Church's witness. I ask all of you to support and assist your bishops, and to work together with them in combating this evil. Victims should receive compassion and care, and those responsible for these evils must be brought to justice. It is an urgent priority to promote a safer and more wholesome environment, especially for young people. In these days marked by the celebration of World Youth Day, we are reminded of how precious a treasure has been entrusted to us in our young people, and how great a part of the Church's mission in this country has been dedicated to their education and care. As the Church in Australia continues, in the spirit of the Gospel, to address effectively this serious pastoral challenge, I join you in praying that this time of purification will bring about healing, reconciliation and ever greater fidelity to the moral demands of the Gospel.

I wish now to turn to the seminarians and young religious in our midst, with a special word of affection and encouragement. Dear friends: with great generosity you have set out on a particular path of consecration, grounded in your baptism and undertaken in response to the Lord's personal call. You have committed yourselves, in different ways, to accepting Christ's invitation to follow him, to leave all behind, and to devote your lives to the pursuit of holiness and the service of his people.

In today's Gospel, the Lord calls us to "believe in the light" (Jn 12:36). These words have a special meaning for you, dear young seminarians and religious. They are a summons to trust in the truth of God's word and to hope firmly in his promises. They invite us to see, with the eyes of faith, the infallible working of his grace all around us, even in those dark times when all our efforts seem to be in vain. Let this altar, with its powerful image of Christ the Suffering Servant, be a constant inspiration to you. Certainly there are times when every faithful disciple will feel the heat and the burden of the day (cf. Mt 20:12), and the struggle of bearing prophetic witness before a world which can appear deaf to the demands of God's word. Do not be afraid! Believe in the light! Take to heart the truth which we have heard in today's second reading: "Jesus Christ is the same, yesterday, today and for ever" (Heb 13:8). The light of Easter continues to dispel the darkness!

The Lord also calls us to walk in the light (cf. Jn 12:35). Each of you has embarked on the greatest and the most glorious of all struggles, to be consecrated in truth, to grow in virtue, to achieve harmony between your thoughts and ideals, and your words and actions. Enter sincerely and deeply into the discipline and spirit of your programs of formation. Walk in Christ's light daily through fidelity to personal and liturgical prayer, nourished by meditation on the inspired word of God. The Fathers of the Church loved to see the Scriptures as a spiritual Eden, a garden where we can walk freely with God, admiring the beauty and harmony of his saving plan as it bears fruit in our own lives, in the life of the Church and in all of history. Let prayer, then, and meditation on God's word, be the lamp which illumines, purifies and guides your steps along the path which the Lord has marked out for you. Make the daily celebration of the Eucharist the centre of your life. At each Mass, when the Lord's Body and Blood are lifted up at the end of the Eucharistic Prayer, lift up your own hearts and lives, through Christ, with him and in him, in the unity of the Holy Spirit, as a loving sacrifice to God our Father.

In this way, dear young seminarians and religious, you yourselves will become living altars, where Christ's sacrificial love is made present as an inspiration and a source of spiritual nourishment to everyone you meet. By embracing the Lord's call to follow him in chastity, poverty and obedience, you have begun a journey of radical discipleship which will make you "signs of contradiction" (cf. Lk 2:34) to many of your contemporaries. Model your lives daily on the Lord's own loving self-oblation in obedience to the will of the Father. You will then discover the freedom and joy which can draw others to the Love which lies beyond all other loves as their source and their ultimate fulfillment. Never forget that celibacy for the sake of the Kingdom means embracing a life completely devoted to love, a love that enables you to commit yourselves fully to God's service and to be totally present to your brothers and sisters, especially those in need. The greatest treasures that you share with other young people — your idealism, your generosity, your time and energy — these are the very sacrifices which you are placing upon the Lord's altar. May you always cherish this beautiful charism which God has given you for his glory and the building up of the Church!

Dear friends, let me conclude these reflections by drawing your attention to the great stained glass window in the chancel of this cathedral. There Our Lady, Queen of Heaven, is represented enthroned in majesty beside her divine Son. The artist has represented Mary, as the new Eve, offering an apple to Christ, the new Adam. This gesture symbolizes her reversal of our first parents' disobedience, the rich fruit which God's grace bore in her own life, and the first fruits of that redeemed and glorified humanity which she has preceded into the glory of heaven. Let us ask Mary, Help of Christians, to sustain the Church in Australia in fidelity to that grace by which the Crucified Lord even now "draws to himself" all creation and every human heart (cf. Jn 12:32). May the power of his Holy Spirit consecrate the faithful of this land in truth, and bring forth abundant fruits of holiness and justice for the redemption of the world. May it guide all humanity into the fullness of life around that Altar, where, in the glory of the heavenly liturgy, we are called to sing God's praises for ever. Amen.

Vigil with the young people at Randwick Racecourse in Sydney (July 19, 2008)

The text is available at:
www.vatican.va/holy_father/benedict_xvi/speeches/2008/july/documents/hf_ben-xvi_spe_20080719_vigil_en.html.

Holy Mass for the 23rd World Youth Day at Randwick Racecourse in Sydney (July 20, 2008)

"You will receive power when the Holy Spirit comes upon you" (*Acts* 1:8). We have seen this promise fulfilled! On the day of Pentecost, as we heard in the first reading, the Risen Lord, seated at the right hand of the Father, sent the Spirit upon the disciples gathered in the Upper Room. In the power of that Spirit, Peter and the Apostles went forth to preach the Gospel to the ends of the earth. In every age, and in every language, the Church throughout the world continues to proclaim the marvels of God and to call all nations and peoples to faith, hope and new life in Christ.

In these days I too have come, as the Successor of Saint Peter, to this magnificent land of Australia. I have come to confirm you, my young brothers and sisters, in your faith and to encourage you to open your hearts to the power of Christ's Spirit and the richness of his gifts. I pray that this great assembly, which unites young people "from every nation under heaven" (cf. Acts 2:5), will be a new Upper Room. May the fire of God's love descend to fill your hearts, unite you ever more fully to the Lord and his Church, and send you forth, a new generation of apostles, to bring the world to Christ!

"You will receive power when the Holy Spirit comes upon you." These words of the Risen Lord have a special meaning for those young people who will be confirmed, sealed with the gift of the Holy Spirit, at today's Mass. But they are also addressed to each of us — to all those who have received the Spirit's gift of reconciliation and new life at Baptism, who have welcomed him into their hearts as their helper and guide at Confirmation, and who daily grow in his gifts of grace through the Holy Eucharist. At each Mass, in fact, the Holy Spirit descends anew, invoked by the solemn prayer of the Church, not only to transform our gifts of bread and wine into the Lord's body and blood, but also to transform our lives, to make us, in his power, "one body, one spirit in Christ."

But what is this "power" of the Holy Spirit? It is the power of God's life! It is the power of the same Spirit who hovered over the waters at the dawn of creation and who, in the fullness of time, raised Jesus from the dead. It is the power which points us, and our world, towards the coming of the Kingdom of God. In today's Gospel, Jesus proclaims that a new age has begun, in which the Holy Spirit will be poured out upon all humanity (cf. Lk 4:21). He himself, conceived by the Holy Spirit and born of the Virgin May, came among us to bring us that Spirit. As the source of our new life in Christ, the Holy Spirit is also, in a very real way, the soul of the Church, the love which binds us to the Lord and one another, and the light which opens our eyes to see all around us the wonders of God's grace.

Here in Australia, this "great south land of the Holy Spirit," all of us have had an unforgettable experience of the Spirit's presence and power in the beauty of nature. Our eyes have been opened to see the world around us as it truly is: "charged," as the poet says, "with the grandeur of God," filled with the glory of his creative love. Here too, in this great assembly of young Christians from all over the world, we have had a vivid experience of the Spirit's presence and power in the life of the Church. We have seen the Church for what she truly is: the Body of Christ, a living community of love, embracing people of every race, nation and tongue, of every time and place, in the unity born of our faith in the Risen Lord.

The power of the Spirit never ceases to fill the Church with life! Through the grace of the Church's sacraments, that power also flows deep within us, like an underground river which nourishes our spirit and draws us ever nearer to the source of our true life, which is Christ. Saint Ignatius of Antioch, who died a martyr in Rome at the beginning of the second century, has left us a splendid description of the Spirit's power dwelling within us. He spoke of the Spirit as a fountain of living water springing up within his heart and whispering: "Come, come to the Father" (cf. *Ad Rom.*, 6:1-9).

Yet this power, the grace of the Spirit, is not something we can merit or achieve, but only receive as pure gift. God's love can only unleash its power when it is allowed to change us from within. We have to let it break through the hard crust of our indifference, our spiritual weariness, our blind conformity to the spirit of this age. Only then can we let it ignite our imagination and shape our deepest desires. That is why prayer is so important: daily prayer, private prayer in the quiet of our hearts and before the Blessed Sacrament, and liturgical prayer in the heart of the Church. Prayer is pure receptivity to God's grace, love in action, communion with the Spirit who dwells within us, leading us, through Jesus, in the Church, to our heavenly Father. In the power of his Spirit, Jesus is always present in our hearts, quietly waiting for us to be still with him, to hear his voice, to abide in his love, and to receive "power from on high," enabling us to be salt and light for our world.

At his Ascension, the Risen Lord told his disciples: "You will be my witnesses … to the ends of the earth" (*Acts* 1:8). Here, in Australia, let us thank the Lord for the gift of faith, which has come down to us like a treasure passed on from generation to generation in the communion of the Church. Here, in Oceania, let us give thanks in a special way for all those heroic missionaries, dedicated priests and religious, Christian parents and grandparents, teachers and catechists who built up the Church in these lands — witnesses like Blessed Mary MacKillop, Saint Peter Chanel, Blessed Peter To Rot, and so many others! The power of the Spirit, revealed in their lives, is still at work in the good they left behind, in the society which they shaped and which is being handed on to you.

Dear young people, let me now ask you a question. What will *you* leave to the next generation? Are you building your lives on firm foundations, building something that will endure? Are you living your lives in a way that opens up space for the Spirit in the midst of a world that wants to forget God, or even rejects him in the name of a falsely-conceived freedom? How are you using the gifts you have been given, the "power" which the Holy Spirit is even now prepared to release within you? What legacy will you leave to young people yet to come? What difference will you make?

The power of the Holy Spirit does not only enlighten and console us. It also points us to the future, to the coming of God's Kingdom. What a magnificent vision of a humanity redeemed and renewed we see in the new age promised by today's Gospel! Saint Luke tells us that Jesus Christ is the fulfillment of all God's promises, the Messiah who fully possesses the Holy Spirit in order to bestow that gift upon all mankind. The outpouring of Christ's Spirit upon humanity is a pledge of hope and deliverance from everything that impoverishes us. It gives the blind new sight; it sets the downtrodden free, and it creates unity in and through diversity (cf. Lk 4:18-19; Is 61:1-2). This power can create a new world: it can "renew the face of the earth" (cf. Ps 104:30)!

Empowered by the Spirit, and drawing upon faith's rich vision, a new generation of Christians is being called to help build a world in which God's gift of life is welcomed, respected and cherished — not rejected, feared as a threat and destroyed. A new age in which love is not greedy or self-seeking, but pure, faithful and genuinely free, open to others, respectful of their dignity, seeking their good, radiating joy and beauty. A new age in which hope liberates us from the shallowness, apathy and self-absorption which deaden our souls and poison our relationships. Dear young friends, the Lord is asking you to be prophets of this new age, messengers of his love, drawing people to the Father and building a future of hope for all humanity.

The world needs this renewal! In so many of our societies, side by side with material prosperity, a spiritual desert is spreading: an interior emptiness, an unnamed fear, a quiet sense of despair. How many of our contemporaries have built broken and empty cisterns (cf. Jer 2:13) in a desperate search for meaning — the ultimate meaning that only love can give? This is the great and liberating gift which the Gospel brings: it reveals our dignity as men and women created in the image and likeness of God. It reveals humanity's sublime calling, which is to find fulfillment in love. It discloses the truth about man and the truth about life.

The Church also needs this renewal! She needs your faith, your idealism and your generosity, so that she can always be young in the Spirit (cf. *Lumen Gentium*, 4)! In today's second reading, the Apostle Paul reminds us that each and every Christian has received a gift meant for building up the Body of Christ. The Church especially needs the gifts of young people, all young people. She needs to grow in the power of the Spirit who even now gives joy to your youth and inspires you to serve the Lord with gladness. Open your hearts to that power! I address this plea in a special way to those of you whom the Lord is calling to the priesthood and the consecrated life. Do not be afraid to say "yes" to Jesus, to find your joy in doing his will, giving yourself completely to the pursuit of holiness, and using all your talents in the service of others!

In a few moments, we will celebrate the sacrament of Confirmation. The Holy Spirit will descend upon the confirmands; they will be "sealed" with the gift of the Spirit and sent forth to be Christ's witnesses. What does it mean to receive the "seal" of the Holy Spirit? It means being indelibly marked, inalterably changed, a new creation. For those who have received this gift, nothing can ever be the same! Being "baptized" in the one Spirit (cf. 1 Cor 12:13) means being set on fire with the love of God. Being "given to drink" of the Spirit means being refreshed by the beauty of the Lord's plan for us and for the world, and becoming in turn a source of spiritual refreshment for others. Being "sealed with the Spirit" means not being afraid to stand up for Christ, letting the truth of the Gospel permeate the way we see, think and act, as we work for the triumph of the civilization of love.

As we pray for the confirmands, let us ask that the power of the Holy Spirit will revive the grace of our own Confirmation. May he pour out his gifts in abundance on all present, on this city of Sydney, on this land of Australia and on all its people! May each of us be renewed in the spirit of wisdom and understanding, the spirit of right judgment and courage, the spirit of knowledge and reverence, the spirit of wonder and awe in God's presence!

Through the loving intercession of Mary, Mother of the Church, may this Twenty-third World Youth Day be experienced as a new Upper Room, from which all of us, burning with the fire and love of the Holy Spirit, go forth to proclaim the Risen Christ and to draw every heart to him! Amen.

Recitation of the *Angelus Domini* at Randwick Racecourse in Sydney (July 20, 2008)

The text is available at:
www.vatican.va/holy_father/benedict_xvi/angelus/2008/documents/hf_ben-xvi_ang_20080720_sydney_en.html.

Meeting with benefactors and organizers of the 23rd World Youth Day at the Reception Hall of the Cathedral House and in the Chapter Hall of St. Mary's Cathedral in Sydney (July 20, 2008)

The text is available at:
www.vatican.va/holy_father/benedict_xvi/speeches/2008/july/documents/hf_ben-xvi_spe_20080720_organiz_en.html.

Greeting to volunteer workers for the 23rd World Youth Day in the Domain of Sydney (July 21, 2008)

The text is available at:
www.vatican.va/holy_father/benedict_xvi/speeches/2008/july/documents/hf_ben-xvi_spe_20080721_volunteers_en.html.

Farewell ceremony at the International Airport of Sydney (July 21, 2008)

Before I take my leave, I wish to say to my hosts how much I have enjoyed my visit here and how grateful I am for your hospitality. I thank the Prime Minister, the Honorable Kevin Rudd, for the kindness he has shown to me and to all the participants at World Youth Day. I also thank the Governor-General, Major-General Michael Jeffery, for his presence here and for graciously receiving me at Admiralty House at the start of my public engagements. The Federal Government and the State Government of New South Wales, as well as the residents and the business community of Sydney, have been most cooperative in their support of World Youth Day. An event of this kind requires an immense amount of preparation and organization, and I know that I speak on behalf of many thousands of young people when I express my appreciation and gratitude to you all. In characteristic Australian style, you have extended a warm welcome to me and to countless young pilgrims who have flocked here from every corner of the globe. To the host families in Australia and New Zealand who have made room for the young people in their homes, I am especially grateful. You have opened your doors and your hearts to the world's youth, and on their behalf I thank you.

The principal actors on the stage over these last few days, of course, have been the young people themselves. World Youth Day is their day. It is they who have made this a global ecclesial event, a great celebration of youth and a great celebration of what it is to be the Church, the people of God throughout the world, united in faith and love and empowered by the Spirit to bear witness to the risen Christ to the ends of the earth. I thank them for coming, I thank them for their participation, and I pray that they will have a safe journey home. I know that the young people, their families and their sponsors have in many cases made great sacrifices to enable them to travel to Australia. For this the entire Church is grateful.

VATICAN DOCUMENTS AND ANNOUNCEMENTS

The Year of St. Paul
Special thanks to Woodeene Koenig-Bricker
In order to commemorate the 2000th anniversary of the birth of St. Paul of Tarsus, Christians all over the world have been invited by Pope Benedict XVI to celebrate "The Year of St. Paul" from June 28, 2008 to June 29, 2009.

As Pope Benedict XVI said in his announcement, this special "Pauline" year is an invitation to join with "The Apostle of the Gentiles, who dedicated himself to the spreading of the good news to all peoples, spent himself for the unity and harmony of all Christians," adding, "May he guide us and protect us in this bimillenary celebration, helping us to advance in the humble and sincere search for the full unity of all the members of the mystical body of Christ."

The year will emphasize meetings and spiritual retreats on St. Paul, a rediscovery of the teachings of Paul through his letters, pilgrimages which trace his missionary journeys, encounters and conversations with other Christian Communities, as well as special liturgies in front of his tomb at the Basilica of St. Paul Outside the Walls in Rome.

Special Events and Celebrations
Pope Benedict XVI presided at the solemn opening of the Pauline Year at the Basilica of St. Paul Outside the Walls. He will preside at the closing ceremony in 2009. In order to celebrate this special year, the Vatican has established five different ways to follow Christ who is "the Way, the Truth and the Life: along with St. Paul: 1. the pontifical way, 2. the pilgrim way, 3. the cultural way, 4. the liturgical way and 5. the media way.

The Pontifical Way includes the opening and closing ceremonies with Pope Benedict XVI, passage through a special door leading to the tomb of St. Paul and a plenary indulgence obtained by praying for the Pope and the Church, making confession and taking communion and visit St. Paul's tomb.

The Pilgrim Way consists of pilgrimages to the tomb of St. Paul, an itinerary through the city of Rome, diocesan pilgrimages, youth pilgrimages and trips and guided tours.

The Cultural Way is marked by exhibitions at the Basilica, guided tours of the Basilica, conferences, a Pauline colloquium and musical concerts.

The Liturgical Way centers on the celebration of Mass and the monastic liturgy.

The Media Way includes such things as the internet site, prayer requests and special Vatican stamps and commemorative medals.

For more information on each of these routes and how you can take part in them, visit the official Year of St. Paul website at www.annopaolino.org; readers are also encouraged to visit the Our Sunday Visit on St. Paul at: www.osv.com/YearofStPaulNav/YearofStPaul/tabid/6133/Default.aspx

Special Faculty
The Congregation for Divine Worship and the Discipline of the Sacraments issued a decree granting a special faculty for the celebration of the Conversion of St. Paul, Apostle in the Jubilee Year bimillennium of his birth. The text follows:
The Apostle St. Paul, who proclaimed the truth of Christ to the entire world and, after having been his persecutor, employed all means to announce the Good News to the peoples, committing himself with zeal for the unity and harmony of all Christians, has always

been and is still now venerated by the faithful, especially in this particular Year, bimillennium of his birth, that the Supreme Pontiff Benedict XVI has willed to institute it as a special Jubilee Year.

Therefore, in force of the faculties attributed to this Congregation by the Supreme Pontiff, Benedict XVI, grants, in an extraordinary way, that next Jan. 25, 2009, the Third Sunday "per annum," the singular churches can celebrate a Mass according to the formula Conversion of St. Paul, Apostle, as found in the Roman Missal. In this case, the Second Reading of the Mass is taken from the Roman Lectionary for the Third Sunday "per annum," and the Creed is recited. This concession, by special mandate of the Supreme Pontiff, is valid only for the Year 2009. CA

Decree on Women's Ordination
On May 30, 2008, *L'Osservatore Romano*, the Vatican newspaper, published a General Decree regarding the delict of attempted sacred ordination of a woman that had been issued by the Congregation of the Doctrine of the Faith on Dec. 19, 2007. The decree was signed by the prefect of the congregation, William Cardinal Levada and the secretary of the congregation, Abp. Angelo Amato, S.D.B. The text follows:
In order to protect the nature and validity of the sacrament of order, the Congregation for the Doctrine of the Faith, in virtue of the special faculty given by the supreme authority of the Church (cf. can. 30, Code of Canon Law), in the Ordinary Session of 19 December 2007, has decreed:
Without prejudice to the prescript of can. 1378 of the Code of Canon Law, both the one who attempts to confer a sacred order on a woman, and the woman who attempts to receive a sacred order, incur an excommunication *latae sententiae* reserved to the Apostolic See.
If, in fact, the one who attempts to confer a sacred order on a woman, or the woman who attempts to receive a sacred order, is one of Christ's faithful subject to the Code of Canons of the Eastern Churches, that person, without prejudice to the prescript of can. 1443 of the same Code, is to be punished with a major excommunication, the remission of which is also reserved to the Apostolic See (cf. can. 1423, Code of Canons of the Eastern Churches).
This decree, once published in *L'Osservatore Romano*, comes into force immediately. CA

Responses to Questions Proposed on the Validity of Baptism
On Feb. 1, 2008, the Congregation of the Doctrine of the Faith issued the document, "On the validity of Baptismal formulas 'I baptize you in the name of the Creator, and of the Redeemer, and of the Sanctifier' and 'I baptize you in the name of the Creator, and of the Liberator, and of the Sustainer.'"
The response was signed by the prefect of the congregation, William Card. Levada and the secretary of the congregation, Abp. Angelo Amato, S.D.B. The text follows:
QUESTIONS
First question: Whether the Baptism conferred with the formulas "I baptize you in the name of the Creator, and of the Redeemer, and of the Sanctifier," and "I

baptize you in the name of the Creator, and of the
Liberator, and of the Sustainer" is valid?

Second question: Whether the persons baptized with
those formulas have to be baptized in forma absoluta?
RESPONSES

To the first question: Negative.

To the second question: Affirmative.

The Supreme Pontiff Benedict XVI, at the Audience
granted to the undersigned Cardinal Prefect of the
Congregation for the Doctrine of the Faith, approved
these Responses, adopted in the Ordinary Session of
the Congregation, and ordered their publication.

Rome, from the Offices of the Congregation for the
Doctrine of the Faith, Feb. 1, 2008. CA

Doctrinal Note on Some Aspects of Evangelization

*On Dec. 3, 2007, the Congregation of the Doctrine of
the Faith issued a Doctrinal Note on Some Aspects of
Evangelization. The note was signed by the prefect of
the congregation, William Card. Levada and the secretary of the congregation, Abp. Angelo Amato, S.D.B.*

At a press conference held on Dec. 14, 2007, the note
was presented publicly, with comments by Card.
Levada and Card. Francis Arinze, the prefect of the
Congregation for Divine Worship and the Discipline of
the Sacraments. The transcript of the press conference
follows:

Address by Card. William Joseph Levada

The Congregation for the Doctrine of the Faith is
very pleased to be able to present our new document,
the *Doctrinal Note on some Aspects of Evangelization*.
I welcome representatives of the media to this press
conference. On behalf of His Excellency, Archbp.
Angelo Amato, Secretary of the Congregation, I
express my gratitude to two of the 18 cardinal and
bishop members of our Congregation, His Eminence,
Card. Francis Arinze, Prefect of the Congregation for
Divine Worship and the Discipline of the Sacraments,
and His Eminence, Card. Ivan Dias, Prefect of the
Congregation for the Evangelization of Peoples, for
their willing participation in this morning's event.

After I give some brief introductory remarks,
Archbp. Amato will offer some theological reflections
on the Doctrinal Note, followed by comments by Card.
Arinze on the missionary situation in Africa, and by
Card. Dias on theologians and evangelization from the
Asian perspective. After these opening remarks, we
will be pleased to respond to your questions.

The Doctrinal Note addresses a central theme in
Catholic and Christian understanding of our belief in
Jesus Christ, that of evangelization. As Jesus was sent
by the Father to bring the good news of salvation to the
world, so He commanded his disciples to proclaim this
good news — the Gospel — to the whole world and to
all people. This work of evangelization belongs to the
very nature of the Church. Because Christians have
received this great gift of God's love in Christ, they
naturally have a desire, indeed a duty, to share this gift
with their families, friends and neighbors.

In this Advent season, when we anticipate once again
this year the beautiful feast of Christmas, we may
recall how the Gospel of St. Luke (chapter 2) tells of
the angel announcing the good news of the birth of
Jesus to the shepherds in the fields around Bethlehem.
We might say that the angel was the first evangelist. In

keeping with the coming feast, the Congregation offers
this new Doctrinal Note as a gift to the Church.

Why a document on evangelization? From its conversations with bishops around the world, and from its
analysis of a certain confusion about whether
Catholics should give testimony about their faith in
Christ, the Congregation decided to address some specific points which seem to undermine the fulfillment
of Christ's missionary mandate. It does so under three
general headings.

The anthropological implications of evangelization
address two key factors of human existence: freedom
and truth. It is the conviction of Christian faith that
God's revelation of his love for us in Christ brings
humanity to the truth of God's purpose and his divine
plan of creation and redemption. To know this truth is
a great blessing for humanity, and for each individual
human being.

At the same time, human dignity requires that the
search for this truth respect human freedom of conscience. In this regard, St. Paul describes "conversion
to the Christian faith as liberation"; thus "belonging to
Christ, who is the Truth, and entering the Church do
not lessen human freedom, but rather exalt it and direct
it towards its fulfillment" (No. 7). It follows then that
evangelization must never resort to "coercion or tac-
tics unworthy of the Gospel" (No. 8). At the same
time, religious liberty requires that evangelization not
be impeded by restrictive measures.

The ecclesiological implications of the Doctrinal
Note remind us that "Since the day of Pentecost ... the
Gospel, in the power of the Holy Spirit, is proclaimed
to all people so that they might believe and become
disciples of Christ and members of his Church.
"Conversion" is a "change in thinking and of acting,"
expressing our new life in Christ; it is an ongoing
dimension of Christian life.

For Christian evangelization, "the incorporation of
new members into the Church is not the expansion of
a power-group, but rather entrance into the network of
friendship with Christ which connects heaven and
earth, different continents and ages." In this sense,
then, "the Church is the bearer of the presence of God
and thus the instrument of the true humanization of
man and the world." (No. 9)

Finally, the importance of Christian witness to holiness and charity is essential if evangelization is to be
credible.

In addressing the ecumenical implications, the
Doctrinal Note stands in the mainstream of the modern
ecumenical movement, whose origins at the beginning
of the last century arose at least in large measure from
the concerns of Christian missionaries who saw their
evangelizing efforts undercut by their multiple and
competing Church structures.

The work of evangelization among various
Christians leads to dialogue and a sharing of gifts leading to deeper conversion to Christ. When individual
persons decide in conscience to enter the Catholic
Church, their decision should be respected without
accusing the Catholic Church of a negative form of
proselytism.

The Doctrinal Note concludes with a beautiful quotation from the first Encyclical Letter of Pope Benedict
XVI: "The love which comes from God unites us to
him and 'makes us a *we* which transcends our divi-

sions and makes us one, until in the end God is *all in all* (1 Cor 15:28).'" I hope that this document can serve as an instrument of a renewal of the evangelizing efforts of Catholics and all Christians, and as a guideline toward unity and brotherhood in the whole human family.

Address by Card. Francis Arinze
"Some Anthropological Implications of Evangelization among People of African Traditional Religion."

Since I come from a country in Africa South of the Sahara, I would like to apply some anthropological implications of evangelization discussed by this Doctrinal Note to areas in Africa South of the great desert. In these regions, African Traditional Religion has been the dominant religious and cultural context for centuries. It is also from that context that most converts to Christianity in these countries in the past two hundred years have come.

African Traditional Religion, making allowance for local variations, is generally marked by belief in one God, in spirits good and bad and in ancestors, with consequent worship which never puts the spirits and ancestors at the same level as the one God who is Creator. This traditional religion permeates a culture which has a marked sense of the sacred, which believes in life after death, which sets high value on marriage, family and human life, and which has a marked sense of community and desire for celebration. The Christian missionaries found this religious context a providential preparation, a fertile ground to bring the Gospel, the good news of salvation in Jesus Christ. Reflecting on this Doctrinal Note of the Congregation for the Doctrine of the Faith, one can make the following four observations on evangelization in these areas marked by African Traditional Religion:

1. Missionary proposal of faith in Jesus Christ pays tribute to the human freedom of the African and to his capacity to know and to love that which is good and true. "The obedience of faith" (Rom 16:26) which is given to God who reveals, not only does not do violence to human intellect and will, but it rather ennobles them. To help another human being who freely listens, reasons and reflects, to accept the Message of salvation in Jesus Christ, is an encounter which does honour both to the missionary and to the convert.

2. Our document rightly notes that the Holy Spirit "animates the maternal action of the Church in the evangelization of cultures" (No. 6). In the multiplicity of languages, cultures and peoples in Africa, this challenging, difficult and delicate work of inculturation has begun. There is still a long way to go. The First African Synod in 1994 underlined its importance. The more the local Churches in Africa have well prepared clerics, theologians, religious, academic and pastoral reflection centres and monasteries, working in union with the Apostolic See, the better the promotion of inculturation will proceed.

3. The sharing of our Catholic faith with others who do not yet know Christ should be regarded as a work of love, provided that it is done with full respect for their human dignity and freedom. Indeed if a Christian did not try to spread the Gospel by sharing the excelling knowledge of Jesus Christ (cf Phil 3:8) with others, we could suspect that Christian either of lack of total conviction on the faith, or of selfishness and lazi-

ness in not wanting to share the full and abundant means of salvation with his fellow human beings.

4. Conversion to Christianity is rightly seen as liberation, as St Paul puts it in his letter to the Colossians. It is entrance into "the kingdom of his (God's) beloved Son in whom we have redemption and the forgiveness of our sins" (Col 1:13-14).

I consider this *Doctrinal Note* of great relevance and actuality.

[The complete text of the Doctrinal Note is available at: http://www.vatican.va/roman_curia/congregations/cfaith/documents/rc_con_cfaith_doc_20071203_nota-evangelizzazione_en.html.] CA

Holy See Finances

On July 3 and 4, 2008, the 42nd meeting of the Council of Cardinals for the Study of the Organizational and Economic Problems of the Holy See, chaired by Card. Tarcisio Bertone, was held in the Vatican City State to make public the 2007 Consolidated Financial Statement of the Holy See and that of the Vatican City State Governorate. The subsequent Consolidated Financial Statement of the Holy See was released and its contents were the subject of a press conference presided over by Card. Bertone.

In the July 9 press conference, Card. Bertone explained that the consolidated financial statement contained the income and the expenses of the various pontifical administrations, including the two Sections of the Secretariat of State, nine Congregations, three Tribunals, 11 Pontifical Councils, the Apostolic Camera, the Prefecture of the Papal Household, the Office for liturgical celebrations of the Supreme Pontiff, the Press Room of the Holy See, the Central Office of Statistics of the Church, five Pontifical Commissions and two Pontifical Committees, three Pontifical Academies and the Institutions connected with the Holy See: the Vatican Secret Archives, the Vatican Library, the Apostolic Almonery, the Synod of Bishops, the Vatican Publishing House, the Vatican Printing Press — *L'Osservatore Romano*, Vatican Radio, the Vatican Television Center; as well as 118 Pontifical Embassies and nine delegations at International Organizations

The primary news in the report was that both the Holy See and Vatican City ended the year with a deficit (in euros) of approximately 9.06 million. The previous three years had reported surpluses of 2.4 million, 9.7 million, 3.1 million respectively. The chief reasons cited for the deficit were the weak American dollar and the subpar performance of the stock market.

The report then focused on the specific areas of activity: institutional, financial, real estate, media institutions connected with the Holy See, and other incomes and expenses.

In the area of institutional activity, meaning all of the dicasteries of the Roman Curia: the Secretariat of State, the Pontifical Representations, the Roman Congregations, Pontifical Councils, the Synod of Bishops and the various Offices, in 2007 the donations that were provided from Episcopal Conferences, dioceses, religious Institutes, faithful and various Entities, in addition to other slight revenues, was essentially unchanged: 86.02 million in 2007 compared to 86 million in 2006. The costs of the sector were also unchanged: 125.4 million in 2007 compared to 126.2 million in 2006 and reflected the cost incurred for personnel for the adjustment both of remunerations to the inflation rate and of the compulsory contributions to the pension funds.

Financial Activity included all financial activities of the consolidated administrations, especially those of APSA Extraordinary Section (Administration of the Patrimony of the Apostolic See). In 2007, this area ended the financial year with a gain of 1.4 million; in 2006 this area ended with a gain of 13.7 million against 43.3 million in 2005. Therefore, a decrease by about 12.3 million occurred, due above all to a sudden, very strong reversal of trend in fluctuations of the rate of exchange, especially of the US Dollar.

The Real Estate concerns of the Holy See and Vatican City State ended the year with a net gain of 36.3 million, higher than that of 2006 which stood at roughly 32.3 million. This positive result can be attributed mostly to appreciated values from the sale of some real estate; in 2005 increased values were equal to only 1.3 million.

When converted into U.S. dollars amounts, the Vatican reported income of approximately $372 million and expenses of $386 million; the expenses outstripped income despite the efforts to reduce the cost of running the Curia offices $1.2 million.

Media Institutions connected with the Holy See—i.e., Vatican Radio, the Vatican Printing Press—L'Osservatore Romano, the Vatican Television Center and the Vatican Publishing House—marked a net deficit of 14.6 million; it is substantially due to the negative results of Vatican Radio and the costs of running L'Osservatore Romano.

The Vatican Printing Press closed its financial statement with a surplus of 1 million, as well as the Vatican Television Centre which closed with a profit of 458 thousand. The Vatican Publishing House closed its 2007 financial statement with a surplus of 1.6 million, a slight improvement over 2006.

The July 3 and 4 meetings were attended by the members of the Council of Cardinals including Cards. Roger Mahony of Los Angeles and Edward M. Egan of New York, as well as Cards. Camillo Ruini, then Vicar General of Rome, Antonio Maria Rouco Varela of Madrid, Anthony Olubunmi Okogie of Lagos, Juan Luis Cipriani Thorne of Lima, Eusébio Oscar Scheid of São Sebastião do Rio de Janeiro, Gaudencio B. Rosales of Manila, and Nicholas Cheong Jinsuk of Seoul.

The Prefecture of the Economic Affairs of the Holy See was represented by its president, Most Rev. Velasio De Paolis, C.S., and the prefecture's secretary, Most Rev. Vincenzo Di Mauro. The Governorate of the Vatican City State was represented by Card. Giovanni Lajolo and Secretary of the Governorate, Most Rev. Domenico Calcagno. CA

SPECIAL REPORTS: INTERNATIONAL NEWS 2007-2008

Fernando Lugo and Paraguay

In Apr. 2008, Fernando Armindo Lugo Méndez, of the Revolutionary Febrerista Party (part of the Patriotic Alliance for Change), won the Paraguayan presidential election. His election was a milestone for several reasons, including the fact that it marked the first defeat of the ruling National Republican Party (the Colorados) in 61 years and that Lugo is only second leftist president in Paraguay's history (the first was Rafael Franco, who served from 1936 to 1937). Most notably, President Lugo is also a bishop.

President Lugo is the former bishop of Paraguayan diocese of San Pedro and a member of the Divine Word Fathers who became known as the "bishop of the poor." The 57 year old bishop left office in 2005 to pursue "other solutions" to the challenges facing his country and in 2007 chose to run for the presidency. Lugo had requested laicization in order to run for president, but the Holy See declined the request on the grounds that Bishops cannot be laicized. Permission was also refused on the basis of canon law's prohibition clergy running for civil elected office.

Lugo was raised in a politically active family; his uncle was a well-known dissident who was persecuted by the General Stroessner regime, and his father was imprisoned twenty times. Lugo discerned a vocation and entered the Society of the Divine Word seminary at the age of 19. Ordained a priest on Aug. 15, 1977, he served for several years as a missionary in Ecuador and there became acquainted with liberation theology. He returned to Paraguay in 1982 and was sent into exile by the government. Church officials sent him to Rome for further academic studies.

Lugo was able to return home in 1987 and was ordained bishop of San Pedro on Apr. 17, 1994, Paraguay's poorest diocese. As his interests in politics increased, Lugo resigned as ordinary on Jan. 11, 2005. Lugo helped to organize a massive demonstration in Mar. 2006 against the government and the seeming movement toward a return to dictatorship under President Nicanor Duarte Frutos. He subsequently became an immensely popular political figure in a country where the Church is revered and the political classes are regarded with suspicion and cynicism. By 2006, he was considered a serious contender for the presidency against the long-standing Colorado party, and in Oct. 2007, he joined the Christian Democratic Party of Paraguay in order to be permitted to run for office. The ensuing coalition, the Patriotic Alliance for Change, was formed, with Federico Franco, from the center-right Authentic Radical Liberal Party, receiving the post of Lugo's running mate.

As a result of his open entrance into politics, Church authorities suspended from the discharge of the ordained ministry; he was not dismissed from the clerical state. Lugo submitted a letter to the Holy See asking to "renounce his ecclesial ministry [...] to take up again the condition of a layperson in the Church."

On Jan. 20, 2007, Cardinal Re, prefect of the Congregation for Bishops, suspended Lugo a divinis, according to Canon 1333 §1 of the Code of Canon Law, for presenting himself as a candidate. The suspension means that Lugo remains in the clerical state but cannot exercise his ministry. The suspension was given, according to Cardinal Re, "With sincere sorrow."

In addition, Article 235 of the Constitution forbids ministers of any religious denomination from holding elective office. This point, however, has not been contested by the Colorado Party. The Paraguayan Bishops' Conference did not issue an official statement in the wake of the election, but there is no question that the bishops acknowledged Lugo's victory.

On Apr. 23, 2008, the president-elect made a formal and public apology for the sorrow that he had caused by his decision to run for political office. He declared in a message delivered on the radio channel Fe y Alegria ("Faith and Joy"), "If my attitude and my disobedience of canon law caused sorrow, I sincerely ask forgiveness to the people of the Church. In particular, I ask pardon to Pope Benedict XVI." Lugo added that it is his hope to enter into dialogue with Church authorities to find a "satisfactory solution" for himself and the Church.

Two days later, the president-elect was visited by Abp. Orlando Antonini, the papal nuncio to Paraguay. The papal ambassador visited Lugo, congratulated him on his victory and presented him with the gift of a pen from Benedict XVI. After the meeting, the nuncio spoke about the Vatican's position on Bishop Lugo's state. The nuncio said, "The Vatican has a position on the case of Bishop Fernando Lugo that will be made known soon through a communiqué."

At a press conference on July 30, 2008, Abp. Antonini announced that Bp. Lugo had had been laicized in order to allow him to take office without violating Church law. Cardinal Re had signed the decree of laicization on June 30. The papal nuncio noted that this was the first case in which a bishop received a dispensation and added, "It's a great pain for the Church to lose a bishop, a priest who we tried to dissuade from the political option up to the last day of his campaign. But the Holy Father recognized that he was elected by the majority of the people to lead Paraguay for the next five years." CA

Christians in Iraq

One of the most unfortunate and unexpected consequences of the Iraq War has been the severe crisis facing the Christian population of Iraq as a result of sectarian and political violence in the country since 2003. As Chaldean archbishop Louis Sako recently declared in an interview with AsiaNews, "In Iraq Christians are dying, the Church is disappearing under continued persecution, threats and violence [are] carried out by extremists who are leaving us no choice: conversion or exile."

The phenomenon of Christians being forced to abandon their lives and abandon their homes, cities, and even countries is a growing one across the globe. It has assumed crisis proportions in the Middle East where in there last decade over three million Christians have left the Holy Land to settle in Europe, the United States, and Canada. They represent between a quarter to a third of all Christians living in the Middle East and the largest exodus of Christians since the 12th and 13th centuries and the fall of the Latin Crusader States. The situation is especially dire for the ancient Christian population of Iraq.

At the start of the Iraq War in 2003, there were nearly 1.5 million Chaldeans, Syro-Catholics, Syro-Orthodox, Assyrians from the East, Catholic and Orthodox Armenians, and Greek-Melkites in Iraq. In the wake of Saddam Hussein's removal, Christians have been targeted for bombings, assassinations, and kidnappings. Emblematic of the situation is the Dora section of Baghdad where in 2003 there were 20,000 Christian families living in relative peace. After four years of chaos and danger, there were only 3,000 families left. In the southern city of Basra, Islamic extremists in 2007 murdered Christian women for not wearing traditional dress and head scarves, known as the hijab. The result of the chaos is that today, there are estimated to be only 500,000 Christians left in Iraq. Most have fled to Syria and Jordan, while others have chosen to settle in Egypt and Lebanon.

The extent of the violence against Christians was reported by the United Nations Assistance Mission in Iraq. The murder and intimidation of Christians escalated steadily from 2003, peaking in 2006 with bloody and savage attacks and bombings on Catholic and a Syrian Orthodox church in Kirkuk, an Anglican church in Baghdad, and the Apostolic Nuncio's residence in Baghdad. Christian clerics were also targeted for kidnapping and assassination, such as a Catholic priest and three deacons who were murdered outside of their church after saying Mass in Mosul.

In the wake of the success of the U.S.-led surge in Iraq and the gradual consolidation and strengthening of the Iraqi government in 2007, conditions in Iraq improved considerably. The number of attacks and bombings declined, and the good relations between the Chaldean Catholic Church and the Iraqi government proved instrumental in preventing even more crimes. The Iraqi prime minister, Nouri al-Maliki, promised greater protection for the country's Christian community, and in December 2007, the Iraqi police arrested a group of Muslim thugs who had been kidnapping Christian doctors. A boost to Iraqi Christian morale came in November 2007 when the Chaldean patriarch of Baghdad, Emmanuel III Delly, was made a cardinal by Pope Benedict, an event celebrated by Christian and Muslim leaders in the country.

The start of 2008, however, brought a downturn in optimism. In early January, a series of attacks was launched against Christian sites in Baghdad, Mosul, and Kirkuk, including Kirkuk's Chaldean cathedral, the Assyrian Christian Maar Afram church, a convent and an orphanage in Mosul, and three churches and a convent in Baghdad.

In a statement issued through Cardinal Tarcisio Bertone, Vatican Secretary of State, Pope Benedict XVI declared, "Mindful that such attacks are also directed against the whole people of Iraq, His Holiness appeals to the perpetrators to renounce the ways of violence, which have caused so much suffering to the civilian population, and he encourages all those in authority to renew efforts toward peaceful negotiation aimed at a just resolution of the country's difficulties, respectful of the rights of all. Praying for a return to the peaceful coexistence of the diverse groups that make up the population of this beloved country, the Holy Father commends all the people of Iraq to the heavenly protection of our almighty and merciful Father."

Adding further to the tragedy, was the kidnapping on Feb. 29, 2008 of archbishop Faraj Raho, Chaldean archbishop of Mosul. Gunmen seized the prelate and murdered three of his companions outside the Holy Spirit cathedral in Mosul after conducting a Stations of the Cross service. The kidnappers demanded a heavy ransom, and Church officials pleaded with the extremists to release the archbishop as his health was poor, he had a heart condition, and he was in need of medication. The archbishop subsequently died while in the hands of the kidnappers who gave instructions on how Church officials could recover the archbishop's body. Informed of the prelate's death, Pope Benedict XVI issued a statement condemning "an act of inhuman

violence that offends the dignity of the human being."
The abduction was a powerful reminder that progress

for Christians continues to have its limitations and
remains precarious. **CA**

SPECIAL REPORTS: NATIONAL NEWS 2007-2008

THE SEX-ABUSE SCANDAL IN THE U.S. CHURCH
By Russell Shaw

Perhaps the year's most important development—
and surely the most moving one—in the ongoing story
of sex abuse of minors by some American priests was
Pope Benedict XVI's meeting with five abuse victims
during his U.S. visit in the spring. His gesture carried
the cause of reconciliation and closure further than
ever before.

The private encounter, which was not announced in
advance, took place Apr. 17 in the chapel of the
Apostolic Nunciature in Washington, DC. On hand
were the five victims, men and women, from the
Archdiocese of Boston and Card. Sean P. O'Malley,
OFM Cap., of Boston, who had asked for the meeting.
People present described the 25-minute session as
spontaneous and emotional, with some of the participants in tears.

Responding to the abuse scandal was a central theme
of Pope Benedict's Apr. 15-20 visit. He spoke about
the issue to reporters on the plane coming to the U.S.,
then several more times in his prepared remarks,
including his Apr. 17 homily at Mass in Washington
and during a meeting with priests and religious Apr. 19
in St. Patrick's Cathedral New York.

Addressing 300 U.S. bishops Apr. 16 at the Basilica of the
National Shrine of the Immaculate Conception in
Washington, the Pope listed sexual abuse of minors among
the "countersigns to the gospel of life" in America and elsewhere. He told the bishops they "rightly...attach priority" to
compassion and care for the victims, but he also urged them
to reach out to their priests. "They have experienced shame
over what has occurred, and there are those who feel they
have lost some of the trust and esteem they once enjoyed," he
said.

The scandal had a prominent place at the spring general meeting of the United States Conference of
Catholic Bishops June 12-14 in Orlando, FL.

Researchers from the John Jay College of Criminal
Justice at the City University of New York presented
another interim report on the study of the "causes and
context" of abuse crisis that they are carrying out on
behalf of USCCB. The project is scheduled for completion in December 2010.

One tentative finding, the bishops were told, concerns correlations between the incidence of clergy sex
abuse and the incidence of things like divorce, premarital sex, and illegal drug use. Abuse, divorce, premarital sex, and the number of new adult users of marijuana all rose 200% in the 1960s, while in the 1980s,
when abuse by priests declined 72%, the divorce rate
was down 40% and premarital sex and new marijuana
use fell 60%. Yet to be determined, said one
researcher, is whether "the same social factors" were
contributing factors in all these areas.

At the USCCB meeting in Baltimore the previous
November, the John Jay researchers said their findings
suggested a link between clergy sex abuse and "over-

all changes in behavior, attitudes, and media representations in American society" in the years when abuse
was peaking.

In Orlando, the bishops also heard that the length of time
between ordination to the priesthood and initial acts of abuse
fell sharply among abusive clergy in the period studied—
from an average of 13 years among those ordained before the
1960s to eight years among those ordained in the 1960s and
four years among those ordained in the 1970s. The study will
examine seminary programs of the era for possible explanations.

Also in Orlando, the USCCB Committee on the
Protection of Children and Young :People held the first
of two scheduled closed-door meetings with representatives of American priests to initiate a dialogue on
issues arising from the abuse scandal, including relations between the bishops and the priests. The first
meeting involved priests from half the USCCB regions
into which the country is divided. A second session
involving priests from the other half of the regions was
scheduled for the USCCB's November general meeting in Baltimore.

In December 2007 the all-lay National Review
Board established by the USCCB to monitor implementation of the bishops' anti-sex abuse policy published a five-year report noting significant progress
overall. But the report cited six challenges that it called
"not easily resolved since they involve extremely
complex issues." They are: better understanding of
victimization and its consequences; the Church's relationship to priests alienated by fallout from the scandal; "appropriate protection and restoration" for those
accused of abuse but later found innocent; greater
speed in determining the credibility of allegations; the
needs of parishes where abuse has occurred; and the
need to keep Church members informed of progress.

In March, the bishops' conference released the 2007
survey covering allegations and costs of sex abuse,
conducted by the Center for Applied Research in the
Apostolate at Georgetown University. The report
showed a continuing decline in the number of new,
credible allegations—599 in 2007, compared with 635
in 2006, 695 in 2005, and 898 in 2004, the first year of
the survey. The vast majority concerned incidents in
past years.

According to CARA, dioceses and religious institutes in 2007 paid out $615 million in legal settle-
ments, therapy, support for offenders, attorneys' fees,
and other expenses, with the cumulative cost to the
Church of the sex abuse scandal passing $2 billion.

An audit by the Gavin Group, released at the same
time as the survey, showed 178 of 190 participating
dioceses in full compliance with the bishops' Charter
for the Protection of Children and Young People, with
12 others complying with all but one or two of 17
items. Ninety-nine percent of the 37,000 priests
included in the study had participated in "safe environment" training as had over 96% of the children
involved in church-sponsored programs. Similarly

high percentages were reported for deacons, educators, seminarians, church employees, and volunteers.

Notable settlements in abuse cases in the past year included: a $50 million settlement by the Oregon province of the Society of Jesus of more than 100 claims involving more a dozen Jesuits who served in Alaska between 1961 and 1987; a $37 million settlement by the Diocese of Davenport, IA, with all but one of 165 complainants, allowing the diocese to emerge from bankruptcy; and a $5.5 million settlement by the Archdiocese of Denver, bringing to $8.2 million the amount it has paid to settle claims involving three priests, all deceased, in incidents occurring between 27 and 54 years ago.

In February, the Diocese of Fairbanks, AK, announced it would become the sixth U.S. diocese to file for bankruptcy in the face of sex abuse claims. The others are the Archdiocese of Portland, OR, and the Dioceses of San Diego, Spokane, Tucson, and Davenport. Portland, Spokane, Tucson, and Davenport have emerged from bankruptcy so far.

During the year, efforts continued in at least nine states to revise civil statute of limitations rules to allow people to sue for sex abuse alleged to have occurred outside the time limit for legal redress. Up to 2008, California and Delaware had taken this step.

On Aug. 12, the Archdiocese of Chicago announced that it had agreed to pay 16 victims of clergy sex abuse more than $12.6 million in a settlement. The archdiocese also agreed to release files related to the cases and other information. Speaking of the settlement, Cardinal George, archbishop of Chicago, stated, "I apologize again today to the survivors and their families and to the whole Catholic community. We must continue to do everything in our power to ensure the safety of the children in our care." CA

CAMPAIGN OF 2008

Special thanks to Russell Shaw for his assistance with this article.

Religion played a prominent and sometimes volatile role in the presidential campaign of 2008.

Seeking to shed their image as the preferred party of the non-religious, Democrats went out of their way to stress religious themes. In particular, Sen. Barack Obama of Illinois and Sen. Hillary Clinton of New York, vying for the party's presidential nomination, spoke often about their own Christian faith and values.

Senator Obama, the eventual nominee, received early and sometimes controversial support from religious figures. These included the Rev. Jeremiah A. Wright Jr., retired pastor of his Chicago congregation, Trinity United Church of Christ, whom Obama described as a friend and mentor. After Rev. Wright drew attention with remarks described as racist and anti-American, however, the candidate severed ties with him. Eventually, too, he quit Trinity United when Fr. Michael Pfleger, a Chicago Catholic pastor, took to its pulpit during the primaries to deliver an attack on Clinton. Another Catholic who was an early and vocal supporter of Obama was Douglas Kmiec, a former dean of the law school at the Catholic University of America now teaching in California.

Religion also figured prominently in the contest for the Republican nomination. Former Massachusetts

Gov. Mitt Romney received sometimes critical attention for being a Mormon, which moved him to deliver a major speech on Dec. 6, 2007, insisting on his right to seek the nomination without being a target of religious discrimination. Meanwhile former Arkansas Gov. Mike Huckabee repeatedly stressed his beliefs as a Southern Baptist minister.

By contrast, Sen. John McCain of Arizona, winner in the GOP contest, said little about his beliefs. Religion nonetheless became an issue for him as a well as a result of controversial remarks by supporters like conservative evangelical Pastor John Hagee. As Obama disavowed Wright, so McCain was moved to disavow Hagee.

For many voters, the difference between McCain and Obama lay especially in their contrasting stands on social issues like abortion and gay marriage. McCain boasted a largely pro-life voting record and had the support of groups like the National Right to Life Committee; Obama was actively pro-choice and had the backing of groups like the Planned Parenthood Action Fund. On same-sex marriage, McCain declared it an issue for states to decide but supported an amendent to the California constitution to bar it. Obama opposed such an amendment. The contrast between the candidates was especially apparent during the Saddleback Civil Forum hosted by Rev. Rick Warren on Aug. 16. Asked when babies are entitled to human rights, McCain replied, "At the moment of conception." Obama answered that the issue was "above my pay grade."

Political analysts said Catholic voters were likely to play a key role in the election of 2008 as they had in previous years. This reflected not only the potential size of the Catholic vote—some 47 million—but also the well-documented fact that the Catholic population contains a significant number of swing voters. In 2000, for instance, 50% of Catholics voted for Democrat Al Gore and 46% for Republican George Bush. In 2004, it was 52% for Bush—61% among those who attend Mass weekly—and 46% for Democrat John Kerry

The American Catholic bishops in 2007 published a statement called *Forming Consciences for Faithful Citizenship* setting out principles for the guidance of Catholic voters. Individual bishops also took similar steps. Archbp. Charles J. Chaput, OFM Cap., of Denver in the summer of 2008 published a widely noted book called *Render Unto Caesar* that discussed the role of Catholics in public life in detail.

Much of the intra-Church debate among Catholics turned once again, as it had in previous years, on the issue of voting for candidates who support legalized abortion or other serious evils morally wrong in themselves.

Forming Consciences for Faithful Citizenship said: "A Catholic cannot vote for a candidate who takes a position in favor of an intrinsic evil, such as abortion or racism, if the voter's intent is to support that position. In such cases a Catholic would be guilty of formal cooperation in grave evil....There may be times when a Catholic who rejects a candidate's unacceptable may decide to vote for that candidate for other morally grave reasons. Voting in this way would be permissible only for truly grave moral reasons, not to advance narrow interests or partisan preferences or to ignore a fundamental moral evil."

Some took this to mean that a Catholic might vote for a pro-choice candidate for a pro-choice candidate for a proportionate reason outweighing the evil of abortion. But in a separate statement of their own issued in August 2008, the four bishops of Kansas said Catholics would "commit moral evil" by voting for candidates who favored abortion, euthanasia, or embryonic stem cell research. If no candidate measures up, they said, Catholics should vote for the least unacceptable one "in order to defeat one who poses an even greater threat to human life and dignity." Archbp. Chaput said he could think of no reason outweighing the serious moral obligation to work for an end to the grave evil of legalized abortion.

Discussion among Catholics also turned on the issue, likewise familiar from previous years, of whether to give or not give communion to pro-choice Catholic politicians. Archbp. Joseph Naumann of Kansas City, KS, disclosed that he had told pro-choice Kansas Gov. Kathleen Sebelius not to receive. The Archbishop rebuked her for nevertheless continuing to receive and told her to desist, lest he be forced to take sterner measures.

The question also came up in another context during Pope Benedict XVI's visit to the United States in April, when some pro-choice Catholic politicians attending papal Masses in Washington, DC, and New York received communion. The incident in Washington passed largely without comment by Church authorities, but in New York, where pro-choice former Mayor Rudolph Giuliani was the politician involved, Cardinal Edward Egan said Giuliani had violated a private agreement with him not to receive and he intended to confront Giuliani about the matter.

The choice of Sen. Joe Biden, a long-time member of the United States Senate from Delaware and a Catholic, was interpreted by many analysts as an effort by the Obama campaign to improve the candidate's standing with Catholic voters. The issue of abortion became one of immediate discussion leading up the Democratic convention because of Sen. Biden's long record of supporting abortion. The choice of Biden was greeted with considerable alarm by the Pro-Life movement.

Adding to the controversy were the comments of House Speaker Nancy Pelosi on the NBC television program "Meet The Press" on Aug. 24, in which she stated, "I would say that as an ardent, practicing Catholic, this is an issue that I have studied for a long time. And what I know is over the centuries, the doctors of the Church have not been able to make that definition. . . ." Her assertion drew a strong rebuttal from many Catholic leaders, including Card. Justin F. Rigali, chairman of the U.S. Bishops' Committee on Pro-Life Activities, Bp. William E. Lori, chairman of the U.S. Bishops' Committee on Doctrine, Abp. Chaput, and Abp. Donald Wuerl of Washington.

On Aug. 29, the Republican presidential nominee announced his surprising choice for running mate, Gov. Sarah Palin of Alaska. Elected governor in 2006, Palin is a strong supporter of the Pro-Life movement. Her fifth child was diagnosed in utero with downs syndrome, but the governor and her husband chose to complete the pregnancy. Her selection sparked immense enthusiasm among social conservatives and members of the Pro-Life movement who had previously expressed some reluctance to support the McCain nomination. CA

LIFE ISSUES 2007-2008

Hydration and the Vegetative State

On Aug. 1, 2007, the Congregation for the Doctrine of the Faith issued the document "Responses to Certain Questions of the United States Conference of Catholic Bishops Concerning Artificial Nutrition and Hydration." The document, in response to a request by the U. S. Conference of Catholic Bishops, reaffirmed the Catholic Church's teaching on providing nutrition and hydration to patients in a persistent "vegetative state."

The initial questions were posed by American bishops in the form a *"dubium,"* or formal question, and the official reply from the congregation was approved by Pope Benedict XVI. The text of the response follows:

First question: Is the administration of food and water (whether by natural or artificial means) to a patient in a "vegetative state" morally obligatory except when they cannot be assimilated by the patient's body or cannot be administered to the patient without causing significant physical discomfort?

Response: Yes. The administration of food and water even by artificial means is, in principle, an ordinary and proportionate means of preserving life. It is therefore obligatory to the extent to which, and for as long as, it is shown to accomplish its proper finality, which is the hydration and nourishment of the patient. In this way suffering and death by starvation and dehydration are prevented.

Second question: When nutrition and hydration are being supplied by artificial means to a patient in a "permanent vegetative state," may they be discontinued when competent physicians judge with moral certainty that the patient will never recover consciousness?

Response: No. A patient in a "permanent vegetative state" is a person with fundamental human dignity and must, therefore, receive ordinary and proportionate care which includes, in principle, the administration of water and food even by artificial means.

The congregation also provided a commentary that discusses and clarifies further the key points of the response. The Commentary states:

The Congregation for the Doctrine of the Faith has formulated responses to questions presented by His Excellency the Most Reverend William S. Skylstad, President of the United States Conference of Catholic Bishops, in a letter of July 11, 2005, regarding the nutrition and hydration of patients in the condition commonly called a "vegetative state." The object of the questions was whether the nutrition and hydration of such patients, especially if provided by artificial means, would constitute an excessively heavy burden for the patients, for their relatives, or for the health-care system, to the point where it could be considered, also in the light of the moral teaching of the Church, a means that is extraordinary or disproportionate and therefore not morally obligatory.

The Address of Pope Pius XII to a Congress on Anesthesiology, given on Nov. 24, 1957, is often invoked in favor of the possibility of abandoning the nutrition and hydration of such patients. In this address, the Pope restated two general ethical principles. On the one hand, natural reason and Christian morality teach that, in the case of a grave illness, the patient and those caring for him or her have the right and the duty to provide the care necessary to preserve health and life. On the other hand, this duty in general includes only the use of those means which, considering all the circumstances, are ordinary, that is to say, which do not impose an extraordinary burden on the patient or on others. A more severe obligation would be too burdensome for the majority of persons and would make it too difficult to attain more important goods. Life, health and all temporal activities are subordinate to spiritual ends. Naturally, one is not forbidden to do more than is strictly obligatory to preserve life and health, on condition that one does not neglect more important duties.

One should note, first of all, that the answers given by Pius XII referred to the use and interruption of techniques of resuscitation. However, the case in question has nothing to do with such techniques. Patients in a "vegetative state" breathe spontaneously, digest food naturally, carry on other metabolic functions, and are in a stable situation. But they are not able to feed themselves. If they are not provided artificially with food and liquids, they will die, and the cause of their death will be neither an illness nor the "vegetative state" itself, but solely starvation and dehydration. At the same time, the artificial administration of water and food generally does not impose a heavy burden either on the patient or on his or her relatives. It does not involve excessive expense; it is within the capacity of an average health-care system, does not of itself require hospitalization, and is proportionate to accomplishing its purpose, which is to keep the patient from dying of starvation and dehydration. It is not, nor is it meant to be, a treatment that cures the patient, but is rather ordinary care aimed at the preservation of life.

What may become a notable burden is when the "vegetative state" of a family member is prolonged over time. It is a burden like that of caring for a quadriplegic, someone with serious mental illness, with advanced Alzheimer's disease, and so on. Such persons need continuous assistance for months or even for years. But the principle formulated by Pius XII cannot, for obvious reasons, be interpreted as meaning that in such cases those patients, whose ordinary care imposes a real burden on their families, may licitly be left to take care of themselves and thus abandoned to die. This is not the sense in which Pius XII spoke of extraordinary means.

Everything leads to the conclusion that the first part of the principle enunciated by Pius XII should be applied to patients in a "vegetative state": in the case of a serious illness, there is the right and the duty to provide the care necessary for preserving health and life. The development of the teaching of the Church's magisterium, which has closely followed the progress of medicine and the questions which this has raised, fully confirms this conclusion.

The Declaration on Euthanasia, published by the Congregation for the Doctrine of the Faith on May 5, 1980, explained the distinction between proportionate and disproportionate means, and between therapeutic treatments and the normal care due to the sick person: "When inevitable death is imminent in spite of the means used, it is permitted in conscience to take the decision to refuse forms of treatment that would only secure a precarious and burdensome prolongation of life, so long as the normal care due to the sick person in similar cases is not interrupted" (Part IV). Still less can one interrupt the ordinary means of care for patients who are not facing an imminent death, as is generally the case of those in a "vegetative state"; for these people, it would be precisely the interruption of the ordinary means of care which would be the cause of their death.

On June 27, 1981, the Pontifical Council Cor Unum published a document entitled Some Ethical Questions Relating to the Gravely Ill and the Dying, in which, among other things, it is stated that "There remains the strict obligation to administer at all costs those means which are called 'minimal': that is, those that normally and in usual conditions are aimed at maintaining life (nourishment, blood transfusions, injections, etc.). The discontinuation of these minimal measures would mean in effect willing the end of the patient's life" (No. 2.4.4.).

In an Address to participants in an international course on

forms of human preleukemia on Nov. 15, 1985, Pope John Paul II, recalling the Declaration on Euthanasia, stated clearly that, in virtue of the principle of proportionate care, one may not relinquish "the commitment to valid treatment for sustaining life nor assistance with the normal means of preserving life," which certainly includes the administration of food and liquids. The Pope also noted that those omissions are not licit which are aimed "at shortening life in order to spare the patient or his family from suffering."

In 1995 the Pontifical Council for Pastoral Assistance to Health Care Workers published the Charter for Health Care Workers, paragraph 120 of which explicitly affirms: "The administration of food and liquids, even artificially, is part of the normal treatment always due to the patient when this is not burdensome for him or her; their undue interruption can have the meaning of real and true euthanasia".

The address of John Paul II to a group of bishops from the United States of America on a visit ad limina, on Oct. 2, 1998, is quite explicit: nutrition and hydration are to be considered as normal care and ordinary means for the preservation of life. It is not acceptable to interrupt them or to withhold them, if from that decision the death of the patient will follow. This would be euthanasia by omission (cf. No. 4).

In his address of Mar. 20, 2004, to the participants of an International Congress on "Life-sustaining Treatments and the Vegetative State: scientific progress and ethical dilemmas," John Paul II confirmed in very clear terms what had been said in the documents cited above, clarifying also their correct interpretation. The Pope stressed the following points:

1) "The term permanent vegetative state has been coined to indicate the condition of those patients whose 'vegetative state' continues for over a year. Actually, there is no different diagnosis that corresponds to such a definition, but only a conventional prognostic judgment, relative to the fact that the recovery of patients, statistically speaking, is ever more difficult as the condition of vegetative state is prolonged in time" (No. 2).[1]

2) In response to those who doubt the "human quality" of patients in a "permanent vegetative state," it is necessary to reaffirm that "the intrinsic value and personal dignity of every human being do not change, no matter what the concrete circumstances of his or her life. A man, even if seriously ill or disabled in the exercise of his highest functions, is and always will be a man, and he will never become a 'vegetable' or an 'animal'" (No. 3).

3) "The sick person in a vegetative state, awaiting recovery or a natural end, still has the right to basic health care (nutrition, hydration, cleanliness, warmth, etc.), and to the prevention of complications related to his confinement to bed. He also has the right to appropriate rehabilitative care and to be monitored for clinical signs of possible recovery. I should like particularly to underline how the administration of water and food, even when provided by artificial means, always represents a natural means of preserving life, not a medical act. Its use, furthermore, should be considered, in principle, ordinary and proportionate, and as such morally obligatory, to the extent to which, and for as long as, it is shown to accomplish its proper finality, which in the present case consists in providing nourishment to the patient and alleviation of his suffering" (No. 4).

4) The preceding documents were taken up and interpreted in this way: "The obligation to provide the 'normal care due to the sick in such cases' (Congregation for the Doctrine of the Faith, Declaration on Euthanasia, p. IV) includes, in fact, the use of nutrition and hydration (cf. Pontifical Council Cor Unum, Some Ethical Questions Relating to the Gravely Ill

and the Dying, No. 2, 4, 4; Pontifical Council for Pastoral Assistance to Health Care Workers, *Charter for Health Care Workers*, No. 120). The evaluation of probabilities, founded on waning hopes for recovery when the vegetative state is prolonged beyond a year, cannot ethically justify the cessation or interruption of *minimal care* for the patient, including nutrition and hydration. Death by starvation or dehydration is, in fact, the only possible outcome as a result of their withdrawal. In this sense it ends up becoming, if done knowingly and willingly, true and proper euthanasia by omission" (No. 4).

Therefore, the Responses now given by the Congregation for the Doctrine of the Faith continue the direction of the documents of the Holy See cited above, and in particular the address of John Paul II of Mar. 20, 2004. The basic points are two. It is stated, first of all, that the provision of water and food, even by artificial means, is in principle an ordinary and proportionate means of preserving life for patients in a "vegetative state": "It is therefore obligatory, to the extent to which, and for as long as, it is shown to accomplish its proper finality, which is the hydration and nourishment of the patient." It is made clear, secondly, that this ordinary means of sustaining life is to be provided also to those in a "permanent vegetative state," since these are persons with their fundamental human dignity.

When stating that the administration of food and water is morally obligatory *in principle*, the Congregation for the Doctrine of the Faith does not exclude the possibility that, in very remote places or in situations of extreme poverty, the artificial provision of food and water may be physically impossible, and then *ad impossibilia nemo tenetur*. However, the obligation to offer the minimal treatments that are available remains in place, as well as that of obtaining, if possible, the means necessary for an adequate support of life. Nor is the possibility excluded that, due to emerging complications, a patient may be unable to assimilate food and liquids, so that their provision becomes altogether useless. Finally, the possibility is not absolutely excluded that, in some rare cases, artificial nourishment and hydration may be excessively burdensome for the patient or may cause significant physical discomfort, for example resulting from complications in the use of the means employed.

These exceptional cases, however, take nothing away from the general ethical criterion, according to which the provision of water and food, even by artificial means, always represents a *natural means* for preserving life, and is not a *therapeutic treatment*. Its use should therefore be considered *ordinary and proportionate*, even when the "vegetative state" is prolonged.

[1] Terminology concerning the different phases and forms of the "vegetative state" continues to be discussed, but this is not important for the moral judgment involved. CA

Stem Cell Research

On Apr. 24, 2008, the U.S. Senate voted to pass the Genetic Information Nondiscrimination Act (GINA).The law prohibits the improper use of genetic information by employers and health insurance providers. It bars group health plans and health insurers from denying coverage to a healthy individual or charging that person higher premiums based solely on a genetic predisposition to developing a disease in the future. The legislation also prohibits employers from using individuals' genetic information when making hiring, firing, job placement, or promotion decisions.

The bill (H.R.493) passed the Senate by a vote of 95-0 and was then sent back to the House of Representatives where it passed by a vote of 414-16 -1 on May 1, 2008 (the lone dissenter was Congressman Ron Paul). President George W. Bush subsequently signed the bill into law on May 21, 2008.

The action by the Senate was praised by the U.S. Bishops' Conference. Deirdre McQuade, of the U.S. conference's Secretariat of Pro-Life Activities, stated: "Today the Senate took a stand for some of the most vulnerable members of the human family, whether born, yet to be born, or placed for adoption. No one should be discriminated against on the basis of genetic testing." McQuade also observed that the bill's protection against discrimination "will cover the families of unborn children with adverse prenatal diagnoses, as well as children being adopted." The bill will likewise "empower families to welcome vulnerable children with special needs into their lives." CA

Bishops' Statement On Embryonic Stem Cell Research

On June 14, 2008, the U.S. Catholic bishops gathered at their spring meeting in Orlando, Florida, at their semi-annual spring meeting, approved by a vote of 191 to 1 a statement concerning embryonic stem cell research. The statement was the first formal statement issued by the bishops that focused exclusively on this increasingly complex and important subject. Following is the text of the statement (courtesy, USCCB):

Stem cell research has captured the imagination of many in our society. Stem cells are relatively unspecialized cells that, when they divide, can replicate themselves and also produce a variety of more specialized cells. Scientists hope these biological building blocks can be directed to produce many types of cells to repair the human body, cure disease, and alleviate suffering.

Stem cells from adult tissues, umbilical cord blood, and placenta (often loosely called "adult stem cells") can be obtained without harm to the donor and without any ethical problem, and these have already demonstrated great medical promise. But some scientists are most intrigued by stem cells obtained by destroying an embryonic human being in the first week or so of development. Harvesting these "embryonic stem cells" involves the deliberate killing of innocent human beings, a gravely immoral act. Yet some try to justify it by appealing to a hoped-for future benefit to others.

The Imperative to Respect Human Life

The Catholic Church "appreciates and encourages the progress of the biomedical sciences which open up unprecedented therapeutic prospects" (Pope Benedict XVI, address of Jan. 31, 2008). At the same time, it affirms that true service to humanity begins with respect for each and every human life. Because life is our first and most basic gift from an infinitely loving God, it deserves our utmost respect and protection. Direct attacks on innocent human life are always gravely wrong. Yet some researchers, ethicists, and policy makers claim that we may directly kill innocent embryonic human beings as if they were mere objects of research—and even that we should make taxpayers complicit in such killing through use of public funds. Thus, while human life is threatened in many ways in our society, the destruction of human embryos for stem cell research confronts us with the issue of respect for life in a stark new way.

Some Arguments and Our Response

Almost everyone agrees with the principle that individuals and governments should not attack the lives of innocent human beings. However, several arguments have been used to justify destroying human embryos to obtain stem cells. It has been argued that (1) any harm done in this case is outweighed by the potential benefits; (2) what is destroyed is not a human life, or at least not a human being with fundamental human rights; and (3) dissecting human embryos for their cells should not be seen as involving a loss of embryonic life. We would like to comment briefly on each of these arguments.

First, the false assumption that a good end can justify direct killing has been the source of much evil in our world. This utilitarian ethic has especially disastrous consequences when used to justify lethal experiments on fellow human beings in the name of progress. No commitment to a hoped-for "greater good" can erase or diminish the wrong of directly taking innocent human lives here and now. In fact, policies undermining our respect for human life can only endanger the vulnerable patients that stem cell research offers to help. The same ethic that justifies taking some lives to help the patient with Parkinson's or Alzheimer's disease today can be used to sacrifice that very patient tomorrow, if his or her survival is viewed as disadvantaging other human beings considered more deserving or productive. The suffering of patients and families affected by devastating illness deserves our compassion and our committed response, but not at the cost of our respect for life itself.

Second, some claim that the embryo in his or her first week of development is too small, immature, or undeveloped to be considered a "human life." Yet the human embryo, from conception onward, is as much a living member of the human species as any of us. As a matter of biological fact, this new living organism has the full complement of human genes and is actively expressing those genes to live and develop in a way that is unique to human beings, setting the essential foundation for further development. Though dependent in many ways, the embryo is a complete and distinct member of the species Homo sapiens, who develops toward maturity by directing his or her own integrated organic functioning. All later stages of life are steps in the history of a human being already in existence. Just as each of us was once an adolescent, a child, a newborn infant, and a child in the womb, each of us was once an embryo. Others, while acknowledging the scientific fact that the embryo is a living member of the human species, claim that life at this earliest stage is too weak or undeveloped, too lacking in mental or physical abilities, to have full human worth or human rights. But to claim that our rights depend on such factors is to deny that human beings have human dignity, that we have inherent value simply by being members of the human family. If fundamental rights such as the right to life are based on abilities or qualities that can appear or disappear, grow or diminish, and be greater or lesser in different human beings, then there are no inherent human rights, no true human equality, only privileges for the strong. As believers who recognize each human life as the gift of an infinitely loving God, we insist that every human being, however small or seemingly insignificant, matters to God—hence everyone, no matter how weak or small, is of concern to us.

This is not only a teaching of the Catholic Church. Our nation's Declaration of Independence took for granted that human beings are unequal in size, strength, and intelligence. Yet it declared that members of the human race who are unequal in all these respects are created equal in their fundamental rights, beginning with the right to life. Tragically, this principle of equal human rights for all has not always been followed in practice, even by the Declaration's signers. But in our nation's proudest moments Americans have realized that we cannot dismiss or exclude any class of humanity—that basic human rights must belong to all members of the human race without distinction. In light of modern knowledge about the continuity of human development from conception onwards, all of us—without regard to religious affiliation—confront this challenge again today when we make decisions about human beings at the embryonic stage of development.

Finally, some claim that scientists who kill embryos for their stem cells are not actually depriving anyone of life, because they are using "spare" or unwanted embryos who will die anyway. This argument is simply invalid. Ultimately each of us will die, but that gives no one a right to kill us. Our society does not permit lethal experiments on terminally ill patients or condemned prisoners on the pretext that they will soon die anyway. Likewise, the fact that an embryonic human being is at risk of being abandoned by his or her parents gives no individual or government a right to directly kill that human being first.

Cloning and Beyond

It is also increasingly clear that such stem cell "harvesting" will not stop with the destruction of "spare" embryos frozen in fertility clinics. The search for a large supply of viable embryos with diverse genetic profiles has already led some researchers to claim a right to create vast numbers of human embryos solely to destroy them for research. Thus human cloning, performed by the same method used to create Dolly the cloned sheep, is now said to be essential for progress in embryonic stem cell research.

Human cloning is intrinsically evil because it reduces human procreation to a mere manufacturing process, producing new human beings in the laboratory to predetermined specifications as though they were commodities. It shows disrespect for human life in the very act of generating it. This is especially clear when human embryos are produced by cloning for research purposes, because new human lives are generated solely in order to be destroyed. Such cloning for research will also inevitably facilitate attempts to produce live-born cloned children, posing a new challenge to each and every child's right to be respected as a unique individual with his or her own future. Some policy makers offer to prevent this result by mandating that all embryos produced by cloning be destroyed at a certain point, so they cannot survive to birth. These proposals wrongly approve human cloning, while compounding the evil further by insisting that the innocent human victim of cloning must die.

Some researchers and lawmakers even propose developing cloned embryos in a woman's womb for some weeks to harvest more useful tissues and organs—a grotesque practice that Congress has acted against through the Fetus Farming Prohibition Act of 2006. Some would solicit women as egg donors for human cloning research, even offering cash payments to overcome these women's qualms about the risk to their own health from the egg harvesting procedure. Other researchers want to use animal eggs for human cloning experiments, creating "hybrid" embryos that disturbingly blur the line between animal and human species. It now seems undeniable that once we cross the fundamental moral line that prevents us from treating any fellow human being as a mere object of research, there is no stopping point. The only moral stance that affirms the human dignity of all of us is to reject the first step down this path. We therefore urge Catholics and all people of good will to join us in reaffirming, precisely in this context of embryonic stem cell research, that "the killing of innocent human creatures, even if carried out to help others, constitutes an absolutely unacceptable act" (Pope John Paul II, The Gospel of Life [*Evangelium Vitae*], No. 63).

A Better Way

Nature in fact provides ample resources for pursuing medical progress without raising these grave moral concerns. Stem cells from adult tissues and umbilical cord blood are now known to be much more versatile than once thought. These cells are now in widespread use to treat many kinds of cancer and other illnesses, and in clinical trials they have already benefited patients suffering from heart disease, corneal damage, sickle-cell anemia, multiple sclerosis, and many other devastating conditions. [In general see the site www.stemcellresearch.org.] CA

UNITED STATES CONFERENCE OF CATHOLIC BISHOPS

MEETINGS OF U.S. BISHOPS 2007-2008

Baltimore, Maryland, Nov. 12-15, 2007

The Bishops of the United States Catholic Conference in Baltimore, gathered for their Nov. 12–15 fall general meeting.

Agenda

The bishops acted on the following issues:

Heard details of Pope Benedict XVI's then planned visit to the United States from Apr. 15-20, 2008. The announcement included the specific dates and locations for the papal visit. [For details on the papal trip, see above in News in Depth.]

Elected Card. Francis E. George of Chicago as the new president of the conference, and Bp. Gerald F. Kicanas of Tucson, AZ, as vice president and secretary, respectively.

Approved by a vote of 221-7 legislation that specified the conditions under which a bishop is required to procure the consent of his diocesan finance·council and college of consultors before making certain financial transactions or commitments. The legislation is subject to Vatican approval.

Approved a document on liturgical music, an English-language version of a document on weekday celebrations of the Liturgy of the Word (with a Spanish-language version), and revised readings during Lent.

Approved by a unanimous vote the curriculum outline for the development of catechetical materials for high school students.

Approved by a vote of 198-6 an English-language version of a document on stewardship and teenagers, "Stewardship and Teenagers: The Challenge of Being a Disciple," and by a vote of 202-5 a Spanish-language version, of the same document.

Approved by a vote of 212-3 with one abstention a 21-page set of guidelines on catechetical instruction to promote chastity among students (kindergarten through 12th grade).

Issued a new version of the conference's statement on the election, "Forming Consciences for Faithful Citizenship: A Call to Political Responsibility."

Approved a $147.7 million conference budget for 2008 and a 16 percent reduction in the diocesan assessment to fund the USCCB.

Authorized a new statement on Iraq, issued in the name of the outgoing conference president, Bp. William S. Skylstad of Spokane, WA.

Heard a briefing from the staff of the John Jay College of Criminal Justice on the continuing study of the "causes and context" of the clerical sexual abuse crisis.

Approved drafting a policy statement on embryonic stem-cell research and a pastoral document on reproductive technologies.

Orlando, Florida, June 12-14, 2008

The Bishops of the United States Catholic Conference gathered in Orlando, FL, for their June 12–14 meeting.

Agenda

The bishops acted on the following issues:

Approved by a vote of 191-1 a brief policy statement, On Embryonic Stem Cell Research.

Approved by a voice vote the request by the Committee on Doctrine to proceed with a revision of the passages in the Ethical and Religious Directives for Catholic Health Care Services that concern medically-assisted nutrition and hydration.

Approved by a vote of 187-3 the use of "*ustedes*" in place of "*vosotros*" and the corresponding verb constructions in the Order of Mass including the verb constructions of the consecration narrative for use in the dioceses of the United States of America.

Approved by a vote of 141-0 for the 2009 for the diocesan assessment to remain at the same overall total amount as in 2008.

Approved by a vote of 191-1 a brief policy statement on embryonic stem cell research.

Approved by a voice vote that Sept. 26, 2010 will be Catholic Charities USA Day.

Sent for a mail ballot approval of the ICEL Gray Book translation of the Proper of the Seasons (of the Roman Missal) for use in the Dioceses of the United States of America.

BISHOP SKYLSTAD'S REMARKS

On Nov. 12 2007, Bp. William S. Skylstad, outgoing president of the USCCB, addressed the bishops. The bishop declared:

It was three years ago that I stood before you, my brother bishops, humbled and with a bit less than fullness of undaunted courage. You had shortly before placed upon me your trust to serve as the president of our conference of bishops. Since then, each time I sat before you to chair our gatherings, I looked with admiration upon all the faces of you, the bishops, the very force and life of this episcopal conference, keenly aware of the task of service I held in support of each of you and all of you. That has been a source of my daily prayers for our strength, prayers for patience for our weaknesses, but most of all prayers of thanksgiving for the grace and goodness that, from long experience, I know characterize this body.

Over the last three years, together, we have continued to live through challenging times in the life of the Church. Our religious liberty is constantly challenged and needs vigilant defense. Our voice for the unborn, the poor, the stranger, the abused—for peace and for justice—is strong, but not always welcome. Our commitment to evangelization and catechesis, so that our people lead lives faithful to all the moral teachings of the Church, confronts the material and spiritual challenges of our time. And our efforts to protect the young and defenseless entrusted to our pastoral care are needed now more than ever. Those challenges have been more than met by your support as a body of brother bishops, by the experienced and prayerful advice of the various committees dealing with so many questions, and by the excellence of our wonderful staff.

For all of this, then, my desire this morning is to say, Thank you for giving me the opportunity to serve as your president for the past three years. To serve you, especially in support of your ministry to God's people, has been an honor and a spiritual fulfillment.

As I complete my own service of leadership to this body, it seems to me that one of the great challenges to our society and culture is increasingly one of just that—leadership. Or perhaps better said, it is a misunderstanding of the meaning of leadership: on the part of many who aspire to it, and also on the part of some who look for leadership. That is probably not a surprise. Leadership has taken a beating in recent years. Our collective history during the past few decades and years is one marked heavily by divisions. Our politics have been very closely contested, and the resulting bitterness has been palpable.

In our age of exploding communications, the rhythm of discourse, of reflection, and of expression has heightened the scrutiny and sometimes the bitterness surrounding many issues and decisions. This, to be sure, is characteristic of both the left and right, believers and not. It has led to a conception of leadership in certain circles, not as a service to the common good, but as a means to victory and dominance. At times, those looking for leadership then become frustrated because their cause or issue is not advanced fully or given clean and total victory.

But here is precisely the paradox we face in our time. Today, Americans often have an image of leadership that equates it to power. We often hear calls in society for strong and decisive leadership. At the same time, however, there is resentment toward those who seem to "lord it over" others—who use power and influence in a manner that conflicts with the strong current of individualism that characterizes our time

and place. Still, the power of leadership is both a reality and a necessity.

And so, the questions for us as Bishops are these: What is the nature of our leadership and authority, and how do we exercise it? To answer, we must look to the true model of leadership: that of Jesus of Nazareth. And we must ask: how did Jesus lead? How did he use his authority? For us as Bishops, a deep and Christ-like vision of leadership must be at the heart of our service. Christ has called us, as successors of the Apostles, to be his voice in our time. And our time needs to hear the voice of Christ. The Old Testament reminds us of a basic truth: without a vision the people will perish (see Prv 29:18). That vision is Christ's. It is carried by the Church; and we, like Jeremiah, must cry out and not hold back. Indeed at a time like this it should be all so clear to us: We cannot shrink from our calling to be shepherds, to be leaders.

Of course the source of Christ's power, and its goal as well, was simply this: Truth. The ultimate basis of all truth, of all understanding, rests in God himself. As Christ made it his mission to show us his Father, to teach us to seek the will of his Father, we cannot in fidelity to him renounce or weaken our proclamation of the truth. In our day, that truth is so often related to questions of the moral life. For that reason, we need to continue to speak out and teach our people joyfully to embrace life, to incorporate fully the Church's vision about chastity and the nature of marriage, and to understand the humanly and spiritually corrosive results of the contraceptive mentality and lifestyle. As shepherds, we will continue to be clear about the fundamental injustice of abortion and of sacrificing sacred human lives at their earliest moments for the sake of progress in medicine and science, or for convenience. We are in a position to speak to those issues not only because our theology holds God's truth, but also because our contributions to health and to the relief of suffering, by means of our Catholic institutions, are second to none.

We can marvel at examples of the mission of those who established these institutions. In the Northwest for example, the early missionary efforts of so many, the network of Catholic health care institutions founded by women religious, the educational institutions founded by both men and women religious, and Catholic Charities organizations in various dioceses are wonderful examples of great, visionary leadership.

As shepherds, we must continue to move minds and hearts to care for those who are needy and disadvantaged. We will continue to speak that truth to all our elected leaders, and to those whose policies affect our society and our world, which so longs for justice and equity.

But even as the basis of our leadership is the moral and doctrinal truth for salvation given by Christ, our leadership is shaped by Christ in a further way. That is, he "did not regard equality with God [as] something to be grasped"; he took on the form of a slave (Phil 2:6-7). He came among us and lived with us in a way that proclaimed the truth, but he did so first and foremost by example. Without compromise, Christ reached out with love and patience. But his leadership was not one that measured success moment to moment. It was a service, summarized by the magnificence of the washing of the feet, of the prayer for unity, and of submission of himself to the Cross for us, in accordance with the will of his Father. Few in our climate today would see that as a successful form of leadership. But with the eyes of faith, and not of the world, it is precisely that. And that is the model we are called to emulate.

That model can have a wide variety of practical circumstances. Just three weeks ago, Cardinal George and I spent twenty-five minutes with our Holy Father on behalf of our Conference. A week ago yesterday, I celebrated Mass with prisoners at the Washington State Penitentiary in Walla Walla. In reflection, I marveled at how the Church calls us as servants to be present in so many and varied circumstances.

Living out such humility does seem paradoxical to many. Consider, for example, the stories that were reported recently, when Mother Teresa's autobiography was published. Here was a person who exercised leadership in a very real way in our Church and our world, even if that leadership is essentially different from what we have been called to. Her leadership was one based in a fundamental and visible humility that challenged, but also attracted, our world. Still, some people were shocked—perhaps even scandalized—by her memoirs. They revealed that, as with many of the greatest of saints, her humility was not only lived externally. It was a deep spiritual reality. God, it seems, gave her periods of dryness during which he hid his face from her.

The example of Mother Teresa should cause us to reflect as bishops. What is the state of our souls? Our leadership must be rooted in the humility of a life of prayer, every day and before the Eucharist. It must embrace Christ in the humbleness of the Sacrament of Penance. Our leadership as shepherds will never be authentic if our souls are not one with Christ the shepherd. The words of Mother Teresa herself are fit for our own meditation as Bishops in service to the God's people: "It is in being humble that our love becomes real, devoted and ardent. If you are humble nothing will touch you, neither praise nor disgrace, because you know what you are. If you are blamed you will not be discouraged. If they call you a saint you will not put yourself on a pedestal."

In a particular way, during the term of my predecessor, Archbishop Wilton Gregory, as well as during my own tenure, the sexual abuse crisis in our Church has given us a tremendous opportunity for a lesson in humility as well as in needed leadership action. We were humbled by the tears of those who had been hurt so profoundly by a small number from among our clergy. We are continually challenged to bring about reconciliation and healing, and to encourage and defend the thousands of exemplary priests and deacons who are faithful to their vows.

While much remains to be done, and we can never forget what has happened in the past, I am most sincerely grateful for all that has been accomplished in the past five years. The steps that the Church has taken have been remarkable. The light that we are shedding on this dark corner of humanity is making a difference. Things will never be the same for the next generation of children. They will be better; and for that, we as a Church can be very proud.

Leadership as called for by Jesus is, at times, painful and transforming. Such moments are never sought, yet they too are redemptive. But this should not be a surprise to us. In the year 411, St. Augustine of Hippo presided at the ordination of a young Bishop. The great saint took the occasion to offer one of his most striking and challenging homilies, this one on the ministry and life of Bishops. "The one who is to preside over the people," Augustine proclaimed, "must first understand that he is the servant of all." And how does the Bishop serve the faithful entrusted to him? Augustine answers in the clearest terms: "Christ said, Feed my sheep: suffer for the sake of my sheep. This must be the good bishop. If he will not do this, he will not be a bishop" (Sermon 340A). Jesus' reminder of the daily cross in our lives is exactly that. We must be faithful to it and accept it gladly, gratefully, and joyfully.

Our meeting this week will offer us other opportunities to practice Christ-like leadership. In the symbolism of the New Testament, a boat often represents the Church. Hopefully, our leadership places us on the prow of the boat looking forward, always mindful of where we have come from. Jesus, in the boat with the Apostles during the storm on the lake, reminds them of who they should be, asking them to trust humbly and be without fear. Our discussions on faithful citizenship, on liturgical reform, even on the efforts to reorganize ourselves, will give us the chance to practice humility during the coming days.

I would be remiss if I did not acknowledge the great work that has been done in moving forward on our reorganization efforts. This truly is a watershed moment for our Conference of Bishops. While it is challenging, it is a time of great blessing as we build a new system of collaboration that should help us proclaim the Gospel of Jesus with a stronger voice, in a more unified and focused way. I look forward with great hope to the fruits of the work being done. I wish to acknowledge and encourage the work of the committees: those that continue as before, and especially those newly formed. Your efforts in the coming year will be a key to our success. But I also want to say a special word of gratitude to each and every member of the Conference staff. We know that this has not been an easy time for you. But your commitment to assisting us in our work, and the excellence with which you carry out that effort, are another key part of this reorganization. Thanks to you as well.

To Card. George, I express my gratitude for his support and wisdom these past three years. It has been an honor to serve with him. I must give special recognition and appreciation to two exceptional General Secretaries of our Conference: Monsignor William Fay in the first year of my term, and then Monsignor Dave Malloy the last two years. Monsignor Malloy: with all the preparation and implementation of the restructuring of our Conference, all of us and especially I owe you a tremendous debt of gratitude.

As we enter into this new style of collaboration, we may have yet more opportunities to practice charity and humility! Of course, we will not always agree on everything. A good leader, however, recognizes that he does not have all of the insights, all of the answers. As leaders, we are called to recognize the value that each person brings to the conversation, and to recognize that our primary role is to bring about unity in truth. That unity often comes at a price: it costs us our egos; it costs us our individualism. It is a pearl purchased at a great price, but it is a pearl that is priceless.

But more important still is our knowledge that what unites us in an unbreakable bond is the vision implanted in our hearts of the Divine Mission entrusted to each one of us: a vision by which we are strengthened, enlivened, and encouraged. We are servants to that Sacred Mission, which has always been and will forever remain as radically simple as this: proclamation of the salvation of humankind through the death and resurrection of Jesus Christ. And I myself, so long as I have served you in this position of President—indeed, so long as I have been a priest and Bishop—have been convinced, in the words of the Prophet Habbakuk, that "the vision still has its time, / presses on to fulfillment, and will not disappoint; / if it delays, wait for it, / it will surely come, it will not be late" (Hab 2:3). That is the joy of the servant, and it is a joy I have known in serving you, an opportunity for which I will remain forever grateful. God bless you all.

Doctrine of the Catholic Church

THE CATECHISM OF THE CATHOLIC CHURCH

By Russell Shaw

"The *Catechism of the Catholic Church* . . . is a statement of the Church's faith and of Catholic doctrine, attested to or illumined by Sacred Scripture, the Apostolic Tradition, and the Church's Magisterium. I declare it to be a sure norm for teaching the faith and thus a valid and legitimate instrument for ecclesial communion."

Thus Pope John Paul II in the Apostolic Constitution *Fidei Depositum* ("The Deposit of Faith") formally presented the first official catechism or compendium of doctrine for the universal Church to have been published since the 16th century.

Fidei Depositum is dated Oct. 11, 1992, the 30th anniversary of the opening of the Second Vatican Council (1962-65), and that date is significant. The predecessor of the *Catechism of the Catholic Church* is the Roman Catechism or Catechism of the Council of Trent, which was published by Pope St. Pius V in 1566 following the great reforming council held from 1545 to 1563. As the Roman Catechism sets forth the doctrine of the Church in light of the Council of Trent, so the *Catechism of the Catholic Church* sets forth the Church's teaching against the background of Vatican Council II.

History of the Catechism

In development since 1986, the definitive text of the *Catechism of the Catholic Church* was officially approved by Pope John Paul on June 25, 1992, with Dec. 8 the date of formal promulgation.

Nine separate drafts of the *Catechism* were prepared. The document was written in French. In Nov. 1989, the commission of cardinals sent a draft text to all the bishops of the world asking for their comments and suggestions. Although this consultation produced a reaction generally favorable to the text, more than 24,000 individual amendments were submitted by the bishops, and these were reviewed by the commission, and helped to shape the further revision of the document.

The pope in *Fidei Depositum* described the *Catechism* as "a sure and authentic reference text" both for the teaching of Catholic doctrine and particularly for the preparation of local catechisms; he said the *Catechism* was presented with these ends in view. Other purposes mentioned included helping Catholics to deepen their knowledge of the faith, supporting ecumenical efforts by "showing carefully the content and wondrous harmony of the Catholic faith," and providing authoritative answers to anyone who wishes to know "what the Catholic Church believes."

Structure and Contents of the Catechism

The *Catechism* adopts the four-fold division of the *Roman Catechism*. The four parts or "pillars" deal with the Creed; the Sacred Liturgy, with special emphasis on the sacraments; the Christian way of life, analyzed according to the Ten Commandments; and prayer, considered in the framework of the petitions of the Our Father.

Describing this organizational scheme, Pope John Paul said: "The four parts are related one to another: the Christian mystery is the object of faith (first part); it is celebrated and communicated in liturgical actions (second part); it is present to enlighten and sustain the children of God in their actions (third part); it is the basis of our prayer, the privileged expression of which is the Our Father, and it represents the object of our supplication, our praise and our intercession (fourth part)."

The Pope also stressed the Christocentric nature of Christian faith as it is presented in the *Catechism*. "In reading the *Catechism of the Catholic Church* we can perceive the wonderful unity of the mystery of God, his saving will, as well as the central place of Jesus Christ, the only-begotten Son of God, sent by the Father, made man in the womb of the Blessed Virgin Mary by the power of the Holy Spirit, to be our Savior.

The text of the *Catechism of the Catholic Church*, with extensive cross-references and sectional summaries, consists of 2,865 numbered paragraphs. Passages in large print set out its more substantive contents, while passages in small print provide background information and explanations; there are numerous cross-references in the margins directing readers to other passages that treat the same theme or related themes. Among the features of the *Catechism* are the "In Brief" sections found throughout, which sum up the teaching of the preceding unit.

Outline of the Catechism

Prologue (1-25)

The nature of catechesis is described, along with the aim of the present *Catechism* and its intended readership, its structure, its use, and the desirability of adaptations for different cultures, age groups, etc.

Part One: The Profession of Faith (26-1065)

Section One discusses the nature of faith. "Faith is man's response to God, who reveals himself and gives himself to man, at the same time bringing man a superabundant light as he searches for the ultimate meaning of his life. Thus we shall consider first that search (Chapter One), then the divine Revelation by which God comes to meet man (Chapter Two), and finally the response of faith (Chapter Three)" (26). The topics discussed include knowledge of God; Divine Revelation and its transmission; Sacred Scripture; and faith as the human response to God. "We do not believe in formulas, but in those realities they express, which faith allows us to touch. . . . All the same, we do approach these realities with the help of formulations of the faith which permit us to express the faith and to hand it on, to celebrate it in community, to assimilate and live on it more and more" (170).

Section Two deals with the profession of Christian faith, with the treatment organized according to the articles of the Creed. The Creed used is the Apostles' Creed; its "great authority," says the Catechism, quoting St. Ambrose, arises from its being "the Creed of the Roman Church, the See of Peter, the first of the apostles" (194). Among the doctrines covered in the three chapters of this section are the Trinity, creation, the angels, the creation of man, original sin, the Incarnation, the virgin birth, redemption, the Resurrection of Christ, the work of the Holy Spirit, the Church, the hierarchical constitution of the Church, the communion of saints, the Virgin Mary as Mother of Christ and Mother of the Church, the resurrection of the dead, judgment, heaven, and hell. "[T]he Creed's final 'Amen' repeats and confirms its first words: 'I believe.' To believe is to say 'Amen' to God's words, promises and commandments; to entrust oneself completely to him who is the 'Amen' of infinite love and perfect faithfulness. The Christian's everyday life will then be the 'Amen' to the 'I believe' of our baptismal profession of faith" (1064).

Part Two: The Celebration of the Christian Mystery (1066-1690)

Section One considers the sacramental economy. It explains that in this present "age of the Church," begun on Pentecost, "Christ now lives and acts in his Church, in a new way appropriate to this new age. He acts through the sacraments in what the common Tradition of the East and the West calls 'the sacramental economy' . . . the communication (or 'dispensation') of the fruits of Christ's Paschal Mystery in the celebration of the Church's 'sacramental' liturgy" (1076). Topics treated here are the Paschal Mystery and its sacramental celebration.

Section Two covers the seven sacraments of the Church. "Christ instituted the sacraments of the new law. . . . The seven sacraments touch all the stages and all the important moments of Christian life: they give birth and increase, healing and mission to the Christian's life of faith. There is thus a certain resemblance between the stages of natural life and the stages of the spiritual life" (1210). The presentation is organized in four chapters. These are: the sacraments of Christian initiation (Baptism, Confirmation, the Eucharist) in chapter one; the sacraments of healing (Penance and Reconciliation, the Anointing of the Sick) in chapter two; the "sacraments at the service of communion" (Holy Orders and Matrimony) in chapter three; and sacramentals and Christian funerals in chapter four.

Part Three: Life in Christ (1691-2557)

Section One is entitled "Man's Vocation: Life in the Spirit." Its three chapters discuss the dignity of the human person, the human community, and "God's Salvation: Law and Grace" (the moral law, grace and justification, the Church as teacher of moral truth). "Catechesis has to reveal in all clarity the joy and the demands of the way of Christ. . . . The first and last point of reference of this catechesis will always be Jesus Christ himself, who is 'they way, and the truth, and the life' " (1697-1698).

Section Two reflects on the contents of Christian moral life. The treatment is organized according to the Ten Commandments, with a chapter devoted to each commandment and its concrete applications. While the commandments admit of what is traditionally called light matter (venial sin), nevertheless, the text says: "Since they express man's fundamental duties toward God and toward his neighbor, the Ten Commandments reveal, in their primordial content, grave obligations. They are fundamentally immutable, and they oblige always and everywhere. No one can dispense from them. The Ten Commandments are engraved by God in the human heart" (2072).

Part Four: Christian Prayer (2558-2865)

Section One considers prayer in Christian life, underlining the relationship of this topic to the rest of the Catechism: "The Church professes this mystery [of faith] in the Apostles' Creed (Part One) and celebrates it in the sacramental liturgy (Part Two), so that the life of the faithful may be conformed to Christ in the Holy Spirit to the glory of God the Father (Part Three). This mystery, then, requires that the faithful believe in it, that they celebrate it, and that they live from it in a vital and personal relationship with the living and true God. This relationship is prayer" (2558). The section then discusses the "revelation of prayer" in the Old Testament and now in the age of the Church, the tradition of prayer, and the life of prayer (kinds of prayer, problems and perseverance in prayer).

Section Two presents an extended reflection on the Our Father, considered as the model of prayer. Quoting Tertullian, the *Catechism* says: "The Lord's Prayer 'is truly the summary of the whole Gospel.' Since the Lord . . . after handing over the practice of prayer, said elsewhere, 'Ask and you will receive,' and since everyone has petitions which are peculiar to his circumstances, the regular and appropriate prayer [the Lord's Prayer] is said first, as the foundation of further desires" (2761).

Reception of the Catechism

Following the publication of the Catechism of the Catholic Church, Pope John Paul established an Interdicasterial Commission for the Catechism, under the chairmanship of Cardinal Ratzinger, responsible for overseeing translations of the volume and reviewing and approving suggested changes in the text. The commission approved the English translation of the Catechism in Feb. 1994, and it was published on June 22 of that year — in the United States, under the auspices of the National Conference of Catholic Bishops (now the United States Conference of Catholic Bishops).

Pope John Paul presented the *editio typica* or normative Latin version of the *Catechism* in a formal ceremony on Sept. 8, 1997.

The following day, Cardinal Ratzinger presented the

editio typica at a Vatican news conference. At the same time, he also introduced more than a hundred changes that had been approved for incorporation into the text.

In the United States, the National Conference of Catholic Bishops in 1994 established an Ad Hoc Committee to Oversee the Use of the Catechism. It has an office and staff at NCCB headquarters in Washington, DC.

Compendium of the Catechism

On June 28, 2005, Pope Benedict XVI issued a *motu proprio* for the approval and publication of the *Compendium of the Catechism of the Catholic Church*.

The Introduction to the Compendium, written by Joseph Cardinal Ratzinger prior to his election as pope, described the process by which the text came about, namely to realize more fully the potential of the Catechism and to provide a synthesis of the vast treasure of its teachings.

Like the Catechism, the Compendium offers four parts, corresponding to the fundamental laws of life in Christ. Part one is "The Profession of Faith"; part two is "The Celebration of the Christian Mystery"; part three is "Life in Christ"; and the fourth part is "Christian Prayer."

DOGMATIC CONSTITUTION ON THE CHURCH — *LUMEN GENTIUM*

Following are excerpts from the first two chapters of the "Dogmatic Constitution on the Church" (*Lumen Gentium*) promulgated by the Second Vatican Council. They describe the relation of the Catholic Church to the Kingdom of God, the nature and foundation of the Church, the People of God, the necessity of membership and participation in the Church for salvation. Additional subjects in the constitution are treated in other *Almanac* entries.

I. MYSTERY OF THE CHURCH

By her relationship with Christ, the Church is a kind of sacrament or sign of intimate union with God, and of the unity of all mankind (No. 1).

He (the eternal Father) planned to assemble in the holy Church all those who would believe in Christ. Already from the beginning of the world the foreshadowing of the Church took place. She was prepared for in a remarkable way throughout the history of the people of Israel and by means of the Old Covenant. Established in the present era of time, the Church was made manifest by the outpouring of the Spirit. At the end of time she will achieve her glorious fulfillment. Then all just men from the time of Adam, "from Abel, the just one, to the last of the elect," will be gathered together with the Father in the universal Church (No. 2).

When the work which the Father had given the Son to do on earth (cf. Jn 17:4) was accomplished, the Holy Spirit was sent on the day of Pentecost in order that he might forever sanctify the Church, and thus all believers would have access to the Father through Christ in the one Spirit (cf. Eph 2:18).

The Spirit dwells in the Church and in the hearts of the faithful as in a temple (cf. 1 Cor 3:16; 6:19).... The Spirit guides the Church into the fullness of truth (cf. Jn 16:13) and gives her a unity of fellowship and service. He furnishes and directs her with various gifts, both hierarchical and charismatic, and adorns her with the fruits of His grace (cf. Eph 4:11-12; 1 Cor 12:4; Gal 5:22). By the power of the Gospel he makes the Church grow, perpetually renews her, and leads her to perfect union with her Spouse (No. 4).

Foundation of the Church

The mystery of the holy Church is manifest in her very foundation, for the Lord Jesus inaugurated her by preaching the Good News, that is, the coming of God's Kingdom, which, for centuries, had been promised in the Scriptures.... In Christ's word, in his works, and in his presence this Kingdom reveals itself to men.

The miracles of Jesus also confirm that the Kingdom has already arrived on earth.

Before all things, however, the Kingdom is clearly visible in the very Person of Christ, Son of God and Son of Man.

When Jesus rose up again after suffering death on the cross for mankind, he manifested that he had been appointed Lord, Messiah, and Priest forever (cf. Acts 2:36; Heb 5:6; 7:17-21), and he poured out on his disciples the Spirit promised by the Father (cf. Acts 2:33). The Church, consequently, equipped with the gifts of her Founder and faithfully guarding his precepts receives the mission to proclaim and to establish among all peoples the Kingdom of Christ and of God. She becomes on earth the initial budding forth of that Kingdom. While she slowly grows, the Church strains toward the consummation of the Kingdom and, with all her strength, hopes and desires to be united in glory with her King (No. 5).

Figures of the Church

In the Old Testament the revelation of the Kingdom had often been conveyed by figures of speech. In the same way the inner nature of the Church was now to be made known to us through various images.

The Church is a sheepfold... a flock... a tract of land to be cultivated, the field of God... his choice vineyard... the true vine is Christ... the edifice of God... the house of God... the holy temple (whose members are) living stones... this holy city... a bride... our Mother... the spotless spouse of the spotless Lamb... an exile (No. 6).

In the human nature which he united to himself, the Son of God redeemed man and transformed him into a new creation (cf. Gal 6:15; 2 Cor 5:17) by overcoming death through his own death and resurrection. By communicating his Spirit to his brothers, called together from all peoples, Christ made them mystically into his own body.

In that body, the life of Christ is poured into the believers, who, through the sacraments, are united in a hidden and real way to Christ who suffered and was glorified. Through baptism we are formed in the likeness of Christ.

Truly partaking of the body of the Lord in the breaking of the eucharistic bread, we are taken up into communion with him and with one another (No. 7).

One Body in Christ

As all the members of the human body, though they are many, form one body, so also are the faithful in Christ (cf. 1 Cor 12:12). Also, in the building up of Christ's body there is a flourishing variety of members and functions. There is only one Spirit who distributes his different gifts for the welfare of the Church (cf. 1 Cor 12:1-11). Among these gifts stands out the grace given to the apostles. To their authority, the Spirit himself subjected even those who were endowed with charisms (cf. 1 Cor 14). The head of this body is Christ (No. 7).

Mystical Body of Christ

Christ, the one Mediator, established and ceaselessly sustains here on earth his holy Church, the community of faith, hope, and charity, as a visible structure. Through her he communicates truth and grace to all. But the society furnished with hierarchical agencies and the Mystical Body of Christ are not to be considered as two realities, nor are the visible assembly and the spiritual community, nor the earthly Church and the Church enriched with heavenly things. Rather they form one interlocked reality which is comprised of a divine and a human element. For this reason, this reality is compared to the mystery of the incarnate Word. Just as the assumed nature inseparably united to the divine Word serves him as a living instrument of salvation, so, in a similar way, does the communal structure of the Church serve Christ's Spirit, who vivifies it by way of building up the body (cf. Eph 4:16).

This is the unique Church of Christ which in the Creed we avow as one, holy, catholic, and apostolic. After his Resurrection our Savior handed her over to Peter to be shepherded (Jn 21:17), commissioning him and the other apostles to propagate and govern her (cf. Mt 28:18, ff.). Her he erected for all ages as "the pillar and mainstay of the truth" (1 Tm 3:15). This Church, constituted and organized in the world as a society, subsists in the Catholic Church, which is governed by the successor of Peter and by the bishops in union with that successor, although many elements of sanctification and of truth can be found outside of her visible structure. These elements, however, as gifts properly belonging to the Church of Christ, possess an inner dynamism toward Catholic unity.

The Church, embracing sinners in her bosom, is at the same time holy and always in need of being purified, and incessantly pursues the path of penance and renewal.

The Church, "like a pilgrim in a foreign land, presses forward, announcing the cross and death of the Lord until he comes" (cf. 1 Cor 11:26) (No. 8).

II. THE PEOPLE OF GOD

At all times and among every people, God has given welcome to whosoever fears him and does what is right (cf. Acts 10:35). It has pleased God, however, to make men holy and save them not merely as individuals without any mutual bonds, but by making them into a single people, a people which acknowledges him in truth and serves him in holiness. He therefore chose the race of Israel as a people unto himself. With it he set up a covenant. Step by step he taught this people by manifesting in its history both himself and the decree of his will, and by making it holy unto himself. All these things, however, were done by way of preparation and as a figure of that new and perfect covenant which was to be ratified in Christ.

Christ instituted this New Covenant, that is to say, the New Testament, in his blood (cf. 1 Cor 11:25), by calling together a people made up of Jew and Gentile, making them one, not according to the flesh but in the Spirit.

This was to be the new People of God... reborn... through the Word of the living God (cf. 1 Pt 1:23). from water and the Holy Spirit (cf. Jn 3:5-6)... "a chosen race, a royal priesthood, a holy nation, a purchased people. You who in times past were not a people, but are now the People of God" (1 Pt 2:9-10).

That messianic people has for its head Christ. Its law is the new commandment to love as Christ loved us (cf. Jn 13:34). Its goal is the Kingdom of God, which has been begun by God himself on earth, and which is to be further extended until it is brought to perfection by him at the end of time.

This messianic people, although it does not actually include all men, and may more than once look like a small flock, is nonetheless a lasting and sure seed of unity, hope, and salvation for the whole human race. Established by Christ as a fellowship of life, charity, and truth, it is also used by him as an instrument for the redemption of all, and is sent forth into the whole world as the light of the world and the salt of the earth (cf. Mt 5:13-16).

Israel according to the flesh...was already called the Church of God (Neh 13:1; cf. Nm 20:4; Dt 23:1, ff.). Likewise the new Israel...is also called the Church of Christ (cf. Mt 16:18). For he has bought it for himself with his blood (cf. Acts 20:28), has filled it with his Spirit, and provided it with those means which befit it as a visible and social unity. God has gathered together as one all those who in faith look upon Jesus as the author of salvation and the source of unity and peace, and has established them as the Church, that for each and all she may be the visible sacrament of this saving unity (No. 9).

Priesthood

The baptized, by regeneration and the anointing of the Holy Spirit, are consecrated into a holy priesthood. [All members of the Church participate in the priesthood of Christ, through the common priesthood of the faithful. (*See* **Priesthood of the Laity**.)]

Though they differ from one another in essence and not only in degree, the common priesthood of the faithful and the ministerial or hierarchical priesthood are nonetheless interrelated. Each of them in its own special way is a participation in the one priesthood of Christ (No. 10).

It is through the sacraments and the exercise of the virtues that the sacred nature and organic structure of the priestly community is brought into operation (No. 11). (*See* **Role of the Sacraments**.)

Prophetic Office

The holy People of God shares also in Christ's prophetic office. It spreads abroad a living witness to him, especially by means of a life of faith and charity and by offering to God a sacrifice of praise.... The body of the faithful as a whole, anointed as they are by the Holy One (cf. Jn 2:20,27), cannot err in matters of belief. Thanks to a supernatural sense of faith which characterizes the People as a whole, it manifests this unerring quality when, "from the bishops down to the last member of the laity," it shows universal agreement in matters of faith and morals.

God's People accepts not the word of men but the very Word of God (cf. 1 Thes 2:13). It clings without fail to the faith once delivered to the saints (cf. Jude 3), penetrates it more deeply by accurate insights, and applies it more thoroughly to life. All this it does under the lead of a sacred teaching authority to which it loyally defers.

It is not only through the sacraments and Church ministries that the same Holy Spirit sanctifies and leads the People of God.... He distributes special graces among the faithful of every rank. By these gifts he makes them fit and ready to undertake the various tasks or offices advantageous for the renewal and upbuilding of the Church. These charismatic gifts ... are to be received with thanksgiving and consolation, for they are exceedingly suitable and useful for the needs of the Church.

Judgment as to their genuineness and proper use belongs to those who preside over the Church, and to whose special competence it belongs... to test all things and hold fast to that which is good (cf. 1 Thes 5:12;19-21) (No. 12).

All Are Called

All men are called to belong to the new People of God. Wherefore this People, while remaining one and unique, is to be spread throughout the whole world and must exist in all ages, so that the purpose of God's will may be fulfilled. In the beginning God made human nature one. After his children were scattered, he decreed that they should at length be united again (cf. Jn 11:52). It was for this reason that God sent his Son.... that he might be Teacher, King, and Priest of all, the Head of the new and universal People of the sons of God. For this God finally sent his Son's Spirit as Lord and Lifegiver. He it is who, on behalf of the whole Church and each and every one of those who believe, is the principle of their coming together and remaining together in the teaching of the apostles and in fellowship, in the breaking of bread and in prayers (cf. Acts 2:42) (No. 13).

One People of God

It follows that among all the nations of earth there is but one People of God, which takes its citizens from every race, making them citizens of a Kingdom which is of a heavenly and not an earthly nature. For all the faithful scattered throughout the world are in communion with each other in the Holy Spirit.... the Church or People of God foster(s) and take(s) to herself, insofar as they are good, the ability, resources and customs of each people. Taking them to herself, she purifies, strengthens, and ennobles them.... This characteristic of universality which adorns the People of God is a gift from the Lord himself. By reason of it, the Catholic Church strives energetically and constantly to bring all humanity with all its riches back to Christ its Head in the unity of his Spirit.

In virtue of this catholicity each individual part of the Church contributes through its special gifts to the good of the other parts and of the whole Church. Thus through the common sharing of gifts. The whole and each of the parts receive increase.

All men are called to be part of this catholic unity of the People of God. And there belong to it or are related to it in various ways, the Catholic faithful as well as all who believe in Christ, and indeed the whole of mankind. For all men are called to salvation by the grace of God (No. 13).

The Catholic Church

This sacred Synod turns its attention first to the Catholic faithful. Basing itself upon sacred Scripture and tradition, it teaches that the Church is necessary for salvation. For Christ, made present to us in his Body, which is the Church, is the one Mediator and the unique Way of salvation. In explicit terms he himself affirmed the necessity of faith and baptism (cf. Mk 16:16; Jn 3:5) and thereby affirmed also the necessity of the Church, for through baptism as through a door men enter the Church. Whosoever, therefore, knowing that the Catholic Church was made necessary by God through Jesus Christ, would refuse to enter her or to remain in her could not be saved.

They are fully incorporated into the society of the Church who, possessing the Spirit of Christ, accepts her entire system and all the means of salvation given to her, and through union with her visible structure are joined to Christ, who rules her through the Supreme Pontiff and the bishops. This joining is effected by the bonds of professed faith, of the sacraments, of ecclesiastical government, and of communion. He is not saved, however, who, though he is part of the body of the Church, does not persevere in charity. He remains indeed in the bosom of the Church, but only in a "bodily" manner and not "in his heart."

Catechumens who, moved by the Holy Spirit, seek with explicit intention to be incorporated into the Church, are by that very intention joined to her. Mother Church already embraces them as her own (No. 14).

Other Christians, The Unbaptized

The Church recognizes that in many ways she is linked with those who, being baptized, are honored with the name of Christian, though they do not profess the faith in its entirety or do not preserve unity of communion with the successor of Peter.

We can say that in some real way they are joined with us in the Holy Spirit, for to them also he gives his gifts and graces, and is thereby operative among them with his sanctifying power (No. 15).

Finally, those who have not yet received the Gospel are related in various ways to the People of God. In the first place there is the people to whom the covenants and the promises were given and from whom Christ was born according to the flesh (cf. Rom 9:4-5). On account of their fathers, this people remains most dear to God, for God does not repent of the gifts he makes nor of the calls he issues (cf. Rom 11:28-29).

But the plan of salvation also includes those who acknowledge the Creator. In the first place among these are the Moslems. Nor is God himself far distant from those who in shadows and images seek the unknown God.

Those also can attain to everlasting salvation who through no fault of their own do not know the Gospel of Christ or his Church, yet sincerely seek God and, moved by grace, strive by their deeds to do his will as it is known to them through the dictates of conscience. Nor does divine Providence deny the help necessary for salvation to those who, without blame on their part, have not yet arrived at an explicit knowledge of God, but who strive to live a good life, thanks to his grace. Whatever goodness or truth is found among them is looked upon by the Church as a preparation for the Gospel. She regards such qualities as given by him who enlightens all men so that they may finally have life (No. l6).

THE POPE, TEACHING AUTHORITY, COLLEGIALITY

The Roman Pontiff—the successor of St. Peter as the bishop of Rome and head of the Church on earth —has full and supreme authority over the universal Church in matters pertaining to faith and morals (teaching authority), discipline and government (jurisdictional authority).

The primacy of the pope is real and supreme power. It is not merely a prerogative of honor—that is, of his being regarded as the first among equals. Neither does primacy imply that the pope is just the presiding officer of the collective body of bishops. The pope is the head of the Church.

Catholic belief in the primacy of the pope was stated in detail in the dogmatic constitution on the Church, *Pastor Aeternus*, approved in 1870 by the fourth session of the First Vatican Council. Some elaboration of the doctrine was made in the Dogmatic Constitution on the Church (*Lumen Gentium*) which was approved and promulgated by the Second Vatican Council Nov. 21, 1964. The entire body of teaching on the subject is based on Scripture and tradition and the centuries-long experience of the Church.

Infallibility

The essential points of doctrine concerning infallibility in the Church and the infallibility of the pope were stated by the Second Vatican Council in the Dogmatic Constitution on the Church, as follows:

"This infallibility with which the divine Redeemer willed his Church to be endowed in defining a doctrine of faith and morals extends as far as extends the deposit of divine revelation, which must be religiously guarded and faithfully expounded. This is the infallibility which the Roman Pontiff, the head of the college of bishops, enjoys in virtue of his office, when, as the supreme shepherd and teacher of all the faithful who confirms his brethren in their faith (cf. Lk 22:32), he proclaims by a definitive act some doctrine of faith or morals. Therefore his definitions, of themselves, and not from the consent of the Church, are justly styled irreformable, for they are pronounced with the assistance of the Holy Spirit, an assistance promised to him in blessed Peter. Therefore they need no approval of others, nor do they allow an appeal to any other judgment. For then the Roman Pontiff is not pronouncing judgment as a private person. Rather, as the supreme teacher of the universal Church, as one in whom the charism of the infallibility of the Church herself is individually present, he is expounding or defending a doctrine of Catholic faith.

"The infallibility promised to the Church resides also in the body of bishops when that body exercises supreme teaching authority with the successor of Peter. To the resultant definitions the assent of the Church can never be wanting, on account of the activity of that same Holy Spirit, whereby the whole flock of Christ is preserved and progresses in unity of faith.

"But when either the Roman Pontiff or the body of bishops together with him defines a judgment, they pronounce it in accord with revelation itself. All are obliged to maintain and be ruled by this revelation, which, as written or preserved by tradition, is transmitted in its entirety through the legitimate succession of bishops and especially through the care of the Roman Pontiff himself.

"Under the guiding light of the Spirit of truth, revelation is thus religiously preserved and faithfully expounded in the Church. The Roman Pontiff and the bishops, in view of their office and of the importance of the matter, strive painstakingly and by appropriate means to inquire properly into that revelation and to give apt expression to its contents. But they do not allow that there could be any new public revelation pertaining to the divine deposit of faith" (No. 25).

Authentic Teaching

The pope rarely speaks *ex cathedra*—that is, "from the chair" of St. Peter—for the purpose of making an infallible pronouncement. More often and in various ways he states authentic teaching in line with Scripture, tradition, the living experience of the Church, and the whole analogy of faith. Of such teaching, the Second Vatican Council said in its Dogmatic Constitution on the Church (No. 25):

"Religious submission of will and of mind must be shown in a special way to the authentic teaching authority of the Roman Pontiff, even when he is not speaking *ex cathedra*. That is, it must be shown in such a way that his supreme magisterium is acknowledged with reverence, the judgments made by him are sincerely adhered to, according to his manifest mind and will. His mind and will in the matter may be known chiefly either from the character of the documents, from his frequent repetition of the same doctrine, or from his manner of speaking."

Bishops "are authentic teachers, that is, teachers endowed with the authority of Christ, who preach to the people committed to them the faith they must believe and put into practice. By the light of the Holy Spirit, they make that faith clear, bringing forth from the treasury of revelation new things and old (cf. Mt 13:52), making faith bear fruit and vigilantly warding off any errors which threaten their flock (cf. 2 Tm 4:1-4).

"Bishops, teaching in communion with the Roman Pontiff, are to be respected by all as witnesses to divine and Catholic truth. In matters of faith and morals, the bishops speak in the name of Christ and the faithful are to accept their teaching and adhere to it with a religious assent of soul."

Magisterium—Teaching Authority

Responsibility for teaching doctrine and judging orthodoxy belongs to the official teaching authority of the Church.

This authority is personalized in the pope, the successor of St. Peter as head of the Church, and in the bishops together and in union with the pope, as it was originally committed to Peter and to the whole college of apostles under his leadership. They are the official teachers of the Church.

Others have auxiliary relationships with the magisterium: theologians, in the study and clarification of doctrine; teachers—priests, religious, lay persons—who cooperate with the pope and bishops in spreading knowledge of religious truth; the faithful, who by their sense of faith and personal witness contribute to the development of doctrine and the establishment of its relevance to life in the Church and the world.

The magisterium, Pope Paul VI noted in an address at a general audience Jan. 11, 1967, "is a subordinate and faithful echo and secure interpreter of the divine word." It does not reveal new truths, "nor is it superior to sacred Scripture." Its competence extends to the limits of divine revelation manifested in Scripture and tradition and the living experience of the Church, with respect to matters of faith and morals and related subjects. Official teaching in these areas is infallible when it is formally defined, for belief and acceptance by all members of the Church, by the pope, acting in the capacity of supreme shepherd of the flock of Christ; also, when doctrine is proposed and taught with moral unanimity of bishops with the pope in a solemn collegial manner, as in an ecumenical council, and/or in the ordinary course of events. Even when not infallibly defined, official teaching in the areas of faith and morals is authoritative and requires religious assent.

The teachings of the magisterium have been documented in creeds, formulas of faith, decrees and enactments of ecumenical and particular councils, various kinds of doctrinal statements, encyclical letters and other teaching instruments. They have also been incorporated into the liturgy, with the result that the law of prayer is said to be a law of belief.

Collegiality

The bishops of the Church, in union with the pope, have supreme teaching and pastoral authority over the whole Church in addition to the authority of office they have for their own dioceses.

This collegial authority is exercised in a solemn manner in an ecumenical council and can be exercised in other ways as well, "provided that the head of the college calls them to collegiate action, or at least so approves or freely accepts the united action of the dispersed bishops that it is made a true collegiate act."

This doctrine is grounded on the fact that: "Just as, by the Lord's will, St. Peter and the other apostles constituted one apostolic college, so in a similar way the Roman Pontiff as the successor of Peter, and the bishops as the successors of the apostles are joined together."

Doctrine on collegiality was stated by the Second Vatican Council in the Dogmatic Constitution on the Church (Nos. 22 and 23).

(For coverage of the *Role of Mary in the Mystery of Christ and the Church,* Chapter VIII, *Lumen Gentium, see the section on the* **Blessed Virgin Mary** *on page 119.*)

REVELATION

Following are excerpts from the "Dogmatic Constitution on Divine Revelation" (*Dei Verbum*) promulgated by the Second Vatican Council on Nov. 18, 1965. They describe the nature and process of divine revelation, inspiration and interpretation of Scripture, the Old and New Testaments, and the role of Scripture in the life of the Church.

I. REVELATION ITSELF

God chose to reveal himself and to make known to us the hidden purpose of his will (cf. Eph 1:9) by which through Christ, the Word made flesh, man has access to the Father in the Holy Spirit and comes to share in the divine nature (cf. Eph 2:18; 2 Pt 1:4). Through this revelation, therefore, the invisible God (cf. Col 1:15; 1 Tm 1:17). speaks to men as friends (cf. Ex 33:11; Jn 15:14-15) and lives among them (cf. Bar 3:38) so that he may invite and take them into fellowship with himself. This plan of revelation is realized by deeds and words having an inner unity: the deeds wrought by God in the history of salvation manifest and confirm the teaching and realities signified by the words, while the words proclaim the deeds and clarify the mystery contained in them. By this revelation then, the deepest truth about God and the salvation of man is made clear to us in Christ, who is the Mediator and at the same time the fullness of all revelation (No. 2).

God from the start manifested himself to our first parents. Then after their fall his promise of redemption aroused in them the hope of being saved (cf. Gn 3:15), and from that time on he ceaselessly kept the human race in his care, in order to give eternal life to those who perseveringly do good in search of salvation (cf. Rom 2:6-7). He called Abraham in order to make of him a great nation (cf. Gn 12:2). Through the patriarchs, and after them through Moses and the prophets, he taught this nation to acknowledge himself as the one living and true God and to wait for the Savior promised by him. In this manner he prepared the way for the Gospel down through the centuries (No. 3).

Revelation in Christ

Then, after speaking in many places and varied ways through the prophets, God "last of all in these days has spoken to us by his Son" (Heb 1:1-2). Jesus perfected revelation by fulfilling it through his whole work of making himself present and manifesting himself: through his words and deeds, his signs and wonders, but especially through his death and glorious resurrection from the dead and final sending of the Spirit of truth. Moreover, he confirmed with divine testimony what revelation proclaimed: that God is with us to free us from the darkness of sin and death, and to raise us up to life eternal.

The Christian dispensation, therefore, as the new and definitive covenant, will never pass away, and we now await no further new public revelation before the glorious manifestation of our Lord Jesus Christ (cf. 1 Tm 6:14; Ti 2:13) (No. 4).

II. TRANSMISSION OF REVELATION

God has seen to it that what he had revealed for the salvation of all nations would abide perpetually in its full integrity and be handed on to all generations. Therefore Christ the Lord, in whom the full revelation of the supreme God is brought to completion (cf. 2 Cor 1:20; 3:16; 4:6), commissioned the apostles to preach to all men that Gospel which is the source of all saving truth and moral teaching, and thus to impart to them divine gifts. This Gospel had been promised in former times through the prophets, and Christ himself fulfilled it and promulgated it with his own lips. This commission was faithfully fulfilled by the apostles who, by their oral preaching, by example, and by ordinances, handed on what they had received from Christ or what they had learned through the prompting of the Holy Spirit. The commission was fulfilled, too, by those apostles and apostolic men who under the inspiration of the same Holy Spirit committed the message of salvation to writing (No. 7).

Tradition

But in order to keep the Gospel forever whole and alive within the Church, the apostles left bishops as their successors, "handing over their own teaching role" to them. This sacred tradition, therefore, and sacred Scripture of both the Old and the New Testament are like a mirror in which the pilgrim Church on earth looks at God (No. 7).

The apostolic preaching, which is expressed in a special way in the inspired books, was to be preserved by a continuous succession of preachers until the end of time. Therefore the apostles, handing on what they themselves had received, warn the faithful to hold fast to the traditions which they have learned. Now what was handed on by the apostles includes everything which contributes to the holiness of life, and the increase in faith of the People of God; and so the Church, in her teaching, life, and worship, perpetuates and hands on to all generations all that she herself is, all that she believes (No. 8).

Development of Doctrine

This tradition which comes from the apostles develops in the Church with the help of the Holy Spirit. For there is a growth in the understanding of the realities and the words which have been handed down. This happens through the contemplation and study made by believers through the intimate understanding of spiritual things they experience, and through the preaching of those who have received through episcopal succession the sure gift of truth. For, as the centuries succeed one another, the Church constantly moves forward toward the fullness of divine truth until the words of God reach their complete fulfillment in her.

The words of the holy Fathers witness to the living presence of this tradition, whose wealth is poured into the practice and life of the believing and praying Church. Through the same tradition the Church's full canon of the sacred books is known, and the sacred writings themselves are more profoundly understood and unceasingly made active in her; ... and the Holy Spirit, through whom the living voice of the Gospel resounds in the Church, and through her, in the world, leads unto all truth those who believe and makes the word of Christ dwell abundantly in them (cf. Col 3:16) (No. 8).

Tradition and Scripture

Hence there exist a close connection and communication between sacred tradition and sacred Scripture. For both of them, flowing from the same divine wellspring, in a certain way merge into a unity and tend toward the same end. For sacred Scripture is the word of God inasmuch as it is consigned to writing under the inspiration of the divine Spirit. To the successors of the apostles, sacred tradition hands on in its full purity

God's word, which was entrusted to the apostles by Christ the Lord and the Holy Spirit. Thus, led by the light of the Spirit of truth, these successors can in their preaching preserve this word of God faithfully, explain it, and make it more widely known. Consequently, it is not from sacred Scripture alone that the Church draws her certainty about every thing which has been revealed. Therefore both sacred tradition and sacred Scripture are to be accepted and venerated with the same sense of devotion and reverence (No. 9).

Sacred tradition and sacred Scripture form one sacred deposit of the word of God, which is committed to the Church (No. 10).

Teaching Authority of Church

The task of authentically interpreting the word of God, whether written or handed on, has been entrusted exclusively to the living teaching office of the Church, whose authority is exercised in the name of Jesus Christ. This teaching office is not above the word of God, but serves it, teaching only what has been handed on ... it draws from this one deposit of faith everything which it presents for belief as divinely revealed.

It is clear, therefore, that sacred tradition, sacred Scripture, and the teaching authority of the Church ... are so linked and joined together that one cannot stand without the others, and that all together and each in its own way under the action of the one Holy Spirit contribute effectively to the salvation of souls (No. 10).

III. INSPIRATION, INTERPRETATION

Those revealed realities contained and presented in sacred Scripture have been committed to writing under the inspiration of the Holy Spirit. Holy Mother Church, relying on the belief of the apostles, holds that the books of both the Old and New Testament in their entirety, with all their parts, are sacred and canonical because, having been written under the inspiration of the Holy Spirit (cf. Jn 20:31; 2 Tm 3:16; 2 Pt 1:19-21, 3:15-16) they have God as their author and have been handed on as such to the Church herself. In composing the sacred books, God chose men and, while employed by him, they made use of their powers and abilities, so that, with him acting in them and through them, they, as true authors, consigned to writing everything and only those things which he wanted (No. 11).

Inerrancy

Therefore, since everything asserted by the inspired authors or sacred writers must be held to be asserted by the Holy Spirit, it follows that the books of Scripture must be acknowledged as teaching firmly, faithfully, and without error that truth which God wanted put into the sacred writings for the sake of our salvation. Therefore "all Scripture is inspired by God and useful for teaching, for reproving, for correcting, for instruction in justice; that the man of God may be perfect, equipped for every good work" (2 Tm 3:16-17) (No. 11).

Literary Forms

However, since God speaks in sacred Scripture through men in human fashion, the interpreter of sacred Scripture, in order to see clearly what God wanted to communicate to us, should carefully investigate what meaning the sacred writers really intended, and what God wanted to manifest by means of their words.

The interpreter must investigate what meaning the sacred writer intended to express and actually expressed in particular circumstances as he used contemporary literary forms in accordance with the situation of his own time and culture. For the correct understanding of what the sacred author wanted to assert, due attention must be paid to the customary and characteristic styles of perceiving, speaking, and narrating which prevailed at the time of the sacred writer, and to the customs men normally followed at that period in their everyday dealings with one another (No. 12).

Analogy of Faith

No less serious attention must be given to the content and unity of the whole of Scripture, if the meaning of the sacred texts is to be correctly brought to light. The living tradition of the whole Church must be taken into account along with the harmony which exists between elements of the faith. All of what has been said about the way of interpreting Scripture is subject finally to the judgment of the Church, which carries out the divine commission and ministry of guarding and interpreting the word of God (No. 12).

IV. THE OLD TESTAMENT

In carefully planning and preparing the salvation of the whole human race, the God of supreme love, by a special dispensation, chose for himself a people to whom he might entrust his promises. First he entered into a covenant with Abraham (cf. Gn 15:18) and, through Moses, with the people of Israel (cf. Ex 24:8). To this people which he had acquired for himself, he so manifested himself through words and deeds as the one true and living God that Israel came to know by experience the ways of God with men. The plan of salvation, foretold by the sacred authors, recounted and explained by them, is found as the true word of God in the books of the Old Testament: these books, therefore, written under divine inspiration, remain permanently valuable (No. 14).

Principal Purpose

The principal purpose to which the plan of the Old Covenant was directed was to prepare for the coming both of Christ, the universal Redeemer, and of the messianic Kingdom. Now the books of the Old Testament, in accordance with the state of mankind before the time of salvation established by Christ, reveal to all men the knowledge of God and of man and the ways in which God deals with men. These books show us true divine pedagogy (No. 15).

The books of the Old Testament with all their parts, caught up into the proclamation of the Gospel, acquire and show forth their full meaning in the New Testament (cf. Mt 5:17; Lk 24:27; Rom 16:25-26; 2 Cor 3:14-16) and in turn shed light on it and explain it (No. 16).

V. THE NEW TESTAMENT

The word of God is set forth and shows its power in a most excellent way in the writings of the New Testament. For when the fullness of time arrived (cf. Gal 4:4), the Word was made flesh and dwelt among us in the fullness of grace and truth (cf. Jn 12:32). This mystery had not been manifested to other generations as it was now revealed to his holy apostles and prophets in the Holy Spirit (cf. Eph 3:4-6), so that they might preach the Gospel, stir up faith in Jesus, Christ and Lord, and gather the Church together. To these

realities, the writings of the New Testament stand as a perpetual and divine witness (No. 17).

The Gospels and Other Writings

The Gospels have a special preeminence for they are the principal witness of the life and teaching of the incarnate Word, our Savior.

The Church has always and everywhere held and continues to hold that the four Gospels are of apostolic origin. For what the apostles preached afterwards they themselves and apostolic men, under the inspiration of the divine Spirit, handed on to us in writing: the foundation of faith, namely, the fourfold Gospel, according to Matthew, Mark, Luke, and John (No. 18).

The four Gospels... whose historical character the Church unhesitatingly asserts, faithfully hand on what Jesus Christ, while living among men, really did and taught for their eternal salvation until the day he was taken up into heaven (see Acts 1:1-2). Indeed, after the ascension of the Lord the apostles handed on to their hearers what he had said and done. The sacred authors wrote the four Gospels, selecting some things from the many which had been handed on by word of mouth or in writing, reducing some of them to a synthesis, explicating some things in view of the situation of their churches, and preserving the form of proclamation but always in such fashion that they told us the honest truth about Jesus. For their intention in writing was that we might know "the truth" concerning those matters about which we have been instructed (cf. Lk 1:2-4) (No. 19).

Besides the four Gospels, the canon of the New Testament also contains the Epistles of St. Paul and other apostolic writings, composed under the inspiration of the Holy Spirit. In these writings those matters which concern Christ the Lord are confirmed, his true teaching is more and more fully stated, the saving power of the divine work of Christ is preached, the story is told of the beginnings of the Church and her marvelous growth, and her glorious fulfillment is foretold (No. 20).

SCRIPTURE IN CHURCH LIFE

The Church has always venerated the divine Scriptures just as she venerates the body of the Lord. She has always regarded the Scriptures together with sacred tradition as the supreme rule of faith, and will ever do so. For, inspired by God and committed once and for all to writing, they impart the word of God himself without change, and make the voice of the Holy Spirit resound in the words of the prophets and apostles. Therefore, like the Christian religion itself, all the preaching of the Church must be nourished and ruled by sacred Scripture (No. 21).

Easy access to sacred Scripture should be provided for all the Christian faithful. That is why the Church from the very beginning accepted as her own that very ancient Greek translation of the Old Testament which is named after seventy men (the Septuagint); and she has always given a place of honor to other translations, Eastern and Latin, especially the one known as the Vulgate. But since the word of God should be available at all times, the Church with maternal concern sees to it that suitable and correct translations are made into different languages, especially from the original texts of the sacred books. And if, given the opportunity and the approval of Church authority, these translations are produced in cooperation with the separated brethren as well, all Christians will be able to use them (No. 22).

Biblical Studies, Theology

The constitution encouraged the development and progress of biblical studies "under the watchful care of the sacred teaching office of the Church."

It also noted: "Sacred theology rests on the written word of God, together with sacred tradition, as its primary and perpetual foundation," and that "the study of the sacred page is, as it were, the soul of sacred theology" (Nos. 23, 24).

(*See separate article,* **Interpretation of the Bible** on page 103.)

THE BIBLE

The Canon of the Bible is the Church's official list of sacred writings. These works, written by men under the inspiration of the Holy Spirit, contain divine revelation and, in conjunction with the tradition and teaching authority of the Church, constitute the rule of Catholic faith. The Canon was fixed and determined by the tradition and teaching authority of the Church.

THE CATHOLIC CANON

The Old Testament Canon of 46 books is as follows.
• **The Pentateuch**, the first five books: Genesis (Gn), Exodus (Ex), Leviticus (Lv), Numbers (Nm), Deuteronomy (Dt).
• **Historical Books**: Joshua (Jos), Judges (Jgs), Ruth (Ru) 1 and 2 Samuel (Sm), 1 and 2 Kings (Kgs), 1 and 2 Chronicles (Chr), Ezra (Ezr), Nehemiah (Neh), Tobit (Tb), Judith (Jdt), Esther (Est), 1 and 2 Maccabees (Mc).
• **Wisdom Books**: Job (Jb), Psalms (Ps), Proverbs (Prv), Ecclesiastes (Eccl), Song of Songs (Song), Wisdom (Wis), Sirach (Sir).
• **The Prophets**: Isaiah (Is), Jeremiah (Jer), Lamentations (Lam), Baruch (Bar), Ezekiel (Ez), Daniel (Dn), Hosea (Hos), Joel (Jl), Amos (Am), Obadiah (Ob), Jonah (Jon), Micah (Mi), Nahum (Na), Habakkuk (Hb), Zephaniah (Zep), Haggai (Hg), Zechariah (Zec) Malachi (Mal).

The New Testament Canon of 27 books is as follows.
• **The Gospels**: Matthew (Mt), Mark (Mk), Luke (Lk), John (Jn).
• **The Acts of the Apostles** (Acts).
• **The Pauline Letters**: Romans (Rom), 1 and 2 Corinthians (Cor), Galatians (Gal), Ephesians (Eph), Philippians (Phil), Colossians (Col), 1 and 2 Thessalonians (Thes) 1 and 2 Timothy (Tm), Titus (Ti), Philemon (Phlm), Hebrews (Heb).
• **The Catholic Letters**: James (Jas), 1 and 2 Peter (Pt), 1, 2, and 3 John (Jn), Jude (Jude).
• **Revelation** (Rv).

Developments

The Canon of the Old Testament was firm by the fifth century despite some questioning by scholars. It was stated by a council held at Rome in 382, by African councils held in Hippo in 393 and in Carthage in 397 and 419, and by Innocent I in 405.

All of the New Testament books were generally known and most of them were acknowledged as inspired by the end of the second century. The Muratorian Fragment, dating from about 200, listed most of the books recognized as canonical in later decrees. Prior to the end of the fourth century, however, there was controversy over the inspired character of several works—the Letter to the Hebrews, James, Jude, 2 Peter, 2 and 3 John and Revelation. Controversy ended in the fourth century and these

books, along with those about which there was no dispute, were enumerated in the canon stated by the councils of Hippo and Carthage and affirmed by Innocent I in 405.

The Canon of the Bible was solemnly defined by the Council of Trent in the dogmatic decree *De Canonicis Scripturis,* Apr. 8, 1546.

HEBREW AND OTHER CANONS

The Hebrew Canon of sacred writings was fixed by tradition and the consensus of rabbis, probably by about A.D. 100 by the Synod or Council of Jamnia and certainly by the end of the second or early in the third century. It consists of the following works in three categories.
• **The Law** (Torah): the five books of Moses: Genesis, Exodus, Leviticus, Numbers, Deuteronomy.
• **The Prophets**: former prophets—Joshua, Judges, 1 and 2 Samuel, 1 and 2 Kings; latter prophets—Isaiah, Jeremiah, Ezekiel; and 12 minor prophets (Hosea, Joel, Amos, Obadiah, Jonah, Micah, Nahum, Habakkuk, Zephaniah, Haggai, Zechariah, Malachi).
• **The Writings**: 1 and 2 Chronicles, Ezra, Nehemiah, Job, Psalms, Proverbs, Ecclesiastes, Song of Songs, Ruth, Esther, Daniel.

This Canon, embodying the tradition and practice of the Palestine community, did not include a number of works contained in the Alexandrian version of sacred writings translated into Greek between 250 and 100 B.C. and in use by Greek-speaking Jews of the Dispersion (outside Palestine). The rejected works, called apocrypha and not regarded as sacred, are: Tobit, Judith, Wisdom, Sirach, Baruch, 1 and 2 Maccabees, the last six chapters of Esther and three passages of Daniel (3:24-90;13;14). These books have also been rejected from the Protestant Canon, although they are included in Bibles under the heading "Apocrypha."

The aforementioned books are held to be inspired and sacred by the Catholic Church. In Catholic usage, they are called deuterocanonical because they were under discussion for some time before questions about their canonicity were settled. Books regarded as canonical with little or no debate were called protocanonical. The status of both categories of books is the same in the Catholic Bible.

The Protestant Canon of the Old Testament is the same as the Hebrew.

The Old Testament Canon of some separated Eastern churches differs from the Catholic Canon. Christians are in agreement on the Canon of the New Testament.

Languages

Hebrew, Aramaic and Greek were the original languages of the Bible. Most of the Old Testament books were written in Hebrew. Portions of Daniel, Ezra, Jeremiah, Esther, and probably the books of Tobit and Judith were written in Aramaic. The Book of Wisdom, 2 Maccabees and all the books of the New Testament were written in Greek.

Manuscripts and Versions

The original writings of the inspired authors have been lost. The Bible has been transmitted through ancient copies called manuscripts and through translations or versions.

Authoritative Greek manuscripts include the Sinaitic and Vatican manuscripts of the fourth century and the Alexandrine of the fifth century A.D. The Septuagint and Vulgate translations are in a class by themselves.

The Septuagint version, a Greek translation of the Old Testament for Greek-speaking Jews, was begun about 250 and completed about 100 B.C. The work of several Jewish translators at Alexandria, it differed from the Hebrew Bible in the arrangement of books and included several, later called deuterocanonical, which were not acknowledged as sacred by the community in Palestine.

The Vulgate was a Latin version of the Old and New Testaments produced from the original languages by St. Jerome from about 383 to 404. It became the most widely used Latin text for centuries and was regarded as basic long before the Council of Trent designated it as authentic and suitable for use in public reading, controversy, preaching and teaching. Because of its authoritative character, it became the basis for many translations into other languages. A critical revision was completed by a pontifical commission in 1977.

Hebrew and Aramaic manuscripts of great antiquity and value have figured more significantly than before in recent scriptural work by Catholic scholars, especially since their use was strongly encouraged, if not mandated, in 1943 by Pius XII in the encyclical *Divino Afflante Spiritu.*

The English translation of the Bible in general use among Catholics until well into the 20th century was the Douay-Rheims, so-called because of the places where it was prepared and published, the New Testament at Rheims in 1582 and the Old Testament at Douay in 1609. The translation was made from the Vulgate text. As revised and issued by Bishop Richard Challoner in 1749 and 1750, it became the standard Catholic English version for about 200 years.

A revision of the Challoner New Testament, made on the basis of the Vulgate text by scholars of the Catholic Biblical Association of America, was published in 1941 in the United States under the sponsorship of the Episcopal Committee of the Confraternity of Christian Doctrine.

New American Bible

A new translation of the entire Bible, the first ever made directly into English from the original languages under Catholic auspices, was projected in 1944 and completed in the fall of 1970 with publication of the *New American Bible.* The Episcopal Committee of the Confraternity of Christian Doctrine sponsored the NAB. The translators were members of the Catholic Biblical Association of America and scholars of other faiths. The typical edition was produced by St. Anthony Guild Press, Paterson, N.J.

The *Jerusalem Bible*, published by Doubleday &

Co., Inc., is an English translation of a French version based on the original languages.

Biblical translations approved for liturgical use by the National Conference of Catholic Bishops and the Holy See are the *New American Bible* (1970 edition), the *Revised Standard Version—Catholic Edition*, and the *Jerusalem Bible* (1966).

The Protestant counterpart of the *Douay-Rheims Bible* was the *King James Bible*, called the *Authorized Version* in England. Originally published in 1611 and in general use for more than three centuries, its several revisions include the *Revised Standard Version* and the *New Revised Standard Version.*

Biblical Federation

In Nov. 1966, Pope Paul VI commissioned the Secretariat for Promoting Christian Unity to start work for the widest possible distribution of the Bible and to coordinate endeavors toward the production of Catholic-Protestant Bibles in all languages.

The World Catholic Federation for the Biblical Apostolate, established in 1969, sponsors a program designed to create greater awareness among Catholics of the Bible and its use in everyday life.

The U. S. Center for the Catholic Biblical Apostolate is related to the Secretariat for Pastoral Research and Practices, United States Conference of Catholic Bishops, 3211 Fourth St. N.E., Washington, DC, 20017.

APOCRYPHA

In Catholic usage, Apocrypha are books which have some resemblance to the canonical books in subject matter and title but which have not been recognized as canonical by the Church. They are characterized by a false claim to divine authority; extravagant accounts of events and miracles alleged to be supplemental revelation; material favoring heresy (especially in New Testament apocrypha); minimal, if any, historical value. Among examples of this type of literature itemized by J. McKenzie, S.J., in *Dictionary of the Bible* are: the Books of Adam and Eve, Martyrdom of Isaiah, Testament of the Patriarchs, Assumption of Moses, Sibylline Oracles, Gospel of James, Gospel of Thomas, Arabic Gospel of the Infancy, History of Joseph the Carpenter, Acts of John, Acts of Paul, Acts of Peter, Acts of Andrew, and numerous epistles.

Books of this type are called "pseudepigrapha" by Protestants.

In Protestant usage, some books of the Catholic Bible (deuterocanonical) are called apocrypha because their inspired character is rejected.

DEAD SEA SCROLLS

The Qumran Scrolls, popularly called the Dead Sea Scrolls, are a collection of manuscripts, all but one of them in Hebrew, found since 1947 in caves in the Desert of Juda west of the Dead Sea.

Among the findings were a complete text of Isaiah dating from the second century, B.C., more or less extensive fragments of other Old Testament texts (including the deuterocanonical Tobit), and a commentary on Habakkuk. Until the discovery of these materials, the oldest known Hebrew manuscripts were from the 10th century A.D.

Also found were messianic and apocalyptic texts, and other writings describing the beliefs and practices of the Essenes, a rigoristic Jewish sect.

The scrolls, dating from about the first century before and after Christ, are important sources of information about Hebrew literature, Jewish history during the period between the Old and New Testaments, and the history of Old Testament texts. They established the fact that the Hebrew text of the Old Testament was fixed before the beginning of the Christian era and have had definite effects in recent critical studies and translations of the Old Testament. Together with other scrolls found at Masada, they are still the subject of intensive study.

BOOKS OF THE BIBLE

OLD TESTAMENT BOOKS

Pentateuch

The Pentateuch is the collective title of the first five books of the Bible. Substantially, they identify the Israelites as Yahweh's Chosen People, cover their history from Egypt to the threshold of the Promised Land, contain the Mosaic Law and Covenant, and disclose the promise of salvation to come. Principal themes concern the divine promise of salvation, Yahweh's fidelity and the Covenant. Work on the composition of the Pentateuch was completed in the sixth century.

Genesis: The book of origins, according to its title in the Septuagint. In two parts, covers: religious prehistory, including accounts of the origin of the world and man, the original state of innocence and the fall, the promise of salvation, patriarchs before and after the deluge, the Tower of Babel narrative, genealogies (first 11 chapters); the covenant with Abraham and patriarchal history from Abraham to Joseph (balance of the 50 chapters). Significant are the themes of Yahweh's universal sovereignty and mercy.

Exodus: Named with the Greek word for departure, is a religious epic which describes the oppression of the 12 tribes in Egypt and their departure, liberation and passover there from under the leadership of Moses; Yahweh's establishment of the covenant with them, making them his chosen people, through the mediation of Moses at Mt. Sinai; instructions concerning the tabernacle, the sanctuary and Ark of the Covenant; the institution of the priesthood. The book is significant because of its theology of liberation and redemption. In Christian interpretation, the Exodus is a figure of baptism.

Leviticus: Mainly legislative in theme and purpose, contains laws regarding sacrifices, ceremonies of ordination and the priesthood of Aaron, legal purity, the holiness code, atonement, the redemption of offerings and other subjects. Summarily, Levitical laws provided directives for all aspects of religious observance and for the manner in which the Israelites were to conduct themselves with respect to Yahweh and each other. Leviticus was the liturgical handbook of the priesthood.

Numbers: Taking its name from censuses recounted at the beginning and near the end, is a continuation of Exodus. It combines narrative of the Israelites' desert pilgrimage from Sinai to the border of Canaan with laws related to and expansive of those in Leviticus.

Deuteronomy: The concluding book of the Pentateuch, recapitulates, in the form of a testament of Moses, the Law and much of the desert history of the Israelites; enjoins fidelity to the Law as the key to good or bad fortune for the people; gives an account of the commissioning of Joshua as the successor of Moses. Notable themes concern the election of Israel by Yahweh, observance of the Law, prohibitions against the worship of foreign gods, worship of and confidence in Yahweh, the power of Yahweh in nature. The Deuteronomic Code or motif, embodying all of these elements, was the norm for interpreting Israelite history.

Joshua, Judges, Ruth

Joshua: Records the fulfillment of Yahweh's promise to the Israelites in their conquest, occupation and division of Canaan under the leadership of Joshua. It also contains an account of the return of Transjordanian Israelites and of a renewal of the Covenant. It was redacted in final form probably in the sixth century or later.

Judges: Records the actions of charismatic leaders, called judges, of the tribes of Israel between the death of Joshua and the time of Samuel, and a crisis of idolatry among the people. The basic themes are sin and punishment, repentance and deliverance; its purpose was in line with the Deuteronomic motif, that the fortunes of the Israelites were related to their observance or non-observance of the Law and the Covenant. It was redacted in final form probably in the sixth century.

Ruth: Named for the Gentile (Moabite) woman who, through marriage with Boaz, became an Israelite and an ancestress of David (her son, Obed, became his grandfather). Themes are filial piety, faith and trust in Yahweh, the universality of messianic salvation. Dates ranging from c. 950 to the seventh century have been assigned to the origin of the book, whose author is unknown.

Historical Books

These books, while they contain a great deal of factual material, are unique in their preoccupation with presenting and interpreting it, in the Deuteronomic manner, in primary relation to the Covenant on which the nation of Israel was founded and in accordance with which community and personal life were judged.

The books are: Samuel 1 and 2, from the end of Judges (c. 1020) to the end of David's reign (c. 961); Kings 1 and 2, from the last days of David to the start of the Babylonian exile and the destruction of the Temple (587); Chronicles 1 and 2, from the reign of Saul (c. 1020-1000) to the return of the people from the exile (538); Ezra and Nehemiah, covering the reorganization of the Jewish community after the exile (458-397); Maccabees 1 and 2, recounting the struggle against attempted suppression of Judaism (168-142).

Three of the books listed below—Tobit, Judith, and Esther—are categorized as religious novels.

Samuel 1 and 2: A single work in concept and contents, containing episodic history of the last two Judges, Eli and Samuel, the establishment and rule of the monarchy under Saul and David, and the political consequences of David's rule. The royal messianic dynasty of David was the subject of Nathan's oracle in 2 Sm 7. The books were edited in final form probably late in the seventh century or during the exile.

Kings 1 and 2: Cover the last days of David and the career of Solomon, including the building of the Temple and the history of the kingdom during his reign; stories of the prophets Elijah and Elisha; the history of the divided kingdom to the fall of Israel in the North (721) and the fall of Judah in the South (587), the destruction of Jerusalem and the Temple. They reflect the Deuteronomic motif in attributing the downfall of the people to corruption of belief and practice in public and private life. They were completed probably in the sixth century.

Chronicles 1 and 2: A collection of historical traditions interpreted in such a way as to present an ideal picture of one people governed by divine law and united in one Temple worship of the one true God. Contents include genealogical tables from Adam to David, the careers of David and Solomon, coverage of the kingdom of Judah to the exile, and the decree of Cyrus permitting the return of the people and rebuilding of Jerusalem. Both are related to and were written about 400 by the same author, the Chronicler, who composed Ezra and Nehemiah.

Ezra and Nehemiah: A running account of the return of the people to their homeland after the exile and of practical efforts, under the leadership of Ezra and Nehemiah, to restore and reorganize the religious and political community on the basis of Israelite traditions, divine worship and observance of the Law. Events of great significance were the building of the second Temple, the building of a wall around Jerusalem and the proclamation of the Law by Ezra. This restored community was the start of Judaism. Both are related to and were written about 400 by the same author, the Chronicler, who composed Chronicles 1 and 2.

Tobit: Written in the literary form of a novel and having greater resemblance to wisdom than to historical literature, narrates the personal history of Tobit, a devout and charitable Jew in exile, and persons connected with him, viz., his son Tobiah, his kinsman Raguel and Raguel's daughter Sarah. Its purpose was to teach people how to be good Jews. One of its principal themes is patience under trial, with trust in divine Providence which is symbolized by the presence and action of the angel Raphael. It was written about 200.

Judith: Recounts, in the literary form of a historical novel or romance, the preservation of the Israelites from conquest and ruin through the action of Judith. The essential themes are trust in God for deliverance from danger and emphasis on observance of the Law. It was written probably during the Maccabean period.

Esther: Relates, in the literary form of a historical novel or romance, the manner in which Jews in Persia were saved from annihilation through the central role played by Esther, the Jewish wife of Ahasuerus; a fact commemorated by the Jewish feast of Purim. Like Judith, it has trust in Divine Providence as its theme and indicates that God's saving will is sometimes realized by persons acting in unlikely ways. It may have been written near the end of the fourth century.

Maccabees 1 and 2: While related to some extent because of common subject matter, are quite different from each other.

The first book recounts the background and events of the 40-year (175-135) struggle for religious and political freedom led by Judas Maccabaeus and his brothers against the Hellenist Seleucid kings and some Hellenophiles among the Jews. Victory was symbolized by the rededication of the Temple. Against the background of opposition between Jews and Gentiles, the author equated the survival of belief in the one true God with survival of the Jewish people, thus identifying religion with patriotism. It was written probably near the year 100.

The second book supplements the first to some extent, covering and giving a theological interpretation to events from 180 to 162. It explains the feast of the dedication of the Temple, a key event in the survival of Judaism which is commemorated in the feast of Hanukkah; stresses the primacy of God's action in the struggle for survival; and indicates belief in an afterlife and the resurrection of the body. It was completed probably about 124.

Wisdom Books

With the exceptions of Psalms and the Song of Songs, the titles listed under this heading are called "wisdom books" because their purpose was to formulate the fruits of human experience in the context of meditation on sacred Scripture and to present them as an aid toward understanding the problems of life. Hebrew wisdom literature was distinctive from pagan literature of the same type, but it had limitations; these were overcome in the New Testament, which added the dimensions of the New Covenant to those of the Old. Solomon was regarded as the archetype of the wise man.

Job: A dramatic, didactic poem consisting mainly of several dialogues between Job and his friends concerning the mystery involved in the coexistence of the just God, evil and the suffering of the just. It describes an innocent man's experience of suffering and conveys the truth that faith in and submission to God rather than complete understanding, which is impossible, make the experience bearable; also, that the justice of God cannot be defended by affirming that it is realized in this world. Of unknown authorship, it was composed between the seventh and fifth centuries.

Psalms: A collection of 150 religious songs or lyrics reflecting Israelite belief and piety dating from the time of the monarchy to the post-Exilic period, a span of well over 500 years. The psalms, which are a compendium of Old Testament theology, were used in temple liturgy and for other occasions. They were of several types suitable for the king, hymns, lamentations, expressions of confidence and thanksgiving, prophecy, historical meditation and reflection, and the statement of wisdom. About one-half of them are attributed to David; many were composed by unknown authors.

Proverbs: The oldest book of the wisdom type in the Bible, consisting of collections of sayings attributed to Solomon and other persons regarding a wide variety of subjects including wisdom and its nature, rules of conduct, duties with respect to one's neighbor, the conduct of daily affairs. It reveals many details of Hebrew life. Its nucleus dates from the period before the exile. The extant form of the book dates probably from the end of the fifth century.

Ecclesiastes: A treatise about many subjects whose unifying theme is the vanity of strictly human efforts and accomplishments with respect to the achievement of lasting happiness; the only things which are not vain are fear of the Lord and observance of his commandments. The pessimistic tone of the book is due to the absence of a concept of afterlife. It was written by an unknown author probably in the third century.

Song of Songs: A collection of love lyrics reflecting various themes, including the love of God for Israel and the celebration of ideal love and fidelity between man and woman. It was written by an unknown author after the exile.

Wisdom: Deals with many subjects including the reward of justice; praise of wisdom, a gift of Yahweh proceeding from belief in him and the practice of his Law; the part played by him in the history of his people, especially in their liberation from Egypt; the folly and shame of idolatry. Its contents are taken from the whole sacred literature of the Jews and represent a distillation of its wisdom based on the law, beliefs and traditions of Israel. The last of the Old Testament books, it was written in the early part of the first century before Christ by a member of the Jewish community at Alexandria.

Sirach: Resembling Proverbs, is a collection of sayings handed on by a grandfather to his grandson. It contains a variety of moral instruction and eulogies of patriarchs and other figures in Israelite history. Its moral maxims apply to individuals, the family and community, relations with God, friendship, education, wealth, the Law, divine worship. Its theme is that true wisdom consists in the Law. (It was formerly called Ecclesiasticus, the Church Book, because of its extensive use by the Church for moral instruction.) It was written in Hebrew between 200 and 175, during a period of strong Hellenistic influence, and was translated into Greek after 132.

The Prophets

These books and the prophecies they contain "express judgments of the people's moral conduct, on the basis of the Mosaic alliance between God and Israel. They teach sublime truths and lofty morals. They contain exhortations, threats, announcements of punishment, promises of deliverance. In the affairs of men, their prime concern is the interests of God, especially in what pertains to the Chosen People through whom the Messiah is to come; hence their denunciations of idolatry and of that externalism in worship which exclude the interior spirit of religion. They are concerned also with the universal nature of the moral law, with personal responsibility, with the person and office of the Messiah, and with the conduct of foreign nations" (*The Holy Bible*, Prophetic Books, CCD Edition, 1961; preface). There are four major (Isaiah, Jeremiah, Ezekiel, Daniel) and twelve minor prophets (distinguished by the length of books), Lamentations and Baruch. Earlier prophets, mentioned in historical books, include Samuel, Gad, Nathan, Elijah, and Elisha.

Before the exile, prophets were the intermediaries through whom God communicated revelation to the people. Afterwards, prophecy lapsed and the written word of the Law served this purpose.

Isaiah: Named for the greatest of the prophets whose career spanned the reigns of three Hebrew kings from 742 to the beginning of the seventh century, in a period of moral breakdown in Judah and threats of invasion by foreign enemies. It is an anthology of poems and oracles credited to him and a number of followers deeply influenced by him. Of special importance are the prophecies concerning Immanuel (6 to 12), including the prophecy of the virgin birth (7:14). Chapters 40 to 55, called Deutero-Isaiah, are attributed to an anonymous poet toward the end of the exile; this portion contains the Songs of the Servant. The concluding part of the book (56-66) contains oracles by later disciples. One of many themes in Isaiah concerned the saving mission of the remnant of Israel in the divine plan of salvation.

Jeremiah: Combines history, biography and prophecy in a setting of crisis caused by internal and external factors, viz., idolatry and general infidelity to the Law among the Israelites and external threats from the Assyrians, Egyptians and Babylonians. Jeremiah prophesied the promise of a new covenant as well as the destruction of Jerusalem and the Temple. His career began in 626 and ended some years after the beginning of the exile. The book, the longest in the Bible, was edited in final form after the exile.

Lamentations: A collection of five laments or elegies over the fall of Jerusalem and the fate of the people in exile, written by an unknown eyewitness. They convey the message that Yahweh struck the people because of their sins and reflect confidence in his love and power to restore his converted people.

Baruch: Against the background of the already-begun exile, it consists of an introduction and several parts: an exile's prayer of confession and petition for forgiveness and the restoration of Israel; a poem praising wisdom and the Law of Moses; a lament in which Jerusalem, personified, bewails the fate of her people and consoles them with the hope of blessings to come; and a polemic against idolatry. Although ascribed to Baruch, Jeremiah's secretary, it was written by several authors, probably in the second century.

Ezekiel: Named for the priest-prophet who prophesied in Babylon from 593 to 571, during the first phase of the exile. To prepare his fellow early exiles for the impending fall of Jerusalem, he reproached the Israelites for past sins and predicted woes to come upon them. After the destruction of the city, the burden of his message was hope and promise of restoration. Ezekiel had great influence on the religion of Israel after the exile.

Daniel: The protagonist is a young Jew, taken early to Babylon where he lived until about 538, who figured in a series of edifying stories which originated in Israelite tradition. The stories, whose characters are not purely legendary but rest on historical tradition, recount the trials and triumphs of Daniel and his three companions, and other episodes including those concerning Susannah, Bel, and the Dragon. The book is more apocalyptic than prophetic: it envisions Israel in glory to come and conveys the message that men of faith can resist temptation and overcome adversity. It states the prophetic themes of right conduct, divine control of men and events, and the final triumph of the kingdom. It was written by an unknown author in the 160s to give moral support to Jews during the persecutions of the Maccabean period.

Hosea: Consists of a prophetic parallel between Hosea's marriage and Yahweh's relations with his people. As the prophet was married to a faithless wife whom he would not give up, Yahweh was bound in Covenant with an idolatrous and unjust Israel whom he would not desert but would chastise for purification. Hosea belonged to the Northern Kingdom of Israel and began his career about the middle of the eighth century. He inaugurated the tradition of describing Yahweh's relation to Israel in terms of marriage.

Joel: Is apocalyptic and eschatological regarding divine judgment, the Day of the Lord, which is symbolized by a ravaging invasion of locusts, the judgment of the nations in the Valley of Josaphat and the outpouring of the Spirit in the messianic era to come. Its message is that God will vindicate and save Israel, in view of the prayer and repentance of the people, and will punish their enemies. It was composed about 400.

Amos: Consists of an indictment against foreign enemies of Israel; a strong denunciation of the people of Israel, whose infidelity, idolatry and injustice made them subject to divine judgment and punishment; and a messianic oracle regarding Israel's restoration. Amos prophesied in the Northern Kingdom of Israel, at Bethel, in the first half of the eighth century; chronologically, he was the first of the canonical prophets.

Obadiah: A 21-verse prophecy, the shortest and one of the sternest in the Bible, against the Edomites, invaders of southern Judah and enemies of those returning from the exile to their homeland. It was probably composed in the fifth century.

Jonah: A parable of divine mercy with the theme that Yahweh wills the salvation of all, not just a few, men who respond to his call. Its protagonist is a disobedient prophet; forced by circumstances beyond his control to preach penance among Gentiles, he is highly successful in his mission but baffled by the divine concern for those who do not belong to the Chosen People. It was written after the exile, probably in the fifth century.

Micah: Attacks the injustice and corruption of priests, false prophets, officials and people; announces judgment and punishment to come; foretells the restoration of Israel; refers to the saving remnant of Israel. Micah was a contemporary of Isaiah.

Nahum: Concerns the destruction of Nineveh in 612 and the overthrow of the Assyrian Empire by the Babylonians.

Habakkuk: Dating from about 605–597, concerns sufferings to be inflicted by oppressors on the people of Judah because of their infidelity to the Lord. It also sounds a note of confidence in the Lord, the Savior, and declares that the just will not perish.

Zephaniah: Exercising his ministry in the second half of the seventh century, during a time of widespread idolatry, superstition and religious degradation, he prophesied impending judgment and punishment for Jerusalem and its people. He prophesied too that a holy remnant of the people (*anawim*, mentioned also by Amos) would be spared. Zephaniah was a forerunner of Jeremiah.

Haggai: One of the first prophets after the exile, Haggai in 520 encouraged the returning exiles to reestablish their community and to complete the second Temple (dedicated in 515), for which he envisioned greater glory, in a messianic sense, than that enjoyed by the original Temple of Solomon.

Zechariah: A contemporary of Haggai, he prophesied in the same vein. A second part of the book, called Deutero-Zechariah and composed by one or more unknown authors, relates a vision of the coming of the Prince of Peace, the Messiah of the Poor.

Malachi: Written by an anonymous author, presents a picture of life in the post-Exilic community between 516 and the initiation of reforms by Ezra and Nehemiah about 432. Blame for the troubles of the community is placed mainly on priests for failure to carry out ritual worship and to instruct the people in the proper manner; other factors were religious indifference and the influence of doubters who were scandalized at the prosperity of the wicked. The vision of a universal sacrifice to be offered to Yahweh (1:11) is interpreted in Catholic theology as a prophecy of the sacrifice of the Mass. Malachi was the last of the minor prophets.

DATES OF THE OLD TESTAMENT

c.1800–c.1600 B.C.: Period of the patriarchs (Abraham, Isaac, Jacob).

c.1600: Israelites in Egypt.

c.1250: Exodus of Israelites from Egypt.

c.1210: Entrance of Israelites into Canaan.

c.1210–c.1020: Period of the Judges.

c.1020–c.1000: Reign of Saul, first king.

c.1000–c.961: Reign of David.

c.961–922: Reign of Solomon. Temple built during his reign.

922: Division of the Kingdom into Israel (North) and Judah (South).

721: Conquest of Israel by Assyrians.

587–538: Conquest of Judah by Babylonians.

Babylonian Captivity and Exile: Destruction of Jerusalem and the Temple, 587. Captivity ended with the return of exiles, following the decree of Cyrus permitting the rebuilding of Jerusalem.

515: Dedication of the second Temple.

458–397: Restoration and reform of the Jewish religious and political community; building of the Jerusalem wall, 439. Leaders in the movement were Ezra and Nehemiah.

168–142: Period of the Maccabees; war against Syrians.

142: Independence granted to Jews by Demetrius II of Syria.

135–37: Period of the Hasmonean dynasty.

63: Beginning of Roman rule.

37–4: Period of Herod the Great.

NEW TESTAMENT BOOKS

Gospels

The term "Gospel" is derived from the Anglo-Saxon *god-spell* and the Greek *euangelion*, meaning good news, good tidings. In Christian use, it means the good news of salvation proclaimed by Christ and the Church, and handed on in written form in the Gospels of Matthew, Mark, Luke and John.

The initial proclamation of the coming of the kingdom of God was made by Jesus in and through his Person, teachings and actions, and especially through his Passion, death and resurrection. This proclamation became the center of Christian faith and the core of the oral Gospel tradition with which the Church spread the good news by apostolic preaching for some 30 years before it was committed to writing by the Evangelists.

Nature of the Gospels

The historical truth of the Gospels was the subject of an instruction issued by the Pontifical Commission for Biblical Studies Apr. 21, 1964.

• The sacred writers selected from the material at their disposal (the oral Gospel tradition, some written collections of sayings and deeds of Jesus, eyewitness accounts) those things which were particularly suitable to the various conditions (liturgical, catechetical, missionary) of the faithful and the aims they had in mind, and they narrated these things in such a way as to correspond with those circumstances and their aims.

• The life and teaching of Jesus were not simply reported in a biographical manner for the purpose of preserving their memory but were "preached" so as to offer the Church the basis of doctrine concerning faith and morals.

• In their works, the Evangelists presented the true sayings of Jesus and the events of his life in the light of the better understanding they had following their enlightenment by the Holy Spirit. They did not transform Christ into a "mythical" Person, nor did they distort his teaching. Passion narratives are the core of all the Gospels, covering the suffering, death and resurrection of Jesus as central events in bringing about and establishing the New Covenant. Leading up to them are accounts of the mission of John the Baptizer and the ministry of Jesus, especially in Galilee and finally in Jerusalem before the Passion. The infancy of Jesus is covered by Luke and Matthew with narratives inspired in part by appropriate Old Testament citations.

Matthew, Mark and Luke, while different in various respects, have so many similarities that they are called Synoptic; their relationships are the subject of the Synoptic Problem.

Matthew: Written probably between 80 and 100 for Jewish Christians with clear reference to Jewish background and identification of Jesus as the divine Messiah, the fulfillment of the Old Testament. Distinctive are the use of Old Testament citations regarding the Person, activity and teaching of Jesus, and the presentation of doctrine in sermons and discourses.

Mark: Most likely the first of the Gospels, dating from about 70. Written for Gentile Christians, it is noted for the realism and wealth of concrete details with which it reveals Jesus as Son of God and Savior more by his actions and miracles than by his discourses. Theologically, it is less refined than the other Gospels.

Luke: Written about 75 for Gentile Christians. It is noted for the universality of its address, the insight it provides into the Christian way of life, the place it gives to women, the manner in which it emphasizes Jesus' friendship with sinners and compassion for the suffering.

John: Edited and arranged in final form probably between 90 and 100, this is the most sublime and theological of the Gospels, and is different from the Synoptics in plan and treatment. Combining accounts of signs with longer discourses and reflections, it progressively reveals the Person and mission of Jesus—as Word, Way, Truth, Life, Light—in line with the purpose, "to help you believe that Jesus is the Messiah, the Son of God, so that through this faith you may have life in his name" (Jn 20:31). There are questions about the authorship but no doubt about the Johannine authority and tradition behind the Gospel.

Acts of the Apostles

Written by Luke about 75 as a supplement to his Gospel. It describes the origin and spread of Christian communities through the action of the Holy Spirit from the resurrection of Christ to the time when Paul was placed in custody in Rome in the early 60s.

Letters (Epistles)

These letters, many of which antedated the Gospels, were written in response to existential needs of the early Christian communities for doctrinal and moral instruction, disciplinary action, practical advice, and exhortation to true Christian living.

Pauline Letters

These letters, which comprise approximately one-fourth of the New Testament, are primary and monumental sources of the development of Christian theology. Several of them may not have had Paul as their actual author, but evidence of the Pauline tradition behind them is strong. The letters to the Colossians, Philippians, Ephesians and Philemon have been called the "Captivity Letters" because of a tradition that they were written while Paul was under house arrest or another form of detention.

Romans: Written about 57, probably from Corinth, on the central significance of Christ and faith in him for salvation, and the relationship of Christianity to Judaism; the condition of mankind without Christ; justification and the Christian life; duties of Christians.

Corinthians 1: Written near the beginning of 57 from Ephesus to counteract factionalism and disorders, it covers community dissension, moral irregularities, marriage and celibacy, conduct at religious gatherings, the Eucharist, spiritual gifts (charisms) and their function in the Church, charity, the resurrection of the body.

Corinthians 2: Written later in the same year as 1 Cor, concerning Paul's defense of his apostolic ministry, and an appeal for a collection to aid poor Christians in Jerusalem.

Galatians: Written probably between 54 and 55 to counteract Judaizing opinions and efforts to undermine his authority, it asserts the divine origin of Paul's authority and doctrine, states that justification is not through Mosaic Law but through faith in Christ, insists on the practice of evangelical virtues, especially charity.

Ephesians: Written probably between 61 and 63, mainly on the Church as the Mystical Body of Christ.

Philippians: Written between 56 and 57 or 61 and 63 to warn the Philippians against enemies of their faith, to urge them to be faithful to their vocation and unity of belief, and to thank them for their kindness to him while he was being held in detention.

Colossians: Written probably while he was under house arrest in Rome from 61 to 63, to counteract the influence of self-appointed teachers who were watering down doctrine concerning Christ. It includes two highly important Christological passages, a warning against false teachers, and an instruction on the ideal Christian life.

Thessalonians 1 and 2: Written within a short time of each other probably in 51 from Corinth, mainly on doctrine concerning the *Parousia*, the second coming of Christ.

Timothy 1 and 2, Titus: Written between 65 and 67, or perhaps in the 70s, giving pastoral counsels to Timothy and Titus, who were in charge of churches in Ephesus and Crete, respectively. 1 Tm emphasizes pastoral responsibility for preserving unity of doctrine; 2 Tm describes Paul's imprisonment in Rome.

Philemon: A private letter written between 61 and 63 to a wealthy Colossian concerning a slave, Onesimus, who had escaped from him; Paul appealed for kind treatment of the man.

Hebrews: Dating from sometime between 70 and 96, a complex theological treatise on Christology, the priesthood and sacrifice of Christ, the New Covenant, and the pattern for Christian living. Critical opinion is divided as to whether it was addressed to Judaeo or Gentile Christians.

Catholic Letters

These seven letters have been called "catholic" because it was thought for some time, not altogether correctly, that they were not addressed to particular communities.

James: Written sometime before 62 in the spirit of Hebrew wisdom literature and the moralism of Tobit.

An exhortation to practical Christian living, it is also noteworthy for the doctrine it states on good works and its citation regarding anointing of the sick.

Peter 1 and 2: The first letter may have been written between 64 and 67 or between 90 and 95; the second may date from 100 to 125. Addressed to Christians in Asia Minor, both are exhortations to perseverance in the life of faith despite trials and difficulties arising from pagan influences, isolation from other Christians and false teaching.

John 1: Written sometime in the 90s and addressed to Asian churches, its message is that God is made known to us in the Son and that fellowship with the Father is attained by living in the light, justice and love of the Son.

John 2: Written sometime in the 90s and addressed to a church in Asia, it commends the people for standing firm in the faith and urges them to perseverance.

John 3: Written sometime in the 90s, it appears to represent an effort to settle a jurisdictional dispute in one of the churches.

Jude: Written probably about 80, it is a brief treatise against erroneous teachings and practices opposed to law, authority and true Christian freedom.

Revelation

Written in the 90s along the lines of Johannine thought, it is a symbolic and apocalyptic treatment of things to come and of the struggle between the Church and evil combined with warning but hope and assurance to the Church regarding the coming of the Lord in glory.

INTERPRETATION OF THE BIBLE

According to the Dogmatic Constitution on Divine Revelation (*Dei Verbum*) issued by the Second Vatican Council, "the interpreter of Sacred Scripture, in order to see clearly what God wanted to communicate to us, should carefully investigate what meaning the sacred writers really intended, and what God wanted to manifest by means of their words" (No. 12).

Hermeneutics, Exegesis

This careful investigation proceeds in accordance with the rules of hermeneutics, the normative science of biblical interpretation and explanation. Hermeneutics in practice is called exegesis.

The principles of hermeneutics are derived from various disciplines and many factors which have to be considered in explaining the Bible and its parts. These include: the original languages and languages of translation of the sacred texts, through philology and linguistics; the quality of texts, through textual criticism; literary forms and genres, through literary and form criticism; cultural, historical, geographical, and other conditions which influenced the writers, through related studies; facts and truths of salvation history; the truths and analogy of faith.

Distinctive to biblical hermeneutics, which differs in important respects from literary interpretation in general, is the premise that the Bible, though written by human authors, is the work of divine inspiration in which God reveals his plan for the salvation of men through historical events and persons, and especially through the Person and mission of Christ.

Textual, Form Criticism

Textual criticism is the study of biblical texts, which have been transmitted in copies several times removed from the original manuscripts, for the purpose of establishing the real state of the original texts. This purpose is served by comparison of existing copies; by application to the texts of the disciplines of philology and linguistics; by examination of related works of antiquity; by study of biblical citations in works of the Fathers of the Church and other authors; and by other means of literary study.

Since about 1920, the sayings of Christ have been a particular object of New Testament study, the purpose being to analyze the forms of expression used by the Evangelists in order to ascertain the words actually spoken by him.

Literary Criticism

Literary criticism aims to determine the origin and kinds of literary composition, called forms or genres, employed by the inspired authors. Such determinations are necessary for decision regarding the nature and purpose and, consequently, the meaning of biblical passages. Underlying these studies is the principle that the manner of writing was conditioned by the intention of the authors, the meaning they wanted to convey, and the then-contemporary literary style, mode or medium best adapted to carry their message—e.g., true history, quasi-historical narrative, poems, prayers, hymns, psalms, aphorisms, allegories, discourses. Understanding these media is necessary for the valid interpretation of their message.

Literal Sense

The key to all valid interpretation is the literal sense of biblical passages. Regarding this matter and the relevance to it of the studies and procedures described above, Pius XII wrote the following in the encyclical *Divino Afflante Spiritu:*

"What the literal sense of a passage is, is not always as obvious in the speeches and writings of ancient authors of the East as it is in the works of our own time. For what they wished to express is not to be determined by the rules of grammar and philology alone nor solely by the context; the interpreter must, as it were, go back wholly in spirit to those remote centuries of the East and with the aid of history, archeology, ethnology, and other sciences accurately determine what modes of writing, so to speak, the authors of that ancient period would be likely to use and in fact did use. In explaining the Sacred Scripture and in demonstrating and proving its immunity from all error [the Catholic interpreter] should make a prudent use of this means, determine to what extent the manner of expression or literary mode adopted by the sacred writer may lead to a correct and genuine interpretation; and let him be convinced that this part of his office cannot be neglected without serious detriment to Catholic exegesis."

The literal sense of the Bible is the meaning in the mind of and intended by the inspired writer of a book or passage of the Bible. This is determined by the application to texts of the rules of hermeneutics. It is not to be confused with word-for-word literalism.

Typological Sense

The typological sense is the meaning which a passage has not only in itself but also in reference to something else of which it is a type or foreshadowing. A clear example is the account of the Exodus of the Israelites: in its literal sense, it narrates the liberation of the Israelites from death and oppression in Egypt; in its typical sense, it foreshadowed the liberation of men from sin through the redemptive death and resurrection of Christ. The typical sense of this and other passages emerged in the working out of God's plan of salvation history. It did not have to be in the mind of the author of the original passage.

Accommodated Senses

Accommodated, allegorical, and consequent senses are figurative and adaptive meanings given to books and passages of the Bible for moral and other purposes. Such interpretations involve the danger of stretching the literal sense beyond proper proportions. Hermeneutical principles require that interpretations like these respect the integrity of the literal sense of the passages in question.

In the Catholic view, the final word on questions of biblical interpretation belongs to the teaching authority of the Church. In other views, generally derived from basic principles stated by Martin Luther, John Calvin and other reformers, the primacy belongs to individual judgment acting in response to the inner testimony of the Holy Spirit, the edifying nature of biblical subject matter, the sublimity and simplicity of the message of salvation, the intensity with which Christ is proclaimed.

Biblical Studies

The first center for biblical studies, in some strict sense of the term, was the School of Alexandria, founded in the latter half of the second century. It was noted for allegorical exegesis. Literal interpretation was a hallmark of the School of Antioch.

St. Jerome, who produced the Vulgate, and St. Augustine, author of numerous commentaries, were the most important figures in biblical studies during the patristic period. By the time of the latter's death, the Old and New Testament canons had been stabilized. For some centuries afterwards, there was little or no progress in scriptural studies, although commentaries were written, collections were made of scriptural excerpts from the writings of the Fathers of the Church, and the systematic reading of Scripture became established as a feature of monastic life.

Advances were made in the 12th and 13th centuries with the introduction of new principles and methods of scriptural analysis stemming from renewed interest in Hebraic studies and the application of dialectics.

By the time of the Reformation, the Bible had become the first book set in movable type, and more than 100 vernacular editions were in use throughout Europe.

The Council of Trent

In the wake of the Reformation, the Council of Trent formally defined the Canon of the Bible; it also reasserted the authoritative role of tradition and the teaching authority of the Church as well as Scripture with respect to the rule of faith. In the heated atmosphere of the 16th and 17th centuries, the Bible was turned into a polemical weapon; Protestants used it to defend their doctrines, and Catholics countered with citations in support of the dogmas of the Church. One result of this state of affairs was a lack of substantial progress in biblical studies during the period.

Rationalists from the 18th century on and later Modernists denied the reality of the supernatural and doctrine concerning inspiration of the Bible, which they generally regarded as a strictly human production expressive of the religious sense and experience of mankind. In their hands, the tools of positive critical research became weapons for biblical subversion. The defensive Catholic reaction to their work had the temporary effect of alienating scholars of the Church from solid advances in archeology, philology, history, textual and literary criticism.

Catholic Developments

Major influences in bringing about a change in Catholic attitude toward use of these disciplines in biblical studies were two papal encyclicals and two institutes of special study, the *École Biblique*, founded in Jerusalem in 1890, and the Pontifical Biblical Institute established in Rome in 1909. The encyclical *Providentissimus Deus*, issued by Leo XIII in 1893, marked an important breakthrough; in addition to defending the concept of divine inspiration and the formal inspiration of the Scriptures, it encouraged the study of allied and ancillary sciences and techniques for a more fruitful understanding of the sacred writings. The encyclical *Divino Afflante Spiritu*, issued by Pope Pius XII 50 years later, gave encouragement for the use of various forms of criticism as tools of biblical research. A significant addition to documents on the subject is "The Interpretation of the Bible in the Church," published by the Pontifical Biblical Commission in

Nov. 1993. It presents an overview of approaches to the Bible and probes the question: "Which hermeneutical theory best enables a proper grasp of the profound reality of which Scripture speaks and its meaningful expression for people today?"

The documents encouraged the work of scholars and stimulated wide communication of the fruits of their study.

Great changes in the climate and direction of biblical studies have occurred in recent years. One of them has been an increase in cooperative effort among Catholic, Protestant, Orthodox, and Jewish scholars. Their common investigation of the Dead Sea Scrolls is well-known. Also productive has been the collaboration of Catholics and Protestants in turning out various editions of the Bible.

The development and results of biblical studies in this century have directly and significantly affected all phases of the contemporary renewal movement in the Church. Their influence on theology, liturgy, catechetics, and preaching indicate the importance of their function in the life of the Church.

APOSTLES AND EVANGELISTS

The Apostles were the men selected, trained, and commissioned by Christ to preach the Gospel, to baptize, and to establish, direct and care for his Church as servants of God and stewards of his mysteries. They were the first bishops of the Church.

St. Matthew's Gospel lists the Apostles in this order: Peter, Andrew, James the Greater, John, Philip, Bartholomew, Thomas, Matthew, James the Less, Jude, Simon, and Judas Iscariot. Matthias was elected to fill the place of Judas. Paul became an Apostle by a special call from Christ. Barnabas was called an Apostle.

Two of the Evangelists, John and Matthew, were Apostles. The other two, Luke and Mark, were closely associated with the apostolic college.

Andrew: Born in Bethsaida, brother of Peter, disciple of John the Baptist, a fisherman, the first Apostle called; according to legend, preached the Gospel in northern Greece, Epirus and Scythia, and was martyred at Patras about 70; in art, is represented with an X-shaped cross, called St. Andrew's Cross; is honored as the patron of Russia and Scotland; Nov. 30.

Barnabas: Originally called Joseph but named Barnabas by the Apostles, among whom he is ranked because of his collaboration with Paul; a Jew of the Diaspora, born in Cyprus; a cousin of Mark and member of the Christian community at Jerusalem, influenced the Apostles to accept Paul, with whom he became a pioneer missionary outside Palestine and Syria, to Antioch, Cyprus, and southern Asia Minor; legend says he was martyred in Cyprus during the Neronian persecution; June 11.

Bartholomew (Nathaniel): A friend of Philip; according to various traditions, preached the Gospel in Ethiopia, India, Persia, and Armenia, where he was martyred by being flayed and beheaded; in art, is depicted holding a knife, an instrument of his death; Aug. 24 (Roman Rite), Aug. 25 (Byzantine Rite).

James the Greater: A Galilean, son of Zebedee, brother of John (with whom he was called a "Son of Thunder"), a fisherman; with Peter and John, witnessed the raising of Jairus's daughter to life, the transfiguration, the agony of Jesus in the Garden of Gethsemane; first of the Apostles to die, by the sword in 44 during the rule of Herod Agrippa; there is doubt about a journey that legend says he made to Spain and also about the authenticity of relics said to be his at Santiago de Compostela; in art, is depicted carrying a pilgrim's bell; July 25 (Roman Rite), Apr. 30 (Byzantine Rite).

James the Less: Son of Alphaeus, called "Less" because he was younger in age or shorter in stature than James the Greater; one of the Catholic Epistles bears his name; was stoned to death in 62 or thrown from the top of the temple in Jerusalem and clubbed to death in 66; in art, is depicted with a club or heavy staff; May 3 (Roman Rite), Oct. 9 (Byzantine Rite).

John: A Galilean, son of Zebedee, brother of James the Greater (with whom he was called a "Son of Thunder"), a fisherman, probably a disciple of John the Baptist, one of the Evangelists, called the "Beloved Disciple"; with Peter and James the Greater, witnessed the raising of Jairus's daughter to life, the transfiguration, the agony of Jesus in the Garden of Gethsemane; Mary was commended to his special care by Christ; the fourth Gospel, three Catholic Epistles, and Revelation bear his name; according to various accounts, lived at Ephesus in Asia Minor for some time and died a natural death about 100; in art, is represented by an eagle, symbolic of the sublimity of the contents of his Gospel; Dec. 27 (Roman Rite), May 8 (Byzantine Rite).

Jude Thaddeus: One of the Catholic Epistles, the shortest, bears his name; various traditions say he preached the Gospel in Mesopotamia, Persia, and elsewhere, and was martyred; in art, is depicted with a halberd, the instrument of his death; Oct. 28 (Roman Rite), June 19 (Byzantine Rite).

Luke: A Greek convert to the Christian community, called "our most dear physician" by Paul, of whom he was a missionary companion; author of the third Gospel and Acts of the Apostles; the place—Achaia, Bithynia, Egypt—and circumstances of his death are not certain; in art, is depicted as a man, a writer, or an ox (because his Gospel starts at the scene of temple sacrifice); Oct. 18.

Mark: A cousin of Barnabas and member of the first Christian community at Jerusalem; a missionary companion of Paul and Barnabas, then of Peter; author of the Gospel that bears his name; according to legend, founded the Church at Alexandria, was bishop there and was martyred in the streets of the city; in art, is depicted with his Gospel and a winged lion, symbolic of the voice of John the Baptist crying in the wilderness, at the beginning of his Gospel; Apr. 25.

Matthew: A Galilean, called Levi by Luke and John and the son of Alphaeus by Mark, a tax collector, one of the Evangelists; according to various accounts, preached the Gospel in Judea, Ethiopia, Persia, and Parthia, and was martyred; in art, is depicted with a spear, the instrument of his death, and as a winged man in his role as Evangelist; Sept. 21 (Roman Rite), Nov. 16 (Byzantine Rite).

Matthias: A disciple of Jesus whom the faithful 11

Apostles chose to replace Judas before the Resurrection; uncertain traditions report that he preached the Gospel in Palestine, Cappadocia, or Ethiopia; in art, is represented with a cross and a halberd, the instruments of his death as a martyr; May 14 (Roman Rite), Aug. 9 (Byzantine Rite).

Paul: Born at Tarsus, of the tribe of Benjamin, a Roman citizen; participated in the persecution of Christians until the time of his miraculous conversion on the way to Damascus; called by Christ, who revealed himself to him in a special way; became the Apostle of the Gentiles, among whom he did most of his preaching in the course of three major missionary journeys through areas north of Palestine, Cyprus, Asia Minor, and Greece; 14 epistles bear his name; two years of imprisonment at Rome, following initial arrest in Jerusalem and confinement at Caesarea, ended with martyrdom, by beheading, outside the walls of the city in 64 or 67 during the Neronian persecution; in art, is depicted in various ways with St. Peter, with a sword, in the scene of his conversion; June 29 (with St. Peter), Jan. 25 (Conversion). Pope Benedict XVI declared 2008-2009 the Year of St. Paul.

Peter: Simon, son of Jonah, born in Bethsaida, brother of Andrew, a fisherman; called Cephas or Peter by Christ, who made him the chief of the Apostles and head of the Church as his vicar; named first in the listings of Apostles in the Synoptic Gospels and the Acts of the Apostles; with James the Greater and John, witnessed the raising of Jairus's daughter to life, the transfiguration, the agony of Jesus in the Garden of Gethsemane; was the first to preach the Gospel in and around Jerusalem and was the leader of the first Christian community there; established a local church in Antioch; presided over the Council of Jerusalem in 51; wrote two Catholic Epistles to the Christians in Asia Minor; established his see in Rome where he spent his last years and was martyred by crucifixion in 64 or 65 during the Neronian persecution; in art, is depicted carrying two keys, symbolic of his primacy in the Church; June 29 (with St. Paul), Feb. 22 (Chair of Peter).

Philip: Born in Bethsaida; according to legend, preached

the Gospel in Phrygia where he suffered martyrdom by crucifixion; May 3 (Roman Rite), Nov. 14 (Byzantine Rite).

Simon: Called the Cananean or the Zealot; according to legend, preached in various places in the Middle East and suffered martyrdom by being sawed in two; in art, is depicted with a saw, the instrument of his death, or a book, symbolic of his zeal for the Law; Oct. 28 (Roman Rite), May 10 (Byzantine Rite).

Thomas (Didymus): Notable for his initial incredulity regarding the Resurrection and his subsequent forthright confession of the divinity of Christ risen from the dead; according to legend, preached the Gospel in places from the Caspian Sea to the Persian Gulf and eventually reached India where he was martyred near Madras; Thomas Christians trace their origin to him; in art, is depicted kneeling before the risen Christ, or with a carpenter's rule and square; July 3 (Roman Rite), Oct. 6 (Byzantine Rite).

Judas: The Gospels record only a few facts about Judas, the Apostle who betrayed Christ. The only non-Galilean among the Apostles, he was from Carioth, a town in southern Judah. He was keeper of the purse in the apostolic band. He was called a petty thief by John. He voiced dismay at the waste of money, which he said might have been spent for the poor, in connection with the anointing incident at Bethany. He took the initiative in arranging the betrayal of Christ. Afterwards, he confessed that he had betrayed an innocent man and cast into the Temple the money he had received for that action. Of his death, Matthew says that he hanged himself; the Acts of the Apostles states that he swelled up and burst open; both reports deal more with the meaning than the manner of his death — the misery of the death of a sinner.

The consensus of speculation over the reason why Judas acted as he did in betraying Christ focuses on disillusionment and unwillingness to accept the concept of a suffering Messiah and his own personal suffering as an Apostle.

APOSTOLIC FATHERS, FATHERS, DOCTORS OF THE CHURCH

The writers listed below were outstanding and authoritative witnesses to authentic Christian belief and practice, and played significant roles in giving them expression.

Apostolic Fathers

The Apostolic Fathers were Christian writers of the first and second centuries whose writings echo genuine apostolic teaching. Chief in importance are: St. Clement (d. c. 97), bishop of Rome and third successor of St. Peter in the papacy; St. Ignatius (50-c. 107), bishop of Antioch and second successor of St. Peter in that see, reputed to be a disciple of St. John; St. Polycarp (69-155), bishop of Smyrna and a disciple of St. John. The authors of the Didache and the Epistle of Barnabas are also numbered among the Apostolic Fathers.

Other early ecclesiastical writers included: St. Justin, martyr (100-165), of Asia Minor and Rome, a layman and apologist; St. Irenaeus (130-202), bishop of Lyons, who opposed Gnosticism; and St. Cyprian (210-258), bishop of Carthage, who opposed Novatianism.

Fathers and Doctors

The Fathers of the Church were theologians and writers of the first eight centuries who were outstanding for sanctity and learning. They were such authoritative witnesses to the belief and teaching of the Church that their unanimous acceptance of doctrines as divinely revealed has been regarded as evidence that such doctrines were so received by the Church in line with apostolic tradition and Sacred Scripture. Their unanimous rejection of doctrines branded them as heretical. Their writings, however, were not necessarily free of error in all respects.

The greatest of these Fathers were: Sts. Ambrose, Augustine, Jerome, and Gregory the Great in the West; Sts. John Chrysostom, Basil the Great, Gregory of Nazianzus, and Athanasius in the East.

The Doctors of the Church were ecclesiastical writers of eminent learning and sanctity who have been given this title because of the great advantage the Church has derived from their work. Their writings, however, were not necessarily free of error in all respects.

Albert the Great, St. (c. 1200-1280): Born in Swabia,

Germany; Dominican; bishop of Regensburg (1260-1262); wrote extensively on logic, natural sciences, ethics, metaphysics, Scripture, systematic theology; contributed to development of Scholasticism; teacher of St. Thomas Aquinas; canonized and proclaimed doctor, 1931; named patron of natural scientists, 1941; called *Doctor Universalis, Doctor Expertus*; Nov. 15.

Alphonsus Liguori, St. (1696-1787): Born near Naples, Italy; bishop of St. Agatha of the Goths (1762-1775); founder of the Redemptorists; in addition to his principal work, *Theologiae Moralis*, wrote on prayer, the spiritual life, and doctrinal subjects in response to controversy; canonized, 1839; proclaimed doctor, 1871; named patron of confessors and moralists, 1950; Aug. 1.

Ambrose, St. (c. 340-397): Born in Trier, Germany; bishop of Milan (374-397); one of the strongest opponents of Arianism in the West; his homilies and other writings—on faith, the Holy Spirit, the Incarnation, the sacraments, and other subjects—were pastoral and practical; influenced the development of a liturgy at Milan which was named for him; Father and Doctor of the Church; Dec. 7.

Anselm, St. (1033-1109): Born in Aosta, Piedmont, Italy; Benedictine; archbishop of Canterbury (1093-1109); in addition to his principal work, *Cur Deus Homo*, on the atonement and reconciliation of man with God through Christ, wrote about the existence and attributes of God and defended the *Filioque* explanation of the procession of the Holy Spirit from the Father and the Son; proclaimed doctor, 1720; called Father of Scholasticism; Apr. 21.

Anthony of Padua, St. (1195-1231): Born in Lisbon, Portugal; first theologian of the Franciscan Order; preacher; canonized, 1232; proclaimed doctor, 1946; called Evangelical Doctor; June 13.

Athanasius, St. (c. 297-373): Born in Alexandria, Egypt; bishop of Alexandria (328-373); participant in the Council of Nicaea I while still a deacon; dominant opponent of Arians, whose errors regarding Christ he refuted in *Apology Against the Arians*, *Discourses against the Arians*, and other works; Father and Doctor of the Church; called Father of Orthodoxy; May 2.

Augustine, St. (354-430): Born in Tagaste, North Africa; bishop of Hippo (395-430) after conversion from Manichaeism; works include the autobiographical and mystical *Confessions*, *City of God*, treatises on the Trinity, grace, passages of the Bible, and doctrines called into question and denied by Manichaeans, Pelagians, and Donatists; had strong and lasting influence on Christian theology and philosophy; Father and Doctor of the Church; called Doctor of Grace; Aug. 28.

Basil the Great, St. (c. 329-379): Born in Caesarea, Cappadocia, Asia Minor; bishop of Caesarea (370-379); wrote three books, *Contra Eunomium*, in refutation of Arian errors, a treatise on the Holy Spirit, many homilies, and several rules for monastic life, on which he had lasting influence; Father and Doctor of the Church; called Father of Monasticism in the East; Jan. 2.

Bede the Venerable, St. (c. 673-735): Born in Northumberland, England; Benedictine; in addition to his principal work, *Ecclesiastical History* of the *English Nation* (covering the period 597-731), wrote scriptural commentaries; regarded as probably the most learned man in Western Europe of his time; called Father of English History; May 25.

Bernard of Clairvaux, St. (c. 1090-1153): Born near Dijon, France; abbot; monastic reformer, called the second founder of the Cistercian Order; mystical theologian with great influence on devotional life; opponent of the rationalism brought forward by Abelard and others; canonized, 1174; proclaimed doctor, 1830; called Mellifluous Doctor because of his eloquence; Aug. 20.

Bonaventure, St. (c. 1217-1274): Born near Viterbo, Italy; Franciscan; bishop of Albano (1273-1274); cardinal; wrote *Itinerarium Mentis in Deum*, *De Reductione Artium ad Theologiam*, *Breviloquium*, scriptural commentaries, additional mystical works affecting devotional life, and a life of St. Francis of Assisi; canonized, 1482; proclaimed doctor, 1588; called Seraphic Doctor; July 15.

Catherine of Siena, St. (c. 1347-1380): Born in Siena, Italy; member of the Third Order of St. Dominic; mystic; authored a long series of letters, mainly concerning spiritual instruction and encouragement, to associates, and *Dialogue*, a spiritual testament in four treatises; was active in support of a crusade against the Turks and efforts to end war between papal forces and the Florentine allies; had great influence in inducing Gregory XI to return himself and the Curia to Rome in 1377, to end the Avignon period of the papacy; canonized, 1461; proclaimed the second woman doctor, Oct. 4, 1970; named a co-patroness of Europe, with St. Edith Stein and St. Bridget of Sweden, on Oct. 1, 1999; Apr. 29.

Cyril of Alexandria, St. (c. 376-444): Born in Egypt; bishop of Alexandria (412-444); wrote treatises on the Trinity, the Incarnation, and other subjects, mostly in refutation of Nestorian errors; made key contributions to the development of Christology; presided at the Council of Ephesus, 431; proclaimed doctor, 1882; June 27.

Cyril of Jerusalem, St. (c. 315-386): Bishop of Jerusalem from 350; vigorous opponent of Arianism; principal work, *Catecheses*, a pre-baptismal explanation of the creed of Jerusalem; proclaimed doctor, 1882; Mar. 18.

Ephraem, St. (c. 306-373): Born in Nisibis, Mesopotamia; counteracted the spread of Gnostic and Arian errors with poems and hymns of his own composition; wrote also on the Eucharist and Mary; proclaimed doctor, 1920; called Deacon of Edessa and Harp of the Holy Spirit; June 9.

Francis de Sales, St. (1567-1622): Born in Savoy; bishop of Geneva (1602-1622); spiritual writer with strong influence on devotional life through treatises such as *Introduction to a Devout Life* and *The Love of God*; canonized, 1665; proclaimed doctor, 1877; patron of Catholic writers and the Catholic press; Jan. 24.

Gregory Nazianzen, St. (c. 330-c. 390): Born in Arianzus, Cappadocia, Asia Minor; bishop of Constantinople (381-390); vigorous opponent of Arianism; in addition to five theological discourses on the Nicene Creed and the Trinity for which he is best known, wrote letters and poetry; Father and Doctor of the Church; called the Christian Demosthenes because of his eloquence and, in the Eastern Church, the Theologian; Jan. 2.

Gregory I, the Great, St. (c. 540-604): Born in Rome; pope (590-604); wrote many scriptural commentaries, a compendium of theology in the *Book of Morals* based on Job, *Dialogues*, concerning the lives of saints, the immortality of the soul, death, purgatory, heaven and hell, and fourteen books of letters; enforced papal supremacy and established the position of the pope vis-á-vis the emperor; worked for clerical and monastic reform and the observance of clerical celibacy; Father and Doctor of the Church; Sept. 3.

Hilary of Poitiers, St. (c. 315-368): Born in Poitiers, France; bishop of Poitiers (c. 353-368); wrote *De Synodis*, with the Arian controversy in mind, and *De Trinitate*, the first lengthy study of the doctrine in Latin; introduced Eastern theology to the West; contributed to the development of hymnology; proclaimed doctor, 1851; called the Athanasius of the West because of his vigorous defense of the divinity of Christ against Arians; Jan. 13.

Isidore of Seville, St. (c. 560-636): Born in Cartagena, Spain; bishop of Seville (c. 600-636); in addition to his principal work, *Etymologiae*, an encyclopedia of the knowledge of his day, wrote on theological and historical subjects; regarded as the most learned man of his time; proclaimed doctor, 1722; Apr. 4.

Jerome, St. (c. 343-420): Born in Stridon, Dalmatia; translated the Old Testament from Hebrew into Latin and revised the existing Latin translation of the New Testament to produce the Vulgate version of the Bible; wrote scriptural commentaries and treatises on matters of controversy; regarded as Father and Doctor of the Church from the eighth century; called Father of Biblical Science; Sept. 30.

John Chrysostom, St. (c. 347-407): Born in Antioch, Asia Minor; archbishop of Constantinople (398-407); wrote homilies, scriptural commentaries, and letters of wide influence, in addition to a classical treatise on the priesthood; proclaimed doctor by the Council of Chalcedon, 451; called the greatest of the Greek Fathers; named patron of preachers, 1909; called Golden-Mouthed because of his eloquence; Sept. 13.

John Damascene, St. (c. 675-c. 749): Born in Damascus, Syria; monk; wrote *Fountain of Wisdom*, a three-part work including a history of heresies and an exposition of the Christian faith, three discourses against the Iconoclasts, homilies on Mary, biblical commentaries, and treatises on moral subjects; proclaimed doctor, 1890; called Golden Speaker because of his eloquence; Dec. 4.

John of the Cross, St. (1542-1591): Born in Old Castile, Spain; Carmelite; founder of Discalced Carmelites; one of the greatest mystical theologians; wrote *The Ascent of Mt. Carmel, The Dark Night of the Soul, The Spiritual Canticle, The Living Flame of Love*; canonized, 1726; proclaimed doctor, 1926; called Doctor of Mystical Theology; Dec. 14.

Lawrence of Brindisi, St. (1559-1619): Born in Brindisi, Italy; Franciscan (Capuchin); vigorous preacher of strong influence in the post-Reformation period; 15 tomes of collected works include scriptural commentaries, sermons, homilies and doctrinal writings; canonized, 1881; proclaimed doctor, 1959; July 21.

Leo I, the Great, St. (c. 400-461): Born in Tuscany, Italy; pope (440-461); wrote the *Tome of Leo*, to explain doctrine concerning the two natures and one Person of Christ, against the background of the Nestorian and Monophysite heresies; other works included sermons, letters, and writings against the errors of Manichaeism and Pelagianism; was instru-

mental in dissuading Attila from sacking Rome in 452; proclaimed doctor, 1574; Nov. 10.

Peter Canisius, St. (1521-1597): Born in Nijmegen, Holland; Jesuit; wrote popular expositions of the Catholic faith in several catechisms which were widely circulated in 20 editions in his lifetime alone; was one of the moving figures in the Counter-Reformation period, especially in southern and western Germany; canonized and proclaimed doctor, 1925; Dec. 21.

Peter Chrysologus, St. (c. 400-450): Born in Imola, Italy; served as archbishop of Ravenna (c. 433-450); his sermons and writings, many of which were designed to counteract Monophysitism, were pastoral and practical; proclaimed doctor, 1729; July 30.

Peter Damian, St. (1007-1072): Born in Ravenna, Italy; Benedictine; cardinal; his writings and sermons, many of which concerned ecclesiastical and clerical reform, were pastoral and practical; proclaimed doctor, 1828; Feb. 21.

Robert Bellarmine, St. (1542-1621): Born in Tuscany, Italy; Jesuit; archbishop of Capua (1602-1605); wrote *Controversies*, a three-volume exposition of doctrine under attack during and after the Reformation, two catechisms, and the spiritual work *The Art of Dying Well*; was an authority on ecclesiology and Church-state relations; canonized, 1930; proclaimed doctor, 1931; Sept. 17.

Teresa of Jesus (Ávila), St. (1515-1582): Born in Ávila, Spain; entered the Carmelite Order, 1535; in the early 1560s, initiated a primitive Carmelite reform which greatly influenced men and women religious, especially in Spain; wrote extensively on spiritual and mystical subjects; principal works included her *Autobiography, Way of Perfection, The Interior Castle, Meditations on the Canticle, The Foundations, Visitation of the Discalced Nuns*; canonized, 1622; proclaimed first woman doctor, Sept. 27, 1970; Oct. 15.

Thérèse of Lisieux, St. (1873-1897): Born in Alençon, Normandy, France; entered the Carmelites at Lisieux in 1888, lived for only nine more years, dying on Sept. 30, 1897, from tuberculosis. Trusting completely in God, a path she described as the "little way," she lived a seemingly ordinary life of a nun, but her spiritual advancement was such that her superiors instructed her to write an autobiography in 1895 (The Story of a Soul). One of the most popular and respected saints throughout the 20th century, she was canonized on May 17, 1925. Pope John Paul II declared her the third woman doctor on Oct. 20, 1997, in the letter *Divini amoris scientia*; her relics also toured the United States, attracting huge crowds; Oct. 1.

Thomas Aquinas, St. (1225-1274): Born near Naples, Italy; Dominican; teacher and writer on virtually the whole range of philosophy and theology; principal works were *Summa contra Gentiles*, a manual and systematic defense of Christian doctrine, and *Summa Theologiae*, a new (at that time) exposition of theology on philosophical principles; canonized, 1323; proclaimed doctor, 1567; called *Doctor Communis, Doctor Angelicus*, the Great Synthesizer because of the way in which he related faith and reason, theology and philosophy (especially that of Aristotle), and systematized the presentation of Christian doctrine; named patron of Catholic schools and education, 1880; Jan. 28.

CREEDS

Creeds are formal and official statements of Christian doctrine. As summaries of the principal truths of faith, they are standards of orthodoxy and are useful for instructional purposes, for actual profession of the faith, and for expression of the faith in the liturgy.

The classical creeds are the Apostles' Creed and the Creed of Nicaea-Constantinople. Two others are the Athanasian Creed and the Creed of Pius IV.

Apostles' Creed

Text: *I believe in God, the Father almighty, Creator of heaven and earth.*

And in Jesus Christ, his only Son, our Lord; who was conceived by the Holy Spirit, born of the Virgin Mary, suffered under Pontius Pilate, was crucified, died, and was buried. He descended into hell; the third day he arose again from the dead; he ascended into heaven, sits at the right hand of God, the Father almighty; from thence he shall come to judge the living and the dead.

I believe in the Holy Spirit, the holy Catholic Church, the communion of saints, the forgiveness of sins, the resurrection of the body, and life everlasting. Amen.

Background: The Apostles' Creed reflects the teaching of the Apostles but is not of apostolic origin. It probably originated in the second century as a rudimentary formula of faith professed by catechumens before the reception of baptism. Baptismal creeds in fourth-century use at Rome and elsewhere in the West closely resembled the present text, which was quoted in a handbook of Christian doctrine written between 710 and 724. This text was in wide use throughout the West by the ninth century. The Apostles' Creed is common to all Christian confessional churches in the West, but is not used in Eastern Churches.

Nicene Creed

The following translation of the Latin text of the Creed was prepared by the International Committee on English in the Liturgy.

Text: *We believe in one God, the Father, the Almighty, maker of heaven and earth, of all that is seen and unseen.*

We believe in one Lord, Jesus Christ, the only Son of God, eternally begotten of the Father, God from God, Light from Light, true God from true God, begotten, not made, one in Being with the Father. Through him all things were made. For us men and for our salvation he came down from heaven: by the power of the Holy Spirit he was born of the Virgin Mary, and became man. For our sake he was crucified under Pontius

Pilate; he suffered, died, and was buried. On the third day he rose again in fulfillment of the Scriptures; he ascended into heaven and is seated at the right hand of the Father. He will come again in glory to judge the living and the dead, and his kingdom will have no end.

We believe in the Holy Spirit, the Lord, the giver of life, who proceeds from the Father and the Son. With the Father and the Son he is worshipped and glorified. He has spoken through the prophets.

We believe in one holy catholic and apostolic Church. We acknowledge one baptism for the forgiveness of sins. We look for the resurrection of the dead, and the life of the world to come. Amen.

Background: The Nicene Creed (Creed of Nicaea-Constantinople) consists of elements of doctrine contained in an early baptismal creed of Jerusalem and enactments of the Council of Nicaea (325) and the Council of Constantinople (381).

Its strong trinitarian content reflects the doctrinal errors, especially of Arianism, it served to counteract. Theologically, it is much more sophisticated than the Apostles' Creed.

Since late in the fifth century, the Nicene Creed has been the only creed in liturgical use in the Eastern Churches. The Western Church adopted it for liturgical use by the end of the eighth century.

The Athanasian Creed

The Athanasian Creed, which has a unique structure, is a two-part summary of doctrine concerning the Trinity and the Incarnation-Redemption bracketed at the beginning and end with the statement that belief in the cited truths is necessary for salvation; it also contains a number of anathemas or condemnatory clauses regarding doctrinal errors. Although attributed to St. Athanasius, it was probably written after his death, between 381 and 428, and may have been authored by St. Ambrose. It is not accepted in the East; in the West, it formerly had place in the Roman-Rite Liturgy of the Hours and in the liturgy for the Solemnity of the Holy Trinity.

Creed of Pius IV

The Creed of Pius IV, also called the Profession of Faith of the Council of Trent, was promulgated in the bull *Injunctum Nobis*, Nov. 13, 1564. It is a summary of doctrine defined by the council concerning Scripture and tradition, original sin and justification, the Mass and sacraments, veneration of the saints, indulgences, and the primacy of the See of Rome. It was slightly modified in 1887 to include doctrinal formulations of the First Vatican Council.

CHRISTIAN MORALITY

By Father Alfred McBride, O.Praem.

"Incorporated into Christ by Baptism, Christians are 'dead to sin and alive in Christ Jesus. . .'" (Rom 6:11).

CHRISTIAN MORALITY IS LIFE IN CHRIST

The third part of the *Catechism* focuses on Christian morality. After the Creed as faith professed, and sacraments as faith celebrated, the *Catechism* turns our attention to the faith lived. It deals with this issue in two major sections. The first section establishes the context for Christian morality. The second section analyzes the Ten Commandments. This approach preserves the *Catechism's* resolute insistence on the primacy of God's initiative through Revelation, salvation, and grace followed by our human response in faith, celebration, and Christian witness. Hence morality does not begin with the rules but with the call to life in Christ and the Holy Spirit. Covenant love comes first, then the response of Christian affection in the life of the commandments. This saves us both from legalism and from piety without practical witness.

The following excerpt from the *Catechism of the Catholic Church* sets the vision for the Christian moral life.

Life In Christ

1691 "Christian, recognize your dignity and, now that you share in God's own nature, do not return to your former base condition by sinning. Remember who is your head and of whose body you are a member. Never forget that you have been rescued from the power of darkness and brought into the light of the Kingdom of God."[1]

1692 The Symbol of the faith confesses the greatness of God's gifts to man in his work of creation, and even more in redemption and sanctification. What faith confesses, the sacraments communicate: by the sacraments of rebirth, Christians have become "children of God,"[2] "partakers of the divine nature."[3] Coming to see in the faith their new dignity, Christians are called to lead henceforth a life "worthy of the gospel of Christ."[4] They are made capable of doing so by the grace of Christ and the gifts of his Spirit, which they receive through the sacraments and through prayer.

1693 Christ Jesus always did what was pleasing to the Father,[5] and always lived in perfect communion with him. Likewise Christ's disciples are invited to live in the sight of the Father "who sees in secret,"[6] in order to become "perfect as your heavenly Father is perfect."[7]

1694 Incorporated into Christ by Baptism, Christians are "dead to sin and alive to God in Christ Jesus" and so participate in the life of the Risen Lord.[8] Following Christ and united with him,[9] Christians can strive to be "imitators of God as beloved children, and walk in love"[10] by conforming their thoughts, words and actions to the "mind... which is yours in Christ Jesus,"[11] and by following his example.[12]

1695 "Justified in the name of the Lord Jesus Christ and in the Spirit of our God," [13] "sanctified... [and] called to be saints,"[14] Christians have become the temple of the Holy Spirit.[15] This "Spirit of the Son" teaches them to pray to the Father[16] and, having become their life, prompts them to act so as to bear "the fruit of the Spirit"[17] by charity in action. Healing the wounds of sin, the Holy Spirit renews us interiorly through a spiritual transformation.[18] He enlightens and strengthens us to live as "children of light" through "all that is good and right and true."[19]

1696 The way of Christ "leads to life"; a contrary way "leads to destruction."[20] The Gospel parable of the two ways remains ever present in the catechesis of the Church; it shows the importance of moral decisions for our salvation: "There are two ways, the one of life, the other of death; but between the two, there is a great difference."[21]

1697 Catechesis has to reveal in all clarity the joy and the demands of the way of Christ.[22] Catechesis for the "newness of life"[23] in him should be:

• a catechesis of the Holy Spirit, the interior Master of life according to Christ, a gentle guest and friend who inspires, guides, corrects, and strengthens this life;

• a catechesis of grace, for it is by grace that we are saved and again it is by grace that our works can bear fruit for eternal life;

• a catechesis of the beatitudes, for the way of Christ is summed up in the beatitudes, the only path that leads to the eternal beatitude for which the human heart longs;

• a catechesis of sin and forgiveness, for unless man acknowledges that he is a sinner he cannot know the truth about himself, which is a condition for acting justly; and without the offer of forgiveness he would not be able to bear this truth;

• a catechesis of the human virtues which causes one to grasp the beauty and attraction of right dispositions towards goodness;

• a catechesis of the Christian virtues of faith, hope, and charity, generously inspired by the example of the saints; a catechesis of the twofold commandment of charity set forth in the Decalogue;

• an ecclesial catechesis, for it is through the manifold exchanges of "spiritual goods" in the "communion of saints" that Christian life can grow, develop, and be communicated.

1698 The first and last point of reference of this catechesis will always be Jesus Christ himself, who is "the way, and the truth, and the life."[24] It is by looking to him in faith that Christ's faithful can hope that he himself fulfills his promises in them, and that, by loving him with the same love with which he has loved them, they may perform works in keeping with their dignity: "I ask you to consider that our Lord Jesus Christ is your true head, and that you are one of his members. He belongs to you as the head belongs to its members; all that is his is yours: his spirit, his heart, his body and soul, and all his faculties. You must make use of all these as of your own, to serve, praise, love, and glorify God. You belong to him, as members belong to their head. And so he longs for you to use all that is in you, as if it were his own, for the service and glory of the Father."[25] "For to me, to live is Christ."[26]

Footnotes

[1] St. Leo the Great, Sermon 22 in nat. Dom 3: PL 54, 192C. [2] Jn 1:12; 1 Jn 3:1. [3] 2 Pt 1:4. [4] Phil 1:27. [5] Cf. Jn 8:29. [6] Mt 6:6. [7] Mt 5:48. [8] Rom 6:11 and cf. 6:5; cf. Col 2:12. [9] Cf. Jn 15:5. [10] Eph 5:1-2. [11] Phil 2:5. [12] Cf. Jn 13:12-16. [13] 1 Cor 6:11. [14] 1 Cor 1:2. [15] Cf. 1 Cor 6:19. [16] Cf. Gal 4:6. [17] Gal 5:22, 25. [18] Cf. Eph 4:23. [19] Eph 5:8, 9. [20] Mt 7:13; cf. Dt 30: 15-20. [21] Didache 1, 1: SCh 248, 140. [22] Cf. John Paul II, CT 29. [23] Rom 6:4. [24] Jn. 14:6. [25] St. John Eudes, Tract. de admirabili corde Jesu, 1, 5. [26] Phil 1:21.

THE TEN COMMANDMENTS

Any discussions of the commandments should begin with the scene at Sinai where God gave them to us. Read Ex 19:3-6; 20:1-17. The first event is a covenant experience. God tells Moses how much he has loved the Israelites, is delivering them from slavery by "raising them up on eagles' wings," and is bringing them to freedom. God then offers them a binding covenant of love. He will be their only God and they will be his chosen people. It's like a marriage experience, an exchange of vows between God and Israel.

The next section shows God telling them how to live out the love they have pledged. He gives them the Ten Commandments as the means to live the covenant, to express the love they have promised. The *Catechism* points out that the Ten Commandments are privileged expressions of the natural law, made known to us by reason as well as Divine Revelation. We are obliged in obedience to observe these laws of love, both in serious and light matters. Love is in the details as well as the large matters. We must remember that what God has commanded, he makes possible by his grace.

Jesus set the tone for understanding the importance of the commandments. When a rich young man came to him and asked him what he should do to enter eternal life, Jesus replied, "if you wish to enter into life, keep the commandments" (Mt 19:17). In another case, someone asked him which were the greatest commandments, Jesus replied, "you shall love the Lord, your God, with all your heart, with all your soul, and with all your mind. This is the greatest and first commandment. The second is like it: You shall love your neighbor as yourself" (Mt 22:37-39). The first three commandments deal with Christ's call to God with all our being. The last seven commandments show us how to love our neighbors as we love ourselves.

The following excerpt from the *Catechism of the Catholic Church* shows how Jesus taught the importance of the Ten Commandments.

"Teacher, what must I do. . .?"

2052 "Teacher, what good deed must I do, to have eternal life?" To the young man who asked this question, Jesus answers first by invoking the necessity to recognize God as the "One there is who is good," as the supreme Good and the source of all good. Then Jesus tells him: "If you would enter life, keep the commandments." And he cites for his questioner the precepts that concern love of neighbor: "You shall not kill, You shall not commit adultery, You shall not steal, You shall not bear false witness, Honor your father and mother." Finally Jesus sums up these commandments positively: "You shall love your neighbor as yourself."[1]

2053 To this first reply Jesus adds a second: "If you

would be perfect, go, sell what you possess and give to the poor, and you will have treasure in heaven; and come, follow me."[2] This reply does not do away with the first: following Jesus Christ involves keeping the Commandments. The Law has not been abolished,[3] but rather man is invited to rediscover it in the person of his Master who is its perfect fulfillment. In the three synoptic Gospels, Jesus' call to the rich young man to follow him, in the obedience of a disciple and in the observance of the Commandments, is joined to the call to poverty and chastity.[4] The evangelical counsels are inseparable from the Commandments.

2054 Jesus acknowledged the Ten Commandments, but he also showed the power of the Spirit at work in their letter. He preached a "righteousness [which] exceeds that of the scribes and Pharisees"[5] as well as that of the Gentiles.[6] He unfolded all the demands of the Commandments. "You have heard that it was said to the men of old, 'You shall not kill.' … But I say to you that every one who is angry with his brother shall be liable to judgment."[7]

2055 When someone asks him, "Which commandment in the Law is the greatest?"[8] Jesus replies: "You shall love the Lord your God with all your heart, and with all your soul, and with all your mind. This is the greatest and first commandment. And a second is like it: You shall love your neighbor as yourself. On these two commandments hang all the Law and the prophets."[9] The Decalogue must be interpreted in light of this twofold yet single commandment of love, the fullness of the Law: "The commandments: 'You shall not commit adultery, You shall not kill, You shall not steal, You shall not covet,' and any other commandment, are summed up in this sentence: 'You shall love your neighbor as yourself.' Love does no wrong to a neighbor; therefore love is the fulfilling of the law."[10]

Footnotes

[1] Mt 19:16-19. [2] Mt 19:21. [3] Cf. Mt 5:17. [4] Cf. Mt 19:6-12, 21, 23-29. [5] Mt 5:20. [6] Cf. Mt 5:46-47. [7] Mt 5:21-22. [8] Mt 22:36. [9] Mt 22:37-40; cf. Dt 6:5; Lv 19:18. [10] Rom 13:9-10.

In the traditional Catholic enumeration and according to Dt 5:6-21, the Commandments are:
1. "I, the Lord, am your God You shall not have other gods besides me. You shall not carve idols."
2. "You shall not take the name of the Lord, your God, in vain."
3. "Take care to keep holy the Sabbath day."
4. "Honor your father and your mother."
5. "You shall not kill."
6. "You shall not commit adultery."
7. "You shall not steal."
8. "You shall not bear dishonest witness against your neighbor."
9. "You shall not covet your neighbor's wife."
10. "You shall not desire your neighbor's house or field, nor his male or female slave, nor his ox or ass, nor anything that belongs to him" (summarily, his goods).

Another version of the Commandments, substantially the same, is given in Ex 20:1-17.

The traditional enumeration of the Commandments in Protestant usage differs from the above. Thus: two commandments are made of the first, as above; the third and fourth are equivalent to the second and third, as above, and so on; and the 10th includes the ninth and 10th, as above.

Love of God and Neighbor

The first three of the commandments deal directly with man's relations with God, viz., acknowledgment of one true God and the rejection of false gods and idols; honor due to God and his name; observance of the Sabbath as the Lord 's Day.

The rest cover interpersonal relationships, viz., the obedience due to parents and, logically, to other persons in authority, and the obligations of parents to children and of persons in authority to those under their care; respect for life and physical integrity; fidelity in marriage, and chastity; justice and rights; truth; internal respect for faithfulness in marriage, chastity, and the goods of others.

Perfection in Christian Life

The moral obligations of the Ten Commandments are complemented by others flowing from the twofold law of love, the whole substance and pattern of Christ's teaching, and everything implied in full and active membership and participation in the community of sal-vation formed by Christ in his Church. Some of these matters are covered in other sections of the *Almanac* under appropriate headings.

Precepts of the Church

The purpose of the precepts of the Church, according to the *Catechism of the Catholic Church*, is "to guarantee to the faithful the indispensable minimum in the spirit of prayer and moral effort, in the growth and love of God and neighbor" (No. 2041).

1. Attendance at Mass on Sundays and holy days of obligation. (Observance of Sundays and holy days of obligation involves refraining from work that hinders the worship due to God.)

2. Confession of sins at least once a year. (Not required by the precept in the absence of serious sin.)

3. Reception of the Eucharist at least during the Easter season (in the U.S., from the first Sunday of Lent to Trinity Sunday).

4. Keep holy the holy days of obligation.

5. Observance of specified days of fasting and abstinence.

There is also an obligation to provide for the material needs of the Church.

CATHOLIC MORAL TEACHINGS OF POPE JOHN PAUL II

On Aug. 6, 1993, Pope John Paul II published his tenth encyclical, Veritatis Splendor *("The Splendor of the Truth") regarding the fundamental truths of the Church's moral teachings. On Mar. 25, 1995, he published his eleventh encyclical,* Evangelium Vitae *("The Gospel of Life"), concerning the value and inviolability of human life. The following material is adapted from* The Encyclicals of John Paul II, *with the kind permission of Most Rev. J. Michael Miller, C.S.B.*

Veritatis Splendor
("The Splendor of the Truth")

On Aug. 6, 1993, John Paul II signed his tenth encyclical, *Veritatis Splendor*, regarding certain fundamental truths of the Church's moral teaching.[1] Undoubtedly it is the pope's most complex and most discussed document. Since its publication, the encyclical has generated a great deal of comment in the media and among theologians. This is not surprising, since *Veritatis Splendor* is the first-ever papal document on the theological and philosophical foundations of Catholic moral teaching. In this encyclical the pope affirms that divine revelation contains "a specific and determined moral content, universally valid and permanent" (§37.1), which the Magisterium has the competence to interpret and teach.

Six years before, in the apostolic letter *Spiritus Domini* (1987), John Paul had publicly announced his intention to publish a document that would treat "more fully and more deeply the issues regarding the very foundations of moral theology" (§5.1). For several reasons the encyclical's preparation took longer than was first anticipated. First, the pope widely consulted bishops and theologians throughout the world, and various drafts were drawn up. Second, he thought that it was fitting for the encyclical "to be preceded by the Catechism of the Catholic Church, which contains a complete and systematic exposition of Christian moral teaching" (§5.3). The Catechism, published in 1992, gives a full presentation of the Church's moral doctrine, including that on particular questions, and expounds it in a positive way. *Veritatis Splendor*, on the other hand, limits itself to dealing with the fundamental principles underlying all moral teaching.

But why does John Paul think that an encyclical on moral issues will serve the Church and the world on the threshold of the third millennium? According to him, reflection on the ethical implications of Christian faith, lived from the beginning as the "way" (Acts 22:4), belongs to the full proclamation of the Gospel. Moreover, he is convinced that society is in the throes of a "crisis of truth" (§32.2). This crisis has the "most serious implications for the moral life of the faithful and for communion in the Church, as well as for a just and fraternal social life" (§5.2).

The deChristianization of many cultures involves not only a loss of faith but also "a decline or obscuring of the moral sense" (§106.2). This new moral situation brings with it "the confusion between good and evil, which makes it impossible to build up and to preserve the moral order" (§93.1). The ethical bewilderment of some Catholics has led to "the spread of numerous doubts and objections of a human and psychological, social and cultural, religious and even properly theological nature, with regard to the Church's moral teachings" (§4.2). In an increasingly secular world, believers are "making judgments and decisions [that] often appear extraneous or even contrary to those of the Gospel" (§88.2). Moreover, dissent from Catholic moral teaching often entails "an overall and systematic calling into question of traditional moral doctrine" (§4.2). Thus, as a service to the ethical and spiritual welfare of individuals and cultures, John Paul addresses the basic moral principles handed down by the

Christian Tradition.

In order to meet his goal, the pope responds in a constructive way to the contemporary moral crisis by proclaiming "the splendor of the truth." When he announced the forthcoming publication of *Veritatis Splendor*, he described the encyclical's purpose: "It reaffirms the dignity of the human person, created in God's image, and proposes anew the genuine concept of human freedom, showing its essential and constitutive relationship with the truth in accordance with Christ's words: 'The truth will make you free!' (Jn 8:32)."[2] On another occasion, John Paul said that he intended the encyclical to be "a proclamation of truth and a hymn to freedom: values felt strongly by contemporary man and deeply respected by the Church."[3] His primary aim, then, is not to censure specific dissident moral opinions but to proclaim that Christ is "the true and final answer to the problem of morality" (§85).

John Paul sets several specific objectives for the encyclical. First, he wishes "to reflect on the whole of the Church's moral teaching, with the precise goal of recalling certain fundamental truths of Catholic doctrine which, in the present circumstances, risk being distorted or denied" (§4.2, cf. §30.1). Second, he aims to show the faithful "the inviting splendor of that truth which is Jesus Christ himself" (§83.2). Christ alone is the answer to humanity's questions, "the only response fully capable of satisfying the desire of the human heart" (§7.1). Third, if the present crisis is to be successfully resolved, the magisterium must authoritatively discern "interpretations of Christian morality which are not consistent with 'sound teaching' (2 Tm 4:3)" (§29.4, cf. §27.4). This pastoral discernment of the pope and bishops is necessary as a way of assuring "the right of the faithful to receive Catholic doctrine in its purity and integrity" (§113.2).

The pope addresses *Veritatis Splendor* specifically to his brother bishops. He intends them to be the first, but not exclusive, recipients of the encyclical. John Paul reminds them of their responsibility to safeguard and find "ever new ways of speaking with love and mercy" about "the path of the moral life" (§3.1,2).

John Paul II's training in ethics and moral theology is clearly evident in *Veritatis Splendor*. The encyclical's exposition is sometimes highly technical, especially in its analyses and responses to opinions contrary to Church teaching. While some commentators have voiced disagreement about the accuracy of the pope's descriptions of the ethical positions with which he disagrees, they respect his desire to be fair-minded. As we shall see, whenever John Paul deals with an opinion he disagrees with, he first takes great pains to point out what is positive in the view. Only after doing this does he then examine its weaknesses. When unmasking theological and philosophical ideas incompatible with revealed truth, he scrupulously avoids imposing "any particular theological system, still less a philosophical one" (§29.4).

Throughout the encyclical the pope repeatedly draws inspiration from the Bible. Chapter one, structured around the encounter of Jesus with the rich young man (Mt 19:16-21), establishes a biblical foundation for fundamental moral principles. In this chapter the pope wishes to apply the theological method proposed by the Second Vatican Council: "Sacred Scripture remains the living and fruitful source of the Church's moral doctrine" (§28.2, cf. §5.3). Chapter two, on the other hand, uses Scripture chiefly to corroborate positions advanced on the basis of the natural moral law. The beginning of chapter three returns to a more biblical approach; it discusses discipleship in terms of the Paschal Mystery and of martyrdom as the supreme expression of following Christ.

More so than in his other encyclicals, in *Veritatis Splendor* John Paul relies considerably on the teaching of St. Thomas Aquinas, referring to him directly at least 20 times, and on the teaching of St. Augustine, citing him 16 times. The pope also mines extensively the documents of Vatican II, especially *Gaudium et Spes*, which he cites more than 25 times. Except for one reference to St. Alphonsus Liguori and a single direct citation of John Henry Newman, the pope mentions no moral philosopher or theologian after the Middle Ages.

Footnotes

1. *Acta Apostolicae Sedis*, 85 (1993), 1133-1228. 2. Angelus, Oct. 3, 1993, *L'Osservatore Romano*, 40 (1993), 1. 3. Angelus, Oct. 17, 1993, *L'Osservatore Romano*, 42 (1993), 1.

Evangelium Vitae ("The Gospel of Life")

"The Gospel of life is at the heart of Jesus' message" (§1.1). With these words Pope John Paul II begins his eleventh encyclical, *Evangelium Vitae*, published on March 25, 1995.[1] He aptly chose the feast of the Annunciation, which celebrates Mary's welcoming of the Son of God who took flesh in her womb, to issue a document dedicated to the value and inviolability of human life. By taking up the cause of the "great multitude of weak and defenseless human beings" (§5.4), especially unborn children and those at the end of life, the pope continues the defense of human dignity dealt with in his three social encyclicals. *Evangelium Vitae* is an anguished and vigorous response to "scientifically and systematically programmed threats" against life (§17.2), assaults which have repercussions on Church teaching, touching upon "the core of her faith in the redemptive Incarnation of the Son of God" (§3.1).

For Pope John Paul II, the cause of life is the cause of the Gospel entrusted to the Church, which is duty-bound to raise her voice in the defense of life. His encyclical is a "pressing appeal addressed to each and every person, in the name of God: respect, protect, love and serve life, every human life!" (§5.5).

Preparations for the encyclical began in Apr. 1991, when the pope called a special meeting in Rome of the College of Cardinals to discuss current threats to human life. After their deliberations, the cardinals asked him "to reaffirm with the authority of the Successor of Peter the value of human life and its inviolability" (§5.1). As a first response to their request, the pope wrote a personal letter to every bishop, seeking contributions to the planned document. They replied with valuable suggestions, and he incorporated many of their proposals into the encyclical. *Evangelium Vitae*, then, is the fruit of genuine episcopal collegiality. By taking an active part in its preparation, the bishops "bore witness to their unanimous desire to share in the doctrinal and pastoral mission of the Church with regard to the Gospel of life" (§5.2).

Unlike *Veritatis Splendor*, which was directed primarily to bishops, John Paul intends *Evangelium Vitae* to be read also by the lay faithful, indeed by all people of good will. Concern for the sacredness of human life is not just a matter for Catholics. "The value at stake," writes the pope, "is one which every human being can grasp by the light of reason" (§101.2). The essential truths of the Gospel of life "are written in the heart of every man and woman," echoing in every human conscience "from the time of creation itself" (§29.3). He insists that anyone who is sincerely open to truth and goodness can discover "the sacred value of human life from its very beginning until its end, and can affirm the right of every human being to have this primary good respected to the highest degree" (§2.2).

The encyclical's style is typically Wojtylan. It intersperses rigorous analysis with prayers and exhortations. As can be seen from the more than three hundred biblical quotations and references, Scripture accompanies the pope's presentation from start to finish, giving *Evangelium Vitae* an inspirational tone and familiar style. He also relies heavily on the Church Fathers. The eighteen patristic quotations that appear in the encyclical reinforce the truths that God is the origin of life, that human beings share in divine life, and that Jesus gave his life so that others might live. As is customary, John Paul frequently cites the documents of the Second Vatican Council — here, more than 25 times. He also makes use of the Catechism of the Catholic Church, citing it on 10 occasions.

Of particular significance in *Evangelium Vitae* are the pope's three authoritative doctrinal pronouncements: on the direct and voluntary killing of innocent human life (cf. §57.4), on abortion (cf. §62.3), and on euthanasia (cf. §65.3). In each of these formal statements John Paul recalls, through his ordinary magisterium, that a specific proposition is taught infallibly by the ordinary and universal Magisterium of the College of Bishops in communion with the Successor of Peter. He does not, therefore, call upon the charism which belongs to the Petrine ministry to teach infallibly, as this was defined at the First Vatican Council (1870). Rather, the pope "confirms" or "declares" (as in the case of abortion) a doctrine already taught by the bishops as belonging to the Catholic faith. Thus, there is nothing "new" in the Pope's affirmations, but merely the reiteration of teaching about which a consensus exists in the Episcopal College.

Footnotes

1. *Acta Apostolicae Sedis*, 87 (1995), 401–522.

CATHOLIC SOCIAL DOCTRINE

Nature of the Doctrine

Writing in *Christianity and Social Progress*, Pope John XXIII made the following statement about the nature and scope of the Church's social doctrine as stated in the encyclicals in particular and related writings in general:

"What the Catholic Church teaches and declares regarding the social life and relationships of men is beyond question for all time valid.

"The cardinal point of this teaching is that individual men are necessarily the foundation, cause, and end of all social institutions insofar as they are social by nature, and raised to an order of existence that transcends and subdues nature.

"Beginning with this very basic principle whereby the dignity of the human person is affirmed and defended, Holy Church—especially during the last century and with the assistance of learned priests and laymen, specialists in the field—has arrived at clear social teachings whereby the mutual relationships of men are ordered. Taking general norms into account, these principles are in accord with the nature of things and the changed conditions of man's social life, or with the special genius of our day. Moreover, these norms can be approved by all."

Background

While social concerns have always been a part of the Church's teachings, Catholic social doctrine has been the subject of much consideration since the end of the last century and has been formulated in a progressive manner in a number of authoritative documents starting with the encyclical *Rerum Novarum* ("On Capital and Labor") issued by Leo XIII in 1891. Owing to its significance, the encyclical was called by Pope John XXIII the *magna carta* of Catholic social doctrine.

Other outstanding examples are the encyclicals: *Quadragesimo Anno* ("On Reconstruction of the Social Order") by Pius XI in 1931; *Mater et Magistra* ("Christianity and Social Progress") and *Pacem in Terris* ("Peace on Earth"), by John XXIII in 1961 and 1963, respectively; *Populorum Progressio* ("Development of Peoples"), by Paul VI in 1967; *Laborem Exercens* ("On Human Work"), *Sollicitudo Rei Socialis* ("On Social Concerns") and *Centesimus Annus* ("The 100th Year") by John Paul II in 1981, 1987, and 1991, respectively. Among many other accomplishments of ideological importance in the social field, Pius XII made a distinctive contribution with his formulation of a plan for world peace and order in Christmas messages from 1939 to 1941, and in other documents.

Of particular significance to the contemporary application of social doctrine are the document *Gaudium et Spes* (Pastoral Constitution on the Church in the Modern World) issued by the Second Vatican Council and Pope John Paul II's encyclical letters, *Laborem Exercens* ("On Human Work"), *Sollicitudo Rei Socialis* ("On Social Concerns"), and *Centesimus Annus* ("The 100th Year").

These documents represent the most serious attempts in modern times to systematize the social implications of divine revelation as well as the socially relevant writings of the Fathers and Doctors of the Church. Their contents are theological penetrations into social life, with particular reference to human rights, the needs of the poor and those in underdeveloped countries, and humane conditions of life, freedom, justice and peace. In some respects, they read like juridical documents; essentially, however, they are Gospel-oriented and pastoral in intention.

Gaudium et Spes

Gaudium et Spes ("Pastoral Constitution on the

Church in the Modern World") was the last document issued by Vatican Council II (Dec. 7, 1965). The document has as its purpose to search out the signs of God's presence and meaning in and through the events of this time in human history. Accordingly, it deals with the situation of men in present circumstances of profound change, challenge and crisis on all levels of life. It is evenly divided into two main parts: the Church's teaching on humanity in the modern era and urgent problems of the times.

Part One

The first part begins: "The joys and the hopes, the griefs and the anxieties of this age" (No. 1)—a clear indication that the Council Fathers were aware both of the positive nature of the modern world and its many dangers and travails. Further, the council places great emphasis throughout on the human existence, a stress that was quite innovative in its presentation: "According to the almost unanimous opinion of believers and unbelievers alike, all things on earth should be related to man as their center and crown" (No. 12). Having developed an analysis of humanity, the document then offered a thorough summary of traditional Church teaching on human life, complete with discussion of sin, the union of body and soul, and the moral conscience.

There is, as well, a genuinely realistic appraisal of contemporary society, noting the pervasiveness of atheism, adding that its spread can be attributed in part to the fault and carelessness of those within the Church whose actions and failures "must be said to conceal rather than reveal the authentic face of God and religion" (No. 19). Toward the fuller understanding of the place of the Church in the modern world, *Gaudium et Spes* emphasizes the harmony that should exist between the Catholic faith and scientific progress because "earthly matters and the concerns of faith derive from the same God" (No. 36). This does not mean, however, that there ought to be no qualifying elements or restraints to science; the Council Fathers add to this positive statement the provision that such research, "within every branch of learning," must be "carried out in a genuinely scientific manner and in accord with moral norms" (No. 36). Finally, the first part makes an ecumenical gesture, noting that the

Church "holds in high esteem the things which other Christian Churches or ecclesial communities have done..." (No. 40).

Part Two

Part Two offers the practical application of the Church's teaching and message enunciated in Part One. Most pressing is the council's concern for the family, and its treatment of family life and marriage is the most detailed and extensive in the history of the councils of the Church. This leads to study of the deeply troubling presence of contraception. The council reiterates Church instruction in an affirmation of opposition to contraception that would receive even fuller expression in three years in the encyclical *Humanae Vitae*. In the matter of abortion, the document states clearly: "... from the moment of its conception life must be guarded with the greatest care, while abortion and infanticide are unspeakable crimes" (No. 51). In its study of culture, in which the council reminds all humanity that culture and civilization are creations of man, it points out his responsibility over it and his duty to seek that which is above, which entails an "obligation to work with all men in constructing a more human world" (No. 57). Here we have a powerful preface or introduction to the next concerns voiced in *Gaudium et Spes*: the questions of economic life, political systems, and war. In building upon earlier social encyclicals, *Gaudium et Spes* discusses economics as vital to human progress and social development, striking the important balance (developed so masterfully in the later writings of Pope John Paul II) between the rights of an individual to possess goods and the obligation to aid the poor (Nos. 63-72). While declaring the autonomous and independent nature of the Church and politics, the Council Fathers do acknowledge: "There are, indeed, close links between earthly affairs and those aspects of man's condition which transcend this world. The Church herself employs the things of time to the degree that her own proper mission demands" (No. 76). The document goes on to state that "the arms race is an utterly treacherous trap for humanity" (No. 81) and "It is our clear duty, then, to strain every muscle as we work for the time when all war can be completely outlawed by international consent" (No. 82).

SOCIAL DOCTRINE UNDER POPE JOHN PAUL II

Background

Throughout his pontificate, Pope John Paul II has traveled the globe speaking out on all matters of the Church's social teachings and has written a number of important encyclicals that are reflective not only of the Church's traditions of social doctrine but that seek to utilize the teachings of the faith to offer specific points of reflection and solutions to the many pressing problems of the late 20th century. Rooted in Christian anthropology and Tradition, Scripture, and

Magisterium, John Paul's writings have encompassed economic ethics, the rights and dignity of the worker, the primacy of the human person, the place of the family in society and the Church, and the integrative teachings of the Church in the areas of moral and pastoral theology.

The three main expressions of his social teachings have been the encyclicals: *Laborem Exercens* (1981); *Sollicitudo Rei Socialis* (1987); and *Centesimus Annus* (1991).

SOCIAL ENCYCLICALS OF POPE JOHN PAUL II

The following material is adapted from The Encyclicals of John Paul II, *with the kind permission of the Most Rev. J. Michael Miller, C.S.B.*

Laborem Exercens

Fascinated as he is by commemorative events, Pope John Paul II marked the 90th anniversary of Leo XIII's *Rerum Novarum* (1891) by publishing his first social encyclical, *Laborem Exercens*, on Sept. 14, 1981.[1] Before him, Pius XI in *Quadragesimo Anno* (1931), John XXIII in *Mater et Magistra* (1961), and Paul VI in *Octogesima Adveniens* (1971) had observed the anniversary of Leo's ground-breaking encyclical with documents of their own.

Laborem Exercens is a very personal document. The encyclical has solid roots in the pope's own experience as a worker. It reflects his familiarity with various worlds of work: in mines and factories, in artistic and literary production, in scholarship and pastoral ministry. More particularly, *Laborem Exercens* has its origins in the long debate carried on by the Archbishop of Krakow with Marxist intellectuals. The topics chosen, which include the struggle between capital and labor, ownership of the means of production, and solidarity, as well as the terminology of the encyclical, bear ample witness to this background of controversy. Here, however, he is less concerned with economic systems than with the human person as a "worker." Furthermore, John Paul intended his letter to encourage the Solidarity union movement, which in the early 1980s was the primary motor for effecting social and political change in a Poland under a totalitarian regime.

The style of encyclical is distinctively Wojtylan. It reveals the pope's preference for combining a phenomenological description of experience with philosophical-theological meditation. While he cites the Second Vatican Council's *Gaudium et Spes*, John Paul never directly quotes from any previous social encyclical, not even from *Rerum Novarum*. The encyclical's footnotes are almost entirely biblical, indicating that its primary inspiration is Sacred Scripture. As in his two previous encyclicals, *Redemptor Hominis* (1979) and *Dives in Misericordia* (1980), the pope relies heavily upon the plastic and descriptive language of the Bible, especially from the opening chapters of Genesis, to develop his theme. The encyclical unfolds the meaning of the human vocation to work in light of the biblical text on "subduing the earth" (cf. Gn 1:28). This call to exercise dominion is to be carried out by those created "in the image of God" (Gn 1:27) through their work, which the pope qualifies as "one of the characteristics that distinguish man from the rest of creatures" (preface).

Unlike earlier social encyclicals which dealt with a wide range of different questions, *Laborem Exercens* is sharply focused. John Paul chooses a very specific theme—the dignity and role of human work—and explores its many ramifications: "Through work man must earn his daily bread and contribute to the continual advance of science and technology and, above all, to elevating unceasingly the cultural and moral level of the society within which he lives in community with those who belong to the same family" (preface). At the present moment, he believes, the world is faced with important choices. It is "on the eve of new developments in technological, economic, and political conditions which, according to many experts, will influence the world of work and production no less than the industrial revolution of the last century" (§1.3).

A crisis in the meaning of human work is a crucial factor contributing to society's current plight. "Work, as human issue, is at the very center of the 'social question' " (§2.1). Moreover, the pope adds, "human work is a key, probably the essential key, to the whole social question" (§3.2). It is a problem with ramifications which extend beyond the so-called "working class"; the dimensions of the crisis are universal. Therefore he does not confine his encyclical to a reflection on the work only of industrial or agricultural workers. Instead, he extends it to encompass the work done by every sector of society: management, white-collar workers, scientists, intellectuals, artists, women in the home. "Each and every individual, to the proper extent and in an incalculable number of ways, takes part in the giant process whereby man 'subdues the earth' through his work" (§4.4). To use a favorite expression of the pope's, the world's "work-bench" includes all those who labor for their daily bread—all men and women.

As in his two previous encyclicals, John Paul takes up the "way" of the human person, this time with regard to his fundamental activity of work. *Laborem Exercens* is yet another chapter in the pope's book on Christian anthropology. Moreover, since work is a great gift and good for humanity, his tone throughout the encyclical is constructive and exhortatory.

Footnote

1. *Acta Apostolicae Sedis*, 73 (1981), 577-647.

Sollicitudo Rei Socialis

Although signed on Dec. 30, 1987, Pope John Paul II's encyclical "on social concern" was not officially published until Feb. 19, 1988.[1] Like *Laborem Exercens* (1981), this second social encyclical commemorates a previous papal document. *Sollicitudo Rei Socialis* marks the twentieth anniversary of Paul VI's *Populorum Progressio* (1967). But more than merely recalling the relevance and doctrine of Paul Paul's encyclical, it highlights new themes and responds to the problems of development in the Third World which had emerged in the intervening 20 years.

John Paul writes as a teacher, explaining why the proclamation of the Church's social doctrine belongs to her evangelizing mission. He also writes as an informed witness to the increasing injustice and poverty in the world. Lastly, he writes as a defender of human dignity and inalienable rights, and of every person's transcendent vocation to communion with the Triune God.

In some ways *Sollicitudo Rei Socialis* echoes *Laborem Exercens* (1981). John Paul's use of Sacred Scripture, for example, is similar in that he frequently quotes from the opening chapters of Genesis. The differences between the two social encyclicals, however, are noteworthy. Whereas in *Laborem Exercens* (1981) the pope never directly cites *Rerum Novarum* (1891), the encyclical of Leo XIII which it commemorates, throughout *Sollicitudo Rei Socialis* John Paul quotes or refers to *Populorum Progressio* more than forty times. It is his constant point of reference. Second, to support his presentation, the pope marshals statements taken from earlier writings and discourses of his own pontificate, as well as the social teaching of the Second Vatican Council expressed in *Gaudium et Spes*. Third, more than in any other encyclical, John Paul makes use of documents published by the Roman Curia. Especially notable are his six references to the Instruction on Christian Freedom and Liberation (1986) issued by the Congregation for the Doctrine of the Faith. He also cites two publications of the Pontifical Commission "Iustitia et Pax": *At the Service of the Human Community: An Ethical Approach to the International Debt Question* (1986) and *The Church and the Housing Problem* (1987).

While *Sollicitudo Rei Socialis* perceptively analyzes the economic, political, social, and cultural dimensions of world development, its perspective is primarily ethical and theological. John Paul rereads *Populorum Progressio* through a moral-spiritual lens. His main concern is to form the consciences of individual men and women, to help them in their task of promoting authentic development "in the light of faith and of the Church's Tradition" (§41.7).

Footnote
1. *Acta Apostolicae Sedis, 80 (1988), 513-586.*

Centesimus Annus

Pope John Paul II issued his ninth encyclical, *Centesimus Annus*, on May 1, 1991.[1] Not surprisingly, the pope chose to mark the centenary of Leo XIII's *Rerum Novarum* (1891) with a document of his own. In the four years since the signing of *Sollicitudo Rei Socialis* (1987) the Berlin Wall had collapsed, and in the light of this event John Paul offers his "rereading" of *Rerum Novarum*. His purpose is twofold. He wishes to recall Leo's contribution to the development of the Church's social teaching and to honor the popes who drew upon the encyclical's "vital energies" in their social teaching.

Centesimus Annus has some interesting peculiarities. First, among all John Paul's encyclicals, it relies the least on citing Sacred Scripture. Its few biblical references are primarily exhortatory or illustrative. For his

sources the pope depends mostly on *Rerum Novarum* and on the social encyclicals of his predecessors, as well as on earlier documents and discourses of his own Magisterium. Second, much of the encyclical's content is conditioned by current geopolitical affairs. Indeed, the encyclical reads as if the pope had *Rerum Novarum* in one hand and a diary of the 1989 events sweeping Eastern Europe in the other.

Despite the opinions of some commentators, John Paul's primary interest is not to pass judgment on either failed socialism or contemporary capitalism. Above all, in keeping with his desire to articulate a Christian anthropology, he recalls the need for Catholic social doctrine to have a "correct view of the human person and of his unique value" (§11.3). Without such a view, he believes, it is impossible to solve today's social, economic, and political problems. The Church's distinctive contribution to meeting these challenges is her vision of the transcendent dignity of the human person created in God's image and redeemed by Christ's blood.

The pope's rereading of Leo XIII encompasses three time frames: "looking back" at *Rerum Novarum* itself, "looking around" at the contemporary situation, and "looking to the future" (§3.1). In looking back, John Paul confirms the enduring principles of Leo's encyclical, principles that belong to the Church's doctrinal inheritance. His "pastoral solicitude" also impels the pope to analyze recent political events from the perspective of the Gospel "in order to discern the new requirements of evangelization" (§3.5).

Even more clearly than in his two previous social encyclicals, *Laborem Exercens* (1981) and *Sollicitudo Rei Socialis* (1987), John Paul clearly distinguishes the authentic doctrine contained in the Church's social teaching from the analysis of contingent historical events. This analysis, he states, "is not meant to pass definitive judgments, since this does not fall per se within the Magisterium's specific domain" (§3.5). Whatever comes within the doctrinal sphere, however, "pertains to the Church's evangelizing mission and is an essential part of the Christian message" (§5.5).

Footnote
1. *Acta Apostolicae Sedis, 83 (1991), 793-867.*

SOCIO-ECONOMIC STATEMENTS BY U.S. BISHOPS

Over a period of nearly 80 years, the bishops of the United States have issued a great number of socio-economic statements reflecting papal documents in a U.S. context.

One such statement, entitled "Economic Justice for All: Social Teaching and the U.S. Economy" was issued in Nov. 1986. Its contents are related in various ways with the subsequently issued encyclical letter, *Centesimus Annus*. Principles drawn from the bishops' document are given in the following excerpt entitled "A Catholic Framework for Economic Life." Another significant statement, entitled "The Harvest of Justice Is Sown in Peace" (1993) follows.

A Catholic Framework for Economic Life

As followers of Jesus Christ and participants in a powerful economy, Catholics in the United States, are called to work for greater economic justice in the face

of persistent poverty, growing income gaps and increasing discussion of economic issues in the United States and around the world. We urge Catholics to use the following ethical framework for economic life as principles for reflection, criteria for judgment and directions for action. These principles are drawn directly from Catholic teaching on economic life.

1. The economy exists for the person, not the person for the economy.

2. All economic life should be shaped by moral principles. Economic choices and institutions must be judged by how they protect or undermine the life and dignity of the human person, support the family and serve the common good.

3. A fundamental moral measure of an economy is how the poor and vulnerable are faring.

4. All people have a right to life and to secure the basic necessities of life (e.g., food, clothing, shelter,

education, health care, safe environment, economic security).

5. All people have the right to economic initiative, to productive work, to just wages and benefits, to decent working conditions as well as to organize and join unions or other associations.

6. All people, to the extent they are able, have a corresponding duty to work, a responsibility to provide for the needs of their families and an obligation to contribute to the broader society.

7. In economic life, free markets have both clear advantages and limits; government has essential responsibilities and limitations; voluntary groups have irreplaceable roles, but cannot substitute for the proper working of the market and the just policies of the state.

8. Society has a moral obligation, including governmental action where necessary, to assure opportunity, meet basic human needs and pursue justice in economic life.

9. Workers, owners, managers, stockholders and consumers are moral agents in economic life. By our choices, initiative, creativity and investment, we enhance or diminish economic opportunity, community life and social justice.

10. The global economy has moral dimensions and human consequences. Decisions on investment, trade, aid and development should protect human life and promote human rights, especially for those most in need wherever they might live on this globe.

The Harvest of Justice Is Sown in Peace

The National Conference of Catholic Bishops, at a meeting Nov. 17, 1993, issued a statement entitled "The Harvest of Justice Is Sown in Peace," marking the 10th anniversary of their earlier pastoral letter, "The Challenge of Peace: God's Promise and Our Response."

The Challenge of Peace

"The challenge of peace today is different, but no less urgent" than in 1983, and the threat of global nuclear war "may seem more remote than at any time in the nuclear age." Questions of peace and war, however, cannot be addressed "without acknowledging that the nuclear question remains of vital political and moral significance."

The statement outlines an agenda for action to guide future advocacy efforts of the bishops' national conference. It also urges that the cause of peace be reflected constantly in liturgical prayers of petition, preaching and Catholic education at all levels.

Confronting the temptation to isolationism in U.S. foreign policy is among "the major challenges peacemakers face in this new era."

Factors in a vision for peace include a commitment to the universal common good and recognition of the imperative of human solidarity.

Nonviolent revolutions in some countries "challenge us to find ways to take into full account the power of organized, active nonviolence."

With respect to just war criteria, the statement says that "important work needs to be done in refining, clarifying and applying the just war tradition to the choices facing our decision-makers in this still violent and dangerous world."

Subjects of concern include humanitarian interven-

tion, deterrence, conscientious objection and the development of peoples.

Presumption against Force

"Our conference's approach, as outlined in 'The Challenge of Peace,' can be summarized in this way:

"1) In situations of conflict our constant commitment ought to be, as far as possible, to strive for justice through nonviolent means.

"2) But when sustained attempts at nonviolent action fail to protect the innocent against fundamental injustice, then legitimate political authorities are permitted as a last resort to employ limited force to rescue the innocent and establish justice."

Lethal Force

"Whether lethal force may be used is governed by the following criteria:

• "Just cause: Force may be used only to correct a grave, public evil, i.e., aggression or massive violation of the basic rights of whole populations.

• "Comparative justice: While there may be rights and wrongs on all sides of a conflict, to override the presumption against the use of force, the injustice suffered by one party must significantly outweigh that suffered by the other.

• "Legitimate authority: Only duly constituted public authorities may use deadly force or wage war.

• "Right intention: Force may be used only in a truly just cause and solely for that purpose.

• "Probability of Success: Arms may not be used in a futile cause or in a case where disproportionate measures are required to achieve success.

• "Proportionality: The overall destruction expected from the use of force must be outweighed by the good to be achieved.

• "Last Resort: Force may be used only after all peaceful alternatives have been seriously tried and exhausted.

"These criteria [of just war], taken as a whole, must be satisfied in order to override the strong presumption against the use of force."

Just War

"The just-war tradition seeks also to curb the violence of war through restraint on armed combat between the contending parties by imposing the following moral standards for the conduct of armed conflict:

• "Noncombatant Immunity: Civilians may not be the object of direct attack, and military personnel must take due care to avoid and minimize indirect harm to civilians.

• "Proportionality: In the conduct of hostilities, efforts must be made to attain military objectives with no more force than is militarily necessary and to avoid disproportionate collateral damage to civilian life and property.

• "Right Intention: Even in the midst of conflict, the aim of political and military leaders must be peace with justice so that acts of vengeance and indiscriminate violence, whether by individuals, military units or governments, are forbidden."

Structures for Justice and Peace

Quoting an address given by Pope John Paul in Aug. 1993 in Denver, the statement said:

"'The international community ought to establish

more effective structures for maintaining and promoting justice and peace. This implies that a concept of strategic interest should evolve which is based on the full development of peoples—out of poverty and toward a more dignified existence, out of injustice and exploitation toward fuller respect for the human person and the defense of universal rights.'

"As we consider a new vision of the international community, five areas deserve special attention: (1) strengthening global institutions; (2) securing human rights; (3) promoting human development; (4) restraining nationalism and eliminating religious violence; and (5) building cooperative security."

Humanitarian Intervention

"Pope John Paul, citing the 'conscience of humanity and international humanitarian law,' has been outspoken in urging that 'humanitarian intervention be obligatory where the survival of populations and entire ethnic groups is seriously compromised. This is a duty for nations and the international community.' He elaborated on this right and duty of humanitarian intervention in his 1993 annual address to the diplomatic corps (accredited to the Holy See):

"'Once the possibilities afforded by diplomatic negotiations and the procedures provided for by international agreements and organizations have been put into effect, and that [sic], nevertheless, populations are succumbing to the attacks of an unjust aggressor, states no longer have a 'right to indifference.' It seems clear that their duty is to disarm this aggressor if all other means have proved ineffective. The principles of the sovereignty of states and of noninterference in their internal affairs—which retain all their value—cannot constitute a screen behind which torture and murder may be carried out.'"

THE BLESSED VIRGIN MARY

ROLE OF MARY IN THE MYSTERY OF CHRIST AND THE CHURCH

The following excerpts are from Chapter VIII of the Second Vatican Council's "Constitution on the Church," Lumen Gentium.

I. Preface

Wishing in his supreme goodness and wisdom to effect the redemption of the world, "when the fullness of time came, God sent his Son, born of a woman, that we might receive the adoption of sons" (Gal 4:4-5). "He for us men, and for our salvation, came down from heaven, and was incarnate by the Holy Spirit from the Virgin Mary." This divine mystery of salvation is revealed to us and continued in the Church, which the Lord established as his own body. In this Church, adhering to Christ the head and having communion with all his saints, the faithful must also venerate the memory "above all of the glorious and perpetual Virgin Mary, Mother of our God and Lord Jesus Christ." (52)

At the message of the angel, the Virgin Mary received the Word of God in her heart and in her body, and gave Life to the world. Hence, she is acknowledged and honored as being truly the Mother of God and Mother of the Redeemer. Redeemed in an especially sublime manner by reason of the merits of her Son, and united to him by a close and indissoluble tie, she is endowed with the supreme office and dignity of being the Mother of the Son of God. As a result, she is also the favorite daughter of the Father and the temple of the Holy Spirit. Because of this gift of sublime grace, she far surpasses all other creatures, both in heaven and on earth.

At the same time, however, because she belongs to the offspring of Adam, she is one with all human beings in their need for salvation. Indeed, she is "clearly the Mother of the members of Christ since she cooperated out of love so that there might be born in the Church the faithful, who are members of Christ their head. Therefore, she is also hailed as a pre-eminent and altogether singular member of the Church, and as the Church's model and excellent exemplar in faith and charity. Taught by the Holy Spirit, the Catholic Church honors her with filial affection and piety as a most beloved Mother. (53)

This sacred synod intends to describe with diligence the role of the Blessed Virgin in the mystery of the Incarnate Word and the Mystical Body. It also wishes to describe the duties of redeemed mankind toward the Mother of God, who is the Mother of Christ and Mother of men, particularly of the faithful.

The synod does not, however, have it in mind to give a complete doctrine on Mary, nor does it wish to decide those questions which have not yet been fully illuminated by the work of theologians. (54)

II. The Role of the Blessed Virgin in the Economy of Salvation

The Father of mercies willed that the consent of the predestined Mother should precede the Incarnation so that, just as a woman contributed to death, so also a woman should contribute to life. This contrast was verified in outstanding fashion by the Mother of Jesus. She gave to the world that very Life which renews all things, and she was enriched by God with gifts befitting such a role.

It is no wonder, then, that the usage prevailed among the holy Fathers whereby they called the Mother of God entirely holy and free from all stain of sin, fashioned by the Holy Spirit into a kind of new substance and new creature. Adorned from the first instant of her conception with the splendors of an entirely unique holiness, the Virgin of Nazareth is, on God's command, greeted by an angel messenger as "full of grace" (cf. Lk 1:28). To the heavenly messenger she replies: "Behold the handmaid of the Lord; be it done to me according to thy word" (Lk 1:38).

By thus consenting to the divine utterance, Mary, a daughter of Adam, became the Mother of Jesus. Embracing God's saving will with a full heart and impeded by no sin, she devoted herself totally as a handmaid of the Lord to the person and work of her Son. In subordination to him and along with him, by the grace of almighty God she served the mystery of redemption.

Rightly, therefore, the holy Fathers see her as used by God not merely in a passive way but as cooperating in the work of human salvation through free faith and obedience. (56)

This union of the Mother with the Son in the work of salvation was manifested from the time of Christ's virginal conception up to his death. It is shown first of all when Mary, arising in haste to go to visit Elizabeth, was greeted by her as blessed because of her belief in the promise of salvation, while the precursor leaped for joy in the womb of his mother (cf. Lk 1:41-45). This association was shown also at the birth of our Lord, who did not diminish his Mother's virginal integrity but sanctified it, when the Mother of God joyfully showed her first-born Son to the shepherds and the Magi.

When she presented him to the Lord in the Temple, making the offering of the poor, she heard Simeon foretelling at the same time that her Son would be a sign of contradiction and that a sword would pierce the Mother's soul, that out of many hearts thoughts might be revealed (cf. Lk 2:34-35). When the Child Jesus was lost and they had sought him sorrowing, his parents found him in the temple, taken up with things which were his Father's business. They did not understand the reply of the Son. But his Mother, to be sure, kept all these things to be pondered over in her heart (cf. Lk 2:41-51). (57)

In the public life of Jesus, Mary made significant appearances. This was so even at the very beginning, when she was moved with pity at the marriage feast of Cana, and her intercession brought about the beginning of the miracles by Jesus the Messiah (Cf. Jn 2:1-11). In the course of her Son's preaching, she received his praise when, in extolling a kingdom beyond the calculations and bonds of flesh and blood, he declared blessed (cf. Mk 3:35 par.; Lk 11:27-28) those who heard and kept the word of the Lord as she was faithfully doing (cf. Lk 2:19, 51).

Thus, the Blessed Virgin advanced in her pilgrimage of faith and loyally persevered in her union with her Son unto the cross. There she stood, in keeping with the divine plan (cf. Jn 19:25), suffering grievously with her only-begotten Son. There she united herself with a maternal heart to his sacrifice, and lovingly consented to the immolation of this Victim whom she herself had brought forth. Finally, the same Christ Jesus dying on the cross gave her as a mother to his disciple. This he did when he said: "Woman, behold your son" (Jn 19:26-27). (58)

But since it pleased God not to manifest solemnly the mystery of the salvation of the human race until he poured forth the Spirit promised by Christ, we see the apostles before the day of Pentecost "continuing with one mind in prayer with the women and Mary, the Mother of Jesus, and with his brethren" (Acts 1:14). We see Mary prayerfully imploring the gift of the Spirit, who had already overshadowed her in the Annunciation.

Finally, preserved free from all guilt of original sin, the Immaculate Virgin was taken up body and soul into heavenly glory upon the completion of her earthly sojourn. She was exalted by the Lord as Queen of all, in order that she might be the more thoroughly conformed to her Son, the Lord of lords (cf. Rv 19:16) and the conqueror of sin and death. (59)

III. The Blessed Virgin and the Church

We have but one Mediator, as we know from the words of the Apostle: "For there is one God, and one Mediator between God and men, himself man, Christ Jesus, who gave himself as a ransom for all" (1 Tm 2:5-6). The maternal duty of Mary toward men in no way obscures or diminishes this unique mediation of Christ, but rather shows its power. For all the saving influences of the Blessed Virgin on men originate, not from some inner necessity, but from the divine pleasure. They flow forth from the superabundance of the merits of Christ, rest on his mediation, depend entirely on it, and draw all their power from it. In no way do they impede the immediate union of the faithful with Christ. Rather, they foster this union. (60)

In an utterly singular way, she (Mary) cooperated by her obedience, faith, hope and burning charity in the Savior's work of restoring supernatural life to souls. For this reason she is a mother to us in the order of grace. (61)

This maternity of Mary in the order of grace began with the consent which she gave in faith at the Annunciation and which she sustained without wavering beneath the cross. This maternity will last without interruption until the eternal fulfillment of all the elect. For, taken up to heaven, she did not lay aside this saving role, but by her manifold acts of intercession continues to win for us gifts of eternal salvation.

By her maternal charity, Mary cares for the brethren of her Son who still journey on earth surrounded by dangers and difficulties until they are led to their happy fatherland. Therefore, the Blessed Virgin is invoked by the Church under the titles of Advocate, *Auxiliatrix, Adjutrix* and *Mediatrix*. These, however, are to be so understood that they neither take away nor add anything to the dignity and efficacy of Christ the one Mediator.

For no creature could ever be classed with the Incarnate Word and Redeemer. But, just as the priesthood of Christ is shared in various ways both by sacred ministers and by the faithful; and as the one goodness of God is in reality communicated diversely to his creatures: so also the unique mediation of the Redeemer does not exclude but rather gives rise among creatures to a manifold cooperation which is but a sharing in this unique source.

The Church does not hesitate to profess this subordinate role of Mary. She experiences it continuously and commends it to the hearts of the faithful so that, encouraged by this maternal help, they may more closely adhere to the Mediator and Redeemer. (62)

Through the gift and role of divine maternity, Mary is united with her Son, the Redeemer, and with his singular graces and offices. By these, the Blessed Virgin is also intimately united with the Church. As St. Ambrose taught, the Mother of God is a model of the Church in the matter of faith, hope and charity, and perfect union with Christ. For in the mystery of the Church, herself rightly called Mother and Virgin, the Blessed Virgin stands out in eminent and singular fashion as exemplar of both virginity and motherhood. (63)

In the most holy Virgin, the Church has already reached that perfection whereby she exists without spot or wrinkle (cf. Eph 5:27). Yet, the followers of Christ still strive to increase in holiness by conquering sin. And so they raise their eyes to Mary who shines forth to the whole community of the elect as a model of the virtues. Devotedly meditating on her and contemplating her in the light of the Word made man, the Church with reverence enters more intimately into the supreme mystery of the Incarnation and becomes ever increasingly like her Spouse. (64)

The Church in her apostolic work looks to her who brought forth Christ, conceived by the Holy Spirit and born of the Virgin, so that through the Church Christ may be born and grow in the hearts of the faithful also. The Virgin Mary in her own life lived as an example of that maternal love by which all should be fittingly animated who cooperate in the apostolic mission of the Church on behalf of the rebirth of men. (65)

IV. Devotion to the Blessed Virgin in the Church

Mary was involved in the mystery of Christ. As the most holy Mother of God she was, after her Son, exalted by divine grace above all angels and men. Hence, the Church appropriately honors her with special reverence. Indeed, from most ancient times the Blessed Virgin has been venerated under the title of "Godbearer." In all perils and needs, the faithful; have fled prayerfully to her protection. Especially after the Council of Ephesus the cult of the people of God toward Mary wonderfully increased in veneration and love, in invocation and imitation, according to her own prophetic words: "All generations shall call me blessed; because he who is mighty has done great things for me" (Lk 1:48).

As it has always existed in the Church, this cult (of Mary) is altogether special, Still, it differs essentially from the cult of adoration which is offered to the Incarnate Word, as well as to the Father and the Holy Spirit. Yet, devotion to Mary is most favorable to this supreme cult. The Church has endorsed many forms of piety toward the Mother of God, provided that they were within the limits of sound and orthodox doctrine. These forms have varied according to the circumstances of time and place, and have reflected the diversity of native characteristics and temperament among the faithful. While honoring Christ's Mother, these devotions cause her Son to be rightly known, loved and glorified, and all his commands observed. Through him all things have their beginning (cf. Col 1: 15-16) and in him "it has pleased (the eternal Father) that all his fullness should dwell" (Col 1:19). (66)

This most Holy Synod deliberately teaches this Catholic doctrine. At the same time, it admonishes all the sons of the Church that the cult, especially the liturgical cult, of the Blessed Virgin, be generously fostered. It charges that practices and exercises of devotion toward her be treasured as recommended by the teaching authority of the Church in the course of centuries.

This synod earnestly exhorts theologians and preachers of the divine word that, in treating of the unique dignity of the Mother of God, they carefully and equally avoid the falsity of exaggeration on the one hand and the excess of narrow-mindedness on the other.

Let the faithful remember, moreover, that true devotion consists neither in fruitless and passing emotion, nor in a certain vain credulity. Rather, it proceeds from the true faith, by which we are led to know the excellence of the Mother of God, and are moved to a filial love toward our Mother and to the imitation of her virtues. (67)

REDEMPTORIS MATER

Redemptoris Mater (Mother of the Redeemer), Pope John Paul II's sixth encyclical letter, is a "reflection on the role of Mary in the mystery of Christ and on her active and exemplary presence in the life of the Church." The letter was published Mar. 25, 1987.

Central to consideration of Mary is the fact that she is the Mother of God (*Theotokos*), since by the power of the Holy Spirit she conceived in her virginal womb and brought into the world Jesus Christ, the Son of God, who is of one being with the Father and the Holy Spirit.

Mary was preserved from original sin in view of her calling to be the Mother of Jesus. She was gifted in grace beyond measure. She fulfilled her role in a unique pilgrimage of faith. She is the Mother of the Church and the spiritual mother of all people.

The following excerpts are from the English text provided by the Vatican and circulated by the CNS Documentary Service, *Origins*, Apr. 9, 1987 (Vol. 16, No. 43). Subheads have been added. Quotations are from pertinent documents of the Second Vatican Council.

Mary's Presence in the Church

Mary, through the same faith which made her blessed, especially from the moment of the Annunciation, is present in the Church's mission, present in the Church's work of introducing into the world the kingdom of her Son.

This presence of Mary finds as many different expressions in our day just as it did throughout the Church's history. It also has a wide field of action: through the faith and piety of individual believers; through the traditions of Christian families or "domestic churches," of parish and missionary communities, religious institutes and dioceses; through the radiance and attraction of the great shrines where not only individuals or local groups, but sometimes whole nations and societies, even whole continents, seek to meet the Mother of the Lord, the one who is blessed because she believed, is the first among believers, and therefore became the Mother of Emmanuel.

This is the message of the land of Palestine, the spiritual homeland of all Christians, because it was the homeland of the Savior of the world and of his Mother.

This is the message of the many churches in Rome and throughout the world which have been raised up in the course of the centuries by the faith of Christians. This is the message of centers like Guadalupe, Lourdes, Fátima and others situated in the various countries. Among them, how could I fail to mention the one in my own native land, Jasna Gora? One could perhaps speak of a specific "geography" of faith and Marian devotion which includes all of these special places of pilgrimage where the people of God seek to meet the Mother of God in order to find, within the radius of the maternal presence of her "who believed," a strengthening of their own faith.

Mary and Ecumenism

"In all of Christ's disciples the Spirit arouses the desire to be peacefully united, in the manner determined by Christ, as one flock under one shepherd." The journey of the Church, especially in our own time, is marked by the sign of ecumenism: Christians are seeking ways to restore that unity which Christ implored from the Father for his disciples on the day before his passion.

Christians must deepen in themselves and each of their communities that "obedience of faith" of which Mary is the first and brightest example.

Christians know that their unity will be truly rediscovered only if it is based on the unity of their faith. They must resolve considerable discrepancies of doctrine concerning the mystery and ministry of the Church, and sometimes also concerning the role of Mary in the work of salvation.

Mary, who is still the model of this pilgrimage, is to lead them to the unity which is willed by their one Lord, and which is so much desired by those who are attentively listening to what "the Spirit is saying to the churches" today.

A Hopeful Sign

Meanwhile, it is a hopeful sign that these churches and ecclesial communities are finding agreement with the Catholic Church on fundamental points of Christian belief, including matters relating to the Virgin Mary. For they recognize her as the Mother of the Lord and hold that this forms part of our faith in Christ, true God and true man. They look to her who at the foot of the cross accepted as her son the Beloved Disciple (John), the one who in his turn accepted her as his Mother.

On the other hand, I wish to emphasize how profoundly the Catholic Church, the Orthodox Church and the ancient churches of the East feel united by love and praise of the *Theotokos*. Not only "basic dogmas of the Christian faith concerning the Trinity and God's Word made flesh of the Virgin Mary were defined in ecumenical councils held in the East," but also in their liturgical worship "the Eastern Christians pay high tribute, in very beautiful hymns, to Mary ever-Virgin. God's most holy Mother."

The churches which profess the doctrine of Ephesus proclaim the Virgin as "true Mother of God" since "our Lord Jesus Christ, born of the Father before time began according to his divinity, in the last days he himself, for our sake and for our salvation, was begotten of Mary the Virgin Mother of God according to his humanity." The Greek Fathers and the Byzantine tradition, contemplating the Virgin in the light of the Word made flesh, have sought to penetrate the depth of that bond which unites Mary, as the Mother of God, to Christ and the Church. The Virgin is a permanent presence in the whole reality of the salvific mystery.

Marian Mediation

The Church knows and teaches with St. Paul that there is only one mediator: "For there is one God, and there is one mediator between God and men, the man Christ Jesus, who gave himself as a ransom for all" (1 Tm 2:5-6). "The maternal role of Mary toward people in no way obscures or diminishes the unique mediation of Christ, but rather shows its power." It is mediation in Christ.

The Church knows and teaches that "all the saving influences of the Blessed Virgin on mankind originate from the divine pleasure. They flow forth from the superabundance of the merits of Christ, rest on his mediation, depend entirely on it and draw all their power from it. In no way do they impede the immediate union of the faithful with Christ. Rather, they foster this union." This saving influence is sustained by the Holy Spirit, who, just as he overshadowed the Virgin Mary when he began in her the divine motherhood, in a similar way constantly sustains her solicitude for the brothers and sisters of her Son.

Mediation and Motherhood

In effect, Mary's mediation is intimately linked with her motherhood. It possesses a specifically maternal character, which distinguishes it from the mediation of the other creatures who in various and always subordinate ways share in the one mediation of Christ, although her own mediation is also a shared mediation. In fact, while it is true that "no creature could ever be classed with the Incarnate Word and Redeemer," at the same time "the unique mediation of the Redeemer does not exclude but rather gives rise among creatures a manifold cooperation which is but a sharing in this unique source." Thus "the one goodness of God is in reality communicated diversely to his creatures."

Subordinate Mediation

The teaching of Vatican II presents the truth of Mary's mediation as "a sharing in the one unique source that is the mediation of Christ himself." Thus we read: "The Church does not hesitate to profess this subordinate role of Mary. She experiences it continuously and commends it to the hearts of the faithful so that, encouraged by this maternal help, they may more closely adhere to the Mediator and Redeemer."

This role is at the same time special and extraordinary. It flows from her divine motherhood and can be understood and lived in faith only on the basis of the full truth of this motherhood. Since by virtue of divine election Mary is the earthly Mother of the Father's consubstantial Son and his "generous companion" in the work of redemption, "she is a Mother to us in the order of grace." This role constitutes a real dimension of her presence in the saving mystery of Christ and the Church.

Mary is honored in the Church "with special reverence. Indeed, from most ancient times the Blessed Virgin Mary has been venerated under the title of 'God-bearer.' In all perils and needs, the faithful have fled prayerfully to her protection." This cult is altogether special; it bears in itself and expresses the profound link which exists between the Mother of Christ and the Church. As Virgin and Mother, Mary remains for the Church a "permanent model." It can therefore be said that, especially under this aspect, namely, as a model or rather as a "figure," Mary, present in the mystery of Christ, remains constantly present also in the mystery of the Church. For the Church too is "called mother and virgin," and these names have a profound biblical and theological justification.

Mary and Women

This Marian dimension of Christian life takes on special importance in relation to women and their status. In fact, femininity has a unique relationship with the Mother of the Redeemer, a subject which can be studied in greater depth elsewhere.... The figure of Mary of Nazareth sheds light on womanhood as such by the very fact that God, in the sublime event of the incarnation of his Son, entrusted himself to the ministry, the free and active ministry, of a woman.

... Women, by looking to Mary, find in her the secret of living their femininity with dignity and of achieving their own true advancement. In the light of Mary, the Church sees in the face of women the reflection of a beauty that mirrors the loftiest sentiments of which the human heart is capable: the self-offering totality of love; the strength that is capable of bearing the greatest sorrows; limitless fidelity and tireless devotion to work; the ability to combine penetrating intuition with words of support and encouragement.

APPARITIONS OF THE BLESSED VIRGIN MARY

Seven of the best-known apparitions are described.

Banneux, near Liège, Belgium: Mary appeared eight times between Jan. 15 and Mar. 2, 1933, to an 11-year-old peasant girl, Mariette Beco, in a garden behind the family cottage in Banneux. She called herself the Virgin of the Poor, and has since been venerated as Our Lady of the Poor, the Sick, and the Indifferent. A small chapel was blessed Aug. 15, 1933. Approval of devotion to Our Lady of Banneux was given in 1949 by Bishop Louis J. Kerkhofs of Liège, and a statue of that title was solemnly crowned in 1956.

Beauraing, Belgium: Mary appeared 33 times between Nov. 29, 1932, and Jan. 3, 1933, to five children in the garden of a convent school in Beauraing. A chapel was erected on the spot. Reserved approval of devotion to Our Lady of Beauraing was given Feb. 2, 1943 and final approbation July 2, 1949, by Bishop Charue of Namur (d. 1977).

Fátima, Portugal: Mary appeared six times between May 13 and Oct. 13, 1917, to three children (Lucia dos Santos, 10, who became a Carmelite nun, and who died Feb. 13, 2005; Francisco Marto, 9, who died in 1919; and his sister Jacinta, 7, who died in 1920; Jacinta and Francisco were beatified by Pope John Paul II in 2000) in a field called Cova da Iria near Fátima. She recommended frequent recitation of the Rosary; urged works of mortification for the conversion of sinners; called for devotion to herself under the title of her Immaculate Heart; asked that the people of Russia be consecrated to her under this title, and that the faithful make a Communion of reparation on the first Saturday of each month. The apparitions were declared worthy of belief in Oct. 1930, and devotion to Our Lady of Fátima was authorized under the title of Our Lady of the Rosary. In Oct. 1942, Pius XII consecrated the world to Mary under the title of her Immaculate Heart. Ten years later, in the first apostolic letter addressed directly to the peoples of Russia, he consecrated them in a special manner to Mary. For more on the Third Secret of Fátima, see the following page.

Guadalupe, Mexico: Mary appeared four times in 1531 to an Indian, Juan Diego (canonized in 2002), on Tepeyac hill outside of Mexico City, and instructed him to tell Bishop Zumarraga of her wish that a church be built there. The bishop complied with the request about two years later, after being convinced of the genuineness of the apparition by the evidence of a miraculously painted life-size figure of the Virgin on the mantle of the Indian. The mantle bearing the picture has been preserved and is enshrined in the Basilica of Our Lady of Guadalupe. The shrine church, originally dedicated in 1709 and subsequently enlarged, has the title of basilica. Benedict XIV, in a 1754 decree, authorized a Mass and Office under the title of Our Lady of Guadalupe for celebration on Dec. 12, and named Mary the patroness of New Spain. Our Lady of Guadalupe was designated patroness of Latin America by St. Pius X in 1910 and of the Americas by Pius XII in 1945.

La Salette, France: Mary appeared as a sorrowing and weeping figure Sept. 19, 1846, to two peasant children, Melanie Matthieu, 15, and Maximin Giraud, 11, at La Salette. The message she confided to them, regarding the necessity of penance, was communicated to Pius IX in 1851 and has since been known as the "secret" of La Salette. Bishop de Bruillard of Grenoble declared in 1851 that the apparition was credible, and devotion to Mary under the title of Our Lady of La Salette was authorized. A Mass and Office with this title were authorized in 1942. The shrine church was given the title of minor basilica in 1879.

Lourdes, France: Mary, identifying herself as the Immaculate Conception, appeared 18 times between Feb. 11 and July 16, 1858, to 14-year-old Bernadette Soubirous (canonized in 1933) at the grotto of Massabielle near Lourdes. Her message concerned the necessity of prayer and penance for the conversion of peoples. Mary's request that a chapel built at the grotto and spring was fulfilled in 1862. Devotion under the title of Our Lady of Lourdes was authorized, and a Feb. 11 feast commemorating the apparitions was instituted by Leo XIII. St. Pius X extended this feast throughout the Church in 1907. The Church of Notre Dame was made a basilica in 1870, and the Church of the Rosary was built later. The underground Church of St. Pius X, with a capacity of 20,000 persons, was consecrated Mar. 25, 1958. Plans were announced in 1994 for renovation and reconstruction of the Lourdes sanctuary.

Notre Dame du Laus, France: Mary appeared to the young girl Benôite Rencurel between 1664 and 1718. After four months of daily apparitions starting in May 1664, the Virgin Mary asked Rencurel to build a church and a sanctuary to receive priests. The apparitions received formal approval on May 4, 2008 after years of study by theologians. The shrine is located in the French Alps, near the southeastern French town of Gap.

Our Lady of the Miraculous Medal, France: Mary appeared three times in 1830 to Catherine Labouré (canonized in 1947) in the chapel of the motherhouse of the Daughters of Charity of St. Vincent de Paul, Rue de Bac, Paris. She commissioned Catherine to have made the medal of the Immaculate Conception, now known as the Miraculous Medal, and to spread devotion to her under this title. In 1832, the medal was struck.

THE THIRD SECRET OF FÁTIMA

Courtesy Vatican Information Service.
On June 26, 2000, the Holy See Press Office issued the document "The Message Of Fátima," which had been prepared by the Congregation for the Doctrine of the Faith and carried the signatures of Cardinal Joseph Ratzinger and Archbishop Tarcisio Bertone, S.D.B., respectively prefect and secretary of the congregation.

The document, which is over 40 pages long, was published in English, French, Italian, Spanish, German, Portuguese and Polish. It was made up of an introduction by Archbishop Bertone; the first and second parts of the "secret" of Fátima in Sr. Lucia's original text dated Aug. 31, 1941, and addressed to the bishop of Leiria-Fátima, and a translation; the photostatic reproduction of the original manuscript of the third part of the "secret" and a translation; John Paul II's letter to Sr. Lucia dated Apr. 19, 2000, and a translation; a summary of Sr. Lucia's conversation with Archbishop Bertone and Bishop Serafim de Sousa Ferreira e Silva of Leiria-Fátima which took place on Apr. 27, 2000, in the Carmel Monastery of St. Teresa of Coimbra, Portugal; the words of Cardinal Secretary of State Angelo Sodano at the end of the beatification of Jacinta and Francisco on May 13, 2000; and a theological commentary by Cardinal Ratzinger.

In his introduction, Archbishop Bertone affirms that "Fátima is undoubtedly the most prophetic of modern apparitions.... In 1917 no one could have imagined all this: the three 'pastorinhos' of Fátima see, listen and remember, and Lucia, the surviving witness, commits it all to paper when ordered to do so by the Bishop of Leiria and with Our Lady's permission."

He continues: "The third part of the 'secret' was written … on Jan. 3, 1944. There is only one manuscript, which is here reproduced photostatically. The sealed envelope was initially in the custody of the Bishop of Leiria. To ensure better protection for the 'secret' the envelope was placed in the secret archives of the Holy Office on Apr. 4, 1957. The Bishop of Leiria informed Sr. Lucia of this."

The secretary of the Congregation for the Doctrine of the Faith indicates that "according to the records of the Archives,

the Commissary of the Holy Office, Fr. Pierre Paul Philippe, O.P., with the agreement of Cardinal Alfredo Ottaviani, brought the envelope containing the third part of the 'secret of Fátima' to Pope John XXIII on Aug. 17, 1959. 'After some hesitation,' His Holiness said: 'We shall wait. I shall pray. I shall let you know what I decide.' In fact Pope John XXIII decided to return the sealed envelope to the Holy Office and not to reveal the third part of the 'secret.' Paul VI read the contents with the Substitute, Archbishop Angelo Dell'Acqua, on Mar. 27, 1965, and returned the envelope to the Archives of the Holy Office, deciding not to publish the text. John Paul II, for his part, asked for the envelope containing the third part of the 'secret' following the assassination attempt on May 13, 1981," and this was given to Archbishop Eduardo Martinez Somalo, Substitute of the Secretariat of State, on July 18 of the same year. On August 11 it was returned to the Archives of the Holy Office.

"As is well known," added Archbishop Bertone, "Pope John Paul II immediately thought of consecrating the world to the Immaculate Heart of Mary and he himself composed a prayer for what he called an 'Act of Entrustment' which was to be celebrated in the Basilica of St. Mary Major on June 7, 1981.

"In order to respond more fully to the requests of 'Our Lady,' the Holy Father desired to make more explicit during the Holy Year of the Redemption the Act of Entrustment of June 7, 1981, which had been repeated in Fátima on May 13, 1982.

"Sr. Lucia," continued the archbishop, "personally confirmed that this solemn and universal act of consecration corresponded to what Our Lady wished. Hence any further discussion or request is without basis."

Sr. Lucia had already hinted at the interpretation of the third part of the "secret" in a letter to the Holy Father dated May 12, 1982. That letter is also published in the document.

Finally, Archbishop Tarcisio Bertone indicates that "the decision of His Holiness Pope John Paul II to make public the third part of the 'secret' of Fátima brings to an end a period of history marked by tragic human lust for power and evil, yet pervaded by the merciful love of God and the watchful care of the Mother of Jesus and of the Church."

TRANSLATION OF THE THIRD SECRET OF FÁTIMA

On June 26, 2000, the Holy See issued the complete translation of the original Portuguese text of the third part of the secret of Fátima, revealed to the three shepherd children at Cova da Iria-Fátima on July 13, 1917, and committed to paper by Sr. Lucia on Jan. 3, 1944:

"I write in obedience to you, my God, who command me to do so through his Excellency the Bishop of Leiria and through your Most Holy Mother and mine.

"After the two parts which I have already explained, at the left of Our Lady and a little above, we saw an Angel with a flaming sword in his left hand; flashing, it gave out flames that looked as though they would set the world on fire; but they died out in contact with the splendor that Our Lady radiated towards him from her right hand: pointing to the earth with his right hand, the Angel cried out in a loud voice: 'Penance, Penance, Penance!' And we saw in an immense light that is God: 'something similar to how people appear in

a mirror when they pass in front of it' a Bishop dressed in White 'we had the impression that it was the Holy Father.' Other Bishops, Priests, men and women Religious going up a steep mountain, at the top of which there was a big Cross of rough-hewn trunks as of a cork-tree with the bark; before reaching there the Holy Father passed through a big city half in ruins and half trembling with halting step, afflicted with pain and sorrow, he prayed for the souls of the corpses he met on his way; having reached the top of the mountain, on his knees at the foot of the big Cross he was killed by a group of soldiers who fired bullets and arrows at him, and in the same way there died one after another the Bishops, Priests, men and women Religious, and various lay people of different ranks and positions. Beneath the two arms of the Cross there were two Angels each with a crystal aspersorium in his hand, in which they gathered up the blood of the Martyrs and with it sprinkled the souls that were making their way to God."

EVENTS AT MEDJUGORJE

The alleged apparitions of the Blessed Virgin Mary to six young people of Medjugorje, Bosnia-Herzogovina, have been the source of interest and controversy since they were first reported in June 1981, initially in the neighboring hillside field, subsequently in the village church of St. James and even in places far removed from Medjugorje.

Reports say the alleged visionaries have seen, heard, and even touched Mary during visions, and that they have variously received several or all of 10 secret messages related to coming world events and urging a quest for peace through penance and personal conversion. An investigative commission appointed by former local Bishop Pavao Zanic of Mostar-Duvno reported in Mar. 1984 that the authenticity of the apparitions had not been verified. He called the apparitions a case of "collective hallucination" exploited by local Franciscan priests at odds with him over control of a parish.

Former Archbishop Frane Franic of Split-Makarska, on the other hand, said in Dec. 1985: "Speaking as a believer and not as a bishop, my personal conviction is that the events at Medjugorje are of supernatural inspiration." He based his conviction on the observations of spiritual benefits related to the reported events, such as the spiritual development of the six young people, the increases in Mass attendance and sacramental practice at the scene of the apparitions, and the incidence of reconciliation among people.

On Jan. 29, 1987, the bishops of Yugoslavia declared: "On the basis of research conducted so far, one cannot affirm that supernatural apparitions are involved" at Medjugorje. Currently, the events at Medjugorje are under on-going investigation by the Holy See to determine their authenticity. Nevertheless, the site of Medjugorje remains a popular destination for Catholic pilgrims from Europe and the United States.

THE CODE OF CANON LAW

Canon Law is the term that denotes the body of laws governing the Catholic Church. The name is derived from the Greek word *kanon* (rule, i.e., rule of practical direction), which, from the fourth century, was used to denote the ordinances and regulations promulgated by the various Church councils that were convened to discuss problems or important topics. The actual term "canon law" (*ius canonicum*) came into use in the 1100s and was intended to differentiate ecclesiastical law from civil law (*ius civile*).

History of Canon Law

In a practical sense, the laws and regulations began to take shape as early as apostolic times and were evident in their nascent form in the Didache, the Didscalia and the Apostolic Tradition. Owing to the persecution of the Church, however, there was little effort to gather laws together, and certainly less time was devoted to systematizing them.

The fourth century brought the Church freedom from persecution and the resulting rapid growth in membership that was a concomitant of the favors bestowed upon the faith by the rulers of the Roman Empire. New laws were naturally needed and desired. Local regulations were soon established through the decrees of the councils, although these most often had only a local authority and adherence. The general (or ecumenical) councils made laws for the whole Church, and the custom developed of carrying on the decrees of previous assemblies by having them read before the start of a new council. Collections of these laws or canons were then undertaken, but these did not bear the weight of being an official code as they were gathered under private authority.

The earliest efforts at collecting Church laws were centered around the private compilation of the decrees of the Eastern councils to which were added those of the Western Church. The councils of the African Church also made lasting contributions, the most significant coming out of the Seventeenth Council of Carthage (419), which accepted the book of canons later adopted into the canon law of both the Eastern and Western Churches. An official Code of Canon Law was recognized in the seventh century under the Isidorian Collection. Other important influences were the writings of monks in England and Ireland. The monks compiled lists of sins and various offenses to which confessors applied the proper fines or penances. The resulting books were called Penitentials, and they offer scholars an invaluable glimpse into the state of Church law in early medieval England and the development of moral theology.

The Carolingian Reforms of the Church under Charlemagne facilitated the enactment of much legislation that was beneficial to the faith, but it also signaled a long period of secular interference in ecclesiastical affairs. Two by-products of this lay intrusion were the creation of the forged but interesting False Decretals (collections of false canons and decrees of the popes used to falsify the Church's position) and the application of legal arguments by Churchmen that could protect the Church from abuse. Efforts at revitalization would become heightened under the Gregorian Reform, in particular with the reign of Pope St. Gregory VII (1073-1085). From that time, throughout the Middle Ages, laws from the Church would be centered in and produced by the papacy, assisted in running the administration of the Church by the Roman Curia.

Gradually, legal experts collected the decrees of popes, enactments of councils, and sources of older, ancient canons. To these were added glosses, or commentaries, to assist in the teaching of the details of the subject. Still, the study of canon law was severely handicapped by the sheer number of collections, the contradiction between many points of law, and the inability to find specific laws because of the chronological arrangements of the material. Thus can be seen the major significance of the *Decretum* of Gratian, published around 1148 in Bologna. Compiled by the legal expert Gratian, the *Decretum* (in full, *Concordantia discordantum canonum*) was not a formal collection of canons but sought to provide a juridical system for its readers. Toward this end, though, Gratian examined (and excerpted) virtually every canon ever published. The *Decretum* was quickly adopted as the textbook of canon law, despite the fact that it was a private collection and not codified.

Over the next centuries, the popes added to the body of laws by giving rulings to those questions posed to them by bishops from around the Church. These decretal letters were then brought together and, for purposes of comprehensiveness, added to the *Decretum Gratiani*. The most important of these was the *Liber extra*, the collection made by St. Raymond Peñafort for Pope Gregory IX. This received official approval and was to be a vital source for the *Corpus Juris Canonici*. Other remarkable contributors to canon law in the late Middle Ages were Zenzelinus de Cassanis, Jean Chappuis, Guido de Baysio, John the Teuton (or Joannes Teutonicus), Stephen of Tournai, and most of all, Joannes Andreae (d. 1348).

Considerable activity was initiated by the Council of Trent (1545-1563), which sought to reform and reinvigorate the Church in the wake of the Protestant Reformation. The same century brought the formation in 1588 of the Sacred Congregation of the Curia by Pope Sixtus V (r. 1585-1590), which became the main means of implementing new laws and examining facets of established ones.

The final decision to codify the laws of the Church was made by Pope St. Pius X who, in 1903, issued *Arduum*, the *motu proprio* ordering the complete reform and codification of all canon law. It was completed and promulgated in 1917 as the *Codex Juris Canonici*, the first official guide to the laws of the Catholic Church. A new Code of Canon Law was issued by Pope John Paul II in 1983, the final result of a call for a new code dating back to Pope John XXIII (r. 1958-1963) and continued by Pope Paul VI (r. 1963-1978).

The 1983 Code of Canon Law

Pope John Paul II promulgated a revised Code of Canon Law for the Latin Rite on Jan. 25, 1983, with the apostolic constitution *Sacrae Disciplinae Legis* ("Of the Sacred Discipline of Law") and ordered it into effect as of the following Nov. 27. Promulgation of the Code marked the completion of the last major reform in the Church stemming from the Second Vatican Council.

The 1983 Code of Canon Law replaced the one which had been in effect since 1918. The new Code incorporates into law the insights of Vatican Council II. These 1,752 canons focus on the People of God and the threefold ministries of sanctifying, teaching and governance. Also included are general norms, temporalities, sanctions and procedures.

Guiding Principles

When Pope John XXIII announced on Jan. 25, 1959, that he was going to convoke the Second Vatican Council, he also called for a revision of the existing Code of Canon Law. His successor, Paul VI, appointed a commission for this purpose in 1963 and subsequently enlarged it. The commission, which began its work after the conclusion of the Council in 1965, was directed by the 1967 Synod of Bishops to direct its efforts in line with 10 guiding principles. The bishops said the revised Code should:

• be juridical in character, not just a set of broad moral principles;

• be intended primarily for the external forum (regarding determinable fact, as opposed to the internal forum of conscience);

• be clearly pastoral in spirit;

• incorporate most of the faculties bishops need in their ministry;

• provide for subsidiarity or decentralization;

• be sensitive to human rights;

• state clear procedures for administrative processes and tribunals;

• be based on the principle of territoriality;

• reduce the number of penalties for infraction of law;

• have a new structure.

The commission carried out its mandate with the collegial collaboration of bishops all over the world and in consultation and correspondence with individuals and experts in canon law, theology, and related disciplines. The group finished its work in 1981 and turned its final draft over to Pope John Paul II at its final plenary meeting in October of that year.

Features

The revised code is shorter (1,752 canons) than the one it replaced (2,414 canons) and has a number of important features:

It is more pastoral and flexible, as well as more theologically oriented than the former Code. It gives greater emphasis than its predecessor to a number of significant facets and concepts in church life.

In the apostolic constitution with which he promulgated the Code, Pope John Paul II called attention to its nature and some of its features, as follows:

Prime Legislative Document

"Since this is so, it seems clear enough that the Code in no way has its scope to substitute for faith, grace, the charisms, and especially charity in the life of the Church of the faithful. On the contrary, its end is rather to create such order in ecclesial society that, assigning primacy to love, grace and charisms, it at the same time renders more active their organic developments in the life both of the ecclesial society and of the individuals belonging to it. Inasmuch as it is the Church's prime legislative document, based on the juridical and legislative heritage of revelation and tradition, the Code must be regarded as the necessary instrument whereby due order is preserved in both individual and social life and in the Church's activity. Therefore, besides containing the fundamental elements of the hierarchical and organic structure of the Church, laid down by her divine Founder and founded on apostolic or at any rate most ancient tradition, and besides outstanding norms concerning the carrying out of the task mandated to the Church herself, the Code must also define a certain number of rules and norms of action."

Suits the Nature of the Church

"The instrument the Code is fully suits the Church's nature, for the Church is presented, especially through the magisterium of the Second Vatican Council, in her universal scope, and especially through the Council's ecclesiological teaching. In a certain sense, indeed, this new Code may be considered as a great effort to transfer that same ecclesiological or conciliar doctrine into canonical language. And, if it is impossible for the image of the Church described by the Council's teaching to be perfectly converted into canonical language, the Code nonetheless must always be referred to that very image, as the primary pattern whose outline the Code ought to express as well as it can by its own nature.

"From this derive a number of fundamental norms by which the whole of the new Code is ruled, of course within the limits proper to it as well as the limits of the very language befitting the material.

"It may rather be rightly affirmed that from this comes that note whereby the Code is regarded as a complement to the magisterium expounded by the Second Vatican Council.

"The following elements are most especially to be noted among those expressing a true and genuine image of the Church: the doctrine whereby the Church is proposed as the People of God and the hierarchical authority is propounded as service; in addition, the doctrine which shows the Church to be a 'communion' and from that lays down the mutual relationships which ought to exist between the particular and universal Church and between collegiality and primacy;

likewise, the doctrine whereby all members of the People of God, each in the manner proper to him, share in Christ's threefold office of priest, prophet and king; to this doctrine is also connected that regarding the duties and rights of the Christian faithful, particularly the laity; then there is the effort which the Church has to make for ecumenism."

Code Necessary for the Church

"Indeed, the Code of Canon Law is extremely necessary for the Church.... The Church needs it for her hierarchichal and organic structure to be visible: so that exercise of the offices and tasks divinely entrusted to her, especially her sacred power and administration of the sacraments, should be rightly ordered; so that mutual relations of the Christian faithful may be carried out according to justice based on charity, with the rights of all being safeguarded and defined; so that we may then prepare and perform our common tasks, and that these, undertaken in order to live a Christian life more perfectly, may be fortified by means of the canonical laws.

"Thus, canonical laws need to be observed because of their very nature. Hence it is of the greatest importance that the norms be carefully expounded on the basis of solid juridical, canonical and theological foundations."

BOOKS OF THE CODE

Book I, General Norms (Canons 1-203): Canons in this book cover Church laws, in general, custom and law, general decrees and instructions, administrative acts, statutes, physical and juridical persons, juridical acts, the power of governing, ecclesiastical offices, prescription (statutes of limitations), the reckoning of time.

Book II, The People of God (Canons 204-746): Canons in Part I cover the obligations and rights of all the faithful, the obligations and rights of lay persons, sacred ministers and clerics, personal prelatures and associations of the faithful.

Canons in Part II cover the hierarchic constitution of the Church under the headings: the supreme authority of the Church and the college of bishops, diocesan churches and the authority constituted in them, councils of diocesan churches and the internal order of diocesan churches.

Canons in Part III cover institutes of consecrated life and societies of apostolic life.

Book III, The Teaching Office of the Church (Canons 747-833): Canons under this heading cover: the ministry of the divine word, the missionary action of the Church, Catholic education, the instruments of social communication and books in particular, and the profession of faith.

Book IV, The Sanctifying Office of the Church (Canons 834-1252): Canons under this heading cover each of the seven sacraments—baptism, confirmation, the Eucharist, penance, anointing of the sick, holy orders and matrimony; other acts of divine worship

including sacramentals, the Liturgy of the Hours, ecclesiastical burial; the veneration of saints, sacred images and relics, vows and oaths.

Book V, Temporal Goods of the Church (Canons 1254-1310): Canons under this heading cover: the acquisition and administration of goods, contracts, the alienation of goods, wills and pious foundations.

Book VI, Sanctions in the Church (Canons 1311-1399): Canons in Part I cover crimes and penalties in general: the punishment of crimes in general, penal law and penal precept, persons subject to penal sanctions, penalties and other punishments, the application and cessation of penalties.

Canons in Part II cover penalties for particular crimes: crimes against religion and the unity of the Church; crimes against the authority of the Church and the liberty of the Church; the usurpation of Church offices and crimes in exercising office; false accusation of a confessor; crimes against special obligations; crimes against human life and liberty; a general norm regarding the punishment of external violations of divine law not specifically covered in the Code.

Book VII, Procedures (Canons 1400-1752): Judicial proceedings are the principal subjects of canons under this heading: tribunals and their personnel, parties to proceedings, details regarding litigation and the manner in which it is conducted, special proceedings—with emphasis on matrimonial cases.

Glossary

A

Abbacy Nullius: A non–diocesan territory whose people are under the pastoral care of an abbot acting in general in the manner of a bishop.

Abbess: The female superior of a monastic community of nuns; e.g., Benedictines, Poor Clares, some others. Elected by members of the community, an abbess has general authority over her community but no sacramental jurisdiction.

Abbey: *See* Monastery.

Abbot: The male superior of a monastic community of men religious; e.g., Benedictines, Cistercians, some others. Elected by members of the community, an abbot has ordinary jurisdiction and general authority over his community. Eastern Rite equivalents of an abbot are a hegumen and an archimandrite. A regular abbot is the head of an abbey or monastery. An abbot general or archabbot is the head of a congregation consisting of several monasteries. An abbot primate is the head of the modern Benedictine Confederation.

Abiogenesis: The term used to describe the spontaneous generation of living matter from non–living matter.

Ablution: A term derived from Latin, meaning washing or cleansing, and referring to the cleansing of the hands of a priest celebrating Mass, after the offering of gifts; and to the cleansing of the chalice with water and wine after Communion.

Abnegation: The spiritual practice of self–denial (or mortification), in order to atone for past sins or in order to join oneself to the passion of Christ. Mortification can be undertaken through fasting, abstinence, or refraining from legitimate pleasure.

Abortion: Abortion is not only "the ejection of an immature fetus" from the womb, but is "also the killing of the same fetus in whatever way at whatever time from the moment of conception it may be procured." (This clarification of Canon 1398, reported in the Dec. 5, 1988, edition of *L'Osservatore Romano*, was issued by the Pontifical Council for the Interpretation of Legislative Texts—in view of scientific developments regarding ways and means of procuring abortion.) Accidental expulsion, as in cases of miscarriage, is without moral fault. Direct abortion, in which a fetus is intentionally removed from the womb, constitutes a direct attack on an innocent human being, a violation of the Fifth Commandment. A person who procures a completed abortion is automatically excommunicated (Canon 1398 of the *Code of Canon Law*); also excommunicated are all persons involved in a deliberate and successful effort to bring about an abortion. Direct abortion is not justifiable for any reason, e.g.: therapeutic, for the physical and/or psychological welfare of the mother; preventive, to avoid the birth of a defective or unwanted child; social, in the interests of family and/or community. Indirect abortion, which occurs when a fetus is expelled during medical or other treatment of the mother for a reason other than procuring expulsion, is permissible under the principle of double effect for a proportionately serious reason; e.g., when a medical or surgical procedure is necessary to save the life of the mother. Such a procedure should not be confused with the purportedly "medical" procedure of the partial-birth abortion, a particularly cruel form of abortion.

Abrogation: The Abolition or elimination of a law by some official action. In Canon Law, abrogation occurs through a direct decree of the Holy See or by the enactment of a later or subsequent law contrary to the former law.

Absolute: (1) A term in philosophy, first introduced at the end of the 18th century and used by Scholasticism, that signifies the "perfect being" (i.e., God), who relies upon no one for existence. Modern philosophical thought has added two new concepts: a) the Absolute is the sum of all being; b) the Absolute has no relationship with any other things; the Absolute is thus unknowable. These concepts are agnostic and contrary to Catholicism, which holds that God is the cause of all being (and hence not the sum) and is knowable by his creatures, at least in part. (2) Certain truths, revealed by God, which are unchanging.

Absolution, Sacramental: The act by which bishops and priests, acting as agents of Christ and ministers of the Church, grant forgiveness of sins in the sacrament of penance. The essential formula of absolution is: "I absolve you from your sins; in the name of the Father, and of the Son, and of the Holy Spirit. Amen." The power to absolve is given with ordination to the priesthood and episcopate. Priests exercise this power in virtue of authorization (faculties) granted by a bishop, a religious superior or canon law. Authorization can be limited or restricted regarding certain sins and penalties or censures. In cases of necessity, and also in cases of the absence of their own confessors, Eastern and Latin Rite Catholics may ask for and receive sacramental absolution from an Eastern or Latin Rite priest; so may Polish National Catholics, according to a Vatican decision issued in May, 1993. Any priest can absolve a person in danger of death; in the absence of a priest with the usual faculties, this includes a laicized priest or a priest under censure. (*See* additional entry under **Sacraments**, p.194.)

Abstinence: 1. The deliberate deprivation by a person of meat or of foods prepared with meat on those days prescribed by the Church as penitential (Ash Wednesday, Good Friday, and all Fridays of the year which are not solemnities—in the United States, not all Fridays of the year but only the Fridays of Lent). Those 14 years of age and above are bound by the discipline. (2) Sexual abstinence is the willing refrain from sexual intercourse; total abstinence is observed in obedience to the Sixth Commandment by single persons and couples whose marriages are not recognized by the Church as valid; periodic abstinence or periodic continence is observed by a married couple for regulating conception by natural means or for ascetical motives.

Adoration: The highest act and purpose of religious worship, which is directed in love and reverence to God alone in acknowledgment of his infinite perfection and goodness, and of his total dominion over creatures. Adoration, which is also called latria, consists of internal and external elements, private and social prayer, liturgical acts and ceremonies, and especially sacrifice.

Adultery: Marital infidelity. Sexual intercourse between a married person and another to whom one is not married, a violation of the obligations of the marital covenant, chastity and justice; any sin of impurity (thought, desire, word, action) involving a married person who is not one's husband or wife has the nature of adultery.

Advent Wreath: A wreath of laurel, spruce, or similar foliage with four candles which are lighted successively in the weeks of Advent to symbolize the approaching celebration of the birth of Christ, the Light of the World, at Christmas. The wreath originated among German Protestants.

Agape: A Greek word, meaning love, love feast, designating the meal of fellowship eaten at some gatherings of early Christians. Although held in some places in connection with the Mass, the agape was not part of the Mass, nor was it of universal institution and observance. It was infrequently observed by the fifth century and disappeared altogether between the sixth and eighth centuries.

Age of Reason: (1) The time of life when one begins to distinguish between right and wrong, to understand an obligation and take on moral responsibility; seven years of age is the presumption in church law. (2) Historically, the 18th century period of Enlightenment in England and France, the age of the Encyclopedists and Deists. According to a basic thesis of the Enlightenment, human experience and reason are the only sources of certain knowledge of truth; consequently, faith and revelation are discounted as valid sources of knowledge, and the reality of supernatural truth is called into doubt and/or denied.

Aggiornamento: An Italian word having the general meaning of bringing up to date, renewal, revitalization, descriptive of the processes of spiritual renewal and institutional reform and change in the Church; fostered by the Second Vatican Council.

Agnosticism: A theory which holds that a person cannot have certain knowledge of immaterial reality, especially the existence of God and things pertaining to him. Immanuel Kant, one of the philosophical fathers of agnosticism, stood for the position that God, as well as the human soul, is unknowable on specula-

tive grounds; nevertheless, he found practical imperatives for acknowledging God's existence, a view shared by many agnostics. The First Vatican Council declared that the existence of God and some of his attributes can be known with certainty by human reason, even without divine revelation. The word agnosticism was first used, in the sense given here, by T. H. Huxley in 1869.

Agnus Dei: A Latin phrase, meaning Lamb of God. (1) A title given to Christ, the Lamb (victim) of the Sacrifice of the New Law (on Calvary and in Mass). (2) A prayer said at Mass before the reception of Holy Communion. (3) A sacramental. It is a round paschal-candle fragment blessed by the pope. On one side it bears the impression of a lamb, symbolic of Christ. On the reverse side, there may be any one of a number of impressions; e.g., the figure of a saint, the name and coat of arms of the reigning pope. The agnus dei may have originated at Rome in the fifth century. The first definite mention of it dates from about 820.

Akathist Hymn: The most profound and famous expression of Marian devotion in churches of the Byzantine Rite. It consists of 24 sections, 12 of which relate to the Gospel of the Infancy and 12 to the mysteries of the Incarnation and the virginal motherhood of Mary. In liturgical usage, it is sung in part in Byzantine churches on the first four Saturdays of Lent and in toto on the fifth Saturday; it is also recited in private devotion. It is of unknown origin prior to 626, when its popularity increased as a hymn of thanksgiving after the successful defense and liberation of Constantinople, which had been under siege by Persians and Avars. Akathist means "without sitting," indicating that the hymn is recited or sung while standing. Pope John Paul II, in a decree dated May 25, 1991, granted a plenary indulgence to the faithful of any rite who recite the hymn in a church or oratory, as a family, in a religious community or in a pious association — in conjunction with the usual conditions of freedom from attachment to sin, reception of the sacraments of penance and the Eucharist, and prayers for the intention of the pope (e.g., an Our Father, the Apostles' Creed and an aspiration). A partial indulgence can be gained for recitation of the hymn in other circumstances.

Alleluia: An exclamation of joy derived from Hebrew, "All hail to him who is, praise God," with various use in the liturgy and other expressions of worship.

Allocution: A formal type of papal address, as distinguished from an ordinary sermon or statement of views.

Alms: An act, gift or service of compassion, motivated by love of God and neighbor, for the help of persons in need; an obligation of charity, which is measurable by the ability of one person to give assistance and by the degree of another's need. Almsgiving, along with prayer and fasting, is regarded as a work of penance as well as an exercise of charity. (*See* **Mercy, Works of.**)

Alpha and Omega: The first and last letters of the Greek alphabet, used to symbolize the eternity of God (Rv 1:8) and the divinity and eternity of Christ, the beginning and end of all things (Rv 21:6; 22:13). Use of the letters as a monogram of Christ originated in the fourth century or earlier.

Amen: A Hebrew word meaning truly, it is true. In

the Gospels, Christ used the word to add a note of authority to his statements. In other New Testament writings, as in Hebrew usage, it was the concluding word to doxologies. As the concluding word of prayers, it expresses assent to and acceptance of God's will.

Anamnesis: A prayer recalling the saving mysteries of the death and resurrection of Jesus, following the consecration at Mass in the Latin Rite.

Anaphora: A Greek term for the Canon or Eucharistic Prayer of the Mass.

Anathema: A Greek word with the root meaning of cursed or separated and the adapted meaning of excommunication, used in church documents, especially the canons of ecumenical councils, for the condemnation of heretical doctrines and of practices opposed to proper discipline.

Anchorite: A kind of hermit living in complete isolation and devoting himself exclusively to exercises of religion and severe penance according to a rule and way of life of his own devising. In early Christian times, anchorites were the forerunners of the monastic life. The closest contemporary approach to the life of an anchorite is that of Carthusian and Camaldolese hermits.

Angels: Purely spiritual beings with intelligence and free will whose name indicates their mission as servants and messengers of God. They were created before the creation of the visible universe. Good angels enjoy the perfect good of the beatific vision. They can intercede for persons. The doctrine of guardian angels, although not explicitly defined as a matter of faith, is rooted in long-standing tradition. No authoritative declaration has ever been issued regarding choirs or various categories of angels: seraphim, cherubim, thrones, dominations, principalities, powers, virtues, archangels and angels. Archangels commemorated in the liturgy are: Michael, leader of the angelic host and protector of the synagogue; Raphael, guide of Tobiah and healer of his father; Gabriel, angel of the Incarnation. Fallen angels, the chief of whom is called the Devil or Satan, rejected the love of God and were therefore banished from heaven to hell. They can tempt persons to commit sin.

Angelus: A devotion which commemorates the Incarnation of Christ. It consists of three versicles, three Hail Marys and a special prayer, and recalls the announcement to Mary by the Archangel Gabriel that she was chosen to be the Mother of Christ, her acceptance of the divine will, and the Incarnation (Lk 1:26-38). The Angelus is recited in the morning, at noon and in the evening. The practice of reciting the Hail Mary in honor of the Incarnation was introduced by the Franciscans in 1263. The *Regina Caeli*, commemorating the joy of Mary at Christ's Resurrection, replaces the Angelus during the Easter season.

Anger (Wrath): Passionate displeasure arising from some kind of offense suffered at the hands of another person, frustration or other cause, combined with a tendency to strike back at the cause of the displeasure; a violation of the Fifth Commandment and one of the capital sins if the displeasure is out of proportion to the cause and/or if the retaliation is unjust.

Anglican Orders: Holy orders conferred according to the rite of the Anglican Church, which Leo XIII declared null and void in the bull *Apostolicae Curae*, Sept. 13, 1896. The orders were declared null because they were conferred according to a rite that was substantially defective in form and intent, and because of a break in apostolic succession that occurred when Matthew Parker became head of the Anglican hierarchy in 1559. In making his declaration, Pope Leo cited earlier arguments against validity made by Julius III in 1553 and 1554 and by Paul IV in 1555. He also noted related directives requiring absolute ordination, according to the Catholic ritual, of convert ministers who had been ordained according to the Anglican Ordinal.

Anglican Use Parishes: In line with Vatican-approved developments since 1980, several Anglican use parishes have been established in the United States with the right to continue using some elements of Anglican usage in their liturgical celebrations. A Vatican document dated Mar. 31, 1981, said: "In June, 1980, the Holy See, through the Congregation for the Doctrine of the Faith, agreed to the request presented by the bishops of the United States of America in behalf of some clergy and laity formerly or actually belonging to the Episcopal (Anglican) Church for full communion with the Catholic Church. The Holy See's response to the initiative of these Episcopalians includes the possibility of a 'pastoral provision' which will provide, for those who desire it, a common identity reflecting certain elements of their own heritage."

Animals: Creatures of God, they are entrusted to human stewardship for appropriate care, use for human needs, as pets, for reasonable experimentation for the good of people. They should not be subject to cruel treatment.

Annulment: A decree issued by an appropriate Church authority or tribunal that a sacrament or ecclesiastical act is invalid and therefore lacking in all legal or canonical consequences.

Antichrist: The "deceitful one," the "antichrist" (2 Jn 7), adversary of Christ and the kingdom of God, especially in the end time before the second coming of Christ. The term is also used in reference to anti-Christian persons and forces in the world.

Antiphon: (1) A short verse or text, generally from Scripture, recited in the Liturgy of the Hours before and after psalms and canticles. (2) Any verse sung or recited by one part of a choir or congregation in response to the other part, as in antiphonal or alternate chanting.

Anti-Semitism: A prejudice against Jews, and often accompanied by persecution. The prejudice has existed historically from the time of the ancient Persian Empire and survives even to the present day. It has been condemned consistently by the Church as being in opposition to scriptural principles and Christian charity.

Apologetics: The science and art of developing and presenting the case for the reasonableness of the Christian faith, by a wide variety of means including facts of experience, history, science, philosophy. The constant objective of apologetics, as well as of the total process of pre-evangelization, is preparation for response to God in faith; its ways and means, however, are subject to change in accordance with the various needs of people and different sets of circumstances.

Apostasy: (1) The total and obstinate repudiation of the Christian faith. An apostate automatically incurs a penalty of excommunication. (2) Apostasy from orders is the unlawful withdrawal from or rejection of the obligations of the clerical state by a man who has received major orders. An apostate from orders is subject to a canonical penalty. (3) Apostasy from the religious life occurs when a Religious with perpetual vows unlawfully leaves the community with the intention of not returning, or actually remains outside the community without permission. An apostate from religious life is subject to a canonical penalty.

Apostolate: The ministry or work of an apostle. In Catholic usage, the word is an umbrella-like term covering all kinds and areas of work and endeavor for the service of God and the Church and the good of people. Thus, the apostolate of bishops is to carry on the mission of the Apostles as pastors of the People of God: of priests, to preach the word of God and to carry out the sacramental and pastoral ministry for which they are ordained; of religious, to follow and do the work of Christ in conformity with the evangelical counsels and their rule of life; of lay persons, as individuals and/or in groups, to give witness to Christ and build up the kingdom of God through practice of their faith, professional competence and the performance of good works in the concrete circumstances of daily life. Apostolic works are not limited to those done within the Church or by specifically Catholic groups, although some apostolates are officially assigned to certain persons or groups and are under the direction of church authorities. Apostolate derives from the commitment and obligation of baptism, confirmation, holy orders, matrimony, the duties of one's state in life, etc.

Apostolic Succession: Bishops of the Church, who form a collective body or college, are successors to the Apostles by ordination and divine right; as such they carry on the mission entrusted by Christ to the Apostles as guardians and teachers of the deposit of faith, principal pastors and spiritual authorities of the faithful. The doctrine of apostolic succession is based on New Testament evidence and the constant teaching of the Church, reflected as early as the end of the first century in a letter of Pope St. Clement to the Corinthians. A significant facet of the doctrine is the role of the pope as the successor of St. Peter, the vicar of Christ and head of the college of bishops. The doctrine of apostolic succession means more than continuity of apostolic faith and doctrine; its basic requisite is ordination by the laying on of hands in apostolic succession.

Archives: Documentary records, and the place where they are kept, of the spiritual and temporal government and affairs of the Church, a diocese, church agencies like the departments of the Roman Curia, bodies like religious institutes, and individual parishes. The collection, cataloguing, preserving, and use of these records are governed by norms stated in canon law and particular regulations. The strictest secrecy is always in effect for confidential records concerning matters of conscience, and documents of this kind are destroyed as soon as circumstances permit.

Ark of the Covenant: The sacred chest of the Israelites in which were placed and carried the tablets of stone inscribed with the Ten Commandments, the basic moral precepts of the Old Covenant (Ex 25: 10-22; 37:1-9). The Ark was also a symbol of God's presence. The Ark was probably destroyed with the Temple in 586 B.C.

Asceticism: The practice of self-discipline. In the spiritual life, asceticism — by personal prayer, meditation, self-denial, works of mortification, and outgoing interpersonal works — is motivated by love of God and contributes to growth in holiness.

Ashes: Religious significance has been associated with their use as symbolic of penance since Old Testament times. Thus, ashes of palm blessed on the previous Sunday of the Passion are placed on the foreheads of the faithful on Ash Wednesday to remind them to do works of penance, especially during the season of Lent, and that they are dust and unto dust will return. Ashes are a sacramental.

Aspergillum: A vessel or device used for sprinkling holy water. The ordinary type is a metallic rod with a bulbous tip which absorbs the water and discharges it at the motion of the user's hand.

Aspersory: A portable metallic vessel, similar to a pail, for carrying holy water.

Aspiration (Ejaculation): Short exclamatory prayer; e.g., My Jesus, mercy.

Atheism: Denial of the existence of God, finding expression in a system of thought (speculative atheism) or a manner of acting (practical atheism) as though there were no God. The Second Vatican Council, in its Pastoral Constitution on the Church in the Modern World (*Gaudium et Spes*, Nos. 19 to 21), noted that a profession of atheism may represent an explicit denial of God, the rejection of a wrong notion of God, an affirmation of man rather than of God, an extreme protest against evil. It said that such a profession might result from acceptance of such propositions as: there is no absolute truth; man can assert nothing, absolutely nothing, about God; everything can be explained by scientific reasoning alone; the whole question of God is devoid of meaning.

Atonement: The redemptive activity of Christ, who reconciled man with God through his Incarnation and entire life, and especially by his suffering and Resurrection. The word also applies to prayer and good works by which persons join themselves with and take part in Christ's work of reconciliation and reparation for sin.

Attributes of God: Perfections of God. God possesses—and is—all the perfections of being, without limitation. Because he is infinite, all of these perfections are one, perfectly united in him. Because of the limited power of human intelligence, divine perfections—such as omnipotence, truth, love, etc.—are viewed separately, as distinct characteristics, even though they are not actually distinct in God.

Authority, Ecclesiastical: The authority exercised by the Church, and particularly by the pope and the bishops; it is delegated by Jesus Christ to St. Peter. This authority extends to all those matters entrusted to the Apostles by Christ, including teaching of the Faith, the liturgy and sacraments, moral guidance, and the administration of discipline.

Avarice (Covetousness): A disorderly and unreasonable attachment to and desire for material things; called a capital sin because it involves preoccupation with material things to the neglect of spiritual goods and obligations of justice and charity.

Ave Maria: *See* **Hail Mary**.

B

Baldacchino: A canopy over an altar.

Baptism: *See* **Sacraments, p. 190.**

Beatification: A preliminary step toward canonization of a saint. It begins with an investigation of the candidate's life, writings and heroic practice of virtue, and, except in the case of martyrs, the certification of one miracle worked by God through his or her intercession. If the findings of the investigation so indicate, the pope decrees that the Servant of God may be called Blessed and may be honored locally or in a limited way in the liturgy. Additional procedures lead to canonization (see separate entry).

Beatific Vision: The intuitive, immediate and direct vision and experience of God enjoyed in the light of glory by all the blessed in heaven. The vision is a supernatural mystery.

Beatitude: A literary form of the Old and New Testaments in which blessings are promised to persons for various reasons. Beatitudes are mentioned 26 times in the Psalms, and in other books of the Old Testament. The best known Beatitudes—identifying blessedness with participation in the kingdom of God and his righteousness, and descriptive of the qualities of Christian perfection—are those recounted in Mt 5:3-12 and Lk 6:20-23. The Beatitudes are of central importance in the teaching of Jesus.

Benedictus: The canticle or hymn of Zechariah at the circumcision of St. John the Baptist (Lk 1:68-79). It is an expression of praise and thanks to God for sending John as a precursor of the Messiah. The Benedictus is recited in the Liturgy of the Hours as part of the Morning Prayer.

Biglietto: A papal document of notification of appointment to the cardinalate.

Biretta: A stiff, square hat with three ridges on top worn by clerics in church and on other occasions.

Blasphemy: Any internal or external expression of hatred, reproach, insult, defiance or contempt with respect to God and the use of his name, principally, and to the Church, saints and sacred things, secondarily; a serious sin, directly opposed to the second commandment. Blasphemy against the Spirit is the deliberate refusal to accept divine mercy, rejection of forgiveness of sins and of the promise of salvation. The sin that is unforgivable because a person refuses to seek or accept forgiveness.

Blessing: Invocation of God's favor, by official ministers of the Church or by private individuals. Blessings are recounted in the Old and New Testaments, and are common in the Christian tradition. Many types of blessings are listed in the Book of Blessings of the Roman Ritual. Private blessings, as well as those of an official kind, are efficacious. Blessings are imparted with the Sign of the Cross and appropriate prayer.

Bride of Christ: A metaphorical title that denotes the intimate union that Christ enjoys with his Church; the title is mentioned specifically in the NT (2 Cor 11:2).

Brief, Apostolic: A papal letter, less formal than a bull, signed for the pope by a secretary and impressed with the seal of the Fisherman's Ring. Simple apostolic letters of this kind are issued for beatifications and with respect to other matters.

Bull, Apostolic: Apostolic letter, a solemn form of papal document, beginning with the name and title of the pope (e.g., John Paul II, Servant of the Servants of God), dealing with an important subject, sealed with a *bulla* or red-ink imprint of the device on the *bulla*. Bulls are issued to confer the titles of bishops and cardinals, to promulgate canonizations, to proclaim Holy Years and for other purposes. A collection of bulls is called a *bullarium*.

Burial, Ecclesiastical: Interment with ecclesiastical rites, a right of the Christian faithful. The Church recommends burial of the bodies of the dead, but cremation is permissible if it does not involve reasons against church teaching. Ecclesiastical burial is in order for catechumens; for unbaptized children whose parents intended to have them baptized before death; and even, in the absence of their own ministers, for baptized non-Catholics unless it would be considered against their will.

Burse, Financial: A special fund maintained by a diocese, religious institute, or private foundation usually endowed by a private benefactor; it often has the purpose of making possible the education of candidates for the priesthood.

C

Calumny (Slander): Harming the name and good reputation of a person by lies; a violation of obligations of justice and truth. Restitution is due for calumny.

Calvary: A knoll about 15 feet high just outside the western wall of Jerusalem where Christ was crucified, so called from the Latin *calvaria* (skull) which described its shape.

Canon: A Greek word meaning rule, norm, standard, measure. (1) The word designates the Canon of Sacred Scripture, which is the list of books recognized by the Church as inspired by the Holy Spirit. (2) The term also designates the canons (Eucharistic Prayers, anaphoras) of the Mass, the core of the eucharistic liturgy. (3) Certain dignitaries of the Church have the title of Canon, and some religious are known as Canons. (*See* **Bible**.)

Canonization: An infallible declaration by the pope that a person, who died as a martyr and/or practiced Christian virtue to a heroic degree, is now in heaven and is worthy of honor and imitation by all the faithful. Such a declaration is preceded by the process of beatification and another detailed investigation concerning the person's reputation for holiness, writings, and (except in the case of martyrs) a miracle ascribed to his or her intercession after death. The pope can dispense from some of the formalities ordinarily required in canonization procedures (equivalent canonization), as Pope John XXIII did in the canonization of St. Gregory Barbarigo on May 26, 1960. A saint is worthy of honor in liturgical worship throughout the universal Church. From its earliest years the Church has venerated saints. Public official honor always required the approval of the bishop of the place. Martyrs were the first to be honored. St. Martin of Tours, who died in 397, was an early non-martyr venerated as a saint. The earliest canonization by a pope with positive documentation was that of St. Ulrich (Uldaric) of Augsburg by John XV in 993. Alexander III reserved the process of canonization to the Holy See in 1171. In 1588 Sixtus V established the Sacred Congregation of Rites for the principal purpose of handling causes for beatification and canonization: this function is now the work of the Congregation for the Causes of Saints. The official listing of saints and blessed is contained in the Roman Martyrology (revised, updated, and published in 2002 by the Congregation for Divine Worship and the Discipline of the Sacraments) and related decrees issued after its last publication. Butler's unofficial *Lives of the Saints* (1956 and recently updated) contains 2,565 entries. The Church regards all persons in heaven as saints, not just those who have been officially canonized. (*See* **Beatification**, **Saints**, **Canonizations by Leo XIII and His Successors**, pp. 251-253.)

Canon Law: *See under* **Canon Law**, pp. 125-127.

Canticle: A scriptural chant or prayer differing from the psalms. Three of the canticles prescribed for use in the Liturgy of the Hours are: the *Magnificat*, the Canticle of Mary (Lk 1:46-55); the *Benedictus*, the Canticle of Zechariah (Lk 1:68-79); and the *Nunc Dimittis*, the Canticle of Simeon (Lk 2:29-32).

Capital Punishment: Punishment for crime by means of the death penalty. The political community, which has authority to provide for the common good, has the right to defend itself and its members against unjust aggression and may in extreme cases punish with the death penalty persons found guilty before the law of serious crimes against individuals and a just social order. Such punishment is essentially vindictive. Its value as a crime deterrent is a matter of perennial debate. The prudential judgment as to whether or not there should be capital punishment belongs to the civic community. The U.S. Supreme Court, in a series of decisions dating from June 29, 1972, ruled against the constitutionality of statutes on capital punishment except in specific cases and with appropriate consideration, with respect to sentence, of mitigating circumstances of the crime. Pope John Paul II, in his encyclical *Evangelium Vitae* ("The Gospel of Life"), wrote: "There is a growing tendency, both in the Church and in civil society, to demand that it (capital punishment) be applied in a very limited way or even that it be abolished completely." Quoting the *Catechism of the Catholic Church*, the pope wrote: "'If bloodless means are sufficient to defend human lives against an aggressor and to protect public order and the safety of persons, public authority must limit itself to such means, because they better correspond to the concrete conditions of the common good and are more in conformity to the dignity of the human person.'"

Capital Sins: Sins which give rise to other sins: pride, avarice, lust, wrath (anger), gluttony, envy, sloth.

Cardinal Virtues: The four principal moral virtues are prudence, justice, temperance and fortitude.

Casuistry: In moral theology, the application of moral principles to specific cases. Casuistry can be of assistance because it takes the abstract and makes it practical in a particular situation. It has definite limitations and does not replace the conscience in the decision-making process; additionally, it must be aligned with the cardinal virtue of prudence.

Catacombs: Underground Christian cemeteries in various cities of the Roman Empire and Italy, especially in the vicinity of Rome; the burial sites of many martyrs and other Christians.

Catechesis: The whole complex of church efforts to make disciples of Christ, involving doctrinal instruction and spiritual formation through practice of the faith.

Catechism: A systematic presentation of the fundamentals of Catholic doctrine regarding faith and morals. Sources are Sacred Scripture, tradition, the magisterium (teaching authority of the Church), the writings of Fathers and Doctors of the Church, liturgy. The new *Catechism of the Catholic Church*, published Oct. 11, 1992, consists of four principal sections: the profession of faith, (the Creed), the sacraments of faith, the life of faith (the Commandments) and the prayer of the believer (the Lord's Prayer). The 16th century Council of Trent mandated publication of the *Roman Catechism*. Catechisms such as these two are useful sources for other catechisms serving particular needs of the faithful and persons seeking admission to the Catholic Church.

Catechumen: A person preparing in a program (catechumenate) of instruction and spiritual formation for baptism and reception into the Church. The Church has a special relationship with catechumens. It invites them to lead the life of the Gospel, introduces them to the celebration of the sacred rites, and grants them various prerogatives that are proper to the faithful (one of which is the right to ecclesiastical burial). (*See* Rite of Christian Initiation of Adults, under Baptism.)

Cathedra: A Greek word for chair, designating the chair or seat of a bishop in the principal church of his diocese, which is therefore called a cathedral.

Cathedraticum: The tax paid to a bishop by all churches and benefices subject to him for the support of episcopal administration and for works of charity.

Catholic: A Greek word, meaning universal, first used in the title Catholic Church in a letter written by St. Ignatius of Antioch about 107 to the Christians of Smyrna.

Celebret: A Latin word, meaning "Let him celebrate," the name of a letter of recommendation issued by a bishop or other superior stating that a priest is in good standing and therefore eligible to celebrate Mass or perform other priestly functions.

Celibacy: The unmarried state of life, required in the Roman Church of candidates for holy orders and of men already ordained to holy orders, for the practice of perfect chastity and total dedication to the service of people in the ministry of the Church. Celibacy is enjoined as a condition for ordination by church discipline and law, not by dogmatic necessity. In the Roman Church, a consensus in favor of celibacy developed in the early centuries while the clergy included both celibates and men who had been married once. The first local legislation on the subject was enacted by a local council held in Elvira, Spain, about 306; it forbade bishops, priests, deacons and other ministers to have wives. Similar enactments were passed by other local councils from that time on, and by the 12th century particular laws regarded marriage by clerics in major orders to be not only unlawful but also null and void. The latter view was translated by the Second Lateran Council in 1139 into what seems to be the first written universal law making holy orders an invalidating impediment to marriage. In 1563 the Council of Trent ruled definitely on the matter and established the discipline in force in the Roman Church. Some exceptions to this discipline have been made in recent years. A number of married Protestant and Episcopalian (Anglican) clergymen who became converts and were subsequently ordained to the priesthood have been permitted to continue in marriage. Married men over the age of 35 can be ordained to the permanent diaconate. Eastern Church discipline on celibacy differs from that of the Roman Church. In line with legislation enacted by the Synod of Trullo in 692 and still in force, candidates for holy orders may marry before becoming deacons and may continue in marriage thereafter, but marriage after ordination is forbidden. Bishops of Eastern Catholic Churches in the U.S., however, do not ordain married candidates for the priesthood. Bishops of Eastern Catholic Churches are unmarried.

Cenacle: The upper room in Jerusalem where Christ ate the Las Supper with his Apostles.

Censer: A metal vessel with a perforated cover and suspended by chains, in which incense is burned. It is used at some Masses, Benediction of the Blessed Sacrament and other liturgical functions.

Censorship of Books: An exercise of vigilance by the Church for safeguarding authentic religious teaching. Pertinent legislation in a decree issued by the Congregation for the Doctrine of the Faith Apr. 9, 1975, is embodied in the Code of Canon Law (Book III, Title IV). The legislation deals with requirements for pre-publication review and clearance of various types of writings on religious subjects. Permission to publish works of a religious character, together with the apparatus of reviewing them beforehand, falls under the authority of the bishop of the place where the writer lives or where the works are published. Clearance for publication is usually indicated by the terms *Nihil obstat* ("Nothing stands in the way") issued by the censor and *Imprimatur* ("Let it be printed") authorized by the bishop. The clearing of works for publication does not necessarily imply approval of an author's viewpoint or his manner of handling a subject.

Censures: Sanctions imposed by the Church on baptized Roman Catholics 18 years of age or older for committing certain serious offenses and for being or remaining obstinate therein: (1) excommunication (exclusion from the community of the faithful, barring a person from sacramental and other participation in the goods and offices of the community of the Church), (2) suspension (prohibition of a cleric to exercise orders) and (3) interdict (deprivation of the sacraments and liturgical activities). The intended purposes of censures are to correct and punish offenders; to deter persons from committing sins which, more seriously and openly than others, threaten the common good of the Church and its members; and to provide for the making of reparation for harm done to the community of the Church. Censures may be incurred automatically (*ipso facto*) on the commission of certain offenses for which fixed penalties have been laid down in church law (*latae sententiae*); or they may be inflicted by sentence of a judge (*ferendae sententiae*). Automatic excommunication is incurred for the offenses of abortion, apostasy, heresy and schism. Obstinacy in crime—also called contumacy, disregard of a penalty, defiance of church authority—is presumed by law in the commission of offenses for which automatic censures are decreed. The presence and degree of contumacy in other cases, for which judicial

sentence is required, is subject to determination by a judge. Absolution can be obtained from any censure, provided the person repents and desists from obstinacy. Absolution may be reserved to the pope, the bishop of a place, or the major superior of an exempt clerical religious institute. In danger of death, any priest can absolve from all censures; in other cases, faculties to absolve from reserved censures can be exercised by competent authorities or given to other priests. The penal law of the Church is contained in Book VI of the Code of Canon Law.

Ceremonies, Master of: One who directs the proceedings of a rite or ceremony during the function.

Chamberlain (*Camerlengo*): (1) The Chamberlain of the Holy Roman Church is a cardinal with special responsibilities, especially during the time between the death of one pope and the election of his successor; among other things, he safeguards and administers the goods and revenues of the Holy See and heads particular congregations of cardinals for special purposes. (*See also* **Papal Election,** pp. 150, 297.) (2) The Chamberlain of the College of Cardinals has charge of the property and revenues of the College and keeps the record of business transacted in consistories. (3) The Chamberlain of the Roman Clergy is the president of the secular clergy of Rome.

Chancellor: Notary of a diocese, who draws up written documents in the government of the diocese; takes care of, arranges and indexes diocesan archives, records of dispensations and ecclesiastical trials.

Chancery: (1) A branch of church administration that handles written documents used in the government of a diocese. (2) The administrative office of a diocese, a bishop's office.

Chant: A type of sacred singing. It is either recitative in nature with a short two-to-six tones for an accentus, or melodic in one of three styles (syllabic, neumatic, or melismatic).

Chapel: A building or part of another building used for divine worship; a portion of a church set aside for the celebration of Mass or for some special devotion.

Chaplain: A priest—or, in some instances, a properly qualified religious or lay person—serving the pastoral needs of particular groups of people and institutions, such as hospitals, schools, correctional facilities, religious communities, the armed forces, etc.

Chaplet: A term, meaning little crown, applied to a rosary or, more commonly, to a small string of beads used for devotional purposes; e.g., the Infant of Prague chaplet.

Chapter: A general meeting of delegates of religious orders for elections and the handling of other important affairs of their communities.

Charismatic Renewal: A movement which originated with a handful of Duquesne University students and faculty members in the 1966-67 academic year and spread from there to Notre Dame, Michigan State University, the University of Michigan, other campuses and cities throughout the U.S., and to well over 125 other countries. Scriptural keys to the renewal are: Christ's promise to send the Holy Spirit upon the Apostles; the description, in the Acts of the Apostles, of the effects of the coming of the Holy Spirit upon the Apostles on Pentecost; St. Paul's explanation, in the Letter to the Romans and 1 Corinthians, of the charismatic gifts (for the good of the Church and persons) the Holy Spirit would bestow on Christians; New Testament evidence concerning the effects of charismatic gifts in and through the early Church. The personal key to the renewal is baptism in the Holy Spirit. This is not a new sacrament but the personally experienced actualization of grace already sacramentally received, principally in baptism and confirmation. The experience of baptism in the Holy Spirit is often accompanied by the reception of one or more charismatic gifts. A characteristic form of the renewal is the weekly prayer meeting, a gathering which includes periods of spontaneous prayer, singing, sharing of experience and testimony, fellowship and teaching. (*See* also Index.)

Charisms: Gifts or graces given by God to persons for the good of others and the Church. Examples are special gifts for apostolic work, prophecy, healing, discernment of spirits, the life of evangelical poverty, here-and-now witness to faith in various circumstances of life. The Second Vatican Council made the following statement about charisms in the Dogmatic Constitution on the Church (No. 12): "It is not only through the sacraments and Church ministries that the same Holy Spirit sanctifies and leads the People of God and enriches it with virtues. Allotting his gifts 'to everyone according as he will' (1 Cor 12:11), he distributes special graces among the faithful of every rank. By these gifts he makes them fit and ready to undertake the various tasks or offices advantageous for the renewal and upbuilding of the Church, according to the words of the Apostle: 'The manifestation of the Spirit is given to everyone for profit' (1 Cor 12:7). These charismatic gifts, whether they be the most outstanding or the more simple and widely diffused, are to be received with thanksgiving and consolation, for they are exceedingly suitable and useful for the needs of the Church. Still, extraordinary gifts are not to be rashly sought after, nor are the fruits of apostolic labor to be presumptuously expected from them. In any case, judgment as to their genuineness and proper use belongs to those who preside over the Church, and to whose special competence it belongs, not indeed to extinguish the Spirit, but to test all things and hold fast to that which is good" (cf. 1 Thes 5:12; 19-21).

Charity: Love of God above all things for his own sake, and love of one's neighbor as oneself because and as an expression of one's love for God; the greatest of the three theological virtues. The term is sometimes also used to designate sanctifying grace.

Chastity: Properly ordered behavior with respect to sex. In marriage, the exercise of the procreative power is integrated with the norms and purposes of marriage. Outside of marriage, the rule is self-denial of the voluntary exercise and enjoyment of the procreative faculty in thought, word or action. The vow of chastity, which reinforces the virtue of chastity with the virtue of religion, is one of the three vows professed publicly by members of institutes of consecrated life.

Chirograph or Autograph Letter: A letter written by a pope himself, in his own handwriting.

Chrism: A mixture of olive or other vegetable oil and balsam (or balm), that is consecrated by a bishop for use in liturgical anointings: Baptism, Confirmation, Holy Orders, the blessing of an altar.

Christ: The title of Jesus, derived from the Greek translation *Christos* of the Hebrew term Messiah, meaning the Anointed of God, the Savior and Deliverer of his people. Christian use of the title is a confession of belief that Jesus is the Savior.

Christianity: The sum total of things related to belief in Christ—the Christian religion, Christian churches, Christians themselves, society based on and expressive of Christian beliefs, culture reflecting Christian values.

Christians: The name first applied about the year 43 to followers of Christ at Antioch, the capital of Syria. It was used by the pagans as a contemptuous term. The word applies to persons who profess belief in the divinity and teachings of Christ and who give witness to him in life.

Circumcision: A ceremonial practice symbolic of initiation and participation in the covenant between God and Abraham.

Circumincession: The indwelling of each divine Person of the Holy Trinity in the others.

Clergy: Men ordained to holy orders and commissioned for sacred ministries and assigned to pastoral and other duties for the service of the people and the Church. (1) Diocesan or secular clergy are committed to pastoral ministry in parishes and in other capacities in a particular church (diocese) under the direction of their bishop, to whom they are bound by a promise of obedience. (2) Regular clergy belong to religious institutes (orders, congregations, societies—institutes of consecrated life) and are so called because they observe the rule (*regula*, in Latin) of their respective institutes. They are committed to the ways of life and apostolates of their institutes. In ordinary pastoral ministry, they are under the direction of local bishops as well as their own superiors.

Clericalism: A term generally used in a derogatory sense to mean action, influence and interference by the Church and the clergy in matters with which they allegedly should not be concerned. Anticlericalism is a reaction of antipathy, hostility, distrust and opposition to the Church and clergy arising from real and/or alleged faults of the clergy, overextension of the role of the laity, or for other reasons.

Cloister: Part of a monastery, convent or other house of religious reserved for use by members of the institute. Houses of contemplative Religious have a strict enclosure.

Code: A digest of rules or regulations, such as the Code of Canon Law.

Code of Canon Law: *See under* **Canon Law**, pp. 125-127.

Collegiality: A term in use especially since the Second Vatican Council to describe the authority exercised by the College of Bishops. The bishops of the Church, in union with and subordinate to the pope—who has full, supreme and universal power over the Church which he can always exercise independently—have supreme teaching and pastoral authority over the whole Church. In addition to their proper authority of office for the good of the faithful in their respective dioceses or other jurisdictions, the bishops have authority to act for the good of the universal Church. This collegial authority is exercised in a solemn manner in an ecumenical council and can also be exercised in other ways sanctioned by the pope. Doctrine on collegiality was set forth by the Second Vatican Council in *Lumen Gentium* (the Dogmatic Constitution on the Church). (*See separate entry.*) By extension, the concept of collegiality is applied to other forms of participation and co-responsibility by members of a community.

Communicatio in Sacris: The reception of the Church's sacraments by non-members or the reception by Catholics of sacraments in non-Catholic Churches.

Communion of Saints: "The communion of all the faithful of Christ, those who are pilgrims on earth, the dead who are being purified, and the blessed in heaven, all together forming one Church; in this communion, the merciful love of God and his saints is always (attentive) to our prayers" (Paul VI, *Creed of the People of God*).

Communism: The substantive principles of modern communism, a theory and system of economics and social organization, were stated about the middle of the 19th century by Karl Marx, author of *The Communist Manifesto* and, with Friedrich Engels, *Das Kapital*. The elements of communist theory include: radical materialism; dialectical determinism; the inevitability of class struggle and conflict, which is to be furthered for the ultimate establishment of a worldwide, classless society; common ownership of productive and other goods; the subordination of all persons and institutions to the dictatorship of the collective; denial of the rights, dignity and liberty of persons; militant atheism and hostility to religion, utilitarian morality. Communism in theory and practice has been the subject of many papal documents and statements. Pius IX condemned it in 1846. Leo XIII dealt with it at length in the encyclical letter *Quod Apostolici Muneris* in 1878 and *Rerum Novarum* in 1891. Pius XI wrote on the same subject in the encyclicals *Quadragesimo Anno* in 1931 and *Divini Redemptoris* in 1937. These writings have been updated and developed in new directions by Pius XII, John XXIII, Paul VI and John Paul II.

Compline: The night prayer of the Church that completes the daily cursus (course) of the Liturgy of the Hours (Divine Office).

Concelebration: The liturgical act in which several priests, led by one member of the group, offer Mass together, all consecrating the bread and wine. Concelebration has always been common in churches of Eastern Rite. In the Roman Rite, it was long restricted, taking place only at the ordination of bishops and the ordination of priests. The Constitution on the Sacred Liturgy issued by the Second Vatican Council set new norms for concelebration, which is now relatively common in the Roman Rite.

Concordance, Biblical: An alphabetical verbal index enabling a user knowing one or more words of a scriptural passage to locate the entire text.

Concordat: A church-state treaty with the force of law concerning matters of mutual concern—e.g., rights of the Church, arrangement of ecclesiastical jurisdictions, marriage laws, education. Approximately 150 agreements of this kind have been negotiated since the Concordat of Worms in 1122.

Concupiscence: Any tendency of the sensitive appetite. The term is most frequently used in reference to desires and tendencies for sinful sense pleasure.

Confession: Sacramental confession is the act by which a person tells or confesses his sins to a priest who is authorized to give absolution in the sacrament of penance.

Confessor: A priest who administers the sacrament of penance. The title of confessor, formerly given to a category of male saints, was suppressed with publication of the calendar reform of 1969.

Confraternity: An association whose members practice a particular form of religious devotion and/or are engaged in some kind of apostolic work.

Congregation: (1) The collective name for the people who form a parish. (2) One of the chief administrative departments of the Roman Curia. (3) An unofficial term for a group of men and women who belong to a religious community or institute of consecrated life.

Conscience: Practical judgment concerning the moral goodness or sinfulness of an action (thought, word, desire). In the Catholic view, this judgment is made by reference of the action, its attendant circumstances and the intentions of the person to the requirements of moral law as expressed in the Ten Commandments, the summary law of love for God and neighbor, the life and teaching of Christ, and the authoritative teaching and practice of the Church with respect to the total demands of divine Revelation. A person is obliged: (1) to obey a certain and correct conscience; (2) to obey a certain conscience even if it is inculpably erroneous; (3) not to obey, but to correct, a conscience known to be erroneous or lax; (4) to rectify a scrupulous conscience by following the advice of a confessor and by other measures; (5) to resolve doubts of conscience before acting. It is legitimate to act for solid and probable reasons when a question of moral responsibility admits of argument (*See* **Probabiliorism** and **Probabilism**).

Conscience, Examination of: Self-examination to determine one's spiritual state before God, regarding one's sins and faults. It is recommended as a regular practice and is practically necessary in preparing for the sacrament of penance. The particular examen is a regular examination to assist in overcoming specific faults and imperfections.

Consequentialism: A moral theory, closely associated with proportionalism and utilitarianism, that holds that the preferable action is one that brings about the best consequences. Preferred results, rather than the objective truth and intentionality, are the object of actions based on consequentialism. While traditional moral theology acknowledges that consequences are important in determining the rightness of an act, importance is also placed on the intrinsic morality of the act and the agent's intention.

Consistory: An assembly of cardinals presided over by the pope.

Constitution: (1) An apostolic or papal constitution is a document in which a pope enacts and promulgates law. (2) A formal and solemn document issued by an ecumenical council on a doctrinal or pastoral subject, with binding force in the whole Church; e.g., the four constitutions issued by the Second Vatican Council on the Church, liturgy, Revelation, and the Church in the modern world. (3) The constitutions of institutes of consecrated life and societies of apostolic life spell out details of and norms drawn from the various rules for the guidance and direction of the life and work of their members.

Consubstantiation: A theory which holds that the Body and Blood of Christ coexist with the substance of bread and wine in the Holy Eucharist. This theory, also called impanation, is incompatible with the doctrine of transubstantiation.

Contraception: Anything done by positive interference to prevent sexual intercourse from resulting in conception. Direct contraception is against the order of nature. Indirect contraception—as a secondary effect of medical treatment or other action having a necessary, good, non-contraceptive purpose—is permissible under the principle of the double effect. The practice of periodic continence is not contraception because it does not involve positive interference with the order of nature. (*See Humanae Vitae*, p. 199 and other entries.)

Contrition: Sorrow for sin coupled with a purpose of amendment. Contrition arising from a supernatural motive is necessary for the forgiveness of sin. (1) Perfect contrition is total sorrow for and renunciation of attachment to sin, arising from the motive of pure love of God. Perfect contrition, which implies the intention of doing all God wants done for the forgiveness of sin (including confession in a reasonable period of time), is sufficient for the forgiveness of serious sin and the remission of all temporal punishment due for sin. (The intention to receive the sacrament of penance is implicit—even if unrealized, as in the case of some persons—in perfect contrition.) (2) Imperfect contrition or attrition is sorrow arising from a quasi-selfish supernatural motive; e.g., the fear of losing heaven, suffering the pains of hell, etc. Imperfect contrition is sufficient for the forgiveness of serious sin when joined with absolution in confession, and sufficient for the forgiveness of venial sin even outside of confession.

Contumely: Personal insult, reviling a person in his presence by accusation of moral faults, by refusal of recognition or due respect; a violation of obligations of justice and charity.

Conversion: In a general sense, the turning away from someone or something and the moving toward another person or thing. In Christian belief, conversion is the embrace of Jesus Christ and a rejection of all that keeps one from God.

Corpus Iuris Canonici: See **Canon Law**, pp. 125-127.

Council: A formal meeting of Church leaders, summoned by a bishop or appropriate Church leader, with the general purpose of assisting the life of the Church through deliberations, decrees, and promulgations. Different councils include: **diocesan** councils (synod), a gathering of the officials of an individual diocese; **provincial** councils, the meeting of the bishops of a province; **plenary** councils, the assembly of the bishops of a country; and **ecumenical** councils, a gathering of all the bishops in the world under the authority of the Bishop of Rome.

Counsels, Evangelical: Gospel counsels of perfection, especially voluntary poverty, perfect chastity and obedience, which were recommended by Christ to those who would devote themselves exclusively and completely to the immediate service of God. Religious (members of institutes of consecrated life) bind themselves by public vows to observe these counsels in a life of total consecration to God and service to people through various kinds of apostolic works.

Counter-Reformation: The period of approximately 100 years following the Council of Trent (1545-63), which witnessed a reform within the Church to stimulate genuine Catholic life and to counteract effects of the Reformation.

Covenant: A bond of relationship between parties pledged to each other. God-initiated covenants in the Old Testament included those with Noah, Abraham, Moses, Levi, David. The Mosaic (Sinai) covenant made Israel God's Chosen People on terms of fidelity to true faith, true worship, and righteous conduct according to the Decalogue. The New Testament covenant, prefigured in the Old Testament, is the bond people have with God through Christ. All people are called to be parties to this perfect and everlasting covenant, which was mediated and ratified by Christ. The marriage covenant seals the closest possible relationship between a man and a woman.

Creation: The production by God of something out of nothing. The biblical account of creation is contained in the first two chapters of Genesis.

Creator: God, the supreme, self-existing Being, the absolute and infinite First Cause of all things.

Creature: Everything in the realm of being is a creature, except God.

Cremation: The reduction of a human corpse to ashes by means of fire. Cremation is not in line with Catholic tradition and practice, even though it is not opposed to any article of faith. The Congregation for the Doctrine of the Faith, under date of May 8, 1963, circulated among bishops an instruction which upheld the traditional practices of Christian burial but modified anti-cremation legislation. Cremation may be permitted for serious reasons, of a private as well as public nature, provided it does not involve any contempt of the Church or of religion, or any attempt to deny, question, or belittle the doctrine of the resurrection of the body. In a letter dated Mar. 21, 1997, and addressed to Bishop Anthony M. Pilla, president of the National Conference of Catholic Bishops, the Congregation for Divine Worship and the Discipline of the Sacraments granted "a particular permission to the diocesan bishops of the United States of America. By this, local Ordinaries (heads of dioceses) are authorized...to permit that the funeral liturgy, including where appropriate the celebration of the Eucharist, be celebrated in the presence of the cremated remains instead of the natural body." Bishop Pilla asked bishops not to use this indult until appropriate texts and ritual directives are approved by the Vatican. (*See* **Burial, Ecclesiastical**).

Crib: Also Crèche, a devotional representation of the birth of Jesus. The custom of erecting cribs is generally attributed to St. Francis of Assisi, who in 1223 obtained from Pope Honorius III permission to use a crib and figures of the Christ Child, Mary, St. Joseph, and others, to represent the mystery of the Nativity.

Crosier: The bishop's staff, symbolic of his pastoral office, responsibility and authority; used at liturgical functions.

Crypt: An underground or partly underground chamber; e.g., the lower part of a church used for worship and/or burial.

Cura Animarum: A Latin phrase, meaning care of souls, designating the pastoral ministry and responsibility of bishops and priests.

Curia: The personnel and offices through which (1) the pope administers the affairs of the universal Church, the Roman Curia (*See p. 255*), or (2) a bishop the affairs of a diocese, diocesan curia. The principal officials of a diocesan curia are the vicar general of the diocese, the chancellor, officials of the diocesan tribunal or court, examiners, consultors, auditors, notaries.

Custos: A religious superior who presides over a number of convents collectively called a custody. In some institutes of consecrated life a custos may be the deputy of a higher superior.

D

Dean: (1) A priest with supervisory responsibility over a section of a diocese known as a deanery. The post-Vatican II counterpart of a dean is an episcopal vicar. (2) The senior or ranking member of a group.

Decision: A judgment or pronouncement on a cause or suit, given by a church tribunal or official with judicial authority. A decision has the force of law for concerned parties.

Declaration: (1) An ecclesiastical document which presents an interpretation of an existing law. (2) A position paper on a specific subject, e.g., the three declarations issued by the Second Vatican Council on religious freedom, non-Christian religions, and Christian education.

Decree: An edict or ordinance issued by a pope and/or by an ecumenical council, with binding force in the whole Church; by a department of the Roman Curia, with binding force for concerned parties; by a territorial body of bishops, with binding force for persons in the area; by individual bishops, with binding force for concerned parties until revocation or the death of the bishop. The nine decrees issued by the Second Vatican Council were combinations of doctrinal and pastoral statements with executive orders for action and movement toward renewal and reform in the Church.

Dedication of a Church: The ceremony whereby a church is solemnly set apart for the worship of God. The custom of dedicating churches had an antecedent in Old Testament ceremonies for the dedication of the Temple, as in the times of Solomon and the Maccabees. The earliest extant record of the dedication of a Christian church dates from early in the fourth century, when it was done simply by the celebration of Mass. Other ceremonies developed later. A church can be dedicated by a simple blessing or a solemn consecration. The rite of consecration is generally performed by a bishop.

Deposit of the Faith: The body of saving truth, entrusted by Christ to the Apostles and handed on by them to the Church to be preserved and proclaimed. As embodied in Revelation and Tradition the term is very nearly coextensive with objective revelation, in that it embraces the whole of Christ's teaching. But the term of deposit highlights particular features of the apostolic teaching implying that this teaching is an inexhaustible store that rewards and promotes reflection and study so that new insights and deeper penetration might be made into the mystery of the divine economy of salvation. Although our understanding of this teaching can develop, it can never be augmented in its substance; the teaching is a divine trust that cannot be altered, modified, or debased. The term *depositum fidei* first entered official Catholic teaching with the Council of Trent, but its substance is well-attested in the Scriptures and the Fathers.

Despair: Abandonment of hope for salvation arising from the conviction that God will not provide the necessary means for attaining it, that following God's way of life for salvation is impossible, or that one's sins are unforgivable; a serious sin against the Holy Spirit and the theological virtues of hope and faith, involving distrust in the mercy and goodness of God and a denial of the truths that God wills the salvation of all persons and provides sufficient grace for it. Real despair is distinguished from unreasonable fear with respect to the difficulties of attaining salvation, from morbid anxiety over the demands of divine justice, and from feelings of despair.

Detraction: Revelation of true but hidden faults of a person without sufficient and justifying reason; a violation of requirements of justice and charity, involving the obligation to make restitution when this is possible without doing more harm to the good name of the offended party. In some cases, e.g., to prevent evil, secret faults may and should be disclosed.

Devil: (1) Lucifer, Satan, chief of the fallen angels who sinned and were banished from heaven. Still possessing angelic powers, he can cause such diabolical phenomena as possession and obsession, and can tempt men to sin. (2) Any fallen angel.

Devotion: (1) Religious fervor, piety; dedication. (2) The consolation experienced at times during prayer; a reverent manner of praying.

Devotions: Pious practices of members of the Church include not only participation in various acts of the liturgy but also in other acts of worship generally called popular or private devotions. Concerning these, the Second Vatican Council said in the Constitution on the Sacred Liturgy (*Sacrosanctum Concilium*, No. 13): "Popular devotions of the Christian people are warmly commended, provided they accord with the laws and norms of the Church. Such is especially the case with devotions called for by the Apostolic See. Devotions proper to the individual churches also have a special dignity. These devotions should be so drawn up that they harmonize with the liturgical seasons, accord with the sacred liturgy, are in some fashion derived from it, and lead the people to it, since the liturgy by its very nature far surpasses any of them." Devotions of a liturgical type are Exposition of the Blessed Sacrament, recitation of Evening Prayer and Night Prayer of the Liturgy of the Hours. Examples of paraliturgical devotion are a Bible Service or Vigil, and the Angelus, Rosary and Stations of the Cross, which have a strong scriptural basis.

Diocese: A particular church, a fully organized ecclesiastical jurisdiction under the pastoral direction of a bishop as local Ordinary.

Discalced: Of Latin derivation and meaning without shoes, the word is applied to religious orders or congregations whose members go barefoot or wear sandals.

Disciple: A term used sometimes in reference to the Apostles but more often to a larger number of followers (70 or 72) of Christ mentioned in Lk 10:1.

Disciplina Arcani: A Latin phrase, meaning discipline of the secret and referring to a practice of the early Church, especially during the Roman persecutions, to: (1) conceal Christian truths from those who, it was feared, would misinterpret, ridicule and profane the teachings, and persecute Christians for believing them; (2) instruct catechumens in a gradual manner, withholding the teaching of certain doctrines until the catechumens proved themselves of good faith and sufficient understanding.

Dispensation: The relaxation of a law in a particular case. Laws made for the common good sometimes work undue hardship in particular cases. In such cases, where sufficient reasons are present, dispensations may be granted by proper authorities. Bishops, religious superiors and others may dispense from certain laws; the pope can dispense from all ecclesiastical laws. No one has authority to dispense from obligations of the divine law.

Divination: Attempting to foretell future or hidden things by means of things like dreams, necromancy, spiritism, examination of entrails, astrology, augury, omens, palmistry, drawing straws, dice, cards, etc. Practices like these attribute to created things a power which belongs to God alone and are violations of the First Commandment.

Divine Praises: Fourteen praises recited or sung at Benediction of the Blessed Sacrament in reparation for sins of sacrilege, blasphemy and profanity. Some of these praises date from the end of the 18th century: *Blessed be God. / Blessed be his holy Name. / Blessed be Jesus Christ, true God and true Man. / Blessed be the Name of Jesus. / Blessed be his most Sacred Heart. / Blessed be his most Precious Blood. / Blessed be Jesus in the most holy Sacrament of the Altar. / Blessed be the Holy Spirit, the Paraclete. / Blessed be the great Mother of God, Mary most holy. / Blessed be her holy and Immaculate Conception. / Blessed be her glorious Assumption. / Blessed be the name of Mary, Virgin and Mother. / Blessed be St. Joseph, her most chaste Spouse. / Blessed be God in his Angels and in his Saints.*

Double Effect Principle: Actions sometimes have two effects closely related to each other, one good and the other bad, and a difficult moral question can arise: Is it permissible to place an action from which two such results follow? It is permissible to place the action, if: the action is good in itself and is directly productive of the good effect; the circumstances are good; the intention of the person is good; the reason for placing the action is proportionately serious to the seriousness of the indirect bad effect.

Doxology: (1) The lesser doxology, or ascription of glory to the Trinity, is the Glory be to the Father. The first part dates back to the third or fourth century, and came from the form of baptism. The concluding words, As it was in the beginning, etc., are of later origin. (2) The greater doxology, Glory to God in the highest, begins with the words of angelic praise at the birth of Christ recounted in the Infancy Narrative (Lk 2:14). It is often recited at Mass. Of early Eastern origin, it is found in the Apostolic Constitutions in a form much like the present. (3) The formula of praise at the end of the Eucharistic Prayer at Mass, sung or said by the celebrant while he holds aloft the paten containing the consecrated host in one hand and the chalice containing the consecrated wine in the other.

Dulia: A Greek term meaning the veneration or homage, different in nature and degree from that given to God, paid to the saints. It includes honoring the saints and seeking their intercession with God.

Duty: A moral obligation deriving from the binding force of law, the exigencies of one's state in life, and other sources.

E

Easter Controversy: A three-phase controversy over the time for the celebration of Easter. Some early Christians in the Near East, called Quartodecimans, favored the observance of Easter on the 14th day of Nisan, the spring month of the Hebrew calendar, whenever it occurred. Against this practice, Pope St. Victor I, in about 190, ordered a Sunday observance of the feast. The Council of Nicaea, in line with usages of the Church at Rome and Alexandria, decreed in 325 that Easter should be observed on the Sunday following the first full moon of spring. Uniformity of practice in the West was not achieved until several centuries later, when the British Isles, in delayed compliance with measures enacted by the Synod of Whitby in 664, accepted the Roman date of observance. Unrelated to the controversy is the fact that some Eastern Christians, in accordance with traditional calendar practices, celebrate Easter at a different time than the Roman and Eastern Churches.

Easter Duty: The serious obligation binding Catholics of Roman Rite, to receive the Eucharist during the Easter season (in the U.S., from the first Sunday of Lent to and including Trinity Sunday).

Easter Water: Holy water blessed with special ceremonies and distributed on the Easter Vigil; used during Easter Week for blessing the faithful and homes.

Ecclesiology: Study of the nature, constitution, members, mission, functions, etc., of the Church.

Ecology: The natural environment of the total range of creation—mineral, vegetable, animal, human—entrusted to people for respect, care and appropriate use as well as conservation and development for the good of present and future generations.

Ecstasy: An extraordinary state of mystical experience in which a person is so absorbed in God that the activity of the exterior senses is suspended.

Economy, Divine: The fulfillment of God's plan of salvation. It was fully developed in his divine mind from eternity, and fully revealed in Jesus Christ. Before the Incarnation it was known only obscurely, but after the ascension of Christ and the coming of the Holy Spirit at Pentecost, it became the substance of apostolic preaching and is preserved in its integrity for each new generation.

Ecumenism: The movement of Christians and their churches toward the unity willed by Christ. The Second Vatican Council called the movement "those activities and enterprises which, according to various needs of the Church and opportune occasions, are started and organized for the fostering of unity among Christians" (Decree on Ecumenism, No. 4). Spiritual ecumenism, i.e., mutual prayer for unity, is the heart of the movement. The movement also involves scholarly and pew-level efforts for the development of mutual understanding and better interfaith relations in general, and collaboration by the churches and their members in the social area. (*See* Index for other entries.)

Elevation: The raising of the host after consecration at Mass for adoration by the faithful. The custom was introduced in the Diocese of Paris about the close of the 12th century to offset an erroneous teaching of the time which held that transubstantiation of the bread did not take place until after the consecration of the wine in the chalice. The elevation of the chalice following the consecration of the wine was introduced in the 15th century.

Encyclical: The highest form of papal teaching document. It is normally addressed to all the bishops and/or to all the faithful.

Envy: Sadness over another's good fortune because it is considered a loss to oneself or a detraction from one's own excellence; one of the seven capital sins, a violation of the obligations of charity.

Epiclesis: An invocation of the Holy Spirit, to bless the offerings consecrated at Mass; before the consecration in the Latin Rite, after the consecration in Eastern usage.

Epikeia: A Greek word meaning reasonableness and designating a moral theory and practice, a mild interpretation of the mind of a legislator who is prudently considered not to wish positive law to bind in certain circumstances.

Episcopate: (1) The office, dignity and sacramental powers bestowed upon a bishop at his ordination. (2) The body of bishops collectively.

Equivocation: (1) The use of words, phrases, or gestures having more than one meaning in order to conceal information which a questioner has no strict right to know. It is permissible to equivocate (have a broad mental reservation) in some circumstances. (2) A lie, i.e., a statement of untruth. Lying is intrinsically wrong. A lie told in joking, evident as such, is not wrong.

Eschatology: Doctrine concerning the last things: death, judgment, heaven and hell, and the final state of perfection of the people and kingdom of God at the end of time.

Eternity: The interminable, perfect possession of life in its totality without beginning or end; an attribute of God, who has no past or future but always is. Man's existence has a beginning but no end and is, accordingly, called immortal.

Ethics: Moral philosophy, the science of the morality of human acts deriving from natural law, the natural end of man, and the powers of human reason. It includes all the spheres of human activity—personal, social, economic, political, etc. Ethics is distinct from but can be related to moral theology, whose primary principles are drawn from divine revelation.

Euthanasia: Mercy killing, the direct causing of death for the purpose of ending human suffering. Euthanasia is murder and is totally illicit, for the natural law forbids the direct taking of one's own life or that of an innocent person. The use of drugs to relieve suffering in serious cases, even when this results in a shortening of life as an indirect and secondary effect, is permissible under conditions of the double-effect principle. It is also permissible for a seriously ill person to refuse to follow—or for other responsible persons to refuse to permit—extraordinary medical procedures even though the refusal might entail shortening of life.

Evangelization: Proclamation of the Gospel, the Good News of salvation in and through Christ, among those who have not yet known or received it; and efforts for the progressive development of the life of faith among those who have already received the Gospel and all that it entails. Evangelization is the primary mission of the Church, in which all members of the Church are called to participate.

Evolution: Scientific theory concerning the development of the physical universe from unorganized matter (inorganic evolution) and, especially, the development of existing forms of vegetable, animal and human life from earlier and more primitive organisms (organic evolution). Various ideas about evolution were advanced for some centuries before scientific evidence in support of the main-line theory of organic evolution, which has several formulations, was discovered and verified in the second half of the 19th century and afterwards. This evidence—from the findings of comparative anatomy and other sciences—confirmed evolution of species and cleared the way to further investigation of questions regarding the processes of its accomplishment. While a number of such questions remain open with respect to human evolution, a point of doctrine not open to question is the immediate creation of the human soul by God. For some time, theologians regarded the theory with hostility, considering it to be in opposition to the account of creation in the early chapters of Genesis and subversive of belief in such doctrines as creation, the early state of man in grace, and the fall of man from grace. This state of affairs and the tension it generated led to considerable controversy regarding an alleged conflict between religion and science.

Gradually, however, the tension was diminished with the development of biblical studies from the latter part of the 19th century onwards, with clarification of the distinctive features of religious truth and scientific truth, and with the refinement of evolutionary concepts. So far as the Genesis account of creation is concerned, the Catholic view is that the writer(s) did not write as a scientist but as the communicator of religious truth in a manner adapted to the understanding of the people of his time. He used anthropomorphic language, the figure of days and other literary devices to state the salvation truths of creation, the fall of man from grace, and the promise of redemption. It was beyond the competency and purpose of the writer(s) to describe creation and related events in a scientific manner.

Excommunication: Severe ecclesiastical penalty imposed by the Church that excludes a member of the faithful from the wider community. Excommunication is today covered in its particulars by Canon 1331 of the new Code of Canon Law, promulgated in 1983. It exists in two contemporary forms, *ferendae sententiae* and *latae sententiae*. The former is a penalty imposed after a formal proceeding presided over by at least three judges. The latter is considered an automatic penalty for certain acts, including the procuring of a successful abortion (Canon 1398), the embrace of heresy (Canon 1364), violation of the Seal of Confession (Canon 1388), and the blasphemous and sacrilegious use of the Eucharist (Canon 1367). A person under the ban of excommunication is unable to take part in all ceremonies of public worship, especially the Eucharist, to receive or celebrate the sacraments, and to discharge any ecclesiastical offices, ministries, or functions. (See **Censures**).

Ex Opere Operantis: A term in sacramental theology meaning that the effectiveness of sacraments depends on the moral rectitude of the minister or participant. This term was applied to rites of the O.T. in contrast with those of the N.T. when it was first advanced in the thirteenth century.

Ex Opere Operato: A term in sacramental theology

meaning that sacraments are effective by means of the sacramental rite itself and not because of the worthiness of the minister or participant.

Exorcism: (1) Driving out evil spirits; a rite in which evil spirits are charged and commanded on the authority of God and with the prayer of the Church to depart from a person or to cease causing harm to a person suffering from diabolical possession or obsession. The sacramental is officially administered by a priest delegated for the purpose by the bishop of the place. Elements of the rite include the Litany of Saints; recitation of the Our Father, one or more creeds, and other prayers; specific prayers of exorcism; the reading of Gospel passages and use of the Sign of the Cross. On Jan. 26, 1999, the Congregation for Divine Worship and the Discipline of the Sacraments published a new rite of exorcism in the Roman Ritual. [*See* Special Report for additional details.] (2) Exorcisms which do not imply the conditions of either diabolical possession or obsession form part of the ceremony of baptism and are also included in formulas for various blessings; e.g., of water.

Exposition of the Blessed Sacrament: "In churches where the Eucharist is regularly reserved, it is recommended that solemn exposition of the Blessed Sacrament for an extended period of time should take place once a year, even though the period is not strictly continuous. Shorter expositions of the Eucharist (Benediction) are to be arranged in such a way that the blessing with the Eucharist is preceded by a reasonable time for readings of the word of God, songs, prayers and a period for silent prayer." So stated Vatican directives issued in 1973.

F

Faculties: Grants of jurisdiction or authority by the law of the Church or superiors (pope, bishop, religious superior) for exercise of the powers of holy orders; e.g., priests are given faculties to hear confessions, officiate at weddings; bishops are given faculties to grant dispensations, etc.

Faith: In religion, faith has several aspects. Catholic doctrine calls faith the assent of the mind to truths revealed by God, the assent being made with the help of grace and by command of the will on account of the authority and trustworthiness of God revealing. The term faith also refers to the truths that are believed (content of faith) and to the way in which a person, in response to Christ, gives witness to and expresses belief in daily life (living faith). All of these elements, and more, are included in the following statement: " 'The obedience of faith' (Rom 16:26; 1:5; 2 Cor 10:5-6) must be given to God who reveals, an obedience by which man entrusts his whole self freely to God, offering 'the full submission of intellect and will to God who reveals' (First Vatican Council, Dogmatic Constitution on the Catholic Faith, Chap. 3), and freely assenting to the truth revealed by him. If this faith is to be shown, the grace of God and the interior help of the Holy Spirit must precede and assist, moving the heart and turning it to God, opening the eyes of the mind, and giving 'joy and ease to everyone in assenting to the truth and believing it'" (Second Council of Orange, Canon 7) (Second Vatican Council, Constitution on Revelation, *Dei Verbum*, No. 5). Faith is necessary for salvation.

Faith, Rule of: The norm or standard of religious belief. The Catholic doctrine is that belief must be professed in the divinely revealed truths in the Bible and tradition as interpreted and proposed by the infallible teaching authority of the Church.

Fast, Eucharistic: Abstinence from food and drink, except water and medicine, is required for one hour before the reception of the Eucharist. Persons who are advanced in age or suffer from infirmity or illness, together with those who care for them, can receive Holy Communion even if they have not abstained from food and drink for an hour. A priest celebrating two or three Masses on the same day can eat and drink something before the second or third Mass without regard for the hour limit.

Father: A title of priests, who are regarded as spiritual fathers because they are the ordinary ministers of baptism, by which persons are born to supernatural life, and because of their pastoral service to people.

Fear: A mental state caused by the apprehension of present or future danger. Grave fear does not necessarily remove moral responsibility for an act, but may lessen it.

First Friday: A devotion consisting of the reception of Holy Communion on the first Friday of nine consecutive months in honor of the Sacred Heart of Jesus and in reparation for sin. (*See* **Sacred Heart, Promises.**)

First Saturday: A devotion tracing its origin to the apparitions of the Blessed Virgin Mary at Fátima in 1917. Those practicing the devotion go to confession and, on the first Saturday of five consecutive months, receive Holy Communion, recite five decades of the Rosary, and meditate on the mysteries for 15 minutes.

Fisherman's Ring: A signet ring (termed in Italian the *pescatorio*) engraved with the image of St. Peter fishing from a boat, and encircled with the name of the reigning pope. It is not worn by the pope. It is used to seal briefs, and is destroyed after each pope's death.

Forgiveness of Sin: Catholics believe that sins are forgiven by God through the mediation of Christ in view of the repentance of the sinner and by means of the sacrament of penance. (*See* **Penance, Contrition**).

Fortitude: Courage to face dangers or hardships for the sake of what is good; one of the four cardinal virtues and one of the seven gifts of the Holy Spirit.

Forty Hours Devotion: A Eucharistic observance consisting of solemn exposition of the Blessed Sacrament coupled with special Masses and forms of prayer, for the purposes of making reparation for sin and praying for God's blessings of grace and peace. The devotion was instituted in 1534 in Milan. St. John Neumann of Philadelphia was the first bishop in the U.S. to prescribe its observance in his diocese. For many years in this country, the observance was held annually on a rotating basis in all parishes of a diocese. Simplified and abbreviated Eucharistic observances have taken the place of the devotion in some places.

Forum: The sphere in which ecclesiastical authority or jurisdiction is exercised. (1) External: Authority is exercised in the external forum to deal with matters affecting the public welfare of the Church and its members. Those who have such authority because of their office (e.g., diocesan bishops) are called ordinaries. (2) Internal: Authority is exercised in the internal forum to deal with matters affecting the private spiritual good of individuals. The sacramental forum is the sphere in which the sacrament of penance is administered; other exercises of jurisdiction in the internal forum take place in the non-sacramental forum.

Freedom, Religious: The Second Vatican Council declared that the right to religious freedom in civil society "means that all men are to be immune from coercion on the part of individuals or of social groups and of any human power, in such wise that in matters religious no one is to be forced to act in a manner contrary to his own beliefs. Nor is anyone to be restrained from acting in accordance with his own beliefs, whether privately or publicly, whether alone or in association with others, within due limits" of requirements for the common good. The foundation of this right in civil society is the "very dignity of the human person" (Declaration on Religious Freedom, *Dignitatis Humanae*, No. 2). The conciliar statement did not deal with the subject of freedom within the Church. It noted the responsibility of the faithful "carefully to attend to the sacred and certain doctrine of the Church" (No. 14).

Freemasons: A fraternal order that originated in London in 1717 with the formation of the first Grand Lodge of Freemasons. From England, the order spread to Europe and elsewhere. Its principles and basic rituals embody a naturalistic religion, active participation in which is incompatible with Christian faith and practice. Grand Orient Freemasonry, developed in Latin countries, is atheistic, irreligious and anticlerical. In some places, Freemasonry has been regarded as subversive of the state; in Catholic quarters, it has been considered hostile to the Church and its doctrine. In the United States, Freemasonry has been widely regarded as a fraternal and philanthropic order. For serious doctrinal and pastoral reasons, Catholics were forbidden to join the Freemasons under penalty of excommunication, according to church law before 1983. Eight different popes in 17 different pronouncements, and at least six different local councils, condemned Freemasonry. The first condemnation was made by Clement XII in 1738. Eastern Orthodox and many Protestant bodies have also opposed the order. In the U.S., there was some easing of the ban against Masonic membership by Catholics in view of a letter written in 1974 by Cardinal Franjo Seper, prefect of the Congregation for the Doctrine of the Faith. The letter was interpreted to mean that Catholics might join Masonic lodges which were not anti-Catholic. This was called erroneous in a declaration issued by the Doctrinal Congregation Feb. 17, 1981. The prohibition against Masonic membership was restated in a declaration issued by the Doctrinal Congregation Nov. 26, 1983, with the approval of Pope John Paul II, as follows. "The Church's negative position on Masonic associations remains unaltered, since their principles have always been regarded as irreconcilable with the Church's doctrine. Hence, joining them remains prohibited by the Church. Catholics enrolled in Masonic associations are involved in serious sin and may not approach Holy Communion. Local ecclesiastical authorities do not have the faculty to pronounce a judgment on the nature of Masonic associations which might include a diminution of the above-mentioned judgment." This latest declaration, like the revised Code of Canon Law, does not include a penalty of excommunication for Catholics who join the Masons. Local bishops are not authorized to grant dispensations from the prohibition. The foregoing strictures against Masonic membership by Catholics were reiterated in a report by the Committee for Pastoral Research and Practice, National Conference of Catholic Bishops, released through Catholic News Service June 7, 1985.

Free Will: The faculty or capability of making a reasonable choice among several alternatives. Freedom of will underlies the possibility and fact of moral responsibility.

Friar: Term applied to members of mendicant orders to distinguish them from members of monastic orders. (*See* **Mendicants**.)

Fruits of the Holy Spirit: Charity, joy, peace, patience, kindness, goodness, generosity, gentleness, faithfulness, modesty, self-control, chastity.

Fruits of the Mass: The spiritual and temporal blessings that result from the celebration of the Holy Sacrifice of the Mass. The general fruits are shared by all the faithful, living and departed, while the special fruits are applied to the priest who celebrates it, to those for whose intention it is offered, and to all those who participate in its celebration.

Fundamental Option: The orientation of one's life either to God by obedience or against Him through disobedience. Catholic Tradition acknowledges that one free and deliberate act with knowledge renders one at odds with God. A prevalent and vague moral theory today asserts that one act cannot change one's option to God—no matter how grave—unless the action comes from the person's "center." Pope John Paul II cautioned against this ambiguous position in the encyclical *Veritatis Splendor* (1993).

G

Gehenna: Greek form of a Jewish name, Gehinnom, for a valley near Jerusalem, the site of Moloch worship; used as a synonym for hell.

Genuflection: Bending of the knee, a natural sign of adoration or reverence, as when persons genuflect with the right knee in passing before the tabernacle to acknowledge the Eucharistic presence of Christ.

Gethsemani: A Hebrew word meaning oil press, designating the place on the Mount of Olives where Christ prayed and suffered in agony the night before he died.

Gifts of the Holy Spirit: Supernatural habits disposing a person to respond promptly to the inspiration of grace; promised by Christ and communicated through the Holy Spirit, especially in the sacrament of confirmation. They are: wisdom, understanding, counsel, knowledge, fortitude, piety, and fear of the Lord.

Glorified Body: The definitive state of humanity in eternity. The risen Christ calls humanity to the glory of his resurrection; this is a theological premise that presupposes that, like Christ, all of his brothers and sisters will be transformed physically.

Gluttony: An unreasonable appetite for food and drink; one of the seven capital sins.

God: The infinitely perfect Supreme Being, uncaused and absolutely self-sufficient, eternal, the Creator and final end of all things. The one God subsists in three equal Persons, the Father and the Son and the Holy Spirit. God, although transcendent and distinct from the universe, is present and active in the world in realization of his plan for the salvation of human beings, principally through Revelation, the operations of the Holy Spirit, the life and ministry of Christ, and the continuation of Christ's ministry in the Church. The existence of God is an article of faith, clearly communicated in divine Revelation. Even without this Revelation, however, the Church teaches, in a declaration by the First Vatican Council, that human beings can acquire certain knowledge of the existence of God and some of his attributes. This can be done on the bases of principles of reason and reflection on human experience. Non-revealed arguments or demonstrations for the existence of God have been developed from the principle of causality; the contingency of human beings and the universe; the existence of design, change and movement in the universe; human awareness of moral responsibility; widespread human testimony to the existence of God.

Goods of Marriage: Three blessings—children, faithful companionship, and permanence—that were first enumerated by St. Augustine in a work on marriage.

Grace: A free gift of God to persons (and angels), grace is a created sharing or participation in the life of God. It is given to persons through the merits of Christ and is communicated by the Holy Spirit. It is necessary for salvation. The principal means of grace are the sacraments (especially the Eucharist), prayer and good works. (1) **Sanctifying or habitual grace** makes persons holy and pleasing to God, adopted children of God, members of Christ, temples of the Holy Spirit, heirs of heaven capable of supernaturally meritorious acts. With grace, God gives persons the supernatural virtues and gifts of the Holy Spirit. The sacraments of baptism and penance were instituted to give grace to those who do not have it; the other sacraments, to increase it in those already in the state of grace. The means for growth in holiness, or the increase of grace, are prayer, the sacraments, and good works. Sanctifying grace is lost by the commission of serious sin. Each sacrament confers sanctifying grace for the special purpose of the sacrament; in this context, grace is called sacramental grace. (2) **Actual grace** is a supernatural help of God which enlightens and strengthens a person to do good and to avoid evil. It is not a permanent quality, like sanctifying grace. It is necessary for the performance of supernatural acts. It can be resisted and refused. Persons in the state of serious sin are given actual grace to lead them to repentance.

Grace at Meals: Prayers said before meals, asking a blessing of God, and after meals, giving thanks to God. In addition to traditional prayers for these purposes, many variations suitable for different occasions are possible, at personal option.

Guilt: The condition of an individual who has committed some moral wrong and is liable to receive punishment.

H

Habit: (1) A disposition to do things easily, given with grace (and therefore supernatural) and/or acquired by repetition of similar acts. (2) The garb worn by Religious.

Hagiography: Writings or documents about saints and other holy persons.

Hail Mary: A prayer addressed to the Blessed Virgin Mary; also called the *Ave Maria* (Latin equivalent of Hail Mary) and the Angelic Salutation. In three parts, it consists of the words addressed to Mary by the Archangel Gabriel on the occasion of the Annunciation, in the Infancy Narrative (*Hail Mary, full of grace, the Lord is with you, blessed are you among women*; Lk 1:28); the words addressed to Mary by her cousin Elizabeth on the occasion of the Visitation (*Blessed is the fruit of your womb*; Lk 1-42); a concluding petition (*Holy Mary, Mother of God, pray for us sinners now and at the hour of our death. Amen.*). The first two salutations were joined in Eastern rite formulas by the sixth century, and were similarly used at Rome in the seventh century. Insertion of the name of Jesus at the conclusion of the salutations was probably made by Urban IV about 1262. The present form of the petition was incorporated into the breviary in 1514.

Heaven: The state of those who, having achieved salvation, are in glory with God and enjoy the beatific vision. The phrase, kingdom of heaven, refers to the order or kingdom of God, grace, salvation.

Hell: The state of persons who die in mortal sin, in a condition of self-alienation from God which will last forever.

Heresy: The obstinate post-baptismal denial or doubt by a Catholic of any truth which must be believed as a matter of divine and Catholic faith (Canon 751, of the Code of Canon Law). Formal heresy involves deliberate resistance to the authority of God who communicates revelation through Scripture and tradition and the teaching authority of the Church. Heretics automatically incur the penalty of excommunication (Canon 1364 of the Code of Canon Law). Heresies have been significant not only as disruptions of unity of faith but also as occasions for the clarification and development of doctrine. Heresies from the beginning of the Church to the 13th century are described in Dates and Events in Church History.

Hermeneutics: *See under the section* **Interpretation of the Bible, pp. 103-105.**

Hermit: *See* **Anchorite**.

Heroic Act of Charity: The completely unselfish offering to God of one's good works and merits for the benefit of the souls in purgatory rather than for oneself. Thus a person may offer to God for the souls in purgatory all the good works he performs during life, all the indulgences he gains, and all the prayers and indulgences that will be offered for him after his death. The act is revocable at will, and is not a vow. Its actual ratification depends on the will of God.

Heroic Virtue: The exemplary practice of the four cardinal virtues and three theological virtues; such virtue is sought in persons considered for sainthood.

Heterodoxy: False doctrine teaching or belief; a departure from truth.

Hierarchy: The hierarchy of order who carry out the sacramental, teaching, and pastoral ministry of the Church; the hierarchy consists of the pope, bishops, priests, and deacons; the pope and the bishops give pastoral governance to the faithful.

Holy Father: A title used for the pope; it is a shortened translation of the Latin title *Beatissimus Pater*, "Most Blessed Father" and refers to his position as the spiritual father of all the Christian faithful.

Holy See: (1) The diocese of the pope, Rome. (2) The pope himself and/or the various officials and bodies of the Church's central administration at Vatican

City— the Roman Curia—which act in the name and by authority of the pope.

Holy Spirit: God the Holy Spirit, third Person of the Holy Trinity, who proceeds from the Father and the Son and with whom he is equal in every respect; inspirer of the prophets and writers of sacred Scripture; promised by Christ to the Apostles as their advocate and strengthener; appeared in the form of a dove at the baptism of Christ and as tongues of fire at his descent upon the Apostles; soul of the Church and guarantor, by his abiding presence and action, of truth in doctrine; communicator of grace to human beings, for which reason he is called the sanctifier.

Holy Water: Water blessed by the Church and used as a sacramental, a practice which originated in apostolic times.

Holy Year: A year during which the pope grants the plenary Jubilee Indulgence to the faithful who fulfill certain conditions. For those who make a pilgrimage to Rome during the year, the conditions are reception of the sacraments of penance and the Eucharist, visits and prayer for the intention of the pope in the basilicas of St. Peter, St. John Lateran, St. Paul and St. Mary Major. For those who do not make a pilgrimage to Rome, the conditions are reception of the sacraments and prayer for the pope during a visit or community celebration in a church designated by the bishop of the locality. Pope Boniface VIII formally proclaimed the first Holy Year on Feb. 22, 1300, and the first three Holy Years were observed in 1300, 1350 and 1390. Subsequent ones were celebrated at 25-year intervals except in 1800 and 1850 when, respectively, the French invasion of Italy and political turmoil made observance impossible. Pope Paul II (1464-1471) set the 25-year timetable. In 1500, Pope Alexander VI prescribed the start and finish ceremonies—the opening and closing of the Holy Doors in the major basilicas on successive Christmas Eves. All but a few of the earlier Holy Years were classified as ordinary. Several—like those of 1933 and 1983-84 to commemorate the 1900th and 1950th anniversaries of the death and resurrection of Christ—were in the extraordinary category. Pope John Paul designated Jubilee Year 2000 to be a Holy Year ending the second and beginning the third millennium of Christianity.

Homosexuality: The condition of a person whose sexual orientation is toward persons of the same rather than the opposite sex. The condition is not sinful in itself. Homosexual acts are seriously sinful in themselves; subjective responsibility for such acts, however, may be conditioned and diminished by compulsion and related factors.

Hope: The theological virtue by which a person firmly trusts in God for the means and attainment salvation. The virtue was the subject of the encyclical *Spe Salvi* by Pope Benedict XVI in 2007.

Hosanna: A Hebrew word, meaning *O Lord, save, we pray.*

Host, The Sacred: The bread under whose appearances Christ is and remains present in a unique manner after the consecration which takes place during Mass. (*See* **Transubstantiation**.)

Human Dignity: The inherent worth of all human persons as they are made in God's image and likeness and they alone—of all God's creatures on earth— have an immortal soul.

Humanism: A world view centered on man. Types of humanism which exclude the supernatural are related to secularism.

Humility: A virtue which induces a person to evaluate himself or herself at his or her true worth, to recognize his or her dependence on God, and to give glory to God for the good he or she has and can do.

Hyperdulia: The special veneration accorded the Blessed Virgin Mary because of her unique role in the mystery of Redemption, her exceptional gifts of grace from God, and her pre-eminence among the saints. Hyperdulia is not adoration; only God is adored.

Hypostatic Union: The union of the human and divine natures in the one divine Person of Christ.

I

Icons: Byzantine-style paintings or representations of Christ, the Blessed Virgin and other saints, venerated in the Eastern Churches where they take the place of statues.

Idolatry: Worship of any but the true God; a violation of the First Commandment.

IHS: In Greek, the first three letters of the name of Jesus—Iota, Eta, Sigma.

Immaculate Conception: The doctrine that affirms that "the Blessed Virgin Mary was preserved, in the first instant of her conception, by a singular grace and privilege of God omnipotent and because of the merits of Jesus Christ the Savior of the human race, free from all stain of Original Sin," as stated by Pope Pius IX in his declaration of the dogma, Dec. 8, 1854. Thus, Mary was conceived in the state of perfect justice, free from Original Sin and its consequences, in virtue of the redemption achieved by Christ on the cross.

Immortality: The survival and continuing existence of the human soul after death.

Imprimatur: *See* **Censorship of Books**.

Impurity: Unlawful indulgence in sexual pleasure. (*See* **Chastity**.)

Imputability: A canonical term for the moral responsibility of a person for an act that he or she has performed.

Incardination: The affiliation of a priest to his diocese. Every secular priest must belong to a certain diocese. Similarly, every priest of a religious community must belong to some jurisdiction of his community; this affiliation, however, is not called incardination.

Incarnation: (1) The coming-into-flesh or taking of human nature by the Second Person of the Trinity. He became human as the Son of Mary, being miraculously conceived by the power of the Holy Spirit, without ceasing to be divine. His divine Person hypostatically unites his divine and human natures. (2) The supernatural mystery coextensive with Christ from the moment of his human conception and continuing through his life on earth; his sufferings and death; his resurrection from the dead and ascension to glory with the Father; his sending, with the Father, of the Holy Spirit upon the Apostles and the Church; and his unending mediation with the Father for the salvation of human beings.

Incense: A granulated substance which, when burnt, emits an aromatic smoke. It symbolizes the zeal with which the faithful should be consumed, the good odor of Christian virtue, the ascent of prayer to God. An incense boat is a small vessel used to hold incense which is to be placed in the censer.

Incest: Sexual intercourse with relatives by blood or marriage; a sin of impurity and also a grave violation of the natural reverence due to relatives. Other sins of impurity desire, etc., concerning relatives have the nature of incest.

Inculturation: The correct and entirely appropriate adaptation of the Catholic liturgy and institutions to the culture, language, and customs of an indigenous or local people among whom the Gospel is first proclaimed. Pope John Paul II, Feb. 15, 1982, at a meeting in Lagos with the bishops of Nigeria proclaimed: "An important aspect of your own evangelizing role is the whole dimension of the inculturation of the Gospel into the lives of your people. The Church truly respects the culture of each people. In offering the Gospel message, the Church does not intend to destroy or to abolish what is good and beautiful. In fact, she recognizes many cultural values and, through the power of the Gospel, purifies and takes into Christian worship certain elements of a people's customs."

Index of Prohibited Books: A list of books which Catholics were formerly forbidden to read, possess or sell, under penalty of excommunication. The books were banned by the Holy See after publication because their treatment of matters of faith and morals and related subjects were judged to be erroneous or serious occasions of doctrinal error. Some books were listed in the Index by name; others were covered under general norms. The Congregation for the Doctrine of the Faith declared June 14, 1966, that the Index and its related penalties of excommunication no longer had the force of law in the Church. Persons are still obliged, however, to take normal precautions against occasions of doctrinal error.

Indifferentism: A theory that any one religion is as true and good—or false—as any other religion, and that it makes no difference, objectively, what religion one professes, if any. The theory is completely subjective, finding its justification entirely in personal choice without reference to or respect for objective validity. It is also self-contradictory, since it regards as equally acceptable—or unacceptable—the beliefs of all religions, which in fact are not only not all the same but are in some cases opposed to each other.

Indulgence: According to The Doctrine and Practice of Indulgences, an apostolic constitution issued by Paul VI Jan. 1, 1967, an indulgence is the remission before God of the temporal punishment due for sins already forgiven as far as their guilt is concerned, which a follower of Christ—with the proper dispositions and under certain determined conditions—acquires through the intervention of the Church. An indulgence is partial or plenary, depending on whether it does away with either part or all of the temporal punishment due for sin. Both types of indulgences can always be applied to the dead by way of suffrage; the actual disposition of indulgences applied to the dead rests with God. Only one plenary indulgence can be gained in a single day. The Apostolic Penitentiary issued a decree Dec. 14, 1985, granting diocesan bishops the right to impart—three times a year on solemn feasts of their choice—the papal blessing with a plenary indulgence to those who cannot be physically present but who follow the sacred rites at which the blessing is imparted by radio or television transmission. In July, 1986, publication was announced of a new and simplified *Enchiridion Indulgentiarum*, in accord with provisions of the revised Code of Canon Law. A revised manual was issued by the Holy See on Sept. 17, 2000.

Indult: A favor or privilege granted by competent ecclesiastical authority, giving permission to do something not allowed by the common law of the Church.

Infallibility: 1) The inability of the Church to err in its teaching, in that she preserves and teaches the deposit of truth as revealed by Christ; 2) The inability of the Roman Pontiff to err when he teaches *ex cathedra* in matters of faith or morals, and indicates that the doctrine is to be believed by all the faithful; and 3) The inability of the college of bishops to err when speaking in union with the pope in matters of faith and morals, agreeing that a doctrine must be held by the universal Church, and the doctrine is promulgated by the Pontiff.

Infused Virtues: The theological virtues of faith, hope, and charity; principles or capabilities of supernatural action, they are given with sanctifying grace by God rather than acquired by repeated acts of a person. They can be increased by practice; they are lost by contrary acts. Natural-acquired moral virtues, like the cardinal virtues of prudence, justice, temperance, and fortitude, can be considered infused in a person whose state of grace gives them supernatural orientation.

Inquisition: A tribunal for dealing with heretics, authorized by Gregory IX in 1231 to search them out, hear and judge them, sentence them to various forms of punishment, and in some cases to hand them over to civil authorities for punishment. The Inquisition was a creature of its time when crimes against faith, which threatened the good of the Christian community, were regarded also as crimes against the state, and when heretical doctrines of such extremists as the Cathari and Albigensians threatened the very fabric of society. The institution, which was responsible for many excesses, was most active in the second half of the 13th century.

Inquisition, Spanish: An institution peculiar to Spain and the colonies in Spanish America. In 1478, at the urging of King Ferdinand, Pope Sixtus IV approved the establishment of the Inquisition for trying charges of heresy brought against Jewish (*Marranos*) and Moorish (*Moriscos*) converts. It acquired jurisdiction over other cases as well, however, and fell into disrepute because of irregularities in its functions, cruelty in its sentences, and the manner in which it served the interests of the Spanish crown more than the accused persons and the good of the Church. Protests by the Holy See failed to curb excesses of the Inquisition, which lingered in Spanish history until early in the 19th century.

I N R I: The first letters of words in the Latin inscription atop the cross on which Christ was crucified: *(I)esus (N)azaraenus, (R)ex (I)udaeorum*—Jesus of Nazareth, King of the Jews.

Insemination, Artificial: The implanting of human semen by some means other than consummation of natural marital intercourse. In view of the principle that procreation should result only from marital intercourse, donor insemination is not permissible.

In Sin: The condition of a person called spiritually dead because he or she does not possess sanctifying grace, the principle of supernatural life, action and merit. Such grace can be regained through repentance.

Instruction: A document containing doctrinal explanations, directive norms, rules, recommendations, admonitions, issued by the pope, a department of the Roman Curia or other competent authority in the Church. To the extent that they so prescribe, instructions have the force of law.

Intercommunion, Eucharistic Sharing: The common celebration and reception of the Eucharist by members of different Christian churches; a pivotal issue in ecumenical theory and practice. Catholic participation and intercommunion in the Eucharistic liturgy of another church without a valid priesthood and with a variant Eucharistic belief is out of order. Under certain conditions, other Christians may receive the Eucharist in the Catholic Church. (*See* additional **Intercommunion** entry, p. 193). Intercommunion is acceptable to some Protestant churches and unacceptable to others.

Interdict: A censure imposed on persons for certain violations of church law. Interdicted persons may not take part in certain liturgical services, administer or receive certain sacraments.

Intinction: A method of administering Holy Communion under the dual appearances of bread and wine, in which the consecrated host is dipped in the consecrated wine before being given to the communicant. The administering of Holy Communion in this manner, which has been traditional in Eastern-Rite liturgies, was authorized in the Roman Rite for various occasions by the Constitution on the Sacred Liturgy promulgated by the Second Vatican Council.

Irenicism: Peace-seeking, conciliation, as opposed to polemics; an important element in ecumenism, provided it furthers pursuit of the Christian unity willed by Christ without degenerating into a peace-at-any-price disregard for religious truth.

Irregularity: A permanent impediment to the lawful reception or exercise of holy orders. The Church instituted irregularities—which include apostasy, heresy, homicide, attempted suicide—out of reverence for the dignity of the sacraments.

J

Jehovah: The English equivalent of the Hebrew *Adonai* ("my Lord") used out of fear and reverence for the Holy Name of Yahweh. *Jehovah* uses the consonants YHWH and the vowels of *Adonai* (a, o, a). Scholars today maintain that *Jehovah* is a false derivation.

Jesus: The name of Jesus, meaning "God saves," expressing the identity and mission of the second Person of the Trinity become man; derived from the Aramaic and Hebrew Yeshua and Joshua, meaning Yahweh is salvation.

Jesus Prayer: A prayer of Eastern origin, dating back to the fifth century: *"Lord Jesus Christ, Son of God, have mercy on me (a sinner)."*

Judgment: (1) **Last or final judgment**: Final judgment by Christ, at the end of the world and the general resurrection. (2) **Particular judgment**: The judgment that takes place immediately after a person's death, followed by entrance into heaven, hell or purgatory.

Jurisdiction: Right, power, authority to rule. Jurisdiction in the Church is of divine institution; has pastoral service for its purpose; includes legislative, judicial and executive authority; can be exercised only by persons with the power of orders. (1) Ordinary jurisdiction is attached to ecclesiastical offices by law; the officeholders, called Ordinaries, have authority over those who are subject to them. (2) Delegated jurisdiction is that which is granted to persons rather than attached to offices. Its extent depends on the terms of the delegation.

Justice: One of the four cardinal virtues by which a person gives to others what is due to them as a matter of right. (*See* **Cardinal Virtues**.)

Justification: The act by which God makes a person just, and the consequent change in the spiritual status of a person, from sin to grace; the remission of sin and the infusion of sanctifying grace through the merits of Christ and the action of the Holy Spirit.

K

Kenosis: A term from the Greek for "emptying" that denotes Christ's emptying of Himself in his free renunciation of his right to divine status, by reason of the Incarnation, particularly as celebrated in the kenotic hymn (Phil 2:6-11), where it is said that Christ "emptied himself," taking the form of a slave, born in the likeness of man totally integrated with his divinity.

Kerygma: Proclaiming the word of God, in the manner of the Apostles, as here and now effective for salvation. This method of preaching or instruction, centered on Christ and geared to the facts and themes of salvation history, is designed to dispose people to faith in Christ and/or to intensify the experience and practice of that faith in those who have it.

Keys, Power of the: Spiritual authority and jurisdiction in the Church, symbolized by the keys of the kingdom of heaven. Christ promised the keys to St. Peter, as head-to-be of the Church (Mt 16:19), and commissioned him with full pastoral responsibility to feed his lambs and sheep (Jn 21:15-17), The pope, as the successor of St. Peter, has this power in a primary and supreme manner. The bishops of the Church also have the power, in union with and subordinate to the pope. Priests share in it through holy orders and the delegation of authority. Examples of the application of the Power of the Keys are the exercise of teaching and pastoral authority by the pope and bishops, the absolving of sins in the sacrament of penance, the granting of indulgences, the imposing of spiritual penalties on persons who commit certain serious sins.

Kingdom of God: God's sovereign lordship or rule over salvation history, leading to the eschatological goal of eternal life with God.

Koinonia: A term from the Greek word for "community, fellowship, or association" that was used by St. Luke for the fellowship of believers who worshipped together and held all their possessions in common (Acts 2:42-47); it is also used of fellowship with God (1 Jn 1:3, 6), with the Son (1 Cor 1:9), and with the Holy Spirit (2 Cor 13:13; Phil 2:1). St. Paul used *koinonia* to denote the intimate union of the believer with Christ and the community that exists among all the faithful themselves (Rom 15:26; 2 Cor 6:14).

L

Laicization: The process by which a man ordained to holy orders is relieved of the obligations of orders and the ministry and is returned to the status of a lay person.

Languages of the Church: The languages in which the Church's liturgy is celebrated. These include Ge'ez, Syriac, Greek, Arabic, and Old Slavonic in the Eastern Churches. In the West, there is, of course, Latin and the various vernaculars. The Eastern Rites have always had the vernacular. The first language in church use, for divine worship and the conduct of ecclesiastical affairs, was Aramaic, the language of the first Christians in and around Jerusalem. As the Church spread westward, Greek was adopted and prevailed until the third century when it was supplanted by Latin for official use in the West. In the Western Church, Latin prevailed as the general official language until the promulgation on Dec. 4, 1963, of the Constitution on the Sacred Liturgy (*Sacrosanctum Concilium*) by the second session of the Second Vatican Council. Since that time, vernacular languages have come into use in the Mass, administration of the sacraments, and the Liturgy of the Hours. Latin, however, remains the official language for documents of the Holy See, administrative and procedural matters.

Latria: Greek-rooted Latin term that refers to that form of praise due to God alone.

Law: An ordinance or rule governing the activity of things. (1) **Natural law**: Moral norms corresponding to man's nature by which he orders his conduct toward God, neighbor, society and himself. This law, which is rooted in human nature, is of divine origin, can be known by the use of reason, and binds all persons having the use of reason. The Ten Commandments are declarations and amplifications of natural law. The primary precepts of natural law, to do good and to avoid evil, are universally recognized, despite differences with respect to understanding and application resulting from different philosophies of good and evil. (2) **Divine positive law**: That which has been revealed by God. Among its essentials are the twin precepts of love of God and love of neighbor, and the Ten Commandments. (3) **Ecclesiastical law**: That which is established by the Church for the spiritual welfare of the faithful and the orderly conduct of ecclesiastical affairs. (*See* **Canon Law**, pp. 125-127.) (4) **Civil law**: That which is established by a socio-political community for the common good.

Liberalism: A multiphased trend of thought and movement favoring liberty, independence and progress in moral, intellectual, religious, social, economic and political life. Traceable to the Renaissance, it developed through the Enlightenment, the rationalism of the 19th century, and modernist- and existentialist-related theories of the 20th century. Evaluations of various kinds of liberalism depend on the validity of their underlying principles. Extremist positions—regarding subjectivism, libertarianism, naturalist denials of the supernatural, and the alienation of individuals and society from God and the Church—were condemned by Gregory XVI in the 1830s, Pius IX in 1864, Leo XIII in 1899, and St. Pius X in 1907. There is, however, nothing objectionable about forms of liberalism patterned according to sound principles of Christian doctrine.

Liberation Theology: Deals with the relevance of Christian faith and salvation—and, therefore, of the mission of the Church—to efforts for the promotion of human rights, social justice and human development. It originated in the religious, social, political and eco-nomic environment of Latin America, with its contemporary need for a theory and corresponding action by the Church, in the pattern of its overall mission, for human rights and integral personal and social development. Some versions of liberation theology are at variance with the body of church teaching because of their ideological concept of Christ as liberator, and also because they play down the primary spiritual nature and mission of the Church. Instructions from the Congregation for the Doctrine of the Faith—"On Certain Aspects of the Theology of Liberation" (Sept. 3, 1984) and "On Christian Freedom and Liberation" (Apr. 5, 1986)—contain warnings against translating sociology into theology and advocating violence in social activism.

Life in Outer Space: Whether rational life exists on other bodies in the universe besides earth, is a question for scientific investigation to settle. The possibility can be granted, without prejudice to the body of revealed truth.

Limbo: The limbo of the fathers was the state of rest and natural happiness after death enjoyed by the just of pre-Christian times until they were admitted to heaven following the Ascension of Christ.

Litany: A prayer in the form of responsive petition; e.g., St. Joseph, pray for us, etc. Examples are the litanies of Loreto (Litany of the Blessed Mother), the Holy Name, All Saints, the Sacred Heart, the Precious Blood, St. Joseph, Litany for the Dying.

Logos: A Greek term for "word, speech, or reason." It is most commonly identified with the title given to Jesus in John's Gospel, though not exclusive to that Gospel; In the NT, however, the term reflects more the influence of Hellenistic philosophy: St. Paul uses logos as interchangeable with *sophia*, wisdom (1 Cor 1:24). The *Logos* is the Wisdom of God made manifest in the Son. As a name for the Second Person of the Trinity, the Incarnate Word, the term receives new meaning in the light of the life, death, and resurrection of Jesus Christ.

Loreto, House of: A Marian shrine in Loreto, Italy, consisting of the home of the Holy Family which, according to an old tradition, was transported in a miraculous manner from Nazareth to Dalmatia and finally to Loreto between 1291 and 1294. Investigations conducted shortly after the appearance of the structure in Loreto revealed that its dimensions matched those of the house of the Holy Family missing from its place of enshrinement in a basilica at Nazareth. Among the many popes who regarded it with high honor was John XXIII, who went there on pilgrimage Oct. 4, 1962. The house of the Holy Family is enshrined in the Basilica of Our Lady.

Love: A devotion to a person or object that has been categorized by Greek philosophy into four types: *storge* (one loves persons and things close to him); *philia* (the love of friends); *eros* (sexual love and that of a spiritual nature); *agape* (a self-giving to one in need). Christian charity is love, but not all love is true charity. The virtue was the subject of the encyclical *Deus Caritas Est* by Pope Benedict XVI in 2005.

Lust: A disorderly desire for sexual pleasure; one of the seven capital sins.

M

Magi: In the Infancy Narrative of St. Matthew's Gospel (2:1-12), three wise men from the East whose visit and homage to the Child Jesus at Bethlehem indicated Christ's manifestation of himself to non-Jewish people. The narrative teaches the universality of salvation. The traditional names of the Magi are Caspar, Melchior and Balthasar.

Magisterium: The Church's teaching authority, instituted by Christ and guided by the Holy Spirit, which seeks to safeguard and explain the truths of the faith. The Magisterium is exercised in two ways. The extraordinary Magisterium is exercised when the pope and ecumenical councils infallibly define a truth of faith or morals that is necessary for one's salvation and that has been constantly taught and held by the Church. Ordinary Magisterium is exercised when the Church infallibly defines truths of the Faith as taught universally and without dissent; which must be taught or the Magisterium would be failing in its duty; is connected with a grave matter of faith or morals; and which is taught authoritatively. Not everything taught by the Magisterium is done so infallibly; however, the exercise of the Magisterium is faithful to Christ and what He taught.

Magnificat: The canticle or hymn of the Virgin Mary on the occasion of her visitation to her cousin Elizabeth (Lk 1:46-55). It is an expression of praise, thanksgiving and acknowledgment of the great blessings given by God to Mary, the Mother of the Second Person of the Blessed Trinity made Man. The *Magnificat* is recited in the Liturgy of the Hours as part of the Evening Prayer.

Martyr: A Greek word, meaning witness, denoting one who voluntarily suffered death for the faith or some Christian virtue.

Martyrology: A catalogue of martyrs and other saints, arranged according to the calendar. The *Roman Martyrology* contains the official list of saints venerated by the Church. Additions to the list are made in beatification and canonization decrees of the Congregation for the Causes of Saints.

Mass for the People: On Sundays and certain feasts throughout the year pastors are required to offer Mass for the faithful entrusted to their care. If they cannot offer the Mass on these days, they must do so at a later date or provide that another priest offer the Mass.

Materialism: Theory that holds that matter is the only reality, and everything in existence is merely a manifestation of matter; there is no such thing as spirit, and the supernatural does not exist. Materialism is incompatible with Christian doctrine.

Meditation: Mental, as distinguished from vocal, prayer, in which thought, affections, and resolutions of the will predominate. There is a meditative element to all forms of prayer, which always involves the raising of the heart and mind to God.

Mendicants: A term derived from Latin and meaning beggars, applied to members of religious orders without property rights; the members, accordingly, worked or begged for their support. The original mendicants were Franciscans and Dominicans in the early 13th century; later, the Carmelites, Augustinians, Servites and others were given the mendicant title and privileges, with respect to exemption from episcopal jurisdiction and wide faculties for preaching and administering the sacrament of penance. The practice of begging is limited at the present time, although it is still allowed with the permission of competent superiors and bishops. Mendicants are supported by free will offerings and income received for spiritual services and other work.

Mercy, Divine: The love and goodness of God, manifested particularly in a time of need.

Mercy, Works of: Works of corporal or spiritual assistance, motivated by love of God and neighbor, to persons in need. (1) **Corporal works**: feeding the hungry, giving drink to the thirsty, clothing the naked, visiting the imprisoned, sheltering the homeless, visiting the sick, burying the dead. (2) **Spiritual works**: counseling the doubtful, instructing the ignorant, admonishing sinners, comforting the afflicted, forgiving offenses, bearing wrongs patiently, praying for the living and the dead.

Merit: In religion, the right to a supernatural reward for good works freely done for a supernatural motive by a person in the state of and with the assistance of grace. The right to such reward is from God, who binds himself to give it. Accordingly, good works, as described above, are meritorious for salvation.

Metanoia: A term from the Greek *metanoein* ("to change one's mind, repent, be converted") that is used in the NT for conversion. It entails the repentance of sin and the subsequent turning toward the Lord. *Metanoia* is fundamental to the Christian life and is necessary for spiritual growth.

Metaphysics: The branch of philosophy (from the Greek *meta* – after + *physika* – physics) dealing with first things, including the nature of being (ontology), the origin and structure of the world (cosmology), and the study of the reality and attributes of God (natural theology). Metaphysics has long been examined by Catholic philosophers, most especially in the writings of St. Augustine and St. Thomas Aquinas.

Millennium: A thousand-year reign of Christ and the just upon earth before the end of the world. This belief of the Millenarians, Chiliasts, and some sects of modern times is based on an erroneous interpretation of Rv 20.

Miracles: Observable events or effects in the physical or moral order of things, with reference to salvation, which cannot be explained by the ordinary operation of laws of nature and which, therefore, are attributed to the direct action of God. They make known, in an unusual way, the concern and intervention of God in human affairs for the salvation of men.

Mission: (1) Strictly, it means being sent to perform a certain work, such as the mission of Christ to redeem mankind, the mission of the Apostles and the Church and its members to perpetuate the prophetic, priestly and royal mission of Christ. (2) A place where: the Gospel has not been proclaimed; the Church has not been firmly established; the Church, although established, is weak. (3) An ecclesiastical territory with the simplest kind of canonical organization, under the jurisdiction of the Congregation for the Evangelization of Peoples. (4) A church or chapel without a resident priest. (5) A special course of sermons and spiritual exercises conducted in parishes for the purpose of renewing and deepening the spiritual life of the faithful and for the conversion of lapsed Catholics.

Modernism: The "synthesis of all heresies," which appeared near the beginning of the 20th century. It undermines the objective validity of religious beliefs and practices which, it contends, are products of the subconscious developed by mankind under the stimulus of a religious sense. It holds that the existence of a personal God cannot be demonstrated, the Bible is not inspired, Christ is not divine, nor did he establish the

Church or institute the sacraments. A special danger lies in modernism, which is still influential, because it uses Catholic terms with perverted meanings. St. Pius X condemned 65 propositions of modernism in 1907 in the decree *Lamentabili* and issued the encyclical *Pascendi* to explain and analyze its errors.

Monastery: The dwelling place, as well as the community thereof, of monks belonging to the Benedictine and Benedictine-related orders like the Cistercians and Carthusians; also, the Augustinians and Canons Regular. Distinctive of monasteries are: their separation from the world; the enclosure or cloister; the permanence or stability of attachment characteristic of their members; autonomous government in accordance with a monastic rule, like that of St. Benedict in the West or of St. Basil in the East; the special dedication of its members to the community celebration of the liturgy as well as to work that is suitable to the surrounding area and the needs of its people. Monastic superiors of men have such titles as abbot and prior; of women, abbess and prioress. In most essentials, an abbey is the same as a monastery.

Monk: A member of a monastic order—e.g., the Benedictines, the Benedictine-related Cistercians and Carthusians, and the Basilians, who bind themselves by religious profession to stable attachment to a monastery, the contemplative life and the work of their community. In popular use, the title is wrongly applied to many men religious who really are not monks.

Monotheism: Belief in and worship of one God.

Morality: Conformity or difformity of behavior to standards of right conduct. (*See* **Moral Obligations, Commandments of God, Precepts of the Church, Conscience, Law.**)

Mortification: Acts of self-discipline, including prayer, hardship, austerities and penances undertaken for the sake of progress in virtue.

Motu Proprio: A Latin phrase designating a document issued by a pope on his own initiative. Documents of this kind often concern administrative matters.

Mystagogy: Experience of the mystery of Christ, especially through participation in the liturgy and the sacraments.

Mysteries of Faith: Supernatural truths whose existence cannot be known without revelation by God and whose intrinsic truth, while not contrary to reason, can never be wholly understood even after revelation. These mysteries are above reason, not against reason. Among them are the divine mysteries of the Trinity, Incarnation and Eucharist. Some mysteries—e.g., concerning God's attributes—can be known by reason without revelation, although they cannot be fully understood.

N

Natural Law: *See* **Law**.

Natural Theology: The field of knowledge that relies upon human reason and the observation of nature, instead of revelation, to determine the existence and attributes of God.

Necromancy: Supposed communication with the dead; a form of divination.

Neo-Scholasticism: A movement begun in the late 19th century that had as its aim the restoration of Scholasticism for use in contemporary philosophy and theology. Great emphasis was placed upon the writings of such Scholastic masters as Peter Lombard, St. Albert the Great, St. Anselm, St. Bonaventure, Bl. John Duns Scotus, and especially St. Thomas Aquinas. The movement began at the Catholic University of Louvain, in Belgium, and then found its way into theological centers in Italy, France, and Germany. Particular attention was given to the philosophical and theological works of St. Thomas Aquinas, from which arose a particular school of neo-Thomism; the movement was strongly reinforced by Pope Leo XIII who issued the encyclical *Aeterni Patris* (1879) mandating that Scholasticism, in particular Thomism, be the foundation for all Catholic philosophy and theology taught in Catholic seminaries, universities, and colleges. Neo-Scholasticism was responsible for a true intellectual renaissance in 20th-century Catholic philosophy and theology. Among its foremost modern leaders were Jacques Maritain, Étienne Gilson, M. D. Chenu, Henri de Lubac, and Paul Claudel.

Nihil Obstat: *See* **Censorship of Books.**

Non-Expedit: A Latin expression. It is not expedient (fitting, proper), used to state a prohibition or refusal of permission.

Novena: A term designating public or private devotional practices over a period of nine consecutive days; or, by extension, over a period of nine weeks, in which one day a week is set aside for the devotions.

Novice: A man or woman preparing, in a formal period of trial and formation called a novitiate, for membership in an institute of consecrated life. The novitiate lasts a minimum of 12 and a maximum of 24 months; at its conclusion, the novice professes temporary promises or vows of poverty, chastity and obedience. Norms require that certain periods of time be spent in the house of novitiate; periods of apostolic work are also required, to acquaint the novice with the apostolate(s) of the institute. A novice is not bound by the obligations of the professed members of the institute, is free to leave at any time, and may be discharged at the discretion of competent superiors. The superior of a novice is a master of novices or director of formation.

Nun: (1) Strictly, a member of a religious order of women with solemn vows (*moniales*). (2) In general, all women religious, even those in simple vows who are more properly called sisters.

Nunc Dimittis: The canticle or hymn of Simeon at the sight of Jesus at the Temple on the occasion of his presentation (Lk 2:29-32). It is an expression of joy and thanksgiving for the blessing of having lived to see the Messiah. It is prescribed for use in the Night Prayer of the Liturgy of the Hours.

O

Oath: Calling upon God to witness the truth of a statement. Violating an oath, e.g., by perjury in court, or taking an oath without sufficient reason, is a violation of the honor due to God.

Obedience: Submission to one in authority. General obligations of obedience fall under the Fourth Commandment. The vow of obedience professed by religious is one of the evangelical counsels.

Obsession, Diabolical: The extraordinary state of one who is seriously molested by evil spirits in an external manner. Obsession is more than just temptation.

Occasion of Sin: A person, place, or thing that is a temptation to sin. An occasion may be either a situation that always leads to sin or one that usually leads to sin.

Octave: A period of eight days given over to the celebration of a major feast such as Easter.

Oils, Holy: The oils blessed by a bishop at the Chrism Mass on Holy Thursday or another suitable day, or by a priest under certain conditions. (1) The oil of catechumens (olive or vegetable oil), used at baptism; also, poured with chrism into the baptismal water blessed in Easter Vigil ceremonies. (2) Oil of the sick (olive or vegetable oil) used in anointing the sick. (3) Chrism (olive or vegetable oil mixed with balm), which is ordinarily consecrated by a bishop, for use at baptism, in confirmation, at the ordination of a priest and bishop, in the dedication of churches and altars.

Ontologism: A philosophical theory (the name is taken from the Greek for being and study) that posits that knowledge of God is immediate and intuitive; it stipulates further that all other human knowledge is dependent upon this. It was condemned in 1861 by Pope Pius IX. (*See also* **Ontology**.)

Ontology: A branch of metaphysics that studies the nature and relations of existence.

Oratory: A chapel.

Ordinariate: An ecclesiastical jurisdiction for special purposes and people. Examples are military ordinariates for armed services personnel (in accord with provisions of the apostolic constitution *Spirituali militum curae*, Apr. 21, 1986) and Eastern-Rite ordinariates in places where Eastern-Rite dioceses do not exist.

Ordination: The consecration of sacred ministers for divine worship and the service of people in things pertaining to God. The power of ordination comes from Christ and the Church, and must be conferred by a minister capable of communicating it.

Organ Transplants: The transplanting of organs from one person to another is permissible provided it is done with the consent of the concerned parties and does not result in the death or essential mutilation of the donor. Advances in methods and technology have increased the range of transplant possibilities in recent years.

Original Sin: The sin of Adam (Gn 2:8-3:24), personal to him and passed on to all persons as a state of privation of grace. Despite this privation and the related wounding of human nature and weakening of natural powers, original sin leaves unchanged all that man himself is by nature. The scriptural basis of the doctrine was stated by St. Paul in 1 Cor 15:21ff., and Rom 5:12-21. Original sin is remitted by baptism and incorporation in Christ, through whom grace is given to persons. Pope John Paul II, while describing original sin during a general audience Oct. 1, 1986, called it "the absence of sanctifying grace in nature which has been diverted from its supernatural end."

O Salutaris Hostia: The first three Latin words, *O Saving Victim*, of a Benediction hymn.

Ostpolitik: Policy adopted by Pope Paul VI in an attempt to improve the situation of Eastern European Catholics through diplomatic negotiations with their governments.

Oxford Movement: A movement in the Church of England from 1833 to about 1845 which had for its objective a threefold defense of the Church as a divine institution, the apostolic succession of its bishops, and the *Book of Common Prayer* as the rule of faith. The movement took its name from Oxford University and involved a number of intellectuals who authored a series of influential Tracts for Our Times. Some of its leading figures—e.g., F. W. Faber, John Henry Newman and Henry Edward Manning—became converts to the Catholic Church. In the Church of England, the movement affected the liturgy, historical and theological scholarship, the status of the ministry, and other areas of ecclesiastical life.

P

Paganism: A term referring to non-revealed religions, i.e., religions other than Christianity, Judaism, and Islam.

Palms: Blessed palms are a sacramental. They are blessed and distributed on the Sunday of the Passion in commemoration of the triumphant entrance of Christ into Jerusalem. Ashes of the burnt palms are used on Ash Wednesday.

Pange Lingua: First Latin words, *Sing, my tongue*, of a hymn in honor of the Holy Eucharist, used particularly on Holy Thursday and in Eucharistic processions.

Pantheism: Theory that all things are part of God, divine, in the sense that God realizes himself as the ultimate reality of matter or spirit through being and/or becoming all things that have been, are, and will be. The theory leads to hopeless confusion of the Creator and the created realm of being, identifies evil with good, and involves many inherent contradictions.

Papal Election: The pope is elected by the College of Cardinals during a secret conclave which begins no sooner than 15 days and no later than 20 days after the death of his predecessor. Cardinals under the age of 80, totaling no more than 120, are eligible to take part in the election by secret ballot. Election is by a two-thirds vote of participating cardinals. New legislation regarding papal elections and church government during a vacancy of the Holy See was promulgated by Pope John Paul Feb. 23, 1996, in the apostolic constitution *Universi Dominici Gregis* ("Shepherd of the Lord's Whole Flock").

Paraclete: A title of the Holy Spirit meaning, in Greek, Advocate, Consoler.

Parental Duties: All duties related to the obligation of parents to provide for the welfare of their children. These obligations fall under the Fourth Commandment.

Parish: A community of the faithful served by a pastor charged with responsibility for providing them with full pastoral service. Most parishes are territorial, embracing all of the faithful in a certain area of a diocese: some are personal or national, for certain classes of people, without strict regard for their places of residence.

Parousia: The coming, or saving presence, of Christ which will mark the completion of salvation history and the coming to perfection of God's kingdom at the end of the world.

Particular Church: A term used since Vatican II that denotes certain divisions of the Universal Church. Examples include dioceses, vicariates, and prelatures.

Paschal Candle: A large candle, symbolic of the risen Christ, blessed and lighted on the Easter Vigil and placed at the altar until Pentecost. It is ornamented with five large grains of incense, representing the wounds of Christ, inserted in the form of a cross; the Greek letters Alpha and Omega, symbolizing Christ the beginning and end of all things, at the top and bottom of the shaft of the cross; and the figures of the current year of salvation in the quadrants formed by the cross.

Paschal Precept: Church law requiring reception of the Eucharist in the Easter season (*See separate entry*) unless, for a just cause, once-a-year reception takes place at another time.

Passion of Christ: Sufferings of Christ, recorded in the four Gospels.

Pastor: An ordained minister charged with responsibility for the doctrinal, sacramental and related service of people committed to his care; e.g., a bishop for the people in his diocese, a priest for the people of his parish.

Pater Noster: The initial Latin words, *Our Father*, of the Lord's Prayer.

Patriarch: (1) The leaders of the Israelite tribes and heads of prominent families who appear in Genesis from Adam to Joseph. Among the most significant patriarchs of the Old Testament are Abraham, Isaac, and Jacob; the patriarchal narratives in Genesis associated with them constitute the prologue to Israel's salvation history, and the period during which they lived is known as the Age of the Patriarchs. It is noted that the title of patriarch that was used for David (Acts 2:29) was simply one of honor. (2) The head of a branch of the Eastern Church, corresponding to a province of the one-time Roman Empire. There are five official traditional patriarchal sees: Rome, Constantinople, Alexandria, Antioch, and Jerusalem. Presently, the autocephalous churches of the Orthodox Church comprise several of these traditional patriarchates.

Peace, Sign of: A gesture of greeting—e.g., a handshake—exchanged by the ministers and participants at Mass.

Pectoral Cross: A cross worn on a chain about the neck and over the breast by bishops and abbots as a mark of their office.

Penance or Penitence: (1) The spiritual change or conversion of mind and heart by which a person turns away from sin, and all that it implies, toward God, through a personal renewal under the influence of the Holy Spirit. Penance involves sorrow and contrition for sin, together with other internal and external acts of atonement. It serves the purposes of reestablishing in one's life the order of God's love and commandments, and of making satisfaction to God for sin. (2) Penance is a virtue disposing a person to turn to God in sorrow for sin and to carry out works of amendment and atonement. (3) The sacrament of penance and sacramental penance.

People of God: A name for the Church in the sense that it is comprised by a people with Christ as its head, the Holy Spirit as the condition of its unity, the law of love as its rule, and the kingdom of God as its destiny. Although it is a scriptural term, it was given new emphasis by the Second Vatican Council's Dogmatic Constitution on the Church (*Lumen Gentium*).

Perjury: Taking a false oath, lying under oath, a violation of the honor due to God.

Persecution, Religious: A campaign waged against a church or other religious body by persons and governments intent on its destruction. The best known campaigns of this type against the Christian Church were the Roman persecutions which occurred intermittently from about 54 to the promulgation of the Edict of Milan in 313. More Catholics have been persecuted in the 20th century than in any other period in history.

Personal Prelature: *See under* **Opus Dei**, p. 507.

Peter's Pence: A collection made each year among Catholics for the maintenance of the pope and his works of charity. It was originally a tax of a penny on each house, and was collected on St. Peter's day, whence the name. It originated in England in the 8th century.

Petition: One of the four purposes of prayer. In prayers of petition, persons ask of God the blessings they and others need.

Pharisees: Influential class among the Jews, referred to in the Gospels, noted for their self-righteousness, legalism, strict interpretation of the Law, acceptance of the traditions of the elders as well as the Law of Moses, and beliefs regarding angels and spirits, the resurrection of the dead and judgment. Most of them were laymen, and they were closely allied with the Scribes; their opposite numbers were the Sadducees. The Pharisaic and rabbinical traditions had a lasting influence on Judaism following the destruction of Jerusalem in 70 A.D.

Pious Fund: Property and money originally accumulated by the Jesuits to finance their missionary work in Lower California. When the Jesuits were expelled from the territory in 1767, the fund was appropriated by the Spanish Crown and used to support Dominican and Franciscan missionary work in Upper and Lower California. In 1842 the Mexican government took over administration of the fund, incorporated most of the revenue into the national treasury, and agreed to pay the Church interest of six per cent a year on the capital so incorporated. From 1848 to 1967 the fund was the subject of lengthy negotiations between the U.S. and Mexican governments because of the latter's failure to make payments as agreed. A lump-sum settlement was made in 1967 with payment by Mexico to the U.S. government of more than $700,000, to be turned over to the Archdiocese of San Francisco.

Polytheism: Belief in and worship of many gods or divinities, especially prevalent in pre-Christian religions.

Poor Box: Alms-box; found in churches from the earliest days of Christianity.

Pope: A title from the Italian word *papa* (from Greek *pappas*, father) used for the Bishop of Rome, the Vicar of Christ and successor of St. Peter, who exercises universal governance over the Church.

Portiuncula: (1) Meaning little portion (of land), the Portiuncula was the chapel of Our Lady of the Angels near Assisi, Italy, which the Benedictines gave to St. Francis early in the 13th century. He repaired the chapel and made it the first church of the Franciscan Order. It is now enshrined in the Basilica of St. Mary of the Angels in Assisi. (2) The plenary Portiuncula Indulgence, or Pardon of Assisi, was authorized by Honorius III. Originally, it could be gained for the souls in purgatory only in the chapel of Our Lady of the Angels; by later concessions, it could be gained also in other Franciscan and parish churches. The indulgence (applicable to the souls in purgatory) can be gained from noon of Aug. 1 to midnight of Aug. 2, once each day. The conditions are, in addition to freedom from attachment to sin: reception of the sacraments of penance and the Eucharist on or near the day and a half; a visit to a parish church within the day and a half, during which the Our Father, the Creed and another prayer are offered for the intentions of the pope.

Positivism: The philosophy that teaches that the only reality is that which is perceived by the senses; the only truth is that which is empirically verified. It asserts that ideas about God, morality, or anything else that cannot be scientifically tested are to be rejected as unknowable.

Possession, Diabolical: The extraordinary state of a person who is tormented from within by evil spirits who exercise strong influence over his powers of mind and body. (*See* also **Exorcism**.)

Postulant: One of several names used to designate a candidate for membership in a religious institute during the period before novitiate.

Poverty: (1) The quality or state of being poor, in actual destitution and need, or being poor in spirit. In the latter sense, poverty means the state of mind and disposition of persons who regard material things in proper perspective as gifts of God for the support of life and its reasonable enrichment, and for the service of others in need. It means freedom from unreasonable attachment to material things as ends in themselves, even though they may be possessed in small or large measure. (2) One of the evangelical counsels professed as a public vow by members of an institute of consecrated life. It involves the voluntary renunciation of rights of ownership and of independent use and disposal of material goods; or, the right of independent use and disposal, but not of the radical right of ownership. Religious institutes provide their members with necessary and useful goods and services from common resources. The manner in which goods are received and/or handled by religious is determined by poverty of spirit and the rule and constitutions of their institute.

Pragmatism: Theory that the truth of ideas, concepts and values depends on their utility or capacity to serve a useful purpose rather than on their conformity with objective standards; also called utilitarianism.

Prayer: The raising of the mind and heart to God in adoration, thanksgiving, reparation and petition. Prayer, which is always mental because it involves thought and love of God, may be vocal, meditative, private and personal, social, and official. The official prayer of the Church as a worshipping community is called the liturgy.

Precepts: Commands or orders given to individuals or communities in particular cases; they establish law for concerned parties. Preceptive documents are issued by the pope, departments of the Roman Curia and other competent authority in the Church.

Presence of God: A devotional practice of increasing one's awareness of the presence and action of God in daily life.

Presumption: A sin against hope, by which a person striving for salvation (1) either relies too much on his own capabilities or (2) expects God to do things which he cannot do, in keeping with his divine attributes, or

does not will to do, according to his divine plan. Presumption is the opposite of despair.

Preternatural Gifts: Exceptional gifts, beyond the exigencies and powers of human nature, enjoyed by Adam in the state of original justice: immunity from suffering and death, superior knowledge, integrity or perfect control of the passions. These gifts were lost as the result of original sin; their loss, however, implied no impairment of the integrity of human nature.

Pride: Unreasonable self-esteem; one of the seven capital sins.

Prie-Dieu: A French phrase, meaning pray God, designating a kneeler or bench suitable for kneeling while at prayer.

Priesthood: (1) The common priesthood of the non-ordained faithful. In virtue of baptism and confirmation, the faithful are a priestly people who participate in the priesthood of Christ through acts of worship, witness to the faith in daily life, and efforts to foster the growth of God's kingdom. (2) The ordained priesthood, in virtue of the sacrament of orders, of bishops, priests and deacons, for service to the common priesthood.

Primary Option: The life-choice of a person for or against God which shapes the basic orientation of moral conduct. A primary option for God does not preclude the possibility of serious sin.

Prior: A superior or an assistant to an abbot in a monastery.

Privilege: A favor, an exemption from the obligation of a law. Privileges of various kinds, with respect to ecclesiastical laws, are granted by the pope, departments of the Roman Curia and other competent authority in the Church.

Probabiliorism: The moral system asserting that the more probable opinion of a varied set of acceptable positions regarding the binding character of a law should be accepted. If the reasons for being free from a law are more probably true, one is freed from the law's obligations. Probabiliorism, however, maintained that if it was probable that the law did not bind, one still had to follow it unless it was more probable that the law did not bind.

Probabilism: A moral system for use in cases of conscience which involve the obligation of doubtful laws. There is a general principle that a doubtful law does not bind. Probabilism, therefore, teaches that it is permissible to follow an opinion favoring liberty, provided the opinion is certainly and solidly probable. Probabilism may not be invoked when there is question of: a certain law or the certain obligation of a law; the certain right of another party; the validity of an action; something which is necessary for salvation.

Pro-Cathedral: A church used as a cathedral.

Promoter of the Faith (*Promotor fidei*): An official of the Congregation for the Causes of Saints, whose role in beatification and canonization procedures is to establish beyond reasonable doubt the validity of evidence regarding the holiness of prospective saints and miracles attributed to their intercession.

Prophecy: (1) The communication of divine revelation by inspired intermediaries, called prophets, between God and his people. Old Testament prophecy was unique in its origin and because of its ethical and religious content, which included disclosure of the saving will of Yahweh for the people, moral censures and warnings of divine punishment because of sin and violations of the Law and Covenant, in the form of promises, admonitions, reproaches and threats. Although Moses and other earlier figures are called prophets, the period of prophecy is generally dated from the early years of the monarchy to about 100 years after the Babylonian Exile. From that time on, the written Law and its interpreters supplanted the prophets as guides of the people. Old Testament prophets are cited in the New Testament, with awareness that God spoke through them and that some of their oracles were fulfilled in Christ. John the Baptist is the outstanding prophetic figure in the New Testament. Christ never claimed the title of prophet for himself, although some people thought he was one. There were prophets in the early Church, and St. Paul mentioned the charism of prophecy in 1 Cor 14:1-5. Prophecy disappeared after New Testament times. Revelation is classified as the prophetic book of the New Testament. (2) In contemporary non-scriptural usage, the term is applied to the witness given by persons to the relevance of their beliefs in everyday life and action.

Proportionalism: The moral theory that asserts that an action is judged on whether the evils resulting are proportionate to the goods that result. If the evils outweigh the goods, the act is objectionable; if the opposite is true, the act is permissible. Proportionalism differs from consequentialism in that the former admits that the inherent morality of the act and the agent's intention must also be considered. Proportionalism is rejected by critics as it does not offer an objective criterion for determining when evils are proportionate or disproportionate. It also fails to consider the intrinsic nature of human acts and does nothing to assist Christians to grow in virtue.

Province: (1) A territory comprising one archdiocese called the metropolitan see and one or more dioceses called suffragan sees. The head of the archdiocese, an archbishop, has metropolitan rights and responsibilities over the province. (2) A division of a religious order under the jurisdiction of a provincial superior.

Prudence: Practical wisdom and judgment regarding the choice and use of the best ways and means of doing good; one of the four cardinal virtues.

Punishment Due for Sin: The punishment which is a consequence of sin. It is of two kinds: (1) Eternal punishment is the punishment of hell, to which one becomes subject by the commission of mortal sin. Such punishment is remitted when mortal sin is forgiven. (2) Temporal punishment is a consequence of venial sin and/or forgiven mortal sin; it is not everlasting and may be remitted in this life by means of penance. Temporal punishment unremitted during this life is remitted by suffering in purgatory.

Purgatory: The state or condition of those who have died in the state of grace but with some attachment to sin, and are purified for a time before they are admitted to the glory and happiness of heaven. In this state and period of passive suffering, they are purified of unrepented venial sins, satisfy the demands of divine justice for temporal punishment due for sins, and are thus converted to a state of worthiness of the beatific vision.

Q

Quadragesima: From the Latin for fortieth, the name given to the forty penitential days of Lent.

Quinquennial Report: A report on the current state of a diocese that must be compiled and submitted by a bishop to the Holy See every five years in anticipation of the *ad liminal* visit.

Quinque Viae: From the Latin for the "five ways," the five proofs for the existence of God that were proposed by St. Thomas Aquinas in his *Summa Theologiae* (Part I, question 2, article 3). The five ways are: 1) all the motion in the world points to an unmoved Prime Mover; 2) the subordinate agents in the world imply the First Agent; 3) there must be a Cause Who is not perishable and Whose existence is underived; 4) the limited goodness in the world must be a reflection of Unlimited Goodness; 5) all things tend to become something, and that inclination must have proceeded from some Rational Planner.

R

Racism: A theory which holds that any one or several of the different races of the human family are inherently superior or inferior to any one or several of the others. The teaching denies the essential unity of the human race, the equality and dignity of all persons because of their common possession of the same human nature, and the participation of all in the divine plan of redemption. It is radically opposed to the virtue of justice and the precept of love of neighbor. Differences of superiority and inferiority which do exist are the result of accidental factors operating in a wide variety of circumstances, and are in no way due to essential defects in any one or several of the branches of the one human race. The theory of racism, together with practices related to it, is incompatible with Christian doctrine.

Rash Judgment: Attributing faults to another without sufficient reason; a violation of the obligations of justice and charity.

Rationalism: A theory which makes the mind the measure and arbiter of all things, including religious truth. A product of the Enlightenment, it rejects the supernatural, divine revelation, and authoritative teaching by any church.

Recollection: Meditation, attitude of concentration or awareness of spiritual matters and things pertaining to salvation and the accomplishment of God's will.

Relativism: Theory which holds that all truth, including religious truth, is relative, i.e., not absolute, certain or unchanging; a product of agnosticism, indifferentism, and an unwarranted extension of the notion of truth in positive science. Relativism is based on the tenet that certain knowledge of any and all truth is impossible. Therefore, no religion, philosophy or science can be said to possess the real truth; consequently, all religions, philosophies and sciences may be considered to have as much or as little of truth as any of the others.

Relics: The physical remains and effects of saints, which are considered worthy of veneration inasmuch as they are representative of persons in glory with God. Catholic doctrine proscribes the view that relics are not worthy of veneration. In line with norms laid down by the Council of Trent and subsequent enactments, discipline concerning relics is subject to control by the Congregations for the Causes of Saints and for Divine Worship and the Discipline of the Sacraments.

Religion: The adoration and service of God as expressed in divine worship and in daily life. Religion is concerned with all of the relations existing between God and human beings, and between humans themselves because of the central significance of God. Objectively considered, religion consists of a body of truth that is believed, a code of morality for the guidance of conduct, and a form of divine worship. Subjectively, it is a person's total response, theoretically and practically, to the demands of faith; it is living faith, personal engagement, self-commitment to God. Thus, by creed, code and cult, a person orders and directs his or her life in reference to God and, through what the love and service of God implies, to all people and all things.

Reliquary: A vessel for the preservation and exposition of a relic; sometimes made like a small monstrance.

Reparation: The making of amends to God for sin committed; one of the four ends of prayer and the purpose of penance.

Requiem: A Mass offered for the repose of the soul of one who has died in Christ. Its name is derived from the first word of the Gregorian (Latin) entrance chant (or Introit) at Masses for the dead: *Requiem aeternam dona eis, Domine* ("Eternal rest grant unto them, O Lord"). The revised Rite for Funerals refers to the requiem as the Mass of Christian Burial; however, it would not be uncommon to hear people employ the former usage.

Rescript: A written reply by an ecclesiastical superior regarding a question or request; its provisions bind concerned parties only. Papal dispensations are issued in the form of rescripts.

Reserved Censure: A sin or censure, absolution from which is reserved to religious superiors, bishops, the pope, or confessors having special faculties. Reservations are made because of the serious nature and social effects of certain sins and censures.

Restitution: An act of reparation for an injury done to another. The injury may be caused by taking and/or retaining what belongs to another or by damaging either the property or reputation of another. The intention of making restitution, usually in kind, is required as a condition for the forgiveness of sins of injustice, even though actual restitution is not possible.

Ring: In the Church a ring is worn as part of the insignia of bishops, abbots, et al.; by sisters to denote their consecration to God and the Church. The wedding ring symbolizes the love and union of husband and wife.

Ritual: A book of prayers and ceremonies used in the administration of the sacraments and other ceremonial functions. In the Roman Rite, the standard book of this kind is the Roman Ritual.

Rogito: The official notarial act or document testifying to the burial of a pope.

Rosary: A form of mental and vocal prayer centered on mysteries or events in the lives of Jesus and Mary. Its essential elements are meditation on the mysteries and the recitation of a number of decades of Hail Marys, each beginning with the Lord's Prayer. Introductory prayers may include the Apostles' Creed, an initial Our Father, three Hail Marys and a Glory be to the Father; each decade is customarily concluded with a Glory be to the Father; at the end, it is customary to say the Hail, Holy Queen and a prayer from the liturgy for the feast of the Blessed Virgin Mary of the Rosary. Traditionally, the Mysteries of the Rosary, which are the subject of meditation, are: (1) Joyful— the Annunciation to Mary that she was to be the Mother of Christ, her visit to Elizabeth, the birth of Jesus, the presentation of Jesus in the Temple, the finding of Jesus in the Temple. (2) Sorrowful—Christ's agony in the Garden of Gethsemani, scourging at the pillar, crowning with thorns, carrying of the cross to Calvary, and crucifixion. (3) Glorious—the Resurrection and Ascension of Christ, the descent of the Holy Spirit upon the Apostles, Mary's Assumption into heaven and her crowning as Queen of angels and men.

The complete Rosary, called the Dominican Rosary, consists of 15 decades. In customary practice, only five decades are usually said at one time. Rosary beads are used to aid in counting the prayers without distraction. The Rosary originated through the coalescence of popular devotions to Jesus and Mary from the 12th century onward. Its present form dates from about the 15th century. Carthusians contributed greatly toward its development; Dominicans have been its greatest promoters. The 15 mysteries were standardized by Pope Pius V in 1569.

In 2002, Pope John Paul II added five new mysteries dedicated to chapters from Jesus' public life. Titled the Mysteries of Light, they are: Christ's baptism in the Jordan River; Christ's self-revelation at the marriage of Cana; Christ's announcement of the kingdom of God with the invitation to conversion; Christ's Transfiguration, when he revealed his glory to his Apostles; and the institution of the Eucharist at the Last Supper as the sacramental expression of the paschal mystery. The pope asked that the Mysteries of Light be recited especially on Thursday.

S

Sabbath: The seventh day of the week, observed by Jews and Sabbatarians as the day for rest and religious observance.

Sacrarium: A basin with a drain leading directly into the ground; standard equipment of a sacristy.

Sacred Heart, Enthronement of the: An acknowledgment of the sovereignty of Jesus Christ over the Christian family, expressed by the installation of an image or picture of the Sacred Heart in a place of honor in the home, accompanied by an act of consecration.

Sacred Heart, Promises: Twelve promises to persons having devotion to the Sacred Heart of Jesus, which were communicated by Christ to St. Margaret Mary Alacoque in a private revelation in 1675.

Sacrilege: Violation of and irreverence toward a person, place or thing that is sacred because of public dedication to God; a sin against the virtue of religion. Personal sacrilege is violence of some kind against a cleric or religious, or a violation of chastity with a cleric or religious. Local sacrilege is the desecration of sacred places. Real sacrilege is irreverence with respect to sacred things, such as the sacraments and sacred vessels.

Sacristy: A utility room where vestments, church furnishings and sacred vessels are kept and where the clergy vest for sacred functions.

Sadducees: The predominantly priestly party among the Jews in the time of Christ, noted for extreme conservatism, acceptance only of the Law of Moses, and rejection of the traditions of the elders. Their opposite numbers were the Pharisees.

Saints, Cult of: The veneration, called *dulia*, of holy persons who have died and are in glory with God in heaven; it includes honoring them and petitioning them for their intercession with God. Liturgical veneration is given only to saints officially recognized by the Church; private veneration may be given to anyone thought to be in heaven. The veneration of saints is essentially different from the adoration given to God alone; by its very nature, however, it terminates in the worship of God. (*See also* **Dulia** and **Latria**.)

Salvation: The liberation of persons from sin and its effects, reconciliation with God in and through Christ, the attainment of union with God forever in the glory of heaven as the supreme purpose of life and as the God-given reward for fulfillment of his will on earth. Salvation-in-process begins and continues in this life through union with Christ in faith professed and in action; its final term is union with God and the whole community of the saved in the ultimate perfection of God's kingdom. The Church teaches that: God wills the salvation of all men; men are saved in and through Christ; membership in the Church established by Christ, known and understood as the community of salvation, is necessary for salvation; men with this knowledge and understanding who deliberately reject this Church, cannot be saved. The Catholic Church is the Church founded by Christ. (*See below*, **Salvation outside the Church**.)

Salvation History: The facts and the record of God's relations with human beings, in the past, present and future, for the purpose of leading them to live in accordance with his will for the eventual attainment after death of salvation, or everlasting happiness with him in heaven. The essentials of salvation history are: God's love for all human beings and will for their salvation; his intervention and action in the world to express this love and bring about their salvation; the revelation he made of himself and the covenant he established with the Israelites in the Old Testament; the perfecting of this revelation and the new covenant of grace through Christ in the New Testament; the continuing action-for-salvation carried on in and through the Church; the communication of saving grace to people through the merits of Christ and the operations of the Holy Spirit in the here-and-now circumstances of daily life and with the cooperation of people themselves.

Salvation outside the Church: The Second Vatican Council covered this subject summarily in the following manner: "Those also can attain to everlasting salvation who through no fault of their own do not know the Gospel of Christ or his Church, yet sincerely seek God and, moved by grace, strive by their deeds to do his will as it is known to them through the dictates of conscience. Nor does divine Providence deny the help necessary for salvation to those who, without blame on their part, have not yet arrived at an explicit knowledge of God, but who strive to live a good life, thanks to his grace. Whatever good or truth is found among them is looked upon by the Church as a preparation for the Gospel. She regards such qualities as given by him who enlightens all men so that they may finally have life" (Dogmatic Constitution on the Church, *Lumen Gentium*, No. 16). The teachings of the Church were reiterated in 2007 by the Congregation for the Doctrine of the Faith's "Doctrinal Note on Some Aspects of Evangelization."

Sanctifying Grace: *See* **Grace**.

Satanism: Worship of the devil, a blasphemous inversion of the order of worship which is due to God alone.

Scandal: Conduct which is the occasion of sin to another person.

Scapular: (1) A part of the habit of some religious orders like the Benedictines and Dominicans; a nearly shoulder-wide strip of cloth worn over the tunic and reaching almost to the feet in front and behind. Originally a kind of apron, it came to symbolize the cross and yoke of Christ. (2) Scapulars worn by lay persons as a sign of association with religious orders and for devotional purposes are an adaptation of monastic scapulars. Approved by the Church as sacramentals, they consist of two small squares of woolen cloth joined by strings and are worn about the neck. They are given for wearing in a ceremony of investiture or enrollment. There are nearly 20 scapulars for devotional use: the five principal ones are generally understood to include those of Our Lady of Mt Carmel (the brown Carmelite Scapular), the Holy Trinity, Our Lady of the Seven Dolors, the Passion, the Immaculate Conception.

Scapular Medal: A medallion with a representation of the Sacred Heart on one side and of the Blessed Virgin Mary on the other. Authorized by St. Pius X in 1910, it may be worn or carried in place of a scapular by persons already invested with a scapular.

Scapular Promise: According to a legend of the Carmelite Order, the Blessed Virgin Mary appeared to St. Simon Stock in 1251 at Cambridge, England, and declared that wearers of the brown Carmelite Scapular would be the beneficiaries of her special intercession. The scapular tradition has never been the subject of official decision by the Church. Essentially, it expresses belief in the intercession of Mary and the efficacy of sacramentals in the context of truly Christian life.

Schism: Derived from a Greek word meaning separation, the term designates formal and obstinate refusal by a baptized Catholic, called a schismatic, to be in communion with the pope and the Church. The canonical penalty is excommunication. One of the most disastrous schisms in history resulted in the definitive separation of the Church in the East from union with Rome about 1054.

Scholasticism: The term usually applied to the Catholic theology and philosophy which developed in the Middle Ages. (*See also* **Neo-Scholasticism**.)

Scribes: Hebrew intellectuals noted for their knowledge of the Law of Moses, influential from the time of the Exile to about A.D. 70. Many of them were Pharisees. They were the antecedents of rabbis and their traditions, as well as those o the Pharisees, had a lasting influence on Judaism following the destruction of Jerusalem in A.D. 70.

Scruple: A morbid, unreasonable fear and anxiety that one's actions are sinful when they are not, or more seriously sinful than they actually are. Compulsive scrupulosity is quite different from the transient scrupulosity of persons of tender or highly sensitive conscience, or of persons with faulty moral judgment.

Seal of Confession: The obligation of secrecy which must be observed regarding knowledge of things learned in connection with the confession of sin in the sacrament of penance. The seal covers matters whose revelation would make the sacrament burdensome. Confessors are prohibited, under penalty of excommunication, from making any direct revelation of confessional matter; this prohibition holds, outside of confession, even with respect to the person who made the confession unless the person releases the priest from the obligation. Persons other than confessors are obliged to maintain secrecy, but not under penalty of excommunication. General, non-specific discussion of confessional matter does not violate the seal.

Secularism: A school of thought, a spirit and manner of action which ignores and/or repudiates the validity or influence of supernatural religion with respect to individual and social life.

See: Another name for diocese or archdiocese.

Seminary: A house of study and formation for men, called seminarians, preparing for the priesthood. Traditional seminaries date from the Council of Trent in the middle of the 16th century; before that time, candidates for the priesthood were variously trained in monastic schools, universities under church auspices, and in less formal ways.

Sermon on the Mount: A compilation of sayings of Our Lord in the form of an extended discourse in Matthew's Gospel (5:1 to 7:27) and, in a shorter discourse, in Luke (6:17-49). The passage in Matthew, called the "Constitution of the New Law," summarizes the living spirit of believers in Christ and members of the kingdom of God. Beginning with the Beatitudes and including the Lord's Prayer, it covers the perfect justice of the New Law, the fulfillment of the Old Law in the New Law of Christ, and the integrity of internal attitude and external conduct with respect to love of God and neighbor, justice, chastity, truth, trust and confidence in God.

Seven Last Words of Christ: The Seven Last Words of Christ on the Cross were: (1) "Father, forgive them; for they do not know what they are doing" (Lk 23:34); (2) To the penitent thief: "I assure you: today you will be with me in Paradise" (Lk 23:24); (3) To Mary and his Apostle John: "Woman, behold thy son! . . . Behold your mother" (Jn 19:26); (4) "Eli Eli, lama sabacthani ["My God, my God, why have you forsaken me?"] (Mt 27:46; cf. Mk 15:34); (5) "I thirst" (Jn 19:28); (6) "It is finished" (Jn 19:30); (7) "Father, into thy hands I commend my spirit"(Lk 23:46).

Shrine, Crowned: A shrine approved by the Holy See as a place of pilgrimage. The approval permits public devotion at the shrine and implies that at least one miracle has resulted from devotion at the shrine. Among the best known crowned shrines are those of the Virgin Mary at Lourdes and Fátima. Shrines with statues crowned by Pope John Paul in 1985 in South America were those of Our Lady of Coromoto, patroness of Venezuela, in Caracas, and Our Lady of Carmen of Paucartambo in Cuzco, Peru.

Shroud of Turin: A strip of brownish linen cloth, 14 feet, three inches in length and three feet, seven inches in width, bearing the front and back imprint of a human body. A tradition dating from the 7th century, which has not been verified beyond doubt, claims that the shroud is the fine linen in which the body of Christ was wrapped for burial. The early history of the shroud is obscure. It was enshrined at Lirey, France, in 1354 and was transferred in 1578 to Turin, Italy, where it has been kept in the cathedral down to the present time. Scientific investigation, which began in 1898, seems to indicate that the markings on the shroud are those of a human body. The shroud, for the first time since 1933, was placed on public view from Aug. 27 to Oct. 8, 1978, and was seen by an estimated 3.3 million people. Scientists conducted intensive studies of it thereafter, finally determining that the material of the shroud dated from between 1260 and 1390. The shroud, which had been the possession of the House of Savoy, was willed to Pope John Paul II in 1983.

Sick Calls: When a person is confined at home by illness or other cause and is unable to go to church for reception of the sacraments, a parish priest should be informed and arrangements made for him to visit the person at home. Such visitations are common in pastoral practice, both for special needs and for providing persons with regular opportunities for receiving the sacraments. If a priest cannot make the visitation, arrangements can be made for a deacon or Eucharistic minister to bring Holy Communion to the homebound or bedridden person.

Sign of the Cross: A sign, ceremonial gesture or movement in the form of a cross by which a person confesses faith in the Holy Trinity and Christ, and intercedes for the blessing of himself or herself, other persons and things. In Roman-Rite practice, a person making the sign touches the fingers of the right hand to forehead, below the breast, left shoulder and right shoulder while saying: "In the name of the Father, and of the Son, and of the Holy Spirit." The sign is also made with the thumb on the forehead, the lips, and the breast. For the blessing of persons and objects, a large sign of the cross is made by movement of the right hand. In Eastern-Rite practice, the sign is made with the thumb and first two fingers of the right hand joined together and touching the forehead, below the breast, the right shoulder and the left shoulder; the formula generally used is the doxology, "O Holy God, O Holy Strong One, O Immortal One." The Eastern manner of making the sign was general until the first half of the 13th century; by the 17th century, Western practice involved the whole right hand and the reversal of direction from shoulder to shoulder.

Signs of the Times: Contemporary events, trends and features in culture and society, the needs and aspirations of people, all the factors that form the context in and through which the Church has to carry on its saving mission. The Second Vatican Council spoke on numerous occasions about these signs and the relationship between them and a kind of manifestation of God's will, positive or negative, and about subjecting them to judgment and action corresponding to the demands of divine revelation through Scripture, Christ, and the experience, tradition and teaching authority of the Church.

Simony: The deliberate intention and act of selling and/or buying spiritual goods or material things so connected with the spiritual that they cannot be separated therefrom; a violation of the virtue of religion, and a sacrilege, because it wrongfully puts a material price on spiritual things, which cannot be either sold or bought. In church law, actual sale or purchase is subject to censure in some cases. The term is derived from the name of Simon Magus, who attempted to buy from Sts. Peter and John the power to confirm people in the Holy Spirit (Acts 8:4-24).

Sin: (1) Actual sin is the free and deliberate violation of God's law by thought, word or action. (a) **Mortal sin** —involving serious matter, sufficient reflection and full consent—results in the loss of sanctifying grace and alienation from God, and renders a person incapable of performing meritorious supernatural acts and subject to everlasting punishment. (b) **Venial sin**— involving less serious matter, reflection and consent— does not have such serious consequences. (2) **Original sin** is the sin of Adam, with consequences for all human beings. (*See separate entry*.)

Sins Against the Holy Spirit: Despair of salvation, presumption of God's mercy, impugning the known truths of faith, envy at another's spiritual good, obstinacy in sin, final impenitence. Those guilty of such sins stubbornly resist the influence of grace and, as long as they do so, cannot be forgiven.

Sins, Occasions of: Circumstances (persons, places, things, etc.) which easily lead to sin. There is an obligation to avoid voluntary proximate occasions of sin, and to take precautions against the dangers of unavoidable occasions.

Sins That Cry to Heaven for Vengeance: Willful murder, sins against nature, oppression of the poor, widows and orphans, defrauding laborers of their wages.

Sister: Any woman religious, in popular speech; strictly, the title applies only to women religious belonging to institutes whose members never professed solemn vows. Most of the institutes whose members are properly called Sisters were established during and since the 19th century. Women religious with solemn vows, or belonging to institutes whose members formerly professed solemn vows, are properly called nuns.

Sisterhood: A generic term referring to the whole institution of the life of women religious in the Church, or to a particular institute of women religious.

Situation Ethics: A subjective, individualistic ethical theory which denies the binding force of ethical principles as universal laws and perceptive norms of moral conduct, and proposes that morality is determined only by situational conditions and considerations and the intention of the person. It has been criticized for ignoring the principles of objective ethics. (*See also* **Consequentialism** *and* **Proportionalism**.)

Slander: Attributing to a person faults which he or she does not have; a violation of the obligations of justice and charity, for which restitution is due.

Sloth (Acedia): One of the seven capital sins; spiritual laziness, involving distaste and disgust for spiritual things; spiritual boredom, which saps the vigor of spiritual life. Physical laziness is a counterpart of spiritual sloth.

Sorcery: A kind of black magic in which evil is invoked by means of diabolical intervention; a violation of the virtue of religion.

Soteriology: The division of theology which treats of the mission and work of Christ as Redeemer.

Species, Sacred: The appearances of bread and wine (color, taste, smell, etc.) which remain after the substance has been changed at the Consecration of the Mass into the Body and Blood of Christ. (*See* **Transubstantiation**.)

Spiritism: Attempts to communicate with spirits and departed souls by means of séances, table tapping, ouija boards, and other methods; a violation of the virtue of religion. Spiritualistic practices are noted for fakery.

Stational Churches, Days: Churches, especially in Rome, where the clergy and lay people were accustomed to gather with their bishop on certain days for the celebration of the liturgy. The 25 early titular or parish churches of Rome, plus other churches, each had their turn as the site of divine worship in practices which may have started in the third century. The observances were rather well developed toward the latter part of the 4th century, and by the fifth they included a Mass concelebrated by the pope and attendant priests. On some occasions, the stational liturgy was preceded by a procession from another church called a *collecta*. There were 42 Roman stational churches in the 8th century, and 89 stational services were scheduled annually in connection with the liturgical seasons. Stational observances fell into disuse toward the end of the Middle Ages. Some revival was begun by John XXIII in 1959 and continued by Paul VI and John Paul II.

Stations (Way) of the Cross: A form of devotion commemorating the Passion and death of Christ, consisting of a series of meditations (stations): (1) his condemnation to death, (2) taking up of the cross, (3) the first fall on the way to Calvary, (4) meeting his Mother, (5) being assisted by Simon of Cyrene and (6) by the woman Veronica who wiped his face, (7) the second fall, (8) meeting the women of Jerusalem, (9) the third fall, (10) being stripped and (11) nailed to the cross, (12) his death, (13) the removal of his body from the cross and (14) his burial. Depictions of these scenes are mounted in most churches, chapels and in some other places, beneath small crosses. A person making the Way of the Cross passes before these stations, or stopping points, pausing at each for meditation. If the stations are made by a group of people, only the leader has to pass from station to station. A plenary indulgence is granted to the faithful who make the stations, under the usual conditions: freedom from all attachment to sin, reception of the sacraments of penance and the Eucharist, and prayers for the intentions of the pope. Those who are impeded from making the stations in the usual manner can gain the same indulgence if, along with the aforementioned conditions, they spend at least a half hour in spiritual reading and meditation on the passion and death of Christ. The stations originated remotely from the practice of Holy Land pilgrims who visited the actual scenes of incidents in the Passion of Christ. Representations elsewhere of at least some of these scenes were known as early as the 5th century. Later, the stations evolved in connection with and as a consequence of strong devotion to the Passion in the 12th and 13th centuries. Franciscans, who were given custody of the Holy Places in 1342, promoted the devotion widely; one of them, St. Leonard of Port Maurice, became known as the greatest preacher of the Way of the Cross in the 18th century. The general features of the devotion were fixed by Clement XII in 1731.

Statutes: Virtually the same as decrees (*See* separate

entry), they almost always designate laws of a particular council or synod rather than pontifical laws.

Stigmata: Marks of the wounds suffered by Christ in his crucifixion, in hands and feet by nails, and side by the piercing of a lance. Some persons, called stigmatists, have been reported as recipients or sufferers of marks like these. The Church, however, has never issued any infallible declaration about their possession by anyone, even in the case of St. Francis of Assisi whose stigmata seem to be the best substantiated and may be commemorated in the Roman-Rite liturgy. Ninety percent of some 300 reputed stigmatists have been women. Judgment regarding the presence, significance, and manner of causation of stigmata would depend, among other things, on irrefutable experimental evidence.

Stipend, Mass: An offering given to a priest for applying the fruits of the Mass according to the intention of the donor. The offering is a contribution to the support of the priest. The disposition of the fruits of the sacrifice, in line with doctrine concerning the Mass in particular and prayer in general, is subject to the will of God. Mass offerings and intentions were the subjects of a decree approved by John Paul II and made public Mar. 22, 1991: (1) Normally, no more than one offering should be accepted for a Mass; the Mass should be offered in accord with the donor's intention; the priest who accepts the offering should celebrate the Mass himself or have another priest do so. (2) Several Mass intentions, for which offerings have been made, can be combined for a "collective" application of a single Mass only if the previous and explicit consent of the donors is obtained. Such Masses are an exception to the general rule.

Stole Fee: An offering given on certain occasions; e.g., at a baptism, wedding, funeral, for the support of the clergy who administer the sacraments and perform other sacred rites.

Stoup: A vessel used to contain holy water.

Suffragan See: Any diocese, except the archdiocese, within a province.

Suicide: The taking of one's own life; a violation of God's dominion over human life. Ecclesiastical burial is denied to persons while in full possession of their faculties; it is permitted in cases of doubt.

Supererogation: Actions which go beyond the obligations of duty and the requirements enjoined by God's law as necessary for salvation. Examples of these works are the profession and observance of the evangelical counsels of poverty, chastity, and obedience, and efforts to practice charity to the highest degree.

Supernatural: Above the natural; that which exceeds and is not due or owed to the essence, exigencies, requirements, powers and merits of created nature. While human beings have no claim on supernatural things and do not need them in order to exist and act on a natural level, they do need them in order to exist and act in the higher order or economy of grace established by God for their salvation. God has freely given them certain things which are beyond the powers and rights of their human nature. Examples of the supernatural are: grace, a kind of participation by human beings in the divine life, by which they become capable of performing acts meritorious for salvation; divine revelation by which God manifests himself to them and makes known truth that is inaccessible to human reason alone; faith, by which they believe divine truth because of the authority of God who reveals it through Sacred Scripture and tradition and the teaching of his Church.

Suspension: A censure by which a cleric is forbidden to exercise some or all of his powers of orders and jurisdiction, or to accept the financial support of his benefices.

Syllabus, The: (1) When not qualified, the term refers to the list of 80 errors accompanying Pope Pius IX's encyclical *Quanta Cura*, issued in 1864. (2) The Syllabus of St. Pius X in the decree *Lamentabili*, issued by the Holy Office July 4, 1907, condemning 65 heretical propositions of modernism. This schedule of errors was followed shortly by that pope's encyclical *Pascendi*, the principal ecclesiastical document against modernism, issued Sept. 8, 1907.

Synod, Diocesan: Meeting of representative persons of a diocese—priests, religious, lay persons—with the bishop, called by him for the purpose of considering and taking action on matters affecting the life and mission of the Church in the diocese. Persons taking part in a synod have consultative status; the bishop alone is the legislator, with power to authorize synodal decrees. According to canon law, every diocese should have a synod every 10 years.

T

Tabernacle: The receptacle in which the Blessed Sacrament is reserved in churches, chapels, and oratories. It is to be immovable, solid, locked, and located in a prominent place.

Te Deum: The opening Latin words, *Thee, God*, of a hymn of praise and thanksgiving prescribed for use in the Office of Readings of the Liturgy of the Hours on many Sundays, solemnities and feasts.

Temperance: Moderation, one of the four cardinal virtues.

Temptation: Any enticement to sin, from any source: the strivings of one's own faculties, the action of the devil, other persons, circumstances of life, etc. Temptation itself is not sin. Temptation can be avoided and overcome with the use of prudence and the help of grace.

Thanksgiving: An expression of gratitude to God for his goodness and the blessings he grants; one of the four ends of prayer.

Theism: A philosophy which admits the existence of God and the possibility of divine revelation; it is generally monotheistic and acknowledges God as transcendent and also active in the world. Because it is a philosophy rather than a system of theology derived from revelation, it does not include specifically Christian doctrines, like those concerning the Trinity, the Incarnation and Redemption.

Theodicy: From the Greek for God (*theos*) and judgment (*dike*), the study of God as he can be known by natural reason, rather than from supernatural revelation. First used by Gottfried Leibnitz (1646-1716), its primary objective is to make God's omnipotence compatible with the existence of evil.

Theological Virtues: The virtues which have God for their direct object: faith, or belief in God's infallible teaching; hope, or confidence in divine assistance; charity, or love of God. They are given to a person with grace in the first instance, through baptism and incorporation in Christ.

Theology: Knowledge of God and religion, deriving from and based on the data of divine Revelation, organized and systematized according to some kind of scientific method. It involves systematic study and presentation of the truths of divine Revelation in Sacred Scripture, tradition, and the teaching of the Church. Theology has been divided under various subject headings. Some of the major fields have been: dogmatic (systematic theology), moral, pastoral, historical, ascetical (the practice of virtue and means of attaining holiness and perfection), sacramental, and mystical (higher states of religious experience). Other subject headings include ecumenism (Christian unity, interfaith relations), ecclesiology (the nature and constitution of the Church), and Mariology (doctrine concerning the Blessed Virgin Mary), etc.

Theotokos: From the Greek for God-bearer, the pre-eminent title given to the Blessed Mother in the Oriental Church. This title has very ancient roots, stretching as far back as the third century but it did not become official in the Church until the Council of Ephesus in 431.

Thomism: The philosophy based on St. Thomas Aquinas (1224/5-1274), which is mandated to be the dominant philosophy used in Catholic educational institutions. (*See also* **Neo-Scholasticism** *and* **Scholasticism**.)

Tithing: Contribution of a portion of one's income, originally one-tenth, for purposes of religion and charity. The practice is mentioned 46 times in the Bible. In early Christian times, tithing was adopted in continuance of Old Testament practices of the Jewish people, and the earliest positive church legislation on the subject was enacted in 567. Catholics are bound in conscience to contribute to the support of their church, but the manner in which they do so is not fixed by law. Tithing, which amounts to a pledged contribution of a portion of one's income, has aroused new attention in recent years in the United States.

Titular Sees: Dioceses where the Church once flourished but which now exist only in name or title. Bishops without a territorial or residential diocese of their own; e.g., auxiliary bishops, are given titular sees. There are more than 2,000 titular sees; 16 of them are in the United States.

Transfinalization, Transignification: Terms coined to express the sign value of consecrated bread and wine with respect to the presence and action of Christ in the Eucharistic sacrifice and the spiritually vivifying purpose of the Eucharistic banquet in Holy Communion. The theory behind the terms has strong undertones of existential and "sign" philosophy, and has been criticized for its openness to interpretation at variance with the doctrine of transubstantiation and the abiding presence of Christ under the appearances of bread and wine after the sacrifice of the Mass and Communion have been completed. The terms, if used as substitutes for transubstantiation, are unacceptable; if they presuppose transubstantiation, they are acceptable as clarifications of its meaning.

Transubstantiation: "The way Christ is made present in this sacrament (Holy Eucharist) is none other than by the change of the whole substance of the bread into his Body, and of the whole substance of the wine into his Blood (in the Consecration at Mass), this

unique and wonderful change the Catholic Church rightly calls transubstantiation" (encyclical *Mysterium Fidei* of Paul VI, Sept. 3, 1965). The first official use of the term was made by the Fourth Council of the Lateran in 1215. Authoritative teaching on the subject was issued by the Council of Trent.

Treasury of the Church: The superabundant merits of Christ and the saints from which the Church draws to confer spiritual benefits, such as indulgences.

Triduum: A three-day series of public or private devotions.

U-Z

Ultramontanism: The movement found primarily in France during the 19th century that advocated a strong sense of devotion and service to the Holy See. Generally considered a reaction to the anti-papal tendencies of Gallicanism, its name was derived from the Latin for "over the mountains," a reference to the Alps, beyond which rested Rome and the Holy See.

Unction: From the Latin, *ungere*, meaning to anoint or smear, a term used to denote the Sacrament of the Sick (or the Anointing of the Sick); it was more commonly termed Extreme Unction and was given as an anointing to a person just before death.

Universal Law: *See* **Law**.

Urbi et Orbi: A Latin phrase meaning "To the City and to the World" that is a blessing given by the Holy Father. Normally, the first *Urbi et Orbi* delivered by a pontiff is immediately after his election by the College of Cardinals. This is a blessing accompanied by a short address to the crowds in St. Peter's Square and to the world; frequently, as with Pope John Paul II in 1978, it is delivered in as many languages as possible. The pope also delivers an *Urbi et Orbi* each year at Christmas and at Easter.

Usury: Excessive interest charged for the loan and use of money; a violation of justice.

Vagi: A Latin word meaning wanderers that is used to describe any homeless person with no fixed residence.

Veni Creator Spiritus: A Latin phrase, meaning "Come, Creator Spirit" that is part of a hymn sung to the Holy Spirit. The hymn invokes the presence of the Holy Spirit and was perhaps first composed by Rabanus Maurus (776-856). The hymn is commonly sung as part of the Divine Office, papal elections, episcopal consecrations, ordinations, councils, synods, canonical elections, and confirmations.

Venial Sin: *See under* **Sin**.

Veronica: A word resulting from the combination of a Latin word for true, *vera*, and a Greek word for image, *eikon*, designating a likeness of the face of Christ or the name of a woman said to have given him a cloth on which he caused an imprint of his face to appear. The veneration at Rome of a likeness depicted on cloth dates from about the end of the 10th century; it figured in a popular devotion during the Middle Ages, and in the Holy Face devotion practiced since the 19th century. A faint, indiscernible likeness said to be of this kind is preserved in St. Peter's Basilica. The origin of the likeness is uncertain, and the identity of the woman is unknown. Before the 14th century, there were no known artistic representations of an incident concerning a woman who wiped the face of Christ with a piece of cloth while he was carrying the cross to Calvary.

Vespers: From the Latin for evening, the evening service of the Divine Office, also known as Evening Prayer, or among Anglicans as Evensong.

Viaticum: Holy Communion given to those in danger of death. The word, derived from Latin, means provision for a journey through death to life hereafter.

Vicar Forane: A Latin term meaning "deputy outside" that is applied to the priest given authority by the local bishop over a certain area or region of the diocese.

Vicar General: A priest or bishop appointed by the bishop of a diocese to serve as his deputy, with ordinary executive power, in the administration of the diocese.

Vicar, Judicial: The title given to the chief judge and head of the tribunal of a diocese.

Virginity: Observance of perpetual sexual abstinence. The state of virginity, which is embraced for the love of God by religious with a public vow or by others with a private vow, was singled out for high praise by Christ (Mt 19:10-12) and has always been so regarded by the Church. In the encyclical *Sacra Virginitas*, Pius XII stated: "Holy virginity and that perfect chastity which is consecrated to the service of God is without doubt among the most perfect treasures which the founder of the Church has left in heritage to the society which he established." Paul VI approved in 1970 a rite in which women can consecrate their virginity "to Christ and their brethren" without becoming members of a religious institute. The *Ordo Consecrationis Virginum*, a revision of a rite promulgated by Clement VII in 1596, is traceable to the Roman liturgy of about 50.

Virtue: A habit or established capability for performing good actions. Virtues are natural (acquired and increased by repeating good acts) and/or supernatural (given with grace by God).

Visions: A charism by which a specially chosen individual is able to behold a person or something that is naturally invisible. A vision should not be confused with an illusion or hallucination. Like other charisms, a vision is granted for the good of people; it should be noted, however, that they are not essential for holiness or salvation. Many saints throughout history have beheld visions, among them St. Thomas Aquinas, St. Teresa of Ávila, St. John of the Cross, and St. Francis of Assisi.

Vocation: A call to a way of life. Generally, the term applies to the common call of all persons, from God, to holiness and salvation. Specifically, it refers to particular states of life, each called a vocation, in which response is made to this universal call; viz., marriage, the religious life and/or priesthood, the single state freely chosen or accepted for the accomplishment of God's will. The term also applies to the various occupations in which persons make a living. The Church supports the freedom of each individual in choosing a particular vocation, and reserves the right to pass on the acceptability of candidates for the priesthood and religious life. Signs or indicators of particular vocations are many, including a person's talents and interests, circumstances and obligations, invitations of grace and willingness to respond thereto.

Vow: A promise made to God with sufficient knowledge and freedom, which has as its object a moral good that is possible and better than its voluntary omission. A person who professes a vow binds himself or herself by the virtue of religion to fulfill the promise. The best known examples of vows are those of poverty, chastity and obedience professed by religious (*See* **Counsels, Evangelical**, individual entries). Public vows are made before a competent person, acting as an agent of the Church, who accepts the profession in the name of the Church, thereby giving public recognition to the person's dedication and consecration to God and divine worship. Vows of this kind are either solemn, rendering all contrary acts invalid as well as unlawful; or simple, rendering contrary acts unlawful. Solemn vows are for life; simple vows are for a definite period of time or for life. Vows professed without public recognition by the Church are called private vows. The Church, which has authority to accept and give public recognition to vows, also has authority to dispense persons from their obligations for serious reasons.

Witness, Christian: Practical testimony or evidence given by Christians of their faith in all circumstances of life—by prayer and general conduct, through good example and good works, etc.; being and acting in accordance with Christian belief; actual practice of the Christian faith.

Zeal: The expression of charity that permits one to serve God and others fully with the objective of furthering the Mystical Body of Christ.

Zucchetto: A small skullcap worn by ecclesiastics, most notably prelates and derived from the popular Italian vernacular term *zucca*, meaning a pumpkin, and used as slang for head. The Holy Father wears a white zucchetto made of watered silk; cardinals use scarlet, and bishops use purple. Priests of the monsignorial rank may wear black with purple piping. All others may wear simple black.

The Church Calendar

The calendar of the Roman Church consists of an arrangement throughout the year of a series of liturgical seasons, commemorations of divine mysteries, and commemorations of saints for purposes of worship.

The key to the calendar is the central celebration of the Easter Triduum, commemorating the supreme saving act of Jesus in his death and resurrection to which all other observances and acts of worship are related.

The purposes of this calendar were outlined in the Constitution on the Sacred Liturgy (*Sacrosanctum Concilium*, Nos. 102-105) promulgated by the Second Vatican Council.

"Within the cycle of a year ... (the Church) unfolds the whole mystery of Christ, not only from his incarnation and birth until his ascension, but also as reflected in the day of Pentecost, and the expectation of a blessed, hoped-for return of the Lord.

"Recalling thus the mysteries of redemption, the Church opens to the faithful the riches of her Lord's powers and merits, so that these are in some way made present at all times, and the faithful are enabled to lay hold of them and become filled with saving grace (No. 102).

"In celebrating this annual cycle of Christ's mysteries, holy Church honors with special love the Blessed Mary, Mother of God" (No. 103).

"The Church has also included in the annual cycle days devoted to the memory of the martyrs and the other saints (who) sing God's perfect praise in heaven and offer prayers for us. By celebrating the passage of these saints from earth to heaven the Church proclaims the paschal mystery as achieved in the saints who have suffered and been glorified with Christ; she proposes them to the faithful as examples who draw all to the Father through Christ, and through their merits she pleads for God's favors (No. 104).

"In the various seasons of the year and according to her traditional discipline, the Church completes the formation of the faithful by means of pious practices for soul and body, by instruction, prayer, and works of penance and mercy (No. 105)."

The Roman Calendar

Norms for a revised calendar for the Western Church as decreed by the Second Vatican Council were approved by Paul VI in the *motu proprio Mysterii Paschalis* dated Feb. 14, 1969. The revised calendar was promulgated a month later by a decree of the Congregation for Divine Worship and went into effect Jan. 1, 1970, with provisional modifications. Full implementation of all its parts was delayed in 1970 and 1971, pending the completion of work on related liturgical texts. The U.S. bishops ordered the calendar into effect for 1972.

The Seasons

Advent: The liturgical year begins with the first Sunday of Advent, which introduces a season of four weeks or slightly less duration with the theme of expectation of the coming of Christ. During the first two weeks, the final coming of Christ as Lord and Judge at the end of the world is the focus of attention. From Dec. 17-24, the emphasis shifts to anticipation of the celebration of his Nativity on the solemnity of Christmas.

Advent has four Sundays. Since the 10th century, the first Sunday has marked the beginning of the liturgical year in the Western Church. In the Middle Ages, a kind of pre-Christmas fast was in vogue during the season.

Christmas Season: The Christmas season begins with the vigil of Christmas and lasts until the Sunday after Jan. 6, inclusive.

The period between the end of the Christmas season and the beginning of Lent belongs to the ordinary time of the year. Of variable length, the pre-Lenten phase of this season includes what were formerly called the Sundays after Epiphany and the suppressed Sundays of Septuagesima, Sexagesima and Quinquagesima.

Lent: The penitential season of Lent begins on Ash Wednesday, which occurs between Feb. 4 and Mar. 11, depending on the date of Easter, and lasts until the Mass of the Lord's Supper (Holy Thursday). It has six Sundays. The sixth Sunday marks the beginning of Holy Week and is known as Passion (formerly called Palm) Sunday.

The origin of Lenten observances dates back to the fourth century or earlier.

Easter Triduum: The Easter Triduum begins with evening Mass of the Lord's Supper and ends with Evening Prayer on Easter Sunday.

Easter Season: The Easter season whose theme is resurrection from sin to the life of grace, lasts for 50 days, from Easter to Pentecost. Easter, the first Sunday after the first full moon following the vernal equinox, occurs between Mar. 22 and Apr. 25. The terminal phase of the Easter season, between the solemnities of the Ascension of the Lord and Pentecost, stresses anticipation of the coming and action of the Holy Spirit.

Ordinary Time: The season of Ordinary Time begins on Monday (or Tuesday if the feast of the Baptism of the Lord is celebrated on that Monday) after the Sunday following Jan. 6 and continues until the day before Ash Wednesday, inclusive. It begins again on the Monday after Pentecost and ends on the Saturday before the first Sunday of Advent. It consists of 33 or 34 weeks. The last Sunday is celebrated as the Solemnity of Christ the King. The overall purpose of the season is to elaborate the themes of salvation history.

The various liturgical seasons are characterized in part by the scriptural readings and Mass prayers assigned to each of them. During Advent, for example, the readings are messianic; during the Easter season, from the Acts of the Apostles, chronicling the Resurrection and the original proclamation of Christ by the Apostles, and from the Gospel of John; during Lent, baptismal and penitential passages. Mass prayers reflect the meaning and purpose of the various seasons.

Commemorations of Saints

The commemorations of saints are celebrated concurrently with the liturgical seasons and feasts of our Lord. Their purpose is to illustrate the paschal mysteries as reflected in the lives of saints, to honor them as heroes of holiness, and to appeal for their intercession.

In line with revised regulations, some former feasts were either abolished or relegated to observance in particular places by local option for one of two reasons: (1) lack of sufficient historical evidence for observance of the feasts; or, (2) lack of universal significance.

The commemoration of a saint, as a general rule, is observed on the day of death (*dies natalis*, day of birth to glory with God in heaven). Exceptions to this rule include the feasts of St. John the Baptist, who is honored on the day of his birth; Sts. Basil the Great and Gregory Nazianzen; and the brother saints, Cyril and Methodius, who are commemorated in joint feasts. Application of this general rule in the revised calendar resulted in date changes of some observances.

Sundays and Other Holy Days

Sunday is the original Christian feast day and holy day of obligation because of the unusually significant events of salvation history which took place and are commemorated on the first day of the week, viz., the Resurrection of Christ, the key event of his life and the fundamental fact of Christianity; and the descent of the Holy Spirit upon the Apostles on Pentecost, the birthday of the Church. The transfer of observance of the Lord's Day from the Sabbath to Sunday was made in apostolic times. The Mass and Liturgy of the Hours (Divine Office) of each Sunday reflect the themes and set the tones of the various liturgical seasons.

Holy days of obligation are special occasions on which Catholics who have reached the age of reason are seriously obliged, as on Sundays, to assist at Mass; they are also to refrain from work and involvement with business that impedes participation in divine worship and the enjoyment of appropriate rest and relaxation.

The holy days of obligation observed in the U.S. are: Christmas, the Nativity of Jesus, Dec. 25; Solemnity of Mary the Mother of God, Jan. 1; Ascension of the Lord; Assumption of Blessed Mary the Virgin, Aug. 15; All Saints' Day, Nov. 1; Immaculate Conception of Blessed Mary the Virgin, Dec. 8.

The precept to attend Mass is abrogated in the U.S.

whenever the Solemnity of Mary, the Assumption, or All Saints falls on a Saturday or Monday (1991 decree of U.S. bishops; approved by Holy See July 4, 1992, and effective Jan. 1, 1993).

In addition to these, there are four other holy days of obligation prescribed in the general law of the Church which are not so observed in the U.S.: Epiphany, Jan. 6; St. Joseph, Mar. 19; Corpus Christi; Sts. Peter and Paul, June 29. The solemnities of Epiphany and Corpus Christi are transferred to a Sunday in countries where they are not observed as holy days of obligation.

Solemnities, Feasts, Memorials

Categories of observances according to dignity and manner of observance are: solemnities, principal days in the calendar (observance begins with Evening Prayer I of the preceding day; some have their own vigil Mass); feasts (celebrated within the limits of the natural day); obligatory memorials (celebrated throughout the Church); optional memorials (observable by choice).

Fixed observances are those that are regularly celebrated on the same calendar day each year.

Movable observances are those that are not observed on the same calendar day each year. Examples of these are Easter (the first Sunday after the first full moon following the vernal equinox), Ascension (40 days after Easter), Pentecost (50 days after Easter), Trinity Sunday (first after Pentecost), Christ the King (last Sunday of the liturgical year).

Weekdays, Days of Prayer

Weekdays are those on which no proper feast or vigil is celebrated in the Mass or Liturgy of the Hours (Divine Office). On such days, the Mass may be that of the preceding Sunday, which expresses the liturgical spirit of the season, an optional memorial, a votive Mass, or a Mass for the dead. Weekdays of Advent and Lent are in a special category of their own.

Days of Prayer: Dioceses, at times to be designated by local bishops, should observe "days or periods of prayer for the fruits of the earth, prayer for human rights and equality, prayer for world justice and peace, and penitential observance outside of Lent." So stated the Instruction on Particular Calendars (No. 331) issued by the Congregation for the Sacraments and Divine Worship June 24, 1970.

These days are contemporary equivalents of what were formerly called ember and rogation days.

Ember days originated at Rome about the fifth century, probably as Christian replacements for seasonal festivals of agrarian cults. They were observances of penance, thanksgiving, and petition for divine blessing on the various seasons; they also were occasions of special prayer for clergy to be ordained. These days were observed four times a year.

Rogation days originated in France about the fifth century. They were penitential in character and also occasions of prayer for a bountiful harvest and protection against evil.

Days and Times of Penance

Fridays throughout the year and the season of Lent are penitential times.

Abstinence: Catholics in the U.S., from the age of 14 throughout life, are obliged to abstain from meat on

Ash Wednesday, the Fridays of Lent and Good Friday. The law forbids the use of meat, but not of eggs, the products of milk or condiments made of animal fat. Permissible are soup flavored with meat, meat gravy and sauces. The obligation to abstain from meat is not in force on days celebrated as solemnities (e.g., Christmas, Sacred Heart).

Fasting: Catholics in the U.S., from the day after their 18th birthday to the day after their 59th birthday, are also obliged to fast on Ash Wednesday and Good Friday. The law allows only one full meal a day, but does not prohibit the taking of some food in the morning and evening, observing as far as quantity and quality are concerned approved local custom. The order of meals is optional, i.e., the full meal may be taken in the evening instead of at midday. Also: (1) The combined quantity of food taken at the two lighter meals should not exceed the quantity taken at the full meal; (2) The drinking of ordinary liquids does not break the fast.

Obligation: There is a general obligation to do penance for sins committed and for the remission of punishment resulting from sin. Substantial observance of fasting and abstinence, prescribed for the community of the Church, is a matter of serious obligation; it allows, however, for alternate ways of doing penance (e.g., works of charity, prayer and prayer-related practices, almsgiving).

Readings at Mass

Scriptural readings for Masses on Sundays and holy days are indicated under the appropriate dates in the calendar pages for the year 2008-09. The Year A cycle is prescribed for Sunday Masses in liturgical year 2008, beginning Dec. 1, 2007. The Year Two cycle of weekday readings is prescribed for the year 2008. The Year B cycle is prescribed for 2009, beginning Nov. 30, 2008. The Year One cycle of weekday readings is prescribed for 2009.

Monthly Prayer Intentions

Intentions chosen and recommended by Pope Benedict XVI to the prayers of the faithful and circulated by the Apostleship of Prayer are given for each month of the calendar. Pope John Paul II expressed his desire that all Catholics make these intentions their own "in the certainty of being united with the Holy Father and praying according to his intentions and desires."

Celebrations in U.S. Particular Calendar

The General Norms for the Liturgical Year and the Calendar, issued in 1969 and published along with the General Roman Calendar for the Universal Church, noted that the calendar consists of the General Roman Calendar used by the entire Church and of particular calendars used in particular churches (nations or dioceses) or in families of religious.

The particular calendar for the U.S. contains the following celebrations. **January:** 4, Elizabeth Ann Seton; 5, John Neumann; 6, Bl. André Bessette. **March:** 3, Katharine Drexel. **May:** 10, Bl. Damien DeVeuster; 15, Isidore the Farmer. **July:** 1, Bl. Junípero Serra; 4, Independence Day; 14, Bl. Kateri Tekakwitha. **August:** 18, Jane Frances de Chantal. **September:** 9, Peter Claver. **October:** 6, Bl. Marie-Rose Durocher; 19, Isaac Jogues and John de Brébeuf and Companions; 20, Paul of the Cross. **November:** 13, Frances Xavier Cabrini; 18, Rose Philippine Duchesne; 23, Bl. Miguel Agustín Pro; fourth Thursday, Thanksgiving Day. **December:** 9, Juan Diego; 12, Our Lady of Guadalupe.

TABLE OF MOVABLE FEASTS

Year	Ash Wed.	Easter	Ascen-sion	Pente-cost	Weeks of Ordinary Time				First Sunday of Advent
					Before Lent		After Pentct.		
					Weeks	Ends	Weeks	Begins	
2008	Feb. 6	Mar. 23	May 1	May 11	4	Feb. 5	29	May 12	Nov. 30
2009	Feb. 25	Apr. 12	May 21	May 31	7	Feb. 24	26	June 1	Nov. 29
2010	Feb. 17	Apr. 4	May 13	May 23	6	Feb. 16	27	May 24	Nov. 28
2011	Mar. 9	Apr. 24	June 2	June 12	9	Mar. 8	24	June 13	Nov. 27
2012	Feb. 22	Apr. 8	May 17	May 27	7	Feb. 21	27	May 28	Dec. 2
2013	Feb. 13	Mar. 31	May 9	May 19	5	Feb. 12	28	May 20	Dec. 1
2014	Mar. 5	Apr. 20	May 29	June 8	8	Mar. 4	25	June 9	Nov. 30
2015	Feb. 18	Apr. 5	May 14	May 24	6	Feb. 17	27	May 25	Nov. 29
2016	Feb. 10	Mar. 27	May 5	May 15	5	Feb. 9	28	May 16	Nov. 27
2017	Mar. 1	Apr. 16	May 25	June 4	8	Feb. 28	26	June 5	Dec. 3
2018	Feb. 14	Apr. 1	May 10	May 20	6	Feb. 13	28	May 21	Dec. 2
2019	Mar. 6	Apr. 21	May 30	June 9	8	Mar. 5	25	June 10	Dec. 1
2020	Feb. 26	Apr. 12	May 21	May 31	7	Feb. 25	26	June 1	Nov. 29
2021	Feb. 17	Apr. 4	May 13	May 23	6	Feb. 16	27	May 24	Nov. 28
2022	Mar. 2	Apr. 17	May 26	June 5	8	Mar. 1	25	June 6	Nov. 27
2023	Feb. 22	Apr. 9	May 18	May 28	7	Feb. 21	27	May 29	Dec. 3
2024	Feb. 14	Mar. 31	May 9	May 19	6	Feb. 13	28	May 20	Dec. 1
2025	Mar. 5	Apr. 20	May 29	June 8	8	Mar. 4	25	June 9	Nov. 30
2026	Feb. 18	Apr. 5	May 14	May 24	6	Feb. 17	27	May 25	Nov. 29
2027	Feb. 10	Mar. 28	May 6	May 16	5	Feb. 9	28	May 17	Nov. 28
2028	Mar. 1	Apr. 16	May 25	June 4	8	Feb. 29	26	June 5	Dec. 3
2029	Feb. 14	Apr. 1	May 10	May 20	6	Feb. 13	28	May 21	Dec. 2
2030	Mar. 6	Apr. 21	May 30	June 9	9	Mar. 7	25	June 10	Dec. 1

2009 CALENDAR

January 2009

General: That the family may become more and more a place of training in charity, personal growth and transmission of the faith.

Mission: That the different Christian confessions may be committed to announcing the Good News and moving toward the full unity of all Christians in order to offer a more credible testimony of the Gospel.

1 Thurs. Octave of Christmas; Solemnity of the Blessed Virgin Mary, Mother of God; Holy (Nm 6: 22-27; Gal 4:4-7; Lk 2:16-21).
2 Fri. Sts. Basil the Great and Gregory Nazianzus, bishops and doctors of the Church; memorial.
3 Sat. Weekday. Christmas Weekday. Most Holy Name of Jesus; optional memorial
4 Sun. Epiphany of Our Lord; solemnity. (Is 60:1-6; Eph 3:2-3a,5-6; Mt 2:1-12).
5 Mon. St. John Neumann, bishop; memorial.
6 Tues. Christmas Weekday. Bl. Andre Bessette; optional memorial
7 Weds. Christmas Weekday. St. Raymond of Peñafort, priest; optional memorial
8 Thurs. Christmas Weekday.
9 Fri. Christmas Weekday.
10 Sat. Christmas Weekday.
11 Sun. Baptism of the Lord; feast. (Is 42:1-4,6-7; Acts 10:34-38; Lk 3:15-16,21-22).
12 Mon. Weekday. (First Week in Ordinary Time.)
13 Tues. Weekday. St. Hilary, optional memorial.
14 Weds. Weekday.
15 Thurs. Weekday.
16 Fri. Weekday. Week of Prayer for Christian Unity begins.
17 Sat. St. Anthony, abbot; memorial.
18 Sun. Second Sunday in Ordinary Time. (1 Sm 3:3b-10,19; 1 Cor 6:13c-15a,17-20; Jn 1:35-42.)
19 Mon. St. Agnes, virgin and martyr; memorial
20 Tues. Weekday. Sts. Fabian and Sebastian, martyrs, optional memorial.
21 Weds. St. Agnes, virgin and martyr; memorial.
22 Thurs. Weekday. St. Vincent, deacon, martyr; optional memorial. DAY OF PENANCE for violations committed through acts of abortion.
23 Fri. Weekday.
24 Sat. St. Francis de Sales, bishop-doctor; memorial.
25 Sun. Third Sunday in Ordinary Time. (Jon 3:1-5,10; 1 Cor 7:29-31; Mk 1:14-20.)
26 Mon. Sts. Timothy and Titus; memorial
27 Tues. Weekday. St. Angela Merici, optional memorial.
28 Weds. St. Thomas Aquinas, priest; memorial
29 Thurs. Weekday.
30 Fri. Weekday.
31 Sat. St. John Bosco, priest; memorial.

Observances:

The year begins with the Solemnity of the Mother of God, a holy day of obligation, and a papal message for the World Day of Peace, Jan. 1; customary ordination of bishops by the Pope on the Solemnity of the Epiphany, Jan. 6. Week of Prayer for Christian Unity, Jan. 18-25; National Prayer Vigil for Life and March for Life in Washington, D.C., in connection with the 1973 Roe vs. Wade and Dole vs. Bolton pro-abortion decisions of the U.S. Supreme Court, Jan. 21-22. On Jan. 22, a Day of Penance shall be observed in all dioceses of the United States.

February 2009

General: That the Pastors of the Church may always be docile to the action of the Holy Spirit in their teaching and in their service to God's people.

Mission: That the Church in Africa may find adequate ways and means to promote reconciliation, justice and peace efficaciously, according to the indications of the Synod of the Bishops' Special Assembly for Africa.

1 Sun. Fourth Sunday in Ordinary Time. (Dt 18:15-20; 1 Cor 7:32-35; Mk 1:21-28.)
2 Mon. Presentation of the Lord, feast (Mal 3:1-4; Heb 2:14-18; Lk 2: 22-40.)
3 Tues. St. Blaise, bishop and martyr; St. Ansgar; optional memorials.
4 Wed. Weekday.
5 Thurs. St. Agatha, virgin and martyr; memorial.
6 Fri. Weekday. St. Paul Miki and companions, martyrs; memorial.
7 Sat. Weekday.
8 Sun. Fifth Sunday in Ordinary Time (Jb 7:1-4,6-7; 1 Cor 9:16-19,22-23; Mk 1:29-39.)
9 Mon. Weekday.
10 Tues. St. Scholastica; memorial.
11 Wed. Weekday. Our Lady of Lourdes; optional memorial.
12 Thurs. Weekday.
13 Fri. Weekday.
14 Sat. Weekday. Sts. Cyril, monk and Methodius, bishop; optional memorial.
15 Sun. Sixth Sunday in Ordinary Time. (Lv 13:1-2,44-46; 1 Cor 10:31-11:1; Mk 1:40-45.)
16 Mon. Weekday. Seven Holy Founders of the Order of Servites; optional memorial.
17 Tues. Weekday.
18 Wed. Weekday.
19 Thurs. Weekday.
20 Fri. Weekday.
21 Sat. St. Peter Damian, bishop-doctor; optional memorial.
22 Sun. Seventh Sunday in Ordinary Time. (Is 43:18-19,21-22,24b-25; 1 Cor 1:18-22; Mk 2:1-12.)
23 Mon. St. Polycarp, bishop and martyr; memorial.
24 Tues. Weekday.
25 Weds. Ash Wednesday. (Jl 2:12-18; 2 Cor 5:20-6:2; Mt 6:1-6,16-18.) Fast and Abstinence.
26 Thurs. Lenten Weekday.
27 Fri. Lenten Weekday. Abstinence.
28 Sat. Lenten Weekday.

Observances:

The Presentation of the Child Jesus in the Temple is the traditional day for the blessings of candles that will be used throughout the year. The Presentation of the Lord is also the World Day for Consecrated Life. Optional memorial of Our Lady of Lourdes which is also World Day of the Sick, a day of prayer, healing and anointing of those who are ill is celebrated on Feb. 11.

The Lenten Season begins with Ash Wednesday (Feb. 25) when ashes are blessed and imposed on the forehead of the faithful to remind them of their obligation to do penance for sins, to seek spiritual renewal by means of prayer, fasting and good works. Catholics are reminded of the serious obligation to fast and abstain on those appointed days during the Lenten season as well as the opportunity for other acts of mortification and sacrifice.

March 2009

General: That the role of women may be more appreciated and used to good advantage in every country in the world.

Mission: That in the light of the letter addressed to them by Pope Benedict XVI, the bishops, priests, consecrated persons, and lay faithful of the Catholic Church in the Popular Republic of China may commit themselves to being the sign and instrument of unity, communion and peace.

1 Sun. First Sunday of Lent. (Gn 9:8-15; 1 Pt 3:18-22; Mk 1:12-15.)
2 Mon. Lenten Weekday.
3 Tues. Lenten Weekday. St. Katherine Drexel, virgin; optional memorial.
4 Weds. Lenten Weekday. St. Casimir; optional memorial.
5 Thurs. Lenten Weekday.
6 Fri. Lenten Weekday. Abstinence.
7 Sat. Lenten Weekday. Sts. Perpetua and Felicity, martyrs; optional memorial.
8 Sun. Second Sunday of Lent. (Gn 22:1-2,9a,10-13,15-18; Rom 8:31b-34; Mk 9:2-10.)
9 Mon. Lenten Weekday. St. Francis of Rome, religious; optional memorial.
10 Tues. Lenten Weekday.
11 Weds. Lenten Weekday.
12 Thurs. Lenten Weekday.
13 Fri. Lenten Weekday. Abstinence.
14 Sat. Lenten Weekday.
15 Sun. Third Sunday of Lent. (Ex 20:1-17; 1 Cor 1:22-25; Jn 2:13-25.)
16 Mon. Lenten Weekday.
17 Tues. Lenten Weekday. St. Patrick; optional memorial.
18 Weds. Lenten Weekday. St. Cyril of Jerusalem; optional memorial.
19 Thurs. St. Joseph, husband of the Blessed Virgin Mary; solemnity.
20 Fri. Lenten Weekday. Abstinence.
21 Sat. Lenten Weekday.
22 Sun. Fourth Sunday of Lent. (2 Chr 36:14-16,19-23; Eph 2: 4-10; Jn 3:14-21.)
23 Mon. Lenten Weekday. St. Toribio de Mogrovejo; optional memorial
24 Tues. Lenten Weekday.
25 Weds. Annunciation of the Lord; solemnity.
26 Thurs. Lenten Weekday.
27 Fri. Lenten Weekday. Abstinence.
28 Sat. Lenten Weekday.
29 Sun. Fifth Sunday of Lent. (Jer 31:31-34; Heb 5:7-9; Jn 12:20-33.)
30 Mon. Lenten Weekday.
31 Tues. Lenten Weekday.

Observances:

The Solemnity of St. Joseph, husband of Mary, is observed March 19. The Solemnity of the Annunciation is observed on March 25. These are the only two feasts days celebrated during the Lenten Season.

April 2009

General: That the Lord may bless the farmers with an abundant harvest and sensitize the richer populations to the drama of hunger in the world

Mission: That the Christians who work in areas where the conditions of the poor, weak and women and children are most tragic, may be signs of hope, thanks to their courageous testimony to the Gospel of solidarity and love.

1 Weds. Lenten Weekday.
2 Thurs. Lenten Weekday. St. Francis of Paola, hermit; optional memorial.
3 Fri. Lenten Weekday.
4 Sat. Lenten Weekday. St. Isidore, bishop and doctor; optional memorial.
5 Sun. Palm Sunday/The Lord's Passion (Mk 11:1-10/Is 50:4-7; Phil 2:6-11; Mk 14:1–15:47.)
6 Mon. Monday of Holy Week.
7 Tues. Tuesday of Holy Week.
8 Weds. Wednesday of Holy Week.
9 Thurs. Holy Thursday. Chrism Mass in the Morning. The Easter Triduum begins with the evening Mass of the Lord's Supper.
10 Fri. Good Friday. The Lord's Passion. Fast and Abstinence.
11 Sat. Holy Saturday. Easter Vigil.
12 Sun. Easter Sunday: Resurrection of the Lord; solemnity (Acts 10:34a,37-43; Col 3:1-4 or 1 Cor 5:6b-8; Jn 20:1-9 or Mk 16:1-7 or [at an afternoon or evening Mass: Lk 24:13-35].)
13 Mon. Easter Monday; solemnity.
14 Tues. Easter Tuesday; solemnity.
15 Weds. Easter Wednesday; solemnity.
16 Thurs. Easter Thursday; solemnity.
17 Fri. Easter Friday; solemnity.
18 Sat. Easter Saturday; solemnity.
19 Sun. Second Sunday of Easter. Divine Mercy Sunday. (Acts 4:32-35; 1 Jn 5:1-6; Jn 20:19-31.)
20 Mon. Easter Weekday.
21 Tues. Easter Weekday. St. Anselm, bishop and doctor; optional memorial.
22 Weds. Easter Weekday.
23 Thurs. Easter Weekday. St. George; St. Adalbert; optional memorials.
24 Fri. Easter Weekday. St. Fidelis, priest; optional memorial.
25 Sat. St. Mark, evangelist, feast.
26 Sun. Third Sunday of Easter. (Acts 3:13-15,17-19; 1 Jn 2:1-5a; Lk 24:35-48.)
27 Mon. Easter Weekday.
28 Tues. Easter Weekday. St. Peter Chanel, priest-martyr; St. Louis Mary de Montfort; optional memorials.
29 Weds. St. Catherine of Siena, virgin-doctor; memorial.
30 Thurs. Easter Weekday. St. Pius V; optional memorial.

Observances: Holy Week — Passion Sunday also called Palm Sunday begins these most solemn and holy celebrations of the Church Year. On this day the Church blesses and distributes palms commemorating our Lord's triumphal entrance into Jerusalem and during this celebration the Passion is read for the first time during Holy Week. Monday, Tuesday, and Wednesday of Holy Week are preparatory days leading to the Sacred Triduum. The Sacred Triduum begins with the Mass of the Lord' Supper on Holy Thursday evening. Good Friday commemorates the Passion of Jesus. Holy Saturday evening begins the Easter Vigil. Easter Sunday is the day when the Holy Father delivers the traditional *Urbi et Orbi* address.

May 2009

General: That the laity and the Christian communities may be responsible promoters of priestly and religious vocations.

Mission: That the recently founded Catholic Churches, grateful to the Lord for the gift of faith, may be ready to share in the universal mission of the Church, offering their availability to preach the Gospel throughout the world.

1 Fri. Easter Weekday. St. Joseph the Worker; optional memorial.
2 Sat. St. Athanasius, bishop-doctor; memorial.
3 Sun. Fourth Sunday of Easter. (Acts 4:8-12; 1 Jn 3:1-2; Jn 10:11-18.)
4 Mon. Easter Weekday.
5 Tues. Easter Weekday.
6 Weds. Weekday.
7 Thurs. Easter Weekday.
8 Fri. Easter Weekday.
9 Sat. Easter Weekday. Bl. Damien Joseph deVeuster of Molokai, priest; optional memorial.
10 Sun. Fifth Sunday of Easter. (Acts 9:26-31; 1 Jn 3:18-24; Jn 15:1-8.)
11 Mon. Easter Weekday.
12 Tues. Easter Weekday. . Sts. Nereus and Achilleus, martyrs; St. Pancras, martyr; optional memorials.
13 Weds. Easter Weekday. Our Lady of Fatima; optional memorial.
14 Thurs. St. Matthias, apostle; feast.
15 Fri. Easter Weekday. . St. Isidore the Farmer; optional memorial.
16 Sat. Easter Weekday.
17 Sun. Sixth Sunday of Easter. (Acts 10:25-26,34-35,44-48; 1 Jn 4:7-10; Jn 15: 9-17.)
18 Mon. Easter Weekday. St. John I; optional memorial.
19 Tues. Easter Weekday.
20 Weds. Easter Weekday. St. Bernardine of Siena, priest; optional memorial.
21 Thurs. Weekday. Ascension of our Lord; solemnity. Holy Day of obligation (Acts 1:1-11; Eph 1:17-23; Mt 28:16-20.) If transferred to Sunday, Easter Weekday.
22 Fri. Easter Weekday. St. Rita of Cascia, religious; optional memorial.
23 Sat. Easter Weekday.
24 Sun. Seventh Sunday of Easter. (Acts 1:15-17,20a,20c-26; 1 Jn 4: 11-16; Mk 17:11b-19.)If transferred from Thursday, then the Ascension of Our Lord.
25 Mon. Easter Weekday. St. Bede; St. Gregory VII; St. Mary Magdalene dePazzi; optional memorials.
26 Tues. St. Philip Neri, priest; memorial.
27 Weds. Easter Weekday. St. Augustine of Canterbury, bishop; optional memorial.
28 Thurs. Easter Weekday.
29 Fri. Easter Weekday.
30 Sat. Easter Weekday.
31 Sun. Pentecost Sunday; solemnity. (Acts 2:1-11; 1 Cor 12: 3b-7,12-13; or Gal 5:16-25; Jn 20:19-23 or Jn 15:26-27; 16:12-15.)

Observances: The Solemnity of the Ascension celebrated May 21 (transferred to Sunday in some dioceses) is a Holy Day of Obligation. The month begins with the celebration of St. Joseph the Worker on May 1 reminding society of the dignity of work dedicated to the honor and glory of God. The Easter Season is completed with the celebration of the Feast of Pentecost on Sunday, May 31. Also, the month of May is traditionally dedicated to our Blessed Mother.

June 2009

General: That international attention towards the poorer countries may give rise to more concrete help, in particular to relieve them of the crushing burden of foreign debt.

Mission: That the particular Churches operating in regions marked by violence may be sustained by the love and concrete closeness of all the Catholics in the world.

1 Mon. St. Justin, martyr; optional memorial.
2 Tues. Weekday. Sts. Marcellinus and Peter, martyrs; optional memorial.
3 Weds. St. Charles Lwanga and Companions, martyrs; memorial
4 Thurs. Weekday.
5 Fri. St. Boniface, bishop and martyr; memorial.
6 Sat. Weekday. St. Norbert, bishop; optional memorial.
7 Sun. Most Holy Trinity; solemnity. (Dt 4:32-34, 39-40; Rom 8:14-17; Mt 28:16-20.)
8 Mon. Weekday.
9 Tues. Weekday. St. Ephrem, deacon and doctor; optional memorial.
10 Weds. Weekday.
11 Thurs. St. Barnabas, apostle; memorial.
12 Fri. Weekday.
13 Sat. St. Anthony of Padua, priest-doctor; memorial.
14 Sun. Most Holy Body and Blood of Christ (Corpus Christi); solemnity (Ex 24:3-8; Heb 9:11-15; Mk 14: 12-16,22-26.)
15 Mon. Weekday.
16 Tues. Weekday.
17 Weds. Weekday.
18 Thurs. Weekday.
19 Fri. Sacred Heart of Jesus; solemnity
20 Sat. Immaculate Heart of Mary; memorial
21 Sun. Twelfth Sunday in Ordinary Time. (Job 38:1, 8-11; 2 Cor 5:14-17; Mk 4:35-41.)
22 Mon. Weekday. St. Paulinus of Nola; Sts. John Fisher and Thomas More; optional memorials.
23 Tues. Weekday.
24 Weds. Nativity of St. John the Baptist; solemnity.
25 Thurs. Weekday.
26 Fri. Weekday.
27 Sat. Weekday. St. Cyril of Alexandria, bishop and doctor; optional memorial.
28 Sun. Thirteenth Sunday of Ordinary Time. (Wis 1:13-15,2:23-24; 2 Cor 8:7,9,13-15; Mk 5:21-43.)
29 Mon. Sts. Peter and Paul, apostles; solemnity.
30 Tues. Weekday. First Martyrs of the Church of Rome; optional memorial.

Observances:
Following the great celebration of Pentecost, the Church celebrates in succession, the Feast of the Most Holy Trinity on June 7, the Feast of Corpus Christi, on June 14 and then the Feast of the Most Sacred Heart of Jesus on Friday, June 19 followed by the Feast of the Immaculate Heart of Mary. All of these celebrations afford us the experience of entering more deeply into the depth of our Lord's Paschal Mystery. It is the custom in certain dioceses to gather for a Corpus Christi procession to venerate the Body of Christ at special altars prepared near the Cathedral or parish church. The procession concludes with Benediction of the Blessed Sacrament. Furthering this experience of the Paschal Mystery, the month of June has several martyrs' feast days: The Feast of the Birth of John the Baptist on June 24 followed by the Feast of Sts. Peter and Paul on June 29. The month concludes with the celebration of the First Martyrs of Rome on June 30.

July 2009

General: That the Christians of the Middle East may live their faith in full freedom and be an instrument of peace and reconciliation.

Mission: That the Church may be the seed and nucleus of a humanity reconciled and reunited in God's one and only family, thanks to the testimony of all the faithful in every country in the world.

1 Weds. Weekday. Bl. Junipero Serra, optional memorial.
2 Thurs. Weekday.
3 Fri. St. Thomas, apostle; feast.
4 Sat. Weekday. St. Elizabeth of Portugal; optional memorial. Proper Mass for Independence Day.
5 Sun. Fourteenth Sunday in Ordinary Time. (Ez 2:2-5; 1 Cor 12:7-10; Mk 6:1-6.)
6 Mon. Weekday. St. Maria Goretti, virgin and martyr; optional memorial.
7 Tues. Weekday.
8 Weds. Weekday.
9 Thurs. Weekday. St. Augustine Zhao Rong and companions, martyrs; optional memorial.
10 Fri. Weekday.
11 Sat. St. Benedict, abbot; memorial.
12 Sun. Fifteenth Sunday in Ordinary Time. (Am 7:12-15; Eph 1:3-14; Mk 6:7-13.)
13 Mon. Weekday. St. Henry; optional memorial.
14 Tues. Bl. Kateri Tekawitha, virgin; memorial.
15 Weds. Weekday. St. Bonaventure, bishop-doctor; memorial.
16 Thurs. Weekday. Our Lady of Mount Carmel; optional memorial.
17 Fri. Weekday.
18 Sat. Weekday. St. Camillus de Lellis, priest; optional memorial.
19 Sun. Sixteenth Sunday in Ordinary. (Jer 23:1-6; Eph 2:13-18; Mk 6:30-34.)
20 Mon. Weekday. St. Apollinaris, martyr; optional memorial.
21 Tues. Weekday. St. Lawrence of Brandisi, priest-doctor; optional memorial
22 Weds. St. Mary Magdalene; memorial.
23 Thurs. Weekday. St. Bridget of Sweden, religious; optional memorial.
24 Fri. Weekday. St. Sharbel Makhluf, priest; optional memorial.
25 Sat. St. James, apostle and martyr; feast.
26 Sun. Seventeenth Sunday in Ordinary Time. (2Kgs 4:42-44; Eph 4:1-6; Jn 6:1-15.)
27 Mon. Weekday.
28 Tues. Weekday.
29 Weds. St. Martha; memorial.
30 Thurs. Weekday. St. Peter Chrysologus, bishop and doctor; optional memorial
31 Fri. St. Ignatius of Loyola, priest; memorial.

Observances:
Blessed Juniper Serra, whose optional memorial may be celebrated July 1, founder of the California Missions who has given his name to the promotion of priestly vocations. St. Thomas the apostles is observed on July 3; St. Maria Goretti, July 6; St. Benedict, the founder of western monasticism and patron saint of Europe, July 11; Blessed Kateri Tekawitha, July 14; St. Bonaventure, called the second founder of the Franciscan Order, July 15; Independence Day, July 4, is observed with a special Mass for celebration in the United States.

August 2009

General: That public opinion may be more aware of the problem of millions of displaced persons and refugees and that concrete solutions may be found for their often tragic situation.

Mission: That those Christians who are discriminated against and persecuted in many Countries because of the name of Christ may have their human rights, equality and religious freedom recognized, in order to be able to live and profess their own faith freely.

1 Sat. Weekday. St. Alphonsus Ligouri, bishop-doctor; memorial.
2 Sun. Eighteenth Sunday in Ordinary Time. (Ex 16:2-4,12-15; Eph 4:17,20-24; Jn 6:24-35.)
3 Mon. Weekday.
4 Tues. St. John Mary Vianney, priest; memorial.
5 Weds. Weekday. Dedication of the Basilica of St. Mary Major in Rome; optional memorial.
6 Thurs. Transfiguration of the Lord; feast.
7 Fri. Weekday. Sts. Cajetan, priest; Sixtus and Companions, martyrs; optional memorials.
8 Sat. St. Dominic, priest; memorial
9 Sun. Nineteenth Sunday in Ordinary Time. (1Kgs 19:4-8; Eph 4:30-5:2; Jn 6:41-51.)
10 Mon. St. Lawrence, deacon; feast.
11 Tues. St. Clare, virgin; memorial.
12 Weds. Weekday. St. Jane Frances de Chantal, religious; optional memorial.
13 Thurs. Weekday. Sts. Pontian, pope, martyr and Hippolytus, priest and martyr; optional memorials.
14 Fri. St. Maximilian Mary Kolbe, priest and martyr; memorial.
15 Sat. Assumption of the Blessed Virgin Mary; solemnity.
16 Sun. Twentieth Sunday in Ordinary. (Prv 9:1-6; Eph 5:15-20; Jn 6:51-58.)
17 Mon. Weekday.
18 Tues. Weekday.
19 Weds. Weekday. St. John Eudes, priest; optional memorial.
20 Thurs. St. Bernard, abbot and doctor; memorial.
21 Fri. St. Pius X, pope; memorial.
22 Sat. Queenship of the Blessed Virgin Mary; memorial.
23 Sun. Twenty-first Sunday of Ordinary Time. (Jos 24:1-2a,15-17,18b; Eph 5:21-32; Jn 6:60-69.)
24 Mon. St. Bartholomew, apostle; feast.
25 Tues. Weekday. Sts. Louis of France and Joseph Calasanz, priest; optional memorials.
26 Weds. Weekday.
27 Thurs. St. Monica; memorial.
28 Fri. St. Augustine, bishop and doctor; memorial.
29 Sat. Martyrdom of St. John the Baptist; memorial.
30 Sun. Twenty-second Sunday in Ordinary Time. (Dt 4:1-2,6-8; Jas 1:17-18,21b-22,27; Mk 7:1-8,14-15,21-23.)
31 Mon. Weekday.

Observances:
St. Alphonsus Liguori, doctor of the Church and moral theologian, Aug. 1; St. John Vianney, patron saint of parish priests, Aug. 4; The Feast of the Transfiguration of the Lord, Aug. 6; St. Dominic, founder of the Dominicans, Aug, 8; St. Clare, foundress of the Poor Clares, Aug. 11; St. Maximilian Mary Kolbe, Aug. 14. The Feast of the Assumption of the Blessed Virgin Mary, Aug. 15; The Queenship of the Blessed Virgin Mary, Aug. 22. St. Monica, Aug. 27, St. Augustine, Aug. 28 and the Martyrdom of St. John the Baptist, Aug. 29.

September 2009

General: That the word of God may be better known, welcomed and lived as the source of freedom and joy.

Mission: That Christians in Laos, Cambodia, and Myanmar, who often meet with great difficulties, may not be discouraged from announcing the Gospel to their brothers, trusting in the strength of the Holy Spirit.

1 Tues. Weekday.
2 Weds. Weekday.
3 Thurs. St. Gregory the Great, pope and doctor; memorial.
4 Fri. Weekday.
5 Sat. Weekday. Bl. Teresa of Calcutta; foundress and religious; optional memorial.
6 Sun. Twenty-third Sunday in Ordinary Time. (Is 35:4-7a; Jas 2:1-5; Mk 7:31-37.)
7 Mon. Weekday.
8 Tues. The Nativity of the Blessed Virgin Mary; feast.
9 Weds. St. Peter Claver, priest; memorial.
10 Thurs. Weekday.
11 Fri. Weekday.
12 Sat. Weekday. Holy Name of Mary; optional memorial.
13 Sun. Twenty-fourth Sunday of Ordinary Time. (Is 50: 5-9a; Jas 2:14-18; Mk 8:27-35.)
14 Mon. Exaltation of the Holy Cross; feast.
15 Tues. Our Lady of Sorrows; memorial.
16 Weds. Weekday. Sts. Cornelius, pope-martyr and Cyprian, bishop-martyr; memorial.
17 Thurs. Weekday. St. Robert Bellarmine, bishop and doctor; optional memorial.
18 Fri. Weekday.
19 Sat. Weekday. St. Januarius, bishop-martyr; optional memorial
20 Sun. Twenty-fifth Sunday in Ordinary Time. (Wis 2:12,17-20; Jas 3:16–4:3; Mk 9:30-37.)
21 Mon. St. Matthew, apostle and evangelist; feast.
22 Tues. Weekday.
23 Weds. St. Pio of Pietrelcina, priest; memorial.
24 Thurs. Weekday.
25 Fri. Weekday.
26 Sat. Weekday. Sts. Cosmas and Damian, martyrs; optional memorial.
27 Sun. Twenty-sixth Sunday in Ordinary Time. (Nm 11:25-29; Jas 5:1-6; Mk 9:38-43,45,47-48.)
28 Mon. Weekday. St. Wenceslaus; St. Lawrence Ruiz and companions; optional memorials.
29 Tues. Sts. Michael, Gabriel, and Raphael, archangels; feast.
30 Weds. St. Jerome, priest and doctor; memorial.

Observances:

The Nativity of the Blessed Virgin Mary, Sept. 8; The Exaltation of the Holy Cross, Sept. 14; Our Lady of Sorrows, Sept. 15; Sts. Cornelius and Cyprian, Sept. 16.; Sts. Michael, Gabriel, and Raphael, archangels, Sept. 29, and St. Jerome, Sept. 30.

Labor Day is celebrated Sept. 7 with a special Mass for the blessing of human labor.

October 2009

General: That Sunday may be lived as the day on which Christians gather to celebrate the risen Lord, participating in the Eucharist.

Mission: That the entire People of God, to whom Christ entrusted the mandate to go and preach the Gospel to every creature, may eagerly assume their own missionary responsibility and consider it the highest service they can offer humanity.

1 Thurs. St. Therese of the Child Jesus; memorial.
2 Fri. The Guardian Angels; memorial.
3 Sat. Weekday.
4 Sun. Twenty-seventh Sunday in Ordinary Time. (Gn 2:18-24; Heb 2:9-11; Mk 10:2-16.)
5 Mon. Weekday.
6 Tues. St. Bruno, priest and Bl. Marie Rose Durocher, virgin; optional memorials.
7 Weds. Our Lady of the Rosary; memorial
8 Thurs. Weekday.
9 Fri. Weekday. St. Denis and Companions, martyrs; St. John Leonardi, priest; optional memorials.
10 Sat. Weekday. .
11 Sun. Twenty-eighth Sunday in Ordinary. (Wis 7:7-11; Heb 4:12-13; Mk 10: 17-30.)
12 Mon. Weekday.
13 Tues. Weekday.
14 Weds. Weekday. Callistus I, pope-martyr; optional memorial.
15 Thurs. St. Teresa of Jesus, virgin and doctor; memorial.
16 Fri. Weekday. Sts. Hedwig, religious; Margaret Mary Alacoque, virgin; optional memorials.
17 Sat. St. Ignatius of Antioch, bishop-martyr; memorial.
18 Sun. Twenty-ninth Sunday in Ordinary Time. (Is 53:10-11; Heb 4:14-16; Mk 10:35-45.)
19 Mon. Sts. John de Brebeuf, Isaac Jogues and companions, martyrs; memorial.
20 Tues. Weekday. St. Paul of the Cross; optional memorial.
21 Weds. Weekday.
22 Thurs. Weekday.
23 Fri. Weekday. St. John of Capistrano, priest; optional memorial
24 Sat. Weekday. St. Anthony Mary Claret, bishop; optional memorial.
25 Sun. Thirtieth Sunday in Ordinary Time. (Jer 31:7-9; Heb 5:1-6; Mk 10:46-52.)
26 Mon. Weekday.
27 Tues. Weekday.
28 Weds. Simon and Jude, apostles; feast.
29 Thurs. Weekday.
30 Fri. Weekday.
31 Sat. Weekday.

Observances: St. Therese of the Child Jesus, doctor of the Church, Oct.1; St. Teresa of Jesus, doctor of the Church, reformer of the Carmelite Order, Oct. 15; St. Ignatius of Antioch, Oct. 17; The North American Martyrs, Oct. 19. St. Paul of the Cross, founder of the Congregation of the Passion, Oct. 20. Sts. Simon and Jude, apostles, Oct. 28.

Respect Life Sunday calls the nation to a deeper respect for all human life from natural conception to natural death. Mission Sunday is observed this month, with appeals for prayer and financial support for the ministry of evangelization at home and abroad. Vocation Awareness Sunday is also celebrated this month calling to mind the various vocations in the life of the Church with particular attention to priestly and religious vocations.

November 2009

General: That all the men and women in the world, especially those who have responsibilities in the field of politics and economics, may never fail in their commitment to safeguard creation.

Mission: That believers in the different religions, through the testimony of their lives and fraternal dialogue, may clearly demonstrate that the name of God is a bearer of peace.

1 Sun. All Saints; solemnity. (Rv 7:2-4,9-14; 1 Jn 3:1-3; Mt 5:1-12a)
2 Mon. Commemoration of All the Faithful Departed. All Souls Day.
3 Tues. Weekday. St. Martin de Porres, religious; optional memorial.
4 Weds. St. Charles Borromeo, bishop; memorial.
5 Thurs. Weekday.
6 Fri. Weekday.
7 Sat. Weekday.
8 Sun. Thirty-second Sunday in Ordinary Time. (1Kgs 17:10-16; Heb 9:24-28; Mk 12:38-44.)
9 Mon. Dedication of the Basilica of St. John Lateran in Rome; feast.
10 Tues. St. Leo the Great, pope-doctor; memorial.
11 Weds. St. Martin of Tours, bishop; memorial.
12 Thurs. St. Josaphat, bishop and martyr; memorial.
13 Fri. St. Frances Xavier Cabrini, virgin; memorial.
14 Sat. Weekday.
15 Sun. Thirty-third Sunday in Ordinary Time. (Dn 12:1-3; Heb 10:11-14, 18; Mk 13:24-32.)
16 Mon. Weekday. St. Margaret of Scotland; St. Gertrude; optional memorials.
17 Tues. St. Elizabeth of Hungary, religious; memorial.
18 Weds. Weekday. St. Rose Philippine Duchesne, virgin; Dedication of the Basilicas of St. Peter and St. Paul, apostles, in Rome; optional memorials.
19 Thurs. Weekday.
20 Fri. Weekday.
21 Sat. Presentation of the Blessed Virgin Mary; memorial.
22 Sun. Our Lord Jesus Christ the King; solemnity. (Dn 7:13-14; Rv 1:5-8; Jn 18:33b-37.)
23 Mon. Weekday. St. Clement I; St. Columban; Bl. Miguel Agustin Pro; optional memorials.
24 Tues. Sts. Andrew Dung-Lac, priest-martyr and Companions, martyrs; memorials.
25 Weds. Weekday. St. Catherine of Alexandria, virgin and martyr; optional memorial.
26 Thurs. Weekday. Thanksgiving Day, proper Mass.
27 Fri. Weekday.
28 Sat. Weekday.
29 Sun. First Sunday of Advent. (Is 63:16b-17,19b;64:2-7; 1 Cor 1:3-9; Mk 13:33-37.)
30 Mon. St. Andrew, apostle; feast.

Observances: All Saints Day, Nov. 1; All Souls Day, Nov. 2; St. Charles Borromeo, Nov. 4; Frances Xavier Cabrini, foundress, first U.S. citizen-saint, Nov. 13; St. Albert the Great, doctor of the Church, Nov. 15; St. Elizabeth of Hungary, Nov. 17. Presentation of the Blessed Virgin Mary, Nov. 21; Christ the King, Nov. 22; St. Andrew Dung-Lac and companions, the Korean Martyrs, Nov. 24.; Thanksgiving Day, Nov. 26. The beginning of the Church Year, the first Sunday of Advent, Nov. 29. The annual fall meeting of the bishops of the U.S. in Washington, D.C. Particular attention will be given to doctrinal, pastoral and educational issues that impact the life of the Church in the United States.

December 2009

General: That children may be respected and loved and never be the victims of exploitation in its various forms.

Mission: That at Christmas the peoples of the earth may recognize in the Word Incarnate the light which illuminates every man and that the Nations may open their doors to Christ, the Savior of the world.

1 Tues. Advent Weekday.
2 Weds. Advent Weekday.
3 Thurs. St. Francis Xavier, priest; memorial.
4 Fri. Advent Weekday. St. John Damascene, priest-doctor; optional memorial.
5 Sat. Advent Weekday.
6 Sun. Second Sunday of Advent. (Is 40:1-5,9-11; 2 Pt 3:8-14; Mk 1:1-8.)
7 Mon. St. Ambrose, bishop; memorial.
8 Tues. Immaculate Conception of the Blessed Virgin Mary; solemnity (Gn 3: 9-15,20; Eph 1:3-6,11-12; Lk 1:26-38.) Holy Day of Obligation.
9 Weds. Advent Weekday. St. Juan Diego; optional memorial.
10 Thurs. Advent Weekday.
11 Fri. Advent Weekday. St. Damasus I, pope; optional memorial.
12 Sat. Our Lady of Guadalupe; feast.
13 Sun. Third Sunday of Advent. (Is 61:1-2a,10-11; 1 Thes 5:16-24; Jn 1:6-8,19-28.)
14 Mon. St. John of the Cross; memorial.
15 Tues. Advent Weekday.
16 Weds. Late Advent Weekday.
17 Thurs. Late Advent Weekday.
18 Fri. Late Advent Weekday.
19 Sat. Late Advent Weekday
20 Sun. Fourth Sunday of Advent. (2 Sm 7:1-5,8b-12,14a,16; Rom 16:25-27; Le 1:26-38.)
21 Mon. Late Advent Weekday.
22 Tues. Late Advent Weekday.
23 Weds. Late Advent Weekday. St. John of Kanty, priest; optional memorial.
24 Thurs. Late Advent Weekday.
25 Fri. Nativity of the Lord, Christmas; solemnity. Holy Day of Obligation. (Vigil Mass – Is 62:1-5; Acts 13:16-17,22-25; Mt 1:1-25 or 1:18-25. Midnight Mass – Is 9:1-6; Ti 2:11-14; Lk 2:1-14. Mass at Dawn – Is 62:11-12; Ti 3:4-7; Lk 2:15-20. Mass during the day – Is 52:7-10; Heb 1:1-6; Jn 1:1-18 or 1:1-5,9-14.)
26 Sat. St. Stephen, first martyr; feast.
27 Sun. Holy Family of Jesus, Mary, and Joseph. (Sir 3:2-7,12-14; Col 3:12-21; Lk 2:22-40.)
28 Mon. Holy Innocents; feast.
29 Tues. Fifth Day in the Octave of Christmas. St. Thomas Becket, bishop-martyr; optional memorial.
30 Weds. Sixth Day in the Octave of Christmas.
31 Thurs. Seventh Day in the Octave of Christmas. St. Sylvester, pope; optional memorial.

Observances:; Sts. John of Damascus, John of the Cross, Peter Canisius, doctors of the Church; Immaculate Conception, Dec. 8; St. Juan Diego, Dec. 9; Our Lady of Guadalupe, Dec. 12; Birth of our Lord, Dec. 25; St. Stephen, proto-martyr, Dec. 26; St. John, apostle-evangelist, Dec. 27; Holy Family, Dec. 28; St. Thomas Becket, Dec. 29; St. Sylvester, Dec. 31.

HOLY DAYS AND OTHER OBSERVANCES

The following list includes the six holy days of obligation observed in the U.S. and additional observances of devotional and historical significance. The dignity or rank of observances is indicated by the terms: solemnity (highest in rank); feast; memorial (for universal observance); optional memorial (for celebration by choice).

All Saints, Nov. 1, Holy Day of Obligation, solemnity. Commemorates all the blessed in heaven, and is intended particularly to honor the blessed who have no special feasts. The background of the feast dates to the fourth century when groups of martyrs, and later other saints, were honored on a common day in various places. In 609 or 610, the Pantheon, a pagan temple at Rome, was consecrated as a Christian church for the honor of Our Lady and the martyrs (later all saints). In 835, Gregory IV fixed Nov. 1 as the date of observance.

All Souls, Commemoration of the Faithful Departed, Nov. 2. The dead were prayed for from the earliest days of Christianity. By the sixth century it was customary in Benedictine monasteries to hold a commemoration of deceased members of the order at Pentecost. A common commemoration of all the faithful departed on the day after All Saints was instituted in 998 by St. Odilo, of the Abbey of Cluny, and an observance of this kind was accepted in Rome in the 14th century.

Annunciation of the Lord (formerly, Annunciation of the Blessed Virgin Mary), Mar. 25, solemnity. A feast of the Incarnation which commemorates the announcement by the Archangel Gabriel to the Virgin Mary that she was to become the Mother of Christ (Lk 1:26-38), and the miraculous conception of Christ by her. The feast was instituted about 430 in the East. The Roman observance dates from the seventh century, when celebration was said to be universal.

Ascension of the Lord, movable observance held 40 days after Easter, holy day of obligation, solemnity. Commemorates the Ascension of Christ into heaven 40 days after his Resurrection from the dead (Mk 16:19; Lk 24:51; Acts 1:2). The feast recalls the completion of Christ's mission on earth for the salvation of all people and his entry into heaven with glorified human nature. The Ascension is a pledge of the final glorification of all who achieve salvation. Documentary evidence of the feast dates from early in the fifth century, but it was observed long before that time in connection with Pentecost and Easter.

Ash Wednesday, movable observance, six and one-half weeks before Easter. It was set as the first day of Lent by Pope St. Gregory the Great (590-604) with the extension of an earlier and shorter penitential season to a total period including 40 weekdays of fasting before Easter. It is a day of fast and abstinence. Ashes, symbolic of penance, are blessed and distributed among the faithful during the day. They are used to mark the forehead with the Sign of the Cross, with the reminder: "Remember you are dust, and to dust you will return," or "Turn away from sin and be faithful to the Gospel."

Assumption, Aug. 15, holy day of obligation, solemnity. Commemorates the taking into heaven of Mary, soul and body, at the end of her life on earth, a truth of faith that was proclaimed a dogma by Pius XII on Nov. 1, 1950. One of the oldest and most solemn feasts of Mary, it has a history dating back to at least the seventh century when its celebration was already established at Jerusalem and Rome.

Baptism of the Lord, movable, usually celebrated on the Sunday after Jan. 6, feast. Recalls the baptism of Christ by John the Baptist (Mk 1:9-11), an event associated with the liturgy of the Epiphany. This baptism was the occasion for Christ's manifestation of himself at the beginning of his public life.

Birth of Mary, Sept. 8, feast. This is a very old feast which originated in the East and found place in the Roman liturgy in the seventh century.

Candlemas Day, Feb. 2. See **Presentation of the Lord**.

Chair of Peter, Feb. 22, feast. The feast, which has been in the Roman calendar since 336, is a liturgical expression of belief in the episcopacy and hierarchy of the Church.

Christmas, Birth of Our Lord Jesus Christ, Dec. 25, holy day of obligation, solemnity. Commemorates the birth of Christ (Lk 2:1-20). This event was originally commemorated in the East on the feast of Epiphany or Theophany. The Christmas feast itself originated in the West; by 354 it was certainly kept on Dec. 25. This date may have been set for the observance to offset pagan ceremonies held at about the same time to commemorate the birth of the sun at the winter solstice. There are texts for three Christmas Masses at midnight, dawn, and during the day.

Christ the King, movable, celebrated on the last Sunday of the liturgical year, solemnity. Commemorates the royal prerogatives of Christ and is equivalent to a declaration of his rights to the homage, service and fidelity of all people in all phases of individual and social life. Pius XI instituted the feast Dec. 11, 1925.

Conversion of St. Paul, Jan. 25, feast. An observance mentioned in some calendars from the 8th and 9th centuries. Pope Innocent III (1198-1216) ordered its observance with great solemnity.

Corpus Christi (The Body and Blood of Christ), movable, celebrated on the Thursday (or Sunday, as in the U.S.) following Trinity Sunday, solemnity. Commemorates the institution of the Holy Eucharist (Mt 26:26-28). The feast originated at Liège in 1246 and was extended throughout the Church in the West by Urban IV in 1264. St. Thomas Aquinas composed the Liturgy of the Hours for the feast.

Cross, The Holy, Sept. 14, feast. Commemorates the finding of the Cross on which Christ was crucified, in 326 through the efforts of St. Helena, mother of Constantine; the consecration of the Basilica of the Holy Sepulcher nearly 10 years later: and the recovery in 628 or 629 by Emperor Heraclius of a major portion of the cross which had been removed by the Persians from its place of veneration at Jerusalem. The feast originated in Jerusalem and spread through the East before being adopted in the West. General adoption followed the building at Rome of the Basilica of the Holy Cross "in Jerusalem," so called because it was the place of enshrinement of a major portion of the cross of crucifixion.

Dedication of St. John Lateran, Nov. 9, feast. Commemorates the first public consecration of a church, that of the Basilica of the Most Holy Savior by

Pope St. Sylvester about 324. The church, as well as the Lateran Palace, was the gift of Emperor Constantine. Since the 12th century it has been known as St. John Lateran, in honor of John the Baptist after whom the adjoining baptistery was named. It was rebuilt by Innocent X (1644-55), reconsecrated by Benedict XIII in 1726, and enlarged by Leo XIII (1878-1903). This basilica is regarded as the church of highest dignity in Rome and throughout the Roman rite.

Dedication of St. Mary Major, Aug. 5, optional memorial. Commemorates the rebuilding and dedication by Pope Sixtus III (432-40) of a church in honor of Blessed Mary the Virgin. This is the Basilica of St. Mary Major on the Esquiline Hill in Rome. An earlier building was erected during the pontificate of Liberius (352-66); according to legend, it was located on a site covered by a miraculous fall of snow seen by a nobleman favored with a vision of Mary.

Easter, movable celebration held on the first Sunday after the full moon following the vernal equinox (between Mar. 22 and Apr. 25), solemnity with an octave. Commemorates the Resurrection of Christ from the dead (Mk 16:1-7). The observance of this mystery, kept since the first days of the Church, extends throughout the Easter season which lasts until the feast of Pentecost, a period of 50 days. Every Sunday in the year is regarded as a "little" Easter. The date of Easter determines the dates of movable feasts, such as Ascension and Pentecost, and the number of weeks before Lent and after Pentecost.

Easter Vigil, called by St. Augustine the "Mother of All Vigils," the night before Easter. Ceremonies are all related to the Resurrection and renewal-in-grace theme of Easter: blessing of the new fire, procession with the Easter Candle, singing of the Easter Proclamation (*Exsultet*), Liturgy of the Word with at least three Old Testament readings, the Litany of Saints, blessing of water, baptism of converts and infants, renewal of baptismal promises, Liturgy of the Eucharist. The vigil ceremonies are held after nightfall on Saturday.

Epiphany of the Lord, Jan. 6 or (in the U.S.) a Sunday between Jan. 2 and 8, solemnity. Commemorates the manifestations of the divinity of Christ. It is one of the oldest Christian feasts, with an Eastern origin traceable to the beginning of the third century and antedating the Western feast of Christmas. Originally, it commemorated the manifestations of Christ's divinity — or Theophany — in his birth, the homage of the Magi, and baptism by John the Baptist. Later, the first two of these commemorations were transferred to Christmas when the Eastern Church adopted that feast between 380 and 430. The central feature of the Eastern observance now is the manifestation or declaration of Christ's divinity in his baptism and at the beginning of his public life. The Epiphany was adopted by the Western Church during the same period in which the Eastern Church accepted Christmas. In the Roman rite, commemoration is made in the Mass of the homage of the wise men from the East (Mt 2:1-12).

Good Friday, the Friday before Easter, the second day of the Easter Triduum. Liturgical elements of the observance are commemoration of the Passion and Death of Christ in the reading of the Passion (according to John), special prayers for the Church and people of all ranks, the veneration of the Cross, and a Communion service. The celebration takes place in the afternoon, preferably at 3:00 p.m.

Guardian Angels, Oct. 2, memorial. Commemorates the angels who protect people from spiritual and physical dangers and assist them in doing good. A feast in their honor celebrated in Spain in the 16th century was placed in the Roman calendar in 1615 and Oct. 2 was set as the date of observance. Earlier, guardian angels were honored liturgically in conjunction with the feast of St. Michael.

Holy Family, movable observance on the Sunday after Christmas, feast. Commemorates the Holy Family of Jesus, Mary and Joseph as the model of domestic society, holiness and virtue. The devotional background of the feast was very strong in the 17th century. In the 18th century, in prayers composed for a special Mass, a Canadian bishop likened the Christian family to the Holy Family. Leo XIII consecrated families to the Holy Family. In 1921, Benedict XV extended the Divine Office and Mass of the feast to the whole Church.

Holy Innocents, Dec. 28, feast. Commemorates the infants who suffered death at the hands of Herod's soldiers seeking to kill the child Jesus (Mt 2:13-18). A feast in their honor has been observed since the fifth century.

Holy Saturday, the day before Easter. The Sacrifice of the Mass is not celebrated, and Holy Communion may be given only as Viaticum. If possible the Easter fast should be observed until the Easter Vigil.

Holy Thursday, the Thursday before Easter. Commemorates the institution of the sacraments of the Eucharist and holy orders, and the washing of the feet of the Apostles by Jesus at the Last Supper. The Mass of the Lord's Supper in the evening marks the beginning of the Easter Triduum. Following the Mass, there is a procession of the Blessed Sacrament to a place of reposition for adoration by the faithful. Usually at an earlier Mass of Chrism, bishops bless oils (of catechumens, chrism, the sick) for use during the year. (For pastoral reasons, diocesan bishops may permit additional Masses, but these should not overshadow the principal Mass of the Lord's Supper.)

Immaculate Conception, Dec. 8, holy day of obligation, solemnity. Commemorates the fact that Mary, in view of her calling to be the Mother of Christ and in virtue of his merits, was preserved from the first moment of her conception from original sin and was filled with grace from the very beginning of her life. She was the only person so preserved from original sin. The present form of the feast dates from Dec. 8, 1854, when Pius IX defined the dogma of the Immaculate Conception An earlier feast of the Conception, which testified to long-existing belief in this truth, was observed in the East by the eighth century, in Ireland in the ninth, and subsequently in European countries. In 1846, Mary was proclaimed patroness of the U.S. under this title.

Immaculate Heart of Mary, Saturday following the second Sunday after Pentecost, memorial. On May 4, 1944, Pius XII ordered this feast observed throughout the Church in order to obtain Mary's intercession for "peace among nations, freedom for the Church, the conversion of sinners, the love of purity and the practice of virtue." Two years earlier, he consecrated the entire human race to Mary under this title. Devotion to Mary under the title of her Most Pure Heart originated during the Middle Ages. It was given great impetus in the 17th century by the preaching of St. John Eudes, who was the first to celebrate a Mass and Divine Office of Mary under this title. A feast, celebrated in various places and on different dates, was authorized in 1799.

Joachim and Ann, July 26, memorial. Commemorates the parents of Mary. A joint feast, celebrated Sept. 9, originated in the East near the end of the sixth century. Devotion to Ann, introduced in the eighth century at Rome, became widespread in Europe in the 14th century; her feast was extended throughout the Latin Church in 1584. A feast of Joachim was introduced in the West in the 15th century.

John the Baptist, Birth of, June 24, solemnity. The precursor of Christ, whose cousin he was, was commemorated universally in the liturgy by the fourth century. He is the only saint, except the Blessed Virgin Mary, whose birthday is observed as a feast. Another feast, on Aug. 29, commemorates his passion and death at the order of Herod (Mk 6:14-29).

Joseph, Mar. 19, solemnity. Joseph is honored as the husband of the Blessed Virgin Mary, the patron and protector of the universal Church and workman. Devotion to him already existed in the eighth century in the East, and in the 11th in the West. Various feasts were celebrated before the 15th century when Mar. 19 was fixed for his commemoration; this feast was extended to the whole Church in 1621 by Gregory XV. In 1955, Pius XII instituted the feast of St. Joseph the Workman for observance May 1; this feast, which may be celebrated by local option, supplanted the Solemnity or Patronage of St. Joseph formerly observed on the third Wednesday after Easter. St. Joseph was proclaimed protector and patron of the universal Church in 1870 by Pius IX.

Michael, Gabriel and Raphael, Archangels, Sept. 29, feast. A feast bearing the title of Dedication of St. Michael the Archangel formerly commemorated on this date the consecration in 530 of a church near Rome in honor of Michael, the first angel given a liturgical feast. For a while, this feast was combined with a commemoration of the Guardian Angels. The separate feasts of Gabriel (Mar. 24) and Raphael (Oct. 24) were suppressed by the calendar in effect since 1970 and this joint feast of the three archangels was instituted.

Octave of Christmas, Jan. 1. See **Solemnity of Mary, Mother of God**.

Our Lady of Guadalupe, Dec. 12, feast (in the U.S.). Commemorates under this title the appearances of the Blessed Virgin Mary in 1531 to an Indian, Juan Diego, on Tepeyac hill outside Mexico City (see Apparitions of the Blessed Virgin Mary). The celebration, observed as a memorial in the U.S., was raised to the rank of feast at the request of the National Conference of Catholic Bishops. Approval was granted in a decree dated Jan. 8, 1988.

Our Lady of Sorrows, Sept. 15, memorial. Recalls the sorrows experienced by Mary in her association with Christ: the prophecy of Simeon (Lk 2:34-35), the flight into Egypt (Mt 2:13-21), the three-day separation from Jesus (Lk 2:41-50), and four incidents connected with the Passion — her meeting with Christ on the way to Calvary, the crucifixion, the removal of Christ's body from the cross, and his burial (Mt 27:31-61; Mk 15:20-47; Lk 23:26-56; Jn 19:17-42). A Mass

and Divine Office of the feast were celebrated by the Servites, especially, in the 17th century, and in 1814 Pius VII extended the observance to the whole Church.

Our Lady of the Rosary, Oct. 7, memorial. Commemorates the Virgin Mary through recall of the mysteries of the Rosary which recapitulate events in her life and the life of Christ. The feast was instituted in 1573 to commemorate a Christian victory over invading the forces of the Ottoman Empire at Lepanto in 1571, and was extended throughout the Church by Clement XI in 1716.

Passion Sunday (formerly called Palm Sunday), the Sunday before Easter. Marks the start of Holy Week by recalling the triumphal entry of Christ into Jerusalem at the beginning of the last week of his life (Mt 21:1-9). A procession and other ceremonies commemorating this event were held in Jerusalem from very early Christian times and were adopted in Rome by the ninth century, when the blessing of palm for the occasion was introduced. Full liturgical observance includes the blessing of palm and a procession before the principal Mass of the day. The Passion, by Matthew, Mark or Luke, is read during the Mass.

Pentecost, also called **Whitsunday**, movable celebration held 50 days after Easter, solemnity. Commemorates the descent of the Holy Spirit upon the Apostles, the preaching of Peter and the other Apostles to Jews in Jerusalem, the baptism and aggregation of some 3,000 persons to the Christian community (Acts 2:1-41). It is regarded as the birthday of the Catholic Church. The original observance of the feast antedated the earliest extant documentary evidence from the third century.

Peter and Paul, June 29, solemnity. Commemorates the martyrdoms of Peter by crucifixion and Paul by beheading during the Neronian persecution. This joint commemoration of the chief Apostles dates at least from 258 at Rome.

Presentation of the Lord (formerly called Purification of the Blessed Virgin Mary, also Candlemas), Feb. 2, feast. Commemorates the presentation of Jesus in the Temple — according to prescriptions of Mosaic Law (Lv 12:2-8; Ex 13:2; Lk 2:22-32) — and the purification of Mary 40 days after his birth. In the East, where the feast antedated fourth century testimony regarding its existence, it was observed primarily as a feast of Our Lord; in the West, where it was adopted later, it was regarded more as a feast of Mary until the calendar in effect since 1970. Its date was set for Feb. 2 after the celebration of Christmas was fixed for Dec. 25, late in the fourth century. The blessing of candles, probably in commemoration of Christ who was the Light to enlighten the Gentiles, became common about the 11th century and gave the feast the secondary name of Candlemas.

Queenship of Mary, Aug. 22, memorial. Commemorates the high dignity of Mary as Queen of heaven, angels and men. Universal observance of the memorial was ordered by Pius XII in the encyclical *Ad Caeli Reginam*, Oct. 11, 1954, near the close of a Marian Year observed in connection with the centenary of the proclamation of the dogma of the Immaculate Conception and four years after the proclamation of the dogma of the Assumption. The original date of the memorial was May 31.

Resurrection. See **Easter**.

Sacred Heart of Jesus, movable observance held on the Friday after the second Sunday after Pentecost (Corpus Christi, in the U.S.), solemnity. The object of the devotion is the divine Person of Christ, whose heart is the symbol of his love for all people — for whom he accomplished the work of Redemption. The Mass and Office now used on the feast were prescribed by Pius XI in 1929. Devotion to the Sacred Heart was introduced into the liturgy in the 17th century through the efforts of St. John Eudes who composed an Office and Mass for the feast. It was furthered as the result of the revelations of St. Margaret Mary Alacoque after 1675 and by the work of St. Claude de la Colombière, S.J. In 1765, Clement XIII approved a Mass and Office for the feast, and in 1856 Pius IX extended the observance throughout the Roman rite.

Solemnity of Mary, Mother of God, Jan. 1, holy day of obligation, solemnity. The calendar in effect since 1970, in accord with Eastern tradition, reinstated the Marian character of this commemoration on the octave day of Christmas. The former feast of the Circumcision, dating at least from the first half of the sixth century, marked the initiation of Jesus (Lk 2:21) in Judaism and by analogy focused attention on the initiation of persons in the Christian religion and their incorporation in Christ through baptism. The feast of the Solemnity supplants the former feast of the Maternity of Mary observed on Oct. 11.

Transfiguration of the Lord, Aug. 6, feast. Commemorates the revelation of his divinity by Christ to Peter, James and John on Mt. Tabor (Mt 17:1-9). The feast, which is very old, was extended throughout the universal Church in 1457 by Callistus III.

Trinity, The Holy, movable observance held on the Sunday after Pentecost, solemnity. Commemorates the most sublime mystery of the Christian faith, i.e., that there are Three Divine Persons — Father, Son and Holy Spirit — in one God (Mt 28:18-20). A votive Mass of the Most Holy Trinity dates from the seventh century; an Office was composed in the 10th century; in 1334, John XXII extended the feast to the universal Church.

Visitation, May 31, feast. Commemorates Mary's visit to her cousin Elizabeth after the Annunciation and before the birth of John the Baptist, the precursor of Christ (Lk 1:39-47). The feast had a medieval origin and was observed in the Franciscan Order before being extended throughout the Church by Urban VI in 1389. It is one of the feasts of the Incarnation and is notable for its recall of the *Magnificat*, one of the few New Testament canticles, which acknowledges the unique gifts of God to Mary because of her role in the redemptive work of Christ. The canticle is recited at Evening Prayer in the Liturgy of the Hours.

Liturgical Life
of the Church

The nature and purpose of the liturgy, along with norms for its revision, were the subject matter of *Sacrosanctum Concilium* (the Constitution on the Sacred Liturgy) promulgated by the Second Vatican Council. The principles and guidelines stated in this document, the first issued by the Council, are summarized here and/or are incorporated in other Almanac entries on liturgical subjects.

NATURE AND PURPOSE OF LITURGY

The paragraphs under this and the following subhead are quoted directly from *Sacrosanctum Concilium* (Constitution on the Sacred Liturgy).

"It is through the liturgy, especially the divine Eucharistic Sacrifice, that 'the work of our redemption is exercised.' The liturgy is thus the outstanding means by which the faithful can express in their lives, and manifest to others, the mystery of Christ and the real nature of the true Church" (No. 2).

"The liturgy is considered as an exercise of the priestly office of Jesus Christ. In the liturgy the sanctification of man is manifested by signs perceptible to the senses, and is effected in a way which is proper to each of these signs; in the liturgy full public worship is performed by the Mystical Body of Jesus Christ, that is, by the Head and his members.

"From this it follows that every liturgical celebration, because it is an action of Christ the priest and of his Body the Church, is a sacred action surpassing all others. No other action of the Church can match its claim to efficacy, nor equal the degree of it" (No. 7).

"The liturgy is the summit toward which the activity of the Church is directed; at the same time it is the fountain from which all her power flows. For the goal of apostolic works is that all who are made sons of God by faith and baptism should come together to praise God in the midst of his Church, to take part in her sacrifice, and to eat the Lord's Supper.

"From the liturgy, therefore, and especially from the Eucharist, as from a fountain, grace is channeled into us; and the sanctification of men in Christ and the glorification of God, to which all other activities of the Church are directed as toward their goal, are most powerfully achieved" (No. 10).

Full Participation

"Mother Church earnestly desires that all the faithful be led to that full, conscious, and active participation in liturgical celebrations which is demanded by the very nature of the liturgy. Such participation by the Christian people as 'a chosen race, a royal priesthood, a holy nation, a purchased people' (1 Pt 2:9; cf. 2:4–5), is their right and duty by reason of their baptism.

"In the restoration and promotion of the sacred liturgy, this full and active participation by all the people is the aim to be considered before all else; for it is the pri-

mary and indispensable source from which the faithful are to derive the true Christian spirit" (No. 14).

"In order that the Christian people may more securely derive an abundance of graces from the sacred liturgy, holy Mother Church desires to undertake with great care a general restoration of the liturgy itself. For the liturgy is made up of unchangeable elements divinely instituted, and elements subject to change. The latter not only may but ought to be changed with the passing of time if features have by chance crept in which are less harmonious with the intimate nature of the liturgy, or if existing elements have grown less functional.

"In this restoration, both texts and rites should be drawn up so that they express more clearly the holy things which they signify. Christian people, as far as possible, should be able to understand them with ease and to take part in them fully, actively, and as befits a community" (No. 21).

Norms

Norms regarding the reforms concern the greater use of Scripture; emphasis on the importance of the sermon or homily on biblical and liturgical subjects; use of vernacular languages for prayers of the Mass and for administration of the sacraments; provision for adaptation of rites to cultural patterns.

Approval for reforms of various kinds — in liturgical texts, rites, etc. — depends on the Holy See, regional conferences of bishops and individual bishops, according to provisions of law. No priest has authority to initiate reforms on his own. Reforms may not be introduced just for the sake of innovation, and any that are introduced in the light of present-day circumstances should embody sound tradition.

To assure the desired effect of liturgical reforms, training and instruction are necessary for the clergy, religious and the laity. The functions of diocesan and regional commissions for liturgy, music and art are to set standards and provide leadership for instruction and practical programs in their respective fields.

Most of the constitution's provisions regarding liturgical reforms have to do with the Roman rite. The document clearly respects the equal dignity of all rites, leaving to the Eastern Churches control over their ancient liturgies.

(For coverage of the Mystery of the Eucharist, *see* **The Mass**; other sacraments, *see* separate entries.)

Sacramentals

Sacramentals, instituted by the Church, "are sacred signs which bear a resemblance to the sacraments: they signify effects, particularly of a spiritual kind, which are obtained through the Church's intercession. By them men are disposed to receive the chief effect of the sacraments, and various occasions in life are rendered holy" (No. 60).

"Thus, for well-disposed members of the faithful, the liturgy of the sacraments and sacramentals sanctifies almost every event in their lives; they are given access to the stream of divine grace which flows from the paschal mystery of the passion, death, and resurrection of Christ, the fountain from which all sacraments and sacramentals draw their power. There is hardly any proper use of material things which cannot thus be directed toward the sanctification of men and the praise of God" (No. 61).

Some common sacramentals are priestly blessings, blessed palm, candles, holy water, medals, scapulars, prayers and ceremonies of the Roman Ritual.

Liturgy of the Hours

The Liturgy of the Hours (Divine Office) is the public prayer of the Church for praising God and sanctifying the day. Its daily celebration is required as a sacred obligation by men in holy orders and by men and women religious who have professed solemn vows. Its celebration by others is highly commended and is to be encouraged in the community of the faithful.

"By tradition going back to early Christian times, the Divine Office is arranged so that the whole course of the day and night is made holy by the praises of God. Therefore, when this wonderful song of praise is worthily rendered by priests and others who are deputed for this purpose by Church ordinance, or by the faithful praying together with the priest in an approved form, then it is truly the voice of the bride addressing her bridegroom; it is the very prayer which Christ himself, together with his Body, addresses to the Father" (No. 84).

"Hence all who perform this service are not only fulfilling a duty of the Church, but also are sharing in the greatest honor accorded to Christ's spouse, for by offering these praises to God they are standing before God's throne in the name of the Church their Mother" (No. 85).

Revised Hours

The Liturgy of the Hours, revised since 1965, was the subject of Pope Paul VI's apostolic constitution *Laudis Canticum*, dated Nov. 1, 1970. The master Latin text was published in 1971; its four volumes have been published in authorized English translation since May 1975.

One-volume, partial editions of the Liturgy of the Hours containing Morning and Evening Prayer and other elements, have been published in approved English translation.

The revised Liturgy of the Hours consists of:

• Office of Readings, for reflection on the word of God. The principal parts are three psalms, biblical and non-biblical readings.

• Morning and Evening Prayer, called the "hinges" of the Liturgy of the Hours. The principal parts are a hymn, two psalms, an Old or New Testament canticle, a brief biblical reading, Zechariah's canticle (the *Benedictus*, morning) or Mary's canticle (the *Magnificat*, evening), responsories, intercessions and a concluding prayer.

• Daytime Prayer. The principal parts are a hymn, three psalms, a biblical reading and one of three concluding prayers corresponding to the time of day.

• Night Prayer. The principal parts are one or two psalms, a brief biblical reading, Simeon's canticle (*Nunc Dimittis*), a concluding prayer and an antiphon in honor of Mary.

In the revised Liturgy of the Hours, the hours are shorter than they had been, with greater textual variety, meditation aids, and provision for intervals of silence and meditation. The psalms are distributed over a four-week period instead of

a week; some psalms, entirely or in part, are not included. Additional canticles from the Old and New Testaments are assigned for Morning and Evening Prayer. Additional scriptural texts have been added and variously arranged for greater internal unity, correspondence to readings at Mass, and relevance to events and themes of salvation history. Readings include some of the best material from the Fathers of the Church and other authors, and improved selections on the lives of the saints.

The book used for recitation of the *Office* is the *Breviary*.

For coverage of the Liturgical Year, see **Church Calendar**.

Sacred Music

"The musical tradition of the universal Church is a treasure of immeasurable value, greater even than that of any other art. The main reason for this pre-eminence is that, as sacred melody united to words, it forms a necessary or integral part of the solemn liturgy.

"Sacred music increases in holiness to the degree that it is intimately linked with liturgical action, winningly expresses prayerfulness, promotes solidarity, and enriches sacred rites with heightened solemnity. The Church indeed approves of all forms of true art, and admits them into divine worship when they show appropriate qualities" (No. 112).

The constitution decreed:

• Vernacular languages for the people's parts of the liturgy, as well as Latin, may be used.

• Participation in sacred song by the whole body of the faithful, and not just by choirs, is to be encouraged and brought about.

• Provisions should be made for proper musical training for clergy, religious and lay persons.

• While Gregorian Chant has a unique dignity and relationship to the Latin liturgy, other kinds of music are acceptable.

• Native musical traditions should be used, especially in mission areas.

• Various instruments compatible with the dignity of worship may be used.

Gregorian Chant: A form and style of chant called Gregorian was the basis and most highly regarded standard of liturgical music for centuries. It originated probably during the formative period of the Roman liturgy and developed in conjunction with Gallican and other forms of chant. Pope St. Gregory I the Great's connection with it is not clear, although it is known that he had great concern for and interest in church music. The earliest extant written versions of Gregorian Chant date from the ninth century. A thousand years later, the Benedictines of Solesmes, France, initiated a revival of chant which gave impetus to the modern liturgical movement.

Sacred Art and Furnishings

"Very rightly the fine arts are considered to rank among the noblest expressions of human genius. This judgment applies especially to religious art and to its highest achievement, which is sacred art. By their very nature both of the latter are related to God's boundless beauty, for this is the reality which these human efforts are trying to express in some way. To the extent that these works aim exclusively at turning men's thoughts to God persuasively and devoutly, they are dedicated to God and to the cause of his greater honor and glory" (No. 122).

The objective of sacred art is "that all things set apart for use in divine worship should be truly worthy, becoming, and beautiful, signs and symbols of heavenly realities. The

Church has always reserved to herself the right to pass judgment upon the arts, deciding which of the works of artists are in accordance with faith, piety, and cherished traditional laws, and thereby suited to sacred purposes. "Sacred furnishings should worthily and beautifully serve the dignity of worship" (No. 122).

According to the constitution:

• Contemporary art, as well as that of the past, shall "be given free scope in the Church, provided that it adorns the sacred buildings and holy rites with due honor and reverence" (No. 123).

• Noble beauty, not sumptuous display, should be sought in art, sacred vestments and ornaments.

• "Let bishops carefully exclude from the house of God and from other sacred places those works of artists which are repugnant to faith, morals, and Christian piety, and which offend true religious sense either by their distortion of forms or by lack of artistic worth, by mediocrity or by pretense.

• "When churches are to be built, let great care be taken that they be suitable for the celebration of liturgical services and for the active participation of the faithful" (No. 124).

• "The practice of placing sacred images in churches so that they may be venerated by the faithful is to be firmly maintained. Nevertheless, their number should be moderate and their relative location should reflect right order. Otherwise they may create confusion among the Christian people and promote a faulty sense of devotion" (No. 125).

• Artists should be trained and inspired in the spirit and for the purposes of the liturgy.

• The norms of sacred art should be revised. "These laws refer especially to the worthy and well-planned construction of sacred buildings, the shape and construction of altars, the nobility, location, and security of the Eucharistic tabernacle, the suitability and dignity of the baptistery, the proper use of sacred images, embellishments, and vestments" (No. 128).

RITES

Rites are the forms and ceremonial observances of liturgical worship coupled with the total expression of the theological, spiritual and disciplinary heritages of particular churches of the East and the West.

Different rites have evolved in the course of church history, giving to liturgical worship and church life in general forms and usages peculiar and proper to the nature of worship and the culture of the faithful in various circumstances of time and place. Thus, there has been development since apostolic times in the prayers and ceremonies of the Mass, in the celebration of the sacraments, sacramentals and the Liturgy of the Hours, and in observances of the liturgical calendar. The principal sources of rites in present use were practices within the patriarchates of Rome (for the West) and Antioch, Alexandria and Constantinople (for the East). Rites are identified as Eastern or Western on the basis of their geographical area of origin in the Roman Empire.

Eastern and Roman Rites

Eastern rites are proper to Eastern Catholic Churches (see separate entry). The principal rites are Byzantine, Alexandrian, Antiochene, Armenian and Chaldean.

The Latin or Roman rite prevails in the Western Church. It was derived from Roman practices and the use of Latin from the third century onward, and has been the rite in general use in the West since the eighth century. Other rites in limited use in the Western Church have been the Ambrosian (in the Archdiocese of Milan), the Mozarabic (in the Archdiocese of Toledo), the Lyonnais, the Braga, and rites peculiar to some religious orders like the Dominicans, Carmelites and Carthusians.

The purpose of the revision of rites in progress since the Second Vatican Council is to renew them, not to eliminate the rites of particular churches or to reduce all rites to uniformity. The Council reaffirmed the equal dignity and preservation of rites as follows.

"It is the mind of the Catholic Church that each individual church or rite retain its traditions whole and entire, while adjusting its way of life to various needs of time and place. Such individual churches, whether of the East or the West, although they differ somewhat among themselves in what are called rites (that is, in liturgy, ecclesiastical discipline and spiritual heritage), are, nevertheless, equally entrusted to the pastoral guidance of the Roman Pontiff, the divinely appointed successor of St. Peter in supreme government over the universal Church. They are, consequently, of equal dignity, so that none of them is superior to the others by reason of rite."

Determination of Rite

Determination of a person's rite is regulated by church law. Through baptism, a child becomes a member of the rite of his or her parents. If the parents are of different rites, the child's rite is decided by mutual consent of the parents; if there is lack of mutual consent, the child is baptized in the rite of the father. A candidate for baptism over the age of 14 can choose to be baptized in any approved rite. Catholics baptized in one rite may receive the sacraments in any of the approved ritual churches; they may transfer to another rite only with the permission of the Holy See and in accordance with other provisions of the Code of Canon Law.

MASS, EUCHARISTIC SACRIFICE AND BANQUET

Declarations of Vatican II

The Second Vatican Council made the following declarations among others with respect to the Mass:

"At the Last Supper, on the night when he was betrayed, our Savior instituted the Eucharistic Sacrifice of his Body and Blood. He did this in order to perpetuate the Sacrifice of the Cross throughout the centuries until he should come again, and so to entrust to his beloved spouse, the Church, a memorial of his death and resurrection: a sacrament of love, a sign of unity, a bond of charity, a paschal banquet in which Christ is consumed, the mind is filled with grace, and a pledge of future glory is given to us" (*Sacrosanctum Concilium*, Constitution on the Sacred Liturgy, No. 47).

"... As often as the Sacrifice of the Cross in which 'Christ, our Passover, has been sacrificed' (1 Cor 5:7) is celebrated on an altar, the work of our redemption is carried on. At the same time, in the sacrament of the Eucharistic bread the unity of all believers who form one body in Christ (cf. 1 Cor 10:17) is both expressed and brought about. All men are called to this union with Christ" (*Lumen Gentium*, Dogmatic Constitution on the Church, No. 3).

"... The ministerial priest, by the sacred power he enjoys, molds and rules the priestly people. Acting in the person of Christ, he brings about the Eucharistic Sacrifice, and offers it to God in the name of all the people. For their part, the faithful join in the offering of the Eucharist by virtue of their royal priesthood" (Ibid, No. 10).

Declarations of Trent

Among its decrees on the Holy Eucharist, the Council of Trent stated the following points of doctrine on the Mass.

1. There is in the Catholic Church a true sacrifice, the Mass instituted by Jesus Christ. It is the sacrifice of his Body and Blood, Soul and Divinity, himself, under the appearances of bread and wine.

2. This Sacrifice is identical with the Sacrifice of the Cross, inasmuch as Christ is the Priest and Victim in both. A difference lies in the manner of offering, which was bloody upon the Cross and is bloodless on the altar.

3. The Mass is a propitiatory Sacrifice, atoning for the sins of the living and dead for whom it is offered.

4. The efficacy of the Mass is derived from the Sacrifice of the Cross, whose superabundant merits it applies to men.

5. Although the Mass is offered to God alone, it may be celebrated in honor and memory of the saints.

6. Christ instituted the Mass at the Last Supper.

7. Christ ordained the Apostles priests, giving them power and the command to consecrate his Body and Blood to perpetuate and renew the Sacrifice.

ORDER OF THE MASS

The Mass consists of two principal divisions called the **Liturgy of the Word**, which features the proclamation of the Word of God, and the **Eucharistic Liturgy**, which focuses on the central act of sacrifice in the Consecration and on the Eucharistic Banquet in Holy Communion. (Formerly, these divisions were called, respectively, the **Mass of the Catechumens** and the **Mass of the Faithful**.) In addition to these principal divisions, there are ancillary introductory and concluding rites.

The following description covers the Mass as celebrated with participation by the people. This Order of the Mass was approved by Pope Paul VI in the apostolic constitution *Missale Romanum* dated Apr. 3, 1969, and promulgated in a decree issued Apr. 6, 1969, by the Congregation for Divine Worship. The assigned effective date was Nov. 30, 1969.

Introductory Rites

Entrance: The introductory rites begin with the singing or recitation of an entrance song consisting of one or more scriptural verses stating the theme of the mystery, season or feast commemorated in the Mass.

Greeting: The priest and people make the Sign of the Cross together. The priest then greets them in one of several alternative ways and they reply in a corresponding manner.

Introductory Remarks: At this point, the priest or another of the ministers may introduce the theme of the Mass.

Penitential Rite: The priest and people together acknowledge their sins as a preliminary step toward worthy celebration of the sacred mysteries.

This rite includes a brief examination of conscience, a general confession of sin and plea for divine mercy in one of several ways, and a prayer for forgiveness by the priest.

Glory to God: A doxology, a hymn of praise to God, sung or said on festive occasions.

Opening Prayer: A prayer of petition offered by the priest on behalf of the worshiping community.

I. Liturgy of the Word

Readings: The featured elements of this liturgy are readings of passages from the Bible. If three readings are in order, the first is usually from the Old Testament, the second from the New Testament (Letters, Acts, Revelation), and the third from one of the Gospels; the final reading is always a selection from a Gospel. The first reading(s) is (are) concluded with the formula, "The Word of the Lord" (effective Feb. 28, 1993; optional before that date), to which the people respond, "Thanks be to God." The Gospel reading is concluded with the formula, "The Gospel of the Lord," (effective as above), to which the people respond, "Praise to you, Lord Jesus Christ." Between the readings, psalm verses are sung or recited. A Gospel acclamation is either sung or omitted.

Homily: An explanation, pertinent to the mystery being celebrated and the special needs of the listeners, of some point in either the readings from sacred Scripture or in another text from the Ordinary or Proper parts of the Mass; it is a proclamation of the Good News for a response of faith.

Creed: The Nicene profession of faith, by priest and people, on certain occasions.

Prayer of the Faithful: Litany-type prayers of petition, with participation by the people. Called general intercessions, they concern needs of the Church, the salvation of the world, public authorities, persons in need, the local community.

II. Eucharistic Liturgy

Presentation and Preparation of Gifts: Presentation to the priest of the gifts of bread and wine, principally, by participating members of the congregation. Preparation of the gifts consists of the prayers and ceremonies with which the priest offers bread and wine as the elements of the sacrifice to take place during the Eucharistic Prayer and of the Lord's Supper to be shared in Holy Communion.

Washing of Hands: After offering the bread and wine, the priest cleanses his fingers with water in a brief ceremony of purification.

Pray, Brothers and Sisters: Prayer that the sacrifice to take place will be acceptable to God. The first part of the prayer is said by the priest; the second, by the people.

Prayer over the Gifts: A prayer of petition offered by the priest on behalf of the worshipping community.

Eucharistic Prayer

Preface: A hymn of praise, introducing the Eucharistic Prayer or Canon, sung or said by the priest following responses by the people. The Order of the Mass contains a variety of prefaces, for use on different occasions.

Holy, Holy, Holy; Blessed is He: Divine praises sung or said by the priest and people.

Eucharistic Prayer (Canon): Its central portion is the Consecration, when the essential act of sacrificial offering takes place with the changing of bread and wine into the Body and Blood of Christ. The various parts of the prayer, which are said by the celebrant only, commemorate principal mysteries of salvation history and include petitions for the Church, the living and dead, and remembrances of saints.

Doxology: A formula of divine praise sung or said by the priest while he holds aloft the chalice containing the consecrated wine in one hand and the paten containing the consecrated host in the other.

Communion Rite

Lord's Prayer: Sung or said by the priest and people.

Prayer for Deliverance from Evil: Called an embolism because it is a development of the final petition of the Lord's Prayer; said by the priest. It concludes with a memorial of the return of the Lord to which the people respond, "For the kingdom, the power, and the glory are yours, now and forever."

Prayer for Peace: Said by the priest, with corresponding responses by the people. The priest can, in accord with local custom, bid the people to exchange a greeting of peace with each other.

Lamb of God (*Agnus Dei*): A prayer for divine mercy sung or said while the priest breaks the consecrated host and places a piece of it into the consecrated wine in the chalice.

Communion: The priest, after saying a preparatory prayer, administers Holy Communion to himself and then to the people, thus completing the sacrifice-banquet of the Mass. (This completion is realized even if the celebrant alone receives the Eucharist.) On giving the Eucharist to each person under both species separately, the priest or eucharistic minister says, "The Body of Christ," "The Blood of Christ." The customary response is "Amen." If the Eucharist is given by intinction (in which the host is dipped into the consecrated wine), the priest says, "The Body and Blood of Christ."

Communion Song: Scriptural verses or a suitable hymn sung or said during the distribution of Holy Communion. After Holy Communion is received, some moments may be spent in silent meditation or in the chanting of a psalm or hymn of praise.

Prayer after Communion: A prayer of petition offered by the priest on behalf of the worshipping community.

Concluding Rite

Announcements: Brief announcements to the people are in order at this time.

Dismissal: Consists of a final greeting by the priest, a blessing, and a formula of dismissal. This rite is omitted if another liturgical action immediately follows the Mass; e.g., a procession, the blessing of the body during a funeral rite.

Some parts of the Mass are changeable with the liturgical season or feast, and are called the proper of the Mass. Other parts are said to be common because they always remain the same.

Additional Mass Notes

Catholics are seriously obliged to attend Mass in a worthy manner on Sundays and holy days of obligation. Failure to do so without a proportionately serious reason is gravely wrong.

It is the custom for priests to celebrate Mass daily whenever possible. To satisfy the needs of the faithful on Sundays and holy days of obligation, they are authorized to say Mass twice (**bination**) or even three times (**trination**). Bination is also permissible on weekdays to satisfy the needs of the faithful. On Christmas every priest may say three Masses.

The **fruits of the Mass**, which in itself is of infinite value, are: **general**, for all the faithful; **special (ministerial)**, for the intentions or persons specifically intended by the celebrant; **most special (personal)**, for the celebrant himself. On Sundays and certain other days pastors are obliged to offer Mass for their parishioners, or to have another priest do so. If a priest accepts a stipend or offering for a Mass, he is obliged in justice to apply the Mass for the intention of the donor. Mass may be applied for the living and the dead, or for any good intention.

Mass can be celebrated in several ways: e.g., with people present, without their presence (privately), with two or more priests as co-celebrants (concelebration), with greater or less solemnity.

Some of the various types of Masses are: **for the dead** (Funeral Mass or Mass of Christian Burial, Mass for the Dead — formerly called Requiem Mass); **ritual**, in connection with celebration of the sacraments, religious profession, etc.; **nuptial**, for married couples, with or after the wedding ceremony; **votive**, to honor a Person of the Trinity, a saint, or for some special intention.

Places, Altars for Mass

The ordinary place for celebrating the Eucharist is a church or other sacred place, at a fixed or movable altar.

The altar is a table at which the Eucharistic Sacrifice is celebrated.

A fixed altar is attached to the floor of the church. It should be of stone, preferably, and should be consecrated. The Code of Canon Law orders observance of the custom of placing under a fixed altar relics of martyrs or other saints.

A movable altar can be made of any solid and suitable material, and should be blessed or consecrated.

Outside of a sacred place, Mass may be celebrated in an appropriate place at a suitable table covered with a linen cloth and corporal. An altar stone containing the relics of saints, which was formerly prescribed, is not required by regulations in effect since the promulgation Apr. 6, 1969, of *Institutio Generalis Missalis Romani.*

LITURGICAL VESTMENTS

In the early years of the Church, vestments worn by the ministers at liturgical functions were the same as the garments in ordinary popular use. They became distinctive when their form was not altered to correspond with later variations in popular style. Liturgical vestments are symbolic of the sacred ministry and add appropriate decorum to divine worship.

Mass Vestments

Alb: A body-length tunic of white fabric; a vestment common to all ministers of divine worship.

Amice: A rectangular piece of white cloth worn about the neck, tucked into the collar and falling over the shoulders; prescribed for use when the alb does not completely cover the ordinary clothing at the neck.

Chasuble: Originally, a large mantle or cloak covering the body, it is the outer vestment of a priest celebrating Mass or carrying out other sacred actions connected with the Mass.

Chasuble-Alb: A vestment combining the features of the chasuble and alb; for use with a stole by concelebrants and, by way of exception, by celebrants in certain circumstances.

Cincture: A cord which serves the purpose of a belt, holding the alb close to the body.

Dalmatic: The outer vestment worn by a deacon in place of a chasuble.

Stole: A long, band-like vestment worn by a priest about the neck and falling to about the knees. A deacon wears a stole over the left shoulder, crossed and fastened at his right side.

The material, form and ornamentation of the aforementioned and other vestments are subject to variation and adaptation, according to norms and decisions of the Holy See and concerned conferences of bishops. The overriding norm is that they should be appropriate for use in divine worship. The customary ornamented vestments are the chasuble, dalmatic and stole.

The minimal vestments required for a priest celebrating Mass are the alb, stole, and chasuble.

Liturgical Colors

The colors of outer vestments vary with liturgical seasons, feasts and other circumstances. The colors and their use are:

Green: For the season of ordinary time; symbolic of hope and the vitality of the life of faith.

Violet (Purple): For Advent and Lent; may also be used in Masses for the dead; symbolic of penance. (See below, Violet for Advent.)

Red: For the Sunday of the Passion, Good Friday, Pentecost; feasts of the Passion of Our Lord, the Apostles and Evangelists, martyrs; symbolic of the supreme sacrifice of life for the love of God.

Rose: May be used in place of purple on the Third Sunday of Advent (formerly called Gaudete Sunday) and the Fourth Sunday of Lent (formerly called Laetare Sunday); symbolic of anticipatory joy during a time of penance.

White: For the seasons of Christmas and Easter; feasts and commemorations of Our Lord, except those of the Passion; feasts and commemorations of the Blessed Virgin Mary, angels, saints who are not martyrs, All Saints (Nov. 1), St. John the Baptist (June 24), St. John the Evangelist (Dec. 27), the Chair of St. Peter (Feb. 22), the Conversion of St. Paul (Jan. 25). White, symbolic of purity and integrity of the life of faith, may generally be substituted for other colors, and can be used for funeral and other Masses for the dead.

Options are provided regarding the color of vestments used in offices and Masses for the dead. The newsletter of the U.S. Bishops' Committee on the Liturgy, in line with No. 308 of the General Instruction of the Roman Missal, announced in July 1970: "In the dioceses of the U.S., white vestments may be used, in addition to violet (purple) and black, in offices and Masses for the dead."

On more solemn occasions, better than ordinary vestments may be used, even though their color (e.g., gold) does not match the requirements of the day.

Violet for Advent: Violet is the official liturgical color for the season of Advent, according to the September 1988 edition of the newsletter of the U.S. Bishops' Committee on the Liturgy. Blue was being proposed in order to distinguish between the Advent season and the specifically penitential season of Lent. The newsletter said, however, that "the same effect can be achieved by following the official color sequence of the Church, which requires the use of violet for Advent and Lent, while taking advantage of the varying shades which exist for violet. Light blue vestments are not authorized for use in the U.S."

Considerable freedom is permitted in the choice of colors of vestments worn for votive Masses.

Other Vestments

Cappa Magna: Flowing vestment with a train, worn by bishops and cardinals.

Cassock: A non-liturgical, full-length, close-fitting robe for use by priests and other clerics under liturgical vestments and in ordinary use; usually black for priests, purple for bishops and other prelates, red for cardinals, white for the pope. In place of a cassock, priests belonging to religious institutes wear the habit proper to their institute.

Cope: A mantle-like vestment open in front and fastened across the chest; worn by sacred ministers in processions and other ceremonies, as prescribed by appropriate directives.

Habit: The ordinary (non-liturgical) garb of members of religious institutes, analogous to the cassock of diocesan priests; the form of habits varies from institute to institute.

Humeral Veil: A rectangular vestment worn about the shoulders by a deacon or priest in Eucharistic processions and for other prescribed liturgical ceremonies.

Mitre: A headdress worn at some liturgical functions by bishops, abbots and, in certain cases, other ecclesiastics.

Pallium: A circular band of white wool about two inches wide, with front and back pendants, marked with six crosses, worn about the neck. It is a symbol of the fullness of the episcopal office. Pope Paul VI, in a document issued July 20, 1978, on his own initiative and entitled *Inter Eximia Episcopalis*, restricted its use to the pope and archbishops of metropolitan sees. In 1984, Pope John Paul II decreed that the pallium would ordinarily be conferred by the pope on the solemnity of Sts. Peter and Paul, June 29. The pallium is made from the wool of lambs blessed by the pope on the feast of St. Agnes (Jan. 21).

Rochet: A knee-length, white linen-lace garment of prelates worn under outer vestments.

Surplice: a loose, flowing vestment of white fabric with wide sleeves. For some functions, it is interchangeable with an alb.

Zucchetto: A skullcap worn by bishops and other prelates.

SACRED VESSELS, LINENS

Vessels

Paten and Chalice: The principal sacred vessels required for the celebration of Mass are the paten (plate) and chalice (cup) in which bread and wine, respectively, are offered, consecrated and consumed. Both should be made of solid and noble material which is not easily breakable or corruptible. Gold coating is required of the interior parts of sacred vessels subject to rust. The cup of a chalice should be made of non-absorbent material.

Vessels for containing consecrated hosts (see below) can be made of material other than solid and noble metal — e.g., ivory, more durable woods — provided the substitute material is locally regarded as noble or rather precious and is suitable for sacred use.

Sacred vessels should be blessed, according to prescribed requirements.

Vessels, in addition to the paten, for containing consecrated hosts are:

Ciborium: Used to hold hosts for distribution to the faithful and for reservation in the tabernacle.

Luna, Lunula, Lunette: A small receptacle which holds the sacred host in an upright position in the monstrance.

Monstrance, Ostensorium: A portable receptacle so made that the sacred host, when enclosed therein, may be clearly seen, as at Benediction or during extended exposition of the Blessed Sacrament.

Pyx: A watch-shaped vessel used in carrying the Eucharist to the sick.

Linens

Altar Cloth: A white cloth, usually of linen, covering the table of an altar. One cloth is sufficient. Three were used according to former requirements.

Burse: A square, stiff flat case, open at one end, in which the folded corporal can be placed; the outside is covered with material of the same kind and color as the outer vestments of the celebrant.

Corporal: A square piece of white linen spread on the altar cloth, on which rest the vessels holding the Sacred Species — the consecrated host(s) and wine — during the Eucharistic Liturgy. The corporal is used whenever the Blessed Sacrament is removed from the tabernacle; e.g., during Benediction the vessel containing the Blessed Sacrament rests on a corporal.

Finger Towel: A white rectangular napkin used by the priest to dry his fingers after cleansing them following the offering of gifts at Mass.

Pall: A square piece of stiff material, usually covered with linen, which can be used to cover the chalice at Mass.

Purificator: A white rectangular napkin used for cleansing sacred vessels after the reception of Communion at Mass.

Veil: The chalice intended for use at Mass can be covered with a veil made of the same material as the outer vestments of the celebrant.

THE CHURCH BUILDING

A church is a building set aside and dedicated for purposes of divine worship, the place of assembly for a worshipping community.

A Catholic church is the ordinary place in which the faithful assemble for participation in the Eucharistic Liturgy and other forms of divine worship.

In the early years of Christianity, the first places of assembly for the Eucharistic Liturgy were private homes (Acts 2:46; Rom 16:5; 1 Cor 16:5; Col 4:15) and, sometimes, catacombs. Church building began in the latter half of the second century during lulls in persecution and became widespread after enactment of the Edict of Milan in 313, when it finally became possible for the Church to emerge completely from the underground. The oldest and basic norms regarding church buildings date from about that time.

The essential principle underlying all norms for church building was reformulated by the Second Vatican Council: "When churches are to be built, let great care be taken that they be suitable for the celebration of liturgical services and for the active participation of the faithful" (*Sacrosanctum Concilium*,

Constitution on the Sacred Liturgy, No. 124).

This principle was subsequently elaborated in detail by the Congregation for Divine Worship in a document entitled *Institutio Generalis Missalis Romani*, which was approved by Paul VI Apr. 3, 1969, and promulgated by a decree of the congregation dated Apr. 6, 1969. Coverage of the following items reflects the norms stated in Chapter V of the *Institutio*.

Main Features

Sanctuary: The part of the church where the altar of sacrifice is located, the place where the ministers of the liturgy lead the people in prayer, proclaim the word of God and celebrate the Eucharist. It is set off from the body of the church by a distinctive structural feature — e.g., elevation above the main floor — or by ornamentation. (The traditional communion rail, removed in recent years in many churches, served this purpose of demarcation.) The customary location of the sanctuary is at the front of the church; it may, however, be centrally located.

Altar: The main altar of sacrifice and table of the Lord is the focal point of the sanctuary and entire church. It stands by itself, so that the ministers can move about it freely, and is so situated that they face the people during the liturgical action. In addition to this main altar, there may also be others; in new churches, these are ideally situated in side chapels or alcoves removed to some degree from the body of the church.

Adornment of the Altar: The altar table is covered with a suitable linen cloth. Required candelabra and a cross are placed upon or near the altar in plain sight of the people and are so arranged that they do not obscure their view of the liturgical action.

Seats of the Ministers: The seats of the ministers should be so arranged that they are part of the seating arrangement of the worshipping congregation and suitably placed for the performance of ministerial functions. The seat of the celebrant or chief concelebrant should be in a presiding position.

Ambo, Pulpit, Lectern: The stand at which scriptural lessons and psalm responses are read, the word of God preached, and the prayer of the faithful offered. It is so placed that the ministers can be easily seen and heard by the people.

Places for the People: Seats and kneeling benches (pews) and other accommodations for the people are so arranged that they can participate in the most appropriate way in the liturgical action and have freedom of movement for the reception of Holy Communion. Reserved seats are out of order.

Place for the Choir: Where it is located depends on the most suitable arrangement for maintaining the unity of the choir with the congregation and for providing its members maximum opportunity for carrying out their proper function and participating fully in the Mass.

Tabernacle: The best place for reserving the Blessed Sacrament is in a chapel suitable for the private devotion of the people. If this is not possible, reservation should be at a side altar or other appropriately adorned place. In either case, the Blessed Sacrament should be kept in a tabernacle, i.e., a safe–like, secure receptacle.

Statues: Images of the Lord, the Blessed Virgin Mary and the saints are legitimately proposed for the veneration of the faithful in churches. Their number and arrangement, however, should be ordered in such a way that they do not distract the people from the central celebration of the Eucharistic Liturgy. There should be only one statue of one and the same saint in a church.

General Adornment and Arrangement of Churches: Churches should be so adorned and fitted out that they serve the direct requirements of divine worship and the needs and reasonable convenience of the people.

Other Items

Ambry: A box containing the holy oils, attached to the wall of the sanctuary in some churches.

Baptistery: The place for administering baptism. Some churches have baptisteries adjoining or near the entrance, a position symbolizing the fact that persons are initiated in the Church and incorporated in Christ through this sacrament. Contemporary liturgical practice favors placement of the baptistery near the sanctuary and altar, or the use of a portable font in the same position, to emphasize the relationship of baptism to the Eucharist, the celebration in sacrifice and banquet of the death and resurrection of Christ.

Candles: Used more for symbolical than illuminative purposes, they represent Christ, the light and life of grace, at liturgical functions. They are made of beeswax. (*See* **Index: Paschal Candle**.)

Confessional, Reconciliation Room: A booth-like structure for the hearing of confessions, with separate compartments for the priest and penitents and a grating or screen between them. The use of confessionals became general in the Roman rite after the Council of Trent. Since the Second Vatican Council, there has been a trend in the U.S. to replace or supplement confessionals with small reconciliation rooms so arranged that priest and penitent can converse face-to-face.

Crucifix: A cross bearing the figure of the body of Christ, representative of the Sacrifice of the Cross.

Cruets: Vessels containing the wine and water used at Mass. They are placed on a credence table in the sanctuary.

Holy Water Fonts: Receptacles containing holy water, usually at church entrances, for the use of the faithful.

Sanctuary Lamp: A lamp which is kept burning continuously before a tabernacle in which the Blessed Sacrament is reserved, as a sign of the Real Presence of Christ.

LITURGICAL DEVELOPMENTS

The principal developments covered in this article are enactments of the Holy See and actions related to their implementation in the U.S.

Modern Movement

Origins of the modern movement for renewal in the liturgy date back to the 19th century. The key contributing factor was a revival of liturgical and scriptural studies. Of special significance was the work of the Benedictine monks of Solesmes, France, who aroused great interest in the liturgy through the restoration of Gregorian Chant. St. Pius X approved their work in a *motu proprio* of 1903 and gave additional encouragement to liturgical study and development.

St. Pius X did more than any other single pope to promote early first Communion and the practice of frequent Communion, started the research behind a revised breviary, and appointed a group to investigate possible revisions in the Mass. The movement attracted some attention in the 1920s and 1930s but made little progress.

Significant pioneering developments in the U.S. during the 1920s, however, were the establishment of the Liturgical Press, the beginning of publication of *Orate Fratres*, and the inauguration of the League of the Divine Office by the Benedictines at St. John's Abbey, Collegeville, MN. Later events of influence were the establishment of the Pius X School of Liturgical Music at Manhattanville College of the Sacred Heart and the organization of a summer school of liturgical music at Mary Manse College by the Gregorian Institute of America. The turning point toward real renewal was reached during and after World War II.

Pius XII gave it impetus and direction, principally through the background teaching in his encyclicals on the Mystical Body (*Mystici Corporis Christi*, 1943), Sacred Liturgy (*Mediator Dei*, 1947), and On Sacred Music (*Musicae Sacrae*, 1955), and by means of specific measures affecting the liturgy itself. His work was continued during the pontificates of his successors. The Second Vatican Council, in virtue of *Sacrosanctum Concilium*, the Constitution on the Sacred Liturgy, inaugurated changes of the greatest significance.

Before and After Vatican II

The most significant liturgical changes made in the years immediately preceding the Second Vatican Council were the following:

1. Revision of the rites of Holy Week for universal observance from 1956.
2. Modification of the Eucharistic fast and permission for afternoon and evening Mass, in effect from 1953 and extended in 1957.
3. The Dialogue Mass, introduced in 1958.
4. Use of popular languages in administration of the sacraments.
5. Calendar-missal-breviary reform, in effect from Jan. 1, 1961.
6. Seven-step administration of baptism for adults, approved in 1962.

The Constitution on the Sacred Liturgy, Sacrosanctum Concilium, approved (2,174 to 4) and promulgated by the Second Vatican Council on Dec. 4, 1963, marked the beginning of a profound renewal in the Church's corporate worship. Implementation of some of its measures was ordered by Paul VI on Jan. 25, 1964, in the motu proprio Sacram Liturgiam. On Feb. 29, a special commission, the Consilium for Implementing the Constitution on the Sacred Liturgy, was formed to supervise the execution of the entire program of liturgical reform. Implementation of the program on local and regional levels was left to bishops acting through their own liturgical commissions and in concert with their fellow bishops in national conferences.

Stages of Development

Liturgical development after the Second Vatican Council proceeded in several stages. It started with the formulation of guidelines and directives, and with the translation into vernacular languages of virtually unchanged Latin ritual texts. Then came structural changes in the Mass, the sacraments, the calendar, the Divine Office and other phases of the liturgy. These revisions were just about completed with the publication of a new order for the sacrament of penance in Feb. 1974. A continuing phase of development, in progress from the beginning, involves efforts to deepen the liturgical sense of the faithful, to increase their participation in worship and to relate it to full Christian life.

RECENT DEVELOPMENTS

"Happy Are Those Who Are Called to His Supper"

On Nov. 14, 2006, during their fall general meeting in Baltimore, the bishops of the United States approved "'Happy Are Those Who Are called to His Supper': On Preparing to Receive Christ Worthily in the Eucharist," a statement on the preparation needed to receive Communion worthily.

The New English Translation of the Order of the Mass

On June 15, 2006, during their spring meeting in Los Angeles, the bishops of the United States approved the new English translations of the Order of the Mass and adopted several U.S. adaptations.

The approved translation included the main parts of the Order of Mass as well as daily prayers, but there are still steps to be taken. For example, the bishops must still receive and approve the other parts of the Order of Mass, including the prefaces and major elements of the Roman Missal with the prayers for each Sunday or feast throughout the liturgical year. These parts are far from being fully translated.

Liturgists have noted that when the new translation of the texts is fully introduced, Catholics in the U.S. will find that many of the prayers and responses that are now so familiar are suddenly different. Among the most discussed changes will be:

When the priest says "The Lord be with you," the current response, "And also with you" will be replaced by "And with your spirit."

The Nicene Creed, that currently begins with "We believe," will start with, "I believe."

Currently, during the offertory prayer that "our sacrifice will be acceptable," will be replaced by "the sacrifice which is mine and yours will be acceptable."

Where people currently confess, "I have sinned through my own fault," they will instead confess "I have sinned greatly ... through my fault, through my fault, through my most grievous fault."

The Sanctus, that now begins with "Holy, holy, holy Lord, God of power and might" will start instead with "Holy, Holy, Holy is the Lord God of hosts."

New U.S. Norms for Distribution of Communion Under Both Species

New norms for the distribution and reception of Communion under the outward signs of both bread and wine by Catholics in the U.S. were approved by the U.S. bishops on June 15, 2001, and confirmed by the Holy See on Mar. 22, 2002; they were subsequently published by Bishop Wilton D. Gregory of Belleville, Ill., president of the USCCB.

The norms, which replaced the U.S. bishops' 1984 directory titled "This Holy and Living Sacrifice," gave specific directives regarding liturgical roles, sacred vessels and the rites to be followed in distributing Communion under both kinds.

The first section of the new norms provided a theological summary of the Church's teaching on Communion under both kinds, while the following section describes the authorized procedures by which such distribution can be accomplished at Mass. The U.S. adaptations were to be incorporated into the new General Instruction of the Roman Missal and have the same force of law in the U.S. as the rest of the general instruction.

The General Instruction of the recently revised Roman Missal permits bishops' conferences to provide norms for the distribution of Communion under both kinds, meaning under the outward signs of both bread and wine.

Included among the norms is an indult — or exception to the general requirement — from the Vatican Congregation for Divine Worship and the Sacraments that provides for the cleansing of sacred vessels by special eucharistic ministers. The indult was promulgated as "particular law" for the dioceses of the U.S. at the same time as the norms and it became effective on Apr. 7, 2002.

However, the Vatican congregation declined to approve an indult authorizing special ministers to assist with the distribution of the consecrated blood to other chalices during the singing of the "Lamb of God."

In the letter confirming the norms, the congregation also made clear that special eucharistic ministers, or indeed any communicant, may assist in the consumption of what remains of the blood after distribution of Communion has been completed.

Texts and Translations

The master texts of all documents on liturgical reform are in Latin. Effective dates of their implementation have depended on the completion and approval of appropriate translations into vernacular languages. English translations were made by the International Committee for English in the Liturgy.

On May 7, 2001, the Congregation for Divine Worship and the Sacraments issued the new instruction, *Liturgiam Authenticam* ("The Authentic Liturgy"). The instruction set stricter rules for the translation of Latin liturgical texts into other languages and bears the subtitle, "On the Use of Vernacular Languages in the Publication of the Books of the Roman Liturgy."

At the bishops' meeting in June 2008, the bishop sent for mail ballot approval the ICEL Gray Book translation of the Proper of the Seasons (of the Roman Missal) for use in the Dioceses of the United States of America. The translation was the source of considerable debate during the bishops' gathering.

General Instruction of the Roman Missal

In spring 2001, Pope John Paul II authorized the publication of an *editio typica tertia* of the *Missale Romanum*. The much anticipated revision included a new edition of the *Institutio Generalis Missalis Romani* (*General Instruction of the Roman Missal*). On Nov. 12, 2002, the Latin Church members of the United States Conference of Catholic Bishops approved a translation of the *Institutio Generalis Missalis Romani* prepared by the International Commission on English in the Liturgy. The translation was confirmed by the Congregation for Divine Worship and the Discipline of the Sacraments on Mar. 17, 2003. This translation of the *General Instruction of the Roman Missal* is the sole translation of the *Institutio Generalis Missalis Romani, editio typica tertia* for use in the dioceses of the United States of America.

Redemptionis Sacramentum

On Apr. 23, 2004, the Congregation for Divine Worship and the Sacraments, in collaboration with the Congregation for the Doctrine of the Faith and at the request of Pope John Paul II issued the instruction "*Redemptionis Sacramentum*: On Certain Matters to Be Observed or to Be Avoided Regarding the Most Holy Eucharist." The instruction states:

"It is not at all the intention here to prepare a compendium of the norms regarding the Most Holy Eucharist, but rather, to take up within this Instruction some elements of liturgical norms that have been previously expounded or laid down and even today remain in force in order to assure a deeper appreciation of the liturgical norms; to establish certain norms by which those earlier ones are explained and complemented; and also to set forth for Bishops, as well as for Priests, Deacons and all the lay Christian faithful, how each should carry them out in accordance with his own responsibilities and the means at his disposal."

The Mass

A new Order of the Mass, supplanting the one authorized by the Council of Trent in the 16th century, was introduced in the U.S. Mar. 22, 1970. It had been approved by Paul VI in the apostolic constitution *Missale Romanum*, dated Apr. 3, 1969.

Preliminary and related to it were the following developments.

Mass in English: Introduced Nov. 29, 1964. In the same year, Psalm 42 was eliminated from the prayers at the foot of the altar.

Incidental Changes: The last Gospel (prologue of John) and vernacular prayers following Mass were eliminated Mar. 7, 1965. At the same time, provision was made for the celebrant to say aloud some prayers formerly said silently.

Rubrics: An instruction entitled *Tres Abhinc Annos*, dated May 4 and effective June 29, 1967, simplified directives for the celebration of Mass, approved the practice of saying the canon aloud, altered the Communion and dismissal rites, permitted purple instead of black vestments in Masses for the dead, discontinued wearing of the maniple, and approved in principle the use of vernacular languages for the canon, ordination rites, and lessons of the Divine Office when read in choir.

Eucharistic Prayers (Canons): The traditional Roman Canon in English was introduced Oct. 22, 1967. Three additional Eucharistic prayers, authorized May 23, 1968, were approved for use in English the following Aug. 15.

The customary Roman Canon, which dates at least from the beginning of the fifth century and has remained substantially unchanged since the seventh century, is the first in the order of listing of the Eucharistic prayers. It can be used at any time, but is the one of choice for most Sundays, some special feasts like Easter and Pentecost, and for feasts of the Apostles and other saints who are commemorated in the canon. Any preface can be used with it.

The second Eucharistic prayer, the shortest and simplest of all, is best suited for use on weekdays and various special circumstances. It has a preface of its own, but others may be used with it. This canon bears a close resemblance to the one framed by St. Hippolytus about 215.

The third Eucharistic prayer is suitable for use on Sundays and feasts as an alternative to the Roman Canon. It can be used with any preface and has a special formula for remembrance of the dead.

The fourth Eucharistic prayer, the most sophisticated of them all, presents a broad synthesis of salvation history. Based on the Eastern tradition of Antioch, it is best suited for use at Masses attended by persons versed in Sacred Scripture. It has an unchangeable preface.

Five additional Eucharistic prayers — three for Masses with children and two for Masses of reconciliation — were approved in 1974 and 1975, respectively, by the Congregation for the Sacraments and Divine Worship.

Use of the Eucharistic Prayers for Various Needs and Occasions, was approved by the U.S. bishops in 1994, con-

firmed by the appropriate Vatican congregations May 9, 1995, and ratified for use beginning Oct. 1, 1995.

Lectionary: A new compilation of scriptural readings and psalm responsories for Mass was published in 1969. The Lectionary contains a three-year cycle of readings for Sundays and solemn feasts, a two-year weekday cycle, and a one-year cycle for the feasts of saints, in addition to readings for a variety of votive Masses, ritual Masses and Masses for various needs. There are also responsorial psalms to follow the first readings and Gospel or alleluia versicles.

A second edition of the Lectionary, substantially the same as the first, was published in 1981. New features included an expanded introduction, extensive scriptural references and additional readings for a number of solemnities and feasts.

Volume One of a new Lectionary for the Mass was decreed by Bishop Anthony Pilla of Cleveland, then president of the NCCB, as permissible for use as of the first Sunday of Advent, Nov. 29, 1998. The first new Lectionary since 1973, Volume One contains the readings for Sundays, solemnities and feasts of the Lord. Volume Two, containing the readings for weekdays, feasts of saints, and various other occasions, was given final approval on June 19, 1998, by the NCCB but still required confirmation by the Holy See.

Sacramentary (Missal): The Vatican Polyglot Press began distribution in June 1970, of the Latin text of a new Roman Missal, the first revision published in 400 years. The English translation was authorized for optional use beginning July 1, 1974; the mandatory date for use was Dec. 1, 1974.

The **Sacramentary** is the celebrant's Mass book of entrance songs, prayers, prefaces and Eucharistic prayers, including special common sets of texts for various commemorations and intentions — dedication of churches, Mary, the apostles, martyrs, doctors of the Church, virgins, holy men and women, the dead, other categories of holy persons, administration of certain sacraments, special intentions.

Study of the Mass: The Bishops' Committee on the Liturgy, following approval by the National Conference of Catholic Bishops in May 1979, began a study of the function and position of elements of the Mass, including the Gloria, the sign of peace, the penitential rite and the readings. Major phases of the study have been completed, and work is still under way toward completion of the project.

Mass for Special Groups: Reasons and norms for the celebration of Mass at special gatherings of the faithful were the subject of an instruction issued May 15, 1969. Two years earlier, the U.S. Bishops' Liturgy Committee went on record in support of the celebration of Mass in private homes under appropriate conditions.

Sunday Mass on Saturday: The Congregation for the Clergy, under date of Jan. 10, 1970, granted the request that the faithful, where bishops consider it pastorally necessary or useful, may satisfy the precept of participating in Mass in the late afternoon or evening hours of Saturdays and the days before holy days of obligation. This provision is stated in Canon 1248 of the Code of Canon Law.

Bination and Trination: Canon 905 of the Code of Canon Law provides that local ordinaries may permit priests to celebrate Mass twice a day (bination), for a just cause; in cases of pastoral need, they may permit priests to celebrate Mass three times a day (trination) on Sundays and holy days of obligation.

Mass in Latin: According to notices issued by the Congregation for Divine Worship June 1, 1971, and Oct. 28, 1974: (1) Bishops may permit the celebration of Mass in Latin for mixed-language groups; (2) bishops may permit the celebration of one or two Masses in Latin on weekdays or

Sundays in any church, irrespective of mixed-language groups involved (1971); (3) priests may celebrate Mass in Latin when people are not present; (4) the approved revised Order of the Mass is to be used in Latin as well as vernacular languages; (5) by way of exception, bishops may permit older and handicapped priests to use the Council of Trent's Order of the Mass in private celebration of the holy Sacrifice. (*See* Permission for **Tridentine Mass**.)

Mass Obligation Waived: The Congregation for Bishops approved July 4, 1992, a resolution of the U.S. bishops to waive the Mass attendance obligation for the holy days of Mary, the Mother of God (Jan. 1), the Assumption of Mary (Aug. 15) and All Saints (Nov. 1) when these solemnities fall on Saturday or Monday.

Inter-Ritual Concelebration: The Apostolic Delegation (now Nunciature) in Washington, DC, announced in June 1971 that it had received authorization to permit priests of Roman and Eastern rites to celebrate Mass together in the rite of the host church. It was understood that the inter-ritual concelebrations would always be "a manifestation of the unity of the Church and of communion among particular churches."

Ordo of the Sung Mass: In a decree dated June 24 and made public Aug. 24, 1972, the Congregation for Divine Worship issued a new *Ordo of the Sung Mass* — containing Gregorian chants in Latin — to replace the *Graduale Romanum.*

Mass for Children: Late in 1973, the Congregation for Divine Worship issued special guidelines for children's Masses, providing accommodations to the mentality and spiritual growth of pre-adolescents while retaining the principal parts and structures of the Mass. The Directory for Masses with Children was approved by Paul VI on Oct. 22 and was dated Nov. 1, 1973. Three Eucharistic prayers for Masses with children were approved by the congregation in 1974; English versions were approved June 5, 1975. Their use, authorized originally for a limited period of experimentation, was extended indefinitely Dec. 15, 1980.

Lectionary for Children: A lectionary for Masses with children, with an announced publication date of September 1993, was authorized for use by choice beginning Nov. 28, 1993. A revised *Lectionary for Masses with Children* was approved by the bishops on Nov. 15, 2006, during their fall general meeting in Washington. The text must also be approved by the Vatican before it can be used in the liturgy in the United States. Assuming approval is given, it will replace the experimental children's Lectionary that has been in use since 1993. The new Lectionary includes stricter rules for its use.

Sacraments

The general use of English in administration of the sacraments was approved for the U.S. Sept. 14, 1964. Structural changes of the rites were subsequently made and introduced in the U.S. as follows.

Pastoral Care of the Sick: Revised rites, covering also administration of the Eucharist to sick persons, were approved Nov. 30, 1972, and published Jan. 18, 1973. The effective date for use of the provisional English prayer formula was Dec. 1, 1974. The mandatory effective date for use of the ritual, Pastoral Care of the Sick in English, was Nov. 27, 1983.

Baptism: New rites for the baptism of infants, approved Mar. 19, 1969, were introduced June 1, 1970.

Rite of Christian Initiation of Adults: Revised rites were issued Jan. 6, 1972, for the Christian initiation of adults — affecting preparation for and reception of baptism, the Eucharist and confirmation; also, for the reception of already baptized adults into full communion with the Church. These rites, which were introduced in the U.S. on the completion of English translation, nullified a seven–step baptismal process approved in 1962. On Mar. 8, 1988, the National Conference of Catholic Bishops was notified that the Congregation for Divine Worship had approved the final English translation of the Rite of Christian Initiation of Adults. The mandatory date for putting the rite into effect was Sept. 1, 1988.

Confirmation: Revised rites, issued Aug. 15, 1971, became mandatory in the U.S. Jan. 1, 1973. The use of a stole by persons being confirmed should be avoided, according to an item in the December 1984 edition of the Newsletter of the Bishops' Committee on the Liturgy. The item said: "The distinction between the universal priesthood of all the baptized and the ministerial priesthood of the ordained is blurred when the distinctive garb (the stole) of ordained ministers is used in this manner."

A decree regarding the proper age for confirmation, approved by the U.S. bishops in June 1993 was ratified by the Congregation for Bishops Feb. 8, 1994. The decree reads: "In accord with prescriptions of canon 891… the sacrament of confirmation in the Latin rite shall be conferred between the age of discretion, which is about the age of seven, and 18 years of age, within the limits determined by the diocesan bishop and with regard for the legitimate exceptions given in canon 891, namely, when there is danger of death or where, in the judgment of the minister, grave cause urges otherwise." The decree became effective July 1, 1994, and continued in effect until July 1, 1999.

Special Ministers of the Eucharist: The designation of lay men and women to serve as special ministers of the Eucharist was authorized by Paul VI in an "Instruction on Facilitating Communion in Particular Circumstances" (*Immensae Caritatis*), dated Jan. 29 and published by the Congregation for Divine Worship Mar. 29, 1973. Provisions concerning them are contained in Canons 230 and 910 of the Code of Canon Law.

Qualified laypersons may serve as special ministers for specific occasions or for extended periods in the absence of a sufficient number of priests and deacons to provide reasonable and appropriate service in the distribution of Holy Communion, during Mass and outside of Mass (to the sick and shut-ins). Appointments of ministers are made by priests with the approval of the appropriate bishop.

The Newsletter of the U.S. Bishops' Committee on the Liturgy stated in its February 1988 edition: "When ordinary ministers (bishops, priests, deacons) are present during a Eucharistic celebration, whether they are participating in it or not, and are not prevented from doing so, they are to assist in the distribution of Communion. Accordingly, if the ordinary ministers are in sufficient number, special ministers of the Eucharist are not allowed to distribute Communion at that Eucharistic celebration." Pope John Paul II approved this decision and ordered it published June 15, 1987.

Holy Orders: Revised ordination rites for deacons, priests and bishops, validated by prior experimental use, were approved in 1970. The sacrament of holy orders underwent further revision in 1972 with the elimination of the Church-instituted orders of porter, reader, exorcist, acolyte and sub-deacon, and of the tonsure ceremony symbolic of entrance into the clerical state. The former minor orders of reader and acolyte were changed from orders to ministries.

Matrimony: A revised rite for the celebration of marriage was promulgated by the Congregation for Divine Worship and the Discipline of the Sacraments Mar. 19, 1969, and went into effect June 1, 1970. A second typical edition of the order of celebration, with revisions in accord with provisions of the Code of Canon Law promulgated in 1983, was approved and published in 1990 (*Notitiae*, Vol. 26, No.6). The date for implementation was reported to be dependent on the completion of required translations and appropriate formalities.

Penance: Ritual revision of the sacraments was completed with approval by Pope Paul VI on Dec. 2, 1973, of new directives for the sacrament of penance or reconciliation. The U.S. Bishops' Committee on the Liturgy set Feb. 27, 1977, as the mandatory date for use of the new rite. The committee also declared that it could be used from Mar. 7, 1976, after adequate preparation of priests and people. The Holy See gave authorization in 1968 for the omission of any reference to excommunication or other censures in the formula of absolution unless there was some indication that a censure had actually been incurred by a penitent.

Additional Developments

Music: An instruction on Music in the Liturgy, dated Mar. 5 and effective May 14, 1967, encouraged congregational singing during liturgical celebrations and attempted to clarify the role of choirs and trained singers. More significantly, the instruction indicated that a major development under way in the liturgy was a gradual erasure of the distinctive lines traditionally drawn between the sung liturgy and the spoken liturgy, between what had been called the high Mass and the low Mass.

In the same year, the U.S. Bishops' Liturgy Committee approved the use of contemporary music, as well as guitars and other suitable instruments, in the liturgy. The Holy See authorized in 1968 the use of musical instruments other than the organ in liturgical services, "provided they are played in a manner suitable to worship."

Calendar: A revised liturgical calendar approved by Paul VI Feb. 14 and made public May 9, 1969, went into effect in the U.S. in 1972. Since that time, memorials and feasts of beatified persons and saints have been added.

Communion in Hand: Since 1969, the Holy See has approved the practice of in-hand reception of the Eucharist in regions and countries where it had the approval of the appropriate episcopal conferences. The first grant of approval was to Belgium, in May 1969. Approval was granted the U.S. in June 1977.

Liturgy of the Hours: The background, contents, scope and purposes of the revised Divine Office, called the Liturgy of the Hours, were described by Paul VI in the apostolic constitution *Laudis Canticum*, dated Nov. 1, 1970. A provisional English version, incorporating basic features of the master Latin text, was published in 1971. The four complete volumes of the Hours in English have been published since May 1975. One-volume, partial editions have also been published in approved form. Nov. 27, 1977, was set by the Congregation for Divine Worship and the National Conference of Catholic Bishops as the effective date for exclusive use in liturgical worship of the translation of the Latin text of the Liturgy of the Hours approved by the International Committee on English in the Liturgy.

Holy Week: The English version of revised Holy Week rites went into effect in 1971. They introduced concelebration of Mass, placed new emphasis on commemorating the institution of the priesthood on Holy Thursday, and modified Good Friday prayers for other Christians, Jews and other non-Christians.

The Congregation for Divine Worship released Feb. 20, 1988, a "Circular Letter concerning the Preparation and Celebration of the Easter Feasts." It called the feasts the "summit of the whole liturgical year," and criticized practices which dilute or change appropriate norms for their celebration. Singled out for blame for the abuse or ignorance of norms was the "inadequate formation given to the clergy and the faithful regarding the paschal mystery as the center of the liturgical year and of Christian life." The document set out the appropriate norms for the Lenten season, Holy Week, the Easter Triduum, Easter and the weeks following. It was particularly insistent on the proper celebration of the Easter Vigil, to take place after nightfall on Saturday and before dawn on Sunday.

Oils: The Congregation for Divine Worship issued a directive in 1971 permitting the use of other oils — from plants, seeds or coconuts — instead of the traditional olive oil in administering some of the sacraments. The directive also provided that oils could be blessed at other times than at the usual Mass of Chrism on Holy Thursday, and authorized bishops' conferences to permit priests to bless oils in cases of necessity.

Dancing and Worship: Dancing and worship was the subject of an essay which appeared in a 1975 edition of *Notitiae* (11, pp. 202–205), the official journal of the Congregation for the Sacraments and Divine Worship. The article was called a "qualified and authoritative sketch," and should be considered "an authoritative point of reference for every discussion of the matter."

The principal points of the essay were:
• "The dance has never been made an integral part of the official worship of the Latin Church."
• "If the proposal of the religious dance in the West is really to be made welcome, care will have to be taken that in its regard a place be found outside of the liturgy, in assembly areas which are not strictly liturgical. Moreover, the priests must always be excluded from the dance."

Mass for Deceased Non-Catholic Christians: The Congregation for the Doctrine of the Faith released a decree June 11, 1976, authorizing the celebration of public Mass for deceased non-Catholic Christians under certain conditions: "(1) The public celebration of the Masses must be explicitly requested by the relatives, friends, or subjects of the deceased person for a genuine religious motive. (2) In the Ordinary's judgment, there must be no scandal for the faithful."

Built of Living Stones: Art, Architecture, and Worship: At their November 2001 meeting in Washington, DC, the Bishops approved this document by the U.S. Bishops' Committee on the Liturgy; it replaces the document *Environment and Art in Catholic Worship* issued in March 1978.

Doxology: The bishops' committee called attention in August 1978, to the directive that the Doxology concluding the Eucharistic Prayer is said or sung by the celebrant (concelebrants) alone, to which the people respond, "Amen."

Churches, Altars, Chalices: The Newsletter of the U.S. Bishops' Committee on the Liturgy reported in November 1978, that the Congregation for Divine Worship had given provisional approval of a new English translation for the rite of dedicating churches and altars, and of a new form for the blessing of chalices.

Eucharistic Worship: This was the subject of two documents issued in 1980. *Dominicae Coenae* was a letter addressed by Pope John Paul to bishops throughout the world in connection with the celebration of Holy Thursday; it was dated Feb. 24 and released Mar.18, 1980. It was more doctrinal in content than the "Instruction on Certain Norms concerning Worship of the Eucharistic Mystery" (*Inaestimabile*

Donum, "The Priceless Gift"), which was approved by the Pope Apr. 17 and published by the Congregation for the Sacraments and Divine Worship May 23. Its stated purpose was to reaffirm and clarify teaching on liturgical renewal contained in enactments of the Second Vatican Council and in several related implementing documents.

Tridentine Mass: The celebration of Mass according to the 1962 typical (master) edition of the Roman Missal — the Tridentine Mass — was authorized by Pope Benedict XVI under certain conditions according to the *motu proprio Summorum Pontificum*, issued on July 7, 2007. **See below.**

The celebration of Mass according to the 1962 typical (master) edition of the Roman Missal — the so-called Tridentine Mass — was authorized by Pope John Paul II under certain conditions.

Pope Benedict XVI issued the Apostolic Letter in the form of a *motu proprio, Summorum Pontificum,* on July 7, 2007. The following are the specific elements that were decreed:

Art. 1. The Roman Missal promulgated by Pope Paul VI is to be regarded as the ordinary expression of the law of prayer (*lex orandi*) of the Catholic Church of Latin Rite, while the Roman Missal promulgated by St. Pius V and published again by Bl. John XXIII as the extraordinary expression of the law of prayer (*lex orandi*) and on account of its venerable and ancient use let it enjoy due honor. These two expressions of the law of prayer (*lex orandi*) of the Church in no way lead to a division in the law of prayer (*lex orandi*) of the Church, for they are two uses of the one Roman Rite.

Hence it is licit to celebrate the Sacrifice of the Mass in accordance with the typical edition of the Roman Missal promulgated by Bl. John XXIII in 1962 and never abrogated, as the extraordinary form of the Liturgy of the Church. The conditions laid down by the previous documents *Quattuor abhinc annos* and *Ecclesia Dei* for the use of this Missal are replaced by what follows:

Art. 2. In Masses celebrated without the people, any priest of Latin rite, whether secular or religious, can use the Roman Missal published by Pope Bl. John XXIII in 1962 or the Roman Missal promulgated by the Supreme Pontiff Paul VI in 1970, on any day except in the Sacred Triduum. For celebration in accordance with one or the other Missal, a priest does not require any permission, neither from the Apostolic See nor his own Ordinary.

Art. 3. If Communities or Institutes of Consecrated Life or Societies of Apostolic Life of either pontifical or diocesan rite desire to have a celebration of Holy Mass in accordance with the edition of the Roman Missal promulgated in 1962 in the conventual or "community" celebration in their own oratories, this is allowed. If an individual community or the entire Institute or Society wants to have such celebrations often or habitually or permanently, the matter is to be decided by the Major Superiors according to the norm of law and the particular laws and statutes.

Art. 4. With due observance of law, even Christ's faithful who spontaneously request it, may be admitted to celebrations of Holy Mass mentioned in art. 2 above.

Art. 5, § 1. In parishes where a group of faithful attached to the previous liturgical tradition exists stably, let the pastor willingly accede to their requests for the celebration of the Holy Mass according to the rite of the Roman Missal published in 1962. Let him see to it that the good of these faithful be harmoniously reconciled with ordinary pastoral care of the parish, under the governance of the bishop according to canon 392, avoiding discord and fostering the unity of the whole Church.

§ 2. Celebration according to the Missal of Bl. John XXIII can take place on weekdays, while on Sundays and on feast days there may be one such celebration.

§ 3. Let the pastor permit celebrations in this extraordinary form for faithful or priests who request it, even in particular circumstances such as weddings, funerals or occasional celebrations, for example pilgrimages.

§ 4. Priests using the Missal of Bl. John XXIII must be worthy and not impeded by law.

§ 5. In churches, which are neither parochial nor conventual, it is the rector of the church who grants the above-mentioned permission.

Art. 6. In Masses celebrated with the people according to the Missal of Bl. John XXIII, the Readings can be proclaimed even in the vernacular, using editions that have received the *recognitio* of the Apostolic See.

Art. 7. Where some group of lay faithful, mentioned in art. 5§1 does not obtain what it requests from the pastor, it should inform the diocesan bishop of the fact. The bishop is earnestly requested to grant their desire. If he cannot provide for this kind of celebration, let the matter be referred to the Pontifical Commission Ecclesia Dei.

Art. 8. A bishop who desires to make provision for requests of lay faithful of this kind, but is for various reasons prevented from doing so, may refer the matter to the Pontifical Commission "Ecclesia Dei," which should give him advice and help.

Art. 9, § 1. Likewise a pastor may, all things duly considered, grant permission to use the older ritual in administering the Sacraments of Baptism, Matrimony, Penance and the Anointing of the Sick, as the good of souls may suggest.

§ 2. Ordinaries are granted the faculty to celebrate the Sacrament of Confirmation using the former Roman Pontifical, as the good of souls may suggest.

§ 3. It is lawful for clerics in holy orders to use even the Roman Breviary promulgated by Bl. John XXIII in 1962.

Art. 10. It is lawful for the local ordinary, if he judges it opportune, to erect a personal parish according to the norm of canon 518 for celebrations according to the older form of the Roman rite or appoint a rector or chaplain, with due observance of the requirements of law.

Art. 11. The Pontifical Commission Ecclesia Dei, erected in 1988 by John Paul II, continues to carry out its function. This Commission is to have the form, duties and norm for action that the Roman Pontiff may wish to assign to it.

Art. 12. The same Commission, in addition to the faculties it already enjoys, will exercise the authority of the Holy See by maintaining vigilance over the observance and application of these dispositions.

Spanish: In accord with decrees of the Congregation for Divine Worship, Spanish was approved as a liturgical language in the U.S. (Jan. 19, 1985). The *texto unico* of the Ordinary of the Mass became mandatory in the U.S. Dec. 3, 1989. Spanish translations of Proper-of-the-Mass texts proper to U.S. dioceses were approved Mar. 12, 1990. An approved Spanish version of the Rite for the Christian Initiation of Adults was published in 1991. The Institute of Hispanic Liturgy opened its national office June 1, 1995, on the campus of the Catholic University of America in Washington. At the bishops' meeting in June 2008, the bishops approved by a vote of 187-3 the use of "*ustedes*" in place of "*vosotros*" and the corresponding verb constructions in the Order of Mass including the verb constructions of the consecration narrative for use in the dioceses of the United States of America.

Funeral Rites: A revised Order of Christian Funerals became mandatory in the U.S. Nov. 2, 1989.

Permission for the presence of cremated human remains in the funeral liturgy, including the Eucharist, was granted in 1997 to local bishops in the U.S. by the Congregation for Divine Worship and the Discipline of the Sacraments. Adaptations to existing rites are under study.

Extended Eucharistic Exposition: In response to queries, the Secretariat of the U.S. bishops' Committee on the Liturgy issued an advisory stating that liturgical law permits and encourages in parish churches:

Exposition of the Blessed Sacrament for an extended period of time once a year, with consent of the local Ordinary and only if suitable numbers of the faithful are expected to be present; Exposition ordered by the local Ordinary, for a grave and general necessity, for a more extended period of supplication when the faithful assemble in large numbers.

With regard to perpetual exposition, this form is generally permitted only in the case of those religious communities of men or women who have the general practice of perpetual Eucharistic adoration or adoration over extended periods of time.

The Secretariat's advisory appeared in the June-July 1986 edition of the Newsletter of the bishops' Committee on the Liturgy.

Native American Languages: The Newsletter of the U.S. Bishops' Committee on the Liturgy reported in Dec. 1986, and May 1987, respectively, that the Congregation for Divine Worship had authorized Mass translations in Navajo and Choctaw. Lakota was approved as a liturgical language in 1989.

Communion Guidelines: In 1986 and again in 1996, the U.S. bishops' approved the insertion of advisories in missalettes and similar publications, stating that: (1) The Eucharist is to be received by Catholics only, except in certain specific cases; (2) To receive Communion worthily, a person must be in the state of grace (i.e., free of serious sin) and observe the eucharistic fast (*See* separate entry).

Unauthorized Eucharistic Prayers: The May 1987 Newsletter of the U.S. Bishops' Committee on the Liturgy restated the standing prohibition against the use of any Eucharistic Prayers other than those contained in the Sacramentary. Specifically, the article referred to the 25 unauthorized prayers in a volume entitled Spoken Visions.

Homilist: According to the Pontifical Commission for the Authentic Interpretation of Canon Law, the diocesan bishop cannot dispense from the requirement of Canon 767, par. 1, that the homily in the liturgy be reserved to a priest or deacon. Pope John Paul approved this decision June 20, 1987.

Concerts in Churches: In a letter released Dec. 5, 1987, the Congregation for Divine Worship declared that churches might be used on a limited basis for concerts of sacred or religious music, but not for concerts featuring secular music.

Blessings: A revised Book of Blessings was ordered into use beginning Dec. 3, 1989.

Litany of the Blessed Virgin Mary: "Queen of Families," a new invocation, was reported by the U.S. bishops in 1996, for insertion between "Queen of the Rosary" and "Queen of Peace."

Inclusive Language: "Criteria for the Evaluation of Inclusive Language Translations of Scriptural Texts Proposed for Liturgical Use" was issued by the U.S. bishops in November 1990. The criteria distinguish between non-use of vertical inclusiveness in references to God and use of horizontal, gender-inclusive terms (he/she, man/woman and the like) where appropriate in references to persons.

The Sacraments of the Church

The sacraments are actions of Christ and his Church (itself a kind of sacrament) that signify grace, cause it in the act of signifying it, and confer it upon persons properly disposed to receive it. They perpetuate the redemptive activity of Christ, making it present and effective. They infallibly communicate the fruit of that activity — namely grace — to responsive persons with faith. Sacramental actions consist of the union of sensible signs (matter of the sacraments) with the words of the minister (form of the sacraments).

Christ himself instituted the seven sacraments of the New Law by determining their essence and the efficacy of their signs to produce the grace they signify.

Christ is the principal priest or minister of every sacrament; human agents — an ordained priest, baptized persons contracting marriage with each other, any person conferring emergency baptism in a proper manner — are secondary ministers. Sacraments have efficacy from Christ, not from the personal dispositions of their human ministers.

Each sacrament confers sanctifying grace for the special purpose of the sacrament; this is, accordingly, called sacramental grace. It involves a right to actual graces corresponding to the purposes of the respective sacraments.

Baptism, confirmation and the Eucharist are sacraments of initiation; penance (reconciliation) and anointing of the sick, sacraments of healing; order and matrimony, sacraments for service.

While sacraments infallibly produce the grace they signify, recipients benefit from them in proportion to their personal dispositions. One of these is the intention to receive sacraments as sacred signs of God's saving and grace-giving action. The state of grace is also necessary for fruitful reception of the Holy Eucharist, confirmation, matrimony, holy orders and anointing of the sick. Baptism is the sacrament in which grace is given in the first instance and original sin is remitted. Penance is the secondary sacrament of reconciliation, in which persons guilty of serious sin after baptism are reconciled with God and the Church, and in which persons already in the state of grace are strengthened in that state.

Role of Sacraments

The Second Vatican Council prefaced a description of the role of the sacraments with the following statement concerning participation by all the faithful in the priesthood of Christ and the exercise of that priesthood by receiving the sacraments (Dogmatic Constitution on the Church, *Lumen Gentium*, Nos. 10 and 11).

"The baptized by regeneration and the anointing of the Holy Spirit are consecrated into a spiritual house and a holy priesthood. Thus through all those works befitting Christian men they can offer spiritual sacrifice and proclaim the power of him who has called them out of darkness into his marvelous light (cf. 1 Pt 2:4-10).

"Though they differ from one another in essence and not only in degree, the common priesthood of the faithful and the ministerial or hierarchical priesthood (of those ordained to holy orders) are nonetheless interrelated. Each of them in its own special way is a participation in the one priesthood of Christ. The ministerial priest, by the sacred power he enjoys, molds and rules the priestly people. Acting in the Person of Christ, he brings about the Eucharistic Sacrifice, and offers it to God in the name of all the people. For their part, the faithful join in the offering of the Eucharist by virtue of their royal priesthood. They likewise exercise that priesthood by receiving the sacraments, by prayer and thanksgiving, by the witness of a holy life, and by self-denial and active charity.

"It is through the sacraments and the exercise of the virtues that the sacred nature and organic structure of the priestly community is brought into operation."

Baptism: "Incorporated into the Church through baptism, the faithful are consecrated by the baptismal character to the exercise of the cult of the Christian religion. Reborn as sons of God, they must confess before men the faith which they have received from God through the Church."

Confirmation: "Bound more intimately to the Church by the sacrament of confirmation, they are endowed by the Holy Spirit with special strength. Hence they are more strictly obliged to spread and defend the faith both by word and by deed as true witnesses of Christ."

Eucharist: "Taking part in the Eucharistic Sacrifice, which is the fount and apex of the whole Christian life, they offer the divine Victim to God, and offer themselves along with It. Thus, both by the act of oblation and through holy Communion, all perform their proper part in this liturgical service, not, indeed, all in the same way but each in that way which is appropriate to himself. Strengthened anew at the holy table by the Body of Christ, they manifest in a practical way that unity of God's People which is suitably signified and wondrously brought about by this most awesome sacrament."

Penance: "Those who approach the sacrament of penance obtain pardon from the mercy of God for offenses committed against him. They are at the same time reconciled with the Church, which they have wounded by their sins, and which by charity, example, and prayer seeks their conversion."

Anointing of the Sick: "By the sacred anointing of the sick and the prayer of her priests, the whole Church commends those who are ill to the suffering and glorified Lord, asking that he may lighten their suffering and save them (cf. Jas 5:14-16). She exhorts them, moreover, to contribute to the welfare of the whole People of God by associating themselves freely with the passion and death of Christ (cf. Rom 8:17; Col 1:24; 2 Tm 2:11-12; 1 Pt 4:13)."

Holy Orders: "Those of the faithful who are consecrated by holy orders are appointed to feed the Church in Christ's name with the Word and the grace of God."

Matrimony: "Christian spouses, in virtue of the sacrament of matrimony, signify and partake of the mystery of that unity and fruitful love which exists between Christ and his Church (cf. Eph 5:32). The spouses thereby help each other to attain to holiness in their married life and by the rearing and education of their children. And so, in their state and way of life, they have their own special gift among the People of God (cf. 1 Cor 7:7).

"For from the wedlock of Christians there comes the family, in which new citizens of human society are born. By the grace of the Holy Spirit received in baptism these are made children of God, thus perpetuating the People of God through the centuries. The family is, so to speak, the domestic Church. In it parents should, by their word and example, be the first preachers of the faith to their children. They should encourage them in the vocation which is proper to each of them, fostering with special care any religious vocation.

"Fortified by so many and such powerful means of salvation, all the faithful, whatever their condition or state, are called by the Lord, each in his own way, to that perfect holiness whereby the Father himself is perfect."

Baptism

Baptism is the sacrament of spiritual regeneration by which a person is incorporated in Christ and made a member of his Mystical Body, given grace, and cleansed of original sin. Actual sins and the punishment owed for them are remitted also if the person baptized was guilty of such sins (e.g., in the case of a person baptized after reaching the age of reason). The theological virtues of faith, hope and charity are given with grace. The sacrament confers a character on the soul and can be received only once.

The matter is the pouring of water. The form is: "I baptize you in the name of the Father and of the Son and of the Holy Spirit."

The minister of solemn baptism is a bishop, priest or deacon, but in case of emergency anyone, including a non-Catholic, can validly baptize. The minister pours water on the forehead of the person being baptized and says the words of the form while the water is flowing. The water used in solemn baptism is blessed during the rite.

Baptism is conferred in the Roman rite by immersion or infusion (pouring of water), depending on the directive of the appropriate conference of bishops, according to the Code of Canon Law. The Church recognizes as valid baptisms properly performed by non-Catholic ministers. The baptism of infants has always been con-

sidered valid and the general practice of infant baptism was well established by the fifth century. Baptism is conferred conditionally when there is doubt about the validity of a previous baptism.

Baptism is necessary for salvation. If a person cannot receive the baptism of water described above, this can be supplied by baptism of blood (martyrdom suffered for the Catholic faith or some Christian virtue) or by baptism of desire (perfect contrition joined with at least the implicit intention of doing whatever God wills that people should do for salvation).

A sponsor is required for the person being baptized. (*See* **Godparents**, below).

A person must be validly baptized before he or she can receive any of the other sacraments.

Christian Initiation of Infants: Infants should be solemnly baptized as soon after birth as conveniently possible. Anyone may baptize an infant in danger of death. If the child survives, the ceremonies of solemn baptism should be supplied.

The sacrament is ordinarily conferred by a priest or deacon of the parents' parish.

Catholics 16 years of age and over who have received the sacraments of confirmation and the Eucharist and are practicing their faith are eligible to be sponsors or godparents. Only one is required. Two, one of each sex, are permitted. A non-Catholic Christian cannot be a godparent for a Catholic child, but may serve as a witness to the baptism. A Catholic may not be a godparent for a child baptized in a non-Catholic religion, but may be a witness.

"Because of the close communion between the Catholic Church and the Eastern Orthodox churches," states the 1993 *Directory on Ecumenism*, "it is permissible for a just cause for an Eastern faithful to act as godparent together with a Catholic godparent at the baptism of a Catholic infant or adult, so long as there is provision for the Catholic education of the person being baptized and it is clear that the godparent is a suitable one.

"A Catholic is not forbidden to stand as godparent in an Eastern Orthodox Church if he/she is so invited. In this case, the duty of providing for the Christian education binds in the first place the godparent who belongs to the church in which the child is baptized."

The role of godparents in baptismal ceremonies is secondary to the role of the parents. They serve as representatives of the community of faith and with the parents request baptism for the child and perform other ritual functions. Their function after baptism is to serve as proxies for the parents if the parents should be unable or fail to provide for the religious training of the child.

At baptism every child should be given a name with Christian significance, usually the name of a saint, to symbolize newness of life in Christ.

Christian Initiation of Adults: According to the *Ordo Initiationis Christianae Adultorum* ("Rite of the Christian Initiation of Adults") issued by the Congregation for Divine Worship on Jan. 6, 1972, and put into effect in revised form Sept. 1, 1988, adults are prepared for baptism and reception into the Church in several stages:

• An initial period of inquiry, instruction and evangelization.

• The catechumenate, a period of at least a year of

formal instruction and progressive formation in and familiarity with Christian life. It starts with a statement of purpose and includes a rite of election.

• Immediate preparation, called a period of purification and enlightenment, from the beginning of Lent to reception of the sacraments of initiation — baptism, confirmation, Holy Eucharist — during ceremonies of the Easter Vigil. The period is marked by scrutinies, formal giving of the creed and the Lord's Prayer, the choice of a Christian name, and a final statement of intention.

• A mystagogic phase whose objective is greater familiarity with Christian life in the Church through observances of the Easter season and association with the community of the faithful, and through extended formation for about a year.

National Statutes for the Catechumenate were approved by the National Conference of Catholic Bishops on Nov. 11, 1986, and were subsequently ratified by the Vatican.

The priest who baptizes a catechumen can also administer the sacrament of confirmation.

A sponsor is required for the person being baptized.

The *Ordo* also provides a simple rite of initiation for adults in danger of death and for cases in which all stages of the initiation process are not necessary, and guidelines for: (1) the preparation of adults for the sacraments of confirmation and Holy Eucharist in cases where they have been baptized but have not received further formation in the Christian life; (2) the formation and initiation of children of catechetical age.

The Church recognizes the right of anyone over the age of seven to request baptism and to receive the sacrament after completing a course of instruction and giving evidence of good will. Practically, in the case of minors in a non-Catholic family or environment, the Church accepts them when other circumstances favor their ability to practice the faith — e.g., well-disposed family situation, the presence of another or several Catholics in the family. Those who are not in such favorable circumstances are prudently advised to defer reception of the sacrament until they attain the maturity necessary for independent practice of the faith.

Reception of Baptized Christians: Procedure for the reception of already baptized Christians into full communion with the Catholic Church is distinguished from the catechumenate, since they have received some Christian formation. Instruction and formation are provided as necessary, however; and conditional baptism is administered if there's reasonable doubt about the validity of the person's previous baptism.

In the rite of reception, the person is invited to join the community of the Church in professing the Nicene Creed and is asked to state: "I believe and profess all that the holy Catholic Church believes, teaches, and proclaims as revealed by God." The priest places his hand on the head of the person, states the formula of admission to full communion, confirms (in the absence of a bishop), gives a sign of peace, and administers Holy Communion during a Eucharistic Liturgy.

Confirmation

Confirmation is the sacrament by which a baptized person, through anointing with chrism and the imposition of hands, is endowed with the fullness of bap-

tismal grace; is united more intimately to the Church; is enriched with the special power of the Holy Spirit; is committed to be an authentic witness to Christ in word and action. The sacrament confers a character on the soul and can be received only once.

According to the apostolic constitution *Divinae Consortium Naturae*, dated Aug. 15, 1971, in conjunction with the *Ordo Confirmationis* ("Rite of Confirmation"): "The sacrament of confirmation is conferred through the anointing with chrism on the forehead, which is done by the imposition of the hand (matter of the sacrament), and through the words: '*N., receive the seal of the Holy Spirit, the Gift of the Father*'" (form of the sacrament). On May 5, 1975, bishops' conferences in English-speaking countries were informed by the Congregation for Divine Worship that Pope Paul VI had approved this English version of the form of the sacrament: "*Be sealed with the gift of the Holy Spirit.*"

The ordinary minister of confirmation in the Roman rite is a bishop. Priests may be delegated for the purpose. A pastor can confirm a parishioner in danger of death, and a priest can confirm in ceremonies of Christian initiation and at the reception of a baptized Christian into union with the Church.

Ideally, the sacrament is conferred during the Eucharistic Liturgy. Elements of the rite include renewal of the promises of baptism, which confirmation ratifies and completes, and the laying on of hands by the confirming bishop and priests participating in the ceremony.

"The entire rite," according to the *Ordo*, "has a twofold meaning. The laying of hands upon the candidates, done by the bishop and the concelebrating priests, expresses the biblical gesture by which the gift of the Holy Spirit is invoked. The anointing with chrism and the accompanying words clearly signify the effect of the Holy Spirit. Signed with the perfumed oil by the bishop's hand, the baptized person receives the indelible character, the seal of the Lord, together with the Spirit who is given and who conforms the person more perfectly to Christ and gives him the grace of spreading the Lord's presence among men."

A sponsor is required for the person being confirmed. Eligible is any Catholic 16 years of age or older who has received the sacraments of confirmation and the Eucharist and is practicing the faith. The baptismal sponsor, preferably, can also be the sponsor for confirmation. Parents may present their children for confirmation but cannot be sponsors.

In the Roman rite, it has been customary for children to receive confirmation within a reasonable time after first Communion and confession. There is a trend, however, to defer confirmation until later when its significance for mature Christian living becomes more evident. In the Eastern rites, confirmation is administered at the same time as baptism.

Eucharist

The Holy Eucharist is a sacrifice (*see* **The Mass**) and the sacrament in which Christ is present and is received under the appearances of bread and wine.

The matter is bread of wheat, unleavened in the Roman rite and leavened in the Eastern rites, and wine of grape. The form consists of the words of consecration said by the priest at Mass: "This is my body. This is the cup of my blood" (according to the traditional usage of the Roman rite).

Only a priest can consecrate bread and wine so they become the body and blood of Christ. After consecration, however, the Eucharist can be administered by deacons and, for various reasons, by religious and lay persons.

Priests celebrating Mass receive the Eucharist under the species of bread and wine. In the Roman rite, others receive under the species of bread only, i.e., the consecrated host, though in some circumstances they may receive under the species of both bread and wine. In Eastern-rite practice, the faithful generally receive a piece of consecrated leavened bread which has been dipped into consecrated wine (i.e., by intinction).

Conditions for receiving the Eucharist, commonly called Holy Communion, are the state of grace, the right intention and observance of the Eucharistic fast.

The faithful of Roman rite are required by a precept of the Church to receive the Eucharist at least once a year, ordinarily during the Easter time.

(See **Eucharistic Fast, Mass, Transubstantiation, Viaticum.**)

First Communion and Confession: Children are to be prepared for and given opportunity for receiving both sacraments (Eucharist and reconciliation, or penance) on reaching the age of discretion, at which time they become subject to general norms concerning confession and Communion. This, together with a stated preference for first confession before first Communion, was the central theme of a document entitled *Sanctus Pontifex* and published May 24, 1973, by the Congregation for the Discipline of the Sacraments and the Congregation for the Clergy, with the approval of Pope Paul VI.

What the document prescribed was the observance of practices ordered by St. Pius X in the decree *Quam Singulari* of Aug. 8, 1910. Its purpose was to counteract pastoral and catechetical experiments virtually denying children the opportunity of receiving both sacraments at the same time. Termination of such experiments was ordered by the end of the 1972-73 school year.

At the time the document was issued, two- or three-year experiments of this kind — routinely deferring reception of the sacrament of penance until after the first reception of Holy Communion — were in effect in more than half of the dioceses of the U.S. They have remained in effect in many places, despite the advisory from the Vatican.

One reason stated in support of such experiments is the view that children are not capable of serious sin at the age of seven or eight, when Communion is generally received for the first time, and therefore prior reception of the sacrament of penance is not necessary. Another reason is the purpose of making the distinctive nature of the two sacraments clearer to children.

The Vatican view reflected convictions that the principle and practice of devotional reception of penance are as valid for children as they are for adults, and that sound catechetical programs can avoid misconceptions about the two sacraments.

A second letter on the same subject and in the same vein was released May 19, 1977, by the aforementioned congregations. It was issued in response to the question:

"'Whether it is allowed after the declaration of May 24, 1973, to continue to have, as a general rule, the reception of first Communion precede the reception of the sacrament of penance in those parishes in which this practice developed in the past few years.'

"The Sacred Congregations for the Sacraments and Divine Worship and for the Clergy, with the approval of the Supreme Pontiff, reply: Negative, and according to the mind of the declaration.

"The mind of the declaration is that one year after the promulgation of the same declaration, all experiments of receiving first Communion without the sacrament of penance should cease so that the discipline of the Church might be restored, in the spirit of the decree, *Quam Singulari.*"

The two letters from the Vatican congregations have not produced uniformity of practice in this country. Simultaneous preparation for both sacraments is provided in some dioceses where a child has the option of receiving either sacrament first, with the counsel of parents, priests and teachers. Programs in other dioceses are geared first to reception of Communion and later to reception of the Sacrament of Reconciliation.

Commentators on the letters note that: they are disciplinary rather than doctrinal in content; they are subject to pastoral interpretation by bishops; they cannot be interpreted to mean that a person who is not guilty of serious sin must be required to receive the sacrament of penance before (even first) Communion.

Canon 914 of the Code of Canon Law states that sacramental confession should precede first Communion.

Holy Communion under the Forms of Bread and Wine (by separate taking of the consecrated bread and wine or by intinction, the reception of the host dipped in the wine): Such reception is permitted under conditions stated in instructions issued by the Congregation for Divine Worship (May 25, 1967; June 29, 1970), the General Instruction on the Roman Missal (No. 242), and directives of bishops' conferences and individual bishops.

Accordingly, Communion can be administered in this way to: persons being baptized, received into communion with the Church, confirmed, receiving anointing of the sick; couples at their wedding or jubilee; religious at profession or renewal of profession; lay persons receiving an ecclesiastical assignment (e.g., lay missionaries); participants at concelebrated Masses, retreats, pastoral commission meetings, daily Masses and, in the U.S., Masses on Sundays and holy days of obligation.

A communicant has the option of receiving the Eucharist under the form of bread alone or under the forms of bread and wine. (See **New U.S. Norms** in the **Liturgy** section.)

Holy Communion More Than Once a Day: A person who has already received the Eucharist may receive it (only) once again on the same day only during a Eucharistic celebration in which the person participates. A person in danger of death who has already received the Eucharist once or twice is urged to receive Communion again as Viaticum. Pope John Paul approved this decision, in accord with Canon 917, and ordered it published July 11, 1984.

Holy Communion and Eucharistic Devotion outside of Mass: These were the subjects of an instruction

(*De Sacra Communione et de Cultu Mysterii Eucharistici extra Missam*) dated June 21 and made public Oct. 18, 1973, by the Congregation for Divine Worship.

Holy Communion can be given outside of Mass to persons unable for a reasonable cause to receive it during Mass on a given day. The ceremonial rite is modeled on the structure of the Mass, consisting of a penitential act, a scriptural reading, the Lord's Prayer, a sign or gesture of peace, giving of the Eucharist, prayer and final blessing. Viaticum and Communion to the sick can be given by extraordinary ministers (authorized lay persons) with appropriate rites.

Forms of devotion outside of Mass are exposition of the Blessed Sacrament (by men or women religious, especially, or lay persons in the absence of a priest; but only a priest can give the blessing), processions and congresses with appropriate rites.

Intercommunion: Church policy on intercommunion was stated in an "Instruction on the Admission of Other Christians to the Eucharist," dated June 1 and made public July 8, 1972, against the background of the Decree on Ecumenism approved by the Second Vatican Council, and the Directory on Ecumenism issued by the Secretariat for Promoting Christian Unity in 1967, 1970 and 1993.

Basic principles related to intercommunion are:

• "There is an indissoluble link between the mystery of the Church and the mystery of the Eucharist, or between ecclesial and Eucharistic communion; the celebration of the Eucharist of itself signifies the fullness of profession of faith and ecclesial communion" (1972 Instruction).

• "Eucharistic communion practiced by those who are not in full ecclesial communion with each other cannot be the expression of that full unity which the Eucharist of its nature signifies and which in this case does not exist; for this reason such communion cannot be regarded as a means to be used to lead to full ecclesial communion" (1972 Instruction).

• The question of reciprocity "arises only with those churches which have preserved the substance of the Eucharist, the sacrament of orders and apostolic succession" (1967 *Directory*).

• "A Catholic cannot ask for the Eucharist except from a minister who has been validly ordained" (1967 *Directory*).

The policy distinguishes between separated Eastern Christians and other Christians.

With Separated Eastern Christians (e.g., Orthodox): These may be given the Eucharist (as well as penance and anointing of the sick) at their request. Catholics may receive these same sacraments from priests of separated Eastern churches if they experience genuine spiritual necessity, seek spiritual benefit, and access to a Catholic priest is morally or physically impossible. This policy (of reciprocity) derives from the facts that the separated Eastern churches have apostolic succession through their bishops, valid priests, and sacramental beliefs and practices in accord with those of the Catholic Church.

With Other Christians (e.g., members of Reformation-related churches, others): Admission to the Eucharist in the Catholic Church, according to the Directory on Ecumenism, "is confined to particular cases of those Christians who have a faith in the sacrament in conformity with that of the Church, who experience a serious spiritual need for the Eucharistic sustenance, who for a prolonged period are unable to have recourse to a minister of their own community and who ask for the sacrament of their own accord; all this provided that they have proper dispositions and lead lives worthy of a Christian." The spiritual need is defined as "a need for an increase in spiritual life and a need for a deeper involvement in the mystery of the Church and its unity."

Circumstances under which Communion may be given to other properly disposed Christians are danger of death, imprisonment, persecution, grave spiritual necessity coupled with no chance of recourse to a minister of their own community.

Catholics cannot ask for the Eucharist from ministers of other Christian churches who have not been validly ordained to the priesthood.

Ecclesia de Eucharistia

On Apr. 17, 2002, Holy Thursday, during the Mass of the Lord's Supper, and within the liturgical setting of the beginning of the Paschal Triduum Pope John Paul II issued the fourteenth encyclical letter of his pontificate, *Ecclesia de Eucharistia.* The encyclical was intended to offer a theological reflection on the mystery of the Eucharist in its relationship with the Church.

Specifically, the pope uses the letter to reaffirm the traditional teaching of the Church on the real presence of Christ in the Eucharist, on the need for validly ordained ministers for its celebration, and on the importance of following the Church's liturgical norms.

The encyclical is organized into five chapters and a conclusion, beginning with the declaration: "The Church draws her life from the Eucharist. This truth does not simply express a daily experience of faith, but recapitulates the heart of the mystery of the Church. In a variety of ways she joyfully experiences the constant fulfillment of the promise." The Eucharistic Sacrifice is thus truly "the source and summit of the Christian life," as the Second Vatican Council proclaimed, and contains the Church's entire spiritual wealth: Jesus Christ, who offers himself to the Father for the redemption of the world. In celebrating this "mystery of faith," the Church presents the Paschal Triduum in a contemporary way, for men and women in every age.

Chapter One, "The Mystery of Faith," describes the sacrificial nature of the Eucharist which, through the ministry of the priest, makes sacramentally present at each Mass the body "given up" and the blood "poured out" by Christ for the salvation of the world.

Chapter Two, "The Eucharist Builds the Church," states that the Church "teaches that the celebration of the Eucharist is at the centre of the process of the Church's growth."

Chapter Three, "The Apostolicity of the Eucharist and of the Church," notes that that just as the Church is apostolic so too is the Eucharist in three ways. First, "The Eucharist too has its foundation in the Apostles, not in the sense that it did not originate in Christ himself, but because it was entrusted by Jesus to the Apostles and has been handed down to us by them and by their successors. It is in continuity with the practice of the Apostles, in obedience to the Lord's command, that the Church has celebrated the Eucharist down the centuries." Second, "it is celebrated in conformity with the faith of the Apostles." Third, just as the full reality of Church does not exist without apostolic succession, so there is no true Eucharist without the Bishop.

Chapter Four, "The Eucharist and Ecclesial Communion," teaches that "the culmination of all the sacraments in perfecting our communion with God the Father by identification with his only-begotten Son through the working of the Holy Spirit."

Chapter Five, "The Dignity of the Eucharistic Celebration" is concerned with the truthful celebration of the Eucharist enunciated in the previous chapter.

Chapter Six, "At the School of Mary, 'Woman of the Eucharist,'" offers a reflection on the analogy between the Mother of God, and the Church.

In his conclusion, the pontiff quotes his Apostolic Letter *Novo Millennio Ineunte* in stating, "it is not a matter of inventing a 'new program.' The program already exists: it is the plan found in the Gospel and in the living Tradition; it is the same as ever." Clearly, the implementation of this process of a renewed impetus in Christian living passes through the Eucharist. He concludes, "In the humble signs of bread and wine, changed into his body and blood, Christ walks beside us as our strength and our food for the journey, and he enables us to become, for everyone, witnesses of hope."

Sacramentum Caritatis

On Mar. 13, 2007, Pope Benedict XVI released the post-synodal apostolic exhortation, *Sacramentum Caritatis* ("The Sacrament of Charity"), a 131-page papal reflection on the discussions and suggestions made during the 2005 world Synod of Bishops on the Eucharist.

Penance

Penance is the sacrament by which sins committed after baptism are forgiven and a person is reconciled with God and the Church.

Individual and integral confession and absolution are the only ordinary means for the forgiveness of serious sin and for reconciliation with God and the Church.

(Other than ordinary means are perfect contrition and general absolution without prior confession, both of which require the intention of subsequent confession and absolution.)

A revised ritual for the sacrament - *Ordo Paenitentiae*, published by the Congregation of Divine Worship Feb. 7, 1974, and made mandatory in the U.S. from the first Sunday of Lent, 1977 - reiterates standard doctrine concerning the sacrament; emphasizes the social (communal and ecclesial) aspects of sin and conversion, with due regard for personal aspects and individual reception of the sacrament; prescribes three forms for celebration of the sacrament; and presents models for community penitential services.

The basic elements of the sacrament are sorrow for sin because of a supernatural motive, confession (of previously unconfessed mortal or grave sins, required; of venial sins also, but not of necessity), and reparation (by means of prayer or other act enjoined by the confessor), all of which comprise the matter of the sacrament; and absolution, which is the form of the sacrament.

The traditional words of absolution — *"I absolve you from your sins in the name of the Father, and of the Son, and of the Holy Spirit"* — remain unchanged at the conclusion of a petition in the new rite that God may grant pardon and peace through the ministry of the Church.

The minister of the sacrament is an authorized priest, i.e., one who, besides having the power of orders to forgive sins, also has faculties of jurisdiction granted by an ecclesiastical superior and/or by canon law.

The sacrament can be celebrated in three ways:

• For individuals, the traditional manner remains acceptable but is enriched with additional elements including: reception of the penitent and making of the Sign of the Cross; an exhortation by the confessor to trust in God; a reading from Scripture; confession of sins; manifestation of repentance; petition for God's forgiveness through the ministry of the Church and the absolution of the priest; praise of God's mercy, and dismissal in peace. Some of these elements are optional.

• For several penitents, in the course of a community celebration including a Liturgy of the Word of God and prayers, individual confession and absolution, and an act of thanksgiving.

• For several penitents, in the course of a community celebration, with general confession and general absolution. In extraordinary cases, reconciliation may be attained by general absolution without prior individual confession as, for example, under these circumstances: (1) danger of death, when there is neither time nor priests available for hearing confessions; (2) grave necessity of a number of penitents who, because of a shortage of confessors, would be deprived of sacramental grace or Communion for a lengthy period of time through no fault of their own. Persons receiving general absolution are obliged to be properly disposed and resolved to make an individual confession of the grave sins from which they have been absolved; this confession should be made as soon as the opportunity to confess presents itself and before any second reception of general absolution.

Norms regarding general absolution, issued by the Congregation for the Doctrine of the Faith in 1972, are not intended to provide a basis for convoking large gatherings of the faithful for the purpose of imparting general absolution, in the absence of extraordinary circumstances. Judgment about circumstances that warrant general absolution belongs principally to the bishop of the place, with due regard for related decisions of appropriate episcopal conferences.

Communal celebrations of the sacrament are not held in connection with Mass.

The place of individual confession, as determined by episcopal conferences in accordance with given norms, can be the traditional confessional or another appropriate setting.

A precept of the Church obliges the faithful guilty of grave sin to confess at least once a year.

The Church favors more frequent reception of the sacrament not only for the reconciliation of persons guilty of serious sins but also for reasons of devotion. Devotional confession — in which venial sins or previously forgiven sins are confessed — serves the purpose of confirming persons in penance and conversion.

Penitential Celebrations: Communal penitential celebrations are designed to emphasize the social dimensions of Christian life — the community aspects and significance of penance and reconciliation.

Elements of such celebrations are community prayer, hymns and songs, scriptural and other readings, examination of conscience, general confession and expression of sorrow for sin, acts of penance and reconciliation, and a form of non-sacramental absolution resembling the one in the penitential rite of the Mass.

If the sacrament is celebrated during the service, there must be individual confession and absolution of sin.

Recent developments: On May 2, 2002, officials of the Roman Curia released a *motu proprio* by Pope John Paul II, *Misericordia Dei* ("Mercy of God, On Certain Aspects of the Celebration of the Sacrament of Penance"). The 15-page document called for a "vigorous revitalization" of the sacrament and asked bishops to adopt stricter observance on Church law's "grave necessity" requirement as a condition for the use of general absolution. It also requested that bishops' conferences submit national norms for general absolution to the Holy See for approval "as soon as possible."

In Feb. 2003, the Bishops' Committee on the Liturgy and the Subcommittee for the Jubilee Year 2000 of the USCCB issued a new booklet, *Celebrating the Sacrament of Penance: Questions and Answers.* The booklet provides answers to some of the frequently asked questions about the Sacrament of Penance, including "Why Do We Need the Sacrament of Penance?" "What Happens in the Sacrament of Penance?" and "What is 'General Absolution'?" The booklet is intended for use in parishes during preparation for the Sacrament of Penance, as a resource for reflection on the sacrament during particular seasons such as Lent, and as a practical tool to aid penitents as they go to confession.

(*See* **Absolution, Confession, Confessional, Confessor, Contrition, Faculties, Forgiveness of Sin, Power of the Keys, Seal of Confession, Sin.**)

Anointing of the Sick

This sacrament, promulgated by St. James the Apostle (Jas 5:13-15), can be administered to the faithful after reaching the age of reason who are in danger because of illness or old age. By the anointing with blessed oil and the prayer of a priest, the sacrament confers on the person comforting grace; the remission of venial sins and inculpably unconfessed mortal sins, together with at least some of the temporal punishment due for sins; and, sometimes, results in an improved state of health.

The matter of this sacrament is the anointing with blessed oil (olive oil, or vegetable oil if necessary) of the forehead and hands; in cases of necessity, a single anointing of another portion of the body suffices. The form is: "Through this holy anointing and his most loving mercy, may the Lord assist you by the grace of the Holy Spirit so that, when you have been freed from your sins, he may save you and in his goodness raise you up."

Anointing of the sick, formerly called extreme unction, may be received more than once, e.g., in new or continuing stages of serious illness. Ideally, the sacrament should be administered while the recipient is conscious and in conjunction with the sacraments of penance and the Eucharist. It should be administered in cases of doubt as to whether the person has reached the age of reason, is dangerously ill or dead.

The sacrament can be administered during a communal celebration in some circumstances, as in a home for the aged.

Holy Orders

Order is the sacrament by which the mission given by Christ to the Apostles continues to be exercised in the Church until the end of time; it is the sacrament of apostolic mission. It has three grades: episcopacy, priesthood and diaconate. The sacrament confers a character on the soul and can be received only once. The minister of the sacrament is a bishop.

Order, like matrimony but in a different way, is a social sacrament. As the Second Vatican Council declared in *Lumen Gentium,* the Dogmatic Constitution on the Church:

"For the nurturing and constant growth of the People of God, Christ the Lord instituted in his Church a variety of ministries, which work for the good of the whole body. For those ministers who are endowed with sacred power are servants of their brethren, so that all who are of the People of God, and therefore enjoy a true Christian dignity, can work toward a common goal freely and in an orderly way, and arrive at salvation" (No. 18).

Bishop: The fullness of the priesthood belongs to those who have received the order of bishop. Bishops, in hierarchical union with the pope and their fellow bishops, are the successors of the Apostles as pastors of the Church: they have individual responsibility for the care of the local churches they serve and collegial responsibility for the care of the universal Church (*see* **Collegiality**). In the ordination or consecration of bishops, the essential form is the imposition of hands by the consecrator(s) and the assigned prayer in the preface of the rite of ordination.

"With their helpers, the priests and deacons, bishops have taken up the service of the community presiding in place of God over the flock whose shepherds they are, as teachers of doctrine, priests of sacred worship, and officers of good order" (No. 20).

Priests: A priest is an ordained minister with the power to celebrate Mass, administer the sacraments, preach and teach the word of God, impart blessings, and perform additional pastoral functions, according to the mandate of his ecclesiastical superior.

Concerning priests, the Second Vatican Council stated in *Lumen Gentium* (No. 28):

"The divinely established ecclesiastical ministry is exercised on different levels by those who from antiquity have been called bishops, priests, and deacons. Although priests do not possess the highest degree of the priesthood, and although they are dependent on the bishops in the exercise of their power, they are nevertheless united with the bishops in sacerdotal dignity. By the power of the sacrament of orders, and in the image of Christ the eternal High Priest (Heb 5:1-10; 7:24; 9:11-28), they are consecrated to preach the Gospel, shepherd the faithful, and celebrate divine worship as true priests of the New Testament.

"Priests, prudent cooperators with the episcopal order as well as its aides and instruments, are called to serve the People of God. They constitute one priesthood with their bishop, although that priesthood is comprised of different functions."

In the ordination of a priest of Roman rite, the essential matter is the imposition of hands on the heads of those being ordained by the ordaining bishop. The essential form is the accompanying prayer in the preface of the ordination ceremony. Other elements in the rite are the presentation of the implements of sacrifice — the chalice containing the wine and the paten containing a host — with accompanying prayers.

Deacon: There are two kinds of deacons: those who receive the order and remain in it permanently, and those who receive the order while advancing to priesthood. The following quotation — from Vatican II's Dogmatic Constitution on the Church (*Lumen Gentium*, No. 29) — describes the nature and role of the diaconate, with emphasis on the permanent diaconate.

"At a lower level of the hierarchy are deacons, upon whom hands are imposed 'not unto the priesthood, but unto a ministry of service.' For strengthened by sacramental grace, in communion with the bishop and his group of priests, they serve the People of God in the ministry of the liturgy, of the word, and of charity. It is the duty of the deacon, to the extent that he has been authorized by competent authority, to administer baptism solemnly, to be custodian and dispenser of the Eucharist, to assist at and bless marriages in the name of the Church, to bring Viaticum to the dying, to read the sacred Scripture to the faithful, to instruct and exhort the people, to preside at the worship and prayer of the faithful, to administer sacramentals, and to officiate at funeral and burial services. (Deacons are) dedicated to duties of charity and administration.

"The diaconate can in the future be restored as a proper and permanent rank of the hierarchy. It pertains to the competent territorial bodies of bishops, of one kind or another, to decide, with the approval of the Supreme Pontiff, whether and where it is opportune for such deacons to be appointed for the care of souls. With the consent of the Roman Pontiff, this diaconate will be able to be conferred upon men of more mature age, even upon those living in the married state. It may also be conferred upon suitable young men. For them, however, the law of celibacy must remain intact" (No. 29).

The Apostles ordained the first seven deacons (Acts 6:1-6): Stephen, Philip, Prochorus, Nicanor, Timon, Parmenas, Nicholas.

Former Orders, Ministries: With the revision of the sacrament of order which began in 1971, the orders of subdeacon, acolyte, exorcist, lector and porter were abolished because they and their respective functions had fallen into disuse or did not require ordination. The Holy See started revision of the sacrament of order in 1971. By virtue of an indult of Oct. 5 of that year, the bishops of the U.S. were permitted to discontinue ordaining porters and exorcists. Another indult, dated three days later, permitted the use of revised rites for ordaining acolytes and lectors.

To complete the revision, Pope Paul VI abolished Sept. 14, 1972, the orders of porter, exorcist and subdeacon; decreed that laymen, as well as candidates for the diaconate and priesthood, can be installed (rather than ordained) in the ministries (rather than orders) of acolyte and lector; reconfirmed the suppression of tonsure and its replacement with a service of dedication to God and the Church; and stated that a man enters the clerical state on ordination to the diaconate.

The abolished orders were:

• Subdeacon, with specific duties in liturgical worship, especially at Mass. The order, whose first extant mention dates from about the middle of the third century, was regarded as minor until the 13th century; afterwards, it was called a major order in the West but not in the East.

• Acolyte, to serve in minor capacities in liturgical worship; a function now performed by Mass servers.

• Exorcist, to perform services of exorcism for expelling evil spirits; a function which came to be reserved to specially delegated priests.

• Lector, to read scriptural and other passages during liturgical worship; a function now generally performed by lay persons.

• Porter, to guard the entrance to an assembly of Christians and to ward off undesirables who tried to gain admittance; an order of early origin and utility but of present insignificance.

Permanent Diaconate

Restoration of the permanent diaconate in the Roman rite — making it possible for men to become deacons permanently, without going on to the priesthood — was promulgated by Pope Paul VI June 18, 1967, in a document entitled *Sacrum Diaconatus Ordinem* ("Sacred Order of the Diaconate").

The Pope's action implemented the desire expressed by the Second Vatican Council for reestablishment of the diaconate as an independent order in its own right not only to supply ministers for carrying on the work of the Church but also to complete the hierarchical structure of the Church of Roman rite.

Permanent deacons have been traditional in the Eastern Church. The Western Church, however, since the fourth or fifth century, generally followed the practice of conferring the diaconate only as a sacred order preliminary to the priesthood, and of restricting the ministry of deacons to liturgical functions.

The pope's document, issued on his own initiative, provided:

• Qualified unmarried men 25 years of age or older may be ordained deacons. They cannot marry after ordination.

• Qualified married men 35 years of age or older may be ordained deacons. The consent of the wife of a prospective deacon is required. A married deacon cannot remarry after the death of his wife.

• Preparation for the diaconate includes a course of study and formation over a period of at least three years.

• Candidates who are not members of religious institutes must be affiliated with a diocese. Reestablishment of the diaconate among religious is reserved to the Holy See.

• Deacons will practice their ministry under the direction of a bishop and with the priests with whom they will be associated. (For functions, *see* the description of deacon, under **Holy Orders**.)

Restoration of the permanent diaconate in the U.S. was approved by the Holy See in October 1968. Shortly afterwards the U.S. bishops established a committee for the permanent diaconate, which was chaired by Bishop Edward U. Kmiec of Nashville in 1997. The current head of the committee is Bishop Frederick F. Campbell of Columbus, Ohio. The committee operates through a secretariat, with offices at 3211 Fourth St. N.E., Washington, DC 20017.

Status and Functions

The 2008 *Official Catholic Directory* reports that in the U.S. there were a total of 16,408 permanent deacons (the highest total by far for any single country), an increase of 540 from the previous year and an increase of 4,161 from 1998. Worldwide, there are currently 34,520 deacons, according to the 2006 edition of the *Annuarium Statisticum Ecclesiae* (the most recent edition).

Training programs of spiritual, theological and pastoral formation are based on guidelines emanating from the USCCB. Deacons have various functions, depending on the nature of their assignments. Liturgically, they can officiate at baptisms, weddings, wake services and funerals, can preach and distribute Holy Communion. Some are engaged in religious education work. All are intended to carry out works of charity and pastoral service of one kind or another.

The majority of deacons, most of whom are married, continue in their secular work. Their ministry of service is developing in three dimensions: of liturgy, of the word, and of charity. Depending on the individual deacon's abilities and preference, he is assigned by his bishop to either a parochial ministry or to another field of service. Deacons are active in a variety of ministries including those to prison inmates and their families, the sick in hospitals, nursing homes and homes for the aged, alienated youth, the elderly and the poor, and in various areas of legal service to the indigent, of education and campus ministry.

National Association of Diaconate Directors: Membership organization of directors, vicars and other staff personnel of diaconate programs. Established in 1977 to promote effective communication and facilitate the exchange of information and resources of members; to develop professional expertise and promote research, training and self evaluation; to foster accountability and seek ways to promote means of implementing solutions to problems. Deacon Thomas R. Dubois, exec. dir. Address: 7625 North High Street, Columbus, OH 43235; (614) 985-2276; www.nadd.org.

Ordination of Women

The Catholic Church believes and teaches that, in fidelity to the will of Christ, it cannot ordain women to the priesthood. This position has been set out over the last quarter-century in a series of authoritative documents published by or with the authority of Pope Paul VI and Pope John Paul II.

The first of these, *Inter Insigniores* ("Among the Characteristics"), was issued by the Congregation for the Doctrine of the Faith in October 1976. Its central statement is: "The Sacred Congregation for the Doctrine of the Faith judges it necessary to recall that the Church, in fidelity to the example of the Lord, does not consider herself authorized to admit women to priestly ordination."

In support of this, the document cited the constant tradition of the Church, the fact that Christ called only men to be Apostles and the continuation of this practice by the Apostles themselves, and the sacramental appropriateness of a male priesthood acting *in persona Christi* — in the person of Christ.

In light of continuing discussion, Pope John Paul II returned to the subject in the apostolic letter *Ordinatio Sacerdotalis* ("Priestly Ordination"), issued May 29, 1994: "Wherefore, in order that all doubt may be removed regarding a matter of great importance, a matter which pertains to the Church's divine constitution itself, in virtue of my ministry of confirming the brethren (cf. Lk 22:32) I declare that the Church has no authority whatsoever to confer priestly ordination on women and that this judgment is to be definitively held by all the Church's faithful."

The Congregation for the Doctrine of the Faith followed this on Oct. 28, 1995, with a response, published over the signature of its Prefect, Cardinal Joseph Ratzinger, to a bishop's inquiry concerning how "to be definitively held" should be understood. The response was:

"This teaching requires definitive assent, since, founded on the written Word of God and from the beginning constantly preserved and applied in the Tradition of the Church, it has been set forth infallibly by the ordinary and universal Magisterium (cf. Second Vatican Council, Dogmatic Constitution on the Church *Lumen Gentium*, 25, 2)."

Concerning the possible ordination of women to the diaconate, the International Theological Commission in 2002 concluded that the permanent diaconate belongs to the sacrament of orders and thus is limited to men only.

MATRIMONY

Marriage Doctrine

The following excerpts, stating key points of doctrine on marriage, are from *Gaudium et Spes*, (Nos. 48 to 51) promulgated by the Second Vatican Council:

Conjugal Covenant

The intimate partnership of married life and love has been established by the Creator and qualified by his laws. It is rooted in the conjugal covenant of irrevocable personal consent.

God himself is the author of matrimony, endowed as it is with various benefits and purposes. All of these have a very decisive bearing on the continuation of the human race, on the personal development and eternal destiny of the individual members of a family, and on the dignity, stability, peace, and prosperity of the family itself and of human society as a whole. By their very nature, the institution of matrimony itself and conjugal love are ordained for the procreation and education of children, and find in them their ultimate crown.

Thus a man and a woman render mutual help and service to each other through an intimate union of their persons and of their actions. Through this union they experience the meaning of their oneness and attain to it with growing perfection day by day. As a mutual gift of two persons, this intimate union, as well as the good of the children, imposes total fidelity on the spouses and argues for an unbreakable oneness between them (No. 48).

Sacrament of Matrimony

Christ the Lord abundantly blessed this many-faceted

love. The Savior of men and the Spouse of the Church comes into the lives of married Christians through the sacrament of matrimony. He abides with them thereafter so that, just as he loved the Church and handed himself over on her behalf, the spouses may love each other with perpetual fidelity through mutual self-bestowal.

Graced with the dignity and office of fatherhood and motherhood, parents will energetically acquit themselves of a duty which devolves primarily on them; namely, education, and especially religious education.

The Christian family, which springs from marriage as a reflection of the loving covenant uniting Christ with the Church, and as a participation in that covenant, will manifest to all men the Savior's living presence in the world, and the genuine nature of the Church (No. 48).

Conjugal Love

The biblical Word of God several times urges the betrothed and the married to nourish and develop their wedlock by pure conjugal love and undivided affection.

This love is an eminently human one since it is directed from one person to another through an affection of the will. It involves the good of the whole person. Therefore it can enrich the expressions of body and mind with a unique dignity, ennobling these expressions as special ingredients and signs of the friendship distinctive of marriage. This love the Lord has judged worthy of special gifts, healing, perfecting, and exalting gifts of grace and of charity.

Such love, merging the human with the divine, leads the spouses to a free and mutual gift of themselves, a gift proving itself by gentle affection and by deed. Such love pervades the whole of their lives. Indeed, by its generous activity it grows better and grows greater. Therefore it far excels mere erotic inclination, which, selfishly pursued, soon enough fades wretchedly away.

This love is uniquely expressed and perfected through the marital act. The actions within marriage by which the couple are united intimately and chastely are noble and worthy ones. Expressed in a manner which is truly human, these actions signify and promote that mutual self-giving by which spouses enrich each other with a joyful and a thankful will.

Sealed by mutual faithfulness and hallowed above all by Christ's sacrament, this love remains steadfastly true in body and mind, in bright days or dark. It will never be profaned by adultery or divorce. Firmly established by the Lord, the unity of marriage will radiate from the equal personal dignity of wife and husband, a dignity acknowledged by mutual and total love.

The steady fulfillment of the duties of this Christian vocation demands notable virtue. For this reason, strengthened by grace for holiness of life, the couple will painstakingly cultivate and pray for constancy of love, largeheartedness, and the spirit of sacrifice (No. 49).

Fruitfulness of Marriage

Marriage and conjugal love are by their nature ordained toward the begetting and educating of children. Children are really the supreme gift of marriage and contribute very substantially to the welfare of their parents. God himself wished to share with man a certain special participation in his own creative work. Thus he blessed male and female, saying: "Increase and multiply" (Gn 1:28).

Hence, while not making the other purposes of matrimony of less account, the true practice of conjugal love, and the whole meaning of the family life which results from it, have this aim: that the couple be ready with stout hearts to cooperate with the love of the Creator and the Savior, who through them will enlarge and enrich his own family day by day.

Parents should regard as their proper mission the task of transmitting human life and educating those to whom it has been transmitted. They should realize that they are thereby cooperators with the love of God the Creator, and are, so to speak, the interpreters of that love. Thus they will fulfill their task with human and Christian responsibility (No. 50).

Norms of Judgment

They will thoughtfully take into account both their own welfare and that of their children, those already born and those who may be foreseen. For this accounting they will reckon with both the material and the spiritual conditions of the times as well as of their state in life. Finally, they will consult the interests of the family group, of temporal society, and of the Church herself.

The parents themselves should ultimately make this judgment in the sight of God. But in their manner of acting, spouses should be aware that they cannot proceed arbitrarily. They must always be governed according to a conscience dutifully conformed to the divine law itself, and should be submissive toward the Church's teaching office, which authentically interprets that law in the light of the Gospel. That divine law reveals and protects the integral meaning of conjugal love, and impels it toward a truly human fulfillment.

Marriage, to be sure, is not instituted solely for procreation. Rather, its very nature as an unbreakable compact between persons, and the welfare of the children, both demand that the mutual love of the spouses, too, be embodied in a rightly ordered manner, that it grow and ripen. Therefore, marriage persists as a whole manner and communion of life, and maintains its value and indissolubility, even when offspring are lacking — despite, rather often, the very intense desire of the couple (No. 50).

Love and Life

This Council realizes that certain modern conditions often keep couples from arranging their married lives harmoniously, and that they find themselves in circumstances where at least temporarily the size of their families should not be increased. As a result, the faithful exercise of love and the full intimacy of their lives are hard to maintain. But where the intimacy of married life is broken off, it is not rare for its faithfulness to be imperiled and its quality of fruitfulness ruined. For then the upbringing of the children and the courage to accept new ones are both endangered.

To these problems there are those who presume to offer dishonorable solutions. Indeed, they do not recoil from the taking of life. But the Church issues the reminder that a true contradiction cannot exist between the divine laws pertaining to the transmission of life and those pertaining to the fostering of authentic conjugal love.

Church Teaching

For God, the Lord of Life, has conferred on men the surpassing ministry of safeguarding life — a ministry which must be fulfilled in a manner which is worthy of men. Therefore from the moment of its conception life must be guarded with the greatest care, while abortion and infanticide are unspeakable crimes. The sexual characteristics of man and the human faculty of reproduction wonderfully exceed the dispositions of lower forms of life. Hence the acts themselves which are proper to conjugal love and which are exercised in accord with genuine human dignity must be honored with great reverence (No. 51).

Therefore when there is question of harmonizing conjugal love with the responsible transmission of life, the moral aspect of any procedure does not depend solely on the sincere intentions or on an evaluation of motives. It must be determined by objective standards. These, based on the nature of the human person and his acts, preserve the full sense of mutual self-giving and human procreation in the context of true love. Such a goal cannot be achieved unless the virtue of conjugal chastity is sincerely practiced. Relying on these principles, sons of the Church may not undertake methods of regulating procreation which are found blameworthy by the teaching authority of the Church in its unfolding of the divine law.

Everyone should be persuaded that human life and the task of transmitting it are not realities bound up with this world alone. Hence they cannot be measured or perceived only in terms of it, but always have a bearing on the eternal destiny of men (No. 51).

Humanae Vitae

Marriage doctrine and morality were the subjects of the encyclical letter *Humanae Vitae* (Of Human Life), issued by Pope Paul VI, July 29, 1968. *Humanae Vitae* was given reaffirmation and its teaching restated and defended by Pope John Paul II in his encyclical *Evangelium Vitae* (The Gospel of Life, 1995). Following are a number of key excerpts from *Humanae Vitae*, which was framed in the pattern of traditional teaching and statements by the Second Vatican Council.

Each and every marriage act ("*quilibet matrimonii usus*") must remain open to the transmission of life (No. 11).

Indeed, by its intimate structure, the conjugal act, while most closely uniting husband and wife, capacitates them for the generation of new lives according to laws inscribed in the very being of man and of woman. By safeguarding both these essential aspects, the unitive and the procreative, the conjugal act preserves in its fullness the sense of true mutual love and its ordination toward man's most high calling to parenthood (No. 12).

It is, in fact, justly observed that a conjugal act imposed upon one's partner without regard for his or her condition and lawful desires is not a true act of love, and therefore denies an exigency of right moral order in the relationships between husband and wife. Hence, one who reflects well must also recognize that a reciprocal act of love which jeopardizes the responsibility to transmit life - which God the Creator, according to particular laws, inserted therein - is in contradiction with the design constitutive of marriage and with the will of the Author of life. To use this divine gift, destroying, even if only partially, its meaning and its purpose, is to contradict the nature both of man and of woman and of their most intimate relationship, and therefore it is to contradict also the plan of God and his will (No. 13).

Forbidden Actions

The direct interruption of the generative process already begun, and, above all, directly willed and procured abortion, even if for therapeutic reasons, are to be absolutely excluded as licit means of regulating birth.

Equally to be excluded is direct sterilization, whether perpetual or temporary, whether of the man or of the woman. Similarly excluded is every action which, either in anticipation of the conjugal act, or in its accomplishment, or in the development of its natural consequences, proposes, whether as an end or as a means, to render procreation impossible.

To justify conjugal acts made intentionally infecund, one cannot invoke as valid reasons the lesser evil, or the fact that such acts would constitute a whole together with the fecund acts already performed or to follow later and hence would share in one and the same moral goodness. In truth, if it is sometimes licit to tolerate a lesser evil in order to avoid a greater evil or to promote a greater good, it is not licit, even for the gravest reasons, to do evil so that good may follow therefrom; that is, to make into the object of a positive act of the will something which is intrinsically disorder, and hence unworthy of the human person, even when the intention is to safeguard or promote individual, family or social well-being.

Consequently, it is an error to think that a conjugal act which is deliberately made infecund, and so is intrinsically dishonest, could be made honest and right by the ensemble of a fecund conjugal life (No. 14).

If, then, there are serious motives to space out births, which derive from the physical or psychological conditions of husband and wife, or from external conditions, the Church teaches that it is then licit to take into account the natural rhythms immanent in the generative functions, for the use of marriage in the infecund periods only, and in this way to regulate birth without offending earlier stated principles (No. 16).

Pastoral Concerns

We do not at all intend to hide the sometimes serious difficulties inherent in the life of Christian married persons; for them, as for everyone else, "the gate is narrow and the way is hard that leads to life." But the hope of that life must illuminate their way, as with courage they strive to live with wisdom, justice and piety in this present time, knowing that the figure of this world passes away.

Let married couples then, face up to the efforts needed, supported by the faith and hope which "do not disappoint because God's love has been poured into our hearts through the Holy Spirit, who has been given to us." Let them implore divine assistance by persevering prayer; above all, let them draw from the source of grace and charity in the Eucharist. And, if sin should still keep its hold over them, let them not be discouraged but rather have recourse with humble perseverance to the mercy of God, which is poured forth in the sacrament of penance (No. 25).

Marriage Laws

The Catholic Church claims jurisdiction over its members in matters pertaining to marriage. Church legislation on the subject is stated principally in 111 canons of the Code of Canon Law.

Marriage laws of the Church provide juridical norms in support of the marriage covenant. In 10 chapters, the revised Code covers: pastoral directives for preparing men and women for marriage; impediments in general and in particular; matrimonial consent; form for the celebration of marriage; mixed marriages; secret celebration of marriage; effects of marriage; separation of spouses; and convalidation of marriage.

Catholics are bound by all marriage laws of the Church. Non-Catholics, whether baptized or not, are not considered bound by these ecclesiastical laws except in cases of marriage with a Catholic. Certain natural laws, in the Catholic view, bind all men and women, irrespective of their religious beliefs; accordingly, marriage is prohibited before the time of puberty, without knowledge and free mutual consent, in the case of an already existing valid marriage bond, in the case of antecedent and perpetual impotence.

Formalities

These include, in addition to arrangements for the time and place of the marriage ceremony, doctrinal and moral instruction concerning marriage and the recording of data which verifies in documentary form the eligibility and freedom of the persons to marry. Records of this kind, which are confidential, are preserved in the archives of the church where the marriage takes place.

Premarital instructions are the subject matter of Pre-Cana Conferences.

Marital Consent

Matrimonial consent can be invalidated by an essential defect, substantial error, the strong influence of force and fear, the presence of a condition or intention against the nature of marriage.

Form of Marriage

A Catholic is required, for validity and lawfulness, to contract marriage — with another Catholic or with a non-Catholic — in the presence of a competent priest or deacon and two witnesses.

There are two exceptions to this law. A Roman-rite Catholic (since Mar. 25, 1967) or an Eastern-rite Catholic (since Nov. 21, 1964) can contract marriage validly in the presence of a priest of a separated Eastern-rite Church, provided other requirements of law are complied with. With permission of the competent Roman-rite or Eastern-rite bishop, this form of marriage is lawful, as well as valid. (*See* **Eastern-rite Laws,** below.)

With these two exceptions, and aside from cases covered by special permission, the Church does not regard as valid any marriages involving Catholics which take place before non-Catholic ministers of religion or civil officials.

(An excommunication formerly in force against Catholics who celebrated marriage before a non-Catholic minister was abrogated in a decree issued by the Sacred Congregation for the Doctrine of the Faith on Mar. 18, 1966.)

The ordinary place of marriage is the parish of either Catholic party or of the Catholic party in case of a mixed marriage.

Church law regarding the form of marriage does not affect non-Catholics in marriages among themselves. The Church recognizes as valid the marriages of non-Catholics before ministers of religion and civil officials, unless they are rendered null and void on other grounds.

The canonical form is not to be observed in the case of a marriage between a non-Catholic and a baptized Catholic who has left the Church by a formal act.

Impediments

Diriment Impediments to marriage are factors that render a marriage invalid.

• age, which obtains before completion of the 14th year for a woman and the 16th year for a man

• impotency, if it is antecedent to the marriage and permanent (this differs from sterility, which is not an impediment)

• the bond of an existing valid marriage

• disparity of worship, which obtains when one party is a Catholic and the other party is unbaptized

• sacred orders

• religious profession of the perpetual vow of chastity

• abduction, which impedes the freedom of the person abducted

• crime, variously involving elements of adultery, promise or attempt to marry, conspiracy to murder a husband or wife

• blood relationship in the direct line (father-daughter, mother-son, etc.) and to the fourth degree inclusive of the collateral line (brother-sister, first cousins)

• affinity, or relationship resulting from a valid marriage, in any degree of the direct line

•public honesty, arising from an invalid marriage or from public or notorious concubinage; it renders either party incapable of marrying blood relatives of the other in the first degree of the direct line

• legal relationship arising from adoption; it renders either party incapable of marrying relatives of the other in the direct line or in the second degree of the collateral line.

Dispensations from impediments: Persons hindered by impediments cannot marry unless they are dispensed therefrom in view of reasons recognized in canon law. Local bishops can dispense from the impediments most often encountered (e.g., disparity of worship) as well as others.

Decision regarding some dispensations is reserved to the Holy See.

Separation

A valid and consummated marriage of baptized persons cannot be dissolved by any human authority or any cause other than the death of one of the persons.

In other circumstances:

1. A valid but unconsummated marriage of baptized persons, or of a baptized and an unbaptized person, can be dissolved:

a. by the solemn religious profession of one of the persons, made with permission of the pope. In such a case, the bond is dissolved at the time of profession, and the other person is free to marry again.

b. by dispensation from the pope, requested for a grave reason by one or both of the persons. If the dispensation is granted, both persons are free to marry again.

Dispensations in these cases are granted for reasons connected with the spiritual welfare of the concerned persons.

2. A legitimate marriage, even consummated, of unbaptized persons can be dissolved in favor of one of them who subsequently receives the sacrament of baptism. This is the Pauline Privilege, so called because it was promulgated by St. Paul (1 Cor 7:12-15) as a means of protecting the faith of converts. Requisites for granting the privilege are:

a. Marriage prior to the baptism of either person;

b. Reception of baptism by one person;

c. Refusal of the unbaptized person to live in peace with the baptized person and without interfering with his or her freedom to practice the Christian faith. The privilege does not apply if the unbaptized person agrees to these conditions.

3. A legitimate and consummated marriage of a baptized and an unbaptized person can be dissolved by the pope in virtue of the Privilege of Faith, also called the Petrine Privilege.

Civil Divorce

Because of the unity and the indissolubility of marriage, the Church denies that civil divorce can break the bond of a valid marriage, whether the marriage involves two Catholics, a Catholic and a non-Catholic, or non-Catholics with each other.

In view of serious circumstances of marital distress, the Church permits an innocent and aggrieved party, whether wife or husband, to seek and obtain a civil divorce for the purpose of acquiring title and right to the civil effects of divorce, such as separate habitation and maintenance, and the custody of children. Permission for this kind of action should be obtained from proper church authority. The divorce, if obtained, does not break the bond of a valid marriage.

Under other circumstances - as would obtain if a marriage was invalid (see **Annulment**, below) - civil divorce is permitted for civil effects and as a civil ratification of the fact that the marriage bond really does not exist.

Annulment

This is a decision by a competent church authority - e.g., a bishop, a diocesan marriage tribunal, the Roman Rota — that an apparently valid marriage was actually invalid from the beginning because of the unknown or concealed existence, from the beginning, of a diriment impediment, an essential defect in consent, radical incapability for marriage, or a condition placed by one or both of the parties against the very nature of marriage.

Eastern-Rite Laws

Marriage laws of the Eastern Church differ in several respects from the legislation of the Roman rite. The regulations in effect since May 2, 1949, were contained in the *motu proprio Crebre Allatae* issued by Pius XII the previous February.

According to both the Roman Code of Canon Law and the Oriental Code, marriages between Roman-rite Catholics and Eastern-rite Catholics ordinarily take place in the rite of the groom and have canonical effects in that rite.

Regarding the form for the celebration of marriages between Eastern Catholics and baptized Eastern non-Catholics, the Second Vatican Council declared:

"By way of preventing invalid marriages between Eastern Catholics and baptized Eastern non-Catholics, and in the interests of the permanence and sanctity of marriage and of domestic harmony, this sacred Synod decrees that the canonical 'form' for the celebration of such marriages obliges only for lawfulness. For their validity, the presence of a sacred minister suffices, as long as the other requirements of law are honored" (Decree on Eastern Catholic Churches, No. 18).

Marriages taking place in this manner are lawful, as well as valid, with permission of a competent Eastern-rite bishop.

The Rota

The Roman Rota is the ordinary court of appeal for marriage, and some other cases, which are appealed to the Holy See from lower church courts. Appeals are made to the Rota if decisions by diocesan and archdiocesan courts fail to settle the matter in dispute. Pope John Paul II, at annual meetings with Rota personnel, speaks about the importance of the court's actions in providing norms of practice for other tribunals.

MIXED MARRIAGES

"Mixed Marriages" (*Matrimonia Mixta*) was the subject of a letter issued under this title by Pope Paul VI, on Mar. 31, 1970, and also a statement, "Implementation of the Apostolic Letter on Mixed Marriages," approved by the National Conference of Catholic Bishops on Nov. 16, 1970.

One of the key points in the bishops' statement referred to the need for mutual pastoral care by ministers of different faiths for the sacredness of marriage and for appropriate preparation and continuing support of parties to a mixed marriage.

Pastoral experience, which the Catholic Church shares with other religious bodies, confirms the fact that marriages of persons of different beliefs involve special problems related to the continuing religious practice of the concerned persons and to the religious education and formation of their children.

Pastoral measures to minimize these problems include instruction of a non-Catholic party in essentials of the Catholic faith for purposes of understanding. Desirably, some instruction should also be given the Catholic party regarding his or her partner's beliefs.

Requirements

The Catholic party to a mixed marriage is required to declare his (her) intention of continuing practice of the Catholic faith and to promise to do all in his (her) power to share his (her) faith with children born of the marriage by having them baptized and raised as Catholics. No declarations or promises are required of the non-Catholic party, but he (she) must be informed of the declaration and promise made by the Catholic.

Notice of the Catholic's declaration and promise is an essential part of the application made to a bishop for permission to marry a baptized non-Catholic, or a dispensation to marry an unbaptized non-Catholic.

A mixed marriage can take place with a Nuptial Mass. (The bishops' statement added this caution: "To the extent that Eucharistic sharing is not permitted by the general discipline of the Church, this is to be considered when plans are being made to have the mixed marriage at Mass or not.")

The ordinary minister at a mixed marriage is an authorized priest or deacon, and the ordinary place is the parish church of the Catholic party. A non-Catholic minister may not only attend the marriage ceremony but may also address, pray with and bless the couple.

For appropriate pastoral reasons, a bishop can grant a dispensation from the Catholic form of marriage and can permit the marriage to take place in a non-Catholic church with a non-Catholic minister as the officiating minister. A priest may not only attend such a ceremony but may also address, pray with and bless the couple.

"It is not permitted," however, the bishops' statement declared, "to have two religious services or to have a single service in which both the Catholic marriage ritual and a non-Catholic marriage ritual are celebrated jointly or successively."

Pastoral Ministry for Divorced and Remarried

Ministry to divorced and remarried Catholics is a difficult field of pastoral endeavor, situated as it is in circumstances tantamount to the horns of a dilemma.

At Issue

On the one side is firm church teaching on the permanence of marriage and norms against reception of the Eucharist and full participation in the life of the Church by Catholics in irregular unions.

On the other side are men and women with broken unions followed by second and perhaps happier attempts at marriage which the Church does not recognize as valid and which may not be capable of being validated because of the existence of an earlier marriage bond.

Factors involved in these circumstances are those of the Church, upholding its doctrine and practice regarding the permanence of marriage, and those of many men and women in irregular second marriages who desire full participation in the life of the Church.

Sacramental participation is not possible for those whose first marriage was valid, although there is no bar to their attendance at Mass, to sharing in other activities of the Church, or to their efforts to have children baptized and raised in the Catholic faith.

An exception to this rule is the condition of a divorced and remarried couple living in a brother-sister relationship.

There is no ban against sacramental participation by separated or divorced persons who have not attempted a second marriage, provided the usual conditions for reception of the sacraments are in order.

Unverified estimates of the number of U.S. Catholics who are divorced and remarried vary between six and eight million.

Tribunal Action

What can the Church do for them and with them in pastoral ministry, is an old question charged with new urgency because of the rising number of divorced and remarried Catholics.

One way to help is through the agency of marriage tribunals charged with responsibility for investigating and settling questions concerning the validity or invalidity of a prior marriage. There are reasons in canon law justifying the Church in declaring a particular marriage null and void from the beginning, despite the short- or long-term existence of an apparently valid union.

Decrees of nullity (annulments) are not new in the history of the Church. If such a decree is issued, a man or woman is free to validate a second marriage and live in complete union with the Church.

The 2006 Statistical Yearbook of the Church (*Annuarium Statisticum Ecclesiae*, the most recent edition) reported in 2006 that U.S. tribunals issued 37,275 annulments (in ordinary and documentary processes). The canonical reasons were: invalid consent (30,075), impotence (4), other impediments (1,670), defect of form (5,526). Worldwide, 59,463 decrees or declarations of nullity were issued in 2006.

On Feb. 8, 2005, Vatican officials issued a new instruction for Church marriage tribunals that was intended clarify Church law, defend the sacrament of marriage, and ensure the efficiency that justice requires. The new handbook for Latin-rite diocesan and interdiocesan tribunals, *Dignitas Connubii* ("The Dignity of Marriage"), details clear procedures for accepting, investigating, assessing, and appealing marriage cases.

Reasons behind Decrees

Pastoral experience reveals that some married persons, a short or long time after contracting an apparently valid marriage, exhibit signs that point back to the existence, at the time of marriage, of latent and serious personal deficiencies which made them incapable of valid consent and sacramental commitment.

Such deficiencies might include gross immaturity and those affecting in a serious way the capacity to love, to have a true interpersonal and conjugal relationship, to fulfill marital obligations, or to accept the faith aspect of marriage.

Psychological and behavioral factors like these have been given greater attention by tribunals in recent years and have provided grounds for numerous decrees of nullity.

Decisions of this type do not indicate any softening of the Church's attitude regarding the permanence of marriage. They affirm, rather, that some persons who have married were really not capable of doing so.

Serious deficiencies in the capacity for real interpersonal relationship in marriage were the reasons behind a landmark decree of nullity issued in 1973 by the Roman Rota, the Vatican high court of appeals in marriage cases. Pope John Paul referred to such deficiencies — the "grave lack of discretionary judgment," incapability of assuming "essential matrimonial rights and obligations," for example, in an address Jan. 26, 1984, to personnel of the Rota.

The tribunal way to a decree of nullity regarding a previous marriage, however, is not open to many persons in second marriages because grounds are either lacking or, if present, cannot be verified in tribunal process.

Unacceptable Solutions

One unacceptable solution of the problem, called "good conscience procedure," involves administration of the sacraments of penance and the Eucharist to divorced and remarried Catholics unable to obtain a decree of nullity for a first marriage who are living in a subsequent marriage "in good faith."

This procedure, despite the fact that it has no standing or recognition in church law, is being advocated and practiced by some priests and remarried Catholics.

This issue was addressed by the Congregation for the Doctrine of the Faith in a letter to bishops dated Oct. 14, 1994, and published with the approval of Pope John Paul II. The letter said in part:

"Pastoral solutions in this area have been suggested according to which divorced-and-remarried members of the faithful could approach holy Communion in specific cases when they considered themselves authorized according to a judgment of conscience to do so. This would be the case, for example, when they had been abandoned completely unjustly although they sincerely tried to save the previous marriage; or when they are convinced of the nullity of their previous marriage although (they are) unable to demonstrate it in the external forum; or when they have gone through a long period of reflection and penance; or also when for morally valid reasons they cannot satisfy the obligation to separate.

"In some places it has also been proposed that, in order objectively to examine their actual situation, the divorced-and-remarried would have to consult a prudent and experienced priest. This priest, however,

would have to respect their eventual decision in conscience to approach holy Communion, without this implying an official authorization.

"In these and similar cases, it would be a matter of a tolerant and benevolent pastoral solution in order to do justice to the different situations of the divorced-and-remarried.

"Even if analogous solutions have been proposed by a few fathers of the Church and in some measure were practiced, nevertheless these never attained the consensus of the fathers and in no way came to constitute the common doctrine of the Church nor to determine her discipline. It falls to the universal magisterium, in fidelity to sacred Scripture and tradition, to teach and to interpret authentically the deposit of faith."

Conditions for Receiving Communion

Practically speaking, "when for serious reasons - for example, for the children's upbringing - a man and a woman cannot satisfy the obligation to separate," they may be admitted to Communion if "they take on themselves the duty to live in complete continence, that is, by abstinence from the acts proper to married couples. In such a case they may receive holy Communion as long as they respect the obligation to avoid giving scandal."

The teaching of the Church on this subject "does not mean that the Church does not take to heart the situation of those faithful who, moreover, are not excluded from ecclesial communion. She is concerned to accompany them pastorally and invite them to share in the life of the Church in the measure that is compatible with the dispositions of divine law, from which the Church has no power to dispense. On the other hand, it is necessary to instruct these faithful so that they do not think their participation in the life of the Church is reduced exclusively to the question of the reception of the Eucharist. The faithful are to be helped to deepen their understanding of the value of sharing in the sacrifice of Christ in the Mass, or spiritual communion, of prayer, of meditation on the word of God, and of works of charity and justice."

The Communion of Saints

SAINTS OF THE CHURCH

Biographical sketches of additional saints and blesseds are found in other *Almanac* entries. See **Index**, under the name of each saint for the apostles, evangelists, Doctors of the Church, and Fathers of the Church. For beatification and canonization procedures, see those entries in the **Glossary**.

An asterisk with a feast date indicates that the saint is listed in the General Roman Calendar or the proper calendar for U.S. dioceses. For rank of observances, see listing in calendar for current year on preceding pages.

Adalbert (956-97): Born in Bohemia; bishop of Prague; Benedictine; missionary in Poland, Prussia and Hungary; martyred by Prussians near Danzig; Apr. 23.*

Adjutor (d. 1131): Norman knight; fought in First Crusade; monk-recluse after his return; Apr. 30.

Agatha (d. c. 250): Sicilian virgin-martyr; her intercession credited in Sicily with stilling eruptions of Mt. Etna; patron of nurses; Feb. 5.*

Agnes (d. c. 304): Roman virgin-martyr; martyred at age of 10 or 12; patron of young girls; Jan. 21.*

Aloysius Gonzaga (1568-91): Italian Jesuit; died while nursing plague-stricken; canonized 1726; patron of youth; June 21.*

Amand (d. c. 676): Apostle of Belgium; b. France; established monasteries throughout Belgium; Feb. 6.

Andre Bessette, Bl. (Bro. Andre) (1845-1937): Canadian Holy Cross Brother; prime mover in building of St. Joseph's Oratory, Montreal; beatified May 23, 1982; Jan. 6* (U.S.).

Andre Grasset de Saint Sauveur, Bl. (1758-92): Canadian priest; martyred in France, Sept. 2, 1792, during the Revolution; one of a group called the Martyrs of Paris who were beatified in 1926; Sept. 2.

Andrew Bobola (1592-1657): Polish Jesuit; joined Jesuits at Vilna; worked for return of Orthodox to union with Rome; martyred; canonized 1938; May 16.

Andrew Corsini (1302-73): Italian Carmelite; bishop of Fiesoli; mediator between quarrelsome Italian states; canonized 1629; Feb. 4.

Andrew Dung-Lac and Companions (d. 18th-19th c.): Martyrs of Vietnam. Total of 117 included 96 Vietnamese, 11 Spanish and 10 French missionaries (8 bishops; 50 priests, including Andrew Dung-Lac; 1 seminarian; 58 lay persons). Canonized June 19, 1988; inscribed in General Roman Calendar, 1989, as a memorial. Nov. 24.*

Andrew Fournet (1752-1834): French priest; co-founder with St. Jeanne Elizabeth Bichier des Anges of the Daughters of the Holy Cross of St. Andrew; canonized 1933; May 13.

Andrew Kim, Paul Chong and Companions (d. between 1839-67): Korean martyrs (103) killed in persecutions of 1839, 1846, 1866, and 1867; among them were Andrew Kim, the first Korean priest, and Paul Chong, lay apostle; canonized May 6, 1984, during Pope John Paul II's visit to Korea. Sept. 20.*

Angela Merici (1474-1540): Italian secular Franciscan; foundress of Company of St. Ursula, 1535, the first teaching order of women Religious in the Church; canonized 1807; Jan. 27.*

Angelico, Bl. (Fra Angelico; John of Faesulis) (1387-1455): Dominican; Florentine painter of early Renaissance; proclaimed blessed by John Paul II, Feb. 3, 1982; patron of artists; Feb. 18.

Anne Marie Javouhey, Bl. (1779-1851): French virgin; foundress of Institute of St. Joseph of Cluny, 1812; beatified 1950; July 15.

Ansgar (801-65): Benedictine monk; b. near Amiens; archbishop of Hamburg; missionary in Denmark, Sweden, Norway, and northern Germany; apostle of Scandinavia; Feb. 3.*

Anthony (c. 251-c. 354): Abbot; Egyptian hermit; patriarch of all monks; established communities for hermits which became models for monastic life, especially in the East; friend and supporter of St. Athanasius in the latter's struggle with the Arians; Jan. 17.*

Anthony Claret (1807-70): Spanish bishop; founder of Missionary Sons of the Immaculate Heart of Mary (Claretians), 1849; archbishop of Santiago, Cuba, 1851-57; canonized 1950; Oct. 24.*

Anthony Gianelli (1789-1846): Italian bishop; founded the Daughters of Our Lady of the Garden, 1829; bishop of Bobbio, 1838; canonized 1951; June 7.

Anthony Zaccaria (1502-39): Italian priest; founder of Barnabites (Clerks Regular of St. Paul), 1530; canonized 1897; July 5.*

Apollonia (d. 249): Deaconess of Alexandria; martyred during persecution of Decius; her patronage of dentists and those suffering from toothaches probably rests on tradition that her teeth were broken by her persecutors; Feb. 9.

Augustine of Canterbury (d. 604 or 605): Italian missionary; apostle of the English; sent by Pope Gregory I with 40 monks to evangelize England; arrived there 597; first archbishop of Canterbury; May 27.*

Bartolomea Capitania (1807-33): Italian foundress with Vincenza Gerosa of the Sisters of Charity of Lovere; canonized 1950; July 26.

Beatrice da Silva Meneses (1424-90): Foundress, b. Portugal; founded Congregation of the Immaculate Conception, 1484, in Spain; canonized 1976; Sept. 1.

Benedict Joseph Labré (1748-83): French layman; pilgrim-beggar; noted for his piety and love of prayer before the Blessed Sacrament; canonized 1883; Apr. 16.

Benedict of Nursia (c. 480-547): Abbot; founder of monasticism in Western Europe; established monastery at Monte Cassino; proclaimed patron of Europe by Paul VI in 1964; July 11.*

Benedict the Black (*il Moro*) (1526-89): Sicilian Franciscan; born a slave; joined Franciscans as lay brother; appointed guardian and novice master; canonized 1807; Apr. 3.

Bernadette Soubirous (1844-79): French peasant girl favored with series of visions of Blessed Virgin Mary at Lourdes (*see* **Lourdes Apparitions**); joined Institute of Sisters of Notre Dame at Nevers, 1866; canonized 1933; Apr. 16.

Bernard of Montjoux (or Menthon) (d. 1081): Augustinian canon; probably born in Italy; founded Alpine hospices near the two passes named for him; patron of mountaineers; May 28.

Bernardine of Feltre, Bl. (1439-94): Italian Franciscan preacher; a founder of *montes pietatis*; Sept. 28.

Bernardine of Siena (1380-1444): Italian Franciscan; noted preacher and missioner; spread of devotion to Holy Name is attributed to him; represented in art holding to his breast the monogram IHS; canonized 1450; May 20.*

Blase (d. c. 316): Armenian bishop; martyr; the blessing of throats on his feast day derives from tradition that he miraculously saved the life of a boy who had half-swallowed a fish bone; Feb. 3.*

Boniface (Winfrid) (d. 754): English Benedictine; bishop; martyr; apostle of Germany; established monastery at Fulda which became center of missionary work in Germany; archbishop of Mainz; martyred near Dukkum in Holland; June 5.*

Brendan (c. 489-583): Irish abbot; founded monasteries; his patronage of sailors probably rests on a legend that he made a seven-year voyage in search of a fabled paradise; called Brendan the Navigator; May 16.

Bridget (Brigid) (c. 450-525): Irish nun; founded religious community at Kildare, the first in Ireland; patron, with Sts. Patrick and Columba, of Ireland; Feb. 1.

Bridget (Birgitta) (c. 1303-73): Swedish mystic; widow; foundress of Order of Our Savior (Brigittines); canonized 1391; patroness of Sweden; named a co-patroness of Europe, with St. Edith Stein and St. Catherine of Siena, on Oct. 1, 1999; July 23.*

Bruno (1030-1101): German monk; founded Carthusians, 1084, in France; Oct. 6.*

Cabrini, Mother: *See* **Frances Xavier Cabrini.**

Cajetan (Gaetano) **of Thiene** (1480-1547): Italian lawyer; religious reformer; a founder of Oratory of Divine Love, forerunner of the Theatines; canonized 1671; Aug. 7.*

Callistus I (d. 222): Pope, 217-22; martyr; condemned Sabellianism and other heresies; advocated a policy of mercy toward repentant sinners; Oct. 14.*

Camillus de Lellis (1550-1614): Italian priest; founder of Camillians (Ministers of the Sick); canonized 1746; patron of the sick and of nurses; July 14.*

Casimir (1458-84): Polish prince; grand duke of Lithuania; noted for his piety; buried at cathedral in Vilna, Lithuania; canonized 1521; patron of Poland and Lithuania; Mar. 4.*

Cassian of Tangier (d. 298): Roman martyr; an official court stenographer who declared himself a Christian; patron of stenographers; Dec. 3.

Catherine Labouré (1806-76): French Religious; favored with series of visions soon after she joined Sisters of Charity of St. Vincent de Paul in Paris in 1830; first Miraculous Medal (*see* **Index**) struck in 1832 in accord with one of the

visions; canonized 1947; Nov. 28.

Catherine of Bologna (1413-63): Italian Poor Clare; mystic, writer, artist canonized 1712; patron of artists; May 9.

Cecilia (2nd-3rd c.): Roman virgin-martyr; traditional patroness of musicians; Nov. 22.*

Charles Borromeo (1538-84): Italian cardinal; nephew of Pope Pius IV; cardinal bishop of Milan; influential figure in Church reform in Italy; promoted education of clergy; canonized 1610; Nov. 4.*

Charles Lwanga and Companions (d. between 1885 and 1887): Twenty-two Martyrs of Uganda, many of them pages of King Mwanga of Uganda, who were put to death because they denounced his corrupt lifestyle; canonized 1964; first martyrs of black Africa; June 3.*

Charles of Sezze (1616-70): Italian Franciscan lay brother who served in humble capacities; canonized 1959; Jan. 6.

Christopher (3rd c.): Early Christian martyr inscribed in Roman calendar about 1550; feast relegated to particular calendars because of legendary nature of accounts of his life; traditional patron of travelers; July 25.

Clare (1194-1253): Foundress of Poor Clares; b. at Assisi; was joined in religious life by her sisters, Agnes and Beatrice, and eventually her widowed mother Ortolana; canonized 1255; patroness of television; Aug. 11.*

Claude de la Colombiere (1641-82): French Jesuit; spiritual director of St. Margaret Mary Alacoque; instrumental in spreading devotion to the Sacred Heart; beatified, 1929; canonized May 31, 1992; Feb. 15.

Clement Hofbauer (1751-1820): Redemptorist priest; missionary; born in Moravia; helped spread Redemptorists north of the Alps; canonized 1909; Mar. 15.

Clement I (d. c. 100): Pope, 88-97; third successor of St. Peter; wrote important letter to Church in Corinth settling disputes there; venerated as a martyr; Nov. 23.*

Columba (521-97): Irish monk; founded monasteries in Ireland; missionary in Scotland; established monastery at Iona which became the center for conversion of Picts, Scots, and Northern English; Scotland's most famous saint; patron saint of Ireland (with Sts. Patrick and Brigid); June 9.

Columban (545-615): Irish monk; scholar; founded monasteries in England and Brittany (famous abbey of Luxeuil), forced into exile because of his criticism of Frankish court; spent last years in northern Italy where he founded abbey at Bobbio; Nov. 23.*

Conrad of Parzham (1818-94): Bavarian Capuchin lay brother; served as porter at the Marian shrine of Altotting in Upper Bavaria for 40 years; canonized 1934; Apr. 21.

Contardo Ferrini, Bl. (1859-1902): Italian secular Franciscan; model of the Catholic professor; beatified 1947; patron of universities; Oct. 20.

Cornelius (d. 253): Pope, 251-53; promoted a policy of mercy with respect to readmission of repentant Christians who had fallen away during the persecution of Decius (*lapsi*); banished from Rome during persecution of Gallus; regarded as a martyr; Sept. 16 (with Cyprian).*

Cosmas and Damian (d. c. 303): Arabian twin brothers, physicians; martyred during Diocletian persecution; patrons of physicians; Sept. 26.*

Crispin and Crispinian (3rd c.): Early Christian martyrs; said to have met their deaths in Gaul; patrons of shoemakers, a trade they pursued; Oct. 25.

Crispin of Viterbo (1668-1750): Capuchin brother; canonized June 20, 1982; May 21.

Cyprian (d. 258): Early ecclesiastical writer; b. Africa; bishop of Carthage, 249-58; supported Pope St. Cornelius concerning the readmission of Christians who had apostatized in time of persecution; erred in his teaching that baptism administered by heretics and schismatics was invalid; wrote *De Unitate*; Sept. 16 (with St. Cornelius).*

Cyril and Methodius (9th c.): Greek missionaries, brothers; venerated as apostles of the Slavs; Cyril (d. 869) and Methodius (d. 885) began their missionary work in Moravia in 863; developed a Slavonic alphabet; used the vernacular in the liturgy, a practice that was eventually approved; declared patrons of Europe with St. Benedict, Dec. 31, 1980; Feb. 14.*

Damasus I (d. 384): Pope, 366-84; opposed Arians and Apollinarians; commissioned St. Jerome to work on Bible translation; developed Roman liturgy; Dec. 11.*

Damian: *See* Cosmas and Damian.

Damien of Molokai, Bl. (d. 1889): The so-called leper priest of Molokai; originally from Belgium, Damien devoted over 20 years to the care of the lepers in Hawaii, ultimately dying from the same disease. He was beatified by Pope John Paul II in 1995.

David (5th or 6th c.): Nothing for certain known of his life; said to have founded monastery at Menevia; patron saint of Wales; Mar. 1.

Denis and Companions (d. 3rd c.): Denis, bishop of Paris, and two companions identified by early writers as Rusticus, a priest, and Eleutherius, a deacon; martyred near Paris; Denis is popularly regarded as the apostle and a patron saint of France; Oct. 9.*

Dismas (1st c.): Name given to repentant thief (Good Thief) to whom Jesus promised salvation (Lk. 23:40-43); regarded as patron of prisoners; Mar. 25 (observed on second Sunday of October in U.S. prison chapels).

Dominic (Dominic de Guzman) (1170-1221): Spanish priest; founded the Order of Preachers (Dominicans), 1215, in France; preached against the Albigensian heresy; a contemporary of St. Francis of Assisi; canonized 1234; Aug. 8.*

Dominic Savio (1842-57): Italian youth; pupil of St. John Bosco; died before his 15th birthday; canonized 1954; patron of choirboys; May 6.

Duns Scotus, John (d. 1308): Scottish Franciscan; theologian; advanced theological arguments for doctrine of the Immaculate Conception; proclaimed blessed; cult solemnly confirmed by John Paul II, Mar. 20, 1993; Nov. 8.

Dunstan (c. 910-88): English monk; archbishop of Canterbury; initiated reforms in religious life; counselor to several kings; considered one of greatest Anglo-Saxon saints; patron of goldsmiths, locksmiths, jewelers (trades in which he is said to have excelled); May 19.

Dymphna (dates unknown): Nothing certain known of her life; according to legend, she was an Irish maiden murdered by her heathen father at Gheel near Antwerp, Belgium, where she had fled to escape his advances; her relics were discovered there in the 13th century; since that time cures of mental illness and epilepsy have been attributed to her intercession; patron of those suffering from mental illness; May 15.

Edith Stein, St. (1891-1942): German Carmelite (Teresa Benedicta of the Cross); born of Jewish parents; author and lecturer; baptized in Catholic Church 1922; arrested with her sister Rosa in 1942 and put to death at Auschwitz; beatified 1987, by Pope John Paul II during his visit to West Germany; was canonized by Pope John Paul II on Oct. 11, 1998, and named a co-patroness of Europe, with St. Bridget of Sweden and St. Catherine of Siena, on Oct. 1, 1999; Aug. 10.

Edmund Campion (1540-81): English Jesuit; convert 1573; martyred at Tyburn; canonized 1970, one of the Forty English and Welsh Martyrs; Dec. 1.

Edward the Confessor (d. 1066): King of England,

1042-66; canonized 1161; Oct. 13.

Eligius (c. 590-660): Bishop; born in Gaul; founded monasteries and convents; bishop of Noyon and Tournai; famous worker in gold and silver; Dec. 1.

Elizabeth Ann Seton (1774-1821): American foundress; convert, 1805; founded Sisters of Charity in the U.S.; beatified 1963; canonized Sept. 14, 1975; the first American-born saint; Jan. 4 (U.S.).*

Elizabeth of Hungary (1207-31): Became secular Franciscan after death of her husband in 1227; devoted life to poor and destitute; a patron of the Secular Franciscan Order; canonized 1235; Nov. 17.*

Elizabeth of Portugal (1271-1336): Queen of Portugal; b. Spain; retired to Poor Clare convent as a secular Franciscan after the death of her husband; canonized 1626; July 4.*

Emily de Rodat (1787-1852): French foundress of the Congregation of the Holy Family of Villefranche; canonized 1950; Sept. 19.

Emily de Vialar (1797-1856): French foundress of the Sisters of St. Joseph of the Apparition; canonized 1951; June 17.

Erasmus (Elmo) (d. 303): Life surrounded by legend; martyred during Diocletian persecution; patron of sailors; June 2.

Ethelbert (552-616): King of Kent, England; baptized by St. Augustine of Canterbury, 597; issued legal code; furthered spread of Christianity; Feb. 26.

Eusebius of Vercelli (283-370): Italian bishop; exiled from his see (Vercelli) for a time because of his opposition to Arianism; considered a martyr because of sufferings he endured; Aug. 2.*

Fabian (d. 250): Pope, 236-50; martyred under Decius; Jan. 20.*

Felicity: *See* Perpetua and Felicity.

Ferdinand III (1198-1252): King of Castile and Leon; waged successful crusade against Muhammadans in Spain; founded university at Salamanca; canonized 1671; May 30.

Fiacre (Fiachra) (d. c. 670): Irish hermit; patron of gardeners; Aug. 30.

Fidelis of Sigmaringen (Mark Rey) (1577-1622): German Capuchin; lawyer before he joined the Capuchins; missionary to Swiss Protestants; stabbed to death by peasants who were told he was an agent of the Austrian emperor; Apr. 24.*

Frances of Rome (1384-1440): Italian model for housewives and widows; happily married for 40 years; after death of her husband in 1436 joined community of Benedictine Oblates she had founded; canonized 1608; patron of motorists; Mar. 9.*

Frances Xavier Cabrini (Mother Cabrini) (1850-1917): American foundress; b. Italy; founded the Missionary Sisters of the Sacred Heart, 1877; settled in the U.S. 1889; became an American citizen at Seattle 1909; worked among Italian immigrants; canonized 1946, the first American citizen so honored; Nov. 13 (U.S.).*

Francis Borgia (1510-72): Spanish Jesuit; joined Jesuits after death of his wife in 1546; became general of the Order, 1565; Oct. 10.

Francis Caracciolo (1563-1608): Italian priest; founder with Father Augustine Adorno of the Clerics Regular Minor (Adorno Fathers); canonized 1807; declared patron of Italian chefs, 1996; June 4.

Francis Fasani (1681-1742): Italian Conventual Franciscan; model of priestly ministry, especially in service to poor and imprisoned; canonized 1986; Nov. 27.

Francis of Assisi (Giovanni di Bernardone) (1181/82-1226): Founder of the Franciscans, 1209; received stigmata

1224; canonized 1228; one of best-known and best-loved saints; patron of Italy, Catholic Action, animals, and ecologists; Oct. 4.*

Francis of Paola (1416-1507): Italian hermit: founder of Minim Friars; Apr. 2.*

Francis Xavier (1506-52): Spanish Jesuit; missionary to Far East; canonized 1602; patron of foreign missions; considered one of greatest Christian missionaries; Dec. 3.*

Francis Xavier Bianchi (1743-1815): Italian Barnabite; acclaimed apostle of Naples because of his work there among the poor and abandoned; canonized 1951; Jan. 31.

Gabriel of the Sorrowful Mother (Francis Possenti) (1838-62): Italian Passionist; died while a scholastic; canonized 1920; Feb. 27.

Gaspar (Caspar) **del Bufalo** (1786-1836): Italian priest; founded Missionaries of the Precious Blood, 1815; canonized 1954; Jan. 2.

Gemma Galgani (1878-1903): Italian laywoman; visionary; subject of extraordinary religious experiences; canonized 1940; Apr. 11.

Genesius (d. c. 300): Roman actor; according to legend, was converted while performing a burlesque of Christian baptism and was subsequently martyred; patron of actors; Aug. 25.

Geneviève (422-500): French nun; a patroness and protectress of Paris; events of her life not authenticated; Jan. 3.

George (d. c. 300): Martyr, probably during Diocletian persecution in Palestine; all other incidents of his life, including story of the dragon, are legendary; patron of England; Apr. 23.*

Gerard Majella (1725-55): Italian Redemptorist lay brother; noted for supernatural occurrences in his life including bilocation and reading of consciences; canonized 1904; patron of mothers; Oct. 16.

Gertrude (1256-1302): German mystic; writer; helped spread devotion to the Sacred Heart; Nov. 16.*

Gregory VII (Hildebrand) (1020?-85): Pope, 1075-85; Benedictine monk; adviser to several popes; as pope, strengthened interior life of Church and fought against lay investiture; driven from Rome by Henry IV; died in exile; canonized 1584; May 25.*

Gregory Barbarigo (1626-97): Italian cardinal; noted for his efforts to bring about reunion of separated Christians; canonized 1960; June 18.

Gregory of Nyssa (c. 335-95): Bishop; theologian; younger brother of St. Basil the Great; Mar. 9.

Gregory Thaumaturgus (c. 213-68): Bishop of Neocaesarea; missionary, famed as wonder worker; Nov. 17.

Gregory the Illuminator (257-332): Martyr; bishop; apostle and patron saint of Armenia; helped free Armenia from the Persians; Sept. 30.

Hedwig (1174-1243): Moravian noblewoman; married duke of Silesia, head of Polish royal family; fostered religious life in country; canonized 1266; Oct. 16.*

Helena (250-330): Empress; mother of Constantine the Great; associated with discovery of the True Cross; Aug. 18.

Henry (972-1024): Bavarian emperor; cooperated with Benedictine abbeys in restoration of ecclesiastical and social discipline; canonized 1146; July 13.*

Herman Joseph (1150-1241): German Premonstratensian; his visions were the subjects of artists; writer; cult approved, 1958; Apr. 7.

Hippolytus (d. c. 236): Roman priest; opposed Pope St. Callistus I in his teaching about the readmission to the Church of repentant Christians who had apostatized during time of persecution; elected antipope; exiled to Sardinia; rec-onciled before his martyrdom; important ecclesiastical writer; Aug. 13* (with Pontian).

Hugh of Cluny (the Great) (1024-1109): Abbot of Benedictine foundation at Cluny; supported popes in efforts to reform ecclesiastical abuses; canonized 1120; Apr. 29.

Ignatius of Antioch (d. c. 107): Early ecclesiastical writer; martyr; bishop of Antioch in Syria for 40 years; Oct. 17.*

Ignatius of Laconi (1701-81): Italian Capuchin lay brother whose 60 years of religious life were spent in Franciscan simplicity; canonized 1951; May 11.

Ignatius of Loyola (1491-1556): Spanish soldier; renounced military career after recovering from wounds received at siege of Pampeluna (Pamplona) in 1521; founded Society of Jesus (Jesuits), 1534, at Paris; wrote *The Book of Spiritual Exercises*; canonized 1622; July 31.*

Irenaeus of Lyons (130-202): Early ecclesiastical writer; opposed Gnosticism; bishop of Lyons; traditionally regarded as a martyr; June 28.*

Isidore the Farmer (d. 1170): Spanish layman; farmer; canonized 1622; patron of farmers; May 15 (U.S.).*

Jane Frances de Chantal (1572-1641): French widow; foundress, under guidance of St. Francis de Sales, of Order of the Visitation; canonized 1767; Dec. 12* (General Roman Calendar); Aug. 18* (U.S.).

Januarius (Gennaro) (d. 304): Bishop of Benevento; martyred during Diocletian persecution; fame rests on liquefaction of some of his blood preserved in a phial at Naples, an unexplained phenomenon which has occurred regularly several times each year for over 400 years; Sept. 19.*

Jeanne Delanoue (1666-1736): French foundress of Sisters of St. Anne of Providence, 1704; canonized 1982; Aug. 16.

Jeanne (Joan) **de Lestonnac** (1556-1640): French foundress; widowed in 1597; founded the Religious of Notre Dame 1607; canonized 1947; Feb. 2.

Jeanne de Valois (Jeanne of France) (1464-1505): French foundress; deformed daughter of King Louis XI; was married in 1476 to Duke Louis of Orleans who had the marriage annulled when he ascended the throne as Louis XII; Jeanne retired to life of prayer; founded contemplative Annonciades of Bourges, 1504; canonized 1950; Feb. 5.

Jeanne-Elizabeth Bichier des Ages (1773-1838): French Religious; co-founder with St. Andrew Fournet of Daughters of the Cross of St. Andrew, 1807; canonized 1947; Aug. 26.

Jeanne Jugan, Bl. (1792-1879): French Religious; foundress of Little Sisters of the Poor; beatified Oct. 3, 1982; Aug. 30.

Jerome Emiliani (1481-1537): Venetian priest; founded Somascan Fathers, 1532, for care of orphans; canonized 1767; patron of orphans and abandoned children; Feb. 8.*

Joan Antida Thouret (1765-1826): French Religious; founded, 1799, congregation now known as Sisters of Charity of St. Joan Antida; canonized 1934; Aug. 24.

Joan of Arc (1412-31): French heroine, called The Maid of Orleans, La Pucelle; led French army in 1429 against English invaders besieging Orleans; captured by Burgundians the following year; turned over to ecclesiastical court on charge of heresy, found guilty and burned at the stake; her innocence was declared in 1456; canonized 1920; patroness of France; May 30.

Joaquina de Vedruna de Mas (1783-1854): Spanish foundress; widowed in 1816; after providing for her children, founded the Carmelite Sisters of Charity; canonized 1959; Aug. 28.

John I (d. 526): Pope, 523-26; martyr; May 18.*

John XXIII, Bl.: see **Popes of the Twentieth**

Century in **Papacy and the Holy See.**

John Baptist de la Salle (1651-1719): French priest; founder of Brothers of the Christian Schools, 1680; canonized 1900; patron of teachers; Apr. 7.*

John Berchmans (1599-1621): Belgian Jesuit scholastic; patron of Mass servers; canonized 1888; Aug. 13.

John (Don) Bosco (1815-88): Italian priest; founded Salesians, 1859, for education of boys; co-founder of Daughters of Mary Help of Christians for education of girls; canonized 1934; Jan. 31.*

John Capistran (1386-1456): Italian Franciscan; preacher; papal diplomat; canonized 1690; declared patron of military chaplains, Feb. 10, 1984; Oct. 23.*

John de Ribera (1532-1611): Spanish bishop and statesman; archbishop of Valencia, 1568-1611, and viceroy of that province; canonized 1960; Jan. 6.

John Eudes (1601-80): French priest; founder of Sisters of Our Lady of Charity of Refuge, 1642, and Congregation of Jesus-Mary (Eudists), 1643; canonized 1925; Aug. 19.*

John Fisher (1469-1535): English prelate; theologian; martyr; bishop of Rochester, cardinal; refused to recognize validity of Henry VIII's marriage to Anne Boleyn; upheld supremacy of the pope; beheaded for refusing to acknowledge Henry as head of the Church; canonized 1935; June 22 (with St. Thomas More).*

John Francis Regis (1597-1640): French Jesuit priest; preached missions among poor and unlettered; canonized 1737; patron of social workers, particularly medical social workers, because of his concern for poor and needy and sick in hospitals; July 2.

John Gualbert (d. 1073): Italian priest; founder of Benedictine congregation of Vallombrosians, 1039; canonized 1193; July 12.

John Kanty (Cantius) (1395-1473): Polish theologian; canonized 1767; Dec. 23.*

John Leonardi (1550-1609): Italian priest; worked among prisoners and the sick; founded Clerics Regular of the Mother of God; canonized 1938; Oct. 9.*

John Nepomucene (1345-93): Bohemian priest; regarded as a martyr; canonized 1729; patron of Czechoslovakia; May 16.

John Nepomucene Neumann (1811-60): American prelate; b. Bohemia; ordained in New York 1836; missionary among Germans near Niagara Falls before joining Redemptorists, 1840; bishop of Philadelphia, 1852; first bishop in U.S. to prescribe Forty Hours devotion in his diocese; beatified 1963; canonized June 19, 1977; Jan. 5 (U.S.).*

John of Ávila (1499-1569): Spanish priest; preacher; ascetical writer; spiritual adviser of St. Teresa of Jesus (Ávila); canonized 1970; May 10.

John of Britto (1647-93): Portuguese Jesuit; missionary in India where he was martyred; canonized 1947; Feb. 4.

John of God (1495-1550): Portuguese founder; his work among the sick poor led to foundation of Brothers Hospitallers of St. John of God, 1540, in Spain; canonized 1690; patron of sick, nurses, hospitals; Mar. 8.*

John of Matha (1160-1213): French priest; founder of the Order of Most Holy Trinity, whose original purpose was the ransom of prisoners from the Muslims; Feb. 8.

John Ogilvie (1579-1615): Scottish Jesuit; martyr; canonized 1976, the first canonized Scottish saint since 1250 (Margaret of Scotland); Mar. 10.

John Vianney (Curé of Ars) (1786-1859): French parish priest; noted confessor, spent 16 to 18 hours a day in confessional; canonized 1925; patron of parish priests; Aug. 4.*

Josaphat Kuncevyc (1584-1623): Basilian monk; b. Poland; archbishop of Polotsk, Lithuania; worked for reunion of separated Eastern Christians with Rome; martyred by mob of schismatics; canonized 1867; Nov. 12.*

Josemaria Escrivá de Balaguer (1902-75) Priest and founder of Opus Dei; the society was designed to promote holiness among individuals in the world; beatified in 1992; canonized on Oct. 6, 2002; May 17.

Joseph Benedict Cottolengo (1786-1842): Italian priest; established Little Houses of Divine Providence (*Piccolo Casa*) for care of orphans and the sick; canonized 1934; Apr. 30.

Joseph Cafasso (1811-60): Italian priest; renowned confessor; promoted devotion to Blessed Sacrament; canonized 1947; June 23.

Joseph Calasanz (1556-1648): Spanish priest; founder of Piarists (Order of Pious Schools); canonized 1767; Aug. 25.*

Joseph of Cupertino (1603-63): Italian Franciscan; noted for remarkable incidents of levitation; canonized 1767; Sept. 18.

Joseph Pignatelli (1737-1811): Spanish Jesuit; left Spain when Jesuits were banished in 1767; worked for revival of the Order; named first superior when Jesuits were reestablished in Kingdom of Naples, 1804; canonized 1954; Nov. 28.

Juan Diego (16th c.): Mexican Indian, convert; indigenous name according to tradition Cuauhtlatohuac ("The eagle who speaks"); favored with apparitions of Our Lady (*see* **Our Lady of Guadalupe**) on Tepeyac hill; beatified 1990; canonized July 30, 2002; Dec. 9* (U.S.).

Julia Billiart (1751-1816): French foundress; founded Sisters of Notre Dame de Namur, 1804; canonized 1969; Apr. 8.

Juliana Falconieri (1270-1341): Italian foundress of the Servite Nuns; the niece of St. Alexis Falconieri; canonized in 1737; June 19.

Justin de Jacobis (1800-60): Italian Vincentian; bishop; missionary in Ethiopia; canonized 1975; July 31.

Justin Martyr (100-65): Early ecclesiastical writer of *Apologies for the Christian Religion, Dialog with the Jew Tryphon*; martyred at Rome; June 1.*

Kateri Tekakwitha, Bl. (1656-80): "Lily of the Mohawks"; Indian maiden born at Ossernenon (Auriesville), NY; baptized Christian, Easter 1676, by Jesuit missionary Father Jacques de Lambertville; lived life devoted to prayer, penitential practices and care of sick and aged in Christian village of Caughnawaga near Montreal where her relics are now enshrined; beatified June 22, 1980; July 14* (in U.S.).

Katharine Drexel, St. (1858-1955): Philadelphia-born heiress; devoted wealth to founding schools and missions for Indians and Blacks; foundress of Sisters of Blessed Sacrament for Indians and Colored People, 1891; beatified 1988; canonized Oct. 1, 2000; Mar. 3* (U.S.).

Ladislaus (1040-1095): King of Hungary; supported Pope Gregory VII against Henry IV; canonized 1192; June 27.

Lawrence (d. 258): Widely venerated martyr who suffered death, according to a long-standing but unverifiable legend, by fire on a gridiron; Aug. 10.*

Lawrence (Lorenzo) **Ruiz and Companions** (d. 1630s): Martyred in or near the city of Nagasaki, Japan; Lawrence Ruiz, first Filipino saint, and 15 companions (nine Japanese, four Spaniards, one Italian and one Frenchman); canonized 1987; Sept. 28.*

Leonard Murialdo (1828-1900): Italian priest; educator; founder of Pious Society of St. Joseph of Turin; 1873; canonized 1970; Mar. 30.

Leonard of Port Maurice (1676-1751): Italian Franciscan; ascetical writer; preached missions throughout Italy; canonized 1867; patron of parish missions; Nov. 26.

Leopold Mandic (1866-1942): Croatian-born Franciscan priest; noted confessor; spent most of his priestly life in Padua, Italy; canonized 1983; July 30.

Louis IX (1215-70): King of France, 1226-70; participated in Sixth Crusade; patron of Secular Franciscan Order; canonized 1297; Aug. 25.*

Louis de Montfort (1673-1716): French priest; founder of Sisters of Divine Wisdom, 1703, and Missionaries of Company of Mary, 1715; wrote *True Devotion to the Blessed Virgin*; canonized 1947; Apr. 28.*

Louis Zepherin Moreau, Bl. (d. 1901): Canadian bishop; headed St. Hyacinthe, Quebec, diocese, 1876-1901; beatified 1987; May 24.

Louise de Marillac (1591-1660): French foundress, with St. Vincent de Paul, of the Sisters of Charity; canonized 1934; Mar. 15.

Lucy (d. 304): Sicilian maiden; martyred during Diocletian persecution; one of most widely venerated early virgin-martyrs; patron of Syracuse, Sicily; invoked by those suffering from eye diseases; Dec. 13.*

Lucy Filippini (1672-1732): Italian educator; helped improve status of women through education; considered a founder of the Religious Teachers Filippini, 1692; canonized 1930; Mar. 25.

Madeleine Sophie Barat (1779-1865): French foundress of the Society of the Sacred Heart of Jesus; canonized 1925; May 25.

Malachy (1095-1148): Irish bishop; instrumental in establishing first Cistercian house in Ireland, 1142; canonized 1190; Nov. 3 (*See* Prophecies of St. Malachy).

Marcellinus and Peter (d. c. 304): Early Roman martyrs; June 2.*

Margaret Clitherow (1556-86): English martyr; convert shortly after her marriage; one of Forty Martyrs of England and Wales; canonized 1970; Mar. 25.

Margaret Mary Alacoque (1647-90): French Religious; spread devotion to Sacred Heart in accordance with revelations made to her in 1675 (*see* **Sacred Heart**); canonized 1920; Oct. 16.*

Margaret of Cortona (1247-97): Secular Franciscan; reformed her life in 1273 following the violent death of her lover; canonized 1728; May 16.

Margaret of Hungary (1242-70): Contemplative; daughter of King Bela IV of Hungary; lived a life of self-imposed penances; canonized 1943; Jan. 18.

Margaret of Scotland (1050-1093): Queen of Scotland; noted for solicitude for the poor and promotion of justice; canonized 1250; Nov. 16.*

Maria Goretti (1890-1902): Italian virgin-martyr; a model of purity; canonized 1950; July 6.*

Mariana Paredes de Jesus (1618-45): South American recluse; Lily of Quito; canonized 1950; May 28.

Marianne Cope, Bl. See *under* **Missionaries to the Americas**.

Marie-Leonie Paradis, Bl. (1840-1912): Canadian Religious; founded Little Sisters of the Holy Family, 1880; beatified 1984; May 4.

Marie-Rose Durocher, Bl. (1811-49): Canadian Religious; foundress of Sisters of Holy Names of Jesus and Mary; beatified 1982; Oct. 6* (in U.S.).

Martha (1st c.): Sister of Lazarus and Mary of Bethany; Gospel accounts record her concern for homely details; patron of cooks; July 29.*

Martin I (d. 655): Pope, 649-55; banished from Rome by emperor in 653 because of his condemnation of Monothelites; considered a martyr; Apr. 13.*

Martin of Tours (316-97): Bishop of Tours; opposed Arianism and Priscillianism; pioneer of Western monasticism, before St. Benedict; Nov. 11.*

Mary Domenica Mazzarello (1837-81): Italian foundress, with St. John Bosco, of the Daughters of Mary Help of Christians, 1872; canonized 1951; May 14.

Mary Josepha Rossello (1811-81): Italian-born foundress of the Daughters of Our Lady of Mercy; canonized 1949; Dec. 7.

Mary Magdalen Postel (1756-1846): French foundress of the Sisters of Christian Schools of Mercy, 1807; canonized 1925; July 16.

Mary Magdalene (1st c.): Gospels record her as devoted follower of Christ to whom he appeared after the Resurrection; her identification with Mary of Bethany (sister of Martha and Lazarus) and the woman sinner (Lk. 7:36-50) has been questioned; July 22.*

Mary Magdalene dei Pazzi (1566-1607): Italian Carmelite nun; recipient of mystical experiences; canonized 1669; May 25.*

Mary Michaeli Desmaisières (1809-65): Spanish-born foundress of the Institute of the Handmaids of the Blessed Sacrament, 1848; canonized 1934; Aug. 24.

Maximilian Kolbe (1894-1941): Polish Conventual Franciscan; prisoner at Auschwitz who heroically offered his life in place of a fellow prisoner; beatified 1971, canonized 1982; Aug. 14.*

Methodius: *See* **Cyril and Methodius.**

Miguel Febres Cordero (1854-1910): Ecuadorean Christian Brother; educator; canonized 1984; Feb. 9.

Miguel Pro, Bl. (1891-1927): Mexican Jesuit; joined Jesuits, 1911; forced to flee because of religious persecution; ordained in Belgium, 1925; returned to Mexico, 1926, to minister to people despite government prohibition; unjustly accused of assassination plot against president; arrested and executed; beatified 1988. Nov. 23* (U.S.).

Monica (332-87): Mother of St. Augustine; model of a patient mother; her feast is observed in the Roman calendar the day before her son's; Aug. 27.*

Nereus and Achilleus (d. c. 100): Early Christian martyrs; soldiers who, according to legend, were baptized by St. Peter; May 12.*

Nicholas of Flüe (1417-87): Swiss layman; at the age of 50, with the consent of his wife and 10 children, he retreated from the world to live as a hermit; called Brother Claus by the Swiss; canonized 1947; Mar. 21.

Nicholas of Myra (4th c.): Bishop of Myra in Asia Minor; one of most popular saints in both East and West; most of the incidents of his life are based on legend; patron of Russia; Dec. 6.*

Nicholas of Tolentino (1245-1305): Italian hermit; famed preacher; canonized 1446; Sept. 10.

Nicholas Tavelic and Companions (Deodatus of Aquitaine, Peter of Narbonne, Stephen of Cuneo) (d. 1391): Franciscan missionaries; martyred by Muslims in the Holy Land; canonized 1970; Nov. 14.

Norbert (1080-1134): German bishop; founded Canons Regular of Premontre (Premonstratensians, Norbertines), 1120; promoted reform of the clergy, devotion to Blessed Sacrament; canonized 1582; June 6.*

Odilia (d. c. 720): Benedictine abbess; according to legend she was born blind, abandoned by her family and adopted by a convent of nuns where her sight was miraculously restored; patroness of blind; Dec. 13.

Oliver Plunket (1629-81): Irish martyr; theologian; archbishop of Armagh and primate of Ireland; beatified 1920; canonized 1975; July 1.

Pancras (d. c. 304): Roman martyr; May 12.*

Paola Frassinetti (1809-82): Italian Religious; foundress, 1834, of Sisters of St. Dorothy; canonized 1984; June 11.

Paschal Baylon (1540-92): Spanish Franciscan lay brother; spent life as door-keeper in various Franciscan friaries; defended doctrine of Real Presence in Blessed Sacrament; canonized 1690; patron of all Eucharistic confraternities and congresses, 1897; May 17.

Patrick (389-461): Famous missionary of Ireland; began missionary work in Ireland about 432; organized the Church there and established it on a lasting foundation; patron of Ireland, with Sts. Bridget and Columba; Mar. 17.*

Paul Miki and Companions (d. 1597): Martyrs of Japan; Paul Miki, Jesuit, and 25 other priests and laymen were martyred at Nagasaki; canonized 1862, the first canonized martyrs of the Far East; Feb. 6.*

Paul of the Cross (1694-1775): Italian Religious; founder of the Passionists; canonized 1867; Oct 19* (Oct. 20, U.S.*).

Paulinus of Nola (d. 451): Bishop of Nola (Spain); writer; June 22.*

Peregrine (1260-1347): Italian Servite; invoked against cancer (he was miraculously cured of cancer of the foot after a vision); canonized 1726; May 1.

Perpetua and Felicity (d. 203): Martyrs; Perpetua was a young married woman; Felicity was a slave girl; Mar. 7.*

Peter Chanel (1803-41): French Marist; missionary to Oceania, where he was martyred; canonized 1954; Apr. 28.*

Peter Fourier (1565-1640): French priest; co-founder with Alice LeClercq (Mother Teresa of Jesus) of the Augustinian Canonesses of Our Lady, 1598; canonized 1897; Dec. 9.

Peter Gonzalez (1190-1246): Spanish Dominican; worked among sailors; court chaplain and confessor of King St. Ferdinand of Castile; patron of sailors; Apr. 14.

Peter Julian Eymard (1811-68): French priest; founder of the Congregation of the Blessed Sacrament (men), 1856, and Servants of the Blessed Sacrament (women), 1864; dedicated to Eucharistic apostolate; canonized 1962; Aug. 2.*

Peter Nolasco (c. 1189-1258): Born in Langueduc area of present-day France; founded the Mercedarians (Order of Our Lady of Mercy), 1218, in Spain; canonized 1628; Jan. 31.

Peter of Alcantara (1499-1562): Spanish Franciscan; mystic; initiated Franciscan reform; confessor of St. Teresa of Jesus (Ávila); canonized 1669; Oct. 22 (in U.S.).

Philip Benizi (1233-85): Italian Servite; noted preacher, peacemaker; canonized 1671; Aug. 23.

Philip Neri (1515-95): Italian Religious; founded Congregation of the Oratory; considered a second apostle of Rome because of his mission activity there; canonized 1622; May 26.*

Philip of Jesus (1517-57): Mexican Franciscan; martyred at Nagasaki, Japan; canonized 1862; patron of Mexico City; Feb. 6.*

Pio, Padre (1887-1968): Pio da Pietrelcina (Francesco Forgione), and Italian Capuchin Franciscan, mystic and stigmatic; assisted souls from all over the world who came to him for counsel and guidance; canonized on June 16, 2002; Sept. 23.

Pius V (1504-72): Pope, 1566-72; enforced decrees of Council of Trent; organized expedition against Turks resulting in victory at Lepanto; canonized 1712; Apr. 30.*

Polycarp (2nd c.): Bishop of Smyrna; ecclesiastical writer; martyr; Feb. 23.*

Pontian (d. c. 235): Pope, 230-35; exiled to Sardinia by the emperor; regarded as a martyr; Aug. 13 (with Hippolytus).*

Rafaela Maria Porras y Ayllon (1850-1925): Spanish Religious; founded the Handmaids of the Sacred Heart, 1877; canonized 1977; Jan. 6.

Raymond Nonnatus (d. 1240): Spanish Mercedarian; cardinal; devoted his life to ransoming captives from the Moors; Aug. 31.

Raymond of Peñafort (1175-1275): Spanish Dominican; confessor of Gregory IX; systematized and codified canon law, in effect until 1917; master general of Dominicans, 1238; canonized 1601; Jan. 7.*

Rita of Cascia (1381-1457): Widow; cloistered Augustinian Religious of Umbria; invoked in impossible and desperate cases; May 22.

Robert Southwell (1561-95): English Jesuit; poet; martyred at Tyburn; canonized 1970, one of the Forty English and Welsh Martyrs; Feb. 21.

Roch (1350-79): French layman; pilgrim; devoted life to care of plague-stricken; widely venerated; invoked against pestilence; Aug. 17.

Romuald (951-1027): Italian monk; founded Camaldolese Benedictines; June 19.*

Rose of Lima (1586-1617): Peruvian Dominican tertiary; first native-born saint of the New World; canonized 1671; Aug. 23.*

Scholastica (d. c. 559): Sister of St. Benedict; regarded as first nun of the Benedictine Order; Feb. 10.*

Sebastian (3rd c.): Roman martyr; traditionally pictured as a handsome youth with arrows; martyred; patron of athletes, archers; Jan. 20.*

Seven Holy Founders of the Servants of Mary (Buonfiglio Monaldo, Alexis Falconieri, Benedict dell'Antello, Bartholomew Amidei, Ricovero Uguccione, Gerardino Sostegni, John Buonagiunta Monetti): Florentine youths who founded Servites, 1233, in obedience to a vision; canonized 1888; Feb. 17.*

Sharbel Makhlouf (1828-98): Lebanese Maronite monk-hermit; canonized 1977; Dec. 24.

Sixtus II and Companions (d. 258): Sixtus, pope 257-58, and four deacons, martyrs; Aug. 7.*

Stanislaus (1030-79): Polish bishop; martyr; canonized 1253; Apr. 11.*

Stephen (d. c. 33): First Christian martyr; chosen by the Apostles as the first of the seven deacons; stoned to death; Dec. 26.*

Stephen (975-1038): King; apostle of Hungary; welded Magyars into national unity; canonized 1083; Aug. 16.*

Sylvester I (d. 335): Pope 314-35; first ecumenical council held at Nicaea during his pontificate; Dec. 31.*

Tarcisius (d. 3rd c.): Early martyr; according to tradition, was martyred while carrying the Blessed Sacrament to some Christians in prison; patron of first communicants; Aug. 15.

Teresa Margaret Redi (1747-70): Italian Carmelite; lived life of prayer and austere penance; canonized 1934; Mar. 11.

Teresa of Jesus Jornet Ibars (1843-97): Spanish Religious; founded the Little Sisters of the Abandoned Aged, 1873; canonized 1974; Aug. 26.

Teresa, Mother (1910-97): Sister, foundress of the Missionaries of Charity, and Nobel Prize winner; called Mother Teresa of Calcutta; beatified by Pope John Paul II on Oct. 19, 2003; Sept. 5.

Thérèse Couderc (1805-85): French Religious; foundress of the Religious of Our Lady of the Retreat in the Cenacle, 1827; canonized 1970; Sept. 26.

Thomas Becket (1118-70): English martyr; archbishop of Canterbury; chancellor under Henry II; murdered for upholding rights of the Church; canonized 1173; Dec. 29.*

Thomas More (1478-1535): English martyr; statesman, chancellor under Henry VIII; author of Utopia; opposed Henry's divorce, refused to renounce authority of the papacy; beheaded; canonized 1935; Pope John Paul II declared him patron of politicians on Oct. 31, 2000; June 22 (with St. John Fisher).*

Timothy (d. c. 97): Bishop of Ephesus; disciple and companion of St. Paul; martyr; Jan. 26.*

Titus (d. c. 96): Bishop; companion of St. Paul; recipient of one of Paul's epistles; Jan. 26.*

Titus Brandsma, Bl. (1881-1942): Dutch Carmelite priest; professor, scholar, journalist; denounced Nazi persecution of Jews; arrested by Nazis, Jan. 19, 1942; executed by lethal injection at Dachau, July 26, 1942; beatified 1985; July 26.

Valentine (d. 269): Priest, physician; martyred at Rome; legendary patron of lovers; Feb. 14.

Vicenta Maria Lopez y Vicuna (1847-96): Spanish foundress of the Daughters of Mary Immaculate for domestic service; canonized 1975; Dec. 26.

Vincent (d. 304): Spanish deacon; martyr; Jan. 22.*

Vincent de Paul (1581?-1660): French priest; founder of Congregation of the Mission (Vincentians, Lazarists) and co-founder of Sisters of Charity; declared patron of all charitable organizations and works by Leo XIII; canonized 1737; Sept. 27.*

Vincent Ferrer (1350-1418): Spanish Dominican; famed preacher; Apr. 5.*

Vincent Pallotti (1795-1850): Italian priest; founded Society of the Catholic Apostolate (Pallottines), 1835; Jan. 22.

Vincent Strambi (1745-1824): Italian Passionist; bishop; reformer; canonized 1950; Sept. 25.

Vitus (d.c. 300): Martyr; died in Lucania, southern Italy; regarded as protector of epileptics and those suffering from St. Vitus Dance (chorea); June 15.

Walburga (d. 779): English-born Benedictine Religious; belonged to group of nuns who established convents in Germany at the invitation of St. Boniface; abbess of Heidenheim; Feb. 25.

Wenceslaus (d. 935): Duke of Bohemia; martyr; patron of Bohemia; Sept. 28.*

Zita (1218-78): Italian maid; noted for charity to poor; patron of domestics; Apr. 27.

SAINTS — PATRONS AND INTERCESSORS

A patron is a saint who is venerated as a special intercessor before God. Most patrons have been so designated as the result of popular devotion and long-standing custom. In many cases, the fact of existing patronal devotion is clear despite historical obscurity regarding its origin. The Church has made official designation of relatively few patrons; in such cases, the dates of designation are given in parentheses in the list below. The theological background of the patronage of saints includes the dogmas of the Mystical Body of Christ and the Communion of Saints. Listed are patron saints of occupations and professions, and saints whose intercession is sought for special needs.

Academics: Thomas Aquinas.
Accomodations: Gertrude of Nivelles.
Accountants: Matthew.
Actors: Genesius.
Adopted children: Clotilde; Thomas More.
Advertisers: Bernardine of Siena (May 20, 1960).
Alcoholics: John of God; Monica.
Alpinists: Bernard of Montjoux (or Menthon) (Aug. 20, 1923).
Altar servers: John Berchmans.
Anesthetists: René Goupil.
Animals: Francis of Assisi.
Archaeologists: Damasus.
Archers: Sebastian.
Architects: Thomas, Apostle.
Art: Catherine of Bologna.
Artists: Luke, Catherine of Bologna, Bl. Angelico (Feb. 21, 1984).
Astronauts: Joseph Cupertino.
Astronomers: Dominic.
Athletes: Sebastian.
Authors: Francis de Sales.
Aviators: Our Lady of Loreto (1920), Thérèse of Lisieux, Joseph of Cupertino.
Bakers: Elizabeth of Hungary, Nicholas.
Bankers: Matthew.

Barbers: Cosmas and Damian, Louis.
Barren women: Anthony of Padua, Felicity.
Basket-makers: Anthony, Abbot.
Bees: Ambrose.
Birth: Margaret.
Beggars: Martin of Tours.
Blacksmiths: Dunstan.
Blind: Odilia, Raphael.
Blood banks: Januarius.
Bodily ills: Our Lady of Lourdes.
Bookbinders: Peter Celestine.
Bookkeepers: Matthew.
Booksellers: John of God.
Boy Scouts: George.
Brewers: Augustine of Hippo, Luke, Nicholas of Myra.
Bricklayers: Stephen.
Brides: Nicholas of Myra.
Bridges: John of Nepomucene.
Broadcasters: Gabriel.
Brushmakers: Anthony, Abbot.
Builders: Vincent Ferrer.
Bus drivers: Christopher.
Butchers: Anthony (Abbot), Luke.
Butlers: Adelelm.
Cabdrivers: Fiacre.
Cabinetmakers: Anne.
Cancer patients: Peregrine.
Canonists: Raymond of Peñafort.
Carpenters: Joseph.
Catechists: Viator, Charles Borromeo, Robert Bellarmine.
Catholic Action: Francis of Assisi (1916).
Catholic Press: Francis de Sales.
Chandlers: Ambrose, Bernard of Clairvaux.
Chaplains: John of Capistrano.
Charitable societies: Vincent de Paul (May 12, 1885).
Chastity: Thomas Aquinas.
Childbirth: Raymond Nonnatus; Gerard Majella.
Children: Nicholas of Myra.

Children of Mary: Agnes, Maria Goretti.
Choirboys: Dominic Savio (June 8, 1956), Holy Innocents.
Church: Joseph (Dec. 8, 1870).
Circus people: Julian the Hospitaller.
Clerics: Gabriel of the Sorrowful Mother.
Colleges: Thomas Aquinas.
Comedians: Vitus.
Communications personnel: Bernardine.
Confessors: Alphonsus Liguori (Apr. 26, 1950), John Nepomucene.
Converts: Helena; Vladimir.
Convulsive children: Scholastica.
Cooks: Lawrence, Martha.
Coopers: Nicholas of Myra.
Coppersmiths: Maurus.
Dairy workers: Brigid.
Dancers: Vitus.
Deaf: Francis de Sales.
Dentists: Apollonia.
Desperate situations: Gregory of Neocaesarea, Jude Thaddeus, Rita of Cascia.
Dietitians (in hospitals): Martha.
Diplomats: Gabriel.
Divorce: Helena.
Drug addiction: Maximilian Kolbe.
Dyers: Maurice, Lydia.
Dying: Joseph.
Ecologists: Francis of Assisi (Nov. 29, 1979).
Ecumenists: Cyril and Methodius.
Editors: John Bosco.
Emigrants: Frances Xavier Cabrini (Sept. 8, 1950).
Endurance: Pantaleon.
Engineers: Ferdinand III.
Epilepsy, Motor Diseases: Vitus, Willibrord.
Eucharistic congresses and societies: Paschal Baylon (Nov. 28, 1897).
Expectant mothers: Raymond Nonnatus, Gerard Majella.
Eye diseases: Lucy.
Falsely accused: Raymond Nonnatus.
Farmers: George, Isidore.
Farriers: John the Baptist.
Firemen: Florian.
Fire prevention: Catherine of Siena.
First communicants: Tarcisius.
Fishermen: Andrew.
Florists: Thérèse of Lisieux.
Forest workers: John Gualbert.
Foundlings: Holy Innocents.
Friendship: John the Divine.
Fullers: Anastasius the Fuller, James the Less.
Funeral directors: Joseph of Arimathea, Dismas.
Gardeners: Adelard, Tryphon, Fiacre, Phocas.
Glassworkers: Luke.
Goldsmiths: Dunstan, Anastasius.
Gravediggers: Anthony, Abbot.
Greetings: Valentine.
Grocers: Michael.
Grooms: King Louis IX of France.
Hairdressers: Martin de Porres.
Happy meetings: Raphael.
Hatters: Severus of Ravenna, James the Less.
Headache sufferers: Teresa of Jesus (Ávila).
Heart patients: John of God.
Homeless: Margaret of Cortona; Benedict Joseph Labré.
Horses: Giles; Hippolytus.
Housekeepers: Zita.
Hospital administrators: Basil the Great, Frances X. Cabrini.
Hospitals: Camillus de Lellis and John of God (June 22, 1886), Jude Thaddeus.
Housewives: Anne.
Hunters: Hubert, Eustachius.
Infantrymen: Maurice.
Innkeepers: Amand, Martha, Julian the Hospitaller.
Innocence: Hallvard.
Invalids: Roch.
Janitors: Theobald.
Jewelers: Eligius, Dunstan.
Journalists: Francis de Sales (Apr. 26, 1923).
Jurists: John Capistran.
Laborers: Isidore, James, John Bosco.
Lawyers: Ivo (Yves Helory), Genesius, Thomas More.
Learning: Ambrose.
Librarians: Jerome.
Lighthouse keepers: Venerius (Mar. 10, 1961).
Linguists: Gottschalk.
Locksmiths: Dunstan.
Lost souls: Nicholas of Tolentino.
Lovers: Raphael; Valentine.
Lunatics: Christina.
Maids: Zita.
Marble workers: Clement I.
Mariners: Michael, Nicholas of Tolentino.
Medical record librarians: Raymond of Peñafort.
Medical social workers: John Regis.
Medical technicians: Albert the Great.
Mentally ill: Dymphna.
Merchants: Francis of Assisi, Nicholas of Myra.
Messengers: Gabriel.
Metal workers: Eligius.
Military chaplains: John Capistran (Feb. 10, 1984).
Millers: Arnulph, Victor.
Missions, foreign: Francis Xavier (Mar. 25, 1904), Thérèse of Lisieux (Dec. 14, 1927).
Missions, black: Peter Claver (1896, Leo XIII), Benedict the Black.
Missions, parish: Leonard of Port Maurice (Mar. 17, 1923).
Monks: Benedict of Nursia.
Mothers: Monica.
Motorcyclists: Our Lady of Grace.
Motorists: Christopher, Frances of Rome.
Mountaineers: Bernard of Montjoux (or Menthon).
Musicians: Gregory the Great, Cecilia, Dunstan.
Mystics: John of the Cross.
Notaries: Luke, Mark.
Nuns: Bridget.
Nurses: Camillus de Lellis and John of God (1930, Pius XI), Agatha, Raphael.
Nursing and nursing service: Elizabeth of Hungary, Catherine of Siena.
Orators: John Chrysostom (July 8, 1908).
Organ builders: Cecilia.
Orphans: Jerome Emiliani.
Painters: Luke.
Paratroopers: Michael.
Pawnbrokers: Nicholas.
Plumbers: Vincent Ferrer.
Pharmacists: Cosmas and Damian, James the Greater.

Pharmacists (in hospitals): Gemma Galgani.
Philosophers: Justin.
Physicians: Pantaleon, Cosmas and Damian, Luke, Raphael.
Pilgrims: James the Greater.
Plasterers: Bartholomew.
Poets: David, Cecilia.
Politicians: Thomas More.
Poison sufferers: Benedict.
Policemen: Michael.
Poor: Lawrence, Anthony of Padua.
Poor souls: Nicholas of Tolentino.
Popes: Gregory I the Great.
Porters: Christopher.
Possessed: Bruno, Denis.
Postal employees: Gabriel.
Priests: Jean-Baptiste Vianney (Apr. 23, 1929).
Printers: John of God, Augustine of Hippo, Genesius.
Prisoners: Dismas, Joseph Cafasso.
Protector of crops: Ansovinus.
Public relations: Bernardine of Siena (May 20, 1960).
Public relations (of hospitals): Paul, Apostle.
Publishers: John the Divine.
Race relations: Martin de Porres.
Radiologists: Michael (Jan. 15, 1941).
Radio workers: Gabriel.
Refugees: Alban.
Retreats: Ignatius Loyola (July 25, 1922).
Rheumatism: James the Greater.
Saddlers: Crispin and Crispinian.
Sailors: Cuthbert, Brendan, Eulalia, Christopher, Peter Gonzalez, Erasmus, Nicholas.
Scholars: Bede the Venerable; Brigid.
Schools, Catholic: Thomas Aquinas (Aug. 4, 1880), Joseph Calasanz (Aug. 13, 1948).
Scientists: Albert (Aug. 13, 1948).
Sculptors: Four Crowned Martyrs.
Seamen: Francis of Paola.
Searchers of lost articles: Anthony of Padua.
Secretaries: Genesius.
Secular Franciscans: Louis of France, Elizabeth of Hungary.
Seminarians: Charles Borromeo.
Servants: Martha, Zita.
Shepherds: Drogo.
Shoemakers: Crispin and Crispinian.
Sick: Michael, John of God and Camillus de Lellis (June 22, 1886).
Silversmiths: Andronicus.
Singers: Gregory, Cecilia.
Single mothers: Margaret of Cortona.
Single women: Catherine of Alexandria.
Skaters: Lidwina.
Skiers: Bernard of Montjoux (or Menthon).
Social workers: Louise de Marillac (Feb. 12, 1960).
Soldiers: Hadrian, George, Ignatius, Sebastian, Martin of Tours, Joan of Arc.
Speleologists: Benedict.
Stamp collectors: Gabriel.
Stenographers: Genesius, Cassian.
Stonecutters: Clement.
Stonemasons: Stephen.
Stress: Walter of Portnoise.
Students: Thomas Aquinas.
Surgeons: Cosmas and Damian, Luke.
Swimmers: Adjutor.

Swordsmiths: Maurice.
Tailors: Homobonus.
Tanners: Crispin and Crispinian, Simon.
Tax collectors: Matthew.
Teachers: Gregory the Great, John Baptist de la Salle (May 15, 1950).
Telecommunications workers: Gabriel (Jan. 12, 1951).
Television: Clare of Assisi (Feb. 14, 1958).
Television workers: Gabriel.
Thieves: Dismas.
Theologians: Augustine, Alphonsus Liguori.
Throat ailments: Blase.
Torture victims: Alban; Eustachius; Regina; Vincent; Victor of Marseilles.
Toymakers: Claude.
Travelers: Anthony of Padua, Nicholas of Myra, Christopher, Raphael.
Travel hostesses: Bona (Mar. 2, 1962).
Truck drivers: Christopher.
Universities: Blessed Contardo Ferrini.
Veterinarians: Blaise.
Vocations: Alphonsus.
Whales: Brendan the Voyager.
Watchmen: Peter of Alcantara.
Weavers: Paul the Hermit, Anastasius the Fuller, Anastasia.
Wine merchants: Amand.
Wineries: Morand; Vincent.
Women in labor: Anne.
Workingmen: Joseph.
Writers: Francis de Sales (Apr. 26, 1923), Lucy.
Yachtsmen: Adjutor.
Young girls: Agnes.
Youth: Aloysius Gonzaga (1729, Benedict XIII; 1926, Pius XI), John Berchmans, Gabriel of the Sorrowful Mother.

Patron Saints of Places

Albania: Our Lady of Good Counsel.
Alsace: Odilia.
Americas: Our Lady of Guadalupe, Rose of Lima.
Angola: Immaculate Heart of Mary (Nov. 21, 1984).
Argentina: Our Lady of Lujan.
Armenia: Gregory Illuminator.
Asia Minor: John, Evangelist.
Australia: Our Lady Help of Christians.
Belgium: Joseph.
Bohemia: Wenceslaus, Ludmilla.
Bolivia: Our Lady of Copacabana, "Virgen de la Candelaria."
Borneo: Francis Xavier.
Brazil: Nossa Señora de Aparecida, Immaculate Conception, Peter of Alcantara.
Canada: Joseph, Anne.
Chile: James the Greater, Our Lady of Mt. Carmel.
China: Joseph.
Colombia: Peter Claver, Louis Bertran.
Corsica: Immaculate Conception.
Cuba: Our Lady of Charity.
Czechoslovakia: Wenceslaus, John Nepomucene, Procopius.
Denmark: Ansgar, Canute.
Dominican Republic: Our Lady of High Grace, Dominic.
East Indies: Thomas, Apostle.
Ecuador: Sacred Heart.

El Salvador: Our Lady of Peace (Oct. 10, 1966).

England: George.

Equatorial Guinea: Immaculate Conception (May 25, 1986).

Europe: Benedict (1964); Cyril and Methodius, co-patrons (Dec. 31, 1980); Sts. Catherine of Siena, Bridget of Sweden, and Edith Stein, co-patronesses (Oct. 1, 1999).

Finland: Henry.

France: Our Lady of the Assumption, Joan of Arc, Thérèse (May 3, 1944).

Germany: Boniface, Michael.

Gibraltar: Blessed Virgin Mary, "Our Lady of Europe" (May 31, 1979).

Greece: Nicholas, Andrew.

Holland: Willibrord.

Hungary: Blessed Virgin, "Great Lady of Hungary," Stephen, king.

Iceland: Thorlac (Jan. 14, 1984).

India: Our Lady of Assumption.

Ireland: Patrick, Brigid and Columba.

Italy: Francis of Assisi, Catherine of Siena.

Japan: Peter Baptist.

Korea: Joseph and Mary, Mother of the Church.

Lesotho: Immaculate Heart of Mary.

Lithuania: Casimir, Bl. Cunegunda.

Luxembourg: Willibrord.

Malta: Paul, Our Lady of the Assumption.

Mexico: Our Lady of Guadalupe.

Monaco: Devota.

Moravia: Cyril and Methodius.

New Zealand: Our Lady Help of Christians.

Norway: Olaf.

Papua New Guinea (including northern Solomon Islands): Michael the Archangel (May 31, 1979).

Paraguay: Our Lady of Assumption (July 13, 1951).

Peru: Joseph (Mar. 19, 1957).

Philippines: Sacred Heart of Mary.

Poland: Casimir, Bl. Cunegunda, Stanislaus of Krakow, Our Lady of Czestochowa.

Portugal: Immaculate Conception, Francis Borgia, Anthony of Padua, Vincent of Saragossa, George.

Russia: Andrew, Nicholas of Myra, Thérèse of Lisieux.

Scandinavia: Ansgar.

Scotland: Andrew, Columba.

Silesia: Hedwig.

Slovakia: Our Lady of Sorrows.

South Africa: Our Lady of Assumption (Mar. 15, 1952).

South America: Rose of Lima.

Solomon Islands: Blessed Virgin Mary, Most Holy Name of Mary (Sept. 4, 1991).

Spain: James the Greater, Teresa.

Sri Lanka (Ceylon): Lawrence.

Sweden: Bridget, Eric.

Tanzania: Immaculate Conception (Dec. 8, 1964).

United States: Immaculate Conception (1846).

Uruguay: Blessed Virgin Mary, "La Virgen de los Treinte y Tres" (Nov. 21, 1963).

Venezuela: Our Lady of Coromoto.

Wales: David.

West Indies: Gertrude.

Emblems, Portrayals of Saints

Agatha: Tongs, veil.

Agnes: Lamb.

Ambrose: Bees, dove, ox, pen.

Andrew: Transverse cross.

Anne, Mother of the Blessed Virgin: Door.

Anthony of Padua: Infant Jesus, bread, book, lily.

Augustine of Hippo: Dove, child, shell, pen.

Bartholomew: Knife, flayed and holding his skin.

Benedict: Broken cup, raven, bell, crosier, bush.

Bernard of Clairvaux: Pen, bees, instruments of the Passion.

Bernardine of Siena: Tablet or sun inscribed with IHS.

Blase: Wax, taper, iron comb.

Bonaventure: Communion, ciborium, cardinal's hat.

Boniface: Oak, ax, book, fox, scourge, fountain, raven, sword.

Bridget of Sweden: Book, pilgrim's staff.

Bridget of Kildare: Cross, flame over her head, candle.

Catherine of Ricci: Ring, crown, crucifix.

Catherine of Siena: Stigmata, cross, ring, lily.

Cecilia: Organ.

Charles Borromeo: Communion, coat of arms with word "Humilitas."

Christopher: Giant, torrent, tree, Child Jesus on his shoulders.

Clare of Assisi: Monstrance.

Cosmas and Damian: A phial, box of ointment.

Cyril of Alexandria: Blessed Virgin holding the Child Jesus, pen.

Cyril of Jerusalem: Purse, book.

Dominic: Rosary, star.

Edmund the Martyr: Arrow, sword.

Elizabeth of Hungary: Alms, flowers, bread, the poor, a pitcher.

Francis of Assisi: Wolf, birds, fish, skull, the Stigmata.

Francis Xavier: Crucifix, bell, vessel.

Genevieve: Bread, keys, herd, candle.

George: Dragon.

Gertrude: Crown, taper, lily.

Gervase and Protase: Scourge, club, sword.

Gregory I (the Great): Tiara, crosier, dove.

Helena: Cross.

Ignatius of Loyola: Communion, chasuble, book, apparition of Our Lord.

Isidore: Bees, pen.

James the Greater: Pilgrim's staff, shell, key, sword.

James the Less: Square rule, halberd, club.

Jerome: Lion.

John Berchmans: Rule of St. Ignatius, cross, rosary.

John Chrysostom: Bees, dove, pen.

John of God: Alms, a heart, crown of thorns.

John the Baptist: Lamb, head on platter, animal skin.

John the Evangelist: Eagle, chalice, kettle, armor.

Josaphat Kuncevyc: Chalice, crown, winged deacon.

Joseph, Spouse of the Blessed Virgin: Infant Jesus, lily, rod, plane, carpenter's square.

Jude: Sword, square rule, club.

Justin Martyr: Ax, sword.

Lawrence: Cross, book of the Gospels, gridiron.

Leander of Seville: Pen.

Liberius: Pebbles, peacock.

Longinus: In arms at foot of the cross.

Louis IX of France: Crown of thorns, nails.

Lucy: Cord, eyes on a dish.

Luke: Ox, book, brush, palette.

Mark: Lion, book.

Martha: Holy water sprinkler, dragon.

Mary Magdalene: Alabaster box of ointment.

Matilda: Purse, alms.
Matthew: Winged man, purse, lance.
Matthias: Lance.
Maurus: Scales, spade, crutch.
Meinrad: Two ravens.
Michael: Scales, banner, sword, dragon.
Monica: Girdle, tears.
Nicholas: Three purses or balls, anchor or boat, child.
Patrick: Cross, harp, serpent, baptismal font, demons, shamrock.
Paul: Sword, book or scroll.
Peter: Keys, boat, cock.
Philip, Apostle: Column.
Philip Neri: Altar, chasuble, vial.

Rita of Cascia: Rose, crucifix, thorn.
Roch: Angel, dog, bread.
Rose of Lima: Crown of thorns, anchor, city.
Sebastian: Arrows, crown.
Simon Stock: Scapular.
Teresa of Jesus (Ávila): Heart, arrow, book.
Thérèse of Lisieux: Roses entwining a crucifix.
Thomas, Apostle: Lance, ax.
Thomas Aquinas: Chalice, monstrance, dove, ox, person trampled under foot.
Vincent de Paul: Children.
Vincent Ferrer: Pulpit, cardinal's hat, trumpet, captives.

CANONIZATIONS AND BEATIFICATIONS 2007-08

Pope Benedict XVI beatified the following individuals from Sept. 2007 to Aug. 2008. Included are the dates of the beatifications, as well as relevant biographical information.

Beatifications

2007

Basile-Antoine Marie Moreau (1799-1873), founder of the Congregation of Holy Cross. Born in Laigné-en-Belin, Sarthe, France, he began studies for the priesthood in 1814 and was ordained on Aug. 12, 1821. To assist the pastoral care of souls, he founded in 1833 the Auxiliary Priests of Le Mans; in 1835, he was named head of the Congregation of the Brothers of St Joseph and united it with the Society to form the Congregation of Holy Cross in 1937. Pontifical approval was granted in 1854. In 1841, he also founded the Marianites of Holy Cross, with pontifical approval granted in 1857. His cause for canonization began in 1955, and he was beatified at Le Mans, France, on Sept. 15, 2007.

Marie-Céline de la Présentation (1878-1897), member of the Order of Poor Clares of Talence. Born Jeanne Germaine Castang at Nojals, France, Marie-Céline suffered from an early age from polio and later tuberculosis. In 1896, she was accepted into the Poor Clare community in Talence. She survived only a year and died from tuberculosis of the bone on May 30, 1897 at the age of 19. Her burial place was soon a popular pilgrim site. She was beatified on Sept. 16, 2007, in Bordeaux, France.

Stanislaw of Jesus and Mary (Jana Papczyñski) (1631-1701), founder of the Congregation of Marian Clerks of the Immaculate Conception. Born in Podegrodzie, Poland, he studied at the Piarist and Jesuit Colleges and entered the Piarist Order in 1654. He made his religious profession in 1656 and was ordained a priest in 1661. He founded the first house in 1673; canonical approval followed that same year. After years of effort, he won papal approbation in 1699, and Fr. Papczyñski pronounced his own solemn vows on June 6, 1701, making the congregation the first Polish order of apostolic right of male religious in the history of Poland. He was beatified on Sept. 16, 2007, in Líchen, Poland.

Maria Luisa Merkert (1817-1872), co-foundress and first Superior General of the Congregation of St. Elizabeth. Born in Nysa in Silesia, Poland, she went on to join Clara Wolff, a Third Order Franciscan, in her charitable labors on behalf of the poor and sick in their homes. From this began the Association of Sisters for the Assistance of Abandoned Sick,

under the Protection of the Most Sacred Heart of Jesus. She entered the novitiate of the Sisters of Mercy of St. Charles Borromeo in Prague in 1846, but Maria and Frances left in 1850 to pursue their original vocation. As they pursued their labors in Nysa, they became known as the Grey Sisters of St. Elizabeth. Ecclesiastic approval was given in 1859, and Maria was elected Superior General. Pontifical approval was granted in 1887. By the time of her death, the congregation had 90 houses in nine dioceses. She was beatified on Sept. 30, 2007, in Nysa, Poland.

Albertina Berkenbrock (1919-1931), Brazilian martyr. Born in São Luís, Imaruí, Santa Catarina, Brazil, she was a model Catholic youth. Tragically, she was attacked by one of her father's employees, Maneco Palhoça. Following her into a wood, he attempted to rape the young girl, and when she refused to cooperate he killed her. Maneco tried to cover up the crime, but he eventually confessed and was sentenced to life in prison. Albertina was honored from the time of her death as a martyr to the faith. Her burial place in the cemetery of São Luís was also quickly a place of pilgrimage. She was beatified on Oct. 20, 2007 in Tubarão, Brazil.

Emmanuel Gómez González (1877-1924), Spanish missionary and martyr. Born in São José de Ribarteme, Spain. Ordained a priest in 1902, he served as a parish priest in his own diocese and then in Braga, Portugal, from this time until 1913. With the start of persecutions of the Church in 1913, he was granted permission to serve in Brazil. Sent in 1915 to a large parish in Nonoai, Brazil, one that required a massive labor to direct, González soon solidified the faith in the region through his zeal. He cared especially for the native Indian people, and he also received the administration over the even more remote parish of Palmeiras das Missões. González made his way to the Três Passos forest, near the border of Uruguay, an area filled with revolutionary groups. Accompanied by a young altar server and student, Adílio Daronch, the priest was martyred by a group of rebels with Daronch on May 21, 1924. The martyrs were tied to two trees and shot to death. Beloved for his zeal and dedication to the faith, Emmanuel was revered as a martyr and his cause for canonization was opened. In 1964, the remains of both martyrs were exhumed and translated to the parish church of Nonoai; a monument was also built at the site of their martyrdom. He was beatified on October 21, 2007, with Adílio in Frederico Westphalen, Brazil.

Adílio Daronch (1908-1924), young Brazilian martyr. Born in Cachoeira do Sul municipality of Rio Grande do Sul, Brazil, he was a young man dedicated to the faith and was active in the parish in Nonoai, Brazil, where he served as an altar server and a student to Fr. Emmanuel Gómez González. Adílio often journeyed with Fr. González on his many pastoral rounds and journeys. On one of those journeys, Adílio was captured with the priest by revolutionaries in the Três Passos forest, near the border of Uruguay. The two of them were executed on May 21, 1924 when they were tied to trees and shot to death. He was beatified on October 21, 2007 in Frederico Westphalen, Brazil, with Father González.

Franz Jägerstätter (1907-1943), German layman and martyr at the hands of the Nazis. Born in St. Radegund, Upper Austria, he grew up in a Catholic environment and married a young woman named Franziska Schwaninger in 1936. Back in Austria, Franz worked as a farmer and was also a sexton. He was the only citizen in his town to vote against the *Anschluss* in 1938, the annexation of Austria by Germany, and he was arrested in 1943 when he refused to join the German Army. He was executed Aug. 9 by beheading and wrote before his death, "Neither prison nor chains nor sentence of death can rob a man of the Faith and his free will. God gives so much strength that it is possible to bear any suffering...."He was beatified on Oct. 26, 2007 in Linz. In attendance were his 94-year-old widow and his four daughters.

498 Martyrs of the Spanish Civil War (d. c. 1936), a large group of martyrs murdered at the start of the Civil War in Spain. The beatification was held on Oct. 26, 2007 with most of Spain's bishops and tens of thousands of pilgrims in attendance. The ceremony for the martyrs followed the release of an apostolic letter by Pope Benedict XVI in June 2007 that approved the decrees of recognition of martyrdom of several groups of Spanish Martyrs from 1934 (in the Asturias Rebellion), 1936, and 1937. Most of the martyrs were clergy and were killed early in the bloody Spanish Civil War in 1936 by anti-Catholic militias fighting for the Republican government. The mass beatification represented the culmination of 23 different causes that carefully and slowly progressed over several decades in Spain and in Rome. The complete list and remarkable stories of the martyrs can be found at: www.conferenciaepiscopal.es/santos/martires/alfabetico.html.

Celine Chludzinska Borzecka (1833-1913), foundress of the Congregation of the Sisters of the Resurrection. Born in Antowil, Orsza, in modern Belarus, she was raised in a devout Catholic family. Obedient to her parents' wishes, she married a young man named Joseph Borzecki, and the couple had four children, two of whom died in their infancy. Her husband suffered a stroke in 1869 and died five years later. Journeying to Rome with her two surviving daughters, Celine met the co-founder of the Resurrectionists, Fr. Peter Semenenko. He served as her spiritual director and assisted her in developing a congregation of women dedicated to the Mystery of the Resurrection. The Congregation of the Sisters of the Resurrection was officially founded in Rome in Jan. 1891, and Celine and her daughter Hedwig professed their final vows. The first house of the congregation was begun near Wadowice, Poland, and Mother Celine served over the next years as head of the community; in 1911, she was elected for life. She was beatified on Oct. 27, 2007, in Basilica of Saint John Lateran in Rome.

Zepherin Namuncurá (1886-1905), seminarian of the Society of St Francis de Sales. Born in Chimpay, Argentina, he was the son of the chief of the Mapuche, Indians of the Argentine Pampas. Zepherin was baptized on Christmas Eve 1887, and at the age of eleven was enrolled in a military school at El Tigre. He was transferred to the Salesian mission school in Buenos Aires. Confirmed in 1899, he soon expressed a desire to enter the seminary. His wish was granted, but in September 1903 he was diagnosed with tuberculosis. His strength proved sufficient to accompany the Salesian bishop to Rome the next year where Zepherin continued his studies and had an audience with Pope St. Pius X on Sept. 27, 1904. His health continued to decline, however, and he died in Rome on May 11, 1905 revered for his holiness and prayerful disposition. His remains were later taken back to Argentina. He was beatified on Nov. 11, 2007, in Chimpay, Argentina.

Antonio Rosmini-Serbati (1797-1855), Italian priest, philosopher, and founder of the Institute of Charity. Born in Rovereto, Italy, that was then part of the Austrian Empire, he studied at the University of Padua, Italy, and earned doctorates in theology and canon law. He then prepared for the priesthood and was ordained Apr. 21, 1821. Two years later, he journeyed to Rome and had an audience with Pope Pius VII at which the elderly pontiff called on him to help reform philosophy. In 1828, he wrote the *Constitutions* to serve as the foundation for his Institute of Charity. Receiving papal approval in 1828 and 1829, he authored several famed works, including *Maxims of Christian Perfection* and *Origin of Ideas*. The Institute spread quickly and reached England in 1835 where it became quite influential among English Catholics. Formal approval was granted in 1838 by Pope Gregory XVI, and the next year Fr. Rosmini was named provost general for life. His efforts to renew the relationship between faith and reason, however, proved controversial (generating the so-called Rosminian Question), and two of his works, The Five Wounds of Holy Church and the Civil Constitution according to Social Justice, were placed on the Index of Prohibited Books in 1849. He was exonerated in 1854, a year before his death. His works remained the source of controversy, but in 2001 they were cleared by the Congregation for the Doctrine of the Faith. Rosmini-Serbati was beatified on Nov. 18, 2007, in Novara, Italy.

Lindalva Justo de Oliveira (1953-1993), Brazilian martyr and member of the Society of the Daughters of Charity of St Vincent de Paul. Born in Sitio Malhada da Areia, Brazil, she was raised in a devout Catholic family and held a variety of jobs, including as a sales clerk and a cashier. After discerning a vocation, she entered the Daughters of Charity in 1988. On Apr. 9, 1993, while serving in a nursing home in Salvador da Bahia, she was stabbed to death by a deranged patient and died forgiving him his terrible crime. Honored as a martyr, her cause was opened, and she was beatified on Dec. 2, 2007, in São Salvador da Bahia, Brazil.

2008

Giuseppina Nicoli (1863-1924), Italian member of the Daughters of Charity of St. Vincent de Paul. Born in Casatisma, Italy, she entered the Daughters of Charity in Turin, Italy in 1883 and was sent two years later to Sardinia. To assist the religious education among the poor children, she started the Associazione dei Figli di Maria (Association of the Sons of Mary) and the Associazione delle Figlie di Maria (Association of the Daughters of Mary); she subsequently began the School of Religion for older students. Called back to Turin in 1910, where she remained until 1913, she served as provincial administrator and then director of education for novices. She returned to Sardinia in 1913 where she was asked by the local bishop to start the Dorotean Society of consecrated lay women; with these lay women, she also began Young Women of Charity in 1917 and opened with them a house for poor children suffering from rickets and tuberculosis. Sr. Giuseppina also helped to launch a variety of other apostolates. She was beatified on Feb. 3, 2008, at Cagliari, Italy.

Celestina of the Mother of God (1848-1925), Italian foundress of the Daughters of the Poor of St Joseph Calasanz. Born Marianna Donati in Marradi, near Florence, Italy, she entered into the spiritual direction of the Piarist priest, Fr. Celestino Zini. In Mar. 1889, under the advice of Fr. Zini, she began with four young women a congregation to serve the poor. Again with Fr. Zini's help — he had since become Archbishop of Siena — she opened a school outside of Florence for poor children. Under her leadership, the congregation expanded. She was beatified on Mar. 30, 2008 in Florence, Italy.

Candelaria de San José Paz Castillo Ramírez (1863-1940), foundress of the Venezuelan Carmelite Sisters. Born in Altagracia de Orituco, Venezuela, she helped raise her family following the death of her mother, but her talents and holiness prompted the founders of St. Anthony's Hospital in Altagracia to ask her to assist them in its administration. With the help of several other young women, in 1910 she began a small diocesan institute for the care of the poor sick that was given the name The Sisters of the Poor of Altagracia de Orituco. Mother Candelaria of St. Joseph soon founded two hospitals and then presided over the continued development of the community. In 1925, she was granted permission for the congregation to be affiliated into the Carmelites; the congregation was then called the Tertiary Carmelite Sisters (today the Venezuelan Carmelite Sisters). Mother Candelaria led the congregation until her death. She was beatified on Apr. 27, 2008 in Caracas, Venezuela.

María Magdalena de la Encarnación (1770-1824) Italian foundress of the Perpetual Adorers of the Blessed Sacrament. Born Caterina Sordini at Grosseto, Italy, she was 17 when she acceded to her father's wishes that she say yes to the marriage proposal of a maritime merchant. When, however, she beheld an image of the Crucified Christ in a mirror, she entered the Franciscan Tertiary Monastery in Ischia di Castro and took the name Sr. Mary Magdalene of the Incarnation. Elected abbess in 1802, she nevertheless was committed to founding a new community and set out for Rome in 1807. She and several sisters moved into a convent near the Trevi Fountain, but the convent was seized by the French forces occupying the Eternal City and she was exiled to Tuscany. Allowed to return to Rome in 1814, and she and her sisters received the approval of Pope Pius VII in 1818 for an institute dedicated to adoration of the Blessed Sacrament. She was beatified in Rome on May 3, 2008.

Margaret Flesch (1826-1906) German foundress of the Franciscan Sisters of St Mary of the Angels. Born in Schönstatt, near Koblenz, Germany, she helped raise her siblings after her parents died. In autumn 1851, Margaret and her sister Marianne moved into the tiny living quarters at the Chapel of the Holy Cross in Waldbreitbach to assist the poor and the sick. In 1856, Margaret was joined by two women, and in 1861 she founded their first formal house. Two years later, Margaret and two other women took her vows and took the name of Rose. She was the first head of the Franciscan Sisters of the Blessed Virgin Mary of the Angels and presided over the swift development of the new congregation. By the

time of her passing, there were 900 Sisters and 72 mission houses. She was beatified on May 4, 2008 in Trier, Germany.

Martha Wiecka (1874-1930) A Polish member of the Daughters of Charity of St. Vincent de Paul. Born in Nowy Wiec in the Polish region of Pomerania, she entered the Daughters of Charity in Cracow at the age of 18 and for the next twelve years ministered in several hospitals. In May 1930, Martha volunteered to disinfect a typhoid patient's room in the hospital of Sniatyn, in the Ukraine to spare a young medical assistant and father from performing the task. Martha contracted the disease and died after a few days. Her grave was soon a place of prayers, especially after the Second World War. Her heroic act was honored by Cardinal Tarcisio Bertone at her beatification with the words that the mission of Christians is "to bear witness to the victory of love at every occasion of life...God is love, and we love him – he who is invisible to our eyes – if we love our neighbor whom we see, to the point of shedding blood, if it is necessary." She was beatified in Lviv, Ukraine, on May 24, 2008.

Maria Giuseppina di Gesù Crocifisso (1894-1948) An Italian Carmelite religious. Born Giuseppina Catanea in Naples, Italy, she entered the Carmelite Community at St. Maria ai Ponti Rossi in 1918 over the objections of her family. Soon after she contracted tuberculosis of the spine which left her paralyzed, but she received a miraculous cure through the intercession of St. Francis Xavier. In 1932, the house at Ponti Rossi entered the Discalced Carmelites, and Maria made her solemn profession in August of that year. In 1934, she was named sub-prioress of the Carmel, and in 1945 she was appointed prioress, an office that she held until her death. As her physical suffering increased in the next years, she offered herself to be conformed to the Crucified Christ. Prior to her death, she wrote her *Autobiography* (1894-1932) and her *Diary* (1925-1945) at the request of her spiritual director. She was beatified in Naples on June 1, 2008.

Jacques Ghazir Haddad (1875-1954) Lebanese founder of the Franciscan Sisters of the Holy Cross. Born in Ghazir, Lebanon, he studied Arabic, French, and Syriac, and went to Alexandria, Egypt, in 1892 to teach Arabic at the Christian Brothers' College. While there, he entered the Capuchin Convent in Khashbau the next year and was ordained a priest on Nov. 1, 1901 in Beirut, Lebanon. He served as an itinerant preacher in Lebanon from 1903 to 1914 and preached in Syria, Palestine, Iraq, and Turkey, and in 1919 built a chapel dedicated to Our Lady of the Sea. The next year, Jacques started the Franciscan Sisters of the Holy Cross of Lebanon to assist him in the care of the poor and the sick. Exhausted from his labors, he died in Lebanon on June 26, 1954. He was beatified in Beirut on June 22, 2008.

Josepha Hendrina Stenmanns (1852-1903) German co-Founder of the Missionary Sisters Servants of the Holy Spirit. Born in Issum, Germany, she joined the Franciscan Third Order at the age of 19, but her desire to enter the religious life was prevented by her mother's poor health and the need for Hendrina to care for her siblings. When she was 32, however, she joined the Mission House established by Fr. Arnold Janssen in Steyl. In Dec. 1889, she and a few other women became postulants in the newly established Missionary Sisters Servants of the Holy Spirit. She professed first vows in Mar. 1894 and took the name Josepha. Aside from her service with postulants, Josepha was noted for her holiness and her heroic sufferings in her later years. She was beatified in Steyl on June 29, 2008.

Dates and Events in Catholic History

FIRST CENTURY

c. 33: First Christian Pentecost; descent of the Holy Spirit upon the disciples; preaching of St. Peter in Jerusalem; conversion, baptism and aggregation of some 3,000 persons to the first Christian community.

St. Stephen, deacon, was stoned to death at Jerusalem; he is venerated as the first Christian martyr.

c. 34: St. Paul, formerly Saul the persecutor of Christians, was converted and baptized. After three years of solitude in the desert, he joined the college of the apostles; he made three major missionary journeys and became known as the Apostle to the Gentiles; he was imprisoned twice in Rome and was beheaded there between 64 and 67.

39: Cornelius (the Gentile) and his family were baptized by St. Peter; a significant event signaling the mission of the Church to all peoples.

42: Persecution of Christians in Palestine broke out during the rule of Herod Agrippa; St. James the Greater, the first apostle to die, was beheaded in 44; St. Peter was imprisoned for a short time; many Christians fled to Antioch, marking the beginning of the dispersion of Christians beyond the confines of Palestine. At Antioch, the followers of Christ were called Christians for the first time.

49: Christians at Rome, considered members of a Jewish sect, were adversely affected by a decree of Claudius which forbade Jewish worship there.

51: The Council of Jerusalem, in which all the apostles participated under the presidency of St. Peter, decreed that circumcision, dietary regulations, and various other prescriptions of Mosaic Law were not obligatory for Gentile converts to the Christian community. The crucial decree was issued in opposition to Judaizers who contended that observance of the Mosaic Law in its entirety was necessary for salvation.

64: Persecution broke out at Rome under Nero, the emperor said to have accused Christians of starting the fire which destroyed half of Rome.

64 or 67: Martyrdom of St. Peter at Rome during the Neronian persecution. He established his see and spent his last years there after preaching in and around Jerusalem, establishing a see at Antioch, and presiding at the Council of Jerusalem.

70: Destruction of Jerusalem by Titus.

88-97: Pontificate of St. Clement I, third successor of St. Peter as bishop of Rome, one of the Apostolic Fathers. The First Epistle of Clement to the Corinthians, with which he has been identified, was addressed by the Church of Rome to the Church at Corinth, the scene of irregularities and divisions in the Christian community.

95: Domitian persecuted Christians, principally at Rome.

c. 100: Death of St. John, apostle and evangelist, marking the end of the Age of the Apostles and the first generation of the Church.

By the end of the century, Antioch, Alexandria and Ephesus in the East and Rome in the West were established centers of Christian population and influence.

SECOND CENTURY

c. 107: St. Ignatius of Antioch was martyred at Rome. He was the first writer to use the expression, "the Catholic Church."

112: Emperor Trajan, in a rescript to Pliny the Younger, governor of Bithynia, instructed him not to search out Christians but to punish them if they were publicly denounced and refused to do homage to the Roman gods. This rescript set a pattern for Roman magistrates in dealing with Christians.

117-38: Persecution under Hadrian. Many acts of martyrs date from this period.

c. 125: Spread of Gnosticism, a combination of elements of Platonic philosophy and Eastern mystery religions. Its adherents claimed that its secret-knowledge principle provided a deeper insight into Christian doctrine than divine revelation and faith. One gnostic thesis denied the divinity of Christ; others denied the reality of his humanity, calling it mere appearance (Docetism, Phantasiasm).

c. 144: Excommunication of Marcion, bishop and heretic, who claimed that there was total opposition and no connection at all between the Old Testament and the New Testament, between the God of the Jews and the God of the Christians; and that the Canon (list of inspired writings) of the Bible consisted only of parts of St. Luke's Gospel and 10 letters of St. Paul. Marcionism was checked at Rome by 200 and was condemned by a council held there about 260, but the heresy persisted for several centuries in the East and had some adherents as late as the Middle Ages.

c. 155: St. Polycarp, bishop of Smyrna and disciple of St. John the Evangelist, was martyred.

c. 156: Beginning of Montanism, a form of religious extremism. Its principal tenets were the imminent second coming of Christ, denial of the divine nature of the Church and its power to forgive sin, and excessively rigorous morality. The heresy, preached by Montanus of Phrygia and others, was condemned by Pope St. Zephyrinus (199-217).

161-80: Reign of Marcus Aurelius. His persecution, launched in the wake of natural disasters, was more violent than those of his predecessors.

165: St. Justin, an important early Christian writer, was martyred at Rome.

c. 180: St. Irenaeus, bishop of Lyons and one of the great early theologians, wrote *Adversus Haereses.* He stated that the teaching and tradition of the Roman See was the standard for belief.

196: Easter Controversy, concerning the day of celebration—a Sunday, according to practice in the West, or the 14th of the month of Nisan (in the Hebrew calendar), no matter what day of the week, according to practice in the East. The controversy was not resolved at this time.

The *Didache*, whose extant form dates from the second century, is an important record of Christian belief, practice and governance in the first century.

Latin was introduced as a liturgical language in the West. Other liturgical languages were Aramaic and Greek.

The Catechetical School of Alexandria, founded about the middle of the century, gained increasing influence on doctrinal study and instruction, and interpretation of the Bible.

THIRD CENTURY

202: Persecution under Septimius Severus, who wanted to establish a simple common religion in the Empire.

206: Tertullian, a convert since 197 and the first great ecclesiastical writer in Latin, joined the heretical Montanists; he died in 230.

215: Death of Clement of Alexandria, teacher of Origen and a founding father of the School of Alexandria.

217-35: St. Hippolytus, the first antipope; he was reconciled to the Church while in prison during persecution in 235.

232-54: Origen established the School of Caesarea after being deposed in 231 as head of the School of Alexandria; he died in 254. A scholar and voluminous writer, he was one of the founders of systematic theology and exerted wide influence for many years.

c. 242: Manichaeism originated in Persia: a combination of errors based on the assumption that two supreme principles (good and evil) are operative in creation and life, and that the supreme objective of human endeavor is liberation from evil (matter). The heresy denied the humanity of Christ, the sacramental system, the authority of the Church (and state), and endorsed a moral code which threatened the fabric of society. In the 12th and 13th centuries, it took on the features of Albigensianism and Catharism.

249-51: Persecution under Decius. Many of those who denied the faith (*lapsi*) sought readmission to the Church at the end of the persecution in 251. Pope St. Cornelius agreed with St. Cyprian that *lapsi* were to be readmitted to the Church after satisfying the requirements of appropriate penance. Antipope Novatian, on the other hand, contended that persons who fell away from the Church under persecution and/or those guilty of serious sin after baptism could not be absolved and readmitted to communion with the Church. The heresy was condemned by a Roman synod in 251.

250-300: Neo-Platonism of Plotinus and Porphyry gained followers.

251: Novatian, an antipope, was condemned at Rome.

256: Pope St. Stephen I upheld the validity of baptism properly administered by heretics, in the Rebaptism Controversy.

257: Persecution under Valerian, who attempted to destroy the Church as a social structure.

258: St. Cyprian, bishop of Carthage, was martyred.

c. 260: St. Lucian founded the School of Antioch, a center of influence on biblical studies.

Pope St. Dionysius condemned Sabellianism, a form of modalism (like Monarchianism and Patripassianism). The heresy contended that the Father, Son and Holy Spirit are not distinct divine persons but are only three different modes of being and self-manifestations of the one God. St. Paul of Thebes became a hermit.

261: Gallienus issued an edict of toleration which ended general persecution for nearly 40 years.

c. 292: Diocletian divided the Roman Empire into East and West. The division emphasized political, cultural and other differences between the two parts of the Empire and influenced different developments in the Church in the East and West. The prestige of Rome began to decline.

FOURTH CENTURY

303: Persecution broke out under Diocletian; it was particularly violent in 304.

305: St. Anthony of Heracles established a foundation for hermits near the Red Sea in Egypt.

c. 306: The first local legislation on clerical celibacy was enacted by a council held at Elvira, Spain; bishops, priests, deacons and other ministers were forbidden to have wives.

311: An edict of toleration issued by Galerius at the urging of Constantine the Great and Licinius officially ended persecution in the West; some persecution continued in the East.

313: The Edict of Milan issued by Constantine and Licinius recognized Christianity as a lawful religion in the Roman Empire.

314: A council of Arles condemned Donatism, declaring that baptism properly administered by heretics is valid, in view of the principle that sacraments have their efficacy from Christ, not from the spiritual condition of their human ministers. The heresy was condemned again by a council of Carthage in 411.

318: St. Pachomius established the first foundation of the cenobitic (common) life, as compared with the solitary life of hermits in Upper Egypt.

325: Ecumenical Council of Nicaea (I). Its principal action was the condemnation of Arianism, the most devastating of the early heresies, which denied the divinity of Christ. The heresy was authored by Arius of Alexandria, a priest. Arians and several kinds of Semi-Arians propagandized their tenets widely, established their own hierarchies and churches, and raised havoc in the Church for several centuries. The council contributed to formulation of the Nicene Creed (Creed of Nicaea-Constantinople); fixed the date for the observance of Easter; passed regulations concerning clerical discipline; adopted the civil divisions of the Empire as the model for the jurisdictional organization of the Church.

326: With the support of St. Helena, the True Cross on which Christ was crucified was discovered.

337: Baptism and death of Constantine.

c. 342: Beginning of a 40-year persecution in Persia.

343-44: A council of Sardica reaffirmed doctrine formulated by Nicaea I and declared also that bishops had the right of appeal to the pope as the highest authority in the Church.

361-63: Emperor Julian the Apostate waged an unsuccessful campaign against the Church in an attempt to restore paganism as the religion of the Empire.

c. 365: Persecution of orthodox Christians under Emperor Valens in the East.

c. 376: Beginning of the barbarian invasion in the West.

379: Death of St. Basil, the Father of Monasticism in the East. His writings contributed greatly to the development of rules for the life of Religious.

381: Ecumenical Council of Constantinople (I). It condemned various brands of Arianism as well as Macedonianism, which denied the divinity of the Holy Spirit; contributed to formulation of the Nicene Creed; approved a canon acknowledging Constantinople as the second see after Rome in honor and dignity.

382: The Canon of Sacred Scripture, the official list of the inspired books of the Bible, was contained in the Decree of Pope St. Damasus and published by a regional council of Carthage in 397; the Canon was formally defined by the Council of Trent in the 16th century.

382-c. 406: St. Jerome translated the Old and New Testaments into Latin; his work is called the Vulgate version of the Bible.

396: St. Augustine became bishop of Hippo in North Africa.

FIFTH CENTURY

410: Visigoths under Alaric sacked Rome and the last Roman legions departed Britain. The decline of imperial Rome dates approximately from this time.

430: St. Augustine, bishop of Hippo for 35 years, died. He was a strong defender of orthodox doctrine against Manichaeism, Donatism and Pelagianism. The depth and range of his writings made him a dominant influence in Christian thought for centuries.

431: Ecumenical Council of Ephesus. It condemned Nestorianism, which denied the unity of the divine and human natures in the Person of Christ; defined *Theotokos* (Bearer of God) as the title of Mary, Mother of the Son of God made Man; condemned Pelagianism. The heresy of Pelagianism, proceeding from the assumption that Adam had a natural right to supernatural life, held that man could attain salvation through the efforts of his natural powers and free will; it involved errors concerning the nature of original sin, the meaning of grace and other matters. Related Semi-Pelagianism was condemned by a council of Orange in 529.

432: St. Patrick arrived in Ireland. By the time of his death in 461 most of the country had been converted, monasteries founded and the hierarchy established.

438: The Theodosian Code, a compilation of decrees for the Empire, was issued by Theodosius II; it had great influence on subsequent civil and ecclesiastical law.

451: Ecumenical Council of Chalcedon. Its principal action was the condemnation of Mono-physitism (also called Eutychianism), which denied the humanity of Christ by holding that he had only one, the divine, nature.

452: Pope St. Leo the Great persuaded Attila the Hun to spare Rome.

455: Vandals under Geiseric sacked Rome.

484: Patriarch Acacius of Constantinople was excommunicated for signing the *Henoticon*, a document which capitulated to the Monophysite heresy. The excommunication triggered the Acacian Schism which lasted for 35 years.

494: Pope St. Gelasius I declared in a letter to Emperor Anastasius that the pope had power and authority over the emperor in spiritual matters.

496: Clovis, King of the Franks, was converted and became the defender of Christianity in the West. The Franks became a Catholic people.

SIXTH CENTURY

520: Irish monasteries flourished as centers for spiritual life, missionary training, and scholarly activity.

529: The Second Council of Orange condemned Semi-Pelagianism.

c. 529: St. Benedict founded the Monte Cassino Abbey. Some years before his death in 543 he wrote a monastic rule which exercised tremendous influence on the form and style of religious life. He is called the Father of Monasticism in the West.

533: John II became the first pope to change his name. The practice did not become general until the time of Sergius IV (1009).

533-34: Emperor Justinian promulgated the *Corpus Iuris Civilis* for the Roman world; like the Theodosian Code, it influenced subsequent civil and ecclesiastical law.

c. 545: Death of Dionysius Exiguus who was the first to date history from the birth of Christ, a practice which resulted in use of the B.C. and A.D. abbreviations. His calculations were at least four years late.

553: Ecumenical Council of Constantinople (II). It condemned the Three Chapters, Nestorian-tainted writings of Theodore of Mopsuestia, Theodoret of Cyrus and Ibas of Edessa.

585: St. Columban founded an influential monastic school at Luxeuil.

589: The most important of several councils of Toledo was held. The Visigoths renounced Arianism, and St. Leander began the organization of the Church in Spain.

590-604: Pontificate of Pope St. Gregory I the Great. He set the form and style of the papacy which prevailed throughout the Middle Ages; exerted great influence on doctrine and liturgy; was strong in support of monastic discipline and clerical celibacy; authored writings on many subjects. Gregorian Chant is named in his honor.

596: Pope St. Gregory I sent St. Augustine of Canterbury and 40 monks to do missionary work in England.

597: St. Columba died. He founded an important monastery at Iona, established schools and did notable missionary work in Scotland. By the end of the century, monasteries of nuns were common; Western monasticism was flourishing; monasticism in the East, under the influence of Monophysitism and other factors, was losing its vigor.

SEVENTH CENTURY

613: St. Columban established the influential monastery of Bobbio in northern Italy; he died there in 615.

622: The *Hegira* (flight) of Mohammed from Mecca to Medina signalled the beginning of Islam which, by the end of the century, claimed almost all of the southern Mediterranean area.

628: Heraclius, Eastern Emperor, recovered the True Cross from the Persians.

649: A Lateran council condemned two erroneous formulas (Ecthesis and Type) issued by emperors Heraclius and Constans II as means of reconciling Monophysites with the Church.

664: Actions of the Synod of Whitby advanced the adoption of Roman usages in England, especially regarding the date for the observance of Easter. (*See* **Easter Controversy,** p. 139.)

680-81: Ecumenical Council of Constantinople (III). It condemned Monothelitism, which held that Christ had only one will, the divine; censured Pope Honorius I for a letter to Sergius, bishop of Constantinople, in which he made an ambiguous but not infallible statement about the unity of will and/or operation in Christ.

692: Trullan Synod. Eastern-Church discipline on clerical celibacy was settled, permitting marriage before ordination to the diaconate and continuation in marriage afterwards, but prohibiting marriage following the death of the wife thereafter. Anti-Roman canons contributed to East-West alienation.

During the century, the monastic influence of Ireland and England increased in Western Europe; schools and learning declined; regulations regarding clerical celibacy became more strict in the East.

EIGHTH CENTURY

711: Muslims began the conquest of Spain.

726: Emperor Leo III, the Isaurian, launched a campaign against the veneration of sacred images and relics; called Iconoclasm (image-breaking), it caused turmoil in the East until about 843.

731: Pope Gregory III and a synod at Rome condemned Iconoclasm, with a declaration that the veneration of sacred images was in accord with Catholic tradition.

Venerable Bede issued his *Ecclesiastical History of the English People.*

732: Charles Martel defeated the Muslims at Poitiers, halting their advance in the West.

744: The Monastery of Fulda was established by St. Sturmi, a disciple of St. Boniface; it was influential in the evangelization of Germany.

754: A council of more than 300 Byzantine bishops endorsed Iconoclast errors. This council and its actions were condemned by the Lateran synod of 769.

Stephen II (III) crowned Pepin ruler of the Franks. Pepin twice invaded Italy, in 754 and 756, to defend the pope against the Lombards. His land grants to the papacy, called the Donation of Pepin, were later extended by Charlemagne (773) and formed part of the States of the Church.

c. 755: St. Boniface (Winfrid) was martyred. He was called the Apostle of Germany for his missionary work and organization of the hierarchy there.

781: Alcuin was chosen by Charlemagne to organize a palace school, which became a center of intellectual leadership.

787: Ecumenical Council of Nicaea (II). It condemned Iconoclasm, which held that the use of images was idolatry, and Adoptionism, which claimed that Christ was not the Son of God by nature but only by adoption. This was the last council regarded as ecumenical by Orthodox Churches.

792: A council at Ratisbon condemned Adoptionism.

The famous *Book of Kells* ("The Great Gospel of Columcille") dates from the early eighth or late seventh century.

NINTH CENTURY

800: Charlemagne was crowned Emperor by Pope Leo III on Christmas Day.

Egbert became king of West Saxons; he unified England and strengthened the See of Canterbury.

813: Emperor Leo V, the Armenian, revived Iconoclasm, which persisted until about 843.

814: Charlemagne died.

843: The Treaty of Verdun split the Frankish kingdom among Charlemagne's three grandsons.

844: A Eucharistic controversy involving the writings of St. Paschasius Radbertus, Ratramnus and Rabanus Maurus occasioned the development of terminology regarding doctrine of the Real Presence.

846: Muslims invaded Italy and attacked Rome.

847-52: Period of composition of the False Decretals, a collection of forged documents attributed to popes from St. Clement (88-97) to Gregory II (714-731). The Decretals, which strongly supported the autonomy and rights of bishops, were suspect for a long time before being repudiated entirely about 1628.

848: The Council of Mainz condemned Gottschalk for heretical teaching regarding predestination. He was also condemned by the Council of Quierzy in 853.

857: Photius displaced Ignatius as patriarch of Constantinople. This marked the beginning of the Photian Schism, a confused state of East-West relations which has not yet been cleared up by historical research. Photius, a man of exceptional ability, died in 891.

865: St. Ansgar, apostle of Scandinavia, died.

869: St. Cyril died and his brother, St. Methodius (d. 885), was ordained a bishop. The Apostles of the Slavs devised an alphabet and translated the Gospels and liturgy into the Slavonic language.

869-70: Ecumenical Council of Constantinople (IV). It issued a second condemnation of Iconoclasm, condemned and deposed Photius as patriarch of Constantinople and restored Ignatius to the patriarchate. This was the last ecumenical council held in the East. It was first called ecumenical by canonists toward the end of the 11th century.

871-c. 900: Reign of Alfred the Great, the only English king ever anointed by a pope at Rome.

TENTH CENTURY

910: William, duke of Aquitaine, founded the

Benedictine Abbey of Cluny, which became a center of monastic and ecclesiastical reform, especially in France.

915: Pope John X played a leading role in the expulsion of Saracens from central and southern Italy.

955: St. Olga, of the Russian royal family, was baptized.

962: Otto I, the Great, crowned by Pope John XII, revived Charlemagne's kingdom, which became the Holy Roman Empire.

966: Mieszko, first of a royal line in Poland, was baptized; he brought Latin Christianity to Poland.

988: Conversion and baptism of St. Vladimir and the people of Kiev which subsequently became part of Russia.

993: John XV was the first pope to decree the official canonization of a saint—Bishop Ulrich (Uldaric) of Augsburg—for the universal Church.

997: St. Stephen became ruler of Hungary. He assisted in organizing the hierarchy and establishing Latin Christianity in that country.

999-1003: Pontificate of Sylvester II (Gerbert of Aquitaine), a Benedictine monk and the first French pope.

ELEVENTH CENTURY

1009: Beginning of lasting East-West Schism in the Church, marked by dropping of the name of Pope Sergius IV from the Byzantine diptychs (the listing of persons prayed for during the liturgy). The deletion was made by Patriarch Sergius II of Constantinople.

1012: St. Romuald founded the Camaldolese Hermits.

1025: The Council of Arras, and other councils later, condemned the Cathari (Neo-Manichaeans, Albigenses).

1027: The Council of Elne proclaimed the Truce of God as a means of stemming violence; it involved armistice periods of varying length, which were later extended.

1038: St. John Gualbert founded the Vallombrosians.

1043-59: Constantinople patriarchate of Michael Cerularius, the key figure in a controversy concerning the primacy of the papacy. His and the Byzantine synod's refusal to acknowledge this primacy in 1054 widened and hardened the East-West Schism in the Church.

1047: Pope Clement II died; he was the only pope ever buried in Germany.

1049-54: Pontificate of St. Leo IX, who inaugurated a movement of papal, diocesan, monastic and clerical reform.

1054: Start of the Great Schism between the Eastern and Western Churches; it marked the separation of Orthodox Churches from unity with the pope.

1055: Condemnation of the Eucharistic doctrine of Berengarius.

1059: A Lateran council issued new legislation regarding papal elections; voting power was entrusted to the Roman cardinals.

1066: Death of St. Edward the Confessor, king of England from 1042 and restorer of Westminster Abbey.

Defeat, at Hastings, of Harold by William, Duke of Normandy (later William I), who subsequently exerted strong influence on the life-style of the Church in England.

1073-85: Pontificate of St. Gregory VII (Hildebrand).

A strong pope, he carried forward programs of clerical and general ecclesiastical reform and struggled against German King Henry IV and other rulers to end the evils of lay investiture. He introduced the Latin liturgy in Spain and set definite dates for the observance of ember days.

1077: Henry IV, excommunicated and suspended from the exercise of imperial powers by Gregory VII, sought absolution from the pope at Canossa. Henry later repudiated this action and in 1084 forced Gregory to leave Rome.

1079: The Council of Rome condemned Eucharistic errors (denial of the Real Presence of Christ under the appearances of bread and wine) of Berengarius, who retracted.

1084: St. Bruno founded the Carthusians.

1097-99: The first of several Crusades undertaken between this time and 1265. Recovery of the Holy Places and gaining free access to them for Christians were the original purposes, but these were diverted to less worthy objectives in various ways. Results included: a Latin Kingdom of Jerusalem, 1099-1187; a military and political misadventure in the form of a Latin Empire of Constantinople, 1204-1261; acquisition, by treaties, of visiting rights for Christians in the Holy Land. East-West economic and cultural relationships increased during the period. In the religious sphere, actions of the Crusaders had the effect of increasing the alienation of the East from the West.

1098: St. Robert founded the Cistercians.

TWELFTH CENTURY

1108: Beginnings of the influential Abbey and School of St. Victor in France.

1115: St. Bernard established the Abbey of Clairvaux and inaugurated the Cistercian Reform.

1118: Christian forces captured Saragossa, Spain; the beginning of the Muslim decline in that country.

1121: St. Norbert established the original monastery of the Praemonstratensians near Laon, France.

1122: The Concordat of Worms (*Pactum Callixtinum*) was formulated and approved by Pope Callistus II and Emperor Henry V to settle controversy concerning the investiture of prelates. The concordat provided that the emperor could invest prelates with symbols of temporal authority but had no right to invest them with spiritual authority, which came from the Church alone, and that the emperor was not to interfere in papal elections. This was the first concordat in history.

1123: Ecumenical Council of the Lateran (I), the first of its kind in the West. It endorsed provisions of the Concordat of Worms concerning the investiture of prelates and approved reform measures in 25 canons.

1139: Ecumenical Council of the Lateran (II). It adopted measures against a schism organized by antipope Anacletus and approved 30 canons related to discipline and other matters; one of the canons stated that holy orders is an invalidating impediment to marriage.

1140: St. Bernard met Abelard in debate at the Council of Sens. Abelard, whose rationalism in theology was condemned for the first time in 1121, died in 1142 at Cluny.

1148: The Synod of Rheims enacted strict disciplinary decrees for communities of women Religious.

1152: The Synod of Kells reorganized the Church in Ireland.

1160: Gratian, whose *Decretum* became a basic text of canon law, died.

Peter Lombard, compiler of the Four Books of Sentences, a standard theology text for nearly 200 years, died.

1170: St. Thomas Becket, archbishop of Canterbury, who clashed with Henry II over church-state relations, was murdered in his cathedral.

1171: Pope Alexander III reserved the process of canonization of saints to the Holy See.

1179: Ecumenical Council of the Lateran (III). It enacted measures against Waldensianism and Albigensianism (see year 242 regarding Manichaeism), approved reform decrees in 27 canons, provided that popes be elected by a two-thirds vote of the cardinals.

1184: Waldenses and other heretics were excommunicated by Pope Lucius III.

THIRTEENTH CENTURY

1198-1216: Pontificate of Innocent III, during which the papacy reached its medieval peak of authority, influence and prestige in the Church and in relations with civil rulers.

1208: Innocent III called for a crusade, the first in Christendom itself, against the Albigensians; their beliefs and practices threatened the fabric of society in southern France and northern Italy.

1209: Verbal approval was given by Innocent III to a rule of life for the Order of Friars Minor, started by St. Francis of Assisi.

1212: The Second Order of Franciscans, the Poor Clares, was founded.

1215: Ecumenical Council of the Lateran (IV). It ordered annual reception of the sacraments of penance and the Eucharist; defined and made the first official use of the term transubstantiation to explain the change of bread and wine into the body and blood of Christ; adopted additional measures to counteract teachings and practices of the Albigensians and Cathari; approved 70 canons.

1216: Formal papal approval was given to a rule of life for the Order of Preachers, started by St. Dominic. The Portiuncula Indulgence was granted by the Holy See at the request of St. Francis of Assisi.

1221: Rule of the Third Order Secular of St. Francis (Secular Franciscan Order) approved verbally by Honorius III.

1226: Death of St. Francis of Assisi.

1231: Pope Gregory IX authorized establishment of the Papal Inquisition for dealing with heretics. It was a creature of its time, when crimes against faith and heretical doctrines of extremists like the Cathari and Albigenses threatened the good of the Christian community, the welfare of the state and the very fabric of society. The institution, which was responsible for excesses in punishment, was most active in the second half of the century in southern France, Italy and Germany.

1245: Ecumenical Council of Lyons (I). It confirmed the deposition of Emperor Frederick II and approved 22 canons.

1247: Preliminary approval was given by the Holy See to a Carmelite rule of life.

1270: St. Louis IX, king of France, died. Beginning of papal decline.

1274: Ecumenical Council of Lyons (II). It accomplished a temporary reunion of separated Eastern Churches with the Roman Church; issued regulations concerning conclaves for papal elections; approved 31 canons.

Death of St. Thomas Aquinas, Doctor of the Church, of lasting influence.

1280: Pope Nicholas III, who made the Breviary the official prayer book for clergy of the Roman Church, died.

1281: The excommunication of Michael Palaeologus by Pope Martin IV ruptured the union effected with the Eastern Church in 1274.

FOURTEENTH CENTURY

1302: Pope Boniface VIII issued the bull *Unam Sanctam*, concerning the unity of the Church and the temporal power of princes, against the background of a struggle with Philip IV of France; it was the most famous medieval document on the subject.

1309-77: For a period of approximately 70 years, seven popes resided at Avignon because of unsettled conditions in Rome and other reasons; see separate entry.

1311-12: Ecumenical Council of Vienne. It suppressed the Knights Templar and enacted a number of reform decrees.

1321: Dante Alighieri died a year after completing the *Divine Comedy*.

1324: Marsilius of Padua completed *Defensor Pacis*, a work condemned by Pope John XXII as heretical because of its denial of papal primacy and the hierarchical structure of the Church, and for other reasons. It was a charter for conciliarism (an ecumenical council is superior to the pope in authority).

1337-1453: Period of the Hundred Years' War, a dynastic struggle between France and England.

1338: Four years after the death of Pope John XXII, who had opposed Louis IV of Bavaria in a years-long controversy, electoral princes declared at the Diet of Rhense that the emperor did not need papal confirmation of his title and right to rule. Charles IV later (1356) said the same thing in a *Golden Bull*, eliminating papal rights in the election of emperors.

1347-50: The Black Death swept across Europe, killing perhaps one-fourth to one-third of the total population; an estimated 40 per cent of the clergy succumbed.

1374: Petrarch, poet and humanist, died.

1377: Return of the papacy from Avignon to Rome. Beginning of the Western Schism; see separate entry.

FIFTEENTH CENTURY

1409: The Council of Pisa, without canonical authority, tried to end the Western Schism but succeeded only in complicating it by electing a third claimant to the papacy; see Western Schism.

1414-18: Ecumenical Council of Constance. It took successful action to end the Western Schism involving rival claimants to the papacy; rejected the teachings of Wycliff; condemned Hus as a heretic. One decree passed in the earlier stages of the council but later rejected—asserted the superiority of an ecumenical council over the pope (conciliarism).

1431: St. Joan of Arc was burned at the stake.

1431-45: Ecumenical Council of Florence (also called Basle-Ferrara-Florence). It affirmed the primacy of the pope against the claims of conciliarists that an ecumenical council is superior to the pope. It also formulated and approved decrees of union with several separated Eastern Churches—Greek, Armenian, Jacobite—which failed to gain general or lasting acceptance.

1438: The Pragmatic Sanction of Bourges was enacted by Charles VII and the French Parliament to curtail papal authority over the Church in France, in the spirit of conciliarism. It found expression in Gallicanism and had effects lasting at least until the French Revolution.

1453: The fall of Constantinople to the Turks.

c. 1456: Gutenberg issued the first edition of the Bible printed from movable type, at Mainz, Germany.

1476: Pope Sixtus IV approved observance of the feast of the Immaculate Conception on Dec. 8 throughout the Church.

1478: Pope Sixtus IV, at the urging of King Ferdinand of Spain, approved establishment of the Spanish Inquisition for dealing with Jewish and Moorish converts accused of heresy. The institution, which was peculiar to Spain and its colonies in America, acquired jurisdiction over other cases as well and fell into disrepute because of its procedures, cruelty and the manner in which it served the Spanish crown, rather than the accused and the good of the Church. Protests by the Holy See failed to curb excesses of the Inquisition, which lingered in Spanish history until early in the 19th century.

1492: Columbus discovered the Americas.

1493: Pope Alexander VI issued a Bull of Demarcation which determined spheres of influence for the Spanish and Portuguese in the Americas. The Renaissance, a humanistic movement which originated in Italy in the 14th century, spread to France, Germany, the Low Countries and England. A transitional period between the medieval world and the modern secular world, it introduced profound changes which affected literature and the other arts, general culture, politics and religion.

SIXTEENTH CENTURY

1512-17: Ecumenical Council of the Lateran (V). It stated the relation and position of the pope with respect to an ecumenical council; acted to counteract the Pragmatic Sanction of Bourges and exaggerated claims of liberty by the Church in France; condemned erroneous teachings concerning the nature of the human soul; stated doctrine concerning indulgences. The council reflected concern for abuses in the Church and the need for reforms but failed to take decisive action in the years immediately preceding the Reformation.

1517: Martin Luther signaled the beginning of the Reformation by posting 95 theses at Wittenberg. Subsequently, he broke completely from doctrinal orthodoxy in discourses and three published works (1519 and 1520); was excommunicated on more than 40 charges of heresy (1521); remained the dominant figure in the Reformation in Germany until his death in 1546.

1519: Zwingli triggered the Reformation in Zurich and became its leading proponent there until his death in combat in 1531.

1524: Luther's encouragement of German princes in putting down the two-year Peasants' Revolt gained political support for his cause.

1528: The Order of Friars Minor Capuchin was approved as an autonomous division of the Franciscan Order; like the Jesuits, the Capuchins became leaders in the Counter-Reformation.

1530: The Augsburg Confession of Lutheran faith was issued; it was later supplemented by the Smalkaldic Articles, approved in 1537.

1533: Henry VIII divorced Catherine of Aragon, married Anne Boleyn, was excommunicated. In 1534 he decreed the Act of Supremacy, making the sovereign the head of the Church in England, under which Sts. John Fisher and Thomas More were executed in 1535. Despite his rejection of papal primacy and actions against monastic life in England, he generally maintained doctrinal orthodoxy until his death in 1547.

1536: John Calvin, leader of the Reformation in Switzerland until his death in 1564, issued the first edition of Institutes of the Christian Religion, which became the classical text of Reformed (non-Lutheran) theology.

1540: The constitutions of the Society of Jesus (Jesuits), founded by St. Ignatius of Loyola, were approved.

1541: Start of the 11-year career of St. Francis Xavier as a missionary to the East Indies and Japan.

1545-63: Ecumenical Council of Trent. It issued a great number of decrees concerning doctrinal matters opposed by the Reformers, and mobilized the Counter-Reformation. Definitions covered the Canon of the Bible, the rule of faith, the nature of justification, grace, faith, original sin and its effects, the seven sacraments, the sacrificial nature of the Mass, the veneration of saints, use of sacred images, belief in purgatory, the doctrine of indulgences, the jurisdiction of the pope over the whole Church. It initiated many reforms for renewal in the liturgy and general discipline in the Church, the promotion of religious instruction, the education of the clergy through the foundation of seminaries, etc. Trent ranks with Vatican II as the greatest ecumenical council held in the West.

1549: The first Anglican Book of Common Prayer was issued by Edward VI. Revised editions were published in 1552, 1559 and 1662 and later.

1553: Start of the five-year reign of Mary Tudor who tried to counteract actions of Henry VIII against the Roman Church.

1555: Enactment of the Peace of Augsburg, an arrangement of religious territorialism rather than toleration, which recognized the existence of Catholicism and Lutheranism in the German Empire and provided that citizens should adopt the religion of their respective rulers.

1558: Beginning of the reign (to 1603) of Queen Elizabeth I of England and Ireland, during which the Church of England took on its definitive form.

1559: Establishment of the hierarchy of the Church of England, with the consecration of Matthew Parker as archbishop of Canterbury.

1563: The first text of the 39 Articles of the Church of England was issued. Also enacted were a new Act of Supremacy and Oath of Succession to the English throne.

1570: Elizabeth I was excommunicated. Penal measures against Catholics subsequently became more severe.

1571: Defeat of the Turkish armada at Lepanto staved off the invasion of Eastern Europe.

1577: The Formula of Concord, the classical statement of Lutheran faith, was issued; it was, generally, a Lutheran counterpart of the canons of the Council of Trent. In 1580, along with other formulas of doctrine, it was included in the Book of Concord.

1582: The Gregorian Calendar, named for Pope Gregory XIII, was put into effect and was eventually adopted in most countries: England delayed adoption until 1752.

SEVENTEENTH CENTURY

1605: The Gunpowder Plot, an attempt by Catholic fanatics to blow up James I of England and the houses of Parliament, resulted in an anti-Catholic Oath of Allegiance.

1610: Death of Matteo Ricci, outstanding Jesuit missionary to China, pioneer in cultural relations between China and Europe.

Founding of the first community of Visitation Nuns by Sts. Francis de Sales and Jane de Chantal.

1611: Founding of the Oratorians.

1613: Catholics were banned from Scandinavia.

1625: Founding of the Congregation of the Mission (Vincentians) by St. Vincent de Paul. He founded the Sisters of Charity in 1633.

1642: Death of Galileo, scientist, who was censured by the Congregation of the Holy Office for supporting the Copernican theory of the sun-centered planetary system. The case against him was closed in his favor in 1992.

Founding of the Sulpicians by Jacques Olier.

1643: Start of publication of the Bollandist *Acta Sanctorum*, a critical work on lives of the saints.

1648: Provisions in the Peace of Westphalia, ending the Thirty Years' War, extended terms of the Peace of Augsburg (1555) to Calvinists and gave equality to Catholics and Protestants in the 300 states of the Holy Roman Empire.

1649: Oliver Cromwell invaded Ireland and began a severe persecution of the Church there.

1653: Pope Innocent X condemned five propositions of Jansenism, a complex theory which distorted doctrine concerning the relations between divine grace and human freedom. Jansenism was also a rigoristic movement which seriously disturbed the Church in France, the Low Countries and Italy in this and the 18th century.

1673: The Test Act in England barred from public office Catholics who would not deny the doctrine of transubstantiation and receive Communion in the Church of England.

1678: Many English Catholics suffered death as a consequence of the Popish Plot, a false allegation by Titus Oates that Catholics planned to assassinate Charles II, land a French army in the country, burn London, and turn over the government to the Jesuits.

1682: The four Gallican articles, drawn up by Bossuet, asserted political and ecclesiastical immunities of France from papal control. The articles, which rejected the primacy of the pope, were declared null and void by Pope Alexander VIII in 1690.

1689: The Toleration Act granted a measure of freedom of worship to other English dissenters but not to Catholics.

EIGHTEENTH CENTURY

1704: Chinese Rites—involving the Christian adaptation of elements of Confucianism, veneration of ancestors and Chinese terminology in religion—were condemned by Clement XI.

1720: The Passionists were founded by St. Paul of the Cross.

1724: Persecution in China.

1732: The Redemptorists were founded by St. Alphonsus Liguori.

1738: Freemasonry was condemned by Clement XII and Catholics were forbidden to join, under penalty of excommunication; the prohibition was repeated by Benedict XIV in 1751 and by later popes.

1760s: Josephinism, a theory and system of state control of the Church, was initiated in Austria; it remained in force until about 1850.

1764: Febronianism, an unorthodox theory and practice regarding the constitution of the Church and relations between Church and state, was condemned for the first of several times. Proposed by an auxiliary bishop of Trier using the pseudonym Justinus Febronius, it had the effects of minimizing the office of the pope and supporting national churches under state control.

1773: Clement XIV issued a brief of suppression against the Jesuits, following their expulsion from Portugal in 1759, from France in 1764 and from Spain in 1767. Political intrigue and unsubstantiated accusations were principal factors in these developments. The ban, which crippled the society, contained no condemnation of the Jesuit constitutions, particular Jesuits or Jesuit teaching. The society was restored in 1814.

1778: Catholics in England were relieved of some civil disabilities dating back to the time of Henry VIII, by an act which permitted them to acquire, own and inherit property. Additional liberties were restored by the Roman Catholic Relief Act of 1791 and subsequent enactments of Parliament.

1789: Religious freedom in the United States was guaranteed under the First Amendment to the Constitution.

Beginning of the French Revolution which resulted in: the secularization of church property and the Civil Constitution of the Clergy in 1790; the persecution of priests, religious and lay persons loyal to papal authority; invasion of the Papal States by Napoleon in 1796; renewal of persecution from 1797-1799; attempts to dechristianize France and establish a new religion; the occupation of Rome by French troops and the forced removal of Pius VI to France in 1798.

This century is called the age of Enlightenment or Reason because of the predominating rational and scientific approach of its leading philosophers, scientists and writers with respect to religion, ethics and natural law. This approach downgraded the fact and significance of revealed religion. Also characteristic of the Enlightenment were subjectivism, secularism and optimism regarding human perfectibility.

NINETEENTH CENTURY

1801: Concordat between Napoleon and Pope Pius VII is signed. It is soon violated by the Organic Articles issued by Napoleon in 1802.

1804: Napoleon crowns himself Emperor of the French with Pope Pius in attendance.

1809: Pope Pius VII was made a captive by Napoleon and deported to France where he remained in exile until 1814. During this time he refused to cooperate with Napoleon who sought to bring the Church in France under his own control, and other leading cardinals were imprisoned.

The turbulence in church-state relations in France at the beginning of the century recurred in connection with the Bourbon Restoration, the July Revolution, the second and third Republics, the Second Empire and the Dreyfus case.

1814: The Society of Jesus, suppressed since 1773, was restored.

1817: Reestablishment of the Congregation for the Propagation of the Faith (Propaganda) by Pius VII was an important factor in increasing missionary activity during the century.

1820: Year's-long persecution, during which thousands died for the faith, ended in China. Thereafter, communication with the West remained cut off until about 1834. Vigorous missionary work got under way in 1842.

1822: The Pontifical Society for the Propagation of the Faith, inaugurated in France by Pauline Jaricot for the support of missionary activity, was established.

1829: The Catholic Emancipation Act relieved Catholics in England and Ireland of most of the civil disabilities to which they had been subject from the time of Henry VIII.

1832: Gregory XVI, in the encyclical *Mirari vos*, condemned indifferentism, one of the many ideologies at odds with Christian doctrine which were proposed during the century.

1833: Start of the Oxford Movement which affected the Church of England and resulted in some notable conversions, including that of John Henry Newman in 1845, to the Catholic Church.

Bl. Frederic Ozanam founded the Society of St. Vincent de Paul in France. The society's objectives are works of charity.

1848: *The Communist Manifesto*, a revolutionary document symptomatic of socio-economic crisis, was issued.

1850: The hierarchy was reestablished in England and Nicholas Wiseman made the first archbishop of Westminster. He was succeeded in 1865 by Henry Manning, an Oxford convert and proponent of the rights of labor.

1853: The Catholic hierarchy was reestablished in Holland.

1854: Pius IX proclaimed the dogma of the Immaculate Conception in the bull *Ineffabilis Deus*.

1858: The Blessed Virgin Mary appeared to St. Bernadette at Lourdes, France.

1864: Pius IX issued the encyclical *Quanta cura* and the Syllabus of Errors in condemnation of some 80 propositions derived from the scientific mentality and rationalism of the century. The subjects in question had deep ramifications in many areas of thought and human endeavor; in religion, they explicitly and/or implicitly rejected divine revelation and the supernatural order.

1867: The first volume of *Das Kapital* was published. Together with the Communist First International, formed in the same year, it had great influence on the subsequent development of communism and socialism.

1869: The Anglican Church was disestablished in Ireland.

1869-70: Ecumenical Council of the Vatican (I). It defined papal primacy and infallibility in a dogmatic constitution on the Church; covered natural religion, revelation, faith, and the relations between faith and reason in a dogmatic constitution on the Catholic faith.

1870-71: Victor Emmanuel II of Sardinia, crowned king of Italy after defeating Austrian and papal forces, marched into Rome in 1870 and expropriated the Papal States after a plebiscite in which Catholics, at the order of Pius IX, did not vote. In 1871, Pius IX refused to accept a Law of Guarantees. Confiscation of church property and hindrance of ecclesiastical administration by the regime followed.

1871: The German Empire, a confederation of 26 states, was formed. Government policy launched a *Kulturkampf* whose May Laws of 1873 were designed to annul papal jurisdiction in Prussia and other states and to place the Church under imperial control. Resistance to the enactments and the persecution they legalized forced the government to modify its anti-Church policy by 1887.

1878: Beginning of the pontificate of Leo XIII, who was pope until his death in 1903. Leo is best known for the encyclical *Rerum novarum*, which greatly influenced the course of Christian social thought and the labor movement. His other accomplishments included promotion of Scholastic philosophy and the impetus he gave to scriptural studies.

1881: The first International Eucharistic Congress was held in Lille, France.

Alexander II of Russia was assassinated. His policies of Russification—as well as those of his two predecessors and a successor during the century—caused great suffering to Catholics, Jews and Protestants in Poland, Lithuania, the Ukraine and Bessarabia.

1882: Charles Darwin died. His theory of evolution by natural selection, one of several scientific highlights of the century, had extensive repercussions in the faith-and-science controversy.

1887: The Catholic University of America was founded in Washington, DC.

1893: The U.S. apostolic delegation was set up in Washington, DC.

TWENTIETH CENTURY

1901: Restrictive measures in France forced the Jesuits, Benedictines, Carmelites and other religious orders to leave the country. Subsequently, 14,000 schools were suppressed; religious orders and congregations were expelled; the concordat was renounced in 1905; church property was confiscated in 1906. For some years the Holy See, refusing to comply with government demands for the control of bishops' appointments, left some ecclesiastical offices vacant.

1903-14: Pontificate of St. Pius X. He initiated the codification of canon law, 1904; removed the ban against participation by Catholics in Italian national elections, 1905; issued decrees calling upon the faithful to receive Holy Communion frequently and daily, and stating that children should begin receiving the Eucharist at the age of seven, 1905 and 1910, respectively; ordered the establishment of the Confraternity of Christian Doctrine in all parishes throughout the world, 1905; condemned Modernism in the decree *Lamentabili* and the encyclical *Pascendi*, 1907.

1908: The United States and England, long under the jurisdiction of the Congregation for the Propagation of the Faith as mission territories, were removed from its control and placed under the common law of the Church.

1910: Laws of separation were enacted in Portugal, marking a point of departure in church-state relations.

1911: The Catholic Foreign Mission Society of America—Maryknoll, the first U.S.-founded society of its type—was established.

1914: Start of World War I, which lasted until 1918.

1914-22: Pontificate of Benedict XV. Much of his pontificate was devoted to seeking ways and means of minimizing the material and spiritual havoc of World War I. In 1917 he offered his services as a mediator to the belligerent nations, but his pleas for settlement of the conflict went unheeded.

1917: The Blessed Virgin Mary appeared to three children at Fatima, Portugal.

A new constitution, embodying repressive laws against the Church, was enacted in Mexico. Its implementation resulted in persecution in the 1920s and 1930s.

Bolsheviks seized power in Russia and set up a communist dictatorship. The event marked the rise of communism in Russian and world affairs. One of its immediate, and lasting, results was persecution of the Church, Jews and other segments of the population.

1918: The Code of Canon Law, in preparation for more than 10 years, went into effect in the Western Church.

1919: Benedict XV stimulated missionary work through the decree *Maximum Illud*, in which he urged the recruiting and training of native clergy in places where the Church was not firmly established.

1920-22: Ireland was partitioned by two enactments of the British government which (1) made the six counties of Northern Ireland part of the United Kingdom in 1920 and (2) gave dominion status to the Irish Free State in 1922. The Irish Free State became an independent republic in 1949.

1922-39: Pontificate of Pius XI. He subscribed to the Lateran Treaty, 1929, which settled the Roman Question created by the confiscation of the Papal States in 1871; issued the encyclical *Casti connubii*, 1930, an authoritative statement on Christian mar-

riage; resisted the efforts of Benito Mussolini to control Catholic Action and the Church, in the encyclical *Non abbiamo bisogno*, 1931; opposed various fascist policies; issued the encyclicals *Quadragesimo anno*, 1931, developing the social doctrine of Leo XIII's *Rerum novarum*, and *Divini Redemptoris*, 1937, calling for social justice and condemning atheistic communism; condemned anti-Semitism, 1937.

1926: The Catholic Relief Act repealed virtually all legal disabilities of Catholics in England.

1931: Leftists proclaimed Spain a republic and proceeded to disestablish the Church, confiscate church property, deny salaries to the clergy, expel the Jesuits and ban teaching of the Catholic faith. These actions were preludes to the civil war of 1936-1939.

1933: Emergence of Adolf Hitler to power in Germany. By 1935 two of his aims were clear, the elimination of the Jews and control of a single national church. Six million Jews were killed in the Holocaust. The Church was subject to repressive measures, which Pius XI protested futilely in the encyclical *Mit brennender sorge* in 1937.

1936-39: Civil war in Spain between the leftist Loyalist and the forces of rightist leader Francisco Franco. The Loyalists were defeated and one-man, one-party rule was established. Many priests, religious and lay persons fell victim to Loyalist persecution and atrocities.

1939-45: World War II.

1939-58: Pontificate of Pius XII. He condemned communism, proclaimed the dogma of the Assumption of Mary in 1950, in various documents and other enactments provided ideological background for many of the accomplishments of the Second Vatican Council. (*See* **Twentieth Century Popes.**)

1940: Start of a decade of communist conquest in more than 13 countries, resulting in conditions of persecution for a minimum of 60 million Catholics as well as members of other faiths.

Persecution diminished in Mexico because of non-enforcement of anti-religious laws still on record.

1950: Pius XII proclaimed the dogma of the Assumption of the Blessed Virgin Mary.

1957: The communist regime of China established the Patriotic Association of Chinese Catholics in opposition to the Church in union with the pope.

1958-63: Pontificate of Bl. John XXIII. His principal accomplishment was the convocation of the Second Vatican Council, the twenty-first ecumenical council in the history of the Church. (*See* **Twentieth Century Popes.**)

1962-65: Ecumenical Council of the Vatican (II). It formulated and promulgated 16 documents—two dogmatic and two pastoral constitutions, nine decrees and three declarations—reflecting pastoral orientation toward renewal and reform in the Church, and making explicit dimensions of doctrine and Christian life requiring emphasis for the full development of the Church and the better accomplishment of its mission in the contemporary world.

1963-78: Pontificate of Paul VI. His main purpose and effort was to give direction and provide guidance for the authentic trends of church renewal set in motion by the Second Vatican Council. (*See* **Twentieth Century Popes.**)

1978: The thirty-four-day pontificate of John Paul I. Start of the pontificate of John Paul II; see Index.

1983: The revised Code of Canon Law, embodying reforms enacted by the Second Vatican Council, went into effect in the Church of Roman Rite.

1985: Formal ratification of a Vatican-Italy concordat replacing the Lateran Treaty of 1929.

1989-91: Decline and fall of communist influence and control in Middle and Eastern Europe and the Soviet Union.

1991: The Code of Canon Law for Eastern Churches went into effect.

1992: Approval of the new *Catechism of the Catholic Church*.

The Vatican officially closed the case against Galileo Galilei.

1994: Initiation of celebration preparations of the start of the third Christian millennium in the year 2000.

1997: Pope John Paul II issued an apology for any anti-Semitism by Catholics; a conference on anti-Semitism was also held in Rome and a number of Catholic leaders in Europe issued apologies for historical anti-Semitism.

1998: Pope John Paul II visited Cuba and secured the release of over 300 political prisoners.

The Vatican issued a white paper on Anti-Semitism, entitled: *We Remember: A Reflection on the Shoah*.

Twentieth anniversary of the pontificate of Pope John Paul II; he became the longest reigning pontiff elected in the 20th century.

TWENTY-FIRST CENTURY

2000: The Catholic Church celebrated the Holy Year 2000 and the Jubilee; commencement of the third Christian millennium.

Pope John Paul II issued apology for the sinful actions of the Church's members in the past. Pope John Paul II traveled to the Holy Land in an historic visit.

2001: Pope John Paul II traveled to Greece and Syria. He also named 44 new members to the College of Cardinals in an unprecedented consistory.

On September 11, the World Trade Center was destroyed and the Pentagon attacked by Islamic terrorists who hijacked several planes and used them as weapons of mass destruction. The attacks launched a global war on terror.

2003: Pope John Paul II appealed for a peaceful resolution to the Iraq War. A coalition headed by the U.S. removed Saddam Hussein.

2004: In March, Pope John Paul II became the third longest reigning pontiff in history, surpassing Pope Leo XIII (r. 1878-1903).

2005: Pope John Paul II died on Apr. 2. Cardinal Joseph Ratzinger was elected pope on Apr. 19 and took the name Benedict XVI.

ECUMENICAL COUNCILS

An ecumenical council is an assembly of the college of bishops, with and under the presidency of the pope, which has supreme authority over the Church in matters pertaining to faith, morals, worship and discipline.

The Second Vatican Council stated: "The supreme authority with which this college (of bishops) is empowered over the whole Church is exercised in a solemn way through an ecumenical council. A council is never ecumenical unless it is confirmed or at least accepted as such by the successor of Peter. It is the prerogative of the Roman Pontiff to convoke these councils, to preside over them, and to confirm them" (Dogmatic Constitution on the Church, *Lumen Gentium*, No. 22).

Pope Presides

The pope is the head of an ecumenical council; he presides over it either personally or through legates. Conciliar decrees and other actions have binding force only when confirmed and promulgated by him. If a pope dies during a council, it is suspended until reconvened by another pope. An ecumenical council is not superior to a pope; hence, there is no appeal from a pope to a council.

Collectively, the bishops with the pope represent the whole Church. They do this not as democratic representatives of the faithful in a kind of church parliament, but as the successors of the Apostles with divinely given authority, care and responsibility over the whole Church.

All and only bishops are council participants with deliberative vote. The supreme authority of the Church can invite others and determine the manner of their participation.

Basic legislation concerning ecumenical councils is contained in Canons 337-41 of the Code of Canon Law. Basic doctrinal considerations were stated by the Second Vatican Council in the Dogmatic Constitution on the Church.

Background

Ecumenical councils had their prototype in the Council of Jerusalem in 51, at which the Apostles under the leadership of St. Peter decided that converts to the Christian faith were not obliged to observe all the prescriptions of Old Testament law (Acts 15). As early as the second century, bishops got together in regional meetings, synods or councils to take common action for the doctrinal and pastoral good of their communities of faithful. The expansion of such limited assemblies to ecumenical councils was a logical and historical evolution, given the nature and needs of the Church.

Emperors Involved

Emperors were active in summoning or convoking the first eight councils, especially the first five and the eighth. Among reasons for intervention of this kind were the facts that the emperors regarded themselves as guardians of the faith; that the settlement of religious controversies, which had repercussions in political and social turmoil, served the cause of peace in the state; and that the emperors had at their disposal ways and means of facilitating gatherings of bishops. Imperial actions, however, did not account for the formally ecumenical nature of the councils.

Some councils were attended by relatively few bishops, and the ecumenical character of several was open to question for a time. However, confirmation and de facto recognition of their actions by popes and subsequent councils established them as ecumenical.

Role in History

The councils have played a highly significant role in

the history of the Church by witnessing to and defining truths of revelation, by shaping forms of worship and discipline, and by promoting measures for the ever-necessary reform and renewal of Catholic life. In general, they have represented attempts of the Church to mobilize itself in times of crisis for self-preservation, self-purification and growth.

The first eight ecumenical councils were held in the East; the other 13, in the West. The majority of separated Eastern Churches—e.g., the Orthodox—recognize the ecumenical character of the first seven councils, which formulated a great deal of basic doctrine. Other separated Eastern Churches acknowledge only the first two or first three ecumenical councils.

The 21 Councils

The 21 ecumenical councils in the history of the Church are listed below, with indication of their names or titles (taken from the names of the places where they were held); the dates; the reigning and/or approving popes; the emperors who were instrumental in convoking the eight councils in the East; the number of bishops who attended, when available; the number of sessions. Significant actions of the first 20 councils are indicated under appropriate dates in **Dates and Events in Church History.**

Nicaea I, 325: St. Sylvester I (Emperor Constantine I); attended by approximately 300 bishops; sessions held between May 20 or June 19 to near the end of August.

Constantinople I, 381: St. Damasus I (Emperor Theodosius I); attended by approximately 150 bishops; sessions held from May to July.

Ephesus, 431: St. Celestine I (Emperor Theodosius II); attended by 150 to 200 bishops; five sessions held between June 22 and July 17.

Chalcedon, 451: St. Leo I (Emperor Marcian); attended by approximately 600 bishops; 17 sessions held between Oct. 8 and Nov. 1.

Constantinople II, 553: Vigilius (Emperor Justinian I); attended by 165 bishops; eight sessions held between May 5 and June 2.

Constantinople III, 680-681: St. Agatho, St. Leo II (Emperor Constantine IV); attended by approximately 170 bishops; 16 sessions held between Nov. 7, 680, and Sept. 6, 681.

Nicaea II, 787: Adrian I (Empress Irene); attended by approximately 300 bishops: eight sessions held between Sept. 24 and Oct. 23.

Constantinople IV, 869-870: Adrian II (Emperor Basil I); attended by 102 bishops; six sessions held between Oct. 5, 869, and Feb. 28, 870.

Lateran I, 1123: Callistus II; attended by approximately 300 bishops; sessions held between Mar. 8 and Apr. 6.

Lateran II, 1139: Innocent II; attended by 900 to 1,000 bishops and abbots; three sessions held in Apr.

Lateran III, 1179: Alexander III; attended by at least 300 bishops; three sessions held between Mar. 5 and 19.

Lateran IV, 1215: Innocent III; sessions held between Nov. 11 and 30.

Lyons I, 1245: Innocent IV; attended by approximately 150 bishops; three sessions held between June 28 and July 17.

Lyons II, 1274: Gregory X; attended by approximately 500 bishops; six sessions held between May 7 and July 17.

Vienne, 1311-1312: Clement V; attended by 132 bishops; three sessions held between Oct. 16, 1311, and May 6, 1312.

Constance, 1414-1418: Gregory XII, Martin V; attended by nearly 200 bishops, plus other prelates and many experts; 45 sessions held between Nov. 5, 1414, and Apr. 22, 1418.

Florence (also called Basel-Ferrara-Florence), 1431-c. 1445: Eugene IV; attended by many Latin-Rite and Eastern-Rite bishops; preliminary sessions were held at Basel and Ferrara before definitive work was accomplished at Florence.

Lateran V, 1512-1517: Julius II, Leo X; 12 sessions held between May 3, 1512, and Mar. 6, 1517.

Trent, 1545-1563: Paul III, Julius III, Pius IV; 25 sessions held between Dec. 13, 1545, and Dec. 4, 1563.

Vatican I, 1869-1870: Pius IX; attended by approximately 800 bishops and other prelates; four public sessions and 89 general meetings held between Dec. 8, 1869, and Sept. 1, 1870.

VATICAN II

The Second Vatican Council, which was forecast by Pope John XXIII Jan. 25, 1959, was held in four sessions in St. Peter's Basilica.

Pope John convoked it and opened the first session, which ran from Oct. 11 to Dec. 8, 1962. Following John's death June 3, 1963, Pope Paul VI reconvened the council for the other three sessions which ran from Sept. 29 to Dec. 4, 1963; Sept. 14 to Nov. 21, 1964; Sept. 14 to Dec. 8, 1965.

A total of 2,860 Fathers participated in council proceedings, and attendance at meetings varied between 2,000 and 2,500. For various reasons, including the denial of exit from Communist-dominated countries, 274 Fathers could not attend.

The council formulated and promulgated 16 documents—two dogmatic and two pastoral constitutions, nine decrees and three declarations—all of which reflect its basic pastoral orientation toward renewal and reform in the Church. Given below are the Latin and English titles of the documents and their dates of promulgation.

Lumen Gentium (Dogmatic Constitution on the Church), Nov. 21, 1964.

Dei Verbum (Dogmatic Constitution on Divine Revelation), Nov. 18, 1965.

Sacrosanctum Concilium (Constitution on the Sacred Liturgy), Dec. 4, 1963.

Gaudium et Spes (Pastoral Constitution on the Church in the Modern World), Dec. 7, 1965.

Christus Dominus (Decree on the Bishops' Pastoral Office in the Church), Oct. 28, 1965.

Ad Gentes (Decree on the Church's Missionary Activity), Dec. 7, 1965.

Unitatis Redintegratio (Decree on Ecumenism), Nov. 21, 1964.

Orientalium Ecclesiarum (Decree on Eastern Catholic Churches), Nov. 21, 1964.

Presbyterorum Ordinis (Decree on the Ministry and Life of Priests), Dec. 7, 1965.

Optatam Totius (Decree on Priestly Formation), Oct. 28, 1965.

Perfectae Caritatis (Decree on the Appropriate Renewal of the Religious Life), Oct. 28, 1965.

Apostolicam Actuositatem (Decree on the

Apostolate of the Laity), Nov. 18, 1965.

Inter Mirifica (Decree on the Instruments of Social Communication), Dec. 4, 1963.

Dignitatis Humanae (Declaration on Religious Freedom), Dec. 7, 1965.

Nostra Aetate (Declaration on the Relationship of the Church to Non-Christian Religions), Oct. 28, 1965.

Gravissimum Educationis (Declaration on Christian Education), Oct. 28, 1965.

The key documents were the four constitutions, which set the ideological basis for all the others. To date, the documents with the most visible effects are those on the liturgy, the Church, the Church in the world, ecumenism, the renewal of religious life, the life and ministry of priests, the lay apostolate.

The main business of the council was to explore and make explicit dimensions of doctrine and Christian life requiring emphasis for the full development of the Church and the better accomplishment of its mission in the contemporary world.

Enactments of the Second Vatican Council have been points of departure for a wide variety of developments in the internal life of the Church and its mission in the world at large. Much effort has been made in the pontificate of Pope John Paul II to provide the interpretation and implementation of the conciliar documents with a more uniform and universal structure.

The Papacy and the Holy See

POPE BENEDICT XVI

Cardinal Joseph Ratzinger of Germany, Prefect of the Congregation for the Doctrine of the Faith since 1981 and one the great theologians in the Church over the last fifty years, was elected Bishop of Rome and the 264th successor of St. Peter as Supreme Pastor of the Universal Church on Apr. 19, 2005, after four ballots over two days. He chose the name Benedict in honor of Pope Benedict XV, an advocate of peace, and St. Benedict of Nursia, who helped to resurrect civilization in Europe during the Dark Ages. Pope Benedict XVI was invested with the pallium, the symbol of his office, on Apr. 24, 2005, in ceremonies attended by more than 500,000 people in St. Peter's Square.

Early Life

Joseph Aloysius Ratzinger was born on April 16, 1927, while the family was living in a three-story house in the little village of Marktl am Inn, situated in eastern Bavaria. His family moved several times in his early years owing to his father's opposition to the Nazis, and young Joseph was forced to join the Hitler Youth. He was adamantly opposed to the Nazis and made every effort to leave at the first opportunity. In 1939, he entered the minor seminary in Traunstein, his first step toward the priesthood. World War II forced a postponement of his studies, until 1945, when he re-entered the seminary with his brother, Georg. In 1947, he entered the *Herzogliches Georgianum*, a theological institute associated with the University of Munich. Finally, on June 29, 1951, both Joseph and his brother were ordained to the priesthood by Cardinal Faulhaber, in the Cathedral at Freising, on the Feast of Sts. Peter and Paul.

Continuing his theological studies at the University of Munich, he received his doctorate in theology in July 1953, with a thesis entitled *Volk und Haus Gottes in Augustins Lehre von der Kirche* ("The People and House of God in Augustine's Doctrine of the Church"). He fulfilled a requirement for teaching at the university level by completing a book-length treatise, "The Theology of History in St. Bonaventure." On April 15, 1959, he began lectures as a full pro-

fessor of fundamental theology at the University of Bonn. From 1962-1965, he was present during all four sessions of the Vatican II as a *peritus,* or chief theological advisor, to Cardinal Josef Frings of Köln (Cologne), Germany.

In 1963, he began teaching at the University of Münster, taking, in 1966, a second chair in dogmatic theology at the University of Tübingen. A wave of student uprisings swept across Europe in 1968, and Marxism quickly became the dominant intellectual system at Tübingen. He found the radicalized environment to be unacceptable, so in 1969 he moved back to Bavaria and took a teaching position at the University of Regensburg. There, he eventually became dean and vice president. He was also a member of the International Theological Commission of the Holy See from 1969 until 1980.

In 1972, together with Hans Urs von Balthasar, Henry De Lubac and others, he launched the Catholic theological journal *Communio,* a quarterly review of Catholic theology and culture. It has been said that this was done in response to the misinterpretation of the Second Vatican Council by various theologians, as represented by the theological journal *Concilium.*

Archbishop and Cardinal

On March 24, 1977, Fr. Ratzinger was appointed Archbishop of Munich and Freising by Pope Paul VI. He was ordained a bishop on May 28, 1977, taking as his Episcopal motto a phrase from 3 John 8, *Cooperatores Veritatis* ("Fellow Worker in the Truth"). On June 27, 1977, he was elevated to Cardinal (Cardinal Priest) by Pope Paul VI, with the titular church of St. Mary of Consolation (in Tiburtina). In 1980, he was named by Pope John Paul II to chair the special Synod on the Laity. Shortly after that, the pope asked him to head the Congregation for Catholic Education. Cardinal Ratzinger declined, feeling he should not leave his post in Munich too soon. On Nov. 25, 1981, he accepted the post of the Prefect for the Congregation for the Doctrine of the Faith, becoming at the same time *ex officio* the president of the Pontifical Biblical Commission,

Coat of Arms of Pope Benedict XVI

and the International Theological Commission.

Cardinal Ratzinger was president of the Commission for the Preparation of the *Catechism of the Catholic Church*, and after 6 years of work (1986-92) he presented the new *Catechism* to the Holy Father. On April 5, 1993, he was transferred to the order of Cardinal Bishops, with the suburbicarian see of Velletri-Signi. On Nov. 9, 1998, his election as Vice-Dean of the Sacred College of Cardinals was approved by Pope John Paul II, and the Holy Father approved his election as Dean of the College of Cardinals on Nov. 30, 2002, with the title of the suburbicarian See of Ostia added to that of Velletri-Segni.

Besides his prefecture at the Doctrine of the Faith, his curial memberships include: the Second Section of the Secretariat of State, the Congregation of Bishops, of Divine Worship and the Discipline of the Sacraments, of Catholic Education, of Evangelization of Peoples, for the Oriental Churches; and the Pontifical Councils for Christian Unity and for Culture; as well as, the Commissions *Ecclesia Dei*, and for Latin America.

As Dean of the College he was a key figure during the *sede vacante* after the death of Pope John Paul II on April 2, 2005, and delivered the funeral homily for the deceased pontiff.

Pontificate

For details on Pope Benedict XVI's pontificate during 2007-2008, *see under* **Special Reports.**

• **Foreign Pastoral Visits**

2005: Cologne, Germany (World Youth Day), Aug. 18-21.
2006: Poland, May 25-28; Valencia, Spain, July 8-9.; Munich, Germany, Sept. 9-14; Turkey, Nov. 28-Dec. 1.

2007: Brazil, May 9-13; Austria, Sept. 7-9.
2008: U.S.A., April 14-20; Australia (World Youth Day); July 12-21; Lourdes, Sept. 12-15.

• **Canonizations and Beatifications**

As of June 29, 2008, Pope Benedict XVI's pontificate witnessed 48 ceremonies of beatification for 571 Servants of God (43 confessors and 528 martyrs). Among them are 48 diocesan priests, 494 men and women religious, and 30 lay people. Pope Benedict XVI has canonized 14 beati (2 bishops, 4 priests, 5 men religious, 3 women religious, 11 men, and 3 women) in 4 ceremonies. The total number of blessed and saints in his pontificate is 586.

• **Encyclicals and Other Writings**

Cardinal Joseph Ratzinger at the time of his election as Pope Benedict XVI was one of the Church's greatest theologians and was the author of a vast body of writings. Since his election, he has issued several documents, including several motu proprio and apostolic letters. His first encyclical, *Deus Caritas Est*, was issued on Dec. 25, 2005. His second encyclical, *Spe Salvi*, was issued on Nov. 30, 2007. On Mar. 13, 2007, he released the post-synodal apostolic exhortation, *Sacramentum Caritatis* ("The Sacrament of Charity"), a 131-page papal reflection on the discussions and suggestions made during the 2005 world Synod of Bishops on the Eucharist. In spring 2007, the pontiff also published his first book as pope, *Jesus of Nazareth*. On July 7, 2007, he issued the long-awaited *Motu Proprio Summorum Pontificum*, on the "Roman liturgy prior to the reform of 1970."

POPE JOHN PAUL II, 1978-2005

Cardinal Karol Wojtyla of Cracow was elected Bishop of Rome and 263rd successor of St. Peter as Supreme Pastor of the Universal Church on Oct. 16, 1978. He chose the name John Paul II in honor of his predecessor, Pope John Paul I, as well as Popes Bl. John XXIII and Paul VI. He was invested with the pallium, symbol of his office, on Oct. 22 in ceremonies attended by more than 250,000 people in St. Peter's Square. He died on Apr. 2, 2005, at 9:37 p.m. in the Apostolic Palace in the Vatican.

From the start, Pope John Paul II labored to keep the Church faithful to its tradition and to the teaching and spirit of Vatican Council II, while positioning it to meet the challenges of the Third Millennium. He was a staunch defender of the sanctity of human life — "from conception to natural death," he often said — and of marriage and the family. Opposition to totalitarianism and support for human rights make this activist, long-reigning pope a major figure on the world political scene.

He was the first non-Italian pope since Adrian VI (1522-23) and the first Polish pope ever. At his election, he was the youngest pope since Pius IX (1846-78). On May 24, 1998, he became the longest-reigning pope elected in the 20th century, surpassing the 19 years, seven months, and seven days of Pius XII (1939-58). (Leo XIII, who died in 1903, was pope for 25 years.) John Paul II's pontificate was also the third longest in the history of the Church. He surpassed Pope Leo XIII (25 years, 5 months), and is behind only Bl. Pius IX (31 years, 7 months, 21 days) and St. Peter (precise dates unknown).

He was the most-traveled pope in history. He covered over

750,000 miles during 104 pastoral visits outside Italy, over 146 within Italy, and 301 to the parishes of Rome. In all, he visited 129 countries and held talks with 1,022 heads of state or government. By the end of his pontificate, the Holy See had diplomatic relations with 174 states, as well as diplomatic relations with the European Union and Sovereign Military Order of Malta, and special relations with the Russian Federation and the PLO.

Certainly he was the pope most prolific in literary output, having issued 14 encyclicals, 14 apostolic exhortations, 11 apostolic constitutions, 45 apostolic letters and 30 *motu proprio*.

John Paul II proclaimed 1,338 Blesseds in 147 ceremonies and had proclaimed 482 Saints in 51 liturgical celebrations; his 17 predecessors from Pope Clement VIII to Pope Paul VI canonized a total of 302 people. He held nine consistories for the creation of cardinals and named a total of 231 cardinals (not including the *in pectore* cardinal. The last consistory was Oct. 2003. The Holy Father presided at 15 synods: the Particular Synod of Bishops of the Netherlands in 1980; six ordinary synods (1980, 1983, 1987, 1990, 1994 and 2001); one extraordinary (1985) and eight special (1980, 1991, 1994, 1995, 1997, two in 1998, and the second synod for Europe in Oct. 1999).

Over the years the pope held over 1,161 weekly general audiences and has welcomed over 17 million faithful from every part of the world. Other audiences, including various groups and heads of state and government, total around 1,600. As pontiff, he consecrated 321 bishops and performed over 1,500 baptisms.

He was also the first pope ever to visit a synagogue

(Rome, Apr. 1986); the first to visit a mosque (Omayyad Great Mosque of Damascus, May 2001); the first to call for a Day of Pardon (Jubilee Year 2000); and the first to add five new mysteries to the Rosary (Oct. 2002).

Early Life

Karol Josef Wojtyla was born May 18, 1920, in Wadowice, an industrial town near Cracow. His parents were Karol Wojtyla, who had been an adminstrative officer in the Austrian army and was a lieutenant in the Polish army until his retirement in 1927, and Emilia Kaczorowska Wojtyla. His mother died in 1929 of kidney and heart failure. His sister died a few days after birth; his older brother Edmund, a physician, died in 1932, and his father in 1941.

He attended schools in Wadowice and in 1938 enrolled in the faculty of philosophy of the Jagiellonian University in Cracow, where he moved with his father. At the university he was active in the Studio 38 experimental theater group.

For young Wojtyla, as for countless others, life changed forever on Sept. 1, 1939, when World War II began. Nazi occupation forces closed the Jagiellonian University and the young man had to work in a quarry as a stone cutter and later in a chemical plant to avoid deportation to Germany. In Feb. 1940, he met Jan Tryanowski, a tailor who became his spiritual mentor and introduced him to the writings of St. John of the Cross and St. Teresa of Ávila. He also participated in underground theater groups, including the Rhapsodic Theater of Mieczyslaw Kotlarczyk.

In Oct. 1942, he began studies for the priesthood in the underground seminary maintained by Cardinal Adam Sapieha of Cracow. He was struck by an automobile Feb. 29, 1944, and hospitalized until Mar. 12. In Aug. of that year Cardinal Sapieha transferred him and the other seminarians to the Archbishop's Residence, where they lived and studied until war's end. Ordained a priest by the Cardinal on Nov. 1, 1946, he left Poland Nov. 15 to begin advanced studies in Rome at the Angelicum University (the Pontifical University of St. Thomas Aquinas).

He subsequently earned doctorates in theology and philosophy and was a respected moral theologian and ethicist.

Bishop and Cardinal

On July 4, 1958, Pope Pius XII named him auxiliary bishop to Archbishop Eugeniusz Baziak, Apostolic Administrator of Cracow. His book *Love and Responsibility* was published in 1960. (Earlier, he had published poetry and several plays.) Following Archbishop Baziak's death in 1962, he became Vicar Capitular and then on Jan. 13, 1964, Archbishop of Cracow — the first residential head of the See permitted by the communist authorities since Cardinal Sapieha's death in 1951.

Archbishop Wojtyla attended all four sessions of the Second Vatican Council, from 1962 to 1965, and helped draft Schema XIII, which became *Gaudium et Spes*, the Pastoral Constitution on the Church in the Modern World. He also contributed to *Dignitatis Humanae* (the "Declaration on Religious Freedom") and on the theology of the laity.

Pope Paul VI created him a cardinal in the consistory of

June 26, 1967, with the titular Roman church of S. Cesario in Palatio. Although scheduled to attend the first general assembly of the Synod of Bishops in Sept. and Oct. of that year, Cardinal Wojtyla did not go, as a sign of solidarity with Cardinal Stefan Wyszynski of Warsaw, Poland's primate, whom the communist government refused a passport. In Oct. 1969, however, he participated in the first extraordinary assembly of the synod. Earlier that year, with approval of the statutes of the Polish bishops' conference, he became its vice president.

In 1971 he took part in the second general assembly of the synod and was elected to the council of the secretary general. He continued to participate in synod assemblies and to serve on the synod council up to his election as pope. May 8, 1972, saw the opening of the archdiocesan of synod of Cracow, which he had convened and would conclude during his visit to Poland as pope in 1979. Also in 1972 he published *Foundations of Renewal: A Study on the Implementation of the Second Vatican Council.*

Pope Paul died Aug. 6, 1978. Cardinal Wojtyla participated in the conclave that chose Cardinal Albino Luciani of Venice his successor on Aug. 26. When the new pope, who had taken the name John Paul I, died unexpectedly on Sept. 28, Cardinal Wojtyla joined 110 other cardinals in that year's second conclave. He emerged on the second day of voting, Oct. 16, as Pope John Paul II.

Pontificate

Pope John Paul set out the major themes and program of his pontificate in his first encyclical, *Redemptor Hominis* (*The Redeemer of Man*), dated Mar. 4, 1979, and published Mar. 15. "The Redeemer of Man, Jesus Christ, is the center of the universe and of history," he wrote. Throughout his pontificate he emphasized preparation for the year 2000 — which he proclaimed a Jubilee Year — and for the Third Millennium of the Christian era, with the aim of fostering a renewed commitment to evangelization among Catholics. He also has produced a significant body of magisterial teaching in such areas as Christian anthropology, sexual morality, and social justice, while working for peace and human rights throughout the world.

His pontificate was uncommonly active and filled with dramatic events. Among the most dramatic are those associated with the fall of communism in Eastern Europe. Many students of that complex event credit John Paul with a central role. His visits to his Polish homeland in 1979 (June 2-10) and 1983 (June 16-23) bolstered Polish Catholicism and kindled Polish resistance to communism, while his determined support for the Solidarity labor movement gave his countrymen a vehicle for their resistance. The result was a growing nonviolent liberation movement leading to the dramatic developments of 1989 — the collapse of communist regimes, the emergence of democracy in Poland and other countries, the fall of the Berlin Wall, and, in time, to the breakup of the Soviet Union and the end of the Cold War.

Dramatic in a much different way was the 1981 attempt on the Pope's life. At 5:19 p.m. on May 13, as he greeted crowds in St. Peter's Square before his Wednesday general audience, a Turkish terrorist named Mehmet Ali Agca shot John Paul at close range.

Whether the assassin acted alone or at the behest of others — and which others — remain unanswered questions. Following a six-hour operation, John Paul was hospitalized for 77 days at Gemelli Hospital. He visited Ali Agca in the Rebibbia prison on Dec. 27, 1983.

Although he resumed his activities vigorously after his recuperation, the pope's health and strength declined over the years. In July 1992, he had colon surgery for the removal of a non-cancerous tumor; in Nov. 1993, his shoulder was dislocated in a fall; he suffered a broken femur in another fall in Apr. 1994; and in Oct. 1996, he had an appendectomy. For several years the effects were apparent of what the Vatican acknowledged to be a neurological condition (Parkinson's disease).

Foreign Pastoral Visits

As noted, his pastoral visits were a striking feature of his pontificate. Many were to nations in the Third World. His 104 trips outside Italy were as follows:

1979 Dominican Republic and Mexico, Jan. 5-Feb. 1; Poland, June 2-10; Ireland and the United States, Sept. 29-Oct. 7; Turkey, Nov. 28-30.

1980 Africa (Zaire, Congo Republic, Kenya, Ghana, Upper Volta, Ivory Coast), May 2-12; France, May 30-June 2; Brazil (13 cities), June 30-July 12; West Germany, Nov. 15-19.

1981 Philippines, Guam, and Japan, with stopovers in Pakistan and Alaska, Feb. 16-27.

1982 Africa (Nigeria, Benin, Gabon, Equatorial Guinea), Feb. 12-19; Portugal, May 12-15; Great Britain, May 28-June 2; Argentina, June 11-12; Switzerland, June 15; San Marino, Aug. 29; Spain, Oct. 31-Nov. 9.

1983 Central America (Costa Rica, Nicaragua, Panama, El Salvador, Guatemala, Belize, Honduras) and Haiti, Mar. 2-10; Poland, June 16-23; Lourdes, France, Aug. 14-15; Austria, Sept. 10-13.

1984 South Korea, Papua New Guinea, Solomon Islands, Thailand, May 12; Switzerland, June 12-17; Canada, Sept. 9-20; Spain, Dominican Republic, and Puerto Rico, Oct. 10-12.

1985 Venezuela, Ecuador, Peru, Trinidad and Tobago, Jan. 26-Feb. 6; Belgium, the Netherlands, and Luxembourg, May 11-21; Africa (Togo, Ivory Coast, Cameroon, Central African Republic, Zaire, Kenya, and Morocco), Aug. 8-19; Liechtenstein, Sept. 8.

1986 India, Feb. 1-10; Colombia and Saint Lucia, July 1-7; France, Oct. 4-7; Oceania (Australia, New Zealand, Bangladesh, Fiji, Singapore, and Seychelles), Nov. 18-Dec. 1.

1987 Uruguay, Chile, and Argentina, Mar. 31-Apr. 12; West Germany, Apr. 30-May 4; Poland, June 8-14; the United States and Canada, Sept. 10-19.

1988 Uruguay, Bolivia, Peru, and Paraguay, May 7-18; Austria, June 23-27; Africa (Zimbabwe, Botswana, Lesotho, Swaziland, and Mozambique), Sept. 10-19; France, Oct. 8-11.

1989 Madagascar, Reunion, Zambia, and Malawi, Apr. 28-May 6; Norway, Iceland, Finland, Denmark, and Sweden, June 1-10; Spain, Aug. 19-21; South Korea, Indonesia, East Timor, and Mauritius, Oct. 6-16.

1990 Africa (Cape Verde, Guinea Bissau, Mali, and Burkna Faso), Jan. 25-Feb. 1; Czechoslovakia, Apr. 21-22; Mexico and Curaçao, May 6-13; Malta, May 25-27; Africa (Tanzania, Burundi, Rwanda, and Ivory Coast), Sept. 1-10.

1991 Portugal, May 10-13; Poland, June 1-9; Poland and Hungary, Aug. 13-20; Brazil, Oct. 12-21.

1992 Africa (Senegal, the Gambia, Guinea), Feb. 10-26; Africa (Angola, São Tome, and Principe), June 4-10; Dominican Republic, Oct. 10-14.

1993 Africa (Benin, Uganda, Sudan), Feb. 2-10; Albania, Apr. 25; Spain, June 12-17; Jamaica, Mexico, Denver (United States), Aug. 9-15; Lithuania, Latvia, Estonia, Sept. 4-10.

1994 Zagreb, Croatia, Sept. 10.

1995 Philippines, Papua New Guinea, Australia, Sri Lanka, Jan. 12-21; Czech Republic and Poland, May 20-22; Belgium, June 3-4; Slovakia, June 30-July 3; Africa (Cameroon, South Africa, Kenya), Sept. 14-20; United Nations and United States, Oct. 4-8.

1996 Central America (Guatemala, Nicaragua, El Salvador), Feb. 5-11; Tunisia, Apr. 17; Slovenia, May 17-19; Germany, June 21-23; Hungary, Sept. 6-7; France, Sept. 19-22.

1997 Sarajevo, Apr. 12-13; Czech Republic, Apr. 25-27; Lebanon, May 10-11; Poland, May 31-June 10; France, Aug. 21-24; Brazil, Oct. 2-5.

1998 Cuba, Jan. 21-25; Nigeria, Mar. 21-23; Austria, June 19-21; Croatia, Oct. 3-4.

1999 Mexico, Jan. 22-25; St. Louis, United States, Jan. 26-27; Romania, May 2-5; Poland June, 5-17; Slovenia, Sept. 19; India, Nov. 6-7; Georgia, Nov. 8-9.

2000 Egypt and Mount Sinai, Feb. 24-26; Holy Land, Mar. 20-26; Fátima, May 12-13.

2001 Greece, Syria, and Malta, May 4-9; Ukraine, June 23-27; Kazakhstan and Armenia, Sept. 22-27.

2002 Azerbaijan and Bulgaria, May 22-26; Toronto, Canada, July 23-28; Guatemala City, July 29-30; Mexico City, July 31-Aug. 2; Poland, Aug. 16-19.

2003 Spain, May 3-4; Croatia, June 5-9; Bosnia-Herzegovina, June 22; Slovak Republic, Sept. 11-14.

2004 Switzerland, May 5-6; Lourdes, France, Aug. 15-16.

Encyclicals and Other Writings

As noted above, Pope John Paul's first encyclical, *Redemptor Hominis* (1979), set the tone for and in general terms indicated the subject matter of many of the documents to follow. These were infused with the pope's distinctive personalism, which emphasizes the dignity and rights of the human person, most truly understood in the light of Christ, as the norm and goal of human endeavor.

His other encyclical letters were: *Dives in Misericordia* ("On the Mercy of God"), 1980; *Laborem Exercens* ("On Human Work"), 1981; *Slavorum Apostoli* ("The Apostles of the Slavs," honoring Sts. Cyril and Methodius), 1985; *Dominum et Vivificantem* ("Lord and Giver of Life," on the Holy Spirit), 1986; *Redemptoris Mater* ("Mother of the Redeemer"), 1987; *Sollicitudo Rei Socialis* ("On Social Concerns"), 1988; *Redemptoris Missio* ("Mission of the Redeemer") and *Centesimus Annus* ("The Hundredth Year," on the anniversary of Leo XIII's *Rerum Novarum*), both 1991; *Veritatis Splendor* ("The Splendor of Truth"), 1993; *Evangelium Vitae*

("The Gospel of Life") and *Ut Unum Sint* ("That All May Be One"), 1995; *Fides et Ratio* ("Faith and Reason"), 1998; and *Ecclesia de Eucharistia* ("Church of the Eucharist"), 2003.

Among his other publications were: *Catechesi Tradendae*, a post-synodal apostolic exhortation on catechesis, 1979; apostolic letter proclaiming Sts. Cyril and Methodius, together with St. Benedict, patrons of Europe, 1980; post-synodal apostolic exhortation *Familiaris Consortio*, on the family, 1981; apostolic letter *Caritatis Christi*, for the Church in China, 1982; letter for the 500th anniversary of the birth of Martin Luther, 1983; apostolic letter *Salvifici Doloris* ("On the Christian Meaning of Suffering"), apostolic exhortation *Redemptionis Donum*, to men and women religious, apostolic letters *Redemptionis Anno*, on Jerusalem, and *Les Grands Mysteres*, on Lebanon, and post-synodal apostolic exhortation *Reconciliatio et Poenitentia* ("Reconciliation and Penance"), all 1984.

Also: apostolic letter *Dilecti Amici*, on the occasion of the United Nations' International Year of Youth, 1985; apostolic letter *Euntes in Mundum*, for the millennium of Christianity in Kievan Rus', and apostolic letter *Mulieris Dignitatem* ("On the Dignity and Vocation of Women"), all 1988; post-synodal apostolic exhortation *Christifideles Laici* ("The Lay Members of Christ's Faithful People") and apostolic exhortation *Redemptoris Custos* ("On St. Joseph"), 1989; post-synodal apostolic exhortation *Pastores Dabo Vobis* ("I Give You Shepherds"), 1992; "Letter to Families," for the International Year of the Family, "Letter on the International Conference on Population and Development" in Cairo, apostolic letter *Ordinatio Sacerdotalis* ("On Reserving Priestly Ordination to Men Alone"), apostolic letter *Tertio Millennio Adveniente*, on preparation for the Jubilee Year 2000, and "Letter to Children in the Year of the Family," all 1994.

Also: apostolic letter *Orientale Lumen* ("The Light of the East"), on Catholic-Orthodox relations, "Letter to Women," post-synodal apostolic exhortations *Ecclesia in Africa*, *Ecclesia in Asia*, and *Ecclesia in Europa*, and apostolic letter for the fourth centenary of the Union of Brest, all 1995; apostolic constitution *Universi Dominici Gregis* ("On the Vacancy of the Apostolic See and the Election of the Roman Pontiff"), post-synodal apostolic exhortation *Vita Consecrata* ("On the Consecrated Life and Its Mission in the Church and in the World"), and apostolic letter on the 350th anniversary of the Union of Uzhorod, all 1996; post-synodal apostolic exhortation, "A New Hope for Lebanon," 1997; *Incarnationis Mysterium*, Bull of Indiction of the Great Jubilee of the Year 2000, 1998; and the apostolic letter *Misericordia Dei* ("On Certain Aspects of the Celebration of the Sacrament of Penance"), 2002.

In his years as pope he published several books, including Crossing the Threshold of Hope (1994), Gift and Mystery: On the Fiftieth Anniversary of My Priestly Ordination (1996), and Alzatevi, Andiamo (Get Up, Let Us Go, 2004), on the pontiff's 20 years as a bishop in Poland.

Issues and Activities

Doctrinal Concerns: The integrity of Catholic doctrine was a major concern of Pope John Paul. On Nov. 25, 1981, he appointed Archbishop — later, Cardinal and Pope Benedict XVI — Joseph Ratzinger of Munich-Freising, a prominent theologian, Prefect of the Congregation for the Doctrine of the Faith. The congregation under Cardinal Ratzinger has published important documents on bioethics, liberation theology (1984 and 1986), the Church's inability to ordain women as priests, the latter affirming that the teaching on this matter has been "set forth infallibly" (1995), and same-sex unions (2003).

Catechism: One of Pope John Paul's most important initiatives was the *Catechism of the Catholic Church*. The idea for this up-to-date compendium was broached at the extraordinary assembly of the Synod of Bishops held in 1985 to evaluate the implementation of Vatican Council II. The pope approved, and the project went forward under a commission of cardinals headed by Cardinal Ratzinger. Published in 1992 by authorization of John Paul II (the original was in French, with the English translation appearing in 1994 and the authoritative Latin *editio typica* in 1997), this first catechism for the universal Church in four centuries is crucial to the hoped-for renewal of catechesis.

Canon Law: John Paul oversaw the completion of the revision of the Code of Canon Law begun in 1959 at the direction of Pope John XXIII. He promulgated the new code on Jan. 25, 1983; it went into effect on Nov. 27 of that year. In *Sacrae Disciplinae Leges*, the apostolic constitution accompanying the revised code, the pope says it has "one and the same intention" as Vatican Council II — whose convening John XXIII announced at the same time — namely, "the renewal of Christian living."

On Apr. 18, 1990, John Paul promulgated the Code of Canons for the Eastern Churches. Although particular sections of the Eastern code appeared at various times dating back to 1949, this was the first time an integrated code of law for the Eastern Churches had been issued in its entirety.

Ecumenical and Interreligious Relations: Ecumenical and interreligious relations received much attention from Pope John Paul II. Two of his major documents, the encyclical *Ut Unum Sint* and the apostolic letter *Orientale Lumen*, both published in 1995, deal with these matters. He met frequently with representatives of other religious bodies, spoke frequently about the quest for unity, and has called for Catholics and others to pray and work to this end.

Among the important actions in this area were the signings of common declarations with the Ecumenical Patriarch of Constantinople His Holiness Dimitrios (Dec. 7, 1987) and his successor Bartholomew I (June 29, 1995), with the Archbishop of Canterbury and Primate of the Anglican Communion, Dr. Robert Runcie (May 29, 1982, in Canterbury Cathedral and again Oct. 2, 1989, in Rome) and his successor Dr. George Leonard Carey (Dec. 6, 1996), with the Supreme Patriarch and Catholicos of All Armenians, His Holiness Karekin I (Dec. 14, 1996), and with His Holiness Aram I Keshishian, Catholicos of Cilicia of the Armenians (Jan. 26, 1997). On Oct. 5, 1991, for the first time since the Reformation, two Lutheran bishops joined the pope and the Catholic bishops of Stockholm and Helsinki in an ecumenical prayer service in St. Peter's Basilica marking the sixth centenary of the canonization of St. Bridget of Sweden.

Pope John Paul II had Jewish friends since boyhood, and he worked hard to strengthen Catholic-Jewish ties. The Holy See formally initiated diplomatic relations with the State of Israel at the level of apostolic nunciature and embassy on June 15, 1994. In Mar. 1998, the

Commission for Religious Relations with the Jews published an important document on the roots of the World War II Jewish Holocaust entitled *We Remember: A Reflection on the Shoah.* In a letter dated Mar. 12 to the commission chairman, Cardinal Edward Idris Cassidy, the Pope expressed "fervent hope" that it would "help to heal the wounds of past misunderstandings and injustices."

On Sunday, Mar. 12, 2000, Pope John Paul II presided over a day of pardon for those sins committed by members of the Church over the centuries. The Holy Father issued a formal apology for the misdeeds of the members of the Church in the past, including a renewed apology for all anti-Semitic actions by Catholics. This apology was given even greater depth by the Holy Father's trip to the Holy Land in Mar. 2000. During his historic visit to Israel, the pope placed a written apology to the Jewish people in the Wailing Wall in Jerusalem. He made further efforts at ecumenical dialogue with the Orthodox Churches during his visits to Greece, Syria, and Ukraine in 2001 and at the Day of Prayer for Peace at Assisi in Jan. 2002.

Women's Concerns: Pope John Paul's insistence that, in fidelity to the will of Christ, the Church is unable to ordain women as priests put him at odds with some feminists, as did his opposition to abortion and contraception. But it is clear from his writings that he was unusually sensitive to women's issues, and he was a strong defender of women's dignity and rights, about which he often had spoken. In 1995 he appointed a woman, Professor Mary Ann Glendon of the Harvard University Law School, head of the Holy See's delegation to the fourth U.N. conference on women, held in Beijing Sept. 4-15, the first time a woman had been named to such a post.

World Affairs: At least since Jan. 1979, when he accepted a request for mediation in a border conflict between Argentina and Chile, John Paul II worked for peace in many parts of the world. He supported efforts to achieve reconciliation between conflicting parties in troubled areas like Lebanon, the Balkans, and the Persian Gulf, where he sought to avert the Gulf War of 1991. He advocated religious liberty and human rights during pastoral visits to many countries, including Cuba and Nigeria in 1998. Among the notable ecumenical and interreligious events of the pontificate was the World Day of Prayer for Peace on Oct. 27, 1986, which he convoked in Assisi and attended along with representatives of numerous other churches and religious groups.

In 1984 the Holy See and the U.S. established diplomatic relations. (The pope has met with Presidents Jimmy Carter, Ronald Reagan, George Bush, Bill Clinton, and George W. Bush.) Relations with Poland were re-established in 1989. Diplomatic relations were established with the Soviet Union in 1990 and with the Russian Federation in 1992. Relations also have been established with other Eastern European countries and countries that were part of the former Soviet Union, with Mexico, and with other nations including Jordan, South Africa, and Libya. Working contacts of a "permanent and official character" were begun with the Palestine Liberation Organization in 1994, leading to the signing of a formal Basic Agreement with the PLO on Feb. 15, 2000. The pope also attempted to prevent the outbreak of hostilities in Iraq in 2003 and welcomed the new sovereign government in 2004.

Administration: Under Pope John Paul II the long-term financial problems of the Holy See were addressed and brought under control. Finances were on the agenda at the first plenary assembly of the College of Cardinals, Nov. 5-9, 1979, and subsequent meetings of that body. A council of cardinals for the study of organizational and economic problems of the Holy See was established in 1981. In 1988, the Holy See's financial report (for 1986) was published for the first time, along with the 1988 budget. In Apr. 1991, a meeting of the presidents of episcopal conferences was held to discuss ways of increasing the Peter's Pence Collection taken in support of the Pope.

A reorganization of responsibilities of Vatican offices was carried out in 1984, and in 1988 an apostolic constitution, *Pastor Bonus,* on reform of the Roman Curia, was issued. A Vatican labor office was instituted in 1989. Pope John Paul established a new Pontifical Academy of Social Sciences in 1994 and Pontifical Academy for Life in 1995. On Apr. 8, 1994, he celebrated Mass in the Sistine Chapel for the unveiling of the Michelangelo frescoes, which had been painstakingly cleaned and restored. The opening presentation of the Holy See's Internet site took place on Mar. 24, 1997.

As Bishop of Rome, John Paul presided over a diocesan synod that concluded May 29, 1993. He also has visited numerous Roman parishes — 301 out of 328 by the time of his passing.

His death on Apr. 2, 2005, came after two months of sharp decline from an infection. He was admitted to Gemelli Clinic, where he had been taken after the assassination attempt in 1981, on Jan. 30. Though released, he never recovered fully, was re-admitted a few weeks later, and eventually needed a tracheotomy to assist his breathing. His voice never returned to normal, and his last two appearances, on Easter Sunday and at his Wednesday audience, proved heartbreaking for those in attendance as he struggled to communicate. His health collapsed completely over the next days, and he journeyed to God at 9:37 p.m. Rome time.

POPES OF THE ROMAN CATHOLIC CHURCH

Information includes the name of the pope, in many cases his name before becoming pope, his birthplace or country of origin, the date of accession to the papacy, and the date of the end of reign that, in all but a few cases, was the date of death. Double dates indicate date of election and date of solemn beginning of ministry as Pastor of the universal Church. *Source*: Annuario Pontificio.

St. Peter (Simon Bar-Jona): Bethsaida in Galilee; d. c.
64 or 67.
St. Linus: Tuscany; 67-76.
St. Anacletus (Cletus): Rome; 76-88.
St. Clement: Rome; 88-97.
St. Evaristus: Greece; 97-105.
St. Alexander I: Rome; 105-115.
St. Sixtus I: Rome; 115-125.
St. Telesphorus: Greece; 125-136.

St. Hyginus: Greece; 136-140.

St. Pius I: Aquileia; 140-155.

St. Anicetus: Syria; 155-166.

St. Soter: Campania; 166-175.

St. Eleutherius: Nicopolis in Epirus; 175-189. Up to the time of St. Eleutherius, the years indicated for the beginning and end of pontificates are not absolutely certain. Also, up to the middle of the 11th century, there are some doubts about the exact days and months given in chronological tables.

St. Victor I: Africa; 189-199.

St. Zephyrinus: Rome; 199-217.

St. Callistus I: Rome; 217-222.

St. Urban I: Rome; 222-230.

St. Pontian: Rome; July 21, 230 to Sept. 28, 235.

St. Anterus: Greece; Nov. 21, 235 to Jan. 3, 236.

St. Fabian: Rome; Jan. 10, 236 to Jan. 20, 250.

St. Cornelius: Rome; Mar. 251 to June 253.

St. Lucius I: Rome; June 25, 253 to Mar. 5, 254.

St. Stephen I: Rome; May 12, 254 to Aug. 2, 257.

St. Sixtus II: Greece; Aug. 30, 257 to Aug. 6, 258.

St. Dionysius: birthplace unknown; July 22, 259 to Dec. 26, 268.

St. Felix I: Rome; Jan. 5, 269 to Dec. 30, 274.

St. Eutychian: Luni; Jan. 4, 275 to Dec. 7, 283.

St. Caius: Dalmatia; Dec. 17, 283 to Apr. 22, 296.

St. Marcellinus: Rome; June 30, 296 to Oct. 25, 304.

St. Marcellus I: Rome; May 27, 308, or June 26, 308, to Jan. 16, 309.

St. Eusebius: Greece; Apr. 18, 309 to Aug. 17, 309 or 310.

St. Melchiades (Miltiades): Africa; July 2, 311 to Jan. 11, 314.

St. Sylvester I: Rome; Jan. 31, 314 to Dec. 31, 335. (Most popes before St. Sylvester I were martyrs.)

St. Marcus: Rome; Jan. 18, 336 to Oct. 7, 336.

St. Julius I: Rome; Feb. 6, 337 to Apr. 12, 352.

Liberius: Rome; May 17, 352 to Sept. 24, 366.

St. Damasus I: Spain; Oct. 1, 366 to Dec. 11, 384.

St. Siricius: Rome; Dec. 15, or 22 or 29, 384 to Nov. 26, 399.

St. Anastasius I: Rome; Nov. 27, 399 to Dec. 19, 401.

St. Innocent I: Albano; Dec. 22, 401 to Mar. 12, 417.

St. Zosimus: Greece; Mar. 18, 417 to Dec. 26, 418.

St. Boniface I: Rome; Dec. 28 or 29, 418 to Sept. 4, 422.

St. Celestine I: Campania; Sept. 10, 422 to July 27, 432.

St. Sixtus III: Rome; July 31, 432 to Aug. 19, 440.

St. Leo I (the Great): Tuscany; Sept. 29, 440 to Nov. 10, 461.

St. Hilary: Sardinia; Nov. 19, 461 to Feb. 29, 468.

St. Simplicius: Tivoli; Mar. 3, 468 to Mar. 10, 483.

St. Felix III (II): Rome; Mar. 13, 483 to Mar. 1, 492. He should be called Felix II, and his successors of the same name should be numbered accordingly. The discrepancy in the numerical designation of popes named Felix was caused by the erroneous insertion in some lists of the name of St. Felix of Rome, a martyr.

St. Gelasius I: Africa; Mar. 1, 492 to Nov. 21, 496.

Anastasius II: Rome; Nov. 24, 496 to Nov. 19, 498.

St. Symmachus: Sardinia; Nov. 22, 498 to July 19, 514.

St. Hormisdas: Frosinone; July 20, 514 to Aug. 6, 523.

St. John I, Martyr: Tuscany; Aug. 13, 523 to May 18, 526.

St. Felix IV (III): Samnium; July 12, 526 to Sept. 22, 530.

Boniface II: Rome; Sept. 22, 530 to Oct. 17, 532.

John II: Rome; Jan. 2, 533 to May 8, 535. John II was the first pope to change his name. His given name was Mercury.

St. Agapitus I: Rome; May 13, 535 to Apr. 22, 536.

St. Silverius, Martyr: Campania; June 1 or 8, 536 to Nov. 11, 537 (d. Dec. 2, 537). St. Silverius was violently deposed in Mar. 537, and abdicated Nov. 11, 537. His successor, Vigilius, was not recognized as pope by all the Roman clergy until his abdication.

Vigilius: Rome; Mar. 29, 537 to June 7, 555.

Pelagius I: Rome; Apr. 16, 556 to Mar. 4, 561.

John III: Rome; July 17, 561 to July 13, 574.

Benedict I: Rome; June 2, 575 to July 30, 579.

Pelagius II: Rome; Nov. 26, 579 to Feb. 7, 590.

St. Gregory I (the Great): Rome; Sept. 3, 590 to Mar. 12, 604.

Sabinian: Blera in Tuscany; Sept. 13, 604 to Feb. 22, 606.

Boniface III: Rome; Feb. 19, 607 to Nov. 12, 607.

St. Boniface IV: Abruzzi; Aug. 25, 608 to May 8, 615.

St. Deusdedit (Adeodatus I): Rome; Oct. 19, 615 to Nov. 8, 618.

Boniface V: Naples; Dec. 23, 619 to Oct. 25, 625.

Honorius I: Campania; Oct. 27, 625 to Oct. 12, 638.

Severinus: Rome; May 28, 640 to Aug. 2, 640.

John IV: Dalmatia; Dec. 24, 640 to Oct. 12, 642.

Theodore I: Greece; Nov. 24, 642 to May 14, 649.

St. Martin I, Martyr: Todi; July 649 to Sept. 16, 655 (in exile from June 17, 653).

St. Eugene I: Rome; Aug. 10, 654 to June 2, 657. St. Eugene I was elected during the exile of St. Martin I, who is believed to have endorsed him as pope.

St. Vitalian: Segni; July 30, 657 to Jan. 27, 672.

Adeodatus II: Rome; Apr. 11, 672 to June 17, 676.

Donus: Rome; Nov. 2, 676 to Apr. 11, 678.

St. Agatho: Sicily; June 27, 678 to Jan. 10, 681.

St. Leo II: Sicily; Aug. 17, 682 to July 3, 683.

St. Benedict II: Rome; June 26, 684 to May 8, 685.

John V: Syria; July 23, 685 to Aug. 2, 686.

Conon: birthplace unknown; Oct. 21, 686 to Sept. 21, 687.

St. Sergius I: Syria; Dec. 15, 687 to Sept. 8, 701.

John VI: Greece; Oct. 30, 701 to Jan. 11, 705.

John VII: Greece; Mar. 1, 705 to Oct. 18, 707.

Sisinnius: Syria; Jan. 15, 708 to Feb. 4, 708.

Constantine: Syria; Mar. 25, 708 to Apr. 9, 715.

St. Gregory II: Rome; May 19, 715 to Feb. 11, 731.

St. Gregory III: Syria; Mar. 18, 731 to Nov. 741.

St. Zachary: Greece; Dec. 10, 741 to Mar. 22, 752.

Stephen II (III): Rome; Mar. 26, 752 to Apr. 26, 757. After the death of St. Zachary, a Roman priest named Stephen was elected but died (four days later) before his consecration as bishop of Rome, which would have marked the beginning of his pontificate. Another Stephen was elected to succeed Zachary as Stephen II. (The first pope with this name was St. Stephen I, 254-57.) The ordinal III appears in parentheses after the name of Stephen II because the name of the earlier elected but deceased priest was included in some lists. Other Stephens have double numbers.

St. Paul I: Rome; Apr. (May 29) 757 to June 28, 767.

Stephen III (IV): Sicily; Aug. 1 (7), 768 to Jan. 24, 772.

Adrian I: Rome; Feb. 1 (9), 772 to Dec. 25, 795.

St. Leo III: Rome; Dec. 26 (27), 795 to June 12, 816.

Stephen IV (V): Rome; June 22, 816 to Jan. 24, 817.

St. Paschal I: Rome; Jan. 25, 817 to Feb. 11, 824.

Eugene II: Rome; Feb. (May) 824 to Aug. 827.

Valentine: Rome; Aug. 827 to Sept. 827.

Gregory IV: Rome; 827 to Jan. 844.

Sergius II: Rome; Jan. 844 to Jan. 27, 847.

St. Leo IV: Rome; Jan. (Apr. 10) 847 to July 17, 855.

Benedict III: Rome; July (Sept. 29), 855,to Apr. 17, 858.

St. Nicholas I (the Great): Rome; Apr. 24, 858 to Nov. 13, 867.

Adrian II: Rome; Dec. 14, 867 to Dec. 14, 872.

John VIII: Rome; Dec. 14, 872 to Dec. 16, 882.

Marinus I: Gallese; Dec. 16, 882 to May 15, 884.

St. Adrian III: Rome; May 17, 884 to Sept. 885. Cult confirmed June 2, 1891.

Stephen V (VI): Rome; Sept. 885 to Sept. 14, 891.

Formosus: Bishop of Porto; Oct. 6, 891 to Apr. 4, 896.

Boniface VI: Rome; Apr. 896 to Apr. 896.

Stephen VI (VII): Rome; May 896 to Aug. 897.

Romanus: Gallese; Aug. 897 to Nov. 897.

Theodore II: Rome; Dec. 897 to Dec. 897.

John IX: Tivoli; Jan. 898 to Jan. 900.

Benedict IV: Rome; Jan. (Feb.) 900 to July 903.

Leo V: Ardea; July 903 to Sept. 903.

Sergius III: Rome; Jan. 29, 904 to Apr. 14, 911.

Anastasius III: Rome; Apr. 911 to June 913.

Landus: Sabina; July 913 to Feb. 914.

John X: Tossignano (Imola); Mar. 914 to May 928.

Leo VI: Rome; May 928 to Dec. 928.

Stephen VII (VIII): Rome; Dec. 928 to Feb. 931.

John XI: Rome; Feb. (Mar.) 931 to Dec. 935.

Leo VII: Rome; Jan. 3, 936 to July 13, 939.

Stephen VIII (IX): Rome; July 14, 939 to Oct. 942.

Marinus II: Rome; Oct. 30, 942 to May 946.

Agapitus II: Rome; May 10, 946 to Dec. 955.

John XII (Octavius): Tusculum; Dec. 16, 955 to May 14, 964 (date of his death).

Leo VIII: Rome; Dec. 4 (6), 963 to Mar. 1, 965.

Benedict V: Rome; May 22, 964 to July 4, 966. Confusion exists concerning the legitimacy of claims to the pontificate by Leo VIII and Benedict V. John XII was deposed Dec. 4, 963, by a Roman council. If this deposition was invalid, Leo was an antipope. If the deposition of John was valid, Leo was the legitimate pope and Benedict was an antipope.

John XIII: Rome; Oct. 1, 965 to Sept. 6, 972.

Benedict VI: Rome; Jan. 19, 973 to June 974.

Benedict VII: Rome; Oct. 974 to July 10, 983.

John XIV (Peter Campenora): Pavia; Dec. 983 to Aug. 20, 984.

John XV: Rome; Aug. 985 to Mar. 996.

Gregory V (Bruno of Carinthia): Saxony; May 3, 996, to Feb. 18, 999.

Sylvester II (Gerbert): Auvergne; Apr. 2, 999 to May 12, 1003.

John XVII (Siccone): Rome; June 1003 to Dec. 1003.

John XVIII (Phasianus): Rome; Jan. 1004 to July 1009.

Sergius IV (Peter): Rome; July 31, 1009 to May 12, 1012. The custom of changing one's name on election to the papacy is generally considered to date from the time of Sergius IV. Before his time, sever-

al popes had changed their names. After his time, it became a regular practice, with few exceptions, e.g., Adrian VI and Marcellus II.

Benedict VIII (Theophylactus): Tusculum; May 18, 1012 to Apr. 9, 1024.

John XIX (Romanus): Tusculum; Apr. (May) 1024 to 1032.

Benedict IX (Theophylactus): Tusculum; 1032 to 1044.

Sylvester III (John): Rome; Jan. 20, 1045 to Feb. 10, 1045.

Sylvester III was an antipope if the forcible removal of Benedict IX in 1044 was not legitimate.

Benedict IX (second time): Apr. 10, 1045 to May 1, 1045.

Gregory VI (John Gratian): Rome; May 5, 1045 to Dec. 20, 1046.

Clement II (Suitger, Lord of Morsleben and Hornburg): Saxony; Dec. 24 (25), 1046 to Oct. 9, 1047. If the resignation of Benedict IX in 1045 and his removal at the Dec. 1046, synod were not legitimate, Gregory VI and Clement II were antipopes.

Benedict IX (third time): Nov. 8, 1047 to July 17, 1048 (d. c. 1055).

Damasus II (Poppo): Bavaria; July 17, 1048 to Aug. 9, 1048.

St. Leo IX (Bruno): Alsace; Feb. 12, 1049 to Apr. 19, 1054.

Victor II (Gebhard): Swabia; Apr. 16, 1055 to July 28, 1057.

Stephen IX (X) (Frederick): Lorraine; Aug. 3, 1057 to Mar. 29, 1058.

Nicholas II (Gerard): Burgundy; Jan. 24, 1059 to July 27, 1061.

Alexander II (Anselmo da Baggio): Milan; Oct. 1, 1061 to Apr. 21, 1073.

St. Gregory VII (Hildebrand): Tuscany; Apr. 22 (June 30), 1073 to May 25, 1085.

Bl. Victor III (Dauferius; Desiderius): Benevento; May 24, 1086 to Sept. 16, 1087. Cult confirmed July 23, 1887.

Bl. Urban II (Otto di Lagery): France; Mar. 12, 1088, to July 29, 1099. Cult confirmed July 14, 1881.

Paschal II (Raniero): Ravenna; Aug. 13 (14), 1099 to Jan. 21, 1118.

Gelasius II (Giovanni Caetani): Gaeta; Jan. 24 (Mar. 10), 1118 to Jan. 28, 1119.

Callistus II (Guido of Burgundy): Burgundy; Feb. 2 (9), 1119 to Dec. 13, 1124.

Honorius II (Lamberto): Fiagnano (Imola); Dec. 15 (21), 1124 to Feb. 13, 1130.

Innocent II (Gregorio Papareschi): Rome; Feb. 14 (23), 1130 to Sept. 24, 1143.

Celestine II (Guido): Citta di Castello; Sept. 26 (Oct. 3), 1143 to Mar. 8, 1144.

Lucius II (Gerardo Caccianemici): Bologna: Mar. 12, 1144 to Feb. 15, 1145.

Bl. Eugene III (Bernardo Paganelli di Montemagno): Pisa; Feb. 15 (18), 1145 to July 8, 1153. Cult confirmed Oct. 3, 1872.

Anastasius IV (Corrado): Rome; July 12, 1153 to Dec, 3, 1154.

Adrian IV (Nicholas Breakspear): England; Dec. 4 (5), 1154 to Sept. 1, 1159.

Alexander III (Rolando Bandinelli): Siena; Sept. 7 (20), 1159 to Aug. 30, 1181.

Lucius III (Ubaldo Allucingoli): Lucca; Sept. 1 (6), 1181 to Sept. 25, 1185.

Urban III (Uberto Crivelli): Milan; Nov. 25 (Dec. 1), 1185 to Oct. 20, 1187.

Gregory VIII (Alberto de Morra): Benevento; Oct. 21 (25), 1187 to Dec. 17, 1187.

Clement III (Paolo Scolari): Rome; Dec. 19 (20), 1187 to Mar. 1191.

Celestine III (Giacinto Bobone): Rome; Mar. 30 (Apr. 14), 1191 to Jan. 8, 1198.

Innocent III (Lotario dei Conti di Segni); Anagni; Jan. 8 (Feb. 22), 1198 to July 16, 1216.

Honorius III (Cencio Savelli): Rome; July 18 (24), 1216 to Mar. 18, 1227.

Gregory IX (Ugolino, Count of Segni): Anagni; Mar. 19 (21), 1227 to Aug. 22, 1241.

Celestine IV (Goffredo Castiglioni): Milan; Oct. 25 (28), 1241 to Nov. 10, 1241.

Innocent IV (Sinibaldo Fieschi): Genoa; June 25 (28), 1243 to Dec. 7, 1254.

Alexander IV (Rinaldo, House of Ienne): Ienne (Rome); Dec. 12 (20), 1254 to May 25, 1261.

Urban IV (Jacques Pantal,on): Troyes; Aug. 29 (Sept. 4), 1261 to Oct. 2, 1264.

Clement IV (Guy Foulques or Guido le Gros): France; Feb. 5 (15), 1265 to Nov. 29, 1268.

Bl. Gregory X (Teobaldo Visconti): Piacenza; Sept. 1, 1271 (Mar. 27, 1272) to Jan. 10, 1276. Cult confirmed Sept. 12, 1713.

Bl. Innocent V (Peter of Tarentaise): Savoy; Jan. 21 (Feb. 22), 1276 to June 22, 1276. Cult confirmed Mar. 13, 1898.

Adrian V (Ottobono Fieschi): Genoa: July 11, 1276 to Aug. 18, 1276.

John XXI (Petrus Juliani or Petrus Hispanus): Portugal; Sept. 8 (20), 1276 to May 20, 1277. There is confusion in the numerical designation of popes named John. The error dates back to the time of John XV.

Nicholas III (Giovanni Gaetano Orsini): Rome; Nov. 25 (Dec. 26), 1277 to Aug. 22, 1280.

Martin IV (Simon de Brie): France; Feb. 22 (Mar. 23), 1281 to Mar. 28, 1285. The names of Marinus 1 (882-84) and Marinus II (942-46) were construed as Martin. In view of these two pontificates and the earlier reign of St. Martin I (649-55), this pope was called Martin IV.

Honorius IV (Giacomo Savelli): Rome; Apr. 2 (May 20), 1285 to Apr. 3, 1287.

Nicholas IV (Girolamo Masci): Ascoli; Feb. 22, 1288, to Apr. 4, 1292.

St. Celestine V (Pietro del Murrone): Isernia; July 5 (Aug. 29), 1294 to Dec. 13, 1294; d. May 19, 1296. Canonized May 5, 1313.

Boniface VIII (Benedetto Caetani): Anagni; Dec. 24, 1294 (Jan. 23, 1295) to Oct. 11, 1303.

Bl. Benedict XI (Niccolo Boccasini): Treviso; Oct. 22 (27), 1303 to July 7, 1304. Cult confirmed Apr. 24, l736.

Clement V (Bertrand de Got): France; June 5 (Nov. 14), 1305 to Apr. 20, 1314. First of Avignon popes.

John XXII (Jacques d'Euse): Cahors; Aug. 7 (Sept. 5), 1316 to Dec. 4, 1334.

Benedict XII (Jacques Fournier): France; Dec. 20, 1334 (Jan. 8, 1335) to Apr. 25, 1342.

Clement VI (Pierre Roger): France; May 7 (19), 1342,

to Dec. 6, 1352.

Innocent VI (Etienne Aubert): France; Dec. 18 (30), 1352 to Sept. 12, 1362.

Bl. Urban V (Guillaume de Grimoard): France; Sept. 28 (Nov. 6), 1362 to Dec. 19, 1370. Cult confirmed Mar. 10, 1870.

Gregory XI (Pierre Roger de Beaufort): France; Dec. 30, 1370 (Jan. 5, 1371) to Mar. 26, 1378. Last of Avignon popes.

Urban VI (Bartolomeo Prignano): Naples; Apr. 8 (18), 1378 to Oct. 15, 1389.

Boniface IX (Pietro Tomacelli): Naples; Nov. 2 (9), 1389 to Oct. 1, 1404.

Innocent VII (Cosma Migliorati): Sulmona; Oct. 17 (Nov. 11), 1404 to Nov. 6, 1406.

Gregory XII (Angelo Correr): Venice; Nov. 30 (Dec. 19), 1406 to July 4, 1415, when he voluntarily resigned from the papacy to permit the election of his successor. He died Oct. 18, 1417. (*See* **Western Schism**.)

Martin V (Oddone Colonna): Rome; Nov. 11 (21), 1417 to Feb. 20, 1431.

Eugene IV (Gabriele Condulmer): Venice; Mar. 3 (11), 1431 to Feb. 23, 1447.

Nicholas V (Tommaso Parentucelli): Sarzana; Mar. 6 (19), 1447 to Mar. 24, 1455.

Callistus III (Alfonso Borgia): Jativa (Valencia); Apr. 8 (20), 1455 to Aug. 6, 1458.

Pius II (Enea Silvio Piccolomini): Siena; Aug. 19 (Sept. 3), 1458 to Aug. 14, 1464.

Paul II (Pietro Barbo): Venice; Aug. 30 (Sept. 16), 1464 to July 26, 1471.

Sixtus IV (Francesco della Rovere): Savona; Aug. 9 (25), 1471 to Aug. 12, 1484.

Innocent VIII (Giovanni Battista Cibo): Genoa; Aug. 29 (Sept. 12), 1484 to July 25, 1492.

Alexander VI (Rodrigo Borgia): Jativa (Valencia); Aug. 11 (26), 1492 to Aug. 18, 1503.

Pius III (Francesco Todeschini-Piccolomini): Siena; Sept. 22 (Oct. 1, 8), 1503 to Oct. 18, 1503.

Julius II (Giuliano della Rovere): Savona; Oct. 31 (Nov. 26), 1503 to Feb. 21, 1513.

Leo X (Giovanni de' Medici): Florence; Mar. 9 (19), 1513 to Dec. 1, 1521.

Adrian VI (Adrian Florensz): Utrecht; Jan. 9 (Aug. 31), 1522 to Sept. 14, 1523.

Clement VII (Giulio de' Medici): Florence; Nov. 19 (26), 1523 to Sept. 25, 1534.

Paul III (Alessandro Farnese): Rome; Oct. 13 (Nov. 3), 1534 to Nov. 10, 1549.

Julius III (Giovanni Maria Ciocchi del Monte): Rome; Feb. 7 (22), 1550 to Mar. 23, 1555.

Marcellus II (Marcello Cervini): Montepulciano; Apr. 9 (10), 1555 to May 1, 1555.

Paul IV (Gian Pietro Carafa): Naples; May 23 (26), 1555 to Aug. 18, 1559.

Pius IV (Giovan Angelo de' Medici): Milan; Dec. 25, 1559 (Jan. 6, 1560) to Dec. 9, 1565.

St. Pius V (Antonio-Michele Ghislieri): Bosco (Alexandria); Jan. 7 (17), 1566 to May 1, 1572. Canonized May 22, 1712.

Gregory XIII (Ugo Buoncompagni): Bologna; May 13 (25), 1572 to Apr. 10, 1585.

Sixtus V (Felice Peretti): Grottammare (Ripa-transone); Apr. 24 (May 1), 1585 to Aug. 27, 1590.

Urban VII (Giambattista Castagna): Rome; Sept. 15,

1590 to Sept. 27, 1590.

Gregory XIV (Niccolo Sfondrati): Cremona; Dec. 5 (8), 1590 to Oct. 16, 1591.

Innocent IX (Giovanni Antonio Facchinetti): Bologna; Oct. 29 (Nov. 3), 1591 to Dec. 30, 1591.

Clement VIII (Ippolito Aldobrandini): Florence; Jan. 30 (Feb. 9), 1592 to Mar. 3, 1605.

Leo XI (Alessandro de' Medici): Florence; Apr. 1 (10), 1605 to Apr. 27, 1605.

Paul V (Camillo Borghese): Rome; May 16 (29), 1605, to Jan. 28, 1621.

Gregory XV (Alessandro Ludovisi): Bologna; Feb. 9 (14), 1621 to July 8, 1623.

Urban VIII (Maffeo Barberini): Florence; Aug. 6 (Sept. 29), 1623 to July 29, 1644.

Innocent X (Giovanni Battista Pamfili): Rome; Sept. 15 (Oct. 4), 1644 to Jan. 7, 1655.

Alexander VII (Fabio Chigi): Siena; Apr. 7 (18), 1655, to May 22, 1667.

Clement IX (Giulio Rospigliosi): Pistoia; June 20 (26), 1667 to Dec. 9, 1669.

Clement X (Emilio Altieri): Rome; Apr. 29 (May 11), 1670 to July 22, 1676.

Bl. Innocent XI (Benedetto Odescalchi): Como; Sept. 21 (Oct. 4), 1676 to Aug. 12, 1689. Beatified Oct. 7, 1956.

Alexander VIII (Pietro Ottoboni): Venice; Oct. 6 (16), 1689 to Feb. 1, 1691.

Innocent XII (Antonio Pignatelli): Spinazzola (Venosa); July 12 (15), 1691 to Sept. 27, 1700.

Clement XI (Giovanni Francesco Albani): Urbino; Nov. 23, 30 (Dec. 8), 1700 to Mar. 19, 1721.

Innocent XIII (Michelangelo dei Conti): Rome; May 8 (18), 1721 to Mar. 7, 1724.

Benedict XIII (Pietro Francesco Vincenzo Maria Orsini): Gravina (Bari); May 29 (June 4), 1724 to Feb. 21, 1730.

Clement XII (Lorenzo Corsini): Florence; July 12 (16), 1730 to Feb. 6, 1740.

Benedict XIV (Prospero Lambertini): Bologna; Aug. 17 (22), 1740 to May 3, 1758.

Clement XIII (Carlo Rezzonico): Venice; July 6 (16), 1758 to Feb. 2, 1769.

Clement XIV (Giovanni Vincenzo Antonio Lorenzo Ganganelli): Rimini; May 19, 28 (June 4), 1769 to Sept. 22, 1774.

Pius VI (Giovanni Angelo Braschi): Cesena; Feb. 15 (22), 1775 to Aug. 29, 1799.

Pius VII (Barnaba Gregorio Chiaramonti): Cesena; Mar. 14 (21), 1800 to Aug. 20, 1823.

Leo XII (Annibale della Genga): Genga (Fabriano); Sept. 28 (Oct. 5), 1823 to Feb. 10, 1829.

Pius VIII (Francesco Saverio Castiglioni): Cingoli; Mar. 31 (Apr. 5), 1829 to Nov. 30, 1830.

Gregory XVI (Bartolomeo Alberto-Mauro-Cappellari): Belluno; Feb. 2 (6), 1831 to June 1, 1846.

Bl. Pius IX (Giovanni M. Mastai-Ferretti): Senigallia; June 16 (21), 1846 to Feb. 7, 1878.

Leo XIII (Gioacchino Pecci): Carpineto (Anagni); Feb. 20 (Mar. 3), 1878 to July 20, 1903.

St. Pius X (Giuseppe Sarto): Riese (Treviso); Aug. 4 (9), 1903 to Aug. 20, 1914. Canonized May 29, 1954.

Benedict XV (Giacomo della Chiesa): Genoa; Sept. 3 (6), 1914 to Jan. 22, 1922.

Pius XI (Achille Ratti): Desio (Milan); Feb. 6 (12),

1922 to Feb. 10, 1939.

Pius XII (Eugenio Pacelli): Rome; Mar. 2 (12), 1939, to Oct. 9, 1958.

Bl. John XXIII (Angelo Giuseppe Roncalli): Sotto il Monte (Bergamo); Oct. 28 (Nov. 4), 1958 to June 3, 1963.

Paul VI (Giovanni Battista Montini): Concessio (Brescia); June 21 (30), 1963 to Aug. 6, 1978.

John Paul I (Albino Luciani): Forno di Canale (Belluno); Aug. 26 (Sept. 3), 1978 to Sept. 28, 1978.

John Paul II (Karol Wojtyla): Wadowice, Poland; Oct. 16 (22), 1978 to Apr. 2, 2005.

Benedict XVI (Joseph Ratzinger): Marktl Am Inn, Germany; Apr. 19 (24), 2005.

ANTIPOPES

This list of men who claimed or exercised the papal office in an uncanonical manner includes names, birthplaces and dates of alleged reigns. Source: Annuario Pontificio.

St. Hippolytus: Rome; 217-235; was reconciled before his death.

Novatian: Rome; 251.

Felix II: Rome; 355 to Nov. 22, 365.

Ursinus: 366-367.

Eulalius: Dec. 27 or 29, 418 to 419.

Lawrence: 498; 501-505.

Dioscorus: Alexandria; Sept. 22, 530 to Oct. 14, 530.

Theodore: ended alleged reign, 687.

Paschal: ended alleged reign, 687.

Constantine: Nepi; June 28 (July 5), 767 to 769.

Philip: July 31, 768; retired to his monastery on the same day.

John: ended alleged reign, Jan. 844.

Anastasius: Aug. 855 to Sept. 855; d. 880.

Christopher: Rome; July or Sept. 903 to Jan. 904.

Boniface VII: Rome; June 974 to July 974; Aug. 984 to July 985.

John XVI: Rossano; Apr. 997 to Feb. 998.

Gregory: ended alleged reign, 1012.

Benedict X: Rome; Apr. 5, 1058 to Jan. 24, 1059.

Honorius II: Verona; Oct. 28, 1061 to 1072.

Clement III: Parma; June 25, 1080 (Mar. 24, 1084) to Sept. 8, 1100.

Theodoric: ended alleged reign, 1100; d. 1102.

Albert: ended alleged reign, 1102.

Sylvester IV: Rome; Nov. 18, 1105 to 1111.

Gregory VIII: France; Mar. 8, 1118 to 1121.

Celestine II: Rome; ended alleged reign, Dec. 1124.

Anacletus II: Rome; Feb. 14 (23), 1130 to Jan. 25, 1138.

Victor IV: Mar. 1138 to May 29, 1138; submitted to Pope Innocent II.

Victor IV: Montecelio; Sept. 7 (Oct. 4), 1159 to Apr. 20, 1164; he did not recognize his predecessor (Victor IV, above).

Paschal III: Apr. 22 (26), 1164 to Sept. 20, 1168.

Callistus III: Arezzo; Sept. 1168 to Aug. 29, 1178; submitted to Pope Alexander III.

Innocent III: Sezze; Sept. 29, 1179 to 1180.

Nicholas V: Corvaro (Rieti); May 12 (22), 1328 to Aug. 25, 1330; d. Oct. 16, 1333.

Four antipopes of the Western Schism:

Clement VII: Sept. 20 (Oct. 31), 1378 to Sept. 16, 1394.

Benedict XIII: Aragon; Sept. 28 (Oct. 11), 1394 to

May 23, 1423.

Alexander V: Crete; June 26 (July 7), 1409 to May 3, 1410.

John XXIII: Naples; May 17 (25), 1410 to May 29, 1415 (date of deposition by Council of Constance which ended the Western Schism); d. Nov. 22, 1419.

Felix V: Savoy; Nov. 5, 1439 (July 24, 1440) to Apr. 7, 1449; d. 1451.

AVIGNON PAPACY

Avignon was the residence (1309-77) of a series of French popes (Clement V, John XXII, Benedict XII, Clement VI, Innocent VI, Urban V and Gregory XI). Prominent in the period were power struggles over the mixed interests of Church and state with the rulers of France (Philip IV, John II), Bavaria (Lewis IV), England (Edward III); factionalism of French and Italian churchmen; political as well as ecclesiastical turmoil in Italy, a factor of significance in prolonging the stay of popes in Avignon. Despite some positive achievements, the Avignon papacy was a prologue to the Western Schism that began in 1378.

GREAT WESTERN SCHISM

The Great Western Schism was a confused state of affairs that divided Christendom into two and then three papal obediences from 1378 to 1417.

It occurred some 50 years after Marsilius theorized that a general (not ecumenical) council of bishops and other persons was superior to a pope and nearly 30 years before the Council of Florence stated definitively that no kind of council had such authority.

It was a period of disaster preceding the even more disastrous period of the Reformation.

Urban VI, following the return of the papal residence to Rome after approximately 70 years at Avignon, was elected pope Apr. 8, 1378, and reigned until his death in 1389. He was succeeded by Boniface IX (1389-1404), Innocent VII (1404-1406), and Gregory XII (1406-1415). These four are considered the legitimate popes of the period.

Some of the cardinals who chose Urban pope, dissatisfied with his conduct of the office, declared that his election was invalid. They proceeded to elect Clement VII, who claimed the papacy from 1378 to 1394. He was succeeded by Benedict XIII.

Prelates seeking to end the state of divided papal loyalties convoked the Council of Pisa (1409) which, without authority, found Gregory XII and Benedict XIII guilty in absentia on 30-odd charges of schism and heresy, deposed them, and elected a third claimant to the papacy, Alexander V (1409-1410). He was succeeded by John XXIII (1410-1415).

The schism was ended by the Council of Constance (1414-1418). Although originally called into session in an irregular manner, the council, acquired authority after being convoked by Gregory XII in 1415. In its early irregular phase, it deposed John XXIII whose election to the papacy was uncanonical anyway. After being formally convoked, it accepted the abdication of Gregory in 1415 and dismissed the claims of Benedict XIII two years later, thus clearing the way for the election of Martin V on Nov. 11, 1417. The Council of Constance also rejected the theories of John Wycliff and condemned John Hus as a heretic.

POPES OF THE TWENTIETH CENTURY

LEO XIII

Leo XIII (Gioacchino Vincenzo Pecci) was born May 2, 1810, in Carpineto, Italy. Although all but three years of his life and pontificate were in the 19th century, his influence extended well into the 20th century.

He was educated at the Jesuit college in Viterbo, the Roman College, the Academy of Noble Ecclesiastics, and the University of the Sapienza. He was ordained to the priesthood in 1837.

He served as an apostolic delegate to two States of the Church, Benevento from 1838 to 1841 and Perugia in 1841 and 1842. Ordained titular archbishop of Damietta, he was papal nuncio to Belgium from Jan. 1843 until May 1846; in the post, he had controversial relations with the government over education issues and acquired his first significant experience of industrialized society.

He was archbishop of Perugia from 1846 to 1878. He became a cardinal in 1853 and chamberlain of the Roman Curia in 1877. He was elected to the papacy Feb. 20, 1878. He died July 20, 1903.

Canonizations: He canonized 18 saints and beatified a group of English martyrs.

Church Administration: He established 300 new dioceses and vicariates; restored the hierarchy in Scotland and set up an English hierarchy, as contrasted with the Portuguese, hierarchy in India; approved the action of the Congregation for the Propagation of

the Faith in reorganizing missions in China.

Encyclicals: He issued 86 encyclicals, on subjects ranging from devotional to social. In the former category were *Annum Sacrum*, on the Sacred Heart, in 1899, and 11 letters on Mary and the Rosary.

Social Questions: Much of Leo's influence stemmed from social doctrine stated in numerous encyclicals, concerning liberalism, liberty, the divine origin of authority; socialism, in *Quod Apostolici Muneris*, 1878; the Christian concept of the family, in *Arcanum*, 1880; socialism and economic liberalism, relations between capital and labor, in *Rerum Novarum*, 1891. Two of his social encyclicals were against the African slave trade.

Interfaith Relations: He was unsuccessful in unity overtures made to Orthodox and Slavic Churches. He declared Anglican orders invalid in the apostolic bull *Apostolicae Curae* Sept. 13, 1896.

International Relations: Leo was frustrated in seeking solutions to the Roman Question arising from the seizure of church lands by the Kingdom of Italy in 1870. He also faced anticlerical situations in Belgium and France and in the *Kulturkampf* policies of Bismarck in Germany.

Scholarship: In the encyclical *Aeterni Patris* of Aug. 4, 1879, he ordered a renewal of philosophical and theological studies in seminaries along scholastic, and especially Thomistic, lines, to counteract influential trends of liberalism and Modernism. He issued guidelines for biblical exegesis in *Providentissimus Deus* Nov. 18, 1893, and established the Pontifical Biblical Commission in 1902.

In other actions affecting scholarship and study, he opened the Vatican Archives to scholars in 1883 and established the Vatican Observatory.

United States: He authorized establishment of the apostolic delegation in Washington, D.C., Jan. 24, 1893. He refused to issue a condemnation of the Knights of Labor. With a document entitled *Testem Benevolentiae*, he eased resolution of questions concerning what was called an American heresy in 1899.

ST. PIUS X

St. Pius X (Giuseppe Melchiorre Sarto) was born in 1835 in Riese, Italy. Educated at the college of Castelfranco and the seminary at Padua, he was ordained to the priesthood Sept. 18, 1858. He served as a curate in Trombolo for nine years before beginning an eight-year pastorate at Salzano. He was chancellor of the Treviso diocese from Nov. 1875, and bishop of Mantua from 1884 until 1893. He was cardinal-patriarch of Venice from that year until his election to the papacy by the conclave held from July 31 to Aug. 4, 1903.

Aims: Pius's principal objectives as pope were "to restore all things in Christ, in order that Christ may be all and in all," and "to teach (and defend) Christian truth and law."

Canonizations, Encyclicals: He canonized four saints and issued 16 encyclicals. One of the encyclicals was issued in commemoration of the 50th anniversary of the proclamation of the dogma of the Immaculate Conception of Mary.

Catechetics: He introduced a whole new era of religious instruction and formation with the encyclical *Acerbo Nimis* of Apr. 15, 1905, in which he called for vigor in establishing and conducting parochial programs of the Confraternity of Christian Doctrine.

Catholic Action: He outlined the role of official Catholic Action in two encyclicals in 1905 and 1906. Favoring organized action by Catholics themselves, he had serious reservations about interconfessional collaboration.

He stoutly maintained claims to papal rights in the anticlerical climate of Italy. He authorized bishops to relax prohibitions against participation by Catholics in some Italian elections.

Church Administration: With the *motu proprio Arduum Sane* of Mar. 19, 1904, he inaugurated the work that resulted in the Code of Canon Law; the code was completed in 1917 and went into effect in the following year. He reorganized and strengthened the Roman Curia with the apostolic constitution *Sapienti Consilio* of June 29, 1908.

While promoting the expansion of missionary work, he removed from the jurisdiction of the Congregation for the Propagation of the Faith the Church in the United States, Canada, Newfoundland, England, Ireland, Holland and Luxembourg.

International Relations: He ended traditional prerogatives of Catholic governments with respect to papal elections, in 1904. He opposed anti-Church and anticlerical actions in several countries: Bolivia in 1905, because of anti-religious legislation; France in 1906, for its 1901 action in annulling its concordat with the Holy See, and for the 1905 Law of Separation by which it decreed separation of Church and state, ordered the confiscation of church property, and blocked religious education and the activities of religious orders; Portugal in 1911, for the separation of Church and state and repressive measures that resulted in persecution later.

In 1912 he called on the bishops of Brazil to work for the improvement of conditions among Indians.

Liturgy: "The Pope of the Eucharist," he strongly recommended the frequent reception of Holy Communion in a decree dated Dec. 20, 1905; in another decree, *Quam Singulari*, of Aug. 8, 1910, he called for the early reception of the sacrament by children. He initiated measures for liturgical reform with new norms for sacred music and the start of work on revision of the Breviary for recitation of the Divine Office.

Modernism: Pius was a vigorous opponent of "the synthesis of all heresies," which threatened the integrity of doctrine through its influence in philosophy, theology and biblical exegesis. In opposition, he condemned 65 of its propositions as erroneous in the decree *Lamentabili*, July 3, 1907; issued the encyclical *Pascendi* in the same vein, Sept. 8, 1907; backed both of these with censures; and published the Oath against Modernism in Sept. 1910, to be taken by all the clergy. Ecclesiastical studies suffered to some extent from these actions, necessary as they were at the time.

Pius followed the lead of Leo XIII in promoting the study of scholastic philosophy. He established the Pontifical Biblical Institute May 7, 1909.

His death, Aug. 20, 1914, was hastened by the outbreak of World War I. He was beatified in 1951 and canonized May 29, 1954. His feast is observed Aug. 21.

BENEDICT XV

Benedict XV (Giacomo della Chiesa) was born Nov. 21, 1854, in Pegli, Italy.

He was educated at the Royal University of Genoa and Gregorian University in Rome. He was ordained to the priesthood Dec. 21, 1878.

He served in the papal diplomatic corps from 1882 to 1907, as secretary to the nuncio to Spain from 1882 to 1887, as secretary to the papal secretary of state from 1887, and as undersecretary from 1901.

He was ordained archbishop of Bologna Dec. 22, 1907, and spent four years completing a pastoral visitation there. He was made a cardinal just three months before being elected to the papacy Sept. 3, 1914. He died Jan. 22, 1922. Two key efforts of his pontificate were for peace and the relief of human suffering caused by World War I.

Canonizations: Benedict canonized three saints; one of them was Joan of Arc.

Canon Law: He published the Code of Canon Law, developed by the commission set up by St. Pius X, May 27, 1917; it went into effect the following year.

Curia: He made great changes in the personnel of the Curia. He established the Congregation for the Oriental Churches May 1, 1917, and founded the Pontifical Oriental Institute in Rome later in the year.

Encyclicals: He issued 12 encyclicals. Peace was the theme of three of them. In another, published two years after the cessation of hostilities, he wrote about child victims of the war. He followed the lead of Leo XIII in *Spiritus Paraclitus*, Sept. 15, 1920, on biblical studies.

International Relations: He was largely frustrated on the international level because of the events and attitudes of the war period, but the number of diplomats accredited to the Vatican nearly doubled, from 14 to 26, between the time of his accession to the papacy and his death.

Peace Efforts: Benedict's stance in the war was one of absolute impartiality but not of uninterested neutrality. Because he would not take sides, he was suspected by both the Allies and the Central Powers, and the seven-point peace plan he offered to all belligerents, Aug. 1, 1917, was turned down. The points of the plan were: recognition of the moral force of right; disarmament; acceptance of arbitration in cases of dispute; guarantee of freedom of the seas; renunciation of war indemnities; evacuation and restoration of occupied territories; examination of territorial claims in dispute.

Relief Efforts: Benedict assumed personal charge of Vatican relief efforts during the war. He set up an international missing persons bureau for contacts between prisoners and their families, but was forced to close it because of the suspicion of warring nations that it was a front for espionage operations. He persuaded the Swiss government to admit into the country military victims of tuberculosis.

Roman Question: Benedict prepared the way for the meetings and negotiations which led to settlement of the question in 1929.

PIUS XI

Pius XI (Ambrogio Damiano Achille Ratti) was born May 31, 1857, in Desio, Italy.

Educated at seminaries in Seviso and Milan, and at the Lombard College, Gregorian University and Academy of St. Thomas in Rome. He was ordained to the priesthood in 1879.

He taught at the major seminary of Milan from 1882 to 1888. Appointed to the staff of the Ambrosian Library in 1888, he remained there until 1911, acquiring a reputation for publishing works on paleography and serving as director from 1907 to 1911. He then moved to the Vatican Library, of which he was prefect from 1914 to 1918. In 1919, he was named apostolic visitor to Poland in Apr. nuncio in June, and was made titular archbishop of Lepanto Oct. 28. He was made archbishop of Milan and cardinal June 13, 1921, before being elected to the papacy Feb. 6, 1922. He died Feb. 10, 1939.

Aims: The objective of his pontificate, as stated in the encyclical *Ubi Arcano*, Dec. 23, 1922, was to establish the reign and peace of Christ in society.

Canonizations: He canonized 34 saints, including the Jesuit Martyrs of North America, and conferred the title of Doctor of the Church on Sts. Peter Canisius, John of the Cross, Robert Bellarmine and Albertus Magnus.

Eastern Churches: He called for better understanding of the Eastern Churches in the encyclical *Rerum Orientalium* of Sept. 8, 1928, and developed facilities for the training of Eastern-Rite priests. He inaugurated steps for the codification of Eastern Church law in 1929. In 1935 he made Syrian Patriarch Tappouni a cardinal.

Encyclicals: His first encyclical, *Ubi Arcano*, in addition to stating the aims of his pontificate, blueprinted Catholic Action and called for its development throughout the Church.

In Quas Primas, Dec. 11, 1925, he established the feast of Christ the King for universal observance. Subjects of some of his other encyclicals were: Christian education, in *Rappresentanti in Terra*, Dec. 31, 1929; Christian marriage, in *Casti Connubii*, Dec. 31, 1930; social conditions and pressure for social change in line with the teaching in *Rerum Novarum*, in *Quadragesimo Anno*, May 15, 1931; atheistic Communism, in *Divini Redemptoris*, Mar. 19, 1937; the priesthood, in *Ad Catholici Sacerdotii*, Dec. 20, 1935.

Missions: Following the lead of Benedict XV, Pius called for the training of native clergy in the pattern of their own respective cultures, and promoted missionary developments in various ways. He ordained six native bishops for China in 1926, one for Japan in 1927, and others for regions of Asia, China and India in 1933. He placed the first 40 mission dioceses under native bishops, saw the number of native priests increase from about 2,600 to more than 7,000, and the number of Catholics in missionary areas more than double from nine million.

In the apostolic constitution *Deus Scientiarum Dominus* of May 24, 1931, he ordered the introduction of missiology into theology courses.

Interfaith Relations: Pius was negative to the ecumenical movement among Protestants but approved the Malines Conversations, 1921 to 1926, between Anglicans and Catholics.

International Relations: Relations with the Mussolini government deteriorated from 1931 on, as indicated in the encyclical *Non Abbiamo Bisogno*, when the regime took steps to curb liberties and activities of the Church; they turned critical in 1938 with the emergence of racist policies. Relations deteriorated in Germany also from 1933 on, resulting finally in condemnation of the Nazis in the encyclical *Mit Brennender Sorge*, March, 1937. Pius sparked a revival of the Church in France by encouraging Catholics to work within the democratic framework of the Republic rather than foment trouble over restoration of a monarchy. Pius was powerless to influence developments related to the civil war that erupted in Spain in July 1936, sporadic persecution and repression by the Calles regime in Mexico, and systematic persecution of the Church in the Soviet Union. Many of the 10 concordats and two agreements reached with European countries after World War I became casualties of World War II.

Roman Question: Pius negotiated for two and a half years with the Italian government to settle the Roman Question by means of the Lateran Agreement of 1929. The agreement provided independent status for the State of Vatican City; made Catholicism the official religion of Italy, with pastoral and educational freedom and state recognition of Catholic marriages, religious orders and societies; and provided a financial payment to the Vatican for expropriation of the former States of the Church.

PIUS XII

Pius XII (Eugenio Maria Giovanni Pacelli) was born Mar. 2, 1876, in Rome.

Educated at the Gregorian University and the Lateran University, in Rome, he was ordained to the priesthood Apr. 2, 1899.

He entered the Vatican diplomatic service in 1901, worked on the codification of canon law, and was appointed secretary of the Congregation for Ecclesiastical Affairs in 1914. Three years later he was ordained titular archbishop of Sardis and made apostolic nuncio to Bavaria. He was nuncio to Germany from 1920 to 1929, when he was made a cardinal, and took office as papal secretary of state in the following year. His diplomatic negotiations resulted in concordats between the Vatican and Bavaria (1924), Prussia (1929), Baden (1932), Austria and the German Republic (1933). He took part in negotiations that led to settlement of the Roman Question in 1929.

He was elected to the papacy Mar. 2, 1939. He died Oct. 9, 1958, at Castel Gandolfo after the 12th longest pontificate in history.

Canonizations: He canonized 34 saints, including Mother Frances X. Cabrini, the first U.S. citizen-saint.

Cardinals: He raised 56 prelates to the rank of cardinal in two consistories held in 1946 and 1953. There were 57 cardinals at the time of his death.

Church Organization and Missions: He increased the number of dioceses from 1,696 to 2,048. He established native hierarchies in China (1946), Burma (1955) and parts of Africa, and extended the native structure of the Church in India. He ordained the first black bishop for Africa.

Communism: In addition to opposing and condemning Communism on numerous occasions, he decreed in 1949 the penalty of excommunication for all Catholics holding formal and willing allegiance to the Communist Party and its policies. During his reign the Church was persecuted in some 15 countries that fell under communist domination.

Doctrine and Liturgy: He proclaimed the dogma of the Assumption of the Blessed Virgin Mary, Nov. 1, 1950 (apostolic constitution, *Munificentissimus Deus*).

In various encyclicals and other enactments, he provided background for the *aggiornamento* introduced by his successor, John XXIII: by his formulations of doctrine and practice regarding the Mystical Body of Christ, the liturgy, sacred music and biblical studies; by the revision of the Rites of Holy Week; by initiation of the work which led to the calendar-missal-breviary reform ordered into effect Jan. 1, 1961; by the first of several modifications of the Eucharistic fast; by extending the time of Mass to the evening. He instituted the feasts of Mary, Queen, and of St. Joseph the Worker, and clarified teaching concerning devotion to the Sacred Heart.

His 41 encyclicals and nearly 1,000 public addresses made Pius one of the greatest teaching popes. His concern in all his communications was to deal with specific points at issue and to bring Christian principles to bear on contemporary world problems.

Peace Efforts: Before the start of World War II, he tried unsuccessfully to get the contending nations — Germany and Poland, France and Italy — to settle their differences peaceably. During the war, he offered his services to mediate the widened conflict, spoke out against the horrors of war and the suffering it caused, mobilized relief work for its victims, proposed a five-point program for peace in Christmas messages from 1939 to 1942, and secured a generally open status for the city of Rome. He has been criticized in some quarters for not doing enough to oppose the Holocaust. This is a matter of historical debate, but it is a fact that through his direct intercession many thousands of Jews in Rome and Italy were saved from certain death, and he resisted wherever possible the threat of Nazism to human rights. Such were his contributions to assisting Jews that the rabbi of Rome, Dr. Abraham Zolli, was converted to Catholicism, and upon his death, Pius was praised by Golda Meir for his efforts. After the war, he endorsed the principles and intent of the U.N. and continued efforts for peace.

United States: Pius appointed more than 200 of the 265 American bishops resident in the U.S. and abroad in 1958, erected 27 dioceses in this country, and raised seven dioceses to archiepiscopal rank.

BL. JOHN XXIII

John XXIII (Angelo Roncalli) was born Nov. 25, 1881, at Sotto il Monte, Italy.

He was educated at the seminary of the Bergamo diocese and the Pontifical Seminary in Rome, where he was ordained to the priesthood Aug. 10, 1904.

He spent the first nine or 10 years of his priesthood as secretary to the bishop of Bergamo and as an instructor in the seminary there. He served as a medic and chaplain in the Italian army during World War I. Afterwards, he resumed duties in his own diocese until he was called to Rome in 1921 for work with the Society for the Propagation of the Faith.

He began diplomatic service in 1925 as titular archbishop of Areopolis and apostolic visitor to Bulgaria. A succession of offices followed: apostolic delegate to Bulgaria (1931-1935); titular archbishop of Mesembria, apostolic delegate to Turkey and Greece, administrator of the Latin vicariate apostolic of Istanbul (1935-1944); apostolic nuncio to France (1944-1953). On these missions, he was engaged in delicate negotiations involving Roman, Eastern Rite and Orthodox relations; the needs of people suffering from the consequences of World War II; and unsettling suspicions arising from wartime conditions.

He was made a cardinal Jan. 12, 1953, and three days later was appointed patriarch of Venice, the position he held until his election to the papacy Oct. 28, 1958. He died of stomach cancer June 3, 1963.

John was a strong and vigorous pope whose influence far outmeasured both his age and the shortness of his time in the papacy. He was beatified by Pope John Paul II on Sept. 3, 2000.

Second Vatican Council: John announced Jan. 25, 1959, his intention of convoking the 21st ecumenical council in history to renew life in the Church, to reform its structures and institutions, and to explore ways and means of promoting unity among Christians. Through the council, which completed its work two and a half years after his death, he ushered in a new era in the history of the Church.

Canon Law: He established a commission Mar. 28, 1963, for revision of the Code of Canon Law. The revised Code was promulgated in 1983.

Canonizations: He canonized 10 saints and beatified Mother Elizabeth Ann Seton, the first native of the U.S. ever so honored. He named St. Lawrence of Brindisi a Doctor of the Church.

Cardinals: He created 52 cardinals in five consistories, raising membership of the College of Cardinals above the traditional number of 70; at one time in 1962, the membership was 87. He made the college more international in representation than it had ever been, appointing the first cardinals from the

Philippines, Japan and Africa. He ordered episcopal ordination for all cardinals. He relieved the suburban bishops of Rome of ordinary jurisdiction over their dioceses so they might devote all their time to business of the Roman Curia.

Eastern Rites: He made all Eastern Rite patriarchs members of the Congregation for the Oriental Churches.

Ecumenism: He assigned to the Second Vatican Council the task of finding ways and means of promoting unity among Christians. He established the Vatican Secretariat for Promoting Christian Unity June 5, 1960. He showed his desire for more cordial relations with the Orthodox by sending personal representatives to visit Patriarch Athenagoras I June 27, 1961; approved a mission of five delegates to the General Assembly of the World Council of Churches which met in New Delhi, India, in Nov. 1961; and removed a number of pejorative references to Jews in the Roman-Rite liturgy for Good Friday.

Encyclicals: Of the eight encyclicals he issued, the two outstanding ones were *Mater et Magistra* ("Christianity and Social Progress"), in which he recapitulated, updated and extended the social doctrine stated earlier by Leo XIII and Pius XI; and *Pacem in Terris* ("Peace on Earth"), the first encyclical ever addressed to all men of good will as well as to Catholics, on the natural law principles of peace.

Liturgy: In forwarding liturgical reforms already begun by Pius XII, he ordered a calendar-missal-breviary reform into effect Jan. 1, 1961. He authorized the use of vernacular languages in the administration of the sacraments and approved giving Holy Communion to the sick in afternoon hours. He selected the liturgy as the first topic of major discussion by the Second Vatican Council.

Missions: He issued an encyclical on the missionary activity of the Church; established native hierarchies in Indonesia, Vietnam and Korea; and called on North American superiors of religious institutes to have one-tenth of their members assigned to work in Latin America by 1971.

Peace: John spoke and used his moral influence for peace in 1961 when tension developed over Berlin, in 1962 during the Algerian revolt from France, and later the same year in the Cuban missile crisis. His efforts were singled out for honor by the Balzan Peace Foundation. In 1963, he was posthumously awarded the U.S. Presidential Medal of Freedom.

PAUL VI

Paul VI (Giovanni Battista Montini) was born Sept. 26, 1897, at Concesio in northern Italy. Educated at Brescia, he was ordained to the priesthood May 29, 1920. He pursued additional studies at the Pontifical Academy for Noble Ecclesiastics and the Pontifical Gregorian University. In 1924 he began 30 years of service in the Secretariat of State; as undersecretary from 1937 until 1954, he was closely associated with Pius XII and was heavily engaged in organizing informational and relief services during and after World War II. He declined the offer of the cardinalate by Pope Pius XII.

Ordained archbishop of Milan Dec. 12, 1954, he was inducted into the College of Cardinals Dec. 15, 1958, by Pope John XXIII. Trusted by John, he was a key figure in organizing the first session of Vatican Council II and was elected to the papacy June 21, 1963, two days after the conclave began. He died of a heart attack Aug. 6, 1978.

Second Vatican Council: He reconvened the Second Vatican Council after the death of John XXIII, presided over its second, third and fourth sessions, formally promulgated the 16 documents it produced, and devoted the whole of his pontificate to the task of putting them into effect throughout the Church. The main thrust of his pontificate — in a milieu of cultural and other changes in the Church and the world — was toward institutionalization and control of the authentic trends articulated and set in motion by the council.

Canonizations: He canonized 84 saints. They included groups of 22 Ugandan martyrs and 40 martyrs of England and Wales, as well as two Americans — Elizabeth Ann Bayley Seton and John Nepomucene Neumann.

Cardinals: He created 144 cardinals, and gave the Sacred College a more international complexion than it ever had before. He limited participation in papal elections to 120 cardinals under the age of 80.

Collegiality: He established the Synod of Bishops in 1965 and called it into session five times. He stimulated the formation and operation of regional conferences of bishops, and of consultative bodies on other levels.

Creed and Holy Year: On June 30, 1968, he issued a Creed of the People of God in conjunction with the celebration of a Year of Faith. He proclaimed and led the observance of a Holy Year from Christmas Eve of 1974 to Christmas Eve of 1975.

Diplomacy: He met with many world leaders, including Soviet President Nikolai Podgorny in 1967, Marshal Tito of Yugoslavia in 1971 and President Nicolai Ceausescu of Romania in 1973. He worked constantly to reduce tension between the Church and the intransigent regimes of Eastern European countries by means of a detente type of policy called *Ostpolitik*. He agreed to significant revisions of the Vatican's concordat with Spain and initiated efforts to revise the concordat with Italy. More than 40 countries established diplomatic relations with the Vatican during his pontificate.

Encyclicals: He issued seven encyclicals, three of which are the best known. In *Populorum Progressio* ("Development of Peoples") he appealed to wealthy countries to take "concrete action" to promote human development and to remedy imbalances between richer and poorer nations; this encyclical, coupled with other documents and related actions, launched the Church into a new depth of involvement as a public advocate for human rights and for humanizing social, political and economic policies. In *Sacerdotalis Caelibatus* ("Priestly Celibacy") he reaffirmed the strict observance of priestly celibacy throughout the Western Church. In *Humanae Vitae* ("Of Human Life") he condemned abortion, sterilization and artificial birth control, in line with traditional teaching and in "defense of life, the gift of God, the glory of the family, the strength of the people."

Interfaith Relations: He initiated formal consultation and informal dialogue on international and national levels between Catholics and non-Catholics — Orthodox, Anglicans, Protestants, Jews, Muslims, Buddhists, Hindus, and unbelievers. He and Greek Orthodox Patriarch Athenagoras I of Constantinople nullified in 1965 the mutual excommunications imposed by their respective churches in 1054.

Liturgy: He carried out the most extensive liturgical reform in history, involving a new Order of the Mass effective in 1969, a revised church calendar in 1970, revisions and translations into vernacular languages of all sacramental rites and other liturgical texts.

Ministries: He authorized the restoration of the permanent diaconate in the Roman Rite and the establishment of new ministries of lay persons.

Peace: In 1968, he instituted the annual observance of a World Day of Peace on New Year's Day as a means of addressing a message of peace to all the world's political leaders and the peoples of all nations. The most dramatic of his many appeals for peace and efforts to ease international tensions was his plea for "No more war!" before the U.N., Oct. 4, 1965.

Pilgrimages: A "Pilgrim Pope," he made pastoral visits to the Holy Land and India in 1964, the U.N. and New York City in 1965, Portugal and Turkey in 1967, Colombia in 1968, Switzerland and Uganda in 1969, and Asia, Pacific islands and Australia in 1970. While in Manila in 1970, he was stabbed by a Bolivian artist.

Roman Curia: He reorganized the central administrative organs of the Church in line with provisions of the apostolic constitution, *Regimini Ecclesiae Universae,* streamlining procedures for more effective service and giving the agencies a more international perspective by drawing officials and consultors from all over the world. He also instituted a number of new commissions and other bodies. Coupled with curial reorganization was a simplification of papal ceremonies.

JOHN PAUL I

John Paul I (Albino Luciani) was born Oct. 17, 1912,

in Forno di Canale (now Canale d'Agordo) in northern Italy. Educated at the minor seminary in Feltre and the major seminary of the Diocese of Belluno, he was ordained to the priesthood July 7, 1935. He pursued further studies at the Pontifical Gregorian University in Rome and was awarded a doctorate in theology. From 1937 to 1947 he was vice rector of the Belluno seminary, where he taught dogmatic and moral theology, canon law and sacred art. He was appointed vicar general of his diocese in 1947 and served as director of catechetics.

Ordained bishop of Vittorio Veneto Dec. 27, 1958, he attended all sessions of the Second Vatican Council, participated in three assemblies of the Synod of Bishops (1971, 1974 and 1977), and was vice president of the Italian Bishops' Conference from 1972 to 1975.

He was appointed archbishop and patriarch of Venice Dec. 15, 1969, and was inducted into the College of Cardinals Mar. 5, 1973.

He was elected to the papacy Aug. 26, 1978, on the fourth ballot cast by the 111 cardinals participating in the largest and one of the shortest conclaves in history. The quickness of his election was matched by the brevity of his pontificate of 33 days, during which he delivered 19 addresses. He died of a heart attack Sept. 28, 1978.

JOHN PAUL II

See separate entry.

BENEDICT XVI

See separate entry.

PAPAL ENCYCLICALS — BENEDICT XIV (1740) TO BENEDICT XVI

(Source: *The Papal Encyclicals* [5 vols.], Claudia Carlen, I.H.M.; Pieran Press, Ann Arbor, Mich. Used with permission.)

An encyclical letter is a pastoral letter addressed by a pope to the whole Church. In general, it concerns matters of doctrine, morals or discipline, or significant commemorations. Its formal title consists of the first few words of the official text. Some encyclicals, notably *Pacem in terris* by John XXIII, *Ecclesiam Suam* by Paul VI and several by John Paul II, have been addressed to people of good will in general as well as to bishops and the faithful in communion with the Church.

An encyclical epistle resembles an encyclical letter but is addressed only to part of the Church. The authority of encyclicals was stated by Pius XII in the encyclical *Humani Generis* Aug. 12, 1950: "Nor must it be thought that what is contained in encyclical letters does not of itself demand assent, on the pretext that the popes do not exercise in them the supreme power of their teaching authority. Rather, such teachings belong to the ordinary magisterium, of which it is true to say: 'He who hears you, hears me' (Lk 10:16); for the most part, too, what is expounded and inculcated in encyclical letters already appertains to Catholic doctrine for other reasons."

The Second Vatican Council declared: "Religious submission of will and of mind must be shown in a special way to the authentic teaching authority of the Roman Pontiff, even when he is not speaking ex cathedra. That is, it must be shown in such a way that his supreme magisterium is acknowledged with reverence, the judgments made by him are sincerely

adhered to, according to his manifest mind and will. His mind and will in the matter may be known chiefly either from the character of the documents (one of which could be an encyclical), from his frequent repetition of the same doctrine, or from his manner of speaking" (Dogmatic Constitution on the Church, *Lumen Gentium*, No. 25).

The following list contains the titles and indicates the subject matter of encyclical letters and epistles. The latter are generally distinguishable by the limited scope of their titles or contents.

Benedict XIV

(1740-58)

1740: *Ubi Primum* (On the duties of bishops), Dec. 3.

1741: *Quanta Cura* (Forbidding traffic in alms), June 30.

1743: *Nimiam Licentiam* (To the bishops of Poland, on validity of marriages), May 18.

1745: *Vix Pervenit* (To the bishops of Italy, on usury and other dishonest profit), Nov. 1.

1748: Magnae Nobis (To the bishops of Poland, on marriage impediments and dispensations), June 29.

1749: *Peregrinantes* (To all the faithful, proclaiming a Holy Year for 1750), May 5.

Apostolica Constitutio (On preparation for the Holy Year), June 26.

1751: *A Quo primum* (To bishops of Poland, on Jews and Christians living in the same place), June 14.

1754: *Cum Religiosi* (To the bishops of the States of the Church, on catechesis), June 26.

Quod Provinciale (To the bishops of Albania, on

Christians using Mohammedan names), Aug. 1.

1755: *Allatae Sunt* (To missionaries of the Orient, on the observance of Oriental rites), July 26.

1756: *Ex quo Primum* (To bishops of the Greek rite, on the Euchologion), Mar. 1.

Ex Omnibus (To the bishops of France, on the apostolic constitution, *Unigenitus*), Oct. 16.

Clement XIII
(1758-69)

1758: *A Quo Die* (Unity among Christians), Sept. 13.

1759: *Cum Primum* (On observing canonical sanctions), Sept. 17.

Appetente Sacro (On the spiritual advantages of fasting), Dec. 20.

1761: *In Dominico Agro* (On instruction in the faith), June 14.

1766: *Christianae Republicae* (On the dangers of anti-Christian writings), Nov. 25.

1768: *Summa Quae* (To the bishops of Poland, on the Church in Poland), Jan. 6.

Clement XIV
(1769-74)

1769: *Decet Quam Maxime* (To the bishops of Sardinia, on abuses in taxes and benefices), Sept. 21.

Inscrutabili Divinae Sapientiae (To all Christians, proclaiming a universal jubilee), Dec. 12.

Cum Summi (Proclaiming a universal jubilee), Dec. 12.

1774: *Salutis Nostra* (To all Christians, proclaiming a universal jubilee), Apr. 30.

Pius VI
(1775-99)

1775: *Inscrutabile* (On the problems of the pontificate), Dec. 25.

1791: *Charitas* (To the bishops of France, on the civil oath in France), Apr. 13.

Pius VII
(1800-1823)

1800: *Diu Satis* (To the bishops of France, on a return to Gospel principles), May 15.

Leo XII
(1823-29)

1824: *Ubi Primum* (To all bishops, on Leo XII's assuming the pontificate), May 5.

Quod Hoc Ineunte (Proclaiming a universal jubilee), May 24.

1825: *Charitate Christi* (Extending jubilee to the entire Church), Dec. 25.

Pius VIII
(1829-30)

1829: *Traditi Humilitati* (On Pius VIII's program for the pontificate), May 24.

Gregory XVI
(1831-46)

1832: *Summo Iugiter Studio* (To the bishops of Bavaria, on mixed marriages), May 27.

Cum Primum (To the bishops of Poland, on civil obedience), June 9.

Mirari Vos (On liberalism and religious indifferentism), Aug. 15.

1833: *Quo Graviora* (To the bishops of the Rhineland, on the "pragmatic Constitution"), Oct. 4.

1834: *Singulari Nos* (On the errors of Lammenais), June 25.

1835: *Commissum Divinitus* (To clergy of Switzerland, on Church and State), May 17.

1840: *Probe Nostis* (On the Propagation of the Faith), Sept. 18.

1841: *Quas Vestro* (To the bishops of Hungary, on mixed marriages), Apr. 30.

1844: *Inter Praecipuas* (On biblical societies), May 8.

Pius IX
(1846-78)

1846: *Qui Pluribus* (On faith and religion), Nov. 9.

1847: *Praedecessores Nostros* (On aid for Ireland), Mar. 25.

Ubi Primum (To religious superiors, on discipline for religious), June 17.

1849: *Ubi Primum* (On the Immaculate Conception), Feb. 2.

Nostis et Nobiscum (To the bishops of Italy, on the Church in the Pontifical States), Dec. 8.

1851: *Exultavit Cor Nostrum* (On the effects of jubilee), Nov. 21.

1852: *Nemo Certe Ignorat* (To the bishops of Ireland, on the discipline for clergy), Mar. 25.

Probe Noscitis Venerabiles (To the bishops of Spain, on the discipline for clergy), May 17.

1853: *Inter Multiplices* (To the bishops of France, pleading for unity of spirit), Mar. 21.

1854: *Neminem Vestrum* (To clergy and faithful of Constantinople, on the persecution of Armenians), Feb. 2.

Optime Noscitis (To the bishops of Ireland, on the proposed Catholic university for Ireland), Mar. 20.

Apostolicae Nostrae Caritatis (Urging prayers for peace), Aug. 1.

1855: *Optime Noscitis* (To the bishops of Austria, on episcopal meetings), Nov. 5.

1856: *Singulari Quidem* (To the bishops of Austria, on the Church in Austria), Mar. 17.

1858: *Cum Nuper* (To the bishops of the Kingdom of the Two Sicilies, on care for clerics), Jan. 20.

Amantissimi Redemptoris (On priests and the care of souls), May 3.

1859: *Cum Sancta Mater Ecclesia* (Pleading for public prayer), Apr. 27.

Qui Nuper (On Pontifical States), June 18.

1860: *Nullis Certe Verbis* (On the need for civil sovereignty), Jan. 19.

1862: *Amantissimus* (To bishops of the Oriental rite, on the care of the churches), Apr. 8.

1863: *Quanto Conficiamur Moerore* (To the bishops of Italy, on promotion of false doctrines), Aug. 10.

Incredibili (To the bishops of Bogota, on persecution in New Granada), Sept. 17.

1864: *Maximae Quidem* (To the bishops of Bavaria, on the Church in Bavaria), Aug. 18.

Quanta Cura (Conedmning current errors), Dec. 8.

1865: *Meridionali Americae* (To bishops of South America, on the seminary for native clergy), Sept. 30.

1867: *Levate* (On the afflictions of the Church), Oct. 27.

1870: *Respicientes* (Protesting the taking of the Pontifical States), Nov. 1.

1871: *Ubi Nos* (To all bishops, on Pontifical States), May 15.

Beneficia Dei (On the 25th anniversary of his pontificate), June 4.

Saepe Venerabiles Fratres (On thanksgiving for 25 years of pontificate), Aug. 5.

1872: *Quae in Patriarchatu* (To bishops and people of Chaldea, on the Church in Chaldea), Nov. 16.

1873: *Quartus Supra* (To bishops and people of the Armenian rite, on the Church in Armenia), Jan. 6.

Etsi Multa (On the Church in Italy, Germany and Switzerland), Nov. 21.

1874: *Vix Dum a Nobis* (To the bishops of Austria, on the Church in Austria), Mar. 7.

Gravibus Ecclesiae (To all bishops and faithful, proclaiming a jubilee for 1875), Dec. 24.

1875: *Quod Nunquam* (To the bishops of Prussia, on the Church in Prussia), Feb. 5.

Graves Ac Diuturnae (To the bishops of Switzerland, on the Church in Switzerland), Mar. 23.

Leo XIII
(1878-1903)

1878: *Inscrutabili Dei Consilio* (On the evils of society), Apr. 21.

Quod Apostolici Muneris (On socialism), Dec. 28.

1879: *Aeterni Patris* (On the restoration of Christian philosophy), Aug. 4.

1880: *Arcanum* (On Christian marriage), Feb. 10.

Grande Munus (On Sts. Cyril and Methodius), Sept. 30.

Sancta Dei Civitas (On mission societies), Dec. 3.

1881: *Diuturnum* (On the origin of civil power), June 29.

Licet Multa (To the bishops of Belgium, on Catholics in Belgium), Aug. 3.

1882: *Etsi Nos* (To the bishops of Italy, on conditions in Italy), Feb. 15.

Auspicato Concessum (On St. Francis of Assisi), Sept. 17.

Cum Multa (To the bishops of Spain, on conditions in Spain), Dec. 8.

1883: *Supremi Apostolatus Officio* (On devotion to the Rosary), Sept. 1.

1884: *Nobilissima Gallorum Gens* (To the bishops of France, on the religious question), Feb. 8.

Humanum Genus (On Freemasonry), Apr. 20.

Superiore Anno (On the recitation of the Rosary), Aug. 30.

1885: *Immortale Dei* (On the Christian constitution of states), Nov. 1.

Spectata Fides (To the bishops of England, on Christian education), Nov. 27.

Quod Auctoritate (Proclamation of extraordinary Jubilee), Dec. 22.

1886: *Iampridem* (To the bishops of Prussia, on Catholicism in Germany), Jan. 6.

Quod Multum (To the bishops of Hungary, on the liberty of the Church), Aug. 22.

Pergrata (To the bishops of Portugal, on the Church in Portugal), Sept. 14.

1887: *Vieben Noto* (To the bishops of Italy, on the Rosary and public life), Sept. 20.

Officio Sanctissimo (To the bishops of Bavaria, on the Church in Bavaria), Dec. 22.

1888: *Quod Anniversarius* (On his sacerdotal jubilee), Apr. 1.

In Plurimis (To the bishops of Brazil, on the abolition of slavery), May 5.

Libertas (On the nature of human liberty), June 20.

Saepe Nos (To the bishops of Ireland, on boycotting in Ireland), June 24.

Paterna Caritas (To the Patriarch of Cilicia and the archbishops and bishops of the Armenian people, on reunion with Rome), July 25.

Quam Aerumnosa (To the bishops of America, on Italian immigrants), Dec. 10.

Etsi Cunctas (To the bishops of Ireland, on the Church in Ireland), Dec. 21.

Exeunte Iam Anno (On the right ordering of Christian life), Dec. 25.

1889: *Magni Nobis* (To bishops of the United States, on the Catholic University of America), Mar. 7.

Quamquam Pluries (On devotion to St. Joseph), Aug. 15.

1890: *Sapientiae Christianae* (On Christians as citizens), Jan. 10.

Dall'Alto Dell'Apostolico Seggio (To the bishops and people of Italy, on Freemasonry in Italy), Oct. 15.

Catholicae Ecclesiae (On slavery in the missions), Nov. 20.

1891: *In Ipso* (To the bishops of Austria, on episcopal reunions in Austria), Mar. 3.

Rerum Novarum (On capital and labor), May 15.

Pastoralis (To the bishops of Portugal, on religious union), June 25.

Pastoralis Officii (To the bishops of Germany and Austria, on the morality of dueling), Sept. 12.

Octobri Mense (On the Rosary), Sept. 22.

1892: *Au Milieu des Sollicitudes* (To the bishops, clergy and faithful of France, on the Church and State in France), Feb. 16.

Quarto Abeunte Saeculo (To the bishops of Spain, Italy, and the two Americas, on the Columbus quadricentennial), July 16.

Magnae Dei Matris (On the Rosary), Sept. 8.

Inimica Vis (To the bishops of Italy, on Freemasonry), Dec. 8.

Custodi di Quella Fede (To the Italian people, on Freemasonry), Dec. 8.

1893: *Ad Extremas* (On seminaries for native clergy), June 24.

Constanti Hungarorum (To the bishops of Hungary, on the Church in Hungary), Sept. 2.

Laetitiae Sanctae (Commending devotion to the Rosary), Sept. 8.

Non Mediocri (To the bishops of Spain, on the Spanish College in Rome), Oct. 25.

Providentissimus Deus (On the study of Holy Scripture), Nov. 18.

1894: *Caritatis* (To the bishops of Poland, on the Church in Poland), Mar. 19.

Inter Graves (To the bishops of Peru, on the Church in Peru), May 1.

Litteras a Vobis (To the bishops of Brazil, on the clergy in Brazil), July 2.

Iucunda Semper Expectatione (On the Rosary), Sept. 8.

Christi Nomen (On the propagation of the Faith and Eastern churches), Dec. 24.

1895: *Longinqua* (To the bishops of the United States, on Catholicism in the United States), Jan. 6.

Permoti Nos (To the bishops of Belgium, on social conditions in Belgium), July 10.

Adiutricem (On the Rosary), Sept. 5.

1896: *Insignes* (To the bishops of Hungary, on the

Hungarian millennium), May 1.

Satis Cognitum (On the unity of the Church), June 29.

Fidentem Piumque Animum (On the Rosary), Sept. 20.

1897: *Divinum Illud Munus* (On the Holy Spirit), May 9.

Militantis Ecclesiae (To the bishops of Austria, Germany, and Switzerland, on St. Peter Canisius), Aug. 1.

Augustissimae Virginis Mariae (On the Confraternity of the Holy Rosary), Sept. 12.

Affari Vos (To the bishops of Canada, on the Manitoba school question), Dec. 8.

1898: *Caritatis Studium* (To the bishops of Scotland, on the Church in Scotland), July 25.

Spesse Volte (To the bishops, priests, and people of Italy, on the suppression of Catholic institutions), Aug. 5.

Quam Religiosa (To the bishops of Peru, on civil marriage law), Aug. 16.

Diuturni Temporis (On the Rosary), Sept. 5.

Quum Diuturnum (To the bishops of Latin America, on Latin American bishops' plenary council), Dec. 25.

1899: *Annum Sacrum* (On consecration to the Sacred Heart), May 25.

Depuis le Jour (To the archbishops, bishops, and clergy of France, on the education of clergy), Sept. 8.

Paternae (To the bishops of Brazil, on the education of the clergy), Sept. 18.

1900: *Omnibus Compertum* (To the Patriarch and bishops of the Greek-Melkite rite, on unity among the Greek Melkites), July 21.

Tametsi Futura Prospicientibus (On Jesus Christ the Redeemer), Nov. 1.

1901: *Graves de Communi Re* (On Christian democracy), Jan. 18.

Gravissimas (To the bishops of Portugal, on religious orders in Portugal), May 16.

Reputantibus (To the bishops of Bohemia and Moravia, on the language question in Bohemia), Aug. 20.

Urbanitatis Veteris (To the bishops of the Latin church in Greece, on the foundation of a seminary in Athens), Nov. 20.

1902: *In Amplissimo* (To the bishops of the United States, on the Church in the United States), Apr. 15.

Quod Votis (To the bishops of Austria, on the proposed Catholic University), Apr. 30.

Mirae Caritatis (On the Holy Eucharist), May 28.

Quae Ad Nos (To the bishops of Bohemia and Moravia, on the Church in Bohemia and Moravia), Nov. 22.

Fin dal Principio (To the bishops of Italy, on the education of the clergy), Dec. 8.

Dum Multa (To the bishops of Ecuador, on marriage legislation), Dec. 24.

St. Pius X

(1903-14)

1903: *E Supremi* (On the restoration of all things in Christ), Oct. 4.

1904: *Ad Diem Illum Laetissimum* (On the Immaculate Conception), Feb. 2.

Iucunda Sane (On Pope Gregory the Great), Mar. 12.

1905: *Acerbo Nimis* (On teaching Christian doctrine), Apr. 15.

Il Fermo Proposito (To the bishops of Italy, on Catholic Action in Italy), June 11.

1906: *Vehementer Nos* (To the bishops, clergy, and people of France, on the French Law of Separation), Feb. 11.

Tribus Circiter (On the Mariavites or Mystic Priests of Poland), Apr. 5.

Pieni l'Animo (To the bishops of Italy, on the clergy in Italy), July 28.

Gravissimo Officio Munere (To the bishops of France, on French associations of worship), Aug. 10.

1907: *Une Fois Encore* (To the bishops, clergy, and people of France, on the separation of Church and State), Jan. 6.

Pascendi Dominici Gregis (On the doctrines of the Modernists), Sept. 8.

1909: *Communium Rerum* (On St. Anselm of Aosta), Apr. 21.

1910: *Editae Saepe* (On St. Charles Borromeo), May 26.

1911: *Iamdudum* (On the Law of Separation in Portugal), May 24.

1912: *Lacrimabili Statu* (To the bishops of Latin America, on the Indians of South America), June 7.

Singulari Quadam (To the bishops of Germany, on labor organizations), Sept. 24.

Benedict XV

(1914-22)

1914: *Ad Beatissimi Apostolorum* (Appeal for peace), Nov. 1.

1917: *Humani Generis Redemptionem* (On preaching the Word of God), June 15.

1918: *Quod Iam Diu* (On the future peace conference), Dec. 1.

1919: *In Hac Tanta* (To the bishops of Germany, on St. Boniface), May 14.

Paterno Iam Diu (On children of central Europe), Nov. 24.

1920: *Pacem, Dei Munus Pulcherrimum* (On peace and Christian reconciliation), May 23.

Spiritus Paraclitus (On St. Jerome), Sept. 15.

Principi Apostolorum Petro (On St. Ephrem the Syrian), Oct. 5.

Annus Iam Plenus (On children of central Europe), Dec. 1.

1921: *Sacra Propediem* (On the Third Order of St. Francis), Jan. 6.

In Praeclara Summorum (To professors and students of fine arts in Catholic institutions of learning, on Dante), Apr. 30.

Fausto Appetente Die (On St. Dominic), June 29.

Pius XI

(1922-39)

1922: *Ubi Arcano Dei Consilio* (On the peace of Christ in the Kingdom of Christ), Dec. 23.

1923: *Rerum Omnium Perturbationem* (On St. Francis de Sales), Jan. 26.

Studiorum Ducem (On St. Thomas Aquinas), June 29.

Ecclesiam Dei (On St. Josaphat), Nov. 12.

1924: *Maximam Gravissimamque* (To the bishops, clergy, and people of France, on French diocesan associations), Jan. 18.

1925: *Quas Primas* (On the feast of Christ the King), Dec. 11.

1926: *Rerum Ecclesiae* (On Catholic missions), Feb. 28.

Rite Expiatis (On St. Francis of Assisi), Apr. 30.

Iniquis Afflictisque (On the persecution of the Church in Mexico), Nov. 18.

1928: *Mortalium Animos* (On religious unity), Jan. 6.

Miserentissimus Redemptor (On reparation to the Sacred Heart), May 8.

Rerum Orientalium (On the promotion of Oriental Studies), Sept. 8.

1929: *Mens Nostra* (On the promotion of Spiritual Exercises), Dec. 20.

Quinquagesimo Ante (On his sacerdotal jubilee), Dec. 23.

Rappresentanti in Terra (On Christian education), Dec. 31. [Latin text, *Divini Illius Magistri*, published several months later with minor changes.]

1930: *Ad Salutem* (On St. Augustine), Apr. 20.

Casti Connubii (On Christian Marriage), Dec. 31.

1931: *Quadragesimo Anno* (Commemorating the fortieth anniversary of Leo XIII's *Rerum Novarum*, on reconstruction of the social order), May 15.

Non Abbiamo Bisogno (On Catholic Action in Italy), June 29.

Nova Impendet (On the economic crisis), Oct. 2.

Lux Veritatis (On the Council of Ephesus), Dec. 25.

1932: *Caritate Christi Compulsi* (On the Sacred Heart), May 3.

Acerba Animi (To the bishops of Mexico, on persecution of the Church in Mexico), Sept. 29.

1933: *Dilectissima Nobis* (To the bishops, clergy, and people of Spain, on oppression of the Church in Spain), June 3.

1935: *Ad Catholici Sacerdotii* (On the Catholic priesthood), Dec. 20.

1936: *Vigilanti Cura* (To the bishops of the United States, on motion pictures), June 29.

1937: *Mit Brennender Sorge* (To the bishops of Germany, on the Church and the German Reich), Mar. 14.

Divini Redemptoris (On atheistic communism), Mar. 19.

Nos es Muy Conocida (To the bishops of Mexico: on the religious situation in Mexico), Mar. 28

Ingravescentibus Malis (On the Rosary) Sept. 29.

Pius XII
(1939-58)

1939: *Summi Pontificatus* (On the unity of human society), Oct. 20.

Sertum Laetitiae (To the bishops of the United States, on the 150th anniversary of the establishment of the hierarchy in the United States), Nov. 1.

1940: *Saeculo Exeunte Octavo* (To the bishops of Portugal and its colonies, on the eighth centenary of the independence of Portugal), June 13.

1943: *Mystici Corporis Christi* (On the Mystical Body of Christ), June 29.

Divino Afflante Spiritu (On promoting biblical studies, commemorating the fiftieth anniversary of *Providentissimus Deus*), Sept. 30.

1944: *Orientalis Ecclesiae* (On St. Cyril, Patriarch of Alexandria), Apr. 9.

1945: *Communium Interpretes Dolorum* (To the bishops of the world, appealing for prayers for peace during May), Apr. 15.

Orientales Omnes Ecclesias (On the 350th anniversary of the reunion of the Ruthenian Church with the Apostolic See), Dec. 23.

1946: *Quemadmodum* (Pleading for the care of the world's destitute children), Jan. 6.

Deiparae Virginis Mariae (To all the bishops of the world, on the possibility of defining the Assumption of the Blessed Virgin Mary as a dogma of faith), May 1.

1947: *Fulgens Radiatur* (On St. Benedict), Mar. 21.

Mediator Dei (On the sacred liturgy), Nov. 20.

Optatissima Pax (Prescribing public prayers for social and world peace), Dec. 18.

1948: *Auspicia Quaedam* (On public prayers for world peace and solution of problem of Palestine), May 1.

In Multiplicibus Curis (On prayers for peace in Palestine), Oct. 24.

1949: *Redemptoris Nostri Cruciatus* (On the holy places in Palestine), Apr. 15.

1950: *Anni Sacri* (On the program for combating atheistic propaganda throughout the world), Mar. 12.

Summi Maeroris (On public prayers for peace), July 19.

Humani Generis (Concerning some false opinions threatening to undermine the foundations of Catholic doctrine), Aug. 12.

Mirabile Illud (On the crusade of prayers for peace), Dec. 6.

1951: *Evangelii Praecones* (On the promotion of Catholic missions), June 2.

Sempiternus Rex Christus (On the Council of Chalcedon), Sept. 8.

Ingruentium Malorum (On reciting the Rosary), Sept. 15.

1952: *Orientales Ecclesias* (On the persecuted Eastern Church), Dec. 15.

1953: *Doctor Mellifluus* (On St. Bernard of Clairvaux, the last of the fathers), May 24.

Fulgens Corona (Proclaiming a Marian Year to commemorate the centenary of the definition of the dogma of the Immaculate Conception), Sept. 8.

1954: *Sacra Virginitas* (On consecrated virginity), Mar. 25.

Ecclesiae Fastos (To the bishops of Great Britain, Germany, Austria, France, Belgium, and Holland, on St. Boniface), June 5.

Ad Sinarum Gentem (To the bishops, clergy, and people of China, on the supranationality of the Church), Oct. 7.

Ad Caeli Reginam (Proclaiming the Queenship of Mary), Oct. 11.

1955: *Musicae Sacrae* (On sacred music), Dec. 25.

1956: *Haurietis Aquas* (On devotion to the Sacred Heart), May 15.

Luctuosissimi Eventus (Urging public prayers for peace and freedom for the people of Hungary), Oct. 28.

Laetamur Admodum (Renewing exhortation for prayers for peace for Poland, Hungary, and especially for the Middle East), Nov. 1.

Datis Nuperrime (Lamenting the sorrowful events in Hungary and condemning the ruthless use of force), Nov. 5.

1957: *Fidei Donum* (On the present condition of the Catholic missions, especially in Africa), Apr. 21.

Invicti Athletae (On St. Andrew Bobola), May 16.

Le Pelerinage de Lourdes (Warning against materialism on the centenary of the apparitions at Lourdes), July 2.

Miranda Prorsus (On the communications field, motion picture, radio, television), Sept. 8.

1958: *Ad Apostolorum Principis* (To the bishops of China, on Communism and the Church in China), June 29.

Meminisse Iuvat (On prayers for persecuted Church), July 14.

Bl. John XXIII
(1958-63)

1959: *Ad Petri Cathedram* (On truth, unity, and peace,

in a spirit of charity), June 29.

Sacerdotii Nostri Primordia (On St. John Vianney), Aug. 1.

Grata Recordatio (On the Rosary, prayer for the Church, missions, international and social problems), Sept. 26.

Princeps Pastorum (On the missions, native clergy, lay participation), Nov. 28.

1961: *Mater et Magistra* (On Christianity and social progress), May 15.

Aeterna Dei Sapientia (On the fifteenth centenary of the death of Pope St. Leo I, the see of Peter as the center of Christian unity), Nov. 11.

1962: *Paenitentiam Agere* (On the need for the practice of interior and exterior penance), July 1.

1963: *Pacem in Terris* (On establishing universal peace in truth, justice, charity, and liberty), Apr. 11.

Paul VI
(1963-78)

1964: *Ecclesiam Suam* (On the Church), Aug. 6.

1965: *Mense Maio* (On prayers during May for the preservation of peace), Apr. 29.

Mysterium Fidei (On the Holy Eucharist), Sept. 3.

1966: *Christi Matri* (On prayers for peace during Oct.), Sept. 15.

1967: *Populorum Progressio* (On the development of peoples), Mar. 26.

Sacerdotalis Caelibatus (On the celibacy of the priest), June 24.

1968: *Humanae Vitae* (On the regulation of birth), July 25.

John Paul II
(1978-2005)

1979: *Redemptor Hominis* (On redemption and dignity of the human race), Mar. 4

1980: *Dives in Misericordia* (On the mercy of God), Nov. 30.

1981: *Laborem Exercens* (On human work), Sept. 14.

1985: *Slavorum Apostoli* (Commemorating Sts. Cyril and Methodius, on the eleventh centenary of the death of St. Methodius), June 2.

1986: *Dominum et Vivificantem* (On the Holy Spirit in the life of the Church and the world), May 18.

1987: *Redemptoris Mater* (On the role of Mary in the mystery of Christ and her active and exemplary presence in the life of the Church), Mar. 25.

Sollicitudo Rei Socialis (On social concerns, on the 20th anniversary of *Populorum Progressio*), Dec. 30.

1991: *Redemptoris Missio* (On the permanent validity of the Church's missionary mandate), Jan. 22.

Centesimus Annus (Commemorating the centenary of *Rerum Novarum* and addressing the social question in a contemporary perspective), May 1.

1993: *Veritatis Splendor* (On fundamental questions on the Church's moral teaching), Aug. 6.

1995: *Evangelium Vitae* (On the value and inviolability of human life), Mar. 25.

Ut Unum Sint (On commitment to ecumenism), May 25.

1998: *Fides et Ratio* (On faith and reason), Oct. 1.

2003: *Ecclesia de Eucharistia* (Church of the Eucharist), April 17.

Benedict XVI (2005-)
2005: *Deus Caritas Est* (God is Love), Dec. 25.
2007: *Spe Salvi* (Saved by hope), Nov. 30.

CANONIZATIONS BY LEO XIII AND HIS SUCCESSORS

"Canonization" (*see* **Glossary**) is an infallible declaration by the pope that a person who suffered martyrdom and/or practiced Christian virtue to a heroic degree is in glory with God in heaven and is worthy of public honor by the universal Church and of imitation by the faithful.

Biographies of some of the saints listed below are given elsewhere in the *Almanac; see* **Index**; for biographies of all new saints for 2007-08, *see* **Saints**.

Leo XIII
(1878-1903)

1881: Clare of Montefalco (d. 1308); John Baptist de Rossi (1698-1764); Lawrence of Brindisi (d. 1619).

1883: Benedict J. Labre (1748-83).

1888: Seven Holy Founders of the Servite Order; Peter Claver (1581-1654); John Berchmans (1599-1621); Alphonsus Rodriguez (1531-1617).

1897: Anthony M. Zaccaria (1502-39); Peter Fourier of Our Lady (1565-1640).

1900: John Baptist de La Salle (1651-1719); Rita of Cascia (1381-1457).

St. Pius X
(1903-14)

1904: Alexander Sauli (1534-93); Gerard Majella (1725-55).

1909: Joseph Oriol (1650-1702); Clement M. Hofbauer (1751-1820).

Benedict XV
(1914-22)

1920: Gabriel of the Sorrowful Mother (1838-62); Margaret Mary Alacoque (1647-90); Joan of Arc (1412-31).

Pius XI
(1922-39)

1925: Thérèse of Lisieux (1873-97); Peter Canisius (1521-97); Mary Magdalen Postel (1756-1846); Mary Magdalen Sophie Barat (1779-1865); John Eudes (1601-80); John Baptist Vianney (Curé of Ars) (1786-1859).

1930: Lucy Filippini (1672-1732); Catherine Tomas (1533-74); Jesuit North American Martyrs; Robert Bellarmine (1542-1621); Theophilus of Corte (1676-1740).

1931: Albert the Great (1206-80) (equivalent canonization).

1933: Andrew Fournet (1752-1834); Bernadette Soubirous (1844-79).

1934: Joan Antida Thouret (1765-1826); Mary Michaeli (1809-65); Louise de Marillac (1591-1660); Joseph Benedict Cottolengo (1786-1842); Pompilius M. Pirotti, priest (1710-56); Teresa Margaret Redi (1747-70); John Bosco (1815-88); Conrad of Parzham (1818-94).

1935: John Fisher (1469-1535); Thomas More (1478-1535).

1938: Andrew Bobola (1592-1657); John Leonardi (c.

1550-1609); Salvatore of Horta (1520-67).

Pius XII
(1939-58)

1940: Gemma Galgani (1878-1903); Mary Euphrasia Pelletier (1796-1868).

1943: Margaret of Hungary (d. 1270) (equivalent canonization).

1946: Frances Xavier Cabrini (1850-1917).

1947: Nicholas of Flüe (1417-87); John of Britto (1647-93); Bernard Realini (1530-1616); Joseph Cafasso (1811-60); Michael Garicoits (1797-1863); Jeanne Elizabeth des Ages (1773-1838); Louis Marie Grignon de Montfort (1673-1716); Catherine Labouré (1806-76).

1949: Jeanne de Lestonnac (1556-1640); Maria Josepha Rossello (1811-80).

1950: Emily de Rodat (1787-1852); Anthony Mary Claret (1807-70); Bartolomea Capitanio (1807-33); Vincenza Gerosa (1784-1847); Jeanne de Valois (1461-1504); Vincenzo M. Strambi (1745-1824); Maria Goretti (1890-1902); Mariana Paredes of Jesus (1618-45).

1951: Maria Domenica Mazzarello (1837-81); Emilie de Vialar (1797-1856); Anthony M. Gianelli (1789-1846); Ignatius of Laconi (1701-81); Francis Xavier Bianchi (1743-1815).

1954: Pope Pius X (1835-1914); Dominic Savio (1842-57); Maria Crocifissa di Rosa (1813-55); Peter Chanel (1803-41); Gaspar del Bufalo (1786-1837); Joseph M. Pignatelli (1737-1811).

1958: Herman Joseph, O. Praem. (1150-1241) (equivalent canonization).

Bl. John XXIII
(1958-63)

1959: Joaquina de Vedruna de Mas (1783-1854); Charles of Sezze (1613-70).

1960: Gregory Barbarigo (1625-97) (equivalent canonization); John de Ribera (1532-1611).

1961: Bertilla Boscardin (1888-1922).

1962: Martin de Porres (1579-1639); Peter Julian Eymard (1811-68); Anthony Pucci, priest (1819-92); Francis Mary of Camporosso (1804-66).

1963: Vincent Pallotti (1795-1850).

Paul VI
(1963-78)

1964: Charles Lwanga and Twenty-one Companions, Martyrs of Uganda (d. between 1885-87).

1967: Benilde Romacon (1805-62).

1969: Julia Billiart (1751-1816).

1970: Maria Della Dolorato Torres Acosta (1826-87); Leonard Murialdo (1828-1900); Therese Couderc (1805-85); John of Ávila (1499-1569); Nicholas Tavelic, Deodatus of Aquitaine, Peter of Narbonne and Stephen of Cuneo, martyrs (d. 1391); Forty English and Welsh Martyrs (d. 16th cent.).

1974: Teresa of Jesus Jornet Ibars (1843-97).

1975: Vicenta Maria Lopez y Vicuna (1847-90); Elizabeth Bayley Seton (1774-1821); John Masias (1585-1645); Oliver Plunket (1629-81); Justin de Jacobis (1800-60); John Baptist of the Conception (1561-1613).

1976: Beatrice da Silva (1424 or 1426-90); John Ogilvie (1579-1615).

1977: Rafaela Maria Porras y Ayllon (1850-1925); John Nepomucene Neumann (1811-60); Sharbel Makhlouf (1828-98).

John Paul II
(1978-2005)

1982: Crispin of Viterbo (1668-1750); Maximilian Kolbe (1894-1941); Marguerite Bourgeoys (1620-1700); Jeanne Delanoue (1666-1736).

1983: Leopold Mandic (1866-1942).

1984: Paola Frassinetti (1809-92); 103 Korean Martyrs (d. between 1839-67); Miguel Febres Cordero (1854-1910).

1986: Francis Anthony Fasani (1681-1742); Giuseppe Maria Tomasi (1649-1713).

1987: Giuseppe Moscati (d. 1927); Lawrence (Lorenzo) Ruiz and Fifteen Companions, Martyrs of Japan (d. 1630s).

1988: Eustochia Calafato (1434-85); 117 Martyrs of Vietnam (96 Vietnamese, 11 Spanish, 10 French, included 8 bishops, 50 priests, 1 seminarian, 58 lay persons); Roque Gonzalez (1576-1628), Alfonso Rodriguez (1598-1628) and Juan de Castillo (1596-1628), Jesuit martyrs of Paraguay; Rose Philippine Duchesne (1796-1852); Simon de Rojas (1552-1624); Magdalen of Canossa (1774-1835); Maria Rosa Molas y Vollve (d. 1876).

1989: Clelia Barbieri (1847-70); Gaspar Bertoni (1777-1853); Richard Pampuri, religious (1897-1930); Agnes of Bohemia (1211-82); Albert Chmielowski (1845-1916); Mutien-Marie Wiaux (1841-1917).

1990: Marguerite D'Youville (1701-77).

1991: Raphael (Jozef) Kalinowski (1835-1907).

1992: Claude La Colombiere (1641-82); Ezequiel Moreno y Diaz (1848-1905).

1993: Marie of St. Ignatius (Claudine Thevenet) (1774-1837); Teresa "de los Andes" (Juana Fernandez Solar) (1900-20); Enrique de Ossó y Cervelló (1840-96).

1995: Jan Sarkander (1576-1620); Zdislava of Lemberk (d. 1252); Marek Krizin (1588-1619), Stefan Pongracz (1582-1619), Melichar Grodziecky (1584-1619), martyrs of Kosice; Eugene de Mazenod (1782-1861).

1996: Jean-Gabriel Perboyre (1802-40); Juan Grande Roman (1546-1600); Bro. Egidio Maria of St. Joseph (1729-1812).

1997: Hedwig (1371-99); John Dukla, O.F.M. (d. 1484).

1998: Edith Stein (d. 1942).

1999: Marcellin Joseph Benoit Champagnat (1789-1840), Giovanni Calabria (1873-1954); Agostina Livia Pietrantonio (1864-94); Sr. Kunegunda Kinga (1224-92); Cirilo Bertrán and Eight Companion Brothers of the Christian Schools (d. Oct. 9, 1934); Inocencio de la Immaculada (d. Oct. 9, 1934); St. Jaime Hilario Barbal (1889-1937); Benedetto Menni (1841-1914); Tommaso da Cori (1655-1729).

2000: Mary Faustina Kowalska (1905-38); María Josefa of the Heart of Jesus Sancho de Guerra (1842-1912); Cristóbal Magallanes and 24 Companions (d. 1915-28); José Maria de Yermo y Parres (1851-1904); Maria de Jesús Sacramentado Venegas (1868-1959); 120 Martyrs of China (17th-20th centuries); Katherine Drexel (1858-1955); Josephine Bakhita (d. 1947).

2001: Luigi Scrosoppi (1804-84); Agostino Roscelli (1818-1902); Bernardo da Corleone (1605-67); Teresa Eustochio Verzeri (1801-52); Rafqa Petra Choboq Ar-Rayes (1832-1914); Giuseppe Marello (1844-95); Paula Montal Fornés de San José de Calasanz (1799-1889); Léonie Françoise de Sales Aviat (1844-1914); Maria Crescentia Höss (1682-1744).

2002: Alonso de Orozco (1500-91); Ignazio da Santhia (Lorenzo Maurizio Belvisotti) (1686-1770); Umile da Bisignano (Luca Antonio Pirozzo) (1582-1637); Paulina do Coracao Agonizante de Jesus (Amabile Visintainer) (1865-1942); Benedetta Cambiagio Frassinello (1791-1858); Pio da Pietrelcina (Padre Pio,1887-1968); Juan Diego Cuauhlatoatzin (16th century); Pedro de San Jose de Betancur (1619-67); Josemaria Escriva (1902-75).

2003: Pedro Poveda Castroverde (1874-1936); José María Rubio y Peralta (1864-1929); Genoveva Torres Morales (1870-1956); Angela de la Cruz (1846-1932); María Maravillas de Jesus (1891-1974); Jozef Sebastian Pelczar (1842-1924); Urszula Ledochowska (1865-1939); Maria de

Mattias (1805-66); Virginia Centurione Bracelli (1587-1651); Daniel Comboni (1831-1881); Arnold Janssen (1837-1909); Josef Freinademetz (1852-1908).

2004: Gianna Beretta Molla (1922-1962); Nimatullah Kassab al-Hardini (1828-1858); Josep Manyanet Vives (1833-1901); Luigi Orione (1872-1940); Annibale Di Francia (1851-1927); Paola Elisabetta Cerioli (1816-1865).

Benedict XVI (2005-)

2005: Józef Bilczewski (1860-1923); Gaetano Catanoso (1879-1963); Zygmunt Gorazdowski (1845-1920); Alberto Hurtado Cruchaga (1901-1952); Felix of Nicosia (1715-1787).

2006: Rafael Guízar Valencia (1878-1938); Filippo Smaldone (1848-1923); Rosa Venerini (1656-1728); Theodore Guérin (1798-1856).

2007: Antoñio de Sant Anna Galváo (1739-1822); George Preca (1880-1962); Simon of Lipnica (c. 1435-1482); Karel Van Sint Andres Houben (1821-1893); Anne Marie Eugenie (1817-1898).

BEATIFICATIONS BY POPE JOHN PAUL II, 1979-2004

For biographical details of all those beatified in 2004, please *see under* **Saints**.

1979: Margaret Ebner (Feb. 24); Francis Coll, O.P., Jacques Laval, S.S.Sp. (Apr. 29); Enrique de Ossó y Cervelló (Oct. 14; canonized June 16, 1993).

1980: José de Anchieta, Peter of St. Joseph Betancurt (canonized July 30, 2002), Francois de Montmorency Laval, Kateri Tekakwitha, Marie Guyart of the Incarnation (June 22); Don Luigi Orione (canonized May 16, 2004), Bartolomea Longo, Maria Anna Sala (Oct. 26).

1981: Sixteen Martyrs of Japan (Lorenzo Ruiz and Companions) (Feb 18; canonized Oct. 18, 1987); Maria Repetto, Alan de Solminihac, Richard Pampuri (canonized Nov. 1, 1989), Claudine Thevenet (canonized Mar. 21, 1993), Aloysius (Luigi) Scrosoppi (canonized June 10, 2001) (Oct. 4).

1982: Peter Donders, C.SS.R., Marie Rose Durocher, Andre Bessette, C.S.C., Maria Angela Astorch, Marie Rivier (May 23); Fra Angelico (equivalent beatification) (July); Jeanne Jugan, Salvatore Lilli and 7 Armenian Companions (Oct. 3); Sr. Angela of the Cross (Nov. 5; canonized May 3, 2003).

1983: Maria Gabriella Sagheddu (Jan. 25); Luigi Versiglia, Callisto Caravario (May 15); Ursula Ledochowska (canonized May 18, 2003) (June 20); Raphael (Jozef) Kalinowski (canonized Nov. 17, 1991), Bro. Albert (Adam Chmielowski), T.O.R. (June 22; canonized Nov. 12, 1989); Giacomo Cusmano, Jeremiah of Valachia, Domingo Iturrate Zubero (Oct. 30); Marie of Jesus Crucified (Marie Bouardy) (Nov. 13).

1984: Fr. William Repin and 98 Companions (Martyrs of Angers during French Revolution), Giovanni Mazzucconi (Feb. 19); Marie Leonie Paradis (Sept. 11); Federico Albert, Clemente Marchisio, Isidore of St. Joseph (Isidore de Loor), Rafaela Ybarra de Villalongo (Sept. 30); José Manyanet y Vives (canonized May 16, 2004), Daniel Brottier, C.S.Sp., Sr. Elizabeth of the Trinity (Elizabeth Catez) (Nov. 25).

1985: Mercedes de Jesus (Feb. 1); Ana de los Angeles Monteagudo (Feb. 2); Pauline von Mallinckrodt, Catherine Troiani (Apr. 14); Benedict Menni (canonized Nov. 21, 1999), Peter Friedhofen (June 23); Anwarite Nangapeta (Aug. 15); Virginae Centurione Bracelli (canonized May 18, 2003) (Sept. 22); Diego Luis de San Vitores, S.J., Jose M. Rubio y Peralta, S.J. (canonized May 4, 2003), Francisco Garate, S.J. (Oct. 6); Titus Brandsma, O.Carm. (Nov. 3); Pio Campidelli, C.P., Marie Teresa of Jesus Gerhardinger, Rafqa Ar-Rayes (canonized June 10, 2001) (Nov. 17).

1986: Alphonsa Mattathupandatu of the Immaculate Conception, Kuriakose Elias Chavara (Feb. 8); Antoine Chevrier (Oct. 4); Teresa Maria of the Cross Manetti (Oct. 19).

1987: Maria Pilar of St. Francis Borgia, Maria Angeles of St. Joseph, Cardinal Marcellis Spinola y Maestre, Emmanuel Domingo y Sol (Mar. 29); Teresa of Jesus "de los Andes" (canonized March 21, 1993) (Apr. 3); Edith Stein (Teresa Benedicta of the Cross) (May 1; canonized, Oct. 11, 1998); Rupert Meyer, S.J. (May 3); Pierre-Francois Jamet, Cardinal Andrea Carlo Ferrari, Benedicta Cambiagio Frassinello, Louis Moreau (May 10); Carolina Kozka, Michal Kozal (June 10); George Matulaitis (Matulewicz) (June 28); Marcel Callo, Pierino Morosini, Antonia Mesina (Oct. 4); Blandina Marten, Ulriche Nische, Jules Reche (Bro. Arnold) (Nov. 1); 85 Martyrs (d. between 1584-1689) of England, Scotland and Wales (Nov. 22).

1988: Giovanni Calabria (canonized Apr. 18, 1999); Joseph Nascimbeni (Apr. 17); Pietro Bonilli, Kaspar Stangassinger, Francisco Palau y Quer, Savina Petrilli (Apr. 24), Laura Vicuna (Sept. 3); Joseph Gerard (Sept. 11); Miguel Pro, Giuseppe Benedetto Dusmet, Francisco Faa di Bruno, Junipero Serra, Frederick Jansoone, Josefa Naval Girbes (Sept. 25); Bernardo Maria Silvestrelli, Charles Houben, Honoratus Kozminski (Oct. 16); Niels Stensen (Nicolaus Steno) (Oct. 23); Katharine Drexel (canonized Oct. 1, 2000), 3 Missionary Martyrs of

Ethiopia (Liberato Weiss, Samuel Marzorati, Michele Pio Fasoli) (Nov. 20).

1989: Martin of Saint Nicholas, Melchior of St. Augustine, Mary of Jesus of the Good Shepherd, Maria Margaret Caiani, Maria of Jesus Siedliska, Maria Catherine of St. Augustine (Apr. 23); Victoria Rasoamanarivo (Apr. 30); Bro. Scubilionis (John Bernard Rousseau) (May 2); Elizabeth Renzi, Antonio Lucci (June 17); Niceforo de Jesus y Maria (Vicente Diez Tejerina and 25 Companions (martyred in Spain), Lorenzo Salvi, Gertrude Caterina Comensoli, Francisca Ana Cirer Carbonell (Oct. 1); 7 Martyrs from Thailand (Philip Sipong, Sr. Agnes Phila, Sr. Lucia Khambang, Agatha Phutta, Cecilia Butsi, Bibiana Khampai, Maria Phon), Timothy Giaccardo, Mother Maria of Jesus Deluil-Martiny (Oct. 22); Giuseppe Baldo (Oct. 31).

1990: 9 Martyrs of Astoria during Spanish Civil War (De la Salle Brothers Cirilo Bertran, Marciano Jose, Julian Alfredo, Victoriano Pio, Benjamin Julian, Augusto Andres, Benito de Jesus, Aniceto Adolfo; and Passionist priest Innocencio Inmaculada; canonized Nov. 21, 1999), Mercedes Prat, Manuel Barbal Cosan (Brother Jaime), Philip Rinaldi, Tommaso da Cori (canonized Nov. 21, 1999) (Apr. 29); Juan Diego (confirmation of Apr. 9 decree; canonized July 31, 2002), 3 Child Martyrs (Cristobal, Antonio and Juan), Fr. Jose Maria de Yermo y Parres (May 6; canonized May 21, 2001); Pierre Giorgio Frassati (May 20); Hanibal Maria Di Francia (canonized May 16, 2004), Joseph Allamano (Oct. 7); Marthe Aimee LeBouteiller, Louise Therese de Montaignac de Chauvance, Maria Schinina, Elisabeth Vendramini (Nov. 4).

1991: Annunciata Cocchetti, Marie Therese Haze, Clara Bosatta (Apr. 21); Jozef Sebastian Pelczar (June 2; canonized May 18, 2003); Boleslava Lament (June 5); Rafael Chylinski (June 9); Angela Salawa (Aug. 13); Edoardo Giuseppe Rosaz (July 14, Susa, Italy); Pauline of the Heart of Jesus in Agony Visentainer (canonized May 19, 2002) (Oct. 18, Brazil); Adolph Kolping (Oct. 27).

1992: Josephine Bakhita (canonized Oct. 1, 2000), Josemaria Escriva de Balaguer (May 17; canonized Oct. 6, 2000); Francesco Spinelli (June 21, Caravaggio, Italy); 17 Irish Martyrs, Rafael Arnáiz Barón, Nazaria Ignacia March Mesa, Léonie Françoise de Sales Aviat (canonized Nov. 25, 2001), and Maria Josefa Sancho de Guerra (canonized Oct. 1, 2000) (Sept. 27); 122 Martyrs of Spanish Civil War, Narcisa Martillo Morán (Oct. 25); Cristóbal Magellanes and 24 companions, Mexican martyrs (), and Maria de Jesús Sacramentado Venegas (Nov. 22; canonized May 21, 2000).

1993: Dina Belanger (Mar. 20); John Duns Scotus (Mar. 20, cult solemnly recognized); Mary Angela Truszkowska, Ludovico of Casoria, Faustina Kowalska (canonized Apr. 30, 2000), Paula Montal Fornés (canonized Nov. 25, 2001) (Apr. 18); Stanislaus Kazimierczyk (Apr. 18, cult solemnly recognized); Maurice Tornay, Marie-Louise Trichet, Columba Gabriel and Florida Cevoli (May 16); Giuseppe Marello (Sept. 26; canonized Nov. 25, 2001); Eleven Martyrs of Almeria, Spain, during Spanish Civil War (2 bishops, 7 brothers, 1 priest, 1 lay person); Victoria Diez y Bustos de Molina,

Maria Francesca (Anna Maria) Rubatto; Pedro Castroverde (canonized May 4, 2003), Maria Crucified (Elisabetta Maria) Satellico (Oct. 10).

1994: Isidore Bakanja, Elizabeth Canori Mora; Dr. Gianna Beretta Molla (Apr. 24; canonized May 16, 2004); Nicolas Roland, Alberto Hurtado Cruchaga, Maria Rafols, Petra of St. Joseph Perez Florida, Josephine Vannini (Oct. 16); Magdalena Caterina Morano (Nov. 5); Hyacinthe Marie Cormier, Marie Poussepin, Agnes de Jesus Galand, Eugenia Joubert, Claudio Granzotto (Nov. 20).

1995: Peter ToRot (Jan. 17); Mother Mary of the Cross MacKillop (Jan. 19); Joseph Vaz (Jan. 21); Rafael Guizar Valencia, Modestino of Jesus and Mary, Genoveva Torres Morales (canonized May 4, 2003), Grimoaldo of the Purification (Jan. 29); Johann Nepomuk von Tschiderer (Apr. 30); Maria Helena Stollenwerk, Maria Alvarado Cordozo, Giuseppina Bonino, Maria Domenica Brun Barbantini, Agostino Roscelli (May 7; canonized June 10, 2001); Damien de Veuster (June 4); 109 Martyrs (64 from French Revolution – Martyrs of La Rochelle – and 45 from Spanish Civil War), Anselm Polanco Fontecha, Felipe Ripoll Morata, and Pietro Casini (Oct. 1); Mary Theresa Scherer, Maria Bernarda Butler and Marguerite Bays (Oct. 29).

1996: Daniel Comboni (canonized Oct. 5, 2003) and Guido Maria Conforti (Mar. 17); Cardinal Alfredo Ildefonso Schuster, O.S.B., Filippo Smaldone and Gennaro Sarnelli (priests) and Candida Maria de Jesus Cipitria y Barriola, Maria Raffaella Cimatti, Maria Antonia Bandres (religious) (May 12), Bernhard Lichtenberg and Karl Leisner (June 23), Wincenty Lewoniuk and 12 companions, Edmund Rice, Maria Ana Mogas Fontcuberta and Marcelina Darowska (Oct 6); Otto Neururer, Jakob Gapp and Catherine Jarrige (Nov. 24).

1997: Bishop Florentino Asensio Barroso, Sr. Maria Encarnacion Rosal of the Sacred Heart, Fr. Gaetano Catanoso, Fr. Enrico Rebuschini and Ceferino Gimenez Malla, first gypsy beatified (May 4); Bernardina Maria Jablonska, Maria Karlowska (June 6); Frédéric Ozanam (Aug. 22); Bartholomew Mary Dal Monte (Sep. 27); Elías del Socorro Nieves, Domenico Lentini, Giovanni Piamarta, Emilie d'Hooghvorst, Maria Teresa Fasce (Oct. 12); John Baptist Scalabrini, Vilmos Apor, María Vicenta of St. Dorothy Chávez Orozco (Nov. 9).

1998: Bishop Vincent Bossilkov, María Sallés, Brigida of Jesus (Mar. 15); Fr. Cyprian Tansi (Mar. 22); Nimatullah al-Hardini (canonized May 16, 2004); 11 Spanish nuns (May 10); Secondo Polla (May 23); Giovanni Maria Boccardo, Teresa Grillo Chavez, Teresa Bracco (May 24); Jakob Kern, Maria Restituta Kafka, and Anton Schwartz (June 21); Giuseppe Tovini (Sept. 20); Cardinal Alojzije Stepinac (Oct. 3); Antônio de Sant'Anna Galvão, Faustino Miguez, Zeferino Agostini, Mother Theodore Guérin (Oct. 25).

1999: Vicente Soler, and six Augustinian Recollect Companions, Manuel Martin Sierra, Nicolas Barre, Anna Schaeffer (Mar. 7); Padre Pio (May 2; canonized June 16, 2002); Fr. Stefan Wincenty Frelichowski (June 7); 108 Polish Martyrs, Regina Protmann, Edmund Bojanowski (June 13); Bishop Anton Slomsek (Sept. 19); Ferdinando Maria

Baccilieri, Edward Maria Joannes Poppe, Arcangelo Tadini, Mariano da Roccacasale, Diego Oddi, Nicola da Gesturi (Oct. 3).

2000: André de Soveral, Ambrósio Francisco Ferro and 28 Companions, Nicolas Bunkerd Kitbamrung, Maria Stella Mardosewicz and 10 Companions, PedroCalungsod and Andrew of Phú Yên (Mar. 5); Mariano de Jesus Euse Hoyos, Francis Xavier Seelos, Anna Rosa Gattorno, Maria Elisabetta Hesselblad, Mariam Thresia Chiramel Mankidiyan (Apr. 9); Jacinta and Francisco Marto of Fatima (May 13); Pope Pius IX, Pope John XXIII, Tommaso Reggio, Guillaume-Joseph Chaminade, Columba Marmion (Sept. 3).

2001: José Aparicio Sanz and 232 Companions of the Spanish Civil War (Mar. 11); Manuel Gonzalez Garcia, Marie-Anne Blondin, Caterina Volpicelli, Caterina Cittadini, Carlos Manuel Cecilio Rodriguez Santiago (Apr. 29); George Preca, Ignatius Falzon, Maria Adeodata Pisani (May 9); Abp. Jósef Bilczewski and Fr. Sygmunt Gorazdowski, Ukrainian martyrs (June 27).

2002: Gaetano Errico, Lodovico Pavoni, Luigi Variara, Maria del Transito de Jesus Sacramentado, Artemide Zatti, Maria Romero Meneses (Apr. 14); Kamen Vitchev, Pavel Djidjov, Josaphat Chichkov (May 26); Juan Bautista and Jacinto de Los Angeles (Aug. 1); Zygmunt Szczęsny Feliński, Jan Balicki, Jan Beyzym, Sancja

Szymkowiak (Aug. 18); Daudi Okelo, Jildo Irwa, Andrea Giacinto Longhin, O.F.M. Cap., Marcantonio Durando, Marie de la Passion Hélène Marie de Chappotin de Neuville, Liduina Meneguzzi (Oct. 20).

2003: Pierre Bonhomme, María Dolores Rodríguez Sopeña, María Caridad Brader, Juana María Condesa Lluch, László Batthyány-Strattmann (Mar. 23); Eugenia Ravasco, Giacomo Alberione, Giulia Salzano, Marco d'Aviano, Maria Cristina Brando, Maria Domenica Mantovani (Apr. 27); Maria of Jesus Crucified *Petkovic* (June 6); Ivan Merz (June 22); Vasil' Hopko, Zdenka Schelingová (Sept. 14); Mother Teresa of Calcutta (Oct. 19); Juan Nepomuceno Zegrí y Moreno, Valentin Paquay, Luigi Maria Monti, Bonifacia Rodríguez Castro, Rosalie Rendu (Nov. 9).

2004: Luigi Talamoni, Matilde del Sagrado Corazón Téllez Robles, Piedad de la Cruz Ortiz Real, Maria Candida of the Eucharist (Mar. 21); Augusto Czartoryski, Laura Montoya, María Guadalupe García Zavala, Giulia Nemesia Valle, Eusebia Palomino Yenes, Alexandrina Maria da Costa (Apr. 25); Pere Tarrés i Claret, Alberto Marvelli, Pina Suriano (Sept. 5); Peter Vigne, Joseph-Marie Cassant, Anna Katharina Emmerick, Maria Ludovica De Angelis, Charles of Austria (Oct. 3).

BEATIFICATIONS UNDER POPE BENEDICT XVI (2005-08)

For biographical details of all those beatified in 2007-2008, please *see* under **Saints**.

2005: Ascension of the Heart of Jesus, Marianne Cope (May 14); Wladyslaw Findysz, Bronislaw Markiewicz, Ignacy Klopotowski (June 19); Cardinal Clemens August von Galen (Oct. 9); Charles de Foucauld, Maria Pia Pastena, Maria Crocifissa Curcio, Eurosia Fabris (Nov. 13); María De Los Ángeles Ginard Martí, Josep Tàpies and six Companions (Oct. 29); Anacleto González Flores and 8 Companions, José Trinidad Rangel, Andrés Solá Molist, Leonardo Pérez, Darío Acosta Zurita (Nov. 20).

2006: Agostino Thevarparampil Kunjachan, Luigi Biraghi, Luigi Monza (Apr. 30); Maria Teresa of Saint Joseph (May 13); Sr. Maria of the Passion (May 14); Rita Amada of Jesus (May 28); Eustáquio von Lieshout (June 15). Euphrasia of the Sacred Heart of Jesus Eluvathingal (Dec. 3).

2007: Luigi Boccardo (Apr. 14); Maria Maddalena of the Passion (Apr. 15); Francesco Spoto (Apr. 21)

Maria Rosa Pellesi (Apr. 29); Carmen del Niño Jesús González Ramos García Prieto (May 6); Carlo Liviero (May 27); Basile-Antoine Marie Moreau (Sept. 15), Marie-Céline de la Présentation (Jeanne Germaine Castang), Stanislaw of Jesus and Mary (Jana Papczyñski) (Sept. 16), Maria Luisa Merkert (Sept. 30), Albertina Berkenbrock (Oct. 20), Emmanuel Gómez González, Adílio Daronch (Oct. 21), Franz Jägerstätter (Oct. 26), Celina Chludziñska v. Borzêcka (Oct. 27), Zepherin Namuncurá (Nov. 11), Antonio Rosmini (Nov. 18), Lindalva Justo de Oliveira (Dec. 2)

2008: Sr. Giuseppina Nicoli (Feb. 3); Celestina of the Mother of God (Marianna Donati) (Mar. 30); Candelaria of St Joseph (Apr. 27); Mary Magdalene of the Incarnation (May 3); Margaret Flesch (May 4); Martha Wiecka (May 24); Maria Giuseppina di Gesù Crocifisso (June 1); Jacques Ghazir Haddad (June 22); Josepha Hendrina Stenmanns (June 29).

ROMAN CURIA

The Roman Curia is the Church's network of central administrative agencies (called dicasteries) serving the Vatican and the local churches, with authority granted by the Pope.

The Curia evolved gradually from advisory assemblies or synods of the Roman clergy with whose assistance the popes directed church affairs during the first 11 centuries. Its original office was the Apostolic Chancery, established in the fourth century to transmit documents. The antecedents of its permanently functioning agencies and offices were special commissions of cardinals and prelates. Its establishment in a form

resembling what it is now dates from the second half of the 16th century.

Pope Paul VI initiated a four-year reorganization study in 1963 that resulted in the constitution *Regimini Ecclesiae Universae.* The document was published Aug. 18, 1967, and went into full effect in March 1968. Pope John Paul II, in the apostolic constitution *Pastor Bonus,* published June 28, 1988, and effective Mar. 1, 1989, ordered modifications of the Curia based on the broad outline of Paul VI's reorganization.

In accordance with Pope John Paul II's reform effective Mar. 1, 1989, and later revisions, the Curia consists of the Secretariat of State, nine congregations (governing agencies), three tribunals (judicial agencies), 11 councils (promotional agencies) and three offices (specialized service agencies). All have equal juridical status with authority granted by the pope.

SECRETARIAT OF STATE

The Secretariat of State, *Palazzo Apostolico Vaticano*, Vatican City. Cardinal Tarcisio Bertone, Secretary of State; Most Rev. Fernando Filoni, Deputy for General Affairs; Dominique Mamberti, Secretary for Relations with States.

The Secretariat of State provides the pope with the closest possible assistance in the care of the universal Church. It consists of two sections:

• The Section for General Affairs assists the pope in expediting daily business of the Holy See. It coordinates curial operations, prepares drafts of documents entrusted to it by the pope, has supervisory duties over the *Acta Apostolicae Sedis, Annuario Pontificio,* the Vatican Press Office and the Central Statistics Office.

• The Section for Relations with States (formerly the Council for Public Affairs of the Church, a separate body) handles diplomatic and other relations with civil governments. Attached to it is a council of Cardinals and Bishops.

Background: Evolved gradually from secretarial offices (dating back to the 15th century) and the Congregation for Extraordinary Ecclesiastical Affairs (dating back to 1793; restructured as the Council for the Public Affairs of the Church by Paul VI in 1967). John Paul II gave it its present form in his June 28, 1988, reform of the Curia.

CONGREGATIONS

Congregation for the Doctrine of the Faith: Piazza del S. Uffizio 11, 00193 Rome, Italy. Cardinal William Levada, prefect; Most Rev. Luis F. Ladaria Ferrer, S.J., secretary.

Has responsibility to safeguard the doctrine of faith and morals. Accordingly, it examines doctrinal questions and promotes studies thereon; evaluates theological opinions and, when necessary and after prior consultation with concerned bishops, reproves those regarded as opposed to principles of the faith; examines books on doctrinal matters and can reprove such works, if the contents so warrant, after giving authors the opportunity to defend themselves. It examines matters pertaining to the Privilege of Faith (Petrine Privilege) in marriage cases, and safeguards the dignity of the sacrament of penance. Attached to the congregation are the Pontifical Biblical Commission and the Theological Commission.

Background: At the beginning of the 13th century, legates of Innocent III were commissioned as the Holy Office of the Inquisition to combat heresy; the same task was entrusted to the Dominican Order by Gregory IX in 1231 and to the Friars Minor by Innocent IV from 1243 to 1254. On July 21, 1542 (apostolic constitution *Licet*), Paul III instituted a permanent congregation of cardinals with supreme and universal competence over matters concerning heretics and those suspected of heresy. Pius IV, St. Pius V and Sixtus V further defined the work of the congregation. St. Pius X changed its name to the Congregation of the Holy

Office. Paul VI (*motu proprio Integrae Servandae,* Dec. 7, 1965), began reorganization of the Curia with this body, to which he gave the new title, Congregation for the Doctrine of the Faith. Its orientation is not merely negative, in the condemnation of error, but positive, in the promotion of orthodox doctrine.

Congregation for the Oriental Churches: Palazzo del Bramante, Via della Conciliazione 34, 00193 Rome, Italy. Cardinal Leonardo Sandri, prefect; Most Rev. Antonio Maria Vegliò, secretary. Members include all patriarchs of the Eastern Catholic Churches and major archbishops.

Has competence in matters concerning the persons and discipline of Eastern Catholic Churches. It has jurisdiction over territories in which the majority of Christians belong to Eastern Churches (i.e., Egypt, the Sinai Peninsula, Eritrea, Northern Ethiopia, Southern Albania, Bulgaria, Cyprus, Greece, Iran, Iraq, Lebanon, Palestine, Syria, Jordan, Turkey, Afghanistan); also, over minority communities of Eastern Church members no matter where they live.

Background: Established by Pius IX Jan. 6, 1862 (apostolic constitution *Romani Pontifices*), and united with the Congregation for the Propagation of the Faith. The congregation was made autonomous by Benedict XV May 1, 1917 (*motu proprio Dei Providentis*), and given wider authority by Pius XI Mar. 25, 1938 (*motu proprio Sancta Dei Ecclesia*).

Congregation for Divine Worship and the Discipline of the Sacraments: Piazza Pio XII 10, 00193 Rome, Italy. Cardinal Francis Arinze, prefect; Most Rev. Albert Malcolm Ranjith Patabendige Don, secretary.

Supervises everything pertaining to the promotion and regulation of the liturgy, primarily the sacraments, without prejudice to the competencies of the Congregation for the Doctrine of the Faith. Attached to the congregation are special commissions treating causes of nullity of sacred ordinations and dispensations from obligations of sacred ordination of deacons and priests.

Background: Originally two separate congregations: the Congregation for Divine Worship (instituted by Paul VI, May 8, 1969) and the Congregation for the Discipline of the Sacraments (established by St. Pius X, June 29, 1908, to replace the Congregation of Rites instituted by Pope Sixtus V in 1588). They were united by Paul VI, July 11, 1975, as the Congregation for the Sacraments and Divine Worship; reestablished as separate congregations by John Paul II in an autograph letter of Apr. 5, 1984, and reunited anew by the same Pope, June 28, 1988 (apostolic constitution *Pastor Bonus*), as the Congregation for Divine Worship and the Discipline of the Sacraments.

Congregation for the Causes of Saints: Piazza Pio XII 10, 00193 Rome, Italy. Most Rev. Angelo Amato, S.D.B., prefect; Most Rev. Michele Di Ruberto, secretary.

Handles matters connected with beatification and canonization causes (in accordance with revised procedures decreed in 1983), and the preservation of relics.

Background: Established by Sixtus V in 1588 as the Congregation of Rites; affected by legislation of Pius XI in 1930; title changed and functions defined by Paul VI, 1969 (apostolic constitution *Sacra Rituum Congregatio*). It was restructured and canonization procedures were revised by John Paul II in 1983 (apostolic constitution *Divinus Perfectionis Magister*).

Congregation for Bishops: Piazza Pio XII 10, 00193 Rome, Italy. Cardinal Giovanni Battista Re, prefect; Most Rev. Francesco Monterisi, secretary.

Has functions related in one way or another to bishops and the jurisdictions in which they serve. It supervises the Pontifical Commission for Latin America. Attached to the congregation are a central coordinating office for Military Vicars (established Feb. 2, 1985) and an office for coordinating ad limina visits (established June 29, 1988).

Background: Established by Sixtus V Jan. 22, 1588 (apostolic constitution *Immensa*); given an extension of powers by St. Pius X June 20, 1908, and Pius XII Aug. 1, 1952 (apostolic constitution *Exsul Familia*); given present title (was known as Consistorial Congregation) by Paul VI (Aug. 1, 1967); competencies redefined by John Paul II, June 28, 1988.

Congregation for the Evangelization of Peoples: Piazza di Spagna 48, 00187 Rome, Italy. Cardinal Ivan Dias, prefect; Most Rev. Robert Sarah, secretary; Most Rev. Piergiuseppe Vacchelli, adjunct secretary.

Directs and coordinates missionary work throughout the world. Accordingly, it has competence over those matters which concern all the missions established for the spread of Christ's kingdom without prejudice to the competence of other congregations. These include: fostering missionary vocations; assigning missionaries to fields of work; establishing ecclesiastical jurisdictions and proposing candidates to serve them as bishops and in other capacities; encouraging the recruitment and development of indigenous clergy; mobilizing spiritual and financial support for missionary activity.

To promote missionary cooperation, the congregation has a Supreme Council for the Direction of Pontifical Missionary Works composed of the Missionary Union of the Clergy and Religious, the Society for the Propagation of the Faith, the Society of St. Peter the Apostle for Native Clergy, the Society of the Holy Childhood, and the International Center of Missionary Animation.

Background: Originated as a commission of cardinals by St. Pius V and Gregory XII for missions in East and West Indies, Italo-Greeks and for ecclesiastical affairs in Protestant territories of Europe; Clement VIII instituted a Congregation of the Propagation of the Faith in 1599 which ceased to exist after several years. Erected as a stable congregation by Gregory XV June 22, 1622 (apostolic constitution *Inscrutabili Divinae*); its functions were redefined by John Paul II, June 28, 1988.

Congregation for the Clergy: Piazza Pio XII 3, 00193 Rome, Italy. Cardinal Cláudio Hummes, O.F.M., prefect; Most Rev. Mauro Piacenza, secretary.

Has three offices with competencies concerning the life, discipline, rights and duties of the clergy; the preaching of the Word, catechetics, norms for religious education of children and adults; preservation and administration of the temporal goods of the Church. Attached to it are the International Council for Catechetics (established in 1973 by Paul VI) and the Institute Sacrum Ministerium for the permanent formation of the clergy (established in line with John Paul II's 1992 apostolic exhortation *Pastores Dabo Vobis*).

Background: Established by Pius IV Aug. 2, 1564 (apostolic constitution *Alias Nos*), under the title Congregation of the Cardinals Interpreters of the Council of Trent; affected by legislation of Gregory

XIII and Sixtus V; known as Congregation of the Council until Aug. 15, 1967, when Paul VI renamed it the Congregation for the Clergy and redefined its competency; John Paul II gave it added responsibilities June 28, 1988.

Congregation for Institutes of Consecrated Life and Societies of Apostolic Life: Piazza Pio XII 3, 00193 Rome, Italy. Cardinal Franc Rodé, C.M., prefect; Most. Rev. Gianfranco Gardin, O.F.M. Conv., secretary.

Has competence over institutes of Religious, secular institutes, societies of the apostolic life and third (secular) orders. With two sections, the congregation has authority in matters related to the establishment, general direction and suppression of the various institutes; general discipline in line with their rules and constitutions; the movement toward renewal and adaptation of institutes in contemporary circumstances; the setting up and encouragement of councils and conferences of major religious superiors for intercommunication and other purposes.

Background: Founded by Sixtus V May 27, 1586, with the title, Congregation for Consultations of Regulars; confirmed by the apostolic constitution *Immensa* Jan. 22, 1588; made part of the Congregation for Consultations of Bishops and other Prelates in 1601; made autonomous by St. Pius X in 1908 as Congregation of Religious; title changed to Congregation for Religious and Secular Institutes by Paul VI in 1967; given present title by John Paul II, June 28, 1988.

Congregation for Catholic Education (for Seminaries and Institutes of Study): Piazza Pio XII 3, 00193 Rome, Italy. Cardinal Zenon Grocholewski, prefect; Most Rev. Jean-Louis Brugués, O.P., secretary.

Has supervisory competence over institutions and works of Catholic education. It carries on its work through three offices. One office handles matters connected with the direction, discipline and temporal administration of seminaries, and with the education of diocesan clergy, religious and members of secular institutes. A second office oversees Catholic universities, faculties of study and other institutions of higher learning inasmuch as they depend on the authority of the Church; encourages cooperation and mutual assistance among Catholic institutions, and the establishment of Catholic hospices and centers on campuses of non-Catholic institutions. A third office is concerned in various ways with all Catholic schools below the college-university level, with general questions concerning education and studies, and with the cooperation of conferences of bishops and civil authorities in educational matters. The congregation supervises Pontifical Works for Priestly Vocations.

Background: The title (Congregation of Seminaries and Universities) and functions of the congregation were defined by Benedict XV Nov. 4, 1915; Pius XI, in 1931 and 1932, and Pius XII, in 1941 and 1949, extended its functions; Paul VI changed its title to Congregation for Catholic Education in 1967; given its present title by Pope John Paul II, June 28, 1988. Its work had previously been carried on by two other congregations erected by Sixtus V in 1588 and Leo XII in 1824.

INTER-AGENCY CURIA COMMISSIONS

In accordance with provisions of the apostolic constitution *Pastor Bonus,* John Paul II established the following interdepartmental permanent commissions to handle matters when more than one agency of the Curia is involved in activities:

• For matters concerning appointments to local Churches and the setting up and alteration of them and their constitution (Mar. 22, 1989). Members include officials of the Secretariat of State and Congregation for Bishops. President, Cardinal Tarcisio Bertone, Secretary of State.

• For matters concerning members, individually or as a community, of Institutes of Consecrated Life founded or working in mission territories (Mar. 22, 1989). Members include officials of the Congregations for the Evangelization of Peoples and for Institutes of Consecrated Life and Societies of Apostolic Life. President, Cardinal Ivan Dias, prefect of the Congregation for the Evangelization of Peoples.

• For the formation of candidates for Sacred Orders (Mar. 22, 1989). Members include officials of the Congregations for Catholic Education, for Institutes of Consecrated Life and Societies of Apostolic Life, for Evangelization of Peoples, for Oriental Churches. President, Cardinal Zenon Grocholewski, prefect of the Congregation for Catholic Education.

• For promoting a more equitable distribution of priests throughout the world (July 20, 1991). Members include secretaries of congregations for Evangelization of Peoples, for the Clergy, Catholic Education, for the Institutes of Consecrated Life and Societies of Apostolic Life; and vice-president of Commission for Latin America. President, Cardinal Zenon Grocholewski, Prefect of the Congregation for Catholic Education.

• For the Church in Eastern Europe (Jan. 15, 1993), replacing the Pontifical Commission for Russia which was terminated. The commission is concerned with both Latin and Eastern-rite churches in territories of the former Soviet Union and other nations affected by the historical circumstances resulting from atheistic communism. It is responsible for promoting the apostolic mission of the Church and fostering ecumenical dialogue with the Orthodox and other Churches of the Eastern tradition. Members, under presidency of Cardinal Secretary of State, include the secretary and undersecretary of the Section for Relations with States and secretaries of Congregations for the Oriental Churches, for the Clergy, for Institutes of Consecrated Life and Societies of Apostolic Life, secretary of the Pontifical Council for Promoting Christian Unity. President, Cardinal Tarcisio Bertone.

TRIBUNALS

Apostolic Penitentiary: Piazza della Cancelleria 1, 00186 Rome, Italy. Cardinal James Francis Stafford, major penitentiary; regent, Rev. P. Gianfranco Girotti, O.F.M. Conv.

Has jurisdiction for the internal forum only (sacramental and non-sacramental). It issues decisions on questions of conscience; grants absolutions, dispensations, commutations, sanations and condonations; has charge of non-doctrinal matters pertaining to indulgences.

Background: Origin dates back to the 12th century; affected by the legislation of many popes; radically reorganized by St. Pius V in 1569; jurisdiction limited to the internal forum by St. Pius X; Benedict XV annexed the Office of Indulgences to it Mar. 25, 1917.

Apostolic Signatura: Piazza della Cancelleria 1, 00186 Rome, Italy. Most Rev. Raymond L. Burke, prefect; Most Rev. Frans Daneels, O. Praem., secretary.

The principal concerns of this supreme court of the Church are to resolve questions concerning juridical procedure and to supervise the observance of laws and rights at the highest level. It decides the jurisdictional competence of lower courts and has jurisdiction in cases involving personnel and decisions of the Rota. It is the supreme court of the State of Vatican City.

Background: A permanent office of the Supreme Tribunal of the Apostolic Signatura has existed since the time of Eugene IV in the 15th century; affected by the legislation of many popes; reorganized by St. Pius X in 1908 and made the supreme tribunal of the Church.

Roman Rota: Piazza della Cancelleria 1, 00186 Rome, Italy. Most Rev. Antoni Stankiewicz, Dean.

The ordinary court of appeal for cases appealed to the Holy See. It is best known for its competence and decisions in cases involving the validity of marriage.

Background: Originated in the Apostolic Chancery; affected by the legislation of many popes; reorganized by St. Pius X in 1908; further revised by Pius XI in 1934; new norms approved and promulgated by John Paul II in 1982 and 1987.

PONTIFICAL COUNCILS

Pontifical Council for the Laity: Piazza S. Calisto 16, 00153 Rome, Italy. Cardinal Stanislaw Rylko, president; Most Rev. Josef Clemens, secretary; Prof. Guzmán Carriquiry, undersecretary.

Its competence covers the apostolate of the laity and their participation in the life and mission of the Church. Members are mostly lay people from different parts of the world and involved in different apostolates.

Background: Established on an experimental basis by Paul VI Jan. 6, 1967; given permanent status Dec. 10, 1976 (*motu proprio Apostolatus Peragendi*).

Pontifical Council for Promoting Christian Unity: Via dell' Erba 1, 00193 Rome, Italy. Cardinal Walter Kasper, president; Most Rev. Brian Farrell, L.C., secretary.

Handles relations with members of other Christian ecclesial communities; deals with the correct interpretation and execution of the principles of ecumenism; initiates or promotes Catholic ecumenical groups and coordinates on national and international levels the efforts of those promoting Christian unity; undertakes dialogue regarding ecumenical questions and activities with churches and ecclesial communities separated from the Apostolic See; sends Catholic observer-representatives to Christian gatherings, and invites to Catholic gatherings observers of other churches; orders into execution conciliar decrees dealing with ecumenical affairs. The **Commission for Religious Relations with the Jews** is attached to the secretariat.

Background: Established by John XXIII June 5, 1960, as a preparatory secretariat of the Second Vatican Council; raised to commission status during the first session of the council in the fall of 1962; status as a secretariat confirmed and functions defined by Paul VI in 1966 and 1967; made a pontifical council by John Paul II, June 28, 1988.

Pontifical Council for the Family: Piazza S. Calisto 16, 00153 Rome, Italy. Cardinal Ennio Antonelli, president; Msgr. Grzegorz Kaszak, secretary.

Is concerned with promoting the pastoral care of families so they may carry out their educative, evangelizing and apostolic mission and make their influence felt in areas such as defense of human life and responsible procreation according to the teachings of the Church. Members, chosen by the Pope, are married couples and men and women from all parts of the world and representing different cultures. They meet in general assembly at least once a year.

Background: Instituted by John Paul II May 9, 1981, replacing the Committee for the Family established by Paul VI Jan. 11, 1973.

Pontifical Council for Justice and Peace: Piazza S. Calisto 16, 00153 Rome, Italy. Cardinal Renato Raffaele Martino, president; Most Rev. Giampaolo Crepaldi, secretary.

Its primary competence is to promote justice and peace in the world according to the Gospels and social teaching of the Church.

Background: Instituted by Paul VI Jan. 6, 1967, on an experimental basis; reconstituted and made a permanent commission Dec. 10, 1976; its competence was redefined and it was made a pontifical council June 28, 1988, by John Paul II.

Pontifical Council "Cor Unum": Piazza S. Calisto 16, 00153 Rome, Italy. Cardinal Paul Josef Cordes, president; Msgr. Karel Kasteel, secretary.

Its principal aims are to provide informational and coordinating services for Catholic aid and human development organizations and projects on a worldwide scale. Attached to the council are the John Paul II Foundation for the Sahel and *"Populorum Progressio."*

Background: Instituted by Paul VI July 15, 1971.

Pontifical Council for Pastoral Care of Migrants and Itinerant Peoples: Piazza S. Calisto 16, 00153 Rome, Italy. Cardinal Renato Raffaele Martino, president; Most Rev. Agostino Marchetto, secretary.

Is concerned with pastoral assistance to migrants, nomads, tourists, sea, and air travelers.

Background: Instituted by Paul VI and placed under general supervision of Congregation for Bishops, Mar. 19, 1970; made autonomous as a pontifical council and renamed by John Paul II, June 28, 1988.

Pontifical Council for Pastoral Assistance to Health Care Workers: Via della Conciliazione 3, 00193 Rome, Italy. Cardinal Javier Lozano Barragán, president; Most Rev. José Luis Redrado Marchite, O.H., secretary.

Its functions are to stimulate and foster the work of formation, study and action carried out by various international Catholic organizations in the health care field.

Background: Established in 1985 as a commission by John Paul II; made a council June 28, 1988.

Pontifical Council for the Interpretation of Legislative Texts: Piazza Pio XII 10, 00193 Rome, Italy. Most Rev. Francesco Coccopalmerio, president; Most Rev. Bruno Bertagna, vice-president; Msgr. Juan Ignacio Arrieta Ochoa de Chinchetru, secretary.

Primary function is the authentic interpretation of the universal laws of the Church.

Background: Established by John Paul II, Jan. 2, 1984, as the Pontifical Commission for the Authentic Interpretation of the Code of Canon Law; name changed and given additional functions June 28, 1988. Its competency was extended in 1991 to include interpretation of Code of Canon Law of Oriental Church that was promulgated in 1990.

Pontifical Council for Interreligious Dialogue: Via dell' Erba 1, 00193 Rome, Italy. Cardinal Jean-Louis Tauran, president; Most Rev. Pier Luigi Celata, secretary.

Its function is to promote studies and dialogue for the purpose of increasing mutual understanding and respect between Christians and non-Christians. The Commission for Religious Relations with Muslims is attached to the council.

Background: Established by Paul VI May 19, 1964, as the Secretariat for Non-Christians; given present title and functions by John Paul II, June 28, 1988.

Pontifical Council for Culture: Piazza S. Calisto 16, 00153 Rome, Italy. Most Rev. Gianfranco Ravasi, president; Very Rev. Bernard Ardura, O. Praem., secretary.

Its functions are to foster the Church's and the Holy See's relations with the world of culture and to establish dialogue with those who do not believe in God or who profess no religion provided these are open to sincere cooperation. It consists of two sections: (1) faith and culture; (2) dialogue with cultures. Attached to it is the **Coordinating Council for Pontifical Academies.**

Background: Present council with expanded functions was instituted by John Paul II (*motu proprio* of Mar. 25, 1993) through the merger of the Pontifical Council for Culture (established May 20, 1982, by John Paul II) and the Pontifical Council for Dialogue with Non-Believers (established by Paul VI Apr. 9, 1965, as the secretariat for Non-Believers).

Pontifical Council for Social Communications: Palazzo S. Carlo, 00120 Vatican City. Most Rev. Claudio M. Celli, president; Msgr. Paul Tighe, secretary; Msgr. Giuseppe Antonio Scotti, adjunct secretary.

Engaged in matters pertaining to instruments of social communication so that through them the message of salvation and human progress is fostered and carried forward in civil culture and mores.

Background: Instituted on an experimental basis by Pius XII in 1948; reorganized three times in the 1950s; made permanent commission by John XXIII Feb. 22, 1959; established as council and functions restated by John Paul II June 28, 1988.

OFFICES

Apostolic Camera: Palazzo Apostolico, 00120 Vatican City. Cardinal Tarcisio Bertone, S.D.B., chamberlain of the Holy Roman Church (Camerlengo); Most Rev. Paolo Sardi, vice-chamberlain.

Administers the temporal goods and rights of the Holy See between the death of one pope and the election of another (*sede vacante*), in accordance with special laws.

Background: Originated in the 11th century; reorganized by Pius XI in 1934; functions redefined (especially of *camerlengo*) by subsequent legislation in 1945, 1962 and 1975.

Administration of the Patrimony of the Apostolic See: Palazzo Apostolico, 00120 Vatican City. Cardinal Attilio Nicora, president; Most Rev. Domenico

Calcagno, secretary.

Handles the estate of the Apostolic See under the direction of papal delegates acting with ordinary or extraordinary authorization.

Background: Some of its functions date back to 1878; established by Paul VI Aug. 15, 1967.

Prefecture for the Economic Affairs of the Holy See: Largo del Colonnato 3, 00193 Rome, Italy. Most Rev. Velasio De Paolis, C.S., president; Most Rev. Vincenzo Di Mauro, secretary.

A financial office that coordinates and supervises administration of the temporalities of the Holy See. Membership includes Cardinal Roger M. Mahony and Cardinal Edward Egan.

Background: Established by Paul VI Aug. 15, 1967; functions redefined by John Paul II, June 28, 1988.

OTHER CURIA AGENCIES

Prefecture of the Papal Household: Most Rev. James M. Harvey, prefect.

Oversees the papal chapel — which is at the service of the pope in his capacity as spiritual head of the Church, and the pontifical family — which is at the service of the pope as a sovereign. It arranges papal audiences, has charge of preparing non-liturgical elements of papal ceremonies, makes all necessary arrangements for papal visits and trips outside the Vatican, and settles questions of protocol connected with papal audiences and other formalities.

Background: Established by Paul VI Aug. 15, 1967, under the title Prefecture of the Apostolic Palace; it supplanted the Sacred Congregation for Ceremonies founded by Sixtus V Jan. 22, 1588. The office was updated and reorganized under the present title by Paul VI, Mar. 28, 1968.

Office for Liturgical Celebrations of the Supreme Pontiff: Palazzo Apostolico Vaticano, 00120 Vatican City. Msgr. Guido Marini, Master of Ceremonies.

Prepares everything necessary for liturgical and other sacred celebrations by the Pope or in his name; directs everything in accordance with prescriptions of liturgical law.

Background: Evolved gradually from the early office of Apostolic Master of Ceremonies; affected by legislation of Pope Paul IV in 1563 and Benedict XV in 1917; restructured by Paul VI in 1967; given its present title (formerly known as Prefecture of Pontifical Ceremonies) and constituted as an autonomous agency of the Roman Curia by John Paul II, June 28, 1988.

Vatican Press Office: Via della Conciliazione 54, 00120 Vatican City. Rev. Federico Lombardi, S.J., director.

Established Feb. 29, 1968, to replace service agencies formerly operated by L'Osservatore Romano and an office created for press coverage of the Second Vatican Council. New directives were issued in 1986.

Vatican Information Service (VIS): Via della Conciliazione 54, 00120 Vatican City.

Established Mar. 28, 1990, within the framework but distinct from the Vatican Press Office. Furnishes information, in English, French and Spanish, on pastoral and magisterial activity of the Pope through use of electronic mail and fax.

Central Statistics Office: Palazzo Apostolico, 00120 Vatican City.

Established by Paul VI Aug. 15, 1967; attached to the Secretariat of State. Compiles, systematizes and analyzes information on the status and condition of the Church.

COMMISSIONS AND COMMITTEES

Listed below are non-curial institutes that assist in the work of the Holy See. Some are attached to curial agencies, as indicated. Other institutes are listed elsewhere in the Almanac; see Index.

Pontifical Commission for the Cultural Heritage of the Church: Established by John Paul II, June 28, 1988, as Pontifical Commission for Preserving the Church's Patrimony of Art and History and attached to the Congregation for the Clergy; made autonomous and given present title Mar. 25, 1993. Most Rev. Gianfranco Ravasi, president.

Pontifical Commission for Sacred Archeology: Instituted by Pius IX Jan, 6, 1852. Most Rev. Gianfranco Ravasi, president.

Pontifical Biblical Commission: Instituted by Leo XIII Oct. 30, 1902; completely restructured by Paul VI June 27, 1971; attached to the Congregation for the Doctrine of the Faith. Cardinal William Levada, president.

Pontifical Commission for Latin America: Instituted by Pius XII Apr. 19, 1958; attached to the Congregation for Bishops July, 1969; restructured by John Paul II in 1988. Cardinal Giovanni Battista Re, president.

Pontifical Commission for the Revision and Emendation of the Vulgate: Established in 1984 by John Paul II to replace the Abbey of St. Jerome instituted by Pius XI in 1933. Rev. Jean Mallet, O.S.B., director.

Pontifical Commission "Ecclesia Dei": Established by John Paul II, July 2, 1988, to facilitate the return to full ecclesial communion of priests, seminarians and religious who belonged to the fraternity founded by Marcel Lefebvre. Cardinal Dario Castrillón Hoyos, president.

International Theological Commission: Instituted by Paul VI Apr. 11, 1969, as an advisory adjunct of no more than 30 theologians to the Congregation for the Doctrine of the Faith; definitive statutes promulgated by John Paul II, Aug. 6, 1982. Cardinal William Levada, president; Most Rev. Luis F. Ladaria Ferrer, S.J., general secretary.

Commission for Religious Relations with the Jews: Instituted by Paul VI, Oct. 22, 1974, to promote and foster relations of a religious nature between Jews and Christians; attached to the Council for Promoting Christian Unity. Cardinal Walter Kasper, president.

Commission for Religious Relations with Muslims: Instituted by Paul VI, Oct. 22, 1974, to promote, regulate and interpret relations between Catholics and Muslims; attached to the Council for Interreligious Dialogue. Cardinal Jean-Louis Tauran, president.

Pontifical Committee for International Eucharistic Congresses: Instituted, 1879, by Pope Leo XIII; established as a pontifical committee with new statutes by John Paul II, Feb. 11, 1986. Most Rev. Piero Marini, president.

Pontifical Committee for Historical Sciences: Instituted by Pius XII Apr. 7, 1954, as a continuation of a commission dating from 1883. Msgr. Walter Brandmüller, president.

Vatican II Archives: Preserves the documents of the Second Vatican Council.

Disciplinary Commission of the Roman Curia: Cardinal Julián Herranz, president.

Commission for the Protection of the Historical and Artistic Monuments of the Holy See: Instituted by Pius XI in 1923, reorganized by Paul VI in 1963. Cardinal Francesco Marchisano, president.

Institute for Works of Religion: Instituted by Pius XII June 27, 1942, to bank and administer funds for works of religion; replaced an earlier administration established by Leo XIII in 1887; reorganized by John Paul II (chirograph of Mar. 1, 1990). Headed by a commission of cardinals, including Cardinal Angelo Sodano and Cardinal Adam Maida.

Fabric of St. Peter: Administration, care and preservation of Vatican Basilica. Cardinal Angelo Comastri, president.

Office of Papal Charities (Apostolic Almoner): Distributes alms and aid to those in need in the name of the pope. Most Rev. Félix del Blanco Prieto, almoner.

Labor Office of the Apostolic See (ULSA - *Ufficio del Lavoro della Sede Apostolica*): Has competence in regard to those who work for the Apostolic See; charged with settling labor issues. Instituted by John Paul II (*motu proprio* of Jan. 1, 1989); functions reaffirmed and definitive text of statutes approved by John Paul II (*motu proprio* of Sept. 30, 1994). Cardinal Francesco Marchisano, president.

INTERNATIONALIZATION

As of May 15, 2008, principal officials of the Roman Curia were from the following countries: Italy (Cards. Antonelli, Antonetti, Bertone, Cacciavillan, Cheli, Comastri, Fagiolo, Farina, Felici, Laghi, Lajolo, Marchisano, Martino, Monduzzi, Nicora, Noè, Pompedda, Ré, Sebastiani, Silvestrini, Sodano, Vallini; Abps. Amato, Bertagna, Calcagno, Celata, Celli, Coccopalmerio Crepaldi, Cunial, de Magistris, di Mauro, di Ruberto, Filoni, Gardin, Marchetto, Marini, Monterisi, Nesti, Piacenza, Pompedda, Salerno, Sardi, Tamburinno, Vegliò; Bps. Lanzani, Pastore, Nicoló, Pagano, Vacchelli); France (Cards. Etchegaray, Poupard, Tauran, Abp. Bruguès, Mamberti); United States (Cards. Baum, Foley, Levada, Stafford, Szoka, Abps. Burke, Harvey); Spain (Card. Martinez Somalo, Herranz; Abps. de Chinchetru, del Blanco Prieto, Gil Hellín, Ladaria, Redrado Marchite); Argentina (Card. Sandri); Belgium (Bp. Daneels), Germany (Cards. Cordes, Kasper, Bp. Clemens); Poland (Cards. Grocholewski, Rylko, Abps. Hoser, Kaszak, Nowak, Bp. Stankiewicz); Brazil (Card. Hummes); Chile (Card. Medina Estévez); French Guinea (Abp. Sarah); Hungary (Abp. Ternyák); Ireland (Farrell), Mexico (Card. Lozano Barrágan); Nigeria (Card. Arinze); Portugal (Card. Saraiva Martins); India (Card. Dias); Slovakia (Card. Tomko); Slovenia (Card. Rodé); Sri Lanka (Abp. Patabendige Don); Switzerland (Card. Agustoni); Syria (Card. Moussa I Daoud); Ukraine, Croatia (Abp. Eterovic).

VATICAN CITY STATE

The State of Vatican City (*Stato della Città del Vaticano*) is the territorial seat of the papacy. The smallest sovereign state in the world, it is situated within the city of Rome, embraces an area of 108.7 acres, and includes within its limits the Vatican Palace, museums, art galleries, gardens, libraries, radio station, post office, bank, astronomical observatory, offices, apartments, service facilities, St. Peter's Basilica, and neighboring buildings between the Basilica and Viale Vaticano. The extraterritorial rights of Vatican City extend to more than 10 buildings in Rome, including the major basilicas and office buildings of various congregations of the Roman Curia, and to the papal villas at **Castel Gandolfo** 15 miles southeast of the City of Rome. Castel Gandolfo is the summer residence of the Holy Father.

The government of Vatican City is in the hands of the reigning pope, who has full executive, legislative and judicial power. The administration of affairs, however, is handled by the **Pontifical Commission for the State of Vatican City** under Cardinal Giovanni Lajolo. The legal system is based on Canon Law; in cases where this code does not obtain, the laws of the City of Rome apply. The City is an absolutely neutral state and enjoys all the rights and privileges of a sovereign power. The citizens of Vatican City, and they alone, owe allegiance to the pope as a temporal head of state. On Nov. 26, 2000, Pope John Paul II promulgated the new Fundamental Law of the Vatican City State. The new law replaced that first established in 1929 by Pope Pius XI.

Cardinals of the Roman Curia residing outside Vatican City enjoy the privileges of extraterritoriality. The Secretary General for the Governatorate of the Vatican City State is Most Rev. Renato Boccardo.

The normal population is approximately 1,000. While the greater percentage is made up of priests and religious, there are several hundred laypersons living in Vatican City. They are housed in their own apartments in the City and are engaged in secretarial, domestic, trade and service occupations. Approximately 3,400 laypersons are employed by the Vatican.

Services of honor and order are performed by the Swiss Guards, who have been charged with responsibility for the personal safety of popes since 1506. The current Captain of the Swiss Guards is Daniel Anrig, who was appointed on August 19, 2008. Additional police and ceremonial functions are under the supervision of a special office. These functions were formerly handled by the Papal Gendarmes, the Palatine Guard of Honor, and the Guard of Honor of the Pope (Pontifical Noble Guard); the units were disbanded by Pope Paul VI on Sept. 14, 1970.

The **Basilica of St. Peter**, built between 1506 and 1626, is the largest church in Christendom (with the exception of the Basilica of Our Lady Queen of Peace in Ivory Coast) and the site of most papal ceremonies. The pope's own patriarchal basilica, however, is **St. John Lateran**, whose origins date back to 324.

St. Ann's, staffed by Augustinian Fathers, is the parish church of Vatican City. Its pastor is appointed by the pope, following the recommendation of the prior general of the Augustinians and the archpriest of the Vatican Basilica.

The Church of **Santa Susanna** was designated as the national church for Americans in Rome by Pope Benedict XV Jan. 10, 1922, and entrusted to the Paulist Fathers, who have served there continuously since then except for several years during World War II.

Pastoral care in Vatican City State, which is separate from

the diocese of Rome, is entrusted to the archpriest of St. Peter's Basilica, who is also vicar general for Vatican City and the papal villas at Castel Gandolfo (chirograph of Pope John Paul II, Jan. 14, 1991). Cardinal Francesco Marchisano was appointed to the posts in April 2002. In February 2005, Abp. (now Cardinal) Angelo Comastri was appointed coadjutor Archpriest of St. Peter's Basilica, vicar general for Vatican City, and President of the Fabric of St. Peter.

The Vatican Library (00120 Vatican City; Msgr. Cesare Pasini, prefect; Dr. Ambrogio Piazzoni, vice-prefect) has among its holdings 150,000 manuscripts, about 1,000,000 printed books, and 7,500 incunabula. **The Vatican Secret Archives** (00120 Vatican City; Most Rev. Sergio Pagano, prefect), opened to scholars by Leo XIII in 1881, contain central church documents dating back to the time of Innocent III (1198-1216). Cardinal Raffaele Farina, S.D.B., is librarian and archivist of the Holy Roman Church.

The independent temporal power of the pope, which is limited to the confines of Vatican City and small areas outside, was for many centuries more extensive than it is now. As late as the 19th century, the pope ruled 16,000 square miles of Papal States across the middle of Italy, with a population of over 3,000,000. In 1870 forces of the Kingdom of Italy occupied these lands that, with the exception of the small areas surrounding the Vatican and Lateran in Rome and the Villas of Castel Gandolfo, became part of the Kingdom by the Italian law of May 13, 1871.

The **Roman Question**, occasioned by this seizure and the voluntary confinement of the pope to the Vatican, was settled with ratification of the Lateran Agreement June 7, 1929, by the Italian government and Vatican City. The agreement recognized Catholicism as the religion of Italy and provided, among other things, a financial indemnity to the Vatican in return for the former Papal States; it became Article 7 of the Italian Constitution, Mar. 26, 1947. The Lateran Agreement was superseded by a new concordat given final approval by the Italian Chamber of Deputies Mar. 20 and formally ratified June 3, 1985.

Papal Flag

The papal flag consists of two equal vertical stripes of yellow and white, charged with the insignia of the papacy on the white stripe — triple crown or tiara over two crossed keys, one of gold and one of silver, tied with a red cord and two tassels. The divisions of the crown represent the teaching, sanctifying and ruling offices of the pope. The keys symbolize his jurisdictional authority.

The papal flag is a national flag inasmuch as it is the standard of the Supreme Pontiff as the sovereign of the state of Vatican City. It is also universally accepted by the faithful as a symbol of the supreme spiritual authority of the Holy Father.

Vatican Radio

The declared purpose of Vatican radio station HVJ is "that the voice of the Supreme Pastor may be heard throughout the world by means of the ether waves, for the glory of Christ and the salvation of souls." Designed by Guglielmo Marconi, the inventor of radio, and supervised by him until his death, the station was inaugurated by Pope Pius XI in 1931. The original purpose has been extended to a wide variety of programming.

Vatican Radio operates on international wave lengths, transmits programs in 37 languages, and serves as a channel of communication between the Vatican, church officials and listeners in general in many parts of the world. The station broadcasts about 400 hours a week throughout the world.

The daily English–language program for North America is broadcast on 6095, 7305, 9600 Khz as well as via satellite INTELSAT 325,5° East (Atlantic) — 4097.75 Mhz — LHCP polarization.

Frequencies, background information and audio files can be obtained at www.radiovaticana.org and www.vatican.va.

The staff of 415 broadcasters and technicians includes 30 Jesuits. Studios and offices are at Palazzo Pio, Piazza Pia, 3, 00193 Rome. The transmitters are situated at Santa Maria di Galeria, a short distance north of Rome. Cardinal Roberto Tucci, S.J., president; Rev. Federico Lombardi, S.J., director-general.

2008 Vatican Stamps and Coins

The Vatican Philatelic and Numismatic Office (00120 Vatican City) published the following list of stamps and coins for the Year 2008:

Stamps

• *Europa 2008* – The Letter • 150th Anniversary of the Lourdes Apparitions • V Centenary of the Sistine Chapel Frescoes of the Vault and Lunettes • 49th International Eucharistic Congress • World Youth Day – Sydney 2008 • V Centenary of the Birth of Andrea Palladio • Visit of His Holiness Benedict XVI to the United Nations (joint issue with U.N.O.) • Year Dedicated to Saint Paul • The International Journeys of Benedict XVI in 2007 • Christmas (joint issue with Germany)

Philatelic and Numismatic Cover

80th Birthday of His Holiness Benedict XVI

Postal Stationery

Aerogram: 350th Anniversary of the Pontificate of Clement XII

Postcards: XII Ordinary General Assembly of the Synod of Bishops.

Publications

Vaticano 2008

Coins

• 2008 Euro Coin Set - BU Version, 8 coins (1 cent, 2 cent, 5 cent, 10 cent, 20 cent, 50 cent, 1euro, 2 euro).
• 2008 Euro Coin Set - Proof Version, 8 coins (1 cent, 2 cent, 5 cent, 10 cent, 20 cent, 50 cent, 1euro, 2 euro) with Silver Medal The Evangelists: Saint Luke.
• 2 Euro Commemorative Bimetallic Coin, Year Dedicated to Saint Paul.
• 5 Euro - Silver Celebrative Coin, World Youth Day – Sydney 2008.
• 10 Euro - Silver Celebrative Coin, 41st World Day of Peace.
• Commemorative 20 and 50 Euro Gold Coins, Masterpieces of Sculpture in Vatican City, "The Torso del Belvedere" and "the Pietà" (Year 1).

Papal Audiences

General audiences are scheduled weekly, on Wednesday.

In Vatican City, they are held in the Audience Hall on the south side of St. Peter's Basilica or, weather permitting, in St. Peter's Square. The hall, which was opened in 1971, has a seating capacity of 6,800 and a total capacity of 12,000. Audiences have been held during the summer at Castel Gandolfo when the pope is there on a working vacation.

General audiences last from about 60 to 90 minutes, during which the pope gives a talk and his blessing. A résumé of the talk, which is usually in Italian, is given in several languages. Arrangements for papal audiences are handled by an office of the Prefecture of the Apostolic Household.

American visitors can obtain passes for general audiences by applying to the Bishops' Office for United States Visitors to the Vatican, Casa Santa Maria, Via dell'Umilita, 30, 00187 Rome. Private and group audiences are reserved for dignitaries of various categories and for special occasions.

Publications

Acta Apostolicae Sedis, 00120 Vatican City: The only "official commentary" of the Holy See, was established in 1908 for the publication of activities of the Holy See, laws, decrees and acts of congregations and tribunals of the Roman Curia. The first edition was published in Jan. 1909. St. Pius X made AAS an official organ in 1908. Laws promulgated for the Church ordinarily take effect three months after the date of their publication in this commentary. The publication, mostly in Latin, is printed by the Vatican Press. The immediate predecessor of this organ was *Acta Sanctae Sedis*, founded in 1865 and given official status by the Congregation for the Propagation of the Faith in 1904.

Activities of the Holy See, an annual documentary volume covering the activities of the pope and of the congregations, commissions, tribunals and offices of the Roman Curia.

Annuario Pontificio, 00120 Vatican City: The yearbook of the Holy See. It is edited by the Central Statistics Office of the Church and is printed in Italian, with some portions in other languages, by the Vatican Press. It covers the worldwide organization of the Church, lists members of the hierarchy, and includes a wide range of statistical information. The publication of a statistical yearbook of the Holy See dates back to 1716, when a volume called *Notizie* appeared. Publication under the present title began in 1860, was suspended in 1870, and resumed again in 1872 under the title *Catholic Hierarchy*. This volume was printed privately at first, but has been issued by the Vatican Press since 1885. The title *Annuario Pontificio* was restored in 1912, and the yearbook was called an "official publication" until 1924.

L'Osservatore Romano, Via del Pellegrino, 00120 Vatican City: The daily newspaper of the Holy See. It began publication July 1, 1861, as an independent enterprise under the ownership and direction of four Catholic laymen headed by Marcantonio Pacelli, vice minister of the interior under Pope Pius IX and a grandfather of the late Pius XII. Leo XIII bought the publication in 1890, making it the "pope's" own newspaper.

The only official material in *L'Osservatore Romano* is what appears under the heading, "*Nostre Informazioni*." This includes notices of appointments by the Holy See, the texts of papal encyclicals and addresses by the Holy Father and others, various types of documents, accounts of decisions and rulings of administrative bodies, and similar items. Additional material includes news and comment on developments in the Church and the world. Italian is the language most used. The editorial board is directed by Prof. Mario Agnes. A staff of about 15 reporters covers Rome news sources. A corps of correspondents provides foreign coverage.

A weekly roundup edition in English was inaugurated in 1968. Other weekly editions are printed in French (1949), Italian (1950), Spanish (1969), Portuguese (1970) and German (1971). The Polish edition (1980) is published monthly. *L'Osservatore della Domenica* is published weekly as a supplement to the Sunday issue of the daily edition.

Statistical Yearbook of the Church (*Annuarium Statisticum Ecclesiae*), issued by the Central Statistics Office of the Church, it contains principal data concerning the presence and work of the Church in the world. The first issue was published in 1972 under the title *Collection of Statistical Tables, 1969*. It is printed in corresponding columns of Italian, French, and Latin.

Vatican Television Center (*Centro Televisivo Vaticano*, CTV), Palazzo Belvedere, 00120 Vatican City: Instituted by John Paul II Oct. 23, 1983, with the rescript, *Ex Audentia*. Dr. Emilio Rossi is president of the administrative council.

Vatican Press, 00120 Vatican City: The official printing plant of the Vatican. The Vatican press was conceived by Marcellus II and Pius IV but was actually founded by Sixtus V on Apr. 27, 1587, to print the Vulgate and the writings of the Fathers of the Church and other authors. A Polyglot Press was established in 1626 by the Congregation for the Propagation of the Faith to serve the needs of the Oriental Church. St. Pius X merged both presses under the title Vatican Polyglot Press. It was renamed Vatican Press in 1991. The plant has facilities for the printing of material in about 30 languages. Dir.: Rev. Elio Torrigiani, S.D.B.

Vatican Publishing House (*Libreria Editrice Vaticana*), Piazza S. Pietro, 00120 Vatican City: Formerly an office of the Vatican Press to assist in the circulation of the liturgical and juridical publications of the Apostolic See, the congregations and later the *Acta Apostolicae Sedis*. In 1926, with the expansion of publishing activities and following the promulgation of the 1917 Code, the office was made an independent entity. An administrative council and editorial commission were instituted in 1983; in 1988 *Pastor Bonus* listed it among institutes joined to the Holy See; new statutes were approved in 1991. President, Msgr. Giuseppe Scotti.

DIPLOMATIC ACTIVITIES OF THE HOLY SEE

REPRESENTATIVES OF THE HOLY SEE

Representatives of the Holy See and their functions were the subject of a document entitled *Sollicitudo Omnium Ecclesiarum* which Pope Paul VI issued on his own initiative under the date of June 24, 1969. As of Jan. 1, 2008 the Holy See maintained full diplomatic relations with 175 states around the world.

Delegates and Nuncios

Papal representatives "receive from the Roman Pontiff the charge of representing him in a fixed way in the various nations or regions of the world.

"When their legation is only to local churches, they are known as apostolic delegates. When to this legation, of a religious and ecclesial nature, there is added diplomatic legation to states and governments, they receive the title of nuncio, pro-nuncio, and internuncio." An apostolic nuncio has the diplomatic rank of ambassador extraordinary and plenipotentiary. Traditionally, because the diplomatic service of the Holy See has the longest uninterrupted history in the world, a nuncio has precedence among diplomats in the country to which he is accredited and serves as dean of the diplomatic corps on state occasions. Since 1965 pro-nuncios, also of ambassadorial rank, have been assigned to countries in which this prerogative is not recognized. In recent years, the Vatican has phased out the title of pro-nuncio. The title of nuncio (with an asterisk denoting he is not dean of the diplomatic corps) has been given to the majority of appointments of ambassadorial rank. See **Other Representatives**.

Service and Liaison

Representatives, while carrying out their general and special duties, are bound to respect the autonomy of local churches and bishops. Their service and liaison responsibilities include the following:

- Nomination of Bishops: To play a key role in compiling, with the advice of ecclesiastics and lay persons, and submitting lists of names of likely candidates to the Holy See with their own recommendations.
- Bishops: To aid and counsel local bishops without interfering in the affairs of their jurisdictions.
- Episcopal Conferences: To maintain close relations with them and to assist them in every possible way. (Papal representatives do not belong to these conferences.)
- Religious Communities of Pontifical Rank: To advise and assist major superiors for the purpose of promoting and consolidating conferences of men and women religious and to coordinate their apostolic activities.
- Church-State Relations: The thrust in this area is toward the development of sound relations with civil governments and collaboration in work for peace and the total good of the whole human family. The mission of a papal representative begins with appointment and assignment by the pope and continues until termination of his mandate. He acts "under the guidance and according to the instructions of the cardinal secretary of state to whom he is directly responsible for the execution of the mandate entrusted to him by the Supreme Pontiff." Normally representatives are required to retire at age 75.

NUNCIOS AND DELEGATES

(*Sources:* Annuario Pontificio, L'Osservatore Romano, Acta Apostolicae Sedis, *Catholic News Service.*) *As of July 30, 2008. Country, rank of legation (corresponding to rank of legate unless otherwise noted), name of legate (archbishop unless otherwise noted) as available. An asterisk (*) indicates a nuncio who is not presently dean of the diplomatic corps.*

Delegate for Papal Legations: Archbishop Carlo M. Viganò, titular archbishop of Ulpiana. The post was

established in 1973 to coordinate papal diplomatic efforts throughout the world. The office entails responsibility for "following more closely through timely visits the activities of papal representatives . . . and encouraging their rapport with the central offices" of the Secretariat of State.

Albania: Tirana, Nunciature; Ramiro Moliner Inglés.*

Algeria: Algiers, Nunciature; Thomas Yeh Shengnan* (also Nuncio* to Tunisia).

Andorra: Nunciature; Manuel Monteiro de Castro (also Nuncio to Spain).

Angola: Luanda, Nunciature; Giovanni Angelo Becciu* (also Nuncio* to São Tome and Principe). (Diplomatic relations established in 1997.)

Antigua and Barbuda: Nunciature; Thomas E. Gullickson* (resides in Port of Spain, Trinidad).

Antilles: Apostolic Delegation; Thomas E. Gullickson (resides in Port of Spain, Trinidad).

Arabian Peninsula: Apostolic Delegation; Luigi Gatti (also Nuncio in Kuwait and Lebanon; resides in Lebanon).

Argentina: Buenos Aires, Nunciature; Adriano Bernardini.

Armenia: Nunciature; Claudio Gugerotti* (resides in Tbilisi, Georgia; also nuncio* to Georgia and Azerbaijan). (Diplomatic relations established in 1992.)

Australia: Canberra, Nunciature; Giuseppe Lazzarotto.

Austria: Vienna, Nunciature; Edmond Farhat.

Azerbaijan: Nunciature; Claudio Gugerotti* (resides in Tbilisi, Georgia; also nuncio* to Georgia and Armenia). (Diplomatic relations established in 1992.)

Bahamas: Nunciature; Thomas E. Gullickson* (resides in Port of Spain, Trinidad).

Bahrain: Manama; Nunciature; Mounged El-Hachem. (Diplomatic relations established Jan. 12, 2000; also nuncio in Kuwait, Qatar, United Arab Emirates, and Yemen).

Bangladesh: Dhaka, Nunciature; Joseph Marino.*

Barbados: Nunciature; Thomas E. Gullickson* (resides in Port of Spain, Trinidad).

Belarus: Nunciature; Martin Vidovic.*

Belgium: Brussels, Nunciature; Karl-Josef Rauber (also Nuncio to Luxembourg).

Belize: Nunciature; Luigi Pezzuto* (resides in Port of Spain, Trinidad).

Benin (formerly Dahomey): Nunciature; Michael A. Blume, S.V.D.* (resides in Accra, Ghana).

Bolivia: La Paz, Nunciature; Luciano Suriani.

Bosnia and Herzegovina: Sarajevo; Nunciature; Alessandro D'Errico.*

Botswana: See **South Africa**.

Brazil: Brasilia, Nunciature; Lorenzo Baldisseri.

Brunei: See **Malaysia and Brunei**.

Bulgaria: Sofia, Nunciature (reestablished in 1990); Janusz Bolonek.*

Burkina Faso: Ouagadougou, Nunciature; Vito Rallo* (also Nuncio* to Niger).

Burma: See **Myanmar.**

Burundi: Bujumbura, Nunciature; Paul Richard Gallagher.*

Cambodia: Nunciature; Salvatore Pennacchio* (resides in Bangkok, Thailand). (Diplomatic relations established in 1994.)

Cameroon: Yaounde, Nunciature; Eliseo Antonio Ariotti (also Nuncio to Equatorial Guinea).

Canada: Ottawa, Nunciature; Luigi Ventura.*

Cape Verde, Republic of: Nunciature; Luis Mariano Montemayor* (resides in Dakar, Senegal).

Central African Republic: Bangui, Nunciature; Jude Thaddeus Okolo* (also Nuncio* to Chad).

Chad: Nunciature; Jude Thaddeus Okolo* (resides in Bangui, Central African Republic).

Chile: Santiago, Nunciature; Giuseppe Pinto.

China, Republic of: Taipei (Taiwan), Nunciature; vacant.

Colombia: Bogota, Nunciature; Aldo Cavalli.

Comoros: See **Madagascar**: (formerly Zaire)

Congo (formerly Zaire): Kinshasa-Gombe, Nunciature; Giovanni d'Aniello.*

Congo: Brazzaville, Nunciature; Andrés Carrascosa Coso* (also Nuncio* to Gabon).

Costa Rica: San Jose, Nunciature; Pierre Nguyên Van Tot.

Côte d'Ivoire (Ivory Coast): Abidjan, Nunciature; Ambrose Madtha.

Croatia: Zagreb, Nunciature; Mario Roberto Cassari.

Cuba: Havana, Nunciature; Luigi Bonazzi.*

Cyprus: Nicosia, Nunciature; Antonio Franco (also Nuncio to Israel).

Czech Republic: Prague, Nunciature; Diego Causero.

Denmark: Copenhagen, Nunciature; Emil Paul Tscherrig* (also Nuncio* to Finland, Iceland, Norway and Sweden).

Djibouti: Nunciature (established May 2000); Vacant (resides in Addis Ababa, Ethiopia).

Dominica: Nunciature; Thomas E. Gullickson* (resides in Port-of-Spain, Trinidad).

Dominican Republic: Santo Domingo, Nunciature; Józef Wesolowski (also serves as Apostolic Delegate to Puerto Rico).

East Timor: Díli, Nunciature (diplomatic relations established on May 20, 2002); Leopoldo Girelli (also Nuncio* to Indonesia).

Ecuador: Quito, Nunciature; Giacomo Ottonello.

Egypt: Cairo, Nunciature; Michael Louis Fitzgerald, M.Afr. (also delegate to the Organization of the League of Arab States).*

El Salvador: San Salvador, Nunciature; Luigi Pezzuto.

Equatorial Guinea: Santa Isabel, Nunciature; Eliseo Antonio Ariotti* (resides in Yaounde, Cameroon).

Eritrea: Nunciature: Leo Boccardi* (resides in Ethiopia). (Diplomatic relations established in 1995.)

Estonia: Nunciature; Peter Stephan Zurbriggen* (resides in Vilna, Lithuania).

Ethiopia: Addis Ababa, Nunciature; Vacant* (also Nuncio* to Djibouti and apostolic delegate to Somalia).

European Community: Brussels, Belgium, Nunciature; André Dupuy.

Fiji: Nunciature; Charles D. Balvo* (resides in Wellington, New Zealand).

Finland: Helsinki, Nunciature; Emil Paul Tscherrig* (resides in Denmark).

France: Paris, Nunciature; Fortunato Baldelli.

Gabon: Libreville, Nunciature; Andrés Carrascosa Coso* (resides in Congo).

Gambia: Nunciature; George Antonysamy* (resides in Freetown, Sierra Leone).

Georgia: Tbilisi, Nunciature; Claudio Gugerotti* (also Nuncio* to Armenia and Azerbaijan). (Diplomatic relations established in 1992.)

Germany: Bonn, Nunciature; Jean-Claude Périsset.

Ghana: Accra, Nunciature; Léon Kalenga Badikebele.*

Great Britain: London, Nunciature; Faustino Sainz Muñoz* (also papal representative to Gibraltar).

Greece: Athens, Nunciature; Patrick Coveney.*

Grenada: Nunciature; Thomas E. Gullickson* (resides in Port of Spain, Trinidad).

Guatemala: Guatemala City, Nunciature; Bruno Musarò.

Guinea: Conakry, Nunciature; George Antonysamy* (resides in Freetown, Sierra Leone).

Guinea Bissau: Nunciature; Luis Mariano Montemayor* (resides at Dakar, Senegal).

Guyana: Nunciature; Thomas E. Gullickson (resides in Port of Spain, Trinidad).

Haiti: Port-au-Prince, Nunciature; Bernardito Auza.

Honduras: Tegucigalpa, Nunciature; Antonio Arcari.

Hungary: Budapest, Nunciature; Juliusz Janusz (also Nuncio* to Moldova).

Iceland: Nunciature; Emil Paul Tscherrig* (resides in Denmark).

India: New Delhi, Nunciature; Pedro López Quintana* (also Nuncio* to Nepal).

Indonesia: Jakarta, Nunciature; Leopoldo Girelli (also nuncio to East Timor).*

Iran: Teheran, Nunciature; Jean-Paul Gobel.*

Iraq: Baghdad, Nunciature; Francis Chullikatt* (also Nuncio to Jordan).

Ireland: Dublin, Nunciature; Giuseppe Leanza.

Israel: Nunciature; Antonio Franco (also Nuncio to Cyprus). (Diplomatic relations established June 1994.)

Italy: Rome, Nunciature; Giuseppe Bertello (also Nuncio to San Marino).

Ivory Coast: See **Côte d'Ivoire**.

Jamaica: Nunciature; Thomas E. Gullickson (resides in Port of Spain, Trinidad).

Japan: Tokyo, Nunciature; Alberto Bottari de Castello*.

Jerusalem and Palestine: Apostolic Delegation (also Nuncio to Israel): Antonio Franco.

Jordan: Nunciature; Francis Chullikatt* (also Nuncio to Iraq).

Kazakstan: Almaty, Nunciature; Miguel Maury Buendía* (also Nuncio* to Kyrgyzstan and Tajikistan).

Kenya: Nairobi, Nunciature; Alain Lebeaupin.*

Kiribati: Nunciature; Charles D. Balvo* (resides in Wellington, New Zealand).

Korea: Seoul, Nunciature; Osvaldo Padilla* (also Nuncio* to Mongolia).

Kuwait: Al Kuwait, Nunciature; Mounged El-Hachem* (also nuncio in Qatar, Bahrain, the United Arab Emirates, and Yemen).

Kyrgyzstan: Nunciature; Miguel Maury Buendía* (resides in Kazakstan; also Nuncio* to Kyrgyzstan and Tajikistan).

Laos: Apostolic Delegation; Salvatore Pennacchio (resides in Bangkok, Thailand).

Latvia: Nunciature; Peter Stephan Zurbriggen* (resides in Vilna, Lithuania).

Lebanon: Beirut, Nunciature; Luigi Gatti (also Nuncio* to Kuwait and apostolic delegate to Arabian Peninsula).

Lesotho: Maseru, Nunciature; James P. Green (also Nuncio to South Africa, Namibia, and Swaziland; resides in Pretoria, South Africa).

Liberia: Monrovia, Nunciature; George Antonysamy* (resides in Freetown, Sierra Leone).

Libya: Nunciature; Tommaso Caputo* (resides in Malta). (Diplomatic relations established in 1997.)

Liechtenstein: Nunciature; Francesco Canalini (resides in Bern, Switzerland).

Lithuania: Vilnius, Nunciature; Peter Stephan Zurbriggen* (also Nuncio to Estonia and Latvia.).

Luxembourg: Nunciature; Karl-Josef Rauber (resides in Brussels, Belgium).

Macedonia: Nunciature; Abril y Castelló Santos* (also Nuncio to Slovenia; resides in Slovenia).

Madagascar: Antananarivo, Nunciature; Augustine Kasujja* (also Nuncio* to Seychelles, and Mauritius and Apostolic Delegate to Comoros and Reunion).

Malawi: Lilongwe, Nunciature; Nicola Girasoli* (resides in Lusaka, Zambia).

Malaysia and Brunei: Apostolic Delegation; Salvatore Pennacchio (resides in Bangkok, Thailand).

Mali: Nunciature; Luis Mariano Montemayor* (resides in Dakar, Senegal).

Malta: La Valletta, Nunciature; Tommaso Caputo (also Nuncio* to Libya).

Marshall Islands: Nunciature; Charles D. Balvo* (resides in Wellington, New Zealand).

Mauritania: Nouakchott, Apostolic Delegation; Luis Mariano Montemayor (resides in Dakar, Senegal).

Mauritius: Port Louis, Nunciature; Augustine Kasujja* (resides in Antananarivo, Madagascar).

Mexico: Mexico City, Nunciature; Christophe Pierre.* (Diplomatic relations established in 1992).

Micronesia, Federated States of: Nunciature; Charles D. Balvo* (resides in Wellington, New Zealand).

Moldova: Nunciature; Francisco-Javier Lozano* (resides in Bucharest, Romania). (Diplomatic relations established in 1992.)

Monaco, Principality of: Nunciature; André Dupuy.

Mongolia: Nunciature; Osvaldo Padilla* (resides in Seoul, South Korea).

Montenegro: Podgorica, Nunciature; Angelo Mottola (Diplomatic relations established Dec. 17, 2006).

Morocco: Rabat, Nunciature; Antonio Sozzo.*

Mozambique: Maputo, nunciature; George Panikulam.* (Diplomatic relations established in 1995.)

Myanmar (formerly Burma): Apostolic Delegation; Salvatore Pennacchio (resides in Bangkok, Thailand).

Namibia: Nunciature; James P. Green* (resides in Pretoria, South Africa).

Nauru: Nunciature; Charles D. Balvo* (resides in Wellington, New Zealand).

Nepal: Nunciature; Pedro López Quintana* (resides in New Delhi, India).

Netherlands: The Hague, Nunciature; François Bacqué.*

New Zealand: Wellington, Nunciature; Charles D.

Balvo* (also Nuncio* to Fiji, Kiribati, Marshall Islands, Federated States of Micronesia, Tonga, Vanuatu and Western Samoa; Apostolic Delegate to Pacific Islands).

Nicaragua: Managua, Nunciature; Henryk Jozef Nowacki.

Niger: Niamey, Nunciature; Vito Rallo* (also Nuncio* to Burkina Faso.)

Nigeria: Lagos, Nunciature; Renzo Fratini.*

Norway: Nunciature; Emil Paul Tscherrig* (resides in Denmark).

Pacific Islands: Nunciature; Charles D. Balvo (resides in Wellington, New Zealand).

Pakistan: Islamabad, Nunciature; Adolfo Tito Yllana.

Palau, Republic of: Palau, Nunciature; Charles D. Balvo.*

Panama: Panama City, Nunciature; Giambattista Diquattro.

Papua New Guinea: Port Moresby; Nunciature; Francisco Padilla* (also Nuncio* to Solomon Islands).

Paraguay: Asuncion, Nunciature; Orlando Antonini.

Peru: Lima, Nunciature; Rino Passigato.

Philippines: Manila, Nunciature; Edward Joseph Adams.

Poland: Warsaw; Nunciature; Józef Kowalczyk.

Portugal: Lisbon, Nunciature; Alfio Rapisarda.

Puerto Rico: See **Dominican Republic**.

Qatar: Dawhah, Nunciature; Mounged El-Hachem (Diplomatic relations established in Nov. 2002; also nuncio in Kuwait, Bahrain, United Arab Emirates, and Yemen).

Reunion: See **Madagascar**.

Romania: Bucharest, Nunciature. Francisco-Javier Lozano.*

Russia (Federation of): Moscow, Nunciature; Antonio Mennini. Nuncio appointed Representative of the Holy See to Russian Federation, 1994.

Rwanda: Kigali, Nunciature. Ivo Scapolo.

Saint Vincent and the Grenadines: Nunciature; Thomas E. Gullickson, Nuncio (resides in Port of Spain, Trinidad).

Samoa: Nunciature; Charles D. Balvo* (resides in Wellington, New Zealand).

San Marino: Nunciature; Giuseppe Bertello.

Santa Lucia: Nunciature; Thomas E. Gullickson* (resides in Port of Spain, Trinidad).

São Tome and Principe: Nunciature; Giovanni Angelo Becciu* (also Nuncio* to Angola, where he resides).

Senegal: Dakar, Nunciature; Luis Mariano Montemayor* (also Nuncio* to Cape Verde, Guinea-Bissau and Mali; Apostolic Delegate to Mauritania.)

Serbia: Belgrade, Nunciature; Eugenio Sbarbaro.

Seychelles Islands: Nunciature; Augustine Kasujja* (resides in Antananrivo, Madagascar).

Sierra Leone: Freetown, Nunciature (1996); George Antonysamy* (also Nuncio* to Gambia, Guinea and Liberia).

Singapore: Nunciature; Salvatore Pennacchio* (He is also Nuncio to Cambodia and Thailand and apostolic delegate to Laos, Malaysia and Brunei and Myanmar.)

Slovakia: Nunciature; Mario Giordana.

Slovenia: Ljubljana, Nunciature; Abril y Castelló

Santos (also Nuncio to Macedonia).
Solomon Islands: Nunciature; Francisco Padilla (resides in Port Moresby, Papua New Guinea).
Somalia: Apostolic Delegation (est. 1992); Vacant (resides in Sudan).
South Africa: Pretoria, Nunciature; James P. Green.* (also Nuncio* to Namibia and Swaziland and apostolic delegate to Botswana.)
Spain: Madrid, Nunciature; Manuel Monteiro de Castro.
Sri Lanka: Colombo, Nunciature; Mario Zenari.*
Sudan: Khartoum, Nunciature; Leo Boccardi* (also Apostolic Delegate to Somalia).
Suriname: Nunciature; Thomas E. Gullickson* (resides in Port of Spain, Trinidad).
Swaziland: Nunciature; James P. Green* (resides in Pretoria, South Africa).
Sweden: Nunciature; Emil Paul Tscherrig* (resides in Denmark).
Switzerland: Bern, Nunciature; Francesco Canalini (also Nuncio to Liechtenstein).
Syria: (Syrian Arab Republic): Damascus, Nunciature, Giovanni Battista Morandini.*
Tajikistan: Nunciature (1996); Miguel Maury Buendía* (resides in Kazakstan; also Nuncio* to Kyrgyzstan and Kazakstan).
Tanzania: Dar-es-Salaam, Nunciature; Joseph Chennoth.*
Thailand: Bangkok, Nunciature; Salvatore Pennacchio* (also Nuncio* to Cambodia and Singapore and Apostolic Delegate to Laos, Malaysia, Brunei, Myanmar).
Togo: Lome, Nunciature; Michael A. Blume, S.V.D.* (resides in Accra, Ghana).
Tonga: Nunciature; Charles D. Balvo* (resides in Wellington, New Zealand).
Trinidad and Tobago: Port of Spain, Trinidad, Nunciature; Thomas E. Gullickson, Nuncio (also Nuncio to Antigua and Barbuda, Bahamas, Barbados, Belize, Dominica, Grenada, Jamaica, Saint Lucia, Saint Vincent and the Grenadines, Suriname and Apostolic Delegate to Antilles).
Tunisia: Tunis, Nunciature; Thomas Yeh Sheng-nan* (resides in Algiers, Algeria).
Turkey: Ankara, Nunciature; Antonio Lucibello.*
Turkmenistan: Nunciature (1996); Antonio Lucibello* (resides in Ankara, Turkey).
Uganda: Kampala, Nunciature; Pro-Nuncio, Paul Tschang In-Nam.
Ukraine: Kiev, Nunciature; Ivan Jurkovic.*
United Arab Emirates: Abu Dhabi, Nunciature (diplomatic relations established May 31, 2007): Mounged El-Hachem* (also nuncio to Kuwait, Bahrain, Qatar, and Yemen).
United States of America: Washington, D.C., Nunciature; Pietro Sambi.*
Uruguay: Montevideo, Nunciature; Anselmo Guido Pecorari.
Uzbekistan: Nunciature; Antonio Mennini * (resides in Russia; also Nuncio* to Russia).
Vanuatu: Nunciature; Charles D. Balvo* (resides in Wellington, New Zealand).
Venezuela: Caracas, Nunciature; Giacinto Berloco.
Vietnam: Apostolic Delegation; Vacant.
Western Samoa: Nunciature; Charles D. Balvo* (resides in Wellington, New Zealand).

Yemen: San'a, Nunciature; Mounged El-Hachem* (relations established in 1998, also nuncio in Kuwait, Bahrain, United Arab Emirate, and Qatar).
Yugoslavia: Belgrade, Nunciature; Eugenio Sbarbaro.
Zaire: See Congo: Lusaka, Nunciature; Giuseppe Leanza* (also Nuncio* to Malawi).
Zambia: Lusaka, Nunciature; Nicola Girasoli* (also Nuncio* to Malawi).
Zimbabwe: Harare, Nunciature; George Kocherry.*

The Current Nuncio to the U.S.

The representative of the Pope to the Church in the United States is Archbishop Pietro Sambi, S.T.D., J.C.D. Archbishop Sambi was born in Sogliano sul Rubicone, Italy, on June 27, 1938, and ordained a priest on Mar. 14, 1964. He holds doctorates in sacred theology and canon law. After studies at the Pontifical Ecclesiastical Academy (the training center for future Vatican diplomats), he began his service in the Diplomatic Corps of the Holy See in April 1969, in Cameroon, and served subsequently in the apostolic nunciatures in Jerusalem in 1971, Cuba in 1974, Algeria in 1978, Nicaragua in 1979, Belgium in 1981, and then in India in 1984, with the rank of counselor. He was ordained as bishop on November 9, 1985 and was named pro-apostolic nuncio in Burundi in October 1985; pro-apostolic nuncio in Indonesia in November 1991; and apostolic nuncio in Israel and Cyprus, and apostolic delegate in Jerusalem and Palestine in June 1998. Archbishop Sambi speaks Italian, English, French and Spanish.

On Dec. 17, 2005, Archbishop Sambi was appointed nuncio to the United States and permanent observer to the Organization of American States, succeeding Archbishop Gabriel Montalvo.

The U.S. Apostolic Nunciature is located at 3339 Massachusetts Ave., N.W., Washington, D.C. 20008-3687; (202) 333-7121.

A Nuncio represents the Holy Father to both the hierarchy and Church of a particular nation and to that nation's civil government.

From 1893 to 1984, papal representatives to the Church in the U.S. were apostolic delegates (all archbishops): Francesco Satolli (1893-96), Sebastiano Martinelli, O.S.A., (1896-1902), Diomede Falconio, O.F.M. (1902-1911), Giovanni Bonzano (1911-22), Pietro Fumasoni-Biondi (1922-33), Amleto Cicognani (1933-58), Egidio Vagnozzi (1958-67), Luigi Raimondi (1967-73), Jean Jadot (1973-80), and Pio Laghi (1980-90) who was the first to hold the title Pro-Nuncio, beginning in 1984 (*See* Index, **U.S.-Vatican Relations**). Archbishop (now Cardinal) Agostino Cacciavillan was Pro-Nuncio and permanent observer to the Organization of American States from 1990 to 1998. Archbishop Gabriel Montalvo was nuncio and permanent observer to the Organization of American States from 1998 to 2005.

Other Representatives

(*Sources*: Annuario Pontificio; Catholic News Service.)

The Holy See has representatives to or is a regular member of a number of quasi-governmental and international organizations. Most Rev. Ernesto Gallina was appointed delegate to International Governmental Organizations Jan. 12, 1991.

Governmental Organizations: U.N. (Abp. Celestino Migliore, permanent observer); U.N. Office in Geneva and Specialized Institutions (Abp. Silvano Maria Tomasi, permanent observer); African Union (Abp. Ramiro Moliner Inglés); League of Arab States (Abp. Michael Fitzgerald, M.Afr.); International Atomic Energy Agency (Msgr. Michael W. Banach, permanent representative); U.N. Office at Vienna and U.N. Organization for Industrial Development (Msgr. Michael W. Banach, permanent observer); U.N. Food and Agriculture Organization (Msgr. Renato Volante, permanent observer); U.N. Educational, Scientific and Cultural Organization (Msgr. Francesco Follo, permanent observer); World Trade Organization (Abp. Silvano Maria Tomasi); Council of Europe (vacant, special representative with function of permanent observer); Council for Cultural Cooperation of the Council of Europe (Msgr. Aldo Giordano, delegate); Organization of American States (Abp. Pietro Sambi, permanent observer, with personal title of Apostolic Nuncio); Organization for Security and Cooperation in Europe (Msgr. Michael W. Banach, permanent representative); International Institute for the Unification of Private Law (Prof. Giuseppe dalla Torre del Tiempo di Sanguinetto Conte, delegate); International Committee of Military Medicine (Rev. Luc De Maere, delegate), World Organization of Tourism (Abp. Manuel Monteiro de Castro, permanent observer).

Non-Governmental Organizations: International Committee of Historical Sciences (Msgr. Walter Brandmüller); International Committee of the History of Art (Dr. Francesco Buranelli); International Committee of Anthropological and Ethnological Sciences; Committee for the Neutrality of Medicine; International Center of Study for the Preservation and Restoration of Cultural Goods (Dr. Francesco Buranelli); International Council of Monuments and Sites (Msgr. Francesco Follo, delegate); International Alliance on Tourism; World Association of Jurists (Abp. Pietro Sambi); International Commission of the Civil State (Msgr. Paul Richard Gallagher); International Astronomical Union; International Institute of Administrative Sciences; International Technical Committee for Prevention and Extinction of Fires; World Medical Association; International Archives Council; World Trade Organization.

DIPLOMATS TO THE HOLY SEE

(*Sources:* Annuario Pontificio, L'Osservatore Romano).
    Listed below are countries maintaining diplomatic relations with the Holy See, dates of establishment (in some cases) and names of Ambassadors (as of Aug. 30, 2008).
Albania (1991): Rrok Logu.
Algeria (1972): Idriss Jazaïry.
Andorra (1995): Antoni Morell Mora.
Angola (1997): José Bernardo Domingos Quiosa.
Antigua and Barbuda (1986): . . . . .
Argentina: Carlos Luis Custer.
Armenia (1992): Edward Nalbandian.
Australia (1973): Anne Maree Plunkett.
Austria: Martin Bolldorf.
Azerbaijan (1992): Elchin Oktyabr Oglu Amirbayov.
Bahamas (1979): . . . . .
Bahrain (2000): . . . .
Bangladesh (1972): Debapriya Bhattacharya.
Barbados (1979): Peter Patrick Kenneth Simmons.

Belarus (1992): Sergei F. Aleinik.
Belgium (1835): Frank De Coninck.
Belize (1983): . . . . .
Benin (formerly Dahomey) (1971): Euloge Hinvi.
Bolivia: Carlos Federico de la Riva Guerra.
Bosnia and Herzegovina (1992): Miroslav Palameta.
Brazil: Vera Barrouin Machado.
Bulgaria (1990): Valentin Vassilev Bozhilov.
Burkina Faso (1973): Felipe Savadogo.
Burundi (1963): Domitille Barancira.
Cambodia (1994): . . . . .
Cameroon (1966): Antoine Zanga.
Canada (1969): Donald Smith.
Cape Verde (1976): Domingos Dias Pereira Mascarenhas.
Central African Republic (1975): . . . . .
Chad (1988): Hissein Brahim Taha.
Chile: Pedro Pablo Cabrera Gaete.
China, Republic of (Taiwan) (1966): Chou-seng Tou.
Colombia: Juan Gómez Martínez.
Congo (formerly Zaire) (1963): . . . . .
Congo (1977): Henri Marie Joseph Lopes.
Costa Rica: Luis París Chaverri.
Côte d'Ivoire (Ivory Coast) (1971): Kouamé Benjamin Konan.
Croatia (1992): Emilio Marin.
Cuba: Raúl Roa Kourí.
Cyprus (1973): Georgios F. Poulides.
Czech Republic (1929-50, reestablished, 1990, with Czech and Slovak Federative Republic; reaffirmed, 1993): Pavel Jajtner.
Denmark (1982): Lars Moller.
Djibouti (2000): Barkat Gourad Hamadou. (Diplomatic relations established May 20, 2000.)
Dominica (1981): . . . . .
Dominican Republic: Carlos Rafael Conrado Marion-Landais Castillo.
East Timor (2002): Justino Maria Aparício Guterres. (Diplomatic relations established on May 20, 2002.)
Ecuador: Fausto Cordovez Chiriboga.
Egypt (1966): Nevine Simaika Halim.
El Salvador: Francisco A. Soler.
Equatorial Guinea (1981): . . . . .
Eritrea (1995): Petros Tseggai Asghedom.
Estonia (1991): Jüri Seilenthal.
Ethiopia (1969): Negash Kebret.
Fiji (1978): Emitat Lausiki Boladuadua.
Finland (1966): Pekka Ojanen.
France: Bernard Kessedjian.
Gabon (1967): Firmin Mboutsou.
Gambia, The (1978): Elizabeth Ya Eli Harding.
Georgia (1992): Princess Khétévane Bagration de Moukhrani.
Germany: Hans-Henning Horstmann.
Ghana (1976): Albert Owusu-Sarpong.
Great Britain (1982): Francis Campbell.
Greece (1980): Miltiadis Hiskakis.
Grenada (1979): . . . . .
Guatemala: Juan Gavarrete Soberón.
Guinea (1986): Alexandre Cécé Loua.
Guinea-Bissau (1986): . . . . .
Guyana (Cooperative Republic of): Laleshwar Kumar Narayan Singh.
Haiti: Carl Henri Guiteau.
Honduras: Alejandro Emilio Valladares Lanza.
Hungary (1990): Gábor Erdödy.

Iceland (1976): Stefan Lárus Stefansson.
India: Amitava Tripathi.
Indonesia (1965): Suprapto Martosetomo.
Iran (1966): Mohammad Javad Faridzadeh.
Iraq (1966): Albert Edward Ismail Yelda.
Ireland: Philip McDonagh.
Israel (1994): Mordechay Lewy.
Italy: Antonio Zanardi Landi.
Ivory Coast: See Côte d'Ivoire.
Jamaica (1979): Marcia Gilbert-Roberts.
Japan (1966): Kagefumi Ueno.
Jordan (1994): Dina Kawar.
Kazakhstan (1992): Nurlan Danenov.
Kenya (1965): Raychelle Awuor Omamo.
Kiribati: Diplomatic relations established Apr. 1995.
Korea (1966): Ji-Young Francesco Kim.
Kuwait (1969): Suhail Khalil Shuhaiber.
Kyrgyzstan (1992): Maratbek Salievec Bakiev.
Latvia (1991): Atis Sjanits.
Lebanon (1966): Naji Abi Assi.
Lesotho (1967): Makase Nyaphisi.
Liberia (1966): Wesley Momo Johnson.
Libya (1997): Abdulhafed Gaddur.
Liechtenstein (1985): Nikolaus de Liechtenstein.
Lithuania: Algirdas Saudargas.
Luxembourg (1955): Georges Santer.
Macedonia (1994): Bartolomej Kajtazi.
Madagascar (1967): Jean-Pierre Razafy-Andriamihaingo.
Malawi (1966): Gilton Bazilio Chiwaula.
Mali (1979): Mohamed Salia Sokona.
Malta (1965): Antonio Ganado.
Marshall Islands (1993): .....
Mauritius: Mohunlall Goburdhun.
Mexico (personal representative, 1990; diplomatic relations, 1992): Luis Felipe Bravo Mena.
Micronesia, Federated States (1994): .....
Moldova (1992): Valeriu Bobuac.
Monaco: Jean- Claude Michel.
Mongolia (1992): Chuluuny Batjargal.
Montenegro (Diplomatic relations established Dec. 17, 2006): Antun Sbutega.
Morocco: Mohammed Sbihi.
Mozambique (diplomatic relations, 1995): Carlos Dos Santos.
Namibia (diplomatic relations established Sept. 1995): Peter Hitjitevi Katjavivi.
Nauru (1992): .....
Nepal (1983): Madan Kumar Bhattarai.
Netherlands (1967): Monique Patricia Antoinette Frank.
New Zealand (1973): Geoffrey Kenyon Ward.
Nicaragua: José Cuadra Chamorro.
Niger (1971): Amadou Touré.
Nigeria (1976): Kingsley Sunny Ebenyi.
Norway (1982): Lars Petter Forberg.
Order of Malta (see Index): Alberto Leoncini Bartoli.
Pakistan (1965): Ayesha Riyaz.
Palau, Republic of (1998): .....
Panama: Lawrence Edward Chewning Fàbrega.
Papua New Guinea (1977): .....
Paraguay: Gerónimo Narváez Torres.
Peru: Alfonso Rivero Monsalve.
Philippines (1951): Leonida L. Vera.
Poland (1989): Hanna Suchocka.

Portugal: Pedro José Ribeiro de Menezes.
Qatar (Diplomatic relations established Nov. 2002): Mohamad Jaham Abdulaziz Al-Kawari.
Romania (1920; broken off, 1948; reestablished, 1990): Marius Gabriel Lazurcã.
Rwanda (1964): Joseph Bonesha.
Saint Lucia (1984): Gilbert Ramez Chagoury.
Saint Vincent and the Grenadines (1990): .....
San Marino (1986): Giovanni Galassi.
São Tome and Principe (1984): .....
Senegal (1966): Félix Oudiane.
Seychelles (1984): Main Butler Payette.
Sierra Leone (Diplomatic relations established July 1996): Fode Maclean Dabor.
Singapore (1981): Barry Desker.
Slovak Republic (1993; when it became independent republic): Jozef Dravecky.
Slovenia (1992): Ivan Rebernik.
Solomon Islands (1984): .....
South Africa (1994): Dr. Konji Sebati.
Spain: Francisco Vázquez Vázquez.
Sri Lanka (1975): Tikiri Bandara Maduwegedera.
Sudan (1972): Ahmed Hamid Elfkah Hamid.
Suriname (1994): Urmila Joella-Sewnundun.
Swaziland (1992): H.R.H. Prince David M. Dlamini.
Sweden (1982): Fredrik Vahlquist.
Switzerland (1992): Jean- François Kammer, Ambassador with special mission to Holy See.
Syria (Arab Republic) (1966): Makram Obeid.
Tajikistan: Diplomatic relations established June 1996.
Tanzania (1968): Ahmada Rweyemamu Ngemera.
Thailand (1969): Chaiyong Satjipanon.
Togo (1981): Félix Kodjo Sagbo.
Tonga (1994): .....
Trinidad and Tobago (1978): Leari E. Rousseau.
Tunisia (1972): Afif Hendaoui.
Turkey (1966): Muammer Akdur.
Turkmenistan: Diplomatic relations established July 1996.
Uganda (1966): Nyine S. Bitahwa.
Ukraine (1992): Tetiana Izhevska.
United States (1984): Mary Ann Glendon.
Uruguay: Mario Juan Bosco Cayota Zappettini.
Uzbekistan (1992): .....
Vanuatu (1994): Michel Rittié.
Venezuela: Iván Guillermo Rincón Urdaneta.
Western Samoa (1994): .....
Yemen: (1998): Yaha Ali Mohamed al-Abiad.
Yugoslavia: Darko Tanaskovic.
Zaire: See Congo.
Zambia (1965): Anderson Kaseba Chibwa.
Zimbabwe (1980): David Douglas Hamadziripi.

Special Representatives

Russia (Federation of) (1989): Nikolay Sadchikov, Ambassador Extraordinary and Plenipotentiary.
United Nations (Center of Information of UN at the Holy See): Shalini Dewan, director.
Office of the League of Arab States: Mohammad Ali Mohammad.
United Nations High Commission for Refugees: Augustine Mahiga, delegate.
Organization for the Liberation of Palestine: Afif E. Safieh, director.

U.S.-HOLY SEE RELATIONS

The U.S. and the Holy See announced Jan. 10, 1984, the establishment of full diplomatic relations, thus ending a period of 117 years in which there was no formal diplomatic relationship. The announcement followed action by the Congress in Nov. 1983 to end a prohibition on diplomatic relations enacted in 1867.

William A. Wilson, President Reagan's personal representative to the Holy See from 1981, was confirmed as the U.S. ambassador by the Senate, on Mar. 7, 1984. He presented his credentials to Pope John Paul II on Apr. 9, 1984, and served until May 1986, when he resigned. He was succeeded by Frank Shakespeare, 1986-89, and Thomas P. Melady, 1989-93. Raymond L. Flynn, Mayor of Boston, was appointed by Bill Clinton and confirmed by the Senate in July 1993. He served until 1997 when he was succeeded by Corinne Claiborne "Lindy" Boggs. She was succeeded by James Nicholson, who served until 2005. On Aug. 1, 2005, Pres. George W. Bush nominated as Nicholson's successor L. Francis Rooney III, an Oklahoma and Florida businessman.

On Nov. 5, 2007, President Bush nominated Prof. Mary Ann Glendon to become Ambassador to the Holy See. The U.S. Senate voted to confirm her on Dec. 19, 2007.

Archbishop (now Cardinal) Pio Laghi, apostolic delegate to the U.S. since 1980, was named first pro-nuncio by the Pope on Mar. 26, 1984. He served until 1990, when he was named prefect of the Congregation for Catholic Education. Archbishop Agostino Cacciavillan was appointed pro-nuncio on June 13, 1990. He served until he was named president of the Administration of the Patrimony of the Apostolic See (APSA) and was succeeded on Dec. 7, 1998, by Archbishop Gabriel Montalvo. Archbishop Montalvo served as nuncio from 1998 to 2005. He was succeeded by Archbishop Pietro Sambi, the current nuncio.

Nature of Relations

The nature of relations was described in nearly identical statements by John Hughes, a State Department spokesman, and the Holy See. Hughes said: "The United States of America and the Holy See, in the desire to further promote the existing mutual friendly relations, have decided by common agreement to establish diplomatic relations between them at the level of embassy on the part of the United States of America, and nunciature on the part of the Holy See, as of today, Jan. 10, 1984."

The Holy See statement said: "The Holy See and the United States of America, desiring to develop the mutual friendly relations already existing, have decided by common accord to establish diplomatic relations at the level of apostolic nunciature on the side of the Holy See and of embassy on the side of the United States beginning today, Jan. 10, 1984."

The establishment of relations was criticized as a violation of the separation-of-church-and-state principle by spokesmen for the National Council of Churches, the National Association of Evangelicals, the Baptist Joint Committee on Public Affairs, Seventh Day Adventists, Americans United for Separation of Church and State, and the American Jewish Congress.

Legal Challenge Dismissed

U.S. District Judge John P. Fullam, ruling May 7, 1985, in Philadelphia, dismissed a legal challenge to U.S.-Holy See relations brought by Americans United for Separation of Church and State. He stated that Americans United and its allies in the challenge lacked legal standing to sue, and that the courts did not have jurisdiction to intervene in foreign policy decisions of the executive branch of the U.S. government. Parties to the suit brought by Americans United were the National Association of Laity, the National Coalition of American Nuns and several Protestant church organizations. Bishop James W. Malone, president of the U.S. Catholic Conference, said in a statement: "This matter has been discussed at length for many years. It is not a religious issue but a public policy question which, happily, has now been settled in this context."

Russell Shaw, a conference spokesman, said the decision to send an ambassador to the Holy See was not a church-state issue and "confers no special privilege or status on the Church."

Earlier Relations

Official relations for trade and diplomatic purposes were maintained by the U.S. and the Papal States while the latter had the character of and acted like other sovereign powers in the international community.

Consular relations developed in the wake of an announcement, made by the papal nuncio in Paris to the American mission there Dec. 15, 1784, that the Papal States had agreed to open several Mediterranean ports to U.S. shipping.

U.S. consular representation in the Papal States began with the appointment of John B. Sartori, a native of Rome, in June 1797. Sartori's successors as consuls were: Felix Cicognani, also a Roman, and Americans George W. Greene, Nicholas Browne, William C. Sanders, Daniel LeRoy, Horatio V. Glentworth, W.J. Stillman, Edwin C. Cushman, David M. Armstrong.

Consular officials of the Papal States who served in the U.S. were: Count Ferdinand Lucchesi, 1826 to 1829, who resided in Washington; John B. Sartori, 1829 to 1841, who resided in Trenton, NJ; Daniel J. Desmond, 1841 to 1850, who resided in Philadelphia; Louis B. Binsse, 1850 to 1895, who resided in New York.

U.S. recognition of the consul of the Papal States did not cease when the states were absorbed into the Kingdom of Italy in 1871, despite pressure from Baron Blanc, the Italian minister. Binsse held the title until his death Mar. 28, 1895. No one was appointed to succeed him.

Diplomatic Relations

The U.S. Senate approved a recommendation, made by President James K. Polk in Dec. 1847 for the establishment of a diplomatic post in the Papal States. Jacob L. Martin, the first charge d'affaires, arrived in Rome Aug. 2, 1848, and presented his credentials to Pius IX Aug. 19. Martin, who died within a month, was succeeded by Lewis Cass, Jr. Cass became minister resident in 1854 and served in that capacity until his retirement in 1858.

John P. Stockton, who later became a U.S. Senator from New Jersey, was minister resident from 1858 to 1861. Rufus King was named to succeed him but, instead, accepted a commission as a brigadier general in the Army. Alexander W. Randall of Wisconsin took the appointment. He was succeeded in Aug. 1862 by Richard M. Blatchford who served until the following year. King was again nominated minister resident and served in that capacity until 1867 when the ministry was ended because of objections from some quarters in the U.S. and failure to appropriate funds for its continuation. J. C. Hooker, a secretary, remained in the Papal States until the end of March, 1868, closing the ministry and performing functions of courtesy.

Personal Envoys

Myron C. Taylor was appointed by President Franklin D. Roosevelt in 1939 to serve as his personal representative to Pope Pius XII and continued serving in that capacity during the presidency of Harry S. Truman until 1951. Henry Cabot Lodge was named to the post by President Richard M. Nixon in 1970, served also during the presidency of Gerald Ford, and represented President Carter at the canonization of St. John Neumann in 1977. Miami attorney David Walters served as the personal envoy of President Jimmy Carter to the Pope from July 1977 until his resignation Aug. 16, 1978. He

was succeeded by Robert F. Wagner who served from Oct. 1978 to the end of the Carter presidency in Jan. 1981. William A. Wilson, appointed by President Ronald Reagan in Feb. 1981, served as his personal envoy until 1984 when he was named ambassador to the Holy See.

None of the personal envoys had diplomatic status. President Harry S. Truman nominated Gen. Mark Clark to be ambassador to the Holy See in 1951, but withdrew the nomination at Clark's request because of controversy over the appointment.

None of Truman's three immediate successors — Dwight D. Eisenhower, John F. Kennedy and Lyndon B. Johnson — had a personal representative to the pope.

PONTIFICAL ACADEMIES

(Sources: Annuario Pontificio, Catholic News Service.*)*

The Pontifical Academy of Sciences was constituted in its present form by Pius XI Oct. 28, 1936, in virtue of *In Multis Solaciis,* a document issued on his own initiative.

The academy is the only supranational body of its kind in the world with a pope -selected, life -long membership of outstanding mathematicians and scientists regardless of creed from many countries. The normal complement of 70 members was increased to 80 in 1985–86 by John Paul II. There are additional honorary members.

The academy traces its origin to the Linceorum Academia (Academy of the Lynxes, its symbol) founded in Rome Aug. 17, 1603. Pius IX reorganized this body and gave it a new name, *Pontificia Accademia dei Nuovi Lincei,* in 1847. It was taken over by the Italian state in 1870 and called the *Accademia Nationale dei Lincei.* Leo XIII reconstituted it with a new charter in 1887. Pius XI designated the Casina of Pope Pius IV in the Vatican Gardens as the site of academy headquarters in 1922 and gave it its present title and status in 1936. In 1940, Pius XII gave the title of Excellency to its members; John XXIII extended the privilege to honorary members in 1961.

Members in U.S.

Scientists in the U.S. who presently hold membership in the Academy are listed below according to year of appointment. Nobel prize-winners are indicated by an asterisk *.

Franco Rasetti, professor emeritus of physics at Johns Hopkins University, Baltimore, MD (Oct. 28, 1936); Christian de Duve,* professor of biochemistry at the International Institute of Cellular and Molecular Pathology at Brussels, Belgium, and Rockefeller University, NY (Apr. 10, 1970); Marshall Warren Nirenberg,* director of Laboratory on genetics and biochemistry at the National Institutes of Health, Bethesda, MD (June 24, 1974). George Palade,* professor of cellular biology at University of California, San Diego and Victor Weisskopf, professor of physics at the Massachusetts Institute of Technology, Cambridge, Mass. (Dec. 2, 1975); David Baltimore,* professor of biology at the Massachusetts Institute of Technology, Cambridge, Mass.; Har Gobind Khorana,* professor of biochemistry, and Alexander Rich, professor of biophysics, both at the Massachusetts Institute of Technology, Cambridge, Mass. (Apr. 17, 1978). Charles Townes,* professor emeritus of physics at the University of California at Berkeley (Jan. 26, 1983); Beatrice Mintz, senior member of the Cancer Research Institute of Philadelphia and Maxine Singer, bio-

chemist, president of Carnegie Institution, Washington, DC (June 9, 1986). Roald Z. Sagdeev, professor of physics at University of Maryland, College Park and Peter Hamilton Raven, professor of biology at the Missouri Botanical Garden of St. Louis, MO (Oct. 4, 1990); Luis Angel Caffarelli, professor of mathematics at New York University and Luigi Luca Cavalli-Sforza, professor of genetics at Stanford University (Aug. 2, 1994). Joshua Lederberg, professor of genetics at Rockefeller University, NY (Mar. 4, 1996); Joseph Edward Murray, professor of plastic surgery at Harvard Medical School, Cambridge, MA; Paul Berg, professor of biochemistry at Stanford Univ. and Vera C. Rubin, professor of astronomy at Carnegie Institution of Washington (June 25, 1996); Gary S. Becker,* professor of economics at the University of Chicago (Mar. 3, 1997); Chen-ning Yang,* professor of physics and director of the Institute of Theoretical Physics at the State University of N.Y. at Stony Brook (Apr. 18, 1997); Frank Press, professor of geophysics and director of the Washington Advisory Group (Sept. 3, 1999); Ahmed Zewail, professor of Chemistry and Physics, California Institute of Technology, Pasadena (Sept. 3, 1999); Mario Jose Molina, professor of atmospheric chemistry at the Massachusetts Institute of Technology (Nov. 9, 2000); Günter Blobel,* professor of cellular biology of the Rockefeller University, NY (Sept. 28, 2001); Fotis C. Kafatos, professor of molecular biology at Harvard University (Jan. 23, 2003); Tsung-Dao Lee, professor of Physics at Columbia University in NY (Apr. 14, 2003); William D. Phillips,* professor of physics at the University of Maryland and the National Institute of Standards and Technology, Gaithersburg, PA (Oct. 23, 2004); Veerabhadran (Ram) Ramanathan, professor of atmospheric science at the University of California, San Diego, and director of the Center for Atmospheric Science at Scripps Institution of Oceanography, La Jolla (Oct. 23, 2004); Edward Witten, professor of Physics at the Institute for Advanced Study, Princeton, NJ (June 21, 2006).

There are also two honorary members from the U.S.: Stanley L. Jaki, O.S.B., professor of physics, history and philosophy at Seton Hall University, N.J. (Sept. 5, 1990); Robert J. White, professor of neurosurgery at Case Western Reserve University, Cleveland (Mar. 29, 1994).

MEMBERS IN OTHER COUNTRIES

Listing includes place and date of selection. Nobel Prize winners are indicated by an asterisk.

Argentina: Antonio M. Battro (Sept. 21, 2002).

Armenia: Rudolf M. Muradian (Oct. 16, 1994).

Austria: Hans Tuppy (Apr. 10, 1970); Walter Thirring (June 9, 1986).
Belgium: Paul Adriaan Jan Janssen (June 25, 1990); Thierry Boon-Falleur (April 9, 2002).
Brazil: Carlos Chagas, former president of the academy (Aug. 18, 1961); Johanna Döbereiner (Apr. 17, 1978); Crodowaldo Pavan (Apr. 17, 1978); Rudolf Muradian (Oct. 16, 1994).
Canada: John Charles Polanyi* (June 9, 1986).
Chile: Héctor Rezzio Croxatto (Dec. 2, 1975); Rafael Vicuna (Nov. 10, 2000).
Congo (formerly Zaire): Felix wa Kalengo Malu (Sept. 26, 1983).
Denmark: Aage Bohr* (Apr. 17, 1978).
France: André Blanc–LaPierre (Apr. 17, 1978); Paul Germain (June 9, 1986); Jacques-Louis Lions (Oct. 4, 1990); Jean–Marie Lehn (May 30, 1996); Claude Cohen-Tannoudji (May 17, 1999); Nicole M. Le Douarin (Sept. 3, 1999); Pierre Jean Léna (Jan. 18, 2001); Yves Quéré (Dec. 20, 2003).
Germany: Rudolf L. Mössbauer* (Apr. 10, 1970); Manfred Eigen* (May 12, 1981); Wolf Joachim Singer (Sept. 18, 1992); Paul Joseph Crutzen (June 25, 1996); Yuri Ivanovich Manin (June 26, 1996); Jürgen Mittelstrass (Sept. 21, 2002); Theodor Wolfgang Hänsch (June 21, 2006); Klaus von Klitzing (Oct. 9, 2007).
Ghana: Daniel Adzei Bekoe (Sept. 26, 1983).
Great Britain: Hermann Alexander Brück (Apr. 5, 1955); George Porter* (June 24, 1974); Max Ferdinand Perutz* (May 12, 1981); Stephen William Hawking (Jan. 9, 1986); Martin John Rees (June 25, 1990); Sir Richard Southwood (Sept. 18, 1992); Raymond Hide (June 25, 1996).
India: Mambillikalathil Govind Kumar Menon (May 12, 1981); Chintamani N.R. Rao (June 25, 1990).
Israel: Michael Sela (Dec. 2, 1975); Aaron J. Ciechanover (March 13, 2007).

Italy: Giampietro Puppi (Apr. 17, 1978); Nicola Cabibbo (June 9, 1986), President; Nicola Dallaporta (Oct. 5, 1989), honorary member; Bernardo Maria Colombo (Sept. 18, 1992); Antonino Zichichi (Nov. 9, 2000); Enrico Berti (Sept. 28, 2001).
Japan: Minoru Oda (Sept. 18, 1992); Ryoji Noyori* (Oct. 1, 2002).
Kenya: Thomas R. Odhiambo (May 12, 1981).
Mexico: Marcos Moshinsky (June 9, 1986).
Nigeria: Thomas Adeoye Lambo (June 24, 1974).
Poland: Stanislaw Lojasiewicz (Jan. 28, 1983); Czeslaw Olech (June 9, 1986); Michal Heller (Oct. 4, 1990); Andrzej Szezeklik (Oct. 16, 1994).
Russia: Vladimir Isaakovich Keilis–Borok (Oct. 16, 1994); Sergei Petrovich Novikov (June 25, 1996), also teaches at University of Maryland).
Spain: Manuel Lora–Tamayo (Sept. 24, 1964); Garcia-Bellido, Antonio (June 24, 2003).
Sweden: Sune Bergström* (Dec. 14, 1985); Kai Siegbahn* (Dec. 14, 1985).
Switzerland: Werner Arber* (May 12, 1981); Carlo Rubbia* (Dec. 14, 1985); Albert Eschenmoser (June 9, 1986).
Taiwan: Te–tzu Chang (Apr. 18, 1997); Yuan Tseh Lee (Oct. 9, 2007).
Vatican City State: Cottier, Rev. George, O.P. (Oct. 28, 1992; honorary member); Rev. Enrico do Rovasenda, O.P. (Nov. 13, 1968), honorary member.
Venezuela: Marcel Roche (Apr. 10, 1970); Ignacio Rodríguez-Iturbe (Jan. 10, 2008).
Ex officio members: Rev. George V. Coyne, S.J., dir. of Vatican Observatory (Sept. 2, 1978); Card. Raffaele Farina, S.D.B., prefect of the Vatican Library (May 24, 1997); Most Rev. Sergio B. Pagano, pref. of the Secret Vatican Archives (Jan. 7, 1997). Pres.: Nicola Cabibbo, professor of physics at University of Rome (app. Apr. 6, 1993). Chancellor: Most Rev. Marcelo Sánchez Sorondo.

PONTIFICAL ACADEMY OF SOCIAL SCIENCES

Founded by John Paul II (*motu proprio Socialium scientiarum investigationes*), Jan. 1, 1994, to promote the study and the progress of social sciences, to advise the Vatican on social concerns and to foster research aimed at improving society. The number of members is not less than 20 or more than 40. Three of the 30 members of the Academy (as of Jan. 1, 2008) were from the United States: Kenneth J. Arrow of Stanford University, Mary Ann Glendon of Harvard University, and Joseph Stiglitz of Columbia University. Chancellor, Most Rev. Marcelo Sánchez Sorondo. Address: Casino Pio IV, Vatican Gardens.

PONTIFICAL ACADEMY FOR LIFE

Established by John Paul II (*motu proprio Vitae Mysterium*), Feb. 11, 1994, "to fulfill the specific task of study, information and formation on the principal problems of biomedicine and law relative to the promotion and defense of life, especially in the direct relationship they have with Christian morality and the directives of the Church's magisterium."

Members, appointed by the pope without regard to religion or nationality, represent the various branches of "the biomedical sciences and those that are most closely related to problems concerning the promotion and protection of life." Membership, as of Jan. 1, 2007, included eight from the United States:

Prof. Carl Anderson, Vice-President of the Pontifical John Paul II Institute for Studies of Marriage and the Family; Mrs. Mercedes Arzu-Wilson, founder and president of the Foundations Family of the Americas and founder and director of the Commission at the World Organization for the Family; Dr. Thomas Hilgers, founder and director of the Institute "Paul VI," Omaha, NB; Mrs. Christine de Vollmer, president of the World Organization for the Family; Dr. Denis Cavanaugh, professor of obstetrics and gynecology at the University of South Florida College of Medicine; Prof. John M. Finnis, professor of philosophy of law, University of Oxford and Notre Dame University; Dr. A.J. Luke Gormally, director emeritus of Linacre Centre for Health Care Ethics in England and research professor at Ave Maria School of Law; Prof. John Haas, professor of Moral Theology and the Pontifical College Josephinum, president of the National Catholic Bioethics Center and the International Institute of Culture; Prof. Edmund Pellegrino, director of the Center for Advanced Studies in Ethics at Georgetown University, honorary member. President: Most Rev. Salvatore Fisichella, titular abp. of Voghenza, rector of the Pontifical Lateran University and aux. bp. of the diocese of Rome.

Hierarchy of the Catholic Church

ORGANIZATION AND GOVERNMENT

As a structured society, the Catholic Church is organized and governed along lines corresponding mainly to the jurisdictions of the pope and bishops. The pope is the supreme head of the Church. He has primacy of jurisdiction as well as honor over the entire Church. Bishops, in union with and in subordination to the pope, are the successors of the Apostles for care of the Church and for the continuation of Christ's mission in the world. They serve the people of their own dioceses, or particular churches, with ordinary authority and jurisdiction. They also share, with the pope and each other, common concern and effort for the general welfare of the whole Church.

Bishops of exceptional status are patriarchs of Eastern Catholic Churches who, subject only to the pope, are heads of the faithful belonging to their rites throughout the world.

Subject to the Holy Father and directly responsible to him for the exercise of their ministry of service to peo-

ple in various jurisdictions or divisions of the Church throughout the world are: resident archbishops and metropolitans (heads of archdioceses), diocesan bishops, vicars and prefects apostolic (heads of vicariates apostolic and prefectures apostolic), certain abbots and prelates, and apostolic administrators. Each of these, within his respective territory and according to the provisions of canon law, has ordinary jurisdiction over pastors (who are responsible for the administration of parishes), priests, religious and lay persons.

Also subject to the Holy Father are titular archbishops and bishops, religious orders and congregations of pontifical right, pontifical institutes and faculties, papal nuncios and apostolic delegates.

Assisting the pope and acting in his name in the central government and administration of the Church are cardinals and other officials of the Roman Curia.

THE HIERARCHY

The ministerial hierarchy is the orderly arrangement of the ranks and orders of the clergy to provide for the spiritual care of the faithful, the government of the Church, and the accomplishment of the Church's total mission in the world.

Persons belong to this hierarchy by virtue of ordination and canonical mission. The term hierarchy is also used to designate an entire body or group of bishops; for example, the hierarchy of the Church, the hierarchy of the United States.

Hierarchy of Order: Consists of the pope, bishops, priests and deacons. Their purpose, for which they are ordained to holy orders, is to carry out the sacramental and pastoral ministry of the Church.

Hierarchy of Jurisdiction: Consists of the pope and bishops by divine institution, and other church officials by ecclesiastical institution and mandate, who have authority to govern and direct the faithful for spiritual ends.

The Pope

His Holiness the Pope is the Bishop of Rome, Vicar of Jesus Christ, successor of St. Peter, Prince of the Apostles, Supreme Pontiff of the Universal Church, Primate of Italy, Archbishop and Metropolitan of the Roman Province, Sovereign of the State of Vatican City, Servant of the Servants of God.

Cardinals
(See **Index**)

Patriarchs
Patriarch, a term which had its origin in the Eastern Church,

is the title of a bishop who, second only to the pope, has the highest rank in the hierarchy of jurisdiction. He is the incumbent of one of the sees listed below. Subject only to the pope, a patriarch of the Eastern Church is the head of the faithful belonging to his rite throughout the world. The patriarchal sees are so called because of their special status and dignity in the history of the Church.

The Council of Nicaea (325) recognized three patriarchs — the Bishops of Alexandria and Antioch in the East, and of Rome in the West. The First Council of Constantinople (381) added the bishop of Constantinople to the list of patriarchs and gave him rank second only to that of the pope, the bishop of Rome and patriarch of the West; this action was seconded by the Council of Chalcedon (451) and was given full recognition by the Fourth Lateran Council (1215). The Council of Chalcedon also acknowledged patriarchal rights of the bishop of Jerusalem.

Eastern patriarchs are as follows: one of Alexandria, for the Copts; three of Antioch, one each for the Syrians, Maronites and Greek Melkites (the latter also has the personal title of Greek Melkite patriarch of Alexandria and of Jerusalem). The patriarch of Babylonia, for the Chaldeans, and the patriarch of Sis, or Cilicia, for the Armenians, should be called, more properly, Katholikos - that is, a prelate delegated for a universality of causes. These patriarchs are elected by bishops of their churches; they receive approval and the pallium, symbol of their office, from the pope.

Latin Rite patriarchates were established for Antioch, Jerusalem, Alexandria and Constantinople during the

Crusades; afterwards, they became patriarchates in name only. Jerusalem, however, was reconstituted as a patriarchate by Pius IX, in virtue of the bull *Nulla Celebrior* of July 23, 1847. In 1964, the Latin titular patriarchates of Constantinople, Alexandria and Antioch, long a bone of contention in relations with Eastern Churches, were abolished.

As of Aug. 15, 2008, the patriarchs in the Church were:

Antonios Naguib, of Alexandria, for the Copts; Gregory III Laham, of Antioch, for the Greek Melkites (the patriarch also has personal titles of Alexandria and Jerusalem for the Greek Melkites); Cardinal Nasrallah Pierre Sfeir, of Antioch, for the Maronites; Nerses Bedros XIX Tarmouni, of Cilicia, for the Armenians; Cardinal Emmanuel III Delly, of Babylon of the Chaldeans. The office of Patriarch of the Syrian Catholic Church is currently vacant. (For biographical information on the patriarchs, see Eastern Catholics; see also Special Reports on the issue of the Pope as the Patriarch of the West.)

The titular patriarchs (in name only) of the Latin Rite were: Cardinal José da Cruz Policarpo of Lisbon; Cardinal Angelo Scola of Venice; Archbishop Filipe Neri António do Rosário Ferrão of the East Indies (archbishop of Goa and Damao, India); and Archbishop Fouad Twal of Jerusalem. The patriarchate of the West Indies has been vacant since 1963.

Major Archbishops

A major archbishop has the prerogatives but not the title of a patriarch. As of May 15, 2008, there were four major archbishops: Cardinal Lubomyr Husar of the major archbishopric of Kiev and Halych of the Ukrainian Catholic Church (Ukraine); Cardinal Varkey Vithayathil, C.SS.R. of the major archbishopric of Ernakulam-Angomaly of the Syro-Malabar Church (India); Abp. Isaac Mar Cleemis Thottunkal of the major archbishopric of Trivandrum of the Syro-Malankara Catholic Church (India), whose election was confirmed on Feb. 8, 2007 by Pope Benedict XVI); and Abp. Lucian Muresan of the major archbishopric of Fagaras and Alba Julia for the Romanian Greek Catholic Church (Romania) who was promoted to the rank of major archbishop on Dec. 16, 2005.

Archbishops, Metropolitans

Archbishop: A bishop with the title of an archdiocese.

Coadjutor Archbishop: An assistant archbishop with right of succession.

Metropolitan: Archbishop of the principal see, an archdiocese, in an ecclesiastical province consisting of several dioceses. He has the full powers of bishop in his own archdiocese and limited supervisory jurisdiction and influence over the other (suffragan) dioceses in the province. The pallium, conferred by the pope, is the symbol of his status as a metropolitan.

Titular Archbishop: Has the title of an archdiocese that formerly existed in fact but now exists in title only. He does not have ordinary jurisdiction over an archdiocese. Examples are archbishops in the Roman Curia, papal nuncios, apostolic delegates.

Archbishop *ad personam*: A title of personal honor and distinction granted to some bishops. They do not have ordinary jurisdiction over an archdiocese.

Primate: A title of honor given to the ranking prelate of some countries or regions.

Bishops

Diocesan Bishop: A bishop in charge of a diocese.

Coadjutor Bishop: An assistant (auxiliary) bishop to a diocesan bishop, with right of succession to the see.

Titular Bishops: A bishop with the title of a diocese that formerly existed in fact but now exists in title only; an assistant (auxiliary) bishop to a diocesan bishop.

Episcopal Vicar: An assistant, who may or may not be a bishop, appointed by a residential bishop as his deputy for a certain part of a diocese, a determined type of apostolic work, or the faithful of a certain rite.

Eparch, Exarch: Titles of bishops of Eastern churches.

Nomination of Bishops: Nominees for episcopal ordination are selected in several ways. Final appointment and/or approval in all cases is subject to decision by the pope.

In the U.S., bishops periodically submit the names of candidates to the archbishop of their province. The names are then considered at a meeting of the bishops of the province, and those receiving a favorable vote are forwarded to the pro-nuncio for transmission to the Holy See. Normally, three names are submitted. Bishops are free to seek the counsel of priests, religious and lay persons with respect to nominees.

Eastern Catholic churches have their own procedures and synodal regulations for nominating and making final selection of candidates for episcopal ordination. Such selection is subject to approval by the pope. The Code of Canon Law concedes no rights or privileges to civil authorities with respect to the election, nomination, presentation or designation of candidates for the episcopate.

Ad Limina Visit: Diocesan bishops and apostolic vicars are obliged to make an *ad limina* visit ("to the threshold" of the Apostles) every five years to the tombs of Sts. Peter and Paul, have audience with the Holy Father and consult with appropriate Vatican officials. They are required to send a report on conditions in their jurisdiction to the Congregation for bishops approximately six - and not less than three - months in advance of the scheduled visit.

Others with Ordinary Jurisdiction

Ordinary: One who has the jurisdiction of an office: the pope, diocesan bishops, vicars general, prelates of missionary territories, vicars apostolic prefects apostolic, vicars capitular during the vacancy of a see, superiors general, abbots primate and other major superiors of men religious.

Some prelates and abbots, with jurisdiction like that of diocesan bishops, are pastors of the people of God in territories (prelatures and abbacies) not under the jurisdiction of diocesan bishops.

Vicar Apostolic: Usually a titular bishop who has ordinary jurisdiction over a mission territory.

Prefect Apostolic: Has ordinary jurisdiction over a mission territory.

Apostolic Administrator: Usually a bishop appointed to administer an ecclesiastical jurisdiction temporarily. Administrators of lesser rank are also appointed on occasion and have more restricted supervisory duties.

Vicar General: A bishop's deputy for the administration of a diocese; does not have to be a bishop.

Prelates Without Jurisdiction

The title of protonotary apostolic was originally given by the fourth century or earlier to clergy who collected accounts of martyrdom and other church documents, or who served the Church with distinction in other ways. Other titles — e.g., domestic prelate, papal chamberlain, prelate of honor — are titles of clergy in service to the pope and the papal household, or of clergy honored for particular reasons. All prelates without jurisdiction are appointed by the pope, and have designated ceremonial privileges and the title of Rev. Monsignor.

SYNOD OF BISHOPS

The Synod of Bishops was chartered by Pope Paul VI, Sept. 15, 1965, in a document he issued on his own initiative under the title *Apostolica Sollicitudo*. Provisions of this motu proprio are contained in Canons 342 to 348 of the Code of Canon Law. According to major provisions of the Synod charter:

• The purposes of the Synod are "to encourage close union and valued assistance between the Sovereign Pontiff and the bishops of the entire world; to insure that direct and real information is provided on questions and situations touching upon the internal action of the Church and its necessary activity in the world of today; to facilitate agreement on essential points of doctrine and on methods of procedure in the life of the Church."

• The Synod is a central ecclesiastical institution, permanent by nature.

• The Synod is directly and immediately subject to the pope, who has authority to assign its agenda, to call it into session, and to give its members deliberative as well as advisory authority.

• In addition to a limited number of ex officio members and a few heads of male religious institutes, the majority of the members are elected by and representative of national or regional episcopal conferences. The pope reserved the right to appoint the general secretary, special secretaries and no more than 15 percent of the total membership.

The pope is president of the Synod. The secretary general is Abp. Nikola Eterovic, of Croatia. Address: Palazzo del Bramante, Via della Concilizione 34, 00193 Rome, Italy.

An advisory council of 15 members (12 elected, three appointed by the pope) provides the secretariat with adequate staff for carrying on liaison with episcopal conferences and for preparing the agenda of synodal assemblies. Cardinal William H, Keeler, Abp. emeritus of Baltimore, is a member of the secretariat.

Assemblies

1. First Assembly: The first assembly was held from Sept. 29 to Oct. 29, 1967. Its objectives, as stated by Pope Paul VI, were "the preservation and strengthening of the Catholic faith, its integrity, its force, its development, its doctrinal and historical coherence." One result was a recommendation for the establishment of an international commission of theologians to assist the Congregation for the Doctrine of the Faith and to broaden approaches to theological research. Pope Paul set up the commission in 1969.

2. Pope-Bishop Relations: The second assembly, held Oct. 11 to 28, 1969, was extraordinary in character. It opened the way toward greater participation by bishops with the pope and each other in the governance of the Church. Proceedings were oriented to three main points: (1) the nature and implications of collegiality; (2) the relationship of bishops and their conferences to the pope; (3) the relationships of bishops and their conferences to each other.

3. Priesthood and Justice: The ministerial priesthood and justice in the world were the principal topics under discussion at the second ordinary assembly, Sept. 30 to Nov. 6, 1971. In one report, the Synod emphasized the primary and permanent dedication of priests in the Church to the ministry of word, sacra-

ment and pastoral service as a full-time vocation. In another report, the assembly stated: "Action on behalf of justice and participation in the transformation of the world fully appear to us as a constitutive dimension of the preaching of the Gospel; or, in other words, of the Church's mission for the redemption of the human race and its liberation from every oppressive situation."

4. Evangelization: The assembly of Sept. 27 to Oct. 26, 1974, produced a general statement on evangelization of the modern world, covering the need for it and its relationship to efforts for total human liberation from personal and social evil. The assembly observed: "The Church does not remain within merely political, social and economic limits (elements which she must certainly take into account) but leads towards freedom under all its forms—liberation from sin, from individual or collective selfishness—and to full communion with God and with men who are like brothers. In this way the Church, in her evangelical way, promotes the true and complete liberation of all men, groups and peoples."

5. Catechetics: The fourth ordinary assembly, Sept. 30 to Oct. 29, 1977, focused attention on catechetics, with special reference to children and young people. The participants issued a "Message to the People of God," the first synodal statement issued since inception of the body, and also presented a set of 34 related propositions and a number of suggestions to Pope Paul VI.

6. Family: "A Message to Christian Families in the Modern World" and a proposal for a "Charter of Family Rights" were produced by the assembly held Sept. 26 to Oct. 25, 1980. The assembly reaffirmed the indissolubility of marriage and the contents of the encyclical letter *Humanae Vitae* (see separate entry), and urged married couples who find it hard to live up to "the difficult but loving demands" of Christ not to be discouraged but to avail themselves of the aid of divine grace. In response to synodal recommendation, Pope John Paul II issued a charter of family rights late in 1983.

7. Reconciliation: Penance and reconciliation in the mission of the Church was the theme of the assembly held Sept. 29 to Oct. 29, 1983. Sixty-three propositions related to this theme were formulated on a wide variety of subjects, including: personal sin and so-called systemic or institutional sin; the nature of serious sin; the diminished sense of sin and of the need of redemption, related to decline in the administration and reception of the sacrament of penance; general absolution; individual and social reconciliation; violence and violations of human rights; reconciliation as the basis of peace and justice in society. In a statement issued Oct. 27, the Synod stressed the need of the world to become increasingly "a reconciled community of peoples," and said that "the Church, as sacrament of reconciliation to the world, has to be an effective sign of God's mercy."

8. Vatican II Review: The second extraordinary assembly was convened Nov. 24 to Dec. 8, 1985, for the purposes of: (1) recalling the Second Vatican Council; (2) evaluating the implementation of its enactments during the 20 years since its conclusion; (3) seeking ways and means of promoting renewal in the Church in accordance with the spirit and letter of the council. At the conclusion of the assembly the bishops issued two documents. (1) In "A Message to the People of God," they noted the need for greater appreciation of the enactments of Vatican II and for greater efforts to put them into effect, so that all members of the Church might discharge their responsibility of proclaiming the good news of salvation. (2) In a "Final Report," the first of its kind published by a synodal assembly, the bishops reflected on lights and shadows since Vatican II, stating that negative developments had come from partial and superficial interpretations of conciliar enactments and from incomplete or ineffective implementation. The report also covered a considerable number of subjects discussed during the assembly, including the mystery of the Church, inculturation, the preferential (but not exclusive) option for the poor, and a suggestion for the development of a new universal catechism of the Catholic faith.

9. Vocation and Mission of the Laity in the Church and in the World 20 years after the Second Vatican Council: The seventh ordinary assembly, Oct. 1 to 30, 1987, said in a "Message to the People of God": "The majority of the Christian laity live out their vocation as followers and disciples of Christ in all spheres of life which we call 'the world': the family, the field of work, the local community and the like. To permeate this day-to-day living with the spirit of Christ has always been the task of the lay faithful; and it should be with still greater force their challenge today. It is in this way that they sanctify the world and collaborate in the realization of the kingdom of God." The assembly produced a set of 54 propositions which were presented to the pope for consideration in the preparation of a document of his own on the theme of the assembly. He responded with the apostolic exhortation, *Christifideles Laici,* "The Christian Faithful Laity," released by the Vatican Jan. 30, 1989.

10. Formation of Priests in Circumstances of the Present Day: The eighth general assembly, Sept. 30 to Oct. 28, 1990, dealt principally with the nature and mission of the priesthood; the identity, multi-faceted formation and spirituality of priests; and, in a "Message to the People of God," the need on all levels of the Church for the promotion of vocations to the priesthood. Forty-one proposals were presented to the Pope for his consideration in preparing a document of his own on the theme of the assembly. Pope John Paul issued an apostolic exhortation entitled *Pastores Dabo Vobis* ("I Will Give You Shepherds") Apr. 7, 1992.

11. The Consecrated Life and Its Role in the Church and in the World: The ninth general assembly was held Oct. 2 to 29, 1994. Pope John Paul's

reflections on the proceedings of the assembly and the recommendations of the bishops were the subjects of his apostolic exhortation entitled *Vita Consecrata* ("Consecrated Life"), issued Mar. 25, 1996. The document dealt with various forms of consecrated life: contemplative institutes, apostolic religious life, secular institutes, societies of apostolic life, mixed institutes and new forms of evangelical life.

12. The Bishop: Servant of the Gospel of Jesus Christ for the Hope of the World: The 10th ordinary general assembly was held from Sept. 30 to Oct. 27, 2001. Pope John Paul II's reflections on the proceedings of the assembly and the recommendations of the Bishops was the subject of the apostolic exhortation *Ecclesia in Europa,* issued on June 28, 2003.

13. The Eucharist: Source and Summit of the Life and Mission of the Church: The 11th ordinary general assembly was held from Oct. 2 to Oct. 23, 2005. Pope Benedict XVI's reflections on the proceedings of the assembly and the recommendations of the Bishops were the subject of an apostolic exhortation, *Sacramentum Caritatis* issued on March 13, 2007.

14. The Word of God in the Life and Mission of the Church: The 12th ordinary general assembly will be held from Oct. 5 to Oct. 26, 2008.

Recent Special Assemblies of the Synod of Bishops: Special Synods have been held for Europe (Nov. 28 to Dec. 14, 1991, on the theme "So that we might be witnesses of Christ who has set us free"); for Africa (Apr. 10 to May 8, 1994, on the theme "The Church in Africa and Her Evangelizing Mission Towards the Year 2000: 'You Shall Be My Witnesses' (Acts 1:8)"); for Lebanon (Nov. 27 to Dec. 14, 1995, on the theme "Christ is Our Hope: Renewed by His Spirit, in Solidarity We Bear Witness to His Love"); the Americas (Nov. 16 to Dec. 12, 1997, on the theme, "Encounter with the Living Jesus Christ: Way to Conversion, Community and Solidarity"); for Asia (Apr. 19 to May 14, 1998, on the theme "Jesus Christ the Savior and His Mission of Love and Service in Asia: '...That They May Have Life, and Have it Abundantly' (Jn 10:10)"); for Oceania (Nov. 12 to Dec. 12, 1998, on the theme "Jesus Christ and the Peoples of Oceania: Walking His Way, Telling His Truth, Living His Life"; and a special assembly for Europe (Oct. 1-23, 1999), on the theme "Jesus Christ, Alive in His Church, Source of Hope for Europe."

COLLEGE OF CARDINALS

Cardinals are chosen by the pope to serve as his principal assistants and advisers in the central administration of church affairs. Collectively, they form the College of Cardinals. Provisions regarding their selection, rank, roles and prerogatives are detailed in Canons 349 to 359 of the Code of Canon Law.

History of the College

The College of Cardinals was constituted in its present form and categories of membership in the 12th century. Before that time the pope had a body of advisers selected from among the bishops of dioceses neighboring Rome, priests and deacons of Rome. The college was given definite form in 1150, and in 1179 the selection of cardinals was reserved exclusively to

the pope. Sixtus V fixed the number at 70, in 1586. John XXIII set aside this rule when he increased membership at the 1959 and subsequent consistories. The number was subsequently raised by Paul VI. The number of cardinals entitled to participate in papal elections was limited to 120 by Paul VI in 1973. The limit on the number of cardinals was set aside by Pope John Paul II three times, in 1998, 2001, and 2003. As of Aug. 24, 2008, 116 of the 194 cardinals were eligible to vote.

In 1567 the title of cardinal was reserved to members of the college; previously it had been used by priests attached to parish churches of Rome and by the leading clergy of other notable churches. The Code of Canon Law promulgated in 1918 decreed that all cardinals must be priests. Previously there had been cardinals who were not priests (e.g., Cardinal Giacomo Antonelli, d. 1876, Secretary of State to Pius IX, was a deacon). John XXIII provided in the *motu proprio Cum Gravissima* Apr. 15, 1962, that cardinals would henceforth be bishops; this provision is included in the revised Code of Canon Law.

Age Limits

Pope Paul VI placed age limits on the functions of cardinals in the apostolic letter *Ingravescentem Aetatem,* dated Nov. 21, 1970, and effective Jan. 1, 1971. At 80, they cease to be members of curial departments and offices, and become ineligible to take part in papal elections. They retain membership in the College of Cardinals, however, with relevant rights and privileges.

Three Categories

All cardinals except Eastern patriarchs are aggregated to the clergy of Rome. This aggregation is signified by the assignment to each cardinal, except the patriarchs, of a titular church in Rome. The three categories of members of the college are cardinal bishops, cardinal priests and cardinal deacons.

Cardinal bishops include the six titular bishops of the suburbicarian sees and Eastern patriarchs. First in rank are the titular bishops of the suburbicarian sees neighboring Rome: Ostia, Palestrina, Porto-Santa Rufina, Albano, Velletri-Segni, Frascati, Sabina-Poggio Mirteto. The dean of the college holds the title of the See of Ostia as well as his other suburbicarian see. These cardinal bishops are engaged in full-time service in the central administration of church affairs in departments of the Roman Curia.

Full recognition is given in the revised Code of Canon Law to the position of Eastern patriarchs as the heads of sees of apostolic origin with ancient liturgies. They are assigned rank among the cardinals in order of seniority, following the suburbicarian titleholders.

Cardinal priests, who were formerly in charge of leading churches in Rome, are bishops whose dioceses are outside Rome.

Cardinal deacons, who were formerly chosen according to regional divisions of Rome, are titular bishops assigned to full-time service in the Roman Curia.

The dean and sub-dean of the college are elected by the cardinal bishops—subject to approval by the pope—from among their number. The dean, or the sub-dean in his absence, presides over the college as the first among equals. Cardinals Angelo Sodano and Roger Etchegeray were elected dean and vice-dean, respectively, on Apr. 30, 2005. The Secretary to the College of Cardinals is Abp. Francesco Monterisi.

Selection and Duties

Cardinals are selected by the pope and are inducted into the college in appropriate ceremonies. Cardinals under the age of 80 elect the pope when the Holy See becomes vacant (see Index: Papal Election, see also below under Conclave); and are major administrators of church affairs, serving in one or more departments of the Roman Curia. Cardinals in charge of agencies of the Roman Curia and Vatican City are asked to submit their resignation from office to the pope on reaching the age of 75. All cardinals enjoy a number of special rights and privileges. Their title, while symbolic of high honor, does not signify any extension of the powers of holy orders. They are called princes of the Church.

A cardinal *in pectore (petto)* is one whose selection has been made by the pope but whose name has not been disclosed; he has no title, rights or duties until such disclosure is made, at which time he takes precedence from the time of the secret selection.

BIOGRAPHIES OF CARDINALS

*Biographies of the cardinals, as of Sept. 15, 2008, are given below in alphabetical order. For historical notes, order of seniority and geographical distribution of cardinals, see separate entries. An * asterisk indicates cardinals ineligible to take part in papal elections.*

Agré,* Bernard: b. Mar. 2, 1926, Monga, Côte d'Ivoire; ord., July 20, 1953; headmaster in Dabou; vicar general of Abidjan archdiocese; app. bp. of Man, June 8, 1968; app. first bp. of Yamoussoukro, Mar. 6, 1992; abp. of Abidjan, 1994-2006; ret. May 2, 2006; pres. of the Episcopal Conferences of Francophone West Africa (CERAO) and chair of the Pan-African Episcopal Committee for Social Communications (CEPACS); cardinal, Feb. 21, 2001; titular church, St. John Chrysostom in Monte Sacro Alto. Abp. emeritus of Abidjan.

Agustoni,* Gilberto: b. July 26, 1922, Schaffhausen, Switzerland; ord., Apr. 20, 1946; called to Rome in 1950 to work under Cardinal Ottaviani in the Congregation for the Holy Office; a Prelate Auditor of the Roman Rota, 1970-86; ord. titular abp. of Caorle Jan. 6, 1987; sec. of the Congregation for the Clergy, 1986-92; pro-prefect of the Apostolic Signatura, 1992-94; cardinal deacon, Nov. 26, 1994; titular church Sts. Urban and Laurence at Prima Porta. Prefect of Supreme Tribunal of Apostolic Signatura, 1994-98. Prefect emeritus of Supreme Tribunal of Apostolic Signatura.

Álvarez Martínez,* Francisco: b. July 14, 1925, Santa Eulalia de Ferroñes Llanera, Spain; ord., June 11, 1950; personal secretary to Abp. Lauzurica y Torralba of Oviedo; chancellor and secretary of archdiocesan curia; chaplain of the university students at Teresian Institute; app. bp. of Tarazona, Apr. 13, 1973; cons., June 3, 1973; bp. of Calahorra and La Calzado-Logroño, Dec. 20, 1976; transferred to Orihuela-Alicante, May 12, 1989; abp. of Toledo, 1995-2002; member of the Standing Committee and the Executive Committee of the Spanish Episcopal Conference; cardinal, Feb. 21, 2001; titular church, St. Mary Regina Pacis in Monte Verde. Abp. emeritus of Toledo.

Ambrozic, Aloysius M.: b. Jan. 27, 1930, Gabrje, Slovenia (emigrated to Austria, 1945, and Canada, 1948); ord., June 4, 1955; taught Scripture, St. Augustine's Seminary, 1960-67; taught NT exegesis, Toronto School of Theology, 1970-76; aux. bp. of Toronto, Mar. 26, 1976; co-adjutor of Toronto, May 22, 1986; abp. of Toronto, 1990-2006; cardinal, Feb. 21, 1998; titular church, Sts. Marcellinus and Peter. Abp. emeritus of Toronto.

Curial membership: Oriental Churches, Sacraments, Clergy (congregation); Pastoral Care of Migrants and Itinerant People, Culture (councils).

Amigo Vallejo, O.F.M., Carlos: b. Aug. 23, 1934, Medina de Rioseco, Spain; joined Order of Friars Minor and ord. Aug. 17, 1960; ord. abp. of Tanger, Morocco, Apr. 28, 1974;

abp. of Toledo, 1974-84; abp. of Seville, May 22, 1984; cardinal, Oct. 21, 2003; titular church, St. Mary of Monserrat of the Spanish. Abp. of Toledo.

Curial membership: Health Care Workers (council); Latin America (commission).

Angelini,* Fiorenzo: b. Aug. 1, 1916, Rome, Italy; ord., Feb. 3, 1940; master of pontifical ceremonies, 1947-54; ord. bp. (titular see of Messene) July 29, 1956, and head of Rome Vicariate's section for apostolate to health care workers; abp, 1985; pres. of newly established Curia agency for health care workers; cardinal deacon, June 28, 1991, deaconry, Holy Spirit (in Sassio). President of Pontifical Council for Pastoral Assistance to Health Care Workers, 1989-96.

Antonelli, Ennio: b. Nov. 18, 1936, Todi, Italy; ord., Apr. 2, 1960; bp. of Gubbio, Aug. 29, 1982; abp. of Perugia-Città della Pieve, 1988-2001; secretary-general of the Italian Episcopal Conference, 1995; abp. of Florence, Mar. 21, 2001-June 7, 2008; app. pres. of the Pont. Council for the Family, June 7, 2008; cardinal, Oct. 21, 2003; titular church, St. Andrew delle Fratte. Pres. of the Pont. Council for the Family.

Curial membership: Laity, Social Communications (councils).

Antonetti,* Lorenzo: b. July 31, 1922, Romagnano Sesia, Italy; ord., May 26, 1945; entered diplomatic service and served in Lebanon, Venezuela, first section for Extraordinary Affairs of the Secretariat of State, U.S., and France; ord. titular abp. of Roselle, May 12, 1968; apostolic nuncio to Nicaragua and Honduras, 1968-1973, and Zaire, 1973-77; secretary of the Administration of the Patrimony of the Apostolic See (APSA), 1977-88; apostolic nuncio to France, 1988-95; pro-president Admin. of the Patrimony of the Apostolic See, 1995-1998; pres. Administration of the Patrimony of the Apostolic See (APSA), Feb. 23, 1998; cardinal deacon, Feb. 21, 1998; cardinal priest, Mar. 2, 2008; titular church, St. Agnes in Agone. President emeritus Administration of the Patrimony of the Apostolic See.

Aponte Martínez,* Luis: b. Aug. 4, 1922, Lajas, Puerto Rico; ord., Apr. 10, 1950; parish priest at Ponce; ord. titular bp. of Lares and aux. of Ponce, Oct. 12, 1960; bp. of Ponce, 1963-64; abp. of San Juan, Nov. 4, 1964-99; cardinal, Mar. 5, 1973; titular church, St. Mary Mother of Providence (in Monte Verde). Abp. emeritus of San Juan.

Arinze, Francis: b. Nov. 1, 1932, Eziowelle, Nigeria; ord., Nov. 23, 1958; ord. titular bp. of Fissiana and aux. bp. of Onitsha, Aug. 29, 1965; abp. of Onitsha, 1967-84; pro-president of Secretariat for Non–Christians (now the Council for Interreligious Dialogue), 1984; cardinal deacon, May 25, 1985; deaconry, St. John (della Pigna); transferred to the order of cardinal priests, Jan. 29, 1996; transferred to the order of cardinal bishops, Apr. 25, 2005, with Suburbicarian See of Veletri-Segni; President of Council for Interreligious Dialogue, 1985-2002; Prefect of the Congregation for Divine Worship and the Discipline of the Sacraments, Oct. 1, 2002.

Curial membership: Doctrine of the Faith, Oriental Churches, Evangelization of Peoples, Causes of Saints (congregations); Laity, Christian Unity, Culture (councils); International Eucharistic Congresses (committee).

Arns,* O.F.M., Paulo Evaristo: b. Sept. 14, 1921, Forquilhinha, Brazil; ord., Nov. 30, 1945; held various teaching posts; director of Sponsa Christi, monthly review for religious, and of the Franciscan publication center in Brazil; ord. titular bp. of Respetta and aux. bp. of São Paulo, July 3, 1966; abp. of São Paulo, 1970-98; cardinal, Mar. 5, 1973; titular church, St. Anthony of Padua (in Via Tuscolana). Abp. emeritus of São Paulo.

Backis, Audrys Juozas: b. Feb. 1, 1937, Kaunas, Lithuania; ord., Mar. 18, 1961; entered Holy See diplomatic service in 1964 and posted to the Philippines, Costa Rica, Turkey, Nigeria, and the Council for the Public Affairs of the Church; underscretary to the Council for the Public Affairs of the Church, 1979-88; app. titular abp. of Meta and nuncio to the Netherlands, Aug. 5, 1988; app. abp. of Vilnius Dec. 24, 1991; pres. of the Lithuanian Bishops' Conference; cardinal, Feb. 21, 2001; titular church, Nativity of Our Lord Jesus Christ in Via Gallia. Abp. of Vilnius.

Curial membership: Education (congregation); Social Communication (council); Cultural Heritage of the Church (commission).

Bagnasco, Angelo: b. Feb. 14, 1943, Pontevico, Italy; ord. June 29, 1966; earned a doctorate in philosophy from the State University of Genoa in 1979 and served in pastoral ministry from 1966-1985; professor of metaphysics and contemporary atheism at the Theological Faculty of Northern Italy, 1980-1998; cons. bp. of Pesaro, Feb. 7, 1998; promoted to archbishop when the diocese was elevated to the rank of metropolitan see, Mar. 11, 2000; app. military ordinary for Italy, June 20, 2003; app. abp. of Genoa, Aug. 29, 2006; app. by Pope Benedict XVI president of the Italian Episcopal Conference on Mar. 7, 2007; cardinal, Nov. 24, 2007, titular church, Great Mother of God.

Curial membership: Bishops, Oriental Churches, Sacraments (congregation).

Barbarin, Philippe: b. Oct. 17, 1950, Rabat, Morocco; ord. Dec. 17, 1977; from 1994 to 1998, served in Madagascar as pastor and professor in the island's seminary; ord. bp. of Moulins, France, Nov. 22, 1998; abp. of Lyon, July 16, 2002, cardinal, Oct. 21, 2003; titular church, Most Holy Spirit al Monte Pincio. Abp. of Lyon.

Curial membership: Sacraments, Consecrated Life and Societies of Apostolic Life (congregations),

Baum,* William Wakefield: b. Nov. 21, 1926, Dallas, TX; moved to Kansas City, MO, at an early age; ord. (Kansas City-St. Joseph diocese), May 12, 1951; executive director of U.S. Bishops' Commission for Ecumenical and Interreligious Affairs, 1964-69; attended Second Vatican Council as peritus (expert adviser); ord. bp. of Springfield-Cape Girardeau, MO, Apr. 6, 1970; abp. of Washington, D.C., 1973-80; cardinal, May 24, 1976; titular church, Holy Cross on the Via Flaminia; prefect of Congregation for Catholic Education (Seminaries and Institutes of Study), 1980-90. Major Penitentiary, 1990-2001; res., Nov. 22, 2001.

Bergoglio, S.J., Jorge Mario: b. Dec. 17, 1936, Buenos Aires, Argentina; ord., priest for the Jesuits, Dec. 13, 1969; novice master in the Theological Faculty of San Miguel; Jesuit provincial for Argentina, 1973-79; rector of the Philosophical and Theological Faculty of San Miguel, 1980-86; completed doctoral dissertation in Germany and served as confessor and spiritual director in Córdoba; app. titular bp. of Auca and aux. bp. of Buenos Aires, May 20, 1992; cons., June 27, 1992; app. coadj. abp. of Buenos Aires, June 3, 1997; succeeded as abp. of Buenos Aires, Feb. 28, 1998; also serves as Ordinary for Eastern-rite faithful in Argentina who lack their own ordinary and second vice-pres. of the Argentine Episcopal Conference; cardinal, Feb. 21, 2001; titular church, St. Robert Bellarmine; pres. of Argentine Episcopal Conference for 2005-2008 Abp. of Buenos Aires.

Curial membership: Sacraments, Clergy, Institutes of Consecrated Life and Societies of Apostolic Life (congregations); Family (council); Latin America (commission).

Bertone, S.D.B., Tarcisio: b. Dec. 2, 1934, Romano

Canavese, entered the Society of St. Francis de Sales of St. John Bosco (Salesians); ord., July 1, 1960; prof. of Special Moral Theology, Pontifical Salesian Athenaeum (later Pontifical Salesian University in 1973), 1967-76; prof. of Canon Law, 1976-1991; vice-rector, Pontifical Salesian University of Rome, 1987-1989; ord. abp. of Vercelli, Aug. 1, 1991; sec. of the Cong. for the Doctrine of the Faith, 1995-2002; abp. of Genoa, Dec. 10, 2002; cardinal, Oct. 21, 2003; titular church, St. Mary, Helper in Via Tuscolana; transferred to the order of cardinal bishops (with the suburbicarian see of Frascati), May 10, 2008; app. Secretary of State, Sept. 15, 2006; app. Chamberlain (Camerlengo) of the Holy Roman Church, Apr. 4, 2007. Secretary of State.

Curial membership: Clergy, Doctrine of the Faith, Eastern Churches, Sacraments (congregations); Synod of Bishops; Institute for Works of Religion (commission).

Betti,* Umberto, O.F.M.: b. Mar. 7, 1922, Pieve San Stefano, Italy; ord. May 4, 1946; entered the Franciscans in 1937 and made his first solemn profession in 1943; earned a doctorate in dogmatic theology in 1951 and served as a professor of theology at the Pontifical Antonian Athenaeum in Rome, from 1964-1991 and rector *magnifico* from 1975-1978; rector *magnifico* of the Pontifical Lateran University, Rome, 1991-1995; cardinal, Nov. 24, 2007; deaconry, Sts. Vitus, Modest, and Crescenzia.

Bevilacqua,* Anthony Joseph: b. June 17, 1923, Brooklyn NY; ord., (Brooklyn diocese), June 11, 1949; ord. titular bp. of Aquae Albae in Byzacena and aux. bp. of Brooklyn, Nov. 24, 1980; bp. of Pittsburgh, Oct. 7, 1983, installed, Dec. 12, 1983; abp. of Philadelphia, Feb. 11, 1988; cardinal, June 28, 1991; titular church, Most Holy Redeemer and St. Alphonsus (on Via Merulana); ret., July 15, 2003. Abp. emeritus of Philadelphia.

Biffi,* Giacomo: b. June 13, 1928, Milan, Italy; ord., Dec. 23, 1950; ord. titular bp. of Fidene and aux. of Milan, Jan. 11, 1976; abp. of Bologna, 1984-2003; cardinal, May 25, 1985; titular church, Sts. John the Evangelist and Petronius. Abp. emeritus of Bologna.

Curial membership: Clergy, Catholic Education (congregations).

Bozanic, Josip: b. Mar. 20, 1949, Rijeka, Yugoslavia; ord., June 29, 1975; prof. of canon law and dogmatic theology in the Seminary of Rijeka, 1988-1997; ord. bp. of Krk, Veglia, June 25, 1989; abp. of Zagreb, Croatia, July 5, 1997; pres. of the Croatian Conference of Bishops and vice-pres. of the Council of European Bishops' Conferences; cardinal, Oct. 21, 2003; titular church, St. Jerome of the Croatians. Abp. of Zagreb.

Curial membership: Sacraments (congregation); Laity (council).

Brady, Seán Baptist: b. Aug. 16, 1939, Drumcalpin, diocese of Kilmore, Ireland; ord. Feb. 22, 1964; served from 1964-1993 as a faculty member in the Minor Seminary, Kilmore and then vice-rector and rector of the Pontifical Irish College in Rome; cons. coadj. abp. of Armagh, Ireland, Feb. 19, 1995 and acceded to the metropolitan and primatial see of Armagh, Oct. 1, 1996; has been a leading voice for peace in Northern Ireland and has warned against secularism in the country; cardinal, Nov. 24, 2007, titular church, Sts. Quirico and Giulitta.

Curial membership: Christian Unity (council); Culture (commission).

Cacciavillan,* Agostino: b. Aug. 14, 1926, Novale de Valdagno (Vicenza), Italy; ord., June 26, 1949; attended Pont. Ecclesiastical Academy; entered Holy See diplomatic service; posted to the Philippines, Spain, Portugal, and Secretariat of State; pro-nuncio in Kenya and apostolic delegate to Seychelles, 1976; titular abp. of Amiternum, Feb. 28, 1976; nuncio to India, 1981; pro-nuncio to Nepal, 1985; nuncio to United States and permanent observer at the Org. of American States, 1990; pres., Admin. of the Patrimony of the Apostolic See (APSA), 1998-2002; cardinal deacon, Feb. 21, 2001; protodeacon, Mar. 2, 2008; deaconry, Holy Guardian Angels in Città Giardino. Pres. emeritus Admin. of the Patrimony of the Apostolic See.

Caffarra, Carlo: b. June 1, 1938, Samboseto di Busseto, in the province of Parma, Italy; ord. July 2, 1961; studied at the Pontifical Lombard Seminary, Gregorian University, where he earned a doctorate in canon law, and the Pontifical Accademia Alfonsiana, with a diploma for a specialization in Moral Theology; after holding a variety of teaching positions, he was named to the International Theological Commission in 1974; founded in 1981 the John Paul II Pontifical Institute for Studies on Marriage and the Family; consultor to the Cong. for the Doctrine of the Faith, 1983-88; app. Sept. 8, 1995, abp. of Ferrara-Comacchio; app. Dec. 16, 2003, abp. of Bologna; pres. of the Episcopal Conference of Emilia Romagna; cardinal Mar. 24, 2006; titular church, San Giovanni Battista dei Fiorentini. Abp. of Bologna.

Curial membership: Evangelization of People (congregation); Family (council); Pontifical Academy of Life; Apostolic Signatura.

Canestri,* Giovanni: b. Sept. 30, 1918, Castelspina, Italy; ord., Apr. 12, 1941; spiritual director of Rome's seminary, 1959; ord. titular bp. of Tenedo and aux. to the cardinal vicar of Rome, July 30, 1961; bp. of Tortona, 1971–75; titular bp. of Monterano (personal title of abp.) and vice regent of Rome, 1975–84; abp. of Cagliari, 1984–87; abp. of Genoa, July 6, 1987–95; cardinal, June 28, 1988; titular church, St. Andrew of the Valley. Abp. emeritus of Genoa.

Cañizares Llovera, Antonio: b. Oct. 10, 1945, Utiel, Spain; after studies in the diocesan seminary of Valencia, he earned a doctorate in theology from the Pontifical University of Salamanca in 1971; ord. June 21, 1970; sec. of the Episcopal Commission for the Doctrine of the Faith, 1985-92; founder and first president of the Spanish Association of Catechists, 1977-89; app. bp. of Ávila, Mar. 6, 1992; contributed to the compilation of the Spanish-language edition of the Catechism of the Catholic Church; app. abp. of Granada, Dec. 10, 1996; founder and first grand chancellor of the Catholic University, "Santa Teresa de Jesús" in Ávila, 1994-97; app. metropolitan abp. of Toledo and primate of Spain, Oct. 24, 2002; cardinal, Mar. 24, 2006; titular church, di San Pancrazio. Abp. of Toledo.

Curial membership: Doctrine of the Faith; Ecclesia Dei (commission).

Carles Gordó,* Ricardo Maria: b. Sept. 24, 1926, Valencia, Spain; ord., June 29, 1951; ord. bp. of Tortosa, Aug. 3, 1969; abp. of Barcelona, 1990-2004; cardinal, Nov. 26, 1994; titular church, St. Mary of Consolation in Tiburtino. Abp. emeritus of Barcelona.

Cassidy,* Edward Idris: b. July 5, 1924, Sydney, Australia; ord., July 23, 1949; entered Vatican diplomatic service in 1955; served in nunciatures in India, Ireland, El Salvador and Argentina; ord. titular bp. of Amantia with personal title of abp., Nov. 15, 1970; pro-nuncio to Republic of China (Taiwan), 1970-79 and pro-nuncio to Bangladesh and apostolic delegate in Burma, 1973-79; pro-nuncio to Lesotho and apostolic delegate to southern Africa, 1979-84; pro-nuncio to the Netherlands, 1984-88; substitute of the Secretary of State for General Affairs, 1988-89; pres. of Pontifical Council for Promoting Christian Unity, 1989-2001; cardinal deacon, June 28, 1991; deaconry, St. Mary (in via Lata). President emeritus of Pontifical Council for Promoting Christian Unity.

Castrillón Hoyos, Darío: b. July 4, 1929, Medellín, Colombia; ord., Oct. 26, 1952; served as curate in two parishes; dir. local Cursillo Movement; delegate for Catholic Action; taught canon law at the Free Civil University; gen. sec. of the Colombian Bishops' Conference; coadj. bp. of Pereira, June 2, 1971; bp. of Pereira, 1976-1992; gen. sec. of Latin American Episcopal Council (CELAM), 1983-87; pres. CELAM, 1987-91; abp. of Bucaramanga, 1992-96; pro-prefect Cong. for the Clergy, 1996-98; Pref. Cong. for the Clergy, 1998-2006; Protodeacon, 2007-2008; cardinal deacon, Feb. 21, 1998; cardinal priest, Mar. 2, 2008; titular church, Holy Name of Mary on the Forum Traiani. Prefect emeritus of the Congregation for the Clergy.

Curial membership: Bishops, Education, Evangelization of Peoples, Sacraments (congregations); Social Communications, Texts (councils); APSA (office); Latin America (commission).

Cé,* Marco: b. July 8, 1925, Izano, Italy; ord., Mar. 27, 1948; taught sacred scripture and dogmatic theology at seminary in his home diocese of Crema; rector of seminary, 1957; presided over diocesan liturgical commission, preached youth retreats; ord. titular bp. of Vulturia, May 17, 1970; aux. bp. of Bologna, 1970-76; gen. ecclesiastical assistant of Italian Catholic Action, 1976-78; patriarch of Venice, 1978-2001; ret., Jan. 5, 2002; cardinal, June 30, 1979; titular church, St. Mark. Patriarch emeritus of Venice.

Cheli,* Giovanni: b. Oct. 4, 1918, Turin, Italy; ord., June 21, 1942; entered Secretariat of State and diplomatic service; second secretary, apostolic nunciature in Guatemala, 1952-55; first secretary, apostolic nunciature in Madrid, Spain, 1955-62; counselor, nunciature in Rome, 1962-67; Council for Public Affairs of the Church, Vatican City, 1967-73; Permanent Observer of the Holy See to the U.N., 1973-86; ord. titular abp. of Santa Giusta, Sept. 16, 1978; pres. Pontifical Council for the Pastoral Care of Migrants and Itinerant People, 1986-98; cardinal deacon, Feb. 21, 1998; cardinal priest, Mar. 2, 2008; titular church, Sts. Cosmas and Damian. President Emeritus Pontifical Council for the Pastoral Care of Migrants and Itinerant People.

Cheong-Jin-Suk, Nicolas: b. Dec. 7, 1931, Supyo Dong, near Seoul, Korea; raised in the faith, he survived the tumult of the Korean War and then entered the Major Seminary of Song Shin; ord. Mar. 18, 1961; after pastoral service, he was sent to Rome for studies in canon law, and earned a doctorate from the Pontifical Urban University; app. bp. of Cheongju, June 25; member of the Executive Committee of the Korean Episcopal Conference, 1975-99; pres. of the Korean Episcopal Conference, 1996-99; app. abp. of Seoul, Apr. 3, 1998 and administrator of the diocese of P'yong-yang; cardinal, Mar. 24, 2006; titular church, Santa Maria Immacolata di Lourdes a Boccea. Abp. of Seoul.

Curial membership: Family, Social Communications (councils).

Cipriani Thorne, Juan Luis: b. Dec. 28, 1943, Lima, Peru; champion basketball player and student in industrial engineering, he joined Opus Dei in 1962; ord. for the prelature, Aug. 21, 1977; after a doctorate in theology at the University of Navarre and pastoral work in Lima, he taught moral theology at the Pontifical Faculty of Theology, Lima, and was regional vicar for Peru and vice-chancellor of the University of Piura; app. titular bp. of Turuzi and aux. bp. of Ayacucho, May 23, 1988; cons. July 3, 1988; app. abp. of Ayacucho, May 13, 1995; tried to negotiate a peaceful reso-

lution to the siege of the Japanese ambassador's residence in Lima, Dec. 1996-Apr. 1997 and ministered to Japanese and Peruvian hostages; app. abp. of Lima, Jan. 9, 1999; cardinal, Feb. 21, 2001; titular church St. Camillus de Lellis. Abp. of Lima.

Curial membership: Causes of Saints, Sacraments (congregation); Latin America (commission); Economic Affairs (office).

Clancy,* Edward Bede: b. Dec. 13, 1923, Lithgow, New South Wales, Australia; ord., July 23, 1949; ord. titular bp. of Ard Carna and aux. of Sydney, Jan. 19, 1974; abp. of Canberra, 1978-83; abp. of Sydney, Feb. 12, 1983; res., Mar. 26, 2001; cardinal, June 28, 1988; titular church, Holy Mary of Vallicella. Abp. emeritus of Sydney.

Comastri, Angelo: b. Sept. 17, 1943, Sorano, diocese of Sovana-Pitigliano (now Pitigliano-Sovana-Orbetello), Italy; ord. Mar. 11, 1967; after many years of pastoral work, served as bp. of Massa Marittima-Piombo, 1990-1994; pres. of the National Italian Committee for the Jubilee of the year 2000; app. prelate of Loreto and pontifical delegate for the Lauretano shrine, and promoted to the rank of archbishop, Nov. 9, 1996; app. coadj. of the archpriest of the papal basilica of St. Peter in the Vatican, vicar general of His Holiness for the State of Vatican City, and pres. of the Fabric of St. Peter's, Feb. 5, 2005; succeeded to the post of archpriest of the papal Vatican basilica, Oct. 31, 2006; cardinal, Nov. 24, 2007, deaconry, San Salvatore in Lauro.

Curial membership: Saints (congregation).

Connell,* Desmond: b. Mar. 24, 1926, Phibsboro, Ireland; ord., May 19, 1951; taught at University College Dublin, 1953-72; dean of the faculty of Philosophy and Sociology, 1983; awarded degree of D.Litt. by National University of Dublin, 1981; chaplain to the Poor Clares in Donnybrook and Carmelites in Drumcondra and Blackrock; app. abp. of Dublin, Jan. 21, 1988; cons., Mar. 6, 1988; ret. Apr. 26, 2004; cardinal, Feb. 21. 2001; titular church, St. Sylvester in Capite. Abp. emeritus of Dublin.

Coppa,* Giovanni: b. Nov. 9, 1925, Alba, Italy; ord. Jan. 2, 1949; earned a doctorate in modern letters from the Catholic University of the Sacred Heart, Milan; entered the Roman Curia in 1952 and held various posts, during the Second Vatican Council, he was an expert for the Latin language; app. titular abp. of Serta and delegate for the pontifical representations in the Secretariat of State, Dec. 1, 1979; cons. Jan. 6, 1980; nuncio to the Czech Republic and Slovakia, Jan. 1, 1993; ceased in his functions of nuncio in Slovakia, Mar. 2, 1994; resigned as nuncio the Czech Republic, May 19, 2001; cardinal, Nov. 24, 2007; deaconry, St. Linus.

Cordero Lanza di Montezemolo,* Andrea: b. Aug. 27, 1925, Turin, Italy; ord. Mar. 13, 1954; entered diplomatic service after studies at the Pontifical Ecclesiastical Academy in 1959; served for 42 years in various diplomatic posts; app. undersecretary and secretary of the Pont. Comm. Justice and Peace; app. nuncio and titular abp. of Anglona, Apr. 5, 1977; nuncio to Papau New Guinea and apostolic delegate to Solomon Islands, 1977; app. apostolic delegate in Jerusalem, Palestine, and Jordan, Apr. 28, 1990; transf. to see of Tuscania, Apr. 13, 1991, and first nuncio to Israel, 1994-98; nuncio to Italy and San Marino, 1998-2001; app. archpriest of the basilica of St. Paul Outside-the-Walls, June 1, 2005; an expert ecclesiastical herald, he assisted the design of the papal coat-of-arms for Pope Benedict XVI in 2005; cardinal, Mar. 24, 2006; titular church, Diaconia di Santa Maria in Portico.

Cordes, Paul-Josef: b. Sept. 5, 1934, Kirchhundem,

Paderborn, Germany; ord. Dec. 21, 1961; served in the seminary for the dioceses of Paderborn and Münster, 1962-1969, and after doctoral studies was in the secretariat of the Episcopal Conference of Germany; titular bp of Naisso and aux. bp. of Paderborn, Oct. 27, 1975; cons., Feb. 1, 1976, vice-president of the Pontifical Council for the Laity, 1980-1995; promoted to abp. and app. pres. of Pontifical Council *Cor Unum*, Dec. 2, 1995; cardinal, Nov. 24, 2007, deaconry, San Lorenzo in Piscibus.

Curial membership: Clergy, Evangelization, Saints (congregations); Justice and Peace (council).

Cottier,* O.P., Georges: b. Apr. 25, 1922; ord. July 2, 1951; theologian of the Papal Household theologian, 1989; secretary general of the International Theological Commission, 1989-2004; cons. Titular abp. of Tullia, Oct. 20, 2003; cardinal, Oct. 21, 2003; titular church, Sts. Dominic and Sixtus.

Daly,* Cahal Brendan: b. Oct. 1, 1917, Loughguile, Northern Ireland; ord., June 22, 1941; earned advanced degrees in philosophy and theology; 30 years of priestly life dedicated to teaching; attended Second Vatican Council as a theological adviser to members of Irish hierarchy; outspoken critic of violence in Northern Ireland; ord. bp. of Ardagh, July 16, 1967; bp. of Down and Connor, 1982-90; abp. of Armagh and primate of All Ireland, 1990-96; cardinal, June 28, 1991; titular church, St. Patrick. Abp. emeritus of Armagh.

Danneels, Godfried: b. June 4, 1933, Kanegem, Belgium; ord., Aug. 17, 1957; professor of liturgy and sacramental theology at Catholic University of Louvain, 1969-77; ord. bp. of Antwerp, Dec. 18, 1977; app. abp. of Mechelen-Brussel, Dec. 19, 1979; installed, Jan. 4, 1980; cardinal, Feb. 2, 1983; titular church, St. Anastasia. Abp. of Mechelen-Brussel, military ordinary of Belgium.

Curial membership: Secretariat of State (second section); Divine Worship and Sacraments, Education, Evangelization of Peoples, Oriental Churches (congregations).

Darmaatmadja, S.J., Julius Riyadi: b. Dec. 20, 1934, Muntilan, Mageland, Central Java, Indonesia; entered Society of Jesus in 1957; ord., Dec. 18, 1969; ord. abp. of Semarang, June 29, 1983 (transferred to Jakarta, Jan. 11, 1996); cardinal, Nov. 26, 1994; titular church, Sacred Heart of Mary. Abp. of Jakarta, military ordinary of Indonesia.

Curial membership: Evangelization of Peoples (congregation); Interreligious Dialogue, Culture (councils).

de Giorgi, Salvatore: b. Sep. 6, 1930 Vernole, Italy; ord., June 28, 1953; diocesan chaplain to the Teachers' Movement of Catholic Action; dir. Diocesan Pastoral Office; app. titular bp. of Tulana and aux. bp. of Oria, Nov. 21, 1973; bp. of Oria, Mar. 17, 1978; abp. of Foggia, Apr. 4, 1981; abp. of Taranto, Oct. 10, 1987 (resigned, 1990); general president of Catholic Action, 1990-96; abp. of Palermo, 1996-2006; president of the Sicilian Episcopal Conference; cardinal, Feb. 21, 1998; titular church, St. Mary in Ara Caeli. Abp. emeritus of Palermo.

Curial membership: Bishops, Clergy, Divine Worship and Sacraments (congregations); Laity, Family (councils).

Delly,* Emmanuel III : b. Oct. 6, 1927, Telkaif, Iraq; ord. Dec. 21, 1952; earned a doctorate in theology from the Pontifical Urbanian University in Rome and a doctorate in canon law form the Pontifical Lateran University; elected titular bp. of Palempoli di Asia and aux. of Babylon of the Chaldeans, Dec. 7, 1962 (confirmed by the pope, Dec. 26, 1962 and cons., Apr. 19, 1963); aux. emeritus of Babylon of the Chaldeans, Oct. 24, 2002; elected patriarch of Babylon of the Chaldeans, Dec. 3, 2003, by the Synod of Bishops of the Chaldean Church, and took the name Emmanuel III; granted

ecclesiastica communio by Pope John Paul II, Dec. 3, 2003; cardinal, Nov. 24, 2007; as a patriarch, he did not receive a titular church.

Curial membership: Eastern Churches.

Deskur,* Andrzej Maria: b. Feb. 29, 1924, Sancygniow, Poland; ord., Aug. 20, 1950, in France; assigned to Vatican secretariat of state, 1952; undersecretary and later secretary of Pontifical Commission for Film, Radio and TV (Social Communications), 1954-73; ord. titular bp. of Tene, June 30, 1974; abp., 1980; president of Pontifical Commission for Social Communications, 1974-84; cardinal deacon, May 25, 1985; deaconry, St. Cesario (in Palatio); transferred to order of cardinal priests, Jan. 29, 1996. President emeritus of Council for Social Communications.

Dias, Ivan: b. Apr. 14, 1936, Bandra, India; ord., Dec. 8, 1958; entered the Holy See diplomatic service and was posted to Indonesia, Madagascar, Reunion, the Comorros, Mauritius, and Secretariat of State; app. titular abp. of Rusubisir and pro-nuncio in Ghana, Togo and Benin, May 8, 1982; cons., June 19, 1982; nuncio in Korea, 1987-91; nuncio in Albania, 1991-97; abp. of Bombay, Jan. 22, 1997-May 22, 2006; cons., Mar. 13, 1997; cardinal, Feb. 21, 2001; titular church, Holy Spirit in Ferratella; app. Prefect of the Cong. for the Evang. of Peoples, May 20, 2006. Prefect of the Cong. for the Evangelization of Peoples.

Curial membership: Doctrine of the Faith, Eastern Churches, Education, Sacraments, (congregations); Culture, Interreligious Dialogue, Laity (councils); Economic Affairs (office); Cultural Heritage of the Church, Latin America (commission); Synod of Bishops.

DiNardo, Daniel N.: b. May 23, 1949, Steubenville, Ohio; ord. July 16, 1977; studied at the Catholic Univ. of America, in Washington, DC, the North American College, Pontifical Gregorian Univ., and the Augustinianum in Rome; served at the Congregation for Bishops in the Roman Curia, 1984 to 1991 and also as director of Villa Stritch and adjunct professor at the Pontifical North American College; app. coadjutor Bp. of Sioux City, Aug. 19, 1997, cons., Oct. 7, 1997; acceded as bp. of Sioux City, Nov. 28, 1998; app. coadjutor bp. of Galveston-Houston, Jan. 16, 2004; inst. Mar. 26, 2004; app. coadjutor abp. of Galveston-Houston, Dec. 29, 2004; abp. of Galveston-Houston, Feb. 28, 2006; cardinal, Nov. 24, 2007; titular church, St. Eusebius.

Curial membership: Migrants (council).

do Nascimento,* Alexandre: b. Mar. 1, 1925, Malanje, Angola; ord., Dec. 20, 1952, in Rome; professor of dogmatic theology in major seminary of Luanda, Angola; editor of *O Apostolada*, Catholic newspaper; forced into exile in Lisbon, Portugal, 1961-71; returned to Angola, 1971; active with student and refugee groups; professor at Pius XII Institute of Social Sciences; ord. bp. of Malanje, Aug. 31, 1975; abp. of Lubango and apostolic administrator of Onjiva, 1977-86; held hostage by Angolan guerrillas, Oct. 15 to Nov. 16, 1982; cardinal, Feb. 2, 1983; titular church, St. Mark in Agro Laurentino. Abp. of Luanda, 1986.

Dulles,* S.J., Avery: b. Aug. 24, 1918, Auburn, NY; the son of U.S. Secretary of State John Foster Dulles; raised a Protestant, he converted to the Catholic faith while a student at Harvard; served in U.S. Navy and then entered the Jesuits; ord. priest for the Jesuits, June 16, 1956; earned a doctorate in theology at the Gregorian University, Rome; taught theology at Woodstock College, 1960-74, and Catholic University of America, 1974-88; visiting professor at numerous other institutions; author of 21 books and over 650 articles; pres. of the Catholic Theological Society of America; member of the International Theological Commission and the U.S.

Lutheran/Roman Catholic Dialogue; consultor to the U.S. Bishops' Committee on Doctrine; currently the Laurence J. McGinley Professor of Religion and Society at Fordham University; cardinal deacon, Feb. 21, 2001; deaconry, Most Holy Names of Jesus and Mary in Via Lata.

Dziwisz, Stanislaw: b. Apr. 27, 1939, in Raba Wyzna, Poland; ord. June 23, 1963; secretary to Cardinal Karol Wojtyla, 1966-78; with election of Wojtyla as Pope John Paul II in 1978, he became papal secretary, a post he held until John Paul II's passing in 2005; named a prelate of his holiness in 1985, titular bishop of San Leone e Prefetto and adjunct prefect of the Papal Household on Feb. 7, 1998, and named titular archbishop on Sept. 29, 2003; app. abp. of Cracow, June 3, 2005; cardinal Mar. 24, 2006; titular church, Titolo di Santa Maria del Popolo. Abp. of Cracow.

Curial membership: Education (Congregation); Laity (Council), Social Communications (Council).

Egan, Edward Michael: b. Apr. 2, 1932, Oak Park, IL; ord., Dec. 15, 1957, in Rome; sec. to Cardinal Albert Meyer, 1958-60; assistant vice-rector of the North American College, 1960-64; vice-chancellor of the archdiocese of Chicago, 1964-68; co-chancellor for human relations and ecumenism, 1968-72; judge of Roman Rota, 1972-85; ord. titular bp. of Allegheny and aux. bp. of New York, May 22, 1985; app. bp. of Bridgeport, Nov. 5, 1988; abp. of New York, May 11, 2000, inst., June 19, 2000; cardinal, Feb. 21, 2001; titular church, St. John and Paul. Abp. of New York.

Curial membership: Family (council); Signatura (tribunal); Economic Affairs (office); Cultural Heritage (commission).

Erdö, Peter: b. June 25, 1952, Budapest, Hungary; ord. June 18, 1975 and earned doctorates in Theology and Canon Law from the Lateran University, Rome; professor of Theology and Canon Law, at the seminary of Esztergom, 1980-1988; guest professor, in Canon Law, Pontifical Gregorian University, 1986; rector of the Catholic University Péter Pázmány, 1998; ord. Jan. 6, 2000 titular bp. of Puppi and aux. bp. of Szikesfehirvar; abp. of Esztergom-Budapest, Dec. 7, 2002; cardinal, Oct. 21, 2003; titular church, St. Balbina. Abp. of Esztergom-Budapest.

Curial membership: Education (congregation); Legislative Texts (council); Supreme Tribunal of the Apostolic Signatura (tribunal).

Errázuriz Ossa, Francisco Javier: b. Sept. 5, 1933, Santiago, Chile; ord. for the Schönstatt Fathers, July 16, 1961; chaplain to students and professionals of the Schönstatt Movement and regional superior; elected superior general of the Schönstatt Fathers, 1974; app. titular abp. of Hólar and sec. of the Cong. For Institutes of Consecrated Life and Societies of Apostolic Life, Dec. 22, 1990; app. abp. of Valparaiso, Sept. 24, 1996; transferred to archdiocese of Santiago, Apr. 24, 1998; pres. of the Episcopal Conference of Chile and first vice-pres. of CELAM; cardinal, Feb. 21, 2001; titular church, St. Mary of Peace. Abp. of Santiago.

Curial membership: Consecrated Life and Societies of Apostolic Life (congregation); Culture, Family (council); Latin America (commission).

Etchegaray,* Roger: b. Sept. 25, 1922, Espelette, France; ord., July 13, 1947; deputy director, 1961-66, and secretary general, 1966-70, of French Episcopal Conference; ord. titular bp. of Gemelle di Numidia and aux. of Paris, May 27, 1969; abp. of Marseilles, 1970-84; prelate of Mission de France, 1975-82; president of French Episcopal Conference, 1979-81; cardinal, June 30, 1979; titular church, St. Leo I. President of Council Cor Unum, 1984-95; president of Council for Justice and Peace (1984-98) and President of Central Committee for the Jubilee of the Holy Year 2000

(1994-98); transferred to order of cardinal bishops, June 24, 1998 (suburbicarian see of Porto-Santa Rufina); Vice-dean of the Sacred College of Cardinals (Apr. 30, 2005).

Falcão,* José Freire: b. Oct. 23, 1925, Erere, Brazil; ord., June 19, 1949; ord. titular bp. of Vardimissa and coadj. of Limoeiro do Norte, June 17, 1967; bp. of Limoeiro do Norte, Aug. 19, 1967; abp. of Teresina, Nov. 25, 1971; abp. of Brasilia, 1984-2004; res. Jan. 28, 2004; cardinal, June 28, 1988; titular church, St. Luke (Via Prenestina). Abp. emeritus of Brasilia.

Farina, S.D.B., Raffaele: b. Sept. 24, 1933, Buonalbergo, Italy; ord. July 1, 1958; entered the Salesians in 1949 and took his final vows in 1954; earned a doctorate in Ecclesiastical History from the Pontifical Gregorian University in Rome and served as a prof. of Church History and also rector at the Theological Faculty of the Pontifical Salesian University; sec. of the Pontifical Committee of Historical Science and under-sec. of the Pontifical Council for Culture; app. prefect of the Apostolic Vatican Library, May 25, 1997; cons. titular bp. of Oderzo, Dec. 16, 2006; app. archivist and librarian of the Holy Roman Church, June 25, 2007; cardinal, Nov. 24, 2007; deaconry, San Giovanni della Pigna.

Curial membership: Education, Saints (congregation); Culture (commission).

Fernandes de Araújo,* Serafim: b. Aug. 13, 1924, Minas Novas, Brazil; ord., Mar. 12, 1949; taught canon law at provincial seminary of Diamantina; titular bp. of Verinopolis and aux. bp. of Belo Horizonte, Jan. 19, 1959; co-adjutor abp. of Belo Horizonte, 1982; abp. Belo Horizonte, 1986-2004; res. Jan. 28, 2004; co-president of the Fourth General Conference of the Latin American Episcopate, 1992; cardinal, Feb. 21, 1998; titular church, St. Louis Marie Grignion de Montfort. Abp. emeritus of Belo Horizonte.

Foley, John P.: b. Nov. 11, 1935, Sharon Hill, Pennsylvania; ord.. May 19, 1962; studied at St. Joseph's Preparatory School, St. Joseph's College (now University), St. Charles Borromeo Seminary, the Univ. of St. Thomas Aquinas in Rome, and the Columbia School of Journalism in New York; served as assistant editor (1967-70) and editor (1970-84) of *The Catholic Standard and Times*, the Philadelphia archdiocesan paper; ord. titular abp. of Neapolis in Proconsulari, 1984 in Philadelphia; pres. of the Pontifical Council for Social Communications, 1984-2007; Pro-Grand Master of the Equestrian Order of the Holy Sepulchre, June 27, 2007; cardinal, Nov. 24, 2007; deaconry, St. Sebastian on the Palatine. Grand Master of the Equestrian Order of the Holy Sepulchre.

Curial membership: Evangelization, Sacraments (congregation).

Furno,* Carlo: b. Dec. 2, 1921, Bairo Canavese, Italy; ord., June 25, 1944; entered diplomatic service of the Holy See in the 1950s; served in Colombia, Ecuador and Jerusalem; worked in Secretariat of State for 11 years and taught at Pontifical Ecclesiastical Academy, 1966-73; ord. titular bp. of Abari with personal title of abp., Sept. 16, 1973; nuncio in Peru, 1973-78; Lebanon, 1978-82; Brazil, 1982-92; Italy, 1992-94; cardinal deacon, Nov. 26, 1994; deaconry, Sacred Heart of Christ the King. Grand Master of the Equestrian Order of the Holy Sepulchre, 1995-2007; pontifical delegate for Patriarchal Basilica of St. Francis in Assisi, 1996; archpriest emeritus of the patriarchal basilica of Santa Maria Maggiore, Rome, 1998-2004.

Garcia-Gasco y Vicente, Agustin: b. Feb. 12, 1931, Corral de Almaguer, Spain; ord. May 26, 1956; after long pastoral service, he was cons. aux. bp. of Madrid-Alcalá, May 11,

1985, sec. gen. of the Spanish Episcopal Conference, 1988-2003; app. abp. of Valencia, July 24, 1992; hosted the Fifth World Day of the Youth in Valencia in 2006; cardinal, Nov. 24, 2007; titular church, St. Marcellus.
Curial membership: Sacraments (congregation); Family (council).

George, O.M.I., Francis E.: b. Jan. 16, 1937, Chicago, IL; ord., Dec. 21, 1963; provincial of central region of Oblates of Mary Immaculate, 1973-74, vicar general, 1974-86; ord. bp. of Yakima, Sept. 21, 1990; abp. of Portland, OR, Apr. 30, 1996, installed, May 27, 1996; abp. of Chicago, Apr. 8, 1997, installed, May 7, 1997; cardinal, Feb. 21, 1998; titular church, St. Bartholomew on Tiber Island. Abp. of Chicago.
Curial membership: Divine Worship and the Discipline of the Sacraments, Institutes of Consecrated Life and Societies of Apostolic Life, Oriental Churches, Evangelization (congregations); Cor Unum, Culture (council); Cultural Heritage of the Church (commission).

Giordano, Michele: b. Sept. 26, 1930, S. Arcangelo, Italy; ord., July 5, 1953; ord. titular bp. of Lari Castello and aux. of Matera, Feb. 5, 1972; abp. of Matera and Irsina, 1974-87; abp. of Naples, May 9, 1987-May 20, 2006; cardinal, June 28, 1988; titular church, St. Joachim. Abp. emeritus of Naples.
Curial membership: Clergy (congregation); Health Care Workers (council).

Glemp, Józef: b. Dec. 18, 1929, Inowroclaw, Poland; assigned to forced labor on German farm in Rycerzow during Nazi occupation; ord., May 25, 1956; studied in Rome, 1958-64; received degree in Roman and canon law from Pontifical Lateran University; secretary of primatial major seminary at Gniezno on his return to Poland, 1964; spokesman for secretariat of primate of Poland and chaplain of primate for archdiocese of Gniezno, 1967; ord. bp. of Warmia, Apr. 21, 1979; abp. of Gniezno, 1981-92, with title of abp. of Warsaw and primate of Poland; cardinal, Feb. 2, 1983; titular church, St. Mary in Trastevere. Abp. of Warsaw, primate of Poland, and ordinary for Eastern-rite faithful in Poland who do not have ordinaries of their own rites 1992-2006. Abp. emeritus of Warsaw.
Curial membership: Oriental Churches (congregation); Signatura (tribunal); Culture (council).

González Zumárraga,* Antonio José: b. Mar. 18, 1925, Pujili (Cotopaxi), Ecuador; ord., June 29, 1951; taught at the Pontifical Catholic University of Ecuador; chancellor of the Curia, 1964; rector of Our Mother of Mercy College; app. titular bp. of Tagarata and aux. bp. of Quito; apostolic admin. of Machala, Mar. 1976; bp. of Machata, Jan. 30, 1978; coadj. abp. of Quito, June 28, 1980; abp. of Quito, June 1, 1985; served two terms as pres. of the Ecuadorean Episcopal Conference; cardinal, Feb. 21, 2001; titular church, St. Mary in Via. Abp. of Quito.

Gracias, Oswald: b. Dec. 24, 1944, Bombay (now Mumbai), India; ord. Dec. 20, 1970; earned a doctorate in canon law and a diploma in jurisprudence from the Pontifical Urbanian University in Rome, 1982; served as chancellor and secretary to the bishop of Jamshedpur, 1971- 1976; chancellor, judge of the metropolitan tribunal, and judicial vicar of Bombay from 1982-1997; cons. titular bp. of Bladia and aux. bp. of Bombay, Sept. 16, 1997; abp. of Agra, 2000-2006; app. abp. of Bombay, Oct. 14, 2006; cardinal, Nov. 24, 2007; titular church, St. Paul of the Cross at Corviale.

Grocholewski, Zenon: b. Oct. 11, 1939, Bródki, Poland; ord., May 26, 1963; earned a doctorate in canon law; served in the Supreme Tribunal of the Apostolic Signatura, 1972-1999; prefect of the Supreme Tribunal of the Apostolic

Signatura; member of the commission studying the 1983 Code of Canon Law; titular bp. of Agropoli, Dec. 21, 1982; titular abp., Dec. 16, 1991; prefect of the Cong. for Catholic Education, Nov. 15, 1999; cardinal deacon, Feb. 21, 2001; titular church, deaconry, St. Nicholas in Carcere. Prefect of the Congregation for Catholic Education.
Curial membership: Bishops, Doctrine of the Faith, Evangelization (congregations); Texts (council); Apostolic Signatura (tribunal).

Gulbinowicz,* Henryk Roman: b. Oct. 17, 1923, Szukiszki, Poland; ord., June 18, 1950; ord. titular bp. of Acci and apostolic administrator of Polish territory in Lithuanian archdiocese of Vilnius (Vilna), Feb. 8, 1970; abp. of Wroclaw, Poland, 1976-2004; cardinal, May 25, 1985; titular church, Immaculate Conception of Mary (a Grottarosa). Abp. of Wroclaw. Abp. emeritus of Wroclaw.

Herranz Casado, Julián: b. Mar. 31, 1930, Baena, Spain; joined the personal prelature of Opus Dei and ord. Aug. 7, 1955; earned doctorates in canon law and medicine; Sec. of the Pontifical Commission for the Interpretation of the Code of Canon Law (later Pontifical Council for the Interpretation of the Legislative Texts), 1984; ord. titular bp. of Vertara, Jan. 6, 1991; pres. of the Pontifical Council for the Interpretation of the Legislative Texts, 1994-2007; president of the Disciplinary Commission of the Roman Curia, Dec. 3, 1999; cardinal deacon, Oct. 21, 2003; titular church, St. Eugene. Pres. emeritus of the Pontifical Council for the Interpretation of Legislative Texts.
Curial membership: Bishops, Causes of Saints, Doctrine of the Faith, Evangelization of Peoples (congregations); Apostolic Signatura (Tribunal); Laity (Council); Ecclesia Dei (commission).

Honoré,* Jean: b. Aug. 13, 1920; ord., June 29, 1943; authored doctoral dissertation under the direction of Jean Daniélou at the Institute Catholique, Paris; taught at St. Vincent's College in Rennes and in Saint-Malo; worked for six years at the National Religious Education Centre (CNEC); rector of the Catholic University of Angers; app. bp. of Evreux, Oct. 24, 1972; cons., Dec. 17, 1972; app. abp. of Tours, Aug. 13, 1981; participated in the preparation of the Catechism, following the 1985 Synod of Bishops; res. as abp. of Tours, July 22, 1997; cardinal, Feb. 21, 2001; titular church, St. Mary of Health in Primavalle. Abp. emeritus of Tours.

Hummes, O.F.M., Cláudio: b. Aug. 8, 1934, Montenegro, Brazil; ord., priest for the Franciscans, Aug. 3, 1958; specialist in ecumenism; taught philosophy at the Franciscan seminary in Garibaldi, at the major seminary of Viamão and the Pontifical Catholic University of Porto Alegre; adviser for ecumenical affairs to the National Bishops' Conference of Brazil; Provincial of Rio Grande do Sul, 1972-75; pres. of the Union of Latin American Conferences of Franciscans; app. coadj. bp. of Santo André, Mar. 22, 1975; cons., May 25, 1975; succeeded to see, Dec. 29, 1975; app. abp. of Fortaleza, July 21, 1996; Abp. of São Paulo, 1998-2006; cardinal, Feb. 21, 2001; titular church, St. Anthony of Padua in Via Merulana; prefect of the Cong. for Clergy, Oct. 31, 2006. Prefect for the Congregation for Clergy.
Curial membership: Bishops, Doctrine of the Faith, Education, Sacraments (congregation); Cor Unum, Culture, Family, Interreligious Dialogue, Laity (councils); Latin America (commission).

Husar, M.S.U., Lubomyr: b. Feb. 26, 1933, Lviv, Ukraine; family fled to Austria because of the war and then to the U.S.; ord. for the eparchy of Stamford for Ukrainians, U.S., Mar. 30, 1958; entered the Studite Monks after completing a doc-

torate in theology in Rome; superior of the Studion in
Grottaferrata, Italy; ord. bp. Apr. 2, 1977; app. archimandrite
of Studite Monks residing outside Ukraine; organized a new
Studite monastery in Ternopil, Ukraine, 1994; elected exarch
of Kyiv-Vyshorod, 1995; app. aux. bp. to major abp. of Lviv,
1996; elected major abp. of Lviv for Ukrainians, Jan. 25,
2001; title changed to major abp. of Kiev and Halych, Aug.
21, 2005; cardinal, Feb. 21, 2001; titular church, Holy
Wisdom in Via Boccea. Major Abp. of Kiev and Halych.
    Curial membership: Oriental Churches (congregation);
Christian Unity, Culture, Texts (councils).
    Innocenti,* Antonio: b. Aug. 23, 1915, Poppi, Italy; ord.,
July 17, 1938; held curial and diplomatic positions; ord. titular bp. of Eclano with personal title of abp., Feb. 18, 1968;
nuncio to Paraguay, 1967-73; secretary of Congregation for
Causes of Saints, 1973-75; secretary of Congregation for
Sacraments and Divine Worship, 1975-80; nuncio to Spain,
1980-85; cardinal deacon, May 25, 1985; transferred to order
of cardinal priests, Jan. 29, 1996; titular church, St. Marie (in
Aquiro); prefect of Congregation for the Clergy, 1986-91;
president of Pontifical Commission for Preservation of
Artistic Patrimony of the Church, 1988-91; president of
Pontifical Commission "Ecclesia Dei," 1991-95.
    Jaworski,* Marian: b. Aug. 21, 1926, Lwów, Poland
(modern Lviv, Ukraine); ord., June 25, 1950; taught at the
Catholic Theological Academy of Warsaw and Pontifical
Theological faculty of Kraków; first rector of the Pontifical
Theological Academy, Kraków, 1981-87; app. titular bp. of
Lambaesis and apostolic admin. of Lubaczów, May 21, 1984;
cons., June 23, 1984; app. abp. of Lviv for Latins, Jan. 16,
1991; pres. of the Ukrainian Episcopal Conference, 1992;
cardinal (in pectore), Feb. 21, 1998; titular church, St. Sixtus.
Abp. of Lviv for Latins.
    Curial membership: Clergy (congregation); Family (coun-
cil).
    Karlic,* Estanislao Esteban: b. Feb. 7, 1926; Oliva,
Argentina; ord. Dec. 8, 1954; completed studies in Rome and
served as a professor in the Major Seminary of Córdoba;
cons. titular bp. of Castro, Aug. 15, 1977; promoted to coadjutor abp. and apostolic administrator of Paraná, Jan. 19,
1983; acceded to the see of Paraná, Apr. 1, 1986; pres. of the
Episcopal Conference of Argentina, 1996-1999 and 1999-
2002; ret., Apr. 29, 2003; cardinal, Nov. 24, 2007; titular
church, Santa Maria Addolorata on Piazza Buenos Aires.
    Kasper, Walter: b. Mar. 5, 1933, Heidenheim/Brenz,
Germany; ord., Apr. 6, 1957; taught theology and was later
dean of the theological faculty in Münster and Tübingen; app.
bp. of Rottenburg-Stuttgart, Apr. 17, 1989, cons., June 17,
1989; co-chair of the International Commission for
Lutheran/Catholic Dialogue, 1994; sec. of the Pontifical
Council for Promoting Christian Unity, June 1, 1999; pres.
Pontifical Council for Promoting Christian Unity, 2001; car-
dinal deacon, Feb. 21, 2001; deaconry, All Saints in Via
Appia Nuova. President of the Pontifical Council for
Promoting Christian Unity.
    Curial membership: Doctrine of the Faith, Oriental
Churches (congregations); Interreligious Dialogue (council);
Apostolic Signatura (tribunal); Culture, Legislative Texts
(council).
    Keeler, William Henry: b. Mar. 4, 1931, San Antonio, TX;
ord., (Harrisburg diocese) July 17, 1955; secretary to Bp.
Leech at Vatican II, named peritus by Pope John XXIII; ord.
titular bp. of Ulcinium and aux. bp. of Harrisburg, Sept. 21,
1979; bp. of Harrisburg, 1983-1989, abp. of Baltimore, 1989-
2007; cardinal, Nov. 26, 1994; titular church, St. Mary of the
Angels. Abp. emeritus of Baltimore.

    Curial membership: Oriental Churches (congregation);
Christian Unity (council).
    Kim Sou-hwan,* Stephen: b. May 8, 1922, Tae Gu,
Korea; ord., Sept. 15, 1951; ord. bp. of Masan, May 31, 1966;
abp. of Seoul, Apr. 9, 1968 (resigned May 29, 1998); cardinal, Apr. 28, 1969; titular church, St. Felix of Cantalice
(Centocelle). Abp. emeritus of Seoul, apostolic administrator
emeritus of Pyeong Yang.
    Kitbunchu, Michael Michai: b. Jan. 25, 1929, Samphran,
Thailand; ord., Dec. 20, 1959, in Rome; rector of metropolitan seminary in Bangkok, 1965-72; ord. abp. of Bangkok,
June 3, 1973; cardinal, Feb. 2, 1983, the first from Thailand;
titular church, St. Laurence in Panisperna. Abp. of Bangkok.
    Curial membership: Evangelization of Peoples (congrega-
tion).
    Korec,* S.J., Ján Chryzostom: b. Jan. 22, 1924, Bosany,
Slovakia; entered Society of Jesus in 1939; ord., Oct. 1, 1950;
ord. bp. secretly, Aug. 24, 1951; sentenced to 12 years in
prison in 1960 for helping seminarians with their study and
ordaining priests; paroled in 1968; appointed bp. of Nitra,
Feb. 6, 1990; ret. June 9, 2005; cardinal, June 28, 1991; titular church, Sts. Fabian and Venantius (a Villa Forelli). Bp.
emeritus of Nitra.
    Laghi,* Pio: b. May 21, 1922, Castiglione, Italy; ord., Apr.
20, 1946; entered diplomatic service of the Holy See in 1952;
served in Nicaragua, the U.S. (as secretary of the apostolic
delegation, 1954-61) and India; recalled to Rome and served
on Council for Public Affairs of the Church; ord. titular abp.
of Mauriana, June 22, 1969; apostolic delegate to Jerusalem
and Palestine, 1969-74; nuncio to Argentina, 1974-80; apostolic delegate, 1980-84, and first pro-nuncio, 1984-90 to the
U.S.; pro-prefect of Congregation for Catholic Education,
1990-91; cardinal deacon, June 28, 1991; deaconry, St. Mary
Auxiliatrix (in Via Tuscolana). Prefect of Congregation for
Catholic Education, 1991-99. Grand chancellor of Pontifical
Gregorian University. Patron of Sovereign Military Order of
Malta, 1993. Protodeacon, 1999-2002.
    Lajolo, Giovanni: b. Jan. 3, 1935, Novara, Italy; ord., Apr.
29, 1960; studied at the Pontifical Gregorian University in
Rome, earned a doctorate in canon law from the University
of Munich, and studied at the Pontifical Ecclesiastical
Academy; entered the service of the Secretariat of State in
1970 and served in the nunciature of Germany and then in the
Secretariat of State; named titular abp. of Cesariana and sec.
of the Administration of the Patrimony of the Apostolic See,
Oct. 3, 1988; cons. Jan. 6, 1989; nuncio in Germany from
1995-2003; sec. of the secretariat of State for the Relations
with the States, 2003-2006; pres. of the Pontifical
Commission for the State of Vatican City and president of the
Governatorato, June 22, 2006; cardinal, Nov. 24, 2007; deaconry, Santa Maria Liberatrice on Monte Testaccio.
    Curial membership: Bishops (congregation); Culture
(council), APSA (office).
    Law, Bernard F.: b. Nov. 4, 1931, Torreon, Mexico, the
son of U.S. Air Force colonel; ord., (Jackson diocese) May
21, 1961; editor of Natchez-Jackson, MS, diocesan paper,
1963-68; director of NCCB Committee on Ecumenical and
Interreligious Affairs, 1968-71; ord. bp. of Springfield-Cape
Girardeau, MO, Dec. 5, 1973; abp. of Boston, Jan. 11, 1984;
cardinal, May 25, 1985; titular church, St. Susanna; res.,
Dec.13, 2002; archpriest of the patriarchal basilica of Santa
Maria Maggiore, Rome, May 27, 2004, Abp. emeritus of
Boston.
    Curial membership: Bishops, Clergy, Consecrated Life and
Societies of Apostolic Life, Divine Worship and Sacraments,
Education, Evangelization of Peoples, Oriental Churches;

(congregations); Family (council).

Lehmann, Karl: b. May 16, 1936, Sigmaringen, Germany; ord., Oct. 10, 1963; earned doctorates in theology and philosophy; assistant to Fr. Karl Rahner at University of Münster; taught dogmatic theology at the Johannes Gutenberg University, Mainz; member of the Central Committee of German Catholics and the Jaeger-Stählin Ecumenical Circle; taught at the Albert Ludwig University, Freiburg im Breisgau; member of the International Theological Commission; edited the official publication of the documents of the Joint Synod of the Dioceses in the Federal Republic of Germany, Synod of Würzburg, 1971-75; app. bp. of Mainz, June 21, 1983; cons., Oct. 2, 1983; pres. of the German Bishops' Conference; cardinal, Feb. 21, 2001; titular church, St. Leo I. Bp. of Mainz.

Curial membership: Bishops, Oriental Churches (congregations); Christian Unity (council); APSA (office).

Levada, William J.: b. June 15, 1936, Long Beach, CA; studied at St. John's College, Camarillo, California, and the Gregorian Univ. in Rome; ord., Dec. 20, 1961; ord. titular bp. of Capri and aux. bp. of Los Angeles, May 12, 1983; app. abp. of Portland, OR, July 3, 1986; coadj. abp. of San Francisco, Aug. 17, 1995; abp. of San Francisco, Dec. 27, 1995; ret. and app. Prefect for the Congregation for the Doctrine of the Faith, May 13, 2005; cardinal, Mar. 24, 2006; titular church, Diaconia di Santa Maria in Dominica. Prefect for the Congregation for the Doctrine of the Faith.

Curial Membership: Bishops, Causes of Saints, Eastern Churches, Education, Evangelization (congregations); Christian Unity (council); Synod of Bishop (special council).

López Rodriguez, Nicolás de Jesús: b. Oct. 31, 1936, Barranca, Dominican Republic; ord., Mar. 18, 1961; sent to Rome for advanced studies at the Angelicum and Gregorian Univ.; served in various diocesan offices after returning to his home diocese of La Vega; ord. first bp. of San Francisco de Macoris, Feb. 25, 1978; abp. of Santo Domingo, Nov. 15, 1981; cardinal, June 28, 1991; titular church, St. Pius X (alla Balduina). Abp. of Santo Domingo and Military Ordinary for Dominican Republic.

Curial membership: Clergy, Institutes of Consecrated Life and Societies of Apostolic Life (congregations); Social Communications (council); Latin America (commission).

Lourdusamy,* D. Simon: b. Feb. 5, 1924, Kalleri, India; ord., Dec. 21, 1951; ord. titular bp. of Sozusa and aux. of Bangalore, Aug. 22, 1962; titular abp. of Filippi and coadj. abp. of Bangalore, Nov. 9, 1964; abp. of Bangalore, 1968-71; associate secretary, 1971-73, and secretary, 1973-85, of Congregation for Evangelization of Peoples; cardinal deacon, May 25, 1985; deaconry, St. Mary of Grace; transferred to the order of cardinal priests, Jan. 29, 1996; prefect of Congregation for Oriental Churches, 1985-91.

Lozano Barragán, Javier: b. Jan. 26, 1933, Toluca, Mexico; ord. Oct. 30, 1955; pres. of the Mexican Theological Society and dir. of the Institute of Pastoral Theology of the Episcopal Conference of Latin America (CELAM); ord. titular bishop of Tinisia di Numidia and aux. bp. of Mexico, Aug. 15, 1979; bp. of Zacatecas, 1984-96; pres. of Pontifical Council for Health Care Workers, Oct. 31, 1996; named abp. 1997; cardinal deacon, Oct. 21, 2003, deaconry, St. Michael the Archangel. Pres. of Pontifical Council for Health Care Workers.

Curial membership: Bishops, Causes of Saints, Evangelization (congregations); Eucharistic Congresses, Latin America (commissions).

McCarrick, Theodore E.: b. July 7, 1930, New York, NY; ord., May 31, 1958; dean of students Catholic Univ. of America, 1961-63; pres., Catholic Univ. of Puerto Rico, 1965-69; secretary to Cardinal Cooke, 1970; ord. titular bp. of Rusubisir and aux. bp. of New York, June 29, 1977; app. first bp. of Metuchen, NJ, Nov. 19, 1981, installed, Jan. 31, 1982; app. abp. of Newark, June 3, 1986, installed, July 25, 1986; abp. of Washington, Nov. 21, 2000; ins., Jan. 3, 2001, cardinal priest, Feb. 21, 2001; titular church, Sts. Nereus and Achilleus; ret. May 16, 2006. Abp. emeritus of Washington.

Curial membership: Christian Unity, Justice and Peace, Migrants and Itinerant People (councils); APSA (office), Latin America (commission).

Macharski,* Franciszek: b. May 20, 1927, Kraków, Poland; ord., Apr. 2, 1950; engaged in pastoral work, 1950-56; continued theological studies in Fribourg, Switzerland, 1956-60; taught pastoral theology at the Faculty of Theology in Kraków; app. rector of archdiocesan seminary at Kraków, 1970; abp. of Kraków, 1979-2005; cardinal, June 30, 1979; titular church, St. John at the Latin Gate. Abp. emeritus of Kraków.

Curial membership: Secretariat of State (second section); Bishops, Clergy, Consecrated Life and Societies of Apostolic Life, Education, Evangelization of Peoples (congregations).

Mahony, Roger M.: b. Feb. 27, 1936, Hollywood, CA; ord., (Fresno diocese) May 1, 1962; ord. titular bp. of Tamascani and aux. bp. of Fresno, Mar. 19,1975; bp. of Stockton, Feb. 15, 1980, installed, Apr. 25, 1980; abp. of Los Angeles, July 16, 1985, installed, Sept. 5, 1985; cardinal, June 28, 1991; titular church, Four Crowned Saints. Abp. of Los Angeles.

Curial membership: Social Communications (council); Economic Affairs (office).

Maida, Adam Joseph: b. Mar. 18, 1930, East Vandergrift, PA; ord., (Pittsburgh diocese), May 26, 1956; ord. bp. of Green Bay, Jan. 25, 1984; app. abp. of Detroit, Apr. 28, 1990, installed, June 12, 1990; cardinal, Nov. 26, 1994; titular church, Sts. Vitalis, Valeria, Gervase and Protase. Abp. of Detroit.

Curial membership: Clergy, Education (congregations); Legislative Texts, Migrants and Itinerant Peoples (council); Institute for Works of Religion (commission).

Majella Agnelo, Geraldo: b. Oct. 19, 1933, Juiz de Fora, Brazil; ord. June 29, 1957; taught at the seminary of Aparecida, Immaculate Conception Seminary, and Pius XI Theological Institute; rector of Our Lady of the Assumption Seminary; bp. of Toledo, May 5, 1978; cons., Aug. 6, 1978; app. abp. of Londrina, Oct. 27, 1982; pres. of the Brazilian Bishops' Liturgical Commission; app. sec. of the Cong. for Divine Worship and the Discipline of Sacraments, Sept. 16, 1991; app. abp. of São Salvador da Bahia, Jan. 13, 1999; cardinal, Feb. 21, 2001; titular church, St. Gregory the Great in Magliana Nuova. Abp. of São Salvador da Bahia.

Curial membership: Pastoral Care of Migrants and Itinerant People (council); Cultural Heritage of the Church (commission).

Marchisano, Francesco, b. June 25, 1929, Racconigi, Italy; ord. June 29, 1952; ord. titular bp. of Populonia, Jan. 6, 1989; secr. of the Pontifical Commission for the Preservation of the Artistic and Cultural Patrimony of the Church, 1988-91; pres. of the Pontifical Commission of Sacred Archeology, 1991; pres. of the Pontifical Commission for the Cultural Patrimony of the Church, 1993-2003; named abp., 1994; archpriest of the Patriarchal Vatican Basilica, vicar general for the State of Vatican City, and president of the Fabric of St. Peter, Apr. 24, 2002; pres. of the Permanent Commission for the Care of the Historical and Artistic Monuments of the Holy See, Mar. 8, 2003; cardinal deacon, Oct. 21, 2003; deaconry, St. Lucy of Gonfalone; pres. of the Labor Office of the Apostolic See, Feb. 5, 2005. Archpriest of the Patriarchal Vatican Basilica, vicar general for the State of Vatican City, and pres. of the Labor Office of the Apostolic See; pres. emeritus of the Fabric of St. Peter.

Curial membership: Education (congregation); Culture (council); Cultural Heritage of the Church (commission).

Margéot,* Jean: b. Feb. 3, 1916, Quatre-Bornes, Mauritius; ord., Dec. 17, 1938; ord. bp. of Port Louis, 1969-93; cardinal, June 28, 1988; titular church, St. Gabriel the Archangel all'Acqua Traversa. Bp. emeritus of Port Louis.

Martínez Sistach, Lluís: b. Apr. 29, 1937, Barcelona, Spain; ord. Sept. 17, 1961; earned a doctorate *in utroque iure*, both canon and civil law, from the Pontifical Lateran University, Rome, in 1967 and served as professor of canon law at the Theological Faculty of Catalonia and at the Superior Institute of Religious Sciences of Barcelona, 1975-1987; cons. titular bp. of Aliezira and aux. bp. of Barcelona, Dec. 27, 1987; bp. of Tortosa, 1991-1997; abp. of Tarragona, 1997-2004; app. abp. of Barcelona, June 15, 2004; cardinal, Nov. 24, 2007; titular church, St. Sebastian in the Catacombs.

Martínez Somalo,* Eduardo: b. Mar. 31, 1927, Baños de Rio Tobia, Spain; ord., Mar. 19, 1950; ord. titular bp. of Tagora with personal title of abp., Dec. 13, 1975; in secretariat of state from 1956; substitute (assistant) secretary of state, 1979-88; cardinal deacon, June 28, 1988; deaconry, Most Holy Name of Jesus (raised pro hac vice to presbyteral title); promoted to cardinal priest, Jan. 9, 1999; prefect of Congregation for Divine Worship and Sacraments, 1988-92. Prefect of Congregation for Institutes of Consecrated Life and Societies of Apostolic Life, 1992-2004; Chamberlain (Camerlengo) of the Holy Roman Church, 1993-2007; Protodeacon, 1996-99.

Curial membership: Secretariat of State (second section); Bishops, Causes of Saints, Clergy, Divine Worship and Sacraments, Education, Evangelization of Peoples (congregations); Legislative Texts (council); Latin America, Institute for Works of Religion (commissions).

Martini,* S.J., Carlo Maria: b. Feb. 15, 1927, Turin, Italy; entered Jesuits, Sept. 25, 1944; ord., July 13, 1952; biblical scholar; seminary professor, Chieri, Italy, 1958-61; professor and later rector, 1969-78, of Pontifical Biblical Institute; rector of Pontifical Gregorian University, 1978-79; author of theological, biblical and spiritual works; abp. of Milan, 1980-2002; cardinal, Feb. 2, 1983; titular church, St. Cecilia. Abp. emeritus of Milan.

Curial membership: Consecrated Life and Societies of Apostolic Life, Education Oriental Churches (congregations); Cultural Heritage of the Church (commission).

Martino, Renato, b. Nov. 23, 1932, Salerno, Italy; ord. June 27, 1957; entered the diplomatic service of the Holy See, July 1, 1962; served in various diplomatic postings, 1962-80; ord. titular abp. of Segerme, Dec. 14, 1980; pronuncio in Thailand and apostolic delegate in Laos, Malaysia and Singapore, 1980-86; permanent observer of the Holy See to the U.N., 1986-2002; pres. of the Pontifical Council Justice and Peace, 2002-2006; cardinal deacon, Oct. 21, 2003, titular church, St. Francis of Paola ai Monti; Pres. of the Pontifical for Council for Pastoral Care of Migrants and Itinerants, Mar. 11, 2006. Curial membership: Evangelization of Peoples (congregation); "Cor Unum" (council); Vatican City State (commission); Administration of the Patrimony of the Apostolic See (APSA).\

Mayer,* O.S.B., Paul Augustin: b. May 23, 1911, Altötting, Germany; ord., Aug. 25, 1935; rector of St. Anselm's Univ., Rome, 1949-66; secretary of Congregation for Religious and Secular Institutes, 1972-84; ord. titular bp. of Satriano with personal title of abp., Feb. 13, 1972; pro-prefect of Congregations for Sacraments and Divine Worship, 1984; cardinal deacon, May 25, 1985; deaconry, St. Anselm; transferred to order of cardinal priests, Jan. 29, 1996. Prefect of Congregation for Divine Worship and Sacraments, 1985-88; president of Pontifical Commission "Ecclesia Dei," 1988-91.

Medina Estévez,* Jorge Arturo: b. Dec. 23, 1926, Santiago, Chile; ord., June 12, 1954; ord. abp., Jan. 6, 1985, Santiago, Chile; appointed pro-Prefect, Congregation for Divine Worship and the Discipline of the Sacraments, 1996-98; prefect of the Congregation for Divine Worship and the Discipline of the Sacraments, 1998-2002; cardinal deacon, Feb. 21, 1998; cardinal priest, Mar. 2, 2008; titular church, St. Sabas; Protodeacon, 2005-2007. Prefect emeritus of the Congregation for Divine Worship and the Discipline of the Sacraments.

Curial membership: Bishops, Clergy, Doctrine of the Faith (congregations); Family (council); Latin America, Ecclesia Dei (commission).

Meisner, Joachim: b. Dec. 25, 1933, Breslau, Silesia, Germany (present-day Wroclaw, Poland); ord., Dec. 22, 1962; regional director of Caritas; ord. titular bp. of Vina and aux. of apostolic administration of Erfurt-Meiningen, E. Germany, May 17, 1975; bp. of Berlin, 1980-88; cardinal, Feb. 2, 1983; titular church, St. Prudenziana. Abp. of Cologne, Dec. 20, 1988.

Curial membership: Bishops, Clergy, Divine Worship and Sacraments (congregations); Legislative Texts (council); Economic Affairs of Holy See (office).

Mejía,* Jorge María: b. Jan. 31, 1923, Buenos Aires, Argentina; ord., Sept. 22, 1945; prof. of Old Testament studies at Catholic University of Buenos Aires; peritus at Second Vatican Council; sec. of CELAM's Department of Ecumenism, 1967-77; sec. of Pontifical Commission for Religious Relations with Jews, 1977-86; vice-president of the Pontifical Commission Justice and Peace and titular bp. of Apollonia, Apr. 12, 1986; sec. of the Cong. for Bishops and titular abp., Mar. 1994; Archivist and Librarian of the Holy Roman Church, 1998-2003; cardinal deacon, Feb. 21, 2001; deaconry, St. Jerome della Carità. Archivist and Librarian emeritus of the Holy Roman Church.

Moussa I Daoud, Ignace: b. Sept. 18, 1930, Meskaneh, Syria; ord., Oct. 17, 1954; elected July 2, 1977, bp. of Cairo, Egypt by Syrian Patriarchal Synod; cons., Sept. 18, 1977; member of the commission for the revision of the Eastern Code of Canon Law and chaired the commission that translated the Code of Canons of the Eastern Churches into Arabic; promoted abp. of Homs for Syrians, Syria, July 6, 1994; elected patriarch of Antioch for Syrians, Oct. 13, 1998; app. prefect of the Cong. for the Oriental Churches, 2000-2007; cardinal, Feb. 21, 2001 (as patriarch, he has no titular church). Prefect emeritus of the Congregation for the Oriental Churches.

Curial membership: Doctrine of the Faith, Causes of Saints (congregations), Christian Unity, Legislative Texts (councils).

Murphy-O'Connor, Cormac: b. Aug. 24, 1932, Reading, Great Britain; ord., Oct. 28, 1956; dir. of vocations and secretary to the bp.; rector of the Venerable English College, Rome, 1971-77; app. bp. of Arundel and Brighton, Nov. 17, 1977; cons., Dec. 21, 1977; co-chairman of the Anglican-Roman Catholic International Commission (ARCIC), 1982-2000; chairman of several committees of the Bishop's Conference of England and Wales; app. abp. of Westminster,

Feb. 15, 2000; cardinal, Feb. 21, 2001; titular church, St. Mary sopra Minerva. Abp. of Westminster.

Curial membership: Sacraments (congregation); Christian Unity, Culture, Family (councils); APSA (office); Cultural Heritage (commission).

Nagy,* Stanislas: b. Sep. 30, 1921, Bieruń Stary, Poland; ord. July 8, 1945; Polish priest of the Sacred Heart of Jesus (Dehonians), Poland; taught with the future Pope John Paul II at Lublin University in Poland; served on Intl., Theological Commission; cons. titular abp. of Hólar, Oct. 13, 2003; cardinal deacon, Oct. 21, 2003; titular church, St. Mary of the Stairs.

Napier, O.F.M., Wilfrid Fox: b. Mar. 8, 1941, Swartberg, South Africa; ord., for the Franciscans, July 25, 1970; app. apostolic admin. of Kokstad, 1978; app. bp. of Kokstad, Nov. 29, 1980; cons., Feb. 28, 1981; deeply involved in the mediation and negotiations surrounding the ending of apartheid in South Africa and subsequent South African politics; pres. of the Southern African Catholic Bishops' Conference, 1987-94; app. abp. of Durban, May 29, 1992; apostolic admin. sede vacante et ad nutum Sanctae Sedis of Umzimkulu, 1994; cardinal, Feb. 21, 2001; titular church, St. Francis of Assisi in Acilia.

Curial membership: Evangelization of Peoples, Institutes of Consecrated Life and Societies of Apostolic Life (congregations); Culture (council); Economic Affairs (office).

Navarrete,* Urbano, S.J.: b. May 25, 1920, Camarena de la Sierra, Teruel, Spain; ord. 1952; entered the Society of Jesus on June 20, 1937 and earned a doctorate in canon law and a licentiate in philosophy and theology; served as dean of the Faculty of Canon Law and rector of the Pontifical Gregorian University in Rome until 1980; granted an honorary doctorate by the Pontifical University of Salmanca, Spain, in 1994 and is a world renowned canonist; cardinal, Nov. 24, 2007; deaconry, San Ponziano.

Nicora, Attilio, b. Mar. 16, 1937, Varese, Italy; ord. June 27, 1964; ord. titular bishop of Fornos minore and aux. bp. of Milan, May 28, 1977; bp. of Verona, 1992-2002; pres. of the Administration of the Patrimony of the Apostolic See (APSA) and abp., Sept. 2002; cardinal deacon, Oct. 21, 2003; deaconry, St. Philip Neri in Eurosia. Pres. of the Administration of the Patrimony of the Apostolic See.

Curial membership: Secretariat of State (second section); Bishops, Evangelization of Peoples (congregation); Apostolic Signatura (tribunal).

Njue, John: b. 1944, Embu, Kenya; ord. Jan. 6, 1973; after studies in Rome, he served as a professor of philosophy and rector at the National Seminary of Bungoma, in the diocese of Kakmega, 1975; cons. the first bp. of Embu, Sept. 20, 1986; app. coadj. abp. of Nyeri, Jan. 23, 2002; app. abp. of Nairobi, Oct. 6, 2007; cardinal, Nov. 24, 2007; titular church, Most Precious Blood of Our Lord Jesus Christ.

Curial Membership: Clergy, Evangelization (congregation).

Noè,* Virgilio: b. Mar. 30, 1922, Zelata di Bereguardo, Italy; ord., Oct. 1, 1944; master of pontifical ceremonies and undersecretary of Congregation for Sacraments and Divine Worship, 1970-82; ord. titular bp. of Voncario with personal title of abp., Mar. 6, 1982; coadj. Archpriest of St. Peter's Basilica, 1989-2002; vicar general of Vatican City State, 1991-2002; cardinal deacon, June 28, 1991; deaconry, St. John Bosco (in Via Tuscolana). Archpriest emeritus of St. Peter's Basilica, Vicar General emeritus of Vatican City State and President emeritus of the Fabric of St. Peter, 1991.

Obando Bravo,* S.D.B., Miguel: b. Feb. 2, 1926, La Libertad, Nicaragua; ord., Aug. 10, 1958; ord. titular bp. of Puzia di Bizacena and aux. of Matagalpa, Mar. 31, 1968; abp. emeritus of Managua, 1970-2005; cardinal, May 25, 1985; titular church, St. John the Evangelist (a Spinaceta).

Curial membership: Clergy, Consecrated Life and Societies of Apostolic Life, Divine Worship and Sacraments, (congregations).

O'Brien, Keith Michael Patrick, b. Mar. 17, 1938, Ballycastle, Ireland; ord. Apr. 3, 1965; ord. abp. of St. Andrews and Edinburgh, May 30, 1985; cardinal, Oct. 21, 2003; titular church, Sts. Joachim and Anne at the Tuscolano. Abp. of St. Andrews and Edinburgh.

Curial membership: Migrants and Itinerant People, Social Communications (councils).

Okogie, Anthony Olubunmi, b. June 16, 1935, Lagos, Nigeria; ord. Dec. 11, 1966; ord. titular bishop of Mascula, June 5, 1971; abp. of Lagos, Apr. 13, 1973; cardinal, Oct. 21, 2003; titular church, Blessed Virgin Mary of Mt. Carmel of Mostacciano. Abp. of Lagos.

Curial membership: Evangelization of Peoples (congregation); Social Communications (council); Economic Affairs (office).

O'Malley, O.F.M. Cap., Sean P.: b. June 29, 1944, Lakewood, OH; studied at St. Fidelis Seminary, Capuchin College, and Catholic University, Washington, DC; ord. Aug. 29, 1970; episcopal vicar of priests serving Spanish speaking in Washington archdiocese, 1974-84; executive director of Spanish Catholic Center, Washington, from 1973; ord. coadjutor bp. of St. Thomas, Virgin Islands, Aug. 2, 1984; bp. of St. Thomas, Oct. 16, 1985; app. bp. of Fall River, June 16, 1992; app. bp. of Palm Beach, Sept. 3, 2002; app. abp. of Boston, July 1, 2003; cardinal, Mar. 24, 2006; titular church, Santa Maria della Vittoria. Abp. of Boston.

Curial membership: Clergy; Consecrated Life (Congregation).

Ortega y Alamino, Jaime Lucas: b. Oct. 18, 1936, Jagüey Grande, Cuba; ord., Aug. 2, 1964 detained in work camps (UMAP), 1966-67; parish priest; ord. bp. of Pinar del Rio, Jan. 14, 1979; app. abp. of Havana, Nov. 20, 1981; cardinal, Nov. 26, 1994; titular church, Sts. Aquila and Priscilla. Abp. of Havana.

Curial membership: Clergy (congregation); Health Care Workers (council); Latin America (commission).

Ouellet, P.S.S., Marc: b. June 8, 1944, Lamotte, Canada; ord. May 25, 1968; entered the Society of Priests of St.-Sulpice, 1972; rector and prof., Major Seminary of Montréal, 1989-1994 and Major Seminary of Edmonton, 1994-1997; prof., John Paul II Institute of Studies on Marriage and the Family, 1997-2001; ord. titular bishop of Agropoli, Mar. 19, 2001; sec. of the Pont. Council for the Promotion of Christian Unity, 2001-2002; abp. of Québec, Nov. 15, 2002; cardinal, Oct. 21, 2003; titular church, St. Mary in Traspontina. Abp. of Quebec.

Curial membership: Education, Sacraments (congregation); Culture (council); Latin America, Eucharistic Congresses (commissions); Economic Affairs (office).

Panafieu, Bernard: b. Jan. 26, 1931, Châtellerault, France; ord. Apr. 22, 1956; ord. titular bishop of Tibili June 9, 1974 and aux. bp. of Annecy, 1974-78; abp. of Aix, 1978-94; coadj. abp. of Marseilles, Aug. 24, 1994; abp. of Marseilles, 1995-2006; metropolitan archbishop when Marseille was elevated to that rank, Dec. 16, 2002; cardinal, Oct. 21, 2003; titular church, St. Gregory Barbarigo alle Tre Fontane. Abp. emeritus of Marseilles.

Curial membership: Interreligious Dialogue, Justice and Peace (councils).

Paskai,* O.F.M., László: b. May 8, 1927, Szeged,

Hungary; ord., Mar. 3, 1951; ord., titular bp. of Bavagaliana and apostolic administrator of Veszprem, Apr. 5, 1978; bp. of Veszprem, Mar. 31, 1979; coadj. abp. of Kalocsa, Apr. 5, 1982; abp. of Esztergom (renamed Esztergom–Budapest, 1993), 1987-2002; cardinal, June 28, 1988; titular church, St. Theresa (al Corso d'Italia). Abp. of Esztergom-Budapest.

Curial membership: Consecrated Life and Societies of Apostolic Life, Oriental Churches (congregations).

Pell, George: b. Apr. 8, 1941, Ballarat, Australia; ord. Dec. 16, 1966; episcopal vicar for Education, diocese of Ballarat, 1973-1984; rector of Corpus Christi College, the Provincial Seminary for Victoria and Tasmania, 1985-1987; ord. titular bishop of Scala, May 21, 1987; aux. bp. of Melbourne, 1987-96; abp. of Melbourne, 1996-2001; abp. of Sydney, Mar. 26, 2001; grand prior of the Equestrian Order of the Holy Sepulchre of Jerusalem, Australian Lieutenancy, Southern, 1998; cardinal, Oct. 21, 2003; titular church, St. Mary Dominic Mazzarello. Abp. of Sydney.

Curial membership: Family, Justice and Peace (councils); Economic Affairs (office).

Pengo, Polycarp: b. Aug. 5, 1944, Mwayze, Tanzania; ord., Aug. 5, 1971; taught moral theology at the major seminary in Kipalapala, Tanzania, 1977; rector of the major seminary in Segerea, 1978-83; ord. bp. of Nachingwea, Jan. 6, 1984; bp. of Tunduru-Masasi 1986-90; co-adjutor abp. of Dar-es-Salaam, Jan. 22, 1990; abp. of Dar-es-Salaam, July 22,1992, in succession to Laurean Cardinal Rugambwa; cardinal, Feb. 21, 1998; titular church, Our Lady of La Salette. Abp. of Dar-es-Salaam.

Curial membership: Doctrine of the Faith, Evangelization of Peoples (congregation); Culture, Family, Interreligious Dialogue (council).

Pham Dinh Tung,* Paul Joseph: b. June 15, 1919, Binh-Hoa, Vietnam; ord., June 6, 1949; ord. bp. of Bac Ninh, Aug. 15, 1963; apostolic administrator of Hanoi, June 18, 1990; abp. of Hanoi, 1994-2005; cardinal, Nov. 26, 1994; titular church, St. Mary Queen of Peace in Ostia mare. Abp. emeritus of Hanoi.

Pham Minh Man, Jean Baptiste: b. 1934, Ca Mau, Vietnam; ord. May 25, 1965; ord. coadjutor bp. of My Tho, Aug. 11, 1993; abp. of Thàn-Phô Hô Chi Minh (Hô Chi Minh City), Mar. 1, 1998; cardinal, Oct. 21, 2003; titular church, St. Justin. Abp. of Thàn-Phô Hô Chi Minh.

Curial membership: Sacraments, Evangelization of Peoples (congregation).

Pimenta,* Simon Ignatius: b. Mar. 1, 1920, Marol, India; ord., Dec. 21, 1949; ord. titular bp. of Bocconia and aux. of Bombay, June 29, 1971; coadj. abp. of Bombay, Feb. 26, 1977; abp. of Bombay, 1978-96; cardinal, June 28, 1988; titular church, Mary, Queen of the World (a Torre Spaccata). Abp. emeritus of Bombay

Piovanelli,* Silvano: b. Feb. 21, 1924, Ronta di Mugello, Italy; ord., July 13, 1947; ord. titular bp. of Tubune di Mauretania and aux. of Florence, June 24, 1982; abp. of Florence, 1983-2001; cardinal, May 25, 1985; titular church, St. Mary of Graces (Via Trionfale).

Poggi,* Luigi: b. Nov. 25, 1917, Piacenza, Italy; ord., July 28, 1940; studied diplomacy at the Pontifical Ecclesiastical Academy, 1944-46; started to work at Secretariat of State; ord. titular bp. of Forontoniana with personal title of abp., May 9, 1965; apostolic delegate for Central Africa, 1965; nuncio in Peru; recalled to Rome, 1973; negotiated with various Eastern bloc governments to improve situation of the Church; named head of Holy See's delegation for permanent contact with government of Poland, 1974; nuncio in Italy, 1986-92; pro-librarian and pro-archivist of the Holy Roman

Church, 1992; cardinal deacon, Nov. 26, 1994; protodeacon, 2002-2005; deaconry, St. Mary in Domnica. Archivist and librarian emeritus of the Holy Roman Church.

Poletto, Severino: b. Mar. 18, 1933, Salgareda (Treviso), Italy; ord., June 29, 1957; pref. of discipline at the diocesan seminary and vocation director; founded the Diocesan Centre for Family Ministry, 1973; coordinated the city mission for the 500th anniversary of the foundation of the diocese of Casale Monferrato; app. coadj. bp. of Fossano, Apr. 3, 1980; cons., May 17, 1980; succeeded to see on Oct. 29, 1980; app. bp. of Asti, Mar. 16, 1989; app. abp. of Turin, June 19, 1999; cardinal, Feb. 21, 2001; titular church, St. Joseph in Via Trionfale. Abp. of Turin.

Curial membership: Clergy (congregation); Economic Affairs of the Holy See (office); Cultural Heritage of the Church (commission).

Policarpo,* José Da Cruz: b. Feb. 26, 1936, Alvorninha, Portugal; ord., priest, Aug. 15, 1961; dir. of the seminary in Penafirme, rector of the seminary in Olivais and dean of the Theological Faculty of the Portuguese Catholic University; served two terms as rector of the Portuguese Catholic University, 1988-96; app. titular bp. of Caliabria and aux. bp. of Lisbon, May 26, 1978; cons., June 29, 1978; app. coadj. abp. of Lisbon, Mar. 5, 1997; succeeded as patriarch of Lisbon, Mar. 24, 1998; grand chancellor of the Portuguese Catholic University, pres. of the Portuguese Episcopal Conference; cardinal, Feb. 21, 2001; titular church, St. Anthony in Campo Formio. Patriarch of Lisbon.

Curial membership: Education (congregation), Culture, Laity (councils).

Poupard, Paul: b. Aug. 30, 1930, Bouzille, France; ord., Dec. 18, 1954; scholar; author of a number of works; ord. titular bp. of Usula and aux. of Paris, Apr. 6, 1979; title of abp. and pro-president of the Secretariat for Non-Believers, 1980; cardinal deacon, May 25, 1985; transferred to order of cardinal priests, Jan. 29, 1996; titular church, St. Praxedes; president of Pontifical Council for Dialogue with Non-Believers, 1985-93. President of Pontifical Council for Culture, 1988; President of the Pontifical Council for Interreligious Dialogue, 2006-2007.

Curial membership: Divine Worship and Sacraments, Education, Evangelization of Peoples (congregations); Christian Unity, Interreligious Dialogue, Laity (council).

Pujats, Janis: b. Nov. 14, 1930, the Rezekne district of Latvia; ord., Mar. 29, 1951; taught art history and liturgy at the catholic Theological Seminary, Riga; vicar general in the Metropolitan Curia, Riga, 1979-84; declared persona non grata by the KGB, 1984; app. abp. of Riga, May 8, 1991, cons., June 1, 1991; pres. of the Latvian Bishops' Conference; cardinal (in pectore), Feb. 21, 1998, titular church, St. Sylvia. Abp. of Riga.

Curial membership: Causes of Saints (congregation).

Puljic, Vinko: b. Sept. 8, 1945, Prijecani, Bosnia–Herzegovina; ord., June 29, 1970; spiritual director of minor seminary of Zadar, 1978-87; parish priest; app. vice–rector of Sarajevo major seminary, 1990; ord. abp. of Vrhbosna (Sarajevo), Jan. 6, 1991, in Rome; cardinal, Nov. 26, 1994; titular church, St. Clare in Vigna Clara. Abp. of Vrhbosna.

Curial membership: Evangelization of Peoples (congregation); Interreligious Dialogue (council).

Quezada Toruño, Rodolfo: b. Mar. 8, 1932, Ciudad de Guatemala, Guatemala; ord. Sept. 21, 1956; ord. titular bishop of Gadiaufala, May 13, 1972; appointed coadjutor, with right of succession of Zacapa, Apr. 5, 1972; succeeded to the see of Zacapa, Feb. 16, 1980; abp. of Guatemala, June 19, 2001; cardinal, Oct. 21, 2003; titular church, St. Saturnius.

Abp. of Guatemala.
Curial membership: Culture (council); Latin America (commission).

Razafindratandra,* Armand Gaétan: b. Aug. 7, 1925, Ambohimalaza, Madagascar; ord., July 27, 1954; ord. bp. of Mahajanga, July 2, 1978; app. abp. of Antananarivo, Feb. 3, 1994; installed, May 15, 1994; cardinal, Nov. 26, 1994; titular church, Sts. Sylvester and Martin ai Monti. Abp. of Antananarivo.
Curial membership: Evangelization of Peoples (congregation).

Re, Giovanni Battista: b. Jan. 30, 1934, Borno (Brescia), Italy; ord., Mar. 3, 1957; earned doctorate in canon law and taught in the Brescia Seminary; entered Holy See diplomatic service, served in Panama and Iran; recalled for service in Secretariat of State; sec. for Cong. for Bishops, 1987; titular abp., Nov. 7, 1987; *sostituto* for Secretariat of State, 1989; prefect of the Cong. of Bishops and pres. of the Pont. Comm. for Latin America, Sept. 16, 2000; cardinal, Feb. 21, 2001; titular church, Twelve Holy Apostles; transferred to order of cardinal bishops as titular bp. of suburbicarian see of Sabina-Poggio Mirteto. Prefect of the Cong. of Bishops.
Curial membership: Secretariat of State (second section); Doctrine of the Faith, Eastern Churches, Evangelization (congregations); Vatican City State (commission); APSA (office).

Ricard, Jean-Pierre: b. Sept. 26, 1944, Marseille, France; studied at Institut Catholique in Paris; ord. Oct. 5, 1968; app. titular bp. of Pulcheriopoli and aux. bp. of Grenoble, Apr. 17, 1993; app. coadjutor bp. of Montpellier, July 4, 1996; bp. of Montpellier, Sept. 6, 1996; promoted close relations with the Church in Africa and visited Peru in 1999 to meet a fidei donum priest of the diocese; visited Lebanon in 2000; major supporter of dialogue with the Jews; elected pres. of the Episcopal Conference of France, Nov. 6, 2001; app. abp. of Bordeaux, Dec 21, 2001; in 2003 authored the book, Sept défis pour l'Eglise (Seven Challenges for the Church); cardinal, Mar. 24, 2006; titular church, Sant'Agostino. Abp. of Bordeaux.
Curial membership: Doctrine of the Faith (congregation); Ecclesia dei (comisison).

Rigali, Justin Francis: b. Apr. 19, 1935, Los Angeles, CA; educ. St. John's Seminary (Camarillo, CA); ord. priest (Los Angeles*), Apr. 25, 1961; in Vatican diplomatic service from 1964; ord. titular abp. of Bolsena, Sept. 14, 1985, by Pope John Paul II; president of the Pontifical Ecclesiastical Academy, 1985-89; secretary of Congregation for Bps., 1989-94, and the College of Cardinals, 1990-94; app. abp. of St. Louis, Jan. 25, 1994, inst., Mar. 16, 1994; app. abp. of Philadelphia, July 15, 2003; cardinal, Oct. 21, 2003; titular church, St. Prisca. Abp. of Philadelphia.
Curial membership: Bishops, Sacraments (congregation); APSA (office).

Rivera Carrera, Norberto: b. June 6, 1942, La Purísima, Mexico; ord., July 3, 1966; taught dogmatic theology at the major seminary of Mexico City; professor of ecclesiology at Pontifical University of Mexico; bp. of Tehuacán, Nov. 5, 1985; abp. of Mexico City, June 13,1995; cardinal, Feb. 21, 1998; titular church, St. Francis of Assisi at Ripa Grande. Abp. of Mexico City.
Curial membership: Clergy, Divine Worship and the Discipline of Sacraments (congregation); Family (council); Latin America (commission).

Robles Ortega, Francisco: b. Mar. 2, 1949, Mascota, México; ord. July 20, 1976; served as vicar general of Autlán and professor of philosophy and theology at its seminary;

cons. titular bp. of Bossa and aux. bp. of Toluca, June 5, 1991; bp. of Toluca, 1996-2003; app. abp. of Monterrey, Jan. 25, 2003; cardinal, Nov. 24, 2007; titular church, St. Mary of the Presentation.
Curial membership: Latin America (commission).

Rodé, C.M., Franc: b. Sept. 23, 1934, Jarse, Ljubljana, Slovenia; the family left for Austria and then Argentina during World War II; entered the Cong. of the Missions (Vincentians), Mar. 6, 1952 and took his perpetual vows in 1957; studied at the Gregorian University in Rome and the Institut Catholique in Paris; ord. June 29, 1960; returned to Slovenia and after parish ministry, he taught at the Faculty of Theology in Ljubljana; his work in support of Catholic education caused him to be placed under surveillance by state authorities; app. undersecretary of the Secretariat for Non-Believers and then secretary of the Pont. Council for Culture; app. abp. of Ljubljana, Mar. 5, 1997; app. prefect of the Cong. for the Institutes of Consecrated Life and Societies of Apostolic Life, Feb. 11, 2004; cardinal Mar. 24, 2006; titular church, Diaconia di San Francesco Saverio alla Garbatella. Prefect of the Cong. for the Institutes of Consecrated Life and Societies of Apostolic Life.
Curial membership: Bishops, Doctrine of the Faith, Education, Evangelization, Sacraments (congregations); Culture (council); Ecclesia Dei (commission).

Rodríguez Maradiaga, S.D.B., Oscar Andrés: b. Dec. 29, 1942, Tegucigalpa, Honduras; ord., for the Salesians June 28, 1870; taught in various Salesian colleges in El Salvador, Honduras and Guatemala; prof. at the Salesian Theological Institute, Guatemala, and rector of the Salesian Philosophical Institute, Guatemala; app. titular bp. of Pudentiana and aux. bp. of Tegucigalpa, Oct. 28, 1978; app. abp. of Tegucigalpa, Jan. 8, 1993; pres. of CELAM, 1995-99; pres. of the Episcopal Conference of Honduras; cardinal priest, Feb. 21, 2001; titular church, St. Mary of Hope. Abp. of Tegucigalpa.
Curial membership: Clergy (congregation); Justice and Peace, Social Communication (councils); Latin America (commission).

Rosales, Gaudencio: b. Aug. 10, 1932, Batangas City; ord. Mar. 23, 1958; app. titular bp. of Esco and aux. bp. of Manila, Aug. 12, 1974; app. coadjutor bp. of Malaybalay, June 9, 1982; bp. of Malaybalay, Sept. 14, 1984; app. abp. of Lipa, Dec. 30, 1992; app. abp. of Manila, Sept. 15, 2003; cardinal, Mar. 24, 1006, titular church, Santissimo Nome di Maria a Via Latina. Abp. of Manila.
Curial membership: Interreligious Dialogue; Social Communications (council); Economic Affairs (office).

Rouco Varela, Antonio María: b. Aug. 24, 1936, Villalba, Spain; ord., Mar. 28, 1959; taught fundamental theology and canon law at the Mondoñedo seminary; adjunct professor at the Univ. of Munich; taught ecclesiastical law at Pontifical Univ. of Salamanca; vice-rector of Pontifical Univ. of Salamanca; titular bp. of Gergis and aux. bp. of Santiago de Compostela, Sep. 17, 1976; abp. of Santiago de Compostela, May 9,1984; abp. of Madrid June 29, 1994; cardinal, Feb. 21, 1998, titular church, St. Laurence in Damaso. Abp. of Santiago de Compostela.
Curial membership: Bishops, Clergy, Education (congregations); "Cor Unum," Culture, Texts (councils); Supreme Tribunal of the Apostolic Signatura (tribunal).

Rubiano Sáenz, Pedro: b. Sept. 13, 1932, Cartago, Colombia; ord., July 8, 1956; chaplain to Marco Fidel Suárez Air Force Academy, St. Liberata National College, and Our Lady of Remedies Clinic; app. bp. of Cúcuta, June 2, 1971; cons., June 11, 1971; app. coadj. abp. of Cali, Mar. 26, 1983; abp. of Cali Feb. 7, 1985; apost. admin. of Popayán; pres. of the Episcopal Conference of Colombia; app., Dec. 27, 1994; cardinal priest, Feb. 21, 2001; titular church, Transfiguration of Our Lord Jesus Christ. Abp. of Cali.

Curial membership: Education (congregation); Pastoral Care of Migrants and Itinerant Peoples (council).

Ruini, Camillo: b. Feb. 19, 1931, Sassuolo, Italy; ord., Dec. 8, 1954; taught at seminaries in central Italy; ord. titular bp. of Nepte and aux. bp. of Reggio Emilia and Guastella, June 29, 1983; secretary general of Italian Bishops' Conference, 1986–91; abp. Jan. 17, 1991 and pro-vicar general of the Pope for the Rome diocese; pro–Archpriest of Patriarchal Lateran Archbasilica; cardinal, June 28, 1991; titular church, St. Agnes outside the Wall. Vicar General of the Pope for the Diocese of Rome and Archpriest of Patriarchal Lateran Basilica, July 1, 1991; Grand Chancellor of Pontifical Lateran University; President of the Peregrinatio ad Petri Sedem, 1992–96.

Curial membership: Bishops (congregation); Laity (council); APSA (office).

Rylko, Stanislaw: b. July 4, 1945, Andrychów, Poland; ord. Mar. 30, 1969; earned a doctorate in social sciences from the Pontifical Gregorian University, Rome and served as a professor at the Pontifical Theological Academy of Kraków; app. titular bp. of Novica and sec. of the Pontifical Council for the Laity, Dec. 20, 1995; pres. of the Pont. Council for the Laity and promoted to the rank of archbishop, Oct. 4, 2003; cardinal, Nov. 24, 2007; deaconry, Sacred Heart of Christ the King.

Curial Membership: Bishops, Saints (congregation); Latin America (commission).

Saldarini,* Giovanni: b. Dec. 11, 1924, Cantu, Italy; ord., May 31, 1947; respected scripture scholar; taught scripture at Milan archdiocesan seminary, 1952-67; ord. titular bp. of Guadiaba and aux. bp. of Milan, Dec. 7, 1984; abp. of Turin, Jan. 31, 1989 (resigned, June 19, 1999); cardinal, June 28, 1991; titular church, Sacred Heart of Jesus (a Castro Pretorio). Abp. emeritus of Turin.

Sales,* Eugênio de Araújo: b. Nov. 8, 1920, Acari, Brazil; ord., Nov. 21, 1943; ord. titular bp. of Tibica and aux. bp. of Natal, Aug. 15, 1954; abp. of São Salvador, 1968-71; cardinal, Apr. 28, 1969; titular church, St. Gregory VII; abp. of Rio de Janeiro (1971), ordinary for Eastern Rite Catholics in Brazil without ordinaries of their own rites. Abp. emeritus of Rio de Janeiro.

Sánchez,* José T.: b. Mar. 17, 1920, Pandan, Philippines; ord., May 12, 1946; ord. titular bp. of Lesvi and coadj. bp. of Lucena, May 12, 1968; bp. of Lucena, 1976–82; abp. of Nueva Segovia, Jan. 12, 1982 (res Mar. 22, 1986); secretary of Congregation for Evangelization of Peoples, 1985–91; cardinal deacon, June 28, 1991; deaconry, St. Pius V (a Villa Carpegna); president of Commission for Preservation of Artistic and Historic Patrimony of the Holy See, 1991–93. Prefect of Congr. for the Clergy, 1991–96.

Sandoval Íñiguez, Juan: b. Mar. 28, 1933, Yahualica, Mexico; ord., Oct. 27, 1957; ord. coadj. bp. of Ciudad Juárez, Apr. 30, 1988; bp. of Ciudad Juarez, July 11, 1992; app. abp. of Guadalajara, Apr. 21, 1994; cardinal, Nov. 26, 1994; titular church, Our Lady of Guadalupe and St. Philip the Martyr on Via Aurelia. Abp. of Guadalajara.

Curial membership: Institutes of Consecrated Life and Societies of Apostolic Life, Catholic Education (congregations); Culture, Latin America (commission); Economic Affairs of the Holy See (office); Works of Religion (commission).

Sandri, Leonardo: b. Nov. 18, 1943, Buenos Aires, Argentina; ord., Dec. 2, 1967; earned a doctorate in canon law at the Pontifical Gregorian University, Rome and studied at the Pontifical Ecclesiastical Academy; entered the diplomatic service of the Holy See in 1974 and served in the nunciatures in Madagascar and Maurice and the U.S.; held several posts in the Secretariat of State; elected titular abp. of Cittanova and nuncio in Venezuela, July 22, 1997; cons., Oct. 11, 1997; nuncio to México, Mar. 1, 2000; *sostituto* of the Secretariat of State for General Affairs, Sept. 16, 2000; cardinal Nov. 24, 2007; deaconry, Sts. Biagio and Carlo at Catinari.

Curial membership: Doctrine, Evangelization (congregations), Christian Unity, Interreligious Dialogue (council), Vatican City (commission).

Santos,* O.F.M., Alexandre José Maria dos: b. Mar. 18, 1924, Zavala, Mozambique; ord., July 25, 1953; first Mozambican black priest; ord. abp. of Maputo, Mar. 9, 1975; cardinal, June 28, 1988; titular church, St. Frumentius (ai Prati Fiscali). Abp. emeritus of Maputo.

Saraiva Martins, C.M.F., José: b. Jan. 6, 1932, Gagos do Jarmelo, Portugal; ord., for the Claretians, Mar. 16, 1957; taught at Claretian seminary in Marino, Italy; taught at Claretianum, Rome; taught at the Pontifical Urbanian University and served as rector, 1977-80, 1980-83, 1986-88; sec. of the Cong. for Catholic Education and titular abp. of Thuburnica, May 26, 1988; cons. abp., July 2, 1988; pref. of Cong. for the Causes of Saints, May 30, 1998; cardinal deacon, Feb. 21, 2001; deaconry of Our Lady of the Sacred Heart. Pref. of Cong. for the Causes of Saints.

Curial membership: Bishops, Sacraments (congregations); Health Care (council).

Sarr, Théodore-Adrien: b. Nov. 28, 1936, Fadiouth, Sénégal; ord. May 28, 1964; served in pastoral ministry and also as professor of the Minor Seminary of N'Gasobil and as its superior, 1970-1974; cons. bp. of Kaolack, Nov. 24, 1974; app. abp. of Dakar, June 2, 2000; he is a well known voice for peace in western Africa; cardinal, Nov. 24, 2007; titular church, St. Lucy at the Piazza d'Armi.

Curial membership: Evangelization, Sacraments (congregation).

Scheid, Eusebio Oscar, b. Dec. 8, 1932, Luzerna, Brazil; ord. July 3, 1960; joined the Congregation of Priests of the Sacred Heart of Jesus (S.C.J.); ord. bp. of São José dos Campos, May 1, 1981; app. abp. of Florianapolis, Jan. 23, 1991; app. abp. of São Sebastião do Rio de Janeiro, July 25, 2001; cardinal, Oct. 21, 2003; titular church, Sts. Boniface and Alexis. Abp. of São Sebastião do Rio de Janeiro.

Curial membership: Social Communications (council); Latin America (commission); Economic Affairs (office).

Scherer, Odilo: b. Sept. 21, 1949, São Francisco, Brazil; ord. Dec. 7, 1976; earned a doctorate in theology from the Pontifical Gregorian University in Rome; served as rector and professor in several seminaries and universities and from 1994 to 2001 was an official of the Congregation for Bishops; cons. titular bp. of Novi and aux. bp. of São Paulo, Nov. 28, 2001; elected sec. general of the National Conference of Bishops of Brazil, 2003; app. abp. of São Paulo, Mar. 21, 2007; cardinal, Nov. 24, 2007; titular church, St. Andrea at the Quirinale.

Curial membership: Clergy (congregation).

Schönborn, O.P., Christoph: b. Jan. 22, 1945, Skalsko, Bohemia (fled to Austria in Sept. 1945); entered Dominican Order in 1963; ord., 1970; student pastor in Graz University, 1973-75; associate professor of dogma in the University of Fribourg, 1976; professor for theology, 1978; professor for dogmatic theology, 1981-91; member of the Orthodox-Roman Catholic Dialogue Commission of Switzerland,

1980-87; member of the International Theological Commission, 1980-; member of the foundation, "Pro Oriente" since 1984; Secretary for the Draft-Commission of the Catechism of the Catholic Church, 1987-1992; ord. aux. bp. (Sutri) of Vienna, Sept. 29, 1991; co-adjutor of Vienna, Apr. 13, 1995; abp. of Vienna, Sept. 14, 1995; cardinal, Feb. 21, 1998; titular church, Jesus the Divine Worker. Abp. of Vienna.

Curial membership: Doctrine of the Faith, Education, Oriental Churches (congregations); Culture (council); Cultural Heritage of the Church (commission).

Schwery, Henri: b. June 14, 1932, Saint-Leonard, Switzerland; ord., July 7, 1957; director of minor seminary and later rector of the College in Sion; bp. of Sion, 1977-95; cardinal, June 28, 1991; titular church, Protomartyrs (a via Aurelia Antica). Bp. emeritus of Sion.

Curial membership: Causes of Saints (congregation).

Scola, Angelo: b. Nov. 7, 1941, Malgrate, Italy; ord., July 18, 1970; served as professor of theological anthropology at the Pontifical John Paul II Institute for Studies on Marriage and the Family at the Pontifical Lateran University, Rome; and later, professor of Contemporary Christology at the Faculty of Theology, Pontifical Lateran University, Rome; ord. bp. of Grosseto, Sep. 21, 1991; rector of the Pontifical Lateran University, 1995-2002; patriarch of Venice, Jan. 5, 2002; cardinal, Oct. 21, 2003; titular church, the Seven Most Holy Apostles. Patriarch of Venice.

Curial membership: Clergy (congregation); Family (council).

Sebastiani, Sergio: b. Apr. 11, 1931, Montemonaco (Ascoli Piceno), Italy; ord., 1956; studied at Lateran University and Pontifical Ecclesiastical Academy; entered Holy See diplomatic service and posted to Peru, Brazil, and Chile; recalled to Secretariat of State; app. titular abp. of Caesarea in Mauretania and pro-nuncio in Madagascar and Mauritius and apostolic delegate to Reunion and Comorros; nuncio to Turkey, 1985; sec. to Central Committee for the Great Jubilee of the Year 2000, 1994; pres. Prefecture for the Economic Affairs of the Holy See, Nov. 3, 1997; cardinal, Feb. 21, 2001; titular church, Deaconry of St. Eustace. Pres. of the Prefecture for the Economic Affairs of the Holy See.

Curial membership: Bishops, Causes of Saints, Clergy, Evangelization (congregations); Christian Unity, Interreligious Dialogue (councils); Apostolic Signatura (tribunal).

Sepe, Crescenzio: b. June 2, 1943, Carinaro (Caserta), Italy; ord., Mar. 12, 1967; taught at Lateran and Urbanian Universities; studied at Pontifical Ecclesiastical Academy; entered Holy See diplomatic service and posted to Brazil; recalled to Secretariat of State, 1987; pres. of Commission for Vatican Telecommunications; app. titular abp. of Grado and sec. of the Cong. for the Clergy, Apr. 2, 1992; cons. Apr. 26, 1992; General Secretary of the Central Committee for the Great Jubilee of the Year 2000, 1997-2001; Pref. Cong. for the Evangelization of Peoples, 2001-2006; cardinal deacon, Feb. 21, 2001; deaconry, God the Merciful Father; app. abp. of Naples, May 20, 2006. Abp. of Naples.

Curial membership: Clergy, Doctrine of the Faith (congregation); Christian Unity, Interreligious Dialogue, Legislative Texts, Social Communication (councils); Latin America (commission).

Sfeir,* Nasrallah Pierre: b. May 15, 1920, Reyfoun, in Maronite diocese of Sarba, Lebanon; ord., May 7, 1950; secretary of Maronite patriarchate, 1956-61; taught Arabic literature and philosophy at Marist Fathers College, Jounieh, 1951–61; ord. titular bp. of Tarsus for the Maronites, July 16,

1961; elected Patriarch of Antioch for Maronites, Apr. 19, 1986; granted ecclesial communion by John Paul II May 7, 1986; cardinal, Nov. 26, 1994. Patriarch of Antioch for Maronites.

Curial membership: Oriental Churches (congregation); Health Care (council).

Shan Kuo-hsi,* S.J., Paul: b. Dec. 2, 1923, Puyang, China; ord., Mar. 18, 1955; director of the Chinese section of the Sacred Heart School in Cebu; socius of the novice master in Thu-duc, Vietnam; novice master and rector of Manresa House, Chanhua, Taiwan; rector of St. Ignatius High School, Taipei, Taiwan; bp. of Hualien, Nov. 15, 1979; bp. of Kaohsiung, Taiwan, 1991; cardinal, Feb. 21, 1998; titular church, St. Chrysogonus. Bp. of Kaohsiung.

Shirayanagi,* Peter Seiichi: b. June 17, 1928, Hachioji City, Japan; ord., Dec. 21, 1954; ord. titular bp. of Atenia and aux. bp. of Tokyo, May 8, 1966; titular abp. of Castro and coadj. abp. of Tokyo, Nov. 15, 1969; abp. of Tokyo, 1970-2000; cardinal, Nov. 26, 1994; titular church, St. Emerentiana in Tor Fiorenza. Abp. emeritus of Tokyo.

Silvestrini,* Achille: b. Oct. 25, 1923, Brisighella, Italy; ord., July 13, 1946; official in Secretariat of State from 1953; ord. titular bp. of Novaliciana with personal title of abp., May 27, 1979; undersecretary, 1973-79, and secretary, 1979-88, of the Council for Public Affairs of the Church (now the second section of the Secretariat of State); cardinal, June 28, 1988; deaconry, St. Benedict Outside St. Paul's Gate, promoted to cardinal priest, Jan. 9, 1999; prefect of Apostolic Signatura, 1988-91. Prefect of Congregation for Oriental Churches, 1991-2001; Grand Chancellor of Pontifical Oriental Institute.

Simonis, Adrianus J.: b. Nov. 26, 1931, Lisse, Netherlands; ord., June 15, 1957; ord. bp. of Rotterdam, Mar. 20, 1971; coadj. abp. of Utrecht, June 27, 1983; abp. of Utrecht, 1983-2007; cardinal, May 25, 1985; titular church, St. Clement. Abp. emeritus of Utrecht.

Curial membership: Consecrated Life and Societies of Apostolic Life, Education (congregations); Christian Unity (council).

Sodano,* Angelo: b. Nov. 23, 1927, Isola d'Asti, Italy; ord., Sept. 23, 1950; entered diplomatic service of the Holy See in 1959; served in Ecuador and Uruguay; ord. titular abp. of Nova di Cesare, Jan. 15, 1978; nuncio to Chile, 1978-88; secretary of the Council for Relations with States, 1988-90; pro-Secretary of State, 1990-1991; cardinal June 28, 1991; titular church, S. Maria Nuova; transferred to order of cardinal bishops, Jan 10, 1994, as titular bp. of suburbicarian see of Albano (while retaining title to S. Maria Nuova). Secretary of State, June 29, 1991-Sept. 15, 2006; Vice-dean of the Sacred College of Cardinals, 2002-05; dean of the College of Cardinals (Apr. 30, 2005). Secretary of State emeritus.

Curial membership: Bishops, Doctrine of the Faith, Oriental Churches (congregations); Vatican City State, Institute for Works of Religion (commission).

Spidlik,* S.J., Thomas: b. Dec. 17, 1919, Boskovice, Czech Republic; Czech theologian and Jesuit; expert in Eastern spirituality; conducted the papal Lenten retreat in 1995; cardinal deacon, Oct. 21, 2003; titular church, St. Agatha of Goti.

Stafford, James Francis: b. July 26, 1932, Baltimore, MD; ord., (Baltimore*) Dec. 15, 1957; ord. titular bp. of Respetta and aux. bp. of Baltimore, Feb. 29, 1976; app. bp. of Memphis, Nov. 17, 1982; app. abp. of Denver, June 3, 1986, installed July 30, 1986; app. President of Pontifical Council for the Laity, 1996-2003; app. Major Penitentiary of the Apostolic Penitentiary, Oct. 4, 2003; cardinal deacon, Feb. 21, 1998; cardinal priest, Mar. 2, 2008; titular church, S.

Pietro in Montorio. Major Penitentiary of the Apostolic Penitentiary.

Curial membership: Bishops, Doctrine of the Faith, Causes of Saints, Evangelization of Peoples (congregations); Texts (council).

Stéphanos II Ghattas, C.M.*: b. Jan. 16, 1920, Sheikh Zein-el-Dine, Egypt; ord., Mar. 25, 1944; taught philosophy and dogmatic theology at the major seminary in Tahta; joined Congregation of the Mission, 1952; worked in Lebanon and served as Vincentian econome and superior in Alexandria; elected by the Coptic Catholic Synod bp. of Thebes-Luxor, May 8, 1967; named apostolic admin. of the patriarchate to substitute for the ailing Patriarch Stéphanos I Sidarous; elected unanimously by the Coptic Catholic Synod patriarch of Alexandria for Copts; changed name from Andraos Ghattas to Stéphanos II in honor of his predecessor; cardinal, Feb. 21, 2001; as a patriarch, he did not receive a titular church. Patriarch of Alexandria for Copts.

Curial membership: Oriental Churches (congregation).

Sterzinsky, Georg Maximilian: b. Feb. 9, 1936, Warlack, Germany; ord., June 29, 1960; vicar general to the apostolic administrator of Erfurt–Meiningen, 1981-89; ord. bp. of Berlin, Sept. 9, 1989; cardinal, June 28, 1991; titular church, St. Joseph (all'Aurelio). Abp. of Berlin.

Curial membership: Catholic Education (congregation); Migrants and Itinerant People (council).

Swiàtek,* Kazimierz: b. Oct. 21, 1914, Walga, in apostolic administration of Estonia; ord., (of Pinsk, Belarus, clergy) Apr. 8, 1939; arrested by KGB Apr. 21, 1941, and imprisoned on death row until June 22, when he escaped during confusion of German invasion and returned to his parish; arrested again by KGB and imprisoned in Minsk until 1945; sentenced to 10 years of hard labor in concentration camps; released June 16, 1954; resumed pastoral work in cathedral parish in Pinsk; ord. abp. of Minsk–Mohilev, Belarus, May 21, 1991, and also appointed apostolic administrator of Pinsk; ret. June 14, 2006; cardinal, Nov. 26, 1994; titular church, St. Gerard Majella. Abp. of Minsk–Mohilev.

Szoka,* Edmund C.: b. Sept. 14, 1927, Grand Rapids, MI; ord., (Marquette diocese) June 5, 1954; ord. first bp. of Gaylord, MI, July 20, 1971; abp. of Detroit, 1981–90; cardinal, June 28, 1988; titular church, Sts. Andrew and Gregory (al Monte Celio). President of Prefecture for Economic Affairs of the Holy See, 1990-97. Pres. Pont. Comm. for Vatican City State, 1997-2006. Pres. emeritus of the Pont. Comm. for Vatican City State.

Curial membership: Secretariat of State (second section); Bishops, Causes of Saints, Clergy, Evangelization of Peoples, Consecrated Life and Societies of Apostolic Life (congregations).

Tauran, Jean-Louis: b. Apr. 3, 1943, Bordeaux, France; ord. Sep. 20, 1969; entered the diplomatic service of the Holy See in 1975; app. titular archbishop of Telepte and appointed secretary of the Secretariat of State for the Relations with the States, 1990-2003; Archivist and Librarian of the Holy Roman Church, 2003; cardinal deacon, Oct. 21, 2003, titular church, St. Apollinaris alle Terme Neroniane-Alessandrine; Pres. of the Pont. Council for Interreligious Dialogue, 2007.

Curial membership: Secretariat of State (second section), Bishops, Doctrine of the Faith, Oriental Churches (Congregations); Culture (council); Supreme Tribunal of the Apostolic Signatura (tribunal); Vatican City State (commission); APSA (office).

Terrazas Sandoval, C.SS.R., Julio: b. Mar. 7, 1936, Vallegrande, Bolivia; ord., for the Redemptorists July 29, 1962; superior of the Redemptorist community in Vallegrande and vicar forane; app. aux. bp. of La Paz and cons., Apr. 15, 1978; transferred to the see of Oruro, Jan. 9, 1982; pres. of the Bolivian Episcopal Conference in 1985 and 1988; app. abp. of Santa Cruz, Feb. 6, 1991; cardinal, Feb. 21, 2001; titular church, St. John Baptist Rossi. Abp. of Santa Cruz.

Curial membership: Laity (council); Latin America (commission).

Tettamanzi, Dionigi: b. Mar. 14, 1934, Renate, Italy; ord., June 28, 1957; taught fundamental theology at the major seminary of Lower Venegono, pastoral theology at the Priestly Institute of Mary Immaculate and the Lombard Regional Institute of Pastoral Ministry, Milan; rector of the Pontifical Lombard Seminary, Rome; abp. of Ancona-Osimo, July 1,1989 (resigned 1991); general secretary of the Italian Episcopal Conference, 1991-95; Vice-President of the Italian Episcopal Conference, May 25, 1995; abp. of Genoa Apr. 20, 1995; cardinal, Feb. 21, 1998; titular church, Sts. Ambrose and Charles; app. abp. of Milan, July 11, 2002. Abp. of Milan.

Curial membership: Clergy, Doctrine of the Faith, Education, Oriental Churches (congregations); Culture (council); Economic Affairs of the Holy See (office).

Tomko,* Jozef: b. Mar. 11, 1924, Udavske, Slovakia; ord., Mar. 12, 1949; ord. titular abp. of Doclea, Sept, 15, 1979; secretary-general of the Synod of Bishops, 1979-85; cardinal deacon, May 25, 1985; transferred to order of cardinal priests, Jan. 29, 1996; titular church, St. Sabina. Prefect of the Congregation for the Evangelization of Peoples, 1985-2001; Grand Chancellor of Pontifical Urban University. President of Pontifical Committee for International Eucharistic Congresses, 2001.

Curial membership: Works of Religion (commission).

Tonini,* Ersilio: b. July 20, 1914, Centovera di San Giorgio Piacentino, Italy; ord., Apr. 18, 1937; vice-rector and later rector of the Piacenza seminary; taught Italian, Latin and Greek; editor of diocesan weekly; ord. bp. of Macerata-Tolentino, June 2, 1969; abp. of Ravenna–Cervia, Nov. 22, 1975-90; cardinal, Nov. 26, 1994; titular church, Most Holy Redeemer in Val Melaina. Abp. of Ravenna-Cervia.

Toppo, Telesphore Placidus: b. Oct. 15, 1939, Chainpur, India, to a tribal family that had converted to Christianity; ord. May 3, 1969; ord. bp. of Dumka, June 8, 1979; abp. of Ranchi, Aug. 7, 1985; supported programs to assist tribes in Jharkhand; cardinal, Oct. 21, 2003; titular church, Sacred Heart of Jesus in Agony at Vitinia. Abp. of Ranchi.

Curial membership: Evangelization of Peoples (congregation); Interreligious Dialogue (council).

Tucci,* S.J., Roberto: b. Apr. 19, 1921, Naples, Italy; ord., for the Jesuits, Aug. 24, 1950; editor of La Civiltà Cattolica; member of the Preparatory Commission on the Apostolate of the Laity for Vatican II and peritus involved in drafting *Ad Gentes* and *Gaudium et Spes*; consultor to the Pontifical Council for Social Communications, 1965-89; member of the editorial committee for the Pastoral Instruction Communio et Progressio; vice-pres. of the Italian Catholic Union of the Press, 1961-82; general sec. of the Italian Province of the Jesuits, 1967-69; app. general manager of Vatican Radio, 1973; since 1982, he has been responsible for all papal visits outside Italy; app. chairman of the Administrative Committee of Vatican Radio, 1986; cardinal, Feb. 21, 2001; titular church, Deaconry of St. Ignatius Loyola in Campo Marzio. Chairman of the Administrative Committee of Vatican Radio.

Tumi, Christian Wiyghan: b. Oct. 15, 1930, Kikaikelaki, Cameroon; ord., Apr. 17, 1966; ord. bp. of Yagoua, Jan. 6, 1980; coadj. abp. of Garoua, Nov. 19, 1982; abp. of Garoua, 1984–91; abp. of Douala, Aug. 31, 1991; cardinal, June 28,

1988; titular church, Martyrs of Uganda (a Poggio Ameno). Abp. of Douala.

Curial membership: Divine Worship and Sacraments, Education, Evangelization of Peoples (congregations); Cor Unum, Family (councils).

Turcotte, Jean–Claude: b. June 26, 1936, Montreal, Canada; ord., May 24, 1959; ord. titular bp. of Suas and aux. of Montreal, June 29, 1982; abp. of Montreal, Mar. 17, 1990; cardinal, Nov. 26, 1994; titular church, Our Lady of the Blessed Sacrament and the Holy Canadian Martyrs. Abp. of Montreal.

Curial membership: Causes of Saints (congregation); Social Communications (council).

Turkson, Peter Kodwo Appiah: b. Oct. 11, 1948, Wassaw Nsuta, Ghana; ord. July 20, 1975; abp. of Cape Coast, Jan. 6, 1992; pres. of the Catholic Bishops' Conference and Chancellor of the Catholic University College of Ghana; cardinal priest, Oct. 21, 2003; titular church, St. Liborius. Abp. of Cape Coast.

Curial membership: Christian Unity (council); Cultural Heritage of the Church (commission).

Urosa Savino, Jorge Liberato: b. Aug. 28, 1942, Caracas, Venezuela; ord. Aug. 15, 1967; earned a doctorate in theology form the Gregorian University in 1971; served as rector of several Venezuelan seminaries, 1974-82 and professor of philosophical anthropology and dogmatic theology; pres. of the organization of Venezuelan Seminries, 1974-77 and vice-pres. of the Organization of Latin American Seminaries, 1976-82; app. titular bishop of Vegesela in Byzacena and aux. bp. of Caracas, July 13, 1982; app. abp. of Valencia in Venezuela, Mar. 17, 1990; app. abp. of Caracas, Sept. 19, 2005; cardinal, Mar. 24, 2006, titular church, Santa Maria ai Monti. Abp. of Caracas.

Curial membership: Justice and Peace (commission); Latin America (commission).

Vallini, Agostino: b. Apr. 17, 1940, Poli, Italy; ord. July 19, 1964; after seminary studies, he progressed to the study of canon law at the Pontifical Lateran University, and earned a doctorate *in utroque iure*; taught in Naples, 1969-71; called back to Rome in 1971 to teach public ecclesiastical law at the lateran, with the task of reorganizing the field in keeping with the Second Vatican Council; rector of the Major Seminary of Naples, 1978; app. titular bp. of Tortibulum and aux. bp. of Naples, Mar. 23, 1989; app. suburbicarian bp. of Albano, Nov. 13, 1999; app. prefect of the Supreme Tribunal of the Apostolic Signatura, May 27, 2004 and elevated to the dignity of archbishop; pres. of the Court of Causation of the Vatican City State; cardinal, Mar. 24, 2006; titular church, Diaconia di San Pier Damiani ai Monti di San Paolo. Prefect of the Supreme Tribunal of the Apostolic Signatura.

Curial membership: Consecrated Life, Evangelization, Saints (Congregation); Texts (council); APSA.

Vanhoye,* S.J., Albert: b. July 24, 1923, Hazebrouck, France; entered the Jesuits, Sept. 11, 1941 and ord. July 24, 1954; earned licentiates in letters, philosophy, and theology, and a doctorate in sacred scripture from the Pontifical Biblical Institute in 1961; professor at the Pontifical Biblical Institute, the Biblicum, in Rome since 1963; dean of the biblical faculty, 1969-75 and rector, 1984-90; taught at the Gregorian University and the Lateran University in Rome; assisted in the preparation of the apostolic constitution, Sapientia Christiana; served as member of the Pontifical Biblical Commission, 1984-2001 and sec. of the commission, 1990-2001; consultor to the Congs. of Catholic Education from 1978 and Doctrine of the Faith from 1990; cardinal, Mar. 24, 2006; titular church, diaconia di Santa Maria della

Mercede e Sant'Adriano a Villa Albani.

Vidal, Ricardo J.: b. Feb. 6, 1931, Mogpoc, Philippines; ord., Mar. 17, 1956; ord. titular bp. of Claterna and coadj. of Melalos, Nov. 30, 1971; abp. of Lipa, 1973-81; coadj. abp. of Cebu, Apr. 13, 1981; abp. of Cebu, Aug. 24, 1982; cardinal, May 25, 1985; titular church, Sts. Peter and Paul (in Via Ostiensi). Abp. of Cebu.

Curial membership: Education, Evangelization of Peoples (congregations); Family, Health Care Workers (councils).

Vingt-Trois, André: b. Nov. 7, 1942, Paris, France; ord. June 28, 1969; served as a professor of theology and in a variety of pastoral positions, including diocesan formation; cons. titular bp. of Tibili and aux. of Paris, Oct. 14, 1988; abp. of Tours, 1999-2005; app. abp. of Paris and ordinary of the Catholics of Oriental rite in France, Feb. 11, 2005; elected pres. of the Episcopal Conference of France, Nov. 5, 2007; cardinal, Nov. 24, 2007; titular church, St. Louis of the French.

Curial Membership: Bishops (congregation); Family, Migrants (councils).

Vithayathil,* C.SS.R., Varkey: b. May 29, 1927, North Paravur, India; ord., for the Redemptorists June 12, 1954; taught canon law for 25 years at the Redemptorist major seminary in Bangalore; served as provincial for Redemptorists in India and Sri Lanka, 1978-84; pres. of the Conference of Religious, India, 1984-85; apostolic administrator of the Asirvanum Benedictine Monastery, Bangalore, 1990-96; app. titular abp. of Ohrid and apostolic administrator of the vacant see of Ernakulam-Angamaly for Syro-Malabars; cons. by the pope, Jan. 6, 1997; app. major abp. of Ernakulam-Angamaly for Syro-Malabars, Dec. 18, 1999; cardinal, Feb. 21, 2001; titular church, St. Bernard at the Baths. Major abp. of Ernakulam-Angamaly for Syro-Malabars.

Curial membership: Oriental Churches (congregation); Christian Unity, Texts (council).

Vlk, Miloslav: b. May 17, 1932, Lisnice, Czech Republic; during communist persecution when theological studies were impossible he studied archival science at Charles University and worked in various archives in Bohemia; ord., June 23, 1968, during "Prague Spring"; sent to isolated parishes in Bohemian Forest by State authorities in 1971; state authorization to exercise his priestly ministry was cancelled in 1978; from then until 1986 he worked as a window-washer in Prague, carrying out his priestly ministry secretly among small groups. In 1989, he was permitted to exercise his priestly ministry for a "trial" year; the situation changed with the "velvet revolution"; ord. bp. of Ceske Budejovice, Mar. 31, 1990; abp. of Prague, Mar. 27, 1991; cardinal, Nov. 26, 1994; titular church, Holy Cross in Jerusalem. Abp. of Prague, President of the Council of European Episcopal Conferences, 1993-. Abp. of Prague.

Curial membership: Oriental Churches (congregation); Social Communications (council).

Wamala,* Emmanuel: b. Dec. 15, 1926, Kamaggwa, Uganda; ord., Dec. 21, 1957; ord. bp. of Kiyinda-Mityana, Nov. 22, 1981; coadj. abp. of Kampala, June 21, 1988; abp. of Kampala, 1990-2006; cardinal, Nov. 26, 1994; titular church, St. Hugh. Abp. emeritus of Kampala.

Curial membership: Evangelization of Peoples (congregation); Cor Unum (council).

Wetter,* Friedrich: b. Feb. 20, 1928, Landau, Germany; ord., Oct. 10, 1953; ord. bp. of Speyer, June 29, 1968; abp. of Munich and Freising, 1982-2007; cardinal, May 25, 1985; titular church, St. Stephen (al Monte Celio). Abp. emeritus of Munich and Freising.

Curial membership: Education, Evangelization of Peoples

(congregations).

Williams, Thomas Stafford: b. Mar. 20, 1930, Wellington, New Zealand; ord., Dec. 20, 1959, in Rome; studied in Ireland after ordination, receiving degree in social sciences; served in various pastoral assignments on his return to New Zealand; missionary in Western Samoa to 1976; abp. of Wellington, New Zealand, 1979-2005; ret. Mar. 20, 2005; cardinal, Feb. 2, 1983; titular church, Jesus the Divine Teacher (at Pineda Sacchetti). Abp. emeritus of Wellington. *Curial membership*: Evangelization of Peoples (congregation).

Zen Ze-Kium, S.D.B., Joseph: b. Jan. 13, 1932, Yang King-pang, Shanghai, China; his parents were converts and survived great hardships during World War II; made his profession in the Salesians on Aug. 16, 1949 and perpetual vows on Aug. 16, 1955; ord. in Turin, Italy on Feb. 11, 1961; taught in several Chinese seminaries from 1989 to 1996; app, coadjutor bp. of Hong Kong, Sept. 13, 1996; bp. of Hong Kong, Sept. 23, 2002; spoke at the 11th Ordinary General Assembly of the Synod of Bishops in Oct. 2005, he spoke of the Church in China; cardinal Mar. 24, 2006; titular church, Santa Maria Madre del Redentore a Tor Bella Monaca. Bp. of Hong Kong. *Curial membership*: Evangelization; Sacraments (congregation); Synod of Bishops.

Zubeir Wako, Gabriel: b. Feb. 27, 1941, Mboro, diocese of Wau, Sudan; ord. July 21, 1963; ord. bp. of Wau, Apr. 6, 1975; coadj. abp. of Khartoum, Oct. 30, 1979; abp. of Khartoum, Oct. 10, 1981; cardinal, Oct. 21, 2003; titular church, St. Anthanasius in Via Tiburtina. Abp. of Khartoum. *Curial membership*: Evangelization of Peoples (congregation); "Cor Unum," Migrants (council).

CATEGORIES OF CARDINALS

(As of Aug. 20, 2008.) Information below includes categories of cardinals listed according to seniority or order of precedence. Seniority or precedence usually depends on order of elevation. It is customary for cardinal deacons to be promoted eventually to the rank of cardinal priest.

Order of Bishops

Titular Bishops of Suburbicarian Sees: Angelo Sodano, dean (June 28, 1991, Albano and Ostia); Roger Etchegaray (June 24, 1998, Porto-Santa Rufina; vice-dean); Giovanni Battista Re (Oct. 1, 2002, Sabina-Poggio Mirteto); Francis Arinze (April 25, 2005, Velletri-Segni); Tarcisio Bertone, (May 10, 2008, Frascati). Eastern Rite Patriarchs: Nasrallah Pierre Sfeir (Nov. 26, 1994); Ignace Moussa I Daoud (Feb. 21, 2001); Stephanos II Ghattas, (Feb. 21, 2001); Emmanuel III Delly (Nov. 24. 2007).

Order of Priests

Stephen Sou-hwan Kim, Eugênio de Araújo Sales, Luis Aponte Martinez, Salvatore Pappalardo, Paulo Evaristo Arns, O.F.M., William W. Baum, Marco Cé, Franciszek Macharski, Michael Michai Kitbunchu, Alexandre do Nascimento, Godfried Danneels, Thomas Stafford Williams, Carlo Maria Martini, Józef Glemp, Joachim Meisner, Simon D. Lourdusamy, Antonio Innocenti, Miguel Obando Bravo, S.D.B., Paul Augustine Mayer, Ricardo Vidal, Henryk Roman Gulbinowicz, Jozef Tomko, Andrzej Maria Deskur, Paul Poupard, Louis-Albert Vachon, Friedrich Wetter, Silvano Piovanelli, Adrianus J. Simonis, Bernard F. Law, Giacomo Biffi, Eduardo Martinez Somalo, Achille Silvestrini, José Freire Falcão, Michele Giordano, Alexandre José Maria dos Santos, O.F.M., Giovanni Canestri, Antonio Maria Javierre Ortas, S.D.B., Simon Ignatius Pimenta, Edward Bede Clancy, Edmund C. Szoka, László Paskai, O.F.M., Christian Wiyghan Tumi, Jean Margéot, Pio Laghi, Edward I. Cassidy, Frédéric Etsou-Nzabi-Bamungwabi, C.I.C.M., Nicolás de Jesús López Rodriguez, José T. Sánchez, Virgilio Noè, Fiorenzo Angelini, Roger Mahony, Anthony J. Bevilacqua, Giovanni Saldarini, Cahal Brendan Daly, Camillo Ruini, Ján Chryzostom Korec, S.J., Henri Schwery, Georg Sterzinsky, Miloslav Vlk, Luigi Poggi, Peter Shirayanagi, Carlo Furno, Julius Riyadi Darmaatmadja, S.J., Jaime Lucas Ortega y Alamino, Gilberto Agustoni, Emmanuel Wamala, William Henry Keeler, Jean-Claude Turcotte, Ricardo Maria Carles Gordó, Adam Joseph Maida, Vinko Puljic, Armand Gaétan Razafindratandra, Paul Joseph Pham Dính Tung, Juan Sandoval Íñiguez, Kazimierz Swiàtek, Ersilio Tonino, Salvatore de Giorgi, Serafim Fernandes de Araújo, Antonio Maria Rouco Varela, Aloysius Ambrozic, Dionigi Tettamanzi, Polycarp Pengo, Christoph Schönborn, O.P., Norberto Rivera Carrera, Francis George, O.M.I., Paul Shan Kuo-his, S.J., Marian Jaworski, Janis Pujats, Antonio Jose Gonzalez Zumarraga, Ivan Dias, Geraldo Majella Agnelo, Pedro Rubiano Sáenz, Theodore E. McCarrick, Desmond Connell, Audrys Juozas Backis, Francisco Javier Errázuriz Ossa, Juan Julio Terrazas Sandoval, C.SS.R., Wilfrid Fox Napier, O.F.M., Oscar Andres Rodríguez Maradiaga, S.D.B., Bernard Agré, Luis Cipriani Thorne, Francisco Álvarez Martínez, Cláudio Hummes, O.F.M., Varkey Vithayathil, C.SS.R., Jorge Mario Bergoglio, S.J., José Da Cruz Policarpo, Severino Poletto, Cormac Murphy-O'Connor, Edward Michael Egan, Lubomyr Husar, Karl Lehmann, Jean Honoré, Angelo Scola, Anthony Olubunmi Okogie, Bernard Panafieu, Gabriel Zubeir Wako, Carlos Amigo Vallejo, Justin Francis Rigali, Keith Michael O'Brien, Eusebio Oscar Scheid, Ennio Antonelli, Tarcisio Bertone, Peter Kodwo Appiah Turkson, Telesphore Placidus Toppo, George Pell, Josip Bozanic, Jean Baptiste Pham Minh Man, Rodolfo Quezada Toruño, Philippe Barbarin, Peter Erdõ, Marc Ouellet, P.S.S., Urosa Savino, Rosales, Ricard, Cañizares Llovera, Cheong-Jin-Suk, O'Malley, Dziwisz, Caffara, Zen Ze-Kiun, Agustin Garcia-Gasco y Vicente, Seán Brady, Lluís Martínez Sistach, André Vingt-Trois, Angelo Bagnasco, Théodore-Adrien Sarr, Oswald Gracias, Francisco Lopez Ortega, Daniel Nicholas DiNardo, Odilo Scherer, John Njue, Dario Castrillón Hoyos, Jorge Medina Estévez, Lorenzo Antonetti, James Francis Stafford, Giovanni Cheli.

Order of Deacons

Agostino Cacciavillan, Sergio Sebastiani, Zenon Grocholewski, José Saraiva Martins, C.M.F., Crescenzio Sepe, Jorge María Mejía, Mario Francesco Pompedda, Walter Kasper, Roberto Tucci, S.J., Avery Dulles, S.J., Jean-Louis Tauran, Renato Martino, Francesco Marchisano, Julián Herranz, Javier Lozano Barragán, Attilio Nicora, Georges Cottier, O.P., Thomas Spidlik, S.J., Stanislas Nagy, Levada, Rodé, Vallini, Montezemolo, Vanhoye, Leonardo Sandri John P. Foley, Giovanni Lajolo, Paul-Josef Cordes, Stanislaw Rylko, Angelo Comastri, Raffaele Farina S.D.B. Giovanni Coppa, Estanislao Esteban Karlic, Urbano Navarrete, S.J., Umberto Betti, O.F.M.

CONSISTORIES

(As of Aug. 15, 2008.) Information below includes dates of consistories at which the current cardinals were created. They are listed according to seniority. Of these 194 cardinals, 5 were named by Paul VI (consistories of Apr. 28, 1969, Mar. 5, 1973, May 24, 1976, and June 27, 1977); 152 by John Paul II (consistories of June 30, 1979, Feb. 2, 1983, May 25, 1985, June 28, 1988, June 28, 1991, Nov. 26, 1994, Feb. 21, 1998, Feb. 21, 2001, and Oct. 21, 2003), and 37 by Pope Benedict XVI (Mar. 24, 2006 and Nov. 24, 2007).

Pope Paul VI

1969 (Apr. 28): Stephen Sou-hwan Kim, Eugênio de Araújo Sales.

1973 (Mar. 5): Luis Aponte Martinez, Paulo Evaristo Arns, O.F.M.

1976 (May 24): William W. Baum.

Pope John Paul II

1979 (June 30): Marco Cé, Roger Etchegaray, Franciszek Macharski.

1983 (Feb. 2): Michael Michai Kitbunchu, Alexandre do Nascimento, Godfried Danneels, Thomas Stafford Williams, Carlo Maria Martini, Józef Glemp, Joachim Meisner.

1985 (May 25): Simon D. Lourdusamy, Francis A. Arinze, Antonio Innocenti, Miguel Obando Bravo, S.D.B., Paul Augustine Mayer, Ricardo Vidal, Henryk Roman Gulbinowicz, Jozef Tomko, Andrzej Maria Deskur, Paul Poupard, Friedrich Wetter, Silvano Piovanelli, Adrianus J. Simonis, Bernard F. Law, Giacomo Biffi.

1988 (June 28): Eduardo Martinez Somalo, Achille Silvestrini, José Freire Falcão, Michele Giordano, Alexandre José Maria dos Santos, O.F.M., Giovanni Canestri, Simon Ignatius Pimenta, Edward Bede Clancy, Edmund C. Szoka, László Paskai, O.F.M., Christian Wiyghan Tumi, Jean Margéot.

1991 (June 28): Angelo Sodano, Pio Laghi, Edward I. Cassidy, Nicolás de Jesús López Rodriguez, José T. Sánchez, Virgilio Noè, Fiorenzo Angelini Roger Mahony, Anthony J. Bevilacqua, Giovanni Saldarini, Cahal Brendan Daly, Camillo Ruini, Ján Chryzostom Korec, S.J., Henri Schwery, Georg Sterzinsky.

1994 (Nov. 26): Nasrallah Pierre Sfeir, Miloslav Vlk, Luigi Poggi, Peter Seiichi Shirayanagi, Carlo Furno, Julius Riyadi Darmaatmadja, S.J., Jaime Lucas Ortega y Alamino, Gilberto Agustoni, Emmanuel Wamala, William Henry Keeler, Jean-Claude Turcotte, Ricardo Maria Carles Gordó, Adam Joseph Maida, Vinko Puljic, Armand Gaétan Razafindratandra, Paul Joseph Pham Dính Tung, Juan Sandoval Íñiguez, Kazimierz Swiàtek, Ersilio Tonino.

1998 (Feb. 21): Jorge Medina Estévez, Darío Castrillón Hoyos, Lorenzo Antonetti, James Francis Stafford, Salvatore de Giorgi, Serafim Fernandes de Araújo, Antonio Maria Rouco Varela, Aloysius Ambrozic, Dionigi Tettamanzi, Polycarp Pengo, Christoph Schönborn, O.P., Norberto Rivera Carrera, Francis George, O.M.I., Paul Shan Kuo-hsi, S.J., Giovanni Cheli, Marian Jaworski, Janis Pujats.

2001 (Feb. 21): Giovanni Battista Re, Agostino Cacciavillan, Sergio Sebastiani, Zenon Grocholewski, José Saraiva Martins, C.M.F., Crescenzio Sepe, Jorge María Mejía, Ignace Moussa I Daoud, Walter Kasper, Antonio Jose Gonzalez Zumarraga, Ivan Dias, Geraldo Majella Agnelo, Pedro Rubiano Sáenz, Theodore E. McCarrick, Desmond Connell, Audrys Juozas Backis, Francisco Javier Errázuriz

Ossa, Juan Julio Terrazas Sandoval, C.SS.R., Wilfrid Fox Napier, O.F.M., Oscar Andres Rodríguez Maradiaga, S.D.B., Bernard Agré, Luis Cipriani Thorne, Francisco Álvarez Martínez, Cláudio Hummes, Varkey Vithayathil, C.SS.R., Jorge Mario Bergoglio, S.J., José Da Cruz Policarpo, Severino Poletto, Cormac Murphy-O'Connor, Edward Michael Egan, Lubomyr Husar, Karl Lehmann, Stephanos II Ghattas, Jean Honoré, O.F.M., Roberto Tucci, S.J., Avery Dulles, S.J.

2003 (Oct. 21): Jean-Louis Tauran, Renato Martino, Francesco Marchisano, Julián Herranz, Javier Lozano Barragán, Attilio Nicora, Angelo Scola, Anthony Olubunmi Okogie, Bernard Panafieu, Gabriel Zubeir Wako, Carlos Amigo Vallejo, Justin Francis Rigali, Keith Michael O'Brien, Eusebio Oscar Scheid, Ennio Antonelli, Tarcisio Bertone, Peter Kodwo Appiah Turkson, Telesphore Placidus Toppo, George Pell, Josip Bozanic, Jean Baptiste Pham Minh Man, Rodolfo Quezada Toruño, Philippe Barbarin, Peter Erdö, Marc Ouellet, P.S.S., Georges Cottier, O.P., Stanislas Nagy, Thomas Spidlik, S.J.

Pope Benedict XVI

2006 (Mar. 24): William Levada, Franc Rodé, C.M., Agostino Vallini, Jorge Liberato Urosa Savino, Gaudencio Rosales, Jean-Pierre Ricard, Antonio Cañizares Llovera, Cheong Jin-Suk, Sean Patrick O'Malley, O.F.M. Cap., Stanislaw Dziwisz, Carlo Caffarra, Joseph Zen Ze-Kiun, S.D.B., Andrea Cordero Lanza di Montezemolo, Albert Vanhoye, S.J.

2007 (Nov. 24): Leonardo Sandri, John P. Foley, Giovanni Lajolo, Paul-Josef Cordes, Stanislaw Rylko, Angelo Comastri, Raffaele Farina SDB, Agustin Garcia-Gasco y Vicente, Seán Brady, Lluís Martínez Sistach, André Vingt-Trois, Angelo Bagnasco, Théodore-Adrien Sarr, Oswald Gracias, Francisco Lopez Ortega, Daniel Nicholas DiNardo, Odilo Scherer, John Njue, Emmanuel III Delly, Giovanni Coppa, Estanislao Esteban Karlic, Urbano Navarrete, S.J., Umberto Betti, O.F.M.

DISTRIBUTION OF CARDINALS

As of Aug. 17, 2008, there were 194 cardinals from 68 countries or areas. Listed below are areas, countries, number and last names. Names with asterisks are cardinals ineligible to vote.

Europe — 103

Italy (42): Angelini,* Antonelli, Antonetti,* Bagnasco, Bertone, Betti,* Biffi,* Cacciavillan,* Caffarra, Canestri,* Cé,* Cheli,* Comastri, Coppa,* Cordero Lanza di Montezemolo,* de Giorgi, Farina, Furno,* Giordano, Innocenti,* Laghi,* Lajolo, Marchisano, Martini,* Martino, Nicora, Noè,* Piovanelli,* Poggi,* Poletto, Re, Ruini, Saldarini,* Scola, Sebastiani, Sepe, Silvestrini,* Sodano,* Tettamanzi, Tonini,* Tucci,* Vallini.

Spain (10): Alvarez Martinez,* Cañizares Llovera, Carles Gordó,* Garcia-Gasco y Vicente, Herranz, Martínez Sistach, Martinez Somalo,* Navarrete,* RoucoVarela, Vallejo.

France (9): Barbarin, Etchegaray,* Honoré,* Panafieu, Poupard, Ricard, Tauran, Vanhoye,* Vingt-Trois.

Poland (8): Deskur,* Dziwisz, Glemp, Grocholewski, Gulbinowicz,* Macharski,* Nagy,* Rylko.

Germany (7): Cordes, Kasper, Lehmann, Mayer,* Meisner, Sterzinsky, Wetter.*

Ireland (3): Brady, Connell,* Daly.*

Switzerland (3): Agustoni,* Cottier,* Schwery.

Czech Republic (2): Spidlik,* Vlk.
Hungary (2): Erdö, Paskai.*
Portugal (2): Policarpo, Saraiva Martins
Slovakia (2): Korec,* Tomko.*
Ukraine (2): Husar, Jaworski.*
One from each of the following countries: Austria, Schönborn; Belarus, Swiatek*; Belgium, Danneels; Bosnia-Herzegovina, Puljic; England, Murphy-O'Connor; Latvia, Pujats; Lithuania, Backis; Netherlands, Simonis; Scotland, O'Brien; Slovenia, Rodé; Yugoslavia, Bozanic.

Asia — 21
India (6): Dias, Gracias, Lourdusamy,* Pimenta,* Toppo, Vithayathil.*
Philippines (3): Rosales, Sánchez,* Vidal.
Korea (2) Cheong Jin-Suk, Kim.*
Vietnam (2): Pham Dinh Tung*, Pham Minh Man.
One from each of the following countries: Hong Kong: Zen Ze-kiun, Indonesia, Darmaatmadja; Iraq, Delly*; Japan, Shirayanagi*; Lebanon, Sfeir,* Syria, Moussa I Daoud; Taiwan, Shan Kuo-hsi,* Thailand, Kitbunchu.

Oceania — 4
Australia (3): Cassidy,* Clancy,* Pell.
One from New Zealand, Williams

Africa — 16
Nigeria (2): Arinze, Okogie.
One from each of the following countries: Angola, do Nascimento*; Cameroon, Tumi; Egypt, Stephanos II Ghattas*; Ghana, Turkson; Ivory Coast, Agre*; Kenya, Njue; Madagascar, Razafindratandra*; Mauritius, Margeot*; Mozambique, Santos*; Senegal, Sarr; South Africa, Napier; Sudan, Wako; Tanzania, Pengo; Uganda, Wamala.*

North America – 25
United States (17): Baum,* Bevilacqua,* DiNardo, Dulles,* Egan, Foley, George, Keeler, Law, Levada, McCarrick, Mahony, Maida, O'Malley, Rigali, Stafford, Szoka.*
Mexico (4): Robles Ortega, Lozano Barragán, Rivera Carrera, Sandoval Iñiguez.
Canada (3): Ambrozic, Ouellet, Turcotte.
Puerto Rico (1): Aponte Martinez.*

Central and South America – 25
Brazil (8): Arns,* Falcão,* Fernandes de Araújo,* Hummes, Majella Agnelo, Sales,* Scheid, Scherer.
Argentina (4): Bergoglio, Karlic,* Mejia,* Sandri.
Chile (2): Errazuriz Ossa, Medina Estévez.*
Colombia (2): Castrillón Hoyos, Rubiano Saenz.
One each from the following countries: Bolivia, Sandoval; Cuba, Ortega y Alamino; Dominican Republic, Lopez Rodriguez; Ecuador, Gonzalez Zumarraga*; Guatemala, Quezada Toruño; Honduras, Rodriguez Maradiaga; Nicaragua, Obando Bravo*; Peru, Cipriani Thorne; Venezuela, Urosa Savino

Cardinal Electors
As of Aug. 24, 2008, there were 194 cardinals from 68 countries or areas.
There were 116 electors from 60 countries: 58 are from Europe, 20 from North America, 16 from South America, 9 from Africa, 11 from Asia and two from Oceania. Of the current cardinal electors, thirty were named by Benedict XVI and 86 by John Paul II.
Ineligible to Vote

As of Aug. 15, 2008, 78 of the 194 cardinals were ineligible to take part in a papal election in line with the apostolic letter *Ingravescentem Aetetem* effective Jan. 1, 1971, which limited the functions of cardinals after completion of their 80th year.
Cardinals affected are: Agré, Agustoni, Álvarez Martínez, Angelini, Antonetti, Aponte Martínez, Arns, Baum, Betti, Bevilacqua, Biffi, Cacciavillan, Canestri, Carles Gordó, Cassidy, Cé, Cheli, Clancy, Connell, Coppa, Cordero Lanza di Montezemolo, Cottier, Daly, Delly, Deskur, do Nascimento, Dulles, Etchegaray, Falcão, Fernandes de Araújo, Furno, Gonzalez Zumarraga, Gulbinowicz, Honoré, Innocenti, Jaworski, Karlic, Kim Sou-hwan, Korec, Laghi, Lourdusamy, Macharski, Margéot, Martinez Somalo, Martini, Mayer, Medina Estévez, Mejia, Nagy, Navarrete, Noè, Obando Bravo, Paskai, Pham Dinh Tung, Pimenta, Piovanelli, Poggi, Razafindratandra, Saldarini, Sales, Sánchez, Santos, Sfeir, Shan Kuo-hsi, Shirayanagi, Silvestrini, Sodano, Spidlik, Stephanos II Ghattas, Swiatek, Szoka, Tomko, Tonini, Tucci, Vanhoye, Vithayathil, Wamala, Wetter.
Cardinals who complete their 80th year in 2009 and who become ineligible to vote: Kitbunchu, Marchisano, Castrillón Hoyos, Glemp.

Cardinals of the United States
As of Aug. 15, 2008, the following cardinals were in service, according to their years of elevation (for biographies, *see* **College of Cardinals** *above*):
1976: **William W. Baum** (major penitentiary emeritus); 1985: **Bernard F. Law** (abp. emeritus of Boston); 1988: **Edmund C. Szoka** (governor emeritus of the Vatican City State); 1991: **Roger M. Mahony** (abp. of Los Angeles), **Anthony M. Bevilacqua** (abp. emeritus of Philadelphia); 1994: **William H. Keeler** (abp. emeritus of Baltimore); **Adam J. Maida** (abp. of Detroit); 1998: **Francis E. George, O.M.I.** (abp. of Chicago), **James F. Stafford** (Major Penitentiary of the Apostolic Penitentiary); 2001: **Edward M. Egan** (abp. of New York), **Theodore E. McCarrick** (abp. emeritus of Washington), **Avery Dulles, S.J.** (theologian); 2003: **Justin F. Rigali** (abp. of Philadelphia); 2006: **William J. Levada** (prefect of the Congregation for the Doctrine of the Faith), **Sean P. O'Malley, O.F.M. Cap.** (abp. of Boston). 2007: **John P. Foley** (Grand Master of the Knights of the Holy Sepulchre); **Daniel N. DiNardo** (abp. of Galveston-Houston). **Cardinal Lubomyr Husar, M.S.U.**, major abp. of Lviv for Ukrainians, is also an American citizen.
U.S. Cardinals of the Past (according to year of elevation; for biographical data, see **American Catholics of the Past** at www.catholicalmanac.com):
1875: John McCloskey; 1886: James Gibbons; 1911: John Farley, William O'Connell; 1921: Dennis Dougherty; 1924: Patrick Hayes, George Mundelein; 1946: John Glennon, Edward Mooney, Francis Spellman, Samuel Stritch; 1953: James F. McIntyre; 1958: John O'Hara, C.S.C., Richard Cushing; 1959: Albert Meyer, Aloysius Muench; 1961: Joseph Ritter; 1965: Lawrence J. Shehan; 1967: Francis Brennan, John P. Cody, Patrick A. O'Boyle, John J. Krol; 1969: John J. Wright, Terence J. Cooke, John F. Dearden, John J. Carberry; 1973: Humberto S. Medeiros, Timothy Manning; 1983: Joseph L. Bernardin; 1985: John J. O'Connor; 1988: James A. Hickey. (Myroslav Lubachivsky, major abp. of Lviv of the Ukrainians

(Ukraine), was made a cardinal in 1985. He was a citizen of the United States and metropolitan of the Philadelphia Ukrainian Rite Archeparchy, from 1979-81.)

Prelates who became cardinals after returning to their native countries: John Lefebvre de Chevrus, first bp. of Boston (1808-23) and apostolic administrator of New York (1810-15), elevated to the cardinalate, 1836, in France. Ignatius Persico, O.F.M. Cap., bp. of Savannah (1870-72), elevated to the cardinalate, 1893, in Italy; Diomede Falconio, O.F.M. ord. a priest in Buffalo, NY, missionary in U.S., apostolic delegate to the U.S. (1902-11), elevated to cardinal, 1911, in Italy.

ELECTING THE POPE: THE CONCLAVE

One of the primary duties of the Cardinals of the Catholic Church is the election of the Bishop of Rome who becomes thereby the Supreme Pontiff of the Church. The election is held in what is termed the conclave. The name is derived from the Latin cum (with) and clavis (key), and implies the fact that the cardinals are locked together in a room until a new pontiff has been chosen. This form of papal election began in 1274 and is considered the third period in the historical evolution of choosing the successor to St. Peter. Central to the full understanding of the conclave is the firm belief that the entire process of election is guided by the Holy Spirit.

In the early Church, new Bishops of Rome were chosen in the manner customarily used in the other dioceses, that is, the clergy, with the people of the diocese, elected or chose the new bishop in the presence of the other bishops in the province. This was a simple method, but it became impractical as the Christian population grew in size and there arose rival claimants and hostility between the upper classes (the patricians) and the lower classes (the plebeians), each of whom had their own candidates. This situation created considerable upheaval in Rome as demonstrated by the riots accompanying the contested elections of Pope St. Damasus I (366-384) and the antipope Ursinus in 366. Such was the violence that the prefect of the city was called in to restore order.

On the basis of these disturbances, the Roman emperors began to involve themselves in the elections by guaranteeing proper procedure and ensuring free voting by the clergy in cases where two claimants had emerged. This intervention launched a long period of secular interference that would continue, to various degrees, until 1903. The so-called barbarian kings often supervised elections until the sixth century when the Byzantines reconquered Italy. The emperors not only demanded tribute from the popes but also retained the right of confirmation, a practice that routinely created long delays, as word would have to be sent to Constantinople (later Ravenna) to request approval. The last pope to seek confirmation from imperial authorities was Gregory III in 731. After this time, the popes sought the protection of the Franks, and in 769, Pope Stephen III convened a synod at Rome that confirmed the decree of 502 (under Symmachus) that laypeople should no longer vote for the popes and that only higher clerics should be considered eligible.

A major reform was achieved in 1059 when Pope Nicholas II decreed that the cardinal bishops should choose the popes, a procedure modified by the Third Lateran Council (1179), which declared an end to distinctions among the three orders of cardinals in terms of voting, and requiring that a candidate receive a two-thirds majority.

The new need of a majority complicated many elections as a two-thirds plurality would often be quite difficult to reach owing to competing international interests among the cardinals. After the death of Pope Clement IV in 1268, for example, three years passed until the 18 cardinals gathered at Viterbo could agree on Pope Gregory X (r. 1271-1276). Gregory introduced changes through the Second Council of Lyons (1272) to speed up elections, inaugurating the system of the conclave. It remained essentially unchanged until 1975. In that year, Pope Paul VI issued the apostolic constitution *Romano Pontifici Eligendo* (Oct. 1) that stipulated various requirements for the conclave. Among these were: only cardinals may be electors; their number is limited to 120, with each cardinal allowed to bring two or three assistants; while not essential for validity, it is the recognized form of election; three forms are acceptable: acclamation (acclamatio); compromise (by which certain cardinals are named delegates and are given power to act on behalf of the others); and balloting; if the person chosen is not a bishop, he is to be ordained to the episcopacy immediately (if a bishop, he is pope at once); secrecy is to be carefully observed; all ecumenical councils are immediately adjourned; and, if no one is elected after three days, one day is to be spent in prayer and meditation.

New legislation regarding papal elections and church government during a vacancy of the Holy See was promulgated by Pope John Paul II on Feb. 23, 1996, in the apostolic constitution *Universi Dominici Gregis* ("Shepherd of the Lord's Whole Flock"). Among the changes that were introduced was the call for heightened security in preventing electronic surveillance and the provision that after a set number of unsuccessful ballots, the cardinals may elect the new pope by a simple majority vote. The constitution was used in the conclave of 2005 that elected Cardinal Joseph Ratzinger as Pope Benedict XVI. On June 26, 2007, Pope Benedict issued a *motu prorio*, written in Latin, with which he restored the traditional norm of a majority of two thirds of the cardinals present.

The last election not held in the Vatican (the Sistine Chapel) was in 1846 (Pius IX), which took place at the Quirinal Palace. The last pope not a cardinal at the time of his election was Urban VI (1378-1389); the last by compromise was John XXII (r. 1316-1334); and the last by acclamation was Gregory XV (1621-1623).

The Universal Church

THE CHURCH IN COUNTRIES THROUGHOUT THE WORLD

(Principal sources for statistics: *Annuarium Statisticum Ecclesiae*, Statistical Yearbook of the Church, 2006 — the most recent edition; *Annuario Pontificio*, 2008; and Agenzia Internazionale FIDES. Figures are as of Jan. 1, 2007, except for cardinals [as of Aug. 30, 2008] and others which are indicated. For 2008 developments, see **Index** entries for individual countries.)

An asterisk indicates that the country has full diplomatic relations with the Holy See (see **Diplomats to the Holy See** in the **Holy See** section).

Abbreviations (in order in which they appear): archd. – archdiocese; dioc. – diocese; ap. ex. – apostolic exarchate; prel. – prelature; abb. – abbacy; v.a. – apostolic vicariate; p.a. – apostolic prefecture; a.a. – apostolic administration; mil. ord. – military ordinariate; card. – cardinal; abp. – archbishops; bp. – bishops (diocesan and titular); priests (dioc. – diocesan or secular priests; rel. – those belonging to religious orders); p.d. – permanent deacons; sem. – major seminarians, diocesan and religious; bros. – brothers; srs. – sisters; bap. – baptisms; Caths. – Catholic population; tot. pop. – total population; (AD) – apostolic delegate (see **Index**: **Papal Representatives**).

Afghanistan

Republic in south-central Asia; capital, Kabul. Christianity antedated Muslim conquest in the seventh century but was overcome by it. All inhabitants are subject to the law of Islam. Under Afghan's Taliban regime, religious freedom was severely restricted, and proselytizing was forbidden. In January 2002, Italian and English chaplains celebrated the first public Mass in nearly 10 years in Kabul, at the Italian Embassy.

Albania*

Archd., 2; dioc., 3; a.a., 1; abp., 3; bp., 6; parishes, 130; priests, 141 (51 dioc., 90 rel.); p.d.,1; sem., 25; bros., 18; srs., 422; bap., 3,514; Caths., 513,000 (16.1%); tot. pop., 3,170,000.

Republic in the Balkans, bordering the Adriatic Sea; capital, Tirana. Christianity was introduced in apostolic times. The northern part of the country remained faithful to Rome while the South broke from unity following the schism of 1054. A large percentage of the population became Muslim following the invasion (15th century) and long centuries of occupation by the Ottoman Turks. Many Catholics fled to southern Italy, Sicily and Greece. In 1945, at the time of the communist takeover, an estimated 68 percent of the population was Muslim; 19 percent was Orthodox and 13 percent Roman Catholic. The Catholic Church prevailed in the north. During 45 years of communist dictatorship, the Church fell victim, as did all religions, to systematic persecution.

In 1967, the government, declaring it had eliminated all religion in the country, proclaimed itself the first atheist state in the world. The right to practice religion was restored in late 1990. In March 1991, a delegation from the Vatican was allowed to go to Albania; later in the year diplomatic relations were established with the Holy See at the request of the Albanian prime minister. Pope John Paul II made a one-day visit to the country Apr. 25, 1993, during which he ordained four bishops appointed by him in December 1992 to fill long-vacant sees. The first Albanian cardinal was named in November 1994. Albanians welcomed hundreds of thousands of ethnic Albanians from Kosovo during Yugoslav persecution in 1999.

Algeria*

Archd., 1; dioc., 3; abp., 2; bp., 3; parishes, 40; priests, 94 (37 dioc., 57 rel.); p.d., 3; sem., 6; bros., 25; srs., 179; bap., 13; Caths., 5,000 (.01%); tot. pop., 33,450,000.

Republic in northwest Africa; capital, Algiers. Christianity, introduced at an early date, succumbed to Vandal devastation in the fifth century and Muslim conquest in 709, but survived in small communities into the 12th century. Missionary work was unsuccessful except in service to traders, military personnel and captives along the coast. Church organization was established after the French gained control of the territory in the 1830s. A large number of Catholics were among the estimated million Europeans who left the country after it secured independence from France July 5, 1962. Islam is the state religion. Armed Islamic militants and guerrillas have caused terror and unrest in Algeria since 1992. Among the more than 80,000 people killed were seven Trappist monks and the Catholic bishop of Oran, all in 1996.

Andorra*

Parishes, 7; priests, 18 (12 dioc., 6 rel.); srs., 10; bap., 367; Caths., 77,000 (99%); tot. pop., 78,000.

Parliamentary state (1993) in the Pyrenees; capital, Andorra la Vella. From 1278-1993, it was a co-principality under the rule of the French head of state and the bishop of Urgel, Spain, who retain their titles. Christianity was introduced at an early date. Catholicism is the state religion. Ecclesiastical jurisdiction is under the Spanish Diocese of Urgel. The constitution calls for freedom of religion, but also guarantees "the Roman Catholic Church free and public exercise of its activities and the preservation of the relations of special cooperation with the state."

Angola*

Archd., 3; dioc., 15; card., 1; abp., 5; bp., 19; parishes, 283;

priests, 749 (410 dioc., 339 rel.); sem., 1,261; bros., 157; srs., 2,204; catechists, 26,341; bap., 204,426; Caths., 8,334,000 (55.6%); tot. pop., 14,993,000.

Republic in southwest Africa; capital, Luanda. Evangelization by Catholic missionaries from Portugal, dating from 1491, reached high points in the 17th and 18th centuries. Independence from Portugal in 1975 and the long civil war that followed (peace accord signed in 1991) left the Church with a heavy loss of personnel resulting from the departure of about half the foreign missionaries and the persecution and martyrdom experienced by the Church during the war. Renewed fighting following elections in late 1992 brought repeated appeals for peace from the nation's bishops and religious in 1993 and 1994.

Despite another peace accord signed by the rebels and the government in late 1994, conditions have remained unsettled. One effect of the fighting was to cut off Church leaders from large groups of the faithful. In an attempt to encourage peace efforts, the Vatican established diplomatic relations with Angola in 1997. Attacks on Church workers, however, continued in 1998 and 1999. In 2000, Church leaders began an active peace movement, holding national and diocesan congresses and beginning a consultation with Angolan political leaders. Government and rebel representatives signed a peace agreement in 2002, after the government killed rebel leader Jonas Savimbi, and the Church offered humanitarian aid and helped to rebuild the country.

Antigua and Barbuda*

Dioc., 1; bp., 1; parishes, 2; priests, 10 (5 dioc., 5 rel.); p.d, 5; sem., 1; srs., 9; bap., 77; Caths., 8,000 (12.5%); tot. pop., 64,000.

Independent (1981) Caribbean island nation; capital, St. John's, Antigua. The Diocese of St. John's-Basseterre includes Antigua and Barbuda, St. Kitts and Nevis, Anguilla, the British Virgin Islands and Montserrat.

Argentina*

Archd., 14; dioc., 50; prel., 3; ap. ex., 3 (for Armenians of Latin America); mil. ord., 1; card., 1; abp., 22; bp., 84; parishes, 2,666; priests, 5,869 (3,859 dioc., 2,010 rel.); p.d., 730; sem., 1,778; bros., 790; srs., 8,687; bap., 549,278; catechists, 92,848; Caths., 35,972,000 (92%); tot. pop., 38,970,000

Republic in southeast South America, bordering on the Atlantic; capital, Buenos Aires. Priests were with the Magellan exploration party and the first Mass in the country was celebrated Apr. 1, 1519. Missionary work began in the 1530s, diocesan organization in the late 1540s, and effective evangelization about 1570. Independence from Spain was proclaimed in 1816. Since its establishment in the country, the Church has been influenced by Spanish cultural and institutional forces, antagonistic liberalism, government interference and opposition; the latter reached a climax during the last five years of the first presidency of Juan Peron (1946-55). Widespread human rights violations, including the disappearance of thousands of people, marked the "Dirty War," the period of military rule from 1976 to December 1983, when an elected civilian government took over. In 1996 the Argentine bishops said they did not do enough to stop human rights violations during the "Dirty War." In the late 1990s, the bishops spoke out against government corruption have worked to find solutions to the country's crises.

Armenia*

Ord., 1 (for Catholic Armenians of Eastern Europe, with seat in Armenia); parishes, 15; abp., 2; priests, 7 (3 dioc., 4 rel.); sem., 10; bros., 1; srs., 21; bap., 573; Caths., 150,000 (4%); tot. pop., 3,220,000.

Republic in Asia Minor; capital Yerevan. Part of the USSR from 1920 until it declared its sovereignty in September 1991. Ancient Armenia, which also included territory annexed by Turkey in 1920, was Christianized in the fourth century. Diplomatic relations were established with the Holy See on May 23, 1992. Pope John Paul II visited Armenia in late September 2001 to help mark the 1,700th anniversary of Christianity in the nation. The small Catholic community in Armenia has good relations with the predominant Armenian Apostolic Church, an Oriental Orthodox Church.

Australia*

Archd., 7; dioc., 24; mil. ord., 1; card., 3; abp., 11; bp., 51; parishes, 1,390; priests, 3,125 (1,883 dioc., 1,242 rel.); p.d., 85; sem., 244; bros., 1,002; srs., 6,948; catechists, 8,192; bap., 68,272; Caths., 5,704,000 (27.5%); tot. pop. 20,700,000.

Commonwealth; island continent southeast of Asia; capital, Canberra. The first Catholics in the country were Irish under penal sentence, 1795-1804; the first public Mass was celebrated May 15, 1803. Official organization of the Church dates from 1820. The country was officially removed from mission status in March 1976.

As the 20th century neared its end, the Church in Australia was rocked by allegations of sexual abuse from previous decades. In 1996 the Australian bishops published a plan for dealing with such cases. In 1998 the bishops also apologized to aboriginal children, saying their support of harsh government policy in the 1970s.

In an unusual move, in mid-November 1998, just before the Synod of Bishops for Oceania at the Vatican and after the Australian bishops' "ad limina" visits, Vatican officials met with Church leaders from Australia to discuss doctrinal and pastoral issues. In December 1998, the Vatican and representatives of Australian Church leaders signed a document, later endorsed by the Australian bishops' conference, that spoke of a "crisis of faith" in the Catholic Church on the continent. The Australian Church, like many others in the late 20th and early 21st century, struggled with cases of clergy sexual abuse.

Austria*

Archd., 2; dioc., 7; abb., 1; ord., 1; mil. ord., 1; card., 2; abp., 5; bp., 20; parishes, 3,072; priests, 4,314 (2,646 dioc., 1,668 rel.); p.d., 542; sem., 300; bros., 487; srs., 4,888; catechists, 1,610; bap., 57,003; Caths., 6,027,000 (73%); tot. pop., 8,290,000.

Republic in central Europe; capital, Vienna. Christianity was introduced by the end of the third century, strengthened considerably by conversion of the Bavarians from about 600, and firmly established in the second half of the eighth century. Catholicism survived and grew stronger as the principal religion in the country in the post-Reformation period, but suffered from Josephinism in the 18th century. Although liberated from much government harassment in the aftermath of the Revolution of 1848, the Church came under pressure again some 20 years later in the Kulturkampf. The Church faced strong opposition from Socialists after World War I and suffered persecution from 1938 to 1945 during the Nazi regime. Some Church-state matters are regulated by a concordat originally concluded in 1934.

At the turn of the century, the Church in Austria was beset by internal difficulties, including a seminary pornography scandal and the launch of a global movement seeking more lay participation in Church decision-making and changes in Church policy on ordination of women and priestly celibacy. In 1995, Cardinal Hans Hermann Gröer resigned as archbishop of Vienna amid charges of sexual misconduct. His successor, Cardinal Christoph Schönborn, worked to restore a sense of unity to the Church.

Azerbaijan*

Independent republic (1991) on the Caspian Sea; formerly part of the USSR; capital, Baku. Islam is the prevailing religion. Soviet rulers destroyed Baku's one Catholic church in the late 1930s; in the 21st century, the church was rebuilt and was dedicated in 2007. A small Catholic community of Polish and Armenian origin near the capital is ministered to by two missionaries. Latin-rite Catholics are under the apostolic administration of Caucasus (seat in Georgia), established in December 1993.

Bahamas*

Dioc., 1; bp., 1; parishes, 30; priests, 26 (13 dioc., 13 rel.); p.d., 14; sem., 5; srs., 15; catechists, 235; bap., 392; Caths., 49,000 (15%); tot. pop., 333,000.

Independent (July 10, 1973) island group consisting of some 700 (30 inhabited) small islands southeast of Florida and north of Cuba; capital, Nassau. On Oct. 12, 1492, Columbus landed on one of these islands, where the first Mass was celebrated in the New World. Organization of the Catholic Church in the Bahamas dates from about the middle of the 19th century. The Church was under the jurisdiction on the Archdiocese of New York until 1960, when Nassau became a diocese. From 1891 to 1981, Benedictines from St. John's Abbey in Collegeville, Minn., were responsible for episcopal leadership. After that time, Benedictine priests and brothers continued working in the Bahamas until 2005; local Benedictine nuns continue their work there. Nassau became an archdiocese in 1999.

Bahrain*

Parish, 1; priests, 4 (rel.); srs., 19; bap., 162; Caths., 41,000 (4.3%); tot. pop., 757,000. (AD)

Island state in Persian Gulf; capital, Manama. Population is Muslim; Catholics are foreign workers, under ecclesiastical jurisdiction of Arabia apostolic vicariate. Diplomatic relations were established between Bahrain and the Holy See in January 2000.

Bangladesh*

Archd., 1; dioc., 5; abp., 3; bp., 8; parishes, 81; priests, 316 (167 dioc., 149 rel.); sem., 120; bros., 92 srs., 1,092; catechists, 1,814; bap., 6,936; Caths., 312,000 (.20%); tot. pop. 140,526,000.

Formerly the eastern portion of Pakistan. Officially constituted as a separate nation Dec. 16, 1971; capital, Dhaka. Jesuit, Dominican and Augustinian missionaries were in the area in the 16th century. An apostolic vicariate (of Bengali) was established in 1834; the hierarchy was erected in 1950. Islam, the principal religion, was declared the state religion in 1988; freedom of religion is granted. Church-run humanitarian and development agencies have been instrumental in responding to natural disasters, such as flooding. The bishops have emphasized inculturation and Church social doctrine.

Barbados*

Dioc., 1; bp., 2; parishes, 6; priests, 9 (5 dioc., 4 rel.); p.d., 1; srs., 11; bap., 144; sem., 1; Caths., 10,000 (3.6%); tot. pop., 274,000.

Parliamentary democracy (independent since 1966), easternmost of the Caribbean islands; capital, Bridgetown. About 70 percent of the population are Anglican.

Belarus*

Archd., 1; dioc., 3; card., 1; abp., 1; bp., 4; parishes, 612; priests, 435 (269 dioc., 166 rel.); sem., 153; bros., 9; srs., 352; bap., 6,933; Caths., 1,405,000 (10%); tot. pop., 10,268,000.

Independent republic (1991) in eastern Europe; former Soviet republic (Byelorussia); capital, Minsk. Slow recovery of the Church was reported after years of repression in the Soviet Union, although in the mid-1990s under the authoritarian rule of President Alexander Lukashenka, the Church encountered tensions, especially in refusal of permits for foreign religious workers. In December 2000, the nation's bishops asked forgiveness for the "human weaknesses" of Church members throughout the centuries and said the Church forgave acts of Soviet-era persecution. In October 2002, Belarus adopted one of the most restrictive religion laws in the former Soviet Union, but by April 2003 government officials had granted the Catholic Church full legal status.

Belgium*

Archd., l; dioc., 7; mil. ord., 1; card., 1; abp., 3; bp., 18; parishes, 3,924; priests, 6,780 (4,016 dioc., 2,764 rel.); p.d., 574; sem., 204; bros., 924; srs., 12,369; catechists, 7,306; bap., 73,694; Caths., 7,705,000 (73%); tot. pop., 10,540,000.

Constitutional monarchy in northwestern Europe; capital, Brussels. Christianity was introduced about the first quarter of the fourth century and major evangelization was completed about 730. During the rest of the medieval period the Church had firm diocesan and parochial organization, generally vigorous monastic life and influential monastic and cathedral schools. Lutherans and Calvinists made some gains during the Reformation period but there was a strong Catholic restoration in the first half of the 17th century, when the country was under Spanish rule. Jansenism disturbed the Church from about 1640 into the 18th century. Josephinism, imposed by an Austrian regime, hampered the Church late in the same century. Repressive and persecutory measures were enforced during the Napoleonic conquest. Freedom came with separation of Church and state in the wake of the Revolution of 1830, which ended the reign of William I. Thereafter, the Church encountered serious problems with philosophical liberalism and political socialism.

Catholics have long been engaged in strong educational, social and political movements. In 1990, in an unprecedented political maneuver, King Baudouin temporarily gave up his throne, saying his Catholic conscience would not allow him to sign a law legalizing abortion. In the mid- and late-1990s, Church leaders expressed concern that Belgians dissented from Church teachings. Therapeutic in vitro fertilization for stable married couples continued at a leading Belgian Catholic hospital despite Vatican objections. The bishops fought a losing battle against the 2002 legalization of euthanasia.

Belize*

Dioc., 1; bp., 2; parishes, 18; priests, 31 (12 dioc., 19 rel.); sem., 2; bros., 5; srs., 63 catechists, 534; bap., 2,501; Caths., 222,000 (76%); tot. pop., 293,000.

Independent (Sept. 21, 1981) republic on eastern coast of Central America; capital, Belmopan. Its history has points in common with Guatemala, where evangelization began in the 16th century. The Church in Belize worked with refugees during the decades of Central American civil wars.

Benin*

Archd., 2; dioc., 8; card., 1; abp., 4; bp., 9; parishes, 247; priests, 643 (506 dioc., 137 rel.); sem., 535; bros., 131; srs., 1,169; catechists, 12,817; bap., 43,060; Caths., 2,038,000 (27%); tot. pop., 7,650,000.

Democratic republic in West Africa, bordering on the Atlantic; capital, Porto Novo. Missionary work was very limited from the 16th to the 18th centuries. Effective evangelization dates from 1861. The hierarchy was established in 1955. In the 1970s, Benin's Marxist-Leninist government nationalized Catholic schools, expelled foreign missionaries and jailed some priests. After the government dropped the one-party system in 1989, Archbishop Isidore de Souza of Cotonou presided over the 1990 national conference that drew up a new constitution and prepared the way for elections. One challenge facing the Church as it entered the 21st century was maintaining peace with people of other faiths.

Bermuda

Dioc., 1; bp., 1; parishes, 7; priests, 8 (1 dioc., 7 rel.); sem., 7; srs., 2; bap., 114; Caths., 9,000 (16%); tot. pop., 67,000. (AD)

British dependency, consisting of 360 islands (20 of them inhabited), nearly 600 miles east of Cape Hatteras; capital, Hamilton. Catholics were not permitted until about 1800. Occasional pastoral care was provided the few Catholics there by visiting priests during the 19th century. Early in the 1900s priests from Nova Scotia began serving the area. An apostolic prefecture was set up in 1953. The first bishop assumed jurisdiction in 1956, when it was made an apostolic vicariate; diocese established, 1967.

Bhutan

Parish; bap., 1; Caths., 1,000 (approx.); tot. pop., 2,451,000.

Kingdom in the Himalayas, northeast of India; capital, Thimphu. Buddhism is the state religion; Christians, including Catholics, are free to worship in private homes but cannot erect religious buildings, proselytize or congregate in public. Jesuits (1963) and Salesians (1965) were invited to the country to direct schools. Salesians were expelled in February 1982, on disputed charges of proselytism. The only Catholic missionary allowed to stay in the country was Canadian Jesuit Father William Mackey, who served Catholics there from 1963 until his death in 1995. Ecclesiastical jurisdiction is under the Darjeeling (India) Diocese, which ordained the first indigenous Bhutanese priest in 1995.

Bolivia*

Archd., 4; dioc., 6; prel., 2; mil. ord., 1; v.a., 5; card., 1; abp., 6; bp., 30; parishes, 605; priests, 1,235 (548 dioc., 687 rel.); p.d., 74; sem., 712; bros., 229; srs., 2,696; catechists, 13,885; bap., 148,688; Caths., 8,019,000 (83%); tot. pop., 9,630,000.

Republic in central South America; capital, Sucre;

seat of government, La Paz. Catholicism, the official religion, was introduced in the 1530s, and the first diocese was established in 1552. Effective evangelization among the Indians, slow to start, reached high points in the middle of the 18th and the beginning of the 19th centuries and was resumed about 1840. Independence from Spain was proclaimed in 1825, at the end of a campaign that started in 1809. Church-state relations are regulated by a 1951 concordat with the Holy See. Catholics have worked against social poverty and corruption. Early in the 21st century, amid social and economic turmoil, surveys showed the Catholic Church was seen as the most credible institution in the country.

Bosnia and Herzegovina*

Archd., 1; dioc., 2; card., 1; abp., 2; bp., 3; parishes, 288; priests, 620 (271 dioc., 349 rel.); sem., 125; bros., 18; srs., 549; bap., 5,230; Caths., 468,000 (12%); tot. pop., 3,860,000.

Independent republic (1992) in southeastern Europe; formerly part of Yugoslavia; capital, Sarajevo. During the three years of fighting that erupted after Bosnia-Herzegovina declared its independence, some 450,000 Catholics were driven from their homes; many fled to Croatia or southern Bosnia. Sarajevo Cardinal Vinko Puljic, named a cardinal in 1994, has led the bishops in calls for the safe return of all refugees from the war and acknowledged that in some areas Croatian Catholics were responsible for atrocities. Although the bishops worked to rebuild the Church, they said ethnic discrimination and violence still plagued the nation more than a decade after the war ended.

Botswana

Dioc., 1; v.a., 1; bp., 2; parishes, 38; priests, 67 (27 dioc., 40 rel.); p.d., 5; sem., 20; bros., 5; srs., 77; catechists, 399; bap., 912; Caths., 85,000 (4.5%); tot. pop., 1,881,000.

Republic (independent since 1966) in southern Africa; capital, Gaborone. The first Catholic mission was opened in 1928 near Gaborone; earlier attempts at evangelization dating from 1879 were unsuccessful. The Church in Botswana gave strong support to tens of thousands of South African refugees from apartheid. As Botswana's diamond industry grew, Church leaders worked to minimize the effects of social changes such as pockets of unemployment and competition for jobs.

Brazil*

Archd., 41; dioc., 212; prel., 13; abb., 1; exarch., 1; mil. ord., 1; card., 8; abp., 66; bp., 354; parishes, 9,685; priests, 18,539 (11,220 dioc., 7,319 rel.); p.d., 1,845; sem., 9,369; bros., 2,715; srs., 33,221; catechists, 491,026; bap., 1,859,828; Caths., 157,816,000 (84%); tot. pop., 186,770,000.

Federal republic in northeastern South America; capital, Brasilia. One of several priests with the discovery party celebrated the first Mass in the country Apr. 26, 1500. Evangelization began some years later, and the first diocese was erected in 1551. During the colonial period, which lasted until 1822, evangelization made some notable progress — especially in the Amazon region between 1680 and 1750 — but was seriously hindered by government policy and the attitude of colonists regarding Amazon Indians the missionaries tried to protect from exploitation and slavery. The Jesuits were suppressed in 1782 and other missionaries expelled as

well. Liberal anti-Church influence grew in strength. The
government exercised maximum control over the Church.
After the proclamation of independence from Portugal in
1822 and throughout the regency, government control was
tightened and the Church suffered greatly from dissident
actions of ecclesiastical brotherhoods, Masonic anticlericalism and general decline in religious life. Church and state
were separated by the constitution of 1891, proclaimed two
years after the end of the empire.

The Church carried into the 20th century problems associated with increasingly difficult political, economic and social
conditions affecting the majority of the population. Many
Afro-Brazilians indiscriminately mixed African-based rites
such as candomble with Catholic rituals. In the second half of
the 20th century, the bishops became known for their liberal
stances on social and some theological issues. In the 1980s,
Vatican officials had a series of meetings with Brazilian bishops to discuss liberation theology and other issues. The
Brazilian bishops' conference took the lead in advocating for
land reform in the country. Members of the Church's Pastoral
Land Commission often faced threats, harassment and murder. The Church-founded Indigenous Missionary Council
worked for the rights of the country's Indians.

Brunei

P.a., 1; parishes, 3; priests, 4 (3 dioc., 1 rel); sem., 1; srs. 2;
bap., 218; Caths., 2,200 (0.6%); tot. pop., 361,000.

Independent state (1984) on the northern coast of Borneo;
formal name, Brunei Darussalam; capital, Bandar Seri
Begawan. Islam is the official religion; other religions are
allowed with some restrictions. Most of the Catholics are
technicians and skilled workers from other countries who are
not permanent residents; under ecclesiastical jurisdiction of
Miri Diocese, Malaysia.

Bulgaria*

Dioc., 2; ap. ex., 1; abp., 1; bp., 3; parishes, 57; priests, 59
(20 dioc., 39 rel.); sem., 7; bros., 7; srs., 89; bap., 339; Caths.,
73,000 (1%); tot. pop., 7,680,000.

Republic in southeastern Europe on the eastern part of the
Balkan peninsula; capital, Sofia. Most of the population is
Orthodox. Christianity was introduced before 343 but disappeared with the migration of Slavs into the territory. The baptism of Boris I about 865 ushered in a new period of
Christianity, which soon became involved in switches of loyalty between Constantinople and Rome. Through it all the
Byzantine, and later Orthodox, element remained stronger
and survived under the rule of Ottoman Turks into the 19th
century.

In 1947 the constitution of the new republic decreed the
separation of Church and state. Catholic schools and institutions were abolished and foreign religious banished in 1948.
A year later the apostolic delegate was expelled. Ivan
Romanoff, vicar general of Plovdiv, died in prison in 1952.
Bishop Eugene Bossilkoff, imprisoned in 1948, was sentenced to death in 1952; his fate remained unknown until
1975, when the Bulgarian government informed the Vatican
that he had died in prison shortly after being sentenced. He
was beatified in 1998. Although Church leaders were permitted to attend the Second Vatican Council, all Church activity
was under surveillance and/or control by the government,
which professed to be atheistic. Pastoral and related activities
were strictly limited. There was some improvement in
Bulgarian-Vatican relations in 1975. In 1979, the Sofia-
Plovdiv apostolic vicariate was raised to a diocese, and a
bishop was appointed for the vacant see of Nicopoli.

Diplomatic relations with the Holy See were established in
1990. In the late 1990s, the government instituted religion
classes in state schools, but Church leaders had no input into
the curriculum and that teachers were mostly Orthodox. In
2002, Pope John Paul II visited Bulgaria.

Burkina Faso*

Archd., 3; dioc., 10; abps., 2; bp., 16; parishes, 152;
priests, 755 (592 dioc., 163 rel.); sem., 430; bros., 245;
srs., 1,405; catechists, 11,042; bap., 67,295; Caths.,
1,734,000 (11.8%); tot. pop., 14,126,000.

Republic inland in West Africa; capital, Ouagadougou.
Missionaries of Africa started the first missions in 1900 and
1901. Their sisters began work in 1911. A minor and a major
seminary were established in 1926 and 1942, respectively.
The hierarchy was established in 1955. The first indigenous
bishop in modern times from West Africa was ordained in
1956 and the first cardinal created in 1965. In 1980 and 1990,
Pope John Paul II's visits to the country were used to launch
appeals for an end to desertification of sub-Saharan Africa
and an end to poverty in the region. In later years, the pope
encouraged increased evangelization and interreligious harmony.

Burma (See Myanmar)

Burundi*

Archd., 2; dioc., 5; abp., 3; bp., 6; parishes, 138;
priests, 523 (441 dioc., 82 rel.); sem., 467; bros., 166;
srs., 1,230; catechists, 4,374; bap., 176,310; Caths.,
5,078,000 (67%); tot. pop., 7,546,000.

Republic (1966), near the equator in east-central Africa;
capital, Bujumbura. The first permanent Catholic mission
station was established late in the 19th century. Large numbers were received into the Church following the ordination
of the first Burundian priests in 1925. The first indigenous
bishop was appointed in 1959.

In 1972-73, the country was torn by tribal warfare between
the Tutsis, the ruling minority, and the Hutus. In 1979, the
government began expelling foreign missionaries, and in
1986, seminaries were nationalized. A gradual resumption of
Church activity since 1987 has been hampered by continuing
ethnic violence, which began in 1993 and left more than
150,000 Burundians dead. The bishops repeatedly have
called for peace and for an end to sanctions imposed by the
Organization of African Unity in 1996. Missionaries continued to be the target of violent attacks, and the papal nuncio
was killed after being shot in an ambush in 2003.

Cambodia*

V.a., 1; p.a., 2; bp., 2; parishes, 40 (there were also 18
mission stations without resident priests); priests, 76
(33 dioc., 43 rel.); sem., 9; bros., 12; srs., 91; catechists, 234; baptisms, 639; Caths., 24,000 (.16%); tot.
pop., 14,287,000.

Republic in Southeast Asia; capital, Phnom Penh.
Evangelization dating from the second half of the 16th century had limited results, more among Vietnamese than Khmers.
Thousands of Catholics of Vietnamese origin were forced to
flee in 1970 because of Khmer hostility. Most indigenous
priests and nuns were killed under the 1975-79 Pol Pot
regime. During those years, the Vietnamese invasion in 1979
and the long civil war that followed, foreign missionaries
were expelled, local clergy and religious were sent to work
the land and a general persecution followed. Religious freedom was re-established in 1990. Diplomatic relations with

the Holy See were established in March 1994. Despite a lack of vocations, many Catholics maintain their faith through small Christian communities led by lay catechists. In the 21st century, Church leaders described their congregations as young and vibrant, involved in such things as AIDS ministry.

Cameroon*

Archd., 5; dioc., 18; card., 1; abp., 7; bp., 22; parishes, 808; priests, 1,732 (1,151 dioc., 581 rel.); p.d., 13; sem., 1,230; bros., 312; srs., 2,155; catechists, 19,597; bap., 94,254; Caths., 4,699,000 (27%); tot. pop., 17,173,000.

Republic in West Africa; capital, Yaounde. Effective evangelization began in 1890, although Catholics had been in the country long before that time. In the 40-year period from 1920 to 1960, the number of Catholics increased from 60,000 to 700,000. The first black priests were ordained in 1935. Twenty years later the first indigenous bishops were ordained and the hierarchy established. The first Cameroonian cardinal (Christian Wiyghan Tumi) was named in 1988. Around that same time, unknown people began persecuting Church personnel. Among those murdered was Archbishop Yves Plumy of Garoua in 1991. Some felt the government did not do enough to investigate.

Canada* (See Catholic Church in Canada; see also Statistics of the Church in Canada)

Cape Verde*

Dioc., 2; bp., 2; parishes, 33; priests, 58 (14 dioc., 44 rel.); sem., 29; bros., 7; srs., 118; catechists, 3,048; bap., 4,610; Caths., 453,000 (93%); tot. pop., 489,000.

Independent (July 5, 1975) island group in the Atlantic 300 miles west of Senegal; formerly a Portuguese overseas province; capital, Praia, São Tiago Island. Evangelization began some years before the establishment of a diocese in 1532. The Church languished from the 17th to the 19th centuries, and for two long periods there was no resident bishop. Portugal's anti-clerical government closed the only minor seminary in 1910. Missionaries returned in the 1940s. Cape Verde has faced massive emigration of youth because of perennial drought and a weak economy.

Central African Republic*

Archd., 1; dioc., 8; abp., 3; bp., 10; parishes, 120; priests, 304 (185 dioc., 119 rel.); sem., 215; bros., 31; srs., 343; catechists, 4,193; bap., 18,506; Caths., 889,000 (21%); tot. pop., 4,013,000.

Former French colony (independent since 1960) in central Africa; capital, Bangui. Effective evangelization dates from 1894. The region was organized as a mission territory in 1909. The first indigenous priest was ordained in 1938. The hierarchy was organized in 1955. The Church in the country has expressed concern about the growing number of sects. Frequent military coups and attempted coups have left the nation divided, and church leaders have worked for reconciliation; including heading the national dialogue coordination team. Hundreds of thousands of people remain displaced, and sporadic fighting continues.

Chad*

Archd., 1; dioc., 6; p.a., 1; abp., 2; bp., 6; parishes, 119; priests, 252 (148 dioc., 104 rel.); sem., 124; bros., 52; srs., 366; catechists, 7,118; bap., 17,166; Caths., 934,000 (9.7%); tot. pop., 9,643,000.

Republic (independent since 1960) in north-central Africa; former French possession; capital, N'Djamena. Evangelization began in 1929, leading to firm organization in 1947 and establishment of the hierarchy in 1955. Many catechists, who often were local community leaders, were killed during Chad's 1982-87 civil war. The Vatican established diplomatic relations with Chad in 1988. After the government established more freedoms in the early 1990s, the Church worked to teach people, including Catholics, that solidarity must extend across religious, ethnic and regional boundaries. Church workers were involved in ministering to hundreds of thousands of refugees displaced during the conflict in the Darfur region of Sudan.

Chile*

Archd., 5; dioc., 18; prel., 2; v.a., 1; mil. ord., 1; card., 2; abp., 10; bp., 39; parishes, 937; priests, 2,400 (1,161 dioc., 1,239 rel.); p.d., 850; sem., 709; bros., 467; srs., 4,877; catechists, 56,727; bap., 149,782; Caths., 12,166,000 (74%); tot. pop., 16,430,000.

Republic on the southwest coast of South America; capital, Santiago. Priests were with the Spanish on their entrance into the territory early in the 16th century. The first parish was established in 1547 and the first diocese in 1561. Overall organization of the Church took place later in the century. By 1650, most of the peaceful Indians in the central and northern areas were evangelized. Missionary work was more difficult in the southern region. Church activity was hampered during the campaign for independence, 1810-18, and through the first years of the new government, to 1830. Later, Church activity increased but was hampered by shortages of indigenous personnel and attempts by the government to control Church administration through the patronage system. Separation of Church and state was decreed in the constitution of 1925.

Church-state relations were strained during the regime of Marxist President Salvador Allende (1970-73). In the mid-1970s, the Archdiocese of Santiago established the Vicariate of Solidarity to counter human-rights abuses under the rule of Gen. Augusto Pinochet. The Chilean bishops issued numerous statements strongly critical of human rights abuses by the military dictator, who remained in power until 1990, when an elected president took office. The Church was praised for its role in educating and registering voters in the 1988 plebiscite that rejected another term for Pinochet. In 1999, when a British court ruled that Pinochet could be extradited from Britain to Spain to face trial for torture and murder, Chilean bishops said the ruling damaged Chilean democracy.

China, People's Republic of

Archd., 20; dioc., 92; p.a., 29. No Roman Catholic statistics are available. In 1949 there were between 3,500,000-4,000,000 Catholics, about .7% of the total population; current total is unknown. Tot. pop. 1,322,502,000. **Hong Kong**: Dioc., 1; card., 1; bps., 2; parishes, 52; priests, 304 (70 dioc., 234 rel.); p.d., 10; sem., 43; bros., 72; srs., 508; catechists, 1,434; bap., 4,288; Caths., 349,000 (5.2%); tot. pop., 6,936,000. **Macau**: Dioc., 1; bp., 2; parishes, 8; priests, 99 (23 dioc., 76 rel.); sem., 4; bros., 13; srs., 163; bap., 289; catechists, 128; Caths., 28,000; tot. pop. 514,000.

People's republic in eastern part of Asia; capital, Beijing. Christianity was introduced by the Church of the East monks called "Nestorians," who had some influence on part of the area from 635 to 845 and again from the 11th century until 1368. John of Monte

Corvino started a Franciscan mission in 1294; he was ordained an archbishop about 1307. Missionary activity involving more priests increased for a while thereafter, but the Franciscan mission ended in 1368. Jesuit Matteo Ricci initiated a remarkable period of activity in the 1580s. In what became known as the Chinese rites controversy, the Jesuits argued that Confucian veneration of ancestors was compatible with Catholicism, but Dominican and Franciscan missionaries viewed it as idolatry. The controversy even was debated in Europe throughout the 17th century, and the Vatican ruled against the rites in the early 1800s.

In the mid-19th century, the Opium War forced China to open its doors, accept free trade and allow Christian missionaries in. Progress in evangelization resumed with an extension of legal and social tolerance. At the turn of the 20th century, however, Christian missionary activity helped provoke the Boxer Rebellion against foreign influence in China.

Missionary work in the 20th century reached a new high. The hierarchy was instituted by Pope Pius XII, Apr. 11, 1946 (Apostolic Constitution *Quotidie Nos*). Then followed persecution initiated by communists, before and especially after they established the republic in 1949. The government outlawed missionary work and pastoral activity; expelled more than 5,000 foreign missionaries; arrested, imprisoned and harassed Chinese Church officials; closed more than 4,000 schools, clinics and social service institutions; denied the free exercise of religion; detained hundreds of priests, religious and lay people in jail or in slave labor; proscribed Catholic movements for "counter-revolutionary activities" and "crimes against the new China."

The government formally established the Chinese Catholic Patriotic Association, independent of the Holy See, in July 1957. Initially, relatively few priests and lay people joined the organization, which was condemned by Pius XII in 1958. Many of the Catholics who then joined the Patriotic Association indicated they chose to cooperate with the government and work within its restrictions, but remained loyal to the Vatican. The government formed the nucleus of what it hoped might become the hierarchy of a national Chinese Catholic Church in 1958 by "electing" 26 bishops and having them consecrated validly but illicitly between Apr. 13, 1958, and Nov. 15, 1959. Additional bishops were subsequently ordained. Catholics continued to practice the faith clandestinely and face persecution.

From 1966 to 1978, the Cultural Revolution declared religions to be dangerous and illegal in China. The Catholic registered communities were forbidden to exist. Total persecution of the Catholics followed for more than 10 years.

In the 1980s, although bishops on the mainland were asked to register with the government and join the Patriotic Association, many began to reconcile secretly with the Vatican. Gradually, and in some regions more than others, clandestine and registered Catholic communities began to mingle. By the early 21st century, nearly all of the government-approved bishops in the Patriotic Association had reconciled with the Vatican. Although Chinese officials continued to insist on the right to name bishops, in most cases bishops also were approved by the Vatican.

In 2007, Pope Benedict XVI issued a historic letter to Chinese Catholics urging reconciliation between the clandestine and registered Catholic communities. The letter said registration with the government was permissible as long as it did not compromise the faith. It also formally revoked all Vatican pastoral directives and special faculties previously granted to address pastoral necessities in difficult times. However, it said the Patriotic Association's idea of an independent Chinese church that self-manages itself democratically was "incompatible with Catholic doctrine," and it criticized government limits on the church's activities. The letter also invited civil authorities to dialogue on issues like the appointment of bishops.

Colombia*

Archd., 13; dioc., 52; v.a., 10; mil. ord., 1; card., 3; abp., 20; bp., 94; parishes, 3,994; priests, 8,312 (6,031 dioc., 2,281 rel.); p.d., 359; sem., 4,827; bros., 1,105 srs., 16,206; catechists, 52,397; bap., 711,662; Caths., 41,019,000 (88%); tot. pop., 46,770,000.

Republic in northwest South America; capital, Bogotá. Evangelization began in 1508. The first two dioceses were established in 1534. Vigorous development of the Church was reported by the middle of the 17th century despite obstacles posed by the multiplicity of Indian languages, government interference through patronage rights, rivalry among religious orders and the small number of native American priests among the predominantly Spanish clergy. Some persecution, including the confiscation of property, followed in the wake of the proclamation of independence from Spain in 1819. Guerrilla warfare aimed at Marxist-oriented radical social reform and redistribution of land, along with violence related to drug traffic, has plagued the country since the 1960s, posing problems for the Church, which backed reforms but rejected actions of radical groups. In the late 20th and early 21st centuries, the Church worked as a mediator between the government and guerrillas, but Church leaders suffered threats, attacks, and sometimes death, including from paramilitaries. For example, on Mar. 16, 2002, Abp. Isaias Duarte Cancino of Cali was shot to death for speaking out about the political situation; he was one of at least 10 Church workers killed in 2002.

Comoros

A.a., 1; parishes, 2; missions, 4; priests, 3 (3 rel.); bros., 2; srs., 5; catechists, 20; bap., 20; Caths., 6,000 (.02%); tot. pop., 835,000. (AD)

Consists of main islands of Grande Comore, Anjouan and Moheli in Indian Ocean off southeast coast of Africa; capital, Moroni, Grande Comore Island. Former French territory; independent (July 6, 1975). The majority of the population is Muslim. An apostolic administration was established in 1975.

Congo, Democratic Republic of *

Archd., 6; dioc., 41; abp., 7; bp., 56; parishes, 1,321; priests, 4,896 (3,030 dioc., 1,836 rel.); p.d., 2, sem., 3,120; bros., 1,301; srs., 8,084; catechists, 74,371; bap., 420,021; Caths., 32,105,000 (53%); tot. pop., 60,679,000.

Republic in south central Africa; capital, Kinshasa. Christianity was introduced in 1484 and evangelization began about 1490. The first bishop from black Africa was ordained in 1518. Subsequent missionary work was hindered by factors including 18th- and

19th-century anticlericalism. Modern evangelization started in the second half of the 19th century. The hierarchy was established in 1959. In the civil disorders that followed independence in 1960, some missions and other Church installations were abandoned, thousands of people reverted to tribal religions and many priests and religious were killed.

Church-state tensions developed in the late 1980s and 1990s because of the Church's criticism of President Mobutu Sese Seko. In 1992, Abp. Laurent Monswengo Pasinya was named president of a council charged with drafting a new constitution and overseeing a transition to democracy, but Mobutu supporters blocked effective change, and the archbishop resigned in 1994. As government and rebel forces battled in the Bukavu region of the country in 1996, Abp. Christophe Munzihirwa Mwene Ngabo was killed in unclear circumstances. In the ensuing years of civil war, Church personnel worked to meet humanitarian needs and to promote peace.

Congo, Republic of *

Archd., 1; dioc., 5; p.a., 1; abp., 2; bp., 6; parishes, 174; priests, 365 (259 dioc., 106 rel.); sem., 315; bros., 62; srs., 389; catechists, 5,477; bap., 28,942; Caths., 2,464,000 (58%); tot. pop., 4,392,000.

Republic (independent since 1960) in west central Africa; former French possession; capital, Brazzaville. Small-scale missionary work with little effect preceded modern evangelization dating from the 1880s. The work of the Church has been affected by political instability, communist influence, tribalism and hostility to foreigners. The hierarchy was established in 1955. In 1992 Bishop Ernest Kombo of Owando was appointed chief organizer of the country's parliamentary elections. In 1994, the Church canceled independence day celebrations after more than 142 Catholics, mostly children, were crushed or suffocated in a rain-induced stampede at a Catholic church in Brazzaville. During renewed violence in the late 1990s, the bishops appealed for peace and stability.

Costa Rica*

Archd., 1; dioc., 7; abp., 3; bp., 10; parishes, 278; priests, 751 (540 dioc., 211 rel.); sem., 202; p.d., 5; bros., 124; srs., 833; catechists, 18,903; bap., 43,134; Caths., 3,713,000 (85%); tot. pop., 4,350,000.

Republic in Central America; capital, San José. Evangelization began about 1520 and proceeded by degrees to real development and organization of the Church in the 17th and 18th centuries. The republic became independent in 1838. Twelve years later Church jurisdiction also became independent with the establishment of a diocese in the present capital.

Côte d'Ivoire (Ivory Coast)*

Archd., 4; dioc., 11; card., 1; abp., 5; bp., 13; parishes, 365; priests, 1,222 (924 dioc., 298 rel.); p.d., 5; sem., 618; bros., 413; srs., 962; catechists, 15,049; bap., 54,595; Caths., 3,147,000 (17%); tot. pop., 19,660,000.

Republic in western Africa; capital, Abidjan. The Holy Ghost Fathers began systematic evangelization in 1895. The first priests from the area were ordained in 1934. The hierarchy was set up in 1955; the first indigenous cardinal (Bernard Yago) was named in 1983. In 1990 Pope John Paul II consecrated the continent's biggest, most costly and most controversial cathedral in Yamoussoukro. The pope only agreed to

accept the cathedral after convincing the country's president to build an adjacent hospital and youth center.

Croatia*

Archd., 4; dioc., 10; mil. ord., 1; abp., 7; bp., 16; parishes, 1,563; priests, 2,391 (1,524 dioc., 867 rel.); p.d., 5; sem., 455; bros., 82; srs., 3,674; catechists, 1,937; bap., 39,190; Caths., 3,910,000 (86%); tot. pop., 4,518,000.

Independent (1991) republic in southeastern Europe; capital Zagreb; formerly a constituent republic of Yugoslavia. Christianity was introduced in the seventh century. On-again, off-again fighting from 1991 to 1995 pitted mostly Catholic Croats against mostly Orthodox Serbs. In 1995, Croatian bishops issued guidelines for rebuilding the nation including suppressing feelings of vengeance toward Serbs. However, in 1996 the head of Croatia's Helsinki human rights committee criticized the bishops for taking a weak stance on Croat abuses after the 1995 Croatian recapture of the Serb-occupied Krajina region. The 1998 beatification of Croatian Cardinal Alojzije Stepinac generated controversy among some Serb and Jewish leaders, who considered the cardinal a Nazi sympathizer.

Cuba*

Archd., 3; dioc., 8; card., 1; abp., 3; bp., 11; parishes, 303; priests, 345 (193 dioc., 152 rel.); p.d., 60; sem., 86; bros., 36; srs., 650; catechists, 4,170; bap., 53,927; Caths. 6,754,000 (59%); tot. pop., 11,320,000.

Republic under Communist dictatorship, south of Florida; capital, Havana. Effective evangelization began about 1514, leading eventually to the predominance of Catholicism on the island. Vocations to the priesthood and religious life were unusually numerous in the 18th century but declined in the 19th. The island became independent of Spain in 1902 following the Spanish-American War.

Fidel Castro took control of the government Jan. 1, 1959. In 1961, after Cuba was officially declared a socialist state, the University of Villanueva was closed, 350 Catholic schools were nationalized and 136 priests expelled. A greater number of foreign priests and religious had already left the country. Freedom of worship and religious instruction were limited to Church premises and no social action was permitted by the Church, which survived under surveillance. A new constitution approved in 1976 guaranteed freedom of conscience but restricted its exercise. Small improvements in Church-state relations occurred in the late 1980s and early 1990s. In December 1997, just before Pope John Paul II's historic visit, the government allowed public celebration of Christmas, banned for 30 years. Although the pope's January 1998 visit was seen as a new dawn for the Church on the islands, Cuban Catholics say change has come slowly. Church leaders say the government has made concessions on public worship and restoration of church buildings. Some progress has been made on visas for foreign Church personnel and in Church-run media. In 2007, representatives of the Latin American bishops' council (CELAM) met on the island for the first time.

Cyprus*

Archd., 1 (Maronite); abp., 1; parishes, 13; priests, 28 (11 dioc., 17 rel.); sem., 1; bros., 13; srs., 51; bap., 68; Caths., 17,000 (2.2%); tot. pop., 791,000.

Republic in the eastern Mediterranean; capital, Nicosia. Christianity was preached on the island in apostolic times and has a continuous history from the fourth century. Latin and Eastern rites were established but the latter prevailed and became Orthodox after the schism of 1054. Christians have suffered under many governments, particularly during the period of Turkish dominion from late in the 16th to late in the 19th centuries, and from differences between the 80 percent Greek majority and the Turkish minority. About 80 percent of the population are Orthodox.

Czech Republic*

Archd., 2; dioc., 6; ap. ex., 1; card., 2; abp., 3; bp., 16; parishes, 2,668; priests, 1,953 (1,356 dioc., 597 rel.); p.d., 171; sem., 211; bros., 109; srs., 1,755; catechists, 1,149; bap., 23,225; Caths., 3,289,000 (32%); tot. pop., 10,291,000.

Independent state (Jan. 1, 1993); formerly part of Czechoslovakia; capital, Prague. The martyrdom of Prince Wenceslaus in 929 triggered the spread of Christianity. Prague has had a continuous history as a diocese since 973. A parish system was organized about the 13th century in Bohemia and Moravia. Mendicant orders strengthened relations with the Latin rite in the 13th century. In the following century the teachings of John Hus in Bohemia brought trouble to the Church in the forms of schism and heresy and initiated a series of religious wars that continued for decades following his death at the stake in 1415. So many of the faithful joined the Bohemian Brethren that Catholics became a minority.

In the 1560s, a Counter-Reformation got under way and led to a gradual restoration through the thickets of Josephinism, the Enlightenment, liberalism and troubled politics. St. Jan Sarkander, a priest accused of helping an invading Polish army, was killed by Protestants in 1620. (His 1995 canonization caused strains with the Protestant community.)

In 1920, two years after the establishment of the Republic of Czechoslovakia, the schismatic Czechoslovak Church was proclaimed at Prague, resulting in numerous defections from the Catholic Church in the Czech region. Following the accession of the Gottwald regime to power early in 1948, persecution began in the Czech part of Czechoslovakia. A number of theatrical trials of bishops and priests were staged in 1950. Pressure was applied on Eastern Catholics in Slovakia to join the Orthodox Church. Diplomatic relations with the Holy See were terminated in 1950. In the following decade, thousands of priests were arrested and hundreds were deported, and attempts were made to force government-approved "peace priests" on the people. Pope Pius XII granted the Czech Church emergency powers to appoint clergy during the communist persecution.

From January to October 1968, Church-state relations improved to some extent under the Dubcek regime: a number of bishops were reinstated; some priests were still barred from priestly work; the "peace priests" organization was disbanded. The Eastern Catholic Church was re-established. In 1969, rehabilitation trials for priests and religious ended, but there was no wholesale restoration of priests and religious to their proper ways of life and work. Government restrictions continued to hamper the work of priests

and nuns. Signatories of the human rights declaration Charter 77 were particular objects of government repression and retribution.

In December 1983, the Czechoslovakian foreign minister met with the pope at Vatican City; it was the first meeting of a high Czech official with a pope since the country had been under communist rule. In 1988, three new bishops were ordained in Czechoslovakia, the first since 1973. The communist government fell in late 1989. In 1990, bishops were appointed to fill vacant sees; diplomatic relations between the Holy See and Czechoslovakia were re-established, and Pope John Paul II visited the country. In 1997 the issue of married Czech priests secretly ordained under communist rule was resolved when they began work in the country's new Eastern Catholic jurisdiction. Under a 1949 communist decree declaring priests Culture Ministry employees, Czech priests were still paid by the state. A Church spokesman said confiscation of Church property under communist rule left priests still financially dependent on the state.

Denmark*

Dioc., 1; bp., 2; parishes, 48; priests, 87 (46 dioc., 41 rel.); p.d., 4; sem., 23; bros., 4; srs., 190; bap., 621; Caths., 37,000 (.6%); tot. pop., 5,363,000.

Includes the Faroe Islands and Greenland. Constitutional monarchy in northwestern Europe; capital, Copenhagen. Christianity was introduced in the ninth century and the first diocese for the area was established in 831. Intensive evangelization and full-scale organization of the Church occurred from the second half of the 10th century and ushered in a period of great development and influence in the 12th and 13th centuries. Decline followed, resulting in almost total loss to the Church during the Reformation, when Lutheranism became the national religion. A few Catholic families practiced the faith secretly until religious freedom was legally assured in the mid-1800s. Since then, immigration has increased the number of Catholics. About 95 percent of the population are Evangelical Lutherans.

Catholicism was introduced in Greenland, a Danish island province northeast of North America, about 1000. The first diocese was established in 1124 and a line of bishops dated from then until 1537. The first known churches in the Western Hemisphere, dating from about the 11th century, were on Greenland. The departure of Scandinavians and spread of the Reformation reduced the Church to nothing. The Moravian Brethren evangelized the Inuit from the 1720s to 1901. By 1930 the Danish Church — Evangelical Lutheran — was in full possession. Since 1930, priests have been in Greenland, which is part of the Copenhagen Diocese.

Djibouti*

Dioc., 1; bp., 1; parishes, 5; priests, 3 (1 dioc., 2 rel.); bros., 6; srs., 23; catechists, 15; sem., 1; bap., 14; Caths., 7,000 (1%); tot. pop., 760,000. (AD)

Independent (1977) republic in East Africa; capital, Djibouti. Christianity in the area, formerly part of Ethiopia, antedated but was overcome by the Arab invasion of 1200. Modern evangelization, begun in the latter part of the 19th century, had meager results. The hierarchy was established in 1955. Formal diplomatic relations with the Holy See were established in May 2000.

Dominica*

Dioc., 1; bp., 1; parishes, 14; priests, 29 (8 dioc., 21 rel.); sem., 10; bros., 7; srs., 20; catechists, 474; bap., 609; Caths., 42,000 (79%); tot. pop., 74,000.

Independent (Nov. 3, 1978) state in Caribbean; capital, Roseau. Evangelization began in 1642.

Dominican Republic*

Archd., 2; dioc., 9; mil. ord., 1; v.a., 1; card., 1; abp., 3; bp., 17; parishes, 596; priests, 960 (486 dioc., 474 rel.); p.d., 422; sem., 734; bros., 182; srs., 2,850; catechists, 47,145; bap., 107,205; Caths., 8,305,000 (88%); tot. pop., 9,420,000.

Caribbean republic on the eastern two-thirds of the island of Hispaniola, bordering on Haiti; capital, Santo Domingo. Evangelization began shortly after discovery by Columbus in 1492 and Church organization, the first in America, was established by 1510. Catholicism is the state religion. Pope John Paul II visited the country in 1992 to mark the quincentennial celebrations of Columbus' discovery. The pope also opened the Fourth General conference of the Latin American Episcopate there. Church leaders worked to end social injustices, including the plight of mistreated sugar cane workers.

East Timor*

Dioc., 2; bp., 2; parishes, 46; priests, 170 (65 dioc., 105 rel.); sem., 159; p.d., 1; bros., 30; srs., 352; catechists, 1,542; bap., 23,752; Caths., 820,000 (89%); tot. pop., 923,000.

Independent (May 2002) state; capital, Dili. The predominantly Catholic former Portuguese colony was invaded by Indonesia in 1975 and annexed the following year. Most countries did not recognize the annexation. The Catholic Church worked to bring peace between the Indonesian government and guerrilla forces seeking independence. Bishop Carlos Filipe Ximenes Belo, former apostolic administrator of Dili, was a co-winner of the 1996 Nobel Peace Prize for his peace efforts. In 1999, dozens of civilians— including more than two dozen at a Catholic church — were killed during a terror campaign waged by pro-Indonesia paramilitaries in the run-up to an August vote on independence for East Timor. Indonesian troops withdrew, and in August 2001, East Timor held elections for a transitional government. The Church has worked on peace and reconciliation issues to raise awareness of social issues.

Ecuador*

Archd., 4; dioc., 11; v.a., 7; p.a., 1; mil. ord., 1; card., 1; abp., 6; bp., 35; parishes, 1,242; priests, 2,078 (1,238 dioc., 840 rel.); p.d., 78; sem., 675; bros., 367; srs., 5,533; catechists, 36,286; bap., 253,191; Caths., 12,255,000 (91%); tot. pop., 13,410,000.

Republic on the west coast of South America, includes Galápagos Islands; capital, Quito. Evangelization began in the 1530s. The first diocese was established in 1545. Multi-phased missionary work, spreading from the coastal and mountain regions into the Amazon, made the Church highly influential during the colonial period. The Church was practically enslaved by the constitution enacted in 1824, two years after Ecuador, as part of Colombia, gained independence from Spain. Some change for the better took place later in the century, but from 1891 until the 1930s the Church labored under serious liabilities imposed by liberal governments. Foreign missionaries were barred from the country for some time; the property of religious orders was confiscated; education was taken over by the state; traditional state support was refused; legal standing was denied; attempts to control Church offices were made through insistence on rights of patronage. A period of harmony and independence for the Church began after agreement was reached on Church-state relations in 1937. In 1998, the Church was actively involved in peace talks that ended a border dispute of some 170 years with Peru. At the beginning of the 21st century, Ecuador's bishops were working to fight social turmoil and the results of severe economic austerity measures. They also were working to support family members left behind as up to 2.5 million of the country's residents emigrated to foreign lands for work.

Egypt*

Patriarchates, 2 (Alexandria for the Copts and for the Melkites); dioc., 11; v.a., 1; ex., 1; patriarch, 1; card., 1; abp., 3; bp., 16; parishes, 203; priests, 468 (223 dioc., 245 rel.); p.d., 7; sem., 129; bros., 62; srs., 1,185; catechists, 2,041; bap., 2,302; Caths., 197,000 (.29%); tot. pop., 75,510,000.

Arab Republic in northeastern Africa; capital, Cairo. Alexandria was the influential hub of a Christian community established by the end of the second century; it became a patriarchate and the center of the Coptic Church and had great influence on the spread of Christianity in various parts of Africa. Monasticism developed from desert communities of hermits in the third and fourth centuries. Arianism was first preached in Egypt in the 320s. In the fifth century, the Coptic Church went Monophysite through failure to accept doctrine formulated by the Council of Chalcedon in 451 with respect to the two natures of Christ. The country was thoroughly Arabized after 640 and was under the rule of Ottoman Turks from 1517 to 1798.

Islam, the religion of some 90 percent of the population, is the state religion. The tiny Catholic minority has a dialogue with the Muslims, but sometimes each side treats the other warily and with mistrust. Pope John Paul II's visit to Cairo and Mount Sinai in 2000 was considered to have given impetus to interreligious dialogue.

El Salvador*

Archd., 1; dioc., 7; mil. ord., 1; abp., 2; bp., 10; parishes, 420, priests, 765 (534 dioc., 231 rel.); p.d., 2; sem., 512; bros., 70; srs., 1,632; catechists, 7,534; bap., 82,689; Cath., 5,593,000 (77%); tot. pop., 7,002,000.

Republic in Central America; capital, San Salvador. Evangelization affecting the whole territory followed Spanish occupation in the 1520s. The country was administered by the captaincy general of Guatemala until 1821, when independence from Spain was declared and it was annexed to Mexico. El Salvador joined the Central American Federation in 1825, declared independence in 1841 and became a republic formally in 1856.

During the country's 1980-92 civil war, Church leaders worked to achieve social justice. The San Salvador Archdiocese's human rights office, Tutela Legal, documented abuses and political killings and offered legal support to victims, despite Church persecution. Archbishop Oscar Romero of San Salvador, peace advocate and outspoken champion of human rights, was murdered Mar. 24, 1980, while celebrating Mass.

Four U.S. Church women were murdered the same year. Six Jesuits and two lay women were assassinated Nov. 16, 1989, at Central American University in El Salvador. Church leaders, particularly Archbishop Romero's successor, Archbishop Arturo Rivera Damas, were active in the peace process. In the 1990s, Church-government relations cooled. Church leaders often urged the U.S. government not to deport the hundreds of thousands of Salvadoran refugees who lived, often illegally, in the United States, and sent money to their families in El Salvador. The situation worsened after the destruction caused by Hurricane Mitch in 1998.

England*

Archd., 4; dioc., 15; ap. ex., 1; mil. ord. (Great Britain), 1; card., 1; abp., 5; bp., 33; parishes, 2,396; priests, 4,194 (3,013 dioc., 1,181 rel.); p.d., 586; sem., 159 bros., 1,559; srs., 5,616; bap., 55,275; Caths., 3,719,519 (8.3%; tot. Catholic pop. for Great Britain: 4,620,490); tot. pop., 44,785,878 (tot. pop. for Great Britain: 53,207,250). Note: England and Wales share a joint Episcopal Conference; see also **Scotland** and **Wales**.

Center of the United Kingdom of Great Britain (England, Scotland, Wales) and Northern Ireland, off the northwestern coast of Europe; capital, London. The arrival of St. Augustine of Canterbury and a band of monks in 597 marked the beginning of evangelization. Real organization of the Church took place some years after the Synod of Whitby, held in 663. Heavy losses were sustained in the wake of the Danish invasion in the 780s, but recovery starting from the time of Alfred the Great and dating especially from the middle of the 10th century led to Christianization of the whole country and close Church-state relations. The Norman Conquest of 1066 opened the Church in England to European influence. The Church began to decline in numbers in the 13th century. In the 14th century, John Wycliff presaged the Protestant Reformation.

Henry VIII, failing in 1529 to gain annulment of his marriage to Catherine of Aragon, refused to acknowledge papal authority over the Church in England, had himself proclaimed its head, suppressed all houses of religious, and persecuted people — Sts. Thomas More and John Fisher, among others — for not subscribing to the Oath of Supremacy and Act of Succession. He held the line on other-than-papal doctrine, however, until his death in 1547. Doctrinal aberrations were introduced during the reign of Edward VI (1547-53), through the Order of Communion, two books of Common Prayer, and the Articles of the Established Church. Mary Tudor's attempted Catholic restoration (1553-58) was a disaster, resulting in the deaths of more than 300 Protestants. Elizabeth (1558-1603) firmed up the established Church with the aid of Matthew Parker, archbishop of Canterbury, with formation of a hierarchy, legal enactments and multiphased persecution. More than 100 priests and 62 lay persons were among the casualties of persecution during the underground Catholic revival that followed the return to England of missionary priests from France and the Lowlands.

Several periods of comparative tolerance ensued after Elizabeth's death. The first of several apostolic vicariates was established in 1685; this form of Church government was maintained until the restoration of the hierarchy and diocesan organization in 1850. The revolution of 1688 and subsequent developments to about 1781 subjected Catholics to a wide variety of penal laws and disabilities in religious, civic and social life. The situation began to improve in 1791, and from 1801 Parliament frequently considered proposals for the repeal of penal laws against Catholics.

The Act of Emancipation restored citizenship rights to Catholics in 1829. Restrictions remained in force for some time afterward, however, on public religious worship and activity. The hierarchy was restored in 1850. Since then the Catholic Church, existing side by side with the established Churches of England and Scotland, has followed a general pattern of growth and development. After the Church of England began ordaining women priests in 1994, hundreds of Anglican priests and four Anglican bishops have been received into the Catholic Church, although many said ordination of women was not their primary reason for leaving. In the late 20th and early 21st centuries, the Church was active in the prolife movement and was outspoken on bioethical issues. (See also **Ireland, Northern**)

Equatorial Guinea*

Archd., 1; dioc., 2; abp., 1; bp., 1; parishes, 68; priests, 126 (69 dioc., 57 rel.); p.d. 1; sem., 64; bros., 33; srs., 293; catechists, 1,686; bap., 17,386; Caths., 499,000 (93%); tot. pop., 535,000.

Republic on the west coast of Africa, consisting of Rio Muni on the mainland and the islands of Bioko and Annobon in the Gulf of Guinea: capital, Malabo. Evangelization began in 1841. The country became independent of Spain in 1968. The Church was severely repressed during the 11-year rule of President Macias Nguema. Developments since his overthrow in 1979 indicated some measure of improvement. An ecclesiastical province was established in October 1982.

In the 1990s, bishops worked to educate Catholics about the need for social justice and respect for human rights. In mid-1998, the government expelled three foreign missionaries involved in development programs partially funded by the United States.

Eritrea*

Dioc., 3; bp., 5; parishes, 118; priests, 388 (85 dioc., 303 rel); sem., 237; p.d., 2, bros., 98; srs., 729; catechists, 195; bap., 3,578; Caths., 141,000 (3.5%); tot. pop., 4,595,000.

Independent state (May 24, 1993) in northeast Africa; formerly a province of Ethiopia. Christianity was introduced in the fourth century. Population is evenly divided between Christians and Muslims. Catholics form a small minority; most of the population is Orthodox or Muslim. In 1995, two new dioceses were established, but because of three decades of civil war, the dioceses had no facilities and little staffing. In 1998 the government announced plans to take over private schools and health clinics, most of which were run by the Church. Eritrean bishops form an episcopal conference with Ethiopia, and the bishops of the two countries frequently appealed for peace during their governments' border war.

Estonia*

A.a., 1; abp., 1 (nuncio is apostolic administrator); parishes, 9; priests, 12 (8 dioc., 4 rel); sem., 1; srs., 20; bap., 83; Caths., 6,000 (.43%); tot. pop., 1,370,000.

Independent (1991) Baltic republic; capital, Tallinn. (Forcibly absorbed by the USSR in 1940, it regained independence in 1991.) Catholicism was introduced in the 11th and 12th centuries. Jurisdiction over the area was made directly subject to the Holy See in 1215. Lutheran penetration was general in the Reformation period, and Russian Orthodox influence was strong from early in the 18th century until 1917, when independence was attained. The first of several apostolic administrators was appointed in 1924. The small Catholic community was hard-hit during the 1940-91 Soviet occupation (not recognized by the Holy See or the United States). Since its independence, the small Catholic community in Estonia has worked to re-establish Catholic theology and education. In 1999 the Holy See and government of Estonia reached agreement on a number of issues, including guarantees that the Church could name its own bishops and that priests from abroad would be able to continue to work in the country.

Ethiopia*

Archd., 1; dioc., 2; v.a., 5; p.a., 2; abp., 2; bp., 8; parishes, 284; priests, 455 (217 dioc., 238 rel.); p.d., 1; sem., 274; bros., 74; srs., 698; catechists, 2,384; bap., 20,986; Caths., 586,000 (.8%); tot. pop., 75,070,000.

People's republic in northeast Africa; capital, Addis Ababa. The country was evangelized by missionaries from Egypt in the fourth century and had a bishop by about 340. Following the lead of its parent body, the Egyptian (Coptic) Church, the Church in the area succumbed to the Monophysite heresy in the sixth century. An apostolic delegation was set up in Addis Ababa in 1937 and several jurisdictions were organized, some under Vatican congregations. The northern Church jurisdictions follow the Alexandrian rite, while the southern part of the country is Latin rite. The small Church has good relations with Orthodox and Protestant Churches, all of which face the task of helping people move from a rural society to a more modern society without losing Christian identity. Although the constitution calls for religious freedom, treatment of the churches can vary in different localities.

Falkland Islands

P.a., 1; parish, 1; srs., 1; bap., 1; Caths., 300 (approx.) (10%); tot. pop., 3,000 (approx).

British colony off the southern tip of South America; capital, Port Stanley. The islands are called Islas Malvinas by Argentina, which also claims sovereignty.

Fiji*

Archd., 1; abp., 1; parishes, 35; priests, 129 (30 dioc., 99 rel.); sem., 61; bros., 39; srs., 142; bap., 1,916; catechists, 550; Caths., 95,000 (9%); tot. pop., 999,000.

Independent island group (100 inhabited) in the southwest Pacific; capital, Suva. Marist missionaries began work in 1844 after Methodism had been firmly established. An apostolic prefecture was organized in 1863. The hierarchy was established in 1966.

Finland*

Dioc., 1; bp., 1; parishes, 7; priests, 22 (11 dioc., 11 rel.); p.d., 1; sem., 14; srs., 40; bap., 179; Caths., 9,000 (.01%); tot. pop., 5,277,000.

Republic in northern Europe; capital, Helsinki. Swedes evangelized the country in the 12th century. The Reformation swept the country, resulting in the prohibition of Catholicism in 1595, general reorganization of ecclesiastical life and affairs, and dominance of the Evangelical Lutheran Church. Catholics were given religious liberty in 1781 but missionaries and conversions were forbidden by law. The first Finnish priest since the Reformation was ordained in 1903 in Paris. An apostolic vicariate for Finland was erected in 1920 (made a diocese in 1955). A law on religious liberty, enacted in 1923, banned the foundation of monasteries.

France*

Archd., 23; dioc., 71; prel., 1; ap. ex., 2; mil. ord., 1; card., 9; abp., 40; bp., 139; parishes, 16,553; priests, 21,074 (15,863 dioc., 5,211 rel.); p.d., 2,099; sem., 1,299; bros., 2,904; srs., 39,521; catechists, 62,831; bap., 346,422; Caths., 46,427,000 (77%); tot. pop., 61,350,000.

Republic in Western Europe; capital, Paris. Christianity was known around Lyons by the middle of the second century. By 250 there were 30 dioceses. The hierarchy reached a fair degree of organization by the end of the fourth century. Vandals and Franks subsequently invaded the territory and caused barbarian turmoil and doctrinal problems because of their Arianism. The Frankish nation was converted following the baptism of Clovis about 496. Christianization was complete by some time in the seventh century. From then on the Church, its leaders and people, figured in virtually every important development — religious, cultural, political and social — through the periods of the Carolingians, feudalism, the Middle Ages and monarchies to the end of the 18th century. The University of Paris became one of the intellectual centers of the 13th century. Churchmen and secular rulers were involved with developments surrounding the Avignon residence of the popes and curia from 1309 until near the end of the 14th century and with the disastrous Western Schism that followed.

Strong currents of Gallicanism and conciliarism ran through ecclesiastical and secular circles in France; the former was an ideology and movement to restrict papal control of the Church in the country, the latter sought to make the pope subservient to a general council. Calvinism entered the country about the middle of the 16th century and won a strong body of converts. Jansenism appeared in the next century, to be followed by the highly influential Enlightenment. The Revolution, which started in 1789 and was succeeded by the Napoleonic period, completely changed the status of the Church, taking a toll of numbers by persecution and defection and disenfranchising the Church in practically every way. Throughout the 19th century the Church was caught up in the whirl of imperial and republican developments and was made the victim of official hostility, popular indifference and liberal opposition.

In the 20th century, the Church struggled with problems involving the heritage of the Revolution and its aftermath. In the 1990s, French bishops fought a racist backlash that resulted from large-scale emigration from Africa.

Gabon*

Archd., 1; dioc., 4; p.a., 1; abp., 1; bp., 4; parishes, 75; priests, 144 (70 dioc., 74 rel.); sem., 86; bros., 19; srs., 175; catechists, 1,541; bap., 9,616; Caths., 750,000 (50%); tot. pop., 1,499,000.

Republic on the west coast of central Africa; capital Libreville. Sporadic missionary effort took place before 1881 when effective evangelization began. The hierarchy was established in 1955. In 1993, Gabon's president defeated a Catholic priest in presidential elections. In the late 1990s, the government and the Holy See signed an agreement setting out the rights of the Church in society.

Gambia*

Dioc., 1; bp., 3; parishes, 56; priests, 29 (16 dioc., 13 rel.); sem., 9; bros., 11; srs., 45; bap., 1,754; Caths., 41,000 (2%); tot. pop., 1,550,000.

Republic (1970) on the northwestern coast of Africa; capital, Banjui. Christianity was introduced by Portuguese explorers in the 15th century; effective evangelization began in 1822. The country was under the jurisdiction of an apostolic vicariate until 1931. The hierarchy was established in 1957.

Georgia*

A.a., 1; parishes, 30; abp., 1; bp., 1; priests, 13 (4 dioc., 9 rel); sem., 12; brs. 2; srs., 29; bap 190; Caths., 90,000 (2%); tot. pop., 4,400,000.

Independent (1991) state in the Caucasus; former Soviet republic; capital, Tbilisi. Christianity came to the area under Roman influence and, according to tradition, was spread through the efforts of St. Nino (or Christiana), a maiden who was brought as a captive to the country and is venerated as its apostle. The apostolic administration of the Caucasus (with seat in Georgia) was established in December 1993 for Latin-rite Catholics of Armenia, Azerbaijan and Georgia. Chaldean- and Armenian-rite Catholics also are present. Differences between Catholicism and Orthodoxy often are blurred on the parish level. The Catholic Church and the Armenian Orthodox Church have been unable to secure the return of Churches closed during the Soviet period, many of which were later given to the Georgian Orthodox Church. Early in the 21st century, many denominations, including Catholics, reported attacks and harassment from Orthodox mobs.

Germany*

Archd., 7; dioc., 20; ap. ex., 1; mil. ord., 1; card., 6; abp., 9; bp., 96; parishes, 11,975; priests, 18,222 (13,867 dioc., 4,355 rel.); p.d., 2,643; sem., 1,223; bros., 1,572; srs., 31,151; catechists, 10,244; bap., 187,873; Caths., 25,711,000 (31.2%); tot. pop., 82,370,000.

Country in northern Europe; capital, Berlin. From 1949-90 it was partitioned into the Communist German Democratic Republic in the East (capital, East Berlin) and the German Federal Republic in the West (capital, Bonn). Christianity was introduced in the third century, if not earlier. Trier, which became a center for missionary activity, had a bishop by 400. Visigoth invaders introduced Arianism in the fifth century but were converted in the seventh century by the East Franks, Celtic and other missionaries. St. Boniface, the apostle of Germany, established real ecclesiastical organization in the eighth century.

Beginning in the Carolingian period, bishops began to act in dual roles as pastors and rulers, a state of affairs that inevitably led to confusion and conflict in Church-state relations and perplexing problems of investiture. The Church developed strength and vitality through the Middle Ages but succumbed to abuses that antedated and prepared the ground for the Reformation. Martin Luther's actions from 1517 made Germany a confessional battleground. Religious strife continued until the conclusion of the Peace of Westphalia at the end of the Thirty Years' War in 1648. Nearly a century earlier the Peace of Augsburg (1555) had been designed, without success, to assure a degree of tranquility by recognizing the legitimacy of different religious confessions in different states, depending on the decisions of princes. The implicit principle that princes should control the churches emerged in practice into the absolutism and Josephinism of subsequent years. St. Peter Canisius and his fellow Jesuits spearheaded a Counter Reformation in the second half of the 16th century. Before the end of the century, however, 70 percent of the population of north and central Germany were Lutheran. Calvinism also had established a strong presence.

The Church suffered some impoverishment as a result of shifting boundaries and the secularization of property shortly after 1800. It came under direct attack in the *Kulturkampf* of the 1870s but helped to generate the opposition that resulted in a dampening of the campaign of Bismarck against it. Despite action by Catholics on the social front and other developments, discrimination against the Church spilled over into the 20th century and lasted beyond World War I. Catholics in politics struggled with others to pull the country through numerous postwar crises. The dissolution of the Center Party, agreed to by the bishops in 1933 without awareness of the ultimate consequences, contributed in part to the rise of Hitler to supreme power. Church officials protested the Nazi anti-Church and anti-Semitic actions, but to no avail.

After World War II East Germany, compelled to communism under Soviet domination, initiated a program of control and repression of the Church. The regime eliminated religious schools, curtailed freedom for religious instruction and formation, and restricted the religious press. Beginning in the mid-1950s, the communists substituted youth initiation and Communist ceremonies for many sacraments. Bishops were generally forbidden to travel outside the Republic. The number of priests decreased, partly because of reduced seminary enrollments ordered by the East German government.

The official reunification of Germany took place Oct. 3, 1990, and the separate episcopal conferences were merged to form one conference in November. During the 1990s, the united German bishops fought against introduction of the former East Germany's more liberal abortion law. When a high-court decision allowed a woman to obtain an abortion after visiting a state-approved counseling center and obtaining proof she had been counseled, German Church leaders searched for a compromise position, since they ran more than 250 such centers. In 1999, Pope John Paul II asked the German bishops to include a line on the proof-of-counseling certificate that said it could not be used for abortion, but some German states said they would not consider the line valid. Eventually, most of the bishops withdrew their centers from the system. As the 20th century came to an end, German Church leaders also spoke on behalf of immigrants, refugees and asylum seekers and against a surge in racist and anti-Semitic attacks. Early in the 21st century, a change in the country's tax rate and growing unemployment led to a severe budget crisis for many German dioceses.

Ghana*

Archd., 4; dioc., 15; p.a., card., 2; abp., 4; bp., 17; parishes, 389; priests, 1,233 (1,009 dioc., 224 rel.); p.d., 2; sem., 652; bros., 202; srs., 895; catechists, 7,218; bap., 56,513; Caths., 2,808,000 (12%); tot. pop., 22,898,000.

Republic on the western coast of Africa; capital, Accra. Priests visited the country in 1482, 11 years after discovery by the Portuguese, but missionary effort, hindered by the slave trade and other factors, was slight until 1880 when systematic evangelization began. An apostolic prefecture was set up in 1879. The hierarchy was established in 1950.

In 1985, the government shut down the Church's newspaper, The Catholic Standard, for criticizing the government; in 1989 the government ordered religious bodies to register. However, in 1992 the paper resumed publication, and five new dioceses were established in 1995. In 1997 the bishops issued a pastoral letter urging an end to political corruption and ethnic tension.

Gibraltar

Dioc., 1; bp., 2; parishes, 5; priests, 14 (13 dioc., 1 rel.); sem., 1; bros., 2; srs., 30; bap., 253; Caths., 21,000 (72%); tot. pop., 27,000.

British dependency on the tip of the Spanish Peninsula on the Mediterranean. Evangelization took place after the Moors were driven out near the end of the 15th century. The Church was hindered by the British, who acquired the colony in 1713. Most of the Catholics were, and are, Spanish and Italian immigrants and their descendants. An apostolic vicariate was organized in 1817. The diocese was erected in 1910.

Great Britain (See separate entries for England, Scotland, Wales, Northern Ireland)

Greece*

Archd., 4; dioc., 4; v.a., 1; ap. ex., 2; abp., 6; bp., 3; parishes, 81; priests, 90 (55 dioc., 35 rel.); p.d., 2; sem., 3; bros., 27; srs., 113; bap., 706; Caths., 130,000 (1%); tot. pop., 11,140,000.

Republic in southeastern Europe on the Balkan Peninsula; capital, Athens. St. Paul preached the Gospel at Athens and Corinth on his second missionary journey and visited the country again on his third tour. Other Apostles may have passed through. Two bishops from Greece attended the First Council of Nicaea. After the division of the Roman Empire, the Church remained Eastern in rite and later broke ties with Rome as a result of the schism of 1054. A Latin-rite jurisdiction was set up during the period of the Latin Empire of Constantinople, 1204-61, but crumbled afterward. Unity efforts of the Council of Florence had poor results and failed to save the Byzantine Empire from conquest by the Ottoman Empire in 1453. The country now has Latin, Byzantine and Armenian rites. The Greek Orthodox Church is predominant. The Catholic Church continues to work to obtain full legal rights. In May 2001, during the first papal visit to Greece since the eighth century, Pope John Paul II apologized for past wrongs against the Orthodox, including the 13th-century sack of Constantinople.

Greenland (Statistics for Greenland are included in Denmark)

Grenada*

Dioc., 1; bp., 2; parishes, 20; priests, 25 (8 dioc., 17 rel.); p.d., 3; sem., 3; bros., 2; srs., 28; catechists, 122; bap., 421; Caths., 55,000 (54%); tot. pop., 100,000.

Independent island state in the West Indies; capital, St. George's.

Guam

Archd., 1; abp., 1; parishes, 24; priests, 45 (35 dioc., 10 rel.); p.d., 20; sem., 22; srs., 100; bap., 1,955; catechists, 471; Caths., 141,000 (85%); tot. pop., 166,000.

Outlying area of U.S. in the southwest Pacific; capital, Agana. The first Mass was offered in the Mariana Islands in 1521. The islands were evangelized by the Jesuits, from 1668, and other missionaries. The first Micronesian bishop was ordained in 1970. The Agana Diocese, which had been a suffragan of San Francisco, was made a metropolitan see in 1984.

Guatemala*

Archd., 2; dioc., 10; prel., 1; v.a., 2; card., 1; abp., 2; bp., 19; parishes, 458; priests, 1,000 (517 dioc., 483 rel.); p.d., 6; sem., 406; bros., 194; srs., 2,641; catechists, 59,735; bap., 179,335; Caths. 10,578,000 (81%); tot. pop. 13,020,000.

Republic in Central America; capital, Guatemala City. Evangelization dates from the beginning of Spanish occupation in 1524. The first diocese, for all Central American territories administered by the captaincy general of Guatemala, was established in 1534. The country became independent in 1839, following annexation to Mexico in 1821, secession in 1823 and membership in the Central American Federation from 1825. In 1870, a government installed by a liberal revolution repudiated the concordat of 1853 and took active measures against the Church. Separation of Church and state was decreed; religious orders were suppressed and their property seized; priests and religious were exiled; schools were secularized. Full freedom was subsequently granted.

During the nation's 36-year civil war, which ended in 1996, Church officials spoke out against atrocities and illegal drafting of youths and often were persecuted. The Guatemala City archbishop's human rights office, established after decades of war, was one of the few agencies able to document abuses. Bishops participated in the country's peace process, at times withdrawing in an effort to force government and guerrilla leaders back to the table.

After the war, the archbishop's human rights office began an extensive project to help document abuses during the war. Two days after the report was released in April 1998, Auxiliary Bishop Juan Gerardi

Conedera of Guatemala City, who headed the project, was murdered. In 2001, a priest who lived with the bishop and three military officers were convicted of involvement in the murder, but said they would appeal the decision. One of the three officers was killed in a Guatemala City prison riot in 2003. Church leaders mobilized to help Guatemalans after mudslides and flooding from Hurricane Stan in 2005 made it the country's worst natural disaster in nearly 30 years.

Guinea*

Archd., 1; dioc., 2; abp. 2; bp., 3; parishes, 64; priests, 113 (93 dioc., 20 rel.); sem., 42; bros., 22; srs., 116; catechists, 782; bap., 1,524; Caths., 240,000 (3%); tot. pop., 8,898,000.

Republic on the west coast of Africa; capital, Conakry. Occasional missionary work followed exploration by the Portuguese about the middle of the 15th century; organized effort dates from 1877. The hierarchy was established in 1955. Following independence from France in 1958, Catholic schools were nationalized, youth organizations banned and missionaries restricted. Foreign missionaries were expelled in 1967. Archbishop Raymond-Marie Tchidimbo of Conakry, sentenced to life imprisonment in 1971 on a charge of conspiring to overthrow the government, was released in August 1979; he resigned his see. Private schools, suppressed by the government for more than 20 years, again were authorized in 1984.

Guinea-Bissau*

Dioc., 2; bp., 2; parishes, 33; priests, 81 (20 dioc., 61 rel.); sem., 27; bros., 13; srs., 129; bap., 1,885; catechists, 925; Caths., 132,000 (9.4%); tot. pop., 1,397,000.

Independent state on the west coast of Africa; capital, Bissau. Catholicism was introduced in the second half of the 15th century but limited missionary work, hampered by the slave trade, had meager results. Missionary work in the 20th century began in 1933. An apostolic prefecture was made a diocese in 1977. In 1998, Bishop Settimio Ferrazzetta of Bissau worked to mediate a crisis between the government and military leaders.

Guyana*

Dioc., 1; bp., 2; parishes, 24; priests, 35 (6 dioc., 29 rel.); p.d., 1; sem., 8; bros., 4; srs., 55; catechists, 585; bap., 1,303; Caths., 61,000 (10.2%); tot. pop., 753,000.

Republic on the north coast of South America; capital, Georgetown. In 1899 the Catholic Church and other churches were given equal status with the Church of England and the Church of Scotland. Most of the Catholics are Portuguese. The Georgetown Diocese was established in 1956, 10 years before Guyana became independent of England. The first indigenous bishop was appointed in 1971. Schools were nationalized in 1976. In the late 1970s and in the 1980s, The Catholic Standard newspaper was cited by the Inter-American Press Association as the "sole independent voice" in Guyana.

Haiti*

Archd., 2; dioc., 7; abp., 5; bp., 13; parishes, 332; priests, 748 (461 dioc., 287 rel.); p.d., 6; sem., 439; bros., 346; srs., 1,796; catechists, 4,844; bap., 101,021; Caths., 6,949,000 (80%); tot. pop., 8,639,000.

Caribbean republic on the western third of Hispaniola adjacent to the Dominican Republic; capital, Port-au-Prince. Evangelization followed discovery by Columbus in 1492. Capuchins and Jesuits did most of the missionary work in the 18th century. From 1804, when independence was declared, until 1860, the country was in schism. Relations were regularized by a concordat concluded in 1860, when an archdiocese and four dioceses were established.

In the second half of the 20th century, the Church worked to develop the small nation, considered among the poorest in the Western Hemisphere. In the 1980s and 1990s, priests and religious often were targets of political violence, which resulted in a series of coups. The Church was sometimes seen as the lone voice for the people and, at times, was seen as backing the government. A Salesian priest, Father Jean-Bertrand Aristide, known for his fiery, anti-government sermons, won the December 1990 president election, considered the first genuinely democratic vote in Haitian history. A 1991 military coup forced him into exile for three years and resulted in an international trade embargo against Haiti. Aristide was laicized by the Vatican and married in January 1996. In the late 1990s, the Church continued its service in the social field through programs in basic literacy and operation of schools and health facilities. Early in the 21st century, Church workers often decried worsening poverty and social injustices.

Honduras*

Archd., 1; dioc., 7; card., 1; abp., 1; bp., 12; parishes, 193; priests, 423 (212 dioc., 211 rel.); p.d., 6; sem., 159; bros., 27; srs., 803; catechists, 14,346; bap., 84,634; Caths., 5,938,000 (82%); tot. pop., 7,232,000.

Republic in Central America; capital, Tegucigalpa. Evangelization preceded establishment of the first diocese in the 16th century. Under Spanish rule and after independence from 1823, the Church held a favored position until 1880, when equal legal status was given to all religions. Harassment of priests and nuns working among indigenous peasants and Salvadoran refugees was reported during the years of Central American civil unrest in the late 20th century. In 1998 Hurricane Mitch killed more than 6,000 Hondurans and forced more than 2 million in the country to evacuate their homes. The Church took a lead role in post-hurricane relief and development efforts.

Hungary*

Archd., 4; dioc., 9; abb., 1; ap. ex., 1; mil. ord. 1; card., 2; abp., 5; bp., 22; parishes, 2,214; priests, 2,341 (1,861 dioc., 480 rel.); p.d., 69; sem., 342; bros., 96; srs., 1,168; catechists, 2,637; bap., 56,042; Caths., 5,977,000 (59%); tot. pop., 10,070,000.

Republic in east central Europe; capital, Budapest. The early origins of Christianity in the country, whose territory was subject to a great deal of change, is not known. Magyars accepted Christianity about the end of the 10th century. St. Stephen I promoted its spread and helped to organize some of its historical dioceses. Bishops became influential in politics as well as in the Church.

For centuries the country served as a buffer for the Christian West against barbarians from the East, notably the Mongols in the 13th century. Hussites and

Waldensians prepared the way for the Reformation, which struck at almost the same time as the Turks. The Reformation made considerable progress after 1526, resulting in the conversion of large numbers to Lutheranism and Calvinism by the end of the century. Turks repressed the Churches, Protestant as well as Catholic, during a reign of 150 years, but they managed to survive. Domination of the Church was one of the objectives of government policy during the reigns of Maria Theresa and Joseph II in the second half of the 18th century; their Josephinism affected Church-state relations until World War I.

Secularization increased in the second half of the 19th century, which also witnessed the birth of many new Catholic organizations and movements. Catholics were involved in the social chaos and anti-religious atmosphere of the years following World War I, struggling with their compatriots for religious as well as political survival.

After World War II, the communist campaign against the Church started with the disbanding of Catholic organizations in 1946. In 1948, Caritas, the Catholic charitable organization, was taken over, and all Catholic institutions were suppressed. Interference in Church administration and attempts to split the bishops preceded the arrest of Cardinal Jozsef Mindszenty Dec. 26, 1948, and his sentence to life imprisonment in 1949. (He was free for a few days during the unsuccessful uprising of 1956. He then took up residence at the U.S. Embassy in Budapest, where he remained until September 1971, when he was permitted to leave the country. He died in 1975 in Vienna.)

In 1950, religious orders and congregations were suppressed and 10,000 religious were interned. Several dozen priests and monks were assassinated, jailed or deported. About 4,000 priests and religious were confined in jail or concentration camps. The government sponsored a national "Progressive Catholic" Church and captive organizations for priests. Despite a 1964 agreement with the Holy See regarding episcopal appointments, bishops remained subject to government surveillance and harassment.

On Feb. 9, 1990, an accord was signed between the Holy See and Hungary re-establishing diplomatic relations. Pope John Paul II reorganized the ecclesiastical structure of the country in May 1993. In 1997, the Vatican and Hungary signed an agreement that restored some Church property confiscated under communism and provided some sources of funding for Church activities. Hungary's bishops have said social conflicts, political changes and economic strains have put new pressures on the Church.

Iceland*

Dioc., 1; bp., 1; parishes, 5; priests, 16 (6 dioc., 10 rel.); sem., 1; bros., 1; srs., 36; bap., 142; Caths., 7,000 (2.2%); tot. pop., 307,000.

Island republic between Norway and Greenland; capital, Rekjavik. Irish hermits were there in the eighth century. Missionaries subsequently evangelized the island and Christianity was officially accepted about 1000. The first bishop was ordained in 1056. The Black Death had dire effects, and spiritual decline set in during the 15th century. Lutheranism was introduced from Denmark between 1537 and 1552 and made the official religion. Some Catholic missionary

work was done in the 19th century. Religious freedom was granted to the few Catholics in 1874. A vicariate was erected in 1929 and was made a diocese in 1968.

India*

Patriarchate, 1 (titular of East Indies); major archbishoprics (Syro-Malabar and Syro-Malankara), 2; archd., 30; dioc., 130; card., 5; patr., 2; abp., 36; bp., 168; parishes, 9,109; priests, 23,408 (12,840 dioc., 10,568 rel.); p.d., 19; sem., 14,028; bros., 3,549; srs., 92,100; catechists, 70,974; bap., 362,580; Caths., 18,408,000 (1.6%); tot. pop. 1,117,730,000.

Republic on the subcontinent of south central Asia; capital, New Delhi. Long-standing tradition credits the Apostle Thomas with the introduction of Christianity in the Kerala area. Evangelization followed the establishment of Portuguese posts and the conquest of Goa in 1510. Jesuits, Franciscans, Dominicans, Augustinians and members of other religious orders figured in the early missionary history. An archdiocese for Goa, with two suffragan sees, was set up in 1558.

Missionaries had some difficulties with the British East India Co., which exercised virtual government control from 1757 to 1858. They also had trouble because of a conflict that developed between policies of the Portuguese government, which pressed its rights of patronage in episcopal and clerical appointments, and the Vatican Congregation for the Propagation of the Faith, which sought greater freedom of action in the same appointments. This struggle resulted in the schism of Goa between 1838 and 1857. In 1886, when the number of Catholics was estimated to be 1 million, the hierarchy for India and Ceylon was restored.

Jesuits contributed greatly to the development of Catholic education from the second half of the 19th century. A large percentage of the Catholic population is located around Goa and Kerala and farther south. The country is predominantly Hindu. Anti-conversion laws in effect in several states have had a restrictive effect on pastoral ministry and social service.

Recent years have seen tensions within the Syro-Malabar rite over liturgy and tradition. In addition, there have been tensions between the Latin-rite and Eastern-rite Catholic churches in India over the care of Catholics outside the traditional boundaries of their rites. In the late 20th and early 21st centuries, Church leaders campaigned for the rights of low-caste Indians. Religious also faced a series of attacks, including murders, by extremist Hindus who claimed they were trying to convert people to Christianity.

Indonesia*

Archd., 10; dioc., 27; mil. ord. 1; card., 1; abp., 11; bps., 32; parishes, 1,184; priests, 3,505 (1,485 dioc., 2,020 rel.); p.d., 15; sem., 2,930; bros., 1,006; srs., 7,443; catechists, 22,559; bap., 218,360; Caths., 6,627,000 (3%); tot. pop. 222,050,000.

Republic in the Malay Archipelago, consisting of some 3,000 islands; capital, Jakarta. Evangelization by the Portuguese began about 1511. St. Francis Xavier spent some 14 months in the area. Christianity was strongly rooted in some parts of the islands by 1600. Islam's rise to dominance began at this time. The Dutch East Indies Co., which gained effective control in the 17th century, banned evangelization by Catholic missionaries for some time, but Dutch secular and religious priests managed to resume the work. A vicariate of Batavia for all the Dutch East Indies was set up in 1841. About 90 percent of the population is Muslim. The hierarchy was established in 1961.

From 1981 to about 1996, Catholics and Protestants clashed more than 40 times over what Catholics perceived as Communion host desecration. At least three Protestants died from beatings by Catholics after the incidents.

In the late 1990s, as the Indonesian economy took a nose-dive, Muslim-Christian violence increased, especially in the Molucca Islands. Church leaders continued to urge calm and dialogue, and at one point a bishop sought U.N. intervention to prevent what he saw as a potential genocide of Christians. A militant Muslim group charged with inciting much of the violence disbanded in late 2002, Church leaders expressed hope for peace. The Church worked for years to help victims of the December 2004 tsunami and subsequent earthquakes and tsunamis, offering its services to people regardless of religious affiliation.

Iran*

Archd., 4; dioc., 2; abp., 4; parishes, 18; priests, 19 (7 dioc., 12 rel.); p.d., 3; sem., 1; srs., 29; bap., 38; Caths., 17,000 (.02%); tot. pop., 70,600,000.

Islamic republic (Persia until 1935) in southwestern Asia; capital, Teheran. Some of the earliest Christian communities were established in this area outside the Roman Empire. They suffered persecution in the fourth century and were then cut off from the outside world. Nestorianism was generally professed in the late fifth century. Islam became dominant after 640. Some later missionary work was attempted but without success. Religious liberty was granted in 1834, but Catholics were the victims of a massacre in 1918. Islam is the religion of perhaps 98 percent of the population. Catholics belong to the Latin, Armenian and Chaldean rites.

After Iran nationalized many Church-run social institutions in 1980, about 75 Catholic missionaries left the country, by force or by choice. In recent years, however, Iranian authorities have shown more cooperation regarding entry visas for Church personnel. Although freedom of worship is guaranteed in Iran, Church sources said Catholic activities are monitored carefully by authorities. Since Pope John Paul II and Iranian President Mohammed Khatami met in 1999, the Holy See and Iran have had several high-level diplomatic exchanges.

Iraq*

Patriarchate, 1; archd., 9; dioc., 5; ap. ex., 2; patriarch, 1; abp., 7; bp., 7; parishes, 100; priests, 145 (110 dioc., 35 rel.); p.d., 10; sem., 54; bros., 15; srs., 318; catechists, 879; bap., 2,732; Caths., 304,000 (1%); tot. pop., 28,810,000.

Republic in southwestern Asia; capital, Baghdad. Some of the earliest Christian communities were established in the area, whose history resembles that of Iran. Catholics belong to the Armenian, Chaldean, Latin and Syrian rites; Chaldeans are most numerous. Islam is the religion of some 90 percent of the population. Iraq's Chaldean Catholic patriarch was outspoken against the international embargo against Iraq, saying it especially hurt children and the sick. In early 2003,

Vatican officials met separately with U.S. and Iraqi leaders in an effort to prevent the U.S.-led war; the Vatican embassy in Baghdad remained open throughout the conflict, and Church aid agencies treated wounded. Catholic aid organizations geared up relief efforts after the war but were frustrated by lawlessness and looting. According to estimates, the Christian population in Iraq has declined from a prewar population of 1.2 million to a current estimate of several hundred thousand. Refugee agencies said Christians, including Catholics, were targeted for persecution marked by violence, murder and restrictions on religious freedom; some Christians in Baghdad were told to convert to Islam, pay higher taxes or leave their homes. The U.N. High Commissioner for Refugees reported over 40% of Iraqi refugees are Christian even though they represent only about 4% of Iraq's total population.

After the war, Catholic leaders were among those expressing alarm at the growing number of Christians leaving the country or fleeing to northern Iraq, where Christians banded together in an effort to gain more of a political voice. Church leaders said Christians in the Baghdad area were threatened with conversion to Islam, paying higher taxes or leaving their homes. The kidnappings and violence led Pope Benedict XVI to say in 2007 that Iraqi Christians were experiencing and "authentic martyrdom." In 2008 the archbishop of Mosul was kidnapped and later found dead.

Ireland*

Archd., 4; dioc., 22; card., 2; abp., 7; bp., 36; parishes, 1,366; priests, 5,120 (3,015 dioc., 2,105 rel.); p.d., 1; sem., 162; bros., 751; srs., 8,121; bap., 67,551 (preceding figures include Northern Ireland); Caths., 5,112,000 (76%); tot. 6,715,000 (population numbers include Northern Ireland; in Republic of Ireland, Catholics comprise 95% of the population).

Republic in the British Isles; capital, Dublin. St. Patrick, who is venerated as the apostle of Ireland, evangelized parts of the island for some years after the middle of the fifth century. Conversion of the island was not accomplished, however, until the seventh century or later. Celtic monks were the principal missionaries. The Church was organized along monastic lines at first, but a movement developed in the 11th century for the establishment of jurisdiction along episcopal lines. The Church gathered strength during the period from the Norman Conquest of England to the reign of Henry VIII despite a wide variety of rivalries, wars, and other disturbances.

Henry introduced an age of repression of the faith, which continued for many years under several of his successors. The Irish suffered from proscription of the Catholic faith, economic and social disabilities, subjection to absentee landlords and a plantation system designed to keep them from owning property, and actual persecution which took an uncertain toll of lives up until about 1714. Some penal laws remained in force until emancipation in 1829. Nearly 100 years later Ireland was divided in two, making Northern Ireland, consisting of six counties, part of the United Kingdom (1920) and giving dominion status to the Irish Free State, made up of the other 26 counties (1922). This state (Eire, in Gaelic) was proclaimed the Republic of Ireland in 1949. The Catholic Church predominates but religious freedom is guaranteed for all. The Irish Republic and Northern Ireland share a bishops' conference, which has worked for peace in Northern Ireland. Recent years have witnessed a decrease in vocations and growing turmoil over issues such as priestly pedophilia, divorce, and abortion.

Ireland, Northern

Tot. pop., 1,610,000; Catholics comprise more than one third. (Other statistics are included in Ireland).

Part of the United Kingdom, it consists of six of the nine counties of Ulster in the northeast corner of Ireland; capital, Belfast. Early history is given under Ireland.

Nationalist-unionist tensions fall primarily along Catholic-Protestant lines, with nationalists, mainly Catholics, advocating an end to British rule. Violence and terrorism began in the late 1960s and, by the late 1990s, more than 3,000 people had been killed.

On Apr. 10, 1998, the governments of the Irish Republic and Great Britain and the political parties of Northern Ireland reached an agreement known as the Good Friday agreement. Irish bishops supported it, and it was endorsed by the voters in Ireland and Northern Ireland. However, the agreement or the coalition government established as a result of the agreement were suspended several times, and Northern Ireland's bishops spoke out in support of continuing democratic structures.

For years, Catholics claimed discrimination in the workplace and harassment from the Royal Ulster Constabulary, Northern Ireland's police force that was disbanded and reformed as the Police Service of Northern Ireland. In 2002 some 40 percent of the new force was Catholic, compared to 8 percent in 2001.

Israel*

Patriarchates, 2 (Jerusalem for Latins; patriarchal vicariate for Greek-Melkites); archd., 2; ap.ex., 5; patriarch, 1; abp., 6; bp., 3; parishes, 80; priests, 404 (102 dioc., 302 rel.); p.d., 4; sem., 95; bros., 225; srs., 983; bap., 1,939; Caths., 128,000 (1.7%); tot. pop., 7,050,000.

Parliamentary democracy in the Middle East; capitals, Jerusalem and Tel Aviv (diplomatic). Israel is the birthplace of Christianity, the site of the first Christian communities. Some persecution was suffered in the early Christian era and again during the several hundred years of Roman control. Muslims conquered the territory in the seventh century and, except for the period of the Kingdom of Jerusalem established by Crusaders, remained in control most of the time up until World War I. The Church survived in the area, sometimes just barely, but it did not prosper greatly or show any notable increase in numbers. The British took over the protectorate of the area after World War I.

Partition into Israel for the Jews and Palestine for the Arabs was approved by the United Nations in 1947. War broke out a year later with the proclamation of the Republic of Israel. The Israelis won the war and 50 percent more territory than they had originally been ceded. War broke out again for six days in June 1967, and in October 1973.

Judaism is the faith professed by about 85 percent of the inhabitants; approximately one-third of them are considered observant. Israeli-Holy See relations improved in 1994 with the implementation of full diplomatic relations, and the Church gained legal status in 1997, although some taxation issues remained unresolved.

The Holy See repeatedly has asked for an internationally guaranteed statute to protect the sacred nature of Jerusalem, which is holy to Christians, Muslims and Jews. It has underlined that this means more than access to specific holy places and that the political and religious dimensions of Jerusalem are interrelated. During the Palestinian intifada, the Vatican and Holy Land Church leaders defended Israeli rights to live without the threat of terrorism and the Palestinians' right to a homeland, saying both would only be achieved through a negotiated settlement.

Italy*

Patriarchate, 1 (Venice); archd. 60 (40 are metropolitan sees); dioc., 156; prel., 3; abb., 6; mil. ord. 1; pat., 1 (Venice); card., 37; abp., 165; bps., 268 (hierarchy includes 216 residential, 22 coadjutors or auxiliaries, 268 in Curia offices, remainder in other offices or retired); parishes, 25,669; priests, 50,854 (33,409 dioc., 17,445 rel.); p.d., 3,372; sem., 5,825; bros., 3,325; srs., 98,965; catechists, 223,804; bap., 443,445; Caths., 56,454,000 (96%); tot. pop., 58,880,000.

Republic in southern Europe; capital, Rome. A Christian community was formed early in Rome, probably by the middle of the first century. St. Peter established his see there. He and St. Paul suffered death for the faith in the 60s. The early Christians were persecuted at various times, as in other parts of the empire, but the Church developed in numbers and influence, gradually spreading out from towns and cities in the center and south to rural areas and the north.

Church organization began in the second century. The Church emerged from underground in 313, with the Edict of Milan, and rose to a position of prestige and lasting influence on politics and culture until well into the 19th century. In the 1870s, the Papal States were annexed by the Kingdom of Italy. The 1929 Lateran Pacts included a treaty recognizing the Vatican as an independent state, a financial agreement by which Italy agreed to compensate the Vatican for loss of the papal states, and a concordat regulating Church-state relations. In 1984 the Vatican and Italy signed a revised concordat, reducing some of the Church's privileges and removing Catholicism as the state religion.

The Church strongly opposed Italy's abortion law in 1978 and forced a 1981 referendum on the issue. Abortion remained legal, and the Italian Church has taken a more low-profile stance. The Church has been active in social issues, including helping unprecedented numbers of illegal immigrants in the late 1990s. Church leaders have expressed concern about Italy's low birth rate.

Jamaica*

Archd., 1; dioc., 2; abp., 1; bp., 2; parishes, 64; priests, 93 (59 dioc., 34 rel.); p.d., 31; sem., 10; bros., 152; srs., 161; catechists, 445; bap., 893; Caths., 116,000 (4.3%); tot. pop., 2,670,000.

Republic in the West Indies; capital, Kingston. Franciscans and Dominicans evangelized the island from about 1512 until 1655. Missionary work was

interrupted after the English took possession but was
resumed by Jesuits about the turn of the 19th century.
An apostolic vicariate was organized in 1837. The
hierarchy was established in 1967. In the late 1990s,
Church leaders spoke out against violence; more than
800 people were murdered in Jamaica in 1997 alone.

Japan*

Archd., 3; dioc., 13; card., 2; abp., 5; bp., 21; parishes, 836; priests, 1,562 (521 dioc., 1,041 rel.); p.d., 19;
sem., 159; bros., 201; srs., 6,065; catechists, 1,746;
bap., 7,687; Caths., 537,000 (.4%); tot. pop.,
127,945,000.

Archipelago in the northwest Pacific; capital, Tokyo.
Jesuits began evangelization in the middle of the 16th
century and about 300,000 converts, most of them in
Kyushu, were reported at the end of the century. The
Nagasaki Martyrs were victims of persecution in 1597.
Another persecution took some 4,000 lives between
1614 and 1651. Missionaries, banned for two centuries, returned about the middle of the 19th century
and found Christian communities still surviving in
Nagasaki and other places in Kyushu. A vicariate was
organized in 1866. Religious freedom was guaranteed
in 1889. The hierarchy was established in 1891.
Several Japanese bishops at the 1998 Synod of
Bishops for Asia said Catholicism has grown slowly in
the region because the Church is too Western.

Since the 1980s, on several occasions Church leaders
have apologized and asked forgiveness for the
Church's complicity in the nation's aggression during
the 1930s and 1940s. At the end of the 20th century,
bishops and religious superiors suggested that during
the 21st century the Japanese Church focus on pastoral
care for migrant workers, concern for the environment
and interreligious dialogue.

Jordan*

Archd., 1; ex. pat., 2; abp., 2; bp., 1; parishes, 64;
priests, 98 (59 dioc., 39 rel.); sem., 3; bros., 10; srs.,
251; bap., 1,160; Caths., 79,000 (1.3%); tot. pop.,
5,600,000.

Constitutional monarchy in the Middle East; capital,
Amman. Christianity there dates from apostolic times.
Survival of the faith was threatened many times under
the rule of Muslims from 636 and Ottoman Turks from
1517 to 1918, and in the Islamic Emirate of Trans-
Jordan from 1918 to 1949. In the years following the
creation of Israel, some 500,000 Palestinian refugees,
including Christians, moved to Jordan. Islam is the
state religion, but religious freedom is guaranteed for
all. The Greek Melkite Archdiocese of Petra and
Filadelfia is located in Jordan. Latin-rite Catholics are
under the jurisdiction of the Latin Patriarchate of
Jerusalem. Jordan established diplomatic relations
with the Holy See in 1994. In the late 20th and especially in the early 21st centuries, an influx of Iraqi
refugees strained the resources of the Jordanian
Catholic community, which offered aid, including
housing, counseling and schooling.

Kazakhstan

Archd. 1, dioc., 2; a.a.; 1; abp., 3; bp., 3; parishes, 66;
priests, 78 (48 dioc., 30 rel.); sem., 11; bros., 8; srs.,
101; bap., 401; Caths., 184,000 (1.3%); tot. pop.,
15,872,000.

Independent republic (1991); formerly part of USSR;
capital, Astana. About 47 percent of the population is
Muslim, and about 44 percent is Orthodox. The
Catholic population is mainly of German, Polish and
Ukrainian origin, descendants of those deported during the Stalin regime. A Latin-rite apostolic administration was established in 1991. In 1998, the Vatican
and the Kazakh government signed an agreement
guaranteeing the Church legal rights. Diocesan structure was established in 1999, and the Vatican created
the first archdiocese and diocese in 2003. The country
had its first priestly ordinations on Kazakh soil in
2006.

Kenya*

Archd. 4; dioc., 20; v.a., 1; mil. ord., 1; abp. 7; bp.
26; parishes, 772; priests, 2,087 (1,292 dioc., 795 rel.);
p.d., 1; sem., 1,676; bros., 722; srs., 4,135; catechists,
10,858; bap., 202,719; Caths., 9,063,000 (25%); tot.
pop., 36,430,000.

Republic in East Africa on the Indian Ocean; capital,
Nairobi. Systematic evangelization by the Holy Ghost
Missionaries began in 1889, nearly 40 years after the
start of work by Protestant missionaries. The hierarchy
was established in 1953. Three metropolitan sees were
established in 1990. Kenyan Catholics were in the
forefront of ministering to victims of the 1998 explo-
sion at the U.S. Embassy in Nairobi. The Kenyan bishops have been outspoken against ethnic violence,
poverty, government corruption and mismanagement,
and the need for a constitutional review. In some rural
areas, Church workers, including foreign missionaries,
were targeted for their work with the poor.

Kiribati*

Dioc., 1; bp., 1; parishes, 21; priests, 27 (17 dioc., 10
rel.); p.d. 2; sem., 13; bros., 17; srs., 96; catechists,
220; bap., 1,894; Caths., 57,000 (54.2%); tot. pop.,
102,000.

Former British colony (Gilbert Islands) in Oceania;
became independent July 12, 1979; capital, Bairiki on
Tarawa. French Missionaries of the Sacred Heart
began work in the islands in 1888. A vicariate for the
islands was organized in 1897. The hierarchy was
established in 1966.

Korea, North

Tot. pop., 23,761,000. No recent Catholic statistics
available; there were an estimated 100,000 Catholics
reported in 1969.

Northern part of peninsula in eastern Asia; formal name
Democratic People's Republic of Korea (May 1, 1948); capital, Pyongyang. See **South Korea** for history before country
was divided. After liberation from Japan in 1945, the Soviet
regime in the North systematically punished all religions.
After the 1950-53 Korean war, Christian worship was not
allowed outside of homes until 1988, when the country's one
Catholic Church was built in Pyongyang. A 1999 South
Korean government report said North Korea clearly restricts
religious practices and churches in the North exist only for
show.

Korea, South*

Archd., 3; dioc., 12; mil. ord. 1; card., 2; abp., 5; bp.,
24; parishes, 1,471; priests, 3,525 (2,947 dioc., 578
rel.); sem., 1,702; bros., 636; srs., 8,828; catechists,

12,824; bap., 158,978; Caths., 4,682,000 (9.6%); tot. pop., 48,500,000.

Southern part of peninsula in eastern Asia; formal name, Republic of Korea (1948); capital, Seoul. Some Catholics may have been in Korea before it became a "hermit kingdom" toward the end of the 16th century and closed its borders to foreigners. The modern introduction to Catholicism came in 1784 through lay converts. A priest arriving in the country in 1794 found 4,000 Catholics there who had never seen a priest. A vicariate was erected in 1831 but was not manned for several years thereafter. There were 15,000 Catholics by 1857. Four persecutions in the 19th century took a terrible toll; several thousand died in the last one, 1866-69. (In 1984, 103 of these martyrs were canonized.) Freedom of religion was granted in 1883, when Korea opened its borders. During World War II, most foreign priests were arrested and expelled, seminaries were closed and churches were taken over. After liberation from Japan in 1945, the Church in the South had religious freedom. Since the 1950-53 Korean war, the Church in South Korea has flourished. Church leaders in the South have worked at reconciliation with the North and to alleviate famine in the North.

Kuwait*

V.a., 1; pat. ex., 1; abp., 1; bp., 1; parishes, 5; priests, 16 (5 dioc., 11 rel.); p.d., 1; bros., 12; bap., 527; Caths., 300,000 (12%); tot. pop., 2,532,000.

Constitutional monarchy (sultanate or sheikdom) in southwest Asia bordering on the Persian Gulf. Remote Christian origins probably date to apostolic times. Islam is the predominant and official religion. Catholics are mostly foreign workers; the Church enjoys religious freedom.

Kyrgyzstan*

A.a., 1; parishes, 3; priests, 8 (2 dioc., 6 rel.); sem., 1; bros., 1; srs., 6; bap., 10; Caths., 1,000; tot. pop., 5,190,000.

Independent republic bordering China; former Soviet republic; capital, Bishkek (former name, Frunze). Most of the people are Sunni Muslim. Established diplomatic relations with the Holy See in August 1992; became apostolic administration in March 2006. The country received its first bishop in July 2006.

Laos

V.a., 4; bp., 3; parishes, 77; priests, 15 (14 dioc., rel. 1); p.d., 1; sem., 20; srs., 96; catechists, 288; bap., 1,208; Caths., 45,000 (.7%); tot. pop., 6,173,000. (AD)

People's republic in southeast Asia; capital, Vientiane. Systematic evangelization by French missionaries started about 1881; earlier efforts ended in 1688. The first mission was established in 1885; an apostolic vicariate was organized in 1899. Most of the foreign missionaries were expelled following the communist takeover in 1975. Catholic schools remain banned, and the government lets foreign missionaries into the country only as "social workers." A Laotian bishop at the 1998 Synod of Bishops for Asia said religious practice was nearly normal in two of the country's four apostolic vicariates, but elsewhere was more controlled and sometimes difficult. Buddhism is the state religion.

Latvia*

Archd., 1; dioc., 3; card., 1; bp., 5; parishes, 274; priests, 138 (112 dioc., 26 rel.); p.d., 1; sem., 43; brs., 26; srs., 101; catechist, 296; bap., 5,937; Caths., 435,000 (19%); tot. pop., 2,298,000.

Independent (1991) Baltic republic; capital, Riga. (Forcibly absorbed by the USSR in 1940; it regained independence in 1991). Catholicism was introduced late in the 12th century. Lutheranism became the dominant religion after 1530. Catholics were free to practice their faith during the long period of Russian control and during independence from 1918 to 1940. The relatively small Catholic community in Latvia was repressed during the 1940-91 Soviet takeover. After Latvia declared its independence, the Church began to flourish, including among people who described themselves as nonreligious. In the late 1990s, one archbishop urged the Russian government not to interfere in disputes over citizenship for the country's ethnic Russians, who make up about one-third of the country's population.

Lebanon*

Patriarchates, 3; achd., 12 (1 Armenian, 4 Maronite, 7 Greek Melkite; dioc., 8 (1 Chaldean, 6 Maronite); v.a., 1 (Latin); card., 1 (patriarch of the Maronites); patriarchs, 3 (patriarchs of Antioch of the Maronites, Antioch of the Syrians and Cilicia of the Armenians who reside in Lebanon); abp., 27; bp., 20; parishes, 1,114; priests, 1,443 (782 dioc., 661 rel.); p.d., 9; sem., 429; bros., 234; srs., 2,919; catechists, 475; bap., 10,609; Caths., 1,836,000 (48%); tot. pop., 3,817,000.

Republic in the Middle East; capital, Beirut. Christianity, introduced in apostolic times, was firmly established by the end of the fourth century and has remained so despite heavy Muslim influence since early in the seventh century. The country is the center of the Maronite rite, and the presidency is reserved for a Maronite Catholic. In the 1980s, the country was torn by violence and often heavy fighting among rival political-religious factions drawn along Christian-Muslim lines. A 1995 Synod of Bishops for Lebanon provoked controversy by directly criticizing Israeli occupation of southern Lebanon and Syria's continued deployment of troops in the area. After Syria withdrew the majority of its troops in 2005, Lebanon's bishops were outspoken in calling for free and fair elections. The Catholic Church has multiple rites in Lebanon and has been seen as influential with politicians.

Lesotho*

Archd., 1; dioc., 3; abp., 1; bp., 3; parishes, 87; priests, 169 (76 dioc., 93 rel.); sem., 73; bros., 31; srs., 714; catechists, 1,502; bap., 23,335; Caths., 1,116,000 (49%); tot. pop., 2,291,000.

Constitutional monarchy, an enclave in the southeastern part of South Africa; capital, Maseru. Oblates of Mary Immaculate, the first Catholic missionaries in the area, started evangelization in 1862. Father Joseph Gerard, beatified in 1988, worked 10 years before he made his first conversion. An apostolic prefecture was organized in 1894. The hierarchy was established in 1951. Under the military government of the late 1980s, Lesotho's Catholics pressed for democratic reforms. In the 1990s, they gave special pastoral care to families whose breadwinners had to travel to South Africa to work, often for weeks at a time.

Liberia*

Archd., 1; dioc., 2; abp., 1; bp., 2; parishes, 58; priests, 56 (40 dioc., 16 rel.); sem., 39; bros., 12; srs., 56; catechists, 917; bap. 961; Caths., 307,000 (8%); tot. pop., 3,636,000.

Republic in West Africa; capital, Monrovia. Missionary work and influence, dating intermittently from the 16th century, were slight before the Society of African Missions undertook evangelization in 1906. The hierarchy was established in 1982. Fighting within the country, which began in 1989, culminated in 1996 and resulted in the evacuation of most Church workers and the archbishop of Monrovia. The war claimed the lives of 150,000 and made refugees of or displaced another million. Most Church institutions in Monrovia were destroyed. Monrovia Archbishop Michael Francis was among leaders calling for U.S.-led intervention to quell chaos in the country in mid-2003.

Libya*

V.a., 3; p.a.; bp., 2; parishes, 6; priests, 11 (2 dioc., 9 rel.); srs., 63; bap., 92; Caths., 104,000 (1.8%); tot. pop., 5,870,000.

Arab state in North Africa; capital, Tripoli. Christianity was probably preached in the area at an early date but was overcome by the spread of Islam from the 630s. Islamization was complete by 1067, and there has been no Christian influence since then. Almost all Catholics are foreign workers. Islam is the state religion. After implementation of a U.N. embargo against the country in 1992, the government removed most limitations on entry of Catholic religious orders, especially health care workers. Libya established diplomatic relations with the Holy See in 1997.

Liechtenstein*

Archd. 1; abp., 1; parishes, 10; priests, 32 (21 dioc., 11 rel); sem., 8; srs., 52; bap., 273; Caths., 27,000 (80%); tot. pop., 34,000.

Constitutional monarchy in central Europe; capital, Vaduz. Christianity in the country dates from the fourth century. The Reformation had hardly any influence in the country. Catholicism is the state religion, but religious freedom for all is guaranteed by law.

Lithuania*

Archd., 2; dioc., 5; mil. ord., 1; card., 1; abp., 1; bp., 12; parishes, 683; priests, 806 (699 dioc., 107 rel.); p.d., 7; sem., 140; bros., 29; srs., 713; catechists, 1,876; bap., 27,652; Caths., 2,757,000 (78%); tot. pop., 3,535,000.

Baltic republic forcibly absorbed and under Soviet domination from 1940; regained independence, 1991; capital, Vilnius. Catholicism was introduced in 1251 and a short-lived diocese was established by 1260. Effective evangelization took place between 1387 and 1417, when Catholicism became the state religion. Efforts of czars to "russify" the Church between 1795 and 1918 were strongly resisted. Concordat relations with the Vatican were established in 1927, nine years after independence from Russia and 13 years before Russia annexed Lithuania. The Russians closed convents and semi-naries; in Kaunas, men needed government approval to attend the seminary. Priests were restricted in pastoral ministry and subject to appointment by government officials; no religious services were allowed outside churches; religious press and instruction were banned. Some bishops and hundreds of priests and laity were imprisoned or detained in Siberia between 1945 and 1955. Two bishops — Vincentas Sladkevicius and Julijonas Steponavicius — were forbidden to act as bishops and relegated to remote parishes in 1957 and 1961, respectively. Despite such conditions, a vigorous underground Church flourished in Lithuania.

In the 1980s, government pressure eased, and some bishops were allowed to return to their dioceses. In 1989, Pope John Paul II appointed bishops in all six Lithuanian dioceses. The Church strongly supported the 1990 independence movement, and Lithuanian independence leaders urged young men to desert the Russian army and seek sanctuary in churches. However, communist rule had nearly destroyed the Church's infrastructure. In 2000 the Church and government signed a series of agreements regularizing the Church's position.

Luxembourg*

Archd., 1; abp., 2; parishes, 275; priests, 228 (163 dioc., 65 rel.); p.d., 8; sem., 5; bros., 12; srs., 566; catechism, 566; bap., 2,779; Caths. 393,000 (85%); tot. pop., 460,000.

Constitutional monarchy in Western Europe; capital, Luxembourg. Christianity, introduced in the fifth and sixth centuries, was firmly established by the end of the eighth century. A full-scale parish system was in existence in the ninth century. Monastic influence was strong until the Reformation, which had minimal influence in the country. The Church experienced some adverse influence from the currents of the French Revolution. In recent years, the Church has restructured its adult formation program to involve more lay workers.

Macedonia*

Dioc., 1; bp., 2; parishes, 8; priests, 19 (13 dioc., 6 rel.); sem., 19; srs., 30; bap., 83; Caths., 19,000 (.9%); tot. pop., 2,350,000.

Former Yugoslav Republic of Macedonia; declared independence in 1992; capital, Skopje. The Diocese of Skopje-Prizren includes the Yugoslav province of Kosovo, so the Macedonian Church helped with ethnic Albanians during the period of ethnic cleansing by Serb forces and retaliatory NATO air strikes.

Madagascar*

Archd., 4; dioc., 17; card., 1; abp., 7; bp., 19; parishes, 312; priests, 1,258 (593 dioc., 665 rel.); p.d., 4; sem., 863; bros., 417; srs., 4,274; catechists, 20,278; bap., 136,418; Caths., 5,576,000 (29%); tot. pop. 18,917,000.

Republic (Malagasy Republic) off the eastern coast of Africa; capital, Antananarivo. Missionary efforts were generally fruitless from early in the 16th century until the Jesuits were permitted to start open evangelization about 1845. An apostolic prefecture was set up in 1850 and an apostolic vicariate in the North was under the charge of the Holy Ghost Fathers in 1898. There were 100,000 Catholics by 1900. The first indigenous bishop was ordained in 1936. The hierarchy was established in 1955. In the late 1980s and early 1990s, the Church joined opposition calls for renewal of social institutions. Today, the Church in Madagascar runs hundreds of schools and dozens of orphanages and is active in the island's social justice concerns; some consider it the largest landowner, after the government.

Malawi*
Archd., 1; dioc., 6; abp., 2; bp., 8; parishes, 145; priests, 406 (299 dioc., 107 rel.); sem., 359; bros., 91; srs., 818; catechists, 2,359; bap., 117,814; Caths., 3,620,000 (28%); tot. pop., 12,760,000.

Republic in the interior of East Africa; capital, Lilongwe. Missionary work, begun by Jesuits in the late 16th and early 17th centuries, was generally ineffective until the end of the 19th century. The Missionaries of Africa (White Fathers) arrived in 1889 and later were joined by others. A vicariate was set up in 1897. The hierarchy was established in 1959. In the late 1980s, the Church in Malawi helped hundreds of thousands of refugees from the war in Mozambique. Malawi's churches, especially the Catholic Church, were instrumental in bringing about the downfall of President Hastings Kamuzu Banda, who ruled for 30 years. A 1992 bishops' pastoral letter criticized Banda's rule and the nation's poverty and galvanized Malawians into pro-democracy protests. Banda responded by summoning the country's bishops, seizing copies of the letter and expelling an Irish member of the Malawi hierarchy. Western donors called off aid, and in 1994 Banda was forced to call multi-party elections, which he lost. In 2002, Church officials were outspoken against plans by Banda's successor, President Bakili Muluzi, to seek a third term of office; Church officials said they were threatened and attacked for that criticism.

Malaysia
Archd., 2; dioc., 6; abp., 5; bp., 7; parishes, 142; priests, 244 (193 dioc., 51 rel.); p.d., 1; sem., 59; bros., 75; srs., 536; catechists, 3,618; bap., 19,150; Caths., 837,000 (3%); tot. pop., 26,640,000. (AD)

Parliamentary democracy in Southeast Asia; capital, Kuala Lumpur. Christianity, introduced by Portuguese colonists about 1511, was confined almost exclusively to Malacca until late in the 18th century. The effectiveness of evangelization increased from then on because of the recruitment and training of indigenous clergy. Singapore (see separate entry), founded in 1819, became a center for missionary work. Effective evangelization in Sabah and Sarawak began in the second half of the 19th century. The hierarchy was established in 1973. In accordance with government wishes for Bahasa Malaysia to be the national language, the Church has tried to introduce it into its liturgies. For more than a decade, Church leaders campaigned against the Internal Security Act, which allows renewable 30-day detentions without trial. Proselytizing Muslims is illegal, but the government allows conversions from other religions.

Maldives
Republic, an archipelago 400 miles southwest of India and Ceylon; capital, Male. No serious attempt was ever made to evangelize the area, which is completely Muslim. Population, 317,000.

Mali*
Archd., 1; dioc., 5; abp., 1; bp., 5; parishes, 43; priests, 169 (101 dioc., 68 rel.); sem., 69; bros., 22; srs., 254; catechists, 1,180; bap., 4,025; Caths., 241,000 (.2%); tot. pop., 14,153,000.

Republic, inland in western Africa; capital, Bamako. Catholicism was introduced late in the second half of the 19th century. Missionary work made little progress in the midst of the predominantly Muslim population. A vicariate was set up in 1921. The hierarchy was established in 1955. In recent years, the Church has promoted the role of women in society. Catholics have cordial relations with Muslims.

Malta*
Archd., 1; dioc., 5; abp., 5; bp., 4; parishes, 85; priests, 855 (472 dioc., 383 rel.); sem., 90; bros., 64; srs., 1,066; catechists, 1,240; bap., 3,440; Caths., 406,000 (94%); tot. pop., 432,000.

Republic south of Sicily; capital, Valletta. Catacombs and inscriptions are evidence of the early introduction of Christianity. St. Paul was shipwrecked on Malta in 60. Saracens controlled the islands from 870 to 1090, a period of difficulty for the Church. The line of bishops extends from 1090 to the present. Late in the 20th century, Church-state conflict developed over passage of government-sponsored legislation affecting Catholic schools and Church-owned property. An agreement reached in 1985 ended the dispute. An influx of several thousand African migrants early in the 21st century strained Maltese hospitality, and Jesuit priests were targeted with arson because of their advocacy for the groups.

Marshall Islands*
P.a., 1; parishes, 4; priests, 7 (6 dioc., 1 rel.); p.d., 1; sem., 2; brs., 1; srs., 12; bap., 177; Caths., 5,000 (12.5%); tot. pop., 56,000.

Island republic in central Pacific Ocean; capital, Majura. Formerly administered by United States as part of U.N. Trust Territory of the Pacific; independent nation, 1991. An apostolic prefecture was erected May 25, 1993 (formerly part of Carolines-Marshall Diocese), with Rev. James Gould, a U.S. Jesuit, as its first apostolic prefect.

Mauritania*
Dioc., 1; bp., 1; parishes, 6; priests, 10 (3 dioc., 7 rel.); brs., 1; srs., 36; sem., 2; bap., 43; Caths., 5,000 (.2%); tot. pop., 3,139,000. (AD)

Islamic republic on the northwest coast of Africa; capital, Nouakchott. With few exceptions, the Catholics in the country are foreign workers. At the 1994 Synod of Bishops for Africa, a bishop from Mauritania reported increasing problems with fundamentalist Muslims, but cautioned Church leaders against generalizing about Muslims.

Mauritius*
Dioc., 1; v.a., 1; card., 1; bp., 2; parishes, 44; priests, 102 (51 dioc., 51 rel.); sem., 13; bros., 28; srs., 227; catechists, 256; bap., 5,996; Caths., 312,000 (26%); tot. pop., 1,250,000.

Island republic in the Indian Ocean; capital, Port Louis. Catholicism was introduced by Vincentians in 1722. Port Louis, made a vicariate in 1819 and a diocesc in 1847, was a jumping-off point for missionaries to Australia, Madagascar and South Africa. During a 1989 visit to Mauritius, Pope John Paul II warned against sins that accompanied its rapid economic development and booming tourism industry.

Mexico* (See Catholic Church in Mexico; see also Statistics of the Church in Mexico)

Micronesia*

Dioc., 1; bp., 1; parishes, 24; priests, 23 (10 dioc., 13 rel.); p.d., 40; sem., 10; bros., 1; srs., 57; catechists, 528; bap., 1,550; Caths., 60,000 (54%); tot. pop., 110,000.

Federated States of Micronesia (Caroline archipelago) in southwest Pacific; capital, Palikir; former U.N. trust territory under U.S. administration; became independent nation September 1991. Effective evangelization began in the late 1880s. The government established diplomatic relations with the Holy See in 1994.

Moldova*

Dioc., 1; bp., 1; parishes, 14; priests, 29 (14 dioc., 15 rel.); p.d., 1; sem., 11; bros., 3; srs., 46; bap., 53; Caths., 20,000 (.5%); tot. pop., 3,590,000.

Independent republic, former constituent republic of the USSR; capital, Kishinev. The majority of people belong to the Orthodox Church. Catholics are mostly of Polish or German descent.

Monaco*

Archd., 1; abp., 1; parishes, 6; priests, 22 (16 dioc., 6 rel.); p.d., 3; sem., 2; srs., 11; bap., 209; Caths., 29,000 (90%); tot. pop., 32,000.

Constitutional monarchy, an enclave on the Mediterranean coast of France; capital, Monaco. Christianity was introduced before 1000. Catholicism is the official religion but religious freedom is guaranteed for all.

Mongolia*

Bp., 1; parishes, 3; priests, 21 (4 dioc., 17 rel.); sem., 4; bros., 3; srs., 53; bap., 49; Caths., 3,000 (.08%); tot. pop., 2,580,000.

Republic in north central Asia; formerly under communist control; capital, Ulan Bator. Christianity was introduced by Oriental Orthodox. Some Franciscans were in the country in the 13th and 14th centuries, en route to China. Freedom of worship is guaranteed under the new constitution, which went into effect in 1992. The government established relations with the Holy See in 1992 and indicated that missionaries would be welcome to help rebuild the country. The first Catholic parish was established in 1994, and by 1997 the Church had extended its work beyond the capital. In 2003 a missionary from the Philippines became Mongolia's first bishop.

Montenegro

Archd. 1, Dioc. 1; abp., 1; bp., 1; parishes, 47; priests, 34 (23 dioc., 11 rel.); sem., 2; brs. 1; srs., 140; bap., 225; Caths., 23,000 (4%); tot. pop., 590,000.

Independent nation (July 2006) in southeastern Europe; formerly part of Yugoslavia and Serbia and Montenegro; capital Podgorica. Church history coincides with much of Serbia. Montenegro and the Vatican announced diplomatic ties in December 2006.

Morocco*

Archd., 2; abp., 2; parishes, 39; priests, 37 (6 dioc., 31 rel.); bros., 12; srs., 231; bap., 38; Caths., 23,000 (.07%); tot. pop., 31,524,000.

Constitutional monarchy in North Africa; capital, Rabat. Christianity was known in the area by the end of the third century. Bishops from Morocco attended a council at Carthage in 484. Catholic life survived under Visigoth and, from 700, Arab rule; later it became subject to influence from the Spanish, Portuguese and French. Islam is the state religion. The hierarchy was established in 1955.

Mozambique*

Archd., 3; dioc., 9; card., 1; abp. 4; bp., 12; parishes, 294; priests, 591 (200 dioc., 391 rel.); sem., 367; bros., 105; srs., 1,130; catechists, 42,574; bap., 98,713; Caths., 4,466,000 (23%); tot. pop., 20,774,000. (AD)

Republic in southeast Africa; capital, Maputo. Christianity was introduced by Portuguese Jesuits about the middle of the 16th century. Evangelization continued from then until the 18th century, when it went into decline largely because of the Portuguese government's expulsion of the Jesuits. Conditions worsened in the 1830s, improved after 1881, but deteriorated again during the anticlerical period from 1910 to 1925.

Conditions improved in 1940, the year Portugal concluded a new concordat with the Holy See and the hierarchy was established. Missionaries' outspoken criticism of Portuguese policies in Mozambique resulted in Church-state tensions in the years immediately preceding independence. The first two indigenous bishops were ordained March 9, 1975. Two ecclesiastical provinces were established in 1984. Mozambican bishops and members of the Rome-based Sant' Egidio Community were official mediators in the talks that ended 16 years of civil war in 1992. Since then, Church participation has flourished, with high attendance at Mass, a boom in vocations and active catechists at the parish level.

Myanmar

Archd., 3; dioc., 10; abp., 4; bp., 15; parishes, 306; priests, 613 (571 dioc., 42 rel.); sem., 399; bros., 111; srs., 1,550; catechists, 3,312; bap., 20,476; Caths., 646,000 (1.2%); tot. pop., 52,650,000. (AD)

Socialist republic in Southeast Asia, formerly Burma; name changed to Myanmar in 1989; capital, Yangon (Rangoon). Christianity was introduced about 1500. Small-scale evangelization had limited results from the middle of the 16th century until the 1850s, when effective organization of the Church began. The hierarchy was established in 1955. Buddhism was declared the state religion in 1961, but the state is now officially secular. In 1965, Church schools and hospitals were nationalized. In 1966, all foreign missionaries who had entered the country for the first time after 1948 were forced to leave when the government refused to renew their work permits. The Church is involved primarily in pastoral and social activities.

Namibia*

Archd., 1; dioc., 1; v.a., 1; abp., 1; bp., 1; parishes, 93; priests, 89 (16 dioc., 73 rel.); p.d., 48; sem., 23;

bros., 17; srs., 495; catechists, 1,328; bap., 16,439; Caths., 405,000 (18%); tot. pop., 2,336,000. (AD) Independent (March 21, 1990) state in southern Africa; capital, Windhoek. The area shares the history of South Africa. The hierarchy was established in 1994. The Church is hindered by a lack of priests.

Nauru*

Parishes, 2; priest, 1 (rel); p.d., 2; srs., 3; bap., 154; Caths., 3,000 (37%); tot. pop., 10,000.

Independent republic in western Pacific; capital, Yaren. Forms part of the Tarawa and Nauru Diocese (Kiribati). Established diplomatic relations with the Holy See in 1992.

Nepal*

P.a., 1; parishes, 7; priests, 62 (12 dioc.; 50 rel.); sem., 24; bros., 4; srs., 132; bap., 349; Caths., 7,000 (.2%); tot. pop., 25,890,000.

Constitutional monarchy in central Asia; capital, Katmandu. Little is known of the country before the 15th century. Some Jesuits passed through from 1628 and some sections were evangelized in the 18th century, with minimal results, before the country was closed to foreigners. Conversions from Hinduism, the state religion, are not recognized in law and are punishable by imprisonment. The Church has established an effective charitable network in Nepal, which officially declared itself a secular state in 2006.

Netherlands*

Archd., 1; dioc., 6; mil ord., 1; card., 2; abp., 2; bp., 15; parishes, 1,428; priests 3,180 (1,289 dioc., 1,891 rel.); p.d., 342; sem., 189; bros., 1,095; srs., 8,441; bap., 33,549; Caths., 4,883,000 (30%); tot. pop., 16,340,000.

Constitutional monarchy in northwestern Europe; capital, Amsterdam (seat of government, The Hague). Evangelization, begun about the turn of the sixth century by Irish, Anglo-Saxon and Frankish missionaries, resulted in Christianization of the country by 800 and subsequent strong influence on the Lowlands. Invasion by French Calvinists in 572 brought serious losses to the Catholic Church and made the Reformed Church dominant. Catholics suffered a practical persecution of official repression and social handicap in the 17th century. The schism of Utrecht occurred in 1724. Only one-third of the population was Catholic in 1726. The Church had only a skeletal organization from 1702 to 1853, when the hierarchy was re-established.

Despite this upturn, cultural isolation was the experience of Catholics until about 1914. From then on new vigor came into the life of the Church, and a whole new climate of interfaith relations began to develop. Before and for some years following the Second Vatican Council, the thrust and variety of thought and practice in the Dutch Church moved it to the vanguard position of "progressive" renewal. A synod of Dutch bishops held at the Vatican in January 1980 discussed ideological differences among Catholics with the aim of fostering unity and restoring some discipline within the nation's Church. However, even into the 1990s Church leaders spoke of a polarization among Catholics over issues such as sexual morality, ministries for women and priestly celibacy. The bishops also spoke out against permissive laws on euthanasia and assisted suicide.

New Zealand*

Archd., 1; dioc., 5; mil. ord., 1; card., 1; abp., 2; bp., 12; parishes, 270; priests, 504 (303 dioc., 201 rel.); p.d., 10; sem., 28; bros., 154; srs., 915; bap., 7,121; Caths. 499,000 (12%); tot. pop., 4,140,000.

Parliamentary democracy in southwestern Pacific Ocean; capital, Wellington. Protestant missionaries were the first evangelizers. On North Island, Catholic missionaries started work before the establishment of two dioceses in 1848; their work among the Maoris was not organized until about 1881. On South Island, whose first resident priest arrived in 1840, a diocese was established in 1869. These three jurisdictions were joined in a province in 1896. The Marists were the predominant Catholic missionaries in the area. The first Maori bishop was named in 1988. In 1998, Pope John Paul II urged New Zealand's bishops not to allow the Church to fall prey to the practices and values of prevailing culture.

Nicaragua*

Archd., 1; dioc., 6; v.a., 1; card., 1; abp., 2; bp., 11; parishes, 288; priests, 536 (376 dioc., 160 rel.); p.d., 29; sem., 298; bros., 47; srs., 1,028; catechists, 23,429; bap., 90,345; Caths., 4,928,000 (89%); tot. pop., 5,530,000.

Republic in Central America: capital, Managua. Evangelization began shortly after the Spanish conquest, about 1524, and eight years later the first bishop took over jurisdiction of the Church in the country. Jesuits were leaders in missionary work during the colonial period, which lasted until the 1820s. Evangelization increased after establishment of the republic in 1838 and extended to the Atlantic coastal area, where Protestant missionaries began work about the middle of the 1900s.

Many Church leaders, clerical and lay, supported the aims but not necessarily all the methods of the Sandinista revolution, which forced the resignation and flight July 17, 1979, of Anastasio Somoza, whose family had controlled the government since the early 1930s. During the Sandinista period that followed, four priests accepted government posts. Some Nicaraguan Catholics threw their energies behind the Sandinista program of land reform and socialism, forming what some called a "popular church" based on liberation theology, while others strongly opposed the government. Managua Cardinal Miguel Obando Bravo helped mediate cease-fire talks during the war between the Sandinistas and U.S.-backed guerrillas. Land distribution, exacerbated by a wide gap in incomes, continued to be an issue, and in the late 1990s the Nicaraguan bishops continued to call for compromise between the government and former government officials. Despite an influx of aid after Hurricane Mitch killed more than 2,500 Nicaraguans and forced 900,000 to evacuate in 1998, Church leaders still cited poverty as a major issue.

Niger*

Archd., 1; dioc.; 1; bp., 3; parishes, 19; priests, 39 (14 dioc., 25 rel.); p.d., 1; sem., 7; bros., 8; srs., 99; catechists, 245; bap., 393; Caths., 19,000 (.13%); tot. pop., 13,039,000.

Republic in west central Africa; capital, Niamey. The first mission was set up in 1831. An apostolic prefecture was organized in 1942, and the first diocese was established in 1961. The country is predominantly Muslim. The Church is active in the fields of health and education.

Nigeria*

Archd., 9; dioc., 41; v.a., 2; card., 1; abp., 10; bp., 48; parishes, 2,435; priests, 4,973 (4,167 dioc., 806 rel.); p.d., 10; sem., 5,734; bros., 425; srs., 4,465; catechists, 31,410; bap., 467,100; Caths., 20,957,000 (15.5%); tot. pop., 138,330,000.

Republic in West Africa; capital, Lagos. The Portuguese introduced Catholicism to the coastal region in the 15th century. Capuchins did some evangelization in the 17th century but systematic missionary work did not get under way along the coast until about 1840. A vicariate for this area was organized in 1870. A prefecture was set up in 1911 for missions in the northern part of the country, where Islam was strongly entrenched. The hierarchy was established in 1950. From 1967, when Biafra seceded, until early in 1970 the country was torn by civil war. Under the 1993-99 rule of Gen. Sani Abacha, Church leaders spoke out on behalf of human rights and democracy. After Abacha announced elections, the bishops said the country needed "new leading actors and fresh vision." As the 21st century began, bishops spoke out against imposition of Islamic law in individual states within the country.

Norway*

Dioc., 1; prel., 2; bp., 3; parishes, 35; priests, 79 (38 dioc., 41 rel.); p.d., 3; sem., 7; bros., 2; srs., 156; bap., 768; Caths., 54,000 (1.1%); tot. pop., 4,650,000.

Constitutional monarchy in northern Europe; capital, Oslo. Evangelization begun in the ninth century by missionaries from England and Ireland put the Church on a firm footing about the turn of the 11th century. The first diocese was set up in 1153 and development of the Church progressed until the Black Death in 1349 inflicted losses from which it never recovered. Lutheranism, introduced from outside in 1537 and furthered cautiously, gained general acceptance by about 1600 and was made the state religion. Legal and other measures crippled the Church, forcing priests to flee the country and completely disrupting normal activity. Changes for the better came in the 19th century, with the granting of religious liberty in 1845 and the repeal of many legal disabilities in 1897. Norway was administered as a single apostolic vicariate from 1892 to 1932, when it was divided into three jurisdictions.

Oman

Parishes, 4; priests, 9 (rel.); bap., 134; Caths., 72,000 (2.7%); tot. pop., 2,580,000.

Independent monarchy in eastern corner of Arabian Peninsula; capital, Muscat. Under ecclesiastical jurisdiction of Arabia apostolic vicariate.

Pakistan*

Archd., 2; dioc., 4; p.a., 1; abp., 3; bp., 5; parishes, 118; priests, 260 (137 dioc., 123 rel.); sem., 102; bros., 67; srs., 795; catechists, 740; bap., 20,023; Caths., 1,044,000 (.07%); tot. pop., 156,250,000.

Islamic republic in southwest Asia; capital, Islamabad. Islam, firmly established in the eighth cen-

tury, is the state religion. Christian evangelization of the native population began about the middle of the 19th century, years after earlier scattered attempts. The hierarchy was established in 1950. A series of death sentences against Christians accused of blasphemy resulted in acquittals during appeal processes, but in 1998 Bishop John Joseph of Faisalabad committed suicide to protest the strict blasphemy laws, which continued to be used as reasons for Christian arrests. In early 2002, the government did away with the system under which religious minorities, such as Catholics, could only vote in elections for members of their religious group. Pakistani Christians, including Catholics, have been the target of several terrorist incidents since the United States attacked Afghanistan in October 2001. The Church has been active in justice and peace work.

Palau*

Parishes, 3; priests, 4 (2 dioc., 2 rel.); p.d., 1; srs., 5; bap., 316; Caths., 10,000 (52%); tot. pop., 19,000.

Independent (1994) nation in western Pacific; capital, Koror; part of Caroline chain of Islands. Under ecclesiastical jurisdiction of diocese of Caroline Islands, Federated States of Micronesia.

Panama*

Archd., 1; dioc., 5; prel., 1; v.a., 1; abp., 2; bp., 10; parishes, 188; priests, 395 (201 dioc., 194 rel.); p.d., 61; sem., 113; bros., 36; srs., 423; catechists, 4,245; bap., 28,599; Caths., 2,757,000 (84%); tot. pop., 3,280,000.

Republic in Central America; capital, Panama City. Catholicism was introduced by Franciscan missionaries and evangelization started in 1514. The Panama Diocese, oldest in the Americas, was set up at the same time. The Catholic Church has favored status and state aid for missions, charities and parochial schools, but freedom is guaranteed to all religions. In May 1989, Panama's bishops accused the government of thwarting the presidential elections and of attempting to intimidate the Church. The elections' legitimate leader, Guillermo Endara, temporarily sought refuge at the Vatican Embassy in Panama City. After increasing unrest and violence, on Dec. 24, 1989, the country's dictator, Gen. Manuel Noriega, sought refuge at the Vatican Embassy. Ten days later, after U.S. troops spent days blasting the embassy with loud rock music and after meetings with Church diplomatic officials, Noriega surrendered.

Papua New Guinea*

Archd., 4; dioc., 15; abp., 6; bp., 21; parishes, 372; priests, 567 (210 dioc., 357 rel.); p.d., 4; sem., 481; bros., 189; srs., 911; catechists, 4,040; bap., 29,967; Caths., 1,776,000 (31%); tot. pop., 5,733,000.

Independent (Sept. 16, 1975) republic in southwest Pacific; capital, Port Moresby. Marists began evangelization about 1844 but were handicapped by many factors, including "spheres of influence" laid out for Catholic and Protestant missionaries. An apostolic prefecture was set up in 1896 and placed in charge of the Divine Word Missionaries. The territory suffered greatly during World War II. Hierarchy was established for New Guinea and adjacent islands in 1966. A decade-long war that began in the Bougainville area in the late 1980s left many churches, schools and health centers destroyed. At the end of the century, the Church fought social disintegration marked by violence, poverty and corruption.

Paraguay*

Archd., 1; dioc., 11; v.a., 2; mil. ord. 1; abp., 4; bp., 18; parishes, 398; priests, 888 (281 dioc., 607 rel.); p.d., 142; sem., 422; bros., 135; srs., 2,158; bap., 90,264; catechists, 58,612; Caths., 5,602,000 (91%); tot. pop., 6,132,000.

Republic in central South America; capital, Asunción. Catholicism was introduced in 1542, evangelization began almost immediately. A diocese erected in 1547 was occupied for the first time in 1556. On many occasions thereafter, dioceses in the country were left unoccupied because of political and other reasons. Jesuits who came into the country after 1609 devised the reductions system for evangelizing the Indians, teaching them agriculture, husbandry, trades and other arts, and giving them experience in property use and community life. The reductions were communes of Indians only, and had an average population of 3,000-4,000, under the direction of the missionaries. At their peak, some 30 reductions had a population of 100,000. Political officials regarded the reductions with disfavor because politicians did not control them and feared that the Indians trained in them might foment revolt and upset the established colonial system under Spanish control. The reductions lasted until about 1768, when the Jesuits were expelled.

Church-state relations following independence from Spain in 1811 were often tense because of government efforts to control the Church through continued exercise of Spanish patronage rights and by other means. The Church as well as the whole country suffered during the War of the Triple Alliance, 1865-70. After that time, the Church had the same kind of experience in Paraguay as in the rest of Latin America, with forces of liberalism, anticlericalism, massive educational needs, poverty, and a shortage of priests and other personnel. In the 1980s, Church-state tensions increased as Catholic leaders spoke out against President Alfredo Stroessner's decades of one-man rule. A 1988 papal visit seemed to increase the Church's confidence, as bishops repeatedly spoke out against Stroessner. The army general who overthrew Stroessner in 1989 said he did so in part to defend the Catholic Church.

Retired Bishop Fernando Lugo, who campaigned on a platform of equality for Paraguay's poor farmers and indigenous people, was elected president of Paraguay in 2008, ending the six-decade rule of the Colorado Party.

Peru*

Archd., 7; dioc., 18; prel., 11; v.a., 8; mil. ord. 1; card., 1; abp., 13; bp., 61; parishes, 1,456; priests, 2,896 (1,636 dioc., 1,260 rel.); p.d., 69; sem., 2,097; bros., 621; srs., 5,738; catechists, 44,648; bap., 346,086; Caths., 24,991,000 (88%); tot. pop., 28,350,000.

Republic on the west coast of South America; capital, Lima. An effective diocese became operational in 1537, five years after the Spanish conquest. Evangelization, already under way, developed for some time after 1570 but deteriorated before the end of the colonial period in the 1820s. The first American

saint of the new world was a Peruvian, Rose of Lima, a Dominican tertiary who died in 1617 and was canonized in 1671.

In the new republic founded after the wars of independence the Church experienced problems of adjustment, government efforts to control it through continuation of the patronage rights of the Spanish crown; suppression of houses of religious and expropriation of Church property; religious indifference and outright hostility. In the 20th century, liberation theology was born in Peru under the leadership of Father Gustavo Gutierrez. In the 1980s and early 1990s, the Maoist Sendero Luminoso guerrillas often targeted Church workers, who also found themselves prone to false charges of terrorism. A Peruvian cardinal was credited with much of the success of an early 1990s government effort to win the surrender of the rebels. When the government initiated a drastic economic program in 1990, Peruvian Church leaders worked to help feed and clothe the poor. In the late '90s, the Church successfully fought a government program of sterilization.

Early in the 21st century, Church leaders became more outspoken on environmental issues and took the lead in reconstruction after the 2007 earthquake hit coastal areas.

Philippines*

Archd., 16; dioc., 56; prel., 6; v.a., 7; mil. ord. 1; card., 3; abp., 19; bp., 107; parishes, 3,018; priests, 8,316 (5,528 dioc., 2,788 rel.); p.d., 9; sem., 7,029; bros., 1,204; srs., 12,579; catechists, 102,495; bap., 1,633,753; Caths., 70,502,000 (81.3%); tot. pop., 86,970,000.

Republic, an archipelago of 7,000 islands off the southeast coast of Asia; capital, Manila. Systematic evangelization was begun in 1564 and resulted in firm establishment of the Church by the 19th century. During the period of Spanish rule, which lasted from the discovery of the islands by Magellan in 1521 to 1898, the Church experienced difficulties with the patronage system under which the Spanish crown tried to control ecclesiastical affairs through episcopal and other appointments. This system ended in 1898 when the United States gained possession of the islands and instituted a policy of separation of Church and state. Anticlericalism flared late in the 19th century. The Aglipayan schism, an attempt to set up a nationalist Church, occurred in 1902.

Church leaders and human rights groups constantly criticized abuses under former president and dictator Ferdinand Marcos. Church newspapers were among those censored or closed after he declared martial law, and religious and lay people were arrested and held without formal charges for long periods of time. After Marcos declared himself the victor in the 1986 elections and international observers declared his win a fraud, the Philippine bishops' call for a nonviolent struggle for justice was seen as the catalyst for the nation's "people power" revolution. Corazon Aquino, Marcos's successor, took refuge with Carmelite nuns during the revolution. At the turn of the century, Church workers often found themselves unintentional victims of violence spurred by Muslim separatists' fight for autonomy in the southern Philippines. Church social action focused on the poor, overseas workers, ecology, corruption, and a fight against the death penalty.

Poland*

Archd., 15; dioc., 28; mil. ord., 1; ordinariate, 1; cards., 8; abps., 22; bps., 106; parishes, 10,198; priests, 28,976 (22,563 dioc., 6,413 rel.); p.d., 13; sem., 6,038; bros., 1,395; srs., 23,039; catechists, 13,593; bap., 353,512; Caths., 36,660,000 (96%); tot. pop., 38,140,000.

Republic in Eastern Europe; capital, Warsaw. The first traces of Christianity date from the second half of the ninth century. Its spread was accelerated by the union of the Slavs in the 10th century. The first diocese was set up in 968. The Reformation, supported mainly by city dwellers and the upper classes, peaked from about the middle of the 16th century, resulting in numerous conversions to Lutheranism, the Reformed Church and the Bohemian Brethren. A successful Counter-Reformation, with the Jesuits in a position of leadership, was completed by about 1632. The movement served a nationalist as well as religious purpose; in restoring religious unity to a large degree, it united the country against potential invaders, the Swedes, Russians and Turks. The Counter-Reformation had bad side effects, leading to the repression of Protestants long after it was over and to prejudice against Eastern-rite Catholics. The Church, in the same manner as the entire country, was adversely affected by the partitions of the 18th and 19th centuries. Russification hurt the Eastern- and Latin-rite Catholics.

In the republic established after World War I the Church reorganized itself, continued to serve as a vital force in national life, and enjoyed generally harmonious relations with the state. Progressive growth was strong until 1939, when German and Russian forces invaded and World War II began. In 1945, seven years before the adoption of a Soviet-type of constitution, the communist-controlled government initiated a policy that included a constant program of atheistic propaganda; a strong campaign against the hierarchy and clergy; the imprisonment in 1948 of 700 priests and even more religious; rigid limitation on the activities of the Catholic press and religious movements.

Regular contacts on a working level were initiated by the Vatican and Poland in 1974; regular diplomatic relations were established in 1989. Cardinal Karol Wojtyla of Krakow was elected to the papacy in 1978. Church and papal support was strong for the independent labor movement, Solidarity, which was recognized by the government in August 1980 but outlawed in December 1981, when martial law was imposed (martial law was suspended in 1982). In May 1989, following recognition of Solidarity and a series of political changes, the Catholic Church was given legal status for the first time since the communists took control of the government in 1944. In 1990, a new constitution was adopted, declaring Poland a democratic state. In 1992, the pope restructured the Church in Poland, adding 13 new dioceses. A new concordat between the Polish government and the Holy See was signed in 1993.

Since the end of communist rule, Poland's Church has struggled with anti-Semitism among some clergy. A dispute over a Carmelite convent outside the former Nazi death camp at Auschwitz resulted in the convent's removal, but several years later the Church was forced to speak against Catholic protesters who posted hundreds of crosses outside the camp. A nearly eight-year national synod process concluded in 1999 with calls for priests to live less luxurious lifestyles and to keep parishes finances open. The Polish Church continued to be a source of missionary priests in more than 90 countries. Church leaders also were dogged by allegations of spying under the communist regime, a charge that led the newly appointed archbishop of Warsaw to resign in early 2007 shortly before his installation.

Portugal*

Patriarchate (Lisbon), 1; archd., 2; dioc., 17; mil. ord., 1; patriarch, 1; card., 2; abp., 6; bp., 42; parishes, 4,386; priests, 3,946 (2,894 dioc., 1,052 rel.); p.d., 198; sem., 475; bros., 327; srs., 5,717; catechists, 63,191; bap., 77,272; Caths., 9,339,000 (88%); tot. pop., 10,660,000.

Republic in the western part of the Iberian peninsula; capital, Lisbon. Christianity was introduced before the fourth century. From the fifth century to early in the eighth century the Church experienced difficulties from the physical invasion of barbarians and the intellectual invasion of doctrinal errors in the forms of Arianism, Priscillianism and Pelagianism. The Church survived under the rule of Arabs from about 711 and of the Moors until 1249. Ecclesiastical life was fairly vigorous from 1080 to 1185, and monastic influence became strong. A decline set in about 1450. Several decades later Portugal became the jumping-off place for many missionaries to newly discovered colonies. The Reformation had little effect in the country.

In the early 1700s, King John V broke relations with Rome and required royal approval of papal acts. His successor, Joseph I, expelled the Jesuits from Portugal and the colonies. Liberal revolutionaries with anti-Church policies made the 19th century a difficult one for the Church. Similar policies prevailed in Church-state relations in the 20th century until the accession to power of Premier Antonio de Oliveira Salazar in 1928; the hierarchy was seen as closely aligned with him. In 1940 Salazar concluded a concordat with the Holy See that regularized Church-state relations but still left the Church in a subservient condition.

In 1930, after lengthy investigation, the Church authorized devotion to Our Lady of Fátima, who appeared to three Portuguese children in 1917. Pope John Paul II, who credited Our Lady of Fátima with saving his life during a 1981 assassination attempt on her feast day, visited Portugal several times, including in May 2000 to beatify two of the Fátima visionaries. At that time, he had his Secretary of State, Cardinal Angelo Sodano, announce that the so-called third secret of Fátima would be published. The following month, the Vatican published the secret and said the message predicted the struggles of the Church with Nazism and communism and foretold the shooting of Pope John Paul.

Puerto Rico

Archd., 1; dioc., 4; card., 1; abp., 1; bp., 7; parishes, 328; priests, 704 (358 dioc., 346 rel.); p.d., 406; sem., 104; bros., 46; srs., 1,153; catechists, 26,571; bap., 29,199; Caths., 3,089,000 (78%); tot. pop., 3,938,000. (AD)

A U.S. commonwealth, the smallest of the Greater Antilles, 885 miles southeast of the southern coast of Florida; capital, San Juan. Following its discovery by Columbus in 1493, the island was evangelized by Spanish missionaries and remained under Spanish ecclesiastical as well as political control until 1898, when it became a possession of the United States. The original diocese, San Juan, was erected in 1511. The present hierarchy was established in 1960.

Qatar

Parish; priest, 7 (7 dioc.); p.d., 1; bap., 247; Caths., 64,000 (10.6%); tot. pop., 679,000.

Independent state in the Persian Gulf; capital, Doha. Under ecclesiastical jurisdiction of Arabia apostolic vicariate.

Réunion

Dioc., 1; bp., 1; parishes, 56; priests, 120 (53 dioc., 67 rel.); p.d., 14; sem., 16; bros., 13; srs., 316; catechists, 3,410; bap., 11,358; Caths., 625,000 (82.6%); tot. pop., 784,000. (AD)

French overseas department, 450 miles east of Madagascar; capital, Saint-Denis. Catholicism was introduced in 1667 and some intermittent missionary work was done through the rest of the century. An apostolic prefecture was organized in 1712. Vincentians began work there in 1817 and were joined later by Holy Ghost Fathers. In 1998 the bishops joined their counterparts in Guadeloupe, French Guiana and Martinique to call slavery "an immense collective sin."

Romania*

Archd., 3; dioc., 8; ord., 1; ex., 1; abp., 6; bp., 12; parishes, 1,883; priests, 1,820 (1,600 dioc., 220 rel.); p.d., 1; sem., 646; bros., 176; srs., 1,317; catechists, 816; bap., 11,133; Caths., 1,886,000 (8.4%); tot. pop., 21,580,000.

Republic in southeastern Europe; capital, Bucharest. Latin Christianity, introduced in the third century, all but disappeared during the barbarian invasions. The Byzantine rite was introduced by the Bulgars about the beginning of the eighth century and established firm roots. It eventually became Orthodox, but a large number of its adherents returned later to union with Rome. Communists took over the government following World War II, forced the abdication of Michael I in 1947, and enacted a Soviet type of constitution in 1952. By that time a campaign against religion was already in progress. In 1948 the government denounced a concordat concluded in 1929, nationalized all schools and passed a law on religions that resulted in the disorganization of Church administration. The 1.5 million-member Romanian Byzantine-rite Church, by government decree, was incorporated into the Romanian Orthodox Church, and Catholic properties were given to the Orthodox. Five of the six Latin-rite bishops were immediately disposed of by the government, and the last was sentenced to 18 years' imprisonment in 1951. Religious orders were suppressed in 1949.

Some change for the better in Church-state relations was reported after the middle of the summer of 1964, although restrictions were still in effect. The Eastern Church regained liberty in 1990 with the change of government. The hierarchy was restored and diplomatic relations with the Holy See were re-established. Today, most Latin-rite Catholics are ethnic Hungarians residing in Transylvania. Pope John Paul II visited Romania May 7-9, 1999. Church leaders said the historic visit led to a deeper openness and understanding between Catholics and Orthodox.

Russia*

Archd., 2; dioc. 3 (2 for European Russia, 1 for Siberia); ap. ex., 1; abp., 2; bp., 2; parish, 408; priests, 328 (126 dioc., 202 rel.); p.d., 4; sem., 99; bros., 17; srs, 357; bap., 1,397; Caths., 955,000 (.07%); tot. pop., 142,480,000.

Federation in Europe and Asia; capital, Moscow. The Orthodox Church has been predominant in Russian history. It developed from the Byzantine Church before 1064. Some of its members subsequently established communion with Rome as the result of reunion movements, but most remained Orthodox. The government has always retained some kind of general or particular control of this Church.

From the beginning of the Communist government in 1917, all churches of whatever kind became the targets of official campaigns designed to negate their influence on society and/or to eliminate them entirely. An accurate assessment of the situation of the Catholic Church in Russia was difficult to make. Research by a Polish priest, reported in 1998, documented the arrests, trials and fabricated confessions of priests in the 1920s and 1930s. A report by a team of research specialists made public by the Judiciary Committee of the U.S. House of Representatives in 1964 said: "The fate of the Catholic Church in the USSR and countries occupied by the Russians from 1917 to 1959 shows the following: (a) the number killed: 55 bishops; 12,800 priests and monks; 2.5 million Catholic believers; (b) imprisoned or deported: 199 bishops; 32,000 priests and 10 million believers; (c) 15,700 priests were forced to abandon their priesthood and accept other jobs; and (d) a large number of seminaries and religious communities were dissolved." Despite repression, Lithuania and Ukraine remained strongholds of Catholicism.

During his 1985-91 presidency, Soviet President Mikhail Gorbachev met twice with Pope John Paul II — meetings later credited with the return of religious freedom in the Soviet Union. In 1991, the pope established two Latin-rite apostolic administrations in the Russian Republic: one in Moscow and one based in Novosibirsk, Siberia.

Catholic communities in Europe and the United States have been instrumental in helping to rebuild the Church in Russia. Under a 1997 religion law, every religious organization in Russia had to register on a national level, then re-register each parish by the end of 1999 to enjoy full legal benefits such as owning property and publishing religious literature. The apostolic administrations registered with no problems, but after the Russian government rejected the Jesuits' registration application, they were forced to take the matter to the country's constitutional court, which ruled that they qualified.

The Vatican's upgrading of Russia's four apostolic administrations to dioceses in early 2002 provoked new tensions with the Orthodox, who accused the

Catholic Church of trying to convert its members. Russian authorities refused to readmit five prominent Church leaders, including one bishop, after they left the country. The Vatican eventually appointed a new bishop for the vacant Russian diocese and transferred the expelled bishop.

Rwanda*

Archd., 1; dioc., 8; abp., 2; bp., 8; parishes, 132; priests, 581 (450 dioc., 131 rel.); sem., 437; bros., 175; srs., 1,527; catechists, 4,563; bap., 135,885; Caths., 4,381,000 (47%); tot. pop., 9,208,000.

Republic in east central Africa; capital, Kigali. Catholicism was introduced about the turn of the 20th century. The hierarchy was established in 1959. Intertribal warfare between the ruling Hutus (90 percent of the population) and the Tutsis (formerly the ruling aristocracy) plagued the country for a number of years. In April 1994, the deaths of the presidents of Rwanda and Burundi in a suspicious plane crash sparked the outbreak of a ferocious civil war. Among the thousands of victims — mostly Tutsis — were three bishops and about 25 percent of the clergy. Thousands more fled the country.

Although in 1996 Pope John Paul II said that all members of the Church who participated in the genocide must face the consequences, in 1997 the Vatican donated $50,000 to help ensure that certain people — including priests and religious — received fair trials. Two nuns accused of participating in the genocide were sent to prison in Belgium, but a bishop was acquitted after a nine-month trial in Rwanda. The bishop later said Marian apparitions in his diocese in the 1980s foretold the genocide.

Saint Lucia*

Archd., 1; abp., 1; parishes, 22; priests, 29 (16 dioc., 13 rel.); sem., 3; bros., 5; srs., 45; catechists, 231; bap., 1,333; Caths., 101,000 (63%); tot. pop., 159,000.

Independent (Feb. 22, 1979) island state in West Indies; capital, Castries.

Saint Vincent and the Grenadines*

Dioc., 1; bp., 1; parishes, 6; priests, 9 (3 dioc., 6 rel.); sem., 1; srs., 16; catechists, 11; bap., 97; Caths., 15,000 (13%); tot. pop., 118,000.

Independent state (1979) in West Indies; capital, Kingstown. The Kingstown diocese (St. Vincent) was established in 1989; it was formerly part of Bridgetown-Kingstown Diocese with see in Barbados. The Vatican established diplomatic relations with St. Vincent and the Grenadines in 1990. The Church is recognized for its role in education and health care.

Samoa, American

Dioc., 1; bp., 1; parishes, 16; priests, 16 (11 dioc., 5 rel.); p.d., 33; sem., 6; srs., 14; bap., 425; Caths., 14,000 (22%); tot. pop., 65,000.

Unincorporated U.S. territory in southwestern Pacific, consisting of six small islands; seat of government, Pago Pago on the Island of Tutuila. Samoa-Pago Pago Diocese established in 1982.

Samoa, Western*

Archd., 1; abp., 1; parishes, 36; priests, 48 (29 dioc., 15 rel.); p.d., 19; sem., 10; bros., 16; srs., 74; cate-chists, 139; bap., 1,495; Caths., 40,000 (19%); tot. pop., 179,000.

Independent state in the southwestern Pacific; capital, Apia. Catholic missionary work began in 1845. Most of the missions now in operation were established by 1870 when the Catholic population numbered about 5,000. Additional progress was made in missionary work from 1896. The first Samoan priest was ordained in 1892. A diocese was established in 1966; elevated to a metropolitan see in 1982.

San Marino*

Parishes, 12; priests, 23 (9 dioc., 14 rel.); p.d. 1; bros., 2; srs 19; bap., 292; Caths., 30,000 (97%); tot. pop., 31,000.

Republic, a 24-square-mile enclave in northeastern Italy; capital, San Marino. The date of initial evangelization is not known, but a diocese was established by the end of the third century. Ecclesiastically, it forms part of the Diocese of San Marino-Montefeltro in Italy.

São Tome and Principe*

Dioc., 1; bp., 2; parishes, 12; priests, 10 (2 dioc., 8 rel.); sem. 8; bros., 4; srs., 42; catechists, 601; bap., 3,051; Caths., 111,000 (73%); tot. pop., 151,000.

Independent republic (July 12, 1975), consisting of two islands off the western coast of Africa in the Gulf of Guinea; former Portuguese territory; capital, São Tome. Evangelization was begun by the Portuguese who discovered the islands in 1471-72. The São Tome Diocese was established in 1534. In a 1992 visit to São Tome, a major transport center for slaves until the mid-1800s, Pope John Paul II condemned slavery as "a cruel offense" to African dignity.

Saudi Arabia

Parishes, 5; priests, 4 (1 dioc., 3 rel.); bap., 536; Caths., 900,000; total pop., 23,680,000.

Monarchy occupying four-fifths of Arabian peninsula; capital, Riyadh. Population is Muslim; all other religions are banned. Christians in the area are workers from other countries. The Church falls under the ecclesiastical jurisdiction of the Arabian apostolic vicariate. In May 1999, Pope John Paul II met with the crown prince of Saudi Arabia at the Vatican. In 2007, Pope Benedict XVI met with King Abdullah in the Vatican; human rights and religious freedom were major topics of discussion.

Scotland*

Archd., 2; dioc., 6; card., 1; abp., 1; bp., 7; parishes, 474; priests, 739 (600 dioc., 139 rel.); p.d., 28; sem., 25; bros., 209; srs., 529; bap., 7,960; Caths., 702,890 (14%); tot. pop., 4,988,993.

Part of the United Kingdom, in the northern British Isles; capital, Edinburgh. St. Ninian's arrival in 397 marked the beginning of Christianity in Scotland. The arrival of St. Columba and his monks in 563 inaugurated a new era of evangelization that reached into remote areas by the end of the sixth century. He was extremely influential in determining the character of the Church, which was tribal, monastic, and in union with Rome. Considerable disruption of Church activity resulted from Scandinavian invasions in the late eighth and ninth centuries. By 1153 the Scottish Church took a turn away from its insularity and was drawn into closer contact with the European community. Anglo-Saxon religious and political relations, complicated by rivalries between princes and ecclesiastical superiors, were not always the happiest.

From shortly after the Norman Conquest of England to 1560 the Church suffered adverse effects from the Hundred Years' War, the Black Death, the Western Schism and other developments. In 1560 Parliament abrogated papal supremacy over the Church in Scotland and committed the country to Protestantism in 1567. The Catholic Church was proscribed, to remain that way for more than 200 years, and the hierarchy was disbanded. Defections made the Church a minority religion from that time on. Presbyterian Church government was ratified in 1690. Priests launched the Scottish Mission in 1653, incorporating themselves as a mission body under an apostolic prefecture and working underground to serve the faithful in much the same way their confreres did in England. Catholics got some relief from legal disabilities in 1793 and more relief later. Many left the country about that time. Some of their numbers were filled subsequently by immigrants from Ireland. About 100 heather priests, trained in clandestine places in the heather country, were ordained by the early 19th century. The hierarchy was restored in 1878. In a 1997 message to celebrations marking 1,600 years of Christianity in Scotland, Pope John Paul II urged Catholics to make new efforts at evangelization and ecumenism.

Senegal*

Archd., 1; dioc., 6; abp., 2; bp., 7; parishes, 130; priests, 425 (300 dioc., 125 rel.); p.d., 2; sem., 170; bros., 158; srs., 776; catechists, 2,747; bap., 10,391; Caths., 551,000 (5%); tot. pop., 11,148,000.

Republic in West Africa; capital, Dakar. The country had its first contact with Catholicism through the Portuguese some time after 1460. Some incidental missionary work was done by Jesuits and Capuchins in the 16th and 17th centuries. A vicariate for the area was placed in charge of the Holy Ghost Fathers in 1779. More effective evangelization efforts were accomplished after the Senegambia vicariate was erected in 1863; the hierarchy was established in 1955. During a 1992 trip to the predominantly Muslim country, Pope John Paul II praised the small Catholic community for its contributions, especially in the areas of health care and education.

Serbia*

Archd., 2; dioc., 3; ex., 1; a.a., 1; abp., 2; bp., 4; parishes, 243; priests, 246 (212 dioc., 34 rel.); p.d., 10; sem., 62; bros., 5; srs., 478; bap., 3,615; Caths., 564,000 (5%); tot. pop., 10,022,000.

Independent nation in southeastern Europe; part of the former Yugoslavia; capital, Belgrade.

Christianity was introduced from the seventh to ninth centuries in the regions combined to form Yugoslavia after World War I. Since these regions straddled the original line of demarcation for the Western and Eastern Empires (and churches), and since the Reformation had little lasting effect, the Christians are nearly all either Latin- or Eastern-rite Catholics or Orthodox. Yugoslavia was proclaimed a Socialist republic in 1945, and persecution of the

Catholic Church began. In an agreement signed June 25, 1966, the government recognized the Holy See's spiritual jurisdiction over the Church in the country and guaranteed to bishops the possibility of maintaining contact with Rome in ecclesiastical and religious matters. During early 1990s the split of the Yugoslav republic, Catholic leaders joined Orthodox and, in some cases, Muslim leaders in calling for peace.

Seychelles*

Dioc., 1; bp., 1; parishes, 17; priests, 19 (8 dioc., 11 rel.); p.d., 1; sem., 4; bros. 2; srs., 45; catechists, 420; bap., 1,062; Caths., 71,000 (85%); tot. pop., 84,000.

Independent (1976) group of 92 islands in the Indian Ocean; capital, Victoria. Catholicism was introduced in the 18th century. An apostolic vicariate was organized in 1852. All education in the islands was conducted under Catholic auspices until 1954. In 1991, Bishop Felix Paul of Port Victoria said the country's one-party socialist government was an affront to the rights and dignity of its people, but President France-Albert René continued to lead the government into the 21st century. Pope John Paul II warned Seychelles to beware of the dark side of tourism, a main industry in the country.

Sierra Leone*

Archd., 1; dioc., 2; abp., 1; bp., 3; parishes, 62; priests, 140 (87 dioc., 53 rel.); p.d., 3; sem., 53; bros., 39; srs., 59; catechists, 637 bap., 12,403; Caths., 264,000 (5%); tot. pop., 5,624,000.

Republic on the west coast of Africa; capital, Freetown. Catholicism was introduced in 1858. Members of the African Missions Society, the first Catholic missionaries in the area, were joined by Holy Ghost Fathers in 1864. Protestant missionaries were active in the area before their Catholic counterparts. Educational work had a major part in Catholic endeavor. The hierarchy was established in 1950. Most of the inhabitants are followers of traditional African religions.

Church leaders suffered at the hands of rebel soldiers in the late 1990s, when a military coup ousted the country's democratically elected government. Although some Church workers fled to neighboring Guinea, some remained. Rebels kidnapped several foreign missionaries and, shortly before West African intervention forces ousted them from power in 1998, rebels forced the archbishop of Freetown to strip naked while they plundered his office. As the war lessened and later ended, the Church worked for reconciliation, to rehabilitate child soldiers and to rebuild damaged Church property.

Singapore*

Archd., 1; abp., 2; parishes, 30; priests, 142 (75 dioc., 67 rel.); sem., 33; bros., 91; srs., 241; catechists, 2,012; bap., 3,886; Caths., 174,000 (3.8%); tot. pop., 4,483,000.

Independent island republic off the southern tip of the Malay Peninsula; capital, Singapore. Christianity was introduced in the area by Portuguese colonists about 1511. Singapore was founded in 1819; the first parish Church was built in 1846. Freedom of religion is generally respected, although in the late 1980s nearly a dozen people involved in Catholic social work were arrested and detained without trial under the Internal Security Act.

Slovakia*

Archd., 2; dioc., 5; ap. ex., 1; card., 2; abp., 3; bp., 20; parishes, 1,520; priests, 2,810 (2,205 dioc., 605 rel.); p.d., 19; sem., 543; bros., 160, srs., 2,603; catechists, 2,169; bap., 39,837; Caths., 4,005,000 (74%); tot. pop., 5,441,000.

Independent state (Jan. 1, 1993); formerly part of Czechoslovakia; capital, Bratislava. Christianity was introduced in Slovakia in the eighth century by Irish and German missionaries, and the area was under the jurisdiction of German bishops. In 863, Sts. Cyril and Methodius began pastoral and missionary work in the region, ministering to the people in their own language. A diocese established at Nitra in 880 had a continuous history (except for one century ending in 1024). The Church in Slovakia was severely tested by the Reformation and political upheavals. After World War I, when it became part of the Republic of Czechoslovakia, it was 75 percent Catholic.

Vigorous persecution of the Church began in Slovakia in 1944, when communists mounted an offensive against bishops, priests and religious. Msgr. Josef Tiso, a Catholic priest who served as president of the Slovak Republic from 1939-45, was tried for "treason" in December 1946 and was executed the following April.

In 1972, the government ordered the removal of nuns from visible but limited apostolates to farms and mental hospitals. In 1973, the government allowed the ordination of three bishops in the Slovak region.

When Slovakia split from Czechoslovakia in 1993, the country slid into economic difficulties. Church-state tensions increased, and the Slovakian government eventually apologized to Bishop Rudolf Balaz of Banska Bystrica, whose house had been raided in a government investigation of stolen art. In an attempt to fight the effects of decades of communism, in 1996 the bishops said all adult Catholics who had not received confirmation must undergo a special two-year catechism course. In 2000, the government and Vatican signed an accord establishing the Church's legal status.

Slovenia*

Archd., 1; dioc., 2; abp., 3; card., 1; bp., 8; parishes, 793; priests, 1,161 (822 dioc., 339 rel.); p.d., 14; sem., 92; bros., 54; srs., 650; catechists, 627; bap., 13,257; Caths., 1,602,000 (79.6%); tot. pop., 2,011,000.

Independent republic (1991) in southeastern Europe; formerly part of Yugoslavia; capital, Ljubljana. Established diplomatic relations with the Holy See in 1992. After independence, Church leaders found themselves in repeated skirmishes with Slovenia's governing coalition over religious education, restitution of Church property and the Church's proper social role.

Solomon Islands*

Archd., 1; dioc., 2; abp., 1; bp., 3; parishes, 27; priests, 69 (40 dioc., 29 rel.); sem., 43; bros., 23; srs., 99; catechists, 719; bap., 3,032; Caths., 99,000 (21%); tot. pop., 467,000.

Independent (July 7, 1978) island group in Oceania; capital, Honiara, on Guadalcanal. After violence inter-

rupted the Marists' evangelization of the Southern Solomons, they resumed their work in 1898. An apostolic vicariate was organized in 1912. A similar jurisdiction was set up for the Western Solomons in 1959. World War II caused a great deal of damage to mission installations.

Somalia

Dioc., 1; parish, 1; priests, 3 (1 dioc., 2 rel.); srs., 4; Caths., 100; tot. pop., 7,815,000. (AD)

Republic on the eastern coast of Africa; capital, Mogadishu. The country has been Muslim for centuries. Pastoral activity has been confined to immigrants. Schools and hospitals were nationalized in 1972, resulting in the departure of some foreign missionaries.

South Africa*

Archd., 5; dioc., 20; v.a., 1; mil. ord., 1; card., 1; abp., 6; bp., 26; parishes, 760; priests, 1,179 (548 dioc., 631 rel.); p.d., 209; p.d., 4; sem., 488; bros., 176; srs., 2,566; catechists, 13,153; bap., 44,953; Caths., 3,234,000 (7%); tot. pop., 47,390,000.

Republic in the southern coast of Africa; capitals, Cape Town (legislative), Pretoria (administrative) and Bloemfontein (judicial). Christianity was introduced by the Portuguese who discovered the Cape of Good Hope in 1488. Boers, who founded Cape Town in 1652, expelled Catholics from the region. There was no Catholic missionary activity from that time until the 19th century. A bishop established residence in 1837, and evangelization got under way thereafter among the Bantus and white immigrants. The hierarchy was established in 1951.

Under South Africa's apartheid regime, the Church found itself the victim of attacks, from the parish level to the headquarters of the bishops' conference in Pretoria. Some Church leaders were detained, tortured and deported, particularly in the 1970s and 1980s. However, in a 1997 statement to South Africa's Truth Commission, the Catholic Church said the complicity of some Catholics with apartheid was an "act of omission rather than commission." Since the end of apartheid, Catholic leaders have spoken out against an increase in violence and anti-Muslim sentiment and have worked to combat the growing AIDS problem. Reports of clergy sexual abuse became public in 2003.

Spain*

Archd., 14; dioc., 55; mil. ord., 1; card., 7; abp., 23; bp., 101; parishes, 22,602; priests, 25,705 (17,464 dioc., 8,241 rel.); p.d., 293; sem., 2,126; bros., 4,354; srs., 53,428; catechists, 100,304; bap., 317,866; Caths., 41,530,000 (94%); tot. pop., 44,100,000.

Constitutional monarchy on the Iberian peninsula in southwestern Europe; capital, Madrid. Christians were on the peninsula by 200; some of them suffered martyrdom during persecutions of the third century. A council held in Elvira about 305 enacted the first legislation on clerical celibacy in the West. Vandals invaded the peninsula in the fifth century, bringing with them an Arian brand of Christianity that they retained until their conversion following the baptism of their king, Reccared, in 589.

In the seventh century, Toledo was established as the primatial see. The Visigoth kingdom lasted to the time of the Arab invasion, 711-14. The Church survived under Muslim rule but experienced some doctrinal and disciplinary irregularities as well as harassment. Re-evangelization of most of the peninsula was accomplished by 1248; unification was achieved during the reign of Ferdinand and Isabella. The discoveries of Columbus and other explorers ushered in an era of colonial expansion in which Spain became one of the greatest missionary-sending countries in history. In 1492, in repetition of anti-Semitic actions of 694, the expulsion of unbaptized Jews was decreed, leading to mass baptisms but a questionable number of real conversions in 1502. Activity by the Inquisition followed. Spain was not seriously affected by the Reformation. Ecclesiastical decline set in about 1650.

Anti-Church actions authorized by a constitution enacted in 1812 resulted in the suppression of religious and other encroachments on the leaders, people and goods of the Church. Political, religious and cultural turmoil recurred during the 19th century and into the 20th. A revolutionary republic was proclaimed in 1931, triggering a series of developments that led to civil war from 1936 to 1939. During the conflict, which pitted leftist Loyalists against the forces of Francisco Franco, more than 6,600 priests and religious and an unknown number of lay people were massacred. One-man, one-party rule, established after the civil war and with rigid control policies with respect to personal liberties and social and economic issues, continued for more than 35 years before giving way after the death of Franco to democratic reforms. Since the 1970s, the Catholic Church has not been the established religion; the constitution guarantees freedom for other religions as well. In the late 20th century, Spanish Church leaders fought a growing feeling of indifference among many Catholics. After the March 2004 al-Qaida bombings led to the election of a Socialist government, Spanish Church leaders were appalled by the series of social policy changes being proposed by the new government.

Sri Lanka*

Archd., 1; dioc., 10; abp., 3; bp., 13; parishes, 398; priests, 1,111 (712 dioc., 399 rel.); p.d., 1; sem., 474; bros., 188; srs., 2,330; catechists, 12,141; bap., 27,650; Caths., 1,381,000 (7%); tot. pop., 20,705,000.
Independent socialist republic, island southeast of India; capital, Colombo. The Portuguese began evangelizing in the 16th century. In 1638, the Dutch began forcing Portuguese from the coastal areas. The Dutch outlawed Catholicism, banished priests and confiscated buildings, forcing people to become Calvinists. Blessed Joseph Vaz, an Oratorian priest, is credited with almost single-handedly reviving the Catholic Church toward the end of the 17th century.
Anti-Catholic laws were repealed by the British in 1806. The hierarchy was established in 1886; the country gained independence in 1948. In an unusual move in January 1998, Archbishop Nicholas M. Fernando of Colombo, authorized by the Vatican Congregation for the Doctrine of the Faith, lifted the excommunication of a prominent Sri Lankan theologian, Oblate Father Tissa Balasuriya. Sri Lankan bishops repeatedly called for reconciliation in the decades-long war between the Liberation Tigers of Tamil Eelam and the Sinhalese-dominated government.

Sudan*

Archd., 2; dioc., 7; ap. ex., 1; card., 1; abp., 1; bp., 11; parishes, 230; priests, 371 (248 dioc., 123 rel.); p.d., 4; sem., 228; bros., 78; srs., 329; catechists, 4,013; bap., 61,529; Caths., 5,050,000 (14%); tot. pop., 36,362,000.
Republic in northeastern Africa, the largest country on the continent; capital Khartoum. Christianity was introduced from Egypt and gained acceptance in the sixth century. Under Arab rule, it was eliminated in the northern region. No Christians were in the country in 1600.
Evangelization attempts begun in the 19th century in the south yielded hard-won results. By 1931 there were nearly 40,000 Catholics there, and considerable progress was made by missionaries after that time. In 1957, a year after the republic was established, Catholic schools were nationalized. An act restrictive of religious freedom went into effect in 1962, resulting in the harassment and expulsion of foreign missionaries. By 1964 all but a few Sudanese missionaries had been forced out of the southern region. The northern area, where Islam predominates, is impervious to Christian influence.
Late in 1971 some missionaries were allowed to return to work in the South. The hierarchy was established in 1974. The most recent fighting, which began in 1983, originally pitted the mostly Arab and Muslim North against the mostly black African Christian and animist South, but it has since evolved into a nationwide conflict fuelled by religion, ethnicity, oil and ideology. The imposition of Islamic penal codes in 1984 was a cause of concern to all Christian Churches. Recent government policies have denied Christians the right to places of worship and authorization to gather for prayer. Bishops from the South have condemned human rights violations — aggravated by famine and war — in their area. They have said they want peace but cannot accept an Islamic state and were hopeful that terms of a 2005 peace agreement would hold. The agreement would allow southerners to vote on independence after a six-year period of power-sharing. A widespread conflict in the western Darfur region resulted in a massive exodus of Sudanese, who were cared for in neighboring countries by international – including church-run – agencies.

Surinam*

Dioc., 1; bp., 1; parishes, 32; priests, 22 (6 dioc., 16 rel.); sem., 1; bros., 4; srs., 9; bap., 1,752; Caths., 126,000 (25%); tot. pop., 506,000.
Independent (Nov. 25, 1975) state in northern South America; capital, Paramaribo. Catholicism was introduced in 1683. Evangelization began in 1817.

Swaziland*

Dioc., 1; bp., 1; parishes, 15; priests, 39 (12 dioc., 27 rel.); sem., 15; bros., 2; srs., 64; bap., 612; Caths., 56,000 (5.1%); tot. pop., 1,100,000.
Monarchy in southern Africa, almost totally surrounded by South Africa; capital, Mbabane. Missionary work was entrusted to the Servites in 1913. An apostolic prefecture was organized in 1923. The hierarchy was established in 1951. Swaziland established diplomatic relations with the Holy See in 1992. In the 1990s, Swazi Catholics worked to help trans-

form the country to a democracy but to retain the traditions of the people.

Sweden*

Dioc., 1; abp., 1; bp., 3; parishes, 43; priests, 154 (73 dioc., 81 rel.); p.d., 22; sem., 5; bros., 8; srs., 197; catechists, 290; bap., 1,200; Caths., 141,000 (1.5%); tot. pop., 9,090,000.

Constitutional monarchy in northwestern Europe; capital, Stockholm. Christianity was introduced by St. Ansgar, a Frankish monk, in 829-830. The Church became well-established in the 12th century and was a major influence at the end of the Middle Ages. Political and other factors favored the introduction and spread of the Lutheran Church, which became the state religion in 1560. The Augsburg Confession of 1530 was accepted by the government; all relations with Rome were severed; monasteries were suppressed; the very presence of Catholics in the country was forbidden in 1617. A decree of tolerance for foreign Catholics was issued about 1781. Two years later an apostolic vicariate was organized for the country. In 1873 Swedes were given the legal right to leave the Lutheran church and join another Christian church. Membership in the Lutheran church is presumed by law unless notice is given of membership in another church.

Since 1952 Catholics have enjoyed almost complete religious freedom. The hierarchy was re-established in 1953. Hindrances to growth of the Church are the strongly entrenched established church, limited resources, a clergy shortage and the size of the country. In the 1960s, an influx of guest workers increased the number of Catholics, and in the 1970s and 1980s, refugees helped increase Church numbers. In 1998, the pope named the first Swedish bishop in more than 400 years. In the early 21st century, the government worked to give the Church and other minority faiths the right to operate as legal entities, including owning property.

Switzerland*

Dioc., 6; abb., 2; card., 3; abp., 3; bp., 18; parishes, 1,650; priests, 2,865 (1,699 dioc., 1,166 rel.); p.d., 217; sem., 204; bros., 351; srs., 5,459; catechists, 1,841; bap., 30,423; Caths., 3,327,000 (44%); tot. pop., 7,480,000.

Confederation in central Europe; capital, Bern. Christianity was introduced in the fourth century or earlier and was established on a firm footing before the barbarian invasions of the sixth century. Constance, established as a diocese in the seventh century, was a stronghold of the faith against the pagan Alamanni, in particular, who were not converted until some time in the ninth century. During this period of struggle with the barbarians, a number of monasteries of great influence were established.

The Reformation in Switzerland was triggered by Zwingli in 1519 and furthered by him at Zurich until his death in battle against the Catholic cantons in 1531. Calvin set in motion the forces that made Geneva the international capital of the Reformation and transformed it into a theocracy. Catholics mobilized a Counter-Reformation in 1570, six years after Calvin's death. Struggle between Protestant and Catholic cantons was a fact of Swiss life for several

hundred years. The Helvetic Constitution enacted at the turn of the 19th century embodied anti-Catholic measures and consequences, among them the dissolution of 130 monasteries. The Church was reorganized later in the century to meet the threats of liberalism, radicalism and the *Kulturkampf.* In the process, the Church, even though on the defensive, gained the strength and cohesion that characterizes it to the present time. In 1973, constitutional articles banning Jesuits from the country and prohibiting the establishment of convents and monasteries were repealed. In the 1990s, Swiss bishops battled internal divisions and sought forgiveness for any anti-Semitism on behalf of the Church.

Syria*

Patriarchates, 1 (Greek Melkites; patriarchs of Antioch of Maronites and Syrians reside in Lebanon); archd., 12 (1 Armenian, 2 Maronite, 5 Greek Melkite, 4 Syrian); dioc., 3 (Armenian, Chaldean, Maronite); v.a., 1 (Latin); ap.ex., 1; patriarch, 1; card., 1; abp., 15; bp., 4; parishes, 216; priests, 273 (197 dioc., 76 rel.); p.d., 12; sem., 87; bros., 25; srs., 470; catechists, 998; bap., 2,245; Caths., 401,000 (2%); tot. pop., 18,870,000.

Arab socialist republic in southwest Asia; capital, Damascus. Christian communities were formed in apostolic times. It is believed that St. Peter established a see at Antioch before going to Rome. Damascus became a center of influence. The area was the place of great men and great events in the early history of the Church. Monasticism developed there in the fourth century; so did the Monophysite and Monothelite heresies to which a portion of the Church succumbed. Byzantine Syrians who remained in communion with Rome were given the name Melkites. Christians of various persuasions — Jacobites, Orthodox and Melkites — were subject to various degrees of harassment from the Arabs who took over in 638 and from the Ottoman Turks who isolated the country and remained in control from 1516 to the end of World War II.

Syrian Catholics are members of the Armenian, Chaldean, Greek-Melkite, Latin, Maronite and Syrian rites. During a visit to Syria in May 2001, Pope John Paul II became the first pontiff in history to enter a mosque. Early in the 21st century, growing instability in neighboring countries, including Iraq, led to an influx of Christians and challenges for the small but flourishing Catholic community.

Taiwan*

Archd., 1; dioc., 7; card., 1; abp., 3; bp., 9; parishes, 448; priests, 691 (257 dioc., 434 rel.); p.d., 1; sem., 84; bros., 112; srs., 1,065; catechists, 553; bap., 2,550; Caths., 306,000 (1.3%); tot. pop., 22,314,000.

Democratic island state, 100 miles off the southern coast of mainland China; capital, Taipei. Attempts to introduce Christianity in the 17th century were unsuccessful. Evangelization in the 19th century resulted in some 1,300 converts in 1895. Missionary endeavor was hampered by the Japanese, who occupied the island following the Sino-Japanese war of 1894-95. Great progress was made in missionary endeavor among the Chinese who emigrated to the island (seat of the Nationalist Government of the Republic of

China) following the Communist takeover of the mainland in 1949. The hierarchy was established in 1952. Many Taiwanese Catholics have worked to form a bridge to Catholics in mainland China.

Tajikistan*

Mission, 3; parishes, 3; priests, 5 (5 rel.); srs., 8; bap., 13; Cath., 3,000; tot. pop. 7,164,000.

Independent republic (1992) in Asia; formerly part of the USSR; capital, Dushanbe. The majority of the population is Sunni Muslim. When the Vatican established diplomatic relations in 1996, Church officials estimated most of the country's Catholics had fled. In 1997, the Vatican established a mission in the country.

Tanzania*

Archd., 5; dioc., 25; card., 1; abp., 5; bp., 31; parishes, 883; priests, 2,340 (1,590 dioc., 750 rel.); p.d. 1; sem., 1,111; bros., 842; srs., 8,456; catechists, 14,453; bap., 273,153; Caths., 11,367,000 (29%); tot. pop., 41,793,000.

Republic on and off the eastern coast of Africa; capital, Dar es Salaam. The first Catholic mission in the former Tanganyikan portion of the republic was manned by Holy Ghost Fathers in 1868. The hierarchy was established there in 1953. Zanzibar was the landing place of Augustinians with the Portuguese in 1499. Some evangelization was attempted between then and 1698 when the Arabs expelled all priests from the territory. There was no Catholic missionary activity from then until the 1860s. The Holy Ghost Fathers arrived in 1863 and were entrusted with the mission in 1872. Zanzibar was important as a point of departure for missionaries to Tanganyika, Kenya and other places in East Africa. A vicariate for Zanzibar was set up in 1906.

In the late 20th century the Church in Tanzania saw an increase in vocations and an active Church life. The bishops assisted hundreds of thousands of refugees from Rwanda, Burundi and Mozambique. More recently, Church leaders worked to stem the AIDS pandemic and to improve education.

Thailand*

Archd., 2; dioc., 8; card., 1; abp., 3; bp., 12; parishes, 402; priests, 759 (469 dioc., 290 rel.); sem., 319; bros., 126; srs., 1,512; catechists, 1,884; bap., 6,407; Caths., 327,000 (.5%); tot. pop., 65,310,000.

Constitutional monarchy in southeast Asia; capital, Bangkok. The first Christians in the region were Portuguese traders who arrived early in the 16th century. A number of missionaries began arriving in the mid-1500s, but pastoral care was confined mostly to the Portuguese until the 1660s, when evangelization began. A seminary was organized in 1665, a vicariate was set up four years later, and a point of departure was established for China. Persecution and death for some of the missionaries ended evangelization efforts in 1688. It was resumed, however, and made progress from 1824 onward. In 1881 missionaries were sent from Siam to neighboring Laos. The hierarchy was established in 1965. Archbishop Michael Michai Kitbunchu was named the first Thai cardinal in 1983. The Church is recognized for its social justice efforts, including work with refugees.

Togo*

Archd., 1; dioc., 6; abp., 1; bp., 5; parishes, 182; priests, 531 (395 dioc., 136 rel.); sem., 378; bros., 225; srs., 830; catechists, 5,242; bap., 31,191; Caths., 1,561,000 (30%); tot. pop., 5,469,000.

Republic on the west coast of Africa; capital, Lome. The first Catholic missionaries in the area, where slave raiders operated for nearly 200 years, were members of the African Missions Society who arrived in 1563. They were followed by Divine Word Missionaries in 1914, when an apostolic prefecture was organized. At that time the Catholic population numbered about 19,000. The African Missionaries returned after their German predecessors were deported following World War I. The first indigenous priest was ordained in 1922. The hierarchy was established in 1955. In the early 1990s, Archbishop Philippe Fanoko Kossi Kpodzro of Lome served as president of the transitional legislative assembly.

Tonga*

Dioc., 1; bp., 1; parishes, 10; priests, 31 (24 dioc., 7 rel.); sem., 27; bros., 3; srs., 40; bap., 498; Caths., 15,000 (14.5%); tot. pop., 94,000.

Polynesian monarchy in the southwestern Pacific, consisting of about 150 islands; capital, Nuku'alofa. Marists started missionary work in 1842, some years after Protestants had begun evangelization. By 1880 the Catholic population numbered about 1,700. A vicariate was organized in 1937. The hierarchy was established in 1966. Tonga established diplomatic relations with the Holy See in 1994.

Trinidad and Tobago*

Archd., 1; abp., 2; bp., 1; parishes, 61; priests, 117 (47 dioc., 70 rel.); sem., 19; bros., 3; srs., 150; catechists, 561; bap., 3,746; Caths., 398,000 (30%); tot. pop., 1,336,000.

Independent nation, consisting of two islands in the Caribbean; capital, Port-of-Spain. The first Catholic Church in Trinidad was built in 1591, years after several missionary ventures had been launched and a number of missionaries killed. Capuchins were there from 1618 until about 1802. Missionary work continued after the British gained control early in the 19th century. Cordial relations have existed between the Church and state, both of which have manifested their desire for the development of indigenous clergy. In 1999, Church leaders protested reinstatement of the death penalty.

Tunisia*

Dioc., 1; abp., 1; parishes, 10; priests, 35 (15 dioc., 20 rel.); bros., 8; sem., 2; srs., 126; bap., 35; Caths., 20,000 (.02%); tot. pop., 10,130,000.

Republic on the northern coast of Africa; capital, Tunis. Ancient Carthage, now a site outside the capital city of Tunis, hosted early Church councils and was home to Church fathers like St. Augustine. Carthage was devastated by Vandals in the fifth century and invaded by Muslims in the seventh century, after which it had few Christians until the 19th century. An apostolic vicariate was organized in 1843, and the Carthage Archdiocese was established in 1884. The Catholic population in 1892 consisted of most of the approximately 50,000 Europeans in the country. When Tunis became a republic in 1956, most of the Europeans left the country. A 1964 agreement with the Vatican and Holy See suppressed the Archdiocese of Carthage and replaced it with the Territorial Prelature of Tunis. In 1995 the prelature was made a diocese.

Today Tunisia's Catholics are predominantly foreign nationals. The Church's social presence is seen in schools, hospitals and institutions for the disabled.

Turkey*

Archd., 3; v.a., 2; ord., 1; ap. ex., 1; abp., 2; bp., 3; parishes, 49; priests, 65 (12 dioc., 53 rel.); p.d., 3; sem., 5; bros., 12; srs., 147; bap., 103; Caths., 32,000 (.05%); tot. pop., 72,970,000.

Republic in Asia Minor and southeastern Europe; capital, Ankara. Christian communities were established in apostolic times, as attested in the Acts of the Apostles, some of the Letters of St. Paul, and Revelation. The territory was the scene of heresies and ecumenical councils, the place of residence of Fathers of the Church, and the area in which ecclesiastical organization reached the dimensions of more than 450 sees in the middle of the seventh century. The region remained generally Byzantine except for the period of the Latin occupation of Constantinople from 1204 to 1261, but was conquered by the Ottoman Turks in 1453 and remained under their domination until establishment of the republic in 1923. Christians, always a minority, numbered more Orthodox than Catholics; they all were under some restrictions during the Ottoman period. They suffered persecution in the 19th and 20th centuries, the Armenians being the most numerous victims. Turkey is overwhelmingly Muslim. Catholics are tolerated to a degree.

Turkmenistan*

Mission, 1; parish, 1; priests, 2 (rel.); bap., 1; Caths., 1,000; tot. pop., 5,000,000.

Former constituent republic of USSR; independent, 1991; capital, Ashgabat. Almost all the population is Sunni Muslim. The Vatican established diplomatic relations with the country in 1996 and set up a mission in 1997.

Tuvalu

Mission, 1; parish, 1; priest, 2 (rel.); bap., 2; Caths., 100; tot. pop., 10,000.

Independent state (1978) in Oceania, consisting of 9 islands; capital, Funafuti.

Uganda*

Archd., 4; dioc., 15; mil. ord., 1; card., 1; abp., 4; bp., 27; parishes, 460; priests, 1,793 (1,462 dioc., 331 rel.); p.d., 2; sem., 1,121; bros., 515; srs., 3,095; catechists, 13,580; bap., 361,998; Caths., 12,274,000 (44%); tot. pop., 28,704,000.

Republic in East Africa; capital, Kampala. The Missionaries of Africa (White Fathers) were the first Catholic missionaries, starting in 1879. Persecution broke out from 1885 to 1887, taking a toll of 22 Catholic martyrs, who were canonized in 1964, and a number of Anglican victims. (Pope Paul VI honored all those who died for the faith during a visit to Kampala in 1969.) By 1888, there were more than 8,000 Catholics. Evangelization was resumed in 1894, after

being interrupted by war, and proceeded thereafter. The first African bishop was ordained in 1939. The hierarchy was established in 1953.

The Church was suppressed during the erratic regime of President Idi Amin, who was deposed in the spring of 1979. Guerrilla activity in northern and southwestern Uganda has hampered Church workers. The Church has devoted much of its resources to caring for the many victims of HIV/AIDS in the country. In northern Uganda as a guerrilla war continued, church officials worked to protect children from being inducted into military or guerrilla service.

Ukraine*

Major archbishopric, 1 (Ukrainian); archd., 3 (Metropolitans); dioc., 14; pat. ex., 2; card., 2; abp., 4; bp., 28; parishes, 4,346; priests, 3,083 (2,604 dioc., 479 rel.); p.d., 28; sem., 1,162; bros., 270; srs., 1,268; catechists, 2,204; bap., 33,981; Caths., 4,826,000 (10%); tot. pop., 46,760,000.

Independent republic bordering on the Black Sea; former USSR republic; capital, Kiev. The baptism of Vladimir and his people in 988 marked the beginning of Christianity in the territory of Kievan Rus, which is included in today's Ukraine. The 1596 Union of Brest brought the Ukrainian Byzantine-rite community back into communion with Rome. The Eastern Catholic Church was officially suppressed and underground in the USSR from the late 1940s; all of its bishops were killed or imprisoned and its property seized by the government and given to the Orthodox. Some Catholic priests continued to minister clandestinely under communist rule.

As the Eastern Church regained its legal status under Soviet President Mikhail Gorbachev, serious tensions arose with the Orthodox over ownership of property and the allegiance of priests and lay people. Latin-rite dioceses were re-established in 1991. In the late 1990s, rising inflation and weakening currency, aggravated by the government's and some companies' failure to pay wages, led Ukrainian Church leaders to fight homelessness and hunger. Despite opposition from Ukraine's largest Orthodox Church, Pope John Paul II visited Ukraine in June 2001. He challenged Ukrainians to talk to each other and focus on unity, despite religious, ethnic and political tensions. Despite Russian Orthodox objections, the Ukrainian Catholic Church moved its headquarters from Lviv to Kiev and Halych in 2005.

United Arab Emirates*

V.a, 1; bp., 2; parishes, 7; priests, 20 (3 dioc., 17 rel.); srs., 42; bap., 1,614; Caths., 459,000 (11%); tot. pop., 4,006,000.

Independent state along Persian Gulf; capital, Abu Dhabi. The apostolic vicariate of Arabia has its seat in Abu Dhabi. It includes the states of Bahrain, Oman, Qatar, Saudi Arabia and Yemen (see separate entries) as well as United Arab Emirates. Diplomatic relations with the Holy See were established in May 2007.

United States*

(See **Catholic Church in the U.S.**; see also **Chronology of American Catholic History**; and **Statistics of the Church in the U.S.**)

Uruguay*

Archd., 1; dioc., 9; abp., 3; bp., 15; parishes, 229; priests, 458 (224 dioc., 234 rel.); p.d., 89; sem., 69; bros., 95; srs., 962; catechists, 4,985; bap., 24,586; Caths., 2,549,000 (75%); tot. pop., 3,310,000.

Republic on the southeast coast of South America; capital, Montevideo. The Spanish established a settlement in 1624 and evangelization followed. Missionaries followed the reduction pattern to reach the Indians, form them in the faith and train them in agriculture, husbandry, other arts, and the experience of managing property and living in community. The constitution of 1830 made Catholicism the religion of the state and subsidized some of its activities, principally the missions to the Indians. Separation of Church and state was provided for in the constitution of 1917. In 1997, despite a court decision halting further investigations, the Church pledged to make one last effort to help search for people who remained missing from the 1973-85 military dictatorship.

Uzbekistan*

A.a, 1; parishes, 5; priests, 9 (9 rel.); bros., 3; sem., 1; srs., 11; bap., 43; Caths. 4,000; tot. pop. 26,468,000.

Former republic of USSR; independent, 1991; capital, Tashkent. The communist government confiscated Catholic properties in 1917 and severely repressed the practice of religion in the country. The country won its independence in 1991. The majority of the population is Sunni Muslim. A small number of Catholics live in Tashkent. The Vatican established a mission in 1997. In 2005 the Church became an apostolic administration and received its first Catholic bishop.

Vanuatu*

Dioc., 1; bp., 1; parishes, 23; priests, 25 (15 dioc., 10 rel.); p.d., 1; sem., 12; bros., 18; srs., 56; catechists, 303; bap., 552; Caths., 33,000 (16%); tot. pop., 220,000.

Independent (July 29, 1980) island group in the southwest Pacific; capital, Vila. Effective, though slow, evangelization by Catholic missionaries began about 1887. An apostolic vicariate was set up in 1904. The hierarchy was established in 1966.

Vatican City State (See separate entry)

Venezuela*

Archd., 9; dioc., 23; ord.; v.a., 4; ap. ex., 2; mil. ord. 1; card., 2; abp., 10; bp., 40; parishes, 1,354; priests, 2,557 (1,613 dioc., 944 rel.); p.d., 169; sem., 1,397; bros., 245; srs., 3,724; catechists, 25,628; bap., 415,586; Caths., 23,526,000 (87%); tot. pop., 27,030,000.

Republic in northern South America; capital, Caracas. Evangelization began in 1513-14 and involved members of a number of religious orders who worked in assigned territories, developing missions into pueblos or villages of Indian converts. Nearly 350 towns originated as missions. The first diocese was established in 1531. Fifty-four missionaries met death by violence from the start of missionary work until 1817. Missionary work was seriously hindered during the wars of independence in the second decade of the 19th century and continued in decline through the rest of the century as dictator followed dictator in a period of political turbulence. Restoration of the missions got under way in 1922. In mid-2005, amid increasing poverty, several surveys found the Catholic Church had the highest respect of any of the nation's institutions. The Church often sparred verbally with the nation's leader, Pres. Hugo Chavez.

Vietnam

Archd., 3; dioc., 22; card., 2; abp., 2; bp., 38; parishes, 2,514; priests, 3,316 (2,609 dioc., 707 rel.); p.d., 22; sem., 2,302; bros., 1,861; srs., 12,817; catechists, 54,565; bap., 153,778, Caths., 5,990,000 (6.8%); tot. pop., 84,110,000.

Country in southeast Asia, reunited officially July 2, 1976, as the Socialist Republic of Vietnam; capital, Hanoi.

Catholicism was introduced in 1533, but missionary work was intermittent until 1615, when Jesuits arrived to stay. Two vicariates were organized in 1659. A seminary was set up in 1666, and two Vietnamese priests were ordained two years later. A congregation of native women religious formed in 1670 is still active. Severe persecution broke out in 1698, three times in the 18th century, and again in the 19th. Up to 300,000 people suffered in some way from persecution during the 50 years before 1883, when the French moved in to secure religious liberty for the Catholics. Most of the 117 beatified Martyrs of Vietnam were killed during this 50-year period. After the French were forced out of Vietnam in 1954, the country was partitioned at the 17th parallel. The North became Communist and the Viet Cong, joined by North Vietnamese regular army troops in 1964, fought to gain control of the South. In 1954 there were approximately 1.1 million Catholics in the North and 480,000 in the South. More than 650,000 fled to the South to avoid the government repression. In South Vietnam, the Church continued to develop during the war years.

After the end of the war in 1975, the government exercised control over virtually all aspects of Church life. In the late 1980s, bishops noted some softening of the government's hard line. In the 1990s, the Vatican and Vietnam held intermittent talks on Church-state issues, with sporadic progress reported, but in 1997, the government censored the section of the "Catechism of the Catholic Church" that dealt with human rights. Although at times the Vatican was forced to wait years for government approval of bishops' appointments, in the late 20th and early 21st century, Vatican delegations made regular visits to Vietnam to discuss the appointments and other Church-related issues. Early in the 21st century, the government approved a series of bishops' appointments in northern Vietnam, and Church leaders said they saw a rejuvenation of the faith there.

Virgin Islands (U.S.)

Dioc., 1 (St. Thomas, suffragan of Washington, D.C.); bp., 2; parishes, 8; priests, 20 (14 dioc., 6 rel.); p.d., 27; sem., 6; bros., 3; srs., 20; bap., 226; Caths., 30,000 (29%); tot. pop., 110,000.

Organized unincorporated U.S. territory in Atlantic Ocean; capital, Charlotte Amalie on St. Thomas (one of the three principal islands). The islands were discovered by Columbus in 1493 and named for St. Ursula and her virgin companions. Missionaries began evangelization in the 16th century. A church on St. Croix dates from about 1660; another, on St. Thomas, from 1774. The Baltimore Archdiocese had jurisdiction over the islands from 1804 to 1820, when it was passed on to the first of several places in the Caribbean area. Some trouble arose over a pastoral appointment in the 19th century, resulting in a small schism. The Redemptorists took over pastoral care in 1858; normal conditions have prevailed since.

Wales*

Archd., 1; dioc., 2; abp., 2; bp., 3; parishes, 168; priests, 211 (133 dioc., 78 rel.); p.d., 23; sem., 7; bros., 99; srs., 338; bap, 1,953; Caths., 198,081 (.5%); tot. pop., 3,432,379.

Part of the United Kingdom, on the western part of the island of Great Britain. Celtic missionaries completed evangelization by the end of the sixth century, the climax of what has been called the age of saints. Welsh Christianity received its distinctive Celtic character at this time. Some conflict developed when attempts were made — and proved successful later — to place the Welsh Church under the jurisdiction of Canterbury; the Welsh opted for direct contact with Rome.

The Church made progress despite the depredations of Norsemen in the eighth and ninth centuries. Norman infiltration occurred near the middle of the 12th century, resulting in a century-long effort to establish territorial dioceses and parishes to replace the Celtic organizational plan of monastic centers and satellite churches. The Western Schism produced split views and allegiances. Actions of Henry VIII in breaking away from Rome had serious repercussions. Proscription and penal laws crippled the Church, resulted in heavy defections and touched off a 150-year period of repression. Methodism prevailed by 1750. Modern Catholicism came to Wales with Irish immigrants in the 19th century, when the number of Welsh Catholics was negligible. Catholic emancipation was granted in 1829. The hierarchy was restored in 1850. Wales shares a bishops' conference with England.

Yemen*

Parishes, 4; priests, 4 (rel.); srs., 23; bap., 2; Caths., 6,000; tot. pop., 22,282,000.

Republic on southern coast of Arabian peninsula; capital, Sana. Formerly North Yemen (Arab Republic of Yemen) and South Yemen (People's Republic of Yemen); formally reunited in 1990. Christians perished in the first quarter of the sixth century. Muslims have been in control since the seventh century. The state religion is Islam; the Church is under the ecclesiastical jurisdiction of Arabia apostolic vicariate. In the early 1990s, Salesians reported some harassment of Church workers in the South. In early 1998, three Missionaries of Charity nuns were murdered. The Vatican established diplomatic relations with Yemen in October 1998.

Zambia*

Archd., 2; dioc., 8; abp., 5; bp., 6; parishes, 268; priests, 759 (362 dioc., 397 rel.); p.d., 1; sem., 448; bros., 177; srs., 1,774; catechists, 8,646; bap., 43,432; Caths., 3,794,000 (31%); tot. pop., 11,800,000.

Republic in central Africa; capital, Lusaka. Portuguese priests did some evangelizing in the 16th and 17th centuries but no results of their work remained in the 19th century. Jesuits began work in the South in the 1880s and White Fathers in the North and East in 1895. Evangelization of the western region began for the first time in 1931. The number of Catholics doubled in the 20 years following World War II.

Zambian Catholics have welcomed tens of thousands of refugees from the region. In the 1990s, Zambian Church leaders worked caring for victims of HIV/AIDS and spoke out against foreign debt. In 2003, the bishops urged parishes to set up civic education programs to help with the nation's constitutional review process.

Zimbabwe*

Archd., 2; dioc., 6; abp., 4; bp., 7; parishes, 218; priests, 461 (210 dioc., 251 rel.); p.d., 32; sem., 444; bros., 91; srs., 1,100; catechists, 8,744; bap., 35,127; Caths., 1,368,000 (9%); tot. pop., 15,217,000.

Independent republic (1980) in south central Africa; capital, Harare. Earlier unsuccessful missionary ventures preceded the introduction of Catholicism in 1879. Missionaries began to make progress after 1893. The hierarchy was established in 1955; the first black bishop was ordained in 1973.

In 1969, four years after the government of Ian Smith made a unilateral declaration of independence from England, a new constitution was enacted for the purpose of assuring continued white supremacy over the black majority. Catholic and Protestant prelates in the country protested. The Smith regime was ousted in 1979 after seven years of civil war in which at least 25,000 people were killed.

In 1997, the bishops published a report detailing more than 7,000 cases of killings, torture and human rights abuses by government troops in western Zimbabwe from 1981-87. As the Church entered the 21st century, it was devoting tremendous resources toward palliative care of AIDS victims and work with AIDS orphans. Some lay Church leaders were outspoken against government-backed campaigns of violence against white landowners and the poor; Bishop Pius Ncube of Bulawayo was targeted for speaking against government abuses. In 2007, the bishops issued a strong pastoral letter condemning Robert Mugabe's regime, and, after Mugabe failed to win a majority in the 2008 presidential election, spoke out against post-election violence.

CATHOLIC WORLD STATISTICS

(Principal sources: Statistical Yearbook of the Church, 2006 (the latest edition); figures are as of Jan. 1, 2007, unless indicated otherwise.)

	Africa	North America[1]	South America	Asia	Europe	Oceania	WORLD TOTALS
Patriarchates[2]	2	2	-	8	2	-	12
Archdioceses	89	91	99	123	175	18	595
Dioceses	392	359	413	339	509	56	2,068
Prelatures	-	7	31	6	6	-	50
Abbacies	-	-	-	-	10	-	10
Exarchates/Ords.	-	-	6	1	17	-	24
Military Ords.	3	4	9	3	14	2	35
Vicariates Apostolic	16	5	37	20	1	-	79
Prefectures	8	-	2	5	-	1	16
Apostolic Admin.	1	-	1	3	4	-	9
Independent Missions	1	2	-	3	1	2	9
Cardinals[3]	16	25	25	21	103	4	194
Patriarchs[2]	1	-	-	7	2	-	10
Archbishops	122	141	159	172	359	27	980[4]
Bishops	498	736	774	524	1,092	98	3,722[4]
Priests	33,478	75,797	45,322	51,281	196,653	4,731	407,262
Diocesan	22,130	50,966	27,835	30,127	137,363	2,670	271,091
Religious	11,348	24,831	17,487	21,154	59,290	2,061	136,171
Perm. Deacons	379	17,945	4,413	143	11,376	264	34,520
Brothers	7,846	9,866	6,778	10,005	19,085	1,527	55,107
Sisters	60,708	127,251	83,908	155,854	315,981	9,698	753,400
Maj. Seminarians	24,034	15,080	22,069	30,702	22,618	976	115,480
Sec. Inst. Mbrs. (Men)	58	46	153	42	391	1	691
Sec. Inst. Mbrs. (Women)	[5]191,734	4,242	1,661	19,149	45	27,350	
Lay Missionaries	4,301	25,376	172,846	9,904	3,929	412	216,768
Catechists	394,036	863,509	879,509	298,170	534,425	16,703	2,986,689
Parishes	12,928	33,805	22,649	22,335	123,995	2,405	218,117[5]
Kindergartens	11,400	8,199	7,117	12,891	23,398	1,405	64,410
Students	1,201,612	584,544	977,788	1,623,466	1,701,596	91,093	6,180,099
Elem./Primary Schools	32,505	13,157	9,684	14,741	17,070	2,995	90,152
Students	12,832,607	3,480,778	3,668,373	4,933,104	3,025,378	655,604	28,595,844
Secondary Schools	8,922	4,131	6,344	9,058	10,214	701	39,370
Students	4,015,172	1,566,102	2,121,580	5,006,881	3,766,964	398,272	16,874,971
Students, Higher Insts[6]	49,964	419,808	143,031	1,056,542	241,607	8,791	1,919,743
Social Service Facilities	15,535	17,411	22,950	22,180	35,456	2,361	115,893
Hospitals	1,077	992	681	1,083	1,255	156	5,244
Dispensaries	5,270	2,923	2,610	3,514	2,779	504	17,600
Leprosariums	178	10	28	308	3	1	528
Homes for Aged/Handic.	769	1,895	1,922	1,976	8,363	450	15,375
Orphanages	879	947	1,548	3,242	2,608	84	9,308
Nurseries	1,276	1,200	2,766	3,197	2,499	96	11,034
Matrimonial Advice Ctrs.	1,608	2,094	2,734	962	5,679	277	13,354
Social Educ. Ctrs.	2,795	5,591	8,164	6,188	9,827	559	33,124
Other Institutions	1,683	1,759	2,497	1,710	2,443	234	10,326
Baptisms	3,345,987	3,848,659	4,553,932	2,696,545	2,340,876	123,755	16,909,754
Under Age 7	2,272,142	3,551,005	3,911,893	2,271,305	2,258,936	109,046	14,374,327
Over Age 7	1,073,845	297,654	642,039	425,240	81,940	14,709	2,535,427
Marriages	344,802	661,072	618,674	602,353	826,913	22,597	3,076,411
Between Catholics	301,390	591,655	601,725	540,925	758,879	13,821	2,808,395
Mixed Marriages	43,412	69,417	16,949	61,428	68,034	8,776	268,016
Catholic Pop[7]	158,313,000	238,779,000	324,256,000	118,466,000	282,108,000	8,828,000	1,130,750,000
World Population	926,878,000	517,797,000	378,269,000	3,981,666,000	704,552,000	33,662,000	6,542,824,000

[1]. Includes Central America. [2]. For listing and description, see Index. [3]. As of Aug. 30, 2008. [4]. Figures for the hierarchy (cardinals, abps. and bps.) includ. 2,704 ordinaries, 606 coadjutors or aux., 267 with offices in the Roman Curia, 14 in other offices, 1,307 ret. [5]. 166,164 have parish priests; 47,490 are administered by other priests; 556 are entrusted to perm. deacons; 163 to bros; 690 to women rel.; 1,544 to lay people; 1,510 vacant. [6]. There are also approximately 345,570 in univs. for ecclesiastical studies and 2,799,856 other univ. students. [7]. Percentages of Catholics in world pop.: Africa, 17.1; North America (Catholics 81,783,000; tot. pop., 332,335,000), 24.6; Central America (Catholics, 156,996,000; tot. pop., 185,462,000), 83.2; South America, 86; Asia, 2.6; Europe, 40; Oceania, 26.2; world, 17.2 (Catholic totals do not include those in areas that could not be surveyed, est. to be approx. 9 million).

EPISCOPAL CONFERENCES

(*Principal sources:* Annuario Pontificio *and* Catholic Almanac *survey.*)

Episcopal conferences, organized and operating under general norms and particular statutes approved by the Holy See, are official bodies in and through which the bishops of a given country or territory act together as pastors of the Church.

Listed according to countries or regions are titles and addresses of conferences, telephone numbers (where possible), and names and sees of presidents.

Africa, Northern: *Conference Episcopale Regionale du Nord de l'Afrique* (CERNA), 13 rue KhelifaBoukhalfa, 16000 Algiers, Algeria; (021) 63-35-62. Abp. Vincent Landel (Rabat).

Africa, Southern: Southern African Catholic Bishops' Conference (SACBC), 140 Visagie St., P.O. Box 941, Pretoria 0001, S. Africa; (021) 65-35-62. Cardinal Wilfrid Napier, O.F.M. (Durban, South Africa).

Albania: *Conferenza Episcopale dell'Albania,* Tirane, Rruga Don Bosco 1, Kulia Postare 2950; (042) 47-159. Abp. Rrok K. Mirdita (Tirane-Durres).

Angola and São Tome: *Conferencia Episcopal de Angola e HR Tome* (CEAST), C.P. 3579 Luanda, Angola; (02) 44-36-86. Archbishop Franklin Damiao (Luanda).

Antilles: Antilles Episcopal Conference (AEC), P.O. Box 3086, St. James (Trinidad and Tobago), W.I.; (868) 622-2932. Abp. Lawrence Burke (Nassau).

Arab Countries: *Conférence des Evêques Latins dans les Régions Arabes* (CELRA), Latin Patriarchate, P.O. Box 14152, Jerusalem (Old City); (02) 628-85-54. Patriarch Michel Sabbah (Jerusalem).

Argentina: *Conferencia Episcopal Argentina* (CEA), C1008AAV, Calle Suipacha 1034, 1008 Buenos Aires; (011) 4328-95-70. Card. Jorge Mario Bergoglio, S.J. (Buenos Aires).

Australia: Australian Catholic Bishops' Conference, 63 Currong St., Braddon, A.C.T. 2601; (02) 6201-9845; www.catholic.org.au. Abp. Philip Wilson (Adelaide, Australia).

Austria: *Österreichische Bischofskonferenz,* Wollzeile 2, A1010 Vienna; 01-516-11-32.80. Cardinal Christoph Schönborn, O.P. (Vienna).

Balkans: Int'l. Conference of Bishops of Sts. Cyril and Methodius, 11000 Beograd (Srbija), Visegradska 23; (011) 303-22-46. Abp. Stanislav Hocevar, S.D.B. (Beograd).

Bangladesh: Catholic Bishops' Conference of Bangladesh (CBCB), P.O. Box 3, Dhaka1000; (02) 40-88-79. Abp. Paulinus Costa (Dhaka).

Belgium: *Bisschoppenconferentie van België — Conférence Episcopale de Belgique,* Rue Guimard 1, B1040 Brussels; (02) 509-96-93; www.catho.be, www.kerknet.be. Card. Godfried Danneels (MechelenBrussel).

Belarus: *Conferentia Episcoporum Catholicorum,* 220030 Minsk, pl. Swobody 9; (017) 26.61.27. Bp. Aleksander Kaszkiewicz (Grodno).

Benin: *Conférence Episcopale du Bénin,* Cotonou, 01 B.P. 491; 30.01.45. Bp. Antoine Ganyé (Dassa-Zoumé).

Bolivia: *Conferencia Episcopal Boliviana* (CEB), Casilla 2309, Calle Potosi 814, La Paz; (02) 40-67-98. Card. Julio Terrazas Sandoval, C.SS.R. (Santa Cruz de la Sierra).

Bosnia and Herzegovina: *Biskupska Konferencija Bosne i Hercegovine* (B.K. B.i.H.), *Nadbiskupski Ordinarijat,* Kaptol 7, 71000 Sarajevo; (071) 47-21-78.

Card. Vinko Puljic (Vrhbosna).

Brazil: *Conferência Nacional dos Bispos do Brasil* (CNBB), C.P. 02067, SE/Sul Quadra 801, Conjunto "B," 70259970 Brasilia, D.F.; (061) 313-8300. Bp. Geraldo Rocha (Mariana).

Bulgaria: *Mejduritual Episcopska Konferenzia vâv Bâlgaria,* Ul. Liulin Planina 5, 1606 Sofia; (0) 540-406. Bp. Christo Proykov (Briula, titular see).

Burkina Faso and Niger: *Conférence des Evêques de Burkina Faso et du Niger,* B.P. 1195, Ouagadougou, Burkina Faso; 30-60-26. Abp. Seraphim François Rouamba (Koupela).

Burma: See **Myanmar**.

Burundi: *Conférence des Evêques catholiques du Burundi* (C.E.CA.B.), B. P. 1390, 5 Blvd. de l'Uprona, Bujumbura; 223-263. Abp. Evariste Ngoyagoye (Bujumbura).

Cameroon: *Conférence Episcopale Nationale du Cameroun* (CENC), BP 1963, Yaoundé; 231-15-92. Bp. Simon-Victor Tonyé Bakot (Yaoundé).

Canada: *See* **Canadian Conference of Catholic Bishops** in Catholic Church in Canada.

Central African Republic: *Conférence Episcopale Centrafricaine* (CECA), B.P. 1518, Bangui; 50-24-84. Bp. François-Xavier Yombandje (Bossangoa).

Chad: *Conférence Episcopale du Tchad,* B.P. 456, N'Djaména; (235) 51-74-44. Bp. Jean-Claude Bouchard, O.M.I. (Pala).

Chile: *Conferencia Episcopal de Chile* (CECH), Casilla 517V, Correo 21, Cienfuegas 47, Santiago; (02) 671-77-33. Bp. Alejandro Goic Karmelic (Rancagua).

China: Chinese Regional Episcopal Conference, 34 Lane 32, KuangFu South Rd., Taipeh 10552, Taiwan; (02) 578-2355. Abp. Jihn Hung Shan-chuan (Taipei).

Colombia: *Conferencia Episcopal de Colombia,* Apartado 7448, Carrera 8ª 47, N. 8485, Santafé de Bogotá D.E.; (91) 311-42-77. Abp. Luis Augusto Castro Quiroga, I.M.C. (Tunja).

Congo: *Conférence Episcopale du Congo,* B.P. 200, Brazzaville; (83) 06-29. Bp. Louis Portella Mbuyu (Kinkala).

Congo, Democratic Republic (formerly Zaire): *Conférence Episcopale du Zaïre* (CEZ), B.P. 3258, KinshasaGombe; 012-33-992. Abp. Laurent Monsengwo Pasinya (Kinshasa).

Costa Rica: *Conferencia Episcopal de Costa Rica* (CECOR), Apartado 497, 1000 San Jose; 221-30-53. Bp. José Francisco Ulloa Rojas (Limon).

Côte d'Ivoire: *Conference Episcopale de la Côte d'Ivoire,* B.P. 1287, Abidjan 01. Bp. Laurent Akran Mandjo (Yopougon).

Croatia: *Hrvatska Biskupska Konferencija,* Kaptol 22, HR10000 Zagreb; 385-01-481-18-93; www.hbk.hr. Bp. Marin Srakic (Djakovo I Srijem).

Cuba: *Conferencia de Obispos Católicos de Cuba* (COCC), Apartado 594, Calle 26 n. 314 Miramar, 10100 Havana 1; (07) 22-3868. Abp. Juan Garcia Rodriguez (Camagüey).

Czech Republic: *Ceská Biskupská Konference,* Sekretariat, Thakurova 3, 160 00 Praha (Prague) 6; (02) 33-15-421. Bp. Jan Graubner (Olomouc).

Dominican Republic: *Conferencia del Episcopado Dominicano* (CED), Apartado 186, Santo Domingo; (809) 685-3141. Abp. Ramon Benito de la Rosa y

Carpio (Santiago de los Caballeros).

Ecuador: *Conferencia Episcopal Ecuatoriana*, Apartado 1081, Avenida América 1805 y Lagasca, Quito; (02) 23-82-21. Bp. Nestor Rafael Herrera Heredia (Machala).

El Salvador: *Conferencia Episcopal de El Salvador* (CEDES). 15 Av. Norte 1420, Col. Layco, Apartado 1310, San Salvador; 25-8997. Abp. Fernando Sáenz Lacalle (San Salvador).

Equatorial Guinea: *Conferencia Episcopal de Guinea Ecuatorial*, Apartado 106, Malabo. Abp. Ildefonso Obama Obono (Malabo).

Ethiopia: Ethiopian Episcopal Conference, P.O. Box 21322, Addis Ababa; (01) 55-03-00. Abp. Berhaneyesus Demerew Souraphiel, C.M. (Addis Ababa).

France: *Conférence des Evêques de France*, 106 rue du Bac, 75341 Paris CEDEX 07; 33-01-45-49-69-70; www.cef.fr. Card. André Vingt-Trois (Paris).

Gabon: *Conférence Episcopale du Gabon*, B.P. 2146, Libreville; 72-20-73. Bp. Timothée Modibo-Nzockena (Franceville).

Gambia, Liberia and Sierra Leone: InterTerritorial Catholic Bishops' Conference of the Gambia, Liberia and Sierra Leone (ITCABIC), Santanno House, P.O. Box 893, Freetown, Sierra Leone; (022) 22-82-40. Bp. George Biguzzi, S.X. (Makeni).

Germany: *Deutsche Bischofskonferenz*, Postfach 2962, Kaiserstrasse 163, D53019 Bonn; (0049) 228-103-290. Card. Karl Lehmann (Mainz).

Ghana: Ghana Bishops' Conference, National Catholic Secretariat, P.O. Box 9712 Airport, Accra; (021) 500-491. Bp. Lucas Abadamloora (Navrongo-Bolgatanga).

Great Britain: Bishops' Conference of England and Wales, General Secretariat, 39 Eccleston Square, London, SWIV IBX; (020) 7630-8220. Card. Cormac Murphy-O'Connor (Westminster).

Greece: *Conferentia Episcopalis Graeciae*, Odos Homirou 9, 106 72 Athens; (01) 3642-311. Bp. Franghiskos Papamanolis, O.F.M. Cap. (Syros and Milos and Santorini).

Guatemala: *Conferencia Episcopal de Guatemala* (CEG), Apartado 1698, 01901 Ciudad de Guatemala; 543-18-27/8. Bp. Leonel Ramazzini Imeri Alvaro (San Marcos).

Guinea: *Conférence Episcopale de la Guinée*, B.P. 1006 bis, Conkary. Abp. Vincent Coulibaly (Conkary).

GuineaBissau: See **Senegal**.

Haiti: *Conférence Episcopale de Haïti* (CEH). B.P. 1572, Angle rues Piquant et Lammarre, Port-au-Prince; 222-5194. Bp. Louis Kébreau, S.D.B. (Hinche).

Honduras: *Conferencia Episcopal de Honduras* (CEH), Apartado 847, Blvd. Estadio Suyapa, Tegucigalpa; (504) 32-40-43. Card. Oscar Andrés Rodríguez Maradiaga (Tegucigalpa).

Hungary: *Magyar Katolikus Püspöki Konferencia*, H-1071 Budapest VII, Városligeti fasor 45; 1-342-69-59. Cardinal Peter Erdö (Esztergom-Budapest).

India: Catholic Bishops' Conference of India (CBCI), CBCI Centre, Ashok Place, Goldakkhana, New Delhi110001; (011) 334-44-70. Bp. Oswald Gracias (Agra). Conference of Catholic Bishops of India – Latin Rite (CCBI L.R.), Divya Deepti Sadan, Second Floor, P.B. 680, 9-10 Bhai Vir Singh Marg; (011) 336-42-22. Card. Placidius Telesphore Toppo (Ranchi).

Indian Ocean: *Conférence Episcopale de l'Océan*

Indien (CEDOI) (includes Islands of Mauritius, Seychelles, Comore and La Réunion), 13 rue Msgr. Gonin, Port Louis, Mauritius; (230) 208-3068. Abp. Oswald Gracias (Bombay).

Indonesia: *Konperensi Waligereja Indonesia* (KWI), Jl. Cut Mutiah 10, Tromolpos 3044, Jakarta 10002; (021) 33-64-22. Bp. Martinus Dogma Situmorang, O.F.M. Cap. (Padang).

Ireland: Irish Episcopal Conference, "*Ara Coeli*," Armagh BT61 7QY; 028-3752-2045. Abp. Sean B. Brady (Armagh).

Italy: *Conferenza Episcopale Italiana* (CEI), Circonvallazione Aurelia, 50, 00165 Rome; 06-663-981. Card. Angelo Bagnasco (Genoa).

Ivory Coast: See **Côte d'Ivoire**.

Japan: Catholic Bishops' Conference of Japan, Shiomi 21010, KotoKu, Tokyo, 135; (03) 56324411. Abp. Peter Takeo Okada (Tokyo).

Kazakstan: Episcopal Conference of Kazakstan, 473003 Astana, 3 Tashenova St., P.O. Box 622; (3172) 37.29.35. Abp. Tomasz Peta (Most Blessed Mary, Astana).

Kenya: Kenya Episcopal Conference (KEC), The Kenya Catholic Secretariat, P.O. Box 13475, Nairobi; (020) 444-3133. Card. John Njue (Nairobi).

Korea: Catholic Bishops' Conference of Korea, Box 16, Seoul 100600; (02) 466-3417. Bp. John Chang Yik (Ch'unch'on).

Laos and Cambodia: *Conférence Episcopale du Laos et du Cambodge*, c/o Msgr. Pierre Bach, Paris Foreign Missions, 254 Silom Rd., Bangkok 10500; (02) 234-1714. Bp. Emile Destombes, M.E.P. (Altava).

Latvia: *Latvijas Biskapu Konference*, Maza Pils iela 2/a, LV-1050, Riga; (7) 22-72-66. Card. Janis Pujats (Riga).

Lesotho: Lesotho Catholic Bishops' Conference, Catholic Secretariat, P.O. Box 200, Maseru 100; (0501) 31-25-25. Bp. Evaristus Thatho Bitsoane (Qacha's Nek).

Liberia: Catholic Bishops' Conference of Liberia, 1000 Monrovia 10, P.O. Box 10-2078; 227-245. Bp. Lewis Zeigler (Gbarnga).

Lithuania: *Conferentia Episcopalis Lituaniae*, Sventaragio, 4, 2001 Vilnius; (5) 212-54-55. Abp. Sigitas Tamkevicius (Kaunas).

Madagascar: *Conférence Episcopale de Madagascar*, 102 bis Av. Maréchal Joffre, Antanimena, B. P 667, Antananrivo; (02) 2220-478. Bp. Fulgence Rabemahafaly (Fianarantsos).

Malawi: Episcopal Conference of Malawi, Catholic Secretariat of Malawi, P.O. Box 30384, Lilongwe 3; 782-066. Bp. Tarcisius Gervazio Ziyaye (Blantyre).

MalaysiaSingaporeBrunei: Catholic Bishops' Conference of Malaysia, Singapore and Brunei (BCMSB), Xavier Selangor Darul Ehsan, 46000 Petaling Jaya, Malaysia; (03) 758-1731. Abp. Nicholas Xavier Pakiam Murphy (Kuala Lumpur).

Mali: *Conférence Episcopale du Mali*, B.P. 298, Bamako; 225-499. Bp. Jean-Gabriel Diarra.

Malta: *Konferenza Episkopali Maltija*, Archbishop's Curia, Floriana; (356) 234317; www.maltachurch.org.mt. Abp. Paul Cremona, O.P. (Malta).

Mexico: See the *Conferencia del Episcopado Mexicano* (CEM), in the section on the **Catholic Church in Mexico**.

Mozambique: *Conferência Episcopal de Moçambique* (CEM), Av. Paulo Samuel Kankhomba

188/RC, C.P. 286; (01) 49-07-66. Abp. Tomé Makhweliha (Nampula).

Myanmar: Myanmar Catholic Bishops' Conference (MCBC), 292 Pyi Rd., P.O. Box 1080, Yangon; (01) 23-71-98. Abp. Paul Zinghtung Grawng (Mandalay).

Namibia: Namibian Catholic Bishops' Conference (NCBC). P.O. Box 11525 W., Windhoek; (061) 22-47-98. Abp. Ndumbukuti Nashenda Liborius, O.M.I. (Windhoek).

Netherlands: *Nederlandse Bisschoppenconferentie*, Postbus 13049, NL3507 LA, Utrecht; (31)-30-232-69-00; www.omroep.nl/rkk. Bp. Herman Luyn Adrianus, S.D.B. (Rotterdam).

New Zealand: New Zealand Catholic Bishops Conference, P.O. Box 1937, Wellington 6015; (04) 496-1747. Bp. Denis George Browne (Hamilton).

Nicaragua: *Conferencia Episcopal de Nicaragua* (CEN), Apartado Postal 2407, de Ferretería Lang 1 cuadro al Norte y 1 cuadro al Este, Managua; (02) 666-292. Abp. Leopoldo José Brenes Solórzano (Managua).

Niger: *See* **Burkina Faso**.

Nigeria: Catholic Bishops Conference of Nigeria, P.O. Box 951, 6 Force Rd., Lagos; (01) 263-58-49. Abp. Adeosin Job Felix (Ibadan).

Pacific: *Conferentia Episcopalis Pacifici* (CE PAC), P.O. Box 289, Suva (Fiji); 300-340. Abp. Anthony Apuron, O.F.M. Cap. (Agana).

Pakistan: Pakistan Episcopal Conference, P.O. Box 909, Lahore 54000; (042) 6366-137. Abp. Lawrence J. Saldanha (Lahore).

Panama: *Conferencia Episcopal de Panamá* (CEP), Apartado 870033, Panama 7; 223-0075. Bp. José Luis Lacunza Maestrojuán, O.A.R. (Goroka).

Papua New Guinea and Solomon Islands: Catholic Bishops' Conference of Papua New Guinea and Solomon Islands, P.O. Box 398, Waigani, N.C.D., Papua New Guinea; 25-9577. Bp. Francesco Sarego, S.V.D. (Goroka).

Paraguay: *Conferencia Episcopal Paraguaya* (CEP), Alberdi 782, Casilla Correo 1436, Asunción; (021) 490-920. Bp. Izaguirre Gogorza Ignacio, S.C.I. (Encarnacion).

Peru: *Conferencia Episcopal Peruana*, Apartado 310, Rio de Janeiro 488, Lima 100; (01) 463-10-10. Bp. Hector Miguel Cabrejos Vidarte, O.F.M. (Trujillo).

Philippines: Catholic Bishops' Conference of the Philippines (CBCP), P.O. Box 3601, 470 General Luna St., 1099 Manila; (02) 527-4054. Abp. Angel N. Lagdameo (Jaro).

Poland: *Konferencja Episkopatu Polski*, Skwer Kardynala Stefana Wyszynskiego 6, 01015 Warsaw; (022) 838-92-51. Jozef Michalik (Przemysl of the Latins).

Portugal: *Conferência Episcopal Portuguesa*, Campo dos Mártires da Pátria, 431 Esq., 1100 Lisbon; 21-885-21-23. Abp. Jorge Ferreira da Costa (Braga).

Puerto Rico: *Conferencia Episcopal Puertorriqueña* (CEP), P.O. Box 40682, Estacion Minillas, San Juan 009400682; (787) 728-1650. Bp. Ruben Antonio Gonzalez Medina, C.M.F. (Caguas).

Romania: *Conferinte Episcopala România*, Via Popa Tatu 58, Bucharest; (01) 311-12-89. Abp. Ioan Robu (Bucharest).

Russian Federation: Conference of Catholic Bishops of the Russian Federation (C.V.C.F.R.),

101031 Moskva, Via Pietrovka, d. 19 str., 5Kv. 35; (095) 923-16-97. Bp. Joseph Werth, S.J. (Transfiguration at Novosibirsk).

Rwanda: *Conférence Episcopale du Rwanda* (C.Ep.R.), B.P. 357, Kigali; 75439. Abp. Alexis Habiyambere, S.J. (Nyundo).

Scandinavia: *Conferentia Episcopalis Scandiae*, Trollbärsvägen 16, S426 55 Västra Frölunda (Sweden); (031) 709-64-87. Bp. Anders Arborelius, O.C.D. (Stockholm).

Scotland: Bishops' Conference of Scotland, 64 Aitken St., Airdrie, ML6; 44-1236-764-061. Card. Keith Michael Patrick O'Brien (St. Andrews and Edinburgh).

Senegal, Mauritania, Cape Verde and Guinea Bissau: *Conférence des Evêques du Sénégal, de la Mauritanie, du CapVert et de GuinéeBissau*, B.P. 941, Dakar, Senegal. Bp. Jean-Noël Diouf (Tambacounda).

Serbia and Montenegro: *Biskupska konferecija Srbije I Crne Gore*, 11000 Beograd, Visegradska 23; (011) 303.22.46. Bp. Stanslav Hocevar, S.D.B. (Beograd).

Sierra Leone: See **Gambia, Liberia and Sierra Leone**.

Slovakia: *Biskupská Konferencia Slovenska*, Kapitulská 11, 81521 Bratislava; (07) 733-54-50. Bp. Frantisek Tondra (Spis).

Slovenia: *Slovenska Skofovska Konferenca*, CirilMetodov trg 4, p.p.1990, 1001 Ljubljana; (386) 1-2342612. Abp. Alojzij Uran (Ljubljana).

Spain: *Conferencia Episcopal Española*, Apartado 29075, Calle Añastro 1, 28080 Madrid; 91-343-96-15. Bp. Perez Ricardo Blazquez (Bilbao).

Sri Lanka: Catholic Bishops' Conference of Sri Lanka, 19 Balcombe Place, Cotta Rd., Borella, Colombo 8; (01) 95-091; 59-70-62. Bp. Joseph Vianney Fernando (Kandy).

Sudan: Sudan Catholic Bishops' Conference (SCBC), P.O. Box 6011, Khartoum; (011) 225-075-9. Bp. Rudolf Deng Majak (Wau).

Switzerland: *Conférence des Evêques Suisses*, Secretariat, C.P. 22, av. Moléson 21, CH1706 Fribourg; (026) 322-47-94; www.kath.ch. Bp. Kurt Koch (Basel).

Tanzania: Tanzania Episcopal Conference (TEC), P.O. Box 2133, Mansfield St., DaresSalaam; (022) 51-075. Bp. Jude Thaddaeus Ruwa'ichi, O.F.M. Cap. (Dodoma).

Thailand: Bishops' Conference of Thailand, 122-67 Soi Naaksuwan, Nonsi Road, Yannawa, Bangkok; 02-6815361-8. Bp. George Yod Phimphisan, C.SS.R. (Udon Thani).

Togo: *Conférence Episcopale du Togo*, B.P. 348, Lomé; 21-22-72. Bp. Ambroise Kotamba Djoliba (Sokode).

Turkey: Turkish Episcopal Conference, Ölçek Sokak 83, Harbiye, 80230 Istanbul; (212) 248-07-75. Bp. Luigi Padovese, O.F.M. Cap. (Monteverde).

Uganda: Uganda Episcopal Conference, P.O. Box 2886, Kampala; (041) 510-398. Bp. Matthias Ssekamanya (Lugazi).

Ukraine: Ukraine Episcopal Conference, 79008 Lviv, Mytropolycha Kuria Latynskoho Obriadu, Pl. Katedralna 1; (0322) 76-94-15. Card. Marian Jaworski (Lviv of Latins).

United States: *See* **National Conference of**

Catholic Bishops.
Uruguay: Conferencia Episcopal Uruguaya (CEU), Avenida Uruguay 1319, 11100 Montevideo; (02) 900-26-42. Bp. Carlos Maria Collazzi Irazabal (Mercedes).
Venezuela: Conferencia Episcopal de Venezuela (CEV), Apartado 4897, Torre a Madrices, Edificio Juan XXIII, Piso 4, Caracas 1010A; (0212) 4432-23-65. Abp. Ubaldo Ramon Santana Sequera (Maracaibo).
Vietnam: Conferenza Episcopale del Viêt Nam, Nha Trang, Khán Hoà, 22 Tran Phu; (058) 822-842. Bp. Pierre Nguyen Van Nhon (Da Lat).
Yugoslavia: Biskupska Konferencija Savezne Republike Jugoslavije, 11000 Beograd, Visegradska 23; (011) 642-280. Abp. Stanislav Hocevar, S.D.B. (Beograd).
Zambia: Zambia Episcopal Conference, P.O. Box 31965, 20201 Lusaka; (01) 212-070. Bp. Telesphore George Mpundu (Mpika).
Zimbabwe: Zimbabwe Catholic Bishops' Conference (ZCBC), Causeway, P.O. Box 8135, Harare; (14) 705-368. Abp. Robert Ndlovu (Harare).

Regional Conferences

(Sources: Almanac survey; Annuario Pontificio.)
Africa: Symposium of Episcopal Conferences of Africa and Madagascar (SECAM) (Symposium des Conférences Episcopales d'Afrique et de Madagascar, SCEAM): Card. Polycarp Pengo, abp. of Dar-es-Salaam, president. Address: Secretariat, P.O. Box 9156 Airport, Accra, Ghana.
Association of Episcopal Conferences of Central Africa (Association des Conférences Episcopales de l'Afrique Centrale, ACEAC): Comprises Burundi, Rwanda and Zaire. Bp. Simon Ntamwana, abp. of Gitega, president. Address: B.P. 20511, Kinshasa, Democratic Republic of Congo.
Association of Episcopal Conferences of the Region of Central Africa (Association des Conférences Episcopales de la Région de l'Afrique Central, ACER-AC): Comprises Cameroon, Chad, Congo, Equatorial Guinea, Central African Republic and Gabon. Bp. François-Xavier Yombandje, bp. of Bossango, president. Address: Secretariat, B.P. 200, Brazzaville, Republic of the Congo.
Association of Episcopal Conferences of Anglophone West Africa (AECAWA): Comprises Gambia, Ghana, Liberia, Nigeria and Sierra Leone. Bp. John Olorunfemi Onaiyekan, abp. of Abuja, president. Address: P.O. Box 11, Santasi, Ghana.
Association of Member Episcopal Conferences in Eastern Africa (AMECEA): Represents Eritrea, Ethiopia, Kenya, Malawi, Sudan, Tanzania, Uganda and Zambia. Affiliate members: Seychelles (1979), Somalia (1994). Bp. Josaphat L. Lebulu, bp. of Arusha, president. Address: P.O. Box 21191, Nairobi, Kenya.
Regional Episcopal Conference of FrenchSpeaking

West Africa (Conférence Episcopale Régionale de l'Afrique de l'Ouest Francophone, CERAO): Comprises Benin, Burkina Faso, Cape Verde, Côte d'Ivoire, Guinea, GuineaBissau, Mali, Mauritania, Niger, Senegal and Togo. Card. Théodore-Adrien Sarr, abp. of Dakar, president. Address: Secretariat General, B.P.470 CIDEX 1, Abidjan — Côte d'Ivoire.
InterRegional Meeting of Bishops of Southern Africa (IMBISA): Bishops of Angola, Botswana, Lesotho, Mozambique, Namibia, São Tome e Principe, South Africa, Swaziland and Zimbabwe. Abp. Gabriel Mbilingi, C.S.Sp., abp. of Lubango, president. Address: 88 Broadlands Rd., Avondale, Harare, Zimbabwe.
Asia: Federation of Asian Bishops' Conferences (FABC): Represents 14 Asian episcopal conferences and four independent jurisdictions (Hong Kong, Macau, Nepal, Mongolia) as regular members (excluding the Middle East). Established in 1970; statutes approved experimentally Dec. 6, 1972. Abp. Orlando B. Quevedeo, O.M.B., abp. of Cotabato, secretary general. Address: 16 Caine Road, Hong Kong; 25258021; www.fabc.org.ph.
Oceania: Federation of Catholic Bishops' Conferences of Oceania (FCBCO). Statutes approved Dec. 25, 1997. Bp. Peter Ingham, bp. of Wollongong in Australia, president. Address: P.O. Box 1937, 22-30 Hill St., Wellington, New Zealand 6015.
Europe: Council of European Bishops' Conferences (Consilium Conferentiarum Episcoporum Europae, CCEE): Reorganized in 1993 in accordance with suggestions made during the 1991 Synod of Bishops on Europe. Card. Peter Erdö, abp. of Esztergom-Budapest, president. Address of secretariat: Gallusstrasse 24, CH9000 Sankt Gallen, Switzerland; (0041) 71-227-33-74; www.kath.ch/ccee.
Commission of the Episcopates of the European Community (Commissio Episcopatuum Com-munitatis Europaeae, COMECE): Established in 1980; represents episcopates of states belonging to European Community. Bp. Adrianus van Luyn, S.D.B., bp. of Rotterdam, president. Address of secretariat: 42, Rue Stévin, B1000 Brussels, Belgium; (02) 230-73-16.
Central and South America: Latin American Bishops' Conference (Consejo Episcopal Latino-Americano, CELAM): Established in 1956; statutes approved Nov. 9, 1974. Represents 22 Latin American national bishops' conferences. Abp. Raymundo Damasceno Assis, president. Address of the secretariat: Carrera 5 No. 11831, Usaquén, Bogotá, Colombia; (91) 612-16-20.
Episcopal Secretariat of Central America and Panama (Secretariado Episcopal de America Central y Panama, SEDAC): Statutes approved experimentally Sept. 26, 1970. Bp. José Francisco Ulloa, bp. of Cartago, president. Address of secretary general: Calle 20 y Av Mexico 24-45, Apartado 6386, Panama 5, Panama; 262-7802.

INTERNATIONAL CATHOLIC ORGANIZATIONS

(Principal sources: Sr. Dorothy Farley, Executive Director, ICO Information Center; Pontifical Council for the Laity; Catholic Almanac survey.)

Guidelines

International organizations wanting to call themselves "Catholic" are required to meet standards set by the Vatican's Council for the Laity and to register with and get the approval of the Papal Secretariat of State, according to guidelines dated Dec. 3 and published in *Acta Apostolicae Sedis* under the date of Dec. 23, 1971.

Among conditions for the right of organizations to "bear the name Catholic" are:
• leaders "will always be Catholics," and candidates for office will be approved by the Secretariat of State
• adherence by the organization to the Catholic Church, its teaching authority and the teachings of the Gospel
• evidence that the organization is really international with a universal outlook and that it fulfills its mission through its own management, meetings and accomplishments.

The guidelines also stated that leaders of the organizations "will take care to maintain necessary reserve as regards taking a stand or engaging in public activity in the field of politics or trade unionism. Abstention in these fields will normally be the best attitude for them to adopt during their term of office."

The guidelines were in line with a provision stated by the Second Vatican Council: "No project may claim the name 'Catholic' unless it has obtained the consent of the lawful Church authority."

They made it clear that all organizations are not obliged to apply for recognition, but that the Church "reserves the right to recognize as linked with her mission and her aims those organizations or movements which see fit to ask for such recognition."

Conference of International Catholic Organizations

A permanent body for collaboration among various organizations the conference seeks to promote the development of international life along the lines of Christian principles. Eleven international Catholic organizations participated in its foundation and first meeting in 1927 at Fribourg, Switzerland. In 1951, the conference established its general secretariat and adopted governing statutes that were approved by the Vatican Secretariat of State in 1953.

The permanent secretariat is located at 37-39 rue de Vermont, CH-1202 Geneva, Switzerland. Other office addresses are: 1 rue Varembe, CH-1211 Geneva 20, Switzerland (International Catholic Center of Geneva); 9, rue Cler, F-75007 Paris, France (International Catholic Center for UNESCO); ICO Information Center, 323 East 47th St., New York, NY 10017.

Charter

According to its charter (adopted in November 1997), the conference "responds to the challenge of *Christifideles Laici*: Open to the saving power of Christ the frontiers of States, economic and political systems, the vast domains of culture, civilization and development (no. 34)."

In a universal vision of those problems, these organizations have the following responsibilities to their members:
• to make them increasingly aware of the complexities of the situations in which they live and work
• to help them to grow in discernment and critical analysis
• to facilitate the search for solutions to concrete difficulties.

The Conference is open to any organization which is acting and is involved recognizably Catholic in its work in the international world, which accepts the present Charter, respects its principles in practice and adheres to its Statutes. The Conference witnesses to the organized presence of Catholics in the international world.

Fundamental Convictions

• Their desire to announce Jesus Christ to the women and men of our time, and their vocation to serve the world, are indivisible; faith calls for action
• Their wish to contribute to the building of the Kingdom of God is demonstrated by solidarity with all women and men of good will
• Their desire for participation in decision-making in the Church in areas which concern their competence and in which they are involved.

A unique spirituality

In its desire to live fully its faith in Jesus Christ, the Conference stresses:
• The need to be rooted in reality, through a relationship with God lived out in the world
• An experience of community nourished by group sharing and exchange
• Openness to the international dimension, validated by experiences at local level to which it gives meaning
• Adaptation to different human groups and to different sensibilities
• The witness of Christian freedom to initiate, as well as willingness to live in "solid and strong communion" with the Church
• Desire to serve the universal Church through insertion in the local Churches by respecting diverse pastoral programs, but also to participate in major events in the life of the universal Church.

Members

Members of the Conference of International Catholic Organizations are listed below. Information includes name, date and place of establishment (when available), address of general secretariat. Approximately 30 of the organizations have consultative status with other international or regional non-governmental agencies.

Caritas Internationalis (1951, Rome, Italy): Piazza San Calisto 16, I-00153, Rome, Italy. Coordinates and represents its 146 national member organizations (in 194 countries) operating in the fields of development, emergency aid, social action.

Catholic International Education Office (1952): 60, rue des Eburons, B-1000 Brussels, Belgium.

Catholic International Union for Social Service (1925, Milan, Italy): rue de la Poste 111, B-1210

Brussels, Belgium (general secretariat).

Christian Life Community (CVX) (1953): Borgo Santo Spirito 8, C.P. 6139, I-00195 Rome, Italy. First Sodality of Our Lady founded in 1563.

International Ascent, The: 84, rue Charles Michels, F-93206 Saint Denis Cedex, France. Member of ICO.

International Association of Charities (1617, Chatillon les Dombes, France): Rue Joseph Brand, 118, B-1030 Brussels, Belgium.

International Catholic Child Bureau (1948, in Paris): 63, rue de Lausanne, CH-1202 Geneva, Switzerland.

International Catholic Committee of Nurses and Medico-Social Assistants (ICCN) (1933): Square Vergote, 43, B-1040 Brussels, Belgium.

International Catholic Conference of Scouting (1948): Piazza Pasquale Paoli, 18, I-00186 Rome, Italy.

International Catholic Migration Commission (1951): 37-39 rue de Vermont, C.P. 96, CH-1211 Geneva 20, Switzerland. Coordinates activities worldwide on behalf of refugees and migrants, both administering programs directly and supporting the efforts of national affiliated agencies.

International Catholic Organization for Cinema and Audiovisual (1928, The Hague, The Netherlands): Rue du Saphir, 15, B-1040 Brussels, Belgium (general secretariat). Federation of National Catholic film offices.

International Catholic Society for Girls (1897): 37-39, rue de Vermont, CH-1202 Geneva, Switzerland.

International Catholic Union of the Press: 37-39 rue de Vermont, Case Postale 197, CH-1211 Geneva 20 CIC, Switzerland. Coordinates and represents at the international level the activities of Catholics and Catholic federations or associations in the field of press and information. Has seven specialized branches: International Federation of Catholic Journalists; International Federation of Dailies; International Federation of Periodicals; International Federation of Catholic News Agencies; International Catholic Federation of Teachers and Researchers in the Science and Techniques of Information; International Federation of Church Press Associations; and International Federation of Book Publishers.

International Conference of Catholic Guiding (1965): c/o Mlle Francoise Parmentier, rue de la Tour 64, 75016 Paris. Founded by member bodies of interdenominational World Association of Guides and Girl Scouts.

International Coordination of Young Christian Workers (YCYCW): via dei Barbieri 22, I-00186 Rome, Italy.

International Council of Catholic Men (ICCM) (Unum Omnes) (1948): Wahringer Str. 2-4, A.1090 Vienna IX, Austria.

International Federation of Catholic Medical Associations (1954): Palazzo San Calisto, I-00120 Vatican City.

International Federation of Catholic Parochial Youth Communities (1962, Rome, Italy): St. Kariliquai 12, 6000 Lucerne 5, Switzerland.

International Federation of Catholic Pharmacists (1954): Bosdorf 180, 9190 Stekene, Belgium.

International Federation of Rural Adult Catholic Movements (1964, Lisbon, Portugal): Rue Jaumain 15, B-5330 Assesse, Belgium.

International Federation of Catholic Universities (1949): 21, rue d'Assas, F-75270 Paris 06, France.

International Federation of the Catholic Associations of the Blind: Avenue Dailly 90, B-1030 Brussels, Belgium. Coordinates actions of Catholic groups and associations for the blind and develops their apostolate.

International Independent Christian Youth (IICY): 11, rue Martin Bernard, 75013 Paris, France.

International Military Apostolate (1967): Breite Strasse 25, D-53111 Bonn, Germany. Comprised of organizations of military men.

International Movement of Apostolate of Children (1929, France): 24, rue Paul Rivet, F-92350 Le Plessis Robinson, France.

International Movement of Apostolate in the Independent Social Milieux (MIAMSI) (1963): Piazza San Calisto 16, 00153 Rome, Italy.

International Movement of Catholic Agricultural and Rural Youth (1954, Annevoie, Belgium): 53, rue J. Coosemans, B-1030 Brussels, Belgium (permanent secretariat).

International Young Catholic Students (1946, Fribourg, Switzerland; present name, 1954): 171 rue de Rennes, F-75006 Paris, France.

Pax Romana (1921, Fribourg, Switzerland, divided into two branches, 1947): **Pax Romana - IMCS (International Movement of Catholic Students)** (1921): 171, rue de Rennes, F-75006, Paris, France, for undergraduates; **Pax Romana - ICMICA (International Catholic Movement for Intellectual and Cultural Affairs)** (1947): rue du Grand Bureau 15, CH-1227 Geneva, Switzerland, for Catholic intellectuals and professionals.

Society of St. Vincent de Paul (1833, Paris): 5, rue du Pré-aux-Clercs, F-75007 Paris, France.

Unda: International Catholic Association for Radio and Television (1928, Cologne, Germany): rue de l'Orme, 12, B-1040 Brussels, Belgium.

World Movement of Christian Workers (1961): Blvd. du Jubilé 124, 1080 Brussels, Belgium.

World Organization of Former Pupils of Catholic Education (1967, Rome): 48, rue de Richelieu, F-75001 Paris, France.

World Union of Catholic Teachers (1951): Piazza San Calisto 16, 00153 Rome, Italy.

World Union of Catholic Women's Organizations (1910): 18, rue Notre Dame des Champs, F-75006 Paris, France.

Other Catholic Organizations

Apostleship of Prayer (1849): Borgo Santo Spirito 5, I-00193 Rome, Italy. National secretariat in most countries.

Apostolatus Maris (Apostleship of the Sea) (1922, Glasgow, Scotland): Pontifical Council for Migrants and Itinerant People, Piazza San Calisto 16, 00153 Rome, Italy. (See Index.)

L'Arche Communities: B.P. 35, 60350 Cuise Lamotte, France.

Associationes Juventutis Salesianae (Associations of Salesian Youth) (1847): Via della Pisana, 1111, 00163 Rome, Italy.

Blue Army of Our Lady of Fatima: P.O. Box 976, Washington, NJ, 07882.

Catholic International Federation for Physical and Sports Education (1911; present name, 1957): 5, rue Cernuschi, 75017 Paris, France.

Christian Fraternity of the Sick and Handicapped: 9, Avenue de la Gare, CH-1630, Bulle, Switzerland.

"Communione e Liberazione" Fraternity (1955, Milan, Italy): Via Marcello Malpighi 2, 00161 Rome, Italy. Catholic renewal movement.

"Focolare Movement" (Work of Mary) (1943, Trent, Italy): Via di Frascati, 306, I-00040 Rocca di Papa (Rome), Italy.

Foi et Lumiere: 8 rue Serret, 75015 Paris, France.

Franciscans International: 345 E. 47th St., New York, NY 10017. A non-governmental organization at the UN.

Inter Cultural Association (ICA, 1937, Belgium) and **Association Fraternelle Internationale** (AFI): 91, rue de la Servette, CH-1202 Geneva, Switzerland.

International Association of Children of Mary (1847): 67 rue de Sèvres, F-75006 Paris, France.

International Catholic Rural Association (1962, Rome): Piazza San Calisto, 00153 Rome, Italy. International body for agricultural and rural organizations. Invited member of ICO.

International Catholic Union of Esperanto: Via Berni 9, 00185 Rome, Italy.

International Centre for Studies in Religious Education LUMEN VITAE (1934-35, Louvain, Belgium, under name Catechetical Documentary Centre; present name, 1956): 184, rue Washington, B-1050 Brussels, Belgium. Also referred to as Lumen Vitae Centre; concerned with all aspects of religious formation.

International Young Christian Workers (1925, Belgium): 11, rue Plantin, B-1070 Brussels, Belgium. Associate member of ICO.

Legion of Mary (1921, Dublin, Ireland): De Montfort House, North Brunswick St., Dublin, Ireland. (See **Index.**)

Medicus Mundi Internationalis (1964, Bensberg, Germany FR): P.O. Box 1547, 6501 BM Nijmegen, Netherlands. To promote health and medico-social services, particularly in developing countries; recruit essential health and medical personnel for developing countries; contribute to training of medical and auxiliary personnel; undertake research in the field of health.

NOVALIS, Marriage Preparation Center: University of St. Paul, 1 rue Stewart, Ottawa 2, ON, Canada.

Our Lady's Teams (Equipes Notre-Dame) (1937, France): 49, rue de la Glacière, 75013 Paris, France.

Movement for spiritual formation of couples.

Pax Christi International (1950): rue du Vieux Marché aux grains 21, B-1000 Brussels, Belgium. International Catholic peace movement. Originated in Lourdes, France, in 1948 by French and German Catholics to reconcile enemies from World War II; spread to Italy and Poland and acquired its international title when it merged with the English organization Pax. Associate member of ICO.

Pro Sanctity Movement: Piazza S. Andrea della Valle 3, 00166 Rome, Italy.

St. Joan's International Alliance (1911, in England, as Catholic Women's Suffrage Society): Quai Churchill 19, Boite 061, B-4020 Liège, Belgium. Associate member of ICO.

Salesian Cooperators (1876, Turin, Italy): **Salesian Cooperators:** Founded by St. John Bosco; for lay men and women and diocesan clergy. A public association of the faithful, members commit themselves to apostolates in the local Church, especially on behalf of the young, in the Salesian spirit and style. Address: 174 Filors Lane, Stony Point, NY 10980-2645; (845) 947-2200.

Secular Franciscan Order (1221, first Rule approved): Via Piemonte, 70, 00187, Rome, Italy.

Secular Fraternity of Charles de Foucauld: Katharinenweg 4, B4700 Eupen, Belgium.

Serra International (1953, in U.S.): 65 E. Wacker Pl. Suite 1210, Chicago, IL 60601.

Unio Internationalis Laicorum in Servitio Ecclesiae (1965, Aachen, Germany): Postfach 990125, Am Kielshof 2, 5000 Cologne, Germany 91. Consists of national and diocesan associations of persons who give professional services to the Church.

Union of Adorers of the Blessed Sacrament (1937): Largo dei Monti Parioli 3, I-00197, Rome, Italy.

World Catholic Federation for the Biblical Apostolate (1969, Rome): Mittelstrasse, 12, P.O. Box 601, D-7000, Stuttgart 1, Germany.

Regional Organizations

European Federation for Catholic Adult Education (1963, Lucerne, Switzerland): Hirschengraben 13, P.B. 2069, CH-6002 Lucerne, Switzerland.

European Forum of National Committees of the Laity (1968): 169, Booterstown Av., Blackrock, Co. Dublin, Ireland.

Movimiento Familiar Cristiano (1949-50, Montevideo and Buenos Aires): Carrera 17 n. 4671, Bogotá, D.E., Colombia. Christian Family Movement of Latin America.

Eastern Catholic Churches

Sources: Rev. Ronald Roberson, C.S.P, Associate Director, Ecumenical and Interreligious Affairs, USCCB.; Annuario Pontificio; Official Catholic Directory.

The Second Vatican Council, in its Decree on Eastern Catholic Churches (*Orientalium Ecclesiarum*), stated the following points regarding Eastern heritage, patriarchs, sacraments and worship.

Venerable Churches: The Catholic Church holds in high esteem the institutions of the Eastern Churches, their liturgical rites, ecclesiastical traditions, and Christian way of life. For, distinguished as they are by their venerable antiquity, they are bright with that tradition which was handed down from the Apostles through the Fathers, and which forms part of the divinely revealed and undivided heritage of the universal Church (No. 1). That Church, Holy and Catholic, which is the Mystical Body of Christ, is made up of the faithful who are organically united in the Holy Spirit through the same faith, the same sacraments, and the same government and who, combining into various groups held together by a hierarchy, form separate Churches or rites. It is the mind of the Catholic Church that each individual Church or rite retain its traditions whole and entire, while adjusting its way of life to the various needs of time and place (No. 2).

Such individual Churches, whether of the East or of the West, although they differ somewhat among themselves in what are called rites (that is, in liturgy, ecclesiastical discipline, and spiritual heritage) are, nevertheless, equally entrusted to the pastoral guidance of the Roman Pontiff, the divinely appointed successor of St. Peter in supreme government over the universal Church. They are consequently of equal dignity, so that none of them is superior to the others by reason of rite (No. 3).

Eastern Heritage: Each and every Catholic, as also the baptized of every non-Catholic Church or community who enters into the fullness of Catholic communion, should everywhere retain his proper rite, cherish it, and observe it to the best of his ability (No. 4). The Churches of the East, as much as those of the West, fully enjoy the right, and are in duty bound, to rule themselves. Each should do so according to its proper and individual procedures (No. 5). All Eastern rite members should know and be convinced that they can and should always preserve their lawful liturgical rites and their established way of life, and that these should not be altered except by way of an appropriate and organic development (No. 6)

Patriarchs: The institution of the patriarchate has existed in the Church from the earliest times and was recognized by the first ecumenical Synods. By the name Eastern Patriarch is meant the bishop who has jurisdiction over all bishops (including metropolitans), clergy, and people of his own territory or rite, in accordance with the norms of law and without prejudice to the primacy of the Roman Pontiff (No. 7). Though some of the patriarchates of the Eastern Churches are of later origin than others, all are equal in patriarchal dignity. Still the honorary and lawfully established order of precedence among them is to be preserved (No. 8). In keeping with the most ancient tradition of the Church, the Patriarchs of the Eastern Churches are to be accorded exceptional respect, since each presides over his patriarchate as father and head.

This sacred Synod, therefore, decrees that their rights and privileges should be re-established in accord with the ancient traditions of each Church and the decrees of the ecumenical Synods. The rights and privileges in question are those which flourished when East and West were in union, though they should be somewhat adapted to modern conditions.

The Patriarchs with their synods constitute the superior authority for all affairs of the patriarchate, including the right to establish new eparchies and to nominate bishops of their rite within the territorial bounds of the patriarchate, without prejudice to the inalienable right of the Roman Pontiff to intervene in individual cases (No. 9).

What has been said of Patriarchs applies as well, under the norm of law, to major archbishops, who preside over the whole of some individual Church or rite (No. 10).

Sacraments: This sacred Ecumenical Synod endorses and lauds the ancient discipline of the sacraments existing in the Eastern Churches, as also the practices connected with their celebration and administration (No. 12).

With respect to the minister of holy chrism (confirmation), let that practice be fully restored which existed among Easterners in most ancient times. Priests, therefore, can validly confer this sacrament, provided they use chrism blessed by a Patriarch or bishop (No. 13).

In conjunction with baptism or otherwise, all Eastern-Rite priests can confer this sacrament validly on all the faithful of any rite, including the Latin; licitly, however, only if the regulations of both common and particular law are observed. Priests of the Latin rite, to the extent of the faculties they enjoy for administering this sacrament, can confer it also on the faithful of Eastern Churches, without prejudice to rite. They do so licitly if the regulations of both common and particular law are observed (No. 14).

The faithful are bound on Sundays and feast days to attend the divine liturgy or, according to the regulations or custom of their own rite, the celebration of the Divine Praises. That the faithful may be able to satisfy their obligation more easily, it is decreed that this obligation can be fulfilled from the Vespers of the vigil to the end of the Sunday or the feast day (No. 15). Because of the everyday intermingling of the communicants of diverse Eastern Churches in the same Eastern region or territory, the faculty for hearing confession, duly and unrestrictedly granted by his proper bishop to a priest of any rite, is applicable to the entire territory of the grantor, also to the places and the faithful belonging to any other rite in the same territory, unless an Ordinary of the place explicitly decides otherwise with respect to the places pertaining to his rite (No. 16).

This sacred Synod ardently desires that where it has fallen into disuse the office of the permanent diaconate be restored. The legislative authority of each individual church should decide about the subdiaconate and the minor orders (No. 17).

By way of preventing invalid marriages between Eastern Catholics and baptized Eastern non-Catholics, and in the interests of the permanence and sanctity of marriage and of domestic harmony, this sacred Synod decrees that the canonical 'form' for the celebration of such marriages obliges only for lawfulness. For their validity, the presence of a sacred minister suffices, as long as the other requirements of law are honored (No. 18).

Worship: Henceforth, it will be the exclusive right of an ecumenical Synod or the Apostolic See to establish, transfer, or suppress feast days common to all the Eastern Churches. To establish, transfer, or suppress feast days for any of the individual Churches is within the competence not only of the Apostolic See but also of a patriarchal or archiepiscopal synod, provided due consideration is given to the entire region and to other individual Churches (No. 19). Until such time as all Christians desirably concur on a fixed day for the celebration of Easter, and with a view meantime to promoting unity among the Christians of a given area or nation, it is left to the Patriarchs or supreme authorities of a place to reach a unanimous agreement, after ascertaining the views of all concerned, on a single Sunday for the observance of Easter (No. 20). With respect to rules concerning sacred seasons, individual faithful dwelling outside the area or territory of their own rite may conform completely to the established custom of the place where they live. When members of a family belong to different rites, they are all permitted to observe sacred seasons according to the rules of any one of these rites (No. 21). From ancient times the Divine Praises have been held in high esteem among all Eastern Churches. Eastern clerics and religious should celebrate these Praises as the laws and customs of their own traditions require. To the extent they can, the faithful too should follow the example of their forebears by assisting devoutly at the Divine Praises (No. 22).

Restoration of Ancient Practices

An "Instruction for the Application of the Liturgical Prescriptions of the Code of Canons of the Eastern Churches" was published in Italian by the Congregation for Eastern-Rite Churches in Jan. 1996. Msgr. Alan Detscher, executive director of the U.S. bishops' Secretariat for the Liturgy, said it was the first instruction on liturgical renewal of the Eastern Catholic Churches since the Second Vatican Council (1962-65).

JURISDICTIONS AND FAITHFUL OF THE EASTERN CATHOLIC CHURCHES

Introduction

The Church originated in Palestine, whence it spread to other regions of the world where certain places became key centers of Christian life with great influence on the local churches in their respective areas. These centers developed into the ancient patriarchates of Constantinople, Alexandria, Antioch and Jerusalem in the East, and Rome in the West. The main lines of Eastern Church patriarchal organization and usages were drawn before the Roman Empire became two empires, East (Byzantine) and West (Roman), in 292. Other churches with distinctive traditions grew up beyond the boundaries of the Roman Empire in Persia, Armenia, Syria, Egypt, Ethiopia, and India. The "nestorian" church in Persia, known today as the Assyrian Church of the East, broke communion with the rest of the church in the wake of the Council of Ephesus (431) whose teachings it did not accept. The "monophysite" churches of Armenia, Syria, Egypt, Ethiopia, Eritrea and India (known today as the Oriental Orthodox Churches) did not accept the christological teachings of the Council of Chalcedon (451) and so broke away from the church within the Roman Empire. And finally, in the wake of the mutual excommunications of 1054 between the Patriarch of Constantinople and the papal legate, the church within the empire divided into what would become the Catholic Church in the West and the Orthodox Church in the East. This was a lengthy process of estrangement that culminated only in 1204 and the sack of Constantinople by the Latin Crusaders.

In the following centuries, attempts to overcome these divisions took place, most notably at the Second Council of Lyons in 1274 and the Council of Ferrara-Florence in 1438-39. Both failed. Subsequently, the Catholic Church began to send missionaries to work with separated Eastern Christians, and some groups within those churches spontaneously asked to enter into full communion with Rome. Thus began the formation of the Eastern Catholic Churches, which retained most of the liturgical, canonical, spiritual and theological patrimony of their non-Catholic counterparts.

The Code of Canons of the Eastern Churches groups these churches today into four categories: patriarchal, major archepiscopal, metropolitan, and other churches *sui iuris*. In common usage, an eparchy is equivalent to a diocese in the Latin rite.

STATISTICS

Principal source: 2007 Annuario Pontificio (the most recent available).

The following statistics are the sum of those reported for Eastern Catholic jurisdictions only, and do not include Eastern Catholics under the jurisdiction of Latin bishops. Some of the figures reported are only approximate. The churches are grouped according to their liturgical traditions.

PATRIARCHS

The current Patriarchs of the Eastern Catholic

Churches (as of July 15, 2008) are as follows:

Naguib, Antonios: b. Mar. 16, 1935; ord. Oct. 30, 1960; cons. bp. Sept. 9, 1977; Patriarch of Alexandria of the Copts, Mar. 30, 2006; granted "ecclesiastical communion" with Pope Benedict XVI, Apr. 7, 2006.

Delly, Emmanuel III: b. Oct. 6, 1927; cons. Apr. 19, 1963; Patriarch of Babylon of the Chaldeans, Dec. 3, 2003; granted "ecclesiastical communion" with Pope John Paul II, Dec. 3, 2003.

Laham, Gregory III: b. Dec. 15, 1933; ord. Feb. 15, 1959; cons. bp., Nov. 27, 1981; patriarch of Greek Melkites, Nov. 29, 2000; granted "ecclesiastical communion" with Pope John Paul II, Dec. 5, 2000.

Sfeir, Nasrallah Pierre: Patriarch of Antioch of the Maronites; for details, see Cardinals, College of.

Tarmouni, Nerses XIX Bedros: b. Jan. 17, 1940, in Cairo, Egypt; ord. Aug. 15, 1965; patriarch of Cilicia of the Armenians, Oct. 7, 1999; granted "ecclesiastical communion" with the Pope John Paul II, Oct. 13, 1999.

The office of Patriarch of the Syrian Catholic Church is currently vacant.

ALEXANDRIAN

The liturgical tradition of Egypt, in particular that of the early Greek Patriarchate of Alexandria. In the Egyptian desert monasteries the rite evolved in a distinctive way and eventually became that of the Coptic Orthodox Church. The Greek Patriarchate of Alexandria adopted the Byzantine rite by the 12th century. The Coptic rite, with its Alexandrian origins, spread to Ethiopia in the fourth century where it underwent substantial modifications under strong Syrian influence. The Catholic Churches in this group are:

The Coptic Catholic Church (Patriarchate): Seven eparchies in Egypt; 161,327.

Catholic missionaries were present since the 17th century. The Patriarchate was established first in 1824 and renewed in 1895. Liturgical languages are Coptic and Arabic.

The Ethiopian Catholic Church (Metropolitanate): Three eparchies in Ethiopia and three in Eritrea; 222,861. Catholic missionary activity began in the 19th century, and the present ecclesiastical structure dates from 1961. The liturgical languages are Ge'ez and Amharic.

ANTIOCHIAN

The liturgical tradition of Antioch, one of the great centers of the early Christian world, also known as West Syrian. In Syria it developed under strong influence of Jerusalem, especially the Liturgy of St. James, into the form used by today's Syrian Orthodox and Catholics in the Middle East and India. The Maronites of Lebanon developed their own liturgical traditions under the influence of both the Antiochian and Chaldean rites.

The Catholic Churches of this group are:

The Syro-Malankara Catholic Church (Major Archbishopric): Five eparchies in India; 412,640. Began in 1930 when two bishops, a priest, a deacon and a layman of the Malankara Orthodox Church were received into full communion with Rome. Raised to Major Archepiscopal status in 2005. The liturgical language is Malayalam.

The Maronite Catholic Church (Patriarchate): Ten eparchies in Lebanon, three in Syria, two in the United States, and one each in Cyprus, Egypt, Argentina, Brazil, Australia, the Holy Land, Canada, and Mexico, plus patriarchal exarchates in Jordan and Jerusalem; 3,105,278.

Founded by St. Maron in the fourth century, the Maronites claim to have always been in communion with Rome. They have no counterpart among the separated Eastern churches. The patriarchate dates to the eigth century, and was confirmed by Pope Innocent III in 1216. Liturgical language is Arabic.

The Syrian Catholic Church (Patriarchate): Four eparchies in Syria, two in Iraq, and one each in Lebanon, Egypt, and North America, and patriarchal exarchates in Turkey, Venezuela, and Iraq/Kuwait; 131,692.

Catholic missionary activity among the Syrian Orthodox began in the 17th century, and there has been an uninterrupted series of Catholic patriarchs since 1783. The liturgical languages are Syriac/Aramaic and Arabic.

ARMENIAN

The liturgical tradition of the Armenian Apostolic and Catholic Churches. It contains elements of the Syriac, Jerusalem, and Byzantine rites. From the fifth to the seventh centuries there was strong influence from Syria and Jerusalem. More Byzantine usages were adopted later, and in the Middle Ages elements of the Latin tradition were added.

The Armenian Catholic Church (Patriarchate): Three eparchies in Syria, one each in Lebanon, Iran, Iraq, Egypt, Turkey, Ukraine, France, Argentina and the United States/Canada, and Ordinariates in Greece, Romania, and Eastern Europe (Armenia); 375,182.

Catholic missionaries had been working among the Armenians since the 14th century, and an Armenian Catholic patriarchate was established in Lebanon in 1742. The liturgical language is classical Armenian. His Beatitude Nerses Bedros XIX Tarmouni, canonically elected as patriarch of Cilicia of the Armenians, by the Synod of Bishops of the Armenian Catholic Church was approved by Pope John Paul II on Oct. 18, 1999.

BYZANTINE

The tradition of the Eastern Orthodox and Byzantine Catholic Churches which originated in the Orthodox Patriarchate of Constantinople (Byzantium). Its present form is a synthesis of Constantinopolitan and Palestinian elements that took place in the monasteries between the ninth and 14th centuries. It is by far the most widely used Eastern liturgical tradition. The Catholic Churches of this group are:

Albanians: One apostolic administration in southern Albania, mostly of the Latin rite; 3,510. Very small groups of Albanian Orthodox became Catholic in 1628 and again in 1900; liturgical language is Albanian.

Belarusans (formerly Byelorussian, also known as White Russian): No hierarchy, Apostolic Visitator. Most Belarusan Orthodox became Catholic with the Union of Brest in 1595-6, but this union was short lived. A modest revival has taken place since the end of communism. The liturgical language is Belarusan.

The Bulgarian Catholic Church: One apostolic exarchate in Bulgaria; 10,107. Originated with a group of Bulgarian Orthodox who became Catholic in 1861;

liturgical language is Old Slavonic.

Greek Catholics in Former Yugoslavia: One eparchy (Krizevci) located in Zagreb with jurisdiction over Slovenia, Croatia, and Bosnia-Herzegovina; Apostolic Exarchates in Serbia-Montenegro and in Macedonia; 55,691. A bishop for former Serbian Orthodox living in Catholic Croatia was first appointed in 1611; liturgical languages are Old Slavonic and Croatian.

The Greek Catholic Church: Apostolic exarchates in Greece and Turkey; 2,325. Catholic missionaries in Constantinople formed a small group of Byzantine Catholics there in the mid-19th century. Most of them moved to Greece in the 1920s. The liturgical language is Greek.

The Hungarian Catholic Church: One eparchy and one apostolic exarchate in Hungary; 290,000.

Descendants of groups of Orthodox in Hungary who became Catholic in the 17th century and after. The liturgical language is Hungarian.

The Italo-Albanian Catholic Church: Two eparchies, one territorial abbey in Italy; 63,240.

Descended mostly from Albanian Orthodox who came to southern Italy and Sicily in the 15th century and eventually became Catholic; liturgical languages are Greek and Italian.

The Melkite Greek Catholic Church (Patriarchate): Five eparchies in Syria, seven in Lebanon, one each in Jordan, Israel, Brazil, US, Canada, Mexico, and Australia. Apostolic Exarchates in Venezuela and Argentina, and patriarchal exarchates in Iraq and Kuwait; 1,346,635.

Catholic missionaries began work within the Greek Orthodox Patriarchate of Antioch in the mid-17th century. In 1724 it split into Catholic and Orthodox counterparts, the Catholics becoming known popularly as Melkites. Liturgical languages are Greek and Arabic.

The Romanian Greek Catholic Church (Major Archbishopric): Five eparchies in Romania and one in the US; 763,083.

Romanian Orthodox in Transylvania formally entered into union with Rome in 1700; the liturgical language is Romanian. In December 2005, the Romanian Greek Catholic Church was raised to the rank of Major Archbishopric.

Russians: No hierarchy. An apostolic exarchate was established for Russia in 1917 and for Russians in China in 1928, but neither is functioning today. There are now at least five parishes in Russia under the local Latin bishops and 13 in the diaspora.

The Ruthenian Catholic Church (Metropolitanate in the United States): One eparchy in Ukraine, four in the United States, and an apostolic exarchate in the Czech Republic. Originated with the reception of 63 Orthodox priests into the Catholic Church at the Union of Uzhhorod in 1646. Liturgical languages are Old Slavonic and English; 594,465.

The Slovak Catholic Church (Metropolitanate): Three eparchies in Slovakia, and one eparchy in Canada; 243,335.

Also originated with the Union of Uzhhorod in 1646; eparchy of Presov was established for them in 1818. Liturgical languages are Old Slavonic and Slovak.

The Ukrainian Greek Catholic Church (Major Archbishopric): Nine eparchies and two archepiscopal exarchates in Ukraine, two eparchies in Poland, five eparchies in Canada, four in the United States, one each in Australia, Brazil and Argentina, apostolic exarchates in Great Britain, Germany, and France; 4,223,425.

Originated with the Union of Brest between the Orthodox Metropolitanate of Kiev and the Catholic Church in 1595-6. Liturgical languages are Old Slavonic and Ukrainian.

CHALDEAN

Also called East Syrian, the liturgical tradition of the Chaldean Catholic and Syro-Malabar Catholic Churches as well as the Assyrian Church of the East. Descends from the ancient rite of the church of Mesopotamia in the Persian Empire. It is celebrated in the eastern dialect of classical Syriac. The Catholic Churches of this tradition are:

The Chaldean Catholic Church (Patriarchate): Ten eparchies in Iraq, three in Iran, two in the U.S., one each in Lebanon, Egypt, Syria, and Turkey; 418,194.

A group of disaffected members of the ("Nestorian") Assyrian Church of the East asked for union with Rome in 1553. In that year Pope Julius III ordained their leader a bishop and named him Patriarch; liturgical languages are Syriac, Arabic.

The Syro-Malabar Catholic Church (Major Archbishopric): 25 eparchies in India, one in the U.S.; 3,902,089.

Descended from Thomas Christians of India who became Catholic in the wake of Portuguese colonization; the diocese of Ernakulam-Angamaly was raised to Major Archepiscopal status in 1993; the liturgical language is Malayalam.

EASTERN JURISDICTIONS

For centuries Eastern Churches were identifiable with a limited number of nationality and language groups in certain countries of the Middle East, Eastern Europe, Asia and Africa. The persecution of religion in the former Soviet Union since 1917 and in communist-controlled countries for more than 40 years following World War II — in addition to decimating and destroying the Church in those places — resulted in the emigration of many Eastern Catholics from their homelands. This forced emigration, together with voluntary emigration, has led to the spread of Eastern Churches to many other countries. As of June 1, 2008.

Europe

Bishop Krikor Ghabroyan, of the Armenian Eparchy of Sainte-Croix-de-Paris, France, is apostolic visitator for Armenian Catholics in Western Europe who do not have their own bishop. Bishop Youssef Ibrahim Sarraf of Cairo of the Chaldeans is apostolic visitator for Chaldeans in Europe. Bishop Samis Mazloum is apostolic visitator for Maronites in Western and Northern Europe. Archimandrite Jan Sergiusz Gajek is Apostolic Visitator for Greek Catholics in Belarus.

Albania: Byzantine apostolic administration.

Austria: Byzantine ordinariate.

Bulgaria: Bulgarian apostolic exarchate.

Croatia: Eparchy of Krizevci.

Czech Republic: Ruthenian apostolic exarchate.

France: Ukrainian apostolic exarchate. Armenian eparchy (1986). Ordinariate for all other Eastern Catholics.

Germany: Ukrainian apostolic exarchate.
Great Britain: Ukrainian apostolic exarchate.
Greece: Byzantine apostolic exarchate. Armenian ordinariate.
Hungary: Hungarian Byzantine eparchy, apostolic exarchate.
Italy: Two Italo-Albanian eparchies, one abbacy.
Macedonia: One apostolic exarchate.
Poland: Ukrainian metropolitan see (1996), one eparchy. Ordinariate for all other Eastern Catholics.
Romania: Romanian Byzantine major archbishopric, four eparchies; Armenian ordinariate.
Russia: Russian apostolic exarchate (for Byzantine Catholics in Moscow).
Serbia and Montenegro: One apostolic exarchate.
Slovakia: Three Slovak Byzantine eparchies.
Ukraine: Armenian archeparchy; Ruthenian eparchy; Ukrainian major archbishopric, eight eparchies, two archepiscopal exarchates.

Asia

Armenia: Armenian ordinariate (for Armenians of Eastern Europe).
China: Russian Byzantine apostolic exarchate.
Cyprus: Maronite archeparchy.
India: Syro-Malankara metropolitan see, five eparchies.
Syro-Malabar major archbishopric (1993), three metropolitan sees (1995), 18 eparchies.
Iran: Two Chaldean metropolitan sees, one archeparchy, one eparchy; Armenian eparchy.
Iraq: Two Syrian archeparchies; Melkite patriarchal exarchate; Chaldean patriarchate, two metropolitan sees, three archeparchies and five eparchies; Armenian archeparchy.
Israel (including Jerusalem): Syrian patriarchal exarchate; Maronite archeparchy; Melkite archeparchy, patriarchal exarchate; Chaldean patriarchal exarchate; Armenian patriarchal exarchate.
Jordan: Melkite archeparchy.
Kuwait: Melkite patriarchal exarchate; Syrian patriarchate exarchate.
Syria: Two Maronite archeparchies, one eparchy; two Syrian metropolitan and two archeparchal sees; Melkite patriarchate, four metropolitan sees, one archeparchy; Chaldean eparchy; Armenian archeparchy, one eparchy .
Turkey: Syrian patriarchal exarchate; Greek apostolic exarchate; Chaldean archeparchy; Armenian archeparchy.

Oceania

Australia: Ukrainian eparchy; Melkite eparchy (1987); Maronite eparchy.

Africa

Egypt: Coptic patriarchate, six eparchies; Maronite eparchy; Syrian eparchy; Melkite patriarchal dependency; Chaldean eparchy; Armenian eparchy.
Eritrea: Three Ethiopian eparchies.
Ethiopia: Ethiopian metropolitan see, two eparchies.
Sudan: Melkite patriarchal dependency.

North America

Canada: One Ukrainian metropolitan, four eparchies; Slovak eparchy; Melkite eparchy; Armenian eparchy for Canada and the U.S. (New York is see city); Maronite eparchy.

United States: Two Maronite eparchies; Syrian eparchy (1995); one Ukrainian metropolitan see, three eparchies; one Ruthenian metropolitan see, three eparchies; Melkite eparchy; Romanian eparchy; Syro-Malabar eparchy based in Chicago; Belarusan apostolic visitator; Armenian eparchy for Canada and U.S. (New York is see city); two Chaldean eparchies; other Eastern Catholics are under the jurisdiction of local Latin bishops. (See **Eastern Catholics in the United States.**)
Mexico: Melkite eparchy; Maronite eparchy (1995).

South America

Armenian Catholics in Latin America (including Mexico and excluding Argentina) are under the jurisdiction of an apostolic exarchate .
Argentina: Ukrainian eparchy; Maronite eparchy; Armenian eparchy; Melkite apostolic exarchate; ordinariate for all other Eastern Catholics.
Brazil: Maronite eparchy; Melkite eparchy; Ukrainian eparchy; ordinariate for all other Eastern Catholics.
Venezuela: Melkite apostolic exarchate.

Synods, Assemblies

These assemblies are collegial bodies that have pastoral authority over members of the Eastern Catholic Churches. (Canons 102-113, 152-153, 322 of Oriental Code of Canon Law.)
Patriarchal Synods:
Synod of the Coptic Catholic Church: Antonios Naguib, patriarch of Alexandria of the Copts.
Synod of the Greek-Melkite Catholic Church: Gregory III Laham, patriarch of Antioch of the Greek Catholics-Melkites.
Synod of the Syrian Catholic Church: (patriarchal office currently vacant)
Synod of the Maronite Church: Cardinal Nasrallah Pierre Sfeir, patriarch of Antioch of the Maronites.
Synod of the Chaldean Church: Emmanuel III Delly, patriarch of Babylonia of the Chaldeans.
Synod of the Armenian Catholic Church: Nerses Bedros XIX Tarmouni, patriarch of Cilicia of the Armenians.

Major Archiepiscopal Synods:

The Synod of the Ukrainian Greek Catholic Church (raised to major archiepiscopal status Dec. 23, 1963): Cardinal Lubomir Husar, major archbishop of Kiev and Halych, president.
The Synod of the Syro-Malabar Catholic Church (raised to major archiepiscopal status, Jan. 29, 1993): Cardinal Varkey Vithayathil, C.SS.R., major archbishop of Ernakulam-Angamaly of the Syro-Malabars, president.
The Synod of the Syro-Malankara Catholic Church (raised to major archiepiscopal status February 10, 2005): Abp. Isaac Mar Cleemis Thottunkal of Trivandrum of the Syro-Malankarese, president.
The Synod of the Romanian Greek Catholic Church (raised to major archiepiscopal status December 16, 2005): Abp. Lucian Muresan of Fagaras and Alba Julia, president.

Councils, Assemblies, Conferences

Council of Ethiopian Churches: Most Rev. Berhane-Yesus Demerew Souraphiel, C.M., Archbishop of Addis Ababa, president.

Council of Ruthenian Churches, U.S.A.: Most Reverend Basil Schott, OFM, Metropolitan of Pittsburgh of the Byzantines, president.

Assembly of the Catholic Hierarchy of Egypt (Dec. 5, 1983): His Beatitude Antonios Naguib, Patriarch of Alexandria of the Copts, president.

Assembly of Catholic Patriarchs and Bishops of Lebanon: Cardinal Nasrallah Pierre Sfeir, patriarch of Antioch of the Maronites, president.

Assembly of Ordinaries of the Syrian Arab Republic: His Beatitude Gregory III Laham, patriarch of Antioch of the Greek Melkites, president.

Assembly of Catholic Ordinaries of the Holy Land (Jan. 27, 1992): His Beatitude Michel Sabbah, patriarch of Jerusalem of the Latins, president.

Interritual Union of the Bishops of Iraq: His Beatitude Emmanuel III Delly, patriarch of Babylonia of the Chaldeans, president.

Iranian Episcopal Conference (Aug. 11, 1977): Most Rev. Ignatius Bedini, SDB, Archbishop of Ispahan of the Latins, president.

Episcopal Conference of Turkey (Nov. 30, 1987): Most Rev. Ruggero Franceschini, O.F.M.Cap., Archbishop of Izmir, president.

EASTERN CATHOLIC CHURCHES IN THE U.S.

Statistics, from the 2007 Annuario Pontificio *(the most recent available)* unless noted otherwise, *are membership figures reported by Eastern jurisdictions. Additional Eastern Catholics are included in statistics for Latin dioceses.*

Byzantine Tradition

Ukrainians: There were 102,678 reported in four jurisdictions in the U.S.: the metropolitan see of Philadelphia (1924, metropolitan 1958) and the suffragan sees of Stamford, CN (1956), St. Nicholas of Chicago (1961) and St. Josaphat in Parma (1983).

Ruthenians: There were 96,761 reported in four jurisdictions in the U.S.: the metropolitan see of Pittsburgh (est. 1924 at Pittsburgh; metropolitan and transferred to Munhall, 1969; transferred to Pittsburgh, 1977) and the suffragan sees of Passaic, NJ (1963), Parma, OH (1969) and Van Nuys, CA (1981). Hungarian and Croatian Byzantine Catholics in the U.S. are also under the jurisdiction of Ruthenian bishops.

Melkites: There were 24,435 reported under the jurisdiction of the Melkite eparchy of Newton, MA (established as an exarchate, 1965; eparchy, 1976).

Romanians: There were 5,000 reported in 15 Romanian Catholic Byzantine Rite parishes in the U.S., under the jurisdiction of the Romanian eparchy of St. George Martyr, Canton, OH (established as an exarchate, 1982; eparchy, 1987).

Russians: In the United States, there are parishes in New York City (Saint Michael) and in El Segundo in the Los Angeles area (Saint Andrew). They are under the jurisdiction of local Latin bishops.

Alexandrian Tradition

Copts: Have a Catholic Chapel—Resurrection, in Brooklyn, NY, and St. Mary's Coptic Catholic parish, Los Angeles, CA.

Antiochian Tradition

Maronites: There were 74,232 reported in two jurisdictions in the U.S.: the eparchy of St. Maron, Brooklyn (established at Detroit as an exarchate, 1966; eparchy, 1972; transferred to Brooklyn, 1977) and the eparchy of Our Lady of Lebanon of Los Angeles (resident in St. Louis, MO, established Mar. 1, 1994).

Syrians: The eparchy of Our Lady of the Deliverance of Newark with 13,270 faithful was established in 1995 for Syrian Catholics of the U.S. and Canada.

Syro-Malankarese: Have twelve mission parishes in the United States under the direction of Most Rev. Dr. Joseph Mar Thomas, Auxiliary Bishop of Trivandrum and Apostolic visitor for Europe and North America.

Armenian Tradition

An apostolic exarchate for Canada and the United States was established July 3, 1981; raised to status of eparchy on Sept. 12, 2005; 36,000 in the two countries.

Chaldean Tradition

Chaldeans: There were 125,200 reported under the jurisdictions of the eparchy of St. Thomas the Apostle of Detroit (established as an exarchate, 1982; eparchy, 1986) and the eparchy of St. Peter the Apostle of San Diego (established on May 21, 2002).

Syro-Malabarese (Malabar): The eparchy of Saint Thomas the Apostle in Chicago (established February 16, 2001) has eight parishes around the country. Estimated 100,000 faithful with 26 diocesan priests.

Eastern Catholic Associates

Eastern Catholic Associates is the association of all Eastern Catholic bishops and their equivalents in law in the United States, representing the Armenian, Chaldean, Maronite, Melkite, Syriac, Romanian, Ruthenian, Syro-Malabar and Ukrainian churches. President: Most Rev. Basil Schott, OFM, Metropolitan Archbishop of Pittsburgh of the Byzantines. Vice President: Most Rev. John Kudrick, Bishop of Parma of the Byzantines.

The association meets at the same time as the United States Conference of Catholic Bishops in the fall of each year.

BYZANTINE DIVINE LITURGY

The Divine Liturgy in all rites is based on the consecration of bread and wine by the narration-reactualization of the actions of Christ at the Last Supper, and the calling down of the Holy Spirit. Aside from this fundamental usage, there are differences between the Roman (Latin) Rite and Eastern Rites, and among the Eastern Rites themselves. Following is a general description of the Byzantine Divine Liturgy which is in widest use in the Eastern Churches.

In the Byzantine, as in all Eastern Rites, the bread and wine are prepared at the start of the Liturgy. The priest does this in a little niche or at a table in the sanctuary. Taking a round loaf of leavened bread stamped with religious symbols, he cuts out a square host and other particles while reciting verses expressing the symbolism of the action. When the bread and wine are ready, he says a prayer of offering and incenses the oblations, the altar, the icons and the people.

Liturgy of the Catechumens: At the altar a litany for all classes of people is sung by the priest. The congregation answers, "Lord, have mercy." The Little Entrance comes next. In procession, the priest leaves the sanctuary carrying the Book of the Gospels, and then returns. He sings prayers especially selected for the day and the feast. These are followed by the solemn singing of the prayer, "Holy God, Holy Mighty One, Holy Immortal One." The Epistle follows. The Gospel is sung or read by the priest facing the people at the middle door of the sanctuary.

An interruption after the Liturgy of the Catechumens, formerly an instructional period for those learning the faith, is clearly marked. Catechumens, if present, are dismissed with a prayer. Following this are a prayer and litany for the faithful.

Great Entrance: The Great Entrance or solemn Offertory Procession then takes place. The priest first says a long silent prayer for himself, in preparation for the great act to come. Again he incenses the oblations, the altar, the icons and people. He goes to the table on the Gospel side for the veil-covered paten and chalice. When he arrives back at the sanctuary door, he announces the intention of the Mass in the prayer: "May the Lord God remember all of you in his kingdom, now and forever." After another litany, the congregation recites the Nicene Creed.

Consecration: The most solemn portion of the sacrifice is introduced by the preface, which is very much like the preface of the Roman Rite. At the beginning of the last phrase, the priest raises his voice to introduce the singing of the Sanctus. During the singing he reads the introduction to the words of consecration. The words of consecration are sung aloud, and the people sing "Amen" to both consecrations. As the priest raises the Sacred Species in solemn offering, he sings: "Thine of Thine Own we offer unto Thee in behalf of all and for all." A prayer to the Holy Spirit is followed by the commemorations, in which special mention is made of the all-holy, most blessed and glorious Lady, the Mother of God and ever-Virgin Mary. The dead are remembered and then the living.

Holy Communion: A final litany for spiritual gifts precedes the Our Father. The Sacred Body and Blood are elevated with the words, "Holy Things for the Holy." The Host is then broken and commingled with the Precious Blood. The priest recites preparatory prayers for Holy Communion, con-

sumes the Sacred Species, and distributes Holy Communion to the people under the forms of both bread and wine. During this time the choir or congregation sings a communion verse.

The Liturgy closes quickly after this. The consecrated Species of bread and wine are removed to the side table to be consumed later by the priest. A prayer of thanksgiving is recited, a prayer for all the people is said in front of the icon of Christ, a blessing is invoked upon all, and the people are dismissed.

BYZANTINE CALENDAR

The Byzantine calendar has many distinctive features of its own, although it shares common elements with the Roman calendar — e.g., general purpose, commemoration of the mysteries of faith and of the saints, identical dates for some feasts. Among the distinctive things are the following. The liturgical year begins on Sept. 1, the Day of Indiction, in contrast with the Latin or Roman start on the First Sunday of Advent late in November or early in December. The Advent season begins on Dec. 10.

Cycles of the Year

As in the Roman usage, the dating of feasts follows the Gregorian Calendar. Formerly, until well into this century, the Julian Calendar was used. (The Julian Calendar, which is now about 13 days late, is still used by some Eastern Churches.) The year has several cycles, which include proper seasons, the feasts of saints, and series of New Testament readings. All of these elements of worship are contained in liturgical books of the rite. The ecclesiastical calendar, called the *Menologion*, explains the nature of feasts, other observances and matters pertaining to the liturgy for each day of the year. In some cases, its contents include the lives of saints and the history and meaning of feasts.

The Divine Liturgy (Mass) and Divine Office for the proper of the saints, fixed feasts, and the Christmas season are contained in the Menaion. The *Triodion* covers the pre-Lenten season of preparation for Easter; Lent begins two days before the Ash Wednesday observance of the Roman Rite. The *Pentecostarion* contains the liturgical services from Easter to the Sunday of All Saints, the first after Pentecost. The *Evangelion* and *Apostolos* are books in which the Gospels, and Acts of the Apostles and the Epistles, respectively, are arranged according to the order of their reading in the Divine Liturgy and Divine Office throughout the year.

The cyclic progression of liturgical music throughout the year, in successive and repetitive periods of eight weeks, is governed by the *Oktoechos*, the *Book of Eight Tones*.

Sunday Names

Many Sundays are named after the subject of the Gospel read in the Mass of the day or after the name of a feast falling on the day — e.g., Sunday of the Publican and Pharisee, of the Prodigal Son, of the Samaritan Woman, of St. Thomas the Apostle, of the Fore-Fathers (Old Testament Patriarchs).

Other Sundays are named in the same manner as in the Roman calendar, e.g., numbered Sundays of Lent and after Pentecost.

Holy Days

The calendar lists about 28 holy days. Many of the major holy days coincide with those of the Roman calendar, but the feast of the Immaculate Conception is observed on Dec. 9 instead of Dec. 8, and the feast of All Saints falls on the Sunday after Pentecost rather than on Nov. 1. Instead of a single All Souls' Day, there are five All Souls' Saturdays. According to regulations in effect in the Byzantine (Ruthenian) Archeparchy of Pittsburgh and its suffragan sees of Passaic, Parma and Van Nuys, holy days are obligatory, solemn and simple, and attendance at the Divine Liturgy is required on five obligatory days — the feasts of the Epiphany, the Ascension, Sts. Peter and Paul, the Assumption of the Blessed Virgin Mary, and Christmas. Although attendance at the liturgy is not obligatory on 15 solemn and seven simple holy days, it is recommended. In the Byzantine (Ukrainian) Archeparchy of Philadelphia and its suffragan sees of St. Josaphat in Parma, St. Nicholas (Chicago) and Stamford, the obligatory feasts are the Epiphany, Annunciation, Ascension, Sts. Peter & Paul, Dormition, and Christmas.

Lent

The first day of Lent — the Monday before Ash Wednesday of the Roman Rite — and Good Friday are days of strict abstinence for persons in the age bracket of obligation. No meat, eggs, or dairy products may be eaten on these days. All persons over the age of 14 must abstain from meat on Fridays during Lent, Holy Saturday, and the vigils of the feasts of Christmas and Epiphany; abstinence is urged, but is not obligatory, on Wednesdays of Lent. The abstinence obligation is not in force on certain "free" or "privileged" Fridays.

Synaxis

An observance without a counterpart in the Roman calendar is the synaxis. This is a commemoration, on the day following a feast, of persons involved with the occasion for the feast — e.g., Sept. 9, the day following the feast of the Nativity of the Blessed Virgin Mary, is the Synaxis of Joachim and Anna, her parents.

Holy Week

In the Byzantine Rite, Lent is liturgically concluded with the Saturday of Lazarus, the day before Palm Sunday, which commemorates the raising of Lazarus from the dead. On the following Monday, Tuesday and Wednesday, the Liturgy of the Presanctified is prescribed.

On Holy Thursday, the Liturgy of St. Basil the Great is celebrated together with Vespers.

The Divine Liturgy is not celebrated on Good Friday. On Holy Saturday, the Liturgy of St. Basil the Great is celebrated along with Vespers.

BYZANTINE FEATURES

Art: Named for the empire in which it developed, Byzantine art is a unique blend of imperial Roman and classic Hellenic culture with Christian inspiration. The art of the Greek Middle Ages, it reached a peak of development in the 10th or 11th century. Characteristic of its products, particularly in mosaic and painting, are majesty, dignity, refinement and grace. Its sacred paintings, called icons, are reverenced highly in all the Eastern Churches of the Byzantine tradition.

Church Building: The classical model of Byzantine church architecture is the Church of the Holy Wisdom (*Hagia Sophia*), built in Constantinople in the first half of the sixth century and still standing. The square structure, extended in some cases in the form of a cross, is topped by a distinctive onion-shaped dome and surmounted by a triple-bar cross. The altar is at the eastern end of building, where the wall bellies out to form an apse. The altar and sanctuary are separated from the body of the church by a fixed or movable screen, the iconostas, to which icons or sacred pictures are attached (see below).

Clergy: The Byzantine Churches have married as well as celibate priests. In places other than the U.S., where married candidates have not been accepted for ordination since about 1929, men already married can be ordained to the diaconate and priesthood and can continue in marriage after ordination. Celibate deacons and priests cannot marry after ordination; neither can a married priest remarry after the death of his wife. Bishops must be unmarried.

Iconostasis: A large screen decorated with sacred pictures or icons that separates the sanctuary from the nave of a church; its equivalent in the Roman Rite, for thus separating the sanctuary from the nave, is an altar rail. An iconostas has three doors through which the sacred ministers enter the sanctuary during the Divine Liturgy: smaller (north and south) Deacons' Doors and a large central Royal Door. The Deacons' Doors usually feature the icons of Sts. Gabriel and Michael; the Royal Door, the icons of the Evangelists — Matthew, Mark, Luke and John. To the right and left of the Royal Door are the icons of Christ the Teacher and of the Blessed Virgin Mary with the Infant Jesus. To the extreme right and left are the icons of the patron of the church and St. John the Baptist (or St. Nicholas of Myra). Immediately above the Royal Door is a picture of the Last Supper. To the right are six icons depicting the major feasts of Christ, and to the left are six icons portraying the major feasts of the Blessed Virgin Mary. Above the picture of the Last Supper is a large icon of Christ the King. Some icon screens also have pictures of the 12 Apostles and the major Old Testament prophets surmounted by a crucifixion scene.

Liturgical Language: In line with Eastern tradition, Byzantine practice has favored the use of the language of the people in the liturgy. Two great advocates of the practice were Sts. Cyril and Methodius, apostles of the Slavs, who devised the Cyrillic alphabet and pioneered the adoption of Slavonic in the liturgy.

Sacraments: Baptism is administered by immersion, and confirmation (Chrismation) is conferred at the same time. The Eucharist is administered by intinction, i.e., by giving the communicant a piece of consecrated leavened bread that has been dipped into the consecrated wine. When giving absolution in the sacrament of penance, the priest holds his stole over the head of the penitent. Distinctive marriage ceremonies include the crowning of the bride and groom. Ceremonies for anointing the sick closely resemble those of the Roman Rite. Holy orders are conferred by a bishop.

Sign of the Cross: The sign of the cross in conjunction with a deep bow expresses reverence for the presence of Christ in the Blessed Sacrament. (*See entry in* **Glossary**.)

VESTMENTS, APPURTENANCES

Antimension: A silk or linen cloth laid on the altar for the Liturgy; it may be decorated with a picture of the burial of Christ and the instruments of his passion; the relics of martyrs are sewn into the front border.

Asteriskos: Made of two curved bands of gold or silver which cross each other to form a double arch; a star depends from the junction, which forms a cross; it is placed over the diskos holding the consecrated bread and is covered with a veil.

Diskos: A shallow plate, which may be elevated on a small stand, corresponding to the Roman-Rite paten.

Eileton: A linen cloth that corresponds to the Roman-Rite corporal.

Epimanikia: Ornamental cuffs; the right cuff symbolizing strength, the left, patience and good will.

Epitrachelion: A stole with ends sewn together, having a loop through which the head is passed; its several crosses symbolize priestly duties.

Lance: A metal knife used for cutting up the bread to be consecrated during the Liturgy.

Phelonion: An ample cape, long in the back and sides and cut away in front; symbolic of the higher gifts of the Holy Spirit.

Poterion: A chalice or cup that holds the wine and Precious Blood.

Spoon: Used in administering Holy Communion by intinction; consecrated leavened bread is dipped into consecrated wine and spooned onto the tongue of the communicant.

Sticharion: A long white garment of linen or silk with wide sleeves and decorated with embroidery; formerly the vestment for clerics in minor orders, acolytes, lectors, chanters, and subdeacons; symbolic of purity.

Veils: Three are used, one to cover the poterion, the second to cover the diskos, and the third to cover both.

Zone: A narrow clasped belt made of the same material as the *epitrachelion*; symbolic of the wisdom of the priest, his strength against enemies of the Church and his willingness to perform holy duties.

CODE OF CANONS OF THE EASTERN CHURCHES

The **Code of Canons of the Eastern Churches** serves as the legal corpus for the Eastern Churches, providing the legal principles for the preservation of the rich heritage of these Churches. The overarching theological structure for the Code was enunciated by the Second Vatican Council in its declaration in *Orientalium Ecclesiarum* (3):

These individual Churches, whether of the East or the West, although they differ somewhat among themselves in rite (to use the current phrase), that is, in liturgy, ecclesiastical discipline, and spiritual heritage, are, nevertheless, each as much as the others, entrusted to the pastoral government of the Roman Pontiff, the divinely appointed successor of St. Peter in primacy over the universal Church. They are consequently of equal dignity, so that none of them is superior to the others as regards rite and they enjoy the same rights and are under the same obligations, also in respect of preaching the Gospel to the whole world (cf. Mk 16:15) under the guidance of the Roman Pontiff.

Background

The creation and promulgation of the Code for the Eastern Churches began during the pontificate of Pope Pius XI (1922-39) when he established a commission of cardinals in 1929 to examine the requirements for a code. This preparatory commission was succeeded in 1935 by a new commission with the task of undertaking the actual composition of the Code. What followed was a gradual process of promulgations. Pope Pius XII (1939-58) issued a series of apostolic letters as different elements of the Eastern Code were completed. This method of promulgation continued until 1972 when Pope Paul VI (1963-78) established the Pontifical Commission for the Revision of the Code of Eastern Canon Law.

The commission approached the initial stages of its work quite deliberately. Extensive consultation was made with canonists as well as many bishops of the Eastern Churches. These efforts culminated in November 1988 with the unanimous vote of the commission's members accepting the draft of the new Code. On Oct. 18, 1990, Pope John Paul II officially promulgated the Code of Canons of the Eastern Churches. The Code became effective on Oct. 1, 1991. As the decree makes clear, in accordance with this universal legislation, each Eastern Catholic Church is to develop its own particular law. This stands in contrast to the Code of Canon Law that applies only to the single Latin Church.

Contents and Structure

The Code of Canons of the Eastern Churches marked a significant milestone in the history of Church law. It represented the long process in the development of Canon Law for the Eastern Churches throughout the 20th century and was an eloquent means of both respecting and preserving the proper discipline of those Churches. It was noted from the start that the Code for the Eastern Catholics was organized differently in comparison with the Code of Canon Law for the Latin Rite. There are different elements to Eastern Law, and the Code presents the independence of these laws from the Latin Rite, save, of course, for those canons that give reference to the Pope. Nevertheless, while safeguarding the centuries' old traditions and heritage of the Eastern Catholic Churches, the differences are not disruptive to the unity of the Church. Rather, the Code is an instrument in moving toward appropriate unity. As the 1996 document, "Applying the Liturgical Prescriptions of the Code of Canons of the Eastern Catholic Churches" (9), by the Congregation for the Eastern Churches states:

The Code of Canons of the Eastern Churches, in can. 28 § 1 which refers to *Lumen Gentium*, no. 23, and *Orientalium Ecclesiarum*, no. 3, elucidates the important areas which articulate the heritage of each of the Churches *sui iuris*: liturgy, theology, spirituality and discipline. It is necessary to note that these particular fields penetrate and condition one another in turn inside a global vision of divine revelation which pervades all life and which culminates in the praise of the most holy Trinity.

The Catholic Church in the United States

CHRONOLOGY OF U.S. CATHOLIC HISTORY

The following are key dates in U.S. Catholic History. Reprinted from *Our Sunday Visitor's Encyclopedia of American Catholic History.*

1492 Christopher Columbus sailed to the New World and reached San Salvador (probably Watlings Island in the Bahamas). He subsequently made three voyages and established a Spanish presence on Santo Domingo (Hispaniola).

1497 John Cabot, a Genoese sailing under the English flag, reached Labrador and Newfoundland.

1499 Alonso de Ojeda and Amerigo Vespucci reached Venezuela and explored the South American coast.

1500 Pedro Cabral reached Brazil.

1511 Diocese of Puerto Rico established as suffragan of Seville, Spain. Bishop Alonso Manso, sailing from Spain in 1512, became first bishop to take up residence in New World.

1513 Juan Ponce de León reached Florida and sailed as far north as the Carolinas.

1519 Hernando Cortes began the conquest of Mexico; by the next year, the Aztec Empire had been conquered and the Spanish rule over Mexico was established.

1521 Missionaries accompanying Ponce de León and other explorers probably said first Masses within present limits of U.S.

1526 Lucas Vázquez de Ayllón attempted to establish a colony in South Carolina; it later failed.

1534-36 Jacques Cartier explored the Newfoundland area and sailed up the St. Lawrence River.

1539 Hernando de Soto journeyed through Florida and as far north as Arkansas.

1540 Francisco Coronado set out to find the Seven Cities of Gold, journeying through Texas, Kansas and New Mexico. Franciscans Juan de Padilla and Marcos de Niza accompanied Coronado expedition through the territory. They celebrated the first Mass within territory of 13 original colonies.

c. 1540 Juan de Padilla, the first martyr of the United States, was murdered on the plains of Kansas by local Indians.

1565 City of St. Augustine, oldest in U.S., founded by Pedro Menendez de Aviles, who was accompanied by four secular priests. America's oldest mission, Nombre de Dios, was established. Fr. Martin Francisco Lopez de Mendoza Grajales became the first parish priest of St. Augustine, where the first parish in the U.S. was established.

1602 Carmelite Anthony of the Ascension offered first recorded Mass in Calif. on shore of San Diego Bay.

1608 Samuel de Champlain established the first permanent French colony at Québec.

1606 Bishop Juan de las Cabeyas de Altamirano, O.P., conducted the first episcopal visitation in the U.S.

1609 Henry Hudson entered New York Bay and sailed up the Hudson River. Santa Fe established as a mission in New Mexico. It later served as a headquarters for missionary efforts in the American Southwest.

1611 Pierre Biard, S.J., and Ennémond Massé, S.J., began missionary labors among the Indians of Maine.

1612 First Franciscan province in U.S. erected under title of Santa Elena; it included Georgia, South Carolina and Florida.

1613 Four Jesuits attempted to establish permanent French settlement near mouth of Kennebec River, Maine.

1619 French Franciscans began work among settlers and Indians. They were driven out by English in 1628.

1620 The Mayflower Compact drawn up by the Pilgrims. The chapel of Nombre de Dios was dedicated to Nuestra Senora de la Leche y Buen Parto (Our Nursing Mother of the Happy Delivery) in Florida; oldest shrine to the Blessed Mother in the U.S.

1622 Pope Gregory XV established the Congregation de Propaganda Fide to oversee all mission territories. The Catholics of America remained under its jurisdiction until 1908.

1630 New England made a prefecture apostolic in charge of French Capuchins.

1634 Ark and Dove reached Maryland with the first settlers. Maryland established by Lord Calvert; two Jesuits were among first colonists. First Mass offered on Island of St. Clement in Lower Potomac by Jesuit Fr. Andrew White.

1638 Jean Nicolet discovered the water route to the Mississippi.

1642 Jesuits Isaac Jogues and René Goupil were mutilated by Mohawks; Goupil was killed shortly afterwards. Dutch Calvinists rescued Fr. Jogues. The colony of Virginia outlawed priests and disenfranchised Catholics.

1646 Jesuit Isaac Jogues and John Lalande were martyred by Iroquois at Ossernenon, now Auriesville.

1647 Massachusetts Bay Company enacted an anti-priest law.

1649 The General Assembly of Maryland passed an act of religious toleration for the colony.

1653 Jesuits opened a school at Newton Manor, the first school in the American English colonies.

1654 Following the English Civil War and the deposition of King Charles I, the installed Puritan regime in Maryland repealed the act of religious toleration in Maryland.

1656 Church of St. Mary erected on Onondaga Lake, in first French settlement within the state. Kateri Tekakwitha, "Lily of the Mohawks," was born at Ossernenon, now Auriesville (d. in Canada, 1680). She was beatified in 1980.

1660 Jesuit René Menard opened first regular mission in Lake Superior region.

1668 Fr. Marquette founded Sainte Marie Mission at Sault Sainte Marie.

1671 Sieur de Lusson and Claude Allouez, S.J., arrived at Mackinac Island and claimed possession of the western country in the name of France.

1673 Louis Joliet and Jacques Marquette, S.J., began their expedition down the Mississippi River.

1674 Fr. Marquette set up a cabin for saying Mass in what later became the city of Chicago.

1675 Fr. Marquette established Mission of the Immaculate Conception among Kaskaskia Indians, near present site of Utica; transferred to Kaskaskia, 1703.

1678 Franciscan Recollect Louis Hennepin, first white man to describe Niagara Falls, celebrated Mass there.

1680 Louis Hennepin followed the Mississippi to its source. The missions of New Mexico were destroyed by a local Indian uprising.

1682 Mission Corpus Christi de Isleta (Ysleta) founded by Franciscans near El Paso, first mission in present-day Texas.

1682 Religious toleration extended to members of all faiths in Pennsylvania.

1683 The New York colony passed the Charter of Liberties providing for religious freedom for believers in Christ.

1687 Eusebio Kino, S.J., launched the missions in Arizona at Pimería Alta.

1688 Maryland became royal colony as a result of the so-called Glorious Revolution in England; Anglican Church became the official religion (1692). Toleration Act repealed; Catholics disenfranchised and persecuted until 1776. Hanging of Ann Glover, an elderly Irish-Catholic widow, who refused to renounce her Catholic religion.

1689 Jesuit Claude Allouez died after 32 years of missionary activity among Indians of Midwest; he had evangelized Indians of 20 different tribes. Jesuit Jacques Gravier succeeded Allouez as vicar general of Illinois.

1690 Mission San Francisco de los Tejas founded in east Texas.

1692 The Church of England officially established in Maryland. New Mexico re-subjugated by the Spanish and the missions re-opened.

1697 Religious liberty granted to all except "papists" in South Carolina.

1700 Jesuit Eusebio Kino, who first visited the area in 1692, established mission at San Xavier del Bac, near Tucson. In 1783, under Franciscan administration, construction was begun of the Mission Church of San Xavier del Bac near the site of the original mission; it is still in use as a parish church. Although the New York Assembly enacted a bill calling for religious toleration for all Christians in 1683, other penal laws were now enforced against Catholics; all

priests were ordered out of the province.

1701 Tolerance granted to all except "papists" in New Jersey.

1703 Mission San Francisco de Solano founded on Rio Grande; rebuilt in 1718 as San Antonio de Valero, or the Alamo.

1704 Destruction of Florida's northern missions by English and Indian troops led by Governor James Moore of South Carolina. Franciscans Juan de Parga, Dominic Criodo, Tiburcio de Osorio, Augustine Ponze de León, Marcos Delgado and two Indians, Anthony Enixa and Amador Cuipa Feliciano, were slain by the invaders.

1709 French Jesuit missionaries obliged to give up their central New York missions.

1716 Antonio de Margil, O.F.M., began his missionary labors in Texas.

1718 The Catholics in Maryland officially disenfranchised. City of New Orleans founded by Jean Baptiste Le Moyne de Bienville.

1727 Ursuline Nuns founded convent in New Orleans, oldest convent in what is now U.S.; they conducted a school, hospital and orphan asylum.

1735 Bishop Francis Martinez de Tejadu Diaz de Velasco, auxiliary of Santiago, was the first bishop to take up residence in U.S., at St. Augustine.

1740s The First Great Awakening among Protestants.

1741 Because of an alleged popish plot to burn the city of New York, four whites were hanged and 11 blacks burned at the stake.

1744 Mission church of the Alamo built in San Antonio.

1751 First Catholic settlement founded among Huron Indians near Sandusky, Ohio, by Jesuit Fr. de la Richardie.

1754-63 The French and Indian War (The Seven Years War in Europe), the first world war; the conflict ended with the defeat of France and the loss of their American colonies.

1755 Fifty-six Catholics of Acadia expelled to the American colonies; those landing in Boston were denied the services of a Catholic priest.

1763 The Jesuits banished from the territories of Louisiana and Illinois Spain ceded Florida to England. The English also gained control of all French territories east of the Mississippi following the cessation of the French and Indian War.

1765 The Quartering Act imposed on the colonies by the British as a means of paying the cost of colonial defense. It was followed by the Stamp Act, sparking the rise of the Sons of Liberty and the convening of the Stamp Act Congress.

1767 Jesuits expelled from Spanish territory. Spanish Crown confiscated their property, including the Pious Fund for Missions. Upper California missions entrusted to Franciscans.

1769 Franciscan Junípero Serra, missionary in Mexico for 20 years, began establishment of Franciscan missions in California, in present San Diego. He was beatified in 1988.

1770 The Boston Massacre resulted in the deaths of five colonists in Boston.

1773 The Tea Act sparked the Boston Tea Party. The British responded with the Intolerable Acts in 1774. Charles Carroll of Carrollton published the "First Citizen" letter in defense of the Church and

Catholics against Daniel Dulany and the royal colonial government in Maryland.

1774 Elizabeth Bayley Seton, foundress of the American Sisters of Charity, was born in New York City on Aug. 28. She was canonized in 1975. The British Parliament passed the Quebec Act granting the French in the region the right to their own religion, language and customs. The first Continental Congress is convened.

1775-1781 The American Revolution, in which Catholics played a major role. In 1790, newly elected President George Washington wrote to American Catholics to thank them for their instrumental role in the war for American freedom.

1775 The Continental Congress denounced the rampant anti-Catholicism of the colonies to King George III. General Washington discouraged Guy Fawkes Day procession, in which pope was carried in effigy.

1776 Charles Carroll received appointment with Samuel Chase and Benjamin Franklin to a commission of the Continental Congress seeking aid from Canada; Fr. John Carroll accompanied them on their mission. Virginia became the first state to vote for full religious freedom in the new state's bill of rights. Similar provisions were passed by Maryland and Pennsylvania. The Continental Congress passed the Declaration of Independence (Charles Carroll was also the longest surviving signer). The New Jersey State Constitution tacitly excluded Catholics from office.

1777 The New York State Constitution gave religious liberty, but the naturalization law required an oath to renounce allegiance to any foreign ruler, ecclesiastical as well as civil.

1778 Fr. Gibault aided George Rogers Clark in campaign against British in conquest of Northwest Territory.

1780 The Massachusetts State Constitution granted religious liberty, but required a religious test to hold public office and provided for tax to support Protestant teachers of piety, religion and morality.

1781 Expedition from San Gabriel Mission founded present city of Los Angeles, Pueblo "de Nuestra Senora de los Angeles." British General Cornwallis surrendered at Yorktown, ending the Revolutionary War.

1783 The Treaty of Paris ended the American Revolution; Great Britain recognized the independence of the United States.

1784 The Vatican appointed Fr. John Carroll to the post of superior of the American Catholic missions. The State Constitution of New Hampshire included a religious test that barred Catholics from public office; local support was provided for public Protestant teachers of religion.

1787 Daniel Carroll of Maryland and Thomas FitzSimons of Pennsylvania signed the Constitution of the United States.

1788 First public Mass said in Boston on Nov. 2 by Abbé de la Poterie, first resident priest.

1789 Pope Pius VI erected the first United States diocese, Baltimore; John Carroll is named the first bishop.

1790 Catholics given right to vote in South Carolina.

1791 French Sulpicians opened the first seminary in the United States, St. Mary's in Baltimore. Georgetown Academy is established and begins holding classes. Bishop Carroll convoked the first synod of the clergy of the diocese. The Bill of Rights ratified by the Congress. Pierre Charles L'Enfant designed the Federal City of Washington. His plans were not fully implemented until the early 1900s.

1792 James Hoban designed the White House.

1793 Rev. Stephen T. Badin first priest ordained by Bishop Carroll; he soon began missionary work in Kentucky.

1799 Prince Demetrius Gallitzin (Fr. Augustine Smith) arrived in the Allegheny Mountains. He labored there for the next 40 years and established the Church in western Pennsylvania, at Loretto.

1800 Jesuit Leonard Neale became first bishop consecrated in present limits of U.S.

1801 Start of the Second Great Awakening among Protestants.

1802 First mayor of Washington, appointed by President Jefferson, was Catholic Judge Robert Brent.

1803 The Louisiana Purchase resulted in the acquisition by the United States of all French lands from the Mississippi River to the Rocky Mountains for $15 million.

1804-06 President Jefferson sponsored the expedition of Lewis and Clark into the Louisiana Territory.

1806 New York anti-Catholic 1777 Test Oath for naturalization repealed.

1808 Pope Pius VII declared Baltimore the first metropolitan see of the United States, erecting at the same time the new dioceses of Bardstown (KY), Boston, New York, and Philadelphia as suffragans.

1809 Mother Elizabeth Ann Seton established the first native American congregation of sisters, at Emmitsburg, Maryland.

1810 The United States annexed West Florida under the pretext that it was included in the Louisiana Purchase.

1811 Catholic Canadian trappers and traders with John J. Astor expedition founded first American settlement, Astoria. Rev. Guy I. Chabrat becomes first priest ordained west of the Allegheny Mountains.

1812 The War of 1812; it was ended by the Treaty of Ghent in 1814.

1814 St. Joseph's Orphanage, Philadelphia, opened, the first Catholic asylum for children in the United States.

1818 Religious freedom established by new constitution in Connecticut, although the Congregational Church remained, in practice, the state church. Bishop DuBourg arrived at St. Louis, with Vincentians Joseph Rosati and Felix de Andreis. Rose Philippine Duchesne arrived at St. Charles; founded first American convent of the Society of the Sacred Heart. She was beatified in 1940 and canonized in 1988.

1822 Bishop John England founded the United States Catholic Miscellany, the first Catholic newspaper in the country of a strictly religious nature. The Society for the Propagation of the Faith is founded in France; it sent missionaries throughout the world. Vicariate Apostolic of Mississippi and Alabama established.

1823 President Monroe proposed the Monroe Doctrine

of foreign policy. Fr. Gabriel Richard elected delegate to Congress from Michigan territory; he was the first priest elected to the House of Representatives.

1828 New York State Legislature enacted a law upholding sanctity of seal of confession. The first hospital opened west of the Mississippi in St. Louis, staffed by the Sisters of Charity from Emmitsburg, Maryland.

1829 The First Provincial Council of Baltimore convoked. The Oblate Sisters of Providence, the first African-American congregation of women religious in the United States was established in Baltimore.

1831 Xavier University founded.

1833 Fr. Frederic Baraga celebrated first Mass in present Grand Rapids.

1834 First native New Yorker to become a secular priest, Rev. John McCloskey, was ordained. Indian missions in Northwest entrusted to Jesuits by Holy See. A mob of Nativists attacked and burned down the Ursuline Convent at Charlestown, Massachusetts.

1835 Samuel F. B. Morse published *The Foreign Conspiracy Against the Liberties of the United States.*

1836 Texans under Stephen F. Austin declared their independence from Mexico; the Battle of the Alamo in San Antonio resulted in the deaths of 188 Texans, including the commander William B. Travis and perhaps Davy Crockett. Texas soon won its independence and was annexed in 1845. John Nepomucene Neumann arrived from Bohemia and was ordained a priest in Old St. Patrick's Cathedral, New York City. He was canonized in 1977. The infamous work of Maria Monk's Awful Disclosures of the Hotel Dieu Nunnery of Montreal, detailing supposed scandals of Catholic religious, was published. President Jackson nominated Roger Brooke Taney as chief justice of the Supreme Court.

1838 Fathers Blanchet and Demers, "Apostles of the Northwest," sent to territory by Abp. of Québec.

1839 Pope Gregory XVI condemned the slave trade in his decree In Supremo Apostolatus.

1840 Mother Theodore Guérin founded the Sisters of Providence of St.-Mary-of-the-Woods in Indiana.

1842 Fr. Augustine Ravoux began ministrations to French and Indians at Fort Pierre, Vermilion and Prairie du Chien; printed devotional book in Sioux language the following year. Henriette Delille and Juliette Gaudin began the Sisters of the Holy Family in New Orleans, the second African-American community of women religious. University of Notre Dame founded by Holy Cross Fr. Edward Sorin and Brothers of St. Joseph on land given the diocese of Vincennes by Fr. Stephen Badin.

1844 Thirteen persons killed, two churches and a school burned in Know-Nothing riots at Philadelphia. Orestes Brownson received into the Church; he subsequently founded *Brownson's Quarterly Review.*

1845 Nativists opposed to Catholics and Irish immigration, established the Native American Party. Issac Hecker received into the Church. The potato famine began in Ireland, causing in part the mass migration of Irish to the United States. The St. Vincent de Paul Society founded in the United States.

1846-48 The Mexican-American War was caused by a border dispute between the United States and Mexico. Catholic chaplains were appointed to the army, to minister to Mexican Catholics.

1846 Peter H. Burnett, who became first governor of California in 1849, received into Catholic Church. First Benedictine Abbey in New World founded near Latrobe by Fr. Boniface Wimmer.

1847 The Bishops of the United States requested Pope Pius IX to name the Immaculate Conception patron of the United States.

1848 The first permanent American Trappist foundation established, in Kentucky. Jacob L. Martin named the first American representative to the Vatican.

1852 The First Plenary Council of Baltimore held. Redemptorist John Nepomucene Neumann became fourth bishop of Philadelphia. He was beatified in 1963 and canonized in 1977.

1853 Calling for the exclusion of Catholics and foreigners from office and a 21-year residence requirement, the American Party was founded, known also as the Know-Nothing Party.

1854 Members of the Benedictine Swiss-American congregation established a community at St. Meinrad in southern Indiana.

1855 The German Catholic Central Verein founded. The "Bloody Monday" Riots in Louisville, Kentucky, leave 20 dead.

1857 The Supreme Court issued the Dred Scott Decision; Chief Justice Roger Taney stated that Congress could not exclude slavery from the territories since, according to the Constitution, slaves were property and could be transported anywhere. The American College at Louvain opened.

1858 Jesuit Fr. De Smet accompanied General Harney as chaplain on expedition sent to settle troubles between Mormons and U.S. government. The Paulists, the first native religious community for men, established. Cornerstone of second (present) St. Patrick's Cathedral, New York City, was laid; the cathedral was completed in 1879.

1859 The North American College founded in Rome as a training center for American seminarians.

1860 South Carolina seceded from the Union.

1861-65 The American Civil War. Catholics participated in large numbers on both sides. There were approximately 40 Catholic chaplains in the Union army and 28 in the Confederate army. More than 500 Catholic nuns ministered to the sick and wounded. Over 20 generals in the Union army and 11 generals in the Confederate army were Catholics.

1861 The Confederacy was formed after 11 states seceded from the Union. Jefferson Davis was elected president of the Confederacy.

1865 *Catholic World* founded. A Test Oath law passed by state legislature (called Drake Convention) to crush Catholicism in Missouri. Law declared unconstitutional by Supreme Court in 1866. Rev. H. H. Spalding, a Protestant missionary, published the Whitman Myth to hinder work of Catholic missionaries in Oregon. President Lincoln was assassinated. The murder sparked anti-Catholicism, including charges that Jesuits orchestrated his death. Congress passed the Thirteenth Amendment abolishing slavery.

1866 The Second Plenary Council of Baltimore.

1867 Reconstruction launched in the South; the presence of Federal troops did not end until 1877. The Ku Klux Klan founded to defeat Reconstruction, oppose Catholicism, and establish white supremacy in the post-war South. The U.S. purchased Alaska for $7.2 million; organized by Secretary of State William Seward, the purchase was called "Seward's Folly."

1869-70 The First Vatican Council convoked. Most of the bishops of the United States took part in the deliberations of the council.

1869 The Transcontinental Railroad completed, with the two tracks meeting at Promontory, near Ogden, Utah. The Knights of Labor founded.

1870 The Holy Name Society organized in the U.S.

1873 Blessed Fr. Damien de Veuster of the Sacred Hearts Fathers arrived in Molokai and spent the remainder of his life working among lepers. He was beatified in 1995.

1875 James A. Healy, first bishop of Negro blood consecrated in U.S., became second Bishop of Portland. Archbishop John McCloskey of New York became the first American prelate to be elevated to the College of Cardinals.

1876 George Armstrong Custer killed at the Battle of Little Bighorn (in the Second Sioux War) in Montana. *The American Catholic Quarterly Review* is established. James Gibbons publishes *Faith of Our Fathers.*

1878 Franciscan Sisters of Allegany becomes first native American community to send members to foreign missions.

1880 William R. Grace becomes the first Catholic mayor of New York City.

1882 Knights of Columbus founded by Fr. Michael J. McGivney.

1884 The Third Plenary Council of Baltimore held. John Gilmary Shea began the U.S. Catholic Historical Society.

1886 Abp. Charles J. Seghers, "Apostle of Alaska," was murdered by a guide; he had surveyed southern and northwest Alaska in 1873 and 1877. Archbishop James Gibbons of Baltimore is named the second American cardinal. Augustus Tolton is ordained the first African-American priest for the United States. The Knights of St. John was established.

1887 The American Protective Association (APA) was established to resist the growth of immigration. The Dawes Act was passed, dissolving all Indian tribes and distributing their lands among their former members, who were not permitted to dispose of their property for 25 years.

1889 The Catholic University of America opened. The first African-American Lay Congress was held in Washington, DC; subsequent congresses held in Cincinnati (1890), Philadelphia (1892), Chicago (1893), and Baltimore (1894). Mother Frances Xavier Cabrini arrived in New York City to begin work among Italian immigrants. She was canonized in 1946. *American Ecclesiastical Review* begun.

1890 Archbishop Ireland delivered an address on public and private schools at the gathering of the National Education Association in St. Paul, Minnesota.

1891 Vicariate Apostolic of Oklahoma and Indian Territory was established. Katharine Drexel founded Sisters of Blessed Sacrament for Indians and Colored Peoples. She was canonized in 2000. The Rosary Society organized.

1893 The Apostolic Delegation under Archbishop Francesco Satolli established in Washington, DC; it became an Apostolic Nunciature in 1984 with the establishment of full diplomatic relations between the U.S. and the Holy See. The first Catholic college for women in the United States, College of Notre Dame of Maryland, was established. *St. Anthony Messenger* launched.

1898 Puerto Rico ceded to U.S. (became self-governing Commonwealth in 1952); inhabitants granted U.S. citizenship in 1917. The United States annexed Hawaii; the monarchy had been overthrown in 1897.

1898 The Spanish-American War.

1899 Pope Leo XIII issued *Testem Benevolentiae.*

1901 President McKinley assassinated.

1904 The National Catholic Education Association (NCEA) founded. First publication of the *Catholic Almanac.*

1905 The Catholic Church Extension Society for home missions established.

1907 The first volume of the *Catholic Encyclopedia* was published by the Catholic University of America.

1908 Pope St. Pius X published *Pascendi Domini Gregis* against Modernism. Pope Pius issued the bull *Sapienti Consilio,* by which the Church in the U.S. was removed from mission status and the jurisdiction of the Congregation de Propaganda Fide. First American Missionary Congress held in Chicago.

1909 The Holy Name Society was established. *America Magazine* founded by the Jesuits.

1911 The Catholic Foreign Mission Society of America (Maryknoll) founded. Katharine Drexel founded the Sisters of the Blessed Sacrament.

1912 *Our Sunday Visitor* founded.

1914-18 World War I.

1917 The United States entered the First World War. The National Catholic War Council was founded. Over one million Catholics served in the Armed Forces (over 20% of the total U.S. military).

1919 The Bishops' Program of Social Reconstruction published. The National Catholic Welfare Council was founded. Peter Guilday began the American Catholic Historical Association.

1920 The National Catholic News Service (NC, now the Catholic News Service, CNS) was established.

1924 The Federated Colored Catholics of the United States was established. *Commonweal Magazine* was founded by Michael Williams.

1925 The Supreme Court declares the Oregon school law unconstitutional. The Scopes Trial, also called the Dayton Monkey Trial, took place in Dayton, Ohio.

1926 The Twenty-Eighth International Eucharistic Congress was held in Chicago.

1928 Alfred E. Smith of New York nominated for president by the Democratic Party; he was the first Catholic ever chosen to head a major-party national ticket. He was defeated by Herbert Hoover, in part because of his opposition to Prohibition and his faith.

1929 The stockmarket crash signaled the start of the

Great Depression. The Catholic Church devoted enormous resources to alleviating the suffering of those afflicted by the global Depression.

1932 Franklin Delano Roosevelt was elected president, launching the New Deal period (1933-45).

1933 The Catholic Worker Movement was established by Dorothy Day and Peter Maurin.

1934 John LaFarge, S.J., begins the first Catholic Interracial Council in New York.

1937 The Association of Catholic Trade Unionists (ACTU) established.

1939 Myron C. Taylor named personal representative of President Roosevelt to Pope Pius XII.

1939-45 World War II.

1941 Pearl Harbor was attacked by Japan; the U.S. entered World War II. Catholics comprised over 25% of the Armed Forces.

1945 End of World War II. Delegates from 50 nations established the Charter of the United Nations.

1947 The Christian Family Movement was begun by Pat and Patty Crowley. The Supreme Court issued the decision *Everson v. Board of Education* approving the use of public school buses to carry Catholic students to parochial schools.

1948 Protestants and Other Americans for Separation of Church and State (POAU) founded.

1951 President Truman nominates General Mark Clark as Ambassador to Vatican City. The nomination later withdrawn in the face of anti-Catholic protests.

1954 The Sisters Formation Conference was founded. The Supreme Court decided *Brown v. Board of Education of Topeka*; the decision declared that segregation in the public schools was unconstitutional.

1955 John Tracy Ellis published *American Catholics and the Intellectual Life*.

1956 Leadership Conference of Women Religious and Conference of Major Superiors of Men founded.

1957 The Civil Rights Act was passed, the first since 1875.

1958 Christopher Dawson was named the first holder of the Chauney Stillman Chair of Roman Catholic Studies at the Harvard Divinity School.

1959 Pope John XXIII announced his intention to convoke the Second Vatican Council.

1960 John F. Kennedy elected president of the United States; he was the first Catholic president.

1962-65 The Second Vatican Council.

1962 Gustave Weigel, S.J., appointed by the Vatican to be one of the five Catholic observers at the third general assembly of the World Council of Churches at New Delhi. Archbishop Joseph Rummel of New Orleans announced the integration of archdiocesan Catholic schools.

1963 The Catholic University of America prohibited Hans Küng, John Courtney Murray, S.J., Gustave Weigel, S.J., and Godfrey Diekmann, O.S.B., from speaking at the school. Elizabeth Ann Seton, the first American to be so honored, was beatified. President Kennedy assassinated in Dallas.

1964 The Civil Rights Act passed.

1965 Pope Paul VI visited the United Nations, the first pope to visit the U.S. Gommar A. De Pauw organizes the Catholic Traditionalist movement.

1966 The National Conference of Catholic Bishops and the United States Catholic Conference were organized. Harold Perry, S.V.D., became the second

African-American to be named a bishop.

1967 The Land O' Lakes Statement issued. The Catholic Charismatic Movement began. The Catholic Committee on Urban Ministry (CCUM) was established.

1968 Pope Paul VI issued *Humanae Vitae*. The National Black Catholic Clergy Caucus, the National Black Sisters' Conference, the National Black Catholic Seminarians Association, and the National Federation of Priests' Council were formed. Catholics United for the Faith established.

1969 The Organization of Priests Associated for Religious, Educational, and Social Rights (PADRES) established. The Campaign for Human Development established.

1970 Patricio Flores, the first modern Latino bishop, ordained.

1971 The Leadership Conference of Women Religious established.

1972 Religious Brothers Conference established.

1973 *Roe v. Wade* decision handed down by the Supreme Court, legalizing abortion.

1975 Pope Paul VI canonized the first American saint, Elizabeth Ann Seton.

1976 The U.S. celebrated the Bicentennial.

1977 Fellowship of Catholic Scholars established.

1979 Pope John Paul II visited the U.S.

1983 The NCCB issued the Challenge of Peace.

1986 The NCCB issued Economic Justice for All. The Vatican and Catholic University of America removed Fr. Charles Curran from teaching theology at the university.

1987 Pope John Paul II visited the U.S. for the second time. The National Black Catholic Congress convoked in Washington, DC.

1991 The U.S. played a major role in the Gulf War.

1992 Council of Major Superiors of Women Religious founded.

1993 World Youth Day held in Denver.

1995 Pope John Paul II visited the United Nations, Baltimore, and New York.

1997 U.S. Bishops took part in a special assembly of the Synod of Bishops on the Church in the Americas.

1999 Pope John Paul II visited St. Louis.

2001 The U.S. attacked on Sept. 11. The NCCB and USSC merged to form the United States Conference of Catholic Bishops (USCCB); Bishop Wilton Gregory of Belleville was elected its first black president of the USCCB.

2002 The pedophilia crisis erupted across the country; the USCCB passed a series of protective norms.

2003 The U.S. launched the Iraq War to topple Saddam Hussein.

2004 Pres. George W. Bush is re-elected. The Democratic nominee, Sen. John Kerry, a Catholic, is the cause of considerable controversy for his pro-abortion position. The issue sparks a national debate over the issue of Catholic politicians and abortion.

2008 Pope Benedict XVI visited Washington, D.C. and New York, his first apostolic voyage to the United States as pope. The bicentennial was also marked of the declaration of Baltimore as the first metropolitan see of the United States and the creation of the suffragan sees Bardstown (KY), Boston, New York, and Philadelphia.

U.S. CATHOLIC HISTORY

Courtesy Rev. Clyde Crews, Ph.D.

The starting point of the mainstream of Catholic history in the U.S. was in Baltimore at the end of the Revolutionary War. Long before that time, however, Catholic explorers had traversed much of the country and missionaries had done considerable work among Indians in the Southeast, Northeast and Southwest. (See **Index, Chronology of Church in U.S.**)

Spanish and French Missions

Missionaries from Spain evangelized Indians in Florida (which included a large area of the Southeast), New Mexico, Texas and California. Franciscan Juan de Padilla, killed in 1542 in what is now central Kansas, was the first of numerous martyrs among the early missionaries. The city of St. Augustine, settled by the Spanish in 1565, was the first permanent settlement in the United States and also the site of the first parish, established the same year with secular Fr. Martin Francisco Lopez de Mendoza Grajales as pastor. Italian Jesuit Eusebio Kino (1645-1711) established Spanish missions in lower California and southern Arizona, where he founded San Xavier del Bac mission in 1700. Bl. Junípero Serra (1713-84), who established nine of the famous chain of 21 Franciscan missions in California, was perhaps the most noted of the Spanish missionaries. He was beatified in 1988.

French missionary efforts originated in Canada and extended to parts of Maine, New York and areas around the Great Lakes and along the Mississippi River as far south as Louisiana. Sts. Isaac Jogues, René Goupil and John de Brébeuf, three of eight Jesuit missionaries of New France martyred between 1642 and 1649 (canonized in 1930), met their deaths near Auriesville, New York. Jesuit explorer Jacques Marquette (1637-75), who founded St. Ignace Mission at the Straits of Mackinac in 1671, left maps and a diary of his exploratory trip down the Mississippi River with Louis Joliet in 1673. Claude Allouez (1622-89), another French Jesuit, worked for 32 years among Indians in the Midwest, baptizing an estimated 10,000. French Catholics founded the colony in Louisiana in 1699. In 1727, Ursuline nuns from France founded a convent in New Orleans, the oldest in the United States.

English Settlements

Catholics were excluded by penal law from English settlements along the Atlantic coast.

The only colony established under Catholic leadership was Maryland, granted to George Calvert (Lord Baltimore) as a proprietary colony in 1632; its first settlement at St. Mary's City was established in 1634 by a contingent of Catholic and Protestant colonists who had arrived from England on the Ark and the Dove. Jesuits Andrew White and John Altham, who later evangelized Indians of the area, accompanied the settlers. The principle of religious freedom on which the colony was founded was enacted into law in 1649 as the Act of Toleration. It was the first such measure passed in the colonies and, except for a four-year period of Puritan control, remained in effect until 1688, when Maryland became a royal colony and the Anglican Church was made the official religion in 1692. Catholics were disenfranchised and persecuted until 1776.

The only other colony where Catholics were assured some degree of freedom was Pennsylvania, founded by the Quaker William Penn in 1681.

One of the earliest permanent Catholic establishments in the English colonies was St. Francis Xavier Mission, Old Bohemia, in northern Maryland, founded by the Jesuits in 1704 to serve Catholics of Delaware, Maryland and southeastern Pennsylvania. Its Bohemia Academy, established in the 1740s, was attended by sons of prominent Catholic families in the area.

Catholics and the Revolution

Despite their small number, which accounted for about one percent of the population, Catholics made significant contributions to the cause for independence from England.

Fr. John Carroll (1735-1815), who would later become the first bishop of the American hierarchy, and his cousin, Charles Carroll (1737-1832), a signer of the Declaration of Independence, were chosen by the Continental Congress to accompany Benjamin Franklin and Samuel Chase to Canada to try to secure that country's neutrality. Fr. Pierre Gibault (1737-1804) gave important aid in preserving the Northwest Territory for the revolutionaries. Thomas FitzSimons (1741-1811) of Philadelphia gave financial support to the Continental Army, served in a number of campaigns and later, with Daniel Carroll of Maryland, became one of the two Catholic signers of the Constitution. John Barry (1745-1803), commander of the *Lexington*, the first ship commissioned by Congress, served valiantly and is considered a founder of the U.S. Navy. There is no record of the number of Catholics who served in Washington's armies, although 38 to 50 percent had Irish surnames.

Casimir Pulaski (1748-79) and Thaddeus Kosciusko (1746-1817) of Poland served the cause of the Revolution. Assisting also were the Catholic nations of France, with a military and naval force, and Spain, with money and the neutrality of its colonies.

Acknowledgment of Catholic aid in the war and the founding of the Republic was made by General Washington in his reply to a letter from prominent Catholics seeking justice and equal rights: "I presume your fellow citizens of all denominations will not forget the patriotic part which you took in the accomplishment of our Revolution and the establishment of our government or the important assistance which they received from a nation [France] in which the Roman Catholic faith is professed."

In 1789, religious freedom was guaranteed under the First Amendment to the Constitution. Discriminatory laws against Catholics remained in force in many of the states, however, until well into the 19th century.

Beginning of Organization

Fr. John Carroll's appointment as superior of the American missions on June 9, 1784, was the first step toward organization of the Church in this country. According to a report he made to Rome the following year, there were 24 priests and approximately 25,000 Catholics, mostly in Maryland and Pennsylvania, in a general population of four million. Many of them had been in the Colonies for several generations. For the most part, however, they were an unknown minority laboring under legal and social handicaps.

Establishment of the Hierarchy

Fr. Carroll was named the first American bishop in 1789 and placed in charge of the Diocese of Baltimore, whose boundaries were coextensive with those of the United States. He was ordained in England on Aug. 15, 1790, and installed in his see the following Dec. 12.

Ten years later, Fr. Leonard Neale became his coadjutor and the first bishop ordained in the U.S. Bishop Carroll became an archbishop in 1808 when Baltimore was designated a metropolitan see and the new dioceses of Boston, New York, Philadelphia and Bardstown (now Louisville) were established. These jurisdictions were later subdivided, and by 1840 there were, in addition to Baltimore, 15 dioceses, 500 priests and 663,000 Catholics in the general population of 17 million.

Priests and First Seminaries

The original number of 24 priests noted in Bishop Carroll's 1785 report was gradually augmented with the arrival of others from France and other countries. Among arrivals from France after the Civil Constitution of the Clergy went into effect in 1790 were Jean Louis Lefebvre de Cheverus and Sulpicians Ambrose Maréchal, Benedict Flaget and William Dubourg, who later became bishops.

The first seminary in the country was St. Mary's, established in 1791 in Baltimore, and placed under the direction of the Sulpicians. French seminarian Stephen T. Badin (1768-1853), who fled to the U.S. in 1792 and became a pioneer missionary in Kentucky, Ohio and Michigan, was the first priest ordained (1793) in the U.S. Demetrius Gallitzin (1770-1840), a Russian prince and convert to Catholicism who did pioneer missionary work in western Pennsylvania, was ordained to the priesthood in 1795; he was the first to receive all his orders in the U.S. By 1815, St. Mary's Seminary had 30 ordained alumni.

Two additional seminaries, Mt. St. Mary's at Emmitsburg, Maryland, and St. Thomas at Bardstown, Kentucky, were established in 1809 and 1811, respectively. These and similar institutions founded later played key roles in the development and growth of the American clergy.

Early Schools

Early educational enterprises included the establishment in 1791 of a school at Georgetown that later became the first Catholic university in the U.S.; the opening of a secondary school for girls, conducted by Visitation Nuns, in 1799 at Georgetown; and the start of a similar school in the first decade of the 19th century at Emmitsburg, Maryland, by St. Elizabeth Ann Seton.

By the 1840s, which saw the beginnings of the present public school system, more than 200 Catholic elementary schools, half of them west of the Alleghenies, were in operation. From this start, the Church subsequently built the greatest private system of education in the world.

Sisterhoods

Institutes of women Religious were largely responsible for the development of educational and charitable institutions. Among them were Ursuline Nuns in Louisiana from 1727 and Visitation Nuns at Georgetown in the 1790s.

The first contemplative foundation in the country was established in 1790 at Fort Tobacco, Maryland, by three American-born Carmelites trained at an English convent in Belgium.

The first community of American origin was the Sisters of Charity of St. Joseph, founded in 1808 at Emmitsburg, Maryland, by Mother Elizabeth Ann Bayley Seton (canonized in 1975). Other early American communities were the Sisters of Loretto and the Sisters of Charity of Nazareth, both founded in 1812 in Kentucky, and the Oblate Sisters of Providence, a black community founded in 1829 in Baltimore by Mother Mary Elizabeth Lange.

Among pioneer U.S. foundresses of European communities were Mother Rose Philippine Duchesne (canonized in 1980), who established the Religious of the Sacred Heart in Missouri in 1818, and Mother Theodore Guérin, who founded the Sisters of Providence of St.-Mary-of-the-Woods in Indiana in 1840.

The number of sisters' communities, most of them branches of European institutes, increased apace with needs for their missions in education, charitable service and spiritual life.

Trusteeism

The initial lack of organization in ecclesiastical affairs, nationalistic feeling among Catholics and the independent action of some priests were factors involved in several early crises.

In Philadelphia, some German Catholics, with the reluctant consent of Bishop Carroll, founded Holy Trinity, the first national parish in the U.S. They refused to accept the pastor appointed by the bishop and elected their own. This and other abuses led to formal schism in 1796, a condition that existed until 1802, when they returned to canonical jurisdiction. Philadelphia was also the scene of the Hogan Schism, which developed in the 1820s when Fr. William Hogan, with the aid of lay trustees, seized control of St. Mary's Cathedral. His movement, for churches and parishes controlled by other than canonical procedures and run in extralegal ways, was nullified by a decision of the Pennsylvania Supreme Court in 1822.

Similar troubles seriously disturbed the peace of the Church in other places, principally New York, Baltimore, Buffalo, Charleston and New Orleans.

Dangers arising from the exploitation of lay control were gradually diminished with the extension and enforcement of canonical procedures and with changes in civil law about the middle of the century.

Anti-Catholicism

Bigotry against Catholics waxed and waned during the 19th century and into the 20th. The first major campaign of this kind, which developed in the wake of the panic of 1819 and lasted for about 25 years, was mounted in 1830 when the number of Catholic immigrants began to increase to a noticeable degree. Nativist anti-Catholicism generated a great deal of violence, represented by loss of life and property in Charlestown, Massachusetts, in 1834, and in Philadelphia 10 years later. Later bigotry was fomented by the Know-Nothings, in the 1850s; the Ku Klux

Klan, from 1866; the American Protective Association, from 1887; and the Guardians of Liberty. Perhaps the last eruption of virulently overt anti-Catholicism occurred during the campaign of Alfred E. Smith for the presidency in 1928. Observers feel the issue was muted to a considerable extent in the political area with the election of John F. Kennedy to the presidency in 1960.

The Catholic periodical press had its beginnings in response to the attacks of bigots. The *U.S. Catholic Miscellany* (1822-61), the first Catholic newspaper in the U.S., was founded by Bishop John England of Charleston to answer critics of the Church. This remained the character of most of the periodicals published in the 19th and into the 20th century.

Growth and Immigration

Between 1830 and 1900, the combined factors of natural increase, immigration and conversion raised the Catholic population to 12 million. A large percentage of the growth figure represented immigrants: some 2.7 million, largely from Ireland, Germany and France, between 1830 and 1880; and another 1.25 million during the 1880s when Eastern and Southern Europeans came in increasing numbers. By the 1860s the Catholic Church, with most of its members concentrated in urban areas, was probably the largest religious body in the country.

The efforts of progressive bishops to hasten the acculturation of Catholic immigrants occasioned a number of controversies, which generally centered around questions concerning national or foreign-language parishes. One of them, called Cahenslyism, arose from complaints that German Catholic immigrants were not being given adequate pastoral care.

Eastern Rite Catholics

The immigration of the 1890s included large numbers of Eastern Rite Catholics with their own liturgies and tradition of a married clergy, but without their own bishops. The treatment of their clergy and people by some of the U.S. (Latin Rite) hierarchy and the prejudices they encountered resulted in the defection of thousands from the Catholic Church.

In 1907, Basilian monk Stephen Ortynsky was ordained the first bishop of Byzantine Rite Catholics in the U.S. Eventually jurisdictions were established for most Byzantine and other Eastern Rite Catholics in the country.

Councils of Baltimore

The bishops of the growing U.S. dioceses met at Baltimore for seven provincial councils between 1829 and 1849.

In 1846, they proclaimed the Blessed Virgin Mary patroness of the United States under the title of the Immaculate Conception, eight years before the dogma was proclaimed in Rome.

After the establishment of the Archdiocese of Oregon City in 1846 and the elevation to metropolitan status of St. Louis, New Orleans, Cincinnati and New York, the first of the three plenary councils of Baltimore was held.

The first plenary assembly was convoked on May 9, 1852, with Abp. Francis P. Kenrick of Baltimore as papal legate. The bishops drew up regulations concerning parochial life, matters of church ritual and ceremonies, the administration of church funds and the teaching of Christian doctrine.

The second plenary council, meeting from Oct. 7 to 21, 1866, under the presidency of Abp. Martin J. Spalding, formulated a condemnation of several current doctrinal errors and established norms affecting the organization of dioceses, the education and conduct of the clergy, the management of ecclesiastical property, parochial duties and general education.

Abp. (later Cardinal) James Gibbons called into session the third plenary council which lasted from Nov. 9 to Dec. 7, 1884. Among highly significant results of actions taken by this assembly were the preparation of the line of Baltimore catechisms that became a basic means of religious instruction in this country; legislation that fixed the pattern of Catholic education by requiring the building of elementary schools in all parishes; the establishment of the Catholic University of America in Washington, DC, in 1889; and the determination of six holy days of obligation for observance in this country.

The enactments of the three plenary councils have had the force of particular law for the Church in the U.S.

The Holy See established the Apostolic Delegation in Washington, DC, on Jan. 24, 1893.

Slavery

In the Civil War period, as before, Catholics reflected attitudes of the general population with respect to the issue of slavery. Some supported it, some opposed it, but none were prominent in the Abolition Movement. Pope Gregory XVI had condemned the slave trade in 1839, but no contemporary pope or American bishop published an official document on slavery itself. The issue did not split Catholics in schism as it did Baptists, Methodists and Presbyterians.

Catholics fought on both sides in the Civil War. Five hundred members of 20 or more sisterhoods served the wounded of both sides.

One hundred thousand of the four million slaves emancipated in 1863 were Catholics; the highest concentrations were in Louisiana, about 60,000, and Maryland, 16,000. Three years later, their pastoral care was one of the subjects covered in nine decrees issued by the Second Plenary Council of Baltimore. The measures had little practical effect with respect to integration of the total Catholic community, predicated as they were on the proposition that individual bishops should handle questions regarding segregation in churches and related matters as best they could in the pattern of local customs.

Long-entrenched segregation practices continued in force through the rest of the 19th century and well into the 20th. The first effective efforts to alter them were initiated by Cardinal Joseph Ritter of St. Louis in 1947, Cardinal (then Abp.) Patrick O'Boyle of Washington in 1948, and Bishop Vincent Waters of Raleigh in 1953.

Friend of Labor

The Church became known during the 19th century as a friend and ally of labor in seeking justice for the working man. Cardinal Gibbons journeyed to Rome in 1887, for example, to defend and prevent a condemnation of the Knights of Labor by Leo XIII. The encyclical *Rerum Novarum* (1891) was hailed by many American bishops as a confirmation, if not vindication, of their own theories. Catholics have always formed a large percentage of union membership, and some have served unions in positions of leadership.

Americanism

Near the end of the century some controversy developed over what was characterized as Americanism or the phantom heresy. It was alleged that Americans were discounting the importance of contemplative virtues, exalting the practical virtues, and watering down the purity of Catholic doctrine for the sake of facilitating convert work.

The French translation of Fr. Walter Elliott's *Life of Isaac Hecker*, which fired the controversy, was one of many factors that led to the issuance of Leo XIII's *Testem Benevolentiae* in January 1899, in an attempt to end the matter. It was the first time the orthodoxy of the Church in the U.S. was called into question.

Schism

In the 1890s, serious friction developed between Poles and Irish in Scranton, Buffalo and Chicago, resulting in schism and the establishment of the Polish National Catholic Church. A central figure in the affair was Fr. Francis Hodur, who was excommunicated by Bishop William O'Hara of Scranton in 1898. Nine years later, his ordination by an Old Catholic Abp. of Utrecht gave the new church its first bishop.

Another schism of the period led to formation of the American Carpatho-Russian Orthodox Greek Catholic Church.

Coming of Age

In 1900, there were 12 million Catholics in the total U.S. population of 76 million, 82 dioceses in 14 provinces, and 12,000 priests and members of about 40 communities of men Religious. Many sisterhoods, most of them of European origin and some of American foundation, were engaged in Catholic educational and hospital work, two of their traditional apostolates.

The Church in the U.S. was removed from mission status with promulgation of the apostolic constitution *Sapienti Consilio* by Pope St. Pius X on June 29, 1908.

Before that time, and even into the early 1920s, the Church in this country received financial assistance from mission-aid societies in France, Bavaria and Austria. Already, however, it was making increasing contributions of its own. At the present time, it is one of the major national contributors to the worldwide Society for the Propagation of the Faith.

American foreign missionary personnel increased from 14 or less in 1906 to an all-time high in 1968 of 9,655 priests, brothers, sisters, seminarians, and lay persons. The first missionary seminary in the U.S. was in operation at Techny, Illinois, in 1909, under the auspices of the Society of the Divine Word. Maryknoll, the first American missionary society, was established in 1911 and sent its first priests to China in 1918. Despite these contributions, the Church in the U.S. has not matched the missionary commitment of some other nations.

Bishops' Conference

A highly important apparatus for mobilizing the Church's resources was established in 1917 under the title of the National Catholic War Council. Its name was changed to National Catholic Welfare Conference several years later, but its objectives remained the same: to serve as an advisory and coordinating agency of the American bishops for advancing works of the Church in fields of social significance and impact—education, communications, immigration, social action, legislation, youth and lay organizations.

The forward thrust of the bishops' social thinking was evidenced in a program of social reconstruction they recommended in 1919. By 1945, all but one of their 12 points had been enacted into legislation—including many later social security programs.

The NCWC was renamed the United States Catholic Conference (USCC) in November 1966, when the hierarchy also organized itself as a territorial conference with pastoral-juridical authority under the title, National Conference of Catholic Bishops. The USCC carried on the functions of the former NCWC until July 2001, when it merged with the National Conference of Catholic Bishops to create the USCCB.

Catholic Press

The establishment of the National Catholic News Service (NC)—now the Catholic News Service (CNS)—in 1920 was an important event in the development of the Catholic press, which had its beginnings about 100 years earlier. Early in the 20th century there were 63 weekly newspapers. The *2008 Catholic Press Directory*, published by the Catholic Press Association, reported a total of 599 periodicals in North America, with a circulation of 26,334,093. The figures included 206 newspapers, with a circulation of 6,586,276; 231 magazines, with a circulation of 14,451,333; 113 newsletters, with a circulation of 4,025,899; and 49 other-language periodicals (newspapers and magazines), with a circulation of 1,270,585.

Lay Organizations

A burst of lay organizational growth occurred from the 1930s onwards with the appearance of Catholic Action types of movements and other groups and associations devoted to special causes, social service and assistance for the poor and needy. Several special apostolates developed under the aegis of the National Catholic Welfare Conference (now the U.S. Catholic Conference); the outstanding one was the Confraternity of Christian Doctrine.

Nineteenth-century organizations of great influence included: The St. Vincent de Paul Society, whose first U.S. office was set up in 1845 in St. Louis; the Catholic Central Union (*Verein*), dating from 1855; the Knights of Columbus, founded in 1882; the Holy Name Society, organized in the U.S. in 1870; the Rosary Society (1891); and scores of chapters of the Sodality of the Blessed Virgin Mary.

Pastoral Concerns

The potential for growth of the Church in this country by immigration was sharply reduced but not entirely curtailed after 1921 with the passage of restrictive federal legislation. As a result, the Catholic population became more stabilized and, to a certain extent and for many reasons, began to acquire an identity of its own.

Some increase from outside has taken place in the past 50 years, however, from Canada, from Central and Eastern European countries, and from Puerto Rico and Latin American countries since World War II. This influx, while not as great as that of the 19th century and early 20th, has enriched the Church here with a sizable body of Eastern Rite Catholics for whom 12 ecclesiastical jurisdictions have been established. It has also created a challenge for pastoral care of millions of Hispanics in urban centers and in agricultural areas where migrant workers are employed.

The Church continues to grapple with serious pastoral problems in rural areas, where about 600 counties have no priests in ministry. The National Catholic Rural Life Conference was established in 1922 in an attempt to make the Catholic presence felt on the land, and the Glenmary Society since its foundation in 1939 has devoted itself to this single apostolate. Religious communities and diocesan priests are similarly engaged.

Other challenges lie in the cities and suburbs, where 75 percent of the Catholic population lives. Conditions peculiar to each segment of the metropolitan area have developed in recent years as the flight to the suburbs has not only altered some traditional aspects of parish life but has also, in combination with many other factors, left behind a complex of special problems in inner city areas.

A Post-War World

In the years after the Second World War, Catholics increasingly assumed a mainline role in American life. This was evidenced especially in the 1960 election of John F. Kennedy as the nation's first Catholic president. Catholic writers and thinkers were making a greater impact in the nation's life. One example of this was Trappist Thomas Merton's runaway best-selling book of 1948, *The Seven Storey Mountain*; another was the early television success of Bishop Fulton Sheen's "Life is Worth Living" series, begun in 1952. Meanwhile, lay leader Dorothy Day, founder of the Catholic Worker movement, continued to challenge American society with her views on pacifism and evangelical poverty.

A Post-Conciliar World

Catholic life in the United States was profoundly affected by the Second Vatican Council (1962-65). In the post-conciliar generation, American Catholicism grew both in numbers and complexity. Lay ministry and participation expanded; extensive liturgical changes (including the use of English) were implemented; and the numbers of priests, vowed religious and seminarians declined.

The Church has taken a high profile in many social issues. This has ranged from opposition to abortion, capital punishments and euthanasia to support for civil rights, economic justice and international peace and cooperation. Meanwhile Catholics have been deeply involved in inter-faith and ecumenical relationships. The bishops have issued landmark pastoral statements, including "The Challenge of Peace" (1983) and "Economic Justice for All" (1986).

In these years after the Council, the Catholics in America have known something of alienation, dissent and polarity. They also found new intensity and maturity. New U.S. saints have been declared by the universal church, such as Elizabeth Ann Seton (1975), John Nepomucene Neumann (1977), and Rose Philippine Duchesne (1988). Especially at the time of visits to America by Pope John Paul II (e.g., in 1979, 1987, 1993, 1995, and 1999), U.S. Catholics have given evidence—in their personal and corporate lives—of the ongoing power of faith, liturgy and the primal call of the Gospel in its many dimensions.

Modern U.S. Catholicism

In the decades after Vatican Council II, the American Church confronted a variety of challenges, including the increasing age of American religious, especially in the Religious Institutes of Women; the decline in vocations; the presence of nominally Catholic organizations that nevertheless work to counter or alter Catholic teaching on such issues as abortion, contraception, papal supremacy, collegiality, women's ordination, clerical celibacy, and homosexuality; the societal decay precipitated by a proliferation of an abortion culture; the weakening of the family structure and the destructive effects of unrestrained materialism and secular humanism; the spread of religious apathy and indifferentism; the needs of Catholic immigrants; and the lamentable state of American education.

The varied difficulties, however, were overshadowed from late 2001 by the sexual scandal involving child molestation by a small number of priests in the country and the resulting legal cases, lawsuits, and media frenzy. While perpetrated by only a few hundred priests over nearly 40 years, the cases of child molestation (the vast majority of cases involved teenage boys) created the most severe scandal faced by the Church in the U.S. in the previous century.

Compounding the legal and financial problems caused by the actions of the priests was the failure on the part of many bishops to recognize the severity of the scandal and the willingness of some bishops to move pedophile priests from one pastoral assignment to another.

At the summer meeting of the USCCB, the American bishops drafted a series of documents to insure the safety of children and to improve oversight of the situation. The bishops approved a Charter for the Protection of Children and Young People and Essential Norms for Diocesan/Eparchial Policies Dealing With Allegations of Sexual Abuse of Minors by Priests, Deacons, or Other Church Personnel. Officials of the Holy See rejected initially certain elements of canonical details of the norms, but the subsequent changes made by the bishops were given full Vatican approval. Nevertheless, the scandal created crushing financial difficulties for many dioceses facing a host of lawsuits, as well as a crisis of confidence among American Catholics.

Even in the face of these problems, there are a number of positive developments that give reason for guarded optimism: the progress in ecumenism; the rise of new religious congregations; the increase in conversions (over 400,000 a year); the marked sophistication of Catholic communications, centered in the USCCB; the Church's active role in social issues (human rights, poverty, health care, race relations, abortion and economic justice); and the greater involvement of the laity —especially women—in the life of the Church. Today, the membership in the U.S. is approximately 23 percent (67 million) of the U.S. population.

MISSIONARIES TO THE AMERICAS

An asterisk with a feast date indicates that the saint or blessed is listed in the General Roman Calendar or the proper calendar for U.S. dioceses.

Allouez, Claude Jean (1622-89): French Jesuit; missionary in Canada and midwestern U.S.; preached to 20 different tribes of Indians and baptized over 10,000; vicar general of Northwest.

Altham, John (1589-1640): English Jesuit; missionary among Indians in Maryland.

Amadeus of the Heart of Jesus (1846-1920): Provincial Superior of the Ursulines in the United States and missionary in Montana, Wyoming, and Alaska; founded 12 Ursuline missions for the Native Americans.

Anchieta, José de, Bl. (1534-97): Portuguese Jesuit, born Canary Islands; missionary in Brazil; writer; beatified 1980; feast, June 9.

Andreis, Felix de (1778-1820): Italian Vincentian; missionary and educator in western U.S.

Aparicio, Sebastian, Bl. (1502-1600): Franciscan brother, born Spain; settled in Mexico, c. 1533; worked as road builder and farmer before becoming Franciscan at about the age of 70; beatified 1787; feast, Feb. 25.

Badin, Stephen T. (1768-1853): French missioner; came to U.S., 1792, when Sulpician seminary in Paris was closed; ordained 1793, Baltimore, the first priest ordained in U.S.; missionary in Kentucky, Ohio and Michigan; bought land on which Notre Dame University now stands; buried on its campus.

Baraga, Frederic (1797-1868): Slovenian missionary bishop in U.S.; studied at Ljubljana and Vienna, ordained 1823; came to U.S., 1830; missionary to Indians of Upper Michigan; first bishop of Marquette, 1857-1868; wrote Chippewa grammar, dictionary, prayer book and other works.

Bauer, Benedicta (1803-65): Missionary Dominican sister who helped establish convents and schools for German-speaking immigrants in New Jersey, California, Missouri, Washington, and Kansas.

Bertran, Louis, St. (1526-81): Spanish Dominican; missionary in Colombia and Caribbean, 1562-69; canonized 1671; feast, Oct. 9.

Betancur, Pedro de San José, Bl. (1626-67): Secular Franciscan, born Canary Islands; arrived in Guatemala, 1651; established hospital, school and homes for poor; beatified 1980; feast, Apr. 25.

Bourgeoys, Marguerite, St. (1620-1700): French foundress, missionary; settled in Canada, 1653; founded Congregation of Notre Dame, 1658; beatified 1950; canonized 1982; feast, Jan. 12.

Brébeuf, Jean de, St. (1593-1649): French Jesuit; missionary among Huron Indians in Canada; martyred by Iroquois, Mar. 16, 1649; canonized 1930; one of Jesuit North American martyrs; feast, Oct. 19* (U.S.).

Cancer de Barbastro, Louis (1500-49): Spanish Dominican; began missionary work in Middle America, 1533; killed at Tampa Bay, Florida.

Castillo, John de, St. (1596-1628): Spanish Jesuit; worked in Paraguay Indian mission settlements (reductions); martyred; beatified 1934; canonized 1988;

feast, Nov. 16.

Catala, Magin (1761-1830): Spanish Franciscan; worked in California mission of Santa Clara for 36 years.

Chabanel, Noel, St. (1613-49): French Jesuit; missionary among Huron Indians in Canada; murdered by renegade Huron, Dec. 8, 1649; canonized 1930; one of Jesuit North American martyrs; feast, Oct. 19* (U.S.).

Chaumonot, Pierre Joseph (1611-93): French Jesuit; missionary among Indians in Canada.

Clarke, Mary Frances (1803-87): Founder of the Sisters of Charity of the Blessed Virgin Mary; went to Iowa to start schools for children of white farmers and Native Americans; in Iowa Women's Hall of Fame.

Claver, Peter, St. (1581-1654): Spanish Jesuit; missionary among Negroes of South America and West Indies; canonized 1888; patron of Catholic missions among black people; feast, Sept. 9*.

Cope, Marianne, Bl. (1838-1918): German-born immigrant; entered Sisters of St. Francis; led sisters to Hawaii to take over a hospital and then to Molokai to care for lepers, including Bl. Damien de Veuster; she cared for women and young girls with the disease; beatified May 2005.

Daniel, Anthony, St. (1601-48): French Jesuit; missionary among Huron Indians in Canada; martyred by Iroquois, July 4, 1648; canonized 1930; one of Jesuit North American martyrs; feast, Oct. 19* (U.S.).

De Smet, Pierre Jean (1801-73): Belgian-born Jesuit; missionary among Indians of northwestern U.S.; served as intermediary between Indians and U.S. government; wrote on Indian culture.

Duchesne, Rose Philippine, St. (1769-1852): French nun; educator and missionary in the U.S.; established first convent of the Society of the Sacred Heart in the U.S., at St. Charles, Missouri; founded schools for girls; did missionary work among Indians; beatified 1940; canonized 1988; feast, Nov. 18* (U.S.).

Farmer, Ferdinand (family name, Steinmeyer) (1720-86): German Jesuit; missionary in Philadelphia, where he died; one of the first missionaries in New Jersey.

Flaget, Benedict J. (1763-1850): French Sulpician bishop; came to U.S., 1792; missionary and educator in U.S.; first bishop of Bardstown, Kentucky (now Louisville), 1810-32; 1833-50.

Frances Xavier Cabrini: *See under* **Saints.**

Friess, Caroline (1824-92): Mother Superior of the School Sisters of Notre Dame in America from 1850-92; through her labors, the sisters opened 265 parochial schools in 29 diocese and four institutes of higher education for women.

Gallitzin, Demetrius (1770-1840): Russian prince, born The Hague; convert, 1787; ordained priest at Baltimore, 1795; frontier missionary, known as Fr. Smith; Gallitzin, PA, named for him.

Garnier, Charles, St. (c. 1606-49): French Jesuit; missionary among Hurons in Canada; martyred by Iroquois, Dec. 7, 1649; canonized 1930; one of Jesuit North American martyrs; feast, Oct. 19* (U.S.).

Gibault, Pierre (1737-1804): Canadian missionary

in Illinois and Indiana; aided in securing states of Ohio, Indiana, Illinois, Michigan and Wisconsin for the Americans during Revolution.

Gonzalez, Roch, St. (1576-1628): Paraguayan Jesuit; worked in Paraguay Indian mission settlements (reductions); martyred; beatified 1934; canonized 1988; feast, Nov. 16.

Goupil, René, St. (1607-42): French lay missionary; had studied surgery at Orleans, France; missionary companion of St. Isaac Jogues among the Hurons; martyred, Sept. 29, 1642; canonized 1930; one of Jesuit North American martyrs; feast, Oct. 19* (U.S.).

Gravier, Jacques (1651-1708): French Jesuit; missionary among Indians of Canada and midwestern U.S.

Guérin, St. Theodore (1798-1856): Pioneer educator and Sister of Providence; arrived in U.S. in 1830 and founded St. Mary-of the-Woods in Vincennes, Indiana. Canonized Oct. 15, 2006.

Hennepin, Louis (d. c. 1701): Belgian-born Franciscan missionary and explorer of Great Lakes region and Upper Mississippi, 1675-81, when he returned to Europe.

Ireland, Seraphine (1842-1930): Mother Superior of the Sisters of St. Joseph in the upper Midwest; opened 30 schools, five hospitals, and the College of St. Catherine, the second Catholic college for women in the U.S.

Jesuit North American Martyrs: Isaac Jogues, Anthony Daniel, John de Brébeuf, Gabriel Lalemant, Charles Garnier, Noel Chabanel (Jesuit priests), and René Goupil and John Lalande (lay missionaries) who were martyred between Sept. 29, 1642, and Dec. 9, 1649, in the missions of New France; canonized June 29, 1930; feast, Oct. 19* (U.S.). See separate entries.

Jogues, Isaac, St. (1607-46): French Jesuit; missionary among Indians in Canada; martyred near present site of Auriesville, NY, by Mohawks, Oct. 18, 1646; canonized 1930; one of Jesuit North American Martyrs; feast, Oct. 19* (U.S.).

Kino, Eusebio (1645-1711): Italian Jesuit; missionary and explorer in U.S.; arrived Southwest, 1681; established 25 Indian missions, took part in 14 exploring expeditions in northern Mexico, Arizona, and southern California; helped develop livestock raising and farming in the area. He was selected in 1965 to represent Arizona in Statuary Hall.

Lalande, John, St. (d. 1646): French lay missionary, companion of Isaac Jogues; martyred by Mohawks at Auriesville, NY, Oct. 19, 1646; canonized 1930; one of Jesuit North American Martyrs; feast, Oct. 19* (U.S.).

Lalemant, Gabriel, St. (1610-49): French Jesuit; missionary among the Hurons in Canada; martyred by the Iroquois, Mar. 17, 1649; canonized 1930; one of Jesuit North American Martyrs; feast, Oct. 19* (U.S.).

Lalor, Teresa (d. 1846): Co-founder, with Bp. Neale of Baltimore, of the Visitation Order in the U.S.; helped establish houses in Mobile, Kaskaskia, and Baltimore.

Lamy, Jean Baptiste (1814-88): French prelate; came to U.S. 1839; missionary in Ohio and Kentucky; bishop in Southwest from 1850; first bishop (later Abp.) of Santa Fe, 1850-85. He was nominated in 1951 to represent New Mexico in Statuary Hall.

Las Casas, Bartolome (1474-1566): Spanish Dominican; missionary in Haiti, Jamaica and Venezuela; reformer of abuses against Indians and

black people; bishop of Chalapas, Mexico, 1544-47; historian.

Laval, Françoise de Montmorency, Bl. (1623-1708): French-born missionary bishop in Canada; named vicar apostolic of Canada, 1658; first bishop of Québec, 1674; jurisdiction extended over all French-claimed territory in New World; beatified 1980; feast, May 6.

Manogue, Patrick (1831-95): Missionary bishop in U.S., born Ireland; migrated to U.S.; miner in California; studied for priesthood at St. Mary's of the Lake, Chicago, and St. Sulpice, Paris; ordained 1861; missionary among Indians of California and Nevada; coadj. bishop, 1881-84, and bishop, 1884-86, of Grass Valley; first bishop of Sacramento, 1886-95, when see was transferred there.

Margil, Antonio, Ven. (1657-1726): Spanish Franciscan; missionary in Middle America; apostle of Guatemala; established missions in Texas.

Marie of the Incarnation, St. (Marie Guyard Martin) (1599-1672): French widow; joined Ursuline Nuns; arrived in Canada, 1639; first superior of Ursulines in Québec; missionary to Indians; writer; beatified 1980; feast, Apr. 30.

Marquette, Jacques (1637-75): French Jesuit; missionary and explorer in America; sent to New France, 1666; began missionary work among Ottawa Indians on Lake Superior, 1668; accompanied Joliet down the Mississippi to mouth of the Arkansas, 1673, and returned to Lake Michigan by way of Illinois River; made a second trip over the same route; his diary and map are of historical significance. He was selected in 1895 to represent Wisconsin in Statuary Hall.

Massias (Macias), John de, St. (1585-1645): Dominican brother, a native of Spain; entered Dominican Friary at Lima, Peru, 1622; served as doorkeeper until his death; beatified 1837; canonized 1975; feast, Sept. 16.

Mazzuchelli, Samuel C. (1806-64): Italian Dominican; missionary in midwestern U.S.; called builder of the West; writer. A decree advancing his beatification cause was promulgated July 6, 1993.

Membre, Zenobius (1645-87): French Franciscan; missionary among Indians of Illinois; accompanied LaSalle expedition down the Mississippi (1681-82) and Louisiana colonizing expedition (1684) that landed in Texas; murdered by Indians.

Mozcygemba, Leopold (1824-91): Polish Franciscan priest and missionary, the patriarch of American Polonia; labored as a missionary in Texas and 11 other states for nearly 40 years; co-founded the Polish seminary of Sts. Cyril and Methodius in Detroit (1885) and served as confessor at Vatican Council I.

Nerinckx, Charles (1761-1824): Belgian priest; missionary in Kentucky; founded Sisters of Loretto at the Foot of the Cross.

Nobrega, Manoel (1517-70): Portuguese Jesuit; leader of first Jesuit missionaries to Brazil, 1549.

Padilla, Juan de (d. 1542): Spanish Franciscan; missionary among Indians of Mexico and southwestern U.S.; killed by Indians in Kansas; proto-martyr of the U.S.

Palou, Francisco (c. 1722-89): Spanish Franciscan; accompanied Junípero Serra to Mexico, 1749; founded Mission Dolores in San Francisco; wrote history of the Franciscans in California.

Pariseau, Mary Joseph (1833-1902): Canadian Sister of Charity of Providence; missionary in state of Washington from 1856; founded first hospitals in Northwest Territory; artisan and architect. Represents Washington in National Statuary Hall.

Peter of Ghent (d. 1572): Belgian Franciscan brother; missionary in Mexico for 49 years.

Porres, Martin de, St. (1579-1639): Peruvian Dominican oblate; his father was a Spanish soldier and his mother a black freedwoman from Panama; called wonder worker of Peru; beatified 1837; canonized 1962; feast, Nov. 3*.

Quiroga, Vasco de (1470-1565): Spanish missionary in Mexico; founded hospitals; bishop of Michoacan, 1537.

Ravalli, Antonio (1811-84): Italian Jesuit; missionary in far-western U.S., mostly Montana, for 40 years.

Raymbaut, Charles (1602-43): French Jesuit; missionary among Indians of Canada and northern U.S.

Richard, Gabriel (1767-1832): French Sulpician; missionary in Illinois and Michigan; a founder of University of Michigan; elected delegate to Congress from Michigan, 1823; first priest to hold seat in the House of Representatives.

Riepp, Benedicta (1825-62): Founder of the first Benedictine community of nuns in the U.S.; by the time of her death, the order had founded convents in Illinois, Kentucky, Minnesota, and New Jersey.

Rodriguez, Alfonso, St. (1598-1628): Spanish Jesuit; missionary in Paraguay; martyred; beatified 1934; canonized 1988; feast, Nov. 16.

Rosati, Joseph (1789-1843): Italian Vincentian; missionary bishop in U.S. (vicar apostolic of Mississippi and Alabama, 1822; coadj. of Louisiana and the Two Floridas, 1823-26; administrator of New Orleans, 1826-29; first bishop of St. Louis, 1826-1843).

Russell, Mary Baptist (1829-98): Mother Superior of the Sisters of Mercy in San Francisco from 1854-98; founded St. Mary's Hospital in 1857, schools, and homes the aged and former prostitutes.

Sahagun, Bernardino de (c. 1500-90): Spanish Franciscan; missionary in Mexico for over 60 years; expert on Aztec archaeology.

Seelos, Francis X. (1819-67): Redemptorist missionary, born Bavaria; ordained 1844, at Baltimore; missionary in Pittsburgh and New Orleans.

Seghers, Charles J. (1839-86): Belgian missionary bishop in North America; Apostle of Alaska; Abp. of Oregon City (now Portland), 1880-84; murdered by berserk companion while on missionary journey.

Serra, Junípero, Bl. (1713-84): Spanish Franciscan, born Majorca; missionary in America; arrived Mexico, 1749, where he did missionary work for 20 years; began work in Upper California in 1769 and established nine of the 21 Franciscan missions along the Pacific coast; baptized some 6,000 Indians and con-

firmed almost 5,000; a cultural pioneer of California Represents California in Statuary Hall. He was declared venerable May 9, 1985, and beatified Sept. 25, 1988; feast, July l* (U.S.).

Solanus, Francis, St. (1549-1610): Spanish Franciscan; missionary in Paraguay, Argentina and Peru; wonder worker of the New World; canonized 1726; feast, July 14.

Sorin, Edward F. (1814-93): French priest; member of Congregation of Holy Cross; sent to U.S. in 1841; founder and first president of the University of Notre Dame; missionary in Indiana and Michigan.

Todadilla, Anthony de (1704-46): Spanish Capuchin; missionary to Indians of Venezuela; killed by Motilones.

Turibius de Mogrovejo, St. (1538-1606): Spanish Abp. of Lima, Peru, c. 1580-1606; canonized 1726; feast, Mar. 23*.

Twelve Apostles of Mexico (early 16th century): Franciscan priests who arrived in Mexico, 1524: Fathers Martin de Valencia (leader), Francisco de Soto, Martin de la Coruna, Juan Suares, Antonio de Ciudad Rodrigo, Toribio de Benevente, Garcia de Cisneros, Luis de Fuensalida, Juan de Ribas, Francisco Ximenes; Brothers Andres de Coroboda, and Juan de Palos.

Valdivia, Luis de (1561-1641): Spanish Jesuit; defender of Indians in Peru and Chile.

Vasques de Espiñosa, Antonio (early 17th century): Spanish Carmelite; missionary and explorer in Mexico, Panama and western coast of South America.

Vieira, Antonio (1608-87): Portuguese Jesuit; preacher; missionary in Peru and Chile; protector of Indians against exploitation by slave owners and traders; considered foremost prose writer of 17th-century Portugal.

Ward, Mary Francis Xavier (1810-84): Established the Sisters of Mercy in U.S.; arrived in Pittsburgh in 1843; founded convents in 10 states to care for the sick and poor and provide education.

White, Andrew (1579-1656): English Jesuit; missionary among Indians in Maryland.

Wimmer, Boniface (1809-87): German Benedictine; missionary among German immigrants in the U.S.

Youville, Marie Marguerite d', St. (1701-71): Canadian widow; foundress of Sisters of Charity (Grey Nuns), 1737, at Montréal: beatified 1959; canonized 1990, first native Canadian saint; feast, Dec. 23.

Zumarraga, Juan de (1468-1548): Spanish Franciscan; missionary; first bishop of Mexico; introduced first printing press in New World; published first book in America, a catechism for Aztec Indians; extended missions in Mexico and Central America; vigorous opponent of exploitation of Indians; approved of devotions at Guadalupe; leading figure in early church history in Mexico.

FRANCISCAN MISSIONS

The 21 Franciscan missions of Upper California were established during the 54-year period from 1769 to 1822. Located along the old El Camino Real, or King's Highway, they extended from San Diego to San Francisco and were the centers of Indian civilization, Christianity and industry in the early history of the state.

Junípero Serra (beatified 1988) was the great pioneer of the missions of Upper California He and his successor as superior of the work, Fermin Lasuen, each directed the establishment of nine missions. One hundred and 46 priests of the Order of Friars Minor, most of them Spaniards, labored in the region from 1769 to 1845; 67 of them died at their posts, two as martyrs.

The regular time of mission service was 10 years.

The missions were secularized by the Mexican government in the 1830s but were subsequently restored to the Church by the U.S. government. They are now variously used as the sites of parish churches, a university, houses of study and museums.

The names of the missions and the order of their establishment were as follows:

San Diego de Alcala, San Carlos Borromeo (El Carmelo), San Antonio de Padua, San Gabriel Arcangel, San Luis Obispo de Tolosa, San Francisco de Asis (Dolores), San Juan Capistrano; Santa Clara de Asis, San Buenaventura, Santa Barbara, La Purisima Concepcion de Maria Santisima, Santa Cruz, Nuestra Señora de la Soledad, San José de Guadalupe, San Juan Bautista, San Miguel Arcangel, San Fernando Rey de España, San Luis Rey de Francia, Santa Înes, San Rafael Arcangel, San Francisco Solano de Sonoma (Sonoma).

Find more material at: www.CatholicAlmanac.com.

CHURCH-STATE RELATIONS IN THE UNITED STATES

CHURCH-STATE DECISIONS OF THE SUPREME COURT

Among sources of this selected listing of U.S. Supreme Court decisions was *The Supreme Court on Church and State*, Joseph Tussman, editor; Oxford University Press, New York, 1962.

Watson v. Jones, 13 Wallace 679 (1872): The Court declared that a member of a religious organization may not appeal to secular courts against a decision made by a church tribunal within the area of its competence.

Reynolds v. United States, 98 US 145 (1879): Davis v. Beason, 133 US 333 (1890); Church of Latter-Day Saints v. United States, 136 US 1 (1890). The Mormon practice of polygamy was at issue in three decisions and was declared unconstitutional.

Bradfield v. Roberts, 175 US 291 (1899): The Court denied that an appropriation of government funds for an institution (Providence Hospital, Washington, DC) run by Roman Catholic sisters violated the No Establishment Clause of the First Amendment.

Pierce v. Society of Sisters, 268 US 510 (1925): The Court denied that a state can require children to attend public schools only. The Court held that the liberty of the Constitution forbids standardization by such compulsion, and that the parochial schools involved had claims to protection under the Fourteenth Amendment.

Cochran v. Board of Education, 281 US 370 (1930): The Court upheld a Louisiana statute providing textbooks at public expense for children attending public or parochial schools. The Court held that the children and state were beneficiaries of the appropriations, with incidental secondary benefit going to the schools.

United States v. MacIntosh, 283 US 605 (1931): The Court denied that anyone can place allegiance to the will of God above his allegiance to the government since such a person could make his own interpretation of God's will the decisive test as to whether he would or would not obey the nation's law. The Court stated that the nation, which has a duty to survive, can require citizens to bear arms in its defense.

Everson v. Board of Education, 330 US 1 (1947): The Court upheld the constitutionality of a New Jersey statute authorizing free school bus transportation for parochial as well as public school students. The Court expressed the opinion that the benefits of public welfare legislation, included under such bus transportation, do not run contrary to the concept of separation of Church and State.

McCollum v. Board of Education, 333 US 203 (1948): The Court declared unconstitutional a program for releasing children, with parental consent, from public school classes so they could receive religious instruction on public school premises from representatives of their own faiths.

Zorach v. Clauson, 343 US 306 (1952): The Court upheld the constitutionality of a New York statute permitting, on a voluntary basis, the release during school time of students from public school classes for religious instruction given off public school premises.

Torcaso v. Watkins, 367 US 488 (1961): The Court declared unconstitutional a Maryland requirement that one must make a declarati on of belief in the existence of God as part of the oath of office for notaries public.

McGowan v. Maryland, 81 Sp Ct 1101; Two Guys from Harrison v. McGinley, 81 Sp Ct 1135; Gallagher v. Crown Kosher Super Market, 81 Sp Ct 1128; Braunfield v. Brown, 81 Sp Ct 1144 (1961): The Court ruled that Sunday closing laws do not violate the No Establishment of Religion Clause of the First Amendment, even though the laws were religious in their inception and still have some religious overtones. The Court held that, "as presently written and administered, most of them, at least, are of a secular rather than a religious character, and that presently they bear no relationship to establishment of religion as those words are used in the Constitution of the United States."

Engel v. Vitale, 370 US 42 (1962): The Court declared that the voluntary recitation in public schools of a prayer composed by the New York State Board of Regents is unconstitutional on the ground that it violates the No Establishment of Religion Clause of the First Amendment.

Abington Township School District v. Schempp and Murray v. Curlett, 83 Sp Ct 1560 (1963): The Court ruled that Bible reading and recitation of the Lord's Prayer in public schools, with voluntary participation by students, are unconstitutional on the ground that they violate the No Establishment of Religion Clause of the First Amendment.

Chamberlin v. Dade County, 83 Sp Ct 1864 (1964): The Court reversed a decision of the Florida Supreme Court concerning the constitutionality of prayer and devotional Bible reading in public schools during the school day, as sanctioned by a state statute which specifically related the practices to a sound public purpose.

Board of Education v. Allen, No. 660 (1968): The Court declared constitutional the New York school-book-loan law that requires local school boards to purchase books with state funds and lend them to parochial and private school students.

Walz v. Tax Commission of New York (1970): The Court upheld the constitutionality of a New York statute exempting church-owned property from taxation.

Earle v. DiCenso, Robinson v. DiCenso, Lemon v. Kurtzman, Tilton v. Richardson (1971): In Earle v. DiCenso and Robinson v. DiCenso, the Court ruled unconstitutional a 1969 Rhode Island statute that provided salary supplements to teachers of secular subjects in parochial schools; in Lemon v. Kurtzman, the Court ruled unconstitutional a 1968 Pennsylvania statute that authorized the state to purchase services for the teaching of secular subjects in nonpublic schools. The principal argument against constitutionality in these cases was that the statutes and programs at issue entailed excessive entanglement of government with religion. In Tilton v. Richardson, the Court held that this argument did not apply to a prohibitive degree with respect to federal grants, under the Higher Education Facilities Act of 1963, for the construction of facilities for nonreligious purposes by four church-related institutions of higher learning, three of which were Catholic, in Connecticut.

Yoder, Miller and Yutzy (1972): In a case appealed on behalf of Yoder, Miller and Yutzy, the Court ruled that Amish parents were exempt from a Wisconsin statute requiring them to send their children to school until the age of 16. The Court said in its decision that secondary schooling exposed Amish children to attitudes, goals and values contrary to their beliefs, and substantially hindered "the religious development of the Amish child and his integration into the way of life of the Amish faith-community at the crucial adolescent state of development."

Committee for Public Education and Religious Liberty, et al., v. Nyquist, et al., No. 72-694 (1973): The Court ruled that provisions of a 1972 New York statute were unconstitutional on the grounds that they were violative of the No Establishment Clause of the First Amendment and had the "impermissible effect" of advancing the sectarian activities of church-affiliated schools. The programs ruled unconstitutional concerned: (1) maintenance and repair grants, for facilities and equipment, to ensure the health, welfare and safety of students in nonpublic, nonprofit elementary and secondary schools serving a high concentration of students from low income families; (2) tuition reimbursement ($50 per grade school child, $100 per high school student) for parents (with income less than $5,000) of children attending nonpublic elementary or secondary schools; tax deduction from adjusted gross income for parents failing to qualify under the above reimbursement plan, for each child attending a nonpublic school.

Sloan, Treasurer of Pennsylvania, et al., v. Lemon, et al., No. 72-459 (1973): The Court ruled unconstitutional a Pennsylvania Parent Reimbursement Act for Nonpublic Education which provided funds to reimburse parents (to a maximum of $150) for a portion of tuition expenses incurred in sending their children to nonpublic schools. The Court held that there was no significant difference between this and the New York tuition reimbursement program (above), and declared that the Equal Protection Clause of the Fourteenth Amendment cannot be relied upon to sustain a program held to be violative of the No Establishment Clause.

Levitt, et al., v. Committee for Public Education and Religious Liberty, et al., No. 72-269 (1973): The Court ruled unconstitutional the Mandated Services Act of 1970 under which New York provided $28 million ($27 per pupil from first to seventh grade, $45 per pupil from seventh to 12th grade) to reimburse nonpublic schools for testing, recording and reporting services required by the state. The Court declared that the act provided "impermissible aid" to religion in contravention of the No Establishment Clause.

In related decisions handed down June 25, 1973, the Court: (1) affirmed a lower-court decision the constitutionality of an Ohio tax credit law benefiting parents with children in nonpublic schools; (2) reinstated an injunction against a parent reimbursement program in New Jersey; (3) affirmed South Carolina's right to grant construction loans to church-affiliated colleges, and (4) dismissed an appeal contesting its right to provide loans to students attending church-affiliated colleges (Hunt v. McNair, Durham v. McLeod).

Wheeler v. Barrera (1974): The Court ruled that nonpublic school students in Missouri must share in federal funds for educationally deprived students on a comparable basis with public school students under Title I of the Elementary and Secondary Education Act of 1965.

Norwood v. Harrison 93 S. Ct. 2804 (1974): The Court ruled that public assistance that avoids the prohibitions of the "effect" and "entanglement" tests (and which therefore does not substantially promote the religious mission of sectarian schools) may be confined to the secular functions of such schools.

Wiest v. Mt. Lebanon School District (1974): The Court upheld a lower court ruling that invocation and benediction prayers at public high school commencement ceremonies do not violate the principle of separation of Church and State.

Meek v. Pittenger (1975): The Court ruled unconstitutional portions of a Pennsylvania law providing auxiliary services for students of nonpublic schools; at the same time, it ruled in favor of provisions of the law permitting textbook loans to students of such schools. In denying the constitutionality of auxiliary services, the Court held that they had the "primary effect of establishing religion" and involved "excessive entanglement" of Church and state officials with respect to supervision; objection was also made against providing such services only on the premises of nonpublic schools and only at the request of such schools.

TWA, Inc., v. Hardison, 75-1126; International Association of Machinists and Aero Space Workers v. Hardison, 75-1385 (1977): The Court ruled that federal civil-rights legislation does not require employers to make more than minimal efforts to accommodate employees who want a particular working day off as their religion's Sabbath Day, and that an employer cannot accommodate such an employee by violating seniority systems determined by a union collective bargaining agreement. The Court noted that its ruling was not a constitutional judgment but an interpretation of existing law.

Wolman v. Walter (1977): The Court ruled constitutional portions of an Ohio statute providing tax-paid textbook loans and some auxiliary services (standardized and diagnostic testing, therapeutic and remedial services, off school premises) for nonpublic school students. It decided that other portions of the law, providing state funds for nonpublic school field trips and instructional materials (audio-visual equipment, maps, tape recorders), were unconstitutional.

Byrne v. Public Funds for Public Schools (1979): The Court decided against the constitutionality of a 1976 New Jersey law providing state income tax deductions for tuition paid by parents of students attending parochial and other private schools.

Student Bus Transportation (1979): The Court upheld a Pennsylvania law providing bus transportation at public expense for students to nonpublic schools up to 10 miles away from the boundaries of the public school districts in which they lived.

Reimbursement (1980): The Court upheld the constitutionality of a 1974 New York law providing direct cash payment to nonpublic schools for the costs of state-mandated testing and record-keeping.

Ten Commandments (1980): The Court struck down a 1978 Kentucky law requiring the posting of the Ten Commandments in public school classrooms in the state.

Widmar v. Vincent (1981): The Court ruled that the University of Missouri at Kansas City could not deny student religious groups the use of campus facilities for worship services. The Court also, in Brandon v. Board of Education of Guilderland Schools, declined without comment to hear an appeal for reversal of lower court decisions denying a group of New York high school students the right to meet for prayer on public school property before the beginning of the school day.

Lubbock v. Lubbock Civil Liberties Union (1983): By refusing to hear an appeal in this case, the Court upheld a lower court ruling against a public policy of permitting student religious groups to meet on public school property before and after school hours.

Mueller v. Allen (1983): The Court upheld a Minnesota law allowing parents of students in public and nonpublic (including parochial) schools to take a tax deduction for the expenses of tuition, textbooks and transportation. Maximum allowable deductions were $500 per child in elementary school and $700 per child in grades seven through 12.

Lynch v. Donnelly (1984): The Court ruled 5-to-4 that the First Amendment does not mandate "complete separation of church and state," and that, therefore, the sponsorship of a Christmas nativity scene by the City of Pawtucket, RI, was not unconstitutional. The case involved a scene included in a display of Christmas symbols sponsored by the city in a park owned by a non-profit group. The majority opinion said "the Constitution (does not) require complete separation of church and state; it affirmatively mandates accommodation, not merely tolerance, of all religions and forbids hostility toward any. Anything less" would entail callous indifference not intended by the Constitution. Moreover, "such hostility would bring us into 'war with our national tradition as embodied in the First Amendment's guaranty of the free exercise of religion.' " (The additional quotation was from the 1948 decision in McCollum v. Board of Education.)

Christmas Nativity Scene (1985): The Court upheld a lower court ruling that the Village of Scarsdale, NY, must make public space available for the display of privately sponsored nativity scenes.

Wallace v. Jaffree, No. 83-812 (1985): The Court ruled against the constitutionality of a 1981 Alabama law calling for a public-school moment of silence that specifically included optional prayer.

Grand Rapids v. Ball, No. 83-990, and **Aguilar v. Felton, No. 84-237** (1985): The Court ruled against the constitutionality of programs in Grand Rapids and New York City allowing public school teachers to teach remedial entitlement subjects (under the Elementary and Secondary Education Act of 1965) in private schools, many of which were Catholic.

Bender v. Williamsport Area School District (1986): The Court let stand a lower federal-court decision allowing a public high school Bible study group the same "equal access" to school facilities as that enjoyed by other extracurricular clubs. A similar decision was handed down in 1990 in Board of Education v. Mergens, involving Westside High School in Omaha.

County of Allegheny v. American Civil Liberties Union (1989): The Court ruled (1) that the display of a Christmas nativity scene in the Allegheny County Courthouse in Pittsburgh, PA, violated the principle of separation of church and state because it appeared to be a government-sponsored endorsement of Christian belief; (2) and that the display of a Hanukkah menorah outside the Pittsburgh-Allegheny city-county building was constitutional because of its "particular physical setting" with secular symbols.

Unemployment Division v. Smith (1990): The Court ruled that religious use of the hallucinogenic cactus peyote is not covered by the First Amendment protection of religious freedom.

Lee v. Weisman (1992): The Court banned officially organized prayer at public school graduation ceremonies.

Lamb's Chapel v. Center Moriches Union School District (1993): The Court reversed a ruling by the 3rd U.S. Circuit Court of Appeals, declaring that the school district was wrong in prohibiting the congregation of Lamb's Chapel from using public school meeting space after hours to show a film series addressing family problems from a religious perspective. In view of the variety of organizations permitted to use school property after school hours, said the Court's opinion: "There would have been no realistic danger that the community would think that the district was endorsing religion or any particular creed, and any benefit to religion or to the church would have been no more than incidental."

5th U.S. Circuit Court of Appeals (1993): The Court let stand a ruling by the 5th U.S. Circuit Court of Appeals, permitting students in Texas, Mississippi and Louisiana to include student-organized and student-led prayers in graduation exercises.

Church of Lukumi Babalu Aye v. City of Hialeah (1993): The Court ruled that municipal laws that effectively prohibit a single church from performing its religious rituals are unconstitutional. The ordinances at issue singled out one religion, Santeria, for the purpose of restricting its members from the practice of ritual animal sacrifices.

Zobrest v. Catalina Foothills School District (1993): The Court ruled that a public school district may provide a sign-language interpreter for a deaf student attending a Catholic school without violating constitutional separation of church and state. The majority opinion said: "Handicapped children, not sectarian schools are the primary beneficiaries of the Disabilities Education Act; to the extent sectarian schools benefit at all from (the act), they are only incidental beneficiaries."

Fairfax County, Va., school district (1994): The Court upheld lower court rulings against a Fairfax County, VA, school district's practice of charging churches more rent than other entities for the use of school buildings.

Board of Education of Kiryas Joel Village School District v. Grumet (1994): The Court ruled in 1994 that a school district created to meet the special education needs of an Hasidic Jewish community violated the Establishment Clause of the Constitution. The Court said the New York Legislature effectively endorsed a particular religion when it established a public school district for the Satmar Hasidic Village of Kiryas Joel.

Agostino v. Felton (1997): The court reversed, 5 to 4, its 1985 Aguilar v. Felton ruling, which had declared it unconstitutional for teachers employed by public school districts to hold Title I remedial programs for low-income students on the property of church-related schools.

Boerne v. Flores (1997): The court ruled, 6 to 3, that the Religious Freedom Restoration Act (1993) was unconstitutional because Congress overstepped its constitutional authority in enacting the law. Congress "has been given the power to 'enforce,' not the power to determine what constitutes a constitutional violation," said the majority opinion.

Mitchell v. Helms (2000): The court ruled, 6 to 3, that a Louisiana parish can distribute money for instructional equipment—including computers, books, maps, and film strip projectors—to private schools as long as it is done in a "secular, neutral and non-ideological" way. The court's decision overturns two previous Supreme Court bans on giving public materials to parochial schools.

Santa Fe Independent School District v. Doe (2000): The court affirmed a lower court ruling that said prayer in public schools must be private and that such prayers at high school football games violate the constitutionally required separation of church and state. At issue in the Santa Fe case was a Texas school policy which permitted students selected by their peers to deliver an inspirational message of their own design at football games and the graduation ceremony. In 1999, the Santa Fe policy was struck down by the U.S. Court of Appeals for the Fifth Circuit. The Court of Appeals held that the policy violated the Establishment Clause of the First Amendment, even though the government played no role in creating the message or selecting the messenger.

Chandler v. Siegelman (2001): The court let stand a lower court ruling that students may participate in group prayers at school functions such as football games or graduations.

The Good News Club v. Milford Central Schools (2001): The court ruled that if the Boy Scouts and 4-H can use a public school as a meeting hall, a children's Bible study class can also.

Brown v. Gilmore (2001): The court declined to hear a challenge to Virginia's mandatory minute of silence in schools.

Children's Health Care is a Legal Duty Inc. v.

McMullan (2001): The court turned down an appeal that claimed Medicare and Medicaid payments to church-run health centers violate the constitutional separation of church and state.

Gentala v. Tucson (2001): The court ordered a federal appeals court to take another look at a case that asked whether taxpayers must cover $340 in expenses from a prayer rally in a city park, saying it should be reconsidered in light of the high court's earlier ruling that a Bible club cannot be excluded from meeting at a public school so long as other groups with a moral viewpoint are allowed to gather there.

Cleveland Voucher Program (2002): By a 5-4 ruling, the court upheld the Cleveland voucher program that had been implemented in 1995 to assist the improvement of one of the worst public school systems in the country.

Ten Commandments (2005): By a 5-4 vote, the court prohibited the posting of the Ten Commandments in court houses; at the same time, the court permitted their posting in state houses.

Gonzales v. Carhart and Gonzales v. Planned Parenthood (2007): By a 5-4 vote, the court upheld the Partial Birth Abortion Ban Act that Congress passed and President George W. Bush signed into law in 2003, saying that the prohibition does not violate the constitutional right to an abortion.

RELIGION IN PUBLIC SCHOOLS

Based on a Catholic News Service article by Carol Zimmermann.

A diverse group of religious and civil rights organizations issued a joint statement Apr. 13, 1995, in an effort to clarify the confusing issue of prayer and religious observances or discussions in public schools. Their six-page statement outlines what is and what is not currently permissible in expressing religious beliefs in public schools.

The statement says, for example: "Students have the right to pray individually or in groups, or to discuss their religious views with their peers so long as they are not disruptive." But, the statement specifies that such prayers or discussions do not include "the right to have a captive audience listen or to compel other students to participate."

Prayer at Graduations

Regarding prayer at graduation ceremonies, the document says school officials may not mandate or organize prayer, but fails to set the record straight about student-led prayer at these services.

"The courts have reached conflicting conclusions under the federal Constitution" in this area, says the statement, recommending that schools consult their lawyers for the rules that apply to them, "until the issue is authoritatively resolved."

Since the Supreme Court's 1992 Lee v. Weisman opinion prohibited school authorities from even arranging for a speaker to present a prayer, lower courts in different states have made various rulings about student-led prayer at commencement exercises.

In Virginia, the state's Attorney General and the Board of Education proposed guidelines in mid-April to allow student-led prayer at graduations, despite a 1994 ruling by a U.S. district judge banning all prayer at graduations.

Religion in the Classroom

"It is both permissible and desirable to teach objectively about the role of religion in the history of the United States and other countries," but public school teachers may not specifically teach religion.

The same rules apply to the recurring controversy surrounding theories of evolution. Teachers may discuss explanations of the beginnings of life, but only within the confines of classes on religion or social studies. Public school teachers are required, according to the statement, to teach only scientific explanations of life's beginnings in science classes. And, just as teachers may not advance a religious view, they should not ridicule a student's religious belief.

Constitutional Protection

The statement says that students' expressions of religious beliefs in reports, homework or artwork are constitutionally protected. Likewise, students have the right to speak to and attempt to persuade their peers on religious topics. "But school officials should intercede to stop student religious speech if it turns into religious harassment aimed at a student or a small group of students."

The statement also says:

• Students have the right to distribute religious literature to their schoolmates, subject to reasonable restrictions for any non-school literature.

• Student religious clubs in secondary schools "must be permitted to meet and to have equal access" to school media for announcing their events.

• Religious messages on T-shirts and the like cannot be singled out for suppression.

• Schools can use discretion about dismissing students for off-site religious instruction.

The 35 organizations that endorsed the statement included the National Association of Evangelicals, the American Jewish Congress, the Christian Legal Society, the National Council of Churches, the Baptist Joint Committee on Public Affairs, the American Muslim Council, the Presbyterian Church (USA) and the American Civil Liberties Union.

Purpose of the Statement

"By making this document available," said Phil Baum, executive director of the American Jewish Congress, "the organizations are attempting to clarify what has become one of the most divisive issues of our time: religion in the public schools."

He said the document attempts to "ensure that the rights of all students are respected in the public schools."

Baum noted that the American Jewish Congress, which initiated the effort to draft the statement, had a long-standing commitment to ensuring that public schools are themselves religiously neutral.

"We believe, however, that it is inconsistent with that historic commitment to ask the public schools to root out private expressions of religious faith."

CHURCH TAX EXEMPTION

The exemption of church-owned property was ruled constitutional by the U.S. Supreme Court May 4, 1970, in the case of Walz v. The Tax Commission of New York.

Suit in the case was brought by Frederick Walz, who

purchased in June 1967, a 22-by-29-foot plot of ground in Staten Island valued at $100 and taxable at $5.24 a year. Shortly after making the purchase, Walz instituted a suit in New York State, contending that the exemption of church property from taxation authorized by state law increased his own tax rate and forced him indirectly to support churches in violation of his constitutional right to freedom of religion under the First Amendment. Three New York courts dismissed the suit, which had been instituted by mail. The Supreme Court, judging that it had probable jurisdiction, then took the case.

In a 7-1 decision affecting Church-state relations in every state in the nation, the Court upheld the New York law under challenge.

For and Against

Chief Justice Warren E. Burger, who wrote the majority opinion, said that Congress from its earliest days had viewed the religion clauses of the Constitution as authorizing statutory real estate tax exemption to religious bodies. He declared: "Nothing in this national attitude toward religious tolerance and two centuries of uninterrupted freedom from taxation has given the remotest sign of leading to an established church or religion, and on the contrary it has operated affirmatively to help guarantee the free exercise of all forms of religious beliefs."

Justice William O. Douglas wrote in dissent that the involvement of government in religion as typified in tax exemption may seem inconsequential but: "It is, I fear, a long step down the establishment path. Perhaps I have been misinformed. But, as I read the Constitution and the philosophy, I gathered that independence was the price of liberty."

Burger rejected Douglas' "establishment" fears. If tax exemption is the first step toward establishment, he said, "the second step has been long in coming."

The basic issue centered on the following question: Is there a contradiction between federal constitutional provisions against the establishment of religion, or the use of public funds for religious purposes, and state statutes exempting church property from taxation? In the Walz decision, the Supreme Court ruled that there is no contradiction.

Legal Background

The U.S. Constitution makes no reference to tax exemption. There was no discussion of the issue in the Constitutional Convention nor in debates on the Bill of Rights.

In the Colonial and post-Revolutionary years, some churches had established status and were state-supported. This changed with enactment of the First Amendment, which laid down no-establishment as the federal norm. This norm was adopted by the states which, however, exempted churches from tax liabilities.

No establishment, no hindrance, was the early American view of Church-State relationships.

This view, reflected in custom law, was not generally formulated in statute law until the second half of the 19th century, although specific tax exemption was provided for churches in Maryland in 1798, in Virginia in 1800, and in North Carolina in 1806.

The first major challenge to church property exemption was initiated by the Liberal League in the 1870s. It reached the point that President Grant included the recommendation in a State of the Union address in 1875, stating that church property should bear its own proportion of taxes. The plea fell on deaf ears in Congress, but there was some support for the idea at state levels. The exemption, however, continued to survive various challenges.

About 36 state constitutions contain either mandatory or permissive provisions for exemption. Statutes provide for exemption in all other states.

There has been considerable litigation challenging this exemption, but most of it focused on whether a particular property satisfied statutory requirements. Few cases before Walz focused on the strictly constitutional question, whether directly under the First Amendment or indirectly under the Fourteenth.

Objections

Objectors to the tax exempt status of churches feel that churches should share, through taxation, in the cost of the ordinary benefits of public services they enjoy, and/or that the amount of "aid" enjoyed through exemption should be proportionate to the amount of social good they do.

According to one opinion, exemption is said to weaken the independence of churches from the political system that benefits them by exemption.

In another view, exemption is said to involve the government in decisions regarding what is and what is not religion.

The Wall of Separation

Thomas Jefferson, in a letter written to the Danbury (Connecticut) Baptist Association Jan. 1, 1802, coined the metaphor, "a wall of separation between Church and State," to express a theory concerning interpretation of the religion clauses of the First Amendment: "Congress shall make no law respecting an establishment of religion or prohibiting the free exercise thereof."

The metaphor was cited for the first time in judicial proceedings in 1879, in the opinion by Chief Justice Waite in Reynolds v. United States. It did not, however, figure substantially in the decision.

Accepted as Rule

In 1947 the wall of separation gained acceptance as a constitutional rule, in the decision handed down in Everson v. Board of Education. Associate Justice Black, in describing the principles involved in the No Establishment Clause, wrote:

"Neither a state nor the Federal Government can set up a church. Neither can pass laws which aid one religion, aid all religions, or prefer one religion over another. Neither can force nor influence a person to go to or to remain away from church against his will or force him to profess a belief or disbelief in any religion. No person can be punished for entertaining or professing religious beliefs or disbeliefs, for church attendance or non-attendance. No tax in any amount, large or small, can be levied to support any religious activities or institutions, whatever they may be called, or whatever form they may adopt to teach or practice religion. Neither a state nor the Federal Government can, openly or secretly, participate in the affairs of any religious organizations or groups and vice versa. In the words of Jefferson, the clause against establishment of religion by law was intended to erect 'a wall of separation between Church and State.' "

Mr. Black's associates agreed with his statement of principles, which were framed without reference to the Freedom of Exercise Clause. They disagreed, however, with respect to application of the principles, as the split decision in the case indicated. Five members of the Court held that the benefits of public welfare legislation—in this case, free bus transportation to school for parochial as well as public school students—did not run contrary to the concept of separation of Church and State embodied in the First Amendment.

(For coverage of the recent Supreme Court decision pertaining to vouchers, see **Education**.)

CATHOLICS IN THE U.S. GOVERNMENT

CATHOLICS IN PRESIDENTS' CABINETS

From 1789 to 1940, nine Catholics were appointed to cabinet posts by six of 32 presidents. The first was Roger Brooke Taney (later named first Catholic Supreme Court Justice) who was appointed in 1831 by Andrew Jackson. Catholics have been appointed to cabinet posts from the time of Franklin D. Roosevelt to the present. Listed below in chronological order are presidents, Catholic cabinet officials, posts held, dates.

Andrew Jackson: Roger B. Taney, Attorney General, 1831-33, Secretary of Treasury, 1833-34.

Franklin Pierce: James Campbell, Postmaster General, 1853-57.

James Buchanan: John B. Floyd, Secretary of War, 1857-61.

William McKinley: Joseph McKenna, Attorney General, 1897-98.

Theodore Roosevelt: Robert J. Wynne, Postmaster General, 1904-05; Charles Bonaparte, Secretary of Navy, 1905-06, Attorney General, 1906-09.

Franklin D. Roosevelt: James A. Farley, Postmaster General, 1933-40; Frank Murphy, Attorney General, 1939-

40; Frank C. Walker, Postmaster General, 1940-45.

Harry S. Truman: Robert E. Hannegan, Postmaster General, 1945-47; J. Howard McGrath, Attorney General, 1949-52; Maurice J. Tobin, Secretary of Labor, 1948-53; James P. McGranery, Attorney General, 1952-53.

Dwight D. Eisenhower: Martin P. Durkin, Secretary of Labor, 1953; James P. Mitchell, Secretary of Labor, 1953-61.

John F. Kennedy: Robert F. Kennedy, Attorney General, 1961-63; Anthony Celebrezze, Secretary of Health, Education and Welfare, 1962-63; John S. Gronouski, Postmaster General, 1963.

Lyndon B. Johnson: Robert F. Kennedy, 1963-64, Anthony Celebrezze, 1963-65, and John S. Gronouski, 1963-65, reappointed to posts held in Kennedy Cabinet; John T. Connor, Secretary of Commerce, 1965-67; Lawrence O'Brien, Postmaster General, 1965-68.

Richard M. Nixon: Walter J. Hickel, Secretary of Interior, 1969-71; John A. Volpe, Secretary of Transportation, 1969-72; Maurice H. Stans, Secretary of Commerce, 1969-72; Peter J. Brennan, Secretary of

Labor, 1973-74; William E. Simon, Secretary of Treasury, 1974.

Gerald R. Ford: Peter J. Brennan, 1974-75, and William E. Simon, 1974-76, reappointed to posts held above.

Jimmy Carter: Joseph Califano, Jr., Secretary of Health, Education and Welfare, 1977-79; Benjamin Civiletti, Attorney General, 1979-81; Moon Landrieu, Secretary of Housing and Urban Development, 1979-81; Edmund S. Muskie, Secretary of State, 1980-81.

Ronald Reagan: Alexander M. Haig, Secretary of State, 1981-82; Raymond J. Donovan, Secretary of Labor, 1981-84; Margaret M. Heckler, Secretary of Health and Human Services, 1983-85; William J. Bennett, Secretary of Education, 1985-88; Ann Dore McLaughlin, Secretary of Labor, 1988-89; Lauro F. Cavazos, Secretary of Education, 1988-89; Nicholas F. Brady, Secretary of Treasury, 1988-89.

George Bush: Lauro F. Cavazos (reappointed), Secretary of Education, 1989-90; Nicholas F. Brady (reappointed), Secretary of Treasury, 1989-93; James D. Watkins, Secretary of Energy, 1989-93; Manuel Lujan, Jr., Secretary of Interior, 1989-93; Edward J. Derwinski, Secretary of Veteran Affairs, 1989-92; Lynn Martin, Secretary of Labor, 1990-93; Edward Madigan, Secretary of Agriculture, 1991-93; William P. Barr, Attorney General, 1991-93.

Bill Clinton: Henry G. Cisneros, Secretary of Housing and Urban Development, 1993-97; Federico F. Peña, Secretary of Transportation, 1993-97; Donna Shalala, Secretary of Health and Human Services, 1993-2001; William M. Daley, Secretary of Commerce, 1997-2000; Andrew Cuomo, Secretary of Housing and Urban Development, 1997-2001; Alexis H. Herman, Secretary of Labor, 1997-2001.

George W. Bush: Paul O'Neill, Secretary of the Treasury, 2001-03; Tommy Thompson, Secretary of Health and Human Services, 2001-05; Mel Martinez, Secretary of Housing and Urban Development, 2001-05; Anthony Principi, Secretary of Veterans Affairs, 2001-05; Jim Nicholson, Secretary of Veterans Affairs, 2005-07; Alberto Gonzalez, Attorney General, 2005-07; Carlos Gutierrez, Commerce Secretary, 2005-.

Cabinet members who became Catholics after leaving their posts were: Thomas Ewing, Secretary of Treasury under William A. Harrison and Secretary of Interior under Zachary Taylor; Luke E. Wright, Secretary of War under Theodore Roosevelt; Albert B. Fall, Secretary of Interior under Warren G. Harding.

Catholics in the 110th Congress

As of the start of the 110th Congress in 2007, there were 155 Catholic members, comprising 30% of the total Congressional membership and therefore the largest faith group in that body (Baptists were second, with 67 House and Senate members, followed by Methodists, with 62 members). There are presently 130 Catholics in the House (42 Republicans and 88 Democrats) and 25 Catholics in the Senate (16 Democrats and 9 Republicans), according to the Congressional Quarterly. There are fewer Catholic Republicans in both houses since the 109th Congress and many more Catholic Democrats. It is noted, however, that Catholic representatives and senators do not vote as a bloc, nor do many vote consistently in line with the teachings of the Church.

There are also 43 members who are of the Jewish faith, as well as two practicing Buddhists, and one Muslim. Six members of the new Congress said they have no religious affiliation.

Catholic Supreme Court Justices

Roger B. Taney, Chief Justice 1836-64; app. by Andrew Jackson.

Edward D. White, Associate Justice 1894-1910, app. by Grover Cleveland; Chief Justice 1910-21; app. by William H. Taft.

Joseph McKenna, Associate Justice 1898-1925; app. by William McKinley.

Pierce Butler, Associate Justice 1923-39; app. by Warren G. Harding.

Frank Murphy, Associate Justice 1940-49; app. by Franklin D. Roosevelt.

William Brennan, Associate Justice 1956-90; app. by Dwight D. Eisenhower.

Antonin Scalia, Associate Justice 1986-; app. by Ronald Reagan.

Anthony M. Kennedy, Associate Justice 1988-; app. by Ronald Reagan.

Clarence Thomas, Associate Justice 1991-; app. by George H. W. Bush.

John Roberts, Chief Justice 2005-; app. by George W. Bush.

Samuel Alito, Associate Justice 2005-; app. George W. Bush.

Sherman Minton, Associate Justice from 1949 to 1956; became a Catholic several years before his death in 1965.

Catholics in Statuary Hall

Statues of 13 Catholics deemed worthy of national commemoration are among those enshrined in National Statuary Hall and other places in the U.S. Capitol. The Hall, formerly the chamber of the House of Representatives, was erected by Act of Congress July 2, 1864.

Donating states, names and years of placement are listed.

Arizona: Rev. Eusebio Kino, S. J., missionary, 1965.

California: Rev. Junípero Serra, O. F. M. missionary, 1931. (Beatified 1988.)

Hawaii: Fr. Damien, missionary, 1969. (Beatified 1995.)

Illinois: Gen. James Shields, statesman, 1893.

Louisiana: Edward D. White, Justice of the U.S. Supreme Court (1894-1921), 1955.

Maryland: Charles Carroll, statesman, 1901.

Nevada: Patrick A. McCarran, statesman, 1960.

New Mexico: Dennis Chavez, statesman, 1966. (Abp. Jean B. Lamy, pioneer prelate of Santa Fe, was nominated for Hall honor in 1951.)

North Dakota: John Burke, U.S. treasurer, 1963.

Oregon: Dr. John McLoughlin, pioneer, 1953.

Washington: Mother Mary Joseph Pariseau, pioneer missionary and humanitarian.

West Virginia: John E. Kenna, statesman, 1901.

Wisconsin: Rev. Jacques Marquette, S.J., missionary, explorer, 1895.

United States Hierarchy

U.S. CATHOLIC JURISDICTIONS, HIERARCHY, STATISTICS

The organizational structure of the Catholic Church in the United States consists of 34 provinces with as many archdioceses (metropolitan sees); 152 suffragan sees (dioceses); five Eastern Church jurisdictions immediately subject to the Holy See — the eparchies of St. Maron and Our Lady of Lebanon of Los Angeles (Maronites), Newton (Melkites), St. Thomas Apostle of Detroit (Chaldeans), St. Thomas of Chicago (Syro-Malabars, created on Mar. 13, 2001), St. George Martyr of Canton, Ohio (Romanians), and eparchy for Armenian Catholics in the United States and Canada; and the Military Services Archdiocese. The current number of archdioceses reflects the creation of the archdiocese of Galveston-Houston on Dec. 29, 2004; the current number of suffragan sees reflects the creation of the new diocese of Laredo, Texas, on July 3, 2000, the eparchy of St. Peter the Apostle of San Diego of the Chaldeans on May 21, 2002, and the elevation of the Apostolic Exarchate for Armenian Catholics in the United States and Canada to the rank of eparchy on Sept. 13, 2005. The eparchy of Our Lady of Deliverance of Newark for Syrian–rite Catholics in the U.S. and Canada has its seat in Newark, N.J. The Armenian apostolic eparchy for the United States and Canada has its seat in New York. Each of these jurisdictions is under the direction of an archbishop or bishop, called an ordinary, who has apostolic responsibility and authority for the pastoral service of the people in his care.

The structure includes the territorial episcopal conference known as the United States Conference of Catholic Bishops (USCCB). In and through this body, which is an amalgamation of the National Conference of Catholic Bishops (NCCB) and the United States Catholic Conference (USCC), the bishops exercise their collegiate pastorate over the Church in the entire country (*see* **Index**).

The representative of the Holy See to the Church in the United States is an apostolic nuncio (presently Abp. Pietro Sambi, J.C.D., S.T.D.)

ECCLESIASTICAL PROVINCES

(Sources: The Official Catholic Directory, *Catholic News Service.*)

The 34 ecclesiastical provinces bear the names of archdioceses, i.e., of metropolitan sees.

Anchorage: Archdiocese of Anchorage and suffragan sees of Fairbanks, Juneau. Geographical area: Alaska.

Atlanta: Archdiocese of Atlanta (GA) and suffragan sees of Savannah (GA); Charlotte and Raleigh (NC), Charleston (SC). Geographical area: Georgia, North Carolina, South Carolina.

Baltimore: Archdiocese of Baltimore (MD) and suffragan sees of Wilmington (DE); Arlington and Richmond (VA); Wheeling–Charleston (WV). Geographical area: Maryland (except five counties), Delaware, Virginia, West Virginia.

Boston: Archdiocese of Boston (MA) and suffragan sees of Fall River, Springfield and Worcester (MA); Portland (ME); Manchester (NH); Burlington (VT). Geographical area: Massachusetts, Maine, New Hampshire, Vermont.

Chicago: Archdiocese of Chicago and suffragan sees of Belleville, Joliet, Peoria, Rockford, Springfield. Geographical area: Illinois.

Cincinnati: Archdiocese of Cincinnati and suffragan sees of Cleveland, Columbus, Steubenville, Toledo, Youngstown. Geographical area: Ohio.

Denver: Archdiocese of Denver (CO) and suffragan sees of Colorado Springs and Pueblo (CO); Cheyenne (WY). Geographical area: Colorado, Wyoming.

Detroit: Archdiocese of Detroit and suffragan sees of Gaylord, Grand Rapids, Kalamazoo, Lansing, Marquette, Saginaw. Geographical area: Michigan.

Dubuque: Archdiocese of Dubuque and suffragan sees of Davenport, Des Moines, Sioux City. Geographical area: Iowa.

Galveston-Houston: Archdiocese of Galveston-Houston and suffragan sees of Austin, Beaumont, Brownsville, Corpus Christi, Tyler, and Victoria. Geographical area: Southeast Texas.

Hartford: Archdiocese of Hartford (CT) and suffragan sees of Bridgeport and Norwich (CT); Providence (RI). Geographical area: Connecticut, Rhode Island.

Indianapolis: Archdiocese of Indianapolis and suffragan sees of Evansville, Fort Wayne–South Bend, Gary, Lafayette. Geographical area: Indiana.

Kansas City (KS): Archdiocese of Kansas City and suffragan sees of Dodge City, Salina, Wichita. Geographical area: Kansas.

Los Angeles: Archdiocese of Los Angeles and suffragan sees of Fresno, Monterey, Orange, San Bernardino, San Diego. Geographical area: Southern and Central California.

Louisville: Archdiocese of Louisville (KY) and suffragan sees of Covington, Lexington and Owensboro (KY); Knoxville, Memphis and Nashville (TN). Geographical area: Kentucky, Tennessee.

Miami: Archdiocese of Miami and suffragan sees of Orlando, Palm Beach, Pensacola-Tallahassee, St. Augustine, St. Petersburg, Venice. Geographical area: Florida.

Milwaukee: Archdiocese of Milwaukee and suffragan sees of Green Bay, La Crosse, Madison, Superior. Geographical area: Wisconsin.

Mobile: Archdiocese of Mobile, AL, and suffragan sees of Birmingham (AL); Biloxi and Jackson (MS). Geographical area: Alabama, Mississippi.

Newark: Archdiocese of Newark and suffragan sees of Camden, Metuchen, Paterson, Trenton. Geographical area: New Jersey.

New Orleans: Archdiocese of New Orleans and suffragan sees of Alexandria, Baton Rouge, Houma-Thibodaux, Lafayette, Lake Charles and Shreveport. Geographical area: Louisiana.

New York: Archdiocese of New York and suffragan sees of Albany, Brooklyn, Buffalo, Ogdensburg, Rochester, Rockville Centre, Syracuse. Geographical area: New York.

Oklahoma City: Archdiocese of Oklahoma City (OK) and suffragan sees of Tulsa (OK) and Little Rock (AR). Geographical area: Oklahoma, Arkansas.

Omaha: Archdiocese of Omaha and suffragan sees of Grand Island, Lincoln. Geographical area: Nebraska.

Philadelphia: Archdiocese of Philadelphia and suffragan sees of Allentown, Altoona-Johnstown, Erie, Greensburg, Harrisburg, Pittsburgh, Scranton. Geographical area: Pennsylvania.

Philadelphia (Byzantine, Ukrainians): Metropolitan See of Philadelphia (Byzantine) and Eparchies of St. Josaphat in Parma (OH), St. Nicholas of the Ukrainians in Chicago and Stamford, CT The jurisdiction extends to all Ukrainian Catholics in the U.S.

from the ecclesiastical province of Galicia in the Ukraine.

Pittsburgh (Byzantine, Ruthenians): Metropolitan See of Pittsburgh, PA and Eparchies of Passaic (NJ), Parma (OH), Van Nuys (CA).

Portland: Archdiocese of Portland (OR) and suffragan sees of Baker (OR); Boise (ID); Great Falls-Billings and Helena (MT). Geographical area: Oregon, Idaho, Montana.

St. Louis: Archdiocese of St. Louis and suffragan sees of Jefferson City, Kansas City-St. Joseph, Springfield-Cape Girardeau. Geographical area: Missouri.

St. Paul and Minneapolis: Archdiocese of St. Paul and Minneapolis (MN) and suffragan sees of Crookston, Duluth, New Ulm, St. Cloud and Winona (MN); Bismarck and Fargo (ND); Rapid City and Sioux Falls (SD). Geographical area: Minnesota, North Dakota, South Dakota.

San Antonio: Archdiocese of San Antonio (TX) and suffragan sees of Amarillo, Dallas, El Paso, Fort Worth, Laredo, Lubbock, and San Angelo. Geographical area: Texas.

San Francisco: Archdiocese of San Francisco (CA) and suffragan sees of Oakland, Sacramento, San Jose, Santa Rosa and Stockton (CA); Honolulu (HI); Reno (NV); Las Vegas (NV); Salt Lake City (UT). Geographical area: Northern California, Nevada, Utah, Hawaii.

Santa Fe: Archdiocese of Santa Fe (NM) and suffragan sees of Gallup and Las Cruces (NM); Phoenix and Tucson (AZ). Geographical area: New Mexico, Arizona.

Seattle: Archdiocese of Seattle and suffragan sees of Spokane, Yakima. Geographical area: Washington.

Washington: Archdiocese of Washington, D.C., and suffragan see of St. Thomas (VI). Geographical area: District of Columbia, five counties of Maryland, Virgin Islands.

ARCHDIOCESES, DIOCESES, ARCHBISHOPS, BISHOPS

(Sources: *Official Catholic Directory*; Catholic News Service; *L'Osservatore Romano*. As of Aug. 20, 2008.) Information includes name of diocese, year of foundation (as it appears on the official document erecting the see), present ordinaries (year of installation), auxiliaries and former ordinaries (for biographies, see Index). Archdioceses are indicated by an asterisk.

Albany, NY (1847): Howard J. Hubbard, bishop, 1977.

Former bishops: John McCloskey, 1847-64; John J. Conroy, 1865-77; Francis McNeirny, 1877-94; Thomas M. Burke, 1894-1915; Thomas F. Cusack, 1915-18; Edmund F. Gibbons, 1919-54; William A. Scully, 1954-69; Edwin B. Broderick, 1969-76.

Alexandria, LA (1853): Ronald P. Herzog, bishop, 2004.

Established at Natchitoches, transferred to Alexandria, 1910; title changed to Alexandria-Shreveport, 1977; redesignated Alexandria, 1986, when Shreveport was made a diocese.

Former bishops: Augustus M. Martin, 1853-75; Francis X. Leray, 1877-79, administrator, 1879-83; Anthony Durier, 1885-1904; Cornelius Van de Ven, 1904-32; Daniel F. Desmond, 1933-45; Charles P. Greco, 1946-73; Lawrence P. Graves, 1973-82;

William B. Friend, 1983-86; John C. Favalora, 1986-89; Sam G. Jacobs, 1989-2003.

Allentown, PA (1961): Edward P. Cullen, 1997.

Former bishop: Joseph McShea, 1961-83; Thomas J. Welsh, 1983-97.

Altoona-Johnstown, PA (1901): Joseph V. Adamec, bishop, 1987.

Established as Altoona, name changed, 1957.

Former bishops: Eugene A. Garvey, 1901-20; John J. McCort, 1920-36; Richard T. Guilfoyle, 1936-57; Howard J. Carroll, 1958-60; J. Carroll McCormick, 1960-66; James J. Hogan, 1966-86.

Amarillo, TX (1926): Patrick J. Zurek, bishop, 2008.

Former bishops; Rudolph A. Gerken, 1927-33; Robert E. Lucey, 1934-41; Laurence J. Fitzsimon, 1941-58; John L. Morkovsky, 1958-63; Lawrence M. De Falco, 1963-79; Leroy T. Matthiesen, 1980-97; John W. Yanta, 1997-2008.

Anchorage,* Alaska (1966): Roger Lawrence Schwietz O.M.I., archbishop, 2001.

Former archbishop: Joseph T. Ryan, 1966-75; Francis T. Hurley, 1976-2001.

Arlington, VA (1974): Paul S. Loverde, bishop, 1999.

Former bishop: Thomas J. Welsh, 1974-83; John R. Keating, 1983-98.

Atlanta,* GA (1956; archdiocese, 1962): Wilton Daniel Gregory, archbishop, 2004.

Former ordinaries: Francis E. Hyland, 1956-61; Paul J. Hallinan, first archbishop, 1962-68; Thomas A. Donnellan, 1968-87; Eugene A. Marino, S.S.J., 1988-90; James P. Lyke, 1991-92; John F. Donoghue, 1993-2004.

Austin, TX (1947): Gregory Michael Aymond, bishop, 2001.

Former bishops: Louis J. Reicher, 1947-71; Vincent M. Harris, 1971-86; John E. McCarthy, 1986-2001.

Baker, OR (1903): Robert Francis Vasa, bishop, 2000. Established as Baker City, name changed, 1952.

Former bishops: Charles J. O'Reilly, 1903-18; Joseph F. McGrath, 1919-50; Francis P. Leipzig, 1950-71; Thomas J. Connolly, 1971-99.

Baltimore,* MD (1789; archdiocese, 1808): Edwin F. O'Brien, archbishop, 2007; Mitchell Thomas Rozanski, Denis James Madden, auxiliaries.

Former ordinaries: John Carroll, 1789-1815, first archbishop; Leonard Neale, 1815-17; Ambrose Marechal, S.S., 1817-28; James Whitfield, 1828-34; Samuel Eccleston, S.S., 1834-51; Francis P. Kenrick, 1851-63; Martin J. Spalding, 1864-72; James R. Bayley, 1872-77; Cardinal James Gibbons, 1877-1921; Michael J. Curley, 1921-47; Francis P. Keough, 1947-61; Cardinal Lawrence J. Shehan, 1961-74; William D. Borders, 1974-89; Cardinal William H. Keeler, 1989-2007.

Baton Rouge, LA (1961): Robert W. Muench, bishop, 2001.

Former bishops: Robert E. Tracy, 1961-74; Joseph V. Sullivan, 1974-82; Stanley J. Ott, 1983-93; Alfred C. Hughes, 1993-2001.

Beaumont, TX (1966): Curtis J. Guillory, S.V.D., bishop, 2000.

Former bishops: Vincent M. Harris, 1966-71; Warren L. Boudreaux, 1971-77; Bernard J. Ganter, 1977-93; Joseph A. Galante, 1994-2000.

Belleville, IL (1887): Edward Braxton, bishop, 2005.

Former bishops: John Janssen, 1888-1913; Henry Althoff, 1914-47; Albert R. Zuroweste, 1948-76; William M. Cosgrove, 1976-81; John N. Wurm, 1981-84; James P. Keleher, 1984-93; Wilton D. Gregory, 1994-2004.

Biloxi, MS (1977): Vacant.

Former bishop: Joseph Lawson Howze, 1977-2001; Thomas John Rodi, 2001-2008.

Birmingham, AL (1969): Robert J. Baker, bishop, 2007.

Former bishops: Joseph G. Vath, 1969-87; Raymond J. Boland, 1988-93; David E. Foley, 1994-2005.

Bismarck, ND (1909): Paul A. Zipfel, bishop, 1996. Former bishops: Vincent Wehrle, O.S.B., 1910-39; Vincent J. Ryan, 1940-51; Lambert A. Hoch, 1952-56; Hilary B. Hacker, 1957-82; John F. Kinney, 1982-95.

Boise, ID (1893): Michael P. Driscoll, 1999.

Former bishops: Alphonse J. Glorieux, 1893-1917; Daniel M. Gorman, 1918-27; Edward J. Kelly, 1928-56; James J. Byrne, 1956-62; Sylvester Treinen, 1962-88; Tod David Brown, 1989-98.

Boston,* MA (1808; archdiocese, 1875): Sean O'Malley, O.F.M. Cap., 2003. Francis Xavier Irwin, Emilio Allué, S.D.B., Walter James Edyvean, John A. Dooher, Robert F. Hennessey, auxiliaries.

Former ordinaries: John L. de Cheverus, 1810-23; Benedict J. Fenwick, S.J., 1825-46; John B. Fitzpatrick, 1846-66; John J. Williams, 1866-1907, first archbishop; Cardinal William O'Connell, 1907-44; Cardinal Richard Cushing, 1944-70; Cardinal Humberto Medeiros, 1970-83; Cardinal Bernard F. Law, 1984-2002.

Bridgeport, CT (1953): William Edward Lori, 2001. Former bishops: Lawrence J. Shehan, 1953-61; Walter W. Curtis, 1961-88; Edward M. Egan, 1988-2000.

Brooklyn, NY (1853): Nicholas A. DiMarzio, 2003. Ignatius Catanello, Octavio Cisneros, Guy Sansaricq, Frank J. Caggiano, auxiliaries.

Former bishops: John Loughlin, 1853-91; Charles E. McDonnell, 1892-1921; Thomas E. Molloy, 1921-56; Bryan J. McEntegart, 1957-68; Francis J. Mugavero, 1968-90; Thomas V. Daily, 1990-2003.

Brownsville, TX (1965): Raymundo J. Peña, bishop, 1995.

Former bishops: Adolph Marx, 1965; Humberto S. Medeiros, 1966-70; John J. Fitzpatrick, 1971-91; Enrique San Pedro, S.J., 1991-94.

Buffalo, NY (1847): Edward U. Kmiec, bishop, 2004. Edward M. Grosz, auxiliary.

Former bishops: John Timon, C.M., 1847-67; Stephen V. Ryan, C.M., 1868-96; James E. Quigley, 1897-1903; Charles H. Colton, 1903-15; Dennis J. Dougherty, 1915-18; William Turner, 1919-36; John A. Duffy, 1937-44; John F. O'Hara, C.S.C., 1945-51; Joseph A. Burke, 1952-62; James McNulty, 1963-72; Edward D. Head, 1973-95 Henry J. Mansell, 1995-2003.

Burlington, VT (1853): Salvatore R. Matano, bishop, 2005.

Former bishops: Louis De Goesbriand, 1853-99; John S. Michaud, 1899-1908; Joseph J. Rice, 1910-38; Matthew F. Brady, 1938-44; Edward F. Ryan, 1945-56; Robert F. Joyce, 1957-71; John A. Marshall, 1972-91. Kenneth A. Angell, bishop, 1992-2005.

Camden, NJ (1937): Joseph Galante, bishop, 2004. Former bishops: Bartholomew J. Eustace, 1938-56; Justin J. McCarthy, 1957-59; Celestine J. Damiano, 1960-67; George H. Guilfoyle, 1968-89; James T. McHugh, 1989-98; Nicholas A.DiMarzio, 1999-2003.

Charleston, SC (1820): Vacant.

Former bishops: John England, 1820-42; Ignatius W. Reynolds, 1844-55; Patrick N. Lynch, 1858-82; Henry P. Northrop, 1883-1916; William T. Russell, 1917-27; Emmet M. Walsh, 1927-49; John J. Russell, 1950-58; Paul J. Hallinan, 1958-62; Francis F. Reh, 1962-64; Ernest L. Unterkoefler, 1964-90; David B. Thompson, 1990-99; Robert J. Baker, 1999-2007.

Charlotte, NC (1971): Peter J. Jugis, bishop, 2003. Former bishops: Michael J. Begley, 1972-84; John F. Donoghue, 1984-93; William G. Curlin, 1994-2002.

Cheyenne, WY (1887): Vacant.

Former bishops: Maurice F. Burke, 1887-93; Thomas M. Lenihan, 1897-1901; James J. Keane, 1902-11; Patrick A. McGovern, 1912-51; Hubert M. Newell, 1951-78; Joseph Hart, 1978-2001; David Laurin Ricken, 2001-2008.

Chicago,* IL (1843; archdiocese, 1880): Cardinal

Francis E. George, archbishop, 1997. John R. Manz, Joseph N. Perry, Francis J. Kane, Thomas J. Paprocki, Gustavo Garcia-Siller, M.Sp.S., George J. Rassas, auxiliaries.

Former ordinaries: William Quarter, 1844-48; James O. Van de Velde, S.J., 1849-53; Anthony O'Regan, 1854-58; James Duggan, 1859-70; Thomas P. Foley, administrator, 1870-79; Patrick A. Feehan, 1880-1902, first archbishop; James E. Quigley, 1903-15; Cardinal George Mundelein, 1915-39; Cardinal Samuel Stritch, 1939-58; Cardinal Albert Meyer, 1958-65; Cardinal John Cody, 1965-82; Cardinal Joseph L. Bernardin, 1982-96.

Cincinnati,* OH (1821; archdiocese, 1850): Daniel E. Pilarczyk, archbishop, 1982.

Former ordinaries: Edward D. Fenwick, O.P., 1822-32; John B. Purcell, 1833-83, first archbishop; William H. Elder, 1883-1904; Henry Moeller, 1904-1925; John T. McNicholas, O.P., 1925-50; Karl J. Alter, 1950-69; Paul F. Leibold, 1969-72; Joseph L. Bernardin, 1972-82.

Cleveland, OH (1847): Richard Gerard Lennon, bishop, 2006. Roger W. Gries, O.S.B., auxiliary.

Former ordinaries: L. Amadeus Rappe, 1847-70; Richard Gilmour, 1872-91; Ignatius F. Horstmann, 1892-1908; John P. Farrelly, 1909-21; Joseph Schrembs, 1921-45; Edward F. Hoban, 1945-66; Clarence G. Issenmann, 1966-74; James A. Hickey, 1974-80; Anthony M. Pilla, 1980-2006.

Colorado Springs, CO (1983): Michael J. Sheridan, bishop, 2003.

Former ordinaries: Richard C. Hanifen, 1984-2003.

Columbus, OH (1868): Frederick Francis Campbell, bishop, 2004.

Former bishops: Sylvester H. Rosecrans, 1868-78; John A. Watterson, 1880-99; Henry Moeller, 1900-03; James J. Hartley, 1904-44; Michael J. Ready, 1944-57; Clarence Issenmann, 1957-64; John J. Carberry, 1965-68; Clarence E. Elwell, 1968-73; Edward J. Herrmann, 1973-82; James A. Griffin, 1983-2004.

Corpus Christi, TX (1912): Edmond Carmody, bishop, 2000.

Former bishops: Paul J. Nussbaum, C.P., 1913-20; Emmanuel B. Ledvina, 1921-49; Mariano S. Garriga, 1949-65; Thomas J. Drury, 1965-83; Rene H. Gracida, 1983-97. Roberto O. Gonzalez, O.F.M., 1997-99.

Covington, KY (1853): Roger J. Foys, bishop, 2002.

Former bishops: George A. Carrell, S.J., 1853-68; Augustus M. Toebbe, 1870-84; Camillus P. Maes, 1885-1914; Ferdinand Brossart, 1916-23; Francis W. Howard, 1923-44; William T. Mulloy, 1945-59; Richard Ackerman, C.S.Sp., 1960-78; William A. Hughes, 1979-95; Robert W. Muench, 1996-2001.

Crookston, MN (1909): Michael J. Hoeppner, bishop, 2007.

Former bishops: Timothy Corbett, 1910-38; John H. Peschges, 1938-44; Francis J. Schenk, 1945-60; Laurence A. Glenn, 1960-70; Kenneth J. Povish, 1970-75; Victor H. Balke, 1976-2007.

Dallas, TX (1890): Kevin J. Farrell, bishop, 2007. Established 1890, as Dallas, title changed to Dallas-Ft. Worth, 1953; redesignated Dallas, 1969, when Ft. Worth was made a diocese.

Former bishops: Thomas F. Brennan, 1891-92; Edward J. Dunne, 1893-1910; Joseph P. Lynch, 1911-54; Thomas K. Gorman, 1954-69; Thomas

Tschoepe, 1969-90; Charles V. Grahmann, 1990-2007.

Davenport, IA (1881): Martin John Amos, bishop, 2006.

Former bishops: John McMullen, 1881-83; Henry Cosgrove, 1884-1906; James Davis, 1906-26; Henry P. Rohlman, 1927-44; Ralph L. Hayes, 1944-66; Gerald F. O'Keefe, 1966-93; William E. Franklin, 1993-2006.

Denver,* CO (1887; archdiocese, 1941): Charles J. Chaput, O.F.M. Cap., archbishop, 1997. James Douglas Conley, auxiliary.

Former ordinaries: Joseph P. Machebeuf, 1887-89; Nicholas C. Matz, 1889-1917; J. Henry Tihen, 1917-31; Urban J. Vehr, 1931-67, first archbishop; James V. Casey, 1967-86; J. Francis Stafford, 1986-96.

Des Moines, IA (1911): Richard Edmund Pates, bishop, 2008.

Former bishops: Austin Dowling, 1912-19; Thomas W. Drumm, 1919-33; Gerald T. Bergan, 1934-48; Edward C. Daly, O.P., 1948-64; George J. Biskup, 1965-67; Maurice J. Dingman, 1968-86; William H. Bullock, 1987-93; Joseph L. Charron, C.PP.S., 1993-2007.

Detroit,* MI (1833; archdiocese, 1937): Cardinal Adam J. Maida, archbishop, 1990. John M. Quinn, Francis R. Reiss, Daniel E. Flores, auxiliaries.

Former ordinaries: Frederic Rese, 1833-71; Peter P. Lefevere, administrator, 1841-69; Caspar H. Borgess, 1871-88; John S. Foley, 1888-1918; Michael J. Gallagher, 1918-37; Cardinal Edward Mooney, 1937-58, first archbishop; Cardinal John F. Dearden, 1958-80; Cardinal Edmund C. Szoka, 1981-90.

Dodge City, KS (1951): Ronald M. Gilmore, bishop, 1998.

Former bishops: John B. Franz, 1951-59; Marion F. Forst, 1960-76; Eugene J. Gerber, 1976-82; Stanley G. Schlarman, 1983-98.

Dubuque,* Iowa (1837; archdiocese, 1893): Jerome Hanus, O.S.B., archbishop, 1995.

Former ordinaries: Mathias Loras, 1837-58; Clement Smyth, O.C.S.O., 1858-65; John Hennessy, 1866-1900, first archbishop; John J. Keane, 1900-11; James J. Keane, 1911-29; Francis J. Beckman, 1930-46; Henry P. Rohlman, 1946-54; Leo Binz, 1954-61; James J. Byrne, 1962-83; Daniel W. Kucera, O.S.B., 1984-95.

Duluth, MN (1889): Dennis M. Schnurr, 2001.

Former bishops: James McGolrick, 1889-1918; John T. McNicholas, O.P., 1918-25; Thomas A. Welch, 1926-59; Francis J. Schenk, 1960-69; Paul F. Anderson, 1969-82; Robert H. Brom, 1983-89; Roger L. Schwietz, O.M.I., 1990-2000.

El Paso, TX (1914): Armando X. Ochoa, bishop, 1996.

Former bishops: Anthony J. Schuler, S.J., 1915-42; Sidney M. Metzger, 1942-78; Patrick F. Flores, 1978-79; Raymundo J. Pena, 1980-95.

Erie, PA (1853): Donald W. Trautman, bishop, 1990.

Former bishops: Michael O'Connor, 1853-54; Josue M. Young, 1854-66; Tobias Mullen, 1868-99; John E. Fitzmaurice, 1899-1920; John M. Gannon, 1920-66; John F. Whealon, 1966-69; Alfred M. Watson, 1969-82; Michael J. Murphy, 1982-90.

Evansville, IN (1944): Gerald A. Gettelfinger, bishop, 1989.

Former bishops: Henry J. Grimmelsman, 1944-65;

Paul F. Leibold, 1966-69; Francis R. Shea, 1970-89.

Fairbanks, Alaska (1962): Donald Kettler, bishop, 2002.

Former bishops: Francis D. Gleeson, S.J., 1962-68; Robert L. Whelan, S.J., 1968-85; Michael J. Kaniecki, S.J., 1985-2000.

Fall River, MA (1904): George William Coleman, bishop, 2003.

Former bishops: William Stang, 1904-07; Daniel F. Feehan, 1907-34; James E. Cassidy, 1934-51; James L. Connolly, 1951-70; Daniel A. Cronin, 1970-91; Sean O'Malley, O.F.M. Cap., 1992-2002.

Fargo, ND (1889): Samuel J. Aquila, bishop, 2002. Established at Jamestown, transferred, 1897.

Former bishops: John Shanley, 1889-1909; James O'Reilly, 1910-34; Aloysius J. Muench, 1935-59; Leo F. Dworschak, 1960-70; Justin A. Driscoll, 1970-84; James S. Sullivan, 1985-2002.

Fort Wayne-South Bend, IN (1857): John M. D'Arcy, bishop, 1985.

Established as Fort Wayne, name changed, 1960.

Former bishops: John H. Luers, 1858-71; Joseph Dwenger, C.Pp. S., 1872-93; Joseph Rademacher, 1893-1900; Herman J. Alerding, 1900-24; John F. Noll, 1925-56; Leo A. Pursley, 1957-76; William E. McManus, 1976-85.

Fort Worth, TX (1969): Kevin W. Vann, bishop, 2005.

Former bishop: John J. Cassata, 1969-80; Joseph P. Delaney, 1981-2005.

Fresno, CA (1967): John T. Steinbock, bishop, 1991. Formerly Monterey-Fresno, 1922.

Former bishops (Monterey-Fresno): John J. Cantwell, administrator, 1922-24; John B. MacGinley, first bishop, 1924-32; Philip G. Sher, 1933-53; Aloysius J. Willinger, 1953-67.

Former bishops (Fresno): Timothy Manning, 1967-69; Hugh A. Donohoe, 1969-80; Joseph J. Madera, M.Pp.S., 1980-91.

Gallup, NM (1939): Vacant.

Former bishops: Bernard T. Espelage, O.F.M., 1940-69; Jerome J. Hastrich, 1969-90; Donald Pelotte, S.S.S., 1990-2008.

Galveston-Houston, TX* (1847; archdiocese, 2004): Cardinal Daniel N. DiNardo, archbishop, 2006. José S. Vasquez, auxiliary.

Established as Galveston, name changed, 1959.

Former bishops: John M. Odin, C.M., 1847-61; Claude M. Dubuis, 1862-92; Nicholas A. Gallagher, 1892-1918; Christopher E. Byrne, 1918-50; Wendelin J. Nold, 1950-75; John L. Morkovsky, 1975-84; Joseph A. Fiorenza, 1985-2004, first archbishop, 2004-2006.

Gary, IN (1956): Dale J. Melczek, bishop, 1996.

Former bishops: Andrew G. Grutka, 1957-84; Norbert F. Gaughan, 1984-96.

Gaylord, MI (1971): Patrick R. Cooney, bishop, 1989, installed 1990.

Former bishops: Edmund C. Szoka, 1971-81; Robert J. Rose, 1981-89.

Grand Island, NE (1912): William J. Dendinger, bishop, 2004.

Established at Kearney, transferred, 1917.

Former bishops: James A. Duffy, 1913-31; Stanislaus V. Bona, 1932-44; Edward J. Hunkeler, 1945-51; John L. Paschang, 1951-72; John J. Sullivan, 1972-77;

Lawrence J. McNamara, 1978-2004.

Grand Rapids, MI (1882): Walter A. Hurley, bishop, 2005.

Former bishops: Henry J. Richter, 1883-1916; Michael J. Gallagher, 1916-18; Edward D. Kelly, 1919-26; Joseph G. Pinten, 1926-40; Joseph C. Plagens, 1941-43; Francis J. Haas, 1943-53; Allen J. Babcock, 1954-69; Joseph M. Breitenbeck, 1969-89; Robert J. Rose, 1989-2003; Kevin M. Britt, 2003-2004.

Great Falls-Billings, MT (1904): Michael W. Warfel, bishop, 2007.

Established as Great Falls, name changed, 1980.

Former bishops: Mathias C. Lenihan, 1904-30; Edwin V. O'Hara, 1930-39; William J. Condon, 1939-67; Eldon B. Schuster, 1968-77; Thomas J. Murphy, 1978-87; Anthony M. Milone, 1988-2006.

Green Bay, WI (1868): David Laurin Ricken, bishop, 2008. Robert F. Morneau, auxiliary.

Former bishops: Joseph Melcher, 1868-73; Francis X. Krautbauer, 1875-85; Frederick X. Katzer, 1886-91; Sebastian G. Messmer, 1892-1903; Joseph J. Fox, 1904-14; Paul P. Rhode, 1915-45; Stanislaus V. Bona, 1945-67; Aloysius J. Wycislo, 1968-83; Adam J. Maida, 1984-90. Robert J. Banks, 1990-2003; David A. Zubic, 2003-2007.

Greensburg, PA (1951): Lawrence E. Brandt, bishop, 2004.

Former bishops: Hugh L. Lamb, 1951-59; Willam G. Connare, 1960-87; Anthony G. Bosco, 1987-2004.

Harrisburg, PA (1868): Kevin C. Rhoades, bishop, 2004.

Former bishops: Jeremiah F. Shanahan, 1868-86; Thomas McGovern, 1888-98; John W. Shanahan,1899-1916; Philip R. McDevitt, 1916-35; George L. Leech, 1935-71; Joseph T. Daley, 1971-83; William H. Keeler, 1984-89; Nicholas C. Dattilo, 1990-2004.

Hartford,* CT (1843; archdiocese, 1953): Henry J. Mansell, archbishop, 2003. Peter A. Rosazza, Christie A. Macaluso, auxiliaries.

Former ordinaries: William Tyler, 1844-49; Bernard O'Reilly, 1850-56; F. P. MacFarland, 1858-74; Thomas Galberry, O.S.A., 1876-78; Lawrence S. McMahon, 1879-93; Michael Tierney, 1894-1908; John J. Nilan, 1910-34; Maurice F. McAuliffe, 1934-44; Henry J. O'Brien, 1945-68, first archbishop; John F. Whealon, 1969-91; Daniel A. Cronin, 1991-2003.

Helena, MT (1884): George L. Thomas, bishop, 2004.

Former bishops: John B. Brondel, 1884-1903; John P. Carroll, 1904-25; George J. Finnigan, C.S.C., 1927-32; Ralph L. Hayes, 1933-35; Joseph M. Gilmore, 1936-62; Raymond Hunthausen, 1962-75; Elden F. Curtiss, 1976-93; Alexander J. Brunett, 1994-97; Robert C. Morlino, 1999-2003.

Honolulu, HI (1941): Clarence L. Silva, bishop, 2005.

Former bishops: James J. Sweeney, 1941-68; John J. Scanlan, 1968-81; Joseph A. Ferrario, 1982-93; Francis X. DiLorenzo (apostolic administrator, 1993), 1994-2004.

Houma-Thibodaux, LA (1977): Sam G. Jacobs, 2003.

Former bishop: Warren L. Boudreaux, 1977-92; C. Michael Jarrell, 1993-2002.

Indianapolis,* IN (1834; archdiocese, 1944): Daniel M. Buechlein, O.S.B., archbishop, 1992.
Established at Vincennes, transferred, 1898.
Former ordinaries: Simon G. Bruté, 1834-39; Celestine de la Hailandiere, 1839-47; John S. Bazin, 1847-48; Maurice de St. Palais, 1849-77; Francis S. Chatard, 1878-1918; Joseph Chartrand, 1918-33; Joseph E. Ritter, 1934-46, first archbishop; Paul C. Schulte, 1946-70; George J. Biskup, 1970-79; Edward T. O'Meara, 1980-92.
Jackson, MS (1837): Joseph Latino, bishop, 2003.
Established at Natchez, title changed to Natchez-Jackson, 1956; transferred to Jackson, 1977 (Natchez made titular see).
Former bishops: John J. Chanche, S.S., 1841-52; James Van de Velde, S.J., 1853-55; William H. Elder, 1857-80; Francis A. Janssens, 1881-88; Thomas Heslin, 1889-1911; John E. Gunn, S.M., 1911-24; Richard O. Gerow, 1924-67; Joseph B. Brunini, 1968-84; William R. Houck, 1984-2003.
Jefferson City, MO (1956): John R. Gaydos, bishop, 1997.
Former bishops: Joseph Marling, C.Pp.S., 1956-69; Michael F. McAuliffe, 1969-97.
Joliet, IL (1948): James Peter Sartain, bishop, 2006. Former bishops: Martin D. McNamara, 1949-66; Romeo Blanchette, 1966-79; Joseph L. Imesch, 1979-2006.
Juneau, Alaska (1951): Vacant.
Former bishops: Dermot O'Flanagan, 1951-68; Joseph T. Ryan, administrator, 1968-71; Francis T. Hurley, 1971-76, administrator, 1976-79; Michael H. Kenny, 1979-95; Michael W. Warfel, 1996-2007.
Kalamazoo, MI (1971): James A. Murray, bishop, 1997.
Former bishop: Paul V. Donovan, 1971-94; Alfred J. Markiewicz, 1995-97.
Kansas City,* KS (1877; archdiocese, 1952): Joseph F. Naumann, archbishop, 2005.
Established as vicariate apostolic, 1850, became Diocese of Leavenworth, 1877, transferred to Kansas City, 1947.
Former ordinaries: J. B. Miege, vicar apostolic, 1851-74; Louis M. Fink, O.S.B., vicar apostolic, 1874-77, first bishop, 1877-1904; Thomas F. Lillis, 1904-10; John Ward, 1910-29; Francis Johannes, 1929-37; Paul C. Schulte, 1937-46; George J. Donnelly, 1946-50; Edward Hunkeler, 1951-69, first archbishop; Ignatius J. Strecker, 1969-93; James P. Keleher, 1993-2005.
Kansas City-St. Joseph, MO (Kansas City, 1880, St. Joseph, 1868, united 1956): Robert W. Finn, bishop, 2005.
Former bishops: John J. Hogan, 1880-1913; Thomas F. Lillis, 1913-38; Edwin V. O'Hara, 1939-56; John P. Cody, 1956-61; Charles H. Helmsing, 1962-77; John J. Sullivan, 1977-93; Raymond J. Boland, 1993-2005.
Former bishops (St. Joseph): John J. Hogan, 1868-80, administrator, 1880-93; Maurice F. Burke, 1893-1923; Francis Gilfillan, 1923-33; Charles H. Le Blond, 1933-56.
Knoxville, TN (1988): Vacant.
Former bishops: Anthony J. O'Connell, bishop, 1988-98; Joseph E. Kurtz, 1999-2007.
La Crosse, WI (1868): Jerome E. Listecki, bishop, 2004.

Former bishops: Michael Heiss, 1868-80; Kilian C. Flasch, 1881-91; James Schwebach, 1892-1921; Alexander J. McGavick, 1921-48; John P. Treacy, 1948-64; Frederick W. Freking, 1965-83; John J. Paul, 1983-94; Raymond L. Burke, 1995-2003.
Lafayette, IN (1944): William L. Higi, bishop, 1984.
Former bishops: John G. Bennett, 1944-57; John J. Carberry, 1957-65; Raymond J. Gallagher, 1965-82; George A. Fulcher, 1983-84.
Lafayette, LA (1918): C. Michael Jarrell, bishop, 2002.
Former bishops: Jules B. Jeanmard, 1918-56; Maurice Schexnayder, 1956-72; Gerard L. Frey, 1973-89; Harry J. Flynn, 1989-94; Edward J. O'Donnell, 1994-2002.
Lake Charles, LA (1980): Glen J. Provost, bishop, 2007
Former bishop: Jude Speyrer, 1980-2000; Edward Braxton, 2000-2005.
Lansing, MI (1937): Earl Boyea, bishop, 2008.
Former bishops: Joseph H. Albers, 1937-65; Alexander Zaleski, 1965-75; Kenneth J. Povish, 1975-95; Carl F. Mengeling, 1995-2008.
Laredo, Tx. (2000): James A. Tamayo, bishop, 2000.
Las Cruces, NM (1982): Ricardo Ramirez, C.S.B., bishop, 1982.
Las Vegas, NV (1995): Joseph Pepe, 2001.
Formerly Reno-Las Vegas, 1976; made separate diocese 1995.
Former bishops: Daniel F. Walsh, 1995-2000.
Lexington, KY (1988): Ronald William Gainer, bishop, 2002.
Former bishops: James Kendrick Williams, 1988-2002.
Lincoln, NE (1887): Fabian W. Bruskewitz, bishop, 1992.
Former bishops: Thomas Bonacum, 1887-1911; J. Henry Tihen, 1911-17; Charles J. O'Reilly, 1918-23; Francis J. Beckman, 1924-30; Louis B. Kucera, 1930-57; James V. Casey, 1957-67; Glennon P. Flavin, 1967-92.
Little Rock, AR (1843): Anthony Basil Taylor, bishop, 2008.
Former bishops: Andrew Byrne, 1844-62; Edward Fitzgerald, 1867-1907; John Morris, 1907-46; Albert L. Fletcher, 1946-72; Andrew J. McDonald, 1972-2000; James Peter Sartain, 2000-2006.
Los Angeles,* CA (1840; archdiocese, 1936): Cardinal Roger M. Mahony, archbishop, 1985. Thomas J. Curry, Gerald E. Wilkerson, Gabino Zavala, Edward William Clark, Oscar Azarcon Solis, Alexander Salazar, auxiliaries.
Founded as diocese of Two Californias, 1840; became Monterey diocese, 1850; Baja California detached from Monterey diocese, 1852; title changed to Monterey-Los Angeles, 1859, Los Angeles-San Diego, 1922; became archdiocese under present title, 1936 (San Diego became separate see).
Former ordinaries: Francisco Garcia Diego y Moreno, O.F.M., 1840-46; Joseph S. Alemany, O.P., 1850-53; Thaddeus Amat, C.M., 1854-78; Francis Mora, 1878-96; George T. Montgomery, 1896-1903; Thomas J. Conaty, 1903-15; John J. Cantwell, 1917-47, first archbishop; Cardinal James McIntyre, 1948-70; Cardinal Timothy Manning, 1970-85.

Louisville,* KY (1808; archdiocese, 1937): Joseph E. Kurtz, archbishop, 2007.

Established at Bardstown, transferred, 1841.

Former ordinaries: Benedict J. Flaget, S.S., 1810-32; John B. David, S.S., 1832-33; Benedict J. Flaget, S.S., 1833-50; Martin J. Spalding, 1850-64; Peter J. Lavialle, 1865-67; William G. McCloskey, 1868-1909; Denis O'Donaghue, 1910-24; John A. Floersh, 1924-67, first archbishop; Thomas J. McDonough, 1967-81; Thomas C. Kelly, O.P., 1982-2007.

Lubbock, TX (1983): Placido Rodriguez, C.M.F., bishop, 1994.

Former bishop: Michael J. Sheehan, 1983-93.

Madison, WI (1946): Robert C. Morlino, bishop, 2003.

Former bishops: William P. O'Connor, 1946-67; Cletus F. O'Donnell, 1967-92, William H. Bullock, 1993-2003.

Manchester, NH (1884): John B. McCormack, bishop, 1998; Francis J. Christian, auxiliary.

Former bishops: Denis M. Bradley, 1884-1903; John B. Delany, 1904-06; George A. Guertin, 1907-32; John B. Peterson, 1932-44; Matthew F. Brady, 1944-59; Ernest J. Primeau, 1960-74; Odore J. Gendron, 1975-90; Leo E. O'Neil, 1990-97.

Marquette, MI (1857): Alexander K. Sample, bishop, 2005.

Founded as Sault Ste. Marie and Marquette; changed to Marquette, 1937.

Former bishops: Frederic Baraga, 1857-68; Ignatius Mrak, 1869-78; John Vertin, 1879-99; Frederick Eis, 1899-1922; Paul J. Nussbaum, C.P., 1922-35; Joseph C. Plagens, 1935-40; Francis Magner, 1941-47; Thomas L. Noa, 1947-68; Charles A. Salatka, 1968-77; Mark F. Schmitt, 1978-92; James H. Garland (1992-2005).

Memphis, TN (1970): J. Terry Steib, S.V.D., bishop, 1993.

Former bishops: Carroll T. Dozier, 1971-82; J. Francis Stafford, 1982-86; Daniel M. Buechlein, O.S.B.,1987-92.

Metuchen, NJ (1981): Paul G. Bootkoski, bishop, 2002.

Former bishops: Theodore E. McCarrick, 1981-86; Edward T. Hughes, 1987-97; Vincent DePaul Breen, 1997-2002.

Miami,* FL (1958; archdiocese, 1968): John C. Favalora, archbishop, 1994. Felipe de Jesús Estevez, John Gerard Noonan, auxiliaries.

Former ordinaries: Coleman F. Carroll, 1958-77, first archbishop; Edward A. McCarthy, 1977-94.

Milwaukee,* WI (1843; archdiocese, 1875): Timothy M. Dolan, archbishop, 2002. Richard J. Sklba, William Callahan, O.F.M. Conv., auxiliaries.

Former ordinaries: John M. Henni, 1844-81, first archbishop; Michael Heiss, 1881-90; Frederick X. Katzer, 1891-1903; Sebastian G. Messmer, 1903-30; Samuel A. Stritch, 1930-39; Moses E. Kiley, 1940-53; Albert G. Meyer, 1953-58; William E. Cousins, 1959-77; Rembert G. Weakland, O.S.B., 1977-2002.

Mobile,* AL (1829; archdiocese, 1980): Thomas John Rodi, archbishop, 2008.

Founded as Mobile, 1829, title changed to Mobile-Birmingham, 1954; redesignated Mobile, 1969.

Former bishops: Michael Portier, 1829-59; John

Quinlan, 1859-83; Dominic Manucy, 1884; Jeremiah O'Sullivan, 1885-96; Edward P. Allen, 1897-1926; Thomas J. Toolen, 1927-69; John L. May, 1969-80; Oscar H. Lipscomb, first archbishop, 1980-2008.

Monterey in California (1967): Richard J. Garcia, bishop, 2006.

Formerly Monterey-Fresno, 1922. (Originally established in 1850, see Los Angeles listing.)

Former bishops (Monterey-Fresno): John J. Cantwell, administrator, 1922-24; John B. MacGinley, first bishop, 1924-32; Philip G. Sher, 1933-53; Aloysius J. Willinger, 1953-67.

Former bishops (Monterey): Harry A. Clinch, 1967-82; Thaddeus A. Shubsda, 1982-91; Sylvester D. Ryan, 1992-2006

Nashville, TN (1837): David Choby, bishop, 2005.

Former bishops: Richard P. Miles, O.P., 1838-60; James Whelan, O.P., 1860-64; Patrick A. Feehan, 1865-80; Joseph Rademacher, 1883-93; Thomas S. Byrne, 1894-1923; Alphonse J. Smith, 1924-35; William L. Adrian, 1936-69; Joseph A. Durick, 1969-75; James D. Niedergeses, 1975-92; Edward U. Kmiec, 1992-2004.

Newark,* NJ (1853; archdiocese, 1937): John J. Myers, 2001. Edgar M. da Cunha, Thomas A. Donato, John W. Flesey, Manuel Cruz, auxiliaries.

Former ordinaries: James R. Bayley, 1853-72; Michael A. Corrigan, 1873-80; Winand M. Wigger, 1881-1901; John J. O'Connor, 1901-27; Thomas J. Walsh, 1928-52, first archbishop; Thomas A. Boland, 1953-74; Peter L. Gerety, 1974-86; Theodore E. McCarrick, 1986-2000.

New Orleans,* LA (1793; archdiocese, 1850): Alfred Hughes, 2002. Roger Paul Morin, Shelton Fabre, auxiliaries.

Former ordinaries: Luis Penalver y Cardenas, 1793-1801; John Carroll, administrator, 1805-15; W. Louis Dubourg, S.S., 1815-25; Joseph Rosati, C.M., administrator, 1826-29; Leo De Neckere, C.M., 1829-33; Anthony Blanc, 1835-60, first archbishop; Jean Marie Odin, C.M., 1861-70; Napoleon J. Perche, 1870-83; Francis X. Leray, 1883-87; Francis A. Janssens, 1888-97; Placide L. Chapelle, 1897-1905; James H. Blenk, S.M., 1906-17; John W. Shaw, 1918-34; Joseph F. Rummel, 1935-64; John P. Cody, 1964-65; Philip M. Hannan, 1965-88; Francis B. Schulte, 1988-2002.

Newton, MA (Melkite) (1966; eparchy, 1976): Cyrille Salim Bustros, S.M.S.P., eparch, 2004.

Former ordinaries: Justin Najmy, exarch, 1966-68; Joseph Tawil, exarch, 1969-76, first eparch, 1976-89; Ignatius Ghattas, B.S.O., 1990-92; John A. Elya, B.S.O., 1993-2004.

New Ulm, MN (1957): John LeVoir, bishop, 2008.

Former bishop: Alphonse J. Schladweiler, 1958-75; Raymond A. Lucker, 1975-2000; John Clayton Nienstedt, 2001-2007.

New York,* NY (1808; archdiocese, 1850): Cardinal Edward M. Egan, archbishop, 2000. Robert J. Iriondo, Dominick J. Lagonegro, Gerald T. Walsh, Dennis J. Sullivan, auxiliaries.

Former ordinaries: Richard L. Concanen, O.P., 1808-10; John Connolly, O.P., 1814-25; John Dubois, S.S., 1826-42; John J. Hughes, 1842-64, first archbishop; Cardinal John McCloskey, 1864-85; Michael A. Corrigan, 1885-1902; Cardinal John Farley, 1902-18;

Cardinal Patrick Hayes, 1919-38; Cardinal Francis Spellman, 1939-67; Cardinal Terence J. Cooke, 1968-83; Cardinal John J. O'Connor, 1984-2000.

Norwich, CT (1953): Michael R. Cote, bishop, 2003.

Former bishops: Bernard J. Flanagan, 1953-59; Vincent J. Hines, 1960-75; Daniel P. Reilly, 1975-94; Daniel A. Hart, 1995-2003.

Oakland, CA (1962): Allen H. Vigneron, bishop, 2003.

Former bishop: Floyd L. Begin, 1962-77; John S. Cummins, 1977-2003.

Ogdensburg, NY (1872): Robert Joseph Cunningham, bishop, 2004.

Former bishops: Edgar P. Wadhams, 1872-91; Henry Gabriels, 1892-1921; Joseph H. Conroy, 1921-39; Francis J. Monaghan, 1939-42; Bryan J. McEntegart, 1943-53; Walter P. Kellenberg, 1954-57; James J. Navagh, 1957-63; Leo R. Smith, 1963; Thomas A. Donnellan, 1964-68; Stanislaus J. Brzana, 1968-93; Paul S. Loverde, 1993-99; Gerald M. Barbarito, 1999-2003.

Oklahoma City,* OK (1905; archdiocese, 1972): Eusebius J. Beltran, archbishop, 1993.

Former ordinaries: Theophile Meerschaert, 1905-24; Francis C. Kelley, 1924-48; Eugene J. McGuinness, 1948-57; Victor J. Reed, 1958-71; John R. Quinn, 1971-77, first archbishop; Charles A. Salatka, 1977-92.

Omaha,* NE (1885; archdiocese, 1945): Elden F. Curtiss, archbishop, 1993.

Former ordinaries: James O'Gorman, O.C.S.O., 1859-74, vicar apostolic; James O'Connor, vicar apostolic, 1876-85, first bishop, 1885-90; Richard Scannell, 1891-1916; Jeremiah J. Harty, 1916-27; Francis Beckman, administrator, 1926-28; Joseph F. Rummel, 1928-35; James H. Ryan, 1935-47, first archbishop; Gerald T. Bergan, 1948-69; Daniel E. Sheehan, 1969-93.

Orange, CA (1976): Tod D. Brown, bishop, 1998; Dominic Mai Luong, auxiliaries.

Former bishop: William R. Johnson, 1976-86; Norman F. McFarland, 1986-98.

Orlando, FL (1968): Thomas G. Wenski, bishop, 2005.

Former bishops: William Borders, 1968-74; Thomas J. Grady, 1974-89.

Our Lady of Deliverance of Newark (for Syrian-rite Catholics of the U.S. and Canada, 1995): Joseph Younan, bishop, 1996.

Our Lady of Lebanon of Los Angeles, CA (Maronite) (1994): Robert J. Shaheen, 2000.

Former eparch: John G. Chedid, 1994-2000.

Owensboro, KY (1937): John J. McRaith, bishop, 1982.

Former bishops: Francis R. Cotton, 1938-60; Henry J. Soenneker, 1961-82.

Palm Beach, FL (1984): Gerald Michael Barbarito, 2003.

Former bishop: Thomas V. Daily, 1984-90; J. Keith Symons, 1990-98; Anthony J. O'Connell, 1998-2002; Sean O'Malley, O.F.M. Cap., 2002-2003.

Parma, OH (Byzantine, Ruthenian) (1969): John Kudrick, bishop, 2002.

Former bishops: Emil Mihalik, 1969-84; Andrew Pataki, 1984-95; Basil Schott, O.F.M., 1996-2002.

Passaic, NJ (Byzantine, Ruthenian) (1963): William C. Skurla, eparch, 2007.

Former bishops: Stephen Kocisko, 1963-68; Michael J. Dudick, 1968-95; Andrew Pataki, 1996-2007.

Paterson, NJ (1937): Arthur J. Serratelli, bishop, 2004.

Former bishops: Thomas H. McLaughlin, 1937-47; Thomas A. Boland, 1947-52; James A. McNulty, 1953-63; James J. Navagh, 1963-65; Lawrence B. Casey, 1966-77; Frank J. Rodimer, 1978-2004.

Pensacola-Tallahassee, FL (1975): John H.Ricard, S.S.J., bishop, 1997.

Former bishops: Rene H. Gracida, 1975-83; J. Keith Symons, 1983-90; John M. Smith, 1991-95.

Peoria, IL (1877): Daniel R. Jenky, C.S.C., bishop, 2002.

Former bishops: John L. Spalding, 1877-1908; Edmund M. Dunne, 1909-29; Joseph H. Schlarman, 1930-51; William E. Cousins, 1952-58; John B. Franz, 1959-71; Edward W. O'Rourke, 1971- 90; John J. Myers, 1990-2001.

Philadelphia,* PA (1808; archdiocese, 1875): Cardinal Justin F. Rigali, archbishop, 2003. Robert P. Maginnis, Joseph Robert Cistone, Joseph Patrick McFadden, Daniel E. Thomas, auxiliaries.

Former ordinaries: Michael Egan, O.F.M., 1810-14; Henry Conwell, 1820-42; Francis P. Kenrick, 1842-51; John N. Neumann, C.SS.R., 1852-60; James F. Wood, 1860-83, first archbishop; Patrick J. Ryan, 1884-1911; Edmond F. Prendergast, 1911-18; Cardinal Dennis Dougherty, 1918-51; Cardinal John O'Hara, C.S.C., 1951-60; Cardinal John Krol, 1961-88; Cardinal Anthony J. Bevilacqua, 1988-2003.

Philadelphia,* PA (Byzantine, Ukrainian) (1924; metropolitan, 1958): Stephen Soroka, archbishop, 2001. John Bura, auxiliary.

Former ordinaries: Stephen Ortynsky, O.S.B.M., 1907-16; Constantine Bohachevsky, 1924-61; Ambrose Senyshyn, O.S.B.M., 1961-76; Joseph Schmondiuk, 1977-78; Myroslav J. Lubachivsky, 1979-80, apostolic administrator, 1980-81; Stephen Sulyk, 1981-2000.

Phoenix, AZ (1969): Thomas J. Olmsted, bishop, 2003.

Former bishops: Edward A. McCarthy, 1969-76; James S. Rausch, 1977-81; Thomas J. O'Brien, 1982-2003.

Pittsburgh,* PA (Byzantine, Ruthenian) (1924; metropolitan, 1969): Basil Schott, O.F.M., archbishop, 2002.

Former ordinaries: Basil Takach 1924-48; Daniel Ivancho, 1948-54; Nicholas T. Elko, 1955-67; Stephen J. Kocisko, 1968-91, first metropolitan; Thomas V. Dolinay, 1991-93; Judson M. Procyk, 1995-2001.

Pittsburgh, PA (1843): David A. Zubic, bishop, 2007. Paul J. Bradley, auxiliary.

Former bishops: Michael O'Connor, 1843-53, 1854-60; Michael Domenec, C.M., 1860-76; J. Tuigg, 1876-89; Richard Phelan, 1889-1904; J.F. Regis Canevin, 1904-20; Hugh C. Boyle, 1921-50; John F. Dearden, 1950-58; John J. Wright, 1959-69; Vincent M. Leonard, 1969-83; Anthony J. Bevilacqua, 1983-88; Donald W. Wuerl, 1988-2006.

Portland, ME (1853): Richard Joseph Malone, bishop, 2004.

Former bishops: David W. Bacon, 1855-74; James A.

Healy, 1875-1900; William H. O'Connell, 1901-06; Louis S. Walsh, 1906-24; John G. Murray, 1925-31; Joseph E. McCarthy, 1932-55; Daniel J. Feeney, 1955-69; Peter L. Gerety, 1969-74; Edward C. O'Leary, 1974-88, Joseph J. Gerry, O.S.B., 1989-2004.

Portland,* OR (1846): John G. Vlazny, archbishop, 1997. Kenneth D. Steiner, auxiliary.
Established as Oregon City, name changed, 1928.
Former ordinaries: Francis N. Blanchet, 1846-80 vicar apostolic, first archbishop; Charles J. Seghers, 1880-84; William H. Gross, C.SS.R., 1885-98; Alexander Christie, 1899-1925; Edward D. Howard, 1926-66; Robert J. Dwyer, 1966-74; Cornelius M. Power, 1974-86; William J. Levada, 1986-95; Francis E. George, 1996-97.

Providence, RI (1872): Thomas J. Tobin, bishop, 2005.
Former bishops: Thomas F. Hendricken, 1872-86; Matthew Harkins, 1887-1921; William A. Hickey, 1921-33; Francis P. Keough, 1934-47; Russell J. McVinney, 1948-71; Louis E. Gelineau, 1972-97; Robert E. Mulvee, 1997-2005.

Pueblo, CO (1941): Arthur N. Tafoya, bishop, 1980.
Former bishops: Joseph C. Willging, 1942-59; Charles A. Buswell, 1959-79.

Raleigh, NC (1924): Michael F. Burbidge, bishop, 2006.
Former bishops: William J. Hafey, 1925-37; Eugene J. McGuinness, 1937-44; Vincent S. Waters, 1945-75.

Rapid City, SD (1902): Blase Cupich, bishop, 1998.
Established at Lead, transferred, 1930.
Former bishops: John Stariha, 1902-09; Joseph F. Busch, 1910-15; John J. Lawler, 1916-48; William T. McCarty, C.SS.R., 1948-69; Harold J. Dimmerling, 1969-87; Charles J. Chaput, O.F.M., Cap., 1988-97.

Reno, NV (1931): Randolph R. Calvo, bishop, 2005.
Established at Reno, 1931; title changed to Reno-Las Vegas, 1976, redesignated Reno, 1995, when Las Vegas was made a separate diocese.
Former bishops (Reno/Reno-Las Vegas): Thomas K. Gorman, 1931-52; Robert J. Dwyer, 1952-66; Joseph Green, 1967-74; Norman F. McFarland, 1976-86; Daniel F. Walsh, 1987-95; Phillip F. Straling, 1995-2005.

Richmond, VA (1820): Francis X. DiLorenzo, 2004.
Former bishops: Patrick Kelly, 1820-22; Ambrose Marechal, S.S., administrator, 1822-28; James Whitfield, administrator, 1828-34; Samuel Eccleston, S.S., administrator, 1834-40; Richard V. Whelan, 1841-50; John McGill, 1850-72; James Gibbons, 1872-77; John J. Keane, 1878-88; Augustine Van de Vyver, 1889-1911; Denis J. O'Connell, 1912-26; Andrew J. Brennan, 1926-45; Peter L. Ireton, 1945-58; John J. Russell, 1958-73; Walter F. Sullivan, 1974-2003.

Rochester, NY (1868): Matthew H. Clark, bishop, 1979.
Former bishops: Bernard J. McQuaid, 1868-1909; Thomas F. Hickey, 1909-28; John F. O'Hern, 1929-33; Edward F. Mooney, 1933-37; James E. Kearney, 1937-66; Fulton J. Sheen, 1966-69; Joseph L. Hogan, 1969-78.

Rockford, IL (1908): Thomas G. Doran, bishop, 1994.
Former bishops: Peter J. Muldoon, 1908-27; Edward

F. Hoban, 1928-42; John J. Boylan, 1943-53; Raymond P. Hillinger, 1953-56; Loras T. Lane, 1956-68; Arthur J. O'Neill, 1968-94.

Rockville Centre, NY (1957): William Francis Murphy, bishop, 2001. John C. Dunne, Paul H. Walsh, Peter Libasci, auxiliaries.
Former bishop: Walter P. Kellenberg, 1957-76; John R. McGann, 1976-2000; James McHugh, 2000.

Sacramento, CA (1886): William K. Weigand, bishop, 1993, installed, 1994; Jaime Soto, coadjutor bishop, 2007.
Former bishops: Patrick Manogue, 1886-95; Thomas Grace, 1896-1921; Patrick J. Keane, 1922-28; Robert J. Armstrong, 1929-57; Joseph T. McGucken, 1957-62; Alden J. Bell, 1962-79; Francis A. Quinn, 1979-93.

Saginaw, MI (1938): Robert J. Carlson, bishop, 2004.
Former bishops: William F. Murphy, 1938-50; Stephen S. Woznicki, 1950-68; Francis F. Reh, 1969-80; Kenneth E. Untener, 1980-2004.

St. Augustine, FL (1870): Victor Benito Galeone, bishop, 2001.
Former bishops: Augustin Verot, S.S., 1870-76; John Moore, 1877-1901; William J. Kenny, 1902-13; Michael J. Curley, 1914-21; Patrick J. Barry, 1922-40; Joseph P. Hurley, 1940-67; Paul F. Tanner, 1968-79; John J. Snyder, 1979-2000.

St. Cloud, MN (1889): John F. Kinney, bishop, 1995.
Former bishops: Otto Zardetti, 1889-94; Martin Marty, O.S.B., 1895-96; James Trobec, 1897-1914; Joseph F. Busch, 1915-53; Peter Bartholome, 1953-68; George H. Speltz, 1968-87; Jerome Hanus, O.S.B.,1987-94.

St. George's in Canton, OH (Byzantine, Romanian) (1982; eparchy, 1987): John Michael Botean, bishop, 1996.
Former bishop: Vasile Louis Puscas, 1983-93.

St. Josaphat in Parma, OH (Byzantine, Ukrainians) (1983): Robert M. Moskal, bishop, 1984.

St. Louis,* MO (1826; archdiocese, 1847): Vacant; Robert J. Hermann, auxiliary.
Former ordinaries: Joseph Rosati, C.M., 1827-43; Peter R. Kenrick, 1843-95, first archbishop; John J. Kain, 1895-1903; Cardinal John Glennon, 1903-46; Cardinal Joseph Ritter, 1946-67; Cardinal John J. Carberry, 1968-79; John L. May, 1980-92; Justin F. Rigali, 1994-2003; Raymond L. Burke, 2003-2008.

St. Maron, Brooklyn, NY (Maronite) (1966; diocese, 1971): Gregory John Mansour, eparch, 2004.
Established at Detroit, transferred to Brooklyn, 1977.
Former eparchs: Francis Zayek, exarch 1966-72, first eparch 1972-97; Hector Y. Doueihi, 1997-2004.

St. Nicholas in Chicago (Byzantine Eparchy of St. Nicholas of the Ukrainians) (1961): Richard Stephen Seminack, 2003.
Former bishops: Jaroslav Gabro, 1961-80; Innocent H. Lotocky, O.S.B.M., 1981-93; Michael Wiwchar, C.SS.R., 1993-2003.

St. Paul and Minneapolis,* MN (1850; archdiocese, 1888): John C. Nienstedt, coadjutor, 2007, archbishop, 2008.
Former ordinaries: Joseph Crétin, 1851-57; Thomas L. Grace, O.P., 1859-84; John Ireland, 1884-1918, first archbishop; Austin Dowling, 1919-30; John G.

Murray, 1931-56; William O. Brady, 1956-61; Leo Binz, 1962-75; John R. Roach, 1975-95; Harry J. Flynn, 1995-2008.

St. Peter the Apostle of San Diego (Chaldean) (2002, eparchy): Sarhad Jammo, first eparch, 2002.

St. Petersburg, FL (1968): Robert N. Lynch, bishop, 1996.

Former bishops: Charles McLaughlin, 1968-78; W. Thomas Larkin, 1979-88; John C. Favalora, 1989-94.

St. Thomas the Apostle of Detroit (Chaldean) (1982; eparchy, 1985): Ibrahim N. Ibrahim, exarch, 1982; first eparch, 1985.

St. Thomas of the Syro-Malabars of Chicago (Syro-Malabars) (2001, eparchy): Jacob Angadiath, first eparch, 2001.

Salina, KS (1887): Paul S. Coakley, bishop, 2004. Established at Concordia, transferred, 1944.

Former bishops: Richard Scannell, 1887-91; John J. Hennessy, administrator, 1891-98; John F. Cunningham, 1898-1919; Francis J. Tief, 1921-38; Frank A. Thill, 1938-57; Frederick W. Freking, 1957-64; Cyril J. Vogel, 1965-79; Daniel W. Kucera, O.S.B., 1980-84; George K. Fitzsimons, 1984-2004.

Salt Lake City, UT (1891): John C. Wester, bishop, 2007.

Former bishops: Lawrence Scanlan, 1891-1915; Joseph S. Glass, C.M., 1915-26; John J. Mitty, 1926-32; James E. Kearney, 1932-37; Duane G. Hunt, 1937-60; J. Lennox Federal, 1960-80; William K. Weigand, 1980-93; George H. Niederauer, 1995-2005.

San Angelo, TX (1961): Michael D. Pfeifer, O.M.I., bishop, 1985.

Former bishops: Thomas J. Drury, 1962-65; Thomas Tschoepe, 1966-69; Stephen A. Leven, 1969-79; Joseph A. Fiorenza, 1979-84.

San Antonio,* TX (1874; archdiocese, 1926): José H. Gomez, archbishop, 2004. Oscar Cantu, auxiliary.

Former ordinaries: Anthony D. Pellicer, 1874-80; John C. Neraz, 1881-94; John A. Forest, 1895-1911; John W. Shaw, 1911-18; Arthur Jerome Drossaerts, 1918-40, first archbishop; Robert E. Lucey, 1941-69; Francis Furey, 1969-79; Patrick F. Flores, 1979-2004.

San Bernardino, CA (1978): Gerald R. Barnes, bishop, 1995. Rutilio J. Del Riego, auxiliaries.

Former bishop: Phillip F. Straling, 1978-95.

San Diego, CA (1936): Robert H. Brom, bishop, 1990. Salvatore Cordileone, auxiliary.

Former bishops: Charles F. Buddy, 1936-66; Francis J. Furey, 1966-69; Leo T. Maher, 1969-90.

San Francisco,* CA (1853): George H. Niederauer, archbishop, 2005. Ignatius Wang, William J. Justice, auxiliaries.

Former ordinaries: Joseph S. Alemany, O.P., 1853-84; Patrick W. Riordan, 1884-1914; Edward J. Hanna, 1915-35; John Mitty, 1935-61; Joseph T. McGucken, 1962-77; John R. Quinn, 1977-95; William J. Levada, 1995-2005.

San Jose, CA (1981): Patrick J. McGrath, bishop, 1999.

Former ordinaries: R. Pierre DuMaine, 1981-98.

Santa Fe*, NM (1850; archdiocese, 1875): Michael J. Sheehan, archbishop, 1993.

Former ordinaries: John B. Lamy, 1850-85; first archbishop; John B. Salpointe, 1885-94; Placide L. Chapelle, 1894-97; Peter Bourgade, 1899-1908; John B. Pitaval, 1909-18; Albert T. Daeger, O.F.M.,

1919-32; Rudolph A. Gerken, 1933-43; Edwin V. Byrne, 1943-63; James P. Davis, 1964-74; Robert F. Sanchez, 1974-93.

Santa Rosa, CA (1962): Daniel Walsh, 2000.

Former bishops: Leo T. Maher, 1962-69; Mark J. Hurley, 1969-86; John T. Steinbock, 1987-91; G. Patrick Ziemann, 1992-99.

Savannah, GA (1850): John Kevin Boland, bishop, 1995.

Former bishops: Francis X. Gartland, 1850-54; John Barry, 1857-59; Augustin Verot, S.S., 1861-70; Ignatius Persico, O.F.M. Cap., 1870-72; William H. Gross, C.SS.R., 1873-85; Thomas A. Becker, 1886-99; Benjamin J. Keiley, 1900-22; Michael Keyes, S.M., 1922-35; Gerald P. O'Hara, 1935-59; Thomas J. McDonough, 1960-67; Gerard L. Frey, 1967-72; Raymond W. Lessard, 1973-95.

Scranton, PA (1868): Joseph F. Martino, bishop, 2003. John M. Dougherty, auxiliary.

Former bishops: William O'Hara, 1868-99; Michael J. Hoban, 1899-1926; Thomas C. O'Reilly, 1928-38; William J. Hafey, 1938-54; Jerome D. Hannan, 1954-65; J. Carroll McCormick, 1966-83; John J. O'Connor, 1983-84; James C. Timlin, 1984-2003.

Seattle,* WA (1850; archdiocese, 1951): Alexander J. Brunett, archbishop, 1997. Joseph J. Tyson, Eusebio Elizondo, M.Sp.S., auxiliaries.

Established as Nesqually, name changed, 1907.

Former ordinaries; Augustin M. Blanchet, 1850-79; Aegidius Junger, 1879-95; Edward J. O'Dea, 1896-1932; Gerald Shaughnessy, S.M., 1933-50; Thomas A. Connolly, first archbishop, 1950-75; Raymond G. Hunthausen, 1975-91; Thomas J. Murphy, 1991-97.

Shreveport, LA (1986): Michael G. Duca, bishop, 2008.

Former bishops: William B. Friend, 1986-2006.

Sioux City, IA (1902): Ralph W. Nickless, bishop, 2005.

Former bishops: Philip J. Garrigan, 1902-19; Edmond Heelan, 1919-48; Joseph M. Mueller, 1948-70; Frank H. Greteman, 1970-83; Lawrence D. Soens, 1983-98; Daniel N. DiNardo, 1998-2004.

Sioux Falls, SD (1889): Paul J. Swain, bishop, 2006.

Former bishops: Martin Marty, O.S.B., 1889-94; Thomas O'Gorman, 1896-1921; Bernard J. Mahoney, 1922-39; William O. Brady, 1939-56; Lambert A. Hoch, 1956-78; Paul V. Dudley, 1978-95; Robert J. Carlson, 1995-2004.

Spokane, WA (1913): William S. Skylstad, bishop, 1990.

Former bishops: Augustine F. Schinner, 1914-25; Charles D. White, 1927-55; Bernard J. Topel, 1955-78; Lawrence H. Welsh, 1978-90.

Springfield, IL (1853): George J. Lucas, 1999.

Established at Quincy, transferred to Alton, 1857; transferred to Springfield, 1923.

Former bishops: Henry D. Juncker, 1857-68; Peter J. Baltes, 1870-86; James Ryan, 1888-1923; James A. Griffin, 1924-48; William A. O'Connor, 1949-75; Joseph A. McNicholas, 1975-83; Daniel L. Ryan, bishop, 1984-99.

Springfield, MA (1870): Timothy A. McDonnell, bishop, 2004.

Former bishops: Patrick T. O'Reilly, 1870-92; Thomas D. Beaven, 1892-1920; Thomas M. O'Leary,

1921-49; Christopher J. Weldon, 1950-77; Joseph F. Maguire, 1977-91; John A. Marshall, 1991-94; Thomas L. Dupre, 1995-2004.

Springfield-Cape Girardeau, MO (1956): James Vann Johnston, Jr., bishop, 2008.

Former bishops: Charles Helmsing, 1956-62; Ignatius J. Strecker, 1962-69; William Baum, 1970-73; Bernard F. Law, 1973-84; John J. Leibrecht, 1984-2008.

Stamford, CT (Byzantine, Ukrainian) (1956): Paul P. Chomnycky, O.S.B.M., eparch, 2006.

Former eparchs: Ambrose Senyshyn, O.S.B.M., 1956-61; Joseph Schmondiuk, 1961-77; Basil Losten, 1977-2006.

Steubenville, OH (1944): Robert Daniel Conlon, 2002.

Former bishops: John K. Mussio, 1945-77; Albert H. Ottenweller, 1977-92; Gilbert I. Sheldon, 1992-2002.

Stockton, CA (1962): Stephen E. Blaire, bishop, 1999.

Former bishops: Hugh A. Donohoe, 1962-69; Merlin J. Guilfoyle, 1969-79; Roger M. Mahony, 1980-85; Donald W. Montrose, 1986-99.

Superior, WI (1905): Peter F. Christensen, bishop, 2007.

Former bishops: Augustine F. Schinner, 1905-13; Joseph M. Koudelka, 1913-21; Joseph G. Pinten, 1922-26; Theodore M. Reverman, 1926-41; William P. O'Connor, 1942-46; Albert G. Meyer, 1946-53; Joseph Annabring, 1954-59; George A. Hammes, 1960-85; Raphael M. Fliss, 1985-2007.

Syracuse, NY (1886): James M. Moynihan, bishop, 1995.

Former bishops: Patrick A. Ludden, 1887-1912; John Grimes, 1912-22; Daniel J. Curley, 1923-32; John A. Duffy, 1933-37; Walter A. Foery, 1937-70; David F. Cunningham, 1970-76; Frank J. Harrison, 1976-87; Joseph T. O'Keefe, 1987-95.

Toledo, OH (1910): Leonard P. Blair, bishop, 2003.

Former bishops: Joseph Schrembs, 1911-21; Samuel A. Stritch, 1921-30; Karl J. Alter, 1931-50; George J. Rehring, 1950-67; John A. Donovan, 1967-80; James R. Hoffman, 1980-2003.

Trenton, NJ (1881): John M. Smith, bishop, 1997.

Former bishops: Michael J. O'Farrell, 1881-94; James A. McFaul, 1894-1917; Thomas J. Walsh, 1918-28; John J. McMahon, 1928-32; Moses E. Kiley, 1934-40; William A. Griffin, 1940-50; George W. Ahr, 1950-79; John C. Reiss, 1980 -97.

Tucson, AZ (1897): Gerald F. Kicanas, bishop, 2003.

Former bishops: Peter Bourgade, 1897-99; Henry Granjon, 1900-22; Daniel J. Gercke, 1923-60; Francis J. Green, 1960-81; Manuel D. Moreno, 1982-2003.

Tulsa, OK (1972): Edward J. Slattery, bishop, 1993.

Former bishops: Bernard J. Ganter, 1973-77; Eusebius J. Beltran, 1978-92.

Tyler, TX (1986): Alvaro Corrada del Rio, S.J., 2000.

Former bishop: Charles E. Herzig, 1987-91; Edmond Carmody, 1992-2000.

Van Nuys, CA (Byzantine, Ruthenian) (1981): Gerald N. Dino, eparch, 2007.

Former bishop: Thomas V. Dolinay, 1982-90; George M. Kuzma, 1991-2000; William C. Skurla, 2002-2007.

Venice, FL (1984): Frank J. Dewane, bishop, 2007.

Former bishops: John J. Nevins, 1984-2007.

Victoria, TX (1982): David E. Fellhauer, bishop, 1990.

Former bishop: Charles V. Grahmann, 1982-89.

Washington,* DC (1939): Donald W. Wuerl, archbishop. Francisco González Valer, S.F., Martin D. Holley, auxiliaries.

Former ordinaries: Michael J. Curley, 1939-47; Cardinal Patrick O'Boyle, 1948-73; Cardinal William Baum, 1973-80; Cardinal James A. Hickey, 1980-2000; Cardinal Theodore E. McCarrick, 2000-2006

Wheeling-Charleston, WV (1850): Michael J. Bransfield, bishop, 2004.

Established as Wheeling, name changed, 1974.

Former bishops: Richard V. Whelan, 1850-74; John J. Kain, 1875-93; Patrick J. Donahue, 1894-1922; John J. Swint, 1922-62; Joseph H. Hodges, 1962-85; Francis B. Schulte, 1985-88; Bernard W. Schmitt, 1989-2004.

Wichita, KS (1887): Michael Owen Jackels, bishop, 2005.

Former bishops: John J. Hennessy, 1888-1920; Augustus J. Schwertner, 1921-39; Christian H. Winkelmann, 1940-46; Mark K. Carroll, 1947-67; David M. Maloney, 1967-82; Eugene J. Gerber, 1982-2001; Thomas J. Olmsted, 2001-2003.

Wilmington, DE (1868): William Francis Malooly, bishop, 2008.

Former bishops: Thomas A. Becker, 1868-86; Alfred A. Curtis, 1886-96; John J. Monaghan, 1897-1925; Edmond Fitzmaurice, 1925-60; Michael Hyle, 1960-67; Thomas J. Mardaga, 1968-84; Robert E. Mulvee, 1985-95; Michael A. Saltarelli, 1995-2008.

Winona, MN (1889): Bernard J. Harrington, 1998.

Former bishops: Joseph B. Cotter, 1889-1909; Patrick R. Heffron, 1910-27; Francis M. Kelly, 1928-49; Edward A. Fitzgerald, 1949-69; Loras J. Watters, 1969-86; John G. Vlazny, 1987-97.

Worcester, MA (1950): Robert McManus, bishop, 2004.

Former bishops: John J. Wright, 1950-59; Bernard J. Flanagan, 1959-83; Timothy J. Harrington, 1983-94; Daniel P. Reilly, 1994-2004.

Yakima, WA (1951): Carlos A. Sevilla, S.J., bishop, 1996.

Former bishops: Joseph P. Dougherty, 1951-69; Cornelius M. Power, 1969-74; Nicolas E. Walsh, 1974-76; William S. Skylstad, 1977-90; Francis E. George, O.M.I., 1990-96.

Youngstown, OH (1943): George V. Murry, S.J., bishop, 2007

Former bishops: James A. McFadden, 1943-52; Emmet M. Walsh, 1952-68; James W. Malone, 1968-95; Thomas J. Tobin, 1995-2005.

Apostolic Eparchy for Armenian Catholics in the United States and Canada, New York, NY (1981, eparchy, 2005): Manuel Batakian, exarch, 2000; first eparch, 2005.

Former exarchs: Nerses Mikael Setian, 1981-93; Hovhannes Tertzakian, O.M. Ven., 1995-2000.

Archdiocese for the Military Services, U.S.A., Washington, DC (1957; restructured, 1985): Timothy M. Broglio, archbishop, 2007. Richard Brendan Higgins, Joseph Walter Estabrook, auxiliaries.

Military vicar appointed, 1917; canonically established, 1957, as U.S. Military Vicariate under jurisdiction of New York archbishop; name changed, restructured as independent jurisdiction, 1985.

Former military vicars: Cardinal Patrick Hayes, 1917-38; Cardinal Francis Spellman, 1939-67; Cardinal Terence J. Cooke, 1968-83; Cardinal John J.

O'Connor, apostolic administrator, 1984-85.

Former military ordinaries: Archbishop Joseph T. Ryan, 1985-91; Joseph T. Dimino, 1991-97; Edwin F. O'Brien, 1997-2007.

(Note: For coverage of Missionary Bishops, see under Missionary Activity of the Church in the U.S.)

CHANCERY OFFICES OF U.S. ARCHDIOCESES AND DIOCESES

A chancery office, under this or another title, is the central administrative office of an archdiocese or diocese. (Archdioceses are indicated by asterisk.)As of

Alexandria, LA: Chancery, 4400 Coliseum Blvd., 71303; (318) 445-2401; www.diocesealex.org.

Allentown, PA: Chancery, P.O. Box F, 18105-1538; (610) 437-0755; www.allentowndiocese.org.

Altoona-Johnstown, PA: Chancery, 126 Logan Blvd., Hollidaysburg, 16648; (814) 695-5579; www.ajdiocese.org.

Amarillo, TX: Pastoral Center, 1800 N. Spring St., P.O. Box 5644, 79117-5644; (806) 383-2243; www.amarillodiocese.org.

Anchorage,* AK: Chancery, 225 Cordova St., 99501; (907) 297-7700; www.archdioceseofanchorage.org

Arlington, VA: Chancery, Suite 914, 200 N. Glebe Rd., 22203; (703) 841-2500; www.arlingtondiocese.org.

Atlanta,* GA: Catholic Center, 680 W. Peachtree St. N.W., 30308; (404) 888-7800; www.archatl.com.

Austin, TX: Chancery, 1600 N. Congress Ave., P.O. Box 13327, 78711; (512) 476-4888; www.austindiocese.org.

Baker, OR: Diocesan Pastoral Office, P.O. Box 5999, Bend, 97708; (541) 388-4004; www.dioceseofbaker.org.

Baltimore,* MD: Chancery, 320 Cathedral St., 21201; (410) 547-5446; www.archbalt.org.

Baton Rouge, LA: Catholic Life Center, P.O. Box 2028. 70821-2028; (225) 387-0561; www.diobr.org.

Beaumont, TX: Diocesan Pastoral Office, 703 Archie St., P.O. Box 3948, 77701; (409) 924-4300; www.dioceseofbmt.org.

Belleville, IL: Chancery, 222 S. Third St. 62220-1985, (618) 235-6601; www.diobelle.org.

Biloxi, MS: Administration Offices, 1790 Popps Ferry Road P.O. Box 6489, 39532; (228) 702-2100; www.biloxidiocese.org.

Birmingham, AL: Catholic Life Center, 2121 3rd Avenue North, 35202-2047; (205) 838-8318; www.bhmdiocese.org.

Bismarck, ND: Chancery, 420 Raymond St., Box 1575, 58502-1575; (701) 223-1347; www.bismarckdiocese.com.

Boise, ID: Chancery, 303 Federal Way; (208) 342-1311; www.catholicidaho.org.

Boston,* MA: Chancery, 66 Brooks Drive, Braintree 02184; (617) 254-0100; www.rcab.org.

Bridgeport, CT: Catholic Center, 238 Jewett Ave., 06606; (203) 416-1340; www.bridgeportdiocese.com.

Brooklyn, NY: Chancery, 75 Greene Ave., P.O. Box C, 11202; (718) 399-5900; www.dioceseofbrooklyn.org.

Brownsville, TX: Catholic Pastoral Center, P.O. Box 2279, 1910 University Blvd., 78520; (956) 542-2501; www.cdob.org.

Aug. 15, 2008.

Albany, NY: Pastoral Center, 40 N. Main Ave., 12203. (518) 453-6600; www.rcda.org.

Buffalo, NY: Chancery, 795 Main St., 14203; (716) 847-5500; www.buffalodiocese.org

Burlington, VT: Chancery, P.O. Box 489,05402; (802) 658-6110; www.vermontcatholic.org.

Camden, NJ: Camden Diocesan Center, 631 Market St., P.O. Box 708, 08102; (609) 756-7900; www.camdendiocese.org.

Charleston, SC: Chancery, 119 Broad St., P.O. Box 818, 29402; (843) 853-2130; www.catholic-doc.org.

Charlotte, NC: Pastoral Center, 1123 South Church Street, 28203; (704) 370-6299; www.charlottediocese.org.

Cheyenne, WY: Chancery, 2121 Capitol Avenue, 82001; (866) 790-0014 or (307) 638-1530; www.dioceseofcheyenne.org.

Chicago,* IL: Pastoral Center, P.O. Box 1979, 60690; (312) 751-8200; www.archdiocese-chgo.org

Cincinnati,* OH: Chancery, 100 E. 8th St. 45202; (513) 421-3131; www.catholiccincinnati.org.

Cleveland, OH: Chancery, 1027 Superior Ave., 44114; (216) 696-6525; www.dioceseofcleveland.org

Colorado Springs, CO: Pastoral Center, 228 N. Cascade, 80903-1498; (719) 636-2345; www.diocs.org.

Columbus, OH: Chancery, 197 E. Gay St., 43215; (614) 228-2457; www.colsdioc.org.

Corpus Christi, TX: Chancery, P.O. Box 2620, 78403-2620; (361) 882-6191; www.diocesecc.org.

Covington, KY: Catholic Center, P.O. Box 15550, 41015; (859) 392-1500; www.covingtondiocese.org.

Crookston, MN: Chancery, 1200 Memorial Dr., 56716; (218) 281-4533; www.crookston.org.

Dallas, TX: Chancery, 3725 Blackburn, 75219; (214) 528-2240; www.cathdal.org.

Davenport, IA: Chancery, 2706 N. Gaines St., 52804-1998; (563) 324-1911; www.davenportdiocese.org.

Denver,* CO: Catholic Pastoral Center, 1300 South Steele St., 80210; (303) 722-4687; www.archden.org.

Des Moines, IA: Chancery, 601 Grand Ave., 50309; (515) 243-7653; www.dmdiocese.org.

Detroit,* MI: Chancery, 305 Michigan Ave., 48226; (313) 237-5800; www.aodonline.org.

Dodge City, KS: Chancery, P.O. Box 137, 67801-0137; (620) 227-1500; www.dcdiocese.org.

Dubuque,* IA: Chancery, 1229 Loretta Ave., 52003; (563) 556-2580; www.arch.pvt.k12.ia.us/archhome.html.

Duluth, MN: Pastoral Center, 2830 E. 4th St., 55812; (218) 724-9111; www.dioceseduluth.org.

El Paso, TX: Chancery, 499 St. Matthews St., 79907; (915) 872-8400; www.elpasodiocese.org.

Erie, PA: St. Mark Catholic Center, P.O. Box 10397, 16514-0397; (814) 824-1135; www.eriercd.org.

Evansville, IN: Chancery, P.O. Box 4169, 47724-0169; (812) 424-5536; www.evansville-diocese.org.

Fairbanks, AK: Chancery, 1316 Peger Rd., 99709; (907) 374-9500; ww.cbna.info/index.shtml.

Fall River, MA: Chancery, Box 2577, 02722; (508) 675-1311; www.fallriverdiocese.org.

Fargo, ND: Chancery, 5201 Bishops Blvd., Suite A, 58104-7605; (701) 356-7900; www.fargodiocese.org.

Fort Wayne-South Bend, IN: Chancery, 1103 S. Calhoun Street, 46801; (260) 422-4611; South Bend Chancery, 114 W. Wayne Street, South Bend, IN 46601; (574) 234-0687; www.diocesefwsb.org.

Fort Worth, TX: Catholic Center, 800 W. Loop 820 South, 76108; (817) 560-3300; www.fwdioc.org.

Fresno, CA: Chancery, 1550 N. Fresno St., 93703-3788; (559) 488-7400; www.dioceseoffresno.org.

Gallup, NM: Chancery, 711 S. Puerco Dr., P.O. Box 1338, 87301; (505) 863-4406; www.dioceseofgallup.org.

Galveston-Houston, TX: Chancery, 1700 San Jacinto, 77001; (713) 659-5461; www.diogh.org.

Gary, IN: Chancery, 9292 Broadway, Merrillville, 46410; (219) 769-9292; www.dcgary.org.

Gaylord, MI: Diocesan Pastoral Center, 611 North St., 49735; (989) 732-5147; www.dioceseofgaylord.org.

Grand Island, NE: Chancery, P.O. Box 1531, 2708 Old Fair Road, 68802; (308) 382.6565; www.gidiocese.org.

Grand Rapids, MI: Chancery, 360 Division Ave. S., 49503-4539; (616) 243-0491; www.dioceseofgrandrapids.org.

Great Falls-Billings, MT: Chancery, P.O. Box 1399, Great Falls, 59403; (406) 727-6683; www.dioceseofgfb.org.

Green Bay, WI: Chancery, P.O. Box 23825, 54305-3825; (920) 437-7531; www.gbdioc.org.

Greensburg, PA: Chancery, 723 E. Pittsburgh St., 15601; (724) 837-0901; www.dioceseofgreensburg.org.

Harrisburg, PA: Chancery, 4800 Union Deposit Rd., 17105; (717) 657-4804; www.hbgdiocese.org.

Hartford,* CT: Chancery, 134 Farmington Ave., 06105; (860) 541-6491; www.archdioceseofhartford.org.

Helena, MT: Chancery, P.O. Box 1729, 59624-1729; (406) 442-5820; www.diocesehelena.org.

Honolulu, HI: Chancery, 1184 Bishop St., 96813; (808) 585-3300; www.catholichawaii.com.

Houma-Thibodaux, LA: Chancery, P.O. Box 505, Schriever, 70395; (504) 850-3132; www.htdiocese.org.

Indianapolis,* IN: Archbishop Edward T. O'Meara Catholic Center, 1400 N. Meridian St., 46202; (317) 236-1405; www.archindy.org.

Jackson, MS: Chancery, 237 E. Amite St., P.O. Box 2248, 39225-2248; (601) 969-1880; www.jacksondiocese.org.

Jefferson City, MO: Chancery, 2207 West Main Street, P.O. Box 104900, 65110-4900; (573) 635-9127; www.diojeffcity.org.

Joliet, IL: Chancery, 425 Summit St., 60435; (815) 722-6606; www.dioceseofjoliet.org

Juneau, AK: Chancery, 414 6th St., No. 300, 99801; (907) 586-2227; www.dioceseofjuneau.org.

Kalamazoo, MI: Chancery, 215 N. Westnedge Ave.,

49007-3760; (269) 349-8714; www.dioceseofkalamazoo.org.

Kansas City,* KS: Chancery, 12615 Parallel Pkwy., 66109; (913) 721-1570; www.archkck.org.

Kansas City-St. Joseph, MO: Chancery, P.O. Box 419037, Kansas City, 64141-6037; (816) 756-1850; www.diocese-kcsj.org.

Knoxville, TN: Chancery, 805 Northshore Dr., SW, 379319; (865) 584-3307; www.dioceseofknoxville.org.

La Crosse, WI: Chancery, 3710 East Ave. S., P.O. Box 4004, 54602; (608) 788-7700; www.dioceseoflacrosse.com

Lafayette, IN: Bishop's Office, P.O. Box 260, 47902-0260; (765) 742-0275; www.dioceseoflafayette.org.

Lafayette, LA: Chancery, P.O. Box 3387, 70502; (337) 261-5614; www.dol-louisiana.org.

Lake Charles, LA: Chancery, P.O. Box 3223, 70602; (337) 439-7400; www.lcdiocese.org.

Lansing, MI: Chancery, 300 W. Ottawa St., 48933-1577; (517) 342-2440; www.dioceseoflansing.org.

Laredo, Tx.: Diocesan Pastoral Center, P.O. Box 2247, 78040; (956) 727-2140; www.dioceseoflaredo.org.

Las Cruces, NM: Chancery, 1280 Med Park Dr., 88005; (575) 523-7577; www.dioceseoflascruces.org.

Las Vegas, NV: Chancery, P.O. Box 18316, 89114; (702) 735-3500; www.lasvegas-diocese.org.

Lexington, KY: Catholic Center, 1310 W. Main St., 40508; (859) 253-1993; www.cdlex.org.

Lincoln, NE: Chancery, P.O. Box 80328, 68501-0328; (402) 488-0921; www.dioceseoflincoln.org.

Little Rock, AR: Chancery, 2500 N. Tyler St., 72207; (501) 664-0340; www.dolr.org.

Los Angeles,* CA: Archdiocesan Catholic Center, 3424 Wilshire Blvd., 90010-2241; (213) 637-7000; www.archdiocese.la.

Louisville,* KY: Chancery, P.O. Box 1073, 40201-1073; (502) 585-3291; www.archlou.org.

Lubbock, TX: Catholic Center, P.O. Box 98700, 79499; (806) 792-3943; www.catholiclubbock.org.

Madison, WI: Bishop O'Connor Catholic Pastoral Center, 702 S. High Point Rd., 53719; (608) 821-3130; www.madisondiocese.org.

Manchester, NH: Chancery, 153 Ash St., P.O. Box 310, 03105-0310; (603) 669-3100; www.catholicchurchnh.org.

Marquette, MI: Chancery, 117 W. Washington Street, Suite 3A, P.O. Box 1000, 49855; (906) 225-1141; www.dioceseofmarquette.org.

Memphis, TN: Catholic Center, 5825 Shelby Oaks Dr., 38134; (901) 373-1200; www.cdom.org.

Metuchen, NJ: Chancery, 146 Metlars Ln, Piscataway, NJ 08854-4303; P.O. Box 191, 08840-0191; (732) 562-1990; www.diometuchen.org.

Miami,* FL: Chancery, 9401 Biscayne Blvd., Miami Shores, 33138; (305) 757-6241; www.miamiarch.org.

Milwaukee,* WI: Archbishop Cousins Catholic Center, P.O. Box 070912, 53207-0912; (414) 769-3300; www.archmil.org.

Mobile,* AL: Chancery, 400 Government St., P.O. Box 1966, 36633; (251) 434-1585; www.mobilearchdiocese.org.

Monterey, CA: Chancery, P.O. Box 2048, 93942;

(831) 373-4345; www.dioceseofmonterey.org.

Nashville, TN: Chancery, 2400 21st Ave. S., 37212-5387; (615) 383-6393; www.dioceseofnashville.com.

Newark,* NJ: Chancery, 171 Clifton Ave., 07104; (973) 497-4000; www.rcan.org.

New Orleans,* LA: Chancery, 7887 Walmsley Ave., 70125; (504) 861-9521; www.arch-no.org.

Newton, MA (Melkite): Chancery, 3 VFW Pkwy., Roslindale, 02131; (617) 323-9922; www.melkite.org.

New Ulm, MN: Catholic Pastoral Center, 1400 Sixth St. N., 56073-2099; (507) 359-2966; www.dnu.org.

New York,* NY: Chancery, 1011 First Ave., 10022-4134; (212) 371-1000; www.ny-archdiocese.org.

Norwich, CT: Chancery, 201 Broadway, 06360-4328; (860) 887-9294; www.norwichdiocese.org.

Oakland, CA: Chancery, 2121 Harrison St., Suite 100, 94612; (510) 893-4711; www.oakdiocese.org.

Ogdensburg, NY: Chancery, 622 Washington St., P.O. Box 369, 13669; (315) 393-2920; www.dioogdensburg.org.

Oklahoma City,* OK: Pastoral Center, 7501 NW Expressway, 73132; (405) 721-5651; www.catharchdioceseokc.org.

Omaha,* NE: Chancery, 100 N. 62nd St., 68132; (402) 558-3100; www.archomaha.com.

Orange, CA: Chancery, 2811 E. Villa Real Dr., P.O. Box 14195, 92867; (714) 282-3000; www.rcbo.org.

Orlando, FL: Chancery, P.O. Box 1800, 32802-1800; (407) 246-4800; www.orlandodiocese.org.

Our Lady of Deliverance of Newark, for Syrian rite Catholics of the U.S. and Canada: P.O. Box 8366, Union City, NJ, 07087-8262; (201) 583-1067; www.syriac-catholic.org.

Our Lady of Lebanon of Los Angeles, CA (Maronite): 1021 South Tenth St., St. Louis, MO 63104; (314) 231-1021; www.usamaronite.org.

Owensboro, KY: Catholic Pastoral Center, 600 Locust St., 42301-2130; (270) 683-1545; www.owensborodio.org.

Palm Beach, FL: Pastoral Center, 9995 N. Military Trail, Palm Beach Gardens, 33410; (561) 775-9500; www.diocesepb.org.

Parma, OH (Byzantine): Chancery, 1900 Carlton Rd., 44134-3129; (216) 741-8773; www.parma.org.

Passaic, NJ (Byzantine): Chancery, 445 Lackawanna Ave., W. Paterson, 07424; (973) 890-7777; www.eparchyofpassaic.com.

Paterson, NJ: Diocesan Pastoral Center, 777 Valley Rd., Clifton, 07013; (973) 777-8818; www.patersondiocese.org.

Pensacola-Tallahassee, FL: Pastoral Center, 11 N. B. St., Pensacola, 32501; (850) 435-3500; www.ptdiocese.org.

Peoria, IL: Chancery, 607 N.E. Madison Ave., 61603; (309) 671-1550; www.cdop.org.

Philadelphia,* PA: Chancery, 222 N. 17th St., 19103; (215) 587-3600; www.archphila.org.

Philadelphia,* PA (Byzantine): Chancery, 827 N. Franklin St., 19123-2097; (215) 627-0143; www.ukrarcheparchy.us.

Phoenix, AZ: Chancery, 400 E. Monroe St., 85004-2376; (602) 354-2000; www.diocesephoenix.org.

Pittsburgh,* PA (Byzantine): Chancery, 66 Riverview Ave., 15214; (412) 231-4000; www.archeparchy.org.

Pittsburgh, PA: Pastoral Center, 111 Blvd. of the

Allies, 15222; (412) 456-3000; www.diopitt.org.

Portland, ME: Chancery, 510 Ocean Ave., P.O. Box 11559, 04104; (207) 773-6471; www.portlanddiocese.net.

Portland, OR*: Pastoral Center, 2838 E. Burnside St., 97214; (503) 234-5334; www.archdpdx.org.

Providence, RI: Chancery, One Cathedral Sq., 02903; (401) 278-4500; www.dioceseofprovidence.org.

Pueblo, CO: Catholic Pastoral Center, 1001 N. Grand Ave., 81003; (719) 544-9861; www.dioceseofpueblo.com.

Raleigh, NC: Catholic Center, 715 Nazareth St., 27606; (919) 821-9700; www.dioceseofraleigh.org.

Rapid City, SD: Chancery, 606 Cathedral Dr., P.O. Box 678, 57709; (605) 343-3541; www.rapidcitydiocese.org.

Reno, NV: Pastoral Center, 290 Arlington Avenue, Ste 200, 89501; (775) 329-9274; www.catholicreno.org.

Richmond, VA: Pastoral Center, 7800 Carousel Lane, 23294-4201; (804)359-5661; www.richmonddiocese.org.

Rochester, NY: The Pastoral Center, 1150 Buffalo Rd., 14624; (585) 328-3210; www.dor.org.

Rockford, IL: Chancery, 1245 N. Court St., P.O. Box 7044, 61125; (815) 399-4300; www.rockforddiocese.org.

Rockville Centre, NY: Chancery, P.O. Box 9023, 11571; (516) 678-5800; www.drvc.org.

Sacramento, CA: Pastoral Center, 2110 Broadway, 95818; (916) 733-0100; www.diocese-sacramento.org.

Saginaw, MI: Chancery, 5800 Weiss St., 48603-2799; (517) 799-7910; www.saginaw.org.

St. Augustine, FL: Catholic Center, 11625 Old St. Augustine Rd., Jacksonville, 32258; (904) 262-3200; staugustine.ml.org/diocese.

St. Cloud, MN: Chancery, P.O. Box 1248, 56302; (320) 251-2340; www.stcdio.org.

St. George's in Canton, OH (Byzantine, Romanian): Chancery, P.O. Box 7189, 44705; (330) 493-9355; www.RomanianCatholic.org.

St. Josaphat in Parma, OH (Byzantine): Chancery, P.O. Box 347180, 44134-7180; (440) 888-1522; www.stjosaphateparchy.org.

St. Louis,* MO: Catholic Center, 4445 Lindell Blvd., 63108-2497; (314) 633-2222; www.archstl.org.

St. Maron of Brooklyn (Maronite): Pastoral Center, 109 Remsen St., 11201; (718) 237-9913; www.stmaron.org.

St. Nicholas in Chicago (Byzantine): Chancery, 2245 W. Rice St., 60622; (773) 276-5080; www.stnicholaseparchy.org.

St. Paul and Minneapolis,* MN: Chancery, 226 Summit Ave., St. Paul, 55102; (651) 291-4400; www.archspm.org.

St. Peter the Apostle of San Diego (Chaldean): Chancery, 1627 Jamacha Way, El Cajon, CA 92019; (619) 590-9028; www.kaldu.org.

St. Petersburg, FL: Chancery, P.O. Box 40200, 33743-0200; (727) 344-1611; www.dioceseofstpete.org.

St. Thomas of Chicago (Syro-Malabar): Diocesan Office, 717 N. Eastland, Elmhurst, IL 60126; (630) 530-8399.

St. Thomas the Apostle of Detroit (Chaldean

Catholic Diocese – USA): Chancery, 25603 Berg Rd., Southfield, MI 48034; (248) 351-0440.
Salina, KS: Chancery, 103 N. 9th St., 67401; (785) 827-8746; www.salinadiocese.org
Salt Lake City, UT: Pastoral Center, 27 C St., 84103; (801) 328-8641; www.utahcatholicdiocese.org.
San Angelo, TX: Chancery, P.O. Box 1829, 76902-1829; (915) 651-7500; www.san-angelo-diocese.org.
San Antonio,* TX: Chancery, 2718 W. Woodlawn, 78228-0410; (210) 734-2620; www.archdiosa.org.
San Bernardino, CA: Chancery, 1201 E. Highland Ave., 92404; (909) 475-5300; www.sbdiocese.org.
San Diego, CA: Pastoral Center, P.O. Box 85728, 92186-5728; (858) 490-8200; www.diocese-sdiego.org.
San Francisco,* CA: Chancery, One Peter Yorke Way, 94109; (415) 614-5500; www.sfarchdiocese.org
San Jose, CA: Chancery, 900 Lafayette St., Suite 301, Santa Clara, 95050-4966; (408) 983-0100; www.dsj.org.
Santa Fe,* NM: Catholic Center, 4000 St. Joseph's Pl. N.W., Albuquerque, 87120; (505) 831-8100; www.archdiocesesantafe.org.
Santa Rosa, CA: Chancery, P.O. Box 1297, 95402; (707) 545-7610; www.santarosacatholic.org.
Savannah, GA: Pastoral Center, 601 E. Liberty St., 31401-5196; (912) 201-4100; www.gamma.diosav.org.
Scranton, PA: Chancery, 300 Wyoming Ave., 18503; (570) 207-2238; www.dioceseofscranton.org.
Seattle,* WA: Chancery, 710 9th Ave., 98104; (206) 382-4560; www.seattlearch.org.
Shreveport, LA: Catholic Center, 3500 Fairfield Ave. 71104; (318) 868-4441; www.dioshpt.org.
Sioux City, IA: Chancery, 1821 Jackson St., P.O. Box 3379, 51102; (712) 255-7933; www.scdiocese.org.
Sioux Falls, SD: Pastoral Center, 523 N. Duluth Ave., 57104; (605) 334-9861; Diocese-of-Sioux-Falls.org.
Spokane, WA: Pastoral Center, Catholic Diocese of Spokane, P.O. Box 1453, 99210; (509) 358-7300; www.dioceseofspokane.org.
Springfield, IL: Pastoral Center, 1615 West Washington, P.O. Box 3187, 62708-3187; (217) 698-8500; www.dio.org.
Springfield, MA: Chancery, P.O. Box 1730, 01101; (413) 452-0800; www.diospringfield.org.
Springfield-Cape Girardeau, MO: Catholic Center, 601 S. Jefferson Ave., Springfield, 65806; (417) 866-0841; home.catholicweb.com/diocspfd-cape/index.cfm.
Stamford, CT (Byzantine): Chancery, 14 Peveril

Rd., 06902-3019; (203) 324-7698; www.stamford-dio.org.
Steubenville, OH: Chancery, P.O. Box 969, 43952; (740) 282-3631; www.diosteub.org.
Stockton, CA: Chancery, 1105 N. Lincoln St., 95203; (209) 466-0636; www.stocktondiocese.org.
Superior, WI: Chancery, 1201 Hughitt Ave., Box 969, 54880; (715) 392-2937; www.catholicdos.org.
Syracuse, NY: Chancery, P.O. Box 511, 13201; (315) 422-7203; wwwsyrdio.org.
Toledo, OH: Chancery, 1933 Spielbusch Ave., 43697-0985; (419) 244-6711; www.toledodiocese.org.
Trenton, NJ: Chancery, 701 Lawrenceville Rd., P.O. Box 5147, 08638; (609) 406-7400; www.diocese-oftrenton.org.
Tucson, AZ: Bishop Moreno Pastoral Center, 111 S. Church Ave., 85702; (520) 792-3410; www.diocese-tuscon.org.
Tulsa, OK: Chancery, P.O. Box 690240, 74169; (918) 294-1904; www.dioceseoftulsa.org.
Tyler, TX: Chancery, 1015 E.S.E. Loop 323, 75701-9663; (903) 534-1077; www.dioceseoftyler.org.
Van Nuys, CA (Byzantine): Chancery, 8105 N. 16th St., Phoenix, AZ 85020; (602) 861-9778; www.eparchy-of-van-nuys.org.
Venice, FL: Catholic Center, P.O. Box 2006, 34284; (941) 484-9543; www.dioceseofvenice.org.
Victoria, TX: Chancery, P.O. Box 4070, 77903; (361) 573-0828; www.victoriadiocese.org.
Washington,* DC: Archdiocesan Pastoral Center, P.O. Box 29260, 20017; (301) 853-4500; www.adw.org.
Wheeling-Charleston, WV: Chancery, 1300 Byron St., P.O. Box 230, Wheeling, 26003; (304) 233-0880; www.dwc.org.
Wichita, KS: Chancery, 424 N. Broadway, 67202; (316) 269-3900; www.cdowk.org.
Wilmington, DE: Chancery, P.O. Box 2030, 19899-2030; (302) 573-3100; www.cdow.org.
Winona, MN: Chancery, P.O. Box 588, 55987; (507) 454-4643; www.dow.org.
Worcester, MA: Chancery, 49 Elm St., 01609-2597; (508) 791-7171; www.worcesterdiocese.org.
Yakima, WA: Chancery, 5301-A Tieton Dr., 98908; (509) 965-7119; www.yakimadiocese.org.
Youngstown, OH: Chancery, 144 W. Wood St., 44503; (330) 744-8451; www.doy.org.
Military Archdiocese: P.O. Box 4469, Washington, DC 20017-0469; 1025 Michigan Ave., Washington, D.C., 20017; (202) 719-3600; www.milarch.org.
Armenian Apostolic Exarchate for the United States and Canada: 110 E. 12th St., New York, NY 10003; (212) 477-2030.

CATHEDRALS, BASILICAS, AND SHRINES IN THE U.S.

CATHEDRALS IN THE UNITED STATES

A cathedral is the principal church in a diocese, the one in which the bishop has his seat (cathedra). He is the actual pastor, although many functions of the church, which usually serves a parish, are the responsibility of a priest serving as the rector. Because of the dignity of a cathedral, the dates of its dedication and its patronal feast are observed throughout a diocese. The pope's cathedral, the Basilica of St. John Lateran, is the highest-ranking church in the world.

(*Archdioceses are indicated by asterisk.*)

Albany, NY: Immaculate Conception.
Alexandria, LA: St. Francis Xavier.
Allentown, PA: St. Catherine of Siena.
Altoona-Johnstown, PA: Blessed Sacrament (Altoona); St. John Gualbert (Johnstown).
Amarillo, TX: St. Laurence.
Anchorage,* AK: Holy Family.
Arlington, VA: St. Thomas More.
Atlanta,* GA: Christ the King.
Austin, TX: St. Mary (Immaculate Conception).
Baker, OR: St. Francis de Sales.
Baltimore,* MD: Mary Our Queen; Basilica of the National Shrine of the Assumption of the Blessed Virgin Mary (Co-Cathedral).
Baton Rouge, LA: St. Joseph.
Beaumont, TX: St. Anthony (of Padua).
Belleville, IL: St. Peter.
Biloxi, MS: Nativity of the Blessed Virgin Mary.
Birmingham, AL: St. Paul.
Bismarck, ND: Holy Spirit.
Boise, ID: St. John the Evangelist.
Boston,* MA: Holy Cross.
Bridgeport, CT: St. Augustine.
Brooklyn, NY: St. James (Minor Basilica).
Brownsville, TX: Immaculate Conception.
Buffalo, NY: St. Joseph.
Burlington, VT: Immaculate Conception; St. Joseph (Co-Cathedral).
Camden, NJ: Immaculate Conception.
Charleston, SC: St. John the Baptist.
Charlotte, NC: St. Patrick.
Cheyenne, WY: St. Mary.
Chicago,* IL: Holy Name (of Jesus).
Cincinnati,* OH: St. Peter in Chains.
Cleveland, OH: St. John the Evangelist.
Colorado Springs, CO: St. Mary.
Columbus, OH: St. Joseph.
Corpus Christi, TX: Corpus Christi.
Covington, KY: Basilica of the Assumption.
Crookston, MN: Immaculate Conception.
Dallas, TX: Cathedral-Santuario de Guadalupe.
Davenport, IA: Sacred Heart.
Denver,* CO: Immaculate Conception (Minor Basilica).
Des Moines, IA: St. Ambrose.
Detroit,* MI: Most Blessed Sacrament.
Dodge City, KS: Our Lady of Guadalupe.
Dubuque,* IA: St. Raphael.
Duluth, MN: Our Lady of the Rosary.
El Paso, TX: St. Patrick.
Erie, PA: St. Peter.
Evansville, IN: Most Holy Trinity (Pro-Cathedral).

Fairbanks, AK: Sacred Heart.
Fall River, MA: St. Mary of the Assumption.
Fargo, N.D.: St. Mary.
Fort Wayne-S. Bend, IN: Immaculate Conception (Fort Wayne); St. Matthew (South Bend).
Fort Worth, TX: St. Patrick.
Fresno, CA: St. John (the Baptist).
Gallup, NM: Sacred Heart.
Galveston-Houston, TX: St. Mary (Minor Basilica, Galveston); Sacred Heart Co-Cathedral (Houston).
Gary, IN: Holy Angels.
Gaylord, MI: St. Mary, Our Lady of Mt. Carmel.
Grand Island, NE: Nativity of Blessed Virgin Mary.
Grand Rapids, MI: St. Andrew.
Great Falls-Billings, MT: St. Ann (Great Falls); St. Patrick Co-Cathedral (Billings).
Green Bay, WI: St. Francis Xavier.
Greensburg, PA: Blessed Sacrament.
Harrisburg, PA: St. Patrick.
Hartford,* CT: St. Joseph.
Helena, MT: St. Helena.
Honolulu, HI: Our Lady of Peace; St. Theresa of the Child Jesus (Co-Cathedral).
Houma-Thibodaux, LA: St. Francis de Sales (Houma); St. Joseph Co-Cathedral (Thibodaux).
Indianapolis,* IN: Sts. Peter and Paul.
Jackson, MS: St. Peter.
Jefferson City, MO: St. Joseph.
Joliet, IL: St. Raymond Nonnatus.
Juneau, AK: Nativity of the Blessed Virgin Mary.
Kalamazoo, MI: St. Augustine.
Kansas City,* KS: St. Peter the Apostle.
Kansas City-St. Joseph, MO: Immaculate Conception (Kansas City); St. Joseph Co-Cathedral (St. Joseph).
Knoxville, TN: Sacred Heart of Jesus.
La Crosse, WI: St. Joseph the Workman.
Lafayette, IN: St. Mary.
Lafayette, LA: St. John the Evangelist.
Lake Charles, LA: Immaculate Conception.
Lansing, MI: St. Mary.
Laredo, TX: San Augustin.
Las Cruces, NM: Immaculate Heart of Mary.
Las Vegas, NV: Guardian Angel.
Lexington, KY: Christ the King.
Lincoln, NE: Cathedral of the Risen Christ.
Little Rock, AR: St. Andrew.
Los Angeles,* CA: Cathedral of Our Lady of the Angels of Los Angeles (opened in 2002).
Louisville,* KY: Assumption.
Lubbock, TX: Christ the King.
Madison, WI: St. Raphael.
Manchester, NH: St. Joseph.
Marquette, MI: St. Peter.
Memphis, TN: Immaculate Conception.
Metuchen, NJ: St. Francis (of Assisi).
Miami,* FL: St. Mary (Immaculate Conception).
Milwaukee,* WI: St. John.
Mobile,* AL: Immaculate Conception (Minor Basilica).
Monterey, CA: San Carlos Borromeo.
Nashville, TN: Incarnation.

Newark,* NJ: Sacred Heart (Minor Basilica).
New Orleans,* LA: St. Louis. (Minor Basilica)
Newton, MA (Melkite): Our Lady of the Annunciation (Boston).
New Ulm, MN: Holy Trinity.
New York,* NY: St. Patrick.
Norwich, CT: St. Patrick.
Oakland, CA: St. Francis de Sales; Christ the Light (dedicated Sept. 25,2008).
Ogdensburg, NY: St. Mary (Immaculate Conception).
Oklahoma City,* OK: Our Lady of Perpetual Help.
Omaha,* NE: St. Cecilia.
Orange, CA: Holy Family.
Orlando, FL: St. James.
Our Lady of Deliverance of Newark, New Jersey for Syrian Rite Catholics in the U.S. and Canada: Our Lady of Deliverance.
Our Lady of Lebanon of Los Angeles, CA (Maronite): Our Lady of Mt. Lebanon-St. Peter.
Owensboro, KY: St. Stephen.
Palm Beach, FL: St. Ignatius Loyola, Palm Beach Gardens.
Parma, OH (Byzantine): St. John the Baptist.
Passaic, NJ (Byzantine): St. Michael.
Paterson, NJ: St. John the Baptist.
Pensacola-Tallahassee, FL: Sacred Heart (Pensacola); Co-Cathedral of St. Thomas More (Tallahassee).
Peoria, IL: St. Mary.
Philadelphia,* PA: Sts. Peter and Paul (Minor Basilica).
Philadelphia,* PA (Byzantine): Immaculate Conception of Blessed Virgin Mary.
Phoenix, AZ: Sts. Simon and Jude.
Pittsburgh,* PA (Byzantine): St. John the Baptist, Munhall.
Pittsburgh, PA: St. Paul.
Portland, ME: Immaculate Conception.
Portland,* OR: Immaculate Conception.
Providence, RI: Sts. Peter and Paul.
Pueblo, CO: Sacred Heart.
Raleigh, NC: Sacred Heart.
Rapid City, SD: Our Lady of Perpetual Help.
Reno, NV: St. Thomas Aquinas.
Richmond, VA: Sacred Heart.
Rochester, NY: Sacred Heart.
Rockford, IL: St. Peter.
Rockville Centre, NY: St. Agnes.
Sacramento, CA: Blessed Sacrament.
Saginaw, MI: St. Mary.
St. Augustine, FL: St. Augustine (Minor Basilica).
St. Cloud, MN: St. Mary.
St. George's in Canton, OH (Byzantine, Romanian): St. George.
St. Josaphat in Parma, OH (Byzantine): St. Josaphat.
St. Louis,* MO: St. Louis.
St. Maron, Brooklyn, NY (Maronite): Our Lady of Lebanon.
St. Nicholas in Chicago (Byzantine): St. Nicholas.
St. Paul and Minneapolis,* MN: St. Paul (St. Paul);

Basilica of St. Mary Co-Cathedral (Minneapolis).
St. Petersburg, FL: St. Jude the Apostle.
St. Thomas the Apostle of Detroit (Chaldean): Our Lady of Chaldeans Cathedral (Mother of God Church), Southfield, MI
St. Thomas of Chicago (Syro-Malabar): Mar Thoma Shleeha Church.
Salina, KS: Sacred Heart.
Salt Lake City, UT: The Madeleine.
San Angelo, TX: Sacred Heart.
San Antonio,* TX: San Fernando.
San Bernardino, CA: Our Lady of the Rosary.
San Diego, CA: St. Joseph.
San Francisco,* CA: St. Mary (Assumption).
San Jose, CA: St. Joseph (Minor Basilica); St. Patrick, Proto-Cathedral.
Santa Fe,* NM: San Francisco de Asis (Minor Basilica).
Santa Rosa, CA: St. Eugene.
Savannah, GA: St. John the Baptist.
Scranton, PA: St. Peter.
Seattle,* WA: St. James.
Shreveport, LA: St. John Berchmans.
Sioux City, IA: Epiphany.
Sioux Falls, SD: St. Joseph.
Spokane, WA: Our Lady of Lourdes.
Springfield, IL: Immaculate Conception.
Springfield, MA: St. Michael.
Springfield-Cape Girardeau, MO: St. Agnes (Springfield); St. Mary (Cape Girardeau).
Stamford, CT (Byzantine): St. Vladimir.
Steubenville, OH: Holy Name.
Stockton, CA: Annunciation.
Superior, WI: Christ the King.
Syracuse, NY: Immaculate Conception.
Toledo, OH: Queen of the Most Holy Rosary.
Trenton, NJ: St. Mary (Assumption).
Tucson, AZ: St. Augustine.
Tulsa, OK: Holy Family.
Tyler, TX: Immaculate Conception.
Van Nuys, CA (Byzantine): St. Mary (Patronage of the Mother of God), Van Nuys; St. Stephen's (Pro-Cathedral), Phoenix, AZ
Venice, FL: Epiphany.
Victoria, TX: Our Lady of Victory.
Washington,* DC: St. Matthew.
Wheeling-Charleston, WV: St. Joseph (Wheeling); Sacred Heart (Charleston).
Wichita, KS: Immaculate Conception.
Wilmington, DE: St. Peter.
Winona, MN: Sacred Heart.
Worcester, MA: St. Paul.
Yakima, WA: St. Paul.
Youngstown, OH: St. Columba.
Apostolic Exarchate for Armenian Catholics in the U.S. and Canada: St. Ann (110 E. 12th St., New York, NY 10003).

BASILICAS IN THE UNITED STATES

Basilica is a title assigned to certain churches because of their antiquity, dignity, historical importance or significance as centers of worship. Major basilicas have the papal altar and holy door, which is opened at the beginning of a Jubilee Year; minor basilicas enjoy certain ceremonial privileges.

Among the major basilicas are the patriarchal basilicas of

St. John Lateran, St. Peter, St. Paul Outside the Walls and St. Mary Major in Rome; St. Francis and St. Mary of the Angels in Assisi, Italy. The patriarchal basilica of St. Lawrence, Rome, is a minor basilica. The dates in the listings below indicate when the churches were designated as basilicas.

Minor Basilicas in U.S., Puerto Rico, Guam
Alabama: Mobile, Cathedral of the Immaculate

Conception (Mar. 10, 1962).

Arizona: Phoenix, St. Mary's (Immaculate Conception) (Sept. 11, 1985).

California: San Francisco, Mission Dolores (Feb. 8, 1952); Carmel, Old Mission of San Carlos (Feb. 5, 1960); Alameda, St. Joseph (Jan. 21, 1972); San Diego, Mission San Diego de Alcala (Nov. 17, 1975); San Jose, St. Joseph (Jan. 28, 1997); San Juan Capistrano, Mission Basilica of San Juan Capistrano (Feb. 14, 2000).

Colorado: Denver, Cathedral of the Immaculate Conception (Nov. 3, 1979).

Connecticut: Waterbury, Basilica of the Immaculate Conception (Feb. 9, 2008).

District of Columbia: National Shrine of the Immaculate Conception (Oct. 12, 1990).

Florida: St. Augustine, Cathedral of St. Augustine (Dec. 4, 1976); Daytona Beach, Basilica of St. Paul (Jan. 25, 2006).

Illinois: Chicago, Our Lady of Sorrows (May 4, 1956); Queen of All Saints (Mar. 26, 1962); Basilica of St. Hyacinth (Nov. 30, 2003).

Indiana: Vincennes, Old Cathedral (Mar. 14, 1970); Notre Dame, Parish Church of Most Sacred Heart, Univ. of Notre Dame (Nov. 23, 1991).

Iowa: Dyersville, St. Francis Xavier (May 11, 1956); Des Moines, St. John the Apostle (Oct. 4, 1989).

Kentucky: Trappist, Our Lady of Gethsemani (May 3, 1949); Covington, Cathedral of Assumption (Dec. 8, 1953); Bardstown, St. Joseph Proto-Cathedral Basilica (2001).

Louisiana: New Orleans, St. Louis King of France (Dec. 9, 1964).

Maine: Lewiston, Basilica of Sts. Peter and Paul (May 22, 2005).

Maryland: Baltimore, Assumption of the Blessed Virgin Mary (Sept. 1, 1937; designated national shrine, 1993); Emmitsburg, Shrine of St. Elizabeth Ann Seton (Feb. 13, 1991).

Massachusetts: Boston, Perpetual Help ("Mission Church") (Sept. 8, 1954); Chicopee, St. Stanislaus (June 25, 1991); Webster, St. Joseph (Oct. 1998).

Michigan: Grand Rapids, St. Adalbert (Aug. 22, 1979).

Minnesota: Minneapolis. St. Mary (Feb. 1, 1926).

Mississippi: Natchez, St. Mary Basilica (Sept. 8, 1998).

Missouri: Conception, Basilica of Immaculate Conception (Sept. 14, 1940); St. Louis, St. Louis King of France (Jan. 27, 1961).

New Jersey: Newark, Cathedral Basilica of the Sacred Heart (Dec. 22, 1995).

New Mexico: Santa Fe, Cathedral Basilica of St. Francis of Assisi (Oct. 4, 2005).

New York: Brooklyn, Our Lady of Perpetual Help (Sept. 5,

1969), Cathedral-Basilica of St. James (June 22, 1982); Buffalo, St. Adalbert's Basilica (1907); Lackawanna, Our Lady of Victory (July 20, 1926); Youngstown, Blessed Virgin Mary of the Rosary of Fatima (Oct. 7, 1975); Syracuse, Sacred Heart of Jesus (Aug. 27, 1998).

North Carolina: Asheville, St. Lawrence (Apr. 6, 1993; ceremonies, Sept. 5, 1993); Belmont, Our Lady Help of Christians (July 27, 1998).

North Dakota: Jamestown, St. James (Oct. 26, 1988).

Ohio: Carey, Shrine of Our Lady of Consolation (Oct. 21, 1971).

Pennsylvania: Latrobe, St. Vincent Basilica, Benedictine Archabbey (Aug. 22, 1955); Conewago, Basilica of the Sacred Heart (June 30, 1962); Philadelphia, Sts. Peter and Paul (Sept. 27, 1976); Danville, Sts. Cyril and Methodius (chapel at the motherhouse of the Sisters of Sts. Cyril and Methodius) (June 30, 1989); Loretto, St. Michael the Archangel (Sept. 9, 1996); Scranton, National Shrine of St. Ann (Oct. 18, 1997).

Texas: Galveston, St. Mary Cathedral (Aug. 11, 1979); San Antonio, Basilica of the National Shrine of the Little Flower (Sept. 27, 1931); Basilica of Our Lady of San Juan del Valle-National Shrine (May 2, 1954); Beaumont, St. Anthony Cathedral Basilica (August 2006).

Virginia: Norfolk, St. Mary of the Immaculate Conception (July 9, 1991).

Wisconsin: Milwaukee, St. Josaphat (Mar. 10, 1929); Hubertus, Holy Hill National Shrine of Mary, Help of Christians (Nov. 19, 2006).

Puerto Rico: San Juan, Cathedral of San Juan (Jan. 25, 1978).

Guam: Agana, Cathedral of Dulce Nombre de Maria (Sweet Name of Mary) (1985).

BASILICA OF THE NATIONAL SHRINE OF THE IMMACULATE CONCEPTION

The Basilica of the National Shrine of the Immaculate Conception is dedicated to the honor of the Blessed Virgin Mary, declared patroness of the United States under this title in 1846, eight years before the proclamation of the dogma of the Immaculate Conception. The church was designated a minor basilica by Pope John Paul II Oct. 12, 1990. The church is the eighth largest religious building in the world and the largest Catholic church in the Western Hemisphere, with numerous special chapels and with normal seating and standing accommodations for 6,000 people. Open daily, it is adjacent to The Catholic University of America, at Michigan Ave. and Fourth St. NE, Washington, D.C. 20017; (202) 526-8300; www.nationalshrine.com. Rev. Msgr. Walter R. Rossi, rector.

SHRINES AND PLACES OF HISTORIC INTEREST IN THE U.S.

(Principal source: Catholic Almanac *survey.)*

Listed below, according to state, are shrines, other centers of devotion and some places of historic interest with special significance for Catholics. The list is necessarily incomplete because of space limitations.

Information includes, where possible: name and location of shrine or place of interest, date of foundation, sponsoring agency or group, and address for more information.

Alabama: Our Lady of the Angels, Hanceville; Birmingham Diocese. Address: Our Lady of the Angels Monastery, 3222 County Road 548, Hanceville, 35077; (256) 352-6267.

• St. Jude Church of the City of St. Jude,

Montgomery (1934; dedicated, 1938); Mobile Archdiocese. Address: 2048 W. Fairview Ave., Montgomery, 36108; (334) 265-1390.

• Shrine of the Most Blessed Trinity, Holy Trinity (1924); Missionary Servants of the Most Blessed Trinity. Address: Holy Trinity, 36859.

Arizona: Chapel of the Holy Cross, Sedona (1956); Phoenix Diocese: P.O. Box 1043, W. Sedona 86339.

• Mission San Xavier del Bac, near Tucson (1692); National Historic Landmark; Franciscan Friars and Tucson Diocese; Address: 1950 W. San Xavier Rd., Tucson, 85746-7409; (520) 294-2624.

• Shrine of St. Joseph of the Mountains, Yarnell (1939); erected by Catholic Action League; currently maintained by Board of Directors. Address: P.O. Box 267, Yarnell, 85362.

California: Mission San Diego de Alcala (July 16, 1769); first of the 21 Franciscan missions of Upper California; Minor Basilica; National Historic Landmark; San Diego Diocese. Address: 10818 San Diego Mission Rd., San Diego, 92108; (619) 283-7319.

• Carmel Mission Basilica (Mission San Carlos Borromeo del Rio Carmelo), Carmel by the Sea (June 3, 1770); Monterey Diocese. Address: 3080 Rio Rd., Carmel, 93923; (831) 624-1271.

• Old Mission San Luis Obispo de Tolosa, San Luis Obispo (Sept. 1, 1772); Monterey Diocese (Parish Church). Address: Old Mission Church, 751 Palm St., San Luis Obispo, 93401.

• San Gabriel Mission, San Gabriel (Sept. 8, 1771); Los Angeles Archdiocese (Parish Church, staffed by Claretians). Address: 537 W. Mission, San Gabriel, 91776.

• Mission San Francisco de Asis (Oct. 9, 1776) and Mission Dolores Basilica (1860s); San Francisco Archdiocese. Address: 3321 Sixteenth St., San Francisco, 94114.

• Old Mission San Juan Capistrano, San Juan Capistrano (Nov. 1, 1776); Orange Diocese. Address: P.O. Box 697, San Juan Capistrano, 92693; (949) 248-2026; www.missionsjc.com.

• Old Mission Santa Barbara, Santa Barbara (Dec. 4, 1786); National Historic Landmark; Parish Church, staffed by Franciscan Friars. Address: 2201 Laguna St., Santa Barbara, 93105; (805) 682-4713.

• Old Mission San Juan Bautista, San Juan Bautista (June 24, 1797); National Historic Landmark; Monterey Diocese (Parish Church). Address: P.O. Box 400, San Juan Bautista, 95045.

• Mission San Miguel, San Miguel (July 25, 1797); Parish Church, Monterey diocese; Franciscan Friars. Address: P.O. Box 69, San Miguel, 93451; (805) 467-3256.

• Old Mission Santa Inés, Solvang (1804); Historic Landmark; Los Angeles Archdiocese (Parish Church, staffed by Capuchin Franciscan Friars). Address: P.O. Box 408, Solvang, 93464; (805) 688-4815; www.missionsantaines.org.

Franciscan Friars founded 21 missions in California. (*See* **Index: Franciscan Missions**.)

• Shrine of Our Lady of Sorrows, Sycamore (1883); Sacramento Diocese. Address: c/o Our Lady of Lourdes Church, 745 Ware Ave., Colusa, 95932.

Colorado: Mother Cabrini Shrine, Golden; Missionary Sisters of the Sacred Heart. Address: 20189 Cabrini Blvd., Golden, 80401.

Connecticut: Shrine of Our Lady of Lourdes, Litchfield (1958); Montfort Missionaries. Address: P.O. Box 667, Litchfield, 06759.

• Shrine of the Infant of Prague, New Haven (1945); Dominican Friars. Address: P.O. Box 1202, 5 Hillhouse Ave., New Haven, 06505.

District of Columbia: Mount St. Sepulchre, Franciscan Monastery of the Holy Land (1897; church dedicated, 1899); Order of Friars Minor. Address: 1400 Quincy St. N.E., Washington, DC 20017.

• Basilica of the National Shrine of the Immaculate Conception. *See* **Index** for separate entry.

Florida: Mary, Queen of the Universe Shrine, Orlando (1986, temporary facilities; new shrine dedicated, 1993); Orlando diocese. Address: 8300 Vineland Ave., Orlando, 32821; (407) 239-6600; www.maryqueenoftheuniverse.org.

• Our Lady of La Leche Shrine (Patroness of Mothers and Mothers-to-be) and Mission of Nombre de Dios, Saint Augustine (1565); Angelus Crusade Headquarters; St. Augustine Diocese. Address: 30 Ocean Ave., St. Augustine 32084.

Illinois: Holy Family Log Church, Cahokia (1799; original log church erected 1699); Belleville Diocese (Parish Church). Address: 116 Church St., Cahokia, 62206; (618) 337-4548.

• Marytown/Shrine of St. Maximilian Kolbe and Retreat Center, Libertyville; Our Lady of the Blessed Sacrament Sanctuary of Perpetual Eucharistic Adoration (1930) and Archdiocesan Shrine to St. Maximilian Kolbe (1989), conducted by Conventual Franciscan Friars, 1600 West Park Ave., Libertyville, 60048; (847) 367-7800.

• National Shrine of Our Lady of the Snows, Belleville (1958); Missionary Oblates of Mary Immaculate. Address: 442 S. De Mazenod Dr., Belleville, 62223.

• National Shrine of St. Jude, Chicago (1929); located in Our Lady of Guadalupe Church, founded and staffed by Claretians. Address: 3200 E. 91st St., Chicago, 60617; (312) 236-7782.

• National Shrine of St. Therese and Museum, Darien (1930), at St. Clara's Church, Chicago; new shrine, 1987, after original destroyed by fire); Carmelites of Most Pure Heart of Mary Province. Address: Carmelite Visitor Center, 8501 Bailey Rd., Darien, 60561; (630) 969-3311; www.saint-therese.org.

• Shrine of St. Jude Thaddeus, Chicago (1929) located in St. Pius V Church; staffed by Dominicans, Central Province. Address: 1909 S. Ashland Ave., Chicago, 60608; (312) 226-0020; www.op.org/domcentral/places/stjude.

Indiana: Our Lady of Monte Cassino Shrine, St. Meinrad (1870); Benedictines. Address: Saint Meinrad Archabbey, Highway 62, St. Meinrad, 47577; (812) 357-6585; www.saintmeinrad.edu/abbey/shrine.

• Old Cathedral (Basilica of St. Francis Xavier), Vincennes (1826, parish records go back to 1749); Evansville Diocese. Minor Basilica, 1970. Address: 205 Church St., Vincennes, 47591; (812) 882-5638.

Iowa: Grotto of the Redemption, West Bend (1912); Sioux City Diocese. Life of Christ in stone. Mailing address: P.O. Box 376, West Bend, 50597; (515) 887-2371; www.aw-cybermail.com/grotto.htm.

Louisiana: National Votive Shrine of Our Lady of Prompt Succor, New Orleans (1810); located in the Chapel of the Ursuline Convent (a National Historic Landmark). Address: 2635 State St., New Orleans, 70118.

• Shrine of St. Ann. Mailing address: 4920 Loveland St., Metaire, 70006; (504) 455-7071.

• Shrine of St. Roch, New Orleans (1876); located in St. Roch's Campo Santo (Cemetery); New Orleans Archdiocese. Address: 1725 St. Roch Ave., New Orleans, 70117.

Maryland: Basilica of the National Shrine of the Assumption of the Blessed Virgin Mary, Baltimore (1806). Mother Church of Roman Catholicism in the U.S. and the first metropolitan cathedral. Designed by Benjamin Henry Latrobe (architect of the Capitol) it is considered one of the finest examples of neoclassical architecture in the world. The church hosted many of the events and personalities central to the growth of Roman Catholicism in the U.S. Address: Cathedral and Mulberry Sts., Baltimore, MD 21201.

• National Shrine Grotto of Our Lady of Lourdes, Emmitsburg (1809, Grotto of Our Lady; 1875, National Shrine Grotto of Lourdes); public oratory, Archdiocese of Baltimore. Address: Mount St. Mary's College and Seminary, Emmitsburg, 21727; (301) 447-5318; www.msmary.edu/grotto/.

• National Shrine of St. Elizabeth Ann Seton, Emmitsburg. Foundation of Sisters of Charity (1809); first parochial school in America (1810); dedicated as Minor Basilica (1991). Address: 333 South Seton Ave., Emmitsburg, 21727; (301) 447-6606; www.seton-shrine.org.

• St. Francis Xavier Shrine, "Old Bohemia," near Warwick (1704); located in Wilmington Diocese; restoration under aupices of Old Bohemia Historical Society, Inc. Address: P.O. Box 61, Warwick, 21912.

• St. Jude Shrine (1873), Archdiocese of Baltimore. Address: 308 N. Paca St., P.O. Box 1455, Baltimore, 21203.

Massachusetts: National Shrine of Our Lady of La Salette, Ipswich (1945); Missionaries of Our Lady of La Salette. Address: 251 Topsfield Rd., Ipswich, 01938.

• Our Lady of Fatima Shrine, Holliston (1950); Xaverian Missionaries. Address: 101 Summer St., Holliston, 01746; (508) 429-2144.

• St. Anthony Shrine, Boston (1947); downtown Service Church with shrine; Boston Archdiocese and Franciscans of Holy Name Province. Address: 100 Arch St., Boston, 02107.

• Saint Clement's Eucharistic Shrine, Boston (1945); Boston Archdiocese, staffed by Oblates of the Virgin Mary. Address: 1105 Boylston St., Boston, 02215.

• National Shrine of the Divine Mercy, Stockbridge (1960); Congregation of Marians. Address: National Shrine of the Divine Mercy, Eden Hill, Stockbridge, 01262.

Michigan: Cross in the Woods-Parish, Indian River (1947); Gaylord diocese; staffed by Franciscan Friars of Sacred Heart Province, St. Louis. Address: 7078 M-68, Indian River, 49749; (231) 238-8973; www.rc.net/gaylord/crossinwoods.

• Shrine of the Little Flower, Royal Oak (c. 1929, by Father Coughlin); Detroit archdiocese. Address: 2123 Roseland, Royal Oak, 48073.

Minnesota: National Shrine of St. Odilia; St. Cloud Diocese. Address: P.O. Box 500, Onamia, 56359.

Missouri: Memorial Shrine of St. Rose Philippine Duchesne, St. Charles; Religious of the Sacred Heart of Jesus. Address: 619 N. Second St., St. Charles, 63301; (314) 946-6127.

• National Shrine of Our Lady of the Miraculous Medal, Perryville; located in St. Mary of the Barrens Church (1837); Vincentians. Address: 1811 W. St. Joseph St., Perryville, 63775; (573) 547-8343; www.amm.org.

• Old St. Ferdinand's Shrine, Florissant (1819, Sacred Heart Convent; 1821, St. Ferdinand's Church); Friends of Old St. Ferdinand's, Inc. Address: No. 1 Rue St. Francois, Florissant, 63031.

• Shrine of Our Lady of Sorrows, Starkenburg (1888; shrine building, 1910); Jefferson City Diocese.

Address: c/o Church of the Risen Savior, 605 Bluff St., Rhineland, 65069; (573) 236-4390.

Nebraska: The Eucharistic Shrine of Christ the King (1973); Lincoln Diocese and Holy Spirit Adoration Sisters. Address: 1040 South Cotner Blvd., Lincoln, 68510; (402) 489-0765.

New Hampshire: Shrine of Our Lady of Grace, Colebrook (1948); Missionary Oblates of Mary Immaculate. Address: R.R. 1, Box 521, Colebrook, 03576-9535; (603) 237-5511.

• Shrine of Our Lady of La Salette, Enfield (1951); Missionaries of Our Lady of La Salette. Address: Rt. 4A, P.O. Box 420, Enfield, 03748.

New Jersey: Blue Army Shrine of the Immaculate Heart of Mary (1978); National Center of the Blue Army of Our Lady of Fatima, USA, Inc. Address: Mountain View Rd. (P.O. Box 976), Washington, 07882-0976; (908) 689-1701; www.bluearmy.com

• Shrine of St. Joseph, Stirling (1924); Missionary Servants of the Most Holy Trinity. Address: 1050 Long Hill Rd., Stirling, 07980; (908) 647-0208; www.STShrine.org.

New Mexico: St. Augustine Mission, Isleta (1613); Santa Fe Archdiocese. Address: P.O. Box 463, Isleta, Pueblo, 87022.

• Santuario de Nuestro Senor de Esquipulas, Chimayo (1816); Santa Fe archdiocese, Sons of the Holy Family; National Historic Landmark, 1970. Address: Santuario de Chimayo, P.O. Box 235; Chimayo, 87522.

• Shrine of St. Bernadette (2003); Santa Fe archdiocese, St. Bernadette parish. Address: 1800 Martha St., N.E., Albuquerque, NM 87112-3161; (505) 298-7557; www.shrineofstbernadette.com.

New York: National Shrine of Bl. Kateri Tekakwitha, Fonda (1938); Order of Friars Minor Conventual. Address: P.O. Box 627, Fonda, 12068.

• Marian Shrine (National Shrine of Mary Help of Christians), West Haverstraw (1953); Salesians of St. John Bosco. Address: 174 Filors Lane, Stony Point, NY 10980-2645; (845) 947-2200; www.MarianShrine.org.

• National Shrine Basilica of Our Lady of Fatima, Youngstown (1954); designated a national shrine in 1994; Barnabite Fathers. Address: 1023 Swann Rd., Youngstown, 14174; (716) 754-7489.

• Original Shrine of St. Ann in New York City (1892); located in St. Jean Baptiste Church; Blessed Sacrament Fathers. Address: 184 E. 76th St., NY 10021; (212) 288-5082.

• Our Lady of Victory National Shrine, Lackawanna (1926); Minor Basilica. Address: 767 Ridge Rd., Lackawanna, 14218.

• Shrine Church of Our Lady of Mt. Carmel, Brooklyn (1887); Brooklyn Diocese (Parish Church). Address: 275 N. 8th St., Brooklyn, 11211; (718) 384-0223.

• Shrine of Our Lady of Martyrs, Auriesville (1885); Society of Jesus. Address: Auriesville, 12016; (518) 853-3033; www.klink.net/~jesuit.

• Shrine of Our Lady of the Island, Eastport (1975); Montfort Missionaries. Address: Box 26, Eastport, 11941; (516) 325-0661.

• Shrine of St. Elizabeth Ann Seton, New York City (1975); located in Our Lady of the Rosary Church. Address: 7 State St., NY 10004.

• Shrine of St. Frances Xavier Cabrini, New York (1938; new shrine dedicated 1960); Missionary Sisters of the Sacred Heart. Address: 701 Fort Washington Ave., 10040; (212) 923-3536; www.cabrinishrineny.org

Ohio: Basilica and National Shrine of Our Lady of Consolation, Carey (1867); Minor Basilica; Toledo Diocese; staffed by Conventual Franciscan Friars. Address: 315 Clay St., Carey, 43316; (419) 396-7107.

• National Shrine of Our Lady of Lebanon, North Jackson (1965); Eparchy of Our Lady of Lebanon of Los Angeles. Address: 2759 N. Lipkey Rd., N. Jackson, 44451; (330) 538-3351; www.national-shrine.org.

• National Shrine and Grotto of Our Lady of Lourdes, Euclid (1926); Sisters of the Most Holy Trinity. Address: 21281 Chardon Rd., Euclid, 44117-2112; (216) 481-8232.

• National Shrine of St. Dymphna, Massillon (1938), Youngstown diocese. Address: 3000 Erie St. S., Massillon, 44648-0004.

• Our Lady of Czestochowa Shrine, Garfield Heights (1939); Sisters of St. Joseph, Third Order of St. Francis. Address: 12215 Granger Rd., Garfield Hts., 44125; (216) 581-3535.

• Our Lady of Fatima, Ironton (1954); Address: Old Rt. 52, Haverhill, OH. Mailing address: St. Joseph Church, P.O. Box 499, Ironton, 45638-0499; (740) 429-2144.

• St. Anthony Shrine, Cincinnati (1888); Franciscan Friars, St. John Baptist Province. Address: 5000 Colerain Ave., Cincinnati, 45223.

• Shrine and Oratory of the Weeping Madonna of Mariapoch, Burton (1956); Social Mission Sisters. Parma Diocese (Byzantine). Address: 17486 Mumford Rd., Burton, 44021.

• Shrine of the Holy Relics (1892); Sisters of the Precious Blood. Address: 2291 St. Johns Rd., Maria Stein, 45860; (419) 925-4532.

• Sorrowful Mother Shrine, Bellevue (1850); Society of the Precious Blood. Address: 4106 State Rt. 269, Bellevue, 44811; (419) 483-3435.

Oklahoma: National Shrine of the Infant Jesus of Prague, Prague (1949); Oklahoma City Archdiocese. Address: P.O. Box 488, Prague ,74864.

Oregon: The Grotto (National Sanctuary of Our Sorrowful Mother), Portland (1924); Servite Friars. Address: P.O. Box 20008, Portland, 97294; www.the-grotto.com.

Pennsylvania: Basilica of the Sacred Heart of Jesus, Conewago Township (1741; present church, 1787); Minor Basilica; Harrisburg Diocese. Address: 30 Basilica Dr., Hanover, 17331.

• National Shrine Center of Our Lady of Guadalupe, Allentown (1974); located in Immaculate Conception Church; Allentown Diocese. Address: 501 Ridge Ave., Allentown, 18102; (610) 433-4404.

• National Shrine of Our Lady of Czestochowa (1955); Order of St. Paul the Hermit (Pauline Fathers). Address: P.O. Box 2049, Doylestown, 18901.

• National Shrine of St. John Neumann, Philadelphia (1860); Redemptorist Fathers, St. Peter's Church. Address: 1019 N. 5th St., Philadelphia, 19123.

• National Shrine of the Sacred Heart, Harleigh (1975); Scranton Diocese. Address: P.O. Box 500,

Harleigh (Hazleton), 18225; (570) 455-1162.

• Old St. Joseph's National Shrine, Philadelphia (1733); Philadelphia Archdiocese (Parish Church). Address: 321 Willings Alley, Philadelphia, 19106; (215) 923-1733; www.oldstjoseph.org.

• St. Ann's Basilica Shrine, Scranton (1902); Passionist Community. Designated a minor basilica Aug. 29, 1996. Address: 1230 St. Ann's St., Scranton, 18504; (570) 347-5691.

• St. Anthony's Chapel, Pittsburgh (1883); Pittsburgh Diocese. Address: 1700 Harpster St., Pittsburgh, 15212.

• Shrine of St. Walburga, Greensburg (1974); Sisters of St. Benedict. Address: 1001 Harvey Ave., Greensburg, 15601; (724) 834-3060.

South Dakota: Fatima Family Shrine, Alexandria; St. Cloud Diocese. Address: St. Mary of Mercy Church, Box 158, Alexandria, 57311.

Texas: Mission Espiritu Santo de Zuniga, Goliad (1749). Victoria Diocese.

• Mission Nuestra Senora de la Purisma Concepcion, San Antonio. San Antonio Archdiocese. Address: 807 Mission Rd., 78210.

• Mission San Francisco de la Espada, San Antonio (1731); San Antonio Archdiocese. Address: 10040 Espada Rd., 78214; (210) 627-2064.

• Mission San Jose y San Miguel de Aguayo, San Antonio (1720); San Antonio Archdiocese. Address: 701 E. Pyron Ave., 78214; (210) 922-0543.

• Mission San Juan Capistrano, San Antonio (1731); San Antonio Archdiocese. Address: 9101 Graf Rd., 78214.

• National Shrine of Our Lady of San Juan Del Valle, San Juan (1949); Brownsville Diocese; staffed by Oblates of Mary Immaculate. Address: P.O. Box 747, San Juan, 78589; (956) 787-0033.

• Nuestra Senora de la Concepcion del Socorro, Socorro, El Paso (1692).

• Oblate Lourdes Grotto Shrine of the Southwest, Tepeyac de San Antonio, San Antonio Archdiocese. Address: P.O. Box 96, San Antonio, 78291-0096; (210) 342-9864; www.oblatemissions.org.

• Old Mission San Francisco de los Tejas, Weches (1690); San Antonio Archdiocese.

• Presidio La Bahia, Goliad (1749); Victoria Diocese. Address: P.O. Box 57, Goliad, 77963; (361) 645-3752.

• San Elizario Presidio Chapel, El Paso (1789); El Paso Diocese. Address: El Paso Co., San Elceario, P.O. Box 398, 79855.

• Ysleta Mission (Nuestra Senora del Carmen), Ysleta, El Paso (1744). El Paso Diocese.

Vermont: St. Anne's Shrine, Isle La Motte (1666); Burlington Diocese, conducted by Edmundites. Address: West Shore Rd., Isle La Motte, 05463; (802) 928-3362.

Wisconsin: Holy Hill — National Shrine of Mary, Help of Christians (1857); Discalced Carmelite Friars. Address: 1525 Carmel Rd., Hubertus, 53033.

• National Shrine of St. Joseph, De Pere (1889); Norbertine Fathers. Address: 1016 N. Broadway, De Pere, 54115.

• Shrine of Mary, Mother Thrice Admirable Queen and Victress of Schoenstatt (1965), Address: W284 N698 Cherry Lane, Waukesha, 53188-9402; (414) 547-7733
.

Biographies of American Bishops

(*Sources:* Catholic Almanac *survey,* The Official Catholic Directory, Annuario Pontificio, *Catholic News Service. As of Aug. 20, 2008. For notable former bishops of the U.S., see* **American Catholics of the Past** *at www.CatholicAlmanac.com.*)

Information includes: date and place of birth; educational institutions attended; date of ordination to the priesthood with, where applicable, name of archdiocese (*) or diocese in parentheses; date of episcopal ordination; episcopal appointments; date of resignation/retirement.

A

Adamec, Joseph V.: b. Aug. 13, 1935, Bannister, MI; educ. Michigan State Univ. (East Lansing), Nepomucene College and Lateran Univ. (Rome); ord. priest (for Nitra diocese, Slovakia), July 3, 1960; served in Saginaw diocese; ord. bp. of Altoona-Johnstown, May 20, 1987.

Adams, Edward J.: b. Aug. 24, 1944, Philadelphia, PA; educ. St. Charles Borromeo Seminary (Philadelphia), Pontifical Ecclesiastical Academy (Rome); ord. priest (Philadelphia*), May 16, 1970; in Vatican diplomatic service from 1976; ord. titular abp. of Scala, Oct. 23, 1996; papal nuncio to Bangladesh.

Ahern, Patrick V.: b. Mar. 8, 1919, New York, NY; educ. Manhattan College and Cathedral College (New York City), St. Joseph's Seminary (Yonkers, NY), St. Louis Univ. (St. Louis, MO), Univ. Notre Dame (Notre Dame, IN); ord. priest (New York*), Jan. 27, 1945; ord. titular bp. of Naiera and aux. bp. of New York, Mar. 19, 1970; ret., Apr. 26, 1994.

Allué, Emilio S., S.D.B.: b. Feb. 18, 1935, Huesca, Spain; educ. Salesain schools (Huesca, Spain) Don Bosco College/Seminary (Newton, NJ); Salesian Pontifical Univ. (Rome), Fordham Univ. (New York); ord. priest Dec. 22, 1966, in Rome; ord. titular bp. of Croe and aux. bp. of Boston, Sept. 17, 1996.

Amos, Martin J.: b. Dec. 8, 1941, Cleveland; educ. St. Mary Seminary Cleveland; ord. priest (Cleveland), May 25, 1968; app. aux. bp. of Cleveland Apr. 3, 2001, ord., June 7, 2001, app. bp. of Davenport Oct. 12, 2006.

Anderson, Moses B., S.S.E.: b. Sept. 9, 1928, Selma, AL; educ. St. Michael's College (Winooski, VT), St. Edmund Seminary (Burlington, VT), Univ. of Legon (Ghana); ord. priest, May 30, 1958; ord. titular bp. of Vatarba and aux. bp. of Detroit, Jan. 27, 1983; ret. Oct. 24, 2003.

Angadiath, Jacob: b. Oct. 26, 1945, Periappuram, Kerala, India; educ. St. Thomas Apostolic Seminary, Vadavathoor, Kottayam, India, Univ. of Kerala, India,

Univ. of Dallas (U.S.); ord. priest (Palai, Kerala) Jan. 5, 1972; Director, Syro-Malabar Catholic Mission, Archdiocese of Chicago, 1999-2001; app. bp. of Eparchy of St. Thomas of Chicago of the Syro-Malabarians and Permanent Apostolic Visitator in Canada, Mar. 13, 2001; inst., July 1, 2001.

Angell, Kenneth A.: b. Aug. 3, 1930, Providence, RI; educ. St. Mary's Seminary (Baltimore, MD); ord. priest (Providence) May 26, 1956; ord. titular bp. of Septimunicia and aux. bp. of Providence, RI, Oct. 7, 1974; bp. of Burlington, Oct. 6, 1992; inst., Nov. 9, 1992; ret. Nov. 9, 2005.

Apuron, Anthony Sablan, O.F.M. Cap.: b. Nov. 1, 1945, Agana, Guam; educ. St. Anthony College and Capuchin Seminary (Hudson, NH), Capuchin Seminary (Garrison, NY), Maryknoll Seminary (NY), Univ. Notre Dame (Notre Dame, IN); ord. priest, Aug. 26, 1972, in Guam; ord. titular bp. of Muzuca in Proconsulari and aux. bp. of Agana, Guam (unincorporated U.S. territory), Feb. 19, 1984; abp. of Agana, Mar. 10, 1986.

Aquila, Samuel J.: b. Sept. 24, 1950, Burbank, CA; educ. St. Thomas Seminary, Denver, San Anselmo (Rome); ord. priest (Denver*), June 5, 1976; rector, St. John Vianney Seminary (Denver), 1999-2001; app. coadjutor bp. of Fargo, June 12, 2001; ord., Aug. 24, 2001; bp. of Fargo, Mar. 19, 2002.

Arias, David, O.A.R.: b. July 22, 1929, Leon, Spain; educ. St. Rita's College (San Sebastian, Spain), Our Lady of Good Counsel Theologate (Granada, Spain), Teresianum Institute (Rome, Italy); ord. priest, May 31, 1952; ord. titular bp. of Badie and aux. bp. of Newark, Apr. 7, 1983; episcopal vicar for Hispanic affairs; ret. May 21, 2004.

Aymond, Gregory M.: b. Nov. 12, 1949, New Orleans, LA; educ. St. Joseph Seminary College, Notre Dame Seminary (New Orleans, LA); ord. priest (New Orleans*), May 10, 1975; ord. titular bp. of Acolla and aux. bp. of New Orleans, Jan. 10, 1997; coadjutor bp. of Austin, June 2, 2000, ins., Aug. 3, 2000; bp. of Austin, Jan. 2, 2001.

Azarcon Solis, Oscar: b. Oct. 13, 1953, San Jose, Philippines; educ: Divine Word Seminary, Tagaytay City, Univ. of St. Thomas Seminary, Manila; ord. Apr. 28, 1979 (Cabanatuan, Philippines); incard. Houma-Thibodaux 1992; app. tit. bp. of Urci and aux. bp. of Los Angeles, Dec. 1, 2003; ord. Feb. 10, 2004.

B

Baker, Robert J.: b. June 4, 1944, Fostoria, OH; educ. Pontifical College Josephinum, Columbus, OH, Gregorian Univ., Rome; ord. (St. Augustine), Mar. 21,

1970; app. bp of Charleston, July 13, 1999; ord., Sept. 29, 1999; app. bp. of Birmingham; inst. Oct. 23, 2007.

Balke, Victor H.: b. Sept. 29, 1931, Meppen, IL; educ. St. Mary of the Lake Seminary (Mundelein, IL), St. Louis Univ. (St. Louis, MO); ord. priest (Springfield, IL), May 24, 1958; ord. bp. of Crookston, Sept. 2, 1976; ret. Sept. 28, 2007.

Baltakis, Paul Antanas, O.F.M.: b. Jan. 1, 1925, Troskunai, Lithuania; educ. seminaries of the Franciscan Province of St. Joseph (Belgium); ord. priest, Aug. 24, 1952, in Belgium; served in U.S. as director of Lithuanian Cultural Center, New York, and among Lithuanian youth; head of U.S. Lithuanian Franciscan Vicariate, Kennebunkport, ME, from 1979; ord. titular bp. of Egara, Sept. 24, 1984; assigned to pastoral assistance to Lithuanian Catholics living outside Lithuania (resides in Brooklyn).

Balvo, Charles Daniel: b. June 29, 1951, Brooklyn, New York; educ. North American College and Pontifical Gregorian University (Rome) and Catholic University of America (Washington, DC); ord. priest (New York*), June 6, 1976; studied at the Pontifical Ecclesiastical Academy and entered the diplomatic service of the Holy See; served in nunciatures in Africa, South America, and Eastern Europe; ord. titular abp. of Castello, June 29, 2005 and appointed apostolic nuncio to New Zealand, Cook Islands, Fiji, Marshall Islands, Kiribati, Fed. States Micronesia, Nauru, Western Samoa, Tonga, Palau and Vanuatu, and Apostolic Delegate to the Pacific Ocean, Apr. 1, 2005.

Banks, Robert J.: b. Feb. 26, 1928, Winthrop, MA; educ. St. John's Seminary (Brighton, MA), Gregorian Univ., Lateran Univ. (Rome); ord. priest (Boston*), Dec. 20, 1952, in Rome; rector of St. John's Seminary, Brighton, MA, 1971-81; vicar general of Boston archdiocese, 1984; ord. titular bp. of Taraqua and aux. bp. of Boston, Sept. 19, 1985; bp. of Green Bay, Oct. 16, 1990, inst., Dec. 5, 1990; ret. Oct. 10, 2003.

Barbarito, Gerald M.: b. Jan. 4, 1950, Brooklyn, NY; educ. Cathedral College (Douglaston, NY), Immaculate Conception Seminary (Huntington, NY), Catholic University (Washington, DC); ord. deacon (Brooklyn), Jan. 31, 1976; ord. titular bp. of Gisipa and aux. bp. of Brooklyn, Aug. 22, 1994; bp. of Ogdensburg, Oct. 27, 1999; inst., Jan. 7, 2000; app. bp. of Palm Beach, July 1, 2003.

Barnes, Gerald R.: b. June 22, 1945, Phoenix, AZ, of Mexican descent; educ. St. Leonard Seminary (Dayton, OH), Assumption-St. John's Seminary (San Antonio, TX); ord. priest (San Antonio*), Dec. 20, 1975; ord. titular bp. of Montefiascone and aux. bp. of San Bernardino, Mar. 18, 1992; bp. of San Bernardino, Dec. 28, 1995.

Batakian, Manuel: b. Nov. 5, 1929, Greece; moved with his family to Lebanon during World War II; educ. philosophy and theology studies in Rome; ord. priest (as a member of the Institute of the Clergy of Bzommar, an Armenian patriarchal religious order), Dec. 8, 1954; patriarchal vicar of the Institute and superior of its motherhouse in Bzommar, 1978-84; pastor of the Armenian Catholic Cathedral, Paris, 1984-90; rector of the Armenian Pontifical College, Rome, 1990-94; elected auxiliary of the patriarchate, Dec. 8, 1994, ordained bishop, Mar. 12, 1995; trans. Our Lady of Nareg in New York Sept. 12, 2005.

Baum, William W.: (*See* **Cardinals, Biographies.**)

Beltran, Eusebius J.: b. Aug. 31, 1934, Ashley, PA; educ. St. Charles Seminary (Philadelphia, PA); ord. priest (Atlanta*), May 14, 1960; ord. bp. of Tulsa, Apr. 20, 1978; app. abp. of Oklahoma City, Nov. 24, 1992; inst., Jan 22, 1993.

Bennett, Gordon D., S.J.: b. Oct. 21, 1946, Denver; educ. Mount St. Michael's (Spokane, WA), Jesuit School of Theology (Berkeley, CA), Fordham Univ. (NY); entered Society of Jesus, 1966; ord priest, June 14, 1975; app. titular bp. of Nesqually and aux. bp. of Baltimore, Dec. 23, 1997, ord. Mar 3, 1998; app. bp. of Mandeville (Jamaica), July 6, 2004; ret. Aug. 6, 2006.

Bevard, Herbert A.: b. Feb. 24, 1946, Baltimore; educ. St. Charles Borromeo Seminary (Wynnewood, Pa.), Dickinson College (Carlisle, Pa.); ord. pr. May 20, 1972 (Philadelphia); app. bp. of St. Thomas July 7, 2008; ord. bp. Sept. 3, 2008.

Bevilacqua, Anthony J.: (*See* **Cardinals, Biographies.**)

Blair, Leonard P.: b. Apr. 12, 1949, Detroit; educ. Sacred Heart Seminary, Detroit, MI; Pontifical North American College, Gregorian University, and the Angelicum, Rome; ord. priest (Detroit*), June 26, 1976; at Vatican Secretariat of State, 1986-1991; Secretary to the President of the Prefecture for the Economic Affairs of the Holy See, 1994-1997; app. aux. of Detroit, July 9, 1999, ord., Aug. 24, 1999; app. bp. of Toledo, Oct. 7, 2003.

Blaire, Stephen E.: b. Dec. 22, 1941, Los Angeles, CA; educ. St. John's Seminary (Camarillo, CA); ord. priest (Los Angeles*), Apr. 29, 1967; ord. titular bp. of Lamzella and aux. of Los Angeles, May 31, 1990; app. bp. of Stockton, Jan. 19, 1999, inst., Mar. 16, 1999.

Blume, Michael A., S.V.D.: b. May 30, 1946, South Bend, Ind.; educ. Gregorian Univ. (Rome); ord. priest Dec. 23, 1972 (Divine Word Fathers); Under-Sec. of the Pont. Council for the Pastoral Care of Migrants and Itinerants, Apr. 6, 2000; app. archbishop (nuncio to Benin and Togo) and titular archbishop of Alessano, Alexanum Aug. 24, 2005; cons. Sept. 30, 2005.

Boland, Ernest B., O.P.: b. July 10, 1925, Providence, RI; educ. Providence College (RI), Dominican Houses of Study (Somerset, OH; Washington, DC); ord. priest, June 9, 1955; ord. bp. of Multan, Pakistan, July 25, 1966; res., Oct. 20, 1984.

Boland, J.(John) Kevin: b. Apr. 25, 1935, Cork, Ireland (brother of Bp. Raymond J. Boland); educ. Christian Brothers School (Cork), All Hallows Seminary (Dublin); ord. priest (Savannah), June 14, 1959; ord. bp. of Savannah, June 18, 1995.

Boland, Raymond J.: b. Feb. 8, 1932, Tipperary, Ireland; educ. National Univ. of Ireland and All Hallows Seminary (Dublin); ord. priest (Washington*), June 16, 1957, in Dublin; vicar general and chancellor of Washington archdiocese; ord. bp. of Birmingham, Mar. 25, 1988; app. bp. of Kansas City-St. Joseph, June 22, 1993; ret. May 24, 2005.

Boles, John P.: b. Jan. 21, 1930, Boston, MA; educ. St. John Seminary, Boston College (Boston, MA); ord. priest (Boston*), Feb. 2, 1955; ord. titular bp. of Nova Sparsa and aux. bp. of Boston, May 21, 1992; ret. Oct. 12, 2006.

Bootkoski, Paul G: b. July 4, 1940, Newark, NJ; educ. Seton Hall Univ. (South Orange, NJ), Immaculate Conception Seminary (Darlington, NJ);

ord. priest, (Newark*), May 29, 1966; ord. titular bp. of Zarna and aux. bp. of Newark, Sept. 5, 1997; app. bp. of Metuchen, Jan. 4, 2002.

Borders, William D.: b. Oct. 9, 1913, Washington, IN; educ. St. Meinrad Seminary (St. Meinrad, IN), Notre Dame Seminary (New Orleans, LA), Univ. Notre Dame (Notre Dame, IN); ord. priest (New Orleans*), May 18, 1940; ord. first bp. of Orlando, June 14, 1968; app. abp. of Baltimore, Apr. 2, 1974, inst., June 26, 1974; ret., Apr. 11, 1989.

Bosco, Anthony G.: b. Aug. 1, 1927, New Castle, PA; educ. St. Vincent Seminary (Latrobe, PA), Lateran Univ. (Rome); ord. priest (Pittsburgh), June 7, 1952; ord. titular bp. of Labicum and aux. of Pittsburgh, June 30, 1970; app. bp. of Greensburg, Apr. 14, 1987, inst., June 30, 1987; ret. Jan. 2.2004.

Botean, John Michael: b. July 9, 1955, Canton, OH; educ. St. Fidelis Seminary (Herman, PA), Catholic University of America (Washington, DC), St. Gregory Melkite Seminary (Newton Centre, MA), Catholic Theological Union (Chicago, IL); ord. priest (Romanian rite St. George's in Canton), May 18, 1986; ord. bp. of St. George's in Canton for Romanians, Aug. 24, 1996.

Boyea, Earl: b. Apr. 10, 1951, Pontiac, MI.; educ. Sacred Heart Seminary (Detroit), North American College and Pontifical Gregorian University (Rome), Wayne State University (Detroit), Catholic University of America (Washington, DC); ord., May 20, 1978 (Detroit*); rector and president of the Pontifical College *Josephinum* (Columbus, Ohio), 2000-2002; app. titular bp. of Siccenna and aux. bp. of Detroit, July 22, 2002, ord., Sept. 13, 2002; app. bp. of Lansing, Feb. 27, 2008; inst. Apr. 29, 2008.

Bradley, Paul J.: b. Oct. 18, 1945, Glassport, PA; educ. St. Meinrad Seminary (St. Meinrad, IN); ord. priest May 1, 1971 (Pittsburgh); app. aux. bp. of Pittsburgh and tit. bp. of Afufenia Dec. 16, 2004; ord. Feb. 2, 2005.

Brandt, Lawrence E.: b. Mar. 27, 1939, Charleston,WV; educ. Pontifical College Josephinum (Worthington, OH), North American College (Rome), University of Innsbruck (Austria), Pontifical Lateran University (Rome); ord. priest (Rapid City), Dec. 19, 1969; after studies in the Pontifical Ecclesiastical Academy, entered into the diplomatic service of the Holy See, 1973 and held posts in Madagascar, Germany, Ecuador and Algeria; incardinated in Erie diocese in 1981; app. bp. of Greensburg of Jan. 2, 2004.

Bransfield, Michael J.: b. Sept. 8, 1943; educ. St. Charles Borromeo Sem. (Wynnewood, PA), The Catholic University of America (Washington); ord. priest May 15, 1971 (Philadelphia); app. bp. of Wheeling-Charleston Dec. 9, 2004; ord. Feb. 22, 2005.

Braxton, Edward K.: b. June 28, 1944, Chicago, IL; educ. Loyola Univ. of Chicago, Univ. of St. Mary of the Lake and Mundelein Seminary (Chicago), Louvain Univ. (Belgium); ord. priest (Chicago*), May 13, 1970; ord. titular bp. of Macomades rusticiana and aux. bp. of St. Louis, May 17, 1995; app. bp. of Lake Charles, Dec. 11, 2000; inst., Feb. 22, 2001; app. bp. of Belleville, Mar. 16, 2005; inst. June 22, 2005.

Broglio, Timothy M.: b. Dec. 22, 1951, Cleveland, OH; educ. Boston College (Boston, MA), North American College and Gregorian Univ. (Rome); ord. May 19, 1977; graduate of the Pontifical Ecclesiastical Academy; entered the diplomatic corps in 1983; chief of staff to the Vatican Secretary of State; app. titular abp. (Amiternum) and papal nuncio to the Dominican Republic and apostolic delegate to Puerto Rico, Feb. 27, 2001; ord., Mar. 19, 2001; app. abp. for Military Services, Nov. 19, 2007; inst. Jan. 25, 2008.

Brom, Robert H.: b. Sept. 18, 1938, Arcadia, WI; educ. St. Mary's College (Winona, MN), Gregorian Univ. (Rome); ord. priest (Winona), Dec. 18, 1963, in Rome; ord. bp. of Duluth, May 23, 1983; coadjutor bp. of San Diego, May, 1989; bp. of San Diego, July 10, 1990.

Brown, Tod D.: b. Nov. 15, 1936, San Francisco, CA; educ. St. John's Seminary (Camarillo, CA), North American College (Rome); ord. priest (Monterey-Fresno), May 1, 1963; ord. bp. of Boise, Apr. 3, 1989; app. bp. of Orange, June 30, 1998.

Brucato, Robert A.: b. Aug. 14, 1931, New York, NY; educ. Cathedral College (Douglaston, NY), St. Joseph's Seminary (Dunwoodie, NY), Univ. of Our Lady of the Lake (San Antonio, TX); ord. priest (New York*), June 1, 1957; air force chaplain for 22 years; ord. titular bp. of Temuniana and aux. of New York, Aug. 25, 1997; ret. Oct. 31, 2006.

Brunett, Alexander J.: b. Jan. 17, 1934, Detroit, MI; educ. Gregorian Univ. (Rome), Sacred Heart Seminary, University of Detroit (Detroit, MI), Marquette Univ. (Milwaukee, WI); ord. priest (Detroit*), July 13, 1958; ord. bp. of Helena, July 6, 1994; app. abp. of Seattle, Oct. 28, 1997, inst., Dec. 18, 1997.

Bruskewitz, Fabian W.: b. Sept. 6, 1935, Milwaukee, WI; educ. North American College, Gregorian Univ. (Rome); ord. priest (Milwaukee*), July 17, 1960; ord. bp. of Lincoln, May 13, 1992.

Buechlein, Daniel M., O.S.B.: b. Apr. 20, 1938; educ. St. Meinrad College and Seminary (St. Meinrad, IN), St. Anselm Univ. (Rome); solemn profession as Benedictine monk, Aug. 15, 1963; ord. priest (St. Meinrad Archabbey) May 3, 1964; ord. bp. of Memphis, Mar. 2, 1987; app. abp. of Indianapolis, July 14, 1992; inst., Sept. 9, 1992.

Bukovsky, John, S.V.D.: b. Jan. 18, 1924, Cerova, Slovakia; educ. Slovakia, Divine Word Seminary (Techny, IL), Catholic Univ. (Washington, DC), Univ. of Chicago, Gregorian Univ. (Rome); ord. priest, Dec. 3, 1950; became U.S. citizen, 1958; worked at East European desk of Secretariat of State; ord. titular abp. of Tabalta, Oct. 13, 1990; nuncio to Romania, 1990-94; app. papal representative to Russia, Dec. 20, 1994-99.

Bullock, William H.: b. Apr. 13, 1927, Maple Lake, MN; educ. St. Thomas College and St. Paul Seminary (St. Paul, MN), Univ. Notre Dame (Notre Dame, IN); ord. priest (St. Paul-Minneapolis*), June 7, 1952; ord. titular bp. of Natchez and aux. bp. of St. Paul and Minneapolis, Aug. 12, 1980; app. bp. of Des Moines, Feb. 10, 1987; app. bp. of Madison, WI, Apr. 13, 1993; ret., May 23, 2003.

Bura, John: b. June 12, 1944, Wegeleben, Germany; educ. St. Basil College Seminary (Stamford), St. Josaphat Ukrainian Catholic Seminary, The Catholic University of America, Washington; ord. priest Feb. 14, 1971 (Philadelphia/Ukrainian); ap. aux. bp. Ukrainian Arch. of Philadelphia and tit. bp. of Limisa Jan. 3, 2006; inst. Feb. 21, 2006.

Burbidge, Michael F.: b. June 16, 1957, Philadelphia; educ. St. Charles Borromeo Seminary; ord. priest (Philadelphia*), May 19, 1984; app. titular bp. of Cluain Iraird and aux. bp. of Philadelphia, June 21, 2002, ord., Sept. 5, 2002; app. bp. of Raleigh, June 8, 2006.

Burke, John J., O.F.M.: b. Mar. 16, 1935, River Edge, NJ; educ. St. Joseph Seminary (Callicoon, NY), St. Bonaventure Univ. (St. Bonaventure, NY), Holy Name College (Washington, DC); solemnly professed in Franciscan Order, Aug. 20, 1958; ord. priest, Feb. 25, 1961; missionary in Brazil from 1964; ord. coadjutor bp. of Miracema do Tocantins, Brazil, Mar. 25, 1995; bp. of Miracema do Tocantins, Feb. 14, 1996.

Burke, Raymond L.: b. June 30, 1948, Richland Center, WI; educ. Holy Cross Seminary (La Crosse, WI), Catholic Univ. (Washington, DC), North American College and Gregorian Univ. (Rome); ord. priest (La Crosse), June 29, 1975; ord. bp. of La Crosse, Jan. 6, 1995, inst., Feb. 22, 1995; app. abp. of St. Louis, Dec. 2, 2003; app. prefect of the Supreme Tribunal of the Apostolic Signatura, June 27, 2008.

Bustros, Cyrille Salim, S.M.S.P.: b. Jan. 26, 1939, Ain-Bourday, Lebanon; educ. Missionaries of St. Paul and Seminary of Sainte-Anne of Jerusalem (Jerusalem), University of Louvain (Louvain, Belgium); ord. June 29, 1962 (Society of the Missionaries of St. Paul); elected abp. of Baalbeck, Lebanon, Oct. 25, 1988; app. eparch of Newton, June 22, 2004.

C

Caggiano, Frank J.: b. Mar. 29, 1959, Brooklyn; educ. Immaculate Conception Seminary (Huntington, NY), Gregorian Univ. (Rome); ord. priest May 16, 1987 (Brooklyn); appointed aux. bp. of Brooklyn and tit. bp. of Inis Cathaig June 6, 2006; ord. Aug. 22, 2006.

Callahan, William P., O.F.M. Conv.: b. June 17, 1950, Chicago, IL; educ. St. Mary Minor Seminary (Crystal Lake, IL), Loyola University (Chicago), University of St. Michael's College, University of Toronto (Toronto, Canada); entered the Conventual Franciscans and made his first profession, Aug. 11, 1970; ord. priest, Apr. 30, 1977; spiritual director of the North American College, 2005-2007; app. titular bp. of Lares and aux. bp. of Milwaukee, Oct. 30, 2007; cons. bp. Dec. 21, 2007.

Calvo, Randolph R.: b. Aug. 28, 1950, Agana, Guam; educ. St. Patrick's Seminary and University (Menlo Park, CA), Angelicum (Rome); ord. priest May 21, 1977 (San Francisco); app. bp of Reno Dec. 23, 2005; ord. bp. Feb. 17, 2006.

Camacho, Tomas Aguon: b. Sept. 18, 1933, Chalon Kanoa, Saipan; educ. St. Patrick's Seminary (Menlo Park, CA); ord. priest, June 14, 1961; ord. first bp. of Chalan Kanoa, Northern Marianas (U.S. Commonwealth), Jan. 13, 1985.

Campbell, Frederick F.: b. Aug. 5, 1943, Elmira, NY; educ. Ohio State Univ., St. Paul Seminary, St. Paul, MN; ord. priest (St. Paul and Minneapolis*), May 31, 1980; app. titular bp. of Afufenia and aux. bp. of St. Paul and Minneapolis, Mar. 2, 1999, ord., May 14, 1999; app. bp. of Columbus, Oct. 14, 2004; inst. Jan. 13, 2005.

Cantú, Oscar: b. Dec. 5, 1966, Houston, TX; educ.

Holy Trinity Seminary and University of Dallas (Dallas, TX), St. Mary's Seminary, (Houston, TX), Gregorian University (Rome); ord. priest, May 21, 1994 (Galveston-Houston*); app. titular bp. of Dardano and aux. bp. of San Antonio, Apr. 10, 2008; ord. bp., June 2, 2008.

Carlson, Robert J.: b. June 30, 1944, Minneapolis, MN; educ. Nazareth Hall and St. Paul Seminary (St. Paul, MN), Catholic Univ. (Washington, DC); ord. priest (St. Paul-Minneapolis*), May 23, 1970; ord. titular bp. of Avioccala and aux. bp. of St. Paul and Minneapolis, Jan. 11, 1984; app. coadjutor bp. of Sioux Falls, Jan. 13, 1994; succeeded as bp. of Sioux Falls, Mar. 21, 1995; app. bp. of Saginaw, Dec. 29, 2004; inst. Feb. 24, 2005.

Carmody, Edmond: b. Jan. 12, 1934, Ahalena, Kerry, Ireland; educ. St. Brendan's College (Killarney), St. Patrick Seminary (Carlow); ord. priest (San Antonio*), June 8, 1957; missionary in Peru 1984-89; ord. titular bp. of Mortlach and aux. bp. of San Antonio, Dec. 15, 1988; app. bp. of Tyler, 1992-2000; app. bp. of Corpus Christi, Feb. 3, 2000; inst., Mar. 17, 2000.

Carmon, Dominic, S.V.D.: b. Dec. 13, 1930, Opelousas, LA; entered Society of Divine Word, 1946; ord. priest, Feb. 2, 1960; missionary in Papua-New Guinea, 1961-68; ord. titular bp. of Rusicade and aux. bp. of New Orleans, Feb. 11, 1993; ret. Dec. 13, 2006.

Casey, Luis Morgan: b. June 23, 1935, Portageville, MO; ord. priest (St. Louis*), Apr. 7, 1962; missionary in Bolivia from 1965; ord. titular bp. of Mibiarca and aux. of La Paz, Jan. 28, 1984; vicar apostolic of Pando, Bolivia, Jan. 18, 1988, and apostolic administrator (1995) of La Paz.

Catanello, Ignatius A.: b. July 23, 1938, Brooklyn, NY; educ. Cathedral Preparatory Seminary and St. Francis College (Brooklyn, NY), Catholic Univ. (Washington, DC); St. John's University (Jamaica, NY), New York University; ord. priest (Brooklyn), May 28, 1966; ord. titular bp. of Deulto and aux. bp. of Brooklyn, Aug. 22, 1994.

Chaput, Charles J., O.F.M. Cap.: b. Sept. 26, 1944, Concordia, KS; educ. St. Fidelis College (Herman, PA), Capuchin College and Catholic Univ. (Washington, DC), Univ. of San Francisco; solemn vows as Capuchin, July 14, 1968; ord. priest, Aug. 29, 1970; ord. bp. of Rapid City, SD, July 26, 1988, the second priest of Native American ancestry (member of Prairie Band Potawatomi Tribe) ordained a bp. in the U.S.; app abp. of Denver, inst., Apr. 7, 1997.

Charron, Joseph L., C.PP.S.: b. Dec. 30, 1939, Redfield, SD; educ. St. John's Seminary (Collegeville, MN); ord. priest, June 3, 1967; ord. titular bp. of Bencenna and aux. bp. of St. Paul and Minneapolis, Jan. 25, 1990; app. bp. of Des Moines, Nov. 12, 1993; res. Apr. 10, 2007.

Chavez, Gilbert Espinoza: b. May 9, 1932, Ontario, CA; educ. St. Francis Seminary (El Cajon, CA), Immaculate Heart Seminary (San Diego), Univ. of CA; ord. priest (San Diego). Mar. 19, 1960; ord. titular bp. of Magarmel and aux. of San Diego, June 21, 1974; ret. June 1, 2007.

Chedid, John: b. July 4, 1923, Eddid, Lebanon; educ. seminaries in Lebanon and Pontifical Urban College (Rome); ord. priest, Dec. 21, 1951, in Rome; ord. titular bp. of Callinico and aux. bp. of St. Maron of Brooklyn for the Maronites, Jan. 25, 1981; app. first bp. of Eparchy of Our Lady of Lebanon of Los Angeles for the Maronites, Mar. 1, 1994; res., Dec. 5, 2000.

Choby, David R.: b. Jan. 17, 1947, Nashville, TN; educ. St. Ambrose College (Davenport, Iowa), The Catholic University of America (Washington, DC), and the Angelicum (Rome); ord. priest Sept. 6, 1974 (Nashville); app. bp of Nashville Dec. 20, 2005; ord. bp. Feb. 27, 2006.

Chomnycky, Paul P.: b. Apr. 5, 2002, Vancouver, B.C; educ. University of British Columbia (Vancouver), Pont. St. Anselm Univ., Pont. Gregorian University (Rome); ord. Oct. 1, 1988 (Basilians); app. bp for Ukrainian Catholics living in Great Britain Apr. 5, 2002; ord. bp. June 11, 2002; trans. Ukrainian Diocese of Stamford Jan. 3, 2006; inst. Feb. 20, 2006.

Christensen, Peter F.: b. Dec. 24, 1952, Pasadena, CA; educ. College of the Redwoods (Eureka, CA), University of Montana (Missoula, MT), St. John Vianney Seminary, Univ. of St. Thomas, and St. Paul Seminary (St. Paul, MN); ord. May 25, 1985 (St. Paul and Minneapolis*); app. bp. of Superior, June 28, 2007; ord. Sept. 14, 2007.

Christian, Francis J.: b. Oct. 8, 1942, Peterborough, NH; educ. St. Anselm College (Manchester, NH), St. Paul Seminary (Ottawa), American College in Louvain (Belgium); ord. priest (Manchester), June 29, 1968; ord titular bp. of Quincy and aux. of Manchester, May 14, 1996.

Cisneros, Octavio: b. July 19, 1945, Cuba; educ.: Immaculate Conception Sem. (Huntington, NY); ord. priest Mary 29, 1971; appointed aux. bp. of Brooklyn and tit. bp. of Eanach Duin June 6, 2006; ord. Aug. 22, 2006.

Cistone, Joseph R.: b. May 18, 1949, Philadelphia, PA; educ. St. Charles Borromeo Seminary (Overbrook, PA); ord. priest (Philadelphia*), May 17, 1975; app. titular bp. of Case mediane and aux. bp. of Philadelphia, June 8, 2004; ord. July 28, 2004.

Clark, Edward W.: b. Nov. 30, 1946, Minneapolis; educ. Our Lady Queen of Angels Seminary (San Fernando, CA), St. John's Seminary College (Camarillo, CA), Gregorian University (Rome); ord. priest (Los Angeles*), May 9, 1972; President/Rector, St. John's Seminary College (Camarillo, CA), 1994-2001; app. titular bp. of Gardar and aux. bp. of Los Angeles, Jan. 16, 2001, ord., Mar. 26, 2001.

Clark, Matthew H.: b. July 15, 1937, Troy, NY; educ. St. Bernard's Seminary (Rochester, NY), Gregorian Univ. (Rome); ord. priest (Albany) Dec. 19, 1962; ord. bp. of Rochester, May 27, 1979; inst., June 26, 1979.

Coakley, Paul S.: b. June 3, 1955, Norfolk, VA; educ. University of Kansas (Lawrence), St. Pius X Seminary (Erlanger, KY), Mount St. Mary's Seminary (Emmitsburg, MD); ord. Priest May 21, 1983 (Wichita); app. bp. of Salina Oct. 21, 2004; ord. Dec. 28, 2004.

Coleman, George W.: b. Feb. 1, 1939, Fall River, MA; educ. Holy Cross College (Worcester, MA), Fall River, St. John's Seminary (Boston, MA), North American College and Gregorian Univ. (Rome), Brown University (Providence, RI); ord. priest, Dec. 16, 1964; app. bp. of Fall River, Apr. 30, 2003; ord. bp., July 22, 2003.

Conley, James Douglas: b. Mar. 19, 1955, Kansas City, MO; educ., University of Kansas (Lawrence, KS), St. Pius X Seminary (Erlanger, KY), Mount St. Mary's Seminary (Emmitsburg, MD), Pontifical North American College and Accademia Alfonsiana (Rome); ord. priest May 18, 1985 (Wichita); served in Congregation for Bishops in Rome, 1996-2006; Chaplain of His Holiness, Feb. 9, 2001; app. titular bp. of Cissa and aux. bp. of Denver, Apr. 10, 2008; ord. bp., May 30, 2008.

Conlon, Robert D.: b. Dec. 4, 1948, Cincinnati; educ. Mount St. Mary's Seminary of the West, University of St. Paul, Ottawa; ord. priest (Cincinnati*), Jan. 15, 1977; app. bp. of Steubenville, May 31, 2002.

Connolly, Thomas J.: b. July 18, 1922, Tonopah, NV; educ. St. Patrick's Seminary (Menlo Park, CA), Catholic Univ. (Washington, DC), Lateran Univ. (Rome); ord. priest (Reno-Las Vegas), Apr. 8, 1947; ord. bp. of Baker, June 30, 1971; res., Nov. 19, 1999.

Connors, Ronald G., C.SS.R.: b. Nov. 1, 1915, Brooklyn, NY; ord. priest, June 22, 1941; ord. titular bp. of Equizetum and coadjutor bp. of San Juan de la Maguana, Dominican Republic, July 20, 1976; succeeded as bp. of San Juan de la Maguana, July 20, 1977; ret., Feb. 20, 1991.

Cooney, Patrick R.: b. Mar. 10, 1934, Detroit, MI; educ. Sacred Heart Seminary (Detroit), Gregorian Univ. (Rome), Univ. Notre Dame (Notre Dame, IN); ord. priest (Detroit*), Dec. 20, 1959; ord. titular bp. of Hodelm and aux. bp. of Detroit, Jan. 27, 1983; app. bp. of Gaylord, Nov. 6, 1989; inst., Jan. 28, 1990.

Cordileone, Salvatore: b. June 5, 1956, San Diego, CA; educ. St. Francis Seminary (San Diego), University of San Diego (San Diego), North American College (Rome), Pontifical Gregorian University (Rome); ord. July 9, 1982; official of the Supreme Tribunal of the Apostolic Signatura in Roma, 1995-2002 and vice-director of Villa Stritch in Rome; app. titular bp. of Natchez and aux. bp. of San Diego, July 5, 2002, ord., Aug. 21, 2002.

Corrada del Rio, Alvaro, S.J.: b. May 13, 1942, Santurce, Puerto Rico; entered Society of Jesus, 1960, at novitiate of St. Andrew-on-Hudson (Poughkeepsie, NY); educ. Jesuit seminaries, Fordham Univ. (NY), Institut Catholique (Paris); ord. priest, July 6, 1974, in Puerto Rico; pastoral coordinator of Northeast Catholic Hispanic Center, New York, 1982-85; ord. titular bp. of Rusticiana and aux. bp. of Washington, DC, Aug. 4, 1985; app. apostolic administrator of Caguas, Puerto Rico, Aug. 5, 1997 (retained his title as aux. bp. of Washington); app. bp. of Tyler, Dec. 5, 2000; inst., Jan. 30, 2001.

Coscia, Benedict Dominic, O.F.M.: b. Aug. 10, 1922, Brooklyn, NY; educ. St. Francis College (Brooklyn, NY), Holy Name College (Washington, DC); ord. priest June 11, 1949; ord. bp. of Jatai, Brazil, Sept. 21, 1961.

Costello, Thomas J.: b. Feb. 23, 1929, Camden, NY; educ. Niagara Univ. (Niagara Falls, NY), St. Bernard's Seminary (Rochester, NY), Catholic Univ. (Washington, DC); ord. priest (Syracuse), June 5, 1954; ord. titular bp. of Perdices and aux. bp. of Syracuse, Mar. 13, 1978; ret. Mar. 23, 2004.

Cote, Michael R.: b. June 19, 1949, Sanford, ME; educ. Our Lady of Lourdes Seminary (Cassadaga,

NY), St. Mary's Seminary College (Baltimore, MD); Gregorian Univ. (Rome), Catholic Univ. (Washington, DC); ord. priest (Portland, ME), June 29, 1975, by Pope Paul VI in Rome; secretary, 1989-94 at apostolic nunciature, Washington; ord. titular bp. of Cebarades and aux. of Portland, ME, July 27, 1995; app. bp. of Norwich, Mar. 11, 2003; inst., May 13, 2003.

Cotey, Arnold R., S.D.S.: b. June 15, 1921, Milwaukee, WI; educ. Divine Savior Seminary (Lanham, MD), Marquette Univ. (Milwaukee, WI); ord. priest, June 7, 1949; ord. first bp. of Nachingwea (now Lindi), Tanzania, Oct. 20, 1963; ret., Nov. 11, 1983.

Cronin, Daniel A.: b. Nov. 14, 1927, Newton, MA; educ. St. John's Seminary (Boston, MA), North American College and Gregorian Univ. (Rome); ord. priest (Boston*), Dec. 20, 1952; attaché apostolic nunciature (Addis Ababa), 1957-61; served in papal Secretariat of State, 1961-68; ord. titular bp. of Egnatia and aux. bp. of Boston, Sept. 12, 1968; bp. of Fall River, Dec. 16, 1970; abp. of Hartford, Dec. 10, 1991; ret. Oct. 23, 2003.

Cruz, Manuel A.: b. Dec. 2, 1953, Havana, Cuba; educ. Seton Hall University (South Orange, NJ), Immaculate Conception Seminary (South Orange, NJ); ord. priest, May 31, 1980 (Newark*), app. aux. bp. of Newark and titular bp. of Gaguari, June 9, 2008; ord. bp. Sept. 9, 2008.

Cullen, Edward P.: b. Mar. 15, 1933, Philadelphia, PA; educ. St. Charles Borromeo Seminary (Overbrook, PA), Univ. of Pennsylvania and LaSalle Univ. (Philadelphia), Harvard Graduate School of Business; ord. priest (Philadelphia*), May 19, 1962; ord. titular bp. of Paria in Proconsolare and aux. of Philadelphia, Feb. 8, 1994; app. bp. of Allentown, Dec. 16, 1997, inst., Feb. 9, 1998.

Cummins, John S.: b. Mar. 3, 1928, Oakland, CA; educ. St. Patrick's Seminary (Menlo Park, CA), Catholic Univ. (Washington, DC), Univ. of CA; ord. priest (San Francisco*), Jan. 24, 1953; executive director of the CA Catholic Conference 1971-76; ord. titular bp. of Lambaesis and aux. bp. of Sacramento, May 16, 1974; app. bp. of Oakland, inst., June 30, 1977; ret. Oct. 1, 2003.

Cunningham, Robert J.: b. June 18, 1943, Buffalo, NY; educ. St. John Vianney Seminary (East Aurora, NY), The Catholic University of America (Washington, DC); ord. May 24, 1969 (Buffalo); bp. of Ogdensburg Mar. 9, 2004; ord. May 18, 2004.

Cupich, Blase: b. Mar. 19, 1949, Omaha, NE; educ. College of St. Thomas (St. Paul, MN), Gregorian Univ. (Rome), Catholic University of America (Washington, DC); ord. priest (Omaha*), Aug. 16, 1975; service at the apostolic nunciature, Washington, DC, 1981-87; rector, Pontifical College Josephinum (Columbus, OH), 1989-97; app. bp. of Rapid City, SD, July 7, 1998; ord., Sept. 21, 1998.

Curlin, William G.: b. Aug. 30, 1927, Portsmouth, VA; educ. Georgetown Univ. (Washington, DC), St. Mary's Seminary (Baltimore, MD); ord. priest (Washington*), May 25, 1957; ord. titular bp. of Rosemarkie and aux. bp. of Washington, Dec. 20, 1988; app. bp. of Charlotte, Feb. 22, 1994, ret., Sept. 16, 2002.

Curry, Thomas J.: b. Jan. 17, 1943, Drumgoon, Ireland; educ. Patrician College (Ballyfin), All Hallows Seminary (Dublin); ord. priest (Los Angeles*), June 17, 1967; ord. titular bp. of Ceanannus Mór and aux. of Los Angeles, Mar. 19, 1994.

Curtiss, Elden F.: b. June 16, 1932, Baker, OR; educ. St. Edward Seminary College and St. Thomas Seminary (Kenmore, WA); ord. priest (Baker), May 24, 1958; ord. bp. of Helena, MT, Apr. 28, 1976; app. abp. of Omaha, NE, May 4, 1993.

D

Da Cunha, Edgar M., S.D.V.: b. Aug. 21, 1953, Riachão do Jacuípe Bahia, Brazil; educ. Catholic University of Salvador (Brazil), Immaculate Conception Seminary (Newark, NJ); professed perpetual vows, Feb. 11, 1979, and ord., priest Mar. 27, 1982; app. titular bp. of Ucres and aux. of Newark, June 27, 2003.

Daily, Thomas V.: b. Sept. 23, 1927, Belmont, MA; educ. Boston College, St. John's Seminary (Brighton, MA); ord. priest (Boston*), Jan. 10, 1952; missionary in Peru for five years as a member of the Society of St. James the Apostle; ord. titular bp. of Bladia and aux. bp. of Boston, Feb. 11, 1975; app. first bp. of Palm Beach, FL, July 17, 1984; app. bp. of Brooklyn, Feb. 20, 1990; inst., Apr. 18, 1990; ret., Aug. 1, 2003.

Daly, James: b. Aug. 14, 1921, New York, NY; educ. Cathedral College (Brooklyn, NY), Immaculate Conception Seminary (Huntington, LI); ord. priest (Brooklyn), May 22, 1948; ord. titular bp. of Castra Nova and aux. bp. of Rockville Centre, May 9, 1977; ret., July 1, 1996.

D'Antonio, Nicholas, O.F.M.: b. July 10, 1916, Rochester, NY; educ. St. Anthony's Friary (Catskill, NY); ord. priest, June 7, 1942; ord. titular bp. of Giufi Salaria and prelate of Olancho, Honduras, July 25, 1966; resigned, 1977; vicar general of New Orleans archdiocese and episcopal vicar for Spanish Speaking, 1977-91.

D'Arcy, John M.: b. Aug. 18, 1932, Brighton, MA; educ. St. John's Seminary (Brighton, MA), Angelicum Univ. (Rome); ord. priest (Boston*), Feb. 2, 1957; spiritual director of St. John's Seminary; ord. titular bp. of Mediana and aux. bp. of Boston, Feb. 11, 1975; app. bp. of Fort Wayne-South Bend, Feb. 26, 1985, inst., May 1, 1985.

Del Riego, Rutilio: b. Sept. 21, 1940, Valdesandinas (Leon), Spain; educ. Diocesan Laborer Priests seminary (Salamanca, Spain), Catholic Univ. of America; ord. priest June 5, 1965, (Diocesan Laborer Priests); app. aux. bp. San Bernardino and tit. bp. of Daimlaig July 26, 2005; ord. Sept. 20, 2005.

Dendinger, William J.: b. May 20, 1939, Omaha; educ. Conception College Seminary (Conception, Missouri), Aquinas Institute (Iowa); ord. priest May 29, 1965; U.S. Air Force chaplain, 1970-2002, achieving the rank of Major General; app. bp. of Grand Island Oct. 14, 2004; ord. Dec. 13, 2004.

De Palma, Joseph A., S.C.J.: b. Sept. 4, 1913, Walton, NY; ord. priest, May 20, 1944; superior general of Congregation of Priests of the Sacred Heart, 1959-67; ord. first bp. of De Aar, South Africa, July 19, 1967; ret., Nov. 18, 1987.

De Simone, Louis A.: b. Feb. 21, 1922, Philadelphia, PA; educ. Villanova Univ. (Villanova, PA), St. Charles Borromeo Seminary (Overbrook, PA); ord. priest

(Philadelphia*), May 10, 1952; ord. titular bp. of Cillium and aux. bp. of Philadelphia, Aug. 12, 1981; ret., Apr. 5, 1997.

DeWane, Frank J.: b. Mar. 9, 1950, Green Bay, Wis.; educ. Univ. of Wisconsin (Oshkosh), American Univ., George Washington Univ. (Washington, DC), North American College, Pont. Gregorian Univ., Angelicum (Rome); ord. priest July 16, 1988 (Green Bay); app. coadj. bp. of Venice Apr. 25, 2006; ord. bp. July 25, 2006; bp. of Venice, Jan. 19, 2007.

Di Lorenzo, Francis X.: b. Apr. 15, 1942, Philadelphia, PA; educ. St. Charles Borromeo Seminary (Philadelphia), Univ. of St. Thomas (Rome); ord. priest (Philadelphia*), May 18, 1968; ord. titular bp. of Tigia and aux. bp. of Scranton, Mar. 8, 1988; app. apostolic administrator of Honolulu, Oct. 12, 1993; bp. of Honolulu, Nov. 29, 1994; app. bp. of Richmond, Mar. 31, 2004.

DiMarzio, Nicholas: b. June 16, 1944, Newark, NJ; educ. Seton Hall University (South Orange, NJ), Immaculate Conception Seminary (Darlington, NJ), Catholic Univ. (Washington, DC), Fordham Univ. (New York), Rutgers Univ. (New Brunswick, NJ); ord. priest (Newark*), May 30, 1970; ord. titular bp. of Mauriana and aux. bp. of Newark, Oct. 31, 1996, app. Bishop of Camden, June 8, 1999, inst., July 22, 1999; app. bp. of Brooklyn, Aug. 1, 2003.

Dimino, Joseph T.: b. Jan. 7, 1923, New York, NY; educ. Cathedral College (Douglaston, NY), St. Joseph's Seminary (Yonkers, NY), Catholic Univ. (Washington, DC); ord. priest (New York*), June 4, 1949; ord. titular bp. of Carini and aux. bp. of the Military Services archdiocese, May 10, 1983; app. ordinary of Military Services archdiocese, May 14, 1991; ret., Aug. 12, 1997.

DiNardo, Daniel N.: (*See* Cardinals' Biographies).

Dino, Gerald N.: b. Jan. 11, 1940, Binghamton, NY; educ. Duquesne University (Pittsburgh, PA), Byzantine Catholic Seminary of Sts. Cyril and Methodius (Pittsburgh, PA), Pontifical Oriental Inst. (Rome); ord. priest, Mar. 21, 1965 (Passaic); app. protosincellus of the eparchy of Passaic of the Ruthenians, U.S.A., and pastor in Linden, New Jersey; app. bishop of the eparchy of Van Nuys of the Ruthenians, Dec. 6, 2007; ord. bp. Mar. 27, 2008.

Dion, George E., O.M.I.: b. Sept. 25, 1911, Central Falls, RI; educ. Holy Cross College (Worcester, MA), Oblate Juniorate (Colebrook, NH), Oblate Scholasticates (Natick, MA, and Ottawa, Ont.); ord. priest, June 24, 1936; ord. titular bp. of Arpaia and vicar apostolic of Jolo, Philippines Apr. 23, 1980; ret., Oct. 11, 1991; titular bp. of Arpaia.

Dolan, Timothy M.: b. Feb. 6, 1950, St. Louis; educ. St. Louis Preparatory Seminary, Cardinal Glennon College, North American College, Pontifical Univ. of St. Thomas (Rome), Catholic University of America (Washington, DC); ord. priest (St. Louis*), June 19, 1976; served on staff of apostolic nunciature (Washington, DC); rector, North American College (Rome), 1994-2001; app. titular bp. of Natchez and aux. bp. of St. Louis, June 19, 2001; ord., Aug. 15, 2001; app. abp. of Milwaukee, June 25, 2002; inst., Aug. 28, 2002.

Donato, Thomas A.: b. Oct. 1, 1940, Jersey City, NJ; educ. Seton Hall Univ. (South Orange, NJ), Immaculate Conception Seminary (Darlington, NJ);

ord. priest (Newark*), May 29, 1965; app. aux. bp. of Newark and tit. bp of Jamestown, May 21, 2004; ord. Aug. 4, 2004.

Donnelly, Robert William: b. Mar. 22, 1931, Toledo, OH; educ. St. Meinrad Seminary College (St. Meinrad, IN), Mount St. Mary's in the West Seminary (Norwood, OH); ord. priest (Toledo), May 25, 1957; ord. titular bp. of Garba and aux. bp. of Toledo, May 3, 1984; ret. May 30, 2006.

Donoghue, John F.: b. Aug. 9, 1928, Washington, DC; educ. St. Mary's Seminary (Baltimore, MD); Catholic Univ. (Washington, DC); ord. priest (Washington*), June 4, 1955; chancellor and vicar general of Washington archdiocese, 1973-84; ord. bp. of Charlotte, Dec. 18, 1984; app. abp. of Atlanta, June 22, 1993; inst., Aug. 19, 1993; ret. Dec. 9, 2004.

Donovan, Paul V.: b. Sept. 1, 1924, Bernard, IA; educ. St. Gregory's Seminary (Cincinnati, OH), Mt. St. Mary's Seminary (Norwood, OH), Lateran Univ. (Rome); ord. priest (Lansing), May 20, 1950; ord. first bp. of Kalamazoo, July 21, 1971; ret., Nov. 22, 1994.

Dooher, John A.: b. May 3, 1943, Dorchester, Mass.; educ. St. John's Seminary (Brighton, Mass.); ord. May 21, 1969 (Boston); app. aux. bp. of Boston and tit. bp. of Teveste Oct. 12, 2006; ord. Dec. 12, 2006.

Doran, Thomas George: b. Feb. 20, 1936, Rockford, IL; educ. Loras College (Dubuque, IA), Gregorian Univ. (Rome), Rockford College (Rockford, IL); ord. priest (Rockford), Dec. 20, 1961; ord. bp. of Rockford, June 24, 1994.

Dorsey, Norbert M., C.P.: b. Dec. 14, 1929, Springfield, MA; educ. Passionist seminaries (eastern U.S. province), Pontifical Institute of Sacred Music and Gregorian Univ. (Rome, Italy); professed in Passionists, Aug. 15, 1949; ord. priest, Apr. 28, 1956; assistant general of Passionists, 1976-86; ord. titular bp. of Mactaris and aux. bp. of Miami, Mar. 19, 1986; app. bp. of Orlando, Mar. 20, 1990, inst., May 25, 1990; ret. Nov. 13, 2004.

Doueihi, Stephen Hector: b. June 25, 1927, Zghorta, Lebanon; educ. University of St. Joseph (Beirut, Lebanon), Propaganda Fide, Gregorian Univ. and Institute of Oriental Study (Rome); ord. priest, Aug. 14, 1955; came to U.S. in 1973; ord. eparch of Eparchy of St. Maron of Brooklyn, Jan 11, 1997; ret. Jan. 10, 2004.

Dougherty, John Martin: b. Apr. 29, 1932, Scranton, PA; educ. St. Charles College (Catonsville, MD), St. Mary's Seminary (Baltimore), Univ. of Notre Dame (South Bend); ord. priest (Scranton), June 15, 1957; ord. titular bp. of Sufetula and aux. bp. of Scranton, Mar. 7, 1995.

Driscoll, Michael P.: b. Aug. 8, 1939, Long Beach, CA; educ. St. John Seminary (Camarillo, CA), Univ. of Southern CA; ord. priest (Los Angeles*), May 1, 1965; ord. titular bp. of Massita and aux. bp. of Orange, Mar. 6, 1990; app. bp. of Boise, Jan. 19, 1999, inst., Mar. 18, 1999.

Duca, Michael Gerard: b. June 5, 1952, Dallas, TX; educ. Holy Trinity Seminary, Irving, TX, Pontifical University of St. Thomas Aquinas, Rome; ord. priest, Apr. 29, 1978 (Dallas); rector of Holy Trinity Seminary (1996-2008); app. bp. of Shreveport, Apr. 1, 2008; cons. May 19, 2008.

Duffy, Paul, O.M.I.: b. July 25, 1932, Norwood, MA; educ Oblate houses of study in Canada and

Washington, DC; ord. priest, 1962; missionary in Zambia from 1984; app. first bp. of Mongu, Zambia, July 1, 1997.

Duhart, Clarence James, C.SS.R.: b. Mar. 23, 1912, New Orleans, LA; ord. priest, June 29, 1937; ord. bp. of Udon Thani, Thailand, Apr. 21, 1966; resigned, Oct. 2, 1975.

DuMaine, (Roland) Pierre: b. Aug. 2, 1931, Paducah, KY; educ. St. Joseph's College (Mountain View, CA), St. Patrick's College and Seminary (Menlo Park, CA), Univ. of CA (Berkeley), Catholic Univ. (Washington, DC); ord. priest (San Francisco), June 15, 1957; ord. titular bp. of Sarda and aux. bp. of San Francisco, June 29, 1978; app. first bp. of San Jose, Jan. 27, 1981; inst., Mar. 18, 1981; res., Nov. 27, 1999.

Dunne, John C.: b. Oct. 30, 1937, Brooklyn, NY; educ. Cathedral College (Brooklyn, NY). Immaculate Conception Seminary (Huntington, NY), Manhattan College (New York); ord. priest (Rockville Centre), June 1, 1963; ord. titular bp. of Abercorn and aux. bp. of Rockville Centre, Dec. 13, 1988. Vicar for Central Vicariate.

Dupre, Thomas L.: b. Nov. 10, 1933, South Hadley Falls, MA; educ. College de Montreal, Assumption College (Worcester, MA), Catholic Univ. (Washington, DC), ord. priest (Springfield, MA), May 23, 1959; ord. titular bp. of Hodelm and aux. bp. of Springfield, MA, May 31, 1990; bp. of Springfield, Mar. 14, 1995; res. Feb.11, 2004.

Durning, Dennis V., C.S.Sp.: b. May 18, 1923, Germantown, PA; educ. St. Mary's Seminary (Ferndale, CT); ord. priest, June 3, 1949; ord. first bp. of Arusha, Tanzania, May 28, 1963; resigned, Mar. 6, 1989.

E

Edyvean, Walter J.: b. Oct. 18, 1938, Medford, MA; educ. Boston College, St. John's Seminary (Brighton, MA), the North American College and the Gregorian Univ. (Rome); ord. priest (Boston*), Dec. 16, 1964; served on staff of Congregation for Catholic Education, 1990-2001; app. titular bp. of Elie and aux. bp. of Boston, June 29, 2001, ord., Sept. 14, 2001

Egan, Edward M.: (See **Cardinals, Biographies).**

Elizondo, Eusebio: b. Aug. 8, 1954, Victoria, Mexico; educ. Missionaries of the Holy Spirit seminary, (Jalisco, Mexico), Gregorian University (Rome); ord. priest (Missionaries of Holy Spirit) Aug. 18, 1984; app. auxiliary bishop of Seattle and titular bishop of Acolla May 12, 2005; ord. bp. June 6, 2005.

Elya, John A., B.S.O.: b. Sept. 16, 1928, Maghdouche, Lebanon; educ. diocesan monastery (Sidon, Lebanon), Gregorian Univ. (Rome, Italy); professed as member of Basilian Salvatorian Order, 1949; ord. priest, Feb. 17, 1952, in Rome; came to U.S., 1958; ord. titular bp. of Abilene of Syria and aux. bp. of Melkite diocese of Newton, MA, June 29, 1986; app. bp. of Newton (Melkites), Nov. 25, 1993, res. Jun. 22, 2004.

Estabrook, Joseph W.: b. May 19, 1944, Kingston, NY; educ. St. Bonaventure University and Christ the King Seminary (St. Bonaventure, NY), Jesuit School of Theology (Berkeley, CA); ord. priest (Albany), May 30, 1969; entered the Archdiocese for the Military Services as a Marine Corps chaplain, 1977; app. titular bp. of Flenucleta and aux. bp. of the Archdiocese

for the Military Ordinariate, May 7, 2004.

Estevez, Felipe de Jesus: b. Feb. 5, 1946, Betancourt, Cuba; educ: Grand Seminary, Montreal, Gregorian Univ., Rome; ord. May 30, 1970 (Matanzas, Cuba); incard. Miami Feb. 1979; app. aux. bp. of Miami and tit. bp. of Kearney Nov. 21, 2003; ord. Jan. 7, 2004.

F

Fabre, Shelton J.: b. Oct. 25, 1963, New Roads, LA; educ. St. Joseph Seminary College (Covington, La.) and American College (Louvain, Belgium);ord. Aug. 5, 1989 (Baton Rouge, LA); app. aux. bp. of New Orleans and tit. bp. of Pudenzuana Dec. 13, 2006; ord. Feb. 28, 2007.

Farrell, Kevin J.: b. Dublin, Ireland, Sept. 2, 1947; educ. University of Salamanca (Spain), Gregorian University and University of St. Thomas Aquinas (Rome), University of Notre Dame (South Bend, IN); ord. priest (of the Legionaries of Christ), Dec. 24, 1978; incardinated into Archdiocese of Washington, 1984; app. titular bp. of Rusuccuru and aux. bp. of Washington, Dec. 28, 2001; app. bp. of Dallas, Mar. 6, 2007.

Favalora, John C.: b. Dec. 5, 1935, New Orleans, LA; educ. St. Joseph Seminary (St. Benedict, LA), Notre Dame Seminary (New Orleans, LA), Gregorian Univ. (Rome), Catholic Univ. of America (Washington, DC), Xavier Univ. and Tulane Univ. (New Orleans); ord. priest (New Orleans*), Dec. 20, 1961; ord. bp. of Alexandria, LA, July 29, 1986; bp. of St. Petersburg, Mar. 14, 1989; app. abp. of Miami, inst., Dec. 20, 1994.

Fellhauer, David E.: b. Aug. 19, 1939, Kansas City, MO; educ. Pontifical College Josephinum (Worthington, OH), St. Paul Univ. (Ottawa); ord. priest (Dallas), May 29, 1965; ord. bp. of Victoria, May 28, 1990.

Fernandez, Gilberto: b. Feb. 13, 1935, Havana, Cuba; educ. El Buen Pastor Seminary (Havana); ord. priest (Havana*), May 15, 1959; came to US, 1967; app. titular bp. of Irina and aux. bp. of Miami, June 24, 1997; ret., Dec. 10, 2002.

Finn, Robert W.: b. Apr. 2, 1953, St. Louis; educ. Kenrick-Glennon Seminary (St. Louis), North American College and Angelicum University (Rome); ord. July 7, 1979 (St. Louis); coad. bp. Kansas City-St. Joseph, Mo., Mar. 9, 2004; ord. May 3, 2004; bp. of Kansas City-St. Joseph, Mo., May 24, 2005.

Fiorenza, Joseph A.: b. Jan. 25, 1931, Beaumont, TX; educ. St. Mary's Seminary (LaPorte, TX); ord. priest (Galveston-Houston), May 29, 1954; ord. bp. of San Angelo, Oct. 25, 1979; app. bp. of Galveston-Houston, Dec. 18, 1984, inst., Feb. 18, 1985; vice president, NCCB/USCC, 1995-1998, President, 1998-2001; app. first abp. of Galveston-Houston, Dec. 29, 2004; ret. Feb. 28, 2006.

Fitzsimons, George K.: b. Sept. 4, 1928, Kansas City, MO; educ. Rockhurst College (Kansas City, MO), Immaculate Conception Seminary (Conception, MO); ord. priest (Kansas City-St. Joseph), Mar. 18, 1961; ord. titular bp. of Pertusa and aux. bp. of Kansas City-St. Joseph, July 3, 1975; app. bp. of Salina, Mar. 28, 1984, inst., May 29, 1984.

Flanagan, Thomas Joseph: b: Oct. 23, 1930, Rathmore, Ireland; educ. St. Patrick's College,

Thurles, Ireland; ord priest (San Antonio*), June 10, 1956; app. titular bp. of Bavagaliana and aux. bp. of San Antonio, Jan. 5, 1998, ord., Feb. 16, 1998; ret. Dec. 15, 2005.

Flesey, John W.: b. Aug. 6, 1942, Jersey City (NJ); educ. St. Peter's College (Jersey City), Immaculate Conception Seminary (South Orange, NJ), Catholic University of America (Washington, DC), Iona College (New Rochelle, NY), Pontifical Gregorian University, Pontifical University of St. Thomas Aquinas (Rome); ord. priest (Newark*), May 31, 1969; dean of the School of Theology, Seton Hall Univ.; app. aux. bp. of Newark and tit. bp. of Allegheny May 21, 2004; ord. Aug. 4, 2004.

Fliss, Raphael M.: b. Oct. 25, 1930, Milwaukee, WI; educ. St. Francis Seminary (Milwaukee, WI), Catholic University (Washington, DC), Pontifical Lateran Univ. (Rome); ord. priest (Milwaukee*), May 26, 1956; ord. coadjutor bp. of Superior with right of succession, Dec. 20, 1979; bp. of Superior, June 27, 1985; ret. June 28, 2007.

Flores, Daniel E.: b. Aug. 28, 1961, Palacios, Texas; educ. University of Dallas, Holy Trinity Seminary (Dallas), Pont. Univ. of St. Thomas Aquinas (Rome); ord. priest Jan. 30, 1988 (Corpus Christi); app. aux. bp. of Detroit and tit. bp. of Cozila Oct. 28, 2006; ord. Nov. 29, 2006.

Flores, Patrick F.: b. July 26, 1929, Ganado, TX; educ. St. Mary's Seminary (Houston, TX); ord. priest (Galveston-Houston), May 26, 1956; ord. titular bp. of Itolica and aux. bp. of San Antonio, May 5, 1970 (first Mexican-American bp.); app. bp. of El Paso, Apr. 4, 1978, inst., May 29, 1978; app. abp. of San Antonio, 1979; inst., Oct. 13, 1979; ret. Dec. 29, 2004.

Flynn, Harry J.: b. May 2, 1933, Schenectady, NY; educ. Siena College (Loudonville, NY), Mt. St. Mary's College (Emmitsburg, MD); ord. priest (Albany), May 28, 1960; ord. coadjutor bp. of Lafayette, LA, June 24, 1986; bp. of Lafayette, LA, May 15, 1989; app. coadjutor abp. of St. Paul and Minneapolis, Feb. 24, 1994, inst., Apr. 27, 1994; abp. of St. Paul and Minneapolis, Sept. 8, 1995; ret. May 2, 2008.

Foley, David E.: b. Feb. 3, 1930, Worcester, MA; educ. St. Charles College (Catonsville, MD), St. Mary's Seminary (Baltimore, MD); ord. priest (Washington*), May 26, 1952; ord. titular bp. of Octaba and aux. bp. of Richmond, June 27, 1986; app. bp. of Birmingham, Mar. 22, 1994; ret. May 10, 2005.

Foley, John Patrick: (See Cardinals' Biographies).

Foys, Roger J.: b. July 27, 1945, Chicago; educ. University of Steubenville, St. John Vianney Seminary, (Bloomingdale, OH), The Catholic University of America, Washington, DC; ord. priest (Steubenville), May 16, 1973; Knight Commander of the Equestrian Order of the Holy Sepulchre of Jerusalem, 1986; app. bp. of Covington, May 31, 2002.

Franklin, William Edwin: b. May 3, 1930, Parnell, IA; educ. Loras College and Mt. St. Bernard Seminary (Dubuque, IA); ord. priest (Dubuque*), Feb. 4, 1956; ord. titular bp. of Surista and aux. bp. of Dubuque, Apr. 1, 1987; app. bp. of Davenport, Nov. 12, 1993, inst., Jan. 20, 1994; ret. Oct. 12, 2006.

Friend, William B.: b. Oct. 22, 1931, Miami, FL; educ. St. Mary's College (St. Mary, KY), Mt. St. Mary Seminary (Emmitsburg, MD), Catholic Univ. (Washington, DC), Notre Dame Univ. (Notre Dame, IN); ord. priest (Mobile*), May 7, 1959; ord. titular bp. of Pomaria and aux. bp. of Alexandria-Shreveport, LA, Oct. 30, 1979; app. bp. of Alexandria-Shreveport, Nov. 17, 1982, inst., Jan 11, 1983; app. first bp. of Shreveport, June, 1986; inst., July 30, 1986; ret. Dec. 20, 2006.

G

Gainer, Ronald W.: b. Aug. 24, 1947, Pottsville, PA; educ. St. Charles Borromeo Seminary (Philadelphia), Gregorian Univ. (Rome); ord. priest (Allentown), May 19, 1973; app. bp. of Lexington, KY, ord. bp., Feb. 22, 2003.

Galante, Joseph A.: b. July 2, 1938, Philadelphia, PA; educ. St. Joseph Preparatory School, St. Charles Seminary (Philadelphia, PA); Lateran Univ., Angelicum, North American College (Rome); ord. priest (Philadelphia*), May 16, 1964; on loan to diocese of Brownsville, TX, 1968-72, where he served in various diocesan posts; returned to Philadelphia, 1972; assistant vicar (1972-79) and vicar (1979-87) for religious; undersecretary of Congregation for Institutes of Consecrated Life and Societies of Apostolic Life (Rome), 1987-92; ord. titular bp. of Equilium and aux. bp. of San Antonio, Dec. 11, 1992; app. bp. of Beaumont, Apr. 5, 1994; app. co-adjutor bp. of Dallas, Nov. 23, 1999; app. bp. of Camden, Mar. 23, 2004.

Galeone, Victor Benito: b. Sept. 13, 1935, Philadelphia; educ. St. Charles College (Baltimore), North American College, Pontifical Gregorian University (Rome), ord. priest (Baltimore*), Dec. 18, 1960; served as missionary in Peru, 1970-75, 1978-85; app. bp. of St. Augustine, June 25, 2001, ord., Aug. 21, 2001.

Garcia, Richard J.: b. Apr. 24, 1947, San Francisco; educ. St. Patrick's Seminary (Menlo Park, CA), Pontifical Univ. of St. Thomas Aquinas (Rome); ord priest (San Francisco*), May 13, 1973; app. Titular bp. of Bapara and aux. bp. of Sacramento, Nov. 25, 1997, ord., Jan. 28, 1998; app. bp. of Monterey in California, Dec. 19, 2006.

Garcia-Siller, Gustavo, M.Sp.S.: b. Dec. 21, 1956, San Luis Potosi, Mexico, educ. St. John's Seminary (Camarillo, CA), Western Jesuit University (Guadalajara, Mexico), Gregorian University (Rome); ord. priest, June 22, 1984; app. aux. bp of Chicago and titular bp. of Esco, Jan. 24, 2003; ord., Mar. 19, 2003.

Garland, James H.: b. Dec. 13, 1931, Wilmington, OH; educ. Wilmington College (OH), Ohio State Univ. (Columbus, OH); Mt. St. Mary's Seminary (Cincinnati, OH), Catholic Univ. (Washington, DC); ord. priest (Cincinnati*), Aug. 15, 1959; ord. titular bp. of Garriana and aux. bp. of Cincinnati, July 25, 1984; app. bp. of Marquette, Oct. 6, 1992; inst., Nov. 11, 1992; ret. Dec. 13, 2005.

Garmo, George: b. Dec. 8, 1921, Telkaif, Iraq; educ. St. Peter Chaldean Patriarchal Seminary (Mossul, Iraq), Pontifical Urban Univ. (Rome); ord. priest, Dec. 8, 1945; pastor of Chaldean parish in Detroit archdiocese, 1960-64, 1966-80; ord. abp. of Chaldean archdiocese of Mosul, Iraq, Sept. 14, 1980.

Gaydos, John R.: b. Aug. 14, 1943, St. Louis, MO; educ Cardinal Glennon College (St. Louis, MO), North American College, Gregorian Univ. (Rome); ord. priest (St. Louis*), Dec. 20, 1968; ord. bp. of Jefferson City, Aug. 27, 1997.

Gelineau, Louis E.: b. May 3, 1928, Burlington, VT; educ. St. Michael's College (Winooski, VT), St. Paul's Univ. Seminary (Ottawa), Catholic Univ. (Washington, DC); ord. priest (Burlington), June 5, 1954; ord. bp. of Providence, RI, Jan. 26, 1972; ret., June 11, 1997.

Gendron, Odore J.: b. Sept. 13, 1921, Manchester, NH; educ. St. Charles Borromeo Seminary (Sherbrooke, QC), Univ. of Ottawa, St. Paul Univ. Seminary (Ottawa, Ont., Canada); ord. priest (Manchester), May 31, 1947; ord. bp. of Manchester, Feb. 3, 1975; res., June 12, 1990.

George, Cardinal Francis E., O.M.I.: (See Cardinals, Biographies).

Gerber, Eugene J.: b. Apr. 30, 1931, Kingman, KS; educ. St. Thomas Seminary (Denver, CO), Wichita State Univ.; Catholic Univ. (Washington, DC), Angelicum (Rome); ord. priest (Wichita), May 19, 1959; ord. bp. of Dodge City, Dec. 14, 1976; app. bp. of Wichita, Nov. 17, 1982, inst., Feb. 9, 1983; res. Oct. 4, 2001.

Gerety, Peter L.: b. July 19, 1912, Shelton, CT; educ. Sulpician Seminary (Paris, France); ord. priest, (Hartford*), June 29, 1939; ord. titular bp. of Crepedula and coadjutor bp. of Portland, ME, with right of succession, June 1, 1966; app. apostolic administrator of Portland, 1967; bp. of Portland, ME, Sept. 15, 1969; app. abp. of Newark, Apr. 2, 1974; inst., June 28, 1974; ret., June 3, 1986.

Gerry, Joseph J., O.S.B.: b. Sept. 12, 1928, Millinocket, ME; educ. St. Anselm Abbey Seminary (Manchester, NH), Univ. of Toronto (Canada), Fordham Univ. (New York); ord. priest, June 12, 1954; abbot of St. Anselm Abbey, Manchester, NH, 1972; ord. titular bp. of Praecausa and aux. of Manchester, Apr. 21, 1986; bp. of Portland, ME, Dec. 27, 1988, inst., Feb. 21, 1989; ret. Feb. 10, 2004.

Gettelfinger, Gerald A.: b. Oct. 20, 1935, Ramsey, IN; educ. St. Meinrad Seminary (St. Meinrad, IN), Butler Univ. (Indianapolis, IN); ord. priest (Indianapolis*), May 7, 1961; ord. bp. of Evansville, Apr. 11, 1989.

Gilbert, Edward J., C.SS.R.: b. Dec. 26, 1936, Brooklyn, NY; educ. Mt. St. Alphonsus Seminary (Esopus, NY), Catholic Univ. (Washington, DC); ord. priest (Redemptorists, Baltimore Province), June 21, 1964; ord. bp. of Roseau, Dominica, Sept. 7, 1994.

Gilmore, Ronald W.: b. Apr. 23, 1942, Wichita, KS; educ. University Seminary (Ottawa), St. Paul University (Ottawa); ord. priest (Wichita), June 7, 1969; app. Bp. of Dodge City, May 11, 1998, ord., July 16, 1998.

Goedert, Raymond E.: b. Oct. 15, 1927, Oak Park, IL; educ. Quigley Preparatory Seminary (Chicago, IL), St. Mary of the Lake Seminary and Loyola Univ. (Chicago, IL), Gregorian Univ. (Rome); ord. priest (Chicago*), May 1, 1952; ord. titular bp. of Tamazeni and aux. bp. of Chicago, Aug. 29, 1991; ret., Jan. 24, 2003.

Gomez, José H.: b. Dec. 26, 1951, Monterrey, Mexico (became U.S. citizen 1995); educ. National University, Mexico, University of Navarre (Spain); ord. priest of the Prelature of Opus Dei, Aug. 15, 1978; Vicar of Opus Dei for State of Texas, 1999-2001; app. titular bp. of Belali and aux. bp of Denver, Jan. 23, 2001, ord., Mar. 26, 2001; app. abp. of San Antonio, Dec. 29, 2004; inst. Feb. 15, 2005.

Gonzalez, Roberto O., O.F.M., b. June 2, 1950, Elizabeth, NJ; educ. St. Joseph Seminary (Callicoon, NY), Siena College, (Loudonville, NY), Washington Theological Union (Silver Spring, MD), Fordham Univ. (New York, NY); solemnly professed in Franciscan Order, 1976; ord. priest, May 8, 1977; ord. titular bp. of Ursona and aux. bp. of Boston, Oct. 3, 1988; app. coadjutor bp. of Corpus Christi, May 16, 1995; bishop of Corpus Christi, Apr. 1, 1997; app. abp. of San Juan de Puerto Rico, Mar. 26, 1999, inst., May 8, 1999.

Gonzalez Valer, S.F., Francisco: b. Arcos de Jalon, Spain, May 22, 1939; educ. Missionary Seminary of the Holy Family, Barcelona (Spain), Catholic University of America (Washington, DC); ord. priest (of the Congregation of the Sons of the Holy Family), May 1, 1964; Episcopal Vicar for Hispanic Catholics, Archdiocese of Washington, 1997; app. titular bp. of Lamfua and aux. bp. of Washington, Dec. 28, 2001.

Gorman, John R.: b. Dec. 11, 1925, Chicago, IL; educ, St. Mary of the Lake Seminary (Mundelein, IL), Loyola Univ. (Chicago, IL); ord. priest (Chicago*), May 1, 1956; ord. titular bp. of Catula and aux. bp. of Chicago, Apr. 11, 1988; ret., Jan. 24, 2003.

Gossman, F. Joseph: b. Apr. 1, 1930, Baltimore, MD; educ. St. Charles College (Catonsville, MD), St. Mary's Seminary (Baltimore, MD), North American College (Rome), Catholic Univ. (Washington, DC); ord. priest (Baltimore*), Dec. 17, 1955; ord. titular bp. of Agunto and aux. bp. of Baltimore, Sept. 11, 1968; app. bp. of Raleigh, Apr. 8, 1975; ret. June 8, 2006.

Gracida, Rene H.: b. June 9, 1923, New Orleans, LA; educ. Rice Univ. and Univ. of Houston (Houston, TX), Univ. of Fribourg (Switzerland); ord. priest (Miami*), May 23, 1959; ord. titular bp. of Masuccaba and aux. bp. of Miami, Jan. 25, 1972; app. first bp. of Pensacola-Tallahassee, Oct. 1, 1975, inst., Nov. 6, 1975; app. bp. of Corpus Christi, May 24, 1983, inst., July 11, 1983; ret., Apr. 1, 1997.

Grahmann, Charles V.: b. July 15, 1931, Halletsville, TX; educ. The Assumption-St. John's Seminary (San Antonio, TX); ord. priest (San Antonio*), Mar. 17, 1956; ord. titular bp. of Equilium and aux. bp. of San Antonio, Aug. 20, 1981; app. first bp. of Victoria, TX, Apr. 13, 1982; app. coadjutor bp. of Dallas, Dec. 9, 1989; bp. of Dallas, July 14, 1990; ret. Mar. 6, 2007.

Green, James P.: b. May 30, 1950, Philadelphia, PA; educ. St. Charles Borromeo Seminary (Overbrook, PA), Pontifical Ecclesiastical Academy (Rome); ord. priest (Philadelphia*), May 15, 1976; after studies at the Pontifical Ecclesiastical Academy, entered the diplomatic service of the Holy See in 1987 and served in Papua New Guinea, Korea, the Netherlands, Spain, Scandinavia, and Taiwan; head of the English-language section in the Secretariat of State 2002-2006; app. nuncio to South Africa, Lesotho, and Namibia, and apostolic delegate in Botswana, Aug. 17, 2006; cons. Sept. 6, 2006.

Gregory, Wilton D.: b. Dec. 7, 1947, Chicago, IL; educ. Quigley Preparatory Seminary South, Niles

College of Loyola Univ. (Chicago, IL), St. Mary of the Lake Seminary (Mundelein, IL), Pontifical Liturgical Institute, Sant'Anselmo (Rome); ord. priest, (Chicago*), May 9, 1973; ord. titular bp. of Oliva and aux. bp. of Chicago, Dec. 13, 1983; app. bp. of Belleville, Dec. 29, 1993; inst., Feb. 10, 1994 vice president, NCCB/USCC, 1998-2001; president, USCCB, 2001-2004; app. abp. of Atlanta, Dec. 9, 2004; inst. Jan. 17, 2005.

Gries, Roger W., O.S.B.: b. Mar. 26, 1937, Cleveland; educ. St. John Univ., (Collegeville, MN), St. Joseph's Seminary, Cleveland, Loyola Univ., Chicago; ord. priest (Order of St. Benedict), May 16, 1963; Abbot, St. Andrew Abbey, Cleveland, 1981-2001; app. aux. bp. of Cleveland, Apr. 3, 2001, ord., June 7, 2001.

Griffin, James A.: b. June 13, 1934, Fairview Park, OH; educ. St. Charles College (Baltimore, MD), Borromeo College (Wicklife, OH); St Mary Seminary (Cleveland, OH); Lateran Univ. (Rome); Cleveland State Univ.; ord. priest (Cleveland), May 28, 1960; ord. titular bp. of Holar and aux. bp. of Cleveland, Aug. 1, 1979; app. bp. of Columbus, Feb. 8, 1983.

Grosz, Edward M.: b. Feb. 16, 1945, Buffalo, NY; educ. St. John Vianney Seminary (East Aurora, NY), Univ. Notre Dame (Notre Dame, IN); ord. priest (Buffalo), May 29, 1971; ord. titular bp. of Morosbisdus and aux. bp. of Buffalo, Feb. 2, 1990.

Guillory, Curtis J., S.V.D.: b. Sept. 1, 1943, Mallet, LA; educ. Divine Word College (Epworth, IA), Chicago Theological Union (Chicago), Creighton Univ. (Omaha, NE); ord. priest, Dec. 16, 1972; ord. titular bp. of Stagno and aux. bp. of Galveston-Houston, Feb. 19, 1988; bp. of Beaumont, June 2, 2000, inst., July 28, 2000.

Gullickson, Thomas E.: b. Aug. 14, 1950, Sioux Falls, SD; educ. North American College and Pontifical Gregorian University (Rome, Italy); ord. priest, June 27, 1976 (Sioux Falls); after studies in the Pontifical Ecclesiastical Academy, he entered the diplomatic service of the Holy See in 1985 and served in the nunciatures in Rwanda, Austria, Czechoslovakia, Jerusalem, and Germany; app. titular abp. of Bomarzo, Oct. 2, 2004; cons. Nov. 11, 2004; Apostolic Nuncio to Trinidad and Tobago, Bahamas, Dominica, St. Kitts and Nevis, Santa Lucia, San Vincenzo and Grenadine.

Gumbleton, Thomas J.: b. Jan. 26, 1930, Detroit, MI; educ. St. John Provincial Seminary (Detroit, MI), Pontifical Lateran Univ. (Rome); ord. priest (Detroit*), June 2, 1956; ord. titular bp. of Ululi and aux. bp. of Detroit, May 1, 1968; ret. Feb. 2, 2006.

H

Hanifen, Richard C.: b. June 15, 1931, Denver, CO; educ. Regis College and St. Thomas Seminary (Denver, CO), Catholic Univ. (Washington, DC), Lateran Univ. (Rome); ord. priest (Denver*), June 6, 1959; ord. titular bp. of Abercorn and aux. bp. of Denver, Sept. 20, 1974; app. first bp. of Colorado Springs, Nov. 10, 1983; inst., Jan. 30, 1984; ret., Jan. 30, 2003.

Hannan, Philip M.: b. May 20, 1913, Washington, DC; educ. St. Charles College (Catonsville, MD), Catholic Univ. (Washington, DC), North American College (Rome); ord. priest (Washington*), Dec. 8, 1939; ord. titular bp. of Hieropolis and aux. bp. of Washington, DC, Aug. 28, 1956; app. abp. of New Orleans, inst., Oct. 13, 1965; ret., Dec. 6, 1988.

Hanus, Jerome George, O.S.B.: b. May 25, 1940, Brainard, NE; educ. Conception Seminary (Conception, MO), St. Anselm Univ. (Rome), Princeton Theological Seminary (Princeton, NJ); ord. priest (Conception Abbey, MO), July 30, 1966; abbot of Conception Abbey, 1977-87; president of Swiss American Benedictine Congregation, 1984-87; ord. bp. of St. Cloud, Aug. 24, 1987; app. coadjutor abp. of Dubuque, Aug. 23, 1994; abp. of Dubuque, Oct. 16, 1995.

Harrington, Bernard J.: b. Sept. 6, 1933, Detroit, MI; educ. Sacred Heart Seminary (Detroit), St. John's Provincial Seminary (Plymouth, MI), Catholic Univ. of America (Washington, DC), University of Detroit; ord. priest (Detroit*), June 6, 1959; ord. titular bp. of Uzali and aux. bp. of Detroit, Jan. 6, 1994; app. Bp. of Winona, Nov. 5, 1998, inst., Jan. 6, 1999.

Hart, Joseph: b. Sept. 26, 1931, Kansas City, MO; educ. St. John Seminary (Kansas City, MO), St. Meinrad Seminary (Indianapolis, IN); ord. priest (Kansas City-St. Joseph), May 1, 1956; ord. titular bp. of Thimida Regia and aux. bp. of Cheyenne, WY, Aug. 31, 1976; app. bp. of Cheyenne, inst., June 12, 1978; ret., Sept. 26, 2001.

Harvey, James M.: b. Oct. 20, 1949, Milwaukee, WI; educ. De Sales Preparatory Seminary and St. Francis De Sales College, Milwaukee, North American College and Gregorian Univ. (Rome); ord. priest (Milwaukee*), June 29, 1975; entered Vatican diplomatic service, 1980; Apostolic Nunciature, Dominican Republic, 1980-82; transferred to the Vatican Secretariat of State, 1982; named assessor of the Secretariat, 1997; named titular bp. of Memphis and prefect of the papal household, Feb. 7, 1998; ordained bp., Mar. 19, 1998; named titular abp. Sept. 29, 2003.

Heim, Capistran F., O.F.M.: b. Jan. 21, 1934, Catskill, NY; educ. Franciscan Houses of Study; ord. priest, Dec. 18, 1965; missionary in Brazil; ord. first bp. of prelature of Itaituba, Brazil, Sept. 17, 1988; inst., Oct. 2, 1988.

Hennessey, Robert F.: b. Apr. 20, 1952 (Boston); educ. St. John's Seminary (Brighton, MA), Moreau Seminary (Notre Dame, IN); ord. May 20, 1978 (Boston); app. aux. bp. of Boston and tit. bp. of Tigia Oct. 12, 2006; ord. Dec. 12, 2006.

Hermann, Robert J.: b. Aug. 12, 1934, Weingarten, MO.; educ. Cardinal Glennon College (Shrewsbury, MO.), St. Louis Univ.; ord. priest (St. Louis), Mar. 30, 1963; aux. bp. St. Louis and tit. bp. of Zerta, Oct. 16, 2002; ord., Dec. 12, 2002.

Hermes, Herbert, O.S.B.: b. May 25, 1933, Scott City, KS; ord. priest (St. Benedict Abbey, Atchison, KS), May 26, 1960; missionary in Brazil; ord. bp. of territorial prelature of Cristalandia, Brazil, Sept. 2, 1990.

Herzog, Ronald P.: b. Apr. 22, 1942, Akron, OH; educ. St. Joseph Seminary (St. Benedict, LA), Pontifical College Josephinum (Worthington, OH); ord. priest June 1, 1968 (Natchez-Jackson, MS; now Biloxi); app. bp. of Alexandria Nov. 4, 2004; ord. Jan. 5, 2005.

Higgins Richard B.: b. Feb. 22, 1944, Longford, Ireland; educ. Pontifical Lateran Univ. (Rome); ord.

priest (Sacramento), Mar. 9, 1968; entered the Air Force as a chaplain, 1974; app. titular bp. of Case Calane and aux. bp. of the Archdiocese for the Military Services, May 7, 2004.

Higi, William L.: b. Aug. 29, 1933, Anderson, IN; educ. Our Lady of the Lakes Preparatory Seminary (Wawasee, IN), Mt. St. Mary of the West Seminary and Xavier Univ. (Cincinnati, OH); ord. priest, (Lafayette, IN) May 30, 1959; ord. bp. of Lafayette, IN, June 6, 1984.

Hoeppner, Michael J.: b. June 1,1949, Winona, MN; educ. Immaculate Heart of Mary Seminary (Winona), Pontifical North American College and Pontifical Gregorian University (Rome), St. Paul University (Ottawa, Canada), Winona State University (Winona); ord. priest, June 29, 1975 (Winona); app. bp. of Crookston, Sept. 28, 2007; inst. Nov. 30, 2007.

Holley, Martin D.: b. Dec. 31, 1954, Pensacola, FL; educ. Alabama State University (Montgomery, AL), Catholic University of America (Washington, DC), St. Vincent de Paul Regional Seminary (Boynton Beach); ord. priest (Pensacola-Tallahassee), May 8, 1987; app. titular bp. of Rusibisir and aux. bp. of Washington, May 18, 2004; ord. July 2, 2004.

Houck, William Russell: b. June 26, 1926, Mobile, AL; educ. St. Bernard Junior College (Cullman, AL), St. Mary's Seminary College and St. Mary's Seminary (Baltimore, MD), Catholic Univ. (Washington, DC); ord. priest (Mobile*), May 19, 1951; ord. titular bp. of Alessano and aux. bp. of Jackson, MS, May 27, 1979, by Pope John Paul II; app. bp. of Jackson, Apr. 11, 1984, inst., June 5, 1984; ret., Jan. 3, 2003.

Howze, Joseph Lawson: b. Aug. 30, 1923, Daphne, AL; convert to Catholicism, 1948; educ. St. Bonaventure Univ. (St. Bonaventure, NY); ord. priest (Raleigh), May 7, 1959; ord. titular bp. of Massita and aux. bp. of Natchez-Jackson, Jan. 28, 1973; app. first bp. of Biloxi, Mar. 8, 1977; inst., June 6, 1977; res. May 15, 2001.

Hubbard, Howard J.: b. Oct. 31, 1938, Troy, NY; educ. St. Joseph's Seminary (Dunwoodie, NY); North American College and Gregorian Univ. (Rome), Catholic Univ. (Washington, DC); ord. priest (Albany), Dec. 18, 1963; ord. bp. of Albany, Mar. 27, 1977.

Hughes, Alfred C.: b. Dec. 2, 1932, Boston, MA; educ. St. John Seminary (Brighton, MA), Gregorian Univ. (Rome); ord. priest (Boston*), Dec. 15, 1957, in Rome; ord. titular bp. of Maximiana in Byzacena and aux. bp. of Boston, Sept. 14, 1981; app. bp. of Baton Rouge, Sept. 7, 1993; co-adj. abp. of New Orleans, Feb. 16, 2001; abp. of New Orleans, Jan. 3, 2002.

Hughes, Edward T.: b. Nov. 13, 1920, Lansdowne, PA; educ. St. Charles Seminary, Univ. of Pennsylvania (Philadelphia); ord. priest (Philadelphia*), May 31, 1947; ord. titular bp. of Segia and aux. bp. of Philadelphia, July 21, 1976; app. bp. of Metuchen, Dec. 11, 1986, inst., Feb. 5, 1987; ret., July 8, 1997.

Hughes, William A.: b. Sept. 23, 1921, Youngstown, OH; educ. St. Charles College (Catonsville, MD), St. Mary's Seminary (Cleveland, OH), Univ. Notre Dame (Notre Dame, IN); ord. priest (Youngstown), Apr. 6, 1946; ord. titular bp. of Inis Cathaig and aux. bp. of Youngstown, Sept. 12, 1974; app. bp. of Covington, inst., May 8, 1979; ret., July 4, 1995.

Hunthausen, Raymond G.: b. Aug. 21, 1921, Anaconda, MT; educ. Carroll College (Helena, MT), St. Edward's Seminary (Kenmore, WA), St. Louis Univ. (St. Louis, MO), Catholic Univ. (Washington, DC), Fordham Univ. (New York City), Univ. Notre Dame (Notre Dame, IN); ord. priest (Helena), June 1, 1946; ord. bp. of Helena, Aug. 30, 1962; app. abp. of Seattle, Feb. 25, 1975; ret., Aug. 21, 1991.

Hurley, Francis T.: b. Jan. 12, 1927, San Francisco, CA; educ. St. Patrick's Seminary (Menlo Park, CA), Catholic Univ. (Washington, DC); ord. priest (San Francisco*), June 16, 1951; assigned to NCWC in Washington, DC, 1957; assistant (1958) and later (1968) associate secretary of NCCB and USCC; ord. titular bp. of Daimlaig and aux. bp. of Juneau, AK, Mar. 19, 1970; app. bp. of Juneau, July 20, 1971, inst., Sept. 8, 1971; app. abp. of Anchorage, May 4, 1976, inst., July 8, 1976; res., Mar. 3, 2001.

Hurley, Walter A.: b. May 30, 1937, Fredericton, New Brunswick; educ. Sacred Heart Seminary, St. John Provincial Seminary, The Catholic University of America; ord. priest, June 5, 1965 (Detroit); app. aux. bp. of Detroit and titular bishop of Cunavia, July 7, 2003; app. bp. of Grand Rapids, June 21, 2005; inst. Aug. 5, 2005.

I-J

Ibrahim, Ibrahim N.: b. Oct. 1, 1937, Telkaif, Mosul, Iraq.; educ. Patriarchal Seminary (Mosul, Iraq), St. Sulpice Seminary (Paris, France); ord. priest, Dec. 30, 1962, in Baghdad, Iraq; ord. titular bp. of Anbar and apostolic exarch for Chaldean Catholics in the United States, Mar. 8, 1982, in Baghdad; inst., in Detroit, Apr. 18, 1982; app. first eparch, Aug. 3, 1985, when exarchate was raised to eparchy of St. Thomas Apostle of Detroit.

Imesch, Joseph L.: b. June 21, 1931, Detroit, MI; educ. Sacred Heart Seminary (Detroit, MI), North American College, Gregorian Univ. (Rome); ord. priest (Detroit*), Dec. 16, 1956; ord. titular bp. of Pomaria and aux. bp. of Detroit, Apr. 3, 1973; app. bp. of Joliet, June 30, 1979; ret. May 16, 2006.

Iriondo, Robert J.: b. Dec. 19, 1938, Legazti, Spain; educ. Collegio San Vittore and Pontifical Gregorian University, Rome; ord. priest (of the Canons Regular of the Lateran), Dec. 22, 1962; incardinated into Archdio. of NY, 1996; Vicar for Hispanics, 1997; ord. titular bp. of Alton and aux. of New York, Dec. 12, 2001.

Irwin, Francis X.: b. Jan 9, 1934, Medford, MA; educ. Boston College High School, Boston College, St. John's Seminary (Brighton, MA), Boston College School of Social Service; ord. priest (Boston*), Feb. 2, 1960; ord. titular bp. of Ubaza and aux. bp. of Boston, Sept. 17, 1996.

Jackels, Michael O.: b. Apr. 13, 1954, Rapid City, SD; educ. University of Nebraska-Lincoln, St. Pius X Seminary (Erlanger, KY), Mount St. Mary's (Emmitburg, MD); ord. priest May 30, 1981 (Lincoln, NE); app. bp. of Wichita Jan. 29, 2005; ord. Apr. 4, 2005.

Jacobs, Sam Gallip: b. Mar. 4, 1938, Greenwood, MS; educ. Immaculata Seminary (Lafayette, LA), Catholic Univ. (Washington, DC); ord. priest (Lafayette), June 6, 1964; became priest of Lake Charles diocese, 1980, when that see was established; ord. bp. of Alexandria, LA, Aug. 24, 1989; app. bp. of Houma-Thibodaux, Aug. 1, 2003.

Jakubowski, Thad J.: b. Apr. 5, 1924, Chicago, IL;

educ. Mundelein Seminary, St. Mary of the Lake Univ., Loyola Univ. (Chicago); ord priest (Chicago*), May 3, 1950; ord. titular bp. of Plestia and aux. bp. of Chicago, Apr. 11, 1988; ret., Jan. 24, 2003.

Jammo, Sarhad: b. Mar. 14, 1941, Baghdad, Iraq; educ. Patriarchal Seminary of Mosul, Urban College of the Propaganda Fide Pontifical Oriental Institute (Rome); ord. priest (Baghdad*), Dec. 19, 1964; rector, Chaldean Seminary, Baghdad; after service in Iraq, transferred in 1977 to the Eparchy of St. Thomas the Apostle of Detroit for Chaldeans; app. first eparch of the eparchy of St. Peter the Apostle of San Diego (Chaldean), May 21, 2002.

Jarrell, C. Michael: b. May 15, 1940, Opelousas, LA; educ. Immaculata Minor Seminary (Lafayette, LA); Catholic Univ. (Washington, DC); ord. priest (Lafayette, LA), June 3, 1967; ord. bp. of Houma-Thibodaux, Mar. 4, 1993; app. bp. of Lafayette, Nov. 8, 2002.

Jenky, Daniel R., C.S.C.: b. Mar. 3, 1947, Chicago; educ. University of Notre Dame; ord. priest, Apr. 6, 1974; Religious Superior of the Holy Cross religious at Notre Dame, 1985-1990; app.Titular Bp. of Amanzia and Aux. of Fort Wayne-South Bend, Oct. 21, 1997, ord., Dec. 16, 1997, bp. of Peoria, Feb. 12, 2002, inst. Apr. 10, 2002.

Johnston, James Vann: b. Oct. 16, 1959, Knoxville, TN; educ. University of Tennessee (Knoxville, TN), St. Meinrad Seminary (St.Meinrad, IN), Catholic University of America (Washington, DC.); ord. priest, June 9, 1990 (Knoxville); app. bp. of Springfield-Cape Girardeau, Jan. 24, 2008; ord. bp., Mar. 31, 2008.

Jugis, Peter J.: b. Mar. 3, 1957, Charlotte, NC; educ. University of North Carolina at Charlotte, North American College and Gregorian Univ. (Rome), Catholic University of America (Washington, DC); ord. priest, June 12, 1983; app. bp. of Charlotte, Aug. 1, 2003; ord. Oct. 24, 2003.

Justice, William J.: b. May 8, 1942; educ., St. Patrick Seminary (Menlo Park, CA), University of San Francisco (San Francisco, CA); ord. priest, May 17, 1968 (San Francisco*); app. titular bp. of Matara di Proconsolare and aux. bp. of San Francisco, Apr. 10, 2008; ord. bp., May 28, 2008.

K

Kaffer, Roger L.: b. Aug. 14, 1927, Joliet, IL; educ. Quigley Preparatory Seminary (Chicago, IL), St. Mary of the Lake Seminary (Mundelein, IL), Gregorian Univ. (Rome); ord. priest (Joliet), May 1, 1954; ord. titular bp. of Dusa and aux. bp. of Joliet, June 26, 1985; res., Aug. 15, 2002, ret., Sept. 1, 2002.

Kalisz, Raymond P., S.V.D.: b. Sept. 25, 1927, Melvindale, MI; educ. St. Mary's Seminary (Techny, IL); ord. priest, Aug. 15, 1954; ord. bp. of Wewak, Papua New Guinea, Aug. 15, 1980; ret. Aug. 14, 2002.

Kane, Francis Joseph: b. Oct. 30, 1942, Chicago, IL; educ. Quigley Preparatory Seminary (Chicago, IL), Niles College Seminary (Chicago, IL), St. Mary of the Lake Seminary (Chicago, IL); ord. priest, May 14, 1969 (Chicago*); app. aux. bp. of Chicago and titular bp. of Sault St. Marie in Michigan Jan. 24, 2003; ord., Mar. 19, 2003.

Keeler, Cardinal William Henry: (*See* **Cardinals, Biographies**.)

Keleher, James P.: b. July 31, 1931, Chicago, IL;

educ. Quigley Preparatory Seminary (Chicago, IL), St. Mary of the Lake Seminary (Mundelein, IL); ord. priest (Chicago*), Apr. 12, 1958; ord. bp. of Belleville, Dec. 11, 1984; app. abp. of Kansas City, KS, June 28, 1993; ret. Jan. 15, 2005.

Kelly, Thomas C., O.P.: b. July 14, 1931, Rochester, NY; educ. Providence College (Providence, RI), Immaculate Conception College (Washington, DC), Angelicum (Rome); professed in Dominicans, Aug. 26, 1952; secretary, apostolic delegation, Washington, DC, 1965-71; associate general secretary, 1971-77, and general secretary, 1977-81, NCCB/USCC; ord. titular bp. of Tusurus and aux. bp. of Washington, DC, Aug. 15, 1977; app. abp. of Louisville, Dec. 28, 1981, inst., Feb. 18, 1982; ret. June 12, 2007.

Kettler, Donald J.: b. Nov. 26, 1944, Minneapolis: educ. St. John's Seminary Collegeville, MN; ord. priest (Sioux Falls), May 29, 1970; app. bp. of Fairbanks, AK, June 7, 2002, ord., Aug. 22, 2002.

Kicanas, Gerald F.: b. Aug. 18, 1941, Chicago, IL; educ. Quigley Preparatory Seminary, St. Mary of the Lake Seminary and Loyola University in Chicago; ord. priest (Chicago*), Apr. 27, 1967; ord. titular bp. of Bela and aux. of Chicago, Mar. 20, 1995; app. coadj. bp. of Tucson, Oct. 30, 2001; inst. as coadj. bp. of Tuscon, Jan. 17, 2002; bp. of Tucson, Mar. 7, 2003.

Kinney, John F.: b. June 11, 1937, Oelwein, IA; educ. Nazareth Hall and St. Paul Seminaries (St. Paul, MN); Pontifical Lateran University (Rome); ord. priest (St. Paul-Minneapolis*), Feb. 2, 1963; ord. titular bp. of Caorle and aux. bp. of St. Paul and Minneapolis, Jan. 25, 1977; app. bp. of Bismarck June 30, 1982; app. bp. of St. Cloud, May 9, 1995.

Kmiec, Edward U.: b. June 4, 1936, Trenton, NJ; educ. St. Charles College (Catonsville, MD), St. Mary's Seminary (Baltimore, MD), Gregorian Univ. (Rome); ord. priest (Trenton), Dec. 20, 1961; ord. titular bp. of Simidicca and aux. bp. of Trenton, Nov. 3, 1982; app. bp. of Nashville, Oct. 13, 1992; inst., Dec. 3, 1992; app. bp. Of Buffalo, Aug. 12, 2004.

Kucera, Daniel W., O.S.B.: b. May 7, 1923, Chicago, IL; educ. St. Procopius College (Lisle, IL), Catholic Univ. (Washington, DC); professed in Order of St. Benedict, June 16, 1944; ord. priest, May 26, 1949; abbot, St. Procopius Abbey, 1964-71; pres. Illinois Benedictine College, 1959-65 and 1971-76; ord. titular bp. of Natchez and aux. bp. of Joliet, July 21, 1977; app. bp. of Salina, Mar. 5, 1980; app. abp. of Dubuque, inst., Feb. 23, 1984; ret., Oct. 16, 1995.

Kuchmiak, Michael, C.SsR.: b. Feb. 5, 1923, Obertyn, Horodenka, Western Ukraine; left during World War II; educ. St. Josaphat Ukrainian Seminary (Rome, Italy), St. Mary's Seminary (Meadowvale, Ont., Canada); ord. priest, May 13, 1956; in the U.S. from 1967; ord. titular bp. of Agathopolis and aux. bp. of Ukrainian metropolitan of Philadelphia, Apr. 27, 1988; exarch of apostolic exarchate for Ukrainian Catholics in Great Britain, June 24, 1989.

Kudrick, John M.: b. Dec. 23, 1947, Lloydell, PA; educ. Third Order Regular of St. Francis, 1967; ord. priest, May 3, 1975; granted bi-ritual faculties for service in the Byzantine Rite, 1978; app. bp. of Parma, May 3, 2002.

Kupfer, William F., M.M.: b. Jan. 28, 1909, Brooklyn, NY; educ. Cathedral College (Brooklyn, NY), Maryknoll Seminary (Maryknoll, NY); ord.

priest, June 11, 1933; missionary in China; app. prefect apostolic of Taichung, Taiwan, 1951; ord. first bp. of Taichung, July 25, 1962; ret., Sept. 3, 1986.

Kurtz, Joseph E.: b. Aug. 18, 1946, Shenandoah, PA.; educ. St. Charles Borromeo Seminary, Philadelphia, Marywood College, Scranton; ord. priest (Allentown), Mar. 18, 1972; app. bishop of Knoxville, Oct. 26, 1999, ord., Dec. 8, 1999; app. abp. of Louisville, June 12, 2007.

Kurtz, Robert, C.R.: b. July 25, 1939, Chicago, IL; ord. priest, Mar. 11, 1967; ord. bp. of Hamilton, Bermuda, Sept. 15, 1995; inst. Aug. 15, 2007.

Kuzma, George M.: b. July 24, 1925, Windber, PA; educ. St. Francis Seminary (Loretto, PA), St. Procopius College (Lisle, IL), Sts. Cyril and Methodius Byzantine Catholic Seminary, Duquesne Univ. (Pittsburgh, PA); ord. priest (Pittsburgh*, Byzantine Rite), May 5, 1955; ord. titular bp. of Telmisso and aux. bp. of Byzantine eparchy of Passaic, 1987; app. bp. of Byzantine diocese of Van Nuys, CA, Oct. 23, 1990, inst., Jan. 15, 1991; res., Dec. 5, 2000.

L

Lagonegro, Dominick J.: b. Mar. 6, 1943, White Plains, NY; educ. Cathedral College, (Douglaston), St. Joseph Seminary, Yonkers; ord. priest (New York*), May 31, 1969; ord. titular bp. of Modrus and aux. of New York, Dec. 12, 2001.

Lambert, Francis, S.M.: b. Feb. 7, 1921, Lawrence, MA; educ. Marist Seminary (Framingham, MA); ord. priest, June 29, 1946; served in Marist missions in Oceania; provincial of Marist Oceania province, 1971; ord. bp. of Port Vila, Vanuatu (New Hebrides), Mar. 20, 1977; ret., Nov. 30, 1996.

Latino, Joseph: b. Oct. 21, 1937, New Orleans, LA; educ. St. Joseph College Seminary (Covington, LA), Notre Dame Seminary (New Orleans, LA); ord. priest, May 25, 1963; app. bp. Jackson, Jan. 3, 2003; ord., Mar. 7, 2003.

Law, Bernard F.: (*See* Cardinals, Biographies.)

Leibrecht, John J.: b. Aug. 30, 1930, Overland, MO; educ. Catholic Univ. (Washington, DC); ord. priest (St. Louis*), Mar. 17, 1956; superintendent of schools of St. Louis archdiocese, 1962-1981; ord. bp. of Springfield-Cape Girardeau, MO, Dec. 12, 1984; ret. Jan. 24, 2008.

Lennon, Richard G.: b. Mar. 26, 1947, Arlington, (MA); educ. St. John's Seminary, Brighton; ord. priest (Boston*), May 19, 1973; rector, St. John's Seminary 1999-2001; app. titular bp. of Sufes and aux. bp. of Boston, June 29, 2001, ord., Sept. 14, 2001; apost. admin. of Boston, 2002-03; app. bp. of Cleveland, Apr. 4, 2006.

Lessard, Raymond W.: b. Dec. 21, 1930, Grafton, ND; educ. St. Paul Seminary (St. Paul, MN), North American College (Rome); ord. priest (Fargo), Dec. 16, 1956; served on staff of the Congregation for Bps. in the Roman Curia, 1964-73; ord. bp. of Savannah, Apr. 27, 1973; ret., Feb. 7, 1995.

Levada, William J.: (*See* Cardinals, Biographies).

LeVoir, John: b. Feb. 7, 1946, Minneapolis, MN; educ. University of St. Thomas (Houston, TX), Dallas University (Dallas, TX), St. Paul Seminary (St. Paul and Minneapolis, MN); ord. priest May 30, 1981 (St. Paul and Minneapolis*); co-author of *Covenant of Love: John Paul II on Sexuality, Marriage, and Family in the Modern World, Faith for Today,* and the series

Image of God; app. bp. of New Ulm, July 14, 2008.

Libasci, Peter A.: b. Nov. 9, 1951, Jackson Heights (NY); educ. St. John's Univ. (Queens, NY), St. Meinrad School of Theology (St. Meinrad, IN); ord. priest (Rockville Center, NY), Apr. 1, 1978; app. titular bp. of Satafis and aux. bp. of Rockville Center, Apr. 3, 2007.

Lipscomb, Oscar H.: b. Sept. 21, 1931, Mobile, AL; educ. McGill Institute, St. Bernard College (Cullman, AL), North American College and Gregorian Univ. (Rome), Catholic Univ. (Washington, DC); ord. priest (Mobile*), July 15, 1956; ord. first abp. of Mobile, Nov. 16, 1980; ret. Apr. 2, 2008.

Listecki, Jerome E.: b. Mar. 12, 1949, Chicago; educ. Loyola University and St. Mary of the Lake Seminary, Mundelein, IL, De Paul University College of Law, University of St. Thomas Aquinas and Pontifical Gregorian University, Rome; ord. priest (Chicago*), June 1, 1975; app. titular bp. of Nara and aux bp. of Chicago, Nov. 7, 2000, ord., Jan. 8, 2001; app. bp. of La Crosse, Dec. 29, 2004; inst. Mar. 1, 2005.

Lohmuller, Martin N.: b. Aug. 21, 1919, Philadelphia, PA; educ. St. Charles Borromeo Seminary (Philadelphia, PA), Catholic Univ. (Washington, DC); ord. priest (Philadelphia*), June 3, 1944; ord. titular bp. of Ramsbury and aux. bp. of Philadelphia, Apr. 2, 1970; ret., Oct. 11, 1994.

Lori, William E.: b. May 6, 1951, Louisville, KY; educ. St. Pius X College (Covington, KY), Mount St. Mary's Seminary (Emmitsburg, MD), Catholic Univ. (Washington, DC); ord. priest (Washington*), May 14, 1977; ord. titular bp. of Bulla and aux. bp. of Washington, DC, Apr. 20, 1995; app. bp. of Bridgeport, Jan. 23, 2001; inst., Mar. 19, 2001.

Losten, Basil: b. May 11, 1930, Chesapeake City, MD; educ. St. Basil's College (Stamford, CT), Catholic University (Washington, DC); ord. priest (Philadelphia* Ukrainian Byzantine), June 10, 1957; ord. titular bp. of Arcadiopolis in Asia and aux. bp. of Ukrainian archeparchy of Philadelphia, May 25, 1971; app. apostolic administrator of archeparchy, 1976; app. bp. of Ukrainian eparchy of Stamford, Sept. 20, 1977; ret. Jan. 3, 2006.

Lotocky, Innocent Hilarius, O.S.B.M.: b. Nov. 3, 1915, Petlykiwci, Ukraine; educ. seminaries in Ukraine, Czechoslovakia and Austria; ord. priest, Nov. 24, 1940; ord. bp. of St. Nicholas of Chicago for the Ukrainians, Mar. 1, 1981; ret., July 15, 1993.

Loverde, Paul S.: b. Sept. 3, 1940, Framingham, MA; educ. St. Thomas Seminary (Bloomfield, CT), St. Bernard Seminary (Rochester, NY), Gregorian Univ. (Rome), Catholic Univ. (Washington, DC); ord. priest (Norwich), Dec. 18, 1965; ord. titular bp. of Ottabia and aux. bp. of Hartford, Apr. 12, 1988; app. bp. of Ogdensburg, Nov. 11, 1993; inst., Jan. 17, 1994; app. bp. of Arlington, Jan. 25, 1999, inst., Mar. 25, 1999.

Lucas, George J.: b. June 12, 1949, St. Louis, MO; educ. Major Seminary of St. Louis, Univ. of St. Louis; ord. priest (St. Louis*), May 24, 1975; rector, Kenrick-Glennon Seminary, 1995-1999; app. bishop of Springfield, IL, Oct. 19, 1999, ord., Dec. 14, 1999.

Luong, Dominic Dinh Mai: b: Dec. 20, 1940, Minh Cuong, Vietnam; educ. seminary (Buffalo, NY), and St. Bernard Seminary (Rochester, NY), Canisius College (Buffalo); ord. priest in Buffalo for Diocese of Danang, Vietnam, May 21, 1966; incardinated into New Orleans 1986; named aux. bp. of Orange, CA, and titular bp. of Cebarades, Apr. 25, 2003; ord., June 11, 2003.

Lynch, Robert N.: b. May 27, 1941, Charleston, WV; educ.

Pontifical College Josephinum (Columbus, OH); John XXIII National Seminary (Weston, MA); ord. priest (Miami*), May 13, 1978; associate general secretary (1984-89) and general secretary (1989-95) of the NCCB/USCC; app. bp. of St. Petersburg, Dec. 5, 1995; ord. and inst., Jan. 26, 1996; app. apostolic administrator of Palm Beach (while continuing as bp. of St. Petersburg), June 2, 1998.

Lyne, Timothy J.: b. Mar. 21, 1919, Chicago, IL; educ. Quigley Preparatory Seminary, St. Mary of the Lake Seminary (Mundelein, IL); ord. priest (Chicago*), May 1, 1943; ord. titular bp. of Vamalla and aux. bp. of Chicago, Dec. 13, 1983; ret., Jan. 24, 1995.

M

Macaluso, Christie Albert: b. June 12, 1945, Hartford, CT; educ. St. Thomas Seminary (Bloomfield, CT), St. Mary's Seminary (Baltimore, Md), Trinity College (Hartford, CT), New York University; ord. priest (Hartford*), May 21, 1971; ord. titular bp. of Grass Valley and aux. bp. of Hartford, June 10, 1997.

McCarrick, Theodore E.: (*See* **Cardinals, Biographies**.)

McCarthy, James F.: b. July 9, 1942, Mount Kisco, NY; educ. Cathedral College and St. Joseph's Seminary, New York; ord. priest (New York*), June 1, 1968; app. titular bp. of Veronna and aux. bp. of New York, May 11, 1999, inst., June 29, 1999; res., June 12, 2002.

McCarthy, John E.: b. June 21, 1930, Houston, TX; educ. Univ. of St. Thomas (Houston, TX); ord. priest (Galveston-Houston), May 26, 1956; assistant director Social Action Dept. USCC, 1967-69; executive director Texas Catholic Conference; ord. titular bp. of Pedena and aux. bp. of Galveston-Houston, Mar. 14, 1979; app. bp. of Austin, Dec. 19, 1985, inst., Feb. 25, 1986; res., Jan. 2, 2001.

McCormack, John B.: b Aug. 12, 1935, Winthrop, MA; educ. St. John Seminary College and St. John Seminary Theologate (Boston, MA); ord. priest (Boston*), Feb. 2, 1960; ord. titular bp. of Cerbali and aux. bp. of Boston, Dec. 27, 1995; app. bp. of Manchester, NH, July 21, 1998, inst., Sept. 22, 1998.

McCormack, William J.: b. Jan. 24, 1924, New York, NY; educ. Christ the King Seminary, St. Bonaventure Univ. (St. Bonaventure, NY); ord. priest (New York*), Feb. 21, 1959; national director of Society for the Propagation of the Faith, 1980; ord. titular bp. of Nicives and aux. bp. of New York, Jan. 6, 1987; res., Oct. 31, 2001.

McDonald, Andrew J.: b. Oct. 24, 1923, Savannah, GA; educ. St. Mary's Seminary (Baltimore, MD), Catholic Univ. (Washington, DC), Lateran Univ. (Rome); ord. priest (Savannah), May 8, 1948; ord. bp. of Little Rock, Sept. 5, 1972; res., Jan. 4, 2000.

McDonnell, Charles J.: b. July 7, 1928, Brooklyn, NY; educ. Seton Hall Univ. (South Orange, NJ), Immaculate Conception Seminary (Darlington, NJ), Long Island Univ. (Brooklyn, NY); ord. priest (Newark*), May 29, 1954; U.S. Army Chaplain, 1965-89; ret., from active duty with rank of Brigadier General; ord. titular bp. of Pocofelto and aux. bp. of Newark, May 12, 1994; ret. May 21, 2004.

McDonnell, Timothy A.: b. Dec. 23, 1937, New York City; educ. St. Joseph Seminary, Yonkers, Iona College, New Rochelle; ord. priest (New York*), June 1, 1963; ord. titular bp. of Semina and aux. bp. of New York, Dec. 12, 2001; app. bp. of Springfield in Massachusetts, Mar. 9, 2004.

McDowell, John B.: b. July 17, 1921, New Castle, PA; educ. St. Vincent College, St. Vincent Theological Seminary (Latrobe, PA), Catholic Univ. (Washington,

DC); ord. priest (Pittsburgh), Nov. 4, 1945; superintendent of schools, Pittsburgh diocese, 1955-70; ord. titular bp. of Tamazuca, and aux. bp. of Pittsburgh, Sept. 8, 1966; ret., Sept. 9, 1996.

McFadden, Joseph P.: b. May 22, 1947, Philadelphia, PA; St. Charles Borromeo Seminary (Overbrook, PA); ord. priest (Philadelphia*), May 16, 1981; app. titular bp. of Orreomargo and aux. bp. of Philadelphia, June 8, 2004; ord. July 28, 2004.

McFarland, Norman F.: b. Feb. 21, 1922, Martinez, CA; educ. St. Patrick's Seminary (Menlo Park, CA), Catholic Univ. (Washington, DC); ord. priest (San Francisco*), June 15, 1946; ord. titular bp. of Bida and aux. bp. of San Francisco, Sept. 8, 1970; apostolic administrator of Reno, 1974; app. bp. of Reno, Feb. 10, 1976, inst., Mar. 31, 1976; title of see changed to Reno-Las Vegas; app. bp. of Orange, CA, Dec. 29, 1986; inst., Mar. 31, 1976; res., June 30, 1998.

McGarry, Urban, T.O.R.: b. Nov. 11, 1911, Warren, PA; ord. priest, Oct. 3, 1942, in India; prefect apostolic of Bhagalpur, Aug. 7, 1956; ord. first bp. of Bhagalpur, India, May 10, 1965; res., Nov. 30, 1987.

McGrath, Patrick J.: b. July 11, 1945, Dublin, Ire.; educ. St. John's College Seminary (Waterford), Lateran Univ. (Rome, Italy); ord. priest in Ireland, June 7, 1970; came to U.S. same year and became San Francisco archdiocesan priest; ord. titular bp. of Allegheny and aux. bp. of San Francisco, Jan. 25, 1989; app. coadj. bp. of San Jose, June 30, 1998; bp. of San Jose, Nov. 29, 1999.

McKinney, Joseph C.: b. Sept. 10, 1928, Grand Rapids, MI; educ. St. Joseph's Seminary (Grand Rapids, MI), Seminaire de Philosophie (Montreal, Canada), Urban Univ. (Rome, Italy); ord. priest (Grand Rapids), Dec. 20, 1953; ord. titular bp. of Lentini and aux. bp. of Grand Rapids, Sept. 26, 1968; res., Oct. 2, 2001.

McLaughlin, Bernard J.: b. Nov. 19, 1912, Buffalo, NY; educ. Urban Univ. (Rome, Italy); ord. priest (Buffalo), Dec. 21, 1935, at Rome; ord. titular bp. of Mottola and aux. bp. of Buffalo, Jan. 6, 1969; res., Jan. 5, 1988.

McManus, Robert J.: b. July 5, 1951, Warwick, RI; educ. Our Lady of Providence Seminary, Catholic Univ. (Washington, DC), Seminary of Toronto, Canada, Pontifical Gregorian Univ. (Rome); ord. priest (Providence), May 27, 1978; diocesan Vicar for Education and Rector of Our Lady of Providence; app. titular bp. of Allegheny and aux. bp. of Providence, Dec. 1, 1998, ord., Feb. 22, 1999; app. bp. of Worcester, Mar. 9, 2004.

McNabb, John C., O.S.A.: b. Dec. 11, 1925, Beloit, WI; educ. Villanova Univ. (Villanova, PA), Augustinian College and Catholic Univ. (Washington, DC), De Paul Univ. (Chicago, IL); ord. priest, May 24, 1952; ord. titular bp. of Saia Maggiore, June 17, 1967 (resigned titular see, Dec. 27, 1977); prelate of Chulucanas, Peru, 1967; first bp. of Chulucanas, Dec. 12, 1988; ret. Oct. 28, 2000).

McNaughton, William J., M.M.: b. Dec. 7, 1926, Lawrence, MA; educ. Maryknoll Seminary (Maryknoll, NY); ord. priest, June 13, 1953; ord. titular bp. of Thuburbo Minus and vicar apostolic of Inchon, Korea, Aug. 24, 1961; first bp. of Inchon, Mar. 10, 1962, when vicariate was raised to diocese; ret. Apr. 25, 2002.

McRaith, John Jeremiah: b. Dec. 6, 1934, Hutchinson, MN; educ. St. John Preparatory School (Collegeville, MN), Loras College, St. Bernard Seminary (Dubuque, IA); ord. priest (New Ulm), Feb. 21, 1960; exec. dir. of Catholic Rural Life Conference, 1971-78; ord. bp. of Owensboro, KY, Dec. 15, 1982.

Madden, Denis J.: b. Mar. 8, 1940, Carbondale, PA; educ. Univ. of Notre Dame, Univ. of Maryland; ord. priest Apr. 1, 1967 (Benedictines); inc. Baltimore Nov. 4, 1976; app. aux. bp. of Baltimore and tit. bp. of Baia, May 10, 2005; ord. bp. Aug. 24, 2005.

Madera, Joseph J., M.Sp.S.: b. Nov. 27, 1927, San Francisco, CA; educ. Domus Studiorum of the Missionaries of the Holy Spirit (Coyoacan, D.F. Mexico); ord. priest, June 15, 1957; ord. coadjutor bp. of Fresno, Mar. 4, 1980; bp. of Fresno, July 1, 1980; app. titular bp. of Orte and aux. of Military Services archdiocese, June 30, 1991; ret. Sept. 15, 2004.

Maginnis, Robert P.: b. Dec. 22, 1933, Philadelphia, PA; educ. St. Charles Borromeo Seminary (Overbrook, PA); ord. priest (Philadelphia*), May 13, 1961; ord. titular bp. of Siminina and aux. bp. of Philadelphia, Mar. 11, 1996.

Maguire, Joseph F.: b. Sept. 4, 1919, Boston, MA; educ. Boston College, St. John's Seminary (Boston, MA); ord. priest (Boston*), June 29, 1945; ord. titular bp. of Macteris and aux. bp. of Boston, Feb. 2, 1972; app. coadjutor bp. of Springfield, MA, Apr. 13, 1976; succeeded as bp. of Springfield, MA, Oct. 15, 1977; ret., Dec. 27, 1991.

Mahony, Roger M.: (*See* **Cardinals, Biographies.**)

Maida, Adam J.: (*See* **Cardinals, Biographies.**)

Malone, Richard J.: b. Mar. 19, 1946, Salem, MA; educ. St. John's Seminary, Brighton, Boston University, ord. priest (Boston*), May 20, 1972; app. titular bp. of Aptuca and aux. bp. of Boston, Jan. 27, 2000, ord., Mar. 1, 2000; app. bp. of Portland, ME, Feb. 10, 2004.

Malooly, William Francis: b. Jan. 18, 1944, Baltimore; educ. St. Charles Minor Seminary, St. Mary's Seminary (Baltimore); ord priest (Baltimore*), May 7, 1970, app. titular bp. of Flumenzer and aux. bp. of Baltimore, Dec. 12, 2000, ord., Mar. 1, 2001; app. bp. of Wilmington, July 7, 2008. .

Manning, Elias (James), O.F.M. Conv.: b. Apr. 14, 1938, Troy, NY; educ. Sao José Seminary (Rio de Janeiro, Brazil); ord. priest, Oct. 30, 1965, in New York; ord. bp. of Valenca, Brazil, May 13, 1990.

Manning, Thomas R., O.F.M.: b. Aug. 29, 1922, Baltimore, MD; educ. Duns Scotus College (Southfield, MI), Holy Name College (Washington, DC); ord. priest, June 5, 1948; ord. titular bp. of Arsamosata, July 14, 1959 (res. titular see, Dec. 30, 1977); prelate of Coroico, Bolivia, July 14, 1959; became first bp., 1983, when prelature was raised to diocese; ret., Oct. 9, 1996.

Mansell, Henry J.: b. Oct. 10, 1937, New York, NY; educ. Cathedral College, St. Joseph's Seminary and College (New York); North American College, Gregorian Univ. (Rome); ord. priest (New York*), Dec. 19, 1962; ord. titular bp. of Marazane and aux. bp. of New York, Jan. 6, 1993, by John Paul II in Vatican City; app. bp. of Buffalo, Apr. 18, 1995; inst., June 12, 1995; app. abp. of Hartford, Oct. 20, 2003.

Mansour, Gregory John: b. Nov. 11, 1955, Flint, MI; educ. University of Michigan (Kalamazoo, MI), Catholic Univ, of America (Washington, DC), North American College and Pontifical Gregorian Univ. (Rome); ord. priest (Eparchy of St. Maron of Brooklyn), Sept. 18, 1982; app. bp. of the Eparchy of St. Maron, Brooklyn, NY, Jan. 10, 2004.

Manz, John R.: b. Nov. 14, 1945, Chicago, IL; educ. Niles College Seminary (Niles, IL), Univ. of St. Mary of the Lake-Mundelein Seminary (Chicago); ord. priest (Chicago*), May 12, 1971; ord. titular bp. of Mulia and aux. bp. of Chicago, Mar. 5, 1996.

Marconi, Dominic A.: b. Mar. 13, 1927, Newark, NJ; educ. Seton Hall Univ. (S. Orange, NJ), Immaculate Conception Seminary (Darlington, NJ), Catholic Univ. (Washington, DC); ord. priest (Newark*), May 30, 1953; ord. titular bp. of Bure and aux. bp. of Newark, June 25, 1976; res., July 1, 2002.

Marino, Joseph: b. Jan. 23, 1953, Birmingham, AL; educ. Pontifical North American College and Pontifical Gregorian University (Rome); ord. priest, Aug. 25, 1979 (Birmingham); completed studies at the Pontifical Ecclesiastical Academy and enered papal diplomatic service in 1988; served in diplomatic posts in the Philippines, Uruguay, Nigeria, Great Britain, and the Secretariat of State in Rome; app. apostolic nuncio to Bangladesh and titular abp. of Natchitoches, Jan. 12, 2008; ord. Mar. 29, 2008.

Martino, Joseph F.: b. May 1, 1946, Philadelphia, PA; educ. St. Charles Borromeo Seminary (Overbrook, PA), Gregorian Univ. (Rome); ord. priest (Philadelphia*), Dec. 18, 1970; ord. titular bp. of Cellae in Mauretania and aux. bp. of Philadelphia, Mar. 11, 1996; app. bp. of Scranton, July 25, 2003.

Matano, Salvatore R.: b. Sept. 15, 1946, Providence, RI; educ. Our Lady of Providence Seminary College (Warwick, RI), Gregorian University (Rome); ord. priest Dec. 17, 1971 (Providence); served on staff of apostolic nunciature (Washington, DC); app. coadjutor bp. of Burlington Mar. 3, 2005; ord. Apr. 19, 2005; bp. of Burlington, Nov. 9, 2005.

Matthiesen, Leroy Theodore: b. June 11, 1921, Olfen, TX; educ. Josephinum College (Columbus, OH), Catholic Univ. (Washington, DC), Register School of Journalism; ord. priest (Amarillo), Mar. 10, 1946; ord. bp. of Amarillo, May 30, 1980; ret., Jan. 21, 1997.

Melczek, Dale J.: b. Nov. 9, 1938, Detroit, MI; educ. St. Mary's College (Orchard Lake, MI), St. John's Provincial Seminary (Plymouth, MI), Univ. of Detroit; ord. priest (Detroit*), June 6, 1964; ord. titular bp. of Trau and aux. bp. of Detroit, Jan. 27, 1983; apostolic administrator of Gary, Aug. 19, 1992; coadjutor bp. of Gary, Oct. 28, 1995; bp. of Gary, June 1, 1996.

Mengeling, Carl F.: b. Oct. 22, 1930, Hammond, IN; educ. St. Meinrad College and Seminary (St. Meinrad, IN), Alphonsianum Univ. (Rome); ord. priest (Gary), May 25, 1957; ord. bp. of Lansing, Jan. 25, 1996; ret. Feb. 27, 2008.

Mestice, Anthony F.: b. Dec. 6, 1923, New York, NY; educ. St. Joseph Seminary (Yonkers, NY); ord. priest (New York*), June 4, 1949; ord. titular bp. of Villa Nova and aux. bp. of New York, Apr. 27, 1973; ret., Oct. 31, 2001.

Michaels, James E., S.S.C.: b. May 30, 1926, Chicago, IL; educ. Columban Seminary (St. Columban, NE), Gregorian Univ. (Rome); ord. priest, Dec. 21, 1951; ord. titular bp. of Verbe and aux. bp. of Kwang Ju, Korea, Apr. 14, 1966; app. aux. bp. of Wheeling, Apr. 3, 1973 (title of see changed to Wheeling-Charleston, 1974); res., Sept. 22, 1987.

Miller, J. Michael, C.S.B.: b. July 9, 1946, Ottawa, Canada; educ. St. Michael's College, Univ. of Toronto (Toronto, Canada), Gregorian Univ. (Rome); ord. priest (Congregation of St. Basil), June 29, 1975, Congregation of St. Basil; official in Secretariat of State, Rome, 1992-97; pres. of Univ. of St. Thomas Aquinas, Houston, TX, 1997-2004; 2004; app.titular abp. of Vertara and sec. of the Cong. for Catholic Education, Rome, Nov. 25, 2003; app. coadj. abp of Vancouver, June 1, 2007.

Milone, Anthony M.: b. Sept. 24, 1932, Omaha, NE; educ. North American College (Rome); ord. priest (Omaha*), Dec. 15, 1957, in Rome; ord. titular bp. of Plestia and aux. bp. of

Omaha, Jan. 6, 1982; app. bp. of Great Falls-Billings, Dec. 14, 1987, inst., Feb. 23, 1988; ret. July 12, 2006.

Minder, John, O.S.F.S.: b. Nov. 1, 1923, Philadelphia, PA; educ. Catholic Univ. (Washington, DC); ord. priest, June 3, 1950; ord. bp. of Keimos (renamed Keimos-Upington, 1985), South Africa, Jan. 10, 1968; ret. June 5, 2000.

Moeddel, Carl K.: b. Dec. 28, 1937, Cincinnati, OH; educ. Athenaeum of Ohio, Mt. St. Mary's Seminary (Cincinnati); ord. priest (Cincinnati*), Aug. 15, 1962; ord. titular bp. of Bistue and aux. bp. of Cincinnati, Aug. 24, 1993; ret. June 20, 2007.

Morin, Roger Paul: b. Mar. 7, 1941, Lowell, MA; educ. Notre Dame Seminary (New Orleans, LA), Tulane University (New Orleans, LA); ord. priest, Apr. 15, 1971 (New Orleans*); app. aux. bp. of New Orleans and titular bishop of Aulona, Feb. 11, 2003; ord., Apr. 22, 2003.

Morlino, Robert C.: b. Dec. 31, 1946, Scranton, PA; educ. Fordham Univ., University of Notre Dame, Weston School of Theology, Cambridge, MA, Gregorian University, Rome; ord. priest for the Society of Jesus, Maryland Province, June 1, 1974, incardinated into the Diocese of Kalamazoo, MI, Oct. 26, 1983, app. bp. of Helena, July 6, 1999, inst,. Sept. 21, 1999; app. bp. of Madison, May 23, 2003.

Morneau, Robert F.: b. Sept. 10, 1938, New London, WI; educ. St. Norbert's College (De Pere, WI), Sacred Heart Seminary (Oneida, WI), Catholic Univ. (Washington, DC); ord. priest (Green Bay), May 28, 1966; ord. titular bp. of Massa Lubrense and aux. bp. of Green Bay, Feb. 22, 1979.

Moskal, Robert M.: b. Oct. 24, 1937, Carnegie, PA; educ. St. Basil Minor Seminary (Stamford, CT), St. Josaphat Seminary and Catholic Univ. (Washington, DC); ord. priest (Philadelphia*, Byzantine Ukrainian), Mar. 25, 1963; ord. titular bp. of Agatopoli and aux. bp. of the Ukrainian archeparchy of Philadelphia, Oct. 13, 1981; app. first bp. of St. Josaphat in Parma, Dec. 5, 1983.

Moynihan, James M.: b. July 16, 1932, Rochester, NY; educ. St. Bernard's Seminary (Rochester, NY), North American College and Gregorian Univ. (Rome); ord. priest (Rochester), Dec. 15, 1957, in Rome; ord. bp. of Syracuse, May 29, 1995.

Muench Robert W.: b. Dec. 28, 1942, Louisville, KY; educ. St. Joseph Seminary and Notre Dame Seminary (New Orleans, LA), Catholic Univ. (Washington, DC); ord. priest (New Orleans*), June 18, 1968; ord. titular bp. of Mactaris and aux. bp. of New Orleans, June 29, 1990; app. bp. of Covington Jan., 1996; inst., Mar. 19, 1996; app. bp. of Baton Rouge, Dec. 15, 2001.

Mulvee, Robert E.: b. Feb. 15, 1930, Boston, MA; educ. St. Thomas Seminary (Bloomfield, CT), University Seminary (Ottawa, ON), American College (Louvain, Belgium), Lateran Univ. (Rome); ord. priest (Manchester), June 30, 1957; ord. titular bp. of Summa and aux. bp. of Manchester, NH, Apr. 14, 1977; app. bp. of Wilmington, DE, Feb. 19, 1985; app. coadjutor bp. of Providence, Feb. 9, 1995; bp. of Providence, June 11, 1997; ret. Mar. 31, 2005.

Mundo, Miguel P.: b. July 25, 1937, New York, NY; educ. Fordham Univ. (Bronx, NY), St. Jerome's College (Kitchener, ON), St Francis Seminary (Loretto, PA); ord. priest (Camden), May 19, 1962; missionary in Brazil from 1963; ord. titular bp. of Blanda Julia and aux. bp. of Jatai, Brazil, June 2, 1978.

Murphy, William F.: b. May 14, 1940, Boston MA; educ. Boston Latin School (Boston), Harvard College, St. John's Seminary (Boston), Gregorian Univ. (Rome); ord. priest (Boston*), Dec. 16, 1964; ord. titular bp. of Saia Maggiore

and aux. bp. of Boston, Dec. 27, 1995; app. bp. of Rockville Centre, June 25, 2001, inst., Sept. 5, 2001.

Murray, James A.: b. July 5, 1932, Jackson, MI; educ. Sacred Heart Seminary Detroit, St. John Provincial Seminary (Plymouth, MI), Catholic Univ. of America; ord. priest (Lansing), June 7, 1958; app. bp. of Kalamazoo, Nov. 18, 1997, ord., Jan. 27, 1998.

Murry, George V., S.J.: b. Dec. 28, 1948, Camden, NJ; educ. St. Joseph's College (Philadelphia, PA), St. Thomas Seminary (Bloomfield, CT), St. Mary Seminary (Baltimore, MD), Jesuit School of Theology (Berkeley, CA), George Washington Univ. (Washington, DC); entered Jesuits 1972; ord. priest, June 9, 1979; ord. titular bp. of Fuerteventura and aux. bp. of Chicago, Mar. 20, 1995; app. co-adjutor of St. Thomas in the Virgin Islands, May 5, 1998; bp. of St. Thomas in the Virgin Islands, June 30, 1999; bp. of Youngstown, Jan. 30, 2007.

Myers, John Joseph: b. July 26, 1941, Ottawa, IL; educ. Loras College (Dubuque, IA), North American College and Gregorian Univ. (Rome), Catholic Univ. of America (Washington, DC); ord. priest (Peoria), Dec. 17, 1966, in Rome; ord. coadjutor bp. of Peoria, Sept. 3, 1987; bp. of Peoria, Jan. 23, 1990; app. abp. of Newark, July 24, 2001.

N

Naumann, Joseph F.: b. June 4, 1949, St. Louis, MO; educ. Cardinal Glennon Seminary College and Kenrick Seminary (St. Louis, MO); ord. priest (St. Louis*), 1975; app. titular bp. of Caput Cilla and aux. bp. of St. Louis, July 9, 1997; app. coadjutor abp. of Kansas City, Jan. 7, 2004; abp. of Kansas City, Jan. 15, 2005.

Nevins, John J.: b. Jan. 19, 1932, New Rochelle, NY; educ. Iona College (New Rochelle, NY), Catholic Univ. (Washington, DC); ord. priest (Miami*), June 6, 1959; ord. titular bp. of Rusticana and aux. bp. of Miami, Mar. 24, 1979; app. first bp. of Venice, FL, July 17, 1984; inst., Oct. 25, 1984; ret. Jan. 19, 2007.

Newman, William C.: b. Aug. 16, 1928, Baltimore, MD; educ. St. Mary Seminary (Baltimore, MD), Catholic Univ. (Washington, DC), Loyola College (Baltimore, MD); ord. priest (Baltimore*), May 29, 1954; ord. titular bp. of Numluli and aux. bp. of Baltimore, July 2, 1984; ret. Aug. 28, 2003.

Nickless, R. Walker: b. May 28, 1947, Denver; educ. St. Thomas Seminary, University of Denver, Gregorian Univ. (Rome); ord. priest Aug. 4, 1973 (Denver); app. bp. of Sioux City, Iowa, Nov. 10, 2005; ord. bp. Jan. 20, 2006.

Niederauer, George H.: b. June 14, 1936, Los Angeles, CA; educ. St. John's Seminary (Camarillo, CA), Catholic Univ. (Washington, DC), Loyola Univ. of Los Angeles, Univ. of Southern CA, Loretta Heights College (Denver, CO); ord. priest (Los Angeles*), Apr. 30, 1962; app. bp. of Salt Lake City, Nov. 3, 1994, ord., Jan. 25, 1995; app. Abp. of San Francisco, Dec. 15, 2005.

Nienstedt, John C.: b. Mar. 18, 1947, Detroit, MI; educ. Sacred Heart Seminary (Detroit), North American College, Gregorian Univ., Alphonsianum (Rome); ord. priest (Detroit*), July 27, 1974; served in Vatican Secretariat of State, 1980-86; rector of Sacred Heart Seminary (Detroit), 1988-94; pastor of the Shrine of the Little Flower (Royal Oak, MI), 1994; ord. titular bp. of Alton and aux. bp. of Detroit, July 9, 1996; app. bp. of New Ulm, June 12, 2001, inst., Aug. 6, 2001; app. coadj. abp. of St. Paul-Minneapolis, Apr. 24, 2007; acceded to the see, May 2, 2008.

Noonan, John G.: b. Feb. 26, 1951, Limerick, Ireland; educ. St. John Vianney College Seminary (Miami), St.

Vincent de Paul Seminary (Boynton Beach, FL); app. aux. bp. Miami June 21, 2005; ord. bp. Aug. 24, 2005.

Novak, Alfred, C.SS.R.: b. June 2, 1930, Dwight, NE; educ. Immaculate Conception Seminary (Oconomowoc, WI); ord. priest, July 2, 1956; ord. titular bp. of Vardimissa and aux. bp. of Sao Paulo, Brazil, May 25, 1979; bp. of Paranagua, Brazil, Mar. 14, 1989.

O

O'Brien, Edwin F.: b. Apr. 8, 1939, Bronx, NY; educ. St. Joseph's Seminary (Yonkers, NY), Angelicum (Rome); ord. priest (New York*), May 29, 1965; ord. titular bp. of Tizica and aux. bp. of New York, Mar. 25, 1996; app. coadjutor abp. for Military Services Archdiocese, Apr. 8, 1997; abp. of Military Services Archdiocese, Aug. 12, 1997; app. abp. of Baltimore, July 12, 2007.

O'Brien, Thomas Joseph: b. Nov. 29, 1935, Indianapolis, IN; educ. St. Meinrad High School Seminary, St. Meinrad College Seminary (St. Meinrad, IN); ord. priest (Tucson), May 7, 1961; ord. bp. of Phoenix, Jan. 6, 1982; res., June 18, 2003.

Ochoa, Armando: b. Apr. 3, 1943, Oxnard, CA; educ. Ventura College (Ventura, CA), St. John's College and St. John's Seminary (Camarillo, CA); ord. priest (Los Angeles*), May 23, 1970; ord. titular bp. of Sitifi and aux. bp. of Los Angeles, Feb. 23, 1987; app. bp. of El Paso, Apr. 1, 1996; inst., June 26, 1996.

O'Connell, Anthony J.: b. May 10, 1938, Lisheen, Co. Clare, Ireland; came to U.S. at age 20; educ. Mt. St. Joseph College (Cork), Mungret College (Limerick), Kenrick Seminary (St. Louis); ord. priest (Jefferson City), Mar. 30, 1963; ord. First bp. of Knoxville, TN, Sept. 8, 1988; app. bp. of Palm Beach, Nov. 12, 1998, inst., Jan. 14, 1999; res., Mar. 8, 2002.

O'Donnell, Edward J.: b. July 4, 1931, St. Louis, MO; educ. St. Louis Preparatory Seminary and Kenrick Seminary (St. Louis, MO); ord. priest (St. Louis*), Apr. 6, 1957; ord. titular bp. of Britania and aux. bp. of St. Louis, Feb. 10, 1984; app. bp. of Lafayette, LA, inst., Dec. 16, 1994; ret. Nov. 8, 2002.

Olivier, Leonard J., S.V.D.: b. Oct. 12, 1923, Lake Charles, LA; educ. St. Augustine Major Seminary (Bay St. Louis, MS), Catholic Univ. (Washington, DC), Loyola Univ. (New Orleans, LA); ord. priest, June 29, 1951; ord. titular bp. of Leges in Numidia and aux. bp. of Washington, Dec. 20, 1988; ret. May 18, 2004.

Olmsted, Thomas J.: b. Jan. 21, 1947, Oketo, KS; educ. St. Thomas Seminary (Denver), North American College and Pontifical Gregorian University (Rome); ord. priest (Lincoln), July 2, 1973; served in Vatican Secretariat of State, 1979-1988; Dean of Formation, Pontifical College Josephinum, Columbus, OH, 1993, President and Rector, Pontifical College, Josephinum, 1997; app. coadjutor bp. of Wichita, Feb. 16, 1999, ord., Apr. 20, 1999; bp. of Wichita, Oct. 4, 2001; app. bp. of Phoenix, Nov. 25, 2003.

O'Malley, Sean, O.F.M.Cap.: (*See* **Cardinals' Biographies**).

O'Neill, Arthur J.: b. Dec. 14, 1917, East Dubuque, IL; educ. Loras Collge (Dubuque, IA), St. Mary's Seminary (Baltimore, MD); ord. priest (Rockford), Mar. 27, 1943; ord. bp. of Rockford, Oct. 11, 1968; ret., Apr. 19, 1994.

Ottenweller, Albert H.: b. Apr. 5, 1916, Stanford, MT; educ. St. Joseph's Seminary (Rensselaer, IN), Catholic Univ. (Washington, DC); ord. priest (Toledo), June 19, 1943; ord. titular bp. of Perdices and aux. bp. of Toledo, May 29, 1974; app. bp. of Steubenville, OH,

Oct. 11, 1977, inst., Nov. 22, 1977; ret., Jan. 28, 1992.

P

Paprocki, Thomas J.: b. Aug. 5, 1952, Chicago, IL; educ. Niles College of Loyola (Chicago, IL), St. Mary of the Lake Seminary (Chicago, IL), DePaul University College of Law (Chicago, IL), Gregorian University (Rome); ord. priest, May 10, 1978 (Chicago); app. aux. bp. of Chicago and titular bishop of Vulturara, Jan. 24, 2003; ord., Mar. 19, 2003.

Paska, Walter: b. Nov. 29, 1923, Elizabeth, NJ; educ. St. Charles Seminary (Catonsville, MD), Catholic Univ. (Washington, DC), Fordham Univ. (New York); ord. priest (Philadelphia of Ukrainians*), June 2, 1947; ord. titular bp. of Tigilava and aux. of Ukrainian archdiocese of Philadelphia, Mar. 19, 1992; res., Nov. 29, 2000.

Pataki, Andrew: b. Aug. 30, 1927, Palmerton, PA; educ. St. Vincent College (Latrobe, PA), St. Procopius College, St. Procopius Seminary (Lisle, IL), Sts. Cyril and Methodius Byzantine Catholic Seminary (Pittsburgh, PA), Gregorian Univ. and Oriental Pontifical Institute (Rome, Italy); ord. priest (Pittsburgh,* Ruthenian Byzantine), Feb. 24, 1952; ord. titular bp. of Telmisso and aux. bp. of Byzantine diocese of Passaic, Aug. 23, 1983; app. bp. of Ruthenian Byzantine diocese of Parma, July 3, 1984; app. bp. of Ruthenian Byzantine diocese of Passaic, Nov. 6, 1995; inst., Feb. 8, 1996; ret. Dec. 6, 2007.

Pates, Richard E.: b. Feb. 12, 1943, St. Paul; educ. St. Paul Seminary, North American College (Rome); ord. priest (St. Paul and Minneapolis*), Dec. 20, 1968; staff, Apostolic Nunciature, Washington, 1975-81; app. titular bp. of Suacia and aux. bp. of St. Paul and Minneapolis, Dec. 22, 2000, ord., Mar. 26, 2001; app. bp. of Des Monies, Apr. 10, 2008; inst. May 29, 2008.

Pearce, George H., S.M.: b. Jan. 9, 1921, Brighton, MA; educ. Marist College and Seminary (Framington, MA); ord. priest, Feb. 2, 1947; ord. titular bp. of Attalea in Pamphylia and vicar apostolic of the Samoa and Tokelau Islands, June 29, 1956; title changed to bp. of Apia, June 21, 1966; app. abp. of Suva, Fiji Islands, June 22, 1967; res., Apr. 10, 1976.

Pelotte, Donald E., S.S.S.: b. Apr. 13, 1945, Waterville, ME; educ. Eymard Seminary and Junior College (Hyde Park, NY), John Carroll Univ. (Cleveland, OH), Fordham Univ. (Bronx, NY); ord. priest, Sept. 2, 1972; ord. coadjutor bp. of Gallup, May 6, 1986 (first priest of Native American ancestry to be named U.S. bp.); bp. of Gallup, Mar. 20, 1990; res. Apr. 30, 2008.

Peña, Raymundo J.: b. Feb. 19, 1934, Robstown, TX; educ. Assumption Seminary (San Antonio, TX); ord. priest (Corpus Christi), May 25, 1957; ord. titular bp. of Trisipa and aux. bp. of San Antonio, Dec. 13, 1976; app. bp. of El Paso, Apr. 29, 1980; app. bp. of Brownsville, May 23, 1995.

Pepe, Joseph A.: b. June 18, 1942, Philadelphia; educ. St. Charles Borromeo Seminary, University of St. Thomas (Rome); ord. priest (Philadelphia*), May 16, 1970; app. bp. of Las Vegas, Apr. 6, 2001, ord., May 31, 2001.

Perry, Joseph N.: b. Apr. 18, 1948, Chicago, IL; educ. Capuchin Seminary of St. Lawrence, (Milwaukee), St. Mary Capuchin Seminary, Crown Point, (IN), St. Francis Seminary (Milwaukee), Catholic Univ. of America (Washington, DC); ord. priest (Milwaukee*), May 24, 1975; app. titular bp. of Lead and aux. bp. of Chicago, May 5, 1998; ord., June 29, 1998.

Pevec, A. Edward: b. Apr. 16, 1925, Cleveland, OH;

educ. St. Mary's Seminary, John Carroll Univ. (Cleveland, OH); ord. priest (Cleveland), Apr. 29, 1950; ord. titular bp. of Mercia and aux. bp. of Cleveland, July 2, 1982; res., Apr. 3, 2001.

Pfeifer, Michael, O.M.I.: b. May 18, 1937, Alamo, TX; educ. Oblate school of theology (San Antonio, TX); ord. priest, Dec. 21, 1964; provincial of southern province of Oblates of Mary Immaculate, 1981; ord. bp. of San Angelo, July 26, 1985.

Pilarczyk, Daniel E.: b. Aug. 12, 1934, Dayton, OH; educ. St. Gregory's Seminary (Cincinnati, OH), Urban Univ. (Rome), Xavier Univ. and Univ. of Cincinnati (Cincinnati, OH); ord. priest (Cincinnati*), Dec. 20, 1959; ord. titular bp. of Hodelm and aux. bp. of Cincinnati, Dec. 20, 1974; app. abp. of Cincinnati, Oct. 30, 1982; inst., Dec. 20, 1982; president of NCCB/USCC, 1989-92.

Pilla, Anthony M.: b. Nov. 12, 1932, Cleveland, OH; educ. St. Gregory College Seminary (Cincinnati, OH), Borromeo College Seminary (Wickliffe, OH), St. Mary Seminary and John Carroll Univ. (Cleveland, OH); ord. priest (Cleveland), May 23, 1959; ord. titular bp. of Scardona and aux. bp. of Cleveland, Aug. 1, 1979; app. apostolic administrator of Cleveland, 1980; bp. of Cleveland, Nov. 13, 1980. President of NCCB/USCC, 1995-98; res. Apr. 4, 2006.

Popp, Bernard F.: b. Dec. 6, 1917, Nada, TX; educ. St. John's Seminary and St. Mary's Univ. (San Antonio, TX); ord. priest (San Antonio*), Feb. 24, 1943; ord. titular bp. of Capsus and aux. bp. of San Antonio, July 25, 1983; ret., Mar. 23, 1993.

Potocnak, Joseph J., S.C.J.: b. May 13, 1933, Berwick, PA; educ. Dehon Seminary (Great Barrington, MA), Kilroe Seminary (Honesdale, PA), Sacred Heart (Hales Corners, WI); ord. priest, Sept 21, 1966; missionary in South Africa from 1973; ord. bp. of De Aar, South Africa, May 1, 1992.

Provost, Glen J.: b. Aug. 9, 1949, Lafayette, LA; educ. Immaculata Seminary (Lafayette), St. Joseph Seminary College (St. Benedict, LA), Pontifical North American College (Rome), University of South Louisiana (Lafayette, LA); ord. June 29, 1975 (Lafayette); app. bp. of Lake Charles Mar. 6, 2007; ord. bp. Apr. 23, 2007.

Puscas, Vasile Louis: b. Sept. 13, 1915, Aurora, IL; educ. Quigley Preparatory Seminary (Chicago, IL), seminary in Oradea-Mare (Romania), Propaganda Fide Seminary (Rome), Illinois Benedictine College (Lisle, IL); ord. priest (Erie), May 14, 1942; ord. titular bp. of Leuce and first exarch of apostolic exarchate for Byzantine Romanians in the U.S., June 26, 1983 (seat of the exarchate, Canton, OH); app. first eparch, Apr. 11, 1987, when exarchate was raised to eparchy of St. George's in Canton; ret., July 15, 1993.

Q

Quinn, Alexander James: b. Apr. 8, 1932, Cleveland, OH; educ. St. Charles College (Catonsville, MD), St. Mary Seminary (Cleveland, OH), Lateran Univ. (Rome), Cleveland State Univ.; ord. priest (Cleveland), May 24, 1958; ord. titular bp. of Socia and aux. bp. of Cleveland, Dec. 5, 1983; ret. June 14, 2008.

Quinn, Francis A.: b. Sept. 11, 1921, Los Angeles, CA; educ. St. Joseph's College (Mountain View, CA), St. Patrick's Seminary (Menlo Park, CA), Catholic Univ. (Washington, DC); Univ. of CA (Berkeley); ord. priest (San Francisco*), June 15, 1946; ord. titular bp. of Numana and aux. bp. of San Francisco, June 29, 1978; app. bp. of Sacramento, Dec. 18,

1979; ret., Nov. 30, 1993.

Quinn, John M.: b. Dec. 17, 1945, Detroit; educ. Sacred Heart Seminary, St. John Provincial Seminary, University of Detroit and the Catholic University of America (Washington, DC); ord. priest, Mar. 17, 1972; app. aux. bp. of Detroit and titular bishop of Ressiana, July 7, 2003.

Quinn, John R.: b. Mar. 28, 1929, Riverside, CA; educ. St. Francis Seminary (El Cajon, CA), North American College (Rome); ord. priest (San Diego), July 19, 1953; ord. titular bp. of Thisiduo and aux. bp. of San Diego, Dec. 12, 1967; bp. of Oklahoma City and Tulsa, Nov. 30, 1971; first abp. of Oklahoma City, Dec. 19, 1972; app. abp. of San Francisco, Feb. 22, 1977, inst., Apr. 26, 1977; president NCCB/USCC, 1977-80; res., see Dec. 27, 1995.

R

Ramirez, Ricardo, C.S.B.: b. Sept. 12, 1936, Bay City, TX; educ. Univ. of St. Thomas (Houston, TX), Univ. of Detroit (Detroit, MI), St. Basil's Seminary (Toronto, ON), Seminario Concilium (Mexico City, Mexico), East Asian Pastoral Institute (Manila, Philippines); ord. priest, Dec. 10, 1966; ord titular bp. of Vatarba and aux. of San Antonio, Dec. 6, 1981; app. first bp. of Las Cruces, NM, Aug. 17, 1982; inst., Oct. 18, 1982.

Rassas, George J.: b. Baltimore May 26, 1942; educ. University of St. Mary of the Lake (Mundelein, IL), Loyola University (Chicago); ord. priest May 2, 1968 (Chicago); app. aux. bp. Chicago and tit. bp. of Reperi Dec. 1, 2005; ord. bp. Feb. 2, 2006.

Raya, Joseph M.: b. July 20, 1917, Zahle, Lebanon; educ. St. Louis College (Paris, France), St. Anne's Seminary (Jerusalem); ord. priest, July 20, 1941; came to U.S., 1949, became U.S. citizen; ord. abp. of Acre, Israel, of the Melkites, Oct. 20, 1968; res., Aug. 20, 1974; assigned titular metropolitan see of Scytopolis (resides in Canada).

Reichert, Stephen J., O.F.M. Cap.: b. May 14, 1943, Leoville, KS; educ. Capuchin minor seminary (Victoria, KS), St. Fidelis College (Hermann, PA), Capuchin College (Washington, DC); ord. priest, Sept. 27, 1969; missionary in Papua New Guinea since 1970; ord. bp. of Mendi, Papua New Guinea, May 7, 1995.

Reilly, Daniel P.: b. May 12, 1928, Providence, RI; educ. Our Lady of Providence Seminary (Warwick, RI), St. Brieuc Major Seminary (Cotes du Nord, France); ord. priest (Providence), May 30, 1953; ord. bp. of Norwich, Aug. 6, 1975; app. bp. of Worcester, Oct. 27, 1994, inst., Nov. 8, 1994; ret. Mar. 9, 2004.

Reiss, Francis R.: b. Nov. 11, 1940, Detroit; educ. Sacred Heart Seminary, St. John Provincial Seminary, University of Detroit, Gregorian University; ord. priest, June 4, 1966; app. aux. bp. of Detroit and titular bishop of Remesiana, July 7, 2003.

Reiss, John C.: b. May 13, 1922, Red Bank, NJ; educ. Catholic Univ. (Washington, DC), Immaculate Conception Seminary (Darlington, NJ); ord. priest (Trenton), May 31, 1947; ord. titular bp. of Simidicca and aux. bp. of Trenton, Dec. 12, 1967; app. bp. of Trenton, Mar. 11, 1980; ret., July 1, 1997.

Rhoades, Kevin C.: b. Nov. 26, 1957, Mahanoy City, PA; educ. Mount St. Mary's College (Emmitsburg, MD), St. Charles Borromeo Seminary (Wynnewood, PA); Gregorian University (Rome); ord. priest July 9, 1983 (Harrisburg); app. bp. of Harrisburg Oct. 14, 2004; ord. Dec. 9, 2004.

Riashi, Georges, B.C.O.: b. Nov. 25, 1933, Kaa-el-Rim, Lebanon; ord. priest, Apr. 4, 1965; parish priest of Our Lady of Redemption Parish, Warren, MI

(Newton Greek-Catholic Melkite eparchy); U.S. citizen; ord. first bp. of eparchy of St. Michael's of Sydney (Australia) for Greek-Catholic Melkites, July 19, 1987; app. abp. of archeparchy of Tripoli of Lebanon for Greek-Melkites, Aug. 5, 1995.

Ricard, John H., S.S.J.: b. Feb. 29, 1940, Baton Rouge, LA; educ. St. Joseph's Seminary (Washington, DC), Tulane Univ. (New Orleans, LA); ord. priest, May 25, 1968; ord. titular bp. of Rucuma and aux. of Baltimore, July 2, 1984; urban vicar, Baltimore; app. bp. of Pensacola-Tallahassee, Jan 21, 1997.

Ricken, David L.: b. Nov. 9, 1952, Dodge City, KS; educ. Conception Seminary College, MO, Univ. of Louvain (Belgium), Pontifical Gregorian Univ., Rome; ord. priest (Pueblo), Sept. 12, 1980; official of the Congregation for the Clergy, 1996-1999; app. Coadjutor Bishop of Cheyenne, Dec. 14, 1999, ord. bp. by Pope John Paul II at the Vatican, Jan. 6, 2000; bp. of Cheyenne, Sept. 26, 2001; app. bp. of Green Bay, July 9, 2008; inst. Aug. 28, 2008.

Rigali, Justin F.: (*See* **Cardinals, Biographies.**)

Rizzotto, Vincent M.: b. Sept. 9, 1931, Houston; educ. St. Mary Seminary (Houston), the Catholic University of America (Washington, DC), ord. priest, (Galveston, now Galveston-Houston) May 26, 1956; Vicar General of Galveston-Houston, 1994; app. titular bp. of Lamasba and aux. bp. of Galveston-Houston June 22, 2001, ord., July 31, 2001; ret. Oct. 30, 2006.

Rodi, Thomas J: b. Mar. 27, 1949, New Orleans; educ. Georgetown University (Washington, DC), Tulane University School of Law (New Orleans), Notre Dame Seminary (New Orleans); ord. priest, (New Orleans*), May 20, 1978; app. bp. of Biloxi, May 15, 2001, ord., July 2, 2001; app. abp. of Mobile, Apr. 2, 2008; inst. June 6, 2008.

Rodimer, Frank J.: b. Oct. 25, 1927, Rockaway, NJ; educ. Seton Hall Prep (South Orange, NJ), St. Charles College (Catonsville, MD), St. Mary's Seminary (Baltimore, MD), Immaculate Conception Seminary (Darlington, NJ), Catholic Univ. (Washington, DC); ord. priest (Paterson), May 19, 1951; ord. bp. of Paterson, Feb. 28, 1978; ret. June 1, 2004.

Rodriguez, Migúel, C.SS.R.: b. Apr. 18, 1931, Mayaguez, P.R.; educ. St. Mary's Minor Seminary (North East, PA), Mt. St. Alphonsus Major Seminary (Esopus, NY); ord. priest, June 22, 1958; ord. bp. of Arecibo, P.R., Mar. 23, 1974; res., Mar. 20, 1990.

Rodriguez, Placido, C.M.F.: b. Oct. 11, 1940, Celaya, Guanajuato, Mexico; educ. Claretian Novitate (Los Angeles, CA), Claretville Seminary College (Calabasas, CA), Catholic Univ. (Washington, DC), Loyola Univ. (Chicago, IL); ord. priest, May 23, 1968; ord. titular bp. of Fuerteventura and aux. bp. of Chicago, Dec. 13, 1983; app. bp. of Lubbock, TX, Apr. 5, 1994.

Roman, Agustin A.: b. May 5, 1928, San Antonio de los Banos, Havana, Cuba; educ. San Alberto Magno Seminary (Matanzas, Cuba), Missions Etrangeres (Montreal, Canada), Barry College (Miami, FL); ord. priest, July 5, 1959, Cuba; vicar for Spanish speaking in Miami archdiocese, 1976; ord. titular bp. of Sertei and aux. bp. of Miami, Mar. 24, 1979; ret., June 7, 2003.

Roque, Francis X.: b. Oct. 9, 1928, Providence RI; educ. St. John's Seminary (Brighton, MA); ord. priest, (Providence) Sept. 19, 1953; became chaplain in U.S. Army 1961; ord. titular bp. of Bagai and aux. bp. of Military Services archdiocese, May 10, 1983; ret. Sept. 15, 2004.

Rosazza, Peter Anthony: b. Feb. 13, 1935, New Haven, CT; educ. St. Thomas Seminary (Bloomfield, CT), Dartmouth College (Hanover, NH), St. Bernard's Seminary (Rochester, NY), St. Sulpice (Issy, France); ord. priest (Hartford*), June 29, 1961; ord. titular bp. of Oppido Nuovo and aux. bp. of Hartford, June 24, 1978.

Rose, Robert John: b. Feb. 28, 1930, Grand Rapids, MI; educ. St. Joseph's Seminary (Grand Rapids, MI), Seminaire de Philosophie (Montreal, Canada), Urban University (Rome), Univ. of Michigan (Ann Arbor); ord. priest (Grand Rapids), Dec. 21, 1955; ord. bp. of Gaylord, Dec. 6, 1981; app. bp. of Grand Rapids, inst., Aug. 30, 1989; ret. Oct. 13, 2003.

Rozanski, Mitchell Thomas: b. Aug. 6, 1958, Baltimore, MD; educ. Catholic University of America (Washington, DC); ord. priest (Baltimore*), Nov. 24, 1984; app. titular bp. of Walla Walla and aux. bp. of Baltimore, July 2, 2004; ord. Aug. 24, 2004.

Rueger, George E.: b. Sept. 3, 1933, Framingham, MA; educ. Holy Cross College (Worcester, MA), St. John's Seminary (Brighton), Harvard University (Cambridge, MA); ord. priest (Worcester), Jan. 6, 1958; ord. titular bp. of Maronana and aux. bp. of Worcester, Feb. 25, 1987; ret. Jan. 25, 2005.

Ryan, Daniel L.: b. Sept. 28, 1930, Mankato, MN; educ. St. Procopius Seminary (Lisle, IL), Lateran Univ. (Rome); ord. priest (Joliet), May 3, 1956; ord. titular bp. of Surista and aux. bp. of Joliet, Sept. 30, 1981; app. bp. of Springfield, IL, Nov. 22, 1983, inst., Jan. 18, 1984; res. Oct. ,19, 1999.

Ryan, Sylvester D.: b. May 3, 1930, Catalina Is., CA; educ. St. John's Seminary (Camarillo, CA); ord. priest (Los Angeles*), May 3, 1957; ord. titular bp. of Remesiana and aux. bp. of Los Angeles, May 31, 1990; app. bp. of Monterey, Jan. 28, 1992; ret. Dec. 19, 2006.

S

Salazar, Alexander: b. Nov. 28, 1949, San Jose, Costa Rica; educ. California State Univ. and Immaculate Heart College (Los Angeles), St. John's Seminary (Camarillo, CA); ord. priest June 16, 1984; appointed auxiliary bishop of Los Angeles and titular bishop of Nesqually Sept. 7, 2004; ord. Nov. 4, 2004.

Saltarelli, Michael A.: b. Jan. 17, 1932, Jersey City, NJ; educ. Seton Hall College and Immaculate Conception Seminary (S. Orange, NJ); ord. priest (Newark*), May 28, 1960; ord. titular bp. of Mesarfelta and aux. bp. of Newark, July 30, 1990; app. bp. of Wilmington, Nov. 21, 1995; inst., Jan. 23, 1996; ret. July 7, 2008.

Sample, Alexander K.: b. Nov. 7, 1960, Kalispell, Mont.; educ. Michigan Technological University (Houghton), St. Thomas College (St. Paul, MN), Pontifical College Josephinum (Columbus, OH), Angelicum (Rome); ord. priest June 1, 1990 (Marquette); app. bp of Marquette Dec. 13, 2005; ord. bp. Jan. 25, 2006.

Samra, Nicholas J.: b. Aug. 15, 1944, Paterson, NJ; educ. St. Anselm College (Manchester, NH), St. Basil Seminary (Methuen, MA), St. John Seminary (Brighton, MA); ord. priest (Newton), May 10, 1970; ord. titular bp. of Gerasa and aux. bp. of Melkite diocese of Newton, July 6, 1989; res. Jan. 11, 2005.

Sanchez, Robert F.: b. Mar. 20, 1934, Socorro, NM; educ. Immaculate Heart Seminary (Santa Fe, NM), Gregorian Univ. (Rome), Catholic Univ. (Washington, DC); ord. priest (Santa Fe*), Dec 20, 1959; ord. abp. of Santa Fe, NM, July 25, 1974; res., Apr. 6, 1993.

Sansaricq, Guy A.: b. Oct. 6, 1934, Jeremie, Haiti;

educ. St. Paul College (Ottawa); ord. priest June 29, 1960 (Les Cayes, Haiti); incard. Brooklyn 1991; appointed aux. bp. of Brooklyn and tit. bp. of Glenndalocha June 6, 2006; ord. Aug. 22, 2006.

Sartain, James P.: b. June 6, 1952, Memphis, TN; educ. St. Meinrad Seminary, (IN), North American College, (Rome), Pontifical University of St. Thomas (the Angelicum), Pontifical Institute of St. Anselm (Rome); ord. priest (Memphis), July 15, 1978; app. bp. of Little Rock, Jan. 4, 2000, ord., Mar. 6, 2000; app. bp. of Joliet, May 16, 2006.

Sartoris, Joseph M.: b. July 1, 1927, Los Angeles, CA; educ. St. John's Seminary (Camarillo, CA); ord. priest (Los Angeles*), May 30, 1953; ord. titular bp. of Oliva and aux. bp. of Los Angeles, Mar. 19, 1994; ret., Dec. 31, 2002.

Scarpone Caporale, Gerald, O.F.M.: b. Oct. 1, 1928, Watertown, MA; ord. priest, June 24, 1956; ord. coadjutor bp. of Comayagua, Honduras, Feb. 21, 1979; succeeded as bp. of Comayagua, May 30, 1979.

Schlarman, Stanley Gerard: b. July 27, 1933, Belleville, IL; educ. St. Henry Prep Seminary (Belleville, IL), Gregorian Univ. (Rome), St. Louis Univ. (St. Louis, MO); ord. priest (Belleville), July 13, 1958, Rome; ord. titular bp. of Capri and aux. bp. of Belleville, May 14, 1979; app. bp. of Dodge City, Mar. 1, 1983; res., May 12, 1998.

Schleck, Charles A., C.S.C.: b. July 5, 1925, Milwaukee, WI; educ. Univ. of Notre Dame (IN), Pontifical Univ. of St. Thomas (Rome); ord. priest, Dec. 22, 1951; ord. titular abp. of Africa (Mehdia), Apr. 1, 1995; adjunct secretary of Congregation for Evangelization of Peoples; president of the superior council of the Pontifical Mission Societies.

Schmitt, Bernard W.: b. Aug. 17, 1928, Wheeling, WV; educ. St. Joseph College (Catonsville, MD), St. Mary's Seminary (Baltimore), Ohio Univ. (Athens, OH); ord. priest (Wheeling-Charleston), May 28, 1955; ord. titular bp. of Walla Walla and bp. of Wheeling-Charleston, Aug. 1, 1988; bp. of Wheeling-Charleston, Mar. 29, 1989; ret. Dec. 9, 2004.

Schmitt, Mark F.: b. Feb. 14, 1923, Algoma, WI; educ. Salvatorian Seminary (St. Nazianz, WI), St. John's Seminary (Collegeville, MN); ord. priest (Green Bay), May 22, 1948; ord. titular bp. of Ceanannus Mor and aux. bp. of Green Bay, June 24, 1970; app. bp. of Marquette, Mar. 21, 1978, inst., May 8, 1978; ret., Oct. 6, 1992.

Schmitz Simon, Paul, O.F.M. Cap.: b. Dec. 4, 1943, Fond du Lac, WI; ord. priest, Sept. 3, 1970; missionary in Nicaragua from 1970; superior of vice province of Capuchins in Central America (headquartered in Managua), 1982-84; ord. titular bp. of Elepla and aux. of the vicariate apostolic of Bluefields, Nicaragua, Sept. 17, 1984; app. bp. of vicariate apostolic of Bluefields, Aug. 17, 1994.

Schnurr, Dennis M.: b. June 21, 1948, Sheldon, IA; educ. Loras College (Dubuque), Gregorian University (Rome), Catholic University of America (Washington, DC); ord. priest (Sioux City), July 20, 1974; Staff, Apostolic Nunciature, Washington, DC, 1985-1989; Associate General Secretary, National Conference of Catholic Bishops/United States Catholic Conference (NCCB/USCC), 1989-1995; National Executive Director, World Youth Day 1993, Denver, 1991-1993; General Secretary, NCCB/USCC, 1995-2001; app. bp. of Duluth, Jan. 18, 2001, ord., Apr. 2, 2001.

Schott, Basil, O.F.M.: b. July 21, 1939, Freeland, PA; entered Byzantine Franciscans, professed Aug. 4, 1959; educ. Immaculate Conception College (Troy, NY), St. Mary's Seminary (Norwalk, CT) and Post Graduate Center (New York, NY); ord. priest, Aug. 29, 1965; ord. bp. of Byzantine eparchy of Parma, July 11, 1996; app. metropolitan abp. of Pittsburgh (Byzantine Ruthenian), May 3, 2002.

Schulte, Francis B.: b. Dec. 23, 1926, Philadelphia, PA; educ. St. Charles Borromeo Seminary (Overbrook, PA); ord. priest (Philadelphia*), May 10, 1952; ord. titular bp. of Afufenia and aux. bp. of Philadelphia, Aug. 12, 1981; app. bp. of Wheeling-Charleston, June 4, 1985; abp. of New Orleans, Dec. 6, 1988, inst., Feb. 14, 1989; ret., Jan. 3, 2002.

Schwietz, Roger L., O.M.I.: b. July 3, 1940, St. Paul, MN; educ. Univ. of Ottawa (Canada), Gregorian Univ. (Rome); ord. priest, Dec. 20, 1967; ord. bp. of Duluth Feb. 2, 1990; bp. of Duluth, 1990-2000; coadj. abp. of Anchorage, Jan. 18, 2000; abp. of Anchorage, Mar. 3, 2001.

Seminack, Richard: b. Mar. 3, 1942, Philadelphia; educ. St. Basil Seminary College (Stamford, CT), St. Josaphat Major Seminary and Catholic University of America (Washington), Oriental Institute (Rome); ord. priest, May 25, 1967 (archeparchy of Philadelphia); incard. Eparchy of St. Josaphat (Parma) 1983; app. bp. of St. Nicholas of Chicago for Ukrainians, Mar. 25, 2003; ord., June 4, 2003.

Serratelli, Arthur J.: b. Apr. 18, 1944, Newark, NJ; educ. Seton Preparatory School (NJ), Seton Hall University (NJ), North American College and Gregorian University (Rome), Pontifical Biblical Institute (Rome); ord. priest (Newark*), Dec. 20, 1968; prof. of Sacred Scripture, Immaculate Conception Seminary; rector of the College Seminary, Seton Hall University; prelate of honor, 1998; app. titular bp. of Enera and aux. bp. of Newark, July 3, 2000; app. bp. of Paterson, June 1, 2004.

Sevilla, Carlos A., S.J.: b. Aug. 9, 1935, San Francisco, CA; entered Jesuits Aug. 14, 1953; educ. Gonzaga Univ. (Spokane, WA), Santa Clara Univ. (Santa Clara, CA), Jesuitenkolleg (Innsbruck, Austria), Catholic Institute of Paris (France); ord. priest, June 3, 1966; ord. titular bp. of Mina and aux. bp. of San Francisco, Jan. 25, 1989; bp. of Yakima, Dec. 31, 1996.

Shaheen, Robert J.: b. June 3, 1937, Danbury, CT; ord., May 2, 1964; elected eparch of Our Lady of Lebanon of Los Angeles of the Maronites (U.S.A.), Dec. 5, 2000.

Sheehan, Michael J.: b. July 9, 1939, Wichita, KS; educ. Assumption Seminary (San Antonio, TX), Gregorian Univ. and Lateran Univ. (Rome); ord. priest (Dallas), July 12, 1964; ord. first bp. of Lubbock, TX, June 17, 1983; apostolic administrator of Santa Fe, Apr. 6, 1993; app. abp. of Santa Fe, Aug. 17, 1993.

Sheldon, Gilbert I.: b. Sept. 20, 1926, Cleveland, OH; educ. John Carroll Univ. and St. Mary Seminary (Cleveland, OH); ord. priest (Cleveland), Feb. 28, 1953; ord. titular bp. of Taparura and aux. bp. of Cleveland, June 11, 1976; app. bp. of Steubenville, Jan. 28, 1992, ret., May 31, 2002.

Sheridan, Michael J.: b. Mar. 4, 1945, St. Louis, MO; educ. Glennon College, Kenrick Seminary (St. Louis, MO), Angelicum (Rome); ord. priest (St. Louis*), 1971; app. titular bp. of Thibiuca and aux. bp. of St. Louis, July 9, 1997; co-adjutor bp. of Colorado Springs, Dec. 4, 2001; bp. of Colorado Springs, Jan. 30, 2003.

Sheridan, Patrick J.: b. Mar. 10, 1922, New York, NY; educ. St. Joseph's Seminary (Yonkers, NY), University of Chicago; ord. priest (New York*), Mar. 1, 1947; ord. titular bp. of Curzola and aux. bp. of New York, Dec. 12, 1990; res., Jan.15, 2001.

Silva, Clarence: b. Aug. 6, 1949, Honolulu; educ. St. Patrick Seminary (Menlo Park, Calif.); ord. priest May 2, 1975 (Oakland); app. bp. of Honolulu May 17,

2005; ord. bp. July 21, 2005.

Sklba, Richard J.: b. Sept. 11, 1935, Racine, WI; educ. Old St. Francis Minor Seminary (Milwaukee, WI), North American College, Gregorian Univ., Pontifical Biblical Institute, Angelicum (Rome); ord. priest (Milwaukee*), Dec. 20, 1959; ord. titular bp. of Castra and aux. bp. of Milwaukee, Dec. 19, 1979.

Skurla, William C.: b. June 1, 1956, Duluth; educ. Columbia Univ., New York, Mary Immaculate Seminary, Northhampton, PA; ord. priest (Franciscan), 1987; incardinated into Eparchy of Van Nuys, 1996; app. bp. of Van Nuys Byzantine Catholic Eparchy in CA, Feb. 19, 2002; app. bp. of Ruthenian Byzantine diocese of Passaic, Dec. 6, 2007.

Skylstad, William S.: b. Mar. 2, 1934, Omak, WA; educ. Pontifical College Josephinum (Worthington, OH), Washington State Univ. (Pullman, WA), Gonzaga Univ. (Spokane, WA); ord. priest (Spokane), May 21, 1960; ord. bp. of Yakima, May 12, 1977; app. bp. of Spokane, Apr. 17, 1990; vice-pres. of USCCB, 2001-.

Slattery, Edward J.: b. Aug. 11, 1940, Chicago, IL; educ. Quigley Preparatory, St. Mary of the Lake Seminary (Mundelein, IL), Loyola Univ. (Chicago); ord. priest (Chicago*), Apr. 26, 1966; vice president, 1971-76, and president, 1976-94, of the Catholic Church Extension Society; ord. bp. of Tulsa, Jan. 6, 1994.

Smith, John M.: b. June 23, 1935, Orange, NJ; educ. Immaculate Conception Seminary (Darlington, NJ), Seton Hall Univ. (South Orange, NJ), Catholic Univ. (Washington, DC); ord. priest (Newark*), May 27, 1961; ord. titular bp. of Tre Taverne and aux. bp. of Newark, Jan. 25, 1988; app. bp. of Pensacola-Tallahassee, FL, June 25, 1991; app. coadjutor bp. of Trenton, Nov. 21, 1995; bp. of Trenton, July 1, 1997.

Snyder, John J.: b. Oct. 25, 1925, New York, NY; educ. Cathedral College (Brooklyn, NY), Immaculate Conception Seminary (Huntington, NY); ord. priest (Brooklyn), June 9, 1951; ord. titular bp. of Forlimpopli and aux. bp. of Brooklyn, Feb. 2, 1973; app. bp. of St. Augustine; inst., Dec. 5, 1979; res., Dec. 11, 2000.

Soens, Lawrence D.: b. Aug. 26, 1926, Iowa City, IA; educ. Loras College (Dubuque, IA), St. Ambrose College (Davenport, IA), Kenrick Seminary (St. Louis, MO), Univ. of Iowa; ord. priest (Davenport), May 6, 1950; ord. bp. of Sioux City, Aug. 17, 1983, res., Nov. 28, 1998.

Soroka, Stephen: b. Nov. 13, 1951, Winnipeg, Manitoba; educ. Univ. of Manitoba, Ukrainian Seminary, Washington, DC, Catholic Univ. of America, ordained (Ukrainian Archdiocese of Winnipeg*), June 13, 1982; Chancellor and financial administrator of the Winnipeg archdiocese, 1994, auxiliary bishop, Winnipeg, 1996; metropolitan abp. of Philadelphia for the Ukrainians, Nov. 29, 2000; inst., Feb. 27, 2001.

Soto, Jaime: b. Dec. 31, 1955, Inglewood, CA; educ. St. John's Seminary, Camarillo, CA, Columbia University School of Social Work, New York; ord. priest (Orange), June 12, 1982; Episcopal Vicar for Hispanic Ministry, 1989; app. titular bp. of Segia and aux. bp. of Orange, Mar. 23, 2000, ord., May 31, 2000; app. coadj. bp. of Sacramento, Oct. 11, 2007; inst. Nov. 19, 2007.

Sowada, Alphonse A., O.S.C.: b. June 23, 1933, Avon, MN; educ. Holy Cross Scholasticate (Fort Wayne, IN), Catholic Univ. (Washington, DC), ord. priest, May 31, 1958; missionary in Indonesia from 1958; ord. bp. of Agats, Indonesia, Nov. 23, 1969.

Speyrer, Jude: b. Apr. 14, 1929, Leonville, LA; educ. St. Joseph Seminary (Covington, LA), Notre Dame Seminary (New Orleans, LA), Gregorian Univ. (Rome), Univ. of Fribourg (Switzerland); ord. priest (Lafayette, LA), July 25, 1953; ord. first bp. of Lake Charles, LA, Apr. 25, 1980; res., Dec. 11, 2000.

Stafford, James Francis: (*See* **Cardinals, Biographies**).

Steib, J. (James) Terry, S.V.D.: b. May 17, 1940, Vacherie, LA; educ. Divine Word seminaries (Bay St. Louis, MS, Conesus, NY, Techny, IL), Xavier Univ. (New Orleans, LA); ord. priest, Jan. 6, 1967; ord. titular bp. of Fallaba and aux. bp. of St. Louis, Feb. 10, 1984; app. bp. of Memphis, Mar. 24, 1993.

Steinbock, John T.: b. July 16, 1937, Los Angeles, CA; educ. Los Angeles archdiocesan seminaries; ord. priest (Los Angeles*), May 1, 1963; ord. titular bp. of Midila and aux. bp. of Orange, CA, July 14, 1984; app. bp. of Santa Rosa, Jan. 27, 1987; app. bp. of Fresno, Oct. 15, 1991.

Steiner, Kenneth Donald: b. Nov. 25, 1936, David City, NE; educ. Mt. Angel Seminary (St. Benedict, OR), St. Thomas Seminary (Seattle, Wash); ord. priest (Portland,* OR), May 19, 1962; ord. titular bp. of Avensa and aux. bp. of Portland, OR, Mar. 2, 1978.

Straling, Phillip F.: b. Apr. 25, 1933, San Bernardino, CA; educ. Immaculate Heart Seminary, St. Francis Seminary, Univ. of San Diego and San Diego State University (San Diego, CA), North American College (Rome); ord. priest (San Diego), Mar. 19, 1959; ord. first bp. of San Bernardino, Nov. 6, 1978; app. first bp. of Reno, Mar. 21, 1995, when Reno-Las Vegas diocese was made two separate dioceses; res. Jun. 21, 2005.

Sullivan, Dennis J.: b. Mar. 17, 1945, New York, NY; educ. Iona College (New Rochelle, NY), St. Joseph Seminary (Dunwoodie, NY); ord. May 29, 1971; app. titular bp. of Enera and aux. bp. of New York, June 28, 2004; ord. Sept. 21, 2004.

Sullivan, Joseph M.: b. Mar. 23, 1930, Brooklyn, NY; educ. Immaculate Conception Seminary (Huntington, NY), Fordham Univ. (New York); ord. priest (Brooklyn), June 2, 1956; ord. titular bp. of Suliana and aux. bp. of Brooklyn, Nov. 24, 1980; ret. May 12, 2005.

Sullivan, Walter F.: b. June 10, 1928, Washington, DC; educ. St. Mary's Seminary (Baltimore, MD), Catholic Univ. (Washington, DC); ord. priest (Richmond), May 9, 1953; ord. titular bp. of Selsea and aux. bp. of Richmond, VA, Dec. 1, 1970; app. bp. of Richmond, June 4, 1974; ret. Sept. 16, 2003.

Sulyk, Stephen: b. Oct. 2, 1924, Balnycia, Western Ukraine; migrated to U.S. 1948; educ. Ukrainian Catholic Seminary of the Holy Spirit (Hirschberg, Germany), St. Josaphat's Seminary and Catholic Univ. (Washington, DC); ord. priest (Philadelphia,* Byzantine), June 14, 1952; ord. abp. of the Ukrainian archeparchy of Philadelphia, Mar. 1, 1981; res., Nov. 29, 2000.

Swain, Paul J.: b. Sept. 12, 1943, Newark, N.Y.; educ. Univ. of Wisc.-Madison, Univ. of Wisc. Law School, John XXIII Seminary (Weston, MA); ord. May 27, 1988 (Madison); app. bp. of Sioux Falls, SD, Aug. 31, 2006; ord. Oct. 26, 2006.

Symons, J. Keith: b. Oct. 14, 1932, Champion, MI; educ. St. Thomas Seminary (Bloomfield, CT), St. Mary Seminary (Baltimore, MD); ord. priest (St. Augustine), May 18, 1958; ord. titular bp. of Siguitanus and aux. bp. of St. Petersburg, Mar. 19, 1981; app. bp. of Pensacola-Tallahassee, Oct. 4, 1983, inst., Nov. 8, 1983; app. bp. of Palm Beach, June 12, 1990; res., June 2, 1998.

Szoka, Edmund C.: (*See* Cardinals, Biographies.)

T

Tafoya, Arthur N.: b. Mar. 2, 1933, Alameda, NM; educ. St. Thomas Seminary (Denver, CO), Conception Seminary (Conception, MO); ord. priest (Santa Fe*), May 12, 1962; ord. bp. of Pueblo, Sept. 10, 1980.

Tamayo, James A.: b. Oct. 23, 1949, Brownsville, TX; educ. Del Mar College (Corpus Christi, TX), Univ. of St. Thomas and Univ. of St. Thomas School of Theology (Houston); ord. priest (Corpus Christi), June 11, 1976; ord. titular bp. of Ita and aux. bp. of Galveston-Houston, Mar. 10, 1993; app. first bp. of Laredo, TX, July 3, 2000, ins., Aug. 9, 2000.

Taylor, Anthony Basil: b. Apr. 24, 1954, Fort Worth, TX; educ. University of Oklahoma (Enid, OK), St. Meinrad Seminary (IN), Pontifical North American College and Gregorian University (Rome, Italy), Fordham University (New York); ord. priest (Oklahoma City*), Aug. 2, 1980; app. bp. of Little Rock, Apr. 10, 2008; inst. June 5, 2008.

Thomas, Daniel E.: b. June 11, 1959, Philadelphia; educ. St. Charles Borromeo Sem. (Philadelphia), Gregorian Univ. (Rome); ord. priest May 18, 1985 (Philadelphia); appointed aux. bp. of Philadelphia and tit. bp. of Bardstown June 8, 2006; ord. July 26, 2006.

Thomas, Elliott G.: b. July 15, 1926, Pittsburgh, PA; educ. Howard Univ. (Washington, DC), Gannon Univ. (Erie, PA), St. Vincent de Paul Seminary (Boynton Beach, FL); ord. priest (St. Thomas, Virgin Islands), June 6, 1986; ord. bp. of St. Thomas in the Virgin Islands, Dec. 12, 1993; res., June 30, 1999.

Thomas, George L.: b. May 19, 1950, Anaconda, MT, educ. St. Thomas Seminary, Seattle, Univ. of Washington, Seattle; ord. priest (Seattle*), May 22, 1976; chancellor and vicar general, 1988-1999, diocesan administrator of Seattle, 1996-1997; app. titular bp. of Vagrauta and aux. bp. of Seattle, Nov. 19, 1999, inst., Jan. 28, 2000; app. bp. of Helena, Mar. 23, 2004.

Thompson, David B.: b. May 29, 1923, Philadelphia, PA; educ. St. Charles Seminary (Overbrook, PA), Catholic Univ. (Washington, DC); ord. priest (Philadelphia*), May 27, 1950; ord. coadjutor bp. of Charleston, May 24, 1989; bp. of Charleston, Feb. 22, 1990; res., July 13, 1999

Tiedemann, Neil, C.P.: b. Mar. 5, 1948, Brooklyn, NY; educ. Passionist seminary; entered Congregation of the Passionists in 1970 and took his perpetual vows on Aug. 22, 1974; ord. priest, May 16, 1975; app. bp. of Mandeville, Jamaica, May 20, 2008.

Timlin, James C.: b. Aug. 5, 1927, Scranton, PA; educ. St. Charles College (Catonville, MD), St. Mary's Seminary (Baltimore, MD), North American College (Rome); ord. priest (Scranton), July 16, 1951; ord. titular bp. of Gunugo and aux. bp. of Scranton, Sept. 21, 1976; app. bp. of Scranton, Apr. 24, 1984; ret., July 25, 2003.

Tobin, Thomas J.: b. Apr. 1, 1948, Pittsburgh, PA; educ. St. Mark Seminary High School, Gannon Univ. (Erie, PA), St. Francis College (Loretto, PA), North American College (Rome); ord. priest (Pittsburgh), July 21, 1973; ord. titular bp. of Novica and aux. bp. of Pittsburgh, Dec. 27, 1992; app. bp. of Youngstown Dec. 5, 1995; inst., Feb. 2, 1996; app. bp. of Providence, Mar. 31, 2005; inst. May 31, 2005.

Trautman, Donald W.: b. June 24, 1936, Buffalo, NY; educ. Our Lady of Angels Seminary (Niagara Falls, NY), Theology Faculty (Innsbruck, Austria), Pontifical Biblical Institute (Rome), Catholic Univ. (Washington, DC); ord. priest (Buffalo), Apr. 7, 1962, in Innsbruck; ord. titular bp. of Sassura and aux. of Buffalo, Apr. 16, 1985; app. bp. of Erie, June 12, 1990.

Tschoepe, Thomas: b. Dec. 17, 1915, Pilot Point, TX; educ. Pontifical College Josephinum (Worthington, OH); ord. priest (Dallas), May 30, 1943; ord. bp. of San Angelo, TX, Mar. 9, 1966; app. bp. of Dallas, TX, Aug. 27, 1969; ret., July 14, 1990.

Turley Murphy, Daniel T. , O.S.A.: b. Jan. 25, 1943, Chicago, IL; ord. priest, Dec. 21, 1961; ord. coadjutor bp. of Chulucanas, Peru, Aug. 17, 1996.

Tyson, Joseph J.: b. Oct. 16, 1957, Moses Lake, WA; educ. University of Washington, The Catholic University of America; ord. priest June 10, 1989 (Seattle); app. auxiliary bishop of Seattle and titular bishop of Migirpa May 12, 2005; ord. bp. June 6, 2005.

U-V

Valero, René A.: b. Aug. 15, 1930, New York, NY; educ. Cathedral College, Immaculate Conception Seminary (Huntington, NY), Fordham Univ. (New York); ord. priest (Brooklyn), June 2, 1956; ord. titular bp. of Turris Vicus and aux. bp. of Brooklyn, Nov. 24, 1980; ret. Oct. 27, 2005.

Vann, Kevin W.: b. May 10, 1951, Springfield, Ill.; educ. Milikin Univ. (Decatur, IL), Immaculate Conception Seminary (Springfield), Kenrick Seminary (St. Louis), Univ. of St. Thomas Aquinas (Rome); ord. May 30, 1981 (Springfield); app. coadjutor bp. Forth Worth May 17, 2005; ord. bp. July 13, 2005.

Vasa, Robert F.: b. May 7, 1951, Lincoln, NE, educ. St. Thomas Seminary, Denver, Holy Trinity Seminary, Dallas, Pontifical Gregorian Univ. (Rome, Italy); ord. priest (Lincoln), May 22,1976; Vicar General and Moderator of the Curia, 1996; app. bp. of Baker, OR Nov. 19, 1999, inst., Jan. 26, 2000.

Vasquez, José S.: b. July 9, 1957, Stamford, Texas; educ. St. Mary Seminary, Houston, University of St. Thomas, North American College and Pontifical Gregorian University (Rome); ord. priest (San Angelo), June 30, 1984; app. titular bp. of Cova and aux. of Galveston-Houston, Nov. 30, 2001, ord., Jan. 23, 2002.

Veigle, Adrian J.M., T.O.R.: b. Sept. 15, 1912, Lilly, PA; educ. St. Francis College (Loretto, PA), Pennsylvania State College; ord. priest, May 22, 1937; ord. titular bp. of Gigthi, June 9, 1966 (res., titular see May 26, 1978); prelate of Borba, Brazil, 1966; ret., July 6, 1988.

Vigneron, Allen H.: b. Oct. 21, 1948, Detroit, MI; educ. Sacred Heart Seminary (Detroit, MI), North American College, Gregorian Univ. (Rome), Catholic Univ.(Washington, DC); ord. priest (Detroit*), July 26, 1975; served in Vatican Secretariat of State, 1991-94; rector of Sacred Heart Seminary (Detroit), 1994; ord. titular bp. of Sault Sainte Marie and aux. bp. of Detroit, July 9, 1996; app. coadjutor bp. of Oakland, Jan. 10, 2003; bp. of Oakland Oct. 1, 2003.

Vlazny, John G.: b. Feb. 22, 1937, Chicago, IL; educ. Quigley Preparatory Seminary (Chicago, IL), St. Mary of the Lake Seminary (Mundelein, IL), Gregorian Univ. (Rome), Univ. of Michigan, Loyola Univ. (Chicago, IL); ord. priest (Chicago*), Dec. 20, 1961; ord. titular bp. of Stagno and aux. bp. of Chicago, Dec. 13, 1983; app. bp. of Winona, MN, May 19, 1987; app. abp. of Portland in Oregon, Oct. 28, 1997, inst., Dec. 19, 1997.

W

Walsh, Daniel Francis: b. Oct. 2, 1937, San Francisco, CA; educ. St. Joseph Seminary (Mountain View, CA), St. Patrick Seminary (Menlo Park, CA) Catholic Univ. (Washington, DC); ord. priest (San Francisco*), Mar. 30, 1963; ord. titular bp. of Tigia and aux. bp. of San Francisco, Sept. 24, 1981; app. bp. of Reno-Las Vegas, June 9, 1987; app. first bp. of Las Vegas, Mar. 21, 1995, when the Reno-Las Vegas diocese was made two separate dioceses; app. bp. Santa Rosa, Apr. 11, 2000.

Walsh, Gerald T.: b. Apr. 25, 1942, New York, NY; educ. Iona College (New Rochelle, NY), St. Joseph Seminary (Dunwoodie, NY), Fordham University (New York, NY); ord. May 27, 1967; app. titular bp. of Altiburo and aux. bp. of New York, June 28, 2004; ord. Sept. 21, 2004.

Walsh, Paul H.: b. Aug. 17, 1937, Brooklyn; educ. Providence College (RI), St. Stephen's College (Dover, MA), Dominican House of Studies (Washington); ord. Dominican, June 9, 1966; incard. Rockville Centre Dec. 13, 1984; app. aux. bp. of Rockville Centre and titular bishop of Abtugni, Apr. 3, 2003; ord. bp., May 29, 2003.

Wang, Ignatius: b. Feb. 27, 1934, Beijing, China; educ. Urbanian Univ. and Gregorian Univ. (Rome); ord. priest (for apostolic vicariate in southern China) July 4, 1959; unable to return home, he served in the Antilles and transferred to San Francisco in 1974; auxiliary bishop of San Francisco and titular bishop of Sitipa, Dec. 13, 2002; ord., Jan. 30, 2003.

Ward, John J.: b. Sept. 28, 1920, Los Angeles, CA; educ. St. John's Seminary (Camarillo, CA), Catholic Univ. (Washington, DC); ord. priest (Los Angeles*), May 4, 1946; ord. titular bp. of Bria and aux. of Los Angeles, Dec. 12, 1963; ret., May 7, 1996; titular bp. of CA.

Warfel, Michael William: b. Sept 16, 1948, Elkhart, IN; educ. Indiana Univ, St. Gregory's College Seminary, Mt. St. Mary's Seminary of the West (Cincinnati, OH); ord. priest, Apr. 26, 1980; ord. bp. of Juneau, Dec. 17, 1996; app. bp. of Great-Fall-Billings, Nov. 20, 2007.

Watters, Loras J.: b. Oct. 14, 1915, Dubuque, IA; educ. Loras College (Dubuque, IA), Gregorian Univ. (Rome), Catholic Univ. (Washington, DC); ord. priest (Dubuque*), June 7, 1941; ord. titular bp. of Fidoloma and aux. bp. of Dubuque, Aug. 26, 1965; bp. of Winona, inst., Mar. 13, 1969; ret., Oct. 14, 1986.

Watty Urquidi, Ricardo, M.Sp.S.: b. July 16, 1938, San Diego, CA; ord. priest, June 8, 1968; ord. titular bp. of Macomedes and aux. bp. of Mexico City, July 19, 1980; app. first bp. of Nuevo Laredo, Mexico, Nov. 6, 1989.

Wcela, Emil A.: b. May 1, 1931, Bohemia, NY; educ. St. Francis College (Brooklyn, NY), Immaculate Conception Seminary (Huntington, NY), Catholic Univ. (Washington, DC), Pontifical Biblical Institute (Rome, Italy); ord. priest (Brooklyn), June 2, 1956; ord. titular bp. of Filaca and aux. bp. of Rockville Centre, Dec. 13, 1988; ret. Apr. 3, 2007.

Weakland, Rembert G., O.S.B.: b. Apr. 2, 1927, Patton, PA; joined Benedictines, 1945; ord. priest, June 24, 1951; abbot-primate of Benedictine Confederation, 1967-77; ord. abp. of Milwaukee, Nov. 8, 1977; res., May 24, 2002.

Weigand, William K.: b. May 23, 1937, Bend, OR; educ. Mt. Angel Seminary (St. Benedict, OR), St. Edward's Seminary and St. Thomas Seminary (Kenmore, WA); ord. priest (Boise), May 25, 1963; ord. bp. of Salt Lake City, Nov. 17, 1980; app. bp. of Sacramento, Nov. 30, 1993, inst., Jan. 27, 1994.

Weitzel, John Quinn, M.M.: b. May 10, 1928, Chicago, IL; educ. Maryknoll Seminary (Maryknoll, NY); ord. priest,

Nov. 5, 1955; missionary to Samoa, 1979; ord. bp. of Samoa-Pago Pago, American Samoa, Oct. 29, 1986.

Welsh, Thomas J.: b. Dec. 20, 1921, Weatherly, PA; educ. St. Charles Borromeo Seminary (Philadelphia, PA), Catholic Univ. (Washington, DC); ord. priest (Philadelphia*), May 30, 1946; ord. titular bp. of Scattery Island and aux. bp. of Philadelphia, Apr. 2, 1970; app. first bp. of Arlington, VA, June 4, 1974; app. bp. of Allentown, Feb. 8, 1983, inst., Mar. 21, 1983; ret.,: Dec. 16, 1997.

Wenski, Thomas G.: b. Oct. 18, 1950, West Palm Beach, FL; educ. St. John Vianney College Seminary, St. Vincent de Paul Regional Seminary, Fordham Univ.; ord. priest (Miami*), May 15, 1976; director of Miami Haitian Apostolate; app. titular bp. of Kearney and aux. of Miami, June 24, 1997; app. coadjutor bp. of Orlando, July 1, 2003; bp. of Orlando, Nov. 13, 2004.

Wester, John Charles: b. Nov. 5, 1950, San Francisco; educ.St. John's Seminary, Camarillo, CA, St. Patrick's Seminary, Menlo Park, CA, Univ. of San Francisco; ord. priest (San Francisco*), May 15, 1976; app. titular bp. of Lamiggiga and aux. bp. of San Francisco, June 30, 1998; app. bp. of Salt Lake City, Jan. 8, 2007.

Wilkerson, Gerald E.: b. Oct. 21, 1939, Des Moines, IA; educ. St. John's Seminary (Camarillo, CA); ord. priest (Los Angeles*), Jan. 5, 1965; app. Titular Bp. of Vincennes and aux. bp. of Los Angeles, Nov. 5, 1997, ord., Jan. 21, 1998.

Williams, James Kendrick: b. Sept. 5, 1936, Athertonville, KY; educ. St. Mary's College (St. Mary's, KY), St. Maur's School of Theology (South Union, KY); ord. priest (Louisville*), May 25, 1963; ord. titular bp. of Catula and aux. bp. of Covington, June 19, 1984; first bp. of Lexington, KY, inst., Mar. 2, 1988; res., June 11, 2002.

Winter, William J.: b. May 20, 1930, Pittsburgh, PA; educ. St. Vincent College and Seminary (Latrobe, PA), Gregorian Univ. (Rome, Italy); ord. priest (Pittsburgh), Dec. 17, 1955; ord. titular bp. of Uthina and aux. bp. of Pittsburgh, Feb. 13, 1989; ret. May 20, 2005.

Wirz, George O.: b. Jan. 17, 1929, Monroe, WI; educ. St. Francis Seminary and Marquette Univ. (Milwaukee, WI); Cath. Univ. (Washington, DC); ord. priest (Madison), May 31, 1952; ord. titular bp. of Municipa and aux. bp. of Madison, Mar. 9, 1978; ret. Feb. 10, 2004.

Wiwchar, Michael, C.SS.R.: b. May 9, 1932, Komarno, Manitoba, Can.; educ. Redemptorist Seminary (Windsor, Ontario); made solemn vows as Redemptorist, 1956; ord. priest, June 28, 1959; pastor St. John the Baptist Parish, Newark, NJ, 1990-93; ord. bp. of St. Nicholas of Chicago for the Ukrainians, Sept. 28, 1993; bp. of Saskatoon of Ukrainians, Nov. 29, 2000.

Wuerl, Donald W.: b. Nov. 12, 1940, Pittsburgh, PA; educ. Catholic Univ. (Washington, DC), North American College, Angelicum (Rome); ord. priest (Pittsburgh), Dec. 17, 1966, in Rome; ord. titular bp. of Rosemarkie Jan. 6, 1986, in Rome; aux. bp. of Seattle, 1986-87; app. bp. of Pittsburgh, Feb. 11, 1988, inst., Mar. 25, 1988; app. Abp. of Washington, May 16, 2006.

Y-Z

Yanta, John W.: b. Oct. 2, 1931, Runge, TX; educ. St. John's Preparatory Seminary and Assumption Seminary (San Antonio); ord. priest (San Antonio*), Mar. 17, 1956; ord. titular bp. of Naratcata and aux. bp. of San Antonio, Dec. 30, 1994; app. bp. of Amarillo, Jan. 21,1997, inst., Mar. 17, 1997; ret. Jan. 3, 2008.

Younan, Joseph: b. Nov. 15, 1944, Hassakeh, Syria; educ. Our Lady of Deliverance Seminary (Charfet, Lebanon), Pontifical College of the Propagation of the Faith (Rome); ord. priest, Sept. 12, 1971; came to U.S., 1986; served Syrian Catholics in U.S.; ord. first bp. Our Lady of Deliverance of Newark for Syrian Catholics in the U.S. and Canada, Jan. 7, 1996, in Kamisly, Syria.

Zavala, Gabino: b. Sept. 7, 1951, Guerrero, Mexico; became U.S. citizen, 1976; educ. St. John's Seminary (Los Angeles), Catholic Univ. (Washington, DC); ord. priest (Los Angeles*), May 28, 1977; ord. titular bp. of Tamascani and aux. bp. of Los Angeles, Mar. 19, 1994.

Zayek, Francis: b. Oct. 18, 1920, Manzanillo, Cuba; ord. priest, Mar. 17, 1946; ord. titular bp. of Callinicum and aux. bp. for Maronites in Brazil, Aug. 5, 1962; named apostolic exarch for Maronites in U.S., with headquarters in Detroit; inst., June 11. 1966; first eparch of St. Maron of Detroit, Mar. 25, 1972; see transferred to Brooklyn, June 27, 1977; given personal title of abp., Dec. 22, 1982; ret., Nov. 23, 1996.

Ziemann, G. Patrick: b. Sept. 13, 1941, Pasadena, CA; educ. St. John's College Seminary and St. John's Seminary (Camarillo, CA), Mt. St. Mary's College (Los Angeles, CA); ord. priest (Los Angeles*), Apr. 29, 1967; ord. titular bp. of Obba and aux. bp. of Los Angeles, Feb. 23, 1987; app. bp. of Santa Rosa, July 14, 1992; res., July 22, 1999.

Zipfel, Paul A.: b. Sept. 22, 1935, St. Louis, MO; educ. Cardinal Glennon College, Kenrick Seminary (St. Louis, MO), Catholic Univ. (Washington, DC), St. Louis Univ. (St. Louis, MO); ord. priest (St. Louis*), Mar. 18, 1961; ord. titular bp. of Walla Walla and aux. bp. of St. Louis, June 29, 1989; app. bp. of Bismarck, Dec. 31, 1996.

Zubic, David A.: b. Sept. 4, 1949, Sewickley, PA; educ. St. Paul Seminary-Duquesne Univ. (Pittsburgh), St. Mary's Seminary (Baltimore), Duquesne Univ. (Pittsburgh); ord. priest (Pittsburgh), May 3, 1975; ord. titular bp. of Jamestown and aux. of Pittsburgh, Apr. 6, 1997; app. bp. of Green Bay, Oct. 10, 2003; app. bp. of Pittsburgh, July 18, 2007.

Zurek, Patrick J.: b. Aug. 17, 1948, Wallis, TX; educ. Univ.of St. Thomas (Houston), Angelicum and Alphonsian Academy (Rome); ord priest (Austin), June 29, 1975; app. titular bp. of Tamugadi and aux. bp. of San Antonio, Jan. 5, 1998, ord., Feb. 16, 1998; app. bp. of Amarillo, Jan. 3, 2008.

BISHOP-BROTHERS

(The asterisk indicates brothers who were bishops at the same time.)

There have been 10 pairs of brother-bishops in the history of the U.S. hierarchy.

Living: Francis T. Hurley,* abp. of Anchorage and Mark J. Hurley,* bp. emeritus of Santa Rosa (deceased). Raymond J. Boland,* bp. emeritus of Kansas City-St. Joseph, MO and John Kevin Boland,* bp. of Savannah.

Deceased: Francis Blanchet* of Oregon City (Portland) and Augustine Blanchet* of Walla Walla; John S. Foley of Detroit and Thomas P. Foley of Chicago; Francis P. Kenrick,* apostolic administrator of Philadelphia, bp. of Philadelphia and Baltimore, and Peter R. Kenrick* of St. Louis; Matthias C. Lenihan of Great Falls and Thomas M. Lenihan of Cheyenne; James O'Connor, vicar apostolic of Nebraska and bp. of Omaha, and Michael O'Connor of Pittsburgh and Erie; Jeremiah F. and John W. Shanahan, both of Harrisburg; Sylvester J. Espelage, O.F.M.* of Wuchang, China, who died 10 days after the ordination of his brother, Bernard T. Espelage, O.F.M.* of Gallup; Coleman F. Carroll* of Miami

and Howard Carroll* of Altoona-Johnstown.

U.S. BISHOPS OVERSEAS

Cardinal William W. Baum, major penitentiary emeritus; Cardinal Edmund C. Szoka, President emeritus, Pontifical Commission for Vatican City State; Cardinal James Francis Stafford, major penitentiary; Card. William Levada, prefect of the Cong. for the Doctrine of the Faith; Card. John P. Foley, Grand Master of the Order of the Holy Sepulchre; Abp. Raymond Burke, prefect of the Apostolic Signatura; Abp. James Harvey, prefect of the Papal Household; Abp. Charles A. Schleck, C.S.C., former adjunct secretary of the Cong. for the Evangelization of Peoples; Abp. Edward Joseph Adams, nuncio to the Philippines; Abp. James P. Green, apostolic nuncio to South Africa and Namibia and apostolic delegate to Botswana; Abp. Thomas E. Gullickson, apostolic nuncio to Trinidad and Tobago, Bahamas, Dominica, St. Kitts and Nevis, Santa Lucia, San Vincenzo and Grenadine; Abp. Charles Daniel Balvo, apostolic nuncio to the Pacific Islands (Oceania), Abp. Michael A. Blume, S.V.D., apostolic nuncio to Benin and Togo; Abp. Joseph Marino, apostolic nuncio to Bangladesh; Abp. George Riashi, B.C.O., abp. of archeparchy of Tripoli of Lebanon (Lebanon) for Greek-Catholic Melkites; Abp. John Bukovsky, S.V.D. (naturalized U.S. citizen), former papal representative to Russia;

Bp. Michael R. Kuchmiak, exarch of apostolic exarchate emeritus of Great Britain for Ukrainian Catholics; Bp. Joseph Pelletier, M.S., bp. of Morondava, Madagascar; Bp. Paul Simon Schmitz, O.F.M.Cap., bp. of Bluefields, Nicaragua; Bp. Ambrose Ravasi, I.M.C., bp. of Marsabit, Kenya; Bp. Caesar Mazzolari, M.C.C.J., bp. of Rumbek, Kenya; Bp. George Biguzzi, S.X., bp. of Makeni, Sierra Leone; Bp. John B. Minder, O.S.F.S., bp. of Keimoes-Upington, South Africa; Bp. Joseph J. Potocnak, S.C.J., bp. of De Aar, South Africa; Bp. Paul Duffy, O.M.I., bp. of Mongu, Zambia; Bp. Henry Howaniec, O.F.M., apostolic admin. of Almaty, Kazakhstan; Bp. William J. McNaughton, M.M. bp. of Inchon., Korea; Bp. Gerald Scarpone Caporale, O.F.M., bp. of: Comayagua, Honduras; Bp. Thomas Maurus Muldoon, O.F.M., bp. of Juticalpa, Honduras; Bp. Edward J. Gilbert, C.SS.R., bp. of Port of Spain, Trinidad and Tobago; Bp. Robert Kurtz, C.R., bp. of Hamilton, Bermuda; Bp. John Quinn Weitzel, M.M., bp. of Samoa-Pago Pago, American Samoa; Bp. Stephen J. Reichert, O.F.M.Cap., bp. of Mendi, Papua New Guinea; Bp. Raymond P. Kalisz, S.V.D., bp. of Wewak Papua New Guinea; Bp. Christopher Cardone, O.P., Gizo, Solomon Islands; Bp. Luis Morgan Casey, vicar apostolic of Pando, Bolivia; Bp. Herbert Hermes, O.S.B., prelate of Cristalandia, Brazil; Bp. Capistran Heim, O.F.M., prelate of Itaituba, Brazil; Bp. John J. Burke, O.F.M., bp. of Miracema do Tocantins Brazil; Bp. Alfred Novak, C.Ss.R., bp. of Paranagua, Brazil; Bp. Elias James Manning, O.F.M. Conv., bp. of Valença, Brazil; Bp. John C. McNabb, O.S.A., bp. of Chulucanas, Peru; Bp. Daniel Thomas Turley Murphy, O.S.A., coadjutor bp. of Chulucanas, Peru; Bp. Michael La Fay Bardi, O.Carm. prelate of Sicuani, Peru. (*See* **Missionary Bishops.**)

RETIRED/RESIGNED U.S. PRELATES

Information, as of Aug. 20, 2008, includes name of the prelate and see held at the time of retirement or resignation; abps. are indicated by an asterisk. Most of the prelates listed below resigned their sees because of age in accordance with church law. See **Index: Biographies, U.S. Bishops.**

Forms of address of retired residential prelates (unless they have a titular see): Abp. or Bp. Emeritus of (last see held); Former Abp. or Bp. of (last see held). Patrick V. Ahern (New York, aux.), Moses B. Anderson (Detroit, aux.), Kenneth A. Angell (Burlington), Juan Arzube (Los Angeles, aux.), Victor H. Balke (Crookston), Robert J. Banks (Green Bay), Gordon D. Bennett (Mandeville, Jamaica), Cardinal Anthony J. Bevilacqua* (Philadelphia), Ernest B. Boland, O.P. (Multan, Pakistan), Raymond J. Boland (Kansas-City-St. Joseph), John P. Boles (Boston, aux.), William D. Borders* (Baltimore), Anthony G. Bosco (Greensburg), Paul M. Boyle, C.P. (Mandeville, Jamaica), Joseph M. Breitenbeck (Grand Rapids), Robert A. Brucato (New York, aux.), William H. Bullock (Madison).

Dominic Carmon (New Orleans, aux.), Joseph L. Charron, C.PP.S. (Des Moines), Gilbert E. Chavez (San Diego, aux.), John Chedid (Our Lady of Lebanon), John W. Comber, M.M. (Foratiano, titular see), Thomas Connolly (Baker), Ronald G. Connors, C.SS.R. (San Juan de la Maguana, Dominican Republic), Thomas J. Costello (Syracuse, aux.), Arnold R. Cotey, S.D.S. (Nachingwea, now Lindi, Tanzania), Daniel A. Cronin* (Hartford), John Stephen Cummins (Oakland), William G. Curlin (Charlotte), James J. Daly (Rockville Centre, aux.), Thomas V. Daily (Brooklyn), Nicholas D'Antonio, O.F.M. (Olancho, Honduras).

Joseph A. DePalma, S.C.J. (DeAar, South Africa), Louis A. DeSimone (Philadelphia, aux.), Joseph T. Dimino* (Military Services archdiocese), George Dion, O.M.I. (titular see, Arpaia), Robert W. Donnelly (Toledo, aux.), John F. Donoghue* (Atlanta), Paul V. Donovan (Kalamazoo), Norbert M. Dorsey, C.P. (Orlando), Stephen Hector Doueihi (St. Maron of Brooklyn), Michael J. Dudick (Passaic, Byzantine rite), Roland Pierre DuMaine (San Jose), Thomas L. Dupre (Springfield), Dennis V. Durning, C.S.Sp. (Arusha, Tanzania), John Elya (Newton), J. Lennox Federal (Salt Lake City), Gilberto Fernandez (Miami, aux.), Joseph A. Fiorenza* (Galveston-Houston), Thomas J. Flanagan (San Antonio, aux.), Raphael M. Fliss (Superior), Patrick F. Flores* (San Antonio), Harry Flynn* (St. Paul-Minneapolis), David E. Foley (Birmingham), Marion F. Forst (Dodge City), William E. Franklin (Davenport), William B. Friend (Shreveport).

James H. Garland (Marquette), Louis E. Gelineau (Providence), Odore Gendron (Manchester), Peter L. Gerety* (Newark), Joseph J. Gerry, O.S.B. (Portland, ME), Raymond E. Goedert (Chicago, aux.), John R. Gorman (Chicago, aux.), F. Joseph Gossman (Raleigh), Rene H. Gracida (Corpus Christi), Charles V. Grahmann (Dallas), Thomas J. Gumbleton (Detroit, aux.), Richard C. Hanifen (Colorado Springs), Philip M. Hannan* (New Orleans), Edward D. Head (Buffalo).

Joseph L. Hogan (Rochester), William Russell Houck (Jackson), Joseph Lawson Howze (Biloxi), Edward T. Hughes (Metuchen), William A. Hughes (Covington), Raymond G. Hunthausen* (Seattle), Joseph L. Imesch (Joliet), Thad J. Jakubowski (Chicago, aux.) Roger L. Kaffer (Joliet, aux.), Raymond Kalisz, S.V.D. (Wewak), Cardinal William Keeler* (Baltimore), James P. Keleher* (Kansas City), Thomas C. Kelly, O.P.* (Louisville), Daniel W. Kucera, O.S.B.* (Dubuque), William F. Kupfer, M.M. (Taichung, Taiwan), George Kuzma (Van Nuys), Francis Lambert, S.M. (Port Vila, Vanuatu), Bernard Cardinal Law* (Boston), John J. Leibrecht (Springfield-Cape Girardeau), Raymond W. Lessard (Savannah), Oscar Lipscomb* (Mobile), Martin N. Lohmuller (Philadelphia, aux.), Basil Losten (Stamford),

Innocent Hilarius Lotocky, O.S.B.M. (St. Nicholas of Chicago for Ukrainians), Timothy J. Lyne (Chicago, aux.). Cardinal Theodore McCarrick* (Washington, DC), James F. McCarthy (New York, aux.) John McCarthy (Austin), William J. McCormack (New York, aux.), Andrew McDonald (Little Rock), Charles J. McDonnell (Newark, aux.), John B. McDowell (Pittsburgh, aux.), Norman McFarland (Orange, CA), Urban McGarry, T.O.R. (Bhagalpur, India), Bernard J. McLaughlin (Buffalo, aux.), John C. McNabb, O.S.A. (Chulucanas), William J. McNaughton (Inchon), Joseph Madera (Military Archdiocese, aux.), Joseph F. Maguire (Springfield, MA), Thomas R. Manning, O.F.M. (Coroico, Bolivia), Dominic Anthony Marconi (Newark, aux.), Leroy T. Matthiesen (Amarillo), Carl F. Mengeling (Lansing), Anthony F. Mestice (New York, aux.), James E. Michaels (Wheeling-Charleston, aux.), Anthony M. Milone (Great Falls-Billings), John B. Minder (Keimos-Upington), C arl K. Moeddel (Cincinnati, aux.), Robert E. Mulvee (Providence), John J. Nevins (Venice), William C. Newman (Baltimore, aux.), Thomas Joseph O'Brien (Phoenix), Anthony J. O'Connell (Palm Beach), Edward J. O'Donnell (Lafayette, LA), Leonard James Olivier, S.V.D. (Washington, aux.), Arthur J. O'Neill (Rockford).

Albert H. Ottenweller (Steubenville), Walter Paska (Philadelphia, Ukrainians, aux.), Andrew Pataki (Passaic), George H. Pearce, S.M.* (Suva, Fiji Islands), Donald Pelotte, S.S.S. (Gallup), Edward Pevec (Cleveland, aux.), Anthony M. Pilla (Cleveland), Bernard F. Popp (San Antonio, aux.), Vasile Louis Puscas (St. George's in Canton of the Romanians), Alexander James Quinn (aux., Cleveland),Francis A. Quinn (Sacramento), John R. Quinn* (San Francisco), Joseph M. Raya* (Acre), Daniel P. Reilly (Worcester), John C. Reiss (Trenton), Vincent M. Rizzotto (Galveston-Houston, aux.), Agustin Roman (Miami, aux.), Francis X. Roque (Military Archdiocese, aux.), Robert John Rose (Grand Rapids), George E. Rueger (Worcester, aux.), Daniel Ryan (Springfield, IL), Sylvester Ryan (Monterey).

Michael A. Saltarelli (Wilmington), Nicholas J. Samra (Melkite eparchy of Newton, aux.), Robert F. Sanchez* (Santa Fe), Joseph Sartoris (Los Angeles, aux.), Stanley G. Schlarman (Dodge City), Bernard W. Schmitt (Wheeling-Charleston), Mark Schmitt (Marquette), Walter J. Schoenherr (Detroit, aux.), Francis B. Schulte* (New Orleans), Daniel E. Sheehan* (Omaha), Gilbert I. Sheldon (Steubenville), Patrick Sheridan (New York, aux.), John Snyder (St. Augustine), Jude Speyrer (Lake Charles), Philip Straling (Reno), Joseph M. Sullivan (Brooklyn, aux.), Walter Francis Sullivan (Richmond), Stephen Sulyk* (Philadelphia, Ukrainians).

Elliott Thomas (Virgin Islands), David B. Thompson (Charleston), Thomas Tschoepe (Dallas), James C. Timlin (Scranton), René A. Valero (Brooklyn, aux.), Adrian Veigle, T.O.R. (Borba, Brazil, Prelate), John J. Ward (Los Angeles, aux.), Loras J. Watters (Winona), Emil A. Wcela (Rockville Center, aux.), Rembert G. Weakland, O.S.B.* (Milwaukee), Thomas J. Welsh (Allentown), James Kendrick Williams (Lexington), George O. Wirz (Madison, aux.), John W. Yanta (Amarillo), Francis Zayek (St. Maron of Brooklyn); G. Patrick Ziemann (Santa Rosa).

American Bishops of the Past: For coverage of the deceased bishops who served in the United States, please visit www.CatholicAlmanac.com.

The United States Conference of Catholic Bishops

Courtesy USCCB

When the Bishops merged their two national organizations into the United States Conference of Catholic Bishops (USCCB) on July 1, 2001, it marked the latest chapter in the evolution of the bishops' national structure, which was established 82 years ago in the aftermath of the First World War. Like its immediate predecessors — the National Conference of Catholic Bishops (NCCB) and United States Catholic Conference (USCC) — the USCCB is an organization staffed by lay people, priests, and members of religious orders, but whose members are the bishops of the United States, and it is the bishops who direct its activities.

The concept of the bishops acting together on matters of mutual interest can be traced back to 1919 when, in their first national meeting since 1884, they agreed to meet annually and to form the National Catholic Welfare Council (NCWC) to serve as their organized voice on the national scene. The word "Council" was replaced by the word "Conference" in 1922.

In 1966, following the Second Vatican Council, NCWC was reorganized into two parallel conferences. The National Conference of Catholic Bishops — sometimes referred to as the canonical arm — would deal with matters connected to the internal life of the Church, such as liturgy and priestly life and ministry. The U.S. Catholic Conference — in effect the civil arm — would represent the bishops as they related to the "secular" world, in areas such as social concerns, education, communications and public affairs.

During the period from 1992 to 1996, a Conference committee on mission and structure, headed by the late Cardinal Joseph L. Bernardin of Chicago, led the bishops in extensive consultation on restructuring. A primary purpose of this undertaking was to provide more of the nation's approximately 300 bishops with an opportunity to be directly involved in the work of the Conference, which operates primarily through a committee structure.

In 1997 the bishops voted to combine NCCB-USCC into one conference, to be called the U.S. Conference of Catholic Bishops. They decided that in the future only bishops would be voting members of committees, but non-bishops could serve on some committees as consultants or advisers. A new committee on statutes and bylaws, headed by Archbishop Daniel E. Pilarczyk of Cincinnati, which was formed to lead the rest of the reorganization process, completed its work last year. The new statutes and bylaws were subsequently approved by the Holy See.

It is unlikely that persons outside the Bishops' Conference will notice any immediate difference in the new structure. Many of the same concerns that motivated the Bishops in 1919 — like the welfare of immigrants, communicating through the Catholic press, and defending the legal rights of the Church — are still pressing today, as evidenced in the departments which carry out these functions, though many others have been added as well.

In a May 23, 2001, letter sent to organizations which have dealings with the Conference, its General Secretary, Monsignor William P. Fay, said the renaming "will not affect any change in the activities or programs of the Conference but simply how the Conference is identified."

USCCB Restructuring

At their fall general meeting on Nov. 14, 2006, the bishops of the USCCB approved a plan to restructure national operations of the USCCB and to cut diocesan assessments by 16 percent, eliminate more than 60 jobs at the USCCB headquarters in Washington and satellite offices, and trim the number of USCCB committees. The comprehensive plan of reorganization and strategic planning for 2008-2011 was approved by a 213-19 vote. Diocesan heads then voted 158-6 to adopt the proposal to reduce diocesan funding of the USCCB in 2008 by 16 percent. Diocesan assessments, covering nearly $11.9 million of the USCCB's overall budget of $139.5 million in 2007, will be reduced in 2008 to just under $10 million.

The restructuring plan was overseen by the bishops' Committee on Priorities and Plans, in the last few years under the chairmanship of Archbishop Michael J. Sheehan of Santa Fe, N.M. who also served as secretary of the conference.

Central to the reorganization was the plan for the conference to concentrate on top priorities discerned by the bishops. Those chosen for the 2008-2011 planning cycle:
· The implementation of the pastoral initiative on marriage.
· Faith formation focused on sacramental practice.
· Priestly and religious vocations.
· The Life and dignity of the human person.
· The recognition of cultural diversity, with special emphasis on Hispanic ministry, "in the spirit of *Encuentro*."

Mission Statement

The United States Conference of Catholic Bishops is a permanent institute composed of Catholic Bishops of the United States of America in and through which the bishops exercise in a communal or collegial manner the pastoral mission entrusted to them by the Lord Jesus of sanctification, teaching, and leadership, especially by devising forms and methods of the apostolate suitably adapted to the circumstances of the times. Such exercise is intended to offer appropriate assistance to each bishop in fulfilling his particular ministry in the local Church, to effect a commonality of ministry addressed to the people of the United States of America, and to foster and express communion with the Church in other nations within the Church universal, under the leadership of its chief pastor, the pope.

Administration

The principal officers of the conference are: Cardinal Francis E. George, OMI, president Bishop Gerald F. Kicanas, vice president; Archbishop Joseph Kurtz, treasurer; Bishop George Murry, S.J., secretary; Msgr. David J. Malloy, general secretary. Headquarters of the conferences are located at 3211 Fourth St. N.E., Washington, DC 20017; (202) 541-3000; www.usccb.org.

USCCB REGIONS

I. Maine, Vermont, New Hampshire, Massachusetts, Rhode Island, Connecticut. II. New York. III. New Jersey, Pennsylvania. IV. Delaware, District of Columbia, Maryland, Virgin Islands, Virginia, West Virginia, Military Archdiocese. V. Alabama, Kentucky, Louisiana, Mississippi, Tennessee. VI. Michigan, Ohio. VII. Illinois, Indiana, Wisconsin. VIII. Minnesota, North Dakota, South Dakota. IX. Iowa, Kansas, Missouri, Nebraska. X. Arkansas, Oklahoma, Texas. XI. California, Hawaii, Nevada. XII. Idaho, Montana, Alaska, Washington, Oregon. XIII. Utah, Arizona, New Mexico, Colorado, Wyoming, including El Paso. XIV. Florida, Georgia, North Carolina, South Carolina. XV. Eastern Catholic Churches (non-geographic; approved on Nov. 14, 2006).

PASTORAL COUNCIL

The conference, one of many similar territorial conferences envisioned in the conciliar Decree on the Pastoral Office of Bishops in the Church (No. 38), is "a council in which the bishops of a given nation or territory [in this case, the United States] jointly exercise their pastoral office to promote the greater good which the Church offers mankind, especially through the forms and methods of the apostolate fittingly adapted to the circumstances of the age."

Its decisions, "provided they have been approved legitimately and by the votes of at least two-thirds of the prelates who have a deliberative vote in the conference, and have been recognized by the Apostolic See, are to have juridically binding force only in those cases prescribed by the common law or determined by a special mandate of the Apostolic See, given either spontaneously or in response to a petition of the conference itself."

All bishops who serve the Church in the U.S., its territories and possessions, have membership and voting rights in the USCCB. Retired bishops cannot be elected to conference offices nor can they vote on matters that by law are binding by two-thirds of the membership. Only diocesan bishops can vote on diocesan quotas, assessments or special collections.

OFFICERS, COMMITTEES

The conference operates through a number of bishops' committees with functions in specific areas of work and concern. Their basic assignments are to prepare materials on the basis of which the bishops, assembled as a conference, make decisions, and to put suitable action plans into effect.

The officers, with several other bishops, hold positions on executive-level committees — Administrative, Executive, the Committee on Budget and Finance, the Committee on Personnel, and the Committee on Priorities and Plans. They also, with other bishops, serve on the USCCB Administrative Committee.

Standing Committees

The standing committees and their chairmen (Cardinals, Archbishops, and Bishops), as of Jan. 1, 2008 are as follows (chairmen elect are in parentheses):

Canonical Affairs: Abp. John Myers (Bp. Thomas Paprocki)

Clergy and Consecrated Life: Cardinal Sean O'Malley, OFM Cap.

Subcommittees: Consecrated Life; Diaconate; Priestly Formation; Priestly Life and Ministry

Communications: Abp. George Niederauer

Areas of responsibility: Office of Media Relations; Catholic News Service; USCCB Publishing; Film and Broadcasting; Office of Digital Media

Subcommittee: Catholic Communication Campaign

Cultural Diversity: Abp. Jose H. Gomez

Subcommittees: African-American Catholics; Asian and Pacific Affairs; Hispanic Affairs; Native American Catholics; Pastoral Care of Migrants, Refugees and Travelers

Divine Worship: Bp. Arthur J. Serratelli

Subcommittee: Spanish Liturgy

Doctrine: Bp. William E. Lori

Subcommittees: Health Care Issues and the Church; Review of Scripture Translations

Domestic Justice and Human Development: Bp. William Murphy

Subcommittee: Catholic Campaign for Human Development:

Ecumenical and Interreligious Affairs: Bp. Richard J. Sklba

Education: Bp. Robert J. McManus

Evangelization and Catechesis: Bp. Richard Malone

Subcommittee: Catechism of the Catholic Church

International Justice and Peace: Bp. Thomas Wenski

Laity Marriage, Family Life, and Youth: Abp. Roger L. Schwietz, OMI

Subcommittee: Marriage and the Family

Migration: Bp. John Wester

National Collections: Abp. John G. Vlazny.

Collections: Aid to the Church in Central & Eastern Europe; Black and Indian Missions; Catholic Campaign for Human Development; Catholic Communication Campaign; Catholic Home Missions Appeal; Catholic Relief Services Collection; Catholic University of America; Church in Latin America; Holy Land; Peter's Pence (Collection for the Holy Father); Retirement Fund for Religious; World Mission Sunday

Pastoral Practices: Bp. Jerome E. Listecki

Pro-Life Activities: Justin Cardinal Rigali
Protection of Children & Young People: Bp. Blaise Cupich

Executive Level and Management Committees

Administrative Committee: Francis Cardinal George, OMI
Budget and Finance: Bp. Dennis Schnurr
  Subcommittee: Audits
Priorities and Plans: Bp. George Murry, SJ
Executive Committee: Francis Cardinal George, OMI
Temporary Task Forces (Temporary)
  Spanish Language Bible

STATE CATHOLIC CONFERENCES

These conferences are agencies of bishops and dioceses in the various states. Their general purposes are to develop and sponsor cooperative programs designed to cope with pastoral and common-welfare needs, and to represent the dioceses before governmental bodies, the public, and in private sectors. Their membership consists of representatives from the dioceses in the states — bishops, clergy and lay persons in various capacities.

The National Association of State Catholic Conference Directors maintains liaison with the general secretariat of the United States Conference of Catholic Bishops. President: Robert J. Castagna, executive director of Oregon Catholic Conference.

Alaska Catholic Conference, 415 6th St., Ste. 300, Juneau. AK 99801; (907) 586-2404; Exec. Dir., Chip Wagoner.

Arizona Catholic Conference, 400 E. Monroe St., Phoenix, AZ 85004-2376; (602) 354-2391; Exec. Dir., Ron Johnson.

California Catholic Conference, 1119 K St., 2nd Floor, Sacramento, CA 95814; (916) 443-4851; Exec. Dir., Edward Dolejsi.

Colorado Catholic Conference, 1535 Logan St., Denver, CO 80203; (303) 894-8808; Exec. Dir. Timothy Dore.

Connecticut Catholic Conference, 134 Farmington Ave., Hartford, CT 06105; (860) 524-7882; Exec. Dir., Dr. Marie T. Hilliard, Ph.D., R.N.

Florida Catholic Conference, 201 W. Park Ave., Tallahassee, FL 32301; (850) 222-3803; Exec. Dir., Dr. D. Michael McCarron, Ph.D.

Georgia Catholic Conference, Office Bldg., 3200 Deans Bridge Rd., Augusta, GA 30906; (706) 798-1719; Exec. Dir., Francis J. Mulcahy, Esq.

Hawaii Catholic Conference, Stephen Diocesan Center, 6301 Pali Hwy., Kaneohe, HI 96744; (808) 585-3341; Exec. Dir., Deacon Walter Yoshimitsu.

Illinois, Catholic Conference of, 65 E. Wacker Pl., Ste. 1620, Chicago, IL 60601; (312) 368-1066. 108 E. Cook, Springfield, IL 62701; (217) 528-9200; Exec. Dir., Robert Gilligan.

Indiana Catholic Conference, 1400 N. Meridian St., P.O. Box 1410, Indianapolis, IN 46206; (317) 236-1455; Exec. Dir., Glenn Tebbe.

Iowa Catholic Conference, 530-42nd St., Des Moines, IA 50312-2707; (515) 243-6256; Exec. Dir., Sara Eide.

Kansas Catholic Conference, 6301 Antioch, Merriam, KS 66202; (913) 722-6633; Exec. Dir., Beatrice E. Swoopes.

Kentucky, Catholic Conference of, 1042 Burlington Lane, Frankfort, KY 40601; (502) 875-4345; Exec. Dir., Edward Monahan.

Louisiana Catholic Conference, 3423 Hundred Oaks Ave., Baton Rouge, LA 70808; (225) 344-7120; Exec. Dir., Daniel J. Loar.

Maryland Catholic Conference, 188 Duke of Gloucester St., Annapolis, MD 21401; (410) 269-1155; Exec. Dir., Richard J. Dowling, Esq.

Massachusetts Catholic Conference, 150 Staniford St., West End Pl., Boston, MA 02114-2511; (617) 367-6060; Exec. Dir., Edward F. Saunders.

Michigan Catholic Conference, 510 N. Capitol Ave., Lansing, MI 48933; (517) 372-9310; President and CEO, Sr. Monica Kostielney, R.S.M.

Minnesota Catholic Conference, 475 University Ave. W., St. Paul, MN 55103; (651) 227-8777; Exec. Dir., Christopher Leifeld.

Missouri Catholic Conference, P.O. Box 1022, 600 Clark Ave., Jefferson City, MO 65102; (573) 635-7239; Exec. Dir., Deacon Lawrence A. Weber.

Montana Catholic Conference, P.O. Box 1708, Helena, MT 59624; (406) 442-5761; www.mt.net/~mcc; Exec. Dir., Moe Wosepka.

Nebraska Catholic Conference, 215 Centennial Mall South, Suite 410, Lincoln, NE 68508-1890; (402) 477-7517; Exec. Dir., James R. Cunningham.

Nevada Catholic Conference, 290 South Arlington Ave., Ste. 200, Reno, NV 89501-1713; (775) 322-7412; Exec. Dir., John Cracchiolo.

New Jersey Catholic Conference, 149 N. Warren St., Trenton, NJ 08608; (609) 989-1120; Exec. Dir., Patrick R. Brannigan.

New York State Catholic Conference, 465 State St., Albany, NY 12203; (518) 434-6195; www.nyscatholicconference.org; Exec. Dir., Richard E. Barnes.

North Dakota Catholic Conference, 103 3rd St., Ste. 2, Bismarck, ND 58501; (701) 223-2519; www.ndcatholic.org; Exec. Dir., Christopher T. Dodson.

Ohio, Catholic Conference of, 9 E. Long St., Suite 201, Columbus, OH 43215; (614) 224-7147; Exec. Dir., Carolyn Jurkowitz.

Oregon Catholic Conference, 2838 E. Burnside, Portland, OR 97214; (503) 233-8387; General Counsel and Exec. Dir., Robert J. Castagna.

Pennsylvania Catholic Conference, 223 North St., Box 2835, Harrisburg, PA 17105; (717) 238-9613; (717) 238-9613; Exec. Dir., Dr. Robert J. O'Hara, Jr.

Texas Catholic Conference, 1625 Rutherford Lane, Bldg. D, Austin, TX 78754; (512) 339-9882; Exec. Dir., Andrew Rivas.

Washington State Catholic Conference, 508 2nd Ave. West, Seattle, WA 98119-3928; (206) 301-0556; Exec. Dir., Sr. Sharon Park, O.P.

West Virginia State Catholic Conference, P.O. Box 230, Wheeling, WV 26003; (304) 233-0880; Dir., Very Rev. John R. Gallagher.

Wisconsin Catholic Conference, 30 W. Mifflin St., Suite 302, Madison, WI 53703; (608) 257-0004; Exec. Dir., John A. Huebscher.

Background

The National Conference of Catholic Bishops (NCCB), was established by action of the U.S. hierarchy Nov. 14, 1966, as a strictly ecclesiastical body with defined juridical authority over the Church in this country. It was set up with the approval of the Holy See and in line with directives from the Second Vatican Council. Its constitution was formally ratified during the November 1967 meeting of the U.S. hierarchy.

The NCCB was a development from the Annual Meeting of the Bishops of the United States, whose pastoral character was originally approved by Pope Benedict XV, Apr. 10, 1919.

The USCC, as of Jan. 1, 1967, took over the general organization and operations of the former National Catholic Welfare Conference, Inc., whose origins dated back to the National Catholic War Council of 1917.

The council underwent some change after World War I and was established on a permanent basis on Sept. 24, 1919, as the National Catholic Welfare Council to serve as a central agency for organizing and coordinating the efforts of U.S. Catholics in carrying out the social mission of the Church in this country.

In 1923, its name was changed to National Catholic Welfare Conference, Inc., and clarification was made of its nature as a service agency of the bishops and the Church rather than as a conference of bishops with real juridical authority in ecclesiastical affairs.

The Official Catholic Directory stated that the USCC assisted "the bishops in their service to the Church in this country by uniting the people of God where voluntary collective action on a broad interdiocesan level is needed. The USCC provided an organizational structure and the resources needed to insure coordination, cooperation, and assistance in the public, educational and social concerns of the Church at the national, regional, state and, as appropriate, diocesan levels."

CATHOLIC RELIEF SERVICES

Catholic Relief Services is the official overseas aid and development agency of U.S. Catholics; it is a separately incorporated organization of the U.S. Conference of Catholic Bishops.

CRS was founded in 1943 by the bishops of the United States to help civilians in Europe and North Africa caught in the disruption and devastation of World War II. As conditions in Europe improved in the late 1940s and early 1950s, the works conducted by CRS spread to other continents and areas — Asia, Africa and Latin America.

Although best known for its record of disaster response, compassionate aid to refugees and commitment to reconstruction and rehabilitation, CRS places primary focus on long-term development projects designed to help people to help themselves and to determine their own future. Administrative funding for CRS comes largely from the American Bishops' Overseas Appeal (ABOA). Major support is derived from private, individual donors and through programs such as Operation Rice Bowl and the new Global Village Project.

Kenneth F. Hackett is Executive Director. CRS headquarters are located at 209 W. Fayette St., Baltimore, MD 21201; (410) 625-2220.

Hispanic, African-American, and Native-American Catholics

HISPANIC CATHOLICS IN THE UNITED STATES

The nation's Hispanic population totaled 35.3 million in 2000, according to figures reported by the U.S. Census Bureau. It is estimated that 73 percent of the Hispanics were baptized Catholics. It was estimated that perhaps 100,000 Catholic Hispanics a year were being lost, principally to fundamentalist and pentecostal sects.

Pastoral Patterns

Pastoral ministry to Hispanics varies, depending on cultural differences and the availability of personnel to carry it out. The pattern in cities with large numbers of Spanish-speaking people is built around special and bilingual churches, centers or other agencies where pastoral and additional forms of service are provided in a manner suited to the needs, language and culture of the people. Services in some places are extensive and include legal advice, job placement, language instruction, recreational and social assistance, specialized counseling, and replacement services. In many places, however, even where there are special ministries, the needs are generally greater than the means available to meet them.

Some urban dwellers have been absorbed into established parishes and routines of church life and activity. Many Spanish-speaking communities remain in need of special ministries. An itinerant form of ministry best meets the needs of the thousands of Hispanic migrant workers who follow the crops.

Pastoral ministry to Hispanics was the central concern of three national meetings, Encuentros, held in 1972, 1977 and 1985.

The third National Encuentro in 1985 produced a master pastoral plan for ministry which the National Conference of Catholic Bishops approved in 1987. Its four keys are collaborative ministry; evangelization; a missionary option regarding the poor, the marginalized, the family, women and youth; and the formation of lay leadership. A National Encuentro was held in 2000. In 2002, the Secretariat published *Encuentro and Mission: A New Pastoral Framework for Hispanic Ministry.*

The U.S. bishops, at their annual meeting in Nov. 1983, approved and subsequently published a pastoral letter on Hispanic Ministry under the title, "The Hispanic Presence: Challenge and Commitment." (For text, see pp. 46-49 of the *1985 Catholic Almanac.*)

Bishops

As of Aug. 1, 2008, there were 37 (28 active) bishops of Hispanic origin in the United States; all were named since 1970 (for biographies, see Index). Twelve were heads of archdioceses or dioceses: Archbishop José H. Gomez (San Antonio); Bishops Raymundo J Peña (Brownsville), James A. Tamayo (Laredo), Ricardo Ramirez, C.S.B. (Las Cruces), Alvaro Corrada del Rio, S.J. (Tyler), Arthur N. Tafoya (Pueblo), Placido Rodriguez, C.M.F. (Lubbock), Gerald R. Barnes (San Bernardino), Armando Ochoa (El Paso), Carlos A. Sevilla, S.J. (Yakima), Victor Benito Galeone (St. Augustine), and Richard J. Garcia (Monterey in California). Bp. Jaime Soto was named coadj. bp. of Sacramento on Oct. 11, 2007.

Fifteen were auxiliary bishops: Gabino Zavala (Los Angeles), Alexander Salazar (Los Angeles), Gilbert Espinoza Chavez (San Diego), Edgar M. Da Cunha, S.D.V. (Newark), Dominick J. Lagonegro (New York), Emilio Simeon Allué (Boston), Francisco Gonzalez Valer, S.F. (Washington, DC), José S. Vasquez (Galveston-Houston), Robert J. Iriondo (New York), Rutilio del Riego (San Bernardino), Felipe de Jesus Estevez (Miami), Gustavo Garcia-Siller, M.Sp.S. (Chicago), Eusebio Elizondo, M.Sp.S. (Seattle), Daniel E. Flores (Detroit), and Octavio Cisneros (Brooklyn).

Resigned/retired prelates: Archbishop Robert F. Sanchez (Santa Fe), Archbishop Patrick F. Flores (San Antonio), Bishop David Arias, O.A.R. (Newark), Bishop Joseph J. Madera (Military Services), Bishop Juan Arzube (Los Angeles), Bishop Rene H. Gracida (Corpus Christi), Bishop Agustin Roman (Miami), Bishop Rene Valero (Brooklyn), Bishop Gilberto Fernandez (Miami). Bishop Roberto O. Gonzalez, O.F.M. (Corpus Christi), was appointed archbishop of San Juan de Puerto Rico on Mar. 26, 1999, by Pope John Paul II.

Hispanic priests and nuns in the U.S. number about 1,600 and 2,900, respectively, according to an estimate made in June 1988 by Father Gary Riebe Estrella, S.V.D., director of a Hispanic vocational recruitment program and recent estimates by the USCCB Secretariat for Hispanic Affairs.

Secretariat for Hispanic Affairs

The national secretariat was established by the U.S. Catholic Conference for service promoting and coordinating pastoral ministry to the Spanish-speaking. Its basic orientation is toward integral evangelization, combining religious ministry with development efforts in programs geared to the culture and needs of Hispanics. Its concerns are urban and migrant Spanish-speaking people; communications and publications in line with secretariat purposes and the service of people; bilingual and bicultural religious and general education; liaison for and representation of Hispanics with church, civic and governmental agencies.

The Secretariat states that its mission is:

"To assist the Catholic Church in its efforts to serve the large Catholic Hispanic/Latino population in the United States and in the New Evangelization as we approach the Great Jubilee of the Year 2000.

"To coordinate Hispanic ministry efforts in the Catholic Church through regional and diocesan offices, pastoral institutes, secular and ecclesial organizations, and apostolic movements.

"To promote the implementation of the National Pastoral Plan for Hispanic Ministry, Ecclesia in America, Many Faces in God's House: A Catholic Vision for the Third Millennium, and other church documents, as well as the development of small ecclesial communities.

"To integrate the Hispanic presence into the life of the Catholic Church and society."

The secretariat publishes a newsletter, En Marcha, available to interested parties.

Ronaldo M. Cruz is executive director of the national office at 3211 Fourth St. N.E., Washington, DC, 20017, (202) 541-3000, www.usccb.org.

The secretariat works in collaboration with regional and diocesan offices and pastoral institutes throughout the country.

The Northeast Regional Office, officially the Northeast Hispanic Catholic Center, was established in 1976 under the auspices of the bishops in 12 states from Maine to Virginia. It has established the Conference of Diocesan Directors of the Hispanic Apostolate, the Association of Hispanic Deacons, a Regional Youth Task Force and a Regional Committee of Diocesan Coordinators of Religious Educators for the Hispanics. The office is the official publishing house for the Hispanic Lectionary approved by the National Conference of Catholic Bishops for the United States. The center has liturgical, evangelization and youth ministry departments and an office of cultural affairs. Rudy Vargas IV is executive director. The center is located at 1011 First Ave., New York, NY 10022, (212) 751-7045.

The Southeast Regional Office serves 26 dioceses in Tennessee, North and South Carolina, Florida, Georgia, Mississippi, Alabama and Louisiana. Father Mario Vizcaíno, Sch. P., is director of the region and institute. The office is located at 7700 S.W. 56 St., Miami, FL 33155, (305) 279-2333. The Southeast Pastoral Institute serves as the educational arm of the regional office by providing formation programs for the development of leadership skills focused on ministry among Hispanics, at the Miami site and in the various dioceses of the region.

The Midwest Regional Office serves dioceses in the following states: Michigan, Ohio, Indiana, Illinois, and Wisconsin. Luis Beteta is director. The office is located at 660 Burton Street, S.E., Grand Rapids, MI 49507, (616) 243-0491, ext. 557.

In the southwest, the Mexican American Cultural Center serves as convener of diocesan directors and representatives of Hispanic ministry in Arkansas, Oklahoma and Texas.

The North Central region covers dioceses in the following states: Iowa, Kansas, Missouri, Nebraska, North Dakota, South Dakota, and Minnesota. Bro. Dale Mooney, FSC, is coordinator. The office is reached at P.O. Box 419037, Kansas City, MO 64141-6037, (816) 756-1850.

The South West region covers dioceses in the following states: Oklahoma, Texas, and Arkansas. Sr. María Elena González is director. The office is contacted at: Mexican American Cultural Center, 3115 W. Ashby, San Antonio, TX 78228; (210) 732-2156.

The Mountain States region covers dioceses in the following states: Arizona, Colorado, New Mexico, Utah, and Wyoming. Rev. Francisco Javier Quezada is director. The office is located at 2715 East Pikes Peak, Colorado Springs, CO 80909; (719) 633-7204.

The Far West region covers dioceses in the following states: California, Nevada and Hawaii. Anibal (Al) Hernandez is director. The office is located at 1119 K Street, 2nd Floor, Sacramento, CA 95814-3904; (916) 313-4014 The North West region covers dioceses in the following states: Alaska, Idaho, Montana, Oregon, and Washington. Sister Diana Quintanilla is director. The office address is 2838 E. Burnside Street, Portland, OR 97214-1895; (503) 234-5334.

The National Pastoral Plan for Hispanic Ministry

The National Pastoral Plan for Hispanic Ministry was approved by the NCCB in November 1987. This plan is addressed to the entire Church in the United States. It focuses on the pastoral needs of the Hispanic Catholic, but it challenges all Catholics as members of the Body of Christ.

General Objective: To live and promote by means of a Pastoral de Conjunto, a model of Church that is: communitarian, evangelizing, and missionary, incarnate in the reality of the Hispanic people and open to the diversity of cultures, a promoter and example of justice . . . that develops leadership through integral education . . . that is leaven for the Kingdom of God in society.

Specific Dimensions: Pastoral de Conjunto: To develop a Pastoral de Conjunto, which through pastoral agents and structures, manifests communion in integration, coordination in servicing, and communication of the Church's pastoral action, in keeping with the general objective of this plan. Evangelization: To recognize, develop, accompany and support small ecclesial communities and other church groups (e.g.,

Cursillos de Cristiandad, Movimiento Familiar Cristiano, RENEW, Charismatic Movement, prayer groups, etc.) which in union with the bishop are effective instruments of evangelization for the Hispanic people. These small ecclesial communities and other groups within the parish framework promote experiences of faith and conversion, prayer life, missionary outreach and evangelization, interpersonal relations and fraternal love, and prophetic questioning and actions for justice. They are a prophetic challenge for the renewal of our Church and humanization of our society. Missionary Option: To promote faith and effective participation in Church and societal structures on the part of priority groups (the poor, women, families, youth) so that they may be agents of their own destiny (self-determination) and capable of progressing and becoming organized. Formation: To provide leadership formation adapted to the Hispanic culture in the United States that will help people to live and promote a style of Church that will be leaven of the Kingdom of God in society.

National Hispanic Priests Association

The National Association of Hispanic Priests of the U.S.A. (ANSH — La Asociación Nacional de Sacerdotes Hispanos, EE. UU.) was established in September 1989 with a representation of about 2,400 Hispanic priests residing and ministering in the U.S. The association came into its present form after a 20-year process of organization by different groups of Hispanic priests around the country. By 1985, the first National Convention of Hispanic Priests was organized in New York City, and in 1989 the Association was established in Miami, FL, as a non-profit corporation for priestly fraternity and support for Hispanic priests in the United States. Among the multiple objectives are: to help members develop their priestly identity in the United States and encourage a genuine spirituality; to provide a national forum of Hispanic priests to help solve the problems that arise in the Hispanic community; to promote vocations to the priesthood among Hispanics; to pray and ask for more Hispanic bishops in the U.S., for the growing needs of the Catholic Hispanic community; and to cooperate with the bishops and the laity in implementing the National Pastoral Plan for Hispanic Ministry. The Association publishes a quarterly newsletter and holds an annual national convention. The president is Rev. José H. Gomez, S.T.D., 2472 Bolsover, Suite 442, Houston, TX 77005, (713) 528-6517.

National Catholic Council for Hispanic Ministry (NCCHM)

The council is a volunteer federation of Roman Catholic organizations, agencies and movements committed to the development of Hispanics/Latinos in Church and society. It was established June 17, 1990, at a gathering at Mundelein College, Chicago; its by-laws were adopted in January 1991 at Mercy Center, Burlingame, CA. The council convokes a national gathering every three years called *Raices y Alas* (Roots and Wings). With funding from foundations NCCHM has designed and piloted a leadership development program that links contemporary understandings of leadership with experiences and insights from faith and Hispanic cultures. NCCHM has 53 member organizations. It publishes *Puentes*, a newsletter. Exec. Dir., Armando A. Contreras, 3131 E. Camelback Rd., Ste. 200, Phoenix, AZ 85016, (602) 266-8623.

Mexican American Cultural Center

This national center, specializing in pastoral studies and language education, was founded in 1972 to provide programs focused on ministry among Hispanics and personnel working with Hispanics in the U.S. Courses—developed according to the see–judge–act methodology—include culture, faith development, Scripture, theology, and praxis; some are offered in Spanish, others in English. Intensive language classes are offered in Spanish, with emphasis on pastoral usage.

The center also conducts workshops for the development of leadership skills and for a better understanding of Hispanic communities. Faculty members serve as resource personnel for pastoral centers, dioceses and parishes throughout the U.S. The center offers master's degree programs in pastoral ministry in cooperation with Incarnate Word College, Boston College, the Oblate School of Theology, St. Mary's University and Loyola University, and other educational institutions.

The center is a distribution agency for the circulation of bilingual pastoral materials in the U.S. and Latin America. Sister Maria Elena Gonzalez, R.S.M., is president of the center, which is located at 3019 W. French Place, San Antonio, TX 78228.

Institute of Hispanic Liturgy

Spanish-speaking communities in the U.S. are served by the Institute of Hispanic Liturgy, a national organization of liturgists, musicians, artists and pastoral agents, funded in part by the U.S. bishops. The institute promotes the study of liturgical texts, art, music and popular religiosity in an effort to develop liturgical spirituality among Hispanics. It works closely with the U.S. Bishops' Committee on the Liturgy, and has published liturgical materials. Rev. Heliodoro Lucatero, is the president; Sr. Doris Mary Turek, S.S.N.D., is executive director. Address: P.O. Box 29387, Washington, DC, 20017, (202) 319-6450.

Statistics

(*Courtesy, Secretariat for Hispanic Affairs, USCCB.*)

The official 2000 Census estimates a population of 35.3 million Hispanics, or about 12.5 percent of the total population. Since 1990, the Hispanic population has increased 58 percent.

The nation's Hispanic Catholic population (not including Puerto Rico) has increased by 71 percent since 1960. The total Hispanic Catholic population as a percentage of the U.S. Catholic population is 39 percent. Of these Hispanic Catholics, 64 percent attend church services regularly.

According to the most recent statistics based on the 2000 Census, there are 4,000 U.S. parishes with Hispanic ministry; 20.6 percent of U.S. parishes have a majority Hispanic presence. There are approximately 2,900 Hispanic priests and 25 active Hispanic bishops.

The 10 metropolitan areas with the largest Hispanic populations are: Los Angeles, New York, Chicago, Miami, Houston, Riverside-San Bernardino, Orange County, Phoenix, San Antonio, and Dallas. Seven states in 2000 had more than one million Hispanic residents: Arizona, California, Florida, Illinois, New Jersey, New York, and Texas. Approximately one half of the Hispanic population lived in just two states:

California and Texas. In New Mexico, Hispanics made up 42 percent of the state's total population, the highest for any state.

Current U.S. Census figures reveal that the Hispanic population increased by 13 million between 1990 and 2000. Hispanics also accounted for 40 percent of the nation's increase in population over the decade. The Hispanic population more than tripled between 1990 and 2000 in Alabama, Arkansas, Georgia, Nevada, North Carolina, South Carolina, and Tennessee.

Data demonstrate that the Hispanic population in the U.S. is young. In 2000, 35.7 percent of Hispanics were less than 18 years old, compared with 23.5 percent of non-Hispanic whites. Only 5.3 percent of Hispanics are older than 65.

The poverty rate in the general population in 1999 was 7.7 percent among non-Hispanic whites; the poverty rate among Hispanics was 21.2 percent or 7.2 million people. This is a record low matching that of the 1970s.

It is projected that in 2020, the Hispanic population will be approximately 52.7 million; by 2040, the population will be about 80.2 million; by 2050 the population will be 96.5 million, comprising approximately 24.5 percent of the U.S. population.

AFRICAN-AMERICAN CATHOLICS IN THE UNITED STATES

Secretariat for African-American Catholics

(Courtesy, Secretariat for African-American Catholics, USCCB.)

The Secretariat for African-American Catholics is the officially recognized voice of the African-American Catholic community as it articulates the needs and aspirations regarding ministry, evangelization, social justice issues, and worship.

The USCCB Secretariat for African-American Catholics supports the Bishops' Committee for African-American Catholics through identification and communication of the socio-cultural dimension of the African-American Community. The vastness of this dimension encompasses historical, social and cultural elements at work within African-American communities. The Secretariat's role is consultative. It is often the voice of conscience, as we, a people of faith, grow toward a truly universal church.

The Secretariat for African-American Catholics serves as the chief advisor to the National Conference of Catholic Bishops and the United States Catholic Conference in fulfilling its ministry to African-American Catholics in the United States. The Secretariat has as its function the coordination of responses regarding ministry, evangelization, and worship in the African-American Community on the national level. The work of the Secretariat is guided by the Bishop's Committee on African-American Catholics whose primary mission is to encourage the development and assist in the implementation of pastoral programs relating to evangelization and incorporation into the local church of racial, ethnic, cultural and language groups within the National Conference of Catholic Bishops.

It also serves as a liaison to the National Black Catholic Clergy Caucus, the National Black Catholic Seminarians Association, the National Black Sisters' Conference, the National Association of Black Catholic Administrators, Knights of St. Peter Claver and Ladies Auxiliary, the National Black Catholic Congress, and the National Black Catholic Theological Society. The Secretariat for African-American Catholics is under the executive direction of Beverly Carroll. The committee and secretariat have offices at 3211 Fourth St. N.E., Washington, DC, 20017, (202) 541-3000, www.usccb.org/saac.

USCCB Committee

The Committee on African-American Catholics, established by the National Conference of Catholic Bishops in 1987, is chaired by Bishop Joseph N. Perry, aux. bp. of Chicago. The purpose of the committee is to assist the bishops in their evangelization efforts to the African-American community by initiating, encouraging and supporting programs that recognize and respect African-American genius and values. Priorities of the committee include implementation of the National Black Catholic Pastoral Plan of 1987, inculturation of liturgy and ministry, and increasing lay leadership and vocations.

The Secretariat for African-American Catholics was established as a service agency to the committee.

National Office for Black Catholics

The National Office for Black Catholics, organized in July 1970, is a central agency with the general purposes of promoting active and full participation by black Catholics in the Church and of making more effective the presence and ministry of the Church in the black community.

Its operations are in support of the aspirations and calls of black Catholics for a number of objectives, including the following:

• representation and voice for blacks among bishops and others with leadership and decision-making positions in the Church

• promoting vocations to the priesthood and religious life

• sponsoring programs of evangelization, pastoral ministry, education and liturgy on a national level

• recognition of the black heritage in liturgy, community life, theology and education.

Walter T. Hubbard is executive director of the NOBC. The NOBC office is located at 3025 Fourth St. N.E., Washington, DC, 20017, (202) 635-1778.

National Black Catholic Clergy Caucus

The National Black Catholic Clergy Caucus, founded in 1968 in Detroit, is a fraternity of several hundred black priests, permanent deacons and brothers pledged to mutual support in their vocations and ministries.

The Caucus develops programs of spiritual, theological, educational and ministerial growth for its members, to counteract the effects of institutionalized racism within the Church and American society. A bimonthly newsletter is published. The NBCCC office is located at 440 W. 36th St., New York, NY 10018, (212) 868-1847, fax (212) 563-0787. Other peer and support groups are the National Black Sisters' Conference and the National Black Catholic Seminarians Association.

National Black Catholic Congress

The National Black Catholic Congress, Inc., was formed in 1985 exclusively to assist in the development of the Roman Catholic Church in the African-

American community and to devise effective means of evangelization of African-American peoples in the United States. Its fundamental purpose is the formation and development of concrete approaches toward the evangelization of African-Americans through revitalization of African-American Catholic life.

The Congress is under the sponsorship of the African-American Roman Catholic bishops of the United States, the National Black Catholic Clergy Caucus, the National Black Sisters' Conference, the National Association of Black Catholic Administrators and the Knights of Peter Claver and Ladies Auxiliary. The Congress is also in consultation with African-American clergy and vowed religious communities of women. The Congress sponsors "Pastoring in African-American Parishes," an annual workshop first held in 1988, and an African-American Catholic Ministries Program, a week-long curriculum presented twice a year, usually in January and June.

The National Black Catholic Congress sponsored the seventh assembly of African-American Catholics and those serving in African-American communities, July 9–12, 1992, in New Orleans. The most recent National Congress convened in Baltimore, Aug. 27 to 31, 1997. The Congress is sponsoring construction of "Our Mother of Africa Chapel" at the Basilica of the National Shrine of the Immaculate Conception in Washington, DC. The office of the Congress is located at the Archdiocese of Baltimore Catholic Center, 320 Cathedral St., 3rd Floor, Baltimore, MD 21201, (410) 547-8496, www.nbccongress.org. The executive director is Valerie E. Washington.

Josephite Pastoral Center

The Josephite Pastoral Center was established in September 1968 as an educational and pastoral service agency for the Josephites in their mission work, specifically in the black community, subsequently to all those who minister in the African–American community. St. Joseph's Society of the Sacred Heart, the sponsoring body, has about 134 priests and 11 brothers in 64 mostly southern parishes in 17 dioceses. Address: Josephite Pastoral Center 1200 Varnum St. N.E., Washington, DC, 20017, (202) 526-9270.

African-American Evangelization

The National Black Catholic Pastoral Plan adopted by the National Black Catholic Congress in May 1987 was approved and recommended for implementation by the National Conference of Catholic Bishops in November 1989.

Following is an account of several points in the bishops' statement, based on coverage by the CNS Documentary Service, Origins, Dec. 28, 1989 (Vol. 19, No. 30).

"Evangelization," wrote the bishops, "would not be complete if it did not take account of the unceasing interplay of the Gospel and of man's concrete life, both personal and social. Evangelization involves an explicit message, adapted to the different situations constantly being realized, about the rights and duties of every human being, about family life, without which personal growth and development are hardly possible, about life in society, about international life, peace, justice and development—a message especially energetic today about liberation."

Three Areas

The pastoral plan "embraces three broad areas: 1) the Catholic identity of African–American Catholics; 2) ministry and leadership within the African-American community; and 3) the responsibility of this community to reach out to the broader society. Within these areas are such issues as culture, family, youth, spirituality, liturgy, ministry, lay leadership, parishes, education, social action and community development."

Reflecting a recommendation of the plan, the bishops encourage African–American Catholics to "discover their past" since "possession of one's history is the first step in an appreciation of one's culture."

Bishops

There were 16 (10 active) black bishops as of Sept. 1, 2008. Six were heads of dioceses: Abp. Wilton D. Gregory (Atlanta, president of the USCCB, 2001-2004); Bishops Curtis J. Guillory, S.V.D. (Beaumont), George V. Murry, S.J. (Youngstown), John H. Ricard, S.S.J. (Pensacola-Tallahassee), Edward K. Braxton (Belleville), J. Terry Steib, S.V.D. (Memphis). Four were auxiliary bishops: Guy A. Sansaricq (Brooklyn), Shelton J. Fabre (New Orleans), Joseph N. Perry (Chicago), and Martin D. Holley (Washington). Elliott G. Thomas, of St. Thomas, Virgin Islands (res., June 30, 1999), Joseph L. Howze of Biloxi (res., May 15, 2001), Moses Anderson, S.S.E. Detroit aux. (ret., Oct. 24, 2003), Leonard J. Olivier, S.V.D. Washington aux. (ret., May 18, 2004), and Dominic Carmon, S.V.D., New Orleans aux. (ret., Dec. 13, 2006), are retired. Bp. Gordon D. Bennett was named Bp. of Mandeville on July 6, 2004; he retired on Aug. 8, 2006.

African-American Bishops of the Past: James August Healy (1830-1900); Joseph A. Francis, S.V.D. (1923-1997); Eugene A. Marino, S.S.J. (1934-2000); Raymond Rodly Caeser, S.V.D. (1932-1987); James Lyke, O.F.M. (1939-1992); Carl A. Fisher, S.S.J. (1945-1993); Emerson J. Moore (1938-1995); Harold R. Perry, S.V.D. (1916-1991).

Statistics

The Secretariat for African-American Catholics reports that there are presently approximately 2.3 million African-American Catholics in the United States out of 36 million total African-Americans. They are served by 798 parishes and 75 African-American pastors. There are approximately 225 African-American priests, 400 African-American sisters, 75 African-American brothers, 437 African-American deacons, and 26 African-American seminarians.

NATIVE-AMERICAN CATHOLICS IN THE UNITED STATES

The Kateri Tekakwitha Conference is so named in honor of Blessed Kateri Tekakwitha, "Lily of the Mohawks," who was born in 1656 at Ossernenon (Auriesville), NY, in 1656, baptized in 1676, lived near Montreal, died in 1680, and was beatified in 1980.

The conference was established in 1939 as a missionary-priest advisory group in the Diocese of Fargo. It was a missionary-priest support group from 1946 to 1977. Since 1977 it has been a gathering of Catholic Native peoples and the men and women—clerical, religious and lay persons—who minister to Native Catholic communities.

The primary focus of conference concern and activity is evangelization, with specific emphasis on development of Native ministry and leadership. Other priorities include catechesis, liturgy, family life, social justice ministry, chemical dependency, youth ministry, spirituality and Native Catholic dialogue. Conferences and local Kateri Circles serve as occasions for the exchange of ideas, prayer and mutual support. Since 1980, the national center has promoted and registered 130 Kateri Circles in the U.S. and Canada. Publications include a quarterly newsletter.

The conference has a board of 12 directors, the majority of whom are Native people. Archbishop Charles Chaput, O.F.M. Cap., is the episcopal moderator. Address: Tekakwitha Conference National Center, P.O. Box 6768, Great Falls, MT 59406, (406) 727-0147.

STATISTICS

On June 19, 2003, the United States Conference of Catholic Bishops issued a report, "Native American Catholics at the Millennium," on the current state of Native American Catholics in the United States. There are 4.1 million people who identify themselves as Native American. Of these, 493,615 Native Americans, or 12 percent of the total population, are considered Catholic.

Bishops

There is presently one Native American bishop in active service in the United States. He is Archbishop Charles J. Chaput, O.F.M. Cap., of Denver; Bishop Donald Pelotte, S.S.S., served from 1990-2008 as bishop of Gallup.

MISSIONARY ACTIVITY OF THE U.S. CHURCH

Sources: U.S. Catholic Mission Handbook 2008: Mission Inventory 2006–2008 *(the most recent issue), reproduced with permission of the United States Catholic Mission Council, 3029 Fourth St. N.E., Washington, DC.*

OVERSEAS MISSIONS

Field Distribution, 2006-2007

Africa: 609 (313 men; 296 women). Largest numbers in Kenya, 172; Tanzania, 77; Zambia, 54; Uganda, 50; Ghana, 40; South Africa, 38; Nigeria, 30.

Asia: 618 (406 men; 212 women). Largest numbers in Philippines, 121; Japan, 108; Taiwan, 82; China PRC-Hong Kong SAR, 66; India, 61; Thailand, 34; Korea, 31. (Those present in China were there for professional services.)

Caribbean: 325 (163 men; 162 women). Largest numbers in Puerto Rico, 76; Jamaica, 65; Dominican Republic 49; Belize, 48; Haiti, 42.

Eurasia (Kazakhstan, Russia, Siberia): 15 (13 men; 2 women). Largest group, Russia, 11.

Europe: 154 (67 men; 87 women). Largest numbers in Italy, 58; Ireland, 27; England, 10; Germany, 10; France, 9; Spain, 7.

Latin America: 1,179 (600 men; 579 women). Largest numbers in Peru, 230; Mexico, 193; Brazil, 187; Bolivia, 116; Guatemala, 96; Chile, 84.

Middle East: 34 (30 men; 4 women). Largest numbers in Israel, 24; Jordan, 4; Lebanon, 3.

North America (Canada and United States): 3,142 (854 men; 2,288 women). Largest number in the United States, 3,095.

Oceania: 125 (70 men; 55 women). Largest numbers in Papua New Guinea, 37; Micronesia, 30; Marshall Island, 14; Australia, 12; Guam, 6.

TOTAL: 6,201 (2,516 men; 3,685 women).

Missionary Personnel, 2006-2007

Bishops: 22.

Religious Priests: 70 mission-sending groups had 1,561 priests in overseas assignments. Listed below are those with 15 or more members abroad.

Jesuits, 283; Maryknoll Fathers and Brothers, 192; Oblates of Mary Immaculate, 102; Society of Divine Word, 90; Redemptorists, 77; Franciscans (O.F.M. Cap), 49; Dominicans, 42; Holy Cross Fathers, 39; Columbans, 27; Legionaries of Christ, 25; Xaverian Missionaries, 19; Carmelites, 17; Spiritans, 16; Comboni Missionaries, 15; Congregation of Sacred Heart, 15; Marianists, 12; LaSalette Fathers, 12.

Diocesan Priests: There were 104 priests from 50 dioceses. The majority were in Latin American countries.

Religious Brothers: 46 mission-sending groups had 342 brothers in overseas assignments. Those with 15 or more members:

Christian Brothers (Brothers of the Christian Schools), 80; Marianists, 32; Franciscans (O.F.M.), 24; Christian Brothers, 26; Maryknoll Priests and Brothers, 15.

Religious Sisters: 174 mission-sending communities of women Religious had 2,717 sisters in overseas missions. Those with 15 or more members:

Maryknoll Mission Sisters, 218; School Sisters of Notre Dame, 149; Franciscan Missionaries of Mary, 119; Blessed Sacrament Sisters, 108; Dominicans, 90; Missionaries of Charity, 87; Marist Missionary Sisters, 77; School Sisters of St. Francis, 71; Society of the Sacred Heart, 56; Congregation of Sisters of St. Agnes, 55; Medical Mission Sisters, 54; Ursulines, 51; Sisters of Mercy (various communities), 46; Providence Sisters, 45; Presentation Sisters, 40; St. Joseph Sisters, 39; Sisters of Notre Dame de Namur, 38; Sisters of Charity of the BVM, 38; Franciscan Sisters, 38; Holy Cross, Cong. of Sisters, 35; Daughters of Charity, 34; Sisters of St. Joseph of Carondelet, 28; Benedictine Sisters, 27; Medical Missionaries of Mary, 26; Franciscan Sisters of Little Falls, 24; Cong. of St. Joseph, 22; Franciscan Sisters of

Charity, 21; Little Sisters of the Poor, 20; Franciscan Sisters of Atonement, 19; IHM Sisters of Immaculata, 19; Sacred Heart of Jesus Sisters, 18; Apostles of the Sacred Heart, 18; Mission Sisters of the Immaculate Heart of Mary, 15; Immaculate Heart of Mary Sisters of Monroe, 13.

Lay Persons: 101 mission-sending groups had 1,442 members in overseas missions. Those with 15 or more members:

Jesuit Volunteer Corps, 417; Maryknoll Mission Associates, 126; Catholic Medical Mission Board, 51; Jesuit Volunteers International, 48; Holy Cross Assoc., 44; Educational Partners, 42; Mercy Corps, 30; Lasallian Volunteers, 28; Salesian Lay Missionaries, 27; Colorado Vincentian Volunteers, 26; Augustinian Volunteers, 23.

Seminarians: There were 10 from 4 groups.

Jesuits, 5; Maryknoll, 2; Redemptorists, 2; Dominicans, 1.

MISSIONARY BISHOPS

The following is a list of missionary bishops in active service around the world. This last does not include retired bishops.

Africa

Kenya: Marsabit (diocese), **Ambrose Ravasi**, I.M.C.; Rumbek (diocese), Caesar Mazzolari, M.C.C.J.

Madagascar: Morondava (diocese), Donald Pelletier, M.S.

Sierra Leone: Makeni (diocese), George Biguzzi, S.X.

South Africa: De Aar (diocese), Joseph J. Potocnak, S.C.J.

Zambia: Mongu (diocese), Paul F. Duffy, O.M.I.

Asia

Kazakhstan: Almaty (diocese), Henry Howaniec, O.F.M.

Central America, West Indies

Honduras: Comayagua (diocese), Gerald Scarpone Caporale, O.F.M.; Juticalpa (diocese), Thomas Maurus Muldoon, O.F.M.

Nicaragua: Bluefields (vicariate apostolic), Paul Simon Schmitz, O.F.M.Cap.

Peru: Chulucanas (diocese): Daniel Turley Murphy, O.S.A.

Trinidad and Tobago: Port of Spain (archdiocese), Edward J. Gilbert, C.SS.R.

North America

Bermuda: Hamilton (diocese), Robert Kurtz, C.R.

Jamaica: Mandeville (diocese), Neil Tiedemann, C.P.

Mexico: Nuevo Laredo (diocese), Ricardo Watty Urquidi, M.Sp.S., first bishop.

Oceania

American Samoa: Samoa-Pago Pago (diocese), John Quinn Weitzel, M.M.

Papua New Guinea: Mendi (diocese), Stephen J. Reichert, O.F.M.Cap.

Solomon Islands: Gizo (diocese), Christopher Cardone, O.P., aux. bp.

South America

Bolivia: Pando (vicariate apostolic), Luis Morgan Casey.

Brazil: Cristalandia (prelacy), Herbert Hermes, O.S.B.; Itaituba (prelacy), Capistran Heim, O.F.M.; Miracema do Tocantins (diocese), John J. Burke, O.F.M.; Paranagua (diocese), Alfred Novak, C.Ss.R.; Valença (diocese), Elias James Manning, O.F.M. Conv.

Peru: Chulucanas (diocese), Daniel Thomas Turley Murphy, O.S.A.; Sicuani (prelacy), Michael La Fay Bardi, O.Carm.

U.S. CATHOLIC MISSION ASSOCIATION

This is a voluntary association of individuals and organizations for whom the missionary presence of the universal Church is of central importance. It is a non-profit religious, educational and charitable organization which exists to promote global missions. Its primary emphasis is on cross–cultural evangelization and the promotion of international justice and peace. The association is also responsible for gathering and publishing annual statistical data on U.S. missionary personnel overseas. President: Joseph Nangle, O.F.M.; Executive Director, Sr. Rosanne Rustemeyer, S.S.N.D. Address: 3029 Fourth St. N.E., Washington, DC, 20017, (202) 832-3112, www.uscatholicmission.org.

Mission Statement

In its 1996–97 handbook, the association included the following in a mission statement.

"In the Church, our understanding of the mission of evangelization is evolving to embrace dialogue, community building, struggles for justice, efforts to model justice and faith in our lifestyles, activities and structures, in addition to the teaching/preaching/witnessing role traditionally at the heart of the mission enterprise. Still, the contemporary 'identity-confusion' about 'mission' stands forth as a major challenge for USCMA as we move toward the 21st century.

"The larger context of mission is the Spirit moving in the Signs of our Times: the liberation movements, the women's movements, the economy movements, the rising awareness and celebration of cultural diversity, the search for ways to live peacefully and creatively with great pluralism, rapid technological change, the emergence of the global economy, the steady increase in poverty and injustice, the realigning of the global political order—and the many ripples radiating out from each of these."

HOME MISSIONS

The expression "home missions" is applied to places in the U.S. where the local church does not have its own resources, human and otherwise. These areas share the name "missions" with their counterparts in foreign lands because they too need outside help to provide the personnel and means for making the Church present and active there in carrying out its mission for the salvation of people.

Dioceses in the southeast, the southwest, and the far west are most urgently in need of outside help to carry on the work of the Church. Millions of people live in counties in which there are no resident priests. Many others live in rural areas beyond the reach and influence of a Catholic center. According to recent statistics compiled by the Glenmary Research Center, there are more than 500 priestless counties in the United States.

Mission Workers

A number of forces are at work to meet the pastoral needs of these missionary areas and to establish permanent churches and operating institutions where they are required. In many dioceses, one or more missions and stations are attended from established parishes and are gradually growing to independent status. Priests, brothers and sisters belonging to scores of religious institutes are engaged full–time in the home missions. Lay persons, some of them in affiliation with special groups and movements, are also involved.

The Society for the Propagation of the Faith, which conducts an annual collection for mission support in all parishes of the U.S., allocates 40 percent of this sum for disbursement to home missions through the American Board of Catholic Missions.

Various mission–aid societies frequently undertake projects on behalf of the home missions.

The Glenmary Home Missioners, founded by Fr. W. Howard Bishop in 1939, is the only home mission society established for the sole purpose of carrying out the pastoral ministry in small towns and rural districts of the U.S. Glenmary serves in many areas where at least 20 percent of the people live in poverty and less than one percent are Catholic. With 61 priests and 19 professed brothers as of January 1998 the Glenmary Missioners had missions in the archdioceses of Atlanta and Cincinnati, and in the dioceses of Birmingham, Charlotte, Covington, Jackson, Lexington, Little Rock, Nashville, Owensboro, Richmond, Savannah, Tulsa, Tyler and Wheeling-Charleston. National headquarters are located at 4119 Glenmary Trace, Fairfield, OH. The mailing address is P.O. Box 465618, Cincinnati, OH 45246, (513) 874-8900.

Organizations

Black and Indian Mission Office (The Commission for Catholic Missions among the Colored People and the Indians): Organized officially in 1885 by decree of the Third Plenary Council of Baltimore. Provides financial support for religious works among Blacks and Native Americans in 133 archdioceses and dioceses through funds raised by an annual collection in all parishes of the U.S. on the first Sunday of Lent, the designated Sunday. In 2005, $9,137,462 was raised; disbursements amounted to $8,700,000 for African-American missions and for Native American evangelization programs.

Bureau of Catholic Indian Missions (1874): Established as the representative of Catholic Indian missions before the federal government and the public; made permanent organization in 1884 by Third Plenary Council of Baltimore. After a remarkable history of rendering important services to the Indian people, the bureau continues to represent the Catholic Church in the U.S. in her apostolate to the American Indian. Concerns are evangelization, catechesis, liturgy, family life, education, advocacy. Address: 2021 H St. NW, Washington, DC 20006-4207, (202) 331-8542.

Catholic Negro–American Mission Board (1907): Supports priests and sisters in southern states and provides monthly support to sisters and lay teachers in the poorest black schools.

Board of Directors of the three organizations above are: Card. Anthony Bevilacqua, president; Cardinal William Keeler; Msgr. Paul A. Lenz, secretary–treasurer; Patricia L. O'Rourke, D.St.G.G., assistant secretary/treasurer. Address: 2021 H St. NW, Washington, DC 20006-4207, (202) 331-8542.

The Catholic Church Extension Society (1905): Established with papal approval for the purpose of preserving and extending the Church in rural and isolated parts of the U.S. and its dependencies through the collection and disbursement of funds for home mission work. Since the time of its founding, more than $300 million has been received and distributed for this purpose. The Society celebrated its 100th anniversary in 2005. Works of the society are supervised by a 14–member board of governors: Cardinal Francis George of Chicago, chancellor; Rev. John Wall, president; three archbishops, three bishops and six lay people. Headquarters: 150 S. Wacker Drive, 20th Floor, Chicago, IL, 60606, (312) 236-7240; www.catholicextension.org.

National Catholic Rural Life Conference: Founded in 1923 through the efforts of Bp. Edwin V. O'Hara. Applies the Gospel message to rural issues through focus on rural parishes and the provision of services including distribution of educational materials development of prayer and worship resources, advocacy for strong rural communities. Bp. Ronald Gilmore, president; James F. Ennis, executive director. National headquarters: 4625 Beaver Ave., Des Moines, IA 50310, (515) 270-2634, www.ncrlc.com.

BISHOPS' COMMITTEE ON THE HOME MISSIONS

Established in 1924, the Committee on the Home Missions of the U.S. Conference of Catholic Bishops provides financial support for missionary activities that strengthen and extend the presence of the Church in the United States and its island territories in the Caribbean and the Pacific. Funding for mission dioceses and national organizations engaged in home mission work is provided through the annual Catholic Home Missions Appeal, which is nationally scheduled on the last weekend of April. For 2004-2005, a record $12 million has been allocated to 90 mission dioceses and 21 mission organizations thanks to the faithfulness and sustained generosity of Catholics. Since 1924, close to $300 million has been collected and disbursed for home missions. The committee's work is supervised by seven bishops and a small national staff. Bp. Michael Warfel (Great Falls-Billings), chairperson; Dr. David J. Suley, exec. dir. National headquarters: U. S. Conference of Catholic Bishops, 3211 4th NE, Washington, DC, 20017-1194, (202) 541-3450, www.usccb.org.

U.S. Catholic Statistics

U.S. STATISTICAL SUMMARY

(Principal sources: The Official Catholic Directory, 2008, Almanac *survey comparisons, where given, are with figures reported in the previous edition of the* Directory. *Totals below do not include statistics for Outlying Areas of U.S. unless otherwise noted. These are given in tables on the preceding pages and elsewhere in the* Catholic Almanac; *see* **Index**.*)*

Catholic Population: 67,117,016; decrease, 398,000. Percent of total population: 22%.

Jurisdictions: In the United States, there are 195 archdioceses and dioceses: 33 Latin Catholic archdioceses, 145 Latin Catholic dioceses, 15 Eastern Catholic dioceses, and 2 Eastern Catholic archdioceses; there is also 1 apostolic exarchate (New York-based Armenian exarchate for U.S. and Canada). The current number of dioceses reflects the elevation of the diocese of Galveston-Houston to an archdiocese on Dec. 29, 2004, and the creation on July 3, 2000, of the new diocese of Laredo. There are also the eparchies of St. Maron and Our Lady of Lebanon of Los Angeles (Maronites), Newton (Melkites), St. Thomas Apostle of Detroit (Chaldeans), St. George Martyr of Canton, Ohio (Romanians), St. Thomas of Chicago (Syro-Malabars) which was created on March 13, 2001, and the Eparchy of St. Peter the Apostle of San Diego which was created on May 21, 2002. The eparchy of Our Lady of Deliverance of Newark has its seat in Newark, NJ. The Armenian apostolic exarchate for the United States and Canada has its seat in New York. Vacant jurisdictions (as of Aug. 15, 2008): Biloxi, Charleston, Cheyenne, Gallup, Juneau, Knoxville, St. Louis.

Cardinals: 18 (7 head archiepiscopal sees in U.S.; 2 are Roman Curia officials; one is grand master; seven are retired, including Puerto Rico, one is a theologian). As of July 10, 2008.

Archbishops: 36. Diocesan, in U.S., 28 (does not include 7 cardinals and military archbishop); retired, 16; there are also 10 archbishops serving outside U.S. As of Feb. 5, 2008.

Bishops: 428. Diocesan, in U.S. (and Virgin Islands), 153; auxiliaries, 79; retired, 141; there are also 25 bishops serving outside U.S. As of Feb. 5, 2008.

Priests: 42,307; decrease, 1. Diocesan, 28,067 (decrease, 395); religious order priests (does not include those assigned overseas), 13,339 (decrease, 506). There were 487 newly ordained priests; decrease, 94.

Permanent Deacons: 16,408; increase, 540

Brothers: 5,040; decrease, 55.

Sisters: 63,032; decrease, 1,845.

Seminarians: 5,029. Diocesan seminarians, 3,248, religious order seminarians, 1,781.

Receptions into Church: 1,039,619. Includes 902,841 infant baptisms; 49,415 adult baptisms and 87,363 already baptized persons received into full communion with the Church.

First Communions: 823,236.

Confirmations: 631,195.

Marriages: 196,420.

Deaths: 442,729.

Parishes: 18,890.

Seminaries, Diocesan: 71.

Religious Seminaries: 110.

Colleges and Universities: 236. Students, 794,321.

High Schools: 1,352. Students, 680,689.

Elementary Schools: 6,622. Students, 1,665,163

Non-Residential Schools for Handicapped: 68. Students, 6,419.

Teachers: 178,288 (priests, 1,427; brothers, 1,040; scholastics, 33; sisters, 5,718; laity, 170,070).

Public School Students in Religious Instruction Programs: 3,834,976. High school students, 689,552; elementary school students, 3,145,424.

Hospitals: 556; patients treated, 84,736,305.

Health Care Centers: 417; patients treated, 7,271,716.

Specialized Homes: 1,538; patients assisted, 756,902.

Residential Care of Children (Orphanages): 163; children assisted, 30,106.

Day Care and Extended Day Care Centers: 1,004; children assisted, 158,922.

Special Centers for Social Services: 2,856; assisted annually, 25,979,422.

PERCENTAGE OF CATHOLICS IN TOTAL POPULATION IN U.S.

(*Source:* The Official Catholic Directory, 2008; figures are as of Jan. 1, 2008. Total general population figures at the end of the table are U.S. Census Bureau estimates for Jan. 1 of the respective years. Archdioceses are indicated by an asterisk; for dioceses marked +, see Dioceses with Interstate Lines.)

State / Diocese	Catholic Pop.	Total Pop.	Cath. Pct.	State / Diocese	Catholic Pop.	Total Pop.	Cath. Pct.
Alabama	151,554	4,407,004	3.4	Indiana	762,076	6,232,337	12.2
*Mobile	66,331	1,697,355	4	*Indianapolis	230,086	2,430,606	9.6
Birmingham	83,223	2,709,649	3	Evansville	86,138	498,973	17.6
Alaska	52,813	636,610	8.3	Ft.Wayne-S.Bend	158,899	1,262,788	12.6
*Anchorage	32,170	401,610	8.0	Gary	186,420	788,055	24
Fairbanks	14,500	161,000	11.2	Lafayette	100,533	1,251,915	8.0
Juneau	6,143	74,000	8.3	Iowa	500,661	2,931,205	17.1
Arizona	1,026,242	6,820,308	15	*Dubuque	209,902	973,488	21.5
Phoenix	644,119	5,130,632	12.5	Davenport	102,096	751,127	13.5
Tucson	382,123	1,689,676	22	Des Moines	102,147	742,190	13.7
Arkansas				Sioux City	86,516	464,400	18.5
Little Rock	116,605	2,810,872	4.1	Kansas	415,103	2,679,143	15.4
California	10,382,988	36,938,015	28.1	*Kansas City	203,741	1,193,425	17.0
*Los Angeles	4,176,296	11,536,079	36.2	Dodge City	45,658	223,507	20.4
*San Francisco	382,500	1,698,282	22.5	Salina	48,527	310,240	15.6
Fresno	317,023	2,584,894	12	Wichita	117,177	951,971	12.3
Monterey	194,550	972,758	19.9	Kentucky	382,521	4,115,957	9.3
Oakland	425,597	2,481,745	17.1	*Louisville	194,547	1,306,847	14.8
Orange	1,197,817	3,002,048	39.8	Covington	89,315	464,629	19.2
Sacramento	557,668	3,474,587	16.0	Lexington	46,878	1,492,784	3.1
San Bernardino	1,217,891	4,059,638	30	Owensboro	51,781	851,697	6.1
San Diego	981,057	3,108,835	31.5	Louisiana	1,188,798	4,230,295	28.4
San Jose	560,000	1,808,056	31	*New Orleans	384,994	1,069,428	36.0
Santa Rosa	165,204	911,678	18.1	Alexandria	48,050	387,701	12.3
Stockton	207,385	1,299,415	16.8	Baton Rouge	212,329	924,844	23.0
Colorado	707,420	4,613,131	15.3	Houma-			
*Denver	407,502	3,071,432	13.2	Thibodaux	112,419	203,000	55.3
Colo. Springs	184,918	920,699	20	Lafayette	317,310	568,154	55.8
Pueblo	115,000	621,000	18.5	Lake Charles	73,972	284,311	28
Connecticut	1,282,153	3,444,660	37.2	Shreveport	39,724	792,857	5
*Hartford	642,375	1,912,290	34	Maine			
Bridgeport	410,304	903,291	45.4	Portland	191,008	1,321,574	15
Norwich+	229,477	629,079	36.4	Maryland			
Delaware+				*Baltimore	504,159	3,081,540	16.3
Wilmington	233,000	1,270,734	18.3	Massachusetts	2,709,552	6,443,038	42
District of Columbia				*Boston	1,855,315	4,020,686	46.1
*Washington+	589,072	2,683,050	21.9	Fall River	324,359	821,799	39.4
Florida	2,366,715	18,250,776	13	Springfield	221,596	817,291	28
*Miami	791,182	4,264,581	18.5	Worcester	308,282	783,262	39.3
Orlando	398,325	3,962,346	9.8	Michigan	2,216,372	10,029,784	22
Palm Beach	278,674	1,967,378	14.1	*Detroit	1,455,664	4,439,490	32.7
Pensacola-				Gaylord	68,178	515,865	13.2
Tallahassee	71,364	1,340,617	5.3	Grand Rapids	176,098	1,283,717	13.7
St. Augustine	164,484	1,905,176	8.6	Kalamazoo	107,700	952,812	11.3
St. Petersburg	425,323	2,873,802	14.8	Lansing	227,346	1,810,728	12.5
Venice	237,363	1,936,876	12.2	Marquette	62,300	308,357	21.8
Georgia	730,005	9,161,283	7.9	Saginaw	119,086	718,815	16.6
*Atlanta	650,000	6,361,283	10.2	Minnesota	1,061,696	5,112,530	20.7
Savannah	80,005	2,800,000	2.9	*St. Paul and			
Hawaii				Minneapolis	623,000	3,015,000	20.6
Honolulu	251,575	1,285,498	19.5	Crookston	35,250	253,262	12.7
Idaho				Duluth	60,532	439,478	13.7
Boise	165,363	1,503,300	11	New Ulm	64,720	283,929	22.7
Illinois	3,871,047	12,830,458	30	St. Cloud	146,914	550,373	26.6
*Chicago	2,341,000	6,002,000	39	Winona	131,280	570,488	23.5
Belleville	100,000	850,076	12	Mississippi	107,098	2,873,011	4.0
Joliet	658,016	1,808,308	36	Biloxi	58,202	761,418	8.2
Peoria	169,375	1,447,418	9.9	Jackson	48,896	2,111,593	2.4
Rockford	441,450	1,604,210	27.5				
Springfield	161,206	1,118,446	14.4				

State / Diocese	Catholic Pop.	Total Pop.	Cath. Pct.
Missouri	**757,319**	**5,770,436**	**13.1**
*St. Louis	476,477	2,205,007	21.6
Jefferson City	80,542	870,832	9.8
Kansas City-			
St. Joseph	134,218	1,468,518	9.1
Springfield-			
C. Girardeau	66,082	1,226,079	5.2
Montana	**104,276**	**1,104,276**	**7.8**
Great Falls-			
Billings	47,804	391,300	12.2
Helena	56,472	944,632	5.9
Nebraska	**366,894**	**1,769,457**	**20.7**
*Omaha	220,430	897,254	24.5
Grand Island	52,475	301,328	17.4
Lincoln	93,988	570,875	16.4
Nevada	**829,675**	**2,517,498**	**33**
Las Vegas	700,000	1,835,000	38.i
Reno	129,675	682,498	19.0
New Hampshire			
Manchester	319,269	1,314,895	24.3
New Jersey	**3,562,389**	**8,707,112**	**40.9**
*Newark	1,318,557	2,809,267	46.9
Camden	467,623	1,385,487	34
Metuchen	568,201	1,352,859	42.0
Paterson	425,000	1,143,647	37.1
Trenton	783,008	2,015,852	39
New Mexico	**498,334**	**2,386,963**	**20.8**
*Santa Fe	307,396	1,397,255	21.9
Gallup	58,292	491,400	11.8
Las Cruces	132,646	498,308	26.5
New York	**7,166,308**	**19,926,453**	**36**
*New York	2,554,454	5,676,566	45
Albany	340,000	1,370,628	24.8
Brooklyn	1,436,312	4,787,708	30
Buffalo	686,355	1,549,334	44.3
Ogdensburg	111,838	492,990	22.6
Rochester	313,582	1,490,905	21
Rockville Ctr.	1,439,510	3,383,435	43
Syracuse	284,257	1,174,887	24
North Carolina	**365,888**	**8,955,408**	**3.9**
Charlotte	161,244	4,678,140	3.4
Raleigh	204,644	4,277,268	4.7
North Dakota	**146,153**	**641,551**	**23.2**
Bismarck	60,583	260,300	23.2
Fargo	85,570	381,251	22
Ohio	**2,068,348**	**11,475,784**	**18.1**
*Cincinnati	485,112	2,988,285	16
Cleveland	766,065	2,828,763	27
Columbus	261,103	2,455,818	11
Steubenville	39,467	509,663	8
Toledo	301,134	1,476,035	21
Youngstown	215,467	1,217,220	19
Oklahoma	**175,006**	**3,725,676**	**5**
*Oklahoma City	115,506	2,125,676	5
Tulsa	59,500	1,600,000	4
Oregon	**442,137**	**3,433,399**	**13**
*Portland	405,293	3,188,180	13
Baker	36,844	245,219	15
Pennsylvania	**3,530,817**	**12,280,840**	**28.7**
*Philadelphia	1,460,758	3,885,395	38
Allentown	272,921	1,161,932	23.6
Altoona-J'town	101,195	640,635	16
Erie	224,220	860,340	26.1
Pennsylvania, cont.			
Greensburg	160,321	675,283	24
Harrisburg	247,492	2,027,835	12.2
Pittsburgh	747,085	1,934,328	38.6
Scranton	316,825	1,095,092	28.9
Rhode Island			
Providence	629,889	1,067,610	59
South Carolina			
Charleston	183,356	4,301,700	4.1
South Dakota	**153,357**	**751,364**	**20**
Rapid City	27,161	227,211	12
Sioux Falls	126,196	524,153	24
Tennessee	**200,268**	**5,998,594**	**3.3**
Knoxville	58,528	2,265,548	2.6
Memphis	70,423	1,532,154	4.6
Nashville	71,317	2,200,892	3
Texas	**6,586,240**	**23,464,854**	**28**
*Galveston			
-Houston	1,073,844	5,494,357	19.5
*San Antonio	687,788	2,171,851	32.4
Amarillo	45,215	422,428	10.7
Austin	464,206	2,513,467	18.4
Beaumont	76,107	601,039	12.6
Brownsville	995,160	1,170,776	85.0
Corpus Christi	392,430	560,614	70
Dallas	1,094,688	3,630,955	30.1
El Paso+	646,340	826,611	78.1
Fort Worth	550,000	3,047,135	18
Laredo	231,560	330,800	70
Lubbock	80,742	451,995	17.8
San Angelo	83,342	691,088	12
Tyler	60,571	1,342,787	4.5
Victoria	104,247	208,931	50
Utah			
Salt Lake City	230,000	2,550,063	9
Vermont			
Burlington	118,000	620,000	19.0
Virginia	**642,064**	**7,686,858**	**8**
Arlington	413,360	2,763,057	15
Richmond	228,704	4,923,801	5
Washington	**746,285**	**6,478,638**	**12**
*Seattle	577,400	5,064,500	11.4
Spokane	97,000	768,838	12.6
Yakima	71,885	645,300	11.1
West Virginia			
Wheeling-			
Charleston	88,974	1,818,470	5
Wisconsin	**1,591,748**	**5,579,892**	**28.5**
*Milwaukee	681,781	2,287,185	29.8
Green Bay	354,153	1,011,867	35
La Crosse	202,103	849,626	23.7
Madison	276,099	979,919	28
Superior	77,617	451,295	17
Wyoming			
Cheyenne	47,119	515,000	9.1
East. Churches	543,985	—	—
Military Arch.('99)	1,194,000	—	—
Outlying Areas	3,057,322	4,301,579	71
Total 2008	67,117,016	305,248,229	21.9
Total 2007	67,515,016	301,107,806	22.4
Total 1998	61,563,769	270,536,283	22.7

CATHOLIC POPULATION OF THE UNITED STATES

(*Source:* The Official Catholic Directory, 2008; *figures as of Jan. 1, 2008. Archdioceses are indicated by an asterisk; for dioceses marked +, see Dioceses with Interstate Lines.*)

State Diocese	Cath. Pop.	Dioc. Priests	Rel. Priests	Total Priests	Perm. Deac.	Bros.	Sisters	Par- ishes
Alabama	151,554	183	68	251	117	28	263	130
*Mobile	68,331	106	37	143	61	11	109	76
Birmingham	83,223	77	31	108	56	17	154	54
Alaska	52,813	33	26	59	44	4	53	77
*Anchorage	32,170	17	12	29	14	2	33	22
Fairbanks	14,500	9	12	21	26	2	15	46
Juneau	6,143	7	2	9	4	—	5	9
Arizona	1,026,242	256	159	415	383	43	409	166
Phoenix	644,119	146	82	228	241	18	202	91
Tucson	382,123	110	77	187	142	25	207	75
Arkansas, Little Rock	116,605	69	47	116	88	32	211	88
California	10,382,988	2,024	1,655	3,679	1,069	424	4,392	1,073
*Los Angeles	4,176,296	527	580	1,107	270	102	1,709	287
*San Francisco	382,500	208	192	400	80	35	777	90
Fresno	317,023	125	31	156	45	2	118	86
Monterey	194,550	83	20	103	—	15	—	46
Oakland	425,597	160	249	409	110	108	390	85
Orange	1,197,817	168	82	250	97	9	317	59
Sacramento	557,668	176	77	253	128	28	179	103
San Bernardino	1,217,891	113	125	238	106	18	154	94
San Diego	981,057	179	68	247	118	22	290	98
San Jose	560,000	146	207	353	17	65	353	49
Santa Rosa	165,204	76	8	84	36	30	48	42
Stockton	207,385	63	16	79	47	5	57	34
Colorado	707,420	285	157	442	258	16	437	206
*Denver	407,502	176	110	286	183	13	282	118
Colo. Springs	184,918	36	27	63	33	1	95	36
Pueblo	115,000	73	20	93	42	2	60	52
Connecticut	1,282,153	695	192	887	452	51	1,292	378
*Hartford	642,375	330	108	438	295	32	757	213
Bridgeport	410,304	248	26	274	85	2	326	87
Norwich+	229,474	117	58	175	72	17	209	78
Delaware, Wilmington+	233,000	126	93	219	92	37	256	58
D.C., *Washington+	589,072	290	382	672	251	82	590	140
Florida	2,366,715	925	386	1,311	690	133	996	470
*Miami	791,182	264	98	362	143	49	291	111
Orlando	398,325	126	55	181	176	13	106	80
Palm Beach	278,674	113	29	142	73	2	126	49
Pensacola-Tallahassee	71,364	75	17	92	56	5	24	49
St. Augustine	164,484	99	20	119	48	2	111	51
St. Petersburg	425,323	132	98	230	102	46	240	74
Venice	237,363	116	69	185	92	16	98	56
Georgia	730,005	278	93	371	213	4	189	139
*Atlanta	650,000	200	71	271	175	—	91	84
Savannah	80,005	78	22	100	38	4	98	55
Hawaii, Honolulu	251,575	61	70	131	64	35	182	66
Idaho, Boise	165,363	77	16	93	65	5	92	51
Illinois	3,871,047	1,646	1,155	2,801	1,155	432	4,106	989
*Chicago	2,341,000	818	888	1,706	650	302	2,249	363
Belleville	100,000	129	46	175	21	7	166	118
Joliet	658,016	178	93	271	198	71	553	120
Peoria	169,375	217	32	249	113	9	217	159
Rockford	441,450	188	44	232	130	13	178	104
Springfield	161,206	116	52	168	23	30	743	125
Indiana	762,076	522	304	826	117	173	1,596	425
*Indianapolis	230,086	148	96	244	4	27	658	139
Evansville	86,138	83	8	91	42	2	254	70
Ft. Wayne-South Bend	158,899	81	147	228	11	127	529	81
Gary	186,420	103	38	141	50	15	83	72
Lafayette	100,533	107	15	122	12	2	72	63

State Diocese	Cath. Pop.	Dioc. Priests	Rel. Priests	Total Priests	Perm. Deac.	Bros.	Sisters	Par- ishes
Iowa	500,661	539	41	580	246	21	1,093	458
*Dubuque	209,902	206	29	235	88	20	773	178
Davenport	102,096	103	2	105	41	1	158	83
Des Moines	102,147	87	8	95	79	—	83	82
Sioux City	86,516	143	2	145	38	—	79	115
Kansas	415,103	316	78	394	13	19	1,094	338
*Kansas City	203,741	99	61	160	3	16	542	111
Dodge City	45,658	33	5	38	9	2	98	48
Salina	48,527	60	10	70	1	1	159	88
Wichita	117,177	124	2	126	4	—	295	91
Kentucky	382,521	369	117	486	182	63	1,372	302
*Louisville	194,547	152	52	204	109	54	750	112
Covington	89,315	94	12	106	31	4	337	47
Lexington	46,878	48	27	75	38	3	100	64
Owensboro	51,781	75	26	101	2	2	185	79
Louisiana*	1,188,798	625	293	918	409	130	830	478
*New Orleans	384,994	210	169	379	179	81	453	137
Alexandria	48,050	61	14	75	5	4	57	48
Baton Rouge	212,329	71	37	108	58	19	105	68
Houma-Thibodaux	112,419	56	—	56	34	5	25	39
Lafayette	317,310	142	51	193	82	16	121	121
Lake Charles	73,972	48	10	58	30	1	16	38
Shreveport	39,724	37	12	49	21	4	53	27
Maine, Portland	191,008	160	32	192	33	18	332	109
Maryland, *Baltimore	504,159	271	248	519	150	65	993	152
Massachusetts	2,709,552	1,318	770	2,088	468	260	3,015	627
*Boston	1,855,315	785	535	1,320	241	153	2,086	294
Fall River	324,359	157	97	254	74	21	189	94
Springfield	221,596	152	32	184	72	13	389	116
Worcester	308,282	224	106	330	81	73	351	123
Michigan	2,216,372	981	306	1,287	427	91	2,505	774
*Detroit	1,455,664	411	204	615	178	78	1,297	281
Gaylord	68,178	63	11	74	18	—	32	81
Grand Rapids	176,098	111	16	127	45	1	316	91
Kalamazoo	107,700	62	9	71	36	1	235	46
Lansing	227,346	152	47	199	95	10	473	95
Marquette	62,300	88	11	99	40	—	49	74
Saginaw	119,086	94	8	102	15	1	103	106
Minnesota	1,016,696	759	223	982	341	132	2,060	708
*St.Paul & Minneapolis	623,000	338	90	428	217	49	878	218
Crookston	35,250	45	3	48	11	1	117	67
Duluth	60,532	77	12	89	40	1	130	93
New Ulm	64,720	71	1	72	3	—	66	78
St. Cloud	146,914	117	110	227	49	60	504	137
Winona	131,280	111	7	118	21	21	365	115
Mississippi	107,098	110	49	159	33	21	232	117
Biloxi	58,202	53	18	71	27	11	37	42
Jackson	48,896	57	31	88	6	10	195	75
Missouri	757,319	636	522	1,158	404	223	2,151	440
*St. Louis	476,477	363	369	732	253	136	1,725	192
Jefferson City	80,542	101	11	112	76	2	68	95
Kansas City-St. Joseph	134,218	106	85	191	62	34	272	87
Springfield-Cape Girardeau	66,082	66	57	123	13	51	86	66
Montana	104,276	139	20	159	38	3	95	116
Great Falls-Billings	47,804	58	14	72	7	—	64	55
Helena	56,472	81	6	87	31	3	31	61
Nebraska	366,894	420	96	516	194	22	530	304
*Omaha	220,430	202	86	288	192	22	327	135
Grand Island	52,475	67	—	67	—	—	68	36
Lincoln	93,989	151	10	161	6	—	135	133
Nevada	829,675	69	28	97	39	9	37	54
Las Vegas	700,000	40	20	60	14	4	3	26
Reno	129,675	29	8	37	25	5	34	28
New Hampshire Manchester	319,269	195	63	258	37	18	500	102

State Diocese	Cath. Pop.	Dioc. Priests	Rel. Priests	Total Priests	Perm. Deac.	Bros.	Sisters	Par- ishes
New Jersey	3,562,389	1,697	441	2,138	1,116	308	2,767	683
*Newark	1,318,557	707	179	886	210	152	1,015	226
Camden	467,623	296	35	331	147	38	314	125
Metuchen	568,201	198	50	248	171	25	320	103
Paterson	425,000	248	139	387	208	28	734	111
Trenton	783,008	248	38	286	380	65	384	118
New Mexico	498,334	197	143	340	275	93	340	191
*Santa Fe	307,396	124	83	207	205	77	203	93
Gallup	58,292	44	20	64	30	12	100	53
Las Cruces	132,646	29	40	69	40	4	37	45
New York	7,166,308	2,681	1,012	3,693	1,299	769	7,945	1,526
*New York	2,554,454	640	482	1,122	375	368	2,911	388
Albany	340,000	220	95	315	106	79	735	165
Brooklyn	1,436,312	548	163	711	165	141	992	206
Buffalo	686,355	357	124	481	108	40	1,019	236
Ogdensburg	111,838	124	3	127	62	7	123	108
Rochester	313,582	184	51	235	145	26	508	136
Rockville Centre	1,439,510	360	53	413	257	88	1,198	133
Syracuse	284,257	248	41	289	81	20	459	154
North Carolina	365,888	188	101	289	147	10	168	154
Charlotte	161,244	95	52	147	108	9	118	73
Raleigh	204,644	93	49	142	39	1	50	81
North Dakota	146,153	206	42	248	121	20	244	198
Bismarck	60,583	63	31	94	76	20	106	62
Fargo	85,570	143	11	154	45	-	138	136
Ohio	2,068,348	1,302	457	1,759	744	203	3,223	871
*Cincinnati	485,112	278	215	493	180	122	965	221
Cleveland	766,065	415	117	532	207	53	1,135	229
Columbus	261,013	168	38	206	86	1	279	106
Steubenville	39,467	93	37	130	8	6	60	69
Toledo	301,134	183	33	216	201	8	578	131
Youngstown	215,467	165	17	182	62	13	206	115
Oklahoma	175,006	161	53	214	157	27	178	148
*Oklahoma City	115,506	89	29	118	93	9	117	70
Tulsa	59,500	72	24	96	64	18	61	78
Oregon	442,137	188	174	362	59	94	448	160
*Portland	405,293	153	171	324	48	94	437	124
Baker	36,844	35	3	38	11	—	11	36
Pennsylvania	3,530,817	2,120	803	2,923	582	201	6,126	1,223
*Philadelphia	1,460,758	617	368	985	236	107	2,953	270
Allentown	272,921	221	71	292	117	11	370	151
Altoona-Johnstown	101,195	129	76	205	31	9	68	97
Erie	224,220	200	7	207	45	1	378	124
Greensburg	160,321	121	78	199	—	29	198	100
Harrisburg	247,492	144	36	180	47	—	357	89
Pittsburgh	747,085	375	107	482	43	36	1,245	214
Scranton	316,825	313	60	373	63	8	557	178
Rhode Island								
Providence	629,889	284	120	404	104	98	536	150
South Carolina								
Charleston	183,356	87	38	125	101	26	131	92
South Dakota	153,357	160	42	202	57	11	370	238
Rapid City	27,161	40	15	55	25	2	52	88
Sioux Falls	126,196	120	27	147	32	9	318	150
Tennessee	200,268	162	57	219	148	49	246	138
Knoxville	58,528	59	13	72	25	11	25	45
Memphis	70,423	62	19	81	49	37	68	42
Nashville	71,317	41	25	66	74	1	153	51
Texas	6,586,240	1,292	786	2,078	1,610	229	2,314	1,060
*Galveston-Houston	1,073,844	201	208	409	378	14	468	150
*San Antonio	687,788	141	197	338	339	84	752	139
Amarillo	45,215	46	13	49	57	1	104	38
Austin	464,206	171	49	220	214	47	105	104
Beaumont	76,107	50	23	73	45	3	18	44
Brownsville	995,160	80	34	114	65	18	126	67

State Diocese	Cath. Pop.	Dioc. Priests	Rel. Priests	Total Priests	Perm. Deac.	Bros.	Sisters	Par- ishes
Texas, cont.								
Corpus Christi	392,430	104	34	138	62	6	172	68
Dallas	1,094,688	95	68	163	143	22	99	67
El Paso	646,340	80	48	128	10	12	147	57
Fort Worth	550,000	66	50	116	76	10	63	89
Laredo	231,560	31	24	55	28	8	74	32
Lubbock	80,742	49	4	53	51	—	25	62
San Angelo	83,342	51	10	61	59	—	15	49
Tyler	60,571	72	15	87	54	3	55	44
Victoria	104,247	55	9	64	29	1	99	50
Utah, Salt Lake City	**230,000**	**59**	**25**	**84**	**60**	**10**	**43**	**48**
Vermont, Burlington	**118,000**	**106**	**29**	**135**	**46**	**19**	**183**	**80**
Virginia	**642,064**	**309**	**97**	**406**	**154**	**52**	**324**	**214**
Arlington	413,360	161	64	225	64	40	145	68
Richmond	228,704	148	33	181	90	12	179	146
Washington	**746,285**	**360**	**193**	**553**	**203**	**28**	**711**	**265**
*Seattle	577,400	196	109	305	122	19	452	142
Spokane	97,000	92	74	166	55	5	219	82
Yakima	71,885	72	10	82	26	4	40	41
West Virginia								
Wheeling-Charleston	**88,974**	**112**	**59**	**171**	**49**	**11**	**177**	**122**
Wisconsin	**1,591,748**	**914**	**461**	**1,375**	**439**	**123**	**3,167**	**774**
*Milwaukee	681,781	355	322	677	180	71	1,584	211
Green Bay	354,153	189	99	288	136	39	530	160
La Crosse	202,103	172	16	188	41	4	442	165
Madison	276,094	134	17	151	24	7	520	133
Superior	77,617	64	7	71	58	2	91	405
Wyoming, Cheyenne+	**47,119**	**49**	**13**	**62**	**20**	**1**	**20**	**36**
EASTERN CHURCHES	**515,958**	**579**	**123**	**702**	**260**	**29**	**285**	**564**
*Philadelphia	22,274	44	5	49	5	1	60	68
St. Nicholas	10,000	31	15	46	7	2	4	38
Stamford	16,600	38	17	55	10	2	33	51
St. Josaphat (Parma)	10,776	45	1	46	10	3	4	38
*Pittsburgh	59,221	60	7	67	16	3	87	79
Parma	8,839	42	1	43	11	—	9	31
Passaic	18,874	70	13	83	27	1	19	86
Van Nuys	2,795	24	2	26	11	2	3	19
St. Maron (Maronites)	30,000	59	11	70	14	4	—	34
Our Lady of Lebanon (Maronites)	44,502	33	16	49	13	—	5	28
Newton (Melkites)	26,704	48	14	62	49	—	3	35
St. Peter the Apostle of San Diego	40,200	9	5	14	—	3	12	8
St. Thomas Apostle of Detroit (Chaldean)	120,000	15	—	15	120	—	11	8
St. Thomas (Syro-Malabrs)	85,000	40	9	49	—	—	16	12
St. George Martyr (Romanian)	5,000	17	3	20	2	4	4	14
Our Lady of Deliverance (Syrians, U.S.-Canada)	18,200	11	—	11	3	—	—	9
Armenian Ex.(U.S.-Canada)	25,000	4	8	12	2	—	—	7
Military Archd. ('99) [1]	**1,194,000**	**—**	**—**	**—**	**—**	**—**	**—**	**—**
Outlying Areas								
Puerto Rico	2,754,537	371	333	704	422	37	1,038	328
Samoa-Pago Pago	14,500	12	5	17	31	—	10	16
Caroline Islands	68,500	14	15	29	40	2	33	27
Chalan Kanoa (N. Mariana Is.)	43,000	15	2	17	—	—	—	12
Guam, *Agana	142,000	40	12	52	21	—	87	24
Marshall Islands	4,785	1	6	7	1	—	9	4
Virgin Islands, St. Thomas	30,000	13	4	17	27	2	21	8
TOTAL 2008	**67,117,016**	**28,067**	**13,339**	**41,406**	**16,408**	**5,040**	**63,032**	**18,890**
TOTAL 2007	**67,515,016**	**28,462**	**13,845**	**42,307**	**15,868**	**5,095**	**64,877**	**19,044**
TOTAL 1998	**61,563,769**	**31,657**	**15,925**	**47,563**	**12,247**	**6,115**	**85,412**	**19,628**

[1] 277 diocesan and 40 religious-order chaplains are on loan to the military (*2008 Annuario Pontificio*).

RECEPTIONS INTO THE CHURCH IN THE UNITED STATES

(Source: The Official Catholic Directory, 2008 figures as of Jan. 1, 2008 Archdioceses are indicated by an asterisk; for dioceses marked +, see Dioceses with Interstate Lines. Information includes infant and adult baptisms and those received into full communion.)

State / Diocese	Infant Baptisms	Adult Bapts.	Rec'd into Full Com.
Alabama	**3,537**	**378**	**611**
*Mobile	1,107	179	289
Birmingham	2,430	199	322
Alaska	**853**	**84**	**102**
*Anchorage	496	63	74
Fairbanks	305	11	13
Juneau	52	10	15
Arizona	**17,511**	**612**	**1,911**
Phoenix	11,251	385	1,656
Tucson	6,260	227	255
Arkansas, Lit. Rock	**2,939**	**201**	**430**
California	**198,910**	**5,314**	**14,304**
*Los Angeles	95,408	1,685	2,626
*San Francisco	6,549	244	570
Fresno	17,725	898	1,999
Monterey	5,818	137	349
Oakland	9,666	315	366
Orange	14,801	564	1,938
Sacramento	9,753	439	1,138
San Bernardino	11,042	363	3,636
San Diego	10,189	109	466
San Jose	8,104	319	626
Santa Rosa	3,302	111	116
Stockton	6,557	130	474
Colorado	**14,174**	**968**	**3,505**
*Denver	10,760	461	1,596
Colorado Springs	1,087	75	151
Pueblo	2,327	432	1,758
Connecticut	**13,938**	**434**	**940**
*Hartford	7,228	185	372
Bridgeport	4,510	160	293
Norwich+	2,200	89	275
Delaware, Wilm.+	**2,843**	**140**	**339**
D.C., *Washington+	**4,377**	**715**	**564**
Florida	**38,038**	**1,597**	**3,421**
*Miami	15,184	542	617
Orlando	6,776	334	566
Palm Beach	4,620	217	236
Pensacola-Tallahassee	936	117	228
St. Augustine	2,285	231	586
St. Petersburg	4,856	-	690
Venice	3,391	156	498
Georgia	**14,039**	**758**	**1,438**
*Atlanta	12,138	538	1,205
Savannah	1,901	220	278
Hawaii, Honolulu	**2,789**	**161**	**173**
Idaho, Boise	**3,121**	**192**	**324**
Illinois	**59,104**	**2,658**	**2,842**
*Chicago	37,049	1,484	761
Belleville	1,040	100	200
Joliet	9,131	386	684
Peoria	2,701	288	435
Rockford	7,331	198	397
Springfield	1,852	202	365
Indiana	**12,024**	**1,039**	**1,695**
*Indianapolis	4,181	430	586
Evansville	1,249	99	144
Ft. Wayne-S. Bend	2,744	208	396
Gary	1,849	75	193
Indiana, cont.			
Lafayette	2,001	227	376
Iowa	**7,667**	**548**	**1,148**
*Dubuque	2,519	87	272
Davenport	1,512	146	184
Des Moines	1,980	198	354
Sioux City	1,656	117	338
Kansas	**8,416**	**691**	**1,190**
*Kansas City	3,902	315	513
Dodge City	1,040	40	63
Salina	927	94	137
Wichita	2,547	242	477
Kentucky	**3,274**	**620**	**931**
*Louisville	2,480	189	390
Covington	1,109	163	135
Lexington	627	166	121
Owensboro	980	102	285
Louisiana	**14,143**	**683**	**1,708**
*New Orleans	3,754	133	335
Alexandria	593	51	122
Baton Rouge	2,531	161	301
Houma-Thibodaux	1,359	40	93
Lafayette	4,424	98	365
Lake Charles	1,031	155	389
Shreveport	451	45	103
Maine, Portland	**1,720**	**149**	**208**
Maryland, *Baltimore	**6,836**	**527**	**766**
Massachusetts	**26,697**	**596**	**649**
*Boston	17,360	329	209
Fall River	3,635	74	119
Springfield	2,648	98	141
Worcester	3,054	95	180
Michigan	**21,115**	**1,834**	**2,986**
*Detroit	11,103	781	1,181
Gaylord	646	65	165
Grand Rapids	2,817	230	461
Kalamazoo	1,398	219	226
Lansing	3,158	392	637
Marquette	743	52	101
Saginaw	1,250	95	215
Minnesota	**15,540**	**611**	**1,712**
*St. Paul and Minneapolis	9,231	317	1,032
Crookston	474	51	60
Duluth	810	79	79
New Ulm	892	99	119
St. Cloud	2,216	46	208
Winona	1,917	72	214
Mississippi	**1,803**	**157**	**434**
Biloxi	933	86	154
Jackson	870	71	280
Missouri	**10,480**	**860**	**1,376**
*St. Louis	6,010	375	541
Jefferson City	1,144	126	241
Ks. City-St. Joe	2,288	217	370
Springfield-Cape Girardeau	1,038	142	224
Montana	**1,428**	**75**	**229**
Great Falls-Billings	699	75	94
Helena	729	-	135

State / Diocese	Infant Baptisms	Adult Bapts.	Rec'd into Full Com.
Nebraska	**6,406**	**366**	**765**
*Omaha	4,234	164	500
Grand Island	972	71	104
Lincoln	1,200	131	161
Nevada	**8,066**	**265**	**486**
Las Vegas	6,096	171	324
Reno	1,970	94	162
New Hampshire			
Manchester	**3,167**	**148**	**119**
New Jersey	**40,098**	**1,596**	**2,189**
*Newark	15,118	317	263
Camden	5,936	462	587
Metuchen	5,473	104	252
Paterson	7,607	146	229
Trenton	5,964	567	858
New Mexico	**8,387**	**398**	**662**
*Santa Fe	5,569	240	466
Gallup	806	114	128
Las Cruces	2,012	44	68
New York	**75,907**	**2,961**	**4,522**
*New York	23,946	1,013	1,235
Albany	3,964	105	210
Brooklyn	16,966	611	1,371
Buffalo	4,869	151	278
Ogdensburg	1,059	76	69
Rochester	3,306	170	527
Rockville Centre	18,069	669	345
Syracuse	3,728	166	487
North Carolina	**12,389**	**440**	**425**
Charlotte	6,686	239	425
Raleigh	5,703	201	-
North Dakota	**2,088**	**130**	**354**
Bismarck	882	64	140
Fargo	1,206	66	214
Ohio	**22,680**	**2,372**	**3,498**
*Cincinnati	6,362	486	801
Cleveland	7,718	836	650
Columbus	3,344	431	604
Steubenville	486	72	633
Toledo	2,846	370	421
Youngstown	1,924	177	389
Oklahoma	**4,153**	**315**	**732**
*Okla. City	2,683	207	463
Tulsa	1,470	108	269
Oregon	**6,770**	**515**	**631**
*Portland	5,985	437	540
Baker	785	78	91
Pennsylvania	**34,174**	**2,257**	**2,843**
*Philadelphia	14,516	1,059	496
Allentown	3,158	118	550
Altoona-Johnstn.	1,151	94	142
Erie	1,752	110	123
Greensburg	1,459	84	314
Harrisburg	2,531	401	446
Pittsburgh	6,032	293	586
Scranton	3,575	98	186
Rhode Island			
Providence	**4,024**	**149**	**94**
South Carolina			
Charleston	3,160	244	500
South Dakota	**2,219**	**87**	**338**
Rapid City	496	22	108
Sioux Falls	1,726	65	230
Tennessee	**4,187**	**356**	**958**
Knoxville	1,006	94	265
Tennessee, cont.			
Memphis	1,592	116	297
Nashville	1,589	146	396
Texas	**78,382**	**4,485**	**7,098**
*Galv.-Houston	11,813	1,811	845
*San Antonio	10,008	405	747
Amarillo	1,112	58	134
Austin	7,433	314	1,050
Beaumont	1,361	96	165
Brownsville	7,596	206	1,129
Corpus Christi	2,739	163	438
Dallas	16,593	711	768
El Paso	4,733	105	137
Fort Worth	5,462	270	517
Laredo	2,912	46	397
Lubbock	958	51	149
San Angelo	1,673	99	173
Tyler	2,551	78	227
Victoria	1,438	72	222
Utah, Salt Lake City	**3,594**	**320**	**358**
Vermont, Burlington	**1,030**	**156**	**88**
Virginia	**10,865**	**588**	**1,660**
Arlington	7,192	519	1,228
Richmond	3,673	69	432
Washington	**11,084**	**224**	**1,417**
*Seattle	6,988	-	617
Spokane	1,163	132	634
Yakima	2,933	92	166
West Virginia			
Wheeling-Chas.	**992**	**212**	**205**
Wisconsin	**17,819**	**671**	**1,560**
*Milwaukee	7,384	241	607
Green Bay	3,916	159	262
La Crosse	2,427	146	302
Madison	3,055	85	283
Superior	1,037	40	106
Wyoming, Chey.+	**919**	**105**	**173**
Eastern Churches	**3,823**	**151**	**320**
*Philadelphia	199	9	34
St. Nicholas	220	5	2
Stamford	169	1	-
St. Josaphat (Parma)	84	1	-
*Pittsburgh	168	9	34
Parma	86	4	26
Passaic	163	13	19
Van Nuys	62	11	11
St. Maron (Maronites)	413	9	40
Our Lady of Lebanon (Maronites)	435	35	41
Newton (Melkites)	315	43	23
St. Peter the Apostle	337	1	-
St. Thomas Apostle of Detroit (Chaldeans)	901	14	-
St. Thomas (Syro-Mal.)	172	9	23
St. George Martyr (Romanian)	36	6	12
Our Lady of Deliverance (Syrians, U.S.-Can.)	54	6	6
Arme. Ex. (U.S.-Can.)	220	5	2
Military Archd.	**3,200**	**753**	**364**
Outlying Areas	**23,910**	**6,517**	**9,065**
Total 2008	**902,841**	**49,415**	**87,363**
Total 2007	953,688	62,464	92,975

The Catholic Church in Canada

Background

The first date in the remote background of the Catholic history of Canada is July 7, 1534, when a priest in the exploration company of Jacques Cartier celebrated Mass on the Gaspe Peninsula.

Successful colonization and the significant beginnings of the Catholic history of the country date from the foundation of Québec in 1608 by Samuel de Champlain and French settlers. Montréal was established in 1642.

The earliest missionaries were Franciscan Récollets (Recollects) and Jesuits who arrived in 1615 and 1625, respectively. They provided some pastoral care for the settlers but worked mainly among the 100,000 Indians —Algonquins, Hurons and Iroquois—in the interior and in the Lake Ontario region. Eight of the Jesuit missionaries, killed in the 1640s, were canonized in 1930. (*See* **Index: Jesuit North American Martyrs.**) Sulpician Fathers, who arrived in Canada late in the 1640s, played a part in the great missionary period, which ended about 1700.

Kateri Tekakwitha, "Lily of the Mohawks," who was baptized in 1676 and died in 1680, was declared "Blessed" on June 22, 1980. Her cause for canonization continues today.

The communities of women religious with the longest histories in Canada are the Canonesses of St. Augustine and the Ursulines, since 1639; and the Hospitallers of St. Joseph, since 1642. Communities of Canadian origin are the Congregation of Notre Dame, founded by St. Marguerite Bourgeoys in 1658, and the Grey Nuns, formed by St. Marie Marguerite d'Youville in 1737.

Mother Marie (Guyard) of the Incarnation, an Ursuline nun, was one of the first three women missionaries to New France; called "Mother of the Church in Canada," she was declared "Blessed" on June 22, 1980.

Start of Church Organization

Ecclesiastical organization began with the appointment in 1658 of François De Montmorency–Laval, "Father of the Church in Canada," as vicar apostolic of New France. He was the first bishop of Québec from 1674 to 1688, with jurisdiction over all French–claimed territory in North America. He was declared "Blessed" on June 22, 1980.

In 1713, the French Canadian population numbered 18,000. In the same year, the Treaty of Utrecht ceded Acadia, Newfoundland and the Hudson Bay Territory to England. The Acadians were scattered among the American colonies in 1755.

The English acquired possession of Canada and its 70,000 French–speaking inhabitants by virtue of the Treaty of Paris in 1763. Anglo–French and Anglican–Catholic differences and tensions developed. The pro–British government at first refused to recognize the titles of church officials, hindered the clergy in their work and tried to install a non–Catholic educational system. Laws were passed that guaranteed religious liberties to Catholics (Québec Act of 1774, Constitutional Act of 1791, legislation approved by Queen Victoria in 1851), but it took some time before actual respect for these liberties matched the legal enactments. The initial moderation of government antipathy toward the Church was caused partly by the loyalty of Catholics to the Crown during the American Revolution and the War of 1812.

Growth

The 15 years following the passage in 1840 of the Act of Union, which joined Upper and Lower Canada, were significant. New communities of men and women religious joined those already in the country. The Oblates of Mary Immaculate, missionaries par excellence in Canada, advanced the penetration of the West that had been started in 1818 by Abbé Provencher. New jurisdictions were established, and Québec became a metropolitan see in 1844. The first Council of Québec was held in 1851. The established Catholic school system enjoyed a period of growth.

Laval University was inaugurated in 1854 and canonically established in 1876.

Abp. Elzear-Alexandre Taschereau of Québec was named Canada's first cardinal in 1886.

The apostolic delegation to Canada was set up in 1899. It became a nunciature October 16, 1969, with the establishment of diplomatic relations with the Vatican. The present Apostolic Nuncio is Abp. Luigi Ventura, appointed on June 22, 2001.

Early in this century, Canada had eight ecclesiastical provinces, 23 dioceses, three vicariates apostolic, 3,500 priests, 2 million Catholics, about 30 communities of men religious, and 70 or more communities of women religious. The Church in Canada was phased out of mission status and removed from the jurisdiction of the Congregation for the Propagation of the Faith in 1908.

Diverse Population

The greatest concentration of Catholics is in the eastern portion of the country. In the northern and western portions, outside metropolitan centers, there are some of the most difficult parish and mission areas in the world. Bilingual (English–French) differences in the general population are reflected in the Church; for example, in the parallel structures of the Canadian

Conference of Catholic Bishops, which was established in 1943. Québec is the center of French cultural influence. Many language groups are represented among Catholics, who include more than 257,000 members of Eastern Rites in one metropolitan see, seven eparchies and an apostolic exarchate.

Education, a past source of friction between the Church and the government, is administered by the civil provinces in a variety of arrangements authorized by the Canadian Constitution. Denominational schools have tax support in one way in Québec and Newfoundland, and in another way in Alberta, Ontario and Saskatchewan. Several provinces provide tax support only for public schools, making private financing necessary for separate church-related schools.

ECCLESIASTICAL JURISDICTIONS OF CANADA

Provinces

Names of ecclesiastical provinces and metropolitan sees in bold face; suffragan sees in parentheses.

Edmonton (Calgary, St. Paul).

Gatineau (Amos, Mont–Laurier, Rouyn Noranda).

Grouard–McLennan (Mackenzie–Ft. Smith, Prince George, Whitehorse).

Halifax (Antigonish, Charlottetown, Yarmouth).

Keewatin–LePas (Churchill–Hudson Bay, Corner Brook and Labrador, Moosonee).

Kingston (Alexandria–Cornwall, Peterborough, Sault Ste. Marie).

Moncton (Bathurst, Edmundston, St. John).

Montréal (Joliette, St. Jean–Longueuil, St. Jerome, Valleyfield).

Ottawa (Hearst, Pembroke, Timmins).

Québec (Chicoutimi, Ste.–Anne–de–la–Pocatiere, Trois Rivieres).

Regina (Prince Albert, Saskatoon, Abbey of St. Peter).

Rimouski (Baie–Comeau, Gaspe).

St. Boniface (no suffragan).

St. John's (Grand Falls, St. George).

Sherbrooke (Nicolet, St. Hyacinthe).

Toronto (Hamilton, London, St. Catharines, Thunder Bay).

Vancouver (Kamloops, Nelson, Victoria).

Winnipeg-Ukrainian (Edmonton, New Westminster, Saskatoon, Toronto).

Jurisdictions immediately subject to the Holy See: Roman–Rite Archdiocese of Winnipeg, Byzantine Eparchy of Sts. Cyril and Methodius for Slovaks, Byzantine Eparchy of St. Sauveur de Montréal for Greek Melkites; Antiochene Eparchy of St. Maron of Montréal for Maronites.

JURISDICTIONS, HIERARCHY

(Principal sources: Information office, Canadian Conference of Catholic Bishops; Rev. Mr. William Kokesch, Dir., Communications Service, Canadian Conference of Catholic Bishops; Annuaire, Conférence des Évêques Catholiques du Canada; Catholic Almanac survey; Annuario Pontificio; L'Osservatore Romano; Catholic News Service. As of June 1, 2008.)

Information includes names of archdioceses (indicated by asterisk) and dioceses, date of foundation, present ordinaries and auxiliaries; addresses of chancery office/bishop's residence; cathedral.

Alexandria-Cornwall, ON (1890 as Alexandria; name changed to Alexandria-Cornwall, 1976): Paul-André Durocher, bishop, 2002.

Diocesan Center: 220, chemin Montréal, C.P. 1388, Cornwall, ON K6H 5V4; (613) 933-1138; www.alexandria-cornwall.ca/. Cathedral: St. Finnans (Alexandria); Nativity Co-Cathedral (Cornwall).

Amos, QC (1938): Eugène Tremblay, bishop, 2004.

Bishop's Residence: 450, rue Principale Nord, Amos, QC J9T 2M1; (819) 732-6515; www.dioceseamos.org. Cathedral: St. Teresa of Ávila.

Antigonish, NS (Arichat, 1844; transferred, 1886): Raymond J. Lahey, bishop, 2003.

Chancery Office: 168 Hawthorne St., P.O. Box 1330, Antigonish, NS B2G 2L7; (902) 863-3335; www.antigonishdiocese.com/title.htm. Cathedral: St. Ninian.

Baie-Comeau, QC (p.a., 1882; v.a., 1905; diocese Gulf of St. Lawrence, 1945; name changed to Hauterive, 1960; present title, 1986): Vacant.

Bishop's Residence: 639, rue de Bretagne, Baie-Comeau, QC G5C 1X2; (418) 589-5744; www.diocese-bc.org. Cathedral: Paroisse St. Jean-Eudes.

Bathurst, NB (Chatham, 1860; transferred, 1938): Valéry Vienneau, bishop, 2002.

Bishop's Residence: 645, avenue Murray, C.P. 460, Bathurst, NB E2A 3Z4; (506) 546-1420; www.diocesebathurst.com. Cathedral: Sacred Heart of Jesus.

Calgary, AB (1912): Frederick Henry, bishop, 1997.

Address: Room 290, The Iona Building, 120 17 Ave. SW, Calgary, AB T2S 2T2; (403) 218-5526; www.rcdiocese-calgary.ab.ca. Cathedral: St. Mary.

Charlottetown, PEI (1829): Joseph Vernon Fougere, bishop, 1992.

Bishop's Residence: P.O. Box 907, Charlottetown, PEI C1A 7L9; (902) 368-8005; www.dioceseofcharlottetown/com. Cathedral: St. Dunstan's.

Chicoutimi, QC (1878): André Rivest, bishop, 2004. Roch Pedneault, aux.

Bishop's Residence: 602, Racine Est, Chicoutimi, QC G7H 6J6; (418) 543-0783; www.evechede chicoutimi.qc.ca. Cathedral: St. Francois-Xavier.

Churchill-Hudson Bay, MB (p.a., 1925; v.a., Hudson Bay, 1931; diocese of Churchill, 1967; present title, 1968): Reynald Rouleau, O.M.I., bishop, 1987.

Diocesan Office: P.O. Box 10, Churchill, MB R0B 0E0; (204) 675-2252. Cathedral: Holy Canadian Martyrs.

Corner Brook and Labrador, QC (formerly Labrador City-Schefferville; v.a. Labrador, 1946; diocese, 1967): Douglas Crosby, O.M.I., bishop, 1997.

Bishop's Residence: Sutton House, 320 avenue Elizabeth, C.P. 545, Labrador City, Labrador, NL A2V 2L3; (709) 944-2046; www.labdiocese.com. Cathedral: Our Lady of Perpetual Help.

Edmonton,* AB (St. Albert, 1871; archdiocese, transferred Edmonton, 1912): Richard W. Smith, archbishop, 2007.

Archdiocesan Office: 8421-101 Avenue, Edmonton,

Alta. T6A 0L1; (780) 469-1010; www.edmonton-catholic-church.com. Cathedral: Basilica of St. Joseph.

Edmonton, AB (Ukrainian Byzantine) (ap. ex. of western Canada, 1948; eparchy, 1956): David Motiuk, bishop, 2007.
Eparch's Residence: 9645 108th Ave., Edmonton, Alta. T5H 1A3; (780) 424-5496. Cathedral: St. Josaphat.

Edmundston, NB (1944): François Thibodeau, C.J.M., bishop, 1994.
Diocesan Center: 60, rue Bouchard, Edmundston, NB E3V 3K1; (506) 735-5578; www.diocese-edmunston.ca. Cathedral: Immaculate Conception.

Gaspé, QC (1922): Jean Gagnon, bishop, 2002.
Bishop's House: 172, rue Jacques-Cartier, Gaspé, QC G4X 1M9; (418) 368-2274; www.gaspesie.net/diocesegaspe. Cathedral: Christ the King.

Gatineau,* QC (1963, as Hull; name changed, 1982; archdiocese, 1990): Roger Ébacher, bishop, 1988; first archbishop, Oct. 31, 1990.
Diocesan Center: 180 Boulevard Mont-Bleu, Hull, QC J8Z 3J5; (819) 771-8391; www.diocesegatineauhull.qc.ca.

Grand Falls, NL (Harbour Grace, 1856; present title, 1964): vacant.
Chancery Office: 8A Church Rd., P.O. Box 771, Grand Falls-Windsor, NL A2A 2M4; (709) 489-2778; www.rcdiocesegrandfalls.ca/. Cathedral: Immaculate Conception.

Grouard-McLennan,* AB (v.a. Athabaska-Mackenzie, 1862; Grouard, 1927; archdiocese Grouard-McLennan, 1967); Gerard Pettipas, C.Ss.R., archbishop, 2006.
Archbishop's Residence: 210-1 Street West, C.P. 388, McLennan, AB T0H 2L0; (780) 324-3820. Cathedral: St. Jean-Baptiste (McLennan).

Halifax,* NS (1842; archdiocese, 1852): Anthony Mancini, archbishop, 2007. Claude Champagne, auxiliary.
Chancery Office: 1531 Grafton St., P.O. Box 1527, Halifax, NS B3J 2Y3; (902) 429-9800; www.catholichalifax.org.

Hamilton, ON (1856): Anthony Tonnos, bishop, 1984. Gerard Paul Bergie, auxiliary
Chancery Office: 700 King St. West, Hamilton, ON L8P 1C7; (905) 528-7988; www.hamiltondiocese.com/. Cathedral: Christ the King.

Hearst, ON (p.a., 1918; v.a., 1920; diocese, 1938): Vincent Cadieux, bishop, 2007.
Bishop's Residence: 76 7e rue, C.P. 1330, Hearst, ON P0L 1N0; (705) 362-4903; www.hearstdiocese.com. Cathedral: Notre Dame de the Assumption.

Joliette, QC (1904): Gilles Lussier, bishop, 1991.
Bishop's Residence: 2 rue Saint-Charles-Borromée Nord, C.P. 470, Joliette, QC J6E 6H6; (450) 753-7596; www.diocesedejoliette.org. Cathedral: St. Charles Borromeo.

Kamloops, BC (1945): David Monroe, bishop, 2002.
Bishop's Residence: 635-A Tranquille Rd., Kamloops, BC V2B 3H5; (250) 376-3351. Cathedral: Sacred Heart.

Keewatin-Le Pas,* MB (v.a., 1910; archdiocese, 1967): Sylvain Lavoie, O.M.I., archbishop, 2006.

Archbishop's Residence: 76 1st St. W., P.O. Box 270, The Pas, MB R9A 1K4; (204) 623-6152. Cathedral: Our Lady of the Sacred Heart.

Kingston,* ON (1826; archdiocese, 1889): Brendan Michael O'Brien, archbishop, 2007.
Chancery Office: 390 Palace Rd., Kingston, ON K7L 4T3; (613) 548-4461; www.romancatholic.kingston.on.ca. Cathedral: St. Mary of the Immaculate Conception.

London, ON (1855; transferred Sandwich, 1859; London, 1869): Ronald P. Fabbro, C.S.B., bishop, 2002. Robert Anthony Daniels, auxiliary.
Bishop's Residence: 1070 Waterloo St., London, ON N6A 3Y2; (519) 433-0658; www.rcec.london.on.ca. Cathedral: St. Peter's Cathedral Basilica.

Mackenzie-Fort Smith, NT (v.a. Mackenzie, 1902; diocese Mackenzie-Fort Smith, 1967): Murray Chatlain, coadjutor bishop, 2007; bishop, 2008.
Diocesan Office: 5117-52nd St., Yellowknife, NT X1A 1T7; (867) 920-2129. Cathedral: St. Joseph (Ft. Smith).

Moncton,* NB (1936): André Richard, C.S.C., archbishop, 2002.
Archbishop's Residence: 452, rue Amirault, Dieppe, NB E1A 1G3; (506) 857-9531. Cathedral: Our Lady of the Assumption.

Mont-Laurier, QC (1913): Vital Massé, bishop, 2001.
Bishop's Residence: 435, rue de la Madone, Mont-Laurier, QC J9L 1S1; (819) 623-5530. Cathedral: Notre Dame de Fourvières.

Montréal,* QC (1836; archdiocese, 1886): Cardinal Jean-Claude Turcotte, archbishop, 1990. Lionel Gendron, P.S.S., André Gazaille, auxiliaries.
Archbishop's Residence: 2000, rue Sherbrooke Ouest, Montréal, QC H3H 1G4; (514) 931-7311; www.diocesemontreal.org. Cathedral: Basilica of Mary Queen of the World and Saint James.

Montréal, QC (Sauveur de Montréal, Eparchy of Greek Melkites) (ap. ex. 1980; eparchy, 1984): Ibrahim M. Ibrahim, 2003.
Address: 34 rue Maplewood, Montréal, QC H2V 2MI; (514) 272-6430.

Montréal, QC (St. Maron of Montréal, Maronites) (1982): Joseph Khoury, eparch, 1996.
Chancery Office: 12 475 rue Grenet, Montréal, QC H4J 2K4; (514) 331-2807. Cathedral: St. Maron.

Moosonee, ON (v.a. James Bay, 1938; diocese Moosonee, 1967): Vincent Cadieux, O.M.I., bishop, 1992.
Bishop's Residence: 2 Bay Rd., C.P. 40, Moosonee, ON P0L 1Y0; (705) 336-2908. Cathedral: Christ the King.

Nelson, BC (1936): John Corriveau, O.F.M. Cap., bishop, 2007.
Bishop's Residence: 402 West Richards St., Nelson, BC VIL 3K3; (250) 354-6921; www.diocese.nelson.bc.ca/. Cathedral: Mary Immaculate.

New Westminster, BC (Ukrainian Byzantine) (1974): Kenneth Nowakowski, eparch, 2007
Eparch's address: 502 5th Ave., New Westminster, BC V3L 1S2; (604) 524-8824; www.vcn.bc.ca/ucepnw.

Nicolet, QC (1885): Raymond Saint-Gelais, bishop, 1989.
Bishop's Residence: 49, rue Mgr Brunault, Nicolet, QC J3T 1X7; (819) 293-4696. Cathedral: St. Jean-Baptiste.

Ottawa,* ON (Bytown, 1847, name changed, 1854; archdiocese, 1886): Terrence Prendergast, S.J., archbishop, 2007.

Archbishop's Residence: 1247 Place Kilborn, Ottawa, ON K1H 6K9; (613) 738-5025; www.ecclesia-ottawa.org. Cathedral: Basilica of Notre Dame-of-Ottawa.

Pembroke, ON (v.a. 1882; diocese, 1898): Michael Mulhall, bishop, 2007. Bishop's Residence: 188 Renfrew St., P.O. Box 7, Pembroke, ON K8A 6X1; (613) 732-7933; www.diocesepembroke.org. Cathedral: St. Columbkille.

Peterborough, ON (1882): Nicola De Angelis, C.F.I.C., bishop 2002.

Bishop's Residence: 350 Hunter St. West, P.O. Box 175, Peterborough, ON K9J 6Y8; (705) 745-5123; www.peterboroughdiocese.org. Cathedral: St. Peter-in-Chains.

Prince Albert, SK (v.a., 1890; diocese, 1907): Albert Thévenot, M. Afr., bishop, 1983.

Address: 1415 4th Ave. West, Prince Albert, SK S6V 5H1; (306) 922-4747; www.padiocese.sk.ca. Cathedral: Sacred Heart.

Prince George, BC (p.a., 1908; v.a. Yukon and Prince Rupert, 1944; diocese Prince George, 1967): Gerald Wiesner, O.M.I., bishop, 1993.

Chancery Office: 6500 Southbridge Ave., P.O. Box 7000, Prince George, BC V2N 3Z2; (250) 964-4424; www.pgdiocese.bc.ca. Cathedral: Sacred Heart.

Québec,* QC (v.a., 1658; diocese, 1674; archdiocese, 1819; metropolitan, 1844; primatial see, 1956): Cardinal Marc Ouellet, P.S.S., archbishop, 2002. Jean Pierre Blais, Pierre-André Fournier, Gilles Lemay, auxiliaries.

Chancery Office: 1073, boul. René-Lévesque ouest, Québec, QC G1S 4R5; (418) 688-1211; www.diocesequebec.qc.ca/. Cathedral: Notre-Dame- de-Québec (Basilica).

Regina,* SK (1910; archdiocese, 1915): Daniel Bohan, archbishop, 2005.

Chancery Office: 445 Broad St. North, Regina, SK S4R 2X8; (306) 352-1651; www.archregina.sk.ca. Cathedral: Our Lady of the Most Holy Rosary.

Rimouski,* QC (1867; archdiocese, 1946): Pierre-André Fournier, archbishop, 2008.

Archbishop's Residence: 34, rue de l'Évêché Ouest, C.P. 730, Rimouski, QC G5L 7C7; (418) 723-3320; www.dioceserimouski.com.

Rouyn-Noranda, QC (1973): Dorylas Moreau, bishop, 2001.

Bishop's Residence: 515, avenue Cuddihy, C.P. 1060, Rouyn-Noranda, QC J9X 4C5; (819) 764-4660; www.dioc-cath-rouyn-noranda.org. Cathedral: St. Michael the Archangel.

Saint-Boniface,* MB (1847; archdiocese, 1871): Émilius Goulet, P.S.S..

Archbishop's Residence: 151, avenue de la Cathédrale, Saint-Boniface, MB R2H 0H6; (204) 237-9851. Cathedral: Basilica of St. Boniface.

St. Catharine's, ON (1958): James M. Wingle, bishop, 2001.

Bishop's Residence: P.O. Box 875, St. Catharines, ON L2R 6Y3; (905) 684-0154; www.romancatholic.niagara.on.ca. Cathedral: St. Catherine of Alexandria.

St. George's, NL (p.a., 1870; v.a., 1890; diocese, 1904): Douglas Crosby, O.M.I., bishop, 2003 (also bp. of Labrador City-Schefferville).

Bishop's Residence: 13 Mount Bernard, Corner Brook, NL A2H 6K6; (709) 639-7073; www.rcchurch. com. Cathedral: Most Holy Redeemer and Immaculate Conception.

Saint-Hyacinthe, QC (1852): François Lapierre, P.M.E., bishop, 1998.

Bishop's Residence: 1900, rue Girouard Ouest, C.P. 190, Saint-Hyacinthe, QC J2S 7B4; (450) 773-8581; www.diocese-st-hyacinthe.qc.ca. Cathedral: St. Hyacinthe the Confessor.

Saint-Jean-Longueuil, QC (1933 as St.-Jean-de-Québec; named changed, 1982): Jacques Berthelet, C.S.V., bishop, 1996. Louis Dicaire, auxiliary.

Bishop's Residence: 740, boulevard Sainte-Foy, C.P. 40, Longueuil, QC J4K 4X8; (450) 679-1100; www.diocese-st-jean-longueuil.org. Cathedral: St. John the Evangelist.

St. Jérôme, QC (1951): Pierre Morissette, bishop, 2008; Donald Lapointe, auxiliary.

Bishop's Residence: 355, Place du Curé Labelle, Saint-Jerome, QC J7Z 5A9; (450) 432-9742; www.diocese-stjerome.qc.ca. Cathedral: St. Jerome.

Saint John, NB (1842): Robert Harris, bishop, 2007.

Chancery Office: 1 Bayard Dr., Saint John, NB E2L 3L5; (506) 653-6800; www.dioceseofsaintjohn.org. Cathedral: Immaculate Conception.

St. John's,* NL (p.a., 1784; v.a., 1796; diocese, 1847; archdiocese, 1904): Martin W. Currie, archbishop, 2007.

Chancery Office: P.O. Box 37, St. John's, NL. A1C 5N5; (709) 726-3660; www.stjohnsarchdiocese.nf.ca. Cathedral: St. John the Baptist.

St. Paul in AB (1948): Joseph Luc André Bouchard, bishop, 2001.

Bishop's Residence: 4410, 51e avenue, Saint Paul, AB T0A 3A2; (780) 645-3277. Cathedral: St. Paul.

Sainte-Anne-de-la-Pocatière, QC (1951): Clément Fecteau, bishop, 1996.

Bishop's Residence: 1200, 4e avenue, C.P. 430, La Pocatière, QC G0R 1Z0; (418) 856-1811. Cathedral: St. Anne.

Saskatoon, SK (1933): Albert LeGatt, bishop, 2001.

Chancery Office: 100-5th Ave. North, Saskatoon, SK S7K 2N7; (306) 242-1500; www.saskatoonrcdiocese. com. Cathedral: St. Paul.

Saskatoon, SK (Ukrainian Byzantine) (ap. ex., 1951; diocese, 1956): P. Bryan Bayda, C.SS.R, 2008.

Address: 866 Saskatchewan Crescent East, Saskatoon, SK S7N 0L4; (306) 653-0138.

Sault Ste. Marie, ON (1904): Jean-Louis Plouffe, bishop, 1990; Brian Joseph Dunn, Noël Simard, auxiliaries.

Chancery Office: 30, chemin Ste. Anne, Sudbury, ON P3C 5E1, (705) 674-2727; www.isys.ca/cathcom.htm. Cathedral: Pro-Cathedral of the Assumption, North Bay.

Sherbrooke,* QC (1874; archdiocese, 1951); André Gaumond, archbishop, 1996.

Archbishop's Residence: 130, rue de la Cathédrale, C.P. 430, Sherbrooke, QC J1H 5K1; (819) 563-9934; www.diosher.org. Cathedral: St. Michel.

Thunder Bay, ON (Ft. William, 1952; transferred, 1970): Frederick J. Colli, bishop, 1999.

Bishop's Office: 1222 Reaume St., P.O. Box 10400, Thunder Bay, ON P7B 6T8; (807) 343-9313;

www.dotb.ca. Cathedral: St. Patrick.
Timmins, ON (v.a. Temiskaming, 1908; diocese Haileybury, 1915; present title, 1938): Paul Marchand, S.M.M., bishop, 1999.
Address: 65, Ave. Jubilee Est, Timmins, ON P4N 5W4; www.nt.net/~dioctims/. Cathedral: St. Anthony of Padua.
Toronto,* **ON** (1841; archdiocese, 1870): Thomas C. Collins, archbishop, 2006. John A. Boissonneau, Richard Grecco, Peter Joseph Hundt, auxiliaries.
Chancery Office: Catholic Pastoral Centre, 1155 Yonge St., Toronto, ON M4T 1W2; (416) 934-0606; www.archtoronto.org. Cathedral: St. Michael.
Toronto, ON (Eparchy for Slovakian Byzantine) (1980): John Pazak, C.Ss.R., 2000.
Eparch's Residence: 223 Carlton Rd., Unionville, ON L3R 3M2; (905) 477-4867.
Toronto, ON (Eparchy for Ukrainian Byzantine) (ap. ex., 1948; eparchy, 1956): Stephen Victor Chmilar eparch, 2003.
Chancery Office: 3100-A Weston Rd., Weston, ON M9M 2S7; (416) 746-0154; www.ucet.ca. Cathedral: St. Josaphat.
Trois-Rivières, QC (1852): Martin Veillette, bishop, 1996.
Bishop's Residence: 362, rue Bonaventure, C.P. 879, Trois-Rivières, QC G9A 5J9; (819) 374-9847; www.diocese-tr.qc.ca/. Cathedral: The Assumption.
Valleyfield, QC (1892): Luc Cyr, bishop, 2001.
Bishop's Residence: 11, rue de l'Eglise, Salaberry-de-Valleyfield, QC J6T 1J5; (450) 373-8122; www.rocler.qc.ca/diocese-valleyfield/. Cathedral: St. Cecilia.
Vancouver,* **BC** (v.a. British Columbia, 1863; diocese New Westminster, 1890; archdiocese Vancouver, 1908): Raymond Roussin, S.M., archbishop, 2004; J. Michael Miller, C.S.B., coadjutor, 2007.
Chancery Office: 150 Robson St., Vancouver, BC V6B 2A7; (604) 683-0281; www.rcav.bc.ca. Cathedral: Holy Rosary.
Victoria, BC (diocese Vancouver Is., 1846; archdiocese, 1903; diocese Victoria, 1908): Richard Gagnon, 2004.
Chancery Office: Diocesan Pastoral Centre, #1-4044 Nelthorpe St., Victoria, BC V8X 2A1; (250) 479-1331; www.rcdvictoria.org. Cathedral: St. Andrew.
Whitehorse, YT (v.a., 1944; diocese 1967): Gary Gordon, bishop, 2006.
Chancery Office: 5119 5th Ave., Whitehorse, YT Y1A 1L5; (867) 667-2052. Cathedral: Sacred Heart.
Winnipeg,* **MB** (1915): V. James Weisgerber, archbishop, 2000.
Chancery Office: Catholic Centre, 1495 Pembina Highway, Winnipeg, MB R3T 2C6; (204) 452-2227; www.archwinnipeg.ca. Cathedral: St. Mary.
Winnipeg,* **MB** (Ukrainian Byzantine) (Ordinariate of Canada, 1912; ap. ex. Central Canada, 1948; ap. ex.

Manitoba, 1951; archeparchy Winnipeg, 1956): Lawrence Huculak, O.S.B.M., archeparch, 1993; David Motiuk, auxiliary.
Archeparchy Office: 233 Scotia St., Winnipeg, MB R2V 1V7; (204) 338-7801; www.archeparchy.ca. Cathedral: Sts. Vladimir and Olga.
Yarmouth, NS (1953): Vacant; Abp. Anthony Mancini, administrator.
Address: C.P. 278, Yarmouth, NS B5A 4B2; (902) 742-7163; www.dioceseyarmouth.org Cathedral: St. Ambrose.
Military Ordinariate of Canada (1951): Donald J. Thériault, bishop, 1998.
Address: Canadian Forces Support Unit (Ottawa), Uplands Site – Bldg. 469, Ottawa, ON K1A 0K2; (613) 990-7824.
An **Apostolic Exarchate for Armenian-Rite Catholics in Canada and the United States** was established in July 1981 with headquarters in New York City (110 E. 12th St., New York, NY 10003); (212) 477-2030. Manuel Batakian, exarch, 1995.
The Eparchy of Our Lady of Deliverance of Newark for Syrian-rite Catholics in the United States and Canada was established Nov. 6, 1995. Address: 502 Palisade Ave., Union City, NJ 08087-5213; (201) 583-1067; www.Syriac-Catholic.org. Joseph Younan, bishop.
Hungarian Emigrants throughout the world, resides in Canada: Most Rev. Attila Mikloshazy, S.J., titular bishop of Cast`el Minore. Address: 2661 Kingston Rd., Scarborough, ON M1M 1M3; (416) 261-7207.
Note: The diocese of **Gravelbourg**, in Saskatchewan, was dissolved in September 1998 as part of a reorganization of Canadian dioceses. The regions under the jurisdiction of **Gravelbourg** were integrated into the neighboring dioceses of **Regina** and **Saskatoon**. The **Territorial Abbacy of St. Peter,** Muenster, SK, was also dissolved.

Dioceses with Interprovincial Lines

The following dioceses, indicated by + in the table, have interprovincial lines.
Churchill–Hudson Bay includes part of Northwest Territories.
Keewatin–LePas includes part of Manitoba and Saskatchewan provinces.
Corner Brook and Labrador City includes the Labrador region of Newfoundland and the northern part of Québec province.
Mackenzie–Fort Smith, Northwest Territories, includes part of Alberta and Saskatchewan provinces.
Moosonee, Ontario, includes part of Québec province.
Pembroke, Ontario, includes one county of Québec province. **Whitehorse**, Yukon Territory, includes part of British Columbia.

CANADIAN CONFERENCE OF CATHOLIC BISHOPS

The Canadian Conference of Catholic Bishops was established Oct. 12, 1943, as a permanent voluntary association of the bishops of Canada, was given official approval by the Holy See in 1948, and acquired the status of an episcopal conference after the Second Vatican Council.

The CCCB acts in two ways: (1) as a strictly ecclesiastical body through which the bishops act together with pastoral authority and responsibility for the Church throughout the country; (2) as an operational secretariat through which the bishops act on a wider scale for the good of the Church and society.

At the top of the CCCB organizational table are the president, an executive committee, a permanent council and a plenary assembly. The membership consists of all the bishops of Canada.

Departments and Offices

The CCCB's work is planned and coordinated by the Programmes and Priorities Committee composed of the six chairmen of the national episcopal commissions and the two general secretaries. It is chaired by the vice-president of the CCCB.

The CCCB's 12 episcopal commissions undertake study and projects in special areas of pastoral work. Six serve nationally (social affairs; canon law/inter–rite; relations with associations of clergy, consecrated life and laity; evangelization of peoples; ecumenism; theology); three relate to French sectors (*communications sociale, éducation Chrétienne, liturgie*); and three relate to corresponding English sectors (social communications, Christian education, liturgy).

The general secretariat consists of a general secretary and assistants and directors of public relations. The current general secretary is Msgr. Mario Paquette, P.H.

Administrative services for purchasing, archives and library, accounting, personnel, publications, printing and distribution are supervised by directors who relate to the general secretaries.

Various advisory councils and committees with mixed memberships of lay persons, religious, priests and bishops also serve the CCCB on a variety of topics.

Operations

Meetings for the transaction of business are held at least once a year by the plenary assembly, six times a year by the executive committee, and four times a year by the permanent council.

Archbishop V. James Weisgerber of Winnipeg is president of the CCCB and Bishop Pierre Morissette of St. Jérôme, is vice president, for the 2007-2009 term.

The Conference headquarters is located at 2500 Don Reid Dr., Ottawa K1N 2J2, Canada; (613) 241-9461; www.cccb.ca.

CANADIAN SHRINES

Our Lady of the Cape (Cap de la Madeleine), Queen of the Most Holy Rosary: The Three Rivers, Québec, parish church, built in 1714 and considered the oldest stone church on the North American continent preserved in its original state, was rededicated June 22, 1888, as a shrine of the Queen of the Most Holy Rosary. The site increased in importance as a pilgrimage and devotional center, and in 1904 St. Pius X decreed the crowning of a statue of the Blessed Virgin which had been donated 50 years earlier to commemorate the dogma of the Immaculate Conception. In 1909, the First Plenary Council of Québec declared the church a shrine of national pilgrimage. In 1964, the church at the shrine was given the status and title of minor basilica.

St. Anne de Beaupre: The devotional history of this shrine in Québec began with the reported cure of a cripple, Louis Guimont, on Mar. 16, 1658, the starting date of construction work on a small chapel of St. Anne. The original building was successively enlarged and replaced by a stone church, which was given the rank of minor basilica in 1888. The present structure, a Romanesque–Gothic basilica, houses the shrine proper in its north transept, including an eight–foot–high oaken statue and a relic of St. Anne, a portion of her forearm.

St. Joseph's Oratory: The massive oratory basilica standing on the western side of Mount Royal and overlooking the city of Montréal had its origin in a primitive chapel erected there by Blessed André Bessette, C.S.C., in 1904. Eleven years later, a large crypt was built to accommodate an increasing number of pilgrims, and in 1924 construction work was begun on the large church. A belfry, housing a 60–bell carillon and standing on the site of the original chapel, was dedicated May 15, 1955, as the first major event of the jubilee year observed after the oratory was given the rank of minor basilica.

Martyrs' Shrine: A shrine commemorating several of the Jesuit Martyrs of North America who were killed between 1642 and 1649 in the Ontario and northern New York area is located on the former site of old Fort Sainte Marie. Before its location was fixed near Midland, ON, in 1925, a small chapel had been erected in 1907 at old Mission St. Ignace to mark the martyrdom of Fathers Jean de Brebeuf and Gabriel Lalemant. This sanctuary has a U.S. counterpart in the Shrine of the North American Martyrs near Auriesville, NY, under the care of the Jesuits.

Others

In Québec City: Basilica of Notre Dame (1650), once the cathedral of a diocese stretching from Canada to Mexico; Notre Dame des Victoires (1690); the Ursuline Convent (1720), on du Parloir St.

Near Montréal: Hermitage of St. Anthony, La Bouchette; Ste. Anne de Micmacs, Restigouche; Chapel of Atonement, Pointe aux Trembles; Our Lady of Lourdes, Rigaud; St. Benoît du Lac, near Magog.

In Montréal: Notre Dame Basilica (1829).

Near Montréal: Chapel of St. Marie Marguerite d'Youville, foundress of the Grey Nuns; Notre Dame de Lourdes, at Rigaud.

STATISTICAL SUMMARY OF THE CATHOLIC CHURCH IN CANADA

(Principal source: 2008 Directory of the Canadian Conference of Catholic Bishops; *figures as of Jan. 2008.)* Catholic population statistics are those reported in the 2001 Canadian Census. Archdioceses are indicated by an asterisk. For dioceses marked +, see Canadian Dioceses with Interprovincial Lines.

Canada's 10 civil provinces and two territories are divided into 18 ecclesiastical provinces consisting of 18 metropolitan sees (archdioceses) and 45 suffragan sees; there are also eight Oriental Rite dioceses, one archdiocese and three eparchies immediately subject to the Holy See, and the Military Ordinariate.

This table presents a regional breakdown of Catholic statistics. In some cases, the totals are approximate because diocesan boundaries fall within several civil provinces.

Civil Province Diocese	Cath. Pop.	Dioc. Priests	Rel. Priests	Total Priests	Perm. Deacs.	Bro-thers	Sis-ters	Lay Assts.	Par-ishes[1]
Newfoundland	191,885	127	18	135	–	7	271	17	263
St. John's*	111,605	40	12	52	–	7	193	1	72
Corner Brook Lab.+	32,060	27	6	28	–	–	28	6	64
Grand Falls	35,850	34	–	34	–	–	25	5	72
St. George's	32,060	26	–	26	–	–	25	5	55
Prince Edward Island									
Charlottetown	63,240	50	1	51	1	–	121	9	58
Nova Scotia	327,945	206	17	223	34	–	530	43	222
Halifax*	161,115	63	12	75	29	–	230	24	68
Antigonish	129,730	118	2	120	1	–	285	15	119
Yarmouth	37,100	25	3	28	4	–	15	4	35
New Brunswick	385,985	186	39	225	3	19	683	124	245
Moncton*	110,895	44	21	65	1	14	291	84	60
Bathurst	107,655	51	7	58	–	5	178	8	62
Edmundston	52,035	27	8	35	–	–	94	12	32
St. John	115,400	64	3	67	2	–	120	20	91
Québec	5,922,385	2,374	1,496	3,870	411	1,284	12,494	942	1,545
Gatineau*	234,725	54	27	81	–	11	175	29	58
Montréal*	1,499,425	495	607	1,102	102	275	4,082	133	237
Québec*	917,045	440	298	738	91	322	3,321	88	223
Rimouski*	143,640	106	10	116	13	28	628	21	105
Sherbrooke*	245,495	186	100	286	20	90	932	54	102
Amos	95,030	19	16	35	–	7	87	0	66
Baie Comeau	86,800	41	11	52	8	2	51	18	49
Chicoutimi	263,950	160	35	195	42	27	505	61	69
Gaspé	85,840	52	5	57	3	3	150	10	65
Joliette	201,735	72	47	119	5	83	198	41	55
Mont Laurier	77,340	30	6	36	–	6	56	19	23
Montréal, St. Maron (Maronites)	4,100	10	7	17	1	–	5	–	14
Montréal, St. Sauveur (Greek-Melkites)	9,200	6	6	12	–	–	–	–	8
Nicolet	184,625	133	22	155	25	91	377	52	78
Rouyn-Noranda	56,380	22	9	31	–	1	83	25	40
Ste-Anne-de-la-Pocatière	87,700	95	–	95	7	–	154	16	58
St.-Hyacinthe	336,445	123	81	204	29	150	625	84	96
St.-Jean-Longueuil	553,470	88	37	125	2	88	340	116	51
St. Jérôme	407,065	75	81	156	18	20	150	79	39
Trois Rivières	232,985	101	81	182	30	63	499	54	67
Valleyfield	199,390	66	10	76	15	17	76	42	42
Ontario	3,575,065	1,394	843	2,237	444	77	2,644	261	1,194
Kingston*	116,845	79	10	89	18	–	183	–	71
Ottawa*	392,635	124	102	226	74	35	701	18	109
Toronto*	1,626,465	380	468	848	112	2	624	61	227
Alexandria-Cornwall	55,570	32	7	39	17	4	26	–	29
Hamilton	559,290	134	90	224	23	10	267	50	150

Civil Province Diocese	Cath. Pop.	Dioc. Priests	Rel. Priests	Total Priests	Perm. Deacs.	Bro- thers	Sis- ters	Lay Assts.	Par- ishes[1]
Ontario, cont.									
Hearst	31,790	31	–	31	3	–	7	15	28
London	444,310	178	65	243	19	6	353	89	136
Moosonee+	3,830	1	3	4	1	1	–	4	18
Pembroke+	67,870	53	2	55	8	4	127	7	57
Peterborough	99,785	95	8	103	11	–	73	1	66
St. Catharine's	153,565	52	34	86	3	4	40	7	46
Sault Ste. Marie	206,405	97	26	123	101	4	190	2	106
Thunder Bay	73,780	26	17	43	28	–	13	–	42
Timmins	50,605	18	2	20	7	5	13	6	26
Toronto (Ukr.)	42,330	89	9	98	19	2	27	1	76
Toronto (Slovaks)	5,000	5	0	5	–	–	–	–	7
Manitoba	346,180	177	96	273	56	15	414	10	372
Keewatin-Le Pas*+	37,380	5	11	16	–	–	8	–	48
St. Boniface*	113,495	80	48	128	24	14	262	9	102
Winnipeg*	158,095	63	25	88	18	1	120	1	92
Winnepeg (Ukrainians)*	29,760	29	12	41	14	–	24	–	130
Churchill-Hud. Bay+	6,115	2	6	8	–	–	1	5	17
Saskatchewan+	301,335	184	82	266	5	20	382	21	438
Regina*#	126,980	94	18	112	1	5	105	4	167
Prince-Albert	55,450	21	8	29	–	1	90	9	87
Saskatoon#	86,645	48	48	96	1	13	170	8	97
Saskatoon (Ukrainians)	17,550	21	8	29	3	1	17	–	87
Alberta	665,870	214	165	379	45	34	508	46	429
Edmonton*	333,545	73	84	157	3	19	329	34	131
Grouard-McLellan*	44,470	8	17	25	2	–	21	4	64
Calgary	320,425	95	42	137	33	11	114	–	85
Edmonton (Ukrainians)	28,845	25	13	38	4	4	26	3	87
St. Paul	56,655	13	9	22	3	–	18	5	62
British Columbia	600,175	189	129	318	5	28	283	4	311
Vancouver*	402,310	89	97	186	1	17	157	–	89
Kamloops	51,435	15	6	21	–	3	13	–	75
Nelson	67,025	30	4	34	–	–	18	–	53
New Westminster (Ukrainians)	7,780	12	2	14	2	–	2	–	15
Prince George	49,500	13	6	19	1	4	20	4	38
Victoria	94,465	30	14	44	1	4	73	–	41
Yukon Territory									
Whitehorse+	8,150	4	6	10	–	–	7	8	20
Northwest Territories									
MacKenzie-Ft. Smith+	20,110	5	3	8	3	1	14	16	40
Military Ordinariate	43,007	42*	2**	44	2	–	–	37	23**
TOTALS	12,986,805[2]	5,133	2,903	8,036	1,009	1,485	18,324	1,530	5,122

[1] Denotes both parishes and missions.
[2] Catholics comprise about 43 percent of the total population. According to the 2006 Annuarium Statisticum *Ecclesiae* (the most recent edition), there were 113,003 baptisms and 25,363 marriages.
* The Canadian Military Ordinariate does not incardinate clerics.
** Not included in the total.

The Catholic Church in Mexico

BACKGROUND

Start of Church Organization

The history of the Catholic Church in Mexico began in 1519 with the capture of Mexico's native civilization, the Aztec Empire, by the Spanish *conquistadores* under Hernándo Cortés. The Spanish army besieged the Aztec capital of Tenochtitlan, massacred most of the inhabitants, strangled the Aztec emperor Montezuma, and crushed the rest of the empire. Mexico City became the chief city of New Spain and the cultural and religious center of colonial Mexico; it was declared a diocese in 1530.

The record of Colonial Spanish treatment of the native peoples of Mexico is a grim one. The Indians suffered exploitation, slavery, and rapid depletion of their population from disease; they were forced to labor in inhuman conditions in mines and endured servitude in the *encomienda* system.

In sharp contrast to the treatment of the natives by the government was the effort to evangelize Mexico by the religious orders, who followed the command of Pope Alexander VI in the 1494 Treaty of Tordesillas to convert all peoples who would be encountered in the coming age of exploration. A papal bull, dated Apr. 25, 1521, gave the Franciscans the permission of the Holy See to preach in New Spain. They were joined by the Dominicans and, later, by the Jesuits. The missionary orders soon distinguished themselves by their resistance to the brutal enslavement of the Indians, their mastery of native languages, and their willingness to endure enormous hardships in bringing the faith to the distant corners of Mexico.

As the Church became more established, however, the missionary priests and friars came increasingly into conflict with the secular clergy, who desired full control over ecclesiastical affairs, resented the extensive powers of religious orders, and normally identified closely with the interests of the crown. The government thus decreed that the missionaries were to have 10 years in which to convert the Indians, after which control would pass to the diocesan clergy. This was protested by the missionary orders, and the conflict was resolved in favor of the diocesan priests in 1640 thanks to the efforts of Bp. Juan de Palafox de Mendoza of Puebla.

The alliance of the secular clergy with the government was a reflection of the control enjoyed by the Spanish Crown over the Church in Mexico. The Holy See had granted to the kings of Spain royal patronage over the Church in Mexico, and the practice of the *Patronato Real* meant that the king nominated all

Church officials in New Spain and held authority over the Church's temporal concerns. A major element in this policy was the forced conversion of the local peoples. Coerced into adopting the faith, many Indians were insincere or hesitant to embrace the faith. To insure the full embrace of the faith, Spanish authorities received permission from King Philip II in 1569 to introduce the Inquisition to Mexico. Indians who had survived the mines, diseases, and brutality of the colonial rulers were now subjected to tribunals to test their faith. This practice was eventually ended when authorities decided that the natives were not culpable because of limited intelligence. Nevertheless, the close identification of the diocesan clergy with the interests and policies of the Spanish crown created a hostility toward the Church in Mexico by the lower classes that endures today.

On the positive side, the Church did much through its missionaries to save many Indians from death and enslavement and to preserve vital portions of Mesoamerican culture, art, and history. Friars also traveled to northern Mexico and beyond, bringing the faith into California, Texas, and New Mexico.

The native peoples were given a profound encouragement to embrace the Catholic faith in 1531 by the appearance of Our Lady of Guadalupe to the farmer Juan Diego (beatified in 1990 by Pope John Paul II) on the Tepeyac hill just outside of Mexico City. The shrine built in her honor remains the most important religious site in Mexico. Enshrined within it is the mantle brought by Juan Diego to Bishop Zumaragga to convince him of the genuine nature of the apparition. Miraculously emblazoned upon it is the life-size image of the Virgin Mary.

Mexican Independence

The Spanish domination of Mexico endured for nearly three centuries, deteriorating gradually throughout the 1700s as the gulf widened between the Spanish ruling class and the native classes that were joined by the *mestizos* and *creoles* (descendants of Native Americans and Europeans). Unrest broke out into a full-scale rebellion in 1810 with the uprising of many priests led by Fr. Miguel Hidalgo y Costilla and, after his execution, by Fr. José Maria Morelos y Pavón. While suppressed in 1816 by the colonial regime with the support of the upper classes and most of the diocesan clergy, it proved only the first of several revolts, culminating in the 1821 declaration of Mexican independence. By the terms of the independence, the

Church received a special status and had enormous sway in political life.

A republic was proclaimed in 1834 and various liberal regimes came to power. Anticlericalism became commonplace, made even more strident by the lingering hostility over the Church's activities with Spanish colonial government. Much influenced by the ideals of the European revolutions then taking place, the Mexican republican movements were strongly anti-Catholic. For more than a decade, power was in the hands of Antonio López de Santa Anna (also known for his victory at the Alamo) and Valentin Gómez Farías. After the Mexican-American War (1846-1848), the political instability led to the dictatorship of Santa Anna.

Santa Anna was toppled in 1855 by a liberal regime whose anti-Church legislation sparked an armed struggle called the War of the Reform (1858-1861). The laws issued by the government included the *Ley Juárez*, abolishing all ecclesiastical courts, and the *Ley Lerdo*, forcing the Church to sell all of its lands. Deprived of its properties, the Church lost control of education and schools, and Mexico's educational system became often bitterly anti-Catholic.

While the liberal forces won the War of the Reform, the conflict had so debilitated Mexico that the French were able to intervene in 1861 and install their puppet, the Austrian duke Maximilian, on the Mexican throne. As the United States was embroiled in its own civil war from 1861-1865, it was unable to respond to French imperialist ambitions in Mexico. Maximilian initially enjoyed the support of the conservative elements and the Church, but his liberal reforms alienated the mistrustful conservatives and he soon clung to power only with French support. When France finally withdrew its troops in 1867, Maximilian was deposed by republican forces and executed.

Modern Mexico

The fall of Emperor Maximilian signaled a restoration of the anticlerical constitution of 1857 and the elevation of Benito Juárez—the republican leader long recognized by the United States—as president. His successor, Sebastián Lerdo de Tijada, was toppled in 1876 by Porfirio Diáz, who remained dictator for thirty-four years. A civil war ended his regime, and more bloodshed ensued. Finally, a constitution was issued in 1917 that placed severe restrictions on the Church: there could be no criticism of the government, only Mexicans could be clergy, the Church was not permitted to own property, and any privileges were stripped away.

The situation became worse after 1923, when the papal legate was expelled. The administration of Plutarco Calles (1924-1928) launched a wave of persecution that sparked a popular but ultimately unsuccessful uprising called the Cristero Rebellion. Coupled with the repressive measures of local governments, the Calles regime and its successors forced the Church into very difficult circumstances, with only a few priests remaining in the country. The tragedy was deepened by the execution of dozens of priests and nuns by republican forces for assorted and imaginary crimes or for speaking out on behalf of the poor or oppressed Catholics. A number of the executed clergy have been beatified and canonized since the tragedy,

most so during the pontificate of Pope John Paul II. The persecution prompted Pope Pius XI to issue the encyclicals *Iniquis afflictisque* (1926) and *Acerba animi* (1932).

An easing of the situation began in 1940 as the rigid anticlerical laws ceased to be enforced with enthusiasm. A rapprochement was visible in the 1958 elections, when the Church received conciliatory gestures from the ruling Revolutionary Party and its presidential candidate Adolfo López Mateos. The Church continued to exist under numerous legal disabilities and was oppressed in a number of the Mexican states.

Gradual improvement in relations between Mexico and the Holy See led to the exchange in 1990 of personal representatives between the Mexican president and Pope John Paul II. The Holy Father's efforts to build a further diplomatic bridge culminated in the establishment of full diplomatic ties in 1992. This was followed by the final easing of many of the handicaps under which the Church had long suffered.

The faith of the Mexican people is profoundly deep, as was seen in the nearly frenzied greeting given to Pope John Paul II in 1979, 1990, 1993, and 1999. However, social unrest, poverty, economic challenges, the violence of drug cartels, and corruption still plague the country. Church leaders—especially religious orders—have been outspoken in their criticism of government human rights abuses and corruption. During the mid-1990s, the Jesuits said they were the target of a "campaign of intimidation" because of their human rights work.

On May 24, 1993, Card. Juan Jesus Posadas Ocampo of Guadalajara was killed during a supposed shoot-out among rival drug cartels. The murder remained unsolved, although Cardinal Posadas' successor, Card. Juan Sandoval Íñiguez, continued to claim that high-ranking officials, including the Mexican attorney general at the time, lied to protect others involved in a plot. In 2001 Card. Sandoval said he would seek a reopening of the case because he had new evidence contradicting the findings of the official investigation; he also claimed he had been almost fatally poisoned in 1999 during a dinner with federal officials angry with his insistence that the murder was not accidental.

In the 1970s and 1980s, one of Mexico's most prominent proponents of liberation theology was Bp. Samuel Ruiz Garcia of San Cristobal de las Casas. In the early 1990s the Vatican began investigating his views, but because he had the trust of indigenous peasants, in 1994 he was thrown into the role of mediator between the government and the mostly native Zapatista National Liberation Army in Chiapas. He continued that role until 1998, when he resigned after accusing the government of "dismantling any possible means or effort to solve the crisis in Chiapas." Mexico's bishops said at that time that they would provide support to the peace process but would not seek to mediate the conflict.

On July 2, 2000, Vicente Fox Quesada, head of the National Action Party and a practicing Catholic, won the Mexican presidential election, marking the first time since 1929 that the country was not ruled by the Institutional Revolutionary Party. Mexico City Cardinal Norberto Rivera Carrera told reporters the election was "not a miracle, as some have suggested, but it is an extraordinary act." Church officials emphasized that they expected no special privileges from the new government, but the general climate was one of optimism for an improvement in church-state relations.

Within weeks, Fox—with news cameras flashing—received Communion in his hometown parish.

However, in July 2001, the Vatican said he failed to have his first marriage annulled before marrying his spokeswoman in a civil ceremony; thus, he would be prohibited from receiving the sacraments. In June 2001, federal and state officials participated in a public Mass at the Basilica of Our Lady of Guadalupe, breaking a taboo on government officials publicly practicing their religion.

On July 31, 2002, during his fifth pastoral visit to Mexico, Pope John Paul II proclaimed Juan Diego a saint. The pope declared at the canonization: "'The Guadalupe Event,' as the Mexican Episcopate has pointed out, 'meant the beginning of evangelization with a vitality that surpassed all expectations. Christ's message, through his Mother, took up the central elements of the indigenous culture, purified them and gave them the definitive sense of salvation.'"

ORGANIZATION

Presently, the Church in Mexico is organized into 18 provinces. There are 18 archdioceses (including the promotion of Tijuana, León, Tuxtla Gutierrez, and Tulancingo as metropolitan sees), 65 dioceses, five prelacies, and two eparchs, for the Greek Melkites and Maronites. In 2006, four new ecclesiastical provinces were established (Baja [Tijuana], Bajia [León], Hidalgo [Tulancingo], and Chiapas [Tuxtla Gutierrez]) as part of the reorganization of Mexico's ecclesiastical structure. As of Aug. 15, 2008, there were four Mexican members of the College of Cardinals: Norberto Rivera Carrera, Juan Sandoval Íñiguez, Javier Lozano Barragán, and Francisco Robles Ortega. (For statistical information on the Church in Mexico, see below.)

The current apostolic delegation to Mexico was set up in 1992 as a nunciature with the establishment of renewed formal diplomatic relations with the Vatican. The present Apostolic Nuncio is Archbishop Christophe Pierre, J.C.D., who was appointed in 2007.

ECCLESIASTICAL JURISDICTIONS OF MEXICO

Provinces

Names of ecclesiastical provinces and metropolitan sees in bold face: suffragan sees in parentheses. The current listing reflects the restructuring of Mexico's provinces in 2006.

Acapulco (Chilpancingo-Chilapa, Ciudad Altamirano, Tlapa).

Antequera, Oaxaca (Puerto Escondido, Tehuantepec, Tuxtepec; Prelacies of Mixes and Huautla).

Chihuahua (Ciudad Juárez, Cuauhtémoc-Madera, Nuevos Casas Grandes, Parral, Tarahumara).

Durango (Mazatlán, Torreón, El Salto,).

Guadalajara (Aguascalientes, Autlán, Ciudad Guzmán, Colima, San Juan de los Lagos, Tepic; Prelature of Jesús Maria del Nayar).

Hermosillo (Ciudad Obregón, Culiacán).

León (Celaya, Irapuato, Querétaro).

México (Atlacomulco, Cuernavaca, Toluca).

Monterrey (Ciudad Victoria, Linares, Matamoros, Nuevo Laredo, Piedras Negras, Saltillo, Tampico).

Morelia (Apatzingán, Ciudad Lázaro Cárdenas, Tacámbaro, Zamora).

Puebla de los Angeles (Huajuapan de León, Tehuacán, Tlaxcala).

San Luis Potosi (Matehuala, Ciudad Valles, Zacatecas).

Tijuana (La Paz, Mexicali, Ensenada).

Tlalnepantla (Texcoco, Cuautitlán, Netzahualcóyotl, Ecatepec, Valle de Chalco).

Tulancingo (Huejutla and Tula).

Tuxtla Gutierrez (San Cristóbal de las Casas and Tapachula).

Xalapa (Papantla, San Andrés Tuxtla, Coatzacoalcos, Tuxpan, Veracruz, Orizaba, Córdoba).

Yucatán (Campeche, Tabasco, Prelacy of Cancún-Chetumal; Eparchy of Nuestra Señora del Paraiso).

Jurisdictions, Hierarchy

(Principal sources: Information office, Mexican Conference of Catholic Bishops; *Catholic Almanac* survey; *Annuario Pontificio*; *L'Osservatore Romano*; Catholic News Service. As of July 1, 2008. Addresses and phone numbers are provided by the *Annuario Pontificio*.)

Information includes names of archdioceses (indicated by asterisk) and dioceses, date of foundation, present ordinaries and auxiliaries; addresses of chancery office/bishop's residence.

Acapulco* (1958; promoted to archdiocese, 1983): Felipe Aguirre Franco, archbishop, 2001; Juan Navarro Castellanos, auxiliary.

Diocesan Address: Apartado Postal 201, Quebrada 16, 39850 Acapulco, Guerrero; (748) 2-07-63.

Aguascalientes (1899): José María De la Torre Martín, bishop, 2008.

Diocesan Address: Apartado 167, Galeana 105 Norte, 20000 Aguascalientes, Aguascalientes; (449) 9-15-32-61.

Apatzingán (1962): Miguel Patiño Velázquez, M.S.F., bishop, 1981.

Diocesan Address: Calle Esteban Vaca Calderón 100, 60600 Apatzingán, Mich.; (453) 5-34-17-87.

Atlacomulco (1984): Constancio Miranda Weckmann, bishop, 1998.

Diocesan Address: Hidalgo Sur 1, Apartado 22, 50450 Atlacomulco, Méx.; (712) 1-22-05-53.

Autlán (1961): Gonzalo Galván Castillo, bishop, 2004.

Diocesan Address: Apartado 8, Hidalgo 74, 48900 Autlán, Jal., Mex.; (317) 3-82-12-28.

Campeche (1895): Ramón Castro Castro, bishop, 2006.

Diocesan Address: Calle 53 # 1-B Entre 8 y 10 Centro Apdo. Postal # 12724000 - Campeche, Camp.; (981) 8-16-25-24.

Cancún-Chetumal, Prelacy of (1970, as Chetumal; name changed in 1996): Pedro Pablo Elizondo Cárdenas, L.C., bishop, 2004.

Diocesan Address: Apartado Postal 165, Othón P. Blanco 150, 77000 Chetumal, Quintana Roo; (983) 2-06-38.

Celaya (1973): Jesús Humberto Velázquez Garay,

bishop, 1988.

Diocesan Address: Curia Diocesana, Apartado 207, Manuel Doblado 110, 38000 Celaya, Gto.; (461) 6-12-48-35.

Chihuahua* (1891; promoted to archdiocese, 1958): José Fernández Arteaga, archbishop, 1991.

Diocesan Address: Av. Cuauhtémoc # 1828 Col. Cuauhtémoc, Apartado Postal 7, 31000 Chihuahua, Chihuahua; (614) 4-10-32-02.

Chilpancingo-Chilapa (1863 as Chilpancingo; name changed to Chilpancingo-Chilapa, 1989): Alejo Zavala Castro, bishop, 2005.

Diocesan Address: Abasolo e Hidalgo, Apartado Postal #185, 39000 Chilpancingo, Gro.; (747) 4-71-05-92.

Ciudad Altamirano (1964): Maximino Martínez Miranda, bishop, 2006.

Diocesan Address: Juárez 18 Oriente, Centro, Apdo 17, 40680 Ciudad Altamirano, Gro.; (767) 6-72-17-74.

Ciudad Guzmán (1972): Braulio Rafael León Villegas, bishop, 1999.

Diocesan Address: Ramón Corona 26, Apartado 86, 49000 Ciudad Guzman, Jal.; (341) 4-12-19-94.

Ciudad Juárez (1957): Renato Ascencio León, bishop, 1994; José Guadalupe Torres Campos, auxiliary.

Diocesan Address: Apartado Postal 188, 32000 Cuidad Juárez, Chih.; (16) 15-09-22.

Ciudad Lázaro Cárdenas (1985): Fabio Martínez Castilla, bishop, 2007.

Diocesan Address: Apartado 500, Andador Ciudad del Carmen #4, Fideicomiso 2° Sector, 60950 Lázaro Cardenas, Mich.; (753) 5-41-64-07.

Ciudad Obregón (1959): Juan Manuel Mancilla Sanchez, bishop, 2005.

Diocesan Address: Apartado 402, Sonora 161 Norte, 85000 Ciudad Obregón, Son.; (644) 4-13-20-98.

Ciudad Valles (1960): Roberto Octavio Balmori Cinta, M.J., bishop, 2002.

Diocesan Address: 16 de Septiembre 726, Apartado 170, 79000 Ciudad Valles, S.L.P.; (138) 2-25-97

Ciudad Victoria (1964): Antonio González Sánchez, bishop, 1995.

Diocesan Address: 15 Hidalgo y Juárez, Centro, Apartado Postal #335, 87000 Ciudad Victoria, Tamps.; (834) 3-12-87-16.

Coatzacoalcos (1984): Rutilo Muñoz Zamora, bishop, 2002.

Diocesan Address: Apartado 513 y 513, Aldama 502, 96400 Coatzacoalcos, Ver.; (921) 2-12-23-99.

Colima (1881): José Luis Amezcua Melgoza, bishop, 2005.

Diocesan Address: Hidalgo 135, Apartado 1, 28000 Colima, Colima; (312) 3-12-02-62.

Cordoba (2000): Eduardo Porfirio Patiño Leal, bishop, 2000.

Diocesan Address: Avenida 11-1300, Esquina con Calle 13, Apartado 154, Zona Centro, 94500 Cordoba, Ver., Mexico; (271) 7-14-91-56.

Cuauhtémoc-Madera (1966): Juan Guillermo López Soto, bishop, 1995.

Diocesan Address: Reforma y 4ª # 479, Apartado Postal 209, 31500 Cuauhtemoc, Chih.; (625) 5-81-57-22.

Cuautitlán (1979): Rodrigo Guillermo Ortiz Mondragón, bishop, 2005.

Diocesan Address: Apartado 14-21, Sor Juana Inés de la Cruz 208, Anexo a Catedral, 54800 Cuautitlán de

Romero Rubio; (55) 58-72-19-96.

Cuernavaca (1891): Florencio Olvera Ochoa, bishop, 2002.

Diocesan Address: Apartado 13, Hidalgo #17, 62000 Cuernavaca, Mor.; (777) 3-18-45-90.

Culiacán (1883 as Sinaloa; name changed 1959): Benjamin Jiménez Hernández, bishop, 1993; Emigdio Duarte Figueroa, auxiliary.

Diocesan Address: Apartado Postal 666, Av. Las Palmas #26 Oriente, 80220 Culiacán, Sinaloa; (667) 7-12-32-72.

Durango* (1620, promoted to archdiocese, 1891): Hector González Martínez, archbishop, 2003; Juan de Dios Caballero Reyes, aux.

Diocesan Address: Apartado Postal 116, 34000 Durango, Durango; (618) 8-11-42-42

Ecatepec (1995): Onésimo Cepeda Silva, bishop, 1995.

Diocesan Address: Plaza Principal s/n, San Cristóbal Centro, Apartado Postal 95, 55000 Ecatepec de Morelos; (5) 116-09-76.

El Salto, Prelacy of (1968): Ruy Rendón Leal, bishop, 2005.

Prelature Address: Mons. Francisco Medina s/n, Apartado Postal 58, 34950 El Salto, Durango; (675) 8-76-00-70.

Ensenada (2007): Noriega Barceló, first bishop, 2007.

Diocesan Address: N/A.

Guadalajara* (1548; promoted to archdiocese, 1863): Cardinal Juan Sandoval Íñiguez, archbishop, 1994; José Trinidad González Rodriguez, Miguel Romano Gómez, Rafael Martínez Sainz, José Leopoldo González González, José Francisco González González, Juan Humberto Gutiérrez Valencia, auxiliaries.

Diocesan Address: Arzobispado, Apartado Postal 1-331, Calle Liceo 17, 44100 Guadalajara, Jal.; (33) 36-14-55-04; www.arquidiocesisgdl.org.mx.

Hermosillo* (1779, as Sonora, promoted to an archdiocese, 1963): José Ulises Macias Salcedo, archbishop, 1996.

Diocesan Address: Apartado 1, Dr. Paliza 81, 83260 Hermosillo, Son.; (662) 2-13-21-38.

Huajuapan de Leon (1903): Teodoro Enrique Pino Miranda, 2000.

Diocesan Address: Apartado 43, Anexos de Catedral, 69000 Huajuapan de León, Oax.; (953) 5-32-07-97.

Huautla, Prelacy of (1972): Héctor Luis Morales Sánchez, bishop, 2005.

Diocesan Address: Casa Prelaticia Calle 5 de Feb. # 15, Apartado 2, 68500 Huautla de Jiménez, Oaxaca; (236) 3-78-00-19.

Huejutla (1922): Salvador Martínez Pérez, bishop, 1994.

Diocesan Address: Obispado, Apartado 8, Ave. Corona del Rosal s/n, Col. Tecoluco, 43000 Huejutla, Hgo.; (789) 8-96-01-85.

Irapuato (2004): José de Jesús Martínez Zepeda, first bishop, 2004.

Diocesan Address: Juarez 138-407, Apatado 13, 36500 Irapuato, Gto.; 462-625-61-04.

Jesús María of Nayar, Prelature of (1962): José Antonio Pérez Sánchez, O.F.M., bishop, 1992.

Diocesan Address: Curia Prelaticia de Jesús María, Belén #24, Apartado 33-B, 63150 Tepic, Nayar; (311) 2-13-88-80.

La Paz en la Baja California Sur (1988): Miguel

Angel Alba Díaz, 2001.
Diocesan Address: Apartado 25, Revolución y 5 de Mayo, 23000 La Paz, B.C.S.; (112) 2-25-96.

León* (1863, promoted to archdiocese, 2006): José Guadalupe Martin Rábago, bishop, 1995-2006, first archbishop, 2006; Juan Frausto Pallares, auxiliary.
Diocesan Address: Pedro Moreno #312, Apartado 108, 37000 León, Gto.; (477) 7-13-27-47; www.diocesisleon.org.mx.

Linares (1962): Ramón Calderón Batres, bishop, 1988.
Diocesan Address: Morelos y Zaragoza s/n, Apartado 70, 67700 Linares, N.L.; (821) 2-00-54.

Matamoros (1958): Faustino Armendáriz Jiménez, bishop, 2005.
Diocesan Address: Apartado 70, Calle 5 y Morelos, 87351 Matamoros, Tamps.; (88) 13-55-11; www.communion.org.mx.

Matehuala (1997): Rodrigo Aguilar Martínez, bishop, 1997.
Diocesan Address: Rayón #200 Centro, Apartado 40, 78700 Matehuala, S.L.P.; (01) 488-2-51-42.

Mazatlán (1958): Mario Espinosa Contreras, bishop, 2005.
Diocesan Address: Apartado Postal 1, Canizales y Benito Juárez s/n, 82000 Mazatlán, Sin.; (69) 81-33-52.

Mexicali (1966): José Isidro Guerrero Macías, bishop, 1997.
Diocesan Address: Av. Morelos #192, Col. Primera sécción, Apartado 3-547, 21100 Mexicali, B.C. Norte; (686) 5-52-40-09.

México* (1530, promoted to an archdiocese, 1546): Cardinal Norberto Rivera Carrera, archbishop, 1995; Abelardo Alvarado Alcántara, José de Jesús Martinez Zepeda, Marcelino Hernández Rodríguez, Luis Fletes Santana, Felipe Tejeda Garcia, M.Sp.S., Francisco Clavel Gil, Rogelio Esquivel Medina, Jonás Guerrero Corona, Antonio Ortega Franco, C.O., Víctor Sánchez Espinosa, Carlos Briseño Arch, O.A.R., auxiliaries.
Diocesan Address: Curia Arzobispal, Apartado Postal 24-433, Durango 90, Col. Roma, 06700 - México, D. F.; (55) 55-25-11-10; www.arzobispadomexico.org.mx.

Mixes, Prelacy of (1964): Don Héctor Guerrero Córdova, S.D.B., bishop, 2007
Diocesan Address: Casa del Señor Obispo, 70283, Ayutla, Mixes, Oax.; (951) 5-58-20-98.

Monterrey* (1777, as Linares o Nuevo León, promoted to an archdiocese, 1891; name changed 1922): Francisco Robles Ortega, archbishop, 2003; José Lizares Estrada, Gustavo Rodríguez Vega, Alfonso Cortés Contreras, auxiliaries.
Diocesan Address: Apartado 7, Zuazua 1110 Sur con Ocampo, 64000 Monterrey, N.L.; (81) 83-45-24-66; www.pixel.com.mx/info-gral/info-nl/religion/catolica/arqui.html.

Morelia* (1536, as Michoacan, promoted to an archdiocese 1863, name changed in 1924): Alberto Suárez Inda, archbishop, 1995; Enrique Díaz Díaz, Octavio Villegas Aguilar, auxiliaries.
Diocesan Address: Apartado 17, 58000 Morelia, Mich.; (443) 3-12-05-23.

Netzahualcóyotl (1979): Carlos Garfias Merlos, bishop, 2003.
Diocesan Address: Apartado 89, 4 Avenida esq. Bellas Artes, Col. Evolución, 57700 Cuidad Netzahualcóyotl; (55) 57-97-61-32.

Nuestra Señora de los Mártires del Libano, Eparchy of (Maronites, 1995): Georges M. Saad Abi Younes, O.L.M., eparch, 2003.
Diocesan address: Ntra. Sra. de Balvarena Correo Mayor # 65, 06060 — México, D. F.; (55) 55-21-20-11.

Nuestra Señora del Paraiso, Eparchy of (Greek Melkites, 1988): vacant.
Diocesan Address: Matías Romero 1014, Dpto. 601, Col. Del Valle, 3100 Mexico, D.F.; (5) 542-0225.

Nuevo Casas Grandes (1977): Gerardo de Jesús Rojas López, bishop, 2004.
Diocesan Address: Apartado Postal 198, Av. Hidalgo #105, 31700 Nuevo Casas Grandes, Chih.; (636) 6-94-05-20.

Nuevo Laredo (1989): Vacant.
Diocesan Address: Saltillo 206, Apartado Postal #20-B, Col. México, 88280 Nuevo Laredo, Tamps.; (867) 7-15-29-28.

Oaxaca* (Also Antequera, 1535, promoted to archdiocese, 1891): José Luis Chávez Botello, archbishop, 2003; Miguel Ángel Alba Díaz, Oscar Campos Contreras, auxiliaries.
Diocesan Address: Apartado Postal # 31, Garcia Vigil #600, 68000 Oaxaca, Oax.; (951) 6-20-49.

Orizaba (2000): Marcelino Hernández Rodríguez, bishop, 2008. Diocesan Address: Templo de Ntra. Sra. del Carmen, Sur 9 # 142 esq. Oriente 4, Apdo. Postal # 151, 94300 - Orizaba, Ver.; (272) 7-24-17-33.

Papantla (1922): Lorenzo Cárdenas Aregullin, bishop, 1980.
Diocesan Address: Apartado 27, Juárez 1102, 73800 Teziutlán, Pue.; (231) 3-24-30.

Parral (1992): José Andrés Corral Arredondo, bishop, 1992.
Diocesan Address: Apartado Postal 313, Fray Bartolomé de las Casas #13, 33800 Parral, Chih.; (152) 2-03-71.

Piedras Negras (2003): Alonso Gerardo Garza Treviño, first bishop, 2003. Diocesan address: Hidalgo Sur # 404 Centro 26000 - Piedras Negras, Coah.; (878) 7-82-94-80.

Puebla de los Angeles* (1525, as Tlaxcala, renamed in 1903): Rosendo Huesca Pacheco, archbishop, 1977.
Diocesan Address: Apartado 235, Av. 2, Sur N. 305, 72000 Puebla, Pue.; (222) 2-32-62-12.

Puerto Escondido (2003): Eduardo Carmona Ortega, O.R.C., first bishop, 2003.
Diocesan Address: Felipe Merklin s/n, Col. Centro Puerto Escondido, Oax; 954-582-36-77.

Querétaro (1863): Mario de Gasperín Gasperín, bishop, 1989.
Diocesan Address: Apartado Postal 49, Reforma #48, 76000 Querétaro, Qro.; (42) 12-10-33.

Saltillo (1891): Raul Vera López, O.P., bishop, 1999.
Diocesan Address: Hidalgo Sur 166, Apartado 25, 25000 Saltillo, Coah.; (844) 4-12-37-84.

San Andrés Tuxtla (1959): José Trinidad Zapata Ortiz, bishop, 2004.
Diocesan Address: Constitución y Morelos, 95700 San Andrés Tuxtla, Ver.; (294) 9-42-03-74.

San Cristóbal de las Casas (1539, as Chiapas, renamed in 1964): Felipe Arizmendi Esquivel, bishop, 2000.
Diocesan Address: 5 de Feb. y 20 de Nov. # 1 Centro 29200 — San Cristóbal las Casas, Chis; (967) 6-78-

00-53; www.laneta.apc.org/curiasc.

San Juan de los Lagos (1972): Felipe Salazar Villagrana, bishop, 2008.
Diocesan Address: Morelos 30, Apartado #1, 47000 San Juan de los Lagos, Jal.; (395) 7-85-05-70; www.redial.com.mx/obispado/index.htm.

San Luis Potosí* (1854, promoted to an archdiocese, 1988): Luis Morales Reyes, archbishop, 1999.
Diocesan Address: Madero # 300, Apartado N. 1, 78000 - San Luis Potosí, S.L.P.; (444) 8-12-45-55.

Tabasco (1880): Benjamin Castillo Plascencia, bishop, 2003.
Diocesan Address: Apartado Postal 97, Fidencia 502, 86000 Villahermosa, Tab.; (93) 12-13-97.

Tacámbaro (1913): Luis Castro Medellín, M.S.F., bishop, 2002.
Diocesan Address: Apartado 4, Professor Enrique Aguilar 49, 61650 Tacámbaro, Mich.; (459) 6-00-44.

Tampico (1870, as Ciudad Victoria o Tamaulipas, renamed in 1958): José Luis Dibildox Martinez, bishop, 2003.
Diocesan Address: Apartado 545, Altamira 116 Oriente, 89000 Tampico, Tamps.; (12) 12-28-02.

Tapachula (1957): Leopoldo González González, bishop, 2005.
Diocesan Address: Apartado 70, Av. Primera Sur 1, 30700 Tapachula, Chiapas; (962) 6-15-03; www.diocesis-tapachula.org.mx.

Tarahumara (1958, as a vicariate apostolic, promoted to diocese, 1993): Rafael Sandoval Sandoval, M.N.M., bishop, 2005.
Diocesan Address: Apartado Postal 11, Av. López Mateos #7, 33190 Guachochi, Chih.; (649) 5-43-02-23.

Tehuacán (1962): Rodrigo Aguilar Martínez, bishop, 2006.
Diocesan Address: Apartado Postal 137, Agustin A. Cacho 107, 75700 Tehuacán, Pue.; (238) 3-83-14-68.

Tehuantepec (1891): Felipe Padilla Cardona, bishop, 2000.
Diocesan Address: Apartado Postal 93, Mina s/n. Anexos de Catedral, 70760 Tehuantepec, Oax.; (971) 7-15-00-60.

Tepic (1891): Ricardo Watty Urquidi, M.Sp.S., bishop, 2008.
Diocesan Address: Apartado 15, Av. de las Flores 10, Fraccionamiento Residencial La Loma, 63137 Tepic, Nay.; (311) 2-14-46-45.

Texcoco (1960): Carlos Aguiar Retes, bishop, 1997; Víctor René Rodríguez Gómez, auxiliary.
Diocesan Address: Apartado Postal 35, Fray Pedro de Gante 2, 56100 Texcoco, Méx.; (595) 4-08-69.

Tijuana* (1963, promoted to archdiocese, 2006): Rafael Romo Muñoz, bishop, 1996-2006, first archbishop, 2006.
Diocesan Address: Apartado 226, Calle 10ª y Av. Ocampo # 1049, 22000 Tijuana, B.C.N.; (664) 6-84-84-11 y 12; www.iglesiatijuana.org.

Tlalnepantla* (1964, promoted to archdiocese, 1989): Ricardo Guizar Díaz, archbishop, 1996; Francisco Ramírez Navarro, auxiliary.
Diocesan Address: Apartado 268 y 270, Av. Juárez 42, 54000 Tlalnepantla, Méx.; (55) 55-65-39-44.

Tlapa (1992): Oscar Roberto Domínguez Couttolenc, M.G., bishop, 2007.
Diocesan Address: Anexo Catedral, Centro, 41300 Tlapa de Comonfort, Gro.; (757) 4-76-08-35.

Tlaxcala (1959): Francisco Moreno Barrón, bishop, 2001.
Diocesan Address: Apartado 84, Lardizábal 45, 90000 Tlaxcala, Tlax.; (246) 4-62-32-43.

Toluca (1950): Francisco Javier Chavolla Ramos, bishop, 2003.
Diocesan Address: Apartado 82, Portal Reforma Norte 104, 50000 Toluca, Méx.; (72) 15-25-35; www.diocesistoluca.org.mx.

Torreón (1957): Vacant.
Diocesan Address: Apartado Postal 430, Av. Morelos 46 Poniente, 27000 Torreón, Coah.; (871) 7-12-30-43.

Tula (1961): Juan Pedro Juárez Meléndez, bishop, 2006.
Diocesan Address: 5 de Mayo, #5, Apartado 31, 42800 Tula de Allende, Hgo.; (773) 7-32-02-75.

Tulancingo* (1863, promoted to archdiocese, 2006): Domingo Díaz Martínez, archbishop, 2008.
Diocesan Address: Apartado #14, Plaza de la Constitución, 43600 Tulancingo, Hgo.; (775) 3-10-10.

Tuxpan (1962): Domingo Díaz Martínez, bishop, 2002.
Diocesan Address: Independencia #56, 92870 Tuxpan, Ver.; (783) 4-16-36.

Tuxtepec (1979): José Antonio Fernández Hurtado, bishop, 2005.
Diocesan Address: Bonfil # 597, entre Juárez y Villa Col. Santa Fe Apartado Postal 9, 68320 — Tuxtepec, Oax.; (287) 5-00-42.

Tuxtla Gutiérrez* (1964, promoted to archdiocese, 2006): Rogelio Cabrera López, bishop, 2004-2006, first archbishop, 2006. José Mendoza Corzo, auxiliary.
Diocesan Address: Uruguay # 500 A Col. El Retiro Apdo. Postal # 36529040 - Tuxtla Gutiérrez, Chis.; (961) 6-04-06-44; www.chisnet.com.mx/~cosi/obispado.

Valle de Chalco (2003): Luis Artemio Flores Calzada, first bishop, 2003.
Diocesan Address: Calle Colorines 12, Col. Granjas, 56600 Chalco, Mex.

Veracruz (1962): Luis Felipe Gallardo Martín del Campo, S.D.B., bishop, 2006.
Diocesan Address: Insurgentes Veracruzanos #470, Paseo del Malecón, 91700 Veracruz, Ver.; (229) 9-31-24-13.

Xalapa* (1962; originally Veracruz and Xalapa, 1863; promoted to archdiocese, 1951): Hipolito Reyes Larios, archbishop, 2007.
Diocesan Address: Apartado 359, Av. Manuel Avila Camacho #73, 91000 Xalapa, Ver.; (228) 8-12-05-79.

Yucatán* (1561, promoted to archdiocese, 1906): Emilio Carlos Berlie Belaunzarán, archbishop, 1995; José Rafael Palma Capetillo, auxiliary.
Diocesan Address: Calle 58 N. 501, 97000 Mérida, Yuc.; (99) 23-79-83; www.geocities.com/SoHo/207/principa.html.

Zacatecas (1863): Fernando Chávez Ruvalcaba, bishop, 1999.
Diocesan Address: Apartado #1, Miguel Auza #219, 98000 Zacatecas, Zacatecas; (492) 9-22-02-32; www.logicnet.com.mx/obispado.

Zamora (1863): Javier Navarro Rodríguez, bishop, 2007.
Diocesan Address: Altos de Catedral (Calle Hidalgo), Apartado Postal #18, 59600 Zamora, Mich.; (351) 5-12-12-08.

CONFERENCIA DEL EPISCOPADO MEXICANO

(Sources: *Annuario Pontificio*; Pbro. Jorge Fco. Vázquez M., Secretario Adjunto, Conferencia del Episcopado Mexicano; Conferencia del Episcopado Mexicano, Directorio, 2008; translation courtesy Suzanne Lea.)

STRUCTURE

The Mexican Conference of Bishops (CEM, Conferencia del Episcopado Mexicano) is the permanent body of Mexican bishops. The bishops adhere to the guidelines of the conference in specific fulfillment of their pastoral labors. They do this in order to obtain the greatest good for the people that the Church can achieve. The conference proposes:
1) To study the problems that occur in pastoral work, and to seek solutions. 2) To initiate, with a common end in mind and a common course of action, the forms and methods of preaching that best suit the needs of the country. 3) In regard to the collective salvific mission of the Church: To look for and to teach the best way in which the respective activities of the deacons, priests, religious, and lay person will be most efficient. 4) To facilitate relations with the civil authority and with other organizations in specific cases. 5) To write to the Episcopal commission regarding patrimonial and proprietary matters, and give counsel on determined financial or labor related points.

All those elected to the body of the CEM will have three years of service and will not be reelected to the same position after two three-year sessions have been completed consecutively.

The address of the conference headquarters is: Prolongación Misterios No. 26, Col. Tepeyac Insurgentes, 07020 México, D.F. Tels. (01-55) 5577-5401; www.cem.org.mx.

Permanent Assembly

The Permanent Assembly is the representative arm of the bishops belonging to the CEM. Its function is to ensure the continuation of the works of the conference and the fulfillment of its accords.

The Permanent Assembly is comprised of the Presidential Assembly and the Assembly of Pastoral Regions. It meets four times per year in ordinary session. It meets in extraordinary sessions whenever the majority of its members or those of the Presidential Assembly determine it to be necessary.

A session is valid if two-thirds of the members are present.

Officers

President: Bishop Carlos Aguiar Retes of Texcoco
Vice-President: Bishop Alberto Suárez Inda of Morelia.
Secretary General: Bishop José Leopoldo González González, aux. bishop of Guadalajara.
General Treasurer: Bishop Alonso Gerardo Garza Treviño of Piedras Negras.
Spokesmen: Archbishop José Luis Chávez Botello Arzobispo de Antequera Oaxaca; Archbishop Rogelio Cabrera López of Tuxtla Gutiérrez.

Commissions

Biblical Studies: Bishop Juan Manuel Mancilla Sánchez.
Doctrine: Bishop Lázaro Pérez Jiménez.
Culture: Bishop Francisco Clavel Gil.
Education: Bishop Alfonso Cortés Contreras.
Evangelization: Bishop Ramón Godínez Flores.
Health Care: Bishop Rafael Martinéz Sainz
Liturgy: Bishop Jonás Guerrero Corona.
Missions: Bishop Florencio Olvera Ochoa.
Pastoral Sanctuaries: Bishop Fernando Chávez Ruvalcaba.
Catechesis: Bishop Benjamin Castillo Plasencia.
Social Justice: Bishop Miguel Ángel Alba Díaz.
Clergy: Bishop Marcelino Hernández.
Social Communications: Bishop Teodor E. Pino Miranda.
Interreligious Dialogue: Bishop Eduardo Patiño.
Consecrated Life: Bishop Roberto Balmori Cinta, M.J.
Lay Apostolates: Bishop Rodrigo Aguilar Martínez.
Lay Ministry and Diaconate: Bishop Luis Felipe Gallardo Martín del Campo, S.D.B.
Military Chaplains: Bishop Hilario Chávez Joya.
Priestly Formation: Bishop Benjamin Jiménez Hernández.
Seminaries and Vocations: Bishop José Luis Amezcua.

STATISTICAL SUMMARY OF THE CATHOLIC CHURCH IN MEXICO

(Principal sources: Annuario Pontificio, 2008; Conferencia del Espicopado Mexicano, Directorio, 2008; *figures as of January 2008. Catholic population statistics are those reported in the most recent* Annuario *population estimates. Archdioceses are indicated by an asterisk.)*

Includes 18 provinces: 18 archdioceses, 65 dioceses, 5 prelacies, and two eparchies. The Catholic population of Mexico comprises approximately 89% of the overall Mexican population of 104,870,000 according to the Conferencia del Episcopado Mexicano, *Directorio, 2008* (the most recent edition). In 2006, there were 1,803,758 baptisms and 321,296 marriages. This table presents a provincial breakdown of Catholic statistics. The population totals are approximate because diocesan estimates are often considered unreliable owing to difficulties in adequate assessment of demographics and population distribution.

Province Diocese	Cath. Pop.	Dioc. Priests	Rel. Priests	Total Priests	Perm. Deacs.	Bro- thers	Sis- sters	Par- ishes
Acapulco	5,194,000	336	62	398	17	91	406	211
Acapulco*	2,972,000	88	23	111	17	35	140	83
Chilpancingo-Chilapa	845,000	138	16	154	–	16	170	73
Ciudad Altamirano	892,000	72	6	78	–	21	62	28
Tlapa	485,000	38	17	55	–	19	34	27
Baja California	4,609,000	355	138	493	17	247	831	210
Tijuana*	2,424,757	172	71	243	11	175	479	98
Ensenada	621,346	25	18	43	–	–	72	23
La Paz	494,000	50	32	82	–	32	148	45
Mexicali	1,068,897	108	17	125	6	40	132	44
Bajío	6,701,170	696	310	1,006	14	413	2,473	332
León*	2,459,000	221	128	349	12	133	755	106
Celaya	1,403,000	162	63	225	–	92	528	65
Irapuato	1,127,170	111	39	150	2	50	160	61
Querétaro	1,712,000	202	80	282	–	138	1,030	100
Chiapas	2,689,000	236	65	301	335	90	533	151
Tuxtla Gutiérrez*	944,000	105	19	124	–	26	224	59
San Cristobal	1,284,000	47	38	85	335	56	212	51
Tapachula	1,460,000	84	8	92	–	8	97	41
Chihuahua	4,790,672	304	107	411	33	153	640	210
Chihuahua*	1,189,000	98	30	128	10	39	181	60
Ciudad Juárez	2,203,000	94	32	126	11	52	164	68
Cuauhtémoc-Madera	336,132	29	10	39	–	12	70	26
Nuevo Casas Grandes	126,700	27	6	34	–	6	29	24
Parral	648,478	42	18	60	12	22	66	18
Tarahumara	287,362	14	21	35	–	22	130	14
Durango	3,112,000	402	77	479	1	109	695	231
Durango*	1,407,000	203	22	225	–	44	434	121
El Salto	321,000	23	–	24	1	4	18	15
Mazatlán	735,000	77	9	86	–	10	126	44
Torreón	649,000	99	46	145	–	51	117	51
Guadalajara	11,358,708	2,121	481	2,602	8	1,124	4,961	833
Guadalajara*	6,231,000	1,029	357	1,386	4	858	3,096	422
Aguascalientes	1,599,000	262	51	313	1	68	680	99
Autlán	323,000	100	–	100	2	–	179	47
Ciudad Guzmán	434,028	103	13	116	–	29	156	52
Colima	595,880	129	6	135	–	13	231	52
San Juan los Lagos	959,000	280	37	317	–	132	324	72
Tepic	1,084,000	206	3	209	–	5	246	73
Jesús Maria of Nayar	1,132,800	12	14	26	1	19	49	16
Hermosillo	4,245,965	1,039	77	1,116	12	154	1,200	510
Hermosillo*	1,014,000	111	8	119	1	12	142	58
Ciudad Obregón	898,000	109	16	125	1	34	159	60
Culiacán	2,333,965	163	5	168	4	10	283	70
Hidalgo	2,843,022	328	24	352	3	49	308	161
Tulancingo*	1,344,921	168	6	174	2	31	167	82
Huejutla	502,000	88	7	95	–	7	56	38
Tula	996,101	72	11	83	1	11	85	41
Mexico	13,388,684	1,162	1,090	2,252	134	2,192	5,950	748
Mexico*	7,580,684	687	985	1,672	130	1,999	5,025	443
Atlacomulco	874,000	90	4	94	1	5	107	63
Cuernavaca	1,874,000	119	56	175	3	119	363	109
Toluca	3,060,000	266	45	311	–	69	453	133

Province Diocese	Cath. Pop.	Dioc. Priests	Rel. Priests	Total Priests	Perm. Deacs.	Bro- thers	Sis- ters	Par- ishes
Monterrey	11,053,733	872	320	1,192	53	509	1,792	484
Monterrey*	5,337,000	381	171	552	33	308	794	180
Ciudad Victoria	391,000	36	14	50	–	20	88	33
Linares	279,000	34	26	60	19	35	97	32
Matamoros	1,727,000	101	14	115	–	23	105	56
Nuevo Laredo	805,000	46	21	66	–	29	106	37
Piedras Negras	467,500	55	19	74	–	10	77	28
Saltillo	1,061,435	116	41	157	1	56	376	56
Tampico	1,123,000	103	14	117	–	18	149	62
Morelia	5,590,215	871	169	1,040	–	395	2,236	455
Morelia*	2,498,500	389	121	510	–	242	1,053	226
Apatzingán	653,000	56	–	56	–	–	132	26
Ciudad Lázaro Cárdenas	733,000	29	12	41	–	16	62	23
Tacámbaro	325,000	92	2	94	–	2	123	40
Zamora	1,380,715	305	34	339	–	135	866	140
Oaxaca	3,841,979	292	100	392	59	120	457	238
Oaxaca*	1,144,000	138	42	180	24	53	230	111
Huautla[1]	126,050	12	4	16	1	7	5	9
Mixes[1]	132,800	7	29	36	16	34	45	17
Puerto Escondido	434,129	29	8	37	1	8	36	29
Tehuantepec	1,335,000	71	7	78	–	8	118	43
Tuxtepec	670,000	35	10	45	17	10	23	29
Puebla de los Angeles	6,890,830	779	182	961	3	259	1,510	437
Puebla de los Angeles*	4,230,000	439	154	593	1	222	970	245
Huajuapan de León	730,000	108	–	108	–	–	145	71
Tehuacán	934,830	91	8	99	–	11	147	57
Tlaxcala	996,000	141	20	161	2	26	248	64
San Luis Potosi	4,272,706	479	96	575	10	224	1,319	261
San Luis Potosi*	1,781,706	201	65	266	10	180	826	95
Ciudad Valles	949,000	58	18	76	–	20	100	42
Matehuala	228,000	32	6	38	–	6	39	17
Zacatecas	1,314,000	188	7	196	–	18	354	107
Tlalnepantla	18,398,760	880	239	1,119	34	395	1,040	592
Tlalnepantla*	3,570,000	265	101	366	13	148	279	198
Cuautitlan	3,791,000	183	56	239	–	149	289	81
Ecatepec	3,400,000	114	17	131	4	21	12	89
Netzahualcóyotl	3,254,760	102	33	135	–	42	97	83
Texcoco	2,135,000	163	9	172	17	10	263	90
Valle de Chalco	2,248,000	53	23	76	–	25	100	51
Xalapa	8,673,981	694	56	750	50	83	1,129	415
Xalapa*	1,031,000	139	9	148	–	18	287	75
Coatzacoalcos	807,776	50	4	54	3	12	95	25
Cordoba	657,447	74	1	75	–	1	156	41
Orizaba	516,758	78	6	84	–	11	158	42
Papantla	1,532,000	88	–	88	1	–	136	54
San Andrés Tuxtla	989,000	82	2	84	34	2	82	51
Tuxpan	1,300,000	94	1	95	3	1	13	58
Veracruz	1,840,000	89	33	122	9	38	202	69
Yucatán	4,567,967	347	136	483	32	228	659	248
Yucatán*	1,700,000	174	51	225	29	106	295	101
Campeche	615,000	51	7	58	–	31	90	42
Tabasco	1,123,000	103	14	117	–	18	149	62
Cancún-Chetumal[1]	977,000	11	57	68	2	66	125	40
Nuestra Sra. de los Mártires[2]	148,267	6	4	10	1	4	–	3
Nuestra Sra. del Paraiso[2]	4,700	2	3	5	–	3	–	–
Totals:	96,370,000[3]	11,537	3,681	15,218	809	8,066	23,232	6,405

Note: [1] Prelacy [2] Eparchy. [3] According to the Conferencia del Episcopado Mexicano.

Consecrated Life

INSTITUTES OF CONSECRATED LIFE

Religious institutes and congregations are special societies in the Church—institutes of consecrated life —whose members, called Religious, commit themselves by public vows to observance of the evangelical counsels of poverty, chastity and obedience in a community kind of life in accordance with rules and constitutions approved by church authority.

Secular institutes (covered in their own *Almanac* entries) are also institutes of consecrated life.

The particular goal of each institute and the means of realizing it in practice are stated in the rule and constitutions proper to the institute. Local bishops can give approval for rules and constitutions of institutes of diocesan rank. Pontifical rank belongs to institutes approved by the Holy See. General jurisdiction over all religious is exercised by the Congregation for Institutes of Consecrated Life and Societies of Apostolic Life. General legislation concerning religious is contained in Canons 573 to 709 in Book II, Part III, of the Code of Canon Law.

All institutes of consecrated life are commonly called religious orders, despite the fact that there are differences between orders and congregations. The best known orders include the Benedictines, Trappists, Franciscans, Dominicans, Carmelites and Augustinians, for men; and the Carmelites, Benedictines, Poor Clares, Dominicans of the Second Order and Visitation Nuns, for women. The orders are older than the congregations, which did not appear until the sixteenth century.

Contemplative institutes are oriented to divine worship and service within the confines of their communities, by prayer, penitential practices, other spiritual activities and self-supporting work. Examples are the Trappists and Carthusians, the Carmelite and Poor Clare nuns. Active institutes are geared for pastoral ministry and various kinds of apostolic work. Mixed institutes combine elements of the contemplative and active ways of life. While most institutes of men and women can be classified as active, all of them have contemplative aspects.

Clerical communities of men are those whose membership is predominantly composed of priests.

Non-clerical or lay institutes of men are the various brotherhoods.

"The Consecrated Life and Its Role in the Church and in the World" was the topic of the ninth general assembly of the Synod of Bishops held Oct. 2-29, 1994.

Societies of Apostolic Life

Some of the institutes listed below have a special kind of status because their members, while living a common life characteristic of religious, do not profess the vows of religious. Examples are the Maryknoll Fathers, the Oratorians of St. Philip Neri, the Paulists and Sulpicians. They are called societies of apostolic life and are the subject of Canons 731 to 746 of the Code of Canon Law.

RELIGIOUS INSTITUTES OF MEN IN THE UNITED STATES

Sources: Annuario Pontificio, The Official Catholic Directory; Catholic Almanac *survey. As of June 1, 2008*

Africa, Missionaries of, M. Afr.: Founded 1868 at Algiers by Cardinal Charles M. Lavigerie; known as White Fathers until 1984. Generalate, Rome, Italy. U.S. headquarters, 1624 21st St. N.W., Washington, DC 20009, (202) 232-5154. Missionary work in Africa.

African Missions, Society of, S.M.A.: Founded 1856, at Lyons, France, by Bishop Melchior de Marion Brésillac. Generalate, Rome, Italy. American province (1941), 23 Bliss Ave., Tenafly, NJ 07670, (201) 567-9085, www.smafathers.com. Missionary work.

Alexian Brothers, C.F.A.: Founded fourteenth century in western Germany and Belgium during the Black Plague. Motherhouse, Aachen, Germany. Generalate, 198 James Blvd., Signal Mountain, TN 37377, (423) 886-0380. Hospital and general health work.

Assumptionists (Augustinians of the Assumption), A.A.: Founded 1845, at Nimes, France, by Rev. Emmanuel d'Alzon; in U.S., 1946. General House, Rome, Italy. U.S. province, 330 Market St., Brighton, MA 02135, (617) 783-0400, www.assumption.us. Educational, parochial, ecumenical, retreat, foreign mission work.

Atonement, Franciscan Friars of the, S.A.: Founded as an Anglican Franciscan community in 1898 at Garrison, NY, by Rev. Paul Wattson. Community corporately received into the Catholic Church in 1909. Generalate, St. Paul's Friary, Graymoor, Rte. 9, P.O. Box 300, Garrison, NY 10524, (914) 424-2113. Ecumenical, mission, retreat and charitable works.

Augustinian Recollects, O.A.R.: Founded 1588; in U.S., 1944. General motherhouse, Rome, Italy. Monastery of St. Cloud (formerly St. Augustine Province, 1944), 29 Ridgeway Ave., W. Orange, NJ 07052-3297, (973) 731-0616, www.augustinianrecollects.org. St. Nicholas of Tolentino Province (U.S.

Delegation), St. Nicholas of Tolentino Monastery, 3201 Central Ave., Union City, NJ 07087, (201) 422-7550. Missionary, parochial, education work.

Augustinians (Order of St. Augustine), O.S.A.: Established canonically in 1256 by Pope Alexander IV; in U.S., 1796. General motherhouse, Rome, Italy. St. Thomas Monastery, 800 Lancaster Ave., Villanova, PA 19085-1687, (610) 519-7548, www.augustinians.org., (1796). Our Mother of Good Counsel Province (1941), Tolentine Center, 20300 Governors Hwy., Olympia Fields, IL 60461-1081, (708) 283-6659, www.midweststaugustinians.org. St. Augustine, Province of (1969), 1605 28th St., San Diego, CA 92102-1417, (619) 235-0247.

Barnabites (Clerics Regular of St. Paul), C.R.S.P.: Founded 1530, in Milan, Italy, by St. Anthony M. Zaccaria; approved 1533; in U.S., 1952. Historical motherhouse, Church of St. Barnabas (Milan). Generalate, Rome, Italy. North American province, 981 Swann Rd, P.O. Box 167, Youngstown, NY 14174, (716) 754-7489, www.catholicchurch.org/barnabites. Parochial, educational, mission work.

Basil the Great, Order of St. (Basilian Order of St. Josaphat), O.S.B.M.: General motherhouse, Rome, Italy. U.S. province, 29 Peacock Ln., Locust Valley, NY 11560, (516) 609-3262. Parochial work among Byzantine Ukrainian Rite Catholics.

Basilian Fathers (Congregation of the Priests of St. Basil), C.S.B.: Founded 1822, at Annonay, France. General motherhouse, Toronto, ON, Canada. U.S. address: 1910 W. Alabama, Houston, TX 77098, (713) 522-1736. Educational, parochial work.

Basilian Salvatorian Fathers, B.S.O.: Founded 1684, at Saida, Lebanon, by Eftimios Saifi; in U.S., 1953. General motherhouse, Saida, Lebanon. American headquarters, 30 East St., Methuen, MA 01844. Educational, parochial work among Eastern Rite peoples.

Benedictine Monks (Order of St. Benedict), O.S.B.: Founded 529, in Italy, by St. Benedict of Nursia; in U.S., 1846.

• **American Cassinese Congregation (1855).** Pres., Rt. Rev. Melvin J. Valvano, O.S.B., Newark Abbey, 528 Dr. Martin Luther King Blvd., Newark, NJ 07102, (973) 733-2822. Abbeys and priories belonging to the congregation:

St. Vincent Archabbey, 300 Fraser Purchase Rd., Latrobe, PA 15650, (724) 805-2503, www.benedictine.stvincent.edu. Saint John's Abbey, P.O. Box 2015, Collegeville, MN 56321, (320) 363-2548, www.saintjohnsabbey.org. St. Benedict's Abbey, 1020 North Second St., Atchison, KS 66002, (913) 367-7853, www.kansasmonks.org. St. Mary's Abbey, 230 Mendham Rd., Morristown, NJ 07960, (973) 538-3231, www.osbmonks.org. Newark Abbey, 528 Dr. Martin Luther King, Jr., Blvd., Newark, NJ 07102, (973) 643-4800. Belmont Abbey, 100 Belmont-Mt. Holly Rd., Belmont, NC 28012, (704) 825-6675, www.belmontabbey.org. St. Bernard Abbey, Cullman, AL 35055, (256) 734-8291. St. Gregory's Abbey, 1900 W. MacArthur, Shawnee, OK 74804, (405) 878-5491, www.stgregorys.edu. St. Leo Abbey, St. Leo, FL 33574, (352) 588-8626, www.saintleoabbey.org. Assumption Abbey, P.O. Box A, Richardton, ND 58652, (701) 974-3315. St. Bede Abbey, Peru, IL 61354, (815) 223-3140, www.theramp.net/stbede/index.html. St. Martin's Abbey, 5300 Pacific Ave. S.E., Lacey, WA 98503-1297, (360) 438-4440, www.stmartin.edu. Holy Cross Abbey, P.O. Box 1510, Canon City, CO 81215, (719) 275-8631, www.holycrossabbey.org. St. Anselm's Abbey, 100 St. Anselm Dr., Manchester, NH, 03102, (603) 641-7651, www.anselm.edu. Holy Trinity

Priory, P.O. Box 990, Butler, PA 16003, (724) 287-4461. Benedictine Priory, 6502 Seawright Dr., Savannah, GA 31406, (912) 356-3520, www.bcsav.net. Woodside Priory, 302 Portola Rd., Portola Valley, CA 94028, (650) 851-6133. Mary Mother of the Church Abbey, 12829 River Rd., Richmond, VA 23233, (804) 784-3508, www.richmondmonks.org. Abadia de San Antonio Abad, P.O. Box 729, Humacao, PR 00792, (787) 852-1616.

• **Swiss-American Congregation (1870).** Abbeys and priory belonging to the congregation:

St. Meinrad Archabbey, 100 Hill Dr., St. Meinrad, IN 47577-1003, (812) 357-6514, www.saintmeinrad.edu. Conception Abbey, 37174 State Hwy., VV, Conception, MO 64433-0501, (660) 944-3100, www.conceptionabbey.org. Mt. Michael Abbey, 22520 Mt. Michael Rd., Elkhorn, NE 68022-3400, (402) 289-2541, www.mountmichael.org. Subiaco Abbey, Subiaco, AR 72865, (479) 934-1001, www.subi.org. St. Joseph's Abbey, St. Benedict, LA 70457, (504) 892-1800. Mt. Angel Abbey, St. Benedict, OR 97373, (503) 845-3030. Marmion Abbey, 850 Butterfield Rd., Aurora, IL 60502 (630) 897-7215.

St. Benedict's Abbey, 12605 224th Ave., Benet Lake, WI 53102, (262) 396-4311, www.benetlake.org. Glastonbury Abbey, 16 Hull St., Hingham, MA 02043, (781) 749-2155, www.glastonburyabbey.org. Blue Cloud Abbey, Marvin, SD 57251-0098, (605) 398-9200, www.bluecloud.org. Corpus Christi Abbey, 101 South Vista Dr., Sandia, TX 78383, (361) 547-3257, www.geocities.com/Athens/styx/8125/ccabbey. html. Prince of Peace Abbey, 650 Benet Hill Rd., Oceanside, CA 92054, (760) 967-4200, www.princeofpeaceabbey.org. St. Benedict Abbey, 254 Still River Rd., PO Box 22, Still River (Harvard), MA 01467, (978) 456-8017.

• **Congregation of St. Ottilien for Foreign Missions:** St. Paul's Abbey, P.O. Box 7, 289 Rt. 206 South, Newton, NJ 07860, (973) 383-2470. Christ the King Priory, P.O. Box 528, Schuyler, NE 68661, (402) 352-2177, www.benedictinemissionhouse.com

• **Congregation of the Annunciation,** St. Andrew Abbey, P.O. Box 40, Valyermo, CA 93563-0040, (661) 944-2178, www.valyermo.com.

• **English Benedictine Congregation:** St. Anselm's Abbey, 4501 S. Dakota Ave. N.E., Washington, DC 20017, (202) 269-2300. Abbey of St. Gregory the Great, Cory's Lane, Portsmouth, RI 02871-1352, (401) 683-2000. Abbey of St. Mary and St. Louis, 500 S. Mason Rd., St. Louis, MO 63141-8500, (314) 434-3690, www.priory.org, www.stlouisabbey.org.

• **Houses Not in Congregations:** Mount Saviour Monastery, 231 Monastery Rd., Pine City, NY 14871-9787, (607) 734-1688, www.servtech.com/~msaviour; Weston Priory, 58 Priory Hill Rd., Weston, VT 05161-6400, (802) 824-5409, www.westonpriory.org.

Benedictines, Camaldolese Hermits of America, O.S.B. Cam.: Founded 1012, at Camaldoli, near Arezzo, Italy, by St. Romuald; in U.S., 1958. General motherhouse, Arezzo, Italy. U.S. foundation, New Camaldoli Hermitage, 62475 Highway 1, Big Sur, CA 93920, (831) 667-2456, www.contemplation.org.

Benedictines, Olivetan, O.S.B.: General motherhouse, Siena, Italy. U.S. monasteries: Our Lady of Guadalupe Abbey, P.O. Box 1080, Pecos, NM 87552, (505) 757-6600, www.pecosabbey.org. Holy Trinity Monastery, P.O. Box 298, St. David, AZ 85630-0298, (520) 720-4642, www.holytrinitymonastery.org. Monastery of the Risen Christ, P.O. Box 3931, San

Luis Obispo, CA 93403-3931, (805) 544-1810. Benedictine Monastery of Hawaii, P.O. Box 490, Waialua, HI 96791, (808) 637-7887, www.catholic hawaii.org/religious/benedictine.

Benedictines, Subiaco Congregation, O.S.B.: Independent priory, 1983. Monastery of Christ in the Desert, Abiquiu, NM 87510, (505) 470-6668, www.christdesert.org. St. Mary's Monastery, P.O. Box 345, Petersham, MA 01366, (978) 724-3350.

Benedictines, Sylvestrine, O.S.B.: Founded 1231, in Italy, by Sylvester Gozzolini. General motherhouse, Rome, Italy. U.S. foundations: 17320 Rosemont Rd., Detroit, MI 48219, (313) 531-0140. 2711 E. Drahner Rd., Oxford, MI 48370, (248) 628-2249, www.benedictinemonks.org. 1697 State Highway 3, Clifton, NJ 07012, (201) 778-1177.

Blessed Sacrament, Congregation of the, S.S.S.: Founded 1856, at Paris, France, by St. Pierre Julien Eymard; in U.S., 1900. General motherhouse, Rome, Italy. U.S. province, 5384 Wilson Mills Rd., Cleveland, OH 44143-3092, (440) 442-6311, www.blessedsacrament.com. Eucharistic apostolate.

Brigittine Monks (Order of the Most Holy Savior), O.Ss.S.: Monastery of Our Lady of Consolation, 23300 Walker Lane, Amity, OR 97101, (503) 835-8080, www.brigittine.org.

Camaldolese Hermits of the Congregation of Monte Corona, Er. Cam.: Founded 1520, from Camaldoli, Italy, by Bl. Paul Giustiniani; in U.S., 1959; motherhouse, Frascati (Rome), Italy. U.S. foundation, Holy Family Hermitage, 1501 Fairplay Rd., Bloomingdale, OH 43910-7971, (740) 765-4511.

Camillian Fathers and Brothers (Order of St. Camillus; Order of Servants of the Sick), O.S.Cam.: Founded 1582, at Rome, by St. Camillus de Lellis; in U.S., 1923. General motherhouse, Rome, Italy. North American province, 3345 South 1st St., Milwaukee, WI 53215, (414) 481-3696, www.camillians.org.

Carmelites (Order of Our Lady of Mt. Carmel), O. Carm.: General motherhouse, Rome, Italy. Most Pure Heart of Mary Province (1864), 1317 Frontage Rd., Darien, IL 60559, (630) 971-0050. North American Province of St. Elias (1931), P.O. Box 3079, Middletown, NY 10940-0890, (845) 344-2225; www.carmelitefriars.org. Mt. Carmel Hermitage, Pineland, R.R. 1, Box 330 C, Bolivar, PA, 15923, (724) 238-0423. Educational, charitable work.

Carmelites, Order of Discalced, O.C.D.: Established 1562, a Reform Order of Our Lady of Mt. Carmel; in U.S., 1924. Generalate, Rome, Italy. Western Province (1983), 926 E. Highland Ave., P.O. Box 2178, Redlands, CA 92373, (909) 793-0424; www.ocdwest.org. Province of St. Thérèse (Oklahoma,1935), 515 Marylake Dr., Little Rock AR 72206, (501) 888-5827. Immaculate Heart of Mary Province (1947), 1233 S. 45th St., Milwaukee, WI 53214, (414) 672-7212. Our Lady of Mt. Carmel Monastery, 1628 Ridge Rd., Munster, IN 46321, (219) 838-7111. Spiritual direction, retreat, parochial work.

Carmelites of Mary Immaculate, C.M.I.: Founded 1831, in India, by Bl. Kuriakose Elias Chavara and two other Syro-Malabar priests; canonically established, 1855. Generalate, Kerala, India. North American headquarters, Holy Family Church, 21 Nassau Ave., Brooklyn, NY 11222, (718) 388-4866.

Carthusians, Order of, O. Cart.: Founded 1084, in France, by St. Bruno; in U.S., 1951. General motherhouse, St. Pierre de Chartreuse, France. U.S., Charterhouse of the Transfiguration, Carthusian Monastery, 1800 Beartown Rd., Arlington, VT 05250, (802) 362-2550, www.chartreux.org. Cloistered contemplatives; semi-eremitic.

Charity, Brothers of, F.C.: Founded 1807, in Belgium, by Canon Peter J. Triest. General motherhouse, Rome, Italy. American District (1963), 7720 Doe Lane, Laverock, PA 19038.

Charity, Servants of (Guanellians), S.C.: Founded 1908, in Italy, by Bl. Luigi Guanella. General motherhouse, Rome, Italy. U.S. headquarters, St. Louis School, 16195 Old U.S. 12, Chelsea, MI 48118, (734) 475-8430, www.stlouiscenter.org.

Christ, Society of, S.Ch.: Founded 1932. General Motherhouse, Poznan, Poland; U.S.-Canadian Province, 3000 Eighteen Mile Rd., Sterling Heights, MI 48311.

Christian Brothers, Congregation of, C.F.C. (formerly Christian Brothers of Ireland): Founded 1802 at Waterford, Ireland, by Bl. Edmund Ignatius Rice; in U.S., 1906. General motherhouse, Rome, Italy. American Province, Eastern U.S. (1916), 33 Pryer Terr., New Rochelle, NY 10804, (914) 712-7580. Brother Rice Province, Western U.S. (1966), 958 Western Ave., Joliet, IL 60435, (815) 723-5464. Educational work.

Christian Instruction, Brothers of (La Mennais Brothers), F.I.C.: Founded 1817, at Ploermel, France, by Abbe Jean Marie de la Mennais and Abbe Gabriel Deshayes. General motherhouse, Rome, Italy. American province, Notre Dame Institute, P.O. Box 159, Alfred, ME 04002, (207) 324-0067, www.ficbrothers.org.

Christian Schools, Brothers of the (Christian Brothers), F.S.C.: Founded 1680, at Reims, France, by St. Jean Baptiste de la Salle. General motherhouse, Rome, Italy. U.S. Conference, 4351 Garden City Dr., Suite 200, Landover, MD 20785, (301) 459-9410, www.cbconf.org. Baltimore Province (1845), Box 29, Adamstown, MD 21710-0029, (301) 874-5188, www.fscbaltimore.org. Brothers of the Christian Schools (Midwest Province) (1995), 7650 S. County Line Rd., Burr Ridge, IL 60527-4718, (630) 323-3725, www.cbmidwest.org. New York Province (1848), 800 Newman Springs Rd., Lincroft, NJ 07738, (732) 842-7420. Long Island-New England Province (1957), Christian Brothers Center, 635 Ocean Rd., Narragansett, RI 02882-1314, (401) 789-0244, www.cbline.org. San Francisco Province (1868), P.O. Box 3720, Napa, CA 94558, (707) 252-0222, www.delasalle.org. Fe Province (1921), De La Salle Christian Brothers, 1522 Carmel Dr., Lafayette, LA 70501, (337) 234-1973. Educational, charitable work.

Cistercians, Order of, O.Cist.: Founded 1098, by St. Robert. Headquarters, Rome, Italy. Our Lady of Spring Bank Abbey, 17304 Havenwood Rd., Sparta, WI 54656-8177, (608) 269-8138. Our Lady of Dallas Abbey, 3550 Cistercian Rd., Irving, TX 75039, (972) 438-2044. Cistercian Monastery of Our Lady of Fatima, 564 Walton Ave., Mt. Laurel, NJ 08054, (856) 235-1330. Cistercian Conventual Priory, St. Mary's Priory, 70 Schuylkill Rd., New Ringgold, PA 17960, (570) 943-2645. www.cistercian.org.

Cistercians of the Strict Observance, Order of (Trappists), O.C.S.O.: Founded 1098, in France, by

St. Robert; in U.S., 1848. Generalate, Rome, Italy. Abbey of Gethsemani (1848), 3642 Monks Rd., KY 40051, (502) 549-3117. Our Lady of New Melleray Abbey (1849), 6632 Melleray Circle, Peosta, IA 52068-7079, (563) 588-2319. Holy Spirit Monastery (1944), 2625 Hwy. 212 S.W., Conyers, GA 30094-4044, (770) 483-8705 (fax), www.trappist.net. Our Lady of Guadalupe Abbey (1947), P.O. Box 97, Lafayette, OR 97127, (503) 852-7174, www.trappistabbey.org. Our Lady of the Holy Trinity Abbey (1947), 1250 South 9500 East, Huntsville, UT 84317, (801) 745-3784, www.xmission.com~hta. Abbey of the Genesee (1951), P.O. Box 900, Piffard, NY 14533, (585) 243-0660, www.geneseeabbey.org. Mepkin Abbey (1949), 1098 Mepkin Abbey Rd., Moncks Corner, SC 29461-4796, (843) 761-8509, www.mepkinabbey.org. Our Lady of the Holy Cross Abbey (1950), 901 Cool Spring Lane, Berryville, VA 22611-2900, (540) 955-4383, www.heava.org. Assumption Abbey (1950), Rt. 5, Box 1056, Ava, MO 65608-9142, (417) 683-5110. Abbey of New Clairvaux (1955), Vina, CA 96092, (530) 839-2161, www.maxinet.com/trappist. St. Benedict's Monastery (1956), 1012 Monastery Rd., Snowmass, CO 81654, (970) 927-3311.

Claretians (Missionary Sons of the Immaculate Heart of Mary), C.M.F.: Founded 1849, at Vich, Spain, by St. Anthony Mary Claret. General headquarters, Rome, Italy. Western Province, 1119 Westchester Pl., Los Angeles, CA 90019-3523, (323) 734-1824. Eastern Province, 400 N. Euclid Ave, Oak Park, IL 60302, (708) 848-2076. Missionary, parochial, educational, retreat work.

Clerics Regular Minor (Adorno Fathers) C.R.M.: Founded 1588, at Naples, Italy, by Ven. Augustine Adorno and St. Francis Caracciolo. General motherhouse, Rome, Italy. U.S. address, 575 Darlington Ave., Ramsey, NJ 07446, (201) 327-7375, members.tripod.com/~adornofathers.

Columban, Missionary Society of St. (St. Columban Foreign Mission Society), S.S.C.: Founded 1918. General headquarters, Dublin, Ireland. U.S. headquarters., P.O. Box 10, St. Columbans, NE 68056, (402) 291-1920, www.columban.org. Foreign mission work.

Comboni Missionaries of the Heart of Jesus (Verona Fathers), M.C.C.J.: Founded 1867, in Italy by Bl. Daniel Comboni; in U.S., 1939. General motherhouse, Rome, Italy. North American headquarters, Comboni Mission Center, 1318 Nagel Rd., Cincinnati, OH 45255, (513) 474-4997. Mission work in Africa and the Americas.

Consolata Missionaries, I.M.C.: Founded 1901, at Turin, Italy, by Bl. Joseph Allamano. General motherhouse, Rome, Italy. U.S. headquarters, P.O. Box 5550, 2301 Rt. 27, Somerset, NJ 08875, (732) 297-9191.

Crosier Fathers (Canons Regular of the Order of the Holy Cross), O.S.C.: Founded 1210, in Belgium by Bl. Theodore De Celles. Generalate, Rome, Italy. U.S. Province of St. Odilia, 3510 Vivian Ave., Shoreview, MN 55126-3852, (651) 486-7456, www.crosier.org. Mission, retreat, educational work.

Cross, Brothers of the Congregation of Holy, C.S.C.: Founded 1837, in France, by Rev. Basil Moreau; U.S. province, 1841. Generalate, Rome, Italy. Midwest Province (1841), Box 460, Notre Dame, IN 46556-0460, (574) 631-2912, www.brothersofholycross.com. Southwest Province (1956), 1101 St. Edward's Dr., Austin, TX 78704-6512, (512) 442-7856, www.holycross-sw.org. Eastern Province (1956), 85 Overlook Circle, New Rochelle, NY 10804,

(914) 632-4468, www.holycrossbrothers.org. Educational, social work, missions.

Cross, Congregation of Holy, C.S.C.: Founded 1837, in France; in U.S., 1841. Generalate, Rome, Italy. Indiana Province (1841), 54515 State Rd. 933, North, P.O. Box 1064, Notre Dame, IN 46556-1064, (574) 631-6196. Eastern Province (1952), 835 Clinton Ave., Bridgeport, CT 06604-2393, (203) 367-7252, www.holycross.org. Southern Province (1968), 2111 Brackenridge St., Austin, TX 78704, (512) 443-3886, www.southerncsc.org. Educational and pastoral work; home missions and retreats; foreign missions; social services and apostolate of the press.

Divine Word, Society of the, S.V.D.: Founded 1875, in Holland, by Bl. Arnold Janssen. General motherhouse, Rome, Italy. North American Province founded 1897 with headquarters in Techny, IL. Province of Bl. Joseph Freinademetz (Chicago Province) (1985, from merger of Eastern and Northern provinces), 1985 Waukegan Rd., Techny, IL 60082, (847) 272-2700. St. Augustine (Southern Province) (1940), 201 Ruella Ave., Bay St. Louis, MS 39520, (228) 467-4322, www.svdsouth.com. St. Therese of the Child Jesus (Western Province) (1964), 2737 Pleasant St., Riverside, CA 92507, (323) 735-8130.

Dominicans (Order of Friars Preachers), O.P.: Founded early 13th century by St. Dominic de Guzman. General headquarters, Santa Sabina, Rome, Italy. Eastern Province of St. Joseph (1805), 869 Lexington Ave., New York, NY 10021-6680, (212) 737-5757, www.op-stjoseph.org. Most Holy Name of Jesus (Western) Province (1912), 5877 Birch Ct., Oakland, CA 94618-1626, (510) 658-8722, www.opwest.org. St. Albert the Great (Central) Province (1939), 1909 S. Ashland Ave., Chicago, IL 60608, (312) 666-3244, www.op.org/domcentral. St. Martin de Porres Province (1979), 1421 N. Causeway Blvd., Suite 200, Metairie, LA 70001-4144, (504) 837-2129, www.opsouth.org. Spanish Province, U.S. foundation (1926), P.O. Box 279, San Diego, TX 78384, (512) 279-3596. Preaching, teaching, missions, research, parishes.

Edmund, Society of St., S.S.E.: Founded 1843, in France, by Fr. Jean Baptiste Muard. General motherhouse, Edmundite Generalate, 270 Winnoski Park, Colchester, VT 05439-0270, (802) 654-3400, www.sse.org. Educational, missionary work.

Eudists (Congregation of Jesus and Mary), C.J.M.: Founded 1643, in France, by St. John Eudes. General motherhouse, Rome, Italy. North American province, 6125 Premiere Ave., Charlesbourg, QC G1H 2V9, Canada, (418) 626-6494; U.S. community, 36 Flohr Ave., W. Seneca, NY 14224, (716) 825-4475; www.eudistes.org. Parochial, educational, pastoral, missionary work.

Francis, Brothers of Poor of St., C.F.P.: Founded 1857. Motherhouse, Aachen, Germany. U.S. province, 239 W. Robbins St., Covington, KY 41011, www.brothersofthepoorofstfrancis.org. Educational work, especially with poor and neglected youth.

Francis, Third Order Regular of St., T.O.R.: Founded 1221, in Italy; in U.S., 1910. General motherhouse, Rome, Italy. Most Sacred Heart of Jesus Province (1910), 128 Woodshire Dr., Pittsburgh, PA 15215-1714, (412) 781-8333. Immaculate Conception Province (1925), 3811 Emerson Ave. N., Minneapolis, MN 55412, (612) 529-7779, www.franciscanfriarstor.com. Franciscan Commissariat of the Spanish

Province (1924), 301 Jefferson Ave., Waco, TX 76701-1419, (254) 752-8434. Educational, parochial, missionary work.

Francis de Sales, Oblates of St., O.S.F.S.: Founded 1871, by Fr. Louis Brisson. General motherhouse, Rome, Italy. Wilmington-Philadelphia Province (1906), 2200 Kentmere Parkway, Wilmington, DE 19806, (302) 656-8529, www.oblates.org. Toledo-Detroit Province (1966), 2043 Parkside Blvd., Toledo, OH 43607, (419) 724-9851. Educational, missionary, parochial work.

Francis Xavier, Brothers of St. (Xaverian Brothers), C.F.X.: Founded 1839, in Belgium, by Theodore J. Ryken. Generalate, 4409 Frederick Ave., Baltimore, MD, 21229, (410) 644-0034; xaverianbrothers.org. Educational work.

Franciscan Brothers of Brooklyn, O.S.F.: Founded in Ireland; established at Brooklyn, 1858. Generalate, 135 Remsen St., Brooklyn, NY 11201, (718) 858-8217, www.franciscanbros.org. Educational work.

Franciscan Brothers of Christ the King, O.S.F.: Founded 1961. General motherhouse, 7329 E. Eastwood Ave., Indianapolis, IN 46239, (317) 862-9211.

Franciscan Brothers of the Holy Cross, F.F.S.C.: Founded 1862, in Germany. Generalate, Hausen, Linz Rhein, Germany; U.S. region, 2500 St. James Rd., Springfield, IL 62707, (217) 528-4757; www.franciscanbrothers.net. Educational work.

Franciscan Brothers of the Third Order Regular, O.S.F.: Generalate, Mountbellew, Ireland. U.S. region, 2117 Spyglass Trail W., Oxnard, CA 93030, (805) 485-5002. (Mailing address: 4522 Gainsborough Ave., Los Angeles, CA 90029.)

Franciscan Friars of the Immaculate, F.F.I: Founded 1990, Italy. General motherhouse, Benevento, Italy. U.S. addresses, 600 Pleasant St., New Bedford, MA. 02740; 22 School Hill Rd., Baltic, CT 06330, (508) 996-8274.

Franciscan Friars of the Renewal, C.F.R.: Community established under jurisdiction of the archbishop of New York. Central House, St. Crispin Friary, 420 E. 156th St., Bronx, NY 10455, (718) 402-8255, www.franciscanfriars.com.

Franciscan Missionary Brothers of the Sacred Heart of Jesus, O.S.F.: Founded 1927, in the St. Louis archdiocese. Motherhouse, St. Joseph Rd., Eureka, MO 63025, (314) 587-3661. Care of aged, infirm, homeless men and boys.

Franciscans (Order of Friars Minor), O.F.M.: A family of the First Order of St. Francis (of Assisi) founded in 1209 and established as a separate jurisdiction in 1517; in U.S., 1844. General headquarters, Rome, Italy. English-speaking conference: 1615 Vine St., Cincinnati, OH 45210-1200, (513) 721-4700.

Immaculate Conception Province (1855), 125 Thompson St., New York, NY 10012, (212) 674-4388. Sacred Heart Province, Franciscan Missionary Union (1858), 3140 Meramec St., St. Louis, MO 63118-4339, (314) 353-7729. Assumption of the Blessed Virgin Mary Province (1887), P.O. Box 100, 165 East Pulaski St., Pulaski, WI 54162-0100. Holy Name Province (1901), 129 W. 31st St., 2nd Floor, New York, NY 10001, (646) 473-0265, www.hnp.org. St. Barbara Province (1915), 1500 34th Ave., Oakland, CA 94601, (510) 536-3722.

Our Lady of Guadalupe Province (1985), 1350 Lakeview Rd. S.W., Albuquerque, NM 87105, (505)

877-5425; OLGofm.org. Commissariat of the Holy Cross (1912), P.O. Box 608, Lemont, IL 60439-0608, (630) 257-2494. Mt. Alverna Friary, 517 S. Belle Vista Ave., Youngstown, OH 44509, (330) 799-1888. Holy Family Croatian Custody (1926), 4851 S. Drexel Blvd., Chicago, IL 60615-1703, (773) 536-0552.

St. Casimir Lithuanian Vice-Province, P.O. Box 980, Kennebunkport, ME 04046, (207) 967-2011. Holy Gospel Province (Mexico), U.S. foundation, 2400 Marr St., El Paso, TX 79903, (915) 565-2921. Commissariat of the Holy Land, Mt. St. Sepulchre, 1400 Quincy St. N.E., Washington, DC 20017, (202) 269-5430. Holy Dormition Friary, Byzantine Slavonic Rite, P.O. Box 270, Rt. 93, Sybertsville, PA 18251, (570) 788-1212, www.hdbf.com. Academy of American Franciscan History, 1712 Euclid Ave., Berkeley, CA 94709. Preaching, missionary, educational, parochial, charitable work.

Franciscans (Order of Friars Minor Capuchin), O.F.M. Cap.: A family of the First Order of St. Francis (of Assisi) founded in 1209 and established as a separate jurisdiction in 1528. St. Joseph Province/St. Bonaventure Monastery (1857), 1740 Mt. Elliott Ave., Detroit, MI 48207-3427, (313) 579-2100. Province of St. Augustine (1873), 220 37th St., Pittsburgh, PA 15201, (412) 682-6011, www.capuchin.com. St. Mary Province (1952), 30 Gedney Park Dr., White Plains, NY 10605, (914) 761-3008. Province of the Stigmata of St. Francis (1918), P.O. Box 809, Union City, NJ 07087-0809, (201) 865-0611. Western American Capuchin Province, Our Lady of the Angels, 1345 Cortez Ave., Burlingame, CA 94010, (650) 342-1489, www.beafriar.com.

St. Stanislaus Friary (1948), 2 Manor Dr., Oak Ridge, NJ 07438, (973) 697-7757. Province of Mid-America (1977), 3553 Wyandot St., Denver, CO 80211, (303) 477-5436, www.midamcaps.org. Vice-Province of Texas, 604 Bernal Dr., Dallas, TX 75212, (214) 631-1937. St. John the Baptist Vice-Province, P.O. Box 21350, Rio Piedras, Puerto Rico 00928-1350, (787) 764-3090. General motherhouse, Rome, Italy. Missionary, parochial work, chaplaincies.

Franciscans (Order of Friars Minor Conventual), O.F.M. Conv.: A family of the First Order of St. Francis (of Assisi) founded in 1209 and established as a separate jurisdiction in 1517; first U.S. foundation, 1852. General curia, Rome, Italy. Immaculate Conception Province (1852), Immaculate Conception Friary, P.O. Box 629, Rensselaer, NY 12144, (518) 472-1000, www.franciscanseast. St. Anthony of Padua Province (1906), 12300 Folly Quarter Rd., Ellicott City, MD 21042, (410) 531-1400,www.stanthonyprovince.org. St. Bonaventure Province (1939), 6107 Kenmore Ave., Chicago, IL 60660, (773) 274-7681. Our Lady of Consolation Province (1926), 101 St. Anthony Dr., Mt. St. Francis, IN 47146, (812) 923-8444. St. Joseph of Cupertino Province (1981), P.O. Box 820, Arroyo Grande, CA 93421-0820, (805) 489-1012. Missionary, educational, parochial work.

Glenmary Missioners (The Home Missioners of America): Founded 1939, in U.S.. General headquarters, P.O. Box 465618, Cincinnati, OH 45246, (513) 881-7442, www.glenmary.org. Home mission work.

Good Shepherd, Little Brothers of the, B.G.S.: Founded 1951, by Bro. Mathias Barrett. Foundation House, P.O. Box 389, Albuquerque, NM 87103, (505)

243-4238. General headquarters, Hamilton, ON, Canada. Operate shelters and refuges for aged and homeless; homes for handicapped men and boys, alcoholic rehabilitation center.

Holy Eucharist, Brothers of the, F.S.E.: Founded in U.S., 1957. Generalate, P.O. Box 25, Plaucheville, LA 71362, (318) 922-3630. Teaching, social, clerical, nursing work.

Holy Family, Congregation of the Missionaries of the, M.S.F.: Founded 1895, in Holland, by Rev. John P. Berthier. General motherhouse, Rome, Italy. U.S. provincialate, 3014 Oregon Ave., St. Louis, MO, 63118-1498, (314) 577-6300, www.msf-america.org. Belated vocations for the missions.

Holy Family, Sons of the, S.F.: Founded 1864, at Barcelona, Spain, by Bl. Jose Mañanet y Vives; in U.S., 1920. General motherhouse, Barcelona, Spain. U.S. address, 401 Randolph Rd., P.O. Box 4138, Silver Spring, MD 20914-4138, (301) 622-1184, www.hometown.aol.com/holyfamsem/index.htm.

Holy Ghost Fathers, C.S.Sp.: Founded 1703, in Paris, France, by Claude Francois Poullart des Places; in U.S., 1872. Generalate, Rome, Italy. Eastern Province (1872), 6230 Brush Run Rd., Bethel Park, PA 15102, (412) 831-0302, www.spiritans.org.Western Province (1964), 1700 W. Alabama St., Houston, TX 77098-2808, (713) 522-2882, www.spiritans.org. Missions, education.

Holy Ghost Fathers of Ireland: Founded 1971. U.S. delegates: 4849 37th St., Long Island City, NY 11101 (East); St. Dunstan's Church, 1133 Broadway, Mill Brae, CA 94030 (West).

Holy Spirit, Missionaries of the, M.Sp.S.: Founded 1914, at Mexico City, Mexico, by Felix Rougier. General motherhouse, Mexico City. U.S. headquarters, 9792 Oma Place, Garden Grove, CA 92841, (714) 534-5476, www.christthepriest.org; charity work.

Immaculate Heart of Mary, Brothers of the, I.H.M.: Founded 1948, at Steubenville, Ohio, by Bishop John K. Mussio. Villa Maria Generalate, 609 N. 7th St., Steubenville, OH 43952, (740) 283-2462. Educational, charitable work.

Jesuits (Society of Jesus), S.J.: Founded 1534, in France, by St. Ignatius of Loyola; received papal approval, 1540; suppressed in 1773 and revived in 1814 by Pope Pius VII; first U.S. province, 1833. The Jesuits remain the largest single order in the Church. Generalate, Rome, Italy. U.S. national office, Jesuit Conference, 1016 16th Street, N.W., Fourth Floor, Washington, DC 20036-1420, (202) 462-0400, www.jesuit.org. Maryland Province (1833), 5704 Roland Ave., Baltimore, MD 21210, (410) 532-1400, www.mdsj.org. New York Province (1943), 39 East 83rd St., New York, NY 10028, (212) 774-5500, www.nysj.org. Missouri Province (1863), 4511 W. Pine Blvd., St. Louis, MO 63108-2191, (314) 361-7765, www.jesuits-mis.org. New Orleans Province (1907), 710 Baronne St., Suite B, New Orleans, LA 70113, (504) 788-1719.

California Province (1909), 300 College Ave., P.O. Box 519, Los Gatos, CA 95031, (408) 884-1600, www.jesuitscalifornia.org. New England Province (1926), 85 School St., Watertown, MA 02472; (617) 607-2800. Chicago Province (1928), 2050 N. Clark St., Chicago, IL 60614, (773) 975-6363, www.jesuits-chi.org. Oregon Province (1932), 2222 N.W. Hoyt,

Portland, OR 97210, (503) 226-6977. Detroit Province (1955), 7303 W. Seven Mile Rd., Detroit, MI 48221-2121, (313) 861-7500, www.jesuitdet.org. Wisconsin Province (1955), PO Box 080288, Milwaukee, WI 53208-0288, (414) 937-6949, www.jesuitwisprov.org. Province of the Antilles (1947), U.S. address, 12725 S.W. 6th St., Miami, FL 33184, (305) 559-9044. Missionary, educational, literary work.

John of God, Brothers of the Hospitaller Order of St., O.H.: Founded 1537, in Spain. General motherhouse, Rome, Italy. American province, 2425 S. Western Ave., Los Angeles, CA 90018, (323) 731-0233, www.hospitallers.org. Nursing and related fields.

Joseph, Congregation of St., C.S.J.: General motherhouse, Rome, Italy. U.S. vice-province, 338 North Grand Ave., San Pedro, CA 90731-2006, (310) 831-5360. Parochial, missionary, educational work.

Joseph, Oblates of St., O.S.J.: Founded 1878, in Italy, by Bl. Joseph Marello; in U.S., 1929. General motherhouse, Rome, Italy. Our Lady of Sorrows Province, 1880 Hwy 315, Pittston, PA 18640, (570) 654-7542. California Province, 544 W. Cliff Dr., Santa Cruz, CA 95060, (831) 457-1868, www.osjoseph.org. Parochial, educational work.

Josephite Fathers, C.J.: General motherhouse, Ghent, Belgium; U.S. foundation, 5075 Harp Rd., Santa Maria, CA 93455, (805) 937-4555; www.josephiteweb.org.

Josephites (St. Joseph's Society of the Sacred Heart), S.S.J.: Established 1893, in U.S. as American congregation (originally established in U.S., in 1871 by Mill Hill Josephites from England). General motherhouse, 1130 N. Calvert St., Baltimore, MD 21202-3802, (410) 727-3386, www.josephite.com. Evangelization in African-American community.

LaSalette, Missionaries of Our Lady of: Province of Mary, Mother of the Americas, 915 Maple Ave., Hartford, CT 06114-2330, (860) 956-8870.

Lateran, Canons Regular of the, C.R.L.: General House, Rome, Italy. U.S. address: 2317 Washington Ave., Bronx, NY 10458, (212) 295-9600.

Legionaries of Christ, L.C.: Founded 1941, in Mexico, by Rev. Marcial Maciel; in U.S., 1965. General headquarters, Rome, Italy. U.S. headquarters, 393 Derby Ave., Orange, CT 06477, (203) 795-2800, novitiate, 475 Oak Ave., Cheshire, CT 06410, (203) 271-0805, www.legionofchrist.org.

Little Brothers of St. Francis, L.B.S.F.: Founded 1970 in Archdiocese of Boston by Bro. James Curran. General fraternity, 785-789 Parker St., Boston, MA 02120-3021, (617) 442-2556, www.littlebrothersofstfrancis.org. Combine contemplative life with evangelical street ministry.

Mariannhill, Congregation of the Missionaries of, C.M.M.: Trappist monastery, begun in 1882 by Abbot Francis Pfanner in Natal, South Africa, became an independent modern congregation in 1909; in U.S., 1920. Generalate, Rome, Italy. U.S.-Canadian province (1938), Our Lady of Grace Monastery, 23715 Ann Arbor Trail, Dearborn Hts., MI 48127-1449, (313) 561-2330, www.rc.net/detroit/marianhill. Foreign mission work.

Marians of the Immaculate Conception, Congregation of, M.I.C.: Founded 1673; U.S. foundation, 1913. General motherhouse, Rome, Italy. St. Casimir Province (1913), 6336 S. Kilbourn Ave.,

Chicago, IL 60629-5588, (773) 582-8191, www.the-marians.org. St. Stanislaus Kostka Province (1948), Eden Hill, Stockbridge, MA 01262, (413) 298-1101. Educational, parochial, mission, publication work.

Marist Brothers, F.M.S.: Co-founded 1817, in France, by St. Marcellin Champagnat. Generalate, Rome, Italy. U.S. Province, 1241 Kennedy Blvd., Bayonne, NJ 07002, (201) 823-1115; www.maristbr.com. Educational, social, catechetical work.

Marist Fathers (Society of Mary), S.M.: Founded 1816, at Lyons, France, by Jean Claude Colin; in U.S., 1863. General motherhouse, Rome, Italy. Atlanta Province, P.O. Box 81144, Atlanta, GA 30366-1144, (770) 458-1435, www.maristsociety.org. Boston Province (1924), 27 Isabella St., Boston, MA 02116, (617) 426-5297. Educational, foreign mission, pastoral work.

Maronite Lebanese Missionaries, Congregation of, C.M.L.M.: Founded in Lebanon 1865; established in the U.S., 1991. U.S. foundation, Our Lady of the Cedars Maronite Mission, 11935 Bellfort Village, Houston, TX 77031, (281) 568-6800.

Maronite Monks of Most Holy Trinity Monastery: Founded in 1978 and canonically approved by John Paul II and established in the Eparchy of St. Maron in 1989. A community of contemplative monks dedicated to a life of prayer and Eucharistic Adoration. Most Holy Trinity Monastery, 67 Dugway Road, Petersham, MA 01366-9725, (978) 724-3347, www.maronitemonks.org.

Mary, Society of (Marianist Fathers and Brothers; Brothers of Mary), S.M.: Founded 1817, at Bordeaux, France, by Rev. William-Joseph Chaminade; in U.S., 1849. General motherhouse, Rome, Italy. Marianist Province of the U.S. (Meribah), 240 Emory Rd., Mineola, NY 11501, (516) 742-5555, www.provinceofmeribah.org. The Marianist provinces of Cincinnati, St. Louis, Pacific, and New York have merged to form one province. Educational work.

Mary Immaculate, Missionary Oblates of, O.M.I.: Founded 1816, in France, by St. Charles Joseph Eugene de Mazenod; in U.S., 1849. General House, Rome, Italy. U.S. Province: 391 Michigan Ave., N.E., Washington, DC, 20017, (202) 529-4505. Southwest Area, 327 Oblate Dr., San Antonio, TX 78216-6602, (210) 349-1475, www.omiusa.org. Parochial, foreign mission, educational work, ministry to marginal.

Maryknoll (Catholic Foreign Mission Society of America), M.M.: Founded 1911, in U.S., by Frs. Thomas F. Price and James A. Walsh. General Center, Maryknoll, NY 10545, (914) 941-7590.

Mercedarians (Order of Our Lady of Mercy), O. de M.: Founded 1218, in Spain, by St. Peter Nolasco. General motherhouse, Rome, Italy. U.S. headquarters, 3205 Fulton Rd., Cleveland, OH 44109 (216) 961-8331.

Mercy, Brothers of, F.M.M.: Founded 1856, in Germany. General motherhouse, Montabaur, Germany. American headquarters, 4520 Ransom Rd., Clarence, NY 14031, (716) 759-8341. Hospital work.

Mercy, Brothers of Our Lady, Mother of, C.F.M.M.: Founded 1844, in the Netherlands by Abp. Jan Zwijsen. Generalate, Tilburg, the Netherlands. U.S. region, 7140 Ramsgate Ave., Los Angeles, CA 90045, (310) 338-5954, www.cmmbrothers.nl.

Mercy, Congregation of Priests of (Fathers of Mercy), C.P.M.: Founded 1808, in France, by Rev. Jean Baptiste Rauzan; in U.S., 1839. General mission house, Auburn, KY 42206, (270) 542-4164; www.fathersofmercy.com. Mission work.

Mill Hill Missionaries (St. Joseph's Society for Foreign Missions), M.H.M.: Founded 1866, in England, by Cardinal Vaughan; in U.S., 1951. International headquarters, London, England. American headquarters, 222 W. Hartsdale Ave., Hartsdale, NY 10530, (914) 682-0645.

Minim Fathers, O.M.: General motherhouse, Rome, Italy. North American delegation (1970), 3431 Portola Ave., Los Angeles, CA 90032, (213) 223-1101.

Missionaries of St. Charles, Congregation of the (Scalabrinians), C.S.: Founded 1887, at Piacenza, Italy, by Bl. John Baptist Scalabrini. General motherhouse, Rome, Italy. St. Charles Borromeo Province (1888), 27 Carmine St., New York, NY 10014, (212) 675-3993. St. John Baptist Province (1903), 546 N. East Ave., Oak Park, IL 60302, (708) 386-4430.

Missionaries of the Holy Apostles, M.Ss.A.: Founded 1962, Washington, DC, by Very Rev. Eusebe M. Menard. North American headquarters, 24 Prospect Hill Rd., Cromwell, CT 06416, (860) 632-3039.

Missionarii Franciscani Verbi Aeterni, Franciscan Missionaries of the Eternal Word, 5821 Old Leeds Rd., Irondale, AL 35210, www.mfva.info.

Missionary Servants of Christ, M.S.C.: Founded 1979 in U.S. by Bro. Edwin Baker. Headquarters, P.O. Box 270, 305 S. Lake St., Aurora, IL 60507-0270, (630) 892-2371, www.misacor-usa.org.

Missionhurst-CICM (Congregation of the Immaculate Heart of Mary): Founded 1862, at Scheut, Brussels, Belgium, by Very Rev. Theophile Verbist. General motherhouse, Rome, Italy. U.S. province, 4651 N. 25th St., Arlington, VA 22207, (703) 528-3800, www.missionhurst.org. Home and foreign mission work.

Montfort Missionaries (Missionaries of the Company of Mary), S.M.M.: Founded 1715, by St. Louis Marie Grignon de Montfort; in U.S., 1948. General motherhouse, Rome, Italy. U.S. province, 101-18 104th St., Ozone Park, NY 11416, (718) 849-5885. Mission work.

Mother Co-Redemptrix, Congregation of, C.M.C.: Founded 1953 at Lein-Thuy, Vietnam (North), by Fr. Dominic Mary Tran Dinh Thu; in U.S., 1975. General house, Hochiminhville, Vietnam. U.S. provincial house, 1900 Grand Ave., Carthage, MO 64836, (417) 358-7787, www.dong-cong.net. Work among Vietnamese Catholics in U.S.

Oblates of the Virgin Mary, O.M.V.: Founded 1815, in Italy; in U.S., 1976; Generalate, Rome, Italy. U.S. provincialate: 2 Ipswich St., Boston, MA 02215, (617) 536-4141.

Oratorians (Congregation of the Oratory of St. Philip Neri), C.O.: Founded 1575, at Rome, by St. Philip Neri. A confederation of autonomous houses. U.S. addresses: P.O. Box 11586, Rock Hill, SC 29731, (803) 327-2097, www.rockhilloratory.org. P.O. Box 1688, Monterey, CA 93940, (831) 373-0476. 4450 Bayard St., Pittsburgh, PA 15213, (412) 681-3181. P.O. Drawer II, Pharr, TX 78577, (956) 843-8217. 109 Willoughby St., Brooklyn, NY 11201, (718) 788-5693.

Pallottines (Society of the Catholic Apostolate), S.A.C.: Founded 1835, at Rome, by St. Vincent Pallotti. Generalate, Rome, Italy. Immaculate Conception Province (1953), P.O. Box 979, South Orange, NJ 07079, (201) 762-2926. Mother of God Province (1946), 5424 W. Blue Mound Rd., Milwaukee, WI 53208, (414) 259-0688. Irish Province (1909), U.S. address: 3352 4th St., Wyandotte, MI 48192, www.irishpallotines.com. Queen of Apostles Province (1909), 448 E. 116th St., New York, NY 10029, (212) 534-0681. Christ the King Province, 3452 Niagara Falls, Blvd., N. Tonawanda, NY 14120, (716) 694-4313. Charitable, educational, parochial, mission work.

Paraclete, Servants of the, S.P.: Founded 1947, Santa Fe, N.M., archdiocese. Generalate and U.S. motherhouse, 13270 Maple Dr., St. Louis, MO 63127, (314) 965-0869; www.theservants.org. Dedicated to ministry to priests and Brothers with personal difficulties.

Paris Foreign Missions Society, M.E.P.: Founded 1662, at Paris, France. Headquarters, Paris, France; U.S. establishment, 930 Ashbury St., San Francisco, CA 94117, (415) 664-6747. Mission work and training of native clergy.

Passionists (Congregation of the Passion), C.P.: Founded 1720, in Italy, by St. Paul of the Cross. General motherhouse, Rome, Italy. St. Paul of the Cross Province (Eastern Province) (1852), 80 David St., South River, NJ 08882, (732) 257-7177, www.thepassionists.org. Holy Cross Province (Western Province), 5700 N. Harlem Ave., Chicago, IL 60631, (773) 631-6336.

Patrician Brothers (Brothers of St. Patrick), F.S.P.: Founded 1808, in Ireland, by Bishop Daniel Delaney. U.S. novitiate, 7820 Bolsa Ave., Midway City, CA 92655, (714) 897-8181. Educational work.

Patrick's Missionary Society, St., S.P.S.: Founded 1932, at Wicklow, Ireland, by Msgr. Patrick Whitney; in U.S., 1953. International headquarters, Kiltegan Co., Wicklow, Ireland. U.S. foundations: 70 Edgewater Rd., Cliffside Park, NJ 07010, (201) 943-6575, 19536 Eric Dr., Saratoga, CA 95070, (408) 253-3135, www.spms.org; 1347 W. Granville Ave., Chicago, IL 60660, (773) 973-3737.

Pauline Fathers (Order of St. Paul the First Hermit), O.S.P.P.E.: Founded 1215; established in U.S., 1955. General motherhouse, Czesto-chowa, Jasna Gora, Poland; U.S. province, P.O. Box 2049, Doylestown, PA 18901, (215) 345-0600; www.czestochowa.us.

Pauline Fathers and Brothers (Society of St. Paul for the Apostolate of Communications), S.S.P.: Founded 1914, by Very Rev. James Alberione; in U.S., 1932. Motherhouse, Rome, Italy. New York province (1932), P.O. Box 139, Ellsworth, OH 44416-0139, (330) 533-7427. Social communications work.

Paulists (Missionary Society of St. Paul the Apostle), C.S.P.: Founded 1858, in New York, by Fr. Isaac Thomas Hecker. Motherhouse: 86-11 Midland Pkwy, Jamaica Estates, NY 11432, (718) 291-5995, www.paulist.org. Missionary, ecumenical, pastoral work.

Piarists (Order of the Pious Schools), Sch.P.: Founded 1617, at Rome, Italy, by St. Joseph Calasanctius. General motherhouse, Rome, Italy. U.S. province, 363 Valley Forge Rd., Devon, PA 19333, (610) 688-7337. New York-Puerto Rico vice-province (Calasanzian Fathers), P.O. Box 7760, Ponce, PR 00732-7760, (787) 840-0610. California vice province, 3940 Perry St., Los Angeles, CA 90063, (323) 261-1386. Educational work.

Pius X, Brothers of St., C.S.P.X.: Founded 1952, at La Crosse, WI, by Bishop John P. Treacy. Motherhouse, P.O. Box 217, De Soto, WI 54624. Education.

Pontifical Institute for Foreign Missions, P.I.M.E.: Founded 1850, in Italy, at request of Pope Pius IX. General motherhouse, Rome, Italy. U.S. province, 17330 Quincy Ave., Detroit, MI 48221, (313) 342-

4066, www.pimeusa.org work.

Precious Blood, Society of, C.P.P.S.: Founded 1815, in Italy, by St. Gaspar del Bufalo. General motherhouse, Rome, Italy. Cincinnati Province, 431 E. Second St., Dayton, OH 45402, (937) 228-9263, www.cpps-preciousblood.org. Kansas City Province, P.O. Box 339, Liberty, MO 64069-0339, (816) 781-4344. Pacific Province, 2337 134th Ave. W., San Leandro, CA 94577, (510) 357-4982, www.rc.net/oakland/cpps. Atlantic Province 100 Pelmo Cres., Toronto, ON M9N 2Y1, (416) 614-7096, www.preciousblood.org.

Premonstratensians (Order of the Canons Regular of Premontre; Norbertines), O. Praem.: Founded 1120, at Premontre, France, by St. Norbert; in U.S., 1893. Generalate, Rome, Italy. St. Norbert Abbey, 1016 N. Broadway, DePere, WI 54114, (920) 337-4300, www.snc.edu/norbertines. Daylesford Abbey, 220 S. Valley Rd., Paoli, PA 19301, (610) 647-2530, www.daylesford.org. St. Michael's Abbey, 19292 El Toro Rd., Silverado, CA 92676, (949) 858-0222, www.abbeynews.com. Immaculate Conception Priory (1997), 3600 Philadelphia Pike, Claymont, DE 19703, (302) 792-2791. Educational, parish work.

Priestly Fraternity of St. Peter, F.S.S.P.: Founded and approved Oct. 18, 1988; first foundation in U.S., 1991. U.S. headquarters, St. Peter's House, Griffin Rd., P.O. Box 196, Elmhurst, PA 18416, (570) 842-4000, www.fssp.com. Pastoral and sacramental ministry using the 1962 liturgical books.

Providence, Sons of Divine, F.D.P.: Founded 1893, at Tortona, Italy, by Bl. Luigi Orione; in U.S., 1933. General motherhouse, Rome, Italy. U.S. address, 111 Orient Ave., E. Boston, MA 02128, (617) 569-2100.

Redemptorist Fathers and Brothers (Congregation of the Most Holy Redeemer), C.SS.R.: Founded 1732, in Italy, by St. Alphonsus Mary Liguori. Generalate, Rome, Italy. Baltimore Province (1850), 7509 Shore Rd., Brooklyn, NY 11209, (718) 833-1900. Redemptorist-Denver Province (1875), Box 300399, Denver, CO 80203-0399, (303) 370-0035, www.redemptorists-denver.org. Richmond Vice-Province (1942), 313 Hillman St., P.O. Box 1529, New Smyrna Beach, FL 32170, (904) 427-3094. Mission work.

Resurrectionists (Congregation of the Resurrection), C.R.: Founded 1836, in France, under direction of Bogdan Janski. Motherhouse, Rome, Italy. U.S. Province, 7050 N. Oakley Ave., Chicago, IL 60645-3426, (773) 465-8320, www.resurrectionists.com. Ontario Kentucky Province, U.S. address, 338 N. 25th St., Louisville, KY 40212, (502) 772-3694.

Rogationist Fathers, R.C.J.: Founded by Bl. Annibale (Hannibal) di Francia, 1887. General motherhouse, Rome, Italy. U.S. delegation: 2688 S. Newmark Ave., Sanger, CA 91343, (209) 875-5808. Charitable work.

Rosary, Brothers of Our Lady of the Holy, F.S.R.: Founded 1956, in U.S. motherhouse and novitiate, 232 Sunnyside Dr., Reno, NV 89503-3510, (775) 326-9429.

Rosminians (Institute of Charity), I.C.: Founded 1828, in Italy, by Antonio Rosmini-Serbati. General motherhouse, Rome, Italy. U.S. address, 2327 W. Heading Ave., Peoria, IL 61604, (309) 676-6341. Charitable work.

Sacred Heart, Brothers of the, S.C.: Founded 1821, in France, by Rev. Andre Coindre. General motherhouse, Rome, Italy. New Orleans Province (1847), 4600 Elysian Fields Ave., New Orleans, LA 70122, (504) 282-5693. New England Province (1945), 159 Earle St., Woonsocket, RI 02895, (401) 769-0313, www.brothersofthesacredheart.org. New York Province (1960), 141-11 123 Ave., South Ozone Park, NY 11436-1426, (718) 322-3309. Educational work.

Sacred Heart, Missionaries of the, M.S.C.: Founded 1854, by Rev. Jules Chevelier. General motherhouse, Rome, Italy. U.S. province, 305 S. Lake St., Aurora, IL 60507-0271, (630) 892-8400.

Sacred Heart of Jesus, Congregation of the (Sacred Heart Fathers and Brothers), S.C.J.: Founded 1877, in France. General motherhouse, Rome, Italy. U.S. provincial office, P.O. Box 289, Hales Corners, WI 53130-0289, (414) 425-6910, www.scj.org. Educational, preaching, mission work.

Sacred Hearts of Jesus and Mary, Congregation of (Picpus Fathers), SS.CC.: Founded 1805, in France, by Fr. Coudrin. General motherhouse, Rome, Italy. Eastern Province (1946), 77 Adams St. (Box 111), Fairhaven, MA 02719, (508) 993-2442, www.sscc.org. Western Province (1970), 2150 Damien Ave., La Verne, CA 91750, (909) 593-5441. Hawaii Province, Box 797, Kaneohe, Oahu, HI 96744, (808) 247-5035. Mission, educational work.

Sacred Hearts of Jesus and Mary, Missionaries of the, M.SS.CC.: Founded 1833, in Naples, Italy, by Cajetan Errico. General motherhouse, Rome, Italy. U.S. headquarters, 2249 Shore Rd., Linwood, NJ 08221, (609) 927-5600.

Salesians of St. John Bosco (Society of St. Francis de Sales), S.D.B.: Founded 1859, by St. John (Don) Bosco. Generalate, Rome, Italy. St. Philip the Apostle Province (1902), 148 Main St., P.O. Box 639, New Rochelle, NY 10802-0639, (914) 636-4225. San Francisco Province (1926), 1100 Franklin St., San Francisco, CA 94109, (415) 441-7144.

Salvatorians (Society of the Divine Savior), S.D.S.: Founded 1881, in Rome, by Fr. Francis Jordan; in U.S., 1896. General headquarters, Rome, Italy. U.S. province, 1735 N. Hi-Mount Blvd., Milwaukee, WI 53208-1720, (414) 258-1735, www.salvatorians.com. Educational, parochial, mission work; campus ministries, chaplaincies.

Scalabrinians: *See* Missionaries of St. Charles.

Servites (Order of Friar Servants of Mary), O.S.M.: Founded 1233, at Florence, Italy, by Seven Holy Founders. Generalate, Rome, Italy. United States Province (1967), 3121 W. Jackson Blvd., Chicago, IL 60612, (773) 533-0360. General apostolic ministry.

Somascan Fathers, C.R.S.: Founded 1534, at Somasca, Italy, by St. Jerome Emiliani. General motherhouse, Rome, Italy. U.S. address, Pine Haven Boys Center, River Rd., P.O. Box 162, Suncook, NH 03275, (603) 485-7141, www.somascans.org.

Society of Our Lady of the Most Holy Trinity, S.O.L.T.: Headquarters, Casa San Jose, 109 W. Avenue F, P.O. Box 152, Robstown, TX 78380, (512) 387-2754.

Sons of Mary (Sons of Mary, Health of the Sick), F.M.S.I.: Founded 1952, in the Boston archdiocese, by Rev. Edward F. Garesche, S.J. Headquarters, 567 Salem End Rd., Framingham, MA 01701-5599, (508) 879-2541, www.sonsofmary.com.

Stigmatine Fathers and Brothers (Congregation of the Sacred Stigmata), C.S.S.: Founded 1816, by St. Gaspar Bertoni. General motherhouse, Rome, Italy. North American Province, 554 Lexington St., Waltham, MA 02452-3097, (781) 209-3100, www.stigmatines.com. Parish work.

Sulpicians (Society of Priests of St. Sulpice), S.S.: Founded 1641, in Paris, by Rev. Jean Jacques Olier. General motherhouse, Paris, France; U.S. province, 5408 Roland Ave., Baltimore, MD 21210, (410) 323-5070, www.sulpicians.org. Education of seminarians and priests.

Theatines (Congregation of Clerics Regular), C.R.: Founded 1524, in Rome, by St. Cajetan. General motherhouse, Rome, Italy. U.S. headquarters, 1050 S. Birch St., Denver, CO 80246, (303) 756-5522.

Trappists: *See* Cistercians of the Strict Observance.

Trinitarians (Order of the Most Holy Trinity), O.SS.T.: Founded 1198, by St. John of Matha; in U.S., 1911. General motherhouse, Rome, Italy. U.S. headquarters, P.O. Box 5742, Baltimore, MD 21282, (410) 486-5171.

Trinity Missions (Missionary Servants of the Most Holy Trinity), S.T.: Founded 1929, by Fr. Thomas Augustine Judge. Generalate, P.O. Box 7130, Silver Springs, MD 20907-7130, (301) 434-6761, www.trinitymissions.org. Home mission work.

Viatorian Fathers (Clerics of St. Viator), C.S.V.: Founded 1831, in France, by Fr. Louis Joseph Querbes. General motherhouse, Rome, Italy. Province of Chicago (1882), 1212 E. Euclid Ave., Arlington Hts., IL 60004, (847) 398-1353. Educational work.

Vincentians (Congregation of the Mission; Lazarists), C.M.: Founded 1625, in Paris, by St. Vincent de Paul; in U.S., 1818. General motherhouse, Rome, Italy. Eastern Province (1867), 500 E. Chelten Ave., Philadelphia, PA 19144, (215) 848-1985. Midwest Province (1888), 13663 Rider Trail North, Earth City, MO 63045, (314) 344-1184; www.vincentian.org. New England Province (1975), 234 Keeney St., Manchester, CT 06040-7048, (860) 643-2828. American Italian Branch, Our Lady of Pompei Church, 3600 Claremont St., Baltimore, MD 21224, (410) 675-7790. American Spanish Branch (Barcelona, Spain), 118 Congress St., Brooklyn, NY 11201-6045, (718) 624-5670. American Spanish Branch (Zaragoza, Spain), Holy Agony Church, 1834 3rd Ave., New York, NY 10029, (212) 289-5589. Western Province (1975), 420 Date St., Montebello, CA 90640, (323) 721-5486. Southern Province (1975), 3826 Gilbert Ave., Dallas, TX 75219, (214) 526-0234, www.cmsouth.org. Educational work.

Vocationist Fathers (Society of Divine Vocations), S.D.V.: Founded 1920, in Italy; in U.S., 1962. Generalate, Rome, Italy. U.S. headquarters, 90 Brooklake Rd., Florham Park, NJ 07932, (973) 966-6262, www.vocationist.org.

Xaverian Missionary Fathers, S.X.: Founded 1895, by Bl. Guido Conforti, at Parma, Italy. General motherhouse, Rome, Italy. U.S. province, 12 Helene Ct., Wayne, NJ 07470, (973) 942-2975, www.xaviermissionaries.org. Foreign mission work.

MEMBERSHIP OF RELIGIOUS INSTITUTES OF MEN

Principal source: Annuario Pontificio. *Statistics as of Jan. 1, 2008 unless indicated otherwise. Listed below are world membership statistics of institutes of men of pontifical right with 500 or more members; the number of priests is in parentheses. Also listed are institutes with less than 500 members with houses in the U.S.*

Jesuits (13,486)	19,216
Salesians (10,954)	16,389
Franciscans (Friars Minor) (10,422)	15,256
Franciscans (Capuchins) (7,037)	11,166
Benedictines (4,239)	7,640
Society of the Divine Word (3,961)	6,096
Dominicans (4,469)	6,044
Redemptorists (4,134)	5,601
Brothers of Christian Schools	5,473
Oblates of Mary Immaculate (3,244)	4,548
Franciscans (Conventuals) (2,925)	4,525
Marist Brothers	4,125
Discalced Carmelites (O.C.D.) (2,724)	4,044
Vincentians (3,110)	3,978
Claretians (2,103)	3,084
Holy Spirit (Holy Ghost), Vincentians Congregation of (2,207)	3,011
Augustinians (2,089)	2,795
Pallottines (1,641)	2,390
Priests of the Sacred Heart (1,627)	2,333
Carmelites of the BVM (1,516)	2,285
Passionists (1,690)	2,229
Trappists (896)	2,162
Legionaries of Christ (713)	2,059
Missionaries of the Sacred Heart of Jesus (1,401)	2,020
Combonian Missionaries of the Heart of Jesus (1,307)	2,018
Carmelites (O.Carm.) (1,337)	1,942
Missionaries of Africa (1,470)	1,788
Holy Cross, Congregation of (747)	1,565
Cistercians (Common Observance) (731)	1,523
Marianists (453)	1,414
Piarists (1,024)	1,405
Christian Brothers	1,360
Missionaries of St. Francis de Sales of Annecy (761)	1,326
Hospitallers of St. John of God (138)	1,291
Premonstratensians (950)	1,290
Brothers of Christian Instruction of St. Gabriel (26)	1,267
Brothers of the Sacred Heart (37)	1,218
Salvatorians (834)	1,211
Augustinians (Recollects) (951)	1,168
Marists (942)	1,149
Ministers of the Sick (Camillians) (679)	1,146
Society of St. Paul (559)	1,054
Little Workers of Divine Providence (692)	1,048
Immaculate Heart of Mary, Congregation of (Missionhurst; Scheut Missionaries)(803)	1,008
Consolata Missionaries (764)	990
Montfort Missionaries (681)	978
Brothers of Christian Instruction of Ploërmel	961
LaSalette Missionaries (700)	956
Society of African Missions (826)	940
Blessed Sacrament, Congregation of (646)	909
Missionaries of the Holy Family (667)	908
Sacred Hearts, Congregation of (Picpus) (722)	905
Assumptionists (564)	887
Servants of Mary (646)	883
Franciscans (Third Order Regular) (369)	883
Xaverian Missionaries (663)	852
Scalabrinians (593)	752
Mercedarians (504)	726
Canons Regular of St. Augustine (572)	681
Most Precious Blood (457)	611
Viatorians (256)	608
St. Joseph, Congregation of (451)	607
Missionaries of the Mill Hill (411)	603
Oblates of St. Francis de Sales (458)	600
Trinitarians (385)	587
Brothers of Charity (Ghent)	570
Order of St. Basil the Great (Basilians of St. Josaphat) (312)	564
Oblates of St. Joseph (355)	563
Columbans (502)	554
Oratorians (413)	537
Pontifical Institute for Foreign Missions (479)	525
Servants of Charity (322)	515
Order of St. Paul the First Hermit (322)	508
Society of Christ (381)	487
Maryknollers (416)	480
Marian Fathers and Brothers (345)	477
Somascans (352)	472
Eudists (371)	445
Crosiers (Order of the Holy Cross) (282)	440
Heralds of Good News (231)	430
Stigmatine Fathers and Brothers (315)	428
Resurrection, Congregation of the (325)	408
Rogationists (263)	399
Mariannhill Missionaries (214)	394
Brothers of the Immaculate Conception (3)	385
Missionaries of the Holy Spirit (248)	381
Vocationist Fathers (172)	379
Barnabites (291)	375
St. Patrick's Mission Society (309)	373
Carthusians (165)	328
Sulpicians (315)	315
Rosminians (203)	313
Priestly Fraternity of St. Peter (191)	313
Paris Foreign Mission Society (275)	285
Little Brothers of Jesus (64)	227
Xaverian Brothers	227
Brothers of St. Patrick	215
Discalced Augustinians (98)	204
Theatines (139)	203
Minim Fathers (108)	195
Sons of the Holy Family (136)	193
Oblates of the Virgin Mary (135)	180
Charitable Schools (90)	176
Paulists (145)	159
Bethlehem Missionaries (109)	148
Missionary Servants of the Most Holy Trinity (90)	145
Mary Immaculate, Sons of (88)	126
Basilian Salvatorian Fathers (97)	114
Franciscan Friars of the Atonement (76)	113

Josephites (C.J.) (84)	113	Clerics Regular of the Mother of God (44)	60
Josephites (St. Joseph's Society of the Sacred		Camaldolese Hermits of Monte Corona (26)	57
Heart—S.S.J.) (87)	106	Sacerdotal Fraternity, Cong. of the (21)	52
Presentation Brothers	106	Brothers of Mercy	40
Franciscan Brothers of Brooklyn	92	Society of St. Edmund (36)	40
Alexian Brothers (3)	89	Franciscan Brothers of the Holy Cross (1)	37
Clerics Regular Minor (Adorno Fathers) (50)	88	Fathers of Mercy	36
Brothers of Our Lady Mother of Mercy (22)	80	Servants of the Holy Paraclete (18)	34
Glenmary Missioners (49)	70	Little Brothers of the Good Shepherd (4)	31

RELIGIOUS INSTITUTES OF WOMEN IN THE UNITED STATES

Sources: The Official Catholic Directory; Catholic Almanac *survey. As of June 1, 2008.*

Adorers of the Blood of Christ, A.S.C.: Founded 1834, in Italy; in U.S., 1870. General motherhouse, Rome, Italy. U.S. region: 4233 Sulphur Ave., St. Louis, MO 63109, (314) 351-6294,; 3950 Columbia Ave., Columbia, PA 17512, (717) 285-4536; www.adorers.org. Education, retreats, social services, pastoral ministry.

Africa, Missionary Sisters of Our Lady of (Sisters of Africa), M.S.O.L.A.: Founded 1869, at Algiers, Algeria, by Cardinal Lavigerie; in U.S., 1929. General motherhouse, Rome, Italy. U.S. headquarters, 47 W. Spring St., Winooski, VT 05404-1397, (802) 655-4003, www.smnda.org. Medical, educational, catechetical and social work in Africa.

Agnes, Sisters of St., C.S.A.: Founded 1858, in U.S., by Rev. Caspar Rehrl. General motherhouse, 320 County Rd., Fond du Lac, WI 54935, (920) 907-2321, www.csasisters.org. Education, health care, social services.

Ann, Sisters of St., S.S.A.: Founded 1834, in Italy; in U.S., 1952. General motherhouse, Rome, Italy. U.S. headquarters, Mount St. Ann, Ebensburg, PA 15931, (814) 472-9354.

Anne, Sisters of St., S.S.A.: Founded 1850, at Vaudreuil, QC, Canada; in U.S., 1866. General motherhouse, Lachine, QC, Canada. U.S. address, 720 Boston Post Rd., Marlborough, MA 01752, (508) 597-0204, www.sistersof-saintanne.org. Retreat work, pastoral ministry, religious education.

Anthony, Missionary Servants of St., M.S.S.A.: Founded 1929, in U.S., by Rev. Peter Basque. General motherhouse, 100 Peter Baque Rd., San Antonio, TX 78209, (210) 824-4553. Social work.

Antonine Maronite Sisters: Founded in Beirut, Lebanon. Motherhouse, Couvent Mar-Doumith, Roumieh, El-Metn, B.P. 84, Borumana, Lebanon. U.S. house, 2691 North Lipkey Rd., North Jackson, OH 44451, (330) 538-9822; www.antoinesisters.com.

Assumption, Little Sisters of the, L.S.A.: Founded 1865, in France; in U.S., 1891. General motherhouse, Paris, France. U.S. provincialate, 100 Gladstone Ave., Walden, NY 12586, (914) 778-0667, www.little-sisters.org. Social work, nursing, family life education.

Assumption, Religious of the, R.A.: Founded 1839, in France; in U.S., 1919. Generalate, Paris, France. North American province, 11 Old English Rd., Worcester, MA 01609, (508) 791-2936; www.assumptionsisters.org.

Assumption of the Blessed Virgin, Sisters of the, S.A.S.V.: Founded 1853, in Canada; in U.S., 1891. General motherhouse, Nicolet, QC, Canada. U.S. province, 316 Lincoln St., Worcester, MA 01605, (508) 856-9450. Education, mission, pastoral ministry.

Augustinian Nuns of Contemplative Life, O.S.A.: Established in Spain in 13th century. U.S. foundation, Convent of Our Mother of Good Counsel, 440 Marley Rd., New Lenox, IL, 60451, (815) 463-9662; www.lampsalight.org.

Augustinian Sisters, Servants of Jesus and Mary, Congregation of, O.S.A.: Generalate, Rome, Italy. U.S. foundation, St. John School, 513 E. Broadway, Brandenburg, KY 40108, (270) 422-2088, www.stjohnonline.org.

Basil the Great, Sisters of the Order of St. (Byzantine Rite), O.S.B.M.: Founded fourth century, in Cappadocia, by St. Basil the Great and his sister, St. Macrina; in U.S., 1911. Generalate, Rome, Italy. U.S. motherhouses: Philadelphia Ukrainian Byzantine Rite, 710 Fox Chase Rd., Philadelphia, PA 19046-4198, (215) 379-3998, www.basilianfoxchase.org. Pittsburgh Ruthenian Byzantine Rite, Mount St. Macrina, P.O. Box 878, Uniontown, PA 15401, (724) 438-8644. Education, health care.

Benedict, Sisters of the Order of St., O.S.B.: Our Lady of Mount Caritas Monastery (founded 1979, Ashford, CT), 54 Seckar Rd., Ashford, CT 06278, (860) 429-7457. Contemplative.

Benedictine Nuns, O.S.B.: St. Scholastica Priory, Box 606, Petersham, MA 01366, (978) 724-3213; www.petershampriory.org. Cloistered.

Benedictine Nuns of the Congregation of Solesmes, O.S.B.: U.S. establishment, 1981, in Burlington diocese. Monastery of the Immaculate Heart of Mary, 4103 Vt. Rte 100, Westfield, VT 05874, (802) 744-6525, www.ihmwest-field.com. Cloistered, papal enclosure.

Benedictine Nuns of the Primitive Observance, O.S.B.: Founded c. 529, in Italy; in U.S., 1948. Abbey of Regina Laudis, Flanders Rd., Bethlehem, CT 06751, (203) 266-7727, www.abbeyofreginalaudis.com. Cloistered.

Benedictine Sisters, O.S.B.: Founded c. 529, in Italy; in U.S., 1852. General motherhouse, Eichstatt, Bavaria, Germany. U.S. addresses: St. Emma Monastery, motherhouse and novitiate, 1001 Harvey Ave., Greensburg, PA 15601, (724) 834-3060, www.stemma.org. Abbey of St. Walburga, 32109 N. U.S. Highway 287, Virginia Dale, CO 80536, (970) 472-0612, www.walburga.org.

Benedictine Sisters, Missionary, O.S.B.: Founded 1885. Generalate, Rome, Italy. U.S. motherhouse, 300 N. 18th St., Norfolk, NE 68701-3687, (402) 371-3438, www.norfolkosb.org.

Benedictine Sisters, Olivetan, O.S.B.: Founded 1887, in U.S. General motherhouse, Holy Angels Convent, P.O. Drawer 130, Jonesboro, AR 72403-0130, (870) 935-5810, www.olivben.org. Educational, hospital work.

Benedictine Sisters of Perpetual Adoration of Pontifical Jurisdiction, Congregation of the, O.S.B.: Founded in U.S., 1874, from Maria Rickenbach, Switzerland. General motherhouse, 8300 Morganford Rd., St. Louis, MO 63123, (314) 638-6427.

Benedictine Sisters of Pontifical Jurisdiction,

O.S.B.: Founded c. 529, in Italy. No general mother-house in U.S. Three federations:
• **Federation of St. Scholastica** (1922). Pres., Sister Esther Fangman, O.S.B., 3741 Forest Ave., Kansas City, MO 64109, (816) 753-2514. Motherhouses belonging to the federation: Mount St. Scholastica, 801 S. 8th St., Atchison, Kans. 66002, (913) 360-6210, www.mountosb.org. Benedictine Sisters of Elk Co., St. Joseph's Monastery, St. Mary's, PA 15857, (814) 834-2267, www.osbnuns.org. Benedictine Sisters of Erie, 6101 E. Lake Rd., Erie, PA 16511, (814) 899-0614, www.eriebenedictines.org. Benedictine Sisters of Chicago, St. Scholastica Priory, 7430 N. Ridge Blvd., Chicago, IL 60645, (773) 764-2413, www.osbchicago.org. Benedictine Sisters of the Sacred Heart, 1910 Maple Ave., Lisle, IL 60532-2164, (630) 725-6000, www.shmlisle.org. Benedictine Sisters of Elizabeth, St. Walburga Monastery, 851 N. Broad St., Elizabeth, NJ 07208-2593, (201) 352-4278, www.catholic-forum.com/bensisnj. Benedictine Sisters of Pittsburgh, 4530 Perrysville Ave., Pittsburgh, PA 15229, (412) 931-2844, www.osbpgh.org.
Red Plains Monastery, 728 Richland Rd. S.W., Piedmont, OK 73078, (405) 373-4565, www.redplainsmonastery.org. St. Joseph's Monastery, 2200 S. Lewis, Tulsa, OK 74114, (918) 742-4989, www.tulsaosb.org. St. Gertrude's Monastery, 14259 Benedictine Lane, Ridgely, MD 21660, (410) 634-2497. St. Walburga Monastery, 2500 Amsterdam Rd., Villa Hills, KY 41017, (859) 331-6771, www.stwalburg.org. Sacred Heart Monastery, P.O. Box 2040, Cullman, AL 35056, (256) 734-4622, www.shmon.org. Benedictine Sisters of Virginia, 9535 Linton Hall Rd., Bristow, VA 20136-1217, (703) 361-0106, www.osbva.org. St. Scholastica Monastery, 416 W. Highland Dr., Boerne, TX 78006, (830) 816-8504, www.boernebenedictines.com. St. Lucy's Priory, 19045 E. Sierra Madre Ave., Glendora, CA 91741, (626) 335-1682. Benedictine Sisters of Florida, Holy Name Monastery, P.O. Box 2450, St. Leo, FL 33574-2450, (352) 588-8320, www.floridabenedictines.com. Benet Hill Monastery, 2555 N. Chelton Rd., Colorado Springs, CO 80909, (719) 633-0655, www.benethillmonastery.org. Queen of Heaven Monastery (Byzantine Rite), 8640 Squires Lane N.E., Warren, OH 44484, (330) 856-1813, www.benedictinebyzantine.org. Queen of Angels Monastery, 23615 N.E. 100th St., Liberty, MO 64068, (816) 750-4618.
• **Federation of St. Gertrude the Great** (1937). Office: St. Benedict of Ferdinand, Indiana, 802 E. 10th St., Ferdinand, IN 47532, (812) 367-1411, www.thedome.org. Pres., Sister Kathryn Huber, O.S.B. Motherhouses belonging to the federation:
Mother of God Monastery, 110 28th Ave., S.E., Watertown, SD 57201, (605) 882-6633, www.watertownbenedictines.org. Sacred Heart Monastery, 1005 W. 8th St., Yankton, SD 57078-3389, (605) 668-6000, www.yanktonbenedictines.org. Mt. St. Benedict Monastery, 620 E. Summit Ave., Crookston, MN 56716, (218) 281-3441, www.msb.net. Sacred Heart Monastery, P.O. Box 364, Richardton, ND 58652, (701) 974-2121, www.sacredheartmonastery.com. St. Martin Monastery, 2110-C St. Martin's Dr., Rapid City, SD 57702-9660, (605) 343-8011, www.blackhillsbenedictine.com. Monastery of Immaculate Conception, 802 E. 10th St., Ferdinand, IN 47532, (812) 367-2313. Monastery of St. Gertrude, 465 Keuterville Rd., Cottonwood, ID 83522-5183, (208) 962-3224, www.stgertrudes.org.
Monastery of St. Benedict Center, Box 5070, Madison, WI 53705-0070, (608) 836-1631, www.sbcenter.org. Queen of Angels Monastery, 840 S. Main St., Mt. Angel, OR 97362,

(503) 845-6141, www.benedictine-srs.org. St. Scholastica Monastery, P.O. Box 3489, Fort Smith, AR 72913-3489, (479) 783-4147, www.stgcho.org. Our Lady of Peace Monastery, 3710 W. Broadway, Columbia, MO 65203, (573) 446-2300, www.benedictinesister.org. Queen of Peace Monastery, Box 370, Belcourt, ND 58316, (701) 477-6167. Our Lady of Grace Monastery, 1402 Southern Ave., Beech Grove, IN 46107, (317) 787-3287, www.benedictine.com. Holy Spirit Monastery, 22791 Pico St., Grand Terrace, CA 92324, (909) 783-4446. Spirit of Life Monastery, 10760 W. Glennon Dr., Lakewood, CO 80226, (303) 986-9234. St. Benedict's Monastery 225 Masters Ave., Winnipeg, MB, R4A 2A1, Canada, (204) 338-4601, www.mts.net/~stbens. The Dwelling Place Monastery, 150 Mt. Tabor Rd., Martin, KY 41649, (606) 886-9624.
• **Federation of St. Benedict** (1947). Pres., Sister Colleen Haggerty, O.S.B., St. Benedict Convent, 104 Chapel Lane, St. Joseph, MN 56374-0220, (320) 363-7100, www.sbm.osb.org. Motherhouses in U.S. belonging to the federation:
St. Benedict's Convent, St. Joseph, MN 56374, (320) 363-7100. St. Scholastica Monasstery, 1001 Kenwood Ave., Duluth, MN 55811-2300, (218) 723-7001, www.duluthbenedictines.org. St. Bede Monastery, 1190 Priory Rd., Eau Claire, WI 54702, (715) 834-3176, www.saintbede.org. St. Mary Monastery, 2200 88th Ave. W., Rock Island, IL 61201, (309) 283-2101, www.smmsisters.org; Annunciation Monastery, 7520 University Dr., Bismarck, ND 58504, (701) 255-1520, www.annunciationmonastery.org. St. Paul's Monastery, 2675 Larpenteur Ave. E., St. Paul, MN 55109, (651) 777-8181, www.osb.org/spm. St. Placid Priory, 500 College St. N.E., Lacey, WA 98516, (360) 438-1771, www.stplacid.org. Mount Benedict Monastery, 6000 South 1075 East, Ogden, UT 84405-4945, (801) 479-6030, www.mbutah.org.

Bethany, Sisters of, C.V.D.: Founded 1928, in El Salvador; in U.S. 1949. General motherhouse, Santa Tecla, El Salvador. U.S. address: 850 N. Hobart Blvd., Los Angeles, CA 90029, (213) 669-9411.

Bethlemita Sisters, Daughters of the Sacred Heart of Jesus (Beth.): Founded 1861, in Guatemala. Motherhouse, Bogota, Colombia. U.S. address, St. Joseph Residence, 330 W. Pembroke St., Dallas, TX 75208, (214) 948-3597.

Bon Secours, Congregation of, C.B.S.: Founded 1824, in France; in U.S., 1881. Generalate, Rome, Italy. U.S. provincial house, 1525 Marriottsville Rd., Marriottsville, MD 21104, (410) 442-1333, www.bonsecours.org. Hospital work.

Brigid, Congregation of St., C.S.B.: Founded 1807, in Ireland; in U.S., 1953. U.S. regional house, 5118 Loma Linda Dr., San Antonio, TX 78201, (210) 733-0701, www.brigidine.org.au.

Brigittine Sisters (Order of the Most Holy Savior), O.S.S.S.: Founded 1344, at Vadstena, Sweden, by St. Bridget; in U.S., 1957. General motherhouse, Rome, Italy. U.S. address, Vikingsborg, 4 Runkenhage Rd., Darien, CT 06820, (203) 655-1068.

Canossian Daughters of Charity (Fd.C.C.): Founded 1808 in Verona, Italy, by St. Magdalen of Canossa. General motherhouse, Rome, Italy. U.S. provincial house, 5625 Isleta Blvd. S.W., Albuquerque, NM 87105, (505) 873-2854, www.fdcc.org.

Carmel, Congregation of Our Lady of Mount, O. Carm.: Founded 1825, in France; in U.S., 1833. Generalate, P.O. Box 476, Lacombe, LA 70445, (504) 882-7577, www.mountcarmel.home.mindspring.com. Education, social services, pastoral ministry, retreat work.

Carmel, Institute of Our Lady of Mount, O. Carm.: Founded 1854, in Italy; in U.S., 1947. General motherhouse, Rome, Italy. U.S. novitiate, 5 Wheatland St., Peabody, MA 01960, (978) 531-4733; www.carmeliteoreschool.com. Apostolic work.

Carmelite Community of the Word, C.C.W.: Motherhouse and novitiate, 394 Bem Rd., Gallitzin, PA 16641, (814) 886-4098 (fax).

Carmelite Nuns, Discalced, O.C.D.: Founded 1562, Spain. First foundation in U.S. in 1790, at Charles County, MD; this monastery was moved to Baltimore. Monasteries in U.S. are listed below by state.

Alabama: 716 Dauphin Island Pkwy., Mobile 36606, (334) 471-3991. Arkansas: 7201 W. 32nd St., Little Rock 72204, (501) 565-5121, www.littlerockcarmel.org. California: 215 E. Alhambra Rd., Alhambra 91801, (626) 282-2387, www.carmelites.org/teresacarmel; 27601 Highway 1, Carmel 93923, (831) 624-3043, www.carmelitesistersbythesea.net; 68 Rincon Rd., Kensington 94707; 6981 Teresian Way, Georgetown 95634, (530) 333-1617; 5158 Hawley Blvd., San Diego 92116, (619) 280-5424, www.carmelsandiego.com; 721 Parker Ave., San Francisco 94118; 530 Blackstone Dr., San Rafael 94903, (415) 479-6872; 1000 Lincoln St., Santa Clara 95050-5285, (408) 296-8412, www.members.aol.com/santaclaracarmel.

Colorado: 6138 S. Gallup St., Littleton 80120, (303) 798-4176. Georgia: Coffee Bluff, 11 W. Back St., Savannah 31419, (912) 925-8505, www.savannahcarmel.org. Hawaii: 6301 Pali Hwy., Kaneohe 96744, (808) 261-6542; Illinois: 1101 N. River Rd., Des Plaines 60016, (847) 298-4241. Indiana: 2500 Cold Spring Rd., Indianapolis 46222-2323, (317) 926-5654, www.praythenews.com; 59 Allendale Pl., Terre Haute 47802, (812) 299-1410; www.heartsawake.org. Iowa: 17937 250th St., Eldridge 52748, (319) 285-8387; 2901 S. Cecilia St., Sioux City 51106, (712) 276-1680. Kentucky: 1740 Newburg Rd., Louisville 40205, (502) 451-6796. Louisiana: 1250 Carmel Ave., Lafayette 70501, (337) 232-4651; 73530 River Rd., Covington 70435, (985) 898-0923.

Maryland: 1318 Dulaney Valley Rd., Towson, Baltimore 21286, (410) 823-7415, www.geocities.com/baltimore-carmel; 5678 Mt. Carmel Rd., La Plata, 20646, (301) 934-1654, www.carmelofporttobacco@erols.com. Massachusetts: 61 Mt. Pleasant Ave., Roxbury, Boston 02119, (617) 442-1411, www.carmelitesofboston.org; 15 Mt. Carmel Rd., Danvers 01923, (978) 774-3008. Michigan: 4300 Mt. Carmel Dr. NE, Ada 49301, (616) 691-7625; 35750 Moravian Dr., Clinton Township 48035, (586) 790-7255, www.rc.net/detroit/carmelite; U.S. 2 Highway, P.O. Box 397, Iron Mountain 49801, (906) 774-0561; 3501 Silver Lake Rd., Traverse City 49684, (231) 946-4960. Minnesota: 8251 De Montreville Trail N., Lake Elmo 55042-9547, (651) 777-3882. Mississippi: 2155 Terry Rd., Jackson 39204, (601) 373-1460.

Missouri: 2201 W. Main St., Jefferson City 65101, (573) 636-3364; 9150 Clayton Rd., Ladue, St. Louis Co. 63124, (314) 993-3494, www.stormpages.com/mtcarmel; 424 E. Monastery Rd., Springfield 65807, (417) 881-2115. Nevada: 1950 La Fond Dr., Reno 89509-3099, (775) 323-3236. New Hampshire: 275 Pleasant St., Concord, 03301-2590, (603) 225-5791. New Jersey: 26 Harmony School Rd., Flemington 08822-2606, www.flemingtoncarmel.org. ingtoncarmel.htm; 189 Madison Ave., Morristown 07960, (973) 538-2886. New Mexico: 49 Mt. Carmel Rd., Santa Fe 87505-0352, (505)

983-7232. New York: c/o Chancery Office, Diocese of Brooklyn, 361 Highland Blvd., Brooklyn 11207, (718) 235-0422; 89 Hiddenbrook Dr., Beacon, 12508, (914) 831-5572; 75 Carmel Rd., Buffalo 14214, (716) 837-6499; 1931 W. Jefferson Rd., Pittsford, NY 14534, (585) 427-7094, www.carmelitesofrochester.org.

Ohio: 3176 Fairmount Blvd., Cleveland Heights 44118, (216) 321-6568; www.clevelandcarmel.org. Oklahoma: 20000 N. County Line Rd., Piedmont 73078, (405) 348-3947, www.okcarmel.org. Oregon: 87609 Green Hill Rd., Eugene 97402, (541) 345-8649. Pennsylvania: 1 Maria Hall Dr., Danville 17821, (570) 275-4682, www.carmelelysburg.org; 510 E. Gore Rd., Erie 16509-3799, (814) 825-0846; 5206 Center Dr., Latrobe 15650, (724) 539-1056, www.latrobecarmel.org; P.O. Box 57, Loretto 15940-0057, (814) 472-8620; Byzantine Rite, 403 West County Rd., Sugarloaf 18249-9998, (570) 788-1205; 66th and Old York Rd., Philadelphia 19126, (215) 424-6143. Rhode Island: 25 Watson Ave., Barrington 02806, (401) 245-3421. South Dakota: 221 5th St., W., Alexandria, 57311, (605) 239-4382. Texas: 600 Flowers Ave., Dallas 75211; 5801 Mt. Carmel Dr., Arlington 76017, (817) 468-1781; 1100 Parthenon Pl., Roman Forest, New Caney 77357-3276, (281) 399-0270, www.icansurf.com/ocdnewcaney; 6301 Culebra and St. Joseph Way, San Antonio 78238-4909, (210) 680-1834, www.carmelsanantonio.com. Utah: 5714 Holladay Blvd., Salt Lake City 84121, (801) 277-6075, www.carmelslc.org. Vermont: 94 Main St., Montpelier, 05601, (914) 831-5572. Washington: 2215 N.E. 147th St., Shoreline 98155, (206) 363-7150. Wisconsin: W267 N2517 Meadowbrook Rd., Pewaukee 53072, (262) 691-0336, www.geocities.com/pewaukeecarmel.org; 6100 Pepper Rd., Denmark 54208, (920) 863-5055.

Carmelite Nuns of the Ancient Observance (Calced Carmelites), O. Carm.: Founded 1452, in the Netherlands; in U.S., 1930, from Naples, Italy, convent (founded 1856). U.S. monasteries: Carmelite Monastery of St. Therese and St. Mary Magdalen di Pazzi, 3551 Lanark Rd., Coopersburg, PA 18036. Carmel of Mary, Wahpeton, ND 58075. Our Lady of Grace Monastery, 6202 CR 339 Via Maria, Christoval, TX 76935 (325) 853-1722. Carmel of the Sacred Heart, 430 Laurel Ave., Hudson, WI 54016, (715) 862-2156, www.pressenter.com/~carmelit. Papal enclosure.

Carmelite Sisters (Corpus Christi), O. Carm.: Founded 1908, in England; in U.S., 1920. General motherhouse, Tunapuna, Trinidad, W.I. U.S. address: Mt. Carmel Home, 412 W. 18th St., Kearney, NE 68845, (308) 237-2287, www.corpuschristi-carmelites.org. Home and foreign mission work.

Carmelite Sisters for the Aged and Infirm, O. Carm.: Founded 1929, at New York, by Mother M. Angeline Teresa, O. Carm. Motherhouse, 600 Woods Rd., Avila-on-Hudson, Germantown, NY 12526, (518) 537-5000, www.carmelitesisters.com. Social work, nursing and educating in the field of gerontology.

Carmelite Sisters of Charity, C.a.Ch.: Founded 1826 at Vich, Spain, by St. Joaquina de Vedruna. Generalate, Rome, Italy. U.S. address, 701 Beacon Rd., Silver Spring, MD 20903, (301) 434-6344.

Carmelite Sisters of St. Therese of the Infant Jesus, C.S.T.: Founded 1917, in U.S. General motherhouse, 1300 Classen Dr., Oklahoma City, OK 73103, (405) 232-7926, www.oksister.com. Educational work.

Carmelite Sisters of the Divine Heart of Jesus, Carmel D.C.J.: Founded 1891, in Germany; in U.S., 1912. General motherhouse, Sittard Netherlands. U.S.

provincial houses: Northern Province, 1230 Kavanaugh Pl., Milwaukee, WI 53213, (414) 453-4040, www.carmelitedcjnorth.org. Central Province, 10341 Manchester Rd., St. Louis, MO 63122, (314) 965-7616, www.carmelitesdcj.org. South Western Province, 8585 La Mesa Blvd., La Mesa, CA 91941-3901, (619) 466-3163. Social services, mission work.

Carmelite Sisters of the Most Sacred Heart of Los Angeles, O.C.D.: Founded 1904, in Mexico. General motherhouse and novitiate, 920 E. Alhambra Rd., Alhambra, CA 91801-2799, (626) 289-1353, wwwcarmel-msh.org. Social services, retreat and educational work.

Carmelites, Calced, O. Carm.: Founded 1856 in Naples, Italy. U.S. address: Carmelite Monastery of St. Therese, 3551 Lanark Rd., Coopersburg, PA 18036.

Carmelites of St. Theresa, Congregation of Missionary, C.M.S.T.: Founded 1903, in Mexico. General motherhouse, Mexico City, Mexico. U.S. foundation, 9548 Deer Trail Dr., Houston, TX 77038, (281) 445-5520.

Casimir, Sisters of St., S.S.C.: Founded 1907, in U.S., by Mother Maria Kaupas. General motherhouse, 2601 W. Marquette Rd., Chicago, IL 60629, (773) 776-1324. Education, missions, social services.

Cenacle, Congregation of Our Lady of the Retreat in the, R.C.: Founded 1826, in France; in U.S., 1892. Generalate, Rome, Italy. Eastern Province, Cenacle Rd., Lake Ronkonkoma, NY 11779, (516) 471-6270. Midwestern Province, 513 Fullerton Pkwy., Chicago, IL 60614-6428, (773) 528-6300, www.cenaclesisters.org.

Charity, Daughters of Divine, F.D.C.: Founded 1868, at Vienna, Austria; in U.S., 1913. General motherhouse, Rome, Italy. U.S. province: 205 Major Ave., Staten Island, NY 10305, (718) 720-4377, www.godslovefdc.org. Education, social services.

Charity, Missionaries of, M.C.: Founded 1950, in Calcutta, India, by Mother Teresa; first U.S. foundation, 1971. General motherhouse, 54A, A.J.C. Bose Rd., Calcutta 700016, India. U.S. address, 335 E. 145th St., Bronx, NY 10451, (718) 292-0019. Service of the poor.

Charity, Religious Sisters of, R.S.C.: Founded 1815, in Ireland; in U.S., 1953. Motherhouse, Dublin, Ireland. U.S. headquarters, 206 N. Edgemont St., Los Angeles, CA 90029, (310) 559-0176.

Charity, Sisters of (of Seton Hill), S.C.: Founded 1870, at Altoona, PA, from Cincinnati foundation. Generalate, De Paul Center, 463 Mt. Thor Rd., Greensburg, PA 15601, (724) 836-0406, www.scsh.org. Educational, hospital, social, foreign mission work.

Charity, Sisters of (Grey Nuns of Montréal), S.G.M.: Founded 1737, in Canada, by St. Marie Marguerite d'Youville; in U.S., 1855. General administration, Montréal, QC H2Y 2L7, Canada. U.S. provincial house, 10 Pelham Rd., Ste. 1000, Lexington, MA 02421, (781) 862-4700, www.sqmlex.org.

Charity, Sisters of (of Leavenworth), S.C.L.: Founded 1858, in U.S. Motherhouse, 4200 S. 4th St., Leavenworth, KS 66048, (913) 758-6508, www.scls.org/.

Charity, Sisters of (of Nazareth), S.C.N.: Founded 1812, in U.S. General motherhouse, SCN Center, P.O. Box 172, Nazareth, KY 40048, (502) 348-1561, www.scnazareth.org. Education, health services.

Charity, Sisters of (of St. Augustine), C.S.A.: Founded 1851, at Cleveland, Ohio. Motherhouse, 5232 Broadview Rd., Richfield, OH 44286, (330) 659-5100, www.srsofcharity.org.

Charity, Sisters of Christian, S.C.C.: Founded 1849, in Paderborn, Germany, by Bl. Pauline von Mallinckrodt; in U.S., 1873. Generalate, Rome, Italy. U.S. provinces: Mallinckrodt Convent, 350 Bernardsville Rd., Mendham, NJ 07945, (973) 543-6528, www.scceast.org. 2041 Elmwood Ave., Wilmette, IL 60091-1431, (847) 920-9341, www.sccwilmette.org. Education, health services, other apostolic work.

Charity, Vincentian Sisters of, V.S.C.: Founded 1835, in Austria; in U.S., 1902. General motherhouse, 8200 McKnight Rd., Pittsburgh, PA 15237, (412) 364-3000, www.vincentiansrspgh.org.

Charity, Vincentian Sisters of, V.S.C.: Founded 1928, at Bedford, Ohio. General motherhouse, 1160 Broadway, Bedford, OH 44146, (440) 232-4755.

Charity of Cincinnati, Ohio, Sisters of, S.C.: Founded 1809; became independent community, 1852. General motherhouse, 5900 Delhi Rd., Mt. St. Joseph, OH 45051, (513) 347-5201, www.srcharitycinti.org. Educational, hospital, social work.

Charity of Ottawa, Sisters of (Grey Nuns of the Cross), S.C.O.: Founded 1845, at Ottawa, Canada; in U.S., 1857. General motherhouse, Ottawa, Canada. U.S. provincial house, 559 Fletcher St., Lowell, MA 01854, (978) 453-4993. Educational, hospital work, extended health care.

Charity of Our Lady, Mother of Mercy, Sisters of, S.C.M.M.: Founded 1832, in Holland; in U.S., 1874. General motherhouse, Den Bosch, the Netherlands. U.S. provincialate, 520 Thompson Ave., East Haven, CT 06512, (203) 469-7872.

Charity of Our Lady, Mother of the Church, S.C.M.C: U.S. foundation, 1970. General motherhouse, 520 Thompson Ave., East Haven, CT 06512, (203) 469-7872.

Charity of Our Lady of Mercy, Sisters of, O.L.M.: Founded 1829, in Charleston, SC. Generalate and motherhouse, 424 Fort Johnson Rd., P. O. Box 12410, Charleston, SC 29422, (843) 795-6083. Education, campus ministry, social services.

Charity of Quebec, Sisters of (Grey Nuns), S.C.Q.: Founded 1849, at Quebec; in U.S., 1890. General motherhouse, 2655 Le Pelletier St., Beauport, QC GIC 3X7, Canada. U.S. address, 359 Summer St., New Bedford, MA 02740, (508) 996-6751. Social work.

Charity of St. Elizabeth, Sisters of (Convent Station, N.J.), S.C.: Founded 1859, at Newark, NJ. General motherhouse, P.O. Box 476, Convent Station, NJ 07961-0476, (973) 290-5000. Education, pastoral ministry, social services.

Charity of St. Hyacinthe, Sisters of (Grey Nuns), S.C.S.H.: Founded 1840, at St. Hyacinthe, Canada; in U.S., 1878. General motherhouse, 16470 Avenue Bourdages, SUD, St. Hyacinthe, QC J2T 4J8, Canada. U.S. regional house, 98 Campus Ave., Lewiston, ME 04240, (207) 797-8607.

Charity of St. Joan Antida, Sisters of, S.C.S.J.A.: Founded 1799, in France; in U.S., 1932. General motherhouse, Rome, Italy. U.S. provincial house, 8560 N. 76th Pl., Milwaukee, WI 53223, (414) 354-9233, www.scsja.org.

Charity of St. Louis, Sisters of, S.C.S.L.: Founded 1803, in France; in U.S., 1910. Generalate, Rome, Italy. U.S. provincialate, 4907 S. Catherine St., Plattsburgh, NY 12901, (518) 563-7410.

Charity of St. Vincent de Paul, Daughters of, D.C.: Founded 1633, in France; in U.S., 1809, at Emmitsburg, MD, by St. Elizabeth Ann Seton. General motherhouse, Paris, France. U.S. provinces: 333 South Seton Ave., Emmitsburg, MD 21727, (301) 447-2900, www.daughtersofcharity-emmitsburg.org. 7800 Natural Bridge Rd., St. Louis, MO 63121, (314) 382-2800. 9400 New Harmony Rd., Evansville, IN 47720-8912, (812) 963-3341, www.doc-ecp.org. 96 Menands Rd., Albany, NY 12204, (518) 462-5593, www.dc-northeast.org. 26000 Altamont Rd., Los Altos Hills, CA 94022, (650) 949-8865, www.daughtersofcharity.com.

Charity of St. Vincent de Paul, Sisters of, V.Z.: Founded 1845, in Croatia. in U.S., 1955. General motherhouse, Zagreb, Croatia; U.S. foundation, 171 Knox Ave., West Seneca, NY 14224, (716) 825-5859.

Charity of St. Vincent de Paul, Sisters of, Halifax, S.C.: Founded 1856, at Halifax, NS, from Emmitsburg foundation. Generalate, Mt. St. Vincent, Halifax, NS, Canada. U.S. addresses: Commonwealth of Massachusetts, 125 Oakland St., Wellesley Hills, MA 02481-5338, (781) 997-1165, www.schalifax.ca. Boston Province, 26 Phipps St., Quincy, MA 02169, (617) 773-6085. New York Province, 84-32 63rd Ave., Middle Village, NY 11379, (718) 651-1685. Educational, hospital, social work.

Charity of St. Vincent de Paul, Sisters of, New York, SC.: Founded 1817, from Emmitsburg foundation. General motherhouse, Mt. St. Vincent on Hudson, 6301 Riverdale Ave., Bronx, NY 10471, (718) 549-9200, www.scny.org. Educational, hospital work.

Charity of the Blessed Virgin Mary, Sisters of, B.V.M.: Founded 1833, in U.S. by Mary Frances Clarke. General motherhouse, BVM Center, 1100 Carmel Dr., Dubuque, IA 52003, (563) 588-2351, www.bvmcong.com. Education, pastoral ministry, social services.

Charity of the Immaculate Conception of Ivrea, Sisters of, S.C.I.C.: Founded 18th century, in Italy; in U.S., 1961. General motherhouse, Rome, Italy. U.S. address, Immaculate Virgin of Miracles Convent, 268 Prittstown Rd., Mt. Pleasant, PA 15666, (724) 887-6753.

Charity of the Incarnate Word, Congregation of the Sisters of, C.C.V.I.: Founded 1869, at San Antonio, TX, by Bishop C. M. Dubuis. Generalate, 3200 McCullough, San Antonio, TX 78212, (210) 734-8310, www.incarnatewordsisters.org.

Charity of the Incarnate Word, Congregation of the Sisters of (Houston, TX), C.C.V.I.: Founded 1866, in U.S., by Bishop C. M. Dubuis. General motherhouse, P.O. Box 230969, Houston, TX 77223, (713) 928-6053. Educational, hospital, social work.

Charity of the Sacred Heart, Daughters of, F.C.S.C.J.: Founded 1823, at La Salle de Vihiers, France; in U.S., 1905. General motherhouse, La Salle de Vihiers, France. U.S. address, Sacred Heart Province, 226 Grove St., P.O. Box 642, Littleton, NH 03561, (603) 444-3970.

Charles Borromeo, Missionary Sisters of St. (Scalabrini Srs.): Founded 1895, in Italy; in U.S., 1941. American novitiate, 1414 N. 37th Ave., Melrose Park, IL 60160; (708) 343-2162.

Child Jesus, Sisters of the Poor, P.C.J.: Founded 1844, at Aix-la-Chapelle, Germany; in U.S., 1924. General motherhouse, Simpelveld, the Netherlands. American provincialate, 4567 Olentangy River Rd., Columbus, OH 43214, (614) 451-3900.

Chretienne, Sisters of Ste., S.S.Ch.: Founded 1807, in France; in U.S., 1903. General motherhouse, Metz, France. U.S. provincial house, 297 Arnold St., Wrentham, MA 02093, (508) 384-8066, www.sistersofstchretienne.org.

Educational, hospital, mission work.

Christ the King, Missionary Sisters of, M.S.C.K.: Founded 1959 in Poland; in U.S., 1978. General motherhouse, Poznan, Poland. U.S. address, 3000 18-Mile Rd., Sterling Heights, MI 48314.

Christ the King, Sister Servants of, S.S.C.K.: Founded 1936, in U.S. General motherhouse, Loretto Convent, N8114 Calvary St., Mt. Calvary, WI 53057, (920) 753-3211. Social services.

Christian Doctrine, Sisters of Our Lady of, R.C.D.: Founded 1910, in New York. Marydell Convent, 110 Larchdale Ave., Nyack, NY 10960; (845) 727-1011.

Christian Education, Religious of, R.C.E.: Founded 1817, in France; in U.S., 1905. General motherhouse, France. U.S. provincial residence, 55 Parkwood Dr., Milton, MA 02186, (617) 696-7732.

Cistercian Nuns, O. Cist.: Headquarters, Rome, Italy. U.S. address, Valley of Our Lady Monastery, E. 11096 Yanke Dr., Prairie du Sac, WI 53578, www.nunocist.org.

Cistercian Nuns of the Strict Observance, Order of, O.C.S.O.: Founded 1125, in France, by St. Stephen Harding; in U.S., 1949. U.S. addresses: Mt. St. Mary's Abbey, 300 Arnold St., Wrentham, MA 02093, (508) 528-1282. HC 1, Box 929, Sonoita, AZ 85637, (520) 455-5595, www.santaritabbey.org. Our Lady of the Redwoods Abbey, 18104 Briceland Thorn Rd., Whitethorn, CA 95589, (707) 986-7419, www.red-woodsabbey.org. Our Lady of the Mississippi Abbey, 8400 Abbey Hill Rd., Dubuque, IA 52003, (563) 582-2595, www.mississippiabbey.org/. Our Lady of the Angels Monastery, 3365 Monastery Dr., Crozet, VA 22932, (434) 823-1452, www.olamonastery.org.

Clare, Sisters of St., O.S.C.: General motherhouse, Dublin, Ireland. U.S. foundation, St. Francis Convent, 1974 Cherrywood St., Vista, CA 92083, (760) 945-8040.

Claretian Missionary Sisters (Religious of Mary Immaculate), R.M.I.: Founded 1855, in Cuba; in U.S., 1956. Generalate, Rome, Italy. U.S. address, 7080 SW 99 Ave., Miami, FL 33173, (305) 274-5695 (fax), www.claretiansisters.org.

Clergy, Congregation of Our Lady, Help of the, C.L.H.C.: Founded 1961, in U.S. Motherhouse, Maryvale Convent, 2522 June Bug Rd., Vale, NC 28168, (704) 276-2626.

Clergy, Servants of Our Lady Queen of the, S.R.C.: Founded 1929, in Canada; in U.S., 1934. General motherhouse, 57 Jules A. Brillant, Rimouski, QC G5L 1X1 Canada, (418) 724-0508. Domestic work.

Colettines: *See* Franciscan Poor Clare Nuns.

Columban, Missionary Sisters of St., S.S.C.: Founded 1922, in Ireland; in U.S., 1930. General motherhouse, Wicklow, Ireland. U.S. region, 73 Mapleton St., Brighton, MA 02135, (617) 782-5683.

Comboni Missionary Sisters (Missionary Sisters of Verona), C.M.S.: Founded 1872, in Italy; in U.S., 1950. U.S. address, 5405 Loch-Raven Blvd., Baltimore, MD 21239, (410) 323-1469, www.combonisrs.com.

Consolata Missionary Sisters, M.C.: Founded 1910, in Italy, by Bl. Giuseppe Allamano; in U.S., 1954. General motherhouse, Turin, Italy. U.S. headquarters, 6801 Belmont Rd., P.O. Box 97, Belmont, MI 49306 (616) 361-9609, www.consolatasisters.org.

Cross, Daughters of the, D.C.: Founded 1640, in France; in U.S., 1855. General motherhouse, 411 E. Flournoy-Lucas Rd., Shreveport, LA 71115, (318) 797-0887. Educational work.

Cross, Daughters of, of Liege, F.C.: Founded 1833, in Liege, Belgium; in U.S., 1958. U.S. address, 165 W. Eaton Ave., Tracy, CA 95376.

Cross, Sisters of the Holy, C.S.C.: Founded 1841, at Le Mans, France; established in Canada, 1847; in U.S., 1881. General motherhouse, St. Laurent, Montreal, QC, Canada. U.S. regional office, 377 Island Pond Rd., Manchester, NH 03109, (603) 622-9504. Educational work.

Cross, Sisters of the Holy, Congregation of, C.S.C.: Founded 1841, at Le Mans, France; in U.S., 1843. General motherhouse, 101 Bertrand Hall – Saint Mary's, Notre Dame, IN 46556, (574) 284-5572, www.cscsisters.org. Education, health care, social services, pastoral ministry.

Cross and Passion, Sisters of the (Passionist Sisters), C.P.: Founded 1852; in U.S., 1924. Generalate, Northampton, England. U.S. address: Holy Family Convent, One Wright Lane, N. Kingstown, RI 02852, (401) 294-3554; www.passionistsisters.org.

Cyril and Methodius, Sisters of Sts., SS.C.M.: Founded 1909, in U.S., by Rev. Matthew Jankola. General motherhouse, Villa Sacred Heart, Danville, PA 17821, (570) 275-4929, www.sscm.org. Education, care of aged.

Disciples of the Lord Jesus Christ, D.L.J.C.: Founded 1972; canonically erected 1991. P.O. Box 17, Channing, TX 79018, (806) 534-2312, www.dljc.org.

Divine Compassion, Sisters of, R.D.C.: Founded 1886, in U.S. General motherhouse, 52 N. Broadway, White Plains, NY 10603, (914) 949-2950. Education, other ministries.

Divine Love, Daughters of, D.D.L.: Founded 1969, in Nigeria; in U.S., 1990. General house, Enugu, Nigeria. U.S. regional house, 140 North Ave., Highwood, IL 60040, (847) 432-4946.

Divine Spirit, Congregation of the, C.D.S.: Founded 1956, in U.S., by Archbishop John M. Gannon. Motherhouse, 409 W. 6th St., Erie, PA 16507, (330) 453-8137. Education, social services.

Divine Zeal, Daughters of, F.D.Z.: Founded 1887 in Italy by Bl. Hannibal Maria DiFrancia; in U.S., 1951. Generalate, Rome. U.S. headquarters, Hannibal House Spiritual Center, 1526 Hill Rd., Reading, PA 19602, (610) 375-1738.

Dominicans

Dominican Nuns: Nuns of the Order of Preachers, O.P.: Founded 1206 by St. Dominic at Prouille, France. Cloistered, contemplative. Two branches in the United States:
• **Dominican Nuns having Perpetual Adoration.** First monastery established 1880, in Newark, NJ, from Oullins, France, foundation (1868). Autonomous monasteries:
Monastery of St. Dominic, 375 13th Ave., Newark, NJ 07103-2124, (973) 622-6622. Corpus Christi Monastery, 1230 Lafayette Ave., Bronx, NY 10474, (718) 328-6996. Blessed Sacrament, 29575 Middlebelt Rd., Farmington Hills, MI 48334-2311, (248) 626-8321, www.opnuns-fh.org. Monastery of the Angels, 1977 Carmen Ave., Los Angeles, CA 90068-4098, (323) 466-2186, www.op-stjoseph.org/nuns/angels/. Corpus Christi Monastery, 215 Oak Grove Ave., Menlo Park, CA 94025-3272, (650) 322-1801, www.nunsmenlo.org. Infant Jesus, 1501 Lotus Lane, Lufkin, TX 75904-2699, (936) 634-4233.

Dominican Nuns devoted to the Perpetual Rosary. First monastery established 1891, in Union City, NJ, from Calais, France, foundation (1880). Autonomous monasteries (some also observe Perpetual Adoration):

Dominican Nuns of Perpetual Rosary, 605 14th and West Sts., Union City, NJ 07087, (201)866-7004. 217 N. 68th St., Milwaukee, WI 53213, (414) 258-0579, www.dsopr.org. Perpetual Rosary, 1500 Haddon Ave., Camden, NJ 08103. Our Lady of the Rosary, 335 Doat St., Buffalo, NY 14211. Our Lady of the Rosary, 543 Spingfield Ave., Summit, NJ 07901, (908) 273-1228, www.op.org/nunsopsummit. Monastery of the Mother of God, 1430 Riverdale St., W. Springfield, MA 01089-4698, (413) 736-3639, www.op-stjoseph.org/nuns/ws. Dominican Monastery of the Perpetual Rosary, 802 Court St., Syracuse, NY 13208-1766. Monastery of the Immaculate Heart of Mary, 1834 Lititz Pike, Lancaster, PA 17601-6585, (717) 569-2104. Mary the Queen, 1310 W. Church St., Elmira, NY 14905, (607) 734-9506, www.oporg/maryqueen. St. Jude, Marbury, AL 36051-0170, (205) 755-1322, www.stjudemonastery.org. Our Lady of Grace Monastery, 11 Race Hill Rd., North Guilford, CT 06437, (203) 345-0599, www.op-stjoseph.org/nuns/olgrace. St. Dominic's Monastery, 4901 16th St. N.W., Washington, DC 20011, (202) 726-2107.

Dominican Sisters of Charity of the Presentation, O.P.: Founded 1696, in France; in U.S., 1906. General motherhouse, Tours, France. U.S. headquarters, 3012 Elm St., Dighton, MA 02715, (508) 669-5425, www.dominicansistersofthepresentation.org. Hospital work.

Dominican Sisters of Hope, O.P.: Formed 1995 through merger of Dominican Sisters of the Most Holy Rosary, Newburgh, NY, Dominican Sisters of the Sick Poor, Ossining, NY, and Dominican Sisters of St. Catherine of Siena, Fall River, MA. General Offices: 299 N. Highland Ave., Ossining, NY 10562, (914) 941-4420, www.ophope.org.

Dominican Sisters of Our Lady of the Rosary and of St. Catherine of Siena (Cabra): Founded 1644 in Ireland. General motherhouse, Cabra, Dublin, Ireland. U.S. regional house, 1930 Robert E. Lee Rd., New Orleans, LA 70122, (504) 288-1593.

Dominican Sisters of the Perpetual Rosary, O.P.: 217 N. 68th St., Milwaukee, WI 53213. Cloistered, contemplative.

Dominican Sisters of the Roman Congregation of St. Dominic, O.P.: Founded 1621, in France; in U.S., 1904. General motherhouse, Rome, Italy. U.S. province, 123 Dumont Ave., Lewiston, ME 04240, (207) 782-3535. Educational work.

Eucharistic Missionaries of St. Dominic, O.P.: Founded 1927, in Louisiana. General motherhouse, 3801 Canal St., Suite 400, New Orleans, LA 70119, (504) 486-1133, (temporary, post-Katrina location: 2645 Bardstown Rd., St. Catharine, KY 40061; 859-336-9303), www.emdsisters.org. Parish work, social services.

Religious Missionaries of St. Dominic, O.P.: General motherhouse, Rome, Italy. U.S. address (Spanish province), 2237 Waldron Rd., Corpus Christi, TX 78418, (361) 939-8102.

Sisters of St. Dominic, O.P.: Names of congregations are given below, followed by the date of foundation, and location of motherhouse. St. Catherine of Siena, 1822. 2645 Bardstown Rd., St. Catharine, KY 40061, (606) 336-9303, www.opkentucky.org. St. Mary of the Springs, 1830. 2320 Airport Dr., Columbus, OH 43219-2098, (614) 416-1038, www.columbusdominicans.org. Most Holy Rosary, 1847. Sinsinawa, WI 53824, (608) 748-4411. Most Holy Name of Jesus, 1850. 1520 Grand Ave., San Rafael, CA 94901, (415) 453-8303, www.sanraelop.org. Holy Cross, 1853. 555 Albany Ave., Amityville, NY 11701, (631) 842-6000, www.amityvilleop.org. St. Cecilia, 1860. 801 Dominican Dr., Nashville, TN 37228, (615) 256-5486, www.nashvilledominican.org.

St. Mary, 1860. 7300 St. Charles Ave., New Orleans, LA 70118, (504) 861-8183, www.dominican-sisters.net/stmarys. St. Catherine of Siena, 1862. 5635 Erie St., Racine, WI 53402, (262) 639-4100, www.racinedominicans.org. Sacred Heart Convent, 1873. 1237 W. Monroe St., Springfield, IL 62704, (217) 787-0481, www.springfieldop.org. Sisters of Our Lady of the Rosary, Dominican Convent, 175 Route 340, Sparkill, NY 10976, (845) 359-6400, www.sparkill.org. Dominican Sisters of Mission San Jose, ____. 43326 Mission Blvd., Mission San Jose, CA 94539, (510) 657-2468, www.msjdominicans.org. Most Holy Rosary, 1892. 1257 Siena Heights Dr., Adrian, MI 49221, (517) 266-3570.

Our Lady of the Sacred Heart, 1877. 2025 E. Fulton St., Grand Rapids, MI 49503, (616) 643-1030. St. Dominic, 1878. 496 Western Hwy., Blauvelt, NY 10913, (845) 359-0696, www.opblauvelt.org. St. Catherine de Ricci, 1880. 131 Copley Rd., Upper Darby, PA 19082, (215) 635-6027. Sisters of St. Dominic, 1881. 1 Ryerson Ave., Caldwell, NJ 07006, (973) 403-3331, www.caldwellop.org. Dominican Sisters of Houston, 1882. 6501 Almeda Rd., Houston, TX 77021-2095, (713) 747-3310, www.houstonop.org. Tacoma Dominican Center, 1888. 935 Fawcett Ave., Tacoma, WA 98402, (253) 272-9688. Holy Cross, 1890. P.O. Box 280, Edmonds, WA 98020, (206) 542-3212, www.opedmonds.org.

St. Rose of Lima (Servants of Relief for Incurable Cancer) 1896. 600 Linda Ave., Hawthorne, NY 10532, (914) 769-0114, www.hawthorne-dominicans.org. Dominican Sisters of Great Bend, 1902. 3600 Broadway, Great Bend, KS 67530, (316) 792-1232, www.ksdom.org. Mission Center, 1911. Box 1288, Kenosha, WI 53141, (262) 694-2067. St. Rose of Lima, 1923. 775 Drahner Rd., #124, Oxford, MI 48371, (248) 628-2872, www.domlife.org. Immaculate Conception, 1929. 9000 W. 81st St., Justice, IL 60458, (708) 458-3040. Immaculate Heart of Mary, 1929. 1230 W. Market St., Akron, OH 44313-7108, (330) 836-4908, www.akrondominicans.org. Dominican Sisters of Oakford (St. Catherine of Siena), 1889. Motherhouse, Oakford, Natal, South Africa; U.S. regional house, 1965. 980 Woodland Ave., San Leandro, CA 94577, (510) 638-2822.

Dorothy, Institute of the Sisters of St., S.S.D.: Founded 1834, in Italy, by St. Paola Frassinetti; in U.S., 1911. General motherhouse, Rome, Italy. U.S. provincialate, St. Dorothy Convent, 1305 Hylan Blvd., Si, NY 10305; (718) 987-2604.

Eucharist, Religious of the, R.E.: Founded 1857, in Belgium; in U.S., 1900. General motherhouse, Belgium. U.S. foundation, 2907 Ellicott Terr., N.W., Washington, DC 20008, (202) 966-3111.

Felix, Congregation of the Sisters of St. (Felician Sisters), C.S.S.F.: Founded 1855, in Poland by Bl. Mary Angela Truszkowska; in U.S., 1874. General motherhouse, Rome, Italy. U.S. provinces: 36800 Schoolcraft Rd., Livonia, MI 48150, (734) 591-1730, www.felicansisters.org. 600 Doat St., Buffalo, NY 14211, (716) 892-4141, www.cssbuffalo.org. 3800 W. Peterson Ave., Chicago, IL 60659-3116, (773) 463-3020, www.felicianschicago.org. 260 South Main St., Lodi, NJ 07644, (973) 473-7447, www.felician.edu/cssf. htm. 1500 Woodcrest Ave., Coraopolis, PA 15108, (412) 264-2890, www.felicianspa.org. 1315 Enfield St., Enfield, CT 06082, (860) 745-7791. 4210 Meadowlark Lane, S.E., Rio Rancho, NM 87124-1021, (505) 892-8862; southwestfeliciansisters.org.

Filippini, Religious Teachers, M.P.F.: Founded 1692, in Italy; in U.S., 1910. General motherhouse, Rome, Italy. U.S. provinces: St. Lucy Filippini Province, Villa Walsh, Morristown, NJ 07960, (973) 538-2886. Queen of Apostles Province, 474 East Rd., Bristol, CT 06010, (860) 584-2138, www.queenofapostles.com. Educational work.

Francis de Sales, Oblate Sisters of St., O.S.F.S.: Founded 1866, in France; in U.S., 1951. General motherhouse, Troyes, France. U.S. headquarters, Villa Aviat Convent, 399 Childs Rd., MD 21916, (410) 398-3699; (410) 398-3699. Educational, social work.

Franciscans

Bernardine Sisters of the Third Order of St. Francis, O.S.F.: Founded 1457, at Cracow, Poland; in U.S., 1894. Generalate, 450 St. Bernardine St., Reading, PA 19607; (484) 334-6976; www.bfranciscan.org. Educational, hospital, social work.

Capuchin Poor Clares, O.S.C. Cap: U.S. establishment, 1981, Amarillo diocese. Convent of the Blessed Sacrament and Our Lady of Guadalupe, 4201 N.E. 18th St., Amarillo, TX 79107, (806) 383-9877. Cloistered.

Congregation of the Servants of the Holy Child Jesus, O.S.F.: Founded 1855, in Germany; in U.S., 1929. General motherhouse, Würzburg, Germany. American motherhouse, Villa Maria, 641 Somerset St., North Plainfield, NJ 07060-4909, (908) 757-3050.

Congregation of the Third Order of St. Francis of Mary Immaculate, O.S.F.: Founded 1865, in U.S., by Fr. Pamphilus da Magliano, O.F.M. General motherhouse, 520 Plainfield Ave., Joliet, IL 60435, (815) 727-3686. Educational and pastoral work.

Daughters of St. Francis of Assisi, D.S.F.: Founded 1894, in Hungary; in U.S., 1946. Provincial motherhouse, 507 N. Prairie St., Lacon, IL 61540, (309) 246-2175. Nursing, CCD work.

Eucharistic Franciscan Missionary Sisters, E.F.M.S.: Founded 1943, in Mexico. Motherhouse, 943 S. Soto St., Los Angeles, CA 90023, (323) 264-6556.

Franciscan Handmaids of the Most Pure Heart of Mary, F.H.M.: Founded 1916, in U.S. General motherhouse, 15 W. 124th St., New York, NY 10027-5634, (212) 289-5655. Educational, social work.

Franciscan Hospitaller Sisters of the Immaculate Conception, F.H.I.C.: Founded 1876, in Portugal; in U.S., 1960. General motherhouse, Lisbon, Portugal. U.S. novitiate, 300 S. 17th St., San Jose, CA 95112, (408) 998-3407.

Franciscan Missionaries of Mary, F.M.M.: Founded 1877, in India; in U.S., 1904. General motherhouse, Rome, Italy. U.S. provincialate, 3305 Wallace Ave., Bronx, NY 10467, (718) 547-4693, www.fmmusa.org. Mission work.

Franciscan Missionaries of Our Lady, O.S.F.: Founded 1854, at Calais, France; in U.S., 1913. General motherhouse, Desvres, France. U.S. provincial house, 4200 Essen Lane, Baton Rouge, LA 70809, (225) 926-1627. Hospital work.

Franciscan Missionaries of St. Joseph (Mill Hill Sisters), F.M.S.J.: Founded 1883, at Rochdale, Lancashire, England; in U.S., 1952. Generalate, Manchester, England. U.S. headquarters, Franciscan House, 1006 Madison Ave., Albany, NY 12208, (518) 482-1991.

Franciscan Missionary Sisters for Africa, O.S.F.: American foundation, 1953. Generalate, Ireland. U.S. headquarters, 172 Foster St., Brighton, MA 02135,

(617) 254-4343.

Franciscan Missionary Sisters of Assisi, F.M.S.A.: First foundation in U.S., 1961. General motherhouse, Assisi, Italy. U.S. address, St. Francis Convent, 1039 Northampton St., Holyoke, MA 01040, (413) 532-8156.

Franciscan Missionary Sisters of Our Lady of Sorrows, O.S.F.: Founded 1939, in China, by Bishop Rafael Palazzi, O.F.M.; in U.S., 1949. 3600 S.W. 170th Ave., Beaverton, OR 97006, (503) 649-7127. Educational, social, domestic, retreat and foreign mission work.

Franciscan Missionary Sisters of the Divine Child, F.M.D.C.: Founded 1927, at Buffalo, NY, by Bishop William Turner. General motherhouse, 6380 Main St., Williamsville, NY 14221, (716) 632-3144. Educational, social work.

Franciscan Missionary Sisters of the Infant Jesus, F.M.I.J.: Founded 1879, in Italy; in U.S., 1961. Generalate, Rome, Italy. U.S. provincialate, 1215 Kresson Rd., Cherry Hill, NJ 08003, (609) 428-8834.

Franciscan Missionary Sisters of the Sacred Heart, F.M.S.C.: Founded 1860, in Italy; in U.S., 1865. Generalate, Rome, Italy. U.S. provincialate, 250 South St., Peekskill, NY 10566-4419, (914) 737-5409. Educational and social welfare apostolates.

Franciscan Poor Clare Nuns (Poor Clares, Order of St. Clare, Poor Clares of St. Colette), P.C., O.S.C., P.C.C.: Founded 1212, at Assisi, Italy, by St. Francis of Assisi; in U.S., 1875. Proto-monastery, Assisi, Italy. Addresses of autonomous motherhouses in U.S. are listed below.

8650 Russell Ave., S., Minneapolis, MN 55431, (952) 881-4766, www.poorclare.com. 3626 N. 65th Ave., Omaha, NE 68104-3299, (402) 558-4916, www.omahapoorclare.org. 720 Henry Clay Ave., New Orleans, LA 70118-5891, (504) 895-2019, www.poorclarenuns.com. 6825 Nurrenbern Rd., Evansville, IN 47712-8518, (812) 425-4396, www.poorclare.org. 1310 Dellwood Ave., Memphis, TN 38127-6399, (901) 357-6662, www.poorclare.org/memphis. 920 Centre St., Jamaica Plain, MA 02130-3099, (617) 524-1760, www.stanthonyshrine.org/poorclares. 327 S. Broad St., Trenton, NJ 08608, (609) 392-7673. 1271 Langhorne-Newtown Rd., Langhorne, PA 19047-1297, (215) 968-5775. 4419 N. Hawthorne St., Spokane, WA 99205, (509) 327-4479. 86 Mayflower Ave., New Rochelle, NY, 10801-1615, (914) 632-5227, www.poorclaresny.com. 421 S. 4th St., Sauk Rapids, MN 56379-1898, (612) 251-3556. 3501 Rocky River Dr., Cleveland, OH 44111, (216) 941-2821.

1671 Pleasant Valley Rd., Aptos, CA 95001, (831) 761-9659. 2111 S. Main St., Rockford, IL 61102, (815) 963-7343, www.poorclare.org/rockford. 215 E. Los Olivos St., Santa Barbara, CA 93105-3605, (805) 682-7670. 445 River Rd., Andover, MA 01810, (978) 683-7599. 809 E. 19th St., Roswell, NM 88201-7514, (575) 622-0868. 28210 Natoma Rd., Los Altos Hills, CA 94022, (650) 948-2947, www.chcweb.com. 1916 N. Pleasantburg Dr., Greenville, SC 29609-4080, (864) 244-4514. 28 Harpersville Rd., Newport News, VA 23601, (804) 596-5942. 1175 N. 300 W., Kokomo, IN 46901-1799, (765) 457-5743, www.thepoorclares.org. 3900 Sherwood Blvd., Delray Beach, FL 33445, (561) 498-3294. 200 Marycrest Dr., St. Louis, MO 63129, (314) 846-2618. 6029 Estero Blvd., Fort Myers Beach, FL 33931, (239) 463-5599, www.poorclares-fmb.org. 9300 Hwy 105, Brenham, TX 77833, (409) 836-2444, www.franciscanpoorclares.org.

Franciscan Sisters, Daughters of the Sacred Hearts of Jesus and Mary, O.S.F.: Founded 1860, in Germany; in U.S., 1872. Generalate, Rome, Italy. U.S. motherhouse, P.O. Box 667, Wheaton, IL 60189-0667,

(630) 462-7422, www.wheatonfranciscan.org. Educational, hospital, foreign mission, social work.

Franciscan Sisters Daughters of Mercy, F.H.M.: Founded 1856, in Spain; in U.S., 1962. General motherhouse, Palma de Mallorca, Spain. U.S. address, 612 N. 3rd St., Waco, TX 76701, (254) 753-5565.

Franciscan Sisters of Allegany, O.S.F.: Founded 1859, at Allegany, NY, by Fr. Pamphilus da Magliano, O.F.M. General motherhouse, P.O. Box W, 115 East Main St., Allegany, NY 14706, (716) 373-0200, www.alleganyfranciscans.org. Hospital, foreign mission work.

Franciscan Sisters of Baltimore, O.S.F.: Founded 1868, in England; in U.S., 1881. General motherhouse, 3725 Ellerslie Ave., Baltimore, MD 21218, (410) 235-0139. Educational work; social services.

Franciscan Sisters of Chicago, O.S.F.: Founded 1894, in U.S., by Mother Mary Therese (Josephine Dudzik). General motherhouse, 11500 Theresa Dr., Lemont, IL 60439, (630) 243-3550. Educational work, social services.

Franciscan Sisters of Christian Charity, O.S.F.: Founded 1869, in U.S. Motherhouse, Holy Family Convent, 2409 S. Alverno Rd., Manitowoc, WI 54220, (920) 682-7728, www.fscc-calledtobe.org. Hospital work.

Franciscan Sisters of Little Falls, MN, O.S.F.: Founded 1891, in U.S. General motherhouse, 116 8th Ave., S.E., Little Falls, MN 56345, (320) 632-0612, www.fslf.org. Health, education, social services, pastoral ministry, mission work.

Franciscan Sisters of Mary, F.S.M.: Established, 1987, through unification of the Sisters of St. Mary of the Third Order of St. Francis (founded 1872, St. Louis) and the Sisters of St. Francis of Maryville, MO (founded 1894). Address of general superior: 1100 Bellevue Ave., St. Louis, MO 63117-1883, (314) 768-1833, www.fsmonline.org. Health care, social services.

Franciscan Sisters of Mary Immaculate of the Third Order of St. Francis of Assisi, F.M.I.: Founded 16th century, in Switzerland; in U.S., 1932. General motherhouse, Bogota, Colombia. U.S. provincial house, 4301 N.E. 18th Ave., Amarillo, TX 79107-7220, (806) 383-5769. Education.

Franciscan Sisters of Our Lady of Perpetual Help, O.S.F.: Founded 1901, in U.S., from Joliet, IL, foundation. General motherhouse, 335 South Kirkwood Rd., St. Louis, MO 63122, (314) 965-3700, www.franciscansisters-olph.org. Educational, hospital work.

Franciscan Sisters of Peace, F.S.P.: Established 1986, in U.S., as archdiocesan community, from Franciscan Missionary Sisters of the Sacred Heart. Congregation Center, 20 Ridge St., Haverstraw, NY 10927, (845) 942-2527, www.fspnet.org.

Franciscan Sisters of Ringwood, F.S.R.: Merged with the Sisters of St. Francis of Philadelphia in 2003.

Franciscan Sisters of St. Elizabeth, F.S.S.E.: Founded 1866, at Naples, Italy, by Bl. Ludovico di Casorio; in U.S., 1919. General motherhouse, Rome, Italy. U.S. delegate house, 499 Park Rd., Parsippany, NJ 07054, (973) 539-3797, www.franciscansisters.com. Educational work, social services.

Franciscan Sisters of St. Joseph, F.S.S.J.: Founded 1897, in U.S. General motherhouse, 5286 S. Park Ave., Hamburg, NY 14075, (716) 649-1205, www.franciscansistershamburg.org. Educational, hospital work.

Franciscan Sisters of St. Joseph (of Mexico): U.S. foundation, St. Paul College, 3015 4th St. N.E., Washington, DC 20017, (202) 832-6262.

Franciscan Sisters of the Atonement (Graymoor Sisters), S.A.: Founded 1898, in U.S., as Anglican community; entered Church, 1909. General motherhouse, St. Francis Convent-Graymoor, 41 Old Highland Turnpike, Garrison, NY 10524, (914) 424-3624. Mission work.

Franciscan Sisters of St. Paul, MN, O.S.F.: Founded 1863, at Neuwied, Germany (Franciscan Sisters of the Blessed Virgin Mary of the Holy Angels); in U.S., 1923. General motherhouse, Rhine, Germany. U.S. motherhouse, 1388 Prior Ave. S., St. Paul, MN 55116, (651) 690-1501; www.askmotherrose.org. Educational, hospital, social work.

Franciscan Sisters of the Immaculate Conception, O.S.F.: Founded in Germany; in U.S., 1928. General motherhouse, Kloster, Bonlanden, Germany. U.S. province, 291 North St., Buffalo, NY 14201, (716) 881-2323.

Franciscan Sisters of the Immaculate Conception, O.S.F.: Founded 1874, in Mexico; in U.S., 1926. U.S. provincial house, 11306 Laurel Canyon Blvd., San Fernando, CA 91340, (818) 365-2582.

Franciscan Sisters of the Immaculate Conception and St. Joseph for the Dying, O.S.F.: Founded 1919, in U.S. General motherhouse, 1249 Joselyn Canyon Rd., Monterey, CA 93940, (408) 372-3579.

Franciscan Sisters of the Poor, S.F.P.: Founded 1845, at Aachen, Germany, by Bl. Frances Schervier; in U.S., 1858. Congregational office, 133 Remsen St., Brooklyn, NY 11201, (718) 643-1919, www.franciscansisters.org. Hospital, social work and foreign missions.

Franciscan Sisters of the Sacred Heart, O.S.F.: Founded 1866, in Germany; in U.S., 1876. General motherhouse, St. Francis Woods, 9201 W. St. Francis Rd., Frankfort, IL 60423-8335, (815) 469-4895. www.fssh.com. Education, health care, other service ministries.

Hospital Sisters of the Third Order of St. Francis, O.S.F.: Founded 1844, in Germany; in U.S., 1875. General motherhouse, Muenster, Germany. U.S. motherhouse, 4849 La Verna Rd., Springfield, IL 62707, (217) 522-3386, www.springfieldfranciscans.org. Hospital work.

Institute of the Franciscan Sisters of the Eucharist, F.S.E.: Founded 1973. Motherhouse, 405 Allen Ave., Meriden, CT 06451, (203) 237-0841, www.fscommunity.org.

Little Franciscans of Mary, P.F.M.: Founded 1889, in U.S. General motherhouse, Baie St. Paul, QC, Canada. U.S. region, 55 Moore Ave., Worcester, MA 01602, (508) 755-0878. Educational, hospital, social work.

Missionary Franciscan Sisters of the Immaculate Conception, M.F.I.C.: Founded 1873, in U.S. General motherhouse, Rome, Italy. U.S. address, 790 Centre St., Newton, MA 02458, (617) 527-1004, www.mficusa.org. Educational work.

Missionary Sisters of the Immaculate Conception of the Mother of God, S.M.I.C.: Founded 1910, in Brazil; in U.S., 1922. U.S. provincialate, P.O. Box 3026, Paterson, NJ 07509, (973) 279-3790, www.smic-missionarysisters.com. Mission, educational, health work, social services.

Mothers of the Helpless, M.D.: Founded 1873, in Spain; in U.S., 1916. General motherhouse, Valencia, Spain. U.S. address, Sacred Heart Residence, 432 W. 20th St., New York, NY 10011, (212) 929-5790; www.sacredheartresidence.com.

Poor Clares of Perpetual Adoration, P.C.P.A.: Founded 1854, at Paris, France; in U.S., 1921, at Cleveland, OH. U.S. monasteries: 4200 N. Market Ave., Canton, OH 44714. 2311 Stockham Lane, Portsmouth, OH 45662-3049, (740) 353-4713. 4108 Euclid Ave., Cleveland, OH 44103, (216) 361-0783. 3900 13th St. N.E., Washington, DC 20017, (202) 526-6808. 5817 Old Leeds Rd., Birmingham, AL 35210, (205) 271-2917. 3222 County Rd. 548, Hanceville, AL 35077, (256) 352-6267, www.olamshrine.com. Contemplative, cloistered, perpetual adoration.

St. Francis Mission Community, O.S.F.: Autonomous province of Franciscan Sisters of Mary Immaculate. 4305 54th St., Lubbock, TX 79413, (806) 793-9859.

School Sisters of St. Francis, O.S.F.: Founded 1874, in U.S. General motherhouse, 1501 S. Layton Blvd., Milwaukee, WI 53215, (414) 384-4105.

School Sisters of St. Francis, (Pittsburgh, PA), O.S.F.: Established 1913, in U.S. Motherhouse, Mt. Assisi Convent, 934 Forest Ave., Pittsburgh, PA 15202-1199, (412) 761-2855, www.franciscansisters-pa.org. Education, health care services and related ministries.

School Sisters of the Third Order of St. Francis (Bethlehem, PA), O.S.F.: Founded in Austria, 1843; in U.S., 1913. General motherhouse, Rome, Italy. U.S. province, 395 Bridle Path Rd., Bethlehem, PA 18017, (610) 866-2597. Educational, mission work.

School Sisters of the Third Order of St. Francis (Panhandle, TX), O.S.F.: Established 1931, in U.S., from Vienna, Austria, foundation (1845). General motherhouse, Vienna, Austria. U.S. center and novitiate, P.O. Box 906, Panhandle, TX 79068, (806) 537-3182, www.panhandlefranciscans.org. Educational, social work.

Sisters of Mercy of the Holy Cross, S.C.S.C.: Founded 1856, in Switzerland; in U.S. 1912. General motherhouse, Ingenbohl, Switzerland. U.S. provincial residence, 1400 O'Day St., Merrill, WI 54452, (715) 539-1460, www.holycrosssisters.org.

Sisters of Our Lady of Mercy (Mercedarians), S.O.L.M.: General motherhouse, Rome, Italy. U.S. address: Most Precious Blood, 133-157 27th Ave., Brooklyn, NY 11214, (718) 373-7343.

Sisters of St. Francis (Clinton, IA), O.S.F.: Founded 1868, in U.S. General motherhouse, 588 N. Bluff Blvd., Clinton, IA 57232-3953, (563) 242-7611, www.clintonfranciscans.com. Educational, hospital, social work.

Sisters of St. Francis (Millvale, PA), O.S.F.: Founded 1865, Pittsburgh. General motherhouse, 146 Hawthorne Rd., Millvale P.O., Pittsburgh, PA 15209, (412) 821-2200. Educational, hospital work.

Sisters of St. Francis (Hastings-on-Hudson), O.S.F.: Founded 1893, in New York. General motherhouse, 49 Jackson Ave., Hastings-on-Hudson, NY 10706-3217, (914) 478-3930. Education, parish ministry, social services.

Sisters of St. Francis of Assisi, O.S.F.: Founded 1849, in U.S. General motherhouse, 3221 S. Lake Dr., St. Francis, WI 53235-3799, (414) 744-3150, www.lakeosfs.org. Education, other ministries.

Sisters of St. Francis of Christ the King, O.S.F.: Founded 1864, in Austria; in U.S., 1909. General motherhouse, Rome, Italy. U.S. provincial house, 13900 Main St., Lemont, IL 60439, (630) 257-7495. Educational work, home for aged.

Sisters of St. Francis of Penance and Christian Charity, O.S.F.: Founded 1835, in Holland; in U.S., 1874. General motherhouse, Rome, Italy. U.S. provinces: 4421 Lower River Rd., Stella Niagara, NY 14144-1001, (716) 754-2193, www.franciscans-stella-niagara.org. 2851 W. 52nd Ave., Denver, CO 80221, (303) 458-6270; 3910 Bret Harte Dr., P.O. Box 1028, Redwood City, CA 94064, (650) 369-1725.

Sisters of St. Francis of Philadelphia, O.S.F.: Founded 1855, at Philadelphia, by Mother Mary Francis Bachmann and St. John N. Neumann. General motherhouse, Convent of Our Lady of the Angels, Aston, PA 19014, (610) 558-7701, www.osfphila.org. Education, health care, social services.

Sisters of St. Francis of Savannah, MO, O.S.F.: Founded 1850, in Austria; in U.S., 1922. Provincial house, La Verna Heights, Box 488, 104 E. Park, Savannah, MO 64485-0488, (816) 324-3179. Educational, hospital work.

Sisters of St. Francis of the Congregation of Our Lady of Lourdes, O.S.F.: Founded 1916, in U.S. General motherhouse, 6832 Convent Blvd., Sylvania, OH 43560-2897, (419) 824-3606, www.sistersosf.org. Education, health care, social services, pastoral ministry.

Sisters of St. Francis of the Holy Cross, O.S.F.: Founded 1881, in U.S., by Rev. Edward Daems, O.S.C. General motherhouse, 3110 Nicolet Dr., Green Bay, WI 54311, (920) 884-2700, www.gbfranciscans.org. Educational, nursing work, pastoral ministry, foreign missions.

Sisters of St. Francis of the Holy Eucharist, O.S.F.: Founded 1378, in Switzerland; in U.S., 1893. General motherhouse, 2100 N. Noland Rd., Independence, MO 64050, (816) 252-1673. Education, health care, social services, foreign missions.

Sisters of St. Francis of the Holy Family, O.S.F.: U.S. foundation, 1875. Motherhouse, Mt. St. Francis, 3390 Windsor Ave., Dubuque, IA 52001, (563) 583-9786, www.osfdbq.org. Varied apostolates.

Sisters of St. Francis of the Immaculate Conception, O.S.F.: Founded 1890, in U.S. General motherhouse, 2408 W. Heading Ave., West Peoria, IL 61604-5096, (309) 674-6168, www.osfsisterswpeoria.org. Education, care of aging, pastoral ministry.

Sisters of St. Francis of the Immaculate Heart of Mary, O.S.F.: Founded 1241, in Bavaria; in U.S., 1913. General motherhouse, Rome, Italy. U.S. motherhouse, 102 6th St., S.E., Hankinson, ND 58041, (701) 242-7195, www.fargodiocese.org/sfc/index.htm. Education, social services.

Sisters of St. Francis of the Martyr St. George, O.S.F.: Founded 1859, in Germany; in U.S., 1923. General motherhouse, Thuine, Germany. U.S. provincial house, St. Francis Convent, 2120 Central Ave., Alton, IL 62002, (618) 463-2750, www.altonfranciscans.org. Education, social services, foreign mission work.

Sisters of St. Francis of the Perpetual Adoration, O.S.F.: Founded 1863, in Germany; in U.S., 1875. General motherhouse, Olpe, Germany. U.S. provinces: Box 766, Mishawaka, IN 46546-0766, (574) 259-5427, www.ssfpa.org. 7665 Assisi Heights, Colorado Springs, CO 80919, (719) 955-7015, www.stfrancis.org.

Sisters of St. Francis of the Providence of God, O.S.F.: Founded 1922, in U.S., by Msgr. M. L. Krusas. General motherhouse, 3603 McRoberts Rd., Pittsburgh, PA 15234, (412) 885-7407. Education, varied apostolates.

Sisters of St. Joseph of the Third Order of St. Francis, S.S.J.: Founded 1901, in U.S. Administrative office, P.O. Box 305, Stevens Pt., WI 54481-0305, (715) 341-8457, www.ssj-tosf.org. Education, health care, social services.

Sisters of the Infant Jesus, I.J.: Founded 1662, at Rouen, France; in U.S., 1950. Motherhouse, Paris, France. Generalate, Rome, Italy. U.S. address: 20 Reiner St., Colma, CA 94014.

Sisters of the Sorrowful Mother (Third Order of St. Francis), S.S.M.: Founded 1883, in Italy; in U.S., 1889. General motherhouse, Rome, Italy. U.S. address: 17600 E. 51st St., Broken Arrow, OK 74012, (918) 355-1148, www.ssmfranciscans.org. Educational, hospital work.

Sisters of the Third Franciscan Order, O.S.F.: Founded 1860, at Syracuse, NY. Generalate offices, 2500 Grant Blvd., Syracuse, NY 13208, (315) 425-0115.

Sisters of the Third Order of St. Francis, O.S.F.: Founded 1877, in U.S., by Bishop John L. Spalding. Motherhouse, 1175 St. Francis Lane, E. Peoria, IL 61611-1299, (309) 699-7215, www.franciscansisterpeoria.org. Hospital work.

Sisters of the Third Order of St. Francis (Oldenburg, IN), O.S.F.: Founded 1851, in U.S. General motherhouse, Sisters of St. Francis, P.O. Box 100, Oldenburg, IN 47036-0100, (812) 934-2475, www.oldenburgfranciscans.org. Education, social services, pastoral ministry, foreign missions.

Sisters of the Third Order of St. Francis of Penance and Charity, O.S.F.: Founded 1869, in U.S., by Rev. Joseph Bihn. Motherhouse, 200 St. Francis Ave., Tiffin, OH 44883, (419) 447-0435, www.tiffinfranciscans.org. Education, social services.

Sisters of the Third Order of St. Francis of the Perpetual Adoration, F.S.P.A.: Founded 1849, in U.S. Generalate, 912 Market St., La Crosse, WI 54601, (608) 782-5610, www.fspa.org. Education, health care.

Sisters of the Third Order Regular of St. Francis of the Congregation of Our Lady of Lourdes, O.S.F.: Founded 1877, in U.S. General motherhouse, Assisi Heights, 1001 14th St., NW, Rochester, MN 55901, (507) 282-7441; www.rochesterfranciscan.org. Education, health care, social services.

Good Shepherd Sisters (Servants of the Immaculate Heart of Mary), S.C.I.M.: Founded 1850, in Canada; in U.S., 1882. General motherhouse, QC, Canada. In U.S., Provincial House, Bay View, 313 Seaside Ave., Saco, Maine 04072, (207) 284-6429. Educational, social work.

Good Shepherd, Sisters of the, R.G.S.: Founded 1835, in France, by St. Mary Euphrasia Pelletier; in U.S., 1843. Generalate, Rome, Italy. U.S. provinces: 2108 Hatmaker St., Cincinnati, OH 45204, (513) 921-5923. 82-31 Doncaster Pl., Jamaica, NY 11432, (718) 380-3270, www.goodshepherdsistersna.org. 504 Hexton Hill Rd., Silver Spring, MD 20904, (301) 384-1169. 7654 Natural Bridge Rd., St. Louis, MO 63121, (314) 381-3400, www.goodshepherdsisters.org. 5100 Hodgson Rd., St. Paul, MN 55126, (651) 484-0221. Active and contemplative (Contemplative Sisters of the Good Shepherd, C.G.S.).

Graymoor Sisters: *See* Franciscan Sisters of the Atonement.

Grey Nuns of the Sacred Heart, G.N.S.H.: Founded 1921, in U.S. General motherhouse, 1750 Quarry Rd., Yardley, PA 19067-3998, (215) 968-4236, www.greynun.org.

Guadalupan Missionaries of the Holy Spirit, M.G.Sp.S.: Founded 1930 in Mexico by Rev. Felix de

Jesus Rougier, M.Sp.S. General motherhouse, Mexico. U.S. delegation: 2483 S.W. 4th St. Miami, FL 33135-2907, (305) 642-9544.

Guardian Angel, Sisters of the, S.A.C.: Founded 1839, in France. General motherhouse, Madrid, Spain. U.S. foundation, 1245 S. Van Ness, Los Angeles, CA 90019, (213) 732-7881.

Handmaids of the Precious Blood, Congregation of, H.P.B.: Founded 1947, at Jemez Springs, NM. Motherhouse and novitiate, Cor Jesu Monastery, P.O. Box 90, Jemez Springs, NM 87025, (505) 829-3906.

Helpers, Society of, H.H.S.: Founded 1856, in France; in U.S., 1892. General motherhouse, Paris, France. American province, 3206 S. Aberdeen, Chicago, IL 60657, (773) 523-8638.

Hermanas Catequistas Guadalupanas, H.C.G.: Founded 1923, in Mexico; in U.S., 1950. General motherhouse, Mexico. 4110 S. Flores, San Antonio, TX 78214, (210) 533-9344.

Hermanas Josefinas, H.J.: General motherhouse, Mexico. U.S. foundation, Assumption Seminary, 2600 W. Woodlawn Ave., P.O. Box 28240, San Antonio, TX 78284, (210) 734-0039. Domestic work.

Holy Child Jesus, Society of the, S.H.C.J.: Founded 1846, in England; in U.S., 1862. General motherhouse, Rome, Italy. U.S. province, 460 Shadeland Ave., Drexel Hill, PA 19026, (610) 626-1400, www.shcj.org.

Holy Faith, Congregation of the Sisters of the, C.H.F.: Founded 1856, in Ireland; in U.S., 1953. General motherhouse, Dublin, Ireland. U.S. province, 12322 S. Paramount Blvd., Downey, CA 90242, (562) 869-6092.

Holy Family, Congregation of the Sisters of the, S.S.F.: Founded 1842, in Louisiana, by Henriette Delille and Juliette Gaudin. General motherhouse, 6901 Chef Menteur Hwy., New Orleans, LA 70126, (504) 242-8315, www.sistersoftheholyfamily. Hospital work.

Holy Family, Sisters of the, S.H.F.: Founded 1872, in U.S. General motherhouse, P.O. Box 3248, Fremont, CA 94539, (510) 624-4500 www.holyfamilysisters.com. Educational, social work.

Holy Family of Nazareth, Sisters of the, C.S.F.N.: Founded 1875, in Italy; in U.S., 1885. General motherhouse, Rome, Italy. U.S. provinces: Sacred Heart, 310 N. River Rd., Des Plaines, IL 60016-1211, (847) 298-6760. Immaculate Conception BVM, 4001 Grant Ave., Philadelphia, PA 19114, (215) 268-1035, www.phila-csfn.org. St. Joseph, 285 Bellevue Rd., Pittsburgh, PA 15229-2195, (412) 931-4778, www.csfn.org. Immaculate Heart of Mary, Marian Heights, 1428 Monroe Turnpike, Monroe, CT 04648, (203) 268-7646. Bl. Frances Siedliska Provincialate, 1814 Egyptian Way, Box 530959, Grand Prairie, TX 75053, (972) 641-4496, www.csfn.org.

Holy Heart of Mary, Servants of the, S.S.C.M.: Founded 1860, in France; in U.S., 1889. General motherhouse, Montreal, QC, Canada. U.S. province, 15 Elmwood Dr., Kankakee, IL 60901, (815) 937-2380, www.sscm-usa.org. Educational, hospital, social work.

Holy Names of Jesus and Mary, Sisters of the, S.N.J.M.: Founded 1843, in Canada by Bl. Marie Rose Durocher; in U.S., 1859. Generalate, Longueuil, QC, Canada. U.S.-Ontario Province was formed in 2006 by uniting the five predominantly English-speaking provinces of the Congregation. Address: Box 25,

Marylhurst, OR 97036, (503) 675-2449, www.snjm.org.

Holy Spirit, Community of the, C.H.S.: Founded 1970 in San Diego, CA. 6151 Rancho Mission Rd., No. 205, San Diego, CA 92108, (619) 584-0809.

Holy Spirit, Daughters of the, D.H.S.: Founded 1706, in France; in U.S., 1902. Generalate, Bretagne, France. U.S. motherhouse, 72 Church St., Putnam, CT 06260-1817, (860) 928-0891. Educational work, district nursing, pastoral ministry.

Holy Spirit, Mission Sisters of the, M.S.Sp.: Founded 1932, at Cleveland, OH. Motherhouse, 1030 N. River Rd., Saginaw, MI 48603, (517) 781-0934.

Holy Spirit, Missionary Sisters, Servants of the: Founded 1889, in Holland; in U.S., 1901. Generalate, Rome, Italy. U.S. motherhouse, Convent of the Holy Spirit, P.O. Box 6026, Techny, IL 60082-6026, (847) 441-0126, www.ssps-usa.org. International congregation for the spread of the Gospel *ad gentes*.

Holy Spirit, Sisters of the, C.S.Sp.: Founded 1890, in Rome, Italy; in U.S. as independent diocesan community, 1929. General motherhouse, 10102 Granger Rd., Garfield Hts., OH 44125, (216) 581-2900, www.sistersoftheholyspirit.org. Educational, social, nursing work.

Holy Spirit, Sisters of the, S.H.S.: Founded 1913, in U.S., by Most Rev. J. F. Regis Canevin. General motherhouse, 5246 Clarwin Ave., Ross Township, Pittsburgh, PA 15229-2208, (412) 931-1917. Educational, nursing work, care of aged.

Holy Spirit and Mary Immaculate, Sisters of, S.H.Sp.: Founded 1893, in U.S. Motherhouse, 301 Yucca St., San Antonio, TX 78203, (210) 533-5149. Education, hospital work.

Holy Spirit of Perpetual Adoration, Sister Servants of the, S.Sp.S.deA.P.: Founded 1896, in Holland; in U.S., 1915. Generalate, Bad Driburg, Germany. U.S. novitiate, 2212 Green St., Philadelphia, PA 19130, (215) 567-0123, www.adorationsisters.org.

Holy Union Sisters, S.U.S.C.: Founded 1826, in France; in U.S., 1886. Generalate, Rome, Italy. U.S. provinces: P.O. Box 410, Milton, MA 02186-0006, (617) 696-8765. Box 993, Main St., Groton, MA 01450, (978) 448-6049. Varied ministries.

Home Mission Sisters of America (Glenmary Sisters), G.H.M.S.: Founded 1952, in U.S. Glenmary Center, P.O. Box 22264, Owensboro, KY 42304-2264, (270) 686-8401; www.glenmarysisters.org.

Home Visitors of Mary, Sisters, H.V.M.: Founded 1949, in Detroit, MI. Motherhouse, 121 E. Boston Blvd., Detroit, MI 48202, (313) 869-2160.

Hospitallers of St. Joseph, Religious, R.H.S.J.: Founded in 1636, in France; in U.S., 1894. Motherhouse, 2450, Chemin de la Côte Sainte-Catherine, Montréal, CanadaH3T 1B1. U.S. address: 644, Langlade Road, Antigo, Wisconsin 54409, (715) 623-4615; www.rhsj.org.

Humility of Mary, Congregation of, C.H.M.: Founded 1854, in France; in U.S., 1864. U.S. address, Humility of Mary Center, Davenport IA, 52804, (319) 323-9466, www.chmiowa.org.

Humility of Mary, Sisters of the, H.M.: Founded 1854, in France; in U.S., 1864. U.S. address, Villa Maria Community Center, Villa Maria, PA 16155, (724) 964-8861, www.humilityofmary.org.

Immaculate Conception, Little Servant Sisters of

the, L.S.I.C.: Founded 1850, in Poland; in U.S., 1926. General motherhouse, Poland. U.S. provincial house, 1000 Cropwell Rd., Cherry Hill, NJ 08003, (609) 424-1962. Education, social services, African missions.

Immaculate Conception, Sisters of the, R.C.M.: Founded 1892, in Spain; in U.S., 1962. General motherhouse, Madrid, Spain. U.S. address, 2230 Franklin, San Francisco, CA 94109, (415) 474-0159, www.rc.net/conception.

Immaculate Conception, Sisters of the, C.I.C.: Founded 1874, in U.S. General motherhouse, P.O. Box 50426, New Orleans, LA 70185, (504) 486-7426.

Immaculate Conception of the Blessed Virgin Mary, Sisters of the (Lithuanian): Founded 1918, at Mariampole, Lithuania; in U.S., 1936. U.S. headquarters, Immaculate Conception Convent, 600 Liberty Hwy., Putnam, CT 06260, (860) 928-7955.

Immaculate Heart of Mary, Missionary Sisters, I.C.M.: Founded 1897, in India; in U.S., 1919. Generalate, Rome, Italy. U.S. province, 283 E. 15th St., New York, NY 10003, (212) 260-8567. Educational social, foreign mission work.

Immaculate Heart of Mary, Sisters of the, I.H.M.: Founded 1848, in Spain; in U.S., 1878. General motherhouse, Rome, Italy. U.S. province, 3820 Sabino Canyon Rd., Tucson, AZ 85750, (520) 886-4273. Educational work.

Immaculate Heart of Mary, Sisters, Servants of the, I.H.M.: Founded 1845. SSIHM Leadership Council, 610 W. Elm, Monroe, MI 48162, (734) 340-9700, www.sistersihm.org.

Immaculate Heart of Mary, Sisters, Servants of the, I.H.M.: Founded 1845; established in Scranton, PA, 1871. General motherhouse, 2300 Adams Ave., Scranton, PA 18509, (570) 346-5404, www.sistersofihm.org.

Immaculate Heart of Mary, Sisters Servants of the, I.H.M.: Founded 1845; established in West Chester, PA, 1872. General motherhouse, Villa Maria, Immaculata, PA 19345, (610) 647-2160, www.ihmimmaculata.org.

Immaculate Heart of Mary of Wichita, Sisters of, I.H.M.: Established at Wichita, KS. 1979. Address: 145 S. Millwood St., Wichita, KS 67213, (316) 722-9316, www.sistersofwichita.org.

Incarnate Word, Religious of, C.V.I.: General motherhouse, Mexico City, Mexico. U.S. address, 153 Rainier Ct., Chula Vista, CA 92011, (619) 420-0231.

Incarnate Word and Blessed Sacrament, Congregation of, C.V.I.: Founded 1625, in France; in U.S., 1853. Incarnate Word Convent, 3400 Bradford Pl., Houston, TX 77025, (713) 668-0423.

Incarnate Word and Blessed Sacrament, Congregation of the, I.W.B.S.: Motherhouse, 1101 Northeast Water St., Victoria, TX 77901, (361) 575-2266, www.iwbsvictoria.org.

Incarnate Word and Blessed Sacrament, Congregation of the, I.W.B.S.: Motherhouse, 2930 S. Alameda, Corpus Christi, TX 78404, (361) 882-5413, www.iwbscc.org.

Incarnate Word and Blessed Sacrament, Sisters of the, S.I.W.: Founded 1625, in France; in U.S. 1853. Motherhouse, 6618 Pearl Rd., Parma Heights, Cleveland, OH 44130, (440) 886-6440, www.incarnatewordorder.org.

Infant Jesus, Congregation of the (Nursing Sisters

of the Sick Poor), C.I.J.: Founded 1835, in France; in U.S., 1905. General motherhouse, 310 Prospect Park W., Brooklyn, NY 11215, (718) 965-7300.

Institute of the Blessed Virgin Mary (Loretto Sisters), I.B.V.M.: Founded 17th century in Belgium; in U.S., 1954. Motherhouse, Rathfarnham, Dublin, Ireland. U.S. address: 2521 W. Maryland Ave., Phoenix, AZ 85017, (602) 242-2544.

Institute of the Blessed Virgin Mary (Loretto Sisters), I.B.V.M.: Founded 1609, in Belgium; in U.S., 1880. Loretto Convent, Box 508, Wheaton, IL 60189, (630) 665-3814. Educational work.

Jesus, Daughters of (*Filles de Jesus*), F.J.: Founded 1834, in France; in U.S., 1904. General motherhouse, Kermaria, Locmine, France. U.S. address, 4209 3rd Ave. S., Great Falls, MT 59405, (406) 452-7231. Educational, hospital, parish and social work.

Jesus, Little Sisters of, L.S.J.: Founded 1939, in Sahara; in U.S., 1952. General motherhouse, Rome, Italy. U.S. headquarters, 400 N. Streeper St., Baltimore, MD 21224, www.rc.net/org/littlesisters.

Jesus, Society of the Sisters, Faithful Companions of, F.C.J.: Founded 1820, in France; in U.S., 1896. General motherhouse, Kent, England. U.S. province, St. Philomena Convent, Cory's Lane, Portsmouth, RI 02871, (401) 683-2222, www.portsmouthabbey.org.

Jesus and Mary, Little Sisters of, L.S.J.M.: Founded 1974 in U.S. Joseph House, P.O. Box 1755, Salisbury, MD 21802, (410) 742-9590, www.thejosephhouse.org.

Jesus and Mary, Religious of, R.J.M.: Founded 1818, at Lyons, France; in U.S., 1877. General motherhouse, Rome, Italy. U.S. province, 6103 Baltimore Ave., Ste. T-5, Riverdale, MD 20713, (301) 277-2535. Educational work.

Jesus Crucified, Congregation of: Founded 1930, in France; in U.S., 1955. General motherhouse, Brou, France. U.S. foundation: Benedictines of Jesus Crucified, Monastery of the Glorious Cross, 61 Burban Dr., Branford, CT 06405-4003, (203) 315-9964, www.benedictinesjc.org.

Jesus Crucified and the Sorrowful Mother, Poor Sisters of, C.J.C.: Founded 1924, in U.S., by Rev. Alphonsus Maria, C.P. Motherhouse, 261 Thatcher St., Brockton, MA 02402. Education, nursing homes, catechetical centers.

Jesus, Mary and Joseph, Missionary Sisters of, M.J.M.J.: Founded 1942, in Spain; in U.S., 1956. General motherhouse, Madrid, Spain. U.S. regional house, 12940 Leopard St., Corpus Christi, TX 78410, (361) 241-1955.

John the Baptist, Sisters of St., C.S.J.B.: Founded 1878, in Italy; in U.S., 1906. General motherhouse, Rome, Italy. U.S. provincialate, 3308 Campbell Dr., Bronx, NY 10465, (718) 518-7820, www.home.att.net/~baptistines. Education, parish and retreat work; social services.

Joseph, Poor Sisters of St., P.S.S.J.: Founded 1880, in Argentina. General motherhouse, Muniz, Buenos Aires, Argentina. U.S. addresses: Casa Belen, 305 E. 4th St., Bethlehem, PA 78015, (610) 867-4030. Casa Nazareth, 5321 Spruce St., Reading, PA 19602, (610) 378-1947. St. Gabriel Convent, 4319 Sano St., Alexandria, VA 22312, (703) 354-0395 .

Joseph, Religious Daughters of St., F.S.J.: Founded 1875, in Spain. General motherhouse, Spain. U.S.

foundation, 319 N. Humphreys Ave., Los Angeles, CA 90022.

Joseph, Servants of St., S.S.J.: Founded 1874, in Spain; in U.S., 1957. General motherhouse, Salamanca, Spain. U.S. address, 203 N. Spring St., Falls Church, VA 22046, (703) 533-8441.

Joseph, Sisters of St., C.S.J. or S.S.J.: Founded 1650, in France; in U.S., 1836, at St. Louis. Independent motherhouses in U.S.: 637 Cambridge St., Brighton, MA 02135, (617) 783-9090. 1515 W. Ogden Ave., La Grange Park, IL, 60526, (708) 354-9200, www.ministryofthearts.org. 480 S. Batavia St., Orange, CA 92868, (714) 633-8121, www.sistersof-stjosephorange.org. St. Joseph Convent, 1725 Brentwood Rd., Brentwood, NY 11717-5587, (516) 273-4531. 23 Agassiz Circle, Buffalo, NY 14214, (716) 838-4400. 3430 Rocky River Dr., Cleveland, OH 44111, (216) 252-0440, www.csjcleveland.org. 1440 W. Division Rd., Tipton, IN 46072, (765) 675-6203, www.csjtipton.org. Motherhouse and novitiate, Nazareth, MI 49074, (616) 381-6290. 1425 Washington St., Watertown, NY 13601, (315) 782-3460, www.ssjwatertown.org. 1020 State St., Baden, PA 15005-1342, (724) 869-2151, www.stjoseph-baden.org. 5031 W. Ridge Rd., Erie, PA 16506, (814) 836-4208, www.ssjerie.org. 150 French Rd., Rochester, NY 14618, (585) 641-8119, www.ssjvolunteers. Mont Marie, 34 Lower Westfield Rd. Holyoke, MA 01040, (413) 536-0853. Pogue Run Rd., Wheeling, WV 26003, (304) 232-8160, www.ssjwhg.org. 3700 E. Lincoln St., Wichita, KS 67218, (316) 686-7171, www.csjoseph.org. 215 Court St., Concordia, KS 66901, (785) 243-2149, www.csjkansas.org.

Joseph, Sisters of St. (Lyons, France), C.S.J.: Founded 1650, in France; in U.S., 1906. General motherhouse, Lyons, France. U.S. provincialate, 93 Halifax St., Winslow, ME 04901, (207) 873-4512, www.e-livingwater.org. Educational, hospital work.

Joseph, Sisters of St., of Peace, C.S.J.P.: Founded 1884, in England; in U.S. 1885. Generalate, 3043 Fourth St., N.E., Washington, DC 20017, (202) 832-5333. Educational, hospital, social service work.

Joseph of Carondelet, Sisters of St., C.S.J.: Founded 1650, in France; in U.S., 1836, at St. Louis, MO. U.S. headquarters, 2311 S. Lindbergh Blvd., St. Louis, MO 63131, (314) 966-4048, www.csjcongregation.org.

Joseph of Chambery, Sisters of St.: Founded 1650, in France; in U.S., 1885. Generalate, Rome, Italy. U.S. provincial house, 27 Park Rd., West Hartford, CT 06119, (860) 233-5126. Educational, hospital, social work.

Joseph of Chestnut Hill, Sisters of St., S.S.J.: Founded 1650; Philadelphia foundation, 1847. Motherhouse, Mt. St. Joseph Convent, 9701 Germantown Ave., Philadelphia, PA 19118, (215) 248-7200, www.ssjphila.org.

Joseph of Cluny, Sisters of St., S.J.C.: Founded 1807, in France. Generalate, Paris, France. U.S. provincial house, 7 Restmere Terrace, Middletown, RI 02842, (401) 846-4826.

Joseph of Medaille, Sisters of, C.S.J.: Founded 1650, in France; in U.S., 1855. Became an American congregation Nov. 30, 1977. Central office, 1821 Summit Rd., Suite 210, Cincinnati, OH 45237, (513) 761-2888.

Joseph of St. Augustine, Florida, Sisters of St., S.S.J.: General motherhouse, 241 St. George St., P.O. Box 3506, St. Augustine, FL 32085, (904) 824-1752. Educational, hospital, pastoral, social work.

Joseph of St. Mark, Sisters of St., S.J.S.M.: Founded 1845, in France; in U.S., 1937. General motherhouse, 21800 Chardon Rd., Euclid, Cleveland, OH 44117, (216) 531-7426. Nursing homes.

Joseph the Worker, Sisters of St., S.J.W.: General motherhouse, St. William Convent, 1 St. Joseph Lane, Walton, KY 41094, (859) 485-4256.

Lamb of God, Sisters of the, A.D.: Founded 1945, in France; in U.S., 1958. General motherhouse, France. U.S. address, 2063 Wyandotte Ave., Owensboro KY 42301, (502) 281-5450.

Life, Sisters of, S.V. (Sorer Vitae): Founded by Cardinal John J. O'Connor, 1991, to protect life. St. Frances de Chantal Convent, 198 Hollywood Ave., Bronx, NY 10465, (718) 863-2264. Our Lady of New York, 1955 Needham Ave., Bronx, NY, 10466, (718) 881-8008. Sacred Heart Convent, 450 W. 51st St., New York, NY, (212) 397-1386.

Little Sisters of the Gospel, L.S.G.: Founded 1963 in France by Rev. Rene Voillaume; in U.S., 1972. Box 305, Mott Haven Sta., Bronx, NY 10454, (718) 292-2867.

Little Workers of the Sacred Hearts, P.O.S.C.: Founded 1892, in Italy; in U.S., 1948. General House, Rome, Italy. U.S. address, Our Lady of Grace Convent, 635 Glenbrook Rd., Stamford, CT 06906, (203) 348-5531.

Living Word, Sisters of the, S.L.W.: Founded 1975, in U.S. Motherhouse, Living Word Center, 800 N. Fernandez Ave. B, Arlington Heights, IL 60004-5316, (847) 577-5972, www.slw.org. Education, hospital, parish ministry work.

Loretto at the Foot of the Cross, Sisters of, S.L.: Founded 1812 in U.S., by Rev. Charles Nerinckx. General motherhouse, 300 E. Hampden Ave., Ste. 400, Englewood, CO 80110-2661, (303) 783-0450, www.lorettocommunity.org. Educational work.

Louis, Juilly-Monaghan, Congregation of Sisters of St., S.S.L.: Founded 1842, in France; in U.S., 1949. General motherhouse, Monaghan, Ireland. U.S. regional house, 22300 Mulholland Dr., Woodland Hills, CA 91364, (818) 883-1678. Educational, medical, parish, foreign mission work.

Lovers of the Holy Cross Sisters (Phat Diem), L.H.C.: Founded 1670, in Vietnam; in U.S. 1976. U.S. address, Holy Cross Convent, 14700 South Van Ness Ave., Gardena, CA 90249, (310) 516-0271.

Mantellate Sisters, Servants of Mary, of Blue Island, O.S.M.: Founded 1861, in Italy; in U.S., 1916. Generalate, Rome, Italy. U.S. motherhouse, 13811 S. Western Ave., Blue Island, IL 60406, (708) 385-2103. Educational work.

Mantellate Sisters Servants of Mary, of Plainfield, O.S.M.: Founded 1861 in Italy; in U.S., 1916. 16949 S. Drauden Rd., Plainfield, IL 60586, (815) 436-5796.

Marian Sisters of the Diocese of Lincoln: Founded 1954. Marycrest Motherhouse, 6905 N. 112th St., Waverly, NE 68462-9690, (402) 786-2750.

Marianites of Holy Cross, Congregation of the Sisters, M.S.C.: Founded 1841, in France; in U.S., 1843. Motherhouse, Le Mans, Sarthe, France. North

American headquarters, 1011 Gallier St., New Orleans, LA 70117-6111, (504) 945-1620, www.marianites.org.

Marist Sisters, Congregation of Mary, S.M.: Founded 1824, in France. General motherhouse, Rome, Italy. U.S. foundation: 810 Peach, Abilene, TX 79602, (915) 675-5806.

Mary, Company of, O.D.N.: Founded 1607, in France; in U.S., 1926. General motherhouse, Rome, Italy. U.S. motherhouse, 16791 E. Main St., Tustin, CA 92680-4034, (714) 541-3125, www.companyof mary.com.

Mary, Daughters of the Heart of, D.H.M.: Founded 1790, in France; in U.S., 1851. Generalate, Paris, France. U.S. provincialate, 1339 Northampton St., Holyoke, MA 01040, (413) 533-6681, www.dhmna.org. Education, retreat work.

Mary, Missionary Sisters of the Society of (Marist Sisters), S.M.S.M.: Founded 1845, at St. Brieuc, France; in U.S., 1922. General motherhouse, Rome, Italy. U.S. provincial house, 349 Grove St., Waltham, MA 02453, (781) 893-0149, www.maristmissionary smsm.org.

Mary, Servants of, O.S.M.: Founded 13th century, in Italy; in U.S., 1893. General motherhouse, England. U.S. provincial motherhouse, 7400 Military Ave., Omaha, NE 68134, (402) 571-2547.

Mary, Servants of (Servite Sisters), O.S.M.: Founded 13th century, in Italy; in U.S., 1912. General motherhouse, Servants of Mary Convent, 1000 College Ave., Ladysmith, WI 54848, (715) 532-3364, www.servitesisters.org.

Mary, Sisters of St., of Oregon, S.S.M.O.: Founded 1886, in Oregon, by Bishop William H. Gross, C.Ss.R. General motherhouse, 4440 S.W. 148th Ave., Beaverton, OR 97007, (503) 644-9181, www.ssmo.org. Educational, nursing work.

Mary, Sisters of the Little Company of, L.C.M.: Founded 1877, in England; in U.S., 1893. Generalate, London, England. U.S. provincial house, 9350 S. California Ave., Evergreen Park, IL 60805, (708) 229-5490, www.lcmglobal.org.

Mary, Sisters Servants of (Trained Nurses), S.M.: Founded 1851, at Madrid, Spain; in U.S., 1914. General motherhouse, Rome, Italy. U.S. motherhouse, 800 N. 18th St., Kansas City, KS 66102, (913) 371-3423. Home nursing.

Mary and Joseph, Daughters of, D.M.J.: Founded 1817, in Belgium; in U.S., 1926. Generalate, Rome, Italy. American provincialate, 5300 Crest Rd., Rancho Palos Verdes, CA 90274, (310) 541-8194.

Mary Help of Christians, Daughters of (Salesian Sisters of St. John Bosco), F.M.A.: Founded 1872, in Italy, by St. John Bosco and St. Mary Dominic Mazzarello; in U.S., 1908. General motherhouse, Rome, Italy. U.S. provinces: 655 Belmont Ave., Haledon, NJ 07508, (937) 790-7963. 6019 Buena Vista St., San Antonio, TX 78237, (210) 432-0090. Education, youth work.

Mary Immaculate, Daughters of (Marianist Sisters), F.M.I.: Founded 1816, in France, by Very Rev. William-Joseph Chaminade. General motherhouse, Rome, Italy. U.S. foundation, 251 W. Ligustrum Dr., San Antonio, TX 78228-4092, (210) 433-5501, www.marianistsisters.org. Educational work.

Mary Immaculate, Religious of, R.M.I.: Founded

1876, in Spain; in U.S., 1954. Generalate, Rome, Italy. U.S. foundation, 719 Augusta St., San Antonio, TX 78215, (210) 226-0025.

Mary Immaculate, Sisters Minor of, S.M.M.I.: Established in U.S., 1989. 138 Brushy Hill Rd., Danbury, CT 06818, (203) 744-8041.

Mary Immaculate, Sisters of, S.M.I.: Founded 1948, in India, by Bishop Louis LaRavoire Morrow; in U.S., 1981. General motherhouse, Bengal, India. U.S. address, 118 Park Rd., Leechburg, PA 15656, (724) 845-2828.

Mary Immaculate, Sisters Servants of, S.S.M.I.: Founded 1878 in Poland. General motherhouse, Mariowka-Opoczynska, Poland; American provincialate, 1220 Tugwell Dr., Catonsville, MD 21228, (410) 747-1353.

Mary Immaculate, Sisters Servants of, S.S.M.I: Founded 1892, in Ukraine; in U.S., 1935. General motherhouse, Rome, Italy. U.S. address, 9 Emmanuel Dr., P.O. Box 9, Sloatsburg, NY 10974-0009, (845) 753-2840. Educational, hospital work.

Mary of Namur, Sisters of St., S.S.M.N.: Founded 1819, at Namur, Belgium; in U.S., 1863. General motherhouse, Namur, Belgium. U.S. provinces: 241 Lafayette Ave., Buffalo, NY 14213-1453, (716) 884-8221, www.ssmn.us. 909 West Shaw St., Ft. Worth, TX 76110, (817) 923-8393, web2.airmail.net/ssmn.

Mary of Providence, Daughters of St., D.S.M.P.: Founded 1872, at Como, Italy; in U.S., 1913. General motherhouse, Rome, Italy. U.S. provincial house, 4200 N. Austin Ave., Chicago, IL 60634, (773) 545-8300. Special education for mentally handicapped.

Mary of the Immaculate Conception, Daughters of, D.M.: Founded 1904, in U.S., by Msgr. Lucian Bojnowski. General motherhouse, 314 Osgood Ave., New Britain, CT 06053, (860) 225-9406. Educational, hospital work.

Mary Queen, Congregation of, C.M.R.: Founded in Vietnam; established in U.S., 1979. U.S. region, 625 S. Jefferson, Springfield, MO 65806.

Mary Reparatrix, Society of, S.M.R.: Founded 1857, in France; in U.S., 1908. Generalate, Rome, Italy. U.S. province, 225 E. 234th St., Bronx NY 10470.

Maryknoll Sisters, M.M.: Founded in 1912 in U.S. by Mother Mary Joseph. General motherhouse: P.O. Box 311, Maryknoll, NY 10545-0311, (914) 941-7575, www.maryknoll.org.

Medical Mission Sisters (Society of Catholic Medical Missionaries, Inc.), M.M.S.: Founded 1925, in U.S., by Mother Anna Dengel. Generalate, London, England. U.S. headquarters, 8400 Pine Rd., Philadelphia, PA 19111, (215) 742-6100, www.medicalmissionsisters.org. Medical work, health education, especially in mission areas.

Medical Missionaries of Mary, M.M.M.: Founded 1937, in Ireland, by Mother Mary Martin; in U.S., 1950. General motherhouse, Dublin, Ireland. U.S. headquarters, 563 Minneford Ave., City Island, Bronx, NY 10464, (718) 885-0945. Medical aid in missions.

Medical Sisters of St. Joseph, M.S.J.: Founded 1946, in India; first U.S. foundation, 1985. General motherhouse, Kerala, S. India. U.S. address, 3435 E. Funston, Wichita, KS 67218, (316) 689-5360. Health care apostolate.

Mercedarian Sisters of the Blessed Sacrament,

H.M.S.S.: Founded 1910, in Mexico; first U.S. foundation, 1926. Regional House, 227 Keller St., San Antonio, TX 78204, (210) 223-5013.

Mercy, Daughters of Our Lady of, D.M.: Founded 1837, in Italy, by St. Mary Joseph Rossello; in U.S., 1919. General motherhouse, Savona, Italy. U.S. motherhouse, Villa Rossello, 1009 Main Rd., Newfield, NJ 08344, (856) 697-2983. Educational, hospital work.

Mercy, Missionary Sisters of Our Lady of, M.O.M.: Founded 1938, in Brazil; in U.S., 1955. General motherhouse, Brazil. U.S. address, 388 Franklin St., Buffalo, NY 14202, (716) 854-5198.

Mercy, Religious Sisters of, R.S.M.: Founded 1973 in U.S. Motherhouse, 1835 Michigan Ave., Alma, MI 48801, (517) 463-6035.

Mercy, Sisters of, of the Americas: Formed in July, 1991, through union of nine provinces and 16 regional communities of Sisters of Mercy which previously were independent motherhouses or houses which formed the Sisters of Mercy of the Union. Mother Mary Catherine McAuley founded the Sisters of Mercy in Dublin, Ireland, in 1831; first established in the U.S., 1843, in Pittsburgh. Administrative office: 8300 Colesville Rd., No. 300, Silver Spring, MD 20910, (301) 587-0423.

Mill Hill Sisters: *See* **Franciscan Missionaries of St. Joseph.**

Minim Daughters of Mary Immaculate, C.F.M.M.: Founded 1886, in Mexico; in U.S., 1926. General motherhouse, Leon, Guanajuato, Mexico. U.S. address, 555 Patagonia Hwy., Nogales, AZ 85621, (520) 287-3377.

Misericordia Sisters, S.M.: Founded 1848, in Canada; in U.S., 1887. General motherhouse, 12435 Ave. Misericorde, Montreal, QC H4J 2G3, Canada. U.S. address, 225 Carol Ave., Pelham, NY 10803. Social work with unwed mothers and their children; hospital work.

Mission Helpers of the Sacred Heart, M.H.S.H.: Founded 1890, in U.S. General motherhouse, 1001 W. Joppa Rd., Baltimore, MD 21204, (410) 823-8585, www.missionhelpers.org. Religious education, evangelization.

Missionary Catechists of the Sacred Hearts of Jesus and Mary (Violetas), M.C.S.H.: Founded 1918, in Mexico; in U.S., 1943. Motherhouse, Tlalpan, Mexico. U.S. address, 805 Liberty St., Victoria, TX 77901, (512) 578-9302.

Missionary Daughters of the Most Pure Virgin Mary, M.D.P.V.M.: Founded in Mexico; in U.S., 1916. 919 N. 9th St., Kingsville, TX 78363, (512) 595-1087.

Mother of God, Missionary Sisters of the, M.S.M.G.: Byzantine, Ukrainian Rite, Stamford. Motherhouse, 711 N. Franklin St., Philadelphia, PA 19123, (215) 627-7808.

Mother of God, Sisters Poor Servants of the, S.M.G.: Founded 1869, in London, England; in U.S., 1947. General motherhouse, Maryfield, Roehampton, London. U.S. address: Maryfield Nursing Home, Greensboro Rd., High Point, NC 27260, (336) 886-2444, www.greensboro.com/mnh. Hospital, educational work.

Nazareth, Poor Sisters of, P.S.N.: Founded in England; U.S. foundation, 1924. General motherhouse, Hammersmith, London, England. U.S. novitiate, 3333 Manning Ave., Los Angeles, CA 90064,

(310) 839-2361. Social services, education.

Notre Dame, School Sisters of, S.S.N.D.: Founded 1833, in Germany; in U.S., 1847. General motherhouse, Rome, Italy. U.S. provinces: 13105 Watertown Plank Rd., Elm Grove, WI 53122-2291, (262) 782-9850, www.ssnd-milw.org. 6401 N. Charles St., Baltimore, MD 21212, (410) 377-7774, www.atlanticmidwest.org; 320 E. Ripa Ave., St. Louis, MO 63125, (314) 633-7000, www.ssnd.org. 170 Good Counsel Dr., Mankato, MN 56001-3138, (507) 389-4208, www.ssndmankato.org. P.O. Box 227275, Dallas, TX 75222, (214) 330-9152, www.ssnddallas.org. 1431 Euclid Ave., Berwyn, IL 60402, (708) 749-1380.

Notre Dame, Sisters of, S.N.D.: Founded 1850, at Coesfeld, Germany; in U.S., 1874. General motherhouse, Rome, Italy. U.S. provinces: 13000 Auburn Rd., Chardon, OH 44024, (440) 286-7101. 1601 Dixie Highway, Covington, KY 41011, (606) 291-2040. 3837 Secor Rd., Toledo, OH 43623, (419) 474-5485. 1776 Hendrix Ave., Thousand Oaks, CA 91360, (805) 496-3243.

Notre Dame, Sisters of the Congregation of, C.N.D.: Founded 1658, in Canada, by St. Marguerite Bourgeoys; in U.S., 1860. General motherhouse, Montréal, QC, Canada. U.S. province, 223 West Mountain Rd., Ridgefield, CT 06877-3627, (203) 438-3115, www.cnd-m.com. Education.

Notre Dame de Namur, Sisters of, S.N.D.deN.: Founded 1804, in France; in U.S., 1840. General motherhouse, Rome, Italy. U.S. provinces: 351 Broadway, Everett, MA 02149, (617) 387-2500, www.SNDdeN.org. 30 Jeffery's Neck Rd., Ipswich, MA 01938, (978) 356-2159. 468 Poquonock Ave., Windsor, CT 06095-2473, (860) 688-1832, www.snd-den.org. 1531 Greenspring Valley Rd., Stevenson, MD 21153, (410) 486-5599. 305 Cable St., Baltimore, MD 21210, (410) 243-1993, www.sndden.org. 701 E. Columbia Ave., Cincinnati, OH 45215, (513) 761-7636. 1520 Ralston Ave., Belmont, CA 94002-1908, (650) 593-2045. SND Base Communities, 125 Michigan Ave., N.E., Washington, DC 20017, (202) 884-9750; www.sndden.org. Educational work.

Notre Dame de Sion, Congregation of, N.D.S.: Founded 1850, in France; in U.S., 1892. Generalate, Rome, Italy. U.S. province, 3823 Locust St., Kansas City, MO 64109, (816) 531-1374. Creation of better understanding between Christians and Jews.

Notre Dame Sisters: Founded 1853, in Czechoslovakia; in U.S., 1910. General motherhouse, Javornik, Czech Republic. U.S. motherhouse, 3501 State St., Omaha, NE 68112, (402) 455-2994, www.notredamesisters.org. Educational work.

Oblates of the Mother of Orphans, O.M.O: Founded 1945, in Italy. General motherhouse, Milan, Italy. U.S. address, 20 E. 72 St., New York, NY 10021.

Our Lady of Charity, North American Union of Sisters of, Eudist Sisters (Sisters of Our Lady of Charity of the Refuge), N.A.U.-O.L.C.: Founded 1641, in Caen, France, by St. John Eudes; in U.S., 1855. Autonomous houses were federated in 1944 and in March 1979 the North American Union of the Sisters of Our Lady of Charity was established. General motherhouse, 154 Edgington Ln., Wheeling, WV 26003, (304) 242-0042. Primarily devoted to re-education and rehabilitation of women and girls in residential and non-residential settings.

Independent houses: 1125 Malvern Ave., Hot Springs, AR 71901, (501) 623-1393, www.adorationchapel.org. 4500 W. Davis St., Dallas, TX 75211, (214) 331-1754.

Our Lady of Sorrows, Sisters of, O.L.S.: Founded 1839, in Italy; in U.S., 1947. General motherhouse, Rome, Italy. U.S. headquarters, 9894 Norris Ferry Rd., Shreveport, LA 71106.

Our Lady of the Holy Rosary, Daughters of, F.M.S.R. (Filiae Mariae Sacri Rosarii): Founded 1946, in North Vietnam; foundation in U.S., 1968. General Motherhouse, Saigon, Vietnam. U.S. Province, 1492 Moss St., New Orleans, LA 70119, (504) 486-0039.

Our Lady of Victory Missionary Sisters, O.L.V.M.: Founded 1922, in U.S. Motherhouse, Victory Noll, 1900 W. Park Dr., P.O. Box 109, Huntington, IN 46750, (260) 356-0628, www.olvm.org. Educational, social work.

Pallottine Missionary Sisters (Missionary Sisters of the Catholic Apostolate), S.A.C.: Founded in Rome, 1838; in U.S., 1912. Generalate, Rome, Italy. U.S. provincialate, 15270 Old Halls Ferry Rd., Florissant, MO 63034, (314) 837-7100, www.geocities.com/pallottinerenewal.

Pallottine Sisters of the Catholic Apostolate, C.S.A.C.: Founded 1843, at Rome, Italy; in U.S., 1889. General motherhouse, Rome. U.S. motherhouse, St. Patrick's Villa, Harriman Heights, Harriman, NY 10926, (914) 783-9007. Educational work.

Parish Visitors of Mary Immaculate, P.V.M.I.: Founded 1920, in New York. General motherhouse, Box 658, Monroe, NY 10950, (845) 783-2251. Mission work.

Passion of Jesus Christ, Religious of (Passionist Nuns), C.P.: Founded 1771, in Italy, by St. Paul of the Cross; in U.S., 1910. U.S. convents: 2715 Churchview Ave., Pittsburgh, PA 15227-2141, (412) 881-1155. 631 Griffin Pond Rd., Clarks Summit, PA 18411-8899, (570) 586-2791, www.intiques.net/cpnuns. 8564 Crisp Rd., Whitesville, KY 42378-9729, (270) 233-4571, www.passionistnuns.org. 1151 Donaldson Hwy., Erlanger, KY 41018, (859) 371-8568. 15700 Clayton Rd., Ellisville, MO 63011, (314) 227-5275. Contemplatives.

Passionist Sisters: *See* Cross and Passion, Sisters of the

Paul, Daughters of St. (Missionary Sisters of the Media of Communication), D.S.P.: Founded 1915, at Alba, Piedmont, Italy; in U.S., 1932. General motherhouse, Rome, Italy. U.S. provincial house, 50 St. Paul's Ave., Boston, MA 02130-3491, (617) 522-8911, www.pauline.org. Apostolate of the communications arts.

Paul of Chartres, Sisters of St., S.P.C.: Founded 1696, in France. General House, Rome, Italy. U.S. address, 2920 Third Ave., So., Escanaba, MI 49828; (906) 399-0420.

Perpetual Adoration of Guadalupe, Sisters of, A.P.G.: U.S. foundation, 2403 W. Travis, San Antonio, TX 78207, (956) 227-7785.

Peter Claver, Missionary Sisters of St., S.S.P.C.: Founded 1894 in Austria by Bl. Maria Teresa Ledochowska; in U.S., 1914. General motherhouse, Rome, Italy. U.S. address, 667 Woods Mill Rd. S.,

Chesterfield, MO 63006, (314) 434-8084.

Pious Disciples of the Divine Master, P.D.D.M.: Founded 1924 in Italy; in U.S., 1948. General motherhouse, Rome, Italy. U.S. headquarters, 60 Sunset Ave., Staten Island, NY 10314, (718) 494-8597.

Pious Schools, Sisters of the, Sch. P.: Founded 1829 in Spain; in U.S., 1954. General motherhouse, Rome, Italy. U.S. headquarters, 17601 Nordhoff St., Northridge, CA 91325, (818) 882-6265.

Poor, Little Sisters of the, L.S.P.: Founded 1839, in France, by Bl. Jeanne Jugan; in U.S., 1868. General motherhouse, St. Pern, France. U.S. provinces: 110-30 221st St., Queens Village, NY 11429, (718) 464-1800. 601 Maiden Choice Lane, Baltimore, MD 21228, (410) 744-9367; www.littlesistersofthepoor.org. 80 W. Northwest Hwy., Palatine, IL 60067, (847) 358-5700. Care of aged.

Poor Clare Missionary Sisters (Misioneras Clarisas), M.C.: Founded in Mexico. General motherhouse, Rome, Italy. U.S. novitiate, 1019 N. Newhope, Santa Ana, CA 92703-1534, (714) 554-8850.

Poor Clare Nuns: *See* Franciscan Poor Clare Nuns.

Poor Handmaids of Jesus Christ (Ancilla Domini Sisters), P.H.J.C.: Founded 1851, in Germany by Bl. Mary Kasper; in U.S., 1868. General motherhouse, Dernbach, Westerwald, Germany. U.S. motherhouse, Ancilla Domini Convent, Donaldson, IN 46513, (219) 936-9936. Educational, hospital work, social services.

Precious Blood, Daughters of Charity of the Most, D.C.P.B.: Founded 1872, at Pagani, Italy; in U.S., 1908. General motherhouse, Rome, Italy. U.S. convent, 1482 North Ave., Bridgeport, CT 06604, (203) 334-7000.

Precious Blood, Missionary Sisters of the, C.P.S.: Founded 1885, at Mariannhill, South Africa; in U.S., 1925. Generalate, Rome, Italy. U.S. novitiate, P.O. Box 97, Reading, PA 19607, (610) 777-1624. Home and foreign mission work.

Precious Blood, Sisters Adorers of the, A.P.B.: Founded 1861, in Canada; in U.S., 1890. General motherhouse, Canada. U.S. autonomous monasteries: 5400 Fort Hamilton Pkwy., Brooklyn, NY 11219, (718) 438-6371, www.sisterspreciousblood.org. 700 Bridge St., Manchester, NH 03104-5495, (603) 623-4264. 166 State St., Portland, ME 04101. 400 Pratt St., Watertown, NY 13601, (315) 788-1669. Cloistered, contemplative.

. **Precious Blood, Sisters of the, C.PP.S.:** Founded 1834, in Switzerland; in U.S., 1844. Generalate, 4000 Denlinger Rd., Dayton, OH 45426, (937) 837-3302. Education, health care, other ministries.

Precious Blood, Sisters of the Most, C.PP.S.: Founded 1845, in Steinerberg, Switzerland; in U.S., 1870. General motherhouse, 204 N. Main St., O'Fallon, MO 63366-2203, (636) 240-3420. Education, other ministries.

Presentation, Sisters of Mary of the, S.M.P.: Founded 1829, in France; in U.S., 1903. General motherhouse, Broons, Côtes-du-Nord, France. U.S. address, Maryvale Novitiate, 11550 River Rd., Valley City, ND 58072, (701) 845-2864, www.smphs.org. Hospital work.

Presentation of Mary, Sisters of the, P.M.: Founded 1796, in France by Bl. Marie Rivier; in U.S., 1873. General motherhouse, Castel Gandolfo, Italy. U.S.

provincial houses: 495 Mammoth Rd., Manchester, NH 03104, (603) 669-1080, www.presentationofmary.com. 209 Lawrence St., Methuen, MA 01844, (978) 687-1369, www.presmarymethuen.org.

Presentation of the B.V.M., Sisters of the, P.B.V.M.: Founded 1775, in Ireland; in U.S., 1854, in San Francisco. U.S. motherhouses: 2360 Carter Rd., Dubuque, IA 52001, (563) 588-2008, www.dubuquepresentations.org. 880 Jackson Ave., New Windsor, NY 12553, (845) 564-0513. 281 Masonic Ave, San Francisco, CA 94118, (415) 422-5013, www.presentationsisterssf.org. St. Colman's Convent, Watervliet, NY 12189, (518) 273-4911. 1101 32nd Ave., S., Fargo ND 58103, (701) 237-4857, www.presetnationsistersfargo.org. Presentation Convent, Aberdeen, SD 57401, (605) 229-8419, Leominster, MA 01453. 419 Woodrow Rd., Staten Island, NY 10312, (718) 966-2365.

Presentation of the Blessed Virgin Mary, Sisters of, of Union: Founded in Ireland, 1775; union established in Ireland, 1976; first U.S. vice province, 1979. Generalate, Kildare, Ireland. U.S. provincialate, 729 W. Wilshire Dr., Phoenix, AZ 85007, (602) 271-9687.

Providence, Daughters of Divine, F.D.P.: Founded 1832, Italy; in U.S., 1964. General motherhouse, Rome, Italy. U.S. address, 74684 Airport Rd., Covington, LA 70435, (985) 809-8836 (fax).

Providence, Missionary Catechists of Divine, M.C.D.P.: Administrative house, 2318 Castroville Rd., San Antonio, TX 78237, (210) 432-0113.

Providence, Oblate Sisters of, O.S.P.: Founded 1829, in U.S., by Mother Mary Elizabeth Lange and Father James Joubert, S.S. First order of black nuns in U.S. General motherhouse, 701 Gun Rd., Baltimore, MD 21227, (410) 242-8500. Educational work.

Providence, Sisters of, S.P.: Founded 1861, in Canada; in U.S., 1873. General motherhouse, Our Lady of Victory Convent, 5 Gamelin St., Holyoke, MA 01040, (413) 536-7511, wwwsisofprov.org.

Providence, Sisters of, S.P.: Founded 1843, in Canada; in U.S., 1854. General motherhouse, Montreal, QC, Canada. U.S. province, Mother Joseph Province, 506 Second Ave., #1200, Seattle, WA 98104, (206) 464-3394, www.sistersofprovidence.net.

Providence, Sisters of (of St. Mary-of-the-Woods), S.P.: Founded 1806, in France; in U.S., 1 Sisters of Providence, St. Mary-of-the-Woods, IN 47876, (812) 535-3131, www.sistersofprovidence.org.

Providence, Sisters of Divine, C.D.P.: Founded 1762, in France; in U.S., 1866. Generalate, 515 SW 24th St., San Antonio, TX 78207, (210) 434-1866. Educational, hospital work.

Providence, Sisters of Divine, C.D.P.: Founded 1851, in Germany; in U.S., 1876. Generalate, Rome, Italy. U.S. provinces: 9000 Babcock Blvd., Allison Park, PA 15101-2793, (412) 931-5241, www.divineprovidenceweb.org. 3415 Bridgeland Dr., Bridgetown, MO 63044, (314) 209-9181. 363 Bishops Hwy., Kingston, MA 02364, (781) 585-7707. Educational, hospital work.

Providence, Sisters of Divine (of Kentucky), C.D.P.: Founded 1762, in France; in U.S., 1889. General motherhouse, Fenetrange, France. U.S. province, St. Bartholomew Parish, Cincinnati, OH 45231, (513) 728-3146, www.cdpkentucky.org. Education, social services, other ministries.

Redeemer, Oblates of the Most Holy, O.SS.R.: Founded 1864, in Spain. General motherhouse, Spain. U.S. foundation, 60-80 Pond St., Jamaica Plain, MA 02130, (617) 524-1640.

Redeemer, Order of the Most Holy, O.SS.R.: Founded 1731, by Ven. Mother Marie Celeste Crostarosa, with the help of St. Alphonsus Liguori; in U.S., 1957. U.S. addresses: Mother of Perpetual Help Monastery, P.O. Box 220, Esopus, NY 12429, (845) 384-6533. Monastery of St. Alphonsus, 200 Ligouri Dr. Liguori, MO 63057, (636) 464-1093.

Redeemer, Sisters of the Divine, S.D.R.: Founded 1849, in Niederbronn, France; in U.S., 1912. General motherhouse, Rome, Italy. U.S. province, 999 Rock Run Road, Elizabeth, PA 15037, (412) 751-8600. Educational, hospital work; care of the aged.

Redeemer, Sisters of the Holy, C.S.R.: Founded 1849, in Alsace; in U.S., 1924. General motherhouse, Wurzburg, Germany. U.S. provincial house, 521 Moredon Rd., Huntingdon Valley, PA 19006, (215) 914-4101. Personalized medical care in hospitals, homes for aged, private homes; retreat work.

Reparation of the Congregation of Mary, Sisters of, S.R.C.M.: Founded 1903, in U.S. Motherhouse, St. Zita's Villa, Monsey, NY 10952, (845) 356-2011.

Reparation of the Sacred Wounds of Jesus, Sisters of, S.R.: Founded 1959 in U.S. General motherhouse, 2120 S.E. 24th Ave., Portland, OR 97214-5504, (503) 236-4207.

Resurrection, Sisters of the, C.R.: Founded 1891, in Italy; in U.S., 1900. General motherhouse, Rome, Italy. U.S. provinces: 7432 Talcott Ave., Chicago, IL 60631, (773) 792-6363. Mt. St. Joseph, 35 Boltwood Ave., Castleton-on-Hudson, NY 12033, (518) 732-2429, www.resurrectionsisters.org. Education, nursing.

Rita, Sisters of St., O.S.A.: General motherhouse, Wurzburg, Germany. U.S. foundation, St. Monica's Convent, 3920 Green Bay Rd., Racine, WI 53404, (262) 639-5050, www.srsofstrita.org.

Rosary, Congregation of Our Lady of the Holy, R.S.R.: Founded 1874, in Canada; in U.S., 1899. General motherhouse, Rimouski, QC, Canada. U.S. regional house, 20 Thomas St., Portland, ME 04102-3638, (207) 774-3756, www.soeursdusaintrosaire.org. Educational work.

Rosary, Missionary Sisters of the Holy, M.S.H.R.: Founded 1924, in Ireland; in U.S., 1954. Motherhouse, Dublin, Ireland. In U.S., 741 Polo Rd., Bryn Mawr, PA 19010, (610) 520-1974, www.holyrosarymissionarysisters.org. African missions.

Sacrament, Missionary Sisters of the Most Blessed, M.SS.S.: General motherhouse, Madrid, Spain. U.S. foundation, 1111 Wordin Ave., Bridgeport, CT 06605.

Sacrament, Nuns of the Perpetual Adoration of the Blessed, A.P.: Founded 1807 in Rome, Italy; in U.S., 1925. U.S. monasteries: 145 N. Cotton Ave., El Paso, TX 79901, (915) 533-5323. 771 Ashbury St., San Francisco, CA 94117, (415) 566-2743.

Sacrament, Oblate Sisters of the Blessed, O.S.B.S.: Founded 1935, in U.S. Motherhouse, St. Sylvester Convent, P.O. Box 217, Marty, SD 57361, (605) 384-3305. Care of American Indians.

Sacrament, Servants of the Blessed, S.S.S.: Founded 1858, in France, by St. Pierre Julien Eymard;

in U.S., 1947. General motherhouse, Rome, Italy. American provincial house, St. Charles Borromeo Parish, 1818 Coal Pl. SE, Albuquerque, NM 87106, (505) 242-3692. Contemplative.

Sacrament, Sisters of the Blessed, for Indians and Colored People, S.B.S.: Founded 1891, in U.S., by St. Katharine Drexel. General motherhouse, 1663 Bristol Pike, P.O. Box 8502, Bensalem, PA 19020, (215) 244-9900, www.katharinedrexel.org.

Sacrament, Sisters of the Most Holy, M.H.S.: Founded 1851, in France; in U.S., 1872. Generalate, 313 Corona Dr. (P.O. Box 90037), Lafayette, LA 70509, (337) 981-8475.

Sacrament, Sisters Servants of the Blessed, S.J.S.: Founded 1904, in Mexico; in U.S., 1926. General motherhouse, Mexico. U.S. address: 215 Lomita St., El Segundo, CA 90245, (310) 615-0766.

Sacramentine Nuns (Religious of the Order of the Blessed Sacrament and Our Lady), O.S.S.: Founded 1639, in France; in U.S., 1912. U.S. monasteries: 235 Bellvale Lakes Rd., Warwick NY 10990. 2798 US 31 N, P.O. Box 86, Conway, MI 49722, (231) 347-0447. Perpetual adoration of the Holy Eucharist.

Sacred Heart, Daughters of Our Lady of the, F.D.N.S.C.: Founded 1882, in France; in U.S., 1955. General motherhouse, Rome, Italy. U.S. address, 424 E. Browning Rd., Bellmawr, NJ 08031, (609) 931-8973. Educational work.

Sacred Heart, Missionary Sisters of the (Cabrini Sisters), M.S.C.: Founded 1880, in Italy, by St. Frances Xavier Cabrini; in U.S., 1889. General motherhouse, Rome, Italy. U.S. provincial office, 222 E. 19th St., 5B, New York, NY 10003. Educational, health, social and catechetical work.

Sacred Heart, Society Devoted to the, S.D.S.H.: Founded 1940, in Hungary; in U.S., 1956. U.S. motherhouse, 9814 Sylvia Ave., Northridge, CA 91324, (818) 831-9710; www.sacredheartsisters.com. Educational work.

Sacred Heart, Society of the, R.S.C.J.: Founded 1800, in France; in U.S., 1818. Generalate, Rome, Italy. U.S. provincial house, 4389 W. Pine Blvd., St. Louis, MO 63108, (314) 652-1500, www.rscj.org. Educational work.

Sacred Heart of Jesus, Apostles of, A.S.C.J.: Founded 1894, in Italy; in U.S., 1902. General motherhouse, Rome, Italy. U.S. motherhouse, 265 Benham St., Hamden, CT 06514, (203) 248-4225, www.ascjus.org. Educational, social work.

Sacred Heart of Jesus, Handmaids of the, A.C.J.: Founded 1877, in Spain. General motherhouse, Rome, Italy. U.S. province, 1242 S. Broad St., Philadelphia, PA 19146, (214) 468-6368. Educational, retreat work.

Sacred Heart of Jesus, Missionary Sisters of the Most (Hiltrup), M.S.C.: Founded 1899, in Germany; in U.S., 1908. General motherhouse, Rome, Italy. U.S. province, 2811 Moyers Lane, Reading, PA 19605, (610) 929-5944; www.mscrdg.org. Education, health care, pastoral ministry.

Sacred Heart of Jesus, Oblate Sisters of the, O.S.H.J.: Founded 1894; in U.S., 1949. General motherhouse, Rome, Italy. U.S. headquarters, 50 Warner Rd., Hubbard, OH 44425, (330) 759-9329, www.oblatesister.com. Educational, social work.

Sacred Heart of Jesus, Servants of the Most, S.S.C.J.: Founded 1894, in Poland; in U.S., 1959.

General motherhouse, Cracow, Poland. U.S. address, 866 Cambria St., Cresson, PA 16630, (814) 886-4223, www.sacredheartsisters.org. Education, health care, social services.

Sacred Heart of Jesus, Sisters of the, S.S.C.J.: Founded 1816, in France; in U.S., 1903. General motherhouse, St. Jacut, Brittany, France. U.S. provincial house, 11931 Radium St., San Antonio, TX 78216, (210) 344-7203. Educational, hospital, domestic work.

Sacred Heart of Jesus and of the Poor, Servants of the (Mexican), S.S.H.J.P.: Founded 1885, in Mexico; in U.S., 1907. General motherhouse, Apartado 92, Puebla, Mexico. U.S. address, 3310 S. Zapata Hwy, Laredo, TX 78046, (956) 723-3343.

Sacred Heart of Jesus and Our Lady of Guadalupe, Missionaries of the, M.S.C.Gpe.: U.S. address, 1212 E. Euclid Ave., Arlington Heights, IL 60004, (708) 398-1350.

Sacred Heart of Jesus for Reparation, Congregation of the Handmaids of the, A.R.: Founded 1918, in Italy; in U.S., 1958. U.S. address, 36 Villa Dr., Steubenville, OH 43953, (740) 282-3801.

Sacred Heart of Mary, Religious of the, R.S.H.M.: Founded 1848, in France; in U.S., 1877. Generalate, Rome, Italy. U.S. provinces; 50 Wilson Park Dr., Tarrytown, NY 10591, (914) 631-8872, www.rshm.org. 441 N. Garfield Ave., Montebello, CA 90640, (323) 887-8821, www.rshm.org.

Sacred Hearts and of Perpetual Adoration, Sisters of the, SS.CC.: Founded 1797, in France; in U.S., 1908. General motherhouse, Rome, Italy. U.S. provinces: 1120 Fifth Ave., Honolulu, Hawaii 96816, (808) 737-5822, www.ssccpicpus.com (Pacific). 35 Huttleston Ave., Fairhaven, MA 02719, (508) 994-9341 (East Coast). Varied ministries.

Sacred Hearts of Jesus and Mary, Sisters of the, S.H.J.M.: Established 1953, in U.S. General motherhouse, Essex, England. U.S. address, 2150 Lake Shore Ave., Oakland CA 94606, (510) 832-2935.

Savior, Company of the, C.S.: Founded 1952, in Spain; in U.S., 1962. General motherhouse, Madrid, Spain. U.S. foundation, 820 Clinton Ave., Bridgeport, CT 06604, (203) 368-1875.

Savior, Sisters of the Divine, S.D.S.: Founded 1888, in Italy; in U.S., 1895. General motherhouse, Rome, Italy. U.S. province, 4311 N. 100th St., Milwaukee, WI 53222, (414) 466-0810, www.salvatoriansisters.org. Educational, hospital work.

Social Service, Sisters of, S.S.S.: Founded in Hungary, 1923, by Sr. Margaret Slachta. U.S. generalate, 296 Summit Ave., Buffalo, NY 14214, (716) 834-0197, www.sistersofsocialservicebuffalo.org. Social work.

Social Service, Sisters of, of Los Angeles, S.S.S.: Founded 1908, in Hungary; in U.S., 1926. General motherhouse, 2303 S. Figueroa Way, Los Angeles, CA 90007, (213) 746-2117.

Teresa of Jesus, Society of St., S.T.J.: Founded 1876, in Spain; in U.S., 1910. General motherhouse, Rome, Italy. U.S. provincial house, 18080 St. Joseph's Way, Covington, LA 70435, (985) 893-1470, www.teresians.org.

Thomas of Villanova, Congregation of Sisters of St., S.S.T.V.: Founded 1661, in France; in U.S., 1948. General motherhouse, Neuilly-sur-Seine, France. U.S.

foundation, W. Rocks Rd., Norwalk, CT 06851, (203) 847-2885.

Trinity, Missionary Servants of the Most Blessed, M.S.B.T.: Founded 1912, in U.S., by Very Rev. Thomas A. Judge. General motherhouse, 3501 Solly Ave., Philadelphia, PA 19136, (215) 335-7550, www.msbt.org. Educational, social work, health services.

Trinity, Sisters Oblates to the Blessed, O.B.T.: Founded 1923, in Italy. U.S. novitiate, Beekman Rd., P.O. Box 98, Hopewell Junction, NY 12533, (914) 226-5671.

Trinity, Sisters of the Most Holy, O.Ss.T.: Founded 1198, in Rome; in U.S., 1920. General motherhouse, Rome, Italy. U.S. address, Immaculate Conception Province, 21281 Chardon Rd., Euclid, OH 44117, (216) 481-8232, www.srstrinity.org. Educational work.

Trinity, Society of Our Lady of the Most Holy, S.O.L.T.: Motherhouse, P.O. Box 189 Skidmore, TX 78389, (361) 287-3256.

Ursula of the Blessed Virgin, Society of the Sisters of St., S.U.: Founded 1606, in France; in U.S., 1902. General motherhouse, France. U.S. novitiate, 50 Linnwood Rd., Rhinebeck, NY 12572, (845) 876-2557, www.societyofstursula.org. Educational work.

Ursuline Nuns (Roman Union), O.S.U.: Founded 1535, in Italy; in U.S., 1727. Generalate, Rome, Italy. U.S. provinces: 1338 North Avenue, New Rochelle, NY 10804, (914) 712-0060. 353 S. Sappington Rd., Kirkwood, MO 63122, (314) 821-6884, www.osucentral.org. 639 Angela Dr., Santa Rosa, CA 95401, (707) 545-6811. 45 Lowder St., Dedham, MA 02026, (781) 326-6219.

Ursuline Sisters of Mount Saint Joseph, O.S.U.: Founded 1535, in Italy; in U.S., 1727, in New Orleans. U.S. motherhouses: 20860 St, Rte. 251, St. Martin, OH 45518-9705, (513) 875-2020. 901 E. Miami St., Paola, KS 66071, (913) 557-2349. 3105 Lexington Rd., Louisville, KY 40206, (502) 896-3948, www.ursuineslou.org. 2600 Lander Rd., Cleveland, OH 44124, (440) 449-1200, www.ursulinesisters.org. 8001 Cummings Rd., Maple Mount, KY 42356, (270) 229-4200, www.ursulinesmsj.org. 4045 Indian Rd., Toledo, OH 43606, (419) 536-9587, www.toledoursulines.org. 4250 Shields Rd., Canfield, OH 44406, (330) 792-7636. 1339 E. McMillan St., Cincinnati, OH 45206, (513) 961-3410.

Ursuline Sisters of the Congregation of Tildonk, Belgium, O.S.U.: Founded 1535, in Italy; Tildonk congregation, 1832; in U.S., 1924. Generalate, Brussels, Belgium. U.S. address, 81-15 Utopia Parkway, Jamaica, NY 11432, (718) 591-0681, www.tressy.tripod.com. Educational, foreign mission work.

Ursuline Sisters of Belleville, O.S.U.: Founded 1535, in Italy; in U.S., 1910; established as diocesan community, 1983. Central house, 1026 N. Douglas Ave., Belleville, IL 62220, (618) 235-3444. Educational work.

Venerini Sisters, Religious, M.P.V.: Founded 1685,

in Italy; in U.S., 1909. General motherhouse, Rome, Italy. U.S. provincialate; 23 Edward St., Worcester, MA 01605, (508) 754-1020, www.venerinisisters.org.

Vietnamese Adorers of the Holy Cross, M.T.G.: Founded 1670 in Vietnam; in U.S. 1976. General motherhouse 7408 S.E. Adler St., Portland, OR 97215, (503) 254-3284.

Vincent de Paul, Sisters: See **Charity of St. Vincent de Paul, Sisters of.**

Visitation Nuns, V.H.M.: Founded 1610, in France; in U.S. (Georgetown, DC), 1799. Contemplative, educational work. Two federations in U.S:

• First Federation of North America. Major pontifical enclosure. Pres., Mother Mary Jozefa Kowalewski, Monastery of the Visitation, 2055 Ridgedale Dr., Snellville, GA 30078, (770) 972-1060. Addresses of monasteries belonging to the federation: 2300 Springhill Ave., Mobile, AL 36607, (251) 473-2321. 14 Beach Rd., Tyringham, MA, 01264, (413) 243-3995. 12221 Bievenue Rd, Rockville, VA 23146, (804) 749-4885. 5820 City Ave., Philadelphia, PA 19131, (215) 473-5888. 1745 Parkside Blvd., Toledo, OH 43607, (419) 536-1343. 2055 Ridgedale Dr., Snellville, GA 30078-2443, (770) 972-1060.

• Second Federation of North America. Constitutional enclosure. Pres., Sr. Anne Madeleine Godefroy, Monastery of the Visitation, 3020 N. Ballas Rd., St. Louis, MO 63131, (314) 432-5353, www.visitationmonastery.org/stlouis. Addresses of monasteries belonging to the federation: 1500 35th St., Washington, DC 20007, (202) 337-0305. 3020 N. Ballas Rd., St. Louis, MO 63131, (314) 432-5353. 200 E. Second St., Frederick, MD 21701, (301) 622-3322. Mt. de Chantal Monastery of the Visitation, 410 Washington Ave., Wheeling, WV 26003, (304) 232-1283; www.mountdechantal.org. 8902 Ridge Blvd., Brooklyn, NY 11209, (718) 745-5151, www.visitationsisters.org. 2455 Visitation Dr., Mendota Heights, MN 55120, (651) 683-1700.

Visitation of the Congregation of the Immaculate Heart of Mary, Sisters of the, S.V.M.: Founded 1952, in U.S. Motherhouse, 2950 Kaufmann Ave., Dubuque, IA 52001, (563) 588-7256. Educational work, parish ministry.

Vocationist Sisters (Sisters of the Divine Vocations), S.V.D.: Founded 1921, in Italy; in U.S., 1967 General motherhouse, Naples, Italy. U.S. foundation, Perpetual Help Nursery, 172 Broad St., Newark, NJ 07104, (973) 484-3535.

Wisdom, Daughters of, D.W.: Founded 1703, in France, by St. Louis Marie Grignion de Montfort; in U.S., 1904. General motherhouse, Vendee, France. U.S. province, 385 Ocean Ave., Islip, NY 11751, (631) 277-2660, www.daughtersofwisdom.org. Education, health care, parish ministry, social services.

Xaverian Missionary Society of Mary, Inc., X.M.M.: Founded 1945, in Italy; in U.S., 1954. General motherhouse, Parma, Italy. U.S. address, 242 Salisbury St., Worcester, MA 01609, (508) 757-0514.

MEMBERSHIP OF RELIGIOUS INSTITUTES OF WOMEN

Principal source: Annuario Pontificio. *Statistics as of Jan. 1, 2008 unless indicated otherwise. Listed below are world membership statistics of institutes of women with 500 or more members. Numbers in parentheses reflect the number of houses. For statistical information of institutes in the United States, see* **Statistics**.

Salesian Srs. (1,488)	14,665
Calced Carmelites (756)	9,857
Claretians (560)	7,463
Franciscan Missionaries of Mary (818)	7,050
Franciscan Clarist Congr. (696)	6,984
Carmel, Srs. of the Mother of (629)	6,428
Charity, Mission. of (751)	5,046
Charity of St. Bartholomew of Capitanio (444)	4,967
Benedictine Nuns (242)	4,613
Ador. of the Bl. Sacrament. (551)	4,583
Our Lady of Charity of Good Sheph. (589)	4,382
Mercy of the Americas, Srs. of (2,034)	4,282
Holy Cross, Srs. of Mercy of the (446)	4,048
Paul of Chartres, Srs. of St. (560)	3,968
Notre Dame, School Srs. of (549)	3,767
Sacred Heart Congregation. (403)	3,568
Holy Spirit, Mission Servants of the (421)	3,540
Immaculate Heart of Mary, Mission. Srs. (2004) (163)	3,248
Dominicans (213)	3,091
Canossian Daught. of Charity (354)	3,049
Joseph, Srs. of St. (Cluny) (424)	2,978
Sacred Heart of Jesus "Sophie Barat," Society of the (410)	2,874
Poor, Little Sisters of the (205)	2,826
Charity of St. Joan Antida, Srs. of (360)	2,811
Dominicans of the Presentation of the Virgin (376)	2,715
Mercy, Srs. of (Ireland) (646)	2,686
Paul, Daught. of St. (248)	2,551
Ancianos Desamparados, Hermanitas de los (208)	2,472
Anne, Srs. of Charity of St. (297)	2,400
Notre Dame, Srs. of (283)	2,354
Ursulines of the Roman Union (250)	2,253
Claretian Capuchins (159)	2,198
Visitandine Nuns (141)	2,188
Cross, Srs. of the (Swiss) (252)	2,111
Holy Family, Srs. of the (Bordeaux) (297)	2,107
Carmelites of Charity of Védruna (287)	2,103
Joseph Benedetto, Srs. of St. (135)	2,049
B.V.M., Inst. of the (English) (246)	2,037
Wisdom, Daught. of (283)	1,934
Holy Family Sisters (210)	1,923
Concezioniste (Franciscan Concessionists) (153)	1,916
Felician Srs. (235)	1,887
Joseph, Srs. of St. (Chambéry) (302)	1,869
Carmelites, Scalced (126)	1,856
Franciscans of the Penance and Christian Charity (234)	1,790
Mission, Carmelites (266)	1,783
Mary Our Lady, Company of (205)	1,727
Notre Dame de Namur, Srs. of (602)	1,720
Mary, Minister of the Infirm, Servants of (113)	1,692
Adorers of the Blood of Christ (329)	1,688
Elizabeth, Srs. of St. (223)	1,670
Cistercian Nuns (Strict Observance) (72)	1,667
Holy Savior, Srs. of the (183)	1,653
Joseph, Srs. of St. (Carondolet) (681)	1,645
Apostolic Carmel, Srs. of (158)	1,643
Comboni Missionary Srs. (216)	1,594
Teresa of Jesus, Society of St. (218)	1,587
Mercy of Australia, Inst. of Srs. (429)	1,570
Dorothy, Srs. of St. (169)	1,531
Franciscan Hospitallers of the Immaculate Conception (165)	1,496
Heart of Mary, Soc. of Daught. of (153)	1,475
Divine Master, Pious Disciples of (183)	1,473
Anne, Daughters of Saint (233)	1,470
Jesus and Mary, Religious of (190)	1,460
Holy Family of Nazareth, Srs. of (154)	1,457
Benedictines, Missionary (141)	1,422
Cross, Srs. of the (194)	1,415
Destitute, Srs. of the (197)	1,399
Divine Providence, Srs. of (St. Maurice) (251)	1,370
Jesus, Mary, and Joseph, Society of (161)	1,360
Salesian Missionaries of Mary Immaculate (163)	1,353
Franciscans of George the Martyr (162)	1,349
Mary Immaculate, Religious of (128)	1,343
Holy Spirit, Daughters of the (186)	1,332
Sacred Heart of Jesus, Apostles of (195)	1,330
Charity of Jesus and Mary, Srs. of (179)	1,329
Immaculate Conception, Little Srs. of the (239)	1,328
Capuchin Tertiaries of the Holy Family (218)	1,327
Presentation of Mary, Srs. of the (185)	1,321
Union of the Srs. of the Pres. (243)	1,311
Notre Dame, Srs. of the Cong. of (148)	1,297
Anne, Srs. of Saint (179)	1,294
Teresian Carmelites of Verapoly (153)	1,293
Jesus, Daught. of (St. Joseph of Kermaria) (171)	1,292
Holy Names of Jesus and Mary, Srs. of the (93)	1,288
Sacred Heart of Jesus, Ancelle (133)	1,280
Our Lady of the Sacred Heart, Daughters of (211)	1,277
Adorers of the Blessed Sacrament and Charity (165)	1,275
Assumption, Religious of the (164)	1,270
Little Flower of Bethany, Srs. of the (156)	1,263
Salvatorians (208)	1,261
Charity, Dtrs. of Divine (169)	1,241
Fraternity of Little Sisters of Jesus (283)	1,229
Mercedarians of Charity (149)	1,202
Infirm of St. Francis, Srs. of (112)	1,175
Hospitallers of the Sacred Heart of Jesus (110)	1,162
Franciscans of Christ, School Srs. (158)	1,148
Franciscans of the Family of Mary (144)	1,139
Servants of Mary, Srs. of Our Lady	

of Sorrows (153)	1,134
School Srs., St. Francis of Milwaukee (364)	1,126
Dorothy of Frassinetti, Srs. of St. (147)	1,103
Mercy, Srs. of (Verona) (111)	1,101
Franciscans of the Immaculate Conception (145)	1,099
Jesus, Daught. of (Salamanca) (145)	1,097
Franciscan Srs. (Pondicherry) (186)	1,090
Religious Dominicans of the Annunciation (142)	1,085
Charity (Ancelle della) (101)	1,073
Caritas Srs. of Miyazaki (171)	1,068
Claretian (Urban) (84)	1,058
Joseph, Srs. of St. (Philadelphia) (145)	1,030
Sacred Heart of Jesus, Daught. of Charity of the (175)	1,027
Ursulines of Tildonk (118)	1,013
Mary Help of Christ., Mission. Srs. (159)	1,011
Cross and Passion, Srs. of the (Passionist Srs.) (157)	1,007
Anne, Srs. of (124)	1,005
Elizabethan Franciscans (112)	997
Our Lady of Mercy, Daught. of (167)	992
Servants of the Imm. Hrt. Of Mary, Srs. (84)	991
Cistercian Nuns, O. Cist. (63)	986
Anne, Daught. of Saint (Ranchi) (154)	982
Servants of Jesus of Charity (97)	980
Our Lady of the Missions, Srs. of (261)	978
B.V.M., Inst. of the (304)	975
Assumption, Little Srs. of the (144)	967
Joseph, Inst. of Srs. of St. (207)	961
Sacramentines (Perp. Ador. of the Blessed Sacrament) (60)	941
Precious Blood, Mission. Srs. of the (102)	939
Mary, Mother of Mercy, Daught. of (175)	939
Joseph of the Sacred Heart of Jesus, Srs. of St. (331)	931
Dominicans of the Most Holy Rosary (290)	926
Mary, Daught. of (137)	926
Our Lady of Africa, Mission. Srs. of (129)	924
Immaculate, Mission. of (110)	924
Franciscan Srs. of Dillingen (95)	913
Joseph of the Apparition, Srs. of St. (154)	912
Imm. Conception, Srs. of Charity (111)	904
Mary Immaculate / Catherine of Siena (154)	903
Sacred Heart of Mary Virgin Immaculate, Srs. of the (148)	896
Providence, Srs. of (95)	892
Sacred Heart of Jesus, Mission. Srs. (152)	892
Imm. Heart of Mary, Mother of Christ (133)	892
Clarist Franciscan Mission. (147)	889
Joseph, Srs. of St. (Lyon) (150)	883
Immaculate Heart of Mary (146)	881
Augustinians (81)	879
Queen of Apostles (121)	873
Carmelite Sisters of St. Teresa (118)	869
Vincent de Paul, Srs. of Charity of (117)	863
Benedictine Srs., Fed. St. Scholastica (22)	859
Medical Srs. of St. Joseph (78)	856
Holy Family, Little Srs. of the (124)	853
Love of God, Sisters of the (111)	853
Poor of the Inst. Palazzolo, Srs. of the (111)	852
Little Srs. of Mary Immaculate (124)	850
Our Lady Mother of Mercy (72)	847
Cross, Daughters of, of Liege (101)	846
Immaculate Conception, Srs. of the (144)	843
Imitation of Christ, Srs. of the (185)	841
Benedictine Srs., Federation of St. Gertrude the Great (17)	839
Baptistine Srs., Srs. of John the Baptist (123)	837
Handmaids of the Holy Child Jesus (125)	835
Franciscan Srs. of Notre Dame de Bon Secours of Madras (120)	835
Camillus, Dtrs. of St. (98)	834
Ursulines of the Sacred Heart of Jesus (96)	827
Charity, Srs. of, Our Lady of Mercy (91)	818
Sacramentine Srs. (103)	815
Divine Love, Daughters of (152)	810
Providence, Srs. of (Portieux) (136)	809
Franciscans Third Order Regular (54)	807
Jesus Crucified, Missionary Sisters of (176)	804
Consolata Missionary Sisters (136)	804
Franciscan Sisters of the Presentation of Mary (134)	800
Mary Imm., Sisters of the B.V.M. (124)	796
Immaculate Conception of the B.V.M. (124)	796
Our Lady of the Apostles, Missionary Sisters of (126)	794
Mary Immaculate of the B.V.M. (149)	791
Charity, Little Mission. Srs. of (119)	789
Dominicans of the Rosary (138)	789
Charity, Srs. of (Thrissur) (91)	789
B.V.M., Religious of the (120)	779
Ursulines of Mary Immaculate (101)	777
Bethlemite Srs., Daughters of the Sacred Heart of Jesus (93)	774
Ursuline Franciscans (107)	772
Franc. Mission. of Mary, Auxiliatrix (123)	771
Mary Most Holy of the Word, Dtrs. of (123)	763
Mary Reparatrix, Society of (103)	757
Divine Providence, Drs. of Mary of the (113)	753
Scalabrinians (157)	749
Franciscan Mission. of Baby Jesus (102)	748
Franciscans of Gonzaga (124)	748
Carmelite Nuns, Discalced, O.C.D. (68)	746
Franciscan Missionaries of the Sacred Heart (105)	740
Providence of S. Gaetano da Thiene (85)	738
Joseph, Srs. of St. (Cantaous) (134)	737
Holy Cross and Seven Dolors, Srs. of the (167)	734
Franciscans of the Bl. Sacrament (43)	733
Charles Borromeo, Srs. of Charity of (90)	731
Teresian Carmelite Mission. (104)	728
Sacred Heart of Jesus and the Poor (81)	724
Pious Schools, Religious of (111)	722
Catherine Virgin and Martyr, Srs. of St. (121)	720
Servants of Jesus Sacramentado (75)	718
Enfant-Jesus, Soeurs de l' (146)	717
Benedictine Srs. Fed. of St. Benedict (12)	717
Jesus Christ, Poor Srs. of (110)	717
Marcellina, Srs. of St. (54)	714
Missionary Srs. of Mary Imm. (108)	713
Mercedarians of the Bl. Sacrament (84)	706
Sacred Hearts and of Perp. Ador., Srs. of the (102)	698
Our Lady of the Consolation, Srs. of (98)	697
Providence of Gap, Srs. of the (123)	696
Sacred Heart of Jesus and the Poor, Srs. of (87)	695
Charity of Ottawa, Srs. of (74)	694
Franciscan Mission., I.H.M., of Egypt (92)	692

Anne, Srs. of (Chennai) (115)	690	Jesus the Good Shepherd, Srs. of (131)	585
Sacred Heart of Jesus and Mary, Srs. of (74)	686	Charity, Sisters of (of QC) (33)	584
Franc. Dtrs. of the Sacred Hearts (74)	686	St. Joseph of St. Mark, Srs. of (80)	579
Dominican Srs. of the Rosary (288)	680	Sacred Heart of Mary, Srs. (86)	577
Franciscan Missionaries of the Mother		Divine Providence, Srs. of (Ribeauville) (76)	576
of the Divine Pastor (109)	677	Franciscan Tertiaries (61)	573
Seraphic Sisters (76)	675	Catherine of Siena, Srs. of (75)	572
Assisi Srs. of Mary Immaculate (92)	675	Joseph, Dtrs. of St. (78)	571
Mary Immaculate of Guadalupe (73)	674	Joseph, Srs. of St. (78)	571
Mary, Dtrs. of (63)	666	Claretians of the Blessed Sacrament (54)	570
Joseph, Servants of St. (94)	664	Holy Redeemer, Oblate Srs. of the (94)	569
Charity of St. Louis, Srs. of (101)	662	Servants of the Poor (80)	569
St. Francis, Srs. of (Glen Riddle) (244)	661	Marianne of Jesus, Inst. of (109)	568
Anne de Lachine, Srs. of Saint (75)	660	Dominicans of Maryknoll (162)	566
Claretian Colettines (57)	660	Brigid, Srs. of St. (51)	564
Francis of Assisi, Srs. (80)	655	Poor Baby Jesus, Srs. of (65)	562
Cross, Srs. of the Company of the (53)	650	Franciscan Missionaries of Our Lord (84)	561
Auxiliatrices des Ames du Purgatoire (120)	649	Virgins of Jesus and Mary (9)	560
Dominican Srs. of the Rosary		Annunciation, Little Sisters of (122)	560
(Sinsinawa) (269)	649	Divine Providence and Imm. Conc. (108)	559
Sacred Heart of Jesus, Srs. of the (108)	647	Franciscans of St. Joseph (89)	559
Srs. of Notre Dame (123)	645	Christian Doctrine, Srs. of (129)	558
Benedictine of the Perpetual Ador. (43)	641	Carmelites of Trivandrum (56)	557
Medical Mission Srs. (111)	640	Franciscan Missionaries of Assisi (85)	556
Immaculate Hrt. of Mary (50)	632	Ursulines of Jesus (91)	555
Missionary Srs. of the Immaculate		Franciscans of the Imm. Conc. (99)	554
Conception (50)	632	Sacred Heart of Jesus, Servants of the (72)	550
Charity, Srs. of (of Nazareth) (242)	630	Martha, Srs. of (63)	549
Mary, Daught. of, Bannabikira Srs. (73)	628	Canonesses of St. Augustine (89)	547
Basil the Great, Srs. of the		Guardian Angel, Srs. of (89)	546
Order of St. (Byzantine Rite) (80)	628	Our Lady of Perp. Help (127)	542
Ann, Srs. of St. (87)	625	Charity of Ireland, Srs. of (73)	541
Holy Family, Srs. of the (Villefranche) (93)	625	Francis de Sales, Srs. of St. (90)	539
Pallottine Srs. of the Catholic Apostolate,		Vincent de Paul, Srs. of Charity (209)	536
Mission. (79)	624	Holy Cross, Srs. of the (109)	534
Albertine Srs. (79)	624	Cenacle, Cong. of Our Lady of the	
Charity of the Blessed		Retreat in the (75)	534
Virgin Mary, Srs. of (255)	623	Franciscan of Perpetual Ador. (56)	533
Ursuline Daught. of Mary Immaculate (79)	619	Mary, Society of (130)	528
Franciscans of Mary Imm. (106)	619	Divine Providence, Srs. of (Mainz) (92)	528
Joseph, Srs. of (Mexico) (85)	618	St. Therese of the Child Jesus, Srs. of (80)	526
Cross, Daught. of, of St. André (120)	617	Oblates of the Assumption (71)	526
Dominican Missionary Srs. (67)	611	Stigmatine Srs. (84)	519
Reparation, Srs. of (85)	607	Concessionist Missionaries (66)	516
Assumption of the Blessed Virgin,		Charles Borromeo, Srs. of (74)	516
Srs. of the (50)	603	Precious Blood, Dtrs. of (57)	508
Dorothy, Srs. of St. (78)	602	Franciscan Srs. of the Imm. Heart (66)	508
Divine Providence, Srs. of		Immaculate Heart of Mary (89)	507
(St.-Jean-de-Bassel) (117)	602	Srs. Servants of the Imm. Hrt. Mary (89)	507
Divine Zeal, Daughters of (75)	601	Mary Immaculate, Claretians (82)	505
Sacred Heart of Jesus, Santa Verzeri (85)	597	Carmelites of the Child Jesus (57)	503
Mary Immaculate, Srs. of (68)	597	Redeemer, Srs. of the (33)	501
Imm. Conc. Srs. of the Mother of God (96)	596	Divine Redeemer, Srs. of (33)	501
Claretians, Sacramentarian (35)	594	Notre Dame de Sion, Cong. of (85)	501
Carmelite Missionaries of St. Teresa (85)	589	Immaculate Conception, Little Srs. of (103)	501

ORGANIZATIONS OF RELIGIOUS

Conferences

Conferences of major superiors of religious institutes, dating from the 1950s, are encouraged by the Code of Canon Law (Code 708) "so that joining forces they can work toward the achievement of the purpose of their individual institutes more fully, transact common business and foster suitable coordination and cooperation with conferences of bishops and also with individual bishops." Statutes of the conferences must be approved by the Holy See "by which alone they are erected" (Canon 709). Conferences have been established in 24 countries of Europe, 14 in North and Central America, 10 in South America, 35 in Africa and 19 in Asia and Oceania.

Listed below are U.S. and international conferences.

Conference of Major Superiors of Men: Founded in 1956; canonically established Sept. 12, 1957. Membership, 269 major superiors representing institutes with a combined membership of approximately 24,000. Pres., Fr. Dominic Izzo, O.P.; Executive director, Rev. Paul Lininger OFM Conv. National office: 8808 Cameron St., Silver Spring, MD 20910, (301) 588-4030, www.cmsm.org.

Leadership Conference of Women Religious: Founded in 1956; canonically established Dec. 12, 1959. Membership, nearly 1,000 (Dec. 31, 1996), representing approximately 400 religious institutes. Pres., Sr. Mary Dacey, S.S.J.; Mary Whited, CPPS, vice president/president elect; executive director, Sister Carole Shinnick, SSND. National office: 8808 Cameron St., Silver Spring, MD 20910, (301) 588-4955, www.lcwr.org.

Council of Major Superiors of Women Religious: Canonically erected June 13, 1992. Membership, 141 superiors of 103 religious congregations. Chairperson, Sister Mary Quentin Sheridan, R.S.M. National office: P.O. Box 4467, Washington, DC 20017-0467, (202) 832-2575, www.cmswr.org.

International Union of Superiors General (Women): Established Dec. 8, 1965; approved, 1967. Pres., Sr. Amelia Kawaji, M.M.B. Address: Piazza Ponte S. Angelo, 28, 00186, Rome, Italy, 06-684-00-20.

Union of Superiors General (Men): Established in 1957. President, Fr. Pascual Chávez Villanueva, S.D.B.; general secretary, Pietro Trabucco, I.M.C. Address: Via dei Penitenzieri 19, 00193 Rome, Italy, 06-686-82-29.

Latin American Confederation of Religious (Confederacion Latinoamericana de Religiosos — CLAR): Established in 1959; statutes reformed in 1984. President, Ignacio Antonio Madera Vargas, S.D.S.; secretary general, Sr. Maria Gonzalez de Castejon, R.S.C.J. Address: Calle 64 No 10-45, Piso 5°, Apartado Aéreo 56804, Santafé de Bogotá, D.C., Colombia, (91) 31-00-481-21-57-774, www.clar.org.

Union of European Conferences of Major Superiors (UCESM): Established Dec. 25, 1983. Permanent secretary, Sr. Ana Maria Garbayo Abascal, O.D.N. Rue de Pascal 4, B-1040, Bruxelles, Belgium, 02-230-86-22.

Other Organizations

Institute on Religious Life (1974). To foster more effective understanding and implementation of teachings of the Church on religious life, promote vocations to religious life and the priesthood, and promote growth in sanctity of all the faithful according to their state in life. Pres., Bishop Thomas Doran. National office, P.O. Box 410007, Chicago, IL 60641, (773) 267-1195, www.religiouslife.com. Publishes *Religious Life* magazine and *Consecrated Life* periodical.

Religious Brothers Conference (1972): To publicize the unique vocations of brothers, to further communication among brothers and provide liaison with various organizations of the Church. Pres., Br. Stephen Synan, F.M.S., 5420 South Cornell, Chicago, IL 60615, (773) 493-2306, www.brothersonline.org.

National Black Sisters' Conference (1968): Black Catholic women religious and associates networking to provide support through prayer, study, solidarity and programs. Address: 101 Q. St., N.E., Washington, DC 20002, (202) 529-9250.

National Conference of Vicars for Religious (1967): National organization of diocesan officials concerned with relations between their respective dioceses and religious communities engaged therein. President, Sr. Therese Sullivan, S.P., 9292 Broadway, Merrillville, IN 46410; secretary, Eymard Flood, O.S.C. Address: 2811 East Villareal Dr., P.O. Box 14195, Orange, CA, 92863-1595, (714) 282-3114.

National Religious Vocation Conference (NRVC) (1988, with merger of National Sisters Vocation Conference and National Conference of Religious Vocation Directors.) Service organization of men and women committed to the fostering and discernment of vocations. Executive director, Br. Paul Bednarczyk, C.S.C. Address: 5420 S. Cornell, #105, Chicago, IL 60615, (773) 363-5454, www.nrvc.net.

Religious Formation Conference (1953): Originally the Sister Formation Conference; membership includes women and men Religious and noncanonical groups. Facilitates the ministry of formation, both initial and ongoing, in religious communities. Executive director, Violet Grennan, M.F.I.C; National office: 8820 Cameron St., Silver Spring, MD 20910-4152, (301) 588-4938, www.relforcon.org.

SECULAR INSTITUTES

Sources: Catholic Almanac survey; United States Conference of Secular Institutes; Annuario Pontificio.

Secular institutes are societies of men and women living in the world who dedicate themselves to observe the evangelical counsels and to carry on apostolic works suitable to their talents and opportunities in the areas of their everyday life.

"Secular institutes are not religious communities but they carry with them in the world a profession of evangelical counsels which is genuine and complete, and recognized as such by the Church. This profession confers a consecration on men and women, laity and clergy, who reside in the world. For this reason they should chiefly strive for total self–dedication to God, one inspired by perfect charity. These institutes should preserve their proper and particular character, a secular one, so that they may everywhere measure up successfully to that apostolate which they were designed

to exercise, and which is both in the world and, in a sense, of the world" ("Decree on the Appropriate Renewal of Religious Life," No. 11; Second Vatican Council).

Secular institutes are under the jurisdiction of the Congregation for Institutes of Consecrated Life and Societies of Apostolic Life. General legislation concerning them is contained in Canons 710 to 730 of the Code of Canon Law.

A secular institute reaches maturity in several stages. It begins as an association of the faithful, technically called a pious union, with the approval of a local bishop. Once it has proved its viability, he can give it the status of an institute of diocesan right, in accordance with norms and permission emanating from the Congregation for Institutes of Consecrated Life and Societies of Apostolic Life. On issuance of a separate decree from this congregation, an institute of diocesan right becomes an institute of pontifical right.

Secular institutes, which originated in the latter part of the 18th century, were given full recognition and approval by Pius XII Feb. 2, 1947, in the apostolic constitution *Provida Mater Ecclesia*. On Mar. 25 of the same year a special commission for secular institutes was set up within the Congregation for Religious. Institutes were commended and confirmed by Pius XII in a motu proprio of Mar. 12, 1948, and were the subject of a special instruction issued a week later, Mar. 19, 1948.

The World Conference of Secular Institutes (CMIS) was approved by the Vatican May 23, 1974. Address: Via Tullio Levi-Civita 5, 00146 Rome, Italy; 0039-06-5410292; www.cmis-int.org.

The United States Conference of Secular Institutes (USCSI) was established following the organization of the World Conference of Secular Institutes in Rome. Its membership is open to all canonically erected secular institutes with members living in the United States. The conference was organized to offer secular institutes an opportunity to exchange experiences, to do research in order to help the Church carry out its mission, and to search for ways and means to make known the existence of secular institutes in the U.S. Address: P.O. Box 4556, 12th St. N.E., Washington, DC 20017, (262) 547-7733, www.secularinstitutes.org. Pres., Rev. George F. Hazler.

Institutes in the U.S.

Apostolic Oblates: Founded in Rome, Italy, 1947; established in the U.S., 1962; for women. Approved as a secular institute of pontifical right Dec. 8, 1994. Addresses: 2125 W. Walnut Ave., Fullerton, CA 92833, (714) 871-3610. 6762 Western Ave., Omaha, NE 68132, (402) 553-4418. 730 E. 87th St., Brooklyn, NY 11236-3621, (718) 649-0324, www.prosanctity.org.

Apostolic Sodales: Founded in Rome, Italy, 1992 by Bp. Guglielmo; for priests. Established to promote a spirit of fraternity among diocesan priests gathered around their bishop in docile availability in the twofold universal vocation — the call to holiness and brotherhood. Address: Rev. Michael F. Murphy, 655 C. Ave. Coronado, CA 92118-2299, (619) 435-3167.

Caritas Christi: Originated in Marseilles, 1937; for women. Established as a secular institute of pontifical right Mar. 19, 1955. Address: P.O. Box 5162, River Forest, IL 60305. International membership.

Catechists of the Heart of Jesus (Ukrainian): Founded in Parana, Brazil, 1940, by Christoforo Myaskiv, OSBM; approved as Secular Institute of Pontifical Right, 1971; for women. Established for religious instruction, to assist clerics in missionary work, to help the Church, and to maintain the Ukrainian rite and culture. Address: 161 Glenbrook Rd., Stamford, CT 06902, (203) 327-6374.

Company of St. Paul: Originated in Milan, Italy, 1920; for lay people and priests. Approved as a secular institute of pontifical right June 30, 1950. Address: Rev. Stuart Sandberg, 52 Davis Ave., White Plains, NY 10605, (914) 946-1019.

Crusaders of St. Mary: Founded 1947 in Madrid, Spain; approved as a secular institute of diocesan right, 1988; for men. Address: 2001 Great Falls St., McLean, VA 22101, (703) 536-5346.

Diocesan Laborer Priests: Founded 1885 in Spain; approved as a secular institute of pontifical right, 1952. The specific aim of the institute is the promotion, sustenance and cultivation of apostolic, religious and priestly vocations. Address: 3706 15th St. N.E., Washington, DC 20017, (202) 832-4217.

Don Bosco Volunteers: Founded 1917 by Bl. Philip Rinaldi; for women. Approved as a secular institute of pontifical right Aug. 5, 1978. Follow spirituality and charism of St. John Bosco. Address: Carol McAvoy, Don Bosco Volunteers, P.O. Box 300H, Scarsdale, NY 10583.

Family of Mary of the Visitation: Founded in Vietnam, 1976. Approved as a Secular Institute of Diocesan Right; intended to promote faith-filled vowed women, to help people protect their faith and to meet social needs. Address: Therese Chan Ngo, P.O. Box 441, Westminster, CA 92684.

Fr. Kolbe Missionaries of the Immaculata: Founded in Bologna, Italy, in 1954, by Fr. Luigi Faccenda, O.F.M. Conv.; for women. Approved as a secular institute of pontifical right Mar. 25, 1992. Live the fullness of baptismal consecration, strive for perfect charity and promote the knowledge and veneration of Mary. Address: 531 E. Merced Ave., West Covina, CA 91790, (626) 917-0040.

Handmaids of Divine Mercy: Founded in Bari, Italy, 1951; for women. Approved as an institute of pontifical right 1972. Address: 2410 Hughes Ave., Bronx, NY 10458, (718) 295-3770.

Holy Family Institute (aggregated to the Society of St. Paul): Founded by Fr. James Alberione in 1963 for married couples who wish to commit themselves to seeking evangelical perfection in marriage; definitively approved by the Holy See, 1993. First Americans professed, 1988. Address: 9531 Akron-Canfield Rd., Box 498, Canfield, OH 44406; www.vocations-holyfamily.com.

Institute of Secular Missionaries: Founded in Vitoria, Spain, 1939; for women. Approved as a secular institute, 1955. Address: 3943 Ruth Ln., Cincinnati, OH 45211. Attn.: E. Dilger.

Institute of the Heart of Jesus (Men): Originated in France Feb. 2, 1791; restored Oct. 29, 1918; for diocesan priests and laity. Received final approval from the Holy See as a secular institute of pontifical right Feb. 2, 1952. U.S. address, Rev. William S. Whelan, Conception Seminary College, Conception, MO 64433, (660) 944-2900.

Institute of the Heart of Jesus (Women): Foundation stems from the Institute of the Heart of Jesus which originated in France Feb. 2, 1791. Established to help lay women live the Gospel radically in the modern world by means of the evangelical counsels, to engage in group discernment and various forms of prayer. Address, Diana Bland, 417 N. Buena Vista St., Burbank, CA 91505-3208.

Jesu Caritas Fraternity: Founded in France, 1952. Approved as a Secular Institute of Diocesan Right, 1996. Established to form members in the contemplative tradition of Brother Charles de Foucauld, bringing God's love especially to his most neglected children; members strive in their daily life to live the Gospel message. Address: Mary D. Christensen, P.O. Box 92, Yonkers, N.Y. 10704.

Lay Missionaries of the Passion: Based in Queens, NY. Address: 311 Leonard St., Brooklyn, NY 11211. Contavt: Constance M. Leist.

Mission of Our Lady of Bethany: Founded in France, 1948; for women. Approved as a secular institute of diocesan right, 1965. Addresses: Estelle Nichols, 109 Rollins Rd., Nottingham, NH 03290.

Missionaries of the Kingship of Christ the King:

Under this title are included three distinct and juridically separate institutes founded by Agostino Gemelli, O.F.M. (1878-1959) and Armida Barelli (1882-1952). Two are active in the U.S.

• **Women Missionaries of the Kingship of Christ**: Founded in 1919, in Italy; definitively approved as an institute of pontifical right 1953. U.S. branch established 1950.

• **Men Missionaries of the Kingship of Christ**: Founded 1928, in Italy, as an institute of diocesan right. U.S. branch established 1962.

Addresses: Rev. Dominic Monti, O.F.M., Spiritual Assistant, 10400 Lorain Ave., Silver Spring, MD 20901 (for Men Missionaries). Rev. Dominic Monti, O.F.M., 10400 Lorain Ave., Silver Spring, MD, 20901 (for Women Missionaries), (301) 593-4479, www.simkc.org.

Nuestra Señora de la Altagracia: Founded in Dominican Republic, 1956; approved as a secular institute of diocesan right, 1964; for women. Address: Ms. Christiana Perez, 129 Van Siclen Ave., Brooklyn, NY 11207.

Oblate Missionaries of Mary Immaculate: Founded, 1952; approved as a secular institute of pontifical right 1984; for women. Address: Oblate Missionaries of Mary Immaculate, P.O. Box 764, Lowell, MA 01853, www.ommi-is.org.

Opus Spiritus Sancti: Originated in West Germany, 1952; for diocesan priests and unmarried permanent deacons. Formally acknowledged by Rome as a secular institute of diocesan right, 1977. Address: Rev. James McCormick, 421 E. Bluff St., Carroll, IA 51401-3099, (712) 792-4386.

Schoenstatt Sisters of Mary: Originated in Schoenstatt, Germany, 1926; for women. Established as a secular institute of diocesan right May 20, 1948; of pontifical right Oct. 18, 1948. Addresses: W. 284 N. 404 Cherry Lane, Waukesha, WI 53188, (262) 522-4200, www.schsrsmary.org. House Schoenstatt, 134 Front St., Rockport, TX 78382, (361) 729-2019.

Secular Institute of Pius X: Originated in Manchester, NH, 1940; for priests and laymen. Approved as a secular institute, 1959. Also admits married couples and unmarried men as associate members. Addresses: C.P. 87731, Succ Charlesbourg, QC G1G 5W6, Canada, (418) 626-5882, www.ispx.org.

Secular Institute of Schoenstatt Fathers: Founded in Germany by Fr. Joseph Kentenich in 1965; for priests serving the International Schoenstatt Movement in over 20 countries. Approved as a secular institute of pontifical right, June 24, 1988. Address: W. 284 N. 746 Cherry Lane, Waukesha, WI 53188, (262) 548-9061.

Secular Institute of St. Francis de Sales: Founded in Vienna, Austria, 1940; for women. Pontifical right, 1964. Address: Thérèse Keyes, Dir., 87 Gerrish Ave., T2, East Haven, CT 06512, (203) 469-3277, www.secularinstitutes.org/sfs.ht.

Society of Our Lady of the Way: Originated, 1936; for women. Approved as a secular institute of pontifical right Jan. 3, 1953. Address: 2339 N. Catalina, Los Angeles, CA 90027, (323) 661-3315, www.execpc.com/uscsi/index.html.

Voluntas Dei Institute: Originated in Canada, 1958, by Father L. M. Parent; for secular priests and laymen (with married couples as associates). Approved as a secular institute of pontifical right, July 12, 1987. Established in 21 countries. Address: Rev. George Hazler, 2104 Eagle pointe, Bloomfield, MI 48304, www.voluntasdeiusa.org.

Volunteers With Don Bosco: Founded in Rome on Sept. 12, 1994, by Fr. Egidio Viganó, rector major of the Salesians of Don Bosco, for celibate men. Recognized as public association of the faithful on May 24, 1998, by Cardinal Ignacio Velasco Garcia, Abp. of Caracas, Venezuela. The association, which follows the spirit and charism of St. John Bosco, intends to become established juridically as a secular institute. Address: P.O. Box 639, New Rochelle, NY 10802-0639, (614) 440-0202; www.secularinstitutes.org/a-dbi.htm. Contact Person: Fr. John Puntino.

The *Annuario Pontificio* lists the following secular institutes of pontifical right that are not established in the U.S.:

For men: Christ the King; Institute of Our Lady of Life; Institute of Prado; Priests of the Sacred Heart of Jesus.

For women: Alliance in Jesus through Mary; Apostles of the Sacred Heart; Catechists of Mary, Virgin and Mother; Company of St. Ursula; Cordimarian Filiation; Daughters of the Nativity of Mary; Daughters of the Queen of the Apostles; Daughters of the Sacred Heart; Evangelical Crusade; Faithful Servants of Jesus; Handmaids of Our Mother of Mercy; Institute of Notre Dame du Travail; Institute of Our Lady of Life; Institute of St. Boniface; Little Apostles of Charity.

Life and Peace in Christ Jesus; Missionaries of Royal Priesthood; Missionaries of the Sick; Oblates of Christ the King; Oblates of the Sacred Heart of Jesus; Servants of Jesus the Priest; Servite Secular Institute; Union of the Daughters of God; Workers of Divine Love; Workers of the Cross; Handmaids of Holy Church; Augustinian Auxiliary Missionaries; Heart of Jesus; Apostolic Missionaries of Charity; Combonian Secular Missionaries; Missionaries of the Gospel; Secular Servants of Jesus Christ Priest; Women of Schoenstatt; Missionaries of Infinite Love.

Associations

Association of Mary Help of Christians: Founded by St. John Bosco in Turin, Italy, in 1869, for men and women. Public association of the faithful. Members encourage participation in the liturgical life of the Church, emphasizing frequent reception of the Eucharist and the Sacrament of Reconciliation. They also live and spread devotion to Mary Help of Christians according to the spirit of St. John Bosco. Address: 148 Main St., P.O. Box 639, New Rochelle, NY 10802, (614) 440-0202.

Caritas: Originated in New Orleans, 1950; for women. Follows guidelines of secular institutes. Small self-supporting groups who live and work with poor and oppressed; in Louisiana and Guatemala. Address: Box 308, Abita Springs, LA 70420, (985) 892-4345.

Daughters of Our Lady of Fatima: Originated in Lansdowne, PA, 1949; for women. Received diocesan approval, Jan. 1952. Address: Fatima House, P.O. Box 116, Bedminster 18910, (215) 795-2947.

Focolare Movement: Founded in Trent, Italy, in 1943, by Chiara Lubich; for men and women. Approved as an association of the faithful, 1962. It is not a secular institute by statute; however, vows are observed by its totally dedicated core membership of 4,000 who live in small communities called Focolare (Italian word for "hearth") centers. There are 17 resident centers in the U.S. and four in Canada. GEN (New Generation) is the youth organization of the movement. An estimated 75,000 are affiliated with the movement in the U.S. and Canada, 2,000,000 worldwide. Publications include *Living City*, monthly; *GEN II* and *GEN III* for young people and children. Five week-long summer conventions, called "Mariapolis" ("City of Mary"), are held annually. Address for information: 204 Cardinal Rd., Hyde Park, NY 12538, (845) 229-0230 (men's or women's branch), www.rc.net/focolare.

Jesus-Caritas Fraternity of Priests: An international association of diocesan priests who strive to combine an active life with a contemplative calling by their membership in small fraternities. U.S. address for information: Rev. Greg Pawloski, St. Patrick's Church, P.O. Box 96, 126 E. 7th St., Imperial, NE 69033-0096, (308) 882-4995, www.rc.net/org/jesuscaritas.

Franciscan Missionaries of Jesus Crucified: Founded in New York in 1987; separate communities for women and men. Approved as an association of the faithful Jan. 7, 1992. To provide an opportunity for persons with disabilities to live a life of total consecration in the pursuit of holiness in the apostolate of service to the Church and to those who suffer in any way. Address: Louise D. Principe, F.M.J.C., 400 Central Ave., Apt. 3D, Albany, NY 12206, (518) 438-5887.

Madonna House Apostolate: Originated in Toronto, Canada, 1930; for priests and lay persons. Public association of the Christian faithful. Address: Madonna House, 2888 Dafoe Rd., Combermere, ON, Canada KOJ ILO, (613) 756-3713, www.madonnahouse.org.

Directors General: Jean Fox (women), Albert Osterberger (men), Fr. Robert Pelton (priests). International membership and missions.

Opus Spiritus Sancti: Originated in Germany; for women. An association of the faithful. Address: 1 Fatima Dr., Cumberland, RI 02864, (401) 723-6719.

Pax Christi: Lay institute of men and women dedicated to witnessing to Christ, with special emphasis on service to the poor in Mississippi. Addresses: St. Francis Center, 709 Ave. I, Greenwood, MS 38930. LaVerna House, 2108 Alta Woods Blvd., Jackson, MS 39204, (601) 373-4463.

Rural Parish Workers of Christ the King: Founded in 1942; for women. A secular institute of the Archdiocese of St. Louis. Dedicated to the glory of God in service of neighbor, especially in rural areas. Address: 15540 Cannon Mines Rd., Cadet, MO 63630, (636) 586-5171; rpwck.com.

Salesian Cooperators: Founded by St. John Bosco in Turin, Italy, in 1876; for lay men and women and diocesan clergy. Public association of the faithful, members commit themselves to apostolates in the local Church, especially on behalf of the young, in the Salesian spirit and style. Address: P.O. Box 639, New Rochelle, NY 10802-0639; (914) 636-4225. Contact person: Fr. Thomas Dunne.

Teresian Institute: Founded in Spain 1911 by Pedro Poveda. Approved as an association of the faithful of pontifical right, Jan. 11, 1924. Mailing Address: 3400 S. W. 99th Ave., Miami, FL 33165, (305) 553-8567.

THIRD ORDERS

Augustine, Third Order Secular of St.: Founded 13th century; approved Nov. 7, 1400.

Carmelites, Lay (Third Order of Our Lady of Mt. Carmel): Rule for laity approved by Pope Nicholas V, Oct. 7, 1452; new statutes, January 1991. Addresses: 8501 Bailey Rd., Darien, IL 60561. P.O. Box 613, Williamston, MA 01267. P.O. Box 27, Tappan, NY 10983-0027, (845) 359-0535. Approximately 270 communities and 10,000 members in the U.S. and Canada.

Carmelites, The Secular Order of Discalced (formerly the Third Order Secular of the Blessed Virgin Mary of Mt. Carmel and of St. Teresa of Jesus): Rule based on the Carmelite reform established by St. Teresa and St. John of the Cross; approved Mar. 23, 1594. Revised rule approved May 10, 1979. Office of National Secretariat, U.S.A.: P.O. Box 3079, San Jose, CA 95156-3079, (408) 251-1361. Approximately 24,445 members throughout the world; 130 groups/communities and 5,200 members in the U.S. and Canada.

Dominican Laity (formerly known as Third Order of St. Dominic): Founded in the 13th century. Addresses of provincial promoters in the United States: St. Dominic Priory, 3601 Lindell Blvd., St. Louis, MO 63108-3393, (314) 977-2588, www.op.org/domcentral. Eastern Province, 487 Michigan Ave., N.E., Washington, DC, 20017, (202) 529-5300. Priory of St. Martin de Porres, P.O. Box 12927, Raleigh, NC 27605, (919) 833-1893. Western Province, 2005 Berryman St., Berkeley, CA 94709, (510) 526-4811. Midwest Province, 3904 Golfside Dr., Ypsilanti, MI 48197, (734) 434-0195.

Franciscan Order, Secular (SFO): Founded 1209 by St.

Francis of Assisi; approved Aug. 30, 1221. Vocation Director, 37430 Stonegate Circle, Clinton Township, MI 48036, (800) FRANCIS, www.NAFRA-SFO.org. International Secretariate, Via Pomponia Grecina, 31, 00145 Rome. *Tau USA*, quarterly. Approximately 780,000 throughout the world; 18,000 in the U.S.

Mary, Third Order of (Marist Laity): Founded, Dec. 8, 1850; rule approved by the Holy See, 1857. Addresses of provincial directors: Marist Laity Center, 1706 Jackson Ave., New Orleans, LA 70113-1510, (504) 524-5192, www.maristlaity.org. Marist Fathers, 698 Beacon St., Boston, MA 02115, (617) 262-2271. Marist Fathers, 2335 Warring St., Berkeley, CA 94704. Approximately 14,000 in world, 5,600 in U.S.

Mary, Secular Order of Servants of (Servite): Founded 1233; approved 1304. Revised rule approved 1995. Address: National Assistant for the Secular Order, 3121 W. Jackson Blvd., Chicago, IL 60612-2729, (773) 638-5800.

Mercy, Secular Third Order of Our Lady of (Mercedarian): Founded 1219 by St. Peter Nolasco; approved the same year.

Norbert, Third Order of St.: Founded 1122 by St. Norbert; approved by Pope Honorius II in 1126.

Oblates of St. Benedict: Lay persons affiliated with a Benedictine abbey, or monastery, who strive to direct their lives, as circumstances permit, according to the spirit and Rule of St. Benedict.

Trinity, Third Order Secular of the Most: Founded 1198; approved 1219.

Apostolates and Ministries

RIGHTS AND OBLIGATIONS OF ALL THE FAITHFUL

The following rights are listed in Canons 208-223 of the revised *Code of Canon Law*; additional rights are specified in other canons.
- Because of their baptism and regeneration, there is equality regarding dignity and action for the building up of the Body of Christ.
- They are bound always to preserve communion with the Church.
- According to their condition and circumstances, they should strive to lead a holy life and promote the growth and holiness of the Church.
- They have the right and duty to work for the spread of the divine message of salvation to all peoples of all times and places.
- They are bound to follow with Christian obedience those things which the bishops, as they represent Christ, declare as teachers of the faith or establish as rulers of the Church.
- They have the right to make known their needs, especially their spiritual needs, to pastors of the Church.
- They have the right, and sometimes the duty, of making known to pastors and others of the faithful their opinions about things pertaining to the good of the Church.
- They have the right to receive help from their pastors, from the spiritual goods of the Church and especially from the word of God and the sacraments.
- They have the right to divine worship performed according to prescribed rules of their rite, and to follow their own form of spiritual life in line with the doctrine of the Church.
- They have the right to freely establish and control

associations for good and charitable purposes, to foster the Christian vocation in the world, and to hold meetings related to the accomplishment of these purposes.
- They have the right to promote and support apostolic action but may not call it "Catholic" unless they have the consent of competent authority.
- They have a right to a Christian education.
- They have a right to freedom of inquiry in sacred studies, in accordance with the teaching authority of the Church.
- They have a right to freedom in the choice of their state of life.
- No one has the right to harm the good name of another person or to violate his or her right to maintain personal privacy.
- They have the right to vindicate the rights they enjoy in the Church, and to defend themselves in a competent ecclesiastical forum.
- They have the obligation to provide for the needs of the Church, with respect to things pertaining to divine worship, apostolic and charitable works, and the reasonable support of ministers of the Church.
- They have the obligation to promote social justice and to help the poor from their own resources.
- In exercising their rights, the faithful should have regard for the common good of the Church and for the rights and duties of others.
- Church authority has the right to monitor the exercise of rights proper to the faithful, with the common good in view.

RIGHTS AND OBLIGATIONS OF LAY PERSONS

In addition to rights and obligations common to all the faithful and those stated in other canons, lay persons are bound by the obligations (224-231) and enjoy the rights specified in these canons.
- Lay persons, like all the faithful, are called by God to the apostolate in virtue of their baptism and confirmation. They have the obligation and right, individually or together in associations, to work for the spread and acceptance of the divine message of salvation among people everywhere; this obligation is more urgent in those circumstances in which people can hear the Gospel and get to know Christ only through them (lay persons).
- They are bound to bring an evangelical spirit to bear on the order of temporal things and to give Christian witness in carrying out their secular pursuits.

- Married couples are obliged to work for the building up of the people of God through their marital and family life.
- Parents have the most serious obligation to provide for the Christian education of their children according to the doctrine handed down by the Church.
- Lay persons have the same civil liberty as other citizens. In the use of this liberty, they should take care that their actions be imbued with an evangelical spirit. They should attend to the doctrine proposed by the magisterium of the Church but should take care that, in questions of opinion, they do not propose their own opinion as the doctrine of the Church.
- Qualified lay persons are eligible to hold and perform the duties of ecclesiastical offices open to them in accord with the provisions of law.

- Properly qualified lay persons can assist pastors of the Church as experts and counselors.
- Lay persons have the obligation and enjoy the right to acquire knowledge of doctrine commensurate with their capacity and condition.
- They have the right to pursue studies in the sacred sciences in pontifical universities or facilities and in institutes of religious sciences, and to obtain academic degrees.
- If qualified, they are eligible to receive from ecclesiastical authority a mandate to teach sacred sciences.
- Laymen can be invested by liturgical rite and in a stable manner in the ministries of lector and acolyte.
- Lay persons, by temporary assignment, can fulfill the office of lector in liturgical actions; likewise, all lay persons can perform the duties of commentator or cantor.

- In cases of necessity and in the absence of the usual ministers, lay persons—even if not lectors or acolytes—can exercise the ministry of the word, lead liturgical prayers, confer baptism and distribute Communion, according to the prescripts of law.
- Lay persons who devote themselves permanently or temporarily to the service of the Church are obliged to acquire the formation necessary for carrying out their duties in a proper manner.
- They have a right to remuneration for their service which is just and adequate to provide for their own needs and those of their families; they also have a right to insurance, social security and health insurance.

(*See* **Canon Law** *for details on the* **Code**.)

DIRECTORY OF LAY GROUPS

In Feb. 2004, the U.S. Conference of Catholic Bishops' Secretariat for Family, Laity, Women and Youth released its 2004-2005 *Directory of Lay Movements, Organizations, and Professional Associations* (the most recent edition).

The directory contains listings for more than 100 national lay movements, professional associations, and organizations. Each listing includes a brief description of the group and the name, address, phone number of a contact person, and web/email information if available. The groups listed are national in scope, but not all are solely lay. Some are included because their work affects the life and mission of the laity and/or because their membership has a significant lay component. The secretariat acknowledges that the listing is a partial one and welcomes suggestions for groups to be included in future editions. Copies may be ordered from the USCCB Secretariat for Family, Laity, Women, and Youth, 3211 4th St., N.E., Washington, DC 20017; (202) 541-3040 (phone); (202) 541-3176 (fax).

SPECIAL APOSTOLATES AND GROUPS

Apostleship of the Sea (1920, Glasgow, Scotland; 1947 in U.S.): 3211 Fourth St. N.E., Washington, DC 20017 (national office); (202) 541-3035; www.aos-usa.org. An international Catholic organization for the moral, social and spiritual welfare of seafarers and those involved in the maritime industry. Formally instituted by the Holy See in 1952 (apostolic constitution *Exul Familia*), it is a sector of the Pontifical Council for Migrants and Itinerant Peoples. Its norms were updated by Pope John Paul II in a *motu proprio* dated Jan. 31, 1997. The U.S. unit, an affiliate of the USCCB, serves port chaplains in 63 U.S. ports. Nat. Dir.: Sr. Myrna Tordillo, MSCS.

Apostleship of the Sea of the United States of America (formerly, National Catholic Conference for Seafarers); affiliated with the Apostleship of the Sea in the U.S.: Apostleship of the Sea, 1500 Jefferson Dr., Pt. Arthur, TX 77642; (409) 985-5111. The membership organization of the Roman Catholic ministry to the people of the sea. Inspired by Pope John Paul II's apostolic letter, *Stella Maris*, AOSUSA brings together chaplains, clergy, religious, laity, and mariners in the common interest of promoting the spiritual and social life of the people of the sea. The people of the sea include fishermen, their families, U.S. and foreign mariners, cadets and trainees and those who have retired from sea service. Pres., Fr. Sinclair Oubre, J.C.L.

Auxiliaries of Our Lady of the Cenacle (1878, France): 18 Sycamore Meadow Rd., Sunderland, MA 01375; www.cenaclesisters.org. An association of consecrated Catholic laywomen, under the direction of the Congregation of Our Lady of the Cenacle. They profess annually the evangelical counsels of celibacy, poverty and obedience and serve God through their own professions and life styles and pursue individual apostolates. Reg. Dir., Dr. Carolyn Jacobs.

Catholic Central Verein (Union) of America (1855): 3835 Westminster Pl., St. Louis, MO 63108; (314) 371-1653; www.socialjusticereview.org. One of the oldest Catholic lay organizations in the U.S. and the first given an official mandate for Catholic Action by a committee of the American bishops (1936); *Social Justice Review*, bimonthly.

Catholic Medical Mission Board (1928): 10 W. 17th Street, New York, NY 10011-5765; (212) 242-7757; www.cmmb.org. A charitable, non-profit organization dedicated to providing health care supplies and support for the medically disadvantaged in developing and transitional countries. CMMB depends upon the financial generosity of over 25,000 individual donors and through product contributions by major pharmaceutical corporations. In 2003, CMMB delivered more than $125 million in medicines, volunteer medical services and healthcare programming to 50 countries and responded to emergencies across the globe. New programs include Born to Live, an international effort to prevent mother-to-child transmission of HIV, especially in Africa. The CMMB also aided Cambodian mothers and children in a Phnom Phen Clinic under the CMMB's Physicians on a Mission Program; assisted over 3,000 refugee families from Liberia and Sierra Leone in the capital city of Monrovia; helped Dominican fathers and families living in the bateyes of Monte Plata; and gave emergency relief to Afghanistan, Haiti, South Africa, and Iraq. CMMB's medical program includes a placement service for health care specialists who volunteer at Catholic medical facilities in developing countries. Pres., John F. Galbraith.

Catholic Movement for Intellectual and Cultural Affairs: 3025 Fourth St., N.E., Washington, DC, 20017; (202) 269-6672. The U.S. affiliate of *Pax Romana*-ICMICA (*see* **International Catholic Organizations**); *The Notebook*, quarterly. Pres., Joseph Kirchner.

Catholic Network of Volunteer Service (1963; formerly, International Liaison of Lay Volunteers in Mission): 6930 Carroll Ave., Suite 820, Takoma Park, MD 201912; (301) 270-0900; www.cnvs.org. Membership organization of 235 faith-based volunteer programs, placing persons in all fifty states and 120 countries; *The Response*, annual directory. Exec. Dir., James Lindsay.

Catholic Volunteers in Florida (1983): P.O. Box 536476, Orlando, FL 32853-6476; (407) 382-7071; www.cvif.org. Co-sponsored by the bishops of Florida to promote values of social justice by direct service to farm workers, homeless, hungry, low-income people, single mothers and others in need. Volunteers, 20 years of age and older, serve for a one-year period in urban and rural settings. Exec. Dir., Richard Galentino.

Center for Applied Research in the Apostolate (CARA): 2300 Wisconsin Ave., N.W., Suite 400, Washington, DC 20007; (202) 687-8080; www.cara.georgetown.edu. A non-profit research center serving the planning needs of the Catholic Church. CARA gathers empirical data for use by bishops, diocesan agencies, parishes, congregations of men and women religious and Catholic organizations. The *CARA Report*, quarterly; *CARA Catholic Ministry Formation Directory*, annually. Exec. Dir., Mary E. Bendyna, R.S.M., Ph.D.

Christian Family Movement (CFM) (1947): National office, P.O. Box 925, Evansville, IN 47706; (812) 962-5508; www.cfm.org. Originated in Chicago to Christianize family life and create communities conducive to Christian family life. Since 1968, CFM in the U.S. has included couples from all Christian churches.

Christian Life Communities (1971, promulgation of revised norms by Pope Paul VI; originated, 1563, as Sodalities of Our Lady, at the Jesuit College in Rome): 3601 Lindell Blvd., Room 202, St. Louis, MO 63108 (national office); (314) 977-7370; www.clc-usa.org. The world CLC office is in Rome. Small communities of primarily lay persons who come together to form committed individuals for service to the world and the Church.

Cursillo Movement (1949, in Spain; in U.S., 1957): National Cursillo Center, P.O. Box 210226, Dallas, TX 75211. An instrument of Christian renewal designed to form and stimulate persons to engage in evangelizing their everyday environments.

Franciscan Mission Service of North America, an Overseas Lay Ministry Program (1990): P.O. Box 29034, Washington, DC 20017; (202) 832-1762; www.franciscanmissionservice.catholic.edu. Lay missioners work with Franciscan sisters, brothers and priests for a minimum of three years in underdeveloped countries. Co-Dir. Joseph Nangle, O.F.M. and Megeen White.

Grail, The (1921, in The Netherlands, by Rev. Jacques van Ginneken, S.J.; 1940, in U.S.): Grailville, 932 O'Bannonville Rd., Loveland, OH 45140 (U. S. headquarters); (513) 683-5750; www.grail-us.org.

Duisburger Strasse 442, 45478 Mulheim, Germany, (international secretariat). An international movement of women concerned about the full development of all peoples, working in education, religious, social, cultural and ecological areas.

Jesuit Volunteer Corps (1956): 18th and Thompson Sts., Philadelphia, PA 19121 (address for information); (215) 232-0300; www.jesuitvolunteers.org. Sponsored by the Society of Jesus in the U.S. Men and women volunteers work throughout the U.S. serving the poor directly and working for structural change.

LAMP Ministries (Lay Apostolic Ministries with the Poor): 2704 Schurz Ave., Bronx, NY 10465; (718) 409-5062; www.lampministries.org. Missionary service of evangelization with the materially poor and homeless in the larger metropolitan New York-New Jersey area. Newsletter, two times a year. Directors, Drs. Tom and Lyn Scheuring.

Lay Mission-Helpers Association (1955): 3435 Wilshire Blvd., #1035, Los Angeles, CA 90010; (213) 368-1870; www.laymissionhelpers.org. Trains and assigns men and women for work in overseas apostolates for periods of two to three years. Approximately 700 members of the association have served in overseas assignments since its founding. Director, Janice England.

The Mission Doctors Association: (same address; (213) 637-7499; www.missiondoctors.org) recruits, trains and sends Catholic physicians and their families to mission hospitals and clinics throughout the world for tours of two to three years. Additionally, MDA has a short-term program for volunteer physicians with a term of service of 1-2 months. Program Dir., Elise Frederick.

Legion of Mary (1921, in Dublin, Ireland, by Frank Duff): Maria Center, 326 E. Ripa, St. Louis, MO 63125 (U.S. address); (314) 631-3447. De Montfort House, Dublin 7, Ireland (headquarters). Membership: active Catholics of all ages, under the direction of local bishops and priests, for the work of conversion, conservation and consolation. Pres., Mary T. Budde.

Movimiento Familiar Cristiano-USA **(MFC)** (1969): St. Mary Seminary, 9845 memorial Dr., Houston, TX 77024; (713) 686-4345. Movement of Catholic Hispanic families united in their efforts to promote the human and Christian virtues of the family so that it may become a force that forms persons, transmits the faith and contributes to the total development of the community. Rev. Rafael Davila, national spiritual director.

Pax Christi **USA** (1972): 532 W. 8th St., Erie, PA 16502; (814) 453-4955; www.paxchristiusa.org. Pax Christi (*see* **International Catholic Organizations**). Founded to establish peacemaking as a priority for the American Catholic Church. *Pax Christi USA*, quarterly.

Schoenstatt Lay Movement (1914): International Schoenstatt Center, W284 N 698 Cherry Lane, Waukesha, WI 53188; (262) 547-7733. Lay movement founded in Germany by Fr. Joseph Kentenich. A Marian and apostolic way of life, Schoenstatt is present on all continents and includes people of all ages and walks of life, men and women, young and old, priests and laity. The Schoenstatt Shrine, dedicated to Mary, Mother Thrice Admirable, Queen and Victress of Schoenstatt, is an integral part of the spirituality of

Schoenstatt. There are over 160 shrines around the world, 6 of them in the U.S., in Minnesota, New York, Texas, and Wisconsin.

Volunteer Missionary Movement (1969): 5980 W. Loomis Rd., Milwaukee, WI 53129; (414) 423-8660; www.vmmusa.org. Independent lay international mission organization with origins in the Catholic tradition but ecumenical and open to all Christian denominations. *Bridges*, quarterly. Exec. Dir., Julie Pagenkopf.

CATHOLIC YOUTH ORGANIZATIONS

Camp Fire Boys and Girls: 4601 Madison Ave., Kansas City, MO 64112; (816) 756-1950; www.campfireusa.org. The National Catholic Committee for Girl Scouts and Camp Fire, a standing committee of the National Federation for Catholic Youth Ministry, cooperates with Camp Fire Boys and Girls.

Catholic Forester Youth Program, Catholic Order of Foresters: Naperville, IL 60566; (800) 552-0145. To develop Christian leadership and promote the moral, intellectual, social and physical growth of its youth members. Membership: youth up to 16 years of age; over 19,046 in 610 local courts in U.S. Catholic Forester. High Chief Ranger-Pres., Robert Ciesla.

Catholic Youth Organization (CYO): Name of parish-centered diocesan Catholic youth programs throughout the country. CYO promotes a program of spiritual, social and physical activities. The original CYO was organized in 1930 by Archbishop Bernard Sheil, auxiliary bishop of Chicago.

Columbian Squires (1925): 1 Columbus Plaza, New Haven, CT 06510-3326; (203) 752-4401; www.kofc.org. The official youth organization of the Knights of Columbus. To train and develop leadership through active participation in a well-organized program of spiritual, service, social, cultural and athletic activities. Membership: Catholic young men, 12-18 years old. More than 25,000 in over 1,000 circles (local units) active in the U.S., Canada, Puerto Rico, Philippines, Mexico, the Bahamas, Virgin Islands and Guam. *Squires Newsletter*, monthly.

Girl Scouts: 830 Third Ave., New York, NY 10022. Girls from archdioceses and dioceses in the U.S. and its possessions participate in Girl Scouting through the collaboration of Girl Scouts of the U.S.A., with the National Catholic Committee for Girl Scouts and Camp Fire, a standing committee of the National Federation for Catholic Youth Ministry.

Holy Childhood Association (Pontifical Association of the Holy Childhood) (1843): 366 Fifth Ave., New York, NY 10001; (212) 563-8700; www.worldmissions-catholic-church.org. The official children's mission-awareness society of the Church. Provides mission awareness for elementary-grade students in parochial schools and religious education programs and financial assistance to children in more than 100 developing countries. Publishes *It's Our World*, three times a year, in two grade levels. Nat. Dir., Rev. Francis W. Wright, C.SS.Sp.

The National Catholic Committee on Scouting: P.O. Box 152079, Irving, TX 75015-2079; (972) 580-2114; www.catholic-church.org/catholicscouting; www.nccs-bsa.org. Works with the Boy Scouts of America in developing the character and spiritual life of members in units chartered to Catholic and non-Catholic organizations. National Committee Chairman, Robert Runnels of Leawood, KS. Admin. Sec., Barbara Nestel.

National Catholic Forensic League (1952): 21 Nancy Rd., Milford, MA 01757; (508) 473-0431. To develop articulate Catholic leaders through an interdiocesan program of speech and debate activities. Newsletter, quarterly. Membership: 925 schools; membership open to Catholic, private and public schools through the local diocesan league. Exec. Sec.-Treas., Richard Gaudette.

National Catholic Young Adult Ministry Association (1982): P.O. Box 32253, Washington, DC 20007; (888) NCYAMA1; www.ncyama.org. A response to the needs of young adults, an invitation to share their gifts with the larger community and a challenge to live Gospel values in the world. A national network for single and married young adults. Exec. Dir., Michelle M. Miller.

National Federation for Catholic Youth Ministry, Inc. (1981): 415 Michigan Ave., N.E., Washington, DC 20017; (202) 636-3825; www.nfcym.org. To foster the development of youth ministry in the United States. Exec. Dir., Robert McCarty.

Young Christian Students: 19666 W. Dunlap Rd., Dennison, IL 62423; (217) 826-5708. A student movement for Christian personal and social change.

CAMPUS MINISTRY

Campus ministry is an expression of the Church's special desire to be present to all who are involved in higher education and to further dialogue between the Church and the academic community. In the words of the U.S. bishops' 1985 pastoral letter entitled "Empowered by the Spirit," this ministry is "the public presence and service through which properly prepared baptized persons are empowered by the Spirit to use their talents and gifts on behalf of the Church in order to be sign and instrument of the Kingdom in the academic world."

Campus ministry, carried on by lay, Religious and ordained ministers, gathers members of the Church on campus to form the faith community, appropriate the faith, form Christian consciences, educate for justice and facilitate religious development.

The dimensions and challenge of this ministry are evident from, among other things, the numbers involved: approximately 550,000 Catholics on more than 230 Catholic college and university campuses; about four million in several thousand non-Catholic private and public institutions; 1,200 or more campus ministers. In many dioceses, the activities of ministers are coordinated by a local diocesan director. Two professional organizations serve the ministry on the national level:

The National Association of Diocesan Directors of Campus Ministry: Ms. Krista Bajoka (contact), 305 Michigan Ave., Detroit, MI 48226; (313) 237-5962.

The Catholic Campus Ministry Association: 1,200 members. 1118 Pendleton St., Suite 300, Cincinnati, OH 45202; (513) 842-0167; www.ccmanet.org. Exec. Dir., Edmund Franchi.

COLLEGE SOCIETIES

Alpha Sigma Nu (1915): Marquette University, Brooks 201, P.O. Box 1881, Milwaukee, WI 53201-1881 (national headquarters); (414) 288-7542; www.alphasigmanu.org. National honor society of the 30 Jesuit institutions of higher education in the U.S. and a chapter at Sogany University in Korea; members chosen on the basis of scholarship, loyalty and service; 1,575 student and 38,000 alumni members. Member, Association of College Honor Societies. Gamma Pi Epsilon (1925) merged with Alpha Sigma Nu in 1973 to form society for men and women. Exec. Dir., Kate Greatner.

Delta Epsilon Sigma (1939): Barry University, 11300 NE Second Ave., Miami Shores, FL 33161; (305) 899-3020; www.des.barry.edu. National scholastic honor society for students, faculty and alumni of colleges and universities with a Catholic tradition. Delta Epsilon Sigma Journal, three times a year. Membership: 60,000 in 116 chapters. Sec., Dr. J. Patrick Lee.

Kappa Gamma Pi (1926): KGP National Office, 10215 Chardon Rd., Chardon, OH, 44024-9700; (440) 286-3764; www.kappagammapi.org. A national Catholic college honor society for graduates who, in addition to academic excellence, have shown outstanding leadership in extra-curricular activities. Also offers Cornaro Scholarship for Graduate Studies.

Kappa Gamma Pi News, five times a year. Membership: more than 37,000 in 139 colleges; 20 alumnae chapters in metropolitan areas. Nat. Coord. Pamela Waitinas.

Phi Kappa Theta: 3901 W. 86th St., Suite 425, Indianapolis, IN 46268. National social fraternity with a Catholic heritage. Merger (1959) of Phi Kappa Fraternity, founded at Brown University in 1889, and Theta Kappa Phi Fraternity, founded at Lehigh University in 1919. The Temple Magazine, semi-annually, and newsletters. Membership: 2,800 undergraduate and 50,500 alumni in 63 collegiate and 40 alumni chapters. Exec. Dir., Mark T. McSweeney.

National Catholic Student Coalition (1988); 45 Lovett Ave., Newark, DE 19717; www.catholicstudent.org. National coalition of Catholic campus ministry groups at public and private institutions of higher education. Formed after National Newman Club Federation and the National Federation of Catholic College Students dissolved in the 1960s. The U.S. affiliate of Pax Romana-IMCS (see International Catholic Organizations). The Catholic Collegian, four times a year. Membership: 200 campus groups. Exec. Dir., Jamie Williams; contact, Kim Zitzner.

ASSOCIATIONS, MOVEMENTS, SOCIETIES IN THE U.S.

Principal source: Catholic Almanac *survey.*

Academy of American Franciscan History (1944): 1712 Euclid Ave., Berkeley, CA 94709; (510) 548-1755; www.aafh.org. To encourage the study of the Franciscan Order in the New World. Dir., Dr. Jeffrey M. Burns.

Adoremus-Society for the Renewal of the Sacred Liturgy (1995): P.O. Box 3286, St. Louis, MO 63130; (314) 863-8385; www.adoremus.org. Promotes authentic renewal of Catholic liturgy. Publishes *Adoremus Bulletin*, 10 times a year; editor, Helen Hull Hitchcock.

Aid to the Church in Need (1947): U.S. office, 725 Leonard St., Brooklyn, N.Y. 11222; (718) 609-0939; www.churchinneed.org. Assists the pastoral activities of the church in Third World countries and Eastern Europe. *Mirror*, newsletter, 9 times a year. Pres./Exec. Dir., Joseph Donnelly.

American Benedictine Academy (1947): Saint Meinrad Archabbey, Guest House, 100 Hill Dr. Saint Meinrad, IN, 47577; (800) 581-6905. To promote Benedictine values in contemporary culture. Pres., Eugene Hensell, O.S.B.

American Catholic Correctional Chaplains Association (1952): 701 Lawrenceville Rd., P.O. Box 1547, Trenton, NJ. 08638; (609) 406-7400. Pres., Rev. Robert R. Schulze.

American Catholic Historical Association (1919): The Catholic University of America, Washington, DC 20064; (202) 319-5079; www.research.cua.edu/acha. *The Catholic Historical Review*, quarterly. Sec.-Treas., Dr. Timothy J. Meagher.

American Catholic Philosophical Association (1926): Administration Building, Fordham University, 441 E. Fordham Rd., Bronx, NY, 10458; (718) 817-3295; www.acpa-main.org. *American Catholic Philosophical Quarterly*; *Proceedings*, annually.

American Committee on Italian Migration (1952): 25 Carmine St., New York, NY 10014; (212) 247-5419; www.acimmigra.org. *ACIM Newsletter*

and *ACIM Nuova Via*, 6 times a year.

American Friends of the Vatican Library (1981): 3535 Indian Trail, Orchard Lake, MI 48324; (248) 683-0311. AMICI, newsletter. Sponsored by the Catholic Library Association. To assist in supporting the Vatican Library. Pres., Rev. Msgr. Charles G. Kosanke.

American Life League, Inc. (1979), P.O. Box 1350, Stafford, VA 22555; (540) 659-4171; www.all.org. *Celebrate Life*, six times a year, and the *ABAC Quarterly*, for the American Bioethics Advisory Commission. Pres., Judie Brown.

Ancient Order of Hibernians in America, Inc. (1836): 31 Logan St., Auburn, NY 13021. National *Hibernian Digest*, bimonthly. 120,000 members. Nat. Sec., Thomas McNabb.

Apostleship of Prayer (1844, France; 1861, U.S.): 3211 South Lake Dr., Suite 216, Milwaukee, WI 53235; (414) 486-1152; www.apostleshipofprayer.org. Promotes Daily Offering and Sacred Heart devotion. Contact: Rev. James Kubicki.

Apostolate for Family Consecration (1975): 3375 County Rd. 36, Bloomingdale, OH 43910; (740) 765-5500; www.familyland.org. Pope John Paul II Holy Family Center, known as Catholic Familyland. To transform families and parishes and nourish families through the Catholic faith. Pres., Jerome F. Coniker.

Archconfraternity of Christian Mothers (Christian Mothers) (1881): 220 37th St., Pittsburgh, PA 15201; (412) 683-2400; www.capuchin.com. Over 3,500 branches. Dir., Rev. Bertin Roll, O.F.M. Cap.

Archconfraternity of the Holy Ghost (1912): Holy Ghost Fathers, 6230 Brush Run Rd., Bethel Park, PA 15102; (412) 831-0302; www.spiritans.org (U.S. headquarters).

Archdiocese for the Military Services Seminary Education Fund (1988): P.O. Box 4469, Washington, D.C., 20017-0469; (202) 269-9100; www.milarch.org.

Association for Social Economics (formerly the Catholic Economic Association) (1941): Marquette University, Milwaukee, WI 53233. *Review of Social Economy*, quarterly. 1,300 members.

Association of Catholic Diocesan Archivists (1979): 711 W. Monroe, Chicago, IL 60661; (312) 831-0711. To work for establishment of an archival program in every American diocese. *ACDA Bulletin*, quarterly. Treas. John J. Treanor.

Association of Marian Helpers (1944): Eden Hill, 2 Prospect Rd., Stockbridge, MA 01263; (413) 298-3691; www.marian.org. *Marian Helpers Bulletin*, quarterly. 900,000 members, mostly in U.S. To promote vocations to Church service and support worldwide apostolates of Marians of the Immaculate Conception. Exec. Dir., Rev. Joseph, M.I.C.

Assumption Guild — Mass Cards: 330 Market St., Brighton, MA 02135; (617) 783-0495; www.mass cardsaa.com.

Beginning Experience (1974): International Ministry Center, 1657 Commerce Dr., Suite 2B, South Bend, IN 46628; (574) 283-0279; www.beginningexperience.org. Programs to help divorced, widowed and separated. Pres., Kathleen Murphy.

Calix Society (1947): 2555 Hazelwood St., St. Paul, MN 55109; www.calixsociety.org. Association of Catholic alcoholics maintaining their sobriety through 12-step program. Sec. Jim Billigmeier.

Canon Law Society of America (1939): Catholic University, Caldwell Hall, 431, Washington, DC 20064; (202) 269-3491; www.clsa.org. To further research and study in canon law. 1,600 members. Exec. Coord., Arthur J. Espelage, O.F.M.

Cardinal Mindszenty Foundation (CMF) (1958): P.O. Box 11321, St. Louis, MO 63105-0121; (314) 727-6279; www.mindszenty.org. To uphold and defend the Catholic Church, family life and freedom for all under God. *The Mindszenty Report*, monthly. Pres., Eleanor Schlafly.

Catholic Aid Association (1878): 3499 N. Lexington Ave. North, St. Paul, MN 55126; (651) 490-0170; www.catholicaid.com. Fraternal life insurance society. *Catholic Aid News*, monthly. Chairman of the Board, Michael McGovern.

Catholic Answers (1982): 2020 Gillespie Way, El Cajon, CA 92020; (619) 387-7200; www.catholic.com. Apologetics and evangelization organization. *This Rock*, monthly. Founder and dir., Karl Keating.

Catholic Biblical Association of America (1936): The Catholic University of America, Washington, DC 20064; (202) 319-5519; www.cba.cua.edu. The *Catholic Biblical Quarterly*, *Old Testament Abstracts*, CBQ monograph series. Exec. Sec., Joseph Jensen, O.S.B.

Catholic Book Publishers Association, Inc. (1987): 8404 Jamesport Dr., Rockford, IL 61108; (815) 332-3245; www.cbpa.org. Exec. Dir., Terry Wessels.

Catholic Cemetery Conference (1949): 1400 S. Wolf Rd., Building 3, Hillside, IL 60162; (888) 850-8131. Exec. Dir., Sidney Cristol.

Catholic Coalition on Preaching: Madonna University, 36600 Schoolcraft Rd. Livonia, MI 48150-1173; (734) 432-5538. Pres., Rev. Francis Tebbe, O.F.M.

Catholic Committee of Appalachia (1970): 885 Orchard Run Rd., Spencer, WV 25276; (304) 927-5798; ccappal.org. Dir., Fr. John Rausch.

Catholic Daughters of the Americas (1903): 10 W. 71st St., New York, NY 10023; (212) 877-3041; www.catholicdaughters.org. *Share Magazine*. 125,000 members. Nat. Regent, M. Joan McKenna.

Catholic Death Row Ministry (1990): P.O. Box 1328, Howe, Texas 75459-1328; (903)892-9411; to share the Catholic Faith with Death Row Inmates; also assist victims and families of Death Row inmates. Founder and director, Michael Denson.

Catholic Familyland (1975): 3375 County Rd. 36, Bloomingdale, OH 43910; (740) 765-5500; www.familyland.org. Canonically named the John Paul II Holy Family Center; functions under the auspices of the Apostolate for Family Consecration. Pres., Jerome F. Coniker.

Catholic Golden Age (1975): P.O. Box 3658, Scranton, PA 18505-0658; (800) 836-5699. *CGA World*, quarterly. For Catholics over 50 years of age.

Catholic Guardian Society and Home Bureau (1913): 1011 First Ave., New York, NY 10022; (212) 371-1000. Exec. Dir., John J. Frein.

Catholic Home Bureau (1899): 1011 First Ave., New York, NY 10022; (212) 371-1000; www.catholichomebureau.com. Exec. Dir., Philip Georgini.

Catholic Home Study Service (1936): P.O. Box 363, Perryville, MO 63775-0363; (573) 547-4084; www.amm.org/chss.htm. Provides instruction in the Catholic faith by mail free of charge. Dir., Rev. Oscar Lukefahr, C.M.

Catholic Interracial Council of New York, Inc. (1934): 899 Tenth Ave., New York, NY 10019; (212) 237-8600; www.amm.org/chss.htm. To promote racial and social justice.

Catholic Knights of America (1877): Publication Office, 1850 Dalton St., Cincinnati, OH 45214. Fraternal insurance society. *CK of A Journal*, monthly. 7,800 members.

Catholic Knights of Ohio (1891): 22005 Mastick Rd., Fairview Park, OH 44126; (440) 777-5355. Fraternal insurance society. *The Messenger*, monthly. 8,000 members in Ohio and Kentucky. Mr. Tom Welsh, General Secretary.

Catholic Kolping Society of America (1849): 9 East 8th St., Clifton, NJ 07011-1101. International society concerned with spiritual and educational development of members. *Kolping Banner*, monthly. Nat. Admin., Edward Farkas.

Catholic Lawyers' Guild: Organization usually on a diocesan basis, under different titles.

Catholic League for Religious Assistance to Poland (1943): 6002 W. Berteau Ave., Chicago, IL 60634-1630; (773) 202-7720. Exec. Dir., Most Rev. Thad Jakubowski.

Catholic League for Religious and Civil Rights (1973): 450 Seventh Ave., 34th Floor, New York, NY 10123; (212) 371-3191; www.catholicleague.org. Local chapters throughout U.S. Serves Catholic community as an anti-defamation and civil rights agency. *Catalyst*, league journal. Pres., William A. Donohue, Ph.D.

Catholic Library Association (1921): 100 North St., Suite 224, Pittsfield, MA 01201-5109; (413) 442-2252. www.cathla.org; *Catholic Library World*, *Catholic Periodical and Literature Index*, quarterlies. Exec.Dir., Jean R. Bostley, S.S.J.

Catholic Marketing Network (1955): 111 Ferguson Court, #102, Irving, TX 75062; (800) 506-6333; www.catholicmarketing.com. A trade association founded to encourage the most effective production and distribution of Catholic goods and provide a common forum for mutual interchange of ideas. *Catholic Marketing Network*, quarterly.

Exec. Dir., Cherylann Tucker.

Catholic Near East Welfare Association (1926): 1011 First Ave., Suite 1552, New York, NY 10022; (212) 826-1480; www.cnewa.org. A papal agency for humanitarian and pastoral support serving the churches and peoples of the Middle East, Northeast Africa, India and Eastern Europe, with offices in New York, Vatican City, Addis Ababa, Amman, Jerusalem and Beirut. Pres., Cardinal Edward Egan; Sec. Gen., Msgr. Robert L. Stern.

Catholic Order of Foresters (1883): 355 Shuman Blvd., P.O. Box 3012, Naperville, IL 60566; (630) 983-4900; www.catholicforester.com. Fraternal insurance society. *The Catholic Forester*, bimonthly. 136,685 members. High Chief Ranger, Robert Ciesla.

Catholic Press Association of the U.S. and Canada, Inc. (1911): 205 W. Monroe, Suite 470, Chicago, IL 60606; (312) 380-6789; (312) 380-6789; www.catholicpress.org. *The Catholic Journalist*, monthly; *Catholic Press Directory*, annually. Exec. Dir., Thomas Conway.

Catholic Theological Society of America (1946), John Carroll University, 20700 North Park Blvd., University Hgts., OH, 44118; (216) 397-1631; www.jcu.edu/ctsa. *Proceedings*, annually. Exec. Sec., Dolores Christie.

Catholic Union of Texas, The K.J.T. (1889): 214 E. Colorado St., La Grange, TX 78945-0297; (979) 968-5877; www.kjtnet.org. Fraternal and insurance society. *Nasinec*, weekly, and *K. J. T. News*, monthly. 18,226 members. Pres., Elo J. Goerig.

Catholic War Veterans (1935): 441 N. Lee St., Alexandria, VA 22314; (703) 549-3622; www.cwv.org. *Catholic War Veteran*, bimonthly. 500 posts.

Catholic Worker Movement (1933): 36 E. 1st St., New York, NY 10003. Lay apostolate founded by Peter Maurin and Dorothy Day; has Houses of Hospitality in over 60 U.S. cities and several communal farms in various parts of the country. *The Catholic Worker*, 8 times a year.

Catholic Workman (Katolicky Delnik) (1891): 111 West Main St., New Prague, MN 56071; (612) 758-2229. Fraternal and insurance society. *Catholic Workman*, monthly. 16,405 members.

Catholics Against Capital Punishment (1992): P.O. Box 5706, Bethesda, MD 20824-5706; (301) 652-1125; www.cacp.org. Promotes greater awareness of papal and episcopal statements against the death penalty. *CACP News Notes*, bimonthly. Nat. Coord., Frank McNeirney.

Catholics United for the Faith (1968): 827 N. Fourth St., Steubenville, OH 43952; (740) 283-2484; www.cuf.org. 23,000 members worldwide. Lay apostolic group concerned with spiritual and doctrinal formation of members. *Lay Witness*, monthly. Mike Sullivan, Dir. of Communications.

Center of Concern (1971): 1225 Otis St., N.E., Washington, DC 20017; (202) 635-2757; www.coc.org. Exec. Dir., Rev. James E. Hug, S.J.

Central Association of the Miraculous Medal (1915): 475 E. Chelten Ave., Philadelphia, PA 19144; (800) 523-3674; www.cammonline.org. *Miraculous Medal*, quarterly. Dir., Rev. James O. Kiernan, C.M.

Chaplains' Aid Association, Inc. (1917): 3311 Toledo Terrace, Hyattsville, MD 20780. To receive and administer funds toward education of seminarians to become priest-chaplains in military services.

Christian Foundation for Children and Aging: One Elmwood Ave., Kansas City, KS 66103; (913) 384-6500; www.cfcusa.org. Grassroots movement dedicated to improving through sponsorship the lives of children and aging at Catholic mission sites around the world. Exec. Dir., Paco Wertin.

Christophers, Inc., The (1945): 12 E. 48th St., New York, NY 10017; (212) 759-4050; www.christophers.org. Founded by Rev. James Keller, M.M. The Christophers stimulate personal initiative and responsible action in line with Judeo-Christian principles through broadcast of Christopher radio and TV programs; free distribution of *Christopher News Notes*, ten times a year; publication of a weekly Christopher column in over 200 newspapers; Spanish literature; annual media awards; youth outreach. Pres., Dennis W. Heaney.

Citizens for Educational Freedom (1959): 9333 Clayton Road, Saint Louis, MO 63124-1511; (314) 997-6361; www.educational-freedom.org. Nonsectarian group concerned with parents' right to educational choice by means of tuition tax credits and vouchers. Exec. Dir., Mae Duggan.

Coming Home Network (1993): P.O. Box 8290, Zanesville, OH 43702; (740) 450-1175; www.chnetwork.org. Founded by Marcus Grodi (a former presbyterian pastor), *The Coming Home Network International* (CHNetwork) provides fellowship, encouragement and support for Protestant pastors and laymen who are somewhere along the journey or have already been received into the Catholic Church. Pres. Marcus Grodi.

Conference of Slovak Clergy (1985): 126 Logan Blvd., Hollidaysburg, PA, 16648; (814) 695-5579. Founded in 1985 and incorporated in 2000, the Conference seeks to associate priests and deacons of Slovak ancestry in the United States and to assist those preparing themselves for priestly ministry in the Church; provides financial assistance to the Slovak Pontifical College of Saints Cyril and Methodius in Rome and scholarships to individual students. Chair., Bishop Joseph V. Adamec.

Confraternity of Bl. Junipero Serra (1989): P.O. Box 7125, Mission Hills, CA 91346. Founded in Monterey (CA) diocese to help promote process of canonization of Bl. Junipero Serra and increase spiritual development of members. 3,500 members in U.S. and foreign countries. Dir., Rev. Thomas L. Davis, Jr.; Spiritual Dir., Rev. Noel F. Moholy, O.F.M.

Confraternity of Catholic Clergy (1976): 4445 W. 64th St., Chicago, IL 60629; (773) 581-8904. Association of priests pledged to pursuit of personal holiness, loyalty to the pope, theological study and adherence to authentic teachings of the Catholic faith. Sec., Rev. L. Dudley Day, O.S.A.

Confraternity of Christian Doctrine, Inc.: 3211 Fourth St., N.E., Washington, DC 20017; (202) 541-3098; www.usccb.org/nab. A distinct entity, separately incorporated and directed by a Board of Trustees from the United States Catholic Conference of Bishops. Its purpose is to foster and promote the teaching of Christ as understood and handed down by the Roman Catholic Church. To this end it licenses use of the Lectionary for Mass and the *New American Bible* (NAB), the *Revised Psalms of the NAB* and the *Revised New Testament of the NAB*, translations made from the original languages in accordance with the papal encyclical *Divino Afflante Spiritu* (1943) of Pope Pius XII.

Confraternity of the Immaculate Conception of Our Lady of Lourdes (1874): Box 561, Notre Dame, IN 46556; (574) 631-6562. Distributors of Lourdes water.

Confraternity of the Most Holy Rosary: *See*

Dominican Rosary Apostolate.
Couple to Couple League (1971), P.O. Box 111184, Cincinnati, OH 45211; (800) 745-8252; www.ccli.org. Founded to teach and promote marital chastity through Natural Family Planning. Exec. Dir., Mark Hayden.
Courage (1980): c/o St. John the Baptist Church and Friary, 210 West 31st St., New York, NY 10001; (212) 268-1010; www.couragerc.org. Ministry to men and women who experience same-sex attractions and desire to live Christian chastity in accordance with the teachings of the Catholic Church. Newsletter, 4 times a year. Nat. Dir., Rev. John F. Harvey, O.S.F.S.
CUSA (Catholics United for Spiritual Action, Inc.) — An Apostolate of the Sick or Disabled (1947): 176 W. 8th St., Bayonne, NJ, 07002-1227; (201) 437-0412; www.cusan.org. A group-correspondence apostolate for the disabled and chronically ill. Admin. Ms. Anna Marie Sopko.

Damien-Dutton Society for Leprosy Aid, Inc. (1944): 616 Bedford Ave., Bellmore, NY 11710; (516) 221-5829; www.damienleprosysociety.org. Provides medicine, rehabilitation and research for conquest of leprosy. *Damien Dutton Call*, quarterly. 25,000 members. Pres., Howard E. Crouch; Vice Pres., Elizabeth Campbell.
Daniel Dajani , S.J., Albanian Catholic Institute (1992): University of San Francisco, Xavier Hall, 650 Parker Ave., San Francisco, CA 94118; (415) 422-6966; www.albanian-catholic-institute.org. To assist the rebuilding of the Catholic Church in Albania and to promote the dissemination of knowledge of Albania's national, religious and cultural heritage. Exec. Dir., Raymond Frost.
Daughters of Isabella (1897): P.O. Box 9585, New Haven, CT 06535; www.daughtersofisabella. To unite Catholic women into a fraternal order for spiritual benefits and to promote higher ideals within society. 100,000 members.
Disaster Response Office (1990): Catholic Charities USA, 1731 King St., Suite 200, Alexandria, VA 22314; (703) 549-1390; www.catholiccharitiesusa.org. Promotes and facilitates Catholic disaster response in the U.S. Dir., Jane A. Gallagher.
Dismas Ministry: P.O. Box 070363, Milwaukee, WI 53207; (414) 977-5064; www.dismasministry.org; outreach to inmates, their families, and the community; services include spiritual ministry to inmates, victim support, and faith-based rehabilitation.
Dominican Rosary Apostolate (1806): Dominican Province of St. Joseph, 280 N. Grant Ave., Columbus, OH 43215, (614) 240-5915. Contact: Rev. André-Joseph LaCasse, O.P., Promoter of the Rosary, Dominican Province of St. Joseph.

Edith Stein Guild, Inc. (1955): Church of St. John the Baptist, 210 W. 31st St., New York, NY 10001-2876; (212) 567-8230. Assists and encourages Jewish Catholics; fosters among Catholics a better understanding of their Jewish heritage; promotes spread of knowledge of life and writings of St. Edith Stein; fosters better understanding between Jews and Christians and supports the Church's spirit of ecumenism. Pres., Sr. Marie Goldstein, R.S.H.M.
Enthronement of the Sacred Heart in the Home (1907): P.O. Box 111, Fairhaven, MA 02719; (508) 999-2680.

Federation of Diocesan Liturgical Commissions (FDLC) (1969): P.O. Box 29039, Washington, DC 20017;

(202) 635-6990; www.fdlc.org. Voluntary association of personnel from diocesan liturgical commissions and worship offices. The main purpose is promotion of the liturgy as the heart of Christian life, especially in the parish community. Exec. Dir., Rev. Michael J. Spillane.
Federation of Seminary Spiritual Directors (1972): Cardinal Muench Seminary, 100 35th Ave., N.E., Fargo, ND 58102; (701) 232-8969. Responsible for priestly spiritual formation in high school and college seminaries, novitiates, theologates and houses of formation in the U.S. and Canada. Pres., Dennis Skonseng.
Fellowship of Catholic Scholars (1977): Ave Maria School of Law, 3475 Plymouth Rd., Ann Arbor, Michigan 48105; (734) 827-8043. Interdisciplinary research and publications of Catholic scholars in accord with the magisterium of the Catholic Church. 1,000 members. Pres., Bernard Dobranski.
First Catholic Slovak Ladies' Association, USA (1892): 24950 Chagrin Blvd., Beachwood, OH 44122; (800) 464-4642; www.fcsla.com. *Fraternally Yours*, monthly. 102,000 members. Fraternal insurance society. Pres., Mary Ann Johanek.
First Catholic Slovak Union (Jednota) (1890): FCSU Corporate Center, 6611 Rockside Rd., Independence, OH 44131; (216) 642-9406; www.fcsu.com. *Jednota*, biweekly. 96,206 members. Nat. Sec., Kenneth A. Arendt.
Foundation for the Family (1986): P.O. Box 111184, Cincinnati, OH 45211; (800) 745-8252; www.ccli.org. Established by Couple to Couple League (see entry above) to provide materials for family not relating to Natural Family Planning, Exec. Dir., Mark Hayden.
Foundations and Donors Interested in Catholic Activities, Inc. (FADICA): 1350 Connecticut Ave. N.W., Suite 303, Washington, DC 20036; (202) 223-3550; www.FADICA.org. A consortium of private foundations providing continuing education and research to members to make church-related philanthropy more effective. Pres., Francis J. Butler.
Franciscan Apostolate of the Way of the Cross (1949): P.O. Box 23, Boston, MA 02112; (617) 542-6659. Distributes religious materials to the sick and shut-in. Dir., Rev. Robert Lynch, O.F.M.
Free The Fathers (1983): 845 Oak St. Chattanooga, TN 37403; (423) 756-9660; www.ftf.org. To work for the freedom of bishops and priests imprisoned in China. Pres., John M. Davies.
Friends of the Holy Land, Inc. (1974): 370 Mile Square Rd., Yonkers, NY 10701. To provide spiritual and material support for the Christian communities in the Holy Land. *Friends of the Holy Land* Newsletter. 300 members. Gen. Dir., Ernest F. Russo.

Gabriel Richard Institute (1949): 3641 Estates Dr., Troy, MI 48084; (248) 643-8887. Conducts Christopher Leadership Course. Exec. Dir., Dolores Ammar.
Guard of Honor of the Immaculate Heart of Mary (1932): 135 West 31st St., New York, NY 10001; (212) 736-8500; www.hnp.org. An archconfraternity approved by the Holy See whose members cultivate devotion to the Blessed Virgin Mary, particularly through a daily Guard Hour of Prayer. Dir., Rev. Cassian A. Miles, O.F.M.

Holy Cross Family Ministries (formerly The Family Rosary, Inc.) (1942): 518 Washington St., North Easton, MA, 02356-1200; (508) 238-4095;

www.hcfm.org. Founded by Father Patrick Peyton, C.S.C. Encourages family prayer, especially the Rosary. Pres., Rev. John Phalen, C.S.C.

Holy Name Society: P.O. Box 12012, Baltimore, MD 21281; (410) 325-1523; www.holynamesociety.info. Founded in 1274 by Blessed John Vercelli, master general of the Dominicans, to promote reverence for the Holy Name of Jesus; this is still the principal purpose of the society, which also develops lay apostolic programs in line with directives of the Second Vatican Council. Introduced in the U.S. in 1870-71 by Dominican Father Charles H. McKenna, the society has about 5 million members on diocesan and parochial levels. With approval of the local bishop and pastor, women as well as men may be members.

Holy Name Society, National Association (NAHNS) (1970): P.O. Box 12012, Baltimore, MD 21281; (410) 276-1166; www.members.aol.com/nahns. Association of diocesan and parochial Holy Name Societies. *Holy Name Newsletter*, monthly.

Hungarian Catholic League of America, Inc. (1945): One Cathedral Sq., Providence, RI 02903-3695; (401) 278-4520. Chair., Rev. Msgr. William I. Varsanyi.

International Catholic Stewardship Council (1962): 1275 K St. N.W., Suite 880, Washington, DC 20005-4083; (800) 352-3452; www.catholicsteward-ship.org. A professional association which fosters an environment in which stewardship is understood, accepted and practiced throughout the church. Moderator, Alex R. Carrion.

International Catholic Charismatic Renewal Services: Palazzo della Cancelleria, 00120 Vatican City; 39 06 698 87538; www.iccrs.org. The ICCRS provides leadership and vision to the Catholic Charismatic Renewal throughout the world in harmony with the Pontifical Council for the Laity which has established ICCRS as a Private Association of the Faithful. See National Catholic Charismatic Renewal Services.

Italian Catholic Federation (1924): 675 Hegenberger Rd., #230, Oakland, CA 94621; (888) 423-1924; www.icf.org. Fraternal organization of Italian-American Catholics. 19,000 members.

John Carroll Society, The (1951): P.O. Box 50188, Washington, DC 20091; (703) 573-3043; www.johncarroll-society.org. Exec. Asst., Mary Ann Dmochowski, Ph.D.

Judean Society, Inc., The (1966): 1075 Space Park Way No. 336, Mountain View, CA 94043.

Knights of Peter Claver (1909), and Knights of Peter Claver, Ladies Auxiliary (1926): 1825 Orleans Ave., New Orleans, LA 70116; (504) 821-4225; www.knightsofpeterclaver.com. Fraternal and aid society. *The Claverite*, biannually. National Chaplain, Most Rev. Curtis J. Guillory, S.V.D.

Knights of St. John, International Supreme Commandery (1886): 89 So. Pine Ave., Albany, N.Y. 12208; (518) 453-5675; www.members.tripod.com/ksji/knights/ksji.html. Supreme Sec., Maj. Gen. Joseph Hauser, Jr.

Ladies of Charity of the United States of America (1960): P.O. Box 31697, St. Louis, MO 63131; (314) 344-1184; www.famvin.org/lcusa. International Association founded by St. Vincent de Paul in 1617. 25,000 members in U.S.; 250,000 worldwide.

Latin Liturgy Association (1975): P. O. Box 3017, Bethlehem, PA, 18017; www.latinliturgy.com. To promote the use of the Latin language and music in the approved rites of the Church. Quarterly journal. 850 members. Pres., James F. Pauer.

Legatus (1987): 30 Frank Lloyd Wright Dr., P.O. Box 997, Ann Arbor, MI 48106; (734) 930-3854. To apply Church's moral teaching in business and personal lives of members. *Legatus Newsletter*, monthly.

LITHUANIAN GROUPS: Ateitininkai, members of Lithuanian Catholic Federation Ateitis (1910), 1209 Country Lane, Lemont, IL 60439. *Ateitis*, bimonthly. Pres., Juozas Polikaitis. **Knights of Lithuania** (1913): Roman Catholic educational-fraternal organization. *Vytis*, monthly. Pres., Evelyn Ozelis, 2533 W. 45th St., Chicago, IL 60632.

Lithuanian Catholic Alliance (1886), 71-73 S. Washington St., Wilkes-Barre, PA 18701. Fraternal insurance organization. Pres., Thomas E. Mack.

Lithuanian Roman Catholic Federation of America (1906): 4545 W. 63rd St., Chicago, IL 60629; (312) 585-9500. Umbrella organization for Lithuanian parishes and organizations. *The Observer*, bimonthly. Pres., Saulius Kuprys.

Lithuanian Catholic Religious Aid, Inc. (1961): 64-25 Perry Ave., Maspeth, NY 11378-2441; (718) 326-5202. To assist Catholics in Lithuania. Chairman and Pres., Most Rev. Paul Baltakis, O.F.M.

Lithuanian Roman Catholic Priests' League (1909): P.O. Box 1025, Humarock, MA 02047-1025; (781) 834-4079. Religious-professional association. Pres., Rev. Albert Contons.

Little Flower Mission League (1957), P.O. Box 25, Plaucheville, LA 71362; (318) 922-3630. Sponsored by the Brothers of the Holy Eucharist. Dir., Bro. André M. Lucia, F.S.E.

Little Flower Society (1923): 1313 Frontage Rd. Darien, IL 60561. 200,000 members. Nat. Dir., Rev. Robert E. Colaresi, O. Carm.

Liturgical Conference, The: 415 Michigan Ave., NE, #65, Washington, DC 20017; (202) 832-6520; www.litconf.org. Liturgy, homily service. Education, research and publication programs for renewing and enriching Christian liturgical life. Ecumenical.

Loyal Christian Benefit Association (1890): P.O. Box 13005, Erie, PA 16514; (814) 453-4331; www.icba.com. Fraternal benefit and insurance society. *The Fraternal Leader,* quarterly. Pres., Jackie Sobania-Robison.

Marian Movement of Priests (1972): P.O. Box 8, St. Francis, ME 04774-0008 (U.S.); (207) 398-3375; www.mmp-usa.net. Via Mercalli, 23, 20122 Milan, Italy (international headquarters). Spiritual renewal through consecration to the Immaculate Heart of Mary. 4,000 clergy members, 53,000 religious and laity (U.S.). Nat. Dir., Rev. Albert G. Roux.

Mariological Society of America (1949): Marian Library, #1390, University of Dayton, Dayton, OH 45469; (937) 229-4214; www.udayton.edu/mary. Founded by Rev. Juniper B. Carol, O.F.M., to promote greater appreciation of and scientific research in Marian theology. Marian Studies, annually. Sec., Rev. Thomas A. Thompson, S.M.

Marriage Encounter, National: 4704 Jamerson Pl., Orlando, FL 32807. The national office of Worldwide Marriage Encounter is located at 2210 East Highland

Ave., #106, San Bernardino, CA 92404; (909) 863-9963. Brings couples together for a weekend program of events directed by a team of several couples and a priest, to develop their abilities to communicate with each other as husband and wife.

Maryheart Crusaders, The (1964): 22 Button St., Meriden, CT 06450; (203) 239-5979; www.maryheartcrusaders.org. Pres., Louise D'Angelo.

Men of the Sacred Heart (1964): National Shrine of the Sacred Heart, P.O. Box 500, Harleigh, PA 18225; (570) 455-1162. Promotes enthronement of Sacred Heart.

Militia Immaculate National Center — Marytown (1917): 1600 W. Park Ave., Libertyville, IL 60048; (847) 367-7800; www.consecration.com. Canonically established with international headquarters in Rome. A pious association to promote total consecration to Mary in the spirit of St. Mximilian Kolbe. Pres., Fr. Patrick Greenough, O.F.M. Conv.

Missionary Association of Catholic Women (1916): 3501 S. Lake Dr., P.O. Box 07212, Milwaukee, WI 53207-0912; (414) 769-3406.

Missionary Vehicle Association, Inc. (MIVA America) (1971): 1400 Michigan Ave., N.E., Washington, DC 20017-7234; (202) 635-3444; www.miva.org. To raise funds and distribute them annually as vehicle grants to missionaries working with the poor in Third World countries. Nat. Dir., Rev. Philip De Rea, M.S.C.; Exec. Dir., Rev. Anthony F. Krisak.

Morality in Media, Inc. (1962): 475 Riverside Dr., Suite 1264, New York, NY 10115; (212) 870-3222; www.moralityinmedia.org. Interfaith national organization. Works by constitutional means to curb the explosive growth of hard-core pornography and to turn back the tide of grossly offensive, indecent media. A major project is the National Obscenity Law Center which provides legal information for prosecutors and other attorneys. Newsletter, bimonthly. Pres., Robert W. Peters.

National Assembly of Religious Women (NARW): 529 S. Wabash Ave., Suite 404, Chicago, IL 60605; (312) 663-1980. Founded as the National Assembly of Women Religious, 1970; title changed, 1980. A movement of feminist women committed to prophetic tasks of giving witness, raising awareness and engaging in public action and advocacy for justice in church and society.

National Association for Lay Ministry (1977): 5420 S. Cornell Ave., Chicago, IL 60615; (773) 241-6050; www.nalm.org. Acts as advocate and support for lay people who respond to a call to ministry in the Church.

National Association of Catholic Family Life Ministers: 300 College Park, Dayton, OH 45469; (937) 229-3324; www.nacflm.org. Strives to be a voice and advocate for families and family ministry in Church and society. Exec. Dir., David Abele.

National Association of Catholic Home Educators (1993): 6102 Saints Hill Lane, Broad Run, VA 20137; (540) 349-4314; www.nache.com. Promotion of home-schooling. *The Catholic Home Educator*, quarterly.

National Association of Church Personnel Administrators (1971): 100 E. 8th St., Cincinnati, OH 45202; (513) 421-3134; www.nacpa.org. Association for human resource and personnel directors dedicated to promotion and development of just personnel practices for all church employees. Exec.

Dir., Sr. Ellen Doyle, O.S.U.

National Association of Diaconate Directors: 1204 N. Church St., Rockford, IL 61103; (815) 965-0075. Deacon Thomas C. Welch, Exec. Dir.

National Association of Diocesan Ecumenical Officers: 7800 Kenrick Rd., St. Louis, MO 63119; (314) 961-4320. Network of Catholics involved in ecumenical and interreligious work. Pres., Vincent A. Heier.

National Association of Pastoral Musicians (1976): 962 Wayne Ave., Suite 210, Silver Spring, MD 20910; (240) 247-3000; www.npm.org. 9,000 members. Dedicated to fostering the art of musical liturgy. *Pastoral Music*, six times a year. Exec. Dir., Dr. J. Michael McMahon.

National Association of Priest Pilots (1964): 481 N. Shore Dr., Apt. 301, Clear Lake IA 50428-1368; (641) 357-4539. Pres., Rev. Msgr. John Hemann.

National Catholic AIDS Network: P.O. Box 422984, San Francisco, CA 94142; (707) 874-3031; www.ncan.org. Exec. dir., Rev. Rodney DeMartini; Board Pres., Rev. Robert J. Vitillo.

National Catholic Band Association (1953): 3334 N. Normandy, Chicago, IL 60634; (773) 282-9153; www.catholicbands.org.

National Catholic Conference for Interracial Justice (NCCIJ) (1960): 1200 Varnum St. N.E., Washington, DC 20017; (202) 529-6480. Exec. Dir., Rev. Mr. Joseph M. Conrad, Jr.

National Catholic Conference for Seafarers: 4219 Constance St., New Orleans, LA 70115; (504) 891-6677. Association of chaplains and laity serving in the pastoral care of seafarers.

National Catholic Council on Alcoholism and Related Drug Problems, Inc.: 1550 Hendrickson St., Brooklyn, NY 11234-3514; (718) 951-7177; P.O. Box 248, Lafayette, IN 47902-0248; (765) 420-0129; www.nccatoday.com. An affiliate of the USCCB. Committed to assisting members in a greater awareness of alcoholism, other chemical addictions and prevention issues. Exec. Dir., Thomas A. Russell.

National Catholic Development Conference (1968): 86 Front St., Hempstead, NY 11550; (516) 481-6000. Professional association of organizations and individuals engaged in raising funds for Catholic charitable activities. Pres., Sr. Georgette Lehmuth, O.S.F.

National Catholic Ministry to the Bereaved (NCMB) (1990): 28700 Euclid Ave., Wickliffe, OH, 44092-2527; (440) 943-3480; www.griefwork.org. Offers ongoing education, resources and assistance to dioceses, parishes and caregivers in their ministry to the bereaved. Pres., Sr. Maureen O'Brien, O.P.

National Catholic Pharmacists Guild of the United States (1962): 1012 Surrey Hills Dr., St. Louis, MO 63117; (314) 645-0085. *The Catholic Pharmacist*. Co-Pres., Exec. Dir. and Editor, John P. Winkelmann.

National Catholic Society of Foresters (1891): 320 S. School St., Mt. Prospect, IL 60056; (847) 342-4500; www.ncsf@enteract.com. A fraternal insurance society. *National Catholic Forester*, quarterly. National Pres., Mary Rausch.

National Catholic Women's Union (1916): 3835 Westminster Pl., St. Louis, MO 63108; (314) 371-1653; www.socialjusticereview.org. 7,000 members.

National Center for the Laity (1977): P.O. Box 291102, Chicago, IL 60629; (708) 974-5221; www.catholiclabor.org/ncl.htm. To promote and implement the vision of Vatican II: That the laity are the Church in the modern world as they attend to their occupational, family and neighborhood responsibilities. *Initiatives*, six times a year.

National Center for Urban Ethnic Affairs (1971): P.O. Box 20, Cardinal Station, Washington, DC 20064; (202) 319-6188. Research and action related to the Church's concern for cultural pluralism and urban neighborhoods. An affiliate of the USCCB. Pres., Dr. John A. Kromkowski.

National Christ Child Society Inc. (1887): 6900 Wisconsin Ave. N.W., Suite 604, Bethesda, MD 20815;   (800)   814-2149; www.NationalChristChildSoc.org. Founder, Mary V. Merrick. A non-profit Catholic association of volunteers of all denominations dedicated to the service of needy children and youth regardless of race or creed. Approximately 7,000 adult members in 38 chapters in U.S. Exec. Dir., Margaret Saffell.

National Committee of Catholic Laymen, The (1977): 215 Lexington Ave., Fourth Floor, New York, NY 10016; (212) 685-6666. Lobbying and publishing organization representing "orthodox" Catholics who strongly support Pope John Paul II. *Catholic Eye*, monthly; editor, Mrs. Anne Conlon.

National Conference of Catechetical Leadership (formerly, National Conference of Diocesan Directors of Religious Education) (1936): 3021 4th St. N.E., Washington, DC 20017; (202) 636-3826. To promote catechetical ministry at the national diocesan and parish levels. 1,300 members. Exec. Dir., Neil A. Parent.

National Conference of Catholic Airport Chaplains (1986): P.O. Box 66353, Chicago, IL 60666; (773) 686-2636. Provides support and communication for Catholics performing pastoral ministry to airport and airline workers and Catholic travelers; affiliated with Bishops' Committee on Migration, USCCB. Pres., Deacon James A. O'Malley, D.Min.

National Conference of Diocesan Vocation Directors (NCDVD) (1961): P.O. Box 1570, Little River, SC 29566; (843) 280-7191. Professional organization for diocesan vocation personnel providing resources and on-going education in their promoting, assessing and forming of candidates for the diocesan priesthood.

National Council for Catholic Evangelization (1983): 415 Michigan Ave, NE, Suite 90, Washington, DC, 20017; 1-800-786-NCCE; www.catholicevangelization.org. To promote evangelization as the "primary and essential mission of the Church," in accordance with *Evangelii Nuntiandi*, the 1975 apostolic exhortation of Pope Paul VI. Exec. Dir., Sr. Priscilla Lemire, R.J.M.

National Council of Catholic Women (1920): 200 N. Glebe Rd., Suite 703, Arlington, VA 22203; (703) 224-0990; www.nccw.org. A federation of some 7,000 organizations of Catholic women in the U.S. NCCW unites Catholic organizations and individual Catholic women of the U.S., develops their leadership potential, assists them to act upon current issues in the Church and society, provides a medium through which Catholic women may speak and act upon matters of common interest, and relates to other national and international organizations in the solution of present-day problems. It is an affiliate of the World Union of Catholic Women's Organizations. *Catholic Woman*, bimonthly. Exec. Dir., Sheila McCarron.

National Evangelization Teams (NET): 110 Crusader Ave., West St. Paul, MN 55118-4427; (651) 450-6833; www.netusa.org. Trains Catholic young adults to be evangelists to peers and high school/junior high youth through traveling retreat teams.

National Federation of Catholic Physicians' Guilds (1927): P.O. Box 757, Pewaukee, WI 53072; (262) 523-6201; www.cathmed.com. *Linacre Quarterly*. Exec. Dir., Robert H. Herzog.

National Federation of Priests' Councils (1968): 1337 West Ohio, Chicago, IL 60622-6490; (312) 226-3334; www.nfpc.org. To give priests' councils a representative voice in matters of presbyteral, pastoral and ministerial concern to the U.S. and the universal Church. *Touchstone*, quarterly. Pres., Rev. Donald J. Wolf; Exec. Dir., Bro. Bernard Stratman, S.M.

National Institute for the Word of God (1972): 487 Michigan Ave. N.E., Washington, DC 20017; (202) 529-0001; www.niwg.op.org/niwg. For renewed biblical preaching, Bible sharing and evangelization. Dir., Rev. John Burke, O.P.

National Life Center, Inc.: 686 N. Broad St., Woodbury, NJ 08096; (856) 848-1819, (800) 848-LOVE; www.nationallifecenter.com. Interdenominational guidance and referral service organization offering pregnant women alternatives to abortion. Pres., Denise F. Cocciolone.

National Organization for Continuing Education of Roman Catholic Clergy, Inc. (1973): 1337 W. Ohio St., Chicago, IL 60622; (312) 226-1890. Membership: 152 dioceses, 66 religious provinces, 46 institutions, 49 individuals in U.S., 18 associates outside U.S. Pres., Rev. Francis S. Tebbe, O.F.M.

National Pastoral Life Center: 18 Bleecker St., New York, NY 10012-2404; (212) 431-7825; www.nplc.org. *Church*, quarterly. Dir., Msgr. Philip Murnion.

National Service Committee of the Catholic Charismatic Renewal: Charismcenter USA, P.O. Box 628, Locust Grove, VA 22508; (540) 972-0225; www.nsc-hariscenter.org, www.iccrs.org. The mission of the National Service Committee is "to stir into flame the grace of Pentecost within and beyond the Church, to broaden and deepen the understanding that baptism in the Holy Spirit is the Christian inheritance of all, and to strengthen the Catholic Charismatic Renewal." Exec. Dir., Walter Matthews.

NETWORK, A Catholic Social Justice Lobby (1971): 22 E St. NW, Suite 200, Washington, DC 20001; (202) 347-9797; www.networklobby.org. A national Catholic social justice lobby. *NETWORK Connection*, bimonthly. Exec. Dir., Simone Campbell.

Nocturnal Adoration Society of the United States (1882): 184 E. 76th St., New York, NY 10021; (212) 288-5082. Nat. Dir., Rev. Mario Marzocchi, S.S.S.

North American Academy of Liturgy: c/o CSSR Executive Office, Valparaiso University, Valparaiso, IN 46383. Foster ecumenical and interreligious liturgical research, publication and dialogue on a scholarly level. Proceedings, annually. Pres., Alan Barthel.

North American Conference of Separated and

Divorced Catholics (1972): P.O. Box 360, Richland, OR 97870; (541) 893-6089; www.nacsdc.com. Exec. Dir., Irene Varley.

North American Forum on the Catechumenate: 125 Michigan Ave. NE, Washington, DC 20017; (202) 884-9758; www.naforum.org. An international network committed to the implementation of the Order of Christian Initiation of Adults. Exec. Dir., James Schellman.

Order of the Alhambra (1904): 4200 Leeds Ave., Baltimore, MD 21229; (410) 242-0660; www.OrderAlhambra.org. Fraternal society dedicated to assisting developmentally disabled and handicapped children. 7,000 members in U.S. and Canada.Exec. Dir., Roger J. Reid.

Our Lady's Rosary Makers (1949): 4611 Poplar Level Rd., Louisville, KY 40233; www.olrm.org. To supply missionaries with free rosaries for distribution throughout the world. *News Bulletin*, monthly. Pres., Michael Ford.

Paulist National Catholic Evangelization Association (1977): 3031 Fourth St., N.E., Washington, DC 20017-1102; (202) 832-5022; www.pncea.org. To work with unchurched and alienated Catholics; to develop, test and document contemporary ways in which Catholic parishes and dioceses can evangelize the unchurched and inactive Catholics. Share the Word, bimonthly magazine; Evangelization Update, bimonthly newsletter. Dir., Rev. Kenneth Boyack, C.S.P.

Philangeli (Friends of the Angels) (1949 in England; 1956 in U.S.): Viatorian Fathers, 1115 E. Euclid St., Arlington Heights, IL 60004.

Pious Union of Prayer (1898): St. Joseph's Home, P.O. Box 288, Jersey City, NJ 07303; (201) 798-4141. *St. Joseph's Messenger* and *Advocate of the Blind*, quarterly.

Polish Roman Catholic Union of America (1887): 984 N. Milwaukee Ave., Chicago, IL 60622; (773) 728-2600; www.prcua.org. Fraternal benefit society. *Narod Polski*, bimonthly. Sec.-Treas. Josephine Szarowicz.

Pontifical Mission for Palestine (1949): 1011 First Ave., New York, NY 10022-4195; (212) 826-1480; www.cnewa.org. A papal relief and development agency of the Holy See for the Middle East, with offices in New York, Vatican City, Amman, Beirut and Jerusalem. Pres., Msgr. Archim; Robert L. Stern, J.C.D.

Pontifical Mission Societies (1916): 366 Fifth Ave., New York, NY 10001; (212) 563-8700; www.world-missions-catholicchurch.org. To promote mission awareness among clergy, religious, candidates, and others engaged in pastoral ministry. Nat. Dir., Msgr. John Kozar.

Population Research Institute (1989): 1190 Progress Drive, Suite 2D, P.O. Box 1559, Front Royal, VA 22630; (540) 622-5240; www.pop.org. Non-profit research and educational organization dedicated to objectively presenting the truth about population-related issues. *PRI Review*, a bimonthly newsletter, which reports on population news of interest from around the world. Pres., Steven W. Mosher.

Priests' Eucharistic League (1887): 5384 Wilson Mills Rd., Highland Heights, OH 44143. *Emmanuel*, 10 issues a year. Nat. Dir., Very Rev. Norman Pelletier, S.S.S.

Pro Ecclesia Foundation (1970): 350 Fifth Ave., New York, NY 10118. *Pro Ecclesia Magazine*. Pres., Dr. Timothy A. Mitchell.

ProLife Across America (1989): P.O. Box 18669, Minneapolis, MN 55418; (612) 781-0410; www.prolifeacrossamerica.org. A non-profit organization that uses various media to promote the culture of life. Contact: Mary Ann Kuharski.

Pro Maria Committee (1952): 112 Norris Rd. Tyngsboro, MA 01879; (978) 649-1813. Promotes devotion to Our Lady of Beauraing (see Index).

Pro Sanctity Movement: Pro Sanctity Spirituality Center, 205 S. Pine Dr., Fullerton, CA 92833; (714) 956-1020. 730 E. 87th St., Brooklyn, NY 11236, (718) 649-0324. 6762 Western Ave., Omaha, NE 68132; (402) 553-4418. 1102 N. 204 St. Elkhorn, NE 68022; (402) 289-2670; www.prosanctity.org. Organized to spread God's call of all persons to holiness.

Project Children (1975): P.O. Box 933, Greenwood Lake, NY 10925; (845) 477-3472; www.interwebinc.com/children. Nonsectarian volunteer group; provides children of Northern Ireland with a six-week summer vacation with host families in the U.S.

The Providence Association of the Ukrainian Catholics in America (Ukrainian Catholic Fraternal Benefit Society) (1912): 817 N. Franklin St., Philadelphia, PA 19123; (215) 627-4984.

Queen of the Americas Guild, Inc. (1979): P.O. Box 851, St. Charles, IL 60174; (630) 584-1822; www.queenoftheamericasguild.org. To build English information center and retreat center near Basilica in Mexico City and spread the message of Guadalupe. 7,000 members. Nat. Coord. Rebecca Nichols.

Raskob Foundation for Catholic Activities, Inc. (1945): P.O. Box 4019, Wilmington, DE 19807-0019; (302) 655-4440; www.rfca.org. Exec. Pres., Frederick Perella, Jr.

Reparation Society of the Immaculate Heart of Mary, Inc. (1946): 100 E. 20th St., Baltimore, MD 21218. *Fatima Findings*, monthly.

Retrouvaille: P.O.Box 25, Kelton, PA 19346. A ministry to hurting marriages, Retrouvaille consists of a weekend experience with follow-up sessions designed to provide couples with ways and means of healing and reconciling. Emphasis is placed on communication, enabling husband and wife to rediscover each other and to examine their lives in a new and positive way. The ministry is neither a retreat nor a sensitivity group, nor does it include group dynamics or discussions. The program is conducted by trained couples and priests, with programs offered under the auspices of diocesan family life agencies. International Coordinating Team: Bill and Peg Swaan.

Sacred Heart League: 6050 Hwy 61 N, P.O. Box 190, Walls, MS 38680. Pres., Rev. Robert Hess, S.C.J.

St. Ansgar's Scandinavian Catholic League (1910): 3 East 28th St., New York, NY 10016; (212) 675-0400. Prayers and financial support for Church in Scandinavia. *St. Ansgar's Bulletin*, annually. 1,000 members. Pres., Astrid M. O'Brien.

St. Anthony's Guild (1924): P.O. 2948, Paterson, NJ

07509-2948; (973) 777-3737. Promotes devotion to St. Anthony of Padua and support for formation programs, infirm friars and ministries of the Franciscans of Holy Name Province. *The Anthonian*, quarterly. Dir., Fr. Joseph Hertel, O.F.M.

St. Bernadette Institute of Sacred Art (1993): P.O. Box 8249, Albuquerque, NM 87198-8249; (505) 265-9126; www.nmia.com/~paulos. To promote, initiate, encourage interest and sustain projects and persons engaged in sacred art.

St. Gregory Foundation for Latin Liturgy (1989): Newman House, 601 Buhler Ct., Pine Beach, NJ 08741; (732) 914-1222. To promote within the Church in the U.S. the use of the Latin language in the Mass in accordance with the teachings of Vatican II. Founder and Pres., Rev. Peter M.J. Stravinskas, Ph.D., S.T.D.

St. Jude League (1929): 205 W. Monroe St., Chicago, IL 60606; (312) 236-7782; www.stjudeleague.org. Promotes devotion to St. Jude; supports work of Claretian Missionaries throughout the world. Dir., Rev. Mark J. Brummel, C.M.F.

St. Margaret of Scotland Guild, Inc. (1938): Graymoor, P.O. Box 300, Garrison, NY 10524-0300; (845) 424-3671. Moderator, Bro. Pius MacIsaac.

St. Martin de Porres Guild (1935): 141 E. 65th St., New York, NY 10021; (212) 744-2410; www.op-stjoseph.org. Dir., Rev. Raymond F. Halligan, O.P.

Serra International (1934): 220 S. State St., Suite 1703, Chicago, IL 60604; (312) 588-0700; www.serrainternational.org. Fosters vocations to the priesthood, and religious life, trains Catholic lay leadership. Formally aggregated to the Pontifical Society for Priestly Vocations, 1951. *Serran*, bimonthly. 21,000 members in 673 clubs in 35 countries. Exec. Dir., John W. Woodward.

Slovak Catholic Federation (1911): 408 North Main St., Taylor, PA 18517-1108; (570) 562-1341; www.slovakcatholicfederation.org. Founded by Rev. Joseph Murgas to promote and coordinate religious activities among Slovak Catholic fraternal societies, religious communities and Slovak ethnic parishes in their effort to address themselves to the special needs of Slovak Catholics in the U.S. and Canada. Pres., Rev. Philip A. Altavilla.

Slovak Catholic Sokol (1905): 205 Madison St., Passaic, NJ 07055; (973) 777-2606; www.slovakcatholicsokol.org. Fraternal benefit society. *Slovak Catholic Falcon*, weekly. 38,000 members.

Society for the Propagation of the Faith (1822): 366 Fifth Ave., New York, NY 10001; (212) 563-8700; www.worldmissions-catholic-church.org. Established in all dioceses. Church's principal instrument for promoting mission awareness and generating financial support for the missions. General fund for ordinary and extraordinary subsidies for all mission dioceses. Is subject to Congregation for the Evangelization of Peoples. Mission, four times a year; *Director's Newsletter*, monthly. Nat. Dir., Rev. John Kozar.

Society of St. Monica (1986): 215 Falls Ave., Cuyahoga Falls, OH 44221. Confident, daily prayer for the return of inactive Catholics and Catholics who have left the Church. More than 10,000 members worldwide. Founder and Spir. Dir., Rev. Dennis M. McNeil.

Society of St. Peter Apostle (1889): 366 Fifth Ave., New York, NY 10001; (212) 563-8700; www.world-missions-catholicchurch.org. Church's central fund for

support of seminaries, seminarians and novices in all mission dioceses. Nat. Dir., Msgr. John Kozar.

Society of the Divine Attributes (1974): 2905 Castlegate Ave., Pittsburgh, PA 15226; (412) 456-3114. Contemplative prayer society. 3,000 members worldwide (lay, clerical and religious). Spir. Dir. Rev. Ronald D. Lawler, O.F.M. Cap.

Spiritual Life Institute of America (1960): Box 219, Crestone, CO 81131; (719) 256-4778; www.spirituallifeinstitute.org. An eremetical movement to foster the contemplative spirit in America. *Forefront*, seasonal. Founder, Rev. William McNamara, O.C.D. Second foundation: Nova Nada, Primitive Wilderness Hermitage, Kemptville, Nova Scotia, Canada B0W 1Y0. Third foundation, Holy Hill Hermitage, Skreen, Co. Sligo, Ireland.

Support Our Aging Religious (SOAR) (1986): 1400 Spring St., Suite 320, Silver Spring, MD 20910-2755; (301) 589-9811; www.soar-usa.org. Laity-led campaign to raise funds for retired religious. Pres., Timothy P. Hamer.

Theresians of the United States (1961): 1237 W. Monroe St., Springfield, IL 62704; (217) 726-5484; www.theresians.org. Spiritual, educational and ministerial organization of Christian women. Exec. Dir., Victoria S. Schmidt. International division: Theresian World Ministry (1971), same address.

United Societies of U.S.A. (1903): 613 Sinclair St., McKeesport, PA 15132. *Prosvita-Enlightenment*, bimonthly newspaper. 3,755 members.

United States Catholic Historical Society (1884): St. Joseph's Seminary, 201 Seminary Ave., Yonkers, NY 10704; (914) 337-8381; www.uschs.com. Exec. Vice-Pres., John T. Gildea.

Western Catholic Union (1877): 510 Maine St., Quincy, IL 62301; (800) 223-4928; www.wculife.com. 19,000 members. A fraternal benefit society. *Western Catholic Union Record*, quarterly. Pres., Mark A. Wiewel.

Women for Faith and Family (1984): P.O. Box 8326, St. Louis, MO 63132; (314) 863-8385; www.wf-f.org. An international movement to promote Catholic teachings especially on all issues involving the family and roles for women. 60,000 signers worldwide of the Affirmation for Catholic Women. Members sign an eight-point statement of fidelity to the Church. *Voices*, quarterly. Dir., Helen Hull Hitchcock.

Word on Fire (1999): 1167 Asbury Ave, Winnetka, IL 60093; (847) 224-4670; www.wordonfire.org; a global media organization in support of Catholic evangelical preaching, particularly the work of Father Robert Barron. Contact: Nancy Ross.

World Apostolate of Fatima, USA (The Blue Army of Our Lady of Fatima, 1947): P.O. Box 976, Washington, NJ 07882; (908) 689-1700; www.bluearmy.com. Soul, bimonthly; Hearts Aflame, quarterly. U.S. branch of the World Apostolate of Fatima. Promote the Fatima Message. Fatima shrine. Exec. Dir.: Michael La Corte.

Young Ladies' Institute (1887): 1111 Gough St., San Francisco, CA 94109-6606; (415) 346-4367. *Voice of YLI*, bimonthly. 13,000 members. Grand Sec., Dolores Williams.

Young Men's Institute (1883): 1625 "C" Palmetto Ave., Pacifica, CA 94044; (650) 738-3007; www.ymiusa.org. *Institute Journal*, bimonthly. 4,500 members. Grand Sec., Clifford C. Smethurst.

PERSONAL PRELATURE OF THE HOLY SEE: OPUS DEI

Founded in Madrid in 1928 by Msgr. Josemaría Escrivá de Balaguer (beatified in 1992 and canonized in October 2002), Opus Dei has the aim of spreading throughout all sectors of society a profound awareness of the universal call to holiness and apostolate (of Christian witness and action) in the ordinary circumstances of life, and, more specifically, through one's professional work. On Nov. 28, 1982, Pope John Paul II established Opus Dei as a personal prelature with the full title, Prelature of the Holy Cross and Opus Dei. The 2008 edition of the *Annuario Pontificio* reported that the prelature had 1,956 priests (37 newly ordained) and 351 major seminarians. Also, there were 86,305 lay persons — men and women, married and single, of every class and social condition — of about 80 nationalities, as well as 1,828 churches and pastoral centers.

Further, the prelature operates the Pontifical University of the Holy Cross in Rome; it was established in 1985 and received approval as a pontifical institution in 1995. Courses of study include theology, philosophy, canon law, and the recently established School of Social Communications.

In the United States, members of Opus Dei, along with cooperators and friends, conduct apostolic works corporately in major cities in the East and Midwest, Texas and on the West Coast. Elsewhere, corporate works include universities, vocational institutes, training schools for farmers and numerous other apostolic initiatives. Opus Dei information offices are located at: 99 Overlook Cir., New Rochelle, NY 10804; (914) 235-6128 (office of the New York chaplain); and 655 Levering Ave., Los Angeles, CA 90024; (310) 208-0941; www.opusdei.org.

KNIGHTS OF COLUMBUS

The Knights of Columbus, a fraternal benefit society of Catholic men, is a family service organization founded by Fr. Michael J. McGivney and chartered by the General Assembly of Connecticut on Mar. 29, 1882. Currently, there are over 1.76 million Knights, more than ever before in the Order's history. Together with their families, the Knights are nearly 6 million strong. From the first local council in New Haven, the Order has grown to more than 13,485 councils in the United States, Canada, Mexico, the Philippines, Puerto Rico, Cuba, the Dominican Republic, Panama, the Virgin Islands, Guatemala, Guam, Saipan, and Poland.

In keeping with their general purpose to be of service to the Church, the Knights and their families are active in many apostolic works and community programs. The Knights cooperate with the U.S. bishops in

pro-life activities and are engaged in other apostolic endeavors as well.

According to the 2008 survey, "Building a Civilization of Love Through Charity, Unity and Fraternity," the Knights raised and donated a record $144.9 million to charity and volunteered more than 68 million hours of service. The total contributions of state and local units were $113 million.

Over the past decade, Knights have donated a grand total of more than 612 million volunteer hours to charitable causes. And the value of that volunteer time, using Independent Sector estimates, is over $10.4 billion.

The Knights of Columbus headquarters address is One Columbus Plaza, New Haven, CT 06510-3326; (203) 752-4350; www.kofc.org. The Grand Knight is Carl Anderson.

REGNUM CHRISTI

Regnum Christi is a lay ecclesial movement associated with the Legionaries of Christ and founded in 1959 Fr. Marcial Maciel, L.C. The Regnum Christi Movement includes lay men and women, as well as deacons and priests, and works to spread Christ's message to humanity by undertaking personal, organized apostolic activity. Its motto is "Love Christ, Serve People, Build the Church." The statutes for the movement were first written by Fr. Maciel and given formal approval on November 25, 2004 by Pope John Paul II. Significantly, the pontiff chose to approve the statutes

on the 60th anniversary of Fr. Maciel's ordination.

Members of Regnum Christi are committed to daily prayers and meditation, weekly meetings, and annual retreats. In addition, they asked to assist the Church through a variety of apostolates including Youth for the Third Millennium, Compass, Helping Hands Medical Missions, Familia, Catholic Kids' Net, Conquest, Challenge, and Pure Fashion.

Contact: R.C. Inquiries, P.O. Box 5425, Hamden, CT 06518-0425; www.regnumchristi.org.

Catholic Social Services

Catholic Charities USA (formerly National Conference of Catholic Charities): 1731 King St., Suite 200, Alexandria, VA 22314; (703) 549-1390; www.catholiccharitiesusa.org. Founded in 1910 by Most Rev. Thomas J. Shahan and Rt. Rev. Msgr. William J. Kerby in cooperation with lay leaders of the Society of St. Vincent de Paul to help advance and promote the charitable programs and activities of Catholic community and social service agencies in the United States. As the central and national organization for this purpose, it services a network of more than 1,400 agencies and institutions by consultation, information and assistance in planning and evaluating social service programs under Catholic auspices.

Diocesan member agencies provide shelter, food, counseling, services to children, teen parents and the elderly, and a variety of other services to people in need — without regard to religion, gender, age or national origin. Each year millions of people receive help from Catholic Charities; in 2005 (the latest statistics available), more than $32 million were spent in activities by Catholic Charities agencies. In addition, Catholic Charities is an advocate for persons and families in need.

Catholic Charities USA serves members through national and regional meetings, training programs, literature and social policy advocacy on the national level. It is charged by the U.S. bishops with responding to disasters in this country. Catholic Charities USA's president represents North America before *Caritas Internationalis*, the international conference of Catholic Charities, and thus maintains contact with the Catholic Charities movement throughout the world. Publications include *Charities USA*, a quarterly membership magazine, and a directory of U.S. Catholic Charities agencies and institutions. Pres., Rev. Larry Snyder.

Society of St. Vincent de Paul, Council of the United States (originally called the Conference of Charity): National Council, 58 Progress Parkway, St. Louis, MO 63043; (314) 576-3993; www. svdpusa.org. An association of Catholic lay men and women devoted to personal service to the poor through the spiritual and corporal works of mercy. The first conference was formed at Paris in 1833 by Bl. Frederic Ozanam and his associates.

The first conference in the U.S. was organized in 1845 at St. Louis. There are now approximately 4,400 units of the society in this country, with a membership of more than 60,000. The society operates world wide in more than 130 countries and has more than 800,000 members.

Besides person-to-person assistance, increasing emphasis is being given to stores and rehabilitation workshops of the society through which persons with marginal income can purchase refurbished goods at minimal cost. Handicapped persons are employed in renovating goods and store opera-

tions. The society also operates food centers, shelters, criminal justice and other programs. Publications include *The Ozanam News*, a biannual membership magazine, and *The United States Councilor*, a quarterly newsletter. Exec. Dir., Roger Playwin.

Catholic Health Association of the United States (CHA): National Headquarters, 4455 Woodson Road, St. Louis, MO 63134; (314) 427-2500; www.chausa.org. Represents more than 1,200 Catholic-sponsored facilities and organizations, works with its members to promote justice and compassion in healthcare, influence public policy, shape a continuum of care through integrated delivery, and strengthen ministry presence and influence in the U.S. healthcare system. CHA supports and strengthens the Catholic health ministry by being a catalyst through research and development (leading edge tools for sustaining a faith-based ministry in price competitive markets), education and facilitation (annual assembly, conferences, and other methods for engaging the ministry), and advocacy (a united ministry voice for public policy). CHA members make up the nation's largest group of not-for-profit healthcare facilities under a single form of sponsorship. Pres., Sr.Carol Keehan, DC.

National Association of Catholic Chaplains: 3501 S. Lake Dr., Milwaukee, WI 53207; (414) 483-4898. Founded in 1965. Membership is over 3,500.

SOCIAL SERVICE ORGANIZATIONS

(See separate article for a listing of facilities for the handicapped.)

The Carroll Center for the Blind (formerly the Catholic Guild for All the Blind): 770 Centre St., Newton, MA 02458; (617) 969-6200; www.carroll. org. The center conducts diagnostic evaluation and rehabilitation programs for blind people over 16 years of age, and provides computer training and other services. Pres., Rachel Rosenbaum.

International Catholic Deaf Association: 8002 S. Sawyer Rd., Darian, IL 60561; TTY (630) 887-9472. Established by deaf adults in Toronto, Canada, in 1949, the association has more than 8,000 members in 130 chapters, mostly in the U.S. It is the only international lay association founded and controlled by deaf Catholic adults. The ICDA publishes *The Deaf Catholic*, bimonthly, sponsors regional conferences, workshops and an annual convention. Pres., Kathleen Kush.

National Apostolate for Inclusion Ministry (NAfIM): P.O. Box 218, Riverdale, MD, 20738; (301) 699-9500; www.nafim.org. Formerly known as the National Apostolate for Persons with Mental Retardation (NAPMR). Established in 1968 to promote the full participation by persons with mental retardation in the life of the Church. Exec. Dir., Barbara Lampe.

National Catholic Office for the Deaf: 7202

Buchanan St., Landover Hills, MD 20784; (301) 577-1684; www.ncod.org. Formally established in 1971, at Washington, DC, to provide pastoral service to those who teach deaf children and adults, to the parents of deaf children, to pastors of deaf persons, and to organizations of the deaf. Publishes *Vision*, a quarterly magazine. Exec. Dir., Consuelo Wild.

National Catholic Office Partnership on Disability (NCPD): 415 Michigan Ave., N.E., Suite 240, Washington, DC 20017; (202) 529-2933; www.ncpd.org. NCPD's mission is to provide resources and consultation to a national network of diocesan directors who oversee access and inclusion at the parish level; to collaborate with other national Catholic organizations, advocating for inclusion within all their programs and initiatives and to work with Catholic organizations addressing the concerns and needs of those with various disabilities. Established in 1982 as a result of the 1978 Pastoral Statement of the U.S. Catholic Bishops on People with Disabilities., the office continues to press for words and actions which promote meaningful participation and inclusion at all levels of the Church. Exec. Dir., Mary Jane Owen, M.S.W.

Xavier Society for the Blind: 154 E. 23rd St., New York, NY 10010-4595; (212) 473-7800. Founded in 1900 by Rev. Joseph Stadelman, S.J., it is a center for publications for the blind and partially sighted. Acting Dir., Kathleen Lynch.

OTHER SOCIAL SERVICES

Cancer Hospitals or Homes: The following homes or hospitals specialize in the care of cancer patients. Capacities are in parentheses.

Our Lady of Perpetual Help Home, Servants of Relief for Incurable Cancer, 760 Pollard Blvd., S.W., Atlanta, GA 30315; (404) 688-9515 (52).

Rose Hawthorne Lathrop Home, Servants of Relief for Incurable Cancer, 1600 Bay St., Fall River, MA 02724; (508) 673-2322 (35).

Our Lady of Good Counsel Home, Servants of Relief for Incurable Cancer, 2076 St. Anthony Ave., St. Paul, MN 55104; (651) 646-2797.

Calvary Hospital, Inc., 1740 Eastchester Rd., Bronx, NY 10461; (718) 863-6900 (200). Operated in connection with Catholic Charities, Department of Health and Hospitals, Archdiocese of New York.

St. Rose's Home, Servants of Relief for Incurable Cancer, 71 Jackson St., New York, NY 10002; (212) 677-8132 (60).

Rosary Hill Home, Servants of Relief for Incurable Cancer, 600 Linda Ave., Hawthorne, NY 10532; (914) 769-0114 (72).

Holy Family Home, Servants of Relief for Incurable Cancer, 6753 State Rd., Parma, OH 44134; (440) 845-7700; www.cle-dioc.org (50).

Sacred Heart Free Home for Incurable Cancer, Servants of Relief for Incurable Cancer, 1315 W. Hunting Park Ave., Philadelphia, PA 19140; (215) 329-3222 (45).

Substance Abuse: Facilities for substance abuse (alcohol and other drugs) include:

Daytop Village, Inc., 54 W. 40th St., New York, NY 10018; (212) 354-6000; www.daytop.org. Twenty-eight residential and ambulatory sites in New York, New Jersey, Pennsylvania, Florida, Texas and California. Msgr. William B. O'Brien, president.

Good Shepherd Gracenter, Convent of the Good

Shepherd, 1310 Bacon St., San Francisco, CA 94134; (415) 586-2822. Residential program for chemically dependent women.

New Hope Manor, 35 Hillside Rd., Barryville, NY 12719; fax (914) 557-6603. Residential substance abuse treatment center for teen-age girls and women ages 13-40. Residential; half-way house and aftercare program totaling 6 months or more.

St. Joseph's Hospital, L.E. Phillips Libertas Center for the Chemically Dependent, 2661 County Road, Hwy. I, Chippewa Falls, WI 54729; (715) 723-1811 (46). Residential and outpatient. Adult and adolescent programs. Hospital Sisters of the Third Order of St. Francis.

St. Joseph's Hospital (Chippewa Falls, WI) Libertas Center for the Treatment of Chemical Dependency, 1701 Dousman St., Green Bay, WI 54302 (23). Residential and outpatient adolescent programs. Hospital Sisters of the Third Order of St. Francis.

St. Luke's Addiction Recovery Services, 7707 NW 2nd Ave., Miami, FL 33150; (305) 795-0077; www.catholiccharitiesadm.org/stluke. A program of Catholic Community Services, Miami. Adult residential and family outpatient recovery services for drug, alcohol addiction and DUI.

Miami Substance Abuse Prevention Programs, 7707 N.W. Second Ave., Miami, FL 33150; (305) 795-0077; www.catholiccharitiesadm.org/stluke. Trains parents, youth, priests and teachers as prevention volunteers in the area of substance abuse.

Transitus House, 1830 Wheaton St., Chippewa Falls, WI 54729; (715) 723-1155. Two programs for chemically dependent: adult intensive residential (15 beds, women); adolescent intensive residential (5 beds, girls 15-18 yrs.). Hospital Sisters of the Third Order of St. Francis.

Matt Talbot Inn, 2270 Professor Ave., Cleveland, OH 44113; (216) 781-0288. Two programs: Chemical dependency Residential Treatment/Halfway House (capacity 27) and outpatient treatment/aftercare. Serves male clients 18 years and over.

Sacred Heart Rehabilitation Center, Inc., 2203 St. Antoine, Detroit, MI 48201 (admissions/assessment, outpatient). 400 Stoddard Rd., P.O. Box 41038, Memphis, MI 48041 (12 beds, detoxification; 70 beds residential treatment). 28573 Schoenherr, Warren, MI 48093 (outpatient). All facilities serve male and female clients 18 and over.

Straight and Narrow, Inc., 396 Straight St., Paterson, NJ 07501. Facilities and services include (at various locations): Straight and Narrow Hospital (Mount Carmel Guild), substance abuse, detoxification (20 beds); Alpha House for Drug and Alcohol Rehabilitation (women; 30 beds — 25 adults, 5 children); Dismas House for Drug and Alcohol Rehabilitation (men; 78 beds); The Guild for Drug and Alcohol Rehabilitation (men, 56 beds); juvenile residential units; outpatient services and facility; three halfway houses; counseling services; employment assistance; intoxicated driver's resource center; medical day care center (available to HIV infected persons and persons diagnosed with AIDS); methadone clinic.

The National Catholic Council on Alcoholism and Related Drug Problems, Inc., 1550 Hendrickson St., Brooklyn, NY 11234. Offers educational material to those involved in pastoral ministry on ways of dealing with problems related to alcoholism and medication dependency.

Convicts: Priests serve as full- or part-time chaplains in penal and correctional institutions throughout the country. Limited efforts have been made to assist in the rehabilitation of released prisoners in Halfway House establishments.

Dining Rooms: Facilities for homeless: Representative of places where meals are provided, and in some cases lodging and other services as well, are:

St. Anthony Foundation, 121 Golden Gate Ave., San Francisco, CA 94102; (415) 241-2600; www.stanthonyfdn.org. Founded in 1950 by the Franciscan Friars. Multi-program social service agency serving people who are poor and homeless. Dining room serves up to 2,100 meals daily; more than 25 million since its founding. Other services include free clothing and furniture; free medical clinic; residential drug and alcohol rehabilitation programs; employment program; emergency shelter, housing and daytime facility for homeless women; residence for low-income senior women; free hygiene services; case management for seniors; social services.

St. Vincent de Paul Free Dining Room, 675 23rd St., Oakland, CA 94612; (510) 451-7676. Administered by Daughters of Charity of St. Vincent de Paul, under sponsorship of St. Vincent de Paul Society. Hot meals served at lunch time 7 days a week. Also provides counseling, referral/information services.

St. Vincent's Dining Room, P.O. Box 5099, Reno, NV 89513; (775) 329-5363.

St. Vincent Dining Room, 1501 Las Vegas Blvd., Las Vegas, NV 89101. Structured program for 275 men in which job development office works with homeless to enable them to find employment. For non-residents, there is a hot meal every day at noon. Emergency overnight shelter facility for families, women and men.

Good Shepherd Center, Little Brothers of the Good Shepherd, 218 Iron St. S.W., P.O. Box 749, Albuquerque, NM 87103; (505) 243-2527.

Holy Name Centre for Homeless Men, Inc., 18 Bleecker St., New York, NY 10012. A shelter for alcoholic, homeless men. Provides social services and aid to transients and those in need. Affiliated with New York Catholic Charities.

St. Francis Inn, 2441 Kensington Ave., Philadelphia, PA 19125. Serves hot meals. Temporary shelter for men. Day center for women. Thrift shop.

St. John's Hospice for Men, staffed by Little Brothers of the Good Shepherd, 1221 Race St., Philadelphia, PA 19107. Hot meals served daily; 36-bed shelter; clothing distribution, showers, mail distribution, drug/alcohol rehabilitation and work programs. Good Shepherd Program of St. John's Hospice, 1225 Race St., Philadelphia, PA 19107. Ten-bed facility for homeless men with AIDS.

Camillus House, Little Brothers of the Good Shepherd, P.O. Box 11829, Miami, FL 33101; (305) 374-1065; www.camillus.org. Free comprehensive services for the poor and homeless including daily dinner; night lodging for 70; clothing distribution; showers; mail distribution; drug/alcohol rehabilitation program. Forty-eight units of single-room housing for employed formerly homeless women and men who have completed drug and alcohol rehabilitation programs.

Camillus Health Concern, P.O. Box 12408, Miami, FL 33101; (305) 577-4840. Free comprehensive medical and social services for the homeless.

Shelters: Facilities for runaways, the abused, exploited and homeless include:

Anthony House, supported by St. Anthony's Guild (*see* **Index**). 38 E. Roosevelt Ave., Roosevelt, NY 11575 (with St. Vincent de Paul Society — for homeless men). 128 W. 112th St., New York, NY 10026 (emergency food and clothing). 6215 Holly St., P.O. Box 880, Zellwood, FL 32798 (for migrant workers and their families).

Good Shepherd Shelter-Convent of the Good Shepherd. Office, 2561 W. Venice Blvd., Los Angeles, CA 90019; (323) 737-6111. Non-emergency long-term shelter for battered women and their children.

Covenant House, 346 W. 17th St., New York, NY 10011; (212) 727-4973. President, Sister Mary Rose McGeady, D.C. Provides crisis care — food, shelter, clothing, medical treatment, job placement and counseling — for homeless youth without regard to race, creed, color and national origin. Locations: New York, New Jersey (Newark, Atlantic City), Houston, Ft. Lauderdale, New Orleans, Anchorage, Los Angeles, Detroit, Orlando, Washington, DC; Toronto (Canada), Tegucigalpa (Honduras), Guatemala City (Guatemala), Mexico City (Mexico).

Crescent House, 1000 Howard Ave., Suite 1200, New Orleans, LA 70113. Provides temporary shelter, counseling and advocacy for battered women and their children.

The Dwelling Place, 409 W. 40th St., New York, NY 10018; (212) 564-7887. For homeless women 30 years of age and over.

Gift of Hope, Missionaries of Charity, 724 N.W. 17th St., Miami, FL 33136; (305) 326-0032. Shelter for women and children; soup kitchen for men.

House of the Good Shepherd, 1114 W. Grace St., Chicago, IL 60613; (773) 935-3434. For abused women with children.

Mercy Hospice, 334 S. 13th St., Philadelphia, PA 19107; (215) 545-5153. Temporary shelter and relocation assistance for homeless women and children.

Mt. Carmel House, Carmelite Sisters, 471 G Pl., N.W., Washington, DC 20001. For homeless women.

Ozanam Inn, 843 Camp St., New Orleans, LA 70130. Under sponsorship of the St. Vincent de Paul Society. Hospice for homeless men.

St. Christopher Inn, P.O. Box 150, Graymoor, Garrison, NY 10524; (845) 424-3616; www.atonementfriars.org. Temporary shelter (21 days) for alcohol- and drug-free homeless and needy men.

Siena-Francis House, Inc., P.O. Box 217 D.T.S., Omaha, NE 68102. Two units, both at 1702 Nicholas St., Omaha, NE 68101; (402) 341-1821. Siena House (for homeless and abused women or women with children; provides 24-hour assistance and advocacy services); and Francis House (temporary shelter for homeless men). Also at this location: a 50-bed residential substance abuse program.

Unwed Mothers: Residential and care services for unwed mothers are available in many dioceses.

FACILITIES FOR RETIRED AND AGED PERSONS

Sources: Catholic Almanac *survey,* The Official Catholic Directory.

This list covers residence, health care and other facilities for the retired and aged under Catholic auspices. Information includes name, type of facility if not evident from the title, address, and total capacity (in parentheses); unless noted otherwise, facilities are for both men and women. Many facilities for the aged offer intermediate nursing care.

Alabama: Allen Memorial Home (skilled nursing), 735 S. Washington Ave., Mobile 36603; (334) 433-2642 (119).

Cathedral Place Apartments (retirement complex), 351 Conti St., Mobile 36602; (334) 434-1590 (184).

Mercy Medical (acute rehabilitation hospital, skilled and post-acute nursing, hospice, home Health and assisted and independent living), P.O. Box 1090, Daphne 36526; (334) 626-2694 (162). Not restricted to elderly.

Sacred Heart Residence Little Sisters of the Poor, 1655 McGill Ave., Mobile 36604; (251) 476-6335 (84).

Seton Haven (retirement complex), 3721 Wares Ferry Rd., Montgomery 36193; (334) 272-4000 (114).

Arizona: Guadalupe Senior Village, 222 W. Thomas Rd., Ste. 214, Phoenix, 85103; (602) 406-6218.

California: Alexis Apartments of St. Patrick's Parish, 756 Mission St. 94103; 390 Clementina St., San Francisco 94103; (415) 495-3690 (240).

Casa Manana Inn, 3700 N. Sutter St., Stockton 95204; (209) 466-4046 (162). Non-profit housing for low-income elderly over 62.

Cathedral Plaza, 1551 Third Ave., San Diego 92101; (619) 234-0093 (222 apartments).

Guadalupe Plaza, 4142 42nd St., San Diego 92105; (619) 584-2414 (147 apartments).

Jeanne d'Arc Manor, 85 S. Fifth St., San Jose 95112; (408) 288-7421 (145). For low income elderly and handicapped.

La Paz Villas, P.O. Box 1962, Palm Desert 92261; (760) 772-1382 (24 units).

Little Flower Haven (residential care facility for retired), 8585 La Mesa Blvd., La Mesa 91941; (619) 466-3163 (85).

Little Sisters of the Poor, St. Anne's Home, 300 Lake St., San Francisco 94118; (415) 751-6510 (90).

Little Sisters of the Poor, Jeanne Jugan Residence, 2100 South Western Ave., San Pedro 90732; (310) 548-0625 (100).

Madonna Senior Center and Residence, St. Anthony Foundation, 350 Golden Gate Ave., San Francisco 94102; (415) 592-2864; www.stanthonysf.org (37).

Marian Residence (retirement home), 124 S. College Dr., Santa Maria 93454; (805) 922-7731 (32).

Mercy McMahon Terrace (residential care facility), 3865 J St., Sacramento 95816; (916) 733-6510; www.mercysacramento.org (118 units).

Mercy Retirement and Care Center, 3431 Foothill Blvd., Oakland 94601; (510) 534-8540; www.mercyretirementcenter.org (59).

Mother Gertrude Home for Senior Citizens, 11320 Laurel Canyon Blvd., San Fernando 91340; (818) 898-1546 (98).

Nazareth House (residential and skilled care), 2121 N. 1st St., Fresno 93703; (559) 237-2257 (65 residential; 39 skilled nursing).

Nazareth House (residential and skilled nursing), 3333 Manning Ave., Los Angeles 90064; (310) 839-2361 (123).

Nazareth House (retirement home), 245 Nova Albion Way, San Rafael 94903; (415) 479-8282 (151).

Nazareth House Retirement Home, 6333 Rancho Mission Rd., San Diego 92108; (619) 563-0480 (354).

O'Connor Woods, 3400 Wagner Heights Rd., Stockton 95209; (209) 956-3464; www.oconnorwoods.org, (48).

Our Lady of Fatima Villa (skilled nursing facility), 20400 Saratoga-Los Gatos Rd., Saratoga 95070; (408) 741-2950; www.fatimavilla.org; (85).

St. Bernardine Plaza (retirement home), 550 W. 5th St., San Bernardino 92401; (909) 888-0153 (150 units).

St. John of God (retirement and care center), 2468 S. St. Andrew Place, Los Angeles 90018; (323) 731-0641; www.hospitallers.org, (215).

Vigil Light Apartments, 1945 Long Dr., Santa Rosa 95405; (707) 544-2810 (54).

Villa Scalabrini (retirement center and skilled nursing Care), 10631 Vinedale St., Sun Valley 91352; (818) 768-6500; www.villascalabrini.com (130 residence; 58 skilled nursing).

Villa Siena (residence and skilled nursing care), 1855 Miramonte Ave., Mountain View 94040; (650) 961-6484; www.vsiena.org (56, residence; 20, skilled nursing care).

Colorado: Francis Heights, Inc., 2626 Osceola St., Denver 80212; (303) 433-6268 (384 units; 411 residents).

Gardens at St. Elizabeth (congregate housing and assisted living), 2835 W. 32nd Ave., Denver 80211; (303) 964-2005 (320).

Little Sisters of the Poor, 3629 W. 29th Ave., Denver 80211; (303) 433-7221 (70).

Connecticut: Augustana Homes (residence), Simeon Rd., Bethel 06801; (203) 743-2508.

Carmel Ridge, 6454 Main St., Trumbull 06611; (203) 261-2229.

Holy Family Home and Shelter, Inc., 88 Jackson St., P.O. Box 884, Willimantic 06226; (860) 423-7719; www.holyfamilywillimantic.org (155).

Monsignor Bojnowski Manor, Inc. (skilled nursing facility), 50 Pulaski St., New Britain 06053; (860) 229-0336 (60).

Notre Dame Convalescent Home, 76 West Rocks Rd., Norwalk 06851; (203) 847-5893 (60).

St. Joseph Living Center, 14 Club Rd., Windham 06280; (860) 456-1107 (120).

St. Joseph's Manor (health care facility; home for aged), Carmelite Srs. for Aged and Infirm, 6448 Main St., Trumbull 06611; (203) 268-6204; www.harborsidehealthcare.com; (297).

St. Joseph's Residence, Little Sisters of the Poor, 1365 Enfield St., Enfield 06082; (860) 741-0791 (84).

St. Lucian's Home for the Aged, 532 Burritt St., New Britain 06053; (860) 223-2123 (42).

St. Mary's Home (residence and health care facility) 2021 Albany Ave., W. Hartford 06117; (860) 570-8200 (26).

Delaware: The Antonian, 1701 W. 10th St., Wilmington 19805; (302) 421-3758 (136 apartments).

Jeanne Jugan Residence, Little Sisters of the Poor, 185 Salem Church Rd., Newark 19713; (302) 368-5886 (80).

Marydale Retirement Village, 135 Jeandell Dr., Newark 19713; (302) 368-2784 (118 apartments).

St. Patrick's House, Inc., 115 E. 14th St., Wilmington 19801; (302) 654-6908 (12).

District of Columbia: Jeanne Jugan Residence-St. Joseph Villa, Little Sisters of the Poor, 4200 Harewood Rd., N.E., Washington 20017; (202) 269-1831; www.lspasa.org (73).

Florida: All Saints Home, 5888 Blanding Blvd., Jacksonville 32244; (904) 772-1220; www.allsaints.org (118).

Casa Calderon, Inc. (retirement apartments), 800 W. Virginia St., Tallahassee 32304; (850) 222-4026 (111).

Haven of Our Lady of Peace (assisted living and nursing home), 5203 N. 9th Ave., Pensacola 32504; (850) 477-0531 (89).

Palmer House, Inc., 1225 S.W. 107th Ave., Miami 33174; (305) 221-9566 (120 apartments).

St. Andrew Towers (retirement apartments), 2700 N.W. 99th Ave., Coral Springs 33065 (432).

St. Catherine Labouré (skilled and intermediate care), 1750 Stockton St., Jacksonville 32204; (904) 308-4700 (239).

St. Dominic Gardens (retirement apartments), 5849 N.W. 7th St., Miami 33126 (149 apartments).

St. Elizabeth Gardens, Inc. (retirement apartments), 801 N.E. 33rd St., Pompano Beach 33064 (150).

St. John's Rehabilitation Hospital and Nursing Center, Inc., 3075 N.W. 35th Ave., Lauderdale Lakes 33311.

Stella Maris House, Inc., 8636 Harding Ave., Miami Beach 33141 (136 apartments).

Illinois: Addolorata Villa (sheltered intermediate, skilled care facility; apartments), 555 McHenry Rd., Wheeling 60090; (847) 808-6168 (100 apartments).

Alvernia Manor (sheltered care), 13950 Main St., Lemont 60439; (630) 257-7721 (50).

Bishop Conway Residence, 1900 N. Karlov Ave., Chicago 60639; (773) 252-9941.

Carlyle Healthcare Center, 501 Clinton St., Carlyle 62231; (618) 594-3112 (131).

Carmelite Carefree Village, 8419 Bailey Rd., Darien 60561; (630) 960-4060 (98).

Cortland Manor Retirement Home, 1900 N. Karlov, Chicago 60639; (773) 235-3670 (48).

Holy Family Nursing and Rehabilitation Center, 2380 Dempster, Des Plaines 60016; (847) 296-3335 (362).

Holy Family Villa (intermediate care facility), 12395 McCarthy Rd., Lemont 60439; (630) 257-7721 (50).

Jugan Terrace, Little Sisters of the Poor, 2300 N. Racine, Chicago 60614; (773) 935-9600 (50 apartments).

Little Sisters of the Poor, St. Joseph's Home for the Elderly, 80 W. Northwest Hwy., Palatine 60067; (847) 358-5700 (61).

Little Sisters of the Poor Center for the Aging, 2325 N. Lakewood Ave., Chicago 60614; (773) 935-9600 (71).

Marian Heights Apartments (elderly, handicapped), 20 Marian Heights Dr., Alton 62002; (618) 462-0363 (130).

Marian Park, Inc., 26 W. 171 Roosevelt Rd.,

Wheaton 60187; (630) 665-9100 (470).

Maryhaven, Inc. (skilled and intermediate care facility), 1700 E. Lake Ave., Glenview 60025; (847) 729-1300 (138).

Mayslake Village (retirement apartments), 1801 35th St., Oak Brook 60523; (630) 850-8232; www.mayslake.com (630 apartments).

Meredith Memorial Home, 16 S. Illinois St., Belleville 62220; (618) 233-8780 (86).

Merkle-Knipprath Countryside (apartments and nursing facility), 1190 E. 2900 N. Rd., Clifton 60927; (815) 694-2306 (130).

Mother Theresa Home (skilled, intermediate and sheltered care), 1270 Franciscan Dr., Lemont 60439; (630) 257-5801; www.franciscancommunities.com. (150).

Nazarethville (intermediate and sheltered care), 300 N. River Rd., Des Plaines 60016; (847) 297-5900; www.nazarethville.com. (83).

Our Lady of Angels Retirement Home, 1201 Wyoming, Joliet 60435; (815) 725-6631; www.olaretirement.org (101).

Our Lady of the Snows, Apartment Community, 9500 West Illinois Highway 15, Belleville 62223; (618) 397-6700 (201).

Our Lady of Victory Nursing Home (intermediate and skilled care), 20 Briarcliff Lane, Bourbonnais 60914; (815) 937-2022 (107).

Pope John Paul Apartments (elderly and handicapped), 1 Pope John Paul Plaza, Springfield 62703; (217) 528-1771; www.dio.org (160).

Provena Cor Mariae Center (assisted living and nursing home), 3330 Maria Linden Dr., Rockford 61107; (815) 877-7416 (146).

Provena St. Anne Center (nursing home), 4405 Highcrest Rd., Rockford 61107; (815) 229-1999 (179).

Provena St. Joseph's Home for the Aged, 659 E. Jefferson St., Freeport 61032; (815) 232-6181 (120).

Provena Villa Franciscan (skilled care), 210 N. Springfield, Joliet 60435; (815) 725-3400; www.provenahealth.com.

Queen of Peace Center, 1910 Maple Ave., Lisle 60532; (630) 852-5360; www.qopc.net (32).

Red Bud Regional Nursing Home (skilled intermediary facility), 350 W. S. First St., Red Bud 62278; (618) 282-3891 (115).

Resurrection Nursing Pavilion (skilled care), 1001 N. Greenwood, Park Ridge 60068; (847) 692-5600 (295).

Resurrection Retirement Community, 7262 W. Peterson Ave., Chicago, 60631; (773) 792-7930; www.reshealth.org (472 apartments).

Rosary Hill Home (women), 9000 W. 81st St., Justice 60458; (708) 458-3040 (48).

St. Andrew Life Center (retirement residence), 7000 N. Newark Ave., Niles 60714; (847) 647-8332 (99).

St. Anne Place (retirement apartments), 4444 Brendenwood Rd., Rockford 61107; (815) 399-6167 (120).

St. Benedict Home, 6930 W. Touhy Ave., Niles 60714; (847) 647-0003. (99).

St. Elizabeth Home (residence), 704 W. Marion St., Joliet 60436; (815) 727-0125 (11). Group living for Senior women.

St. James Manor, 1251 East Richton Rd., Crete 60417; (708) 672-6700 (110).

St. Joseph's Home (sheltered and intermediate care), 3306 S. 6th St. Rd., Springfield 62703; (217) 529-5596 (110).

St. Joseph's Home (sheltered and intermediate care), 2223 W. Heading Ave., Peoria 61604; (309) 673-7425; www.stjhome.org (200).

St. Joseph Home of Chicago, Inc. (skilled care), 2650 N. Ridgeway Ave., Chicago 60647; (773) 235-8600; www.franciscancommunities.com (173).

St. Patrick's Residence, 1400 Brookdale Rd., Naperville 60563-2125; (630) 416-6565; www.stpatricksresidence.org

Villa Scalabrini (sheltered, intermediate and skilled), 480 N. Wolf Rd., Northlake 60164; (708) 562-0040 (259).

Indiana: Albertine Home, 1501 Hoffman St., Hammond 46327; (219) 937-0575 (35).

Provena LaVerna Terrace, 517 N. Main St., Avilla 46710; (260) 897-2093 (51).

Provena Sacred Heart Home (comprehensive nursing), 515 N. Main St., Avilla 46710; (260) 897-2841, (133).

Regina Continuing Care Center (intermediate care Facility), 3900 Washington Ave., Evansville 47714; (812) 485-4226; www.stmarys.org (137).

St. Anne Home (Residential and Comprehensive nursing), 1900 Randallia Dr., Ft. Wayne 46805; (219) 484-5555 (254).

St. Anthony Home, Inc., 203 Franciscan Rd., Crown Point 46307; (219) 661-5100 (219).

St. Augustine Home for the Aged, Little Sisters of the Poor, 2345 W. 86th St., Indianapolis 46260; (317) 872-6420 (92).

St. John's Home for the Aged, Little Sisters of the Poor, 1236 Lincoln Ave., Evansville 47714; (812) 464-3607 (70).

St. Paul Hermitage (residential and intermediate care nursing), 501 N. 17th Ave., Beech Grove 46107; (317) 786-2261 (100).

Iowa: The Alverno Health Care Facility (nursing care), 849 13th Ave. N., Clinton 52732; (563) 242-1521; www.alvernohealthcare.com (194).

Bishop Drumm Retirement Center, 5837 Winwood Dr., Johnston 50131; (515) 270-1100 (64).

Hallmar-Mercy Medical Center, 701 Tenth St. S.E., Cedar Rapids 52403; (319) 369-4638 (57).

Holy Spirit Retirement Home (intermediate care), 1701 W. 25th St., Sioux City 51103; (712) 252-2726 (95).

Kahl Home for the Aged and Infirm (skilled and intermediate care facility), 1101 W. 9th St., Davenport 52804; (319) 324-1621 (135).

The Marian Home, 2400 6th Ave. North, Fort Dodge 50501; (515) 576-1138 (116).

St. Anthony Nursing Home (intermediate care), 406 E. Anthony St., Carroll 51401; (712) 792-3581 (79).

St. Francis Continuation Care and Nursing Home Center, Burlington 52601; (319) 752-4564 (170).

Stonehill Adult Center (day care), 3485 Windsor, Dubuque 52001; (319) 557-7180 (35).

Kansas: Catholic Care Center (skilled and intermediate care facility), 6700 E. 45th St, Wichita 67226; (316) 744-2020 (294).

Mt. Joseph Senior Village (intermediate care facility), 1110 W. 11, Concordia 66901; (785) 143-1347 (16 apartments).

St. John Rest Home (nursing facility), 701 Seventh St., Victoria 67671; (785) 735-2208 (90).

St. John's New Horizons, 2225 Canterbury, Hays 67601; (785) 628-8742 (43).

Villa Maria, Inc. (intermediate care facility), 116 S. Central, Mulvane 67110; (316) 777-1129 (99).

Kentucky: Bishop Soenneker Personal Care Home, 9545 Ky. 144, Knottsville, KY 42366; (270) 281-4881 (55).

Carmel Home (residence, adult day care, respite care and nursing care), 2501 Old Hartford Rd., Owensboro 42303; (270) 683-0227 (101).

Carmel Manor (skilled, intermediate and personal care home), 100 Carmel Manor Rd., Ft. Thomas, 41075; (859) 781-5111; (145).

Madonna Manor Nursing Home, 2344 Amsterdam Rd., Villa Hills 41017; (606) 341-3981 (60).

Marian Home, 3105 Lexington Rd., Louisville 40206; (502) 893-0121 (69).

Nazareth Home, 2000 Newburg Rd., Louisville 40205; (502) 459-9681; www.nazhome.org (168).

St. Charles Care Center and Village, 500 Farrell Dr., Covington 41011; (606) 331-3224; www.stcharlescare.org (149). Nursing home; adult day health program. Independent living cottages (44); assisted living (60); independent living apartments (12).

Louisiana: Annunciation Inn, 1220 Spain St., New Orleans 70117; (504) 944-0512 (111).

Bethany M.H.S. Health Care Center (women), P.O. Box 2308, Lafayette 70502; (337) 234-2459. (200).

Château de Notre Dame (residence and nursing home), 2832 Burdette St., New Orleans 70125; (504) 866-2741 (103).

Christopher Inn Apartments, 2110 Royal St., New Orleans 70116; (504) 949-0312 (144).

Christus St. Joseph's Home (nursing home), 2301 Sterlington Rd., Monroe 71211; (318) 323-3426 (150).

Consolata Home (nursing home), 2319 E. Main St., New Iberia 70560; (337) 365-8226 (114).

Haydel Heights Apartments, 4402 Reynes St., New Orleans 70126; (504) 242-4438 (65 units).

Lafon Nursing Home of the Holy Family, 6900 Chef Menteur Hwy., New Orleans 70126; (504) 246-1100 (171).

Metairie Manor, 4929 York St., Metairie 70001; (504) 456-1467 (287).

Nazareth Inn, 9630 Hayne Blvd., New Orleans 70127; (504) 241-9630 (158).

Ollie Steele Burden Manor (nursing home), 4250 Essen Lane, Baton Rouge 70809; (225) 926-0091 (184).

Our Lady of Prompt Succor Home, 954 East Prudhomme St., Opelousas 70570; (337) 948-3634 (80).

Our Lady's Manor, Inc., 402 Monroe St., Alexandria 71301; (318) 473-2560 (114).

Place Dubourg, 201 Rue Dubourg, LaPlace 70068; (504) 652-1981 (115).

Rouquette Lodge, 4300 Hwy 22, Mandeville 70471; (504) 626-5217 (51).

St. John Berchmans Manor, 3400 St. Anthony Ave., New Orleans 70122; (504) 943-9342 (157).

St. Margaret's Daughters Home (nursing home), 3419 St. Claude Ave., New Orleans 70117; (504) 279-6414; www.stmargaretno.org; (139).

St. Martin Manor, 1501 N. Johnson St., New Orleans 70116; (504) 945-7728 (145).

Villa St. Maurice 500 St. Maurice Ave., New Orleans 70117; (504) 277-8477 (193).

Villa St. Maurice II, 6101 Douglas St., New Orleans 70117; (504) 277-8731 (80).

Village du Lac, Inc., 1404 Carmel Ave., Lafayette 70501; (337) 234-5106 (200).

Wynhoven Apartments and Wynhoven II (residence for senior citizens), 4600-10th St., Marrero; (504) 347-8442 (375).

Maine: Deering Pavilion (apartments for senior citizens), 880 Forest Ave., Portland 04103; (207) 797-8777 (232 units).

Maison Marcotte (independent living community), 100 Campus Ave., Lewiston 04240; (207) 786-0062 (128 apartments).

Mt. St. Joseph Holistic Care Community, Highwood St., Waterville 04901; (207) 873-0705 (138).

St. Andre Health Care Facility, Inc. (nursing facility), 407 Pool St., Biddeford 04005; (207) 282-5171 (96).

St. Joseph's Manor (nursing care facility), 1133 Washington Ave., Portland 04103; (207) 797-0600; www.saintjosephsmanor.org. (200).

St. Marguerite D'Youville Pavilion, 102 Campus Ave., Lewiston 04240; (207) 777-4200 (280).

St. Xavier's Home (apartments), 199 Somerset St., Bangor 04401; (207) 942-4815 (19 units).

Seton Village, Inc., 1 Carver St., Waterville 04901; (207) 873-0178 (140 housing units).

Maryland: Little Sisters of the Poor, St. Martin's Home (for the aged), 601 Maiden Choice Lane, Baltimore 21228; (410) 744-9367 (104).

Sacred Heart Home, 5805 Queens Chapel Rd., Hyattsville 20782; (301) 277-6500; www.sacredhearthome.org (102).

St. Joseph Nursing Home, 1222 Tugwell Dr., Baltimore 21228; (410) 747-0026 (51).

Villa Rosa Nursing Home, 3800 Lottsford Vista Rd., Mitchellville 20721; (301) 459-4700 (100).

Massachusetts: Catholic Memorial Home (nursing home), 2446 Highland Ave., Fall River 02720; (508) 679-0011 (300).

Don Orione Nursing Home, 111 Orient Ave., East Boston 02128; (617) 569-2100 (185).

D'Youville Manor (nursing home), 981 Varnum Ave., Lowell 01854; (978) 454-5681; www.dyouville.com (203).

Jeanne Jugan Pavilion, 190 Highland Ave., Somerville 02143; (617) 776-4420 (30).

Jeanne Jugan Residence, Little Sisters of the Poor (home for the elderly), 186 Highland Ave., Somerville 02143; (617) 776-4420 (84).

Madonna Manor (nursing home), 85 N. Washington St., N. Attleboro 02760; (508) 699-2740; www.dhfo.org (129).

Marian Manor, for the Aged and Infirm (nursing home), 130 Dorchester St., S. Boston, 02127; (617) 268-3333; www.marianmanor.org (366).

Marian Manor of Taunton (nursing home), 33 Summer St., Taunton 02780; (508) 822-4885 (184).

Maristhill Nursing Home, 66 Newton St., Waltham 02154; (781) 893-0240 (154).

MI Nursing/Restorative Center, 172 Lawrence St., Lawrence 01841; (978) 685-6321; www.mihcs.com (335).

MI Residential Community, 189 Maple St., Lawrence 01841; (978) 682-7575; www.mihcs.com (35).

Our Lady's Haven (nursing home), 71 Center St., Fairhaven 02719; (508) 999-4561; www.dhfo.org (158).

Sacred Heart Home (nursing home), 359 Summer St., New Bedford 02740; (508) 996-6751; www.dhfo.org (217).

St. Joseph Manor Health Care, Inc., 215 Thatcher St., Brockton 02302; (508) 583-5834 (118).

St. Joseph's Nursing Care Center, 321 Centre St., Dorchester, Boston 02122; (617) 825-6320 (191).

St. Patrick's Manor (nursing home), 863 Central St., Framingham 01701; (508) 879-8000; www.stpatricksmanor.org (460).

Michigan: Bishop Noa Home for Senior Citizens (nursing home and residence), 2900 3rd Ave. S., Escanaba 49829; (906) 786-5810 (123).

Lourdes Nursing Home (skilled facility), 2300 Watkins Lake Rd., Waterford 48328; (248) 674-2241; www.lourdescampus.com (108).

Marycrest Manor (skilled nursing facility), 15475 Middlebelt Rd., Livonia 48154; (313) 427-9175 (55).

Ryan Senior Residences of the Archdiocese of Detroit: Casa Maria, 600 Maple Vista, Imlay City 48444; (810) 724-6300 (84). Kundig Center, 3300 Jeffries Freeway, Detroit 48208; (313) 894-0555 (160). Lourdes Assisted Living Home, Inc. (residence), 2450 Watkins Lake Rd., Waterford 48328; (248) 618-6361; www.lourdescampus.com (6). Marian-Oakland West, 29250 W. Ten Mile Rd., Farmington Hills 48336; (248) 474-7204 (87). Marian Place, 408 W. Front St., Monroe 48161; (734) 241-2414 (53). Marydale Center, 3147 Tenth Ave., Port Huron 48060; (810) 985-9683 (56). Maryhaven, 11350 Reeck Rd., Southgate 48195; (734) 287-2111 (90). Mercy Madonna Villa 17825 Fifteen Mile Rd., Clinton Twp. 48035; (810) 792-0358 (86). Stapleton Center, 9341 Agnes St., Detroit 48214; (313) 822-0397 (59). Villa Marie, 15131 Newburgh Rd., Livonia 48154; (734) 464-9494 (86). St. Ann's Home, (residence and nursing home), 2161 Leonard St. N.W., Grand Rapids 49504; (616) 453-7715; www.stannshome.com (140). St. Catherine House, 1641 Webb Ave., Detroit 48206; (313) 868-4505 (12). St. Elizabeth Briarbank (women, residence), 1315 N. Woodward Ave., Bloomfield Hills 48304; (248) 644-1011 (44).

St. Francis Home (nursing home), 915 N. River Rd., Saginaw 48609; (989) 781-3150 (100).

St. Joseph's Home, 4800 Cadieux Rd., Detroit 48224; (313) 882-3800 (104).

Minnesota: Alverna Apartments, 300 8th Ave. S.E., Little Falls 56345; (320) 632-1246 (68).

Assumption Home, 715 North First St., Cold Spring 56320; (320) 685-4110 (34).

Benedictine Health Center, 935 Kenwood Ave., Duluth, MN 55811; (218) 723-6408; www.benedictinehealthcenter.org.

Divine Providence Community Home (skilled nursing care) and Lake Villa Maria Senior Housing, 702 Third Ave. N.W., Sleepy Eye 56085; (507) 794-5333 (58).

Franciscan Health Community, 1925 Norfolk Ave., St. Paul 55116; (651) 696-8400 (223).

John Paul Apartments, 200 8th Ave. N., Cold Spring 56320; (320) 685-4429 (61).

Little Sisters of the Poor, Holy Family Residence (skilled nursing and intermediate care), 330 S. Exchange St., St. Paul 55102; (651) 227-0336 (73). Independent living apartments (32).

Madonna Towers (retirement apartments and nursing home), 4001 19th Ave. N.W., Rochester 55901; (507) 288-3911 (184).

Mary Rondorf Retirement Home of Sacred Heart Parish, Inc., 222 5th St., N.E., Staples 56479; (218) 894-2124 (45). Board and lodging with special services.

Mother of Mercy Nursing Home and Retirement Center, 230 Church Ave., Box 676, Albany 56307; (320) 845-2195 (114).

Regina Nursing Home and Retirement Residence Center, 1175 Nininger Rd., Hastings 55033; (651) 480-6836; www.reginamedical.com. Nursing home (61); retirement home (43); boarding care (32). Admin., Juliane M. Saxon.

Sacred Heart Hospice (skilled nursing home, adult day care, home health care) 1200 Twelfth St. S.W., Austin 55912; (507) 433-1808 (59).

St. Ann's Residence, 330 E. 3rd St., Duluth 55811; (218) 727-8831; www.stanns.com (185).

St. Anne of Winona (skilled nursing home), 1347 W. Broadway, Winona 55987; (507) 454-3621; www.saintannehosp.homestead.com (74).

St. Benedict's Center, 1810 Minnesota Blvd. S.E., St. Cloud 56304; (320) 252-0010; www.centracare.com (198 bed skilled nursing care; adult day care, respite care). Benedict Village(retirementt apartments), 2000 15th Ave. S.E., St. Cloud 56304; (320) 252-0010; www.centracare.com. Benedict Homes (Alzheimer residential care) and Benedict Court (assisted living), 1980 15th Ave. S.E., St. Cloud 56304; (320) 252-0010.

St. Benedict's Senior Community (independent and assisted living), 1301 East 7th St., Monticello, MN 55362; (763) 295-4051; www.centracare.com.

St. Elizabeth's Health Care Center, 1200 Grant Blvd., Wabasha 55981; (651) 565-4531; www.stelizabethswabasha.org (106).

St. Elizabeth's Medical Center, 626 Shields Ave., Wabasha, MN 55981; (651) 565-4581; www.stelizabethswabasha.org.

St. Francis Home, 2400 St. Francis Dr., Breckenridge 56520; (218) 643-3000; www.sfcare.org (124).

St. Mary's Regional Health Center, 1027 Washington Ave., Detroit Lakes 56501; (218) 847-5611 (100).

St. Otto's Care Center (nursing home), 920 S.E. 4th St., Little Falls 56345; (320) 632-9281 (150).

St. William's Nursing Home, P.O. Box 30, Parkers Prairie 56361; (218) 338-4671 (90).

Villa of St. Francis Nursing Home, 1001 Scott Ave., Morris 56267; (320) 589-1133 (128).

Villa St. Vincent (skilled nursing home and residence), 516 Walsh St., Crookston 56716; (218) 281-3424. Skilled nursing home (80); special care unit (24); apartments (27); board and care (34).

Westwood Senior Apartments, 925 Kenwood Ave., Duluth 55811; (218) 733-2238; www.westwoodduluth.org (70).

Mississippi: Notre Dame de la Mer Retirement Apartments, 292 Hwy. 90, Bay St. Louis 39520; (228) 467-2885 (61).

Santa Maria Retirement Apartments, 674 Beach Blvd., Biloxi, 39530; (228) 432-1289 (223).

Villa Maria Retirement Apartments, 921 Porter Ave., Ocean Springs 39564; (228) 875-8811 (225).

Missouri: Cathedral Square Towers, 444 W. 12th St.,

Kansas City 64105; (816) 471-6555 (167).

Chariton Apartments (retirement apartments), 4249 Michigan Ave., St. Louis 63111; (314) 352-7600 (122 units; 143 residents).

LaVerna Village Nursing Home, 904 Hall Ave., Savannah 64485; (816) 324-3185 (133).

Little Sisters of the Poor (home for aged), 3225 N. Florissant Ave., St. Louis 63107; (314) 421-6022 (114).

Mary, Queen and Mother Center (nursing care), 7601 Watson Rd., St. Louis 63119; (314) 961-8000; www.cardinalcarberry.org (230).

Mother of Good Counsel Home (skilled nursing, women), 6825 Natural Bridge Rd., Northwoods, 63121; (314) 383-4765 (114).

Our Lady of Mercy Country Home, 2205 Hughes Rd., Liberty 64068; (816) 781-7276; www.ourladyofmercy.net (105).

Price Memorial skilled nursing facility, Forby Rd., P.O. Box 476, Eureka 63025; (636) 587-3200 (120).

St. Agnes Home for the Elderly, 10341 Manchester Rd., Kirkwood 63122; (314) 965-7616 (124).

St. Joseph Hill Infirmary, Inc., (nursing care facility, men), St. Joseph Road, Eureka 63025; (636) 587-3661 (120).

St. Joseph's Home (residential and intermediate care), 723 First Capitol Dr., St. Charles 63301; (314) 946-4140; (110).

St. Joseph's Home (residential and intermediate care facility), 1306 W. Main St., Jefferson City 65109; (573) 635-0166 (90).

Nebraska: Madonna Rehabilitation Hospital, 5401 South St., Lincoln 68506; (402) 489-7102; www.madonna.org (252).

Mercy Care Center (skilled nursing facility for chronic, complex and subacute levels of care and rehabilitation), 1870 S. 75th St., Omaha 68124; (402) 343-8500 (246).

Mercy Villa, 1845 S. 72nd St., Omaha 68124; (402) 391-6224.

Mt. Carmel Home, Keens Memorial (nursing home), 412 W. 18th St., Kearney 68847; (308) 237-2287 (75).

New Cassel Retirement Center, 900 N. 90th St., Omaha 68114; (402) 393-2277; www.newcassel.org (165).

St. Joseph's Rehabilitation and Care Center, 401 N. 18th St., Norfolk 68701; (402) 644-7375 (99).

St. Joseph's Retirement Community, 320 E. Decatur St., West Point 68788; (402) 372-3477 (90).

St. Joseph's Villa (nursing home), 927 7th St., David City 68632; (402) 367-3045; www.saintjoseph villa.org (65).

New Hampshire: Mount Carmel Healthcare Center, 235 Myrtle St., Manchester 03104; (603) 627-3811 (120).

St. Ann Home (nursing home), 195 Dover Point Rd., Dover 03820; (603) 742-2612 (54).

St. Francis Home (nursing home), 406 Court St., Laconia 03246; (603) 524-0466 (51).

St. Teresa Rehabilitation and Nursing Center (nursing home), 519 Bridge St., Manchester 03104; (603) 668-2373; www.nh-cc.org; (5).

St. Vincent de Paul Healthcare Center, 29 Providence Ave., Berlin 03570; (603) 752-1820 (80).

New Jersey: McCarrick Care Center, 15 Dellwood Lane, Somerset 08873; (732) 545-4200 (142).

Mater Dei Nursing Home, 176 Rt. 40, Newfield 08344; (856) 358-2061 (64).

Morris Hall (St. Joseph Skilled Nursing Center, St. Mary Residence), 1 Bishops' Dr., Lawrenceville 08648-2050; (609) 896-0006; www.morrishall.org (100).

Mount St. Andrew Villa (residence), 55 W. Midland Ave., Paramus 07652; (201) 261-5950 (55).

Our Lady's Residence (nursing home), 1100 Clematis Ave., Pleasantville 08232; (609) 646-2450 (236).

St. Ann's Home for the Aged (akilled and intermediate nursing care home, women), 198 Old Bergen Rd., Jersey City 07305; (201) 433-0950; www.saintannshome.com; (106).

St. Francis Health Resort (residence), 122 Diamond Spring Rd., Denville 07834; (973) 627-5560; www.saintfrancisres.com (150).

St. Joseph's Home for the Elderly, Little Sisters of the Poor, 140 Shepherd Lane, Totowa 07512; (973) 942-0300 (134).

St. Joseph's Rest Home for Aged Women, 46 Preakness Ave., Paterson 07522; (973) 956-1921 (35).

St. Joseph's Assisted Living Residence, 1 St. Joseph Terr., Woodbridge, 07095; (732) 634-0004 (60).

St. Joseph's Nursing Home, 3 St. Joseph Terr., Woodbridge, 07095; (732) 750-0077.

St. Mary's Nursing Home, 210 St. Mary's Dr., Cherry Hill 08003; (856) 424-9521 (215). The Manor at St. Mary's, 220 St. Mary's Dr., Cherry Hill 08003; (856) 424-3817 (739).

St. Vincent's Nursing Home, 45 Elm St., Montclair 07042; (973) 754-4800 (220).

Villa Maria (residence and infirmary, women), 641 Somerset St., N. Plainfield 07061; (908) 757-3050 (86).

New York: Bernardine Apartments, 417 Churchill Ave., Syracuse 13205; (315) 469-7786.

Brothers of Mercy Sacred Heart Home (residence) 4520 Ransom Rd., Clarence 14031; (716) 759-2644 (80). Brothers of Mercy Nursing Home, 10570 Bergtold Rd., Clarence 14031; (716) 759-6985; www.brothersofmercy.org (240). Brothers of Mercy Housing Co., Inc. (apartments), 10500 Bergtold Rd., Clarence 14031; (716) 759-2122 (110).

Carmel Richmond Nursing Home, 88 Old Town Rd., Staten Island 10304; (718) 979-5000 (300).

Ferncliff Nursing Home, 21 Ferncliff Dr., Rhinebeck 12572; (845) 876-2011 (328).

Franciscan Health System of New York, 2975 Independence Ave., Bronx 10463; (718) 548-1700.

Good Samaritan Nursing Home (skilled nursing), 101 Elm St., Sayville 11782; (631) 244-2400 (100).

The Heritage (apartments with skilled nursing care), 1450 Portland Ave., Rochester 14621; (716) 342-1700; www.stannsrochester.org (237)

Holy Family Home, 1740-84th St., Brooklyn 11214; (718) 232-3666 (200).

Kateri Residence (skilled nursing), 150 Riverside Dr., New York 10024; (646) 505-3500; www.catholichealthcaresystem.org/kateri (610).

Little Sisters of the Poor, Jeanne Jugan Residence (Skilled Nursing and Health Related; Adult Care), 3200 Baychester Ave., Bronx 10475; (718) 671-2120 (60).

Little Sisters of the Poor, Queen of Peace Residence, 110-30 221st St., Queens Village 11429; (718) 464-1800.

Mary Manning Walsh Home (nursing home), 1339 York Ave., New York 10021; (212) 628-2800 (362).

Mercy Healthcare Center (skilled nursing facility), 114 Wawbeek Ave., Tupper Lake 12986; (518) 359-3355; www.muhc.org (80).

Mt. Loretto Nursing Home, (skilled nursing home), Sisters of the Resurrection, 302 Swart Hill Rd., Amsterdam 12010; (518) 842-6790 (120).

Nazareth Nursing Home (women), 291 W. North St., Buffalo 14201; (716) 881-2323 (125).

Our Lady of Consolation Nursing and Rehabilitation Care Center (skilled nursing) 111 Beach Dr., West Islip 11795; (631) 587-1600; www.olc.chsli.org (450).

Our Lady of Hope Residence (home for the aged), Little Sisters of the Poor, 1 Jeanne Jugan Lane, Latham 12210; (518) 785-4551 (117).

Ozanam Hall of Queens Nursing Home, Inc., 42-41 201st St., Bayside 11361; (718) 423-2000 (432).

Providence Rest , 3304 Waterbury Ave., Bronx 10465; (718) 931-30000; www.chcn.org/providence (242).

Resurrection Nursing Home (skilled nursing facility), Castleton 12033; (518) 732-7617 (80).

St. Ann's Community (skilled nursing facility), 1500 Portland Ave., Rochester 14621; (585) 697-6000; www.stannscommunity.com (354).

St. Cabrini Nursing Home, 115 Broadway, Dobbs Ferry 10522; (914) 693-6800 (304).

St. Clare Manor (nursing home), 543 Locust St., Lockport 14094; (716) 434-4718 (28).

St. Columban's on the Lake (retirement home), 2546 Lake Rd., Silver Creek 14136; (716) 934-4515 (50).

St. Elizabeth Home (adult home), 5539 Broadway, Lancaster 14086; (716) 683-5150 (117).

St. Francis Home (skilled nursing facility), 147 Reist St., Williamsville 14221; (716) 633-5400 (142).

St. Joseph Manor (nursing home), 2211 W. State St., Olean 14760; (716) 372-7810 (22).

St. Joseph Nursing Home, 2535 Genesee St., Utica 13501; (315) 797-1230; www.stjosephnh.org.

St. Joseph's Guest Home, Missionary Sisters of St. Benedict, 350 Cuba Hill Rd., Huntington 11743; (631) 368-9528.

St. Joseph's Home (nursing home), 420 Lafayette St., Ogdensburg 13669; (315) 393-3780; www.stjh.org (117).

St. Joseph's Villa (adult home), 38 Prospect Ave., Catskill 12414; (518) 943-5701.

St. Luke Manor, 17 Wiard St., Batavia 14020; (585) 343-8806 (20).

St. Mary's Manor, 515 Sixth St., Niagara Falls 14301; (716) 285-3236 (165).

St. Patrick's Home for the Aged and Infirm, 66 Van Cortlandt Park S., Bronx NY 10463; (718) 304-1832; www.stpatrickshome.org (264).

St. Teresa Nursing Home, 120 Highland Ave., Middletown 10940; (914) 342-1033 (98).

St. Vincent's Home for the Aged, 319 Washington Ave., Dunkirk 14048; (716) 366-2066 (40).

Terence Cardinal Cooke Health Care Center (skilled nursing), 1249 Fifth Ave., New York 10029; (212) 360-1000 (523).

Teresian House, 200 Washington Ave. Extension, Albany 12203; (518) 456-2000; www.teresianhouse.com (300).

Uihlein Mercy Center (nursing home), 185 Old Military Rd., Lake Placid 12946; (518) 523-2464

(220).

North Carolina: Mayfield Nursing Home, 1315 Greensboro Rd., High Point 27260; (336) 886-2444 (115).

North Dakota: Manor St. Joseph (basic care facility), 404 Fourth Ave., Edgeley 58433; (701) 493-2477 (40).

Marillac Manor Retirement Center, 1016 28th St., Bismarck 58501-3139; (701) 258-8702; www.marillac-manor.org (78 apartments).

St. Anne's Guest Home, 524 N. 17th St., Grand Forks 58203; (701) 746-9401 (86).

St. Vincent's Care Center (nursing facility), 1021 N. 26th St., Bismarck 58501; (701) 323-1999 (101).

Ohio: Archbishop Leibold Home for the Aged, Little Sisters of the Poor, 476 Riddle Rd., Cincinnati 45220; (513) 281-8001 (100).

The Assumption Village, 9800 Market St., North Lima 44452; (330) 549-0740 (120).

Francesca Residence (retirement), 39 N. Portage Path, Akron 44303; (330) 867-6334 (40).

House of Loreto (nursing home), 2812 Harvard Ave. N.W., Canton 44709; (330) 453-8137 (76).

Jennings Center for Older Adults (nursing care), 10204 Granger Rd., Cleveland 44125; (216) 581-2900; www.jenningscenter.org (150).

Little Sisters of the Poor, Sacred Heart Home, 930 Wynn Rd. Oregon 43616; (419) 698-4331 (81).

Little Sisters of the Poor, Sts. Mary and Joseph Home for Aged, 4291 Richmond Rd., Cleveland 44122; (216) 464-1222 (125).

The Maria-Joseph Living Care Center, 4830 Salem Ave., Dayton 45416; (937) 278-2692; www.maria-joseph.org (440).

Mercy Franciscan Terrace, 100 Compton Rd., Cincinnati 45215; (513) 761-9036 (148).

Mercy St. Theresa Center, 7010 Rowan Hill Dr., Cincinnati 45227; (513) 527-0105; www.e-mercy.com (157).

Mercy Siena Retirement Community, 6125 N. Main St., Dayton 45415; (937) 278-8211; www.mercysiena.com; (99).

Mount Alverna Village (intermediate care nursing facility), 6765 State Rd., Cleveland 44134; (440) 843-7800; www.franciscanservices.com/facilities/ (203).

Mt. St. Joseph (skilled nursing facility, dual certified), 21800 Chardon Rd., Euclid 44117; (216) 531-7426 (100).

Nazareth Towers, 300 E. Rich St., Columbus 43215; (614) 464-4780 (229).

St. Augustine Manor (skilled nursing facility), 7801 Detroit Ave., Cleveland 44102; (216) 634-7400 (248).

St. Francis Health Care Centre, 401 N. Broadway St., Green Springs 44836; (419) 639-2626; www.sfhcc.org (186).

St. Francis Home, Inc. (residence and nursing care), 182 St. Francis Ave., Tiffin 44883; (419) 447-2723 (173).

St. Joseph's Care Center, 2308 Reno Dr., Louisville 44641; (330) 875-5562 (100, nursing home; 40 assisted living).

St. Margaret Hall (rest home and nursing facility), Carmelite Sisters for the Aged and Infirm, 1960 Madison Rd., Cincinnati 45206; (513) 751-5880

(133).

St. Raphael Home (nursing home), 1550 Roxbury Rd., Columbus 43212; (614) 486-0436 (78).

St. Rita's Home (skilled nursing home), 880 Greenlawn Ave., Columbus 43223; (614) 443-9433 (100).

Schroder Manor Retirement Community (residential care, skilled nursing care and independent living units), Franciscan Sisters of the Poor, 1302 Millville Ave., Hamilton 45013; (513) 867-1300 (125).

The Villa Sancta Anna Home for the Aged, Inc., 25000 Chagrin Blvd., Beachwood 44122; (216) 464-9250 (68).

The Village at St. Edward (apartments, nursing care and assisted living), 3131 Smith Rd., Fairlawn 44333; (330) 666-1183; www.vased.org (160).

Oklahoma: St. Ann's Home, 9400 St. Ann's Dr., Oklahoma City 73162; (405) 728-7888 (120).

Westminster Village, Inc. (residence), 1601 Academy, Ponca City 74604; (580) 762-0927 (131).

Oregon: Benedictine Nursing Center, 540 S. Main St., Mt. Angel 97362; (503) 845-6841 (75). Home Health Agency, Outpatient Therapies. Benedictine Institute for Long Term Care. Child Development Center.

Evergreen Court Independent Retirement Living, 451 O'Connell St., North Bend 97459; (541) 751-7658; www.baycrest-village.com.

Maryville Nursing Home, 14645 S.W. Farmington, Beaverton 97007; (503) 643-8626; www.ssmo.org.

Mt. St. Joseph, 3060 S.E. Stark St., Portland 97214; (503) 535-4700 (347).

St. Catherine's Residence and Nursing Center, 3959 Sheridan Ave., North Bend 97459; (541) 756-4151 (200).

Pennsylvania: Antonian Towers, 1318 Spring St., Bethlehem, PA 18018; (610) 865-3963.

Ascension Manor I (senior citizen housing), 911 N. Franklin St., Philadelphia 19123; (215) 922-1116.

Ascension Manor II (senior citizen housing), 970 N. 7th St., Philadelphia 19123; (215) 922-1116.

Benetwood Apartments, Benedictine Sisters of Erie, 641 Troupe St., Harborcreek 16421; (814) 899-0088 (80).

Bethlehem Retirement Village, 100 W. Wissahickon Ave., Flourtown 19031; (215) 233-0998.

Catholic Senior Housing Development and Management, 1318 Spring St., Bethlehem 18018; (610) 865-3963; hfmanor.com/html/independent_living.html (50).

Christ the King Manor, 1100 W. Long Ave., Du Bois 15801; (814) 371-3180 (160).

D'Youville Manor (residential care facility), 1750 Quarry Rd., Yardley 19067; (215) 579-1750 (49).

Garvey Manor and Our Lady of the Allegheny Residence (nursing home), 128 Logan Blvd., Hollidaysburg 16648-2693; (814) 695-5571; www.garveymanor.org (150).

Grace Mansion (personal care facility), Holy Family Residential Services, 1200 Spring St., Bethlehem; (610) 865-6748; www.hfmanor.com (33).

Holy Family Home, Little Sisters of the Poor, 5300 Chester Ave., Philadelphia 19143; (215) 729-5153 (105).

Holy Family Manor (skilled and intermediate nursing facility), 1200 Spring St., Bethlehem 18018; (610) 865-5595; www.hfmanor.com (208).

Holy Family Residence (personal care facility), 900 W. Market St., Orwigsburg 17961; (570) 366-2912 (85).

Immaculate Mary Home (nursing care facility), 2990 Holme Ave., Philadelphia 19136; (215) 335-2100 (296).

John XXIII Home (skilled, intermediate and personal care), 2250 Shenango Freeway, Hermitage 16148; (724) 981-3200; www.johnxxiiihome.org (196).

Little Flower Manor (residence, women), 1215 Springfield Rd., Darby 19023; (610) 534-6000 (180).

Little Flower Manor Nursing Home (skilled nursing), 1201 Springfield Rd., Darby 19023; (610) 534-6000 (185).

Little Flower Manor of Diocese of Scranton, (longterm skilled nursing care facility), 200 S. Meade St., Wilkes-Barre 18702; (570) 823-6131.

Little Sisters of the Poor, 1028 Benton Ave., Pittsburgh 15212; (412) 307-1100; www.littlsesistersofthepoor-pittsburgh.org (40).

Little Sisters of the Poor, Holy Family Residence, 2500 Adams Ave., Scranton 18509; (570) 343-4065 (58).

Maria Joseph Manor (skilled nursing, personal care facility and independent living cottages), 875 Montour Blvd., Danville 17821; (570) 275-4221 (135).

Marian Hall Home for the Aged (women), 934 Forest Ave., Pittsburgh 15202; (412) 761-1999 (49).

Marian Manor (intermediate care), 2695 Winchester Dr., Pittsburgh 15220; (412) 563-6866 (194).

Mount Macrina Manor (skilled nursing facility), 520 W. Main St., Uniontown 15401; (724) 437-1400 (141).

Neumann Apartments (low income), 25 N. Nichols St., St. Clair 17970; (570) 429-0699 (25).

Queen of Angels Apartments, 22 Rothermel St., Hyde Park, Reading 19605; (610) 921-3115 (45 units).

Queen of Peace Apartments (low income), 1318 Spring St., Bethlehem 18018; (610) 865-3963 (65).

Redeemer Village II, 1551 Huntingdon Pike, Huntingdon Valley 19006; (215) 947-8168; www.holyredeemer.com (151).

Sacred Heart Manor (nursing home and independent living), 6445 Germantown Ave., Philadelphia 19119; (215) 438-5268 (171 nursing home; 48 personal care; 48 independent living).

St. Anne's Home and Village, 3952 Columbia Ave., Columbia 17512; (717) 285-5443 (121).

St. Anne Home (nursing facility), 685 Angela Dr., Greensburg 15601; (724) 837-6070 (125).

St. Ignatius Nursing Home, 4401 Haverford Ave., Philadelphia 19104; (215) 349-8800 (176).

St. John Neumann Nursing Home, 10400 Roosevelt Blvd., Philadelphia 19116; (215) 248-7200 (107).

St. Joseph Home for the Aged (Residential and skilled nursing facility), 1182 Holland Rd., Holland 18966; (215) 357-5511 (76).

St. Joseph Nursing and Health Care Center (skilled nursing facility), 5324 Penn Ave., Pittsburgh 15224; (412) 665-5100 (153).

St. Leonard's Home Inc. (personal care facility), 601 N. Montgomery St., Hollidaysburg 16648; (814) 695-9581 (30).

St. Mary of Providence Center, R.D. 2, Box 145, Elverson 19520; (610) 942-4166 (52).

Saint Mary's Home of Erie, 607 E. 26th St., Erie 16504-2813; (814) 459-0621; www.stmaryshome.org (131).

Saint Mary's at Asbury Ridge, 4855 West Ridge Rd., Erie, PA 16506; (814) 836-5300.

Saint Mary's Manor (residential, personal care, short-term rehabilitation and nursing care), 701 Lansdale Ave., Lansdale 19446; (215) 368-0900; www.smmphl.org (200).

St. Mary's Villa Nursing Home, 675 St. Mary's Villa Rd., Moscow 18444; (570) 842-7621 (176).

Trexler Pavilion (personal care facility), 1220 Prospect Ave., Bethlehem 18018; (610) 868-7776 (30).

Vincentian de Marillac Nursing Home, 5300 Stanton Ave., Pittsburgh 15206; (412) 361-2833 (52).

Vincentian Home (nursing facility), 111 Perrymont Rd., Pittsburgh 15237; (412) 366-5600 (217).

Rhode Island: Jeanne Jugan Residence of the Little Sisters of the Poor, 964 Main St., Pawtucket 02860; (401) 723-4314 (95).

Saint Antoine Residence (skilled nursing facility), 10 Rhodes Ave., North Smithfield 02896; (401) 767-3500; www.stantoine.net (416).

St. Clare Home (nursing facility), 309 Spring St., Newport 02840; (401) 849-3204 (47).

St. Francis House, 167 Blackstone St., Woonsocket 02895; (401) 762-5255 (59).

Scalabrini Villa (convalescent, rest-nursing home). 860 N. Quidnessett Rd., North Kingstown 02852; (401)   884-1802; www.freeyellow.com/members3/scalabrini (175).

South Carolina: Carter-May Home/St. Joseph Residence, 1660 Ingram Rd., Charleston 29407; (843) 556-8314 (15).

South Dakota: Avera Brady Health and Rehabilitation (skilled nursing facility), 500 S. Ohlman St., Mitchell 57301; (605) 966-7701 (83).

Mother Joseph Manor (skilled nursing facility), 1002 N. Jay St., Aberdeen 57401; (605) 622-5850 (81).

Prince of Peace Retirement Community, 4500 Prince of Peace Pl., Sioux Falls 57103; (605) 322-5600 (204).

St. William's Care Center (intermediate care, 60), and Angela Hall (assisted living center for developmentally handicapped women, 22), 100 South 9th St., Milbank 57252; (605) 432-5811.

Tekakwitha Nursing Home (skilled and intermediate care), 6 E. Chestnut St., Sisseton 57262; (605) 698-7693 (101).

Tennessee: Alexian Village of Tennessee, 100 James Blvd., Signal Mountain 37377; (423) 886-0100 (277).

St. Mary Manor, 1771 Highway 45 Bypass, Jackson 38305; (731) 668-5633.

St. Peter Manor (retirement community), 108 N. Auburndale, Memphis 38104; (901) 278-8200.

St. Peter Villa (intermediate and skilled care), 141 N. McLean, Memphis 38104; (901) 276-2021.

Villa Maria Manor, 32 White Bridge Rd., Nashville 37205; (615) 352-3084 (230).

Texas: Casa, Inc., Housing for Elderly and Handicapped, 3201 Sondra Dr., Fort Worth 76107;

(817) 332-7276 (200).

Casa Brendan Housing for the Elderly and Handicapped (56 apartments) and Casa II, Inc. (30 apartments), 1300 Hyman St., Stephenville 76401; (254) 965-6964 (83).

John Paul II Nursing Home (intermediate care and personal care), 209 S. 3rd St., Kenedy 78119; (830) 583-9841.

Mother of Perpetual Help Home (intermediate care facility), 519 E. Madison Ave., Brownsville 78520; (956) 546-6745 (38).

Mt. Carmel Home (personal care home), 4130 S. Alameda St., Corpus Christi 78411; (512) 855-6243 (92).

Nuestro Hogar Housing for Elderly and Handicapped, 709 Magnolia St., Arlington 76012; (817) 261-0608 (63).

St. Ann's Nursing Home, P.O. Box 1179, Panhandle 79068; (806) 537-3194 (56).

St. Dominic Residence Hall, 2401 Holcombe Blvd., Houston 77021; (713) 741-8700 (149).

St. Francis Nursing Home (intermediate care facility), 630 W. Woodlawn, San Antonio 78212; (210) 736-3177 (152).

St. Francis Village, Inc. (retired and elderly), 1 Chapel Plaza, Crowley 76036; (817) 292-5786 (420).

San Juan Nursing Home, Inc. (skilled and intermediate care facility), P.O. Box 1238, San Juan 78589; (956) 787-1771 (127).

Villa Maria (home for aged women-men), 920 S. Oregon St., El Paso 79901; (915) 533-5152 (17 units).

Villa Maria, Inc. (apartment complex), 3146 Saratoga Blvd., Corpus Christi 78415; (361) 857-6171 (59).

Utah: Christus Health Utah (Christus St. Joseph Villa and Christus Marian Center), 451 Bishop Federal Lane, Salt Lake City 84115; (801) 487-7557; www.stjosephvilla.com (300).

Vermont: Loretto Home, 59 Meadow St., Rutland 05701; (802) 773-8840 (57).

Michaud Memorial Manor (residential home for elderly), Derby Line 05830; (802) 873-3152 (34).

St. Joseph's Residential Care Home, 243 N. Prospect St., Burlington 05401; (802) 864-0264 (32).

Virginia: Madonna Home (home for aged), 814 W. 37th St., Norfolk 23508; (757) 623-6662 (16).

Marian Manor (assisted living, nursing care), 5345 Marian Lane, Virginia Beach 23462; (757) 456-5018 (100).

Marywood Apartments, 1261 Marywood Lane, Richmond 23229; (804) 740-5567 (126).

McGurk House Apartments, 2425 Tate Springs Rd., Lynchburg 24501; (434) 846-2425 (89).

Our Lady of the Valley Retirement Community, 650 N. Jefferson St., Roanoke 24016; (540) 345-5111.

Russell House Apartments, 900 First Colonial Rd., Virginia Beach 23454; (757) 481-0770 (126).

St. Francis Home, 2511 Wise St., Richmond 23225; (804) 231-1043 (34).

St. Joseph's Home for the Aged, Little Sisters of the Poor, 1503 Michael Rd., Richmond 23229; (804) 288-6245 (72).

St. Mary's Woods (independent and assisted living apartments), 1257 Marywood Lane, Richmond 23229;

(804) 741-8624; www.stmaryswood.com (118 apartments).

Seton Manor (apartments), 215 Marcella Rd., Hampton 23666; (757) 827-6512 (112).

Washington: Cathedral Plaza Apartments (retirement apartments), W. 1120 Sprague Ave., Spokane 99204 (150).

Chancery Place (retirement apartments), 910 Marion, Seattle 98104; (206) 343-9415; www.ccsww.org.

The Delaney, W. 242 Riverside Ave., Spokane 99201; (509) 747-5081 (83).

Elbert House, 16000 N.E. 8th St., Bellevue 98008; (206) 747-5111.

Emma McRedmond Manor, 7960-169th N.E., Redmond 98052; (206) 869-2424 (31).

Fahy Garden Apartments, W. 1403-11 Dean Ave., Spokane 99201 (31).

Fahy West Apartments, W. 1523 Dean Ave., Spokane 99201 (55).

The Franciscan (apartments), 15237-21stAve. S.W., Seattle 98166; (206) 431-8001.

Providence Mt. St. Vincent (nursing center and retirement apartments), 4831 35th Ave. S.W., Seattle 98126; (206) 937-3700 (174).

Tumwater Apartments, 5701-6th Ave. S.W., Tumwater 98501; (360) 352-4321.

West Virginia: Welty Home for the Aged, 21 Washington Ave., Wheeling 26003; (304) 242-5233 (46).

Wisconsin: Alexian Village of Milwaukee (retirement community/skilled nursing home), 9301 N. 76th St., Milwaukee 53223; (414) 355-9300; www.alexianvillage.org (327).

Bethany-St. Joseph Health Care Center, 2501 Shelby Rd., La Crosse 54601; (608) 788-5700 (226).

Clement Manor (retirement community and skilled nursing), 3939 S. 92nd St., Greenfield 53228; (414) 321-1800 (162).

Divine Savior Nursing Home, 715 W. Pleasant St., Portage 53901; (608) 742-4131 (124).

Felician Village (independent living), 1700 S. 18th St., Manitowoc 54020; (920) 683-8811 (134 apartments).

Franciscan Care Center, 500 S. Oakwood Rd., Oshkosh, WI 54901; (920) 223-0110.

Franciscan Skemp Healthcare, Mayo Health System: Arcadia Campus Nursing Home, 464 S. St. Joseph Ave., Arcadia 54612; (608) 323-3341 (75).

McCormick Memorial Home, 212 Iroquois St., Green Bay 54301; (920) 437-0883 (60).

Marian Catholic Home (skilled care nursing home), 3333 W. Highland Blvd., Milwaukee 53208; (414) 344-8100 (215).

Marian Franciscan Center, 9632 W. Appleton Ave., Milwaukee 53225; (414) 461-8850 (310).

Marian Housing Center (independent living), 4105 Spring St., Racine 53405; (262) 633-5807 (40).

Maryhill Manor Nursing Home (skilled nursing facility), 501 Madison Ave., Niagara 54151; (715) 251-3178 (75).

Milwaukee Catholic Home (continuing care retirement community), 2462 N. Prospect Ave., Milwaukee

53211-4462; (414) 224-9700; www.milwau-keecatholichome.org (131).

Nazareth House (skilled nursing facility), 814 Jackson St., Stoughton 53589; (608) 873-6448 (99).

St. Ann Rest Home (intermediate care facility, women), 2020 S. Muskego Ave., Milwaukee 53204; (414) 383-2630 (50).

St. Anne's Home for the Elderly, 3800 N. 92nd St., Milwaukee 53222; (414) 463-7570; www.wahsa.org/st.anne (106).

St. Camillus Campus (continuing care retirement community), 10100 West Blue Mound Road, Wauwatosa 53226; (414) 258-1814; www.stcam.com (386).

St. Elizabeth Nursing Home, 502 St. Lawrence Ave., Janesville 53545; (608) 752-6709 (43).

St. Francis Home (skilled nursing facility), 1416 Cumming Ave., Superior 54880; (715) 394-5591.

St. Francis Home (skilled nursing), 33 Everett St., Fond du Lac 54935; (920) 923-7980 (106).

St. Joseph's Home, 9244 29th Ave., Kenosha 53143; (262) 925-8124; www.stjosephs.com (93).

St. Joseph's Rehabilitation Center, 2902 East Ave. S., La Crosse 54601; (608) 788-9870; www.crsinc.org (80).

St. Joseph's Nursing Home of St. Joseph Community Health Services, Inc. P.O. Box 527, Hillsboro 54634; (608) 489-8000.

St. Joseph Residence, Inc. (nursing home), 107 E. Beckert Rd., New London 54961; (920) 982-5354 (107).

St. Mary's Home for the Aged (skilled nursing, Alzheimer's unit, respite care), 2005 Division St., Manitowoc 54220; (920) 684-7171; www.felician-community.com (266).

St. Mary's Nursing Home, 3515 W. Hadley St., Milwaukee 53210; (414) 873-9250 (88).

St. Monica's Senior Citizens Home, 3920 N. Green Bay Rd., Racine 53404; (262) 639-5050; www.srsof-strita.org (110).

St. Paul Home, Inc. (intermediate and skilled nursing home), 1211 Oakridge Ave., Kaukauna 54130; (920) 766-6020 (129).

Villa Loretto Nursing Home, N8114 Calvary St., Mount Calvary 53057; (920) 753-3211 (52).

Villa St. Francis, Inc., 1910 W. Ohio Ave., Milwaukee 53215; (414) 649-2888 (142).

FACILITIES FOR CHILDREN AND ADULTS WITH DISABILITIES

Sources: Catholic Almanac *survey;* The Official Catholic Directory.

This listing covers facilities and programs with educational and training orientation. Information about other services for the handicapped can generally be obtained from the Catholic Charities Office or its equivalent (c/o Chancery Office) in any diocese. (*See* **Index** for listing of addresses of chancery offices in the U.S.)

Abbreviation code: b, boys; c, coeducational; d, day; g, girls; r, residential. Other information includes age for admission. The number in parentheses at the end of an entry indicates total capacity or enrollment.

Deaf and Hearing Impaired

California: St. Joseph's Center for Deaf and Hard of Hearing, 3880 Smith St., Union City 94587.

Louisiana: Chinchuba Institute (d,c; birth through 18 yrs.), 1131 Barataria Blvd., Marrero 70072.

Missouri: St. Joseph Institute for the Deaf (r,d,c; birth to 14 years), 1809 Clarkson Rd., Chesterfield, MO 63107; (636) 532-3211 (Voice/TDD).

New York: Cleary School for the Deaf (d,c; infancy through 21), 301 Smithtown Blvd., Nesconset, NY 11767-2077; (516) 588-0530; www.clearyschool.org (70).

St. Francis de Sales School for the Deaf (d,c; infant through elementary grades), 260 Eastern Parkway, Brooklyn 11225; (718) 636-4573 (150).

St. Joseph's School for the Deaf (d,c; parent-infant through 14 yrs.), 1000 Hutchinson River Pkwy, Bronx 10465; (718) 828-9000 (140).

Ohio: St. Rita School for the Deaf (r,d,c; birth to 12th grade), 1720 Glendale-Milford Rd., Cincinnati 45215; (513) 771-7600; www.srsdeaf.org (130).

Pennsylvania: Archbishop Ryan School for Hearing Impaired Children (d,c; parent-infant programs through 8th grade), 233 Mohawk Ave., Norwood, PA 19074; (610) 586-7044 (49).

De Paul Institute (d,c; birth through 21 yrs.), 2904 Castlegate Ave., Pittsburgh 15226; (412) 561-4848 (77).

Emotionally and/or Socially Maladjusted

This listing includes facilities for abused, abandoned and neglected as well as emotionally disturbed children and youth.

Alabama: St. Mary's Home for Children (r,c; referred from agencies), 4350 Moffat Rd., Mobile 36618; (251) 344-7733.

California: Hanna Boys Center (r,b; 10-15 yrs. at intake; school, 4th to 10th grade), Box 100, Sonoma 95476; (707)996-6767 (107). Treatment center and therapeutic special school for boys with emotional problems, behavior disorders, learning disabilities.

Rancho San Antonio (r,b; 13-17 yrs.), 21000 Plummer St., Chatsworth 91311; (818) 882-6400.

St. Vincent's (r,d,g; 12-17 yrs.), 4200 Calle Real, Santa Barbara 93110-1454; (805) 683-6381.

Colorado: Mt. St. Vincent Home (r,c; 5-13 yrs.), 4159 Lowell Blvd., Denver 80211; (303) 458-7220; www.nahse.org/member/st.vincent.

Connecticut: St. Francis Home for Children (r,d,c; 4-17 yrs.), 651 Prospect St., New Haven 06511; (203) 777-5513. Exec. Dir., Peter Salerno.

Mt. St. John Home and School for Boys (r,b; 11-16 yrs.), 135 Kirtland St., Deep River 06417; (860) 526-5391; www.mtstjohn.org (77).

Delaware: Our Lady of Grace Home for Children (r,d,c; 6-12 yrs.), 487 E. Chestnut Hill Rd., Newark 19713; (302) 738-4658.

Seton Villa, Siena Hall and Children's Home (r,c; group home; 12-18 yrs,; mothers and their children), c/o 2307 Kentmere Pkwy, Wilmington 19806; (302) 656-2183.

Florida: Boystown of Florida (r,b; 12-16 yrs.; group home), 11400 S.W. 137th Ave., Miami 33186.

Georgia: Village of St. Joseph (r,c; 6-16 yrs.), 1961 Druid Hills Rd., Ste. 205-B, 30329; (404) 321-2900.

Illinois: Guardian Angel Community Services (d,c; r,b), 1550 Plainfield Rd., Joliet 60435; (815) 729-0930 (35).

Maryville Academy (r,c; 6-18 yrs.), 1150 North

River Rd., Des Plaines 60016; (708) 824-1893.

Mission of Our Lady of Mercy, Mercy Home for Boys and Girls (r,d,c; 15-18 yrs.), 1140 W. Jackson Blvd., Chicago 60607; (312) 738-7560; www.mercyhome.org.

Indiana: Gibault School for Boys (r; 10-18 yrs.), 6301 South U.S. Highway 41, Terre Haute 47802; (812) 298-3120.

Campagna Academy (r; 10-18 yrs.), 7403 Cline Ave., Schererville 46375; (219) 322-8614.

Kentucky: Boys' Haven (r; 12-18 yrs.), 2301 Goldsmith Lane, Louisville 40218; (502) 458-1171; www.boyshaven.org.

Louisiana: Hope Haven Center (r,c; 5-18 yrs.), 1101 Barataria Blvd., Marrero 70072; (504) 347-5581.

Maryland: Good Shepherd Center (r,g; 13-18 yrs.), 4100 Maple Ave., Baltimore, 21227; (410) 247-2770; www.goodshepherdcenter.com.

Massachusetts: The Brightside for Families and Children (r,d,c; 6-16 yrs.), 2112 Riverdale St., W. Springfield 01089; (413) 827-4255; www.mercycares.com. Vice-Pres. James Bastien.

McAuley Nazareth Home for Boys (r; 6-13 yrs.), 77 Mulberry St., Leicester 01524; (508) 892-4886 (16). Residential treatment center.

St. Vincent Home (r,c 5-22 yrs.), 2425 Highland Ave., Fall River 02720; (508) 679-8511.

Michigan: Don Bosco Hall (r,b; 13-17 years.), 10001 Petoskey Ave., Detroit 48204; (313) 834-8677.

Holy Cross Children's Services (r,d,c; 13-17 yrs.), 8759 Clinton-Macon Rd., Clinton 49236; (517) 423-7451; www.hccsnet.org (650). Facilities located throughout the state and northern Ohio.

Vista Maria (r,g; 11-18 yrs.), 20651 W. Warren Ave., Dearborn Heights 48127; (313) 271-6250; www.community.milive.com/cc/girls.

Minnesota: St. Cloud Children's Home (r,c; 8-18 yrs.), RTC Campus, Bld. 4-D, P.O. Box 1006, Fergus Falls, MN 56538; (218) 739-9325. Day Treatment Program (d,c; 7-14 yrs.), same address.

St. Elizabeth Home (r,c; 18 yrs. and older), 306 15th Ave. N., St. Cloud 56301; (320) 252-8350.

Missouri: Child Center of Our Lady (r,d,c; 5-14 yrs.), 7900 Natural Bridge Rd., St. Louis 63121; (314) 383-0200.

Marygrove (r,d,c; 6-21 yrs.) (97); intense treatment unit (r,b; 13-18 yrs) (13); overnight crises care (r,d,c; birth to 18 yrs.) (8), 2705 Mullanphy Lane, Florissant, 63031; (314) 837-1702; www.marygroveonline.org.

St. Joseph's Home for Boys (r,d,b; 6-14 yrs.), 4753 S. Grand Blvd., St. Louis 63111; (314) 481-9121.

Nebraska: Father Flanagan's Boys' Home (r,c; 10-16 yrs.), 14100 Crawford St., Boys Town 68010; (402) 498-1000; www.boystown.org (556). Boys Town National Research Hospital (r,d,c; 1-18 yrs.), 555 N. 30th St., Omaha 68131; (402) 498-6362; www.boystownhospital.org. Center for abused handicapped children, diagnosis of speech, language and hearing problems in children. Boys Town also has various facilities or programs in Brooklyn, NY; Portsmouth, RI; Philadelphia, PA; Washington, DC; Tallahassee, Orlando and Delray Beach, FL; Atlanta, GA; New Orleans, LA; San Antonio, TX; Las Vegas, NV; and southern CA.

New Jersey: Catholic Community Services/Mt. Carmel Guild, 1160 Raymond Blvd., Newark 07102;

(973) 596-4084.

Collier High School (d,c; 13-18 yrs.), 160 Conover Rd., Wickatunk 07765; (732) 946-4771; www.collierservices.com.

Collier Group Home, 180 Spring St., Red Bank, NJ 07701; (732) 842-8337.

Collier House (transitional living), 386 Maple Pl., Keyport, NJ 07735; (732) 264-3222.

New York: The Astor Home for Children (r,d,c; 5-12 yrs.), 6339 Mill St., P.O. Box 5005, Rhinebeck 12572-5005; (845) 871-1000; www.astorservices.org. Child Guidance Clinics/Day Treatment (Rhinebeck, Poughkeepsie, Beacon, Bronx). Head Start - Day Care (Poughkeepsie, Beacon, Red Hook, Dover, Millerton).

Baker Victory Services, 780 Ridge Rd. Lackawanna 14218; (716) 828-9500; www.ourladyofvictory.org.

Good Shepherd Services (r,d,c), 305 Seventh Ave., New York, NY 10001; (212) 243-7070; www.goodshepherds.org. City-wide residential programs or adolescents (12-21 yrs.); foster care and adoption services (infant-21 yrs.); training institute for human services workers; day treatment program (13-18 yrs.); community-based neighborhood family services in South Brooklyn Community (infant-adult),

LaSalle School (r,d,b; 12-18 yrs.), 391 Western Ave., Albany 12203; (518) 242-4731.

Madonna Heights Services (r,d,g; 12-18 yrs.), 151 Burrs Lane, Dix Hills 11746; (631) 643-8800; www.sco.org (110). Also conducts group homes on Long Island and outpatient programs.

Saint Anne Institute (r,d,g; 12-18 yrs.), 160 N. Main Ave., Albany 12206; (518) 437-6500.

St. Catherine's Center for Children (r,d,c; birth through 12 yrs.), 40 N. Main Ave., Albany 12203; (518) 453-6700; www.st-cath.org.

St. John's of Rockaway Beach (r,b; 9-21 yrs.), 144 Beach 111th St., Rockaway Park 11694; (718) 945-2800. Programs include diagnostic centers and independent living programs.

North Dakota: Home on the Range (r,c; 10-18 yrs.), 16351 I-94, Sentinel Butte 58654; (701) 872-3745; www.gohotr.org (79). Residential and emergency shelter therapeutic programs.

Home on the Range-Red River Victory Ranch (r,b; 10-18 yrs.), P.O. Box 9615, Fargo 58106; (701) 293-6321; www.hotr.org (12). Residential chemical addictions program.

Ohio: St. Vincent Family Centers (d,c; preschool) Outpatient counseling program (c; 2-18 yrs.), 1490 East Main St., Columbus 43205; (614) 252-0731; www.svfc.org.

Marycrest (r,g; 13-18 yrs.), 7800 Brookside Rd., Independence 44131.

Catholic Charities Services/Parmadale (r,c; 12-18 yrs.), 6753 State Rd., Parma 44134; (440) 845-7700.

Rosemont (r,g;d,c; 11-18 yrs.), 2440 Dawnlight Ave., Columbus 43211; (614) 471-2626.

Oregon: St. Mary's Home for Boys (r; 10-18 yrs.), 16535 S.W. Tualatin Valley Highway, Beaverton 97006; (503) 649-5651.

Pennsylvania: Auberle (r,c; 7-18 yrs.), 1101 Hartman St., McKeesport 15132-1500; (412) 673-5800; www.auberle.org (181). Residential treatment for boys; emergency shelter care, foster care, group home for girls and family preservation program.

De LaSalle in Towne (d,b; 14-17 yrs.), 25 S. Van Pelt

522   FACILITIES FOR CHILDREN AND ADULTS WITH DISABILITIES

St., Philadelphia 19103; (215) 567-5500.

De LaSalle Vocational Day Treatment (b; 15-18 yrs.), P.O. Box 344, Bensalem 19020; (215) 464-0344.

Gannondale (r,g; 12-17 yrs.), 4635 E. Lake Rd., Erie 16511; (814) 899-7659.

Harborcreek Youth Services (r,d,c; 10-17 yrs.), 5712 Iroquois Ave., Harborcreek 16421; (814) 899-7664; www.hys-erie.org.

Holy Family Institute (r,d,c; 0-18 yrs.), 8235 Ohio River Blvd., Emsworth 15202; (412) 766-4030; www.hfi-pgh.org.

Lourdesmont Good Shepherd Youth and Family Services (r,g;d,c; 12-17 yrs.), 537 Venard Rd., Clarks Summit 18411; (507) 587-4741; www.lourdesmont. com. Sponsored by the Sisters of the Good Shepherd. John A. Antognoli.

St. Gabriel's Hall (r,b; 10-18 yrs.), P.O. Box 7280, Audubon 19407; (215) 247-2776.

St. Michael's School (r,b; d,c; 12-17 yrs.), Box 370, Tunkhannock 18657; (570) 388-6155.

Texas: St. Joseph Adolescent and Family Counseling Center (c; 13-17 yrs.), 5415 Maple Ave., #320, Dallas 75235; (214) 631-TEEN.

Washington: Morning Star Boys Ranch (Spokane Boys' Ranch, Inc.) (r,b; 10-18 yrs.), Box 8087, Spokane 99203-0087; (509) 448-1411; www.morningstarboysranch.org. Dir. Joseph M. Weitensteiner.

Wisconsin: North American Union Sisters of Our Lady of Charity (r,c; 10-17 yrs.), 154 Edgington Lane, Wheeling, WV 26003-1535; (304) 242-0042.

St. Charles Youth and Family Services (r,d,b; 12-18 yrs.), 151 S. 84th St., Milwaukee 53214; (414) 476-3710; www.stcharlesinc.org.

Wyoming: St. Joseph's Children's Home (r,c; 6-18 yrs.), P.O. Box 1117, Torrington 82240; (307) 532-4197.

Developmentally Challenged

This listing includes facilities for children, youth, and adults with learning disabilities.

Alabama: Father Purcell Memorial Exceptional Children's Center (r, c; birth to 10 yrs.), 2048 W. Fairview Ave., Montgomery 36108; (334) 834-5590; www.mnw.net/fpm.

Father Walter Memorial Child Care Center (r,c; birth-12 yrs.), 2815 Forbes Dr., Montgomery 36110; (334) 262-6421.

California: Child Study Center of St. John's Hospital (d,c; birth-18 yrs.), 1339-20th St., Santa Monica 90404; (310) 829-8921.

St. Madeleine Sophie's Center (d,c; 18 yrs. and older), 2111 E. Madison Ave., El Cajon 92019.

Tierra del Sol Foundation (d,c; 18 yrs. and older), 9919 Sunland Blvd., Sunland 91040; (818) 352-1419. 14547 Gilmore St., Van Nuys 91411; (818) 904-9164.

Connecticut: Gengras Center (d,c; 3-21 yrs.), St. Joseph College, 1678 Asylum Ave., W. Hartford 06117.

Villa Maria Education Center (d,c; 6-14 yrs.), 161 Sky Meadow Dr., Stamford 06903-3400; (203) 322-5886; www.villamariaedcenter.org.

District of Columbia: Lt. Joseph P. Kennedy, Jr., Institute (d,c; 6 weeks to 5 yrs. for Kennedy Institute for Child Development Center; 6-21 yrs. for Kennedy School; 18 yrs. and older for training and employment, therapeutic and residential services). Founded in 1959

for people of all ages with developmental disabilities and their families in the Washington archdiocese. Heaquarters: 801 Buchanan St. N.E., Washington 20017; (202) 529-7600; www.kennedyinstitute.org. Other locations in D.C. and Maryland. No enrollment limit.

Florida: L'Arche Harbor House, (c; 20 yrs. and older; community home), 700 Arlington Rd., Jacksonville 32211; (904) 721-5992.

Marian Center Services for Developmentally Handicapped and Mentally Retarded (r,d,c; 2-21 yrs.), 15701 Northwest 37th Ave., Opa Locka 33054; (305) 625-8354; www.mariancenterschool.org. Pre-school, school, workshop residence services.

Morning Star School (d,c; 4-16 yrs.), 725 Mickler Rd., Jacksonville, 32211; (904) 421-2144.

Morning Star School (d,c; school age), 954 Leigh Ave., Orlando 32804.

Morning Star School (d,c; 6-14 yrs.), 4661-80th Ave. N., Pinellas Park 33781; (727) 544-6036; www.morningstarschool.org.

Morning Star School (d,c; 6-16 yrs.), 210 E. Linebaugh Ave., Tampa 33612; (813) 935-0232; www.tampa-morningstar.org..

Georgia: St. Mary's Home (r,c), 2170 E. Victory Dr., Savannah 31404; (912) 236-7164.

Illinois: Bartlett Learning Center (r,d,c; 3-21 yrs.), 801 W. Bartlett Rd., Bartlett 60103; (630) 289-4221.

Brother James Court (r, men over 18 yrs.), 2508 St. James Rd., Springfield 62707; (217) 544-4878.

Good Shepherd Manor (men; 18 yrs. and older), Little Brothers of the Good Shepherd, P.O. Box 260, Momence 60954; (815) 472-3700; www.goodshepherdmanor.org. Resident care for developmentally disabled men.

Misericordia Home South (r,c), 2916 W. 47th St., Chicago 60632; (773) 254-9595. For severely and profoundly impaired children.

Misericordia Home — Heart of Mercy Village (r,c; 6-45 yrs.), 6300 North Ridge, Chicago 60660; (773) 973-6300; www.misericordia.com.

Mt. St. Joseph (developmentally disabled women; over age 21), 24955 N. Highway 12, Lake Zurich 60047; (847) 438-5050.

Provena St. Vincent Community Living Facility (r,c; adults, over 18 yrs.) (20), and St. Vincent Supported Living Arrangement (r,c; adults, over 18 yrs.) (20), 659 E. Jefferson St., Freeport 61032; (815) 232-6181.

St. Coletta's of Illinois (r,d,; 6 to adult), 123rd and Wolf Rd., Palos Park 60464; (708) 448-6520.

St. Mary of Providence (r,women; 18 yrs. and older), 4200 N. Austin Ave., Chicago 60634; (773) 545-8300.

Springfield Developmental Center (m; 21 yrs. and over), 4595 Laverna Rd., Springfield 62707; (217) 525-8271.

Massachusetts: Cardinal Cushing Centers (d,c; 3-22 yrs.), 85 Washington St., Braintree 02184; (781) 848-6250; www.coletta.org.

Vocational Training

Indiana: Marian Day School (d,c; 6-16 yrs.), 700 Herndon Dr., Evansville 47711; (812) 422-5346.

Kansas: Lakemary Center, Inc. (r,d,c), 100 Lakemary Dr., Paola 66071; (913) 557-4000.

Kentucky: Pitt Academy (d,c), 6010 Preston Hwy., Louisville 40219; (502) 966-6979; www.pitt.com.

Louisiana: Department of Special Education, Archdiocese of New Orleans, St. Michael Special School (d,c; 6-21 yrs.), 1522 Chippewa St., New Orleans 70130.

Holy Angels Residential Facility (r,c; teenage, 14 yrs. and older), 10450 Ellerbe Rd., Shreveport 71106; (318) 797-8500.

Ocean Avenue Community Home, 361 Ocean Ave., Gretna 70053; (504) 361-0674.

Padua Community Services (r,c; birth-25 yrs.), 200 Beta St., Belle Chasse 70037.

St. Jude the Apostle, 1430 Claire Ave., Gretna 70053; (504) 361-8457.

St. Mary's Residential Training School (r,c: 3-22 yrs.), P.O. Drawer 7768, Alexandria 71306; (318) 445-6443.

St. Peter the Fisherman, 62269 Airport Dr., Slidell 70458; (504) 641-4914.

St. Rosalie (r; men 18 and up), 119 Kass St., Gretna 70056; (504) 361-8320.

Sts. Mary and Elizabeth, 720 N. Elm St., Metairie 70003; (504) 738-6959.

Maryland: The Benedictine School for Exceptional Children (r,c; 6-21 yrs.), 14299 Benedictine Lane, Ridgely 21660; (410) 634-2112; www.benschool.com.

Francis X. Gallagher Services (r), 2520 Pot Spring Rd., Timonium 21093.

St. Elizabeth School and Habilitation Center (d,c; 11-21 yrs.), 801 Argonne Dr., Baltimore 21218; (410) 889-5054; www.stelizabeth-school.org.

Massachusetts: Cardinal Cushing School and Training Center (r,d,c; 16-22 yrs.), Hanover 02339 (116 r; 28 d).

Mercy Centre (d,c; 3-22 yrs. and over), 25 West Chester St., Worcester 01605-1136; (508) 852-7165; www.mercycentre.com.

Michigan: Our Lady of Providence Center (r,g; 11-30 yrs., d,c; 26 yrs. and older), 16115 Beck Rd., Northville 48118; (734) 453-1300.

St. Louis Center and School (r,d,b; 6-18 yrs. child care; 18-36 yrs. adult foster care), 16195 Old U.S. 12, Chelsea 48118-9646; (734) 475-8430; www.stlouiscenter.org.

Minnesota: Mother Teresa Home (r,c; 18 yrs. and older), 101-10th Ave. N., Cold Spring 56320.

St. Francis Home (r,c; 18 yrs. and older), P.O. Box 326, Waite Park 56387; (320) 251-7630.

St. Luke's Home (r; 18 yrs. and older), 411 8th Ave. N., Cold Springs 56320.

Missouri: Department of Special Education, Archdiocese of St. Louis, 4472 Lindell Blvd., St. Louis. 63108; (314) 533-3454. Serves children with developmental disabilities, mental retardation or learning disabilities; services include special ungraded day classes in 8 parish schools.

Good Shepherd Homes (residential for developmentally disabled men; 18 yrs. and up), The Community of the Good Shepherd, 10101 James A. Reed Rd., Kansas City 64134; (816) 767-8090.

St.Mary's Special School (r,c; 5-21 yrs.), 1724 Redman, St. Louis 63138; (314) 653-2591. St. Mary's Supported Living (r,c) (24); supervised homes for adolescents or adults. St. Mary's Early Intervention (d,c) (30); early intervention for toddlers.

Nebraska: Madonna School for Exceptional Children (d,c; 5-21 yrs.), 2537 N. 62nd St., Omaha 68104; (402) 556-1883; www.madonnaschool.org. Children with learning problems.

Villa Marie School and Home for Exceptional Children (r,d,c; 6-18 yrs.), 3700 Sheridan Blvd., Ste. 3, Lincoln 68506; (402) 488-2040.

New Jersey: Archbishop Damiano School (d,c; 3-21 yrs.), 1145 Delsea Dr., Westville Grove 08093.

Catholic Community Services, Archdiocese of Newark, 1160 Raymond Blvd., Newark 07102.

Department of Special Education, Diocese of Camden, 5609 Westfield Ave., Pennsauken, NJ 08110-1836; (609) 488-7123; www.catholiccharities.org. Services include: Archbishop Damiano School (above), and full time programs (d,c; 6-21 yrs.) at 4 elementary (96) and 2 high schools (60) and some religious education programs.

Department for Persons with Disabilities, Diocese of Paterson, 1049 Weldon Rd., Oak Ridge, N.J. 07438; (973) 406-1100; www.dpd.org. Services include 8 residential programs for adults, one adult training center, family support services.

Felician School for Exceptional Children (d,c; 5-21 yrs.), 260 S. Main St., Lodi 07644; (973) 777-5355.

McAuley School for Exceptional Children (d,c; 5-21 yrs.), 1633 Rt. 22 at Terrill Rd., Watchung 07069; (908) 754-4114.

Mt. Carmel Guild Special Education School (d,c ; 6-21 yrs.), 60 Kingsland Ave., Kearny 07032; (201) 995-3280.

St. Anthony's Special Education School (d,c), 25 N. 7th St., Belleville 07109; (973) 844-3700.

Sister Georgine School (d,c; 6-17 yrs.), 544 Chestnut Ave., Trenton 08611; (609) 396-5444.

St. Patrick's Special Education School (d,c), 72 Central Ave., Newark 07102.

New York: Baker Victory Services (r), 780 Ridge Rd., Lackawanna, N.Y. 14218; (716) 828-9500; www.bakervictoryservices.org. Residential care for handicapped and retarded children; nursery school program for emotionally disturbed pre-school children.

Bishop Patrick V. Ahern High School (d,c; 15-21 yrs.), 100 Merrill Ave., Staten Island 10314.

Cantalician Center for Learning (d,c; birth-21 yrs.), 3233 Main St., Buffalo 14214; (716) 833-5353; www.cantalician.org. Infant and pre-school; elementary and secondary; workshop (426). Three group homes. Rehabilitation; day treatment and senior rehabilitation programs.

Catholic Charities Residential Services, Rockville Centre Diocese, 269 W. Main St., Bay Shore 11706. Residences for developmentally disabled adults (88).

Cobb Memorial School (r,d,c; 5-21 yrs.), 100-300 Mt. Presentation Way, Altamont 12009; (518) 861-6446.

Joan Ann Kennedy Memorial Preschool (d,c; 3-5 yrs.), 26 Sharpe Ave., Staten Island 10302.

L'Arche Syracuse (r, adults), 1232 Teall Ave., Syracuse 13206-3468; (315) 479-8088; www.larchesyracuse.com (12). Homes where assistants and persons with developmental disabilities share life, following the philosophy of Jean Vanier. Member of International L'Arche Federation, Exec. Dir., Frank Woolever.

Maryhaven Center of Hope (r,d,c; school age to adult), 51 Terryville Rd., Port Jefferson 11776; (631) 474-4120; www.maryhaven.org.

Mercy Home for Children (r,c), 243 Prospect Park West, Brooklyn 11215; (718) 832-1075. Residences for adolescents and young adults who are developmentally disabled: Visitation, Warren, Vincent Haire, Santulli and Littlejohn residences (Brooklyn), Kevin Keating Residence (Queens).

Office for Disabled Persons, Catholic Charities, Diocese of Brooklyn, 191 Joralemon St., Brooklyn 11201; (718) 722-6000; www.ccbg.org. Services include: adult day treatment center; community residences for mentally retarded adults; special events for disabled children (from age 3) and adults.

Office for Disabled Persons, Archdiocese of New York, 1011 First Ave., New York 10022; (212) 371-1000. Services include consultation and referral, variety of services for deaf, blind, mentally retarded, mentally ill.

Seton Foundation for Learning (d,c; 5-15 yrs.), 104 Gordon St., Staten Island 10304; (718) 447-1750.

North Carolina: Holy Angels (r,c; birth to adult), 6600 Wilkinson Blvd., P.O. Box 710, Belmont 28012; (704) 825-4161; www.holyangelsnc.org.

North Dakota: Friendship, Inc. (r,d,c; all ages), 3004 11th St. South, Fargo 58103; (701) 235-8217.

Ohio: Julie Billiart School (d,c; 6-12 yrs.), 4982 Clubside Rd., Cleveland 44124; (216) 381-1191; www.juliebilliartschool.org.

Mary Immaculate School (d,c; 6-14 yrs.), 3835 Secor Rd., Toledo 43623; (419) 474-1688; www.maryimmaculatetoledo.org

OLA/St. Joseph Center (d,c; 6-16 yrs.), 2346 W. 14th St., Cleveland 44113; (216) 621-3451.

Rose Mary, The Johanna Graselli Rehabilitation and Education Center (r,c; 5 yrs. and older), 19350 Euclid Ave., Cleveland 44117.

St. John's Villa (r,c; continued care and training, 15 yrs. and over), P.O. Box 457, Carrollton 44615; (330) 627-9789.

Oregon: Providence Montessori School Early Intervention Program (d,c; 3-5 yrs.), 830 N.E. 47th Ave., Portland 97213; (503) 215-2409.

Pennsylvania: Clelian Heights School for Exceptional Children (r,d,c; 5-21 yrs.), R.D. 9, Box 607, Greensburg 15601; (724) 837-8120 (95). Also conducts re-socialization program (r,d,c; young adults).

Divine Providence Village (adults), 686 Old Marple Rd., Springfield 19064; (610) 328-7730. Admin., Sr. Esther Leroux.

Don Guanella Village: Don Guanella School (r,d,b; 6-21 yrs.) and Cardinal Krol Center (r; adults, post-school age), 1797 S. Sproul Rd., Springfield 19602; (610) 543-3380. Admin. Rev. Dennis Weber, S.C.

John Paul II Center (d,c; 3-21 yrs.), 1092 Welsh Rd., Shillington, PA 19607; (610) 777-0605; www.John PaulIICenter.org.

McGuire Memorial (r,d,c; 18 mos. to adult.), 2119 Mercer Rd., New Brighton 15066; (724) 843-3400; www.mcguirememorial.org.

Mercy Special Learning Center (d,c; 3-21 yrs. and early intervention), 830 S. Woodward St., Allentown 18103; (610) 797-8242.

Our Lady of Confidence Day School (d,c; 4-21 yrs.),

10th and Lycoming Sts., Philadelphia 19140.

Queen of the Universe Day Center (d,c; 4-16 yrs.), 2479 Trenton Rd., Levittown 19056; (215) 945-6090; www.qudaycenter.org.

St. Anthony School Programs (d,c; 5-21 yrs.), 2718 Custer Ave., Pittsburgh 15227; (412) 882-1333.

St. Joseph Center for Special Learning (d,c; 4-21 yrs.), 2075 W. Norwegian St., Pottsville 17901; (570) 622-4638; www.pottsville.com/stjosephctr.

St. Joseph's Center (r,d,c; birth-10 yrs.), 2010 Adams Ave., Scranton 18509; (570) 342-8379; www.stjosephcenter.org.

St. Katherine Day School (d,c; 4-21 yrs.), 930 Bowman Ave., Wynnewood 19096; (610) 667-3958.

Tennessee: Madonna Learning Center, Inc., for Retarded Children (d,c; 5-16 yrs.), 7007 Poplar Ave., Germantown 38138.

Texas: Notre Dame of Dallas School (d,c; 3-21 yrs.), 2018 Allen St., Dallas 75204; (214) 720-3911.

Virginia: St. Coletta School (d,c; 5-22 yrs.), 207 S. Peyton St., Alexandria, 22314; (703) 683-3686. For developmentally disabled. Services include: occupational, physical and language therapy; vocational program with job search, placement, training and follow-up services.

St. Mary's Infant Home (r,c; birth to 14 yrs.), 317 Chapel St., Norfolk 23504; (757) 622-2208. For multiple handicapped.

Wisconsin: St Coletta of Wisconsin, W4955 Hwy 18, Jefferson 53549; (920) 674-4330; www.stcolettawi.org. Year-round special education programs for adolescents and adults; pre-vocational and vocational skills training; residential living alternatives. Young adult population. Employment opportunities for those who qualify.

St. Coletta Day School (c; 8-17 yrs.), 1740 N. 55th St., Milwaukee 53208; (414) 453-1850.

Orthopedically/Physically Challenged

Pennsylvania: St. Edmond's Home for Children (r,c; 1-21 yrs.)., 320 S. Roberts Rd., Rosemont 19010; (610) 525-8800.

Virginia: St. Joseph Villa Housing Corp. (adults), 8000 Brook Rd., Richmond 23227; (804) 553-3283.

Visually Challenged

Maine: Educational Services for Blind and Visually Impaired Children (Catholic Charities, Maine), 1066 Kenduskeag Ave., Bangor 04401. 66 Western Ave., Fairfield 04937. 15 Westminster St., Lewiston 04240. P.O. Box 378, Fairfield, ME 04937; (800) 660-5231. Itinerant teachers, instructional materials center.

New Jersey: St. Joseph's School for the Blind (r,d,c; 3-21 yrs.), 257 Baldwin Ave., Jersey City 07306; (201) 653-0578; www.sjsb.net.

New York: Lavelle School for the Blind (d,c; 3-21 yrs.), East 221st St. and Paulding Ave., Bronx 10469; (718) 882-1212. For visually impaired, multiple handicapped.

Pennsylvania: St. Lucy Day School (d,c; pre-K to 8th grade), 130 Hampden Rd., Upper Darby 19082; (610) 352-4550; www.stlucydayschool.org. For children with visual impairments.

HOUSES OF RETREAT AND RENEWAL

There is great variety in retreat and renewal programs, with orientations ranging from the traditional to teen encounters. Central to all of them are celebration of the liturgy and deepening of a person's commitment to faith and witness in life.

Features of many of the forms are as follows.

Traditional Retreats: Centered around conferences and the direction of a retreat master; oriented to the personal needs of the retreatants; including such standard practices as participation in Mass, reception of the sacraments, private and group prayer, silence and meditation, discussions.

Team Retreat: Conducted by a team of several leaders or directors (priests, religious, lay persons) with division of subject matter and activities according to their special skills and the nature and needs of the group.

Closed Retreat: Involving withdrawal for a period of time—overnight, several days, a weekend—from everyday occupations and activities.

Open Retreat: Made without total disengagement from everyday involvements, on a part-time basis.

Private Retreat: By one person, on a kind of do-it-yourself basis with the one-to-one assistance of a director.

Special Groups: With formats and activities geared to particular groups; e.g., members of Alcoholics Anonymous, vocational groups and apostolic groups.

Marriage Encounters: Usually weekend periods of husband-wife reflection and dialogue; introduced into the U.S. from Spain in 1967.

Charismatic Renewal: Featuring elements of the movement of the same name; "Spirit-oriented," communitarian and flexible, with spontaneous and shared prayer, personal testimonies of faith and witness.

Christian Community: Characterized by strong community thrust.

Teens Encounter Christ (TEC), SEARCH: Formats adapted to the mentality and needs of youth, involving experience of Christian faith and commitment in a community setting.

Christian Maturity Seminars: Similar to teen encounters in basic concept but different to suit persons of greater maturity.

RENEW International: Spiritual renewal process involving the entire parish. Office, 1232 George St., Plainfield, NJ 07062; (908) 769-5400. Director, Msgr. Thomas A. Kleissler.

Cursillo: *See separate entry.*

Conference

Retreats International Inc.: National Office, Box 1067, Notre Dame, IN 46556; (574) 247-4443. An organization for promoting retreats in the U.S. was started in 1904 in New York. Its initial efforts and the gradual growth of the movement led to the formation in 1927 of the National Catholic Laymen's Retreat Conference, the forerunner of the men's division of Retreats International. The women's division developed from the National Laywomen's Retreat Movement that was founded in Chicago in 1936. The men's and women's divisions merged July 9, 1977. The services of the organization include an annual summer institute for retreat and pastoral ministry, regional conferences for retreat center leadership and area meetings of directors and key leadership in the retreat movement. Exec. Dir., Anne M. Luther.

Houses of Retreat and Renewal

Principal sources: Catholic Almanac *survey;* The Official Catholic Directory.

Abbreviation code: m, men; w, women; mc, married couples; y, youth. Houses and centers without code generally offer facilities to most groups. An asterisk after an abbreviation indicates that the facility is primarily for the group designated but that special groups are also accommodated. Houses furnish information concerning the types of programs they offer.

Alabama: Blessed Trinity Shrine Retreat and Cenacle, 107 Holy Trinity Rd., Holy Trinity 36856, (334) 855-4474; Visitation Sacred Heart Retreat House, 2300 Spring Hill Ave., Mobile 36607, (334) 473-2321.

Alaska: Holy Spirit Center, 10980 Hillside Dr., Anchorage 99507, (907) 346-2343, home.gci.net/~hsrh.

Arizona: Franciscan Renewal Center, 5802 E. Lincoln Dr., Scottsdale 85253, (480) 948-7460; Holy Trinity Monastery, P.O. Box 298, St. David 85630, Benedictine community, self-directed/Spirit-directed monastic retreat, (520) 720-4642; Mount Claret Retreat Center, 4633 N. 54th St., Phoenix 85018, (602) 840-5066; Our Lady of Solitude House of Prayer, P.O. Box 1140, Black Canyon City 85324, (623) 374-9204; Redemptorist Picture Rocks Retreat House, 7101 W. Picture Rocks Rd., Tucson 85743, (520) 744-3400, www.desertrenewal.org.

Arkansas: Brothers and Sisters of Charity, Little Portion Hermitage, 350 CR 248, Berryville, 72616-8505, (479) 253-7710, www.johnmichaeltalbot.com; Little Portion Retreat and Training Center, Rt. 4, Box 430, Eureka Springs 72632, (501) 253-7379; St. Scholastica Retreat Center, P.O. Box 3489, Ft. Smith 72913, (479) 783-1135, www. scholasticafortsmith. org; Hesychia House of Prayer, 204 St. Scholastica Rd., New Blaine, Shoal Creek, 72851, (501) 938-7375.

California: Angela Center, 535 Angela Dr., Santa Rosa 95403, (707) 528-8578; Christ the King Retreat Center, 6520 Van Maren Lane, Citrus Heights 95621, (916) 725-4720, www.passionist.org; Claretian Retreat Center, 1119 Westchester Pl., Los Angeles 90019, (323) 737-8464; El Carmelo Retreat House, P.O. Box 446, Redlands 92373, (909) 792-1047, www.elcarmelo.org; Heart of Jesus Retreat Center, 2927 S. Greenville St., Santa Ana 92704, (714) 557-4538; Holy Spirit Retreat Center, 4316 Lanai Rd., Encino 91436, (818) 784-4515; Holy Transfiguration Monastery (m*), Monks of Mt. Tabor (Byzantine Ukrainian), 17001 Tomki Rd., P.O. Box 217, Redwood Valley 95470, (707) 485-8959; Jesuit Retreat House, 300 Manresa Way, Los Altos 94022, (650) 948-4491, www.elretiro.org; Madonna of Peace Renewal Center (y), P.O. Box 71, Copperopolis 95228, (209) 785-2157; Marian Retreat Center, 535 Sacramento St., Auburn 95603, (916) 887-2019; Mary and Joseph Retreat Center, 5300 Crest Rd., Rancho Palos Verdes 90275, (310) 377-4867, www.maryjoseph.org.

Marywood Retreat Center, 2811 E. Villa Real Dr.,

Orange 92863-1595, (714) 282-3000, www.rcbo.org; Mater Dolorosa Retreat Center, 700 N. Sunnyside Ave., Sierra Madre 91024, (626) 355-7188, www.passionist.org; Mercy Center, 2300 Adeline Dr., Burlingame 94010, (650) 340-7474, www.mercy-center.org; Mission San Luis Rey Retreat, 4050 Mission Ave., Oceanside, 92057-6402, (760) 757-3659, www.sanluisrey.org; Mount Alverno Retreat and Conference Center, 3910 Bret Harte Dr., Redwood City 94061, (650) 369-0798, www.mountalverno.com; New Camaldoli Hermitage, Big Sur 93920, (831) 667-2456, www.contemplation.com; Our Lady of the Oaks Villa, P.O. Box 128, Applegate 95703, (530) 878-2776.

Poverello of Assisi Retreat House, 1519 Woodworth St., San Fernando 91340, (818) 365-1071; Presentation Education and Retreat Center, 19480 Bear Creek Rd., Los Gatos 95033, (408) 354-2346, www.prescenter.org; Prince of Peace Abbey, 650 Benet Hill Rd., Oceanside 92054, (760) 430-1305; Pro Sanctity Spirituality Center, 205 S. Pine St., Fullerton 92633 (for day use); Sacred Heart Retreat House (w*), 920 E. Alhambra Rd., Alhambra 91801, (626) 289-1353; St. Andrew's Abbey Retreat House, P.O. Box 40, Valyermo 93563, (661) 944-2178, www.valyermo.com; St. Anthony Retreat, P.O. Box 249, Three Rivers 93271, (559) 561-4595, www.stanthonyretreat.org; St. Clare's Retreat, 2381 Laurel Glen Rd., Soquel 95073, (831) 423-8093, www.infoteam.com/nonprofit/stclaresretreat/index.html; St. Francis Retreat, P.O. Box 970, San Juan Bautista 95045, (831) 623-4234,www.stfrancisretreat.com; St. Francis Youth Center (y), 2400 E. Lake Ave., Watsonville 95076; St. Joseph's Salesian Youth Center, P.O. Box 1639, 8301 Arroyo Dr., Rosemead 91770, (626) 280-8622, www.stjoescenter.org; St. Mary's Seminary and Retreat House, 1964 Las Canoas Rd., Santa Barbara 93105, (805) 966-4829; San Damiano Retreat, P.O. Box 767, Danville 94526, (925) 837-9141, www.san damiano.org.

San Miguel Retreat House, P.O. Box 69, San Miguel 93451, (805) 467-3256; Santa Sabina Center, 25 Magnolia Ave., San Rafael 94901, (415) 457-7727; Serra Retreat, 3401 S. Serra Rd., Box 127, Malibu 90265, (310) 456-6631, www.serraretreat.com; Starcross Community, 34500 Annapolis Rd., Annapolis 95412, (707) 886-1919, www.starcross.org; Villa Maria del Mar, Santa Cruz, 2-1918 E. Cliff Dr., Santa Cruz 95062, (831) 475-1236, www.villamariadelmar.org; Villa Maria – House of Prayer (w), 1252 N. Citrus Dr., La Habra 90631, (562) 691-5838.

Colorado: Benet Pines Retreat Center, 15880 Highway 83, Colorado Springs 80921, (719) 495-2574, www.geocities.com; Camp St. Malo Religious Retreat and Conference Center, 10758, Hwy. 7, Allenspark 80510, (303) 747-2892; Sacred Heart Retreat House, Box 185, Sedalia 80135, (303) 688-4198, www.gabrielmedia.org/shjrh; Spiritual Life Institute (individuals only), Nada Hermitage, P.O. Box 219, Crestone 81131, (719) 256-4778. www.spirituallifeinstitute.org.

Connecticut: St. Edmund's Retreat, P.O. Box 399, Mystic 06355, (860) 536-0565, www.sse.org/enders; Emmaus Spiritual Life Center, 24 Maple Ave., Uncasville 06382, (860) 848-3427; Holy Family Retreat, 303 Tunxis Rd., Farmington 06107, (860)

521-0440; Immaculata Retreat House, P.O. Box 55, Willimantic 06226, (860) 423-8484, www.immaculateretreat.org; Mercy Center at Madison, P.O. Box 191, 167 Neck Rd., Madison 06443, (203) 245-0401, www.mercybythesea.org; My Father's House, Box 22, 39 North Moodus Rd., Moodus 06469, (860) 873-1906, www.myfathershouse.com; Our Lady of Calvary Retreat (w*), 31 Colton St., Farmington 06032, (860) 677-8519, www.ourladyofcalvary.com; Trinita Retreat Center, 595 Town Hill Rd., Rt. 219, New Hartford 06057, (860) 379-4329; Villa Maria Guadalupe Retreat House, 159 Sky Meadow Dr., Stamford 06903, (203) 329-1492; Wisdom House Retreat Center, 229 E. Litchfield Rd., 06759, (860) 567-3163, www.wisdomhouse.org.

Delaware: St. Francis Renewal Center, 1901 Prior Rd., Wilmington 19809, (302) 798-1454.

District of Columbia: Washington Retreat House, 4000 Harewood Rd. N.E., Washington 20017, (202) 529-1111.

Florida: Cenacle Retreat House, 1400 S. Dixie Highway, Lantana 33462-5492, (561) 582-2534, www.cenaclesisters.org; Dominican Retreat House, Inc., 7275 S.W. 124th St., Miami 33156-5324, (305) 238-2711; Franciscan Center, 3010 Perry Ave., Tampa 33603, (813) 229-2695, www.slleganyfranciscans.org/franciscancenter.htm; John Paul II Retreat House, 720 N.E. 27th St., Miami 33137, (305) 576-2748, www.acu-adsum.org; Our Lady of Divine Providence, 702 S. Bayview Ave., Clearwater, 33759, (727) 797-7412, www.divineprovidence.org; Our Lady of Perpetual Help Retreat and Spirituality Center, 3989 S. Moon Dr., Venice 34292, (941) 486-0233, www.olphretreat.org; Saint John Neumann Renewal Center, 685 Miccosukee Rd., Tallahassee 32308, (850) 224-2971; St. Leo Abbey Retreat Center, P.O. Box 2350, St. Leo 33574, (352) 588-2009.

Georgia: Ignatius House, 6700 Riverside Dr. N.W., Atlanta 30328, (404) 255-0503.

Idaho: Nazareth Retreat Center, 4450 N. Five Mile Rd., Boise 83713, (208) 375-2932.

Illinois: Bellarmine Jesuit Retreat House (mc), 175 W. County Line Rd, Barrington 60010, (847) 381-1261, www.bellarminehall.org; Bishop Lane Retreat House, 7708 E. McGregor Rd., Rockford 61102, (815) 965-5011; Cabrini Retreat Center, 9430 Golf Rd., Des Plaines 60016, (847) 297-6530; Carmelite Spiritual Center, 8433 Bailey Rd., Darien 60561, (630) 969-4141; Cenacle Retreat House, 513 Fullerton Parkway, Chicago 60614, (773) 528-6300; Cenacle Retreat House, P.O. Box 797, Warrenville 60555, (630) 393-1231, www.cenacle.org; King's House Retreat and Renewal Center, 700 N. 66th St., Belleville 62223-3949, (618) 397-0584;

La Salle Manor, Christian Brothers Retreat House, 12480 Galena Rd., Plano 60545, (630) 552-3224, www.lasallemanor.org; St. Mary's Retreat House, P.O. Box 608, 14230 Main St., Lemont 60439, (630) 257-5102; Tolentine Center, 20300 Governors Highway, Olympia Fields 60461, (708) 748-9500.

Indiana: Archabbey Guest House, St. Meinrad Archabbey, St. Meinrad 47577, (800) 581-6905, www.saintmeinrad.edu; Benedict Inn Retreat and Conference Center, 1402 Southern Ave., Beech Grove 46107, (317) 788-7581, www.benedictinn.org; Bethany Retreat House, 2202 Lituanica Ave., 46312,

(219) 398-5047; Fatima Retreat House, 5353 E. 56th St., Indianapolis 46226-1486, (317) 545-7681, www.archindy.org; John XXIII Retreat Center, 407 W. McDonald St., Hartford City 47348, (765) 348-4008, www.netusa1.net/~john23rd; Kordes Retreat Center, 841 E. 14th St., Ferdinand 47532, (812) 367-1411, www.thedome.org/kordes.

Lindenwood, PHJC Ministry Center, P.O. Box 1, Donaldson 46513, (574) 935-1780; Mary's Solitude, St.Mary's, 100 Lourdes Hall, Notre Dame 46556, (219) 284-5599; Mount Saint Francis Retreat Center and Friary, 101 St. Anthony Dr., Mount Saint Francis 47146, (812) 923-8817, www.mountsaintfrancis.org; Sarto Retreat House, 4200 N. Kentucky Ave., Evansville 47724, (812) 424-5536.

Iowa: American Martyrs Retreat House, 2209 N. Union Rd., P.O. Box 605, Cedar Falls 50613-0605, (319) 266-3543, www.americanmartyrs.tripod.com; Emmanuel House of Prayer Country Retreat and Solitude Center, 4427 Kotts Rd. N.E., Iowa City 52240; New Melleray Guest House, 6500 Melleray Circle, Dubuque 52068, (319) 588-2319; Shalom Retreat Center, 1001 Davis Ave., Dubuque 52001, (319) 582-3592, members.aol.com/dbqshalom.

Kansas: Heartland Center for Spirituality, 3600 Broadway, Great Bend 67530, (316) 792-1232; Manna House of Prayer, 323 East 5th St., Box 675, Concordia 66901, (785) 243-4428; Spiritual Life Center, 7100 E. 45th St., N. Wichita 67226, (316) 744-0167, www.slcwichita.org.

Kentucky: Bethany Spring, 115 Dee Head Rd., New Haven, 40051, (502) 549-8277; Flaget Center, 1935 Lewiston Dr., Louisville 40216, (502) 448-8581; Marydale Retreat Center, 945 Donaldson Hwy., Erlanger 41018, (606) 371-4224; Mt. St. Joseph Retreat Center, 8001 Cummings Rd., Maple Mount 42356-9999, (229) 229-0200, www.msjcenter.org; Our Lady of Gethsemani (m, w, private), The Guestmaster, Abbey of Gethsemani, Trappist, 40051; Passionist Nuns, 8564 Crisp Rd, Whitesville 42378, (270) 233-4571.

Louisiana: Abbey Christian Life Center, St. Joseph's Abbey, St. Benedict 70457, (504) 892-3473; Ave Maria Retreat House, 8089 Barataria Blvd., Crown Point, 70072, (504) 689-3837; Cenacle Retreat House (w*), 5500 St. Mary St., P.O. Box 8115, Metairie 70006, (504) 887-1420, www.cenaclesisters.org/ metairie.htm; Jesuit Spirituality Center (m,w; directed), P.O. Box C, Grand Coteau 70541-1003, (337) 662-5251, www.jesuitspiritualitycenter.org; Lumen Christi Retreat Center, 100 Lumen Christi Lane, Hwy. 311, Schriever 70395, (504) 868-1523; Magnificat Center of the Holy Spirit, 23629 Faith Rd., Ponchatoula 70454, (504) 362-4356.

Manresa House of Retreats (m), P.O. Box 89, Convent 70723, (225) 562-3596; Maryhill Renewal Center, 600 Maryhill Rd., Pineville 71360, (318) 640-1378, www.diocesealex.org; Our Lady of the Oaks Retreat House, P.O. Box D, 214 Church St., Grand Coteau 70541, (318) 662-5410; Regina Coeli Retreat Center, 17225 Regina Coeli Rd., Covington 70433, (504) 892-4110; Sophie Barat House, 1719 Napoleon Ave., New Orleans 70115, (504) 899-6027.

Maine: Bay View Villa, 187 Bay View Rd., Saco 04072, (207) 286-8762; Marie Joseph Spiritual Center,

10 Evans Rd., Biddeford 04005, (207) 284-5671, www.mariejosephspiritual.org; Mother of the Good Shepherd Monastery by the Sea, 235 Pleasant Ave., Peaks Island 04108, (207) 766-2717; Notre Dame Retreat & Spiritual Center, P.O. Box 159, Alfred 04002, (207) 324-6160; St. Paul Retreat and Cursillo Center, 136 State St., Augusta 04330, (207) 622-6235.

Maryland: Bon Secours Spiritual Center, Marriottsville 21104, (410) 442-1320, www.bonsecours.org/bssc; Christian Brothers Spiritual Center (m,w,y), P.O. Box 29, 2535 Buckeyestown Pike, Adamstown 21710, (301) 874-5180; Loyola on the Potomac Retreat House, Faulkner 20632, (301) 870-3515, www.loyolaretreat.org; Msgr. Clare J. O'Dwyer Retreat House (y*), 15523 York Rd., P.O. Box 310, Sparks 21152, (410) 666-2400; Our Lady of Mattaponi Youth Retreat and Conference Center, 11000 Mattaponi Rd., Upper Marlboro 20772, (301) 952-9074; Seton Retreat Center, 333 S. Seton Ave., Emmitsburg 21727, (301) 447-6021.

Massachusetts: Boston Cenacle Society, 25 Avery St., Dedham 02026; Calvary Retreat Center, 59 South St., P.O. Box 219, Shrewsbury 01545, (508) 842-8821, www.calvaryretreat.org; Campion Renewal Center, 319 Concord Rd., Weston 02193, (781) 788-6810; Community of Teresian Carmelites, 30 Chrome St., 01613, (508) 752-5734; Don Orione Center, P.O. Box 205, Old Groveland Rd., Bradford 01835, (508) 373-0461; Eastern Point Retreat House, Gonzaga Hall, 37 Niles Pond Rd., Gloucester 01930, (978) 283-0013; Espousal Center, 554 Lexington St., Waltham 02452, (781) 209-3120, www.espousal.org; Esther House of Spiritual Renewal, Sisters of St. Anne, 1015 Pleasant St., Worcester 01602-1338.

Franciscan Center — Retreat House, 459 River Rd., Andover 01810, (978) 851-3391, www.franrcent.org; Genesis Spiritual Life Center, 53 Mill St., Westfield 01085, (413) 562-3627; Glastonbury Abbey (Benedictine Monks), 16 Hull St., Hingham 02043, (701) 749-2155, www.glastonburyabbey.org; Holy Cross Fathers Retreat House, 490 Washington St., N. Easton 02356, (508) 238-2051; La Salette Center for Christian Living, 947 Park St., Attleboro 02703, (508) 222-8530, www.lasalette.shrine.tripod.com; Marian Center, 1365 Northampton St., Holyoke 01040-1913, (413) 534-4502 (day and evening programs); Marist House, 518 Pleasant St., 01701, (508) 879-1620; Miramar Retreat Center, P.O. Box M, Duxbury, 02331-0614, (781) 585-2460; Mt. Carmel Christian Life Center, Oblong Rd., Box 613, Williamstown 01267, (413) 458-3164.

Sacred Heart Retreat Center, Salesians of St. John Bosco, P.O. Box 567, Ipswich 01938; St. Benedict Abbey (Benedictine Monks), 252 Still River Rd., P.O. Box 67, Still River 01467, (978) 456-3221; St. Joseph Villa Retreat Center, Sisters of St. Joseph, 339 Jerusalem Rd., Cohasset 02025, (781) 383-6024; St. Joseph's Abbey Retreat House (m) (Trappist Monks), 167 North Spencer Rd., Spencer 01562, (508) 885-8710, www.spencerabbey.org; St. Stephen Priory Spiritual Life Center (Dominican), 20 Glen St., Box 370, Dover 02030, (508) 785-0124, www.ststephenpriory.org.

Michigan: Augustine Center, 2798 U.S. 31 North, Box 84, Conway 49722, (231) 347-3657, www.dioceseofgaylord.org; Capuchin Retreat, 62460 Mt. Vernon,

Box 396, Washington 48094, (248) 651-4826; Colombiere Conference and Retreat Center, 9075 Big Lake Rd., Clarkston 48346, (248) 620-2534, www.colombiere.com; Manresa Jesuit Retreat House, 1390 Quarton Rd., Bloomfield Hills 48304, (248) 644-4933; Marygrove Retreat Center, Garden 49835, (906) 644-2771; Queen of Angels Retreat, 3400 S. Washington Rd., P.O. Box 2026, Saginaw 48605, (517) 755-2149, www.rc.net/saginaw/retreat.

St. Francis Retreat Center, 703 E. Main St., De Witt 48820-9499, (517) 669-8321, www.stfrancis.ws; St. Lazare Retreat House, 18600 W. Spring Lake Rd., Spring Lake 49456, (616) 842-3370; St. Mary's Retreat House (w*), 775 W. Drahner Rd., Oxford 48371, (248) 628-3894, www.op.org/oxford; St. Paul of the Cross Retreat Center (m*), 23333 Schoolcraft, Detroit 48223, (313) 535-9563; Weber Retreat Center, 1257 Siena Hghts. Dr., Adrian 49221, (517) 266-4000.

Minnesota: Benedictine Center, St. Paul's Monastery, 2675 Larpenteur Ave. East, St. Paul 55109, (651) 777-7251, www.osb.org/spm; The Cenacle, 1221 Wayzata Blvd., Wayzata 55391; Center for Spiritual Development, 211 Tenth St. S., P.O. Box 538, Bird Island 55310, (320) 365-3644, www.centerbi.com; Christ the King Retreat Center, 621 First Ave. S., Buffalo 55313, (763) 682-1394, www.kingshouse. com; Dunrovin Christian Brothers Retreat Center, 15525 St. Croix Trail North, Marine-on-St. Croix 55047, (651) 433-2486, www.dunrovin.org.

Franciscan Retreats, Conventual Franciscan Friars, 16385 St. Francis Lane, Prior Lake 55372, (952) 447-2182, www.franciscanretreats.net; Holy Spirit Retreat House, 3864 420th Ave., Janesville, 56048, (507) 234-5712; Jesuit Retreat House (m), 8243 DeMontreville Trail North, Lake Elmo 55042, (651) 777-1311; Maryhill (m,w*), 1988 Summit Ave., St. Paul 55105, (651) 696-2970, www.sdhm.net; Villa Maria Center, Villa Maria Center, 29847 County 2 Blvd., Frontenac 55026, (651) 345-4582.

Missouri: Assumption Abbey, Rte. 5, Box 1056, Ava 65608, (417) 683-5110, www.assumptionabbey.org; The Cenacle, 3393 McKelvey Rd., Apt. 211, Bridgeton, 63044-2544, (314) 387-2211; Cordis House, 648 S. Assisi Way, Republic 65738, (417) 732-6684; Il Ritiro - The Little Retreat, P.O. Box 38, Eime Rd., Dittmer 63023, (636) 274-0554; La Salle Institute, 2101 Rue de la Salle, Wildwood 63038, (636) 938-5374; Maria Fonte Solitude (private; individual hermitages), P.O. Box 322, High Ridge 63049, (314) 677-3235.

Marianist Retreat and Conference Center, P.O. Box 718, Eureka 63025-0718, (636) 938-5390; Mercy Center, 2039 N. Geyer Rd., St. Louis 63131, (314) 909-4629; Our Lady of Assumption Abbey (m,w), Trappists, Rt. 5, Box 1056, Ava 65608-9142, (417) 683-5110; Pallottine Renewal Center, 15270 Old Halls Ferry Rd., Florissant 63034, (314) 837-7100, members.aol.com/prcrenewal/home.html; Society of Our Mother of Peace (private, individual hermitages), 6150 Antire Rd., High Ridge 63049, (636) 677-3235; White House Retreat, 3601 Lindell Blvd., St. Louis 63108, (314) 846-2575, www.whretreat.org; Windridge Solitude, 1932 W. Linda Lane, Lonedell 63060; (636) 629-4449.

Montana: Sacred Heart Retreat Center, 26 Wyoming

Ave., P.O. Box 153, Billings 59103, (406) 252-0322; Ursuline Retreat Centre, 2300 Central Ave., Great Falls 59401, (406) 452-8585.

Nebraska: Our Lady of Good Counsel retreat House, R.R. 1, Box 110, 7303 N. 112th St., Waverly 68462, (402) 786-2705.

New Hampshire: Epiphany Monastery, 96 Scobie Rd., P.O. Box 60, New Boston 03070; La Salette Shrine (private and small groups), 410 NH, Route 4A, P.O. Box 420, Enfield 03748, (603) 632-7087.

New Jersey: Bethany Ridge, P.O. Box 241, Little York 08834, (908) 995-9758; Bethlehem Hermitage, 82 Pleasant Hill Rd., Chester 07930-2135, (908) 879-7059; Carmel Retreat House, 1071 Ramapo Valley Rd., Mahwah 07430, (201) 327-7090, www.carmelretreat.com; Cenacle Retreat House, 411 River Rd., Highland Park 08904, (732) 249-8100, www.cenacle.sisters.org; Emmaus House, 101 Center St., Perth Amboy 08861, (732) 442-7688; Father Judge Apostolic Center (young adults), 1292 Long Hill Rd., Stirling 07980; Felician Retreat House, 35 Windemere Ave., Mt. Arlington 07856, (973) 398-9806; John Paul II Retreat Center, 414 S. 8th St., Vineland 08360; Loyola House of Retreats, 161 James St., Morristown 07960, (973) 539-0740, www.loyola.org.

Marianist Family Retreat Center (families*), 417 Yale Ave., Box 488, Cape May Point 08212-0488; Maris Stella (Retreat and Vacation Center), 7201 Long Beach Blvd., P.O. Box 3135, Harvey Cedars 08008, (609) 474-1182; Mount Paul Retreat Center, 243 Mt. Paul Rd., Oak Ridge 07438, (973) 697-6341; Franciscan Spiritual Center, 474 Sloatsburg Rd., Ringwood 07456-1978, (973) 962-9778; Queen of Peace Retreat House, St. Paul's Abbey, P.O. Box 7, Newton 07860, (973) 383-2470, www.newtonsb.org; Sacred Heart Renewal Center, P.O. Box 68, Belvidere 07823, (908) 475-4694; Sacred Heart Retreat Center (y*, m,w), 20 Old Swartswood Rd., Newton 07860, (973) 383-2620; St. Joseph by the Sea Retreat House, 400 Rte. 35 N., South Mantoloking 08738-1309, (732) 892-8494, www.filippiniusa.org.

St. Pius X Spiritual Life Center, P.O. Box 216, Blackwood 08012, (856) 227-1436; San Alfonso Retreat House, P.O. Box 3098, 755 Ocean Ave., Long Beach 07740, (732) 222-2731, www.sanalfonsoretreats.org; Sanctuary of Mary, Pilgrimage Place, Branchville 07826, (973) 875-7625; Stella Maris Retreat House, 981 Ocean Ave., Elberon 07740, (732) 229-0602, www.stellamarisretreatcenter.org; Villa Pauline Retreat House, 350 Bernardsville Rd., Mendham 07945, (973) 543-9058; Vincentian Renewal Center, 75 Mapleton Rd., P.O. Box 757, Plainsboro 08536, (609) 520-9626; Vocationist Fathers Retreat, 90 Brooklake Rd., Florham Park 07932, (973) 966-6262, www.vocationist.org; Xavier Retreat and Conference Center, P.O. Box 211, Convent Station 07961, (973) 290-5100, www.xaviercenter.org.

New Mexico: Holy Cross Retreat, Conventual Franciscan Friars, P.O. Box 158, Mesilla Park 88047, (505) 524-3688, www.zianet.com/franciscan; Immaculate Heart of Mary Retreat and Conference Center, Mt. Carmel Rd., Santa Fe 87501, (505) 988-1975; Madonna Retreat Center, Inc., 4040 St. Joseph Pl., N.W., 87120, (505) 831-8196; Pecos Benedictine Monastery, Pecos 87552, (505) 757-6600, www.pecosabbey.org; Spiritual Renewal Center, 6400 Coors Rd., NW, Albuquerque 87120; (505) 890-4110; www.spiritualretreats.com; Sacred Heart Retreat, P.O. Box 1989, Gallup 87301.

New York: Bethany Spirituality Center, 202 County Road 105, Box 1003, Highland Mills 10930, (845) 460-3061, www.bthanysiritualitycnter.org. Bethlehem Retreat House, Abbey of the Genesee, Piffard 14533; Bishop Molloy Retreat House, 86-45 Edgerton Blvd., Jamaica 11432, (718) 739-1229, www.bishopmolloy. org; Blessed Kateri Retreat House, National Kateri Shrine, P.O. Box 627, Fonda 11432, (518) 853-3646; Cardinal Spellman Retreat House, Passionist Community, 5801 Palisade Ave., Bronx (Riverdale) 10471, (718) 549-6500, www.passionists.org; Cenacle Center for Spiritual Renewal, 310 Cenacle Rd., Ronkonkoma 11779-2203, (631) 588-8366, www.cenaclesisters.org.

Cenacle Retreat House, State Rd., P.O. Box 467, Bedford Village 10506, (914) 234-3344; Christ the King Retreat and Conference Center, 500 Brookford Rd., Syracuse 13224, (315) 446-2680; Cormaria Retreat House, Sag Harbor, L.I. 11963, (631) 725-4206; Dominican Retreat and Conference Center, 1945 Union St., Niskayuma, (518) 393-4169, www.dslcny.org; Don Bosco Retreat Center, 174 Filors Lane, Stony Point, 10980-2645, (845) 947-2200, www.marianshrine.org; Graymoor Spiritual Life Center, Graymoor, Route 9, P.O. Box 300, Garrison 10524, (845) 424-3671, www.graymoorcenter.org; Jesuit Retreat House, Auriesville, (518) 853-3033; Monastery of the Precious Blood (w), Ft. Hamilton Parkway and 54th St., Brooklyn 11219 (single day retreats); Mount Alvernia Retreat Center, Box 858, Wappingers Falls 12590, (845) 297-5706, www.mtalvernia.org.

Mount Irenaeus Franciscan Mountain Retreat, Holy Peace Friary, P.O. Box 100, West Clarksville, NY 14786, (716) 973-2470; Mount Manresa Retreat House, 239 Fingerboard Rd., Staten Island 10305, (718) 727-3844; Mt. St. Alphonsus Redemptorist Retreat Ministry, P.O. Box 219, Esopus 12429, (845) 384-8000, www.msaretreat.org; Notre Dame Retreat House, Box 342, 5151 Foster Rd., Canandaigua 14424, (585) 394-5700, www.notredameretreathouse.org; Our Lady of Hope Center, 434 River Rd., Newburgh 12550, (914) 568-0780; Regina Maria Retreat House, 77 Brinkerhoff St., Plattsburgh 12901-2701, (518) 561-3421; St. Andrew's House, 257 St. Andrew's Rd., Walden 12586, (845) 778-5941; St. Columban Center, Diocese of Buffalo, 6892 Lake Shore Rd., P.O. Box 816, Derby 14047, (716) 947-4708, www.stcolumbancenter.org.

St. Francis Retreat, 1 Pryer Manor Rd., Larchmont 10538, (914) 235-6839; St. Francis Center for Spirituality, 500 Todt Hill Rd., Staten Island, NY 10304, (718) 981-3131, www.st-francis-center-for-spirituality.org; St. Gabriel's Spiritual Center for Youth (y, mc), 64 Burns Rd., P.O. Box 3015, Shelter Island Heights 11965, (631) 749-3154 (fax); St. Ignatius Retreat House, 251 Searingtown Rd., Manhasset 11030, (516) 621-8300, www.inisfada.net; St. Josaphat's Retreat House, Basilian Monastery, 1 East Beach Dr., Glen Cove 11542, (516) 671-8980; St. Joseph Center (Spanish Center), 275 W. 230th St., Bronx 10463, (718) 796-4340; St. Mary's Villa, 150 Sisters Servants Lane, P.O. Box 9, Sloatsburg 10974-0009, (914) 753-5100; St. Paul Center, 21-35 Crescent St., Astoria 11105, (718) 932-0752; St. Ursula Retreat Center, 186 Middle Rd., Blue Point 11715, (631) 363-2422, www.ursulinesofbluepoint.org; Stella Maris Retreat Center, 130 E. Genesee St., Skaneateles 13152, (315) 685-6836; Tagaste Monastery, 220 Lafayette Ave., Suffern 10901; Trinity Retreat, 1 Pryer Manor Rd., Larchmont 10538, (914) 235-6839.

North Carolina: Avila Retreat Center, 711 Mason Rd., Durham 27712, (919) 477-1285; Madonna House, 424 Rose Ln., Raleigh 27610.

North Dakota: Presentation Prayer Center, 1101 32nd Ave. S., Fargo 58103, (701) 237-4857; Queen of Peace Retreat, 1310 Broadway, Fargo 58102, (701) 293-9286.

Ohio: Bergamo Center for Lifelong Learning, 4400 Shakertown Rd., Dayton 45430, (937) 426-2363, www.bergamocenter.org; Friarhurst Retreat House, 8136 Wooster Pike, Cincinnati 45227, (513) 561-2270; Jesuit Retreat House, 5629 State Rd., Cleveland 44134-2292, (440) 884-9300, www.jrh-cleveland.org; Jesuit Spiritual Center at Milford, 5361 S. Milford Rd., Milford 45150, (513) 248-3500, www.milfordspiritualcenter.org; Loyola of the Lakes, 700 Killinger Rd., Clinton 44216-9653, (330) 896-2315, www.loyolaofthelakes.com; Maria Stein Spiritual Center, 2365 St. Johns Rd., Maria Stein 45860, (419) 925-7625, www.spiritualcenter.net; Our Lady of Consolation Retreat House, 321 Clay St., Carey 43316, (419) 396-7970, www.olcshrine.com; Our Lady of the Pines, 1250 Tiffin St., Fremont 43420, (419) 332-6522, www.pinesretreat.org.

Sacred Heart Retreat and Renewal Center, 3128 Logan Ave., P.O. Box 6074, Youngstown 44501, (330) 759-9539; St. Joseph Christian Life Center, 18485 Lake Shore Blvd., Cleveland 44119, (216) 531-7370, www.enterthecenter.org; St. Francis Spirituality Center, 200 St. Francis Ave., Tiffin 44883, (419) 443-1485, www.stfrancisspiritualitycenter.org; St. Therese Retreat Center, 5277 E. Broad St., Columbus, OH 43213, (614) 866-1611, www.cathedralbookshop.com.

Oklahoma: St. Gregory's Abbey, 1900 W. MacArthut, Shawnee 74804, (405) 878-5491, www.sgc.edu.

Oregon: The Jesuit Spirituality Center, 424 S.W. Mill St., Portland 97201, (503) 242-1973; Mount Angel Abbey Retreat House, 1 Abbey Dr., St. Benedict 97373, (503) 845-3027, www.mtangel.edu; Our Lady of Peace Retreat, 3600 S. W. 170th Ave., Beaverton 97006, (503) 649-7127, www.geocities.com/ourladyofpeaceretreat; St. Rita Retreat Center, P.O. Box 310, Gold Hill 97525, (541) 855-1333; Shalom Prayer Center, Benedictine Sisters, 840 S. Main St., Mt. Angel 97362-9527, (503) 845-6773, www.benedictsrs.org; St. Benedict Lodge, 56630 North Bank Rd., McKenzie Bridge 97413, (541) 822-3572; Trappist Abbey Guesthouse (m,w), 9200 N.E. Abbey Rd., Lafayette 97127, (503) 852-0107; www.trappistabbey.org.

Pennsylvania: Avila Retreat Center, 61 E. High St., Union City 16438, (814) 438-7020; Dominican Retreat House, 750 Ashbourne Rd., Elkins Park 19027, (215) 782-8520; Ecclesia Center, 9101 Ridge Rd., Erie 16417, (814) 774-9691; Fatima Renewal

Center, 1000 Seminary Rd., Dalton 18414, (570) 563-8500; Fatima House Retreat Center, P.O. Box 116, Bedminster 18910, (215) 579-2947.

Franciscan Spirit and Life Center, 3605 McRoberts Rd., Pittsburgh 15234, (412) 881-9207; Gilmary Diocesan Center, 601 Flaugherty Run Rd., Coraopolis 15108-3899, (412) 264-8400, www.diopitt.org.

Jesuit Center, 501 N. Church Rd., Wernersville 19565, (610) 670-3676, www.jesuitcenter.org; Kearns Spirituality Center, 9000 Babcock Blvd., Allison Park 15101, (412) 366-1124, www.divineprovidenceweb.org; Mariawald Renewal Center, P.O. Box 97 (1094 Welsh Rd.), Reading 19607, (610) 777-0135, www.hometown.aol.com/mariawald/index.html; Martina Spiritual Renewal Center, 5244 Clarwin Ave., Pittsburgh 15229, (412) 931-9766; Mt. Saint Macrina House of Prayer, 510 W. Main St., Box 878, Uniontown 15401, (724) 438-7149, www.sistersofst-basil.org; St. Emma Guest House and St. Emma Retreat House, 1001 Harvey Ave., Greensburg 15601-1494, (724) 834-3060, www.stemm.org; St. Francis Center for Renewal, Monocacy Manor, 395 Bridle Path Rd., Bethlehem 18017, (610) 867-8890, www.catholic-church.org/stfrancis-cfn; St. Francis Retreat House, 3918 Chipman Rd., Easton 18045, (610) 258-3053; St. Gabriel's Retreat House, 631 Griffin Pond Rd., Clarks Summit 18411-8899, (570) 586-4957, www.intiques.com/cpnuns.

St. Joseph's in the Hills, 315 S. Warren Ave., Malvern 19355-0315, (610) 644-0400, www.malvern-retreat. com; St. Paul of the Cross Retreat Center, 148 Monastery Ave., Pittsburgh 15203, (412) 381-7676, www.catholic-church.org/stpaulsretreatcenter; Saint Raphaela Center, 616 Coopertown Rd., Haverford 19041, (610) 642-5715; St. Vincent Summer Retreat Program (m,w,mc; summers only), Latrobe 15650, (724) 805-2139; Urban House of Prayer, 1919 Cambridge St., Philadelphia 19130, (215) 236-8328; Villa of Our Lady Retreat Center (w, mc, y), HCR No. 1, Box 41, Mt. Pocono 18344, (570) 839-7217.

Rhode Island: Bethany Renewal Center, 397 Fruit Hill Ave., N. Providence 02911, (401) 353-5860; Father Marot CYO Center (y), 53 Federal St., Woonsocket 02895, (401) 762-3252; Our Lady of Peace Spiritual Life Center, 333 Ocean Rd., Box 507, Narragansett 02882, (401) 884-7676; St. Paul Priory Guest House, 61 Narrangansett Ave., Newport 02840, (401) 847-2423.

South Carolina: Sea of Peace House of Prayer, 59 Palmetto Pointe Rd., Edisto Island 29438, (843) 869-0513; Springbank Retreat for Eco-Spirituality and the Arts, 1345 Springbank Rd., Kingstree 29556, (800) 671-0361, www.springbankspirit.org.

South Dakota: St. Martin's Community Center, 2110C St. Martin's Dr., Rapid City 57702, (605) 343-8011; Sioux Spiritual Center, 20100 Center Rd., Howes, SD 57748, (605) 985-5906.

Tennessee: Carmelites of Mary Immaculate Center of Spirituality, 610 Bluff Rd., Liberty 37095, (615) 536-5177.

Texas: Benedictine Retreat Center, HC#2, Box 6300, Sandia 78383; Bishop DeFalco Retreat Center, 2100 N. Spring, Amarillo 79107-7274, (806) 383-1811, www.bdrc.org; Bishop Rene H. Gracida Retreat Center, 3036 Saratoga Blvd., Corpus Christi 78415, (512) 851-1443; Catholic Renewal Center of North

Texas, 4503 Bridge St., Ft. Worth 76103, (817) 429-2920; Cenacle Retreat House, 420 N. Kirkwood, Houston 77079, (281) 497-3131, www.cenaclere-treathouse.org; Christian Renewal Center (Centro de Renovacion Cristiana), Oblates of Mary Immaculate, P.O. Box 699, Dickinson 77539, (281) 337-1312, www.retreatcentercrc.org.

Holy Family Retreat Center, 9920 N. Major Dr., Beaumont 77713-7618, (409) 899-5617, www.dioce-seofbmt.org/holyfamily/index/html; Holy Name Retreat Center, 430 Bunker Hill Rd., Houston 77024, (713) 464-0211; Holy Spirit Retreat and Conference Center, 501 Century Dr. S., Laredo 78040, (956) 726-4352, www.stjean.com/laredo/hsrc/holy.htm; Lebh Shomea House of Prayer, La Parra Ranch, P.O. Box 9, Sarita 78385; Montserrat Retreat House, P.O. Box 1390, Lake Dallas 75065, (940) 321-6020, www.montserratretreat.org; Moye Center, 600 London, Castroville 78009, (830) 931-2233, www.moyecenter.org; Oblate Renewal Center, 5700 Blanco Rd., San Antonio 78216, (210) 349-4173.

Omega Retreat Center, 216 W. Highland Dr., Boerne 78006, (830) 816-8471; Our Lady of Mercy Retreat Center, P.O. Box 744, 19th & Division, Slaton 79364, (806) 828-6428; Prayer Town Emmanuel Retreat House, P.O. Box 17, Channing 79018, (806) 534-2312; San Juan Retreat House (St. Eugene de Mazenod Retreat Center), P.O. Box 747, San Juan 78589, (956) 787-0033.

Utah: Abbey of Our Lady of the Holy Trinity (m), 1250 S 9500 E, Huntsville 84317, (801) 745-3784, www.xmission.com/~hta; Our Lady of the Mountains, 1794 Lake St., Ogden 84401, (801) 392-9231.

Virginia: Benedictine Retreat and Conf. Center, Mary Mother of the Church Abbey, 12829 River Rd., 23233, (804) 784-3508; Dominican Retreat, 7103 Old Dominion Dr., McLean 22101-2799, (703) 356-4243, www.dominicanretreat.org; The Dwelling Place, 601 Holly Grove Ln., Richmond 23235, (804) 323-3360; Holy Family Retreat House, P.O. 3151, 1414 N. Mallory St., Hampton 23663, (757) 722-3997; Madonna House, 828 Campbell Ave., S.W., Roanoke 24016, (540) 343-8464.

Retreat House, Holy Cross Abbey, 901 Cool Spring Lane, Berryville 22611, (540) 955-4383; Shalom House, P.O. Box 196, Montpelier 23192, (804) 883-6149; Tabor Retreat Center, 2125 Langhorne Rd., Lynchburg 24501, (804) 846-6475; The Well, 18047 Quiet Way, Smithfield 23430, (757) 255-2366, www.thewellretreatcenter.org.

Washington: Immaculate Heart Retreat Center, 6910 S. Ben Burr Rd., Spokane 99223, (509) 448-1224, www.ihrc.net; House of the Lord Retreat Center, P.O. Box 1034, Tum Tum 99034, (509) 276-2219; KAIROS House of Prayer, 1714 W. Stearns Rd., Spokane 99208, (509) 466-2187; Palisades Retreat House, 4700 SW Dash Point Rd., #100, Federal Way 98023, (206) 748-7991, www.seattlearch.org/forma-tionandeducation; St. Peter Retreat Center, 15880 Summitview Rd., Cowiche 98923, (509) 678-4935.

West Virginia: Bishop Hodges Pastoral Center, Rt. 1, Box 9D, Huttonsville, 26273, (304) 335-2165; Good Counsel Friary, 493 Tyrone Rd., Morgantown 26508, (304) 594-1714; John XXIII Pastoral Center, 100 Hodges Rd., Charleston 25314, (304) 342-0507; Paul VI Pastoral Center, 667 Stone and Shannon Rd.,

Wheeling 26003, (304) 277-3300; Priest Field Pastoral Center, Rt. 51, Box 133, Kearneysville 25430, (304) 725-1435; West Virginia Institute for Spirituality, 1414 Virginia St. E., Charleston, WV 25301, (304) 345-0926, www.wvis.ws. **Wisconsin:** Archdiocesan Retreat Center, 3501 S. Lake Dr., P.O. Box 07912, Milwaukee 53207, (414) 769-3491, www.archmil.org; The Dwelling Place, 528 N. 31st St., Milwaukee 53208, (414) 933-1100; Franciscan Spirituality Center, 920 Market St., La Crosse 54601, (608) 791-5295, www.fspa.org; Holy Name Retreat House, Chambers Island, mailing address: 1825 Riverside Drive, P.O. Box 23825, Green Bay 54305, (920) 437-7531; Jesuit Retreat House, 4800 Fahrnwald Rd., Oshkosh 54902, (920) 231-9060, www.jesuitretreathouse.org; Marywood Franciscan Spirituality Center (FSPA), 3560 Hwy. 51 N., Arbor Vitae 54568, (715) 385-3750, www.fspa.org. Monte Alverno Retreat Center, 1000 N. Ballard Rd., Appleton 54911, (920) 733-8526; Mount Carmel Hermitage, 897 U.S. Hwy. 8, 54001, (715) 268-9313; Mount Tabor, 522 2 St., Menasha 54952, (920) 722-8918; Norbertine Center for Spirituality, St. Norbert Abbey, 1016 N. Broadway, De Pere 54115, (920) 337-4315, www.norbertines.org; Redemptorist Retreat Center, 1800 N. Timber Trail Lane, Oconomowoc 53066-4897, (262) 567-6900, www.redemptoristretreat.org; St. Anthony Retreat Center, 300 E. 4th St., Marathon 54448, (715) 443-2236, www.sarcenter.com. St. Bede Retreat and Conference Center, 1190 Priory Rd., P.O. Box 66, Eau Claire 54702, (715) 834-8642, www.saintbede.org; Saint Benedict Center (monastery and ecumenical retreat and conference center), P.O. Box 5070, Madison 53705-0070, (608) 836-1631, www.sbcenter.org; St. Benedict's Retreat Center, 12605 224th Avenue, Benet Lake, WI 53102-0333, (262) 396-4311, www.benetlake.org; St. Clare Center for Spirituality, 7381 Church St., Custer 54423, (715) 592-4099; St. Joseph's Retreat Center, 3035 O'Brien Rd., Bailey's Harbor 54202, (920) 839-2391, www.stjosephretreat.org; St. Vincent Pallotti Center, N6409 Bowers Rd., Elkhorn 53121, (262) 723-2108, (877) 220-3306, www.elknet.net/vpallelk; Schoenstatt Center, W. 284 N. 698 Cherry Lane, Waukesha 53188, (262) 522-4300.

Catholic Education

LEGAL STATUS OF CATHOLIC EDUCATION

The right of private schools to exist and operate in the United States is recognized in law. It was confirmed by the U.S. Supreme Court in 1925 when the tribunal ruled (Pierce v. Society of Sisters, see Church-State Decisions of the Supreme Court) that an Oregon state law requiring all children to attend public schools was unconstitutional.

Private schools are obliged to comply with the education laws in force in the various states regarding such matters as required basic curricula, periods of attendance, and standards for proper accreditation.

The special curricula and standards of private schools are determined by the schools themselves. Thus, in Catholic schools, the curricula include not only the subject matter required by state educational laws but also other fields of study, principally, education in the Catholic faith.

The Supreme Court has ruled that the First Amendment to the U.S. Constitution, in accordance with the No Establishment of Religion Clause of the First Amendment, prohibits direct federal and state aid from public funds to church-affiliated schools. (See several cases in **Church-State Decisions of the Supreme Court.**)

Public Aid

This prohibition does not extend to all child-benefit and public-purpose programs of aid to students of non-public elementary and secondary schools.

Statutes authorizing such programs have been ruled constitutional on the grounds that they:
• have a "secular legislative purpose"
• neither inhibit nor advance religion as a "principal or primary effect"
• do not foster "excessive government entanglement with religion."

Aid programs considered constitutional have provided bus transportation, textbook loans, school lunches and health services, and "secular, neutral or non-ideological services, facilities and materials provided in common to all school children," public and non-public.

The first major aid to education program in U.S. history containing provisions benefiting non-public school students was enacted by the 89th Congress and signed into law by President Lyndon B. Johnson on Apr. 11, 1965. The Elementary and Secondary Education Act was designed to avoid the separation of Church and state impasse which had blocked all earlier aid proposals pertaining to non-public, and especially church-affiliated, schools. The objective of the program, under public control, is to serve the public purpose by aiding disadvantaged pupils in non-public as well as public schools.

With respect to college and university education in church-affiliated institutions, the Supreme Court has upheld the constitutionality of statutes providing student loans and, under the Federal Higher Education Facilities Act of 1963, construction loans and grants for secular-purpose facilities.

Catholic schools are exempt from real estate taxation in all of the states. Since Jan. 1, 1959, nonprofit parochial and private schools have also been exempt from several federal excise taxes.

NCEA

The National Catholic Educational Association, founded in 1904, is a voluntary organization of educational institutions and individuals concerned with Catholic education in the U.S. Its objectives are to promote and encourage the principles and ideals of Christian education and formation by suitable service and other activities. The NCEA serves approximately 200,000 Catholic educators at all levels from pre-K through university. Its official publication is *Momentum*. Numerous service publications are issued to members. Abp. Donald Wuerl of Washington, D.C., chairman of the Board of Directors; Dr. Karen Ristau, president. Address: 1077 30th St. N.W., Washington, DC 20007, (202) 337-6232, www.ncea.org.

EDUCATIONAL VOUCHERS

Although 41 educational voucher programs funded by private philanthropy were operating in the United States by 1998-99, discussion of vouchers as a political, legal, and educational issue primarily concerns publicly-funded plans allowing parents to send their children to the school of their choice. At present there are three educational voucher programs of this kind — in Milwaukee, Cleveland, and the state of Florida.

The Vouchers Debate

Proponents of vouchers argue that they are not merely consistent with parental rights but an appropriate, even necessary, practical means of realizing them. In particular, it is said, they enable low-income parents to exercise a choice about schools. Another pro-vouchers argument is that they create an incentive for self-improvement by public schools that is lacking when they enjoy a near monopoly.

Arguments against vouchers are that they take funds away from public schools and encourage highly motivated parents and competent students to abandon failing public institutions in favor of private ones. Using vouchers at church-related schools also is said to violate the First Amendment ban on an establishment of religion. The chief opponents of educational vouchers are teacher unions — the National Education Association, the American Federation of Teachers, and their affiliates — and other public school groups, church-state separationists, and some mainline African-American organizations. Phi Delta Kappa/Gallup polls in 1998 and 1999 found 51% of the respondents, including 60% of public school parents in the latter year, were in favor of total or partial government-paid tuition for children in private or church-related schools, although support declined when vouchers were specified.

Recent Developments

On June 27, 2002, the U.S. Supreme Court upheld the Cleveland voucher program in a 5-4 ruling, saying it is "entirely neutral with respect to religion." The majority opinion, written by Chief Justice William Rehnquist, said the program is therefore "a program of true private choice" and does not violate the Establishment Clause of the First Amendment.

Cleveland established the voucher program in 1995 to help address problems in what was considered one of the worst public school systems in the country. The state Legislature created the system after a federal judge declared the schools were being mismanaged and put them under the authority of the state superintendent of public instruction. The program provides for vouchers of up to $4,000 annually for children in low-income families to attend other public or private schools or pay for tutors. The vast majority of participants use their vouchers to pay tuition at church-affiliated schools, nearly all of them Catholic.

The case came to the Supreme Court after the 6th U.S. Circuit Court of Appeals ruled in 2000 that the program was unconstitutional because the vouchers are primarily used at religious schools. The U.S. Conference of Catholic Bishops in a friend-of-the-court brief argued that the program should not be considered unconstitutional because most voucher recipients choose to attend church schools.

Opponents of the program who filed briefs included

the National Association for the Advancement of Colored People, an association of Ohio school boards and several groups of public schools from around the country. Opponents call vouchers a fraud meant to siphon tax money from struggling public schools. The Ohio school boards argued that the state has ignored its responsibility to provide a good education and is merely shifting the burden to religious schools.

Central to the court's reasoning was that children in the Cleveland program have a theoretical choice of attending religious schools, secular private academies, suburban public schools, or charter schools run by parents or others outside the education establishment. The fact that only a handful of secular schools and no suburban public schools have signed up to accept voucher students is not the fault of the program itself, Ohio authorities say. "We believe that the program challenged here is a program of true private choice," Chief Justice William H. Rehnquist wrote for himself and Justices Sandra Day O'Connor, Antonin Scalia, Anthony M. Kennedy and Clarence Thomas.

The Cleveland program goes too far toward state-sponsored religion, the dissenting justices said. It does not treat religion neutrally, as Rehnquist contended, wrote Justice David H. Souter. The majority is also wrong about the question of whether parents have a true choice among schools, Souter wrote for himself and Justices John Paul Stevens, Ruth Bader Ginsburg and Stephen Breyer. "There is, in any case, no way to interpret the 96.6 percent of current voucher money going to religious schools as reflecting a free and genuine choice by the families that apply for vouchers," Souter wrote.

President George W. Bush has been a staunch advocate of school vouchers, and emphasized the issue in his campaign for the White House. Congress last year shelved that effort, but Bush resurrected the idea, proposing in his 2003 budget to give families up to $2,500 per child in tax credits if they choose a private school rather than a failing neighborhood public school. Following the court's hearing on arguments in Feb. 2002, Education Secretary Rod Paige said he would continue advocating on behalf of both improved public schools and school choice. Republican lawmakers in Congress agreed with Bush's stance. The Bush administration sided with Ohio, arguing that the program is constitutional because parents control where the money goes. In Cleveland, the public money flows to parents, not directly to the church-run schools, the program's supporters noted.

EX CORDE ECCLESIAE

On Nov. 17, 1999, the Catholic Bishops of the Unites States approved The Application of Ex Corde Ecclesiae for the United States, implementing the Apostolic Constitution Ex Corde Ecclesiae. This action received the recognitio from the Congregation for Bishops on May 3, 2000. Bishop Joseph Fiorenza, President of the National Conference of Catholic Bishops, decreed that the application would have the force of particular law for the United States on May 3, 2001. Guidelines concerning the academic mandatum in Catholic universities were subsequently issued, based on Canon 812. The following are the first guidelines.

Pope John Paul II's Constitution Ex Corde Ecclesiae

of 1990 fostered a productive dialogue between the Bishops of the United States and the leaders of our Catholic colleges and universities. It is anticipated that this recently approved Application of Ex Corde Ecclesiae for the United States would further that dialogue and build a community of trust between bishops and theologians. Both bishops and theologians are engaged in a necessary though complementary service to the Church that requires ongoing and mutually respectful conversation.

Article 4, 4, e, iv of the Application states that "a detailed procedure will be developed outlining the process of requesting and granting (or withdrawing) the *mandatum*." These guidelines are intended to explain and serve as a resource for the conferral of the *mandatum*. Only those guidelines herein which repeat a norm of the *Application* have the force of particular law. They were approved for distribution to the members of NCCB by the Conference's general membership.

Nature of the *mandatum*

• The *mandatum* is fundamentally an acknowledgment by Church authority that a Catholic professor of a theological discipline is a teacher within the full communion of the Catholic Church (*Application*: Article 4,4,e,i).

• The *mandatum*, therefore, recognizes the professor's commitment and responsibility to teach authentic Catholic doctrine and to refrain from putting forth as Catholic teaching anything contrary to the Church's magisterium (cf. *Application*: Article 4,4,e, iii).

• The *mandatum* should not be construed as an appointment, authorization, delegation or approbation of one's teaching by Church authorities. Those who have received a *mandatum* teach in their own name in virtue of their baptism and their academic and professional competence, not in the name of the bishop or of the Church's magisterium (*Application*: Article 4,4,e,ii).

Cardinal Newman Society

The Cardinal Newman Society is a national organization established in 1993 and dedicated to the renewal of Catholic identity in Catholic higher education in the United States. CNS has more than 18,000 members nationwide who share a common concern for the future of Catholic higher education and urge fidelity to the magisterium. The society seeks to: promote discussion and understanding of the message of the Catholic Church concerning the nature and value of Catholic higher education; assist college leaders, educators, students, and alumni in their efforts to preserve the religious identity of Catholic institutions of higher learning; and advocate the faithful implementation of *Ex Corde Ecclesiae* by facilitating an active dialogue among members of the Catholic university community. J. Laurence McCarty, Chairman of the Board; Patrick J. Reilly, president. Address: 10562 Associates Court, Manassas, VA 20109; (703) 367-0333; www.cardinalnew mansociety.org.

SUMMARY OF SCHOOL STATISTICS

Status and figures (as of Jan. 1, 2008) reported by The Official Catholic Directory.

Colleges and Universities: 236 (U.S., 231; outlying areas, 5).

College and University Students: 794,321 (U.S., 773,459; outlying areas, 20,862).

High Schools: 1,350 (771 diocesan and parochial; 579 private). U.S., 1,239 (706 diocesan and parochial; 533 private). Outlying areas, 111 (65 diocesan and parochial; 46 private).

High School Students: 680,689 (374,496 diocesan and parochial; 306,193 private). U.S., 653,401 (358,391 diocesan and parochial; 295,010 private). Outlying areas, 27,288 (16,105 diocesan and parochial; 11,183 private).

Public High School Students Receiving Religious Instruction: 689,552 (U.S., 680,366; outlying areas, 9,186).

Elementary Schools: 6,622 (6,266 diocesan and parochial; 356 private). U.S., 6,470 (6,170 diocesan and parochial; 300 private). Outlying areas, 152 (96 diocesan and parochial; 56 private).

Elementary School Students: 1,665,163 (1,576,301 diocesan and parochial; 88,862 private) U.S., 1,616,561 (1,546,038 diocesan and parochial; 70,523 private). Outlying areas, 48,602 (30,263 diocesan and parochial; 18,339 private).

Public Elementary School Students Receiving Religious Instruction: 3,145,424 (U.S., 3,112,593; outlying areas, 32,831).

Non-Residential Schools for Handicapped: 68 (U.S.). Students: 6,419 (U.S.).

Teachers: 178,288 U.S., 173,199 (lay persons 165,278; sisters, 5,517; priests, 1,353; brothers, 1,021; scholastics, 30). Outlying areas, 5,089 (lay persons, 4,792; sisters, 201; priests, 74; brothers, 19; scholastics, 3).

Seminaries: 181 (71 diocesan; 110 religious). U.S.: 168 (65 diocesan; 103 religious). Outlying areas: 13 (6 diocesan; 7 religious).

Seminarians: 5,029 (3,248 diocesan; 1,781 religious). U.S.: 4,922 (3,156 diocesan; 1,766 religious). Outlying areas: 107 (92 diocesan; 15 religious).

CATHOLIC SCHOOLS AND STUDENTS IN THE UNITED STATES

(*Source:* Official Catholic Directory, 2008; *figures as of Jan. 1, 2008. Archdioceses are indicated by an asterisk.*)

State Diocese	Universities/ Colleges	Students	High Schools	Students	Elem. Schools	Students
Alabama	1	1,867	9	3,497	35	10,024
*Mobile	1	1,867	3	2,024	16	4,983
Birmingham	-	-	6	1,473	19	5,041
Alaska	-	-	3	328	6	754
*Anchorage	-	-	2	132	4	411
Fairbanks	-	-	1	196	1	264
Juneau	-	-	-	-	1	79
Arizona	-	-	12	7,225	51	15,840
Phoenix	-	-	6	3,875	29	10,176
Tucson	-	-	6	2,106	22	5,664
Arkansas						
Little Rock	-	-	6	1,750	27	5,955
California	15	45,679	123	77,854	581	156,499
*Los Angeles	5	11,845	50	30,574	224	58,040
*San Francisco	3	12,177	14	8,316	62	17,460
Fresno	-	-	2	1,324	22	5,180
Monterey	-	-	5	1,794	14	3,541
Oakland	3	5,460	9	6,160	48	12,371
Orange	-	-	7	6,871	35	12,955
Sacramento	1	139	14	7,448	45	10,690
San Bernardino	-	-	3	1,077	31	6,856
San Diego	2	7,568	5	4,215	45	13,405
San Jose	1	8,490	6	6,621	31	10,187
Santa Rosa	-	-	6	1,851	13	2,627
Stockton	-	-	2	1,603	11	3,187
Colorado	1	15,741	8	4,438	50	12,722
*Denver	1	15,741	7	4,053	39	10,002
Colorado Springs	-	-	1	385	7	1,698
Pueblo	-	-	-	-	4	1,022
Connecticut	4	15,176	21	11,125	117	25,432
*Hartford	2	4,441	9	4,855	61	13,479
Bridgeport	2	10,735	7	3,846	35	8,816
Norwich	-	-	5	2,424	21	3,137
Delaware, Wilmington	-	-	8	4,780	29	9,401
District of Columbia *Wash., DC	3	15,108	18	10,112	80	21,478
Florida	4	26,952	36	25,151	179	65,516
*Miami	2	15,568	13	12,929	60	23,779
Orlando	-	-	5	2,276	31	12,139
Palm Beach	-	-	3	1,920	14	5,288
Pensacola-Tallahassee	-	-	2	724	9	2,214
St. Augustine	-	-	4	2,469	27	8,673
St. Petersburg	1	13,790	6	3,255	27	9,525
Venice	1	594	3	1,578	9	3,316
Georgia	1	185	12	5,836	35	11,676
*Atlanta	1	185	7	3,634	19	7,412
Savannah	-	-	5	2,202	16	4,264
Hawaii, Honolulu	1	2,547	7	3,547	37	7,617
Idaho, Boise	-	-	1	672	13	2,489
Illinois	13	63,379	71	46,001	430	122,147
*Chicago	6	47,789	39	27,828	216	68,236
Belleville	-	-	3	1,302	33	5,321
Joliet	3	13,105	8	5,785	56	18,262
Peoria	1	434	7	2,770	40	9,658
Rockford	1	115	8	4,309	41	11,130
Springfield	2	1,936	6	4,007	44	9,540
Indiana	11	28,554	25	12,889	166	44,234
*Indianapolis	2	3,450	11	5,907	60	17,497
Evansville	-	-	4	1,574	24	5,807

State Diocese	Universities/ Colleges	Students	High Schools	Students	Elem. Schools	Students
Indiana, cont.						
Ft.Wayne-S. Bend	5	15,853	4	3,224	40	10,570
Gary	1	1,275	4	1,465	22	6,001
Lafayette	3	7,976	2	719	20	4,359
Iowa	6	9,933	22	7,330	93	22,969
*Dubuque	3	4,246	7	2,629	44	10,321
Davenport	1	3,870	5	1,264	14	3,635
Des Moines	1	679	2	1,464	16	4,888
Sioux City	1	1,138	8	1,973	19	4,125
Kansas	4	6,915	17	6,735	94	22,867
*Kansas City	3	4,715	7	3,526	41	11,722
Dodge City	-	-	-	-	7	1,067
Salina	-	-	6	740	11	1,740
Wichita	1	2,200	4	2,468	35	8,338
Kentucky	5	7,437	23	11,514	99	29,619
*Louisville	3	5,147	9	6,334	40	15,540
Covington	1	1,400	9	3,410	28	7,623
Lexington	-	-	2	986	15	3,390
Owensboro	1	890	3	784	16	3,066
Louisiana	4	11,221	50	26,147	149	59,202
*New Orleans	3	9,175	23	14,184	63	26,440
Alexandria	-	-	3	563	8	2,291
Baton Rouge	1	2,046	8	4,285	24	11,733
Houma-Thib.	-	-	3	1,872	10	4,025
Lafayette	-	-	10	4,012	32	11,347
Lake Charles	-	-	1	582	7	2,140
Shreveport	-	-	2	649	5	1,226
Maine, Portland	1	3,972	3	1,062	15	3,332
Maryland,*Baltimore	4	12,024	22	12,057	63	22,122
Massachusetts	12	36,578	50	25,873	165	43,585
*Boston	7	24,400	34	17,918	99	28,542
Fall River	1	2,389	5	2,973	24	5,255
Springfield	1	1,249	4	1,422	20	4,661
Worcester	3	8,540	7	3,560	21	5,127
Michigan	6	21,323	41	16,621	228	50,836
*Detroit	3	16,860	22	10,598	87	26,726
Gaylord	-	-	4	560	16	2,491
Grand Rapids	1	2,250	4	1,771	32	5,328
Kalamazoo	-	-	3	672	20	3,082
Lansing	2	2,213	5	2,278	41	8,757
Marquette	-	-	-	-	9	1,393
Saginaw	-	-	3	742	23	3,059
Minnesota	7	26,099	24	11,306	185	45,850
*St.Paul and Minn.	3	17,323	14	8,637	96	32,500
Crookston	-	-	1	159	9	1,473
Duluth	1	3,259	-	-	12	1,679
New Ulm	-	-	3	418	16	2,167
St. Cloud	2	4,167	2	1,007	31	4,694
Winona	1	1,350	4	1,085	21	3,337
Mississippi	2	44	9	2,722	27	6,266
Biloxi	-	-	5	1,583	12	2,909
Jackson	2	44	4	1,139	15	3,357
Missouri	4	23,503	42	19,990	214	51,848
*St.Louis	2	15,136	29	14,316	122	34,558
Jefferson City	-	-	2	1,122	37	6,190
Kansas City-St. Joseph	2	8,367	8	3,557	32	7,427
Springfield-Cape Girar.	-	-	3	995	23	3,673
Montana	2	2,153	5	887	16	3,034
Great Falls-Billings	1	725	3	561	12	1,996
Helena	1	1,428	2	326	4	1,038
Nebraska	2	7,992	28	8,093	91	20,818
*Omaha	2	7,992	18	5,867	58	14,549
Grand Island	-	-	4	482	6	952
Lincoln	-	-	6	1,744	27	5,317

State Diocese	Universities/ Colleges	Students	High Schools	Students	Elem. Schools	Students
Nevada	-	-	2	1,727	11	3,805
Las Vegas	-	-	1	1,050	7	2,746
Reno	-	-	1	677	4	1,059
New Hampshire Manchester	4	4,425	5	2,543	25	5,281
New Jersey	7	21,661	70	38,494	487	75,640
*Newark	4	15,956	34	15,489	302	23,322
Camden	-	-	10	8,033	54	13,220
Metuchen	-	-	7	3,429	38	10,768
Paterson	2	2,079	8	3,977	51	12,610
Trenton	1	3,626	11	7,566	42	15,728
New Mexico	1	2,614	4	2,122	30	5,575
*Santa Fe	1	2,614	2	1,828	14	3,900
Gallup	-	-	2	294	11	1,158
Las Cruces	-	-	-	-	5	517
New York	26	115,525	123	74,541	574	156,614
*New York	10	61,268	55	29,624	231	63,001
Albany	4	6,400	7	2,557	28	5,871
Brooklyn	3	23,630	20	16,984	117	37,741
Buffalo	7	17,194	15	5,673	61	14,318
Ogdensburg	-	-	2	455	15	2,114
Rochester	-	-	7	3,432	42	7,307
Rockville Centre	1	3,533	11	12,821	58	21,490
Syracuse	1	3,500	6	2,955	23	4,772
North Carolina	1	1,337	4	3,121	48	14,401
Charlotte	1	1,337	2	1,903	16	6,487
Raleigh	-	-	2	1,218	32	7,914
North Dakota	2	3,264	4	998	22	3,516
Bismarck	1	2,784	3	666	10	1,641
Fargo	1	480	1	332	12	1,875
Ohio	13	48,312	78	45,786	382	111,069
*Cincinnati	4	29,656	22	17,736	98	34,563
Cleveland	3	6,796	22	13,986	116	39,555
Columbus	2	3,761	11	5,006	41	11,888
Steubenville	1	2,347	3	543	14	1,709
Toledo	2	2,962	14	6,054	73	15,758
Youngstown	1	2,703	6	2,464	38	7,291
Oklahoma	1	740	4	2,500	31	7,383
*Oklahoma City	1	740	2	1,000	17	3,427
Tulsa	-	-	2	1,500	11	3,200
Oregon	2	5,420	10	5,476	45	9,789
*Portland	2	5,420	10	5,476	41	9,182
Baker	-	-	-	-	4	607
Pennsylvania	26	87,600	80	46,610	493	125,170
*Philadelphia	11	40,462	35	27,705	205	64,770
Allentown	2	6,075	8	3,780	48	10,262
Altoona-Johnstown	2	4,125	3	1,011	23	3,197
Erie	2	7,436	7	2,579	35	6,188
Greensburg	2	3,645	2	767	15	3,246
Harrisburg	-	-	7	3,979	39	9,087
Pittsburgh	3	12,909	12	4,049	101	20,774
Scranton	4	12,948	6	2,740	24	7,414
Rhode Island, Providence	2	7,604	12	6,258	44	10,408
South Carolina Charleston	-	-	4	1,380	28	5,973
South Dakota	2	1,992	5	1,466	22	4,647
Rapid City	-	-	2	488	2	943
Sioux Falls	2	1,992	3	978	20	3,704
Tennessee	2	3,513	12	6,068	49	12,667
Knoxville	-	-	2	1,228	8	2,379
Memphis	1	1,871	6	3,057	22	5,676
Nashville	1	1,642	3	1,783	19	4,612
Texas	9	25,244	52	18,284	370	62,301
*Galveston-Houston	1	4,721	9	4,139	190	13,956
*San Antonio	4	12,832	9	2,508	36	11,108
Amarillo	-	-	1	124	6	649

State Diocese	Universities/ Colleges	Students	High Schools	Students	Elem. Schools	Students
Texas, cont.						
Austin	1	4,651	5	1,104	17	4,090
Beaumont	-	-	1	469	5	1,313
Brownsville	-	-	3	932	11	3,204
Corpus Christi	1	18	2	510	16	2,992
Dallas	1	2,972	9	4,348	34	10,649
El Paso	-	-	3	1,242	11	3,219
Fort Worth	1	50	4	1,520	16	4,929
Laredo	-	-	1	595	6	1,709
Lubbock	-	-	1	35	2	337
San Angelo	-	-	-	-	3	804
Tyler	-	-	1	211	4	853
Victoria	-	-	3	547	12	2,279
Utah, Salt Lake City	-	-	3	1,802	12	3,868
Vermont, Burlington	2	2,940	2	489	12	1,837
Virginia	4	5,639	15	6,255	64	20,514
Arlington	4	5,639	7	4,246	39	13,558
Richmond	-	-	8	2,009	25	6,956
Washington	3	16,257	13	7,525	81	22,070
*Seattle	2	9,400	9	6,139	60	16,773
Spokane	1	6,857	3	1,196	15	3,589
Yakima	-	-	1	190	6	1,708
West Virginia, Wheeling-Charleston	1	1,420	8	1,738	26	5,030
Wisconsin	9	32,646	28	11,192	317	52,350
*Milwaukee	5	23,302	13	6,870	123	26,228
Green Bay	2	3,803	6	2,019	57	8,520
La Crosse	1	2,991	7	1,653	74	8,282
Madison	1	2,550	2	650	47	6,785
Superior	-	-	-	-	16	2,535
Wyoming, Cheyenne	-	-	1	28	7	854
EASTERN CHURCHES	1	805	3	656	18	2,845
*Philadelphia	1	924	1	403	5	661
St. Nicholas (Chicago)	-	-	1	40	1	350
Stamford	-	-	1	100	2	202
St. Josaphat (Parma)	-	-	-	-	1	98
*Pittsburgh	-	-	-	-	1	155
Parma	-	-	-	-	1	180
Passaic	-	-	-	-	-	-
Van Nuys	-	-	-	-	-	-
St. Maron (Maronites)	-	-	-	-	-	-
Our Lady of Deliverance (Syriacs)	-	-	-	-	-	-
Our Lady of Lebanon (Maronites)	-	-	-	-	1	13
Newton (Melkites)	-	-	-	-	-	-
St. George Martyr (Romanians)	-	-	-	-	-	-
St. Peter the Apostle (Chaldeans)	-	-	-	-	-	-
St. Thomas Apostle of Detroit (Chaldeans)	-	-	-	-	-	-
St. Thomas (Syro-Malabars)	-	-	-	-	-	-
Armenians (Ap. Ex.)	-	-	-	-	4	960
SCHOOLS AND STUDENTS IN OUTLYING AREAS						
American Samoa	-	-	1	196	2	333
Caroline Islands	-	-	4	825	5	1,480
Guam	-	-	3	1,257	7	2,899
Marshall Islands	-	-	2	268	5	997
Marianas	-	-	1	153	3	306
Puerto Rico	5	20,862	99	24,360	127	41,927
Virgin Islands	-	-	2	229	3	660
TOTAL 2008	236	794,321	1,352	680,689	6,622	1,665,163
TOTAL 2007	236	785,619	1,350	672,426	6,562	1,724,761
TOTAL 1998	240	692,951	1,347	660,583	7,151	2,052,948

CATHOLIC UNIVERSITIES AND COLLEGES IN THE UNITED STATES

(*Sources:* Catholic Almanac *survey;* The Official Catholic Directory.)

Listed below are institutions of higher learning established under Catholic auspices. Some of them are now independent.

Information includes: name of each institution; indication of male (m), female (w), coeducational (c) student body; name of founding group or group with which the institution is affiliated; year of foundation; total number of students, in parentheses.

Albertus Magnus College (c): 700 Prospect St., New Haven, CT 06511; (203) 773-8550; www.albertus.edu. Dominican Sisters; 1925; independent (2,065).

Alvernia College (c): 400 Saint Bernardine St., Reading, PA 19607; (610) 796-8200; www.alvernia.edu. Bernardine Sisters; 1958 (2,457).

Alverno College (w): 3400 S. 43th St., P.O. Box 343922, Milwaukee, WI 53234; (414) 382-6000; www.alverno.edu. School Sisters of St. Francis; 1887; independent (2,000).

Anna Maria College (c): 50 Sunset Lane, Paxton, MA 01612; (508) 849-3300; www.annamaria.edu. Sisters of St. Anne; 1946; independent (1,244).

Aquinas College (c): 1607 Robinson Rd. S.E., Grand Rapids, MI 49506; (616) 459-8281. Sisters of St. Dominic; 1922; independent (2,571).

Aquinas College (c): 4210 Harding Rd., Nashville, TN 37205; (615) 297-7545; www.aquinas-tn.edu. Dominican Sisters; 1961 (506).

Aquinas Institute of Theology (c): 3642 Lindell Boulevard, St. Louis, MO 63108; (314) 977-3869; www.op.org/aquinas. Dominicans, 1961; graduate theology; offers distance learning program in pastoral studies and specializations in preaching (200).

Assumption College (c): 500 Salisbury St., Worcester, MA 01615-0005; (508) 767-7000; www.assumption.edu. Assumptionist Religious; 1904 (2,766).

Ave Maria School of Law (c): 3475 Plymouth Rd., Ann Arbor, MI 48105; (734) 930-4408.

Avila University (c): 11901 Wornall Rd., Kansas City, MO 64145-1698; (816) 942-8400; www.avila.edu. Sisters of St. Joseph of Carondelet; 1916 (2,658).

Barry University (c): 11300 N.E. 2nd Ave., Miami Shores, FL 33161; (305) 899-3000; www.barry.edu. Dominican Sisters (Adrian, MI); 1940 (8,691).

Bellarmine College (c): 2001 Newburg Rd., Louisville, KY 40205; (502) 452-8211; www.bellarmine.edu. Louisville archdiocese; independent (2,323).

Belmont Abbey College (c): 100 Belmont-Mt. Holly Rd., Belmont, NC 28012; (704) 825-6700; www.belmontabbeycollege.edu. Benedictine Fathers; 1876 (883).

Benedictine College (c): 1020 N. Second St., Atchison, KS 66002; (913) 367-5340; www.benedictine.edu. Benedictines; 1859; independent (1,375).

Benedictine University (formerly Illinois Benedictine College) (c): 5700 College Rd., Lisle, IL 60532-0900; (630) 829-600 0; www.ben.edu. Benedictine Monks of St. Procopius Abbey; 1887 (2,809).

Boston College (University status) (c): Chestnut Hill, MA 02167; (617) 552-8000; www.bc.edu. Jesuit

Fathers; 1863 (14,297).

Brescia University (c): 717 Frederica St., Owensboro, KY 42301; (270) 685-3131; www.brescia.edu. Ursuline Sisters; 1950 (820).

Briar Cliff College (c): 3303 Rebecca St., Sioux City, IA 51104; (712) 279-5405; www.briarcliff.edu. Sisters of St. Francis of the Holy Family; 1930 (994).

Cabrini College (c): 610 King of Prussia Rd., Radnor, PA 19087; (610) 902-8100; www.cabrini.edu. Missionary Srs. of Sacred Heart; 1957; private (2,669).

Caldwell College (c): 9 Ryerson Ave., Caldwell, NJ 07006; (973) 618-3000; www.caldwell.edu. Dominican Sisters; 1939 (2,270).

Calumet College of St. Joseph (c): 2400 New York Ave., Whiting, IN 46394; (219) 473-7770; www.ccsj.edu. Society of the Precious Blood, 1951 (1,141).

Canisius College (c): 2001 Main St., Buffalo, NY 14208; (716) 883-7000; www.canisius.edu. Jesuit Fathers; 1870; independent (4,995).

Cardinal Stritch University (c): 6801 N. Yates Rd., Milwaukee, WI 53217; (414) 410-4000; www.stritch.edu. Sisters of St. Francis of Assisi; 1937 (5,855).

Carlow College (w): 3333 5th Ave., Pittsburgh, PA 15213; (412) 578-6059; www.carlow.edu. Sisters of Mercy; 1929 (2,199).

Carroll College (c): 1601 N. Benton Ave., Helena, MT 59625; (406) 447-4300. Diocesan; 1909 (1,400).

Catholic Distance University (c): 120 East Colonial Highway, Hamilton, VA 20158-9012; www.cdu.edu. Offers External Degree programs, including Masters degrees in Religious Studies (7,000).

Catholic Theological Union (c): 5401 South Cornell Ave., Chicago, IL 60615; (773) 324-8000; www.ctu.edu (348). Offers Graduate theological programs, including M.Div., M.A., M.A.P.S., and D.Min.

Catholic University of America, The (c): Michigan Ave. & Fourth St., NE, Washington, DC 20064; (202) 319-5000; www.cua.edu. Hierarchy of the United States; 1887. Pontifical University (5,777).

Chaminade University of Honolulu (c): 3140 Waialae Ave., Honolulu, HI 96816; (808) 735-4711; www.chaminade.edu. Marianists; 1955 (2,788).

Chestnut Hill College (w): 9601 Germantown Ave., Philadelphia, PA 19118; (215) 248-7000; www.chc.edu. Sisters of St. Joseph; 1924 (1,645).

Christendom College (c): 134 Christendom Dr., Front Royal, VA 22630; (540) 636-2900. Independent, 1977 (477).

Christian Brothers University (c): 650 E. Parkway S., Memphis, TN 38104; (901) 321-3000. Brothers of the Christian Schools; 1871 (2,027).

Clarke College (c): 1550 Clarke Dr., Dubuque, IA 52001; (563) 588-6300; www.clarke.edu. Sisters of Charity, BVM; 1843; independent (1,126).

Creighton University (c): 2500 California Plaza, Omaha, NE 68178; (402) 280-2700; www.creighton.edu. Jesuit Fathers; 1878; independent (6,297).

Dallas, University of (c): 1845 E. Northgate, Irving, TX 75062; (972) 721-5000. Dallas diocese; 1956; independent (3,518).

Dayton, University of (c): 300 College Park, Dayton, OH 45469-1660; (937) 229-1000; www.udayton.edu. Marianists; 1850 (10,248).

DePaul University (c): One E. Jackson Blvd., Chicago, IL 60604; (312) 362-8000; www.depaul.edu. Vincentians; 1898 (23,174).

De Sales University (c): 2755 Station Ave., Center Valley, PA 18034; (610) 282-1100; www.desales.edu. Oblates of St. Francis de Sales; 1965 (1,339).

Detroit Mercy, University of (c): 4001 W. McNichols Rd., Detroit, MI, 48221; 8200 W. Outer Dr., Detroit MI 48219; (313) 993-1000. Society of Jesus and Sisters of Mercy; 1877; independent (5,843).

Dominican College (c): 470 Western Hwy., Orangeburg, NY 10962; (845) 359-7800; www.dc.edu. Dominican Sisters; 1952; independent (1,700).

Dominican University of California (c): 50 Acacia Ave., San Rafael, CA 94901-2298; (415) 457-4440; www.dominican.edu. Dominican Sisters; 1890; independent (1,578).

Dominican University (formerly Rosary College) (c): 7900 W. Division St., River Forest, IL 60305; (708) 366-2490; www.dom.edu. Sinsinawa Dominican Sisters; 1901 (2,533).

Duquesne University (c): 600 Forbes Ave., Pittsburgh, PA 15282; (412) 396-6000; www.duq.edu. Congregation of the Holy Ghost; 1878 (9,600).

D'Youville College (c): 320 Porter Ave., Buffalo, NY 14201; (716) 881-3200; www.dyc.edu. Grey Nuns of the Sacred Heart; 1908; independent (2,453).

Edgewood College (c): 1000 Edgewood College Dr., Madison, WI 53711; (608) 663-4861. Sinsinawa Dominican Sisters; 1927 (2,258).

Emmanuel College (w): 400 The Fenway, Boston, MA 02115; (617) 735-9715; www.emmanuel.edu. Sisters of Notre Dame de Namur; 1919; independent (1,549).

Fairfield University (c): 1073 North Benson Rd., Fairfield, CT 06430; (203) 254-4000; www.fairfield.edu. Jesuits; 1942 (6,001).

Felician College (c): 262 S. Main St., Lodi, NJ 07644; (201) 559-6000; www.felician.edu. Felician Sisters; 1942; independent (1,400).

Fontbonne University (c): 6800 Wydown Blvd., St. Louis, MO 63105; (314) 862-3456; www.fontbonne.edu. Sisters of St. Joseph of Carondelet; 1917; independent (2,344).

Fordham University (c): Fordham Rd. and Third Ave., New York, NY 10458; (718) 817-3040. Society of Jesus (Jesuits); 1841; independent (13,800).

Franciscan University of Steubenville (c): 1235 University Blvd., Steubenville, OH 43952; (740) 283-3771; www.franuniv.edu. Franciscan TOR Friars; 1946 (2,208). Also offers distance learning programs.

Gannon University (c): 109 University Square, Erie, PA 16541-0001; (814) 871-7000; www.gannon.edu. Diocese of Erie; 1933 (3,404).

Georgetown University (c): 37th and O Sts. N.W., Washington, DC 20057; (202) 687-0100; www.georgetown.edu. Jesuit Fathers; 1789 (12,688).

Georgian Court College (w/c): 900 Lakewood Ave., Lakewood, NJ 08701; (732) 364-2200; www.georgian.edu. Sisters of Mercy; 1908 (3,561).

Gonzaga University (c): E. 502 Boone Ave., Spokane, WA 99258; (509) 328-4220. Jesuit Fathers; 1887 (4,515).

Graduate School of Theology (c): 5890 Birch Ct., Oakland, CA 94618; (510) 652-1651; www.satgtu.org. Affiliate of the Graduate Theological Union.

Great Falls, University of (c): 1301 20th St. S., Great Falls, MT 59405; (406) 761-8210; www.ugf.edu. Sisters of Providence; 1932; independent (825).

Gwynedd-Mercy College (c): Gwynedd Valley, PA 19437; (215) 646-7300; www.gmc.edu. Sisters of Mercy; 1948; independent (2,198).

Hilbert College (c): 5200 S. Park Ave., Hamburg, NY 14075; (716) 649-7900; www.hilbert.edu. Franciscan Sisters of St. Joseph; 1957; independent (970).

Holy Cross, College of the (c): Worcester, MA 01610; (508) 793-2011; www.holycross.edu. Jesuits; 1843 (2,811).

Holy Family College (c): Grant and Frankford Aves., Philadelphia, PA 19114 and One Campus Dr., Newtown, PA 18940; (215) 637-7700; www.hfc.edu. Sisters of Holy Family of Nazareth; 1954; independent (2,559).

Holy Names College (c): 3500 Mountain Blvd., Oakland, CA 94619; (510) 436-1000; www.hnc.edu. Sisters of the Holy Names of Jesus and Mary; 1868; independent (947).

Immaculata College (w): Immaculata, PA 19345; (610) 647-4400; www.immaculata.edu. Sisters, Servants of the Immaculate Heart of Mary; 1920 (3,062).

Incarnate Word, University of the (c): 4301 Broadway, San Antonio, TX 78209; (210) 829-6000; www.uiw.edu. Sisters of Charity of the Incarnate Word; 1881 (4,264).

Iona College (c): 715 North Ave., New Rochelle, NY 10801; (914) 633-2000; www.iona.edu. Congregation of Christian Brothers; 1940; independent (4,897).

John Carroll University (c): 20700 N. Park Blvd., Cleveland, OH 44118; (216) 397-1886; www.jcu.edu. Jesuits; 1886 (4,294).

King's College (c): 133 North River St., Wilkes-Barre, PA 18711; (570) 208-5900; www.kings.edu. Holy Cross Fathers; 1946 (2,178).

La Roche College (c): 9000 Babcock Blvd., Pittsburgh, PA 15237; (412) 367-9300; www.laroche.edu. Sisters of Divine Providence; 1963 (1,981).

La Salle University (c): 1900 W. Olney Ave., Philadelphia, PA 19141; (215) 951-1000. Christian Brothers; 1863 (5,567).

Le Moyne College (c): 1419 Salt Springs Rd., Syracuse, NY 13214; (315) 445-4100; www.lemoyne.edu. Jesuit Fathers; 1946; independent (approx. 3,129, full-time, part-time, graduate)

Lewis University (c): Romeoville, IL 60446; (815) 838-0500; www.lewisu.edu. Christian Brothers; 1932 (4,348).

Loras College (c): 1450 Alta Vista St., Dubuque, IA 52004; (563) 588-7100. Archdiocese of Dubuque; 1839 (1,736).

Lourdes College (c): 6832 Convent Blvd., Sylvania, OH 43560; (419) 885-3211; www.lourdes.edu. Sisters of St. Francis; 1958 (1,356).

Loyola College (c): 4501 N. Charles St., Baltimore, MD 21210; (410) 617-2000; www.loyola.edu. Jesuits; 1852; combined with Mt. St. Agnes College, 1971 (6,144).

Loyola Marymount University (c): 7900 Loyola Blvd., Los Angeles, CA 90045-2699; (310) 338-2700; www.lmu.edu. Society of Jesus; Religious of Sacred Heart of Mary, Sisters of St. Joseph of Orange, 1911 (6,591).

Loyola University (c): 6363 St. Charles Ave., New Orleans, LA 70118; (504) 865-2011. Jesuit Fathers;

1912 (5,842).

Loyola University Chicago (c): 820 N. Michigan Ave., Chicago, IL 60611; (312) 915-6000; www.luc.edu. Society of Jesus; 1870 (12,604).·

Madonna University (c): 36600 Schoolcraft Rd., Livonia, MI 48150; (734) 432-5300. Felician Sisters; 1947 (3,979).

Magdalen College (c): 511 Kearsarge Mountain Rd., Warner, NH 03278; (603) 456-2656; www.magdalen.edu. Magdalen College Corporation; 1973 (81).

Manhattan College (c): Manhattan College Pkwy., Bronx, NY 11201; (718) 862-7200; www.manhattan.edu. De La Salle Christian Brothers; 1835; independent (2,744). Cooperative program with College of Mt. St. Vincent.

Marian College of Fond du Lac (c): 45 S. National Ave., Fond du Lac, WI 54935; (920) 923-7600; www.mariancollege.edu. Sisters of St. Agnes; 1936 (2,558).

Marian College (c): 3200 Cold Spring Rd., Indianapolis, IN 46222; (317) 955-6000; www.marian.edu. Sisters of St. Francis (Oldenburg, IN); 1851; independent (1,425).

Marquette University (c): P.O. Box 1881, Milwaukee, WI 53201-1881; (414) 288-7250; www.marquette.edu. Jesuit Fathers; 1881; independent (10,832).

Mary, University of (c): 7500 University Dr., Bismarck, ND 58504; (701) 255-7500; www.umary.edu. Benedictine Sisters; 1959 (2,546).

Marygrove College (c): 8425 W. McNichols Rd., Detroit, MI 48221; (313) 927-1200. Sisters, Servants of the Immaculate Heart of Mary; 1905; independent (6,459).

Marylhurst College (c): P.O. Box 261, Marylhurst, OR 97036-0261; (503) 636-8141; www.marylhurst.edu. Sisters of Holy Names of Jesus and Mary; 1893; independent (1,579).

Marymount College (w): Tarrytown, NY 10591; (914) 631-3200; www.marymt.edu. Religious of the Sacred Heart of Mary; 1907; independent (842). Coed in weekend degree programs.

Marymount University (c): 2807 N. Glebe Rd., Arlington, VA 22207; (703) 522-5600; www.marymount.edu. Religious of the Sacred Heart of Mary; 1950; independent (3,672).

Marywood College (c): Scranton, PA 18509; (570) 348-6211; www.marywood.edu. Sisters, Servants of the Immaculate Heart of Mary; 1915; independent (3,087).

Mercy College of Health Sciences (c): 928-6th Ave., Des Moines, IA 50309-1239; (515) 643-3180; www.mchs.edu. Sisters of Mercy of the Americas (552).

Mercyhurst College (c): 501 E. 38th St., Erie, PA 16546; (814) 824-2000; www.mercyhurst.edu. Sisters of Mercy; 1926 (3,404).

Merrimack College (c): North Andover, MA 01845; (978) 837-5000; www.merrimack.edu. Augustinians;1947 (2,108).

Misericordia (College Misericordia) (c): 301 Lake St., Dallas, PA 18612-1098; (570) 674-6400; www.miseri.edu. Religious Sisters of Mercy of the Union; 1924 (1,983).

Molloy College (c): 1000 Hempstead Ave., P.O. Box 5002, Rockville Centre, NY 11570-5002; (516) 678-5000. Dominican Sisters; 1955; independent (2,500).

Mount Aloysius College (c): 7373 Admiral Peary Hwy., Cresson, PA 16630; (814) 886-4131; www.mtaloy.edu. Sisters of Mercy; 1939 (2,000).

Mount Marty College (c): 1105 W. 8th St., Yankton, SD

57078; (800) 658-4552; www.mtmc.edu. Benedictine Sisters; 1936 (1,168).

Mount Mary College (w): 2900 N. Menomonee River Pkwy., Milwaukee, WI 53222; (414) 258-4810. School Sisters of Notre Dame; 1913 (1,368).

Mount Mercy College (c): 1330 Elmhurst Dr. N.E., Cedar Rapids, IA 52402; (319) 363-8213; www.mtmercy.edu. Sisters of Mercy; 1928; independent (1,432).

Mount St. Clare College (c): 400 N. Bluff Blvd., Clinton, IA 52732; (319) 242-4023; www.clare.edu. Sisters of St. Francis of Clinton, Iowa; 1918 (appr. 497).

Mount St. Joseph, College of (c): 5701 Delhi Rd., Cincinnati, OH 45233-1670; (513) 244-4200; www.msj.edu. Sisters of Charity; 1920 (5,527).

Mount Saint Mary College (c): Newburgh, NY 12550; (914) 561-0800; www.msmc.edu. Dominican Sisters; 1954; independent (2,541).

Mount St. Mary's College (c): Emmitsburg, MD 21727; (301) 447-6122; www.msmary.edu. Founded by Fr. John DuBois, 1808; independent (1,821).

Mount St. Mary's College (w/c): 12001 Chalon Rd., Los Angeles, CA 90049 and 10 Chester Pl., Los Angeles, CA 90007 (Doheny Campus); (310) 954-4010; www.msmc.la.edu. Sisters of St. Joseph of Carondelet; 1925. Coed in music, nursing and graduate programs (1,965).

Mount Saint Vincent, College of (c): 6301 Riverdale Ave., New York, NY 10471; (718) 405-3200; www.cmsv.edu. Sisters of Charity; 1847; independent (1,515). Cooperative program with Manhattan College.

Neumann College (c): One Neumann Dr., Aston, PA 19014; (610) 459-0905; www.neumann.edu. Sisters of St. Francis; 1965; independent (2,221).

Newman University (c): 3100 McCormick Ave., Wichita, KS 67213; (316) 942-4291; www.newmanu.edu. Sisters Adorers of the Blood of Christ; 1933 (1,929).

New Rochelle, College of (w/c): 29 Castle Pl., New Rochelle, NY 10805 (main campus); (914) 654-5000; www.cnr.edu. Ursuline Order; 1904; independent (6,084). Coed in nursing, graduate, new resources divisions.

Niagara University (c): Lewiston Rd. Niagara Univ., NY 14109-2015; (716) 285-1212; www.niagara.edu. Vincentian Fathers and Brothers; 1856 (3,446).

Notre Dame de Namur University (c): 1500 Ralston Ave., Belmont, CA 94002; (650) 593-1601; www.cnd.edu. Sisters of Notre Dame de Namur; 1851; independent (1,799).

Notre Dame, University of (c): (University of Notre Dame du Lac) Notre Dame, IN 46556; (219) 631-5000; www.nd.edu. Congregation of Holy Cross; 1842 (11,054).

Notre Dame College of Ohio (w): 4545 College Rd., Cleveland, OH 44121; (216) 381-1680; www.ndc.edu. Sisters of Notre Dame; 1922 (1,093).

Notre Dame of Maryland, College of (w): 4701 N. Charles St., Baltimore, MD 21210; (410) 435-0100; www.ndm.edu. School Sisters of Notre Dame; 1873 (3,077).

Oblate School of Theology (c): 285 Oblate Dr., San Antonio, TX 78216-6693; (210) 341-1366; www.ost.edu. Oblates of Mary Immaculate; 1903 (264). Graduate theology programs.

Ohio Dominican College (c): 1216 Sunbury Rd., Columbus, OH 43219-2099; (614) 253-2741; www.odc.edu.

Dominican Sisters of St. Mary of the Springs; 1911 (2,300).

Our Lady of Holy Cross College (c): 4123 Woodland Dr., New Orleans, LA 70131; (504) 394-7744; www.olhcc.edu. Congregation of Sisters Marianites of Holy Cross; 1916 (3,994).

Our Lady of the Elms, College of (w): Chicopee, MA 01013; (413) 594-2761; www.elms.edu. Sisters of St. Joseph; 1928 (866).

Our Lady of the Lake College (c): 5345 Brittany Dr., Baton Rouge, LA 70808-4398; (225) 768-1710; www.ololcollege. Independent (1,421).

Our Lady of the Lake University (c): 411 S.W. 24th St., San Antonio, TX 78207; (210) 434-6711; www.ollusa.edu. Sisters of Divine Providence; 1895 (3,324).

Pontifical Catholic University of Puerto Rico (c): 2250 Avenida de las Americas, Ponce, PR 00717-0777; (787) 841-2000; www.pucpr.edu. Hierarchy of Puerto Rico; 1948; Pontifical University (9,912).

Portland, University of (c): 5000 N. Willamette Blvd., Portland, OR 97203; (503) 943-7911; www.up.edu. Holy Cross Fathers; 1901; independent (3,234).

Presentation College (c): Aberdeen, SD 7401; (605) 225-1634. Sisters of the Presentation; 1951 (615).

Providence College (c): 549 River Ave., Providence, RI 02918; (401) 865-1000; www.providence.edu. Dominican Friars; 1917 (5,742, day, evening, and graduate).

Queen of the Holy Rosary College (c): P.O. Box 3908, Mission San Jose, CA 94539; (510) 657-2468. Dominican Sisters of Mission San Jose, independent (200).

Quincy University (c): 1800 College Ave., Quincy, IL 62301; (217) 222-8020; www.quincy.edu. Franciscan Friars; 1860 (1,146).

Regis College (w): 235 Wellesley St., Weston, MA 02493-1571; (781) 768-7000; www.regiscollege.edu. Sisters of St. Joseph; 1927; independent (1,300).

Regis University (c): 3333 Regis Blvd. Denver, CO 80221; (303) 458-4100. Jesuits; 1887 (11,240).

Rivier College (c): Nashua, NH 03060; (603) 888-1311; www.rivier.edu. Sisters of the Presentation of Mary; 1933; independent (2,572).

Rockhurst College (c): 1100 Rockhurst Rd., Kansas City, MO 64110; (816) 501-4000; www.rockhurst.edu. Jesuit Fathers; 1910 (3,536).

Rosemont College of the Holy Child Jesus (w): Rosemont, PA 19010-1699; (610) 526-2984; www.rose mont.edu. Society of the Holy Child Jesus; 1921 (1,210).

Sacred Heart University (c): 5151 Park Ave., Fairfield, CT 06432; (203) 371-7999; www.sacred-heart.edu. Diocese of Bridgeport; 1963; independent (6,001).

St. Ambrose University (c): Davenport, IA 52803; (319) 333-6300; www.sau.edu. Diocese of Davenport; 1882 (3,500).

Saint Anselm College (c): Manchester NH 03102-1030; (603) 641-7000; www.anselm.edu. Benedictines; 1889 (1,985).

St. Basil College (m): 195 Glenbrook Rd., Stamford, CT 06902; (203) 324-4578; UkrCathSem@aol.com. The Ukrainian Catholic Diocese of Stamford.

Saint Benedict, College of (w): 37 S. College Ave., St. Joseph, MN 56374; (320) 363-5407; www.csbsju.edu. Benedictine Sisters; 1913 (2,072). Sister college of St. John's University, Collegeville

St. Bonaventure University (c): St. Bonaventure,

NY 14778; (716) 375-2000; www.sbu.edu. Franciscan Friars; 1858; independent (2,719).

St. Catherine, College of (w): St. Paul: 2004 Randolph Ave., St. Paul, MN 55105; (651) 690-6000; Minneapolis; www.stkate.edu. Sisters of St. Joseph of Carondelet; 1905 (4,622).

St. Edward's University (c): 3001 S. Congress Ave., Austin, TX 78704; (512) 448-8400; www.stedwards.edu. Holy Cross Brothers; 1881; independent (4,267).

Saint Elizabeth, College of (w): 2 Convent Rd., Morristown, NJ 07960-6989; (973) 290-4000; www.st-eliza beth.edu. Sisters of Charity; 1899; independent (1,766). Coed in adult undergraduate and graduate programs.

St. Francis College (c): 180 Remsen St., Brooklyn Heights, NY 11201; (718) 489-5200. Franciscan Brothers; 1884; private, independent in the Franciscan tradition (2,505).

St. Francis University (c): P.O. Box 600, Loretto, PA 15940-0600; (814) 472-3000; www.sfcpa.edu. Franciscan Friars; 1847; independent (2,012).

St. Francis, University of (c): 500 N. Wilcox, Joliet, IL 60435; (815) 740-3360; www.stfrancis.edu. Sisters of St. Francis of Mary Immaculate (3,920).

St. Francis, University of (c): 2701 Spring St., Fort Wayne, IN 46808-3994; (219) 434-3100; www.sf.edu. Sisters of St. Francis; 1890 (1,740).

St. Gregory's University (c): 1900 W. MacArthur, Shawnee, OK 74801; (405) 878-5100; www.sgc.edu. Benedictine Monks; 1876 (805).

St. John's University (c): 8000 Utopia Pkwy., Jamaica, NY 11439 (Queens Campus); 300 Howard Ave., Staten Island, NY 10301 (Staten Island Campus); (718) 990-6161; www.stjohns.edu. Vincentians; 1870 (18,523).

St. John's University (m): Collegeville, MN 56321; (320) 363-2011; www.csbsju.edu. Benedictines; 1857 (2,072). All classes and programs are coeducational with College of St. Benedict.

St. Joseph in Vermont, College of (c): 71 Clement Rd., Rutland, VT 05701; (802) 773-5900; www.csj.edu. Sisters of St. Joseph; 1950; independent (482).

Saint Joseph College (w/c): 1678 Asylum Ave., West Hartford, CT 06117-2700; (860) 232-4571; www.sjc.edu. Sisters of Mercy; 1932 (1,965). Women's college in undergraduate liberal arts. Coed in graduate school and Weekend College.

Saint Joseph's College (c): 278 Whites Bridge Rd., Standish, ME 04084-5263; (207) 893-7711; www.sjcme.edu. Sisters of Mercy; 1912 (4,197 total; 1,609 graduate). Offers extensive distance education programs.

Saint Joseph's College (c): P.O. Box 909, Rensselaer, IN 47978; (219) 866-6000; www.stjoe.edu. Society of the Precious Blood; 1891 (1,101).

St. Joseph's College (c): 245 Clinton Ave., Brooklyn, NY 11205; (718) 636-6800 and 155 W. Roe Blvd., Patchogue, NY 11772; (631) 447-3200; www.sjcny.edu. Sisters of St. Joseph; 1916; independent (3,444).

St. Joseph's University (c): 5600 City Ave., Philadelphia, PA 19131; (610) 660-1000; www.sju.edu. Jesuit Fathers; 1851 (6,850).

Saint Leo University (c): P.O. Box 6665, MC 2186, Saint Leo, FL 33574; (352) 588-8200; www.saintleo.edu. Order of St. Benedict; 1889; independent (9,931).

Saint Louis University (c): 221 N. Grand Blvd., St. Louis, MO 63103; (314) 977-2222; www.slu.edu. Society of Jesus; 1818; independent (11,274).

Saint Martin's College (c): 5300 Pacific Ave. SE, Lacey, WA 98503-1297; (360) 438-4311; www.stmartin.edu. Benedictine Monks; 1895 (1,474 main and extension campuses).

Saint Mary, College of (w): 1901 S. 72nd St., Omaha, NE 68124; (402) 399-2400; www.csm.edu. Sisters of Mercy; 1923; independent (981).

Saint Mary College (c): Leavenworth, KS 66048; (913) 682-5151. Sisters of Charity of Leavenworth; 1923 (888).

Saint Mary-of-the-Woods College (w): St. Mary-of-the-Woods, IN 47876; (812) 535-5151; www.smwc.edu. Sisters of Providence; 1840 (1,510).

Saint Mary's College (w): Notre Dame, IN 46556; (219) 284-4556; www.saintmarys.edu. Sisters of the Holy Cross; 1844 (1,473).

Saint Mary's College (c): 3535 Indian Trail, Orchard Lake, MI 48324; (248) 683-0521; www.stmarys-avemaria.edu. 1885 (510).

St. Mary's College (c): Moraga, CA 94575; (510) 631-4000. Brothers of the Christian Schools; 1863 (4,127).

Saint Mary's University of Minnesota (c): 700 Terrace Heights, Winona, MN 55987-1399; (507) 452-4430; www.smumn.edu. Brothers of the Christian Schools; 1912 (1,376).

St. Mary's University of San Antonio (c): One Camino Santa Maria, San Antonio, TX 78228-8607; (210) 436-3011; www.stmarytx.edu. Society of Mary (Marianists). 1852 (4,264).

Saint Meinrad School of Theology (c): 200 Hill Dr., St. Meinrad, IN 47577; (812) 357-6611; www.saint-meinrad.edu. Benedictines (91 full- and part-time lay students.) Graduate-level theological studies.

St. Michael's College (c): Winooski Park, Colchester, VT 05439; (802) 654-2211; www.smcvt.edu. Society of St. Edmund; 1904 (2,630).

St. Norbert College (c): De Pere, WI 54115; (920) 403-3181; www.snc.edu. Norbertine Fathers; 1898; independent (2,045).

Saint Peter's College (c): 2641 Kennedy Blvd., Jersey City, NJ 07306; (201) 915-9000; www.spc.edu. Society of Jesus; 1872; independent (4,201).

Saint Rose, College of (c): 432 Western Ave., Albany, NY 12203; (518) 454-5111. Sisters of St. Joseph of Carondelet; 1920; independent (4,441).

St. Scholastica, The College of (c): 1200 Kenwood Ave., Duluth, MN 55811; (218) 723-6000. Benedictine Sisters; 1912; independent (2,518).

St. Thomas, University of (c): 2115 Summit Ave., St. Paul, MN 55105; (651) 962-5000; www.stthomas.edu. Archdiocese of St. Paul and Minneapolis; 1885 (11,366).

St. Thomas, University of (c): 3800 Montrose Blvd., Houston, TX 77006-4696; (713) 522-7911; www.stthom.edu. Basilian Fathers; 1947 (7,174).

St. Thomas Aquinas College (c): Sparkill, NY 10976; (914) 398-4000; www.stac.edu. Dominican Sisters of Sparkill; 1952; independent, corporate board of trustees (2,200).

St. Thomas University (c): 16400 N.W. 32nd Ave., Miami, FL 33054; (305) 625-6000; www.stu.edu. Archdiocese of Miami; 1962 (3,677).

Saint Vincent College (c): 300 Fraser Purchase Rd., Latrobe, PA 15650-2690; (724) 539-9761; www.bene-dictine.stvincent.edu/seminary. Benedictine Fathers; 1846 (1,222).

Saint Vincent's College (c): 2800 Main St., Bridgeport, CT 06606; (203) 576-5235; www.stvin-centscollege.edu. (345).

St. Xavier University (c): 3700 W. 103rd St., Chicago, IL 60655; (773) 298-3000. Sisters of Mercy; chartered 1847 (4,100).

Salve Regina University (c): Ochre Point Ave., Newport, RI 02840-4192; (401) 847-6650; www.salve.edu. Sisters of Mercy; 1934 (1,542). Offers distance learning programs in graduate studies.

San Diego, University of (c): 5998 Alcala Park, San Diego, CA 92110; (619) 260-4600. San Diego diocese and Religious of the Sacred Heart; 1949; independent (7,062).

San Francisco, University of (c): 2130 Fulton St., San Francisco, CA 94117; (415) 422-5555. Jesuit Fathers; 1855 (8,130).

Santa Clara University (c): 500 El Camino Real, Santa Clara, CA 95053; (408) 554-4000; www.scu.edu. Jesuit Fathers; 1851; independent (7,368).

Santa Fe, College of (c): 1600 St. Michael's Dr., Santa Fe, NM 87505; (505) 473-6011. Brothers of the Christian Schools; 1947 (1,588).

Scranton, University of (c): Scranton, PA 18510; (570) 941-7533; www.uofs.edu. Society of Jesus; 1888; independent (4,728).

Seattle University (c): 900 Broadway, Seattle, WA 98122; (206) 296-6000; www.seattleu.edu. Society of Jesus; 1891 (6,337).

Seton Hall University (c): 400 South Orange Ave., South Orange, NJ 07079; (973) 761-9000. Diocesan Clergy; 1856 (9,760).

Seton Hill College (w): Seton Hill Dr., Greensburg, PA 15601-1599; (724) 834-2200; www.setonhill.edu. Sisters of Charity of Seton Hill; 1883 (1,521).

Siena College (c): 515 Loudon Rd., Loudonville, NY 12211; (518) 783-2300; www.siena.edu. Franciscan Friars; 1937 (3,379).

Siena Heights University (c): 1247 E. Siena Heights Dr., Adrian, MI 49221; (517) 263-0731; www.sien-ahts.edu. Adrian Dominican Sisters; 1919 (2,124).

Silver Lake College of the Holy Family (c): 2406 S. Alverno Rd., Manitowoc, WI 54220-9319; (920) 684-6691. Franciscan Sisters of Christian Charity; 1935 (2,969).

Spalding University (c): 851 S. 4th Ave., Louisville, KY 40203; (502) 585-9911; www.spalding.edu. Sisters of Charity of Nazareth; 1814; independent (1,670).

Spring Hill College (c): 4000 Dauphin St., Mobile, AL 36608; (334) 380-4000; www.shc.edu. Jesuit Fathers; 1830 (1,050).

Stonehill College (c): North Easton, MA 02357; (508) 565-1000; www.stonehill.edu. Holy Cross Fathers; 1948; independent (2,550).

Thomas Aquinas College (c): 10000 N. Ojai Rd., Santa Paula, CA 93060; (805) 525-4417; www.thomasaquinas.edu. Founded 1971 (331).

Thomas More College (c): 333 Thomas More Pkwy., Crestview Hills, Covington, KY 41017; (859) 341-5800; www.thomasmore.edu. Diocese of Covington; 1921 (1,555).

Trinity College of Vermont (w): 208 Colchester Ave., Burlington, VT 05401; (802) 658-0337; www.trinityvt.edu. Sisters of Mercy; 1925 (200). May be closed.

Trinity College (w): 125 Michigan Ave. NE, Washington, DC 20017; (202) 939-5000. Sisters of

Notre Dame de Namur; 1897 (1,600). Coed graduate school.

Ursuline College (w): 2550 Lander Rd., Pepper Pike, OH 44124; (440) 449-4200; www.ursuline.edu. Ursuline Nuns; 1871 (1,319).

Villanova University (c): Villanova, PA 19085; (610) 519-7499; www.villanova.edu. Order of St. Augustine; 1842 (10,396).

Viterbo College (c): 815 S. 9th, La Crosse, WI 54601; (608) 796-3000; www.viterbo.org. Franciscan Sisters of Perpetual Adoration; 1890 (2,200).

Walsh University (c): 2020 Easton St. N.W., North Canton, Ohio 44720-3396; (330) 490-7090; www.walsh.edu. Brothers of Christian Instruction; 1958 (1,648).

Washington Theological Union (c): 6896 Laurel Street N.W., Washington, DC 20012-2016; (202) 726-8800; www.wtu.edu. Coalition of Religious Seminaries; 1968 (263).

Wheeling Jesuit University (c): 316 Washington Ave., Wheeling, WV 26003-6295; (304) 243-2000; www.wju.edu. Jesuit Fathers; 1954 (1,703).

Xavier University (c): 3800 Victory Pkwy., Cincinnati, OH 45207; (513) 745-3000; www.xu.edu. Jesuit Fathers; 1831 (2,631).

Xavier University of Louisiana (c): 1 Drexel Dr., New Orleans, LA 70125; (504) 486-7411; www.xula.edu. Sisters of Blessed Sacrament; 1925 (3,787).

Catholic Two-Year Colleges

Ancilla Domini College (c): P.O. Box 1, Donaldson, IN 46513; (219) 936-8898; www.ancilla.edu. Poor Handmaids of Jesus Christ Sisters; 1937 (546).

Assumption College for Sisters: Mendham, NJ 07945; (973) 543-6528. Sisters of Christian Charity; 1953 (24).

Chatfield College (c): St. Martin, OH 45118; (937) 875-3344; www.chatfield.edu. Ursulines; 1971 (273).

The College of St. Catherine-Minneapolis (c): 601 25th Ave. S., Minneapolis, MN 55454; (651) 690-7702. Sisters of St. Joseph of Carondelet (918).

Donnelly College (c): 608 N. 18th St., Kansas City, KS 66102; (913) 621-6070; www.donnelly.cc.ks.us. Archdiocesan College; 1949 (645).

Don Bosco Technical Institute (m): 1151 San Gabriel Blvd., Rosemead, CA 91770; (626) 307-6500; www.boscotech.tec.ca.us. Salesians; 1969 (994).

Holy Cross College (c): 54515 State Rd., 933 N., Notre Dame, IN 46556-0308; (219) 239-8400; www.hcc-nd.edu. Brothers of Holy Cross; 1966 (503).

Manor College (c): 700 Fox Chase Road, Jenkintown, PA 19046; (215) 885-2360; www.manor.edu. Sisters of St. Basil the Great; 1947.

Maria College (c): 700 New Scotland Ave., Albany, NY 12208. Sisters of Mercy; 1963 (1,048).

Marymount College Palos Verdes (c): 30800 Palos Verdes Dr., E., Rancho Palos Verdes, CA 90275-6299; (310) 377-5501; www.marymountpv.edu. Religious of the Sacred Heart of Mary; independent (840).

St. Catharine College (c): 2735 Bardstown Rd., St. Catharine, KY 40061; (859) 336-5082. Dominican Sisters; 1931 (742).

Springfield College in Illinois (c): 1500 N. Fifth St., Springfield, IL 62702-2694; (217) 525-1420; www.sci.edu. Ursuline Sisters; 1929 (300).

Trocaire College (c): 360 Choate Ave., Buffalo, NY 14220; (716) 827-2423; www.trocaire.edu. Sisters of Mercy; 1958; independent (780).

Villa Maria College of Buffalo (c): 240 Pine Ridge Rd., Buffalo, NY 14225; (716) 896-0700; www.villa.edu. Felician Sisters 1960; independent (475).

DIOCESAN AND INTERDIOCESAN SEMINARIES

(Sources: Catholic Almanac *survey;* The Official Catholic Directory; *Catholic News Service.)*

Information, according to states, includes names of archdioceses and dioceses, and names and addresses of seminaries. Types of seminaries, when not clear from titles, are indicated in most cases. Interdiocesan seminaries are generally conducted by religious orders for candidates for the priesthood from several dioceses. The list does not include houses of study reserved for members of religious communities. Archdioceses are indicated by an asterisk.

California: Los Angeles* — St. John's Seminary (major), 5118 Seminary Rd., Camarillo 93012-2599; (805) 482-2755; www.stjohnsem.edu.

San Diego — St. Francis Seminary (college and pre-theology formation program), 1667 Santa Paula Dr., 92111; (619) 291-7446.

San Francisco* — St. Patrick's Seminary (major), 320 Middlefield Rd., Menlo Park 94025; (650) 325-5621; www.stpatricksseminary.org..

Colorado: Denver* — St. John Vianney Theological Seminary (college and pre-theology formation program), 1300 S. Steele St., 80210; (303) 282-3427.

Connecticut: Hartford* — St. Thomas Seminary (college formation program), 467 Bloomfield Ave.,

Bloomfield 06002-2999; (860) 242-5573.

Norwich — Holy Apostles College and Seminary (adult vocations; minor and major), 33 Prospect Hill Rd., Cromwell 06416; (860) 632-3000; www.holyapostles.edu.

Stamford — Byzantine Rite: Ukrainian Catholic Seminary: St. Basil College Seminary (minor), 195 Glenbrook Rd., Stamford 06902-3099; (203) 324-4578.

District of Columbia: Washington, DC* — Theological College (national, major), The Catholic University of America, 401 Michigan Ave., N.E., 20017; (202) 756-4900; www.theologicalcollege.org.

St. Josaphat's Seminary, 201 Taylor St. N.E., 20017; (202) 529-1177. Major house of formation serving the four Ukrainian Byzantine-rite dioceses in the U.S.

Florida: Miami* — St. John Vianney College Seminary, 2900 S.W. 87th Ave., 33165; (305) 223-4561.

Palm Beach — St. Vincent de Paul Regional Seminary (major), 10701 S. Military Trail, Boynton Beach 33436; (561) 732-4424; www.svdp.edu.

Illinois: Chicago* — Archbishop Quigley Preparatory Seminary (high school), 103 East Chestnut St., Chicago 60611; (312) 787-9343; www.quigley.org. St. Joseph Seminary (college), 6551

N. Sheridan Rd., Chicago 60626; (773) 973-9700; www.stjoseph.luc.edu. University of St. Mary of the Lake Mundelein Seminary (School of Theology), 1000 E. Maple Ave., Mundelein 60060; (847) 566-6401; www.vocations.org.

Indiana: Indianapolis* — Saint Meinrad Seminary, College and School of Theology (interdiocesan), St. Meinrad 47577; (812) 357-6611; www.saintmeinrad.edu.

Iowa: Davenport — St. Ambrose University Seminary (interdiocesn), 518 W. Locust St., 52803; (319) 333-6151; www.davenportdiocese.org.

Dubuque* — Seminary of St. Pius X (interdiocesan), Loras College, 52004-0178; (319) 588-7782.

Louisiana: New Orleans* — Notre Dame Seminary Graduate School of Theology, 2901 S. Carrollton Ave., 70118; (504) 866-7426. St. Joseph Seminary College (interdiocesan), St. Benedict 70457-9999; (504) 892-1800; www.stjosephabbey.org.

Maryland: Baltimore* — Mount St. Mary's Seminary and University, 5400 Roland Ave., 21210; (410) 864-4000; www.stmarys.edu. Mount St. Mary's Seminary, Emmitsburg 21727-7797; (301) 447-5295; www.msmary.edu.

Massachusetts: Boston* — St. John's Seminary, School of Theology, 127 Lake St., Brighton 02135; (617) 254-2610. St. John's Seminary, College of Liberal Arts, 127 Lake St., Brighton 02135; (617) 746-5450. Pope John XXIII National Seminary (for ages 30-60), 558 South Ave., Weston 02943; (781) 899-5500; www.blessedjohnXXIII.org.

Newton — Melkite Greek Catholic: St. Gregory the Theologian Seminary, 3 VFW Parkway, Roslindale, MA 02131; (617) 323-9922. Seminary of St. Basil the Great, 30 East St., 01844; (978) 683-2471.

Michigan: Detroit* — Sacred Heart Major Seminary (college/theologate and institute for ministry), 2701 Chicago Blvd., Detroit 48206; (313) 883-8500. Sts. Cyril and Methodius Seminary, St. Mary's College (theologate and college) independent, primarily serving Polish-American community, 3535 Indian Trail, Orchard Lake 48324; (248) 683-0311.

Grand Rapids — Christopher House, 723 Rosewood Ave., S.E., East Grand Rapids 49506; (616) 243-6538.

Minnesota: St. John's School of Theology and Seminary, St. John's University, P.O. Box 7288, Collegeville 56321-7288; (320) 363-2100; www.csbsju.edu/sot.

St. Paul and Minneapolis* — St. Paul Seminary School of Divinity, University of St. Thomas, St. Paul 55101; (612) 962-5050; www.stthomas.edu. St. John Vianney Seminary (college residence), 2115 Summit Ave., St. Paul 55105; (651) 962-6825; www.stthomas.edu/sjv.

Winona — Immaculate Heart of Mary Seminary, St. Mary's University, No. 43, 700 Terrace Heights, 55987; (507) 457-7373; www.ihmseminary.org.

Missouri: St. Louis* — Kenrick — Glennon Seminary (St. Louis Roman Catholic Theological Seminary). Kenrick School of Theology and Cardinal Glennon College, 5200 Glennon Dr., 63119; (314) 792-6100.

Nebraska: Seward — St. Gregory the Great Seminary (pre-theology), 1301 280th Rd., 68434; (402) 643-4052, www.stgregoryseminary.org. Our Lady of Guadalupe Seminary, P.O. Box 147, Denton, NE 68339; (402) 797-7700; www.fssp.com.

New Jersey: Newark* — Immaculate Conception Seminary — college seminary; major seminary; graduate school — Seton Hall University, 400 South Orange Ave., South Orange 07079; (973) 761-9575; www.shu.edu. Redemptoris Mater, Archdiocesan Missionary Seminary, 672 Passaic Ave., 07032; (201) 997-3220.

New York: Brooklyn — Cathedral Seminary Residence of the Immaculate Conception (college and pre-theology), 7200 Douglaston Parkway, Douglaston 11362; (718) 229-8001. Cathedral Preparatory Seminary, 56-25 92nd St., Elmhurst 11373; (718) 592-6800. St. Alphonsus Formation Residence, 22-04 Parsons Blvd., 11357-3440; (718) 321-1096.

Buffalo — Christ the King Seminary (interdiocesan theologate), P.O. Box 607, 711 Knox Rd., East Aurora 14052; (716) 652-8900. Pope John Paul II Residence, 217 Winston Rd., 14216; (716) 836-5526.

New York* — St. Joseph's Seminary (major), 201 Seminary Ave., Dunwoodie, Yonkers 10704; (914) 968-6200. St. John Neumann Residence (college and pre-theology), 201 Seminary Ave., Yonkers N.Y., 10704-1896; (914) 964-3025. Cathedral Preparatory Seminary, 946 Boston Post Rd., Rye 10580; (914) 968-6200; www.cathedralprep.com.

Rockville Centre — Seminary of the Immaculate Conception (major), 440 West Neck Rd., Huntington, 11743; (631) 423-2346.

St. Maron Eparchy, Brooklyn — Our Lady of Lebanon Maronite Seminary, 7164 Alaska Ave. N.W., Washington, DC 20012; (202) 723-8831; www.maroniteseminary.org.

North Dakota: Fargo — Cardinal Muench Seminary (interdiocesan high school, college and pre-theology), 100 35th Ave. N.E., Fargo 58102; (701) 232-8969; www.cardinalmuench.org.

Ohio: Cincinnati* — Mt. St. Mary's Seminary of the West (division of the Athenaeum of Ohio), 6616 Beechmont Ave., 45230; (513) 231-2223; www.mtsm..

Cleveland — St. Mary Seminary and Graduate School of Theology, 28700 Euclid Ave. Wickliffe 44092; (440) 943-7600. Borromeo Seminary, 28700 Euclid Ave., 44092-2585; (440) 943-7600; www.a-full-life.com.

Columbus — Pontifical College Josephinum (national), theologate and college, 7625 North High St., 43235-1498; (614) 885-5585; www.pcj.edu.

Oregon: Portland* — Mount Angel Seminary (interdiocesan, college, pre-theology program, graduate school of theology), 1 Abbey Dr., St. Benedict 97373; (503) 845-3951. Felix Rougier House of Studies, 585 E. College St., 97362. Jesuit Novitiate of St. Francis Xavier, 3301 S.E. 45th Ave., 97206.

Pennsylvania: Erie — St. Mark Seminary, P.O. Box 10397, Erie 16514; (814) 824-1200.

Greensburg — St. Vincent Seminary (interdiocesan; pre-theology program; theologate; graduate programs in theology; religious education), 300 Fraser Purchase Rd., Latrobe 15650-2690; (724) 539-9761; www.stvincent.edu.

Philadelphia* — Theological Seminary of St. Charles Borromeo (College, pre-theology program, spirituality year program, theologate), 100 East Wynnewood Rd., Wynnewood 19096; (610) 667-3394; www.scs.edu.

Pittsburgh* (Byzantine-Ruthenian) — Byzantine Catholic Seminary of Sts. Cyril and Methodius (college, pre-theology program, theologate), 3605 Perrysville Ave., 15214; (412) 321-8383; www.byzcath.org/seminary.

Pittsburgh — St. Paul Seminary (interdiocesan, college and pre-theology), 2900 Noblestown Rd., 15205; (412) 921-5800; www.diopitt.org.

Scranton — St. Pius X Seminary (college and pre-theology formation; interdiocesan), 1000 Seminary Rd., Dalton 18414; (570) 563-1131. Affiliated with the University of Scranton.

Rhode Island: Providence — Seminary of Our Lady of Providence (House of Formation; college students and pre-theology), 485 Mount Pleasant Ave., 02908; (401) 331-1316; www.catholicpriest.com.

Texas: Dallas — Holy Trinity Seminary (college and pre-theology; English proficiency and academic foundation programs), P.O. Box 140309, Irving 75014; (972) 438-2212.

El Paso — St. Charles Seminary College, P.O. Box 17548, 79917; (915) 591-9821.

Galveston-Houston — St. Mary's Seminary (theologate), 9845 Memorial Dr., Houston 77024; (713) 686-4345.

San Antonio* — Assumption Seminary (theologate and pre-theology, Hispanic ministry emphasis), 2600 W. Woodlawn Ave., 78228; (210) 734-2324.

Washington: Spokane — Bishop White Seminary, College Formation Program, E. 429 Sharp Ave., 99202; (509) 326-3255; www.bishopwhiteseminary.org.

Wisconsin: Milwaukee* — St. Francis Seminary, 3257 S. Lake Dr., St. Francis 53235; (414) 747-6400; www.sfs.edu. College Program, 2497 N. Murray Ave., Milwaukee, 53211; (414) 964-6982. Sacred Heart School of Theology (interdiocesan seminary for sec-ond-career vocations), P.O. Box 429, Hales Corners, 53130-0429; (414) 425-8300.

North American College

Founded by the U.S. Bishops in 1859, the North American College serves as a residence and house of formation for U.S. seminarians and graduate students in Rome. The first ordination of an alumnus took place June 14, 1862. Pontifical status was granted the college by Pope Leo XIII Oct. 25, 1884. Students pursue theological and related studies principally at the Pontifical Gregorian University and at the Pontifical University of St. Thomas Aquinas (the Angelicum). The current rector is Msgr. James F. Checcio, J.C.D., M.B.A. Address: 00120 Città del Vaticano; 011-39-06-684-931; www.pnac.org.

American College of Louvain

Founded by U.S. Bishops in 1857, the American College of Louvain, Belgium, is a seminary for U.S. students. It also serves as a community for English-speaking graduate-student priests and religious priests pursuing studies at the Catholic University of Louvain (*Université Catholique de Louvain*, founded 1425). The college is administered by an American rector and faculty, and operates under the auspices of a committee of the national Conference of Catholic Bishops. The rector is Rev. Msgr. Ross A. Shecterle, STL, PhD. Address: The American College, Catholic University of Louvain, Naamsestraat 100, B-3000, Leuven, Belgium; 32-16-32-00-11; www.acl.be.

PONTIFICAL UNIVERSITIES

(*Principal source:* Annuario Pontificio.)

These universities, listed according to country of location, have been canonically erected and authorized by the Congregation for Catholic Education to award degrees in stated fields of study. New laws and norms governing ecclesiastical universities and faculties were promulgated in the apostolic constitution *Sapientia Christiana*, issued Apr. 15, 1979. Phone numbers are listed where possible.

Argentina: Pontifical Catholic University of S. Maria of Buenos Aires (June 16, 1960): Av. Alicia Moreau de Justo 1400, 1107 Buenos Aires.

Belgium: Catholic University of Louvain (founded Dec. 9, 1425; canonically erected, 1834), with autonomous institutions for French- (Louvain) and Flemish-(Leuven) speaking: Place de l'Universite I, B-1348 Louvain-La-Neuve (French); Naamsestraat 22/b, B-3000 Leuven (Flemish).

Brazil: Pontifical Catholic University of Rio de Janeiro (Jan. 20, 1947): Rua Marquês de São Vicente 225, 22451-000 Rio de Janeiro, RJ.

Pontifical Catholic University of Minas Gerais (June 5, 1983): Av. Dom José Gaspar 500, C.P. 2686, 30161-000 Belo Horizonte, MG.; (031) 319-1127.

Pontifical Catholic University of Parana (Aug. 6, 1985): Rua Imaculada Conceição, 1155, Prado Velho, C.P. 670, 80001-000 Curitiba, PR; (041) 223-0922.

Pontifical Catholic University of Rio Grande do Sul (Nov. 1, 1950): Av. Ipiranga 6681, C.P.1429,90001-000 Porto Alegre, RS.

Pontifical Catholic University of São Paulo (Jan. 25, 1947): Rua Monte Alegre 984, 05014-901 São Paulo SP.

Pontifical University of Campinas (Sept. 8, 1956): Rua Marechal Deodoro 1099, 13020-000 Campinas, SP.; (0192) 27-001.

Canada: Laval University (Mar. 15, 1876): Case Postale 460, QC G1K 7P4.

St. Paul University (formerly University of Ottawa) (Feb. 5, 1889): 223 Rue Main, Ottawa, ON K1S 1C4;

University of Sherbrooke (Nov. 21, 1957): Chemin Ste.-Catherine, 2500, boulevard de l'Université, Sherbrooke, QC J1K 12R1.

Chile: Pontifical Catholic University of Chile (June 21, 1888): Avenida Bernardo O'Higgins, 340, Casilla 114D, Santiago.

Catholic University of Valparaíso (Nov. 1, 1961): Avenida Brasil 2950, Casilla 4059, Valparaíso.

Colombia: Bolivarian Pontifical Catholic University (Aug. 16, 1945): Circular 1a, N.70-01, Apartado 56006, Medellín.

Pontifical Xaverian University (July 31, 1937): Carrera 7, N. 40-62, Apartado 56710, Santafé de Bogota D.C.; Apartado 26239, Calle 18, N. 118-250, Cali (Cali campus).

Cuba: Catholic University of St. Thomas of Villanueva (May 4, 1957): Avenida Quenta 16,660, Marianao.

Dominican Republic: Pontifical Catholic University "Mother and Teacher" (Sept. 9, 1987): Apartado 822, Santiago de Los Caballeros.

Ecuador: Pontifical Catholic University of Ecuador (July 16, 1954): Doce de Octubre, N. 1076, Apartado 17-01-2184, Quito.

France: Catholic University of Lille (Nov. 18, 1875):

Boulevard Vauban 60, 59016 Lille.

Catholic Faculties of Lyon (Nov. 22, 1875): 25, Rue du Plat, 69288 Lyon 02.

Catholic Institute of Paris (Aug. 11, 1875): 21, Rue d'Assas, 75270 Paris 06.

Catholic Institute of Toulouse (Nov. 15, 1877): Rue de la Fonderie 31, 31068 Toulouse.

Catholic University of the West (Sept. 16, 1875): 3, Place André Leroy, B.P. 808, 49005 Angers; 2-41-81-66-00.

Germany: Catholic University Eichstätt (Apr. 1, 1980): Ostenstrasse 26, D-85072, Eichstätt, Federal Republic of Germany; (08421) 201.

Guatemala: Rafael Landívar University (Oct. 18, 1961): Vista Hermosa III, Zona 16, Guatemala; (02) 69-21-51.

Hungary: Catholic University Pázmány Péter (March 25, 1999): Papnövelde Utea 7, H-1053 Budapest, Hungary; (01) 11-73-701.

Ireland: St. Patrick's College (Mar. 29, 1896): Maynooth, Co. Kildare.

Italy: Catholic University of the Sacred Heart (Dec. 25, 1920): Largo Gemelli 1, 20123 Milan.

Libera University Mary of the Assumption (Oct. 26, 1939): Via della Transpontina 21, 00193 Rome, Italy.

Japan: Jochi Daigaku (Sophia University) (Mar. 29, 1913): Chiyoda-Ku, Kioi-cho 7, Tokyo 102.

Lebanon: St. Joseph University of Beirut (Mar. 25, 1881): Rue de l'Université St.-Joseph, Boite Postale 293, Beyrouth (Beirut), Liban; (01) 42-64-56.

Netherlands: Catholic University of Nijmegen (June 29, 1923): P.B. 9102, Comeniuslaam 4, 6500 HC, Nijmegen.

Panama: University of S. Maria La Antigua (May 27, 1965): Apartado 6-1696, Panama 6.

Paraguay: Catholic University of Our Lady of the Assumption (Feb. 2, 1965): Independencia Nacional y Comuneros, Casilla 1718, Asunción; (021) 44-10-44.

Peru: Pontifical Catholic University of Peru (Sept. 30, 1942): Av. Universitaria, s/n. San Miguel, Apartado 1761, Lima 100.

Philippines: Pontifical University of Santo Tomás (Nov. 20, 1645): España Street, 1008 Manila.

Poland: Catholic University of Lublin (July 25, 1920): Aleje Racùawickie 14, Skr. Poczt. 129, 20-950, Lublin.

Catholic Theological Academy (June 29, 1989): Ul. Dewajtis 5, 01-815, Warsaw.

Pontifical Academy of Theology of Krakow (Dec. 8, 1981): Ul. Kanonicza, 25, 31-002 Kraków; (014) 22-33-31.

Portugal: Portuguese Catholic University (Nov. 1, 1967): Palma de Cima, 1 600 Lisbon.

Puerto Rico: Pontifical Catholic University of Puerto Rico (Aug. 15, 1972): 2250 Ave. Las Américas Suite 523, Ponce, Puerto Rico 00731-6382.

Spain: Catholic University of Navarra (Aug. 6, 1960): Campus Universitario, E-31080 Pamplona.

Pontifical University "Comillas" (Mar. 29, 1904): Campus de Cantoblanco, 28049 Madrid.

Pontifical University of Salamanca (Sept. 25, 1940): Compañia 5, 37002 Salamanca.

University of Deusto (Aug. 10, 1963): Avenida de las Universidades, 28, 48007 Bilbao o Apartado 1, 48080 Bilbao; 94-445-31-00.

Taiwan (China): Fu Jen Catholic University (Nov. 15, 1923, at Peking; reconstituted at Taipeh, Sept. 8, 1961): Hsinchuang, Taipeh Hsien 24205.

United States: The Catholic University of America (Mar. 7, 1889): 620 Michigan Ave. N.E., Washington, DC 20064.

Georgetown University (Mar. 30, 1833): 37th and O Sts. N.W., Washington, DC 20057.

Niagara University (June 21, 1956): Lewiston Rd., Niagara Falls, NY 14109.

Uruguay: Catholic University of Uruguay "Dámaso Antonio Larrañaga" (Jan. 25, 1985): Avda. 8 de Octubre 2738, 11.600 Montevideo.

Venezuela: Catholic University "Andrés Bello" (Sept. 29, 1963): Esquina Jesuitas, Apartado 29068, Caracas 1021; (02) 442-21-20.

WORLD AND U.S. SEMINARY STATISTICS

The *2006 Statistical Yearbook of the Church* (the most recent edition) reports the following comparative statistics for the years 1990 to 2006 of candidates in Philosophy and Theology (major seminarians). World totals are given first; U.S. statistics are given in parentheses.

Year	Total Major Seminarians	Diocesan	Religious
1990	96,155 (5,552)	64,629 (3,676)	31,526 (1,876)
1991	99,668 (5,487)	66,305 (3,777)	33,363 (1,710)
1992	102,000 (5,380)	67,960 (3,645)	34,040 (1,735)
1993	103,709 (5,123)	68,829 (3,505)	34,880 (1,618)
1994	105,075 (5,100)	69,613 (3,526)	35,462 (1,574)
1995	106,346 (4,831)	69,777 (3,234)	36,569 (1,597)
1996	105,870 (4,785)	70,034 (3,268)	35,836 (1,517)
1997	108,517 (4,729)	70,534 (3,311)	37,983 (1,418)
1998	109,171 (4,830)	70,564 (3,436)	38,607 (1,394)
1999	110,021 (5,024)	70,989 (3,428)	39,032 (1,596)
2000	110,583 (5,109)	71,756 (3,479)	38,827 (1,630)
2001	112,244 (5,080)	72,241 (3,404)	40,003 (1,676)
2002	113,199 (5,169)	72,977 (3,578)	40,222 (1,591)
2003	112,373 (4,676)	72,266 (3,181)	40,107 (1,495)
2004	113,044 (5,642)	71,841 (3,929)	41,203 (1,713)
2005	114,439 (5,180)	72,188 (3,383)	42,251 (1,797)
2006	115,480 (4,913)	71,878 (3,214)	43,602 (1,699)

ECCLESIASTICAL FACULTIES

(*Principal source*: Annuario Pontificio.)

These faculties in Catholic seminaries and universities, listed according to country of location, have been canonically erected and authorized by the Congregation for Catholic Education to award degrees in stated fields of study.

Argentina: Faculties of Philosophy and Theology, San Miguel (Sept. 8, 1932).

Australia: Catholic Institute of Sydney, Sydney (Feb. 2, 1954).

Austria: Theological Faculty, Linz (Dec. 25, 1978). International Theological Institute for Family Studies (Oct. 1, 1996).

Brazil: Philosophical and Theological Faculties of the Company of Jesus, Belo Horizonte (July 15, 1941 and Mar. 12, 1949).

Ecclesiastical Faculty of Philosophy "John Paul II," Rio de Janeiro (Aug. 6, 1981).

Cameroon: Catholic Institute of Yaoundé (Nov. 15, 1991).

Canada: College of Immaculate Conception — Montréal Section of Jesuit Faculties in Canada (Sept. 8, 1932). Suspended.

Pontifical Institute of Medieval Studies, Toronto (Oct. 18, 1939).

Dominican Faculty of Theology of Canada, Ottawa (1965; Nov. 15, 1975).

Regis College, Toronto Section of the Jesuit Faculty of Theology in Canada, Toronto (Feb. 17, 1956; Dec. 25, 1977).

Congo (formerly Zaire): Catholic Faculties of Kinshasa, Kinshasa (theology, Apr. 25, 1957; philosophy, Nov. 25, 1987).

Côte d'Ivoire (Ivory Coast): Catholic Institute of West Africa, Abidjan (Aug. 12, 1975).

Croatia: Philosophical Faculty, Zagreb (July 31, 1989).

France: Centre Sèvres, Faculties of Theology and Philosophy of the Jesuits, Paris (Sept. 8, 1932).

Germany: Theological Faculty of the Major Episcopal Seminary, Trier (Sept. 8, 1955).

Theological Faculty, Paderborn (June 11, 1966).

Theological-Philosophical Faculty, Frankfurt (1932; June 7, 1971).

Philosophical Faculty, Munich (1932; Oct. 25, 1971).

Theological Faculty, Fulda (Dec. 22, 1978).

Philosophical-Theological School of Salesians, Benediktbeuern (May 24, 1992).

Philosophical-Theological School, Vallendar (Oct. 7, 1993).

Great Britain: Heythrop College, University of London, London (Nov. 1, 1964). Theology, philosophy.

Hungary: Faculty of Theology (1635), Institute on Canon Law (Nov. 30, 1996), Budapest.

India: *Jnana Deepa Vidyapeeth* (Pontifical Atheneaum), Institute of Philosophy and Religion, Poona (July 27, 1926).

Vidyajyoti, Institute of Religious Studies, Faculty of Theology, Delhi (1932; Dec. 9, 1974).

Satya Nilayam, Institute of Philosophy and Culture. Faculty of Philosophy, Madras (Sept. 8, 1932; Dec. 15, 1976).

Pontifical Institute of Theology and Philosophy at the Pontifical Interritual Seminary of St. Joseph, Alwaye, Kerala (Feb. 24, 1972).

Dharmaram Vidya Kshetram, Pontifical Athenaeum of Theology and Philosophy, Bangalore (theology, Jan. 6, 1976; philosophy, Dec. 8, 1983).

Pontifical Oriental Institute of Religious Studies, Kottayam (July 3, 1982).

Faculty of Theology, Ranchi (Aug. 15, 1982).

St. Peter's Pontifical Institute of Theology, Bangalore (Jan. 6, 1985).

Indonesia: Wedabhakti Pontifical Faculty of Theology, Yogyakarta (Nov. 1, 1984).

Ireland: The Milltown Institute of Theology and Philosophy, Dublin (1932).

Israel: French Biblical and Archeological School, Jerusalem (founded 1890; approved Sept. 17, 1892; canonically approved to confer Doctorate in Biblical Science, June 29, 1983).

Italy: Theological Faculty of Southern Italy, Naples. Two sections: St. Louis Posillipo (Mar. 16, 1918) and St. Thomas Aquinas Capodimonte (Oct. 31, 1941).

Pontifical Theological Faculty of Sardinia, Cagliari, (Aug. 5, 1927).

Interregional Theological Faculty, Milan (Aug. 8, 1935; restructured 1969).

Faculty of Philosophy "Aloisianum," Gallarate (1937; Mar. 20, 1974).

Pontifical Ambrosian Institute of Sacred Music, Milan (Mar. 12, 1940).

Theological Faculty of Sicily, Palermo (Dec. 8, 1980).

Theological Institute Pugliese, Molfetta (June 24, 1992).

Theological Institute Calabro, Catanzaro (Jan. 28, 1993).

Theological Faculty of Central Italy, Florence (Sep. 9, 1997).

Japan: Faculty of Theology, Nagoya (May 25, 1984).

Kenya: Catholic Higher Institute of Eastern Africa, Nairobi (May 2, 1984).

Lebanon: Faculty of Theology, University of the Holy Spirit, Kaslik (May 30, 1982).

Madagascar: Superior Institute of Theology and Philosophy, at the Regional Seminary of Antananarivo, Ambatoroka-Antananarivo (Apr. 21, 1960).

Malta: Faculty of Theology, Tal-Virtù (Nov. 22, 1769), with Institute of Philosophy and Human Studies (Sept. 8, 1984).

Mexico: Theological Faculty of Mexico (June 29, 1982) and Philosophy (Jan. 6, 1986), Institute of Canon Law (Sept. 4, 1995), Mexico City.

Nigeria: Catholic Institute of West Africa, Port Harcourt (May 9, 1994).

Peru: Pontifical and Civil Faculty of Theology, Lima (July 25, 1571).

Poland: Pontifical Theological Faculty, Warsaw (May 3, 1988) with two sections: St. John Baptist (1837, 1920, Nov. 8, 1962) at the Metropolitan Seminary Duchowne, and St. Andrew Bobola – Bobolanum (Sept. 8, 1932).

Philosophical Faculty, Krakow (1932; Sept. 20, 1984).

Theological Faculty, Poznan (1969; pontifical designation, June 2, 1974).

Spain: Theological Faculty, Granada (1940; July 31, 1973).

Theological Faculty of San Esteban, Salamanca (1947; Oct. 4, 1972).

Theological Faculty of the North, of the Metropolitan

Seminary of Burgos and the Diocesan Seminary of Vitoria (Feb. 6, 1967).

Theological Faculty of Catalunya, (Mar. 7, 1968), with the Institutes of Fundamental Theology (Dec. 28, 1984), Liturgy (Aug. 15, 1986) and Philosophy (July 26, 1988), Barcelona.

Theological Faculty "San Vicente Ferrer" (two sections), Valencia (Jan. 23, 1974).

Theological Faculty "San Damaso" (Sept. 19, 1996), Madrid.

Switzerland: Theological Faculty, Lucerne (Dec. 25, 1973).

Theological Faculty, Chur (Jan. 1, 1974).

Theological Faculty, Lugano (Nov. 20, 1993).

United States: St. Mary's Seminary and University, School of Theology, Baltimore (May 1, 1822).

St. Mary of the Lake Faculty of Theology, Mundelein, IL (Sept. 30, 1929).

Weston Jesuit School of Theology, Cambridge, MA (Oct. 18, 1932).

The Jesuit School of Theology, Berkeley, CA (Feb. 2, 1934, as "Alma College," Los Gatos, CA).

Faculty of Philosophy and Letters, St. Louis, MO (Feb. 2, 1934).

St. Michael's Institute, Jesuit School of Philosophy and Letters, Spokane, WA (Feb. 2, 1934).

Pontifical Faculty of Theology of the Immaculate Conception, Dominican House of Studies, Washington, DC (Nov. 15, 1941).

Also located in the **United States** are:

The Marian Library/International Marian Research Institute (IMRI), U.S. branch of Pontifical Theological Faculty "Marianum," University of Dayton, Dayton, OH 45469 (affil. 1976, inc. 1983).

John Paul II Institute for Studies on Marriage and the Family, U.S. section of Pontifical John Paul II Institute for Studies on Marriage and Family at the Pontifical Lateran University, 487 Michigan Ave. N.E., Washington, DC 20017 (Aug. 22, 1988).

Pontifical College Josephinum (Theologate and College) at Columbus, OH, is a national pontifical seminary. Established Sept. 1, 1888, it is directly under the auspices of the Vatican through the Apostolic Nuncio to the U.S., who serves as the seminary's chancellor.

Vietnam: Theological Faculty of the Pontifical National Seminary of St. Pius X, Dalat (July 31, 1965). Activities suppressed.

In addition to those listed above, there are other faculties of theology or philosophy in state universities and for members of certain religious orders only. These include:

Austria: Katholisch-Theologische Fakultät (1619), Universitätsstrasse, 1, A-5010 Salzburg, Österreich.

Katholisch-Theologische Fakultät (1365), Dr. Karl-Lueger-Ring, 1, A-1010 Wien, Österreich.

Theologische Fakultät (1586), Karl-Franzens-Universität, Universitätsplatz, 3, A-8010 Graz, Österreich.

Theologische Fakultät (1669), Leopold-Franzens-Universität, Karl-Rahner-Platz 1, A-6020 Innsbruck, Österreich.

Canada: Faculté de Theologie et Institut Supérieur de Science Religieuses (1878), University of Montreal, 3034, Bd. Edouard-Montpetit, C.P. 6128,

Montral, QC H3C 3J7, Canada.

Croatia: Facolta di Teologia Cattolica nell'Università Statale de Split (1999), Zrinsko-Frankopanska, 19, 21000 Split, Hrvatska.

Katolicki Bogoslovni Fakultet u Zagrebu (1669), Vlaska 38, 10000 Zagreb, Hrvatska.

Czech Republic: Cyrilometodejska teologicka fakulta (1570), Univerzitni 22, 771-11 Olomouc, Ceska Republika.

Katolicka teologicka fakulta University Karlovy (1347), Thakurova 3, 160 00 Praha 6/Dejvice, Ceska Republika.

France: Faculté de Theologie Catholique (1567), 9, Place de l'Université, 67084 Strasbourg, France.

Germany: Katholisch-Theologische Fakultät, Universität Augsburg (1970), Universitätsstrasse 10, D-86159 Augsburg.

Katholisch-Theologische Fakultät, Universität Bamberg (1972), An der Universität 2, D-96045 Bamberg.

Katholisch-Theologische Fakultät (1965), Universität Ruhr, Universitätsstrasse 150, Postfach 102148, D-44801 Bochum.

Katholisch-Theologische Fakultät Universität Bonn (1818), Am Hof 1, D-53113 Bonn.

Theologische Fakultät (1657), Albert-Ludwigs Universität, Erbprinzstrasse 13, D-79098 Freiburg im Breisgau.

Fachbereich Katholische Theologie (1946), Johannes Gutenberg-Universität, Saarstrasse 21, D-55122, Mainz.

Katholisch-Theologische Fakultät (1472), Ludwig-Maximilians-Universität, Geschw.-Scholl-Platz 1, D-80539, München.

Katholisch-Theologische Fakultät (1780), WestfälischeWilhelms-Universität, Johannisstrasse 8-10, D-48143, Münster.

Katholisch-Theologische Fakultät (1978), Michaeligasse 13, D-94032, Passau.

Fachbereich Katholische Theologie (1962), Universitätsstrasse 31, D-93053 Regensburg.

Katholisch-Theologische Fakultät (1477), Eberhard-Karls-Universität Tübingen, Libermeisterstr., 18, D-72076 Tübingen.

Katholisch-Theologische Fakultät (1402), Bayerische Julius-Maximilians-Universität, Sanderring 2, D-97070 Würzburg.

Lithuania: Kataliku Teologijos Fakultetas (1922), Vilniaus 29, LT-3000 Kaunas, Lietuva.

Poland: Wydzial Teologiczny, Wydzial Prawa Kanonicznego, Wydzial Filozofii Chrzescijanskiej (1999), ul. Dewajtis, 5, 01-815 Warszawa.

Wydzial Teologiczny Uniwersytetu Slaskiego w Katowicach (2000), ul. Wita Stwosza 17 A, 40-042 Katowice.

Wydzial Teologii Uniwersytetu Warminsko-Mazurskiego w Olsztynie (1999), ul. Stanislawa Kard. Hozjusza, 15, 11-041 Olsztyn.

Wydzial Teologiczny (1994), ul. Drzymaly, 1/a, 45-342 Opole.

Wydzial Teologiczny Uniwersytetu Mikolaja Kopernika w. Toruniu (2001), pl. Bl. Ks. S. Frelichowskiego 1, 87-100, Torun.

Slovakia: Rimskokatolicka cyrilo-metodska bohoslovecka fakulta (1919), Archdiocese of Bratislava-Trnava, Kapitulska 26, 814-58 Bratislava.

Slovenia: Teoloska Fakulteta v. Ljublana (1920), p.p.

2007, 1001 Ljubljana.

Switzerland: Theologische Fakultät (1889), University of Fribourg, Misericorde, CH-1700 Fribourg.

PONTIFICAL UNIVERSITIES AND INSTITUTES IN ROME

(*Source*: Annuario Pontificio.)

Pontifical Gregorian University (*Gregorian*) (1552): Piazza della Pilotta, 4, 00187 Rome. Associated with the university are: **Pontifical Biblical Institute** (May 7, 1909): Via della Pilotta, 25, 00187 Rome; **Pontifical Institute of Oriental Studies** (Oct. 15, 1917): Piazza S. Maria Maggiore, 7, 00185 Rome.

Pontifical Lateran University (1773): Piazza S. Giovanni in Laterano, 4, 00184 Rome. Attached to the university is the **Pontifical Institute of Studies of** Marriage and the Family, erected by Pope John Paul II, Oct 7, 1982; a section of the Institute was established at the Dominican House of Studies, Washington, DC, by a decree dated Aug. 22, 1988; sections were opened in Mexico in 1992 and Valencia, Spain, in 1994.

Pontifical Urbaniana University (1627): Via Urbano VIII, 16, 00165 Rome.

Pontifical University of St. Thomas Aquinas (*Angelicum*) (1580), of the Order of Preachers: Largo Angelicum, 1, 00184 Rome.

Pontifical University *Salesianum* (May 3, 1940; university designation May 24, 1973), of the Salesians of Don Bosco: Piazza dell'Ateneo Salesiano, 1, 00139 Rome. Associated with the university is the **Pontifical Institute of Higher Latin Studies**, known as the Faculty of Christian and Classical Letters (June 4, 1971).

Pontifical University *della Santa Croce* (of the Holy Cross) (Jan. 9, 1985), of the Personal Prelature of Opus Dei: Piazza S. Apollinare, 49, 00186 Rome.

Pontifical University *Antonianum* (of St. Anthony) (May 17, 1933), of the Order of Friars Minor: Via Merulana, 124, 00185 Rome. Pontifical University status granted in 2005.

Pontifical Athenaeum of St. Anselm (1687) of the Benedictines: Piazza Cavalieri di Malta, 5, 00153 Rome.

Pontifical Athenaeum *Regina Apostolorum* (Queen of the Apostles), of the Legionaries of Christ: Via Aurelia Antica, 460, 00165 Rome.

Pontifical Institute of Sacred Music (1911; May 24, 1931): Via di Torre Rossa, 21, 00165 Rome.

Pontifical Institute of Christian Archeology (Dec. 11, 1925): Via Napoleone III, 1, 00185 Rome.

Pontifical Theological Faculty St. Bonaventure (Dec. 18, 1587), of the Order of Friars Minor Conventual: Via del Serafico, 1, 00142 Rome.

Pontifical Theological Faculty, Pontifical Institute of Spirituality *Teresianum* (1935), of the Discalced Carmelites: Piazza San Pancrazio, 5-A, 00152 Rome.

Pontifical Theological Faculty *Marianum* (1398), of the Servants of Mary: Viale Trente Aprile, 6, 00153 Rome. Attached to the university is **The Marian Library/International Marian Research Institute** (IMRI): U.S. branch of Pontifical Theological Faculty *Marianum*, University of Dayton, Dayton, OH, 45469 (affil. 1976, inc. 1983).

Pontifical Institute of Arabic and Islamic Studies (1926), of the Missionaries of Africa: Viale di Trastevere, 89, 00153 Rome.

Pontifical Faculty of Educational Science *Auxilium* (June 27, 1970), of the Daughters of Mary, Help of Christians: Via Cremolino, 141, 00166 Rome.

Catholic Communications

CATHOLIC PRESS

The 2008 Catholic Press Directory, published by the Catholic Press Association, reported a total of 599 periodicals in North America, with a circulation of 26,334,093. The figures included 206 newspapers, with a circulation of 6,586,276; 231 magazines, with a circulation of 14,451,333; 113 newsletters, with a circulation of 4,025,899; and 49 other-language periodicals (newspapers and magazines), with a circulation of 1,270,585.

Newspapers in the U.S.

There were 198 newspapers in the United States, with a circulation 6,462,926. Five of these had national circulation totaling 184,661; 170 were diocesan newspapers with a total circulation of 5,996,297; 10 were Eastern Catholic Church publications with a total circulation of 67,948. Fourteen other publications were classified by the CPA as Other Diocesan Newspaper and Other Newspapers, to classify them correctly based on their actual format; they had a total circulation of 224,020.

National papers included: *National Catholic Register*, founded 1900; *Our Sunday Visitor*, founded 1912; *National Catholic Reporter*, founded 1964; *The Wanderer*, founded 1867. In addition there were *The Adoremus Bulletin*, founded 1995; and the English-language weekly edition of *L'Osservatore Romano*, established in the U.S. in 1998.

The oldest U.S. Catholic newspaper is *The Pilot* of Boston, established in 1829 (under a different title).

Other diocesan newspapers: There were three other diocesan newspapers located outside continental North America (Samoa, U.S. Virgin Islands, West Indies), with a circulation of 62,575.

Magazines in the U.S.

The Catholic Press Directory reported 231 magazines in the U.S., with a circulation of 14,451,333. In addition, there were 111 newsletters, with a circulation of 4,013,399.

America and *Commonweal* are the only weekly and biweekly magazines, respectively, of general interest.

The monthly magazines with the largest circulation are *Columbia* (1,554,248), the official organ of the Knights of Columbus, *Catholic Digest* (285,000) and *St. Anthony's Messenger* (298,000).

Other-language publications: There were an additional 36 publications (newspapers and magazines) in the U.S. in languages other than English, with a circulation of 1,060,985.

Canadian Statistics

There were eight newspapers in Canada with a circulation of 123,350. These included three national newspapers (*The Catholic Register*, founded 1893; *Restoration*, founded 1947; and *Catholic New Times*, founded 1976) and seven diocesan. There were 13 magazines, with a circulation of 771,584; two newsletters, with a circulation of 12,500; and 13 publications in languages other than English, with a circulation of 209,600.

CATHOLIC NEWSPAPERS, MAGAZINES, AND NEWSLETTERS IN THE U.S.

(Sources: *Catholic Press Directory; The Catholic Journalist; Catholic Almanac* survey; Catholic News Service.) Abbreviation code: a, annual; bm, bimonthly; m, monthly; q, quarterly; w, weekly; bw, bi-weekly.

Newspapers

Our Sunday Visitor, w; 200 Noll Plaza, Huntington, IN 46750; (260) 356-8400; www.osv.com; national.

Acadiana Catholic, m; 1408 Carmel Ave., Lafayette, LA 70501; (337) 261-5511; Lafayette diocese.

A.D. Times, bw; P.O. Box F, Allentown, PA 18105-1538; (610) 871-5200; Allentown diocese.

Adoremus Bulletin, The, 10 times a year; P.O. Box 3286, St. Louis, MO 63130; (314) 863-8385; www.adoremus.org; national liturgical journal.

Agua Viva, m; 1280 Med Park Dr., Las Cruces, NM 88005-3239; (505) 523-7577; www.diocese-

oflascruces.org; Las Cruces diocese.

Alaskan Shepherd, bm; 1312 Peger Rd., Fairbanks, AK 99709; (904) 374-9532; www.cbna.info; Fairbanks diocese.

America (Ukrainian-English), 2 times a week; 817 N. Franklin St., Philadelphia, PA 19123; (215) 627-4519; Providence Association of Ukrainian Catholics in America.

Anchor, The, w; P.O. Box 7, Fall River, MA 02722; (508) 675-7151; Fall River diocese.

Arkansas Catholic, w; P.O. Box 7417, Little Rock, AR 72217; (501) 664-0125; www.arkansas-catholic.org. Little Rock diocese.

Arlington Catholic Herald, w; 200 N. Glebe Rd., Suite 607, Arlington, VA 22203; (703) 841-2590; www.catholicherald.com; Arlington diocese.

Bayou Catholic, The, w; P.O. Box 505, Schriever, LA 70395; (985) 850-3132; Houma-Thibodaux diocese.

Beacon, The, w; P.O. Box 1887, Clifton, NJ 07015-1887;

(973) 279-8845; www.patersondiocese.org; Paterson diocese.

Bishop's Bulletin, m; 523 N. Duluth Ave., Sioux Falls, SD 57104-2714; (605) 988-3791; www.sfcatholic.org; Sioux Falls diocese.

Bolletino, m; 675 Hegenberger Rd., Suite 110, Oakland, CA 94621; (510) 633-9058; www.icf.org; Italian Catholic Federation.

Byzantine Catholic World, bw; 66 Riverview Ave., Pittsburgh, PA 15214; (412) 231-4000; Pittsburgh Byzantine archdiocese.

Catholic Accent, 40 times a year; 725 E. Pittsburgh St., Greensburg, PA 15601; (724) 834-4010; www.dioceseofgreensburg.org; Greensburg diocese.

Catholic Advance, The, w; 424 N. Broadway, Wichita, KS 67202-2377; (316) 269-3965; www.catholic advance.org; Wichita diocese.

Catholic Advocate, The, w; 171 Clifton Ave., Newark, NJ 07104-9500; (973) 497-4200; www.rcan.org/advocate; Newark archdiocese.

Catholic Aid News, m; 3499 N. Lexington Ave., St. Paul, MN 55126; (651) 490-0170; www.catholicaid.com.

Catholic Anchor, w; 225 Cordova St., Anchorage, AK 99501; (907) 297-7708; Anchorage diocese.

Catholic Calendar, semi-monthly; 411 Iris St., Lake Charles, LA 70601; (337) 439-7426; www.lcdiocese.org; one page in local newspaper semi-monthly; Lake Charles diocese.

Catholic Chronicle, bw; P.O. Box 1866, Toledo, OH 43603-1866; (419) 244-6711; www.catholicchronicle.org; Toledo diocese.

Catholic Commentator, The, bw; P.O. Box 14746, Baton Rouge, LA 70898-4746; (225) 387-0983; www.diobr.com; Baton Rouge diocese.

Catholic Connector, The, m; 660 Burton, SE, Grand Rapids, MI 49507; (616) 243-0491; www.dioceseofgrandrapids.org; Grand Rapids diocese.

Catholic Courier, w; P.O. Box 24379, Rochester, NY 14624-0379; (585) 529-9530; www.catholiccourier.com; Rochester diocese.

Catholic East Texas, bw; 1015 ESE Loop 323, Tyler, TX 75701-9663; (903) 534-1077; Tyler diocese.

Catholic Explorer, w (bw July, Aug.); 402 S. Independence Blvd., Romeoville, IL 60446-2264; (815) 838-6475; www.dioceseofjoliet.org/explorer; Joliet diocese.

Catholic Exponent, bw; P.O. Box 6787, Youngstown, OH 44501-6787; (330) 744-5251; www.doy.org; Youngstown diocese.

Catholic Free Press, w; 51 Elm St., Worcester, MA 01609; (508) 757-6387; www.catholicfreepress.org; Worcester diocese.

Catholic Health World, semi-monthly; 4455 Woodson Rd., St. Louis, MO 63134-3797; (314) 427-2500; www.chausa.org; Catholic Health Association.

Catholic Herald, The Colorado, m; 228 N. Cascade Ave., Colorado Springs, CO 80903; (719) 636-2345; www.coloradocatholicherald.com; Colorado Springs diocese.

Catholic Herald, w; P.O. Box 070913, Milwaukee, WI 53207-0913; (414) 769-3500; www.chnonline.org; Milwaukee archdiocese; also publishes editions for Madison and Superior dioceses.

Catholic Herald: Madison Edition, w; P.O. Box 44985, Madison, WI 53744-4985; (608) 821-3070; www.madisoncatholicherald.org; Madison diocese.

Catholic Herald: Superior Edition, w; P.O. Box 969, Superior, WI 54880; (715) 392-8268; www.catholicherald.org; Superior diocese.

Catholic Herald, bw; 5890 Newman Ct., Sacramento, CA 95819; (916) 452-3344; www.diocese-sacramento.org; Sacramento diocese.

Catholic Islander, m; P.O. Box 301825, St. Thomas, USVI, 00803-1825; (340) 774-3166; www.catholicislander.com; Virgin Islands diocese.

Catholic Journalist, The, m; 3555 Veterans Highway, Unit O, Ronkonkoma, NY 11779; (631) 471-4730; www.catholicpress.org; Catholic Press Association.

Catholic Key, 44 times a year; P.O. Box 419037, Kansas City, MO 64141-6037; (816) 756-1850; www.catholickey.org; Kansas City-St. Joseph diocese.

Catholic Light, bw; 300 Wyoming Ave., Scranton, PA 18503; (570) 207-2229; www.dioceseofscranton.org; Scranton diocese.

Catholic Lighthouse, m; P.O. Box 4070, Victoria, TX 77903; (361) 573-0828; www.victoriadiocese.org; Victoria diocese.

Catholic Messenger, w; P.O. Box 460, Davenport, IA 52805; (563) 323-9959; home.catholicweb.com/cathmessdavdio; Davenport diocese.

Catholic Mirror, The, m; 601 Grand Ave., Des Moines, IA 50309; (515) 244-6234; www.dmdiocese.org; Des Moines diocese.

Catholic Miscellany, The, w; 119 Broad St., Charleston, SC 29401; (843) 724-8375; www.catholicdoc.org; Charleston diocese.

Catholic Missourian, The, w; P.O. Box 104900, Jefferson City, MO 65110-4900; (573) 635-9127; Jefferson City diocese.

Catholic Moment, The, w; P.O. Box 1603, Lafayette, IN 47902; (765) 742-2050; www.thecatholicmoment.org; Lafayette diocese.

Catholic New World, The, w; 640 N. La Salle St., Ste. 390, Chicago, IL 60610; (312) 655-7777; www.catholicnewworld.com; Chicago archdiocese.

Catholic New York, w; 1011 First Ave., New York, NY 10022; (212) 688-2399; www.cny.org; New York archdiocese.

Catholic News, w; P.O. Box 85, Independence Square, Port-of-Spain, Trinidad, West Indies; (868) 623-6093; www.catholicnews-tt.net.

Catholic News and Herald, The, w; P.O. Box 37267, Charlotte, NC 28237; (704) 370-3333; www.charlottediocese.org; Charlotte diocese.

Catholic Northwest Progress, The, w; 910 Marion St., Seattle, WA 98104; (206) 382-4850; www.seattlearch.org;/progress; Seattle archdiocese.

Catholic Observer, bw; Box 1730, Springfield, MA 01101-1730; (413) 737-4744; www.iobserve.org; Springfield diocese.

Catholic Peace Voice, q.; 532 W. Eighth St., Erie, PA 16502-1343; (814) 453-4955; www.paxchristiusa.org; published by Pax Christi.

Catholic Post, The, w; P.O. Box 1722, Peoria, IL 61656; (309) 673-3603; www.cdop.org/post; Peoria diocese.

Catholic Register, bw; P.O. Box 413, Hollidaysburg, PA 16648; (814) 695-7563; www.cathregaj.org; Altoona-Johnstown diocese.

Catholic Review, w; P.O. Box 777, Baltimore, MD 21203; (443) 524-3150; www.catholicreview.org; Baltimore archdiocese.

Catholic San Francisco, bw; One Peter Yorke Way, San Francisco, CA 94109; (415) 614-5630; www.catholic-sf.org; San Francisco archdiocese.

Catholic Sentinel, w; P.O. Box 18030, Portland, OR 97218-0030; (503) 281-1191; www.sentinel.org; Portland archdiocese, Baker diocese.

Catholic Spirit, The, w; 244 Dayton Ave., Ste. 2, St. Paul, MN 55102-1893; (651) 291-4444; www.thecatholicspirit.com; St. Paul and Minneapolis archdiocese.

Catholic Spirit, The, w; P.O. Box 191, Metuchen, NJ 08840-0969; (732) 562-1990; www.catholicspirit.com; Metuchen diocese.

Catholic Spirit, The, m; P.O. Box 13327, Austin, TX 78711; (512) 476-4888; www.austindiocese.org; Austin diocese.

Catholic Spirit, The, m; P.O. Box 951, Wheeling, WV 26003-0119; (304) 233-0880; www.dwc.org; Wheeling–Charleston diocese.

Catholic Standard, w; P.O. Box 4464, Washington, DC, 20017; (202) 281-2410; www.cathstan.org; Washington archdiocese.

Catholic Standard and Times, w; 222 N. 17th St., Philadelphia, PA 19103; (215) 587-3660; www.cstphl.com; Philadelphia archdiocese.

Catholic Star Herald, w; 15 North 7th St., Camden, NJ 08102; (856) 756-7900; Camden diocese.

Catholic Sun, The, semi-monthly; P.O. Box 13549, Phoenix, AZ 85002; (602) 354-2139; www.catholicsun.org; Phoenix diocese.

Catholic Sun, The, w; 421 S. Warren St., Syracuse, NY 13202; (315) 422-8153; www.syrdio.org; Syracuse diocese.

Catholic Telegraph, w; 100 E. 8th St., Cincinnati, OH 45202; (513) 421-3131; www.catholiccincinnati.org; Cincinnati archdiocese.

Catholic Times, w; 197 E. Gay St., Columbus, OH 43215-3229; (614) 224-5195; www.ctonline.org; Columbus diocese.

Catholic Times, The, w; P.O. Box 1405, Saginaw, MI 48605; (810) 659-4670; www.catholictimesmi.org; Lansing diocese.

Catholic Times, The, w; P.O. Box 4004, La Crosse, WI 54602-4004; (608) 788-1524; www.dioceseoflacrosse.com; La Crosse diocese.

Catholic Times, w; P.O. Box 3187, Springfield, IL 62708-3187; (217) 698-8500; www.dio.org/catholictimes; Springfield diocese.

Catholic Transcript, w; 467 Bloomfield Ave., Bloomfield, CT 06002; (860) 286-2828; Hartford archdiocese, Bridgeport and Norwich dioceses.

Catholic Universe Bulletin, bw; 1027 Superior Ave. NE, Cleveland, OH 44114-2556; (216) 696-6525; www.catholicuniversebulletin.org; Cleveland diocese.

Catholic Virginian, bw; Box 26843, Richmond, VA 23220; (804) 359-5654; www.catholicvirginia.org; Richmond diocese.

Catholic Vision, m.; P.O. Box 31, Tucson, AZ 85702; (520) 792-3410; www.catholicvision.org; Tuscon diocese.

Catholic Voice, The, bw; 3014 Lakeshore Ave., Oakland, CA 94610; (510) 893-5339; www.catholicvoiceoakland.org; Oakland diocese.

Catholic Voice, The, bw; P.O. Box 4010, Omaha, NE 68104-0010; (402) 558-6611; www.tcvomaha.com; Omaha archdiocese.

Catholic War Veteran, bm; 441 N. Lee St., Alexandria, VA 22314-2344; (703) 549-3622; www.cwv.org.

Catholic Week, The, w; P.O. Box 349, Mobile, AL 36601; (251) 434-1544; Mobile archdiocese.

Catholic Weekly, The, w; P.O. Box 1405, Saginaw, MI 48605; (989) 793-7661; www.catholicweekly.org;

Saginaw diocese.

Catholic Weekly, The, w; P.O. Box 1405, Saginaw, MI 48602; (989) 793-7661; Gaylord diocese.

Catholic Witness, The, bw; P.O. Box 2555, Harrisburg, PA 17105; (717) 657-4804; Harrisburg diocese.

Catholic Workman, m; P.O. Box 47, New Prague, MN 56071; (952) 758-2229; www.catholicworkman.com.

Central Washington Catholic, bm; 5301-A Tieton Dr., Yakima, WA 98908; (509) 965-7117; Yakima diocese.

Chicago Catolico (Spanish), m; 721 N. La Salle St., 4th Floor, Chicago, IL 60610; (312) 655-7880; Chicago archdiocese.

Chronicle of Catholic Life, bm; 1001 North Grand Ave., Pueblo, CO 81003; (719) 685-5202; www.dioceseofpueblo.com; Pueblo diocese.

Church Today, twice a month; P.O. Box 7417, Alexandria, LA 71306-0417; (318) 445-2401; www.diocesealex.org; Alexandria diocese.

Clarion Herald, bw; P.O. Box 53247, New Orleans, LA 70153; (504) 596-3035; www.clarionherald.org; New Orleans archdiocese.

Compass, The, w; P.O. Box 23825, Green Bay, WI 54305-3825; (920) 437-7531; www.thecompassnews.org; Green Bay diocese.

Courier, The, m; 55 W. Sanborn St., P.O. Box 949, Winona, MN 55987-0949; (507) 454-4643; www.dow.org; Winona diocese.

Criterion, The, w; P.O. Box 1717, Indianapolis, IN 46206; (317) 236-1570; www.criteriononline.com; Indianapolis archdiocese.

Cross Roads, bw; 1310 W. Main St., Lexington, KY 40508-2040; (859) 253-1993; Lexington diocese.

Dakota Catholic Action, m (except July); P.O. Box 1137, Bismarck, ND 58502-1137; (701) 222-3035; www.bismarckdiocese.com; Bismarck diocese.

Denver Catholic Register, w; 1300 S. Steele St., Denver, CO 80210-2599; (303) 715-3121; www.archden.org; Denver archdiocese.

Dialog, The, w; P.O. Box 2208, Wilmington, DE 19899; (302) 573-3109; www.cdow.org/dialog.html; Wilmington diocese.

East Tennessee Catholic, The, bw; P.O. Box 11127, Knoxville, TN 37939-1127; (865) 584-3307; www.etcatholic.com; Knoxville diocese.

East Texas Catholic, semi-monthly; P.O. Box 3948, Beaumont, TX 77704-3948; (409) 832-3944; Beaumont diocese.

Eastern Catholic Life, bw; 445 Lackawanna Ave., W. Paterson, NJ 07424; (201) 890-7794; Passaic Byzantine eparchy.

Eastern Oklahoma Catholic, bw; Box 690240, Tulsa, OK 74169-0240; (918) 294-1904; www.dioceseoftulsa.org; Tulsa diocese.

Eternal Flame (Armenian-English), 110 E. 12th St., New York, NY 10003; (212) 477-2030; Armenian exarchate.

Evangelist, The, w; 40 N. Main Ave., Albany, NY 12203; (518) 453-6688; www.evangelist.org; Albany diocese.

Fairfield County Catholic, m; 238 Jewett Ave., Bridgeport, CT 06606; (203) 372-4301; www.bridgeportdiocese.org; Bridgeport diocese.

Florida Catholic, The, w; P.O. Box 609512, Orlando, FL 32860-9512; (407) 660-9141; www.thefloridacatholic.org; Orlando diocese; publishes editions for Miami archdiocese and Palm Beach, Pensacola-Tallahassee, St. Petersburg and Venice dioceses.

Florida Catholic: Miami Edition, w; 9401 Biscayne Blvd., Miami, FL 33138; (305) 762-1131; www.thefloridacatholic.org.

Florida Catholic: Palm Beach Edition, w; P.O. Box 109650, Palm Beach Gardens, FL 33410-9650; (561) 775-9528; www.thefloridacatholic.org; Palm Beach diocese.

Florida Catholic: Pensacola-Tallahassee Edition, w; 11 North B St., Pensacola, FL 32501; (850) 435-3500; www.thefloridacatholic.org.

Florida Catholic: St. Petersburg Edition, w; P.O. Box 43022, St. Petersburg, FL 33743; (727) 345-3338.

Florida Catholic: Venice Edition, w; 1000 Pinebrook Rd., Venice, FL 34292; (941) 484-9543; www.thefloridacatholic.org.

Four County Catholic, m; 1595 Norwich New London Turnpike, Uncasville, CT 06382; (860) 848-2237; www.norwichdiocese.org; Norwich diocese.

Georgia Bulletin, w; 680 W. Peachtree St. NW, Atlanta, GA 30308; (404) 877-5500; www.archatl.com; Atlanta archdiocese.

Glasilo KSKJ Amerikanski Slovenec (Slovenian), bw; 708 E. 159th, Cleveland, OH 44110; (216) 541-7243; American Slovenian Catholic Union.

Globe, The, w; P.O. Box 5079, Sioux City, IA 51102; (712) 255-2550; www.catholicglobe.org; Sioux City diocese.

Good News for the Diocese of Kalamazoo, The, m; 215 N. Westnedge, Kalamazoo, MI 49007-3760; (269) 349-8714; www.dioceseofkalamazoo.org; Kalamazoo diocese.

Gulf Pine Catholic, w; P.O. Box 1189, Biloxi, MS 39533-1189; (228) 702-2127; Biloxi diocese.

Harvest, The, 121 23rd St. South, Great Falls, MT 59405; (406) 727-6683; www.dioceseofgfb.org; Great Falls diocese.

Hawaii Catholic Herald, bw; 1184 Bishop St., Honolulu, HI 96813; (808) 533-1791; Honolulu diocese.

Hlas Naroda (Voice of the Nation) (Czech-English), bw; 2340 61st Ave., Cicero, IL 60650; (708) 484-0583.

Horizons, twice a month; 1900 Carlton Rd., Parma, OH 44134-3129; (216) 741-3312; www.parma.org; Parma Byzantine eparchy.

Idaho Catholic Register, twice a month; 303 Federal Way, Boise, ID 83705; (208) 342-1311; www.catholicidaho.org/icr.cfm; Boise diocese.

Inland Register, every 3 weeks; P.O. Box 48, Spokane, WA 99210; (509) 358-7340; www.dioceseofspokane.org; Spokane diocese.

Inside Passage, bw; 415 6th St., Juneau, AK 99801; (907) 586-2227; www.dioceseofjuneau.org; Juneau diocese.

Intermountain Catholic, w; P.O. Box 2489, Salt Lake City, UT 84110-2489; (801) 328-8641; www.icnp.com; Salt Lake City diocese.

Jednota (Slovak-Eng.), w; 6611 Rockside Rd., Independence, OH 44131; (216) 642-9406; First Catholic Slovak Union.

Leaven, The, w; 12615 Parallel Parkway, Kansas City, KS 66109; (913) 721-1570; www.theleaven.com; Kansas City archdiocese.

Long Island Catholic, The, w; P.O. Box 9000, Rockville Centre, NY 11575-9000; (516) 594-1000; www.licatholic.org; Rockville Centre diocese.

L'Osservatore Romano, w; P.O. Box 777, The Cathedral Foundation, Baltimore, MD, 21203; (443) 263-0248; www.catholicreview.org. English edition of the Vatican newspaper.

Maronite Voice, The, m; 4611 Sadler Rd., Glen Allen, VA 23060; (804) 270-7234; www.stmaron.org; Eparchy of St. Maron of Brooklyn.

Message, The, w; P.O. Box 4169, Evansville, IN 47724-0169; (812) 424-5536; Evansville diocese.

Messenger, The, w; 2620 Lebanon Ave., Belleville, IL 62221; (618) 233-8670; www.bellevillemessenger.org; Belleville diocese.

Messenger, The, 45 times a year; P.O. Box 15550, Erlanger, KY 41018; (859) 392-1570; www.covingtondiocese.org; Covington diocese.

Michigan Catholic, The, w; 305 Michigan Ave., 4th Floor, Detroit, MI 48226; (313) 224-8000; Detroit archdiocese.

Mirror, The, w; 601 S. Jefferson Ave., Springfield, MO 65806-3143; (417) 866-0841; www.themirror.org; Springfield-Cape Girardeau diocese.

Mississippi Catholic, w; P.O. Box 2130, Jackson, MS 39225-2130; (601) 969-1880; www.mississippicatholic.com; Jackson diocese.

Monitor, The, w; P.O. Box 5147, Trenton, NJ 08638-0147; (609) 406-7404; www.dioceseoftrenton.org; Trenton diocese.

Montana Catholic, The, 16 times a year; P.O. Box 1729, Helena, MT 59624; (406) 442-5820; www.diocesehelena.org; Helena diocese.

Narod Polski (Polish Nation) (Polish-Eng.) semi-monthly; 984 Milwaukee Ave., Chicago, IL 60622-4101; (773) 782-2600; www.prcua.com; Polish Roman Catholic Union of America.

National Catholic Register, w; 432 Washington Ave., North Haven, CT 06473; (203) 230-3800; www.ncregister.com; national.

National Catholic Reporter, w; P.O. Box 419281, Kansas City, MO 64141; (816) 531-0538; www.ncronline.org; national.

National Jesuit News, m; 1616 P St. NW, Suite 300, Washington, DC 20036; (202) 462-0400; www.jesuit.org.

New Earth, The, m; 5201 Bishops Blvd., Ste. A, Fargo, ND 58104; (701) 356-7958; www.fargidiocese.org; Fargo diocese.

New Star, The, every 3 weeks; 2208 W. Chicago Ave., Chicago, IL 60622; (312) 772-1919; St. Nicholas of Chicago Ukrainian diocese.

NC Catholic, bw; 715 Nazareth St., Raleigh, NC 27606; (919) 821-9736; www.nccatholic.org; Raleigh diocese.

North Country Catholic, w; P.O. Box 326, Ogdensburg, NY 13669; (315) 393-2540; www.northcountrycatholic.org; Ogdensburg diocese.

North Texas Catholic, w; 800 West Loop 820 South, Fort Worth, TX 76108; (817) 560-3300; www.fwdioc.org; Fort Worth diocese.

Northern Cross, The, m; 2830 E. 4th St., Duluth, MN 55812; (218) 724-9111; www.dioceseduluth.org; Duluth diocese.

Northern Nevada Catholic, m; 290 S. Arlington Ave., #200, Reno, NV 89501; (775) 826-1010; Reno diocese.

Northwest Indiana Catholic, w; 9292 Broadway, Merrillville, IN 46410-7088; (219) 769-9292; www.nwicatholic.com; Gary diocese.

Northwestern Kansas Register, w; P.O. Box 1038,

Salina, KS 67402; (785) 827-8746; www.salinadiocese.org; Salina diocese.

Oblate World, The and Voice of Hope, twice a month; P.O. Box 680, Tewksbury, MA 01876; (978) 851-7258; www.omiusa.org; published by the Missionary Oblates of Mary Immaculate.

Observer, The, m; P.O. Box 2079, Monterey, CA 93942; (831) 373-2919; www.dioceseofmonterey.org; Monterey diocese.

Observer, The, m; 4545 W. 63rd St., Chicago, IL 60629; (312) 585-9500; Lithuanian Roman Catholic Federation of America.

Observer, The, twice a month; P.O. Box 7044, Rockford, IL 61125; (815) 399-4300; www.rockforddiocese.org; Rockford diocese.

One Voice, w; P.O. Box 10822, Birmingham, AL 35202; (205) 838-8305; Birmingham diocese.

Orange County Catholic, m.; P.O. Box 14195, Orange, CA 92863-1595; (714) 282-3022; Orange diocese.

Our Lady's Messenger/Our Lady of the Hills Church, six times a year; 2700 Ashland Rd., Columbia, SC 29210; (803) 772-7400.

Our Northland Diocese, semi-monthly; P.O. Box 610, Crookston, MN 56716; (218) 281-4553; www.crookston.org; Crookston diocese.

People of God, m; 4000 St. Joseph Pl. NW, Albuquerque, NM 87120; (505) 831-8188; Santa Fe archdiocese.

Pilot, The, w; 2121 Commonwealth Ave., Brighton, MA 02135-3193; (617) 746-5889; www.rcab.org; Boston archdiocese.

Pittsburgh Catholic, w; 135 First Ave., Suite 200, Pittsburgh, PA 15222-1506; (412) 471-1252; www.pittsburghcatholic.org; Pittsburgh diocese.

Prairie Catholic, m; 1400 6th St. North, New Ulm, MN 56073-2099; (507) 359-2966; www.dnu.org; New Ulm diocese.

Praxis Press, 10 times a year; P.O. Box 508, San Jose, CA 95103; (408) 370-4748.

Providence Visitor, The, w; 184 Broad St., Providence, RI 02903; (401) 272-1010; www.providencevisitor.com; Providence diocese.

Record, The, w; Maloney Center, 1200 S. Shelby St., Louisville, KY 40203-2600; (502) 636-0296; Louisville archdiocese.

Rio Grande Catholic, The, m; 499 St. Matthews St., El Paso, TX 79907; (915) 872-8414; www.elpasodiocese.org; El Paso diocese.

Saint Cloud Visitor, The, w; P. O. Box 1068, St. Cloud, MN 56302-1066; (320) 251-3022; www.stclouddiocese.org/visitor; St. Cloud diocese.

St. Louis Review, w; 20 Archbishop May Dr., St. Louis, MO 63119; (314) 792-7500; www.stlouisreview.com; St. Louis archdiocese.

Seasons, q; 5800 Weiss St., Saginaw, MI 48603-2799; (989) 797-6666; www.dioceseofsaginaw.org; Saginaw diocese.

Slovak Catholic Falcon (Slovak-English), w; 205 Madison St., P.O.Box 899, Passaic, NJ 07055; (973) 777-4010; Slovak Catholic Sokol.

Sooner Catholic, The, bw; P.O. Box 32180, Oklahoma City, OK 73123; (405) 721-1810; www.catharchdioceseok.org; Oklahoma City archdiocese.

Sophia, q; 200 E. North Ave., Northlake, IL 60164; (708) 865-7050; Newton Melkite eparchy.

South Plains Catholic, twice a month; P.O. Box 98700, Lubbock, TX 79499-8700; (806) 792-3943; www.catholiclubbock.org; Lubbock diocese.

South Texas Catholic, twice a month; P.O. Box 2620, Corpus Christi, TX 78403-2620; (361) 882-6191; www.goccn.org; Corpus Christi diocese.

Southern Cross, semi-monthly; P.O. Box 81869, San Diego, CA 92138; (858) 490-8266; www.thesoutherncross.org; San Diego diocese.

Southern Cross, The, w; 601 E. Liberty St., Savannah, GA 31401-5196; (912) 201-4100; www.diosav.org; Savannah diocese.

Southern Nebraska Register, w; P.O. Box 80329, Lincoln, NE 68501; (402) 488-0090; Lincoln diocese.

Southwest Catholic, The, m; P.O. 411 Iris St., Lake Charles, LA 70601; (337) 439-7426; www.lcdiocese.org; Lake Charles diocese.

Southwest Kansas Register, bw; P.O. Box 137, Dodge City, KS 67801; (620) 227-1519; www.dcdiocese.org/swkregister; Dodge City diocese.

Sower (Ukrainian and English), bw; 14 Peveril Rd., Stamford, CT 06902; (203) 324-7698; www.thesower@adcus.com; Stamford Ukrainian diocese.

Star of Chaldeans (Arabic and English), bm; 25585 Berg Rd., Southfield, MI 48034; St. Thomas the Apostle Chaldean diocese.

Steubenville Register, bw; P.O. Box 160, Steubenville, OH 43952; (740) 282-3631; www.diosteub.org; Steubenville diocese.

Tablet, The, w; 310 Prospect Park West, Brooklyn, NY 11215-6214; (718) 965-7333; www.dioceseofbrooklyn.org/tablet; Brooklyn diocese.

Tautai, bw; P.O. Box 532, Feiloaimauso Hall, Apia, Samoa; Samoa-Apia archdiocese.

Tennessee Register, The, bw; 2400 21st Ave. S., Nashville, TN 37212; (615) 783-0770; www.dioceseofnashville.org; Nashville diocese.

Texas Catholic, The, bw; P.O. Box 190346, Dallas, TX 75219; (214) 528-8792; www.texascatholic.com; Dallas diocese.

Texas Catholic Herald, The, twice a month; 1700 San Jacinto St., Houston, TX 77001-0907; (713) 659-5461; Galveston-Houston diocese.

Tidings, The, w; 3424 Wilshire Blvd, Los Angeles, CA 90010; (213) 637-7360; www.the-tidings.com; Los Angeles archdiocese.

Today's Catholic, w; P.O. Box 11169, Fort Wayne, IN 46856; (260) 456-2824; www.diocesefwsb.org; Fort Wayne–South Bend diocese.

Today's Catholic, bw; P.O. Box 28410, San Antonio, TX 78228-0410; (210) 734-2620; www.satodaycatholic.org; San Antonio archdiocese.

UNIREA (The Union) (Romanian) 10 times a year; 2654 Glen Ave., Altadena, CA 91001; (626) 797-3851; Romanian diocese of Canton.

U. P. Catholic, The, semi-monthly; P.O. Box 548, Marquette, MI 49855; (906) 227-9131; www.upcatholic.org; Marquette diocese.

Valley Catholic, m; 900 Lafayette St., Suite 301, Santa Clara, CA 95050-4966; (408) 983-0260; www.dsj.org/community/valley.asp; San Jose diocese.

Vermont Catholic Tribune, bw; P.O. Box 489,

Burlington, VT 05402; (802) 658-6110; www.vermontcatholic.org; Burlington diocese.

Vida Nueva; 3424 Wilshire Blvd., Los Angeles, CA 90010-2241; (213) 637-7310.

Voice of the Southwest, m; 711 S. Puerco, Gallup, NM 87301; (505) 863-4406; Gallup diocese.

Wanderer, The, w; 201 Ohio St., St. Paul, MN 55107; (651) 224-5733; national.

Way, The (Ukrainian-Eng.), bw; 827 N. Franklin St., Philadelphia, PA 19123; (215) 922-5231; Philadelphia archeparchy.

West Nebraska Register, w; P.O. Box 608, Grand Island, NE 68802; (308) 382-4660; Grand Island diocese.

West River Catholic, m; P.O. Box 678, Rapid City, SD 57709; (605) 343-3541; Rapid City diocese.

West Tennessee Catholic, w; P.O. Box 341669, Memphis, TN 38184-1669; (901) 373-1213; www.cdom.org; Memphis diocese.

West Texas Angelus, m; P.O. Box 1829, San Angelo, TX 76902; (915) 651-7500; www.san-angelo-diocese.org; San Angelo diocese.

West Texas Catholic, bw; P.O. Box 5644, Amarillo, TX 79117-5644; (806) 383-2243; www.amarillodiocese.org; Amarillo diocese.

Western Kentucky Catholic, m; 600 Locust St., Owensboro, KY 42301; (270) 683-1545; Owensboro diocese.

Western New York Catholic, m; 795 Main St., Buffalo, NY 14203-1250; (716) 847-8727; www.wnycatholic.org; Buffalo diocese.

Witness, The, w; P.O. Box 917, Dubuque, IA 52004-0917; (319) 588-0556; Dubuque archdiocese.

Wyoming Catholic Register, m; P.O. Box 227, Cheyenne, WY 82003; (307) 638-1530; www.wyocathregister.org; Cheyenne diocese.

Magazines

Abbey Banner, The, 3 times a year; Saint John's Abbey, Collegeville, MN 56321; (320) 363-3875; www.sja.osb/abbeybanner.

AIM: Liturgy Resources, q; 3708 River Rd., Ste. 400, Franklin Park, IL 60131; (800) 566-6150.

America, w; 106 W. 56th St., New York, NY 10019; (212) 581-4640; www.americamagazine.org; Jesuits of U.S. and Canada.

American Benedictine Review, q; Assumption Abbey, Box A, Richardton, ND 58652; (701) 974-3315.

American Catholic Philosophical Quarterly (formerly **The New Scholasticism**), Fordham University, Bronx, NY 10458; (718) 817-4081; www.acpamain.org; American Catholic Philosophical Assn.

American Catholic Studies; Villanova University, 800 Lancaster Ave., Villanova, PA 19085; (610) 519-5470.

The Annals of St. Anne de Beaupre, m; P.O. Box 1000, St. Anne de Beaupre, Quebec, GOA 3CO; (418) 827-4538.

Anthonian, The, q; c/o St. Anthony's Guild, Paterson, NJ 07509; (212) 924-1451; www.hnp.org/publications; St. Anthony's Guild.

Apostolate of the Little Flower, bm; P.O. Box 5280, San Antonio, TX 78201-0280; (210) 736-3889; Discalced Carmelite Fathers.

Augustinian Journey, q; P.O. Box 340, Villanova, PA 19085; (610) 527-3330; www.augustinian.org; published by the Province of St. Thomas of Villanova.

Barry Magazine, 2 times a year; 11300 NE 2nd Ave., Miami Shores, FL 33161; (305) 899-3188; Barry University.

Benedictines, m., 44 N. Mill St., Kansas City, KS 66101; (913) 342-0938; www.mountosb.com.

Bible Today, The, bm; Liturgical Press, Collegeville, MN 56321-7500; (320) 363-2218; www.litpress.org.

Bright Ideas; P.O. Box 510817, New Berlin, WI, 53151-0817; (800) 876-4574; www.lpiresourcecenter.com.

Carmelite Digest, q; P.O. Box 2178, Relands, CA 92373-0701; (909) 793-0424; www.carmelitedigest.org.

Carmelite Review, twice a month; 6725 Reed Rd., Houston, TX 77087-6830; (713) 644-8400; www.carmelnet.org/publications.htm; published by the Province of the Most Pure Heart of Mary of the Carmelite Order.

Catechist, The, 7 times a year; 2621 Dryden Rd., Dayton, OH 45439; (937) 293-1415; www.pflaum.com.

Catechumenate: A Journal of Christian Initiation, bm; 1800 N. Hermitage Ave., Chicago, IL 60622-1101; (773) 486-8970; www.ltp.org.

Catholic Answer, The, bm; 200 Noll Plaza, Huntington, IN 46750; (260) 356-8400; www.osv.com; Our Sunday Visitor, Inc.

Catholic Biblical Quarterly; Catholic University of America, Washington, DC 20064; (202) 319-5519; www.cba.cua.edu; Catholic Biblical Assn.

Catholic Cemetery, The, m; 710 N. River Rd., Des Plaines, IL 60016; (847) 824-8131; National Catholic Cemetery Conference.

Catholic Connection, The, m.; 3500 Fairfield Ave., Shreveport, LA 71104; (318) 868-4441; www.dioshpt.org; diocese of Shreveport.

Catholic Digest, m 1 Montauk Ave., Ste. 200, New London, CT 06320; (860) 437-3012; www.catholicdigest.org.

Catholic Family News, m.; MPO Box 743, Niagara Falls, NY 14302; (905) 871-6292.

Catholic Historical Review, q; 620 Michigan Ave. N.E., Washington, DC 20064; (202) 319-5079; research.cua.edu/acha.

Catholic Knights of America Journal, m; 1850 Dalton St., Cincinnati, OH 45214; (513) 721-0781; Catholic Knights of America.

Catholic Lawyer, q; St. John's University, 8000 Utopia Parkway, Jamaica, NY 11439; (718) 990-6655; St. Thomas More Institute for Legal Research.

Catholic Library World, q; 100 North St., #224, Pittsfield, MA 01201-5109; (413) 443-2252; www.cathla.org; Catholic Library Association.

Catholic Near East Magazine, bm; 1011 First Ave., New York, NY 10022; (212) 826-1480; www.cnewa.org; Catholic Near East Welfare Assn.

Catholic Outlook, m; 2830 E. 4th St., Duluth, MN 55812; (218) 724-9111; www.dioceseduluth.org; Duluth diocese.

Catholic Pharmacist, q; 1012 Surrey Hills Dr., St. Louis, MO 63117-1438; (314) 645-0085; National Catholic Pharmacists Guild.

Catholic Press Directory, a; 3555 Veterans Highway, Unit O, Ronkonkoma, NY 11779; (631) 471-4730; www.catholicpress.com; Catholic Press Assn.

Catholic Response, m.; 21 Fairview Ave., Mt. Pocono, PA 18344; (570) 839-2185; www.jhcnewman.org.

Catholic Review (Braille, tape, large print), bm; 154 E. 23rd St., New York, NY 10010; (212) 473-7800; Xavier Society for the Blind.

Catholic Southwest: A Journal of History and

Culture, a; 1625 Rutherford Lane, Bldg. D, Austin, TX, 78754-5105; (512) 339-9882.

Catholic Woman, bm; 200 N. Glebe Rd., Suite 703, Arlington, VA 22203; (202) 224-0990; www.nccw.org; National Council of Catholic Women.

Catholic Worker, 7 times a year; 36 E. First St., New York, NY 10003; (212) 677-8627; Catholic Worker Movement.

Catholic Workman, bi-monthly, P.O. Box 47, New Prague, MN 56071; (952) 758-2229; www.catholicworkmen.org; official publication of the Catholic Workmen.

Catholic World Report, The, 11 times a year; P.O. Box 1328, Dedham, MA 02027 (editorial office); Ignatius Press.

Celebration, m; 115 E. Armour Blvd., Kansas City, MO 64111; (816) 968-2266; National Catholic Reporter Publishing Co.

Charities USA, q; 1731 King St., Suite 200, Alexandria, VA 22314; (703) 549-1390; www.catholiccharitiesusa.org.

Chesterton Review, The, q; Seton Hall University, 400 South Orange Ave., South Orange, NJ 07079; (973) 275-2430; G.K. Chesterton Society.

Chicago Studies, 3 times a year; 1800 N. Hermitage Ave., Chicago, IL 60622-1101; (800) 933-1800.

Christian Renewal News, q.; P.O. Box 6164, Santa Maria, CA 93456; (805) 524-5890; www.theservants andhandmaids.net; published by The Servants and Handmaids of the Sacred Heart of Jesus.

Christianity and the Arts, q; P.O. Box 118088, Chicago, IL 60611; (312) 642-8606; www.christianarts.net.

Church, q; 18 Bleeker St., New York, NY 10012; (212) 431-7825; www.nplc.org; National Pastoral Life Center.

CMMB Today, q., 10 West 17th St., New York, N.Y. 10011; (212) 242-7757; www.cmmb.org; Catholic Medical Mission Board publication.

CNEWA World, bm; 1011 First Ave., New York, NY 10022; (212) 826-1480; www.cnewa.org; Catholic Near East Welfare.

Columban Mission, 8 times a year; St. Columbans, NE 68056; (402) 291-1920; www.columban.org; Columban Fathers.

Columbia, m; One Columbus Plaza, New Haven, CT 06510; (203) 752-4398; www.kofc.org; Knights of Columbus.

Commonweal, bw; 475 Riverside Dr., Room 405, New York, NY 10115; (212) 662-4200; www.commonwealmagazine.org.

Communio: International Catholic Review, q; P.O. Box 4557, Washington, DC 20017-0557; (202) 526-0251; www.communio-icr.org.

Company, q; P.O. Box 60790, Chicago, IL 60660-0790; (773) 760-9432; www.companymagazine.com; Jesuit magazine.

Consecrated Life, semi-annually; P.O. Box 41007, Chicago, IL 60641; (773) 267-1195; www.religiouslife.com; Institute on Religious Life. English edition of *Informationes*, official publication of Congregation for Institutes of Consecrated Life and Societies of Apostolic Life.

Consolata Missionaries, bm; P.O. Box 5550, Somerset, NJ 08875-5550; (732) 297-9191; www.consolata.org.

Cord, The, m; Franciscan Institute, St. Bonaventure University, St. Bonaventure, NY 14778; (716) 375-2160; franinst@sbu.edu; Franciscan Institute.

Counseling and Values, 3 times a year; College of Educational, Southern Illinois University, Carbondale, IL 62901; (618) 537-7791.

Crescat, 3 times a year; Belmont Abbey, Belmont,

NC 28012; (704) 825-6707; Benedictine Monks.

Crisis, 11 times a year; 1814 N St. NW, Washington, DC 20036; (202) 861-7790; www.crisismagazine.com; journal of lay Catholic opinion.

Cross Currents, q; College of New Rochelle, New Rochelle, NY 10805; (914) 235-1439; www.aril.org; interreligious; Assn. for Religion and Intellectual Life.

Crusade Magazine, bm; P.O. Box 341, Hanover, PA 17331; (717) 225-9177; Foundation for a Christian Civilization, Inc.

CUA Magazine, 3 times a year; 620 Michigan Ave. N.E., Washington, DC 20064; (202) 319-5600; www.cua.edu; Catholic University of America.

Darbininkas (The Worker) (Lithuanian), w; 341 Highland Blvd., Brooklyn, NY 11207; (718) 827-1352; Lithuanian Franciscans.

Desert Call, q.; P.O. Box 219, Crestone, CO 81131-0219; (719) 256-4778; www.spirituallifeinstitute.org; published by the Spiritual Life Institute.

Desert Clarion, 10 times a year; 4519 Simmons St., North Las Vegas, NV 89031; (702) 657-0200; Las Vegas diocese.

Diakonia, 3 times a year; University of Scranton, Scranton, PA 18510-4643; (570) 941-6141; www.nyssa.cecs.uofs.edu/diaktoc.html; Center for Eastern Christian Studies.

Divine Word Missionaries, q; P.O. Box 6099, Techny, IL 60082-6099; (847) 272-7600; www.svdmissions.org.

Don Bosco Alive/The Salesian Bulletin; 148 Main Street, New Rochelle, NY 10802-0639; (914) 636-4225; www.salesians.org.

Ecumenical Trends, m (except Aug.); Graymoor, Route 9, P.O. Box 306, Garrison, NY 10524-0306; (845) 424-2109; www.atonementfriars.org; Graymoor Ecumenical Institute.

Eglute (The Little Fir Tree) (Lithuanian), m; 13648 Kikapoo Trail, Lockport, IL 60441; (708) 301-6410; for children ages 5-10.

Emmanuel, 10 times a year; 5384 Wilson Mills Rd., Cleveland, OH 44143; (440) 449-2103; www.blessedsacrament.com; Congregation of Blessed Sacrament.

Envoy, bm; P.O. Box 585, Granville, OH 43023; (740) 587-2292; www.envoymagazine.com; journal of Catholic apologetics and evangelization.

EWTN Religious Catalogue, two times a year; 5817 Old Leeds Rd., Irondale, AL 35210; 205-271-2900; www.ewtn.com; printed catalogue of select new and favorite "holy reminders" for the Easter and Christmas seasons. Circ. 700,000.

Extension, m; 150 S. Wacker Dr., 20th Floor, Chicago, IL 60606; (312) 236-7240; www.catholicextension.org; Catholic Church Extension Society.

Faith, 209 Seymour Ave., Lansing, MI 48933-1577; (517) 342-2595; www.faithmag.com.

Faith-Diocese of Erie, 429 E. Grandview Blvd., Erie, PA 16504; (814) 824-1160; www.faitherie.com.

Faith and Family, bm; 432 Washington Ave., North Haven, CT 06473; (203) 230-3800; formerly *Catholic Twin Circle*.

Faith and Reason, q; 134 Christendom Dr., Front Royal, VA 22630; (540) 636-2900.

Family Digest, The, bm; P.O. Box 40137, Fort

Wayne, IN 46804 (editorial address); (952) 929-6765.

Family Foundations Magazine, P.O. Box 111184, Cincinnati, OH 45211; (513) 471-2000; www.ccli.org; published by the Couple to Couple League.

Family Friend, q; P.O. Box 11563, Milwaukee, WI 53211; (414) 961-0500; www.cfli.org; Catholic Family Life Insurance.

Fidelity, m; 206 Marquette Ave., South Bend, IN 46617; (219) 289-9786.

F.M.A. Focus, q; P.O. Box 598, Mt. Vernon, NY 10551; (914) 664-5604; Franciscan Mission Associates.

Forum Focus, q.; P.O. Box 542, Hudson, WI 54016-0542; (651) 276-1429; www.wandererforum.org.

Franciscan Studies, a; Franciscan Institute, St. Bonaventure, NY 14778; (716) 375-2105; www.franinst.sbu.edu; Franciscan Institute.

Franciscan Way, q; 1235 University Blvd., Steubenville, OH 43952; (740) 283-6450; www.franuniv.edu.

Fraternal Leader, q; P.O. Box 13005; Erie, PA 16514-1302; (814) 453-4331; Loyal Christian Benefit Association.

Fraternally Yours (English-Slovak), m; 24950 Chagrin Blvd., Beachwood, OH 44122; (216) 464-8015; First Catholic Slovak Ladies Assn.

Fuente de Misericordia, q; Eden Hill, Stockbridge, MA 01263; (413) 298-3691; www.marian.org; Congregation of Marians of the Immaculate Conception.

Glenmary Challenge, The, q; P.O. Box 465618, Cincinnati, OH 45246-5618; (513) 874-8900; www.glenmary.org; Glenmary Home Missioners.

God's Word Today, m; 185 Willow St., Mystic, CT 06355; (860) 536-2611; www.godswordtoday.org; Daily Scripture readings.

Good News, m; P.O. Box 432, Milwaukee, WI 53201-0432; (800) 876-4574; www.execpc.com/~lpi; Liturgical Publications.

Good News for Children, 32 times during school year; 2621 Dryden Rd., Suite 300, Dayton, OH 45439; (937) 293-1415; www.pflaum.com.

Good Shepherd (Dobry Pastier) (Slovak-English), a; 8200 McKnight Rd., Pittsburgh, PA 15237; (412) 364-3000.

Greyfriars Review, 3 times a year; Franciscan Institute, St. Bonventure University, St. Bonaventure, NY 14778; (716) 375-2105; www.franinst.sbu.edu; Franciscan Institute.

Growing with the Gospel, w; Liturgical Publications, P.O. Box 510817, New Berlin, WI, 53151; (800) 950-9952.

Guide to Religious Ministries for Catholic Men and Women, A, a; 210 North Ave., New Rochelle, NY 10801; (914) 632-1220; www.religiousministries.com.

Health Progress, bm; 4455 Woodson Rd., St. Louis, MO 63134-3797; (314) 427-2500; www.chausa.org; Catholic Health Association.

Heart, 4389 West Pine Blvd., St. Louis, MO 63108; (314) 652-1500; www.rscj.org.

Hearts Aflame, q; P.O. Box 976, Washington, NJ 07882; (210) 689-1700; www.ewtn.com/Bluearmy/; for youth ages 13-23.

Homiletic and Pastoral Review, m; P.O. Box 591810, San Francisco, CA 94159-1810; (415) 387-2324.

Horizon, q; 5420 S. Cornell Ave., #105, Chicago, IL 60615-5604; (773) 363-5454.

Horizons, 2 times a year; Villanova University, Villanova, PA 19085; (610) 519-7302; College Theology Society.

Human Development, q; 1353 Boston Post Rd., Suite 11, Madison, CT 06443; (203) 318-1886; www.ctu.edu/cishs.html.

ICSC Resource; 1275 K St. N.W., Suite 980, Washington, DC, 20005-4006; (202) 289-1093; www.catholicstewardship.org; published by International Catholic Stewardship Council.

Immaculata, bm; 1600 W. Park Ave., Libertyville, IL 60048; (847) 367-7800; www.marytown.com.

Immaculate Heart Messenger, q; 1224 County Rd. 548, Hanceville, AL 35077; (800) 721-6279; www.fatimafamily.org.

In a Word, m; 199 Seminary Dr., Bay Saint Louis, MS 39520-4626; (601) 467-1097; www.inaword.com; Society of the Divine Word.

Inside the Vatican, 10 times a year; Rome office: Via della Mura Aurelio 7c, 00165 Rome, Italy; U.S. office: St. Martin de Porres Lay Dominican Community, 3050 Gap Knob Rd., New Hope, KY 40052; (270) 325-5499; www.insidethevatican.com. The only current journal that focuses exclusively on Rome, the impact of the papacy worldwide, and the functioning, travels, and activities of the Holy Father and the Roman Curia.

Jesuit Bulletin, 3 times a year; 3601 Lindell Blvd., St. Louis, MO 63108; (314) 977-7363; www.jesuits-mis.org; Jesuit Seminary Aid Association.

Jesuit Journeys, 3 times a year; 3400 W. Wisconsin Ave., Milwaukee, WI 53208-0288; (414) 937-6949; www.jesuitswisprov.org.

Josephinum Journal of Theology, twice a year; 7625 N. High St., Columbus, OH 43235; (614) 985-2278; www.pcj.edu.

Josephite Harvest, The, q; 1130 N. Calvert St., Baltimore, MD 21202-3802; (410) 727-2233; www.josephite.com; Josephite Missionaries.

Journal of Catholic Legal Studies, St. John's University, 8000 Utopia Parkway, Jamaica, NY 11439; (718) 890-6655.

Jurist, The, semi-annually; Catholic University of America, Washington, DC 20064; (202) 319-5439; Department of Canon Law.

Kinship, q; P.O. Box 22264, Owensboro, KY 42304; (270) 686-8401; www.glenmarysisters.org; Glenmary Sisters.

Knights of St. John International, q; 89 South Pine Ave., Albany, NY 12208; (518) 453-5675; www.members.tripod.com/ksji/knights/ksji.html.

Law Briefs, m; 3211 Fourth St. NE, Washington DC 20017; (202) 541-3300; Office of General Counsel, USCCB.

Lay Witness, m; 827 North Fourth St., Steubenville, OH, 43952; (740) 283-2484; www.cuf.org; Catholics United for the Faith.

Leaflet Missal, 16565 South State St., S. Holland, IL 60473; (708) 331-5485; www.leafletmissal.com.

Leaves, bm; P.O. Box 87, Dearborn, MI 48121-0087; (313) 561-2330; www.rc.net/detroit/marianhill/leaves.htm; Marianhill Mission Society.

Legatus, ten times a year, 2640 Golden Gate Pkwy, #118, Naples, FL 34105; (239) 435-3852; www.legatus.org. Published by Legatus International.

Liguorian, m; 1 Liguori Dr., Liguori, MO 63057;

(636) 464-2500; www.liguorian.org; Redemptorists.

Linacre Quarterly; P.O. Box 757, Pewaukee, WI 53072; (262) 523-6201; www.cathmed.org; Catholic Medical Association (National Federation of Catholic Physicians Guilds).

Liturgia y Cancion (Spanish and English), q; 5536 NE Hassalo, Portland, OR 97213; (800) 548-8749; Oregon Catholic Press.

Liturgical Catechesis, 6 times a year; 160 E. Virginia St., #290, San Jose, CA 95112; (408) 286-8505; www.rpinet.com/lc.

Liturgy Planner, The, semi-annual; P.O. Box 13071, Portland, OR 97213; (503) 331-2965.

Living City, m; P.O. Box 837, Bronx, NY 10465; (718) 828-2932; www.livingcitymagazine.com; Focolare Movement.

Living Faith: Daily Catholic Devotions, q; 1564 Fencorp Dr., Fenton, MO 63026-2942; (636) 305-9777; www.livingfaith.com.

Living Light, The, q; 3211 Fourth St. NE, Washington, DC 20017; (202) 541-3453; www.usccb.org/education/catechetics/livinglt.htm; Department of Education, USCCB.

Magnificat, m.; Dunwoodie, 201 Seminary Ave., Yonkers, NY 10704; (914) 377-8513; www.magnificat.net.

Marian Helper, q.; Eden Hill, Stockbridge, MA 01263; (413) 298-3691; www.marian.org.

Marriage, bm; 955 Lake Dr., St. Paul, MN 55120; (651) 454-7947; www.marriagemagazine; International Marriage Encounter.

Mary's Shrine, 2 times a year; 400 Michigan Ave. NE, Washington, DC 20017-1566; (202) 526-8300; www.nationalshrine.com; Basilica of National Shrine of the Immaculate Conception.

Maryknoll, m; Maryknoll, NY 10545-0308; (914) 941-7590; www.maryknoll.org; Catholic Foreign Mission Society.

Matrimony, q; 215 Santa Rosa Pl., Santa Barbara, CA 93109; (805) 965-9541; Worldwide Marriage Encounter.

Medjugorje Magazine, q; 317 W. Ogden Ave., Westmont, IL 60559; (630) 968-4684; www.medjugor.com.

Migration World, 5 times a year; 209 Flagg Pl., Staten Island, NY 10304; (718) 351-8800; www.cmsny.org; Center for Migration Studies.

Ministry & Liturgy, m.; 160 E. Virginia St., #290, San Jose, CA 95112; (408) 286-8505; www.rpinet.com.

Miraculous Medal, q; 475 E. Chelten Ave., Philadelphia, PA 19144; (215) 848-1010; www.cammonline.org; Central Association of the Miraculous Medal.

Mission, q; 1663 Bristol Pike, Bensalem, PA 19020-8502; (215) 244-9900; www.katharinedrexel.org; Sisters of the Blessed Sacrament.

Mission, q., 10582 Associates Court, Manassas, VA 20109; (703) 367-0333; www.cardinalnewmansociety.org; Cardinal Newman Society to promote Catholic higher education.

MISSION Magazine, q; 366 Fifth Ave., New York, NY 10001; (212) 563-8700; www.worldmissions-catholicchurch.org; Society for Propagation of the Faith.

Mission Helper, The, q; 1001 W. Joppa Rd., Baltimore, MD 21204-3787; (410) 823-8585; Mission Helpers of the Sacred Heart.

Missionhurst, bm; 4651 N. 25th St., Arlington, VA 22207; (703) 528-3804; www.missionhurst.org.

Modern Schoolman, The, q; St. Louis University,

P.O. Box 56907, St. Louis, MO 63156; (314) 997-3149; St. Louis University Philosophy Department.

Momento Catolico, El; 205 W. Monroe St., Chicago, IL, 60606; (312) 236-7782; www.hmrc.claretianpubs.org.

Momentum, q; Suite 100, 1077 30th St. NW, Washington, DC 20007-3852; (202) 337-6232; www.ncea.org; National Catholic Educational Association.

Mountain Spirit, The, bm; P.O. Box 459, Hagerhill, KY 41222; (606) 789-9791; www.chrisapp.org; Christian Appalachian Project.

My Daily Visitor, bm; 200 Noll Plaza, Huntington, IN 46750; (260) 356-8400; www.osv.com; Our Sunday Visitor, Inc.

My Friend—The Catholic Magazine for Kids, 10 times a year; 50 St. Paul's Ave., Jamaica Plain, Boston, MA 02130; (617) 522-8911; www.myfriendmagazine.org; for children ages 6-12.

National Apostolate for Inclusion Ministry, q; P.O. Box 218, Riverdale, MD, 20738-0218; (301) 699-9500; www.nafim.org.

National Catholic Forester, q; 320 S. School St., Mt. Prospect, IL 60056; (847) 342-4500; www.ncsf.com.

National Catholic Rural Life, bi-annual; 4625 Beaver Ave., Des Moines, IA 50310; (515) 270-2634; www.ncrlc.com.

NC Catholic, 715 Nazareth, Raleigh, NC 27606; (919) 821-9736; www.nccatholics.org; diocese of Raleigh.

NETWORK Connection, bm; 801 Pennsylvania Ave. SE, #460, Washington, DC 20003; (202) 547-5556; www.networklobby.org; Network.

New Oxford Review, 10 issues a year; 1069 Kains Ave., Berkeley, CA 94706; (510) 526-5374; www.newoxfordreview.org.

Notebook, The, q; CMICA-USA, 3049 4 St. NE, Washington, DC 20017; (202) 269-6672; www.paxromana.org; Catholic Movement for Intellectual and Cultural Affairs.

Notre Dame Magazine, q; University of Notre Dame, Notre Dame, IN 46556; (574) 631-5335; www.nd.edu/~mdmag.

Nova-Voice of Ministry, bm; P.O. Box 432, Milwaukee, WI 53201; (800) 876-4574; www.execpc.com/~lpi; Liturgical Publications.

Oblates Magazine, six times a year, 9480 North De Mazenod Dr., Belleville, IL 62223-1160; (618) 398-4848; www.oblatesusa.org.

Old Testament Abstracts, 3 times a year; 320 Caldwell Hall, Catholic University of America, Washington, DC 20064; (202) 319-5519.

ONE, bm., 1011 First Ave., New York, NY 10022; (212) 826-1480; www.cnewa.org. Catholic Near East Welfare Association.

Origins, 48 times a year; 3211 4th St. NE, Washington, DC 20017; (202) 541-3284; documentary service.

Ozanam News, The, twice a year; 58 Progress Parkway, St. Louis, MO 63043-3706; (314) 576-3993; www.svdpuscouncil.org; Society of St. Vincent de Paul.

Palabra Entre Nosotros, La, bm; 9639 Dr. Perry Rd., Unit 126N, Jamesville, MD, 21754; (301) 831-1262; www.wau.org.

Parish Liturgy, q; 16565 S. State St., S. Holland, IL

60473; (708) 331-5485; www.parishliturgy.com.

Partners Magazine: Chicago Province of the Society of Jesus, 3 times a year; 2059 N. Sedgwick St., Chicago, IL 60614; (773) 975-8181; www.jesuits-chi.org.

Passionists' Compassion, The, q; 526 Monastery Pl., Union City, NJ 07087; (201) 864-0018; www.cptryon.org.

Pastoral Life, m; Box 595, Canfield, OH 44406; (330) 533-5503; www.albahouse.org; Society of St. Paul.

Pastoral Music, bm; 962 Wayne Ave., Suite 210, Silver Spring, MD 20910-4433; (240) 247-3000; www.npm.org; National Association of Pastoral Musicians.

Pax Romana/CMICA-USA, q; 3049 4th St., NE, Washington, DC 20017; (202) 269-6672; www.pax-romana.org.

Philosophy Today, q; De Paul University, 2219 N. Kenmore Ave., Chicago, IL 60614-3504; (773) 325-7267; Philosophy Department.

PIME World, m (except July-Aug.); 17330 Quincy St., Detroit, MI 48221; (313) 342-4066; www.pimeysa.org; PIME Missionaries.

Poverello, The, 10 times a year; 6832 Convent Blvd., Sylvania, OH 43560; (419) 824-3627; www.sistersosf; Sisters of St. Francis of Sylvania.

Prayers for Worship, q; P.O. Box 510817, New Berlin, WI 532151-0817; (800) 950-9952; www.execpc.com/~lpi.

Preach: Enlivening the Pastoral Art, 6 times a year, 3708 River Rd., Ste. 400, Franklin Park, IL 60131; (800) 566-6150; www.wlpmusic.com; published by World Library Publications.

Priest, The, m; 200 Noll Plaza, Huntington, IN 46750; (260) 356-8400; www.osv.com; Our Sunday Visitor, Inc.

Proceedings, a; Fordham University, Adm. Bldg., Bronx, NY 10458; (718) 817-4081; www.acpa-main.org; Journal of the American Catholic Philosophical Association.

Promise, 32 times a year; 2621 Dryden Rd., Suite 300, Dayton, OH 45439; (937) 293-1415; www.pflaum.com.

Queen of All Hearts, bm; 26 S. Saxon Ave., Bay Shore, NY 11706; (631) 665-0726; www.montfortmissionaries.com; Montfort Missionaries.

Reign of the Sacred Heart, q; 6889 S. Lovers Lane, Hales Corners, WI 53130; (414) 425-3383; www.poshusa.org.

Religion Teacher's Journal, m (Sept.-May); P.O. Box 180, Mystic, CT 06355; (860) 536-2611; www.twentythirdpublications.com.

Religious Life, bm., P.O. Box 410007, Chicago, IL 60641; (773) 267-1195; www.religiouslife.com.

Renascence, q; P.O. Box 1881, Marquette University, Milwaukee, WI 53201-1881; (414) 288-6725.

Report on U.S. Catholic Overseas Mission, bi-annually; 3029 Fourth St. N.E., Washington, DC 20017; (202) 832-3112; www.catholicmission.org; United States Catholic Mission Association.

Response: Directory of Volunteer Opportunities, a; 6930 Carroll Ave., Suite 506, Takoma Park, MD 20912; (301) 270-0900; www.cnvs.org; Catholic Network of Volunteer Service.

Review for Religious, bm; Room 428, 3601 Lindell Blvd., St. Louis, MO 63108; (314) 977-7363; www.reviewforreligious.org.

Review of Politics, q; Box B, Notre Dame, IN 46556; (574) 631-6623; www.nd.edu/~rop.

Review of Social Economy, q; Marquette University, Milwaukee, WI 53233; (414) 288-5438; Association for Social Economics.

Revista Maryknoll (Spanish-English), m; Maryknoll, NY 10545; (914) 941-7590; www.maryknoll.org; Catholic Foreign Mission Society of America.

RITE, 8 times a year; 1800 North Hermitage Ave., Chicago, IL 60622-1101; (773) 486-8970; www.ltp.org.

Roze Maryi (Polish), m; Eden Hill, Stockbridge, MA 01263; (413) 298-3691; www.marian.org; Marian Helpers Center.

Sacred Music, q; 134 Christendom Dr., c/o K. Poterack, Front Royal, VA 22630; (540) 636-2900.

St. Anthony Messenger, m; 28 W. Liberty St., Cincinnati, OH 45210-1298; (513) 241-5615; www.americancatholic.org; Franciscan Friars.

St. Augustine Catholic, bm (Sept-May); 11625 Old St. Augustine Rd., Jacksonville, FL 32258; (904) 262-3200; www.staugcatholic.org; St. Augustine diocese.

St. Joseph's Messenger and Advocate of the Blind, bi-annual; St. Joseph Home, 537 Pavonia Ave., Jersey City, NJ 07303; (201) 798-4141.

St. Paul's Family Magazine, q; 14780 W. 159th St., Olathe, KS 66062; (913) 780-0405.

Salesian Missions of St. John Bosco, q; 2 Lefevre Lane, New Rochelle, NY 10801-5710; (914) 633-8344; www.salesianmissions.org; Salesians of Don Bosco.

SALT/Sisters of Charity, BVM, q; 1100 Carmel Dr., Dubuque, IA 52001; (563) 588-2351; www.bvmcong.org.

Scalabrinians, q; 209 Flagg Pl., Staten Island, NY 10304; (718) 351-0257.

School Guide, a; 210 North Ave., New Rochelle, NY 10801; (914) 632-7771; www.schoolguides.com.

SCN Journey, bm; SCN Office of Communications, P.O. Box 9, Nazareth, KY 40048; (502) 348-1564; www.scnazarethky.org; Sisters of Charity of Nazareth.

Seeds, 32 times a year; 2621 Dryden Rd., Dayton, OH 45439; (937) 293-1415; www.pflaum.com.

Serenity, q; 601 Maiden Choice Lane, Baltimore, MD 21228; (410) 744-9367; Little Sisters of the Poor.

SerraUSA, The, bm; 65 E. Wacker Pl., #802, Chicago, IL 60601-7203; (312) 201-6549; www.serraus.org; Serra International.

Share Magazine, q; 10 W. 71st St., New York, NY 10023; (212) 877-3041; www.catholicdaughters.com; Catholic Daughters of the Americas.

Share the Word, bm; 3031 Fourth St. NE, Washington, DC 20017-1102; (202) 832-5022; www.sharetheword.net; Paulist Catholic Evangelization Association.

Silent Advocate, q; St. Rita School for the Deaf, 1720 Glendale-Milford Rd., Cincinnati, OH 45215; (513) 771-7600; www.srsdeaf.org.

Social Justice Review, bm; 3835 Westminster Pl., St. Louis, MO 63108-3409; (314) 371-1653; www.socialjusticereview.com; Catholic Central Union of America.

SOUL Magazine, bm; P.O. Box 976, Washington, NJ 07882; (908) 213-2223; www.bluearmy.com; The Blue Army of Our Lady of Fatima, USA, Inc.

Spirit, w; 1884 Randolph Ave., St. Paul, MN 55105; (612) 690-7012; www.goodgroundpress.com; for teens.

Spirit, bi-annually; Seton Hall University, South Orange, NJ 07079; (201) 761-9000.

Spirit & Life, bm; 800 N. Country Club Rd., Tucson, AZ 85716; (520) 325-6401; www.benedictinesisters.org; Benedictine Srs. of Perpetual Adoration.

Spiritual Life, q; 2131 Lincoln Rd. NE, Washington, DC 20002; (800) 832-8489; Discalced Carmelite Friars.

Star, 10 times a year; 22 W. Kiowa, Colorado Springs, CO 80903.

Studies in the Spirituality of Jesuits, 5 times a year; 3601 Lindell Blvd., St. Louis, MO 63108; (314) 977-7257.

Sunday by Sunday, w; 1884 Randolph Ave., St. Paul, MN 55105; (651) 690-7012; www.goodground-press.com.

Sword Magazine, 2 times a year; 2097 Town Hall Terrace, #3, Grand Island, NY 14072-1737; (716) 773-0992; Carmelite Fathers.

Take Out, 10 times a year; 200 Noll Plaza, Huntington, IN 46750; (260) 356-8400; www.osv.com; Our Sunday Visitor, Inc.

Theological Studies, q; Marquette University, 100 Coughlin Hall, Milwaukee, WI 53201-1881; (414) 288-3164; www.ts.mu.edu.

Theology Digest, q; P.O. Box 56907, St. Louis, MO 63156-0907; (314) 977-3410; St. Louis University.

This Rock Magazine, 10 times a year; 2020 Gillespie Way, El Cajon, CA 92020; (619) 387-7200; www.catholic.com; Catholic apologetics.

Thomist, The, q; 487 Michigan Ave. NE, Washington, DC 20017; (202) 529-5300; www.thomist.org; Dominican Fathers.

Today's Catholic Teacher, m (Sept.–April); 2621 Dryden Rd., Dayton, OH 45439; (937) 293-1415; www.catholicteacher.com.

Today's Liturgy, q; 5536 NE Hassalo, Portland, OR 97213; (800) 548-8749.

Today's Parish, m (Sept.-May); P.O. Box 180, Mystic, CT 06355; (860) 536-2611; www.twentythird-publications.com.

Together in the Word, bi-annual; Box 577, Techny, IL 60082-0577; (708) 272-2700; www.divineword.org; Chicago province, Society of Divine Word.

The Tower, w; The Catholic University of America, University Center, 127 Pryzbyla Center, Washington, DC 20064; (202) 319-5778.

Tracings, q; 5 Gamelin St., Holyoke, MA 01040; (413) 536-7511; www.sisofprov.org; Sisters of Providence.

Ultreya Magazine, bm; 4500 W. Davis St., P.O. Box 210226, Dallas, TX 75211; (214) 339-6321; Cursillo Movement.

L'Union (French and English), q; P.O. Box F, Woonsocket, RI 02895; (401) 769-0520.

Universitas, q; 221 N. Grand, Room 39, St. Louis, MO 63103; (314) 977-2537; www.slu.edu; St. Louis University.

U.S. Catholic, m; 205 W. Monroe St., Chicago, IL 60606; (312) 236-7782; www.uscatholic.org; Claretians.

Venture, 32 times during school year; 2621 Dryden Rd., Suite 300, Dayton, OH 45439; (937) 293-1415; www.pflaum.com; intermediate grades.

Vida Catolica, La, m.; 40 Green St., Lynn, MA 01902; (781) 586-0197; www.la-vida.org/catolica; Boston archdiocese Hispanic community.

Vincentian Heritage, twice a year; 2233 N. Kenmore Ave., Chicago, IL 60614; (773) 325-7348;

www.depaul.edu/~vstudies.

Vision, a, 205 W. Monroe St., Chicago, IL 60606; (312) 236-7782; www.visionguide.org; Claretian Publications in conjunction with National Religious Vocation Conference.

Vision, 3 times a year; 7202 Buchanan St., Landover Hills, MD 20784; (301) 577-1684; www.ncod.org; National Catholic Office for the Deaf.

Vision (Spanish-English), P.O. Box 28185, San Antonio, TX 78228; (210) 732-2156; www.maccsa.org; Mexican American Cultural Center.

Visions, 32 times during school year; 2621 Dryden Rd., Suite 300, Dayton, OH 45439; (937) 293-1415; www.pflaum.com; for students in grades 7-9.

Vocations and Prayer, q; 6635 Tobias Ave., Van Nuys, CA 91405; (818) 782-1765; www.rcj.org; Rogationist Fathers.

Voice Crying in the Wilderness, A, q; 4425 Schneider Rd., Filmore, NY 14735; (716) 567-4433; Most Holy Family Monastery.

Waif's Messenger, q; 1140 W. Jackson Blvd., Chicago, IL 60607; (312) 738-9522; Mission of Our Lady of Mercy.

Way of St. Francis, bm; 1500 34th Ave., Oakland, CA 94601; (916) 443-5717; www.sbfranciscans.org; Franciscan Friars of California, Inc.

Wheeling Jesuit University Chronicle, 3 times a year; 316 Washington Ave., Wheeling, WV 26003; (304) 243-2296.

Word Among Us, The, m; 9639 Dr. Perry Rd., No. 126N, Jamesville, MD 21754; (301) 831-1262; www.wau.org.

Word and Witness, P.O. Box 510817, New Berlin, WI, 53151-0817; (800) 950-9952; www.lpiresource-center.com.

World Lithuanian Catholic Directory, P.O. Box 1025, Humarock, MA 02407; (781) 834-4079.

Worship, bm; St. John's Abbey, Collegeville, MN 56321; (612) 363-3883.

Newsletters

ACT, 10 times a year; Box 925, Evansville, IN 47706-0925; (812) 962-5508; www.cfm.org; Christian Family Movement.

Action News, q; Pro-Life Action League, 6160 N. Cicero Ave., Chicago, IL 60646; (773) 777-2900; www.prolifeaction.org.

Annual Report, The, 2021 H St. NW, Washington, DC 20006; (202) 331-8542; Black and Indian Mission Office.

Archdiocesan Bulletin, bm; 827 N. Franklin St., Philadelphia, PA 19123; (215) 627-0143; Philadelphia archeparchy.

Baraga Bulletin, The, q; P.O. Box 550, Marquette, MI 49855; (906) 227-9117; www.dioceseofmar-quette.org; Bishop Baraga Association.

Bringing Home the Word, w; 28 W. Liberty St., Cincinnati, OH 45202; (513) 241-5615; www.ameri-cancatholic.org; lectionary-based resource from St. Anthony's Messenger Press.

Brothers' Voice, 5420 South Cornell Ave., #205, Chicago, IL 60615-5604; (773) 493-2306.

Called By Joy, three times a year; 4419 N. Hawthorne St., Spokane, WA 99205; (509) 327-4479;

Franciscan Monastery of St. Clare.

Campaign Update, bm; 1513 Sixteenth St. NW, Ste. 400, Washington, DC 20036; (202) 833-4999; www.cathcamp.org; Catholic Campaign for America.

Canticle, The, four times a year, 146 Hawthorne Rd., Pittsburgh, PA 15209; (412) 821-2200; www.millvale-franciscans.org; Sisters of St. Francis of Millvale.

Capuchin Chronicle, q.; P.O. Box 15099, Pittsburgh, PA 15237-0099; (412) 367-2222; www.capuchin.org.

CARA Report, The, bm; Georgetown University, Washington, DC 20057-1203; (202) 687-8080; www.cara.georgetown.edu; Center for Applied Research in the Apostolate.

Caring Community, The, m; 115 E. Armour Blvd., Kansas City, MO 64111; (816) 968-2278; www.ncrpub.com.

Catalyst, 10 times a year; 450 Seventh Ave., New York, NY, 10123; (212) 371-3191; www.catholicleague.org; Catholic League for Civil and Religious Rights.

Catechist's Connection, The, 10 times a year; 115 E. Armour Blvd., Kansas City, MO 64111; (816) 968-2278; www.ncrpub.com.

Catholic Communicator, The, q; 120 East Colonial Hgwy., Hamilton, VA 20158-9012; (540) 338-2700; Catholic Distance University Newsletter.

Catholic Trends, bw; 3211 Fourth St. NE, Washington, DC 20017; (202) 541-3290; Catholic News Service.

Catholic Update, m; 28 W. Liberty St., Cincinnati, OH 45202-6498; (513) 241-5615; www.americancatholic.org.

CCHD News, q; 3211 Fourth St. NE, Washington, DC 20017-1194; (202) 541-3210; www.povertyusa.org; Catholic Campaign for Human Development.

Celebration, Sisters of Charity of Seaton Hill, q; DePaul Center, 463 Mount Thor Rd., Greensburg, PA 15601; (724) 836-0406; www.scsh.org.

C.F.C. Newsletter, 5 times a year; 145 Huguenot Ave., Suite 402, New Rochelle, NY 10801; (914) 712-7580; Christian Brothers.

Christ the King Seminary Newsletter, 3 times a year; 711 Knox Rd., Box 607, E. Aurora, NY 14052; (716) 652-8900.

Christian Response Newsletter, P.O. Box 125, Staples, MN 56479-0125; (218) 894-1165.

Christopher News Notes, 10 times a year; 12 E. 48th St., New York, NY 10017; (212) 759-4050; www.christophers.org; The Christophers.

Clarion, The, 5 times a year; Box 159, Alfred, ME 04002-0159; (207) 324-0067; Brothers of Christian Instruction.

CMSM Bulletin, m; 8808 Cameron St., Silver Spring, MD 20910; (301) 588-4030; www.cmsm.org.

Comboni Mission Newsletter, q; 1318 Nagel Rd., Cincinnati, OH 45255-3194; (513) 474-4997; www.combonimissionaries.org.

Connections, five times a year, 610 W. Elm, Monroe, MI 48161; (734) 240-9745; IHM Sisters.

Context, 22 issues a year; 205 W. Monroe St., Chicago, IL 60606; (312) 236-7782; www.contexton-line.org; Claretians.

CPN Newsletter, twice a month; 1318 Nagel Rd., Cincinnati, OH, 45255-3120; (513) 474-4997; www.combonimissionaries.org.

Cross and Feathers (Tekakwitha Conference Newsletter), q; P.O. Box 6768, Great Falls, MT 59406; (406) 727-0147; www.tekconf.org; Tekakwitha Conference.

Crossroads, 8 times a year; 1118 Pendleton St., #300, Cincinnati, OH 45202; (888) 714-6631; www.ccmanet.org;

Catholic Campus Ministry Association.

CRUX of the News, w; P.O. Box 758, Latham, NY 12110-0758; (518) 783-0058.

Cycles of Faith, P.O. Box 510817, New Berlin, WI 53201; (800) 950-9952; www.lpiresourcecenter.com.

Damien-Dutton Call, q; 616 Bedford Ave., Bellmore, NY 11710.

Dimensions, m; 86 Front St., Hempstead, NY 11550; (516) 481-6000; www.ncdc.org; National Catholic Development Conference.

Diocesan Dialogue, two times a year; 16565 South State St., South Holland, IL 60473; (708) 331-5485; www.acpress.org.

Diocesan Newsletter, The, m; P.O. Box 2147, Harlingen, TX 78551; (956) 421-4111; www.cdob.org; Brownsville diocese.

Environment and Art Letter, m; 1800 N. Hermitage Ave., Chicago, IL 60622-1101; (773) 486-8970; www.ltp.org; Liturgy Training Publications.

E-Proclaim, 10 times a year; 3211 Fourth St., NE, Washington, DC, 20017-1194; (202) 541-3204; www.usccb.org/ccc.

Ethics and Medics, m; 6399 Drexel Rd., Philadelphia, PA 19151; (215) 877-2660; www.ncb-center.org; National Catholic Bioethics Center.

Eucharistic Minister, m; 115 E. Armour, Kansas City, MO 64111; (816) 968-2278; www.ncrpub.com.

Every Day Catholic, m; 28 W. Liberty St., Cincinnati, OH 45202-6498; (513) 241-5615; www.everydaycatholic.org; St. Anthony Messenger Press.

EWTN Family Newsletter, 13 times a year; 5817 Leeds Rd., Irondale, AL 35210; (205) 271-2900; www.ewtn.com; Eternal Word Television Network.

EWTN Monthly Programming Guide, 13 times a year for each satellite; 5817 Old Leeds Rd., Irondale, AL 35210; 205-271-2900; www.ewtn.com; EWTN Global Catholic Network, lists monthly programming and schedule for each satellite coverage area, including additional special end-of-year Christmas schedule.

Explorations, q; American Interfaith Institute, 321 Chestnut St., Philadelphia, PA, 19106; (215) 238-5345.

Faith Extra, 26 times a year; P.O. Box 10668, Erie, PA 16514; www.eriecd.org; diocese of Erie.

Family Connection, The, bm; 3753 MacBeth Dr., San Jose, CA 95127; (408) 258-8534.

Father Flood, q; P.O. Box 51087, New Berlin, WI 53151-0817; (800) 950-9952; www.lpireseourcecen-ter.com; Liturgical Publications.

Fellowship of Catholic Scholars Newsletter Quarterly, P.O. Box 495, Notre Dame, IN 46556; www.catholicscholars.org.

Fonda Tekakwitha News, P.O. Box 627, Fonda, NY 12068; (518) 853-3636; www.katerishrine.com; Order Minor Conventuals.

Food for the Poor, 3 times a year; 550 SW 12th Ave., Deerfield Beach, FL 33442; (954) 427-2222; www.foodforthepoor.org.

FOOTSTEPS: Walking with Edmund, q; 145 Huguenot Ave., Ste. 402; (914) 712-7580; Christian Brothers Foundation.

Forum Focus, q; P.O. Box 542, Hudson, WI 54016; (651) 276-1429; www.focusonfaith.org; The Wanderer Forum Foundation.

Foundations Newsletter for Newly Married Couples, bm; P.O. Box 1632, Portland, ME, 04104-1632; (207) 775-4757.

Franciscan Foundation for the Holy Land, three or four times a year; 910 Oakwood Trail, Indianapolis, IN 46260; (317) 726-1679; www.ffhl.org.

Franciscan World Care, q; P.O. Box 29034, Washington, DC 20017; (202) 832-1762; www.franciscanmissionservice.catholic.edu; Franciscan Mission Service.

Frontline Report, bm; 23 Bliss Ave., Tenafly, NJ 07670; (201) 567-0450; www.smafathers.org; Society of African Missions.

Graymoor Today, m; P.O. Box 301, Garrison, NY 10524-0301; (845) 424-3671; www.atonementfriars.org.

Harmony, 3 times a year; 800 N. Country Club Rd., Tucson, AZ 85716; (520) 325-6401; Benedictine Srs. of Perpetual Adoration.

Healing & Hope, 9480 North De Mazenod Dr., Belleville, IL 62223-1160; (618) 398-4848; www.snows.org.

Heart Beats, 169 Cummins Hwy., Roslindale, MA 02131; (617) 325-3322.

Heart to Heart, twice a year; St. Vincent Archabbey, 300 Fraser Purchase Rd., Latrobe, PA 15650; (724) 805-2601; www.stvincentstore.com; Benedictines of St. Vincent Archabbey.

HLI Reports, m; 4 Family Life, Front Royal, VA 22630; Human Life International.

HN People, bm; 158 W. 27th St., New York, NY 10001; (212) 924-1451; www.hnp.org/publications; Franciscans of Holy Name Province.

HNP Today, w; 158 W. 27th St., New York, NY 10001; (212) 924-1451; www.hnp.org/publications; Franciscans of Holy Name Province.

ICSC Commitment, 1275 K St. NW, Suite 980, Washington, DC 20005-4006; (202) 289-1093; www.catholicstewardship.org.

Immaculate Heart of Mary Shrine Bulletin, 3 times a year; Mountain View Rd., P.O. Box 976, Washington, NJ 07882-0976; (908) 689-1700; www.ewtn.com/bluearmy.

Initiatives, bm; P.O. Box 291102, Chicago, IL 60629; (773) 776-9036; www.centerforlaity.org; National Center for the Laity.

Interchange, Assisi Heights, 1001 14 St., NW, #100, Rochester, MN 55901-2525; (507) 529-3523; www.rochesterfranciscan.org; Rochester Franciscan Sisters.

It's Our World, 4 times during school year; 366 Fifth Ave., New York, NY 10001; (212) 563-8700; www.holychildhoodusa.org; Young Catholics in Mission.

Journey, The, q; 210 W. 31st St., New York, NY 10001-2876; (212) 714-0950; www.capuchin.org; Province of St. Mary of Capuchin Order.

Joyful Noiseletter, The, m; P.O. Box 895, Portage, MI 49081-0895; (616) 324-0990; www.joyfulnoiseletter.com; Fellowship of Merry Christians.

Jubilee, q; 3900 Harewood Rd., NE, Washington, DC 20017; (202) 635-5400; www.jp2cc.org; John Paul II Cultural Center.

Knightline, 18 times a year; 1 Columbus Plaza, New Haven, CT 06510-3326; (203) 772-2130; www.kofc.org; Knights of Columbus Supreme Council.

Laity and Family Life Updates, bm; 20 Archbishop May Dr., St. Louis, MO, 63119; (314) 792-7173; www.stlcatholics.org.

Land of Cotton, q; 2048 W. Fairview Ave., Montgomery, AL 39196; (205) 265-6791; City of St. Jude.

Law Reports, q; 4455 Woodson Rd., St. Louis, MO 63134; (314) 427-2500; Catholic Health Association.

LCWR Update, m; 8808 Cameron St., Silver Spring, MD 20910; (301) 588-4955; www.lcwr.org; Leadership Conference of Women Religious.

Legatus, m; P.O. Box 511, Ann Arbor, MI 48106; (734) 930-3854; www.legatus.org; Legatus.

Let's Talk! (English edition), **Hablemos!** (Spanish edition), bm; 3031 Fourth St. NE, Washington, DC 20017-1102; (202) 832-5022; www.prisonministry.org; prison ministries of Paulist National Catholic Evangelization Assn.

Letter to the Seven Churches, bm; 1516 Jerome St., Lansing, MI 48912; (517) 372-6222; Catholic Charismatics.

Life at Risk, 10 times a year; 3211 Fourth St. NE, Washington, DC 20017; (202) 541-3070; Pro-Life Activities Committee, USCCB.

Life Insight, m; 3211 Fourth St. NE, Washington, DC 20017; (202) 541-3070; Committee for Pro-Life Activities, USCCB.

Liturgical Images, m; P.O. Box 2225, Hickory, NC 28603; (828) 327-3225.

Loyola World, 22 times a year; 820 North Michigan Ave., Chicago, IL, 60611; (312) 915-6157; www.luc.edu.

Magnificat, three times a year; Star Route 1, Box 226, Eagle Harbor, MI, 49950; (906) 289-4388 (fax); www.societystjohn.com.

Malvern Retreat House, q; P.O. Box 315, Malvern, PA 19355-0315; (610) 644-0400; www.malvernretreat.org; Laymen's Retreat League.

Maronites Today, m; P.O. Box 1891, Austin, TX 78767-1891; (512) 458-3693; www.eparchyla.org; Eparchy of Our Lady of Los Angeles.

Medical Mission Sisters News, q; 8400 Pine Rd., Philadelphia, PA 19111; (215) 742-6100; www.medicalmissionsisters.org.

Messenger of St. Joseph's Union, The, 3 times a year; 108 Bedell St., Staten Island, NY 10309; (718) 984-9296.

Mission, The, three times a year; 90 Cherry Lane, Hicksville, NY 11801-6299; (516) 733-7042; www.catholiccharities.cc; Catholic Charities.

Mission Messenger, The, q; P.O. Box 610, Thoreau, NM, 87323; (505) 862-7847; www.stbonaventuremission.org; St. Bonaventure Indian Mission and School.

Missionaries of Africa Report, q; 1624 21st St. NW, Washington, DC 20009; (202) 232-5154; Society of Missionaries of Africa (White Fathers).

Mission Update, bm; 3029 Fourth St. NE, Washington, DC 20017; (202) 832-3112; www.uscatholicmission.org.

Mountain View, q.; 8501 Bailey Rd., Darien, IL 60561; (630) 969-5050; Lay Carmelite Headquarters.

National Holy Name Newsletter, bm; 53 Laux St., Buffalo, NY 14206-2218; (716) 847-6419; www.members.aol.com/nahns.

NCPD National Update, q; 415 Michigan Ave. NE, #240, Washington, DC 20017; (202) 529-2933;

www.ncpd.org; National Catholic Office for Persons with Disabilities.

Neighbors, Committee on Home Missions, q.; 3211 Fourth St. NE, Washington, D.C. 20017; (202) 541-5400; Bishops' Committee on Home Missions.

News and Ideas, q.; 9480 North De Mazenod Dr., Belleville, IL 62223; (618) 398-4848; www.snows.org; Missionary Oblates of Mary Immaculate.

News and Views, q; 3900 Westminster Pl., St. Louis, MO 63108; (314) 533-0320; www.sacredheartprogram.org; Sacred Heart Program.

Newsletter of the Bureau of Catholic Indian Missions, 10 times a year; 2021 H St. NW, Washington, DC 20006; (202) 331-8542.

North Coast Catholic, bi-monthly; P.O. Box 1297, Santa Rosa, CA 95402; (707) 566-3302; www.santarosacatholic.org; Santa Rosa diocese.

Nuestra Parroquia (Spanish-English), m; 205 W. Monroe St., Chicago, IL 60606; (312) 236-7782; www.hmrc.claretianpubs.org; Claretians.

Oblates, six times a year; 9480 North De Mazenod Dr., Belleville, IL 62223-1160; (618) 398-4848; www.snows.org; Missionary Oblates of Mary Immaculate.

Origins, 48 times a year; 3211 Fourth St. NE, Washington, DC 20017; (202) 541-3284; Catholic News Service.

Overview, m; 205 W. Monroe St., 6th Floor, Chicago, IL 60606; (312) 609-8880; Thomas More Assn.

Paulist, Today, q; 415 W. 59th St., New York, NY 10019; (212) 265-3209; www.paulist.org.

Peace Times, 3-4 times a year; P.O. Box 248, Bellevue, WA 98009-0248; (425) 451-1770.

Pentecost Today, q; P.O. Box 628, Locust Grove, VA 22508-0628;   (540)   972-0628;   www.nscchariscenter.org.

Perspectives, q; 912 Market St., La Crosse, WI 54601; (608) 791-5289; www.fspa.org.

Pilgrim, The, q; 136 Shrine Rd., Auriesville, NY 12016; (518) 853-3033; Shrine of North American Martyrs.

Poverello, q; 220 37th St., Pittsburgh, PA 15201; (412) 682-1300; www.capuchin.com; Capuchin Franciscans.

Priests for Life, bm; P.O. Box 141172, Staten Island, NY 10314; (718) 980-4400; www.priestsforlife.org.

Proclaim, 10 times a year; 3211 Fourth St. NE, Washington, DC 20017-1194; (202) 541-3237; www.usccb.org.

Quarterly, The, q; 209 W. Fayette St., Baltimore, MD 21201; (410) 951-7455; www.catholicrelief.org; Catholic Relief Services.

Religious Life, m (bm, May-Aug.); P.O. Box 41007, Chicago, IL 60641; (312) 267-1195; www.ewtn.com/religious life; Institute on Religious Life.

RSCJ Newsletter, m; 1235 Otis St. NE, Washington, DC 20017-2516; (202) 526-6258; www.rscj.org; Religious of Sacred Heart.

St. Anthony's Newsletter, m; 103 St. Francis Blvd., Mt. St. Francis, IN 47146; (812) 923-5250; Conventual Franciscans.

St. Joseph's Parish Life Quarterly, q; 1382 Highland Ave., Needham, MA 02192; (617) 444-0245.

Sacred Ground, three times a year; 1 Elmwood Ave.,

Kansas City, KS 66103-3719; (913) 384-6500; www.cfcusa.org; Christian Foundation for Children and Aging.

San Francisco Charismatics, m; 2555 17th Ave., San Francisco, CA 94116; (415) 664-8481; www.sfspirit.com.

SCJ News, 9 times a year; P.O. Box 289, Hales Corners, WI 53130-0289; (414) 427-4266; Sacred Heart Fathers and Brothers.

SCRC Spirit, The, bm; 9795 Cabrini Dr., #105, Burbank, CA, 91504-1739; (818) 771-1361; www.scrc.org.

Spirit & The Bride, The, m; 8300 Morganford Rd., St. Louis, MO 63123; (314) 792-7070; www.stlcharismatic.org.

Spiritual Book Associates, 8 times a year; Notre Dame, IN 46556-0428; (219) 287-2838; www.spiritualbookassoc.org.

Squires Newsletter, m; One Columbus Plaza, New Haven, CT 06510-3326; (203) 752-4402; Columbian Squires.

SSpS Mission, q; P.O. Box 6026, Techny, IL 60082-6026; (847) 441-0126; Holy Spirit Missionary Sisters.

Tidings, Washington Theological Union, 3 times a year; 6896 Laurel St. NW, Washington, DC 20012; (202) 726-8800; www.wtu.edu.

Touchstone, q; NFPC Office, 1337 W. Ohio St., Chicago, IL 60622; (312) 226-3334; www.nfpc.org; National Federation of Priests' Councils.

Trinity Missions Report, q; 9001 New Hampshire Ave., Silver Spring, MD 20903; (301) 434-6761.

Triumph of the Past, m.; P.O. Box 29535, Columbus, OH 43229; (614) 261-1300.

Unda USA Newsletter, q; 901 Irving Ave., Dayton, OH 45409-2316; (937) 229-2303; www.undausa.org.

Vision: National Association of Catholic Chaplains, 10 times a year; P.O. Box 070473, Milwaukee, WI 53207-0473; (414) 483-4898; www.nacc.org.

Voices, 2 times a year; 1625 Rutherford Ln., Bldg. D, Austin, TX 78754-5105; (512) 339-7123; Volunteers for Educational and Social Services.

Voices in Mission and Ministry, q.; 1257 E. Siena Heights Dr., Adrian, MI 49221; (517) 266-3400; www.adriansisters.org; Adrian Dominicans.

Woodstock Report, q; Georgetown University, Box 571137, Washington, DC 20057; (202) 687-3532; www.georgetown.edu/centers/woodstock; Woodstock Theological Center.

Word One, 5 times a year; 205 W. Monroe St., Chicago, IL 60606; (312) 236-7782; www.wordone.org; Claretians.

Xaverian Missions Newsletter, bm; 101 Summer St., P.O. Box 5857, Holliston, MA 01746; (508) 429-2144; Xaverian Missionary Fathers.

Your Edmundite Missions Newsletter, bm; 1428 Broad St., Selma, AL 36701; (334) 872-2359; www.edmunditemissions.com; Southern Missions of Society of St. Edmund.

Youth Update, m; 28 W. Liberty St., Cincinnati, OH 45210; (513) 241-5615; www.americancatholic.org.

Zeal Newsletter, 3 times a year; P.O. Box 86, Allegany, NY 14706; (716) 373-1130; Franciscan Sisters of Allegany.

BOOKS

The Catholic Almanac, a; Our Sunday Visitor, Inc., 200 Noll Plaza, Huntington, IN 46750, editorial offices, 6105 Chapel Pines Run, Fort Wayne, IN 46804; (260) 444-4398; www.catholicalmanac.com; first edition, 1904.

The Official Catholic Directory, a; P.J. Kenedy & Sons in association with R.R. Bowker, a Reed Reference Publishing Company, 121 Chanlon Rd., New Providence, NJ 07974; (847) 966-8278; first edition, 1817.

BOOK CLUBS

Catholic Book Club (1928), 106 W. 56th St., New York, NY 10019; (212) 581-4640; www.americapress.org/cbc.htm; sponsors the Campion Award.

Catholic Digest Book Club (1954), 2115 Summit Ave., St. Paul, MN 55105-1081; (651) 962-6748.

Spiritual Book Associates (1934), Ave Maria Press Building, P.O. Box 428, Notre Dame, IN 46556; (219) 287-2838.

Thomas More Book Club (1939), Thomas More Association, 205 W. Monroe St., Sixth Floor, Chicago, IL 60606; (312) 609-8880.

GENERAL PUBLISHERS

(*Source:* Catholic Press Directory, Almanac *Survey*.)

Our Sunday Visitor Publishing: 200 Noll Plaza, Huntington IN 46750; (800) 348-2440, (260) 356-8400; e-mail: booksed@osv.com.

Abbey Press: One Caring Place, Saint Meinrad, IN 47577; (812) 357-8215; www.carenotes.com.

Abingdon Press: 201 8th Ave. South, Nashville, TN 37202; (615) 749-6347; www.abingdonpress.com.

ACTA Publications: 4848 N. Clark St., Chicago, IL 60640; (773) 271-1030; www.actapublications.com.

Alba House/St. Pauls: 2187 Victory Blvd., Staten Island, NY 10314; (718) 698-2759; www.alba-house.com

Alleluia Press: P.O. Box 103, Allendale, NJ 07401; (201) 327-3513.

American Catholic Press: 16565 South State St., South Holland, IL 60473; (708) 331-5485; www.acpress.org.

AMI Press, The Blue Army of Our Lady of Fatima: Mountain View Rd., Washington, NJ 07882; (908) 213-2223.

Ave Maria Press, Inc.: PO Box 428, Notre Dame IN 46556; (800) 282-1865, (219) 287-2831; e-mail: avemariapress.1@nd.edu.

Angelus Press: 2915 Forest Ave., Kansas City, MO 64109; (816) 753-3150; www.angeluspress.org.

Ave Maria Press: P.O. Box 428, Notre Dame, IN 46556; (219) 287-2831.

Cathedral Foundation Press: P.O. Box 777, Baltimore, MD 21203; (443) 263-0248; www.catholicfoundation.org.

Catholic News Service: 3211 Fourth St. NE, Washington DC 20017; (202) 541-3250; www.catholicnews.com.

Catholic Relief Services: 209 West Fayette St., Baltimore, MD 21201; (410) 625-2220.

Catholic University of America Press: 620 Michigan Ave. NE, Washington, DC 20064; (202) 319-5052; www.cuapress.cua.edu.

The Christophers: 12 East 48th St., New York, NY 10017; (212) 759-4050; www.christophers.org.

Claretian Publications: 205 West Monroe St.,

Chicago, IL 60606; (800) 328-6515, (312) 236-7782; e-mail: editors@uscatholic.org.

Clarity Publishing, Inc.: PO Box 758, Latham, NY 12110-3510; (518) 783-0058.

Doubleday: 1540 Broadway, New York, NY 10036; (212) 782-9392; www.randomhouse.com.

Eerdmans: 255 Jefferson Ave. SE, Grand Rapids, MI 49503; (616) 459-4591; www.eerdmans.com.

Emmaus Road: 827 N. Fourth St., Steubenville, OH 43952; (740) 283-2880.

Franciscan Mission Associates: PO Box 598, Mount Vernon, NY 10551-0598; (914) 664-5604.

Franciscan Press: Quincy University, 1800 College Ave., Quincy, IL 62301; (217) 228-5670; www.qufranciscanpress.com.

Georgetown University Press: 3240 Prospect St., NW, Washington, DC 20007; (202) 687-5889; www.press.georgetown.edu.

Ignatius Press: 2515 McAllister St., San Francisco, CA 94118; (415) 387-2324; www.ignatius.com.

Liguori Publications: One Liguori Dr., Liguori, MO 63057; (636) 464-2500.

Liturgical Press: St. John's Abbey, P.O. Box 7500, Collegeville, MN 56321; (320) 363-2213; www.litpress.org.

Loyola Press: 3441 North Ashland Avenue, Chicago, IL 60657; (800) 621-1008; www.loyolapress.org.

Marquette University Press: 1415 West Wisconisn Ave., Milwaukee, WI 53233; (414) 288-1564; www.marquette.edu/mupress/.

Missionary Oblates of Mary Immaculate: 9480 North De Mazenod Dr., Belleville, IL 62223-1160; (888) 330-6264; e-mail: mami@oblatesusa.org.

National Catholic Bioethics Center (NCBC): 159 Washington St., Boston, MA 02135; (617) 787-1900; e-mail: ChadM@ncbcenter.org.

Notre Dame Press, University of: 310 Flanner Hall, Notre Dame, IN 46556; (219) 631-6346; www.undpress.edu.

Orbis Books: P.O. Box 308, Maryknoll, NY 10545; (914) 941-7636; www.orbisbooks.com.

Pauline Books & Media: 50 St. Paul's Ave., Boston, MA 02130; (617) 522-8911; www.pauline.org.

Paulist National Catholic Evangelization Association: 3031 Fourth St. NE, Washington, DC 20017; (800) 237-5515, (202) 832-5022; e-mail: pncea@pncea.org.

Paulist Press: 997 Macarthur Blvd., Mahwah, NJ 07430; (201) 825-7300; www.paulistpress.com.

Pittsburgh Press, University of: 3400 Forbes Ave., 5th Floor Eureka, Pittsburgh, PA 15260; (412) 383-2456; www.pitt.edu/~press.

Pontifical Mission Societies in the United States: 366 Fifth Ave., New York, NY 10001; (800) 431-2222, (212) 563-8700; e-mail: propfaith@aol.com.

St. Anthony Messenger Press: 28 W Liberty St, Cincinnati, OH 45210; (513) 241-5615; www.americancatholic.org.

St. Joseph's University Press: 5600 City Ave., Philadelphia, PA 19131; (610) 660-3400; www.sju.edu/sjupress.

Scepter: P.O. Box 211, New York, NY 10018; (212) 354-0670; www.scepterpublishers.org.

Servant Publications: 1143 Highland Dr., Suite E, Ann Arbor, MI 48108; (734) 677-6490; www.servantpub.com.

Sophia Institute Press: Box 5284, Manchester, NH 03108; (603) 641-9344; www.sophiainstitute.com.

Twenty-Third Publications: P.O. Box 180, Mystic, CT 06355; (860) 437-3012; www.twentythirdpublications.com.

CANADIAN CATHOLIC PUBLICATIONS
(*Principal source*: 2007 Catholic Press Directory.)

Newspapers
Atlantic Catholic, The, bw; 88 College St., Antigonish, NS B2G 2L7; (902) 863-4370.

B. C. Catholic, The, w; 150 Robson St., Vancouver, BC V6B 2A7; (604) 683-0281; www.bcc.rcav.org.

Casket, The, w; 88 College St., Antigonish, NS B2G 2L7; (902) 863-4370.

Catholic New Times (national), bw; 80 Sackville St., Toronto, ON M5A 3E5; (416) 361-0761; www.catholicnewtimes.org.

Catholic Register, The (national), w; 1155 Younge St., Suite 401, Toronto, ON M4T 1W2; (416) 934-3410; www.catholicregister.org; lay edited.

Catholic Times, 10 times a year; 2005 St. Marc St., Montreal, QC H3H 2G8; (514) 937-2301.

Monitor, The, m; P.O. Box 986, St. John's, NF A1C 5M3; (709) 739-6553; www.stjohnsarchdiocese.nf.ca.

New Freeman, The, w; 1 Bayard Dr., St. John, NB E2L 3L5; (506) 653-6806.

Northwest Ontario Catholic, eight times a year, P.O. Box 10400, Thunder Bay, Ontario P7B 6T8; (807) 343-9313; www.dotb.ca.

Prairie Messenger, w; Box 190, Muenster, SK S0K 2Y0; (306) 682-1772; www.stpeters.sk.ca/prairie_messenger.

Restoration, 10 times a year; 2888 Dafoe Rd., Combemere, ON K0J 1L0; (613) 756-3713; www.madonnahouse.org.

St. Vladimir's College Gazette, q; Box 789, Roblin, MB, R0L 1PO; (204) 937-2173.

***Teviskes Ziburiai* (The Lights of the Homeland)** (Lithuanian), w; 2185 Stavebank Rd., Mississauga, ON L5C 1T3; (905) 275-4672.

Western Catholic Reporter, w.; 8421 101 Ave. NW, Edmonton, AB T6A 0L1; (780) 465-8030; www.wcr.ab.ca.

Magazines, Other Periodicals
L'Almanach Populaire Catholique, a; P.O. Box 1000, St. Anne de Beaupre, QC G0A3C0; (418) 827-4538.

ANNALS of St. Anne de Beaupre, The, m; Box 1000, Ste. Anne de Beaupre, QC G0A 3C0; (418) 827-4538; Basilica of St. Anne.

Apostolat, bm; 8844 Notre-Dame Est, Montréal, QC H1L 3M4; (514) 351-9310; Oblates of Mary Immaculate, CMO (*Centre Missionnaire Oblat*).

Bread of Life, The, bm; P.O. Box 395, Hamilton, ON L8N 3H8; (905) 529-4496; www.breadoflife.ca.

Canadian Catholic Review, The, St. Joseph's College, University of Alberta, Edmonton, AB T6G 2J5; (403) 492-7681.

Canadian League, The, q; 1-160 Murray Park Rd., Winnipeg, MB R3J 3X5; (204) 927-2310; www.cwl.ca; Catholic Women's League of Canada.

Caravan, q; 90 Parent Ave., Ottawa, ON K1N 7B1; (613) 241-9461; www.cccb.ca; Canadian Conference of Catholic Bishops.

Celebrate! (Novalis), bm; St. Paul University, 223 Main St., Ottawa, ON K1S 1C4; (780) 451-2228.

Companion Magazine, m; 695 Coxwell Ave., Suite 600, Toronto, ON M4C 5R6; (416) 690-5611;

www.franciscan.on.ca; Conventual Franciscan Fathers.

Compass—A Jesuit Journal, bm (Jan.-Nov.); Box 400, Stn. F, 50 Charles St. East, Toronto, ON M4Y 2L8; (416) 921-0653; www.io.org/ngvanv/compass/com-phome.html.

CRC Bulletin (French-English), q; 219 Argyle Ave., Ottawa, ON K2P 2H4; (613) 236-0824; www.crcn.ca; Canadian Religious Conference.

L'Église Canadienne (French), 11 times a year; 6255 rue Hutchison, Bureau 103, Montreal, QC H2V 4C7; (514) 278-3020; www.novalis.ca.

Fatima Crusader, q; P.O. Box 602, Fort Erie, ON L2A 4M7; (905) 871-7607; www.fatima.org.

Global Village Voice, The, q; 10 St. Mary St., Suite 420, Toronto, ON M4Y 1P9; (416) 922-1592; Canadian Organization for Development and Peace.

Kateri (English-French), q; P.O. Box 70, Kahnawake, QC J0L 1B0; (450) 638-1546.

Le Messager de Saint Antoine (French), 10 times a year; Lac-Bouchette, QC G0W 1V0; (418) 348-6344.

Messenger of the Sacred Heart, m; 661 Greenwood Ave., Toronto, ON M4J 4B3; (416) 466-1195; Apostleship of Prayer.

Mission Canada, q; 201-1155 Younge St., Toronto, ON M4T 1W2; (416) 934-3424; www.missioncanada.ca.

Missions Étrangères (French), bm; 180 Place Juge-Desnoyers, Laval, QC H7G 1A4; (450) 667-4190; www.smelaval.org.

Nouvel Informateur Catholiqué, Le, semi-monthly; 6550 Rte 125, Rawdon, QC J0K 1S0; (450) 834-8503.

Oratory, bm; 3800 Ch. Queen Mary, Montreal, QC H3V 1H6; (514) 733-8211; www.saint-joseph.org.

Our Family, m; P.O. Box 249, Battleford, SK; S0M 0E0; (306) 937-7771; www.ourfamilymagazine.com; Oblates of Mary Immaculate.

Prêtre et Pasteur (French), m; 4450 St. Hubert St., #500, Montreal, QC H2J 2W9; (514) 525-6210.

Prieres Missionaire, m; Missionaires de la Consolata, 2505 Boulevard Gouin ouest, Montréal, QC H3M 1B5; (514) 334-1910; www.consolata.org.

Relations (French), 10 times a year; 25 Rue Jarry Ouest, Montreal, QC H2P 1S6; (514) 387-2541.

Reveil Missionaire, bm; Missionaire de la Consolata, 2505 Boulevard Gouin ouest, Montréal, QC H3M 1B5; (514) 334-1910; www.consolata.org.

La Revue d'Sainte Anne de Beaupre (French), m; P.O. Box 1000, Ste. Anne de Beaupre, Québec G0A 3C0; (418) 827-4538.

Scarboro Missions, 9 times a year; 2685 Kingston Rd., Scarboro, ON M1M 1M4; (416) 261-7135; www.web.net/~sfms.

Spiritan Missionary News, q; 121 Victoria Park Ave., Toronto, ON M4E 3S2; (416) 698-2003; www.spiritans.com.

Unity, q; 308 Young St., Montréal, QC H3C 2G2; (514) 937-5973.

INTERNATIONAL CATHOLIC PERIODICALS
(*Principal source*: Catholic Almanac *survey. Included are English-language Catholic periodicals published outside the U.S.*)

African Ecclesial Review (AFER), bm; Gaba Publications, P.O. Box 4002, Eldoret, Kenya.

Australasian Catholic Record, q; 99 Albert Rd., Strathfield 2135, New South Wales, Australia.

Christ to the World, 5 times a year; Via di Propaganda 1-C, 00187, Rome, Italy.

Christian Orient, q; P.B. 1 Vadavathoor, Kottayam 686010, Kerala, India.

Doctrine and Life, m; Dominican Publications, 42 Parnell Sq., Dublin 1, Ireland.

Downside Review, q; Downside Abbey, Stratton on the Fosse, Bath, BA3 4RH, England.

East Asian Pastoral Review, q; East Asian Pastoral Institute, P.O. Box 221, U.P. Campus, 1101 Quezon City, Philippines.

Furrow, The, m; St. Patrick's College, Maynooth, Ireland.

Heythrop Journal, q; Heythrop College, Kensington Sq., London W8 5HQ, England (editorial office); published by Blackwell Publishers, 108 Cowley Rd., Oxford, OX4 1JF, England.

Holy Land Magazine, q; P.O. Box 186, 91001 Jerusalem, Israel; illustrated.

Irish Biblical Studies, The, q; Union Theological College, 108 Botanic Ave., Belfast BT7 1JT, N. Ireland.

Irish Journal of Sociology, The, a; St. Patrick's College, Maynooth, Ireland.

Irish Theological Quarterly, q; St. Patrick's College, Maynooth, Ireland.

L'Osservatore Romano, w; Vatican City. (*See above under* U.S. Newspapers.)

Louvain Studies, q; Peeters Publishers, Bondgenotenlaan 153, B-3000, Leuven, Belgium.

Lumen Vitae (French, with English summaries), q; International Center for Studies in Religious Education, 186, rue Washington, B-1050 Brussels, Belgium.

Mediaeval Studies, a; Pontifical Institute of Mediaeval Studies, 59 Queen's Park Crescent East, Toronto, ON M5S 2C4, Canada.

Month, m; 114 Mount St., London WIY 6AH, England.

Music and Liturgy, bm; The Editor, 33 Brockenhurst Rd., Addiscombe Croydan, Surrey CRO 7DR, England.

New Blackfriars, m; edited by English Dominicans, Blackfriars, Oxford OX1 3LY, England.

Omnis Terra (English Edition), m; Pontifical Missionary Union, Congregation for the Evangelization of Peoples, Via di Propaganda 1/c, 00187 Rome, Italy.

One in Christ, q; Edited at Turvey Abbey, Turvey, Bedfordshire MK43 8DE, England.

Priests & People (formerly **The Clergy Review**), 11 times a year; Blackfriars, Buckingham Rd., Cambridge CB3 0DD, England.

Recusant History, bi-annual; Catholic Record Society, 12 Melbourne Pl., Wolsingham, Durham DL13 3EH, England.

Religious Life Review, bm; Dominican Publications, 42 Parnell Sq., Dublin 1, Ireland.

Scripture in Church, q; Dominican Publications, 42 Parnell Sq., Dublin 1, Ireland.

Southwark Liturgy Bulletin, q; The Editor, 10 Claremont Rd., Maidstone, Kent ME14 5L2, England.

Spearhead, 5 times a year; Gaba Publications, P.O. Box 4002, Eldoret, Kenya.

Spirituality, bm; Dominican Publications, 42 Parnell Sq., Dublin 1, Ireland.

Tablet, The, w; 1 King St. Cloisters, Clifton Walk, London W60QZ, England; 44(1)-20-8748-8484.

Way, The, q; 114 Mount St., London W1Y6AN, England.

CATHOLIC NEWS AGENCIES

(*Sources: International Catholic Union of the Press, Geneva; Catholic Press Association, U.S.*)

Argentina: *Agencia Informativa Catolica Argentina* (AICA), av. Rivadavia, 413, 40 Casilla de Correo Central 2886, 1020 Buenos Aires.

Austria: *Katholische Presse-Agentur* (Kathpress), Singerstrasse 7/6/2, 1010 Vienna 1.

Belgium: *Centre d'Information de Presse* (CIP), 35 Chausée de Haecht, 1030 Brussels.

Bolivia: *Agencia Noticias Fides*, ANF, Casilla 5782, La Paz.

ERBOL, Casilla 5946, La Paz.

Chile: *Agencia informativa y de comunicaciones* (AIC Chile), Brasil 94, Santiago.

Croatia: *Christian Information Service*, Marulicev 14, PP 434, 410001 Zagreb.

Germany: *Katholische Nachrichten Agentur* (KNA), Adenauer Allee 134, 5300 Bonn 1.

Greece: *Agence TYPOS*, Rue Acharnon 246, Athens 815.

Hong Kong: *UCA-News*, P.O. Box 69626, Kwun Tong (Hong Kong).

Hungary: *Magyar Kurir*, Milkszath ter 1, 1088, Budapest.

India: *South Asian Religious News* (SAR-News), PB 6236, Mazagaon, Bombay 400 010.

Italy: *Servizio Informazioni Religiosa* (SIR), Via di Porta Cavalleggeri 143, I-00165 Roma.

Centrum Informationis Catolicae (CIC-Roma), via Delmonte de la Farina, 30/4, 00186 Roma.

Peru: ACI-PRENSA, A.P. 040062, Lima.

Switzerland: *Katholische Internationale Presse-Agentur* (KIPA), Case Postale 1054 CH 1701, Fribourg.

Centre International de Reportages et d'Information Culturelle (CIRIC), Chemin Clochetons 8, P.O. Box 1000, Lausanne.

United States of America: *Catholic News Service* (CNS), 3211 Fourth St. NE, Washington, DC 20017; (202) 541-3250; www.catholicnews.com.

U.S. PRESS SERVICES

Catholic News Service (CNS), established in 1920 (NC News Service), provides a worldwide daily news report by satellite throughout the U.S. and Canada and by wire and computer links into several foreign countries, and by mail to other clients, serving Catholic periodicals and broadcasters including Vatican Radio in about 40 countries. CNS also provides feature and photo services and a weekly religious education package, "Faith Alive!" It publishes "Origins," a weekly documentary service, and *Catholic Trends*, a fortnightly newsletter, the weekly *TV and Movie Guide* and *Movie Guide Monthly*. CNS maintains a full-time bureau in Rome. It is a division of the United States Catholic Conference, with offices at 3211 Fourth St. NE, Washington, DC 20017; (202) 541-3250; www.catholicnews.com.

EWTNews, 5817 Old Leeds Rd., Irondale, AL 35210; 205-271-2900; www.ewtn.com. Exclusive interviews, investigative reports, live coverage of special events and cultural reporting weekly on the *World Over Live* newsmagazine. Daily coverage of world news from a Catholic perspective.

Spanish-Language Service: A weekly news summary provided by Catholic News Service, used by a number of Catholic newspapers. Some papers carry features of their own in Spanish.

Religion News Service (RNS) provides coverage of all

religions as well as ethics, spirituality and moral issues. Founded in 1934 (as the Religious News Service) by the National Conference of Christian and Jews as an independent agency, RNS became an editorially independent subsidiary of the United Methodist Reporter, an interfaith publishing company, in 1983. It was acquired by Newhouse News Service in 1994. Address: 1101 Connecticut Ave. NW, Suite 350, Washington, DC 20036.

RADIO, TELEVISION, THEATER

(The following listings are as of June 1, 2008. Sources, Catholic Almanac survey. Telephone and web addresses are listed as available.)

Radio
Catholic Radio Association: an association comprised primarily of the majority of Catholic radio stations in the United States and Catholic program providers united to advance the apostolate of Catholic radio. The Mission Statement states: "The Catholic Radio Association seeks to bring together Catholic radio apostolates, program providers and the hierarchy of the Catholic Church in order that this means of social communication be used effectively and in obedience to the decrees of the Second Vatican Council and the magisterium of the Church, especially as expressed in the words of Pope John Paul II." The Catholic Radio Association, 121 Broad StreetCharleston, SC 29401; (843) 853-2300; www.catholicradioassociation.org.

Ave Maria Radio: Ave Maria Radio employs radio, internet and other media to offer news, analysis, teaching, devotions and music. Programs include Teresa Tomeo and Al Kresta. Ave Maria Radio, P.O. Box 504, Ann Arbor, MI 48106; (734) 930-5200; www.avemariaradio.com.

Catholic Answers Radio: Produced by Catholic Answers; programming includes "Catholic Answers Live" is a two hour, daily, call–in radio program, hosted by Jerry Usher. Catholic Answers, 2020 Gillespie Way, El Cajon, CA 92020 USAMain: 619-387-7200; www.catholic.com.

EWTN Global Catholic Radio Network (formerly known as WEWN), 5817 Old Leeds Road, Irondale, AL 35210; 205-271-2900; www.ewtn.com; the first 24-hour U.S. Catholic radio network, launched in 1996.

Relevant Radio: Relevant Radio exists to assist the Church in the New Evangelization by providing relevant programming through a media platform to help people bridge the gap between faith and everyday life. Programming includes "Searching the Word," "The Drew Mariani Show," and "On Call with Dr. Ray." Relevant Radio PO Box 10707, Green Bay, WI 54307-0707; (920) 884-1460; www.relevantradio.com.

Vatican Radio: See under Vatican City State.

Stations and Programs
Catholic Views Broadcasts, Inc.: 10 Audrey Place, Fairfield, NJ 07004; (973) 882-8700. Produces weekly 15-minute program "Views of the News." Also operates Catholic community TV stations in Chicago and Minneapolis.

Christopher Radio Program: 14-minute interview series, "Christopher Closeup" weekly and "Christopher Minutes" daily, on 400 stations. 12 E. 48th St., New York, NY 10017; (212) 759-4050; www.christophers.org.

Father Justin Rosary Hour: P.O. Box 454, Athol Springs, NY 14010; (716) 627-3861; www.franciszkanie.com/rosary.hour. Founded in 1931. Polish Catechetical Radio Network. Rev. Marion M. Tolczyk, O.F.M. Conv., director.

Journeys Thru Rock: Produced in cooperation with the Department of Communication, USCCB. A 15-minute weekly program currently employing a youth-oriented music and commentary format (ABC).

KVSS Radio: A Catholic radio station broadcasting throughout the Omaha Archdiocese. Founded in 1999 to employ broadcast media to transmit the Gospel of Jesus Christ with the fullness of the living Tradition as preserved, revered and proclaimed by the Catholic Church for 2000 years. Programming includes Spirit Morning Show and Loving Life. 5829 N. 60th Street, Omaha, NE 68104; (402) 571-0200; www.kvss.com

Radio Maria (Italian): Italian Catholic radio station founded in 1992. 352 W. 44th St., New York, NY 10036. Rev. Mariano Cisco, C.S., executive director.

Redeemer Radio: A Catholic radio station broadcasting throughout northern Indiana and parts of Ohio; its mission is to (a) to evangelize, educate, and inspire both Catholics and non-Catholics to draw closer to Jesus Christ through His Church—and (b) to serve the Catholic community. Redeemer Radio, 4705 Illinois Rd., Suite 104, Fort Wayne, IN 46804; (260) 436- 9598; www.redeemerradio.com.

Sirius Satellite Radio: Offers the Catholic Channel through the Archdiocese of New York; programs include, "Busted Halo with Father Dave Dwyer," "The Catholic Guy with Lino Rulli," "Speak Now... with Dave and Susan Konig," and "Across the Nation with Bob Dunning."

Television and Communications Services
Catholic Familyland: A ministry of the Apostolate for Family Consecration. Established in 1975, FL-TV produces television and video programs and operates in Asia, Latin America, Europe and Africa. Familyland Television Network, 3375 County Rd. 36, Bloomingdale, OH 43910; (740) 765-5500; www.familyland.org.

Catholic Academy for Communication Arts Professionals: The U.S. affiliate of SIGNIS, a Vatican-approved organization for Catholic communication professionals; membership is open to those professionally involved in Catholic church-related communications and to Catholic communicators working in secular organizations. President: Frank Morock, Catholic Academy for Communication Arts Professionals, Irving Ave., Dayton, OH 45409-2316; (937) 229-2303; www.catholicacademy.org.

Catholic Communication Campaign (CCC): A U.S. Catholic bishops' program that produces, distributes and supports Catholic media projects, including a weekly television talk show, "Personally Speaking," television documentaries and public service messages. Ellen McCloskey, 3211 4th St. NE, Washington, DC 20017; (202) 541-3204; www.usccb.org/ccc.

Catholic Communications Foundation (CCF): A foundation established by the Catholic Fraternal Benefit Societies in 1966 to lend support and assistance to development of the communications apostolate of the Church. The CCF promotes diocesan communications capabilities and funds a scholarship program at the Annual Institute for Religious Communications. 303 W. Lancaster Ave., PMB 333, Wayne, PA 19087.

Christopher TV Series, "Christopher Closeup": Originated in 1952. Half-hour interviews, weekly, on commercial TV and numerous cable outlets. 12 E. 48th St., New

York, NY 10017; (212) 759-4050; www.christophers.org.

Clemons Productions, Inc.: Produces "That's the Spirit," a family show for television; "Thoughts for the Week," on the ABC Satellite Network, and "Spirituality for Today" on the internet. Available to dioceses, organizations or channels. P.O. Box 7466, Greenwich, CT 06830; www.spirituality.org.

EWTN Global Catholic Network (EWTN): 5817 Old Leeds Rd., Irondale, AL 35210; 205-271-2900; www.ewtn.com. America's largest religious cable network, features 24 hours of spiritual growth programming for the entire family. Offers documentaries, weekly teaching series and talk shows, including the award-winning "Mother Angelica Live." Nightly live programs include "The Journey Home," "Threshold of Hope," "EWTN Live," "Life on the Rock" and "The World Over." Daily live radio programming includes the popular call-in shows, Open Line. Also features live Church events from around the world and devotional programs such as "The Holy Rosary." Mother M. Angelica, P.C.P.A., Foundress.

Family Theater Productions: Founded by Father Patrick Peyton, C.S.C. Videocassettes, films for TV. 7201 Sunset Blvd., Hollywood, CA 90046; (323) 874-6633; www.familytheater.org. Nat. Dir., Rev. Wilfred J. Raymond, C.S.C.

Franciscan Communications: Producer of video and print resources for pastoral ministry; St. Anthony Messenger Press, 28 W. Liberty St., Cincinnati, OH 45210; (513) 241-5615; www.AmericanCatholic.org.

Hispanic Telecommunications Network, Inc. (HTN): Produces "Nuestra Familia," a national weekly Spanish-language TV series; 1405 N. Main, Suite 240, San Antonio, TX 78212.

Mary Productions: Originated in 1950. Offers royalty-free scripts for stage, film, radio and tape production. Audio and video tapes of lives of the saints and historical characters. Traveling theater company; Mary Productions, 212 Oakdale Dr., Tomaso Plaza, Middletown, NJ 07748; (732) 617-8144.

National Interfaith Cable Coalition: A 28-member consortium representing 64 faith groups from Roman Catholic, Jewish, Protestant and Eastern Orthodox traditions; works with faith groups to present programming on the Faith and Values Media; 74 Trinity Place, Suite 1550, New York, NY 10006; (212) 406-4121; www.faithandvalues.com.

Oblate Media and Communication Corporation: Producers, Broadcast syndicators and distributors of Catholic and value-centered video programming. 7315 Manchester Rd., St. Louis, MO 63143.

Passionist Communications, Inc.: Presents Sunday Mass on TV seen in U.S. and available to dioceses and channels; publishes "TV Prayer Guide," semi-annually. P.O. Box 440, Pelham, NY 10803-0440.

Paulist Media Works: Full service audio production in syndication to dioceses, religious communities and church groups; 3055 4th St. NE, Washington, DC 20017; (202) 269-6064. Pres., Sue Donovan.

Paulist Productions: Producers and distributors of the INSIGHT Film Series (available for TV) and educational film series. 17575 Pacific Coast Hwy., Pacific Palisades, CA 90272; (310) 454-0688; www.paulistproductions.org.

Sacred Heart Program, Inc.: Produces and distributes free of charge the weekly "CONTACT" program in 30-, 15-, and 5-minute formats to more than 300 stations in North America; 3900 Westminster Pl., St. Louis, MO 63108; (341) 533-0320; www.sacredheartprogram.org/www.contactradio.org.

SIGNIS (World Catholic Association for Communication): A Vatican approved non-governmental organization that includes members from 140 countries and brings together radio, television, cinema, video, media education, Internet, and new technology professionals. SIGNIS was established in November 2001 from the merger between Unda (for radio and television) and OCIC (for cinema and audiovisual); both had been created in 1928. Its varied initiatives cover fields such as the promotion of films or television programs (including juries at festivals such as Cannes, Berlin, Monte Carlo, Venice, etc.), the creation of radio, video, and television studios, production and distribution of programs, training professionals in the field, and supplying specialized equipment. General Secretariat, 15, rue du Saphir, 1030 Brussels, Belgium; 00 32 (0)2 7349708; www.signis.net/.

Telecare: non-profit, state-of-the-art television and production facility of the Diocese of Rockville Centre. Broadcasts seven days a week to almost a million homes served by Cablevision, Telecare works through a partnership with WLNY/Channel 55. Programming includes the popular God Squad program that reaches 12 million viewers in New York, New Jersey and Connecticut every weekday. Rev. Msgr. Thomas Hartman, Director. 1200 Glen Curtiss Blvd., Uniondale, 11553; (516) 538-4108; www.telecaretv.org.

Theater

Catholic Actors' Guild of America, Inc.: Established in 1914 to provide material and spiritual assistance to people in the theater. Has more than 500 members; publishes *The Call Board*. 1501 Broadway, Suite 510, New York, NY 10036; (212) 398-1868 (fax).

FILM

Best Films of 2007

(Courtesy, U.S. Bishops' Office of Film and Broadcasting, OFB). The U.S. Bishops' Office of Film and Broadcasting (OFB) announced its 2007 Ten Best Films List.

The following are the best films, in alphabetical order: *Amazing Grace; Bella/Juno; Beyond the Gates; Into Great Silence; The Kite Runner; Lars and the Real Girl; The Lives of Others; The Namesake; The Rape of Europa; Ratatouille.*

The top 10 best family films of 2007, in alphabetical order: *Arctic Tale; Bee Movie; Bridge to Terabithia; Enchanted; Evan Almighty; Fred Claus; Mr. Bean's Holiday; Martian Child; Shrek the Third; Underdog.*

The following films received honorable mention honors, in alphabetical order: *Away From Her; The Death of Mr. Lazarescu; December Boys; The Diving Bell and the Butterfly; The Great Debaters; Once; Rescue Dawn; Reservation Road; Resurrecting the Champ; Things We Lost in the Fire.*

The Office for Film and Broadcasting (OFB) has the responsibility of reviewing and rating theatrical motion pictures, previewing and evaluating television programming, and providing the Catholic public with information about the role of the entertainment and news media in influencing societal and personal values. The Office is supported by the U.S. Bishops' Catholic Communication Campaign (CCC). Weekly movie reviews, brief capsules, and film classifications of new film releases can be heard on the office's toll-free movieline at 1-800-311-4222, sponsored by the CCC. Movie reviews are available online at www.usccb.org/movies.

Vatican List of the Greatest Films of the 20th Century

On the occasion of the 100th anniversary of cinema in 1995, the Vatican compiled this list of "great films." The 45 movies are divided into three categories: "Religion," "Values," and "Art."

Religion

"Andrei Rublev" (1969); "Babette's Feast" (1988); "Ben-Hur" (1959); "The Flowers of St. Francis" (1950); "Francesco" (1989); "The Gospel According to St. Matthew" (1966); "La Passion de Notre Seigneur Jesus-Christ" (1905); "A Man for All Seasons" (1966); "The Mission" (1986); "Monsieur Vincent" (1947); "Nazarin" (1958); "Ordet" (1954); "The Passion of Joan of Arc" (1928); "The Sacrifice" (1986); "Thérèse" (1986).

Values

"Au Revoir les Enfants" (1988); "The Bicycle Thief" (1949); "The Burmese Harp" (1956); "Chariots of Fire" (1981); "Decalogue" (1988); "Dersu Uzala" (1978); "Gandhi" (1982); "Intolerance" (1916); "It's a Wonderful Life" (1946); "On the Waterfront" (1954); "Open City" (1945); "Schindler's List" (1993); "The Seventh Seal" (1956); "The Tree of Wooden Clogs" (1978); "Wild Strawberries" (1958).

Art

"Citizen Kane" (1941); "8-1/2" (1963); "Fantasia" (1940); "Grand Illusion" (1937); "La Strada" (1956); "The Lavender Hill Mob" (1951); "The Leopard" (1963); "Little Women" (1933); "Metropolis" (1926); "Modern Times" (1936); "Napoleon" (1927); "Nosferatu" (1922); "Stagecoach" (1939); "2001: A Space Odyssey" (1968); "The Wizard of Oz" (1939).

CATHOLIC INTERNET SITES

Web site addresses change periodically. Find this list online at www.CatholicAlmanac.com. Visit Our Sunday Visitor's web site at www.osv.com.

Holy See Sites
Vatican: www.vatican.va
L'Osservatore Romano: www.vatican.va/news_services/or/or_eng/index.html
Vatican Radio: www.vatican.va/news_services/radio

Catholic Megasites, Directories and Links
Catholic Almanac: www.CatholicAlmanac.com
Catholic Canada: www.catholicanada.com
Catholic Community Forum: www:catholic-forum.com
Catholic Goldmine!: www.catholicgoldmine.com
Catholic Hotlinks: www.cathinsight.com
Catholic Information Center on the Internet: www.catholic.net
Catholic Information Network: www.cin.org
Catholic Internet Directory: www.catholic-church.org
Catholic Internet Yellow Pages: www.monksofadoration.org/directory.html
Catholic Kiosk: www.aquinas-multimedia.com/arch
Catholic.Net Periodicals: www.catholic.net/RCC/Periodicals
Catholic Pages: www.catholic-pages.com
Catholic Press Association: www.catholicpress.org
Catholicity Internet Directory: www.catholicity.com
Catholic Exchange: www.catholicexchange.com
Ecclesia Web Service for Catholics: www.catholicchurch.org
El Directorio Catolico en Internet: www.iglesia.org
New Advent: www.newadvent.org
Our Sunday Visitor: www.OSV.com
PetersNet: www.catholicculture.org
RCNet: www.rc.net
St. Jane's: www.stjane.org
The Internet Padre: www.internetpadre.com
Theology Library Search Engines: www.shc.edu/theolibrary/engines.htm

Catholic Internet Service Providers

Catholic Families Network: www.catholicfamilies.net
Catholic Online: www.catholiconline.com
FamiLink (ISP for the family): www.familink.com

Catholic Movements and Organizations
Adoremus: www.adoremus.org
Catholic Charismatic Center: www.garg.com/ccc
Catholic Doctrinal Concordance: www.infpage.com/concordance
Catholic Family and Human Rights Institute: www.c-fam.org
Catholic Health Association USA: www.chausa.org
Catholic League: www.catholicleague.org
Focolare Movement: www.rc.net/focolare
Madonna House: www.madonnahouse.org
Nat'l Bioethics Center: www.ncbcenter.org
Opus Dei: www.opusdei.org
Pax Christi International: www.paxchristi.net
Pax Christi USA: www.paxchristiusa.org
Saints Alive: www.ichrusa.com/saintsalive
Schoenstatt (information): www.catholiclinks.org/schoenstattunitedstates.htm
Seton Home Study School: www.setonhome.org

Catholic Newspapers and Magazines
Catholic Digest: www.catholicdigest.org
Catholic New York Online: www.cny.org
Catholic Worker: www.catholicworker.org
First Things: www.firstthings.com
Houston Catholic Worker: www.cjd.org
Our Sunday Visitor: www.osv.com
The Tablet, U.K.: www.thetablet.co.uk
The Universe, U.K.: www.totalcatholic.com
The Wanderer: www.thewandererpress.com

Religious Orders and Apostolates
Apostolates/Orders: www.catholic-forum.com/links/pages/Religious_Orders
EWTN: www.ewtn.com
RCNet-Apostolates: www.rc.net/org

Colleges and Universities (Links To)

Colleges: www.shc.edu/theolibrary/edu.htm

Assocation of Catholic Colleges and Universities: www.accunet.org

Useful and Informative Sites

Mass Times: www.masstimes.org

Mass in Transit: www.massintransit.com

Christworld: www.christworld.com

Catholic-Pages: www.catholic-pages.com

PetersVoice: www.petersvoice.com

Rosary Center: www.rosary-center.org

Daily E-pistle (e-newsletter) Signup Page: www.catholic forum.com/e-pistle.html

Grace In Action Stewardship: www.GraceInAction.org

For Kids and Families

Catholic Kids Net: www.catholickidsnet.org

Global Schoolhouse: www.gsn.org

My Friend: www.myfriendmagazine.com

Teaching Catholic Kids: www.TeachingCatholicKids.com

Apostolate for Family Consecration: www.family land.org

Catholic Family and Human Rights Institute: www.c fam.org

Catholic Fathers: www.dads.org

Catholic Parent Magazine: www.CatholicParent.com

Natural Family Planning: www.ccli.org

Domestic Church: www.domestic-church.com

DEVELOPMENTS IN COMMUNICATIONS 2007-08

The following are significant developments or documents in the field of Catholic communications in 2007-2008.

MESSAGE OF THE HOLY FATHER FOR THE 42nd WORLD COMMUNICATIONS DAY

On Jan. 24, 20078, Pope Benedict XVI issued his 2008 message for the 40th World Communications Day, held May 4. The theme was: "The Media: At the Crossroads between Self-Promotion and Service. Searching for the Truth in order to Share it with Others." Following is the text of the message:

Dear Brothers and Sisters!

1. The theme of this year's World Communications Day — "The Media: At the Crossroads between Self-Promotion and Service. Searching for the Truth in order to Share it with Others" — sheds light on the important role of the media in the life of individuals and society. Truly, there is no area of human experience, especially given the vast phenomenon of globalization, in which the media have not become an integral part of interpersonal relations and of social, economic, political and religious development. As I said in my Message for this year's World Day of Peace (Jan. 1, 2008): "The social communications media, in particular, because of their educational potential, have a special responsibility for promoting respect for the family, making clear its expectations and rights, and presenting all its beauty" (No. 5).

2. In view of their meteoric technological evolution, the media have acquired extraordinary potential, while raising new and hitherto unimaginable questions and problems. There is no denying the contribution they can make to the diffusion of news, to knowledge of facts and to the dissemination of information: they have played a decisive part, for example, in the spread of literacy and in socialization, as well as the development of democracy and dialogue among peoples. Without their contribution it would truly be difficult to foster and strengthen understanding between nations, to breathe life into peace dialogues around the globe, to guarantee the primary good of access to information, while at the same time ensuring the free circulation of ideas, especially those promoting the ideals of solidarity and social justice. Indeed, the media, taken overall, are not only vehicles for spreading ideas: they can and should also be instruments at the service of a world of greater justice and solidarity. Unfortunately, though, they risk being transformed into systems aimed at subjecting humanity to agendas dictated by the dominant interests of the day. This is what happens when communication is used for ideological purposes or for the aggressive advertising of consumer products. While claiming to represent reality, it can tend to legitimize or impose distorted models of personal, family or social life. Moreover, in order to attract listeners and increase the size of audiences, it does not hesitate at times to have recourse to vulgarity and violence, and to overstep the mark. The media can also present and support models of development which serve to increase rather than reduce the technological divide between rich and poor countries.

3. Humanity today is at a crossroads. One could properly apply to the media what I wrote in the Encyclical *Spe Salvi* concerning the ambiguity of progress, which offers new possibilities for good, but at the same time opens up appalling possibilities for evil that formerly did not exist (cf. No. 22). We must ask, therefore, whether it is wise to allow the instruments of social communication to be exploited for indiscriminate "self-promotion" or to end up in the hands of those who use them to manipulate consciences. Should it not be a priority to ensure that they remain at the service of the person and of the common good, and that they foster "man's ethical formation … man's inner growth" (ibid.)? Their extraordinary impact on the lives of individuals and on society is widely acknowledged, yet today it is necessary to stress the radical shift, one might even say the complete change of role, that they are currently undergoing. Today, communication seems increasingly to claim not simply to represent reality, but to determine it, owing to the power and the force of suggestion that it possesses. It is clear, for example, that in certain situations the media are used not for the proper purpose of disseminating information, but to "create" events. This dangerous change in function has been noted with concern by many Church leaders. Precisely because we are dealing with realities that have a profound effect on all those dimensions of human life (moral, intellectual, religious, relational, affective, cultural) in which the good of the person is at stake, we must stress that not everything that is technically possible is also ethically permissible. Hence, the impact of the communications media on modern life raises unavoidable questions, which require choices and solutions that can no longer be deferred.

4. The role that the means of social communication have acquired in society must now be considered an integral part of the "anthropological" question that is emerging as the key challenge of the third millennium. Just as we see happening in areas such as human life, marriage and the family, and in the great contemporary issues of peace, justice and protection of creation, so too in the sector of social communications there are essential dimensions of the human person and the

truth concerning the human person coming into play. When communication loses its ethical underpinning and eludes society's control, it ends up no longer taking into account the centrality and inviolable dignity of the human person. As a result it risks exercising a negative influence on people's consciences and choices and definitively conditioning their freedom and their very lives. For this reason it is essential that social communications should assiduously defend the person and fully respect human dignity. Many people now think there is a need, in this sphere, for "info-ethics," just as we have bioethics in the field of medicine and in scientific research linked to life.

5. The media must avoid becoming spokesmen for economic materialism and ethical relativism, true scourges of our time. Instead, they can and must contribute to making known the truth about humanity, and defending it against those who tend to deny or destroy it. One might even say that seeking and presenting the truth about humanity constitutes the highest vocation of social communication. Utilizing for this purpose the many refined and engaging techniques that the media have at their disposal is an exciting task, entrusted in the first place to managers and operators in the sector. Yet it is a task which to some degree concerns us all, because we are all consumers and operators of social communications in this era of globalization. The new media — telecommunications and internet in particular — are changing the very face of communication; perhaps this is a valuable opportunity to reshape it, to make more visible, as my venerable predecessor Pope John Paul II said, the essential and indispensable elements of the truth about the human person (cf. Apostolic Letter, The Rapid Development, No. 10).

6. Man thirsts for truth, he seeks truth; this fact is illustrated by the attention and the success achieved by so many publications, programs or quality fiction in which the truth, beauty and greatness of the person, including the religious dimension of the person, are acknowledged and favorably presented. Jesus said: "You will know the truth and the truth will make you free" (Jn 8:32). The truth which makes us free is Christ, because only he can respond fully to the thirst for life and love that is present in the human heart. Those who have encountered him and have enthusiastically welcomed his message experience the irrepressible desire to share and communicate this truth. As Saint John writes, "That which was from the beginning, which we have heard, which we have seen with our eyes, which we have looked upon and touched with our hands, concerning the word of life … we proclaim also to you, so that you may have fellowship with us. And our fellowship is with the Father and with his Son Jesus Christ. And we are writing this that our joy may be complete" (1 Jn 1:1-3).

Let us ask the Holy Spirit to raise up courageous communicators and authentic witnesses to the truth, faithful to Christ's mandate and enthusiastic for the message of the faith, communicators who will "interpret modern cultural needs, committing themselves to approaching the communications age not as a time of alienation and confusion, but as a valuable time for the quest for the truth and for developing communion between persons and peoples" (John Paul II, Address to the Conference for those working in Communications and Culture, Nov. 9, 2002).

From the Vatican, Jan. 24, 2008, the Feast of Saint Francis de Sales.

BENEDICTUS PP. XVI

Identity and Mission in Communications

On May 23, 2008, Pope Benedict XVI addressed the participants of a congress on social communication in Catholic universities. The theme of the congress was "Identity and Mission of a Communications' Faculty in a Catholic University." Following are excerpts (courtesy Vatican Information Service):Venerable Brothers in the Episcopate and in the Priesthood, Distinguished Ladies and Gentlemen, I am very pleased to address my welcome to all of you, academicians and educators of Catholic Institutions of higher culture, gathered in Rome to reflect, together with members of the Pontifical Council for Social Communications, on the identity and mission of the Communications Faculty in Catholic Universities. Through you I wish to greet your colleagues, your students and all those who are part of the Faculty that you represent. A particular thanks goes to your President, Archbishop Claudio Maria Celli, for the kind words of tribute that he addressed to me. Along with him I greet the Secretaries and the Undersecretary of the Pontifical Council for Social Communications.

The diverse forms of communication — dialogue, prayer, teaching, witness, proclamation — and their different instruments — the press, electronics, the visual arts, music, voice, gestural art and contact — are all manifestations of the fundamental nature of the human person. It is communication that reveals the person, that creates authentic and community relationships, and which permits human beings to mature in knowledge, wisdom and love. However, communication is not the simple product of a pure and fortuitous chance or of our human capacity. In the light of the biblical message, it reflects, rather, our participation in the creative, communicative and unifying Trinitarian Love which is the Father, the Son and the Holy Spirit. God has created us to be united to him and he has given us the gift and the duty of communication, because he wants us to obtain this union, not alone, but through our knowledge, our love and our service to him and to our brothers and sisters in a communicative and loving relationship.

It is self-evident that at the heart of any serious reflection on the nature and purpose of human communications there must be an engagement with questions of truth. A communicator can attempt to inform, to educate, to entertain, to convince, to comfort; but the final worth of any communication lies in its truthfulness. In one of the earliest reflections on the nature of communication, Plato highlighted the dangers of any type of communication that seeks to promote the aims and purposes of the communicator or those by whom he or she is employed without consideration for the truth of what is communicated. No less worth recalling is Cato the Elder's sober definition of the orator; "vir bonus dicendi peritus" a good or honest man skilled in communicating.

The art of communication is by its nature linked to an ethical value, to the virtues that are the foundation of morality. In the light of that definition, I encourage you, as educators, to nourish and reward that passion for truth and goodness that is always strong in the young. Help them give themselves fully to the search for truth. Teach them as well, however, that their passion for truth, which can be well served by a certain methodological skepticism, particularly in matters affecting the public interest, must not be distorted to become a relativistic cynicism in which all claims to truth and beauty are routinely rejected or ignored.

I encourage you to give more attention to academic programs in the area of the means of social communication, in particular to the ethical dimensions of communication between people, in a period in which the phenomenon of communication is occupying an ever greater place in all social contexts. It is important that this formation is never considered as a simple technical exercise, or a mere wish to give information. Primarily it should be more like an invitation to promote the truth in information and to help our contemporaries reflect on events in order to be educators of humankind today and to build a better world. It is likewise necessary to promote justice and solidarity, and to respect in whatever circumstance the value and dignity of every person, who also has a right not to be wounded in what concerns his private life.

It would be a tragedy for the future of humanity if the new instruments of communication, which permit the sharing of knowledge and information in a more rapid and effective manner, were not made accessible to those who are already economically and socially marginalized, or if it would contribute only to increasing the gap that separates those people from the new network that is developing at the service of human socialization, of information and of understanding. On the other hand, it would be equally grave if the tendency toward globalization in the world of communications were to weaken or eliminate the traditional customs and the local cultures, particularly those which are able to strengthen family and social values: love, solidarity, and respect for life. In this context I desire to express my esteem to those religious communities who, notwithstanding the heavy financial burden or the generous human input, have opened Catholic universities in developing countries and I am pleased that many of these institutions are represented here today. Their efforts will ensure the countries where they are present the benefits of young men and women who receive a deep professional formation, inspired by the Christian ethic which promotes education and teaching as a service to the whole community. I appreciate, in a particular way, their commitment to offer a sound education to all, independent of race, social condition or creed, which constitutes the mission of the Catholic University.

In these days you will examine together the question of the identity of a university or a Catholic school. In this regard, I would like to recall that such an identity is not simply a question of the number of Catholic students. It is above all a question of conviction: it concerns truly believing that only in the mystery of the Word made flesh does the mystery of man become clear. The consequence is that the Catholic identity lies, in the first place, in the decision to entrust oneself, intellect and will, mind and heart, to God. As experts in the theory and in the practice of communication and as educators who are forming a new generation of communicators, you have a privileged role, not only in the life of your students, but also in the mission of your local Churches and of your Pastors to make the Good News of God's love known to all peoples.

Dear friends, in confirming my appreciation for this, your interesting meeting that opens the heart to hope, I wish to assure you that I follow your precious activity with prayer and accompany it with a special Apostolic Blessing, which I extend to all those who are dear to you.

PONTIFICAL HONORS AND AWARDS

Pontifical Orders

The Pontifical Orders of Knighthood are secular orders of merit whose membership depends directly on the pope.

Supreme Order of Christ (Militia of Our Lord Jesus Christ): The highest of the five pontifical orders of knighthood, the Supreme Order of Christ was approved Mar. 14, 1319, by John XXII as a continuation in Portugal of the suppressed Order of Templars. Members were religious with vows and a rule of life until the order lost its religious character toward the end of the 15th century. Since that time it has existed as an order of merit. Paul VI, in 1966, restricted awards of the order to Christian heads of state.

Order of the Golden Spur (Golden Militia): Although the original founder is not certainly known, this order is one of the oldest knighthoods. Indiscriminate bestowal and inheritance diminished its prestige, however, and in 1841 Gregory XVI replaced it with the Order of St. Sylvester and gave it the title of Golden Militia. In 1905 St. Pius X restored the Order of the Golden Spur in its own right, separating it from the Order of St. Sylvester. Paul VI, in 1966, restricted awards of the order to Christian heads of state.

Order of Pius IX: Founded by Pius IX June 17, 1847, the order is awarded for outstanding services for the Church and society, and may be given to non-Catholics as well as Catholics. The title to nobility formerly attached to membership was abolished by Pius XII in 1939. In 1957 Pius XII instituted the Class of the Grand Collar as the highest category of the order; in 1966, Paul VI restricted this award to heads of state "in solemn circumstances." The other three classes are of Knights of the Grand Cross, Knight Commanders with and without emblem, and Knights. The new class was created to avoid difficulties in presenting papal honors to Christian or non-Christian leaders of high merit.

Order of St. Gregory the Great: First established by Gregory XVI in 1831 to honor citizens of the Papal States, the order is conferred on persons who are distinguished for personal character and reputation, and for notable accomplishment. The order has civil and military divisions, and three classes of knights.

Order of St. Sylvester: Instituted Oct. 31, 1841, by Gregory XVI to absorb the Order of the Golden Spur, this order was divided into two by St. Pius X in 1905, one retaining the name of St. Sylvester and the other assuming the title of Golden Militia. Membership consists of three degrees: Knights of the Grand Cross, Knight Commanders with and without emblem, and Knights.

Papal Medals

Pro Ecclesia et Pontifice: This decoration ("For the Church and the Pontiff") had its origin in 1888 as a token of the golden sacerdotal jubilee of Leo XIII; he bestowed it on those who had assisted in the observance of his jubilee and on persons responsible for the success of the Vatican Exposition. The medal, cruciform in shape, bears the likenesses of Sts. Peter and Paul, the tiara and the papal keys, the words *Pro Ecclesia et Pontifice*, and the name of the present pontiff, all on the same side; it is attached to a ribbon of yellow and white, the papal colors. Originally, the medal was issued in gold, silver or bronze. It is awarded in recognition of service to the Church and the papacy.

Benemerenti: Several medals ("To a well-deserving person") have been conferred by popes for exceptional accomplishment and service. The medals, which are made of gold, silver or bronze, bear the likeness and name of the reigning pope on one side; on the other, a laurel crown and the letter "B." These two medals may be given by the pope to both men and women. Their bestowal does not convey any title or honor of knighthood.

Ecclesiastical Orders

Equestrian Order of the Holy Sepulchre of Jerusalem: The order traces its origin to Godfrey de Bouillon who instituted it in 1099. It took its name from the Basilica of the Holy Sepulchre where its members were knighted. After the fall of the Latin Kingdom of Jerusalem and the consequent departure of the knights from the Holy Land, national divisions were established in various countries.

The order was re-organized by Pius IX in 1847 when he reestablished the Latin Patriarchate of Jerusalem and placed the order under the jurisdiction of its patriarch. In 1888, Leo XIII confirmed permission to admit women—Ladies of the Holy Sepulchre—to all degrees of rank. Pius X reserved the office of grand master to himself in 1907; Pius XII gave the order a cardinal patron in 1940 and, in 1949, transferred the office of grand master from the pope to the cardinal patron. Pope John XXIII approved updated constitutions in 1962; the latest statutes were approved by Paul VI in 1977.

The purposes of the order are strictly religious and charitable. Members are committed to sustain and aid the charitable, cultural and social works of the Catholic Church in the Holy Land, particularly in the Latin Patriarchate of Jerusalem.

The order is composed of knights and ladies grouped in three classes: class of Knights of the Collar and Ladies of the Collar; Class of Knights (in four grades); Class of Ladies (in four grades). Members are appointed by the cardinal grand master according to procedures outlined in the constitution.

Under the present constitution the order is divided into national lieutenancies, largely autonomous, with international headquarters in Rome. Cardinal John P. Foley is the grand master of the order.

There are nine lieutenancies of the order in the United States and one in Puerto Rico. Vice Governor General, F. Russell Kendall, 309 Knipp Rd., Houston, TX 77024; (713) 468-5602; www.holysepulchre.net.

Order of Malta: The Sovereign Military Hospitaller Order of St. John of Jerusalem of Rhodes and of Malta traces its origin to a group of men who maintained a Christian hospital in the Holy Land in the 11th century. The group was approved as a religious order—the Hospitallers of St. John—by Paschal II in 1113.

The order, while continuing its service to the poor, principally in hospital work, assumed military duties in the 12th century and included knights, chaplains and sergeants-at-arms among its members. All the knights were professed monks with the vows of poverty, chastity and obedience. Headquarters were located in the Holy Land until the last decade of the 13th century and on Rhodes after 1308 (whence the title, Knights of Rhodes).

After establishing itself on Rhodes, the order became a sovereign power like the sea republics of Italy and the Hanseatic cities of Germany, flying its own flag, coining its own money, floating its own navy, and maintaining diplomatic relations with many nations.

The order was forced to abandon Rhodes in 1522 after the third siege of the island by the Turks under Sultan Suleyman I. Eight years later, the Knights were given the island of Malta, where they remained as a bastion of Christianity until near the end of the 18th century. Headquarters have been located in Rome since 1834.

The title of Grand Master of the Order, in abeyance for some time, was restored by Leo XIII in 1879. A more precise definition of both the religious and the sovereign status of the order was embodied in a new constitution of 1961 and a code issued in 1966.

The four main classifications of members are: Knights of Justice, who are religious with the vows of poverty, chastity and obedience; Knights of Obedience, who make a solemn promise to strive for Christian perfection; Knights of Honor and Devotion and of Grace and Devotion, all of noble lineage; and Knights of Magistral Grace. There are also chaplains, Dames and Donats of the order.

The order, with six grand priories, three sub-priories and 40 national associations, is devoted to hospital and charitable works of all kinds in some 100 countries.

Under the provisions of international law, the order maintains full diplomatic relations with the Holy See —on which, in its double nature, it depends as a religious Order, but of which, as a sovereign Order of Knighthood, it is independent—and 68 countries throughout the world.

The Grand Master, who is the head of the order, has the title of Most Eminent Highness with the rank of Cardinal. He must be of noble lineage and under solemn vows for a minimum period of 10 years, if under 50.

Fra' Andrew Willoughby Ninian Bertie, member of the British aristocracy who was elected for life as Grand Master on Apr. 8, 1988 by the Council of State, died on February 7, 2008. [See under Obituaries, 2007-2008.]

The present and 79th Grand Master is Fra' Matthew Festing, 58, an Englishman. He was the first Grand Prior of England since the Priory's re-establishment in 1993 after an abeyance of 450 years. He became a member of the Order of Malta, taking solemn religious vows in 1991.

Daniel J. Kelly, from Michigan and Chairman and CEO of Rose Hill Center, a rehabilitation center for the seriously mentally ill, was elected President of the American Association of the Knights of Malta for a three year term commencing January 1, 2004.

The headquarters of the order is at Via Condotti, 68, Palazzo Malta, 00187 Rome, Italy; (011) 3906-679-8851. U.S. addresses: American Association, 1011 First Ave., New York, NY 10022; Western Association of U.S.A., 465 California St., Suite 524, San Francisco, CA 94104; Federal Association of U.S.A., 1730 M St. N.W., Suite 403, Washington, D.C. 20036; (202) 331-2494; www.smom.org.

Order of St. George: The Sacred Military Constantinian Order of St. George was established by Pope Clement XI in 1718. The purposes of the order are to work for the preaching and defense of the Catholic faith and to promote the spiritual and physical welfare of sick, disabled, homeless and other unfortunate persons. The principal officer is Prince Carlo of Bourbon-Two Sicilies, duke of Calabria. Addresses: Via Sistina 121, 00187 Rome, Italy; Via Duomo 149, 80138 Naples, Italy; American Delegation, 302 Gessner Rd., Houston, TX 77024; (713) 888-0242.

2008 CATHOLIC PRESS ASSOCIATION AWARDS

The winners of the 2008 Catholic Press Awards were announced on Friday, May 30, 2008 at the Catholic Media Convention in Toronto, Canada.

Newspapers — General Excellence

National Newspapers: First Place: *National Catholic Reporter,* Kansas City, MO.; Second Place: *The Catholic Register,* Toronto, Ont.; Third Place: *National Catholic Register,* North Haven, CT.

Diocesan Newspapers, 40,001+ Circulation: First Place: *Catholic Courier,* Rochester, NY; Second Place: *The Catholic Spirit,* St. Paul, MN; Third Place: *Catholic Standard,* Washington, Washington, DC; Honorable Mention: *Catholic New York,* New York, NY.

Diocesan Newspapers, 17,001-40,000: First Place: *Florida Catholic,* Miami Edition, Orlando, FL; Second Place: *The Rhode Island Catholic,* Providence, RI; Third Place: *The Michigan Catholic,* Detroit, MI; Honorable Mention: *The Southern Cross,* San Diego, CA.

Diocesan Newspapers, 1-17,000: First Place: *The Catholic Northwest Progress,* Seattle, WA; Second Place: *Today's Catholic,* Fort Wayne, IN; Third Place: *The Catholic Spirit,* Metuchen, NJ.

Magazines

General Excellence: First Place: *America,* New York, NY; Second Place: *U.S. Catholic,* Chicago, IL; Third Place: *Liguorian,* Liguori, MO.

Mission Magazines: First Place: *ONE,* New York, NY; Second Place: *Maryknoll Magazine,* Maryknoll, NY; Third Place: *Columban Mission,* St. Columbans, NE.

Religious Order: First Place: *Marian Helper,* Stockbridge, MA; Second Place: *The Anthonian,* East Rutherford, NJ; Third Place: *Jesuit Journeys,* Milwaukee, WI.

Professional/Special Interest: First Place: *CHURCH,* New York, NY; Second Place: *Faith Magazine,* Lansing, MI; Third Place: *Momentum,* Washington, DC; Honorable Mention: *Legatus Magazine,* Naples, FL.

Scholarly: First Place: *National Catholic Bioethics Quarterly,* Philadelphia, PA; Second Place: *American Catholic Studies,* Villanova, PA; Third Place: *Horizons,* Villanova, PA; Honorable Mention: *Catholic Southwest,* Pflugerville, TX.

Prayer and Spirituality: First Place: *Magnificat,* Yonkers, NY; Second Place: *Spiritual Life,* Washington, DC.

Newsletters

General Interest: First Place: *Sacred Ground,* Kansas City, KS; Second Place: *Comboni Mission Newsletter,* Cincinnati, OH; Third Place: *SCJ News,* Hales Corners, Wis.; Honorable Mention: *Focus on Future Church,* Lakewood, OH.

Special Interest Newsletters: First Place: *The CARA Report,* Washington, DC; Second Place: *Dimensions,* Hempstead, N.Y.; Third Place: *CNS Documentary Service/Origins,* Washington, DC.

Books

Popular Presentation of the Catholic Faith: First Place: *A Jesuit Off Broadway,* by James Martin, SJ, Loyola Press, Chicago, IL; Second Place: *A Faith That Frees,* by Richard Malloy, Orbis Books, Maryknoll, NY; Third Place: *Created for Joy,* by Sidney Callahan, The Crossroad Publishing Co., New York, NY; *Broken Trust,* by Patrick Fleming, et. al., The Crossroad Publishing Co., New York, NY; *A Concise Guide to the Documents of Vatican II,* by Edward P. Hahnenberg, St. Anthony Messenger Press, Cincinnati, OH.

Spirituality – Soft Cover: First Place: *Teilhard de Chardin, The Divine Milieu Explained: A Spirituality for the 21st Century,* by Louis M. Savary, Paulist Press, Mahwah, NJ; Second Place: *Finding Francis, Following Christ,* by Michael Crosby, Orbis Books, Maryknoll, NY; Third Place: *The Developing Christian: Spiritual Growth Through the Life Cycle,* by Peter Feldmeier, Paulist Press, Mahwah, NJ; Honorable Mention: *Lourdes: Font of Faith, Hope and Charity,* by Elizabeth Ficocelli, Paulist Press, Mahwah NJ.

Spirituality – Hard Cover: First Place: *Welcome to the Wisdom of the World,* by Joan Chittister, Wm. B. Eerdmans Publishing Co, Grand Rapids, MI; Second Place: *Broken Trust,* by Patrick Fleming et. al., The Crossroad Publishing Co., New York, NY; Third Place: *Crossing the Desert, Learning to Let Go, See Clearly and Live Simply,* by Robert J. Wicks, Sorin Books (an imprint of Ave Maria Press), Notre Dame, IN.

Theology: First Place: *The Quest for the Living God,* by Elizabeth Johnson, Continuum, New York, NY; Second Place: *Faith and Force: A Christian Debate About War,* by David L. Clough & Brian Stiltner, Georgetown University Press, Washington, DC; Third Place: *Gathered for the Journey,* by David Matzko McCarthy & M. Therese Lysaught, Wm. B. Eerdmans Publishing Co., Grand Rapids, MI; Honorable Mention: *The Option for the Poor in Christian Theology,* by Daniel Groody, University of Notre Dame Press, Notre Dame, IN; *With the Silent Glimmer of God's Spirit,* by Lambert J. Leijssen, Paulist Press, Mahwah NJ; *Creation, Grace and Redemption,* by Neil Ormerod, Orbis Books, Maryknoll, NY.

Scripture: First Place: *Introduction to the Synoptic Gospels,* by Pheme Perkins, Wm. B. Eerdmans Publishing Co., Grand Rapids, MI; Second Place: *Biblical Human Failures,* by Walter Vogels, Novalis, Ottawa, Ontario; *Sacra Pagina Series: Hebrews,* by Alan C. Mitchell, Liturgical Press, Collegeville, MN; Third Place: *The One Who is to Come,* by Joseph A. Fitzmeyer, Wm. B. Eerdmans Publishing Co., Grand Rapids, MI.

Liturgy: First Place: *A Commentary on the General Instruction of the Roman Missal,* by Ed Foley, et. al., Liturgical Press, Collegeville, MN; Second Place: *Sacred Music and Liturgical Reform: Treasures and Transformations,* by Anthony Ruff, OSB, Liturgy Training Publications, Chicago, IL; Third Place: *Liturgy: Sacrosanctum Concilium,* by Rita Ferrone, Paulist Press, Mahwah, NJ.

Pastoral Ministry: First Place: *Turning the Wheel,* by Jonathan Bengtson & Gabrielle Earnshaw, Orbis

Books, Maryknoll, NY; Second Place: *Mexican American Catholics,* by Eduardo C. Fernandez, Paulist Press, Mahwah, NJ; Third Place: *Mission Driven Parish,* by Patrick Brennan, Orbis Books, Maryknoll, NY; Honorable Mention: *Broken Trust,* by Patrick Fleming, et. al., The Crossroad Publishing Co., New York, NY; *The Practical Prophet: Pastoral Writings,* by Bishop Ken Untener, Paulist Press, Mahwah, NJ; *I Don't Want to Go to Church,* by Scott Cooper, Paulist Press, Mahwah, NJ.

Professional Books: First Place: *Keeping the Covenant,* by Thomas Sweetser, The Crossroad Publishing Co., New York, NY; Second Place: *The Emerging Diaconate,* by William T. Ditewig, Paulist Press, Mahwah, NJ; *Welcoming the Word in Year A: Building on a Rock,* by Verna Holyhead, S.G.S., Liturgical Press, Collegeville, MN; Third Place: *Battle for Rights in the United States Catholic Church,* by Kevin E. McKenna, Paulist Press, Mahwah, NJ; Honorable Mention: *A Commentary on the General Instruction of the Roman Missal,* by Ed Foley, et. al., Liturgical Press, Collegeville, MN.

Educational Books: First Place: *Bendecidos,* RCL Benziger, Allen, Texas; Second Place: *Love That Does Justice,* by Thomas Schubeck, Orbis Books, Maryknoll, NY; Third Place: *From Sand to Solid Ground,* by Michael Morwood, The Crossroad Publishing Co., New York, NY; Honorable Mention: *Spiritual Leadership: The Quest for Integrity,* by Leonard Doohan, Paulist Press, Mahwah NJ; *Christianity 101: A Textbook of Catholic Theology,* by Gregory C. Higgins, Paulist Press, Mahwah, NJ.

Design & Production: First Place: *A Reflection of Faith: Saint Paul Cathedral 1906 to 2006,* by David G. Wilkins, Ph.D, St. Paul Cathedral Centennial Book Committee, Pittsburgh, PA; Second Place: *Saint John's Bible: Prophets, Liturgical Press,* Collegeville, Minn.; Third Place: *Portraits of Grace,* by Patricia A. Lynch, ACTA Publications, Skokie, IL; Third Place: *The Work of Our Hands: The Art of Martin Srspamer, OSB,* by Bari Colombari, Pastoral Press (An imprint of Oregon Catholic Press), Portland, OR; Honorable Mention: *In Shining Splendor: Easter Season Meditations on the Exsultet,* by Richard N. Fragomeni, Work Library Publication, Franklin Park, IL; *The Great Catholic Reformers,* by C. Colt Anderson, Paulist Press, Mahwah, NJ.

Children's Books: First Place: *He Said Yes,* by Kelly Ann Lynch, Paulist Press, Mahwah, NJ; Second Place: *Easter Swallows,* by Vicki Howie, Pauline Books and Media, Boston, MA; Second Place: *Living the 10 Commandments for Children,* by Rosemarie Gortler & Donna Piscitelli, Our Sunday Visitor Publishing, Huntington, IN; Third Place: *More Saints, Lives and Illuminations,* by Ruth Sanderson, Wm. B. Eerdmans Publishing Co., Grand Rapids, MI.

First Time Author of a Book: First Place: *Wake Up to God's Word: Exercises for Spiritual Transformation,* by Mary Reaman, St. Anthony Messenger Press, Cincinnati, OH; Second Place: *Make Room for God: Clearing Out the Clutter,* by Susan K. Rowland, St. Anthony Messenger Press, Cincinnati, OH; Third Place: *Jesus of Israel: Finding Christ in the Old Testament,* by Fr. Richard Veras, Servant Books, Cincinnati, OH; Honorable Mention: *John Cuthbert Ford, SJL Moral Theologian at the End of the*

Manualist Era, by Eric Marcelo O. Genilo, SJ, Georgetown University Press, Washington, DC.

Family Life: First Place: *Jesus in the House: Gospel Reflections on Christ's Presence in the Home,* by Allan F. Wright, St. Anthony Messenger Press, Cincinnati, OH; Second Place: *Christian Marriage: The New Challenge,* by David Thomas, Liturgical Press, Collegeville, MN; Third Place: *Good Discipline, Great Teens,* by Dr. Ray Guarendi, Servant Books, Cincinnati, OH.

History: First Place: *As it was in the Beginning,* by Robert McClory, The Crossroad Publishing Co., New York, NY; Second Place: *Voices of the Faithful,* by D'Antonio & Pogorelc, EDS, The Crossroad Publishing Co., New York, NY; Third Place: *The Great Catholic Reformers,* by C. Colt Anderson, Paulist Press, Mahwah, NJ; Honorable Mention: *A Concise Guide to the Documents of Vatican II,* by Edward P. Hahnenberg, St. Anthony Messenger Press, Cincinnati, OH.

Biography: First Place: *Mother Teresa,* by Brian Kolodieschuk M.C. & Trace Murphy, Doubleday Religious Publishing Group, New York, NY; Second Place: *A Life Poured Out,* by Jean Jacques Perennes, Orbis Books, Maryknoll, NY; Third Place: *Women in Church History: 21 Stories for 21 Centuries,* by Joanne Turpin, St. Anthony Messenger Press, Cincinnati, OH.

Gender Issues: First Place: *Green Sisters: A Spiritual Ecology,* by Sarah McFarland Taylor, Harvard University Press, Evanston, IL; Second Place: *Created in God's Image,* by Michelle Gonzalez, Orbis Books, Maryknoll, N.Y.; Third Place: *Women in Mission,* by Susan Smith, Orbis Books, Maryknoll, NY; Honorable Mention: *Feminist Intercultural Theology,* by Maria Pilar Aquino & Maria Rosado Nunes, Orbis Books, Maryknoll, NY.

Spanish Language Titles: First Place: *Santos Americanos,* Arturo Perez Rodriguez & Miguel Arias, Loyola Press, Chicago, IL; *Introducion a la Bible,* by Stephen J. Binz, Liturgical Press, Collegeville, MN; Second Place: *Jesus de Nazaret,* by Joseph Ratzinger Papa Benedicto XVI & Bill Barry, Doubleday Religious Publishing Group, New York, NY; Third Place: *Palabra Vida y Fe,* by Miguel Arias, Oregon Catholic Press, Portland, OR.

Reference Books: First Place: *An Introductory Dictionary of Theology and Religious Studies,* by Orlando O. Espin & James B. Nickoloff, Liturgical Press, Collegeville, MN; Second Place: *A New Dictionary of Saint: East and West,* by Michael Walsh, Liturgical Press, Collegeville, MN; Third Place: *St. Joseph Atlas of the Bible,* by Tim Dowley, Catholic Book Publishing Corp, Totowa, NJ; Honorable Mention: *Encyclopedia of Mary,* by Monica & Bill Dodds, Our Sunday Visitor Publishing, Huntington, IN.

Diocesan Directory: First Place: *Archdiocese of Newark 2007 Directory & Almanac,* by Msgr. Francis R. Seymour, Marge McCue, Fred Bauer, & Paula Blackman, SVO, Advocate Publishing Corporation, Newark, NJ; Second Place: *Archdiocesan Review,* by Patti Medinger, The Catholic Review, Baltimore, MD; Third Place: *Catholic Directory, Diocese of San Diego,* by Donna Moore, Diocese of San Diego, Bishop Robert H. Brom, San Diego, CA; Third Place:

Official Catholic Directory, by Jordan McMorrough & Patsy Pelton, Today's Catholic-Archdiocese of San Antonio, San Antonio, TX.

Francis de Sales Award: Chic Richards Davis,

advertising director for *The Catholic Review,* newspaper of the Archdiocese of Baltimore, and for the Cathedral Foundation.

2008 CHRISTOPHER AWARDS

Christopher Awards recognize the creative writers, producers and directors who have achieved artistic excellence in films, books and television specials. The 2008 awards were presented Apr. 10, 2008, in New York.

Books: Brother, I'm Dying, by Edwidge Danticat (Alfred A. Knopf/Random House, Inc.); The Florist's Daughter, by Patricia Hempl (Harcourt, Inc.); The Invisible Wall: A Love Story That Broke Barriers, by Harry Bernstein (Ballatine Books/Random House, Inc.); The Lonely Patient: How We Experience Illness, by Michael Stein, M.D. (William Morrow/HarperCollins Publishers); A Long Way Gone: Memoirs of a Boy Soldier, by Ishmael Beah (Sarah Crichton Books/Farrar, Straus and Giroux); A Slave No More: Two Men Who Escaped to Freedom, by David W. Blight (Harcourt, Inc.).

Books for Young People: **Preschool**: Taking a Bath with the Dog and Other Things That Make Me Happy, by Scott Menchin (Candlewick Press); **Ages 6-8**: How Many Seeds in a Pumpkin?, by Margaret McNamara; Illustrated by G. Brian Karas (Schwartz & Wade Books/Random House Children's Books); **Ages 8-10**: Owen & Mzee: The Language of Friendship, by

Isabella Hatkoff, Craig Hatkoff & Dr. Paula Kahumbu; Photographs by Peter Greste (Scholastic Press/Scholastic, Inc.); **Ages 10-12**: The Wild Girls, by Pat Murphy (Viking/Penguin Young Readers Group); **Young Adult**: Diamonds in the Shadow, by Caroline B. Cooney (Delacorte Press/Random House Children's Books)

Films: Amazing Grace (Walden Media, Samuel Goldwyn Films & Roadside Attractions); The Diving Bell and the Butterfly (Miramax Films & Pathe Renn); The Great Debaters (The Weinstein Company & MGM); Juno (Fox Searchlight Pictures); The Kite Runner (Paramount Classics); Ratatouille (Walt Disney Pictures & Pixar Animation Studios).

Television and Cable: Flashpoint: Kimberly Dozier and the Army's 4th I.D. - A Story of Bravery, Recovery and Loss (CBS-TV); In God's Name (CBS-TV); Longford (HBO); Pictures of Hollis Woods (CBS-TV); The War miniseries (PBS/WETA Washington, DC).

Christopher Leadership Award: John Cardinal Foley.

Christopher Life Achievement Award: David McCullogh.

Special Award: American Masters

Ecumenism and Interreligious Dialogue

ECUMENISM

Sources: Brother Jeffrey Gros, F.S.C. and Fr. Ronald Roberson, C.S.P., associate directors, Secretariat for Ecumenical and Interreligious Affairs, USCCB.

The modern ecumenical movement, with roots in 19th-century scholars and individuals began its institutional life in 1910 among Protestants and Orthodox and led to formation of the World Council of Churches in 1948, developed outside the mainstream of Catholic interest until the 1950s. It has now become for Catholics as well one of the great religious facts of our time.

The *magna carta* of ecumenism for Catholics is a complex of several documents which include, in the first place, *Unitatis Redintegratio,* the "Decree on Ecumenism," promulgated by the Second Vatican Council Nov. 21, 1964. Other enactments underlying and expanding this decree are *Lumen Gentium* ("Dogmatic Constitution on the Church"), *Orientalium Ecclesiarum* ("Decree on Eastern Catholic Churches"), and *Gaudium et Spes* ("Pastoral Constitution on the Church in the Modern World").

The Holy See has more recently brought together Catholic ecumenical priorities in Directory for the Application of Principles and Norms on Ecumenism (1993) and The Ecumenical Dimension in the Formation of Pastoral Workers (1998). These, in addition to Pope John Paul II's encyclical letter, *Ut Unum Sint* (1995), provide a guide for Catholic ecumenical initiatives. Pope Benedict XVI reiterated this irreversible commitment at his installation, and during his meeting with the ecumenical guests the day following his installation (2005).

POPE BENEDICT XVI

Pope Benedict XVI has reaffirmed the commitment of the Catholic Church to the ecumenical movement, and stated that ecumenism would be the "primacy task" of his pontificate. This is an excerpt from his address to the Cardinals at the end of a Mass he celebrated with them the day after his election, on Apr. 20, 2005:

"Nourished and sustained by the Eucharist, Catholics cannot but feel encouraged to strive for the full unity for which Christ expressed so ardent a hope in the Upper Room. The Successor of Peter knows that he must make himself especially responsible for his Divine Master's supreme aspiration. Indeed, he is entrusted with the task of strengthening his brethren (cf. Lk 22: 32).

With full awareness, therefore, at the beginning of his ministry in the Church of Rome which Peter bathed in his blood, Peter's current Successor takes on as his primary task the duty to work tirelessly to rebuild the full and visible unity of all Christ's followers. This is his ambition, his impelling duty. He is aware that good intentions do not suffice for this. Concrete gestures that enter hearts and stir consciences are essential, inspiring in everyone that inner conversion that is the prerequisite for all ecumenical progress.

Theological dialogue is necessary; the investigation of the historical reasons for the decisions made in the past is also indispensable. But what is most urgently needed is that 'purification of memory,' so often recalled by John Paul II, which alone can dispose souls to accept the full truth of Christ. Each one of us must come before him, the supreme Judge of every living person, and render an account to him of all we have done or have failed to do to further the great good of the full and visible unity of all his disciples. The current Successor of Peter is allowing himself to be called in the first person by this requirement and is prepared to do everything in his power to promote the fundamental cause of ecumenism. Following the example of his Predecessors, he is fully determined to encourage every initiative that seems appropriate for promoting contacts and understanding with the representatives of the different Churches and Ecclesial Communities. Indeed, on this occasion he sends them his most cordial greeting in Christ, the one Lord of us all."

VATICAN II DECREE

The following excerpts from *Unitatis Redintegratio* cover the broad theological background and principles and indicate the thrust of the Church's commitment to ecumenism.

Men who believe in Christ and have been properly baptized are brought into a certain, though imperfect, communion with the Catholic Church. Undoubtedly, the differences that exist in varying degrees between them and the Catholic Church — whether in doctrine and sometimes in discipline, or concerning the structure of the Church — do indeed create many and sometimes serious obstacles to full ecclesiastical communion. These the ecumenical movement is striving to overcome (No. 3).

Elements Common to Christians

Moreover some, even very many, of the most significant elements or endowments which together go to build up and give life to the Church herself can exist outside the visible boundaries of the Catholic Church: the written word of God; the life of grace; faith, hope, and charity, along with other interior gifts of the Holy Spirit and visible elements. All of these, which come from Christ and lead back to Him, belong by right to the one Church of Christ (No. 3).

[In a later passage, the decree singled out a number of elements which the Catholic Church and other churches have in common but not in complete agreement: confession of Christ as Lord and God and as mediator between God and man; belief in the Trinity; reverence for Scripture as the revealed word of God; baptism and the Lord's Supper; Christian life and worship; faith in action; concern with moral questions.]

The brethren divided from us also carry out many of the sacred actions of the Christian religion. Undoubtedly, in ways that vary according to the condition of each church or community, these actions can truly engender a life of grace, and can be rightly described as capable of providing access to the community of salvation.

It follows that these separated Churches and Communities, though we believe they suffer from defects already mentioned, have by no means been deprived of significance and importance in the mystery of salvation. For the Spirit of Christ has not refrained from using them as means of salvation which derive their efficacy from the very fullness of grace and truth entrusted to the Catholic Church (No. 3).

Unity Lacking

Nevertheless, our separated brethren, whether considered as individuals or as Communities and Churches, are not blessed with that unity which Jesus Christ wished to bestow on all those whom he has regenerated and vivified into one body and newness of life — that unity which the holy Scriptures and the revered tradition of the Church proclaim. For it is through Christ's Catholic Church alone, which is the all-embracing means of salvation, that the fullness of the means of salvation can be obtained. It was to the apostolic college alone, of which Peter is the head, that we believe our Lord entrusted all the blessings of the New Covenant, in order to establish on earth the one Body of Christ into which all those should be fully incorporated who already belong in any way to God's People (No. 3).

What the Movement Involves

Today, in many parts of the world, under the inspiring grace of the Holy Spirit, multiple efforts are being expended through prayer, word, and action to attain that fullness of unity which Jesus Christ desires. This sacred Synod, therefore, exhorts all the Catholic faithful to recognize the signs of the times and to participate skillfully in the work of ecumenism.

The "ecumenical movement" means those activities and enterprises which, according to various needs of the Church and opportune occasions, are started and organized for the fostering of unity among Christians. These are:

• First, every effort to eliminate words, judgments, and actions which do not respond to the condition of separated brethren with truth and fairness and so make mutual relations between them more difficult.

• Then, "dialogue" between competent experts from different Churches and Communities [scholarly ecumenism].

• In addition, these Communions cooperate more closely in whatever projects a Christian conscience demands for the common good [social ecumenism].

• They also come together for common prayer, where this is permitted [spiritual ecumenism].

• Pope John Paul urged that the results of (now) forty years of dialogue become a "common heritage," therefore all Catholic catechetical and ministry formation programs are to be informed by the progress of ecumenical relations.

• Finally, all are led to examine their own faithfulness to Christ's will for the Church and, wherever necessary, undertake with vigor the task of renewal and reform.

It is evident that the work of preparing and reconciling those individuals who wish for full Catholic communion is of its nature distinct from ecumenical action. But there is no opposition between the two, since both proceed from the wondrous providence of God (No. 4).

Primary Duty of Catholics

In ecumenical work, Catholics must assuredly be concerned for their separated brethren, praying for them, keeping them informed about the Church, making the first approaches toward them. But their primary duty is to make an honest and careful appraisal of whatever needs to be renewed and achieved in the Catholic household itself, in order that its life may bear witness more loyally and luminously to the teachings and ordinances which have been handed down from Christ through the Apostles.

Every Catholic must aim at Christian perfection (cf. Jas 1:4; Rom 12:1-2) and, each according to his station, play his part so that the Church may daily be more purified and renewed, against the day when Christ will present her to himself in all her glory, without spot or wrinkle (cf. Eph 5:27).

Catholics must joyfully acknowledge and esteem the truly Christian endowments from our common heritage which are to be found among our separated brethren.

Nor should we forget that whatever is wrought by the grace of the Holy Spirit in the hearts of our separated brethren can contribute to our own edification. Whatever is truly Christian never conflicts with the genuine interests of the faith; indeed, it can always result in a more ample realization of the very mystery of Christ and the Church (No. 4).

Participation in Worship

Norms concerning participation by Catholics in the worship of other Christian Churches were sketched in this conciliar decree and elaborated in a number of other documents such as: the Decree on Eastern Catholic Churches, promulgated by the Second Vatican Council in 1964; Interim Guidelines for Prayer in Common, issued June 18, 1965, by the U.S. Bishops' Committee for Ecumenical and Interreligious Affairs; a Directory on Ecumenism, published in 1967, 1970 and 1993 by the Pontifical Council for Promoting Christian Unity; additional communications from the U.S. Bishops' Committee, and numerous sets of guidelines issued locally by and for dioceses throughout the U.S.

The norms encourage common prayer services for Christian unity and other intentions. Beyond that, they draw a distinction between separated churches of the Reformation tradition and of the Anglican Communion, and separated Eastern churches, in view of doctrine and practice the Catholic Church has in common with the separated Eastern churches concerning the apostolic succession of bishops, holy orders, liturgy and other creedal matters.

Full participation by Catholics in official Protestant liturgies is prohibited, because it implies profession of the faith expressed in the liturgy. Intercommunion by Catholics at Protestant liturgies is prohibited. Under certain conditions, Protestants may be given Holy Communion in the Catholic Church (see Intercommunion). A Catholic may stand as a witness, but not as a sponsor, in baptism, and as a witness in the marriage of separated Christians. Similarly, a Protestant may stand as a witness, but not as a sponsor, in a Catholic baptism, and as a witness in the marriage of Catholics.

The principal norms regarding liturgical participations with separated Eastern Churches are included under Eastern Ecumenism.

DIRECTORY ON ECUMENISM

A "Directory for the Application of the Principles and Norms of Ecumenism" was approved by Pope John Paul II on Mar. 25, 1993, and published early in June. The Pontifical Council for Promoting Christian Unity said on release of the document that revision of Directories issued in 1967 and 1970 was necessary in view of subsequent developments. These included promulgation of the Code of Canon Law for the Latin Church in 1983 and of the Code of Canons of the Eastern Churches in 1990; publication of the Catechism of the Catholic Church in 1992; additional documents and the results of theological dialogues. In 1998, The Ecumenical Dimension in the Formation of Pastoral Workers was published by the Holy See to give practical and detailed guidance in the implementation of Chapter 3 of the Directory.

The following excerpts are from the text published in the June 16, 1993, English edition of L'Osservatore Romano.

Address and Purpose

"The Directory is addressed to the pastors of the Catholic Church, but it also concerns all the faithful, who are called to pray and work for the unity of Christians, under the direction of their bishops."

"At the same time, it is hoped that the Directory will also be useful to members of churches and ecclesial communities that are not in full communion with the Catholic Church."

"The new edition of the Directory is meant to be an instrument at the service of the whole Church, and especially of those who are directly engaged in ecumenical activity in the Catholic Church. The Directory intends to motivate, enlighten and guide this activity, and in some particular cases also to give binding directives in accordance with the proper competence of the Pontifical Council for Promoting Christian Unity."

Outline

Principles and norms of the document are covered in five chapters.

I. The Search for Christian Unity. The ecumenical commitment of the Catholic Church based on the doctrinal principles of the Second Vatican Council.

II. Organization in the Catholic Church at the Service of Christian Unity. Persons and structures involved in promoting ecumenism at all levels, and the norms that direct their activity.

III. Ecumenical Formation in the Catholic Church. Categories of people to be formed, those responsible for formation; the aims and methods of formation; its doctrinal and practical aspects.

IV. Communion in Life and Spiritual Activity among the Baptized. The communion that exists with other Christians on the basis of the sacramental bond of baptism, and the norms for sharing in prayer and other spiritual activities, including, in particular cases, sacramental sharing.

V. Ecumenical Cooperation, Dialogue and Common Witness. Principles, different forms and norms for cooperation between Christians with a view to dialogue and common witness in the world.

ECUMENICAL AGENCIES

Pontifical Council

The top-level agency for Catholic ecumenical efforts is the Pontifical Council for Promoting Christian Unity (formerly the Secretariat for Promoting Christian Unity), which originated in 1960 as a preparatory commission for the Second Vatican Council. Its purposes are to provide guidance and, where necessary, coordination for ecumenical endeavor by Catholics, and to establish and maintain relations with representatives of other Christian Churches for ecumenical dialogue and action.

The council, under the direction of Card. Walter Kasper (successor to Card. Edward I. Cassidy), has established firm working relations with representative agencies of other churches and the World Council of Churches. It has joined in dialogue with the Eastern and Oriental Orthodox, the Anglican Communion, the Lutheran World Federation, the World Alliance of Reformed Churches, the World Methodist Council, Baptist World Alliance, World Evangelical Alliance, the Pentecostals, Mennonites and other religious bodies. In the past several years, staff members and representatives of the council have been involved in one way or another in nearly every significant ecumenical enterprise and meeting held throughout the world.

While the council and its counterparts in other churches have focused primary attention on theological and other related problems of Christian unity, they have also begun, and in increasing measure, to emphasize the responsibilities of the churches for greater unity of witness and effort in areas of humanitarian need. With the Congregation of the Doctrine of the Faith, the Council carries responsibility for official Catholic action on the results of the dialogue and shepherding the process of reception in the Catholic Church.

Bishops' Committee

The U.S. Bishops' Committee for Ecumenical and Interreligious Affairs was established by the American hierarchy in 1964. Its purposes are to maintain relationships with other Christian churches and other religious communities at the national level, to help other offices of the Conference do their work ecumenically, to advise and assist dioceses in developing and applying ecumenical policies, and to maintain liaison with corresponding Vatican offices — the Pontifical Councils for Christian Unity and for Interreligious Dialogue and other bishops conferences when needed.

This standing committee of the United States

Conference of Catholic Bishops is chaired by Bp. Richard Sklba of the Archdiocese of Milwaukee. Operationally, the committee is assisted by a secretariat with Rev. James Massa, executive director; Rev. Francis Tiso, executive secretary for Interreligious Relations, and the Rev. Ronald Roberson, C.S.P.

The committee co-sponsors several national consultations with other churches and confessional families. These bring together Catholic representatives and their counterparts from the Episcopal Church, Evangelical Lutheran Church in America and Lutheran Church — Missouri Synod, the Polish National Catholic Church, the United Methodist Church, the Orthodox Churches, the Oriental Orthodox Churches, the Reformed Churches: the United Church of Christ, the Presbyterian Church, Christian Reformed Church and Reformed Church in America. There are dialogues with the National Association of Evangelicals, a regular Pentecostal Catholic dialogue in the context of the Society for Pentecostal Studies, and — until 2001 — a 30-year conversation with the Southern Baptist Convention. (See Ecumenical Dialogues.)

The committee relates with the National Council of Churches of Christ, through membership in the Faith and Order Commission, producing the annual Week of Prayer for Christian Unity, and has sponsored a joint study committee investigating the possibility of Roman Catholic membership in that body in the 1970's. Collaboration in multiple areas of Church life has proved to be more fruitful than membership given the disparity of numbers and diversity of program priorities of the Bishop's Conference and the Council.

The USCCB participates in a new ecumenical entity, Christian Churches Together in the USA. It includes representatives from the five major families of Christian churches in the United States which, in addition to the Catholic Church, include the historic Protestant, Orthodox, Evangelical/Pentecostal, and Racial/Ethnic churches.

Advisory and other services are provided by the committee to ecumenical commissions and agencies in dioceses throughout the country.

Through its Section for Catholic-Jewish Relations, the committee is in contact with several national Jewish agencies and bodies. Issues of mutual interest and shared concern are reviewed for the purpose of furthering deeper understanding between the Catholic and Jewish communities.

The committee also co-sponsors dialogues with Muslims, Buddhists and Hindus and other interreligious activities and programs. By the end of 2003, there were three regional dialogues with Muslims and one with Buddhists meeting annually and an annual ecumenical consultation with Hindus.

Offices of the committee are located at 3211 Fourth St. N.E., Washington, DC 20017; www.usccb.org/seia.

World Council of Churches

The World Council of Churches is a fellowship of churches which acknowledge "Jesus Christ as Lord and Savior." It is a permanent organization providing constituent members — 330 churches with some 450 million communicants in 100 countries — with opportunities for meeting, consultation and cooperative action with respect to doctrine, worship, practice, social mission, evangelism and missionary work, and other matters of mutual concern.

The WCC was formally established Aug. 23, 1948, in Amsterdam with ratification of a constitution by 147 communions. This action merged two previously existing movements — Life and Work (social mission), Faith and Order (doctrine) — which had initiated practical steps toward founding a fellowship of Christian churches at meetings held in Oxford, Edinburgh and Utrecht in 1937 and 1938. A third movement for cooperative missionary work, which originated about 1910 and, remotely, led to formation of the WCC, was incorporated into the council in 1971 under the title of the International Missionary Council.

Additional general assemblies of the council have been held since the charter meeting of 1948: in Evanston, IL (1954), New Delhi, India (1961), Uppsala, Sweden (1968), Nairobi, Kenya (1975), Vancouver, British Columbia, Canada (1983) and Canberra, Australia (1991). The 1998 general assembly was held in Harare, Zimbabwe, with the regular Catholic delegation in attendance, led by Abp. Mario Conti from Glasgow, Scotland. The Ninth General Assembly took place in Porto Alegre, Brazil, from Feb. 14–23, 2006. A Catholic delegation headed by Cardinal Walter Kasper, President of the Pontifical Council for Promoting Christian Unity, was present.

The council continues the work of the International Missionary Council, the Commission on Faith and Order, and the Commission on Church and Society. The work of the council is carried out through four program units: unity and renewal; mission, education and witness; justice, peace and creation; sharing and service.

Liaison between the council and the Vatican has been maintained since 1966 through a joint working group. Roman Catholic membership in the WCC is a question officially on the agenda of this body. The Joint Commission on Society, Development and Peace (SODEPAX) was an agency of the council and the Pontifical Commission for Justice and Peace from 1968 to Dec. 31, 1980, after which another working group was formed. Roman Catholics serve individually as full members of the Commission on Faith and Order and in various capacities on other program committees of the council.

WCC headquarters are located in Geneva, Switzerland. The United States Conference for the World Council of Churches at 475 Riverside Dr., Room 915, New York, NY 10115, provides liaison between the U.S. churches and Geneva, a communications office for secular and church media relations, and a publications office. The WCC also maintains fraternal relations with regional, national and local councils of churches throughout the world. Web site: www.wcc-coe.org/wcc/english.html.

National Council of Churches

The National Council of the Churches of Christ in the U.S.A., the largest ecumenical body in the United States, is an organization of 36 Protestant, Orthodox and Anglican communions, with an aggregate membership of about 50 million in 140,000 congregations.

The NCC, established by the churches in 1950, was structured through the merger of 12 separate cooperative agencies. Presently, the NCC carries on work in behalf of member churches in overseas ministries, Christian education, domestic social action, communications, disaster relief, refugee assistance, rehabilitation and development, biblical translation, international affairs, theological dialogue, interfaith activities, worship and evangelism, and other areas.

Policies of the NCC are determined by a general board of approximately 270 members appointed by the constituent churches. The board meets once a year.

NCC president: Archbishop Vicken Aykazian. General Secretary: Rev. Dr. Michael Kinnamon. NCC headquarters are located at 475 Riverside Drive, New York, NY 10115; (212) 870-2141; www.ncccusa.org.

Christian Churches Together in the USA

In early 2001, discussions began in earnest among church leaders in the United States about the possibility of forming a new ecumenical organization. There was an acute awareness that since the members of the current National Council of Churches (NCC) represent only about one third of the Christians in the United States, a much broader ecumenical witness was needed. Thus in the summer of 2001 letters were sent out to various American church leaders inviting them to attend a meeting at St. Mary's Seminary and University in Baltimore on Sept. 7-8. The letter was signed by Bishop Tod Brown, Cardinal William Keeler, Rev. Wesley Granberg-Michaelson (General Secretary of the Reformed Church in America), and Rev. Dr. Robert Edgar (NCC General Secretary). The meeting was to explore whether or not the time had come to "create a new, more inclusive ecumenical table and/or body." The most striking result was the unanimous strong desire among the participants for a broader structure of some kind that would include all the major groupings of churches, including the Catholic Church and major Evangelical and Pentecostal groups that do not now belong to the NCC. Subsequent organizational meetings were held in Chicago (April 2002), Pasadena (January 2003), and Navasota, TX (January 2004). The name chosen for the new entity is "Christian Churches Together in the USA" (CCT).

In November 2004, the Catholic Bishops of the United States took an historic ecumenical step by voting to participate in CCT. Bishop Stephen E. Blaire of Stockton, California, chairman of the Committee on Ecumenical and Interreligious Affairs, presented the proposal to the body of bishops and urged its adoption, calling CCT a "fresh and creative initiative to broaden the ecumenical table." The bishops approved the proposal to join CCT by a vote of 151-73, slightly more than a 2-to-1 margin.

From June 1 to 3, 2005, 67 national Christian leaders from five Christian families — Evangelical/Pentecostal, Historic Protestant, Historic Racial/Ethnic, Orthodox and Catholic— met in their fifth and largest CCT organizational meeting at the Jesuit Conference Center in Los Altos, CA. The gathering at Los Altos brought together a wider, more diverse circle of Christian church leaders than at any of the previous four meetings.

Thirty-one churches and national Christian organizations have now formally decided to join Christian Churches Together. Twenty additional church leaders attended as observers from denominations that are actively considering joining. Through two and a half days of sharing, prayer and worship, the participants wrestled with difficult and complex issues in a spirit of love and good will. Relationships with the Historic Black Churches were deepened through intensive dialogue and sharing.

It was decided at Los Altos to delay a formal launch planned for September 2005 in order to continue the productive and positive conversation with churches and organizations actively considering joining. Participants enthusiastically reaffirmed their commitment to "grow closer together in Christ in order to strengthen our Christian witness in the world." The Rev. Wesley Granberg-Michaelson was unanimously reelected as moderator to lead an expanded Steering Committee.

Another plenary meeting of CCT took place at Simpsonwood Conference and Retreat Center near Atlanta, GA, from Mar. 28–31, 2006. At this meeting the new By-laws of CCT were adopted and the new organization formally came into existence. Subsequent plenaries have been held in Pasadena, CA, in February 2007 and in Baltimore, MD, in January 2008. Forty-three churches and national Christian organizations currently participate in CCT (and 13 more are in the decision-making process), making it the broadest, most inclusive fellowship of Christian churches and traditions in the USA. The main focus of recent meetings has been poverty in the United States and evangelization.

Moderator (elected 2008): Rev. Leonid Kishkovsky; Catholic President: Archbp. Wilton D. Gregory of Atlanta; Executive Administrator: Dr. Richard L "Dick" Hamm; www.christianchurchestogether.org

Churches Uniting in Christ

Churches Uniting in Christ (CUIC) is a relationship among ten Christian communions that have pledged to live more closely together in expressing their unity in Christ and to combat racism together. CUIC is both an outgrowth of and successor to the Consultation on Church Union (COCU), an organization that worked for more than 40 years toward the day when Christians can become more fully reconciled to each other.

The eight marks of communion membership in the CUIC partnership are: mutual recognition of each other as authentic expressions of the one church of Jesus Christ, mutual recognition of members in one Baptism, mutual recognition that each affirms the apostolic faith of Scripture and tradition which is expressed in the Apostles' and Nicene Creeds, and that each seeks to give witness to the apostolic faith in its life and mission, provision for celebration of the Eucharist together with intentional regularity, engagement together in Christ's mission on a regular and intentional basis, especially a shared mission to combat racism, intentional commitment to promote unity with wholeness and to oppose marginalization and exclusion in church and society based on such things as race, age, gender, forms of disability, sexual orientation, and class, appropriate structures of accountability and appropriate means for consultation and decision making, an ongoing process of theological dialogue.

The member communions, representing 25 million Christians, are the African Methodist Episcopal Church, the African Methodist Episcopal Zion Church, the Christian Church (Disciples of Christ), the Christian Methodist Episcopal Church, the Episcopal Church, the Presbyterian Church (U.S.A), the United Church of Christ, the United Methodist Church, the Moravian Church Northern Province, and the International Council of Community Churches. The Evangelical Lutheran Church in America is a partner in mission and dialogue, and the Catholic Church is an official observer.

Three task forces were created to carry out the mission of CUIC. The Local and Regional Task Force was responsible for developing strategies to encourage and facilitate the formation of CUIC partnerships among local congregations and between regional governing bodies. The Ministry Task Force was responsible for providing a foundation for the mutual recognition and reconciliation of the ordained ministry of the member churches of Churches Uniting in Christ. The Racial Justice Task Force was responsible for promoting an open dialogue about racial justice within the life of the member churches and of society in general. It was also to develop strategies that would enable the churches to confront and eradicate the sin of racism. Though the participating churches have achieved broad consensus on matters of faith and sacramental worship, agreement about the mutual recognition of ministry remains elusive. Disagreements about ordained ministry are rooted in the distinctive histories, theologies, and polities of the member churches. In 2006 CUIC examined the historic episcopacy to assess whether it is a "pathway" or "barrier" to unity.

Catholic participation includes a staff representative to the CUIC coordinating council, with a voice but no vote, and Catholic membership on the task forces, with a voice and a vote. Catholic theologians have made a significant contribution by serving on the ministry task force and offering insights from the Catholic perspective. CUIC is presently working to reconcile with two of its member communions, the African Methodist Episcopal Church and the African Methodist Episcopal Zion Church, which have both suspended participation in its activities. At the January 2008 plenary meeting in St. Louis, CUIC set forth a plan to seek reconciliation with the separated churches. It also formed a consultative group, made up of representatives from each of the member communions, to assess the efficacy of CUIC's governance and programmatic structure in serving its mission and to reassess the role of racial justice work in relationship to the task of the mutual recognition of ordained ministries.

In the coming months, while efforts at reconciliation and a renewal of CUIC's mission are addressed, the work of the task forces has been suspended.

President: The Rev. Dr. Suzanne Webb, Union Avenue Christian Church (Disciples of Christ), 733 Union Blvd, St. Louis, MO 63108, (314-361-8844). The CUIC office is maintained on the Eden Theological Seminary campus, 475 Lockwood Ave., Webster Groves, MO, 63119, (314-252-3160), www.cuicinfo.org.

Graymoor Institute

The Graymoor Ecumenical and Interreligious Institute is a forum where issues that confront the Christian Churches are addressed, the spiritual dimensions of ecumenism are fostered, and information, documentation and developments within the ecumenical movement are published through *Ecumenical Trends*, a monthly journal. GEII also produces annual materials for the Week of Prayer for Christian Unity.

Director: The Rev. James Lougran. Address: 475 Riverside Dr., Rm. 1960, New York, NY 10115-1999.

INTERNATIONAL BILATERAL COMMISSIONS

Anglican-Roman Catholic International Commission, sponsored by the Pontifical Council for Promoting Christian Unity and the Lambeth Conference, from 1970 to 1981; succeeded by a Second Anglican-Roman Catholic International Commission, called into being by the Common Declaration of Pope John Paul and the Archbishop of Canterbury in 1982.

The International Theological Colloquium between Baptists and Catholics, established in 1984 by the Pontifical Council for Promoting Christian Unity and the Commission for Faith and Interchurch Cooperation of the Baptist World Alliance.

The Disciples of Christ-Roman Catholic Dialogue, organized by the Council of Christian Unity of the Christian Church (Disciples of Christ) and the U.S. Bishops' Committee for Ecumenical and Interreligious Affairs, along with participation by the Disciples' Ecumenical Consultative Council and the Unity Council; since 1977.

The Evangelical-Roman Catholic Dialogue on Mission, organized by Evangelicals and the Pontifical Council for Promoting Christian Unity; from 1977. This dialogue is now sponsored by the World Evangelical Alliance, on the evangelical side.

The Lutheran-Roman Catholic Commission on Unity, established by the Pontifical Council for Promoting Christian Unity and the Lutheran World Federation; from 1967.

The Joint International Commission for Theological Dialogue between the Orthodox Church and the Catholic Church, established by the Holy See and 14 autocephalous Orthodox Churches, began its work at a first session held at Patmos/Rhodes in 1980. Subsequent sessions have been held at Munich (1982), Crete (1984), Bari (1987), Valamo (1988), Freising (1990), Balamand (1993), and Emmitsburg, MD (2000); Belgrade, Serbia (2006); Ravenna, Italy (2007).

Pentecostal-Roman Catholic Conversations, since 1966.

The Reformed-Roman Catholic Conversations, inaugurated in 1970 by the Pontifical Council for Promoting Christian Unity and the World Alliance of Reformed Churches.

The International Joint Commission between the Catholic Church and the Coptic Orthodox Church, since 1974. Established officially in the Common Declaration signed by Pope Paul VI and Coptic Pope Shenouda III in Rome in 1973. Superseded in 2003 by the international dialogue with the Oriental Orthodox.

The Joint International Commission between the Roman Catholic Church and the Malankara Orthodox Syrian Church, since 1989.

The Joint Commission between the Catholic Church and the Malankara Jacobite Syrian Orthodox Church, since 1990.

The Assyrian Church of the East-Roman Catholic Dialogue, officially established in the Common Declaration signed by Pope John Paul II and Mar Dinkha IV in November 1994.

A new Catholic Church-Oriental Orthodox Churches International Joint Commission for Dialogue was planned at a Preparatory Meeting held in Rome in January 2003. The first meeting of the Joint Commission took place in Cairo in January 2004. Subsequent meetings have taken place in Rome (2005), Etchmiadzin, Armenia (2006), Rome (2007) and near Damascus, Syria (2008).

Dialogue between the World Evangelical Alliance and the Catholic Church begun in 1990 issued a statement in 2002.

Dialogue with the Mennonite World Conference begun in 1998 produced an agreed statement in 2003.

U.S. ECUMENICAL DIALOGUES

Representatives of the Bishops' Committee for Ecumenical and Interreligious Affairs, National Conference of Catholic Bishops, have met in dialogue with representatives of other churches since the 1960s, for discussion of a wide variety of subjects related to the quest for unity among Christians. Following is a list of dialogue groups and the years in which dialogue began.

Anglican-Roman Catholic Consultation, 1965; North American Orthodox-Catholic Theological Consultation, 1965; Joint Committee of Orthodox and Catholic Bishops, 1981; Lutheran Consultation, 1965; Oriental Orthodox Consultation (with Armenian, Coptic, Ethiopian, Indian Malabar and Syrian Orthodox Churches), 1978; Polish National-Catholic Consultation, 1984; Presbyterian/Reformed Consultation, 1965; Southern Baptist Conversations, 1969; United Methodist Consultation, 1966; Faith and Order National Council of Churches, 1968; National Association of Evangelicals, 2003.

COMMON DECLARATIONS OF POPES, OTHER CHURCH LEADERS

(Source: Secretariat of the Bishops' Committee for Ecumenical and Interreligious Affairs, United States Conference of Catholic Bishops.)

The following Common Declarations, issued by several popes and heads, carry the authority given them by their signators.

Paul VI and Orthodox Ecumenical Patriarch Athenagoras I, First Common Declaration, Dec. 7, 1965: They hoped the differences between the churches would be overcome with the help of the Holy Spirit, and that their "full communion of faith, brotherly concord and sacramental life" would be restored.

Paul VI and Anglican Archbishop Michael Ramsey of Canterbury, Mar. 24, 1966: They stated their intention "to inaugurate between the Roman Catholic Church and the Anglican Communion a serious dialogue which, founded on the Gospels and on the ancient common traditions, may lead to that unity in truth for which Christ prayed."

Paul VI and Patriarch Athenagoras I, Second Common Declaration, Oct. 27, 1967: They wished "to emphasize their conviction that the restoration of full communion (between the churches) is to be found within the framework of the renewal of the Church and of Christians in fidelity to the traditions of the Fathers and to the inspirations of the Holy Spirit who remains always with the Church."

Paul VI and Vasken I, Orthodox Catholicos-Patriarch of All Armenians, May 12, 1970: They called for closer collaboration "in all domains of Christian life…. This collaboration must be based on the mutual recognition of the common Christian faith and the sacramental life, on the mutual respect of persons and their churches."

Paul VI and Mar Ignatius Jacob III, Syrian Orthodox Patriarch of Antioch, Oct. 27, 1971: They declared themselves to be "in agreement that there is no difference in the faith they profess concerning the mystery of the Word of God made flesh and become really man, even if over the centuries difficulties have arisen out of the different theological expressions by which this faith was expressed."

Paul VI and Shenouda III, Coptic Orthodox Pope of Alexandria, May 10, 1973: Their common declaration recalls the common elements of the Catholic and Coptic Orthodox faith in the Trinity, the divinity and humanity of Christ, the seven sacraments, the Virgin Mary, the Church founded upon the Apostles, and the Second Coming of Christ. It recognizes that the two churches "are not able to give more perfect witness to this new life in Christ because of existing divisions which have behind them centuries of difficult history" dating back to the year A.D. 451. In spite of these difficulties, they expressed "determination and confidence in the Lord to achieve the fullness and perfection of that unity which is his gift."

Paul VI and Anglican Archbishop Donald Coggan of Canterbury, Apr. 29, 1977: They stated many points on which Anglicans and Roman Catholics hold the faith in common and called for greater cooperation between Anglicans and Roman Catholics.

John Paul II and Orthodox Ecumenical Patriarch Dimitrios I, First Common Declaration, Nov. 30, 1979: "Purification of the collective memory of our churches is an important fruit of the dialogue of charity and an indispensable condition of future progress." They announced the establishment of the Catholic-Orthodox Theological Commission.

John Paul II and Anglican Archbishop Robert Runcie of Canterbury, May 29, 1982: They agreed to establish a new Anglican-Roman Catholic commission with the task of continuing work already begun toward the eventual resolution of doctrinal differences.

John Paul II and Ignatius Zakka I, Syrian Orthodox Patriarch of Antioch, June 23, 1984: They recalled and solemnly reaffirmed the common profession of faith made by their predecessors, Paul VI and Mar Ignatius Jacob III, in 1971. They said: "The confusions and the schisms that occurred between the churches, they realize today, in no way affect or touch the substance of their faith, since these arose only because of differences in terminology and culture, and in the various formulae adopted by different theological schools to express the same matter. Accordingly, we find today no real basis for the sad divisions which arose between us concerning the doctrine of the Incarnation." On the pastoral level, they declared: "It is not rare for our faithful to find access to a priest of their own church materially or morally impossible. Anxious to meet their needs and with their spiritual benefit in mind, we authorize them in such cases to ask for the sacraments of penance, Eucharist and anointing of the sick from lawful priests of either of our two sister churches, when they need them."

John Paul II and Orthodox Ecumenical Patriarch Dimitrios I, Second Common Declaration, Dec. 7, 1987: Dialogue conducted since 1979 indicated that the churches can already profess together as common faith about the mystery of the Church and the connection between faith and the sacraments. They also stated that, "when unity of faith is assured, a certain diversity of expressions does not create obstacles to unity, but enriches the life of the Church and the understanding, always imperfect, of the revealed mystery."

John Paul II and Anglican Archbishop Robert Runcie of Canterbury, Oct. 2, 1989: They said: "We solemnly re-commit ourselves and those we represent to the restoration of visible unity and full ecclesial communion in the confidence that to seek anything less would be to betray our Lord's intention for the unity of his people."

John Paul II and His Holiness Mar Dinkha IV, Catholicos-Patriarch of the Assyrian Church of the East, Nov. 11, 1994: Following is the text of the "Common

Christological Declaration" between the Catholic Church and the Assyrian Church of the East, signed Nov. 11, 1994, by Pope John Paul II and His Holiness Mar Dinkha IV, Catholicos-Patriarch of the Assyrian Church of the East. The declaration acknowledges that, despite past differences, both churches profess the same faith in the real union of divine and human natures in the divine Person of Christ. Providing background to the declaration was the Assyrian Church's adherence to the teaching of Nestorius who, in the fifth century, denied the real unity of divine and human natures in the single divine Person of Christ.

Pope John Paul II with Ecumenical Orthodox Patriarch Bartholomew I, June 29, 1995: Pope John Paul and Ecumenical Orthodox Patriarch Bartholomew I, after several days of meetings, signed a common declaration June 29, 1995, declaring: "Our meeting has followed other important events which have seen our Churches declare their desire to relegate the excommunications of the past to oblivion and to set out on the way to establishing full communion." This dialogue — through the Joint International (Catholic-Orthodox) Commission — has proved fruitful and has made substantial progress.

Pope John Paul II with Anglican Archbishop George Carey, Common Ecumenical Declaration, Dec. 5, 1996: The pontiff and archbishop praised the work of the Anglican-Roman Catholic International Commission and stated that "In many parts of the world Anglicans and Catholics attempt to witness together in the face of growing secularism, religious apathy and moral confusion."

Pope John Paul II with Karekin I, Catholicos of All Armenians, Dec. 13, 1996.

Pope John Paul and His Holiness Karekin I, Supreme Patriarch and Catholicos of All Armenians, signed Dec. 13, 1996, signed a common declaration in which they said in part: "Pope John Paul II and Catholicos Karekin I recognize the deep spiritual communion which already unites them and the bishops and clergy and lay faithful of their churches. It is a communion which finds its roots in the common faith in the holy and life-giving Trinity proclaimed by the Apostles and transmitted down the centuries. . . . They rejoice in the fact that recent developments of ecumenical relations and theological discussions . . . have dispelled many misunderstandings inherited from the controversies and dissensions of the past. Such dialogues and encounters have prepared a healthy situation of mutual understanding and recovery of the deeper spiritual communion based on the common faith in the holy Trinity that they have been given through the Gospel of Christ and in the holy tradition of the Church.

Pope John Paul II with Aram I, Armenian Catholicos of Cilicia, Jan. 25, 1997: The common declaration stated, "the two spiritual leaders stress the vital importance of sincere dialogue. The Catholic Church and the Catholicate of Cilicia also have an immense field of constructive cooperation before them."

Cardinal Edward Cassidy with Bishop Christian Krause, President of the Lutheran World Federation, Oct. 31, 1999: "Joint Declaration on Justification by Faith."

Pope John Paul II with Karekin II, Catholicos of All Armenians, Nov. 10, 2000 in Rome: His Holiness Pope John Paul II, Bishop of Rome, and His Holiness Karekin II, Supreme Patriarch and Catholicos of All Armenians, give thanks to the Lord and Savior Jesus Christ, for enabling them to meet together on the occasion of the Jubilee of the Year 2000 and on the threshold of the 1700th anniversary of the proclamation of Christianity as the state religion of Armenia.

Pope John Paul II with Christodoulos, Archbishop of Athens, May 4, 2001: The common declaration stated: We are anguished to see that wars, massacres, torture and martyrdom constitute a terrible daily reality for millions of our brothers. We commit ourselves to struggle for the prevailing of peace throughout the whole world, for the respect of life and human dignity, and for solidarity towards all who are in need.

John Paul II and Karekin II, Catholicos of All Armenians, Sept. 27, 2001, in Etchmiadzin, Armenia:

The celebration of the 1700th anniversary of the proclamation of Christianity as the religion of Armenia has brought us together — John Paul II, Bishop of Rome and Pastor of the Catholic Church, and Karekin II, the Supreme Patriarch and Catholicos of All Armenians — and we thank God for giving us this joyous opportunity to join again in common prayer, in praise of his all-holy Name. Blessed be the Holy Trinity — Father, Son and Holy Spirit — now and forever.

Pope John Paul II and Ecumenical Patriarch Bartholomew I signed a Common Declaration on Environmental Ethics, June 10, 2002: We are gathered here today in the spirit of peace for the good of all human beings and for the care of creation. At this moment in history, at the beginning of the third millennium, we are saddened to see the daily suffering of a great number of people from violence, starvation, poverty and disease. We are also concerned about the negative consequences for humanity and for all creation resulting from the degradation of some basic natural resources such as water, air and land, brought about by an economic and technological progress which does not recognize and take into account its limits. Rome — Venice, June 10, 2002.

Pope John Paul II and Patriarch Teoctist of the Romanian Orthodox Church signed a Joint Declaration in Rome on Oct. 12, 2002: The glory which you have given me I have given to them, that they may be one even as we are one, I in them and you in me, that they may become perfectly one, so that the world may know that you have sent me and have loved them even as you have loved me" (Jn 17:22-23).

In the deep joy of being together again in the city of Rome, close to the tombs of the holy Apostles Peter and Paul, we exchange the kiss of peace under the gaze of the One who watches over his Church and guides our steps; and we meditate anew on these words, which the Evangelist John transmitted to us and which constitute Christ's heartfelt prayer on the eve of his Passion.

Pope John Paul II and Ecumenical Patriarch Bartholomew I signed a Common Declaration in Rome on June 29, 2004: Unity and Peace! The hope kindled by that historic encounter has lit up our journey in these last decades. Aware that the Christian world has suffered the tragedy of separation for centuries, our Predecessors and we ourselves have persevered in the 'dialogue of charity,' our gaze turned to that blessed, shining day on which it will be possible to communicate with the same cup of the precious Blood and the holy Body of the Lord (cf. Patriarch Athenagoras I, Address to Pope Paul VI [Jan. 5, 1964], ibid., no. 48, p. 109).

Despite our firm determination to journey on towards full communion, it would have been unrealistic not to expect obstacles of various kinds: doctrinal, first of all, but also the result of conditioning by a troubled history. In addition, the new problems which have emerged from the radical changes that have occurred in political and social structures have not failed to make themselves felt in relations between the Christian Churches. With the return to freedom of Christians in Central and Eastern Europe, old fears have also been reawakened, making dialogue difficult. Nonetheless, St

Paul's exhortation to the Corinthians: let all things be done in charity, must always be vibrant within us and between us...

Pope Benedict XVI and Ecumenical Patriarch Bartholomew I signed a Common Declaration in Constantinople (Istanbul) on Nov. 30, 2006:

This fraternal encounter which brings us together, Pope Benedict XVI of Rome and Ecumenical Patriarch Bartholomew I, is God's work, and in a certain sense his gift. We give thanks to the Author of all that is good, who allows us once again, in prayer and in dialogue, to express the joy we feel as brothers and to renew our commitment to move towards full communion. This commitment comes from the Lord's will and from our responsibility as Pastors in the Church of Christ. May our meeting be a sign and an encouragement for us to share the same sentiments and the same attitudes of fraternity, cooperation and communion in charity and truth. The Holy Spirit will help us to prepare the great day of the re-establishment of full unity, whenever and however God wills it. Then we shall truly be able to rejoice and be glad.

1. We have recalled with thankfulness the meetings of our venerable predecessors, blessed by the Lord, who showed the world the urgent need for unity and traced sure paths for attaining it, through dialogue, prayer and the daily life of the Church. Pope Paul VI and Patriarch Athenagoras I went as pilgrims to Jerusalem, to the very place where Jesus Christ died and rose again for the salvation of the world, and they also met again, here in the Phanar and in Rome. They left us a common declaration which retains all its value; it emphasizes that true dialogue in charity must sustain and inspire all relations between individuals and between Churches, that it "must be rooted in a total fidelity to the one Lord Jesus Christ and in mutual respect for their own traditions" (Tomos Agapis, 195). Nor have we forgotten the reciprocal visits of His Holiness Pope John Paul II and His Holiness Dimitrios I. It was during the visit of Pope John Paul II, his first ecumenical visit, that the creation of the Mixed Commission for Theological Dialogue between the Roman Catholic Church and the Orthodox Church was announced. This Commission brought our Churches together with the declared aim of re-establishing full communion.

As far as relations between the Church of Rome and the Church of Constantinople are concerned, we cannot fail to recall the solemn ecclesial act effacing the memory of the ancient anathemas which for centuries have had a negative effect on relations between our Churches. We have not yet drawn from this act all the positive consequences which can flow from it in our progress towards full unity, to which the mixed Commission is called to make an important contribution. We exhort our faithful to take an active part in this process, through prayer and through significant gestures.

2. At the time of the plenary session of the mixed Commission for theological dialogue, which was recently held in Belgrade through the generous hospitality of the Serbian Orthodox Church, we expressed our profound joy at the resumption of the theological dialogue. This had been interrupted for several years because of various difficulties, but now the Commission has been able to work afresh in a spirit of friendship and cooperation. In treating the topic "Conciliarity and Authority in the Church" at local, regional and universal levels, the Commission undertook a phase of study on the ecclesiological and canonical consequences of the sacramental nature of the Church. This will permit us to address some of the principal questions that are still unresolved. We are committed to offer unceasing support, as in the past, to the work entrusted to this Commission and we

accompany its members with our prayers.

3. As Pastors, we have first of all reflected on the mission to proclaim the Gospel in today's world. This mission, "Go, make disciples of all nations" (Mt 28:19), is today more timely and necessary than ever, even in traditionally Christian countries. Moreover, we cannot ignore the increase of secularization, relativism, even nihilism, especially in the Western world. All this calls for a renewed and powerful proclamation of the Gospel, adapted to the cultures of our time. Our traditions represent for us a patrimony which must be continually shared, proposed, and interpreted anew. This is why we must strengthen our cooperation and our common witness before the world.

4. We have viewed positively the process that has led to the formation of the European Union. Those engaged in this great project should not fail to take into consideration all aspects affecting the inalienable rights of the human person, especially religious freedom, a witness and guarantor of respect for all other freedoms. In every step towards unification, minorities must be protected, with their cultural traditions and the distinguishing features of their religion. In Europe, while remaining open to other religions and to their cultural contributions, we must unite our efforts to preserve Christian roots, traditions and values, to ensure respect for history, and thus to contribute to the European culture of the future and to the quality of human relations at every level. In this context, how could we not evoke the very ancient witnesses and the illustrious Christian heritage of the land in which our meeting is taking place, beginning with what the Acts of the Apostles tells us in evoking the figure of Saint Paul, Apostle of the Gentiles? In this land, the Gospel message and the cultural tradition of the ancient world met. This link, which has contributed so much to the Christian heritage that we share, remains timely and will bear more fruit in the future for evangelization and for our unity.

5. Our concern extends to those parts of today's world where Christians live and to the difficulties they have to face, particularly poverty, wars and terrorism, but equally to various forms of exploitation of the poor, of migrants, women and children. We are called to work together to promote respect for the rights of every human being, created in the image and likeness of God, and to foster economic, social and cultural development. Our theological and ethical traditions can offer a solid basis for a united approach in preaching and action. Above all, we wish to affirm that killing innocent people in God's name is an offence against him and against human dignity. We must all commit ourselves to the renewed service of humanity and the defence of human life, every human life.

We take profoundly to heart the cause of peace in the Middle East, where our Lord lived, suffered, died and rose again, and where a great multitude of our Christian brethren have lived for centuries. We fervently hope that peace will be re-established in that region, that respectful coexistence will be strengthened between the different peoples that live there, between the Churches and between the different religions found there. To this end, we encourage the establishment of closer relationships between Christians, and of an authentic and honest interreligious dialogue, with a view to combating every form of violence and discrimination.

6. At present, in the face of the great threats to the natural environment, we want to express our concern at the negative consequences for humanity and for the whole of creation which can result from economic and technological progress that does not know its limits. As religious leaders, we consider it one of our duties to encourage and to support all efforts

made to protect God's creation, and to bequeath to future generations a world in which they will be able to live.

7. Finally, our thoughts turn towards all of you, the faithful of our Churches throughout the world, Bishops, priests, deacons, men and women religious, lay men and women engaged in ecclesial service, and all the baptized. In Christ we greet other Christians, assuring them of our prayers and our openness to dialogue and cooperation. In the words of the Apostle of the Gentiles, we greet all of you: "Grace to you and peace from God our Father and the Lord Jesus Christ" (2 Cor 1:2). — From the Phanar, Nov. 30, 2006.

Common Declaration Signed By Pope Benedict XVI and H.B. Christodoulos, Archbishop of Athens and All of Greece.

The Common Declaration was signed by Pope Benedict XVI and Archbishop Christodoulos of Athens and All Greece during the Archbishop's visit to Rome on Dec. 14, 2006:

1. We, Benedict XVI, Pope and Bishop of Rome, and Christodoulos, Archbishop of Athens and All Greece, in this sacred place of Rome, renowned for the preaching of the Gospel and the martyrdom of the Apostles Peter and Paul, desire to live ever more intensely our mission to offer an apostolic witness, to pass on the faith to those both near and far and to proclaim to them the Good News of the Savior's birth, which we will both be celebrating shortly. It is also our common responsibility to overcome the many problems and painful experiences of the past in love and truth, for the glory of God, the Blessed Trinity, and of his Holy Church.

2. Our meeting in charity makes us ever more conscious of our common task: to travel together along the arduous route of a dialogue in truth with a view to re-establishing the full communion of faith in the bond of love. Thus, we will be obeying the divine commandment and will put into practice the prayer of Our Lord Jesus Christ. In addition, enlightened by the Holy Spirit, who accompanies Christ's Church and never abandons her, we will persevere in our commitment on this path, following the example of the Apostles and demonstrating our mutual love and spirit of reconciliation.

3. With regard to our relations, we recognize the important steps that have been taken in the dialogue of charity and by the decisions of the Second Vatican Council. Furthermore, we hope that the bilateral theological dialogue will carry forward these positive elements to formulate proposals accepted by both parties in a spirit of reconciliation, after the example of our illustrious Father of the Church, Saint Basil the Great, who, in a period of manifold divisions in the Ecclesial Body, declared his conviction "that by extended communication and mutual experience without strife, if anything more requires to be added by way of explanation, the Lord, who works all things together for the good of those who love him, will grant it" (cf. Letter, 113).

4. We unanimously declare the need to persevere on the path of constructive theological dialogue. Despite the difficulties noted, this path is one of the essential means we have at our disposal to re-establish around the altar of the Lord the unity so longed for by the Ecclesial Body, and likewise, to strengthen the credibility of the Christian message in this period of social upheaval in which we live, amid the great spiritual hunger of many of our contemporaries who are anxious about the increasing globalization that sometimes even threatens man's existence and his relationship to God and to the world.

5. In a very special way, we solemnly renew our desire to proclaim the Gospel of Jesus Christ to the world, especially to the new generations because "the love of Christ impels us" (2 Cor 5:14), and to enable them to discover the Lord, who came into our world so that all might have life and have it abundantly. This is particularly important in our societies where many currents of thought distance people from God and fail to give life meaning. We desire to proclaim the Gospel of grace and love so that all people may also be in communion with the Father, the Son and the Holy Spirit, and that their joy may be complete.

6. We believe that religions have a role to play in guaranteeing the spread of peace in the world and in ensuring that they themselves in no way foster intolerance or violence. As Christian religious leaders, together we urge all religious leaders to pursue and to strengthen interreligious dialogue and to strive to create a society of peace and brotherhood between individuals and peoples. This is one of the tasks of religions. In this regard, Christians are working and wish to continue working in the world with all people of good will in a spirit of solidarity and brotherhood.

7. We wish to pay tribute to the impressive progress achieved in all areas of science, especially with regard to the human being. However, we invite governments and scientists to respect the sacredness of the human person and his dignity, because his life is a divine gift. We are concerned to see that some branches of science are experimenting on the human being, without respect for either the dignity or the integrity of the person in all the stages of his life, from conception to his natural end.

8. Furthermore, we ask for greater sensitivity in order to protect more effectively in our countries, in Europe and internationally, the fundamental human rights that are based on the dignity of the human being created in God's image.

9. We look forward to a fruitful collaboration to enable our contemporaries to rediscover the Christian roots of the European Continent which forged the different nations and contributed to developing increasingly harmonious links between them. This will help them live and promote the fundamental human and spiritual values for all people, as well as the development of their own societies.

10. We recognize the merits of the progress of technology and economics for a great number of modern societies. Nevertheless, we also invite rich countries to pay greater attention to developing and poorer countries in a spirit of generous solidarity, recognizing that all people are our brothers and sisters and that we are duty bound to come to the aid of the lowliest and the poorest who are the beloved of the Lord. In this regard, it is also important not to exploit or abuse creation, which is the work of God. In this regard, we appeal to social leaders and to all people of good will to engage in a reasonable and respectful stewardship of creation, so that it may be correctly administered in a spirit of solidarity, especially for the sake of peoples afflicted by famine, so as to bequeath to future generations a world that is truly inhabitable for everyone.

11. Our common convictions impel us to repeat our wish to work together in the development of society with constructive cooperation for the service of humanity and of peoples, bearing witness to the faith and hope that motivate us.

12. Especially mindful of the Orthodox and Catholic faithful, we offer them our greeting and entrust them to Christ the Saviour, so that they may be tireless witnesses of God's love, and we make it our fervent prayer that the Lord will grant peace to all people, in the charity and unity of the human family. — From the Vatican, Dec. 14, 2006.

Common Declaration Signed By Pope Benedict XVI and Chrysostomos II, Archbishop of Nea Justiniana and All Cyprus

"Blessed be God and Father of Our Lord Jesus Christ, who

has blessed us in Christ with every spiritual blessing in the heavenly places" (Eph 1: 3).1. We, Benedict XVI, Pope and Bishop of Rome, and Chrysostomos II, Archbishop of Nea Justiniana and All Cyprus, full of hope for the future of our Churches' relations, thank God with joy for this fraternal meeting in our common faith in the Risen Christ. This visit has enabled us to observe how these relations have increased, both at a local level and in the context of the theological dialogue between the Catholic Church and the Orthodox Church as a whole. The Delegation of the Church of Cyprus has always made a positive contribution to this dialogue; among other things, for instance, in 1983 it hosted the Coordination Committee of the International Joint Commission for Theological Dialogue, so that in addition to doing the demanding preparatory work, the Catholic and Orthodox Members were able to visit and admire the great spiritual riches and wealth of art works of the Church of Cyprus.

2. On the happy occasion of our fraternal encounter at the tombs of Sts Peter and Paul, the "coryphaei of the Apostles," as liturgical tradition says, we would like to declare of common accord our sincere and firm willingness, in obedience to the desire of Our Lord Jesus Christ, to intensify our search for full unity among all Christians, making every possible effort deemed useful to the life of our Communities. We desire that the Catholic and Orthodox faithful of Cyprus live a fraternal life in full solidarity, based on our common faith in the Risen Christ. We also wish to sustain and encourage the theological dialogue which is preparing through the competent International Commission to address the most demanding issues that marked the historical event of the division. For full communion in the faith, the sacramental life and the exercise of the pastoral ministry, it is necessary to reach substantial agreement. To this end, we assure our faithful of our fervent prayers as Pastors in the Church and ask them to join us in a unanimous invocation "that they may all be one... so that the world may believe" (Jn 17: 21).

3. At our meeting, we reviewed the historical situations in which our Churches are living. In particular, we examined the situation of division and tensions that have marked the Island of Cyprus for more than 30 years, with its tragic daily problems which impair the daily life of our communities and of individual families. More generally, we considered the situation in the Middle East, where the war and conflicts between peoples risk spreading with disastrous consequences. We prayed for the peace that "comes from the heavenly places." It is the intention of our Churches to play a role of peacemaking in justice and solidarity and, to achieve all this, it is our constant wish to foster fraternal relations among all Christians and loyal dialogue between the different religions present and active in the Region. May faith in the one God help the people of these ancient and celebrated regions to rediscover friendly coexistence, in reciprocal respect and constructive collaboration.

4. We therefore address this appeal to all those who, everywhere in the world, raise their hand against their own brethren, exhorting them firmly to lay down their weapons and to take steps to heal the injuries caused by war. We also ask them to spare no effort to ensure that human rights are always defended in every nation: respect for the human person, an image of God, is in fact a fundamental duty for all. Thus, among the human rights to be safeguarded, freedom of religion should be at the top of the list. Failure to respect this right constitutes a very serious offence to the dignity of the human being, who is struck deep within his heart where God dwells. Consequently, to profane, destroy or sack the places of worship of any religion is an act against humanity and the civilization of the peoples.

5. We did not omit to reflect on a new opportunity that is opening for more intense contact and more concrete collaboration between our Churches. In fact, the building of the European Union is progressing, and Catholics and Orthodox are called to contribute to creating a climate of friendship and cooperation. At a time when secularization and relativism are growing, Catholics and Orthodox in Europe are called to offer a renewed common witness to the ethical values, ever ready to account for their faith in Jesus Christ, Lord and Savior. The European Union, which will not be able to restrict itself to merely economic cooperation, needs sound cultural foundations, shared ethical references and openness to the religious dimension. It is essential to revive the Christian roots of Europe which made its civilization great down the centuries and to recognize that in this regard the Western and Eastern Christian traditions have a common task to achieve.

6. At our encounter, therefore, we considered our Churches' long journey through history and the great tradition which has come down to our day, starting with the proclamation of the first disciples, who came to Cyprus from Jerusalem after the persecution of Stephen, and reviewing Paul's voyage from the coasts of Cyprus to Rome as it is recounted in the Acts of the Apostles (Acts 11: 19; 27: 4ff.). The rich patrimony of faith and the solid Christian tradition of our lands should spur Catholics and Orthodox to a renewed impetus in proclaiming the Gospel in our age, in being faithful to our Christian vocation and in responding to the demands of the contemporary world.

7. The treatment of bioethical issues gives rise to serious concern. Indeed, there is a risk that certain techniques, applied to genetics, intentionally conceived to meet legitimate needs, actually go so far as to undermine the dignity of the human being created in the image of God. The exploitation of human beings, abusive experimentation and genetic experiments which fail to respect ethical values are an offence against life and attack the safety and dignity of every human person, in whose existence they can never be either justified or permitted.

8. At the same time, these ethical considerations and a shared concern for human life prompt us to invite those nations which, with God's grace, have made significant progress in the areas of the economy and technology, not to forget their brothers and sisters who live in countries afflicted by poverty, hunger and disease. We therefore ask the leaders of nations to encourage and promote an equitable distribution of the goods of the earth in a spirit of solidarity with the poor and with all those who are destitute in the world.

9. We also concurred in our anxiety about the risk of destroying the creation. Man received it so that he might implement God's plan. However, by setting himself up at the centre of the universe, forgetting the Creator's mandate and shutting himself in a selfish search for his own well-being, the human being has managed the environment in which he lives by putting into practice decisions that threaten his own existence, whereas the environment requires the respect and protection of all who dwell in it.

10. Let us address together this prayer to the Lord of history, so that he will strengthen our Churches' witness in order that the Gospel proclamation of salvation may reach the new generations and be a light for all men and women. To this end, we entrust our desires and commitments to the Theotokos, the Mother of God Hodegetria, who points out the way to Our Lord Jesus Christ. — From the Vatican, June 16, 2007.

ECUMENICAL STATEMENTS

The ecumenical statements listed below, and others like them, reflect the views of participants in the dialogues which produced them. They have not been formally accepted by the respective churches as formulations of doctrine or points of departure for practical changes in discipline. (For other titles, see U.S. Ecumenical Dialogues, Ecumenical Reports.)

• The "Windsor Statement" on Eucharistic doctrine, published Dec. 31, 1971, by the Anglican-Roman Catholic International Commission of theologians. (For text, see pages 132-33 of the 1973 *Catholic Almanac*.)

• The "Canterbury Statement" on ministry and ordination, published Dec. 13, 1973, by the same commission. (For excerpts, see pages 127-30 of the 1975 *Catholic Almanac*.)

• "Papal Primacy/Converging Viewpoints," published Mar. 4, 1974, by the dialogue group sanctioned by the U.S.A. National Convention of the World Lutheran Federation and the U.S. Bishops' Committee for Ecumenical and Interreligious Affairs. (For excerpts, see pages 130-31 of the 1975 *Catholic Almanac*.)

• An "Agreed Statement on the Purpose of the Church," published Oct. 31, 1975, by the Anglican-Roman Catholic Consultation in the U.S.

• "Christian Unity and Women's Ordination," published Nov. 7, 1975, by the same consultation, in which it was said that the ordination of women (approved in principle by the Anglican Communion but not by the Catholic Church) would "introduce a new element" in dialogue but would not mean the end of consultation nor the abandonment of its declared goal of full communion and organic unity.

• "Holiness and Spirituality of the Ordained Ministry," issued early in 1976 by theologians of the Catholic Church and the United Methodist Church; the first statement resulting from dialogue begun in 1966.

• "Mixed Marriages," published in the spring of 1976 by the Anglican-Roman Catholic Consultation in the U.S.

• "Bishops and Presbyters," published in July 1976, by the Orthodox-Roman Catholic Consultation in the U.S. on the following points of common understanding: (1) Ordination in apostolic succession is required for pastoral office in the Church. (2) Presiding at the Eucharistic Celebration is a task belonging to those ordained to pastoral service. (3) The offices of bishop and presbyter are different realizations of the sacrament of order. (4) Those ordained are claimed permanently for the service of the Church.

• "The Principle of Economy," published by the body named above at the same time, concerning God's plan and activities in human history for salvation.

• "Venice Statement" on authority in the Church, published Jan. 20, 1977, by the Anglican-Roman Catholic International Commission of theologians.

• "Response to the Venice Statement," issued Jan. 4, 1978, by the Anglican-Roman Catholic Consultation in the U.S.A., citing additional questions.

• "An Ecumenical Approach to Marriage," published in January 1978, by representatives of the Catholic Church, the Lutheran World Federation and the World Alliance of Reformed Churches.

• "Teaching Authority and Infallibility in the Church," released in October 1978, by the Catholic-Lutheran dialogue group in the U.S.

• "The Eucharist," reported early in 1979, in which the Roman Catholic-Lutheran Commission indicated developing convergence of views.

• "The Holy Spirit," issued Feb. 12, 1979, by the International Catholic-Methodist Commission.

• A statement on "Ministry in the Church," published in March 1981, by the International Roman Catholic-Lutheran Joint Commission, regarding possible mutual recognition of ministries.

• The Final Report of the Anglican-Roman Catholic International Commission, 1982, on the results of 12 years of dialogue.

• "The Mystery of the Church and of the Eucharist in the Light of the Mystery of the Holy Trinity," issued by the Mixed International Commission for Theological Dialogue between the Catholic Church and the Orthodox Church at Munich, Germany, in July 1982.

• The Final Report of the Anglican-Roman Catholic International Commission, 1982, on the results of 12 years of dialogue.

• "Justification by Faith," issued Sept. 30, 1983, by the U.S. Lutheran-Roman Catholic dialogue group, claiming a "fundamental consensus on the Gospel."

• "Images of God: Reflections on Christian Anthropology," released Dec. 22, 1983, by the Anglican-Roman Catholic Dialogue in the United States.

• "The Journeying Together in Christ — The Report of the Polish National Catholic-Roman Catholic Dialogue (1984-89)."

• "Salvation and the Church," issued Jan. 22, 1987, by the Second Anglican-Roman Catholic International Commission.

• "Faith, Sacraments and the Unity of the Church," issued by the Mixed International Commission for Theological Dialogue between the Catholic Church and the Orthodox Churches in June 1987.

• "The Sacrament of Order in the Sacramental Structure of the Church, with Particular Reference to the Importance of Apostolic Succession for the Sanctification and Unity of the People of God," issued by the Mixed International Commission for Theological Dialogue between the Catholic Church and the Orthodox Church in Valamo, Finland, in 1988.

• "The Presence of Christ in Church and World" and "Toward a Common Understanding of the Church" (developed between 1984 and 1990), by the Reformed-Roman Catholic Conversations, under the auspices of the Pontifical Council for Promoting Christian Unity and the World Alliance of Reformed Churches.

• "The Church as Communion," issued by the Second Anglican-Roman Catholic International Commission, 1991.

• "Uniatism, Method of Union of the Past, and the Present Search for Full Communion," issued by the Joint International Commission for Theological Dialogue between the Catholic Church and the Orthodox Church at Balamand, Lebanon, in 1993.

• "Life in Christ: Morals, Communion and the Church," issued by the Second Anglican-Roman Catholic International Commission, 1994.

• "Common Response to the Aleppo Statement on the Date of Easter/Pacha," issued by the North American Orthodox-Catholic Theological Consultation in Washington, DC, Oct. 31, 1998.

• "The Gift of Authority," issued by the Second Anglican-Roman Catholic International Commission, May 12, 1999.

• "Baptism and 'Sacramental Economy,'" issued by the North American Orthodox-Catholic Theological Consultation at Crestwood, NY, in June 1999.
• "Guidelines Concerning the Pastoral Care of Oriental Orthodox Students in Catholic Schools," issued by the Oriental Orthodox-Roman Catholic Theological Consultation in the United States at New Rochelle, NY, in June 1999.
• "Joint Declaration of the Catholic Church and the Lutheran World Federation on the Doctrine of Justification," issued July 8, 1999, by the International Roman Catholic-Lutheran Joint Commission.
• "Agreed Report on the Local/Universal Church," issued by the United States Anglican-Roman Catholic Consultation, Nov. 12, 1999.
• "Communion in Mission" and "Action Plan to Implement 'Communion in Mission,'" issued by a special consultation of Anglican and Roman Catholic bishops in Mississauga, Ontario, Canada, May 19, 2000.
• "Sharing the Ministry of Reconciliation: A Statement on the Orthodox-Catholic Dialogue and the Ecumenical Movement," issued June 1, 2000, by the North American Orthodox-Catholic Theological Consultation in Brookline, MA.
• "Methodist-Catholic Dialogues: Thirty Years of Mission and Witness," issued by the U.S. dialogue in 2001.
• "Doing the Truth in Charity," issued in July 2001 by the World Methodist Council and the Pontifical Council for Promoting Unity's Methodist-Catholic International Commission.
• "Interchurch Families: Resources for Ecumenical Hope," issued by the Catholic/Reformed Dialogue in the United States in 2002.
• Response of the Anglican-Roman Catholic Consultation

in the USA to the Anglican-Roman Catholic International Commission's "The Gift of Authority" (Mar. 29, 2003).
• "Called Together to be Peacemakes," Mennonite World Conference Catholic Dialogue 2003.
• "Church, Evangelization, and *Koinonia*," World Evangelical Alliance – Pontifical Council for Promoting Christian Unity 2003.
• "The *Filioque*: A Church-Dividing Issue?" issued by the North American Orthodox-Catholic Theological Consultation, October 2003.
• "The Church as *Koinonia* of Salvation: Its Structures and Ministries," May 2004, Lutheran Catholic Dialogue in the U.S.
• "Mary: Grace and Hope in Christ," Anglican Roman Catholic Commission, 2004.
• "Journey in Faith: Forty Years of Reformed-Catholic Dialogue: 1965-2005," 2005.
• "Through Divine Love: The Church in Each Place and All Places," April 2005, United Methodist Roman Catholic Dialogue in the U.S.
• "Joint Declaration on Unity," by the Polish National Catholic – Roman Catholic Dialogue (May 17, 2006).
•ARCUSA Response to "Mary: Grace & Hope in Christ," October 2007, Anglican-Roman Catholic Consultation in the USA.
• "Ecclesiological and Canonical Consequences of the Sacramental Nature of the Church: Ecclesial Communion, Conciliarity and Authority," issued by the Joint International Commission for Theological Dialogue between the Catholic Church and the Orthodox Church at Ravenna, Italy, on Oct. 13, 2007. See online: www.prounione.urbe.it/dia-int/e_dialogues.html, or http://www.usccb.org/seia/.

SEPARATED EASTERN CHURCHES

This is a group of Eastern churches of the Byzantine tradition that were in full communion with Rome during the first millennium, and which all recognize the Patriarch of Constantinople as the first Orthodox bishop. In spite of the division between Catholics and Orthodox, often symbolized by the mutual excommunications of 1054, the Catholic Church considers itself to be in almost full communion with the Orthodox Churches. According to Vatican II, they "are still joined to us in closest intimacy" in various ways, especially in the priesthood and Eucharist. The Orthodox Churches recognize the first seven ecumenical councils as normative for their faith, along with the Scriptures and other local councils that took place in later centuries.
The Orthodox Churches are organized in approximately 15 autocephalous (independent) churches that correspond in most cases to nations or ethnic groups. The Ecumenical Patriarch of Constantinople (modern Istanbul) has a primacy of honor among the patriarchs, but his actual jurisdiction is limited to his own patriarchate. As the spiritual head of worldwide Orthodoxy, he serves as a point of unity, and has the right to call Pan-Orthodox assemblies.
Top-level relations between the Churches have improved in recent years through the efforts of Ecumenical Patriarch Athenagoras I, Bl. John XXIII, Paul VI and Patriarch

Dimitrios I. Pope Paul met with Athenagoras three times before the latter's death in 1972. The most significant action of both spiritual leaders was their mutual nullification of excommunications imposed by the two Churches on each other in 1054. Development of better relations with the Orthodox was a priority of John Paul II, as well as Benedict XVI. Both Pope Benedict and Orthodox Ecumenical Patriarch Bartholomew have made known their commitment to better relations, despite contentions between Eastern Catholic and Orthodox Churches over charges of proselytism and rival property claims in places liberated from anti-religious communist control in the recent past.
The largest Orthodox body in the United States is the Greek Orthodox Archdiocese of America consisting of nine dioceses; it has an estimated membership of 1.9 million. The second largest is the Orthodox Church in America, with more than one million members; it was given autocephalous status by the Patriarchate of Moscow May 18, 1970, without the consent of the Patriarchate of Constantinople. An additional 650,000 or more Orthodox belong to smaller national and language jurisdictions. Heads of orthodox jurisdictions in this hemisphere hold membership in the Standing Conference of Canonical Orthodox Bishops in the Americas.

JURISDICTIONS

The Autocephalous Orthodox Churches

Patriarchate of Constantinople (Ecumenical Patriarchate), with jurisdiction in Turkey, Crete, the Dodecanese, and Greeks in the rest of the world outside Greece and Africa. Autonomous churches linked to the Ecumenical Patriarchate exist in Finland and Estonia. Several other jurisdictions of various ethnicities in the diaspora are also directly under the Patriarchate.

Patriarchate of Alexandria, with jurisdiction in Egypt and the rest of Africa; it includes a native African Orthodox Church centered in Kenya and Uganda.

Patriarchate of Antioch, with jurisdiction in Syria, Lebanon, Iraq, Australia, the Americas.

Patriarchate of Jerusalem, with jurisdiction in Israel and Jordan. The autonomous church of Mount Sinai is linked to the Jerusalem Patriarchate.

Russian Orthodox Church, the Patriarchate of Moscow with jurisdiction over most of the former Soviet Union. Autonomous churches in Japan and China are linked to the Moscow Patriarchate, and since the breakup of the Soviet Union, a certain autonomy has been granted to the Orthodox churches in the newly independent republics of Ukraine, Belarus, Estonia, Moldova and Latvia.

The Serbian Orthodox Church, a patriarchate with jurisdiction in all of former Yugoslavia, Western Europe, North America and Australia.

The Romanian Orthodox Church, a patriarchate with jurisdiction in Romania, Western Europe and North America.

The Bulgarian Orthodox Church, a patriarchate with jurisdiction in Bulgaria, Western Europe and North America.

The Georgian Orthodox Church, a patriarchate with jurisdiction in the republic of Georgia.

The Orthodox Church of Cyprus, an archbishopric with jurisdiction in Cyprus.

The Orthodox Church of Greece, an archbishopric with jurisdiction in most of Greece.

The Orthodox Church of Poland, a metropolitanate with jurisdiction in Poland.

The Orthodox Church of Albania, an archbishopric with jurisdiction in Albania.

The Orthodox Church in the Czech and Slovak Republics, a metropolitanate with jurisdiction in the Czech and Slovak Republics. Its autocephalous status was granted by Moscow in 1951 but by Constantinople only in 1998.

The Orthodox Church in America, a metropolitanate with jurisdiction in North America and a few parishes in Latin America and Australia. Its autocephalous status was granted by Moscow in 1970; Constantinople and most other Orthodox churches have not recognized this.

Population

The Center for the Study of Global Christianity estimates that in 2004 there were a total of 216,574,000 Orthodox Christians worldwide. Some Orthodox claim a total membership of as many as 300 million.

Standing Conference of Orthodox Bishops

The Standing Conference of Canonical Orthodox Bishops in the Americas was established in 1960 to achieve cooperation among the various Orthodox jurisdictions in the Americas. Office: 8-10 East 79th St., New York, NY 10021.

Member churches are the: Albanian Orthodox Diocese of America (Ecumenical Patriarchate), American Carpatho-Russian Orthodox Diocese in the U.S.A. (Ecumenical Patriarchate), Antiochian Orthodox Christian Archdiocese of North America, Bulgarian Eastern Orthodox Church, Greek Orthodox Archdiocese of America (Ecumenical Patriarchate), Orthodox Church in America, Romanian Orthodox Archdiocese in America and Canada, Serbian Orthodox Church in the United States and Canada, Ukrainian Orthodox Church in the United States (Ecumenical Patriarchate), and the Representation of the Moscow Patriarchate in the United States of America.

EASTERN ECUMENISM

The Second Vatican Council, in *Orientalium Ecclesiarum*, the "Decree on Eastern Catholic Churches," pointed out the special role they have to play "in promoting the unity of all Christians." The document also stated in part as follows.

The Eastern Churches in communion with the Apostolic See of Rome have a special role to play in promoting the unity of all Christians, particularly Easterners, according to the principles of this sacred Synod's Decree on Ecumenism first of all by prayer, then by the example of their lives, by religious fidelity to ancient Eastern traditions, by greater mutual knowledge, by collaboration, and by a brotherly regard for objects and attitudes (No. 24).

If any separated Eastern Christian should, under the guidance of grace of the Holy Spirit, join himself to Catholic unity, no more should be required of him than what a simple profession of the Catholic faith demands. A valid priesthood is preserved among Eastern clerics. Hence, upon joining themselves to the unity of the Catholic Church, Eastern clerics are permitted to exercise the orders they possess, in accordance with the regulations established by the competent authority (No. 25).

Divine Law forbids any common worship (*communicatio in sacris*) that would damage the unity of the Church, or involve formal acceptance of falsehood or the danger of deviation in the faith, of scandal, or of indifferentism. At the same time, pastoral experience clearly shows that with respect to our Eastern brethren there should and can be taken into consideration various circumstances affecting individuals, wherein the unity of the Church is not jeopardized nor are intolerable risks involved, but in which salvation itself and the spiritual profit of souls are urgently at issue.

Hence, in view of special circumstances of time, place, and personage, the Catholic Church has often adopted and now adopts a milder policy, offering to all the means of salvation and an example of charity among Christians through participation in the sacraments and in other sacred functions and objects. With these considerations in mind, and "lest because of the harshness of our judgment we prove an obstacle to those seeking salvation," and in order to promote closer union with the Eastern Churches separated from us, this sacred Synod lays down the following policy:

In view of the principles recalled above, Eastern Christians who are separated in good faith from the Catholic Church, if they ask of their own accord and have the right dispositions, may be granted the sacraments of penance, the Eucharist, and the anointing of the sick. Furthermore, Catholics may ask for these same sacraments from those non-Catholic ministers whose Churches possess valid sacraments, as often as necessity or a genuine spiritual benefit recommends such a course of action, and when access to a Catholic priest is physically or morally impossible (Nos. 26, 27). Again, in view of these very same principles, Catholics may for a just cause join with their separated Eastern brethren in sacred functions, things, and places (No. 28). Bishops decide when and if to follow this policy.

RELATIONS WITH THE ORTHODOX CHURCHES

DOCUMENTS

Two documents of great importance with respect to relations between the Catholic and separated Eastern Churches are the apostolic letter, *Orientale Lumen*, issued May 5, 1995; and the encyclical letter, *Ut Unum Sint*, issued May 30, 1995, especially paragraphs 50-63.

In addition, the Pontifical Council for Promoting Christian Unity issued *Guidelines for Admission to the Eucharist between the Chaldean Church and the Assyrian Church of the East* on July 20, 2001, and made public on Oct. 25, 2001.

All the documents produced by the international and North American dialogues between the Catholic and Orthodox churches up to 1995 can be found in J. Borelli and J. Erickson, eds., *The Quest for Unity: Orthodox and Catholics in Dialogue*, US Conference of Catholic Bishops, 1996.

RELATIONS WITH THE MOSCOW PATRIARCHATE

The following Report on Russian Orthodox-Catholic Church Relations was written by Fr. Jozef M. Maj, SJ, of the Pontifical Council for Promoting Christian Unity and appeared on May 5, 2004, in the English-language edition of L'Osservatore Romano.

A look at the events that unfolded on the scene of interecclesial relations in the course of the year 2003, and particularly on relations between the Holy See and the Patriarchate of Moscow, could lead observers who are awaiting decisive and courageous steps in common witness from the Catholic and Orthodox Churches to think that it is a slow and ascending journey.

Such impressions, nonetheless, can be disproved in a certain way by the announcement made last Jan. 22: "Cardinal Walter Kasper, President of the Pontifical Council for Promoting Christian Unity, receiving the invitation of the Conference of Catholic Bishops of the Russian Federation, will visit Moscow this Feb. 16, (2004)."

The Cardinal was set to meet Catholic Bishops present in the Russian Federation as well as the Catholic Community at Moscow and, as the announcement revealed, "during this visit, which is animated also by heartfelt respect for the Russian Orthodox Church, he will be received in audience by His Holiness Alexis II, Patriarch of Moscow and All Russia, and will have a meeting with the Metropolitan of Smolensk and Kaliningrad, Kirill, the President of the Department for Ecclesiastical Foreign Relations of the Patriarchate of Moscow, in view of the ecumenical dialogue between the two Churches."

This announcement opens new prospects for all contacts between the Catholic Church and the Russian Orthodox Church and for the quality of their relations internationally and locally.

Spirit of Exchange and Enrichment

These last relations have had a noteworthy force in the course of the past year. The initiatives promoted by the Pontifical Representative in the Russian Federation are especially remembered, thanks to which the climate of such relations has notably improved on the local level and reciprocal trust has grown, an indispensable condition for every further bilateral contact.

In this context the regular meetings of the Pontifical Representative with the Primate of the Russian Orthodox Church, His Holiness Alexis II, are recorded, together with the other institutions of the Patriarchate, such as the Department for Ecclesiastical Foreign Relations, led by the Metropolitan of Smolensk and Kaliningrad, Kirill.

The Nuncio's visits to Catholic communities spread throughout the territory of this great country are no less important. In the course of such visits, alongside meetings with the civil Authorities, there is also among the priorities a visit to the local Orthodox bishop. In many cases such encounters foster the already-existing collaboration or favor the start of other forms of meeting and collaboration between the Orthodox and Catholic communities; aimed at eliminating and overcoming mutual prejudices inherited form the past or that have arisen following misunderstandings and interpretations of events that' have affected both Churches.

At the level of contacts between the Holy See and the Patriarchate of I Moscow, we note the regular exchange of epistles between Pope John Paul II: and Patriarch Alexis II, or that of the Pontifical Council for Promoting Christian Unity and the Department for Ecclesiastical Foreign Relations of the Patriarchate of Moscow. The Presidents of these bodies, Cardinal Walter Kasper and the Metropolitan Kirill, respectively, have met on two occasions: Mar. 19, 2003 at Geneva and in the first days of September at Aachen, Germany.

The Catholic Committee of Cultural Collaboration has continued to provide monetary support for the educational institutions of the Patriarchate of Moscow stationed in various countries of the Community of the Independent States, and support has been maintained for those institutions that, by preserving their autonomy and maintaining their own Orthodox inspiration through editorial and educational activity and conferences and summer courses on theology, work with the participation of Catholic experts for Orthodoxy in Russia, Belarus and Ukraine and for a meeting and collaboration between Catholics and Orthodox in a spirit of mutual exchange and enrichment.

The Russian Orthodox Church

Throughout 2003, various Catholic organizations continued to offer their fraternal support and help for the Russian Orthodox Church, including such agencies as *Kirche in Not* and *Renovabis*. These agencies' activity cannot be interpreted as an isolated and independent choice; rather, they express the entire solidarity of the Catholic faithful which arises and is nourished from the teaching of the Catholic Church and the Holy Father. Any sort of attempt to deny the intrinsic, ecclesial dimension of the solidarity that the agencies or the Catholic faithful promote would mean that one is trying to reduce it to a mere act which, noble as it may be, would be left void of its testimonial value to brotherly love, respect and high regard for .the Russian Orthodox Church.

The brief overview just presented of relations between the Catholic Church and the Russian Orthodox Church does not desire to close with a statement, but rather, desires to open itself up to those testimonies that the Catholic Church and the Russian Orthodox Church are called to give today to Europe and the World.

The recent Address delivered by Pope John Paul II on Jan. 12, 2004 to the Diplomatic Corps accredited to the Holy See offers some ideas that could serve as a point for common reflection and an eventual and more meaningful cooperation with the Patriarchate of Moscow. Obviously, it is not collaboration dictated by any sort of pragmatism; rather, it is that ecumenical commitment which aims at overcoming divisions and permits the respective faithful to live and experience the, numerous bonds of communion by which they are already united between themselves.

Only by this reality will a living witness be able to spring up in a position to extend itself at every level of ecclesial life; a witness that will more convincingly spread those Christian values on which Europe's identity is founded.

The Common Commitment

It is precisely our Continent which is above all in need of a renewal and a common commitment by the Catholic and Orthodox Churches. The Christian identity of Europe and the values that have formed it through the centuries are today having a difficult time finding a place in the area of the important European structures and social life of certain Countries.

Although, as the Holy Father affirmed in the aforementioned Address, "Everyone may agree to respect the religious sentiment of individuals, but the same cannot be said of the 'religious factor,' that is, the social dimension of religions; here the engagements made in the context of what was formerly known as the 'Conference on Security and Cooperation in Europe' have been forgotten" *(Address to the Diplomatic Corps Accredited to the Holy See*, Jan. 12, 2004; *L'Osservatore Romano* English edition *[ORE]*, Jan. 21, 2004, p. 3).

Such a tendency, which wishes to ignore "what Christianity has contributed to the culture and institutions of the Continent: the dignity of the human being, freedom, the sense of the universal, schools and universities, social services," addresses in a particular way the Churches regarding their presence and role in affirming Gospel values in today's Europe.

This commitment becomes more urgent in the face of the tendency towards laicism that wishes to reduce the presence of religion to the private sector and to propose life models that are inconsistent with a religious view on life.

Under the various atheistic regimes and ideologies, the Russian Orthodox Church and the Catholic Church, together with other Christian communities, have already undergone long periods of limitations and restrictions accompanied by persecutions, whose devastating consequences on life have been felt up to our day-by many societies. Among these consequences, it is enough to mention: signs of social injustice, the break-down of families, and the loss of moral values and propagation of alternative lifestyles that attempt to present as a way of life a modern society free from any bond with natural law.

In the face of these challenges, the Holy Father has said that as Christians: "All together, we can effectively contribute to respect for life, to safeguarding the dignity of the human person and his or her inalienable rights, to social justice and to the preservation of the environment."

Bond between unity and peace

Lastly, in the perspective of common action between the Catholic Church and the Russian Orthodox Church, a concern for world peace cannot be lacking.

Peace always remains an imperative or Christians, and wherever it is threatened, in the Middle East or elsewhere, these same people cannot shrink from heir duty to act together by investing all their spiritual forces to achieve it.

But there also exists here interdependence between the unity of Christians tend their commitment to peace. In fact, as the Holy Father notes: "We do not give sufficient importance to the pacifying influence that Christians could have, were they united, on their own community as well as on civil society."

And he adds, "If I say this, it is not only to remind all who claim to be followers of Christ of the pressing need to set out with determination on the road that leads to the unity that Christ desired, but also to point out to the leaders of societies the resources they could find in the Christian heritage as well as among those who practice it."

Unity, therefore, is not an optional accessory; rather, it is an essential quality of the vocation of Christians and their presence in the world. This calling in a certain way conditions the Lord's ardent prayer: "so that the world may believe" (Jn 17:21), and the efficacy of that particular mission which they must complete towards humanity as a whole. In order for such a mission to proceed, the unique contribution that both the Catholic Church and Russian Orthodox Church can offer must not be lacking.

NOTABLE DEVELOPMENTS

North American Orthodox-Catholic Theological Consultation Issues Agreed Statement on *Filioque*, a Question that Divided the Two Communions for Many Centuries

(Courtesy, USCCB.) The North American Orthodox-Catholic Theological Consultation concluded a four-year study of the *Filioque* on Oct. 25, 2003, when it unanimously adopted an agreed text on this difficult question that has divided the two communions for many centuries. This important development took place at the 65th meeting of the Consultation, held at St. Paul's College in Washington, DC, under the joint chairmanship of Metropolitan Maximos of the Greek Orthodox Metropolis of Pittsburgh and Archbishop Daniel E. Pilarczyk of Cincinnati.

The original version of the Creed most Christian churches accept as the standard expression of their faith dates from the First Council of Constantinople, in 381, and has been used by Orthodox Christians since that time. Toward the end, this Creed states that the Holy Spirit "proceeds from the Father." The word *Filioque* ("and the Son") was later added to the Latin version of this Creed used in the West, so that the phrase as most western Christians know it reads that the Holy Spirit "proceeds from the Father and the Son." This modification appeared in some areas of Western Europe as early as the 6th century but was accepted in Rome only in the 11th century. This change in the wording of the Creed and the underlying variations in understanding the origin and procession of the Holy Spirit within the Trinity have long been considered a church-dividing issue between Catholics and Orthodox. The Consultation had been studying this question since 1999 in the hope of eventually releasing an agreed statement.

Entitled "The *Filioque*: A Church-Dividing Issue?" the ten-thousand word text has three major sections. The first, "The Holy Spirit in the Scriptures," summarizes references to the Spirit in both the Old and New Testaments. The more lengthy second section, "Historical Considerations," provides an overview of the origins of the two traditions concerning the eternal procession of the Spirit and the slow process by which the *Filioque* was added to the Creed in the West. It also shows how this question concerning Trinitarian theology became entwined with disputes regarding papal jurisdiction and primacy, and reviews recent developments in the Catholic Church which point to a greater awareness of the unique and normative character of the original Greek version of the Creed as an expression of the faith that unites the Orthodox East and Catholic West. The third section, "Theological Reflections," emphasizes our limited ability to speak of the inner life of God, points out that both sides of the debate have often caricatured the positions of the other, and lists areas in which the traditions agree. It then explores the differences that have developed regarding terminology, and identifies both theological and ecclesiological divergences that have arisen over the centuries.

In a final section, the Consultation makes eight recommendations to the members and bishops of the two churches. It recommends that they "enter into a new and earnest dialogue concerning the origin and person of the Holy Spirit." It also proposes that in the future both Catholics and Orthodox "refrain from labeling as heretical the traditions of the other side" on this subject, and that the theologians of both traditions make a clearer distinction between the divinity of the Spirit, and the manner of the Spirit's origin, "which still awaits full and final ecumenical resolution." The text also urges theologians to distinguish, as far as possible, the theological issues concerning the origin of the Holy Spirit from ecclesiological issues, and suggests that attention be paid in the future to the status of councils of both our churches that took place after the seven ecumenical councils of the first millennium. And finally, in view of the fact that the Vatican has affirmed the "normative and irrevocable dogmatic value" of the Creed of 381" in its original Greek version, the Consultation recommends that the Catholic Church use the same text (without the *Filioque*) "in making translations of that Creed for catechetical and liturgical use," and declare that the anathema pronounced by the Second Council of Lyons against those who deny that the Spirit proceeds eternally from the Father and the Son is no longer applicable.

The North American Orthodox-Catholic Theological Consultation is sponsored jointly by the Standing Conference of Canonical Orthodox Bishops of the Americas (SCOBA), the Bishops' Committee for Ecumenical and Interreligious Affairs of the USCCB, and the Canadian Conference of Catholic Bishops. Since its establishment in 1965, the Consultation has now issued 22 agreed statements on various topics. All these texts are now available on the website of the US Catholic Conference at: www.usccb.org/seia/dialogues.htm. The full text of the document is available on the USCCB website at: www.usccb.org/seia/filioque.htm.

Pope John Paul II Returns Icon of the Mother of God of Kazan to the Russian Orthodox Church

In August 2004 Pope John Paul II returned to the Russian Orthodox Church an icon of the Mother of God of Kazan that had hung over his desk in his personal study for eleven years. The icon was believed to have been taken out of Russia at the time of the Bolshevik Revolution, and had been given to the Holy Father by the Blue Army in 1993.

Pope John Paul II Returns Relics of Sts John Chrysostom and Gregory Nazianzen to the Patriarchate of Constantinople

In November 2004 Pope John Paul II returned relics of Sts. John Chrysostom and Gregory Nazianzus to the Ecumenical Patriarchate. Patriarch Bartholomew traveled to Rome to receive the relics in a special service in St Peter's Basilica on Nov. 27.

RECENT DEVELOPMENTS

Joint International Commission for Theological Dialogue

The tenth meeting of the Joint International Commission for the Theological Dialogue between the Orthodox Church and the Roman Catholic Church met in Ravenna, Italy, a city marked by its historical and artistic monuments many from the Byzantine era. The meeting took place from Oct. 8- 4, 2007, generously hosted by the Archdiocese of Ravenna-Cervia.

Twenty seven of the thirty Catholic members (cardinals, archbishops, bishops, priests and lay theologians) were present. The Orthodox members (metropolitans, bishops; priests and lay theologians) represented the Ecumenical Patriarchate, the Patriarchate of Alexandria, the Patriarchate of Antioch, the Patriarchate of Jerusalem, the Patriarchate of Moscow, the Patriarchate of Serbia, the Patriarchate of Romania, the Patriarchate of Georgia, the Church of Cyprus, the Church of Greece, the Church of Poland, the Church of Albania, the Church of Czech Lands and Slovakia, the Church of Finland and the Apostolic Church of Estonia. The representatives of the Patriarchate of Bulgaria were unable to attend.

The Commission worked under the direction of the two co-presidents, Cardinal Walter Kasper and Metropolitan John of Pergamon, helped by the two co-secretaries, Metropolitan Gennadios of Sassima, (Ecumenical Patriarchate) and Msgr. Eleuterio Fortino from the Pontifical Council for Promoting Christian Unity.

The session began in the Basilica of Sant'Apollinare in Classe on the evening of Oct. 8, with the celebration of Vespers, presided over by the Archbishop of Ravenna, the Most Reverend Giuseppe Verucchi, and with a prayer on the part of the Orthodox members.

In addressing those present, the Archbishop of Ravenna stated: "We are happy that you are here. You have the prayers of our two contemplative communities, of the religious men and women, the priests and the parish communities. While you are busy with the dialogue, searching for the path that will lead us closer to full communion, we will not disturb you, but we will embrace you with our affection and prayer."

The Commission was welcomed in the prefecture by the Prefect, Her Excellency Floriana De Sanctis, who expressed the hope that "the desire for dialogue, to understand and to be understood, which characterizes the Joint Commission might be a sign copied by all of us in our daily lives." Also present at this meeting were the mayor of the city, the president of the region and the president of the province, together with other civil authorities.

The Commission has been working on the theme of "The Ecclesiological and Canonical Consequences of the Sacramental Nature of the Church: Ecclesial Communion, Conciliarity and Authority in the Church." This study had already begun in the previous session in Belgrade, from Sept. 18-25 2006, on the basis of a draft elaborated by the Joint Coordinating Committee in Moscow in 1990, but which had not yet been discussed in plenary session. At this meeting this study has been completed and an agreed common document was approved. The document offers a solid basis for the future work of the Commission.

On the first day of the meeting, as is customary in this Commission, the Roman Catholic and Orthodox members met separately to coordinate their work. At the Orthodox meeting the delegate of the Moscow Patriarchate presented a decision of that Church to withdraw from the meeting because of the presence of delegates from the Church of Estonia, declared "autonomous" by the Ecumenical Patriarchate, a status not recognized by the Patriarchate of Moscow, and in spite of the fact that the Ecumenical Patriarchate with the agreement of all the Orthodox members offered a compromise that would have acknowledged the Moscow Patriarchate's non-recognition of the Autonomous Church of Estonia.

The theme for the next plenary session will be: "The role of the Bishop of Rome in the communion of the Church in the first millennium."

The place and time for the next Coordinating Committee will be decided at a later date.

The tenth plenary session ended with prayer. On Saturday, Oct. 13, the Catholic members celebrated the Eucharist in the Cathedral of Ravenna, in the presence of the Orthodox members. On Sunday, Oct. 14, the Orthodox members celebrated the Divine Liturgy in the Basilica of St. Vitalis, in the presence of the Catholic members. On both of these occasions the Archbishop of Ravenna and members of the clergy and laity of Ravenna attended.

The meeting of the Joint Commission was marked by a spirit of friendship and trustful collaboration. The members of the Commission greatly appreciated the generous hospitality of the Archdiocese of Ravenna, and they strongly commend the continuing work of the dialogue to the prayers of the faithful.

Ravenna, Italy, Oct. 14, 2007.

THE ORIENTAL ORTHODOX CHURCHES

Relations with the Oriental Orthodox Churches

(By Johan Bonny)

The Oriental Orthodox Churches were the subject of an article by Johan Bonny in the Italian-language edition of L'Osservatore Romano *in early 2004. The following is an approved English-language translation of the article. Thanks are expressed to Fr. Ron Roberson, C.S.P., for his kind assistance in providing the translation.*

A family of Churches

The Oriental Orthodox family of churches is composed of four different traditions: Coptic, Syriac, Malankara and Armenian. The Coptic tradition, first of all, originated in the ancient Patriarchate of Alexandria. It gave birth to three autocephalous churches, each of them distinct from each other in terms of language, liturgy and culture: The Coptic Orthodox Church in Egypt, the Orthodox Church of Ethiopia and the Orthodox Church of Eritrea. The Syriac tradition originated in the ancient Patriarchate of Antioch. It also gave birth to a number of local churches, including the Syriac Orthodox Church with its patriarchal see in Damascus, Syria. The Malankara tradition, situated in Kerala in southern India, has roots in the great missionary outreach of the east Syriac Church that developed in the first centuries of the Christian era under the patronage of the Apostle Thomas. In the 16th century, following ecclesiastical and social problems due to the presence of new colonial authorities in southern India, a part of this local church entered into canonical communion with the Syriac Orthodox Church while maintaining a certain level of autonomy; this church is usually called the Malankara Syrian Orthodox Church. And finally, the Armenian tradition grew out of the evangelization of the Armenian people around the year 301 through the efforts of St. Gregory the Illuminator. For a number of centuries the Armenian Apostolic Church has included two catholicossates, one with its seat in Etchmiadzin, Armenia, and the other in Antelias, Lebanon.

There is a great diversity among these particular churches, each of them having its own language, its own theological, liturgical and canonical tradition, and its own artistic and cultural patrimony. As churches linked to particular ethnic groups or nations, each of them over the course of the centuries has developed close relations with the people or nation to which it belongs. This is why these churches and their leaders, until these more recent ecumenical times, were unable to develop closer relations, and even less on the official level.

But then, what do these churches have in common? First of all there is a theological factor of the greatest importance: the non-recognition of certain doctrinal formulas of the Council of Chalcedon (451). Certainly this was due to theological disputes, but also and perhaps above all there were political factors related to the marginal position these churches had in relation to the Roman Empire with its center in Constantinople. Some of these communities, such as the Armenian, Syrian and Malankara, were for the most part located outside the borders of the empire. These churches also have in common a certain sensitivity and a certain standpoint, determined by the non-chalcedonian character of their Christology, that places greater emphasis on the divine rather than the human aspect, especially in the areas of spirituality and liturgy. Finally, another element that brings them together in this ecumenical era is the desire to work together more closely in various fields, above all in the Middle East, the cradle and homeland of most of these churches. Alongside the three Orthodox, Catholic and Protestant families that are working for greater integration and collaboration in the region, the fourth family, that of the Oriental Orthodox Churches, does not want to be left behind.

A New Phase of Ecumenical Dialogue

Since the time of the Second Vatican Council, the Catholic Church has been engaged in a bilateral dialogue with each of the Oriental Orthodox Churches. The effectiveness of these bilateral dialogues is shown by the publication of a series of impressive Common Declarations, approved and signed by the highest authorities of the Catholic Church and the Oriental Orthodox Churches. These declarations focus on Christology, the theology of the sacraments, and ecclesiology.

A new initiative has just been taken to integrate this dialogue and its results more thoroughly into the lives of our churches. During a preparatory meeting organized in Rome by the Pontifical Council for Promoting Christian Unity in January 2003, representatives of the East and the West decided to establish a new international commission for dialogue between the Catholic Church and the Oriental Orthodox Churches. The first plenary meeting will take place from Jan. 26–31, 2002, in Cairo, at the St. Mark Center of the Coptic Orthodox Church, under the co-presidency of Cardinal Walter Kasper and Metropolitan Anba Bishoy. The Orthodox delegation will be composed of 14 representatives (two from each particular church); the Catholic delegation will include the same number of persons, including bishops and theologians of the Latin and Eastern traditions. This first meeting will study the results of the various official and unofficial bilateral dialogues that have taken place over the course of the last 30 years between the Catholic Church and the Oriental Orthodox Churches. In this way it should be possible to identify the doctrinal questions that remain open and the best way to deal with them. This new multilateral dialogue could also create a favorable atmosphere for the growth of a common initiative among theologians and pastors of the churches involved, allowing the Catholic Church and the Oriental Orthodox Churches to move forward together along the path toward full communion.

This new prospect should not prevent the theological dialogue between the Catholic Church and the Malankara Church in India from taking its own course. In fact, the two joint dialogue commissions with the Malankara Syrian Orthodox Church and the Malankara Orthodox Syrian Church held their annual meetings in Kottayam in October 2003. The meeting of the latter dialogue was dedicated to the study of various themes related to the history of the Church in Kerala, the ecclesiology of communion and common witness. Moreover, a common declaration was published that rules out all forms of proselytism and offensive publications by any of the various Christian communities of the region. As for common witness, some initiatives were taken with regard to the continuing formation of clergy and religious.

The Assyrian Church of the East

In the context of the Oriental Orthodox Churches mentioned above, the Assyrian Church of the East is a special case. Its origins go back to another doctrinal controversy, one that preceded the Council of Chalcedon (451) by about 20 years, and which concerned the Christological definitions of the Council of Ephesus (431). Along with the Chaldean Catholic Church, the Assyrian Church of the East derives from Christian communities in the ancient territory of Mesopotamia or Babylon which, at the time, were opposed to the definitions of the Council of Ephesus. The bilateral dialogue between the Catholic Church and the Assyrian Church of the East followed its normal course in 2003. From Oct. 28 until Nov. 1, 2003, the ninth annual meeting of this dialogue took place in Rome. The two major themes on the program concerned Christology and ecclesiology. In Christology, the contributions of certain theologians of the ancient Mesopotamian tradition to the development of Christian dogma were examined. In ecclesiology, the discussion centered on the relationship between the local church and the universal church, a key question in the ecumenical debate.

Aleppo and the Middle East

In conclusion, we need to remember the city of Aleppo in Syria, since it was there that the material for the 2004 Week of Prayer for Christian Unity was prepared. Aleppo is a typical example of a Middle Eastern city where almost all the churches and ecclesial communities have lived next to each another for centuries. Situated at the crossroads of the most ancient commercial routes of the Middle East, Aleppo is home to the great Christian traditions: Greek, Syriac, Armenian and Assyro-Chaldean, in their Orthodox or Catholic expressions, as well as several Protestant communities. The bishops and pastors of all these communities meet each month to coordinate their pastoral activity and to give witness to their common commitment to Christian unity. The project of drafting the brochure for this year's Week of Prayer reflects the ecumenical hopes that are held by the churches and ecclesial communities of Aleppo and the entire Middle East. From Jan. 18–25, 2004, Christians around the world will join the churches of the Middle East in a common prayer that "the Lord's peace" will overcome our divisions and lead us towards full communion.

REFORMATION CHURCHES

LEADERS AND DOCTRINES OF THE REFORMATION

Some of the leading figures, doctrines and churches of the Reformation are covered below. A companion article covers major Protestant Churches in the U.S.

LEADERS

John Wycliff (c. 1320–1384): English priest and scholar who advanced one of the leading Reformation ideas nearly 200 years before Martin Luther — that the Bible alone is the sufficient rule of faith — but had only an indirect influence on the 16th century Reformers. Supporting belief in an inward and practical religion, he denied the divinely commissioned authority of the pope and bishops of the Church; he also denied the Real Presence of Christ in the Holy

Eucharist, and wrote against the sacrament of penance and the doctrine of indulgences. Nearly 20 of his propositions were condemned by Gregory XI in 1377; his writings were proscribed more extensively by the Council of Constance in 1415. His influence was strongest in Bohemia and Central Europe.

John Hus (c. 1369-1415): A Bohemian priest and preacher of reform who authored 30 propositions condemned by the Council of Constance. Excommunicated in 1411 or 1412, he was burned at the stake in 1415. His principal errors concerned the nature of the Church and the origin of papal authority. He spread some of the ideas of Wycliff but did not subscribe to his views regarding faith alone as the condition for justification and salvation, the sole sufficiency of Scripture as the rule of faith, the Real Presence of Christ in the Eucharist, and the sacramental system. In 1457 some of his followers founded the Church of the Brotherhood which later became known as the United Brethren or Moravian Church and is considered the earliest independent Protestant body.

Martin Luther (1483-1546): An Augustinian friar, priest and doctor of theology, the key figure in the Reformation. In 1517, as a special indulgence was being preached in Germany, and in view of needed reforms within the Church, he published at Wittenberg 95 theses concerning matters of Catholic belief and practice. Leo X condemned 41 statements from Luther's writings in 1520. Luther, refusing to recant, was excommunicated the following year. His teachings strongly influenced subsequent Lutheran theology; its statements of faith are found in the Book of Concord (1580).

Luther's doctrines included the following: The sin of Adam, which corrupted human nature radically (but not substantially), has affected every aspect of man's being. Justification, understood as the forgiveness of sins and the state of righteousness, is by grace for Christ's sake through faith. Faith involves not merely intellectual assent but an act of confidence by the will. Good works are indispensably necessary concomitants of faith, but do not merit salvation. Of the sacraments, Luther retained baptism, penance and the Holy Communion as effective vehicles of the grace of the Holy Spirit; he held that in the Holy Communion the consecrated bread and wine are the Body and Blood of Christ. The rule of faith is the divine revelation in the Sacred Scriptures. He rejected purgatory, indulgences and the invocation of the saints, and held that prayers for the dead have no efficacy. Calvin's clarified their positions at the Council of Trent. The 1999 Joint Declaration indicates that the condemnations of doctrine by the Council of Trent and the Book of Concord do not apply to present day Catholic and Lutheran teaching respectively.

Ulrich Zwingli (1484-1531): A priest who triggered the Reformation in Switzerland with a series of New Testament lectures in 1519, later disputations and by other actions. He held the Gospel to be the only basis of truth; rejected the Mass (which he suppressed in 1525 at Zurich), penance and other sacraments; denied papal primacy and doctrine concerning purgatory and the invocation of saints; rejected celibacy, monasticism and many traditional practices of piety. His symbolic view of the Eucharist, which was at odds with Catholic doctrine, caused an irreconcilable controver-

sy with Luther and his followers. Zwingli was killed in a battle between the forces of Protestant and Catholic cantons in Switzerland.

John Calvin (1509-64): French leader of the Reformation in Switzerland, whose key tenet was absolute predestination of some persons to heaven and others to hell. He rejected Catholic doctrine in 1533 after becoming convinced of a personal mission to reform the Church. In 1536 he published the first edition of Institutes of the Christian Religion, a systematic exposition of his doctrine which became the classic textbook of Reformed — as distinguished from Lutheran — theology. To Luther's principal theses — regarding Scripture as the sole rule of faith, the radical corruption of human nature, and justification by faith alone — he added absolute predestination, certitude of salvation for the elect, and the incapability of the elect to lose grace. Calvin's Eucharist teaching, while affirming Christ's true presence, was not able to find agreement with that of Luther. However, in our own time, agreement has been reached between Lutherans and Reformed (Calvinists), and considerable progress has been made with Catholics and Orthodox toward a common understanding of Christ's presence in Communion.

CHURCHES AND MOVEMENTS

Adventists: Members of several Christian groups whose doctrines are dominated by belief in a more or less imminent second advent or coming of Christ upon earth for a glorious 1,000-year reign of righteousness. This reign, following victory by the forces of good over evil in a final Battle of Armageddon, will begin with the resurrection of the chosen and will end with the resurrection of all others and the annihilation of the wicked. Thereafter, the just will live forever in a renewed heaven and earth. A sleep of the soul takes place between the time of death and the day of judgment. There is no hell. The Bible, in literalist interpretation, is regarded as the only rule of faith and practice. About six churches have developed in the course of the Adventist movement which originated with William Miller (1782–1849) in the United States. Miller, on the basis of calculations made from the Book of Daniel, predicted that the second advent of Christ would occur between 1843 and 1844. After the prophecy went unfulfilled, divisions occurred in the movement and the Seventh Day Adventists, whose actual formation dates from 1860, emerged as the largest single body. The observance of Saturday instead of Sunday as the Lord's Day dates from 1844.

Anabaptism: Originated in Saxony in the first quarter of the 16th century and spread rapidly through southern Germany. Its doctrine included several key Lutheran tenets but was not regarded with favor by Luther, Calvin or Zwingli. Anabaptists believed that baptism is for adults only and that infant baptism is invalid. Their doctrine of the Inner Light, concerning the direct influence of the Holy Spirit on the believer, implied rejection of Catholic doctrine concerning the sacraments and the nature of the Church. Eighteen articles of faith were formulated in 1632 in Holland. Mennonites are Anabaptists.

Arminianism: A modification of the rigid predestinationism of Calvin, set forth by Jacob Arminius (1560-1609) and formally stated in the Remonstrance of 1610. Arminianism influenced some Calvinist bodies.

Baptists: So called because of their doctrine concerning baptism. They reject infant baptism and consider only baptism by immersion as valid. Leaders in the formation of the church were John Smyth (d. 1612) in England and Roger Williams (d. 1683) in America.

Congregationalists: Evangelical in spirit and seeking a return to forms of the primitive church, they uphold individual freedom in religious matters, do not require the acceptance of a creed as a condition for communion, and regard each congregation as autonomous. Robert Browne influenced the beginnings of Congregationalism.

Disciples: From a 19th century revival movement and desire for the unity of the Christian churches, a network of congregations developed which desired to be called simply "Christian churches." These churches opened their communion and membership to all, celebrated the Eucharist each Sunday and baptized only adults. From this movement the Christian Church/Disciples of Christ, the Churches of Christ and the independent Christian Churches emerged.

Methodists: A group who broke away from the Anglican Communion under the leadership of John Wesley (1703–1791), although some Anglican beliefs were retained. Doctrines include the witness of the Spirit to the individual and personal assurance of salvation. The largest Methodist body in the United States is the United Methodist Church. There are three Black Methodist bodies: African Methodist Episcopal, African Methodist Episcopal Zion, and Christian Methodist Episcopal Churches. There are also several Holiness Churches in the Wesleyan tradition: i.e., Nazarene, Free Methodist, Wesleyan Church.

Pentecostals: Churches that grew up after the 1906 enthusiastic revival, accompanied by the phenomena of speaking in foreign tongues and the experience of baptism in the Holy Spirit. From this revival churches of a Methodist or Baptist theological emphasis emerged, such as the Church of God in Christ or the Assemblies of God. In the mid-20th century, the charismatic experience began to be shared by some members of the classical churches, including Roman Catholic.

Puritans: Congregationalists who sought church reform along Calvinist lines in severe simplicity. (Use of the term was generally discontinued after 1660.)

Presbyterians: Basically Calvinistic, called Presbyterian because church polity centers around assemblies of presbyters or elders. John Knox (c. 1513–1572) established the church in Scotland.

Quakers: Their key belief is in internal divine illumination, the inner light of the living Christ, as the only source of truth and inspiration. George Fox (1624–1691) was one of their leaders in England. Called the Society of Friends, the Quakers are noted for their pacifism.

Unitarianism: A 16th century doctrine which rejected the Trinity and the divinity of Christ in favor of a uni–personal God. It claimed scriptural support for a long time but became generally rationalistic with respect to "revealed" doctrine as well as in ethics and its world–view. One of its principal early proponents was Faustus Socinus (1539–1604), a leader of the Polish Brethren. A variety of communions developed in England in the Reformation and post–Reformation periods.

Universalism: A product of 18th–century liberal Protestantism in England. The doctrine is not Trinitarian and includes a tenet that all men will ultimately be saved.

Anglican Communion: This communion, which regards itself as the same apostolic Church as that which was established by early Christians in England, derived not from Reformation influences but from the renunciation of papal jurisdiction by Henry VIII (1491–1547). His Act of Supremacy in 1534 called Christ's Church an assembly of local churches subject to the prince, who was vested with fullness of authority and jurisdiction. In spite of Henry's denial of papal authority, this Act did not reject substantially other principal articles of faith. Notable changes, proposed and adopted for the reformation of the church, took place in the subsequent reigns of Edward VI and Elizabeth, with respect to such matters as Scripture as the rule of faith, the sacraments, the nature of the Mass, and the constitution of the hierarchy. There are more than 27 provinces in the Anglican Communion. (*See* **Episcopal Church, Anglican Orders, Anglican-Catholic Final Report**.)

MAJOR PROTESTANT CHURCHES IN THE UNITED STATES

There are more than 250 Protestant Church bodies in the U.S. The majority of U.S. Protestants belong to the following denominations: Baptist, Methodist, Lutheran, Presbyterian, Protestant Episcopal, the United Church of Christ, the Christian Church (Disciples of Christ), Evangelicals. *See* **Ecumenical Dialogues, Reports.**

Baptist Churches

Baptist churches, comprising the largest of all American Protestant denominations, were first established by John Smyth near the beginning of the 17th century in England. The first Baptist church in America was founded at Providence by Roger Williams in 1639. Largest of the nearly 30 Baptist bodies in the U.S. are: The Southern Baptist Convention, 901 Commerce St., Suite 750, Nashville, TN 37203, with 15.7 million members. The National Baptist Convention, U.S.A., Inc., 915 Spain St., Baton Rouge, LA 70802, with 8 million members. The National Baptist Convention of America, Inc., 1320 Pierre Ave., Shreveport, LA 71103, with 4.5 million members. The American Baptist Churches in the U.S.A., P.O. Box 851, Valley Forge, PA 19482, with 1.5 million members. The total number of U.S. Baptists is more than 29 million. The world total is 33 million.

Proper to Baptists is their doctrine on baptism. Called an "ordinance" rather than a sacrament, baptism by immersion is a sign that one has experienced and decided in favor of the salvation offered by Christ. It is administered only to persons who are able to make a responsible decision. Baptism is not administered to infants. Baptists do not have a formal creed but generally subscribe to two professions of faith formulated in 1689 and 1832 and are in general agreement with classical Protestant theology. Their local churches are autonomous. Worship services differ in form from one congregation to another.

Christian Church (Disciples of Christ)

The Christian Church (Disciples of Christ) originated early in the 1800s from two movements against rigid denominationalism led by Presbyterians Thomas and Alexander Campbell in western Pennsylvania and Barton W. Stone in Kentucky. The two movements developed separately for about 25 years before being merged in 1832. The church has nearly one million members in almost 4,000 congregations in the U.S. and Canada. The greatest concentration of members in the U.S. is located in an arc sweeping from Ohio and Kentucky into Oklahoma and Texas. The general offices of the church are located at 130 E. Washington St., Indianapolis, IN 46204. The church's persistent concern for Christian unity is based on a conviction expressed in a basic document, Declaration and Address, dating from its founding. The Disciples have no official doctrine or dogma. Membership is granted after a simple statement of belief in Jesus Christ and baptism by immersion; most congregations admit un-immersed transfers from other denominations. The Lord's Supper or Eucharist, generally called Communion, is always open to Christians of all persuasions. Distinction between ordained and non-ordained members is blurred.

The Christian Church is oriented to congregational government, with three sections of polity (general, regional and congregational) operate as equals rather than in a pyramid of authority. At the national or international level, it is governed by a general assembly.

Episcopal Church

The Episcopal Church, which includes over 100 dioceses in the United States, Central and South America, and elsewhere overseas, regards itself as part of the same apostolic church which was established by early Christians in England. Established in this country during the colonial period, it became independent of the jurisdiction of the Church of England when a new constitution and Prayer Book were adopted at a general convention held in 1789. It has approximately 2.5 million members worldwide. Offices of the presiding bishop and the executive council are located at 815 Second Ave., New York, NY 10017.

The presiding bishop is chief pastor and primate; he or she is elected by the House of Bishops and confirmed by the House of Deputies for a term of nine years. The Episcopal Church, which is a part of the Anglican Communion, regards the Archbishop of Canterbury as the "First among Equals," though not under his authority. The Anglican Communion, worldwide, has 70 million members in 36 self-governing churches.

Official statements of belief and practice are found in the Book of Common Prayer. Scripture has primary importance with respect to the rule of faith, and authority is also attached to tradition. The levels of government are the general convention, and executive council, dioceses, and local parishes. Liturgical worship is according to the Book of Common Prayer as adopted in 1979, but details of ceremonial practice vary from one congregation to another.

Lutheran Churches

The origin of Lutheranism is generally traced to Oct. 31, 1517, when Martin Luther — Augustinian friar, priest, doctor of theology — tacked "95 Theses" to the door of the castle church in Wittenberg, Germany and began the Protestant Reformation. The world's 61 million Lutherans form the third largest grouping of Christians, after Roman Catholics and Orthodox. About 57 million of them belong to church bodies which make up the Lutheran World Federation, headquartered in Geneva. There are about 8.5 million Lutherans in the United States, making them the fourth largest Christian grouping, after Roman Catholics, Baptists and Methodists. Although there are nearly 20 U.S. Lutheran church bodies, all but 100,000 Lutherans belong to either the Evangelical Lutheran Church in America (with 5.2 million members and headquarters at 8765 W. Higgins Rd., Chicago, IL 60631), The Lutheran Church-Missouri Synod (with 2.61 million members and headquarters at 1333 S. Kirkwood Rd., St. Louis, MO 63122), or the Wisconsin Evangelical Lutheran Synod (with 420,000 members and headquarters at 2929 N. Mayfair Rd., Milwaukee, WI 53222).

The Evangelical Lutheran Church in America and the Lutheran Church-Missouri Synod carry out some work together through inter-Lutheran agencies such as Lutheran World Relief and Lutheran Immigration and Refugee Services; both agencies have offices at 390 Park Ave. South, New York, NY 10010.

The statements of faith which have shaped the confessional life of Lutheranism are found in the Book of Concord. This 1580 collection includes the three ancient ecumenical creeds (Apostles', Nicene and Athanasian), Luther's Large and Small Catechisms (1529), the Augsburg Confession (1530) and the Apology in defense of it (1531), the Smalkald Articles (including the "Treatise on the Power and Primacy of the Pope") (1537), and the Formula of Concord (1577).

The central Lutheran doctrinal proposition is that Christians "receive forgiveness of sins and become righteous before God by grace, for Christ's sake." Baptism and the Lord's Supper (Holy Communion, the Eucharist) are universally celebrated. Lutherans also treasure the Word proclaimed in the reading of the Scriptures, preaching and absolution.

In the ELCA, the bishop is the minister of ordination. Much of Lutheranism continues what it understands as the historic succession of bishops (though without considering the historic episcopate essential to the church). Lutheran churches in Scandinavia and the Baltics, in the U.S., and in Canada have moved into full communion with their Anglican counterparts.

Lutheran jurisdictions corresponding to dioceses are called districts or synods in North America. There are more than 100 of them; each of them is headed by a bishop or president. The Evangelical Lutheran Church in America moved into full communion with the three Reformed Churches (Presbyterian Church, United Church of Christ and Reformed Church in America) in 1997, and in 2000 into full communion with the Episcopal Church, all of its bishops being ordained by bishops including those in the apostolic succession as understood by Anglicans. It also moved into full communion with the Moravian Church in 1999.

Methodist Churches

John Wesley (1703-1791), an Anglican clergyman, was the founder of Methodism. In 1738, following a period of missionary work in America, he experienced a new conversion to Christ and shortly thereafter became a leader in a religious awakening in England. By the end of the 18th century, Methodism was strongly rooted also in America.

The United Methodist Church, formed in 1968 by a merger of the Methodist Church and the Evangelical United Brethren Church, is the second largest Protestant denomination in the U.S., with more than nine million members; its principal agencies are located in New York, Evanston, IL, Nashville, TN, Washington, DC, Dayton, OH, and Lake Junaluska, NC (World Methodist Council, P.O. Box 518 28745). The second largest body, with just under two million communicants, is the African Methodist Episcopal Church. Four other major churches in the U.S. are the African Methodist Episcopal Zion, Christian Methodist Episcopal, Free Methodist Church and the Wesleyan Church. The total Methodist membership in the U.S. is about 15.5 million. Worldwide, there are more than 73 autonomous Methodist/Wesleyan churches in 107 countries, with a membership of more than 33 million. All of them participate in the World Methodist Council.

Methodism rejects absolute predestination and maintains that Christ offers grace freely to all men, not just to a select elite. Wesley's distinctive doctrine was the "witness of the Spirit" to the individual soul and personal assurance of salvation. He also emphasized the central themes of conversion and holiness. Methodists are in general agreement with classical Protestant theology. Church polity is structured along episcopal lines in America, with ministers being appointed to local churches by a bishop; churches stemming from British Methodism do not have bishops but vest appointive powers within an appropriate conference. Congregations are free to choose various forms of worship services.

Presbyterian Churches

Presbyterians are so called because of their tradition of governing the church through a system of representative bodies composed of elders (presbyters).

Presbyterianism is a part of the Reformed Family of Churches that grew out of the theological work of John Calvin following the Lutheran Reformation, to which it is heavily indebted. Countries in which it acquired early strength and influence were Switzerland, France, Holland, Scotland and England.

Presbyterianism spread widely in this country in the latter part of the 18th century and afterwards. Presently, it has approximately 4.5 million communicants in nine bodies.

The two largest Presbyterian bodies in the country — the United Presbyterian Church in the U.S.A. and the Presbyterian Church in the United States — were reunited in June 1983, to form the Presbyterian Church (U.S.A.), with a membership of 2.7 million. Its national offices are located at 100 Witherspoon St., Louisville, KY 40202.

These churches, now merged, are closely allied with the Reformed Church in America, the United Church of Christ, the Cumberland Presbyterian Churches, the Korean Presbyterian Church in America and the Associate Reformed Presbyterian Church.

In Presbyterian doctrine, baptism and the Lord's Supper, viewed as seals of the covenant of grace, are regarded as sacraments. Baptism, which is not necessary for salvation, is conferred on infants and adults The Lord's Supper is celebrated as a covenant of the Sacrifice of Christ. In both sacraments, a doctrine of the real presence of Christ is central.

The Church is twofold, being invisible and also visible; it consists of all of the elect and all those Christians who are united in Christ as their immediate head. Presbyterians are in general agreement with classical Protestant theology regarding Scripture, sal-

vation by grace, and justification.

Presbyterian congregations are governed by a session composed of elders elected by the communicant membership. On higher levels there are presbyteries, synods and a general assembly with various degrees of authority over local bodies; all such representative bodies are composed of elected elders and ministers in approximately equal numbers. The church annually elects a moderator who presides at the General Assembly and travels throughout the church to speak to and hear from the members.

Worship services, simple and dignified, include sermons, prayer, reading of the Scriptures and hymns. The Lord's Supper is celebrated at intervals.

Doctrinal developments of the past several years included approval in May, 1967, by the General Assembly of the United Presbyterian Church of a contemporary confession of faith to supplement the historic Westminster Confession. A statement entitled "The Declaration of Faith" was approved in 1977 by the Presbyterian Church in the U.S. for teaching and liturgical use. The reunited church adopted "A Brief Statement of Reformed Faith" in 1991 regarding urgent concerns of the church. The Presbyterian Church, USA, has moved into full communion with the Evangelical Lutheran Church in America in 1997.

United Church of Christ

The 1,501,310-member (in 1994) United Church of Christ was formed in 1957 by a union of the Congregational Christian and the Evangelical and Reformed Churches. Its headquarters are located at 700 Prospect, Cleveland, OH 44115.

Its statement of faith recognizes Jesus Christ as "our crucified and risen Lord (who) shared our common lot, conquering sin and death and reconciling the world to himself." It believes in the life after death, the fact that God "judges men and nations by his righteous will, that Christ calls its members to share in his baptism "and eat at his table." Each local church is free to adopt its own methods of worship and to formulate its own covenants and confessions of faith. Like other Calvinistic bodies, it believes that Christ is spiritually present in the sacrament. The United Church is governed along congregational lines, with a biennial General Synod. A 44-member executive council oversees the daily work of the church. In 1989 the UCC moved into full communion with the Christian Church (Disciples of Christ) and in 1997 with the Evangelical Lutheran Church in America.

Evangelicalism

Evangelicalism, dating from 1735 in England (the Evangelical Revival) and after 1740 in the United States (the Great Awakening), has had and continues to have widespread influence in Protestant churches. It has been estimated that about 45 million American Protestants are evangelicals. The Bible is their rule of faith and religious practice. Being born again in a life-changing experience through faith in Christ is the promise of salvation. Fundamentalists, numbering perhaps 4.5 million, comprise an extreme right-wing subculture of evangelicalism. Fundamentalism developed early in the 20th century in reaction against liberal theology and secularizing trends in mainstream and other Protestant denominations. The Holiness or Perfectionist wing of evangelicalism evolved from Methodist efforts to preserve the personal-piety and inner-religion concepts of John Wesley. There are at least 30 Holiness bodies in the U.S. Pentecostals, probably the most demonstrative of evangelicals. There are strong charismatic movements within many of the historic Protestant churches and Roman Catholicism. Black and white Pentecostal churches belong to the Pentecostal and Charismatic Fellowship of North America. Over forty Pentecostal, Holiness and evangelical churches belong to the US National Association of Evangelicals. Internationally, these national evangelical associations collaborate in the World Evangelical Alliance.

Assemblies of God

Assemblies (Churches) of God form the largest body (more than 2 million members) in the Pentecostal Movement which developed from (1) the Holiness Revival in the Methodist Church after the Civil War and (2) the Apostolic Faith Movement at the beginning of the 20th century. Members share with other Pentecostals belief in the religious experience of conversion and in the baptism by the Holy Spirit that sanctifies. Distinctive is the emphasis placed on the charismatic gifts of the apostolic church, healing and speaking in tongues. The Assemblies are conservative and biblicist in theology and are loosely organized.

ANGLICAN-CATHOLIC DIALOGUE

Anglican and Catholic leaders in the United States met Oct. 18-20, 2007, in dialogue on the role of the Virgin Mary and the progress in ecumenical relations between the two church bodies.

The 63rd meeting of the Anglican-Roman Catholic Theological Consultation (ARCUSA) took place at Virginia Theological Seminary, Alexandria, Virginia. The meeting completed work on two documents. The first was a response to the 2004 "Seattle Document" of the Anglican-Roman Catholic International Commission, entitled "Mary: Grace and Hope in Christ." The response, which is both a commentary on the document and a meditation on the meaning of the Blessed Virgin for the faithful of the two churches, is attached below.

The second task was to finish drafting a Spanish-language pastoral tool to be used to clarify the distinctions between the two churches and illustrate progress that has been made in their ecumenical relationship in recent decades. The completed text will be submitted for consideration to the U.S. bishops' Committee for Ecumenical and Interreligious Affairs and the Episcopal Church's Standing Commission for Ecumenical and Interreligious Relations, as well as the relevant offices for Hispanic affairs of the two churches. This meeting closed the current phase of the dialogue between the two churches. To commemorate the end of the current phase of the dialogue, a public event took place at Georgetown University on Oct. 18.

The Anglican-Roman Catholic Consultation in the United States was established in 1965 and has ordinarily met twice each year.

Anglican-Catholic Relations

The article below appeared in L'Osservatore Romano *in early 2008, and was written by Fr. Donald Bolen of the staff of the Pontifical Council for Promoting Christian Unity in the Vatican:*

For some years now, the Provinces (member churches) of the Anglican Communion have been struggling with deep internal tensions focused on questions of human sexuality, tensions which have threatened the unity of the communion. Efforts to address the moral issues have given rise to serious questions about the structures of authority and decision-making within Anglicanism, the nature of the Anglican Communion, the ministry of bishops, and the interpretation of Scripture. These questions, and the way in which they will eventually be resolved, have clear implications for the Anglican Communion's ecumenical relations, including their relations with the Catholic Church.

Throughout this period of Anglican discernment, the Pontifical Council for Promoting Christian Unity has maintained close communication with our Anglican dialogue partners — with the Archbishop of Canterbury and his office at Lambeth Palace, with the Anglican Communion Office in London, and with the Anglican Centre in Rome. Long-established relations of friendship and trust have resulted in frequent conversations, and a readiness to reflect together on questions as they emerge.

At times, our Anglican dialogue partners have also looked to the Catholic Church, and to their other ecumenical partners, for advice and support; they have not been afraid to ask open and honest questions and to hear what the Catholic Church has to say. Open and clear lines of communication have been especially helpful given that the secular media has at times sensationalized internal Anglican disputes, making it difficult to gain a clear understanding of the current situation within the Anglican Communion.

The Dialogue Commissions

The Anglican-Roman Catholic International Commission (ARCIC), which is the principal means by which the Anglican Communion and Catholic Church have entered into dialogue about doctrinal differences, completed its second phase of work in 2005 with the publication of the agreed statement Mary: Grace and Hope in Christ. A preparatory group has met to explore possible themes which could fruitfully be addressed in the future, but a third round of ARCIC dialogue has not yet been initiated.

In 2001, a second international commission was established, entitled the International Anglican-Roman Catholic Commission for Unity and Mission (IARCCUM). Constituted principally but not exclusively of bishops, IARCCUM was asked to produce a synthesis of the work of ARCIC, which has produced statements on Eucharist (1971), Ministry (1973), Authority in the Church (1976, 1981, 1999), Salvation and Justification (1987), Ecclesiology (1991), Morals (1994) and Mary, the Mother of God (2005). IARCCUM's text was finalized in late 2006 and published in 2007, with the title Growing Together in Unity and Mission: Building on 40 Years of Anglican-Roman Catholic Dialogue.

As the Co-Chair's Preface notes, the document is not an authoritative declaration by the Catholic Church or the Anglican Communion; similar to ARCIC statements, it has been published to foster discussion and reflection. Growing Together in Unity and Mission attempts to identify the degree to which Anglicans and Catholics have come to doctrinal agreement, as well as naming the areas where further theological dialogue is needed. Convinced that steps towards doctrinal agreement should translate into an increase in common witness and mission, IARCCUM members have also included a section proposing a range of practical initiatives, largely drawn from and aiming to be consistent with authorized texts and norms for Catholic ecumenical engagement; the text notes, however, that assessing these proposals will require discernment in light of local circumstances, given that "the context and dynamics of relationship between Anglicans and Roman Catholics differ widely across the world" (§99).

On the Catholic side, the IARCCUM text has been published alongside a commentary by Bishop Bernard Longley, Auxiliary Bishop of the Archdiocese of Westminster. Bishop Longley's commentary offers an initial assessment of the document from the perspective of the Catholic Church, assessing both its strengths and weaknesses. Both the IARCCUM text and the accompanying commentary are available on the Vatican's website.

The Lambeth Conference

Every ten years, the Archbishop of Canterbury invites Anglican bishops throughout the world to gather together for the Lambeth Conference. The current Archbishop of Canterbury, Dr Rowan Williams, has invited bishops to join him for such a conference from July 16 to Aug. 4, 2008. The Conference is not a lawmaking body; each of the 38 Provinces of the Anglican Communion have their own codes of canon law, and there is no overarching legislative body. But as Archbishop Williams recently noted, there is a long history of Lambeth Conferences seeking ways to ensure that Anglicans worldwide "acted in a responsible way toward each other and stayed faithful to the common inheritance of biblical and doctrinal faith".

The forthcoming Lambeth Conference will have two principle points of focus: strengthening Anglican identity, and equipping bishops for their role as leaders in mission. Both of these themes should assist in addressing current tensions within Anglican Communion. A key draft text which has been prepared for study at the Lambeth Conference is a proposal for an Anglican covenant, which is to be revised in light of further discussion, with the intention that it will eventually be signed by all the member churches of the Anglican Communion, and serve as a constructive bond of union.

While there has been much discussion within the Anglican world about the possible delay of the Lambeth Conference until current points of dispute are settled, Archbishop Williams has indicated that about 70% of Anglican bishops worldwide have already formally registered for the Conference, with a number of others signaling that they will attend. In addition to the 881 Anglican bishops invited to the Lambeth Conference, Archbishop Williams has also invited nearly 100 ecumenical guests, including a group of representatives from the Catholic Church.

For constructive ecumenical dialogue it is important for the Catholic Church to have a clear sense of where its dialogue partners stand, and a strengthening of the interdependence of Anglican Provinces, particularly if that means a stronger and united affirmation of the apostolic faith, would certainly have positive repercussions for our relations.

The Anglican Centre in Rome

Established in 1966, the Anglican Centre in Rome has been a valuable means of fostering close communication and mutual understanding between the Catholic Church and the Anglican Communion. The Director of the Anglican Centre is also the representative of the Archbishop of Canterbury to the Holy See, and for the past five years, this role has been generously filled by Bishop John Flack from England. Bishop Flack will be returning to episcopal ministry in England in early February. The gracious, calm and dedicated leadership of Bishop Flack has been greatly appreciated, among many others, by the officials of the Pontifical Council for Promoting Christian Unity; he will be sincerely missed. The Pontifical Council looks forward to welcoming his successor, the Very Reverend David Richardson of Melbourne, Australia, in April of this year.

Conclusion

Four years ago, during the course of a visit of Archbishop Rowan Williams to the Holy See, Cardinal Kasper noted that internal tensions in the ecclesial life of a dialogue partner do not signal an end to ecumenical relations: "Precisely when there are problems there is ever greater need of dialogue." When Archbishop Williams visited the Holy See just over a year ago, he and Pope Benedict XVI signed a Common Declaration which, while giving thanks for what has been achieved through dialogue and identifying possible areas for common witness, also directly acknowledged recent developments which, "besides being divisive for Anglicans, present serious obstacles to our ecumenical progress." The Common Declaration proceeded to state: "It is a matter of urgency, therefore, that in renewing our commitment to pursue the path towards full visible communion in the truth and love of Christ, we also commit ourselves in our continuing dialogue to address the important issues involved in the emerging ecclesiological and ethical factors making that journey more difficult and arduous."

Ecumenical relations are not simply a strategy or a means to an end which we ourselves orchestrate; they are fostered in obedience to the Lord's desire that His disciples be one, and they grow out of the recognition that those baptized into the death and resurrection of Christ are sisters and brothers in Him, who cannot simply be put aside when we face tensions or disagreements, old or new. In the present context, the Holy Spirit has been present amidst challenges and difficulties, calling forth honest conversation, prayerful support, and joint discernment about what it means to be faithful to the apostolic faith which has been handed down to us.

LUTHERAN-CATHOLIC RELATIONS

JOINT DECLARATION ON JUSTIFICATION WITH THE LUTHERAN WORLD FEDERATION

By Russell Shaw

Hailed by Pope John Paul II as a "milestone" on the road to Christian unity, a Lutheran-Catholic Joint Declaration on the Doctrine of Justification was signed Oct. 31, 1999, in Augsburg, Germany, by representatives of the Catholic Church and the Lutheran World Federation.

"This document represents a sound basis for continuing the ecumenical theological research and for addressing the remaining problems with a better founded hope of resolving them in the future," Pope John Paul said the same day in Rome in a talk accompanying the recitation of the Angelus. "It is also a valuable contribution to the purification of historical memory and to our common witness."

The Joint Declaration states a "consensus" shared by the signers regarding the doctrine of justification. The key passage formulating this consensus says:

"In faith we together hold the conviction that justification is the work of the triune God. The Father sent his Son into the world to save sinners. The foundation and presupposition of justification is the incarnation, death, and resurrection of Christ. Justification thus means that Christ himself is our righteousness, in which we share through the Holy Spirit in accord with the will of the Father.

"Together we confess: By grace alone, in faith in Christ's saving work and not because of any merit on our part, we are accepted by God and receive the Holy Spirit, who renews our hearts while equipping and calling us to good works."

The signers of the Joint Declaration were Card. Edward I. Cassidy, President of the Vatican's Pontifical Council for Promoting Christian Unity, and Bp. Christian Krause, President of the Lutheran World Federation, which represents 58 million of the world's 61 million Lutherans. Most, but not all, of the churches within the federation have accepted the Joint Declaration.

The Joint Declaration stresses that the churches "neither take the condemnations lightly nor do they disavow their own past." But, it insists, as a result of ecumenical dialogue during the last 30 years, they have come to "new insights" that transcend the mutual polemics of the Reformation era and make it clear that neither party's understanding of justification, as it is expressed in the Joint Declaration, now merits condemnation by the other, while the differences about the doctrine that continue to exist between them "are acceptable."

Despite the harmonious tone of the document and the various statements that accompanied its signing, the Joint Declaration has been, and to some extent remains, a controversial document. Some Lutheran bodies, including the Lutheran churches of several countries, have not accepted it. Nor has an unknown number of individual Lutherans, theologians among them.

On the Catholic side, there has been criticism that the document does not go far enough in coming to terms with Lutheranism and, on the other hand, that it goes too far in papering-over serious theological differences. According to the theologian Fr. Avery Dulles, SJ, it is "a bold statement,

difficult to defend" to claim that the differing views still held by Catholics and Lutherans on various questions relating to the doctrine of justification really do "escape the condemnations" pronounced by each side on the other in the 16th century.

"But notwithstanding all the theological reservations on both sides," Fr. Dulles added in an October 1999, lecture at Fordham University, New York, reprinted in the magazine First Things, the signing of the Joint Declaration "can be a powerful symbolic event."

"It says clearly to a world that hovers on the brink of unbelief that the two churches that split Western Christendom on the issue of justification nearly five centuries ago are still united on truths of the highest import," he said.

The Joint Declaration has been hailed as the fruit of some 30 years of ecumenical dialogue between Lutherans and Catholics. The doctrine of justification was an issue in these conversations from the start. The 1972 report of the international Lutheran-Catholic dialogue included five paragraphs on the topic, and observed that "today...a far-reaching consensus is developing." This emerging consensus also was noted in 1980 and 1981 reports by the international dialogue.

The doctrine of justification was considered in reports from national Lutheran-Catholic dialogues in the United States ("Justification by Faith," 1985) and Germany ("The Condemnations of the Reformation Era. Do They Still Divide?" 1986). These reports from national dialogues contributed to a lengthy report developed by the third phase of the international dialogue and published in 1993 as "Church and Justification: Understanding the Church in the Light of the Doctrine of Justification." In 1993, at the request of the Lutheran World Federation and the Council for Promoting Christian Unity, a small Lutheran-Catholic working group was formed to begin work on what became the Joint Declaration.

While the document first of all marks a significant new stage in Lutheran-Catholic relations, it also has broader ecumenical significance, Cardinal Cassidy said in an article published in the Vatican newspaper *L'Osservatore Romano*.

"What has been achieved in this mutual agreement of the Joint Declaration surely is an historic development of particular importance in the history of Western Christianity, and indeed for the whole ecumenical movement as well, since it illustrates that ecumenical progress can be made on questions that are of central importance, and have long been seen as church-dividing issues," he wrote.

Cardinal Cassidy listed "three basic truths" that he said were central to the doctrine of justification and to the Lutheran-Catholic consensus expressed in the Joint Declaration. They are:

"Firstly, justification is a free gift bestowed by the Trinitarian God and centers on the person of Christ who became incarnate, died and rose. In being related to the person of Christ through the work of the Holy Spirit, we enter into a condition of righteousness....

"Secondly, we receive this salvation in faith....[T]he reality of justification is linked to faith, but not simply as an intellectual assent of the mind. Rather the believer is to give him/herself over to Christ in the renewal of life.

"Thirdly, justification points to the heart of the Gospel message, but must be seen in an organic unity with all the other truths of faith: Trinity, Christology, Ecclesiology and Sacraments."

The Joint Declaration begins with a Preamble that includes this statement of the document's intention: "...to show that on the basis of their dialogue the subscribing Lutheran churches and the Roman Catholic Church are now able to articulate a common understanding of our justification by God's grace through faith in Christ. It does not cover all that either church teaches about justification; it does encompass a consensus on basic truths of the doctrine of justification and shows that the remaining differences in its explication are no longer the occasion for doctrinal condemnations."

Following an overview of significant scriptural passages on the doctrine (section one), the document notes that, historically, justification has been an ecumenical problem between the Catholic Church and the Reformation churches and that differences focusing on it were the "principal cause" of their division and mutual condemnations in the 16th century. But in the ecumenical dialogue since the Second Vatican Council (1962-1965), it says, a "notable convergence" has emerged (section two).

The Joint Declaration then states the "consensus" on the basic truths of the doctrine, quoted above (section three). Justification is said to be "more than just one part of Christian doctrine. It stands in an essential relation with all truths of faith, which are to be seen as internally related to each other."

The fourth section of the Declaration ("Explicating the Common Understanding of Justification") is the document's longest section. It identifies, one by one, seven particular questions relating to the doctrine, states the consensus shared by Lutherans and Catholics regarding these seven questions, and then sets out distinctive Catholic and Lutheran perspectives on each.

The seven topics treated in this manner are: "Human Powerlessness and Sin in Relation to Justification," "Justification as Forgiveness of Sins and Making Righteous," "Justification by Faith and through Grace," "The Justified as Sinner," "Law and Gospel," "Assurance of Salvation," and "The Good Works of the Justified."

The Joint Declaration closes by once again underlining the "consensus in basic truths" regarding justification and stating its "significance and scope" (section five):

"In light of this consensus the remaining differences of language, theological elaboration, and emphasis in the understanding described in paras. 18 to 39 [section four] are acceptable. Therefore the Lutheran and Catholic explications of justification are in their difference open to one another and do not destroy the consensus regarding the basic truths.

"Thus the doctrinal condemnations of the 16th century, in so far as they relate to the doctrine of justification, appear in a new light. The teaching of the Lutheran churches presented in this Declaration does not fall under the condemnations from the Council of Trent. The condemnations of the Lutheran Confessions do not apply to the teaching of the Roman Catholic Church presented in this Declaration."

The document lists a number of other questions between Catholics and Lutherans that need clarification: the relationship between the Word of God and church doctrine, ecclesiology, ecclesial authority, church unity, ministry, the sacraments, and the relation between justification and social ethics. "We are confident that the consensus we have reached offers a solid basis for this clarification," it says.

An "Official Common Statement" of the Lutheran World Federation and the Catholic Church, issued at the time of the signing in Augsburg, commits both to continued ecumenical dialogue on outstanding questions regarding justification as well as the matters just mentioned. Such dialogue is necessary, it says, "in order to reach full church communion, a unity in diversity, in which remaining differences would be 'reconciled' and no longer have a divisive force."

In his article in *L'Osservatore Romano*, Cardinal Cassidy linked the signing of the Joint Declaration to the preparations for the third millennium of Christianity and the Great Jubilee of the Year 2000. In his 1994 apostolic letter *Tertio Millennio Adveniente* ("On the Coming of the Third Millennium"), he pointed out, Pope John Paul spoke of the scandal of Christian division and the need to work for unity in the new millennium. The Lutheran-Catholic accord marks important progress toward this goal, he suggested.

At the same time, the Cardinal acknowledged "the limits of our achievement" as represented in the Joint Declaration: "The declaration brings the Catholic Church and the member churches of the Lutheran World Federation which affirmed it a clear step closer to unity. They have not yet, however, achieved the goal of full, visible unity."

In particular, he said, "Catholics are not able to share the Eucharist with their Lutheran brothers and sisters....Our common participation in the Eucharist awaits the full ecclesial communion which we seek."

Nevertheless, Cardinal Cassidy added, the limitations of what has been accomplished in reaching this agreement should not cause it to be underestimated. "Serious difficulties remain, but they are secondary to what we hold in common. No longer may we look upon our different expressions of faith as being like two huge cannons drawn up in battle line and facing each other....We need, above all, to give thanks to God for this achievement."

RELATIONS WITH THE POLISH NATIONAL CATHOLIC CHURCH

The Roman Catholic-Polish National Catholic Dialogue issued a Joint Declaration on Unity on May 17, 2006, in Fall River, MA. Excerpts follow:

With thankfulness to God, the members of the Roman Catholic-Polish National Catholic dialogue in the United States look back on twenty-two years of theological and canonical reflection concerning the nature of our division and the possibility of reaching full communion. Because of a new outpouring of the Holy Spirit that affected both our churches following the celebration of the Second Vatican Council (1962-1965) and a similar renewal within the Polish National Catholic Church, our faithful have been rediscovering one another increasingly as brothers and sisters in the Lord. At this time we wish to review the progress that we have achieved over the past two decades, and reaffirm our intention to continue our efforts to achieve that unity for which Christ prayed.

Calls for a dialogue between our churches go back as far as 1966, when the Most Rev. Leon Grochowski, Prime Bishop of the Polish National Catholic Church, courageously proposed such a dialogue to the Roman Catholic Bishop of Scranton. Later, in 1980, His Holiness Pope John Paul II of blessed memory expressed the desire that the conference of bishops of the United States examine the relationship that exists with the Polish National Catholic Church and explore the possibility of dialogue. This resulted in an exchange of correspondence between the leaders of our churches that would culminate in the first meeting of an official dialogue in Passaic, NJ, on Oct. 23, 1984.

In view of the fact that most of the ecumenical dialogues began in the 1960s and 1970s, the establishment of our dialogue was late in coming. This was the result of the particularly painful history of our relationship and the circumstances of the origins of the Polish National Catholic Church among ethnic Polish and other Roman Catholics in the United States at the end of the 19th and the beginning of the 20th century. The disputes of that time, we now realize, were more concerned with matters of church governance than points of doctrine. Nevertheless, the complicated series of events that led to our division caused much hurt and anguish even within families whose members often found themselves on opposite sides of the dispute. The consequences of those events can still be felt among us more than a century later, and must be addressed.

For this purpose, a number of highly symbolic gestures of reconciliation have taken place, perhaps most notably at the Service of Healing that was held in St. Stanislaus Polish National Catholic Cathedral in Scranton, PA, on Feb. 15, 1992. Leaders of our two churches, including Card. Edward I. Cassidy (President of the Pontifical Council for Promoting Christian Unity), His Grace John F. Swantek, Prime Bishop of the Polish National Catholic Church, and the two co-chairmen of the dialogue, asked for forgiveness, and pledged to work to overcome our divisions definitively. In 1997 Bp. James C. Timlin, then the Roman Catholic Co-Chairman of the dialogue, reiterated this request for forgiveness in a letter he issued on the occasion of the centenary of the organization of the Polish National Catholic Church.

Our dialogue has achieved much. For example, in a 1989 report summarizing the first five years of the dialogue's progress, we affirmed our agreement on the seven sacraments of the Church, in spite of some differences in practice that do not touch upon our basic common faith. The report also examined two areas of divergence — our understandings of the Word of God and the life to come — and discovered that here too there are broad areas of agreement. In sum, the report was able to look back over five years of dialogue and state that "we have thus far discovered no doctrinal obstacle that would impede the further growth of our churches toward that unity which we believe is Christ's will." A second report dealing with developments in our dialogue from 1989 to 2002 was published in 2003.

In view of this progress, concrete steps have been taken. In response to an inquiry from the Archbishop of Baltimore, His Excellency William Keeler, then President of the National Conference of Catholic Bishops, His Eminence Edward Card. Cassidy, President of the Pontifical Council for Promoting Christian Unity, stated in 1993 that members of the Polish National Catholic Church in the United States and Canada may receive the sacraments of Penance, Holy Communion and Anointing of the Sick from Roman Catholic priests if they ask for them on their own, are properly disposed and not otherwise excluded from the sacraments in line with the provisions of canon 844 §3 of The Code of Canon Law. This was followed in 1996 by a letter by Archbishop Oscar H. Lipscomb, the Chairman of the Bishops' Committee for Ecumenical and Interreligious Affairs, to the bishops of the United States spelling out in more detail the conditions under which Polish National Catholics may receive the aforementioned sacraments in the Roman Catholic Church. In 1998 the Polish National Catholic Church issued Guidelines for the Reception by Polish National Catholics of Sacraments in the Roman Catholic Church. Canon 844 §2 of The Code of Canon Law also specifies conditions under which Roman Catholics may receive the sacraments in the Polish National Catholic Church.

In light of these concrete steps towards unity, we have much for which to be thankful. Furthermore, we recognize each other's ecclesial character and sacraments, allow a certain amount of sacramental sharing, and maintain many of the same traditions. These facts bear witness to how much we have rediscovered as our common heritage. Our mutual esteem clearly rules out inappropriate actions such as proselytism among each other's faithful or the re-ordination of clergy who pass from one church to the other.

During our century-long division we have grown apart in ways that at first glance make reconciliation appear to be difficult. The Polish National Catholic Church, which during most of its existence was a member of the Union of Utrecht, has developed a strong sense of autonomy and the desire to preserve its distinctive traditions, including the vital role played by the laity in church governance. Even though the primacy and infallibility of the Bishop of Rome was not an issue at the time of our division, our churches today have different understandings of the Pope's role in the Church. Another complicating factor is the presence of a significant number of former Roman Catholic priests in the ranks of the Polish National Catholic clergy. Such is the legacy of the divisions of the past that remain with us today.

At this point in our relationship, therefore, we the members of the Polish National Catholic-Roman Catholic dialogue wish to reaffirm our resolve to overcome what still divides us, and to state clearly that our goal is full communion between our churches. We wish to emphasize that "full communion" does not imply absorption or uniformity, but a unity that fully recognizes differing traditions that are consistent with our common apostolic faith. It must still be determined if any of our divergent traditions are truly church-dividing, or simply examples of legitimate diversity which, in the words of Pope John Paul II, "is in no way opposed to the Church's unity, but rather enhances her splendor and contributes greatly to the fulfillment of her mission" (*Ut Unum Sint*, No. 50). We plan to give further consideration to other concrete steps concerning reciprocity in regard to the sacraments, acting as godparents, and the requirement of canonical form for lawfulness only in mixed marriages. We are equally committed to a thorough examination of the theological concepts of primacy and conciliarity. This will include searching for a common understanding of the ministry of the Bishop of Rome in the Church.

As members of a commission authorized to engage in this ecumenical dialogue, our role is not to speak definitively for either of our churches. Nevertheless, we hope to propose new incremental steps that will make concrete the growing unity between us, and we wish our faithful to know of our conviction that a way can be found to overcome this regrettable division that took place among Catholics here in the United States. We know that the goal of unity is nothing less than the will of Christ for us. Therefore we ask the faithful of both our churches to join us in fervent prayer that, with a new outpouring of the Holy Spirit, the barriers between us will fall and we will one day soon find ourselves joined again in that perfect unity that befits the disciples of our Lord Jesus Christ.

INTERRELIGIOUS DIALOGUE

JUDAISM

Judaism is the religion of the Hebrew Bible and of contemporary Jews. Divinely revealed and with a patriarchal background (Abraham and Sarah, Isaac and Jacob), it originated with the Mosaic Covenant, was identified with the Israelites, and achieved distinctive form and character as the religion of the Torah (Law, "The Teaching") from this Covenant and reforms initiated by Ezra and Nehemiah after the Babylonian Exile.

Judaism does not have a formal creed but its principal points of belief are clear. Basic is belief in one transcendent God who reveals himself through the Torah, the prophets, the life of his people and events of history. The fatherhood of God involves the brotherhood of all humanity. Religious faith and practice are equated with just living according to God's Law. Moral conviction and practice are regarded as more important than precise doctrinal formulation and profession. Formal worship, whose principal act was sacrifice from the Exodus times to A.D. 70, is by prayer, reading and meditating upon the sacred writings, and observance of the Sabbath and festivals.

Judaism has messianic expectations of the complete fulfillment of the Covenant, the coming of God's kingdom, the ingathering of his people, and final judgment and retribution for all. Views differ regarding the manner in which these expectations will be realized — through a person, the community of God's people, an evolution of historical events, an eschatological act of God himself. Individual salvation expectations also differ, depending on views about the nature of immortality, punishment and reward, and related matters.

Sacred Books

The sacred books are the 24 books of the Masoretic Hebrew Text of The Law, the Prophets and the Writings (see The Bible). Together, they contain the basic instruction or norms for just living. In some contexts, the term Law or Torah refers only to the Pentateuch (Genesis, Exodus, Leviticus, Numbers, Deuteronomy); in others, it denotes all the sacred books and/or the whole complex of written and oral tradition. Also of great authority are two Talmuds, which were composed in Palestine and Babylon in the fourth and fifth centuries A.D., respectively. They consist of the Mishna, a compilation of oral laws, and the Gemara, a collection of rabbinical commentary on the Mishna. Midrash are collections of scriptural comments and moral counsels.

Priests were the principal religious leaders during the period of sacrificial and temple worship. Rabbis were originally teachers; today they share with cantors the function of leaders of prayer. The synagogue is the place of community worship. The family and home are focal points of many aspects of Jewish worship and practice.

Of the various categories of Jews, Orthodox are the most conservative in adherence to strict religious traditions. Others — Reformed, Conservative, Reconstructionist — are liberal in comparison with the Orthodox. They favor greater or less modification of religious practices in accommodation to contemporary culture and living conditions.

Principal events in Jewish life include the circumcision of males, according to prescriptions of the Covenant; the bar and bat mitzvah that marks the coming–of–age of boys and girls in Judaism at age 13; marriage; and observance of the Sabbath and festivals.

Observances of the Sabbath and festivals begin at sundown of the previous calendar day and continue until the following sundown.

Sabbath: Saturday, the weekly day of rest prescribed in the Decalogue.

Sukkoth (Tabernacles): A seven-to-nine-day festival in the month of Tishri (Sept.-Oct.), marked by some Jews with Covenant-renewal and reading of The Law. It originated as an agricultural feast at the end of the harvest and got its name from the temporary shelters used by workers in the fields.

Hanukkah (The Festival of Lights, the Feast of Consecration and of the Maccabees): Commemorates the dedication of the new altar in the Temple at Jerusalem by Judas Maccabeus in 165 B.C. The eight-day festival, during which candles in an eight-branch candelabra are lighted in succession, one each day, occurs near the winter solstice, close to Christmas time.

Pesach (Passover): A seven-day festival commemorating the liberation of the Israelites from Egypt. The narrative of the Exodus, the Haggadah, is read at ceremonial Seder meals on the first and second days of the festival, which begins on the 14th day of Nisan (Mar.-Apr.).

Shavuoth, Pentecost (Feast of Weeks): Observed 50 days after Passover, commemorating the anniversary of the revelation of the Law to Moses.

Purim: A joyous festival observed on the 14th day of Adar (Feb.-Mar.), commemorating the rescue of the Israelites from massacre by the Persians through the intervention of Esther. The festival is preceded by a day of fasting. A gift and alms giving custom became associated with it in medieval times.

Rosh Hashana (Feast of Trumpets, New Year): Observed on the first day of Tishri (Sept.-Oct.), the festival focuses attention on the ways of life and the ways of death. It is second in importance only to the most solemn observance of Yom Kippur.

Yom Kippur (Day of Atonement): The highest holy day, observed with strict fasting. It occurs 10 days after Rosh Hashana.

Yom HaShoah (Holocaust Memorial Day): Observed in the week after Passover; increasingly observed with joint Christian-Jewish services of remembrance.

CATHOLIC-JEWISH RELATIONS

The Second Vatican Council, in addition to the *Decree on Ecumenism* (concerning the movement for unity among Christians, stated the mind of the Church on a similar matter in *Nostra Aetate*, a" Declaration on the Relationship of the Church to Non-Christian Religions." This document, as the following excerpts indicate, backgrounds the reasons and directions of the Church's regard for the Jews. (Other portions of the document refer to Hindus, Buddhists and Muslims.)

Spiritual Bond

As this sacred Synod searches into the mystery of the Church, it recalls the spiritual bond linking the people of the New Covenant with Abraham's stock.

For the Church of Christ acknowledges that, according to the mystery of God's saving design, the beginnings of her faith and her election are already found among the patriarchs, Moses, and the prophets. She professes that all who believe in Christ, Abraham's sons according to faith (cf. Gal 3:7), are included in the same patriarch's call, and likewise that the salvation of the Church was mystically foreshadowed by the Chosen People's exodus from the land of bondage.

The Church, therefore, cannot forget that she received the revelation of the Old Testament through the people with whom God in his inexpressible mercy deigned to establish the Ancient Covenant. Nor can she forget that she draws sustenance from the root of that good olive tree onto which have been grafted the wild olive branches of the Gentiles (cf. Rom 11:17-24). Indeed, the Church believes that by his cross Christ, our Peace, reconciled Jew and Gentile, making them both one in himself (cf. Eph 2:14-16).

The Jews still remain most dear to God because of their fathers, for he does not repent of the gifts he makes nor of the calls he issues (cf. Rom 11:28-29). In company with the prophets and the same Apostle (Paul), the Church awaits that day, known to God alone, on which all peoples will address the Lord in a single voice and "serve him with one accord" (Zeph 3:9; cf. Is 66:23; Ps 65:4; Rom 11:11-32).

Since the spiritual patrimony common to Christians and Jews is thus so great, this sacred Synod wishes to foster and recommend that mutual understanding and respect which is the fruit above all of biblical and theological studies, and of brotherly dialogues.

No Anti-Semitism

True, authorities of the Jews and those who followed their lead pressed for the death of Christ (cf. Jn 19:6); still, what happened in his passion cannot be blamed upon all the Jews then living, without distinction, nor upon the Jews of today. Although the Church is the new People of God, the Jews should not be presented as repudiated or cursed by God, as if such views followed from the holy Scriptures. All should take pains, then, lest in catechetical instruction and in the preaching of God's Word they teach anything out of harmony with the truth of the Gospel and the spirit of Christ.

The Church repudiates all persecutions against any person. Moreover, mindful of her common patrimony with the Jews, and motivated by the Gospel's spiritual love and by no political considerations, she deplores the hatred, persecutions, and displays of anti-Semitism directed against the Jews at any time and from any source (No. 4).

The Church rejects, as foreign to the mind of Christ, any discrimination against men or harassment of them because of their race, color, condition of life, or religion (No. 5).

Bishops' Secretariat

The American hierarchy's first move toward implementation of the Vatican II "Declaration on the Relationship of the Church to Non-Christian Religions" (*Nostra Aetate*) was to establish, in 1965, a Subcommission for Catholic-Jewish Relations in the framework of its Commission for Ecumenical and Interreligious Affairs. Its moderator is Cardinal William H. Keeler. The Secretariat for Ecumenical and Interreligious Relations is located at 3211 Fourth St. N.E., Washington, DC 20017. Its Catholic-Jewish efforts were directed by Dr. Eugene J. Fisher from 1977 until his retirement in 2007.

According to the key norm of a set of guidelines issued by the secretariat Mar. 16, 1967, and updated Apr. 9, 1985: "The general aim of all Catholic-Jewish meetings (and relations) is to increase our understanding both of Judaism and the Catholic faith, to eliminate sources of tension and misunderstanding, to initiate dialogue or conversations on different levels, to multiply intergroup meetings between Catholics and Jews, and to promote cooperative social action."

Vatican Guidelines

In a document issued Jan. 3, 1975, the Vatican Commission for Religious Relations with the Jews offered a number of suggestions and guidelines for implementing the Christian-Jewish portion of the Second Vatican Council's Declaration on Relations with Non-Christian Religions.

Among "suggestions from experience" were those concerning dialogue, liturgical links between Christian and Jewish worship, the interpretation of biblical texts, teaching and education for the purpose of increasing mutual understanding, and joint social action.

Notes on Preaching and Catechesis

On June 24, 1985, the Vatican Commission for Religious Relations with the Jews promulgated its "Notes on the Correct Way to Present Jews and Judaism in Preaching and Catechesis in the Roman Catholic Church," with the intent of providing "a helpful frame of reference for those who are called upon in the course of their teaching assignments to speak about Jews and Judaism and who wish to do so in keeping with the current teaching of the Church in this area."

The document states emphatically that, since the relationship between the Church and the Jewish people is one "founded on the design of the God of the Covenant," Judaism does not occupy "an occasional and marginal place in catechesis," but an "essential" one that "should be organically integrated" throughout the curriculum on all levels of Catholic education.

The Notes discuss the relationship between the Hebrew Scriptures and the New Testament, focusing especially on typology, which is called "the sign of a problem unresolved." Underlined is the "eschatological dimension," that "the people of God of the Old and the New Testament are tending toward a like end in the future: the coming or return of the Messiah." Jewish witness to God's Kingdom, the

Notes declare, challenges Christians to "accept our responsibility to prepare the world for the coming of the Messiah by working together for social justice and reconciliation."

The Notes emphasize the Jewishness of Jesus' teaching, correct misunderstandings concerning the portrayal of Jews in the New Testament and describe the Jewish origins of Christian liturgy. One section addresses the "spiritual fecundity" of Judaism to the present, its continuing "witness —

often heroic — of its fidelity to the one God," and mandates the development of Holocaust curricula and a positive approach in Catholic education to the "religious attachment which finds its roots in biblical tradition " between the Jewish people and the Land of Israel, affirming the "existence of the State of Israel" on the basis of "the common principles of international law."

WE REMEMBER: A REFLECTION ON THE SHOAH

On Mar. 16, 1998, the Commission for Religious Relations with the Jews under Card. Edward Idris Cassidy, issued a long-awaited white paper on the Holocaust, entitled "We Remember: Reflections on the Shoah."

The document offered repentance for the failures of many Christians to oppose the policies of Nazi Germany and to resist the extermination of the Jews during the years of the Third Reich. It analyzed the history of anti-Semitism in the Church, while distinguishing between the historical anti-Judaism of Christian teaching over the centuries and the modern, racial ideology of Nazism that climaxed with the Holocaust.

"We Remember" defends Pope Pius XII and his efforts on behalf of the Jews during World War II, and at the same time acknowledges the need for a "call to penitence" by the Church as a whole "for the failures of her sons and daughters in every age." Card. Cassidy, in an address given in May 1998 to the American Jewish Committee responding to criticisms of the text, stated clearly that terms such as "sons and daughters" and "members of the Church" are not restricted to a single category, "but can include popes cardinals, bish-

ops, priests and laity," and he acknowledged that Christian anti-Judaism paved the way for Nazi anti-Semitism, though distinct from it.

We Remember begins with a letter from Pope John Paul II expressing his hope that the document will indeed help to heal the wounds of past misunderstandings and injustices and enable memory to play its necessary part in the process of shaping a future in which the unspeakable iniquity of the Shoah will never again be possible."

The U.S. Conference of Catholic Bishops' Committee for Ecumenical and Interreligious Relations in 1998 published the text of "We Remember" along with the statements of European and American bishops' conferences similarly expressing repentance for Christian sins of omission and commission during the Shoah in a volume entitled, *Catholics Remember the Holocaust.* In 2001 the U.S. Bishops issued *Catholic Teaching on the Shoah: Implementing the Holy See's "We Remember"* urging and giving guidelines for Holocaust education in all Catholic schools, from elementary through college and university education.

PAPAL STATEMENTS

(Courtesy Bishops' Committee for Ecumenical and Interreligious Affairs.)

Pope John Paul II

Pope John Paul II was deeply loved and admired by the Jewish people worldwide over his long tenure. The Jewish outpouring of grief and condolence was deep and widespread, and save for that when the beloved Bl. John XXIII died, entirely without precedent. The prayers and statements of Jewish groups can be seen on their websites. Pope John Paul II, in a remarkable series of addresses beginning in 1979, sought to promote and give shape to the development of dialogue between Catholics and Jews.

In a homily delivered June 7, 1979, at Auschwitz, which he called the "Golgotha of the Modern World," he prayed movingly for "the memory of the people whose sons and daughters were intended for total extermination."

In a key address delivered Nov. 17, 1980, to the Jewish community in Mainz, the Pope articulated his vision of the three "dimensions" of the dialogue: (1) "the meeting between the people of God of the Old Covenant and the people of the New Covenant"; (2) the encounter of "mutual esteem between today's Christian churches and today' s people of the Covenant concluded with Moses"; (3) the "holy duty" of witnessing to the one God in the world and "jointly to work for peace and justice."

During his historic visit to the Great Synagogue in Rome Apr. 13, 1986, the Holy Father affirmed that

God's covenant with the Jewish people is "irrevocable," and stated: "The Jewish religion is not 'extrinsic' to us, but in a certain way is 'intrinsic' to our own religion. With Judaism, therefore, we have a relationship which we do not have with any other religion."

Meeting with the Jewish community in Sydney, Australia, Nov. 26, 1986, the Holy Father termed the 20th century "the century of the Shoah" (Holocaust) and called "sinful" any "acts of discrimination or persecution against Jews."

On June 14, 1987, meeting with the Jewish community of Warsaw, the pope called the Jewish witness to the Shoah (Holocaust) a "saving warning before all of humanity" which reveals "your particular vocation, showing you (Jews) to be still the heirs of that election to which God is faithful."

Meeting with Jewish leaders Sept. 11, 1987, in Miami, the Pope praised the efforts in theological dialogue and educational reform implemented in the U.S. since the Second Vatican Council; affirmed the existence of the State of Israel "according to international law," and urged "common educational programs on the Holocaust so that never again will such a horror be possible. Never again!"

On Apr. 7, 1994, the eve of Yom HaShoah, the Jewish day of prayer commemorating the victims of the Holocaust, Pope John Paul II hosted a memorial concert at the Vatican. It was, he noted, a moment of "common meditation and shared prayer," as the Kaddish, the prayer for the dead, and the Kol Nidre, the prayer for forgiveness and atonement, were recited.

Pope Benedict XVI

Because he had already built up an impressive series of positive reflections on Catholic-Jewish relations over the years, including a book, the election of Cardinal Joseph Ratzinger to the papacy was greeted with joy by all involved in Catholic-Jewish relations. In a major article in *L'Osservatore Romano* in December 2000, for example, Cardinal Ratzinger clarified and synthesized Catholic teaching on Jews and Judaism. With regard to the Shoah, for example, he stated: "Even if the most recent, loathsome experience of the Shoah was perpetrated in the name of an anti-Christian ideology, which tried to strike the Christian faith at its Abrahamic roots in the people of Israel, it cannot be denied that a certain insufficient resistance to this atrocity on the part of Christians can be explained by an inherited anti-Judaism present in the hearts of not a few Christians." The dialogue, he said, "must begin with a prayer to our God, first of all that he might grant to us Christians a greater esteem and love for that people, the people of Israel, to whom belong 'the adoption as sons, the glory, the covenants, the giving of the law, the worship, and the promises; theirs are the patriarchs, and from them comes Christ according to the flesh, he who is over all, God, blessed forever. Amen' (Rom 9:4-5), and this not only in the past, but still today, 'for the gifts and the call of God are irrevocable' (Rom 11:29)."

In his first meeting with the International Jewish Committee for Interreligious Consultations, Benedict reassured many by affirming the direction of his predecessor: "At the very beginning of my Pontificate, I wish to assure you that the Church remains firmly committed, in her catechesis and in every aspect of her life, to implementing this decisive teaching."

Similarly, in his meeting with Jews in the Synagogue in Cologne, Benedict stated that "I make my own the words written by my venerable Predecessor on the occasion of the 60th anniversary of the liberation of Auschwitz and I too say: 'I bow my head before all those who experienced this manifestation of the *mysterium iniquitatis*.' The terrible events of that time must 'never cease to rouse consciences, to resolve conflicts, to inspire the building of peace.'"

In his review of the year 2005 with the Vatican Curia in December of that year, the Pope discussed the proper understanding of the Second Vatican Council. He spoke of the "hermeneutics of continuity and discontinuity" in three key areas: faith and science, Church and State (religious freedom), and "the relationship between the Church and the faith of Israel."

Greeting the chief rabbi of Rome in January 2006, Benedict, in a remarkable formulation, emphasized God's enduring and saving love for the Jewish People: "Your visit brings me great joy, and induces me to renew with you this song of gratitude for the salvation we have received. The people of Israel have been liberated many times from the hands of their enemies and, in times of anti-Semitism, in the dramatic moments of the Shoah, the hand of the Almighty has supported and guided them. The favor of the God of the Covenant has always accompanied them, giving them the strength to overcome trials. To this divine loving attention your Jewish community, present in the city of Rome for more than 2,000 years, can also render testimony."

While affirming the necessity of Jewish, Christian, Muslim dialogue, Benedict emphasized in meeting with the American Jewish Committee in March 2007 that "Jews and Christians have a rich common patrimony. In many ways this distinguishes our relationship as unique among the religions of the world. The Church can never forget that chosen people with whom God entered into a holy covenant (cf. *Nostra Aetate*, 4)."

In May 2006, Benedict visited Auschwitz. "In a place like this," he said, "words fail; in the end, there can only be a dread silence — a silence which is itself a heartfelt cry to God: Why, Lord, did you remain silent? How could you tolerate all this? In silence, then, we bow our heads before the endless line of those who suffered and were put to death here; yet our silence becomes in turn a plea for forgiveness and reconciliation, a plea to the living God never to let this happen again." Returning to Rome and reflecting on the visit at the General Audience, he stated that "At the death camp of Auschwitz-Birkenau, a place of horror and godless inhumanity, I paid homage to the victims, including over a million Jews and many Poles.... May modern humanity not forget Auschwitz and the other 'factories of death' where the Nazi regime attempted to eliminate God in order to take his place."

MILLENNIUM EVENTS

During 2000 the London Philharmonic conducted by Maestro Gilbert Levine played a special series of concerts of Haydn's "Creation" for interreligious audiences in Baltimore, Paris, Jerusalem and, finally in Rome to celebrate the Holy Father's 80th birthday. In London, the Holy See and the World Union for Progressive Judaism sponsored a theological dialogue, papers of which have been published as *He Kissed Him and They Wept* (London: SCM Press) co-edited by Tony Bayfield, Sydney Brichto and Eugene Fisher. A second theological conference on Revelation and Covenant was held in London in 2003.

Pope John Paul II determined that the year marking the beginning of the third millennium would be a year of repentance by the Church for the sins of its members during the secondnd millennium. On the first Sunday of Lent, during Mass in St. Peter's, he lead the Church in a liturgy of repentance in seven categories of Christian sins, one of which was the mistreatment of Jews and Judaism over the centuries including, especially the Shoah in the 20th century.

A high point of the millennium year was the Pope's pilgrimage to the Holy Land. In Israel, he visited not only Christian holy places, but places central to Jewish memory as well. At Yad VaShem in Jerusalem, Israel's memorial to the six million Jews murdered by Nazi Germany, he prayed for the deceased and embraced Jewish survivors, some of them from his own home town of Wadowice. The prime minister of Israel, Ehud Barak, spoke movingly for his people and his country in a warm response. At the Western Wall (the Kotel, the last remnant of the ancient Temple of Jerusalem), the Pope not only prayed but inserted into the Wall a written petition just as the humblest of Jews have done ever since the Temple's destruction in 70 C.E. Its wording summarizes one of the major themes of the millennium year and of the remarkable pontificate of Karol Wojtyla. Addressing the "God of our fathers," the Pope prayed in the name of the whole Church: "We are deeply saddened by the behavior of those who in the course of history have caused these children of yours to suffer and, asking your forgiveness, we wish to commit ourselves to genuine brotherhood with the People of the Covenant." The note was reverently taken from the wall for permanent display at Yad VaShem.

Pontifical Biblical Commission

In 2002 the Pontifical Biblical Commission issued "The Jewish People and Their Sacred Scriptures in the Christian Bible," a 205-page volume fulfilling the pope's 1997 mandate to the Commission. The first section of the report stresses, contrary to Marcionism, that the Jewish Scriptures are a fundamental part of the Christian Bible. The second section shows how the New Testament attests "conformity" (continuity) to the Jewish Bible in "fulfilling the Scriptures" but also presents a "newness" ("discontinuity, progression") in the life and certain teachings of Christ (IIA). Still, major "fundamental themes" of revelation are shared by both testaments (IIB). Jewish readings of the Bible, from rabbinic times to the present, maintain their own integrity and validity based upon the integrity and validity of the Jewish Scriptures understood in their own terms.

The third section outlines the historical setting of the New Testament as a document of "post-exilic Judaism" (IIIA) and describes the portrait of Jews in each gospel (IIIB) and of Judaism in the Pauline Letters and other apostolic writings (IIIC). The document concludes with "pastoral orientations" urging Jews and Christians to continued dialogue over the "inexhaustible riches" of our shared sacred texts.

INTERNATIONAL LIAISON COMMITTEE

The International Catholic-Jewish Liaison Committee (ILC) was formed in 1971 and is the official link between the Commission for Religious Relations with the Jewish People and the International Jewish Committee for Interreligious Consultations. The committee meets every 18 months to examine matters of common interest.

Topics under discussion have included: mission and witness (Venice, 1977), religious education (Madrid, 1978), religious liberty and pluralism (Regensburg, 1979), religious commitment (London, 1981), the sanctity of human life in an age of violence (Milan, 1982), youth and faith (Amsterdam, 1984), the Vatican Notes on Preaching and Catechesis (Rome, 1985), the Holocaust (Prague, 1990), education and social action (Baltimore, 1992), family and ecology (Jerusalem, 1994), the Catholic Church and the Shoah (Rome, 1998), theological understandings of one another (New York, 2001), and theology (Buenos Aires, 2004).

Pope John Paul, addressing in Rome a celebration of *Nostra Aetate* (the Second Vatican Council's "Declaration on the Relationship of the Church to Non-Christian Religions") by the Liaison Committee, stated: "What you are celebrating is nothing other than the divine mercy which is guiding Christians and Jews to mutual awareness, respect, cooperation and solidarity. The universal openness of *Nostra Aetate* is anchored in and takes its orientation from a high sense of the absolute singularity of God's choice of a particular people. The Church is fully aware that Sacred Scripture bears witness that the Jewish people, this community of faith and custodian of a tradition thousands of years old, is an intimate part of the mystery of revelation and of salvation."

Family Rights and Obligations

The Liaison Committee, at its May 1994, meeting in Jerusalem, issued its first joint statement, on the family, in anticipation of the UN Cairo Conference subsequently held in September.

The statement affirmed that "the rights and obligations of the family do not come from the State but exist prior to the State and ultimately have their source in God the Creator. The family is far more than a legal, social or economic unit. For both Jews and Christians, it is a stable community of love and solidarity based on God's covenant."

Caring for God's Creation

During its Mar. 23-26, 1998, meeting in the Vatican, the Liaison Committee issued its second joint statement, on the environment. Drawing deeply on the shared sacred text of Genesis, the Committee affirmed that "concern for the environment has led both Catholics and Jews to reflect on the concrete implications of their belief in God, creator of all things," especially "a recognition of the mutual dependence between the land and the human person." "Care for creation," the document concluded "is also a religious act."

In its April 2001, meeting, the Liaison Committee issued two statements, one affirming the need to preserve the sacred character of Christian and Jewish holy places, as well as the communities who give witness to them, and one urging review and revision where necessary of curriculum and course materials teaching about each other's traditions especially in institutions of theological education.

Protecting Religious Freedom and Holy Sites

At its May 2001, meeting in New York, the Liaison Committee issued a joint declaration on a subject of increasing concern, not only in the Middle East, but in Asia and Africa as well. With regard to the obligation of states, the document notes: "Government and political authorities bear special responsibility for protecting human and religious rights. Those responsible for law, order, and public security should feel themselves obligated to defend religious minorities and to use available legal remedies against those who commit crimes against religious liberty and the sanctity of holy places. Just as they are prohibited from engaging in anti-religious acts, governments must also be vigilant lest by inaction they effectively tolerate religious hatred or provide impunity for the perpetrators of anti-religious actions."

On Education in Catholic and Jewish Seminaries and Theological Schools

Also in New York, the Liaison Committee issued a statement calling on Catholic and Jewish seminaries to provide understanding of the other. In addition to expanding course work and examining existing courses for the treatment of the other, the statement concluded that "educational institutions in both our communities should make every effort to expose students to living Jewish and Christian communities through guest lecturers, field trips, involvement in local national and international dialogue groups and conferences."

Tzedeq and Tzedaqah

The 18th International Catholic-Jewish Liaison Committee Meeting was held in Buenos Aires, from July 5-8, 2004. This encounter, convened for the first time in Latin America, was devoted to the subject of Tzedeq and Tzedaqah (Justice and

Charity). The group renewed its "total rejection of anti-Semitism in all its forms, including anti-Zionism as a more recent manifestation of anti-Semitism," noting that while anti-Zionism can be distinguished from anti-Semitism, it can serve as a "screen" for it and lead to it.

Dialogue with the Chief Rabbinate of Israel

After two meetings, in Jerusalem (June 2002) and Grottaferrata/Rome (February 2003) the respective high ranking delegations convened in Jerusalem to discuss the theme of "The Relevance Of Central Teachings In The Holy Scriptures Which We Share For Contemporary Society And The Education Of Future Generations Accordingly." The Feb. 27, 2003 meeting in Rome issued statements on "The Sanctity of Human Life" and "Family Values." In Jerusalem in June, 2005, the Bi-Lateral Commission discussed "The Relationship between Religious and Civil Authority in the Jewish and Christian Traditions," agreeing on the following principles based upon biblical values:

1. Religious values are crucial for the wellbeing of the individual and society
2. The purpose of civil authority is to serve and provide for the welfare of the people through respecting the life and dignity of every individual
3. While emphasizing the importance of democracy in this regard, at the same time it is essential to legally protect society from extreme individualism, exploitation by vested interest groups and insensitivity to the cultural and moral values of religious tradition
4. Freedom of religion must be guaranteed to both individuals and communities by the religious and civil authorities
5. The relationship between religion and state must be based on reciprocity, mutual respect and cooperation
6. Legislation for the promotion of particular religious values is legitimate when done in harmony with the principles of human rights

We have an ethical obligation to demonstrate religious responsibility in these regards, and especially to educate future generations through engaging media opinion makers as well as through conventional educational channels.

At the February 2006 meeting in Rome, the Commission issued a statement on "human Life and Technology," stating among other principle that "The conviction that we share, that life on earth is but one stage in the soul's existence, must only lead us to a greater respect for the vessel — the human form — in which the soul resides in this world. Accordingly we totally reject the idea that the temporary nature of human existence on earth allows us to instrumentalise it. In this regard we strongly condemn any kind of bloodshed to promote any ideology — especially if this is done in the name of Religion. Such action is nothing less than a desecration of the Divine Name."

Vatican-Israel Accord

On Dec. 30, 1993, a year of dramatic developments in the Middle East was capped by the signing in Jerusalem of a "Fundamental Agreement" between representatives of the Holy See and the State of Israel. The agreement acknowledged in its preamble that the signers were "aware of the unique nature of the relationship between the Catholic Church and the Jewish people, and of the historic process of reconciliation and growth in mutual understanding and friendship between Catholics and Jews." Abp. (later Cardinal) William H. Keeler, president of the National Conference of Catholic Bishops, welcomed the accord together with the Israeli Ambassador to the United States at a ceremony at the NCCB headquarters in Washington. In 1996, the Anti-Defamation League published a set of documents related to the accord, entitled "A Challenge Long Delayed," edited by Eugene Fisher and Rabbi Klenicki.

U.S. DIALOGUE

The National Workshop on Christian–Jewish Relations, begun in 1973 by the NCCB Secretariat, draws more than 1,000 participants from around the world. Recent workshops have been held in Baltimore (1986), Minneapolis (1987), Charleston, SC (1989), Chicago (1990), Pittsburgh (1992), Tulsa (1994), Stamford (1996), and Houston (1999).

In October 1987, the Bishops' Committee for Ecumenical and Interreligious Affairs began a series of twice-yearly consultations with representatives of the Synagogue Council of America. Topics of discussion have included education, human rights, respect for life, the Middle East. The consultation has issued several joint statements: "On Moral Values in Public Education" (1990), "On Stemming the Proliferation of Pornography" (1993), "On Dealing with Holocaust Revisionism" (1994).

Ongoing relationships are maintained by the USCCB Secretariat with such Jewish agencies as the American Jewish Committee, the Anti–Defamation League, B'nai B'rith International, and the National Jewish Council for Public Affairs.

In June, 1988, the Bishops' Committee for Ecumenical and Interreligious Affairs published in Spanish and English Criteria for the Evaluation of Dramatizations of the Passion, providing for the first time Catholic guidelines for passion plays.

In January 1989, the Bishops' Committee for the Liturgy issued guidelines for the homiletic presentation of Judaism

under the title, "God's Mercy Endures Forever."

When the Synagogue Council of America dissolved in 1995, the Bishops' Committee for Ecumenical and Interreligious Affairs initiated separate consultations with the new National Council of Synagogues (Reform and Conservative), chaired by Card. William H. Keeler, and the Orthodox Union/Rabbinical Council, chaired by Card. John J. O'Connor, of blessed memory. The bishops have issued several joint statements with the National Council of Synagogues: "Reflections on the Millennium" (1998), "To End the Death Penalty" (1999), "Children and the Environment" (2001), "Filled with Sadness, Charged with Hope" (2001), and "Reflections on Covenant and Mission" (2002). Joint communiqués on issues of common concern, such as the Middle East and Catholic teaching on the Jews and the death of Jesus, were issued in 2003 and 2004. Bp. William Murphy of the Rockville Center diocese has succeeded Card. O'Connor as co-chair of the dialogue with Orthodox Judaism. This ongoing consultation has also issued joint communiqués and is working on a joint statement on aid for private education.

Recent Developments

In December 1999, the Holy See's Commission and the International Jewish Committee for Interreligious Consultations announced the establishment of a committee of three Catholic and three Jewish scholars to look into the many complex historical and moral issues involving the Church and the Shoah beginning with an analysis of the thousands of archival documents for the period of World War II already made public by the Holy See in its 12-volume *Actes et Documents* (1965-80). The Committee met in New York in December 1999, in London in May of 2000, in Baltimore in July 2000, and finally in Rome in October 2000, where it issued its "Preliminary Report." The report affirmed the objectivity of the original team of four Jesuit scholars who selected the tens of thousands of texts from the Vatican archives for inclusion in the 11 volumes of the *Actes et Documents du Saint Siege Relatives a la Seconde Guerre Mondiale* (*Libreria Editrice Vaticana*, 1965-80), but also raised numerous questions for further study and documentation. The Joint Commission's Catholic Coordinator, Dr. Eugene Fisher praised the group's "achievement of so much consensus between Catholic and Jewish scholars on what are the questions that need to be faced today. Such solid consensus could by no means be presumed when the group started its work, so emotional and complex are the issues. . . .The scholarly successors of this group will be forever in their debt" (*Catholic International*, May 2002, p. 68). Card. Jorge Mejia, then Vatican Archivist, announced a major increase in the number of archivists working on preparing the remaining material for scholarly review, a process that already resulted in the release of tens of thousands of documents in 2003.

In 2004, the film, *The Passion of the Christ*, precipitated great controversy in the media. Jews, given the often violent history of Passion Plays, with which *The Passion* has much in common, expressed various concerns. Catholic leaders, whatever their personal feelings on the artistic merits of the movie, were strong in condemning any possible anti-Semitic use of it, pointing teachers and preachers to resources where the full and accurate teaching of the Church can be found, such as the BCEIA's *The Bible, the Jews and the Death of Jesus*.

40th Anniversary of Nostra Aetate

Card. Keeler, Fr. Kennedy, and Dr. Fisher represented the BCEIA at the meeting of representatives of Bishops conferences held at the Pontifical Commission on Religious Relations with the Jews on Oct. 27, in conjunction with its celebration of the 40th anniversary of *Nostra Aetate*. The group reported on current efforts and future hopes for the implementation of the document, especially in the area of education. The celebration that evening featured addresses by Cardinals Kasper and Lustiger, and Rabbi David Rosen, International Interfaith Affairs Director of the American Jewish Committee. Ancillary to the main event were dinners hosted by the Ambassador of Great Britain to the Quirinale and the Ambassador of Israel to the Holy See.

The Nov. 2, 2005, meeting of the ongoing Consultation between representatives of the National Council of Synagogues and the BCEIA was held at St. Mary's Seminary and University, Baltimore. In a public session celebrating the 40th anniversary, Card. Keeler recalled being a *peritus* at the Council. In response to concerns from the Jewish side that the Church might be stepping back from the her commitment to the ongoing nature of God's covenant with the Jews, Card. Keeler responded that we are in a new age and Pope Benedict XVI has reaffirmed John Paul II's teachings and the church's stand on this matter. Prof. Byron Sherwin of Spertus College of Judaica challenged the Jewish community, in the light of the Catholic Church's reappraisal of its theological understanding of Judaism, to reappraise its own historic attitude toward the Church and Christianity, replacing its largely defensive posture with a positive assessment of the spiritual reality and integrity of Christianity from a Jewish point of view.

On Nov. 14, 2005, a concert in celebrating the 40th anniversary of *Nostra Aetate* took place at the Basilica of the Shrine of the Immaculate Conception. A dinner beforehand sponsored by the Pope John Paul II Cultural Center was attended by many bishops and representatives of the Jewish community. The concert, sponsored by the Knights of Columbus, featured the world premiere of American composer Richard Danielpour's "Washington Speaks" with Ted Koppel as Narrator. Maestro Gilbert Levine conducted the Baltimore Symphony and the Morgan State University Choir.

On Dec. 7, 2005, a panel was held at the U.S. Holocaust Memorial Museum in Washington on *Nostra Aetate* featuring members of the Advisory Committee to the BCEIA on Catholic-Jewish relations. On Dec. 19, 2005, Bp. Richard Sklba presented a paper, "New Beginnings: Catholic-Jewish Relations after 40 Years," to a special session of the annual meeting of the National Association of Jewish Studies in Washington, with Jewish and Protestant respondents (*Origins*, Jan. 19, 2006, vol. 35, no. 31, pp. 509-514. Similar events honoring *Nostra Aetate* and reflecting on its ongoing influence took place in dioceses across the country as well.

UPDATE OF GUIDELINES

In 2007, the BCEIA issued an updated version of its *Guidelines for Catholic-Jewish Relations*. The *Guidelines* were first published in 1967, and were the first guidelines issued after the Second Vatican Council. The Vatican's own *Guidelines for Implementing Nostra Aetate, no. 4* did not come out until 1975, so the U.S. bishops' were the first such guidelines ever issued in the history of the Church. The 2007 version takes into account the numerous statements of the Holy See and the USCCB.

ISLAM

(Fr. Francis Tiso, Associate Director of the USCCB Secretariat for Ecumenical and Interreligious Dialogue.)

Islam literally means submission (to God). As a distinct religion, Islam originated with Muhammad (570-633 C.E.) and with the revelation he is believed to have received. Muslims acknowledge that this revelation, recorded in the Qur'ân, is from the one God and do not view Islam as a new religion. They profess that Muhammad was the last in a long series of prophets, most of whom are named in the Hebrew Bible and the New Testament, beginning with Adam and continuing through Noah, Abraham, Moses, Jesus and down to Muhammad. Muslims believe in the immaculate birth of Jesus Christ and have great reverence for Mary, the mother of Jesus, to whom an entire chapter of the Qur'ân is devoted.

Muslims believe in the one God, Allah in Arabic, and cognate with the Hebrew Elohim and the ancient Aramaic Elah. According to the Qur'ân, God is one and transcendent, Creator and Sustainer of the universe, all-merciful and all-compassionate Ruler and Judge. God possesses numerous other titles, known collectively by His 99 attributes. The profession of faith states: "There is no god but the God and Muhammad is the messenger of God."

There are five pillars of Islam, the essential duties of Muslims: to witness the faith in one God and the prophethood of Muhammad and of the prophets who came before him; to worship five times a day facing in the direction of the holy Kaaba in Mecca, a sanctuary believed to have been dedicated by Abraham to belief in one God; give alms; fast daily from dawn to dusk during the month of Ramadan; make a pilgrimage to Mecca once in a lifetime if affordable.

Muslims believe in the final judgment, the resurrection of the body, and heaven and hell. Following divinely prescribed moral norms are extremely important to Muslims. Some dietary regulations (e.g. avoiding alcoholic beverages and pork) are in effect. On Fridays, the noon prayer is a congregational (*juma*) prayer. The general themes of prayer are adoration and thanksgiving. The imam gives a sermon to the congregation, but unlike Judeo-Christian tradition, the day is not a "day of rest." Muslims do not have an ordained ministry.

The basis of Islamic belief is the Qur'ân, believed to be the word of God revealed to Muhammad through the angel Gabriel over a period of 23 years. The contents of this sacred book are supplemented by the *Sunna*, a collection of sacred traditions from the life of the prophet Muhammad, and reinforced by *Ijma*, the consensus of scholars of Islamic Law (*Shariah*) which shields them against errors in matters of belief and practice.

Conciliar Statement

The attitude of the Church toward Islam was stated in the Second Vatican Council's "Constitution on the Church" (*Lumen Gentium*, No. 16): "But the plan of salvation also includes those who acknowledge the Creator, in the first place among whom are the Muslims: these profess to hold the faith of Abraham, and together with us they adore the one, merciful God, mankind's judge on the last day." The Council's "Declaration on the Relation of the Church to Non-Christian Religions" (*Nostra Aetate*, No. 3) stated the position in further detail:

"The Church has a high regard for the Muslims. They worship God, who is one, living and subsistent, merciful and almighty, the Creator of heaven and earth, who has also spoken to men. They strive to submit themselves without reserve to the hidden decrees of God, just as Abraham submitted himself to God's plan, to whose faith Muslims eagerly link their own. Although not acknowledging him as God, they venerate Jesus as a prophet, his virgin Mother they also honor, and even at times devoutly invoke. Further, they await the day of judgment and the reward of God following the resurrection of the dead. For this reason, they highly esteem an upright life and worship God, especially by way of prayer, alms-deeds and fasting.

Over the centuries many quarrels and dissensions have arisen between Christians and Muslims. The sacred Council now pleads with all to forget the past, and urges that a sincere effort be made to achieve mutual understanding; for the benefit of all men, let them together preserve and promote peace, liberty, social justice and moral values."

Dialogue

Pope John Paul II met with Muslim leaders and delegations both in Rome and during his trips abroad. He addressed large gatherings of Muslims in Morocco, Indonesia, Mali and elsewhere. In *Tertio Millennio Adveniente* (1999), he recommended that "the dialogue with Jews and the Muslims ought to have a pre-eminent place" involving "meetings in places of significance for the great monotheistic religions." On Feb. 24, 2000, John Paul II traveled to Egypt as part of his Jubilee Year pilgrimages and was received by Grand Sheik Mohammed Sayyid Tantawi at al-Azhar University, the most influential Islamic university in the world. On a pastoral visit to Syria in May 2001, John Paul II spoke of the significant relationship that exists between Muslims and Christians citing his first letter of the new millennium. On the same trip to Syria, on May 6, 2001, John Paul II made the first papal visit to a mosque when he was received at the Umayyad Mosque in Damascus by the Minister of the Waqf and the Grand Mufti of Syria. On Nov. 18, 2001, John Paul II asked Catholics to fast and pray for peace on Friday, Dec. 14, the last Friday of the Ramadan fast that year. He also announced that he was intending to invite representatives of various world religions to Assisi for a day of prayer which was held on Jan. 24, 2002.

The Pontifical Council for Interreligious Dialogue holds formal dialogues with several Islamic organizations on a regular basis; these are regularly reported in the official bulletin, Pro Dialogo and in Islamochristiana, a journal published by the Pontifical Institute for Arabic and Islamic Studies.

At the beginning of the pontificate of Pope Benedict XVI, a meeting with Muslims in Cologne, France, was added to the Holy Father's participation in the 2005 World Youth Day. In a university lecture at Regensburg, Germany, on Sept. 12, 2006, Pope Benedict caused controversy by quoting a fourteenth century Byzantine Emperor, Manuel Palaeologos regarding Mohammed. Although the actual subject of this lecture was an analysis of the intellectual crisis of European civilization, and the need to recover both faith and reason in contemporary discourse, unfortunately, the quote about Muhammad attracted world media attention. Violent protests broke out in Muslim-majority countries, churches were burned, and several people lost their lives, in spite of the fact that the Pope had not expressed any personal agreement with the citation. A group of 39 Muslim scholars responded to the crisis in October of 2006 with an insightful written discussion of some points in the Pope's lecture. The Holy Father visited Turkey from Nov. 28 – December 1, 2006; in the course of his visit he met several times with Muslim leaders and prayed silently in the Blue Mosque in Istanbul. The visit to Turkey considerably improved Muslim responses to the current pontificate.

In October of 2007, a group of 138 Muslim scholars convened by the Royal Academy of The Royal Aal al-Bayt Institute for Islamic Thought in Jordan, under the Patronage of H.M. King Abdullah II, composed "A Common Word Between Us and You" addressed to Christian leaders of various churches and ecclesial communities around the world. The theme of this document is the love of God and the love of neighbor, known to Christians from the words of Jesus in the New Testament. The Muslim scholars cited texts from the Qur'ân and from the Bible to show how love of God and neighbor can constitute a common ground for Muslims and Christians to work together for mutual understanding and world peace. A number of Christian scholars have replied to "A Common Word" on the website: www.acommonword.com. The Holy See has formed The Catholic-Muslim Forum which will be meeting on Nov. 4-6, 2008 with Muslim signatories in order to formulate together an in-depth response to "A Common Word."

During the visit of Pope Benedict XVI to the United States (April 15-20, 2008), the Pope John Paul II Cultural Center hosted an interreligious gathering for over 180 Jews, Muslims, Hindus, Buddhists, and Jains entitled "Peace Our Hope." Pope Benedict also pointed out that dialogue not only serves the members of the respective religious communities, but also bears valuable witness to the larger society of the perennial value of religious faith.

In the U.S., the Bishops' Committee for Ecumenical and Interreligious Affairs holds regular regional bilateral dialogues with Muslims. Dialogue on a national level with the participation of Catholics and Muslims from several U.S. cities was initiated in October 1991. A series of conversations with Muslims on international and domestic issues were co-sponsored with the American Muslim Council. In the late 1990s, the bishops' committee initiated the following three regional dialogues with Muslims.

In 1996, an annual regional dialogue in the Midwest with the co-sponsorship of the Islamic Society of North America in Plainfield, Indiana was initiated. This dialogue concluded several years of discussion on revelation with a report,

Revelation: Catholic and Muslim Perspectives, published by USCCB Publishing (2006). This dialogue has continued to examine the role of virtues and values in our communities in view of the challenges that Catholics and Muslims face in American society. A mission statement was adopted in 2007.

In 1998, an annual dialogue in the Mid-Atlantic region with the co-sponsorship of the Islamic Circle of North America in Queens, New York held its first meeting. The group has been working on a common document on marriage, which should be of great value for mosque and parish leaders responsible for marriage preparation. In 2007, a new round of this dialogue began work on a study of interreligious education in order to make recommendations to the education communities that serve our churches and mosques.

In 2000, the West Coast Dialogue of Muslims and Catholics began meeting in Orange, CA, with the co-sponsorship of several Islamic councils. The West Coast Dialogue issued a report in December 2003, Friends and Not Adversaries, a Catholic-Muslim Spiritual Journey. Since 2004, the West Coast dialogue has focused on a study of comparative narratives from the Bible and from the Qur'ân; in each case, the moral, cultural, and catechetical principles of these narratives have allowed us to explore the immigrant experience of Catholics and Muslims in American society.

All three regional dialogues are co-chaired by Bishops and Islamic leaders. Also in 1995 a dialogue between representatives of the ministry of W.D. Mohammed and the United States Conference of Catholic Bishops began. Since then, the relationship between Imam W. D. Mohammad's American Society of Muslims and the Catholic Church has been served by the Focolare Movement. The Pope John Paul II Cultural Center in Washington, DC, has also been the at the service of Muslim-Catholic dialogue, hosting a dialogue on "The Primordial Relationship Between God and the Human Person in Catholicism and Islam" on Jan. 16, 2007, with Cardinal Angelo Scola, Patriarch of Venice, and Dr. Muzammil Siddiqi, head of the Islamic Society of Orange County, California. On May 16, 2007, the Center sponsored a one-day dialogue on "Sin, Forgiveness, Repentance, Reparation, and Mercy" with Professor Zeki Saritoprak of John Carroll University and Fr. Francis Tiso of the Secretariat for Ecumenical and Interreligious Affairs of the USCCB.

MESSAGE FOR THE END OF RAMADAN 'ID AL-FITR 1428 A.H./A.D. 2007

This message was issued by Cardinal Jean-Louis Tauran, President of the Pontifical Council for Interreligious Dialogue, and was addressed to the Muslim community on the observance of the Muslim feast of 'Id al-Fitr at the end of Ramadan, the month of fasting.

"Christians and Muslims: Called to Promote a Culture of Peace"

Dear Muslim Friends,

1. It gives me special pleasure to send you for the first time friendly and warmest greetings from the Pontifical Council for Interreligious Dialogue on the occasion of your joyful feast of 'Id al-Fitr, with which the month-long fasting and prayer of Ramadan ends. This month is always an important time for the Muslim community and gives to each individual member a new strength for their personal, family and social existence. It matters that all of us witness to our religious beliefs with a life increasingly integrated and in conformity with the Creator's plan, a life concerned with serving our brothers and sisters in ever increasing solidarity and fraternity with members of other religions and all men of good will, in the desire to work together for the common good.

2. In the troubled times we are passing through, religious believers have, as servants of the Almighty, a duty above all to work in favor of peace, by showing respect for the convictions of individuals and communities everywhere through freedom of religious practice. Religious freedom, which must not be reduced to mere freedom of worship, is one of the essential aspects of freedom of conscience, which is the right of every individual and a cornerstone of human rights. It takes into account the requirement that a culture of peace and solidarity between men can be built in which everybody can be firmly engaged in the construction of an increasingly fraternal society, doing everything one can to reject, denounce and refuse every recourse to violence which can never be motivated by religion, since it wounds the very image of God in man. We know that violence, especially terrorism which strikes blindly and claims countless innocent victims, is incapable of resolving conflicts and leads only to a deadly chain of destructive hatred, to the detriment of mankind and of societies.

3. As religious believers, it's up to us all to be educators of peace, of human rights, of a freedom which respects each

person, but also to ensure increasingly strong social bonds, because man must take care of his human brothers and sisters without discrimination. No individual in the national community should be excluded on the grounds of his or her race, religion, or any other personal characteristic. Together, as members of different religious traditions, we are called to spread a teaching which honors all human creatures, a message of love between individuals and peoples. We are particularly responsible for ensuring that our young people, who will be in charge of tomorrow's world, are formed in this spirit. It is above all the responsibility of families and then of those involved in the educational world, and of civic and religious authorities, all of whom have a duty to pay attention to the spread of a just teaching. They must provide everyone an education appropriate to his or her particular circumstances, especially a civic education which invites each young person to respect those around him or her, and to consider them as brothers and sisters with whom he or she is daily called to live, not in indifference, but in fraternal care. It is thus more urgent than ever to teach to the younger generations, those fundamental human, moral and civic values which are necessary to both personal and community life. All instances of incivility must be made use of to remind the young of what is waiting for them in social life. It is the common good of every society and of the entire world which is at stake.

4. In this spirit, the pursuit and intensification of dialogue between Christians and Muslims must be considered important, in both educational and cultural dimensions. Thus all forces can be mobilized in the service of mankind and humanity so that the younger generations do not become cultural or religious blocs opposed to one another, but genuine brothers and sisters in humanity. Dialogue is the tool which can help us to escape from the endless spiral of conflict and multiple tensions which mark our societies, so that all peoples can live in serenity and peace and with mutual respect and harmony among their component groups.

To achieve this, I appeal to you with all my heart to heed my words, so that, by means of encounters and exchanges, Christians and Muslims will work together in mutual respect for peace and for a better future for all people; it will provide an example for the young people of today to follow and imitate. They will then have a renewed confidence in society and will see the advantage in belonging and taking part in its transformation. Education and example will also be a source of hope in the future for them.

5. This is the ardent hope I share with you: that Christians and Muslims continue to develop increasingly friendly and constructive relationships in order to share their specific riches, and that they will pay particular attention to the quality of the witness of their believers.

Dear Muslim Friends, once again I give you my warmest greetings on the occasion of your festival and I ask the God of Peace and Mercy to give you all, good health, serenity and prosperity.

Jean Louis Cardinal Tauran, President

HINDUISM AND BUDDHISM

(Fr. Francis Tiso, Associate Director of the USCCB Secretariat for Ecumenical and Interreligious Dialogue.)

In its Declaration on the Relation of the Church to Non-Christian Religions, the Second Vatican Council stated: "In Hinduism men explore the divine mystery and express it both in the limitless riches of myth and the accurately defined insights of philosophy. They seek release from the trials of the present life by ascetical practices, profound meditation and recourse to God in confidence and love" (No. 2).

Catholics, especially in India, have sought good relations with Hindus and have engaged in numerous dialogues and conferences. In visits to India, Paul VI in 1964 and John Paul II in 1986 and 1999, popes have addressed words of respect for Indian, particularly Hindu, religious leaders. Pope John Paul II said to Hindus in India in 1986: "Your overwhelming sense of the primacy of religion and of the greatness of the Supreme Being has been a powerful witness against a materialistic and atheistic view of life." In 1987, he said of Hinduism: "I hold in esteem your concern for inner peace and for the peace of the world, based not on purely mechanistic or materialistic political considerations, but on self-purification, unselfishness, love and sympathy for all."

In 1995, the Pontifical Council for Interreligious Dialogue began sending a general message to Hindus on the occasion of Diwali, a feast commemorating the victory of light over darkness. When Pope John Paul II was in India during Diwali in 1999, he addressed the religious leaders of India: "On the occasion of Diwali, the festival of lights, which symbolizes the victory of life over death, good over evil, I express the hope that this meeting will speak to the world of the things that unite us all: our common human origin and destiny, our shared responsibility for people's well-being and progress, our need of the light and strength that we seek in our religious convictions." Pope John Paul II also encouraged an intellec-

tual exchange with Indian philosophy in his encyclical, *Fides et Ratio* (1998): "A great spiritual impulse leads Indian thought to seek an experience which would liberate the spirit from the shackles of time and space and would therefore acquire absolute value. The dynamic of this quest for liberation provides the context for great metaphysical systems" (sections 72-73).

In the United States, dialogues between Catholics and Hindus focus on common themes of spirituality and theological philosophy. A series of informal consultations with the Vaishnava Hindu traditions over the past ten years, since 1998, has explored the problem of evil, the mystical expression of divine love, and the theological rationales in our traditions for interreligious dialogue. New consultations have germinated since the April 15-20, 2008, visit of Pope Benedict XVI, involving the Swadhyaya Pariwar activist movement, founded by Rev. Pandurang Shastri Athavale, and with the Vishwa Madhva Sangha in New Jersey. Leaders from the Hindu Temple Society and from the InterFaith Conference of Metropolitan Washington, D.C. have been available to assist with Hindu-Catholic relations in recent years.

The Second Vatican Council, in its Declaration on the Relation of the Church to Non-Christian Religions, stated: "Buddhism in its multiple forms acknowledges the radical insufficiency of this shifting world. It teaches a path by which men, in a devout and confident spirit, can either reach a state of absolute freedom or attain supreme enlightenment by their own efforts or by higher assistance."

Numerous delegations of Buddhists and leading monks have been received by the popes, and John Paul II has met with Buddhist leaders on many of his trips. Paul VI said to a group of Japanese Buddhists in 1973: "Buddhism is one of the riches of Asia: you teach men to seek truth and peace in the kingdom of the Eternal, beyond the horizon of visible things. You likewise strive to encourage the qualities of goodness, meekness and non-violence." In 1995, while in Sri Lanka, John Paul II said to Buddhists: "I express my highest regard for the followers of Buddhism, . .. with its four great values of loving kindness, compassion, sympathy, and equanimity; with its ten transcendental virtues and the joys of the Sangha [the monastic community]. . . At the 1986 World Day of Prayer for Peace at Assisi, the Dalai Lama, principal teacher of the Gelugpa lineage, was placed immediately to the Holy Father's left. Numerous dialogues and good relations between Catholics and Buddhists exist in many countries.

In 1995, the Pontifical Council for Interreligious Dialogue organized a Buddhist-Christian colloquium hosted by the Fo Kuang Shan Buddhist order in Taiwan. A second colloquium was held in Bangalore, India, in 1998. A third was held in Tokyo in 2002. These grew out of the perceived need for greater ongoing contact between the Pontifical Council and Buddhist leaders and scholars. Each of these meetings has produced a report. Also in 1995, the council began sending a message to Buddhists on the feast of Vesakh, the celebration of Gautama Buddha's birth, enlightenment, and final entry into Nirvana.

A meeting of great significance between Buddhist and Catholic monastics took place at Our Lady of Gethsemani Abbey, Kentucky, in July 1996, which was organized and facilitated by Monastic Interreligious Dialogue, a network formed in 1981 mostly of monasteries of men and women following the rule of St. Benedict. The Gethsemani Encounter, the result of several formal visits and hospitality between Catholic and Buddhist monks and nuns, focused on various aspects of monastic life. There were twenty-five participants on each side with numerous observers. The Buddhists represented the Theravada, Tibetan, and Zen traditions. A second Gethsemani Encounter took place in April 2002, the proceedings of which have been published as Transforming Suffering: Reflections on Finding Peace in Troubled Times. In 2008, a third Gethsemani Encounter on "Monasticism and the Environment" addressed ethical concerns raised by the world ecological and food crisis, taking into consideration the witness value to the wider world of simplicity of life as practiced by monastic communities.

In 1998, an ongoing dialogue between Buddhists and Catholics in Los Angeles hosted a retreat dialogue for 50 Catholic and Buddhist participants from different regions of the U.S. The retreat/dialogue was co-planned with the Faiths in the World Committee of the National Association of Diocesan Ecumenical Officers (now called CADEIO), a network of Catholic diocesan staff responsible for ecumenical and interreligious relations. A second retreat/dialogue, co-planned by the Faiths in the World Committee, met at Graymoor, a spiritual life center at the headquarters of the Society of the Atonement, in Garrison, New York, in 2003. This second retreat/dialogue was a "two monastery dialogue," co-hosted by Graymoor and Chuang Yen Buddhist Monastery in nearby Carmel, New York.

Formal dialogues continue in the Archdiocese of Los Angeles and formal relations are developing in a few other dioceses. In 1989 and 1990, the Bishops' Committee for Ecumenical and Interreligious Affairs convened its earliest national consultations on relations with Buddhists. After a series of meetings in the San Francisco area, the Bishops' Committee inaugurated a Buddhist-Catholic dialogue in March 2003, following the model of its regional dialogues, with the Dharma Realm Buddhist Association and the San Francisco Zen Center as partners. The theme of the first dialogue was "Walking the Bodhisattva Path/Walking the Christ Path." The Northern California Chan/Zen-Catholic Dialogue met again in March 2004 to discuss the theme "Transformation of Hearts and Minds: Chan/Zen-Catholic Approaches to Precepts." In 2005, the theme was "Practice: Means Towards Transformation," at the San Francisco Zen Center. The theme of the 2006 meeting was "Meeting on the Path." The theme for the 2007 meeting was "Taking Refuge in the Buddha / Abiding in Christ," with particular attention to the stages of initiation into Buddhist and Christian life. In 2008, the dialogue topic, "Abiding in Christ; Taking Refuge in the Buddha: Then What?" focused on the stages of the spiritual life from the perspective of the training programs for lay and ordained religious teachers. Attention was directed not only to the stages formation in contemplative communities, but also in active religious orders, lay associations such as the St. Vincent de Paul Society, and the Engaged Buddhist movement.

In an effort to further the Bishops' interest in interreligious dialogue, planning for a new outreach to the Sikh community began in 2005. In May 2006 the first meeting of a Sikh-Catholic Consultation comprised of representatives of the World Sikh Council - America Region and the U.S. Conference of Catholic Bishops was held in New York. At the consultation, the Sikh and Catholic communities expressed shared concerns over the challenges faced by immigrant communities in the US, the curtailment of religious freedom and human rights in South Asia, and the challenges of secularism to both religious communities. The consultation has also explored the spiritual teachings of Sikhism and Christianity and discussed personal paths to holiness as exemplified by Catholic saints and Sikhs revered as holy people.

The new consultation with the Sikhs arose in part from previous years of collaboration with religious organizations working together for world peace. The World Conference on Religions for Peace and Religions for Peace-USA have provided a vital forum for peace making. Religions for Peace-USA has fostered closer ties with the Sikh, Hindu, Buddhist, and Jain communities, as well as our ecumenical partners and non-governmental organizations addressing issues of the international community.

INDEX

A

Aachen, 342, 458, 461, 476, 592
Aaron, 98
Abbacies, 274, 335
Abbacy, 128, 298, 347, 445
Abbess, 128, 149, 210, 217
Abbot, 52, 107, 128, 149, 152, 165, 168, 204, 205, 207, 211, 212, 403, 404, 406, 463
Abbott, Walter, 51
Abelard, Peter, 107, 222
Abortion, 3, 8, 12, 16, 36, 40, 63, 79, 80, 85, 114, 115, 128, 134, 140, 165, 199, 236, 245, 300, 311, 315, 316, 357, 362, 363, 369, 504
Abraham, 93, 95, 98, 101, 606, 607, 613
Absolution, 128, 134, 136, 137, 154, 186, 194, 195, 222, 275, 350, 599
Abstinence, 112, 128, 129, 141, 160, 162, 163, 165, 166, 171, 203, 350
Acacian Schism, 220
Academies Pontifical, 271-273
Academy of Noble Ecclesiastics, 241
Acadia, 353, 441
Acclamatio, 297
Accommodated Senses, 104
Acolyte, 185, 196, 495
Act of Emancipation, 308
Act of Supremacy, 224, 225, 598
Act of Toleration, 358
Acta Apostolicae Sedis, 113, 114, 116, 117, 256, 263, 264, 340
Acta Sanctae Sedis, 263
Acts of the Apostles, 96, 102, 105, 106, 134, 162, 332, 349, 586, 588
Ad Gentes, 229, 292, 478
Ad Limina Visit, 274
Adam, 89, 97, 99, 119, 150-152, 157, 597, 613
Adamec, Bp. Joseph V., 374, 394, 500
Adams, Abp. Edward, 266, 394, 418
Addiction Recovery Services, 509
Adeodatus I, Pope, 237
Adeodatus II, Pope, 237
Adjutor, 204, 213
Adjutrix, 120
Administration of the Patrimony of the Apostolic See (APSA), 76, 270, 278-280, 284-287, 289, 290, 292, 293
Adoptionism, 221
Adorno Fathers, 206, 461, 468
Adrian Dominican Sisters, 543
Adrian Dominicans, 565
Adrian I, Pope, 229, 237
Adrian II, Pope, 229, 238
Adrian III, Pope, 238
Adrian IV, Pope, 238
Adrian V, Pope, 239
Adrian VI, Pope, 232, 238, 239
Adultery, 111, 129, 198, 200
Advent, 17, 18, 74, 129, 161, 162, 164, 170, 180, 184, 349, 570, 597
Aeterni Patris, 149, 241, 248
Afghanistan, 256, 298, 322, 495
Africa, 13, 19, 21, 23, 40, 42, 43, 52, 57, 60, 67, 74, 75, 107, 165, 205, 206, 214, 220, 234-237, 244, 250, 264, 266, 267, 269, 276, 277, 279, 287-290, 296, 298, 299, 301-312, 316, 318-322, 326-332, 334-336, 339, 346, 347, 395, 400, 404, 410, 412, 414, 418, 419, 423, 428-430, 458, 461, 463, 467, 468, 474, 475, 484, 488, 490, 495, 500, 548, 550, 564, 568, 591, 610
African Missions Society, 327, 331, 458
African-American Catholics, 3, 421, 427, 428
Agape, 129, 147
Agapitus I, Pope, 237
Agapitus II, Pope, 238
Aggiornamento, 129, 244
Agnosticism, 129, 153
Agnus Dei, 129, 179
Agré, Card. Bernard, 277, 294, 296
Agustoni, Card. Gilberto, 261, 277, 294, 296
Ahern, Bp. Patrick, 394, 419
AIDS, 17, 23, 176, 303, 328, 331, 332, 334, 503, 509, 510
Akathist Hymn, 129
Alabama, 354, 365, 368, 374, 389, 390, 405, 421, 425, 427, 433, 435, 439, 459, 463, 470, 511, 520, 522, 525, 535
Alaska, 28, 79, 80, 234, 356, 363, 365, 373, 374, 376, 378, 421, 422, 425, 433, 435, 439, 525, 535, 545
Alb, 179, 180
Albania, 15, 17, 213, 234, 246, 256, 264, 268, 281, 298, 336, 345, 346, 501, 591, 594
Albertus Magnus, 243, 539
Albigensianism, 219, 223
Alcohol Rehabilitation, 509, 510
Alcoholism, 503, 509, 510
Alexander I, Pope, 236
Alexander II, Pope, 226, 238
Alexander III, Pope, 132, 223, 229, 238, 240
Alexander IV, Pope, 239, 459
Alexander V, Pope, 241
Alexander VI, Pope, 144, 224, 239, 449
Alexander VII, Pope, 240
Alexander VIII, Pope, 225, 240
Alexandrian Rite, 309
Alexandrian Tradition, 348
Alexian Brothers, 458, 468
Alexy II, Patriarch, 7, 17, 34
Algeria, 27, 264, 267, 268, 298, 336, 396, 468
All Saints, 13, 147, 162, 170, 171, 180, 185, 284, 349, 350, 390, 512
All Souls, 170, 171, 350
Allah, 613
Alleluia, 129, 184, 565
Allocution, 129
Allouez, Claude, 363
Allué, Bp. Emilio, 375, 394, 424
Alms, 129, 214, 215, 246, 261, 606, 613
Alphonsianum, 410, 411
Alphonsus Liguori, St., 107, 113, 168, 212, 213, 225, 484
Altar, 178, 179, 181, 182, 184, 211, 215, 216, 349-351, 389, 587, 606
Altar Cloth, 181
Álvarez Martínez, Card. Francisco, 277, 294, 296
Alzheimers, 81, 83, 515, 520
Amato, Abp. Angelo, 8, 39, 73, 74, 256, 261

Ambassadors of the Holy See, 264-268
Ambassadors to the Holy See, 18, 268-269
Ambo, 181
Ambrose of Milan, 11, 88, 106, 107, 109, 120
Ambrozic, Card. Aloysius, 277, 294-296
Amen, 25, 66, 68, 70, 72, 88, 109, 128, 129, 143, 179, 186, 349, 609
American College of Louvain, 546
American Friends of the Vatican Library, 498
American Samoa, 417, 419, 430, 538
Americanism, 361
Amice, 180
Amigo Vallejo, Card. Carlos, 277, 294, 295
Amos, 96, 101
Amos, Bp. Martin, 376, 394, 442, 447
Anabaptism, 597
Anacletus I, Pope, 222
Anacletus II, Pope, 222, 240
Analogy of Faith, 92, 95, 103
Anamnesis, 130
Anaphora, 130
Anastasius I, Pope, 237
Anastasius II, Pope, 237
Anastasius III, Pope, 238
Anastasius IV, Pope, 238
Anathema, 130, 594
Anchor, 36, 54, 215, 551, 552
Anchorite, 130, 143
Ancient Churches of the East, 122
Ancient Order of Hibernians, 498
Anderson, Bp. Moses S.S.E., 394, 428
Anderson, Carl Supreme Knight, 16, 32, 507
Andorra, 30, 264, 268, 298
Andrew, St., 97, 105, 106
Angadiath, Bp. Jacob, 382, 394
Angel, 88, 99, 108, 119, 121, 124, 130, 138, 613
Angelico, Fra, 204, 211, 253
Angelicum, 233, 285, 395, 397-403, 406, 411, 414, 415, 418, 546, 550
Angelini, Card. Fiorenzo, 278, 294-296
Angell, Bp. Kenneth, 375, 394, 419
Angelus, 6, 7, 13, 17, 21-23, 25, 29, 35, 41, 43, 45, 49, 62, 67, 72, 113, 130, 138, 391, 556, 565, 603
Anger, 57, 130, 133
Anglican Church, 77, 130, 226, 353, 358
Anglican-Catholic Final Report, 598
Anglican-Roman Catholic Dialogue, 578, 584, 589, 601
Angola, 15, 213, 234, 264, 266, 268, 281, 296, 299, 336, 339
Anguilla, 299
Animals, 18, 22, 46, 50, 130, 207, 211
Anne, Srs. of St., 468, 487
Annuario Pontificio, 26, 236, 240, 256, 263, 264, 267, 268, 271, 298, 336, 339, 343, 344, 348, 394, 438, 442, 451, 455, 456, 458, 467, 487, 490, 492, 507, 546, 548, 550
Annuarium Statisticum Ecclesiae, 197, 202, 263, 298, 448
Annulment, 130, 201, 308
Annum Sacrum, 241, 249
Annunciation, 113, 120, 121, 143, 154,

166, 171, 174, 350, 389, 459, 469, 488, 489, 513
Anointing the Sick, 150, 350
Anrig, Col. Daniel, 261
Anthony of Padua, St., 107
Anti-Catholicism, 354, 355, 359, 360
Antichrist, 130
Anticlericalism, 135, 302, 305, 323, 450
Antigua, 264, 267, 268, 299, 547
Antilles Netherlands, 33, 264, 267, 325, 336, 417, 463
Antimension, 351
Antiochene Rite, 177, 442
Antiphon, 130, 176
Antipope, 207, 219, 222, 238, 297
Anti-Semitism, 130, 227, 228, 324, 330, 607-609, 611
Antonelli, Card. Ennio, 259, 278, 294, 295
Antonetti, Card. Lorenzo, 259, 261, 277, 278, 294, 295
Antonianum, Pontifical University, 53, 550
Antonio Rosmini-Serbati, 216, 466
Apocrypha, 96, 97
Apologetics, 130, 499, 557, 561
Aponte Martinez, Card. Luis,
Apostasy, 130, 131, 134, 146
Apostles and Evangelists, 105-106, 180
Apostle's Creed, 109
Apostleship of Prayer, 17, 21, 25, 33, 163, 341, 498, 566
Apostleship of the Sea, 341, 495
Apostolic Almoner, 261
Apostolic Camera, 75, 259
Apostolic Delegate, 13, 52, 241, 244, 265-267, 270, 279, 280, 284, 286, 288, 291, 297, 298, 302, 395, 396, 404, 418
Apostolic Fathers, 3, 106-108, 218
Apostolic Signatura, 258, 277, 279, 282-284, 287, 289, 291-293, 397, 398
Apostolic Succession, 130, 131, 150, 193, 579, 589, 599
Apostolicam Actuositatem, 229
Apparitions of the Blessed Virgin Mary, 123-125, 141, 173
Apuron, Bp. Anthony, 338, 394
Aquila, Bp. Samuel, 8, 287, 377, 394
Aramaic, 96, 97, 146, 147, 219, 345, 613
Archaeology, 24, 365
Archangel, 130, 143, 171, 173, 214, 285, 286, 390, 444
Archbishop, 273, 274
Archbishop ad personam, 274
Archconfraternity, 498, 501
Archdiocese for Military Services,
Archdioceses, U.S., 374-384
Archdioceses, U.S., Statistics, 431-433, 435
Arche (L') Communities, 341, 522-524
Archives, Secret Vatican, 262
Archives, Vatican II, 260
Archpriest, 39, 60, 261, 262, 280, 282, 284, 285, 287, 290
ARCIC, 286, 601, 602
Argentina, 10, 15, 25, 27, 60, 61, 213, 216, 234, 236, 261, 264, 268, 271, 278, 279, 284, 286, 289, 290, 296, 299, 309, 336, 345-347, 365, 480, 546, 548, 567
Arianism, 107, 109, 206, 209, 219, 220, 307, 309, 310, 324
Arias, Bp. David O.A.R., 394, 424, 576
Arinze, Card. Francis, 21, 74, 75, 256, 261, 278, 294-296,

Arizona, 79, 353, 358, 364, 372, 374, 390, 421, 422, 425, 426, 433, 435, 439, 511, 525, 535
Ark of the Covenant, 60, 98, 131
Arkansas, 8, 79, 352, 364, 374, 421, 425, 427, 433, 435, 439, 470, 525, 535, 551
Armenia, 26, 34, 105, 207, 213, 234, 248, 264, 265, 268, 271, 299, 310, 344, 345, 347, 583, 585, 595
Arminianism, 597, 598
Arns, Card. Paulo E., 278, 294-296
Artificial Insemination, 145
Arzube, Bp. Juan, 51, 419, 424
Ascension of Christ, 37, 139, 147, 154, 171
Ascension of the Lord (Feast), 161, 162, 164, 167
Asceticism, 68, 131
Ash Wednesday, 24, 25, 129, 131, 150, 161, 163, 165, 171, 349, 350
Asia, 17, 21, 41, 46, 60, 64, 67, 103, 105-108, 209, 213, 235, 243, 246, 276, 281, 296, 298, 299, 302, 304, 313, 314, 316, 317, 319-323, 325, 330-333, 335, 339, 346, 347, 407, 423, 429, 430, 490, 568, 610, 615, 616
Aspergillum, 131
Aspersory, 131
Aspiration, 57, 68, 129, 131, 578
Assemblies of God, 598, 601
Assisi, 10, 15, 20, 53, 65, 107, 137, 151, 158, 160, 205-207, 211-214, 223, 236, 248, 249, 282, 287, 289, 388-390, 462, 474-477, 489, 493, 526, 528, 539, 563, 613, 616
Associations U.S. Catholic, 498-507
Assumption of Blessed Mary, 162
Assumptionists Religious of, 458, 467
Athanasian Creed, 109
Athanasius St., 107
Atheism, 115, 131, 136, 278
Atonement, 98, 107, 131, 151, 430, 446, 458, 467, 476, 478, 606, 609, 616
Atonement Franciscan Friars of the, 458
Audiences Papal, 5-7, 10, 11, 13-15, 17-19, 22, 23, 25, 26, 29-31, 33-35, 37-39, 41-43, 45, 46, 74, 93, 150, 216, 233, 236, 262, 263, 274, 369, 571, 592, 609
Augsburg Confession, 224, 330, 599
Augustine of Canterbury, 167, 204, 206, 220, 308
Augustine of Hippo, 23, 26, 59, 86, 107, 211, 213, 214, 220
Augustinian Fathers, 261
Augustinian Nuns of Contemplative Life, 468
Augustinian Recollects, 458
Augustinian Sisters, 468
Augustinians, 148, 149, 261, 313, 331, 458, 459, 467, 488, 541
Auschwitz, 49, 53, 206, 209, 324, 608, 609
Australia, 11, 13, 33, 45-48, 52, 67-72, 213, 232, 234, 246, 264, 268, 279, 280, 288, 296, 299, 320, 336, 339, 345-347, 413, 429, 487, 548, 567, 581, 591, 602, 608
Austria, 6-8, 16, 45, 54, 62-64, 66, 216, 225, 232, 234, 244, 247-250, 255, 264, 268, 271, 277, 283, 289, 290, 296, 299, 300, 336, 341, 346, 361, 396, 404, 407, 414, 416, 471, 476, 477,

483, 492, 548, 549, 567
Authentic Teaching, 92, 246
Authority (Magisterium), 81, 87, 92, 93, 112-115, 117, 126, 127, 133, 148, 197, 203, 246, 272, 494, 501, 534, 568
Autocephalous Orthodox Churches, 583, 591
Autograph (Chirograph), 135, 261, 262
Auxiliary Bishop, 51, 225, 233, 274, 312, 348, 401, 414-417, 443, 444, 497, 602
Auxiliatrix, 120, 284, 488
Ave Maria, 131, 143, 272, 501, 527, 539, 565, 568, 575
Avignon Papacy, 241
Awards, 51, 53, 54, 500, 573-577
Awards, Communications, 575-577
Aymond, Bp. Gregory, 375, 394
Azerbaijan, 31, 34, 234, 264, 265, 268, 300, 310

B
Babylonian Captivity, 101
Babylonian Exile, 98, 153, 606
Backis, Card. Audrys, 278, 294-296
Baghdad, 33, 47, 60, 77, 265, 314, 405, 406
Bagnasco, Card. Angelo, 60, 61, 278, 294, 295, 337
Bahamas, 264, 267, 268, 300, 352, 404, 418, 497
Bahrain, 45, 46, 264-268, 300, 333
Baker, Bp. Robert, 375, 394-395
Baldacchino, 132
Balke, Bp. Victor, 376, 395, 419
Baltakis, Bp. Paul, 395, 502
Baltimore Councils of, 355-356
Balvo, Abp. Charles, 265-267, 395, 418
Bangladesh, 21, 41, 234, 264, 268, 279, 300, 336, 394, 409, 418
Banks, Bp. Robert J., 377, 395, 419
Banneux, 123
Baptism, 189-191, 194, 196
Baptism of the Lord (Feast), 165
Baptists, 17, 360, 372, 583, 598, 599
Barbados, 264, 267, 268, 300, 326
Barbarin, Card. Philippe, 278, 294, 295
Barbarito, Bp. Gerald, 380, 395
Barbuda, 264, 267, 268, 299
Barnabas St., 105, 106
Barnabite Fathers, 392
Barnes, Bp. Gerald, 382, 395, 422
Bartholomew, 105, 590, 594
Baruch, 96, 100
Basel-Ferrara Florence Council of, 229
Basil the Great Order of Srs., 468, 489
Basilian Fathers, 459, 543
Basilian Order of St. Josaphat, 459
Basilian Salvatorian Fathers, 459, 467
Basilian Salvatorian Order, 401
Basilians, 149, 398, 467
Basilians of St. Josaphat, 467
Basilica of the National Shrine of the Immaculate Conception, 16, 24, 36, 78, 390, 428, 559
Basilicas, 144, 170, 261, 389-390
Basilicas, U.S., 389-390
Batakian, Bp. Manuel, 383, 395, 445
Baum, Card. William, 261, 278, 294-296, 370, 382, 383, 395, 418
Beatific Vision, 130, 132, 143, 153
Beatifications, 3, 19, 42, 132, 215-217,

232, 253-255
Beatissimus Pater, 143
Beatitude, 110, 132, 345, 348
Bede the Venerable, 107, 213
Beeswax, 182
Belarus, 8, 11, 27, 29, 32, 216, 264, 268, 292, 296, 300, 336, 346, 591, 592
Belgium, 8, 44, 51, 123, 149, 186, 204, 206, 209, 213, 234, 241, 248, 250, 261, 264-268, 271, 272, 281, 296, 300, 326, 336, 339-342, 359, 395-398, 401, 410, 413, 458, 460-464, 473, 474, 479, 481, 486, 490, 546, 567, 569
Belize, 234, 264, 267, 268, 301, 429
Beltran, Abp. Eusebius, 12, 380, 383, 395
Benedict I, Pope, 237
Benedict II, Pope, 237
Benedict III, Pope, 238
Benedict IV, Pope, 238
Benedict V, Pope, 238
Benedict VI, Pope, 238
Benedict VII, Pope, 238
Benedict VIII, Pope, 238
Benedict IX, Pope, 238
Benedict X, Pope, 240
Benedict XI, Pope, 239
Benedict XII, Pope, 239, 241
Benedict XIII, Pope, 172, 213, 240, 241
Benedict XIV, Pope, 123, 225, 240, 246
Benedict XV, Pope, 17, 172, 227, 231, 240, 242-243, 249, 251, 256-258, 260, 261, 423
Benedict XVI, Pope, 5-53, 55-58, 59-60, 62-72, 104, 112-117, 132, 136, 231-232, 253, 255, 262, 274, 276, 278, 280, 295-297, 304, 314, 326, 345, 357, 571, 572, 578, 586-588, 590, 602, 609, 612-615
  Beatifications, 19, 42, 232, 253
  Canonizations, 232, 253
  Encyclicals, 59-60, 232, 251
  Islam, 61-62, 613-614
  Life, 231-232
  Travels, 55-58, 62-72, 232
  Writings, 59-60, 232
Benedict of Nursia, 59, 205, 212, 231, 459
Benedictine Confederation, 128, 417
Benedictine Fathers, 539, 543
Benedictine Nuns, 300, 468, 487
Benedictine Oblates, 206
Benedictine Sisters, 429, 468, 469, 517, 529, 541-543
Benedictines, 15, 52, 128, 149, 151, 155, 176, 182, 210, 226, 300, 391, 409, 417, 458-460, 467, 480, 487, 539, 542, 543, 550, 556, 563
Benediction, 15, 134, 139, 141, 150, 167, 181, 367
Benin, 6, 22, 52, 234, 264, 268, 281, 301, 336, 339, 395, 418
Bennett, Bp. Gordon, 372, 378, 395, 419, 428
Bergoglio, Card. Jorge, 278, 294-296, 336
Bermuda, 301, 407, 419, 430
Bernadette Soubirous, 20, 123, 205, 251
Bernard of Clairvaux, 59, 107, 211, 214, 250
Bernardin, Card. Joseph, 52, 296, 376, 420
Bernardine of Siena, 167, 205, 211, 213, 214

Bernardine Sisters, 474, 539
Bertagna, Abp. Bruno, 259, 261
Bertie, Fra Andrew, 51, 574
Bertone, Card. Tarcisio, 5, 6, 10, 11, 13-15, 17-19, 22, 25-27, 30, 31, 33, 37, 46, 61, 75, 77, 124, 217, 256, 258, 259, 261, 278, 294, 295
Betancur, Pedro de San Jose, 253, 363
Bethany Sisters, 469
Bethlehem, 21, 24, 74, 147, 467, 468, 476, 480, 502, 517, 518, 528-530
Bethlemita Sisters, 469
Betti, Card. Umberto, 61, 279, 294-296
Bevard, Bp. Herbert, 395
Bevilacqua, Card. Anthony, 279, 294-296, 380, 395, 419, 431
Bhutan, 301
Bible, 3, 11, 18, 20, 38, 42, 50, 51, 69, 96-105, 107, 108, 113, 116, 132, 138, 141, 143, 148, 159, 178, 206, 218-220, 224, 366, 368, 369, 422, 500, 504, 556, 576, 596, 597, 600, 606, 610, 612-614
Biblical Commission Pontifical, 231, 242, 256, 260, 293
Biblical Institute, Pontifical, 242, 286, 293, 550
Biblicism, 601
Biffi, Card. Giacomo, 279, 294-296
Biglietto, 132
Bination, 179, 184
Bioethics, 37, 54, 235, 272, 498, 562, 565, 570, 572, 575
Biographies of American Bishops, 394-417
Biographies of Cardinals, 277-292
Biographies of New Blesseds and Saints, 215-217
Biretta, 14, 132
Birth Control, 245
Birth of Mary (Feast), 171, 173
Birth of Our Lord (Feast), 171
Bishop, 274
Bishop Brothers, 418
Bishops, Biographies of, 394-417
Bishops' Conferences, 27, 28, 35, 46, 60, 183, 186, 191, 192, 195, 279, 339, 580, 608, 612
Bishops, Canadian, 442-446
Bishops, Congregation for, 257
Bishops, Mexican, 451-455
Bishops in Foreign Countries, 418
Bishops, National Conference of Bishops, **See** USCCB
Bishops, Retired/Resigned, 419
Bishops, Synod of, 275
Bishops, U.S. Overseas, 418
Blair, Bp. Leonard, 383, 395
Blaire, Bp. Stephen, 383, 395, 582
Blasphemy, 132, 139, 322
Blessed Sacrament Exposition, 181, 188, 193
Blessed Virgin Mary, See Mary, Blessed Virgin
Blessings, 40, 57, 58, 64, 100, 132, 141-143, 148, 151, 158, 165, 176, 188, 195, 579
Blind Catholic Facilities and Organizations, 508, 509, 524
Blue Army, 342, 392, 506, 561, 565, 594
Boland, Bp. Ernest, 395
Boland, Bp. J. Kevin, 382, 395
Boland, Bp. Raymond, 375, 378, 395

Boles, Bp. John, 395, 419
Bolivia, 25, 30, 213, 234, 242, 264, 268, 292, 296, 301, 336, 397, 409, 419, 429, 430, 567
Bollandist Acta Sanctorum, 225
Bon Secours Congr., 469, 488, 527
Bonaventure, St., 107
Boniface I, Pope, 237
Boniface II, Pope, 237
Boniface III, Pope, 237
Boniface IV, Pope, 237
Boniface V, Pope, 237
Boniface VI, Pope, 238
Boniface VII, Pope, 240
Boniface VIII, Pope, 144, 223, 239
Boniface IX, Pope, 239, 241
Boniface, St., 444
Book of Blessings, 132, 188
Book of Common Prayer, 150, 224, 599
Books of the Bible, 98-102, 220
Bootkoski, Bp. Paul, 379, 396
Borders, Bp. William, 375, 380, 396
Bosco, Bp. Anthony, 377, 396, 419
Bosnia Herzegovina, 288
Botean, Bp. John, 10, 11, 234, 264, 268, 288, 296, 301, 336, 364
Botswana, 234, 264, 267, 301, 339, 404, 418
Boyea, Bp. Earl, 378, 396
Boyle, Bp. Paul, 51
Boy Scouts, 38, 211, 369, 497
Boys Town, 521
Bozanic, Card. Josip, 279, 294-296
Brady, Card. Seán, 60, 279, 294, 295
Bradley, Bp. Paul J., 379, 380, 396
Brandt, Bp. Lawrence, 377, 396
Bransfield, Bp. Michael J., 383, 396
Braxton, Bp. Edward K., 375, 378, 396, 428
Brazil, 10, 15, 29, 32, 38, 46, 53, 60, 61, 213, 215, 216, 232, 234, 242, 248, 249, 254, 261, 264, 268, 272, 278, 282, 283, 285, 290, 291, 296, 301, 336, 345-347, 352, 363, 364, 397-399, 404, 405, 409-411, 417-419, 429, 430, 476, 482, 491, 546, 548, 581
Breviary, 143, 176, 182, 187, 223, 242
Brigid, Congr. of, 469, 489
Brigittine Monks, 460
Brigittine Sisters, 469
Brigittines, 205
Broglio, Abp. Timothy, 32, 383, 396
Brom, Bp. Robert, 376, 382, 396, 577
Brothers, 427-429, 431, 432, 458, 460-468
Brothers Hospitallers of St. John of God, 208
Brothers of Charity, 467
Brothers of Christian Instruction, 467, 544, 562
Brothers of Christian Instruction of Ploërmel, 467
Brothers of Christian Instruction of St. Gabriel, 467
Brothers of Christian Schools, 467
Brothers of Holy Cross, 544
Brothers of Mary, 464
Brothers of Mercy, 468, 516
Brothers of Our Lady, 464, 466, 468
Brothers of Our Lady Mother of Mercy, 468
Brothers of St. Patrick, 465, 467
Brown, Bp. Tod, 380, 396, 582,

Brucato, Bp. Robert, 396, 419
Brunei, 41, 264, 266, 267, 302, 337
Brunett, Bp. Alexander, 377, 382, 396
Bruno of Carinthia, 238
Bruskewitz, Bp. Fabian, 378, 396
Buckley, William F., 51
Buddhism, 4, 301, 317, 321, 578, 615, 616
Buechlein, Abp. Daniel O.S.B., 377, 379, 396
Bukovsky, Abp. John S.V.D., 396, 418
Bulgaria, 234, 244, 256, 264, 268, 302, 336, 345, 346, 591, 594
Bull, 109, 130, 132, 223, 224, 226, 235, 241, 274, 356, 449
Bulla, 132, 407
Bullock, Bp. William, 376, 379, 396, 419
Bura, Bp. John, 380, 396
Burbidge, Bp. Michael, 381, 397
Burghardt, Father Walter, 51
Burial, 49, 127, 132, 133, 137, 154, 156-158, 173, 179, 196, 215, 351
Burke, Abp. Raymond, 28, 40, 48, 258, 261, 378, 381, 397, 418
Burke, Bp. John, 397, 418
Burkina Faso, 264, 266, 268, 302, 336, 338, 339
Burma, 37, 244, 264, 266, 279, 302, 321, 336
Burse, 132, 181
Burundi, 234, 264, 267, 268, 302, 326, 331, 336, 339
Bush Pres. George W., 16, 20, 24, 32, 36, 40, 42, 50, 54, 56, 79, 82, 214, 236, 270
Bustros, Bp. Cyrille, 379, 397
Buswell, Bp. Charles, 51, 381
Byzantine Catholics, 346-348
Byzantine Divine Liturgy, 349-350
Byzantines, Ukrainian, 347, 350, 380, 382, 407, 410, 416, 443-445, 459, 468, 482, 525, 544

C

Cabrini Sisters, 485
Cabrini, Mother, 205, 206
Cacciavillan, Card. Agostino, 261, 267, 270, 279, 294-296
Caffarra, Card. Carlo, 279, 294-295
Caggiano, Bp. Frank J., 375, 397
Cajetan, 168, 205
Calendar, Church, 161-164, 165-170
California, 53, 79, 151, 168, 271, 285, 353, 355, 358, 363-365, 372-374, 378, 379, 390, 391, 402, 414, 421, 422, 424-426, 433, 435, 439, 449, 452, 456, 463, 465, 470, 481, 509, 511, 520, 522, 525, 535, 539, 540, 544, 561, 574, 582, 614, 616
Callahan, Bp. William P., 379, 397
Callistus I, Pope, 169, 205, 207, 237
Callistus II, Pope, 222, 229, 238
Callistus III, Pope, 174, 239, 240
Calumny, 132
Calvary, 129, 132, 154, 157, 159, 173, 472, 509, 520, 526, 527
Calvinism, 309, 310, 313
Calvo, Bp. Randolph, 381, 397
Camacho, Bp. Thomas, 397, 454
Camaldolese, 130, 210, 222, 459, 460, 468

Camaldolese Benedictines, 210
Cambodia, 6, 169, 264, 266-268, 302, 337
Camerlengo, 134, 259, 279, 286
Cameroon, 234, 265, 267, 268, 292, 296, 303, 336, 339, 548
Camillian Fathers, 460
Campbell, Bp. Frederick, 376, 397
Camp Fire Boys and Girls, 497
Campus Ministry, 197, 471, 497, 498, 562
Cana, 120, 154
Canada, 7, 13, 32, 45, 47, 52, 53, 77, 213, 234, 242, 249, 265, 268, 272, 277, 287, 293, 296, 303, 336, 342, 345-348, 353, 354, 358, 362-365, 373, 380, 383, 386, 387, 389, 394, 397, 401, 403, 405, 407-410, 412-414, 418, 429, 432, 438, 441-443, 445-448, 459, 461, 463, 468, 469, 471-473, 476, 478, 482-485, 492, 493, 497, 500, 501, 505-508, 510, 546, 548, 549, 551, 556, 566, 567, 570, 575, 581, 590, 591, 599, 605
Canadian Catholic Publications, 566-567
Canadian Conference of Catholic Bishops, 336, 442, 446-447
Canary Islands, 363
Cancer Homes and Hospitals, 474, 509
Candlemas, 171, 173
Candles, 129, 165, 173, 176, 182, 606
Canestri, Card. Giovanni, 279, 294-296
Cañizares Llovera, Card. Antonio, 279, 294, 295
Canon Law, 18, 25, 35, 38, 51-54, 73, 76, 77, 125-128
Canon Law Society of America, 499
Canon of the Bible, 96, 104, 224
Canonizations by Leo XIII and His Successors, 251-253
Canonizations by Pope Benedict XVI, 253
Canonizations by Pope John Paul II, 252-253
Canons of Eastern Churches, 351
Canons Regular, 149, 210, 405, 461, 463, 465, 467
Canossian Daughters of Charity, 469
Canterbury, 10, 37, 107, 167, 204, 206, 211, 220, 221, 223, 225, 235, 308, 334, 513, 583, 584, 589, 599, 601, 602
Canticle, 133
Cantú, Bp. Oscar, 382, 397
Cape Verde, 234, 265, 266, 268, 303, 338, 339
Capital Punishment, 15, 133, 500
Capital Sins, 130, 133, 140, 142, 147, 152, 157
Cappa Magna, 180
Capuchins, 206, 224, 312, 322, 327, 331, 352, 414, 467, 487
CARA, 78, 496, 562, 575
Carberry, Card. John, 296, 376, 378, 381
Cardinal Bishops, 52, 232, 277-279, 282, 289, 291, 297
Cardinal Deacons, 277, 294
Cardinal in Pectore, 277, 284, 288
Cardinal Priests, 51, 52, 54, 277, 278, 281, 284-286, 288, 292
Cardinal Secretary of State, 6, 61, 124, 258, 264
Cardinal Virtues, 133, 141, 143, 145, 146, 153, 158
Cardinals, 60, 276-297

Cardinals, Biographies, 277-294
Cardinals of the Past, U.S., 296-297
Carey, Abp. George of Canterbury, 529, 585
Caribbean, 28, 29, 32, 33, 38, 299, 300, 307, 312, 331, 334, 363, 429, 431
Carles Gordó, Card. Ricardo, 279, 294-296
Carlson, Bp. Robert, 381, 382, 397
Carmelite Nuns, 324, 470, 488
Carmelite Order, 14, 108, 155, 169, 556
Carmelite Sisters, 208, 217, 470, 471, 488, 510, 517
Carmelite Sisters of Charity, 208, 470
Carmelite Sisters of St. Therese, 471
Carmelites, 108, 148, 177, 217, 226, 280, 359, 391, 429, 458, 460, 467, 470, 471, 487, 489, 493, 527, 530, 550
Carmelites of Mary Immaculate, 460, 530
Carmelites of St. Theresa, 471
Carmody, Bp. Edmond, 376, 383, 397
Carmon, Bp. Dominic, 397, 419, 428
Carter, Pres. Jimmy, 236, 271, 372
Carthusians, 149, 154, 177, 205, 222, 458, 460, 467
Casa Santa Maria, 263
Casimir, 166, 205, 214
Cassock, 180
Castel Gandolfo, 5-7, 45, 46, 49, 244, 261-263, 484
Castillo Lara, Card. Rosalio, 51
Castrillón Hoyos, Card. Dario, 260, 280, 294-296
Casuistry, 133
Catacombs, 133, 181, 286, 319
Catanello, Bp. Ignatius, 375, 397
Catechesi Tradendae, 235
Catechesis, 44, 48, 57, 85, 87, 88, 110, 133, 235, 246, 421, 429, 431, 455, 559, 607, 609, 610
Catechism of the Catholic Church, 3, 38, 87-89, 110-112, 114, 133, 228, 232, 235, 279, 290, 333, 421, 580, 616
Catechists World Statistics, 335
Catechumenate (RCIA), 133, 190, 191, 505, 556
Categories of Cardinals, 293-294
Cathari, 145, 222, 223
Cathedra, 92, 133, 145, 246, 388
Cathedrals in the U.S., 388-389
Cathedraticum, 133
Catherine of Siena, 107, 166, 205, 206, 212, 214, 388, 473, 474, 488, 489
Catholic Action, 207, 211, 227, 242, 243, 249, 250, 280, 281, 361, 390, 495, 553, 580
Catholic Associations, 341
Catholic Biblical Association of America, 97, 499
Catholic Book Publishers Association, 499
Catholic Charities Services, 521
Catholic Church Extension Society, 356, 415, 431, 557
Catholic Daughters of the Americas, 499, 561
Catholic Organizations, 495-507
Catholic Population of the United States, 435-438
Catholic Population World, 335
Catholic Press Association Awards, 575-577
Catholic Relief Services, 8, 421, 423, 564, 565

Catholic Schools and Students in the United States, 535-538
Catholic Theological Society of America, 51, 281, 500
Catholic Universities and Colleges in the United States, 539-544
Catholic University of America, 20, 28, 32, 52, 54, 79, 187, 226, 248, 281, 356, 357, 360, 390, 395-400, 402, 403, 405, 406, 412-414, 416, 421, 498, 499, 539, 544, 547, 556-558, 560, 561, 565
Catholic World Statistics, 335
Catholic Youth Organizations, 497
Catholicos, 235, 585
Causes of Saints, Congr. of the, 6, 19, 26, 152, 256
Cé, Card. Marco, 280, 294-296
CELAM, 53, 60, 280, 282, 285, 286, 289, 306, 339
Celebret, 133
Celestine I, Pope, 229, 237
Celestine II, Pope, 238, 240
Celestine III, Pope, 239
Celestine IV, Pope, 239
Celestine V, Pope, 239
Celibacy, 10, 70, 102, 108, 133, 134, 196, 219-221, 245, 251, 300, 321, 329, 362, 495, 597
Celli, Abp. Claudio, 37, 259, 261, 572
Cenacle, 37, 134, 211, 471, 489, 495, 525-530
Censorship of Books, 134, 144, 149
Censures, 128, 134, 140, 152, 154, 186, 242
Centesimus Annus, 114, 115, 117, 234, 251
Central African Republic, 234, 265, 268, 303, 336, 339
Central America, 21, 32, 234, 301, 305, 307, 311, 312, 321, 322, 335, 414, 430, 490
Central Statistics Office, 256, 260, 263
Ceylon, 214, 313, 319
Chad, 265, 268, 303, 336, 339
Chair of Peter, 28, 106, 171
Chalcedon, Council of, 108, 220, 229, 250, 273, 307, 344, 595, 596
Chaldean Catholics, 60, 77, 314, 345, 346, 386, 596
Chalice, 32, 128, 139, 179-181, 196, 214, 215, 349, 351
Champlin, Msgr. Joseph, 51
Chancery Offices of U.S. Archdioceses and Dioceses, 384-387
Chant, Gregorian, 176, 182, 220
Chapel, 134
Chaplain, 134
Chaplains' Aid Assoc., 500
Chaplet, 134
Chaput, Abp. Charles O.F.M. Cap., 16, 79, 80, 376, 381, 397, 429
Charismatic Movement, 357, 425
Charismatic Renewal, 37, 134, 502, 504, 525
Charisms, 90, 102, 126, 135, 160
Charities Catholic, 501, 508
Charities, Office of Papal, 261
Charity, Srs. of, 488, 489
Charles Borromeo, 170, 205, 211, 213-215, 249, 282, 394-400, 402-404, 407-409, 412-414, 416, 417, 443, 464, 472, 485, 488, 489, 545

Charles Borromeo, Srs. of, 488, 489
Charron, Bp. Joseph, 376, 397, 419
Chastity, 135
Chasuble, 180, 214, 215
Chavez, Bp. Gilbert, 397, 419
Chedid, Bp. John, 380, 398, 419
Cheli, Card. Giovanni, 261, 280, 294-296
Cheong Jin-Suk , Card., 280, 294, 295, 296
Chile, 10, 15, 28, 33, 34, 213, 234, 236, 261, 265, 268, 272, 282, 286, 291, 296, 303, 336, 365, 429, 546, 567
China, 37, 38, 41, 43, 49, 166, 213, 225-227, 235, 241, 243, 244, 250, 252, 265, 268, 279, 291, 294, 303, 304, 317, 320, 331, 336, 346, 347, 361, 407, 417, 418, 429, 475, 501, 547, 591
Chirograph, 135, 261, 262
Choby, Bp. David, 379, 398
Choir, 176, 181, 186
Chomnycky, Bp. Paul, 383, 398
Chretienne Srs. of, 472
Chrism, 31, 135, 150, 166, 172, 186, 191, 343
Chrism Mass, 31, 150, 166
Christ Society of, 460
Christ the King (Feast), 162, 170, 171
Christ the King Missionary Sisters of, 472
Christ the King Rural Parish Workers, 493
Christ the King Sister Servants, 472
Christ the King Sisters of St. Francis, 472
Christensen, Bp. Peter, 383, 398, 491
Christian, Bp. Francis, 379, 398
Christian Brothers, 217, 395, 429, 460, 467, 526-528, 539-541, 562, 563
Christian Church, U.S., 599
Christian Doctrine, Sisters of Our Lady of, 472
Christian Education, Religious of, 472
Christian Initiation, 32, 88, 133, 185, 187, 190, 191, 505, 556
Christian Instruction, Brothers of, 460
Christian Schools, Brothers of the, 460
Christian Unity, Pontifical Council, 232, 258
Christians Baptized, Reception into Church, 439-440
Christifideles Laici, 235, 276, 340
Christmas, 17-20, 23, 35, 60, 74, 114, 129, 144, 159, 161-163, 165, 170-174, 179, 180, 216, 221, 244, 245, 262, 305, 349, 350, 368, 557, 562, 606
Christodoulos, Archbishop, 51, 585, 587
Christopher Awards, 577
Christophers, 500, 562, 565, 568, 569
Christus Dominus, 229
Chronicles, 96, 98, 99
Church Tax Exemption, 370
Chronology of Church History, 218-227
Chronology of U.S. Church History, 352-357
Church State Decisions of the Supreme Court, 366-370
Church State Relations, 366-370
Church Tax Exemption, 370
Ciborium, 181, 214
Cincture, 180
Cipriani Thorne, Card. Luis, 76, 280, 294-296
Circumcision, 132, 135, 174, 218, 606
Circumincession, 135
Cisneros, Bp. Octavio, 365, 372, 375, 398,

424
Cistercian Nuns, 472, 487, 488
Cistercian Order, 107
Cistone, Bp. Joseph, 380, 398
Civil Rights, 12, 51, 357, 362, 369, 499
Clancy, Card. Edward, 280, 294-296
Clare of Assisi, 53, 65, 213, 214
Claretian Missionary Sisters, 472
Claretians, 204, 290, 391, 461, 467, 487, 489, 561, 562, 564, 565
Claretianum, 290
Clark, Bp. Edward, 378, 398
Clark, Bp. Matthew, 381, 398
Clemens, Abp. Josef, 258, 261
Clement I, Pope, 170, 205, 212, 218
Clement II, Pope, 222, 238
Clement III, Pope, 239, 240
Clement IV, Pope, 239, 297
Clement V, Pope, 229, 239, 241
Clement VI, Pope, 239, 241
Clement VII, Pope, 37, 160, 239-241
Clement VIII, Pope, 232, 240, 257
Clement IX, Pope, 240
Clement X, Pope, 240
Clement XI, Pope, 173, 225, 240, 574
Clement XII, Pope, 142, 157, 225, 240, 262
Clement XIII, Pope, 174, 240, 247
Clement XIV, Pope, 225, 240, 247
Clergy, Congregation of the, 257
Clergy Sex Abuse, 50, 78-79
Clericalism, 135
Clerics of St. Viator, 466
Clerics Regular, 206, 208, 459, 461, 466, 468
Clerics Regular Minor, 206, 461, 468
Clerics Regular of St. Paul, 459
Clinton, Bill, 53, 236, 270, 372
Cloister, 135, 149
Cluny, 171, 204, 207, 222, 480, 487
Coakley, Bp. Paul S., 382, 398
Coccopalmerio, Abp. Francesco, 259, 261
Coadjutor Bishop, 274, 381, 413, 443
Code of Canon Law, 18, 25, 35, 38, 51-54, 73, 76, 77, 125-128
Code of Canon Law of Oriental Church, 259, 344, 351
Coins, Vatican, 262
Coleman, Bp. George, 377, 379, 398, 418
Colettines, 472, 489
Collegiality, 92, 93, 113, 127, 135, 195, 245, 275, 362
Colombia, 34, 45, 53, 213, 234, 246, 265, 268, 280, 282, 289, 296, 304, 307, 336, 339, 363, 469, 475, 490, 546
Colorado, 16, 76, 77, 323, 373, 376, 384, 388, 390, 391, 404, 415, 419, 421, 422, 425, 430, 433, 435, 439, 469, 470, 477, 500, 511, 520, 526, 535, 544, 552, 561
Color, Liturgical, 180
Colossians, 75, 96, 102
Columban, Bp., Society of, 461, 467
Columban St., Missionary Sisters, 472
Columbian Squires, 497, 564
Columbus, Knights of, 497, 507
Comastri, Card. Angelo, 18, 39, 60, 261, 262, 280, 294, 295
Comboni Missionaries, 429, 461
Comboni Missionary Sisters, 472
Combonian Missionaries, 467
Commandments of God, 149

Commissions, Pontifical, 260-261
Communion of Saints, 88, 109, 110, 136, 204, 211
Communism, 24, 59, 136, 226, 227, 233, 243, 244, 250, 258, 310, 313, 325, 328, 345
Company of Mary, 209, 464
Company of St. Paul, 491
Company of St. Ursula, 204, 492
Compline, 136
Conclave, 33, 60, 61, 150, 233, 242, 245, 277, 297
Concluding Rite, 179
Concordat of Worms, 136, 222
Concupiscence, 136
Confederation of Latin American Religious (CLAR), 490
Conference of Major Superiors in U.S., 490
Conference of Major Superiors of Men in U.S., 490
Conference of Major Superiors, U.S., 490
Conferences, Episcopal, 336-338
Confessional, 182
Confirmation, 16, 21, 71, 72, 88, 127, 131, 135, 142, 150, 152, 184, 185, 187, 189-191, 223, 228, 254, 297, 328, 343, 350, 361, 494
Confraternity of Christian Doctrine, 97, 227, 242, 361, 500
Congo, 10, 33, 35, 42, 43, 234, 265, 267-269, 272, 304, 305, 336, 339, 548
Congo Republic, 234, 305
Congregation of Blessed Sacrament, 557
Congregation of Christian Brothers, 540
Congregation of Clerics Regular, 466
Congregation of Divine Worship, 232, 256, 278
Congregation of Marians, 392, 558
Congregation of Mary, 481, 485
Congregation of Missionary, 471
Congregation of Monte Corona, 460
Congregation of Notre Dame, 363, 441
Congregation of Our Lady, 470-472, 477, 485, 495
Congregation of Our Lady of Lourdes, 477
Congregation of Sacred Heart, 429
Congregation of Sisters Marianites of Holy, 542
Congregation of St. Joseph, 463, 467
Congregation of St. Ottilien, 459
Congregationalists, 598
Congresses, Eucharistic, 260
Conjugal Covenant, 197
Conjugal Love, 197-199
Conley, Bp. James, 376, 398
Conlon, Bp. Robert, 383, 398, 504
Connecticut, 32, 354, 367, 371, 373, 390, 391, 421, 422, 433, 435, 439, 501, 507, 511, 520, 522, 526, 535, 544, 569
Connell, Card. Desmond, 280, 294-296
Connolly, Bp. Thomas, 375, 398, 419
Connors, Bp. Ronald, 398, 419
Conscience, 30, 43, 47, 49, 56, 74, 75, 81, 91, 114, 115, 119, 126, 131, 133, 136, 149, 152, 155, 159, 178, 194, 198, 203, 258, 300, 305, 427, 579, 614
Consecrated Life, 4, 7, 25, 72, 127, 135-138, 149, 152, 165, 187, 235, 257, 258, 276, 278, 282-293, 402, 421, 446, 455, 458, 490, 491, 557
Consistory, 9, 10, 60, 136, 228, 232, 233
Consolata Missionaries, 461, 467, 557

Consolata Missionary Sisters, 473, 488
Constantinople I Council of, 220, 229
Constantinople II, Council of, 220, 229
Constantinople III, Council of, 221, 229
Constantinople IV, Council of, 221, 229
Consubstantiation, 136
Contemplative Sisters, 478
Contraception, 115, 136, 137, 236, 362
Contrition, 137, 141, 151, 190, 194, 195
Contumely, 137
Conventual Franciscan Fathers, 566
Conventual Franciscan Friars, 391, 393, 528
Conventual Franciscans, 397, 564
Cooney, Bp. Patrick, 377, 398, 577
Cope, 64, 180, 209, 255, 363, 422
Coppa, Card. Giovanni, 61, 280, 294-296
Coptic Catholic Church, 345, 347
Cor Unum, Pontifical Council, 25, 52, 60, 81, 82, 259, 281-283, 286, 289, 292-294
Cordes, Card. Paul-Josef, 60, 259, 261, 280, 294, 295
Cordileone, Bp. Salvatore, 382, 398
Corinthians, 96, 102, 131, 134, 218, 586
Corporal Works of Mercy, 508
Corpus Christi (Feast), 162, 167, 169
Corpus Iuris Canonici, 126; see also Code of Canon Law
Corpus Iuris Civilis, 220
Corrada del Rio, Bp. Alvaro, 383, 398, 424
Corripio Ahumada, Card. Ernesto, 51
Corsica, 213
Coscia, Bp. Benedict, 398
Costa Rica, 25, 234, 265, 268, 278, 305, 336, 414
Costello, Bp. Thomas, 398, 419
Cote, Bp. Michael, 379, 399
Côte d'Ivoire, 265, 268, 269, 277, 305, 336, 337, 339, 548
Cotey, Bp. Arnold, 399, 419
Cottier, Card. George, 272, 281, 294-296
Council of European Bishops Conferences, 279, 339
Council of Major Superiors, 357, 490
Council of Major Superiors of Women Religious, 357, 490
Counsels Evangelical, 137, 160
Countries of the World Catholic Church (Statistics), 335
Countries of the World, Catholic Church in, 298-335
Creeds, 35, 93, 109, 141, 582, 599
Cremation, 132, 137
Crepaldi, Abp. Giampaolo, 259, 261
Crete, 103, 241, 512, 583, 591
Crib, 137
Croatia, 15, 234, 261, 265, 268, 275, 279, 301, 305, 336, 346, 472, 548, 549, 567
Cronin, Abp. Daniel, 377, 399, 419
Crosier, 137, 214, 461
Crosier Fathers, 461
Crucifix, 182, 214, 215
Cruets, 182
Crusades, 222, 273
Cruz, Bp. Manuel, 379, 399
Cuba, 27, 29, 33, 37, 204, 213, 228, 234, 236, 265, 267, 268, 287, 296, 300, 305, 336, 398, 399, 401, 413, 418, 472, 507, 516, 546
Cullen, Bp. Edward, 374, 399
Cultural Heritage of the Church, 260, 278,

281, 283, 285, 286, 288, 291, 293
Culture, Pontifical Council, 259
Cummins, Bp. John, 380, 399, 419
Cunningham, Bp. Robert, 380, 399
Cupich, Bp. Blaise, 381, 399, 422
Cura Animarum, 137
Curia, Diocesan, 137-138
Curia, Roman, 255-261
Curlin, Bp. William, 375, 399, 419
Curry, Bp. Thomas, 378, 399
Cursillo Movement, 280, 496, 561
Curtiss, Bp. Elden, 377, 380, 399
Custos, 27, 137, 138, 235
Cyprian, 106, 169, 205, 206, 219, 254
Cyprus, 105, 106, 256, 265, 267, 268, 306, 345, 347, 588, 591, 594
Cyril and Methodius, 6, 162, 206, 209, 212, 214, 234, 235, 248, 251, 328, 336, 350, 364, 390, 400, 407, 411, 442, 473, 500, 545
Cyril of Alexandria, 11, 107, 167, 214
Cyril of Jerusalem, 107, 166, 214
Czech Republic, 61, 234, 265, 268, 280, 291, 293, 295, 306, 336, 346, 483, 549

D

D'Antonio, Bp. Nicholas, 399, 419
D'Arcy, Bp. John, 377, 399
Da Cunha, Bp. Edgar M. S.V.D., 379, 399, 424
Dachau, 53, 211
Daily, Bp. Thomas, 375, 399, 419
Dalai Lama, 616
Dalmatic, 180
Daly, Bp. James, 376, 399, 419
Daly, Card. Cahal, 281, 294-296
Damasus I, Pope, 170, 206, 229, 237, 297
Damasus II, Pope, 238
Damien de Veuster, 13, 44, 45, 254, 356, 363
Dancing and Worship, 186
Danneels, Card. Godfried, 8, 281, 294-296, 336
Darmaatmadja, Card. Julius S.J., 281, 294-296
Dates and Events in Catholic History, 218-227
Daughters of Charity, 123, 216, 217, 429, 469, 484, 510
Daughters of Charity of St. Vincent de Paul, 123, 216, 217, 510
Daughters of Divine Love, 473, 488
Daughters of Mary, 28, 208, 209, 211, 216, 482
Daughters of Mary Help of Christians, 208, 209
Daughters of Mary Immaculate, 211, 482
Daughters of Our Lady, 204, 209, 482, 485, 492
Daughters of Our Lady of Fatima, 492
Daughters of Our Lady of Mercy, 209
Daughters of St. Francis of Assisi, 474
Day of Atonement, 606
Day of Prayer, 26, 32, 34, 38, 48, 165, 236, 608, 613, 616
De Giorgi Card. Salvatore, 281, 294, 295
De Palma, Bp. Joseph, 399, 419
De Paoli, Bp. Ambrose, 52
De Paolis, Abp. Velasio, 76, 260
De Simone, Bp. Louis, 399-400, 419
Deacon, 51-54, 107, 156, 165, 167, 168,

180, 188, 190, 196-197, 200, 202, 206, 211, 214, 218, 277-288, 290-292, 335, 345, 422, 503, 504
Deacon, U.S. Statistics, 197, 335
Deacons, Permanent, 196-197
Dead Sea Scrolls, 97, 105
Deaf, 28, 70, 212, 369, 371, 508, 509, 520, 524, 561
Dean of Cardinals, 277, 291
Death Penalty, 15, 133, 324, 332, 500, 611
Decalogue, 110, 111, 137, 570, 606
Decretals, 125, 221
Decretum, 125, 126, 223
Dei Verbum, 93, 103, 141, 229
Deiss, Father Lucien, 52
Delaney, Bp. Joseph, 377
Delaware, 79, 80, 358, 373, 421, 433, 435, 439, 512, 520, 526, 535
Del Blanco Prieto, Abp. Félix, 261
Delegates, Apostolic, 263-264
Delly, Card. Emmanuel III, 30, 60, 61, 77, 274, 281, 294-296, 345, 347, 348
Del Riego, Bp. Rutilio, 382, 399, 424
Dendinger, Bp. William J., 377, 399
Denmark, 204, 213, 234, 265-268, 272, 306, 311, 313, 470
Deposit of Faith, 87, 92, 94, 131, 203
Dery, Card. Peter Poreku, 52
Deskur, Card. Andres, 281, 294-296
Deus Caritas Est, 14, 59, 147, 232, 251
Deutero-Isaiah, 100
Deuteronomic Code, 98
Deuteronomy, 96, 98, 606
Deutero-Zechariah, 101
DeWane, Bp. Frank, 383, 400
Diaconate, 48, 134, 195-197, 221, 246, 344, 350, 421, 455, 503, 576
Dialogue, Ecumenical, See Ecumenical Dialogue
Dialogue, Interreligious, See Interreligious Dialogue
Dias, Card. Ivan, 20, 32, 74, 257, 258, 261, 268, 281, 294-296
Diaspora, 105, 346, 591
Didache, 106, 111, 125, 219
Didascalia, 125
Didymus (Thomas), 106
Diego, Juan, 123, 163, 170, 173, 208, 253, 254, 449, 451
Dignitas Connubii, 202
Dignitatis Humanae, 142, 230, 233
Dilecti Amici, 235
Diabolic Obsession, 141, 149
Diabolic Possession, 141, 152
Di Lorenzo, Bp. Francis, 377, 381, 400
Di Marzio, Bp. Nicholas, 375, 400
Di Mauro, Abp. Vincenzo, 76, 260, 261
Dimino, Bp. Joseph, 383, 400, 419
DiNardo, Card. Daniel, 10, 14, 36, 60, 61, 281, 294-296, 377, 382, 400
Dino, Bp. Gerald N., 383, 400
Diocesan and Interdiocesan Seminaries, 544, 545
Diocesan Bishops, 137, 141, 145, 172, 273, 274, 421
Diocesan Curia, 137
Diocesan Newspapers, 551, 575
Diocesan Synod, 236
Dioceses, Canadian, 442-445
Dioceses Mexico, 451-454
Dioceses U.S., 373-383

Dioceses World, 335
Diocletian, 205-207, 209, 219
Dion, Bp. George E., 400, 419
Directory on Ecumenism, 190, 193, 579, 580
Di Ruberto, Abp. Michele, 256, 261
Disabilities, 22, 58, 225-227, 308, 315, 322, 327, 369, 450, 493, 509, 520-524, 564
Discalced Augustinians, 467
Discalced Carmelite Fathers, 556
Discalced Carmelite Friars, 393, 561
Discalced Carmelites, 108, 217, 467, 550
Disciple, 65, 70, 84, 105, 106, 111, 120, 122, 138, 211, 218, 221
Disciples of Christ, 34, 67, 74, 133, 276, 582, 583, 598-600
Diskos, 351
District of Columbia, 12, 374, 390, 391, 421, 433, 512, 522, 526, 535, 544
Divine Compassion Sisters, 473
Divine Love, Daughters of, 473, 488
Divine Office, 66, 136, 159, 162, 172, 173, 176, 182, 184, 186, 242, 349
Divine Zeal Daughters, 473, 489
Divino Afflante Spiritu, 97, 104, 250, 500
Divorce, 78, 198, 201, 202-203, 211, 212, 315
Divorced and Remarried Catholics and Reception of Communion, 202-203
Diwali, 615
Djibouti, 265, 268, 306
Doctors of the Church, 18, 80, 106-108, 114, 133, 165, 170, 184, 204
Doctrine of Justification, 590, 603, 604
Doctrine of the Faith, Congr. for the, 7, 8, 9, 20, 26, 39, 40, 46, 55, 73, 74-75, 80-82, 231, 232, 235, 256, 260, 285
Doctrine of the Faith, Congr. for the (Functions), 256
Dolan, Abp. Timothy, 379, 400
Dominic, St., 206, 223; See also Dominicans
Dominican Nuns, 473
Dominican Nuns of Perpetual Rosary, 473
Dominican Republic, 33, 213, 234, 265, 266, 268, 285, 296, 307, 312, 336, 396,
Dominican Sisters, 24, 473, 474, 539-543
Dominican Sisters of Charity, 473
Dominican Sisters of Hope, 473
Dominican Sisters of Our Lady, 473
Dominican Sisters of Sparkill, 543
Dominican Sisters of St. Catherine of Siena, 473
Dominican Sisters of St. Mary, 542
Dominicans, 148, 154, 155, 168, 177, 206, 210, 313, 316, 391, 406, 429, 430, 449, 458, 461, 467, 473, 487-489, 502, 539, 565, 567
Do Nascimento, Card. Alexandre, 281, 294-296
Donatism, 219, 220
Donato, Bp. Thomas, 379, 400
Donnelly, Bp. Robert, 400, 419
Donoghue, Abp. John, 375, 400, 419
Donovan, Bp. Paul, 378, 400, 419
Dooher, Bp. John , 375, 400
Doran, Bp. Thomas, 381, 400, 490
Dormition, 350, 462
Dorothy, Inst. of, 487-489
Dorsey, Bp. Norbert, 400, 419

Douay-Rheims Bible, 97
Double Effect Principle, 139
Doueihi, Bp. Stephen, 381, 400, 419
Dougherty, Bp. John, 382, 400
Doxology, 139, 156, 178, 179, 186
Driscoll, Bp. Michael, 375, 377, 400
Duca, Bp. Michael, 382, 400
Duffy, Bp. Paul, 400-401
Duhart, Bp. Clarence, 401
Dulia, 139, 155
Dulles, Card. Avery, S.J., 281, 294-296, 603
Du Maine, Bp. Pierre, 382, 401, 419
Dunne, Bp. John, 381, 401
Dupre, Bp. Thomas, 382, 401, 419
Durning, Bp. Dennis, 401, 419
Dziwisz, Card. Stanislaw, 33, 282, 294, 295

E

Easter, 23, 24, 31, 34, 44, 69, 70, 112, 130, 139, 150, 151, 159, 161, 162, 164, 166, 167, 171-174, 180, 184, 186, 191, 192, 208, 219, 221, 236, 344, 349, 557, 576, 589
Easter Candle, 172
Easter Controversy, 139, 219, 221
Easter Duty, 139
Easter Triduum, 31, 161, 166, 172, 186
Easter Vigil, 44, 139, 150, 166, 172, 186, 191
Eastern Catholic Churches, 134, 177, 201, 229, 256, 273, 274, 343-348, 351, 421, 578, 579, 591
Eastern Code of Canon Law, 286
Eastern Jurisdictions, 346-348
Ecclesia de Eucharistia, 193, 235, 251
Ecclesia Dei, 35, 47, 187, 232, 260, 279, 283, 284, 286, 289
Ecclesiastes, 96, 99
Ecclesiastical Faculties, 548-550
Ecclesiasticus, 100
Economic Affairs of Holy See, 286
Economy of Salvation, 119, 138
Ecstasy, 139
Ecthesis, 221
Ecuador, 25, 29, 32, 38, 51, 76, 213, 234, 249, 265, 268, 282, 283, 291, 296, 307, 337, 396, 546
Ecumenical Agencies, 580-582
Ecumenical Councils, 122, 125, 130, 137, 148, 228-230, 297, 332, 590, 594
Ecumenical Patriarchate, 591, 594-595
Ecumenical Statements, 587-589
Ecumenism, 22, 51, 68, 122, 127, 139, 146, 159, 190, 193, 229, 230, 245, 251, 258, 282, 283, 286, 327, 362, 446, 501, 578-580, 583, 591, 595, 607
Education, Catholic, Congregation, 257-258
Education, Catholic, U.S., 534-544
Education, Catholic, World Statistics, 335
Education, Religious (Statistics), 534, 535-538
Edyvean, Bp. Walter, 375, 401
Egan, Card. Edward, 24, 36, 40, 76, 80, 260, 282, 294-296, 375, 379, 380, 401, 500
Egypt, 15, 61, 77, 98, 100, 101, 104, 105, 107, 173, 217, 219, 234, 256, 265, 268, 286, 292, 296, 307, 309, 329,

344-348, 489, 591, 595, 606, 613
Ehringer, Abbot Claude, 52
Eileton, 351
Ejaculation (Aspiration), 131
El Salvador, 26, 214, 234, 265, 268, 279, 289, 307, 308, 337, 469
Electing the Pope, 297
Elijah, 99, 100
Elizabeth Ann Seton, 163, 206, 244, 354, 357, 359, 362, 390, 392, 472
Elizondo, Bp. Eusebio, 382, 401, 424, 451
Elya Bp. John, 379, 401, 419
Emblems of Saints, 214-215
Emmanuel III Delly, 30, 60, 61, 77, 274, 294, 295, 347, 348
Enchiridion Indulgentiarum, 145
Encyclicals, 2, 3, 38, 42, 104, 112-117, 136, 182, 227, 232, 234, 241-250, 263, 450
Encyclicals, Pope Benedict XVI, 232, 251
Encyclicals, Pope John Paul II, 251, 234-235
England, 8, 13, 35, 45, 47, 50, 97, 107, 125, 129, 142, 150, 151, 155, 204-207, 209, 214, 216, 220-227, 238, 241, 242, 245, 248, 253, 272, 286, 296, 308, 311, 312, 314, 322, 327, 334, 337, 342, 352-354, 358-360, 375, 429, 441, 460, 463, 464, 466, 470, 473, 475, 478-482, 486, 496, 505, 567, 574, 598-600, 602
Enthronement of the Sacred Heart, 501
Envy, 133, 140, 157
Eparch, 274, 379-383, 397, 400, 405, 406, 412, 415, 418, 443, 445, 453
Ephesians, 59, 96, 102
Epiclesis, 140
Epikeia, 140
Epilepsy, 206, 212
Epimanikia, 351
Epiphany, 21, 161, 162, 165, 171, 172, 350, 389, 528
Epiphany (Feast), 162, 165, 172
Episcopal Church, 37, 47, 581-583, 598-601
Episcopal Conferences, 3, 21, 29, 35, 48, 76, 186, 194, 236, 264, 275, 277, 293, 311, 336-339
Episcopal Vicar, 138, 274, 287, 288, 394, 399, 403, 415
Epistles of St. Paul, 95
Equestrian Order, 10, 282, 288, 402, 418, 574
Erdò, Card. Peter, 8, 282, 294-296, 337, 339
Eritrea, 256, 265, 268, 308, 339, 344, 345, 347, 595
Errázuriz Ossa, Card. Francisco, 282, 294, 295, 296
Eschatology, 140
Estabrook Bp. Joseph, 383, 401
Estevez, Bp. Felipe, 379, 401, 424
Estonia, 234, 265, 266, 268, 292, 309, 591, 594, 595
Etchegaray, Card. Roger, 7, 261, 282, 294-296
Eternal Word Television Network (EWTN), 28, 562
Ethiopia, 105, 106, 208, 253, 256, 265, 268, 306, 308, 309, 337, 339, 344, 345, 347, 595
Eucharist, 178-179, 183-185, 191-194

Eucharist, Religious of, 474
Eucharistic Banquet, 159, 178
Eucharistic Celebration, 31, 48, 185, 192, 194, 589
Eucharistic Devotion, 192
Eucharistic Franciscan Missionary Sisters, 474
Eucharistic Minister, 156, 179, 562
Eucharistic Missionaries of St. Dominic, 24, 473
Eucharistic Prayer, 70, 130, 139, 178, 179, 184, 186
Eucharistic Sacrifice and Banquet, 178-181
Eudist Sisters, 483
Eudists, 208, 461, 467
Europe, 6, 15, 19, 23, 24, 29, 42, 53, 60, 62-64, 67, 77, 104, 107, 117, 125, 142, 168, 173, 205, 206, 214, 221, 223, 225, 228, 231-233, 235, 249, 257, 258, 268, 276, 295, 296, 299-302, 304-306, 308-311, 313, 315, 318, 320-322, 324-330, 332, 335, 339, 345-348, 353, 364, 395, 421, 423, 429, 490, 498, 500, 568, 586-588, 591, 593, 594, 597
Eusebio Kino, 353, 358, 372
Euthanasia, 12, 14, 26, 29, 80-82, 114, 140, 301, 321, 362
Eutychianism, 220
Evangelists, 102-105, 180, 204, 262, 350, 504
Evangelium Vitae, 84, 112-114, 133, 199, 234, 251
Evangelization of Peoples Congr. of, 14, 20, 23, 32, 52, 257
Evening Prayer, 138, 148, 159, 161, 162, 176
Ex Opere Operantis, 140
Ex Opere Operatio, 140
Exarch, 274, 284, 301, 379, 381-383, 405, 407, 412, 418, 445
Excommunication, 7, 39, 40, 48, 73, 130, 131, 134, 140, 142, 143, 145, 155, 156, 186, 200, 218, 220, 223, 225, 244, 329
Exegesis, 52, 103, 104, 242, 277
Exodus, 23, 77, 96, 98, 101, 104, 329, 606, 607
Exorcism, 141, 152, 196
Exsultet, 172, 576
Extension Society, 356, 415, 431, 557
Extreme Unction, 159, 195
Ezekiel, 96, 100
Ezra, 96-99, 101, 606

F

Fabre, Bp. Shelton, 379, 401, 428
Fabric of St. Peter, 261, 262, 280, 285-287
Facilities for Children and Adults with, 520-524
Facilities for Retired and Aged Persons, 511-519
Falcão, Card. José Freire, 282, 294-296
Family, Pontifical Council for the, 259
Farina, Card. Raffaele, 60, 261, 262, 272, 282, 294, 295
Farrell, Bp. Kevin, 376, 401
Fasting, 23, 25, 48, 112, 128, 129, 163, 165, 171, 247, 606, 613, 614
Fátima, 121, 123, 124, 141, 156, 234, 325
Favalora, Abp. John, 374, 379, 381, 401

Feast Days and Holy Days, 171-174
Federation of St. Benedict, 469
Federation of St. Gertrude, 469, 488
Federation of St. Scholastica, 469
Felician Sisters, 474, 540, 541
Felix, Congr. of, 474
Felix of Nicosia, 253
Fellhauer, Bp. David, 383, 401
Fernandes de Araújo, Card. Serafim, 282, 294-296
Fernandez, Bp. Gilberto, 401, 419, 424
Festing, Fra Matthew, 574
Fidei Depositum, 87
Fidei donum, 250, 289
Fides et Ratio, 234, 251, 615
Fiji, 234, 265, 266, 268, 309, 338, 395, 412
Filioque, 107, 590, 593, 594
Filippini Religious, 474
Films, 54, 569-570, 577
Filoni, Abp. Fernando, 26, 33, 256, 261
Finland, 22, 214, 234, 265, 268, 309, 589, 591, 594
Finn, Bp. Robert, 378, 401
Fiorenza, Abp. Joseph, 377, 382, 401, 419, 533
Fisherman's Ring, 132, 141
Fitzsimons, Bp. George, 382, 401
Flanagan, Bp. Thomas, 401-402
Flesey, Bp. John W., 379, 402
Fliss, Bp. Patrick, 383, 402, 419
Flores, Bp. Daniel, 376, 402
Flores, Bp. Patrick, 376, 382, 402
Florida, 50, 82, 84, 254, 270, 272, 300, 305, 325, 352-354, 358, 363, 366, 374, 390, 391, 421, 422, 425, 426, 433, 435, 439, 469, 480, 496, 509, 512, 520, 522, 526, 532, 535, 544, 553, 554, 575
Flynn, Bp. Harry, 69, 378, 381, 402, 419
Foley, Card. John P., 9, 10, 14, 48, 60, 261, 282, 294, 296, 418, 574, 577
Foley, Bp. David, 375, 402
Foreign Missions, 207, 337, 356, 459, 461, 464, 465, 467, 476, 477
Foreign Missions, U.S. Personnel, 429-430
Formosus, Pope, 238
Forst, Bp. Marion, 376, 419
Forty Hours Devotion, 141, 208
Foys, Bp. Roger, 376, 402
France, 10, 19, 20, 29, 32, 34, 35, 39, 43, 52, 53, 61, 107, 108, 123, 129, 149, 156, 159, 162, 168, 176, 182, 204-210, 212-215, 222-226, 234, 238-245, 247-250, 261, 265, 268, 272, 278, 281, 282, 287-289, 292, 293, 295, 297, 298, 308, 309, 312, 320, 337, 340-342, 345-347, 353, 354, 358-361, 364, 390, 403, 405, 412, 413, 415, 429, 441, 450, 458-461, 463-464, 468-487, 491, 492, 495, 498, 546, 548, 549, 600, 613
Francis de Sales, 107, 165, 207, 211-213, 216, 225, 249, 279, 388, 389, 404, 462, 466, 467, 474, 489, 492, 520, 540, 572
Francis de Sales Oblates, 462
Francis of Assisi, 15, 20, 107, 137, 158, 160, 206, 207, 211, 212, 214, 223, 248, 249, 287, 289, 388, 390, 462, 474, 475, 477, 489, 493, 539
Francis Xavier, 170, 207, 212-214, 217, 224, 252, 255, 314, 358, 365, 375,

388, 390-392, 462, 545
Franciscan Brothers, 462, 468, 542
Franciscan Brothers of Brooklyn, 462, 468
Franciscan Brothers of Christ, 462
Franciscan Handmaids, 474
Franciscan Hospitaller Sisters, 474
Franciscan Mission Service, 496, 563
Franciscan Missionaries of Jesus Crucified, 493
Franciscan Missionaries of Mary, 429, 474, 487
Franciscan Missionaries of Our Lady, 475
Franciscan Missionaries of St. Joseph, 475, 482
Franciscan Missionary Brothers, 462
Franciscan Missionary Sisters, 474-476
Franciscan Missionary Sisters of Assisi, 475
Franciscan Missionary Sisters of Our Lady of Sorrows, 475
Franciscan Missions, 353, 358, 365, 391
Franciscan Order, 107, 151, 168, 174, 206, 209, 223, 224, 342, 397, 403, 477, 493, 498
Franciscans (Men), 462, 467-468
Franciscans (Women), 474-477, 487-489
Franklin, Bp. William, 376,
Free Will, 130, 142, 148, 216, 220
Freemasonry, 142, 225, 248
French Guinea, 261
Frey, Bp. Gerald, 52
Friar, 31, 46, 142, 466, 597, 599
Friars Minor, Order of, See Franciscans
Friars of the Atonement, 467
Friars of the Renewal, 462
Friars Preachers Order of, See Dominicans.
Friend, Bp. William, 374, 402
Fruits of the Holy Spirit, 142
Fruits of the Mass, 142, 158, 179
Fundamental Option, 142
Fundamentalists, 24, 600
Funeral Mass, 179
Funeral Rites, 188
Furnishings, 154, 176, 177
Furno, Card. Carlo, 282, 294-296

G
Gabon, 15, 43, 234, 265, 268, 310, 337, 339
Gabriel (feast), 169, 173
Gainer, Bp. Ronald W., 378, 402
Galante, Bp. Joseph, 375, 402
Galatians, 96, 102
Galeone, Bp. Victor, 381, 402, 424
Gallagher, Father Joseph, 52
Gallicanism, 159, 224, 309
Gambia, 18, 234, 265, 266, 268, 310, 337-339
Gantin, Card. Bernardin, 52
Garcia, Bp. Richard, 379, 402
Garcia-Gasco y Vicente, Card. Agustin, 60, 282, 294, 295
Garcia Siller Bp. Gustavo M.Sp.S., 376, 402, 424
Garey, Gerard S., 52
Garland, Bp. James, 379, 402, 419
Garmo, Bp. George, 402
Gaudium et Spes, 69, 113-117, 131, 197, 229, 233, 292, 578
Gaydos, Bp. John, 378, 403
Gelasius I, Pope, 220, 237
Gelasius II, Pope, 238

Gelineau, Bp. Louis, 381, 403, 419
Gendron, Bp. Odore, 379, 403, 419, 443
General Instruction of the Roman Missal, 180, 183, 575, 576
Genuflection, 142
George, Cardinal Francis E., 16, 84, 283, 296, 375, 381, 383, 403, 421
Georgia, 34, 49, 234, 264, 265, 268, 300, 310, 352, 373, 421, 422, 425, 427, 433, 435, 439, 470, 520, 522, 526, 535, 554, 591, 594
Gerber, Bp. Eugene, 376, 383, 403
Gerety, Bp. Peter, 379, 380, 403, 419
Germany, 6, 10, 35, 45, 60, 106-108, 149, 204-206, 214, 216, 217, 221-224, 227, 231-234, 240, 241, 243, 244, 248-250, 261, 262, 265, 268, 272, 278, 280, 281, 284-286, 292, 293, 295, 310, 311, 337, 341, 342, 346, 347, 360, 396, 397, 404, 416, 429, 458, 461, 462, 464, 468, 471, 472, 474-477, 479, 482, 484, 485, 492, 493, 496, 547-549, 567, 574, 589, 592, 597, 599, 603, 608, 609, 613
Gerry, Bp. Joseph, 380, 403, 419
Gettelfinger, Bp. Gerald, 376, 403
Ghana, 52, 234, 264, 265, 267, 268, 272, 281, 293, 296, 311, 337, 339, 394, 429
Gibraltar, 214, 265, 311
Gift of Authority, 590
Gilbert, Bp. Edward, 403
Gilmore, Bp. Ronald, 376, 403
Giordano, Card. Michele, 268, 283, 294, 295
Girl Scouts, 341, 497
Glemp, Card. Józef, 283, 294-296
Glendon, Mary Ann, 16, 20, 42, 236, 269, 270, 272
Glenmary Home Missioners, 431, 558
Glenmary Sisters, 479, 558
Glenmary Society, 362
Gluttony, 133, 142
Gnosticism, 106, 207, 218
Goedert, Bp. Raymond, 403, 419
Gomez, Abp. José, 382, 403, 424
Gonzalez, Bp. Roberto, 376, 403, 424
Gonzalez Valer, Bp. Francisco, 383, 403, 424
González Zumarraga, Card. Antonio José, 283, 294-296
Good Friday, 23, 25, 129, 163, 166, 172, 180, 186, 245, 315, 350
Good Shepherd Sisters, 478
Goods of Marriage, 143
Gorman, Bp. John, 403, 419
Gospels, 95, 96, 101, 102, 106, 111, 130, 151, 178, 209, 214, 221, 259, 349, 575, 584
Gossman, Bp. Joseph, 403, 419
Goulet, Robert, 52
Grace, 88-92, 95, 107, 110, 111, 119-122, 126, 135, 138, 140-146, 148, 150, 153, 155, 157, 158, 160, 161, 172, 175, 176, 178, 182, 188-192, 194-196, 198, 569, 571, 574-579, 587, 588, 590, 591, 597, 599-601, 603-605
Gracias, Card. Oswald, 61, 283, 294-296, 337
Gracida, Bp. Rene, 376, 380, 403, 419, 424
Graduale Romanum, 185
Grahmann, Bp. Charles, 376, 383, 403,

419
Graymoor, 458, 476, 478, 506, 510, 529, 557, 563, 583, 616
Graymoor Sisters, 476, 478
Great Western Schism, 241
Greece, 6, 30, 51, 105, 106, 214, 228, 234, 236, 237, 244, 249, 256, 265, 268, 298, 311, 337, 345-347, 395, 567, 587, 591, 594
Green, Abp. James, 266, 267, 404, 418
Gregorian Calendar, 225, 349
Gregorian Chant, 176, 182, 220
Gregorian University, 52-54, 61, 242, 243, 245, 246, 279, 281, 282, 284, 286, 287, 289, 290, 293, 395-398, 401, 402, 404, 405, 407, 409-411, 413, 414, 416, 417, 546, 550
Gregory I, Pope, 107, 176, 204, 213, 214, 220, 237
Gregory II, Pope, 221, 237
Gregory III, Pope, 221, 237, 274, 297, 345, 347, 348
Gregory IV, Pope, 171, 238
Gregory V, Pope, 238
Gregory VI, Pope, 238
Gregory VII, Pope, 125, 167, 207, 208, 222, 238, 290
Gregory VIII, 239, 240
Gregory VIII (Antipope),
Gregory IX, Pope, 126, 145, 210, 223, 239, 256
Gregory X, Pope, 729, 239, 297
Gregory XI, Pope, 107, 239, 241, 597
Gregory XII, Pope, 229, 239, 241, 257
Gregory XIII, Pope, 225, 239, 257
Gregory XIV, Pope, 240
Gregory XV, Pope, 173, 240, 257, 297, 352
Gregory XVI, Pope, 147, 216, 226, 240, 247, 355, 360, 573
Gregory III Laham, 274, 347, 348
Gregory, Abp. Wilton, 183, 375, 404, 428, 582
Grey Nuns, 365, 441, 446, 471, 478, 540
Grey Nuns of Montréal, 471
Gries, Bp. Roger, 376, 404
Griffin, Bp. James, 376, 382, 404
Grocholewski, Card. Zenon, 9, 257, 258, 261, 283, 294, 295
Grosz, Bp. Edward, 375, 404
Guadalupe Our Lady of (Feast), 163, 170
Guam, 32, 234, 311, 389, 390, 394, 397, 429, 438, 497, 507, 538
Guardian Angel, 388, 478, 489, 521
Guardian Angels (Feast), 169, 172, 173
Guardian Angel, Sisters of, 478
Guatemala, 29, 234, 265, 268, 280, 288, 289, 296, 301, 307, 311, 312, 337, 363, 364, 429, 469, 492, 507, 510, 547
Guérin, St. Théodore, 253, 254, 355, 359, 364
Guillory, Bp. Curtis, 375, 404, 428
Guinea, 214, 234, 261, 265-269, 280, 308, 312, 323, 326, 328, 337-339, 397, 404, 406, 413, 419, 429, 430
Guinea Bissau, 234, 265, 338
Gulbinowicz, Card. Henryk, 283, 294-296
Gullickson, Abp. Thomas E., 264-267, 404, 418
Gumbleton, Bp. Thomas, 404, 419
Guyana, 265, 268, 312

H

Habakkuk, 96, 97, 101
Habit, 143, 155, 160, 180
Habitual Grace, 143
Haggai, 96, 101
Hail Mary, 37, 130, 131, 143
Haiti, 33, 34, 234, 265, 268, 307, 312, 337, 364, 414, 429, 495
Hamao, Card. Stephen Fumio, 53
Handmaids of Divine Mercy, 491
Hanifen, Bp. Richard, 376, 404, 419
Hannan, Abp. Philip, 379, 382, 404, 419
Hanukkah, 99, 368, 606
Hanus, Abp. Jerome, 376, 381, 404
Harrington, Bp. Bernard, 383, 404
Hart, Bp. Daniel, 53
Hart, Bp. Joseph, 375, 404, 419
Harvey, Abp. James, 260, 404, 418
Hawaii, 44, 206, 356, 363, 372, 374, 421, 422, 425, 433, 435, 439, 460, 466, 470, 486, 535, 554
Hawthorne Dominicans, 474, 509
Health Care, 335, 508-510
Hearing Impaired Children, 520
Hedwig, 65, 169, 207, 214, 216, 252
Heim, Bp. Capistran, 404, 419, 430
Hell, 44, 88, 108, 109, 130, 137, 140, 142, 143, 146, 153, 597, 613
Helpers, Society of, 478
Hennessey, Bp. Robert, 375, 404
Henoticon, 220
Heresy, 97, 134, 140, 143, 145, 146, 206, 208, 218-220, 224, 241, 242, 256, 306, 309, 361
Hermanas Catequistas, 478
Hermanas Josefinas, 478
Hermann, Bp. Robert J., 381, 404
Hermeneutics, 103, 104, 143, 609
Hermes, Bp. Herbert, 405, 419, 430
Heroic Virtue, 31, 32, 143
Herranz, Card. Julián, 260, 261, 283, 294, 295
Herzog, Bp. Ronald P., 374, 405
Hickey, Card. James, 296, 376, 383
Hierarchy of the Catholic Church, 273-275
Higgins, Bp. Richard, 16, 385, 404-405
High Schools Catholic U.S., 432, 534-538
Higi, Bp. William, 378, 405
Hinduism, 4, 321, 578, 615
Hippolytus, 168, 184, 207, 210, 212, 219, 240
Hispanic Catholics in the United States, 424-426
Historical Books, 96, 98, 100
Hoeppner, Bp. Michael, 376, 405
Holland, 108, 205, 214, 226, 242, 250, 461, 463, 471, 477-479, 518, 559, 560, 562, 565, 597, 600
Holley, Bp. Martin, 383, 405, 428
Holocaust, 6, 39, 227, 236, 244, 606, 608, 610-612
Holy Cross Fathers, 429, 527, 540, 542
Holy Days and Other Observances, 3, 171-174
Holy Door, 389
Holy Family of Nazareth, Srs. of, 487
Holy Ghost Fathers, 305, 319, 325, 327, 331, 463, 498
Holy Ghost Fathers of Ireland, 463
Holy Land, 5, 6, 11, 22, 24, 27, 31, 36, 39, 77, 157, 210, 222, 228, 234, 236,

246, 315, 345, 348, 391, 421, 462, 501, 563, 567, 574, 609
Holy Name Society, 356, 361, 502
Holy Names of Jesus and Mary, Srs. of, 487
Holy Office, 56, 124, 158, 225, 256, 277
Holy Orders, 34, 39, 40, 88, 127, 130, 131, 133-135, 141, 146, 172, 176, 185, 187, 189, 190, 195, 196, 222, 273, 277, 350, 580
Holy Saturday, 32, 166, 172, 350
Holy See, 5, 6, 8-10, 13, 15-21, 29, 30, 35, 36, 41-48, 51, 52, 56, 57, 63, 75-76, 231-271
Holy See Finances, 75-76, 260
Holy See, Representatives of the, 263-268
Holy See, Representatives in the, 268-269
Holy Sepulchre of Jerusalem, 60, 288, 402, 574
Holy Sepulchre Order, 9, 10, 14, 48, 60, 261, 282, 294, 296, 418, 574, 577
Holy Spirit, 87-96, 102, 104, 107, 109, 110, 119, 121, 122, 128, 132, 134, 135, 138-144, 146, 148, 150, 151, 154-157, 159, 161, 162, 165, 169, 173, 174, 189-191, 194, 195, 199
Holy Spirit Missionary Sisters, 478, 564
Holy Spirit of Perpetual Adoration, 479
Holy Thursday, 30, 31, 150, 161, 166, 172, 186, 193, 350
Holy Water, 131, 139, 144, 158, 176, 182, 214
Holy Water Fonts, 182
Holy Year, 124, 144, 228, 245, 246, 282
Home Mission Sisters, 479
Home Missions, 356, 421, 430, 431, 461, 564
Home Visitors of Mary Srs. of, 478
Homilist, 188
Homosexuality, 55, 144, 362
Honduras, 43, 234, 265, 268, 278, 289, 296, 312, 337, 399, 414, 419, 430, 510
Hong Kong, 23, 31, 43, 294, 296, 303, 339, 567
Honoré, Card. Jean, 283, 294-296
Honorius I, Pope, 221, 237
Honorius II, Pope, 238, 240, 493
Honorius III, Pope, 137, 151, 223, 239
Honorius IV, Pope, 239
Hosanna, 144
Hosea, 96, 100, 101
Hoser, Abp. Henryk, 261
Hospice, 63, 510, 511, 515
Hospital Sisters, 476, 509
Hospitallers of St. John, 208, 467, 574
Hospitals, 33, 50, 134, 197, 208, 212, 213, 217, 321, 328, 332, 335, 364, 365, 432, 485, 496, 509
Houck, Bp. William, 378, 405, 419
Howze, Bp. Joseph, 375, 405, 419, 428
Hubbard, Bp. Howard, 374, 405
Hughes, Abp. Alfred, 375, 379, 405
Hughes, Bp. Edward, 379, 405, 419
Hughes, Bp. William A., 376, 405, 419
Humanae Vitae, 115, 137, 199, 245, 251, 275, 357
Humeral Veil, 180
Humility of Mary Congr., 478
Humility of Mary Srs., 478-479
Hummes, Card. Claudio O.F.M., 34, 257, 261, 283, 294-296
Hungary, 65, 170, 204, 206, 208-214, 222, 234, 247, 248, 250, 252, 261,

265, 268, 282, 287, 296, 312, 313, 337, 346, 347, 474, 485, 486, 547, 548, 567
Hunthausen, Abp. Raymond, 377, 382, 405, 419
Hurley, Abp. Francis, 374, 378, 405,419
Hurley, Bp. Walter A., 377, 405
Husar, Card. Lubomyr, 274, 283, 294-296, 347
Hyde, Henry, 53
Hymn, 19, 113, 129, 132, 146, 148-150, 158, 159, 176, 178, 179
Hyperdulia, 144
Hypostatic Union, 144

I

Ibrahim, Bp. Ibrahim, 382, 405
Iceland, 11, 214, 234, 265, 268, 313
Icon, 349, 350, 594
Iconoclasm, 221
Iconostasis, 350
Idaho, 374, 421, 425, 433, 435, 439, 526, 535, 554
Idolatry, 30, 98, 100, 101, 144, 221, 304
Ignatius Loyola, 213, 292, 389
IHM Sisters, 430, 562
IHS, 144, 205, 214
Illinois, 53, 79, 353, 361, 364, 365, 372, 373, 390, 391, 406, 412, 421, 422, 425, 426, 433, 435, 439, 470, 512, 521, 522, 526, 535, 539, 544, 557, 568
Imesch, Bp. Joseph, 378, 405, 419
Immaculate Conception, 12, 16-18, 20, 24, 31, 36, 55, 56, 78, 123, 139, 144, 155, 162, 170, 172, 174, 204, 206, 213-215, 224, 226, 242, 247, 249, 250, 253, 283, 285, 350, 353, 355, 360, 388-391, 393, 395-402, 406, 408, 409, 411, 413-417, 428, 443, 444, 446, 462, 464, 465, 467, 469, 472, 474, 476-479, 482, 486-489, 499, 500, 545, 548, 549, 558, 559, 612
Immaculate Conception, Srs. of, 488
Immaculate Heart of Mary, Sisters of, 430, 479
Immortality, 107, 144, 606
Impediments, 200, 202, 246
Impotency, 200
Imprimatur, 134, 144
Imputability, 144
Incardination, 144
Incense, 134, 144, 150
Incest, 144, 145
Inclusive Language, 188
Inculturation, 52, 75, 145, 276, 300, 427
Incurable Cancer, 474, 509
Index of Prohibited Books, 145, 216
India, 10, 13, 34, 43, 46, 50, 61, 105, 106, 208, 214, 234, 241, 243-246, 261, 265-267, 269, 272, 274, 279, 281, 283-285, 288, 292, 293, 296, 301, 313, 319, 329, 337, 344-347, 394, 408, 419, 429, 460, 471, 474, 482, 500, 548, 567, 581, 595, 596, 615, 616
Indiana, 355, 359, 364, 365, 373, 390, 391, 417, 421, 422, 425, 433, 435, 439, 461, 469, 470, 513, 521, 522, 526, 535, 536, 545, 554, 568, 614
Indissolubility of Marriage, 201, 275
Indonesia, 13, 27, 50, 234, 245, 265, 267, 269, 281, 296, 307, 314, 337, 415,

548, 613
Indulgence, 17, 73, 129, 144, 145, 151, 157, 223, 597
Indult, 137, 145, 183, 196
Inerrancy, 94
Infallibility, 92, 145, 226, 589, 605
Infancy Narrative, 139, 143, 147
Infused Virtues, 145
Innocent I, Pope, 96, 237
Innocent II, Pope, 229, 238, 240
Innocent III, Pope, 171, 223, 229, 239, 240, 256, 262, 345
Innocent IV, Pope, 229, 239, 256
Innocent V, Pope, 239
Innocent VI, Pope, 239, 241
Innocent VII, Pope, 239, 241
Innocent VIII, Pope, 239
Innocent IX, Pope, 240
Innocent X, Pope, 172, 225, 240
Innocent XII, Pope, 240
Innocent XIII, Pope, 240
Innocenti, Card. Antonio, 284, 294-296
Inquisition, 145, 223, 224, 256, 329, 449
Insemination, 145
Institutes of Consecrated Life, 7, 25, 127, 135-138, 187, 257, 258, 278, 282, 283, 285-287, 289, 290, 402, 458, 490, 491, 557
Inter Insigniores, 197
Inter Mirifica, 230
Inter-Agency Curia Commissions, 258
Interdict, 134, 146
Interment, 132
International Catholic Organizations, 259, 340-342, 496, 498
International Catholic Periodicals, 567, 568
International Eucharistic Congresses, 52, 260, 278, 292
Internet, 28, 73, 236, 568-572
Interpretations of the Bible, 94-95
Interreligious Dialogue, 4, 11, 14, 35, 41, 43, 46, 51, 58, 259, 260, 278, 281, 283, 284, 287-292, 307, 316, 455, 578, 580, 586, 587, 606, 613-616
Intinction, 146, 179, 192, 350, 351
Iowa, 363, 373, 376, 390, 391, 398, 399, 411, 415, 421, 422, 425, 433, 436, 439, 470, 513, 527, 536, 541, 545
Iran, 6, 61, 256, 265, 269, 289, 314, 345-347
Iraq, 10, 13, 15, 22, 23, 29-31, 34, 36, 46, 47, 60, 61, 77, 84, 217, 228, 236, 256, 265, 269, 281, 296, 314, 331, 345-348, 357, 403, 405, 406, 495, 591
Ireland, 10, 11, 13, 32, 60, 125, 172, 205, 209, 210, 214, 220, 221, 223-227, 234, 242, 247, 248, 261, 265, 269, 279-281, 287, 293, 295, 308, 311, 314, 315, 322, 327, 337, 342, 355, 356, 360, 364, 381, 395, 397, 399, 401, 402, 405, 408, 411, 429, 460-463, 465, 469, 471-473, 475, 478, 479, 481, 482, 484, 485, 487, 489, 496, 505, 506, 547, 548, 567
Irenicism, 146
Iriondo, Bp. Robert, 379, 405, 424
Isaac, 24, 44, 101, 151, 163, 169, 274, 347, 352, 358, 361, 364, 465, 606
Isaac Jogues, 163, 169, 352, 358, 364
Isaiah, 96, 97, 100, 101
Islam, 13, 27, 35, 43, 45, 61, 63, 64, 150, 221, 298, 300, 302, 307, 314, 316-318,

320, 322, 329, 334, 578, 613-614
Islam, Benedict XVI and, 61-62, 613-614
Israel, 6, 22, 24, 25, 28, 64, 89, 90, 95, 98-101, 111, 137, 151, 235, 236, 265, 267, 269, 272, 280, 315, 316, 346, 347, 412, 429, 548, 567, 576, 591, 608, 609, 611, 612
Italo-Albanian Catholic Church, 346
Italy, 5-8, 10, 13, 14, 18, 29, 32, 34, 35, 37, 41, 42, 45, 46, 51, 53, 55, 60, 61, 107, 108, 133, 144, 147, 149, 151, 156, 205-207, 209, 214, 216, 217, 221-226, 232, 234, 241-250, 254, 256-262, 265, 267, 269, 270, 272, 273, 275, 278-295, 297, 298, 315, 316, 326, 337, 340-342, 346, 347, 389, 394, 400, 401, 404, 407, 408, 411, 416-418, 429, 458-486, 490-493, 502, 547, 548, 558, 567, 574, 583, 590, 594, 595
Ivory Coast, 234, 261, 265, 268, 269, 296, 305, 337, 548

J

Jackels, Michael O., 44, 383, 406
Jacob, 101, 584, 597, 606
Jacobs, Bp. Sam, 374, 377, 406
Jadot, Abp. Jean, 267
Jakubowski, Bp. Thad, 406, 419, 499
Jamaica, 33, 51, 234, 265, 267, 269, 316, 364, 395, 397, 416, 419, 429, 430, 465, 475, 478, 484, 486, 529, 542, 556, 558, 559
Jammo, Bp. Sarhad, 381, 406
Japan, 18, 53, 209, 210, 214, 224, 234, 243, 244, 252, 253, 265, 269, 272, 291, 296, 316, 317, 337, 357, 429, 547, 548, 591
Jarrell, Bp. C. Michael, 377, 378, 406
Jaworski, Card. Marian, 284, 294-296, 339
Jenky, Bp. Daniel, 380, 406
Jeremiah, 69, 79, 85, 96, 97, 100, 101, 253, 377, 379, 380, 409, 418
Jerome, St., 108, 563
Jerusalem, 10, 11, 22, 38, 39, 41, 60, 65, 97, 99-102, 104-107, 109, 132, 134, 142, 147, 150, 151, 155, 157, 166, 171, 173, 214, 218, 222, 228, 235, 236, 265, 267, 273, 274, 280, 282, 284, 288, 293, 315, 316, 336, 344, 345, 347, 348, 397, 402, 404, 412, 500, 505, 527, 548, 567, 574, 586, 588, 591, 594, 606, 609-611
Jerusalem Bible, 97
Jerusalem Patriarchate, 591
Jesuit Martyrs of North America, 243, 446
Jesuits (Society of Jesus), 53, 151, 207, 208, 224-227, 262, 278, 281, 292, 293, 301, 302, 304, 308, 310-313, 316, 319-321, 323, 324, 326, 327, 330, 334, 352, 353, 355, 356, 358, 430, 441, 446, 449, 450, 463, 467, 540, 548, 561
Jesus Prayer, 146
Jews, Judaism, 38, 90, 99, 100, 105, 208, 607-612; See also Israel
Joan of Arc, 207, 213, 214, 224, 242, 251, 570
Job, 96, 99, 107
Joel, 96, 101
John Chrysostom, 6, 7, 106, 108, 212, 214, 277, 594
John Damascene, 108, 170

John Fisher, 167, 208, 211, 224, 251, 308
John I, Pope, 167, 208, 237
John II, Pope, 220, 237, 241
John III, Pope, 237
John IV, Pope, 237
John V, Pope, 237, 324
John VI, Pope, 237
John VII, Pope, 237
John VIII, Pope, 238
John IX, Pope, 238
John X, Pope, 222, 238
John XI, Pope, 238
John XII, Pope, 222, 238
John XIII, Pope, 238
John XIV, Pope, 238
John XV, Pope, 132, 222, 238, 239
John XVI, Antipope, 240
John XVII, Pope, 238
John XVIII, Pope, 238
John XIX, Pope, 238
John XXI, Pope, 239
John XXII, Pope, 174, 223, 239, 241, 297, 573
John XXIII, Antipope, 241
John XXIII, Bl., Pope, 114, 116, 124, 208, 232, 235, 240, 244-245, 251, 252
Canonizations, 244, 252
Encyclicals, 114, 116, 245, 251
Life, 244-245
Writings, 114, 116, 245, 251
John XXIII National Seminary, 408, 416, 545
John Vianney, 168, 208, 251, 394, 398, 399, 402, 404, 411, 417, 544, 545
John Nepomucene Neumann, 208, 245, 252, 355, 362
John Paul I, Pope, 228, 232, 233, 240, 246
John Paul II, Pope, 7, 11, 14, 16, 18-20, 23, 25, 27, 28, 31, 33, 35, 36, 39, 44-48, 51, 53, 56-58, 60, 63, 81, 82, 84, 87, 108, 111-117, 121, 123, 124, 126, 129, 132, 133, 136, 142, 145, 150, 154, 156-159, 163, 180, 183, 185, 187, 193, 195, 197, 199, 201, 203, 204, 206, 211, 228, 230-236, 240, 244, 246, 251-263, 270-272, 275, 276, 279, 281, 282, 287, 289, 291, 295-299, 302, 305-307, 311, 313, 314, 318, 320, 321, 325-327, 330, 332, 345, 351, 357, 362, 390, 405, 407, 409, 413, 424, 449-451, 464, 495, 498, 499, 504, 507, 519, 524, 526, 528, 533, 545, 548-550, 563, 568, 572, 578, 580, 583-586, 590, 592-594, 603, 605, 608, 609, 612-616
Beatifications, 25, 28, 42, 132, 253-254
Canonizations, 132, 133, 215-217, 232, 252-253
Encyclicals, 38, 42, 104, 112-114, 121-123, 136, 182, 227, 232, 234, 251
Life, 31, 232-233
Moral Teachings, 112-114
Pontificate, 233-234
Writings, 112-114, 121-123, 234-235, 251
Travels, 233-234
Johnston, Bp. James, 383, 406
Joint Declaration on Justification, 585, 589, 603
Jonah, 96, 101, 106
Josemaria Escrivá de Balaguer, St., 208, 253, 254, 507

Josephinism, 225, 299, 300, 306, 310, 313
Josephite Fathers, 463
Joshua, 96, 98, 146, 271
Juan Diego, 123, 163, 170, 173, 208, 253, 254, 449, 451
Jubilee, 17, 20, 21, 36, 41-43, 73, 144, 192, 195, 228, 233, 235, 247, 248, 250, 280, 282, 291, 389, 425, 445, 446, 563, 573, 585, 604, 613
Judah, 99-101, 106
Judaism, 38, 90, 99, 100, 105, 208, 607-612; See also Israel
Judas Iscariot, 105
Jude, 91, 96, 103, 105
Jude Thaddeus, 105
Judges, 96, 98, 101
Judith, 96-99
Jugis, Bp. Peter J., 375, 406
Julian Calendar, 34, 349
Julius I, Pope, 237
Julius II, Pope, 229, 239
Julius III, Pope, 130, 229, 239, 346
Junípero Serra, 163, 353, 358, 365, 372
Jurisdictions and Faithful of the Eastern, 344-347
Just War, 118
Justice, Bp. William, 382, 406
Justification, 88, 102, 109, 122, 145, 146, 224, 585, 589, 590, 597, 600-604
Justin Martyr, 106, 167, 208, 214

K

Kaddish, 608
Kaffer, Bp. Roger, 406, 419
Kalisz, Bp. Raymond, 406, 419
Kane, Bp. Francis, 375, 406
Kansas, 40, 80, 278, 352, 358, 363, 364, 368, 373, 374, 378, 385, 388, 395, 398, 401, 402, 404, 406, 410, 418, 419, 421, 422, 425, 433, 434, 436, 439, 465, 469, 481, 483, 497, 500, 513, 515, 523, 527, 536, 539, 542, 544, 552, 554-557, 562, 564, 565, 575
Kappa Gamma Pi, 498
Karcher, Carl, 53
Karekin I Catholicos, 585
Karekin II Catholicos, 585
Karlic, Card. Estanislao Esteban, 61, 284, 294-296
Kasper, Card. Walter, 6, 14, 47, 49, 258, 260, 261, 284, 294, 295, 484, 580, 581, 592, 594, 596, 602, 612
Kateri Tekakwitha, 163, 168, 208, 253, 353, 392, 429, 441
Katharine Drexel, 28, 163, 208, 253, 356, 485
Kazakstan, 265, 267, 337, 419
Keeler, Card. William, 8, 275, 284, 294-296, 375, 377, 406, 419, 431, 582, 605, 607, 611, 612
Keleher, Bp. James, 375, 378, 406, 419
Kelly, Abp. Thomas, 379, 406, 419
Kentucky, 354, 355, 359, 363-365, 368, 374, 390, 421, 422, 433, 436, 439, 465, 470, 484, 499, 513, 521, 523, 527, 536, 556, 599, 616
Kenya, 10, 35, 61, 234, 265, 269, 272, 279, 287, 296, 316, 331, 337, 339, 418, 419, 429, 430, 548, 567, 581, 591
Kerygma, 146

Kettler, Abp. Donald, 28, 376, 406
Keys, Power of the, 146
Kicanas, Bp. Gerald, 16, 84, 383, 406, 421
Kim Sou- hwan, Card. Stephen, 284, 294-296
Kings, 96, 98-100
Kingship of Christ (Feast), 162, 170, 171
Kingship of Christ Women Missionaries, 492
Kinney, Bp. John, 375, 381, 406
Kitbunchu, Card. Michael, 284, 294-296, 331
Kmiec, Bp. Edward, 375, 379, 406
Knights of Columbus, 16, 32, 356, 361, 497, 507, 551, 557, 563, 612
Knights of Labor, 242, 356, 361
Knights of Lithuania, 502
Knights of Malta, 51, 574
Knights of Peter Claver, 428, 502
Knights of Rhodes, 574
Knights of St. John, 356, 502, 558
Knights Templar, 11, 223
Koinonia, 17, 146, 590
Korea, 9, 44, 45, 204, 214, 234, 245, 265, 266, 269, 280, 281, 284, 296, 316, 317, 337, 404, 409, 410, 419, 429, 498
Korec, Card. Jan, 284, 294-296
Kozlowiecki, Card. Adam, 53
Kucera, Bp. Daniel, 376, 378, 382, 406, 419
Kuchmiak, Bp. Michael, 407, 418
Kudrick, Bp. John, 348, 380, 407
Ku Klux Klan, 356
Kulturkampf, 226, 241, 299, 310, 330
Kupfer, Bp. William, 407, 419
Kurtz, Abp. Joseph, 378, 379,
Kurtz, Bp. Robert, 407, 421, 430
Kuwait, 13, 18, 264-267, 269, 317, 345-347
Kuzma, Bp. George, 383, 407, 419
Kyrgyzstan, 265, 267, 269, 317

L

La Civiltà Cattolica, 292
La Mennais Brothers, 460
Laborem Exercens, 114-117, 234, 251
Ladaria Ferrer, Abp. Luis, 256, 260, 261
Laetare Sunday, 180
Laghi, Card. Pio, 267, 270, 284, 294, 295
Lagonegro, Bp. Dominick, 379, 407, 424
Laicization, 76, 77, 146
Laity, 27, 28, 43, 48, 60, 69, 90, 127, 130, 135, 167, 175, 230, 231, 233, 258, 270, 276, 278, 279, 281-283, 288, 290-292, 318, 340, 342, 363, 421, 426, 432, 446, 490, 491, 493, 495, 496, 502-504, 563, 595, 605, 608
Laity Pontifical Council for the, 259
Lajolo, Card. Giovanni, 18, 60, 76, 261, 284, 294, 295
Lamb of God, 129, 179, 183, 480
Lambaesis, 284, 399
Lambert, Bp. Francis, 407, 419
Lambeth Conference, 46, 47, 49, 583, 602
Lamentations, 96, 99, 100
Languages of the Church, 146
Lanza Di Montezemolo, Card. Andrea Cordero, 280, 294-296
LaSalette Missionaries, 463, 467
Last Supper, 12, 154, 172, 178, 349, 350

Lateran Basilica, 290
Lateran, Councils of, 222, 223, 224, 229
Lateran University, 15, 42, 61, 243, 272, 279, 281-283, 286, 290, 291, 293, 396, 406, 549, 550
Latin American Bishops, 16, 28, 38, 60, 249, 306, 339; see also CELAM
Latin Liturgy, 176, 222, 502, 506
Latin Patriarchate of Jerusalem, 316, 574
Latino, Bp. Joseph, 378, 407, 425
Latria, 129, 147, 155
Latvia, 234, 265, 266, 269, 288, 296, 317, 337, 591
Law, Cardinal Bernard, 284, 294-296, 375, 382, 407
Lay Ministry, 362, 455, 496, 503
Lay Mission Helpers Association, 496
Lay Organizations, 361, 495
Lazarists, 211, 466
Lazarus, 209, 350
Lebanon, 13, 31, 35, 40, 77, 217, 234-236, 256, 264, 266, 269, 276, 278, 282, 289, 291, 292, 296, 317, 330, 345, 346, 348, 367, 373, 380, 386, 389, 393, 395, 397, 398, 400, 401, 412, 413, 415, 418, 419, 429, 432, 438, 440, 459, 464, 468, 538, 545, 547, 548, 554, 589, 591, 595
Lectern, 181
Lectionary, 52, 73, 184, 185, 425, 500
Lector, 196, 495
Legal Status of Catholic Education, 532
Legion of Mary, 342, 496
Legionaries of Christ, 53, 401, 429, 463, 467, 507, 550
Lehmann, Card. Karl, 284, 294, 295, 337
Leibrecht, Bp. John, 382, 407, 419
Lennon, Bp. Richard, 376, 407
Lent, 24, 25, 32, 84, 112, 129, 131, 139, 153, 161-164, 166, 171, 172, 180, 191, 194, 195, 349, 350, 431, 609
Leo I, Pope, 108, 229, 237, 251, 282, 285
Leo II, Pope, 229, 237
Leo III, Pope, 221, 238
Leo IV, Pope, 238
Leo V, Pope, 221, 238
Leo VI, Pope, 238
Leo VII, Pope, 238
Leo VIII, Pope, 238
Leo X, Pope, 229, 239, 597
Leo XI, Pope, 240
Leo XII, Pope, 240, 247, 257
Leo XIII, Pope, 14, 29, 35, 104, 114, 116, 117, 123, 130, 133, 136, 147, 149, 172, 212, 226-228, 232, 234, 240-242, 245, 248, 250-252, 260-263, 271, 356, 361, 546, 573, 574
Lepanto, Battle of, 173, 210, 225, 243
Lesotho, 52, 214, 234, 266, 269, 279, 318, 337, 339, 404
Lessard, Bp. Raymond, 382, 407, 419
Levada, Card. William, 26, 39, 46, 73, 74, 256, 260, 261, 285, 294-296, 381, 382, 407, 418
Leviticus, 96, 98, 606
LeVoir, Bp. John, 379, 407
Libasci, Bp. Peter, 381, 407
Liberation Theology, 59, 76, 147, 235, 302, 321, 323, 450
Liberia, 266, 269, 318, 337-339, 495
Libreria Editrice Vaticana, 45, 263, 612
Libya, 236, 266, 269, 318

Liechtenstein, 234, 266, 267, 269, 318
Life, Sisters of, 480
Limbo, 147
Linceorum Academia, 271
Lindalva Justo de Oliveira, 216, 255
Linus, 236, 280
Lipscomb, Abp. Oscar, 379, 407, 419, 605
Lisbon, 8, 107, 266, 274, 281, 288, 324, 338, 341, 474, 547
Listecki, Bp. Jerome, 378, 407, 421
Litany of Saints, 141, 172
Literary Criticism, 103-104
Literary Forms, 94-95, 103
Lithuania, 205, 208, 214, 226, 234, 265, 266, 269, 278, 296, 318, 325, 337, 395, 479, 502, 549
Lithuanian Groups, 502
Little Brothers of St. Francis, 463
Little Flower Society, 502
Little Franciscans of Mary, 476
Liturgiam Authenticam, 12, 183
Liturgical Celebrations, 19, 75, 130, 175, 186, 232, 260
Liturgical Colors and Vestments, 180
Liturgical Developments, 182-188
Liturgical Year, 161-163; see also Calendar
Logos, 12, 147
Lohmuller, Bp. Martin, 407, 419
Lopez Ortega, Card. Francisco Robles, 61, 289, 294-296
López Rodríguez, Card. Nicolás de Jesús, 285, 294, 295, 296
Lopez Trujillo, Card. Alfonso, 53
Loretto Sisters, 479
Lori, Bp. William, 80, 375, 407, 421
Lorscheider, Card. Aloisio O.F.M., 53
Losten, Bp. Basil, 383, 407, 419
Lotocky, Bp. Hilarius O.S.B.M., 381, 407, 419
Louis de Montfort, 209
Louise de Marillac, 209, 213, 251
Louisiana, 353, 354, 358-360, 364-366, 368, 369, 372, 374, 390, 391, 412, 421, 422, 425, 433, 436, 439, 470, 473, 478, 492, 513, 520, 521, 523, 527, 536, 544, 545
Lourdes, 17, 20, 27, 36, 42, 49, 121, 123, 156, 165, 205, 211, 226, 232, 234, 250, 262, 280, 342, 389, 391-393, 399, 446, 477, 500, 514, 527, 540, 575
Lourdusamy, Card. D. Simon, 285, 294-296
Louvain, 51, 149, 281, 342, 355, 396-398, 401, 410, 413, 546, 567
Loverde, Bp. Paul, 374, 380, 408
Lozano Barragan, Card. Javier, 259, 261, 285, 294-296, 451
Lubich, Chiara, 53
Lucas, Bp. George, 382, 407
Lucia, Sr., of Fátima, 25, 35, 123-124
Lucius I, Pope, 237
Lucius II, Pope, 238
Lucius III, Pope, 223, 238
Lugo, Fernando, 76-77, 323
Luigi Scrosoppi, 252, 253
Luigi Versiglia, 253
Luke, 71, 74, 95, 96, 101, 102, 105
Lumen Gentium, 72, 89-93, 119, 135, 151, 155, 178, 189, 195-197, 228, 229, 246, 351, 578, 613
Lumen Vitae Centre, 342
Luong, Bp. Dominic, 380, 408

Luther, Martin, 104, 224, 235, 310, 525, 596, 597, 599
Lutheran Church, 22, 309, 330, 581, 582, 599, 600
Lutheran World Federation, 580, 583, 585, 589, 590, 599, 603, 604
Lutheran-Catholic Joint Declaration, 603-604
Luxembourg, 29, 214, 234, 242, 264, 266, 269, 318
Lynch, Bp. Robert, 382, 407-408
Lyne, Bp. Timothy, 408, 419

M

Macaluso, Bp. Christie, 377, 408
Macau, 303, 339
Maccabees, 96-99, 101, 138, 606
Macharski, Card. Franciszek, 285, 294-296
Maciel Degollado, Father Marcial, 53
Madagascar, 234, 265, 266, 269, 278, 281, 289-291, 296, 319, 320, 325, 337, 339, 396, 418, 430, 548
Madden, Denis J., 375, 409
Madeleine Sophie Barat, 209
Madera, Bp. Joseph, 377, 409, 419, 424, 490
Magi, 120, 147, 172
Maginnis, Bp. Robert, 380, 409
Magisterium, 81, 87, 92, 93, 112-115, 117, 126, 127, 133, 148, 197, 203, 246, 272, 494, 501, 534, 568
Maguire, Bp. Joseph, 382, 409, 419
Mahony, Card. Roger, 76, 260, 285, 294-296, 378, 383, 409
Maida, Card. Adam, 40, 261, 285, 294-296, 376, 377, 409
Maine, 352, 358, 373, 390, 421, 425, 433, 436, 439, 478, 506, 514, 524, 527, 536
Majella Agnelo, Card. Geraldo, 285, 294-296
Major Protestant Churches in the United States, 578, 598-601
Malabar Rite, 348, 584
Malachi, 96, 101
Malankara Orthodox Church, 345
Malawi, 234, 266, 267, 269, 319, 337, 339
Malaysia, 27, 41, 264, 266, 267, 286, 302, 319, 337
Maldives, 319
Mali, 234, 266, 269, 319, 337, 339, 613
Malloy, Msgr. David, 421
Malone, Bp. Richard, 380, 409
Malooly, Bp. W. Francis, 383, 409
Malta, 51, 214, 232, 234, 266, 269, 284, 319, 337, 548, 550, 574
Malta Knights of, 51, 574
Mamberti, Abp. Dominique, 5, 10, 11, 13, 15, 17-19, 22, 25, 29, 45, 46, 256, 261
Mandatum, 533-534
Manichaeism, 107, 108, 219, 220, 223
Manning, Bp. Elias, 409, 430
Manning, Bp. Thomas, 409, 419
Manning, Timothy Cardinal, 296, 377, 378
Mansell, Abp. Henry, 375, 377, 409
Mansour, Bp. Gregory, 381, 409
Mantellate Sisters, 481
Mantellate Sisters Servants of Mary, 481
Manz, Bp. John, 375, 409
Mar Dinkha IV, 583-585

Mar Ignatius, Jacob III, 584
Marcellin, Joseph Benoit Champagnat, 252
Marcellus I, Pope, 237
Marcellus II, Pope, 238, 239, 263
Marchetto, Abp. Agostino, 259, 261
Marchisano, Card. Francesco, 261, 262, 285, 294-296
Marcionism, 218, 610
Marconi, Bp. Dominic, 262, 409, 419
Margaret Clitherow, 209
Margaret Flesch, 217, 255
Margaret Mary Alacoque, 154, 169, 174, 205, 209, 251
Margaret of Cortona, 209, 212, 213
Margaret of Hungary, 209, 252
Margaret of Scotland, 170, 208, 209, 506
Margéot, Card. Jean, 286, 294-296
Marguerite Bourgeoys, 252, 441, 483
María De Los Ángeles Ginard Martí, 255
Maria Giuseppina di Gesù Crocifisso, 217, 255
Maria Goretti, 168, 209, 212, 252
Maria Luisa Merkert, 215, 255
María Magdalena de la Encarnación, 217
Maria of the Passion, 255
Maria Teresa of Saint Joseph, 255
Marian Movement of Priests, 502
Marian Shrine, 6, 9, 38, 147, 205, 392
Marian Year, 250
Mariana Islands, 311
Mariana Paredes of Jesus, 209, 252
Marianist Fathers, 464
Marianist Sisters, 481
Marianists, 429, 467, 539, 540, 543
Marianites of Holy Cross, 215, 481, 542
Marianne Cope, 209, 255
Mariannhill Mission Society, 559
Mariannhill Missionaries, 467
Marie Leonie Paradis, 253
Marie-Céline de la Présentation, 215, 255
Marie-Rose Durocher, 163, 209
Marini, Msgr. Guido, 260
Marini, Abp. Piero, 260, 294, 409
Marino, Bp. Joseph, 264, 409
Marinus I, Pope, 238
Marinus II, Pope, 238, 239
Mariological Society of America, 51, 502
Mariology, 159
Marist Brothers, 464, 467
Marist Fathers, 291, 464, 493
Marist Missionary Sisters, 429
Marist Sisters, 481
Mark, 95, 96, 101, 102, 105, 117
Maronites, 273, 274, 291, 317, 330, 345-348, 373, 398, 415, 418, 432, 438, 440, 442, 443, 447, 451, 453, 538, 563
Marriage Doctrine, 197, 199
Marriage Encounter, 502, 559
Marshall Islands, 266, 269, 319, 395, 438, 538
Martha Wiecka, 217, 255
Martin de Porres, 170, 212, 213, 252, 461, 493, 506, 558
Martin I, Pope, 209, 237, 239
Martin II, Pope, See Marinus I
Martin III, Pope, See Marinus II
Martin IV, Pope, 223, 239
Martin V, Pope, 229, 239, 241
Martin of Tours, 132, 170, 209, 211, 213
Martínez Sistach, Card. Lluís, 60, 286, 294, 295

Martinez Somalo, Card. Eduardo, 124, 261, 286, 294-296
Martini, Card. Carlo Maria, 286, 294-296
Martinique, 325
Martino, Bp. Joseph, 382, 409
Martino, Card. Renato, 7, 11, 259, 261, 268, 286, 294, 295, 452
Martyr, 7, 50, 71, 106, 132, 148, 165, 167, 168, 170, 205-211, 214-216, 218, 237, 290, 348, 352, 373, 432, 438, 440, 477, 487, 488, 538
Martyrdom, 21, 49, 65, 97, 106, 113, 168, 169, 190, 207, 215, 216, 218, 251, 274, 299, 306, 314, 329, 446, 585, 587
Martyrology, 133, 148
Martyrs of the Spanish Civil War, 216
Mary Blessed Virgin, 6, 7, 17, 25, 26, 31, 37, 39, 47, 49, 87, 88, 93, 109, 119-125, 141, 143, 144, 148, 154-156, 159, 165, 166, 168-171, 173, 180, 181, 188, 205, 214, 217, 226, 227, 244, 250, 287, 350, 360, 361, 363, 388-392, 449, 462, 464, 467, 472, 476, 479, 482, 484, 489, 493, 501, 584, 601
   Apparitions of, 123-125, 141, 173
   Redemptoris Mater, 121-123
   Role of Mary, 119-121
Mary Faustina Kowalska, 252
Mary Help of Christians, 70, 208, 209, 390, 392, 393, 481, 492
Mary Magdalen Sophie Barat, 251
Mary Magdalene, 167, 168, 209, 214, 217, 255
Mary Reparatrix, 482, 488
Maryheart Crusaders, 503
Maryknoll, 227, 356, 361, 394, 407, 409, 417, 429, 430, 458, 464, 482, 489, 559, 560, 566, 575, 576
Maryknoll Fathers, 429, 458
Maryknoll Mission Sisters, 429
Maryknoll Priests, 429
Maryknoll Sisters, 482
Maryland, 84, 271, 272, 352-356, 358-360, 363, 365, 366, 371-374, 390, 391, 409, 410, 421, 422, 433, 436, 439, 463, 470, 479, 514, 521-523, 527, 536, 541, 545
Mass, 175-177, 178-182,191-194
Mass of Chrism, 172, 186
Mass of Christian Burial, 154, 179
Mass Vestments, 179
Massachusetts, 79, 267, 271, 352, 354, 355, 359, 373, 390, 392, 408, 421, 422, 433, 436, 439, 470, 472, 514, 521-523, 527, 536, 545
Matano, Bp. Salvatore R., 375, 409
Matrimonia Mixta, 201
Matthew, 95, 96, 101, 102, 105, 106
Matthiesen, Bp. Leroy, 374, 409, 419
Mauretaina, 288, 291, 409
Mauritania, 52, 266, 319, 320, 338, 339
Maximilian Kolbe, 49, 209, 212, 252, 391
Mayer, Card. Paul, 286, 294-296
McCain, Sen. John, 79-80
McCarrick, Card. Theodore, 285, 294-296, 379, 383, 408, 419
McCarthy, Bp. James, 379, 380, 408, 419
McCarthy, Bp. John, 375, 408, 419
McCormack, Bp. John, 379, 408
McCormack, Bp. William, 408, 419
McDonald, Bp. Andrew J., 378, 408, 419
McDonnell, Bp. Charles, 408, 419

McDonnell, Bp. Timothy, 382, 408
McDowell, Bp. John, 408, 419
McFadden, Bp. Joseph, 380, 408
McFarland, Bp. Norman, 380, 381, 408, 419
McGarry, Bp. Urban, 408, 419
McGrath, Bp. Patrick, 382, 408
McKinney, Bp. Joseph, 408, 419
McLaughlin, Bp. Bernard, 408, 419
McManus, Bp. Robert, 377, 383, 408
McNabb, Bp. John, 409, 419
McNaughton, Bp. William, 409, 419
McRaith, Bp. John, 380, 409
Mediator Dei, 182, 250
Mediatrix, 120
Medical Mission Sisters, 429, 482, 563
Medical Missionaries of Mary, 429, 482
Medical Sisters of St. Joseph, 482
Medina Estévez, Card. Jorge, 261, 286, 294-296
Meditations, 31, 108, 157, 576
Medjugorje, 125, 559
Meisner, Card. Joachim, 286, 294, 295
Mejía, Card. Jorge María, 286, 295, 296, 612
Melczek, Bp. Dale, 377, 409
Melkites, 249, 273, 274, 307, 330, 345, 346, 348, 373, 401, 412, 413, 418, 432, 438, 440, 442, 443, 449, 451, 453, 538
Membership of Religious Institutes of Men, 467-468
Membership of Religious Institutes of Women, 487-489
Men of the Sacred Heart, 503
Men Religious, 458-467
Men Religious (Statistics), 467-468
Men Religious Institutes U.S., 458-467
Menaion, 349
Mendicants, 142, 148
Mengeling, Bp. Carl, 378, 410, 419
Menologion, 349
Mentally Retarded, 522-524
Mercedarian Sisters, 482
Mercedarians, 210, 464, 467, 476, 487, 488
Merit, 71, 145, 148, 573, 597, 603
Messiah, 71, 89, 100-102, 106, 120, 132, 135, 149, 608
Mestice, Bp. Anthony, 410, 419
Metanoia, 148
Methodist Church, 581, 582, 589, 598, 600, 601
Methodist-Catholic International Commission, 590
Mexico, 10, 15, 16, 21, 28, 29, 32, 38, 51, 52, 54, 60, 61, 123, 151, 173, 209, 210, 214, 227, 234, 236, 243, 250, 261, 266, 269, 272, 284, 285, 289, 290, 296, 307, 311, 320, 337, 338, 345-347, 352, 353, 355, 358, 363-365, 372, 374, 390, 392, 401-403, 409, 412, 413, 417, 418, 421, 425, 426, 429, 430, 434, 437, 440, 446, 449-453, 456, 457, 462, 463, 470, 471, 474, 476, 478, 479, 482, 483, 485, 486, 489, 497, 505, 507, 510, 528, 537, 548, 550
Micah, 64, 96, 101
Michael (Feasts), 169, 173
Michaels, Bp. James, 410, 419
Michelangelo, 18, 236, 240
Michigan, 134, 355, 359, 363-365, 373, 384, 387, 390, 392, 394, 406, 409,

413, 414, 417, 421, 422, 425, 433, 436, 439, 464, 470, 482, 483, 493, 497, 501-505, 509, 514, 515, 521, 523, 527, 536, 539, 541, 544, 545, 547, 549, 554, 556, 557, 559, 561, 563-565, 574, 575
Micronesia, 266, 269, 320, 322, 395, 429
Midnight Mass, 19, 20, 60, 170
Midrash, 606
Migliore Abp. Celestino, 15, 268
Migrant and Itinerant Peoples, Pontifical Council, 259
Migration, 13, 302, 341, 355, 421, 498, 504, 559
Miguel Febres Cordero, 209, 252
Miguel Pro, 209, 253
Military Services Archdiocese, 373, 400, 409, 411, 413, 419
Militia Immaculate, 503
Mill Hill Missionaries, 464
Miller, Abp. Michael, 409
Milone, Bp. Anthony, 377, 410, 419
Minder, Bp. John, 410, 419
Minim Daughters of Mary Immaculate, 482
Minim Fathers, 464, 467
Minim Friars, 207
Minnesota, 48, 356, 365, 368, 374, 390, 392, 421, 422, 425, 433, 436, 439, 470, 497, 514, 515, 521, 523, 528, 536, 543, 545
Miracle, 44, 132, 156, 450
Miraculous Medal, 47, 123, 205, 392, 500, 559
Misericordia Dei, 195, 235
Misericordia Sisters, 482
Missal, 13, 21, 25, 35, 48, 50, 73, 84, 180, 183, 184, 187, 192, 559, 575, 576
Missale Romanum, 48, 178, 183, 184
Mission Helpers, 482, 559
Mission Workers, 431
Missionaries of Africa, 302, 319, 332, 467, 550, 564
Missionaries to the Americas, 3, 209, 363, 364
Missionary Association of Catholic Women, 503
Missionary Daughters, 482
Missionary Oblates of Mary Immaculate, 391, 392, 555, 564, 565
Missionary Sisters of Our Lady, 468, 475, 482
Missionary Sisters of St. Benedict, 516
Missionary Sisters of Verona, 472
Missionary Society of St. Paul, 44, 465
Mississippi, 352-355, 358, 364, 365, 368, 374, 390, 421, 425, 433, 436, 439, 470, 472, 493, 515, 536, 554
Missouri, 271, 355, 359, 363, 367, 368, 374, 390, 392, 399, 421, 422, 425, 434, 436, 439, 463, 470, 515, 520, 521, 523, 528, 536, 545, 581
Mit Brennender Sorge, 227, 243, 250
Mitre, 180
Mixed Marriages, 35, 200, 201, 247, 335, 589, 605
Modernism, 148, 149, 158, 227, 242, 356
Moeddel, Bp. Carl, 410, 419
Monarchianism, 219
Monasticism, 107, 168, 205, 209, 220, 221, 307, 330, 597, 616
Mongolia, 17, 27, 265, 266, 269, 320,

339

Monica, 168, 169, 209, 211, 212, 215, 422, 485, 506, 520, 522, 576

Monophysitism, 108, 221

Monotheism, 149

Monothelitism, 221

Monstrance,, 154, 181, 214, 215

Montalvo Abp. Gabriel, 267, 270

Montana, 356, 363, 365, 374, 398, 421, 422, 425, 434, 436, 439, 528, 536, 554

Monterisi, Abp. Francesco, 257, 261, 277

Montfort Missionaries, 391, 392, 464, 467, 560

Montrose, Bp. Donald, 54

Moraczewski, Father Albert, 54

Moral Teachings, 3, 85, 112-113

Moral Teachings of the Church, 85, 112-113

Moravian Brethren, 306

Morin, Bp. Roger, 379, 410

Morlino, Bp. Robert, 377, 379, 410

Morneau, Bp. Robert, 377, 410

Morocco, 234, 266, 269, 277, 278, 320, 613

Mosaic Covenant, 606

Mosaic Law, 98, 102, 173, 218

Moscow Patriarchate, 16, 17, 591, 592, 595, 596

Moses, 93, 95-98, 100, 111, 606-608, 613

Moskal, Bp. Robert, 381, 410

Mother of God, 19, 21, 23, 34, 62, 64, 119-122, 139, 143, 161, 162, 165, 173, 174, 185, 194, 208, 217, 255, 278, 349, 389, 465, 468, 469, 473, 476, 482, 489, 588, 594, 601

Mother of God Sisters of, 482

Motu Proprio, 47, 89, 126, 149, 161, 182, 187, 195, 201, 232, 242, 256, 258, 259, 261, 272, 275, 277, 491, 495; See also under individual titles

Moussa I Daoud, Card. Ignace, 261, 286, 294-296

Movimiento Familiar Cristiano, 425

Mozambique, 13, 234, 266, 269, 290, 296, 319, 320, 331, 338, 339

Mozarabic, 177

Mozcygemba, Leopold, 364

Moynihan, Bp. James, 383, 410

Muench, Bp. Robert W., 375, 376, 410

Mulieris Dignitatem, 235

Mulvee, Bp. Robert, 381, 383, 410, 419

Mundo, Bp. Miguel, 410

Munificentissimus Deus, 244

Muratorian Fragment, 96

Murphy, Bp. William, 381, 410

Murphy-O'Connor, Card. Cormac, 20, 286, 294-296, 337

Murry, Bp. George, 383, 410, 421, 422, 428

Music, 5, 9, 12, 46, 50, 52, 84, 175, 176, 182, 186, 188, 242, 244, 250, 322, 349, 400, 426, 502, 503, 541, 548, 550, 560, 567, 568, 572, 575

Muslims, See Islam

Myanmar, 37, 41, 169, 264, 266, 267, 302, 320, 321, 336, 338

Myers, Abp. John, 48, 379, 380, 410

Mystagogy, 149

Mysterium Fidei, 159, 251

Mystery of the Church, 89, 120, 122, 193, 276, 584, 589, 607

Mystic, 107, 205, 207, 210, 249, 526,

558, 560, 561, 566

Mystical Body of Christ, 73, 90, 102, 160, 211, 244, 250, 343

Mystici Corporis Christi, 182, 250

N

Nagy, Card. Stanislas, 287, 294-296

Namibia, 18, 266, 267, 269, 321, 338, 339, 404, 418

Napier, Card. Wilfrid O.F.M., 287, 294-296, 336

Nathan, 98, 100

Nathaniel, 105

National Assembly of Religious Women, 503

National Assembly of Women Religious, 503

National Association for Lay Ministry, 503

National Association of Catholic Family Life, 503

National Association of Catholic Home Educators, 503

National Association of Church Personnel Administrators, 503

National Association of Diaconate Directors, 197, 503

National Association of Diocesan Ecumenical Officers, 503, 616

National Association of Pastoral Musicians, 503, 560

National Association of Priest Pilots, 503

National Catholic AIDS Network, 503

National Catholic Band Association, 503

National Catholic Cemetery, 556

National Catholic Forensic League, 497

National Catholic Rural Life Conference, 362, 431

National Catholic Welfare Conference, 361, 423

National Catholic Welfare Council, 356, 420, 423

National Christ Child Society, 504

National Conference of Catholic Bishops, See USCCB

National Council for Catholic Evangelization, 504

National Council of Catholic Women, 504, 557

National Federation for Catholic Youth Ministry, 497

National Federation of Priests' Councils, 504, 564

National Life Center, 504

National News, 78-80

National Pastoral Life Center, 504, 557

Native American Catholics in the United States, 429

Nativity, 18, 24, 62, 137, 161, 162, 167, 169, 170, 278, 350, 368, 388, 442, 492

Natural Family Planning, 501

Natural Law, 111, 140, 147, 149, 225, 245, 593

Naumann, Bp. Joseph, 40, 80, 378, 410

Navarrete, Card. Urbano, 61, 287, 294-296

Nazareth, 9, 15, 24, 69, 85, 119, 123, 145, 147, 232, 359, 386, 397, 406, 471, 478, 480, 482, 487, 489, 511, 513, 516, 517, 520, 521, 526, 540, 543, 554, 559, 560

Nebraska, 374, 392, 418, 421, 422, 425,

434, 436, 440, 515, 521, 523, 528, 536, 545, 555, 556

Necromancy, 139, 149

Nehemiah, 96, 98, 99, 101, 606

Neo-Scholasticism, 149, 155, 159

Nepal, 46, 265, 266, 269, 279, 321, 339

Nerinckx, Charles, 364

Nerses Bedros XIX Tarmouni, 274, 345, 347

Nestorian Churches, 304

Nestorianism, 220, 304, 314

Netherlands, 232, 234, 266, 269, 278, 279, 291, 296, 321, 338, 341, 342, 404, 464, 470-472, 496, 547

NETWORK, 504

Nevada, 364, 372, 374, 421, 422, 425, 427, 434, 436, 440, 470, 537, 554

Nevins, Bp. John, 383, 410, 419

New American Bible, 97, 500

New Evangelization, 8, 425, 568

New Hampshire, 354, 373, 392, 421, 434, 436, 440, 470, 515, 528, 537, 564

New Jersey, 270, 353, 354, 363, 365-368, 374, 389, 390, 392, 400, 421, 422, 426, 434, 437, 440, 470, 509, 510, 515, 521, 523, 524, 528, 537, 545, 569, 615

New Mexico, 352, 353, 358, 364, 372, 374, 390, 392, 421, 425, 426, 434, 437, 440, 449, 470, 528, 537

New Testament, 59, 61, 86, 90, 94-97, 99, 101-104, 108, 130, 131, 134, 137, 153, 155, 176, 178, 195, 218, 349, 500, 597, 607, 608, 610, 613, 614

New Zealand, 13, 15, 72, 214, 234, 265-267, 269, 293, 294, 296, 321, 338, 339, 395

Newman, Bp. William, 410, 419

Newman John Henry, 50, 113, 150, 226

Newsletters, 561-564, 575

Newspapers, 551-556, 575

Nicaea, Councils of, 107, 109, 139, 219-221, 273, 311

Nicaragua, 234, 266, 267, 269, 278, 284, 287, 296, 321, 338, 414, 418, 430

Nicene Creed, 107, 109, 183, 191, 219, 220, 349

Nicholas I, Pope, 238

Nicholas II, Pope, 238, 297

Nicholas III, Pope, 223, 239

Nicholas IV, Pope, 239

Nicholas V, Pope, 239, 240, 270, 419, 493

Nicholas of Flüe, 209, 252

Nicholas of Myra, 209, 211-214, 350

Nicholas of Tolentino, 210, 212, 213, 459

Nicholson, Amb. James, 270

Nickless, Bp. R. Walker, 382, 411

Nicora, Card. Attilio, 259, 261, 287, 294, 295

Niederauer, Abp. George, 382, 411, 421

Niedergeses, Bp. James, 54

Nienstedt, Bp. John, 379, 381, 411

Niger, 264, 266, 269, 322, 336, 338, 339

Nigeria, 145, 234, 236, 261, 266, 269, 272, 278, 287, 296, 322, 338, 339, 409, 429, 473, 548

Night Prayer, 136, 138, 149, 176

Nihil Obstat, 134, 149

Njue, Card. John, 61, 287, 294-296, 337

Noah, 137, 613

Nobel Peace Prize, 307

Noè, Card. Virgilio, 261, 287, 294-296

Nomination of Bishops, 264, 274
Non Abbiamo Bisogno, 227, 243, 250
Non Expedit, 149
Non-Believers Council for Dialogue, 259, 288, 289
Noonan, Bp. John G., 379, 411
Norbertine Fathers, 393, 543
Norms of Ecumenism, 580
Norms of Judgment, 198
North American College, 52, 281, 282, 355, 395-407, 409-412, 414-418, 546
North American Martyrs, 169, 251, 363, 364, 441, 446, 564
North Carolina, 371, 373, 390, 406, 421, 427, 434, 437, 440, 517, 524, 529, 537
North Dakota, 8, 372, 374, 390, 421, 422, 425, 434, 437, 440, 517, 521, 524, 529, 537, 545
North Korea, 317
Norway, 204, 214, 234, 265, 266, 269, 313, 322
Nostra Aetate, 230, 607, 609, 610, 612, 613
Novak, Bp. Alfred, 411, 419, 430
NOVALIS, 342, 566, 575
Novatianism, 106
Novena, 149
Novice, 149, 205, 278, 291
Numismatic Office, 262
Nunc Dimittis, 133, 149, 176
Nuncios and Delegates, 263-268

O

O Salutaris Hostia, 150
O'Brien Abp. Edwin, 8, 375, 378, 382, 383, 411
O'Brien Bp. Thomas, 380, 411, 419
O'Brien, Card. Keith, 43, 287, 294, 295, 338, 380
O'Connell, Bp. Anthony, 380, 419
O'Donnell, Bp. Edward, 378, 411
O'Malley, Card. Sean, 40, 78, 287, 295, 296, 375, 377, 380, 411
O'Neill, Bp. Arthur, 381, 411, 419
Oath, 14, 149, 151, 225, 242, 247, 308, 354, 355, 366
Oath of Succession, 225
Oath of Supremacy, 308
Obadiah, 96, 101
Obama, Sen. Barack, 79-80
Obando Bravo, Card. Miguel, 287, 294-296, 322
Obituaries, 53-54
Oblate Sisters, 355, 359, 474, 484, 485
Oblate Sisters of Providence, 355, 359
Oblates of Mary Immaculate, 283, 318, 391-393, 412, 429, 441, 467, 530, 542, 555, 564-567
Observance of Sundays, 112
Oceania, 21, 60, 67, 71, 210, 234, 276, 296, 299, 316, 328, 332, 335, 339, 347, 407, 418, 429, 430, 490
Ochoa, Bp. Armando, 376, 411, 424
Octave, 31, 150, 165, 170, 172-174
Office of Papal Charities, 261
Ohio, 196, 281, 353, 356, 359, 363, 364, 367, 368, 373, 390, 393, 396, 397, 403, 410, 414, 421, 422, 425, 432, 434, 437, 440, 463, 470, 471, 499, 504, 517, 520-522, 524, 529, 533, 537, 541, 542, 544, 545, 556, 564, 568, 599

Oils, Holy, 150
Oklahoma, 12, 51, 270, 356, 374, 380, 386, 389, 393, 395, 412, 416, 421, 425, 434, 437, 440, 460, 470, 471, 517, 529, 537, 553, 555, 599
Okogie, Card. Anthony, 76, 287, 294-296
Old Testament, 59, 85, 88, 89, 95-102, 108, 131, 132, 137, 138, 151-153, 155, 159, 172, 178, 218, 228, 286, 349, 350, 499, 559, 576, 607
Olivetans, 459, 468
Olivier, Bp. Leonard, 411, 419, 428
Olmsted, Bp. Thomas, 380, 383, 411
Oman, 322, 333
Omega, 69, 129, 150, 530
Ontology, 148, 150
Optatam Totius, 229
Opus Dei, 32, 151, 208, 280, 283, 403, 507, 550, 570
Oratorians, 225, 458, 464, 467
Oratory of St. Philip Neri, 464
Ordained Ministry, 76, 582, 583, 589, 613
Order of Christian Funerals, 188
Order of Christian Initiation of Adults, 505
Order of the Alhambra, 505
Orders of Knighthood, 573-574
Orders, Religious, 458-467, 468-486
Orders, Religious (Statistics), 467-468
Orders, Religious, Men, 458-467
Orders, Religious, Women, 468-486
Ordinary, 273, 274
Ordinatio Sacerdotalis, 197, 235
Ordination, 185, 195-196,
Ordination of Women, 37, 39, 45-47, 49, 197, 300, 308, 589
Ordo Confirmationis, 191
Ordo Consecrationis Virginum, 160
Ordo Initiationis Christianae Adultorum, 190
Ordo Paenitentiae, 194
Oregon, 79, 355, 356, 360, 365, 372, 374, 381, 393, 417, 418, 421, 422, 425, 434, 437, 440, 463, 470, 481, 517, 519, 521, 524, 529, 532, 537, 545, 559, 576
Organizations, Catholic, 494-507
Oriental Orthodox Churches, 344, 581, 593-596
Orientale Lumen, 235, 592
Orientalium Ecclesiarum, 229, 343, 351, 578, 591
Origen, 219
Ortega y Alamino, Card. Jaime Lucas, 287, 294-296
Orthodox Churches, 6, 190, 221, 222, 236, 344, 581, 583, 584, 589-596
Orthodox-Roman Catholic Consultation, 589-590
Osservatore Romano, L', 22, 35, 43, 56, 73, 75, 76, 113, 128, 260, 263, 264, 268, 374, 442, 451, 551, 554, 567, 570, 580, 592, 593, 595, 601, 603, 604, 609
Ostensorium, 181
Ostpolitik, 150, 245
Ottenweller, Bp. Albert, 383, 411, 419
Ouellet, Card. Marc, 7, 287, 294-296, 444
Our Father, 70, 87, 88, 129, 141, 151, 152, 154, 349, 587
Overseas Missions, 429, 430

P

Pactum Callixtinum, 222
Padre Pio of Pietrelcina, 31, 65, 210, 253, 254
Paganism, 150, 220
Pago Pago, 326
Pakistan, 13, 15, 27, 42, 61, 234, 266, 269, 300, 322, 338, 395, 419
Palatine Guard of Honor, 261
Palau, 253, 266, 269, 322, 395
Palazzo Apostolico Vaticano, 256, 260
Palestine, 96, 97, 105, 106, 121, 207, 217, 218, 236, 250, 256, 265, 267, 269, 280, 284, 315, 344, 505, 606
Palin, Gov. Sarah, 80
Pallium, 22, 43, 180, 231, 232, 273, 274
Pallottine Sisters, 483
Palm Sunday, 30, 161, 166, 173, 350
Panafieu, Card. Bernard, 287, 294, 295
Panama, 234, 266, 269, 289, 322, 338, 365, 507, 547
Pancras, 167, 210
Pange Lingua, 150
Paola Frassinetti, 210, 252, 474
Papacy, 38, 46, 55, 106, 107, 125, 208, 211, 220-223, 231, 236, 238, 239, 241-246, 261, 262, 324, 558, 573, 609
Papal Flag, 262
Papal Gendarmes, 261
Papal Household Prefecture, 75, 260, 274, 281, 282, 404, 418
Papal Medals, 573
Papal Primacy, 14, 34, 92, 99, 104, 106, 109, 110, 115, 126, 127, 222-226, 273, 343, 351, 578, 589, 590, 594, 597, 599, 605, 615
Papal Representatives, 263-268
Papal States, 225-227, 262, 270, 315, 573
Papal Trips, 55-58, 62-72, 232
Paprocki, Bp. Thomas J., 375, 411, 421
Papua New Guinea, 214, 234, 266, 267, 269, 323, 338, 404, 406, 413, 419, 429, 430
Paraclete, 139, 150, 465, 468
Paraclete, Servants of the, 465
Paraguay, 11, 16, 34, 76, 77, 214, 234, 252, 266, 269, 284, 323, 338, 363-365, 547
Paris Foreign Mission Society, 467
Parishes (Statistics), 335, 435-438
Parousia, 103, 150
Partial-Birth Abortion Ban Act, 369
Paschal Baylon, 210, 212
Paschal Candle, 150, 182
Paschal I, Pope, 238
Paschal II, Pope, 238, 574
Paschal III, Pope, 240
Paschal Mystery, 13, 88, 113, 154, 161, 167, 176, 186
Paschal Precept, 151
Paska, Bp. Walter, 411, 419
Paskai, Card. László, 287, 294-296
Passion of Christ, 128, 151, 157
Passion Sunday, 166, 173
Passionist Nuns, 483, 527
Passionist Sisters, 473, 483
Passionists, 40, 51, 210, 225, 400, 416, 465, 467, 529, 560
Passover, 98, 178, 606
Pastor Aeternus, 92
Pastor Bonus, 236, 255, 256, 258, 263

Pastoral Care, 7, 14, 29, 45, 49, 53, 54, 56, 85, 128, 185, 187, 201, 215, 259, 261, 277, 280, 285, 286, 289, 301, 316, 318, 331, 334, 360, 362, 395, 421, 441, 503, 590
Pastoral Ministry, 116, 131, 135, 137, 143, 202, 273, 278, 290, 292, 313, 318, 424-427, 431, 458, 468, 470-473, 475, 477, 478, 485, 504, 505, 509, 525, 569, 576, 588
Pastoral Office of Bishops, 421
Pastores Dabo Vobis, 235, 257, 276
Pataki, Bp. Andrew, 380, 411
Paten, 139, 179-181, 196, 349, 351
Pater Noster, 70, 87, 88, 129, 141, 151, 152, 154, 349, 587
Pates, Bp. Richard, 376, 411
Patriarch, 7, 8, 10, 17, 22, 26, 29, 30, 34, 36, 38, 40, 42, 60, 61, 77, 151, 204, 220-222, 235, 243-246, 248-250, 273, 274, 280, 281, 286, 288, 291, 292, 307, 314, 315, 317, 324, 330, 336, 343-348, 364, 574, 584-586, 590, 592, 594, 607, 614
Patriarchal Lateran Archbasilica, 290
Patriarchal Vatican Basilica, 285
Patriarchs, Eastern Catholic, 274, 344-345
Patriarchs, Orthodox, 10, 17, 29, 42, 590, 592
Patron Saints of Places, 213-214
Patrons and Intercessors, 211-213
Paul, 81, 82, 84, 87, 88, 93, 95, 97, 102, 103, 105, 106, 108, 111-119
Paul I, Pope, 228, 232, 233, 237, 240, 246
Paul II, Pope, 239
Paul III, Pope, 229, 239, 256
Paul IV, Pope, 130, 239, 260
Paul V, Pope, 240, 378, 382, 400, 419
Paul VI, Pope 15, 45, 57, 60, 93, 97, 114, 116, 124, 126, 136, 145, 150, 157, 159-161, 176, 178, 180-182, 184-187, 191, 192, 196, 197, 199, 201, 205, 227, 229, 231-233, 240, 245, 246, 251, 252, 255-261, 263, 272, 275-277, 295, 297, 332, 351, 357, 399, 496, 504, 530, 573, 574, 583-586, 590, 615
    Canonizations, 245, 252
    Encyclicals, 245, 251
    Life, 245-246
    Pontificate, 245-246
Paul Miki, 165, 210
Paul of Tarsus, 73
Paula Montal Fornés, 253, 254
Pauline Fathers, 393, 465
Pauline Letters, 96, 102, 610
Pauline Privilege, 201
Paulinus of Nola, 167, 210
Paulists, 52, 355, 458, 465, 467
Pax Christi, 54, 342, 493, 496, 552, 570
Pax Christi International, 342, 570
Pax Christi USA, 54, 496, 570
Peace of Augsburg, 224, 225, 310
Peace of Westphalia, 225, 310
Pearce, Bp. George, 411, 419
Pectoral Cross, 151
Pedophilia, See Sex Abuse Scandal
Pedro de San Jose Betancur, 253
Pelagianism, 108, 220, 324
Pelagius I, Pope, 237
Pelagius II, Pope, 237
Pell, Card. George, 46, 288, 294-296

Pelotte, Bp. Donald, 377, 412, 429
Peña, Bp. Raymundo, 375, 411
Penance, 189, 192-195, 200, 203
Penance, Sacrament of, 194-195
Pengo, Card. Polycarp, 288, 294-296, 339
Penitence, 151, 608
Penitential Celebrations, 194
Penitential Rite, 178, 184, 195
Pennsylvania, 54, 58, 282, 353, 354, 358, 359, 367, 368, 374, 390, 393, 399, 405, 417, 421, 422, 434, 437, 440, 470, 509, 517, 520, 521, 524, 529, 537, 545, 559, 599
Pentateuch, 96, 98, 606
Pentecost, 38, 39, 71, 74, 88, 89, 120, 134, 139, 150, 161, 162, 164, 167, 171-174, 180, 184, 218, 349, 350, 504, 564, 606
Pentecost (Feast), 606
Pentecostals, 580, 598, 601
Pentecostarion, 349
People of God, 6, 9, 38, 72, 89-91, 94, 121, 126, 127, 131, 135, 136, 151, 169, 190, 195, 196, 245, 274-276, 423, 494, 555, 589, 607, 608
Pepe, Bp. Joseph, 378, 412
Percentage of Catholics in Total Population, 433-434
Percentage of Catholics in World Population, 335
Perfectae Caritatis, 229
Permanent Deacons, 196-197, 298, 427, 432, 492
Permanent Deacon, U.S. Statistics, 197, 432, 435-436
Permanent Deacons, World, 335
Permanent Observer, 15, 19, 267, 268, 279, 280, 286
Perpetual Eucharistic Adoration, 188, 391
Perry, Bp. Joseph, 376, 411
Persecution of Christians, 15, 106, 218
Persian Empire, 130, 346
Personal Envoys, 271
Personal Prelature, 32, 151, 283, 507, 550
Peru, 24, 156, 214, 234, 248, 249, 266, 269, 280, 282, 288, 289, 291, 296, 307, 323, 338, 364, 365, 397, 399, 402, 409, 416, 419, 429, 430, 459, 547, 548, 568
Pesach (Passover), 606
Peter, 88, 90-93, 96, 97, 103, 105, 106, 108, 113, 114
Peter, Primacy of, 14, 34, 92, 99, 104, 106, 109, 110, 115, 126, 127, 222-226, 273, 343, 351, 578, 589, 590, 594, 597, 599, 605, 615
Peter Canisius, 108, 170, 243, 249, 251, 310
Peter Celestine, 211
Peter Chanel, 71, 166, 210, 252
Peter Chrysologus, 108, 168
Peter Claver, 163, 169, 212, 213, 251, 427, 428, 483, 502
Peter Damian, 108, 165
Peter Donders, 253
Peter Julian Eymard, 210, 252
Peter Lombard, 149, 223
Peter Nolasco, 210, 464, 493
Peter of Alcantara, 210, 213
Peter of Ghent, 365
Peter of Narbonne, 210, 252
Peter of Tarentaise, 239

Petrarch, 223
Petrine Privilege, 201, 256
Pevec, Bp. A. Edward, 412, 419
Pfeifer, Bp. Michael, 382, 412
Pham Dinh Tung, Card. Paul, 288, 296
Pham Minh Mân Card. JeanBaptiste, 288, 294-296
Pharisees, 111, 151, 155
Phelonion, 351
Phi Delta Kappa, 533
Phi Kappa Theta, 498
Philangeli, 505
Philemon, 96, 102, 103
Philip, 105, 106
Philip Benizi, 210
Philip Neri, 167, 210, 215, 287, 458, 464
Philippians, 96, 102
Philippines, 5, 13, 15, 27, 32, 33, 214, 234, 244, 266, 269, 278, 279, 290, 293, 296, 320, 323, 324, 338, 394, 400, 409, 412, 418, 429, 497, 507, 547, 567
Philosophy, 5, 41, 52-54, 59, 63, 107, 108, 128, 130, 140, 147-149, 152, 153, 155, 158, 159, 216, 218, 226, 233, 242, 248, 271, 272, 278, 280, 281, 283, 285, 287, 289, 291-293, 370, 395, 507, 523, 547-549, 559, 560, 615; See also Scholasticism
Photian Schism, 221
Physically Challenged, 524
Piacenza, Abp. Mauro, 257, 261
Piarists, 208, 465, 467
Picpus Fathers, 466
Pierce, Franklin, 371
Pilarczyk, Abp. Daniel, 376, 412, 420, 593
Pilgrimages, 13, 27, 73, 187, 246, 613
Pilgrims, 5, 6, 9, 13, 15, 17, 18, 27, 38, 39, 44, 46, 49, 50, 62, 64, 67, 72, 125, 136, 157, 213, 216, 352, 446, 586
Pilla, Bp. Anthony, 137, 184, 376, 412
PIME Missionaries, 560
Pimenta, Card. Ignatius, 288, 294-296
Pio, Padre, 31, 65, 210, 253, 254
Pious Schools, 208, 465, 483, 488
Pious Union of Prayer, 505
Piovanelli, Card. Silvano, 288, 294-296
Pius I, Pope, 237
Pius II, Pope, 239
Pius III, Pope, 239
Pius IV, Pope, 109, 205, 229, 239, 256, 257, 263, 271
Pius VI, Pope, 225, 240, 247, 354
Pius VII, Pope, 173, 216, 217, 226, 240, 247, 354, 463
Pius VIII, Pope, 240, 247
Pius X, St., Pope, 47, 123, 126, 147, 148, 155, 158, 168, 182, 192, 216, 227, 240, 242, 249, 251, 252, 256-258, 263, 285, 356, 361, 398, 406, 407, 446, 465, 492, 528, 545, 546, 549, 573, 574
    Canonizations, 242, 251
    Encyclicals, 242, 249
    Life, 242
    Pontificate, 242
Pius XI, Pope, 14, 35, 114, 116, 136, 171, 174, 212, 213, 227, 240, 243, 245, 249, 251, 256-262, 271, 285, 351, 450
    Canonizations, 243, 251-252
    Encyclicals, 243, 249-250
    Life, 243
    Pontificate, 243

Pius XII, Pope, 42, 81, 97, 104, 114, 123, 136, 160, 171-173, 182, 201, 227, 232, 233, 240, 243, 245, 246, 250, 252, 257, 259-261, 263, 271, 281, 304, 306, 351, 357, 491, 500, 573, 574, 608
Canonizations, 244, 252
Encyclicals, 244, 250
Life, 243-244
Pontificate, 243-244
PLO, 232, 236
Poggi, Card. Luigi, 288, 294-296
Poland, 6, 10, 11, 17, 32, 39, 53, 60, 116, 204, 205, 208, 214-216, 222, 226, 232-236, 240, 243, 244, 246-250, 261, 266, 269, 272, 281-288, 290, 295, 324, 338, 342, 346, 347, 358, 460, 465, 472, 474, 479, 481, 485, 499, 507, 547-549, 591, 594
Poletto, Card. Severino, 288, 294, 295
Policarpo, Card. José, 8, 274, 288, 294-296
Polish National Catholic Church, 361, 581, 604, 605
Polish National Catholic-Roman Catholic Dialogue, 589, 605
Polycarp, 106
Pompedda, Card. Mario, 261, 294
Pontian, 168, 207, 210, 237
Pontiff, 11, 14, 17, 19, 22, 25, 26, 30-33, 41, 42, 55-59, 61, 67, 73-75, 91-93, 145, 159, 177, 187, 192, 194, 196, 216, 228, 232, 235, 246, 260, 262, 264, 273, 275, 297, 330, 343, 351, 507, 573, 585
Pontifical Academies, 75, 259, 271
Pontifical Academy of Sciences, 271
Pontifical Academy of Social Sciences, 16, 20, 37, 236, 272
Pontifical Biblical Commission, 104, 231, 242, 256, 260, 293, 610
Pontifical Biblical Institute, 104, 242, 286, 293, 414-417, 550
Pontifical College Josephinum, 272, 395, 396, 399, 401, 405, 408, 411, 414-416, 545, 549
Pontifical Commissions, 75
Pontifical Councils, 11, 75, 76, 232, 258, 580
Pontifical Ecclesiastical Faculties, 548-550
Pontifical Mission Societies, 414, 505, 566
Pontifical Missionary Union, 567
Pontifical Noble Guard, 261
Pontifical Orders, 573
Pontifical Orders of Knighthood, 573-574
Pontifical Universities, 495, 546-550
Pontifical Universities and Institutes in Rome, 550
Pontificio, L'Annuario, 26, 236, 240, 256, 263, 264, 267, 268, 271, 298, 336, 339, 343, 344, 348, 394, 438, 442, 451, 455, 456, 458, 467, 487, 490, 492, 507, 546, 548, 550
Pontius Pilate, 109
Poor Clare Nuns, 458, 472, 475, 484
Poor Clares, 128, 168, 205, 215, 223, 280, 458, 474-476
Poor Clares of Perpetual Adoration, 476
Poor Clares of St. Colette, 475
Poor Handmaids of Jesus Christ, 484, 544
Popes of the Roman Catholic Church, 236-240
Popish Plot, 225, 353

Popp, Bp. Bernard, 412, 419
Population, Catholic, World, 335
Population, Catholic, U.S., 432, 433-434
Population Research Institute, 505
Populorum Progressio, 114, 116, 117, 245, 251, 259
Pornography, 300, 503, 611
Porphyry, 219
Portiuncula Indulgence, 151, 223
Portugal, 8, 15, 25, 107, 123, 124, 168, 204, 206, 214, 215, 225, 227, 234, 239, 242, 246, 248-250, 261, 266, 269, 279, 281, 288, 290, 296, 299, 302, 303, 320, 324, 325, 338, 341, 365, 474, 547, 573
Potocnak, Bp. Joseph, 412, 419, 430
Poupard, Card. Paul, 261, 288, 294, 295
Power of the Keys, 146, 195
Pragmatic Sanction of Bourges, 224
Pragmatism, 152, 593
Precious Blood Sisters, 484
Precious Blood, Society of, 465
Prefect Apostolic, 17, 274, 407, 408
Prefecture of Economic Affairs of the Holy See, 260
Prelates U.S. Retired, 418-419
Prelature of Opus Dei, 283, 403, 550
Premonstratensians, 210, 465, 467
Preparation of Gifts, 178
Presbyterian Churches, 600
Presbyterorum Ordinis, 229
Presentation (Feast), 165, 173
Presentation (Religious), 484, 487
Press Association, Catholic, 552
Press Association Catholic (Awards), 575-576
Press Office, 5, 11, 14, 18, 33, 124, 256, 260
Press, Catholic (Statistics), 551
Press, Vatican, 5, 11, 14, 32, 33, 75, 76, 124, 184, 256, 260, 263, 575, 576
Preternatural Gifts, 152
Prie Dieu, 152
Priestly Celibacy, 245, 300, 321
Priestly Formation, 229, 421, 455
Priestly Fraternity of St. Peter, 465, 467
Primacy of Pope, 14, 34, 92, 99, 104, 106, 109, 110, 115, 126, 127, 222-226, 273, 343, 351, 578, 589, 590, 594, 597, 599, 605, 615
Primary Option, 152
Primate, 51, 128, 210, 233, 235, 273, 274, 279, 281, 283, 592, 599
Prior, 46, 52, 55, 67, 89, 96, 129, 149, 152, 185, 192, 194, 201, 202, 217, 232, 256, 261, 288, 476, 526, 528, 574, 610
Priscillianism, 209, 324
Privilege of Faith (Petrine Privilege), 256
Pro-Cathedral, 152, 388-389, 444
Pro Ecclesia Foundation, 505
Pro Sanctity Movement, 342, 505
Probabiliorism, 136, 152
Probabilism, 136, 152
Profession of Faith, 14, 43, 87-89, 109, 127, 133, 178, 193, 584, 613
Pro-Life Activities, 8, 12, 21, 39, 53, 79, 80, 82, 421, 507, 561, 563
Pro-Life Activities United States Conference of Catholic Bishops, 8, 12, 39, 80, 563
Pro-Nuncio, 52, 264, 267, 270, 274, 279, 281, 284, 286, 291

Propaganda Fide, 352, 356, 400, 406, 412
Proportionalism, 136, 153, 157
Protestant Churches, 146, 309, 578, 596, 598, 600, 601, 603-605
Protestant Reformation, 126, 308, 599
Protocanonical, 96
Protodeacon, 279, 280, 284, 286, 288
Protomartyrs, 291
Protonotary, 274
Proverbs, 96, 99, 100
Providentissimus Deus, 104, 242, 248, 250
Provost, Bp. Glen, 216, 378, 412
Psalms, 66, 96, 99, 103
Publications, Vatican, 263
Publishers, Catholic, 565-566
Puerto Rico, 12, 33, 234, 265, 266, 278, 285, 296, 325, 338, 352, 356, 362, 389, 390, 396, 398, 403, 424, 426, 429, 432, 438, 462, 497, 507, 538, 542, 547, 574
Pujats, Card. Janis, 288, 294-296, 337
Puljic, Card. Vinko, 288, 294-296, 301, 336
Pulpit, 51, 79, 181, 215
Purgatory, 107, 143, 146, 151, 153, 224, 597
Purification, 30, 70, 101, 173, 178, 191, 254, 578, 584, 603
Purim, 99, 606
Purse, 106, 214, 215
Pyx, 181

Q

Qatar, 32, 40, 264-267, 269, 325, 333
Quadragesima, 153
Quadragesimo Anno, 114, 116, 136, 227, 243, 250
Quakers, 598
Quam Singulari, 192, 242
Quanta Cura, 158, 226, 246, 247
Quartodecimans, 139
Quebec, 7, 42, 44, 52, 209, 287, 354, 471, 556
Queen of Peace, 188, 261, 288, 469, 512, 516, 518, 528, 529
Queenship of Mary, 173, 250
Quezada Toruño, Card. Rodolfo, 288, 294-296
Quinn, Abp. John, 380, 382, 412, 419
Quinn Bp. Alexander, 412,
Quinn Bp. Francis, 381, 412, 419
Quinn Bp. John M., 376, 412
Quinque Viae, 153
Qumran, 97

R

Racism, 49, 79, 153, 427, 582, 583
Radio, Catholic, 262, 568-570
Radio, Vatican, 262
Ramadan, 14, 23, 578, 613, 614
Ramirez Bp. Ricardo, 378, 412, 424
Raphael (Feast), 169, 173
Rash Judgment, 153
Rassas, Bp. George, 376, 412
Rationalism, 107, 147, 153, 222, 226
Ratzinger, Card. Joseph, See Benedict XVI
Ravasi, Abp. Gianfranco, 259, 260
Ravenna, 8, 14, 108, 212, 238, 292, 297, 583, 590, 594, 595

Raya, Bp. Joseph, 412
Raymond Nonnatus, 210-212, 388
Raymond of Peñafort, 165, 210-212
Razafindratandra, Card. Armand, 288, 294-296
RCIA, 32, 133, 185, 187, 190
Re, Card. Giovanni Battista, 76-77, 257, 260, 289, 294, 295
Reader (Lector), 196
Reagan, Pres. Ronald, 54, 270, 271
Reception of Communion, 181, 183, 192
Receptions into Church, 432, 439-440
Receptions into the Church in the United States, 432, 439-440
Recollects, 441, 458, 467
Reconciliation Sacrament of, See Penance, Sacrament of
Redemptionis Donum, 235
Redemptionis Sacramentum, 183
Redemptor Hominis, 116, 233, 234, 251
Redemptoris Custos, 235
Redemptoris Mater, 121, 122, 234, 251, 545
Redemptoris Missio, 234, 251
Redemptorist Fathers, 393, 465
Redemptorists, 47, 107, 205, 208, 225, 292, 293, 334, 403, 429, 430, 467, 559
Reformation, Catholic, 108, 137, 224-225, 306, 310, 324, 330
Reformation Protestant, 126, 224-225, 308, 327, 578, 579, 596, 601-604
Refugees, 21, 22, 34, 46, 168, 213, 269, 301, 303, 308, 311, 312, 314, 316, 318, 319, 330, 331, 334, 341, 421, 423
Rehabilitation Center, 463, 509, 512, 520, 574
Reichert, Bp. Stephen, 412, 419, 430
Reilly, Bp. Daniel, 383, 412, 419
Reiss, Bp. Francis, 376, 413
Reiss Bp. John, 383, 413
Relativism, 20, 153, 572, 586, 588
Relics, 14, 105, 108, 127, 153, 179, 206, 208, 221, 256, 351, 393, 594
Religion in Public Schools, 369-370
Religious Freedom, 15, 27, 61, 138, 142, 168, 225, 230, 233, 298, 303, 306, 309, 313-318, 320, 326, 327, 329, 330, 353, 354, 358, 368, 369, 586, 609, 610, 614, 616
Religious Orders, Religious Orders (Statistics), 335, 467-468, 487-489
Religious Orders, Men, 335, 467-468
Religious Orders, Women, 335, 468-486
Reliquary, 154
Renewal, 37, 43, 55, 64, 67, 69, 70, 72, 75, 90, 91, 98, 105, 129, 134, 135, 138, 151, 165, 172, 182, 187, 191, 192, 224, 225, 227, 229, 230, 233, 235, 241, 257, 275, 319, 321, 342, 344, 426, 462, 490, 496, 498, 502, 504, 525-531, 534, 557, 579, 581, 583, 584, 593, 603, 604
Renner, Gerald, 54
Representatives of the Holy See, 29, 264-268
Representatives to the Holy See, 18, 268-269
Requiem Mass, 179
Rerum Novarum, 114, 116, 117, 136, 226, 227, 234, 241, 243, 248, 250, 251, 361
Rescript, 154, 218, 263

Resurrection of Christ, 31, 88, 102, 104, 144, 162, 172, 176, 182, 602, 603
Resurrectionists, 216, 465
Retarded Children, 523-524
Retired Bishops, 418-419
Retired, Facilities for, 511-520
Retreats, 525-531
Retreats International, 525
Retrouvaille, 505
Revelation, 88, 89, 92-97, 100, 103, 105, 110-112, 114
Revelation, Dogmatic Constitution, See Dei Verbum
Revelation, Book of, 103
Revised Standard Version, 97
Rhoades, Kevin C., 377, 413
Rhode Island, 367, 373, 421, 434, 437, 440, 470, 518, 530, 537, 546, 575
Riashi, Bp. Georges, 413, 418
Ricard, Card. Jean-Pierre, 289, 294, 295
Ricard, Bp. John, 380, 413, 428
Ricken, Bp. David, 375, 377, 413
Rigali, Card. Justin, 8, 12, 24, 28, 39, 80, 289, 294-296, 380, 381, 413, 421
Rights and Obligations of the Faithful, 494
Rights and Obligations of the Laity, 494-495
Risen Christ, 38, 49, 65, 72, 106, 142, 150, 388, 460, 588
Rita Amada of Jesus, 255
Rita of Cascia, 167, 210, 212, 215, 251
Rite of Christian Initiation of Adults (RCIA), 32, 133, 185, 187, 190
Rivera Carrera, Card. Norberto, 289, 294-296, 450, 451, 453
Rizzotto, Bp. Vincent, 413, 419
Robert Bellarmine, 108, 169, 211, 243, 251, 278
Roberts, John, Chief Justice, 372
Rochet, 180
Rodé, Card. Franc, 257, 261, 289, 294-296
Rodi, Bp. Thomas, 375, 379, 413
Rodimer, Bp. Frank, 380, 413
Rodriguez, Bp. Miguel, 413, 419
Rodriguez Bp. Placido, 379, 413
Rodríguez Maradiaga, Card. Oscar, 289, 294, 295, 337
Rogationists, 467
Rogito, 154
Roman, Bp. Agustin, 413, 424
Roman Curia, 3, 38, 75, 117, 125, 131, 136-138, 143, 145, 152, 195, 236, 241, 242, 245, 246, 255-261, 263, 273, 274, 277, 280, 281, 283, 335, 407, 432, 558
Roman Empire, 125, 133, 151, 177, 219, 222, 225, 311, 314, 344, 595
Roman Martyrology, 133, 148
Roman Missal, 13, 21, 25, 48, 73, 84, 180, 183, 184, 187, 192, 575, 576
Roman Question, 227, 241, 243, 244, 262
Roman Rite, 35, 105, 106, 136, 139, 146, 154, 172, 174, 175, 177, 182, 187, 190-192, 195, 196, 201, 228, 246, 349, 350, 442
Romani Pontifices, 256
Romania, 15, 29, 32, 234, 245, 266, 269, 274, 325, 338, 345-347, 396, 412, 591, 594
Romanian Catholics, 348
Romanian Orthodox Church, 325, 585,

591
Romano Pontifici Eligendo, 297
Romans, 59, 96, 102
Rome, 6, 7, 9, 11, 13-15, 17-23, 25, 26, 29, 31, 33-35, 37, 38, 40-44, 46, 48, 49, 51-54, 60, 61, 63, 71, 73, 74, 76, 92, 96, 102-104, 106-109, 113, 121, 129, 133, 134, 137, 139, 143, 144, 151, 155, 157, 159, 162, 166-168, 170-173, 177, 204-212, 216-223, 225, 226, 228, 231-233, 235-246, 248, 256-263, 265, 270-273, 275-293, 297, 298, 302, 311, 315, 324, 325, 327, 330, 332, 334, 337, 340-342, 344-346, 355, 358, 360, 389, 394-418, 458-466, 468-486, 490-493, 496, 500, 503, 507, 546, 547, 550, 558, 567, 572, 574, 578, 583, 585-588, 590, 591, 594-596, 601-603, 605, 608-613
Rooney III, L. Francis, 16, 20, 270
Roosevelt, Franklin D., 271
Roosevelt, Theodore, 371, 372
Roque, Bp. Francis, 413, 419
Roque Gonzalez, 252
Rosales, Card. Gaudencio, 76, 289, 294-296
Rosary, 7, 24, 27, 29, 32, 37, 123, 134, 138, 141, 154, 169, 173, 188, 214, 233, 241, 248-251, 356, 361, 388-390, 392, 444-446, 466, 473, 474, 483, 485, 488, 489, 500-502, 505, 509, 512, 540, 542, 568, 569, 571
Rosazza, Bp. Peter, 377, 413
Rose, Bp. Robert, 377, 413, 419
Rose Hawthorne Lathrop Home, 509
Rose of Lima, 24, 210, 213-215, 323, 474
Rose Philippine Duchesne, 163, 170, 252, 354, 359, 362, 392
Rosh Hashana, 606
Rosminians, 466, 467
Rota Roman, 201-203, 258, 277, 282
Rouco Varela, Card. Antonio, 76, 289, 294, 295
Rozanski, Bp. Mitchell, 48, 375, 413
Rubiano Sáenz, Card. Pedro, 289, 294, 295, 296
Rubrics, 184
Ruini, Card. Camillo, 21, 22, 33, 41, 76, 290, 294, 295
Rule of St. Benedict, 493, 616
Russert, Tim, 54
Russia, 7, 11, 17, 24, 34, 49, 105, 123, 209, 214, 222, 226, 227, 258, 266, 267, 269, 272, 318, 325, 326, 346, 347, 396, 418, 429, 592, 594
Russian Orthodox Church, 591-594
Ruthenian Byzantine Catholics, 346
Rwanda, 234, 266, 269, 326, 331, 338, 339, 404
Ryan, Bp. Daniel, 382, 413, 419
Ryan, Bp. Sylvester, 379, 413, 419
Rylko, Card. Stanislaw, 43, 60, 258, 261, 290, 294, 295

S
Sabbath Day, 111, 367
Sabellianism, 205, 219
Sacerdotalis Caelibatus, 245, 251
Sacrae Disciplinae Leges, 235
Sacramental Economy, 88, 590
Sacramentals, 39, 40, 88, 127, 155, 175-

177, 196
Sacramentary, 184, 188
Sacramentine Nuns, 485
Sacraments, Congregation for the, 256
Sacraments, 189-203; See also individual Sacraments.
Sacraments Congregation for the Discipline of, 256
Sacramentum Caritatis, 194, 232, 276
Sacred Heart Missionaries, 466
Sacred Heart of Jesus and Our Lady of, 486
Sacred Heart of Jesus and Our Lady of Guadalupe, 485
Sacred Heart of Jesus Oblate Sisters, 485
Sacred Heart of Jesus, Apostles of, 485, 487
Sacred Heart of Jesus, Congr. of, 485, 487
Sacred Heart of Jesus, Handmaids of, 485
Sacred Heart of Jesus, Missionary Sisters of, 485
Sacred Heart of Jesus Oblate Sisters, 485
Sacred Heart of Jesus, Servants of, 485, 489, 492
Sacred Heart of Jesus, Sisters of the, 485
Sacred Heart of Jesus and the Poor, Sisters of, 485
Sacred Heart of Mary Religious, 486
Sacred Heart Society, Devoted to, 485
Sacred Heart, Brothers of the, 466
Sacred Heart, Daughters of, 472, 485, 487
Sacred Heart, Missionary Sisters of the, 485
Sacred Heart, Society of, 485
Sacred Liturgy, 175-188
Sacred Music, 176, 182, 242, 244, 250, 400, 548, 550, 560, 575
Sacred Vessels, 154, 180, 181, 183
Sacrilege, 139, 154, 156
Sacristy, 154
Sacrosanctum Concilium, 138, 147, 161, 175, 178, 181, 182, 229, 576
Sadducees, 151, 154
Saints, 204-211
Saints, Patrons and Intercessors, 211-213
Saints, Patrons of Places, 213-214
Saints Congregation for the Causes of, 6, 19, 26, 152, 256
Salazar, Bp. Alexander, 378, 413, 424
Saldarini, Card. Giovanni, 290, 294-296
Sales, Card. Eugênio de Araújo, 290, 295, 296
Salesian Congregation, 15, 29, 46, 51, 54, 60, 216, 279, 282, 289, 312, 342, 394, 430, 481, 487, 493, 526, 557, 560
Salesian Cooperators, 342, 493
Salesian Lay Missionaries, 430
Salesian Srs. of St. John Bosco, 481
Salesians of Don Bosco, 54, 492, 550, 560
Salesians, See Salesian Congregation
Saltarelli, Bp. Michael, 383, 414
Salvation History, 103, 104, 146, 150, 151, 155, 162, 176, 179, 184
Salvation Outside the Church, 155
Salvatorians, 466, 467, 487
Salvifici Doloris, 235
Samoa, 266, 267, 269, 293, 326, 395, 412, 417, 419, 430, 538, 551, 555
Sample, Bp. Alexander, 379, 414
Samra, Bp. Nicholas, 414, 419
Samuel, 96, 98, 100
Sanchez, Bp. Robert, 382, 413, 419
Sánchez Card. José T., 290, 294-296

Sanctification, 34, 90, 110, 175, 176, 421, 589
Sanctifying Grace, 135, 143, 145, 146, 150, 155, 157, 189
Sanctions, 126, 127, 134, 247, 302
Sanctuary Lamp, 182
Sanctuary of Mary, 528
Sandoval Iñiguez, Card. Juan, 290, 294, 295, 296, 450-452
Sandri, Card. Leonardo, 27, 60, 256, 261, 290, 294-296
Sansaricq, Bp. Guy, 375, 414, 428
Santos, Card. Alexandre José Maria dos, 290, 294-296
Sapienti Consilio, 242, 356, 361
Sapientia Christiana, 293, 546
Sarah, Abp. Robert, 257, 261
Saraiva Martins, Card. José, 6, 26, 45, 261, 290, 294-296
Sardi, Abp. Paolo, 259, 261
Sardinia, 207, 210, 216, 226, 237, 247, 548
Sarr, Card. Théodore-Adrien, 60, 61, 290, 294-296, 339
Sartain, Bp. James, 378, 414
Sartoris, Bp. Joseph, 414, 419
Satan, 130, 138
Satanism, 155
Saturday, Holy, 166, 172
Saudi Arabia, 13, 22, 32, 43, 46, 61, 326, 333
Saul, 98, 101, 218
Scalabrini Srs., 472
Scalabrinians, 464, 466, 467, 488, 560
Scandinavia, 204, 214, 221, 225, 338, 404, 505, 599
Scapular Medal, 155
Scapular Promise, 155
Scarboro Missions, 567
Scarpone Caporale, Bp. Gerald, 414, 419, 430
Scheid, Card. Oscar, 76, 290, 294-296
Scherer, Card. Odilo, 60, 61, 254, 290, 294-296
Scheut Missionaries, 467
Schism, 40, 45, 47, 134, 155, 220-222, 298, 306, 309, 311-313, 321, 324, 327, 334, 359-361
Schism, Eastern, 40, 45, 47, 134, 155, 220-223, 298, 306, 309, 311-313, 321, 324, 327, 334, 359-361
Schism Great Western, 223-224, 239, 240, 241
Schlarman, Bp. Stanley, 376, 380, 414
Schleck, Abp. Charles, 414, 419
Schmitt, Bp. Bernard, 383, 414
Schmitt, Bp. Mark, 379, 414
Schmitz Simon, Bp. Paul O.F.M., 414, 418, 430
Schnurr, Bp. Dennis, 376, 414, 422
Schoenstatt, 16, 393, 492, 496, 497, 531, 570
Schoenstatt Center, 496, 531
Schoenstatt Srs. of Mary, 492
Scholasticism, 107, 128, 149, 155, 159, 556
Schönborn, Card. Christoph, 6, 8, 33, 290, 294-296, 300, 336
Schönstatt Fathers, 282
Schönstatt Movement, 282
Schools, Catholic, U.S., 534, 535-538, 539-544

Schools, Catholic, World Statistics, 335
Schools, Religious (Statistics), 534, 535-538
Schools and Students in Outlying Areas, 538
Schott, Abp. Basil, 348, 380, 414
Schulte, Abp. Francis, 378, 379, 383, 414
Schwery, Card. Henry, 291, 294, 295
Schwietz, Abp. Roger, O.M.I., 374, 376, 414, 421
Scola, Card. Angelo, 61, 274, 291, 294, 295, 614
Scotland, 7, 13, 47, 105, 170, 205, 208, 209, 214, 221, 241, 249, 253, 296, 308, 311, 312, 327, 338, 341, 495, 506, 544, 581, 598, 600
Scripture, 10, 17, 24, 52, 67, 68, 87, 88, 91-95, 99, 103-107, 109, 113-117, 597-601, 610
Scripture in Church Life, 95
Scruple, 155
Seal of Confession, 140, 155, 195, 355
Season of Advent, 17, 180
Season of Lent, 25, 131, 161, 162, 180
Season of Ordinary Time, 161, 180
Seasons, 21, 48, 84, 138, 157, 161, 162, 180, 183, 195, 344, 349, 555, 557, 570
Sebastian, 165, 210, 211, 213, 215, 253, 254, 282, 286, 363, 377, 379, 394
Sebastiani, Card. Sergio, 261, 291, 294, 295
Second Coming of Christ, 103, 130, 218, 584
Secret Vatican Archives, 272
Secretariat of State, Vatican, 15, 25, 33, 75, 124, 232, 245, 256, 258, 260, 264, 278-282, 284-292, 340, 395, 396, 399, 404, 409-411, 417, 422
Secular Franciscan Order, 206, 209, 223, 342
Secular Franciscans, 213
Secular Institutes, 257, 276, 286, 458, 490-492
Secular Order, 493
Secularism, 23, 60, 144, 156, 226, 279, 585, 616
Seder, 606
Seelos Francis Xavier, 255, 365
Selection of Bishops, 274
Semi-Arians, 219
Seminack, Bp. Richard, 381, 414
Seminarians, 27, 36, 46, 54, 55, 58, 62, 64, 67, 69, 70, 79, 544-546
Seminaries, 335, 534, 544-546, 547
Seminary (Statistics), 335, 534, 547
Seminary Enrollment, 335, 534, 547
Semi-Pelagianism, 220
Senegal, 10, 60, 61, 234, 265, 266, 269, 296, 303, 327, 337-339
Sepe, Card. Crescenzio, 291, 294, 295
Septuagint, 95, 97-98
Serbia, 266, 320, 327, 338, 347, 583, 594
Sergius I, Pope, 237
Sergius II, Pope, 222, 238
Sergius III, Pope, 238
Sergius IV, Pope, 220, 222, 238
Sermon, 86, 111, 129, 156, 175, 613
Serra International, 12, 342, 506, 560
Serratelli, Bp. Arthur, 50, 380, 414, 421
Servite Friars, 393
Servite Sisters, 481
Servites Order, 466
Seventh Day Adventists, 270, 597

Sevilla, Bp. Carlos, 383, 414, 424
Sexual Abuse Scandal, 12, 55, 67, 78-79
Seychelles, 18, 234, 266, 269, 279, 327, 337, 339
Sfeir, Card. Nasrallah, 35, 40, 274, 291, 294-296, 345, 347, 348
Shaheen, Bp. Robert, 380, 415
Shan Kuo-hsi Card. Paul, S.J., 291, 295, 296
Sharbel Makhlouf, 210, 252
Sheehan, Abp. Michael, 379, 380, 382, 415, 420
Sheen, Abp. Fulton, 28, 362, 381
Sheldon, Bp. Gilbert, 383, 414, 415
Shelters, 463, 508, 510, 606
Sheridan, Bp. Michael, 376, 415
Sheridan, Bp. Patrick, 414, 419
Shirayanagi, Card. Peter, 291, 294-296
Shoah, 228, 236, 578, 608-610, 612
Shrine, 121, 156, 387, 388, 390-393, 446, 497
Shrines and Places of Historic Interest in the, 390-393
Shroud of Turin, 156
Siberia, 318, 325, 326, 429
Sick Calls, 156
Sierra Leone, 265, 266, 269, 327, 337-339, 419, 430, 495
Signatura, Apostolic, 258, 277, 279, 282-284, 287, 289, 291-293, 397, 398
Silva, Bp. Clarence, 377, 415
Silvestrini, Card. Achille, 261, 291, 294-296
Simonis, Card. Adrianus, 291, 294-296
Simony, 156
Sin, 31, 47, 64, 69, 70, 88, 93, 98, 104, 109, 110, 112, 115, 119-121, 129-132, 137, 138, 141-146, 148-159, 161, 163, 171, 172, 178, 188-190, 192, 194, 195
Sinai, 98, 111, 137, 234, 256, 307, 591
Singapore, 18, 41, 234, 266, 267, 269, 286, 319, 328, 337
Sirach, 96, 100
Sisters Adorers, 484, 541
Sisters Oblates, 486
Sisters of Africa, 468
Sisters of Blessed Sacrament, 208, 356, 544
Sisters of Charity, 204-209, 211, 225, 354, 355, 359, 363, 365, 392, 429, 470, 473, 525, 539-543, 560, 562
Sisters of Charity of Leavenworth, 543
Sisters of Charity of Nazareth, 359, 543, 560
Sisters of Charity of Seton Hill, 543
Sisters of Charity of St. Joan Antida, 207
Sisters of Charity of St. Vincent de Paul, 205
Sisters of Christian Charity, 475, 543, 544
Sisters of Divine Providence, 540, 542
Sisters of Holy Family of Nazareth, 540
Sisters of Holy Names of Jesus, 209, 541
Sisters of Loretto, 359, 364
Sisters of Mary, 475, 476, 484, 492
Sisters of Mercy, 215, 365, 429, 476, 482, 539-544
Sisters of Notre Dame, 205, 208, 363, 429, 540, 541, 544
Sisters of Notre Dame de Namur, 208, 429, 540, 541, 544
Sisters of Our Lady, 208, 468, 472-476, 482, 483, 522
Sisters of Our Lady of Charity, 208, 483, 522
Sisters of Our Lady of Charity of Refuge, 208
Sisters of Our Lady of Mercy, 476
Sisters of Providence, 12, 355, 359, 484, 540, 543, 561
Sisters of St. Agnes, 429, 541
Sisters of St. Anne, 207, 527, 539
Sisters of St. Basil, 544
Sisters of St. Benedict, 393, 516
Sisters of St. Dominic, 24, 474, 539
Sisters of St. Dorothy, 210
Sisters of St. Francis, 363, 429, 475-477, 539-542, 560, 562
Sisters of St. Francis of Assisi, 477, 539
Sisters of St. Francis of Christ, 477
Sisters of St. Francis of Clinton, 541
Sisters of St. Francis of Mary Immaculate, 542
Sisters of St. Francis of Maryville, 475
Sisters of St. Francis of Penance, 477
Sisters of St. Francis of Philadelphia, 476, 477
Sisters of St. Francis of Savannah, 477
Sisters of St. Francis of Sylvania, 560
Sisters of St. Joseph, 206, 364, 393, 429, 476, 477, 482, 527, 539-544
Sisters of St. Joseph of Carondelet, 429, 539-544
Sisters of St. Mary, 217, 475, 542
Sisters of Ste. Chretienne, 472
Sisters of Sts. Cyril & Methodius, 477
Sistine Chapel, 21, 42, 236, 262, 297
Sixtus I, Pope, 236
Sixtus II, Pope, 210, 237
Sixtus III, Pope, 172, 237
Sixtus IV, Pope, 145, 224, 239
Sixtus V, Pope, 126, 132, 239, 256, 257, 260, 263, 276
Skilled Care, 511-513, 518, 519
Skilled Nursing Facilities, 511-520
Sklba, Bp. Richard, 379, 415, 421, 581, 612
Skurla, Bp. William, 380, 383, 415
Skylstad, Bp. William, 80, 84, 85, 382, 383, 415
Slander, 132, 157
Slattery, Bp. Edward, 383, 415
Slavery, 31, 111, 248, 302, 325, 326, 355, 356, 360, 449
Slavorum Apostoli, 234, 251
Slovak Catholic Federation, 506
Slovak Catholic Sokol, 506, 555
Slovakia, 6, 61, 214, 234, 261, 266, 280, 284, 292, 296, 306, 328, 338, 346, 347, 394, 396, 549, 594
Slovenia, 15, 23, 25, 234, 261, 266, 269, 277, 289, 296, 328, 338, 346, 550
Smith, Bp. John, 380, 383, 415
Snow, Tony, 54
Snyder, Bp. John, 381, 415
Social Communications, Catholic, 22, 127, 230, 259, 278, 289, 291, 568, 571-572
Social Doctrine, 15, 114-117, 227, 241, 245, 300
Social Encyclicals of Pope John Paul II, 116-117
Social Justice, 63, 118, 147, 216, 227, 233, 308, 319, 331, 427, 429, 455, 494-496, 499, 504, 561, 571, 593, 608, 613
Social Mission Sisters, 393
Social Service Facilities, 335
Social Service Organizations, 508
Societies of Apostolic Life, 7, 14, 127, 136, 187, 257, 258, 276, 278, 282-292, 402, 458, 490, 491, 557
Society for the Propagation of the Faith, 226, 244, 257, 354, 361, 408, 431, 506
Society of African Missions, 318, 467, 563
Society of Christ, 467
Society of Divine Word, 397, 429, 561
Society of Jesus, 51, 79, 207, 224, 226, 281, 284, 287, 392, 395, 398, 410, 463, 496, 540, 541, 543, 560
Society of Mary, 464, 543
Society of Missionaries of Africa, 564
Society of Priests of St. Sulpice, 287, 466
Society of St. Edmund, 468, 543, 565
Society of St. Francis de Sales, 216, 279, 466
Society of St. Monica, 506
Society of St. Paul, 44, 465, 467, 491, 560
Society of St. Peter Apostle, 506
Society of St. Vincent de Paul, 226, 341, 508, 560
Socio-Economic Statements by U.S. Bishops, 117-118
Sodalities of Our Lady, 496
Sodano, Card. Angelo, 7, 124, 261, 277, 291, 294-296, 325
Soens, Bp. Lawrence, 382, 415
Solemnity of Christ, 9, 162
Solemnity of Mary, 19, 21, 162, 173, 174
Solemnity of St. Joseph, 166
Sollicitudo Omnium Ecclesiarum, 263
Sollicitudo Rei Socialis, 57, 114-117, 234, 251
Solomon, 99, 101
Somalia, 265, 267, 328, 339
Somascan Fathers, 207, 466
Song of Songs, 96, 99, 100
Sorcery, 157
Soroka, Abp. Stephen, 380, 415
Soteriology, 157
Soto, Bp. Jaime, 381, 415, 424
Soul, 30, 49, 59, 71, 92, 96, 107, 108, 110, 111, 115, 120, 129, 140, 144, 154, 161, 171, 178, 190, 191, 195, 224
South Africa, 13, 23, 40, 52, 214, 234, 236, 264, 266, 267, 269, 287, 296, 318, 320, 321, 328, 330, 336, 339, 400, 404, 410, 412, 418, 419, 429, 430, 463, 474, 484, 495
South America, 53, 60, 156, 214, 247, 249, 296, 299, 301, 303, 304, 307, 309, 312, 323, 330, 333, 335, 339, 347, 363, 365, 395, 430, 490, 599
South Carolina, 352-355, 367, 373, 421, 425, 427, 434, 437, 440, 518, 530, 537
South Dakota, 374, 393, 421, 425, 434, 437, 440, 470, 518, 530, 537
South Korea, 9, 234, 266, 317
Southern Baptist Convention, 581, 598
Sovereign Military Hospitaller Order of St. John of Jerusalem of Rhodes, 574
Soviet Union, 34, 228, 233, 236, 243, 258, 300, 326, 346, 591
Spain, 9, 10, 21, 29, 32, 42-46, 60, 61, 105, 108, 123, 133, 145, 172, 204, 206, 208, 210, 214-216, 219-222, 224, 225, 227, 232, 234, 237, 242, 243, 245, 247, 248, 250, 254, 261, 264-267, 269, 272, 277, 279, 280, 282-284, 286,

287, 289, 295, 298, 299, 301, 303-305, 307, 308, 323, 329, 338, 352, 353, 358, 363, 364, 394, 399, 401, 403-405, 419, 429, 430, 449, 461, 463, 464, 466-468, 470, 475, 476, 478-481, 483-486, 491, 493, 496, 513, 525, 547, 548, 550, 598
Spanish Inquisition, 224
Spe Salvi, 14, 17, 56, 59, 144, 232, 251, 571
Special Apostolates and Groups, 495-496
Spellman, Card. Francis, 296, 379, 383
Speyrer, Bp. Jude, 378, 415
Spidlik, Card. Tomás, 291, 294-296
Spiritual Exercises, 148, 207, 250
Spiritual Renewal Programs, 37, 129, 165, 502, 525, 527-530
Spoon, 351
Sri Lanka, 8, 27, 52, 214, 234, 261, 267, 269, 293, 329, 338, 616
St. Ansgar's Scandinavian Catholic League, 505
St. Anthony's Guild, 505, 510, 556
St. Jude League, 506
St. Margaret of Scotland, 170, 506
St. Martin de Porres Guild, 506
Stafford, Card. James, 258, 261, 291, 293-296, 376, 379, 415, 418, 498
Stamps, Vatican, 73, 262
Stanislaw of Jesus and Mary, 215, 255
State Catholic Conferences, 422
Stational Churches, 157
Stations of the Cross, 77, 138
Statistical Yearbook of the Church, 202, 263, 298, 335, 547
Statistics Catholic, Canada, 447-448
Statistics, Catholic, Education, 335, 534, 535-539
Statistics, Catholic, Mexico, 456-457
Statistics, Catholic, U.S., 432, 433-441
Statistics, International Church, 335
Statuary Hall, 364, 365, 372
Steib, Bp. J. Terry, 379, 415, 428
Steinbock, Bp. John, 377, 382, 415
Steiner, Bp. Kenneth, 380, 415
Stephanos II Ghattas, Card., 291, 292, 294-296
Stephen, St., 218
Stephen I, Pope, 219, 237, 313
Stephen II, Pope, 221, 237
Stephen II., Pope, 221, 237
Stephen III, Pope, 237, 297
Stephen IV, Pope, 238
Stephen V, Pope, 238, 375
Stephen VI, Pope, 238
Stephen VII, Pope, 238
Stephen VIII, Pope, 238
Stephen IX, Pope, 238
Sterzinsky, Card. Georg, 292, 294, 295
Stewardship, 84, 130, 502, 558, 571, 587
Sticharion, 351
Stickler, Card. Alfons S.D.B., 54
Stigmata, 31, 157, 158, 207, 214, 462, 466
Stigmatine Fathers, 466, 467
Stipend, 158, 179
Stole, 158, 180, 185, 350, 351
Straling, Bp. Philip, 381, 382, 415
Strict Observance, 245, 461, 466, 472, 487
Stridon, 108
Studion, 283

Studite Monks, 283, 284
Suárez Rivera, Card. Adolfo, 54
Subdeacon, 185, 196
Subiaco Congregation, 460
Substance Abuse, 509-510
Successor of Peter, 6, 14, 43, 70, 90-93, 113, 114, 228, 578
Sudan, 21, 234, 267, 269, 294, 296, 303, 329, 338, 339, 347
Suffragan See, 158, 374
Sullivan, Bp. Dennis, 379, 415
Sullivan, Bp. Joseph, 375, 415, 419
Sullivan, Bp. Walter, 381, 415, 419
Sulpicians, 52, 225, 354, 359, 458, 466, 467
Sulyk, Abp. Stephen, 380, 415
Summa Theologiae, 108, 153
Summary of School Statistics, 534
Summorum Pontificum, 47, 187, 232
Sunday Mass, 30, 56, 184, 569
Sundays of Lent, 349
Supererogation, 158
Support our Aging Religious, 506
Supreme Court U.S., 355-357, 359, 366, 369, 370, 372
Supreme Pontiff, 19, 42, 73-75, 91, 187, 192, 196, 260, 262, 264, 273, 297
Supreme Tribunal of Apostolic Signatura, 258, 277, 279, 282-284, 287, 289, 291-293, 397, 398
Suriname, 18, 267, 269
Surplice, 180
Susannah, 100
Swain, Bp. Paul, 382, 415
Swaziland, 234, 266, 267, 269, 330, 339
Sweden, 107, 168, 204-206, 214, 234, 235, 265, 267, 269, 272, 330, 338, 469, 581
Swiątek, Card. Kazimierz, 292, 294, 295,296
Swiss American Benedictine Congregation, 404
Swiss Guards, 9, 37, 261
Switzerland, 18, 224, 234, 246-249, 261, 266, 267, 269, 272, 277, 285, 290, 291, 295, 330, 338-342, 403, 415, 469, 475-477, 484, 549, 550, 568, 581, 597, 600
Syllabus of Errors, 226
Sylvester I, Pope, 211, 229, 237
Sylvester II, Pope, 222, 238
Sylvester III, Pope, 238
Sylvester IV, Pope, 240
Symons, Bp. J. Keith, 380, 415
Synaxis, 350
Synod of Bishops, 21, 75, 76, 126, 194, 232, 233, 235, 245, 246, 262, 275-276, 279, 281, 283, 292, 294, 299, 316, 317, 320, 339, 345, 357, 458
Synoptic Gospels, 106, 111, 575
Synoptic Problem, 102
Syria, 5, 49, 61, 77, 101, 105, 108, 135, 207, 217, 228, 234, 236, 237, 256, 261, 267, 269, 286, 296, 317, 330, 344-347, 401, 418, 583, 591, 595, 596, 613
Syrian Catholics, 330, 348, 418
Syrian Orthodox Church, 77, 583, 595, 596
Syro-Malabar, 274, 313, 346-348, 386, 389, 394, 460
Syro-Malankara, 274, 313, 345, 347

Szoka, Card. Edmund, 261, 292, 294-296, 376, 377, 416, 418

T
Tabernacle, 69, 98, 142, 158, 177, 181
Table of Movable Feasts, 164
Tafoya, Bp. Arthur, 16, 381, 416, 424
Taiwan, 265, 268, 272, 279, 291, 296, 331, 336, 404, 407, 419, 429, 547, 616
Tajikistan, 265, 267, 269, 331
Talmuds, 606
Tamayo, Bp. James, 378, 416, 424
Tanzania, 10, 42, 214, 234, 267, 269, 288, 296, 331, 338, 339, 399, 401, 419, 429
Tarmouni, Nerses XIX Bedros, 274, 345, 347
Tauran, Card. Jean-Louis, 41, 43, 46, 61, 259-261, 292, 294, 295, 614, 615
Taylor, Bp. Anthony, 378, 416
Te Deum, 19, 158
Teaching Authority (*Magisterium*), 81, 87, 92, 93, 112-115, 117, 126, 127, 133, 148, 197, 203, 246, 272, 494, 501, 534, 568
Teaching Office, 94, 96, 127, 198
Tekakwitha Conference National Center, 429
Television, 4, 15, 23, 28, 31, 34, 41, 53, 54, 75, 76, 80, 145, 205, 213, 250, 263, 341, 362, 562, 568, 569, 577
Temporal Goods, 127, 257, 259
Temptation, 7, 14, 49, 100, 118, 149, 158
Ten Commandments, 87, 88, 110-112, 131, 136, 147, 368, 369
Tennessee, 54, 374, 406, 421, 425, 427, 434, 437, 440, 518, 524, 530, 537, 553, 555, 556
Teresa of Ávila, 160, 233, 442
Teresa, Mother, 211
Terrazas Sandoval, Card., 292, 294, 295, 336
Tertio Millennio Adveniente, 235, 604, 613
Tertullian, 88, 219
Test Act, 225
Testem Benevolentiae, 242, 356, 361
Tettamanzi, Card. Dionigi, 292, 294, 295
Texas, 9, 10, 16, 36, 50, 60, 352, 353, 355, 358, 364, 368, 369, 373, 374, 390, 393, 402, 403, 408, 417, 421, 422, 425, 426, 434, 437, 438, 440, 449, 462, 470, 497, 499, 500, 507, 509, 518, 522, 524, 530, 537, 538, 546, 552-556, 576, 599
Thailand, 18, 27, 234, 254, 264-267, 269, 284, 286, 296, 331, 338, 401, 429
Theatines, 205, 466, 467
Theism, 158
Theodicy, 158
Theodore I, Pope, 237
Theodore II, Pope, 238
Theologian of the Papal Household, 281
Theological Commission, International, 9, 14, 197, 231, 232, 256, 260, 275, 279, 281, 285, 287, 290, 583, 584, 586, 588-590, 594
Theological Virtues, 14, 135, 138, 143, 145, 158, 190
Theophany, 171, 172
Theotokos, 6, 121, 122, 159, 220, 588
Thérèse of Lisieux, St., 108

Theresians, 506
Thessalonians, 22, 96, 103
Theta Kappa Phi Fraternity, 498
Third Order, 107, 215, 217, 223, 249, 393, 407, 461, 462, 467, 474-477, 488, 493, 509
Third Orders, 493
Thomas (Didymus), 106
Thomas Aquinas, 53, 107, 108, 113, 148, 149, 153, 159, 160, 165, 171, 211-213, 215, 223, 233, 249, 282, 389, 401, 402, 407, 410, 416, 543, 544, 546, 548, 550
Thomas Becket, 170, 211, 223
Thomas, Bp. Daniel E., 380, 416
Thomas, Elliott, 416, 419
Thomas, Bp. George, 377, 416
Thomas Christians, 106, 346
Thomas More, 167, 208, 211-213, 224, 251, 308, 388, 389, 544, 556, 564, 565
Thomism, 149, 159
Throne, 176, 207, 225, 300, 450
Tiedemann, Bp. Neil, 416, 430
Timlin, Bp. James, 382, 416, 605
Timor, East, 234, 265, 268, 307
Timothy, 96, 103
Tithing, 159
Titular Archbishop, 241, 243, 244, 264, 274, 282, 292, 395
Titular Sees, 159
Titus, 96, 103
Titus Brandsma, 211, 253
Tobin, Bp. Thomas, 381, 416
Tobit, 96-99, 103
Togo, 22, 234, 267, 269, 281, 331, 338, 339, 395, 418
Tokelau, 412
Tomko, Card. Jozef, 44, 261, 292, 294-296
Tonga, 266, 267, 269, 331, 395
Tonini, Card. Ersilio, 292, 295, 296
Toppo, Card. Telesphore, 292, 294-296, 337
Torah, 61, 96, 606
Tradition, 91-96, 100-102
Transfiguration of Our Lord Jesus Christ, 289
Transfinalization, 159
Transignification, 159
Translation of Latin liturgical texts, 183
Translations, 18, 21, 48, 51, 88, 95, 97, 98, 153, 186-188, 246, 421, 500, 594
Transubstantiation, 136, 139, 144, 157, 159, 192, 223, 225
Trappists, 458, 461, 466, 467, 528
Trautman, Bp. Donald, 376, 416
Travelers and Migrants Council, 259
Trent, Council of, 53, 87, 96, 97, 104, 109, 126, 133, 137, 138, 153, 156, 159, 178, 182, 184, 185, 210, 220, 224, 225, 229, 257, 342, 492, 597, 604
Tribunal Action, 202
Tridentine Mass, 185, 187
Triduum, 31, 159, 161, 166, 172, 186, 187, 193
Trination, 179, 184
Trinity Sunday, 112, 139, 162, 171
Truce of God, 222
True Cross, 207, 220, 221
Truman, Harry S., 271, 371
Trusteeism, 359
Tschoepe, Bp. Thomas, 376, 382, 416
Tucci, Card. Roberto S.J., 262, 292, 294-296

Tumi, Card. Christian, 292, 294-296, 303
Tunisia, 65, 234, 264, 267, 269, 332
Turcotte, Card. Jean-Claude, 292, 294-296, 443
Turkey, 20, 29, 52, 61, 217, 232, 234, 244, 246, 256, 267, 269, 278, 291, 299, 332, 338, 345-347, 591, 613
Turkmenistan, 267, 269, 332
Turkson, Card. Peter, 293-296
Turley, Bp. Murphy, 416, 419, 430
Typological Sense, 104
Tyson, Bp. Joseph J., 382, 416

U

Ubi Arcano, 243, 249
Uganda, 35, 205, 234, 246, 252, 267, 269, 292, 293, 296, 332, 338, 339, 429, 591
Ukraine, 7, 25, 217, 226, 234, 236, 261, 267, 269, 274, 283, 284, 296, 325, 332, 339, 345-347, 374, 407, 416, 481, 591, 592
Ukrainian Byzantine Catholics, 347, 374, 398, 407, 418, 459, 505, 551
Ukrainian Orthodox Church, 591
Ultramontanism, 159

Unam Sanctam, 223
Unauthorized Eucharistic Prayers, 188
Unction, 159, 195
Unda, 341, 564, 569
UndaUSA, 564
Uniatism, 589
Union of Brest, 235, 332, 345, 346
Union of European Conferences of Major Superiors, 490
Union of Superiors General, 26, 490
UNIREA, 555
Unitatis Redintegratio, 68, 229, 578
United Church of Christ, 79, 581, 582, 598-600
United Nations (U.N.), 13, 57, 77, 269
United States Catholic Conference, 84, 357, 361, 373, 414, 420, 427, 500
United States Catholic Historical Society, 506
United States Catholic Mission Association, 560
United States Conference of Catholic Bishops (USCCB), 3, 78-80, 84-86, 88, 97, 183, 357, 373, 420-422, 429, 584, 614
United States Dioceses, 373-384
United States Hierarchy, 273, 373-384
United States Social Services, 508-531
United States Statistics, 432-440
United States Statistics, Catholic, Education, 534-538
Universal Law, 133, 159
Universi Dominici Gregis, 150, 235, 297
Universities, 9, 28, 29, 42, 45, 53, 68, 539-544, 546-550
Universities, Pontifical, 546-550
Universities, U.S. Catholic (Statistics), 534-538
Urban I, Pope, 237
Urban II, Pope, 238
Urban III, Pope, 239
Urban IV, Pope, 143, 171, 239
Urban V, Pope, 239, 241

Urban VI, Pope, 174, 239, 241, 297
Urban VII, Pope, 239
Urban VIII, Pope, 29, 240
Ursuline Nuns, 353, 358, 359, 364, 486, 544
Ursuline Order, 541
Ursuline Sisters, 486, 539
Ursuline Sisters of Belleville, 486
Ursuline Sisters of Mount Saint Joseph, 486
Ursulines, 363, 364, 429, 441, 487-489, 544
Uruguay, 214-216, 234, 267, 269, 291, 333, 339, 409, 454, 547
USCCB, 78, 80, 84, 88, 89, 183, 357, 373, 420-422, 425, 427, 429, 500, 584, 614
USCCB Administrative Committee, 421
USCCB Committees, 420
USCCB Regions, 78, 421
Use of Vernacular Languages, 175, 183, 184, 245
Usury, 159, 246
Ut Unum Sint, 23, 68, 234, 235, 251, 578, 592, 605
Utah, 356, 374, 421, 425, 434, 438, 440, 470, 519, 530, 538
Uzbekistan, 267, 269, 333

V

Vagi, 159
Valero, Bp. René, 353, 416, 424
Vallini, Card. Agostino, 261, 293-295
Vanhoye, Card. Albert, 293-296
Vann, Bp. Kevin W., 377, 382, 406, 416
Vanuatu, 266, 267, 269, 333, 395, 407, 419
Vasa, Bp. Robert, 375, 416
Vasquez, Bp. José, 377, 417, 424
Vatican Archives, 242, 272, 612
Vatican Bank, 260
Vatican City State, 3, 5, 7, 18, 51, 60, 75, 76, 261, 262, 272, 286, 287, 289, 291-293, 296, 333, 418, 568
Vatican Council I, 119, 126, 226, 364, 603
Vatican Council II, 38, 51, 52, 87, 89, 92, 93, 103, 113, 114, 116, 117, 119, 121, 126, 127, 129, 131, 135, 136, 138, 139, 141, 142, 146, 147, 151, 155, 156, 161, 175, 177, 178, 181, 182, 187, 189, 193, 195-197, 199, 201, 227-231, 233, 244-246, 258, 260, 275, 276, 278, 280, 281, 286, 293, 302, 321, 340, 343, 351, 357, 362, 420, 423, 446, 490, 502, 568, 578-580, 587, 591, 596, 604, 607-610, 612, 613, 615
Vatican Gardens, 42, 271, 272
Vatican Information Service, 124, 260, 572
Vatican Library, 54, 60, 75, 243, 262, 272, 282, 498
Vatican Observatory, 9, 242, 272
Vatican Polyglot Press, 184, 263
Vatican Press Office, 11, 14, 33, 256, 260
Vatican Publishing House, 45, 75, 76, 263
Vatican Radio, 17, 49, 51, 75, 76, 262, 292, 568, 570
Vatican Secret Archives, 11, 75, 262
Vatican Secretariat of State, 25, 33, 281, 340, 395, 404, 411, 417
Vatican Stamps, 73, 262
Vatican Television Center, 75, 76, 263
Vegliò, Abp. Antonio, 261
Veigle, Bp Adrian, 417, 419

Venerable Churches, 343
Venezuela, 15, 27, 34, 47, 51, 52, 156, 214, 217, 234, 267, 269, 272, 278, 290, 293, 296, 333, 339, 345-347, 352, 364, 365, 492, 547
Veni Creator Spiritus, 159
Venial Sin, 88, 137, 153, 157, 159
Veritatis Splendor, 112, 113, 142, 234, 251
Vermont, 340, 341, 373, 393, 421, 434, 438, 440, 470, 519, 538, 542, 544, 556
Vernacular, 104, 147, 160, 175, 176, 182-185, 187, 206, 245, 246
Verona Fathers, 461
Veronica, 157, 159
Vesakh, 616
Vessels, 46, 154, 180-183
Vestments, 25, 154, 177, 179-181, 184, 350
Viaticum, 159, 172, 192, 193, 196
Viator, 211, 466
Viatorian Fathers, 466, 505
Viatorians, 467
Vicar Apostolic, 51, 274, 364, 365, 378, 380, 381, 397, 400, 409, 412, 418, 419, 441
Vicar General, 76, 137, 160, 246, 262, 274, 277, 280, 283, 285, 287-290, 292, 302, 353, 363, 395, 399, 400, 413, 416, 417
Vicar of Christ, 131, 151
Vicariates Apostolic, 273, 335, 441
Vidal, Card. Ricardo, 293-296
Vietnam, 26, 27, 44, 204, 245, 252, 267, 288, 291, 296, 333, 334, 339, 408, 464, 481-483, 487, 491, 549
Vigil Mass, 24, 162, 170
Vigilanti Cura, 250
Vigneron, Bp. Allen, 380, 417
Vincent de Paul, 123, 205, 209, 211, 215-217, 225, 226, 341, 355, 361, 405, 411, 416, 417, 466, 472, 487-489, 502, 508, 510, 515, 544, 560, 616
Vincent Ferrer, 211, 212, 215
Vincent Pallotti, 18, 252, 465, 531
Vincentians, 211, 225, 289, 320, 325, 354, 392, 466, 467, 540, 542
Vingt-Trois, Card. André, 8, 61, 293-295, 337
Virgin Islands, 287, 299, 334, 374, 410, 416, 421, 428, 432, 438, 497, 507, 538, 551, 552
Virgin Mary, See Mary, Blessed Virgin
Virginia, 253, 352, 354, 369-373, 390, 421, 422, 425, 434, 438, 440, 468, 469, 512, 519, 524, 530, 531, 538, 559, 601
Virginity, 120, 160, 250
Virtues, 13, 14, 28, 31, 90, 102, 110, 121, 130, 133, 135, 138, 141, 143, 145, 146, 153, 158, 160, 189, 190, 361, 496, 572, 614, 616
Visually Challenged, 524
Vithayathil, Card. Varkey C.SS.R., 274, 293-296, 347
Vlazny, Abp. John, 380, 383, 417, 421
Vlk, Card. Miloslav, 293-295
Vocationist Fathers, 467, 528
Vocations Awareness Sunday, 169
Vouchers, 500, 532, 533
Vow, 135, 143, 149, 152, 160, 200
Vulgate, 95, 97, 104, 108, 220, 260, 263

W
Wako, Card. Gabriel, 294-296
Walburga, 393, 468, 469
Waldensians, 313
Wales, 13, 35, 47, 72, 206, 209, 214, 245, 253, 280, 286, 308, 311, 334, 337, 567
Walsh, Bp. Daniel, 378, 381, 382, 416-417
Walsh, Bp. Gerald, 379, 417
Walsh, Bp. Paul H., 381, 417
Wamala, Card. Emmanuel, 293-296
Wang, Bp. Ignatius, 382, 417
Ward, Bp. John, 417, 419
Warfel, Bp. Michael, 377, 378, 417, 431
Washing of Hands, 178
Washington, 8, 16, 24, 28, 29, 32, 33, 36, 39, 44, 52-57, 66, 78, 80, 86, 89, 97, 165, 170, 185-187, 197, 226, 242, 267, 270, 271, 278, 281, 285, 287, 296, 334, 342, 354, 356-358, 360, 363, 365, 366, 372, 374, 383, 385-387, 389-393, 395-422, 424-431, 433-435, 438-440, 458, 459, 462-464, 470, 473, 474, 476, 480, 483, 490, 491, 493, 495-506, 509-516, 519, 521, 522, 526-528, 530, 532, 538-540, 544-547, 549, 550, 553, 554, 556-569, 574-577, 581, 590, 593, 599, 600, 607, 611, 612, 614, 615
Washington, D.C., 57, 165, 170, 242, 267, 278, 334, 357, 374, 387, 390, 498, 532, 564, 574, 615
Water, 35, 44, 70, 71, 80-82, 90, 128, 131, 139, 141, 144, 150, 158, 172, 176, 178, 182, 190, 214, 352, 479, 500, 585
Watters, Bp. Lucas, 383, 417
Watty Urquidi, Bp. Ricardo, 417, 430, 454
Way of the Cross, 29, 31, 67, 157, 501
Wcela, Bp. Emil, 417, 419
Weakland, Abp. Rembert, 379, 417
Weigand, Bp. William, 381, 382, 417
Weitzel Bp. John, 417, 419, 430
Welsh, Bp. Thomas, 374, 417, 419
Wenski, Bp. Thomas, 380, 417, 421
West Virginia, 372, 373, 421, 422, 434, 438, 440, 519, 530, 531, 538
Wester, Bp. John, 382, 417, 421
Wetter, Card. Friedrich, 293-296
White Fathers, 319, 332, 334, 458, 564
Whitsunday, 173
Wilkerson, Bp. Gerald, 378, 417
Williams, Bp. James, 378, 417
Williams, Card. Thomas, 293-296
Willibrord, 212, 214
Wine, 71, 128, 136, 139, 146, 157, 159, 178-183, 191, 192, 194, 196, 213, 222, 223, 349-351, 597
Winter, Bp. William, 418, 419
Wirz, Bp. George, 418, 419
Wisconsin, 270, 364, 367, 372, 374, 390, 393, 400, 421, 422, 425, 434, 438, 440, 463, 470, 479, 496, 497, 504, 519, 522, 524, 531, 538, 546, 558, 599
Wisdom Books, 96, 99
Wiseman, Card. Nicholas, 226
Wiwchar, Bp. Michael C.SSR, 381, 418
Women for Faith and Family, 506
Women Missionaries, 441, 492
Women Religious, 8, 15, 24, 42, 43, 46, 58, 64, 85, 108, 335, 468-488

Women Religious U.S., 468-488
Word, Liturgy of, 178
Works of Religion Institute for, 260
World Communications Day, 22, 37, 571
World Conference of Secular Institutes, 491
World Council of Churches, 23, 245, 357, 578, 580, 581
World Day of Prayer, 26, 34, 236, 616
World Statistics, 335
World War I, 227, 242-244, 299, 310, 313, 315, 324, 327, 328, 331, 356, 423
World War II, 52-54, 182, 227, 231, 233, 236, 243-245, 261, 289, 294, 310, 313, 317, 323-325, 328, 330, 334, 342, 346, 357, 362, 395, 407, 423, 608, 612
World Youth Day, 45, 46, 48, 67, 70-72, 232, 262, 357, 414, 613
Wuerl, Abp. Donald, 32, 39, 40, 44, 80, 380, 383, 418, 532
Wyman, Jane, 54
Wyoming, 363, 373, 387, 421, 425, 434, 438, 440, 512, 522, 528, 538, 552, 556

XYZ
Xaverian Brothers, 462, 467
Xaverian Missionary Fathers, 565
Yad Va Shem, 609-610
Yanta, Bp. John, 374, 417
Yemen, 264-267, 269, 333, 334
YHWH, 50, 98, 100, 101, 146, 152
Yom HaShoah, 606, 608
Yom Kippur, 606
Younan, Bp. Joseph, 380, 418, 445
Young Ladies' Institute, 506
Young Men's Institute, 507
Youth Day, 45, 46, 48, 67, 70-72, 232, 262, 357, 414, 613
Youth Ministry, 425, 429, 497
Youth Organizations, 312, 497
Yugoslavia, 125, 245, 267, 269, 279, 296, 301, 305, 320, 327, 328, 339, 346, 591
Zahn, Gordon, 54
Zaire, 234, 265, 267-269, 272, 278, 336, 339, 548
Zambia, 53, 234, 266, 267, 269, 334, 339, 401, 419, 429, 430
Zavala, Bp. Gabino, 378, 418, 424, 452
Zayek, Bp. Francis, 381, 418
Zeal, 30, 73, 106, 144, 160, 215, 473, 489, 565
Zebedee, 105
Zechariah, 64, 96, 101, 132, 133, 176
Zen Zekiun, Card. Joseph, 23, 294-296
Zephaniah, 96, 101
Ziemann, Bp. G. Patrick, 382, 418
Zimbabwe, 234, 267, 269, 334, 339, 581
Zipfel, Bp. Paul, 375, 418
Zone, 351
Zubic, Bp. David, 377, 380, 418
Zucchetto, 160, 180
Zurek, Bp. Patrick, 374, 418
Zwingli, Huldrych, 224, 330, 597